America's Top-Rated Cities: A Statistical Handbook

Volume 1

2015

Twenty-Second Edition

America's Top-Rated Cities: A Statistical Handbook

Volume 1: Southern Region

A UNIVERSAL REFERENCE BOOK

Grey House Publishing

PUBLISHER: Leslie Mackenzie
EDITORIAL DIRECTOR: Laura Mars
EDITOR: David Garoogian

RESEARCHER & WRITER: Sebastian Marturana
PRODUCTION MANAGER: Kristen Thatcher
MARKETING DIRECTOR: Jessica Moody

A Universal Reference Book
Grey House Publishing, Inc.
4919 Route 22
Amenia, NY 12501
518.789.8700
Fax 845.373.6390
www.greyhouse.com
e-mail: books @greyhouse.com

Twenty-second Edition
Printed in Canada

Publisher's Cataloging-in-Publication Data
(Prepared by The Donohue Group, Inc.)

America's top-rated cities. Vol. I, Southern region : a statistical handbook. — 1992-

v. : ill. ; cm.
Annual, 1995-
Irregular, 1992-1993
ISSN: 1082-7102

1. Cities and towns--Ratings--Southern States--Statistics--Periodicals. 2. Cities and towns--Southern States--Statistics--Periodicals. 3. Social indicators--Southern States--Periodicals. 4. Quality of life--Southern States--Statistics--Periodicals. 5. Southern States--Social conditions--Statistics--Periodicals. I. Title: America's top rated cities. II. Title: Southern region

HT123.5.S6 A44
307.76/0973/05 95644648

4-Volume Set ISBN: 978-1-61925-552-4
Volume 1 **ISBN: 978-1-61925-553-1**
Volume 2 ISBN: 978-1-61925-554-8
Volume 3 ISBN: 978-1-61925-555-5
Volume 4 ISBN: 978-1-61925-556-2

Athens, Georgia

Atlanta, Georgia

Austin, Texas

Cape Coral, Florida

Charleston, South Carolina

Clarksville, Tennessee

Dallas, Texas

El Paso, Texas

Fort Worth, Texas

Gainesville, Florida

Houston, Texas

Huntsville, Alabama

Jacksonville, Florida

Lafayette, Louisiana

Lubbock, Texas

McAllen, Texas

Miami, Florida

Midland, Texas

Nashville, Tennessee

New Orleans, Louisiana

Orlando, Florida

Palm Bay, Florida

San Antonio, Texas

Savannah, Georgia

Tallahassee, Florida

Tampa, Florida

Tyler, Texas

Introduction

This twenty-second edition of *America's Top-Rated Cities* is a concise, statistical, 4-volume work identifying America's top-rated cities with populations of at least 100,000. It profiles 100 cities that have received high marks for business and living from prominent sources such as *Forbes, U.S. News & World Report, BusinessWeek, Inc., Fortune, Men's Health, The Wall Street Journal, Cosmopolitan,* and *CNNMoney.*

Each volume covers a different region of the country—Southern, Western, Central and Eastern—and includes a detailed Table of Contents, City Chapters, Appendices, and Maps. Each City Chapter incorporates information from hundreds of resources to create the following major sections:

- **Background**—lively narrative of significant, up-to-date news for both businesses and residents. These combine historical facts with current developments, "known-for" annual events, and climate data.
- **Rankings**—fun-to-read, bulleted survey results from over 300 books, magazines, and online articles, ranging from general (Great Places to Live), to specific (Best Cities for Newlyweds), and everything in between.
- **Statistical Tables**—122 tables and detailed topics—several new and expanded—that offer an unparalleled view of each city's Business and Living Environments. They are carefully organized with data that is easy to read and understand.
- **Appendices**—five in all, follow each volume of City Chapters. These range from listings of Metropolitan Statistical Areas to Comparative Statistics for all 100 cities.

This new edition of *America's Top-Rated Cities* includes cities that not only surveyed well, but ranked highest using our unique weighting system. We looked at violent crime, property crime, population growth, median household income, housing affordability, poverty, educational attainment, and unemployment. You'll find that a number of American cities remain "top-rated" despite less-than-stellar numbers. Miami, for example, is known for high crime and unemployment, but also for its unique location—as both a valuable business port and popular vacation spot. New York and Los Angeles have relatively low high school graduation rates, but both of these cities make up for it in other ways. A final consideration is location—we strive to include as many states in the country as possible.

Part of this year's city criteria is that it be the "primary" city in a given metropolitan area. For example, if the metro area is Raleigh-Cary, NC, we would consider Raleigh, not Cary. This allows for a more equitable core city to core city comparison. In general, the core city of a metro area is defined as having substantial influence on neighboring cities.

The following five cities have never before appeared as a top-rated city:

- SOUTHERN: Tyler, TX; Palm Bay, FL
- CENTRAL: Springfield, IL
- EASTERN: Roanoke, VA; Winston-Salem, NC

The following city has regained its top-city status after being removed from the list for several years:

- WESTERN: Sacramento, CA

Praise for previous editions:

> *"...[ATRC] has...proven its worth to a wide audience...from businesspeople and corporations planning to launch, relocate, or expand their operations to market researchers, real estate professionals, urban planners, job-seekers, students...interested in...reliable, attractively presented statistical information about larger U.S. cities."*
>
> —ARBA

> *"...For individuals or businesses looking to relocate, this resource conveniently reports rankings from more than 300 sources for the top 100 US cities. Recommended..."*
>
> —Choice

> *"...While patrons are becoming increasingly comfortable locating statistical data online, there is still something to be said for the ease associated with such a compendium of otherwise scattered data. A well-organized and appropriate update...*
>
> —Library Journal

BACKGROUND

Each city begins with an informative Background that combines history with current events. These narratives often reflect changes that have occurred during the past year, and touch on the city's environment, politics, employment, cultural offerings, and climate, often including interesting trivia. For example: The unique craft of cowboy boot making is demonstrated at the Abilene Historical Museum; Peregrine Falcons were rehabilitated and released into the wild from Boise City's World Center for Birds of Prey; Gainesville is home to a 6,800 square-foot living Butterfly Rainforest, and Grand Rapids was the first city to introduce fluoride into its drinking water in 1945.

RANKINGS
This section has rankings from a possible 316 books, articles, and reports. For easy reference, these Rankings are categorized into 16 topics including Business/Finance, Dating/Romance, and Health/Fitness.

The Rankings are presented in an easy-to-read, bulleted format and include results from both annual surveys and one-shot studies. **Fastest-Growing Wages . . . Most Well-Read . . . Most Playful . . . Most Wired. . . Healthiest for Women . . . Best for Minority Entrepreneurs . . . Safest . . . Best to Grow Old . . . Most Polite . . . Best for Moviemakers . . . Most Frugal . . . Noisiest . . . Most Vegetarian-Friendly . . . Least Stressful . . . Hottest Cities of the Future . . . Most Political . . . Most Charitable . . . Most Tax Friendly . . . Best for Telecommuters . . . Best for Singles . . . Gayest . . . Best for Dogs . . . Most Tattooed . . . Best for Wheelchair Users,** and more.

Sources for these Rankings include both well-known magazines and other media, including *Forbes, Fortune, Inc. Magazine, Working Mother, BusinessWeek, Kiplinger's Personal Finance, Men's Journal,* and *Travel + Leisure,* as well as resources not as well known, such as the *Asthma & Allergy Foundation of America, Christopher & Dana Reeve Foundation, The Advocate, Black Enterprise, National Civic League, The National Coalition for the Homeless, MovieMaker Magazine, Center for Digital Government, U.S. Conference of Mayors,* and the *Milken Institute.*

Since rankings cover a variety of geographic areas-metropolitan statistical areas, metropolitan divisions, cities, etc.-rankings can apply to one or all of these areas; see Appendix B for full geographic definitions.

STATISTICAL TABLES
Each city chapter includes a possible 122 tables and detailed topics—68 in BUSINESS and 54 in LIVING. Over 90% of statistical data has been updated. New topics include *Disability Status.* Expanded topics include the addition of gender and gender identity bias to *Hate Crimes* and best medical schools to *Higher Education.*

Business Environment includes hard facts and figures on 10 topics, including City Finances, Demographics, Income, Economy, Employment, and Taxes. *Living Environment* includes 11 topics, such as Cost of Living, Housing, Health, Education, Safety, Recreation, and Climate.

To compile the Statistical Tables, our editors have again turned to a wide range of sources, some well known, such as the *U.S. Census Bureau, U.S. Environmental Protection Agency, Bureau of Labor Statistics, Centers for Disease Control and Prevention,* and the *Federal Bureau of Investigation,* and some more obscure, like *The Council for Community and Economic Research, Texas Transportation Institute,* and *Federation of Tax Administrators.*

APPENDICES: Data for all cities appear in all volumes.

- **Appendix A**—*Comparative Statistics*
- **Appendix B**—*Metropolitan Area Definitions*
- **Appendix C**—*Government Type and County*
- **Appendix D**—*Chambers of Commerce and Economic Development Organizations*
- **Appendix E**—*State Departments of Labor and Employment*

Material provided by public and private agencies and organizations was supplemented by original research, numerous library sources and Internet sites. *America's Top-Rated Cities, 2015,* is designed for a wide range of readers: private individuals considering relocating a residence or business; professionals considering expanding their businesses or changing careers; corporations considering relocation, opening up additional offices or creating new divisions; government agencies; general and market researchers; real estate consultants; human resource personnel; urban planners; investors; and urban government students.

Customers who purchase the four-volume set receive free online access to *America's Top-Rated Cities* to: download city reports; sort and rank by 50-plus data points; and access data for 200 more cities than in the print version.

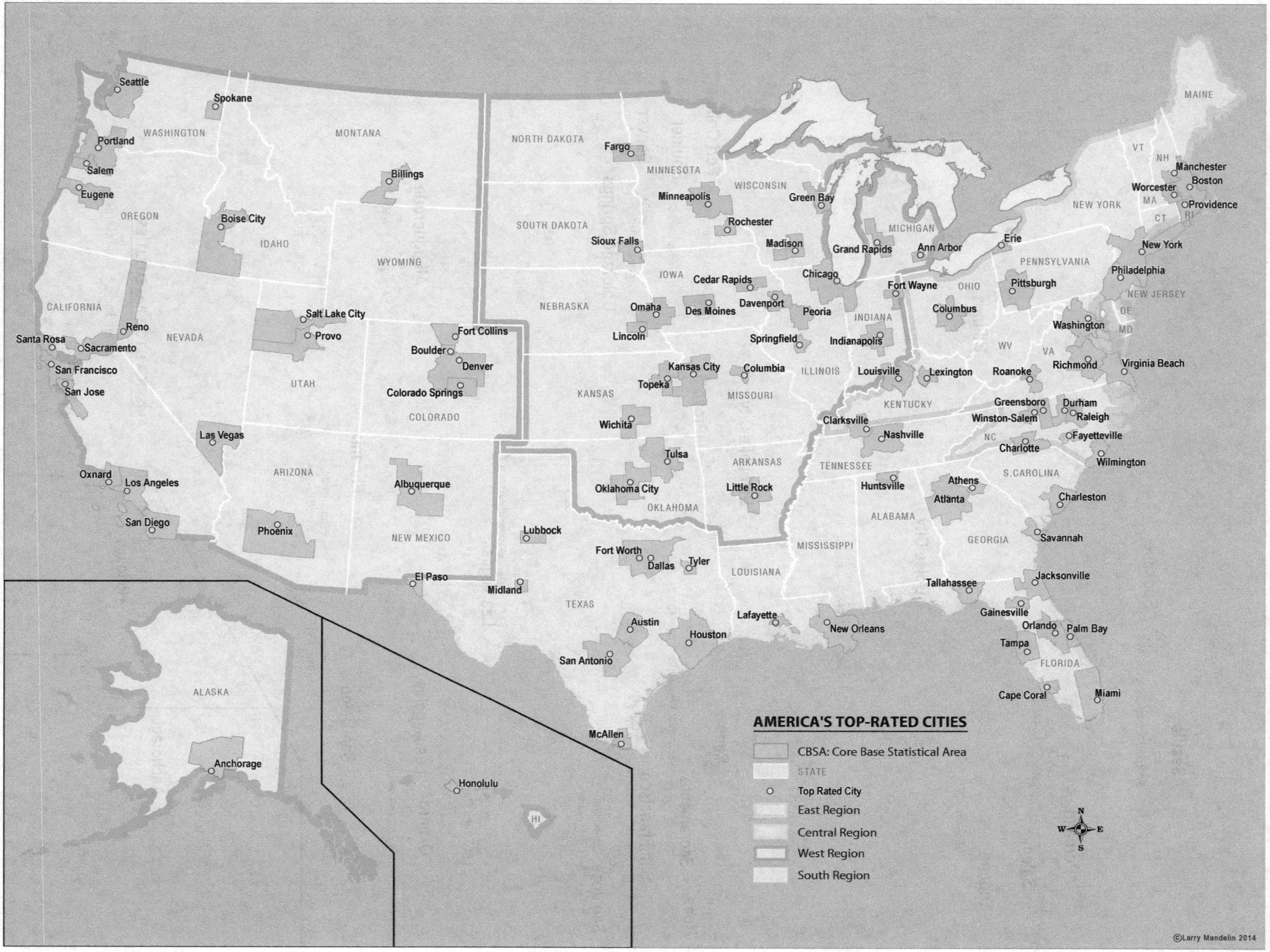
AMERICA'S TOP-RATED CITIES
CBSA: Core Base Statistical Area
STATE
Top Rated City
East Region
Central Region
West Region
South Region
N
S
E
W
WASHINGTON
OREGON
CALIFORNIA
NEVADA
IDAHO
MONTANA
WYOMING
UTAH
ARIZONA
COLORADO
NEW MEXICO
NORTH DAKOTA
SOUTH DAKOTA
NEBRASKA
KANSAS
OKLAHOMA
TEXAS
MINNESOTA
IOWA
MISSOURI
ARKANSAS
LOUISIANA
WISCONSIN
ILLINOIS
MICHIGAN
INDIANA
OHIO
KENTUCKY
TENNESSEE
MISSISSIPPI
ALABAMA
GEORGIA
FLORIDA
S.CAROLINA
NC
VA
WV
PENNSYLVANIA
NEW YORK
NEW JERSEY
DE
MD
VT
NH
MA
CT
RI
MAINE
ALASKA
HI
Seattle
Spokane
Portland
Salem
Eugene
Billings
Boise City
Reno
Santa Rosa
Sacramento
San Francisco
San Jose
Salt Lake City
Provo
Fort Collins
Boulder
Denver
Colorado Springs
Las Vegas
Oxnard
Los Angeles
San Diego
Phoenix
Albuquerque
El Paso
Lubbock
Midland
Fargo
Minneapolis
Rochester
Sioux Falls
Green Bay
Madison
Grand Rapids
Ann Arbor
Erie
Chicago
Cedar Rapids
Omaha
Des Moines
Davenport
Peoria
Lincoln
Springfield
Indianapolis
Fort Wayne
Columbus
Pittsburgh
Kansas City
Topeka
Columbia
Louisville
Lexington
Wichita
Tulsa
Oklahoma City
Little Rock
Clarksville
Nashville
Huntsville
Fort Worth
Dallas
Tyler
Austin
San Antonio
Houston
Lafayette
New Orleans
McAllen
Atlanta
Athens
Tallahassee
Jacksonville
Gainesville
Orlando
Palm Bay
Tampa
Cape Coral
Miami
Savannah
Charleston
Charlotte
Greensboro
Winston-Salem
Durham
Raleigh
Fayetteville
Wilmington
Roanoke
Richmond
Virginia Beach
Washington
Philadelphia
New York
Worcester
Manchester
Boston
Providence
Anchorage
Honolulu
©Larry Mandelin 2014

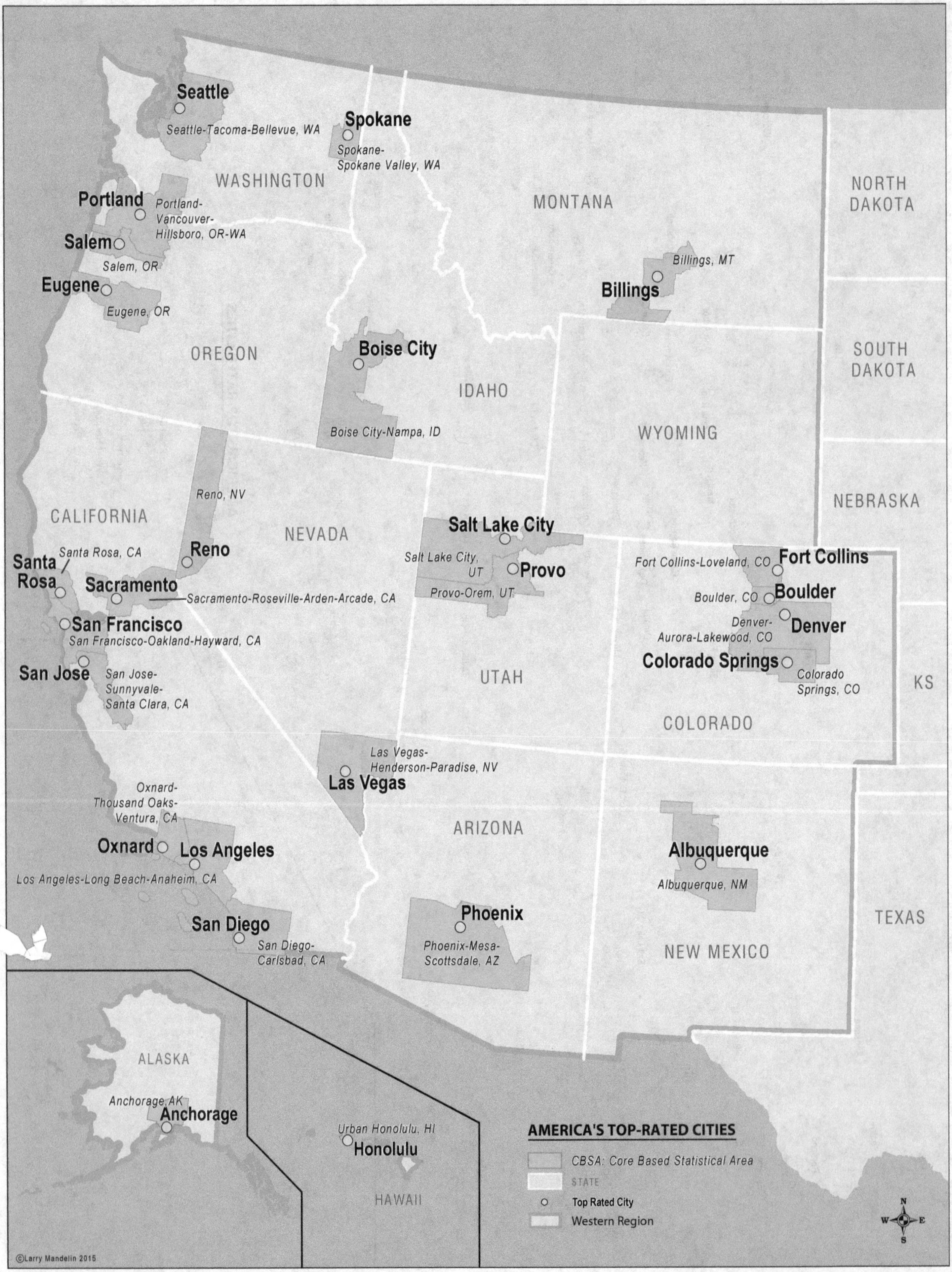
Seattle
Seattle-Tacoma-Bellevue, WA
Spokane
Spokane-
Spokane Valley, WA
WASHINGTON
MONTANA
NORTH DAKOTA
Portland
Portland-
Vancouver-
Hillsboro, OR-WA
Salem
Salem, OR
Eugene
Eugene, OR
Billings, MT
Billings
OREGON
Boise City
IDAHO
SOUTH DAKOTA
Boise City-Nampa, ID
WYOMING
Reno, NV
CALIFORNIA
NEBRASKA
NEVADA
Salt Lake City
Santa Rosa, CA
Reno
Santa Rosa
Salt Lake City, UT
Provo
Fort Collins-Loveland, CO
Fort Collins
Sacramento
Sacramento-Roseville-Arden-Arcade, CA
Provo-Orem, UT
Boulder, CO
Boulder
San Francisco
San Francisco-Oakland-Hayward, CA
Denver-
Aurora-Lakewood, CO
Denver
Colorado Springs
San Jose
San Jose-
Sunnyvale-
Santa Clara, CA
UTAH
Colorado Springs, CO
KS
COLORADO
Las Vegas-
Henderson-Paradise, NV
Las Vegas
Oxnard-
Thousand Oaks-
Ventura, CA
ARIZONA
Oxnard
Los Angeles
Albuquerque
Los Angeles-Long Beach-Anaheim, CA
Albuquerque, NM
Phoenix
San Diego
TEXAS
San Diego-
Carlsbad, CA
Phoenix-Mesa-
Scottsdale, AZ
NEW MEXICO
ALASKA
Anchorage, AK
Anchorage
Urban Honolulu, HI
Honolulu
HAWAII
AMERICA'S TOP-RATED CITIES
CBSA: Core Based Statistical Area
STATE
Top Rated City
Western Region
N
W
E
S
©Larry Mandelin 2015

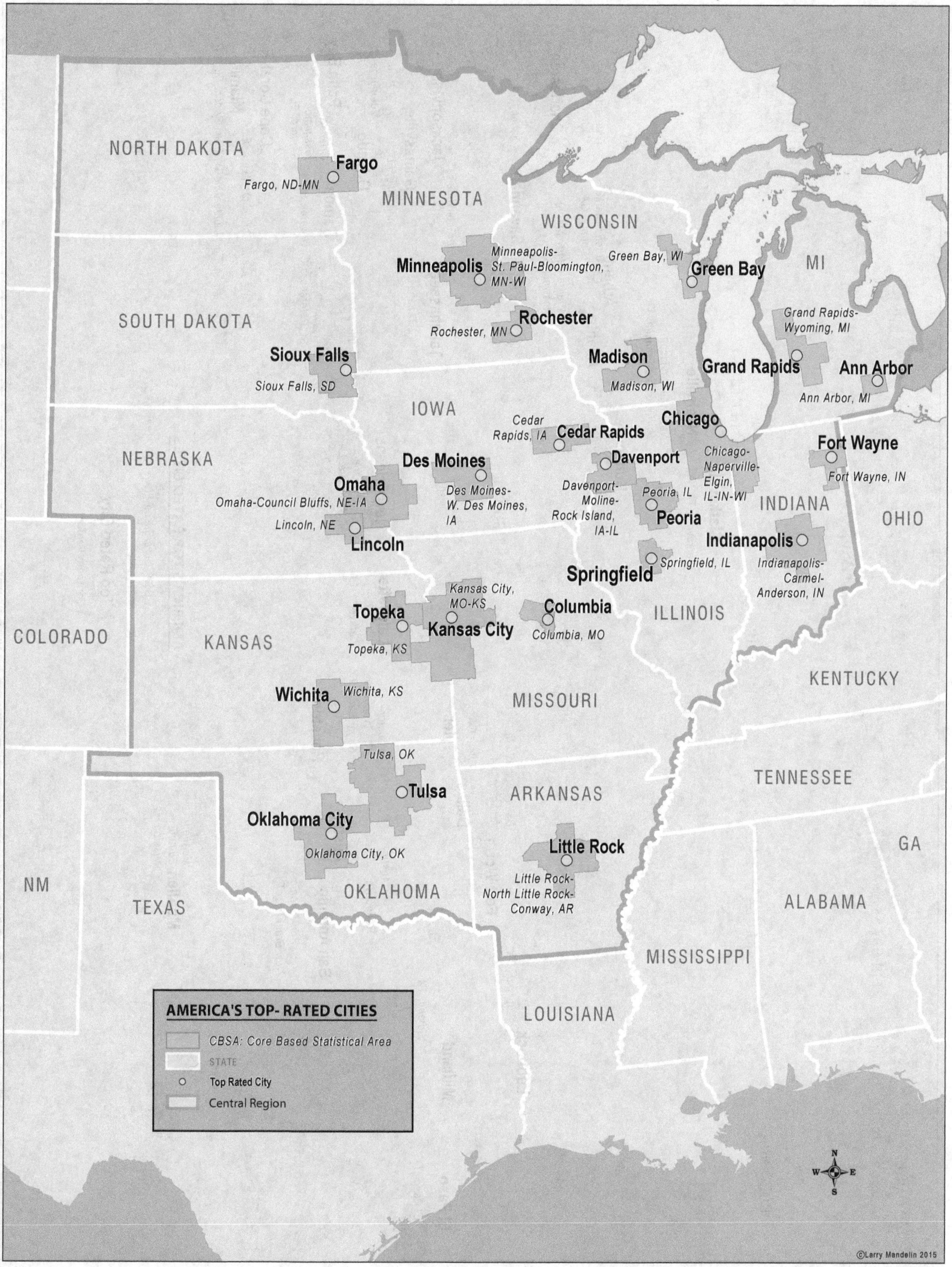

NORTH DAKOTA
MINNESOTA
WISCONSIN
SOUTH DAKOTA
MI
IOWA
NEBRASKA
INDIANA
OHIO
ILLINOIS
COLORADO
KANSAS
KENTUCKY
MISSOURI
TENNESSEE
ARKANSAS
GA
NM
TEXAS
OKLAHOMA
ALABAMA
MISSISSIPPI
LOUISIANA
Fargo
Fargo, ND-MN
Minneapolis
Minneapolis-St. Paul-Bloomington, MN-WI
Green Bay, WI
Green Bay
Rochester
Rochester, MN
Grand Rapids-Wyoming, MI
Sioux Falls
Sioux Falls, SD
Madison
Madison, WI
Grand Rapids
Ann Arbor
Ann Arbor, MI
Cedar Rapids, IA
Cedar Rapids
Chicago
Chicago-Naperville-Elgin, IL-IN-WI
Fort Wayne
Fort Wayne, IN
Des Moines
Des Moines-W. Des Moines, IA
Davenport
Davenport-Moline-Rock Island, IA-IL
Omaha
Omaha-Council Bluffs, NE-IA
Peoria, IL
Peoria
Lincoln, NE
Lincoln
Indianapolis
Indianapolis-Carmel-Anderson, IN
Springfield, IL
Springfield
Kansas City, MO-KS
Kansas City
Topeka
Topeka, KS
Columbia
Columbia, MO
Wichita
Wichita, KS
Tulsa, OK
Tulsa
Oklahoma City
Oklahoma City, OK
Little Rock
Little Rock-North Little Rock-Conway, AR
AMERICA'S TOP- RATED CITIES
CBSA: Core Based Statistical Area
STATE
Top Rated City
Central Region
N
W
E
S
©Larry Mandelin 2015

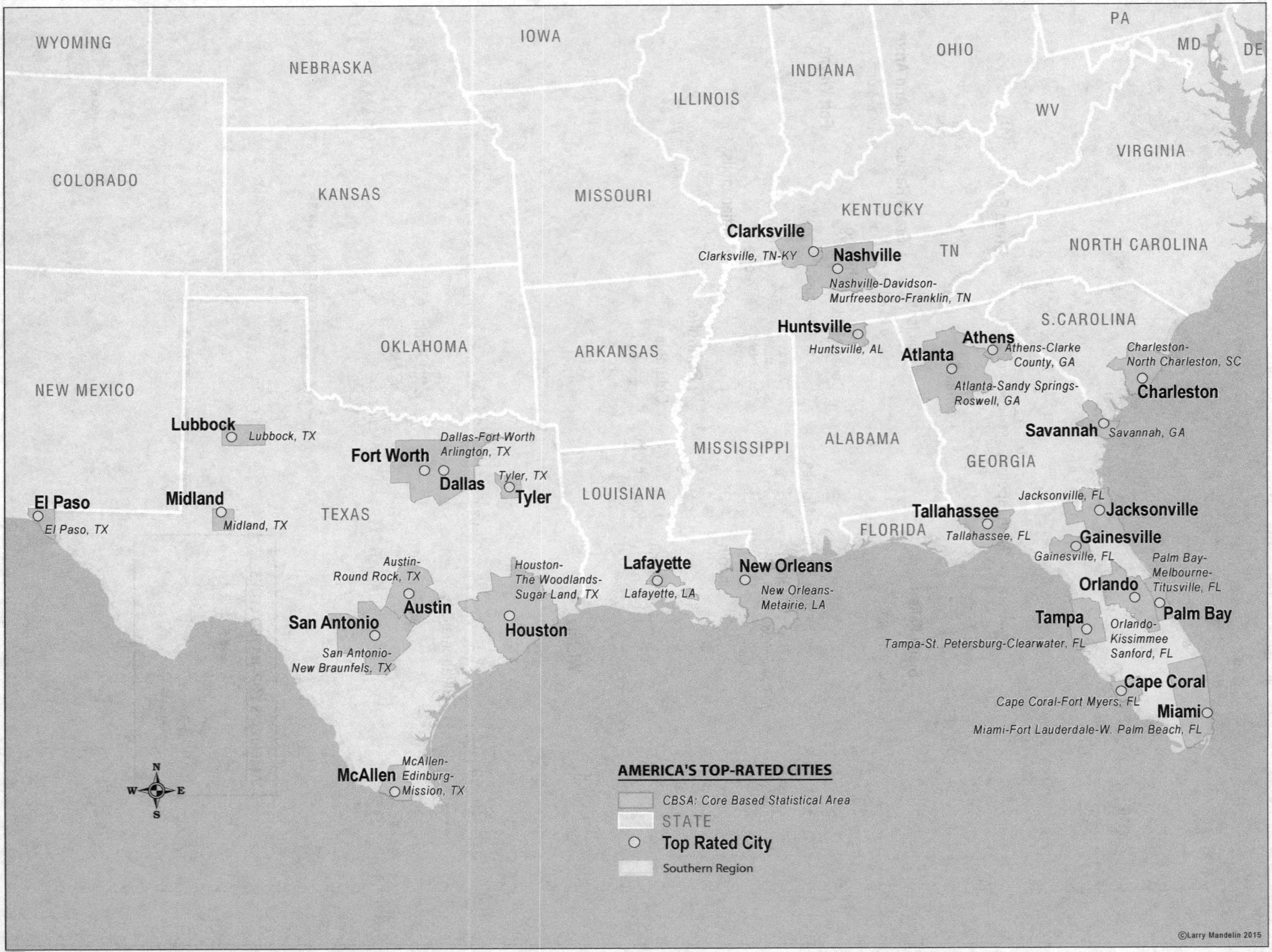
AMERICA'S TOP-RATED CITIES
CBSA: Core Based Statistical Area
STATE
Top Rated City
Southern Region
El Paso
El Paso, TX
Lubbock
Lubbock, TX
Midland
Midland, TX
Fort Worth
Dallas
Dallas-Fort Worth Arlington, TX
Tyler
Tyler, TX
Austin
Austin-Round Rock, TX
San Antonio
San Antonio-New Braunfels, TX
Houston
Houston-The Woodlands-Sugar Land, TX
McAllen
McAllen-Edinburg-Mission, TX
Lafayette
Lafayette, LA
New Orleans
New Orleans-Metairie, LA
Clarksville
Clarksville, TN-KY
Nashville
Nashville-Davidson-Murfreesboro-Franklin, TN
Huntsville
Huntsville, AL
Atlanta
Atlanta-Sandy Springs-Roswell, GA
Athens
Athens-Clarke County, GA
Savannah
Savannah, GA
Charleston
Charleston-North Charleston, SC
Tallahassee
Tallahassee, FL
Jacksonville
Jacksonville, FL
Gainesville
Gainesville, FL
Orlando
Orlando-Kissimmee Sanford, FL
Palm Bay
Palm Bay-Melbourne-Titusville, FL
Tampa
Tampa-St. Petersburg-Clearwater, FL
Cape Coral
Cape Coral-Fort Myers, FL
Miami
Miami-Fort Lauderdale-W. Palm Beach, FL
WYOMING
NEBRASKA
IOWA
ILLINOIS
INDIANA
OHIO
PA
MD
DE
WV
VIRGINIA
COLORADO
KANSAS
MISSOURI
KENTUCKY
TN
NORTH CAROLINA
S.CAROLINA
NEW MEXICO
OKLAHOMA
ARKANSAS
MISSISSIPPI
ALABAMA
GEORGIA
TEXAS
LOUISIANA
FLORIDA
N
E
S
W
©Larry Mandelin 2015

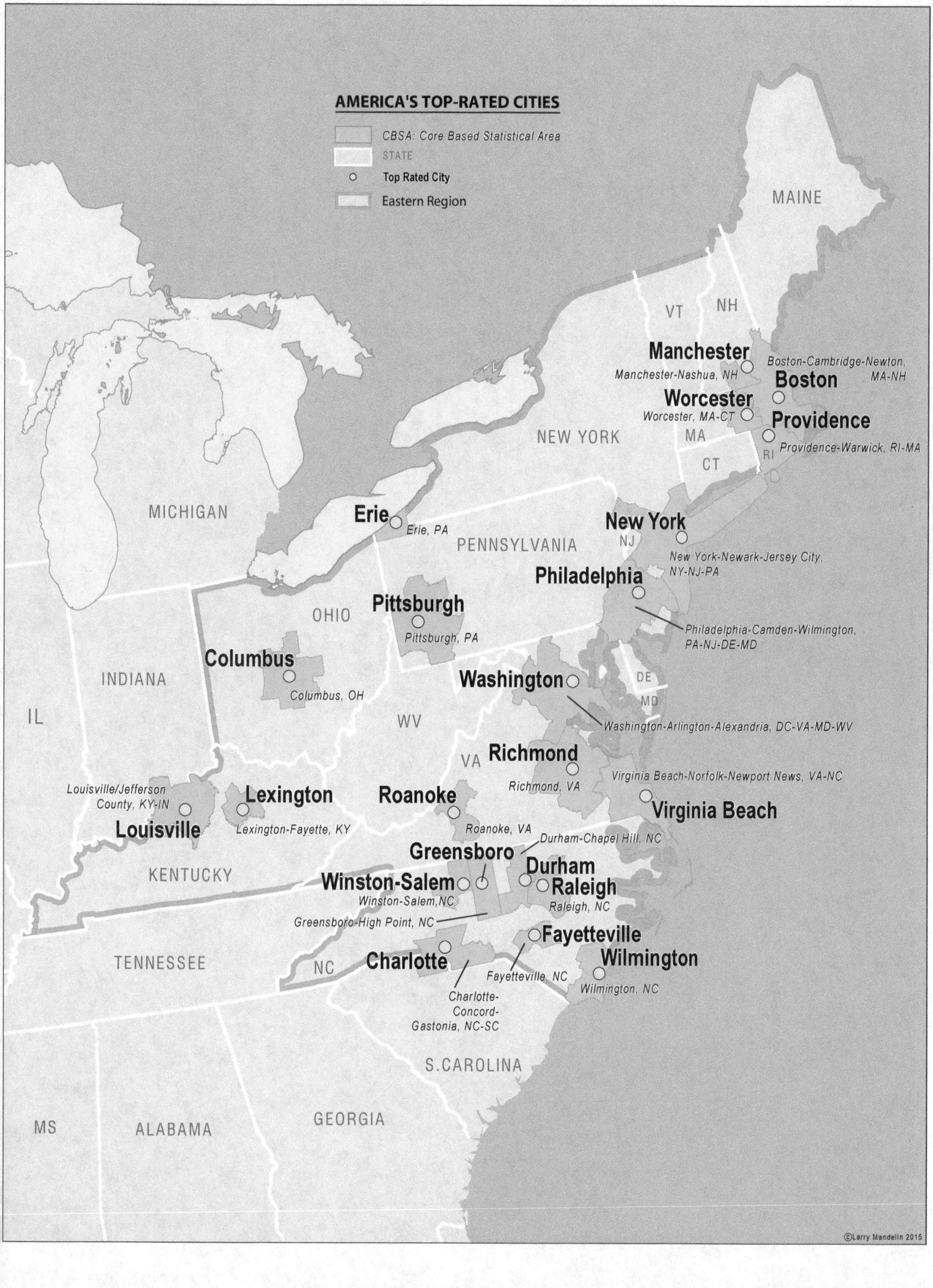
AMERICA'S TOP-RATED CITIES
CBSA: Core Based Statistical Area
STATE
Top Rated City
Eastern Region
MAINE
VT
NH
MA
CT
RI
NEW YORK
MICHIGAN
PENNSYLVANIA
NJ
OHIO
INDIANA
IL
WV
DE
MD
VA
KENTUCKY
TENNESSEE
NC
S.CAROLINA
GEORGIA
ALABAMA
MS
Manchester
Manchester-Nashua, NH
Boston
Boston-Cambridge-Newton, MA-NH
Worcester
Worcester, MA-CT
Providence
Providence-Warwick, RI-MA
Erie
Erie, PA
New York
New York-Newark-Jersey City, NY-NJ-PA
Philadelphia
Philadelphia-Camden-Wilmington, PA-NJ-DE-MD
Pittsburgh
Pittsburgh, PA
Columbus
Columbus, OH
Washington
Washington-Arlington-Alexandria, DC-VA-MD-WV
Richmond
Richmond, VA
Virginia Beach
Virginia Beach-Norfolk-Newport News, VA-NC
Louisville
Louisville/Jefferson County, KY-IN
Lexington
Lexington-Fayette, KY
Roanoke
Roanoke, VA
Greensboro
Greensboro-High Point, NC
Durham
Durham-Chapel Hill, NC
Raleigh
Raleigh, NC
Winston-Salem
Winston-Salem,NC
Fayetteville
Fayetteville, NC
Wilmington
Wilmington, NC
Charlotte
Charlotte-Concord-Gastonia, NC-SC
©Larry Mandelin 2015

Athens, Georgia

Background

Athens, home to the University of Georgia, retains its old charms while cultivating the new. Antebellum homes that grace the city still stand because Gen. William Tecumseh Sherman's March to the Sea took a route that left this northeast Georgia town intact (while burning Atlanta, about 60 miles to the southwest). The Athens Music History Walking Tour, available through the local convention and visitors' bureau, stops at Weaver D's soul food restaurant with the slogan, "Automatic for the People," that went national as the name of locally-grown REM's 1992 album. The college music scene that spawned the B-52s and the Indigo Girls in the 1970s and 1980s, continues to support a thriving music industry. In 2002, the *New York Times* called Athens "Live Music Central."

Present-day Athens started as a small settlement where an old Cherokee trail crossed the Oconee River. In 1785 the state's General Assembly chartered the university, which established a campus here in 1801. Three years later, the school held its first graduation ceremony. The city was named for the ancient Greece's center of learning.

Undoubtedly the major influence in the city and surrounding Clarke County, the University of Georgia is also the area's largest employer. The comprehensive land grant and sea-grant institution offers all levels of degree programs in numerous disciplines. Other educational institutions in Athens are the Navy Supply School, Athens Technical College, and branches of Piedmont College and Old Dominion University.

Other major employers are focused on health care, government, and manufacturing. They include Athens Regional Medical Center and St. Mary's Health Care System, which have enlarged their facilities and specialized in areas including oncology, pediatrics and heart disease. In March 2010, St. Mary's was the first area hospital to implement the next generation of minimally invasive surgery using a hi-tech assistive robot. Manufacturing is a major employment sector.

The city's official government merged with its home county in 1991, creating the Unified Government of Athens-Clark County.

With its shops, boutiques and restaurants, Athens offers plenty to do. The Georgia State Museum of Art, Museum of Natural History, and the State Botanical Garden here are affiliated with the university. The restored 1910 Morton Theater once hosted Cab Calloway, Duke Ellington, and Louis Armstrong, and now hosts dramatic and musical performances. Undoubtedly the strong presence of young people in Athens has contributed to the burgeoning artistic scene there. The city center is home to bars, galleries, cafes, and music venues that cater to the city's creative climate. The annual AthFest in June, hosts 120 bands to support local education. The city's charms, attractive to all ages, have not gone unnoticed by the media. Athens has been named one of the best places for small business, the best college town for retirees, and the best place to recapture your youth. The city also has a lively bicycle culture, and hosts several annual bicycle races.

The climate is mild, with average temperatures about 20 degrees warmer than the U.S. average. Snowfall is next to nothing, but precipitation is at its highest from January-March. Spring is lovely, with three to four inches of rain, sunshine up to 70 percent of the time starting in April, and temperatures averaging in the 70s.

Rankings

Business/Finance Rankings

- Athens was identified as one of "America's Hardest-Working Towns." The city ranked #15 out of 25. Criteria: average hours worked per capita; willingness to work during personal time; number of dual income households; local employment rate. *Parade, "What is America's Hardest-Working Town?," April 15, 2012*
- The Athens metro area appeared on the Milken Institute "2013 Best Performing Cities" list. Rank: #103 out of 179 small metro areas. Criteria: job growth; wage and salary growth; high-tech output growth.*Milken Institute, "Best-Performing Cities 2014," January 2015*
- *Forbes* ranked 184 smaller metro areas to determine the nation's "Best Small Places for Business and Careers." The Athens metro area was ranked #36. Criteria: costs (business and living); job growth (past and projected); income growth; educational attainment (college and high school); projected economic growth; cultural and recreational opportunities; net migration patterns; number of highly ranked colleges. *Forbes, "The Best Small Places for Business and Careers 2014," July 23, 2014*

Culture/Performing Arts Rankings

- Athens was selected as one of America's top cities for the arts. The city ranked #13 in the mid-sized city (population 100,000 to 499,999) category. Criteria: readers' top choices for arts travel destinations based on the richness and variety of visual arts sites, activities and events. *American Style, "2012 Top 25 Arts Destinations," June 2012*

Environmental Rankings

- The Athens metro area came in at #257 for the relative comfort of its climate on Sperling's list of "chill cities," as measured by the Sperling Heat Index. All 361 metro areas are included. Criteria included daytime high temperatures, nighttime low temperatures, dew point, and relative humidity at the high temperatures. *www.bertsperling.com, "Sperling's Chill Cities," July 18, 2013*
- Sperling's BestPlaces assessed 379 metropolitan areas of the United States for the likelihood of dangerously extreme weather events or earthquakes. In general the Southeast and South-Central regions have the highest risk of weather extremes and earthquakes, while the Pacific Northwest enjoys the lowest risk. Of the least risky metropolitan areas, the Athens metro area was ranked #323. *www.bestplaces.net, "Safest Places from Natural Disasters," April 2011*

Real Estate Rankings

- Athens was ranked #82 out of 275 metro areas in terms of house price appreciation in 2014 (#1 = highest rate). *Federal Housing Finance Agency, House Price Index, 4th Quarter 2014*

Safety Rankings

- The National Insurance Crime Bureau ranked 380 metro areas in the U.S. in terms of per capita rates of vehicle theft. The Athens metro area ranked #210 (#1 = highest rate). Criteria: number of vehicle theft offenses per 100,000 inhabitants in 2012. *National Insurance Crime Bureau, "Hot Spots 2012," June 26, 2013*

Seniors/Retirement Rankings

- From its Best Cities for Successful Aging indexes, the Milken Institute generated rankings for metropolitan areas, weighing data in eight categories—health care, wellness, living arrangements, transportation, financial characteristics, education and employment opportunities, community engagement, and overall livability. The Athens metro area was ranked #29 overall in the small metro area category. *Milken Institute, "Best Cities for Successful Aging, 2014"*

- Athens was chosen in the "College Town" category of CNNMoney's list of the 25 best places to retire." Criteria include: type of location (big city, small town, resort area, college town); median home prices; top state income tax rate. *CNNMoney, "25 Best Places to Retire," December 17, 2012*
- Athens was identified as one of the most popular places to retire by *Topretirements.com*. The list reflects the 100 cities (out of 900+ total cities reviewed) that visitors to the website are most interested in for retirement. *Topretirements.com, "Most Popular Places to Retire for 2014," February 25, 2014*

Sports/Recreation Rankings

- Athens was chosen as a bicycle friendly community by the League of American Bicyclists. A "Bicycle Friendly Community" welcomes cyclists by providing safe accommodation for cycling and encouraging people to bike for transportation and recreation. There are four award levels: Platinum; Gold; Silver; and Bronze. The community achieved an award level of Bronze. *League of American Bicyclists, "Bicycle Friendly Community Master List," Fall 2013*

Business Environment

CITY FINANCES

City Government Finances

Component	2012 ($000)	2012 ($ per capita)
Total Revenues	231,812	2,008
Total Expenditures	292,175	2,531
Debt Outstanding	263,425	2,282
Cash and Securities[1]	207,409	1,796

Note: (1) Cash and security holdings of a government at the close of its fiscal year, including those of its dependent agencies, utilities, and liquor stores.
Source: U.S Census Bureau, State & Local Government Finances 2012

City Government Revenue by Source

Source	2012 ($000)	2012 ($ per capita)
General Revenue		
From Federal Government	4,824	42
From State Government	17,980	156
From Local Governments	46,305	401
Taxes		
Property	48,208	418
Sales and Gross Receipts	18,874	163
Personal Income	0	0
Corporate Income	0	0
Motor Vehicle License	0	0
Other Taxes	4,091	35
Current Charges	44,139	382
Liquor Store	0	0
Utility	25,307	219
Employee Retirement	0	0

Source: U.S Census Bureau, State & Local Government Finances 2012

City Government Expenditures by Function

Function	2012 ($000)	2012 ($ per capita)	2012 (%)
General Direct Expenditures			
Air Transportation	2,776	24	1.0
Corrections	15,621	135	5.3
Education	0	0	0.0
Employment Security Administration	0	0	0.0
Financial Administration	4,099	36	1.4
Fire Protection	12,332	107	4.2
General Public Buildings	15,635	135	5.4
Governmental Administration, Other	23,823	206	8.2
Health	12,960	112	4.4
Highways	11,073	96	3.8
Hospitals	0	0	0.0
Housing and Community Development	4,551	39	1.6
Interest on General Debt	943	8	0.3
Judicial and Legal	10,048	87	3.4
Libraries	9,566	83	3.3
Parking	3,890	34	1.3
Parks and Recreation	13,660	118	4.7
Police Protection	27,346	237	9.4
Public Welfare	479	4	0.2
Sewerage	20,519	178	7.0
Solid Waste Management	8,264	72	2.8
Veterans' Services	0	0	0.0
Liquor Store	0	0	0.0
Utility	42,821	371	14.7
Employee Retirement	0	0	0.0

Source: U.S Census Bureau, State & Local Government Finances 2012

DEMOGRAPHICS

Population Growth

Area	1990 Census	2000 Census	2010 Census	Population Growth (%) 1990-2000	Population Growth (%) 2000-2010
City	86,561	100,266	115,452	15.8	15.1
MSA[1]	136,025	166,079	192,541	22.1	15.9
U.S.	248,709,873	281,421,906	308,745,538	13.2	9.7

Note: (1) Figures cover the Athens-Clarke County, GA Metropolitan Statistical Area—see Appendix B for areas included
Source: U.S. Census Bureau, Census 1990, 2000, 2010

Household Size

Area	Persons in Household (%) One	Two	Three	Four	Five	Six	Seven or More	Average Household Size
City	34.3	33.9	14.6	11.5	3.4	1.5	0.8	2.63
MSA[1]	29.2	34.5	15.7	13.2	4.6	1.7	1.1	2.70
U.S.	27.7	33.6	15.7	13.1	6.0	2.3	1.5	2.64

Note: (1) Figures cover the Athens-Clarke County, GA Metropolitan Statistical Area—see Appendix B for areas included
Source: U.S. Census Bureau, 2011-2013 American Community Survey 3-Year Estimates

Race

Area	White Alone[2] (%)	Black Alone[2] (%)	Asian Alone[2] (%)	AIAN[3] Alone[2] (%)	NHOPI[4] Alone[2] (%)	Other Race Alone[2] (%)	Two or More Races (%)
City	65.5	26.4	4.3	0.2	0.0	1.5	2.1
MSA[1]	73.4	19.5	3.4	0.3	0.0	1.4	2.0
U.S.	73.9	12.6	5.0	0.8	0.2	4.7	2.9

Note: (1) Figures cover the Athens-Clarke County, GA Metropolitan Statistical Area—see Appendix B for areas included; (2) Alone is defined as not being in combination with one or more other races; (3) American Indian and Alaska Native; (4) Native Hawaiian and Other Pacific Islander
Source: U.S. Census Bureau, 2011-2013 American Community Survey 3-Year Estimates

Hispanic or Latino Origin

Area	Total (%)	Mexican (%)	Puerto Rican (%)	Cuban (%)	Other (%)
City	10.6	7.2	0.4	0.4	2.7
MSA[1]	8.2	5.6	0.5	0.3	1.9
U.S.	16.9	10.8	1.6	0.6	3.8

Note: Persons of Hispanic or Latino origin can be of any race; (1) Figures cover the Athens-Clarke County, GA Metropolitan Statistical Area—see Appendix B for areas included
Source: U.S. Census Bureau, 2011-2013 American Community Survey 3-Year Estimates

Segregation

Type	Segregation Indices[1] 1990	2000	2010	2010 Rank[2]	Percent Change 1990-2000	1990-2010	2000-2010
Black/White	n/a	n/a	n/a	n/a	n/a	n/a	n/a
Asian/White	n/a	n/a	n/a	n/a	n/a	n/a	n/a
Hispanic/White	n/a	n/a	n/a	n/a	n/a	n/a	n/a

Note: All figures cover the Metropolitan Statistical Area—see Appendix B for areas included; Figures are based on an analysis of 1990, 2000, and 2010 Census Decennial Census tract data by William H. Frey, Brookings Institution and the University of Michigan Social Science Data Analysis Network. In this analysis all racial groups (whites, blacks, and asians) are non-Hispanic members of those races. Hispanics are shown as a separate category;
(1) Segregation Indices are Dissimilarity Indices that measure the degree to which the minority group is distributed differently than whites across census tracts. They range from 0 (complete integration) to 100 (complete segregation) where the value indicates the percentage of the minority group that needs to move to be distributed exactly like whites; (2) Ranges from 1 (most segregated) to 102 (least segregated); n/a not available.
Source: www.CensusScope.org

Ancestry

Area	German	Irish	English	American	Italian	Polish	French[2]	Scottish	Dutch
City	9.2	7.9	9.1	8.6	2.5	1.8	1.5	3.2	0.7
MSA[1]	9.3	8.9	9.7	13.0	2.5	1.3	1.6	2.9	0.7
U.S.	14.9	10.8	8.0	7.4	5.5	3.0	2.7	1.7	1.4

Note: Figures are the percentage of the total population reporting a particular ancestry. The nine most commonly reported ancestries in the U.S. are shown. Figures include multiple ancestries (e.g. if a person reported being Irish and Italian, they were included in both columns); (1) Figures cover the Athens-Clarke County, GA Metropolitan Statistical Area—see Appendix B for areas included; (2) Excludes Basque
Source: U.S. Census Bureau, 2011-2013 American Community Survey 3-Year Estimates

Foreign-Born Population

Area	Percent of Population Born in								
	Any Foreign Country	Mexico	Asia	Europe	Carribean	South America	Central America[2]	Africa	Canada
City	n/a	n/a	n/a	n/a	n/a	n/a	n/a	n/a	n/a
MSA[1]	7.5	2.6	2.6	0.7	0.2	0.4	0.7	0.2	0.1
U.S.	13.0	3.7	3.8	1.5	1.2	0.9	1.0	0.6	0.3

Note: (1) Figures cover the Athens-Clarke County, GA Metropolitan Statistical Area—see Appendix B for areas included; (2) Excludes Mexico.
Source: U.S. Census Bureau, 2011-2013 American Community Survey 3-Year Estimates

Marital Status

Area	Never Married	Now Married[2]	Separated	Widowed	Divorced
City	56.8	29.6	1.4	4.3	7.8
MSA[1]	44.7	39.4	1.6	5.4	8.9
U.S.	32.7	48.1	2.2	6.0	11.0

Note: Figures are percentages and cover the population 15 years of age and older; (1) Figures cover the Athens-Clarke County, GA Metropolitan Statistical Area—see Appendix B for areas included; (2) Excludes separated
Source: U.S. Census Bureau, 2011-2013 American Community Survey 3-Year Estimates

Disability Status

Area	All Ages	Under 18 Years Old	18 to 64 Years Old	65 Years and Over
City	9.9	2.9	8.6	34.5
MSA[1]	11.4	3.2	9.8	36.8
U.S.	12.3	4.1	10.2	36.3

Note: Figures show percent of the civilian noninstitutionalized population that reported having a disability. Disability status is determined from from six types of difficulty: vision, hearing, cognitive, ambulatory, self-care, and independent living. For children under 5 years old, hearing and vision difficulty are used to determine disability status. For children between the ages of 5 and 14, disability status is determined from hearing, vision, cognitive, ambulatory, and self-care difficulties. For people aged 15 years and older, they are considered to have a disability if they have difficulty with any one of the six difficulty types; (1) Figures cover the Athens-Clarke County, GA Metropolitan Statistical Area—see Appendix B for areas included.
Source: U.S. Census Bureau, 2011-2013 American Community Survey 3-Year Estimates

Age

Area	Percent of Population									Median Age
	Under Age 5	Age 5–19	Age 20–34	Age 35–44	Age 45–54	Age 55–64	Age 65–74	Age 75–84	Age 85+	
City	5.9	21.3	36.8	10.3	8.8	8.2	5.0	2.5	1.3	26.2
MSA[1]	5.7	21.4	28.6	11.6	11.5	10.3	6.5	3.1	1.3	30.7
U.S.	6.4	19.9	20.7	12.9	14.1	12.3	7.6	4.2	1.9	37.4

Note: (1) Figures cover the Athens-Clarke County, GA Metropolitan Statistical Area—see Appendix B for areas included
Source: U.S. Census Bureau, 2011-2013 American Community Survey 3-Year Estimates

Gender

Area	Males	Females	Males per 100 Females
City	56,490	62,221	90.8
MSA[1]	94,417	101,892	92.7
U.S.	154,451,010	159,410,713	96.9

Note: (1) Figures cover the Athens-Clarke County, GA Metropolitan Statistical Area—see Appendix B for areas included
Source: U.S. Census Bureau, 2011-2013 American Community Survey 3-Year Estimates

Religious Groups by Family

Area	Catholic	Baptist	Non-Den.	Methodist[2]	Lutheran	LDS[3]	Pente-costal	Presby-terian[4]	Muslim[5]	Judaism
MSA[1]	4.4	16.3	2.3	8.4	0.4	0.8	2.8	2.0	0.4	0.2
U.S.	19.1	9.3	4.0	4.0	2.3	2.0	1.9	1.6	0.8	0.7

Note: Figures are the number of adherents as a percentage of the total population; (1) Figures cover the Athens-Clarke County, GA Metropolitan Statistical Area—see Appendix B for areas included; (2) Methodist/Pietist; (3) Latter Day Saints; (4) Reformed; (5) Figures are estimates
Source: Association of Statisticians of American Religious Bodies, 2010 U.S. Religion Census: Religious Congregations & Membership Study

Religious Groups by Tradition

Area	Catholic	Evangelical Protestant	Mainline Protestant	Other Tradition	Black Protestant	Orthodox
MSA[1]	4.4	21.1	9.8	1.7	2.5	0.1
U.S.	19.1	16.2	7.3	4.3	1.6	0.3

Note: Figures are the number of adherents as a percentage of the total population; (1) Figures cover the Athens-Clarke County, GA Metropolitan Statistical Area—see Appendix B for areas included
Source: Association of Statisticians of American Religious Bodies, 2010 U.S. Religion Census: Religious Congregations & Membership Study

ECONOMY

Gross Metropolitan Product

Area	2012	2013	2014	2015	Rank[2]
MSA[1]	6.8	7.1	7.4	7.7	224

Note: Figures are in billions of dollars; (1) Figures cover the Athens-Clarke County, GA Metropolitan Statistical Area—see Appendix B for areas included; (2) Rank is based on 2015 data and ranges from 1 to 363
Source: The U.S. Conference of Mayors, U.S. Metro Economies: GMP and Employment 2013-2015, June 2014

Economic Growth

Area	2010-12 (%)	2013 (%)	2014 (%)	2015 (%)	Rank[2]
MSA[1]	0.2	2.8	2.1	2.7	220
U.S.	2.1	2.0	2.3	3.2	–

Note: Figures are real gross metropolitan product (GMP) growth rates and represent annual average percent change; (1) Figures cover the Athens-Clarke County, GA Metropolitan Statistical Area—see Appendix B for areas included; (2) Rank is based on 2015 data and ranges from 1 to 363
Source: The U.S. Conference of Mayors, U.S. Metro Economies: GMP and Employment 2013-2015, June 2014

Metropolitan Area Exports

Area	2008	2009	2010	2011	2012	2013	Rank[2]
MSA[1]	171.4	214.6	194.6	221.6	229.7	286.0	271

Note: Figures are in millions of dollars; (1) Figures cover the Athens-Clarke County, GA Metropolitan Statistical Area—see Appendix B for areas included; (2) Rank is based on 2013 data and ranges from 1 to 387
Source: U.S. Department of Commerce, International Trade Administration, Office of Trade & Industry Information, Manufacturing & Services, data extracted April 3, 2015

Building Permits

Area	Single-Family			Multi-Family			Total		
	2013	2014	Pct. Chg.	2013	2014	Pct. Chg.	2013	2014	Pct. Chg.
City	143	116	-18.9	351	422	20.2	494	538	8.9
MSA[1]	698	502	-28.1	381	428	12.3	1,079	930	-13.8
U.S.	620,802	634,597	2.2	370,020	411,766	11.3	990,822	1,046,363	5.6

Note: (1) Figures cover the Athens-Clarke County, GA Metropolitan Statistical Area—see Appendix B for areas included; Figures represent new, privately-owned housing units authorized (unadjusted data); All permit data are based on estimates with imputation.
Source: U.S. Census Bureau, Manufacturing, Mining, and Construction Statistics, Building Permits, 2013, 2014

Bankruptcy Filings

Area	Business Filings			Nonbusiness Filings		
	2013	2014	% Chg.	2013	2014	% Chg.
Clarke County	18	7	-61.1	383	381	-0.5
U.S.	33,212	26,983	-18.8	1,038,720	909,812	-12.4

Note: Business filings include Chapter 7, Chapter 11, Chapter 12, and Chapter 13; Nonbusiness filings include Chapter 7, Chapter 11, and Chapter 13
Source: Administrative Office of the U.S. Courts, Business and Nonbusiness Bankruptcy, County Cases Commenced by Chapter of the Bankruptcy Code, During the 12- Month Period Ending December 31, 2013 and Business and Nonbusiness Bankruptcy, County Cases Commenced by Chapter of the Bankruptcy Code, During the 12- Month Period Ending December 31, 2014

Housing Vacancy Rates

Area	Gross Vacancy Rate[2] (%)			Year-Round Vacancy Rate[3] (%)			Rental Vacancy Rate[4] (%)			Homeowner Vacancy Rate[5] (%)		
	2012	2013	2014	2012	2013	2014	2012	2013	2014	2012	2013	2014
MSA[1]	n/a	n/a	n/a	n/a	n/a	n/a	n/a	n/a	n/a	n/a	n/a	n/a
U.S.	13.8	13.6	13.4	10.8	10.7	10.4	8.7	8.3	7.6	2.0	2.0	1.9

Note: (1) Figures cover the Athens-Clarke County, GA Metropolitan Statistical Area—see Appendix B for areas included; (2) The percentage of the total housing inventory that is vacant; (3) The percentage of the housing inventory (excluding seasonal units) that is year-round vacant; (4) The percentage of rental inventory that is vacant for rent; (5) The percentage of homeowner inventory that is vacant for sale; n/a not available
Source: U.S. Census Bureau, Housing Vacancies and Homeownership Annual Statistics: 2014

INCOME

Income

Area	Per Capita ($)	Median Household ($)	Average Household ($)
City	18,885	31,884	49,581
MSA[1]	21,588	39,291	57,764
U.S.	27,884	52,176	72,897

Note: (1) Figures cover the Athens-Clarke County, GA Metropolitan Statistical Area—see Appendix B for areas included
Source: U.S. Census Bureau, 2011-2013 American Community Survey 3-Year Estimates

Household Income Distribution

Area	Percent of Households Earning							
	Under $15,000	$15,000 -24,999	$25,000 -34,999	$35,000 -49,999	$50,000 -74,999	$75,000 -99,000	$100,000 -149,999	$150,000 and up
City	28.6	13.2	11.7	12.4	14.0	8.3	6.6	5.4
MSA[1]	21.7	12.7	11.3	13.2	15.5	10.0	9.2	6.7
U.S.	13.0	10.9	10.3	13.6	17.9	11.9	12.7	9.6

Note: (1) Figures cover the Athens-Clarke County, GA Metropolitan Statistical Area—see Appendix B for areas included
Source: U.S. Census Bureau, 2011-2013 American Community Survey 3-Year Estimates

Poverty Rate

Area	All Ages	Under 18 Years Old	18 to 64 Years Old	65 Years and Over
City	36.9	37.0	40.2	11.6
MSA[1]	27.0	26.1	30.1	10.1
U.S.	15.9	22.4	14.8	9.5

Note: Figures are percentage of people whose income during the past 12 months was below the poverty level; (1) Figures cover the Athens-Clarke County, GA Metropolitan Statistical Area—see Appendix B for areas included
Source: U.S. Census Bureau, 2011-2013 American Community Survey 3-Year Estimates

EMPLOYMENT

Labor Force and Employment

Area	Civilian Labor Force			Workers Employed		
	Dec. 2013	Dec. 2014	% Chg.	Dec. 2013	Dec. 2014	% Chg.
City	58,098	58,233	0.2	54,164	54,791	1.2
MSA[1]	94,913	95,298	0.4	88,840	90,012	1.3
U.S.	154,408,000	155,521,000	0.7	144,423,000	147,190,000	1.9

Note: Data is not seasonally adjusted and covers workers 16 years of age and older; (1) Figures cover the Athens-Clarke County, GA Metropolitan Statistical Area—see Appendix B for areas included
Source: Bureau of Labor Statistics, Local Area Unemployment Statistics

Unemployment Rate

Area	2014											
	Jan.	Feb.	Mar.	Apr.	May	Jun.	Jul.	Aug.	Sep.	Oct.	Nov.	Dec.
City	6.8	6.8	6.9	6.3	7.0	8.0	8.2	7.6	6.9	6.4	6.1	5.9
MSA[1]	6.5	6.5	6.5	5.9	6.6	7.4	7.7	7.1	6.4	6.0	5.7	5.5
U.S.	7.0	7.0	6.8	5.9	6.1	6.3	6.5	6.3	5.7	5.5	5.5	5.4

Note: Data is not seasonally adjusted and covers workers 16 years of age and older; (1) Figures cover the Athens-Clarke County, GA Metropolitan Statistical Area—see Appendix B for areas included
Source: Bureau of Labor Statistics, Local Area Unemployment Statistics

Employment by Occupation

Occupation Classification	City (%)	MSA[1] (%)	U.S. (%)
Management, Business, Science, and Arts	38.1	38.0	36.2
Natural Resources, Construction, and Maintenance	5.4	7.2	9.0
Production, Transportation, and Material Moving	12.3	13.1	12.1
Sales and Office	22.2	22.6	24.4
Service	22.0	19.1	18.3

Note: Figures cover employed civilians 16 years of age and older; (1) Figures cover the Athens-Clarke County, GA Metropolitan Statistical Area—see Appendix B for areas included
Source: U.S. Census Bureau, 2011-2013 American Community Survey 3-Year Estimates

Employment by Industry

Sector	MSA[1] Number of Employees	MSA[1] Percent of Total	U.S. Percent of Total
Construction, Mining, and Logging	n/a	n/a	5.0
Education and Health Services	n/a	n/a	15.5
Financial Activities	n/a	n/a	5.7
Government	31,000	33.1	15.8
Information	n/a	n/a	2.0
Leisure and Hospitality	9,800	10.5	10.3
Manufacturing	n/a	n/a	8.7
Other Services	n/a	n/a	4.0
Professional and Business Services	7,200	7.7	13.8
Retail Trade	10,600	11.3	11.4
Transportation, Warehousing, and Utilities	n/a	n/a	3.9
Wholesale Trade	n/a	n/a	4.2

Note: Figures are non-farm employment as of December 2014. Figures are not seasonally adjusted and include workers 16 years of age and older; (1) Figures cover the Athens-Clarke County, GA Metropolitan Statistical Area—see Appendix B for areas included; n/a not available
Source: Bureau of Labor Statistics, Current Employment Statistics, Employment, Hours, and Earnings

Occupations with Greatest Projected Employment Growth: 2012 – 2022

Occupation[1]	2012 Employment	2022 Projected Employment	Numeric Employment Change	Percent Employment Change
Combined Food Preparation and Serving Workers, Including Fast Food	169,450	192,830	23,380	13.8
Customer Service Representatives	95,900	115,410	19,510	20.3
Laborers and Freight, Stock, and Material Movers, Hand	85,460	104,150	18,690	21.9
Elementary School Teachers, Except Special Education	42,300	56,170	13,870	32.8
General and Operations Managers	71,410	84,890	13,480	18.9
Sales Representatives, Wholesale and Manufacturing, Except Technical and Scientific Products	56,220	67,450	11,230	20.0
Secretaries and Administrative Assistants, Except Legal, Medical, and Executive	51,850	63,030	11,180	21.6
Office Clerks, General	79,920	91,010	11,090	13.9
Janitors and Cleaners, Except Maids and Housekeeping Cleaners	52,860	63,600	10,740	20.3
Childcare Workers	37,650	48,280	10,630	28.2

Note: Projections cover Georgia; (1) Sorted by numeric employment change
Source: www.projectionscentral.com, State Occupational Projections, 2012–2022 Long-Term Projections

Fastest Growing Occupations: 2012 – 2022

Occupation[1]	2012 Employment	2022 Projected Employment	Numeric Employment Change	Percent Employment Change
Physician Assistants	2,820	4,740	1,920	67.9
Health Specialties Teachers, Postsecondary	4,870	8,060	3,190	65.5
Agents and Business Managers of Artists, Performers, and Athletes	430	700	270	62.6
Personal Care Aides	16,440	26,630	10,190	62.0
Interpreters and Translators	1,650	2,630	980	58.9
Nursing Instructors and Teachers, Postsecondary	1,420	2,200	780	55.5
Psychiatric Aides	1,390	2,150	760	55.3
Home Health Aides	7,950	12,340	4,390	55.1
Nurse Practitioners	3,260	5,010	1,750	53.9
Nurse Midwives	250	380	130	53.6

Note: Projections cover Georgia; (1) Sorted by percent employment change and excludes occupations with numeric employment change less than 100
Source: www.projectionscentral.com, State Occupational Projections, 2012–2022 Long-Term Projections

Average Wages

Occupation	$/Hr.	Occupation	$/Hr.
Accountants and Auditors	27.70	Maids and Housekeeping Cleaners	9.44
Automotive Mechanics	17.29	Maintenance and Repair Workers	16.76
Bookkeepers	15.39	Marketing Managers	52.97
Carpenters	14.66	Nuclear Medicine Technologists	n/a
Cashiers	9.12	Nurses, Licensed Practical	19.18
Clerks, General Office	12.14	Nurses, Registered	29.28
Clerks, Receptionists/Information	12.72	Nursing Assistants	10.65
Clerks, Shipping/Receiving	14.88	Packers and Packagers, Hand	10.21
Computer Programmers	26.72	Physical Therapists	39.78
Computer Systems Analysts	28.85	Postal Service Mail Carriers	23.71
Computer User Support Specialists	19.61	Real Estate Brokers	n/a
Cooks, Restaurant	9.20	Retail Salespersons	10.84
Dentists	n/a	Sales Reps., Exc. Tech./Scientific	25.40
Electrical Engineers	37.44	Sales Reps., Tech./Scientific	26.49
Electricians	21.17	Secretaries, Exc. Legal/Med./Exec.	15.47
Financial Managers	52.53	Security Guards	13.58
First-Line Supervisors/Managers, Sales	18.71	Surgeons	n/a
Food Preparation Workers	9.46	Teacher Assistants	8.80
General and Operations Managers	44.55	Teachers, Elementary School	26.10
Hairdressers/Cosmetologists	13.01	Teachers, Secondary School	27.70
Internists	n/a	Telemarketers	n/a
Janitors and Cleaners	10.90	Truck Drivers, Heavy/Tractor-Trailer	21.06
Landscaping/Groundskeeping Workers	13.31	Truck Drivers, Light/Delivery Svcs.	16.84
Lawyers	48.77	Waiters and Waitresses	8.47

Note: Wage data covers the Athens-Clarke County, GA Metropolitan Statistical Area—see Appendix B for areas included; Hourly wages for elementary/secondary school teachers and teacher assistants were calculated by the editors from annual wage data assuming a 40 hour work week; n/a not available.
Source: Bureau of Labor Statistics, Metro Area Occupational Employment and Wage Estimates, May 2014

TAXES

State Corporate Income Tax Rates

State	Tax Rate (%)	Income Brackets ($)	Num. of Brackets	Financial Institution Tax Rate (%)[a]	Federal Income Tax Ded.
Georgia	6.0	Flat rate	1	6.0	No

Note: Tax rates as of January 1, 2015; (a) Rates listed are the corporate income tax rate applied to financial institutions or excise taxes based on income. Some states have other taxes based upon the value of deposits or shares.
Source: Federation of Tax Administrators, "State Corporate Income Tax Rates, 2015"

State Individual Income Tax Rates

State	Tax Rate (%)	Income Brackets ($)	Num. of Brackets	Personal Exempt. ($)[1]		Fed. Inc. Tax Ded.
				Single	Dependents	
Georgia	1.0 - 6.0	750 - 7,001 (h)	6	2,700	3,000	No

Note: Tax rates as of January 1, 2015; Local- and county-level taxes are not included; n/a not applicable; (1) Married joint filers generally receive double the single exemption; (h) The Georgia income brackets reported are for single individuals. For married couples filing jointly, the same tax rates apply to income brackets ranging from $1,000, to $10,000.
Source: Federation of Tax Administrators, "State Individual Income Tax Rates, 2015"

Various State and Local Tax Rates

State	State and Local Sales and Use (%)	State Sales and Use (%)	Gasoline[1] (¢/gal.)	Cigarette[2] ($/pack)	Spirits[3] ($/gal.)	Wine[4] ($/gal.)	Beer[5] ($/gal.)
Georgia	7.0	4.0	26.53	0.37	3.79 (f)	1.51	1.01 (q)

Note: All tax rates as of January 1, 2015; (1) The American Petroleum Institute has developed a methodology for determining the average tax rate on a gallon of fuel. Rates may include any of the following: excise taxes, environmental fees, storage tank fees, other fees or taxes, general sales tax, and local taxes. In states where gasoline is subject to the general sales tax, or where the fuel tax is based on the average sale price, the average rate determined by API is sensitive to changes in the price of gasoline. States that fully or partially apply general sales taxes to gasoline: CA, CO, GA, IL, IN, MI, NY; (2) The federal excise tax of $1.0066 per pack and local taxes are not included; (3) Rates are those applicable to off-premise sales of 40% alcohol by volume (a.b.v.) distilled spirits in 750ml containers. Local excise taxes are excluded; (4) Rates are those applicable to off-premise sales of 11% a.b.v. non-carbonated wine in 750ml containers; (5) Rates are those applicable to off-premise sales of 4.7% a.b.v. beer in 12 ounce containers; (f) Different rates are also applicable according to alcohol content, place of production, size of container, or place purchased (on- or off-premise or onboard airlines); (q) Includes statewide local tax in Alabama ($0.52) and Georgia ($0.53).
Source: Tax Foundation, 2015 Facts & Figures: How Does Your State Compare?

State Business Tax Climate Index Rankings

State	Overall Rank	Corporate Tax Index Rank	Individual Income Tax Index Rank	Sales Tax Index Rank	Unemployment Insurance Tax Index Rank	Property Tax Index Rank
Georgia	36	8	42	17	36	30

Note: The index is a measure of how each state's tax laws affect economic performance. The lower the rank, the more favorable a state's tax system is for business. States without a given tax are given a ranking of 1. The scores/rankings for the District of Columbia do not affect other states. The 2015 index represents the tax climate as of July 1, 2014.
Source: Tax Foundation, State Business Tax Climate Index 2015

COMMERCIAL UTILITIES

Typical Monthly Electric Bills

Area	Commercial Service ($/month)		Industrial Service ($/month)	
	1,500 kWh	40 kW demand 14,000 kWh	1,000 kW demand 200,000 kWh	50,000 kW demand 32,500,000 kWh
City	n/a	n/a	n/a	n/a
Average[1]	201	1,653	26,124	2,639,743

Note: Figures are based on annualized 2014 rates; (1) Average based on 180 utilities surveyed; n/a not available
Source: Edison Electric Institute, Typical Bills and Average Rates Report, Summer 2014

TRANSPORTATION

Means of Transportation to Work

Area	Car/Truck/Van		Public Transportation			Bicycle	Walked	Other Means	Worked at Home
	Drove Alone	Car-pooled	Bus	Subway	Railroad				
City	76.3	9.6	3.1	0.0	0.0	1.7	5.1	1.6	2.5
MSA[1]	80.1	8.9	1.9	0.0	0.0	1.1	3.4	1.3	3.3
U.S.	76.4	9.6	2.6	1.8	0.6	0.6	2.8	1.3	4.3

Note: Figures are percentages and cover workers 16 years of age and older; (1) Figures cover the Athens-Clarke County, GA Metropolitan Statistical Area—see Appendix B for areas included
Source: U.S. Census Bureau, 2011-2013 American Community Survey 3-Year Estimates

Travel Time to Work

Area	Less Than 10 Minutes	10 to 19 Minutes	20 to 29 Minutes	30 to 44 Minutes	45 to 59 Minutes	60 to 89 Minutes	90 Minutes or More
City	17.8	48.7	16.6	8.2	3.3	3.5	1.9
MSA[1]	14.2	40.8	21.2	13.4	4.1	3.7	2.6
U.S.	13.3	29.7	20.9	20.2	7.7	5.7	2.6

Note: Figures are percentages and include workers 16 years old and over; (1) Figures cover the Athens-Clarke County, GA Metropolitan Statistical Area—see Appendix B for areas included
Source: U.S. Census Bureau, 2011-2013 American Community Survey 3-Year Estimates

Travel Time Index

Area	1985	1990	1995	2000	2005	2010	2011
Urban Area[1]	n/a	n/a	n/a	n/a	n/a	n/a	n/a
Average[2]	1.09	1.14	1.16	1.19	1.23	1.18	1.18

Note: Travel Time Index—the ratio of travel time in the peak period to the travel time at free-flow conditions. For example, a value of 1.30 indicates a 20-minute free-flow trip takes 26 minutes in the peak. Free-flow speeds (60 mph on freeways and 35 mph on principal arterials) are used as the comparison threshold; (1) Data for the Athens-Clarke County, GA urban area was not available; (2) average of 498 urban areas
Source: Texas Transportation Institute, Urban Mobility Report 2012, December 2012

Public Transportation

Agency Name / Mode of Transportation	Vehicles Operated in Maximum Service	Annual Unlinked Passenger Trips (in thous.)	Annual Passenger Miles (in thous.)
Athens Transit System			
Bus (directly operated)	22	1,725.7	5,403.4
Demand Response (directly operated)	3	7.8	43.0

Source: Federal Transit Administration, National Transit Database, 2013

Air Transportation

Airport Name and Code / Type of Service	Passenger Airlines[1]	Passenger Enplanements	Freight Carriers[2]	Freight (lbs.)
Athens Municipal (AHN)				
Domestic service (U.S. carriers - 2014)	3	1,519	1	732
International service (U.S. carriers - 2013)	0	0	0	0

Note: (1) Includes all U.S.-based major, minor and commuter airlines that carried at least one passenger during the year; (2) Includes all U.S.-based airlines and freight carriers that transported at least one lb. of freight during the year.
Source: Bureau of Transportation Statistics, The Intermodal Transportation Database, Air Carriers: T-100 Domestic Market (U.S. Carriers), 2014; Bureau of Transportation Statistics, The Intermodal Transportation Database, Air Carriers: T-100 International Market (U.S. Carriers), 2013

Other Transportation Statistics

Major Highways:	CR-82 connecting to I-85 (18 miles)
Amtrak Service:	No
Major Waterways/Ports:	None

Source: Amtrak.com; Google Maps

BUSINESSES

Major Business Headquarters

Company Name	Rankings	
	Fortune[1]	Forbes[2]
No companies listed	-	-

Note: (1) Fortune 500—companies that produce a 10-K are ranked 1 to 500 based on 2013 revenue; (2) all private companies with at least $2 billion in annual revenue through the end of their most current fiscal year are ranked 1 to 221; companies listed are headquartered in the city; dashes indicate no ranking
Source: Fortune, "Fortune 500," June 16, 2014; Forbes, "America's Largest Private Companies," November 5, 2014

Minority- and Women-Owned Businesses

Group	All Firms		Firms with Paid Employees			
	Firms	Sales ($000)	Firms	Sales ($000)	Employees	Payroll ($000)
Asian	330	285,670	161	280,037	1,813	40,491
Black	(s)	(s)	(s)	(s)	(s)	(s)
Hispanic	311	22,829	16	11,624	81	2,166
Women	2,687	605,533	366	562,480	4,810	119,645
All Firms	10,181	8,756,927	2,435	8,454,434	48,844	1,391,992

Note: Figures cover firms located in the city; minority- and women-owned business are defined as firms in which the corresponding group own 51% or more of the stock or equity of the company; (s) estimates are suppressed when publication standards are not met
Source: U.S. Census Bureau, 2007 Economic Census, Survey of Business Owners (2012 Survey of Business Owners data will be released starting in June 2015)

HOTELS & CONVENTION CENTERS

Hotels/Motels

Area	5 Star		4 Star		3 Star		2 Star		1 Star		Not Rated	
	Num.	Pct.[3]	Num.	Pct.[3]	Num.	Pct.[3]	Num.	Pct.[3]	Num.	Pct.[3]	Num.	Pct.[3]
City[1]	0	0.0	2	2.4	10	11.9	65	77.4	3	3.6	4	4.8
Total[2]	166	0.9	1,264	7.0	5,718	31.8	9,340	52.0	411	2.3	1,070	6.0

Note: (1) Figures cover Athens and vicinity; (2) Figures cover all 100 cities in this book; (3) Percentage of hotels which have a given star rating; Star ratings are determined by expedia.com and offer an indication of the general quality of a particular hotel.
Source: expedia.com, April 2, 2015

Major Convention Centers

Name	Overall Space (sq. ft.)	Exhibit Space (sq. ft.)	Meeting Space (sq. ft.)	Meeting Rooms
The Classic Center	104,540	56,000	n/a	35

Note: Table includes convention centers located in the Athens-Clarke County, GA metro area; n/a not available
Source: Original research

Living Environment

COST OF LIVING

Cost of Living Index

Composite Index	Groceries	Housing	Utilities	Trans-portation	Health Care	Misc. Goods/ Services
n/a	n/a	n/a	n/a	n/a	n/a	n/a

Note: The Cost of Living Index measures regional differences in the cost of consumer goods and services, excluding taxes and non-consumer expenditures, for professional and managerial households in the top income quintile. It is based on more than 50,000 prices covering almost 60 different items for which prices are collected three times a year by chambers of commerce, economic development organizations or university applied economic centers in each participating urban area. The numbers shown should be read as a percentage above or below the national average of 100. For example, a value of 115.4 in the groceries column indicates that grocery prices are 15.4% higher than the national average. Small differences in the index numbers should not be interpreted as significant; n/a not available.
Source: The Council for Community and Economic Research, ACCRA Cost of Living Index, 2014

Grocery Prices

Area[1]	T-Bone Steak ($/pound)	Frying Chicken ($/pound)	Whole Milk ($/half gal.)	Eggs ($/dozen)	Orange Juice ($/64 oz.)	Coffee ($/11.5 oz.)
City[2]	n/a	n/a	n/a	n/a	n/a	n/a
Avg.	10.40	1.37	2.40	1.99	3.46	4.27
Min.	8.48	0.93	1.37	1.30	2.83	2.99
Max.	14.20	2.44	3.62	4.02	6.42	6.96

Note: (1) Values for the local area are compared with the average, minimum and maximum values for all 308 areas in the Cost of Living Index; (2) Figures cover the Athens GA urban area; n/a not available; **T-Bone Steak** *(price per pound);* **Frying Chicken** *(price per pound, whole fryer);* **Whole Milk** *(half gallon carton);* **Eggs** *(price per dozen, Grade A, large);* **Orange Juice** *(64 oz. Tropicana or Florida Natural);* **Coffee** *(11.5 oz. can, vacuum-packed, Maxwell House, Hills Bros, or Folgers).*
Source: The Council for Community and Economic Research, ACCRA Cost of Living Index, 2014

Housing and Utility Costs

Area[1]	New Home Price ($)	Apartment Rent ($/month)	All Electric ($/month)	Part Electric ($/month)	Other Energy ($/month)	Telephone ($/month)
City[2]	n/a	n/a	n/a	n/a	n/a	n/a
Avg.	305,838	919	181.00	93.66	73.14	27.95
Min.	183,142	480	112.00	42.06	23.42	17.16
Max.	1,358,576	3,851	594.00	180.03	440.99	40.42

Note: (1) Values for the local area are compared with the average, minimum and maximum values for all 308 areas in the Cost of Living Index; (2) Figures cover the Athens GA urban area; n/a not available; **New Home Price** *(2,400 sf living area, 8,000 sf lot, in urban area with full utilities);* **Apartment Rent** *(950 sf 2 bedroom/1.5 or 2 bath, unfurnished, excluding all utilities except water);* **All Electric** *(average monthly cost for an all-electric home);* **Part Electric** *(average monthly cost for a part-electric home);* **Other Energy** *(average monthly cost for natural gas, fuel oil, coal, wood, and any other forms of energy except electricity);* **Telephone** *(price includes basic monthly rate for a private residential line plus additional local usage charges incurred by a family of four).*
Source: The Council for Community and Economic Research, ACCRA Cost of Living Index, 2014

Health Care, Transportation, and Other Costs

Area[1]	Doctor ($/visit)	Dentist ($/visit)	Optometrist ($/visit)	Gasoline ($/gallon)	Beauty Salon ($/visit)	Men's Shirt ($)
City[2]	n/a	n/a	n/a	n/a	n/a	n/a
Avg.	102.86	87.89	97.66	3.44	34.37	26.74
Min.	67.47	65.78	51.18	3.00	17.43	12.79
Max.	173.50	150.14	235.00	4.33	64.28	49.50

Note: (1) Values for the local area are compared with the average, minimum and maximum values for all 308 areas in the Cost of Living Index; (2) Figures cover the Athens GA urban area; n/a not available; **Doctor** *(general practitioners routine exam of an established patient);* **Dentist** *(adult teeth cleaning and periodic oral examination);* **Optometrist** *(full vision eye exam for established adult patient);* **Gasoline** *(one gallon regular unleaded, national brand, including all taxes, cash price at self-service pump if available);* **Beauty Salon** *(woman's shampoo, trim, and blow-dry);* **Men's Shirt** *(cotton/polyester dress shirt, pinpoint weave, long sleeves).*
Source: The Council for Community and Economic Research, ACCRA Cost of Living Index, 2014

HOUSING

House Price Index (HPI)

Area	National Ranking[2]	Quarterly Change (%)	One-Year Change (%)	Five-Year Change (%)
MSA[1]	82	-0.57	6.20	-2.89
U.S.[3]	–	1.35	4.91	11.59

Note: The HPI is a weighted repeat sales index. It measures average price changes in repeat sales or refinancings on the same properties. This information is obtained by reviewing repeat mortgage transactions on single-family properties whose mortgages have been purchased or securitized by Fannie Mae or Freddie Mac in January 1975; (1) Athens-Clarke County Metropolitan Statistical Area—see Appendix B for areas included; (2) Rankings are based on annual percentage change for all metro areas containing at least 15,000 transactions over the last 10 years and ranges from 1 to 275; (3) figures based on a weighted average of Census Division estimates using a seasonally adjusted, purchase-only index; all figures are for the period ending December 31, 2014

Source: Federal Housing Finance Agency, House Price Index, February 26, 2015

Median Single-Family Home Prices

Area	2012	2013	2014p	Percent Change 2013 to 2014
MSA[1]	n/a	n/a	n/a	n/a
U.S. Average	177.2	197.4	209.0	5.9

Note: Figures are median sales prices of existing single-family homes in thousands of dollars; (p) preliminary; n/a not available; (1) Athens-Clarke County, GA Metropolitan Statistical Area—see Appendix B for areas included

Source: National Association of Realtors, Median Sales Price of Existing Single-Family Homes for Metropolitan Areas, 4th Quarter 2014

Qualifying Income Based on Median Sales Price of Existing Single-Family Homes

Area	With 5% Down ($)	With 10% Down ($)	With 20% Down ($)
MSA[1]	n/a	n/a	n/a
U.S. Average	45,863	43,449	38,621

Note: Figures are preliminary; Qualifying income is based on a mortgage rate of 4.0%. Monthly principal and interest payment is limited to 25% of income; n/a not available; (1) Athens-Clarke County, GA Metropolitan Statistical Area—see Appendix B for areas included

Source: National Association of Realtors, Qualifying Income Based on Median Sales Price of Existing Single-Family Homes for Metropolitan Areas, 4th Quarter 2014

Median Apartment Condo-Coop Home Prices

Area	2012	2013	2014p	Percent Change 2013 to 2014
MSA[1]	n/a	n/a	n/a	n/a
U.S. Average	173.7	194.9	205.1	5.2

Note: Figures are median sales prices of existing apartment condo-coop homes in thousands of dollars; (p) preliminary; n/a not available; (1) Athens-Clarke County, GA Metropolitan Statistical Area—see Appendix B for areas included

Source: National Association of Realtors, Median Sales Price of Existing Apartment Condo-Coop Homes for Metropolitan Areas, 4th Quarter 2014

Gross Monthly Rent

Area	Under $200	$200 -299	$300 -499	$500 -749	$750 -999	$1,000 -1,499	$1,500 and up	Median ($)
City	2.4	2.5	8.5	37.1	27.2	16.5	5.9	747
MSA[1]	2.1	2.6	8.6	36.8	27.0	17.1	5.8	749
U.S.	1.7	3.2	7.8	22.1	24.3	26.0	14.9	900

Note: Figures are percentages except for Median; Gross rent is the contract rent plus the estimated average monthly cost of utilities (electricity, gas, and water and sewer) and fuels (oil, coal, kerosene, wood, etc.) if these are paid by the renter (or paid for the renter by someone else); (1) Figures cover the Athens-Clarke County, GA Metropolitan Statistical Area—see Appendix B for areas included

Source: U.S. Census Bureau, 2011-2013 American Community Survey 3-Year Estimates

Homeownership Rate

Area	2007 (%)	2008 (%)	2009 (%)	2010 (%)	2011 (%)	2012 (%)	2013 (%)	2014 (%)
MSA[1]	n/a	n/a	n/a	n/a	n/a	n/a	n/a	n/a
U.S.	68.1	67.8	67.4	66.9	66.1	65.4	65.1	64.5

Note: (1) Figures cover the Athens-Clarke County, GA Metropolitan Statistical Area—see Appendix B for areas included; n/a not available
Source: U.S. Census Bureau, Housing Vacancies and Homeownership Annual Statistics: 2014

Year Housing Structure Built

Area	2010 or Later	2000 -2009	1990 -1999	1980 -1989	1970 -1979	1960 -1969	1950 -1959	1940 -1949	Before 1940	Median Year
City	0.8	18.3	19.5	19.3	17.9	10.4	6.2	3.1	4.5	1984
MSA[1]	0.8	20.2	20.2	18.7	17.4	9.6	5.5	2.7	5.0	1985
U.S.	0.9	15.0	13.9	13.8	15.8	11.0	10.9	5.4	13.3	1976

Note: Figures are percentages except for Median Year; (1) Figures cover the Athens-Clarke County, GA Metropolitan Statistical Area—see Appendix B for areas included
Source: U.S. Census Bureau, 2011-2013 American Community Survey 3-Year Estimates

HEALTH

Health Risk Data

Category	MSA[1] (%)	U.S. (%)
Adults aged 18–64 who have any kind of health care coverage	n/a	79.6
Adults who reported being in good or excellent health	n/a	83.1
Adults who are current smokers	n/a	19.6
Adults who are heavy drinkers[2]	n/a	6.1
Adults who are binge drinkers[3]	n/a	16.9
Adults who are overweight (BMI 25.0 - 29.9)	n/a	35.8
Adults who are obese (BMI 30.0 - 99.8)	n/a	27.6
Adults who participated in any physical activities in the past month	n/a	77.1
Adults 50+ who have ever had a sigmoidoscopy or colonoscopy	n/a	67.3
Women aged 40+ who have had a mammogram within the past two years	n/a	74.0
Men aged 40+ who have had a PSA test within the past two years	n/a	45.2
Adults aged 65+ who have had flu shot within the past year	n/a	60.1
Adults who always wear a seatbelt	n/a	93.8

Note: Data as of 2012 unless otherwise noted; n/a not available; (1) Figures cover the Athens-Clarke County, GA Metropolitan Statistical Area—see Appendix B for areas included; (2) Heavy drinkers are classified as males having more than two drinks per day or females having more than one drink per day; (3) Binge drinkers are classified as males having five or more drinks on one occasion or females having four or more drinks on one occasion
Source: Centers for Disease Control and Prevention, Behaviorial Risk Factor Surveillance System, SMART: Selected Metropolitan/Micropolitan Area Risk Trends, 2012 (Note: the CDC has discontinued this dataset but will be releasing a replacement in late 2015)

Chronic Health Indicators

Category	MSA[1] (%)	U.S. (%)
Adults who have ever been told they had a heart attack	n/a	4.5
Adults who have ever been told they had a stroke	n/a	2.9
Adults who have been told they currently have asthma	n/a	8.9
Adults who have ever been told they have arthritis	n/a	25.7
Adults who have ever been told they have diabetes[2]	n/a	9.7
Adults who have ever been told they had skin cancer	n/a	5.7
Adults who have ever been told they had any other types of cancer	n/a	6.5
Adults who have ever been told they have COPD	n/a	6.2
Adults who have ever been told they have kidney disease	n/a	2.5
Adults who have ever been told they have a form of depression	n/a	18.0

Note: Data as of 2012 unless otherwise noted; n/a not available; (1) Figures cover the Athens-Clarke County, GA Metropolitan Statistical Area—see Appendix B for areas included; (2) Figures do not include pregnancy-related, borderline, or pre-diabetes
Source: Centers for Disease Control and Prevention, Behaviorial Risk Factor Surveillance System, SMART: Selected Metropolitan/Micropolitan Area Risk Trends, 2012 (Note: the CDC has discontinued this dataset but will be releasing a replacement in late 2015)

Mortality Rates for the Top 10 Causes of Death in the U.S.

ICD-10[a] Sub-Chapter	ICD-10[a] Code	Age-Adjusted Mortality Rate[1] per 100,000 population	
		County[2]	U.S.
Malignant neoplasms	C00-C97	162.7	166.2
Ischaemic heart diseases	I20-I25	74.5	105.7
Other forms of heart disease	I30-I51	66.1	49.3
Chronic lower respiratory diseases	J40-J47	39.7	42.1
Organic, including symptomatic, mental disorders	F01-F09	65.2	38.1
Cerebrovascular diseases	I60-I69	43.7	37.0
Other external causes of accidental injury	W00-X59	26.5	26.9
Other degenerative diseases of the nervous system	G30-G31	20.3	25.6
Diabetes mellitus	E10-E14	29.5	21.3
Hypertensive diseases	I10-I15	34.1	19.4

Note: (a) ICD-10 = International Classification of Diseases 10th Revision; (1) Mortality rates are a three year average covering 2011-2013; (2) Figures cover Clarke County
Source: Centers for Disease Control and Prevention, National Center for Health Statistics. Compressed Mortality File 1999-2013 on CDC WONDER Online Database, released October 2014. Data are compiled from the Compressed Mortality File 1999-2013, Series 20 No. 2S, 2014.

Mortality Rates for Selected Causes of Death

ICD-10[a] Sub-Chapter	ICD-10[a] Code	Age-Adjusted Mortality Rate[1] per 100,000 population	
		County[2]	U.S.
Assault	X85-Y09	*3.0	5.2
Diseases of the liver	K70-K76	16.0	13.2
Human immunodeficiency virus (HIV) disease	B20-B24	Suppressed	2.2
Influenza and pneumonia	J09-J18	10.7	15.4
Intentional self-harm	X60-X84	15.7	12.5
Malnutrition	E40-E46	Suppressed	0.9
Obesity and other hyperalimentation	E65-E68	Suppressed	1.8
Renal failure	N17-N19	12.2	13.1
Transport accidents	V01-V99	6.3	11.7
Viral hepatitis	B15-B19	Suppressed	2.2

Note: (a) ICD-10 = International Classification of Diseases 10th Revision; (1) Mortality rates are a three year average covering 2011-2013; (2) Figures cover Clarke County; (*) Unreliable data as per CDC
Source: Centers for Disease Control and Prevention, National Center for Health Statistics. Compressed Mortality File 1999-2013 on CDC WONDER Online Database, released October 2014. Data are compiled from the Compressed Mortality File 1999-2013, Series 20 No. 2S, 2014.

Health Insurance Coverage

Area	With Health Insurance	With Private Health Insurance	With Public Health Insurance	Without Health Insurance	Population Under Age 18 Without Health Insurance
City	82.4	66.8	23.1	17.6	9.5
MSA[1]	83.8	67.2	25.1	16.2	7.2
U.S.	85.2	65.2	31.0	14.8	7.3

Note: Figures are percentages that cover the civilian noninstitutionalized population; (1) Figures cover the Athens-Clarke County, GA Metropolitan Statistical Area—see Appendix B for areas included
Source: U.S. Census Bureau, 2011-2013 American Community Survey 3-Year Estimates

Number of Medical Professionals

Area[1]	MDs[2]	DOs[2,3]	Dentists	Podiatrists	Chiropractors	Optometrists
Local (number)	335	11	66	6	24	21
Local (rate[4])	278.5	9.1	54.5	5.0	19.8	17.3
U.S. (rate[4])	270.0	20.2	63.1	5.7	25.2	14.9

Note: Data as of 2013 unless noted; (1) Local data covers Clarke County; (2) Data as of 2012 and includes all active, non-federal physicians; (3) Doctor of Osteopathic Medicine; (4) rate per 100,000 population
Source: U.S. Department of Health and Human Services, Health Resources and Services Administration, Bureau of Health Professions, Area Resource File (ARF) 2013-2014

EDUCATION

Public School District Statistics

District Name	Schls	Pupils	Pupil/ Teacher Ratio	Minority Pupils[1] (%)	Free Lunch Eligible[2] (%)	IEP[3] (%)
Clarke County	21	12,682	12.9	80.8	76.3	12.3

Note: Table includes school districts with 2,000 or more students; (1) Percentage of students that are not non-Hispanic white; (2) Percentage of students that are eligible for the free lunch program; (3) Percentage of students that have an Individualized Education Program.

Source: U.S. Department of Education, National Center for Education Statistics, Common Core of Data, Local Education Agency (School District) Universe Survey: School Year 2012-2013; U.S. Department of Education, National Center for Education Statistics, Common Core of Data, Public Elementary/Secondary School Universe Survey: School Year 2012-2013

Highest Level of Education

Area	Less than H.S.	H.S. Diploma	Some College, No Deg.	Associate Degree	Bachelor's Degree	Master's Degree	Prof. School Degree	Doctorate Degree
City	13.6	22.6	20.2	4.8	19.0	11.9	2.5	5.3
MSA[1]	14.1	26.5	20.6	5.2	17.1	10.4	2.5	3.7
U.S.	13.7	28.0	21.2	7.9	18.2	7.7	1.9	1.3

Note: Figures cover persons age 25 and over; (1) Figures cover the Athens-Clarke County, GA Metropolitan Statistical Area—see Appendix B for areas included

Source: U.S. Census Bureau, 2011-2013 American Community Survey 3-Year Estimates

Educational Attainment by Race

Area	High School Graduate or Higher (%)					Bachelor's Degree or Higher (%)				
	Total	White	Black	Asian	Hisp.[2]	Total	White	Black	Asian	Hisp.[2]
City	86.4	90.3	80.0	91.5	53.0	38.7	50.5	10.5	69.9	9.9
MSA[1]	85.9	88.7	78.2	88.7	53.6	33.5	39.0	10.9	63.1	10.3
U.S.	86.3	88.3	83.1	85.7	64.0	29.1	30.4	18.8	50.7	13.7

Note: Figures shown cover persons 25 years old and over; (1) Figures cover the Athens-Clarke County, GA Metropolitan Statistical Area—see Appendix B for areas included; (2) People of Hispanic origin can be of any race

Source: U.S. Census Bureau, 2011-2013 American Community Survey 3-Year Estimates

School Enrollment by Grade and Control

Area	Preschool (%)		Kindergarten (%)		Grades 1 - 4 (%)		Grades 5 - 8 (%)		Grades 9 - 12 (%)	
	Public	Private	Public	Private	Public	Private	Public	Private	Public	Private
City	67.4	32.6	84.6	15.4	93.5	6.5	90.1	9.9	89.3	10.7
MSA[1]	67.9	32.1	88.5	11.5	93.3	6.7	89.8	10.2	87.4	12.6
U.S.	57.7	42.3	87.9	12.1	89.9	10.1	90.0	10.0	90.7	9.3

Note: Figures shown cover persons 3 years old and over; (1) Figures cover the Athens-Clarke County, GA Metropolitan Statistical Area—see Appendix B for areas included

Source: U.S. Census Bureau, 2011-2013 American Community Survey 3-Year Estimates

Average Salaries of Public School Classroom Teachers

Area	2013-14		2014-15		Percent Change 2013-14 to 2014-15	Percent Change 2004-05 to 2014-15
	Dollars	Rank[1]	Dollars	Rank[1]		
GEORGIA	52,924	24	53,382	24	0.87	14.7
U.S. Average	56,610	–	57,379	–	1.36	20.8

Note: (1) State rank ranges from 1 to 51 where 1 indicates highest salary.

Source: National Education Association, Rankings & Estimates: Rankings of the States 2014 and Estimates of School Statistics 2015, March 2015

Higher Education

Four-Year Colleges			Two-Year Colleges			Medical Schools[1]	Law Schools[2]	Voc/ Tech[3]
Public	Private Non-profit	Private For-profit	Public	Private Non-profit	Private For-profit			
1	0	0	1	0	0	0	1	1

Note: Figures cover institutions located within the city limits and include main campuses only; (1) includes schools accredited by the Liaison Committee on Medical Education and the American Osteopathic Association's Commission on Osteopathic College Accreditation; (2) includes ABA-accredited schools, schools with provisional ABA accreditation, and state accredited schools; (3) includes all schools with programs that are less than 2 years.

Source: National Center for Education Statistics, Integrated Postsecondary Education System (IPEDS), 2013-14; Association of American Medical Colleges, Member List, May 1, 2015; American Osteopathic Association, Member List, May 1, 2015; Law School Admission Council, Official Guide to ABA-Approved Law Schools Online, May 1, 2015; Wikipedia, List of Medical Schools in the United States, May 1, 2015; Wikipedia, List of Law Schools in the United States, May 1, 2015

According to *U.S. News & World Report,* the Athens-Clarke County, GA metro area is home to one of the best national universities in the U.S.: **University of Georgia** (#62). The indicators used to capture academic quality fall into a number of categories: assessment by administrators at peer institutions; retention of students; faculty resources; student selectivity; financial resources; alumni giving; high school counselor ratings of colleges; and graduation rate. *U.S. News & World Report, "America's Best Colleges 2015"*

According to *U.S. News & World Report,* the Athens-Clarke County, GA metro area is home to one of the top 100 law schools in the U.S.: **University of Georgia** (#31). The rankings are based on a weighted average of 12 measures of quality: peer assessment score; assessment score by lawyers/judges; median LSAT scores; median undergrad GPA; acceptance rate; employment rates for graduates; placement success; bar passage rate; faculty resources; expenditures per student; student/faculty ratio; and library resources. *U.S. News & World Report, "America's Best Graduate Schools, Law, 2016"*

According to *U.S. News & World Report,* the Athens-Clarke County, GA metro area is home to one of the top 75 business schools in the U.S.: **University of Georgia (Terry)** (#53). The rankings are based on a weighted average of the following nine measures: quality assessment; peer assessment; recruiter assessment; placement success; mean starting salary and bonus; student selectivity; mean GMAT and GRE scores; mean undergraduate GPA; and acceptance rate. *U.S. News & World Report, "America's Best Graduate Schools, Business, 2016"*

PRESIDENTIAL ELECTION

2012 Presidential Election Results

Area	Obama (%)	Romney (%)	Other (%)
Clarke County	63.3	34.4	2.4
U.S.	51.0	47.2	1.8

Note: Results may not add to 100% due to rounding

Source: Dave Leip's Atlas of U.S. Presidential Elections

EMPLOYERS

Major Employers

Company Name	Industry
Agricultural Research Service	Regulation of agricultural marketing
Athens Regional Medical Center	General medical and surgical hospitals
Athens-Clarke County, Unified Govt of	Executive offices, local government
Athens-Clarke County, Unified Govt of	Air, water, & solid waste management, county govt
Carrier Corporation	Refrigeration equipment, complete
Certainteed Corporation	Insulation: rock wool, slag, and silica minerals
Flowers	Gifts and novelties
Georgia Power Company	Electric services
Island Apparel	Men's and boy's trousers and slacks
McLane/Southeast	Groceries, general line
Power Partners	Power, distribution and specialty transformers
St Mary's Health Care System	General medical and surgical hospitals
The University of Georgia	Colleges and universities
The University of Georgia	Vocational schools
United States Postal Service	U.s. postal service
University of Georgia Athletic Assn	Athletic organizations
Wal-Mart Stores	Department stores, discount

Note: Companies shown are located within the Athens-Clarke County, GA Metropolitan Statistical Area.
Source: Hoovers.com; Wikipedia

PUBLIC SAFETY

Crime Rate

Area	All Crimes	Violent Crimes				Property Crimes		
		Murder	Forcible Rape	Robbery	Aggrav. Assault	Burglary	Larceny -Theft	Motor Vehicle Theft
City	3,727.9	1.7	30.8	104.1	199.8	805.0	2,424.2	162.3
Suburbs[1]	2,766.6	0.0	19.4	11.6	141.0	539.4	1,953.0	102.2
Metro[2]	3,351.4	1.0	26.3	67.9	176.8	701.0	2,239.7	138.8
U.S.	3,098.6	4.5	25.2	109.1	229.1	610.0	1,899.4	221.3

Note: Figures are crimes per 100,000 population; (1) All areas within the metro area that are located outside the city limits; (2) Figures cover the Athens-Clarke County, GA Metropolitan Statistical Area—see Appendix B for areas included
Source: FBI Uniform Crime Reports, 2013

Hate Crimes

Area	Number of Quarters Reported	Number of Incidents per Bias Motivation						
		Race	Religion	Sexual Orientation	Ethnicity	Disability	Gender	Gender Identity
City	4	0	0	0	0	0	0	0
U.S.	4	2,871	1,031	1,233	655	83	18	31

Source: Federal Bureau of Investigation, Hate Crime Statistics 2013

Identity Theft Consumer Complaints

Area	Complaints	Complaints per 100,000 Population	Rank[2]
MSA[1]	120	60.6	250
U.S.	332,646	104.3	-

Note: (1) Figures cover the Athens-Clarke County, GA Metropolitan Statistical Area—see Appendix B for areas included; (2) Rank ranges from 1 to 380 where 1 indicates greatest number of identity theft complaints per 100,000 population
Source: Federal Trade Commission, Consumer Sentinel Network Data Book for January–December 2014

Fraud and Other Consumer Complaints

Area	Complaints	Complaints per 100,000 Population	Rank[2]
MSA[1]	560	283.0	340
U.S.	2,250,205	705.7	-

Note: (1) Figures cover the Athens-Clarke County, GA Metropolitan Statistical Area—see Appendix B for areas included; (2) Rank ranges from 1 to 380 where 1 indicates greatest number of identity theft complaints per 100,000 population
Source: Federal Trade Commission, Consumer Sentinel Network Data Book for January–December 2014

RECREATION

Culture

Dance[1]	Theatre[1]	Instrumental Music[1]	Vocal Music[1]	Series and Festivals	Museums and Art Galleries[2]	Zoos and Aquariums[3]
2	2	0	0	1	13	0

Note: (1) Professional perfoming groups; (2) Based on organizations with SIC code 8412; (3) AZA-accredited
Source: The Grey House Performing Arts Directory, 2015-16; Association of Zoos & Aquariums, AZA Member Zoos & Aquariums, April 2015; www.AccuLeads.com, April 2015

Professional Sports Teams

Team Name	League	Year Established
No teams are located in the metro area		

Source: Wikipedia, Major Professional Sports Teams of the United States and Canada, April 2015

CLIMATE

Average and Extreme Temperatures

Temperature	Jan	Feb	Mar	Apr	May	Jun	Jul	Aug	Sep	Oct	Nov	Dec	Yr.
Extreme High (°F)	79	80	85	93	95	101	105	102	98	95	84	77	105
Average High (°F)	52	56	64	73	80	86	88	88	82	73	63	54	72
Average Temp. (°F)	43	46	53	62	70	77	79	79	73	63	53	45	62
Average Low (°F)	33	36	42	51	59	66	70	69	64	52	42	35	52
Extreme Low (°F)	-8	5	10	26	37	46	53	55	36	28	3	0	-8

Note: Figures cover the years 1945-1990
Source: National Climatic Data Center, International Station Meteorological Climate Summary, 9/96

Average Precipitation/Snowfall/Humidity

Precip./Humidity	Jan	Feb	Mar	Apr	May	Jun	Jul	Aug	Sep	Oct	Nov	Dec	Yr.
Avg. Precip. (in.)	4.7	4.6	5.7	4.3	4.0	3.5	5.1	3.6	3.4	2.8	3.8	4.2	49.8
Avg. Snowfall (in.)	1	1	Tr	Tr	0	0	0	0	0	0	Tr	Tr	2
Avg. Rel. Hum. 7am (%)	79	77	78	78	82	83	88	89	88	84	81	79	82
Avg. Rel. Hum. 4pm (%)	56	50	48	45	49	52	57	56	56	51	52	55	52

Note: Figures cover the years 1945-1990; Tr = Trace amounts (<0.05 in. of rain; <0.5 in. of snow)
Source: National Climatic Data Center, International Station Meteorological Climate Summary, 9/96

Weather Conditions

Temperature			Daytime Sky			Precipitation		
10°F & below	32°F & below	90°F & above	Clear	Partly cloudy	Cloudy	0.01 inch or more precip.	0.1 inch or more snow/ice	Thunder-storms
1	49	38	98	147	120	116	3	48

Note: Figures are average number of days per year and cover the years 1945-1990
Source: National Climatic Data Center, International Station Meteorological Climate Summary, 9/96

HAZARDOUS WASTE

Superfund Sites

Athens has no sites on the EPA's Superfund Final National Priorities List. There are a total of 1,322 Superfund sites on the list in the U.S. *U.S. Environmental Protection Agency, Final National Priorities List, April 14, 2015*

AIR & WATER QUALITY

Air Quality Trends: Ozone

	2004	2005	2006	2007	2008	2009	2010	2011	2012	2013
MSA[1]	0.078	0.082	0.086	0.083	0.077	0.067	0.073	0.075	0.071	0.060

Note: (1) Data covers the Athens-Clarke County, GA Metropolitan Statistical Area—see Appendix B for areas included. The values shown are the composite ozone concentration averages among trend sites based on the highest fourth daily maximum 8-hour concentration in parts per million. These trends are based on sites having an adequate record of monitoring data during the trend period. Data from exceptional events are included.
Source: U.S. Environmental Protection Agency, Air Quality Monitoring Information, "Air Quality Trends by City, 2000-2013"

Air Quality Index

Area	Percent of Days when Air Quality was...[2]					AQI Statistics[2]	
	Good	Moderate	Unhealthy for Sensitive Groups	Unhealthy	Very Unhealthy	Maximum	Median
MSA[1]	70.1	29.9	0.0	0.0	0.0	92	41

Note: (1) Data covers the Athens-Clarke County, GA Metropolitan Statistical Area—see Appendix B for areas included; (2) Based on 358 days with AQI data in 2014. Air Quality Index (AQI) is an index for reporting daily air quality. EPA calculates the AQI for five major air pollutants regulated by the Clean Air Act: ground-level ozone, particle pollution (aka particulate matter), carbon monoxide, sulfur dioxide, and nitrogen dioxide. The AQI runs from 0 to 500. The higher the AQI value, the greater the level of air pollution and the greater the health concern. There are six AQI categories: "Good" AQI is between 0 and 50. Air quality is considered satisfactory; "Moderate" AQI is between 51 and 100. Air quality is acceptable; "Unhealthy for Sensitive Groups" When AQI values are between 101 and 150, members of sensitive groups may experience health effects; "Unhealthy" When AQI values are between 151 and 200 everyone may begin to experience health effects; "Very Unhealthy" AQI values between 201 and 300 trigger a health alert; "Hazardous" AQI values over 300 trigger warnings of emergency conditions (not shown).
Source: U.S. Environmental Protection Agency, Air Quality Index Report, 2014

Air Quality Index Pollutants

Area	Percent of Days when AQI Pollutant was...[2]					
	Carbon Monoxide	Nitrogen Dioxide	Ozone	Sulfur Dioxide	Particulate Matter 2.5	Particulate Matter 10
MSA[1]	0.0	0.0	21.8	0.0	78.2	0.0

Note: (1) Data covers the Athens-Clarke County, GA Metropolitan Statistical Area—see Appendix B for areas included; (2) Based on 358 days with AQI data in 2014. The Air Quality Index (AQI) is an index for reporting daily air quality. EPA calculates the AQI for five major air pollutants regulated by the Clean Air Act: ground-level ozone, particle pollution (also known as particulate matter), carbon monoxide, sulfur dioxide, and nitrogen dioxide. The AQI runs from 0 to 500. The higher the AQI value, the greater the level of air pollution and the greater the health concern.
Source: U.S. Environmental Protection Agency, Air Quality Index Report, 2014

Maximum Air Pollutant Concentrations: Particulate Matter, Ozone, CO and Lead

	Particulate Matter 10 (ug/m^3)	Particulate Matter 2.5 Wtd AM (ug/m^3)	Particulate Matter 2.5 24-Hr (ug/m^3)	Ozone (ppm)	Carbon Monoxide (ppm)	Lead (ug/m^3)
MSA[1] Level	n/a	9.7	28	0.06	n/a	n/a
NAAQS[2]	150	15	35	0.075	9	0.15
Met NAAQS[2]	n/a	Yes	Yes	Yes	n/a	n/a

Note: (1) Data covers the Athens-Clarke County, GA Metropolitan Statistical Area—see Appendix B for areas included; Data from exceptional events are included; (2) National Ambient Air Quality Standards; ppm = parts per million; ug/m^3 = micrograms per cubic meter; n/a not available.
Concentrations: Particulate Matter 10 (coarse particulate)—highest second maximum 24-hour concentration; Particulate Matter 2.5 Wtd AM (fine particulate)—highest weighted annual mean concentration; Particulate Matter 2.5 24-Hour (fine particulate)—highest 98th percentile 24-hour concentration; Ozone—highest fourth daily maximum 8-hour concentration; Carbon Monoxide—highest second maximum non-overlapping 8-hour concentration; Lead—maximum running 3-month average
Source: U.S. Environmental Protection Agency, Air Quality Monitoring Information, "Air Quality Statistics by City, 2013"

Maximum Air Pollutant Concentrations: Nitrogen Dioxide and Sulfur Dioxide

	Nitrogen Dioxide AM (ppb)	Nitrogen Dioxide 1-Hr (ppb)	Sulfur Dioxide AM (ppb)	Sulfur Dioxide 1-Hr (ppb)	Sulfur Dioxide 24-Hr (ppb)
MSA[1] Level	n/a	n/a	n/a	n/a	n/a
NAAQS[2]	53	100	30	75	140
Met NAAQS[2]	n/a	n/a	n/a	n/a	n/a

Note: (1) Data covers the Athens-Clarke County, GA Metropolitan Statistical Area—see Appendix B for areas included; Data from exceptional events are included; (2) National Ambient Air Quality Standards; ppm = parts per million; ug/m^3 = micrograms per cubic meter; n/a not available.

Concentrations: Nitrogen Dioxide AM—highest arithmetic mean concentration; Nitrogen Dioxide 1-Hr—highest 98th percentile 1-hour daily maximum concentration; Sulfur Dioxide AM—highest annual mean concentration; Sulfur Dioxide 1-Hr—highest 99th percentile 1-hour daily maximum concentration; Sulfur Dioxide 24-Hr—highest second maximum 24-hour concentration

Source: U.S. Environmental Protection Agency, Air Quality Monitoring Information, "Air Quality Statistics by City, 2013"

Drinking Water

Water System Name	Pop. Served	Primary Water Source Type	Violations[1] Health Based	Violations[1] Monitoring/ Reporting
Athens-Clarke Co. Water System	120,266	Surface	0	0

Note: (1) Based on violation data from January 1, 2014 to December 31, 2014 (includes unresolved violations from earlier years)

Source: U.S. Environmental Protection Agency, Office of Ground Water and Drinking Water, Safe Drinking Water Information System (based on data extracted January 27, 2015)

Atlanta, Georgia

Background

Atlanta was born of a rough-and-tumble past, first as a natural outgrowth of a thriving railroad network in the 1840s, and second as a resilient go-getter that proudly rose again above the rubble of the Civil War.

Blanketed over the rolling hills of the Piedmont Plateau, at the foot of the Blue Ridge Mountains, Georgia's capital stands 1,000 feet above sea level. Atlanta is located in the northwest corner of Georgia where the terrain is rolling to hilly, and slopes downward to the east, west, and south.

Atlanta proper begins at the "terminus," or zero mile mark, of the now defunct Western and Atlantic Railroad Line. However its metropolitan area comprises 28 counties that include Fulton, DeKalb, Clayton and Gwinnet, among others. Population-wise, Atlanta is the largest city in the southeast United States, and has been growing at a steady rate for the last decade. In 2007, the census bureau declared Atlanta the fastest growing metropolitan area in the nation. Understandably, the city contributes to nearly two thirds of the state's economy.

Within the city itself, Atlanta's has a diversified economy that allows for employment in a variety of sectors such as manufacturing, retail, and government. The city hosts many of the nation's Fortune 500 company headquarters, including CNN headquarters, as well as the nation's Centers for Disease Control and Prevention (CDC).

These accomplishments are the result of an involved city government that seeks to work closely with its business community, due in part to a change in the city charter in 1974, when greater administrative powers were vested in the mayoral office, and the city inaugurated its first black mayor.

As middle class residents, both white and black, continue to move to the suburbs separating themselves from Atlanta's old downtown, the city faces the complex issue of where it plans to move as an urban center in light of the conflict between the city and its surroundings.

While schools in the city remain predominantly black and schools in its suburbs predominantly white, Atlanta boasts a racially progressive climate. The Martin Luther King, Jr. Historic Site and Preservation District is located in the Sweet Auburn neighborhood, which includes King's birth home and the Ebenezer Baptist Church, where both he and his father preached. The city's consortium of black colleges that includes Morehouse College and the Interdenominational Theological Center testifies to the city's appreciation for a people who have always been one-third of Atlanta's population. Atlanta has become a major regional center for film and television production in recent years, with Tyler Perry Studios, TurnerStudios and EVE/ScreenGems Studio in the city.

Indeed, King is one of Atlanta's two Nobel Peace Prize winners. The second, former President Jimmy Carter, famously of Plains, Georgia, also brings his name to Atlanta as namesake to the Carter Center. Devoted to human rights, the center is operated with neighboring Emory University, and sits adjacent to the Jimmy Carter Library and Museum on a hill overlooking the city. Habitat for Humanity, also founded by Carter, moved its international administrative headquarters to Atlanta in 2006.

Hartsfield-Jackson Atlanta International Airport, the world's busiest passenger airport, underwent significant expansion in recent years. MARTA, the city's public transport system, is the nation's 9th largest and transports on average 500,000 passengers daily on a 48-mile, 38-station rapid rail system with connections to hundreds of bus routes.

The Appalachian chain of mountains, the Gulf of Mexico, and the Atlantic Ocean influence Atlanta's climate. Temperatures are moderate to hot throughout the year, but extended periods of heat are unusual and 100-degree heat is rarely experienced. Atlanta winters are mild with a few, short-lived cold spells. Summers can be humid. A rare event occurred in March 2008, when a tornado caused considerable damage to the city.

Rankings

General Rankings

- Atlanta appeared on *Business Insider's* list of the "15 Hottest American Cities for 2015." Criteria: job and population growth; demographics; affordability; livability; residents' health and welfare; technological innovation; sustainability; culture favoring youth and creativity. *www.businessinsider.com, "The Fifteen Hottest American Cities for 2015," November 19, 2014*
- Atlanta was selected as one of America's best cities by *Bloomberg Businessweek.* The city ranked #16 out of 50. Criteria: leisure attributes (the number of restaurants, bars, libraries, museums, professional sports teams, and park acres by population); educational attributes (public school performance, the number of colleges, and graduate degree holders); economic factors (2011 income and June and July 2012 unemployment); crime; and air quality. *Bloomberg BusinessWeek, "America's Best Cities," September 26, 2012*
- Atlanta was selected as one of "America's Favorite Cities." The city ranked #5 in the "Type of Trip: Gay-friendly Vacation" category. Respondents to an online survey were asked to rate 38 top urban destinations in the United States from a visitor's perspective. Criteria: gay-friendly. *Travel + Leisure, "America's Favorite Cities 20143"*
- The human resources consulting firm Mercer ranked 230 cities worldwide in terms of overall quality of life. Atlanta ranked #66. Criteria: political, social, economic, and socio-cultural factors; medical and health considerations; schools and education; public services and transportation; recreation; consumer goods; housing; and natural environment. *Mercer, "Mercer 2015 Quality of Living Survey," March 4, 2015*

Business/Finance Rankings

- Measuring indicators of "tolerance"—the nonjudgmental environment that "attracts open-minded and new-thinking kinds of people"— as well as concentrations of technological and economic innovators, analysts identified the most creative American metro areas. On the resulting 2012 Creativity Index, the Atlanta metro area placed #19. *www.thedailybeast.com, "Boulder, Ann Arbor, Tucson & More: 20 Most Creative U.S. Cities," June 26, 2012*
- The personal finance site NerdWallet scored the nation's 50 largest American cities according to how friendly a business climate they offer to would-be entrepreneurs. Criteria included access to funding, human capital, local economy, and business-friendliness as judged by small business owners. On the resulting list of most welcoming cities, Atlanta ranked #6. *www.nerdwallet.com, "Best Cities to Start a Business," May 7, 2014*
- Based on metro area social media reviews, the employment opinion group Glassdoor surveyed 50 of the largest U.S. metro areas on measures including compensation and benefits, satisfaction with management, business outlook, and number of employers hiring. The Atlanta metro area was ranked #18 in overall employee satisfaction. *www.glassdoor.com, "Employment Satisfaction Report Card by City," June 13, 2014*
- In its Competitive Alternatives report, consulting firm KPMG analyzed the 27 largest metropolitan statistical areas according to 26 cost components (such as taxes, labor costs, and utilities) and 30 non-cost-related variables (such as crime rates and number of universities). The business website 24/7 Wall Street examined the KPMG findings, adding to the mix current unemployment rates, GDP, median income, and employment decline during the last recession and "projected" recovery. It identified the Atlanta metro area as #2 among the ten best American cities for business. *247wallst.com, "Best American Cities for Business," April 4, 2012*
- In a survey of economic confidence in the nation's 50 largest metropolitan areas conducted January–December 2014, the Atlanta metro area placed #21, according to Gallup's 2014 Economic Confidence Index. *Gallup, "San Jose and San Francisco Lead in Economic Confidence," March 19, 2015*
- The Brookings Institution ranked the 50 largest cities in the U.S. based on income inequality. Atlanta was ranked #1. (#1 = greatest ineqality). Criteria: the cities were ranked based on the "95/20 ratio," a figure representing the income at which a household earns more than 95 percent of all other households, divided by the income at which a household earns more than only 20 percent of all other households. *Brookings Institution, "Income Inequality in America's 50 Largest Cities, 2007-2013," March 17, 2015*

- Atlanta was ranked #39 out of 100 metro areas in terms of economic performance (#1 = best) during the recession and recovery from trough quarter through the second quarter of 2013. Criteria: percent change in employment; percentage point change in unemployment rate; percent change in gross metropolitan product; percent change in House Price Index. *Brookings Institution, MetroMonitor: Tracking Economic Recession and Recovery in America's 100 Largest Metropolitan Areas, September 2013*
- Payscale.com ranked the 20 largest metro areas in terms of wage growth. The Atlanta metro area ranked #14. Criteria: private-sector wage growth between the 1st quarter of 2014 and the 1st quarter of 2015. *PayScale, "Wage Trends by Metro Area," 1st Quarter, 2015*
- The Atlanta metro area was identified as one of the most debt-ridden places in America by the finance site Credit.com. The metro area was ranked #8. Criteria: residents' average personal debt load and average credit scores. *Credit.com, "The Most Debt-Ridden Cities," May 1, 2014*
- Atlanta was identified as one of America's most frugal metro areas by *Coupons.com.* The city ranked #6 out of 25. Criteria: online coupon usage. *Coupons.com, "Top 25 Most Frugal Cities of 2013," April 10, 2014*
- Atlanta was identified as one of America's most frugal metro areas by *Coupons.com.* The city ranked #3 out of 25. Criteria: Grocery IQ and coupons.com mobile app usage. *Coupons.com, "Top 25 Most On-the-Go Frugal Cities of 2013," April 10, 2014*
- Atlanta was cited as one of America's top metros for new and expanded facility projects in 2014. The area ranked #4 in the large metro area category (population over 1 million). *Site Selection, "Top Metros of 2014," March 2015*
- Atlanta was identified as one of the best cities for college graduates to find work—and live. The city ranked #6 out of 15. Criteria: job availability; average salary; average rent. *CareerBuilder.com, "15 Best Cities for College Grads to Find Work—and Live," June 5, 2012*
- The Atlanta metro area appeared on the Milken Institute "2013 Best Performing Cities" list. Rank: #50 out of 200 large metro areas. Criteria: job growth; wage and salary growth; high-tech output growth. *Milken Institute, "Best-Performing Cities 2014," January 2015*
- *Forbes* ranked the 200 most populous metro areas to determine the nation's "Best Places for Business and Careers." The Atlanta metro area was ranked #14. Criteria: costs (business and living); job growth (past and projected); income growth; educational attainment (college and high school); projected economic growth; cultural and recreational opportunities; net migration patterns; number of highly ranked colleges. *Forbes, "The Best Places for Business and Careers 2014," July 23, 2014*
- Mercer Human Resources Consulting ranked 211 urban areas worldwide in terms of cost-of-living. Atlanta ranked #147 (the lower the ranking, the higher the cost-of-living). The survey measured the comparative cost of over 200 items (such as housing, food, clothing, household goods, transportation, and entertainment) in each location.*Mercer, "2014 Cost of Living Survey," July 10, 2014*

Culture/Performing Arts Rankings

- Atlanta was selected as one of the ten best large U.S. cities in which to be a moviemaker. Of cities with a population over 400,000, the city was ranked #6. Criteria: film community; access to new films; access to equipment; cost of living; tax incentives. *MovieMaker Magazine, "Best Places to Live and Work as a Moviemaker: 2013," January 22, 2015*
- Atlanta was selected as one of America's top cities for the arts. The city ranked #8 in the mid-sized city (population 100,000 to 499,999) category. Criteria: readers' top choices for arts travel destinations based on the richness and variety of visual arts sites, activities and events. *American Style, "2012 Top 25 Arts Destinations," June 2012*

Dating/Romance Rankings

- CreditDonkey, a financial education website, sought out the ten best U.S. cities for newlyweds, considering the number of married couples, divorce rate, average credit score, and average number of hours worked per week in metro areas with a million or more residents. The Atlanta metro area placed #1. *www.creditdonkey.com, "Study: Best Cities for Newlyweds," November 30, 2013*

- Atlanta took the #8 spot on NerdWallet's list of best cities for singles wanting to date, based on the availability of singles; "date-friendliness," as determined by a city's walkability and the number of bars and restaurants per thousand residents; and the affordability of dating in terms of the cost of movie tickets, pizza, and wine for two. *www.nerdwallet.com, "Best Cities for Singles," February 2, 2015*

- Of the 100 U.S. cities surveyed by *Men's Health* in its quest to identify the nation's best cities for dating and forming relationships, Atlanta was ranked #1 for online dating (#1 = best). *Men's Health, "The Best and Worst Cities for Online Dating," January 30, 2013*

- Atlanta was selected as one of America's best cities for singles by the readers of *Travel + Leisure* in their annual "America's Favorite Cities" survey. The city was ranked #5 out of 20. Criteria included good-looking locals, cool shopping, and hipster-magnet coffee bars. *Travel + Leisure, "America's Best Cities for Singles," January 23, 2015*

Education Rankings

- Personal finance website *WalletHub* analyzed the 150 largest U.S. metropolitan statistical areas to determine where the most educated Americans are choosing to settle. Criteria: educational attainment; percentage of workers with jobs in computer, engineering, and science fields; quality and size of each metro area's universities. Atlanta was ranked #17 (#1 = most educated city). *www.WalletHub.com, "2014's Most and Least Educated Cities*

- Atlanta was selected as one of the most well-read cities in America by Amazon.com. The city ranked #15 among the top 20. Cities with populations greater than 100,000 were evaluated based on per capita sales of books, magazines and newspapers. *Amazon.com, "The 20 Most Well-Read Cities in America," May 20, 2014*

- The real estate website *MovoTo.com* selected Atlanta as one of the "Nerdiest Cities in America." The city ranked #1 among the top 10 derived from data on the 50 most populous cities in the United States. Criteria: Number of annual comic book, video game, anime, and sci-fi/fantasy conventions; people per comic book store, video game store, and traditional gaming store; people per LARPing ("live action role-playing") group; people per science museum. Also factored in: distance to the nearest Renaissance faire. *MovoTo.com, "The 10 Nerdiest Cities in America," April 10, 2013*

- Atlanta was selected as one of America's most literate cities. The city ranked #5 out of the 77 largest U.S. cities. Criteria: number of booksellers; library resources; Internet resources; educational attainment; periodical publishing resources; newspaper circulation. *Central Connecticut State University, "America's Most Literate Cities, 2014," April 8, 2015*

Environmental Rankings

- The Atlanta metro area came in at #246 for the relative comfort of its climate on Sperling's list of "chill cities," as measured by the Sperling Heat Index. All 361 metro areas are included. Criteria included daytime high temperatures, nighttime low temperatures, dew point, and relative humidity at the high temperatures. *www.bertsperling.com, "Sperling's Chill Cities," July 18, 2013*

- Sperling's BestPlaces assessed 379 metropolitan areas of the United States for the likelihood of dangerously extreme weather events or earthquakes. In general the Southeast and South-Central regions have the highest risk of weather extremes and earthquakes, while the Pacific Northwest enjoys the lowest risk. Of the least risky metropolitan areas, the Atlanta metro area was ranked #358. *www.bestplaces.net, "Safest Places from Natural Disasters," April 2011*

- The U.S. Environmental Protection Agency (EPA) released a list of large U.S. metropolitan areas with the most ENERGY STAR certified buildings in 2014. The Atlanta metro area was ranked #3 out of 25. *U.S. Environmental Protection Agency, "Top Cities With the Most ENERGY STAR Certified Buildings in 2014," March 25, 2015*

Food/Drink Rankings

- *Men's Health* ranked 100 major U.S. cities in terms of alcohol intoxication. Atlanta ranked #13 (#1 = most sober).Criteria: binge drinking; alcohol-related traffic accidents, arrests, and fatalities. *Men's Health, "The Drunkest Cities in America," November 19, 2013*

Health/Fitness Rankings

- For each of the 50 most populous metro areas in the United States, the American College of Sports Medicine's American Fitness Index evaluated infrastructure, community assets, and policies that encourage healthy and fit lifestyles, including preventive health behaviors, levels of chronic disease conditions, health care access, and community resources and policies that support physical activity. The Atlanta metro area ranked #21 for "community fitness." Personal health indicators were considered as well as community and environmental indicators. *www.americanfitnessindex.org, "ACSM American Fitness Index Health and Community Fitness Status of the 50 Largest Metropolitan Areas," May 2013*
- The Atlanta metro area was identified as one of the worst cities for bed bugs in America by pest control company Orkin. The area ranked #15 out of 50 based on the number of bed bug treatments Orkin performed from January to December 2013. *Orkin, "Chicago Tops Bed Bug Cities List for Second Year in a Row," January 16, 2014*
- Atlanta was selected as one of the 25 fattest cities in America by *Men's Fitness Online*. It ranked #20 out of America's 50 largest cities. Criteria: fitness centers and sport stores; nutrition; sports participation; TV viewing; overweight/sedentary; junk food; air quality; geography; commute; parks and open space; city recreational facilities; access to healthcare; motivation; mayor and city initiatives; state obesity initiatives. *Men's Fitness, "The Fittest and Fattest Cities in America," March 5, 2012*
- Atlanta was identified as a "2013 Spring Allergy Capital." The area ranked #72 out of 100. Three groups of factors were used to identify the most severe cities for people with allergies during the spring season: annual pollen levels; medicine utilization; access to board-certified allergists. *Asthma and Allergy Foundation of America, "Spring Allergy Capitals 2013"*
- Atlanta was identified as a "2013 Fall Allergy Capital." The area ranked #74 out of 100. Three groups of factors were used to identify the most severe cities for people with allergies during the fall season: annual pollen levels; medicine utilization; access to board-certified allergists. *Asthma and Allergy Foundation of America, "Fall Allergy Capitals 2013"*
- Atlanta was identified as a "2013 Asthma Capital." The area ranked #9 out of the nation's 100 largest metropolitan areas. Twelve factors were used to identify the most challenging places to live for people with asthma: estimated prevalence; self-reported prevalence; crude death rate for asthma; annual pollen score; annual air quality; public smoking laws; number of board-certified asthma specialists; school inhaler access laws; rescue medication use; controller medication use; uninsured rate; poverty rate. *Asthma and Allergy Foundation of America, "Asthma Capitals 2013"*
- *Men's Health* ranked 100 major U.S. cities in terms of the best and worst cities for men. Atlanta ranked #28. Criteria: thirty-three data points were examined covering health, fitness, and quality of life. *Men's Health, "The Best & Worst Cities for Men 2014," December 6, 2013*
- Atlanta was selected as one of the best metropolitan areas for hospital care in America by *HealthGrades.com.* The rankings are based on a comprehensive study of patient death and complication rates in the nation's nearly 5,000 hospitals. Hospitals performing in the top 5% nationwide across 26 different medical procedures and diagnoses were identified. *HealthGrades.com* then ranked cities by the highest percentage of these Distinguished Hospitals for Clinical Excellence™. The Atlanta metro area ranked #50. *HealthGrades.com, "America's Top 50 Cities for Hospital Care," January 21, 2012*
- The Atlanta metro area appeared in the 2013 Gallup-Healthways Well-Being Index. The area ranked #42 out of 189. The Gallup-Healthways Well-Being Index score is an average of six sub-indexes, which individually examine life evaluation, emotional health, work environment, physical health, healthy behaviors, and access to basic necessities. Results are based on telephone interviews conducted as part of the Gallup-Healthways Well-Being Index survey January 2–December 29, 2012, and January 2–December 30, 2013, with a random sample of 531,630 adults, aged 18 and older, living in metropolitan areas in the 50 U.S. states and the District of Columbia. *Gallup-Healthways, "State of American Well-Being," March 25, 2014*
- The Atlanta metro area was identified as one of "America's Most Stressful Cities" by *Sperling's BestPlaces.* The metro area ranked #15 out of 50. Criteria: unemployment rate; suicide rate; commute time; mental health; poor rest; alcohol use; violent crime rate; property crime rate; cloudy days annually. *Sperling's BestPlaces, www.BestPlaces.net, "Stressful Cities 2012*

- Atlanta was selected as one of the "20 Most Livable U.S. Cities for Wheelchair Users" by the Christopher & Dana Reeve Foundation. The city ranked #20. Criteria: Medicaid eligibility and spending; access to physicians and rehabilitation facilities; access to fitness facilities and recreation; access to paratransit; percentage of people living with disabilities who are employed; clean air; climate. *Christopher & Dana Reeve Foundation, "20 Most Livable U.S. Cities for Wheelchair Users," July 26, 2010*

Real Estate Rankings

- On the list compiled by Penske Truck Rental, the Atlanta metro area was named the #1 moving destination in 2014, based on one-way consumer truck rental reservations made through Penske's website and reservations call center. *blog.gopenske.com, "Penske Truck Rental's 2014 Top Moving Destinations List," February 4, 2015*
- The Atlanta metro area appeared on Realtor.com's list of the hottest housing markets to watch in 2015. Criteria: strong housing growth; affordable prices; and fast-paced sales. *Realtor.com®, "Top 10 Hot Housing Markets to Watch in 2015," December 4, 2014*
- The Atlanta metro area was identified as one of the top 20 housing markets to invest in for 2015 by *Forbes*. The area ranked #13. Criteria: strong population and job growth; relatively low home prices which are below equilibrium home price (EHP). The EHP is what the average price for a market should be, if speculation, weird distortions in local income, and other factors (like the housing collapse) weren't present in the market. *Forbes.com, "Best Buy Cities: Where to Invest in Housing in 2015," January 9, 2015*
- Atlanta was ranked #40 out of 275 metro areas in terms of house price appreciation in 2014 (#1 = highest rate). *Federal Housing Finance Agency, House Price Index, 4th Quarter 2014*
- The Atlanta metro area was identified as one of the 20 best housing markets in the U.S. in 2014. The area ranked #4 out of 178 markets with a home price appreciation of 14.3%. Criteria: year-over-year change of median sales price of existing single-family homes between the 4th quarter of 2013 and the 4th quarter of 2014. *National Association of Realtors®, Median Sales Price of Existing Single-Family Homes for Metropolitan Areas, 4th Quarter 2014*
- The Atlanta metro area was identified as one of the 10 best condo markets in the U.S. in 2014. The area ranked #5 out of 66 markets with a price appreciation of 16.2%. Criteria: year-over-year change of median sales price of existing apartment condo-coop homes between the 4th quarter of 2013 and the 4th quarter of 2014. *National Association of Realtors®, Median Sales Price of Existing Apartment Condo-Coop Homes for Metropolitan Areas, 4th Quarter 2014*
- Atlanta was ranked #121 out of 226 metro areas in terms of housing affordability in 2014 by the National Association of Home Builders (#1 = most affordable). The NAHB-Wells Fargo Housing Opportunity Index (HOI) for a given area is defined as the share of homes sold in that area that would have been affordable to a family earning the local median income, based on standard mortgage underwriting criteria. *National Association of Home Builders®, NAHB-Wells Fargo Housing Opportunity Index, 4th Quarter 2014*

Safety Rankings

- Business Insider looked at the FBI's Uniform Crime Report to identify the U.S. cities with the most violent crime per capita, excluding localities with fewer than 100,000 residents. To judge by its relatively high murder, rape, and robbery data, Atlanta was ranked #23 (#1 = worst) among the 25 most dangerous cities. *www.businessinsider.com, "The 25 Most Dangerous Cities in America," June 13, 2013*
- Symantec, in partnership with Sperling's BestPlaces, ranked the 50 largest cities in the U.S. in terms of their vulnerability to cybercrime. The city ranked #4. Criteria: number of cyberattacks and potential infections; level of Internet access; expenditures on smartphones and computer hardware/software; wireless hotspots; broadband connectivity; Internet usage; online purchases. *Symantec, "Riskiest Online Cities of 2012" February 15, 2012*
- Allstate ranked the 200 largest cities in America in terms of driver safety. Atlanta ranked #179. Allstate researchers analyzed internal property damage claims over a two-year period from January 2011 to December 2012. A weighted average of the two-year numbers determined the annual percentages. *Allstate, "Allstate America's Best Drivers Report, 2014"*

- The Atlanta metro area was identified as one of "America's Most Dangerous Cities" by *Forbes*. The area ranked #9 out of 10. Criteria: violent crime (murder and non-negligent manslaughter, forcible rape, robbery, and aggravated assault) rates per capita. The editors only considered metropolitan areas with populations above 200,000. *Forbes, "America's Most Dangerous Cities 2013," October 22, 2013*

- Atlanta was identified as one of the most dangerous cities in America by *The Business Insider.* Criteria: cities with 100,000 residents or more were ranked by violent crime rate in 2011. Violent crimes include for murder, rape, robbery, and aggravated assault. The city ranked #8 out of 25. *The Business Insider, "The 25 Most Dangerous Cities in America," November 4, 2012*

- The National Insurance Crime Bureau ranked 380 metro areas in the U.S. in terms of per capita rates of vehicle theft. The Atlanta metro area ranked #48 (#1 = highest rate). Criteria: number of vehicle theft offenses per 100,000 inhabitants in 2012. *National Insurance Crime Bureau, "Hot Spots 2012," June 26, 2013*

Seniors/Retirement Rankings

- From its Best Cities for Successful Aging indexes, the Milken Institute generated rankings for metropolitan areas, weighing data in eight categories—health care, wellness, living arrangements, transportation, financial characteristics, education and employment opportunities, community engagement, and overall livability. The Atlanta metro area was ranked #83 overall in the large metro area category. *Milken Institute, "Best Cities for Successful Aging, 2014"*

Sports/Recreation Rankings

- Atlanta was selected as one of "America's Most Miserable Sports Cities" by *Forbes.* The city was ranked #2. Criteria: postseason losses; years since last title; ratio of cumulative seasons to championships won. Contenders were limited to cities with at least 75 total seasons of NFL, NBA, NHL and MLB play. *Forbes, "America's Most Miserable Sports Cities," July 31, 2013*

- Atlanta was selected as one of the most playful cities in the U.S. by KaBOOM! The organization's Playful City USA initiative honors cities and towns across the nation for a vision, plan and commitment to creating an agenda for play. Criteria: creating a local play commission or task force; designing an annual action plan for play; conducting a play space audit; outlining a financial investment in play for the current fiscal year; and proclaiming and celebrating an annual "play day." *KaBOOM! National Campaign for Play, "2013 Playful City USA Communities"*

Transportation Rankings

- NerdWallet surveyed average annual car insurance premiums in 125 U.S. cities to identify the least expensive U.S. cities in which to insure a car. Locations with no-fault insurance laws was a strong determinant. Atlanta came in at #26 for the most expensive rates. *www.nerdwallet.com, "Best Cities for Cheap Car Insurance," February 3, 2014*

- Atlanta was identified as one of the most congested metro areas in the U.S. The area ranked #7 out of 10. Criteria: yearly delay per auto commuter in hours. *Texas A&M Transportation Institute, "2012 Urban Mobility Report," December 2012*

- The Atlanta metro area appeared on *Forbes* list of places with the most extreme commutes. The metro area ranked #7 out of 10. Criteria: average travel time; percentage of mega commuters. Mega-commuters travel more than 90 minutes and 50 miles each way to work. *Forbes.com, "The Cities with the Most Extreme Commutes," March 5, 2013*

Women/Minorities Rankings

- The Daily Beast surveyed the nation's cities for highest percentage of singles and lowest divorce rate, plus other measures, to determine "emotional intelligence"—happiness, confidence, kindness—which, researchers say, has a strong correlation with people's satisfaction with their romantic relationships. Atlanta placed #4. *www.thedailybeast.com, "Best Cities to Find Love and Stay in Love," February 14, 2014*

- *Women's Health* examined U.S. cities and identified the 100 best cities for women. Atlanta was ranked #39. Criteria: 30 categories were examined from obesity and breast cancer rates to commuting times and hours spent working out. *Women's Health, "Best Cities for Women 2012"*

- Atlanta was selected as one of the gayest cities in America by *The Advocate.* The city ranked #5 out of 15. This year's criteria include points for a city's LGBT elected officials (and fractional points for the state's elected officials), points for the percentage of the population comprised by lesbian-coupled households, a point for a gay rodeo association, points for bars listed in *Out* magazine's 200 Best Bars list, a point per women's college, and points for concert performances by Mariah Carey, Pink, Lady Gaga, or the Jonas Brothers. The raw score is divided by the population to provide a ranking based on a per capita LGBT quotient. *The Advocate, "2014's Gayest Cities in America" January 6, 2014*

Miscellaneous Rankings

- The watchdog site Charity Navigator conducts an annual study of charities in the nation's major markets both to analyze statistical differences in their financial, accountability, and transparency practices and to track year-to-year variations in individual communities. The Atlanta metro area was ranked #27 among the 30 metro markets. *www.charitynavigator.org, "Metro Market Study 2013," June 1, 2013*

- The Harris Poll's Happiness Index survey revealed that of the top ten U.S. markets, the Atlanta metro area residents ranked #4 in happiness. Criteria included strong assent to positive statements and strong disagreement with negative ones, and degree of agreement with a series of statements about respondents' personal relationships and general outlook. The online survey was conducted between July 14 and July 30, 2013. *www.harrisinteractive.com, "Dallas/Fort Worth Is "Happiest" City among America's Top Ten Markets," September 4, 2013*

- Market analyst Scarborough Research surveyed adults who had done volunteer work over the previous 12 months to find out where volunteers are concentrated. The Atlanta metro area made the list for highest volunteer participation. *Scarborough Research, "Salt Lake City, UT; Minneapolis, MN; and Des Moines, IA Lend a Helping Hand," November 27, 2012*

- Atlanta was selected as one of America's funniest cities by the Humor Research Lab at the University of Colorado. The city ranked #3 out of 10. Criteria: frequency of visits to comedy websites; number of comedy clubs per square mile; traveling comedians' ratings of each city's comedy-club audiences; number of famous comedians born in each city per capita; number of famous funny tweeters living in each city per capita; number of comedy radio stations available in each city; frequency of humor-related web searches originating in each city. *The New York Times, "So These Professors Walk Into a Comedy Club…," April 20, 2014*

- Energizer Personal Care, the makers of Edge® shave gel, in partnership with Sperling's BestPlaces, ranked 50 major metro areas in terms of everyday irritations. The Atlanta metro area ranked #5. Criteria: high male-to-female ratio; poor sports team performance and high ticket prices; slow traffic; lack of job availability; unaffordable housing; extreme weather; lack of nightlife and fitness options. *Energizer Personal Care, "Most Irritatng Cities for Guys," August 26, 2013*

- Mars Chocolate North America, the makers of COMBOS®, in partnership with Sperling's BestPlaces, ranked 50 major metro areas in terms of their "manliness." The Atlanta metro area ranked #17. Criteria: number of professional sports teams; number of nearby NASCAR tracks and racing events; manly lifestyle; concentration of manly retail stores; manly occupations per capita; salty snack sales; "Board of Manliness" rankings. *Mars Chocolate North America, "America's Manliest Cities 2012"*

- The Atlanta metro area was selected as one of "America's Most Miserable Cities" by *Forbes.com.* The metro area ranked #16 out of 20. Criteria: violent crime; unemployment; foreclosures; income and property taxes; home prices; commute times; climate. *Forbes.com, "America's Most Miserable Cities" February 22, 2013*

- The National Alliance to End Homelessness ranked the 100 most populous metro areas in terms the rate of homelessness. The Atlanta metro area ranked #61. Criteria: number of homeless people per 10,000 population in 2011. *National Alliance to End Homelessness, The State of Homelessness in America 2012*

Business Environment

CITY FINANCES

City Government Finances

Component	2012 ($000)	2012 ($ per capita)
Total Revenues	2,123,297	5,055
Total Expenditures	2,237,556	5,327
Debt Outstanding	7,446,495	17,730
Cash and Securities[1]	5,726,229	13,634

Note: (1) Cash and security holdings of a government at the close of its fiscal year, including those of its dependent agencies, utilities, and liquor stores.
Source: U.S Census Bureau, State & Local Government Finances 2012

City Government Revenue by Source

Source	2012 ($000)	2012 ($ per capita)
General Revenue		
From Federal Government	43,295	103
From State Government	22,641	54
From Local Governments	216,271	515
Taxes		
Property	312,518	744
Sales and Gross Receipts	146,908	350
Personal Income	0	0
Corporate Income	0	0
Motor Vehicle License	0	0
Other Taxes	61,536	147
Current Charges	923,535	2,199
Liquor Store	0	0
Utility	285,417	680
Employee Retirement	48,504	115

Source: U.S Census Bureau, State & Local Government Finances 2012

City Government Expenditures by Function

Function	2012 ($000)	2012 ($ per capita)	2012 (%)
General Direct Expenditures			
Air Transportation	588,579	1,401	26.3
Corrections	27,248	65	1.2
Education	0	0	0.0
Employment Security Administration	0	0	0.0
Financial Administration	37,186	89	1.7
Fire Protection	85,874	204	3.8
General Public Buildings	19,236	46	0.9
Governmental Administration, Other	40,571	97	1.8
Health	945	2	0.0
Highways	35,117	84	1.6
Hospitals	0	0	0.0
Housing and Community Development	15,044	36	0.7
Interest on General Debt	162,464	387	7.3
Judicial and Legal	12,144	29	0.5
Libraries	0	0	0.0
Parking	0	0	0.0
Parks and Recreation	63,592	151	2.8
Police Protection	171,937	409	7.7
Public Welfare	19,476	46	0.9
Sewerage	176,593	420	7.9
Solid Waste Management	39,669	94	1.8
Veterans' Services	0	0	0.0
Liquor Store	0	0	0.0
Utility	422,093	1,005	18.9
Employee Retirement	248,006	590	11.1

Source: U.S Census Bureau, State & Local Government Finances 2012

DEMOGRAPHICS

Population Growth

Area	1990 Census	2000 Census	2010 Census	Population Growth (%) 1990-2000	Population Growth (%) 2000-2010
City	394,092	416,474	420,003	5.7	0.8
MSA[1]	3,069,411	4,247,981	5,268,860	38.4	24.0
U.S.	248,709,873	281,421,906	308,745,538	13.2	9.7

Note: (1) Figures cover the Atlanta-Sandy Springs-Marietta, GA Metropolitan Statistical Area—see Appendix B for areas included
Source: U.S. Census Bureau, Census 1990, 2000, 2010

Household Size

Area	Persons in Household (%)							Average Household Size
	One	Two	Three	Four	Five	Six	Seven or More	
City	46.6	29.9	11.2	7.5	2.9	1.3	0.7	2.26
MSA[1]	26.6	31.4	16.6	14.8	6.5	2.5	1.5	2.78
U.S.	27.7	33.6	15.7	13.1	6.0	2.3	1.5	2.64

Note: (1) Figures cover the Atlanta-Sandy Springs-Roswell, GA Metropolitan Statistical Area—see Appendix B for areas included
Source: U.S. Census Bureau, 2011-2013 American Community Survey 3-Year Estimates

Race

Area	White Alone[2] (%)	Black Alone[2] (%)	Asian Alone[2] (%)	AIAN[3] Alone[2] (%)	NHOPI[4] Alone[2] (%)	Other Race Alone[2] (%)	Two or More Races (%)
City	40.5	52.8	3.7	0.2	0.0	1.0	1.7
MSA[1]	56.2	32.9	5.1	0.3	0.0	3.4	2.2
U.S.	73.9	12.6	5.0	0.8	0.2	4.7	2.9

Note: (1) Figures cover the Atlanta-Sandy Springs-Roswell, GA Metropolitan Statistical Area—see Appendix B for areas included; (2) Alone is defined as not being in combination with one or more other races; (3) American Indian and Alaska Native; (4) Native Hawaiian and Other Pacific Islander
Source: U.S. Census Bureau, 2011-2013 American Community Survey 3-Year Estimates

Hispanic or Latino Origin

Area	Total (%)	Mexican (%)	Puerto Rican (%)	Cuban (%)	Other (%)
City	5.3	2.8	0.7	0.4	1.5
MSA[1]	10.5	6.0	1.0	0.4	3.1
U.S.	16.9	10.8	1.6	0.6	3.8

Note: Persons of Hispanic or Latino origin can be of any race; (1) Figures cover the Atlanta-Sandy Springs-Roswell, GA Metropolitan Statistical Area—see Appendix B for areas included
Source: U.S. Census Bureau, 2011-2013 American Community Survey 3-Year Estimates

Segregation

Type	Segregation Indices[1]				Percent Change		
	1990	2000	2010	2010 Rank[2]	1990-2000	1990-2010	2000-2010
Black/White	66.3	64.3	59.0	41	-2.0	-7.2	-5.3
Asian/White	42.5	46.9	48.5	10	4.4	6.0	1.5
Hispanic/White	35.3	51.6	49.5	27	16.3	14.1	-2.1

Note: All figures cover the Metropolitan Statistical Area—see Appendix B for areas included; Figures are based on an analysis of 1990, 2000, and 2010 Census Decennial Census tract data by William H. Frey, Brookings Institution and the University of Michigan Social Science Data Analysis Network. In this analysis all racial groups (whites, blacks, and asians) are non-Hispanic members of those races. Hispanics are shown as a separate category;
(1) Segregation Indices are Dissimilarity Indices that measure the degree to which the minority group is distributed differently than whites across census tracts. They range from 0 (complete integration) to 100 (complete segregation) where the value indicates the percentage of the minority group that needs to move to be distributed exactly like whites; (2) Ranges from 1 (most segregated) to 102 (least segregated); n/a not available.
Source: www.CensusScope.org

Ancestry

Area	German	Irish	English	American	Italian	Polish	French[2]	Scottish	Dutch
City	5.9	5.2	6.7	7.4	2.1	1.2	1.4	2.2	0.6
MSA[1]	7.5	7.6	7.4	10.2	2.5	1.3	1.5	1.7	0.8
U.S.	14.9	10.8	8.0	7.4	5.5	3.0	2.7	1.7	1.4

Note: Figures are the percentage of the total population reporting a particular ancestry. The nine most commonly reported ancestries in the U.S. are shown. Figures include multiple ancestries (e.g. if a person reported being Irish and Italian, they were included in both columns); (1) Figures cover the Atlanta-Sandy Springs-Roswell, GA Metropolitan Statistical Area—see Appendix B for areas included; (2) Excludes Basque
Source: U.S. Census Bureau, 2011-2013 American Community Survey 3-Year Estimates

Foreign-Born Population

Area	Percent of Population Born in								
	Any Foreign Country	Mexico	Asia	Europe	Carribean	South America	Central America[2]	Africa	Canada
City	7.8	1.4	2.7	1.3	0.6	0.4	0.3	0.7	0.1
MSA[1]	13.2	3.1	3.9	1.2	1.5	0.9	1.0	1.3	0.2
U.S.	13.0	3.7	3.8	1.5	1.2	0.9	1.0	0.6	0.3

Note: (1) Figures cover the Atlanta-Sandy Springs-Roswell, GA Metropolitan Statistical Area—see Appendix B for areas included; (2) Excludes Mexico.
Source: U.S. Census Bureau, 2011-2013 American Community Survey 3-Year Estimates

Marital Status

Area	Never Married	Now Married[2]	Separated	Widowed	Divorced
City	54.0	27.3	2.4	5.4	10.9
MSA[1]	34.4	47.4	2.3	4.8	11.2
U.S.	32.7	48.1	2.2	6.0	11.0

Note: Figures are percentages and cover the population 15 years of age and older; (1) Figures cover the Atlanta-Sandy Springs-Roswell, GA Metropolitan Statistical Area—see Appendix B for areas included; (2) Excludes separated
Source: U.S. Census Bureau, 2011-2013 American Community Survey 3-Year Estimates

Disability Status

Area	All Ages	Under 18 Years Old	18 to 64 Years Old	65 Years and Over
City	11.4	3.3	9.6	39.4
MSA[1]	9.9	3.3	8.7	35.1
U.S.	12.3	4.1	10.2	36.3

Note: Figures show percent of the civilian noninstitutionalized population that reported having a disability. Disability status is determined from from six types of difficulty: vision, hearing, cognitive, ambulatory, self-care, and independent living. For children under 5 years old, hearing and vision difficulty are used to determine disability status. For children between the ages of 5 and 14, disability status is determined from hearing, vision, cognitive, ambulatory, and self-care difficulties. For people aged 15 years and older, they are considered to have a disability if they have difficulty with any one of the six difficulty types; (1) Figures cover the Atlanta-Sandy Springs-Roswell, GA Metropolitan Statistical Area—see Appendix B for areas included.
Source: U.S. Census Bureau, 2011-2013 American Community Survey 3-Year Estimates

Age

Area	Percent of Population									Median Age
	Under Age 5	Age 5–19	Age 20–34	Age 35–44	Age 45–54	Age 55–64	Age 65–74	Age 75–84	Age 85+	
City	6.2	16.3	30.7	14.8	12.3	9.6	5.7	3.0	1.3	33.2
MSA[1]	6.9	21.8	20.6	15.2	14.6	11.0	6.1	2.8	1.0	35.4
U.S.	6.4	19.9	20.7	12.9	14.1	12.3	7.6	4.2	1.9	37.4

Note: (1) Figures cover the Atlanta-Sandy Springs-Roswell, GA Metropolitan Statistical Area—see Appendix B for areas included
Source: U.S. Census Bureau, 2011-2013 American Community Survey 3-Year Estimates

Gender

Area	Males	Females	Males per 100 Females
City	220,467	220,597	99.9
MSA[1]	2,648,950	2,801,341	94.6
U.S.	154,451,010	159,410,713	96.9

Note: (1) Figures cover the Atlanta-Sandy Springs-Roswell, GA Metropolitan Statistical Area—see Appendix B for areas included
Source: U.S. Census Bureau, 2011-2013 American Community Survey 3-Year Estimates

Religious Groups by Family

Area	Catholic	Baptist	Non-Den.	Methodist[2]	Lutheran	LDS[3]	Pente-costal	Presby-terian[4]	Muslim[5]	Judaism
MSA[1]	7.5	17.5	6.9	7.9	0.5	0.8	2.6	1.8	0.8	0.6
U.S.	19.1	9.3	4.0	4.0	2.3	2.0	1.9	1.6	0.8	0.7

Note: Figures are the number of adherents as a percentage of the total population; (1) Figures cover the Atlanta-Sandy Springs-Marietta, GA Metropolitan Statistical Area—see Appendix B for areas included; (2) Methodist/Pietist; (3) Latter Day Saints; (4) Reformed; (5) Figures are estimates
Source: Association of Statisticians of American Religious Bodies, 2010 U.S. Religion Census: Religious Congregations & Membership Study

Religious Groups by Tradition

Area	Catholic	Evangelical Protestant	Mainline Protestant	Other Tradition	Black Protestant	Orthodox
MSA[1]	7.5	26.1	9.8	2.9	3.2	0.3
U.S.	19.1	16.2	7.3	4.3	1.6	0.3

Note: Figures are the number of adherents as a percentage of the total population; (1) Figures cover the Atlanta-Sandy Springs-Marietta, GA Metropolitan Statistical Area—see Appendix B for areas included
Source: Association of Statisticians of American Religious Bodies, 2010 U.S. Religion Census: Religious Congregations & Membership Study

ECONOMY

Gross Metropolitan Product

Area	2012	2013	2014	2015	Rank[2]
MSA[1]	294.0	306.2	321.1	339.9	10

Note: Figures are in billions of dollars; (1) Figures cover the Atlanta-Sandy Springs-Roswell, GA Metropolitan Statistical Area—see Appendix B for areas included; (2) Rank is based on 2015 data and ranges from 1 to 363
Source: The U.S. Conference of Mayors, U.S. Metro Economies: GMP and Employment 2013-2015, June 2014

Economic Growth

Area	2010-12 (%)	2013 (%)	2014 (%)	2015 (%)	Rank[2]
MSA[1]	2.6	2.7	3.3	3.9	35
U.S.	2.1	2.0	2.3	3.2	–

Note: Figures are real gross metropolitan product (GMP) growth rates and represent annual average percent change; (1) Figures cover the Atlanta-Sandy Springs-Roswell, GA Metropolitan Statistical Area—see Appendix B for areas included; (2) Rank is based on 2015 data and ranges from 1 to 363
Source: The U.S. Conference of Mayors, U.S. Metro Economies: GMP and Employment 2013-2015, June 2014

Metropolitan Area Exports

Area	2008	2009	2010	2011	2012	2013	Rank[2]
MSA[1]	14,432.9	13,405.9	15,009.7	17,229.1	18,169.1	18,827.9	18

Note: Figures are in millions of dollars; (1) Figures cover the Atlanta-Sandy Springs-Roswell, GA Metropolitan Statistical Area—see Appendix B for areas included; (2) Rank is based on 2013 data and ranges from 1 to 387
Source: U.S. Department of Commerce, International Trade Administration, Office of Trade & Industry Information, Manufacturing & Services, data extracted April 3, 2015

Building Permits

Area	Single-Family			Multi-Family			Total		
	2013	2014	Pct. Chg.	2013	2014	Pct. Chg.	2013	2014	Pct. Chg.
City	473	545	15.2	5,070	3,960	-21.9	5,543	4,505	-18.7
MSA[1]	14,824	16,984	14.6	9,473	9,699	2.4	24,297	26,683	9.8
U.S.	620,802	634,597	2.2	370,020	411,766	11.3	990,822	1,046,363	5.6

Note: (1) Figures cover the Atlanta-Sandy Springs-Roswell, GA Metropolitan Statistical Area—see Appendix B for areas included; Figures represent new, privately-owned housing units authorized (unadjusted data); All permit data are based on estimates with imputation.
Source: U.S. Census Bureau, Manufacturing, Mining, and Construction Statistics, Building Permits, 2013, 2014

Bankruptcy Filings

Area	Business Filings			Nonbusiness Filings		
	2013	2014	% Chg.	2013	2014	% Chg.
Fulton County	256	161	-37.1	5,143	5,080	-1.2
U.S.	33,212	26,983	-18.8	1,038,720	909,812	-12.4

Note: Business filings include Chapter 7, Chapter 11, Chapter 12, and Chapter 13; Nonbusiness filings include Chapter 7, Chapter 11, and Chapter 13
Source: Administrative Office of the U.S. Courts, Business and Nonbusiness Bankruptcy, County Cases Commenced by Chapter of the Bankruptcy Code, During the 12- Month Period Ending December 31, 2013 and Business and Nonbusiness Bankruptcy, County Cases Commenced by Chapter of the Bankruptcy Code, During the 12- Month Period Ending December 31, 2014

Housing Vacancy Rates

Area	Gross Vacancy Rate[2] (%)			Year-Round Vacancy Rate[3] (%)			Rental Vacancy Rate[4] (%)			Homeowner Vacancy Rate[5] (%)		
	2012	2013	2014	2012	2013	2014	2012	2013	2014	2012	2013	2014
MSA[1]	12.5	12.4	11.0	12.2	11.8	10.3	10.6	10.2	8.8	2.6	2.1	2.5
U.S.	13.8	13.6	13.4	10.8	10.7	10.4	8.7	8.3	7.6	2.0	2.0	1.9

Note: (1) Figures cover the Atlanta-Sandy Springs-Roswell, GA Metropolitan Statistical Area—see Appendix B for areas included; (2) The percentage of the total housing inventory that is vacant; (3) The percentage of the housing inventory (excluding seasonal units) that is year-round vacant; (4) The percentage of rental inventory that is vacant for rent; (5) The percentage of homeowner inventory that is vacant for sale
Source: U.S. Census Bureau, Housing Vacancies and Homeownership Annual Statistics: 2014

INCOME

Income

Area	Per Capita ($)	Median Household ($)	Average Household ($)
City	36,091	46,783	82,895
MSA[1]	28,166	55,295	76,582
U.S.	27,884	52,176	72,897

Note: (1) Figures cover the Atlanta-Sandy Springs-Roswell, GA Metropolitan Statistical Area—see Appendix B for areas included
Source: U.S. Census Bureau, 2011-2013 American Community Survey 3-Year Estimates

Household Income Distribution

Area	Percent of Households Earning							
	Under $15,000	$15,000 -24,999	$25,000 -34,999	$35,000 -49,999	$50,000 -74,999	$75,000 -99,000	$100,000 -149,999	$150,000 and up
City	20.5	10.8	9.5	11.2	15.1	9.2	10.4	13.3
MSA[1]	11.9	9.8	10.0	13.7	18.5	12.0	13.4	10.7
U.S.	13.0	10.9	10.3	13.6	17.9	11.9	12.7	9.6

Note: (1) Figures cover the Atlanta-Sandy Springs-Roswell, GA Metropolitan Statistical Area—see Appendix B for areas included
Source: U.S. Census Bureau, 2011-2013 American Community Survey 3-Year Estimates

Poverty Rate

Area	All Ages	Under 18 Years Old	18 to 64 Years Old	65 Years and Over
City	25.4	38.7	22.9	16.9
MSA[1]	16.3	23.0	14.6	9.6
U.S.	15.9	22.4	14.8	9.5

Note: Figures are percentage of people whose income during the past 12 months was below the poverty level; (1) Figures cover the Atlanta-Sandy Springs-Roswell, GA Metropolitan Statistical Area—see Appendix B for areas included
Source: U.S. Census Bureau, 2011-2013 American Community Survey 3-Year Estimates

EMPLOYMENT

Labor Force and Employment

Area	Civilian Labor Force			Workers Employed		
	Dec. 2013	Dec. 2014	% Chg.	Dec. 2013	Dec. 2014	% Chg.
City	230,075	232,034	0.9	211,965	215,889	1.9
MSA[1]	2,791,270	2,815,375	0.9	2,598,666	2,647,261	1.9
U.S.	154,408,000	155,521,000	0.7	144,423,000	147,190,000	1.9

Note: Data is not seasonally adjusted and covers workers 16 years of age and older; (1) Figures cover the Atlanta-Sandy Springs-Roswell, GA Metropolitan Statistical Area—see Appendix B for areas included
Source: Bureau of Labor Statistics, Local Area Unemployment Statistics

Unemployment Rate

Area	2014											
	Jan.	Feb.	Mar.	Apr.	May	Jun.	Jul.	Aug.	Sep.	Oct.	Nov.	Dec.
City	8.0	8.0	7.9	7.2	7.8	8.3	8.6	8.3	7.5	7.4	7.1	7.0
MSA[1]	7.1	7.1	7.0	6.4	6.9	7.3	7.6	7.3	6.7	6.5	6.1	6.0
U.S.	7.0	7.0	6.8	5.9	6.1	6.3	6.5	6.3	5.7	5.5	5.5	5.4

Note: Data is not seasonally adjusted and covers workers 16 years of age and older; (1) Figures cover the Atlanta-Sandy Springs-Roswell, GA Metropolitan Statistical Area—see Appendix B for areas included
Source: Bureau of Labor Statistics, Local Area Unemployment Statistics

Employment by Occupation

Occupation Classification	City (%)	MSA[1] (%)	U.S. (%)
Management, Business, Science, and Arts	50.8	39.2	36.2
Natural Resources, Construction, and Maintenance	3.3	8.0	9.0
Production, Transportation, and Material Moving	6.8	11.0	12.1
Sales and Office	22.9	25.6	24.4
Service	16.2	16.3	18.3

Note: Figures cover employed civilians 16 years of age and older; (1) Figures cover the Atlanta-Sandy Springs-Roswell, GA Metropolitan Statistical Area—see Appendix B for areas included
Source: U.S. Census Bureau, 2011-2013 American Community Survey 3-Year Estimates

Employment by Industry

Sector	MSA[1] Number of Employees	MSA[1] Percent of Total	U.S. Percent of Total
Construction	102,300	4.0	4.4
Education and Health Services	313,900	12.2	15.5
Financial Activities	163,000	6.4	5.7
Government	328,000	12.8	15.8
Information	89,600	3.5	2.0
Leisure and Hospitality	264,100	10.3	10.3
Manufacturing	153,500	6.0	8.7
Mining and Logging	1,300	0.1	0.6
Other Services	96,300	3.8	4.0
Professional and Business Services	472,500	18.4	13.8
Retail Trade	285,500	11.1	11.4
Transportation, Warehousing, and Utilities	141,000	5.5	3.9
Wholesale Trade	155,700	6.1	4.2

Note: Figures are non-farm employment as of December 2014. Figures are not seasonally adjusted and include workers 16 years of age and older; (1) Figures cover the Atlanta-Sandy Springs-Roswell, GA Metropolitan Statistical Area—see Appendix B for areas included
Source: Bureau of Labor Statistics, Current Employment Statistics, Employment, Hours, and Earnings

Occupations with Greatest Projected Employment Growth: 2012 – 2022

Occupation[1]	2012 Employment	2022 Projected Employment	Numeric Employment Change	Percent Employment Change
Combined Food Preparation and Serving Workers, Including Fast Food	169,450	192,830	23,380	13.8
Customer Service Representatives	95,900	115,410	19,510	20.3
Laborers and Freight, Stock, and Material Movers, Hand	85,460	104,150	18,690	21.9
Elementary School Teachers, Except Special Education	42,300	56,170	13,870	32.8
General and Operations Managers	71,410	84,890	13,480	18.9
Sales Representatives, Wholesale and Manufacturing, Except Technical and Scientific Products	56,220	67,450	11,230	20.0
Secretaries and Administrative Assistants, Except Legal, Medical, and Executive	51,850	63,030	11,180	21.6
Office Clerks, General	79,920	91,010	11,090	13.9
Janitors and Cleaners, Except Maids and Housekeeping Cleaners	52,860	63,600	10,740	20.3
Childcare Workers	37,650	48,280	10,630	28.2

Note: Projections cover Georgia; (1) Sorted by numeric employment change
Source: www.projectionscentral.com, State Occupational Projections, 2012–2022 Long-Term Projections

Fastest Growing Occupations: 2012 – 2022

Occupation[1]	2012 Employment	2022 Projected Employment	Numeric Employment Change	Percent Employment Change
Physician Assistants	2,820	4,740	1,920	67.9
Health Specialties Teachers, Postsecondary	4,870	8,060	3,190	65.5
Agents and Business Managers of Artists, Performers, and Athletes	430	700	270	62.6
Personal Care Aides	16,440	26,630	10,190	62.0
Interpreters and Translators	1,650	2,630	980	58.9
Nursing Instructors and Teachers, Postsecondary	1,420	2,200	780	55.5
Psychiatric Aides	1,390	2,150	760	55.3
Home Health Aides	7,950	12,340	4,390	55.1
Nurse Practitioners	3,260	5,010	1,750	53.9
Nurse Midwives	250	380	130	53.6

Note: Projections cover Georgia; (1) Sorted by percent employment change and excludes occupations with numeric employment change less than 100
Source: www.projectionscentral.com, State Occupational Projections, 2012–2022 Long-Term Projections

Average Wages

Occupation	$/Hr.	Occupation	$/Hr.
Accountants and Auditors	37.98	Maids and Housekeeping Cleaners	9.24
Automotive Mechanics	19.46	Maintenance and Repair Workers	18.51
Bookkeepers	18.75	Marketing Managers	65.68
Carpenters	20.59	Nuclear Medicine Technologists	35.15
Cashiers	9.33	Nurses, Licensed Practical	19.12
Clerks, General Office	13.71	Nurses, Registered	31.27
Clerks, Receptionists/Information	13.81	Nursing Assistants	11.22
Clerks, Shipping/Receiving	14.24	Packers and Packagers, Hand	11.08
Computer Programmers	47.23	Physical Therapists	39.00
Computer Systems Analysts	39.53	Postal Service Mail Carriers	25.21
Computer User Support Specialists	25.60	Real Estate Brokers	54.71
Cooks, Restaurant	11.41	Retail Salespersons	12.20
Dentists	91.62	Sales Reps., Exc. Tech./Scientific	30.23
Electrical Engineers	42.31	Sales Reps., Tech./Scientific	38.88
Electricians	22.92	Secretaries, Exc. Legal/Med./Exec.	17.11
Financial Managers	64.95	Security Guards	11.76
First-Line Supervisors/Managers, Sales	20.49	Surgeons	119.43
Food Preparation Workers	9.97	Teacher Assistants	10.60
General and Operations Managers	58.17	Teachers, Elementary School	25.90
Hairdressers/Cosmetologists	13.23	Teachers, Secondary School	26.90
Internists	125.05	Telemarketers	14.51
Janitors and Cleaners	11.63	Truck Drivers, Heavy/Tractor-Trailer	20.07
Landscaping/Groundskeeping Workers	12.39	Truck Drivers, Light/Delivery Svcs.	16.69
Lawyers	66.91	Waiters and Waitresses	9.20

Note: Wage data covers the Atlanta-Sandy Springs-Marietta, GA Metropolitan Statistical Area—see Appendix B for areas included; Hourly wages for elementary/secondary school teachers and teacher assistants were calculated by the editors from annual wage data assuming a 40 hour work week; n/a not available.
Source: Bureau of Labor Statistics, Metro Area Occupational Employment and Wage Estimates, May 2014

TAXES

State Corporate Income Tax Rates

State	Tax Rate (%)	Income Brackets ($)	Num. of Brackets	Financial Institution Tax Rate (%)[a]	Federal Income Tax Ded.
Georgia	6.0	Flat rate	1	6.0	No

Note: Tax rates as of January 1, 2015; (a) Rates listed are the corporate income tax rate applied to financial institutions or excise taxes based on income. Some states have other taxes based upon the value of deposits or shares.
Source: Federation of Tax Administrators, "State Corporate Income Tax Rates, 2015"

State Individual Income Tax Rates

State	Tax Rate (%)	Income Brackets ($)	Num. of Brackets	Personal Exempt. ($)[1]		Fed. Inc. Tax Ded.
				Single	Dependents	
Georgia	1.0 - 6.0	750 - 7,001 (h)	6	2,700	3,000	No

Note: Tax rates as of January 1, 2015; Local- and county-level taxes are not included; n/a not applicable; (1) Married joint filers generally receive double the single exemption; (h) The Georgia income brackets reported are for single individuals. For married couples filing jointly, the same tax rates apply to income brackets ranging from $1,000, to $10,000.
Source: Federation of Tax Administrators, "State Individual Income Tax Rates, 2015"

Various State and Local Tax Rates

State	State and Local Sales and Use (%)	State Sales and Use (%)	Gasoline[1] (¢/gal.)	Cigarette[2] ($/pack)	Spirits[3] ($/gal.)	Wine[4] ($/gal.)	Beer[5] ($/gal.)
Georgia	8.0	4.0	26.53	0.37	3.79 (f)	1.51	1.01 (q)

Note: All tax rates as of January 1, 2015; (1) The American Petroleum Institute has developed a methodology for determining the average tax rate on a gallon of fuel. Rates may include any of the following: excise taxes, environmental fees, storage tank fees, other fees or taxes, general sales tax, and local taxes. In states where gasoline is subject to the general sales tax, or where the fuel tax is based on the average sale price, the average rate determined by API is sensitive to changes in the price of gasoline. States that fully or partially apply general sales taxes to gasoline: CA, CO, GA, IL, IN, MI, NY; (2) The federal excise tax of $1.0066 per pack and local taxes are not included; (3) Rates are those applicable to off-premise sales of 40% alcohol by volume (a.b.v.) distilled spirits in 750ml containers. Local excise taxes are excluded; (4) Rates are those applicable to off-premise sales of 11% a.b.v. non-carbonated wine in 750ml containers; (5) Rates are those applicable to off-premise sales of 4.7% a.b.v. beer in 12 ounce containers; (f) Different rates are also applicable according to alcohol content, place of production, size of container, or place purchased (on- or off-premise or onboard airlines); (q) Includes statewide local tax in Alabama ($0.52) and Georgia ($0.53).
Source: Tax Foundation, 2015 Facts & Figures: How Does Your State Compare?

State Business Tax Climate Index Rankings

State	Overall Rank	Corporate Tax Index Rank	Individual Income Tax Index Rank	Sales Tax Index Rank	Unemployment Insurance Tax Index Rank	Property Tax Index Rank
Georgia	36	8	42	17	36	30

Note: The index is a measure of how each state's tax laws affect economic performance. The lower the rank, the more favorable a state's tax system is for business. States without a given tax are given a ranking of 1. The scores/rankings for the District of Columbia do not affect other states. The 2015 index represents the tax climate as of July 1, 2014.
Source: Tax Foundation, State Business Tax Climate Index 2015

COMMERCIAL REAL ESTATE

Office Market

Market Area	Inventory (sq. ft.)	Vacancy Rate (%)	Under Construction (sq. ft.)	YTD Net Absorption (sq. ft.)	Total Average Asking Rent ($/sq. ft./year)
Atlanta	144,321,653	19.4	500,000	2,301,916	20.99
National	4,745,108,508	14.3	71,190,461	51,084,126	27.40

Source: Newmark Grubb Knight Frank, National Office Market Report, 4th Quarter 2014

Industrial/Warehouse/R&D Market

Market Area	Inventory (sq. ft.)	Vacancy Rate (%)	Under Construction (sq. ft.)	YTD Net Absorption (sq. ft.)	Total Average Asking Rent ($/sq. ft./year)
Atlanta	600,048,125	9.7	8,102,731	11,957,759	4.10
National	14,238,613,765	7.2	134,387,407	185,246,438	5.64

Source: Newmark Grubb Knight Frank, National Industrial Market Report, 4th Quarter 2014

COMMERCIAL UTILITIES

Typical Monthly Electric Bills

Area	Commercial Service ($/month)		Industrial Service ($/month)	
	1,500 kWh	40 kW demand 14,000 kWh	1,000 kW demand 200,000 kWh	50,000 kW demand 32,500,000 kWh
City	254	1,610	31,246	2,340,613
Average[1]	201	1,653	26,124	2,639,743

Note: Figures are based on annualized 2014 rates; (1) Average based on 180 utilities surveyed
Source: Edison Electric Institute, Typical Bills and Average Rates Report, Summer 2014

TRANSPORTATION

Means of Transportation to Work

Area	Car/Truck/Van		Public Transportation			Bicycle	Walked	Other Means	Worked at Home
	Drove Alone	Car-pooled	Bus	Subway	Railroad				
City	68.5	7.5	6.2	3.0	0.1	0.9	4.9	1.2	7.7
MSA[1]	77.9	10.4	2.2	0.7	0.1	0.2	1.4	1.3	5.8
U.S.	76.4	9.6	2.6	1.8	0.6	0.6	2.8	1.3	4.3

Note: Figures are percentages and cover workers 16 years of age and older; (1) Figures cover the Atlanta-Sandy Springs-Roswell, GA Metropolitan Statistical Area—see Appendix B for areas included
Source: U.S. Census Bureau, 2011-2013 American Community Survey 3-Year Estimates

Travel Time to Work

Area	Less Than 10 Minutes	10 to 19 Minutes	20 to 29 Minutes	30 to 44 Minutes	45 to 59 Minutes	60 to 89 Minutes	90 Minutes or More
City	9.0	31.4	27.6	19.4	6.1	4.3	2.3
MSA[1]	8.0	23.5	20.4	24.9	11.8	8.5	2.9
U.S.	13.3	29.7	20.9	20.2	7.7	5.7	2.6

Note: Figures are percentages and include workers 16 years old and over; (1) Figures cover the Atlanta-Sandy Springs-Roswell, GA Metropolitan Statistical Area—see Appendix B for areas included
Source: U.S. Census Bureau, 2011-2013 American Community Survey 3-Year Estimates

Travel Time Index

Area	1985	1990	1995	2000	2005	2010	2011
Urban Area[1]	1.10	1.13	1.21	1.26	1.29	1.24	1.24
Average[2]	1.09	1.14	1.16	1.19	1.23	1.18	1.18

Note: Travel Time Index—the ratio of travel time in the peak period to the travel time at free-flow conditions. For example, a value of 1.30 indicates a 20-minute free-flow trip takes 26 minutes in the peak. Free-flow speeds (60 mph on freeways and 35 mph on principal arterials) are used as the comparison threshold; (1) Covers the Atlanta GA urban area; (2) average of 498 urban areas
Source: Texas Transportation Institute, Urban Mobility Report 2012, December 2012

Public Transportation

Agency Name / Mode of Transportation	Vehicles Operated in Maximum Service	Annual Unlinked Passenger Trips (in thous.)	Annual Passenger Miles (in thous.)
Metropolitan Atlanta Rapid Transit Authority (MARTA)			
Bus (directly operated)	446	59,689.8	230,560.8
Demand Response (directly operated)	153	581.7	7,707.9
Heavy Rail (directly operated)	182	69,629.9	444,043.2

Source: Federal Transit Administration, National Transit Database, 2013

Air Transportation

Airport Name and Code / Type of Service	Passenger Airlines[1]	Passenger Enplanements	Freight Carriers[2]	Freight (lbs.)
Hartsfield-Jackson Atlanta International Airport (ATL)				
Domestic service (U.S. carriers - 2014)	35	41,353,329	20	272,199,434
International service (U.S. carriers - 2013)	17	4,316,316	9	108,664,646

Note: (1) Includes all U.S.-based major, minor and commuter airlines that carried at least one passenger during the year; (2) Includes all U.S.-based airlines and freight carriers that transported at least one lb. of freight during the year.
Source: Bureau of Transportation Statistics, The Intermodal Transportation Database, Air Carriers: T-100 Domestic Market (U.S. Carriers), 2014; Bureau of Transportation Statistics, The Intermodal Transportation Database, Air Carriers: T-100 International Market (U.S. Carriers), 2013

Other Transportation Statistics

Major Highways:	I-20; I-75; I-85
Amtrak Service:	Yes
Major Waterways/Ports:	None

Source: Amtrak.com; Google Maps

BUSINESSES

Major Business Headquarters

Company Name	Rankings	
	Fortune[1]	Forbes[2]
Coca-Cola Enterprises	348	-
Cox Enterprises	-	18
Delta Air Lines	81	-
First Data Corporation	261	31
Genuine Parts Company	205	-
HD Supply Holdings	317	-
Home Depot	33	-
Newell Rubbermaid	436	-
RaceTrac Petroleum	-	41
SunTrust Banks	314	-
The Coca-Cola Company	58	-
The Southern Company	170	-
United Parcel Service	50	-

Note: (1) Fortune 500—companies that produce a 10-K are ranked 1 to 500 based on 2013 revenue; (2) all private companies with at least $2 billion in annual revenue through the end of their most current fiscal year are ranked 1 to 221; companies listed are headquartered in the city; dashes indicate no ranking
Source: Fortune, "Fortune 500," June 16, 2014; Forbes, "America's Largest Private Companies," November 5, 2014

Fast-Growing Businesses

According to *Inc.*, Atlanta is home to eight of America's 500 fastest-growing private companies: **Residential Capital Management** (#147); **Futurewave Systems** (#180); **Expert Technical Solutions** (#239); **Caduceus Healthcare** (#334); **StandBy Talent Staffing Services** (#396); **Patientco** (#405); **Cloud Sherpas** (#458); **Mashburn Outdoor** (#467). Criteria: must be an independent, privately-held, for-profit, U.S. corporation, proprietorship or partnership; revenues must be at least $100,000 in 2010 and $2 million in 2013; must have four-year operating/sales history. Holding companies, regulated banks, and utilities were excluded. *Inc., "America's 500 Fastest-Growing Private Companies," September 2014*

According to *Fortune*, Atlanta is home to one of the 100 fastest-growing companies in the world: **Ocwen Financial** (#8). Companies were ranked by their revenue growth rate; their EPS growth rate; and their three-year annualized total return to investors for the period ending June 30, 2014. Criteria for inclusion: a company, foreign or domestic, must trade on a major U.S. stock exchange; must file quarterly reports with the SEC; must have a minimum market capitalization of $250 million; must have a stock price of at least $5 on June 30, 2014; must have been trading continuously since June 30, 2010; must have revenue and net income for the four quarters ended on or before April 30, 2014, of at least $50 million and $10 million, respectively; and must have posted a compound annual growth in revenue and earnings per share of at least 20% annually over the three years ending on or before April 30, 2014. Real estate investment trusts, limited-liability companies, limited parterships, business development companies, closed end investment firms, and companies that lost money in the quarter ending April 30, 2014 were excluded. *Fortune, "100 Fastest-Growing Companies," August 28, 2014*

According to Deloitte, Atlanta is home to three of North America's 500 fastest-growing high-technology companies: **Damballa** (#170); **LogFire** (#236); **AirSage** (#244). Companies are ranked by percentage growth in revenue over a five-year period. Criteria for inclusion: company must be headquartered within North America; must own proprietary intellectual property or proprietary technology that contributes to a significant portion of the company's operating revenue, or devote a significant proportion of revenues to research and development of technology; must have been in business for a minumum of five years with 2009 operating revenues of at least $50,000 USD/CD and 2013 operating revenues of at least $5 million USD/CD. *Deloitte Touche Tohmatsu, 2014 Technology Fast 500™*

Minority Business Opportunity

Atlanta is home to four companies which are on the *Black Enterprise* Industrial/Service 100 list (100 largest companies based on gross sales): **H. J. Russell & Co.** (#13); **The Gourmet Cos.** (#24); **Jackmont Hospitality** (#36); **B & S Electric Supply Co.** (#72). Criteria: operational in previous calendar year; at least 51% black-owned and manufactures/owns the product it sells or provides industrial or consumer services. Brokerages, real estate firms and firms that provide professional services are not eligible. *Black Enterprise, B.E. 100s, 2014*

Atlanta is home to one company which is on the *Black Enterprise* Auto Dealer 60 list (60 largest dealers based on gross sales): **Mercedes-Benz of Buckhead** (#11). Criteria: company must be operational in previous calendar year and be at least 51% black-owned. *Black Enterprise, B.E. 100s, 2014*

Atlanta is home to two companies which are on the *Black Enterprise* Bank 20 list (20 largest banks based on total assets, capital, deposits and loans, including mortgage-backed securities for the calendar year): **Citizens Bancshares Corp. (Citizens Trust Bank)** (#5); **Capitol City Bank & Trust Co. (Capitol City Bank)** (#9). Only commercial banks or savings and loans that are classified by the Federal Reserve as black institutions and have been fully operational for the previous calendar year were considered. *Black Enterprise, B.E. 100s, 2014*

Atlanta is home to one company which is on the *Black Enterprise* Asset Manager 15 list (15 largest asset management firms based on assets under management): **Herndon Capital Management** (#2). Criteria: company must have been operational in previous calendar year and be at least 51% black-owned. *Black Enterprise, B.E. 100s, 2014*

Atlanta is home to three companies which are on the *Hispanic Business* 500 list (500 largest U.S. Hispanic-owned companies based on 2012 revenue): **Precision 2000** (#293); **Caduceus Healthcare** (#406); **GSB Architects** (#468). Companies included must show at least 51 percent ownership by Hispanic U.S. citizens, and must maintain headquarters in one of the 50 states or Washington, D.C. *Hispanic Business, "Hispanic Business 500," June 20, 2013*

Atlanta is home to two companies which are on the *Hispanic Business* Fastest-Growing 100 list (greatest sales growth from 2008 to 2012): **Precision 2000** (#75); **GSB Architects** (#85). Companies included must show at least 51 percent ownership by Hispanic U.S. citizens, and must maintain headquarters in one of the 50 states or Washington, D.C. In addition, companies must have minimum revenues of $200,000 for calendar year 2008. *Hispanic Business, June 20, 2013*

Minority- and Women-Owned Businesses

Group	All Firms		Firms with Paid Employees			
	Firms	Sales ($000)	Firms	Sales ($000)	Employees	Payroll ($000)
Asian	2,257	1,178,708	1,025	1,131,161	5,837	164,452
Black	15,738	1,256,723	981	895,035	7,367	230,657
Hispanic	1,240	415,116	200	356,231	2,051	78,188
Women	17,047	5,316,681	2,348	4,800,357	24,541	851,096
All Firms	50,966	105,935,888	12,824	103,541,309	347,658	19,829,323

Note: Figures cover firms located in the city; minority- and women-owned business are defined as firms in which the corresponding group own 51% or more of the stock or equity of the company
Source: U.S. Census Bureau, 2007 Economic Census, Survey of Business Owners (2012 Survey of Business Owners data will be released starting in June 2015)

HOTELS & CONVENTION CENTERS

Hotels/Motels

Area	5 Star		4 Star		3 Star		2 Star		1 Star		Not Rated	
	Num.	Pct.[3]	Num.	Pct.[3]	Num.	Pct.[3]	Num.	Pct.[3]	Num.	Pct.[3]	Num.	Pct.[3]
City[1]	6	1.1	24	4.5	153	28.5	301	56.1	22	4.1	31	5.8
Total[2]	166	0.9	1,264	7.0	5,718	31.8	9,340	52.0	411	2.3	1,070	6.0

Note: (1) Figures cover Atlanta and vicinity; (2) Figures cover all 100 cities in this book; (3) Percentage of hotels which have a given star rating; Star ratings are determined by expedia.com and offer an indication of the general quality of a particular hotel.
Source: expedia.com, April 2, 2015

The Atlanta-Sandy Springs-Roswell, GA metro area is home to four of the best hotels in the U.S. according to *Travel & Leisure*: **InterContinental Buckhead Atlanta**; **Ritz-Carlton, Atlanta**; **St. Regis Atlanta**; **Ritz-Carlton Lodge, Reynolds Plantation**. Criteria: service; location; rooms; food; and value. The list includes the top 236 hotels in the U.S. *Travel & Leisure, "T+L 500, The World's Best Hotels 2015"*

Major Convention Centers

Name	Overall Space (sq. ft.)	Exhibit Space (sq. ft.)	Meeting Space (sq. ft.)	Meeting Rooms
AmericasMart Atlanta	n/a	441,000	n/a	38
Cobb Galleria Centre	320,000	144,000	20,000	20
Georgia International Convention Center	n/a	150,000	16,000	n/a
Georgia World Congress Center	3,900,000	1,400,000	n/a	106

Note: Table includes convention centers located in the Atlanta-Sandy Springs-Roswell, GA metro area; n/a not available
Source: Original research

Living Environment

COST OF LIVING

Cost of Living Index

Composite Index	Groceries	Housing	Utilities	Trans-portation	Health Care	Misc. Goods/ Services
99.4	104.3	96.5	90.9	102.0	101.2	101.3

Note: The Cost of Living Index measures regional differences in the cost of consumer goods and services, excluding taxes and non-consumer expenditures, for professional and managerial households in the top income quintile. It is based on more than 50,000 prices covering almost 60 different items for which prices are collected three times a year by chambers of commerce, economic development organizations or university applied economic centers in each participating urban area. The numbers shown should be read as a percentage above or below the national average of 100. For example, a value of 115.4 in the groceries column indicates that grocery prices are 15.4% higher than the national average. Small differences in the index numbers should not be interpreted as significant; Figures cover the Atlanta GA urban area.
Source: The Council for Community and Economic Research, ACCRA Cost of Living Index, 2014

Grocery Prices

Area[1]	T-Bone Steak ($/pound)	Frying Chicken ($/pound)	Whole Milk ($/half gal.)	Eggs ($/dozen)	Orange Juice ($/64 oz.)	Coffee ($/11.5 oz.)
City[2]	11.61	1.26	2.45	1.80	3.48	4.84
Avg.	10.40	1.37	2.40	1.99	3.46	4.27
Min.	8.48	0.93	1.37	1.30	2.83	2.99
Max.	14.20	2.44	3.62	4.02	6.42	6.96

Note: (1) Values for the local area are compared with the average, minimum and maximum values for all 308 areas in the Cost of Living Index; (2) Figures cover the Atlanta GA urban area; **T-Bone Steak** *(price per pound);* **Frying Chicken** *(price per pound, whole fryer);* **Whole Milk** *(half gallon carton);* **Eggs** *(price per dozen, Grade A, large);* **Orange Juice** *(64 oz. Tropicana or Florida Natural);* **Coffee** *(11.5 oz. can, vacuum-packed, Maxwell House, Hills Bros, or Folgers).*
Source: The Council for Community and Economic Research, ACCRA Cost of Living Index, 2014

Housing and Utility Costs

Area[1]	New Home Price ($)	Apartment Rent ($/month)	All Electric ($/month)	Part Electric ($/month)	Other Energy ($/month)	Telephone ($/month)
City[2]	286,196	948	-	92.54	62.77	25.06
Avg.	305,838	919	181.00	93.66	73.14	27.95
Min.	183,142	480	112.00	42.06	23.42	17.16
Max.	1,358,576	3,851	594.00	180.03	440.99	40.42

Note: (1) Values for the local area are compared with the average, minimum and maximum values for all 308 areas in the Cost of Living Index; (2) Figures cover the Atlanta GA urban area; **New Home Price** *(2,400 sf living area, 8,000 sf lot, in urban area with full utilities);* **Apartment Rent** *(950 sf 2 bedroom/1.5 or 2 bath, unfurnished, excluding all utilities except water);* **All Electric** *(average monthly cost for an all-electric home);* **Part Electric** *(average monthly cost for a part-electric home);* **Other Energy** *(average monthly cost for natural gas, fuel oil, coal, wood, and any other forms of energy except electricity);* **Telephone** *(price includes basic monthly rate for a private residential line plus additional local usage charges incurred by a family of four).*
Source: The Council for Community and Economic Research, ACCRA Cost of Living Index, 2014

Health Care, Transportation, and Other Costs

Area[1]	Doctor ($/visit)	Dentist ($/visit)	Optometrist ($/visit)	Gasoline ($/gallon)	Beauty Salon ($/visit)	Men's Shirt ($)
City[2]	97.13	100.61	83.70	3.44	42.80	24.27
Avg.	102.86	87.89	97.66	3.44	34.37	26.74
Min.	67.47	65.78	51.18	3.00	17.43	12.79
Max.	173.50	150.14	235.00	4.33	64.28	49.50

Note: (1) Values for the local area are compared with the average, minimum and maximum values for all 308 areas in the Cost of Living Index; (2) Figures cover the Atlanta GA urban area; **Doctor** *(general practitioners routine exam of an established patient);* **Dentist** *(adult teeth cleaning and periodic oral examination);* **Optometrist** *(full vision eye exam for established adult patient);* **Gasoline** *(one gallon regular unleaded, national brand, including all taxes, cash price at self-service pump if available);* **Beauty Salon** *(woman's shampoo, trim, and blow-dry);* **Men's Shirt** *(cotton/polyester dress shirt, pinpoint weave, long sleeves).*
Source: The Council for Community and Economic Research, ACCRA Cost of Living Index, 2014

HOUSING

House Price Index (HPI)

Area	National Ranking[2]	Quarterly Change (%)	One-Year Change (%)	Five-Year Change (%)
MSA[1]	40	0.55	8.87	2.55
U.S.[3]	–	1.35	4.91	11.59

Note: The HPI is a weighted repeat sales index. It measures average price changes in repeat sales or refinancings on the same properties. This information is obtained by reviewing repeat mortgage transactions on single-family properties whose mortgages have been purchased or securitized by Fannie Mae or Freddie Mac in January 1975; (1) Atlanta-Sandy Springs-Roswell Metropolitan Statistical Area—see Appendix B for areas included; (2) Rankings are based on annual percentage change for all metro areas containing at least 15,000 transactions over the last 10 years and ranges from 1 to 275; (3) figures based on a weighted average of Census Division estimates using a seasonally adjusted, purchase-only index; all figures are for the period ending December 31, 2014

Source: Federal Housing Finance Agency, House Price Index, February 26, 2015

Median Single-Family Home Prices

Area	2012	2013	2014p	Percent Change 2013 to 2014
MSA[1]	101.4	139.5	159.5	14.3
U.S. Average	177.2	197.4	209.0	5.9

Note: Figures are median sales prices of existing single-family homes in thousands of dollars; (p) preliminary; n/a not available; (1) Atlanta-Sandy Springs-Roswell, GA Metropolitan Statistical Area—see Appendix B for areas included

Source: National Association of Realtors, Median Sales Price of Existing Single-Family Homes for Metropolitan Areas, 4th Quarter 2014

Qualifying Income Based on Median Sales Price of Existing Single-Family Homes

Area	With 5% Down ($)	With 10% Down ($)	With 20% Down ($)
MSA[1]	34,655	32,831	29,183
U.S. Average	45,863	43,449	38,621

Note: Figures are preliminary; Qualifying income is based on a mortgage rate of 4.0%. Monthly principal and interest payment is limited to 25% of income; n/a not available; (1) Atlanta-Sandy Springs-Roswell, GA Metropolitan Statistical Area—see Appendix B for areas included

Source: National Association of Realtors, Qualifying Income Based on Median Sales Price of Existing Single-Family Homes for Metropolitan Areas, 4th Quarter 2014

Median Apartment Condo-Coop Home Prices

Area	2012	2013	2014p	Percent Change 2013 to 2014
MSA[1]	76.9	117.3	136.3	16.2
U.S. Average	173.7	194.9	205.1	5.2

Note: Figures are median sales prices of existing apartment condo-coop homes in thousands of dollars; (p) preliminary; n/a not available; (1) Atlanta-Sandy Springs-Roswell, GA Metropolitan Statistical Area—see Appendix B for areas included

Source: National Association of Realtors, Median Sales Price of Existing Apartment Condo-Coop Homes for Metropolitan Areas, 4th Quarter 2014

Gross Monthly Rent

Area	Under $200	$200 -299	$300 -499	$500 -749	$750 -999	$1,000 -1,499	$1,500 and up	Median ($)
City	3.5	4.4	5.2	14.7	27.4	33.3	11.6	953
MSA[1]	1.1	1.7	3.0	17.9	33.3	33.7	9.3	946
U.S.	1.7	3.2	7.8	22.1	24.3	26.0	14.9	900

Note: Figures are percentages except for Median; Gross rent is the contract rent plus the estimated average monthly cost of utilities (electricity, gas, and water and sewer) and fuels (oil, coal, kerosene, wood, etc.) if these are paid by the renter (or paid for the renter by someone else); (1) Figures cover the Atlanta-Sandy Springs-Roswell, GA Metropolitan Statistical Area—see Appendix B for areas included

Source: U.S. Census Bureau, 2011-2013 American Community Survey 3-Year Estimates

Homeownership Rate

Area	2007 (%)	2008 (%)	2009 (%)	2010 (%)	2011 (%)	2012 (%)	2013 (%)	2014 (%)
MSA[1]	66.4	67.5	67.7	67.2	65.8	62.1	61.6	61.6
U.S.	68.1	67.8	67.4	66.9	66.1	65.4	65.1	64.5

Note: (1) Figures cover the Atlanta-Sandy Springs-Roswell, GA Metropolitan Statistical Area—see Appendix B for areas included
Source: U.S. Census Bureau, Housing Vacancies and Homeownership Annual Statistics: 2014

Year Housing Structure Built

Area	2010 or Later	2000 -2009	1990 -1999	1980 -1989	1970 -1979	1960 -1969	1950 -1959	1940 -1949	Before 1940	Median Year
City	1.2	24.9	10.8	8.4	8.6	13.4	12.3	6.8	13.7	1974
MSA[1]	0.9	26.9	22.6	18.2	13.1	8.0	5.1	2.1	3.3	1990
U.S.	0.9	15.0	13.9	13.8	15.8	11.0	10.9	5.4	13.3	1976

Note: Figures are percentages except for Median Year; (1) Figures cover the Atlanta-Sandy Springs-Roswell, GA Metropolitan Statistical Area—see Appendix B for areas included
Source: U.S. Census Bureau, 2011-2013 American Community Survey 3-Year Estimates

HEALTH

Health Risk Data

Category	MSA[1] (%)	U.S. (%)
Adults aged 18–64 who have any kind of health care coverage	74.3	79.6
Adults who reported being in good or excellent health	86.5	83.1
Adults who are current smokers	17.3	19.6
Adults who are heavy drinkers[2]	4.6	6.1
Adults who are binge drinkers[3]	14.6	16.9
Adults who are overweight (BMI 25.0 - 29.9)	34.4	35.8
Adults who are obese (BMI 30.0 - 99.8)	26.5	27.6
Adults who participated in any physical activities in the past month	81.0	77.1
Adults 50+ who have ever had a sigmoidoscopy or colonoscopy	70.3	67.3
Women aged 40+ who have had a mammogram within the past two years	75.7	74.0
Men aged 40+ who have had a PSA test within the past two years	54.7	45.2
Adults aged 65+ who have had flu shot within the past year	57.2	60.1
Adults who always wear a seatbelt	96.3	93.8

Note: Data as of 2012 unless otherwise noted; (1) Figures cover the Atlanta-Sandy Springs-Marietta, GA Metropolitan Statistical Area—see Appendix B for areas included; (2) Heavy drinkers are classified as males having more than two drinks per day or females having more than one drink per day; (3) Binge drinkers are classified as males having five or more drinks on one occasion or females having four or more drinks on one occasion
Source: Centers for Disease Control and Prevention, Behaviorial Risk Factor Surveillance System, SMART: Selected Metropolitan/Micropolitan Area Risk Trends, 2012 (Note: the CDC has discontinued this dataset but will be releasing a replacement in late 2015)

Chronic Health Indicators

Category	MSA[1] (%)	U.S. (%)
Adults who have ever been told they had a heart attack	3.7	4.5
Adults who have ever been told they had a stroke	2.9	2.9
Adults who have been told they currently have asthma	8.0	8.9
Adults who have ever been told they have arthritis	20.7	25.7
Adults who have ever been told they have diabetes[2]	8.9	9.7
Adults who have ever been told they had skin cancer	5.2	5.7
Adults who have ever been told they had any other types of cancer	5.2	6.5
Adults who have ever been told they have COPD	5.2	6.2
Adults who have ever been told they have kidney disease	3.0	2.5
Adults who have ever been told they have a form of depression	14.5	18.0

Note: Data as of 2012 unless otherwise noted; (1) Figures cover the Atlanta-Sandy Springs-Marietta, GA Metropolitan Statistical Area—see Appendix B for areas included; (2) Figures do not include pregnancy-related, borderline, or pre-diabetes
Source: Centers for Disease Control and Prevention, Behaviorial Risk Factor Surveillance System, SMART: Selected Metropolitan/Micropolitan Area Risk Trends, 2012 (Note: the CDC has discontinued this dataset but will be releasing a replacement in late 2015)

Mortality Rates for the Top 10 Causes of Death in the U.S.

ICD-10[a] Sub-Chapter	ICD-10[a] Code	Age-Adjusted Mortality Rate[1] per 100,000 population	
		County[2]	U.S.
Malignant neoplasms	C00-C97	161.2	166.2
Ischaemic heart diseases	I20-I25	66.0	105.7
Other forms of heart disease	I30-I51	57.9	49.3
Chronic lower respiratory diseases	J40-J47	27.0	42.1
Organic, including symptomatic, mental disorders	F01-F09	56.1	38.1
Cerebrovascular diseases	I60-I69	38.8	37.0
Other external causes of accidental injury	W00-X59	23.5	26.9
Other degenerative diseases of the nervous system	G30-G31	17.1	25.6
Diabetes mellitus	E10-E14	18.3	21.3
Hypertensive diseases	I10-I15	38.9	19.4

Note: (a) ICD-10 = International Classification of Diseases 10th Revision; (1) Mortality rates are a three year average covering 2011-2013; (2) Figures cover Fulton County
Source: Centers for Disease Control and Prevention, National Center for Health Statistics. Compressed Mortality File 1999-2013 on CDC WONDER Online Database, released October 2014. Data are compiled from the Compressed Mortality File 1999-2013, Series 20 No. 2S, 2014.

Mortality Rates for Selected Causes of Death

ICD-10[a] Sub-Chapter	ICD-10[a] Code	Age-Adjusted Mortality Rate[1] per 100,000 population	
		County[2]	U.S.
Assault	X85-Y09	9.7	5.2
Diseases of the liver	K70-K76	10.3	13.2
Human immunodeficiency virus (HIV) disease	B20-B24	10.4	2.2
Influenza and pneumonia	J09-J18	12.6	15.4
Intentional self-harm	X60-X84	11.5	12.5
Malnutrition	E40-E46	*0.7	0.9
Obesity and other hyperalimentation	E65-E68	0.9	1.8
Renal failure	N17-N19	18.8	13.1
Transport accidents	V01-V99	7.7	11.7
Viral hepatitis	B15-B19	2.1	2.2

Note: (a) ICD-10 = International Classification of Diseases 10th Revision; (1) Mortality rates are a three year average covering 2011-2013; (2) Figures cover Fulton County; (*) Unreliable data as per CDC
Source: Centers for Disease Control and Prevention, National Center for Health Statistics. Compressed Mortality File 1999-2013 on CDC WONDER Online Database, released October 2014. Data are compiled from the Compressed Mortality File 1999-2013, Series 20 No. 2S, 2014.

Health Insurance Coverage

Area	With Health Insurance	With Private Health Insurance	With Public Health Insurance	Without Health Insurance	Population Under Age 18 Without Health Insurance
City	81.7	61.6	27.6	18.3	7.1
MSA[1]	81.2	64.9	24.3	18.8	9.6
U.S.	85.2	65.2	31.0	14.8	7.3

Note: Figures are percentages that cover the civilian noninstitutionalized population; (1) Figures cover the Atlanta-Sandy Springs-Roswell, GA Metropolitan Statistical Area—see Appendix B for areas included
Source: U.S. Census Bureau, 2011-2013 American Community Survey 3-Year Estimates

Number of Medical Professionals

Area[1]	MDs[2]	DOs[2,3]	Dentists	Podiatrists	Chiropractors	Optometrists
Local (number)	4,718	98	641	40	464	137
Local (rate[4])	482.4	10.0	65.1	4.1	47.1	13.9
U.S. (rate[4])	270.0	20.2	63.1	5.7	25.2	14.9

Note: Data as of 2013 unless noted; (1) Local data covers Fulton County; (2) Data as of 2012 and includes all active, non-federal physicians; (3) Doctor of Osteopathic Medicine; (4) rate per 100,000 population
Source: U.S. Department of Health and Human Services, Health Resources and Services Administration, Bureau of Health Professions, Area Resource File (ARF) 2013-2014

Best Hospitals

According to *U.S. News,* the Atlanta-Sandy Springs-Roswell, GA metro area is home to three of the best hospitals in the U.S.: **Emory University Hospital** (9 specialties); **Emory Wesley Woods Geriatric Hospital** (1 specialty); **Shepherd Center** (1 specialty). The hospitals listed were nationally ranked in at least one adult specialty. Only 144 hospitals nationwide were nationally ranked in one or more specialties. Seventeen hospitals in the U.S. made the Honor Roll with high scores in at least six specialties. *U.S. News Online, "America's Best Children's Hospitals 2014-15"*

According to *U.S. News,* the Atlanta-Sandy Springs-Roswell, GA metro area is home to one of the best children's hospitals in the U.S.: **Children's Healthcare of Atlanta** (10 specialties). The hospital listed was highly ranked in at least one pediatric specialty. Eighty-nine children's hospitals in the U.S. were nationally ranked in at least one specialty. Ten children's hospitals in the U.S. made the Honor Roll with high scores in at least three specialties. *U.S. News Online, "America's Best Children's Hospitals 2014-15"*

EDUCATION

Public School District Statistics

District Name	Schls	Pupils	Pupil/ Teacher Ratio	Minority Pupils[1] (%)	Free Lunch Eligible[2] (%)	IEP[3] (%)
Atlanta Public Schools	103	49,558	13.4	85.9	72.6	9.1
Fulton County	104	93,907	15.0	67.9	40.8	10.2

Note: Table includes school districts with 2,000 or more students; (1) Percentage of students that are not non-Hispanic white; (2) Percentage of students that are eligible for the free lunch program; (3) Percentage of students that have an Individualized Education Program.
Source: U.S. Department of Education, National Center for Education Statistics, Common Core of Data, Local Education Agency (School District) Universe Survey: School Year 2012-2013; U.S. Department of Education, National Center for Education Statistics, Common Core of Data, Public Elementary/Secondary School Universe Survey: School Year 2012-2013

Highest Level of Education

Area	Less than H.S.	H.S. Diploma	Some College, No Deg.	Associate Degree	Bachelor's Degree	Master's Degree	Prof. School Degree	Doctorate Degree
City	11.1	19.5	16.6	4.6	28.3	12.9	4.8	2.2
MSA[1]	12.2	24.8	20.8	7.1	22.7	8.9	2.2	1.3
U.S.	13.7	28.0	21.2	7.9	18.2	7.7	1.9	1.3

Note: Figures cover persons age 25 and over; (1) Figures cover the Atlanta-Sandy Springs-Roswell, GA Metropolitan Statistical Area—see Appendix B for areas included
Source: U.S. Census Bureau, 2011-2013 American Community Survey 3-Year Estimates

Educational Attainment by Race

Area	High School Graduate or Higher (%)					Bachelor's Degree or Higher (%)				
	Total	White	Black	Asian	Hisp.[2]	Total	White	Black	Asian	Hisp.[2]
City	88.9	96.5	82.0	96.8	76.8	48.2	74.1	23.3	82.5	42.0
MSA[1]	87.8	89.0	88.4	86.5	60.0	35.1	38.7	27.4	52.9	15.6
U.S.	86.3	88.3	83.1	85.7	64.0	29.1	30.4	18.8	50.7	13.7

Note: Figures shown cover persons 25 years old and over; (1) Figures cover the Atlanta-Sandy Springs-Roswell, GA Metropolitan Statistical Area—see Appendix B for areas included; (2) People of Hispanic origin can be of any race
Source: U.S. Census Bureau, 2011-2013 American Community Survey 3-Year Estimates

School Enrollment by Grade and Control

Area	Preschool (%)		Kindergarten (%)		Grades 1 - 4 (%)		Grades 5 - 8 (%)		Grades 9 - 12 (%)	
	Public	Private	Public	Private	Public	Private	Public	Private	Public	Private
City	55.1	44.9	81.2	18.8	84.3	15.7	83.7	16.3	78.2	21.8
MSA[1]	54.0	46.0	87.6	12.4	90.5	9.5	89.9	10.1	90.6	9.4
U.S.	57.7	42.3	87.9	12.1	89.9	10.1	90.0	10.0	90.7	9.3

Note: Figures shown cover persons 3 years old and over; (1) Figures cover the Atlanta-Sandy Springs-Roswell, GA Metropolitan Statistical Area—see Appendix B for areas included
Source: U.S. Census Bureau, 2011-2013 American Community Survey 3-Year Estimates

Average Salaries of Public School Classroom Teachers

Area	2013-14		2014-15		Percent Change 2013-14 to 2014-15	Percent Change 2004-05 to 2014-15
	Dollars	Rank[1]	Dollars	Rank[1]		
GEORGIA	52,924	24	53,382	24	0.87	14.7
U.S. Average	56,610	–	57,379	–	1.36	20.8

Note: (1) State rank ranges from 1 to 51 where 1 indicates highest salary.
Source: National Education Association, Rankings & Estimates: Rankings of the States 2014 and Estimates of School Statistics 2015, March 2015

Higher Education

Four-Year Colleges			Two-Year Colleges			Medical Schools[1]	Law Schools[2]	Voc/ Tech[3]
Public	Private Non-profit	Private For-profit	Public	Private Non-profit	Private For-profit			
3	10	12	2	0	8	2	3	5

Note: Figures cover institutions located within the city limits and include main campuses only; (1) includes schools accredited by the Liaison Committee on Medical Education and the American Osteopathic Association's Commission on Osteopathic College Accreditation; (2) includes ABA-accredited schools, schools with provisional ABA accreditation, and state accredited schools; (3) includes all schools with programs that are less than 2 years.
Source: National Center for Education Statistics, Integrated Postsecondary Education System (IPEDS), 2013-14; Association of American Medical Colleges, Member List, May 1, 2015; American Osteopathic Association, Member List, May 1, 2015; Law School Admission Council, Official Guide to ABA-Approved Law Schools Online, May 1, 2015; Wikipedia, List of Medical Schools in the United States, May 1, 2015; Wikipedia, List of Law Schools in the United States, May 1, 2015

According to *U.S. News & World Report,* the Atlanta-Sandy Springs-Roswell, GA metro area is home to two of the best national universities in the U.S.: **Emory University** (#21); **Georgia Institute of Technology** (#35). The indicators used to capture academic quality fall into a number of categories: assessment by administrators at peer institutions; retention of students; faculty resources; student selectivity; financial resources; alumni giving; high school counselor ratings of colleges; and graduation rate. *U.S. News & World Report, "America's Best Colleges 2015"*

According to *U.S. News & World Report,* the Atlanta-Sandy Springs-Roswell, GA metro area is home to four of the best liberal arts colleges in the U.S.: **Agnes Scott College** (#73); **Spelman College** (#81); **Morehouse College** (#133); **Oglethorpe University** (#148). The indicators used to capture academic quality fall into a number of categories: assessment by administrators at peer institutions; retention of students; faculty resources; student selectivity; financial resources; alumni giving; high school counselor ratings of colleges; and graduation rate. *U.S. News & World Report, "America's Best Colleges 2015"*

According to *U.S. News & World Report,* the Atlanta-Sandy Springs-Roswell, GA metro area is home to two of the top 100 law schools in the U.S.: **Emory University** (#19); **Georgia State University** (#56). The rankings are based on a weighted average of 12 measures of quality: peer assessment score; assessment score by lawyers/judges; median LSAT scores; median undergrad GPA; acceptance rate; employment rates for graduates; placement success; bar passage rate; faculty resources; expenditures per student; student/faculty ratio; and library resources. *U.S. News & World Report, "America's Best Graduate Schools, Law, 2016"*

According to *U.S. News & World Report,* the Atlanta-Sandy Springs-Roswell, GA metro area is home to one of the top 75 medical schools for research in the U.S.: **Emory University** (#23). The rankings are based on a weighted average of 11 measures of quality: quality assessment; peer assessment score; assessment score by residency directors; research activity; total research activity; average research activity per faculty member; student selectivity; median MCAT total score; median undergraduate GPA; acceptance rate; and faculty resources. *U.S. News & World Report, "America's Best Graduate Schools, Medical, 2016"*

According to *U.S. News & World Report,* the Atlanta-Sandy Springs-Roswell, GA metro area is home to two of the top 75 business schools in the U.S.: **Emory University (Goizueta)** (#21); **Georgia Institute of Technology (Scheller)** (#30). The rankings are based on a weighted average of the following nine measures: quality assessment; peer assessment; recruiter assessment; placement success; mean starting salary and bonus; student selectivity; mean GMAT and GRE scores; mean undergraduate GPA; and acceptance rate. *U.S. News & World Report, "America's Best Graduate Schools, Business, 2016"*

PRESIDENTIAL ELECTION

2012 Presidential Election Results

Area	Obama (%)	Romney (%)	Other (%)
Fulton County	64.3	34.5	1.2
U.S.	51.0	47.2	1.8

Note: Results may not add to 100% due to rounding
Source: Dave Leip's Atlas of U.S. Presidential Elections

EMPLOYERS

Major Employers

Company Name	Industry
Apartments.Com	Apartment locating service
Aquilex Holdings	Facilities support services
AT&T Corp.	Engineering services
Behavioral Health, Georgia Department of	Administration of public health programs
Clayton County Board of Education	Public elementary and secondary schools
County of Gwinnett	County commissioner
Delta Air Lines	Air transportation, scheduled
Georgia Department of Human Resoures	Administration of public health programs
Georgia Department of Transportation	Regulation, administration of transportation
Internal Revenue Service	Taxation department, government
Lockheed Martin Aeronautical Company	Aircraft
NCR Corporation	Calculating and accounting equipment
Progressive Logistics Services	Labor organizations
Robert Half International	Employment agencies
The Army, United States Department of	Army
The Coca-Cola Company	Bottled and canned soft drinks
The Fulton-Dekalb Hospital Authority	General medical and surgical hospitals
The Home Depot	Hardware stores
WellStar Kennestone Hospital	General medical and surgical hospitals
World Travel Partners Group	Travel agencies

Note: Companies shown are located within the Atlanta-Sandy Springs-Roswell, GA Metropolitan Statistical Area.
Source: Hoovers.com; Wikipedia

Best Companies to Work For

Alston & Bird; Children's Healthcare of Atlanta, headquartered in Atlanta, are among "The 100 Best Companies to Work For." To pick the best companies, *Fortune* partnered with the Great Place to Work Institute. Two-thirds of a company's score is based on the results of the Institute's Trust Index survey, which is sent to a random sample of employees from each company. The questions related to attitudes about management's credibility, job satisfaction, and camaraderie. The other third of the scoring is based on the company's responses to the Institute's Culture Audit, which includes detailed questions about pay and benefit programs, and a series of open-ended questions about hiring practices, internal communication, training, recognition programs, and diversity efforts. Any company that is at least five years old with more than 1,000 U.S. employees is eligible. *Fortune, "The 100 Best Companies to Work For," 2015*

Children's Healthcare of Atlanta; Turner Broadcasting System, headquartered in Atlanta, are among the "100 Best Companies for Working Mothers." Criteria: leave policies, workforce representation, benefits, child care, advancement programs, and flexibility policies. This year *Working Mother* gave particular weight to representation of women, advancement programs and flex. *Working Mother, "100 Best Companies 2014"*

Southern Company, headquartered in Atlanta, is among the "50 Best Employers for Workers Over 50." Criteria: recruiting practices; opportunities for training, education, and career development; workplace accommodations; alternative work options, such as flexible scheduling, job sharing, and phased retirement; employee health and pension benefits; and retiree benefits. Employers with at least 50 employees based in the U.S. are eligible, including for-profit companies, not-for-profit organizations, and government employers. *AARP, "2013 AARP Best Employers for Workers Over 50"*

Coca-Cola Enterprises; Southern Co, headquartered in Atlanta, are among the "100 Best Places to Work in IT." To qualify, companies, both public and private, had to have a minimum of 50 IT employees and were selected based on average salary and bonus increases, the percentage of IT staffers promoted, IT staff turnover rates, training and development programs, and the percentage of women and minorities in IT staff and management positions. In addition, *Computerworld* looked at retention efforts, programs for recognizing and rewarding outstanding performances, and benefits such as flextime, elder care and child care, and reimbursement for college tuition and the cost of pursuing technology certifications. *Computerworld, "100 Best Places to Work in IT 2014"*

PUBLIC SAFETY

Crime Rate

Area	All Crimes	Violent Crimes: Murder	Violent Crimes: Forcible Rape	Violent Crimes: Robbery	Violent Crimes: Aggrav. Assault	Property Crimes: Burglary	Property Crimes: Larceny -Theft	Property Crimes: Motor Vehicle Theft
City	7,326.7	18.6	23.3	523.9	657.4	1,316.6	3,804.3	982.7
Suburbs[1]	3,398.5	4.7	19.2	125.5	165.3	763.9	2,040.0	279.9
Metro[2]	3,719.9	5.9	19.5	158.1	205.6	809.1	2,184.4	337.4
U.S.	3,098.6	4.5	25.2	109.1	229.1	610.0	1,899.4	221.3

Note: Figures are crimes per 100,000 population; (1) All areas within the metro area that are located outside the city limits; (2) Figures cover the Atlanta-Sandy Springs-Roswell, GA Metropolitan Statistical Area—see Appendix B for areas included
Source: FBI Uniform Crime Reports, 2013

Hate Crimes

Area	Number of Quarters Reported	Race	Religion	Sexual Orientation	Ethnicity	Disability	Gender	Gender Identity
		Number of Incidents per Bias Motivation						
City	4	5	1	12	2	1	0	0
U.S.	4	2,871	1,031	1,233	655	83	18	31

Source: Federal Bureau of Investigation, Hate Crime Statistics 2013

Identity Theft Consumer Complaints

Area	Complaints	Complaints per 100,000 Population	Rank[2]
MSA[1]	7,809	141.4	15
U.S.	332,646	104.3	-

Note: (1) Figures cover the Atlanta-Sandy Springs-Roswell, GA Metropolitan Statistical Area—see Appendix B for areas included; (2) Rank ranges from 1 to 380 where 1 indicates greatest number of identity theft complaints per 100,000 population
Source: Federal Trade Commission, Consumer Sentinel Network Data Book for January–December 2014

Fraud and Other Consumer Complaints

Area	Complaints	Complaints per 100,000 Population	Rank[2]
MSA[1]	25,593	463.4	42
U.S.	2,250,205	705.7	-

Note: (1) Figures cover the Atlanta-Sandy Springs-Roswell, GA Metropolitan Statistical Area—see Appendix B for areas included; (2) Rank ranges from 1 to 380 where 1 indicates greatest number of identity theft complaints per 100,000 population
Source: Federal Trade Commission, Consumer Sentinel Network Data Book for January–December 2014

RECREATION

Culture

Dance[1]	Theatre[1]	Instrumental Music[1]	Vocal Music[1]	Series and Festivals	Museums and Art Galleries[2]	Zoos and Aquariums[3]
5	22	5	8	9	81	2

Note: (1) Professional perfoming groups; (2) Based on organizations with SIC code 8412; (3) AZA-accredited
Source: The Grey House Performing Arts Directory, 2015-16; Association of Zoos & Aquariums, AZA Member Zoos & Aquariums, April 2015; www.AccuLeads.com, April 2015

Professional Sports Teams

Team Name	League	Year Established
Atlanta Braves	Major League Baseball (MLB)	1966
Atlanta Falcons	National Football League (NFL)	1966
Atlanta Hawks	National Basketball Association (NBA)	1968

Note: Includes teams located in the Atlanta-Sandy Springs-Roswell, GA Metropolitan Statistical Area.
Source: Wikipedia, Major Professional Sports Teams of the United States and Canada, April 2015

CLIMATE

Average and Extreme Temperatures

Temperature	Jan	Feb	Mar	Apr	May	Jun	Jul	Aug	Sep	Oct	Nov	Dec	Yr.
Extreme High (°F)	79	80	85	93	95	101	105	102	98	95	84	77	105
Average High (°F)	52	56	64	73	80	86	88	88	82	73	63	54	72
Average Temp. (°F)	43	46	53	62	70	77	79	79	73	63	53	45	62
Average Low (°F)	33	36	42	51	59	66	70	69	64	52	42	35	52
Extreme Low (°F)	-8	5	10	26	37	46	53	55	36	28	3	0	-8

Note: Figures cover the years 1945-1990
Source: National Climatic Data Center, International Station Meteorological Climate Summary, 9/96

Average Precipitation/Snowfall/Humidity

Precip./Humidity	Jan	Feb	Mar	Apr	May	Jun	Jul	Aug	Sep	Oct	Nov	Dec	Yr.
Avg. Precip. (in.)	4.7	4.6	5.7	4.3	4.0	3.5	5.1	3.6	3.4	2.8	3.8	4.2	49.8
Avg. Snowfall (in.)	1	1	Tr	Tr	0	0	0	0	0	0	Tr	Tr	2
Avg. Rel. Hum. 7am (%)	79	77	78	78	82	83	88	89	88	84	81	79	82
Avg. Rel. Hum. 4pm (%)	56	50	48	45	49	52	57	56	56	51	52	55	52

Note: Figures cover the years 1945-1990; Tr = Trace amounts (<0.05 in. of rain; <0.5 in. of snow)
Source: National Climatic Data Center, International Station Meteorological Climate Summary, 9/96

Weather Conditions

Temperature			Daytime Sky			Precipitation		
10°F & below	32°F & below	90°F & above	Clear	Partly cloudy	Cloudy	0.01 inch or more precip.	0.1 inch or more snow/ice	Thunder-storms
1	49	38	98	147	120	116	3	48

Note: Figures are average number of days per year and cover the years 1945-1990
Source: National Climatic Data Center, International Station Meteorological Climate Summary, 9/96

HAZARDOUS WASTE

Superfund Sites

Atlanta has no sites on the EPA's Superfund Final National Priorities List. There are a total of 1,322 Superfund sites on the list in the U.S. *U.S. Environmental Protection Agency, Final National Priorities List, April 14, 2015*

AIR & WATER QUALITY

Air Quality Trends: Ozone

	2004	2005	2006	2007	2008	2009	2010	2011	2012	2013
MSA[1]	0.081	0.085	0.092	0.091	0.080	0.072	0.074	0.078	0.077	0.065

Note: (1) Data covers the Atlanta-Sandy Springs-Roswell, GA Metropolitan Statistical Area—see Appendix B for areas included. The values shown are the composite ozone concentration averages among trend sites based on the highest fourth daily maximum 8-hour concentration in parts per million. These trends are based on sites having an adequate record of monitoring data during the trend period. Data from exceptional events are included.
Source: U.S. Environmental Protection Agency, Air Quality Monitoring Information, "Air Quality Trends by City, 2000-2013"

Air Quality Index

Area	Percent of Days when Air Quality was...[2]					AQI Statistics[2]	
	Good	Moderate	Unhealthy for Sensitive Groups	Unhealthy	Very Unhealthy	Maximum	Median
MSA[1]	38.4	58.9	2.5	0.0	0.3	214	54

Note: (1) Data covers the Atlanta-Sandy Springs-Roswell, GA Metropolitan Statistical Area—see Appendix B for areas included; (2) Based on 365 days with AQI data in 2014. Air Quality Index (AQI) is an index for reporting daily air quality. EPA calculates the AQI for five major air pollutants regulated by the Clean Air Act: ground-level ozone, particle pollution (aka particulate matter), carbon monoxide, sulfur dioxide, and nitrogen dioxide. The AQI runs from 0 to 500. The higher the AQI value, the greater the level of air pollution and the greater the health concern. There are six AQI categories: "Good" AQI is between 0 and 50. Air quality is considered satisfactory; "Moderate" AQI is between 51 and 100. Air quality is acceptable; "Unhealthy for Sensitive Groups" When AQI values are between 101 and 150, members of sensitive groups may experience health effects; "Unhealthy" When AQI values are between 151 and 200 everyone may begin to experience health effects; "Very Unhealthy" AQI values between 201 and 300 trigger a health alert; "Hazardous" AQI values over 300 trigger warnings of emergency conditions (not shown).
Source: U.S. Environmental Protection Agency, Air Quality Index Report, 2014

Air Quality Index Pollutants

Area	Percent of Days when AQI Pollutant was...[2]					
	Carbon Monoxide	Nitrogen Dioxide	Ozone	Sulfur Dioxide	Particulate Matter 2.5	Particulate Matter 10
MSA[1]	0.0	1.1	22.2	0.0	76.7	0.0

Note: (1) Data covers the Atlanta-Sandy Springs-Roswell, GA Metropolitan Statistical Area—see Appendix B for areas included; (2) Based on 365 days with AQI data in 2014. The Air Quality Index (AQI) is an index for reporting daily air quality. EPA calculates the AQI for five major air pollutants regulated by the Clean Air Act: ground-level ozone, particle pollution (also known as particulate matter), carbon monoxide, sulfur dioxide, and nitrogen dioxide. The AQI runs from 0 to 500. The higher the AQI value, the greater the level of air pollution and the greater the health concern.
Source: U.S. Environmental Protection Agency, Air Quality Index Report, 2014

Maximum Air Pollutant Concentrations: Particulate Matter, Ozone, CO and Lead

	Particulate Matter 10 (ug/m^3)	Particulate Matter 2.5 Wtd AM (ug/m^3)	Particulate Matter 2.5 24-Hr (ug/m^3)	Ozone (ppm)	Carbon Monoxide (ppm)	Lead (ug/m^3)
MSA[1] Level	34	9.7	20	0.071	1	0.01
NAAQS[2]	150	15	35	0.075	9	0.15
Met NAAQS[2]	Yes	Yes	Yes	Yes	Yes	Yes

Note: (1) Data covers the Atlanta-Sandy Springs-Roswell, GA Metropolitan Statistical Area—see Appendix B for areas included; Data from exceptional events are included; (2) National Ambient Air Quality Standards; ppm = parts per million; ug/m^3 = micrograms per cubic meter; n/a not available.
Concentrations: Particulate Matter 10 (coarse particulate)—highest second maximum 24-hour concentration; Particulate Matter 2.5 Wtd AM (fine particulate)—highest weighted annual mean concentration; Particulate Matter 2.5 24-Hour (fine particulate)—highest 98th percentile 24-hour concentration; Ozone—highest fourth daily maximum 8-hour concentration; Carbon Monoxide—highest second maximum non-overlapping 8-hour concentration; Lead—maximum running 3-month average
Source: U.S. Environmental Protection Agency, Air Quality Monitoring Information, "Air Quality Statistics by City, 2013"

Maximum Air Pollutant Concentrations: Nitrogen Dioxide and Sulfur Dioxide

	Nitrogen Dioxide AM (ppb)	Nitrogen Dioxide 1-Hr (ppb)	Sulfur Dioxide AM (ppb)	Sulfur Dioxide 1-Hr (ppb)	Sulfur Dioxide 24-Hr (ppb)
MSA[1] Level	9	43	n/a	9	n/a
NAAQS[2]	53	100	30	75	140
Met NAAQS[2]	Yes	Yes	n/a	Yes	n/a

Note: (1) Data covers the Atlanta-Sandy Springs-Roswell, GA Metropolitan Statistical Area—see Appendix B for areas included; Data from exceptional events are included; (2) National Ambient Air Quality Standards; ppm = parts per million; ug/m^3 = micrograms per cubic meter; n/a not available.
Concentrations: Nitrogen Dioxide AM—highest arithmetic mean concentration; Nitrogen Dioxide 1-Hr—highest 98th percentile 1-hour daily maximum concentration; Sulfur Dioxide AM—highest annual mean concentration; Sulfur Dioxide 1-Hr—highest 99th percentile 1-hour daily maximum concentration; Sulfur Dioxide 24-Hr—highest second maximum 24-hour concentration
Source: U.S. Environmental Protection Agency, Air Quality Monitoring Information, "Air Quality Statistics by City, 2013"

Drinking Water

Water System Name	Pop. Served	Primary Water Source Type	Violations[1]	
			Health Based	Monitoring/ Reporting
Atlanta	650,000	Surface	1	0

Note: (1) Based on violation data from January 1, 2014 to December 31, 2014 (includes unresolved violations from earlier years)

Source: U.S. Environmental Protection Agency, Office of Ground Water and Drinking Water, Safe Drinking Water Information System (based on data extracted January 27, 2015)

Austin, Texas

Background

Starting out in 1730 as a peaceful Spanish mission on the north bank of the Colorado River in south-central Texas, Austin soon engaged in an imbroglio of territorial wars, beginning when the "Father of Texas," Stephen F. Austin, annexed the territory from Mexico in 1833 as his own. Later, the Republic of Texas named the territory Austin in honor of the colonizer, and conferred upon it state capital status. Challenges to this decision ensued, ranging from an invasion by the Mexican government to reclaim its land, to Sam Houston's call that the capital ought to move from Austin to Houston.

During peaceful times, however, Austin has been called the "City of the Violet Crown." Coined by the short story writer, William Sydney Porter, or O. Henry, the name refers to the purple mist that circles the surrounding hills of the Colorado River Valley.

This city of technological innovation is home to a strong computer and electronics industry. Austin offers more free wireless spots—including its city parks—per capita than any other city in the nation, and its technology focus has traditionally drawn numerous high-tech companies. Samsung Electronics' major computer chip plant was built in Austin in the late 1990s with expansions and a new facility, nine football fields big, since. Along with this technology growth has come the problem of increased traffic, especially on Interstate 35, the main highway linking the U.S. and Mexico. A recently developed 89-mile bypass has helped to relieve some of the traffic difficulties long associated with I-35. In May 2010, Facebook opened a sales and operations facility in the city.

In addition to its traditional business community, Austin is home to the main campus of the University of Texas. The university provides Austin with even further diverse lifestyles; today there is a solid mix of white-collar workers, students, professors, blue-collar workers, musicians and artists, and members of the booming tech industry who all call themselves Austinites.

The influx of young people centered on university life has contributed to the city's growth as a thriving live music scene. It is so important to the city that its local government maintains the Austin Music Commission to promote the local music industry.

A notable industry conference takes place here each spring. The South by Southwest Conference (SXSW) showcases more than 2,000 performers at 90+ venues throughout the city. The growing film and interactive industries have been added to the conference in recent years.

The civic-minded city, whose mayor is working toward making Austin the nation's fittest city, is operating from a new city hall, which was completed in late 2004. The building, at about 115,000 square feet, is also home to a public plaza facing Town Lake. One of the town's cultural hubs, the Long Center for the Performing Arts, underwent renovation in 2006, and reopened in 2008.

It is most likely Austinites' pride in their creative and independent culture that has spawned a movement to keep the city from too much corporate development. The slogan "Keep Austin Weird" was adopted by the Austin Independent Business Alliance in 2003 as a way to promote local and alternative business.

The city sits at a desirable location along the Colorado River, and many recreational activities center on the water. For instance, Austin boasts three spring-fed swimming pools enjoyed by its residents, as well as the Lance Armstrong Crosstown Bikeway. The city has more than 100 miles of bike paths.

The climate of Austin is subtropical with hot summers. Winters are mild, with below-freezing temperatures occurring on an average of 25 days a year. Cold spells are short, seldom lasting more than two days. Daytime temperatures in summer are hot, while summer nights are usually pleasant.

Rankings

General Rankings

- Austin appeared on *Business Insider's* list of the "15 Hottest American Cities for 2015." Criteria: job and population growth; demographics; affordability; livability; residents' health and welfare; technological innovation; sustainability; culture favoring youth and creativity. *www.businessinsider.com, "The Fifteen Hottest American Cities for 2015," November 19, 2014*

- The Austin metro area was identified as one of America's fastest-growing areas in terms of population and economy by *Forbes*. The area ranked #2 out of 20. The 100 most populous metro areas in the U.S. were evaluated on the following criteria: estimated population growth; job growth; gross metropolitan product growth; unemployment; median salaries for college-educated workers. *Forbes, "America's Fastest-Growing Cities 2015," January 27, 2015*

- Austin was identified as one of America's fastest-growing major metropolitan areas in terms of population growth by CNNMoney.com. The area ranked #1 out of 10. Criteria: population growth between July 2012 and July 2013. *CNNMoney, "10 Fastest-Growing Cities," March 28, 2014*

- Among the 50 largest U.S. cities, Austin placed #5 in Vocativ's "semi-exhaustive, mostly scientific" city Livability Index for people aged 35 and under. Average salary, unemployment rates, rents, and other living costs were considered, along with crime rates, weather, public transportation, access to music and sports, and "lifestyle metrics" such as the price of dinner at Buffalo Wild Wings and an ounce of high-quality weed. *vocative.com, "The Livability Index: The Best U.S. Cities for People 35 and Under," December 9, 2014*

- Austin was selected as one of America's best cities by *Bloomberg Businessweek*. The city ranked #8 out of 50. Criteria: leisure attributes (the number of restaurants, bars, libraries, museums, professional sports teams, and park acres by population); educational attributes (public school performance, the number of colleges, and graduate degree holders); economic factors (2011 income and June and July 2012 unemployment); crime; and air quality. *Bloomberg BusinessWeek, "America's Best Cities," September 26, 2012*

Business/Finance Rankings

- Measuring indicators of "tolerance"—the nonjudgmental environment that "attracts open-minded and new-thinking kinds of people"— as well as concentrations of technological and economic innovators, analysts identified the most creative American metro areas. On the resulting 2012 Creativity Index, the Austin metro area placed #16. *www.thedailybeast.com, "Boulder, Ann Arbor, Tucson & More: 20 Most Creative U.S. Cities," June 26, 2012*

- The personal finance site NerdWallet scored the nation's 50 largest American cities according to how friendly a business climate they offer to would-be entrepreneurs. Criteria included access to funding, human capital, local economy, and business-friendliness as judged by small business owners. On the resulting list of most welcoming cities, Austin ranked #7. *www.nerdwallet.com, "Best Cities to Start a Business," May 7, 2014*

- Recognizing the sizeable percentage of American workers who are self-employed, NerdWallet editors assessed the country's cities according to percentage of freelancers, median rental costs, and affordability of median healthcare costs. By these criteria, Austin placed #4 among the best cities for independent workers. *www.nerdwallet.com, "Best Cities for Freelancers," February 25, 2014*

- The editors of *Kiplinger's Personal Finance Magazine* named Austin to their list of ten of the best metro areas for start-ups. The area rank #5.Criteria: well-educated workforce; low living costs for self-employed people, as measured by the Council for Community and Economic Research; a strong existing community of small business; low unemployment; low business costs. *www.kiplinger.com, "10 Great Cities for Starting a Business," October 2014*

- To help veterans transition to civilian life, USAA and Hiring Our Heroes worked with Sperlings's BestPlaces and the Institute for Veterans and Military Families at Syracuse University to develop a list of the major metropolitan areas where military-skills-related employment is strongest. Criteria for veterans *starting out* included G.I. Bill enrollment, job prospects, unemployment rate, military skills jobs and certification/license transfers, recent job growth, and accessible health resources. Metro areas with a violent crime rate or high cost of living were excluded. At #2, the Austin metro area made the top ten. *www.usaa.com, "2014 Best Places for Veterans"*

- To help veterans transition to civilian life, USAA and Hiring Our Heroes worked with Sperlings's BestPlaces and the Institute for Veterans and Military Families at Syracuse University to develop a list of the major metropolitan areas where military-skills-related employment is strongest. Criteria for *mid-career* veterans included veteran wage growth; military skills, defense contractor, and government jobs; recent job growth; supervisor/manager jobs; and accessible health resources. Metro areas with a violent crime rate or high cost of living were excluded. At #5, the Austin metro area made the top ten. *www.usaa.com, "2014 Best Places for Veterans"*

- The finance website Wall St. Cheat Sheet reported on the prospects for high-wage job creation in the nation's largest metro areas over the next five years and ranked them accordingly, drawing on in-depth analysis by CareerBuilder and Economic Modeling Specialists International (EMSI). The Austin metro area placed #2 on the Wall St. Cheat Sheet list. *wallstcheatsheet.com, "Top 10 Cities for High-Wage Job Growth," December 8, 2013*

- Austin was the #7-ranked city in a Seedtable analysis of the world's most active cities for start-up companies, as reported by Statista. *www.statista.com, "San Francisco Has the Most Active Start-Up Scene," August 21, 2013*

- The business website 24/7 Wall Street drew on Brookings Institution research on 50 advanced industries to identify the proportion of workers in the nation's largest metropolitan areas that were employed in jobs requiring knowledge in the science, technology, engineering, or math (STEM) fields. The Austin metro area was #11. *247wallst.com, "15 Cities with the Most High-Tech Jobs," March 13, 2015*

- Based on metro area social media reviews, the employment opinion group Glassdoor surveyed 50 of the largest U.S. metro areas on measures including compensation and benefits, satisfaction with management, business outlook, and number of employers hiring. The Austin metro area was ranked #10 in overall employee satisfaction. *www.glassdoor.com, "Employment Satisfaction Report Card by City," June 13, 2014*

- In a survey of economic confidence in the nation's 50 largest metropolitan areas conducted January–December 2014, the Austin metro area placed #9, according to Gallup's 2014 Economic Confidence Index. *Gallup, "San Jose and San Francisco Lead in Economic Confidence," March 19, 2015*

- The financial literacy site NerdWallet.com set out to identify the 10 most promising cities for job seekers, analyzing data for the nation's 100 largest cities. Austin was ranked #6. Criteria: job availability; workforce growth; affordability. *NerdWallet.com, "Best Cities for Job Seekers in 2015," January 12, 2015*

- The Brookings Institution ranked the 50 largest cities in the U.S. based on income inequality. Austin was ranked #28. (#1 = greatest ineqality). Criteria: the cities were ranked based on the "95/20 ratio," a figure representing the income at which a household earns more than 95 percent of all other households, divided by the income at which a household earns more than only 20 percent of all other households. *Brookings Institution, "Income Inequality in America's 50 Largest Cities, 2007-2013," March 17, 2015*

- *Forbes* ranked the largest metro areas in the U.S. in terms of the "Best Cities for Young Professionals." The Austin metro area ranked #8 out of 15. Criteria: job growth; unemployment rate; median salary of college graduates age 24 to 34; cost of living; number of small businesses per capita; number of large companies; percentage of population 25 years of age and older with college degrees. *Forbes.com, "America's 15 Best Cities for Young Professionals," August 18, 2014*

- Austin was ranked #2 out of 100 metro areas in terms of economic performance (#1 = best) during the recession and recovery from trough quarter through the second quarter of 2013. Criteria: percent change in employment; percentage point change in unemployment rate; percent change in gross metropolitan product; percent change in House Price Index. *Brookings Institution, MetroMonitor: Tracking Economic Recession and Recovery in America's 100 Largest Metropolitan Areas, September 2013*
- Austin was identified as one of the best places for finding a job by *U.S. News & World Report.* The city ranked #5 out of 10. Criteria: strong job market. *U.S. News & World Report, "The 10 Best Cities to Find Jobs," June 17, 2013*
- The Austin metro area was identified as one of the most affordable metropolitan areas in America by *Forbes.* The area ranked #19 out of 20. Criteria: the 100 largest metro areas in the U.S. were analyzed based on the National Association of Home Builders/Wells Fargo Housing Affordability Index and Sperling's Best Places' cost-of-living index. Some major cities were omitted for lack of data. *Forbes.com, "America's Most Affordable Cities in 2015," March 12, 2015*
- Austin was identified as one of America's most frugal metro areas by *Coupons.com.* The city ranked #22 out of 25. Criteria: Grocery IQ and coupons.com mobile app usage. *Coupons.com, "Top 25 Most On-the-Go Frugal Cities of 2013," April 10, 2014*
- Austin was identified as one of America's "10 Best Cities to Find Jobs" by *U.S. News & World Report.* The city ranked #5. Criteria: Bureau of labor Statistics unemployment rates; employment data from Indeed.com and juju.com. *U.S. News & World Report, "10 Best Cities to Find Jobs," June 17, 2013*
- The lifestyle website Livability.com rated Austin as #3 among its list of ten cities where new college grads' job prospects are brightest. Criteria included: number of 25- to 34-year olds; unemployment rate; rental vacancies; rental costs; nonservice jobs; public transportation users; educational attainment; bars and restaurants per capita. *Livability.com, "10 Best Cities for New College Grads, 2014" February 10, 2014*
- *Forbes* reports that Austin was identified as one of the unhappiest cities to work in by CareerBliss.com, an online community for career advancement. The city ranked #5 out of 10. Criteria: work-life balance; an employee's relationship with his or her boss and co-workers; general work environment; compensation; opportunities for advancement; company culture; and resources. *Forbes.com, "The 10 Happiest and Unhappiest Cities to Work in Right Now," January 16, 2015*
- The Austin metro area appeared on the Milken Institute "2013 Best Performing Cities" list. Rank: #2 out of 200 large metro areas. Criteria: job growth; wage and salary growth; high-tech output growth. *Milken Institute, "Best-Performing Cities 2014," January 2015*
- *Forbes* ranked the 200 most populous metro areas to determine the nation's "Best Places for Business and Careers." The Austin metro area was ranked #19. Criteria: costs (business and living); job growth (past and projected); income growth; educational attainment (college and high school); projected economic growth; cultural and recreational opportunities; net migration patterns; number of highly ranked colleges. *Forbes, "The Best Places for Business and Careers 2014," July 23, 2014*

Culture/Performing Arts Rankings

- Austin was selected as one of the ten best large U.S. cities in which to be a moviemaker. Of cities with a population over 400,000, the city was ranked #1. Criteria: film community; access to new films; access to equipment; cost of living; tax incentives. *MovieMaker Magazine, "Best Places to Live and Work as a Moviemaker: 2013," January 22, 2015*
- Austin was selected as one of "America's Favorite Cities." The city ranked #2 in the "Culture: Concerts " category. Respondents to an online survey were asked to rate 38 top urban destinations in the U.S. from a visitor's perspective. Criteria: number and quality of concerts. *Travelandleisure.com, "America's Favorite Cities," October 7, 2014*
- Austin was selected as one of "America's Favorite Cities." The city ranked #2 in the "Culture: Music Scene " category. Respondents to an online survey were asked to rate 38 top urban destinations in the U.S. from a visitor's perspective. *Travelandleisure.com, "America's Favorite Cities," October 7, 2014*

- Austin was selected as one of America's top cities for the arts. The city ranked #9 in the big city (population 500,000 and over) category. Criteria: readers' top choices for arts travel destinations based on the richness and variety of visual arts sites, activities and events. *American Style, "2012 Top 25 Arts Destinations," June 2012*

Dating/Romance Rankings

- A *Cosmopolitan* magazine article surveyed the gender balance and other factors to arrive at a list of the best and worst cities for women to meet single guys. Austin was #8 among the best for single women looking for dates. *www.cosmopolitan.com, "Working the Ratio," October 1, 2013*
- Of the 100 U.S. cities surveyed by *Men's Health* in its quest to identify the nation's best cities for dating and forming relationships, Austin was ranked #11 for online dating (#1 = best). *Men's Health, "The Best and Worst Cities for Online Dating," January 30, 2013*
- Austin ranked #5 among cities congenial to singles, according to Kiplinger, which searched for "dating scenes as financially attractive as they are romantically promising." High percentages of unmarried people, above-average household incomes, and cost-of-living factors determined the rankings. *Kiplinger.com, "10 Best Cities for Singles," February 2014*
- Austin was selected as one of America's best cities for singles by the readers of *Travel + Leisure* in their annual "America's Favorite Cities" survey. The city was ranked #4 out of 20. Criteria included good-looking locals, cool shopping, and hipster-magnet coffee bars. *Travel + Leisure, "America's Best Cities for Singles," January 23, 2015*
- Austin was selected as one of the best cities for post grads by *Rent.com*. The city ranked #6 of 10. Criteria: millenial population; jobs per capita; unemployment rate; median rent; number of bars and restaurants; access to nightlife and entertainment. *Rent.com, "Top 10 Best Cities for Post Grads," April 3, 2015*
- Austin was selected as one of "America's Best Cities for Dating" by *Yahoo! Travel*. Criteria: high proportion of singles; excellent dating venues and/or stunning natural settings. *Yahoo! Travel, "America's Best Cities for Dating," February 7, 2012*

Education Rankings

- Based on a Brookings Institution study, *24/7 Wall St.* identified the ten U.S. metropolitan areas with the most average patent filings per million residents between 2007 and 2011. Austin ranked #9. *24/7 Wall St., "America's Most Innovative Cities," February 1, 2013*
- The Austin metro area was selected as one of America's most innovative cities" by *The Business Insider*. The metro area was ranked #9 out of 20. Criteria: patents per capita. *The Business Insider, "The 20 Most Innovative Cities in the U.S.," February 1, 2013*
- Personal finance website *WalletHub* analyzed the 150 largest U.S. metropolitan statistical areas to determine where the most educated Americans are choosing to settle. Criteria: educational attainment; percentage of workers with jobs in computer, engineering, and science fields; quality and size of each metro area's universities. Austin was ranked #11 (#1 = most educated city). *www.WalletHub.com, "2014's Most and Least Educated Cities*
- Austin was selected as one of America's most literate cities. The city ranked #22 out of the 77 largest U.S. cities. Criteria: number of booksellers; library resources; Internet resources; educational attainment; periodical publishing resources; newspaper circulation. *Central Connecticut State University, "America's Most Literate Cities, 2014," April 8, 2015*

Environmental Rankings

- The Austin metro area came in at #346 for the relative comfort of its climate on Sperling's list of "chill cities," as measured by the Sperling Heat Index. All 361 metro areas are included. Criteria included daytime high temperatures, nighttime low temperatures, dew point, and relative humidity at the high temperatures. *www.bertsperling.com, "Sperling's Chill Cities," July 18, 2013*

- Sperling's BestPlaces assessed 379 metropolitan areas of the United States for the likelihood of dangerously extreme weather events or earthquakes. In general the Southeast and South-Central regions have the highest risk of weather extremes and earthquakes, while the Pacific Northwest enjoys the lowest risk. Of the least risky metropolitan areas, the Austin metro area was ranked #373. *www.bestplaces.net, "Safest Places from Natural Disasters," April 2011*
- The U.S. Environmental Protection Agency (EPA) released a list of large U.S. metropolitan areas with the most ENERGY STAR certified buildings in 2014. The Austin metro area was ranked #23 out of 25. *U.S. Environmental Protection Agency, "Top Cities With the Most ENERGY STAR Certified Buildings in 2014," March 25, 2015*
- The U.S. Environmental Protection Agency (EPA) released a list of mid-size U.S. metropolitan areas with the most ENERGY STAR certified buildings in 2014. The Austin metro area was ranked #3 out of 10. *U.S. Environmental Protection Agency, "Top Cities With the Most ENERGY STAR Certified Buildings in 2014," March 25, 2015*
- Austin was highlighted as one of the top 25 cleanest metro areas for short-term particle pollution (24-hour PM 2.5) in the U.S. during 2011 through 2013. Monitors in these cities reported no days with unhealthful PM 2.5 levels. *American Lung Association, State of the Air 2015*

Food/Drink Rankings

- According to Fodor's Travel, Austin placed #3 among the best U.S. cities for food-truck cuisine. *www.fodors.com, "America's Best Food Truck Cities," December 20, 2013*
- *Men's Health* ranked 100 major U.S. cities in terms of alcohol intoxication. Austin ranked #93 (#1 = most sober).Criteria: binge drinking; alcohol-related traffic accidents, arrests, and fatalities. *Men's Health, "The Drunkest Cities in America," November 19, 2013*
- Austin was identified as one of the most vegetarian-friendly cities in America by GrubHub.com, the nation's largest food ordering service. The city ranked #6 out of 10. Criteria: percentage of vegetarian restaurants. *GrubHub.com, "Top Vegetarian-Friendly Cities," July 18, 2012*
- Austin was selected as one of the seven best cities for barbeque by *U.S. News & World Report.* The city was ranked #5. *U.S. New & World Report, "America's Best BBQ Cities," February 29, 2012*
- Austin was selected as one of America's 10 most vegan-friendly cities. The city was ranked #1. *People for the Ethical Treatment of Animals, "Top Vegan-Friendly Cities of 2013," June 11, 2013*

Health/Fitness Rankings

- For each of the 50 most populous metro areas in the United States, the American College of Sports Medicine's American Fitness Index evaluated infrastructure, community assets, and policies that encourage healthy and fit lifestyles, including preventive health behaviors, levels of chronic disease conditions, health care access, and community resources and policies that support physical activity. The Austin metro area ranked #11 for "community fitness." Personal health indicators were considered as well as community and environmental indicators. *www.americanfitnessindex.org, "ACSM American Fitness Index Health and Community Fitness Status of the 50 Largest Metropolitan Areas," May 2013*
- Austin was selected as one of the 25 fittest cities in America by *Men's Fitness Online*. It ranked #12 out of America's 50 largest cities. Criteria: fitness centers and sport stores; nutrition; sports participation; TV viewing; overweight/sedentary; junk food; air quality; geography; commute; parks and open space; city recreational facilities; access to healthcare; motivation; mayor and city initiatives; state obesity initiatives. *Men's Fitness, "The Fittest and Fattest Cities in America," March 5, 2012*
- Austin was identified as a "2013 Spring Allergy Capital." The area ranked #64 out of 100. Three groups of factors were used to identify the most severe cities for people with allergies during the spring season: annual pollen levels; medicine utilization; access to board-certified allergists. *Asthma and Allergy Foundation of America, "Spring Allergy Capitals 2013"*

- Austin was identified as a "2013 Fall Allergy Capital." The area ranked #45 out of 100. Three groups of factors were used to identify the most severe cities for people with allergies during the fall season: annual pollen levels; medicine utilization; access to board-certified allergists. *Asthma and Allergy Foundation of America, "Fall Allergy Capitals 2013"*
- Austin was identified as a "2013 Asthma Capital." The area ranked #93 out of the nation's 100 largest metropolitan areas. Twelve factors were used to identify the most challenging places to live for people with asthma: estimated prevalence; self-reported prevalence; crude death rate for asthma; annual pollen score; annual air quality; public smoking laws; number of board-certified asthma specialists; school inhaler access laws; rescue medication use; controller medication use; uninsured rate; poverty rate. *Asthma and Allergy Foundation of America, "Asthma Capitals 2013"*
- *Men's Health* ranked 100 major U.S. cities in terms of the best and worst cities for men. Austin ranked #7. Criteria: thirty-three data points were examined covering health, fitness, and quality of life. *Men's Health, "The Best & Worst Cities for Men 2014," December 6, 2013*
- Austin was selected as one of the best metropolitan areas for hospital care in America by *HealthGrades.com.* The rankings are based on a comprehensive study of patient death and complication rates in the nation's nearly 5,000 hospitals. Hospitals performing in the top 5% nationwide across 26 different medical procedures and diagnoses were identified. *HealthGrades.com* then ranked cities by the highest percentage of these Distinguished Hospitals for Clinical Excellence™. The Austin metro area ranked #45. *HealthGrades.com, "America's Top 50 Cities for Hospital Care," January 21, 2012*
- The Austin metro area appeared in the 2013 Gallup-Healthways Well-Being Index. The area ranked #30 out of 189. The Gallup-Healthways Well-Being Index score is an average of six sub-indexes, which individually examine life evaluation, emotional health, work environment, physical health, healthy behaviors, and access to basic necessities. Results are based on telephone interviews conducted as part of the Gallup-Healthways Well-Being Index survey January 2–December 29, 2012, and January 2–December 30, 2013, with a random sample of 531,630 adults, aged 18 and older, living in metropolitan areas in the 50 U.S. states and the District of Columbia. *Gallup-Healthways, "State of American Well-Being," March 25, 2014*
- The Austin metro area was identified as one of "America's Most Stressful Cities" by *Sperling's BestPlaces.* The metro area ranked #38 out of 50. Criteria: unemployment rate; suicide rate; commute time; mental health; poor rest; alcohol use; violent crime rate; property crime rate; cloudy days annually. *Sperling's BestPlaces, www.BestPlaces.net, "Stressful Cities 2012*

Pet Rankings

- Austin was selected as one of the best cities for dogs by real estate website Estately.com. The city was ranked #4. Criteria: weather; walkability; yard sizes; dog activities; meetup groups; availability of dogsitters. *Estately.com, "17 Best U.S. Cities for Dogs," May 14, 2013*

Real Estate Rankings

- The Austin metro area was identified as one of the nations's 20 hottest housing markets in 2015. Criteria: listing views relative to the number of listings. The area ranked #13. *Realtor.com, "These Are the 20 Hottest Housing Markets in the U.S. Right Now," April 8, 2015*
- The Austin metro area was identified as one of the nation's 20 hottest housing markets in 2015.Criteria: median number of days homes were spending on the market in March 2015. The area ranked #17. *Realtor.com, "These Are the 20 Hottest Housing Markets in the U.S. Right Now," April 8, 2015*
- The Austin metro area was identified as one of the top 20 housing markets to invest in for 2015 by *Forbes*. The area ranked #1. Criteria: strong population and job growth; relatively low home prices which are below equilibrium home price (EHP). The EHP is what the average price for a market should be, if speculation, weird distortions in local income, and other factors (like the housing collapse) weren't present in the market. *Forbes.com, "Best Buy Cities: Where to Invest in Housing in 2015," January 9, 2015*
- Austin was ranked #18 out of 275 metro areas in terms of house price appreciation in 2014 (#1 = highest rate). *Federal Housing Finance Agency, House Price Index, 4th Quarter 2014*

- The Austin metro area was identified as one of the 15 worst housing markets for the next five years." Criteria: projected annualized change in home prices between the fourth quarter 2012 and the fourth quarter 2017. *The Business Insider, "The 15 Worst Housing Markets for the Next Five Years," May 22, 2013*

- Austin was ranked #165 out of 226 metro areas in terms of housing affordability in 2014 by the National Association of Home Builders (#1 = most affordable). The NAHB-Wells Fargo Housing Opportunity Index (HOI) for a given area is defined as the share of homes sold in that area that would have been affordable to a family earning the local median income, based on standard mortgage underwriting criteria. *National Association of Home Builders®, NAHB-Wells Fargo Housing Opportunity Index, 4th Quarter 2014*

Safety Rankings

- Symantec, in partnership with Sperling's BestPlaces, ranked the 50 largest cities in the U.S. in terms of their vulnerability to cybercrime. The city ranked #10. Criteria: number of cyberattacks and potential infections; level of Internet access; expenditures on smartphones and computer hardware/software; wireless hotspots; broadband connectivity; Internet usage; online purchases. *Symantec, "Riskiest Online Cities of 2012" February 15, 2012*

- Farmers Insurance, in partnership with Sperling's BestPlaces, ranked metro areas in the U.S. and identified the "Most Secure Places to Live." The Austin metro area ranked #4 out of the top 20 in the large metro area category (500,000 or more residents). Criteria: economic stability; crime statistics; extreme weather; risk of natural disasters; housing depreciation; foreclosures; air quality; environmental hazards; life expectancy; motor vehicle fatalities; and employment numbers. *Farmers Insurance Group of Companies, "Most Secure U.S. Places to Live in the U.S.," June 25, 2013*

- Allstate ranked the 200 largest cities in America in terms of driver safety. Austin ranked #159. Allstate researchers analyzed internal property damage claims over a two-year period from January 2011 to December 2012. A weighted average of the two-year numbers determined the annual percentages. *Allstate, "Allstate America's Best Drivers Report, 2014"*

- Austin was identified as one of the safest large cities in America by CQ Press. All 32 cities with populations of 500,000 or more that reported crime rates in 2012 for murder, rape, robbery, aggravated assault, burglary, and motor vehicle thefts were ranked. The city ranked #3 out of the top 10. *CQ Press, City Crime Rankings 2014*

- The National Insurance Crime Bureau ranked 380 metro areas in the U.S. in terms of per capita rates of vehicle theft. The Austin metro area ranked #134 (#1 = highest rate). Criteria: number of vehicle theft offenses per 100,000 inhabitants in 2012. *National Insurance Crime Bureau, "Hot Spots 2012," June 26, 2013*

Seniors/Retirement Rankings

- From its Best Cities for Successful Aging indexes, the Milken Institute generated rankings for metropolitan areas, weighing data in eight categories—health care, wellness, living arrangements, transportation, financial characteristics, education and employment opportunities, community engagement, and overall livability. The Austin metro area was ranked #9 overall in the large metro area category. *Milken Institute, "Best Cities for Successful Aging, 2014"*

- Austin made the 2014 *Forbes* list of "25 Best Places to Retire." Criteria include: housing and living costs; tax climate for retirees; weather and air quality; crime rates; doctor availability; active-lifestyle rankings for walkability, bicycling and volunteering. *Forbes.com, "The Best Places to Retire in 2014," January 16, 2014*

- Austin was chosen in the "Big City" category of CNNMoney's list of the 25 best places to retire." Criteria include: type of location (big city, small town, resort area, college town); median home prices; top state income tax rate. *CNNMoney, "25 Best Places to Retire," December 17, 2012*

- Austin was identified as one of the most popular places to retire by *Topretirements.com*. The list reflects the 100 cities (out of 900+ total cities reviewed) that visitors to the website are most interested in for retirement. *Topretirements.com, "Most Popular Places to Retire for 2014," February 25, 2014*

Sports/Recreation Rankings

- Austin was chosen as a bicycle friendly community by the League of American Bicyclists. A "Bicycle Friendly Community" welcomes cyclists by providing safe accommodation for cycling and encouraging people to bike for transportation and recreation. There are four award levels: Platinum; Gold; Silver; and Bronze. The community achieved an award level of Silver. *League of American Bicyclists, "Bicycle Friendly Community Master List," Fall 2013*
- Austin was selected as one of the most playful cities in the U.S. by KaBOOM! The organization's Playful City USA initiative honors cities and towns across the nation for a vision, plan and commitment to creating an agenda for play. Criteria: creating a local play commission or task force; designing an annual action plan for play; conducting a play space audit; outlining a financial investment in play for the current fiscal year; and proclaiming and celebrating an annual "play day." *KaBOOM! National Campaign for Play, "2013 Playful City USA Communities"*
- Austin was chosen as one of America's best cities for bicycling. The city ranked #13 out of 50. Criteria: robust cycling infrastructure; vibrant bike culture. The editors only considered cities with populations of 95,000 or more. *Bicycling, "America's Top 50 Bike-Friendly Cities," May 23, 2012*

Transportation Rankings

- Austin appeared on *Trapster.com's* list of the 10 most-active U.S. cities for speed traps. The city ranked #10 of 10. *Trapster.com* is a community platform accessed online and via smartphone app that alerts drivers to traps, hazards and other traffic issues nearby. *Trapster.com, "Speeders Beware: Cities With the Most Speed Traps," February 10, 2012*

Women/Minorities Rankings

- To determine the best metro areas for working women, the personal finance website NerdWallet considered city size as well as relevant economic metrics—high salaries, narrow pay differential by gender, prevalence of women in the highest-paying industries, and population growth over 2010–2012. Of the large U.S. cities examined, the Austin metro area held the #4 position. *www.nerdwallet.com, "Best Places for Women in the Workforce," May 19, 2013*
- *Women's Health* examined U.S. cities and identified the 100 best cities for women. Austin was ranked #9. Criteria: 30 categories were examined from obesity and breast cancer rates to commuting times and hours spent working out. *Women's Health, "Best Cities for Women 2012"*
- Austin was selected as one of the best cities for young Latinos in 2013 by mun2, a national cable television broadcast network. The city ranked #2. Criteria: U.S. cities with populations over 500,000 residents were evaluated on the following criteria: number of young latinos; jobs; friendliness; cost of living; fun. *mun2.tv, "Best Cities for Young Latinos 2013*

Miscellaneous Rankings

- Austin was selected as a 2013 Digital Cities Survey winner. The city ranked #6 in the large city (250,000 or more population) category. The survey examined and assessed how city governments are utilizing information technology to operate and deliver quality service to their customers and citizens. Survey questions focused on implementation and adoption of online service delivery; planning and governance; and the infrastructure and architecture that make the transformation to digital government possible. *Center for Digital Government, "2013 Digital Cities Survey," November 7, 2013*
- *Travel + Leisure* invited readers to rate cities on indicators such as aloofness, "smarty-pants residents," highbrow cultural offerings, high-end shopping, artisanal coffeehouses, conspicuous eco-consciousness, and more in order to identify the nation's snobbiest cities. Cities large and small made the list; among them was Austin, at #19. *www.travelandleisure.com, "America's Snobbiest Cities, June 2013*
- In *Condé Nast Traveler* magazine's 2013 Readers' Choice Survey, Austin made the top ten list of friendliest American cities, at #5. *www.cntraveler.com, "The Friendliest and Unfriendliest Cities in the U.S.," July 30, 2013*

- Ink Army reported on a survey by the website TotalBeauty calculating the number of tattoo shops per 100,000 residents in order to determine the U.S. cities with the most tattoo acceptance. Austin took the #6 slot. *inkarmy.com, "Most Tattoo Friendly Cities in the United States," November 1, 2013*

- Market analyst Scarborough Research surveyed adults who had done volunteer work over the previous 12 months to find out where volunteers are concentrated. The Austin metro area made the list for highest volunteer participation. *Scarborough Research, "Salt Lake City, UT; Minneapolis, MN; and Des Moines, IA Lend a Helping Hand," November 27, 2012*

- Austin was selected as one of the 10 best run cities in America by *24/7 Wall St.* The city ranked #8. Criteria: the 100 largest cities in the U.S. were ranked in terms of economy, job market, crime, and the welfare of its residents. *24/7 Wall St., "The Best and Worst Run Cities in America," January 15, 2013*

- The Austin metro area was selected as one of "The Best U.S. Cities for Bargain Shopping" by *Forbes.* The area ranked #2 out of 10. Criteria: number of outlet stores; gross leasable retail space in major malls; low consumer price index; low sales tax rate. Indicators were examined in the nation's 50 largest metropolitan areas. *Forbes, "The Best U.S. Cities for Bargain Shopping," January 20, 2012*

- Austin was selected as one of the most tattooed cities in America by *Lovelyish.com.* The city was ranked #6. Criteria: number of tattoo shops per capita. *Lovelyish.com, "Top Ten: Most Tattooed Cities in America," October 17, 2012*

- The National Alliance to End Homelessness ranked the 100 most populous metro areas in terms the rate of homelessness. The Austin metro area ranked #57. Criteria: number of homeless people per 10,000 population in 2011. *National Alliance to End Homelessness, The State of Homelessness in America 2012*

Business Environment

CITY FINANCES

City Government Finances

Component	2012 ($000)	2012 ($ per capita)
Total Revenues	3,147,884	3,983
Total Expenditures	3,194,297	4,041
Debt Outstanding	5,572,826	7,051
Cash and Securities[1]	4,679,762	5,921

Note: (1) Cash and security holdings of a government at the close of its fiscal year, including those of its dependent agencies, utilities, and liquor stores.
Source: U.S Census Bureau, State & Local Government Finances 2012

City Government Revenue by Source

Source	2012 ($000)	2012 ($ per capita)
General Revenue		
From Federal Government	59,258	75
From State Government	25,125	32
From Local Governments	8,441	11
Taxes		
Property	355,262	449
Sales and Gross Receipts	239,678	303
Personal Income	0	0
Corporate Income	0	0
Motor Vehicle License	0	0
Other Taxes	18,653	24
Current Charges	603,126	763
Liquor Store	0	0
Utility	1,471,819	1,862
Employee Retirement	265,306	336

Source: U.S Census Bureau, State & Local Government Finances 2012

City Government Expenditures by Function

Function	2012 ($000)	2012 ($ per capita)	2012 (%)
General Direct Expenditures			
Air Transportation	87,710	111	2.7
Corrections	0	0	0.0
Education	0	0	0.0
Employment Security Administration	0	0	0.0
Financial Administration	29,813	38	0.9
Fire Protection	127,792	162	4.0
General Public Buildings	0	0	0.0
Governmental Administration, Other	30,481	39	1.0
Health	104,198	132	3.3
Highways	113,832	144	3.6
Hospitals	0	0	0.0
Housing and Community Development	49,798	63	1.6
Interest on General Debt	89,771	114	2.8
Judicial and Legal	27,120	34	0.8
Libraries	28,954	37	0.9
Parking	24	< 1	< 0.1
Parks and Recreation	124,455	157	3.9
Police Protection	269,199	341	8.4
Public Welfare	0	0	0.0
Sewerage	189,017	239	5.9
Solid Waste Management	84,528	107	2.6
Veterans' Services	0	0	0.0
Liquor Store	0	0	0.0
Utility	1,484,805	1,879	46.5
Employee Retirement	197,997	251	6.2

Source: U.S Census Bureau, State & Local Government Finances 2012

DEMOGRAPHICS

Population Growth

Area	1990 Census	2000 Census	2010 Census	Population Growth (%) 1990-2000	Population Growth (%) 2000-2010
City	499,053	656,562	790,390	31.6	20.4
MSA[1]	846,217	1,249,763	1,716,289	47.7	37.3
U.S.	248,709,873	281,421,906	308,745,538	13.2	9.7

Note: (1) Figures cover the Austin-Round Rock-San Marcos, TX Metropolitan Statistical Area—see Appendix B for areas included
Source: U.S. Census Bureau, Census 1990, 2000, 2010

Household Size

Area	Persons in Household (%)							Average Household Size
	One	Two	Three	Four	Five	Six	Seven or More	
City	33.8	33.1	14.8	10.7	4.7	1.6	1.2	2.46
MSA[1]	27.8	33.1	15.9	13.5	6.1	2.3	1.4	2.68
U.S.	27.7	33.6	15.7	13.1	6.0	2.3	1.5	2.64

Note: (1) Figures cover the Austin-Round Rock, TX Metropolitan Statistical Area—see Appendix B for areas included
Source: U.S. Census Bureau, 2011-2013 American Community Survey 3-Year Estimates

Race

Area	White Alone[2] (%)	Black Alone[2] (%)	Asian Alone[2] (%)	AIAN[3] Alone[2] (%)	NHOPI[4] Alone[2] (%)	Other Race Alone[2] (%)	Two or More Races (%)
City	74.9	7.7	6.6	0.6	0.1	6.8	3.3
MSA[1]	78.6	7.3	4.9	0.5	0.1	5.7	2.9
U.S.	73.9	12.6	5.0	0.8	0.2	4.7	2.9

Note: (1) Figures cover the Austin-Round Rock, TX Metropolitan Statistical Area—see Appendix B for areas included; (2) Alone is defined as not being in combination with one or more other races; (3) American Indian and Alaska Native; (4) Native Hawaiian and Other Pacific Islander
Source: U.S. Census Bureau, 2011-2013 American Community Survey 3-Year Estimates

Hispanic or Latino Origin

Area	Total (%)	Mexican (%)	Puerto Rican (%)	Cuban (%)	Other (%)
City	33.9	28.5	0.6	0.5	4.3
MSA[1]	31.7	26.9	0.6	0.4	3.9
U.S.	16.9	10.8	1.6	0.6	3.8

Note: Persons of Hispanic or Latino origin can be of any race; (1) Figures cover the Austin-Round Rock, TX Metropolitan Statistical Area—see Appendix B for areas included
Source: U.S. Census Bureau, 2011-2013 American Community Survey 3-Year Estimates

Segregation

Type	Segregation Indices[1]				Percent Change		
	1990	2000	2010	2010 Rank[2]	1990-2000	1990-2010	2000-2010
Black/White	54.1	52.1	50.1	70	-1.9	-4.0	-2.1
Asian/White	39.4	42.3	41.2	49	2.9	1.8	-1.2
Hispanic/White	41.7	45.6	43.2	51	3.9	1.5	-2.4

Note: All figures cover the Metropolitan Statistical Area—see Appendix B for areas included; Figures are based on an analysis of 1990, 2000, and 2010 Census Decennial Census tract data by William H. Frey, Brookings Institution and the University of Michigan Social Science Data Analysis Network. In this analysis all racial groups (whites, blacks, and asians) are non-Hispanic members of those races. Hispanics are shown as a separate category;
(1) Segregation Indices are Dissimilarity Indices that measure the degree to which the minority group is distributed differently than whites across census tracts. They range from 0 (complete integration) to 100 (complete segregation) where the value indicates the percentage of the minority group that needs to move to be distributed exactly like whites; (2) Ranges from 1 (most segregated) to 102 (least segregated); n/a not available.
Source: www.CensusScope.org

Ancestry

Area	German	Irish	English	American	Italian	Polish	French[2]	Scottish	Dutch
City	12.8	8.4	8.3	4.2	3.0	1.6	3.0	2.2	0.9
MSA[1]	14.6	8.7	8.8	5.1	3.0	1.6	2.8	2.2	1.0
U.S.	14.9	10.8	8.0	7.4	5.5	3.0	2.7	1.7	1.4

Note: Figures are the percentage of the total population reporting a particular ancestry. The nine most commonly reported ancestries in the U.S. are shown. Figures include multiple ancestries (e.g. if a person reported being Irish and Italian, they were included in both columns); (1) Figures cover the Austin-Round Rock, TX Metropolitan Statistical Area—see Appendix B for areas included; (2) Excludes Basque
Source: U.S. Census Bureau, 2011-2013 American Community Survey 3-Year Estimates

Foreign-Born Population

Area	Percent of Population Born in								
	Any Foreign Country	Mexico	Asia	Europe	Carribean	South America	Central America[2]	Africa	Canada
City	18.3	8.7	5.0	1.2	0.4	0.5	1.6	0.6	0.3
MSA[1]	14.8	7.3	3.7	1.1	0.3	0.4	1.1	0.5	0.3
U.S.	13.0	3.7	3.8	1.5	1.2	0.9	1.0	0.6	0.3

Note: (1) Figures cover the Austin-Round Rock, TX Metropolitan Statistical Area—see Appendix B for areas included; (2) Excludes Mexico.
Source: U.S. Census Bureau, 2011-2013 American Community Survey 3-Year Estimates

Marital Status

Area	Never Married	Now Married[2]	Separated	Widowed	Divorced
City	43.6	39.1	2.4	3.4	11.5
MSA[1]	35.9	47.4	2.1	3.6	11.0
U.S.	32.7	48.1	2.2	6.0	11.0

Note: Figures are percentages and cover the population 15 years of age and older; (1) Figures cover the Austin-Round Rock, TX Metropolitan Statistical Area—see Appendix B for areas included; (2) Excludes separated
Source: U.S. Census Bureau, 2011-2013 American Community Survey 3-Year Estimates

Disability Status

Area	All Ages	Under 18 Years Old	18 to 64 Years Old	65 Years and Over
City	9.2	4.3	8.1	35.5
MSA[1]	9.5	4.0	8.5	33.1
U.S.	12.3	4.1	10.2	36.3

Note: Figures show percent of the civilian noninstitutionalized population that reported having a disability. Disability status is determined from from six types of difficulty: vision, hearing, cognitive, ambulatory, self-care, and independent living. For children under 5 years old, hearing and vision difficulty are used to determine disability status. For children between the ages of 5 and 14, disability status is determined from hearing, vision, cognitive, ambulatory, and self-care difficulties. For people aged 15 years and older, they are considered to have a disability if they have difficulty with any one of the six difficulty types; (1) Figures cover the Austin-Round Rock, TX Metropolitan Statistical Area—see Appendix B for areas included.
Source: U.S. Census Bureau, 2011-2013 American Community Survey 3-Year Estimates

Age

Area	Percent of Population									Median Age
	Under Age 5	Age 5–19	Age 20–34	Age 35–44	Age 45–54	Age 55–64	Age 65–74	Age 75–84	Age 85+	
City	6.8	18.1	31.0	15.4	12.1	9.3	4.2	2.1	1.0	31.9
MSA[1]	7.1	20.6	25.0	15.4	13.0	10.2	5.3	2.5	1.0	33.2
U.S.	6.4	19.9	20.7	12.9	14.1	12.3	7.6	4.2	1.9	37.4

Note: (1) Figures cover the Austin-Round Rock, TX Metropolitan Statistical Area—see Appendix B for areas included
Source: U.S. Census Bureau, 2011-2013 American Community Survey 3-Year Estimates

Gender

Area	Males	Females	Males per 100 Females
City	434,273	428,603	101.3
MSA[1]	918,435	914,909	100.4
U.S.	154,451,010	159,410,713	96.9

Note: (1) Figures cover the Austin-Round Rock, TX Metropolitan Statistical Area—see Appendix B for areas included
Source: U.S. Census Bureau, 2011-2013 American Community Survey 3-Year Estimates

Religious Groups by Family

Area	Catholic	Baptist	Non-Den.	Methodist[2]	Lutheran	LDS[3]	Pente-costal	Presby-terian[4]	Muslim[5]	Judaism
MSA[1]	16.0	10.3	4.5	3.6	2.0	1.2	0.8	1.1	1.2	0.3
U.S.	19.1	9.3	4.0	4.0	2.3	2.0	1.9	1.6	0.8	0.7

Note: Figures are the number of adherents as a percentage of the total population; (1) Figures cover the Austin-Round Rock-San Marcos, TX Metropolitan Statistical Area—see Appendix B for areas included; (2) Methodist/Pietist; (3) Latter Day Saints; (4) Reformed; (5) Figures are estimates
Source: Association of Statisticians of American Religious Bodies, 2010 U.S. Religion Census: Religious Congregations & Membership Study

Religious Groups by Tradition

Area	Catholic	Evangelical Protestant	Mainline Protestant	Other Tradition	Black Protestant	Orthodox
MSA[1]	16.0	16.1	6.3	3.9	1.4	0.1
U.S.	19.1	16.2	7.3	4.3	1.6	0.3

Note: Figures are the number of adherents as a percentage of the total population; (1) Figures cover the Austin-Round Rock-San Marcos, TX Metropolitan Statistical Area—see Appendix B for areas included
Source: Association of Statisticians of American Religious Bodies, 2010 U.S. Religion Census: Religious Congregations & Membership Study

ECONOMY

Gross Metropolitan Product

Area	2012	2013	2014	2015	Rank[2]
MSA[1]	98.7	104.4	110.6	117.5	31

Note: Figures are in billions of dollars; (1) Figures cover the Austin-Round Rock, TX Metropolitan Statistical Area—see Appendix B for areas included; (2) Rank is based on 2015 data and ranges from 1 to 363
Source: The U.S. Conference of Mayors, U.S. Metro Economies: GMP and Employment 2013-2015, June 2014

Economic Growth

Area	2010-12 (%)	2013 (%)	2014 (%)	2015 (%)	Rank[2]
MSA[1]	5.1	4.6	3.9	4.7	8
U.S.	2.1	2.0	2.3	3.2	–

Note: Figures are real gross metropolitan product (GMP) growth rates and represent annual average percent change; (1) Figures cover the Austin-Round Rock, TX Metropolitan Statistical Area—see Appendix B for areas included; (2) Rank is based on 2015 data and ranges from 1 to 363
Source: The U.S. Conference of Mayors, U.S. Metro Economies: GMP and Employment 2013-2015, June 2014

Metropolitan Area Exports

Area	2008	2009	2010	2011	2012	2013	Rank[2]
MSA[1]	7,405.5	5,963.7	8,867.8	8,626.3	8,976.6	8,870.8	38

Note: Figures are in millions of dollars; (1) Figures cover the Austin-Round Rock, TX Metropolitan Statistical Area—see Appendix B for areas included; (2) Rank is based on 2013 data and ranges from 1 to 387
Source: U.S. Department of Commerce, International Trade Administration, Office of Trade & Industry Information, Manufacturing & Services, data extracted April 3, 2015

Building Permits

Area	Single-Family			Multi-Family			Total		
	2013	2014	Pct. Chg.	2013	2014	Pct. Chg.	2013	2014	Pct. Chg.
City	2,573	2,800	8.8	9,261	6,642	-28.3	11,834	9,442	-20.2
MSA[1]	8,941	11,515	28.8	11,911	8,434	-29.2	20,852	19,949	-4.3
U.S.	620,802	634,597	2.2	370,020	411,766	11.3	990,822	1,046,363	5.6

Note: (1) Figures cover the Austin-Round Rock, TX Metropolitan Statistical Area—see Appendix B for areas included; Figures represent new, privately-owned housing units authorized (unadjusted data); All permit data are based on estimates with imputation.
Source: U.S. Census Bureau, Manufacturing, Mining, and Construction Statistics, Building Permits, 2013, 2014

Bankruptcy Filings

Area	Business Filings			Nonbusiness Filings		
	2013	2014	% Chg.	2013	2014	% Chg.
Travis County	141	112	-20.6	1,062	838	-21.1
U.S.	33,212	26,983	-18.8	1,038,720	909,812	-12.4

Note: Business filings include Chapter 7, Chapter 11, Chapter 12, and Chapter 13; Nonbusiness filings include Chapter 7, Chapter 11, and Chapter 13
Source: Administrative Office of the U.S. Courts, Business and Nonbusiness Bankruptcy, County Cases Commenced by Chapter of the Bankruptcy Code, During the 12- Month Period Ending December 31, 2013 and Business and Nonbusiness Bankruptcy, County Cases Commenced by Chapter of the Bankruptcy Code, During the 12- Month Period Ending December 31, 2014

Housing Vacancy Rates

Area	Gross Vacancy Rate[2] (%)			Year-Round Vacancy Rate[3] (%)			Rental Vacancy Rate[4] (%)			Homeowner Vacancy Rate[5] (%)		
	2012	2013	2014	2012	2013	2014	2012	2013	2014	2012	2013	2014
MSA[1]	12.7	12.5	12.4	11.9	11.9	11.6	9.6	12.1	10.9	1.3	1.1	0.8
U.S.	13.8	13.6	13.4	10.8	10.7	10.4	8.7	8.3	7.6	2.0	2.0	1.9

Note: (1) Figures cover the Austin-Round Rock, TX Metropolitan Statistical Area—see Appendix B for areas included; (2) The percentage of the total housing inventory that is vacant; (3) The percentage of the housing inventory (excluding seasonal units) that is year-round vacant; (4) The percentage of rental inventory that is vacant for rent; (5) The percentage of homeowner inventory that is vacant for sale
Source: U.S. Census Bureau, Housing Vacancies and Homeownership Annual Statistics: 2014

INCOME

Income

Area	Per Capita ($)	Median Household ($)	Average Household ($)
City	32,091	54,331	77,898
MSA[1]	31,255	60,443	82,338
U.S.	27,884	52,176	72,897

Note: (1) Figures cover the Austin-Round Rock, TX Metropolitan Statistical Area—see Appendix B for areas included
Source: U.S. Census Bureau, 2011-2013 American Community Survey 3-Year Estimates

Household Income Distribution

Area	Percent of Households Earning							
	Under $15,000	$15,000 -24,999	$25,000 -34,999	$35,000 -49,999	$50,000 -74,999	$75,000 -99,000	$100,000 -149,999	$150,000 and up
City	12.5	9.5	10.2	14.3	17.7	11.6	13.2	11.0
MSA[1]	10.3	8.7	9.2	13.7	18.1	12.8	15.1	12.2
U.S.	13.0	10.9	10.3	13.6	17.9	11.9	12.7	9.6

Note: (1) Figures cover the Austin-Round Rock, TX Metropolitan Statistical Area—see Appendix B for areas included
Source: U.S. Census Bureau, 2011-2013 American Community Survey 3-Year Estimates

Poverty Rate

Area	All Ages	Under 18 Years Old	18 to 64 Years Old	65 Years and Over
City	19.0	26.6	17.7	8.9
MSA[1]	15.0	19.4	14.4	6.8
U.S.	15.9	22.4	14.8	9.5

Note: Figures are percentage of people whose income during the past 12 months was below the poverty level; (1) Figures cover the Austin-Round Rock, TX Metropolitan Statistical Area—see Appendix B for areas included
Source: U.S. Census Bureau, 2011-2013 American Community Survey 3-Year Estimates

EMPLOYMENT

Labor Force and Employment

Area	Civilian Labor Force			Workers Employed		
	Dec. 2013	Dec. 2014	% Chg.	Dec. 2013	Dec. 2014	% Chg.
City	520,901	531,265	2.0	501,106	515,399	2.9
MSA[1]	1,032,725	1,052,087	1.9	988,473	1,016,673	2.9
U.S.	154,408,000	155,521,000	0.7	144,423,000	147,190,000	1.9

Note: Data is not seasonally adjusted and covers workers 16 years of age and older; (1) Figures cover the Austin-Round Rock, TX Metropolitan Statistical Area—see Appendix B for areas included
Source: Bureau of Labor Statistics, Local Area Unemployment Statistics

Unemployment Rate

Area	2014											
	Jan.	Feb.	Mar.	Apr.	May	Jun.	Jul.	Aug.	Sep.	Oct.	Nov.	Dec.
City	4.1	4.0	3.8	3.3	3.6	3.9	4.0	3.9	3.6	3.4	3.3	3.0
MSA[1]	4.6	4.6	4.4	3.8	4.1	4.4	4.5	4.4	4.1	3.8	3.7	3.4
U.S.	7.0	7.0	6.8	5.9	6.1	6.3	6.5	6.3	5.7	5.5	5.5	5.4

Note: Data is not seasonally adjusted and covers workers 16 years of age and older; (1) Figures cover the Austin-Round Rock, TX Metropolitan Statistical Area—see Appendix B for areas included
Source: Bureau of Labor Statistics, Local Area Unemployment Statistics

Employment by Occupation

Occupation Classification	City (%)	MSA[1] (%)	U.S. (%)
Management, Business, Science, and Arts	45.7	43.6	36.2
Natural Resources, Construction, and Maintenance	7.8	8.7	9.0
Production, Transportation, and Material Moving	6.0	7.2	12.1
Sales and Office	22.7	23.8	24.4
Service	17.9	16.7	18.3

Note: Figures cover employed civilians 16 years of age and older; (1) Figures cover the Austin-Round Rock, TX Metropolitan Statistical Area—see Appendix B for areas included
Source: U.S. Census Bureau, 2011-2013 American Community Survey 3-Year Estimates

Employment by Industry

Sector	MSA[1]		U.S.
	Number of Employees	Percent of Total	Percent of Total
Construction, Mining, and Logging	50,400	5.4	5.0
Education and Health Services	109,500	11.8	15.5
Financial Activities	52,600	5.7	5.7
Government	170,600	18.4	15.8
Information	25,800	2.8	2.0
Leisure and Hospitality	105,600	11.4	10.3
Manufacturing	57,900	6.2	8.7
Other Services	39,900	4.3	4.0
Professional and Business Services	152,200	16.4	13.8
Retail Trade	101,400	10.9	11.4
Transportation, Warehousing, and Utilities	16,300	1.8	3.9
Wholesale Trade	46,600	5.0	4.2

Note: Figures are non-farm employment as of December 2014. Figures are not seasonally adjusted and include workers 16 years of age and older; (1) Figures cover the Austin-Round Rock, TX Metropolitan Statistical Area—see Appendix B for areas included; n/a not available
Source: Bureau of Labor Statistics, Current Employment Statistics, Employment, Hours, and Earnings

Occupations with Greatest Projected Employment Growth: 2012 – 2022

Occupation[1]	2012 Employment	2022 Projected Employment	Numeric Employment Change	Percent Employment Change
Combined Food Preparation and Serving Workers, Including Fast Food	285,480	378,000	92,520	32.4
Personal Care Aides	199,230	283,980	84,750	42.5
Retail Salespersons	378,330	439,340	61,010	16.1
Registered Nurses	189,380	242,860	53,480	28.2
Customer Service Representatives	214,240	262,770	48,530	22.7
Waiters and Waitresses	196,390	240,390	44,000	22.4
Janitors and Cleaners, Except Maids and Housekeeping Cleaners	172,120	213,340	41,220	23.9
Laborers and Freight, Stock, and Material Movers, Hand	185,770	226,470	40,700	21.9
Elementary School Teachers, Except Special Education	141,030	180,920	39,890	28.3
Secretaries and Administrative Assistants, Except Legal, Medical, and Executive	190,470	230,220	39,750	20.9

Note: Projections cover Texas; (1) Sorted by numeric employment change
Source: www.projectionscentral.com, State Occupational Projections, 2012–2022 Long-Term Projections

Fastest Growing Occupations: 2012 – 2022

Occupation[1]	2012 Employment	2022 Projected Employment	Numeric Employment Change	Percent Employment Change
Diagnostic Medical Sonographers	4,380	6,900	2,520	57.6
Computer Numerically Controlled Machine Tool Programmers, Metal and Plastic	1,740	2,700	960	54.8
Interpreters and Translators	4,510	6,720	2,210	49.0
Skincare Specialists	5,130	7,620	2,490	48.3
Agents and Business Managers of Artists, Performers, and Athletes	310	450	140	47.4
Petroleum Engineers	19,280	28,010	8,730	45.3
Information Security Analysts	6,640	9,630	2,990	45.0
Insulation Workers, Mechanical	4,460	6,460	2,000	44.6
Cardiovascular Technologists and Technicians	3,950	5,700	1,750	44.3
Physician Assistants	5,470	7,880	2,410	44.2

Note: Projections cover Texas; (1) Sorted by percent employment change and excludes occupations with numeric employment change less than 100
Source: www.projectionscentral.com, State Occupational Projections, 2012–2022 Long-Term Projections

Average Wages

Occupation	$/Hr.	Occupation	$/Hr.
Accountants and Auditors	32.55	Maids and Housekeeping Cleaners	9.32
Automotive Mechanics	18.74	Maintenance and Repair Workers	17.30
Bookkeepers	19.22	Marketing Managers	68.82
Carpenters	18.19	Nuclear Medicine Technologists	35.23
Cashiers	10.31	Nurses, Licensed Practical	22.40
Clerks, General Office	16.13	Nurses, Registered	31.42
Clerks, Receptionists/Information	13.51	Nursing Assistants	11.92
Clerks, Shipping/Receiving	13.79	Packers and Packagers, Hand	11.54
Computer Programmers	42.31	Physical Therapists	36.27
Computer Systems Analysts	38.17	Postal Service Mail Carriers	25.51
Computer User Support Specialists	24.07	Real Estate Brokers	56.11
Cooks, Restaurant	10.96	Retail Salespersons	13.21
Dentists	82.77	Sales Reps., Exc. Tech./Scientific	31.05
Electrical Engineers	52.24	Sales Reps., Tech./Scientific	39.30
Electricians	22.44	Secretaries, Exc. Legal/Med./Exec.	16.04
Financial Managers	65.24	Security Guards	12.59
First-Line Supervisors/Managers, Sales	20.91	Surgeons	102.01
Food Preparation Workers	10.58	Teacher Assistants	10.50
General and Operations Managers	57.92	Teachers, Elementary School	23.00
Hairdressers/Cosmetologists	16.16	Teachers, Secondary School	23.70
Internists	n/a	Telemarketers	11.84
Janitors and Cleaners	10.70	Truck Drivers, Heavy/Tractor-Trailer	18.81
Landscaping/Groundskeeping Workers	11.84	Truck Drivers, Light/Delivery Svcs.	17.42
Lawyers	63.59	Waiters and Waitresses	9.85

Note: Wage data covers the Austin-Round Rock-San Marcos, TX Metropolitan Statistical Area—see Appendix B for areas included; Hourly wages for elementary/secondary school teachers and teacher assistants were calculated by the editors from annual wage data assuming a 40 hour work week; n/a not available.
Source: Bureau of Labor Statistics, Metro Area Occupational Employment and Wage Estimates, May 2014

TAXES

State Corporate Income Tax Rates

State	Tax Rate (%)	Income Brackets ($)	Num. of Brackets	Financial Institution Tax Rate (%)[a]	Federal Income Tax Ded.
Texas	(y)	–	–	(y)	No

Note: Tax rates as of January 1, 2015; (a) Rates listed are the corporate income tax rate applied to financial institutions or excise taxes based on income. Some states have other taxes based upon the value of deposits or shares; (y) Texas imposes a Franchise Tax, otherwise known as margin tax, imposed on entities with more than $1,030,000 total revenues at rate of 1%, or 0.5% for entities primarily engaged in retail or wholesale trade, on lesser of 70% of total revenues or 100%of gross receipts after deductions for either compensation or cost of goods sold.
Source: Federation of Tax Administrators, "State Corporate Income Tax Rates, 2015"

State Individual Income Tax Rates

State	Tax Rate (%)	Income Brackets ($)	Num. of Brackets	Personal Exempt. ($)[1]		Fed. Inc. Tax Ded.
				Single	Dependents	
Texas	None	–	–	–	–	–

Note: Tax rates as of January 1, 2015; Local- and county-level taxes are not included; n/a not applicable; (1) Married joint filers generally receive double the single exemption
Source: Federation of Tax Administrators, "State Individual Income Tax Rates, 2015"

Various State and Local Tax Rates

State	State and Local Sales and Use (%)	State Sales and Use (%)	Gasoline[1] (¢/gal.)	Cigarette[2] ($/pack)	Spirits[3] ($/gal.)	Wine[4] ($/gal.)	Beer[5] ($/gal.)
Texas	8.25	6.25	20	1.41	2.40 (f)	0.20	0.20 (p)

Note: All tax rates as of January 1, 2015; (1) The American Petroleum Institute has developed a methodology for determining the average tax rate on a gallon of fuel. Rates may include any of the following: excise taxes, environmental fees, storage tank fees, other fees or taxes, general sales tax, and local taxes. In states where gasoline is subject to the general sales tax, or where the fuel tax is based on the average sale price, the average rate determined by API is sensitive to changes in the price of gasoline. States that fully or partially apply general sales taxes to gasoline: CA, CO, GA, IL, IN, MI, NY; (2) The federal excise tax of $1.0066 per pack and local taxes are not included; (3) Rates are those applicable to off-premise sales of 40% alcohol by volume (a.b.v.) distilled spirits in 750ml containers. Local excise taxes are excluded; (4) Rates are those applicable to off-premise sales of 11% a.b.v. non-carbonated wine in 750ml containers; (5) Rates are those applicable to off-premise sales of 4.7% a.b.v. beer in 12 ounce containers; (f) Different rates are also applicable according to alcohol content, place of production, size of container, or place purchased (on- or off-premise or onboard airlines); (p) Local excise taxes are excluded.
Source: Tax Foundation, 2015 Facts & Figures: How Does Your State Compare?

State Business Tax Climate Index Rankings

State	Overall Rank	Corporate Tax Index Rank	Individual Income Tax Index Rank	Sales Tax Index Rank	Unemployment Insurance Tax Index Rank	Property Tax Index Rank
Texas	10	39	6	36	15	36

Note: The index is a measure of how each state's tax laws affect economic performance. The lower the rank, the more favorable a state's tax system is for business. States without a given tax are given a ranking of 1. The scores/rankings for the District of Columbia do not affect other states. The 2015 index represents the tax climate as of July 1, 2014.
Source: Tax Foundation, State Business Tax Climate Index 2015

COMMERCIAL REAL ESTATE

Office Market

Market Area	Inventory (sq. ft.)	Vacancy Rate (%)	Under Construction (sq. ft.)	YTD Net Absorption (sq. ft.)	Total Average Asking Rent ($/sq. ft./year)
Austin	60,262,988	10.7	2,568,758	1,286,311	29.08
National	4,745,108,508	14.3	71,190,461	51,084,126	27.40

Source: Newmark Grubb Knight Frank, National Office Market Report, 4th Quarter 2014

Industrial/Warehouse/R&D Market

Market Area	Inventory (sq. ft.)	Vacancy Rate (%)	Under Construction (sq. ft.)	YTD Net Absorption (sq. ft.)	Total Average Asking Rent ($/sq. ft./year)
Austin	83,923,813	8.7	969,214	-100,770	8.12
National	14,238,613,765	7.2	134,387,407	185,246,438	5.64

Source: Newmark Grubb Knight Frank, National Industrial Market Report, 4th Quarter 2014

COMMERCIAL UTILITIES

Typical Monthly Electric Bills

Area	Commercial Service ($/month)		Industrial Service ($/month)	
	40 kW demand 5,000 kWh	500 kW demand 100,000 kWh	5,000 kW demand 1,500,000 kWh	70,000 kW demand 50,000,000 kWh
City	833	12,848	141,305	3,300,700

Note: Figures are based on rates in effect January 2, 2014
Source: Memphis Light, Gas and Water, 2014 Utility Bill Comparisons for Selected U.S. Cities

TRANSPORTATION

Means of Transportation to Work

Area	Car/Truck/Van		Public Transportation			Bicycle	Walked	Other Means	Worked at Home
	Drove Alone	Car-pooled	Bus	Subway	Railroad				
City	73.3	10.3	3.9	0.0	0.1	1.6	2.6	1.5	6.6
MSA[1]	76.0	10.6	2.2	0.0	0.1	0.9	1.9	1.4	6.9
U.S.	76.4	9.6	2.6	1.8	0.6	0.6	2.8	1.3	4.3

Note: Figures are percentages and cover workers 16 years of age and older; (1) Figures cover the Austin-Round Rock, TX Metropolitan Statistical Area—see Appendix B for areas included
Source: U.S. Census Bureau, 2011-2013 American Community Survey 3-Year Estimates

Travel Time to Work

Area	Less Than 10 Minutes	10 to 19 Minutes	20 to 29 Minutes	30 to 44 Minutes	45 to 59 Minutes	60 to 89 Minutes	90 Minutes or More
City	10.6	33.9	24.5	21.4	5.0	3.1	1.5
MSA[1]	10.8	28.9	22.2	23.0	8.2	5.0	2.0
U.S.	13.3	29.7	20.9	20.2	7.7	5.7	2.6

Note: Figures are percentages and include workers 16 years old and over; (1) Figures cover the Austin-Round Rock, TX Metropolitan Statistical Area—see Appendix B for areas included
Source: U.S. Census Bureau, 2011-2013 American Community Survey 3-Year Estimates

Travel Time Index

Area	1985	1990	1995	2000	2005	2010	2011
Urban Area[1]	1.12	1.16	1.22	1.26	1.35	1.31	1.32
Average[2]	1.09	1.14	1.16	1.19	1.23	1.18	1.18

Note: Travel Time Index—the ratio of travel time in the peak period to the travel time at free-flow conditions. For example, a value of 1.30 indicates a 20-minute free-flow trip takes 26 minutes in the peak. Free-flow speeds (60 mph on freeways and 35 mph on principal arterials) are used as the comparison threshold; (1) Covers the Austin TX urban area; (2) average of 498 urban areas
Source: Texas Transportation Institute, Urban Mobility Report 2012, December 2012

Public Transportation

Agency Name / Mode of Transportation	Vehicles Operated in Maximum Service	Annual Unlinked Passenger Trips (in thous.)	Annual Passenger Miles (in thous.)
Capital Metropolitan Transportation Authority (CMTA)			
Bus (purchased transportation)	292	34,094.0	133,207.5
Commuter Bus (purchased transportation)	34	641.5	9,728.6
Demand Response (purchased transportation)	122	592.0	4,772.6
Demand Response Taxi (purchased transportation)	109	20.1	138.4
Hybrid Rail (purchased transportation)	4	834.7	13,281.9
Vanpool (directly operated)	101	219.9	5,825.0

Source: Federal Transit Administration, National Transit Database, 2013

Air Transportation

Airport Name and Code / Type of Service	Passenger Airlines[1]	Passenger Enplanements	Freight Carriers[2]	Freight (lbs.)
Austin-Bergstrom International (AUS)				
Domestic service (U.S. carriers - 2014)	29	5,141,191	17	67,632,564
International service (U.S. carriers - 2013)	8	26,067	5	11,126,007

Note: (1) Includes all U.S.-based major, minor and commuter airlines that carried at least one passenger during the year; (2) Includes all U.S.-based airlines and freight carriers that transported at least one lb. of freight during the year.
Source: Bureau of Transportation Statistics, The Intermodal Transportation Database, Air Carriers: T-100 Domestic Market (U.S. Carriers), 2014; Bureau of Transportation Statistics, The Intermodal Transportation Database, Air Carriers: T-100 International Market (U.S. Carriers), 2013

Other Transportation Statistics

Major Highways:	I-35
Amtrak Service:	Yes
Major Waterways/Ports:	None

Source: Amtrak.com; Google Maps

BUSINESSES

Major Business Headquarters

Company Name	Rankings	
	Fortune[1]	Forbes[2]
Whole Foods Market	218	-

Note: (1) Fortune 500—companies that produce a 10-K are ranked 1 to 500 based on 2013 revenue; (2) all private companies with at least $2 billion in annual revenue through the end of their most current fiscal year are ranked 1 to 221; companies listed are headquartered in the city; dashes indicate no ranking
Source: Fortune, "Fortune 500," June 16, 2014; Forbes, "America's Largest Private Companies," November 5, 2014

Fast-Growing Businesses

According to *Inc.*, Austin is home to seven of America's 500 fastest-growing private companies: **Simpler Trading** (#21); **Main Street Hub** (#73); **Phunware** (#82); **Jobs2Careers** (#131); **Kohana Coffee** (#171); **LocalSearchForDentists.com** (#357); **Gossett Jones Homes** (#427). Criteria: must be an independent, privately-held, for-profit, U.S. corporation, proprietorship or partnership; revenues must be at least $100,000 in 2010 and $2 million in 2013; must have four-year operating/sales history. Holding companies, regulated banks, and utilities were excluded. *Inc., "America's 500 Fastest-Growing Private Companies," September 2014*

According to *Fortune*, Austin is home to three of the 100 fastest-growing companies in the world: **Multimedia Games** (#36); **Forestar Group** (#45); **SolarWinds** (#94). Companies were ranked by their revenue growth rate; their EPS growth rate; and their three-year annualized total return to investors for the period ending June 30, 2014. Criteria for inclusion: a company, foreign or domestic, must trade on a major U.S. stock exchange; must file quarterly reports with the SEC; must have a minimum market capitalization of $250 million; must have a stock price of at least $5 on June 30, 2014; must have been trading continuously since June 30, 2010; must have revenue and net income for the four quarters ended on or before April 30, 2014, of at least $50 million and $10 million, respectively; and must have posted a compound annual growth in revenue and earnings per share of at least 20% annually over the three years ending on or before April 30, 2014. Real estate investment trusts, limited-liability companies, limited parterships, business development companies, closed end investment firms, and companies that lost money in the quarter ending April 30, 2014 were excluded. *Fortune, "100 Fastest-Growing Companies," August 28, 2014*

According to *Initiative for a Competitive Inner City (ICIC)*, Austin is home to five of America's 100 fastest-growing "inner city" companies: **Origen Biomedical** (#37); **PetRelocation.com** (#64); **Home Trends & Design** (#71); **Aztec Promotional Group** (#85); **PrintGlobe** (#88). Criteria for inclusion: company must be headquartered in or have 51 percent or more of its physical operations in an economically distressed urban area; must be an independent, for-profit corporation, partnership or proprietorship; must have 10 or more employees and have a five-year sales history that includes sales of at least $200,000 in the base year and at least $1 million in the current year with no decrease in sales over the two most recent years. This year, for the first time in the list's 16-year history, the Inner City 100 consists of 10 fast-growing businesses in 10 industry categories. Companies were ranked overall by revenue growth over the five-year period between 2009 and 2013 as well as within their respective industry categories. *Initiative for a Competitive Inner City (ICIC), "Inner City 100 Companies, 2014"*

According to Deloitte, Austin is home to 12 of North America's 500 fastest-growing high-technology companies: **Phunware** (#4); **Q1Media** (#69); **One Source Networks** (#160); **Kinnser Software** (#181); **Bazaarvoice** (#186); **SailPoint** (#233); **Cirrus Logic** (#266); **Zenoss** (#299); **HomeAway** (#404); **SolarWinds** (#405); **Asure Software** (#459); **Starmount** (#498). Companies are ranked by percentage growth in revenue over a five-year period. Criteria for inclusion: company must be headquartered within North America; must own proprietary intellectual property or proprietary technology that contributes to a significant portion of the company's operating revenue, or devote a significant proportion of revenues to research and development of technology; must have been in business for a minumum of five years with 2009 operating revenues of at least $50,000 USD/CD and 2013 operating revenues of at least $5 million USD/CD. *Deloitte Touche Tohmatsu, 2014 Technology Fast 500™*

Minority Business Opportunity

Austin is home to two companies which are on the *Black Enterprise* Auto Dealer 60 list (60 largest dealers based on gross sales): **JMC Auto Group** (#30); **Davis Automotive** (#32). Criteria: company must be operational in previous calendar year and be at least 51% black-owned. *Black Enterprise, B.E. 100s, 2014*

Austin is home to one company which is on the *Black Enterprise* Private Equity 15 list (15 largest private equity firms based on capital under management): **Vista Equity Partners** (#1). Criteria: company must be operational in previous calendar year and be at least 51% black-owned. *Black Enterprise, B.E. 100s, 2014*

Austin is home to two companies which are on the *Hispanic Business* 500 list (500 largest U.S. Hispanic-owned companies based on 2012 revenue): **Venta Financial Group** (#187); **Tramex Travel** (#233). Companies included must show at least 51 percent ownership by Hispanic U.S. citizens, and must maintain headquarters in one of the 50 states or Washington, D.C. *Hispanic Business, "Hispanic Business 500," June 20, 2013*

Minority- and Women-Owned Businesses

Group	All Firms		Firms with Paid Employees			
	Firms	Sales ($000)	Firms	Sales ($000)	Employees	Payroll ($000)
Asian	3,970	4,402,119	1,293	4,268,417	10,160	271,171
Black	3,118	505,907	240	450,953	2,879	71,712
Hispanic	10,546	1,468,542	1,233	1,059,525	10,337	295,270
Women	22,714	4,016,054	3,107	3,369,162	26,252	885,256
All Firms	80,570	127,872,644	18,383	124,575,830	424,724	19,184,572

Note: Figures cover firms located in the city; minority- and women-owned business are defined as firms in which the corresponding group own 51% or more of the stock or equity of the company
Source: U.S. Census Bureau, 2007 Economic Census, Survey of Business Owners (2012 Survey of Business Owners data will be released starting in June 2015)

HOTELS & CONVENTION CENTERS

Hotels/Motels

Area	5 Star		4 Star		3 Star		2 Star		1 Star		Not Rated	
	Num.	Pct.[3]	Num.	Pct.[3]	Num.	Pct.[3]	Num.	Pct.[3]	Num.	Pct.[3]	Num.	Pct.[3]
City[1]	0	0.0	26	9.8	70	26.3	149	56.0	5	1.9	16	6.0
Total[2]	166	0.9	1,264	7.0	5,718	31.8	9,340	52.0	411	2.3	1,070	6.0

Note: (1) Figures cover Austin and vicinity; (2) Figures cover all 100 cities in this book; (3) Percentage of hotels which have a given star rating; Star ratings are determined by expedia.com and offer an indication of the general quality of a particular hotel.
Source: expedia.com, April 2, 2015

The Austin-Round Rock, TX metro area is home to one of the best hotels in the U.S. according to *Travel & Leisure*: **Four Seasons Hotel Austin**. Criteria: service; location; rooms; food; and value. The list includes the top 236 hotels in the U.S. *Travel & Leisure, "T+L 500, The World's Best Hotels 2015"*

Major Convention Centers

Name	Overall Space (sq. ft.)	Exhibit Space (sq. ft.)	Meeting Space (sq. ft.)	Meeting Rooms
Austin Convention Center	881,400	246,097	37,170	54

Note: Table includes convention centers located in the Austin-Round Rock, TX metro area; n/a not available
Source: Original research

Living Environment

COST OF LIVING

Cost of Living Index

Composite Index	Groceries	Housing	Utilities	Transportation	Health Care	Misc. Goods/ Services
94.4	85.6	87.4	103.4	96.0	99.5	100.2

Note: The Cost of Living Index measures regional differences in the cost of consumer goods and services, excluding taxes and non-consumer expenditures, for professional and managerial households in the top income quintile. It is based on more than 50,000 prices covering almost 60 different items for which prices are collected three times a year by chambers of commerce, economic development organizations or university applied economic centers in each participating urban area. The numbers shown should be read as a percentage above or below the national average of 100. For example, a value of 115.4 in the groceries column indicates that grocery prices are 15.4% higher than the national average. Small differences in the index numbers should not be interpreted as significant; Figures cover the Austin TX urban area.
Source: The Council for Community and Economic Research, ACCRA Cost of Living Index, 2014

Grocery Prices

Area[1]	T-Bone Steak ($/pound)	Frying Chicken ($/pound)	Whole Milk ($/half gal.)	Eggs ($/dozen)	Orange Juice ($/64 oz.)	Coffee ($/11.5 oz.)
City[2]	9.82	1.09	2.18	1.95	3.22	3.79
Avg.	10.40	1.37	2.40	1.99	3.46	4.27
Min.	8.48	0.93	1.37	1.30	2.83	2.99
Max.	14.20	2.44	3.62	4.02	6.42	6.96

Note: (1) Values for the local area are compared with the average, minimum and maximum values for all 308 areas in the Cost of Living Index; (2) Figures cover the Austin TX urban area; **T-Bone Steak** *(price per pound);* **Frying Chicken** *(price per pound, whole fryer);* **Whole Milk** *(half gallon carton);* **Eggs** *(price per dozen, Grade A, large);* **Orange Juice** *(64 oz. Tropicana or Florida Natural);* **Coffee** *(11.5 oz. can, vacuum-packed, Maxwell House, Hills Bros, or Folgers).*
Source: The Council for Community and Economic Research, ACCRA Cost of Living Index, 2014

Housing and Utility Costs

Area[1]	New Home Price ($)	Apartment Rent ($/month)	All Electric ($/month)	Part Electric ($/month)	Other Energy ($/month)	Telephone ($/month)
City[2]	239,151	1,037	-	103.58	41.87	35.66
Avg.	305,838	919	181.00	93.66	73.14	27.95
Min.	183,142	480	112.00	42.06	23.42	17.16
Max.	1,358,576	3,851	594.00	180.03	440.99	40.42

Note: (1) Values for the local area are compared with the average, minimum and maximum values for all 308 areas in the Cost of Living Index; (2) Figures cover the Austin TX urban area; **New Home Price** *(2,400 sf living area, 8,000 sf lot, in urban area with full utilities);* **Apartment Rent** *(950 sf 2 bedroom/1.5 or 2 bath, unfurnished, excluding all utilities except water);* **All Electric** *(average monthly cost for an all-electric home);* **Part Electric** *(average monthly cost for a part-electric home);* **Other Energy** *(average monthly cost for natural gas, fuel oil, coal, wood, and any other forms of energy except electricity);* **Telephone** *(price includes basic monthly rate for a private residential line plus additional local usage charges incurred by a family of four).*
Source: The Council for Community and Economic Research, ACCRA Cost of Living Index, 2014

Health Care, Transportation, and Other Costs

Area[1]	Doctor ($/visit)	Dentist ($/visit)	Optometrist ($/visit)	Gasoline ($/gallon)	Beauty Salon ($/visit)	Men's Shirt ($)
City[2]	89.86	91.64	122.67	3.33	41.49	29.72
Avg.	102.86	87.89	97.66	3.44	34.37	26.74
Min.	67.47	65.78	51.18	3.00	17.43	12.79
Max.	173.50	150.14	235.00	4.33	64.28	49.50

Note: (1) Values for the local area are compared with the average, minimum and maximum values for all 308 areas in the Cost of Living Index; (2) Figures cover the Austin TX urban area; **Doctor** *(general practitioners routine exam of an established patient);* **Dentist** *(adult teeth cleaning and periodic oral examination);* **Optometrist** *(full vision eye exam for established adult patient);* **Gasoline** *(one gallon regular unleaded, national brand, including all taxes, cash price at self-service pump if available);* **Beauty Salon** *(woman's shampoo, trim, and blow-dry);* **Men's Shirt** *(cotton/polyester dress shirt, pinpoint weave, long sleeves).*
Source: The Council for Community and Economic Research, ACCRA Cost of Living Index, 2014

HOUSING

House Price Index (HPI)

Area	National Ranking[2]	Quarterly Change (%)	One-Year Change (%)	Five-Year Change (%)
MSA[1]	18	1.20	10.57	27.37
U.S.[3]	–	1.35	4.91	11.59

Note: The HPI is a weighted repeat sales index. It measures average price changes in repeat sales or refinancings on the same properties. This information is obtained by reviewing repeat mortgage transactions on single-family properties whose mortgages have been purchased or securitized by Fannie Mae or Freddie Mac in January 1975; (1) Austin-Round Rock Metropolitan Statistical Area—see Appendix B for areas included; (2) Rankings are based on annual percentage change for all metro areas containing at least 15,000 transactions over the last 10 years and ranges from 1 to 275; (3) figures based on a weighted average of Census Division estimates using a seasonally adjusted, purchase-only index; all figures are for the period ending December 31, 2014

Source: Federal Housing Finance Agency, House Price Index, February 26, 2015

Median Single-Family Home Prices

Area	2012	2013	2014p	Percent Change 2013 to 2014
MSA[1]	206.0	222.9	240.7	8.0
U.S. Average	177.2	197.4	209.0	5.9

Note: Figures are median sales prices of existing single-family homes in thousands of dollars; (p) preliminary; n/a not available; (1) Austin-Round Rock, TX Metropolitan Statistical Area—see Appendix B for areas included

Source: National Association of Realtors, Median Sales Price of Existing Single-Family Homes for Metropolitan Areas, 4th Quarter 2014

Qualifying Income Based on Median Sales Price of Existing Single-Family Homes

Area	With 5% Down ($)	With 10% Down ($)	With 20% Down ($)
MSA[1]	53,576	50,756	45,117
U.S. Average	45,863	43,449	38,621

Note: Figures are preliminary; Qualifying income is based on a mortgage rate of 4.0%. Monthly principal and interest payment is limited to 25% of income; n/a not available; (1) Austin-Round Rock, TX Metropolitan Statistical Area—see Appendix B for areas included

Source: National Association of Realtors, Qualifying Income Based on Median Sales Price of Existing Single-Family Homes for Metropolitan Areas, 4th Quarter 2014

Median Apartment Condo-Coop Home Prices

Area	2012	2013	2014p	Percent Change 2013 to 2014
MSA[1]	168.8	195.8	215.4	10.0
U.S. Average	173.7	194.9	205.1	5.2

Note: Figures are median sales prices of existing apartment condo-coop homes in thousands of dollars; (p) preliminary; n/a not available; (1) Austin-Round Rock, TX Metropolitan Statistical Area—see Appendix B for areas included

Source: National Association of Realtors, Median Sales Price of Existing Apartment Condo-Coop Homes for Metropolitan Areas, 4th Quarter 2014

Gross Monthly Rent

Area	Under $200	$200 -299	$300 -499	$500 -749	$750 -999	$1,000 -1,499	$1,500 and up	Median ($)
City	1.0	0.9	2.2	15.8	32.1	33.9	14.1	984
MSA[1]	0.9	0.9	2.5	15.2	32.2	34.0	14.3	987
U.S.	1.7	3.2	7.8	22.1	24.3	26.0	14.9	900

Note: Figures are percentages except for Median; Gross rent is the contract rent plus the estimated average monthly cost of utilities (electricity, gas, and water and sewer) and fuels (oil, coal, kerosene, wood, etc.) if these are paid by the renter (or paid for the renter by someone else); (1) Figures cover the Austin-Round Rock, TX Metropolitan Statistical Area—see Appendix B for areas included

Source: U.S. Census Bureau, 2011-2013 American Community Survey 3-Year Estimates

Homeownership Rate

Area	2007 (%)	2008 (%)	2009 (%)	2010 (%)	2011 (%)	2012 (%)	2013 (%)	2014 (%)
MSA[1]	66.4	65.5	64.0	65.8	58.4	60.1	59.6	61.1
U.S.	68.1	67.8	67.4	66.9	66.1	65.4	65.1	64.5

Note: (1) Figures cover the Austin-Round Rock, TX Metropolitan Statistical Area—see Appendix B for areas included
Source: U.S. Census Bureau, Housing Vacancies and Homeownership Annual Statistics: 2014

Year Housing Structure Built

Area	2010 or Later	2000 -2009	1990 -1999	1980 -1989	1970 -1979	1960 -1969	1950 -1959	1940 -1949	Before 1940	Median Year
City	1.5	22.7	16.2	21.1	19.0	8.1	5.8	2.7	3.0	1985
MSA[1]	2.4	30.7	19.4	19.1	14.3	5.5	4.1	2.0	2.6	1991
U.S.	0.9	15.0	13.9	13.8	15.8	11.0	10.9	5.4	13.3	1976

Note: Figures are percentages except for Median Year; (1) Figures cover the Austin-Round Rock, TX Metropolitan Statistical Area—see Appendix B for areas included
Source: U.S. Census Bureau, 2011-2013 American Community Survey 3-Year Estimates

HEALTH

Health Risk Data

Category	MSA[1] (%)	U.S. (%)
Adults aged 18–64 who have any kind of health care coverage	71.9	79.6
Adults who reported being in good or excellent health	84.2	83.1
Adults who are current smokers	15.2	19.6
Adults who are heavy drinkers[2]	7.5	6.1
Adults who are binge drinkers[3]	17.6	16.9
Adults who are overweight (BMI 25.0 - 29.9)	35.8	35.8
Adults who are obese (BMI 30.0 - 99.8)	25.5	27.6
Adults who participated in any physical activities in the past month	80.2	77.1
Adults 50+ who have ever had a sigmoidoscopy or colonoscopy	68.3	67.3
Women aged 40+ who have had a mammogram within the past two years	71.1	74.0
Men aged 40+ who have had a PSA test within the past two years	40.1	45.2
Adults aged 65+ who have had flu shot within the past year	64.0	60.1
Adults who always wear a seatbelt	97.3	93.8

Note: Data as of 2012 unless otherwise noted; (1) Figures cover the Austin-Round Rock, TX Metropolitan Statistical Area—see Appendix B for areas included; (2) Heavy drinkers are classified as males having more than two drinks per day or females having more than one drink per day; (3) Binge drinkers are classified as males having five or more drinks on one occasion or females having four or more drinks on one occasion
Source: Centers for Disease Control and Prevention, Behaviorial Risk Factor Surveillance System, SMART: Selected Metropolitan/Micropolitan Area Risk Trends, 2012 (Note: the CDC has discontinued this dataset but will be releasing a replacement in late 2015)

Chronic Health Indicators

Category	MSA[1] (%)	U.S. (%)
Adults who have ever been told they had a heart attack	2.1	4.5
Adults who have ever been told they had a stroke	1.6	2.9
Adults who have been told they currently have asthma	8.4	8.9
Adults who have ever been told they have arthritis	17.6	25.7
Adults who have ever been told they have diabetes[2]	7.4	9.7
Adults who have ever been told they had skin cancer	5.8	5.7
Adults who have ever been told they had any other types of cancer	4.0	6.5
Adults who have ever been told they have COPD	4.0	6.2
Adults who have ever been told they have kidney disease	2.1	2.5
Adults who have ever been told they have a form of depression	15.6	18.0

Note: Data as of 2012 unless otherwise noted; (1) Figures cover the Austin-Round Rock, TX Metropolitan Statistical Area—see Appendix B for areas included; (2) Figures do not include pregnancy-related, borderline, or pre-diabetes
Source: Centers for Disease Control and Prevention, Behaviorial Risk Factor Surveillance System, SMART: Selected Metropolitan/Micropolitan Area Risk Trends, 2012 (Note: the CDC has discontinued this dataset but will be releasing a replacement in late 2015)

Mortality Rates for the Top 10 Causes of Death in the U.S.

ICD-10[a] Sub-Chapter	ICD-10[a] Code	Age-Adjusted Mortality Rate[1] per 100,000 population	
		County[2]	U.S.
Malignant neoplasms	C00-C97	140.6	166.2
Ischaemic heart diseases	I20-I25	71.3	105.7
Other forms of heart disease	I30-I51	35.7	49.3
Chronic lower respiratory diseases	J40-J47	31.4	42.1
Organic, including symptomatic, mental disorders	F01-F09	54.7	38.1
Cerebrovascular diseases	I60-I69	33.8	37.0
Other external causes of accidental injury	W00-X59	36.9	26.9
Other degenerative diseases of the nervous system	G30-G31	21.5	25.6
Diabetes mellitus	E10-E14	14.8	21.3
Hypertensive diseases	I10-I15	15.9	19.4

Note: (a) ICD-10 = International Classification of Diseases 10th Revision; (1) Mortality rates are a three year average covering 2011-2013; (2) Figures cover Travis County
Source: Centers for Disease Control and Prevention, National Center for Health Statistics. Compressed Mortality File 1999-2013 on CDC WONDER Online Database, released October 2014. Data are compiled from the Compressed Mortality File 1999-2013, Series 20 No. 2S, 2014.

Mortality Rates for Selected Causes of Death

ICD-10[a] Sub-Chapter	ICD-10[a] Code	Age-Adjusted Mortality Rate[1] per 100,000 population	
		County[2]	U.S.
Assault	X85-Y09	2.8	5.2
Diseases of the liver	K70-K76	12.7	13.2
Human immunodeficiency virus (HIV) disease	B20-B24	2.1	2.2
Influenza and pneumonia	J09-J18	9.5	15.4
Intentional self-harm	X60-X84	12.0	12.5
Malnutrition	E40-E46	1.9	0.9
Obesity and other hyperalimentation	E65-E68	1.0	1.8
Renal failure	N17-N19	12.0	13.1
Transport accidents	V01-V99	10.4	11.7
Viral hepatitis	B15-B19	2.1	2.2

Note: (a) ICD-10 = International Classification of Diseases 10th Revision; (1) Mortality rates are a three year average covering 2011-2013; (2) Figures cover Travis County
Source: Centers for Disease Control and Prevention, National Center for Health Statistics. Compressed Mortality File 1999-2013 on CDC WONDER Online Database, released October 2014. Data are compiled from the Compressed Mortality File 1999-2013, Series 20 No. 2S, 2014.

Health Insurance Coverage

Area	With Health Insurance	With Private Health Insurance	With Public Health Insurance	Without Health Insurance	Population Under Age 18 Without Health Insurance
City	80.3	64.5	22.3	19.7	9.3
MSA[1]	81.9	68.0	22.0	18.1	9.9
U.S.	85.2	65.2	31.0	14.8	7.3

Note: Figures are percentages that cover the civilian noninstitutionalized population; (1) Figures cover the Austin-Round Rock, TX Metropolitan Statistical Area—see Appendix B for areas included
Source: U.S. Census Bureau, 2011-2013 American Community Survey 3-Year Estimates

Number of Medical Professionals

Area[1]	MDs[2]	DOs[2,3]	Dentists	Podiatrists	Chiropractors	Optometrists
Local (number)	3,244	174	721	55	338	169
Local (rate[4])	295.7	15.9	64.2	4.9	30.1	15.1
U.S. (rate[4])	270.0	20.2	63.1	5.7	25.2	14.9

Note: Data as of 2013 unless noted; (1) Local data covers Travis County; (2) Data as of 2012 and includes all active, non-federal physicians; (3) Doctor of Osteopathic Medicine; (4) rate per 100,000 population
Source: U.S. Department of Health and Human Services, Health Resources and Services Administration, Bureau of Health Professions, Area Resource File (ARF) 2013-2014

EDUCATION

Best Hospitals

According to *U.S. News,* the Austin-Round Rock, TX metro area is home to one of the best children's hospitals in the U.S.: **Dell Children's Medical Center of Central Texas** (1 specialty). The hospital listed was highly ranked in at least one pediatric specialty. Eighty-nine children's hospitals in the U.S. were nationally ranked in at least one specialty. Ten children's hospitals in the U.S. made the Honor Roll with high scores in at least three specialties. *U.S. News Online, "America's Best Children's Hospitals 2014-15"*

Public School District Statistics

District Name	Schls	Pupils	Pupil/ Teacher Ratio	Minority Pupils[1] (%)	Free Lunch Eligible[2] (%)	IEP[3] (%)
Austin ISD	129	86,516	14.7	75.2	57.3	10.1
Eanes ISD	9	7,865	14.3	28.4	2.4	7.4
Harmony Science Academy (Austin)	5	2,960	15.2	82.7	40.1	5.0
Kipp Austin Public Schools Inc	7	2,081	15.7	98.4	82.0	7.0
Lake Travis ISD	9	7,809	15.7	28.2	10.4	7.0

Note: Table includes school districts with 2,000 or more students; (1) Percentage of students that are not non-Hispanic white; (2) Percentage of students that are eligible for the free lunch program; (3) Percentage of students that have an Individualized Education Program.

Source: U.S. Department of Education, National Center for Education Statistics, Common Core of Data, Local Education Agency (School District) Universe Survey: School Year 2012-2013; U.S. Department of Education, National Center for Education Statistics, Common Core of Data, Public Elementary/Secondary School Universe Survey: School Year 2012-2013

Best High Schools

According to *The Daily Beast,* Austin is home to four of the best high schools in the U.S.: **Liberal Arts and Science Academy** (#14); **NYOS Charter School** (#93); **L.C. Anderson High School** (#245); **Westlake High School** (#277); *The Daily Beast* used six indicators culled from school surveys to compare public high schools in the U.S., with graduation and college acceptance rates weighed most heavily. Other criteria included: college-level courses/exams and SAT/ACT scores. *The Daily Beast, "Top High Schools 2014"*

Highest Level of Education

Area	Less than H.S.	H.S. Diploma	Some College, No Deg.	Associate Degree	Bachelor's Degree	Master's Degree	Prof. School Degree	Doctorate Degree
City	12.9	16.4	19.5	5.3	29.3	11.5	2.8	2.2
MSA[1]	11.8	19.3	21.5	6.5	26.9	9.9	2.3	1.7
U.S.	13.7	28.0	21.2	7.9	18.2	7.7	1.9	1.3

Note: Figures cover persons age 25 and over; (1) Figures cover the Austin-Round Rock, TX Metropolitan Statistical Area—see Appendix B for areas included

Source: U.S. Census Bureau, 2011-2013 American Community Survey 3-Year Estimates

Educational Attainment by Race

Area	High School Graduate or Higher (%)					Bachelor's Degree or Higher (%)				
	Total	White	Black	Asian	Hisp.[2]	Total	White	Black	Asian	Hisp.[2]
City	87.1	89.0	88.1	92.0	64.6	45.8	49.0	21.6	67.8	19.6
MSA[1]	88.2	89.7	89.0	92.1	67.1	40.8	42.6	24.1	65.8	17.8
U.S.	86.3	88.3	83.1	85.7	64.0	29.1	30.4	18.8	50.7	13.7

Note: Figures shown cover persons 25 years old and over; (1) Figures cover the Austin-Round Rock, TX Metropolitan Statistical Area—see Appendix B for areas included; (2) People of Hispanic origin can be of any race

Source: U.S. Census Bureau, 2011-2013 American Community Survey 3-Year Estimates

School Enrollment by Grade and Control

Area	Preschool (%)		Kindergarten (%)		Grades 1 - 4 (%)		Grades 5 - 8 (%)		Grades 9 - 12 (%)	
	Public	Private	Public	Private	Public	Private	Public	Private	Public	Private
City	47.4	52.6	87.8	12.2	91.3	8.7	90.2	9.8	92.6	7.4
MSA[1]	50.2	49.8	88.8	11.2	92.2	7.8	92.2	7.8	93.5	6.5
U.S.	57.7	42.3	87.9	12.1	89.9	10.1	90.0	10.0	90.7	9.3

Note: Figures shown cover persons 3 years old and over; (1) Figures cover the Austin-Round Rock, TX Metropolitan Statistical Area—see Appendix B for areas included
Source: U.S. Census Bureau, 2011-2013 American Community Survey 3-Year Estimates

Average Salaries of Public School Classroom Teachers

Area	2013-14		2014-15		Percent Change 2013-14 to 2014-15	Percent Change 2004-05 to 2014-15
	Dollars	Rank[1]	Dollars	Rank[1]		
TEXAS	49,690	30	50,576	29	1.78	23.3
U.S. Average	56,610	–	57,379	–	1.36	20.8

Note: (1) State rank ranges from 1 to 51 where 1 indicates highest salary.
Source: National Education Association, Rankings & Estimates: Rankings of the States 2014 and Estimates of School Statistics 2015, March 2015

Higher Education

Four-Year Colleges			Two-Year Colleges			Medical Schools[1]	Law Schools[2]	Voc/ Tech[3]
Public	Private Non-profit	Private For-profit	Public	Private Non-profit	Private For-profit			
1	6	9	1	0	8	0	1	11

Note: Figures cover institutions located within the city limits and include main campuses only; (1) includes schools accredited by the Liaison Committee on Medical Education and the American Osteopathic Association's Commission on Osteopathic College Accreditation; (2) includes ABA-accredited schools, schools with provisional ABA accreditation, and state accredited schools; (3) includes all schools with programs that are less than 2 years.
Source: National Center for Education Statistics, Integrated Postsecondary Education System (IPEDS), 2013-14; Association of American Medical Colleges, Member List, May 1, 2015; American Osteopathic Association, Member List, May 1, 2015; Law School Admission Council, Official Guide to ABA-Approved Law Schools Online, May 1, 2015; Wikipedia, List of Medical Schools in the United States, May 1, 2015; Wikipedia, List of Law Schools in the United States, May 1, 2015

According to *U.S. News & World Report,* the Austin-Round Rock, TX metro area is home to one of the best national universities in the U.S.: **University of Texas-Austin** (#53). The indicators used to capture academic quality fall into a number of categories: assessment by administrators at peer institutions; retention of students; faculty resources; student selectivity; financial resources; alumni giving; high school counselor ratings of colleges; and graduation rate. *U.S. News & World Report, "America's Best Colleges 2015"*

According to *U.S. News & World Report,* the Austin-Round Rock, TX metro area is home to one of the best liberal arts colleges in the U.S.: **Southwestern University** (#87). The indicators used to capture academic quality fall into a number of categories: assessment by administrators at peer institutions; retention of students; faculty resources; student selectivity; financial resources; alumni giving; high school counselor ratings of colleges; and graduation rate. *U.S. News & World Report, "America's Best Colleges 2015"*

According to *U.S. News & World Report,* the Austin-Round Rock, TX metro area is home to one of the top 100 law schools in the U.S.: **University of Texas-Austin** (#15). The rankings are based on a weighted average of 12 measures of quality: peer assessment score; assessment score by lawyers/judges; median LSAT scores; median undergrad GPA; acceptance rate; employment rates for graduates; placement success; bar passage rate; faculty resources; expenditures per student; student/faculty ratio; and library resources. *U.S. News & World Report, "America's Best Graduate Schools, Law, 2016"*

According to *U.S. News & World Report,* the Austin-Round Rock, TX metro area is home to one of the top 75 business schools in the U.S.: **University of Texas-Austin (McCombs)** (#17). The rankings are based on a weighted average of the following nine measures: quality assessment; peer assessment; recruiter assessment; placement success; mean starting salary and bonus; student selectivity; mean GMAT and GRE scores; mean undergraduate GPA; and acceptance rate. *U.S. News & World Report, "America's Best Graduate Schools, Business, 2016"*

PRESIDENTIAL ELECTION

2012 Presidential Election Results

Area	Obama (%)	Romney (%)	Other (%)
Travis County	60.1	36.2	3.6
U.S.	51.0	47.2	1.8

Note: Results may not add to 100% due to rounding
Source: Dave Leip's Atlas of U.S. Presidential Elections

EMPLOYERS

Major Employers

Company Name	Industry
3M Company	Tape, pressure sensitive: made from purchased materials
Attorney General, Texas	Attorney general's office
Dell	Electronic computers
Dell USA Corporation	Business management
Environmental Quality, Texas Comm On	Air, water, & solid waste management
Freescale Semiconductor	Semiconductors and related devices
Hospital Housekeeping Systems GP	Cleaning service, industrial or commercial
Internal Revenue Service	Taxation department, government
Legislative Office, Texas	Legislative bodies
Nextel of Texas	Radiotelephone communication
Pleasant Hill Preservation LP	Apartment building operators
State Farm	Automobile insurance
Texas Department of Public Safety	Public order and safety statistics centers
Texas Department of State Health Services	Administration of public health programs
Texas State University-San Marcos	Colleges and universities
Texas Workforce Commission	Administration of social and manpower programs
Univ of Texas System	Generation, electric power
University of Texas at Austin	University

Note: Companies shown are located within the Austin-Round Rock, TX Metropolitan Statistical Area.
Source: Hoovers.com; Wikipedia

Best Companies to Work For

Whole Foods Market, headquartered in Austin, is among "The 100 Best Companies to Work For." To pick the best companies, *Fortune* partnered with the Great Place to Work Institute. Two-thirds of a company's score is based on the results of the Institute's Trust Index survey, which is sent to a random sample of employees from each company. The questions related to attitudes about management's credibility, job satisfaction, and camaraderie. The other third of the scoring is based on the company's responses to the Institute's Culture Audit, which includes detailed questions about pay and benefit programs, and a series of open-ended questions about hiring practices, internal communication, training, recognition programs, and diversity efforts. Any company that is at least five years old with more than 1,000 U.S. employees is eligible. *Fortune, "The 100 Best Companies to Work For," 2015*

PUBLIC SAFETY

Crime Rate

Area	All Crimes	Violent Crimes: Murder	Violent Crimes: Forcible Rape	Violent Crimes: Robbery	Violent Crimes: Aggrav. Assault	Property Crimes: Burglary	Property Crimes: Larceny -Theft	Property Crimes: Motor Vehicle Theft
City	5,213.1	3.0	25.3	88.8	246.4	762.4	3,834.8	252.5
Suburbs[1]	1,964.6	2.5	21.6	23.3	146.3	341.6	1,349.4	79.8
Metro[2]	3,449.8	2.8	23.3	53.3	192.0	534.0	2,485.7	158.7
U.S.	3,098.6	4.5	25.2	109.1	229.1	610.0	1,899.4	221.3

Note: Figures are crimes per 100,000 population; (1) All areas within the metro area that are located outside the city limits; (2) Figures cover the Austin-Round Rock, TX Metropolitan Statistical Area—see Appendix B for areas included
Source: FBI Uniform Crime Reports, 2013

Hate Crimes

Area	Number of Quarters Reported	Number of Incidents per Bias Motivation						
		Race	Religion	Sexual Orientation	Ethnicity	Disability	Gender	Gender Identity
City	4	0	0	1	3	0	0	0
U.S.	4	2,871	1,031	1,233	655	83	18	31

Source: Federal Bureau of Investigation, Hate Crime Statistics 2013

Identity Theft Consumer Complaints

Area	Complaints	Complaints per 100,000 Population	Rank[2]
MSA[1]	1,771	94.0	74
U.S.	332,646	104.3	-

Note: (1) Figures cover the Austin-Round Rock, TX Metropolitan Statistical Area—see Appendix B for areas included; (2) Rank ranges from 1 to 380 where 1 indicates greatest number of identity theft complaints per 100,000 population
Source: Federal Trade Commission, Consumer Sentinel Network Data Book for January–December 2014

Fraud and Other Consumer Complaints

Area	Complaints	Complaints per 100,000 Population	Rank[2]
MSA[1]	8,457	449.1	60
U.S.	2,250,205	705.7	-

Note: (1) Figures cover the Austin-Round Rock, TX Metropolitan Statistical Area—see Appendix B for areas included; (2) Rank ranges from 1 to 380 where 1 indicates greatest number of identity theft complaints per 100,000 population
Source: Federal Trade Commission, Consumer Sentinel Network Data Book for January–December 2014

RECREATION

Culture

Dance[1]	Theatre[1]	Instrumental Music[1]	Vocal Music[1]	Series and Festivals	Museums and Art Galleries[2]	Zoos and Aquariums[3]
5	8	3	4	4	62	0

Note: (1) Professional perfoming groups; (2) Based on organizations with SIC code 8412; (3) AZA-accredited
Source: The Grey House Performing Arts Directory, 2015-16; Association of Zoos & Aquariums, AZA Member Zoos & Aquariums, April 2015; www.AccuLeads.com, April 2015

Professional Sports Teams

Team Name	League	Year Established
No teams are located in the metro area		

Source: Wikipedia, Major Professional Sports Teams of the United States and Canada, April 2015

CLIMATE

Average and Extreme Temperatures

Temperature	Jan	Feb	Mar	Apr	May	Jun	Jul	Aug	Sep	Oct	Nov	Dec	Yr.
Extreme High (°F)	90	97	98	98	100	105	109	106	104	98	91	90	109
Average High (°F)	60	64	72	79	85	91	95	96	90	81	70	63	79
Average Temp. (°F)	50	53	61	69	75	82	85	85	80	70	60	52	69
Average Low (°F)	39	43	50	58	65	72	74	74	69	59	49	41	58
Extreme Low (°F)	-2	7	18	35	43	53	64	61	47	32	20	4	-2

Note: Figures cover the years 1948-1990
Source: National Climatic Data Center, International Station Meteorological Climate Summary, 9/96

Average Precipitation/Snowfall/Humidity

Precip./Humidity	Jan	Feb	Mar	Apr	May	Jun	Jul	Aug	Sep	Oct	Nov	Dec	Yr.
Avg. Precip. (in.)	1.6	2.3	1.8	2.9	4.3	3.5	1.9	1.9	3.3	3.5	2.1	1.9	31.1
Avg. Snowfall (in.)	1	Tr	Tr	0	0	0	0	0	0	0	Tr	Tr	1
Avg. Rel. Hum. 6am (%)	79	80	79	83	88	89	88	87	86	84	81	79	84
Avg. Rel. Hum. 3pm (%)	53	51	47	50	53	49	43	42	47	47	49	51	48

Note: Figures cover the years 1948-1990; Tr = Trace amounts (<0.05 in. of rain; <0.5 in. of snow)
Source: National Climatic Data Center, International Station Meteorological Climate Summary, 9/96

Weather Conditions

Temperature			Daytime Sky			Precipitation		
10°F & below	32°F & below	90°F & above	Clear	Partly cloudy	Cloudy	0.01 inch or more precip.	0.1 inch or more snow/ice	Thunder-storms
< 1	20	111	105	148	112	83	1	41

Note: Figures are average number of days per year and cover the years 1948-1990
Source: National Climatic Data Center, International Station Meteorological Climate Summary, 9/96

HAZARDOUS WASTE

Superfund Sites

Austin has no sites on the EPA's Superfund Final National Priorities List. There are a total of 1,322 Superfund sites on the list in the U.S. *U.S. Environmental Protection Agency, Final National Priorities List, April 14, 2015*

AIR & WATER QUALITY

Air Quality Trends: Ozone

	2004	2005	2006	2007	2008	2009	2010	2011	2012	2013
MSA[1]	0.081	0.081	0.083	0.073	0.072	0.073	0.072	0.074	0.075	0.070

Note: (1) Data covers the Austin-Round Rock, TX Metropolitan Statistical Area—see Appendix B for areas included. The values shown are the composite ozone concentration averages among trend sites based on the highest fourth daily maximum 8-hour concentration in parts per million. These trends are based on sites having an adequate record of monitoring data during the trend period. Data from exceptional events are included.
Source: U.S. Environmental Protection Agency, Air Quality Monitoring Information, "Air Quality Trends by City, 2000-2013"

Air Quality Index

Area	Percent of Days when Air Quality was...[2]					AQI Statistics[2]	
	Good	Moderate	Unhealthy for Sensitive Groups	Unhealthy	Very Unhealthy	Maximum	Median
MSA[1]	71.8	28.2	0.0	0.0	0.0	93	42

Note: (1) Data covers the Austin-Round Rock, TX Metropolitan Statistical Area—see Appendix B for areas included; (2) Based on 365 days with AQI data in 2014. Air Quality Index (AQI) is an index for reporting daily air quality. EPA calculates the AQI for five major air pollutants regulated by the Clean Air Act: ground-level ozone, particle pollution (aka particulate matter), carbon monoxide, sulfur dioxide, and nitrogen dioxide. The AQI runs from 0 to 500. The higher the AQI value, the greater the level of air pollution and the greater the health concern. There are six AQI categories: "Good" AQI is between 0 and 50. Air quality is considered satisfactory; "Moderate" AQI is between 51 and 100. Air quality is acceptable; "Unhealthy for Sensitive Groups" When AQI values are between 101 and 150, members of sensitive groups may experience health effects; "Unhealthy" When AQI values are between 151 and 200 everyone may begin to experience health effects; "Very Unhealthy" AQI values between 201 and 300 trigger a health alert; "Hazardous" AQI values over 300 trigger warnings of emergency conditions (not shown).
Source: U.S. Environmental Protection Agency, Air Quality Index Report, 2014

Air Quality Index Pollutants

Area	Percent of Days when AQI Pollutant was...[2]					
	Carbon Monoxide	Nitrogen Dioxide	Ozone	Sulfur Dioxide	Particulate Matter 2.5	Particulate Matter 10
MSA[1]	0.0	3.6	40.3	0.0	55.9	0.3

Note: (1) Data covers the Austin-Round Rock, TX Metropolitan Statistical Area—see Appendix B for areas included; (2) Based on 365 days with AQI data in 2014. The Air Quality Index (AQI) is an index for reporting daily air quality. EPA calculates the AQI for five major air pollutants regulated by the Clean Air Act: ground-level ozone, particle pollution (also known as particulate matter), carbon monoxide, sulfur dioxide, and nitrogen dioxide. The AQI runs from 0 to 500. The higher the AQI value, the greater the level of air pollution and the greater the health concern.
Source: U.S. Environmental Protection Agency, Air Quality Index Report, 2014

Maximum Air Pollutant Concentrations: Particulate Matter, Ozone, CO and Lead

	Particulate Matter 10 (ug/m³)	Particulate Matter 2.5 Wtd AM (ug/m³)	Particulate Matter 2.5 24-Hr (ug/m³)	Ozone (ppm)	Carbon Monoxide (ppm)	Lead (ug/m³)
MSA[1] Level	57	7.2	24	0.07	0	n/a
NAAQS[2]	150	15	35	0.075	9	0.15
Met NAAQS[2]	Yes	Yes	Yes	Yes	Yes	n/a

Note: (1) Data covers the Austin-Round Rock, TX Metropolitan Statistical Area—see Appendix B for areas included; Data from exceptional events are included; (2) National Ambient Air Quality Standards; ppm = parts per million; ug/m³ = micrograms per cubic meter; n/a not available.
Concentrations: Particulate Matter 10 (coarse particulate)—highest second maximum 24-hour concentration; Particulate Matter 2.5 Wtd AM (fine particulate)—highest weighted annual mean concentration; Particulate Matter 2.5 24-Hour (fine particulate)—highest 98th percentile 24-hour concentration; Ozone—highest fourth daily maximum 8-hour concentration; Carbon Monoxide—highest second maximum non-overlapping 8-hour concentration; Lead—maximum running 3-month average
Source: U.S. Environmental Protection Agency, Air Quality Monitoring Information, "Air Quality Statistics by City, 2013"

Maximum Air Pollutant Concentrations: Nitrogen Dioxide and Sulfur Dioxide

	Nitrogen Dioxide AM (ppb)	Nitrogen Dioxide 1-Hr (ppb)	Sulfur Dioxide AM (ppb)	Sulfur Dioxide 1-Hr (ppb)	Sulfur Dioxide 24-Hr (ppb)
MSA[1] Level	5	n/a	n/a	5	n/a
NAAQS[2]	53	100	30	75	140
Met NAAQS[2]	Yes	n/a	n/a	Yes	n/a

Note: (1) Data covers the Austin-Round Rock, TX Metropolitan Statistical Area—see Appendix B for areas included; Data from exceptional events are included; (2) National Ambient Air Quality Standards; ppm = parts per million; ug/m³ = micrograms per cubic meter; n/a not available.
Concentrations: Nitrogen Dioxide AM—highest arithmetic mean concentration; Nitrogen Dioxide 1-Hr—highest 98th percentile 1-hour daily maximum concentration; Sulfur Dioxide AM—highest annual mean concentration; Sulfur Dioxide 1-Hr—highest 99th percentile 1-hour daily maximum concentration; Sulfur Dioxide 24-Hr—highest second maximum 24-hour concentration
Source: U.S. Environmental Protection Agency, Air Quality Monitoring Information, "Air Quality Statistics by City, 2013"

Drinking Water

Water System Name	Pop. Served	Primary Water Source Type	Violations[1] Health Based	Violations[1] Monitoring/ Reporting
Austin Water & Wastewater	903,570	Surface	0	0

Note: (1) Based on violation data from January 1, 2014 to December 31, 2014 (includes unresolved violations from earlier years)
Source: U.S. Environmental Protection Agency, Office of Ground Water and Drinking Water, Safe Drinking Water Information System (based on data extracted January 27, 2015)

Cape Coral, Florida

Background

Tucked along Florida's Gulf Coast 71 miles south of Sarasota, Cape Coral is a mid-twentieth century community grown from a development launched in 1957. Today, at 115 square miles, it is Florida's third-largest city by land mass and the most populous city between Tampa and Miami. To the east across the Caloosahatchie River lies Fort Myers, and to the west across Pine Island and Pine Island sound lie the fabled barrier islands of Captiva and Sanibel by Pine Island and Pine Island Sound.

Baltimore brothers Leonard and Jack Rosen purchased the former Redfish Point for $678,000 and renamed the property Cape Coral. By June of the following year "the Cape," as it is known, was receiving its first residents. The city incorporated in 1970 when its population reached 11,470.

Despite the city's relative youth, this self-named "Waterfront Wonderland" has developed an interest in its roots. It fosters a Cape Coral Historical Museum that is housed in the original snack bar from the local country club, and one of its oldest historical documents is the Cape's 1961 phone book.

Four hundred precious miles of salt water and fresh water canals slice through the city, providing water access to abundant recreational boaters and numerous opportunities for waterfront living.

Following the economic downturn, Cape Coral is rebounding nicely. It was named a "most improved" housing market in a National Association of Builders report, and Realty Trac showed improvement in the area's foreclosures at the same time. The Army Reserve purchased a 15-acre Cape Coral site for use as an Army Reserve Training Center for local reservists.

Industry-wise, Cape Coral has Foreign Trade Zones in two of its three industrial parks, the 92.5 acre North Cape Industrial Park—home to light manufacturers, service industry and warehouses—and the Mid Cape Commerce Park which, at 143.37 acres, is comprised of service industries and warehouses. In addition, a VA Clinic was recently built by the U.S. Dept. of Veteran's Affairs at the Hancock Creek Commerce Park and Indian Oaks Trade Centre.

The VA Clinic provides a full range of services ranging from mental health and diagnostic radiology to urology and a full complement of imaging services such as CT scans and nuclear medicine. It is the centerpiece of a Veterans Investment Zone initiative that is proposed to draw office, medical parks, assisted living facilities and the like.

Today the U.S. Bureau of Labor Statistics tracks Cape Coral's success in conjunction with that of nearby Fort Myers, and the region boasts trade, transportation and utilities as its largest economic sector. Essentially, this is a retirement and tourism destination.

Significant recreational opportunities are available in the area, and include the Four Mile Cove Ecological Preserve with its nature trail, picnic area, and warm weather kayak rentals. The Cape Coral Yacht Club, located where the city first began, includes a fishing pier, beach, and community pool. The 18-hole public Coral Oaks Golf Course (replete with pro shop and pub), the Northwest Softball Complex, the William Bill Austen Youth Center Eagle Skate Park, the Strausser BMX Sports Complex, and even the Pelican Sport Soccer Complex show the city's diverse recreational opportunities.

To the east of Cape Coral—on the other side of Fort Myers—is both the Florida Gulf Coast University and Southwest Florida International Airport.

Cape Coral's climate borders on perfect, with an average 335 days per year of sunshine (albeit hot and humid ones in summer time). Annual rainfall is 53.37 inches, with the most rain coming in summer. The city dries out from October into May.

Rankings

Business/Finance Rankings

- Building on the U.S. Department of Labor's Occupational Information Network Data Collection Program, the Brookings Institution defined STEM occupations and job opportunities for STEM workers at various levels of educational attainment. The Cape Coral metro area was one of the ten metro areas where workers in low-education-level STEM jobs earn the highest relative wages. *www.brookings.edu, "The Hidden Stem Economy," June 10, 2013*

- Building on the U.S. Department of Labor's Occupational Information Network Data Collection Program, the Brookings Institution defined STEM occupations and job opportunities for STEM workers at various levels of educational attainment. The Cape Coral metro area was placed among the ten large metro areas with the lowest demand for high-level STEM knowledge. *www.brookings.edu, "The Hidden Stem Economy," June 10, 2013*

- Cape Coral was ranked #10 out of 100 metro areas in terms of economic performance (#1 = best) during the recession and recovery from trough quarter through the second quarter of 2013. Criteria: percent change in employment; percentage point change in unemployment rate; percent change in gross metropolitan product; percent change in House Price Index. *Brookings Institution, MetroMonitor: Tracking Economic Recession and Recovery in America's 100 Largest Metropolitan Areas, September 2013*

- The Cape Coral metro area appeared on the Milken Institute "2013 Best Performing Cities" list. Rank: #88 out of 200 large metro areas. Criteria: job growth; wage and salary growth; high-tech output growth. *Milken Institute, "Best-Performing Cities 2014," January 2015*

- *Forbes* ranked the 200 most populous metro areas to determine the nation's "Best Places for Business and Careers." The Cape Coral metro area was ranked #81. Criteria: costs (business and living); job growth (past and projected); income growth; educational attainment (college and high school); projected economic growth; cultural and recreational opportunities; net migration patterns; number of highly ranked colleges. *Forbes, "The Best Places for Business and Careers 2014," July 23, 2014*

Education Rankings

- Personal finance website *WalletHub* analyzed the 150 largest U.S. metropolitan statistical areas to determine where the most educated Americans are choosing to settle. Criteria: educational attainment; percentage of workers with jobs in computer, engineering, and science fields; quality and size of each metro area's universities. Cape Coral was ranked #111 (#1 = most educated city). *www.WalletHub.com, "2014's Most and Least Educated Cities*

Environmental Rankings

- The Cape Coral metro area came in at #347 for the relative comfort of its climate on Sperling's list of "chill cities," as measured by the Sperling Heat Index. All 361 metro areas are included. Criteria included daytime high temperatures, nighttime low temperatures, dew point, and relative humidity at the high temperatures. *www.bertsperling.com, "Sperling's Chill Cities," July 18, 2013*

- Sperling's BestPlaces assessed 379 metropolitan areas of the United States for the likelihood of dangerously extreme weather events or earthquakes. In general the Southeast and South-Central regions have the highest risk of weather extremes and earthquakes, while the Pacific Northwest enjoys the lowest risk. Of the least risky metropolitan areas, the Cape Coral metro area was ranked #335. *www.bestplaces.net, "Safest Places from Natural Disasters," April 2011*

- Cape Coral was highlighted as one of the cleanest metro areas for ozone air pollution in the U.S. during 2011 through 2013. The list represents cities with no monitored ozone air pollution in unhealthful ranges. *American Lung Association, State of the Air 2015*

- Cape Coral was highlighted as one of the top 25 cleanest metro areas for year-round particle pollution (Annual PM 2.5) in the U.S. during 2011 through 2013. The area ranked #13. *American Lung Association, State of the Air 2015*

- Cape Coral was highlighted as one of the top 25 cleanest metro areas for short-term particle pollution (24-hour PM 2.5) in the U.S. during 2011 through 2013. Monitors in these cities reported no days with unhealthful PM 2.5 levels. *American Lung Association, State of the Air 2015*

Health/Fitness Rankings

- Cape Coral was identified as a "2013 Spring Allergy Capital." The area ranked #73 out of 100. Three groups of factors were used to identify the most severe cities for people with allergies during the spring season: annual pollen levels; medicine utilization; access to board-certified allergists. *Asthma and Allergy Foundation of America, "Spring Allergy Capitals 2013"*
- Cape Coral was identified as a "2013 Fall Allergy Capital." The area ranked #65 out of 100. Three groups of factors were used to identify the most severe cities for people with allergies during the fall season: annual pollen levels; medicine utilization; access to board-certified allergists. *Asthma and Allergy Foundation of America, "Fall Allergy Capitals 2013"*
- Cape Coral was identified as a "2013 Asthma Capital." The area ranked #95 out of the nation's 100 largest metropolitan areas. Twelve factors were used to identify the most challenging places to live for people with asthma: estimated prevalence; self-reported prevalence; crude death rate for asthma; annual pollen score; annual air quality; public smoking laws; number of board-certified asthma specialists; school inhaler access laws; rescue medication use; controller medication use; uninsured rate; poverty rate. *Asthma and Allergy Foundation of America, "Asthma Capitals 2013"*
- Cape Coral was selected as one of the best metropolitan areas for hospital care in America by *HealthGrades.com.* The rankings are based on a comprehensive study of patient death and complication rates in the nation's nearly 5,000 hospitals. Hospitals performing in the top 5% nationwide across 26 different medical procedures and diagnoses were identified. *HealthGrades.com* then ranked cities by the highest percentage of these Distinguished Hospitals for Clinical Excellence™. The Cape Coral metro area ranked #11. *HealthGrades.com, "America's Top 50 Cities for Hospital Care," January 21, 2012*
- The Cape Coral metro area appeared in the 2013 Gallup-Healthways Well-Being Index. The area ranked #149 out of 189. The Gallup-Healthways Well-Being Index score is an average of six sub-indexes, which individually examine life evaluation, emotional health, work environment, physical health, healthy behaviors, and access to basic necessities. Results are based on telephone interviews conducted as part of the Gallup-Healthways Well-Being Index survey January 2–December 29, 2012, and January 2–December 30, 2013, with a random sample of 531,630 adults, aged 18 and older, living in metropolitan areas in the 50 U.S. states and the District of Columbia. *Gallup-Healthways, "State of American Well-Being," March 25, 2014*

Real Estate Rankings

- Cape Coral was ranked #14 out of 275 metro areas in terms of house price appreciation in 2014 (#1 = highest rate). *Federal Housing Finance Agency, House Price Index, 4th Quarter 2014*
- The Cape Coral metro area was identified as one of the 20 best housing markets in the U.S. in 2014. The area ranked #6 out of 178 markets with a home price appreciation of 13.6%. Criteria: year-over-year change of median sales price of existing single-family homes between the 4th quarter of 2013 and the 4th quarter of 2014. *National Association of Realtors®, Median Sales Price of Existing Single-Family Homes for Metropolitan Areas, 4th Quarter 2014*
- The Cape Coral metro area was identified as one of the 10 best condo markets in the U.S. in 2014. The area ranked #7 out of 66 markets with a price appreciation of 13.9%. Criteria: year-over-year change of median sales price of existing apartment condo-coop homes between the 4th quarter of 2013 and the 4th quarter of 2014. *National Association of Realtors®, Median Sales Price of Existing Apartment Condo-Coop Homes for Metropolitan Areas, 4th Quarter 2014*

- Cape Coral was ranked #151 out of 226 metro areas in terms of housing affordability in 2014 by the National Association of Home Builders (#1 = most affordable). The NAHB-Wells Fargo Housing Opportunity Index (HOI) for a given area is defined as the share of homes sold in that area that would have been affordable to a family earning the local median income, based on standard mortgage underwriting criteria. *National Association of Home Builders®, NAHB-Wells Fargo Housing Opportunity Index, 4th Quarter 2014*

Safety Rankings

- Allstate ranked the 200 largest cities in America in terms of driver safety. Cape Coral ranked #15. Allstate researchers analyzed internal property damage claims over a two-year period from January 2011 to December 2012. A weighted average of the two-year numbers determined the annual percentages. *Allstate, "Allstate America's Best Drivers Report, 2014"*
- The National Insurance Crime Bureau ranked 380 metro areas in the U.S. in terms of per capita rates of vehicle theft. The Cape Coral metro area ranked #217 (#1 = highest rate). Criteria: number of vehicle theft offenses per 100,000 inhabitants in 2012. *National Insurance Crime Bureau, "Hot Spots 2012," June 26, 2013*

Seniors/Retirement Rankings

- From its Best Cities for Successful Aging indexes, the Milken Institute generated rankings for metropolitan areas, weighing data in eight categories—health care, wellness, living arrangements, transportation, financial characteristics, education and employment opportunities, community engagement, and overall livability. The Cape Coral metro area was ranked #93 overall in the large metro area category. *Milken Institute, "Best Cities for Successful Aging, 2014"*
- Cape Coral made the 2014 *Forbes* list of "25 Best Places to Retire." Criteria include: housing and living costs; tax climate for retirees; weather and air quality; crime rates; doctor availability; active-lifestyle rankings for walkability, bicycling and volunteering. *Forbes.com, "The Best Places to Retire in 2014," January 16, 2014*

Miscellaneous Rankings

- The National Alliance to End Homelessness ranked the 100 most populous metro areas in terms the rate of homelessness. The Cape Coral metro area ranked #43. Criteria: number of homeless people per 10,000 population in 2011. *National Alliance to End Homelessness, The State of Homelessness in America 2012*

Business Environment

CITY FINANCES

City Government Finances

Component	2012 ($000)	2012 ($ per capita)
Total Revenues	326,567	2,116
Total Expenditures	320,044	2,074
Debt Outstanding	907,596	5,882
Cash and Securities[1]	442,618	2,868

Note: (1) Cash and security holdings of a government at the close of its fiscal year, including those of its dependent agencies, utilities, and liquor stores.
Source: U.S Census Bureau, State & Local Government Finances 2012

City Government Revenue by Source

Source	2012 ($000)	2012 ($ per capita)
General Revenue		
From Federal Government	7,547	49
From State Government	38,322	248
From Local Governments	1,852	12
Taxes		
Property	69,271	449
Sales and Gross Receipts	19,665	127
Personal Income	0	0
Corporate Income	0	0
Motor Vehicle License	0	0
Other Taxes	3,355	22
Current Charges	61,664	400
Liquor Store	0	0
Utility	29,927	194
Employee Retirement	50,955	330

Source: U.S Census Bureau, State & Local Government Finances 2012

City Government Expenditures by Function

Function	2012 ($000)	2012 ($ per capita)	2012 (%)
General Direct Expenditures			
Air Transportation	0	0	0.0
Corrections	0	0	0.0
Education	24,982	162	7.8
Employment Security Administration	0	0	0.0
Financial Administration	19,385	126	6.1
Fire Protection	26,775	174	8.4
General Public Buildings	0	0	0.0
Governmental Administration, Other	3,542	23	1.1
Health	0	0	0.0
Highways	26,218	170	8.2
Hospitals	0	0	0.0
Housing and Community Development	7,166	46	2.2
Interest on General Debt	11,657	76	3.6
Judicial and Legal	993	6	0.3
Libraries	0	0	0.0
Parking	26	< 1	< 0.1
Parks and Recreation	16,760	109	5.2
Police Protection	36,233	235	11.3
Public Welfare	0	0	0.0
Sewerage	13,044	85	4.1
Solid Waste Management	0	0	0.0
Veterans' Services	0	0	0.0
Liquor Store	0	0	0.0
Utility	55,553	360	17.4
Employee Retirement	23,890	155	7.5

Source: U.S Census Bureau, State & Local Government Finances 2012

DEMOGRAPHICS

Population Growth

Area	1990 Census	2000 Census	2010 Census	Population Growth (%) 1990-2000	Population Growth (%) 2000-2010
City	75,507	102,286	154,305	35.5	50.9
MSA[1]	335,113	440,888	618,754	31.6	40.3
U.S.	248,709,873	281,421,906	308,745,538	13.2	9.7

Note: (1) Figures cover the Cape Coral-Fort Myers, FL Metropolitan Statistical Area—see Appendix B for areas included
Source: U.S. Census Bureau, Census 1990, 2000, 2010

Household Size

Area	Persons in Household (%)							Average Household Size
	One	Two	Three	Four	Five	Six	Seven or More	
City	22.0	41.5	15.7	11.2	6.5	1.8	1.2	2.87
MSA[1]	28.1	43.7	11.9	9.6	4.2	1.7	0.8	2.64
U.S.	27.7	33.6	15.7	13.1	6.0	2.3	1.5	2.64

Note: (1) Figures cover the Cape Coral-Fort Myers, FL Metropolitan Statistical Area—see Appendix B for areas included
Source: U.S. Census Bureau, 2011-2013 American Community Survey 3-Year Estimates

Race

Area	White Alone[2] (%)	Black Alone[2] (%)	Asian Alone[2] (%)	AIAN[3] Alone[2] (%)	NHOPI[4] Alone[2] (%)	Other Race Alone[2] (%)	Two or More Races (%)
City	91.0	3.4	1.8	0.4	0.0	2.1	1.4
MSA[1]	84.1	8.3	1.6	0.4	0.0	3.9	1.7
U.S.	73.9	12.6	5.0	0.8	0.2	4.7	2.9

Note: (1) Figures cover the Cape Coral-Fort Myers, FL Metropolitan Statistical Area—see Appendix B for areas included; (2) Alone is defined as not being in combination with one or more other races; (3) American Indian and Alaska Native; (4) Native Hawaiian and Other Pacific Islander
Source: U.S. Census Bureau, 2011-2013 American Community Survey 3-Year Estimates

Hispanic or Latino Origin

Area	Total (%)	Mexican (%)	Puerto Rican (%)	Cuban (%)	Other (%)
City	19.1	1.9	5.3	5.6	6.3
MSA[1]	18.9	5.8	4.2	3.5	5.4
U.S.	16.9	10.8	1.6	0.6	3.8

Note: Persons of Hispanic or Latino origin can be of any race; (1) Figures cover the Cape Coral-Fort Myers, FL Metropolitan Statistical Area—see Appendix B for areas included
Source: U.S. Census Bureau, 2011-2013 American Community Survey 3-Year Estimates

Segregation

Type	Segregation Indices[1]				Percent Change		
	1990	2000	2010	2010 Rank[2]	1990-2000	1990-2010	2000-2010
Black/White	76.8	69.4	61.6	35	-7.5	-15.3	-7.8
Asian/White	23.3	28.5	25.3	96	5.3	2.0	-3.3
Hispanic/White	36.1	40.8	40.2	63	4.7	4.1	-0.6

Note: All figures cover the Metropolitan Statistical Area—see Appendix B for areas included; Figures are based on an analysis of 1990, 2000, and 2010 Census Decennial Census tract data by William H. Frey, Brookings Institution and the University of Michigan Social Science Data Analysis Network. In this analysis all racial groups (whites, blacks, and asians) are non-Hispanic members of those races. Hispanics are shown as a separate category;
(1) Segregation Indices are Dissimilarity Indices that measure the degree to which the minority group is distributed differently than whites across census tracts. They range from 0 (complete integration) to 100 (complete segregation) where the value indicates the percentage of the minority group that needs to move to be distributed exactly like whites; (2) Ranges from 1 (most segregated) to 102 (least segregated); n/a not available.
Source: www.CensusScope.org

Ancestry

Area	German	Irish	English	American	Italian	Polish	French[2]	Scottish	Dutch
City	18.9	14.5	8.6	9.9	11.1	4.5	3.3	1.4	1.0
MSA[1]	15.5	11.9	9.0	13.6	7.7	3.5	3.1	1.5	1.3
U.S.	14.9	10.8	8.0	7.4	5.5	3.0	2.7	1.7	1.4

Note: Figures are the percentage of the total population reporting a particular ancestry. The nine most commonly reported ancestries in the U.S. are shown. Figures include multiple ancestries (e.g. if a person reported being Irish and Italian, they were included in both columns); (1) Figures cover the Cape Coral-Fort Myers, FL Metropolitan Statistical Area—see Appendix B for areas included; (2) Excludes Basque
Source: U.S. Census Bureau, 2011-2013 American Community Survey 3-Year Estimates

Foreign-Born Population

Area	Percent of Population Born in								
	Any Foreign Country	Mexico	Asia	Europe	Carribean	South America	Central America[2]	Africa	Canada
City	n/a	n/a	n/a	n/a	n/a	n/a	n/a	n/a	n/a
MSA[1]	15.1	2.7	1.2	2.2	4.4	1.8	1.6	0.1	1.0
U.S.	13.0	3.7	3.8	1.5	1.2	0.9	1.0	0.6	0.3

Note: (1) Figures cover the Cape Coral-Fort Myers, FL Metropolitan Statistical Area—see Appendix B for areas included; (2) Excludes Mexico.
Source: U.S. Census Bureau, 2011-2013 American Community Survey 3-Year Estimates

Marital Status

Area	Never Married	Now Married[2]	Separated	Widowed	Divorced
City	24.6	52.6	2.3	6.9	13.6
MSA[1]	26.0	50.3	2.1	8.2	13.4
U.S.	32.7	48.1	2.2	6.0	11.0

Note: Figures are percentages and cover the population 15 years of age and older; (1) Figures cover the Cape Coral-Fort Myers, FL Metropolitan Statistical Area—see Appendix B for areas included; (2) Excludes separated
Source: U.S. Census Bureau, 2011-2013 American Community Survey 3-Year Estimates

Disability Status

Area	All Ages	Under 18 Years Old	18 to 64 Years Old	65 Years and Over
City	12.8	2.9	10.6	31.9
MSA[1]	14.2	3.6	10.8	29.8
U.S.	12.3	4.1	10.2	36.3

Note: Figures show percent of the civilian noninstitutionalized population that reported having a disability. Disability status is determined from from six types of difficulty: vision, hearing, cognitive, ambulatory, self-care, and independent living. For children under 5 years old, hearing and vision difficulty are used to determine disability status. For children between the ages of 5 and 14, disability status is determined from hearing, vision, cognitive, ambulatory, and self-care difficulties. For people aged 15 years and older, they are considered to have a disability if they have difficulty with any one of the six difficulty types; (1) Figures cover the Cape Coral-Fort Myers, FL Metropolitan Statistical Area—see Appendix B for areas included.
Source: U.S. Census Bureau, 2011-2013 American Community Survey 3-Year Estimates

Age

Area	Percent of Population									Median Age
	Under Age 5	Age 5–19	Age 20–34	Age 35–44	Age 45–54	Age 55–64	Age 65–74	Age 75–84	Age 85+	
City	5.7	19.8	14.8	12.3	14.5	14.2	10.9	5.4	2.5	43.0
MSA[1]	5.1	16.2	16.0	10.9	12.8	14.1	14.0	7.8	3.1	46.5
U.S.	6.4	19.9	20.7	12.9	14.1	12.3	7.6	4.2	1.9	37.4

Note: (1) Figures cover the Cape Coral-Fort Myers, FL Metropolitan Statistical Area—see Appendix B for areas included
Source: U.S. Census Bureau, 2011-2013 American Community Survey 3-Year Estimates

Gender

Area	Males	Females	Males per 100 Females
City	79,085	82,607	95.7
MSA[1]	316,615	329,066	96.2
U.S.	154,451,010	159,410,713	96.9

Note: (1) Figures cover the Cape Coral-Fort Myers, FL Metropolitan Statistical Area—see Appendix B for areas included
Source: U.S. Census Bureau, 2011-2013 American Community Survey 3-Year Estimates

Religious Groups by Family

Area	Catholic	Baptist	Non-Den.	Methodist[2]	Lutheran	LDS[3]	Pente-costal	Presby-terian[4]	Muslim[5]	Judaism
MSA[1]	16.2	5.0	3.0	2.5	1.2	0.5	4.4	1.4	0.9	0.2
U.S.	19.1	9.3	4.0	4.0	2.3	2.0	1.9	1.6	0.8	0.7

Note: Figures are the number of adherents as a percentage of the total population; (1) Figures cover the Cape Coral-Fort Myers, FL Metropolitan Statistical Area—see Appendix B for areas included; (2) Methodist/Pietist; (3) Latter Day Saints; (4) Reformed; (5) Figures are estimates
Source: Association of Statisticians of American Religious Bodies, 2010 U.S. Religion Census: Religious Congregations & Membership Study

Religious Groups by Tradition

Area	Catholic	Evangelical Protestant	Mainline Protestant	Other Tradition	Black Protestant	Orthodox
MSA[1]	16.2	14.3	4.6	2.0	0.3	0.2
U.S.	19.1	16.2	7.3	4.3	1.6	0.3

Note: Figures are the number of adherents as a percentage of the total population; (1) Figures cover the Cape Coral-Fort Myers, FL Metropolitan Statistical Area—see Appendix B for areas included
Source: Association of Statisticians of American Religious Bodies, 2010 U.S. Religion Census: Religious Congregations & Membership Study

ECONOMY

Gross Metropolitan Product

Area	2012	2013	2014	2015	Rank[2]
MSA[1]	20.9	21.9	23.1	24.6	95

Note: Figures are in billions of dollars; (1) Figures cover the Cape Coral-Fort Myers, FL Metropolitan Statistical Area—see Appendix B for areas included; (2) Rank is based on 2015 data and ranges from 1 to 363
Source: The U.S. Conference of Mayors, U.S. Metro Economies: GMP and Employment 2013-2015, June 2014

Economic Growth

Area	2010-12 (%)	2013 (%)	2014 (%)	2015 (%)	Rank[2]
MSA[1]	1.3	3.4	3.8	4.3	19
U.S.	2.1	2.0	2.3	3.2	–

Note: Figures are real gross metropolitan product (GMP) growth rates and represent annual average percent change; (1) Figures cover the Cape Coral-Fort Myers, FL Metropolitan Statistical Area—see Appendix B for areas included; (2) Rank is based on 2015 data and ranges from 1 to 363
Source: The U.S. Conference of Mayors, U.S. Metro Economies: GMP and Employment 2013-2015, June 2014

Metropolitan Area Exports

Area	2008	2009	2010	2011	2012	2013	Rank[2]
MSA[1]	282.8	237.5	298.0	305.1	509.8	442.6	225

Note: Figures are in millions of dollars; (1) Figures cover the Cape Coral-Fort Myers, FL Metropolitan Statistical Area—see Appendix B for areas included; (2) Rank is based on 2013 data and ranges from 1 to 387
Source: U.S. Department of Commerce, International Trade Administration, Office of Trade & Industry Information, Manufacturing & Services, data extracted April 3, 2015

Building Permits

Area	Single-Family			Multi-Family			Total		
	2013	2014	Pct. Chg.	2013	2014	Pct. Chg.	2013	2014	Pct. Chg.
City	492	663	34.8	6	0	-100.0	498	663	33.1
MSA[1]	2,531	3,112	23.0	645	983	52.4	3,176	4,095	28.9
U.S.	620,802	634,597	2.2	370,020	411,766	11.3	990,822	1,046,363	5.6

Note: (1) Figures cover the Cape Coral-Fort Myers, FL Metropolitan Statistical Area—see Appendix B for areas included; Figures represent new, privately-owned housing units authorized (unadjusted data); All permit data are based on estimates with imputation.
Source: U.S. Census Bureau, Manufacturing, Mining, and Construction Statistics, Building Permits, 2013, 2014

Bankruptcy Filings

Area	Business Filings			Nonbusiness Filings		
	2013	2014	% Chg.	2013	2014	% Chg.
Lee County	79	74	-6.3	1,833	1,619	-11.7
U.S.	33,212	26,983	-18.8	1,038,720	909,812	-12.4

Note: Business filings include Chapter 7, Chapter 11, Chapter 12, and Chapter 13; Nonbusiness filings include Chapter 7, Chapter 11, and Chapter 13
Source: Administrative Office of the U.S. Courts, Business and Nonbusiness Bankruptcy, County Cases Commenced by Chapter of the Bankruptcy Code, During the 12- Month Period Ending December 31, 2013 and Business and Nonbusiness Bankruptcy, County Cases Commenced by Chapter of the Bankruptcy Code, During the 12- Month Period Ending December 31, 2014

Housing Vacancy Rates

Area	Gross Vacancy Rate[2] (%)			Year-Round Vacancy Rate[3] (%)			Rental Vacancy Rate[4] (%)			Homeowner Vacancy Rate[5] (%)		
	2012	2013	2014	2012	2013	2014	2012	2013	2014	2012	2013	2014
MSA[1]	n/a	n/a	n/a	n/a	n/a	n/a	n/a	n/a	n/a	n/a	n/a	n/a
U.S.	13.8	13.6	13.4	10.8	10.7	10.4	8.7	8.3	7.6	2.0	2.0	1.9

Note: (1) Figures cover the Cape Coral-Fort Myers, FL Metropolitan Statistical Area—see Appendix B for areas included; (2) The percentage of the total housing inventory that is vacant; (3) The percentage of the housing inventory (excluding seasonal units) that is year-round vacant; (4) The percentage of rental inventory that is vacant for rent; (5) The percentage of homeowner inventory that is vacant for sale; n/a not available
Source: U.S. Census Bureau, Housing Vacancies and Homeownership Annual Statistics: 2014

INCOME

Income

Area	Per Capita ($)	Median Household ($)	Average Household ($)
City	22,251	48,095	59,217
MSA[1]	26,690	46,587	66,302
U.S.	27,884	52,176	72,897

Note: (1) Figures cover the Cape Coral-Fort Myers, FL Metropolitan Statistical Area—see Appendix B for areas included
Source: U.S. Census Bureau, 2011-2013 American Community Survey 3-Year Estimates

Household Income Distribution

Area	Percent of Households Earning							
	Under $15,000	$15,000 -24,999	$25,000 -34,999	$35,000 -49,999	$50,000 -74,999	$75,000 -99,000	$100,000 -149,999	$150,000 and up
City	11.2	11.9	12.8	16.1	21.6	11.7	9.8	5.0
MSA[1]	12.0	12.5	12.6	16.0	18.9	10.7	9.8	7.4
U.S.	13.0	10.9	10.3	13.6	17.9	11.9	12.7	9.6

Note: (1) Figures cover the Cape Coral-Fort Myers, FL Metropolitan Statistical Area—see Appendix B for areas included
Source: U.S. Census Bureau, 2011-2013 American Community Survey 3-Year Estimates

Poverty Rate

Area	All Ages	Under 18 Years Old	18 to 64 Years Old	65 Years and Over
City	14.9	21.3	14.6	7.9
MSA[1]	16.0	27.1	16.3	6.8
U.S.	15.9	22.4	14.8	9.5

Note: Figures are percentage of people whose income during the past 12 months was below the poverty level; (1) Figures cover the Cape Coral-Fort Myers, FL Metropolitan Statistical Area—see Appendix B for areas included
Source: U.S. Census Bureau, 2011-2013 American Community Survey 3-Year Estimates

EMPLOYMENT

Labor Force and Employment

Area	Civilian Labor Force			Workers Employed		
	Dec. 2013	Dec. 2014	% Chg.	Dec. 2013	Dec. 2014	% Chg.
City	80,176	82,969	3.5	75,135	78,825	4.9
MSA[1]	304,065	315,307	3.7	285,502	299,521	4.9
U.S.	154,408,000	155,521,000	0.7	144,423,000	147,190,000	1.9

Note: Data is not seasonally adjusted and covers workers 16 years of age and older; (1) Figures cover the Cape Coral-Fort Myers, FL Metropolitan Statistical Area—see Appendix B for areas included
Source: Bureau of Labor Statistics, Local Area Unemployment Statistics

Unemployment Rate

Area	2014											
	Jan.	Feb.	Mar.	Apr.	May	Jun.	Jul.	Aug.	Sep.	Oct.	Nov.	Dec.
City	6.5	6.4	6.4	5.7	6.1	6.3	6.6	6.5	5.9	5.6	5.5	5.0
MSA[1]	6.3	6.2	6.1	5.5	6.0	6.3	6.7	6.6	6.0	5.6	5.4	5.0
U.S.	7.0	7.0	6.8	5.9	6.1	6.3	6.5	6.3	5.7	5.5	5.5	5.4

Note: Data is not seasonally adjusted and covers workers 16 years of age and older; (1) Figures cover the Cape Coral-Fort Myers, FL Metropolitan Statistical Area—see Appendix B for areas included
Source: Bureau of Labor Statistics, Local Area Unemployment Statistics

Employment by Occupation

Occupation Classification	City (%)	MSA[1] (%)	U.S. (%)
Management, Business, Science, and Arts	29.4	29.9	36.2
Natural Resources, Construction, and Maintenance	9.8	10.9	9.0
Production, Transportation, and Material Moving	7.9	7.8	12.1
Sales and Office	31.5	28.6	24.4
Service	21.3	22.9	18.3

Note: Figures cover employed civilians 16 years of age and older; (1) Figures cover the Cape Coral-Fort Myers, FL Metropolitan Statistical Area—see Appendix B for areas included
Source: U.S. Census Bureau, 2011-2013 American Community Survey 3-Year Estimates

Employment by Industry

Sector	MSA[1] Number of Employees	MSA[1] Percent of Total	U.S. Percent of Total
Construction, Mining, and Logging	21,200	8.9	5.0
Education and Health Services	27,200	11.4	15.5
Financial Activities	11,800	4.9	5.7
Government	40,200	16.8	15.8
Information	3,100	1.3	2.0
Leisure and Hospitality	39,200	16.4	10.3
Manufacturing	5,200	2.2	8.7
Other Services	9,900	4.1	4.0
Professional and Business Services	30,400	12.7	13.8
Retail Trade	39,500	16.5	11.4
Transportation, Warehousing, and Utilities	4,700	2.0	3.9
Wholesale Trade	7,000	2.9	4.2

Note: Figures are non-farm employment as of December 2014. Figures are not seasonally adjusted and include workers 16 years of age and older; (1) Figures cover the Cape Coral-Fort Myers, FL Metropolitan Statistical Area—see Appendix B for areas included; n/a not available
Source: Bureau of Labor Statistics, Current Employment Statistics, Employment, Hours, and Earnings

Occupations with Greatest Projected Employment Growth: 2012 – 2022

Occupation[1]	2012 Employment	2022 Projected Employment	Numeric Employment Change	Percent Employment Change
Retail Salespersons	326,380	380,120	53,740	16.5
Combined Food Preparation and Serving Workers, Including Fast Food	196,980	237,340	40,360	20.5
Customer Service Representatives	191,210	228,620	37,410	19.6
Registered Nurses	164,020	201,140	37,120	22.6
Waiters and Waitresses	191,370	227,810	36,440	19.0
Office Clerks, General	142,710	170,300	27,590	19.3
Cashiers	206,660	230,190	23,530	11.4
Landscaping and Groundskeeping Workers	92,510	115,540	23,030	24.9
Receptionists and Information Clerks	75,780	95,680	19,900	26.2
Nursing Assistants	86,990	106,200	19,210	22.1

Note: Projections cover Florida; (1) Sorted by numeric employment change
Source: www.projectionscentral.com, State Occupational Projections, 2012–2022 Long-Term Projections

Fastest Growing Occupations: 2012 – 2022

Occupation[1]	2012 Employment	2022 Projected Employment	Numeric Employment Change	Percent Employment Change
Helpers—Carpenters	1,280	2,450	1,170	90.7
Helpers—Brickmasons, Blockmasons, Stonemasons, and Tile and Marble Setters	1,050	1,890	840	79.5
Biomedical Engineers	760	1,300	540	70.7
Reinforcing Iron and Rebar Workers	520	870	350	67.5
Glaziers	2,890	4,710	1,820	62.8
Solar Photovoltaic Installers	170	270	100	58.7
Brickmasons and Blockmasons	2,820	4,430	1,610	57.1
Stonemasons	450	710	260	56.4
Helpers—Pipelayers, Plumbers, Pipefitters, and Steamfitters	2,420	3,750	1,330	54.8
Cement Masons and Concrete Finishers	10,390	16,050	5,660	54.4

Note: Projections cover Florida; (1) Sorted by percent employment change and excludes occupations with numeric employment change less than 100
Source: www.projectionscentral.com, State Occupational Projections, 2012–2022 Long-Term Projections

Average Wages

Occupation	$/Hr.	Occupation	$/Hr.
Accountants and Auditors	32.71	Maids and Housekeeping Cleaners	10.18
Automotive Mechanics	19.81	Maintenance and Repair Workers	16.36
Bookkeepers	16.61	Marketing Managers	54.42
Carpenters	18.60	Nuclear Medicine Technologists	31.55
Cashiers	9.83	Nurses, Licensed Practical	20.35
Clerks, General Office	13.22	Nurses, Registered	30.64
Clerks, Receptionists/Information	13.00	Nursing Assistants	12.52
Clerks, Shipping/Receiving	12.90	Packers and Packagers, Hand	9.31
Computer Programmers	45.16	Physical Therapists	44.59
Computer Systems Analysts	40.73	Postal Service Mail Carriers	24.80
Computer User Support Specialists	19.77	Real Estate Brokers	22.86
Cooks, Restaurant	11.59	Retail Salespersons	11.99
Dentists	50.97	Sales Reps., Exc. Tech./Scientific	26.37
Electrical Engineers	32.32	Sales Reps., Tech./Scientific	43.19
Electricians	18.53	Secretaries, Exc. Legal/Med./Exec.	14.95
Financial Managers	51.28	Security Guards	11.25
First-Line Supervisors/Managers, Sales	21.86	Surgeons	n/a
Food Preparation Workers	9.84	Teacher Assistants	13.30
General and Operations Managers	55.15	Teachers, Elementary School	23.80
Hairdressers/Cosmetologists	15.98	Teachers, Secondary School	24.60
Internists	99.55	Telemarketers	10.01
Janitors and Cleaners	11.93	Truck Drivers, Heavy/Tractor-Trailer	17.41
Landscaping/Groundskeeping Workers	11.41	Truck Drivers, Light/Delivery Svcs.	15.51
Lawyers	42.74	Waiters and Waitresses	9.55

Note: Wage data covers the Cape Coral-Fort Myers, FL Metropolitan Statistical Area—see Appendix B for areas included; Hourly wages for elementary/secondary school teachers and teacher assistants were calculated by the editors from annual wage data assuming a 40 hour work week; n/a not available.
Source: Bureau of Labor Statistics, Metro Area Occupational Employment and Wage Estimates, May 2014

TAXES

State Corporate Income Tax Rates

State	Tax Rate (%)	Income Brackets ($)	Num. of Brackets	Financial Institution Tax Rate (%)[a]	Federal Income Tax Ded.
Florida	5.5 (f)	Flat rate	1	5.5 (f)	No

Note: Tax rates as of January 1, 2015; (a) Rates listed are the corporate income tax rate applied to financial institutions or excise taxes based on income. Some states have other taxes based upon the value of deposits or shares; (f) An exemption of $50,000 is allowed. Florida's Alternative Minimum Tax rate is 3.3%.
Source: Federation of Tax Administrators, "State Corporate Income Tax Rates, 2015"

State Individual Income Tax Rates

State	Tax Rate (%)	Income Brackets ($)	Num. of Brackets	Personal Exempt. ($)[1]		Fed. Inc. Tax Ded.
				Single	Dependents	
Florida	None	–	–	–	–	–

Note: Tax rates as of January 1, 2015; Local- and county-level taxes are not included; n/a not applicable; (1) Married joint filers generally receive double the single exemption
Source: Federation of Tax Administrators, "State Individual Income Tax Rates, 2015"

Various State and Local Tax Rates

State	State and Local Sales and Use (%)	State Sales and Use (%)	Gasoline[1] (¢/gal.)	Cigarette[2] ($/pack)	Spirits[3] ($/gal.)	Wine[4] ($/gal.)	Beer[5] ($/gal.)
Florida	6.0	6.0	36.42	1.339	6.50 (f)	2.25	0.48 (p)

Note: All tax rates as of January 1, 2015; (1) The American Petroleum Institute has developed a methodology for determining the average tax rate on a gallon of fuel. Rates may include any of the following: excise taxes, environmental fees, storage tank fees, other fees or taxes, general sales tax, and local taxes. In states where gasoline is subject to the general sales tax, or where the fuel tax is based on the average sale price, the average rate determined by API is sensitive to changes in the price of gasoline. States that fully or partially apply general sales taxes to gasoline: CA, CO, GA, IL, IN, MI, NY; (2) The federal excise tax of $1.0066 per pack and local taxes are not included; (3) Rates are those applicable to off-premise sales of 40% alcohol by volume (a.b.v.) distilled spirits in 750ml containers. Local excise taxes are excluded; (4) Rates are those applicable to off-premise sales of 11% a.b.v. non-carbonated wine in 750ml containers; (5) Rates are those applicable to off-premise sales of 4.7% a.b.v. beer in 12 ounce containers; (f) Different rates are also applicable according to alcohol content, place of production, size of container, or place purchased (on- or off-premise or onboard airlines); (p) Local excise taxes are excluded.
Source: Tax Foundation, 2015 Facts & Figures: How Does Your State Compare?

State Business Tax Climate Index Rankings

State	Overall Rank	Corporate Tax Index Rank	Individual Income Tax Index Rank	Sales Tax Index Rank	Unemployment Insurance Tax Index Rank	Property Tax Index Rank
Florida	5	14	1	12	3	16

Note: The index is a measure of how each state's tax laws affect economic performance. The lower the rank, the more favorable a state's tax system is for business. States without a given tax are given a ranking of 1. The scores/rankings for the District of Columbia do not affect other states. The 2015 index represents the tax climate as of July 1, 2014.
Source: Tax Foundation, State Business Tax Climate Index 2015

COMMERCIAL UTILITIES

Typical Monthly Electric Bills

Area	Commercial Service ($/month)		Industrial Service ($/month)	
	1,500 kWh	40 kW demand 14,000 kWh	1,000 kW demand 200,000 kWh	50,000 kW demand 32,500,000 kWh
City	n/a	n/a	n/a	n/a
Average[1]	201	1,653	26,124	2,639,743

Note: Figures are based on annualized 2014 rates; (1) Average based on 180 utilities surveyed; n/a not available
Source: Edison Electric Institute, Typical Bills and Average Rates Report, Summer 2014

TRANSPORTATION

Means of Transportation to Work

Area	Car/Truck/Van: Drove Alone	Car/Truck/Van: Car-pooled	Public Transportation: Bus	Public Transportation: Subway	Public Transportation: Railroad	Bicycle	Walked	Other Means	Worked at Home
City	83.2	9.3	0.5	0.0	0.0	0.4	0.8	1.5	4.4
MSA[1]	77.8	11.1	1.1	0.0	0.0	0.7	1.0	2.6	5.7
U.S.	76.4	9.6	2.6	1.8	0.6	0.6	2.8	1.3	4.3

Note: Figures are percentages and cover workers 16 years of age and older; (1) Figures cover the Cape Coral-Fort Myers, FL Metropolitan Statistical Area—see Appendix B for areas included
Source: U.S. Census Bureau, 2011-2013 American Community Survey 3-Year Estimates

Travel Time to Work

Area	Less Than 10 Minutes	10 to 19 Minutes	20 to 29 Minutes	30 to 44 Minutes	45 to 59 Minutes	60 to 89 Minutes	90 Minutes or More
City	7.2	25.3	19.5	30.1	11.0	4.6	2.3
MSA[1]	8.4	27.5	20.7	26.4	9.4	4.9	2.7
U.S.	13.3	29.7	20.9	20.2	7.7	5.7	2.6

Note: Figures are percentages and include workers 16 years old and over; (1) Figures cover the Cape Coral-Fort Myers, FL Metropolitan Statistical Area—see Appendix B for areas included
Source: U.S. Census Bureau, 2011-2013 American Community Survey 3-Year Estimates

Travel Time Index

Area	1985	1990	1995	2000	2005	2010	2011
Urban Area[1]	1.10	1.13	1.21	1.15	1.18	1.15	1.15
Average[2]	1.09	1.14	1.16	1.19	1.23	1.18	1.18

Note: Travel Time Index—the ratio of travel time in the peak period to the travel time at free-flow conditions. For example, a value of 1.30 indicates a 20-minute free-flow trip takes 26 minutes in the peak. Free-flow speeds (60 mph on freeways and 35 mph on principal arterials) are used as the comparison threshold; (1) Covers the Cape Coral FL urban area; (2) average of 498 urban areas

Source: Texas Transportation Institute, Urban Mobility Report 2012, December 2012

Public Transportation

Agency Name / Mode of Transportation	Vehicles Operated in Maximum Service	Annual Unlinked Passenger Trips (in thous.)	Annual Passenger Miles (in thous.)
Lee County Transit (LeeTran)			
Bus (directly operated)	48	4,075.3	23,636.5
Demand Response (directly operated)	35	104.3	1,119.1
Vanpool (purchased transportation)	11	44.6	1,747.9

Source: Federal Transit Administration, National Transit Database, 2013

Air Transportation

Airport Name and Code / Type of Service	Passenger Airlines[1]	Passenger Enplanements	Freight Carriers[2]	Freight (lbs.)
Southwest Florida International Airport (RSW)				
Domestic service (U.S. carriers - 2014)	23	3,791,348	11	10,341,511
International service (U.S. carriers - 2013)	3	363	0	0

Note: (1) Includes all U.S.-based major, minor and commuter airlines that carried at least one passenger during the year; (2) Includes all U.S.-based airlines and freight carriers that transported at least one lb. of freight during the year.

Source: Bureau of Transportation Statistics, The Intermodal Transportation Database, Air Carriers: T-100 Domestic Market (U.S. Carriers), 2014; Bureau of Transportation Statistics, The Intermodal Transportation Database, Air Carriers: T-100 International Market (U.S. Carriers), 2013

Other Transportation Statistics

Major Highways:	I-75
Amtrak Service:	Bus service only (station is in Ft. Myers)
Major Waterways/Ports:	Gulf of Mexico; Caloosahatchee River

Source: Amtrak.com; Google Maps

BUSINESSES

Major Business Headquarters

Company Name	Rankings: Fortune[1]	Rankings: Forbes[2]
No companies listed	-	-

Note: (1) Fortune 500—companies that produce a 10-K are ranked 1 to 500 based on 2013 revenue; (2) all private companies with at least $2 billion in annual revenue through the end of their most current fiscal year are ranked 1 to 221; companies listed are headquartered in the city; dashes indicate no ranking

Source: Fortune, "Fortune 500," June 16, 2014; Forbes, "America's Largest Private Companies," November 5, 2014

Minority- and Women-Owned Businesses

Group	All Firms		Firms with Paid Employees			
	Firms	Sales ($000)	Firms	Sales ($000)	Employees	Payroll ($000)
Asian	374	46,704	(s)	(s)	(s)	(s)
Black	741	36,991	65	16,996	322	4,468
Hispanic	3,487	149,403	(s)	(s)	(s)	(s)
Women	5,213	365,051	505	252,724	2,110	58,541
All Firms	18,476	4,711,956	3,366	4,140,517	26,555	820,005

Note: Figures cover firms located in the city; minority- and women-owned business are defined as firms in which the corresponding group own 51% or more of the stock or equity of the company; (s) estimates are suppressed when publication standards are not met
Source: U.S. Census Bureau, 2007 Economic Census, Survey of Business Owners (2012 Survey of Business Owners data will be released starting in June 2015)

HOTELS & CONVENTION CENTERS

Hotels/Motels

Area	5 Star		4 Star		3 Star		2 Star		1 Star		Not Rated	
	Num.	Pct.[3]	Num.	Pct.[3]	Num.	Pct.[3]	Num.	Pct.[3]	Num.	Pct.[3]	Num.	Pct.[3]
City[1]	0	0.0	5	5.6	34	38.2	42	47.2	1	1.1	7	7.9
Total[2]	166	0.9	1,264	7.0	5,718	31.8	9,340	52.0	411	2.3	1,070	6.0

Note: (1) Figures cover Cape Coral and vicinity; (2) Figures cover all 100 cities in this book; (3) Percentage of hotels which have a given star rating; Star ratings are determined by expedia.com and offer an indication of the general quality of a particular hotel.
Source: expedia.com, April 2, 2015

The Cape Coral-Fort Myers, FL metro area is home to one of the best hotels in the U.S. according to *Travel & Leisure*: **Gasparilla Inn**. Criteria: service; location; rooms; food; and value. The list includes the top 236 hotels in the U.S. *Travel & Leisure, "T+L 500, The World's Best Hotels 2015"*

Major Convention Centers

Name	Overall Space (sq. ft.)	Exhibit Space (sq. ft.)	Meeting Space (sq. ft.)	Meeting Rooms
Harborside Events Center (Fort Myers)	n/a	42,000	n/a	n/a

Note: Table includes convention centers located in the Cape Coral-Fort Myers, FL metro area; n/a not available
Source: Original research

Living Environment

COST OF LIVING

Cost of Living Index

Composite Index	Groceries	Housing	Utilities	Transportation	Health Care	Misc. Goods/ Services
98.6	107.0	87.6	86.5	112.9	103.7	102.4

Note: The Cost of Living Index measures regional differences in the cost of consumer goods and services, excluding taxes and non-consumer expenditures, for professional and managerial households in the top income quintile. It is based on more than 50,000 prices covering almost 60 different items for which prices are collected three times a year by chambers of commerce, economic development organizations or university applied economic centers in each participating urban area. The numbers shown should be read as a percentage above or below the national average of 100. For example, a value of 115.4 in the groceries column indicates that grocery prices are 15.4% higher than the national average. Small differences in the index numbers should not be interpreted as significant; Figures cover the Cape Coral-Fort Myers FL urban area.
Source: The Council for Community and Economic Research, ACCRA Cost of Living Index, 2014

Grocery Prices

Area[1]	T-Bone Steak ($/pound)	Frying Chicken ($/pound)	Whole Milk ($/half gal.)	Eggs ($/dozen)	Orange Juice ($/64 oz.)	Coffee ($/11.5 oz.)
City[2]	11.36	1.42	2.83	2.11	3.84	4.12
Avg.	10.40	1.37	2.40	1.99	3.46	4.27
Min.	8.48	0.93	1.37	1.30	2.83	2.99
Max.	14.20	2.44	3.62	4.02	6.42	6.96

Note: (1) Values for the local area are compared with the average, minimum and maximum values for all 308 areas in the Cost of Living Index; (2) Figures cover the Cape Coral-Fort Myers FL urban area; **T-Bone Steak** *(price per pound);* **Frying Chicken** *(price per pound, whole fryer);* **Whole Milk** *(half gallon carton);* **Eggs** *(price per dozen, Grade A, large);* **Orange Juice** *(64 oz. Tropicana or Florida Natural);* **Coffee** *(11.5 oz. can, vacuum-packed, Maxwell House, Hills Bros, or Folgers).*
Source: The Council for Community and Economic Research, ACCRA Cost of Living Index, 2014

Housing and Utility Costs

Area[1]	New Home Price ($)	Apartment Rent ($/month)	All Electric ($/month)	Part Electric ($/month)	Other Energy ($/month)	Telephone ($/month)
City[2]	260,323	925	165.00	-	-	19.97
Avg.	305,838	919	181.00	93.66	73.14	27.95
Min.	183,142	480	112.00	42.06	23.42	17.16
Max.	1,358,576	3,851	594.00	180.03	440.99	40.42

Note: (1) Values for the local area are compared with the average, minimum and maximum values for all 308 areas in the Cost of Living Index; (2) Figures cover the Cape Coral-Fort Myers FL urban area; **New Home Price** *(2,400 sf living area, 8,000 sf lot, in urban area with full utilities);* **Apartment Rent** *(950 sf 2 bedroom/1.5 or 2 bath, unfurnished, excluding all utilities except water);* **All Electric** *(average monthly cost for an all-electric home);* **Part Electric** *(average monthly cost for a part-electric home);* **Other Energy** *(average monthly cost for natural gas, fuel oil, coal, wood, and any other forms of energy except electricity);* **Telephone** *(price includes basic monthly rate for a private residential line plus additional local usage charges incurred by a family of four).*
Source: The Council for Community and Economic Research, ACCRA Cost of Living Index, 2014

Health Care, Transportation, and Other Costs

Area[1]	Doctor ($/visit)	Dentist ($/visit)	Optometrist ($/visit)	Gasoline ($/gallon)	Beauty Salon ($/visit)	Men's Shirt ($)
City[2]	107.90	92.31	93.93	3.58	39.87	23.17
Avg.	102.86	87.89	97.66	3.44	34.37	26.74
Min.	67.47	65.78	51.18	3.00	17.43	12.79
Max.	173.50	150.14	235.00	4.33	64.28	49.50

Note: (1) Values for the local area are compared with the average, minimum and maximum values for all 308 areas in the Cost of Living Index; (2) Figures cover the Cape Coral-Fort Myers FL urban area; **Doctor** *(general practitioners routine exam of an established patient);* **Dentist** *(adult teeth cleaning and periodic oral examination);* **Optometrist** *(full vision eye exam for established adult patient);* **Gasoline** *(one gallon regular unleaded, national brand, including all taxes, cash price at self-service pump if available);* **Beauty Salon** *(woman's shampoo, trim, and blow-dry);* **Men's Shirt** *(cotton/polyester dress shirt, pinpoint weave, long sleeves).*
Source: The Council for Community and Economic Research, ACCRA Cost of Living Index, 2014

HOUSING

House Price Index (HPI)

Area	National Ranking[2]	Quarterly Change (%)	One-Year Change (%)	Five-Year Change (%)
MSA[1]	14	4.12	10.98	30.10
U.S.[3]	–	1.35	4.91	11.59

Note: The HPI is a weighted repeat sales index. It measures average price changes in repeat sales or refinancings on the same properties. This information is obtained by reviewing repeat mortgage transactions on single-family properties whose mortgages have been purchased or securitized by Fannie Mae or Freddie Mac in January 1975; (1) Cape Coral-Fort Myers Metropolitan Statistical Area—see Appendix B for areas included; (2) Rankings are based on annual percentage change for all metro areas containing at least 15,000 transactions over the last 10 years and ranges from 1 to 275; (3) figures based on a weighted average of Census Division estimates using a seasonally adjusted, purchase-only index; all figures are for the period ending December 31, 2014

Source: Federal Housing Finance Agency, House Price Index, February 26, 2015

Median Single-Family Home Prices

Area	2012	2013	2014[p]	Percent Change 2013 to 2014
MSA[1]	128.1	166.1	188.7	13.6
U.S. Average	177.2	197.4	209.0	5.9

Note: Figures are median sales prices of existing single-family homes in thousands of dollars; (p) preliminary; n/a not available; (1) Cape Coral-Fort Myers, FL Metropolitan Statistical Area—see Appendix B for areas included

Source: National Association of Realtors, Median Sales Price of Existing Single-Family Homes for Metropolitan Areas, 4th Quarter 2014

Qualifying Income Based on Median Sales Price of Existing Single-Family Homes

Area	With 5% Down ($)	With 10% Down ($)	With 20% Down ($)
MSA[1]	41,753	39,556	35,161
U.S. Average	45,863	43,449	38,621

Note: Figures are preliminary; Qualifying income is based on a mortgage rate of 4.0%. Monthly principal and interest payment is limited to 25% of income; n/a not available; (1) Cape Coral-Fort Myers, FL Metropolitan Statistical Area—see Appendix B for areas included

Source: National Association of Realtors, Qualifying Income Based on Median Sales Price of Existing Single-Family Homes for Metropolitan Areas, 4th Quarter 2014

Median Apartment Condo-Coop Home Prices

Area	2012	2013	2014[p]	Percent Change 2013 to 2014
MSA[1]	n/a	146.9	167.3	13.9
U.S. Average	173.7	194.9	205.1	5.2

Note: Figures are median sales prices of existing apartment condo-coop homes in thousands of dollars; (p) preliminary; n/a not available; (1) Cape Coral-Fort Myers, FL Metropolitan Statistical Area—see Appendix B for areas included

Source: National Association of Realtors, Median Sales Price of Existing Apartment Condo-Coop Homes for Metropolitan Areas, 4th Quarter 2014

Gross Monthly Rent

Area	Under $200	$200 -299	$300 -499	$500 -749	$750 -999	$1,000 -1,499	$1,500 and up	Median ($)
City	0.0	0.2	0.8	11.5	32.1	42.1	13.5	1,046
MSA[1]	0.4	1.0	3.5	22.0	33.1	29.1	10.9	923
U.S.	1.7	3.2	7.8	22.1	24.3	26.0	14.9	900

Note: Figures are percentages except for Median; Gross rent is the contract rent plus the estimated average monthly cost of utilities (electricity, gas, and water and sewer) and fuels (oil, coal, kerosene, wood, etc.) if these are paid by the renter (or paid for the renter by someone else); (1) Figures cover the Cape Coral-Fort Myers, FL Metropolitan Statistical Area—see Appendix B for areas included

Source: U.S. Census Bureau, 2011-2013 American Community Survey 3-Year Estimates

Homeownership Rate

Area	2007 (%)	2008 (%)	2009 (%)	2010 (%)	2011 (%)	2012 (%)	2013 (%)	2014 (%)
MSA[1]	n/a	n/a	n/a	n/a	n/a	n/a	n/a	n/a
U.S.	68.1	67.8	67.4	66.9	66.1	65.4	65.1	64.5

Note: (1) Figures cover the Cape Coral-Fort Myers, FL Metropolitan Statistical Area—see Appendix B for areas included; n/a not available
Source: U.S. Census Bureau, Housing Vacancies and Homeownership Annual Statistics: 2014

Year Housing Structure Built

Area	2010 or Later	2000 -2009	1990 -1999	1980 -1989	1970 -1979	1960 -1969	1950 -1959	1940 -1949	Before 1940	Median Year
City	0.5	43.3	14.4	22.7	11.9	5.9	0.8	0.3	0.2	1996
MSA[1]	0.5	34.4	17.9	21.8	15.8	5.5	2.8	0.6	0.7	1992
U.S.	0.9	15.0	13.9	13.8	15.8	11.0	10.9	5.4	13.3	1976

Note: Figures are percentages except for Median Year; (1) Figures cover the Cape Coral-Fort Myers, FL Metropolitan Statistical Area—see Appendix B for areas included
Source: U.S. Census Bureau, 2011-2013 American Community Survey 3-Year Estimates

HEALTH

Health Risk Data

Category	MSA[1] (%)	U.S. (%)
Adults aged 18–64 who have any kind of health care coverage	n/a	79.6
Adults who reported being in good or excellent health	n/a	83.1
Adults who are current smokers	n/a	19.6
Adults who are heavy drinkers[2]	n/a	6.1
Adults who are binge drinkers[3]	n/a	16.9
Adults who are overweight (BMI 25.0 - 29.9)	n/a	35.8
Adults who are obese (BMI 30.0 - 99.8)	n/a	27.6
Adults who participated in any physical activities in the past month	n/a	77.1
Adults 50+ who have ever had a sigmoidoscopy or colonoscopy	n/a	67.3
Women aged 40+ who have had a mammogram within the past two years	n/a	74.0
Men aged 40+ who have had a PSA test within the past two years	n/a	45.2
Adults aged 65+ who have had flu shot within the past year	n/a	60.1
Adults who always wear a seatbelt	n/a	93.8

Note: Data as of 2012 unless otherwise noted; n/a not available; (1) Figures cover the Cape Coral-Fort Myers, FL Metropolitan Statistical Area—see Appendix B for areas included; (2) Heavy drinkers are classified as males having more than two drinks per day or females having more than one drink per day; (3) Binge drinkers are classified as males having five or more drinks on one occasion or females having four or more drinks on one occasion
Source: Centers for Disease Control and Prevention, Behaviorial Risk Factor Surveillance System, SMART: Selected Metropolitan/Micropolitan Area Risk Trends, 2012 (Note: the CDC has discontinued this dataset but will be releasing a replacement in late 2015)

Chronic Health Indicators

Category	MSA[1] (%)	U.S. (%)
Adults who have ever been told they had a heart attack	n/a	4.5
Adults who have ever been told they had a stroke	n/a	2.9
Adults who have been told they currently have asthma	n/a	8.9
Adults who have ever been told they have arthritis	n/a	25.7
Adults who have ever been told they have diabetes[2]	n/a	9.7
Adults who have ever been told they had skin cancer	n/a	5.7
Adults who have ever been told they had any other types of cancer	n/a	6.5
Adults who have ever been told they have COPD	n/a	6.2
Adults who have ever been told they have kidney disease	n/a	2.5
Adults who have ever been told they have a form of depression	n/a	18.0

Note: Data as of 2012 unless otherwise noted; n/a not available; (1) Figures cover the Cape Coral-Fort Myers, FL Metropolitan Statistical Area—see Appendix B for areas included; (2) Figures do not include pregnancy-related, borderline, or pre-diabetes
Source: Centers for Disease Control and Prevention, Behaviorial Risk Factor Surveillance System, SMART: Selected Metropolitan/Micropolitan Area Risk Trends, 2012 (Note: the CDC has discontinued this dataset but will be releasing a replacement in late 2015)

Mortality Rates for the Top 10 Causes of Death in the U.S.

ICD-10[a] Sub-Chapter	ICD-10[a] Code	Age-Adjusted Mortality Rate[1] per 100,000 population	
		County[2]	U.S.
Malignant neoplasms	C00-C97	142.4	166.2
Ischaemic heart diseases	I20-I25	97.9	105.7
Other forms of heart disease	I30-I51	24.3	49.3
Chronic lower respiratory diseases	J40-J47	32.8	42.1
Organic, including symptomatic, mental disorders	F01-F09	33.5	38.1
Cerebrovascular diseases	I60-I69	20.9	37.0
Other external causes of accidental injury	W00-X59	28.5	26.9
Other degenerative diseases of the nervous system	G30-G31	12.3	25.6
Diabetes mellitus	E10-E14	13.6	21.3
Hypertensive diseases	I10-I15	17.4	19.4

Note: (a) ICD-10 = International Classification of Diseases 10th Revision; (1) Mortality rates are a three year average covering 2011-2013; (2) Figures cover Lee County
Source: Centers for Disease Control and Prevention, National Center for Health Statistics. Compressed Mortality File 1999-2013 on CDC WONDER Online Database, released October 2014. Data are compiled from the Compressed Mortality File 1999-2013, Series 20 No. 2S, 2014.

Mortality Rates for Selected Causes of Death

ICD-10[a] Sub-Chapter	ICD-10[a] Code	Age-Adjusted Mortality Rate[1] per 100,000 population	
		County[2]	U.S.
Assault	X85-Y09	7.5	5.2
Diseases of the liver	K70-K76	15.1	13.2
Human immunodeficiency virus (HIV) disease	B20-B24	2.7	2.2
Influenza and pneumonia	J09-J18	5.3	15.4
Intentional self-harm	X60-X84	15.5	12.5
Malnutrition	E40-E46	Suppressed	0.9
Obesity and other hyperalimentation	E65-E68	1.3	1.8
Renal failure	N17-N19	7.0	13.1
Transport accidents	V01-V99	13.8	11.7
Viral hepatitis	B15-B19	1.6	2.2

Note: (a) ICD-10 = International Classification of Diseases 10th Revision; (1) Mortality rates are a three year average covering 2011-2013; (2) Figures cover Lee County
Source: Centers for Disease Control and Prevention, National Center for Health Statistics. Compressed Mortality File 1999-2013 on CDC WONDER Online Database, released October 2014. Data are compiled from the Compressed Mortality File 1999-2013, Series 20 No. 2S, 2014.

Health Insurance Coverage

Area	With Health Insurance	With Private Health Insurance	With Public Health Insurance	Without Health Insurance	Population Under Age 18 Without Health Insurance
City	79.6	56.1	35.9	20.4	10.5
MSA[1]	79.2	56.0	40.4	20.8	13.2
U.S.	85.2	65.2	31.0	14.8	7.3

Note: Figures are percentages that cover the civilian noninstitutionalized population; (1) Figures cover the Cape Coral-Fort Myers, FL Metropolitan Statistical Area—see Appendix B for areas included
Source: U.S. Census Bureau, 2011-2013 American Community Survey 3-Year Estimates

Number of Medical Professionals

Area[1]	MDs[2]	DOs[2,3]	Dentists	Podiatrists	Chiropractors	Optometrists
Local (number)	1,150	170	300	49	174	88
Local (rate[4])	178.3	26.4	45.4	7.4	26.3	13.3
U.S. (rate[4])	270.0	20.2	63.1	5.7	25.2	14.9

Note: Data as of 2013 unless noted; (1) Local data covers Lee County; (2) Data as of 2012 and includes all active, non-federal physicians; (3) Doctor of Osteopathic Medicine; (4) rate per 100,000 population
Source: U.S. Department of Health and Human Services, Health Resources and Services Administration, Bureau of Health Professions, Area Resource File (ARF) 2013-2014

EDUCATION

Public School District Statistics

District Name	Schls	Pupils	Pupil/ Teacher Ratio	Minority Pupils[1] (%)	Free Lunch Eligible[2] (%)	IEP[3] (%)
Lee County School District	125	85,765	15.7	53.6	57.2	13.4

Note: Table includes school districts with 2,000 or more students; (1) Percentage of students that are not non-Hispanic white; (2) Percentage of students that are eligible for the free lunch program; (3) Percentage of students that have an Individualized Education Program.

Source: U.S. Department of Education, National Center for Education Statistics, Common Core of Data, Local Education Agency (School District) Universe Survey: School Year 2012-2013; U.S. Department of Education, National Center for Education Statistics, Common Core of Data, Public Elementary/Secondary School Universe Survey: School Year 2012-2013

Highest Level of Education

Area	Less than H.S.	H.S. Diploma	Some College, No Deg.	Associate Degree	Bachelor's Degree	Master's Degree	Prof. School Degree	Doctorate Degree
City	9.0	38.9	23.6	7.9	13.5	5.2	1.0	0.8
MSA[1]	13.2	32.5	21.5	7.8	15.8	6.2	1.9	1.2
U.S.	13.7	28.0	21.2	7.9	18.2	7.7	1.9	1.3

Note: Figures cover persons age 25 and over; (1) Figures cover the Cape Coral-Fort Myers, FL Metropolitan Statistical Area—see Appendix B for areas included

Source: U.S. Census Bureau, 2011-2013 American Community Survey 3-Year Estimates

Educational Attainment by Race

Area	High School Graduate or Higher (%)					Bachelor's Degree or Higher (%)				
	Total	White	Black	Asian	Hisp.[2]	Total	White	Black	Asian	Hisp.[2]
City	91.0	91.2	93.1	79.5	76.0	20.6	20.9	11.2	24.5	17.3
MSA[1]	86.8	89.1	73.1	86.0	63.2	25.0	26.5	12.6	34.9	11.9
U.S.	86.3	88.3	83.1	85.7	64.0	29.1	30.4	18.8	50.7	13.7

Note: Figures shown cover persons 25 years old and over; (1) Figures cover the Cape Coral-Fort Myers, FL Metropolitan Statistical Area—see Appendix B for areas included; (2) People of Hispanic origin can be of any race

Source: U.S. Census Bureau, 2011-2013 American Community Survey 3-Year Estimates

School Enrollment by Grade and Control

Area	Preschool (%)		Kindergarten (%)		Grades 1 - 4 (%)		Grades 5 - 8 (%)		Grades 9 - 12 (%)	
	Public	Private	Public	Private	Public	Private	Public	Private	Public	Private
City	64.1	35.9	94.4	5.6	94.1	5.9	95.7	4.3	93.0	7.0
MSA[1]	59.9	40.1	94.5	5.5	94.1	5.9	91.5	8.5	93.6	6.4
U.S.	57.7	42.3	87.9	12.1	89.9	10.1	90.0	10.0	90.7	9.3

Note: Figures shown cover persons 3 years old and over; (1) Figures cover the Cape Coral-Fort Myers, FL Metropolitan Statistical Area—see Appendix B for areas included

Source: U.S. Census Bureau, 2011-2013 American Community Survey 3-Year Estimates

Average Salaries of Public School Classroom Teachers

Area	2013-14		2014-15		Percent Change 2013-14 to 2014-15	Percent Change 2004-05 to 2014-15
	Dollars	Rank[1]	Dollars	Rank[1]		
FLORIDA	47,780	39	48,992	36	2.54	17.8
U.S. Average	56,610	–	57,379	–	1.36	20.8

Note: (1) State rank ranges from 1 to 51 where 1 indicates highest salary.

Source: National Education Association, Rankings & Estimates: Rankings of the States 2014 and Estimates of School Statistics 2015, March 2015

Higher Education

Four-Year Colleges			Two-Year Colleges			Medical Schools[1]	Law Schools[2]	Voc/ Tech[3]
Public	Private Non-profit	Private For-profit	Public	Private Non-profit	Private For-profit			
0	0	0	0	0	0	0	0	1

Note: Figures cover institutions located within the city limits and include main campuses only; (1) includes schools accredited by the Liaison Committee on Medical Education and the American Osteopathic Association's Commission on Osteopathic College Accreditation; (2) includes ABA-accredited schools, schools with provisional ABA accreditation, and state accredited schools; (3) includes all schools with programs that are less than 2 years.
Source: National Center for Education Statistics, Integrated Postsecondary Education System (IPEDS), 2013-14; Association of American Medical Colleges, Member List, May 1, 2015; American Osteopathic Association, Member List, May 1, 2015; Law School Admission Council, Official Guide to ABA-Approved Law Schools Online, May 1, 2015; Wikipedia, List of Medical Schools in the United States, May 1, 2015; Wikipedia, List of Law Schools in the United States, May 1, 2015

PRESIDENTIAL ELECTION

2012 Presidential Election Results

Area	Obama (%)	Romney (%)	Other (%)
Lee County	41.4	57.9	0.7
U.S.	51.0	47.2	1.8

Note: Results may not add to 100% due to rounding
Source: Dave Leip's Atlas of U.S. Presidential Elections

EMPLOYERS

Major Employers

Company Name	Industry
Aris Horticulture	Flowers: grown under cover
Chico's FAS	Women's clothing stores
Christian & Missionary Alliance Fndn	Retirement hotel operation
City of Cape Coral	City and town managers' office
County of Lee	Sheriffs' office
Crowther Roofing & Sheet Metal of FL	Roofing contractor
Doctors Osteopathic Medical Center	General medical and surgical hospitals
Edison State College	Community college
Florida Department of Military	National guard
General Electric Company	Aircraft engines and engine parts
K Corp Lee	Restaurant management
Lee Memorial Health System	General medical and surgical hospitals
Lee Memorial Health System Foundation	Health systems agency
MCI Communications Services	Telephone communication, except radio
Raymond Building Supply Corporation	Lumber plywood, and millwork
Robby & Stucky Limited	Furniture stores
Schear Corp.	Multi-family dwellings, new construction
Sunshine Masonry	Concrete block masonry laying
United States Postal Service	U.s. postal service
Wal-Mart Stores	Department stores, discount

Note: Companies shown are located within the Cape Coral-Fort Myers, FL Metropolitan Statistical Area.
Source: Hoovers.com; Wikipedia

PUBLIC SAFETY

Crime Rate

Area	All Crimes	Violent Crimes				Property Crimes		
		Murder	Forcible Rape	Robbery	Aggrav. Assault	Burglary	Larceny -Theft	Motor Vehicle Theft
City	2,185.2	1.8	4.3	24.5	89.9	491.2	1,484.8	88.7
Suburbs[1]	2,640.5	4.5	29.0	109.0	260.8	603.9	1,497.8	135.6
Metro[2]	2,527.1	3.8	22.9	87.9	218.2	575.9	1,494.6	123.9
U.S.	3,098.6	4.5	25.2	109.1	229.1	610.0	1,899.4	221.3

Note: Figures are crimes per 100,000 population; (1) All areas within the metro area that are located outside the city limits; (2) Figures cover the Cape Coral-Fort Myers, FL Metropolitan Statistical Area—see Appendix B for areas included
Source: FBI Uniform Crime Reports, 2013

Hate Crimes

Area	Number of Quarters Reported	Number of Incidents per Bias Motivation						
		Race	Religion	Sexual Orientation	Ethnicity	Disability	Gender	Gender Identity
City	4	0	0	0	0	0	0	0
U.S.	4	2,871	1,031	1,233	655	83	18	31

Source: Federal Bureau of Investigation, Hate Crime Statistics 2013

Identity Theft Consumer Complaints

Area	Complaints	Complaints per 100,000 Population	Rank[2]
MSA[1]	988	149.4	11
U.S.	332,646	104.3	-

Note: (1) Figures cover the Cape Coral-Fort Myers, FL Metropolitan Statistical Area—see Appendix B for areas included; (2) Rank ranges from 1 to 380 where 1 indicates greatest number of identity theft complaints per 100,000 population
Source: Federal Trade Commission, Consumer Sentinel Network Data Book for January–December 2014

Fraud and Other Consumer Complaints

Area	Complaints	Complaints per 100,000 Population	Rank[2]
MSA[1]	2,812	425.3	98
U.S.	2,250,205	705.7	-

Note: (1) Figures cover the Cape Coral-Fort Myers, FL Metropolitan Statistical Area—see Appendix B for areas included; (2) Rank ranges from 1 to 380 where 1 indicates greatest number of identity theft complaints per 100,000 population
Source: Federal Trade Commission, Consumer Sentinel Network Data Book for January–December 2014

RECREATION

Culture

Dance[1]	Theatre[1]	Instrumental Music[1]	Vocal Music[1]	Series and Festivals	Museums and Art Galleries[2]	Zoos and Aquariums[3]
0	0	0	0	0	4	0

Note: (1) Professional perfoming groups; (2) Based on organizations with SIC code 8412; (3) AZA-accredited
Source: The Grey House Performing Arts Directory, 2015-16; Association of Zoos & Aquariums, AZA Member Zoos & Aquariums, April 2015; www.AccuLeads.com, April 2015

Professional Sports Teams

Team Name	League	Year Established
No teams are located in the metro area		

Source: Wikipedia, Major Professional Sports Teams of the United States and Canada, April 2015

CLIMATE

Average and Extreme Temperatures

Temperature	Jan	Feb	Mar	Apr	May	Jun	Jul	Aug	Sep	Oct	Nov	Dec	Yr.
Extreme High (°F)	88	91	93	96	99	103	98	98	96	95	95	90	103
Average High (°F)	75	76	80	85	89	91	91	92	90	86	80	76	84
Average Temp. (°F)	65	65	70	74	79	82	83	83	82	77	71	66	75
Average Low (°F)	54	54	59	62	68	73	74	75	74	68	61	55	65
Extreme Low (°F)	28	32	33	39	52	60	66	67	64	48	34	26	26

Note: Figures cover the years 1948-1995
Source: National Climatic Data Center, International Station Meteorological Climate Summary, 9/96

Average Precipitation/Snowfall/Humidity

Precip./Humidity	Jan	Feb	Mar	Apr	May	Jun	Jul	Aug	Sep	Oct	Nov	Dec	Yr.
Avg. Precip. (in.)	2.0	2.2	2.6	1.7	3.6	9.3	8.9	8.9	8.2	3.5	1.4	1.5	53.9
Avg. Snowfall (in.)	0	0	0	0	0	0	0	0	0	0	0	0	0
Avg. Rel. Hum. 7am (%)	90	89	89	88	87	89	90	91	92	90	90	90	90
Avg. Rel. Hum. 4pm (%)	56	54	52	50	53	64	68	67	66	59	58	57	59

Note: Figures cover the years 1948-1995; Tr = Trace amounts (<0.05 in. of rain; <0.5 in. of snow)
Source: National Climatic Data Center, International Station Meteorological Climate Summary, 9/96

Weather Conditions

Temperature			Daytime Sky			Precipitation		
32°F & below	45°F & below	90°F & above	Clear	Partly cloudy	Cloudy	0.01 inch or more precip.	0.1 inch or more snow/ice	Thunder-storms
1	18	115	93	220	52	110	0	92

Note: Figures are average number of days per year and cover the years 1948-1995
Source: National Climatic Data Center, International Station Meteorological Climate Summary, 9/96

HAZARDOUS WASTE

Superfund Sites

Cape Coral has no sites on the EPA's Superfund Final National Priorities List. There are a total of 1,322 Superfund sites on the list in the U.S. *U.S. Environmental Protection Agency, Final National Priorities List, April 14, 2015*

AIR & WATER QUALITY

Air Quality Trends: Ozone

	2004	2005	2006	2007	2008	2009	2010	2011	2012	2013
MSA[1]	0.072	0.070	0.070	0.069	0.068	0.062	0.064	0.062	0.063	0.065

Note: (1) Data covers the Cape Coral-Fort Myers, FL Metropolitan Statistical Area—see Appendix B for areas included. The values shown are the composite ozone concentration averages among trend sites based on the highest fourth daily maximum 8-hour concentration in parts per million. These trends are based on sites having an adequate record of monitoring data during the trend period. Data from exceptional events are included.
Source: U.S. Environmental Protection Agency, Air Quality Monitoring Information, "Air Quality Trends by City, 2000-2013"

Air Quality Index

Area	Percent of Days when Air Quality was...[2]					AQI Statistics[2]	
	Good	Moderate	Unhealthy for Sensitive Groups	Unhealthy	Very Unhealthy	Maximum	Median
MSA[1]	88.5	11.5	0.0	0.0	0.0	81	35

Note: (1) Data covers the Cape Coral-Fort Myers, FL Metropolitan Statistical Area—see Appendix B for areas included; (2) Based on 365 days with AQI data in 2014. Air Quality Index (AQI) is an index for reporting daily air quality. EPA calculates the AQI for five major air pollutants regulated by the Clean Air Act: ground-level ozone, particle pollution (aka particulate matter), carbon monoxide, sulfur dioxide, and nitrogen dioxide. The AQI runs from 0 to 500. The higher the AQI value, the greater the level of air pollution and the greater the health concern. There are six AQI categories: "Good" AQI is between 0 and 50. Air quality is considered satisfactory; "Moderate" AQI is between 51 and 100. Air quality is acceptable; "Unhealthy for Sensitive Groups" When AQI values are between 101 and 150, members of sensitive groups may experience health effects; "Unhealthy" When AQI values are between 151 and 200 everyone may begin to experience health effects; "Very Unhealthy" AQI values between 201 and 300 trigger a health alert; "Hazardous" AQI values over 300 trigger warnings of emergency conditions (not shown).
Source: U.S. Environmental Protection Agency, Air Quality Index Report, 2014

Air Quality Index Pollutants

Area	Percent of Days when AQI Pollutant was...[2]					
	Carbon Monoxide	Nitrogen Dioxide	Ozone	Sulfur Dioxide	Particulate Matter 2.5	Particulate Matter 10
MSA[1]	0.0	0.0	55.9	0.0	42.7	1.4

Note: (1) Data covers the Cape Coral-Fort Myers, FL Metropolitan Statistical Area—see Appendix B for areas included; (2) Based on 365 days with AQI data in 2014. The Air Quality Index (AQI) is an index for reporting daily air quality. EPA calculates the AQI for five major air pollutants regulated by the Clean Air Act: ground-level ozone, particle pollution (also known as particulate matter), carbon monoxide, sulfur dioxide, and nitrogen dioxide. The AQI runs from 0 to 500. The higher the AQI value, the greater the level of air pollution and the greater the health concern.
Source: U.S. Environmental Protection Agency, Air Quality Index Report, 2014

Maximum Air Pollutant Concentrations: Particulate Matter, Ozone, CO and Lead

	Particulate Matter 10 (ug/m3)	Particulate Matter 2.5 Wtd AM (ug/m3)	Particulate Matter 2.5 24-Hr (ug/m3)	Ozone (ppm)	Carbon Monoxide (ppm)	Lead (ug/m3)
MSA[1] Level	49	5.8	15	0.066	n/a	n/a
NAAQS[2]	150	15	35	0.075	9	0.15
Met NAAQS[2]	Yes	Yes	Yes	Yes	n/a	n/a

Note: (1) Data covers the Cape Coral-Fort Myers, FL Metropolitan Statistical Area—see Appendix B for areas included; Data from exceptional events are included; (2) National Ambient Air Quality Standards; ppm = parts per million; ug/m³ = micrograms per cubic meter; n/a not available.
Concentrations: Particulate Matter 10 (coarse particulate)—highest second maximum 24-hour concentration; Particulate Matter 2.5 Wtd AM (fine particulate)—highest weighted annual mean concentration; Particulate Matter 2.5 24-Hour (fine particulate)—highest 98th percentile 24-hour concentration; Ozone—highest fourth daily maximum 8-hour concentration; Carbon Monoxide—highest second maximum non-overlapping 8-hour concentration; Lead—maximum running 3-month average
Source: U.S. Environmental Protection Agency, Air Quality Monitoring Information, "Air Quality Statistics by City, 2013"

Maximum Air Pollutant Concentrations: Nitrogen Dioxide and Sulfur Dioxide

	Nitrogen Dioxide AM (ppb)	Nitrogen Dioxide 1-Hr (ppb)	Sulfur Dioxide AM (ppb)	Sulfur Dioxide 1-Hr (ppb)	Sulfur Dioxide 24-Hr (ppb)
MSA[1] Level	n/a	n/a	n/a	n/a	n/a
NAAQS[2]	53	100	30	75	140
Met NAAQS[2]	n/a	n/a	n/a	n/a	n/a

Note: (1) Data covers the Cape Coral-Fort Myers, FL Metropolitan Statistical Area—see Appendix B for areas included; Data from exceptional events are included; (2) National Ambient Air Quality Standards; ppm = parts per million; ug/m³ = micrograms per cubic meter; n/a not available.
Concentrations: Nitrogen Dioxide AM—highest arithmetic mean concentration; Nitrogen Dioxide 1-Hr—highest 98th percentile 1-hour daily maximum concentration; Sulfur Dioxide AM—highest annual mean concentration; Sulfur Dioxide 1-Hr—highest 99th percentile 1-hour daily maximum concentration; Sulfur Dioxide 24-Hr—highest second maximum 24-hour concentration
Source: U.S. Environmental Protection Agency, Air Quality Monitoring Information, "Air Quality Statistics by City, 2013"

Drinking Water

Water System Name	Pop. Served	Primary Water Source Type	Violations[1]	
			Health Based	Monitoring/ Reporting
City of Cape Coral	124,051	Ground	0	0

Note: (1) Based on violation data from January 1, 2014 to December 31, 2014 (includes unresolved violations from earlier years)
Source: U.S. Environmental Protection Agency, Office of Ground Water and Drinking Water, Safe Drinking Water Information System (based on data extracted January 27, 2015)

Charleston, South Carolina

Background

Charleston is located on the state's Atlantic coastline, 110 miles southeast of Columbia and 100 miles north of Savannah, Georgia. The city, named for King Charles II of England, is the county seat of Charleston County. Charleston is located on a bay at the end of a peninsula between the Ashley and Cooper rivers. The terrain is low-lying and coastal with nearby islands and inlets.

In 1670, English colonists established a nearby settlement, and subsequently moved to Charleston's present site. Charleston became an early trading center for rice, indigo, cotton and other goods. As the plantation economy grew, Charleston became a slave-trading center. In 1861, the Confederacy fired the cannon shot that launched the Civil War from the city's Battery, aimed at the Union's Fort Sumter in Charleston Harbor. Charleston was under siege during the Civil War, and experienced many difficulties during Reconstruction. Manufacturing industries including textiles and ironwork became important in the nineteenth century.

Charleston is part of a larger metropolitan area that includes North Charleston and Mount Pleasant and covers Charleston, Berkley and Dorchester counties. This area is a regional commercial and cultural center and a southern transportation hub whose port is among the nation's busiest shipping facilities. Charleston's other contemporary economic sectors include manufacturing, health care, business and professional services, defense activity, retail and wholesale trade, tourism, education and construction.

Charleston is a popular tourist area, based on its scenery, history and recreation. The city's center is well known for its historic neighborhoods with distinctive early southern architecture and ambiance. As one of the first American cities in the early twentieth century to actively encourage historic restoration and preservation, Charleston has more recently undertaken numerous revitalization initiatives, including the Charleston Place Hotel and retail complex, and Waterfront Park. North Charleston and other communities are also growing with industry and suburban development.

The founding of the Charleston Naval Shipyard stimulated a military-based economy after 1901. Numerous other defense facilities were later established, including the Charleston Air Force Base, located in North Charleston. Several military facilities were closed in the 1990s, including the shipyard, although other defense-related operations have remained.

In 2000, the Confederate submarine the *HL Hunley,* which sank in 1864, was raised, and brought to a conservation laboratory at the old Charleston Naval Base. Author Patricia Cornwell has taken a great interest in the project, and is involved in the creation of a museum to house the submarine. Also, an International Museum of African American History, will sit across from Liberty Square.

Charleston is a center for health care and medical research. SPAWAR (US Navy Space and Naval Warfare Systems Command) is the area's largest single employer followed by the Medical University of South Carolina, founded in 1824, with approximately 8,000 employees. Other area educational institutions include The College of Charleston, The Citadel Military College, Trident Technical College, Charleston Southern University, and a campus of Johnson and Wales University offering culinary and hospitality education.

The Charleston area has numerous parks, including one with a skateboard center, and public waterfront areas. Coastal recreation activities such as boating, swimming, fishing and beaches are popular, as are golf and other land sports.

The Charleston Museum is the nation's oldest, founded in 1773. There are also several former plantations in the area, including Boone Hall Plantation, Drayton Hall, Magnolia Plantation, and Middleton Place. Other attractions include the South Carolina Aquarium with its IMAX Theater, the American Military Museum, the Drayton Hall Plantation Museum, the Gibbes Museum of Art and the Karpeles Manuscript Museum. A North Charleston Convention Center and Performing Arts Center complex opened in 1999. Cultural organizations include the Spoleto Festival USA annual summer arts festival. The fifth annual Charleston International Film Festival, CIFF, was held in 2011.

The Arthur Ravenel Jr. Bridge is the longest cable-stayed bridge in all of the Americas, running across Charleston's Cooper River.

The nearby Atlantic Ocean moderates the climate, especially in winter, and keeps summer a bit cooler than expected. Expect Indian summers in fall, and a possible hurricane, while spring sharply turns from the cold winds of March to lovely May. Severe storms are possible.

Rankings

General Rankings

- Charleston was selected as one the best places to live in America by *Outside Magazine.* The city ranked #12. Criteria included nearby adventure, healthy eating options, bike lanes, green spaces, number of outfitters and bike shops, miles of trails, median income, and unemployment rate. *Outside Magazine, "Outside's Best 16 Best Places to Live in the U.S. 2014," September 2014*
- Charleston was selected as one of "America's Favorite Cities." The city ranked #4 in the "Quality of Life: Cleanliness" category. Respondents to an online survey were asked to rate 38 top urban destinations in the United States from a visitor's perspective. Criteria: cleanliness. *Travel + Leisure, "America's Favorite Cities 2014"*
- The U.S. Conference of Mayors and Waste Management sponsor the City Livability Awards Program. The awards recognize and honor mayors for exemplary leadership in developing and implementing specific programs that improve the quality of life in America's cities. Charleston was one of 17 second round finalists in the large cities (population 100,000 or more) category. *U.S. Conference of Mayors, "2015 City Livability Awards"*
- Charleston appeared on *Travel + Leisure's* list of the ten best cities in the United States and Canada. The city was ranked #1. Criteria: activities/attractions; culture/arts; restaurants/food; people; and value. *Travel + Leisure, "The World's Best Awards 2014"*
- Based on nearly 77,000 responses, *Condé Nast Traveler* ranked its readers' favorite cities worldwide. Charleston ranked #2. *Condé Nast Traveler, Readers' Choice Awards 2014, "Top 10 Cities in the World"*
- In their second annual survey, analysts for the small- and mid-sized city lifestyle site Livability.com looked at data for more than 2,000 U.S. cities to determine the rankings for Livability's "Top 100 Best Places to Live" in 2015. Charleston ranked #92. Criteria: vibrant economy; low cost of living; abundant lifestyle amenities. *Livability.com, "Top 100 Best Places to Live 2015"*

Business/Finance Rankings

- Using data from the Council for Community and Economic Research's 2013 Annual Report, NerdWallet ranked the 100 U.S. cities with the most expensive cost of living. Cities in California and in the Northeast topped the list. Of the cities with the highest cost of living, Charleston ranked #77. *NerdWallet.com, "Most Expensive Cities in America," June 4, 2014*
- Charleston was ranked #17 out of 100 metro areas in terms of economic performance (#1 = best) during the recession and recovery from trough quarter through the second quarter of 2013. Criteria: percent change in employment; percentage point change in unemployment rate; percent change in gross metropolitan product; percent change in House Price Index. *Brookings Institution, MetroMonitor: Tracking Economic Recession and Recovery in America's 100 Largest Metropolitan Areas, September 2013*
- The Charleston metro area appeared on the Milken Institute "2013 Best Performing Cities" list. Rank: #39 out of 200 large metro areas. Criteria: job growth; wage and salary growth; high-tech output growth. *Milken Institute, "Best-Performing Cities 2014," January 2015*
- *Forbes* ranked the 200 most populous metro areas to determine the nation's "Best Places for Business and Careers." The Charleston metro area was ranked #59. Criteria: costs (business and living); job growth (past and projected); income growth; educational attainment (college and high school); projected economic growth; cultural and recreational opportunities; net migration patterns; number of highly ranked colleges. *Forbes, "The Best Places for Business and Careers 2014," July 23, 2014*

Children/Family Rankings

- Charleston was chosen as one of America's 100 best communities for young people. The winners were selected based upon detailed information provided about each community's efforts to fulfill five essential promises critical to the well-being of young people: caring adults who are actively involved in their lives; safe places in which to learn and grow; a healthy start toward adulthood; an effective education that builds marketable skills; and opportunities to help others. *America's Promise Alliance, "100 Best Communities for Young People, 2012"*

Culture/Performing Arts Rankings

- Charleston was selected as one of "America's Favorite Cities." The city ranked #3 in the "Culture: Historical Sites " category. Respondents to an online survey were asked to rate 38 top urban destinations in the U.S. from a visitor's perspective. *Travelandleisure.com, "America's Favorite Cities," October 7, 2014*

- Charleston was selected as one of America's top cities for the arts. The city ranked #10 in the mid-sized city (population 100,000 to 499,999) category. Criteria: readers' top choices for arts travel destinations based on the richness and variety of visual arts sites, activities and events. *American Style, "2012 Top 25 Arts Destinations," June 2012*

Education Rankings

- Personal finance website *WalletHub* analyzed the 150 largest U.S. metropolitan statistical areas to determine where the most educated Americans are choosing to settle. Criteria: educational attainment; percentage of workers with jobs in computer, engineering, and science fields; quality and size of each metro area's universities. Charleston was ranked #39 (#1 = most educated city). *www.WalletHub.com, "2014's Most and Least Educated Cities*

Environmental Rankings

- The Charleston metro area came in at #307 for the relative comfort of its climate on Sperling's list of "chill cities," as measured by the Sperling Heat Index. All 361 metro areas are included. Criteria included daytime high temperatures, nighttime low temperatures, dew point, and relative humidity at the high temperatures. *www.bertsperling.com, "Sperling's Chill Cities," July 18, 2013*

- Sperling's BestPlaces assessed 379 metropolitan areas of the United States for the likelihood of dangerously extreme weather events or earthquakes. In general the Southeast and South-Central regions have the highest risk of weather extremes and earthquakes, while the Pacific Northwest enjoys the lowest risk. Of the least risky metropolitan areas, the Charleston metro area was ranked #250. *www.bestplaces.net, "Safest Places from Natural Disasters," April 2011*

- Charleston was highlighted as one of the cleanest metro areas for ozone air pollution in the U.S. during 2011 through 2013. The list represents cities with no monitored ozone air pollution in unhealthful ranges. *American Lung Association, State of the Air 2015*

Health/Fitness Rankings

- Charleston was identified as a "2013 Spring Allergy Capital." The area ranked #32 out of 100. Three groups of factors were used to identify the most severe cities for people with allergies during the spring season: annual pollen levels; medicine utilization; access to board-certified allergists. *Asthma and Allergy Foundation of America, "Spring Allergy Capitals 2013"*

- Charleston was identified as a "2013 Fall Allergy Capital." The area ranked #26 out of 100. Three groups of factors were used to identify the most severe cities for people with allergies during the fall season: annual pollen levels; medicine utilization; access to board-certified allergists. *Asthma and Allergy Foundation of America, "Fall Allergy Capitals 2013"*

- Charleston was identified as a "2013 Asthma Capital." The area ranked #71 out of the nation's 100 largest metropolitan areas. Twelve factors were used to identify the most challenging places to live for people with asthma: estimated prevalence; self-reported prevalence; crude death rate for asthma; annual pollen score; annual air quality; public smoking laws; number of board-certified asthma specialists; school inhaler access laws; rescue medication use; controller medication use; uninsured rate; poverty rate. *Asthma and Allergy Foundation of America, "Asthma Capitals 2013"*
- The Charleston metro area appeared in the 2013 Gallup-Healthways Well-Being Index. The area ranked #111 out of 189. The Gallup-Healthways Well-Being Index score is an average of six sub-indexes, which individually examine life evaluation, emotional health, work environment, physical health, healthy behaviors, and access to basic necessities. Results are based on telephone interviews conducted as part of the Gallup-Healthways Well-Being Index survey January 2–December 29, 2012, and January 2–December 30, 2013, with a random sample of 531,630 adults, aged 18 and older, living in metropolitan areas in the 50 U.S. states and the District of Columbia. *Gallup-Healthways, "State of American Well-Being," March 25, 2014*

Real Estate Rankings

- Using data from the housing-market research firm RealtyTrac, Yahoo! Finance researchers listed the housing markets in which housing affordability is deteriorating most, factoring in interest rates as well as median home prices. The Charleston metro area was among the least affordable housing markets according to the percentage difference in the income required to buy a home in December 2013 as opposed to in December 2012. *news.yahoo.com, "10 Cities Where Ordinary People Can No Longer Afford Homes," March 5, 2014*
- Charleston was ranked #60 out of 275 metro areas in terms of house price appreciation in 2014 (#1 = highest rate). *Federal Housing Finance Agency, House Price Index, 4th Quarter 2014*
- Charleston was ranked #166 out of 226 metro areas in terms of housing affordability in 2014 by the National Association of Home Builders (#1 = most affordable). The NAHB-Wells Fargo Housing Opportunity Index (HOI) for a given area is defined as the share of homes sold in that area that would have been affordable to a family earning the local median income, based on standard mortgage underwriting criteria. *National Association of Home Builders®, NAHB-Wells Fargo Housing Opportunity Index, 4th Quarter 2014*

Safety Rankings

- The National Insurance Crime Bureau ranked 380 metro areas in the U.S. in terms of per capita rates of vehicle theft. The Charleston metro area ranked #75 (#1 = highest rate). Criteria: number of vehicle theft offenses per 100,000 inhabitants in 2012. *National Insurance Crime Bureau, "Hot Spots 2012," June 26, 2013*

Seniors/Retirement Rankings

- From its Best Cities for Successful Aging indexes, the Milken Institute generated rankings for metropolitan areas, weighing data in eight categories—health care, wellness, living arrangements, transportation, financial characteristics, education and employment opportunities, community engagement, and overall livability. The Charleston metro area was ranked #36 overall in the large metro area category. *Milken Institute, "Best Cities for Successful Aging, 2014"*
- Charleston made the 2014 *Forbes* list of "25 Best Places to Retire." Criteria include: housing and living costs; tax climate for retirees; weather and air quality; crime rates; doctor availability; active-lifestyle rankings for walkability, bicycling and volunteering. *Forbes.com, "The Best Places to Retire in 2014," January 16, 2014*
- Charleston was identified as one of the most popular places to retire by *Topretirements.com*. The list reflects the 100 cities (out of 900+ total cities reviewed) that visitors to the website are most interested in for retirement. *Topretirements.com, "Most Popular Places to Retire for 2014," February 25, 2014*

Sports/Recreation Rankings

- Charleston was chosen as a bicycle friendly community by the League of American Bicyclists. A "Bicycle Friendly Community" welcomes cyclists by providing safe accommodation for cycling and encouraging people to bike for transportation and recreation. There are four award levels: Platinum; Gold; Silver; and Bronze. The community achieved an award level of Bronze. *League of American Bicyclists, "Bicycle Friendly Community Master List," Fall 2013*
- Charleston was chosen as one of America's best cities for bicycling. The city ranked #48 out of 50. Criteria: robust cycling infrastructure; vibrant bike culture. The editors only considered cities with populations of 95,000 or more. *Bicycling, "America's Top 50 Bike-Friendly Cities," May 23, 2012*

Miscellaneous Rankings

- *Travel + Leisure* invited readers to rate cities on indicators such as aloofness, "smarty-pants residents," highbrow cultural offerings, high-end shopping, artisanal coffeehouses, conspicuous eco-consciousness, and more in order to identify the nation's snobbiest cities. Cities large and small made the list; among them was Charleston, at #10. *www.travelandleisure.com, "America's Snobbiest Cities, June 2013*
- In *Condé Nast Traveler* magazine's 2013 Readers' Choice Survey, Charleston made the top ten list of friendliest American cities, at #1. *www.cntraveler.com, "The Friendliest and Unfriendliest Cities in the U.S.," July 30, 2013*
- Charleston appeared on *Travel + Leisure's* list of America's most attractive people. Criteria: cities were selected by readers in their annual America's Favorite Cities survey. The city ranked #10 out of 10. *Travel + Leisure, "America's Most and Least Attractive People," November 2013*
- Charleston was selected as one of "America's Best Cities for Hipsters" by *Travel + Leisure.* The city was ranked #7 out of 20. Criteria: live music; coffee bars; independent boutiques; best microbrews; offbeat and tech-savvy locals. *Travel + Leisure, "America's Best Cities for Hipsters," November 2013*
- The National Alliance to End Homelessness ranked the 100 most populous metro areas in terms the rate of homelessness. The Charleston metro area ranked #91. Criteria: number of homeless people per 10,000 population in 2011. *National Alliance to End Homelessness, The State of Homelessness in America 2012*
- Charleston was selected as one of America's best-mannered cities. The area ranked #1. The general public determined the winners by casting votes online. *The Charleston School of Protocol and Etiquette, "2012 Most Mannerly City in America Contest," January 31, 2013*

Business Environment

CITY FINANCES

City Government Finances

Component	2012 ($000)	2012 ($ per capita)
Total Revenues	314,541	2,619
Total Expenditures	230,094	1,916
Debt Outstanding	74,311	619
Cash and Securities[1]	153,540	1,279

Note: (1) Cash and security holdings of a government at the close of its fiscal year, including those of its dependent agencies, utilities, and liquor stores.
Source: U.S Census Bureau, State & Local Government Finances 2012

City Government Revenue by Source

Source	2012 ($000)	2012 ($ per capita)
General Revenue		
From Federal Government	7,746	65
From State Government	20,056	167
From Local Governments	0	0
Taxes		
Property	56,039	467
Sales and Gross Receipts	35,361	294
Personal Income	0	0
Corporate Income	0	0
Motor Vehicle License	0	0
Other Taxes	40,871	340
Current Charges	33,802	281
Liquor Store	0	0
Utility	106,980	891
Employee Retirement	0	0

Source: U.S Census Bureau, State & Local Government Finances 2012

City Government Expenditures by Function

Function	2012 ($000)	2012 ($ per capita)	2012 (%)
General Direct Expenditures			
Air Transportation	0	0	0.0
Corrections	0	0	0.0
Education	0	0	0.0
Employment Security Administration	0	0	0.0
Financial Administration	13,127	109	5.7
Fire Protection	21,780	181	9.5
General Public Buildings	1,785	15	0.8
Governmental Administration, Other	4,561	38	2.0
Health	0	0	0.0
Highways	5,479	46	2.4
Hospitals	0	0	0.0
Housing and Community Development	6,865	57	3.0
Interest on General Debt	2,972	25	1.3
Judicial and Legal	2,860	24	1.2
Libraries	0	0	0.0
Parking	9,190	77	4.0
Parks and Recreation	23,767	198	10.3
Police Protection	40,002	333	17.4
Public Welfare	804	7	0.3
Sewerage	2,992	25	1.3
Solid Waste Management	5,147	43	2.2
Veterans' Services	0	0	0.0
Liquor Store	0	0	0.0
Utility	51,310	427	22.3
Employee Retirement	0	0	0.0

Source: U.S Census Bureau, State & Local Government Finances 2012

DEMOGRAPHICS

Population Growth

Area	1990 Census	2000 Census	2010 Census	Population Growth (%) 1990-2000	Population Growth (%) 2000-2010
City	96,102	96,650	120,083	0.6	24.2
MSA[1]	506,875	549,033	664,607	8.3	21.1
U.S.	248,709,873	281,421,906	308,745,538	13.2	9.7

Note: (1) Figures cover the Charleston-North Charleston-Summerville, SC Metropolitan Statistical Area—see Appendix B for areas included
Source: U.S. Census Bureau, Census 1990, 2000, 2010

Household Size

Area	Persons in Household (%) One	Two	Three	Four	Five	Six	Seven or More	Average Household Size
City	36.8	35.9	14.1	9.3	2.9	0.5	0.4	2.28
MSA[1]	28.3	35.3	16.7	12.5	4.8	1.6	0.8	2.58
U.S.	27.7	33.6	15.7	13.1	6.0	2.3	1.5	2.64

Note: (1) Figures cover the Charleston-North Charleston, SC Metropolitan Statistical Area—see Appendix B for areas included
Source: U.S. Census Bureau, 2011-2013 American Community Survey 3-Year Estimates

Race

Area	White Alone[2] (%)	Black Alone[2] (%)	Asian Alone[2] (%)	AIAN[3] Alone[2] (%)	NHOPI[4] Alone[2] (%)	Other Race Alone[2] (%)	Two or More Races (%)
City	71.8	24.4	1.4	0.2	0.1	0.5	1.6
MSA[1]	67.3	27.2	1.7	0.4	0.1	1.2	2.2
U.S.	73.9	12.6	5.0	0.8	0.2	4.7	2.9

Note: (1) Figures cover the Charleston-North Charleston, SC Metropolitan Statistical Area—see Appendix B for areas included; (2) Alone is defined as not being in combination with one or more other races; (3) American Indian and Alaska Native; (4) Native Hawaiian and Other Pacific Islander
Source: U.S. Census Bureau, 2011-2013 American Community Survey 3-Year Estimates

Hispanic or Latino Origin

Area	Total (%)	Mexican (%)	Puerto Rican (%)	Cuban (%)	Other (%)
City	2.9	1.0	1.0	0.4	0.7
MSA[1]	5.3	2.9	0.8	0.1	1.4
U.S.	16.9	10.8	1.6	0.6	3.8

Note: Persons of Hispanic or Latino origin can be of any race; (1) Figures cover the Charleston-North Charleston, SC Metropolitan Statistical Area—see Appendix B for areas included
Source: U.S. Census Bureau, 2011-2013 American Community Survey 3-Year Estimates

Segregation

Type	Segregation Indices[1] 1990	2000	2010	2010 Rank[2]	Percent Change 1990-2000	1990-2010	2000-2010
Black/White	47.4	44.2	41.5	88	-3.2	-5.9	-2.7
Asian/White	34.4	34.2	33.4	84	-0.3	-1.1	-0.8
Hispanic/White	26.6	32.2	39.8	66	5.6	13.2	7.6

Note: All figures cover the Metropolitan Statistical Area—see Appendix B for areas included; Figures are based on an analysis of 1990, 2000, and 2010 Census Decennial Census tract data by William H. Frey, Brookings Institution and the University of Michigan Social Science Data Analysis Network. In this analysis all racial groups (whites, blacks, and asians) are non-Hispanic members of those races. Hispanics are shown as a separate category;
(1) Segregation Indices are Dissimilarity Indices that measure the degree to which the minority group is distributed differently than whites across census tracts. They range from 0 (complete integration) to 100 (complete segregation) where the value indicates the percentage of the minority group that needs to move to be distributed exactly like whites; (2) Ranges from 1 (most segregated) to 102 (least segregated); n/a not available.
Source: www.CensusScope.org

Ancestry

Area	German	Irish	English	American	Italian	Polish	French[2]	Scottish	Dutch
City	12.0	11.4	11.4	13.9	4.2	2.1	2.7	3.2	1.0
MSA[1]	11.4	10.4	9.0	13.5	3.6	1.7	2.6	2.6	1.0
U.S.	14.9	10.8	8.0	7.4	5.5	3.0	2.7	1.7	1.4

Note: Figures are the percentage of the total population reporting a particular ancestry. The nine most commonly reported ancestries in the U.S. are shown. Figures include multiple ancestries (e.g. if a person reported being Irish and Italian, they were included in both columns); (1) Figures cover the Charleston-North Charleston, SC Metropolitan Statistical Area—see Appendix B for areas included; (2) Excludes Basque
Source: U.S. Census Bureau, 2011-2013 American Community Survey 3-Year Estimates

Foreign-Born Population

Area	Percent of Population Born in								
	Any Foreign Country	Mexico	Asia	Europe	Carribean	South America	Central America[2]	Africa	Canada
City	n/a	n/a	n/a	n/a	n/a	n/a	n/a	n/a	n/a
MSA[1]	5.2	1.4	1.3	1.0	0.3	0.4	0.4	0.1	0.2
U.S.	13.0	3.7	3.8	1.5	1.2	0.9	1.0	0.6	0.3

Note: (1) Figures cover the Charleston-North Charleston, SC Metropolitan Statistical Area—see Appendix B for areas included; (2) Excludes Mexico.
Source: U.S. Census Bureau, 2011-2013 American Community Survey 3-Year Estimates

Marital Status

Area	Never Married	Now Married[2]	Separated	Widowed	Divorced
City	42.5	38.5	2.5	5.3	11.2
MSA[1]	33.7	45.9	3.2	5.9	11.2
U.S.	32.7	48.1	2.2	6.0	11.0

Note: Figures are percentages and cover the population 15 years of age and older; (1) Figures cover the Charleston-North Charleston, SC Metropolitan Statistical Area—see Appendix B for areas included; (2) Excludes separated
Source: U.S. Census Bureau, 2011-2013 American Community Survey 3-Year Estimates

Disability Status

Area	All Ages	Under 18 Years Old	18 to 64 Years Old	65 Years and Over
City	10.1	2.9	7.8	32.9
MSA[1]	11.4	3.5	9.6	35.7
U.S.	12.3	4.1	10.2	36.3

Note: Figures show percent of the civilian noninstitutionalized population that reported having a disability. Disability status is determined from from six types of difficulty: vision, hearing, cognitive, ambulatory, self-care, and independent living. For children under 5 years old, hearing and vision difficulty are used to determine disability status. For children between the ages of 5 and 14, disability status is determined from hearing, vision, cognitive, ambulatory, and self-care difficulties. For people aged 15 years and older, they are considered to have a disability if they have difficulty with any one of the six difficulty types; (1) Figures cover the Charleston-North Charleston, SC Metropolitan Statistical Area—see Appendix B for areas included.
Source: U.S. Census Bureau, 2011-2013 American Community Survey 3-Year Estimates

Age

Area	Percent of Population									Median Age
	Under Age 5	Age 5–19	Age 20–34	Age 35–44	Age 45–54	Age 55–64	Age 65–74	Age 75–84	Age 85+	
City	6.2	15.6	30.0	12.1	11.6	11.7	7.5	3.6	1.7	33.9
MSA[1]	6.6	18.9	23.3	12.8	13.8	12.2	7.5	3.5	1.3	35.7
U.S.	6.4	19.9	20.7	12.9	14.1	12.3	7.6	4.2	1.9	37.4

Note: (1) Figures cover the Charleston-North Charleston, SC Metropolitan Statistical Area—see Appendix B for areas included
Source: U.S. Census Bureau, 2011-2013 American Community Survey 3-Year Estimates

Gender

Area	Males	Females	Males per 100 Females
City	59,351	66,304	89.5
MSA[1]	341,017	356,099	95.8
U.S.	154,451,010	159,410,713	96.9

Note: (1) Figures cover the Charleston-North Charleston, SC Metropolitan Statistical Area—see Appendix B for areas included
Source: U.S. Census Bureau, 2011-2013 American Community Survey 3-Year Estimates

Religious Groups by Family

Area	Catholic	Baptist	Non-Den.	Methodist[2]	Lutheran	LDS[3]	Pente-costal	Presby-terian[4]	Muslim[5]	Judaism
MSA[1]	6.2	12.4	7.1	10.0	1.1	1.0	2.0	2.4	0.2	0.3
U.S.	19.1	9.3	4.0	4.0	2.3	2.0	1.9	1.6	0.8	0.7

Note: Figures are the number of adherents as a percentage of the total population; (1) Figures cover the Charleston-North Charleston-Summerville, SC Metropolitan Statistical Area—see Appendix B for areas included; (2) Methodist/Pietist; (3) Latter Day Saints; (4) Reformed; (5) Figures are estimates
Source: Association of Statisticians of American Religious Bodies, 2010 U.S. Religion Census: Religious Congregations & Membership Study

Religious Groups by Tradition

Area	Catholic	Evangelical Protestant	Mainline Protestant	Other Tradition	Black Protestant	Orthodox
MSA[1]	6.2	19.7	11.2	1.9	7.3	0.1
U.S.	19.1	16.2	7.3	4.3	1.6	0.3

Note: Figures are the number of adherents as a percentage of the total population; (1) Figures cover the Charleston-North Charleston-Summerville, SC Metropolitan Statistical Area—see Appendix B for areas included
Source: Association of Statisticians of American Religious Bodies, 2010 U.S. Religion Census: Religious Congregations & Membership Study

ECONOMY

Gross Metropolitan Product

Area	2012	2013	2014	2015	Rank[2]
MSA[1]	31.0	31.9	33.3	35.2	74

Note: Figures are in billions of dollars; (1) Figures cover the Charleston-North Charleston, SC Metropolitan Statistical Area—see Appendix B for areas included; (2) Rank is based on 2015 data and ranges from 1 to 363
Source: The U.S. Conference of Mayors, U.S. Metro Economies: GMP and Employment 2013-2015, June 2014

Economic Growth

Area	2010-12 (%)	2013 (%)	2014 (%)	2015 (%)	Rank[2]
MSA[1]	3.5	1.6	2.7	3.6	61
U.S.	2.1	2.0	2.3	3.2	–

Note: Figures are real gross metropolitan product (GMP) growth rates and represent annual average percent change; (1) Figures cover the Charleston-North Charleston, SC Metropolitan Statistical Area—see Appendix B for areas included; (2) Rank is based on 2015 data and ranges from 1 to 363
Source: The U.S. Conference of Mayors, U.S. Metro Economies: GMP and Employment 2013-2015, June 2014

Metropolitan Area Exports

Area	2008	2009	2010	2011	2012	2013	Rank[2]
MSA[1]	2,005.5	1,455.7	2,120.0	2,299.4	2,429.8	3,464.3	71

Note: Figures are in millions of dollars; (1) Figures cover the Charleston-North Charleston, SC Metropolitan Statistical Area—see Appendix B for areas included; (2) Rank is based on 2013 data and ranges from 1 to 387
Source: U.S. Department of Commerce, International Trade Administration, Office of Trade & Industry Information, Manufacturing & Services, data extracted April 3, 2015

Building Permits

Area	Single-Family 2013	Single-Family 2014	Single-Family Pct. Chg.	Multi-Family 2013	Multi-Family 2014	Multi-Family Pct. Chg.	Total 2013	Total 2014	Total Pct. Chg.
City	576	600	4.2	351	378	7.7	927	978	5.5
MSA[1]	3,779	4,144	9.7	1,638	2,011	22.8	5,417	6,155	13.6
U.S.	620,802	634,597	2.2	370,020	411,766	11.3	990,822	1,046,363	5.6

Note: (1) Figures cover the Charleston-North Charleston, SC Metropolitan Statistical Area—see Appendix B for areas included; Figures represent new, privately-owned housing units authorized (unadjusted data); All permit data are based on estimates with imputation.
Source: U.S. Census Bureau, Manufacturing, Mining, and Construction Statistics, Building Permits, 2013, 2014

Bankruptcy Filings

Area	Business Filings 2013	Business Filings 2014	Business Filings % Chg.	Nonbusiness Filings 2013	Nonbusiness Filings 2014	Nonbusiness Filings % Chg.
Charleston County	22	29	31.8	480	448	-6.7
U.S.	33,212	26,983	-18.8	1,038,720	909,812	-12.4

Note: Business filings include Chapter 7, Chapter 11, Chapter 12, and Chapter 13; Nonbusiness filings include Chapter 7, Chapter 11, and Chapter 13
Source: Administrative Office of the U.S. Courts, Business and Nonbusiness Bankruptcy, County Cases Commenced by Chapter of the Bankruptcy Code, During the 12- Month Period Ending December 31, 2013 and Business and Nonbusiness Bankruptcy, County Cases Commenced by Chapter of the Bankruptcy Code, During the 12- Month Period Ending December 31, 2014

Housing Vacancy Rates

Area	Gross Vacancy Rate[2] (%) 2012	2013	2014	Year-Round Vacancy Rate[3] (%) 2012	2013	2014	Rental Vacancy Rate[4] (%) 2012	2013	2014	Homeowner Vacancy Rate[5] (%) 2012	2013	2014
MSA[1]	n/a	n/a	n/a	n/a	n/a	n/a	n/a	n/a	n/a	n/a	n/a	n/a
U.S.	13.8	13.6	13.4	10.8	10.7	10.4	8.7	8.3	7.6	2.0	2.0	1.9

Note: (1) Figures cover the Charleston-North Charleston, SC Metropolitan Statistical Area—see Appendix B for areas included; (2) The percentage of the total housing inventory that is vacant; (3) The percentage of the housing inventory (excluding seasonal units) that is year-round vacant; (4) The percentage of rental inventory that is vacant for rent; (5) The percentage of homeowner inventory that is vacant for sale; n/a not available
Source: U.S. Census Bureau, Housing Vacancies and Homeownership Annual Statistics: 2014

INCOME

Income

Area	Per Capita ($)	Median Household ($)	Average Household ($)
City	32,832	52,066	75,238
MSA[1]	27,162	51,580	68,685
U.S.	27,884	52,176	72,897

Note: (1) Figures cover the Charleston-North Charleston, SC Metropolitan Statistical Area—see Appendix B for areas included
Source: U.S. Census Bureau, 2011-2013 American Community Survey 3-Year Estimates

Household Income Distribution

Area	Percent of Households Earning: Under $15,000	$15,000 -24,999	$25,000 -34,999	$35,000 -49,999	$50,000 -74,999	$75,000 -99,000	$100,000 -149,999	$150,000 and up
City	17.2	9.4	9.3	12.2	17.2	11.6	11.6	11.5
MSA[1]	13.6	10.6	10.1	14.1	19.2	12.4	12.0	8.1
U.S.	13.0	10.9	10.3	13.6	17.9	11.9	12.7	9.6

Note: (1) Figures cover the Charleston-North Charleston, SC Metropolitan Statistical Area—see Appendix B for areas included
Source: U.S. Census Bureau, 2011-2013 American Community Survey 3-Year Estimates

Poverty Rate

Area	All Ages	Under 18 Years Old	18 to 64 Years Old	65 Years and Over
City	20.1	26.0	20.4	10.1
MSA[1]	16.1	23.1	14.9	8.9
U.S.	15.9	22.4	14.8	9.5

Note: Figures are percentage of people whose income during the past 12 months was below the poverty level; (1) Figures cover the Charleston-North Charleston, SC Metropolitan Statistical Area—see Appendix B for areas included
Source: U.S. Census Bureau, 2011-2013 American Community Survey 3-Year Estimates

EMPLOYMENT

Labor Force and Employment

Area	Civilian Labor Force			Workers Employed		
	Dec. 2013	Dec. 2014	% Chg.	Dec. 2013	Dec. 2014	% Chg.
City	66,385	68,271	2.8	63,572	65,182	2.5
MSA[1]	338,882	348,192	2.7	321,313	329,245	2.5
U.S.	154,408,000	155,521,000	0.7	144,423,000	147,190,000	1.9

Note: Data is not seasonally adjusted and covers workers 16 years of age and older; (1) Figures cover the Charleston-North Charleston, SC Metropolitan Statistical Area—see Appendix B for areas included
Source: Bureau of Labor Statistics, Local Area Unemployment Statistics

Unemployment Rate

Area	2014											
	Jan.	Feb.	Mar.	Apr.	May	Jun.	Jul.	Aug.	Sep.	Oct.	Nov.	Dec.
City	4.5	4.3	4.2	3.8	4.4	5.1	5.2	5.5	5.1	4.8	4.8	4.5
MSA[1]	5.3	5.3	5.0	4.5	5.1	5.8	6.0	6.3	5.9	5.7	5.6	5.4
U.S.	7.0	7.0	6.8	5.9	6.1	6.3	6.5	6.3	5.7	5.5	5.5	5.4

Note: Data is not seasonally adjusted and covers workers 16 years of age and older; (1) Figures cover the Charleston-North Charleston, SC Metropolitan Statistical Area—see Appendix B for areas included
Source: Bureau of Labor Statistics, Local Area Unemployment Statistics

Employment by Occupation

Occupation Classification	City (%)	MSA[1] (%)	U.S. (%)
Management, Business, Science, and Arts	44.6	35.4	36.2
Natural Resources, Construction, and Maintenance	4.1	9.6	9.0
Production, Transportation, and Material Moving	7.3	11.4	12.1
Sales and Office	23.7	24.8	24.4
Service	20.3	18.8	18.3

Note: Figures cover employed civilians 16 years of age and older; (1) Figures cover the Charleston-North Charleston, SC Metropolitan Statistical Area—see Appendix B for areas included
Source: U.S. Census Bureau, 2011-2013 American Community Survey 3-Year Estimates

Employment by Industry

Sector	MSA[1]		U.S.
	Number of Employees	Percent of Total	Percent of Total
Construction, Mining, and Logging	16,000	4.9	5.0
Education and Health Services	37,300	11.4	15.5
Financial Activities	13,700	4.2	5.7
Government	62,900	19.2	15.8
Information	5,300	1.6	2.0
Leisure and Hospitality	41,400	12.7	10.3
Manufacturing	25,200	7.7	8.7
Other Services	13,300	4.1	4.0
Professional and Business Services	50,000	15.3	13.8
Retail Trade	40,100	12.3	11.4
Transportation, Warehousing, and Utilities	13,800	4.2	3.9
Wholesale Trade	8,200	2.5	4.2

Note: Figures are non-farm employment as of December 2014. Figures are not seasonally adjusted and include workers 16 years of age and older; (1) Figures cover the Charleston-North Charleston, SC Metropolitan Statistical Area—see Appendix B for areas included; n/a not available
Source: Bureau of Labor Statistics, Current Employment Statistics, Employment, Hours, and Earnings

Occupations with Greatest Projected Employment Growth: 2012 – 2022

Occupation[1]	2012 Employment	2022 Projected Employment	Numeric Employment Change	Percent Employment Change
Registered Nurses	43,690	51,940	8,250	18.9
Retail Salespersons	68,460	75,150	6,690	9.8
Combined Food Preparation and Serving Workers, Including Fast Food	43,640	50,180	6,540	15.0
Laborers and Freight, Stock, and Material Movers, Hand	37,500	43,340	5,840	15.6
Customer Service Representatives	38,720	44,170	5,450	14.1
Home Health Aides	10,730	15,720	4,990	46.5
Team Assemblers	40,280	45,140	4,860	12.1
Personal Care Aides	11,490	16,300	4,810	41.9
Heavy and Tractor-Trailer Truck Drivers	22,960	27,280	4,320	18.8
Nursing Assistants	19,030	23,210	4,180	22.0

Note: Projections cover South Carolina; (1) Sorted by numeric employment change
Source: www.projectionscentral.com, State Occupational Projections, 2012–2022 Long-Term Projections

Fastest Growing Occupations: 2012 – 2022

Occupation[1]	2012 Employment	2022 Projected Employment	Numeric Employment Change	Percent Employment Change
Insulation Workers, Mechanical	390	580	190	47.6
Home Health Aides	10,730	15,720	4,990	46.5
Interpreters and Translators	500	720	220	43.7
Diagnostic Medical Sonographers	780	1,120	340	43.3
Helpers—Brickmasons, Blockmasons, Stonemasons, and Tile and Marble Setters	310	440	130	43.2
Personal Care Aides	11,490	16,300	4,810	41.9
Information Security Analysts	1,030	1,450	420	40.4
Skincare Specialists	550	770	220	39.8
Physician Assistants	770	1,070	300	38.8
Health Specialties Teachers, Postsecondary	480	660	180	38.6

Note: Projections cover South Carolina; (1) Sorted by percent employment change and excludes occupations with numeric employment change less than 100
Source: www.projectionscentral.com, State Occupational Projections, 2012–2022 Long-Term Projections

Average Wages

Occupation	$/Hr.	Occupation	$/Hr.
Accountants and Auditors	28.39	Maids and Housekeeping Cleaners	9.55
Automotive Mechanics	19.80	Maintenance and Repair Workers	18.73
Bookkeepers	16.44	Marketing Managers	50.87
Carpenters	18.76	Nuclear Medicine Technologists	33.40
Cashiers	9.48	Nurses, Licensed Practical	19.89
Clerks, General Office	12.52	Nurses, Registered	31.98
Clerks, Receptionists/Information	13.73	Nursing Assistants	11.57
Clerks, Shipping/Receiving	14.81	Packers and Packagers, Hand	10.97
Computer Programmers	35.48	Physical Therapists	38.61
Computer Systems Analysts	33.17	Postal Service Mail Carriers	24.42
Computer User Support Specialists	23.47	Real Estate Brokers	27.17
Cooks, Restaurant	11.26	Retail Salespersons	11.27
Dentists	88.43	Sales Reps., Exc. Tech./Scientific	29.99
Electrical Engineers	36.59	Sales Reps., Tech./Scientific	34.28
Electricians	21.15	Secretaries, Exc. Legal/Med./Exec.	15.48
Financial Managers	53.06	Security Guards	13.90
First-Line Supervisors/Managers, Sales	19.67	Surgeons	131.24
Food Preparation Workers	10.77	Teacher Assistants	11.10
General and Operations Managers	48.40	Teachers, Elementary School	24.50
Hairdressers/Cosmetologists	12.98	Teachers, Secondary School	25.50
Internists	95.46	Telemarketers	9.50
Janitors and Cleaners	10.36	Truck Drivers, Heavy/Tractor-Trailer	20.52
Landscaping/Groundskeeping Workers	11.51	Truck Drivers, Light/Delivery Svcs.	14.54
Lawyers	48.27	Waiters and Waitresses	9.67

Note: Wage data covers the Charleston-North Charleston-Summerville, SC Metropolitan Statistical Area—see Appendix B for areas included; Hourly wages for elementary/secondary school teachers and teacher assistants were calculated by the editors from annual wage data assuming a 40 hour work week; n/a not available.
Source: Bureau of Labor Statistics, Metro Area Occupational Employment and Wage Estimates, May 2014

TAXES

State Corporate Income Tax Rates

State	Tax Rate (%)	Income Brackets ($)	Num. of Brackets	Financial Institution Tax Rate (%)[a]	Federal Income Tax Ded.
South Carolina	5.0	Flat rate	1	4.5 (x)	No

Note: Tax rates as of January 1, 2015; (a) Rates listed are the corporate income tax rate applied to financial institutions or excise taxes based on income. Some states have other taxes based upon the value of deposits or shares; (x) South Carolina taxes savings and loans at a 6% rate.
Source: Federation of Tax Administrators, "State Corporate Income Tax Rates, 2015"

State Individual Income Tax Rates

State	Tax Rate (%)	Income Brackets ($)	Num. of Brackets	Personal Exempt. ($)[1]		Fed. Inc. Tax Ded.
				Single	Dependents	
South Carolina (a)	0.0 - 7.0	2,910 - 14,550	6	4,000 (d)	4,000 (d)	No

Note: Tax rates as of January 1, 2015; Local- and county-level taxes are not included; n/a not applicable; (1) Married joint filers generally receive double the single exemption; (a) 17 states have statutory provision for automatically adjusting to the rate of inflation the dollar values of the income tax brackets, standard deductions, and/or personal exemptions. Massachusetts, Michigan, and Nebraska index the personal exemptiononly. Oregon does not index the income brackets for $125,000 and over. Maine has suspended indexing for 2014 and 2015; (d) These states use the personal exemption amounts provided in the federal Internal Revenue Code.
Source: Federation of Tax Administrators, "State Individual Income Tax Rates, 2015"

Various State and Local Tax Rates

State	State and Local Sales and Use (%)	State Sales and Use (%)	Gasoline[1] (¢/gal.)	Cigarette[2] ($/pack)	Spirits[3] ($/gal.)	Wine[4] ($/gal.)	Beer[5] ($/gal.)
South Carolina	8.5	6.0	16.75	0.57	5.42 (i)	1.08	0.77

Note: All tax rates as of January 1, 2015; (1) The American Petroleum Institute has developed a methodology for determining the average tax rate on a gallon of fuel. Rates may include any of the following: excise taxes, environmental fees, storage tank fees, other fees or taxes, general sales tax, and local taxes. In states where gasoline is subject to the general sales tax, or where the fuel tax is based on the average sale price, the average rate determined by API is sensitive to changes in the price of gasoline. States that fully or partially apply general sales taxes to gasoline: CA, CO, GA, IL, IN, MI, NY; (2) The federal excise tax of $1.0066 per pack and local taxes are not included; (3) Rates are those applicable to off-premise sales of 40% alcohol by volume (a.b.v.) distilled spirits in 750ml containers. Local excise taxes are excluded; (4) Rates are those applicable to off-premise sales of 11% a.b.v. non-carbonated wine in 750ml containers; (5) Rates are those applicable to off-premise sales of 4.7% a.b.v. beer in 12 ounce containers; (i) Includes case fees and/or bottle fees which may vary with the size of container.
Source: Tax Foundation, 2015 Facts & Figures: How Does Your State Compare?

State Business Tax Climate Index Rankings

State	Overall Rank	Corporate Tax Index Rank	Individual Income Tax Index Rank	Sales Tax Index Rank	Unemployment Insurance Tax Index Rank	Property Tax Index Rank
South Carolina	37	13	41	18	40	21

Note: The index is a measure of how each state's tax laws affect economic performance. The lower the rank, the more favorable a state's tax system is for business. States without a given tax are given a ranking of 1. The scores/rankings for the District of Columbia do not affect other states. The 2015 index represents the tax climate as of July 1, 2014.
Source: Tax Foundation, State Business Tax Climate Index 2015

COMMERCIAL REAL ESTATE

Office Market

Market Area	Inventory (sq. ft.)	Vacancy Rate (%)	Under Construction (sq. ft.)	YTD Net Absorption (sq. ft.)	Total Average Asking Rent ($/sq. ft./year)
Charleston	15,892,312	7.1	0	383,545	19.84
National	4,745,108,508	14.3	71,190,461	51,084,126	27.40

Source: Newmark Grubb Knight Frank, National Office Market Report, 4th Quarter 2014

Industrial/Warehouse/R&D Market

Market Area	Inventory (sq. ft.)	Vacancy Rate (%)	Under Construction (sq. ft.)	YTD Net Absorption (sq. ft.)	Total Average Asking Rent ($/sq. ft./year)
Charleston	59,995,268	7.4	0	865,846	4.36
National	14,238,613,765	7.2	134,387,407	185,246,438	5.64

Source: Newmark Grubb Knight Frank, National Industrial Market Report, 4th Quarter 2014

COMMERCIAL UTILITIES

Typical Monthly Electric Bills

Area	Commercial Service ($/month)		Industrial Service ($/month)	
	1,500 kWh	40 kW demand 14,000 kWh	1,000 kW demand 200,000 kWh	50,000 kW demand 32,500,000 kWh
City	212	1,771	26,017	2,445,050
Average[1]	201	1,653	26,124	2,639,743

Note: Figures are based on annualized 2014 rates; (1) Average based on 180 utilities surveyed
Source: Edison Electric Institute, Typical Bills and Average Rates Report, Summer 2014

TRANSPORTATION

Means of Transportation to Work

Area	Car/Truck/Van		Public Transportation			Bicycle	Walked	Other Means	Worked at Home
	Drove Alone	Car-pooled	Bus	Subway	Railroad				
City	76.5	6.5	2.2	0.0	0.0	2.5	5.8	1.5	4.9
MSA[1]	80.5	9.2	1.5	0.0	0.0	0.9	2.7	0.9	4.3
U.S.	76.4	9.6	2.6	1.8	0.6	0.6	2.8	1.3	4.3

Note: Figures are percentages and cover workers 16 years of age and older; (1) Figures cover the Charleston-North Charleston, SC Metropolitan Statistical Area—see Appendix B for areas included
Source: U.S. Census Bureau, 2011-2013 American Community Survey 3-Year Estimates

Travel Time to Work

Area	Less Than 10 Minutes	10 to 19 Minutes	20 to 29 Minutes	30 to 44 Minutes	45 to 59 Minutes	60 to 89 Minutes	90 Minutes or More
City	14.7	35.3	26.5	16.5	3.6	2.4	1.1
MSA[1]	10.5	30.1	24.3	22.9	7.7	3.0	1.4
U.S.	13.3	29.7	20.9	20.2	7.7	5.7	2.6

Note: Figures are percentages and include workers 16 years old and over; (1) Figures cover the Charleston-North Charleston, SC Metropolitan Statistical Area—see Appendix B for areas included
Source: U.S. Census Bureau, 2011-2013 American Community Survey 3-Year Estimates

Travel Time Index

Area	1985	1990	1995	2000	2005	2010	2011
Urban Area[1]	1.10	1.12	1.14	1.15	1.16	1.15	1.15
Average[2]	1.09	1.14	1.16	1.19	1.23	1.18	1.18

Note: Travel Time Index—the ratio of travel time in the peak period to the travel time at free-flow conditions. For example, a value of 1.30 indicates a 20-minute free-flow trip takes 26 minutes in the peak. Free-flow speeds (60 mph on freeways and 35 mph on principal arterials) are used as the comparison threshold; (1) Covers the Charleston-North Charleston SC urban area; (2) average of 498 urban areas
Source: Texas Transportation Institute, Urban Mobility Report 2012, December 2012

Public Transportation

Agency Name / Mode of Transportation	Vehicles Operated in Maximum Service	Annual Unlinked Passenger Trips (in thous.)	Annual Passenger Miles (in thous.)
Charleston Area Regional Transportation (CARTA)			
Bus (purchased transportation)	81	4,793.0	21,568.6
Demand Response (purchased transportation)	23	73.3	792.7

Source: Federal Transit Administration, National Transit Database, 2013

Air Transportation

Airport Name and Code / Type of Service	Passenger Airlines[1]	Passenger Enplanements	Freight Carriers[2]	Freight (lbs.)
Charleston International Airport (CHS)				
Domestic service (U.S. carriers - 2014)	25	1,538,952	12	16,168,145
International service (U.S. carriers - 2013)	2	109	5	296,894

Note: (1) Includes all U.S.-based major, minor and commuter airlines that carried at least one passenger during the year; (2) Includes all U.S.-based airlines and freight carriers that transported at least one lb. of freight during the year.
Source: Bureau of Transportation Statistics, The Intermodal Transportation Database, Air Carriers: T-100 Domestic Market (U.S. Carriers), 2014; Bureau of Transportation Statistics, The Intermodal Transportation Database, Air Carriers: T-100 International Market (U.S. Carriers), 2013

Other Transportation Statistics

Major Highways:	I-26; I-95
Amtrak Service:	Yes (station is located in North Charleston)
Major Waterways/Ports:	Atlantic Ocean

Source: Amtrak.com; Google Maps

BUSINESSES

Major Business Headquarters

Company Name	Rankings	
	Fortune[1]	Forbes[2]
No companies listed	-	-

Note: (1) Fortune 500—companies that produce a 10-K are ranked 1 to 500 based on 2013 revenue; (2) all private companies with at least $2 billion in annual revenue through the end of their most current fiscal year are ranked 1 to 221; companies listed are headquartered in the city; dashes indicate no ranking
Source: Fortune, "Fortune 500," June 16, 2014; Forbes, "America's Largest Private Companies," November 5, 2014

Fast-Growing Businesses

According to *Inc.*, Charleston is home to one of America's 500 fastest-growing private companies: **PureCars** (#141). Criteria: must be an independent, privately-held, for-profit, U.S. corporation, proprietorship or partnership; revenues must be at least $100,000 in 2010 and $2 million in 2013; must have four-year operating/sales history. Holding companies, regulated banks, and utilities were excluded. *Inc., "America's 500 Fastest-Growing Private Companies," September 2014*

According to Deloitte, Charleston is home to one of North America's 500 fastest-growing high-technology companies: **BoomTown** (#78). Companies are ranked by percentage growth in revenue over a five-year period. Criteria for inclusion: company must be headquartered within North America; must own proprietary intellectual property or proprietary technology that contributes to a significant portion of the company's operating revenue, or devote a significant proportion of revenues to research and development of technology; must have been in business for a minumum of five years with 2009 operating revenues of at least $50,000 USD/CD and 2013 operating revenues of at least $5 million USD/CD. *Deloitte Touche Tohmatsu, 2014 Technology Fast 500™*

Minority- and Women-Owned Businesses

Group	All Firms		Firms with Paid Employees			
	Firms	Sales ($000)	Firms	Sales ($000)	Employees	Payroll ($000)
Asian	230	97,937	57	89,149	866	16,742
Black	1,081	64,190	114	37,962	479	11,292
Hispanic	(s)	(s)	(s)	(s)	(s)	(s)
Women	3,766	640,119	657	544,193	4,477	108,612
All Firms	13,392	11,088,365	3,844	10,554,855	62,244	2,129,311

Note: Figures cover firms located in the city; minority- and women-owned business are defined as firms in which the corresponding group own 51% or more of the stock or equity of the company; (s) estimates are suppressed when publication standards are not met
Source: U.S. Census Bureau, 2007 Economic Census, Survey of Business Owners (2012 Survey of Business Owners data will be released starting in June 2015)

HOTELS & CONVENTION CENTERS

Hotels/Motels

Area	5 Star		4 Star		3 Star		2 Star		1 Star		Not Rated	
	Num.	Pct.[3]	Num.	Pct.[3]	Num.	Pct.[3]	Num.	Pct.[3]	Num.	Pct.[3]	Num.	Pct.[3]
City[1]	1	0.6	19	11.4	69	41.3	73	43.7	2	1.2	3	1.8
Total[2]	166	0.9	1,264	7.0	5,718	31.8	9,340	52.0	411	2.3	1,070	6.0

Note: (1) Figures cover Charleston and vicinity; (2) Figures cover all 100 cities in this book; (3) Percentage of hotels which have a given star rating; Star ratings are determined by expedia.com and offer an indication of the general quality of a particular hotel.
Source: expedia.com, April 2, 2015

The Charleston-North Charleston, SC metro area is home to eight of the best hotels in the U.S. according to *Travel & Leisure*: **Belmond Charleston Place**; **French Quarter Inn**; **HarbourView Inn**; **Market Pavilion Hotel**; **Planters Inn**; **Vendue Inn**; **Wentworth Mansion**; **Sanctuary at Kiawah Island Golf Resort**. Criteria: service; location; rooms; food; and value. The list includes the top 236 hotels in the U.S. *Travel & Leisure, "T+L 500, The World's Best Hotels 2015"*

Major Convention Centers

Name	Overall Space (sq. ft.)	Exhibit Space (sq. ft.)	Meeting Space (sq. ft.)	Meeting Rooms
Charleston Area Convention Center Complex	n/a	76,960	n/a	n/a

Note: Table includes convention centers located in the Charleston-North Charleston, SC metro area; n/a not available
Source: Original research

Living Environment

COST OF LIVING

Cost of Living Index

Composite Index	Groceries	Housing	Utilities	Trans-portation	Health Care	Misc. Goods/ Services
100.6	108.7	94.2	112.8	95.9	105.1	99.8

Note: The Cost of Living Index measures regional differences in the cost of consumer goods and services, excluding taxes and non-consumer expenditures, for professional and managerial households in the top income quintile. It is based on more than 50,000 prices covering almost 60 different items for which prices are collected three times a year by chambers of commerce, economic development organizations or university applied economic centers in each participating urban area. The numbers shown should be read as a percentage above or below the national average of 100. For example, a value of 115.4 in the groceries column indicates that grocery prices are 15.4% higher than the national average. Small differences in the index numbers should not be interpreted as significant; Figures cover the Charleston-N Charleston SC urban area.
Source: The Council for Community and Economic Research, ACCRA Cost of Living Index, 2014

Grocery Prices

Area[1]	T-Bone Steak ($/pound)	Frying Chicken ($/pound)	Whole Milk ($/half gal.)	Eggs ($/dozen)	Orange Juice ($/64 oz.)	Coffee ($/11.5 oz.)
City[2]	11.45	1.44	2.72	1.98	3.72	4.48
Avg.	10.40	1.37	2.40	1.99	3.46	4.27
Min.	8.48	0.93	1.37	1.30	2.83	2.99
Max.	14.20	2.44	3.62	4.02	6.42	6.96

Note: (1) Values for the local area are compared with the average, minimum and maximum values for all 308 areas in the Cost of Living Index; (2) Figures cover the Charleston-N Charleston SC urban area; **T-Bone Steak** *(price per pound);* **Frying Chicken** *(price per pound, whole fryer);* **Whole Milk** *(half gallon carton);* **Eggs** *(price per dozen, Grade A, large);* **Orange Juice** *(64 oz. Tropicana or Florida Natural);* **Coffee** *(11.5 oz. can, vacuum-packed, Maxwell House, Hills Bros, or Folgers).*
Source: The Council for Community and Economic Research, ACCRA Cost of Living Index, 2014

Housing and Utility Costs

Area[1]	New Home Price ($)	Apartment Rent ($/month)	All Electric ($/month)	Part Electric ($/month)	Other Energy ($/month)	Telephone ($/month)
City[2]	263,355	1,078	202.00	-	-	28.92
Avg.	305,838	919	181.00	93.66	73.14	27.95
Min.	183,142	480	112.00	42.06	23.42	17.16
Max.	1,358,576	3,851	594.00	180.03	440.99	40.42

Note: (1) Values for the local area are compared with the average, minimum and maximum values for all 308 areas in the Cost of Living Index; (2) Figures cover the Charleston-N Charleston SC urban area; **New Home Price** *(2,400 sf living area, 8,000 sf lot, in urban area with full utilities);* **Apartment Rent** *(950 sf 2 bedroom/1.5 or 2 bath, unfurnished, excluding all utilities except water);* **All Electric** *(average monthly cost for an all-electric home);* **Part Electric** *(average monthly cost for a part-electric home);* **Other Energy** *(average monthly cost for natural gas, fuel oil, coal, wood, and any other forms of energy except electricity);* **Telephone** *(price includes basic monthly rate for a private residential line plus additional local usage charges incurred by a family of four).*
Source: The Council for Community and Economic Research, ACCRA Cost of Living Index, 2014

Health Care, Transportation, and Other Costs

Area[1]	Doctor ($/visit)	Dentist ($/visit)	Optometrist ($/visit)	Gasoline ($/gallon)	Beauty Salon ($/visit)	Men's Shirt ($)
City[2]	108.95	101.00	97.24	3.31	35.29	33.13
Avg.	102.86	87.89	97.66	3.44	34.37	26.74
Min.	67.47	65.78	51.18	3.00	17.43	12.79
Max.	173.50	150.14	235.00	4.33	64.28	49.50

Note: (1) Values for the local area are compared with the average, minimum and maximum values for all 308 areas in the Cost of Living Index; (2) Figures cover the Charleston-N Charleston SC urban area; **Doctor** *(general practitioners routine exam of an established patient);* **Dentist** *(adult teeth cleaning and periodic oral examination);* **Optometrist** *(full vision eye exam for established adult patient);* **Gasoline** *(one gallon regular unleaded, national brand, including all taxes, cash price at self-service pump if available);* **Beauty Salon** *(woman's shampoo, trim, and blow-dry);* **Men's Shirt** *(cotton/polyester dress shirt, pinpoint weave, long sleeves).*
Source: The Council for Community and Economic Research, ACCRA Cost of Living Index, 2014

HOUSING

House Price Index (HPI)

Area	National Ranking[2]	Quarterly Change (%)	One-Year Change (%)	Five-Year Change (%)
MSA[1]	60	0.93	7.63	4.92
U.S.[3]	–	1.35	4.91	11.59

Note: The HPI is a weighted repeat sales index. It measures average price changes in repeat sales or refinancings on the same properties. This information is obtained by reviewing repeat mortgage transactions on single-family properties whose mortgages have been purchased or securitized by Fannie Mae or Freddie Mac in January 1975; (1) Charleston-North Charleston Metropolitan Statistical Area—see Appendix B for areas included; (2) Rankings are based on annual percentage change for all metro areas containing at least 15,000 transactions over the last 10 years and ranges from 1 to 275; (3) figures based on a weighted average of Census Division estimates using a seasonally adjusted, purchase-only index; all figures are for the period ending December 31, 2014

Source: Federal Housing Finance Agency, House Price Index, February 26, 2015

Median Single-Family Home Prices

Area	2012	2013	2014p	Percent Change 2013 to 2014
MSA[1]	207.5	221.7	228.2	2.9
U.S. Average	177.2	197.4	209.0	5.9

Note: Figures are median sales prices of existing single-family homes in thousands of dollars; (p) preliminary; n/a not available; (1) Charleston-North Charleston, SC Metropolitan Statistical Area—see Appendix B for areas included

Source: National Association of Realtors, Median Sales Price of Existing Single-Family Homes for Metropolitan Areas, 4th Quarter 2014

Qualifying Income Based on Median Sales Price of Existing Single-Family Homes

Area	With 5% Down ($)	With 10% Down ($)	With 20% Down ($)
MSA[1]	47,357	44,865	39,880
U.S. Average	45,863	43,449	38,621

Note: Figures are preliminary; Qualifying income is based on a mortgage rate of 4.0%. Monthly principal and interest payment is limited to 25% of income; n/a not available; (1) Charleston-North Charleston, SC Metropolitan Statistical Area—see Appendix B for areas included

Source: National Association of Realtors, Qualifying Income Based on Median Sales Price of Existing Single-Family Homes for Metropolitan Areas, 4th Quarter 2014

Median Apartment Condo-Coop Home Prices

Area	2012	2013	2014p	Percent Change 2013 to 2014
MSA[1]	n/a	n/a	n/a	n/a
U.S. Average	173.7	194.9	205.1	5.2

Note: Figures are median sales prices of existing apartment condo-coop homes in thousands of dollars; (p) preliminary; n/a not available; (1) Charleston-North Charleston, SC Metropolitan Statistical Area—see Appendix B for areas included

Source: National Association of Realtors, Median Sales Price of Existing Apartment Condo-Coop Homes for Metropolitan Areas, 4th Quarter 2014

Gross Monthly Rent

Area	Under $200	$200 -299	$300 -499	$500 -749	$750 -999	$1,000 -1,499	$1,500 and up	Median ($)
City	2.4	3.8	4.5	13.8	28.4	31.9	15.1	975
MSA[1]	0.9	2.1	4.6	17.5	30.4	32.5	11.9	956
U.S.	1.7	3.2	7.8	22.1	24.3	26.0	14.9	900

Note: Figures are percentages except for Median; Gross rent is the contract rent plus the estimated average monthly cost of utilities (electricity, gas, and water and sewer) and fuels (oil, coal, kerosene, wood, etc.) if these are paid by the renter (or paid for the renter by someone else); (1) Figures cover the Charleston-North Charleston, SC Metropolitan Statistical Area—see Appendix B for areas included

Source: U.S. Census Bureau, 2011-2013 American Community Survey 3-Year Estimates

Homeownership Rate

Area	2007 (%)	2008 (%)	2009 (%)	2010 (%)	2011 (%)	2012 (%)	2013 (%)	2014 (%)
MSA[1]	n/a	n/a	n/a	n/a	n/a	n/a	n/a	n/a
U.S.	68.1	67.8	67.4	66.9	66.1	65.4	65.1	64.5

Note: (1) Figures cover the Charleston-North Charleston, SC Metropolitan Statistical Area—see Appendix B for areas included; n/a not available
Source: U.S. Census Bureau, Housing Vacancies and Homeownership Annual Statistics: 2014

Year Housing Structure Built

Area	2010 or Later	2000 -2009	1990 -1999	1980 -1989	1970 -1979	1960 -1969	1950 -1959	1940 -1949	Before 1940	Median Year
City	1.4	24.7	12.8	13.1	10.9	10.9	7.1	4.3	14.7	1982
MSA[1]	1.7	26.5	15.9	17.4	15.6	9.3	6.0	2.8	4.7	1987
U.S.	0.9	15.0	13.9	13.8	15.8	11.0	10.9	5.4	13.3	1976

Note: Figures are percentages except for Median Year; (1) Figures cover the Charleston-North Charleston, SC Metropolitan Statistical Area—see Appendix B for areas included
Source: U.S. Census Bureau, 2011-2013 American Community Survey 3-Year Estimates

HEALTH

Health Risk Data

Category	MSA[1] (%)	U.S. (%)
Adults aged 18–64 who have any kind of health care coverage	77.7	79.6
Adults who reported being in good or excellent health	84.5	83.1
Adults who are current smokers	20.2	19.6
Adults who are heavy drinkers[2]	8.2	6.1
Adults who are binge drinkers[3]	21.1	16.9
Adults who are overweight (BMI 25.0 - 29.9)	33.9	35.8
Adults who are obese (BMI 30.0 - 99.8)	28.5	27.6
Adults who participated in any physical activities in the past month	79.0	77.1
Adults 50+ who have ever had a sigmoidoscopy or colonoscopy	70.1	67.3
Women aged 40+ who have had a mammogram within the past two years	75.7	74.0
Men aged 40+ who have had a PSA test within the past two years	49.9	45.2
Adults aged 65+ who have had flu shot within the past year	68.1	60.1
Adults who always wear a seatbelt	93.5	93.8

Note: Data as of 2012 unless otherwise noted; (1) Figures cover the Charleston-North Charleston, SC Metropolitan Statistical Area—see Appendix B for areas included; (2) Heavy drinkers are classified as males having more than two drinks per day or females having more than one drink per day; (3) Binge drinkers are classified as males having five or more drinks on one occasion or females having four or more drinks on one occasion
Source: Centers for Disease Control and Prevention, Behaviorial Risk Factor Surveillance System, SMART: Selected Metropolitan/Micropolitan Area Risk Trends, 2012 (Note: the CDC has discontinued this dataset but will be releasing a replacement in late 2015)

Chronic Health Indicators

Category	MSA[1] (%)	U.S. (%)
Adults who have ever been told they had a heart attack	4.0	4.5
Adults who have ever been told they had a stroke	3.5	2.9
Adults who have been told they currently have asthma	8.0	8.9
Adults who have ever been told they have arthritis	24.8	25.7
Adults who have ever been told they have diabetes[2]	11.7	9.7
Adults who have ever been told they had skin cancer	6.6	5.7
Adults who have ever been told they had any other types of cancer	6.6	6.5
Adults who have ever been told they have COPD	6.1	6.2
Adults who have ever been told they have kidney disease	2.1	2.5
Adults who have ever been told they have a form of depression	17.3	18.0

Note: Data as of 2012 unless otherwise noted; (1) Figures cover the Charleston-North Charleston, SC Metropolitan Statistical Area—see Appendix B for areas included; (2) Figures do not include pregnancy-related, borderline, or pre-diabetes
Source: Centers for Disease Control and Prevention, Behaviorial Risk Factor Surveillance System, SMART: Selected Metropolitan/Micropolitan Area Risk Trends, 2012 (Note: the CDC has discontinued this dataset but will be releasing a replacement in late 2015)

Mortality Rates for the Top 10 Causes of Death in the U.S.

ICD-10[a] Sub-Chapter	ICD-10[a] Code	Age-Adjusted Mortality Rate[1] per 100,000 population	
		County[2]	U.S.
Malignant neoplasms	C00-C97	166.3	166.2
Ischaemic heart diseases	I20-I25	83.2	105.7
Other forms of heart disease	I30-I51	46.2	49.3
Chronic lower respiratory diseases	J40-J47	37.8	42.1
Organic, including symptomatic, mental disorders	F01-F09	55.8	38.1
Cerebrovascular diseases	I60-I69	44.5	37.0
Other external causes of accidental injury	W00-X59	25.7	26.9
Other degenerative diseases of the nervous system	G30-G31	34.0	25.6
Diabetes mellitus	E10-E14	20.2	21.3
Hypertensive diseases	I10-I15	15.6	19.4

Note: (a) ICD-10 = International Classification of Diseases 10th Revision; (1) Mortality rates are a three year average covering 2011-2013; (2) Figures cover Charleston County
Source: Centers for Disease Control and Prevention, National Center for Health Statistics. Compressed Mortality File 1999-2013 on CDC WONDER Online Database, released October 2014. Data are compiled from the Compressed Mortality File 1999-2013, Series 20 No. 2S, 2014.

Mortality Rates for Selected Causes of Death

ICD-10[a] Sub-Chapter	ICD-10[a] Code	Age-Adjusted Mortality Rate[1] per 100,000 population	
		County[2]	U.S.
Assault	X85-Y09	8.8	5.2
Diseases of the liver	K70-K76	15.4	13.2
Human immunodeficiency virus (HIV) disease	B20-B24	4.0	2.2
Influenza and pneumonia	J09-J18	8.7	15.4
Intentional self-harm	X60-X84	12.1	12.5
Malnutrition	E40-E46	*1.6	0.9
Obesity and other hyperalimentation	E65-E68	*1.4	1.8
Renal failure	N17-N19	11.0	13.1
Transport accidents	V01-V99	15.6	11.7
Viral hepatitis	B15-B19	2.4	2.2

Note: (a) ICD-10 = International Classification of Diseases 10th Revision; (1) Mortality rates are a three year average covering 2011-2013; (2) Figures cover Charleston County; (*) Unreliable data as per CDC
Source: Centers for Disease Control and Prevention, National Center for Health Statistics. Compressed Mortality File 1999-2013 on CDC WONDER Online Database, released October 2014. Data are compiled from the Compressed Mortality File 1999-2013, Series 20 No. 2S, 2014.

Health Insurance Coverage

Area	With Health Insurance	With Private Health Insurance	With Public Health Insurance	Without Health Insurance	Population Under Age 18 Without Health Insurance
City	87.2	73.4	24.8	12.8	8.7
MSA[1]	83.4	66.6	28.0	16.6	9.3
U.S.	85.2	65.2	31.0	14.8	7.3

Note: Figures are percentages that cover the civilian noninstitutionalized population; (1) Figures cover the Charleston-North Charleston, SC Metropolitan Statistical Area—see Appendix B for areas included
Source: U.S. Census Bureau, 2011-2013 American Community Survey 3-Year Estimates

Number of Medical Professionals

Area[1]	MDs[2]	DOs[2,3]	Dentists	Podiatrists	Chiropractors	Optometrists
Local (number)	2,852	86	381	19	156	71
Local (rate[4])	780.4	23.5	102.2	5.1	41.8	19.0
U.S. (rate[4])	270.0	20.2	63.1	5.7	25.2	14.9

Note: Data as of 2013 unless noted; (1) Local data covers Charleston County; (2) Data as of 2012 and includes all active, non-federal physicians; (3) Doctor of Osteopathic Medicine; (4) rate per 100,000 population
Source: U.S. Department of Health and Human Services, Health Resources and Services Administration, Bureau of Health Professions, Area Resource File (ARF) 2013-2014

Best Hospitals

According to *U.S. News,* the Charleston-North Charleston, SC metro area is home to two of the best children's hospitals in the U.S.: **MUSC Children's Heart Program of South Carolina** (1 specialty); **Medical University of South Carolina Children's Hospital** (1 specialty). The hospitals listed were highly ranked in at least one pediatric specialty. Eighty-nine children's hospitals in the U.S. were nationally ranked in at least one specialty. Ten children's hospitals in the U.S. made the Honor Roll with high scores in at least three specialties. *U.S. News Online, "America's Best Children's Hospitals 2014-15"*

EDUCATION

Public School District Statistics

District Name	Schls	Pupils	Pupil/ Teacher Ratio	Minority Pupils[1] (%)	Free Lunch Eligible[2] (%)	IEP[3] (%)
Charleston 01	78	44,599	13.6	54.2	47.0	10.1

Note: Table includes school districts with 2,000 or more students; (1) Percentage of students that are not non-Hispanic white; (2) Percentage of students that are eligible for the free lunch program; (3) Percentage of students that have an Individualized Education Program.
Source: U.S. Department of Education, National Center for Education Statistics, Common Core of Data, Local Education Agency (School District) Universe Survey: School Year 2012-2013; U.S. Department of Education, National Center for Education Statistics, Common Core of Data, Public Elementary/Secondary School Universe Survey: School Year 2012-2013

Highest Level of Education

Area	Less than H.S.	H.S. Diploma	Some College, No Deg.	Associate Degree	Bachelor's Degree	Master's Degree	Prof. School Degree	Doctorate Degree
City	6.9	18.5	18.4	7.4	30.4	11.1	4.4	2.9
MSA[1]	11.5	25.8	22.4	8.8	20.1	7.9	2.0	1.3
U.S.	13.7	28.0	21.2	7.9	18.2	7.7	1.9	1.3

Note: Figures cover persons age 25 and over; (1) Figures cover the Charleston-North Charleston, SC Metropolitan Statistical Area—see Appendix B for areas included
Source: U.S. Census Bureau, 2011-2013 American Community Survey 3-Year Estimates

Educational Attainment by Race

Area	High School Graduate or Higher (%)					Bachelor's Degree or Higher (%)				
	Total	White	Black	Asian	Hisp.[2]	Total	White	Black	Asian	Hisp.[2]
City	93.1	96.7	81.3	n/a	89.4	48.7	58.8	15.5	n/a	32.2
MSA[1]	88.5	91.8	81.1	81.6	69.4	31.4	38.2	13.7	34.3	20.9
U.S.	86.3	88.3	83.1	85.7	64.0	29.1	30.4	18.8	50.7	13.7

Note: Figures shown cover persons 25 years old and over; (1) Figures cover the Charleston-North Charleston, SC Metropolitan Statistical Area—see Appendix B for areas included; (2) People of Hispanic origin can be of any race
Source: U.S. Census Bureau, 2011-2013 American Community Survey 3-Year Estimates

School Enrollment by Grade and Control

Area	Preschool (%)		Kindergarten (%)		Grades 1 - 4 (%)		Grades 5 - 8 (%)		Grades 9 - 12 (%)	
	Public	Private	Public	Private	Public	Private	Public	Private	Public	Private
City	39.3	60.7	79.4	20.6	77.8	22.2	72.7	27.3	82.1	17.9
MSA[1]	44.5	55.5	84.8	15.2	88.3	11.7	88.2	11.8	89.8	10.2
U.S.	57.7	42.3	87.9	12.1	89.9	10.1	90.0	10.0	90.7	9.3

Note: Figures shown cover persons 3 years old and over; (1) Figures cover the Charleston-North Charleston, SC Metropolitan Statistical Area—see Appendix B for areas included
Source: U.S. Census Bureau, 2011-2013 American Community Survey 3-Year Estimates

Average Salaries of Public School Classroom Teachers

Area	2013-14		2014-15		Percent Change 2013-14 to 2014-15	Percent Change 2004-05 to 2014-15
	Dollars	Rank[1]	Dollars	Rank[1]		
SOUTH CAROLINA	48,430	37	48,709	38	0.58	15.5
U.S. Average	56,610	–	57,379	–	1.36	20.8

Note: (1) State rank ranges from 1 to 51 where 1 indicates highest salary.
Source: National Education Association, Rankings & Estimates: Rankings of the States 2014 and Estimates of School Statistics 2015, March 2015

Higher Education

Four-Year Colleges			Two-Year Colleges			Medical Schools[1]	Law Schools[2]	Voc/ Tech[3]
Public	Private Non-profit	Private For-profit	Public	Private Non-profit	Private For-profit			
3	1	2	1	0	1	1	1	2

Note: Figures cover institutions located within the city limits and include main campuses only; (1) includes schools accredited by the Liaison Committee on Medical Education and the American Osteopathic Association's Commission on Osteopathic College Accreditation; (2) includes ABA-accredited schools, schools with provisional ABA accreditation, and state accredited schools; (3) includes all schools with programs that are less than 2 years.
Source: National Center for Education Statistics, Integrated Postsecondary Education System (IPEDS), 2013-14; Association of American Medical Colleges, Member List, May 1, 2015; American Osteopathic Association, Member List, May 1, 2015; Law School Admission Council, Official Guide to ABA-Approved Law Schools Online, May 1, 2015; Wikipedia, List of Medical Schools in the United States, May 1, 2015; Wikipedia, List of Law Schools in the United States, May 1, 2015

According to *U.S. News & World Report,* the Charleston-North Charleston, SC metro area is home to one of the top 75 medical schools for research in the U.S.: **Medical University of South Carolina** (#60). The rankings are based on a weighted average of 11 measures of quality: quality assessment; peer assessment score; assessment score by residency directors; research activity; total research activity; average research activity per faculty member; student selectivity; median MCAT total score; median undergraduate GPA; acceptance rate; and faculty resources. *U.S. News & World Report, "America's Best Graduate Schools, Medical, 2016"*

PRESIDENTIAL ELECTION

2012 Presidential Election Results

Area	Obama (%)	Romney (%)	Other (%)
Charleston County	50.4	48.0	1.6
U.S.	51.0	47.2	1.8

Note: Results may not add to 100% due to rounding
Source: Dave Leip's Atlas of U.S. Presidential Elections

EMPLOYERS

Major Employers

Company Name	Industry
Allergy Centers of America	Ears, nose, and throat specialist, physician/surgeon
Alternative Staffing	Help supply services
Behr Heat Transfer Systems	Radiators & radiator shells & cores, motor vehicle
Campground At James Island	Trailer parks and campsites
CELLCO Partnership	Cellular telephone services
College of Charleston	Colleges and universities
County of Charleston	Marshals' office, police
CUMMINS	Internal combustion engines
Kiawah Island Inn Company	Resort hotel
Medical University Hospital Authority	General medical and surgical hospitals
Medical University of South Carolina	General medical and surgical hospitals
Six Continents Hotels	Hotels and motels
The Boeing Company	Airplanes, fixed or rotary wing
Trident Medical Center	General medical and surgical hospitals
United States Department of the Navy	Navy
Veterans Health Administration	General medical and surgical hospitals

Note: Companies shown are located within the Charleston-North Charleston, SC Metropolitan Statistical Area.
Source: Hoovers.com; Wikipedia

PUBLIC SAFETY

Crime Rate

Area	All Crimes	Violent Crimes				Property Crimes		
		Murder	Forcible Rape	Robbery	Aggrav. Assault	Burglary	Larceny -Theft	Motor Vehicle Theft
City	2,690.9	5.5	22.8	56.6	96.7	239.8	2,142.2	127.4
Suburbs[1]	3,688.7	7.5	29.6	74.2	286.8	705.4	2,321.0	264.2
Metro[2]	3,510.2	7.2	28.4	71.0	252.8	622.1	2,289.0	239.7
U.S.	3,098.6	4.5	25.2	109.1	229.1	610.0	1,899.4	221.3

Note: Figures are crimes per 100,000 population; (1) All areas within the metro area that are located outside the city limits; (2) Figures cover the Charleston-North Charleston, SC Metropolitan Statistical Area—see Appendix B for areas included
Source: FBI Uniform Crime Reports, 2013

Hate Crimes

Area	Number of Quarters Reported	Number of Incidents per Bias Motivation						
		Race	Religion	Sexual Orientation	Ethnicity	Disability	Gender	Gender Identity
City	4	2	0	0	0	0	0	0
U.S.	4	2,871	1,031	1,233	655	83	18	31

Source: Federal Bureau of Investigation, Hate Crime Statistics 2013

Identity Theft Consumer Complaints

Area	Complaints	Complaints per 100,000 Population	Rank[2]
MSA[1]	640	89.9	90
U.S.	332,646	104.3	-

Note: (1) Figures cover the Charleston-North Charleston, SC Metropolitan Statistical Area—see Appendix B for areas included; (2) Rank ranges from 1 to 380 where 1 indicates greatest number of identity theft complaints per 100,000 population
Source: Federal Trade Commission, Consumer Sentinel Network Data Book for January–December 2014

Fraud and Other Consumer Complaints

Area	Complaints	Complaints per 100,000 Population	Rank[2]
MSA[1]	3,050	428.2	96
U.S.	2,250,205	705.7	-

Note: (1) Figures cover the Charleston-North Charleston, SC Metropolitan Statistical Area—see Appendix B for areas included; (2) Rank ranges from 1 to 380 where 1 indicates greatest number of identity theft complaints per 100,000 population
Source: Federal Trade Commission, Consumer Sentinel Network Data Book for January–December 2014

RECREATION

Culture

Dance[1]	Theatre[1]	Instrumental Music[1]	Vocal Music[1]	Series and Festivals	Museums and Art Galleries[2]	Zoos and Aquariums[3]
2	5	2	0	4	34	1

Note: (1) Professional perfoming groups; (2) Based on organizations with SIC code 8412; (3) AZA-accredited
Source: The Grey House Performing Arts Directory, 2015-16; Association of Zoos & Aquariums, AZA Member Zoos & Aquariums, April 2015; www.AccuLeads.com, April 2015

Professional Sports Teams

Team Name	League	Year Established
No teams are located in the metro area		

Source: Wikipedia, Major Professional Sports Teams of the United States and Canada, April 2015

CLIMATE

Average and Extreme Temperatures

Temperature	Jan	Feb	Mar	Apr	May	Jun	Jul	Aug	Sep	Oct	Nov	Dec	Yr.
Extreme High (°F)	83	87	90	94	98	101	104	102	97	94	88	83	104
Average High (°F)	59	62	68	76	83	88	90	89	85	77	69	61	76
Average Temp. (°F)	49	51	57	65	73	78	81	81	76	67	58	51	66
Average Low (°F)	38	40	46	53	62	69	72	72	67	56	46	39	55
Extreme Low (°F)	6	12	15	30	36	50	58	56	42	27	15	8	6

Note: Figures cover the years 1945-1995
Source: National Climatic Data Center, International Station Meteorological Climate Summary, 9/96

Average Precipitation/Snowfall/Humidity

Precip./Humidity	Jan	Feb	Mar	Apr	May	Jun	Jul	Aug	Sep	Oct	Nov	Dec	Yr.
Avg. Precip. (in.)	3.5	3.1	4.4	2.8	4.1	6.0	7.2	6.9	5.6	3.1	2.5	3.1	52.1
Avg. Snowfall (in.)	Tr	Tr	Tr	0	0	0	0	0	0	0	Tr	Tr	1
Avg. Rel. Hum. 7am (%)	83	81	83	84	85	86	88	90	91	89	86	83	86
Avg. Rel. Hum. 4pm (%)	55	52	51	51	56	62	66	66	65	58	56	55	58

Note: Figures cover the years 1945-1995; Tr = Trace amounts (<0.05 in. of rain; <0.5 in. of snow)
Source: National Climatic Data Center, International Station Meteorological Climate Summary, 9/96

Weather Conditions

Temperature			Daytime Sky			Precipitation		
10°F & below	32°F & below	90°F & above	Clear	Partly cloudy	Cloudy	0.01 inch or more precip.	0.1 inch or more snow/ice	Thunder-storms
< 1	33	53	89	162	114	114	1	59

Note: Figures are average number of days per year and cover the years 1945-1995
Source: National Climatic Data Center, International Station Meteorological Climate Summary, 9/96

HAZARDOUS WASTE

Superfund Sites

Charleston has one hazardous waste site on the EPA's Superfund Final National Priorities List: **Koppers Co., Inc. (Charleston Plant).** There are a total of 1,322 Superfund sites on the list in the U.S. *U.S. Environmental Protection Agency, Final National Priorities List, April 14, 2015*

AIR & WATER QUALITY

Air Quality Trends: Ozone

	2004	2005	2006	2007	2008	2009	2010	2011	2012	2013
MSA[1]	0.072	0.073	0.071	0.065	0.069	0.059	0.067	0.066	0.063	0.059

Note: (1) Data covers the Charleston-North Charleston, SC Metropolitan Statistical Area—see Appendix B for areas included. The values shown are the composite ozone concentration averages among trend sites based on the highest fourth daily maximum 8-hour concentration in parts per million. These trends are based on sites having an adequate record of monitoring data during the trend period. Data from exceptional events are included.
Source: U.S. Environmental Protection Agency, Air Quality Monitoring Information, "Air Quality Trends by City, 2000-2013"

Air Quality Index

Area	Percent of Days when Air Quality was...[2]					AQI Statistics[2]	
	Good	Moderate	Unhealthy for Sensitive Groups	Unhealthy	Very Unhealthy	Maximum	Median
MSA[1]	80.8	19.2	0.0	0.0	0.0	74	39

Note: (1) Data covers the Charleston-North Charleston, SC Metropolitan Statistical Area—see Appendix B for areas included; (2) Based on 365 days with AQI data in 2014. Air Quality Index (AQI) is an index for reporting daily air quality. EPA calculates the AQI for five major air pollutants regulated by the Clean Air Act: ground-level ozone, particle pollution (aka particulate matter), carbon monoxide, sulfur dioxide, and nitrogen dioxide. The AQI runs from 0 to 500. The higher the AQI value, the greater the level of air pollution and the greater the health concern. There are six AQI categories: "Good" AQI is between 0 and 50. Air quality is considered satisfactory; "Moderate" AQI is between 51 and 100. Air quality is acceptable; "Unhealthy for Sensitive Groups" When AQI values are between 101 and 150, members of sensitive groups may experience health effects; "Unhealthy" When AQI values are between 151 and 200 everyone may begin to experience health effects; "Very Unhealthy" AQI values between 201 and 300 trigger a health alert; "Hazardous" AQI values over 300 trigger warnings of emergency conditions (not shown).
Source: U.S. Environmental Protection Agency, Air Quality Index Report, 2014

Air Quality Index Pollutants

Area	Percent of Days when AQI Pollutant was...[2]					
	Carbon Monoxide	Nitrogen Dioxide	Ozone	Sulfur Dioxide	Particulate Matter 2.5	Particulate Matter 10
MSA[1]	0.0	0.8	23.3	0.3	75.6	0.0

Note: (1) Data covers the Charleston-North Charleston, SC Metropolitan Statistical Area—see Appendix B for areas included; (2) Based on 365 days with AQI data in 2014. The Air Quality Index (AQI) is an index for reporting daily air quality. EPA calculates the AQI for five major air pollutants regulated by the Clean Air Act: ground-level ozone, particle pollution (also known as particulate matter), carbon monoxide, sulfur dioxide, and nitrogen dioxide. The AQI runs from 0 to 500. The higher the AQI value, the greater the level of air pollution and the greater the health concern.
Source: U.S. Environmental Protection Agency, Air Quality Index Report, 2014

Maximum Air Pollutant Concentrations: Particulate Matter, Ozone, CO and Lead

	Particulate Matter 10 (ug/m^3)	Particulate Matter 2.5 Wtd AM (ug/m^3)	Particulate Matter 2.5 24-Hr (ug/m^3)	Ozone (ppm)	Carbon Monoxide (ppm)	Lead (ug/m^3)
MSA[1] Level	34	7.1	16	0.059	n/a	n/a
NAAQS[2]	150	15	35	0.075	9	0.15
Met NAAQS[2]	Yes	Yes	Yes	Yes	n/a	n/a

Note: (1) Data covers the Charleston-North Charleston, SC Metropolitan Statistical Area—see Appendix B for areas included; Data from exceptional events are included; (2) National Ambient Air Quality Standards; ppm = parts per million; ug/m^3 = micrograms per cubic meter; n/a not available.
Concentrations: Particulate Matter 10 (coarse particulate)—highest second maximum 24-hour concentration; Particulate Matter 2.5 Wtd AM (fine particulate)—highest weighted annual mean concentration; Particulate Matter 2.5 24-Hour (fine particulate)—highest 98th percentile 24-hour concentration; Ozone—highest fourth daily maximum 8-hour concentration; Carbon Monoxide—highest second maximum non-overlapping 8-hour concentration; Lead—maximum running 3-month average
Source: U.S. Environmental Protection Agency, Air Quality Monitoring Information, "Air Quality Statistics by City, 2013"

Maximum Air Pollutant Concentrations: Nitrogen Dioxide and Sulfur Dioxide

	Nitrogen Dioxide AM (ppb)	Nitrogen Dioxide 1-Hr (ppb)	Sulfur Dioxide AM (ppb)	Sulfur Dioxide 1-Hr (ppb)	Sulfur Dioxide 24-Hr (ppb)
MSA[1] Level	7	37	n/a	15	n/a
NAAQS[2]	53	100	30	75	140
Met NAAQS[2]	Yes	Yes	n/a	Yes	n/a

Note: (1) Data covers the Charleston-North Charleston, SC Metropolitan Statistical Area—see Appendix B for areas included; Data from exceptional events are included; (2) National Ambient Air Quality Standards; ppm = parts per million; ug/m^3 = micrograms per cubic meter; n/a not available.
Concentrations: Nitrogen Dioxide AM—highest arithmetic mean concentration; Nitrogen Dioxide 1-Hr—highest 98th percentile 1-hour daily maximum concentration; Sulfur Dioxide AM—highest annual mean concentration; Sulfur Dioxide 1-Hr—highest 99th percentile 1-hour daily maximum concentration; Sulfur Dioxide 24-Hr—highest second maximum 24-hour concentration
Source: U.S. Environmental Protection Agency, Air Quality Monitoring Information, "Air Quality Statistics by City, 2013"

Drinking Water

Water System Name	Pop. Served	Primary Water Source Type	Violations[1]	
			Health Based	Monitoring/ Reporting
Charleston Water System	219,665	Surface	0	0

Note: (1) Based on violation data from January 1, 2014 to December 31, 2014 (includes unresolved violations from earlier years)
Source: U.S. Environmental Protection Agency, Office of Ground Water and Drinking Water, Safe Drinking Water Information System (based on data extracted January 27, 2015)

Clarksville, Tennessee

Background

Located just south of the Kentucky border and 47 miles north of Nashville, Clarksville is Tennessee's fifth-largest town and has seen significant growth in recent years. Named for Gen. George Rogers Clark, a decorated veteran of the Indian and Revolutionary Wars, the city was found in 1784, and became incorporated by the state of Tennessee when it joined the union in 1796.

Located near the confluence of Red and Cumberland rivers, Clarksville was the site of three Confederate forts that the Union defeated in 1862. Fort Defiance transferred hands and became known as a place where fleeing or freed slaves could find refuge—and jobs. In the 1980s the well-preserved fort passed from the private hands of a local judge to the city itself, and in 2011 an interpretive center and walking trails were unveiled at what is now called Fort Defiance Civil War Park and Interpretive Center. The site features walking trails as well as the 1,500+ square foot center.

Clarksville is home to the 105,000-acre Fort Campbell, established as Camp Campbell in 1942, with nearly two-thirds of its land mass in Tennessee and the rest—including the post office—located in Kentucky. It is home to the world's only air assault division, known as the Screaming Eagles. Two special ops command units, a combat support hospital, and far more make this home to the U.S. Army's most-deployed contingency forces and the its fifth-largest military population. With more than 4,000 civilian jobs, it's the area's largest employer with services on the post ranging from bowling to the commissary to the Fort Campbell Credit Union, as well as medical services and child care.

Austin Peay State University's main campus is in Clarksville, another of the city's major employers, and named for a local son who became governor. The four-year public master's-level university saw its enrollment climb throughout the 2000's, crossing the 10,000 mark in 2009. Austin Peay also operates a center at Fort Campbell with fifteen associate, bachelor and master's level programs.

In 2012, Hemlock Semiconductor Corp, a subsidiary of Dow Corning, opened a $1.2 billion plant to generate polycrystalline silicon used in semiconductor chips and solar products. The state committed $6.4 million to create a new educational center at APSU to train workers, and also is spending $5 million to support Hemlock's worker training.

A 146-acre Liberty Park and Marina redevelopment project was completed in 2012, replete with pavilions, sports fields, picnic shelters, a dog park, and a ten-acre pond with a boardwalk and fishing piers. The Wilma Rudolph Pavilion and Great lawn is named for the great Olympic runner, Clarksville's native daughter. Another recent development came when the city created an Indoor Aquatic Center with an inflatable dome that allows for water sports in winter.

On the cultural side of Clarksville's quality of life, the popular Clarksville Downtown Market—with produce and arts and crafts—is enjoying significant popularity after opening in the summer of 2009.

Clarksville is also home to the state's second largest general museum, called the Customs House Museum and Cultural Center, which has seen a recent facelift. Model trains, a gallery devoted to sports champions, and even a bubble cave are all part of the experience.

The climate in Clarksville means hot summers but relatively moderate winters with average lows reaching 25 degrees in January. Precipitation stays fairly steady year round, getting no higher than 5.39 in March and bottoming out at 3.27 inches in October.

Rankings

Business/Finance Rankings

- The Clarksville metro area appeared on the Milken Institute "2013 Best Performing Cities" list. Rank: #101 out of 200 large metro areas. Criteria: job growth; wage and salary growth; high-tech output growth. *Milken Institute, "Best-Performing Cities 2014," January 2015*
- *Forbes* ranked the 200 most populous metro areas to determine the nation's "Best Places for Business and Careers." The Clarksville metro area was ranked #180. Criteria: costs (business and living); job growth (past and projected); income growth; educational attainment (college and high school); projected economic growth; cultural and recreational opportunities; net migration patterns; number of highly ranked colleges. *Forbes, "The Best Places for Business and Careers 2014," July 23, 2014*

Environmental Rankings

- The Clarksville metro area came in at #247 for the relative comfort of its climate on Sperling's list of "chill cities," as measured by the Sperling Heat Index. All 361 metro areas are included. Criteria included daytime high temperatures, nighttime low temperatures, dew point, and relative humidity at the high temperatures. *www.bertsperling.com, "Sperling's Chill Cities," July 18, 2013*
- Sperling's BestPlaces assessed 379 metropolitan areas of the United States for the likelihood of dangerously extreme weather events or earthquakes. In general the Southeast and South-Central regions have the highest risk of weather extremes and earthquakes, while the Pacific Northwest enjoys the lowest risk. Of the least risky metropolitan areas, the Clarksville metro area was ranked #197. *www.bestplaces.net, "Safest Places from Natural Disasters," April 2011*

Health/Fitness Rankings

- Analysts who tracked obesity rates in 189 of the nation's metro areas found that the Clarksville metro area was one of the ten communities where residents were most likely to be obese, defined as a BMI score of 30 or above. *www.gallup.com, "Boulder, Colo., Residents Still Least Likely to Be Obese," April 4, 2014*
- The Clarksville metro area appeared in the 2013 Gallup-Healthways Well-Being Index. The area ranked #146 out of 189. The Gallup-Healthways Well-Being Index score is an average of six sub-indexes, which individually examine life evaluation, emotional health, work environment, physical health, healthy behaviors, and access to basic necessities. Results are based on telephone interviews conducted as part of the Gallup-Healthways Well-Being Index survey January 2–December 29, 2012, and January 2–December 30, 2013, with a random sample of 531,630 adults, aged 18 and older, living in metropolitan areas in the 50 U.S. states and the District of Columbia. *Gallup-Healthways, "State of American Well-Being," March 25, 2014*

Safety Rankings

- Allstate ranked the 200 largest cities in America in terms of driver safety. Clarksville ranked #110. Allstate researchers analyzed internal property damage claims over a two-year period from January 2011 to December 2012. A weighted average of the two-year numbers determined the annual percentages. *Allstate, "Allstate America's Best Drivers Report, 2014"*
- The National Insurance Crime Bureau ranked 380 metro areas in the U.S. in terms of per capita rates of vehicle theft. The Clarksville metro area ranked #251 (#1 = highest rate). Criteria: number of vehicle theft offenses per 100,000 inhabitants in 2012. *National Insurance Crime Bureau, "Hot Spots 2012," June 26, 2013*

Seniors/Retirement Rankings

- From its Best Cities for Successful Aging indexes, the Milken Institute generated rankings for metropolitan areas, weighing data in eight categories—health care, wellness, living arrangements, transportation, financial characteristics, education and employment opportunities, community engagement, and overall livability. The Clarksville metro area was ranked #179 overall in the small metro area category. *Milken Institute, "Best Cities for Successful Aging, 2014"*

Business Environment

CITY FINANCES

City Government Finances

Component	2012 ($000)	2012 ($ per capita)
Total Revenues	387,951	2,918
Total Expenditures	350,048	2,633
Debt Outstanding	870,078	6,545
Cash and Securities[1]	371,000	2,791

Note: (1) Cash and security holdings of a government at the close of its fiscal year, including those of its dependent agencies, utilities, and liquor stores.
Source: U.S Census Bureau, State & Local Government Finances 2012

City Government Revenue by Source

Source	2012 ($000)	2012 ($ per capita)
General Revenue		
From Federal Government	4,372	33
From State Government	19,835	149
From Local Governments	14,594	110
Taxes		
Property	28,193	212
Sales and Gross Receipts	5,660	43
Personal Income	0	0
Corporate Income	0	0
Motor Vehicle License	0	0
Other Taxes	3,657	28
Current Charges	31,965	240
Liquor Store	0	0
Utility	250,577	1,885
Employee Retirement	0	0

Source: U.S Census Bureau, State & Local Government Finances 2012

City Government Expenditures by Function

Function	2012 ($000)	2012 ($ per capita)	2012 (%)
General Direct Expenditures			
Air Transportation	0	0	0.0
Corrections	0	0	0.0
Education	0	0	0.0
Employment Security Administration	0	0	0.0
Financial Administration	3,406	26	1.0
Fire Protection	13,905	105	4.0
General Public Buildings	637	5	0.2
Governmental Administration, Other	1,409	11	0.4
Health	0	0	0.0
Highways	10,985	83	3.1
Hospitals	0	0	0.0
Housing and Community Development	1,693	13	0.5
Interest on General Debt	6,904	52	2.0
Judicial and Legal	432	3	0.1
Libraries	0	0	0.0
Parking	323	2	0.1
Parks and Recreation	6,378	48	1.8
Police Protection	23,498	177	6.7
Public Welfare	0	0	0.0
Sewerage	27,161	204	7.8
Solid Waste Management	0	0	0.0
Veterans' Services	0	0	0.0
Liquor Store	0	0	0.0
Utility	246,145	1,852	70.3
Employee Retirement	0	0	0.0

Source: U.S Census Bureau, State & Local Government Finances 2012

DEMOGRAPHICS

Population Growth

Area	1990 Census	2000 Census	2010 Census	Population Growth (%) 1990-2000	Population Growth (%) 2000-2010
City	78,569	103,455	132,929	31.7	28.5
MSA[1]	189,277	232,000	273,949	22.6	18.1
U.S.	248,709,873	281,421,906	308,745,538	13.2	9.7

Note: (1) Figures cover the Clarksville, TN-KY Metropolitan Statistical Area—see Appendix B for areas included
Source: U.S. Census Bureau, Census 1990, 2000, 2010

Household Size

Area	Persons in Household (%)							Average Household Size
	One	Two	Three	Four	Five	Six	Seven or More	
City	22.0	32.0	19.2	15.5	6.8	2.3	2.0	2.72
MSA[1]	22.1	32.9	18.6	14.4	7.1	2.9	2.0	2.72
U.S.	27.7	33.6	15.7	13.1	6.0	2.3	1.5	2.64

Note: (1) Figures cover the Clarksville, TN-KY Metropolitan Statistical Area—see Appendix B for areas included
Source: U.S. Census Bureau, 2011-2013 American Community Survey 3-Year Estimates

Race

Area	White Alone[2] (%)	Black Alone[2] (%)	Asian Alone[2] (%)	AIAN[3] Alone[2] (%)	NHOPI[4] Alone[2] (%)	Other Race Alone[2] (%)	Two or More Races (%)
City	66.5	22.7	2.2	1.0	0.4	2.2	5.0
MSA[1]	73.0	18.5	1.7	0.6	0.4	1.6	4.2
U.S.	73.9	12.6	5.0	0.8	0.2	4.7	2.9

Note: (1) Figures cover the Clarksville, TN-KY Metropolitan Statistical Area—see Appendix B for areas included; (2) Alone is defined as not being in combination with one or more other races; (3) American Indian and Alaska Native; (4) Native Hawaiian and Other Pacific Islander
Source: U.S. Census Bureau, 2011-2013 American Community Survey 3-Year Estimates

Hispanic or Latino Origin

Area	Total (%)	Mexican (%)	Puerto Rican (%)	Cuban (%)	Other (%)
City	10.2	5.2	2.8	0.1	2.1
MSA[1]	7.9	4.4	1.7	0.1	1.7
U.S.	16.9	10.8	1.6	0.6	3.8

Note: Persons of Hispanic or Latino origin can be of any race; (1) Figures cover the Clarksville, TN-KY Metropolitan Statistical Area—see Appendix B for areas included
Source: U.S. Census Bureau, 2011-2013 American Community Survey 3-Year Estimates

Segregation

Type	Segregation Indices[1]				Percent Change		
	1990	2000	2010	2010 Rank[2]	1990-2000	1990-2010	2000-2010
Black/White	n/a	n/a	n/a	n/a	n/a	n/a	n/a
Asian/White	n/a	n/a	n/a	n/a	n/a	n/a	n/a
Hispanic/White	n/a	n/a	n/a	n/a	n/a	n/a	n/a

Note: All figures cover the Metropolitan Statistical Area—see Appendix B for areas included; Figures are based on an analysis of 1990, 2000, and 2010 Census Decennial Census tract data by William H. Frey, Brookings Institution and the University of Michigan Social Science Data Analysis Network. In this analysis all racial groups (whites, blacks, and asians) are non-Hispanic members of those races. Hispanics are shown as a separate category;
(1) Segregation Indices are Dissimilarity Indices that measure the degree to which the minority group is distributed differently than whites across census tracts. They range from 0 (complete integration) to 100 (complete segregation) where the value indicates the percentage of the minority group that needs to move to be distributed exactly like whites; (2) Ranges from 1 (most segregated) to 102 (least segregated); n/a not available.
Source: www.CensusScope.org

Ancestry

Area	German	Irish	English	American	Italian	Polish	French[2]	Scottish	Dutch
City	13.6	11.5	6.9	7.0	3.3	2.5	2.2	1.6	1.3
MSA[1]	12.4	10.5	8.2	13.2	3.0	2.0	1.8	1.9	1.3
U.S.	14.9	10.8	8.0	7.4	5.5	3.0	2.7	1.7	1.4

Note: Figures are the percentage of the total population reporting a particular ancestry. The nine most commonly reported ancestries in the U.S. are shown. Figures include multiple ancestries (e.g. if a person reported being Irish and Italian, they were included in both columns); (1) Figures cover the Clarksville, TN-KY Metropolitan Statistical Area—see Appendix B for areas included; (2) Excludes Basque
Source: U.S. Census Bureau, 2011-2013 American Community Survey 3-Year Estimates

Foreign-Born Population

Area	Percent of Population Born in								
	Any Foreign Country	Mexico	Asia	Europe	Carribean	South America	Central America[2]	Africa	Canada
City	n/a	n/a	n/a	n/a	n/a	n/a	n/a	n/a	n/a
MSA[1]	n/a	n/a	n/a	n/a	n/a	n/a	n/a	n/a	n/a
U.S.	13.0	3.7	3.8	1.5	1.2	0.9	1.0	0.6	0.3

Note: (1) Figures cover the Clarksville, TN-KY Metropolitan Statistical Area—see Appendix B for areas included; (2) Excludes Mexico.
Source: U.S. Census Bureau, 2011-2013 American Community Survey 3-Year Estimates

Marital Status

Area	Never Married	Now Married[2]	Separated	Widowed	Divorced
City	28.1	52.8	3.3	3.9	12.0
MSA[1]	26.8	54.2	2.7	5.1	11.2
U.S.	32.7	48.1	2.2	6.0	11.0

Note: Figures are percentages and cover the population 15 years of age and older; (1) Figures cover the Clarksville, TN-KY Metropolitan Statistical Area—see Appendix B for areas included; (2) Excludes separated
Source: U.S. Census Bureau, 2011-2013 American Community Survey 3-Year Estimates

Disability Status

Area	All Ages	Under 18 Years Old	18 to 64 Years Old	65 Years and Over
City	13.8	5.8	14.2	42.8
MSA[1]	13.9	5.1	14.1	38.9
U.S.	12.3	4.1	10.2	36.3

Note: Figures show percent of the civilian noninstitutionalized population that reported having a disability. Disability status is determined from from six types of difficulty: vision, hearing, cognitive, ambulatory, self-care, and independent living. For children under 5 years old, hearing and vision difficulty are used to determine disability status. For children between the ages of 5 and 14, disability status is determined from hearing, vision, cognitive, ambulatory, and self-care difficulties. For people aged 15 years and older, they are considered to have a disability if they have difficulty with any one of the six difficulty types; (1) Figures cover the Clarksville, TN-KY Metropolitan Statistical Area—see Appendix B for areas included.
Source: U.S. Census Bureau, 2011-2013 American Community Survey 3-Year Estimates

Age

Area	Percent of Population									Median Age
	Under Age 5	Age 5–19	Age 20–34	Age 35–44	Age 45–54	Age 55–64	Age 65–74	Age 75–84	Age 85+	
City	9.2	21.4	30.4	13.3	10.9	7.7	4.2	2.1	0.7	28.7
MSA[1]	8.8	21.4	27.1	12.8	11.4	9.1	5.5	2.9	1.0	30.3
U.S.	6.4	19.9	20.7	12.9	14.1	12.3	7.6	4.2	1.9	37.4

Note: (1) Figures cover the Clarksville, TN-KY Metropolitan Statistical Area—see Appendix B for areas included
Source: U.S. Census Bureau, 2011-2013 American Community Survey 3-Year Estimates

Gender

Area	Males	Females	Males per 100 Females
City	69,555	71,073	97.9
MSA[1]	135,821	134,884	100.7
U.S.	154,451,010	159,410,713	96.9

Note: (1) Figures cover the Clarksville, TN-KY Metropolitan Statistical Area—see Appendix B for areas included
Source: U.S. Census Bureau, 2011-2013 American Community Survey 3-Year Estimates

Religious Groups by Family

Area	Catholic	Baptist	Non-Den.	Methodist[2]	Lutheran	LDS[3]	Pente-costal	Presby-terian[4]	Muslim[5]	Judaism
MSA[1]	4.1	30.9	2.3	6.2	0.6	1.5	1.8	1.1	0.1	<0.1
U.S.	19.1	9.3	4.0	4.0	2.3	2.0	1.9	1.6	0.8	0.7

Note: Figures are the number of adherents as a percentage of the total population; (1) Figures cover the Clarksville, TN-KY Metropolitan Statistical Area—see Appendix B for areas included; (2) Methodist/Pietist; (3) Latter Day Saints; (4) Reformed; (5) Figures are estimates
Source: Association of Statisticians of American Religious Bodies, 2010 U.S. Religion Census: Religious Congregations & Membership Study

Religious Groups by Tradition

Area	Catholic	Evangelical Protestant	Mainline Protestant	Other Tradition	Black Protestant	Orthodox
MSA[1]	4.1	35.4	7.3	1.7	2.4	<0.1
U.S.	19.1	16.2	7.3	4.3	1.6	0.3

Note: Figures are the number of adherents as a percentage of the total population; (1) Figures cover the Clarksville, TN-KY Metropolitan Statistical Area—see Appendix B for areas included
Source: Association of Statisticians of American Religious Bodies, 2010 U.S. Religion Census: Religious Congregations & Membership Study

ECONOMY

Gross Metropolitan Product

Area	2012	2013	2014	2015	Rank[2]
MSA[1]	11.8	11.8	12.2	12.7	167

Note: Figures are in billions of dollars; (1) Figures cover the Clarksville, TN-KY Metropolitan Statistical Area—see Appendix B for areas included; (2) Rank is based on 2015 data and ranges from 1 to 363
Source: The U.S. Conference of Mayors, U.S. Metro Economies: GMP and Employment 2013-2015, June 2014

Economic Growth

Area	2010-12 (%)	2013 (%)	2014 (%)	2015 (%)	Rank[2]
MSA[1]	3.6	-1.1	1.2	2.8	194
U.S.	2.1	2.0	2.3	3.2	–

Note: Figures are real gross metropolitan product (GMP) growth rates and represent annual average percent change; (1) Figures cover the Clarksville, TN-KY Metropolitan Statistical Area—see Appendix B for areas included; (2) Rank is based on 2015 data and ranges from 1 to 363
Source: The U.S. Conference of Mayors, U.S. Metro Economies: GMP and Employment 2013-2015, June 2014

Metropolitan Area Exports

Area	2008	2009	2010	2011	2012	2013	Rank[2]
MSA[1]	311.4	158.4	238.3	328.8	326.3	315.9	263

Note: Figures are in millions of dollars; (1) Figures cover the Clarksville, TN-KY Metropolitan Statistical Area—see Appendix B for areas included; (2) Rank is based on 2013 data and ranges from 1 to 387
Source: U.S. Department of Commerce, International Trade Administration, Office of Trade & Industry Information, Manufacturing & Services, data extracted April 3, 2015

Building Permits

Area	Single-Family			Multi-Family			Total		
	2013	2014	Pct. Chg.	2013	2014	Pct. Chg.	2013	2014	Pct. Chg.
City	779	850	9.1	580	137	-76.4	1,359	987	-27.4
MSA[1]	1,256	1,276	1.6	586	231	-60.6	1,842	1,507	-18.2
U.S.	620,802	634,597	2.2	370,020	411,766	11.3	990,822	1,046,363	5.6

Note: (1) Figures cover the Clarksville, TN-KY Metropolitan Statistical Area—see Appendix B for areas included; Figures represent new, privately-owned housing units authorized (unadjusted data); All permit data are based on estimates with imputation.
Source: U.S. Census Bureau, Manufacturing, Mining, and Construction Statistics, Building Permits, 2013, 2014

Bankruptcy Filings

Area	Business Filings			Nonbusiness Filings		
	2013	2014	% Chg.	2013	2014	% Chg.
Montgomery County	14	14	0.0	773	808	4.5
U.S.	33,212	26,983	-18.8	1,038,720	909,812	-12.4

Note: Business filings include Chapter 7, Chapter 11, Chapter 12, and Chapter 13; Nonbusiness filings include Chapter 7, Chapter 11, and Chapter 13
Source: Administrative Office of the U.S. Courts, Business and Nonbusiness Bankruptcy, County Cases Commenced by Chapter of the Bankruptcy Code, During the 12- Month Period Ending December 31, 2013 and Business and Nonbusiness Bankruptcy, County Cases Commenced by Chapter of the Bankruptcy Code, During the 12- Month Period Ending December 31, 2014

Housing Vacancy Rates

Area	Gross Vacancy Rate[2] (%)			Year-Round Vacancy Rate[3] (%)			Rental Vacancy Rate[4] (%)			Homeowner Vacancy Rate[5] (%)		
	2012	2013	2014	2012	2013	2014	2012	2013	2014	2012	2013	2014
MSA[1]	n/a	n/a	n/a	n/a	n/a	n/a	n/a	n/a	n/a	n/a	n/a	n/a
U.S.	13.8	13.6	13.4	10.8	10.7	10.4	8.7	8.3	7.6	2.0	2.0	1.9

Note: (1) Figures cover the Clarksville, TN-KY Metropolitan Statistical Area—see Appendix B for areas included; (2) The percentage of the total housing inventory that is vacant; (3) The percentage of the housing inventory (excluding seasonal units) that is year-round vacant; (4) The percentage of rental inventory that is vacant for rent; (5) The percentage of homeowner inventory that is vacant for sale; n/a not available
Source: U.S. Census Bureau, Housing Vacancies and Homeownership Annual Statistics: 2014

INCOME

Income

Area	Per Capita ($)	Median Household ($)	Average Household ($)
City	21,017	46,100	55,585
MSA[1]	21,868	46,183	58,156
U.S.	27,884	52,176	72,897

Note: (1) Figures cover the Clarksville, TN-KY Metropolitan Statistical Area—see Appendix B for areas included
Source: U.S. Census Bureau, 2011-2013 American Community Survey 3-Year Estimates

Household Income Distribution

Area	Percent of Households Earning							
	Under $15,000	$15,000 -24,999	$25,000 -34,999	$35,000 -49,999	$50,000 -74,999	$75,000 -99,000	$100,000 -149,999	$150,000 and up
City	13.4	10.8	12.1	17.6	23.2	11.2	8.7	2.9
MSA[1]	13.6	11.8	12.1	16.2	21.5	11.6	9.0	4.1
U.S.	13.0	10.9	10.3	13.6	17.9	11.9	12.7	9.6

Note: (1) Figures cover the Clarksville, TN-KY Metropolitan Statistical Area—see Appendix B for areas included
Source: U.S. Census Bureau, 2011-2013 American Community Survey 3-Year Estimates

Poverty Rate

Area	All Ages	Under 18 Years Old	18 to 64 Years Old	65 Years and Over
City	18.1	26.7	15.5	7.9
MSA[1]	17.8	25.8	15.5	8.8
U.S.	15.9	22.4	14.8	9.5

Note: Figures are percentage of people whose income during the past 12 months was below the poverty level; (1) Figures cover the Clarksville, TN-KY Metropolitan Statistical Area—see Appendix B for areas included
Source: U.S. Census Bureau, 2011-2013 American Community Survey 3-Year Estimates

EMPLOYMENT

Labor Force and Employment

Area	Civilian Labor Force			Workers Employed		
	Dec. 2013	Dec. 2014	% Chg.	Dec. 2013	Dec. 2014	% Chg.
City	56,955	56,613	-0.6	53,150	53,062	-0.2
MSA[1]	108,531	107,539	-0.9	100,928	101,055	0.1
U.S.	154,408,000	155,521,000	0.7	144,423,000	147,190,000	1.9

Note: Data is not seasonally adjusted and covers workers 16 years of age and older; (1) Figures cover the Clarksville, TN-KY Metropolitan Statistical Area—see Appendix B for areas included
Source: Bureau of Labor Statistics, Local Area Unemployment Statistics

Unemployment Rate

Area	2014											
	Jan.	Feb.	Mar.	Apr.	May	Jun.	Jul.	Aug.	Sep.	Oct.	Nov.	Dec.
City	6.6	6.7	6.7	6.0	6.6	7.6	7.9	7.6	6.9	6.9	6.7	6.3
MSA[1]	7.2	7.4	7.3	6.4	6.9	7.5	7.8	7.3	6.7	6.5	6.4	6.0
U.S.	7.0	7.0	6.8	5.9	6.1	6.3	6.5	6.3	5.7	5.5	5.5	5.4

Note: Data is not seasonally adjusted and covers workers 16 years of age and older; (1) Figures cover the Clarksville, TN-KY Metropolitan Statistical Area—see Appendix B for areas included
Source: Bureau of Labor Statistics, Local Area Unemployment Statistics

Employment by Occupation

Occupation Classification	City (%)	MSA[1] (%)	U.S. (%)
Management, Business, Science, and Arts	30.7	31.2	36.2
Natural Resources, Construction, and Maintenance	8.4	9.4	9.0
Production, Transportation, and Material Moving	13.5	16.0	12.1
Sales and Office	25.9	24.6	24.4
Service	21.5	18.7	18.3

Note: Figures cover employed civilians 16 years of age and older; (1) Figures cover the Clarksville, TN-KY Metropolitan Statistical Area—see Appendix B for areas included
Source: U.S. Census Bureau, 2011-2013 American Community Survey 3-Year Estimates

Employment by Industry

Sector	MSA[1]		U.S.
	Number of Employees	Percent of Total	Percent of Total
Construction, Mining, and Logging	3,200	3.6	5.0
Education and Health Services	11,600	13.0	15.5
Financial Activities	3,100	3.5	5.7
Government	20,300	22.7	15.8
Information	1,200	1.3	2.0
Leisure and Hospitality	11,100	12.4	10.3
Manufacturing	10,100	11.3	8.7
Other Services	3,000	3.4	4.0
Professional and Business Services	9,300	10.4	13.8
Retail Trade	11,800	13.2	11.4
Transportation, Warehousing, and Utilities	2,400	2.7	3.9
Wholesale Trade	n/a	n/a	4.2

Note: Figures are non-farm employment as of December 2014. Figures are not seasonally adjusted and include workers 16 years of age and older; (1) Figures cover the Clarksville, TN-KY Metropolitan Statistical Area—see Appendix B for areas included; n/a not available
Source: Bureau of Labor Statistics, Current Employment Statistics, Employment, Hours, and Earnings

Occupations with Greatest Projected Employment Growth: 2012 – 2022

Occupation[1]	2012 Employment	2022 Projected Employment	Numeric Employment Change	Percent Employment Change
Combined Food Preparation and Serving Workers, Including Fast Food	57,280	69,200	11,920	20.8
Laborers and Freight, Stock, and Material Movers, Hand	73,340	84,450	11,110	15.1
Heavy and Tractor-Trailer Truck Drivers	58,030	66,640	8,610	14.8
Janitors and Cleaners, Except Maids and Housekeeping Cleaners	44,250	52,850	8,600	19.4
Customer Service Representatives	48,050	56,410	8,360	17.4
Team Assemblers	39,680	47,700	8,020	20.2
Registered Nurses	56,400	64,290	7,890	14.0
Security Guards	22,050	29,280	7,230	32.8
Secretaries and Administrative Assistants, Except Legal, Medical, and Executive	42,120	49,220	7,100	16.8
General and Operations Managers	40,120	46,280	6,160	15.4

Note: Projections cover Tennessee; (1) Sorted by numeric employment change
Source: www.projectionscentral.com, State Occupational Projections, 2012–2022 Long-Term Projections

Fastest Growing Occupations: 2012 – 2022

Occupation[1]	2012 Employment	2022 Projected Employment	Numeric Employment Change	Percent Employment Change
Computer Numerically Controlled Machine Tool Programmers, Metal and Plastic	490	740	250	49.8
Paralegals and Legal Assistants	4,820	7,170	2,350	48.7
Skincare Specialists	560	830	270	46.5
Physician Assistants	1,300	1,880	580	44.6
Interpreters and Translators	690	1,000	310	44.4
Diagnostic Medical Sonographers	1,450	2,060	610	42.0
Ambulance Drivers and Attendants, Except Emergency Medical Technicians	270	380	110	41.6
Meeting, Convention, and Event Planners	1,180	1,670	490	41.1
Veterinary Technologists and Technicians	1,620	2,250	630	39.4
Helpers—Brickmasons, Blockmasons, Stonemasons, and Tile and Marble Setters	420	580	160	39.0

Note: Projections cover Tennessee; (1) Sorted by percent employment change and excludes occupations with numeric employment change less than 100
Source: www.projectionscentral.com, State Occupational Projections, 2012–2022 Long-Term Projections

Average Wages

Occupation	$/Hr.	Occupation	$/Hr.
Accountants and Auditors	27.33	Maids and Housekeeping Cleaners	9.53
Automotive Mechanics	19.77	Maintenance and Repair Workers	18.16
Bookkeepers	15.70	Marketing Managers	36.81
Carpenters	17.69	Nuclear Medicine Technologists	n/a
Cashiers	9.16	Nurses, Licensed Practical	18.91
Clerks, General Office	13.49	Nurses, Registered	27.70
Clerks, Receptionists/Information	11.35	Nursing Assistants	12.03
Clerks, Shipping/Receiving	16.19	Packers and Packagers, Hand	9.71
Computer Programmers	24.00	Physical Therapists	37.99
Computer Systems Analysts	36.80	Postal Service Mail Carriers	24.87
Computer User Support Specialists	18.85	Real Estate Brokers	n/a
Cooks, Restaurant	9.70	Retail Salespersons	12.04
Dentists	n/a	Sales Reps., Exc. Tech./Scientific	22.17
Electrical Engineers	36.18	Sales Reps., Tech./Scientific	44.78
Electricians	19.36	Secretaries, Exc. Legal/Med./Exec.	13.70
Financial Managers	29.83	Security Guards	14.07
First-Line Supervisors/Managers, Sales	18.14	Surgeons	n/a
Food Preparation Workers	10.10	Teacher Assistants	11.00
General and Operations Managers	39.05	Teachers, Elementary School	27.40
Hairdressers/Cosmetologists	11.03	Teachers, Secondary School	26.40
Internists	n/a	Telemarketers	n/a
Janitors and Cleaners	10.97	Truck Drivers, Heavy/Tractor-Trailer	15.19
Landscaping/Groundskeeping Workers	11.95	Truck Drivers, Light/Delivery Svcs.	13.62
Lawyers	38.00	Waiters and Waitresses	8.80

Note: Wage data covers the Clarksville, TN-KY Metropolitan Statistical Area—see Appendix B for areas included; Hourly wages for elementary/secondary school teachers and teacher assistants were calculated by the editors from annual wage data assuming a 40 hour work week; n/a not available.
Source: Bureau of Labor Statistics, Metro Area Occupational Employment and Wage Estimates, May 2014

TAXES

State Corporate Income Tax Rates

State	Tax Rate (%)	Income Brackets ($)	Num. of Brackets	Financial Institution Tax Rate (%)[a]	Federal Income Tax Ded.
Tennessee	6.5	Flat rate	1	6.5	No

Note: Tax rates as of January 1, 2015; (a) Rates listed are the corporate income tax rate applied to financial institutions or excise taxes based on income. Some states have other taxes based upon the value of deposits or shares.
Source: Federation of Tax Administrators, "State Corporate Income Tax Rates, 2015"

State Individual Income Tax Rates

State	Tax Rate (%)	Income Brackets ($)	Num. of Brackets	Personal Exempt. ($)[1] Single	Personal Exempt. ($)[1] Dependents	Fed. Inc. Tax Ded.
Tennessee	State income tax of 6% on dividends and interest income only					

Note: Tax rates as of January 1, 2015; Local- and county-level taxes are not included; n/a not applicable; (1) Married joint filers generally receive double the single exemption
Source: Federation of Tax Administrators, "State Individual Income Tax Rates, 2015"

Various State and Local Tax Rates

State	State and Local Sales and Use (%)	State Sales and Use (%)	Gasoline[1] (¢/gal.)	Cigarette[2] ($/pack)	Spirits[3] ($/gal.)	Wine[4] ($/gal.)	Beer[5] ($/gal.)
Tennessee	9.5	7.0	21.4	0.62	4.46 (i)	1.27 (m)	1.29 (t)

Note: All tax rates as of January 1, 2015; (1) The American Petroleum Institute has developed a methodology for determining the average tax rate on a gallon of fuel. Rates may include any of the following: excise taxes, environmental fees, storage tank fees, other fees or taxes, general sales tax, and local taxes. In states where gasoline is subject to the general sales tax, or where the fuel tax is based on the average sale price, the average rate determined by API is sensitive to changes in the price of gasoline. States that fully or partially apply general sales taxes to gasoline: CA, CO, GA, IL, IN, MI, NY; (2) The federal excise tax of $1.0066 per pack and local taxes are not included; (3) Rates are those applicable to off-premise sales of 40% alcohol by volume (a.b.v.) distilled spirits in 750ml containers. Local excise taxes are excluded; (4) Rates are those applicable to off-premise sales of 11% a.b.v. non-carbonated wine in 750ml containers; (5) Rates are those applicable to off-premise sales of 4.7% a.b.v. beer in 12 ounce containers; (i) Includes case fees and/or bottle fees which may vary with the size of container; (m) Includes case fees and/or bottle fees which may vary with size of container; (t) Includes the wholesale tax rate of 17%, converted into a gallonage excise tax rate.
Source: Tax Foundation, 2015 Facts & Figures: How Does Your State Compare?

State Business Tax Climate Index Rankings

State	Overall Rank	Corporate Tax Index Rank	Individual Income Tax Index Rank	Sales Tax Index Rank	Unemployment Insurance Tax Index Rank	Property Tax Index Rank
Tennessee	15	15	8	47	26	37

Note: The index is a measure of how each state's tax laws affect economic performance. The lower the rank, the more favorable a state's tax system is for business. States without a given tax are given a ranking of 1. The scores/rankings for the District of Columbia do not affect other states. The 2015 index represents the tax climate as of July 1, 2014.
Source: Tax Foundation, State Business Tax Climate Index 2015

COMMERCIAL UTILITIES

Typical Monthly Electric Bills

Area	Commercial Service ($/month)		Industrial Service ($/month)	
	1,500 kWh	40 kW demand 14,000 kWh	1,000 kW demand 200,000 kWh	50,000 kW demand 32,500,000 kWh
City	n/a	n/a	n/a	n/a
Average[1]	201	1,653	26,124	2,639,743

Note: Figures are based on annualized 2014 rates; (1) Average based on 180 utilities surveyed; n/a not available
Source: Edison Electric Institute, Typical Bills and Average Rates Report, Summer 2014

TRANSPORTATION

Means of Transportation to Work

Area	Car/Truck/Van		Public Transportation			Bicycle	Walked	Other Means	Worked at Home
	Drove Alone	Car-pooled	Bus	Subway	Railroad				
City	84.0	9.2	0.9	0.0	0.0	0.1	2.8	1.1	1.9
MSA[1]	81.2	9.9	0.7	0.0	0.0	0.1	4.1	1.6	2.3
U.S.	76.4	9.6	2.6	1.8	0.6	0.6	2.8	1.3	4.3

Note: Figures are percentages and cover workers 16 years of age and older; (1) Figures cover the Clarksville, TN-KY Metropolitan Statistical Area—see Appendix B for areas included
Source: U.S. Census Bureau, 2011-2013 American Community Survey 3-Year Estimates

Travel Time to Work

Area	Less Than 10 Minutes	10 to 19 Minutes	20 to 29 Minutes	30 to 44 Minutes	45 to 59 Minutes	60 to 89 Minutes	90 Minutes or More
City	12.7	34.5	27.0	15.7	5.4	4.0	0.7
MSA[1]	15.9	32.6	24.3	16.3	5.6	4.0	1.1
U.S.	13.3	29.7	20.9	20.2	7.7	5.7	2.6

Note: Figures are percentages and include workers 16 years old and over; (1) Figures cover the Clarksville, TN-KY Metropolitan Statistical Area—see Appendix B for areas included
Source: U.S. Census Bureau, 2011-2013 American Community Survey 3-Year Estimates

Travel Time Index

Area	1985	1990	1995	2000	2005	2010	2011
Urban Area[1]	n/a	n/a	n/a	n/a	n/a	n/a	n/a
Average[2]	1.09	1.14	1.16	1.19	1.23	1.18	1.18

Note: Travel Time Index—the ratio of travel time in the peak period to the travel time at free-flow conditions. For example, a value of 1.30 indicates a 20-minute free-flow trip takes 26 minutes in the peak. Free-flow speeds (60 mph on freeways and 35 mph on principal arterials) are used as the comparison threshold; (1) Data for the Clarksville, TN-KY urban area was not available; (2) average of 498 urban areas
Source: Texas Transportation Institute, Urban Mobility Report 2012, December 2012

Public Transportation

Agency Name / Mode of Transportation	Vehicles Operated in Maximum Service	Annual Unlinked Passenger Trips (in thous.)	Annual Passenger Miles (in thous.)
Clarksville Transit System (CTS)			
Bus (directly operated)	16	844.9	5,115.3
Demand Response (directly operated)	8	28.5	223.5

Source: Federal Transit Administration, National Transit Database, 2013

Air Transportation

Airport Name and Code / Type of Service	Passenger Airlines[1]	Passenger Enplanements	Freight Carriers[2]	Freight (lbs.)
Outlaw Field (CKV)				
Domestic service (U.S. carriers - 2014)	0	0	0	0
International service (U.S. carriers - 2013)	0	0	0	0

Note: (1) Includes all U.S.-based major, minor and commuter airlines that carried at least one passenger during the year; (2) Includes all U.S.-based airlines and freight carriers that transported at least one lb. of freight during the year.
Source: Bureau of Transportation Statistics, The Intermodal Transportation Database, Air Carriers: T-100 Domestic Market (U.S. Carriers), 2014; Bureau of Transportation Statistics, The Intermodal Transportation Database, Air Carriers: T-100 International Market (U.S. Carriers), 2013

Other Transportation Statistics

Major Highways:	I-24; SR-79; SR-41A
Amtrak Service:	No
Major Waterways/Ports:	Cumberland River

Source: Amtrak.com; Google Maps

BUSINESSES

Major Business Headquarters

Company Name	Rankings	
	Fortune[1]	Forbes[2]
No companies listed	-	-

Note: (1) Fortune 500—companies that produce a 10-K are ranked 1 to 500 based on 2013 revenue; (2) all private companies with at least $2 billion in annual revenue through the end of their most current fiscal year are ranked 1 to 221; companies listed are headquartered in the city; dashes indicate no ranking
Source: Fortune, "Fortune 500," June 16, 2014; Forbes, "America's Largest Private Companies," November 5, 2014

Minority- and Women-Owned Businesses

Group	All Firms		Firms with Paid Employees			
	Firms	Sales ($000)	Firms	Sales ($000)	Employees	Payroll ($000)
Asian	260	74,105	117	68,699	1,187	9,011
Black	760	26,591	44	15,759	233	3,835
Hispanic	(s)	(s)	(s)	(s)	(s)	(s)
Women	2,355	301,725	271	268,592	2,465	51,824
All Firms	7,044	5,624,589	1,770	5,453,404	30,502	781,365

Note: Figures cover firms located in the city; minority- and women-owned business are defined as firms in which the corresponding group own 51% or more of the stock or equity of the company; (s) estimates are suppressed when publication standards are not met
Source: U.S. Census Bureau, 2007 Economic Census, Survey of Business Owners (2012 Survey of Business Owners data will be released starting in June 2015)

HOTELS & CONVENTION CENTERS

Hotels/Motels

Area	5 Star		4 Star		3 Star		2 Star		1 Star		Not Rated	
	Num.	Pct.[3]	Num.	Pct.[3]	Num.	Pct.[3]	Num.	Pct.[3]	Num.	Pct.[3]	Num.	Pct.[3]
City[1]	0	0.0	0	0.0	4	8.9	39	86.7	0	0.0	2	4.4
Total[2]	166	0.9	1,264	7.0	5,718	31.8	9,340	52.0	411	2.3	1,070	6.0

Note: (1) Figures cover Clarksville and vicinity; (2) Figures cover all 100 cities in this book; (3) Percentage of hotels which have a given star rating; Star ratings are determined by expedia.com and offer an indication of the general quality of a particular hotel.
Source: expedia.com, April 2, 2015

Major Convention Centers

Name	Overall Space (sq. ft.)	Exhibit Space (sq. ft.)	Meeting Space (sq. ft.)	Meeting Rooms

There are no major convention centers located in the metro area
Source: Original research

Living Environment

COST OF LIVING

Cost of Living Index

Composite Index	Groceries	Housing	Utilities	Trans-portation	Health Care	Misc. Goods/ Services
n/a	n/a	n/a	n/a	n/a	n/a	n/a

Note: The Cost of Living Index measures regional differences in the cost of consumer goods and services, excluding taxes and non-consumer expenditures, for professional and managerial households in the top income quintile. It is based on more than 50,000 prices covering almost 60 different items for which prices are collected three times a year by chambers of commerce, economic development organizations or university applied economic centers in each participating urban area. The numbers shown should be read as a percentage above or below the national average of 100. For example, a value of 115.4 in the groceries column indicates that grocery prices are 15.4% higher than the national average. Small differences in the index numbers should not be interpreted as significant; n/a not available.
Source: The Council for Community and Economic Research, ACCRA Cost of Living Index, 2014

Grocery Prices

Area[1]	T-Bone Steak ($/pound)	Frying Chicken ($/pound)	Whole Milk ($/half gal.)	Eggs ($/dozen)	Orange Juice ($/64 oz.)	Coffee ($/11.5 oz.)
City[2]	n/a	n/a	n/a	n/a	n/a	n/a
Avg.	10.40	1.37	2.40	1.99	3.46	4.27
Min.	8.48	0.93	1.37	1.30	2.83	2.99
Max.	14.20	2.44	3.62	4.02	6.42	6.96

Note: (1) Values for the local area are compared with the average, minimum and maximum values for all 308 areas in the Cost of Living Index; (2) Figures cover the Clarksville TN urban area; n/a not available; **T-Bone Steak** *(price per pound);* **Frying Chicken** *(price per pound, whole fryer);* **Whole Milk** *(half gallon carton);* **Eggs** *(price per dozen, Grade A, large);* **Orange Juice** *(64 oz. Tropicana or Florida Natural);* **Coffee** *(11.5 oz. can, vacuum-packed, Maxwell House, Hills Bros, or Folgers).*
Source: The Council for Community and Economic Research, ACCRA Cost of Living Index, 2014

Housing and Utility Costs

Area[1]	New Home Price ($)	Apartment Rent ($/month)	All Electric ($/month)	Part Electric ($/month)	Other Energy ($/month)	Telephone ($/month)
City[2]	n/a	n/a	n/a	n/a	n/a	n/a
Avg.	305,838	919	181.00	93.66	73.14	27.95
Min.	183,142	480	112.00	42.06	23.42	17.16
Max.	1,358,576	3,851	594.00	180.03	440.99	40.42

Note: (1) Values for the local area are compared with the average, minimum and maximum values for all 308 areas in the Cost of Living Index; (2) Figures cover the Clarksville TN urban area; n/a not available; **New Home Price** *(2,400 sf living area, 8,000 sf lot, in urban area with full utilities);* **Apartment Rent** *(950 sf 2 bedroom/1.5 or 2 bath, unfurnished, excluding all utilities except water);* **All Electric** *(average monthly cost for an all-electric home);* **Part Electric** *(average monthly cost for a part-electric home);* **Other Energy** *(average monthly cost for natural gas, fuel oil, coal, wood, and any other forms of energy except electricity);* **Telephone** *(price includes basic monthly rate for a private residential line plus additional local usage charges incurred by a family of four).*
Source: The Council for Community and Economic Research, ACCRA Cost of Living Index, 2014

Health Care, Transportation, and Other Costs

Area[1]	Doctor ($/visit)	Dentist ($/visit)	Optometrist ($/visit)	Gasoline ($/gallon)	Beauty Salon ($/visit)	Men's Shirt ($)
City[2]	n/a	n/a	n/a	n/a	n/a	n/a
Avg.	102.86	87.89	97.66	3.44	34.37	26.74
Min.	67.47	65.78	51.18	3.00	17.43	12.79
Max.	173.50	150.14	235.00	4.33	64.28	49.50

Note: (1) Values for the local area are compared with the average, minimum and maximum values for all 308 areas in the Cost of Living Index; (2) Figures cover the Clarksville TN urban area; n/a not available; **Doctor** *(general practitioners routine exam of an established patient);* **Dentist** *(adult teeth cleaning and periodic oral examination);* **Optometrist** *(full vision eye exam for established adult patient);* **Gasoline** *(one gallon regular unleaded, national brand, including all taxes, cash price at self-service pump if available);* **Beauty Salon** *(woman's shampoo, trim, and blow-dry);* **Men's Shirt** *(cotton/polyester dress shirt, pinpoint weave, long sleeves).*
Source: The Council for Community and Economic Research, ACCRA Cost of Living Index, 2014

HOUSING

House Price Index (HPI)

Area	National Ranking[2]	Quarterly Change (%)	One-Year Change (%)	Five-Year Change (%)
MSA[1]	(a)	n/a	2.66	1.19
U.S.[3]	–	1.35	4.91	11.59

Note: The HPI is a weighted repeat sales index. It measures average price changes in repeat sales or refinancings on the same properties. This information is obtained by reviewing repeat mortgage transactions on single-family properties whose mortgages have been purchased or securitized by Fannie Mae or Freddie Mac in January 1975; (1) Clarksville Metropolitan Statistical Area—see Appendix B for areas included; (2) Rankings are based on annual percentage change for all metro areas containing at least 15,000 transactions over the last 10 years and ranges from 1 to 275; (3) figures based on a weighted average of Census Division estimates using a seasonally adjusted, purchase-only index; all figures are for the period ending December 31, 2014; n/a not available; (a) Not ranked because of increased index variability due to smaller sample size
Source: Federal Housing Finance Agency, House Price Index, February 26, 2015

Median Single-Family Home Prices

Area	2012	2013	2014p	Percent Change 2013 to 2014
MSA[1]	n/a	n/a	n/a	n/a
U.S. Average	177.2	197.4	209.0	5.9

Note: Figures are median sales prices of existing single-family homes in thousands of dollars; (p) preliminary; n/a not available; (1) Clarksville, TN-KY Metropolitan Statistical Area—see Appendix B for areas included
Source: National Association of Realtors, Median Sales Price of Existing Single-Family Homes for Metropolitan Areas, 4th Quarter 2014

Qualifying Income Based on Median Sales Price of Existing Single-Family Homes

Area	With 5% Down ($)	With 10% Down ($)	With 20% Down ($)
MSA[1]	n/a	n/a	n/a
U.S. Average	45,863	43,449	38,621

Note: Figures are preliminary; Qualifying income is based on a mortgage rate of 4.0%. Monthly principal and interest payment is limited to 25% of income; n/a not available; (1) Clarksville, TN-KY Metropolitan Statistical Area—see Appendix B for areas included
Source: National Association of Realtors, Qualifying Income Based on Median Sales Price of Existing Single-Family Homes for Metropolitan Areas, 4th Quarter 2014

Median Apartment Condo-Coop Home Prices

Area	2012	2013	2014p	Percent Change 2013 to 2014
MSA[1]	n/a	n/a	n/a	n/a
U.S. Average	173.7	194.9	205.1	5.2

Note: Figures are median sales prices of existing apartment condo-coop homes in thousands of dollars; (p) preliminary; n/a not available; (1) Clarksville, TN-KY Metropolitan Statistical Area—see Appendix B for areas included
Source: National Association of Realtors, Median Sales Price of Existing Apartment Condo-Coop Homes for Metropolitan Areas, 4th Quarter 2014

Gross Monthly Rent

Area	Under $200	$200 -299	$300 -499	$500 -749	$750 -999	$1,000 -1,499	$1,500 and up	Median ($)
City	1.2	1.3	4.8	28.0	31.9	26.9	6.0	857
MSA[1]	1.0	2.2	9.4	28.8	31.0	22.9	4.8	823
U.S.	1.7	3.2	7.8	22.1	24.3	26.0	14.9	900

Note: Figures are percentages except for Median; Gross rent is the contract rent plus the estimated average monthly cost of utilities (electricity, gas, and water and sewer) and fuels (oil, coal, kerosene, wood, etc.) if these are paid by the renter (or paid for the renter by someone else); (1) Figures cover the Clarksville, TN-KY Metropolitan Statistical Area—see Appendix B for areas included
Source: U.S. Census Bureau, 2011-2013 American Community Survey 3-Year Estimates

Homeownership Rate

Area	2007 (%)	2008 (%)	2009 (%)	2010 (%)	2011 (%)	2012 (%)	2013 (%)	2014 (%)
MSA[1]	n/a	n/a	n/a	n/a	n/a	n/a	n/a	n/a
U.S.	68.1	67.8	67.4	66.9	66.1	65.4	65.1	64.5

Note: (1) Figures cover the Clarksville, TN-KY Metropolitan Statistical Area—see Appendix B for areas included; n/a not available
Source: U.S. Census Bureau, Housing Vacancies and Homeownership Annual Statistics: 2014

Year Housing Structure Built

Area	2010 or Later	2000 -2009	1990 -1999	1980 -1989	1970 -1979	1960 -1969	1950 -1959	1940 -1949	Before 1940	Median Year
City	3.9	28.4	21.2	13.3	13.0	9.1	5.9	2.5	2.7	1992
MSA[1]	3.0	23.7	21.3	12.9	14.7	10.2	6.9	2.6	4.8	1988
U.S.	0.9	15.0	13.9	13.8	15.8	11.0	10.9	5.4	13.3	1976

Note: Figures are percentages except for Median Year; (1) Figures cover the Clarksville, TN-KY Metropolitan Statistical Area—see Appendix B for areas included
Source: U.S. Census Bureau, 2011-2013 American Community Survey 3-Year Estimates

HEALTH

Health Risk Data

Category	MSA[1] (%)	U.S. (%)
Adults aged 18–64 who have any kind of health care coverage	n/a	79.6
Adults who reported being in good or excellent health	n/a	83.1
Adults who are current smokers	n/a	19.6
Adults who are heavy drinkers[2]	n/a	6.1
Adults who are binge drinkers[3]	n/a	16.9
Adults who are overweight (BMI 25.0 - 29.9)	n/a	35.8
Adults who are obese (BMI 30.0 - 99.8)	n/a	27.6
Adults who participated in any physical activities in the past month	n/a	77.1
Adults 50+ who have ever had a sigmoidoscopy or colonoscopy	n/a	67.3
Women aged 40+ who have had a mammogram within the past two years	n/a	74.0
Men aged 40+ who have had a PSA test within the past two years	n/a	45.2
Adults aged 65+ who have had flu shot within the past year	n/a	60.1
Adults who always wear a seatbelt	n/a	93.8

Note: Data as of 2012 unless otherwise noted; n/a not available; (1) Figures cover the Clarksville, TN-KY Metropolitan Statistical Area—see Appendix B for areas included; (2) Heavy drinkers are classified as males having more than two drinks per day or females having more than one drink per day; (3) Binge drinkers are classified as males having five or more drinks on one occasion or females having four or more drinks on one occasion
Source: Centers for Disease Control and Prevention, Behaviorial Risk Factor Surveillance System, SMART: Selected Metropolitan/Micropolitan Area Risk Trends, 2012 (Note: the CDC has discontinued this dataset but will be releasing a replacement in late 2015)

Chronic Health Indicators

Category	MSA[1] (%)	U.S. (%)
Adults who have ever been told they had a heart attack	n/a	4.5
Adults who have ever been told they had a stroke	n/a	2.9
Adults who have been told they currently have asthma	n/a	8.9
Adults who have ever been told they have arthritis	n/a	25.7
Adults who have ever been told they have diabetes[2]	n/a	9.7
Adults who have ever been told they had skin cancer	n/a	5.7
Adults who have ever been told they had any other types of cancer	n/a	6.5
Adults who have ever been told they have COPD	n/a	6.2
Adults who have ever been told they have kidney disease	n/a	2.5
Adults who have ever been told they have a form of depression	n/a	18.0

Note: Data as of 2012 unless otherwise noted; n/a not available; (1) Figures cover the Clarksville, TN-KY Metropolitan Statistical Area—see Appendix B for areas included; (2) Figures do not include pregnancy-related, borderline, or pre-diabetes
Source: Centers for Disease Control and Prevention, Behaviorial Risk Factor Surveillance System, SMART: Selected Metropolitan/Micropolitan Area Risk Trends, 2012 (Note: the CDC has discontinued this dataset but will be releasing a replacement in late 2015)

Mortality Rates for the Top 10 Causes of Death in the U.S.

ICD-10[a] Sub-Chapter	ICD-10[a] Code	Age-Adjusted Mortality Rate[1] per 100,000 population	
		County[2]	U.S.
Malignant neoplasms	C00-C97	187.9	166.2
Ischaemic heart diseases	I20-I25	132.4	105.7
Other forms of heart disease	I30-I51	43.0	49.3
Chronic lower respiratory diseases	J40-J47	71.3	42.1
Organic, including symptomatic, mental disorders	F01-F09	49.9	38.1
Cerebrovascular diseases	I60-I69	52.6	37.0
Other external causes of accidental injury	W00-X59	33.0	26.9
Other degenerative diseases of the nervous system	G30-G31	31.3	25.6
Diabetes mellitus	E10-E14	30.6	21.3
Hypertensive diseases	I10-I15	17.1	19.4

Note: (a) ICD-10 = International Classification of Diseases 10th Revision; (1) Mortality rates are a three year average covering 2011-2013; (2) Figures cover Montgomery County
Source: Centers for Disease Control and Prevention, National Center for Health Statistics. Compressed Mortality File 1999-2013 on CDC WONDER Online Database, released October 2014. Data are compiled from the Compressed Mortality File 1999-2013, Series 20 No. 2S, 2014.

Mortality Rates for Selected Causes of Death

ICD-10[a] Sub-Chapter	ICD-10[a] Code	Age-Adjusted Mortality Rate[1] per 100,000 population	
		County[2]	U.S.
Assault	X85-Y09	5.3	5.2
Diseases of the liver	K70-K76	15.2	13.2
Human immunodeficiency virus (HIV) disease	B20-B24	Suppressed	2.2
Influenza and pneumonia	J09-J18	17.5	15.4
Intentional self-harm	X60-X84	15.2	12.5
Malnutrition	E40-E46	Suppressed	0.9
Obesity and other hyperalimentation	E65-E68	4.2	1.8
Renal failure	N17-N19	12.2	13.1
Transport accidents	V01-V99	12.7	11.7
Viral hepatitis	B15-B19	*2.4	2.2

Note: (a) ICD-10 = International Classification of Diseases 10th Revision; (1) Mortality rates are a three year average covering 2011-2013; (2) Figures cover Montgomery County; (*) Unreliable data as per CDC
Source: Centers for Disease Control and Prevention, National Center for Health Statistics. Compressed Mortality File 1999-2013 on CDC WONDER Online Database, released October 2014. Data are compiled from the Compressed Mortality File 1999-2013, Series 20 No. 2S, 2014.

Health Insurance Coverage

Area	With Health Insurance	With Private Health Insurance	With Public Health Insurance	Without Health Insurance	Population Under Age 18 Without Health Insurance
City	86.4	69.3	29.8	13.6	4.5
MSA[1]	85.7	68.7	29.6	14.3	6.5
U.S.	85.2	65.2	31.0	14.8	7.3

Note: Figures are percentages that cover the civilian noninstitutionalized population; (1) Figures cover the Clarksville, TN-KY Metropolitan Statistical Area—see Appendix B for areas included
Source: U.S. Census Bureau, 2011-2013 American Community Survey 3-Year Estimates

Number of Medical Professionals

Area[1]	MDs[2]	DOs[2,3]	Dentists	Podiatrists	Chiropractors	Optometrists
Local (number)	200	36	75	4	28	26
Local (rate[4])	107.9	19.4	40.6	2.2	15.2	14.1
U.S. (rate[4])	270.0	20.2	63.1	5.7	25.2	14.9

Note: Data as of 2013 unless noted; (1) Local data covers Montgomery County; (2) Data as of 2012 and includes all active, non-federal physicians; (3) Doctor of Osteopathic Medicine; (4) rate per 100,000 population
Source: U.S. Department of Health and Human Services, Health Resources and Services Administration, Bureau of Health Professions, Area Resource File (ARF) 2013-2014

EDUCATION

Public School District Statistics

District Name	Schls	Pupils	Pupil/ Teacher Ratio	Minority Pupils[1] (%)	Free Lunch Eligible[2] (%)	IEP[3] (%)
Montgomery County	37	30,622	15.2	42.5	38.3	13.1

Note: Table includes school districts with 2,000 or more students; (1) Percentage of students that are not non-Hispanic white; (2) Percentage of students that are eligible for the free lunch program; (3) Percentage of students that have an Individualized Education Program.
Source: U.S. Department of Education, National Center for Education Statistics, Common Core of Data, Local Education Agency (School District) Universe Survey: School Year 2012-2013; U.S. Department of Education, National Center for Education Statistics, Common Core of Data, Public Elementary/Secondary School Universe Survey: School Year 2012-2013

Highest Level of Education

Area	Less than H.S.	H.S. Diploma	Some College, No Deg.	Associate Degree	Bachelor's Degree	Master's Degree	Prof. School Degree	Doctorate Degree
City	8.6	29.0	28.9	9.4	16.6	6.0	0.8	0.8
MSA[1]	11.4	31.2	26.9	8.9	14.7	5.3	1.0	0.6
U.S.	13.7	28.0	21.2	7.9	18.2	7.7	1.9	1.3

Note: Figures cover persons age 25 and over; (1) Figures cover the Clarksville, TN-KY Metropolitan Statistical Area—see Appendix B for areas included
Source: U.S. Census Bureau, 2011-2013 American Community Survey 3-Year Estimates

Educational Attainment by Race

Area	High School Graduate or Higher (%)					Bachelor's Degree or Higher (%)				
	Total	White	Black	Asian	Hisp.[2]	Total	White	Black	Asian	Hisp.[2]
City	91.4	92.9	88.0	84.2	86.2	24.1	26.4	16.6	26.3	18.7
MSA[1]	88.6	89.3	86.2	84.5	81.9	21.6	23.0	14.8	32.5	15.8
U.S.	86.3	88.3	83.1	85.7	64.0	29.1	30.4	18.8	50.7	13.7

Note: Figures shown cover persons 25 years old and over; (1) Figures cover the Clarksville, TN-KY Metropolitan Statistical Area—see Appendix B for areas included; (2) People of Hispanic origin can be of any race
Source: U.S. Census Bureau, 2011-2013 American Community Survey 3-Year Estimates

School Enrollment by Grade and Control

Area	Preschool (%)		Kindergarten (%)		Grades 1 - 4 (%)		Grades 5 - 8 (%)		Grades 9 - 12 (%)	
	Public	Private	Public	Private	Public	Private	Public	Private	Public	Private
City	67.0	33.0	96.4	3.6	94.5	5.5	94.8	5.2	90.8	9.2
MSA[1]	71.4	28.6	94.8	5.2	90.8	9.2	92.3	7.7	90.2	9.8
U.S.	57.7	42.3	87.9	12.1	89.9	10.1	90.0	10.0	90.7	9.3

Note: Figures shown cover persons 3 years old and over; (1) Figures cover the Clarksville, TN-KY Metropolitan Statistical Area—see Appendix B for areas included
Source: U.S. Census Bureau, 2011-2013 American Community Survey 3-Year Estimates

Average Salaries of Public School Classroom Teachers

Area	2013-14		2014-15		Percent Change 2013-14 to 2014-15	Percent Change 2004-05 to 2014-15
	Dollars	Rank[1]	Dollars	Rank[1]		
TENNESSEE	47,742	40	48,503	39	1.59	15.3
U.S. Average	56,610	–	57,379	–	1.36	20.8

Note: (1) State rank ranges from 1 to 51 where 1 indicates highest salary.
Source: National Education Association, Rankings & Estimates: Rankings of the States 2014 and Estimates of School Statistics 2015, March 2015

Higher Education

Four-Year Colleges			Two-Year Colleges			Medical Schools[1]	Law Schools[2]	Voc/ Tech[3]
Public	Private Non-profit	Private For-profit	Public	Private Non-profit	Private For-profit			
1	0	1	0	0	2	0	0	1

Note: Figures cover institutions located within the city limits and include main campuses only; (1) includes schools accredited by the Liaison Committee on Medical Education and the American Osteopathic Association's Commission on Osteopathic College Accreditation; (2) includes ABA-accredited schools, schools with provisional ABA accreditation, and state accredited schools; (3) includes all schools with programs that are less than 2 years.

Source: National Center for Education Statistics, Integrated Postsecondary Education System (IPEDS), 2013-14; Association of American Medical Colleges, Member List, May 1, 2015; American Osteopathic Association, Member List, May 1, 2015; Law School Admission Council, Official Guide to ABA-Approved Law Schools Online, May 1, 2015; Wikipedia, List of Medical Schools in the United States, May 1, 2015; Wikipedia, List of Law Schools in the United States, May 1, 2015

PRESIDENTIAL ELECTION

2012 Presidential Election Results

Area	Obama (%)	Romney (%)	Other (%)
Montgomery County	44.0	54.5	1.5
U.S.	51.0	47.2	1.8

Note: Results may not add to 100% due to rounding
Source: Dave Leip's Atlas of U.S. Presidential Elections

EMPLOYERS

Major Employers

Company Name	Industry
ABMA	Motor vehicle brake systems and parts
Army & Air Force Exchange Service	Army-navy goods stores
AT&T Corp.	Engineering services
Austin Peay State University	University
Bridgestone Metalpha U.S.A.	Steel tire cords and tire cord fabrics
Flynn Enterprises	Dungarees: men's, youths', and boys'
Gateway Health System	General medical and surgical hospitals
Jennie Stuart Medical Center	General medical and surgical hospitals
Jostens	Rings, finger: precious metal
Martinrea Industries	Body parts, automobile: stamped metal
Metalsa, S.A. De C.V.	Motor vehicle parts and accessories
TG Automotive Sealing Kentucky	Automotive stampings
The Army, United States Department of	General medical and surgical hospitals
The Army, United States Department of	Army
Trigg County Board of Education	Elementary and secondary schools
Wal-Mart Stores	Department stores, discount

Note: Companies shown are located within the Clarksville, TN-KY Metropolitan Statistical Area.
Source: Hoovers.com; Wikipedia

PUBLIC SAFETY

Crime Rate

Area	All Crimes	Violent Crimes				Property Crimes		
		Murder	Forcible Rape	Robbery	Aggrav. Assault	Burglary	Larceny -Theft	Motor Vehicle Theft
City	3,357.9	4.1	57.7	79.0	372.9	700.6	2,036.4	107.1
Suburbs[1]	2,365.5	6.0	36.8	36.8	132.0	602.3	1,460.3	91.5
Metro[2]	2,883.5	5.0	47.7	58.8	257.8	653.6	1,761.0	99.7
U.S.	3,098.6	4.5	25.2	109.1	229.1	610.0	1,899.4	221.3

Note: Figures are crimes per 100,000 population; (1) All areas within the metro area that are located outside the city limits; (2) Figures cover the Clarksville, TN-KY Metropolitan Statistical Area—see Appendix B for areas included
Source: FBI Uniform Crime Reports, 2013

Hate Crimes

Area	Number of Quarters Reported	Number of Incidents per Bias Motivation						
		Race	Religion	Sexual Orientation	Ethnicity	Disability	Gender	Gender Identity
City	4	0	0	5	6	0	0	0
U.S.	4	2,871	1,031	1,233	655	83	18	31

Source: Federal Bureau of Investigation, Hate Crime Statistics 2013

Identity Theft Consumer Complaints

Area	Complaints	Complaints per 100,000 Population	Rank[2]
MSA[1]	172	63.1	234
U.S.	332,646	104.3	-

Note: (1) Figures cover the Clarksville, TN-KY Metropolitan Statistical Area—see Appendix B for areas included; (2) Rank ranges from 1 to 380 where 1 indicates greatest number of identity theft complaints per 100,000 population
Source: Federal Trade Commission, Consumer Sentinel Network Data Book for January–December 2014

Fraud and Other Consumer Complaints

Area	Complaints	Complaints per 100,000 Population	Rank[2]
MSA[1]	1,116	409.4	123
U.S.	2,250,205	705.7	-

Note: (1) Figures cover the Clarksville, TN-KY Metropolitan Statistical Area—see Appendix B for areas included; (2) Rank ranges from 1 to 380 where 1 indicates greatest number of identity theft complaints per 100,000 population
Source: Federal Trade Commission, Consumer Sentinel Network Data Book for January–December 2014

RECREATION

Culture

Dance[1]	Theatre[1]	Instrumental Music[1]	Vocal Music[1]	Series and Festivals	Museums and Art Galleries[2]	Zoos and Aquariums[3]
0	1	0	0	1	3	0

Note: (1) Professional perfoming groups; (2) Based on organizations with SIC code 8412; (3) AZA-accredited
Source: The Grey House Performing Arts Directory, 2015-16; Association of Zoos & Aquariums, AZA Member Zoos & Aquariums, April 2015; www.AccuLeads.com, April 2015

Professional Sports Teams

Team Name	League	Year Established
No teams are located in the metro area		

Source: Wikipedia, Major Professional Sports Teams of the United States and Canada, April 2015

CLIMATE

Average and Extreme Temperatures

Temperature	Jan	Feb	Mar	Apr	May	Jun	Jul	Aug	Sep	Oct	Nov	Dec	Yr.
Extreme High (°F)	78	84	86	91	95	106	107	104	105	94	84	79	107
Average High (°F)	47	51	60	71	79	87	90	89	83	72	60	50	70
Average Temp. (°F)	38	41	50	60	68	76	80	79	72	61	49	41	60
Average Low (°F)	28	31	39	48	57	65	69	68	61	48	39	31	49
Extreme Low (°F)	-17	-13	2	23	34	42	54	49	36	26	-1	-10	-17

Note: Figures cover the years 1948-1990
Source: National Climatic Data Center, International Station Meteorological Climate Summary, 9/96

Average Precipitation/Snowfall/Humidity

Precip./Humidity	Jan	Feb	Mar	Apr	May	Jun	Jul	Aug	Sep	Oct	Nov	Dec	Yr.
Avg. Precip. (in.)	4.4	4.2	5.0	4.1	4.6	3.7	3.8	3.3	3.2	2.6	3.9	4.6	47.4
Avg. Snowfall (in.)	4	3	1	Tr	0	0	0	0	0	Tr	1	1	11
Avg. Rel. Hum. 6am (%)	81	81	80	81	86	86	88	90	90	87	83	82	85
Avg. Rel. Hum. 3pm (%)	61	57	51	48	52	52	54	53	52	49	55	59	54

Note: Figures cover the years 1948-1990; Tr = Trace amounts (<0.05 in. of rain; <0.5 in. of snow)
Source: National Climatic Data Center, International Station Meteorological Climate Summary, 9/96

Weather Conditions

Temperature			Daytime Sky			Precipitation		
10°F & below	32°F & below	90°F & above	Clear	Partly cloudy	Cloudy	0.01 inch or more precip.	0.1 inch or more snow/ice	Thunder-storms
5	76	51	98	135	132	119	8	54

Note: Figures are average number of days per year and cover the years 1948-1990
Source: National Climatic Data Center, International Station Meteorological Climate Summary, 9/96

HAZARDOUS WASTE

Superfund Sites

Clarksville has no sites on the EPA's Superfund Final National Priorities List. There are a total of 1,322 Superfund sites on the list in the U.S. *U.S. Environmental Protection Agency, Final National Priorities List, April 14, 2015*

AIR & WATER QUALITY

Air Quality Trends: Ozone

	2004	2005	2006	2007	2008	2009	2010	2011	2012	2013
MSA[1]	n/a	n/a	n/a	n/a	n/a	n/a	n/a	n/a	n/a	n/a

Note: (1) Data covers the Clarksville, TN-KY Metropolitan Statistical Area—see Appendix B for areas included; n/a not available. The values shown are the composite ozone concentration averages among trend sites based on the highest fourth daily maximum 8-hour concentration in parts per million. These trends are based on sites having an adequate record of monitoring data during the trend period. Data from exceptional events are included.
Source: U.S. Environmental Protection Agency, Air Quality Monitoring Information, "Air Quality Trends by City, 2000-2013"

Air Quality Index

Area	Percent of Days when Air Quality was...[2]					AQI Statistics[2]	
	Good	Moderate	Unhealthy for Sensitive Groups	Unhealthy	Very Unhealthy	Maximum	Median
MSA[1]	75.1	24.9	0.0	0.0	0.0	87	42

Note: (1) Data covers the Clarksville, TN-KY Metropolitan Statistical Area—see Appendix B for areas included; (2) Based on 365 days with AQI data in 2014. Air Quality Index (AQI) is an index for reporting daily air quality. EPA calculates the AQI for five major air pollutants regulated by the Clean Air Act: ground-level ozone, particle pollution (aka particulate matter), carbon monoxide, sulfur dioxide, and nitrogen dioxide. The AQI runs from 0 to 500. The higher the AQI value, the greater the level of air pollution and the greater the health concern. There are six AQI categories: "Good" AQI is between 0 and 50. Air quality is considered satisfactory; "Moderate" AQI is between 51 and 100. Air quality is acceptable; "Unhealthy for Sensitive Groups" When AQI values are between 101 and 150, members of sensitive groups may experience health effects; "Unhealthy" When AQI values are between 151 and 200 everyone may begin to experience health effects; "Very Unhealthy" AQI values between 201 and 300 trigger a health alert; "Hazardous" AQI values over 300 trigger warnings of emergency conditions (not shown).
Source: U.S. Environmental Protection Agency, Air Quality Index Report, 2014

Air Quality Index Pollutants

Area	Percent of Days when AQI Pollutant was...[2]					
	Carbon Monoxide	Nitrogen Dioxide	Ozone	Sulfur Dioxide	Particulate Matter 2.5	Particulate Matter 10
MSA[1]	0.0	0.0	48.2	2.2	49.6	0.0

Note: (1) Data covers the Clarksville, TN-KY Metropolitan Statistical Area—see Appendix B for areas included; (2) Based on 365 days with AQI data in 2014. The Air Quality Index (AQI) is an index for reporting daily air quality. EPA calculates the AQI for five major air pollutants regulated by the Clean Air Act: ground-level ozone, particle pollution (also known as particulate matter), carbon monoxide, sulfur dioxide, and nitrogen dioxide. The AQI runs from 0 to 500. The higher the AQI value, the greater the level of air pollution and the greater the health concern.
Source: U.S. Environmental Protection Agency, Air Quality Index Report, 2014

Maximum Air Pollutant Concentrations: Particulate Matter, Ozone, CO and Lead

	Particulate Matter 10 (ug/m^3)	Particulate Matter 2.5 Wtd AM (ug/m^3)	Particulate Matter 2.5 24-Hr (ug/m^3)	Ozone (ppm)	Carbon Monoxide (ppm)	Lead (ug/m^3)
MSA[1] Level	26	9.8	22	0.064	n/a	n/a
NAAQS[2]	150	15	35	0.075	9	0.15
Met NAAQS[2]	Yes	Yes	Yes	Yes	n/a	n/a

Note: (1) Data covers the Clarksville, TN-KY Metropolitan Statistical Area—see Appendix B for areas included; Data from exceptional events are included; (2) National Ambient Air Quality Standards; ppm = parts per million; ug/m^3 = micrograms per cubic meter; n/a not available.

Concentrations: Particulate Matter 10 (coarse particulate)—highest second maximum 24-hour concentration; Particulate Matter 2.5 Wtd AM (fine particulate)—highest weighted annual mean concentration; Particulate Matter 2.5 24-Hour (fine particulate)—highest 98th percentile 24-hour concentration; Ozone—highest fourth daily maximum 8-hour concentration; Carbon Monoxide—highest second maximum non-overlapping 8-hour concentration; Lead—maximum running 3-month average

Source: U.S. Environmental Protection Agency, Air Quality Monitoring Information, "Air Quality Statistics by City, 2013"

Maximum Air Pollutant Concentrations: Nitrogen Dioxide and Sulfur Dioxide

	Nitrogen Dioxide AM (ppb)	Nitrogen Dioxide 1-Hr (ppb)	Sulfur Dioxide AM (ppb)	Sulfur Dioxide 1-Hr (ppb)	Sulfur Dioxide 24-Hr (ppb)
MSA[1] Level	n/a	n/a	n/a	28	n/a
NAAQS[2]	53	100	30	75	140
Met NAAQS[2]	n/a	n/a	n/a	Yes	n/a

Note: (1) Data covers the Clarksville, TN-KY Metropolitan Statistical Area—see Appendix B for areas included; Data from exceptional events are included; (2) National Ambient Air Quality Standards; ppm = parts per million; ug/m^3 = micrograms per cubic meter; n/a not available.

Concentrations: Nitrogen Dioxide AM—highest arithmetic mean concentration; Nitrogen Dioxide 1-Hr—highest 98th percentile 1-hour daily maximum concentration; Sulfur Dioxide AM—highest annual mean concentration; Sulfur Dioxide 1-Hr—highest 99th percentile 1-hour daily maximum concentration; Sulfur Dioxide 24-Hr—highest second maximum 24-hour concentration

Source: U.S. Environmental Protection Agency, Air Quality Monitoring Information, "Air Quality Statistics by City, 2013"

Drinking Water

Water System Name	Pop. Served	Primary Water Source Type	Violations[1]	
			Health Based	Monitoring/ Reporting
Clarksville Water Department	174,740	Surface	0	0

Note: (1) Based on violation data from January 1, 2014 to December 31, 2014 (includes unresolved violations from earlier years)

Source: U.S. Environmental Protection Agency, Office of Ground Water and Drinking Water, Safe Drinking Water Information System (based on data extracted January 27, 2015)

Dallas, Texas

Background

Dallas is one of those cities that offer everything. Founded in 1841 by Tennessee lawyer and trader, John Neely Bryan, Dallas has come to symbolize in modern times all that is big, exciting, and affluent. The city itself is home to 15 billionaires, placing it ninth worldwide among cities with the most billionaires. When combined with the eight billionaires who live in Dallas's neighboring city of Fort Worth, the area has one of the greatest concentrations of billionaires in the world.

Originally one of the largest markets for cotton in the U.S., Dallas moved on to become one of the largest markets for oil in the country. In the 1930s, oil was struck on the eastern fields of Texas. As a result, oil companies were founded and millionaires were made. The face we now associate with Dallas and the state of Texas had emerged.

Today, oil still plays a dominant role in the Dallas economy. Outside of Alaska, Texas holds most of the U.S. oil reserves. For that reason, many oil companies choose to headquarter in the silver skyscrapers of Dallas.

In addition to employment opportunities in the oil industry, the Dallas branch of the Federal Reserve Bank, and a host of other banks and investment firms clustering around the Federal Reserve hub employ thousands. Other opportunities are offered in the aircraft, advertising, motion picture, and publishing industries.

Major employers in the Dallas area include American Airlines (Dallas-Fort Worth Airport); Lockheed Martin (in nearby Fort Worth); University of North Texas in Denton; Parkland Memorial Hospital; and Baylor University Medical center. Vought Aircraft Industries, a major supplier of aircraft components to Boeing, Sikorsky and other aircraft manufacturers, continues to expand its local operations. The city is sometimes referred to as Texas's "Silicon Prairie" because of a high concentration of telecommunications companies.

The Dallas Convention Center, with more than two million square feet of space, is the largest convention center in Texas with more than 1 million square feet of exhibit area, including nearly 800,000 square feet of same level, contiguous prime exhibit space with more than 3.8 million people attending more than 3,600 conventions and spending more than $4.2 billion annually.

Dallas also is busy culturally. A host of independent theater groups is sponsored by Southern Methodist University. The Museum of Art houses an excellent collection of modern art, especially American paintings. The Winspear Opera House, along with 3 other venues that make up the AT&T Performing Arts Center was dedicated in 2009. The Dallas Opera has showcased Maria Callas, Joan Sutherland, and Monserrat Caballe. The city also contains many historical districts such as the Swiss Avenue District, and elegant buildings such as the City Hall Building designed by I.M. Pei. The most notable event held in Dallas is the State Fair of Texas, which has been held annually at Fair Park since 1886. The fair is a massive event for the state of Texas and brings an estimated $350 million to the city's economy annually.

The area's high concentration of wealth undoubtedly contributes to Dallas's wide array of shopping centers and high-end boutiques. Downtown Dallas is home to many cafes, restaurants and clubs. The city's centrally located "Arts District" is appropriately named for the independent theaters and art galleries located in the neighborhood. While northern districts of the city and the central downtown have seen much urban revival in the last 30 years, neighborhoods south of downtown have not experienced the same growth.

Colleges and universities in the Dallas area include Southern Methodist University, University of Dallas, and University of Texas at Dallas. In 2006, University of North Texas opened a branch in the southern part of the city, in part, to help accelerate development south of downtown Dallas.

The city maintains around 21,000 acres of park land, with over 400 parks.

The climate of Dallas is generally temperate. Occasional periods of extreme cold are short-lived, and extremely high temperatures that sometimes occur in summer usually do not last for extended periods.

Rankings

General Rankings

- The Dallas metro area was identified as one of America's fastest-growing areas in terms of population and economy by *Forbes*. The area ranked #3 out of 20. The 100 most populous metro areas in the U.S. were evaluated on the following criteria: estimated population growth; job growth; gross metropolitan product growth; unemployment; median salaries for college-educated workers. *Forbes, "America's Fastest-Growing Cities 2015," January 27, 2015*
- Dallas was selected as one of America's best cities by *Bloomberg Businessweek*. The city ranked #41 out of 50. Criteria: leisure attributes (the number of restaurants, bars, libraries, museums, professional sports teams, and park acres by population); educational attributes (public school performance, the number of colleges, and graduate degree holders); economic factors (2011 income and June and July 2012 unemployment); crime; and air quality. *Bloomberg BusinessWeek, "America's Best Cities," September 26, 2012*
- The human resources consulting firm Mercer ranked 230 cities worldwide in terms of overall quality of life. Dallas ranked #62. Criteria: political, social, economic, and socio-cultural factors; medical and health considerations; schools and education; public services and transportation; recreation; consumer goods; housing; and natural environment. *Mercer, "Mercer 2015 Quality of Living Survey," March 4, 2015*

Business/Finance Rankings

- The finance website Wall St. Cheat Sheet reported on the prospects for high-wage job creation in the nation's largest metro areas over the next five years and ranked them accordingly, drawing on in-depth analysis by CareerBuilder and Economic Modeling Specialists International (EMSI). The Dallas metro area placed #9 on the Wall St. Cheat Sheet list. *wallstcheatsheet.com, "Top 10 Cities for High-Wage Job Growth," December 8, 2013*
- Based on metro area social media reviews, the employment opinion group Glassdoor surveyed 50 of the largest U.S. metro areas on measures including compensation and benefits, satisfaction with management, business outlook, and number of employers hiring. The Dallas metro area was ranked #23 in overall employee satisfaction. *www.glassdoor.com, "Employment Satisfaction Report Card by City," June 13, 2014*
- In its Competitive Alternatives report, consulting firm KPMG analyzed the 27 largest metropolitan statistical areas according to 26 cost components (such as taxes, labor costs, and utilities) and 30 non-cost-related variables (such as crime rates and number of universities). The business website 24/7 Wall Street examined the KPMG findings, adding to the mix current unemployment rates, GDP, median income, and employment decline during the last recession and "projected" recovery. It identified the Dallas metro area as #5 among the ten best American cities for business. *247wallst.com, "Best American Cities for Business," April 4, 2012*
- In a survey of economic confidence in the nation's 50 largest metropolitan areas conducted January–December 2014, the Dallas metro area placed #14, according to Gallup's 2014 Economic Confidence Index. *Gallup, "San Jose and San Francisco Lead in Economic Confidence," March 19, 2015*
- The Brookings Institution ranked the 50 largest cities in the U.S. based on income inequality. Dallas was ranked #7. (#1 = greatest ineqality). Criteria: the cities were ranked based on the "95/20 ratio," a figure representing the income at which a household earns more than 95 percent of all other households, divided by the income at which a household earns more than only 20 percent of all other households. *Brookings Institution, "Income Inequality in America's 50 Largest Cities, 2007-2013," March 17, 2015*
- CareerBliss, an employment and careers website, analyzed U.S. Bureau of Labor Statistics data, more than 30,000 company reviews from employees and former employees, and job openings over a 12-month period to arrive at its list of the best and worst places in the United States to look for a job. Dallas was #10 among the best places. *CareerBliss.com, "CareerBliss 2013 Best and Worst Cities to Find a Job," January 8, 2013*

- Dallas was ranked #20 out of 100 metro areas in terms of economic performance (#1 = best) during the recession and recovery from trough quarter through the second quarter of 2013. Criteria: percent change in employment; percentage point change in unemployment rate; percent change in gross metropolitan product; percent change in House Price Index. *Brookings Institution, MetroMonitor: Tracking Economic Recession and Recovery in America's 100 Largest Metropolitan Areas, September 2013*

- Payscale.com ranked the 20 largest metro areas in terms of wage growth. The Dallas metro area ranked #8. Criteria: private-sector wage growth between the 1st quarter of 2014 and the 1st quarter of 2015. *PayScale, "Wage Trends by Metro Area," 1st Quarter, 2015*

- The Dallas metro area was identified as one of the most debt-ridden places in America by the finance site Credit.com. The metro area was ranked #1. Criteria: residents' average personal debt load and average credit scores. *Credit.com, "The Most Debt-Ridden Cities," May 1, 2014*

- Dallas was identified as one of America's most frugal metro areas by *Coupons.com.* The city ranked #19 out of 25. Criteria: online coupon usage. *Coupons.com, "Top 25 Most Frugal Cities of 2013," April 10, 2014*

- Dallas was identified as one of America's most frugal metro areas by *Coupons.com.* The city ranked #11 out of 25. Criteria: Grocery IQ and coupons.com mobile app usage. *Coupons.com, "Top 25 Most On-the-Go Frugal Cities of 2013," April 10, 2014*

- Dallas was identified as one of "America's Hardest-Working Towns." The city ranked #25 out of 25. Criteria: average hours worked per capita; willingness to work during personal time; number of dual income households; local employment rate. *Parade, "What is America's Hardest-Working Town?," April 15, 2012*

- Dallas was cited as one of America's top metros for new and expanded facility projects in 2014. The area ranked #5 in the large metro area category (population over 1 million). *Site Selection, "Top Metros of 2014," March 2015*

- Dallas was identified as one of the best cities for college graduates to find work—and live. The city ranked #5 out of 15. Criteria: job availability; average salary; average rent. *CareerBuilder.com, "15 Best Cities for College Grads to Find Work—and Live," June 5, 2012*

- The Dallas metro area appeared on the Milken Institute "2013 Best Performing Cities" list. Rank: #9 out of 200 large metro areas. Criteria: job growth; wage and salary growth; high-tech output growth. *Milken Institute, "Best-Performing Cities 2014," January 2015*

- *Forbes* ranked the 200 most populous metro areas to determine the nation's "Best Places for Business and Careers." The Dallas metro area was ranked #13. Criteria: costs (business and living); job growth (past and projected); income growth; educational attainment (college and high school); projected economic growth; cultural and recreational opportunities; net migration patterns; number of highly ranked colleges. *Forbes, "The Best Places for Business and Careers 2014," July 23, 2014*

- Mercer Human Resources Consulting ranked 211 urban areas worldwide in terms of cost-of-living. Dallas ranked #125 (the lower the ranking, the higher the cost-of-living). The survey measured the comparative cost of over 200 items (such as housing, food, clothing, household goods, transportation, and entertainment) in each location.*Mercer, "2014 Cost of Living Survey," July 10, 2014*

Children/Family Rankings

- Dallas was selected as one of the best cities for families to live by *Parenting* magazine. The city ranked #4 out of 100. Criteria: education ratings; FBI crime statistics, Bureau of Labor statistics, U.S. Census data. *Parenting.com, " Top Ten Best Cities for Families 2014"*

Culture/Performing Arts Rankings

- Dallas was selected as one of America's top cities for the arts. The city ranked #19 in the big city (population 500,000 and over) category. Criteria: readers' top choices for arts travel destinations based on the richness and variety of visual arts sites, activities and events. *American Style, "2012 Top 25 Arts Destinations," June 2012*

Dating/Romance Rankings

- A *Cosmopolitan* magazine article surveyed the gender balance and other factors to arrive at a list of the best and worst cities for women to meet single guys. Dallas was #6 among the best for single women looking for dates. *www.cosmopolitan.com, "Working the Ratio," October 1, 2013*
- *Forbes* reports that the Dallas metro area made Rent.com's Best Cities for Newlyweds survey for 2013, based on Bureau of Labor Statistics and Census Bureau data on number of married couples, percentage of families with children under age six, average annual income, cost of living, and availability of rentals. *www.forbes.com, "The 10 Best Cities for Newlyweds to Live and Work In," May 30, 2013*
- Of the 100 U.S. cities surveyed by *Men's Health* in its quest to identify the nation's best cities for dating and forming relationships, Dallas was ranked #18 for online dating (#1 = best). *Men's Health, "The Best and Worst Cities for Online Dating," January 30, 2013*
- Dallas was selected as one of America's best cities for singles by the readers of *Travel + Leisure* in their annual "America's Favorite Cities" survey. The city was ranked #14 out of 20. Criteria included good-looking locals, cool shopping, and hipster-magnet coffee bars. *Travel + Leisure, "America's Best Cities for Singles," January 23, 2015*
- Dallas was selected as one of the best cities for newlyweds by *Rent.com*. The city ranked #3 of 10. Criteria: cost of living; availability of rental inventory; annual mean wages; percentage of married couples; percentage of children under the age of six. *Rent.com, "10 Best Cities for Newlyweds," May 10, 2013*

Education Rankings

- Personal finance website *WalletHub* analyzed the 150 largest U.S. metropolitan statistical areas to determine where the most educated Americans are choosing to settle. Criteria: educational attainment; percentage of workers with jobs in computer, engineering, and science fields; quality and size of each metro area's universities. Dallas was ranked #80 (#1 = most educated city). *www.WalletHub.com, "2014's Most and Least Educated Cities*
- Dallas was selected as one of America's most literate cities. The city ranked #44 out of the 77 largest U.S. cities. Criteria: number of booksellers; library resources; Internet resources; educational attainment; periodical publishing resources; newspaper circulation. *Central Connecticut State University, "America's Most Literate Cities, 2014," April 8, 2015*

Environmental Rankings

- The Dallas metro area came in at #350 for the relative comfort of its climate on Sperling's list of "chill cities," as measured by the Sperling Heat Index. All 361 metro areas are included. Criteria included daytime high temperatures, nighttime low temperatures, dew point, and relative humidity at the high temperatures. *www.bertsperling.com, "Sperling's Chill Cities," July 18, 2013*
- Sperling's BestPlaces assessed 379 metropolitan areas of the United States for the likelihood of dangerously extreme weather events or earthquakes. In general the Southeast and South-Central regions have the highest risk of weather extremes and earthquakes, while the Pacific Northwest enjoys the lowest risk. Of the least risky metropolitan areas, the Dallas metro area was ranked #379. *www.bestplaces.net, "Safest Places from Natural Disasters," April 2011*
- The U.S. Environmental Protection Agency (EPA) released a list of large U.S. metropolitan areas with the most ENERGY STAR certified buildings in 2014. The Dallas metro area was ranked #7 out of 25. *U.S. Environmental Protection Agency, "Top Cities With the Most ENERGY STAR Certified Buildings in 2014," March 25, 2015*
- Dallas was highlighted as one of the 25 most ozone-polluted metro areas in the U.S. during 2011 through 2013. The area ranked #7. *American Lung Association, State of the Air 2015*

Food/Drink Rankings

- *Men's Health* ranked 100 major U.S. cities in terms of alcohol intoxication. Dallas ranked #16 (#1 = most sober).Criteria: binge drinking; alcohol-related traffic accidents, arrests, and fatalities. *Men's Health, "The Drunkest Cities in America," November 19, 2013*
- Dallas was identified as one of the most vegetarian-friendly cities in America by GrubHub.com, the nation's largest food ordering service. The city ranked #5 out of 10. Criteria: percentage of vegetarian restaurants. *GrubHub.com, "Top Vegetarian-Friendly Cities," July 18, 2012*

Health/Fitness Rankings

- For each of the 50 most populous metro areas in the United States, the American College of Sports Medicine's American Fitness Index evaluated infrastructure, community assets, and policies that encourage healthy and fit lifestyles, including preventive health behaviors, levels of chronic disease conditions, health care access, and community resources and policies that support physical activity. The Dallas metro area ranked #44 for "community fitness." Personal health indicators were considered as well as community and environmental indicators. *www.americanfitnessindex.org, "ACSM American Fitness Index Health and Community Fitness Status of the 50 Largest Metropolitan Areas," May 2013*
- The Dallas metro area was identified as one of the worst cities for bed bugs in America by pest control company Orkin. The area ranked #13 out of 50 based on the number of bed bug treatments Orkin performed from January to December 2013. *Orkin, "Chicago Tops Bed Bug Cities List for Second Year in a Row," January 16, 2014*
- Dallas was identified as one of 15 cities with the highest increase in bed bug activity in the U.S. by pest control provider Terminix. The city ranked #13.Criteria: cities with the largest percentage gains in bed bug customer calls from January–May 2013 compared to the same time period in 2012. *Terminix, "Cities with Highest Increases in Bed Bug Activity," July 9, 2013*
- Dallas was selected as one of the 25 fattest cities in America by *Men's Fitness Online*. It ranked #25 out of America's 50 largest cities. Criteria: fitness centers and sport stores; nutrition; sports participation; TV viewing; overweight/sedentary; junk food; air quality; geography; commute; parks and open space; city recreational facilities; access to healthcare; motivation; mayor and city initiatives; state obesity initiatives. *Men's Fitness, "The Fittest and Fattest Cities in America," March 5, 2012*
- Dallas was identified as a "2013 Spring Allergy Capital." The area ranked #23 out of 100. Three groups of factors were used to identify the most severe cities for people with allergies during the spring season: annual pollen levels; medicine utilization; access to board-certified allergists. *Asthma and Allergy Foundation of America, "Spring Allergy Capitals 2013"*
- Dallas was identified as a "2013 Fall Allergy Capital." The area ranked #18 out of 100. Three groups of factors were used to identify the most severe cities for people with allergies during the fall season: annual pollen levels; medicine utilization; access to board-certified allergists. *Asthma and Allergy Foundation of America, "Fall Allergy Capitals 2013"*
- Dallas was identified as a "2013 Asthma Capital." The area ranked #49 out of the nation's 100 largest metropolitan areas. Twelve factors were used to identify the most challenging places to live for people with asthma: estimated prevalence; self-reported prevalence; crude death rate for asthma; annual pollen score; annual air quality; public smoking laws; number of board-certified asthma specialists; school inhaler access laws; rescue medication use; controller medication use; uninsured rate; poverty rate. *Asthma and Allergy Foundation of America, "Asthma Capitals 2013"*
- *Men's Health* ranked 100 major U.S. cities in terms of the best and worst cities for men. Dallas ranked #50. Criteria: thirty-three data points were examined covering health, fitness, and quality of life. *Men's Health, "The Best & Worst Cities for Men 2014," December 6, 2013*

- The Dallas metro area appeared in the 2013 Gallup-Healthways Well-Being Index. The area ranked #54 out of 189. The Gallup-Healthways Well-Being Index score is an average of six sub-indexes, which individually examine life evaluation, emotional health, work environment, physical health, healthy behaviors, and access to basic necessities. Results are based on telephone interviews conducted as part of the Gallup-Healthways Well-Being Index survey January 2–December 29, 2012, and January 2–December 30, 2013, with a random sample of 531,630 adults, aged 18 and older, living in metropolitan areas in the 50 U.S. states and the District of Columbia. *Gallup-Healthways, "State of American Well-Being," March 25, 2014*

- The Dallas metro area was identified as one of "America's Most Stressful Cities" by *Sperling's BestPlaces*. The metro area ranked #43 out of 50. Criteria: unemployment rate; suicide rate; commute time; mental health; poor rest; alcohol use; violent crime rate; property crime rate; cloudy days annually. *Sperling's BestPlaces, www.BestPlaces.net, "Stressful Cities 2012*

Real Estate Rankings

- On the list compiled by Penske Truck Rental, the Dallas metro area was named the #3 moving destination in 2014, based on one-way consumer truck rental reservations made through Penske's website and reservations call center. *blog.gopenske.com, "Penske Truck Rental's 2014 Top Moving Destinations List," February 4, 2015*

- The Dallas metro area appeared on Realtor.com's list of the hottest housing markets to watch in 2015. Criteria: strong housing growth; affordable prices; and fast-paced sales. *Realtor.com®, "Top 10 Hot Housing Markets to Watch in 2015," December 4, 2014*

- The Dallas metro area was identified as one of the nation's 20 hottest housing markets in 2015.Criteria: median number of days homes were spending on the market in March 2015. The area ranked #15. *Realtor.com, "These Are the 20 Hottest Housing Markets in the U.S. Right Now," April 8, 2015*

- The Dallas metro area was identified as one of the top 20 housing markets to invest in for 2015 by *Forbes*. The area ranked #5. Criteria: strong population and job growth; relatively low home prices which are below equilibrium home price (EHP). The EHP is what the average price for a market should be, if speculation, weird distortions in local income, and other factors (like the housing collapse) weren't present in the market. *Forbes.com, "Best Buy Cities: Where to Invest in Housing in 2015," January 9, 2015*

- Dallas was ranked #32 out of 275 metro areas in terms of house price appreciation in 2014 (#1 = highest rate). *Federal Housing Finance Agency, House Price Index, 4th Quarter 2014*

- The Dallas metro area was identified as one of the 10 worst condo markets in the U.S. in 2014. The area ranked #7 out of 66 markets with a price appreciation of -2.2%. Criteria: year-over-year change of median sales price of existing apartment condo-coop homes between the 4th quarter of 2013 and the 4th quarter of 2014. *National Association of Realtors®, Median Sales Price of Existing Apartment Condo-Coop Homes for Metropolitan Areas, 4th Quarter 2014*

- Dallas was ranked #182 out of 226 metro areas in terms of housing affordability in 2014 by the National Association of Home Builders (#1 = most affordable). The NAHB-Wells Fargo Housing Opportunity Index (HOI) for a given area is defined as the share of homes sold in that area that would have been affordable to a family earning the local median income, based on standard mortgage underwriting criteria. *National Association of Home Builders®, NAHB-Wells Fargo Housing Opportunity Index, 4th Quarter 2014*

Safety Rankings

- Symantec, in partnership with Sperling's BestPlaces, ranked the 50 largest cities in the U.S. in terms of their vulnerability to cybercrime. The city ranked #15. Criteria: number of cyberattacks and potential infections; level of Internet access; expenditures on smartphones and computer hardware/software; wireless hotspots; broadband connectivity; Internet usage; online purchases. *Symantec, "Riskiest Online Cities of 2012" February 15, 2012*

- Farmers Insurance, in partnership with Sperling's BestPlaces, ranked metro areas in the U.S. and identified the "Most Secure Places to Live." The Dallas metro area ranked #10 out of the top 20 in the large metro area category (500,000 or more residents). Criteria: economic stability; crime statistics; extreme weather; risk of natural disasters; housing depreciation; foreclosures; air quality; environmental hazards; life expectancy; motor vehicle fatalities; and employment numbers. *Farmers Insurance Group of Companies, "Most Secure U.S. Places to Live in the U.S.," June 25, 2013*

- Allstate ranked the 200 largest cities in America in terms of driver safety. Dallas ranked #174. Allstate researchers analyzed internal property damage claims over a two-year period from January 2011 to December 2012. A weighted average of the two-year numbers determined the annual percentages. *Allstate, "Allstate America's Best Drivers Report, 2014"*

- Dallas was identified as one of the most dangerous large cities in America by CQ Press. All 32 cities with populations of 500,000 or more that reported crime rates in 2012 for murder, rape, robbery, aggravated assault, burglary, and motor vehicle thefts were ranked. The city ranked #10 out of the top 10. *CQ Press, City Crime Rankings 2014*

- The National Insurance Crime Bureau ranked 380 metro areas in the U.S. in terms of per capita rates of vehicle theft. The Dallas metro area ranked #70 (#1 = highest rate). Criteria: number of vehicle theft offenses per 100,000 inhabitants in 2012. *National Insurance Crime Bureau, "Hot Spots 2012," June 26, 2013*

Seniors/Retirement Rankings

- From its Best Cities for Successful Aging indexes, the Milken Institute generated rankings for metropolitan areas, weighing data in eight categories—health care, wellness, living arrangements, transportation, financial characteristics, education and employment opportunities, community engagement, and overall livability. The Dallas metro area was ranked #40 overall in the large metro area category. *Milken Institute, "Best Cities for Successful Aging, 2014"*

Sports/Recreation Rankings

- According to the personal finance website NerdWallet, the Dallas metro area, at #1, is one of the nation's top dozen metro areas for sports fans. Criteria included the presence of all four major sports—MLB, NFL, NHL, and NBA, fan enthusiasm (as measured by game attendance), ticket affordability, and "sports culture," that is, number of sports bars. *www.nerdwallet.com, "Best Cities for Sports Fans," May 5, 2013*

- The sports site Bleacher Report named Dallas as one of the nation's top ten golf cities. Criteria included the concentration of public and private golf courses in a given city and the favored locations of PGA tour events. *BleacherReport.com, "Top 10 U.S. Cities for Golf," September 16, 2013*

Women/Minorities Rankings

- To determine the best metro areas for working women, the personal finance website NerdWallet considered city size as well as relevant economic metrics—high salaries, narrow pay differential by gender, prevalence of women in the highest-paying industries, and population growth over 2010–2012. Of the large U.S. cities examined, the Dallas metro area held the #5 position. *www.nerdwallet.com, "Best Places for Women in the Workforce," May 19, 2013*

- *Women's Health* examined U.S. cities and identified the 100 best cities for women. Dallas was ranked #53. Criteria: 30 categories were examined from obesity and breast cancer rates to commuting times and hours spent working out. *Women's Health, "Best Cities for Women 2012"*

- Dallas was selected as one of the best cities for young Latinos in 2013 by mun2, a national cable television broadcast network. The city ranked #8. Criteria: U.S. cities with populations over 500,000 residents were evaluated on the following criteria: number of young latinos; jobs; friendliness; cost of living; fun. *mun2.tv, "Best Cities for Young Latinos 2013*

Miscellaneous Rankings

- The watchdog site Charity Navigator conducts an annual study of charities in the nation's major markets both to analyze statistical differences in their financial, accountability, and transparency practices and to track year-to-year variations in individual communities. The Dallas metro area was ranked #14 among the 30 metro markets. *www.charitynavigator.org, "Metro Market Study 2013," June 1, 2013*

- The Harris Poll's Happiness Index survey revealed that of the top ten U.S. markets, the Dallas metro area residents ranked #1 in happiness. Criteria included strong assent to positive statements and strong disagreement with negative ones, and degree of agreement with a series of statements about respondents' personal relationships and general outlook. The online survey was conducted between July 14 and July 30, 2013. *www.harrisinteractive.com, "Dallas/Fort Worth Is "Happiest" City among America's Top Ten Markets," September 4, 2013*

- Mars Chocolate North America, the makers of COMBOS®, in partnership with Sperling's BestPlaces, ranked 50 major metro areas in terms of their "manliness." The Dallas metro area ranked #15. Criteria: number of professional sports teams; number of nearby NASCAR tracks and racing events; manly lifestyle; concentration of manly retail stores; manly occupations per capita; salty snack sales; "Board of Manliness" rankings. *Mars Chocolate North America, "America's Manliest Cities 2012"*

- The National Alliance to End Homelessness ranked the 100 most populous metro areas in terms the rate of homelessness. The Dallas metro area ranked #87. Criteria: number of homeless people per 10,000 population in 2011. *National Alliance to End Homelessness, The State of Homelessness in America 2012*

Business Environment

CITY FINANCES

City Government Finances

Component	2012 ($000)	2012 ($ per capita)
Total Revenues	2,973,519	2,482
Total Expenditures	3,295,436	2,751
Debt Outstanding	7,943,610	6,632
Cash and Securities[1]	9,674,807	8,077

Note: (1) Cash and security holdings of a government at the close of its fiscal year, including those of its dependent agencies, utilities, and liquor stores.
Source: U.S Census Bureau, State & Local Government Finances 2012

City Government Revenue by Source

Source	2012 ($000)	2012 ($ per capita)
General Revenue		
From Federal Government	68,982	58
From State Government	98,085	82
From Local Governments	5,638	5
Taxes		
Property	677,258	565
Sales and Gross Receipts	370,135	309
Personal Income	0	0
Corporate Income	0	0
Motor Vehicle License	0	0
Other Taxes	36,962	31
Current Charges	1,125,160	939
Liquor Store	0	0
Utility	321,997	269
Employee Retirement	106,738	89

Source: U.S Census Bureau, State & Local Government Finances 2012

City Government Expenditures by Function

Function	2012 ($000)	2012 ($ per capita)	2012 (%)
General Direct Expenditures			
Air Transportation	583,725	487	17.7
Corrections	1,201	1	0.0
Education	0	0	0.0
Employment Security Administration	0	0	0.0
Financial Administration	31,181	26	0.9
Fire Protection	189,559	158	5.8
General Public Buildings	21,778	18	0.7
Governmental Administration, Other	16,303	14	0.5
Health	25,594	21	0.8
Highways	139,428	116	4.2
Hospitals	0	0	0.0
Housing and Community Development	47,280	39	1.4
Interest on General Debt	423,687	354	12.9
Judicial and Legal	23,130	19	0.7
Libraries	30,980	26	0.9
Parking	120	< 1	< 0.1
Parks and Recreation	181,472	152	5.5
Police Protection	355,359	297	10.8
Public Welfare	18,299	15	0.6
Sewerage	227,498	190	6.9
Solid Waste Management	58,950	49	1.8
Veterans' Services	0	0	0.0
Liquor Store	0	0	0.0
Utility	344,373	288	10.4
Employee Retirement	408,045	341	12.4

Source: U.S Census Bureau, State & Local Government Finances 2012

DEMOGRAPHICS

Population Growth

Area	1990 Census	2000 Census	2010 Census	Population Growth (%) 1990-2000	Population Growth (%) 2000-2010
City	1,006,971	1,188,580	1,197,816	18.0	0.8
MSA[1]	3,989,294	5,161,544	6,371,773	29.4	23.4
U.S.	248,709,873	281,421,906	308,745,538	13.2	9.7

Note: (1) Figures cover the Dallas-Fort Worth-Arlington, TX Metropolitan Statistical Area—see Appendix B for areas included
Source: U.S. Census Bureau, Census 1990, 2000, 2010

Household Size

Area	Persons in Household (%) One	Two	Three	Four	Five	Six	Seven or More	Average Household Size
City	34.6	28.4	14.0	11.5	6.6	3.0	2.0	2.62
MSA[1]	25.2	30.8	16.6	15.0	7.5	3.0	1.8	2.80
U.S.	27.7	33.6	15.7	13.1	6.0	2.3	1.5	2.64

Note: (1) Figures cover the Dallas-Fort Worth-Arlington, TX Metropolitan Statistical Area—see Appendix B for areas included
Source: U.S. Census Bureau, 2011-2013 American Community Survey 3-Year Estimates

Race

Area	White Alone[2] (%)	Black Alone[2] (%)	Asian Alone[2] (%)	AIAN[3] Alone[2] (%)	NHOPI[4] Alone[2] (%)	Other Race Alone[2] (%)	Two or More Races (%)
City	58.5	24.6	3.0	0.2	0.0	11.6	2.1
MSA[1]	69.6	15.0	5.6	0.5	0.1	6.5	2.7
U.S.	73.9	12.6	5.0	0.8	0.2	4.7	2.9

Note: (1) Figures cover the Dallas-Fort Worth-Arlington, TX Metropolitan Statistical Area—see Appendix B for areas included; (2) Alone is defined as not being in combination with one or more other races; (3) American Indian and Alaska Native; (4) Native Hawaiian and Other Pacific Islander
Source: U.S. Census Bureau, 2011-2013 American Community Survey 3-Year Estimates

Hispanic or Latino Origin

Area	Total (%)	Mexican (%)	Puerto Rican (%)	Cuban (%)	Other (%)
City	41.8	37.2	0.4	0.2	4.0
MSA[1]	27.8	23.7	0.6	0.2	3.3
U.S.	16.9	10.8	1.6	0.6	3.8

Note: Persons of Hispanic or Latino origin can be of any race; (1) Figures cover the Dallas-Fort Worth-Arlington, TX Metropolitan Statistical Area—see Appendix B for areas included
Source: U.S. Census Bureau, 2011-2013 American Community Survey 3-Year Estimates

Segregation

Type	Segregation Indices[1] 1990	2000	2010	2010 Rank[2]	Percent Change 1990-2000	1990-2010	2000-2010
Black/White	62.8	59.8	56.6	48	-3.1	-6.2	-3.2
Asian/White	41.8	45.6	46.6	19	3.8	4.8	1.0
Hispanic/White	48.8	52.3	50.3	24	3.5	1.5	-2.0

Note: All figures cover the Metropolitan Statistical Area—see Appendix B for areas included; Figures are based on an analysis of 1990, 2000, and 2010 Census Decennial Census tract data by William H. Frey, Brookings Institution and the University of Michigan Social Science Data Analysis Network. In this analysis all racial groups (whites, blacks, and asians) are non-Hispanic members of those races. Hispanics are shown as a separate category;
(1) Segregation Indices are Dissimilarity Indices that measure the degree to which the minority group is distributed differently than whites across census tracts. They range from 0 (complete integration) to 100 (complete segregation) where the value indicates the percentage of the minority group that needs to move to be distributed exactly like whites; (2) Ranges from 1 (most segregated) to 102 (least segregated); n/a not available.
Source: www.CensusScope.org

Ancestry

Area	German	Irish	English	American	Italian	Polish	French[2]	Scottish	Dutch
City	5.9	4.4	5.0	3.2	1.4	0.9	1.4	1.1	0.5
MSA[1]	10.3	8.2	7.5	6.9	2.2	1.1	2.0	1.7	0.9
U.S.	14.9	10.8	8.0	7.4	5.5	3.0	2.7	1.7	1.4

Note: Figures are the percentage of the total population reporting a particular ancestry. The nine most commonly reported ancestries in the U.S. are shown. Figures include multiple ancestries (e.g. if a person reported being Irish and Italian, they were included in both columns); (1) Figures cover the Dallas-Fort Worth-Arlington, TX Metropolitan Statistical Area—see Appendix B for areas included; (2) Excludes Basque
Source: U.S. Census Bureau, 2011-2013 American Community Survey 3-Year Estimates

Foreign-Born Population

Area	Percent of Population Born in								
	Any Foreign Country	Mexico	Asia	Europe	Carribean	South America	Central America[2]	Africa	Canada
City	24.4	16.8	2.6	0.8	0.1	0.4	2.0	1.4	0.2
MSA[1]	17.5	9.1	4.3	0.8	0.2	0.5	1.3	1.0	0.2
U.S.	13.0	3.7	3.8	1.5	1.2	0.9	1.0	0.6	0.3

Note: (1) Figures cover the Dallas-Fort Worth-Arlington, TX Metropolitan Statistical Area—see Appendix B for areas included; (2) Excludes Mexico.
Source: U.S. Census Bureau, 2011-2013 American Community Survey 3-Year Estimates

Marital Status

Area	Never Married	Now Married[2]	Separated	Widowed	Divorced
City	40.9	39.6	3.5	4.8	11.2
MSA[1]	31.4	50.4	2.5	4.5	11.2
U.S.	32.7	48.1	2.2	6.0	11.0

Note: Figures are percentages and cover the population 15 years of age and older; (1) Figures cover the Dallas-Fort Worth-Arlington, TX Metropolitan Statistical Area—see Appendix B for areas included; (2) Excludes separated
Source: U.S. Census Bureau, 2011-2013 American Community Survey 3-Year Estimates

Disability Status

Area	All Ages	Under 18 Years Old	18 to 64 Years Old	65 Years and Over
City	9.4	2.9	8.0	38.1
MSA[1]	9.5	3.3	8.2	35.8
U.S.	12.3	4.1	10.2	36.3

Note: Figures show percent of the civilian noninstitutionalized population that reported having a disability. Disability status is determined from from six types of difficulty: vision, hearing, cognitive, ambulatory, self-care, and independent living. For children under 5 years old, hearing and vision difficulty are used to determine disability status. For children between the ages of 5 and 14, disability status is determined from hearing, vision, cognitive, ambulatory, and self-care difficulties. For people aged 15 years and older, they are considered to have a disability if they have difficulty with any one of the six difficulty types; (1) Figures cover the Dallas-Fort Worth-Arlington, TX Metropolitan Statistical Area—see Appendix B for areas included.
Source: U.S. Census Bureau, 2011-2013 American Community Survey 3-Year Estimates

Age

Area	Percent of Population									Median Age
	Under Age 5	Age 5–19	Age 20–34	Age 35–44	Age 45–54	Age 55–64	Age 65–74	Age 75–84	Age 85+	
City	8.1	20.2	26.4	14.0	12.4	9.8	5.1	2.8	1.3	32.2
MSA[1]	7.4	22.4	21.4	14.7	14.0	10.4	5.7	2.8	1.1	34.1
U.S.	6.4	19.9	20.7	12.9	14.1	12.3	7.6	4.2	1.9	37.4

Note: (1) Figures cover the Dallas-Fort Worth-Arlington, TX Metropolitan Statistical Area—see Appendix B for areas included
Source: U.S. Census Bureau, 2011-2013 American Community Survey 3-Year Estimates

Gender

Area	Males	Females	Males per 100 Females
City	621,146	618,122	100.5
MSA[1]	3,301,095	3,393,794	97.3
U.S.	154,451,010	159,410,713	96.9

Note: (1) Figures cover the Dallas-Fort Worth-Arlington, TX Metropolitan Statistical Area—see Appendix B for areas included
Source: U.S. Census Bureau, 2011-2013 American Community Survey 3-Year Estimates

Religious Groups by Family

Area	Catholic	Baptist	Non-Den.	Methodist[2]	Lutheran	LDS[3]	Pente-costal	Presby-terian[4]	Muslim[5]	Judaism
MSA[1]	13.3	18.7	7.8	5.3	0.8	1.2	2.2	1.0	2.4	0.4
U.S.	19.1	9.3	4.0	4.0	2.3	2.0	1.9	1.6	0.8	0.7

Note: Figures are the number of adherents as a percentage of the total population; (1) Figures cover the Dallas-Fort Worth-Arlington, TX Metropolitan Statistical Area—see Appendix B for areas included; (2) Methodist/Pietist; (3) Latter Day Saints; (4) Reformed; (5) Figures are estimates
Source: Association of Statisticians of American Religious Bodies, 2010 U.S. Religion Census: Religious Congregations & Membership Study

Religious Groups by Tradition

Area	Catholic	Evangelical Protestant	Mainline Protestant	Other Tradition	Black Protestant	Orthodox
MSA[1]	13.3	28.3	7.0	4.8	1.8	0.2
U.S.	19.1	16.2	7.3	4.3	1.6	0.3

Note: Figures are the number of adherents as a percentage of the total population; (1) Figures cover the Dallas-Fort Worth-Arlington, TX Metropolitan Statistical Area—see Appendix B for areas included
Source: Association of Statisticians of American Religious Bodies, 2010 U.S. Religion Census: Religious Congregations & Membership Study

ECONOMY

Gross Metropolitan Product

Area	2012	2013	2014	2015	Rank[2]
MSA[1]	418.6	440.1	464.7	491.4	6

Note: Figures are in billions of dollars; (1) Figures cover the Dallas-Fort Worth-Arlington, TX Metropolitan Statistical Area—see Appendix B for areas included; (2) Rank is based on 2015 data and ranges from 1 to 363
Source: The U.S. Conference of Mayors, U.S. Metro Economies: GMP and Employment 2013-2015, June 2014

Economic Growth

Area	2010-12 (%)	2013 (%)	2014 (%)	2015 (%)	Rank[2]
MSA[1]	3.8	3.7	3.3	4.5	14
U.S.	2.1	2.0	2.3	3.2	–

Note: Figures are real gross metropolitan product (GMP) growth rates and represent annual average percent change; (1) Figures cover the Dallas-Fort Worth-Arlington, TX Metropolitan Statistical Area—see Appendix B for areas included; (2) Rank is based on 2015 data and ranges from 1 to 363
Source: The U.S. Conference of Mayors, U.S. Metro Economies: GMP and Employment 2013-2015, June 2014

Metropolitan Area Exports

Area	2008	2009	2010	2011	2012	2013	Rank[2]
MSA[1]	22,503.7	19,881.8	22,500.4	26,648.7	27,820.9	27,596.0	9

Note: Figures are in millions of dollars; (1) Figures cover the Dallas-Fort Worth-Arlington, TX Metropolitan Statistical Area—see Appendix B for areas included; (2) Rank is based on 2013 data and ranges from 1 to 387
Source: U.S. Department of Commerce, International Trade Administration, Office of Trade & Industry Information, Manufacturing & Services, data extracted April 3, 2015

Building Permits

Area	Single-Family			Multi-Family			Total		
	2013	2014	Pct. Chg.	2013	2014	Pct. Chg.	2013	2014	Pct. Chg.
City	1,075	1,181	9.9	7,559	6,675	-11.7	8,634	7,856	-9.0
MSA[1]	21,224	22,550	6.2	16,686	18,868	13.1	37,910	41,418	9.3
U.S.	620,802	634,597	2.2	370,020	411,766	11.3	990,822	1,046,363	5.6

Note: (1) Figures cover the Dallas-Fort Worth-Arlington, TX Metropolitan Statistical Area—see Appendix B for areas included; Figures represent new, privately-owned housing units authorized (unadjusted data); All permit data are based on estimates with imputation.
Source: U.S. Census Bureau, Manufacturing, Mining, and Construction Statistics, Building Permits, 2013, 2014

Bankruptcy Filings

Area	Business Filings			Nonbusiness Filings		
	2013	2014	% Chg.	2013	2014	% Chg.
Dallas County	310	379	22.3	5,162	4,779	-7.4
U.S.	33,212	26,983	-18.8	1,038,720	909,812	-12.4

Note: Business filings include Chapter 7, Chapter 11, Chapter 12, and Chapter 13; Nonbusiness filings include Chapter 7, Chapter 11, and Chapter 13
Source: Administrative Office of the U.S. Courts, Business and Nonbusiness Bankruptcy, County Cases Commenced by Chapter of the Bankruptcy Code, During the 12- Month Period Ending December 31, 2013 and Business and Nonbusiness Bankruptcy, County Cases Commenced by Chapter of the Bankruptcy Code, During the 12- Month Period Ending December 31, 2014

Housing Vacancy Rates

Area	Gross Vacancy Rate[2] (%)			Year-Round Vacancy Rate[3] (%)			Rental Vacancy Rate[4] (%)			Homeowner Vacancy Rate[5] (%)		
	2012	2013	2014	2012	2013	2014	2012	2013	2014	2012	2013	2014
MSA[1]	8.7	9.0	9.2	8.4	8.8	9.0	9.2	8.2	9.8	2.1	1.9	1.5
U.S.	13.8	13.6	13.4	10.8	10.7	10.4	8.7	8.3	7.6	2.0	2.0	1.9

Note: (1) Figures cover the Dallas-Fort Worth-Arlington, TX Metropolitan Statistical Area—see Appendix B for areas included; (2) The percentage of the total housing inventory that is vacant; (3) The percentage of the housing inventory (excluding seasonal units) that is year-round vacant; (4) The percentage of rental inventory that is vacant for rent; (5) The percentage of homeowner inventory that is vacant for sale
Source: U.S. Census Bureau, Housing Vacancies and Homeownership Annual Statistics: 2014

INCOME

Income

Area	Per Capita ($)	Median Household ($)	Average Household ($)
City	27,380	42,026	69,885
MSA[1]	29,110	57,630	80,048
U.S.	27,884	52,176	72,897

Note: (1) Figures cover the Dallas-Fort Worth-Arlington, TX Metropolitan Statistical Area—see Appendix B for areas included
Source: U.S. Census Bureau, 2011-2013 American Community Survey 3-Year Estimates

Household Income Distribution

Area	Percent of Households Earning							
	Under $15,000	$15,000 -24,999	$25,000 -34,999	$35,000 -49,999	$50,000 -74,999	$75,000 -99,000	$100,000 -149,999	$150,000 and up
City	16.3	13.2	12.4	14.9	16.6	8.5	8.9	9.3
MSA[1]	10.4	9.5	10.1	13.5	18.3	12.1	14.5	11.6
U.S.	13.0	10.9	10.3	13.6	17.9	11.9	12.7	9.6

Note: (1) Figures cover the Dallas-Fort Worth-Arlington, TX Metropolitan Statistical Area—see Appendix B for areas included
Source: U.S. Census Bureau, 2011-2013 American Community Survey 3-Year Estimates

Poverty Rate

Area	All Ages	Under 18 Years Old	18 to 64 Years Old	65 Years and Over
City	24.4	38.1	20.2	15.9
MSA[1]	15.1	21.8	13.1	9.1
U.S.	15.9	22.4	14.8	9.5

Note: Figures are percentage of people whose income during the past 12 months was below the poverty level; (1) Figures cover the Dallas-Fort Worth-Arlington, TX Metropolitan Statistical Area—see Appendix B for areas included
Source: U.S. Census Bureau, 2011-2013 American Community Survey 3-Year Estimates

EMPLOYMENT

Labor Force and Employment

Area	Civilian Labor Force			Workers Employed		
	Dec. 2013	Dec. 2014	% Chg.	Dec. 2013	Dec. 2014	% Chg.
City	628,877	644,851	2.5	594,858	618,008	3.9
MD[1]	2,331,802	2,392,061	2.6	2,210,843	2,296,944	3.9
U.S.	154,408,000	155,521,000	0.7	144,423,000	147,190,000	1.9

Note: Data is not seasonally adjusted and covers workers 16 years of age and older; (1) Figures cover the Dallas-Plano-Irving, TX Metropolitan Division—see Appendix B for areas included
Source: Bureau of Labor Statistics, Local Area Unemployment Statistics

Unemployment Rate

Area	2014											
	Jan.	Feb.	Mar.	Apr.	May	Jun.	Jul.	Aug.	Sep.	Oct.	Nov.	Dec.
City	5.8	5.8	5.5	5.0	5.3	5.5	5.6	5.5	5.0	4.7	4.6	4.2
MD[1]	5.6	5.6	5.4	4.8	5.0	5.3	5.4	5.2	4.8	4.5	4.4	4.0
U.S.	7.0	7.0	6.8	5.9	6.1	6.3	6.5	6.3	5.7	5.5	5.5	5.4

Note: Data is not seasonally adjusted and covers workers 16 years of age and older; (1) Figures cover the Dallas-Plano-Irving, TX Metropolitan Division—see Appendix B for areas included
Source: Bureau of Labor Statistics, Local Area Unemployment Statistics

Employment by Occupation

Occupation Classification	City (%)	MSA[1] (%)	U.S. (%)
Management, Business, Science, and Arts	32.6	37.5	36.2
Natural Resources, Construction, and Maintenance	11.9	9.4	9.0
Production, Transportation, and Material Moving	12.1	11.5	12.1
Sales and Office	23.4	25.5	24.4
Service	19.9	16.1	18.3

Note: Figures cover employed civilians 16 years of age and older; (1) Figures cover the Dallas-Fort Worth-Arlington, TX Metropolitan Statistical Area—see Appendix B for areas included
Source: U.S. Census Bureau, 2011-2013 American Community Survey 3-Year Estimates

Employment by Industry

Sector	MD[1] Number of Employees	MD[1] Percent of Total	U.S. Percent of Total
Construction, Mining, and Logging	126,500	5.4	5.0
Education and Health Services	287,700	12.2	15.5
Financial Activities	215,000	9.1	5.7
Government	278,600	11.8	15.8
Information	68,500	2.9	2.0
Leisure and Hospitality	226,000	9.6	10.3
Manufacturing	166,200	7.0	8.7
Other Services	78,400	3.3	4.0
Professional and Business Services	438,500	18.6	13.8
Retail Trade	238,600	10.1	11.4
Transportation, Warehousing, and Utilities	89,200	3.8	3.9
Wholesale Trade	147,100	6.2	4.2

Note: Figures are non-farm employment as of December 2014. Figures are not seasonally adjusted and include workers 16 years of age and older; (1) Figures cover the Dallas-Plano-Irving, TX Metropolitan Division—see Appendix B for areas included; n/a not available
Source: Bureau of Labor Statistics, Current Employment Statistics, Employment, Hours, and Earnings

Occupations with Greatest Projected Employment Growth: 2012 – 2022

Occupation[1]	2012 Employment	2022 Projected Employment	Numeric Employment Change	Percent Employment Change
Combined Food Preparation and Serving Workers, Including Fast Food	285,480	378,000	92,520	32.4
Personal Care Aides	199,230	283,980	84,750	42.5
Retail Salespersons	378,330	439,340	61,010	16.1
Registered Nurses	189,380	242,860	53,480	28.2
Customer Service Representatives	214,240	262,770	48,530	22.7
Waiters and Waitresses	196,390	240,390	44,000	22.4
Janitors and Cleaners, Except Maids and Housekeeping Cleaners	172,120	213,340	41,220	23.9
Laborers and Freight, Stock, and Material Movers, Hand	185,770	226,470	40,700	21.9
Elementary School Teachers, Except Special Education	141,030	180,920	39,890	28.3
Secretaries and Administrative Assistants, Except Legal, Medical, and Executive	190,470	230,220	39,750	20.9

Note: Projections cover Texas; (1) Sorted by numeric employment change
Source: www.projectionscentral.com, State Occupational Projections, 2012–2022 Long-Term Projections

Fastest Growing Occupations: 2012 – 2022

Occupation[1]	2012 Employment	2022 Projected Employment	Numeric Employment Change	Percent Employment Change
Diagnostic Medical Sonographers	4,380	6,900	2,520	57.6
Computer Numerically Controlled Machine Tool Programmers, Metal and Plastic	1,740	2,700	960	54.8
Interpreters and Translators	4,510	6,720	2,210	49.0
Skincare Specialists	5,130	7,620	2,490	48.3
Agents and Business Managers of Artists, Performers, and Athletes	310	450	140	47.4
Petroleum Engineers	19,280	28,010	8,730	45.3
Information Security Analysts	6,640	9,630	2,990	45.0
Insulation Workers, Mechanical	4,460	6,460	2,000	44.6
Cardiovascular Technologists and Technicians	3,950	5,700	1,750	44.3
Physician Assistants	5,470	7,880	2,410	44.2

Note: Projections cover Texas; (1) Sorted by percent employment change and excludes occupations with numeric employment change less than 100
Source: www.projectionscentral.com, State Occupational Projections, 2012–2022 Long-Term Projections

Average Wages

Occupation	$/Hr.	Occupation	$/Hr.
Accountants and Auditors	37.39	Maids and Housekeeping Cleaners	9.34
Automotive Mechanics	20.77	Maintenance and Repair Workers	17.74
Bookkeepers	19.04	Marketing Managers	68.82
Carpenters	14.87	Nuclear Medicine Technologists	33.63
Cashiers	9.56	Nurses, Licensed Practical	23.73
Clerks, General Office	16.19	Nurses, Registered	34.57
Clerks, Receptionists/Information	13.04	Nursing Assistants	12.31
Clerks, Shipping/Receiving	14.53	Packers and Packagers, Hand	10.63
Computer Programmers	39.61	Physical Therapists	47.84
Computer Systems Analysts	41.45	Postal Service Mail Carriers	25.37
Computer User Support Specialists	23.89	Real Estate Brokers	n/a
Cooks, Restaurant	11.58	Retail Salespersons	12.97
Dentists	107.16	Sales Reps., Exc. Tech./Scientific	36.59
Electrical Engineers	44.24	Sales Reps., Tech./Scientific	35.52
Electricians	19.95	Secretaries, Exc. Legal/Med./Exec.	16.76
Financial Managers	67.69	Security Guards	13.07
First-Line Supervisors/Managers, Sales	22.06	Surgeons	107.42
Food Preparation Workers	9.68	Teacher Assistants	10.90
General and Operations Managers	66.25	Teachers, Elementary School	25.40
Hairdressers/Cosmetologists	12.48	Teachers, Secondary School	26.10
Internists	82.59	Telemarketers	14.68
Janitors and Cleaners	10.05	Truck Drivers, Heavy/Tractor-Trailer	20.00
Landscaping/Groundskeeping Workers	11.91	Truck Drivers, Light/Delivery Svcs.	15.74
Lawyers	69.58	Waiters and Waitresses	10.42

Note: Wage data covers the Dallas-Plano-Irving, TX Metropolitan Division—see Appendix B for areas included; Hourly wages for elementary/secondary school teachers and teacher assistants were calculated by the editors from annual wage data assuming a 40 hour work week; n/a not available.
Source: Bureau of Labor Statistics, Metro Area Occupational Employment and Wage Estimates, May 2014

TAXES

State Corporate Income Tax Rates

State	Tax Rate (%)	Income Brackets ($)	Num. of Brackets	Financial Institution Tax Rate (%)[a]	Federal Income Tax Ded.
Texas	(y)	–	–	(y)	No

Note: Tax rates as of January 1, 2015; (a) Rates listed are the corporate income tax rate applied to financial institutions or excise taxes based on income. Some states have other taxes based upon the value of deposits or shares; (y) Texas imposes a Franchise Tax, otherwise known as margin tax, imposed on entities with more than $1,030,000 total revenues at rate of 1%, or 0.5% for entities primarily engaged in retail or wholesale trade, on lesser of 70% of total revenues or 100%of gross receipts after deductions for either compensation or cost of goods sold.
Source: Federation of Tax Administrators, "State Corporate Income Tax Rates, 2015"

State Individual Income Tax Rates

State	Tax Rate (%)	Income Brackets ($)	Num. of Brackets	Personal Exempt. ($)[1]		Fed. Inc. Tax Ded.
				Single	Dependents	
Texas	None	–	–	–	–	–

Note: Tax rates as of January 1, 2015; Local- and county-level taxes are not included; n/a not applicable; (1) Married joint filers generally receive double the single exemption
Source: Federation of Tax Administrators, "State Individual Income Tax Rates, 2015"

COMMERCIAL REAL ESTATE

Various State and Local Tax Rates

State	State and Local Sales and Use (%)	State Sales and Use (%)	Gasoline[1] (¢/gal.)	Cigarette[2] ($/pack)	Spirits[3] ($/gal.)	Wine[4] ($/gal.)	Beer[5] ($/gal.)
Texas	8.25	6.25	20	1.41	2.40 (f)	0.20	0.20 (p)

Note: All tax rates as of January 1, 2015; (1) The American Petroleum Institute has developed a methodology for determining the average tax rate on a gallon of fuel. Rates may include any of the following: excise taxes, environmental fees, storage tank fees, other fees or taxes, general sales tax, and local taxes. In states where gasoline is subject to the general sales tax, or where the fuel tax is based on the average sale price, the average rate determined by API is sensitive to changes in the price of gasoline. States that fully or partially apply general sales taxes to gasoline: CA, CO, GA, IL, IN, MI, NY; (2) The federal excise tax of $1.0066 per pack and local taxes are not included; (3) Rates are those applicable to off-premise sales of 40% alcohol by volume (a.b.v.) distilled spirits in 750ml containers. Local excise taxes are excluded; (4) Rates are those applicable to off-premise sales of 11% a.b.v. non-carbonated wine in 750ml containers; (5) Rates are those applicable to off-premise sales of 4.7% a.b.v. beer in 12 ounce containers; (f) Different rates are also applicable according to alcohol content, place of production, size of container, or place purchased (on- or off-premise or onboard airlines); (p) Local excise taxes are excluded.
Source: Tax Foundation, 2015 Facts & Figures: How Does Your State Compare?

State Business Tax Climate Index Rankings

State	Overall Rank	Corporate Tax Index Rank	Individual Income Tax Index Rank	Sales Tax Index Rank	Unemployment Insurance Tax Index Rank	Property Tax Index Rank
Texas	10	39	6	36	15	36

Note: The index is a measure of how each state's tax laws affect economic performance. The lower the rank, the more favorable a state's tax system is for business. States without a given tax are given a ranking of 1. The scores/rankings for the District of Columbia do not affect other states. The 2015 index represents the tax climate as of July 1, 2014.
Source: Tax Foundation, State Business Tax Climate Index 2015

Office Market

Market Area	Inventory (sq. ft.)	Vacancy Rate (%)	Under Construction (sq. ft.)	YTD Net Absorption (sq. ft.)	Total Average Asking Rent ($/sq. ft./year)
Dallas-Fort Worth	228,035,737	18.7	5,305,025	3,986,942	21.76
National	4,745,108,508	14.3	71,190,461	51,084,126	27.40

Source: Newmark Grubb Knight Frank, National Office Market Report, 4th Quarter 2014

Industrial/Warehouse/R&D Market

Market Area	Inventory (sq. ft.)	Vacancy Rate (%)	Under Construction (sq. ft.)	YTD Net Absorption (sq. ft.)	Total Average Asking Rent ($/sq. ft./year)
Dallas-Fort Worth	759,512,156	7.5	17,360,899	7,955,734	5.28
National	14,238,613,765	7.2	134,387,407	185,246,438	5.64

Source: Newmark Grubb Knight Frank, National Industrial Market Report, 4th Quarter 2014

COMMERCIAL UTILITIES

Typical Monthly Electric Bills

Area	Commercial Service ($/month)		Industrial Service ($/month)	
	1,500 kWh	40 kW demand 14,000 kWh	1,000 kW demand 200,000 kWh	50,000 kW demand 32,500,000 kWh
City	n/a	n/a	n/a	n/a
Average[1]	201	1,653	26,124	2,639,743

Note: Figures are based on annualized 2014 rates; (1) Average based on 180 utilities surveyed; n/a not available
Source: Edison Electric Institute, Typical Bills and Average Rates Report, Summer 2014

TRANSPORTATION

Means of Transportation to Work

Area	Car/Truck/Van: Drove Alone	Car/Truck/Van: Car-pooled	Public Transportation: Bus	Public Transportation: Subway	Public Transportation: Railroad	Bicycle	Walked	Other Means	Worked at Home
City	76.6	11.2	3.3	0.3	0.4	0.2	1.9	1.8	4.3
MSA[1]	80.8	10.2	1.0	0.2	0.3	0.2	1.2	1.4	4.8
U.S.	76.4	9.6	2.6	1.8	0.6	0.6	2.8	1.3	4.3

Note: Figures are percentages and cover workers 16 years of age and older; (1) Figures cover the Dallas-Fort Worth-Arlington, TX Metropolitan Statistical Area—see Appendix B for areas included
Source: U.S. Census Bureau, 2011-2013 American Community Survey 3-Year Estimates

Travel Time to Work

Area	Less Than 10 Minutes	10 to 19 Minutes	20 to 29 Minutes	30 to 44 Minutes	45 to 59 Minutes	60 to 89 Minutes	90 Minutes or More
City	9.0	29.0	22.8	25.2	7.3	4.8	2.0
MSA[1]	9.9	26.5	21.2	24.8	9.8	5.9	1.9
U.S.	13.3	29.7	20.9	20.2	7.7	5.7	2.6

Note: Figures are percentages and include workers 16 years old and over; (1) Figures cover the Dallas-Fort Worth-Arlington, TX Metropolitan Statistical Area—see Appendix B for areas included
Source: U.S. Census Bureau, 2011-2013 American Community Survey 3-Year Estimates

Travel Time Index

Area	1985	1990	1995	2000	2005	2010	2011
Urban Area[1]	1.08	1.12	1.16	1.22	1.30	1.25	1.26
Average[2]	1.09	1.14	1.16	1.19	1.23	1.18	1.18

Note: Travel Time Index—the ratio of travel time in the peak period to the travel time at free-flow conditions. For example, a value of 1.30 indicates a 20-minute free-flow trip takes 26 minutes in the peak. Free-flow speeds (60 mph on freeways and 35 mph on principal arterials) are used as the comparison threshold; (1) Covers the Dallas-Fort Worth-Arlington TX urban area; (2) average of 498 urban areas
Source: Texas Transportation Institute, Urban Mobility Report 2012, December 2012

Public Transportation

Agency Name / Mode of Transportation	Vehicles Operated in Maximum Service	Annual Unlinked Passenger Trips (in thous.)	Annual Passenger Miles (in thous.)
Dallas Area Rapid Transit Authority (DART)			
Bus (directly operated)	527	37,937.2	154,490.4
Commuter Rail (purchased transportation)	23	2,092.8	40,170.3
Demand Response (purchased transportation)	148	517.3	7,218.2
Demand Response Taxi (purchased transportation)	79	315.0	4,635.2
Light Rail (directly operated)	102	29,471.9	238,107.3
Vanpool (directly operated)	192	947.0	37,017.4

Source: Federal Transit Administration, National Transit Database, 2013

Air Transportation

Airport Name and Code / Type of Service	Passenger Airlines[1]	Passenger Enplanements	Freight Carriers[2]	Freight (lbs.)
Dallas-Fort Worth International (DFW)				
Domestic service (U.S. carriers - 2014)	31	27,243,474	16	356,351,117
International service (U.S. carriers - 2013)	11	2,667,707	7	74,412,988
Dallas Love Field (DAL)				
Domestic service (U.S. carriers - 2014)	21	4,517,138	8	9,809,404
International service (U.S. carriers - 2013)	7	3,031	5	78,450

Note: (1) Includes all U.S.-based major, minor and commuter airlines that carried at least one passenger during the year; (2) Includes all U.S.-based airlines and freight carriers that transported at least one lb. of freight during the year.
Source: Bureau of Transportation Statistics, The Intermodal Transportation Database, Air Carriers: T-100 Domestic Market (U.S. Carriers), 2014; Bureau of Transportation Statistics, The Intermodal Transportation Database, Air Carriers: T-100 International Market (U.S. Carriers), 2013

Other Transportation Statistics

Major Highways:	I-20; I-30; I-35E; I-45
Amtrak Service:	Yes
Major Waterways/Ports:	None

Source: Amtrak.com; Google Maps

BUSINESSES

Major Business Headquarters

Company Name	Rankings	
	Fortune[1]	Forbes[2]
AT&T	11	-
Dean Foods Company	285	-
Energy Future Holdings Corp.	438	60
Energy Transfer Equity	54	-
Glazer's	-	108
HollyFrontier Corporation	145	-
Hunt Consolidated/Hunt Oil	-	88
Neiman Marcus Group	-	82
Sammons Enterprises	-	81
Southwest Airlines Co.	160	-
Tenet Healthcare Corporation	229	-
Texas Instruments Incorporated	227	-

Note: (1) Fortune 500—companies that produce a 10-K are ranked 1 to 500 based on 2013 revenue; (2) all private companies with at least $2 billion in annual revenue through the end of their most current fiscal year are ranked 1 to 221; companies listed are headquartered in the city; dashes indicate no ranking
Source: Fortune, "Fortune 500," June 16, 2014; Forbes, "America's Largest Private Companies," November 5, 2014

Fast-Growing Businesses

According to *Inc.*, Dallas is home to six of America's 500 fastest-growing private companies: **CPSG Partners** (#24); **CenseoHealth** (#174); **Apex Resources** (#303); **Wingspan Portfolio Advisors** (#322); **Think Tech Labs** (#344); **Gadberry Construction Company** (#374). Criteria: must be an independent, privately-held, for-profit, U.S. corporation, proprietorship or partnership; revenues must be at least $100,000 in 2010 and $2 million in 2013; must have four-year operating/sales history. Holding companies, regulated banks, and utilities were excluded. *Inc., "America's 500 Fastest-Growing Private Companies," September 2014*

According to *Fortune*, Dallas is home to three of the 100 fastest-growing companies in the world: **Eagle Materials** (#17); **Trinity Industries** (#23); **HollyFrontier** (#78). Companies were ranked by their revenue growth rate; their EPS growth rate; and their three-year annualized total return to investors for the period ending June 30, 2014. Criteria for inclusion: a company, foreign or domestic, must trade on a major U.S. stock exchange; must file quarterly reports with the SEC; must have a minimum market capitalization of $250 million; must have a stock price of at least $5 on June 30, 2014; must have been trading continuously since June 30, 2010; must have revenue and net income for the four quarters ended on or before April 30, 2014, of at least $50 million and $10 million, respectively; and must have posted a compound annual growth in revenue and earnings per share of at least 20% annually over the three years ending on or before April 30, 2014. Real estate investment trusts, limited-liability companies, limited parterships, business development companies, closed end investment firms, and companies that lost money in the quarter ending April 30, 2014 were excluded. *Fortune, "100 Fastest-Growing Companies," August 28, 2014*

Minority Business Opportunity

Dallas is home to two companies which are on the *Black Enterprise* Industrial/Service 100 list (100 largest companies based on gross sales): **Parrish Restaurants Ltd.** (#55); **On-Target Supplies & Logistics Ltd.** (#85). Criteria: operational in previous calendar year; at least 51% black-owned and manufactures/owns the product it sells or provides industrial or consumer services. Brokerages, real estate firms and firms that provide professional services are not eligible. *Black Enterprise, B.E. 100s, 2014*

Dallas is home to one company which is on the *Black Enterprise* Auto Dealer 60 list (60 largest dealers based on gross sales): **Freedom Enterprises** (#12). Criteria: company must be operational in previous calendar year and be at least 51% black-owned. *Black Enterprise, B.E. 100s, 2014*

Dallas is home to two companies which are on the *Black Enterprise* Private Equity 15 list (15 largest private equity firms based on capital under management): **Pharos Capital Group** (#5); **21st Century Group** (#13). Criteria: company must be operational in previous calendar year and be at least 51% black-owned. *Black Enterprise, B.E. 100s, 2014*

Dallas is home to eight companies which are on the *Hispanic Business* 500 list (500 largest U.S. Hispanic-owned companies based on 2012 revenue): **Sun Holdings** (#21); **Pinnacle Technical Resources** (#33); **Gilbert May** (#113); **Aguirre Roden** (#175); **ROC Construction** (#271); **Alman Electric** (#285); **Pursuit of Excellence HR** (#330); **Carrco Painting Contractor** (#341). Companies included must show at least 51 percent ownership by Hispanic U.S. citizens, and must maintain headquarters in one of the 50 states or Washington, D.C. *Hispanic Business, "Hispanic Business 500," June 20, 2013*

Dallas is home to one company which is on the *Hispanic Business* Fastest-Growing 100 list (greatest sales growth from 2008 to 2012): **Sun Holdings** (#40). Companies included must show at least 51 percent ownership by Hispanic U.S. citizens, and must maintain headquarters in one of the 50 states or Washington, D.C. In addition, companies must have minimum revenues of $200,000 for calendar year 2008. *Hispanic Business, June 20, 2013*

Minority- and Women-Owned Businesses

Group	All Firms		Firms with Paid Employees			
	Firms	Sales ($000)	Firms	Sales ($000)	Employees	Payroll ($000)
Asian	5,977	3,165,560	2,181	3,012,132	15,033	478,254
Black	16,319	1,212,849	770	906,803	7,562	204,412
Hispanic	18,162	3,358,739	1,989	2,603,364	27,163	712,610
Women	33,387	9,048,065	4,057	8,115,528	47,614	1,543,965
All Firms	121,276	185,276,034	26,420	179,315,299	723,706	36,948,202

Note: Figures cover firms located in the city; minority- and women-owned business are defined as firms in which the corresponding group own 51% or more of the stock or equity of the company
Source: U.S. Census Bureau, 2007 Economic Census, Survey of Business Owners (2012 Survey of Business Owners data will be released starting in June 2015)

HOTELS & CONVENTION CENTERS

Hotels/Motels

Area	5 Star		4 Star		3 Star		2 Star		1 Star		Not Rated	
	Num.	Pct.[3]	Num.	Pct.[3]	Num.	Pct.[3]	Num.	Pct.[3]	Num.	Pct.[3]	Num.	Pct.[3]
City[1]	3	0.6	34	6.2	179	32.8	293	53.8	10	1.8	26	4.8
Total[2]	166	0.9	1,264	7.0	5,718	31.8	9,340	52.0	411	2.3	1,070	6.0

Note: (1) Figures cover Dallas and vicinity; (2) Figures cover all 100 cities in this book; (3) Percentage of hotels which have a given star rating; Star ratings are determined by expedia.com and offer an indication of the general quality of a particular hotel.
Source: expedia.com, April 2, 2015

The Dallas-Plano-Irving, TX metro area is home to five of the best hotels in the U.S. according to *Travel & Leisure*: **Hotel ZaZa, Dallas; Ritz-Carlton, Dallas; Rosewood Crescent Hotel; Rosewood Mansion on Turtle Creek; Four Seasons Resort and Club Dallas at Las Colinas**. Criteria: service; location; rooms; food; and value. The list includes the top 236 hotels in the U.S. *Travel & Leisure, "T+L 500, The World's Best Hotels 2015"*

Major Convention Centers

Name	Overall Space (sq. ft.)	Exhibit Space (sq. ft.)	Meeting Space (sq. ft.)	Meeting Rooms
Dallas Convention Center	2,000,000	929,726	n/a	96
Fort Worth Convention Center	n/a	253,226	58,849	41
Frisco Conference Center	90,000	n/a	n/a	14

Note: Table includes convention centers located in the Dallas-Fort Worth-Arlington, TX metro area; n/a not available
Source: Original research

Living Environment

COST OF LIVING

Cost of Living Index

Composite Index	Groceries	Housing	Utilities	Trans-portation	Health Care	Misc. Goods/ Services
95.5	101.2	75.0	103.0	100.1	99.9	106.4

Note: The Cost of Living Index measures regional differences in the cost of consumer goods and services, excluding taxes and non-consumer expenditures, for professional and managerial households in the top income quintile. It is based on more than 50,000 prices covering almost 60 different items for which prices are collected three times a year by chambers of commerce, economic development organizations or university applied economic centers in each participating urban area. The numbers shown should be read as a percentage above or below the national average of 100. For example, a value of 115.4 in the groceries column indicates that grocery prices are 15.4% higher than the national average. Small differences in the index numbers should not be interpreted as significant; Figures cover the Dallas TX urban area.
Source: The Council for Community and Economic Research, ACCRA Cost of Living Index, 2014

Grocery Prices

Area[1]	T-Bone Steak ($/pound)	Frying Chicken ($/pound)	Whole Milk ($/half gal.)	Eggs ($/dozen)	Orange Juice ($/64 oz.)	Coffee ($/11.5 oz.)
City[2]	9.53	1.35	2.34	1.81	4.01	4.09
Avg.	10.40	1.37	2.40	1.99	3.46	4.27
Min.	8.48	0.93	1.37	1.30	2.83	2.99
Max.	14.20	2.44	3.62	4.02	6.42	6.96

Note: (1) Values for the local area are compared with the average, minimum and maximum values for all 308 areas in the Cost of Living Index; (2) Figures cover the Dallas TX urban area; **T-Bone Steak** *(price per pound);* **Frying Chicken** *(price per pound, whole fryer);* **Whole Milk** *(half gallon carton);* **Eggs** *(price per dozen, Grade A, large);* **Orange Juice** *(64 oz. Tropicana or Florida Natural);* **Coffee** *(11.5 oz. can, vacuum-packed, Maxwell House, Hills Bros, or Folgers).*
Source: The Council for Community and Economic Research, ACCRA Cost of Living Index, 2014

Housing and Utility Costs

Area[1]	New Home Price ($)	Apartment Rent ($/month)	All Electric ($/month)	Part Electric ($/month)	Other Energy ($/month)	Telephone ($/month)
City[2]	214,204	825	-	126.22	50.81	28.15
Avg.	305,838	919	181.00	93.66	73.14	27.95
Min.	183,142	480	112.00	42.06	23.42	17.16
Max.	1,358,576	3,851	594.00	180.03	440.99	40.42

Note: (1) Values for the local area are compared with the average, minimum and maximum values for all 308 areas in the Cost of Living Index; (2) Figures cover the Dallas TX urban area; **New Home Price** *(2,400 sf living area, 8,000 sf lot, in urban area with full utilities);* **Apartment Rent** *(950 sf 2 bedroom/1.5 or 2 bath, unfurnished, excluding all utilities except water);* **All Electric** *(average monthly cost for an all-electric home);* **Part Electric** *(average monthly cost for a part-electric home);* **Other Energy** *(average monthly cost for natural gas, fuel oil, coal, wood, and any other forms of energy except electricity);* **Telephone** *(price includes basic monthly rate for a private residential line plus additional local usage charges incurred by a family of four).*
Source: The Council for Community and Economic Research, ACCRA Cost of Living Index, 2014

Health Care, Transportation, and Other Costs

Area[1]	Doctor ($/visit)	Dentist ($/visit)	Optometrist ($/visit)	Gasoline ($/gallon)	Beauty Salon ($/visit)	Men's Shirt ($)
City[2]	100.80	86.99	102.48	3.36	39.23	31.16
Avg.	102.86	87.89	97.66	3.44	34.37	26.74
Min.	67.47	65.78	51.18	3.00	17.43	12.79
Max.	173.50	150.14	235.00	4.33	64.28	49.50

Note: (1) Values for the local area are compared with the average, minimum and maximum values for all 308 areas in the Cost of Living Index; (2) Figures cover the Dallas TX urban area; **Doctor** *(general practitioners routine exam of an established patient);* **Dentist** *(adult teeth cleaning and periodic oral examination);* **Optometrist** *(full vision eye exam for established adult patient);* **Gasoline** *(one gallon regular unleaded, national brand, including all taxes, cash price at self-service pump if available);* **Beauty Salon** *(woman's shampoo, trim, and blow-dry);* **Men's Shirt** *(cotton/polyester dress shirt, pinpoint weave, long sleeves).*
Source: The Council for Community and Economic Research, ACCRA Cost of Living Index, 2014

HOUSING

House Price Index (HPI)

Area	National Ranking[2]	Quarterly Change (%)	One-Year Change (%)	Five-Year Change (%)
MD[1]	32	1.10	9.51	17.75
U.S.[3]	–	1.35	4.91	11.59

Note: The HPI is a weighted repeat sales index. It measures average price changes in repeat sales or refinancings on the same properties. This information is obtained by reviewing repeat mortgage transactions on single-family properties whose mortgages have been purchased or securitized by Fannie Mae or Freddie Mac in January 1975; (1) Dallas-Plano-Irving Metropolitan Division—see Appendix B for areas included; (2) Rankings are based on annual percentage change for all metro areas containing at least 15,000 transactions over the last 10 years and ranges from 1 to 275; (3) figures based on a weighted average of Census Division estimates using a seasonally adjusted, purchase-only index; all figures are for the period ending December 31, 2014

Source: Federal Housing Finance Agency, House Price Index, February 26, 2015

Median Single-Family Home Prices

Area	2012	2013	2014p	Percent Change 2013 to 2014
MSA[1]	159.3	175.6	188.3	7.2
U.S. Average	177.2	197.4	209.0	5.9

Note: Figures are median sales prices of existing single-family homes in thousands of dollars; (p) preliminary; n/a not available; (1) Dallas-Fort Worth-Arlington, TX Metropolitan Statistical Area—see Appendix B for areas included

Source: National Association of Realtors, Median Sales Price of Existing Single-Family Homes for Metropolitan Areas, 4th Quarter 2014

Qualifying Income Based on Median Sales Price of Existing Single-Family Homes

Area	With 5% Down ($)	With 10% Down ($)	With 20% Down ($)
MSA[1]	41,665	39,473	35,087
U.S. Average	45,863	43,449	38,621

Note: Figures are preliminary; Qualifying income is based on a mortgage rate of 4.0%. Monthly principal and interest payment is limited to 25% of income; n/a not available; (1) Dallas-Fort Worth-Arlington, TX Metropolitan Statistical Area—see Appendix B for areas included

Source: National Association of Realtors, Qualifying Income Based on Median Sales Price of Existing Single-Family Homes for Metropolitan Areas, 4th Quarter 2014

Median Apartment Condo-Coop Home Prices

Area	2012	2013	2014p	Percent Change 2013 to 2014
MSA[1]	142.1	155.7	152.3	-2.2
U.S. Average	173.7	194.9	205.1	5.2

Note: Figures are median sales prices of existing apartment condo-coop homes in thousands of dollars; (p) preliminary; n/a not available; (1) Dallas-Fort Worth-Arlington, TX Metropolitan Statistical Area—see Appendix B for areas included

Source: National Association of Realtors, Median Sales Price of Existing Apartment Condo-Coop Homes for Metropolitan Areas, 4th Quarter 2014

Gross Monthly Rent

Area	Under $200	$200 -299	$300 -499	$500 -749	$750 -999	$1,000 -1,499	$1,500 and up	Median ($)
City	1.2	2.0	4.7	31.9	29.2	22.2	8.9	828
MSA[1]	0.9	1.3	3.7	25.0	30.4	27.9	10.9	896
U.S.	1.7	3.2	7.8	22.1	24.3	26.0	14.9	900

Note: Figures are percentages except for Median; Gross rent is the contract rent plus the estimated average monthly cost of utilities (electricity, gas, and water and sewer) and fuels (oil, coal, kerosene, wood, etc.) if these are paid by the renter (or paid for the renter by someone else); (1) Figures cover the Dallas-Fort Worth-Arlington, TX Metropolitan Statistical Area—see Appendix B for areas included

Source: U.S. Census Bureau, 2011-2013 American Community Survey 3-Year Estimates

Homeownership Rate

Area	2007 (%)	2008 (%)	2009 (%)	2010 (%)	2011 (%)	2012 (%)	2013 (%)	2014 (%)
MSA[1]	60.9	60.9	61.6	63.8	62.6	61.8	59.9	57.7
U.S.	68.1	67.8	67.4	66.9	66.1	65.4	65.1	64.5

Note: (1) Figures cover the Dallas-Fort Worth-Arlington, TX Metropolitan Statistical Area—see Appendix B for areas included
Source: U.S. Census Bureau, Housing Vacancies and Homeownership Annual Statistics: 2014

Year Housing Structure Built

Area	2010 or Later	2000 -2009	1990 -1999	1980 -1989	1970 -1979	1960 -1969	1950 -1959	1940 -1949	Before 1940	Median Year
City	1.1	12.5	9.3	17.4	19.6	14.6	13.4	6.3	5.8	1975
MSA[1]	1.7	23.2	16.6	19.6	15.5	9.5	7.7	3.1	3.0	1986
U.S.	0.9	15.0	13.9	13.8	15.8	11.0	10.9	5.4	13.3	1976

Note: Figures are percentages except for Median Year; (1) Figures cover the Dallas-Fort Worth-Arlington, TX Metropolitan Statistical Area—see Appendix B for areas included
Source: U.S. Census Bureau, 2011-2013 American Community Survey 3-Year Estimates

HEALTH

Health Risk Data

Category	MD[1] (%)	U.S. (%)
Adults aged 18–64 who have any kind of health care coverage	63.9	79.6
Adults who reported being in good or excellent health	83.3	83.1
Adults who are current smokers	15.8	19.6
Adults who are heavy drinkers[2]	5.0	6.1
Adults who are binge drinkers[3]	16.0	16.9
Adults who are overweight (BMI 25.0 - 29.9)	36.5	35.8
Adults who are obese (BMI 30.0 - 99.8)	26.1	27.6
Adults who participated in any physical activities in the past month	75.1	77.1
Adults 50+ who have ever had a sigmoidoscopy or colonoscopy	63.6	67.3
Women aged 40+ who have had a mammogram within the past two years	70.3	74.0
Men aged 40+ who have had a PSA test within the past two years	44.4	45.2
Adults aged 65+ who have had flu shot within the past year	56.2	60.1
Adults who always wear a seatbelt	n/a	93.8

Note: Data as of 2012 unless otherwise noted; n/a not available; (1) Figures cover the Dallas-Plano-Irving, TX Metropolitan Division—see Appendix B for areas included; (2) Heavy drinkers are classified as males having more than two drinks per day or females having more than one drink per day; (3) Binge drinkers are classified as males having five or more drinks on one occasion or females having four or more drinks on one occasion
Source: Centers for Disease Control and Prevention, Behaviorial Risk Factor Surveillance System, SMART: Selected Metropolitan/Micropolitan Area Risk Trends, 2012 (Note: the CDC has discontinued this dataset but will be releasing a replacement in late 2015)

Chronic Health Indicators

Category	MD[1] (%)	U.S. (%)
Adults who have ever been told they had a heart attack	3.8	4.5
Adults who have ever been told they had a stroke	2.2	2.9
Adults who have been told they currently have asthma	8.0	8.9
Adults who have ever been told they have arthritis	19.3	25.7
Adults who have ever been told they have diabetes[2]	9.9	9.7
Adults who have ever been told they had skin cancer	4.6	5.7
Adults who have ever been told they had any other types of cancer	5.9	6.5
Adults who have ever been told they have COPD	4.2	6.2
Adults who have ever been told they have kidney disease	4.3	2.5
Adults who have ever been told they have a form of depression	13.3	18.0

Note: Data as of 2012 unless otherwise noted; (1) Figures cover the Dallas-Plano-Irving, TX Metropolitan Division—see Appendix B for areas included; (2) Figures do not include pregnancy-related, borderline, or pre-diabetes
Source: Centers for Disease Control and Prevention, Behaviorial Risk Factor Surveillance System, SMART: Selected Metropolitan/Micropolitan Area Risk Trends, 2012 (Note: the CDC has discontinued this dataset but will be releasing a replacement in late 2015)

Mortality Rates for the Top 10 Causes of Death in the U.S.

ICD-10[a] Sub-Chapter	ICD-10[a] Code	Age-Adjusted Mortality Rate[1] per 100,000 population	
		County[2]	U.S.
Malignant neoplasms	C00-C97	162.2	166.2
Ischaemic heart diseases	I20-I25	94.7	105.7
Other forms of heart disease	I30-I51	52.5	49.3
Chronic lower respiratory diseases	J40-J47	39.4	42.1
Organic, including symptomatic, mental disorders	F01-F09	47.5	38.1
Cerebrovascular diseases	I60-I69	42.4	37.0
Other external causes of accidental injury	W00-X59	22.5	26.9
Other degenerative diseases of the nervous system	G30-G31	29.2	25.6
Diabetes mellitus	E10-E14	19.2	21.3
Hypertensive diseases	I10-I15	30.1	19.4

Note: (a) ICD-10 = International Classification of Diseases 10th Revision; (1) Mortality rates are a three year average covering 2011-2013; (2) Figures cover Dallas County
Source: Centers for Disease Control and Prevention, National Center for Health Statistics. Compressed Mortality File 1999-2013 on CDC WONDER Online Database, released October 2014. Data are compiled from the Compressed Mortality File 1999-2013, Series 20 No. 2S, 2014.

Mortality Rates for Selected Causes of Death

ICD-10[a] Sub-Chapter	ICD-10[a] Code	Age-Adjusted Mortality Rate[1] per 100,000 population	
		County[2]	U.S.
Assault	X85-Y09	7.5	5.2
Diseases of the liver	K70-K76	12.9	13.2
Human immunodeficiency virus (HIV) disease	B20-B24	4.1	2.2
Influenza and pneumonia	J09-J18	12.2	15.4
Intentional self-harm	X60-X84	10.5	12.5
Malnutrition	E40-E46	1.3	0.9
Obesity and other hyperalimentation	E65-E68	1.9	1.8
Renal failure	N17-N19	17.2	13.1
Transport accidents	V01-V99	10.2	11.7
Viral hepatitis	B15-B19	2.6	2.2

Note: (a) ICD-10 = International Classification of Diseases 10th Revision; (1) Mortality rates are a three year average covering 2011-2013; (2) Figures cover Dallas County
Source: Centers for Disease Control and Prevention, National Center for Health Statistics. Compressed Mortality File 1999-2013 on CDC WONDER Online Database, released October 2014. Data are compiled from the Compressed Mortality File 1999-2013, Series 20 No. 2S, 2014.

Health Insurance Coverage

Area	With Health Insurance	With Private Health Insurance	With Public Health Insurance	Without Health Insurance	Population Under Age 18 Without Health Insurance
City	69.6	44.9	30.5	30.4	15.9
MSA[1]	78.1	60.8	24.3	21.9	12.9
U.S.	85.2	65.2	31.0	14.8	7.3

Note: Figures are percentages that cover the civilian noninstitutionalized population; (1) Figures cover the Dallas-Fort Worth-Arlington, TX Metropolitan Statistical Area—see Appendix B for areas included
Source: U.S. Census Bureau, 2011-2013 American Community Survey 3-Year Estimates

Number of Medical Professionals

Area[1]	MDs[2]	DOs[2,3]	Dentists	Podiatrists	Chiropractors	Optometrists
Local (number)	7,589	481	1,851	96	790	299
Local (rate[4])	308.9	19.6	74.5	3.9	31.8	12.0
U.S. (rate[4])	270.0	20.2	63.1	5.7	25.2	14.9

Note: Data as of 2013 unless noted; (1) Local data covers Dallas County; (2) Data as of 2012 and includes all active, non-federal physicians; (3) Doctor of Osteopathic Medicine; (4) rate per 100,000 population
Source: U.S. Department of Health and Human Services, Health Resources and Services Administration, Bureau of Health Professions, Area Resource File (ARF) 2013-2014

Best Hospitals

According to *U.S. News,* the Dallas-Plano-Irving, TX metro area is home to two of the best hospitals in the U.S.: **Baylor University Medical Center** (6 specialties); **UT Southwestern Medical Center** (2 specialties). The hospitals listed were nationally ranked in at least one adult specialty. Only 144 hospitals nationwide were nationally ranked in one or more specialties. Seventeen hospitals in the U.S. made the Honor Roll with high scores in at least six specialties. *U.S. News Online, "America's Best Children's Hospitals 2014-15"*

According to *U.S. News,* the Dallas-Plano-Irving, TX metro area is home to three of the best children's hospitals in the U.S.: **Children's Medical Center Dallas** (6 specialties); **Children's Medical Center Dallas-Parkland Memorial Hospital** (1 specialty); **Children's Medical Center-Texas Scottish Rite Hospital for Children** (1 specialty). The hospitals listed were highly ranked in at least one pediatric specialty. Eighty-nine children's hospitals in the U.S. were nationally ranked in at least one specialty. Ten children's hospitals in the U.S. made the Honor Roll with high scores in at least three specialties. *U.S. News Online, "America's Best Children's Hospitals 2014-15"*

EDUCATION

Public School District Statistics

District Name	Schls	Pupils	Pupil/ Teacher Ratio	Minority Pupils[1] (%)	Free Lunch Eligible[2] (%)	IEP[3] (%)
Dallas Can Academy Charter	4	2,109	18.2	98.1	88.1	11.6
Dallas ISD	234	158,932	16.0	95.2	84.2	7.4
Highland Park ISD	7	6,848	15.8	11.2	0.0	7.7

Note: Table includes school districts with 2,000 or more students; (1) Percentage of students that are not non-Hispanic white; (2) Percentage of students that are eligible for the free lunch program; (3) Percentage of students that have an Individualized Education Program.
Source: U.S. Department of Education, National Center for Education Statistics, Common Core of Data, Local Education Agency (School District) Universe Survey: School Year 2012-2013; U.S. Department of Education, National Center for Education Statistics, Common Core of Data, Public Elementary/Secondary School Universe Survey: School Year 2012-2013

Best High Schools

According to *The Daily Beast,* Dallas is home to 11 of the best high schools in the U.S.: **School for the Talented and Gifted** (#3); **School of Science/Engineering** (#9); **Highland Park High School** (#84); **Rosie Sorrells School of Education and Social Services** (#102); **School of Business and Management** (#109); **Uplift Peak Preparatory** (#253); **Uplift Williams Preparatory** (#285); **Trinidad Garza Early College High School** (#366); **Uplift Hampton Preparatory** (#401); **School of Health Professions** (#592); **Dallas Skyline High School and Career Development Center** (#753); *The Daily Beast* used six indicators culled from school surveys to compare public high schools in the U.S., with graduation and college acceptance rates weighed most heavily. Other criteria included: college-level courses/exams and SAT/ACT scores. *The Daily Beast, "Top High Schools 2014"*

Highest Level of Education

Area	Less than H.S.	H.S. Diploma	Some College, No Deg.	Associate Degree	Bachelor's Degree	Master's Degree	Prof. School Degree	Doctorate Degree
City	25.8	22.0	18.1	4.6	18.5	7.3	2.7	1.1
MSA[1]	15.9	22.8	22.9	6.6	21.3	7.9	1.6	1.0
U.S.	13.7	28.0	21.2	7.9	18.2	7.7	1.9	1.3

Note: Figures cover persons age 25 and over; (1) Figures cover the Dallas-Fort Worth-Arlington, TX Metropolitan Statistical Area—see Appendix B for areas included
Source: U.S. Census Bureau, 2011-2013 American Community Survey 3-Year Estimates

Educational Attainment by Race

Area	High School Graduate or Higher (%)					Bachelor's Degree or Higher (%)				
	Total	White	Black	Asian	Hisp.[2]	Total	White	Black	Asian	Hisp.[2]
City	74.2	74.6	82.9	84.1	45.4	29.6	37.2	16.0	58.9	8.4
MSA[1]	84.1	85.3	88.8	88.0	55.2	31.9	33.4	23.7	55.9	11.0
U.S.	86.3	88.3	83.1	85.7	64.0	29.1	30.4	18.8	50.7	13.7

Note: Figures shown cover persons 25 years old and over; (1) Figures cover the Dallas-Fort Worth-Arlington, TX Metropolitan Statistical Area—see Appendix B for areas included; (2) People of Hispanic origin can be of any race
Source: U.S. Census Bureau, 2011-2013 American Community Survey 3-Year Estimates

School Enrollment by Grade and Control

Area	Preschool (%)		Kindergarten (%)		Grades 1 - 4 (%)		Grades 5 - 8 (%)		Grades 9 - 12 (%)	
	Public	Private	Public	Private	Public	Private	Public	Private	Public	Private
City	70.4	29.6	89.5	10.5	92.3	7.7	89.6	10.4	90.7	9.3
MSA[1]	56.4	43.6	89.9	10.1	92.6	7.4	92.2	7.8	92.4	7.6
U.S.	57.7	42.3	87.9	12.1	89.9	10.1	90.0	10.0	90.7	9.3

Note: Figures shown cover persons 3 years old and over; (1) Figures cover the Dallas-Fort Worth-Arlington, TX Metropolitan Statistical Area—see Appendix B for areas included
Source: U.S. Census Bureau, 2011-2013 American Community Survey 3-Year Estimates

Average Salaries of Public School Classroom Teachers

Area	2013-14		2014-15		Percent Change 2013-14 to 2014-15	Percent Change 2004-05 to 2014-15
	Dollars	Rank[1]	Dollars	Rank[1]		
TEXAS	49,690	30	50,576	29	1.78	23.3
U.S. Average	56,610	–	57,379	–	1.36	20.8

Note: (1) State rank ranges from 1 to 51 where 1 indicates highest salary.
Source: National Education Association, Rankings & Estimates: Rankings of the States 2014 and Estimates of School Statistics 2015, March 2015

Higher Education

Four-Year Colleges			Two-Year Colleges			Medical Schools[1]	Law Schools[2]	Voc/ Tech[3]
Public	Private Non-profit	Private For-profit	Public	Private Non-profit	Private For-profit			
1	7	5	3	1	11	1	2	14

Note: Figures cover institutions located within the city limits and include main campuses only; (1) includes schools accredited by the Liaison Committee on Medical Education and the American Osteopathic Association's Commission on Osteopathic College Accreditation; (2) includes ABA-accredited schools, schools with provisional ABA accreditation, and state accredited schools; (3) includes all schools with programs that are less than 2 years.
Source: National Center for Education Statistics, Integrated Postsecondary Education System (IPEDS), 2013-14; Association of American Medical Colleges, Member List, May 1, 2015; American Osteopathic Association, Member List, May 1, 2015; Law School Admission Council, Official Guide to ABA-Approved Law Schools Online, May 1, 2015; Wikipedia, List of Medical Schools in the United States, May 1, 2015; Wikipedia, List of Law Schools in the United States, May 1, 2015

According to *U.S. News & World Report,* the Dallas-Plano-Irving, TX metro division is home to two of the best national universities in the U.S.: **Southern Methodist University** (#58); **University of Texas-Dallas** (#145). The indicators used to capture academic quality fall into a number of categories: assessment by administrators at peer institutions; retention of students; faculty resources; student selectivity; financial resources; alumni giving; high school counselor ratings of colleges; and graduation rate. *U.S. News & World Report, "America's Best Colleges 2015"*

According to *U.S. News & World Report,* the Dallas-Plano-Irving, TX metro division is home to one of the top 100 law schools in the U.S.: **Southern Methodist University (Dedman)** (#46). The rankings are based on a weighted average of 12 measures of quality: peer assessment score; assessment score by lawyers/judges; median LSAT scores; median undergrad GPA; acceptance rate; employment rates for graduates; placement success; bar passage rate; faculty resources; expenditures per student; student/faculty ratio; and library resources. *U.S. News & World Report, "America's Best Graduate Schools, Law, 2016"*

According to *U.S. News & World Report,* the Dallas-Plano-Irving, TX metro division is home to one of the top 75 medical schools for research in the U.S.: **University of Texas Southwestern Medical Center** (#25). The rankings are based on a weighted average of 11 measures of quality: quality assessment; peer assessment score; assessment score by residency directors; research activity; total research activity; average research activity per faculty member; student selectivity; median MCAT total score; median undergraduate GPA; acceptance rate; and faculty resources. *U.S. News & World Report, "America's Best Graduate Schools, Medical, 2016"*

According to *U.S. News & World Report,* the Dallas-Plano-Irving, TX metro division is home to two of the top 75 business schools in the U.S.: **University of Texas-Dallas** (#33); **Southern Methodist University (Cox)** (#48). The rankings are based on a weighted average of the following nine measures: quality assessment; peer assessment; recruiter assessment; placement success; mean starting salary and bonus; student selectivity; mean GMAT and GRE scores; mean undergraduate GPA; and acceptance rate. *U.S. News & World Report, "America's Best Graduate Schools, Business, 2016"*

PRESIDENTIAL ELECTION

2012 Presidential Election Results

Area	Obama (%)	Romney (%)	Other (%)
Dallas County	57.1	41.7	1.2
U.S.	51.0	47.2	1.8

Note: Results may not add to 100% due to rounding
Source: Dave Leip's Atlas of U.S. Presidential Elections

EMPLOYERS

Major Employers

Company Name	Industry
AMR Corporation	Air transportation, scheduled
Associates First Capital Corporation	Mortgage bankers
Baylor University Medical Center	General medical and surgical hospitals
Children's Medical Center Dallas	Specialty hospitals, except psychiatric
Combat Support Associates	Engineering services
County of Dallas	County supervisors' and executives' office
Dallas County Hospital District	General medical and surgical hospitals
Fort Worth Independent School District	Public elementary and secondary schools
Housewares Holding Company	Toasters, electric: household
HP Enterprise Services	Computer integrated systems design
J.C. Penney Company	Department stores
JCP Publications Corp.	Department stores
L-3 Communications Corporation	Business economic service
Odyssey HealthCare	Home health care services
Romano's Macaroni Grill	Italian restaurant
SFG Management Limited Liability	Milk processing (pasteurizing, homogenizing, bottling)
Texas Instruments Incorporated	Semiconductors and related devices
University of North Texas	Colleges and universities
University of Texas SW Medical Center	Accident and health insurance
Verizon Business Global	Telephone communication, except radio

Note: Companies shown are located within the Dallas-Fort Worth-Arlington, TX Metropolitan Statistical Area.
Source: Hoovers.com; Wikipedia

Best Companies to Work For

Ryan; TDIndustries, headquartered in Dallas, are among "The 100 Best Companies to Work For." To pick the best companies, *Fortune* partnered with the Great Place to Work Institute. Two-thirds of a company's score is based on the results of the Institute's Trust Index survey, which is sent to a random sample of employees from each company. The questions related to attitudes about management's credibility, job satisfaction, and camaraderie. The other third of the scoring is based on the company's responses to the Institute's Culture Audit, which includes detailed questions about pay and benefit programs, and a series of open-ended questions about hiring practices, internal communication, training, recognition programs, and diversity efforts. Any company that is at least five years old with more than 1,000 U.S. employees is eligible. *Fortune, "The 100 Best Companies to Work For," 2015*

Ryan, headquartered in Dallas, is among the "100 Best Companies for Working Mothers." Criteria: leave policies, workforce representation, benefits, child care, advancement programs, and flexibility policies. This year *Working Mother* gave particular weight to representation of women, advancement programs and flex. *Working Mother, "100 Best Companies 2014"*

AT&T, headquartered in Dallas, is among the "100 Best Places to Work in IT." To qualify, companies, both public and private, had to have a minimum of 50 IT employees and were selected based on average salary and bonus increases, the percentage of IT staffers promoted, IT staff turnover rates, training and development programs, and the percentage of women and minorities in IT staff and management positions. In addition, *Computerworld* looked at retention efforts, programs for recognizing and rewarding outstanding performances, and benefits such as flextime, elder care and child care, and reimbursement for college tuition and the cost of pursuing technology certifications. *Computerworld, "100 Best Places to Work in IT 2014"*

AT&T; Texas Instruments, headquartered in Dallas, are among the "Top Companies for Executive Women." To be named to the list, companies with a minimum of two women on the board complete a comprehensive application that focuses on the number of women in senior ranks. In addition to assessing corporate programs and policies dedicated to advancing women, NAFE examined the number of women in each company overall, in senior management, and on its board of directors, paying particular attention to the number of women with profit-and-loss responsibility. *National Association for Female Executives, "2015 NAFE Top 50 Companies for Executive Women"*

PUBLIC SAFETY

Crime Rate

Area	All Crimes	Violent Crimes				Property Crimes		
		Murder	Forcible Rape	Robbery	Aggrav. Assault	Burglary	Larceny -Theft	Motor Vehicle Theft
City	4,828.9	11.4	43.3	334.8	274.3	1,156.6	2,420.2	588.4
Suburbs[1]	2,583.7	2.2	24.0	54.8	103.5	504.5	1,722.1	172.7
Metro[2]	3,209.0	4.7	29.4	132.8	151.1	686.1	1,916.5	288.4
U.S.	3,098.6	4.5	25.2	109.1	229.1	610.0	1,899.4	221.3

Note: Figures are crimes per 100,000 population; (1) All areas within the metro area that are located outside the city limits; (2) Figures cover the Dallas-Plano-Irving, TX Metropolitan Division—see Appendix B for areas included

Source: FBI Uniform Crime Reports, 2013

Hate Crimes

Area	Number of Quarters Reported	Number of Incidents per Bias Motivation						
		Race	Religion	Sexual Orientation	Ethnicity	Disability	Gender	Gender Identity
City	4	3	2	9	4	0	0	0
U.S.	4	2,871	1,031	1,233	655	83	18	31

Source: Federal Bureau of Investigation, Hate Crime Statistics 2013

Identity Theft Consumer Complaints

Area	Complaints	Complaints per 100,000 Population	Rank[2]
MSA[1]	8,158	119.8	27
U.S.	332,646	104.3	-

Note: (1) Figures cover the Dallas-Fort Worth-Arlington, TX Metropolitan Statistical Area—see Appendix B for areas included; (2) Rank ranges from 1 to 380 where 1 indicates greatest number of identity theft complaints per 100,000 population

Source: Federal Trade Commission, Consumer Sentinel Network Data Book for January–December 2014

Fraud and Other Consumer Complaints

Area	Complaints	Complaints per 100,000 Population	Rank[2]
MSA[1]	32,064	470.8	35
U.S.	2,250,205	705.7	-

Note: (1) Figures cover the Dallas-Fort Worth-Arlington, TX Metropolitan Statistical Area—see Appendix B for areas included; (2) Rank ranges from 1 to 380 where 1 indicates greatest number of identity theft complaints per 100,000 population

Source: Federal Trade Commission, Consumer Sentinel Network Data Book for January–December 2014

RECREATION

Culture

Dance[1]	Theatre[1]	Instrumental Music[1]	Vocal Music[1]	Series and Festivals	Museums and Art Galleries[2]	Zoos and Aquariums[3]
3	18	8	3	6	54	2

Note: (1) Professional perfoming groups; (2) Based on organizations with SIC code 8412; (3) AZA-accredited
Source: The Grey House Performing Arts Directory, 2015-16; Association of Zoos & Aquariums, AZA Member Zoos & Aquariums, April 2015; www.AccuLeads.com, April 2015

Professional Sports Teams

Team Name	League	Year Established
Dallas Cowboys	National Football League (NFL)	1960
Dallas Mavericks	National Basketball Association (NBA)	1980
Dallas Stars	National Hockey League (NHL)	1993
FC Dallas	Major League Soccer (MLS)	1996
Texas Rangers	Major League Baseball (MLB)	1972

Note: Includes teams located in the Dallas-Fort Worth-Arlington, TX Metropolitan Statistical Area.
Source: Wikipedia, Major Professional Sports Teams of the United States and Canada, April 2015

CLIMATE

Average and Extreme Temperatures

Temperature	Jan	Feb	Mar	Apr	May	Jun	Jul	Aug	Sep	Oct	Nov	Dec	Yr.
Extreme High (°F)	85	90	100	100	101	112	111	109	107	101	91	87	112
Average High (°F)	55	60	68	76	84	92	96	96	89	79	67	58	77
Average Temp. (°F)	45	50	57	66	74	82	86	86	79	68	56	48	67
Average Low (°F)	35	39	47	56	64	72	76	75	68	57	46	38	56
Extreme Low (°F)	-2	9	12	30	39	53	58	58	42	24	16	0	-2

Note: Figures cover the years 1945-1993
Source: National Climatic Data Center, International Station Meteorological Climate Summary, 9/96

Average Precipitation/Snowfall/Humidity

Precip./Humidity	Jan	Feb	Mar	Apr	May	Jun	Jul	Aug	Sep	Oct	Nov	Dec	Yr.
Avg. Precip. (in.)	1.9	2.3	2.6	3.8	4.9	3.4	2.1	2.3	2.9	3.3	2.3	2.1	33.9
Avg. Snowfall (in.)	1	1	Tr	Tr	0	0	0	0	0	Tr	Tr	Tr	3
Avg. Rel. Hum. 6am (%)	78	77	75	77	82	81	77	76	80	79	78	77	78
Avg. Rel. Hum. 3pm (%)	53	51	47	49	51	48	43	41	46	46	48	51	48

Note: Figures cover the years 1945-1993; Tr = Trace amounts (<0.05 in. of rain; <0.5 in. of snow)
Source: National Climatic Data Center, International Station Meteorological Climate Summary, 9/96

Weather Conditions

Temperature			Daytime Sky			Precipitation		
10°F & below	32°F & below	90°F & above	Clear	Partly cloudy	Cloudy	0.01 inch or more precip.	0.1 inch or more snow/ice	Thunder-storms
1	34	102	108	160	97	78	2	49

Note: Figures are average number of days per year and cover the years 1945-1993
Source: National Climatic Data Center, International Station Meteorological Climate Summary, 9/96

HAZARDOUS WASTE

Superfund Sites

Dallas has one hazardous waste site on the EPA's Superfund Final National Priorities List: **RSR Corp.** There are a total of 1,322 Superfund sites on the list in the U.S. *U.S. Environmental Protection Agency, Final National Priorities List, April 14, 2015*

AIR & WATER QUALITY

Air Quality Trends: Ozone

	2004	2005	2006	2007	2008	2009	2010	2011	2012	2013
MSA[1]	0.087	0.093	0.089	0.081	0.077	0.080	0.076	0.085	0.083	0.078

Note: (1) Data covers the Dallas-Fort Worth-Arlington, TX Metropolitan Statistical Area—see Appendix B for areas included. The values shown are the composite ozone concentration averages among trend sites based on the highest fourth daily maximum 8-hour concentration in parts per million. These trends are based on sites having an adequate record of monitoring data during the trend period. Data from exceptional events are included.

Source: U.S. Environmental Protection Agency, Air Quality Monitoring Information, "Air Quality Trends by City, 2000-2013"

Air Quality Index

Area	Percent of Days when Air Quality was...[2]					AQI Statistics[2]	
	Good	Moderate	Unhealthy for Sensitive Groups	Unhealthy	Very Unhealthy	Maximum	Median
MSA[1]	53.2	43.0	3.8	0.0	0.0	132	49

Note: (1) Data covers the Dallas-Fort Worth-Arlington, TX Metropolitan Statistical Area—see Appendix B for areas included; (2) Based on 365 days with AQI data in 2014. Air Quality Index (AQI) is an index for reporting daily air quality. EPA calculates the AQI for five major air pollutants regulated by the Clean Air Act: ground-level ozone, particle pollution (aka particulate matter), carbon monoxide, sulfur dioxide, and nitrogen dioxide. The AQI runs from 0 to 500. The higher the AQI value, the greater the level of air pollution and the greater the health concern. There are six AQI categories: "Good" AQI is between 0 and 50. Air quality is considered satisfactory; "Moderate" AQI is between 51 and 100. Air quality is acceptable; "Unhealthy for Sensitive Groups" When AQI values are between 101 and 150, members of sensitive groups may experience health effects; "Unhealthy" When AQI values are between 151 and 200 everyone may begin to experience health effects; "Very Unhealthy" AQI values between 201 and 300 trigger a health alert; "Hazardous" AQI values over 300 trigger warnings of emergency conditions (not shown).

Source: U.S. Environmental Protection Agency, Air Quality Index Report, 2014

Air Quality Index Pollutants

Area	Percent of Days when AQI Pollutant was...[2]					
	Carbon Monoxide	Nitrogen Dioxide	Ozone	Sulfur Dioxide	Particulate Matter 2.5	Particulate Matter 10
MSA[1]	0.0	6.8	41.9	0.3	50.1	0.8

Note: (1) Data covers the Dallas-Fort Worth-Arlington, TX Metropolitan Statistical Area—see Appendix B for areas included; (2) Based on 365 days with AQI data in 2014. The Air Quality Index (AQI) is an index for reporting daily air quality. EPA calculates the AQI for five major air pollutants regulated by the Clean Air Act: ground-level ozone, particle pollution (also known as particulate matter), carbon monoxide, sulfur dioxide, and nitrogen dioxide. The AQI runs from 0 to 500. The higher the AQI value, the greater the level of air pollution and the greater the health concern.

Source: U.S. Environmental Protection Agency, Air Quality Index Report, 2014

Maximum Air Pollutant Concentrations: Particulate Matter, Ozone, CO and Lead

	Particulate Matter 10 (ug/m^3)	Particulate Matter 2.5 Wtd AM (ug/m^3)	Particulate Matter 2.5 24-Hr (ug/m^3)	Ozone (ppm)	Carbon Monoxide (ppm)	Lead (ug/m^3)
MSA[1] Level	93	10.6	26	0.085	2	0.08
NAAQS[2]	150	15	35	0.075	9	0.15
Met NAAQS[2]	Yes	Yes	Yes	No	Yes	Yes

Note: (1) Data covers the Dallas-Fort Worth-Arlington, TX Metropolitan Statistical Area—see Appendix B for areas included; Data from exceptional events are included; (2) National Ambient Air Quality Standards; ppm = parts per million; ug/m^3 = micrograms per cubic meter; n/a not available.

Concentrations: Particulate Matter 10 (coarse particulate)—highest second maximum 24-hour concentration; Particulate Matter 2.5 Wtd AM (fine particulate)—highest weighted annual mean concentration; Particulate Matter 2.5 24-Hour (fine particulate)—highest 98th percentile 24-hour concentration; Ozone—highest fourth daily maximum 8-hour concentration; Carbon Monoxide—highest second maximum non-overlapping 8-hour concentration; Lead—maximum running 3-month average

Source: U.S. Environmental Protection Agency, Air Quality Monitoring Information, "Air Quality Statistics by City, 2013"

Maximum Air Pollutant Concentrations: Nitrogen Dioxide and Sulfur Dioxide

	Nitrogen Dioxide AM (ppb)	Nitrogen Dioxide 1-Hr (ppb)	Sulfur Dioxide AM (ppb)	Sulfur Dioxide 1-Hr (ppb)	Sulfur Dioxide 24-Hr (ppb)
MSA[1] Level	12	49	n/a	16	n/a
NAAQS[2]	53	100	30	75	140
Met NAAQS[2]	Yes	Yes	n/a	Yes	n/a

Note: (1) Data covers the Dallas-Fort Worth-Arlington, TX Metropolitan Statistical Area—see Appendix B for areas included; Data from exceptional events are included; (2) National Ambient Air Quality Standards; ppm = parts per million; ug/m^3 = micrograms per cubic meter; n/a not available.
Concentrations: Nitrogen Dioxide AM—highest arithmetic mean concentration; Nitrogen Dioxide 1-Hr—highest 98th percentile 1-hour daily maximum concentration; Sulfur Dioxide AM—highest annual mean concentration; Sulfur Dioxide 1-Hr—highest 99th percentile 1-hour daily maximum concentration; Sulfur Dioxide 24-Hr—highest second maximum 24-hour concentration
Source: U.S. Environmental Protection Agency, Air Quality Monitoring Information, "Air Quality Statistics by City, 2013"

Drinking Water

Water System Name	Pop. Served	Primary Water Source Type	Violations[1]	
			Health Based	Monitoring/ Reporting
Dallas Water Utility	1,253,000	Surface	1	0

Note: (1) Based on violation data from January 1, 2014 to December 31, 2014 (includes unresolved violations from earlier years)
Source: U.S. Environmental Protection Agency, Office of Ground Water and Drinking Water, Safe Drinking Water Information System (based on data extracted January 27, 2015)

El Paso, Texas

Background

El Paso is so named because it sits in a spectacular pass through the Franklin Mountains, at an average elevation of 3,700 feet and in direct view of peaks that rise to 7,200 feet. El Paso is the fourth-largest city in Texas. It lies just south of New Mexico on the Rio Grande and just north of Juarez, Mexico.

The early Spanish explorer Alvar Nunez Cabeza de Vaca (circa 1530) probably passed through this area, but the city was named in 1598 by Juan de Onante, who dubbed it El Paso del Rio del Norte, or The Pass at the River of the North. It was also Onante who declared the area Spanish, on the authority of King Philip II, but a mission was not established until 1649. For some time, El Paso del Norte was the seat of government for northern Mexico, but settlement in and around the present-day city was sparse for many years.

This changed considerably by 1807, when Zebulon A. Pike, a United States Army officer, was interned in El Paso after being convicted of trespassing on Spanish territory. He found the area pleasant and well tended, with many irrigated fields and vineyards and a thriving trade in brandy and wine. In spite of Pike's stay there, though, El Paso remained for many years a largely Mexican region, escaping most of the military action connected to the Texas Revolution.

In the wake of the Mexican War (1846-1848) and in response to the California gold rush in 1849, El Paso emerged as a significant way station on the road West. A federal garrison, Fort Bliss, was established there in 1849, and was briefly occupied by Confederate sympathizers in 1862. Federal forces quickly reoccupied the fort, however, and the area was firmly controlled by Union armies. El Paso was incorporated in 1873, and after 1881, growth accelerated considerably with the building of rail links through the city, giving rise to ironworks, mills, and breweries.

During the Mexican Revolution (1911), El Paso was an important and disputed city, with Pancho Villa himself a frequent visitor, and many of his followers residents of the town. Mexico's national history, in fact, continued to affect El Paso until 1967 when, by way of settling a historic border dispute, 437 acres of the city was ceded to Mexico. Much of the disputed area on both sides of the border was made into parkland. The U.S. National Parks Service maintains the Chamizal Park on the U.S. side and it plays host to a variety of community events during the year including the Chamizal Film Festival and the summer concert series, Music Under the Stars.

One of the major points of entry to the U.S. from Mexico, El Paso is a vitally important international city and a burgeoning center of rail, road, and air transportation. During the 1990s, the city's economy shifted more toward a service-oriented economy and away from a manufacturing base.

Transportation services and motor freight transportation and warehousing has been increasing, and tourism is becoming a growing segment of the economy. Government and military are also sources of employment, with Ft. Bliss being the largest Air Defense Artillery Training Center in the world. The city hosts the University of Texas at El Paso, and a community college. Cultural amenities include the Tigua Indian Cultural Center, a Wilderness Park Museum, the El Paso Zoo, museums, a symphony orchestra, a ballet company, and many theaters. The city's "Wild West" qualities have long made it a popular destination for musicians-many of whom have recorded albums at El Paso's Sonic Ranch recording studio.

El Paso 2015 downtown renovation project began in 2006, with the goal of increasing El Paso's aesthetic appeal. Completed are an open-air mall and "lifestyle center" in the city's central area, Doubletree by Hilton Hotel, and renovations of several historic downtown buildings.

In August 2007, El Paso became the site of the world's largest inland desalination plant, designed to produce 27.5 million gallons of fresh water daily making it a critical component of the region's water portfolio.

The weather in El Paso is of the mountain-desert type, with very little precipitation. Summers are hot, humidity is low and winters are mild. However, temperatures in the flat Rio Grande Valley nearby are notably cooler at night year-round. There is plenty of sunshine and clear skies 202 days of the year.

Rankings

Business/Finance Rankings

- TransUnion ranked the nation's metro areas by average credit score, calculated on the VantageScore system, developed by the three major credit-reporting bureaus—TransUnion, Experian, and Equifax. The El Paso metro area was among the ten cities with the lowest collective credit score, meaning that its residents posed the highest average consumer credit risk. *www.usatoday.com, "Metro Areas' Average Credit Rating Revealed," February 7, 2013*
- Building on the U.S. Department of Labor's Occupational Information Network Data Collection Program, the Brookings Institution defined STEM occupations and job opportunities for STEM workers at various levels of educational attainment. The El Paso metro area was one of the ten metro areas where workers in low-education-level STEM jobs earn the lowest relative wages. *www.brookings.edu, "The Hidden Stem Economy," June 10, 2013*
- Using data from the Council for Community and Economic Research's 2013 Annual Report, NerdWallet ranked the 100 most affordable cities in America. States from the central and southern United States dominate the list. On the affordability scale, El Paso ranked #93. *NerdWallet.com, "Most Affordable Cities in America," June 4, 2014*
- The Brookings Institution ranked the 50 largest cities in the U.S. based on income inequality. El Paso was ranked #35. (#1 = greatest ineqality). Criteria: the cities were ranked based on the "95/20 ratio," a figure representing the income at which a household earns more than 95 percent of all other households, divided by the income at which a household earns more than only 20 percent of all other households. *Brookings Institution, "Income Inequality in America's 50 Largest Cities, 2007-2013," March 17, 2015*
- CareerBliss, an employment and careers website, analyzed U.S. Bureau of Labor Statistics data, more than 30,000 company reviews from employees and former employees, and job openings over a 12-month period to arrive at its list of the best and worst places in the United States to look for a job. El Paso was #6 among the worst places. *CareerBliss.com, "CareerBliss 2013 Best and Worst Cities to Find a Job," January 8, 2013*
- El Paso was ranked #38 out of 100 metro areas in terms of economic performance (#1 = best) during the recession and recovery from trough quarter through the second quarter of 2013. Criteria: percent change in employment; percentage point change in unemployment rate; percent change in gross metropolitan product; percent change in House Price Index. *Brookings Institution, MetroMonitor: Tracking Economic Recession and Recovery in America's 100 Largest Metropolitan Areas, September 2013*
- The El Paso metro area appeared on the Milken Institute "2013 Best Performing Cities" list. Rank: #53 out of 200 large metro areas. Criteria: job growth; wage and salary growth; high-tech output growth. *Milken Institute, "Best-Performing Cities 2014," January 2015*
- *Forbes* ranked the 200 most populous metro areas to determine the nation's "Best Places for Business and Careers." The El Paso metro area was ranked #89. Criteria: costs (business and living); job growth (past and projected); income growth; educational attainment (college and high school); projected economic growth; cultural and recreational opportunities; net migration patterns; number of highly ranked colleges. *Forbes, "The Best Places for Business and Careers 2014," July 23, 2014*

Dating/Romance Rankings

- Of the 100 U.S. cities surveyed by *Men's Health* in its quest to identify the nation's best cities for dating and forming relationships, El Paso was ranked #83 for online dating (#1 = best). *Men's Health, "The Best and Worst Cities for Online Dating," January 30, 2013*

Education Rankings

- Personal finance website *WalletHub* analyzed the 150 largest U.S. metropolitan statistical areas to determine where the most educated Americans are choosing to settle. Criteria: educational attainment; percentage of workers with jobs in computer, engineering, and science fields; quality and size of each metro area's universities. El Paso was ranked #124 (#1 = most educated city). *www.WalletHub.com, "2014's Most and Least Educated Cities*

- El Paso was selected as one of America's most literate cities. The city ranked #75 out of the 77 largest U.S. cities. Criteria: number of booksellers; library resources; Internet resources; educational attainment; periodical publishing resources; newspaper circulation. *Central Connecticut State University, "America's Most Literate Cities, 2014," April 8, 2015*

Environmental Rankings

- The El Paso metro area came in at #273 for the relative comfort of its climate on Sperling's list of "chill cities," as measured by the Sperling Heat Index. All 361 metro areas are included. Criteria included daytime high temperatures, nighttime low temperatures, dew point, and relative humidity at the high temperatures. *www.bertsperling.com, "Sperling's Chill Cities," July 18, 2013*

- Sperling's BestPlaces assessed 379 metropolitan areas of the United States for the likelihood of dangerously extreme weather events or earthquakes. In general the Southeast and South-Central regions have the highest risk of weather extremes and earthquakes, while the Pacific Northwest enjoys the lowest risk. Of the least risky metropolitan areas, the El Paso metro area was ranked #86. *www.bestplaces.net, "Safest Places from Natural Disasters," April 2011*

- El Paso was highlighted as one of the 25 metro areas most polluted by year-round particle pollution (Annual PM 2.5) in the U.S. during 2011 through 2013. The area ranked #23. *American Lung Association, State of the Air 2015*

- El Paso was highlighted as one of the 25 metro areas most polluted by short-term particle pollution (24-hour PM 2.5) in the U.S. during 2011 through 2013. The area ranked #17. *American Lung Association, State of the Air 2015*

Food/Drink Rankings

- *Men's Health* ranked 100 major U.S. cities in terms of alcohol intoxication. El Paso ranked #84 (#1 = most sober).Criteria: binge drinking; alcohol-related traffic accidents, arrests, and fatalities. *Men's Health, "The Drunkest Cities in America," November 19, 2013*

Health/Fitness Rankings

- El Paso was selected as one of the 25 fattest cities in America by *Men's Fitness Online*. It ranked #7 out of America's 50 largest cities. Criteria: fitness centers and sport stores; nutrition; sports participation; TV viewing; overweight/sedentary; junk food; air quality; geography; commute; parks and open space; city recreational facilities; access to healthcare; motivation; mayor and city initiatives; state obesity initiatives. *Men's Fitness, "The Fittest and Fattest Cities in America," March 5, 2012*

- El Paso was identified as a "2013 Spring Allergy Capital." The area ranked #80 out of 100. Three groups of factors were used to identify the most severe cities for people with allergies during the spring season: annual pollen levels; medicine utilization; access to board-certified allergists. *Asthma and Allergy Foundation of America, "Spring Allergy Capitals 2013"*

- El Paso was identified as a "2013 Fall Allergy Capital." The area ranked #52 out of 100. Three groups of factors were used to identify the most severe cities for people with allergies during the fall season: annual pollen levels; medicine utilization; access to board-certified allergists. *Asthma and Allergy Foundation of America, "Fall Allergy Capitals 2013"*

- El Paso was identified as a "2013 Asthma Capital." The area ranked #45 out of the nation's 100 largest metropolitan areas. Twelve factors were used to identify the most challenging places to live for people with asthma: estimated prevalence; self-reported prevalence; crude death rate for asthma; annual pollen score; annual air quality; public smoking laws; number of board-certified asthma specialists; school inhaler access laws; rescue medication use; controller medication use; uninsured rate; poverty rate. *Asthma and Allergy Foundation of America, "Asthma Capitals 2013"*

- *Men's Health* ranked 100 major U.S. cities in terms of the best and worst cities for men. El Paso ranked #60. Criteria: thirty-three data points were examined covering health, fitness, and quality of life. *Men's Health, "The Best & Worst Cities for Men 2014," December 6, 2013*

- The El Paso metro area appeared in the 2013 Gallup-Healthways Well-Being Index. The area ranked #68 out of 189. The Gallup-Healthways Well-Being Index score is an average of six sub-indexes, which individually examine life evaluation, emotional health, work environment, physical health, healthy behaviors, and access to basic necessities. Results are based on telephone interviews conducted as part of the Gallup-Healthways Well-Being Index survey January 2–December 29, 2012, and January 2–December 30, 2013, with a random sample of 531,630 adults, aged 18 and older, living in metropolitan areas in the 50 U.S. states and the District of Columbia. *Gallup-Healthways, "State of American Well-Being," March 25, 2014*

Real Estate Rankings

- El Paso was ranked #222 out of 275 metro areas in terms of house price appreciation in 2014 (#1 = highest rate). *Federal Housing Finance Agency, House Price Index, 4th Quarter 2014*
- El Paso was ranked #172 out of 226 metro areas in terms of housing affordability in 2014 by the National Association of Home Builders (#1 = most affordable). The NAHB-Wells Fargo Housing Opportunity Index (HOI) for a given area is defined as the share of homes sold in that area that would have been affordable to a family earning the local median income, based on standard mortgage underwriting criteria. *National Association of Home Builders®, NAHB-Wells Fargo Housing Opportunity Index, 4th Quarter 2014*

Safety Rankings

- In search of the nation's safest cities, Business Insider looked at the FBI's preliminary Uniform Crime Report, excluding localities with fewer than 200,000 residents. To judge by its low murder, rape, and robbery data, El Paso made the 20 safest cities list, at #14. *www.businessinsider.com, "The 20 Safest Cities in America," July 25, 2013*
- Symantec, in partnership with Sperling's BestPlaces, ranked the 50 largest cities in the U.S. in terms of their vulnerability to cybercrime. The city ranked #49. Criteria: number of cyberattacks and potential infections; level of Internet access; expenditures on smartphones and computer hardware/software; wireless hotspots; broadband connectivity; Internet usage; online purchases. *Symantec, "Riskiest Online Cities of 2012" February 15, 2012*
- Farmers Insurance, in partnership with Sperling's BestPlaces, ranked metro areas in the U.S. and identified the "Most Secure Places to Live." The El Paso metro area ranked #17 out of the top 20 in the large metro area category (500,000 or more residents). Criteria: economic stability; crime statistics; extreme weather; risk of natural disasters; housing depreciation; foreclosures; air quality; environmental hazards; life expectancy; motor vehicle fatalities; and employment numbers. *Farmers Insurance Group of Companies, "Most Secure U.S. Places to Live in the U.S.," June 25, 2013*
- Allstate ranked the 200 largest cities in America in terms of driver safety. El Paso ranked #56. Allstate researchers analyzed internal property damage claims over a two-year period from January 2011 to December 2012. A weighted average of the two-year numbers determined the annual percentages. *Allstate, "Allstate America's Best Drivers Report, 2014"*
- El Paso was identified as one of the safest large cities in America by CQ Press. All 32 cities with populations of 500,000 or more that reported crime rates in 2012 for murder, rape, robbery, aggravated assault, burglary, and motor vehicle thefts were ranked. The city ranked #1 out of the top 10. *CQ Press, City Crime Rankings 2014*
- The National Insurance Crime Bureau ranked 380 metro areas in the U.S. in terms of per capita rates of vehicle theft. The El Paso metro area ranked #129 (#1 = highest rate). Criteria: number of vehicle theft offenses per 100,000 inhabitants in 2012. *National Insurance Crime Bureau, "Hot Spots 2012," June 26, 2013*

Seniors/Retirement Rankings

- From its Best Cities for Successful Aging indexes, the Milken Institute generated rankings for metropolitan areas, weighing data in eight categories—health care, wellness, living arrangements, transportation, financial characteristics, education and employment opportunities, community engagement, and overall livability. The El Paso metro area was ranked #61 overall in the large metro area category. *Milken Institute, "Best Cities for Successful Aging, 2014"*

Women/Minorities Rankings

- To determine the best metro areas for working women, the personal finance website NerdWallet considered city size as well as relevant economic metrics—high salaries, narrow pay differential by gender, prevalence of women in the highest-paying industries, and population growth over 2010–2012. Of the medium-sized U.S. cities examined, the El Paso metro area held the #7 position. *www.nerdwallet.com, "Best Places for Women in the Workforce," May 19, 2013*
- *Women's Health* examined U.S. cities and identified the 100 best cities for women. El Paso was ranked #42. Criteria: 30 categories were examined from obesity and breast cancer rates to commuting times and hours spent working out. *Women's Health, "Best Cities for Women 2012"*

Miscellaneous Rankings

- The National Alliance to End Homelessness ranked the 100 most populous metro areas in terms the rate of homelessness. The El Paso metro area ranked #37. Criteria: number of homeless people per 10,000 population in 2011. *National Alliance to End Homelessness, The State of Homelessness in America 2012*

Business Environment

CITY FINANCES

City Government Finances

Component	2012 ($000)	2012 ($ per capita)
Total Revenues	900,377	1,387
Total Expenditures	871,844	1,343
Debt Outstanding	1,534,086	2,363
Cash and Securities[1]	1,964,584	3,027

Note: (1) Cash and security holdings of a government at the close of its fiscal year, including those of its dependent agencies, utilities, and liquor stores.
Source: U.S Census Bureau, State & Local Government Finances 2012

City Government Revenue by Source

Source	2012 ($000)	2012 ($ per capita)
General Revenue		
From Federal Government	67,105	103
From State Government	22,836	35
From Local Governments	2,056	3
Taxes		
Property	193,854	299
Sales and Gross Receipts	177,857	274
Personal Income	0	0
Corporate Income	0	0
Motor Vehicle License	0	0
Other Taxes	14,917	23
Current Charges	203,504	314
Liquor Store	0	0
Utility	100,739	155
Employee Retirement	56,110	86

Source: U.S Census Bureau, State & Local Government Finances 2012

City Government Expenditures by Function

Function	2012 ($000)	2012 ($ per capita)	2012 (%)
General Direct Expenditures			
Air Transportation	40,889	63	4.7
Corrections	0	0	0.0
Education	0	0	0.0
Employment Security Administration	0	0	0.0
Financial Administration	6,934	11	0.8
Fire Protection	85,039	131	9.8
General Public Buildings	22,579	35	2.6
Governmental Administration, Other	6,621	10	0.8
Health	20,822	32	2.4
Highways	22,688	35	2.6
Hospitals	0	0	0.0
Housing and Community Development	13,743	21	1.6
Interest on General Debt	52,858	81	6.1
Judicial and Legal	8,699	13	1.0
Libraries	7,971	12	0.9
Parking	0	0	0.0
Parks and Recreation	28,673	44	3.3
Police Protection	116,718	180	13.4
Public Welfare	2,622	4	0.3
Sewerage	67,846	105	7.8
Solid Waste Management	32,864	51	3.8
Veterans' Services	0	0	0.0
Liquor Store	0	0	0.0
Utility	153,368	236	17.6
Employee Retirement	96,883	149	11.1

Source: U.S Census Bureau, State & Local Government Finances 2012

DEMOGRAPHICS

Population Growth

Area	1990 Census	2000 Census	2010 Census	Population Growth (%)	
				1990-2000	2000-2010
City	515,541	563,662	649,121	9.3	15.2
MSA[1]	591,610	679,622	800,647	14.9	17.8
U.S.	248,709,873	281,421,906	308,745,538	13.2	9.7

Note: (1) Figures cover the El Paso, TX Metropolitan Statistical Area—see Appendix B for areas included
Source: U.S. Census Bureau, Census 1990, 2000, 2010

Household Size

Area	Persons in Household (%)							Average Household Size
	One	Two	Three	Four	Five	Six	Seven or More	
City	23.2	26.6	18.9	16.6	8.9	3.6	2.2	3.01
MSA[1]	21.4	25.9	19.1	17.2	9.8	4.0	2.8	3.13
U.S.	27.7	33.6	15.7	13.1	6.0	2.3	1.5	2.64

Note: (1) Figures cover the El Paso, TX Metropolitan Statistical Area—see Appendix B for areas included
Source: U.S. Census Bureau, 2011-2013 American Community Survey 3-Year Estimates

Race

Area	White Alone[2] (%)	Black Alone[2] (%)	Asian Alone[2] (%)	AIAN[3] Alone[2] (%)	NHOPI[4] Alone[2] (%)	Other Race Alone[2] (%)	Two or More Races (%)
City	83.2	3.6	1.2	0.5	0.2	9.1	2.2
MSA[1]	82.1	3.4	1.1	0.6	0.2	10.4	2.2
U.S.	73.9	12.6	5.0	0.8	0.2	4.7	2.9

Note: (1) Figures cover the El Paso, TX Metropolitan Statistical Area—see Appendix B for areas included; (2) Alone is defined as not being in combination with one or more other races; (3) American Indian and Alaska Native; (4) Native Hawaiian and Other Pacific Islander
Source: U.S. Census Bureau, 2011-2013 American Community Survey 3-Year Estimates

Hispanic or Latino Origin

Area	Total (%)	Mexican (%)	Puerto Rican (%)	Cuban (%)	Other (%)
City	79.7	75.7	1.1	0.3	2.7
MSA[1]	81.2	77.4	1.0	0.2	2.6
U.S.	16.9	10.8	1.6	0.6	3.8

Note: Persons of Hispanic or Latino origin can be of any race; (1) Figures cover the El Paso, TX Metropolitan Statistical Area—see Appendix B for areas included
Source: U.S. Census Bureau, 2011-2013 American Community Survey 3-Year Estimates

Segregation

Type	Segregation Indices[1]				Percent Change		
	1990	2000	2010	2010 Rank[2]	1990-2000	1990-2010	2000-2010
Black/White	37.5	36.2	30.7	100	-1.3	-6.8	-5.5
Asian/White	23.8	21.9	22.2	100	-1.9	-1.7	0.2
Hispanic/White	49.7	45.2	43.3	50	-4.5	-6.5	-1.9

Note: All figures cover the Metropolitan Statistical Area—see Appendix B for areas included; Figures are based on an analysis of 1990, 2000, and 2010 Census Decennial Census tract data by William H. Frey, Brookings Institution and the University of Michigan Social Science Data Analysis Network. In this analysis all racial groups (whites, blacks, and asians) are non-Hispanic members of those races. Hispanics are shown as a separate category;
(1) Segregation Indices are Dissimilarity Indices that measure the degree to which the minority group is distributed differently than whites across census tracts. They range from 0 (complete integration) to 100 (complete segregation) where the value indicates the percentage of the minority group that needs to move to be distributed exactly like whites; (2) Ranges from 1 (most segregated) to 102 (least segregated); n/a not available.
Source: www.CensusScope.org

Ancestry

Area	German	Irish	English	American	Italian	Polish	French[2]	Scottish	Dutch
City	3.5	2.9	1.7	4.2	1.0	0.4	0.6	0.4	0.2
MSA[1]	3.3	2.6	1.6	3.9	1.0	0.4	0.6	0.4	0.2
U.S.	14.9	10.8	8.0	7.4	5.5	3.0	2.7	1.7	1.4

Note: Figures are the percentage of the total population reporting a particular ancestry. The nine most commonly reported ancestries in the U.S. are shown. Figures include multiple ancestries (e.g. if a person reported being Irish and Italian, they were included in both columns); (1) Figures cover the El Paso, TX Metropolitan Statistical Area—see Appendix B for areas included; (2) Excludes Basque
Source: U.S. Census Bureau, 2011-2013 American Community Survey 3-Year Estimates

Foreign-Born Population

Area	Percent of Population Born in								
	Any Foreign Country	Mexico	Asia	Europe	Carribean	South America	Central America[2]	Africa	Canada
City	24.9	22.2	1.0	0.5	0.2	0.3	0.4	0.1	0.1
MSA[1]	25.8	23.4	0.9	0.4	0.2	0.2	0.4	0.1	0.1
U.S.	13.0	3.7	3.8	1.5	1.2	0.9	1.0	0.6	0.3

Note: (1) Figures cover the El Paso, TX Metropolitan Statistical Area—see Appendix B for areas included; (2) Excludes Mexico.
Source: U.S. Census Bureau, 2011-2013 American Community Survey 3-Year Estimates

Marital Status

Area	Never Married	Now Married[2]	Separated	Widowed	Divorced
City	31.9	47.0	3.8	5.7	11.6
MSA[1]	32.5	47.4	3.9	5.4	10.9
U.S.	32.7	48.1	2.2	6.0	11.0

Note: Figures are percentages and cover the population 15 years of age and older; (1) Figures cover the El Paso, TX Metropolitan Statistical Area—see Appendix B for areas included; (2) Excludes separated
Source: U.S. Census Bureau, 2011-2013 American Community Survey 3-Year Estimates

Disability Status

Area	All Ages	Under 18 Years Old	18 to 64 Years Old	65 Years and Over
City	12.6	3.6	10.6	45.3
MSA[1]	12.6	3.7	11.1	46.2
U.S.	12.3	4.1	10.2	36.3

Note: Figures show percent of the civilian noninstitutionalized population that reported having a disability. Disability status is determined from from six types of difficulty: vision, hearing, cognitive, ambulatory, self-care, and independent living. For children under 5 years old, hearing and vision difficulty are used to determine disability status. For children between the ages of 5 and 14, disability status is determined from hearing, vision, cognitive, ambulatory, and self-care difficulties. For people aged 15 years and older, they are considered to have a disability if they have difficulty with any one of the six difficulty types; (1) Figures cover the El Paso, TX Metropolitan Statistical Area—see Appendix B for areas included.
Source: U.S. Census Bureau, 2011-2013 American Community Survey 3-Year Estimates

Age

Area	Percent of Population									Median Age
	Under Age 5	Age 5–19	Age 20–34	Age 35–44	Age 45–54	Age 55–64	Age 65–74	Age 75–84	Age 85+	
City	7.9	23.3	22.4	12.5	12.5	10.0	6.2	3.9	1.4	32.2
MSA[1]	8.2	24.3	22.4	12.8	12.1	9.6	5.7	3.5	1.3	31.2
U.S.	6.4	19.9	20.7	12.9	14.1	12.3	7.6	4.2	1.9	37.4

Note: (1) Figures cover the El Paso, TX Metropolitan Statistical Area—see Appendix B for areas included
Source: U.S. Census Bureau, 2011-2013 American Community Survey 3-Year Estimates

Gender

Area	Males	Females	Males per 100 Females
City	324,421	346,637	93.6
MSA[1]	405,065	423,307	95.7
U.S.	154,451,010	159,410,713	96.9

Note: (1) Figures cover the El Paso, TX Metropolitan Statistical Area—see Appendix B for areas included
Source: U.S. Census Bureau, 2011-2013 American Community Survey 3-Year Estimates

Religious Groups by Family

Area	Catholic	Baptist	Non-Den.	Methodist[2]	Lutheran	LDS[3]	Pente-costal	Presby-terian[4]	Muslim[5]	Judaism
MSA[1]	43.2	3.8	5.0	0.9	0.3	1.6	1.4	0.2	0.1	0.2
U.S.	19.1	9.3	4.0	4.0	2.3	2.0	1.9	1.6	0.8	0.7

Note: Figures are the number of adherents as a percentage of the total population; (1) Figures cover the El Paso, TX Metropolitan Statistical Area—see Appendix B for areas included; (2) Methodist/Pietist; (3) Latter Day Saints; (4) Reformed; (5) Figures are estimates
Source: Association of Statisticians of American Religious Bodies, 2010 U.S. Religion Census: Religious Congregations & Membership Study

Religious Groups by Tradition

Area	Catholic	Evangelical Protestant	Mainline Protestant	Other Tradition	Black Protestant	Orthodox
MSA[1]	43.2	10.9	1.3	2.1	0.2	0.1
U.S.	19.1	16.2	7.3	4.3	1.6	0.3

Note: Figures are the number of adherents as a percentage of the total population; (1) Figures cover the El Paso, TX Metropolitan Statistical Area—see Appendix B for areas included
Source: Association of Statisticians of American Religious Bodies, 2010 U.S. Religion Census: Religious Congregations & Membership Study

ECONOMY

Gross Metropolitan Product

Area	2012	2013	2014	2015	Rank[2]
MSA[1]	29.6	29.9	31.1	32.6	78

Note: Figures are in billions of dollars; (1) Figures cover the El Paso, TX Metropolitan Statistical Area—see Appendix B for areas included; (2) Rank is based on 2015 data and ranges from 1 to 363
Source: The U.S. Conference of Mayors, U.S. Metro Economies: GMP and Employment 2013-2015, June 2014

Economic Growth

Area	2010-12 (%)	2013 (%)	2014 (%)	2015 (%)	Rank[2]
MSA[1]	2.4	-0.3	1.9	3.1	134
U.S.	2.1	2.0	2.3	3.2	–

Note: Figures are real gross metropolitan product (GMP) growth rates and represent annual average percent change; (1) Figures cover the El Paso, TX Metropolitan Statistical Area—see Appendix B for areas included; (2) Rank is based on 2015 data and ranges from 1 to 363
Source: The U.S. Conference of Mayors, U.S. Metro Economies: GMP and Employment 2013-2015, June 2014

Metropolitan Area Exports

Area	2008	2009	2010	2011	2012	2013	Rank[2]
MSA[1]	9,390.5	7,748.0	10,315.9	11,615.9	12,796.9	14,359.7	22

Note: Figures are in millions of dollars; (1) Figures cover the El Paso, TX Metropolitan Statistical Area—see Appendix B for areas included; (2) Rank is based on 2013 data and ranges from 1 to 387
Source: U.S. Department of Commerce, International Trade Administration, Office of Trade & Industry Information, Manufacturing & Services, data extracted April 3, 2015

Building Permits

Area	Single-Family			Multi-Family			Total		
	2013	2014	Pct. Chg.	2013	2014	Pct. Chg.	2013	2014	Pct. Chg.
City	2,271	2,021	-11.0	1,408	777	-44.8	3,679	2,798	-23.9
MSA[1]	2,613	2,260	-13.5	1,484	783	-47.2	4,097	3,043	-25.7
U.S.	620,802	634,597	2.2	370,020	411,766	11.3	990,822	1,046,363	5.6

Note: (1) Figures cover the El Paso, TX Metropolitan Statistical Area—see Appendix B for areas included; Figures represent new, privately-owned housing units authorized (unadjusted data); All permit data are based on estimates with imputation.
Source: U.S. Census Bureau, Manufacturing, Mining, and Construction Statistics, Building Permits, 2013, 2014

Bankruptcy Filings

Area	Business Filings			Nonbusiness Filings		
	2013	2014	% Chg.	2013	2014	% Chg.
El Paso County	82	68	-17.1	2,108	2,035	-3.5
U.S.	33,212	26,983	-18.8	1,038,720	909,812	-12.4

Note: Business filings include Chapter 7, Chapter 11, Chapter 12, and Chapter 13; Nonbusiness filings include Chapter 7, Chapter 11, and Chapter 13
Source: Administrative Office of the U.S. Courts, Business and Nonbusiness Bankruptcy, County Cases Commenced by Chapter of the Bankruptcy Code, During the 12- Month Period Ending December 31, 2013 and Business and Nonbusiness Bankruptcy, County Cases Commenced by Chapter of the Bankruptcy Code, During the 12- Month Period Ending December 31, 2014

Housing Vacancy Rates

Area	Gross Vacancy Rate[2] (%)			Year-Round Vacancy Rate[3] (%)			Rental Vacancy Rate[4] (%)			Homeowner Vacancy Rate[5] (%)		
	2012	2013	2014	2012	2013	2014	2012	2013	2014	2012	2013	2014
MSA[1]	4.3	8.8	9.3	4.3	8.6	8.4	8.2	7.9	9.2	0.1	2.9	1.5
U.S.	13.8	13.6	13.4	10.8	10.7	10.4	8.7	8.3	7.6	2.0	2.0	1.9

Note: (1) Figures cover the El Paso, TX Metropolitan Statistical Area—see Appendix B for areas included; (2) The percentage of the total housing inventory that is vacant; (3) The percentage of the housing inventory (excluding seasonal units) that is year-round vacant; (4) The percentage of rental inventory that is vacant for rent; (5) The percentage of homeowner inventory that is vacant for sale
Source: U.S. Census Bureau, Housing Vacancies and Homeownership Annual Statistics: 2014

INCOME

Income

Area	Per Capita ($)	Median Household ($)	Average Household ($)
City	19,895	41,657	58,012
MSA[1]	18,563	40,595	56,031
U.S.	27,884	52,176	72,897

Note: (1) Figures cover the El Paso, TX Metropolitan Statistical Area—see Appendix B for areas included
Source: U.S. Census Bureau, 2011-2013 American Community Survey 3-Year Estimates

Household Income Distribution

Area	Percent of Households Earning							
	Under $15,000	$15,000 -24,999	$25,000 -34,999	$35,000 -49,999	$50,000 -74,999	$75,000 -99,000	$100,000 -149,999	$150,000 and up
City	17.2	13.7	11.7	15.6	17.3	9.9	9.2	5.4
MSA[1]	17.7	13.9	12.2	15.5	17.4	9.7	8.7	4.9
U.S.	13.0	10.9	10.3	13.6	17.9	11.9	12.7	9.6

Note: (1) Figures cover the El Paso, TX Metropolitan Statistical Area—see Appendix B for areas included
Source: U.S. Census Bureau, 2011-2013 American Community Survey 3-Year Estimates

Poverty Rate

Area	All Ages	Under 18 Years Old	18 to 64 Years Old	65 Years and Over
City	21.7	30.4	18.3	18.6
MSA[1]	23.6	32.7	19.8	19.4
U.S.	15.9	22.4	14.8	9.5

Note: Figures are percentage of people whose income during the past 12 months was below the poverty level; (1) Figures cover the El Paso, TX Metropolitan Statistical Area—see Appendix B for areas included
Source: U.S. Census Bureau, 2011-2013 American Community Survey 3-Year Estimates

EMPLOYMENT

Labor Force and Employment

Area	Civilian Labor Force			Workers Employed		
	Dec. 2013	Dec. 2014	% Chg.	Dec. 2013	Dec. 2014	% Chg.
City	291,236	288,097	-1.1	272,823	274,124	0.5
MSA[1]	350,534	346,011	-1.3	326,299	327,831	0.5
U.S.	154,408,000	155,521,000	0.7	144,423,000	147,190,000	1.9

Note: Data is not seasonally adjusted and covers workers 16 years of age and older; (1) Figures cover the El Paso, TX Metropolitan Statistical Area—see Appendix B for areas included
Source: Bureau of Labor Statistics, Local Area Unemployment Statistics

Unemployment Rate

Area	2014											
	Jan.	Feb.	Mar.	Apr.	May	Jun.	Jul.	Aug.	Sep.	Oct.	Nov.	Dec.
City	6.7	6.7	6.3	5.7	5.9	6.4	6.5	6.3	5.8	5.5	5.3	4.9
MSA[1]	7.3	7.2	6.8	6.2	6.5	7.0	7.1	6.8	6.3	5.9	5.7	5.3
U.S.	7.0	7.0	6.8	5.9	6.1	6.3	6.5	6.3	5.7	5.5	5.5	5.4

Note: Data is not seasonally adjusted and covers workers 16 years of age and older; (1) Figures cover the El Paso, TX Metropolitan Statistical Area—see Appendix B for areas included
Source: Bureau of Labor Statistics, Local Area Unemployment Statistics

Employment by Occupation

Occupation Classification	City (%)	MSA[1] (%)	U.S. (%)
Management, Business, Science, and Arts	32.1	29.9	36.2
Natural Resources, Construction, and Maintenance	8.6	10.1	9.0
Production, Transportation, and Material Moving	11.2	12.6	12.1
Sales and Office	26.8	26.0	24.4
Service	21.3	21.5	18.3

Note: Figures cover employed civilians 16 years of age and older; (1) Figures cover the El Paso, TX Metropolitan Statistical Area—see Appendix B for areas included
Source: U.S. Census Bureau, 2011-2013 American Community Survey 3-Year Estimates

Employment by Industry

Sector	MSA[1]		U.S.
	Number of Employees	Percent of Total	Percent of Total
Construction, Mining, and Logging	12,500	4.2	5.0
Education and Health Services	41,700	14.0	15.5
Financial Activities	11,800	4.0	5.7
Government	69,200	23.2	15.8
Information	5,900	2.0	2.0
Leisure and Hospitality	32,600	10.9	10.3
Manufacturing	17,100	5.7	8.7
Other Services	9,600	3.2	4.0
Professional and Business Services	31,800	10.7	13.8
Retail Trade	40,800	13.7	11.4
Transportation, Warehousing, and Utilities	14,300	4.8	3.9
Wholesale Trade	11,100	3.7	4.2

Note: Figures are non-farm employment as of December 2014. Figures are not seasonally adjusted and include workers 16 years of age and older; (1) Figures cover the El Paso, TX Metropolitan Statistical Area—see Appendix B for areas included; n/a not available
Source: Bureau of Labor Statistics, Current Employment Statistics, Employment, Hours, and Earnings

Occupations with Greatest Projected Employment Growth: 2012 – 2022

Occupation[1]	2012 Employment	2022 Projected Employment	Numeric Employment Change	Percent Employment Change
Combined Food Preparation and Serving Workers, Including Fast Food	285,480	378,000	92,520	32.4
Personal Care Aides	199,230	283,980	84,750	42.5
Retail Salespersons	378,330	439,340	61,010	16.1
Registered Nurses	189,380	242,860	53,480	28.2
Customer Service Representatives	214,240	262,770	48,530	22.7
Waiters and Waitresses	196,390	240,390	44,000	22.4
Janitors and Cleaners, Except Maids and Housekeeping Cleaners	172,120	213,340	41,220	23.9
Laborers and Freight, Stock, and Material Movers, Hand	185,770	226,470	40,700	21.9
Elementary School Teachers, Except Special Education	141,030	180,920	39,890	28.3
Secretaries and Administrative Assistants, Except Legal, Medical, and Executive	190,470	230,220	39,750	20.9

Note: Projections cover Texas; (1) Sorted by numeric employment change
Source: www.projectionscentral.com, State Occupational Projections, 2012–2022 Long-Term Projections

Fastest Growing Occupations: 2012 – 2022

Occupation[1]	2012 Employment	2022 Projected Employment	Numeric Employment Change	Percent Employment Change
Diagnostic Medical Sonographers	4,380	6,900	2,520	57.6
Computer Numerically Controlled Machine Tool Programmers, Metal and Plastic	1,740	2,700	960	54.8
Interpreters and Translators	4,510	6,720	2,210	49.0
Skincare Specialists	5,130	7,620	2,490	48.3
Agents and Business Managers of Artists, Performers, and Athletes	310	450	140	47.4
Petroleum Engineers	19,280	28,010	8,730	45.3
Information Security Analysts	6,640	9,630	2,990	45.0
Insulation Workers, Mechanical	4,460	6,460	2,000	44.6
Cardiovascular Technologists and Technicians	3,950	5,700	1,750	44.3
Physician Assistants	5,470	7,880	2,410	44.2

Note: Projections cover Texas; (1) Sorted by percent employment change and excludes occupations with numeric employment change less than 100
Source: www.projectionscentral.com, State Occupational Projections, 2012–2022 Long-Term Projections

TAXES

Average Wages

Occupation	$/Hr.	Occupation	$/Hr.
Accountants and Auditors	28.34	Maids and Housekeeping Cleaners	8.55
Automotive Mechanics	15.87	Maintenance and Repair Workers	13.50
Bookkeepers	15.25	Marketing Managers	57.93
Carpenters	13.88	Nuclear Medicine Technologists	n/a
Cashiers	8.96	Nurses, Licensed Practical	21.28
Clerks, General Office	12.73	Nurses, Registered	31.21
Clerks, Receptionists/Information	10.04	Nursing Assistants	10.30
Clerks, Shipping/Receiving	11.36	Packers and Packagers, Hand	9.13
Computer Programmers	36.58	Physical Therapists	46.97
Computer Systems Analysts	32.53	Postal Service Mail Carriers	24.27
Computer User Support Specialists	21.75	Real Estate Brokers	n/a
Cooks, Restaurant	9.26	Retail Salespersons	11.34
Dentists	107.28	Sales Reps., Exc. Tech./Scientific	21.16
Electrical Engineers	45.16	Sales Reps., Tech./Scientific	37.74
Electricians	18.67	Secretaries, Exc. Legal/Med./Exec.	13.05
Financial Managers	48.33	Security Guards	10.13
First-Line Supervisors/Managers, Sales	20.84	Surgeons	116.07
Food Preparation Workers	8.55	Teacher Assistants	11.00
General and Operations Managers	50.94	Teachers, Elementary School	24.40
Hairdressers/Cosmetologists	8.93	Teachers, Secondary School	24.70
Internists	118.46	Telemarketers	10.43
Janitors and Cleaners	9.89	Truck Drivers, Heavy/Tractor-Trailer	17.44
Landscaping/Groundskeeping Workers	10.00	Truck Drivers, Light/Delivery Svcs.	12.44
Lawyers	71.19	Waiters and Waitresses	8.85

Note: Wage data covers the El Paso, TX Metropolitan Statistical Area—see Appendix B for areas included; Hourly wages for elementary/secondary school teachers and teacher assistants were calculated by the editors from annual wage data assuming a 40 hour work week; n/a not available.
Source: Bureau of Labor Statistics, Metro Area Occupational Employment and Wage Estimates, May 2014

State Corporate Income Tax Rates

State	Tax Rate (%)	Income Brackets ($)	Num. of Brackets	Financial Institution Tax Rate (%)[a]	Federal Income Tax Ded.
Texas	(y)	–	–	(y)	No

Note: Tax rates as of January 1, 2015; (a) Rates listed are the corporate income tax rate applied to financial institutions or excise taxes based on income. Some states have other taxes based upon the value of deposits or shares; (y) Texas imposes a Franchise Tax, otherwise known as margin tax, imposed on entities with more than $1,030,000 total revenues at rate of 1%, or 0.5% for entities primarily engaged in retail or wholesale trade, on lesser of 70% of total revenues or 100%of gross receipts after deductions for either compensation or cost of goods sold.
Source: Federation of Tax Administrators, "State Corporate Income Tax Rates, 2015"

State Individual Income Tax Rates

State	Tax Rate (%)	Income Brackets ($)	Num. of Brackets	Personal Exempt. ($)[1] Single	Personal Exempt. ($)[1] Dependents	Fed. Inc. Tax Ded.
Texas	None	–	–	–	–	–

Note: Tax rates as of January 1, 2015; Local- and county-level taxes are not included; n/a not applicable; (1) Married joint filers generally receive double the single exemption
Source: Federation of Tax Administrators, "State Individual Income Tax Rates, 2015"

Various State and Local Tax Rates

State	State and Local Sales and Use (%)	State Sales and Use (%)	Gasoline[1] (¢/gal.)	Cigarette[2] ($/pack)	Spirits[3] ($/gal.)	Wine[4] ($/gal.)	Beer[5] ($/gal.)
Texas	8.25	6.25	20	1.41	2.40 (f)	0.20	0.20 (p)

Note: All tax rates as of January 1, 2015; (1) The American Petroleum Institute has developed a methodology for determining the average tax rate on a gallon of fuel. Rates may include any of the following: excise taxes, environmental fees, storage tank fees, other fees or taxes, general sales tax, and local taxes. In states where gasoline is subject to the general sales tax, or where the fuel tax is based on the average sale price, the average rate determined by API is sensitive to changes in the price of gasoline. States that fully or partially apply general sales taxes to gasoline: CA, CO, GA, IL, IN, MI, NY; (2) The federal excise tax of $1.0066 per pack and local taxes are not included; (3) Rates are those applicable to off-premise sales of 40% alcohol by volume (a.b.v.) distilled spirits in 750ml containers. Local excise taxes are excluded; (4) Rates are those applicable to off-premise sales of 11% a.b.v. non-carbonated wine in 750ml containers; (5) Rates are those applicable to off-premise sales of 4.7% a.b.v. beer in 12 ounce containers; (f) Different rates are also applicable according to alcohol content, place of production, size of container, or place purchased (on- or off-premise or onboard airlines); (p) Local excise taxes are excluded.
Source: Tax Foundation, 2015 Facts & Figures: How Does Your State Compare?

State Business Tax Climate Index Rankings

State	Overall Rank	Corporate Tax Index Rank	Individual Income Tax Index Rank	Sales Tax Index Rank	Unemployment Insurance Tax Index Rank	Property Tax Index Rank
Texas	10	39	6	36	15	36

Note: The index is a measure of how each state's tax laws affect economic performance. The lower the rank, the more favorable a state's tax system is for business. States without a given tax are given a ranking of 1. The scores/rankings for the District of Columbia do not affect other states. The 2015 index represents the tax climate as of July 1, 2014.
Source: Tax Foundation, State Business Tax Climate Index 2015

COMMERCIAL UTILITIES

Typical Monthly Electric Bills

Area	Commercial Service ($/month)		Industrial Service ($/month)	
	1,500 kWh	40 kW demand 14,000 kWh	1,000 kW demand 200,000 kWh	50,000 kW demand 32,500,000 kWh
City	214	1,411	28,058	2,175,903
Average[1]	201	1,653	26,124	2,639,743

Note: Figures are based on annualized 2014 rates; (1) Average based on 180 utilities surveyed
Source: Edison Electric Institute, Typical Bills and Average Rates Report, Summer 2014

TRANSPORTATION

Means of Transportation to Work

Area	Car/Truck/Van		Public Transportation			Bicycle	Walked	Other Means	Worked at Home
	Drove Alone	Car-pooled	Bus	Subway	Railroad				
City	79.2	11.3	2.0	0.0	0.0	0.1	2.0	2.5	2.8
MSA[1]	78.7	11.3	1.7	0.0	0.0	0.1	2.4	2.8	3.0
U.S.	76.4	9.6	2.6	1.8	0.6	0.6	2.8	1.3	4.3

Note: Figures are percentages and cover workers 16 years of age and older; (1) Figures cover the El Paso, TX Metropolitan Statistical Area—see Appendix B for areas included
Source: U.S. Census Bureau, 2011-2013 American Community Survey 3-Year Estimates

Travel Time to Work

Area	Less Than 10 Minutes	10 to 19 Minutes	20 to 29 Minutes	30 to 44 Minutes	45 to 59 Minutes	60 to 89 Minutes	90 Minutes or More
City	8.8	34.0	28.9	21.2	3.6	2.0	1.5
MSA[1]	9.6	32.3	27.8	22.0	4.0	2.6	1.6
U.S.	13.3	29.7	20.9	20.2	7.7	5.7	2.6

Note: Figures are percentages and include workers 16 years old and over; (1) Figures cover the El Paso, TX Metropolitan Statistical Area—see Appendix B for areas included
Source: U.S. Census Bureau, 2011-2013 American Community Survey 3-Year Estimates

Travel Time Index

Area	1985	1990	1995	2000	2005	2010	2011
Urban Area[1]	1.05	1.08	1.12	1.21	1.23	1.21	1.21
Average[2]	1.09	1.14	1.16	1.19	1.23	1.18	1.18

Note: Travel Time Index—the ratio of travel time in the peak period to the travel time at free-flow conditions. For example, a value of 1.30 indicates a 20-minute free-flow trip takes 26 minutes in the peak. Free-flow speeds (60 mph on freeways and 35 mph on principal arterials) are used as the comparison threshold; (1) Covers the El Paso TX-NM urban area; (2) average of 498 urban areas
Source: Texas Transportation Institute, Urban Mobility Report 2012, December 2012

Public Transportation

Agency Name / Mode of Transportation	Vehicles Operated in Maximum Service	Annual Unlinked Passenger Trips (in thous.)	Annual Passenger Miles (in thous.)
Mass Transit Department-City of El Paso (Sun Metro)			
Bus (directly operated)	124	12,485.7	62,584.5
Demand Response (directly operated)	41	38.6	465.0
Demand Response (purchased transportation)	59	178.5	2,126.0
Demand Response Taxi (purchased transportation)	60	7.5	51.3

Source: Federal Transit Administration, National Transit Database, 2013

Air Transportation

Airport Name and Code / Type of Service	Passenger Airlines[1]	Passenger Enplanements	Freight Carriers[2]	Freight (lbs.)
El Paso International (ELP)				
Domestic service (U.S. carriers - 2014)	22	1,350,552	14	88,134,360
International service (U.S. carriers - 2013)	4	10,978	5	1,151,841

Note: (1) Includes all U.S.-based major, minor and commuter airlines that carried at least one passenger during the year; (2) Includes all U.S.-based airlines and freight carriers that transported at least one lb. of freight during the year.
Source: Bureau of Transportation Statistics, The Intermodal Transportation Database, Air Carriers: T-100 Domestic Market (U.S. Carriers), 2014; Bureau of Transportation Statistics, The Intermodal Transportation Database, Air Carriers: T-100 International Market (U.S. Carriers), 2013

Other Transportation Statistics

Major Highways:	I-10
Amtrak Service:	Yes
Major Waterways/Ports:	Rio Grande

Source: Amtrak.com; Google Maps

BUSINESSES

Major Business Headquarters

Company Name	Rankings	
	Fortune[1]	Forbes[2]
Western Refining	281	-

Note: (1) Fortune 500—companies that produce a 10-K are ranked 1 to 500 based on 2013 revenue; (2) all private companies with at least $2 billion in annual revenue through the end of their most current fiscal year are ranked 1 to 221; companies listed are headquartered in the city; dashes indicate no ranking
Source: Fortune, "Fortune 500," June 16, 2014; Forbes, "America's Largest Private Companies," November 5, 2014

Minority Business Opportunity

El Paso is home to 28 companies which are on the *Hispanic Business* 500 list (500 largest U.S. Hispanic-owned companies based on 2012 revenue): **Fred Loya Insurance** (#19); **Bravo Southwest LP** (#71); **R. M. Personnel** (#155); **Integrated Human Capital/Santana Group** (#157); **dmDickason Personnel Services** (#195); **JACO General Contractors** (#254); **Miratek Corp.** (#275); **Thrifty Car Sales** (#312); **LGA Trucking** (#339); **Mike Garcia Merchant Security** (#354); **Aztec Contractors** (#402); **MFH Environmental Corp.** (#416); **Milvian Solutions** (#426); **Five Star Automatic Fire Protection** (#431); **American Packaging and Supply Co.** (#436); **Cesar-Scott** (#437); **El Paso Sanitation Systems** (#449); **Dynatec Scientific Laboratories** (#451); **H.G. Arias & Associates LP** (#462); **Servpro of West El Paso** (#464);

DataXport.Net (#472); **Arrow Discount Automotive** (#474); **Accurate Collision Center** (#479); **ASEO** (#480); **Paul Meza CPA Firm** (#483); **The Saucedo Co.** (#487); **ENCON International** (#494); **Kuzzy Industrial Supplier** (#498). Companies included must show at least 51 percent ownership by Hispanic U.S. citizens, and must maintain headquarters in one of the 50 states or Washington, D.C. *Hispanic Business, "Hispanic Business 500," June 20, 2013*

El Paso is home to six companies which are on the *Hispanic Business* Fastest-Growing 100 list (greatest sales growth from 2008 to 2012): **LGA Trucking** (#28); **Integrated Human Capital/Santana Group** (#30); **Bravo Southwest** (#70); **Milvian Solutions** (#80); **Fred Loya Insurance** (#81); **dmDickason Personnel Services** (#96). Companies included must show at least 51 percent ownership by Hispanic U.S. citizens, and must maintain headquarters in one of the 50 states or Washington, D.C. In addition, companies must have minimum revenues of $200,000 for calendar year 2008. *Hispanic Business, June 20, 2013*

Minority- and Women-Owned Businesses

Group	All Firms		Firms with Paid Employees			
	Firms	Sales ($000)	Firms	Sales ($000)	Employees	Payroll ($000)
Asian	1,115	189,485	432	173,094	2,805	43,016
Black	1,197	57,643	(s)	(s)	(s)	(s)
Hispanic	31,640	5,521,058	3,924	4,565,644	29,777	798,704
Women	14,792	1,952,682	1,609	1,638,631	17,694	375,970
All Firms	52,897	45,727,653	9,346	44,068,193	181,930	5,012,823

Note: Figures cover firms located in the city; minority- and women-owned business are defined as firms in which the corresponding group own 51% or more of the stock or equity of the company; (s) estimates are suppressed when publication standards are not met
Source: U.S. Census Bureau, 2007 Economic Census, Survey of Business Owners (2012 Survey of Business Owners data will be released starting in June 2015)

HOTELS & CONVENTION CENTERS

Hotels/Motels

Area	5 Star		4 Star		3 Star		2 Star		1 Star		Not Rated	
	Num.	Pct.[3]	Num.	Pct.[3]	Num.	Pct.[3]	Num.	Pct.[3]	Num.	Pct.[3]	Num.	Pct.[3]
City[1]	0	0.0	1	1.1	31	34.1	55	60.4	0	0.0	4	4.4
Total[2]	166	0.9	1,264	7.0	5,718	31.8	9,340	52.0	411	2.3	1,070	6.0

Note: (1) Figures cover El Paso and vicinity; (2) Figures cover all 100 cities in this book; (3) Percentage of hotels which have a given star rating; Star ratings are determined by expedia.com and offer an indication of the general quality of a particular hotel.
Source: expedia.com, April 2, 2015

Major Convention Centers

Name	Overall Space (sq. ft.)	Exhibit Space (sq. ft.)	Meeting Space (sq. ft.)	Meeting Rooms
Judson F. Williams Convention Center	n/a	80,000	14,900	17

Note: Table includes convention centers located in the El Paso, TX metro area; n/a not available
Source: Original research

Living Environment

COST OF LIVING

Cost of Living Index

Composite Index	Groceries	Housing	Utilities	Transportation	Health Care	Misc. Goods/ Services
92.9	100.2	85.6	88.3	96.8	88.8	96.7

Note: The Cost of Living Index measures regional differences in the cost of consumer goods and services, excluding taxes and non-consumer expenditures, for professional and managerial households in the top income quintile. It is based on more than 50,000 prices covering almost 60 different items for which prices are collected three times a year by chambers of commerce, economic development organizations or university applied economic centers in each participating urban area. The numbers shown should be read as a percentage above or below the national average of 100. For example, a value of 115.4 in the groceries column indicates that grocery prices are 15.4% higher than the national average. Small differences in the index numbers should not be interpreted as significant; Figures cover the El Paso TX urban area.
Source: The Council for Community and Economic Research, ACCRA Cost of Living Index, 2014

Grocery Prices

Area[1]	T-Bone Steak ($/pound)	Frying Chicken ($/pound)	Whole Milk ($/half gal.)	Eggs ($/dozen)	Orange Juice ($/64 oz.)	Coffee ($/11.5 oz.)
City[2]	10.65	1.30	2.26	1.78	3.22	4.43
Avg.	10.40	1.37	2.40	1.99	3.46	4.27
Min.	8.48	0.93	1.37	1.30	2.83	2.99
Max.	14.20	2.44	3.62	4.02	6.42	6.96

Note: (1) Values for the local area are compared with the average, minimum and maximum values for all 308 areas in the Cost of Living Index; (2) Figures cover the El Paso TX urban area; **T-Bone Steak** *(price per pound);* **Frying Chicken** *(price per pound, whole fryer);* **Whole Milk** *(half gallon carton);* **Eggs** *(price per dozen, Grade A, large);* **Orange Juice** *(64 oz. Tropicana or Florida Natural);* **Coffee** *(11.5 oz. can, vacuum-packed, Maxwell House, Hills Bros, or Folgers).*
Source: The Council for Community and Economic Research, ACCRA Cost of Living Index, 2014

Housing and Utility Costs

Area[1]	New Home Price ($)	Apartment Rent ($/month)	All Electric ($/month)	Part Electric ($/month)	Other Energy ($/month)	Telephone ($/month)
City[2]	244,332	930	-	99.97	39.65	26.95
Avg.	305,838	919	181.00	93.66	73.14	27.95
Min.	183,142	480	112.00	42.06	23.42	17.16
Max.	1,358,576	3,851	594.00	180.03	440.99	40.42

Note: (1) Values for the local area are compared with the average, minimum and maximum values for all 308 areas in the Cost of Living Index; (2) Figures cover the El Paso TX urban area; **New Home Price** *(2,400 sf living area, 8,000 sf lot, in urban area with full utilities);* **Apartment Rent** *(950 sf 2 bedroom/1.5 or 2 bath, unfurnished, excluding all utilities except water);* **All Electric** *(average monthly cost for an all-electric home);* **Part Electric** *(average monthly cost for a part-electric home);* **Other Energy** *(average monthly cost for natural gas, fuel oil, coal, wood, and any other forms of energy except electricity);* **Telephone** *(price includes basic monthly rate for a private residential line plus additional local usage charges incurred by a family of four).*
Source: The Council for Community and Economic Research, ACCRA Cost of Living Index, 2014

Health Care, Transportation, and Other Costs

Area[1]	Doctor ($/visit)	Dentist ($/visit)	Optometrist ($/visit)	Gasoline ($/gallon)	Beauty Salon ($/visit)	Men's Shirt ($)
City[2]	83.67	79.14	75.22	3.31	32.50	24.55
Avg.	102.86	87.89	97.66	3.44	34.37	26.74
Min.	67.47	65.78	51.18	3.00	17.43	12.79
Max.	173.50	150.14	235.00	4.33	64.28	49.50

Note: (1) Values for the local area are compared with the average, minimum and maximum values for all 308 areas in the Cost of Living Index; (2) Figures cover the El Paso TX urban area; **Doctor** *(general practitioners routine exam of an established patient);* **Dentist** *(adult teeth cleaning and periodic oral examination);* **Optometrist** *(full vision eye exam for established adult patient);* **Gasoline** *(one gallon regular unleaded, national brand, including all taxes, cash price at self-service pump if available);* **Beauty Salon** *(woman's shampoo, trim, and blow-dry);* **Men's Shirt** *(cotton/polyester dress shirt, pinpoint weave, long sleeves).*
Source: The Council for Community and Economic Research, ACCRA Cost of Living Index, 2014

HOUSING

House Price Index (HPI)

Area	National Ranking[2]	Quarterly Change (%)	One-Year Change (%)	Five-Year Change (%)
MSA[1]	222	-0.06	1.99	-0.86
U.S.[3]	–	1.35	4.91	11.59

Note: The HPI is a weighted repeat sales index. It measures average price changes in repeat sales or refinancings on the same properties. This information is obtained by reviewing repeat mortgage transactions on single-family properties whose mortgages have been purchased or securitized by Fannie Mae or Freddie Mac in January 1975; (1) El Paso Metropolitan Statistical Area—see Appendix B for areas included; (2) Rankings are based on annual percentage change for all metro areas containing at least 15,000 transactions over the last 10 years and ranges from 1 to 275; (3) figures based on a weighted average of Census Division estimates using a seasonally adjusted, purchase-only index; all figures are for the period ending December 31, 2014
Source: Federal Housing Finance Agency, House Price Index, February 26, 2015

Median Single-Family Home Prices

Area	2012	2013	2014p	Percent Change 2013 to 2014
MSA[1]	138.6	141.2	140.8	-0.3
U.S. Average	177.2	197.4	209.0	5.9

Note: Figures are median sales prices of existing single-family homes in thousands of dollars; (p) preliminary; n/a not available; (1) El Paso, TX Metropolitan Statistical Area—see Appendix B for areas included
Source: National Association of Realtors, Median Sales Price of Existing Single-Family Homes for Metropolitan Areas, 4th Quarter 2014

Qualifying Income Based on Median Sales Price of Existing Single-Family Homes

Area	With 5% Down ($)	With 10% Down ($)	With 20% Down ($)
MSA[1]	31,579	29,917	26,593
U.S. Average	45,863	43,449	38,621

Note: Figures are preliminary; Qualifying income is based on a mortgage rate of 4.0%. Monthly principal and interest payment is limited to 25% of income; n/a not available; (1) El Paso, TX Metropolitan Statistical Area—see Appendix B for areas included
Source: National Association of Realtors, Qualifying Income Based on Median Sales Price of Existing Single-Family Homes for Metropolitan Areas, 4th Quarter 2014

Median Apartment Condo-Coop Home Prices

Area	2012	2013	2014p	Percent Change 2013 to 2014
MSA[1]	n/a	n/a	n/a	n/a
U.S. Average	173.7	194.9	205.1	5.2

Note: Figures are median sales prices of existing apartment condo-coop homes in thousands of dollars; (p) preliminary; n/a not available; (1) El Paso, TX Metropolitan Statistical Area—see Appendix B for areas included
Source: National Association of Realtors, Median Sales Price of Existing Apartment Condo-Coop Homes for Metropolitan Areas, 4th Quarter 2014

Gross Monthly Rent

Area	Under $200	$200 -299	$300 -499	$500 -749	$750 -999	$1,000 -1,499	$1,500 and up	Median ($)
City	4.1	4.5	13.3	29.2	25.0	19.7	4.2	742
MSA[1]	4.0	4.2	14.2	29.2	24.6	19.4	4.4	738
U.S.	1.7	3.2	7.8	22.1	24.3	26.0	14.9	900

Note: Figures are percentages except for Median; Gross rent is the contract rent plus the estimated average monthly cost of utilities (electricity, gas, and water and sewer) and fuels (oil, coal, kerosene, wood, etc.) if these are paid by the renter (or paid for the renter by someone else); (1) Figures cover the El Paso, TX Metropolitan Statistical Area—see Appendix B for areas included
Source: U.S. Census Bureau, 2011-2013 American Community Survey 3-Year Estimates

Homeownership Rate

Area	2007 (%)	2008 (%)	2009 (%)	2010 (%)	2011 (%)	2012 (%)	2013 (%)	2014 (%)
MSA[1]	68.2	64.8	63.8	70.1	72.0	67.4	69.3	66.7
U.S.	68.1	67.8	67.4	66.9	66.1	65.4	65.1	64.5

Note: (1) Figures cover the El Paso, TX Metropolitan Statistical Area—see Appendix B for areas included
Source: U.S. Census Bureau, Housing Vacancies and Homeownership Annual Statistics: 2014

Year Housing Structure Built

Area	2010 or Later	2000 -2009	1990 -1999	1980 -1989	1970 -1979	1960 -1969	1950 -1959	1940 -1949	Before 1940	Median Year
City	2.8	16.9	12.8	14.8	18.3	12.9	12.7	4.1	4.7	1979
MSA[1]	3.1	18.6	14.1	15.8	17.6	11.6	11.2	3.7	4.3	1981
U.S.	0.9	15.0	13.9	13.8	15.8	11.0	10.9	5.4	13.3	1976

Note: Figures are percentages except for Median Year; (1) Figures cover the El Paso, TX Metropolitan Statistical Area—see Appendix B for areas included
Source: U.S. Census Bureau, 2011-2013 American Community Survey 3-Year Estimates

HEALTH

Health Risk Data

Category	MSA[1] (%)	U.S. (%)
Adults aged 18–64 who have any kind of health care coverage	52.1	79.6
Adults who reported being in good or excellent health	76.6	83.1
Adults who are current smokers	15.1	19.6
Adults who are heavy drinkers[2]	5.2	6.1
Adults who are binge drinkers[3]	21.0	16.9
Adults who are overweight (BMI 25.0 - 29.9)	36.6	35.8
Adults who are obese (BMI 30.0 - 99.8)	29.4	27.6
Adults who participated in any physical activities in the past month	68.0	77.1
Adults 50+ who have ever had a sigmoidoscopy or colonoscopy	50.0	67.3
Women aged 40+ who have had a mammogram within the past two years	65.8	74.0
Men aged 40+ who have had a PSA test within the past two years	36.5	45.2
Adults aged 65+ who have had flu shot within the past year	50.9	60.1
Adults who always wear a seatbelt	n/a	93.8

Note: Data as of 2012 unless otherwise noted; n/a not available; (1) Figures cover the El Paso, TX Metropolitan Statistical Area—see Appendix B for areas included; (2) Heavy drinkers are classified as males having more than two drinks per day or females having more than one drink per day; (3) Binge drinkers are classified as males having five or more drinks on one occasion or females having four or more drinks on one occasion
Source: Centers for Disease Control and Prevention, Behaviorial Risk Factor Surveillance System, SMART: Selected Metropolitan/Micropolitan Area Risk Trends, 2012 (Note: the CDC has discontinued this dataset but will be releasing a replacement in late 2015)

Chronic Health Indicators

Category	MSA[1] (%)	U.S. (%)
Adults who have ever been told they had a heart attack	n/a	4.5
Adults who have ever been told they had a stroke	n/a	2.9
Adults who have been told they currently have asthma	7.5	8.9
Adults who have ever been told they have arthritis	19.6	25.7
Adults who have ever been told they have diabetes[2]	14.1	9.7
Adults who have ever been told they had skin cancer	n/a	5.7
Adults who have ever been told they had any other types of cancer	5.8	6.5
Adults who have ever been told they have COPD	4.1	6.2
Adults who have ever been told they have kidney disease	n/a	2.5
Adults who have ever been told they have a form of depression	17.2	18.0

Note: Data as of 2012 unless otherwise noted; n/a not available; (1) Figures cover the El Paso, TX Metropolitan Statistical Area—see Appendix B for areas included; (2) Figures do not include pregnancy-related, borderline, or pre-diabetes
Source: Centers for Disease Control and Prevention, Behaviorial Risk Factor Surveillance System, SMART: Selected Metropolitan/Micropolitan Area Risk Trends, 2012 (Note: the CDC has discontinued this dataset but will be releasing a replacement in late 2015)

Mortality Rates for the Top 10 Causes of Death in the U.S.

ICD-10[a] Sub-Chapter	ICD-10[a] Code	Age-Adjusted Mortality Rate[1] per 100,000 population	
		County[2]	U.S.
Malignant neoplasms	C00-C97	142.1	166.2
Ischaemic heart diseases	I20-I25	72.8	105.7
Other forms of heart disease	I30-I51	31.3	49.3
Chronic lower respiratory diseases	J40-J47	33.6	42.1
Organic, including symptomatic, mental disorders	F01-F09	39.4	38.1
Cerebrovascular diseases	I60-I69	34.4	37.0
Other external causes of accidental injury	W00-X59	19.2	26.9
Other degenerative diseases of the nervous system	G30-G31	27.1	25.6
Diabetes mellitus	E10-E14	33.8	21.3
Hypertensive diseases	I10-I15	40.7	19.4

Note: (a) ICD-10 = International Classification of Diseases 10th Revision; (1) Mortality rates are a three year average covering 2011-2013; (2) Figures cover El Paso County
Source: Centers for Disease Control and Prevention, National Center for Health Statistics. Compressed Mortality File 1999-2013 on CDC WONDER Online Database, released October 2014. Data are compiled from the Compressed Mortality File 1999-2013, Series 20 No. 2S, 2014.

Mortality Rates for Selected Causes of Death

ICD-10[a] Sub-Chapter	ICD-10[a] Code	Age-Adjusted Mortality Rate[1] per 100,000 population	
		County[2]	U.S.
Assault	X85-Y09	2.6	5.2
Diseases of the liver	K70-K76	28.1	13.2
Human immunodeficiency virus (HIV) disease	B20-B24	2.0	2.2
Influenza and pneumonia	J09-J18	8.7	15.4
Intentional self-harm	X60-X84	8.2	12.5
Malnutrition	E40-E46	1.3	0.9
Obesity and other hyperalimentation	E65-E68	2.0	1.8
Renal failure	N17-N19	13.9	13.1
Transport accidents	V01-V99	13.1	11.7
Viral hepatitis	B15-B19	2.3	2.2

Note: (a) ICD-10 = International Classification of Diseases 10th Revision; (1) Mortality rates are a three year average covering 2011-2013; (2) Figures cover El Paso County
Source: Centers for Disease Control and Prevention, National Center for Health Statistics. Compressed Mortality File 1999-2013 on CDC WONDER Online Database, released October 2014. Data are compiled from the Compressed Mortality File 1999-2013, Series 20 No. 2S, 2014.

Health Insurance Coverage

Area	With Health Insurance	With Private Health Insurance	With Public Health Insurance	Without Health Insurance	Population Under Age 18 Without Health Insurance
City	73.7	48.3	32.7	26.3	12.7
MSA[1]	72.2	45.7	33.0	27.8	13.2
U.S.	85.2	65.2	31.0	14.8	7.3

Note: Figures are percentages that cover the civilian noninstitutionalized population; (1) Figures cover the El Paso, TX Metropolitan Statistical Area—see Appendix B for areas included
Source: U.S. Census Bureau, 2011-2013 American Community Survey 3-Year Estimates

Number of Medical Professionals

Area[1]	MDs[2]	DOs[2,3]	Dentists	Podiatrists	Chiropractors	Optometrists
Local (number)	1,458	115	308	30	67	65
Local (rate[4])	175.4	13.8	37.0	3.6	8.1	7.8
U.S. (rate[4])	270.0	20.2	63.1	5.7	25.2	14.9

Note: Data as of 2013 unless noted; (1) Local data covers El Paso County; (2) Data as of 2012 and includes all active, non-federal physicians; (3) Doctor of Osteopathic Medicine; (4) rate per 100,000 population
Source: U.S. Department of Health and Human Services, Health Resources and Services Administration, Bureau of Health Professions, Area Resource File (ARF) 2013-2014

EDUCATION

Public School District Statistics

District Name	Schls	Pupils	Pupil/ Teacher Ratio	Minority Pupils[1] (%)	Free Lunch Eligible[2] (%)	IEP[3] (%)
Canutillo ISD	10	6,068	16.1	95.8	63.0	8.9
Clint ISD	15	11,762	18.3	96.1	75.6	6.3
El Paso ISD	96	63,210	15.3	89.4	61.2	8.9
Socorro ISD	45	44,259	19.3	94.7	59.1	8.0
Ysleta ISD	63	43,680	14.3	97.3	69.9	10.2

Note: Table includes school districts with 2,000 or more students; (1) Percentage of students that are not non-Hispanic white; (2) Percentage of students that are eligible for the free lunch program; (3) Percentage of students that have an Individualized Education Program.
Source: U.S. Department of Education, National Center for Education Statistics, Common Core of Data, Local Education Agency (School District) Universe Survey: School Year 2012-2013; U.S. Department of Education, National Center for Education Statistics, Common Core of Data, Public Elementary/Secondary School Universe Survey: School Year 2012-2013

Best High Schools

According to *The Daily Beast,* El Paso is home to one of the best high schools in the U.S.: **Franklin High School** (#658); *The Daily Beast* used six indicators culled from school surveys to compare public high schools in the U.S., with graduation and college acceptance rates weighed most heavily. Other criteria included: college-level courses/exams and SAT/ACT scores. *The Daily Beast, "Top High Schools 2014"*

Highest Level of Education

Area	Less than H.S.	H.S. Diploma	Some College, No Deg.	Associate Degree	Bachelor's Degree	Master's Degree	Prof. School Degree	Doctorate Degree
City	22.7	23.5	23.4	7.5	15.6	5.5	1.2	0.7
MSA[1]	25.2	23.8	22.8	7.3	14.3	5.0	1.0	0.7
U.S.	13.7	28.0	21.2	7.9	18.2	7.7	1.9	1.3

Note: Figures cover persons age 25 and over; (1) Figures cover the El Paso, TX Metropolitan Statistical Area—see Appendix B for areas included
Source: U.S. Census Bureau, 2011-2013 American Community Survey 3-Year Estimates

Educational Attainment by Race

Area	High School Graduate or Higher (%)					Bachelor's Degree or Higher (%)				
	Total	White	Black	Asian	Hisp.[2]	Total	White	Black	Asian	Hisp.[2]
City	77.3	77.6	92.0	89.6	72.2	23.0	22.8	27.9	48.4	18.6
MSA[1]	74.8	75.4	92.6	90.6	69.5	21.0	20.9	28.3	48.9	16.7
U.S.	86.3	88.3	83.1	85.7	64.0	29.1	30.4	18.8	50.7	13.7

Note: Figures shown cover persons 25 years old and over; (1) Figures cover the El Paso, TX Metropolitan Statistical Area—see Appendix B for areas included; (2) People of Hispanic origin can be of any race
Source: U.S. Census Bureau, 2011-2013 American Community Survey 3-Year Estimates

School Enrollment by Grade and Control

Area	Preschool (%)		Kindergarten (%)		Grades 1 - 4 (%)		Grades 5 - 8 (%)		Grades 9 - 12 (%)	
	Public	Private	Public	Private	Public	Private	Public	Private	Public	Private
City	81.6	18.4	94.1	5.9	95.0	5.0	94.3	5.7	96.7	3.3
MSA[1]	84.6	15.4	95.2	4.8	95.9	4.1	95.3	4.7	97.2	2.8
U.S.	57.7	42.3	87.9	12.1	89.9	10.1	90.0	10.0	90.7	9.3

Note: Figures shown cover persons 3 years old and over; (1) Figures cover the El Paso, TX Metropolitan Statistical Area—see Appendix B for areas included
Source: U.S. Census Bureau, 2011-2013 American Community Survey 3-Year Estimates

Average Salaries of Public School Classroom Teachers

Area	2013-14		2014-15		Percent Change 2013-14 to 2014-15	Percent Change 2004-05 to 2014-15
	Dollars	Rank[1]	Dollars	Rank[1]		
TEXAS	49,690	30	50,576	29	1.78	23.3
U.S. Average	56,610	–	57,379	–	1.36	20.8

Note: (1) State rank ranges from 1 to 51 where 1 indicates highest salary.
Source: National Education Association, Rankings & Estimates: Rankings of the States 2014 and Estimates of School Statistics 2015, March 2015

Higher Education

Four-Year Colleges			Two-Year Colleges			Medical Schools[1]	Law Schools[2]	Voc/ Tech[3]
Public	Private Non-profit	Private For-profit	Public	Private Non-profit	Private For-profit			
1	0	1	1	0	8	1	0	6

Note: Figures cover institutions located within the city limits and include main campuses only; (1) includes schools accredited by the Liaison Committee on Medical Education and the American Osteopathic Association's Commission on Osteopathic College Accreditation; (2) includes ABA-accredited schools, schools with provisional ABA accreditation, and state accredited schools; (3) includes all schools with programs that are less than 2 years.
Source: National Center for Education Statistics, Integrated Postsecondary Education System (IPEDS), 2013-14; Association of American Medical Colleges, Member List, May 1, 2015; American Osteopathic Association, Member List, May 1, 2015; Law School Admission Council, Official Guide to ABA-Approved Law Schools Online, May 1, 2015; Wikipedia, List of Medical Schools in the United States, May 1, 2015; Wikipedia, List of Law Schools in the United States, May 1, 2015

PRESIDENTIAL ELECTION

2012 Presidential Election Results

Area	Obama (%)	Romney (%)	Other (%)
El Paso County	65.6	33.0	1.3
U.S.	51.0	47.2	1.8

Note: Results may not add to 100% due to rounding
Source: Dave Leip's Atlas of U.S. Presidential Elections

EMPLOYERS

Major Employers

Company Name	Industry
AHAC	Employmant agencies
Automatic Data Processing	Data processing service
Bureau of Customs and Border Protection	Customs
City of El Paso	Executive/legislative combined
Delphi Automotive Systems	Motor vehicle parts/accessories
Delphi Automotive Systems Corporation	Automotive, electrical equipment
El paso County Hospital Direct	General medical/surgical hospitals
El Paso Electric Company	Electric services
Elcom	Electrical circuits
Furukawa Wiring Systems America	Public building /related furniture
Genpact	Data processing/preparation
Justin Brands	Boots/dress or casual mens
Philips Consumer Electronic Company	Cameras/televisions
Redcats USA, LP	Catalog/mail order house
Tenet Hospitals Limited	General medical/surgical hospitals
Texas Tech University	University
Time Warner, Advance Newhouse Prtnrshp	Cable television services
United States Postal Service	Postal service
University of Texas at El Paso	Colleges/universities

Note: Companies shown are located within the El Paso, TX Metropolitan Statistical Area.
Source: Hoovers.com; Wikipedia

PUBLIC SAFETY

Crime Rate

Area	All Crimes	Violent Crimes				Property Crimes		
		Murder	Forcible Rape	Robbery	Aggrav. Assault	Burglary	Larceny -Theft	Motor Vehicle Theft
City	2,660.0	1.5	25.9	67.2	276.4	260.6	1,911.6	116.8
Suburbs[1]	1,953.6	1.2	36.9	24.0	185.8	364.8	1,238.2	102.7
Metro[2]	2,523.7	1.4	28.0	58.9	258.9	280.7	1,781.6	114.1
U.S.	3,098.6	4.5	25.2	109.1	229.1	610.0	1,899.4	221.3

Note: Figures are crimes per 100,000 population; (1) All areas within the metro area that are located outside the city limits; (2) Figures cover the El Paso, TX Metropolitan Statistical Area—see Appendix B for areas included
Source: FBI Uniform Crime Reports, 2013

Hate Crimes

Area	Number of Quarters Reported	Number of Incidents per Bias Motivation						
		Race	Religion	Sexual Orientation	Ethnicity	Disability	Gender	Gender Identity
City	4	0	0	3	0	0	0	0
U.S.	4	2,871	1,031	1,233	655	83	18	31

Source: Federal Bureau of Investigation, Hate Crime Statistics 2013

Identity Theft Consumer Complaints

Area	Complaints	Complaints per 100,000 Population	Rank[2]
MSA[1]	614	73.9	159
U.S.	332,646	104.3	-

Note: (1) Figures cover the El Paso, TX Metropolitan Statistical Area—see Appendix B for areas included; (2) Rank ranges from 1 to 380 where 1 indicates greatest number of identity theft complaints per 100,000 population
Source: Federal Trade Commission, Consumer Sentinel Network Data Book for January–December 2014

Fraud and Other Consumer Complaints

Area	Complaints	Complaints per 100,000 Population	Rank[2]
MSA[1]	2,314	278.4	346
U.S.	2,250,205	705.7	-

Note: (1) Figures cover the El Paso, TX Metropolitan Statistical Area—see Appendix B for areas included; (2) Rank ranges from 1 to 380 where 1 indicates greatest number of identity theft complaints per 100,000 population
Source: Federal Trade Commission, Consumer Sentinel Network Data Book for January–December 2014

RECREATION

Culture

Dance[1]	Theatre[1]	Instrumental Music[1]	Vocal Music[1]	Series and Festivals	Museums and Art Galleries[2]	Zoos and Aquariums[3]
0	2	2	1	4	17	1

Note: (1) Professional perfoming groups; (2) Based on organizations with SIC code 8412; (3) AZA-accredited
Source: The Grey House Performing Arts Directory, 2015-16; Association of Zoos & Aquariums, AZA Member Zoos & Aquariums, April 2015; www.AccuLeads.com, April 2015

Professional Sports Teams

Team Name	League	Year Established

No teams are located in the metro area

Source: Wikipedia, Major Professional Sports Teams of the United States and Canada, April 2015

CLIMATE

Average and Extreme Temperatures

Temperature	Jan	Feb	Mar	Apr	May	Jun	Jul	Aug	Sep	Oct	Nov	Dec	Yr.
Extreme High (°F)	80	83	89	98	104	114	112	108	104	96	87	80	114
Average High (°F)	57	63	70	79	87	96	95	93	88	79	66	58	78
Average Temp. (°F)	44	49	56	64	73	81	83	81	75	65	52	45	64
Average Low (°F)	31	35	41	49	58	66	70	68	62	50	38	32	50
Extreme Low (°F)	-8	8	14	23	31	46	57	56	42	25	1	5	-8

Note: Figures cover the years 1948-1995
Source: National Climatic Data Center, International Station Meteorological Climate Summary, 9/96

Average Precipitation/Snowfall/Humidity

Precip./Humidity	Jan	Feb	Mar	Apr	May	Jun	Jul	Aug	Sep	Oct	Nov	Dec	Yr.
Avg. Precip. (in.)	0.4	0.4	0.3	0.2	0.3	0.7	1.6	1.5	1.4	0.7	0.3	0.6	8.6
Avg. Snowfall (in.)	1	1	Tr	Tr	0	0	0	0	0	Tr	1	2	6
Avg. Rel. Hum. 6am (%)	68	60	50	43	44	46	63	69	72	66	63	68	59
Avg. Rel. Hum. 3pm (%)	34	27	21	17	17	17	28	30	32	29	30	36	26

Note: Figures cover the years 1948-1995; Tr = Trace amounts (<0.05 in. of rain; <0.5 in. of snow)
Source: National Climatic Data Center, International Station Meteorological Climate Summary, 9/96

Weather Conditions

Temperature			Daytime Sky			Precipitation		
10°F & below	32°F & below	90°F & above	Clear	Partly cloudy	Cloudy	0.01 inch or more precip.	0.1 inch or more snow/ice	Thunder-storms
1	59	106	147	164	54	49	3	35

Note: Figures are average number of days per year and cover the years 1948-1995
Source: National Climatic Data Center, International Station Meteorological Climate Summary, 9/96

HAZARDOUS WASTE

Superfund Sites

El Paso has no sites on the EPA's Superfund Final National Priorities List. There are a total of 1,322 Superfund sites on the list in the U.S. *U.S. Environmental Protection Agency, Final National Priorities List, April 14, 2015*

AIR & WATER QUALITY

Air Quality Trends: Ozone

	2004	2005	2006	2007	2008	2009	2010	2011	2012	2013
MSA[1]	0.074	0.077	0.077	0.074	0.074	0.068	0.068	0.069	0.067	0.066

Note: (1) Data covers the El Paso, TX Metropolitan Statistical Area—see Appendix B for areas included. The values shown are the composite ozone concentration averages among trend sites based on the highest fourth daily maximum 8-hour concentration in parts per million. These trends are based on sites having an adequate record of monitoring data during the trend period. Data from exceptional events are included.
Source: U.S. Environmental Protection Agency, Air Quality Monitoring Information, "Air Quality Trends by City, 2000-2013"

Air Quality Index

Area	Percent of Days when Air Quality was...[2]					AQI Statistics[2]	
	Good	Moderate	Unhealthy for Sensitive Groups	Unhealthy	Very Unhealthy	Maximum	Median
MSA[1]	55.3	43.6	0.8	0.3	0.0	158	48

Note: (1) Data covers the El Paso, TX Metropolitan Statistical Area—see Appendix B for areas included; (2) Based on 365 days with AQI data in 2014. Air Quality Index (AQI) is an index for reporting daily air quality. EPA calculates the AQI for five major air pollutants regulated by the Clean Air Act: ground-level ozone, particle pollution (aka particulate matter), carbon monoxide, sulfur dioxide, and nitrogen dioxide. The AQI runs from 0 to 500. The higher the AQI value, the greater the level of air pollution and the greater the health concern. There are six AQI categories: "Good" AQI is between 0 and 50. Air quality is considered satisfactory; "Moderate" AQI is between 51 and 100. Air quality is acceptable; "Unhealthy for Sensitive Groups" When AQI values are between 101 and 150, members of sensitive groups may experience health effects; "Unhealthy" When AQI values are between 151 and 200 everyone may begin to experience health effects; "Very Unhealthy" AQI values between 201 and 300 trigger a health alert; "Hazardous" AQI values over 300 trigger warnings of emergency conditions (not shown).
Source: U.S. Environmental Protection Agency, Air Quality Index Report, 2014

Air Quality Index Pollutants

Area	Percent of Days when AQI Pollutant was...[2]					
	Carbon Monoxide	Nitrogen Dioxide	Ozone	Sulfur Dioxide	Particulate Matter 2.5	Particulate Matter 10
MSA[1]	0.0	9.9	32.1	0.0	55.3	2.7

Note: (1) Data covers the El Paso, TX Metropolitan Statistical Area—see Appendix B for areas included; (2) Based on 365 days with AQI data in 2014. The Air Quality Index (AQI) is an index for reporting daily air quality. EPA calculates the AQI for five major air pollutants regulated by the Clean Air Act: ground-level ozone, particle pollution (also known as particulate matter), carbon monoxide, sulfur dioxide, and nitrogen dioxide. The AQI runs from 0 to 500. The higher the AQI value, the greater the level of air pollution and the greater the health concern.
Source: U.S. Environmental Protection Agency, Air Quality Index Report, 2014

Maximum Air Pollutant Concentrations: Particulate Matter, Ozone, CO and Lead

	Particulate Matter 10 (ug/m^3)	Particulate Matter 2.5 Wtd AM (ug/m^3)	Particulate Matter 2.5 24-Hr (ug/m^3)	Ozone (ppm)	Carbon Monoxide (ppm)	Lead (ug/m^3)
MSA[1] Level	233	10.8	30	0.073	3	0.03
NAAQS[2]	150	15	35	0.075	9	0.15
Met NAAQS[2]	No	Yes	Yes	Yes	Yes	Yes

Note: (1) Data covers the El Paso, TX Metropolitan Statistical Area—see Appendix B for areas included; Data from exceptional events are included; (2) National Ambient Air Quality Standards; ppm = parts per million; ug/m^3 = micrograms per cubic meter; n/a not available.
Concentrations: Particulate Matter 10 (coarse particulate)—highest second maximum 24-hour concentration; Particulate Matter 2.5 Wtd AM (fine particulate)—highest weighted annual mean concentration; Particulate Matter 2.5 24-Hour (fine particulate)—highest 98th percentile 24-hour concentration; Ozone—highest fourth daily maximum 8-hour concentration; Carbon Monoxide—highest second maximum non-overlapping 8-hour concentration; Lead—maximum running 3-month average
Source: U.S. Environmental Protection Agency, Air Quality Monitoring Information, "Air Quality Statistics by City, 2013"

Maximum Air Pollutant Concentrations: Nitrogen Dioxide and Sulfur Dioxide

	Nitrogen Dioxide AM (ppb)	Nitrogen Dioxide 1-Hr (ppb)	Sulfur Dioxide AM (ppb)	Sulfur Dioxide 1-Hr (ppb)	Sulfur Dioxide 24-Hr (ppb)
MSA[1] Level	14	56	n/a	9	n/a
NAAQS[2]	53	100	30	75	140
Met NAAQS[2]	Yes	Yes	n/a	Yes	n/a

Note: (1) Data covers the El Paso, TX Metropolitan Statistical Area—see Appendix B for areas included; Data from exceptional events are included; (2) National Ambient Air Quality Standards; ppm = parts per million; ug/m^3 = micrograms per cubic meter; n/a not available.
Concentrations: Nitrogen Dioxide AM—highest arithmetic mean concentration; Nitrogen Dioxide 1-Hr—highest 98th percentile 1-hour daily maximum concentration; Sulfur Dioxide AM—highest annual mean concentration; Sulfur Dioxide 1-Hr—highest 99th percentile 1-hour daily maximum concentration; Sulfur Dioxide 24-Hr—highest second maximum 24-hour concentration
Source: U.S. Environmental Protection Agency, Air Quality Monitoring Information, "Air Quality Statistics by City, 2013"

Drinking Water

Water System Name	Pop. Served	Primary Water Source Type	Violations[1]	
			Health Based	Monitoring/ Reporting
El Paso Water Utilities	631,253	Surface	0	2

Note: (1) Based on violation data from January 1, 2014 to December 31, 2014 (includes unresolved violations from earlier years)
Source: U.S. Environmental Protection Agency, Office of Ground Water and Drinking Water, Safe Drinking Water Information System (based on data extracted January 27, 2015)

Fort Worth, Texas

Background

Fort Worth lies in north central Texas near the headwaters of the Trinity River. Despite its modern skyscrapers, multiple freeways, shopping malls, and extensive industry, the city is known for its easygoing, Western atmosphere.

The area has seen many travelers. Nomadic Native Americans of the plains rode through on horses bred from those brought by Spanish explorers. The 1840s saw American-Anglos settle in the region. On June 6, 1849, Major Ripley A. Arnold and his U.S. Cavalry troop established an outpost on the Trinity River to protect settlers moving westward. The fort was named for General William J. Worth, Commander of the U.S. Army's Texas department. When the fort was abandoned in 1853, settlers moved in and converted the vacant barracks into trading establishments and homes, stealing the county seat from Birdville (an act made legal in the 1860 election).

In the 1860s, Fort Worth, which was close to the Chisholm Trail, became an oasis for cowboys traveling to and from Kansas. Although the town's growth virtually stopped during the Civil War, Fort Worth was incorporated as a city in 1873. In a race against time, the final 26 miles of the Texas & Pacific Line were completed and Fort Worth survived to be a part of the West Texas oil boom in 1917.

Real prosperity followed at the end of World War II, when the city became a center for a number of military installations. Aviation has been the city's principal source of economic growth. The city's leading industries include the manufacture of aircraft, automobiles, machinery, and containers, as well as food processing and brewing. Emerging economic sectors in the new century include semiconductor manufacturing, communications equipment manufacturing, corporate offices, and distribution.

Since it first began testing DNA samples in 2003, the DNA Identity Laboratory at the University of North Texas Health Science Center has made nearly 100 matches, helping to solve missing-persons cases and closing criminal cases. The university is also home to the national Osteopathic Research Center, the only academic DNA Lab qualified to work with the FBI, the Texas Center for Health Disparities and the Health Institutes of Texas. Other colleges in Fort Worth include Texas Christian University, Southwestern Baptist Seminary, and Texas Wesleyan University.

Fort Worth's most comprehensive mixed-use project at Walsh Ranch, is nearing completion. With designs for residential, commercial, office and retail development, the 7,275-acre planned community is named after the original owners of the property, F. Howard and Mary D. Walsh, who were well-known ranchers, philanthropists and civic leaders.

The Omni Fort Worth Hotel opened in January of 2009, and is the first new hotel in the city in over 20 years. It was host to the 2011 AFC champion Pittsburgh Steelers during Super Bowl XLV.

The city also boasts the 3,600-acre Greer Island Nature Center and Refuge, which celebrates its 50th anniversary in 2014.

Winter temperatures and rainfall are both modified by the northeast-northwest mountain barrier, which prevents shallow cold air masses from crossing over from the west. Summer temperatures vary with cloud and shower activity, but are generally mild. Summer precipitation is largely from local thunderstorms and varies from year to year. Damaging rains are infrequent. Hurricanes have produced heavy rainfall, but are usually not accompanied by destructive winds.

Rankings

General Rankings

- The Fort Worth metro area was identified as one of America's fastest-growing areas in terms of population and economy by *Forbes.* The area ranked #8 out of 20. The 100 most populous metro areas in the U.S. were evaluated on the following criteria: estimated population growth; job growth; gross metropolitan product growth; unemployment; median salaries for college-educated workers. *Forbes, "America's Fastest-Growing Cities 2015," January 27, 2015*

- Among the 50 largest U.S. cities, Fort Worth placed #14 in Vocativ's "semi-exhaustive, mostly scientific" city Livability Index for people aged 35 and under. Average salary, unemployment rates, rents, and other living costs were considered, along with crime rates, weather, public transportation, access to music and sports, and "lifestyle metrics" such as the price of dinner at Buffalo Wild Wings and an ounce of high-quality weed. *vocative.com, "The Livability Index: The Best U.S. Cities for People 35 and Under," December 9, 2014*

Business/Finance Rankings

- To help veterans transition to civilian life, USAA and Hiring Our Heroes worked with Sperlings's BestPlaces and the Institute for Veterans and Military Families at Syracuse University to develop a list of the major metropolitan areas where military-skills-related employment is strongest. Criteria for *mid-career* veterans included veteran wage growth; military skills, defense contractor, and government jobs; recent job growth; supervisor/manager jobs; and accessible health resources. Metro areas with a violent crime rate or high cost of living were excluded. At #9, the Fort Worth metro area made the top ten. *www.usaa.com, "2014 Best Places for Veterans"*

- The finance website Wall St. Cheat Sheet reported on the prospects for high-wage job creation in the nation's largest metro areas over the next five years and ranked them accordingly, drawing on in-depth analysis by CareerBuilder and Economic Modeling Specialists International (EMSI). The Dallas metro area placed #9 on the Wall St. Cheat Sheet list. *wallstcheatsheet.com, "Top 10 Cities for High-Wage Job Growth," December 8, 2013*

- Based on metro area social media reviews, the employment opinion group Glassdoor surveyed 50 of the largest U.S. metro areas on measures including compensation and benefits, satisfaction with management, business outlook, and number of employers hiring. The Fort Worth metro area was ranked #23 in overall employee satisfaction. *www.glassdoor.com, "Employment Satisfaction Report Card by City," June 13, 2014*

- In its Competitive Alternatives report, consulting firm KPMG analyzed the 27 largest metropolitan statistical areas according to 26 cost components (such as taxes, labor costs, and utilities) and 30 non-cost-related variables (such as crime rates and number of universities). The business website 24/7 Wall Street examined the KPMG findings, adding to the mix current unemployment rates, GDP, median income, and employment decline during the last recession and "projected" recovery. It identified the Fort Worth metro area as #5 among the ten best American cities for business. *247wallst.com, "Best American Cities for Business," April 4, 2012*

- In a survey of economic confidence in the nation's 50 largest metropolitan areas conducted January–December 2014, the Dallas metro area placed #14, according to Gallup's 2014 Economic Confidence Index. *Gallup, "San Jose and San Francisco Lead in Economic Confidence," March 19, 2015*

- The financial literacy site NerdWallet.com set out to identify the 10 most promising cities for job seekers, analyzing data for the nation's 100 largest cities. Fort Worth was ranked #2. Criteria: job availability; workforce growth; affordability. *NerdWallet.com, "Best Cities for Job Seekers in 2015," January 12, 2015*

- The Brookings Institution ranked the 50 largest cities in the U.S. based on income inequality. Fort Worth was ranked #38. (#1 = greatest ineqality). Criteria: the cities were ranked based on the "95/20 ratio," a figure representing the income at which a household earns more than 95 percent of all other households, divided by the income at which a household earns more than only 20 percent of all other households. *Brookings Institution, "Income Inequality in America's 50 Largest Cities, 2007-2013," March 17, 2015*

- Dallas was ranked #20 out of 100 metro areas in terms of economic performance (#1 = best) during the recession and recovery from trough quarter through the second quarter of 2013. Criteria: percent change in employment; percentage point change in unemployment rate; percent change in gross metropolitan product; percent change in House Price Index. *Brookings Institution, MetroMonitor: Tracking Economic Recession and Recovery in America's 100 Largest Metropolitan Areas, September 2013*

- Payscale.com ranked the 20 largest metro areas in terms of wage growth. The Dallas metro area ranked #8. Criteria: private-sector wage growth between the 1st quarter of 2014 and the 1st quarter of 2015. *PayScale, "Wage Trends by Metro Area," 1st Quarter, 2015*

- The Dallas metro area was identified as one of the most debt-ridden places in America by the finance site Credit.com. The metro area was ranked #1. Criteria: residents' average personal debt load and average credit scores. *Credit.com, "The Most Debt-Ridden Cities," May 1, 2014*

- Dallas was identified as one of America's most frugal metro areas by *Coupons.com.* The city ranked #19 out of 25. Criteria: online coupon usage. *Coupons.com, "Top 25 Most Frugal Cities of 2013," April 10, 2014*

- Dallas was identified as one of America's most frugal metro areas by *Coupons.com.* The city ranked #11 out of 25. Criteria: Grocery IQ and coupons.com mobile app usage. *Coupons.com, "Top 25 Most On-the-Go Frugal Cities of 2013," April 10, 2014*

- Fort Worth was cited as one of America's top metros for new and expanded facility projects in 2014. The area ranked #5 in the large metro area category (population over 1 million). *Site Selection, "Top Metros of 2014," March 2015*

- The Fort Worth metro area appeared on the Milken Institute "2013 Best Performing Cities" list. Rank: #8 out of 200 large metro areas. Criteria: job growth; wage and salary growth; high-tech output growth. *Milken Institute, "Best-Performing Cities 2014," January 2015*

- *Forbes* ranked the 200 most populous metro areas to determine the nation's "Best Places for Business and Careers." The Fort Worth metro area was ranked #24. Criteria: costs (business and living); job growth (past and projected); income growth; educational attainment (college and high school); projected economic growth; cultural and recreational opportunities; net migration patterns; number of highly ranked colleges. *Forbes, "The Best Places for Business and Careers 2014," July 23, 2014*

Dating/Romance Rankings

- *Forbes* reports that the Dallas metro area made Rent.com's Best Cities for Newlyweds survey for 2013, based on Bureau of Labor Statistics and Census Bureau data on number of married couples, percentage of families with children under age six, average annual income, cost of living, and availability of rentals. *www.forbes.com, "The 10 Best Cities for Newlyweds to Live and Work In," May 30, 2013*

- Of the 100 U.S. cities surveyed by *Men's Health* in its quest to identify the nation's best cities for dating and forming relationships, Fort Worth was ranked #54 for online dating (#1 = best). *Men's Health, "The Best and Worst Cities for Online Dating," January 30, 2013*

Education Rankings

- Personal finance website *WalletHub* analyzed the 150 largest U.S. metropolitan statistical areas to determine where the most educated Americans are choosing to settle. Criteria: educational attainment; percentage of workers with jobs in computer, engineering, and science fields; quality and size of each metro area's universities. Dallas was ranked #80 (#1 = most educated city). *www.WalletHub.com, "2014's Most and Least Educated Cities*

- Fort Worth was selected as one of America's most literate cities. The city ranked #53 out of the 77 largest U.S. cities. Criteria: number of booksellers; library resources; Internet resources; educational attainment; periodical publishing resources; newspaper circulation. *Central Connecticut State University, "America's Most Literate Cities, 2014," April 8, 2015*

Environmental Rankings

- The Dallas metro area came in at #350 for the relative comfort of its climate on Sperling's list of "chill cities," as measured by the Sperling Heat Index. All 361 metro areas are included. Criteria included daytime high temperatures, nighttime low temperatures, dew point, and relative humidity at the high temperatures. *www.bertsperling.com, "Sperling's Chill Cities," July 18, 2013*
- Sperling's BestPlaces assessed 379 metropolitan areas of the United States for the likelihood of dangerously extreme weather events or earthquakes. In general the Southeast and South-Central regions have the highest risk of weather extremes and earthquakes, while the Pacific Northwest enjoys the lowest risk. Of the least risky metropolitan areas, the Fort Worth metro area was ranked #371. *www.bestplaces.net, "Safest Places from Natural Disasters," April 2011*
- The U.S. Environmental Protection Agency (EPA) released a list of large U.S. metropolitan areas with the most ENERGY STAR certified buildings in 2014. The Fort Worth metro area was ranked #7 out of 25. *U.S. Environmental Protection Agency, "Top Cities With the Most ENERGY STAR Certified Buildings in 2014," March 25, 2015*
- Dallas was highlighted as one of the 25 most ozone-polluted metro areas in the U.S. during 2011 through 2013. The area ranked #7. *American Lung Association, State of the Air 2015*

Food/Drink Rankings

- *Men's Health* ranked 100 major U.S. cities in terms of alcohol intoxication. Fort Worth ranked #74 (#1 = most sober).Criteria: binge drinking; alcohol-related traffic accidents, arrests, and fatalities. *Men's Health, "The Drunkest Cities in America," November 19, 2013*

Health/Fitness Rankings

- For each of the 50 most populous metro areas in the United States, the American College of Sports Medicine's American Fitness Index evaluated infrastructure, community assets, and policies that encourage healthy and fit lifestyles, including preventive health behaviors, levels of chronic disease conditions, health care access, and community resources and policies that support physical activity. The Dallas metro area ranked #44 for "community fitness." Personal health indicators were considered as well as community and environmental indicators. *www.americanfitnessindex.org, "ACSM American Fitness Index Health and Community Fitness Status of the 50 Largest Metropolitan Areas," May 2013*
- The Fort Worth metro area was identified as one of the worst cities for bed bugs in America by pest control company Orkin. The area ranked #13 out of 50 based on the number of bed bug treatments Orkin performed from January to December 2013. *Orkin, "Chicago Tops Bed Bug Cities List for Second Year in a Row," January 16, 2014*
- Fort Worth was identified as one of 15 cities with the highest increase in bed bug activity in the U.S. by pest control provider Terminix. The city ranked #13.Criteria: cities with the largest percentage gains in bed bug customer calls from January–May 2013 compared to the same time period in 2012. *Terminix, "Cities with Highest Increases in Bed Bug Activity," July 9, 2013*
- Dallas was identified as a "2013 Spring Allergy Capital." The area ranked #23 out of 100. Three groups of factors were used to identify the most severe cities for people with allergies during the spring season: annual pollen levels; medicine utilization; access to board-certified allergists. *Asthma and Allergy Foundation of America, "Spring Allergy Capitals 2013"*
- Dallas was identified as a "2013 Fall Allergy Capital." The area ranked #18 out of 100. Three groups of factors were used to identify the most severe cities for people with allergies during the fall season: annual pollen levels; medicine utilization; access to board-certified allergists. *Asthma and Allergy Foundation of America, "Fall Allergy Capitals 2013"*

- Dallas was identified as a "2013 Asthma Capital." The area ranked #49 out of the nation's 100 largest metropolitan areas. Twelve factors were used to identify the most challenging places to live for people with asthma: estimated prevalence; self-reported prevalence; crude death rate for asthma; annual pollen score; annual air quality; public smoking laws; number of board-certified asthma specialists; school inhaler access laws; rescue medication use; controller medication use; uninsured rate; poverty rate. *Asthma and Allergy Foundation of America, "Asthma Capitals 2013"*

- *Men's Health* ranked 100 major U.S. cities in terms of the best and worst cities for men. Fort Worth ranked #35. Criteria: thirty-three data points were examined covering health, fitness, and quality of life. *Men's Health, "The Best & Worst Cities for Men 2014," December 6, 2013*

- The Fort Worth metro area appeared in the 2013 Gallup-Healthways Well-Being Index. The area ranked #54 out of 189. The Gallup-Healthways Well-Being Index score is an average of six sub-indexes, which individually examine life evaluation, emotional health, work environment, physical health, healthy behaviors, and access to basic necessities. Results are based on telephone interviews conducted as part of the Gallup-Healthways Well-Being Index survey January 2–December 29, 2012, and January 2–December 30, 2013, with a random sample of 531,630 adults, aged 18 and older, living in metropolitan areas in the 50 U.S. states and the District of Columbia. *Gallup-Healthways, "State of American Well-Being," March 25, 2014*

- The Fort Worth metro area was identified as one of "America's Most Stressful Cities" by *Sperling's BestPlaces.* The metro area ranked #33 out of 50. Criteria: unemployment rate; suicide rate; commute time; mental health; poor rest; alcohol use; violent crime rate; property crime rate; cloudy days annually. *Sperling's BestPlaces, www.BestPlaces.net, "Stressful Cities 2012"*

- Fort Worth was selected as one of the "20 Most Livable U.S. Cities for Wheelchair Users" by the Christopher & Dana Reeve Foundation. The city ranked #14. Criteria: Medicaid eligibility and spending; access to physicians and rehabilitation facilities; access to fitness facilities and recreation; access to paratransit; percentage of people living with disabilities who are employed; clean air; climate. *Christopher & Dana Reeve Foundation, "20 Most Livable U.S. Cities for Wheelchair Users," July 26, 2010*

Real Estate Rankings

- Based on the home-price forecasts compiled by the real-estate valuation firm CoreLogic Case-Shiller, the finance website CNNMoney reported that in 2014, the Fort Worth metro area is expected to place #2 among American metro areas in terms of increases in residential real estate prices. *money.cnn.com, "10 Hottest Housing Markets for 2014," January 23, 2014*

- On the list compiled by Penske Truck Rental, the Fort Worth metro area was named the #3 moving destination in 2014, based on one-way consumer truck rental reservations made through Penske's website and reservations call center. *blog.gopenske.com, "Penske Truck Rental's 2014 Top Moving Destinations List," February 4, 2015*

- The Dallas metro area appeared on Realtor.com's list of the hottest housing markets to watch in 2015. Criteria: strong housing growth; affordable prices; and fast-paced sales. *Realtor.com®, "Top 10 Hot Housing Markets to Watch in 2015," December 4, 2014*

- The Dallas metro area was identified as one of the nation's 20 hottest housing markets in 2015.Criteria: median number of days homes were spending on the market in March 2015. The area ranked #15. *Realtor.com, "These Are the 20 Hottest Housing Markets in the U.S. Right Now," April 8, 2015*

- The Fort Worth metro area was identified as one of the top 20 housing markets to invest in for 2015 by *Forbes*. The area ranked #10. Criteria: strong population and job growth; relatively low home prices which are below equilibrium home price (EHP). The EHP is what the average price for a market should be, if speculation, weird distortions in local income, and other factors (like the housing collapse) weren't present in the market. *Forbes.com, "Best Buy Cities: Where to Invest in Housing in 2015," January 9, 2015*

- Fort Worth was ranked #74 out of 275 metro areas in terms of house price appreciation in 2014 (#1 = highest rate). *Federal Housing Finance Agency, House Price Index, 4th Quarter 2014*

- The Fort Worth metro area was identified as one of the 10 worst condo markets in the U.S. in 2014. The area ranked #7 out of 66 markets with a price appreciation of -2.2%. Criteria: year-over-year change of median sales price of existing apartment condo-coop homes between the 4th quarter of 2013 and the 4th quarter of 2014. *National Association of Realtors®, Median Sales Price of Existing Apartment Condo-Coop Homes for Metropolitan Areas, 4th Quarter 2014*
- Fort Worth was ranked #154 out of 226 metro areas in terms of housing affordability in 2014 by the National Association of Home Builders (#1 = most affordable). The NAHB-Wells Fargo Housing Opportunity Index (HOI) for a given area is defined as the share of homes sold in that area that would have been affordable to a family earning the local median income, based on standard mortgage underwriting criteria. *National Association of Home Builders®, NAHB-Wells Fargo Housing Opportunity Index, 4th Quarter 2014*

Safety Rankings

- Symantec, in partnership with Sperling's BestPlaces, ranked the 50 largest cities in the U.S. in terms of their vulnerability to cybercrime. The city ranked #32. Criteria: number of cyberattacks and potential infections; level of Internet access; expenditures on smartphones and computer hardware/software; wireless hotspots; broadband connectivity; Internet usage; online purchases. *Symantec, "Riskiest Online Cities of 2012" February 15, 2012*
- Farmers Insurance, in partnership with Sperling's BestPlaces, ranked metro areas in the U.S. and identified the "Most Secure Places to Live." The Dallas metro area ranked #10 out of the top 20 in the large metro area category (500,000 or more residents). Criteria: economic stability; crime statistics; extreme weather; risk of natural disasters; housing depreciation; foreclosures; air quality; environmental hazards; life expectancy; motor vehicle fatalities; and employment numbers. *Farmers Insurance Group of Companies, "Most Secure U.S. Places to Live in the U.S.," June 25, 2013*
- Allstate ranked the 200 largest cities in America in terms of driver safety. Fort Worth ranked #147. Allstate researchers analyzed internal property damage claims over a two-year period from January 2011 to December 2012. A weighted average of the two-year numbers determined the annual percentages. *Allstate, "Allstate America's Best Drivers Report, 2014"*
- The National Insurance Crime Bureau ranked 380 metro areas in the U.S. in terms of per capita rates of vehicle theft. The Fort Worth metro area ranked #70 (#1 = highest rate). Criteria: number of vehicle theft offenses per 100,000 inhabitants in 2012. *National Insurance Crime Bureau, "Hot Spots 2012," June 26, 2013*

Seniors/Retirement Rankings

- From its Best Cities for Successful Aging indexes, the Milken Institute generated rankings for metropolitan areas, weighing data in eight categories—health care, wellness, living arrangements, transportation, financial characteristics, education and employment opportunities, community engagement, and overall livability. The Fort Worth metro area was ranked #40 overall in the large metro area category. *Milken Institute, "Best Cities for Successful Aging, 2014"*
- *Forbes* selected the Fort Worth metro area as one of 25 "Best Places for a Working Retirement." Criteria: affordability; improving, above-average economies and job prospects; and a favorable tax climate for retirees. *Forbes.com, "Best Places for a Working Retirement in 2013," February 4, 2013*

Sports/Recreation Rankings

- According to the personal finance website NerdWallet, the Dallas metro area, at #1, is one of the nation's top dozen metro areas for sports fans. Criteria included the presence of all four major sports—MLB, NFL, NHL, and NBA, fan enthusiasm (as measured by game attendance), ticket affordability, and "sports culture," that is, number of sports bars. *www.nerdwallet.com, "Best Cities for Sports Fans," May 5, 2013*

Women/Minorities Rankings

- To determine the best metro areas for working women, the personal finance website NerdWallet considered city size as well as relevant economic metrics—high salaries, narrow pay differential by gender, prevalence of women in the highest-paying industries, and population growth over 2010–2012. Of the large U.S. cities examined, the Fort Worth metro area held the #5 position. *www.nerdwallet.com, "Best Places for Women in the Workforce," May 19, 2013*
- *Women's Health* examined U.S. cities and identified the 100 best cities for women. Fort Worth was ranked #43. Criteria: 30 categories were examined from obesity and breast cancer rates to commuting times and hours spent working out. *Women's Health, "Best Cities for Women 2012"*

Miscellaneous Rankings

- The watchdog site Charity Navigator conducts an annual study of charities in the nation's major markets both to analyze statistical differences in their financial, accountability, and transparency practices and to track year-to-year variations in individual communities. The Dallas metro area was ranked #14 among the 30 metro markets. *www.charitynavigator.org, "Metro Market Study 2013," June 1, 2013*
- The Harris Poll's Happiness Index survey revealed that of the top ten U.S. markets, the Fort Worth metro area residents ranked #1 in happiness. Criteria included strong assent to positive statements and strong disagreement with negative ones, and degree of agreement with a series of statements about respondents' personal relationships and general outlook. The online survey was conducted between July 14 and July 30, 2013. *www.harrisinteractive.com, "Dallas/Fort Worth Is "Happiest" City among America's Top Ten Markets," September 4, 2013*
- Mars Chocolate North America, the makers of COMBOS®, in partnership with Sperling's BestPlaces, ranked 50 major metro areas in terms of their "manliness." The Dallas metro area ranked #15. Criteria: number of professional sports teams; number of nearby NASCAR tracks and racing events; manly lifestyle; concentration of manly retail stores; manly occupations per capita; salty snack sales; "Board of Manliness" rankings. *Mars Chocolate North America, "America's Manliest Cities 2012"*
- The National Alliance to End Homelessness ranked the 100 most populous metro areas in terms the rate of homelessness. The Dallas metro area ranked #87. Criteria: number of homeless people per 10,000 population in 2011. *National Alliance to End Homelessness, The State of Homelessness in America 2012*

Business Environment

CITY FINANCES

City Government Finances

Component	2012 ($000)	2012 ($ per capita)
Total Revenues	1,372,592	1,852
Total Expenditures	1,448,368	1,954
Debt Outstanding	2,401,798	3,240
Cash and Securities[1]	3,691,637	4,981

Note: (1) Cash and security holdings of a government at the close of its fiscal year, including those of its dependent agencies, utilities, and liquor stores.
Source: U.S Census Bureau, State & Local Government Finances 2012

City Government Revenue by Source

Source	2012 ($000)	2012 ($ per capita)
General Revenue		
From Federal Government	37,423	50
From State Government	43,786	59
From Local Governments	0	0
Taxes		
Property	362,932	490
Sales and Gross Receipts	222,116	300
Personal Income	0	0
Corporate Income	0	0
Motor Vehicle License	0	0
Other Taxes	24,558	33
Current Charges	270,253	365
Liquor Store	0	0
Utility	204,005	275
Employee Retirement	60,073	81

Source: U.S Census Bureau, State & Local Government Finances 2012

City Government Expenditures by Function

Function	2012 ($000)	2012 ($ per capita)	2012 (%)
General Direct Expenditures			
Air Transportation	14,330	19	1.0
Corrections	0	0	0.0
Education	0	0	0.0
Employment Security Administration	0	0	0.0
Financial Administration	10,470	14	0.7
Fire Protection	107,720	145	7.4
General Public Buildings	6,547	9	0.5
Governmental Administration, Other	16,712	23	1.2
Health	14,424	19	1.0
Highways	102,205	138	7.1
Hospitals	0	0	0.0
Housing and Community Development	34,404	46	2.4
Interest on General Debt	64,155	87	4.4
Judicial and Legal	20,239	27	1.4
Libraries	19,834	27	1.4
Parking	2,923	4	0.2
Parks and Recreation	85,024	115	5.9
Police Protection	234,711	317	16.2
Public Welfare	0	0	0.0
Sewerage	168,705	228	11.6
Solid Waste Management	43,536	59	3.0
Veterans' Services	0	0	0.0
Liquor Store	0	0	0.0
Utility	219,180	296	15.1
Employee Retirement	112,488	152	7.8

Source: U.S Census Bureau, State & Local Government Finances 2012

DEMOGRAPHICS

Population Growth

Area	1990 Census	2000 Census	2010 Census	Population Growth (%) 1990-2000	Population Growth (%) 2000-2010
City	448,311	534,694	741,206	19.3	38.6
MSA[1]	3,989,294	5,161,544	6,371,773	29.4	23.4
U.S.	248,709,873	281,421,906	308,745,538	13.2	9.7

Note: (1) Figures cover the Dallas-Fort Worth-Arlington, TX Metropolitan Statistical Area—see Appendix B for areas included
Source: U.S. Census Bureau, Census 1990, 2000, 2010

Household Size

Area	Persons in Household (%)							Average Household Size
	One	Two	Three	Four	Five	Six	Seven or More	
City	27.1	28.4	15.2	15.0	8.3	3.5	2.4	2.87
MSA[1]	25.2	30.8	16.6	15.0	7.5	3.0	1.8	2.80
U.S.	27.7	33.6	15.7	13.1	6.0	2.3	1.5	2.64

Note: (1) Figures cover the Dallas-Fort Worth-Arlington, TX Metropolitan Statistical Area—see Appendix B for areas included
Source: U.S. Census Bureau, 2011-2013 American Community Survey 3-Year Estimates

Race

Area	White Alone[2] (%)	Black Alone[2] (%)	Asian Alone[2] (%)	AIAN[3] Alone[2] (%)	NHOPI[4] Alone[2] (%)	Other Race Alone[2] (%)	Two or More Races (%)
City	66.2	18.7	3.6	0.8	0.2	7.5	3.0
MSA[1]	69.6	15.0	5.6	0.5	0.1	6.5	2.7
U.S.	73.9	12.6	5.0	0.8	0.2	4.7	2.9

Note: (1) Figures cover the Dallas-Fort Worth-Arlington, TX Metropolitan Statistical Area—see Appendix B for areas included; (2) Alone is defined as not being in combination with one or more other races; (3) American Indian and Alaska Native; (4) Native Hawaiian and Other Pacific Islander
Source: U.S. Census Bureau, 2011-2013 American Community Survey 3-Year Estimates

Hispanic or Latino Origin

Area	Total (%)	Mexican (%)	Puerto Rican (%)	Cuban (%)	Other (%)
City	34.5	31.1	0.7	0.1	2.6
MSA[1]	27.8	23.7	0.6	0.2	3.3
U.S.	16.9	10.8	1.6	0.6	3.8

Note: Persons of Hispanic or Latino origin can be of any race; (1) Figures cover the Dallas-Fort Worth-Arlington, TX Metropolitan Statistical Area—see Appendix B for areas included
Source: U.S. Census Bureau, 2011-2013 American Community Survey 3-Year Estimates

Segregation

Type	Segregation Indices[1]				Percent Change		
	1990	2000	2010	2010 Rank[2]	1990-2000	1990-2010	2000-2010
Black/White	62.8	59.8	56.6	48	-3.1	-6.2	-3.2
Asian/White	41.8	45.6	46.6	19	3.8	4.8	1.0
Hispanic/White	48.8	52.3	50.3	24	3.5	1.5	-2.0

Note: All figures cover the Metropolitan Statistical Area—see Appendix B for areas included; Figures are based on an analysis of 1990, 2000, and 2010 Census Decennial Census tract data by William H. Frey, Brookings Institution and the University of Michigan Social Science Data Analysis Network. In this analysis all racial groups (whites, blacks, and asians) are non-Hispanic members of those races. Hispanics are shown as a separate category;
(1) Segregation Indices are Dissimilarity Indices that measure the degree to which the minority group is distributed differently than whites across census tracts. They range from 0 (complete integration) to 100 (complete segregation) where the value indicates the percentage of the minority group that needs to move to be distributed exactly like whites; (2) Ranges from 1 (most segregated) to 102 (least segregated); n/a not available.
Source: www.CensusScope.org

Ancestry

Area	German	Irish	English	American	Italian	Polish	French[2]	Scottish	Dutch
City	8.9	7.1	5.4	6.8	1.9	1.2	1.5	1.5	0.7
MSA[1]	10.3	8.2	7.5	6.9	2.2	1.1	2.0	1.7	0.9
U.S.	14.9	10.8	8.0	7.4	5.5	3.0	2.7	1.7	1.4

Note: Figures are the percentage of the total population reporting a particular ancestry. The nine most commonly reported ancestries in the U.S. are shown. Figures include multiple ancestries (e.g. if a person reported being Irish and Italian, they were included in both columns); (1) Figures cover the Dallas-Fort Worth-Arlington, TX Metropolitan Statistical Area—see Appendix B for areas included; (2) Excludes Basque
Source: U.S. Census Bureau, 2011-2013 American Community Survey 3-Year Estimates

Foreign-Born Population

Area	Percent of Population Born in								
	Any Foreign Country	Mexico	Asia	Europe	Carribean	South America	Central America[2]	Africa	Canada
City	17.8	11.5	3.2	0.7	0.2	0.4	0.8	0.7	0.2
MSA[1]	17.5	9.1	4.3	0.8	0.2	0.5	1.3	1.0	0.2
U.S.	13.0	3.7	3.8	1.5	1.2	0.9	1.0	0.6	0.3

Note: (1) Figures cover the Dallas-Fort Worth-Arlington, TX Metropolitan Statistical Area—see Appendix B for areas included; (2) Excludes Mexico.
Source: U.S. Census Bureau, 2011-2013 American Community Survey 3-Year Estimates

Marital Status

Area	Never Married	Now Married[2]	Separated	Widowed	Divorced
City	33.9	46.1	3.0	4.6	12.5
MSA[1]	31.4	50.4	2.5	4.5	11.2
U.S.	32.7	48.1	2.2	6.0	11.0

Note: Figures are percentages and cover the population 15 years of age and older; (1) Figures cover the Dallas-Fort Worth-Arlington, TX Metropolitan Statistical Area—see Appendix B for areas included; (2) Excludes separated
Source: U.S. Census Bureau, 2011-2013 American Community Survey 3-Year Estimates

Disability Status

Area	All Ages	Under 18 Years Old	18 to 64 Years Old	65 Years and Over
City	10.6	3.4	10.1	39.8
MSA[1]	9.5	3.3	8.2	35.8
U.S.	12.3	4.1	10.2	36.3

Note: Figures show percent of the civilian noninstitutionalized population that reported having a disability. Disability status is determined from from six types of difficulty: vision, hearing, cognitive, ambulatory, self-care, and independent living. For children under 5 years old, hearing and vision difficulty are used to determine disability status. For children between the ages of 5 and 14, disability status is determined from hearing, vision, cognitive, ambulatory, and self-care difficulties. For people aged 15 years and older, they are considered to have a disability if they have difficulty with any one of the six difficulty types; (1) Figures cover the Dallas-Fort Worth-Arlington, TX Metropolitan Statistical Area—see Appendix B for areas included.
Source: U.S. Census Bureau, 2011-2013 American Community Survey 3-Year Estimates

Age

Area	Percent of Population									Median Age
	Under Age 5	Age 5–19	Age 20–34	Age 35–44	Age 45–54	Age 55–64	Age 65–74	Age 75–84	Age 85+	
City	8.6	23.2	23.4	14.3	12.5	9.3	4.8	2.6	1.1	31.7
MSA[1]	7.4	22.4	21.4	14.7	14.0	10.4	5.7	2.8	1.1	34.1
U.S.	6.4	19.9	20.7	12.9	14.1	12.3	7.6	4.2	1.9	37.4

Note: (1) Figures cover the Dallas-Fort Worth-Arlington, TX Metropolitan Statistical Area—see Appendix B for areas included
Source: U.S. Census Bureau, 2011-2013 American Community Survey 3-Year Estimates

Gender

Area	Males	Females	Males per 100 Females
City	377,614	399,898	94.4
MSA[1]	3,301,095	3,393,794	97.3
U.S.	154,451,010	159,410,713	96.9

Note: (1) Figures cover the Dallas-Fort Worth-Arlington, TX Metropolitan Statistical Area—see Appendix B for areas included
Source: U.S. Census Bureau, 2011-2013 American Community Survey 3-Year Estimates

Religious Groups by Family

Area	Catholic	Baptist	Non-Den.	Methodist[2]	Lutheran	LDS[3]	Pente-costal	Presby-terian[4]	Muslim[5]	Judaism
MSA[1]	13.3	18.7	7.8	5.3	0.8	1.2	2.2	1.0	2.4	0.4
U.S.	19.1	9.3	4.0	4.0	2.3	2.0	1.9	1.6	0.8	0.7

Note: Figures are the number of adherents as a percentage of the total population; (1) Figures cover the Dallas-Fort Worth-Arlington, TX Metropolitan Statistical Area—see Appendix B for areas included; (2) Methodist/Pietist; (3) Latter Day Saints; (4) Reformed; (5) Figures are estimates
Source: Association of Statisticians of American Religious Bodies, 2010 U.S. Religion Census: Religious Congregations & Membership Study

Religious Groups by Tradition

Area	Catholic	Evangelical Protestant	Mainline Protestant	Other Tradition	Black Protestant	Orthodox
MSA[1]	13.3	28.3	7.0	4.8	1.8	0.2
U.S.	19.1	16.2	7.3	4.3	1.6	0.3

Note: Figures are the number of adherents as a percentage of the total population; (1) Figures cover the Dallas-Fort Worth-Arlington, TX Metropolitan Statistical Area—see Appendix B for areas included
Source: Association of Statisticians of American Religious Bodies, 2010 U.S. Religion Census: Religious Congregations & Membership Study

ECONOMY

Gross Metropolitan Product

Area	2012	2013	2014	2015	Rank[2]
MSA[1]	418.6	440.1	464.7	491.4	6

Note: Figures are in billions of dollars; (1) Figures cover the Dallas-Fort Worth-Arlington, TX Metropolitan Statistical Area—see Appendix B for areas included; (2) Rank is based on 2015 data and ranges from 1 to 363
Source: The U.S. Conference of Mayors, U.S. Metro Economies: GMP and Employment 2013-2015, June 2014

Economic Growth

Area	2010-12 (%)	2013 (%)	2014 (%)	2015 (%)	Rank[2]
MSA[1]	3.8	3.7	3.3	4.5	14
U.S.	2.1	2.0	2.3	3.2	–

Note: Figures are real gross metropolitan product (GMP) growth rates and represent annual average percent change; (1) Figures cover the Dallas-Fort Worth-Arlington, TX Metropolitan Statistical Area—see Appendix B for areas included; (2) Rank is based on 2015 data and ranges from 1 to 363
Source: The U.S. Conference of Mayors, U.S. Metro Economies: GMP and Employment 2013-2015, June 2014

Metropolitan Area Exports

Area	2008	2009	2010	2011	2012	2013	Rank[2]
MSA[1]	22,503.7	19,881.8	22,500.4	26,648.7	27,820.9	27,596.0	9

Note: Figures are in millions of dollars; (1) Figures cover the Dallas-Fort Worth-Arlington, TX Metropolitan Statistical Area—see Appendix B for areas included; (2) Rank is based on 2013 data and ranges from 1 to 387
Source: U.S. Department of Commerce, International Trade Administration, Office of Trade & Industry Information, Manufacturing & Services, data extracted April 3, 2015

Building Permits

Area	Single-Family 2013	Single-Family 2014	Single-Family Pct. Chg.	Multi-Family 2013	Multi-Family 2014	Multi-Family Pct. Chg.	Total 2013	Total 2014	Total Pct. Chg.
City	3,321	3,121	-6.0	2,334	2,802	20.1	5,655	5,923	4.7
MSA[1]	21,224	22,550	6.2	16,686	18,868	13.1	37,910	41,418	9.3
U.S.	620,802	634,597	2.2	370,020	411,766	11.3	990,822	1,046,363	5.6

Note: (1) Figures cover the Dallas-Fort Worth-Arlington, TX Metropolitan Statistical Area—see Appendix B for areas included; Figures represent new, privately-owned housing units authorized (unadjusted data); All permit data are based on estimates with imputation.
Source: U.S. Census Bureau, Manufacturing, Mining, and Construction Statistics, Building Permits, 2013, 2014

Bankruptcy Filings

Area	Business Filings 2013	Business Filings 2014	Business Filings % Chg.	Nonbusiness Filings 2013	Nonbusiness Filings 2014	Nonbusiness Filings % Chg.
Tarrant County	214	177	-17.3	4,694	4,302	-8.4
U.S.	33,212	26,983	-18.8	1,038,720	909,812	-12.4

Note: Business filings include Chapter 7, Chapter 11, Chapter 12, and Chapter 13; Nonbusiness filings include Chapter 7, Chapter 11, and Chapter 13
Source: Administrative Office of the U.S. Courts, Business and Nonbusiness Bankruptcy, County Cases Commenced by Chapter of the Bankruptcy Code, During the 12- Month Period Ending December 31, 2013 and Business and Nonbusiness Bankruptcy, County Cases Commenced by Chapter of the Bankruptcy Code, During the 12- Month Period Ending December 31, 2014

Housing Vacancy Rates

Area	Gross Vacancy Rate[2] (%)			Year-Round Vacancy Rate[3] (%)			Rental Vacancy Rate[4] (%)			Homeowner Vacancy Rate[5] (%)		
	2012	2013	2014	2012	2013	2014	2012	2013	2014	2012	2013	2014
MSA[1]	8.7	9.0	9.2	8.4	8.8	9.0	9.2	8.2	9.8	2.1	1.9	1.5
U.S.	13.8	13.6	13.4	10.8	10.7	10.4	8.7	8.3	7.6	2.0	2.0	1.9

Note: (1) Figures cover the Dallas-Fort Worth-Arlington, TX Metropolitan Statistical Area—see Appendix B for areas included; (2) The percentage of the total housing inventory that is vacant; (3) The percentage of the housing inventory (excluding seasonal units) that is year-round vacant; (4) The percentage of rental inventory that is vacant for rent; (5) The percentage of homeowner inventory that is vacant for sale
Source: U.S. Census Bureau, Housing Vacancies and Homeownership Annual Statistics: 2014

INCOME

Income

Area	Per Capita ($)	Median Household ($)	Average Household ($)
City	24,059	51,168	67,578
MSA[1]	29,110	57,630	80,048
U.S.	27,884	52,176	72,897

Note: (1) Figures cover the Dallas-Fort Worth-Arlington, TX Metropolitan Statistical Area—see Appendix B for areas included
Source: U.S. Census Bureau, 2011-2013 American Community Survey 3-Year Estimates

Household Income Distribution

Area	Percent of Households Earning							
	Under $15,000	$15,000 -24,999	$25,000 -34,999	$35,000 -49,999	$50,000 -74,999	$75,000 -99,000	$100,000 -149,999	$150,000 and up
City	13.5	11.0	10.9	13.4	19.3	12.4	12.1	7.4
MSA[1]	10.4	9.5	10.1	13.5	18.3	12.1	14.5	11.6
U.S.	13.0	10.9	10.3	13.6	17.9	11.9	12.7	9.6

Note: (1) Figures cover the Dallas-Fort Worth-Arlington, TX Metropolitan Statistical Area—see Appendix B for areas included
Source: U.S. Census Bureau, 2011-2013 American Community Survey 3-Year Estimates

Poverty Rate

Area	All Ages	Under 18 Years Old	18 to 64 Years Old	65 Years and Over
City	20.1	27.8	17.4	12.9
MSA[1]	15.1	21.8	13.1	9.1
U.S.	15.9	22.4	14.8	9.5

Note: Figures are percentage of people whose income during the past 12 months was below the poverty level; (1) Figures cover the Dallas-Fort Worth-Arlington, TX Metropolitan Statistical Area—see Appendix B for areas included
Source: U.S. Census Bureau, 2011-2013 American Community Survey 3-Year Estimates

EMPLOYMENT

Labor Force and Employment

Area	Civilian Labor Force			Workers Employed		
	Dec. 2013	Dec. 2014	% Chg.	Dec. 2013	Dec. 2014	% Chg.
City	386,122	393,410	1.9	366,908	377,987	3.0
MD[1]	1,177,281	1,198,013	1.8	1,117,300	1,150,482	3.0
U.S.	154,408,000	155,521,000	0.7	144,423,000	147,190,000	1.9

Note: Data is not seasonally adjusted and covers workers 16 years of age and older; (1) Figures cover the Fort Worth-Arlington, TX Metropolitan Division—see Appendix B for areas included
Source: Bureau of Labor Statistics, Local Area Unemployment Statistics

Unemployment Rate

Area	2014											
	Jan.	Feb.	Mar.	Apr.	May	Jun.	Jul.	Aug.	Sep.	Oct.	Nov.	Dec.
City	5.4	5.4	5.2	4.6	4.9	5.3	5.4	5.2	4.7	4.4	4.3	3.9
MD[1]	5.6	5.5	5.3	4.7	4.9	5.3	5.4	5.2	4.7	4.5	4.4	4.0
U.S.	7.0	7.0	6.8	5.9	6.1	6.3	6.5	6.3	5.7	5.5	5.5	5.4

Note: Data is not seasonally adjusted and covers workers 16 years of age and older; (1) Figures cover the Fort Worth-Arlington, TX Metropolitan Division—see Appendix B for areas included
Source: Bureau of Labor Statistics, Local Area Unemployment Statistics

Employment by Occupation

Occupation Classification	City (%)	MSA[1] (%)	U.S. (%)
Management, Business, Science, and Arts	33.7	37.5	36.2
Natural Resources, Construction, and Maintenance	9.7	9.4	9.0
Production, Transportation, and Material Moving	14.7	11.5	12.1
Sales and Office	23.9	25.5	24.4
Service	18.0	16.1	18.3

Note: Figures cover employed civilians 16 years of age and older; (1) Figures cover the Dallas-Fort Worth-Arlington, TX Metropolitan Statistical Area—see Appendix B for areas included
Source: U.S. Census Bureau, 2011-2013 American Community Survey 3-Year Estimates

Employment by Industry

Sector	MD[1] Number of Employees	MD[1] Percent of Total	U.S. Percent of Total
Construction, Mining, and Logging	72,700	7.3	5.0
Education and Health Services	125,900	12.6	15.5
Financial Activities	57,200	5.7	5.7
Government	132,800	13.3	15.8
Information	13,000	1.3	2.0
Leisure and Hospitality	108,300	10.8	10.3
Manufacturing	96,800	9.7	8.7
Other Services	37,000	3.7	4.0
Professional and Business Services	115,700	11.6	13.8
Retail Trade	116,200	11.6	11.4
Transportation, Warehousing, and Utilities	75,800	7.6	3.9
Wholesale Trade	47,600	4.8	4.2

Note: Figures are non-farm employment as of December 2014. Figures are not seasonally adjusted and include workers 16 years of age and older; (1) Figures cover the Fort Worth-Arlington, TX Metropolitan Division—see Appendix B for areas included; n/a not available
Source: Bureau of Labor Statistics, Current Employment Statistics, Employment, Hours, and Earnings

Occupations with Greatest Projected Employment Growth: 2012 – 2022

Occupation[1]	2012 Employment	2022 Projected Employment	Numeric Employment Change	Percent Employment Change
Combined Food Preparation and Serving Workers, Including Fast Food	285,480	378,000	92,520	32.4
Personal Care Aides	199,230	283,980	84,750	42.5
Retail Salespersons	378,330	439,340	61,010	16.1
Registered Nurses	189,380	242,860	53,480	28.2
Customer Service Representatives	214,240	262,770	48,530	22.7
Waiters and Waitresses	196,390	240,390	44,000	22.4
Janitors and Cleaners, Except Maids and Housekeeping Cleaners	172,120	213,340	41,220	23.9
Laborers and Freight, Stock, and Material Movers, Hand	185,770	226,470	40,700	21.9
Elementary School Teachers, Except Special Education	141,030	180,920	39,890	28.3
Secretaries and Administrative Assistants, Except Legal, Medical, and Executive	190,470	230,220	39,750	20.9

Note: Projections cover Texas; (1) Sorted by numeric employment change
Source: www.projectionscentral.com, State Occupational Projections, 2012–2022 Long-Term Projections

Fastest Growing Occupations: 2012 – 2022

Occupation[1]	2012 Employment	2022 Projected Employment	Numeric Employment Change	Percent Employment Change
Diagnostic Medical Sonographers	4,380	6,900	2,520	57.6
Computer Numerically Controlled Machine Tool Programmers, Metal and Plastic	1,740	2,700	960	54.8
Interpreters and Translators	4,510	6,720	2,210	49.0
Skincare Specialists	5,130	7,620	2,490	48.3
Agents and Business Managers of Artists, Performers, and Athletes	310	450	140	47.4
Petroleum Engineers	19,280	28,010	8,730	45.3
Information Security Analysts	6,640	9,630	2,990	45.0
Insulation Workers, Mechanical	4,460	6,460	2,000	44.6
Cardiovascular Technologists and Technicians	3,950	5,700	1,750	44.3
Physician Assistants	5,470	7,880	2,410	44.2

Note: Projections cover Texas; (1) Sorted by percent employment change and excludes occupations with numeric employment change less than 100
Source: www.projectionscentral.com, State Occupational Projections, 2012–2022 Long-Term Projections

Average Wages

Occupation	$/Hr.	Occupation	$/Hr.
Accountants and Auditors	34.66	Maids and Housekeeping Cleaners	9.40
Automotive Mechanics	19.75	Maintenance and Repair Workers	16.75
Bookkeepers	18.03	Marketing Managers	56.57
Carpenters	15.44	Nuclear Medicine Technologists	34.54
Cashiers	9.96	Nurses, Licensed Practical	22.81
Clerks, General Office	15.42	Nurses, Registered	34.32
Clerks, Receptionists/Information	12.59	Nursing Assistants	11.86
Clerks, Shipping/Receiving	14.49	Packers and Packagers, Hand	11.20
Computer Programmers	39.65	Physical Therapists	40.58
Computer Systems Analysts	42.08	Postal Service Mail Carriers	25.27
Computer User Support Specialists	23.54	Real Estate Brokers	42.75
Cooks, Restaurant	11.18	Retail Salespersons	12.49
Dentists	80.18	Sales Reps., Exc. Tech./Scientific	34.57
Electrical Engineers	45.23	Sales Reps., Tech./Scientific	35.89
Electricians	20.19	Secretaries, Exc. Legal/Med./Exec.	14.87
Financial Managers	59.62	Security Guards	13.96
First-Line Supervisors/Managers, Sales	23.34	Surgeons	123.79
Food Preparation Workers	9.79	Teacher Assistants	9.20
General and Operations Managers	56.63	Teachers, Elementary School	26.00
Hairdressers/Cosmetologists	12.43	Teachers, Secondary School	26.60
Internists	102.25	Telemarketers	11.23
Janitors and Cleaners	10.54	Truck Drivers, Heavy/Tractor-Trailer	18.98
Landscaping/Groundskeeping Workers	11.63	Truck Drivers, Light/Delivery Svcs.	15.83
Lawyers	56.57	Waiters and Waitresses	9.08

Note: Wage data covers the Fort Worth-Arlington, TX Metropolitan Division—see Appendix B for areas included; Hourly wages for elementary/secondary school teachers and teacher assistants were calculated by the editors from annual wage data assuming a 40 hour work week; n/a not available.
Source: Bureau of Labor Statistics, Metro Area Occupational Employment and Wage Estimates, May 2014

TAXES

State Corporate Income Tax Rates

State	Tax Rate (%)	Income Brackets ($)	Num. of Brackets	Financial Institution Tax Rate (%)[a]	Federal Income Tax Ded.
Texas	(y)	–	–	(y)	No

Note: Tax rates as of January 1, 2015; (a) Rates listed are the corporate income tax rate applied to financial institutions or excise taxes based on income. Some states have other taxes based upon the value of deposits or shares; (y) Texas imposes a Franchise Tax, otherwise known as margin tax, imposed on entities with more than $1,030,000 total revenues at rate of 1%, or 0.5% for entities primarily engaged in retail or wholesale trade, on lesser of 70% of total revenues or 100%of gross receipts after deductions for either compensation or cost of goods sold.
Source: Federation of Tax Administrators, "State Corporate Income Tax Rates, 2015"

State Individual Income Tax Rates

State	Tax Rate (%)	Income Brackets ($)	Num. of Brackets	Personal Exempt. ($)[1]		Fed. Inc. Tax Ded.
				Single	Dependents	
Texas	None			–	–	–

Note: Tax rates as of January 1, 2015; Local- and county-level taxes are not included; n/a not applicable; (1) Married joint filers generally receive double the single exemption
Source: Federation of Tax Administrators, "State Individual Income Tax Rates, 2015"

Various State and Local Tax Rates

State	State and Local Sales and Use (%)	State Sales and Use (%)	Gasoline[1] (¢/gal.)	Cigarette[2] ($/pack)	Spirits[3] ($/gal.)	Wine[4] ($/gal.)	Beer[5] ($/gal.)
Texas	8.25	6.25	20	1.41	2.40 (f)	0.20	0.20 (p)

Note: All tax rates as of January 1, 2015; (1) The American Petroleum Institute has developed a methodology for determining the average tax rate on a gallon of fuel. Rates may include any of the following: excise taxes, environmental fees, storage tank fees, other fees or taxes, general sales tax, and local taxes. In states where gasoline is subject to the general sales tax, or where the fuel tax is based on the average sale price, the average rate determined by API is sensitive to changes in the price of gasoline. States that fully or partially apply general sales taxes to gasoline: CA, CO, GA, IL, IN, MI, NY; (2) The federal excise tax of $1.0066 per pack and local taxes are not included; (3) Rates are those applicable to off-premise sales of 40% alcohol by volume (a.b.v.) distilled spirits in 750ml containers. Local excise taxes are excluded; (4) Rates are those applicable to off-premise sales of 11% a.b.v. non-carbonated wine in 750ml containers; (5) Rates are those applicable to off-premise sales of 4.7% a.b.v. beer in 12 ounce containers; (f) Different rates are also applicable according to alcohol content, place of production, size of container, or place purchased (on- or off-premise or onboard airlines); (p) Local excise taxes are excluded.
Source: Tax Foundation, 2015 Facts & Figures: How Does Your State Compare?

State Business Tax Climate Index Rankings

State	Overall Rank	Corporate Tax Index Rank	Individual Income Tax Index Rank	Sales Tax Index Rank	Unemployment Insurance Tax Index Rank	Property Tax Index Rank
Texas	10	39	6	36	15	36

Note: The index is a measure of how each state's tax laws affect economic performance. The lower the rank, the more favorable a state's tax system is for business. States without a given tax are given a ranking of 1. The scores/rankings for the District of Columbia do not affect other states. The 2015 index represents the tax climate as of July 1, 2014.
Source: Tax Foundation, State Business Tax Climate Index 2015

COMMERCIAL REAL ESTATE

Office Market

Market Area	Inventory (sq. ft.)	Vacancy Rate (%)	Under Construction (sq. ft.)	YTD Net Absorption (sq. ft.)	Total Average Asking Rent ($/sq. ft./year)
Dallas-Fort Worth	228,035,737	18.7	5,305,025	3,986,942	21.76
National	4,745,108,508	14.3	71,190,461	51,084,126	27.40

Source: Newmark Grubb Knight Frank, National Office Market Report, 4th Quarter 2014

Industrial/Warehouse/R&D Market

Market Area	Inventory (sq. ft.)	Vacancy Rate (%)	Under Construction (sq. ft.)	YTD Net Absorption (sq. ft.)	Total Average Asking Rent ($/sq. ft./year)
Dallas-Fort Worth	759,512,156	7.5	17,360,899	7,955,734	5.28
National	14,238,613,765	7.2	134,387,407	185,246,438	5.64

Source: Newmark Grubb Knight Frank, National Industrial Market Report, 4th Quarter 2014

COMMERCIAL UTILITIES

Typical Monthly Electric Bills

Area	Commercial Service ($/month)		Industrial Service ($/month)	
	1,500 kWh	40 kW demand 14,000 kWh	1,000 kW demand 200,000 kWh	50,000 kW demand 32,500,000 kWh
City	n/a	n/a	n/a	n/a
Average[1]	201	1,653	26,124	2,639,743

Note: Figures are based on annualized 2014 rates; (1) Average based on 180 utilities surveyed; n/a not available
Source: Edison Electric Institute, Typical Bills and Average Rates Report, Summer 2014

TRANSPORTATION

Means of Transportation to Work

Area	Car/Truck/Van		Public Transportation			Bicycle	Walked	Other Means	Worked at Home
	Drove Alone	Car-pooled	Bus	Subway	Railroad				
City	81.9	11.1	0.7	0.0	0.2	0.2	1.2	1.6	3.2
MSA[1]	80.8	10.2	1.0	0.2	0.3	0.2	1.2	1.4	4.8
U.S.	76.4	9.6	2.6	1.8	0.6	0.6	2.8	1.3	4.3

Note: Figures are percentages and cover workers 16 years of age and older; (1) Figures cover the Dallas-Fort Worth-Arlington, TX Metropolitan Statistical Area—see Appendix B for areas included
Source: U.S. Census Bureau, 2011-2013 American Community Survey 3-Year Estimates

Travel Time to Work

Area	Less Than 10 Minutes	10 to 19 Minutes	20 to 29 Minutes	30 to 44 Minutes	45 to 59 Minutes	60 to 89 Minutes	90 Minutes or More
City	9.3	29.1	23.1	23.1	8.1	5.6	1.7
MSA[1]	9.9	26.5	21.2	24.8	9.8	5.9	1.9
U.S.	13.3	29.7	20.9	20.2	7.7	5.7	2.6

Note: Figures are percentages and include workers 16 years old and over; (1) Figures cover the Dallas-Fort Worth-Arlington, TX Metropolitan Statistical Area—see Appendix B for areas included
Source: U.S. Census Bureau, 2011-2013 American Community Survey 3-Year Estimates

Travel Time Index

Area	1985	1990	1995	2000	2005	2010	2011
Urban Area[1]	1.08	1.12	1.16	1.22	1.30	1.25	1.26
Average[2]	1.09	1.14	1.16	1.19	1.23	1.18	1.18

Note: Travel Time Index—the ratio of travel time in the peak period to the travel time at free-flow conditions. For example, a value of 1.30 indicates a 20-minute free-flow trip takes 26 minutes in the peak. Free-flow speeds (60 mph on freeways and 35 mph on principal arterials) are used as the comparison threshold; (1) Covers the Dallas-Fort Worth-Arlington TX urban area; (2) average of 498 urban areas
Source: Texas Transportation Institute, Urban Mobility Report 2012, December 2012

Public Transportation

Agency Name / Mode of Transportation	Vehicles Operated in Maximum Service	Annual Unlinked Passenger Trips (in thous.)	Annual Passenger Miles (in thous.)
Fort Worth Transportation Authority (The T)			
Bus (directly operated)	129	7,454.3	23,444.1
Bus (purchased transportation)	4	79.4	308.8
Demand Response (directly operated)	29	161.7	1,858.5
Demand Response (purchased transportation)	44	234.2	2,697.2

Source: Federal Transit Administration, National Transit Database, 2013

Air Transportation

Airport Name and Code / Type of Service	Passenger Airlines[1]	Passenger Enplanements	Freight Carriers[2]	Freight (lbs.)
Dallas-Fort Worth International (DFW)				
Domestic service (U.S. carriers - 2014)	31	27,243,474	16	356,351,117
International service (U.S. carriers - 2013)	11	2,667,707	7	74,412,988
Dallas Love Field (DAL)				
Domestic service (U.S. carriers - 2014)	21	4,517,138	8	9,809,404
International service (U.S. carriers - 2013)	7	3,031	5	78,450

Note: (1) Includes all U.S.-based major, minor and commuter airlines that carried at least one passenger during the year; (2) Includes all U.S.-based airlines and freight carriers that transported at least one lb. of freight during the year.
Source: Bureau of Transportation Statistics, The Intermodal Transportation Database, Air Carriers: T-100 Domestic Market (U.S. Carriers), 2014; Bureau of Transportation Statistics, The Intermodal Transportation Database, Air Carriers: T-100 International Market (U.S. Carriers), 2013

Other Transportation Statistics

Major Highways:	I-20; I-35W; I-30
Amtrak Service:	Yes
Major Waterways/Ports:	None

Source: Amtrak.com; Google Maps

BUSINESSES

Major Business Headquarters

Company Name	Rankings	
	Fortune[1]	Forbes[2]
American Airlines Group	112	-
Ben E Keith	-	139
D.R. Horton	418	-

Note: (1) Fortune 500—companies that produce a 10-K are ranked 1 to 500 based on 2013 revenue; (2) all private companies with at least $2 billion in annual revenue through the end of their most current fiscal year are ranked 1 to 221; companies listed are headquartered in the city; dashes indicate no ranking
Source: Fortune, "Fortune 500," June 16, 2014; Forbes, "America's Largest Private Companies," November 5, 2014

Fast-Growing Businesses

According to *Inc.*, Fort Worth is home to one of America's 500 fastest-growing private companies: **PMG Worldwide** (#61). Criteria: must be an independent, privately-held, for-profit, U.S. corporation, proprietorship or partnership; revenues must be at least $100,000 in 2010 and $2 million in 2013; must have four-year operating/sales history. Holding companies, regulated banks, and utilities were excluded. *Inc., "America's 500 Fastest-Growing Private Companies," September 2014*

According to *Fortune*, Fort Worth is home to two of the 100 fastest-growing companies in the world: **D.R. Horton** (#43); **AZZ** (#93). Companies were ranked by their revenue growth rate; their EPS growth rate; and their three-year annualized total return to investors for the period ending June 30, 2014. Criteria for inclusion: a company, foreign or domestic, must trade on a major U.S. stock exchange; must file quarterly reports with the SEC; must have a minimum market capitalization of $250 million; must have a stock price of at least $5 on June 30, 2014; must have been trading continuously since June 30, 2010; must have revenue and net income for the four quarters ended on or before April 30, 2014, of at least $50 million and $10 million, respectively; and must have posted a compound annual growth in revenue and earnings per share of at least 20% annually over the three years ending on or before April 30, 2014. Real estate investment trusts, limited-liability companies, limited parterships, business development companies, closed end investment firms, and companies that lost money in the quarter ending April 30, 2014 were excluded. *Fortune, "100 Fastest-Growing Companies," August 28, 2014*

Minority Business Opportunity

Fort Worth is home to one company which is on the *Black Enterprise* Asset Manager 15 list (15 largest asset management firms based on assets under management): **American Beacon Advisors** (#1). Criteria: company must have been operational in previous calendar year and be at least 51% black-owned. *Black Enterprise, B.E. 100s, 2014*

Fort Worth is home to four companies which are on the *Hispanic Business* 500 list (500 largest U.S. Hispanic-owned companies based on 2012 revenue): **Thos. S. Byrne Ltd.** (#32); **Elite Staffing Services** (#320); **Ponce Contractors** (#405); **Open Integration Consulting** (#481). Companies included must show at least 51 percent ownership by Hispanic U.S. citizens, and must maintain headquarters in one of the 50 states or Washington, D.C. *Hispanic Business, "Hispanic Business 500," June 20, 2013*

Fort Worth is home to two companies which are on the *Hispanic Business* Fastest-Growing 100 list (greatest sales growth from 2008 to 2012): **Open Integration Consulting** (#53); **Thos. S. Byrne Ltd** (#66). Companies included must show at least 51 percent ownership by Hispanic U.S. citizens, and must maintain headquarters in one of the 50 states or Washington, D.C. In addition, companies must have minimum revenues of $200,000 for calendar year 2008. *Hispanic Business, June 20, 2013*

Minority- and Women-Owned Businesses

Group	All Firms		Firms with Paid Employees			
	Firms	Sales ($000)	Firms	Sales ($000)	Employees	Payroll ($000)
Asian	2,530	1,131,325	588	1,054,655	2,854	114,999
Black	7,643	209,790	172	92,162	1,219	31,476
Hispanic	8,168	828,355	625	556,625	7,700	171,154
Women	16,515	3,158,441	1,533	2,784,740	13,109	395,861
All Firms	54,911	85,076,401	10,416	83,106,496	311,610	13,842,330

Note: Figures cover firms located in the city; minority- and women-owned business are defined as firms in which the corresponding group own 51% or more of the stock or equity of the company
Source: U.S. Census Bureau, 2007 Economic Census, Survey of Business Owners (2012 Survey of Business Owners data will be released starting in June 2015)

HOTELS & CONVENTION CENTERS

Hotels/Motels

Area	5 Star		4 Star		3 Star		2 Star		1 Star		Not Rated	
	Num.	Pct.[3]	Num.	Pct.[3]	Num.	Pct.[3]	Num.	Pct.[3]	Num.	Pct.[3]	Num.	Pct.[3]
City[1]	0	0.0	4	2.6	36	23.5	99	64.7	5	3.3	9	5.9
Total[2]	166	0.9	1,264	7.0	5,718	31.8	9,340	52.0	411	2.3	1,070	6.0

Note: (1) Figures cover Fort Worth and vicinity; (2) Figures cover all 100 cities in this book; (3) Percentage of hotels which have a given star rating; Star ratings are determined by expedia.com and offer an indication of the general quality of a particular hotel.
Source: expedia.com, April 2, 2015

Major Convention Centers

Name	Overall Space (sq. ft.)	Exhibit Space (sq. ft.)	Meeting Space (sq. ft.)	Meeting Rooms
Dallas Convention Center	2,000,000	929,726	n/a	96
Fort Worth Convention Center	n/a	253,226	58,849	41
Frisco Conference Center	90,000	n/a	n/a	14

Note: Table includes convention centers located in the Dallas-Fort Worth-Arlington, TX metro area; n/a not available
Source: Original research

Living Environment

COST OF LIVING

Cost of Living Index

Composite Index	Groceries	Housing	Utilities	Trans-portation	Health Care	Misc. Goods/ Services
99.5	95.3	93.2	96.7	99.4	101.6	107.6

Note: The Cost of Living Index measures regional differences in the cost of consumer goods and services, excluding taxes and non-consumer expenditures, for professional and managerial households in the top income quintile. It is based on more than 50,000 prices covering almost 60 different items for which prices are collected three times a year by chambers of commerce, economic development organizations or university applied economic centers in each participating urban area. The numbers shown should be read as a percentage above or below the national average of 100. For example, a value of 115.4 in the groceries column indicates that grocery prices are 15.4% higher than the national average. Small differences in the index numbers should not be interpreted as significant; Figures cover the Fort Worth TX urban area.
Source: The Council for Community and Economic Research, ACCRA Cost of Living Index, 2014

Grocery Prices

Area[1]	T-Bone Steak ($/pound)	Frying Chicken ($/pound)	Whole Milk ($/half gal.)	Eggs ($/dozen)	Orange Juice ($/64 oz.)	Coffee ($/11.5 oz.)
City[2]	10.05	1.13	2.01	1.89	3.53	4.12
Avg.	10.40	1.37	2.40	1.99	3.46	4.27
Min.	8.48	0.93	1.37	1.30	2.83	2.99
Max.	14.20	2.44	3.62	4.02	6.42	6.96

Note: (1) Values for the local area are compared with the average, minimum and maximum values for all 308 areas in the Cost of Living Index; (2) Figures cover the Fort Worth TX urban area; **T-Bone Steak** *(price per pound);* **Frying Chicken** *(price per pound, whole fryer);* **Whole Milk** *(half gallon carton);* **Eggs** *(price per dozen, Grade A, large);* **Orange Juice** *(64 oz. Tropicana or Florida Natural);* **Coffee** *(11.5 oz. can, vacuum-packed, Maxwell House, Hills Bros, or Folgers).*
Source: The Council for Community and Economic Research, ACCRA Cost of Living Index, 2014

Housing and Utility Costs

Area[1]	New Home Price ($)	Apartment Rent ($/month)	All Electric ($/month)	Part Electric ($/month)	Other Energy ($/month)	Telephone ($/month)
City[2]	228,573	1,332	-	125.46	51.44	23.97
Avg.	305,838	919	181.00	93.66	73.14	27.95
Min.	183,142	480	112.00	42.06	23.42	17.16
Max.	1,358,576	3,851	594.00	180.03	440.99	40.42

Note: (1) Values for the local area are compared with the average, minimum and maximum values for all 308 areas in the Cost of Living Index; (2) Figures cover the Fort Worth TX urban area; **New Home Price** *(2,400 sf living area, 8,000 sf lot, in urban area with full utilities);* **Apartment Rent** *(950 sf 2 bedroom/1.5 or 2 bath, unfurnished, excluding all utilities except water);* **All Electric** *(average monthly cost for an all-electric home);* **Part Electric** *(average monthly cost for a part-electric home);* **Other Energy** *(average monthly cost for natural gas, fuel oil, coal, wood, and any other forms of energy except electricity);* **Telephone** *(price includes basic monthly rate for a private residential line plus additional local usage charges incurred by a family of four).*
Source: The Council for Community and Economic Research, ACCRA Cost of Living Index, 2014

Health Care, Transportation, and Other Costs

Area[1]	Doctor ($/visit)	Dentist ($/visit)	Optometrist ($/visit)	Gasoline ($/gallon)	Beauty Salon ($/visit)	Men's Shirt ($)
City[2]	98.71	97.50	90.58	3.44	44.90	35.77
Avg.	102.86	87.89	97.66	3.44	34.37	26.74
Min.	67.47	65.78	51.18	3.00	17.43	12.79
Max.	173.50	150.14	235.00	4.33	64.28	49.50

Note: (1) Values for the local area are compared with the average, minimum and maximum values for all 308 areas in the Cost of Living Index; (2) Figures cover the Fort Worth TX urban area; **Doctor** *(general practitioners routine exam of an established patient);* **Dentist** *(adult teeth cleaning and periodic oral examination);* **Optometrist** *(full vision eye exam for established adult patient);* **Gasoline** *(one gallon regular unleaded, national brand, including all taxes, cash price at self-service pump if available);* **Beauty Salon** *(woman's shampoo, trim, and blow-dry);* **Men's Shirt** *(cotton/polyester dress shirt, pinpoint weave, long sleeves).*
Source: The Council for Community and Economic Research, ACCRA Cost of Living Index, 2014

HOUSING

House Price Index (HPI)

Area	National Ranking[2]	Quarterly Change (%)	One-Year Change (%)	Five-Year Change (%)
MD[1]	74	0.28	6.65	11.53
U.S.[3]	–	1.35	4.91	11.59

Note: The HPI is a weighted repeat sales index. It measures average price changes in repeat sales or refinancings on the same properties. This information is obtained by reviewing repeat mortgage transactions on single-family properties whose mortgages have been purchased or securitized by Fannie Mae or Freddie Mac in January 1975; (1) Fort Worth-Arlington Metropolitan Division—see Appendix B for areas included; (2) Rankings are based on annual percentage change for all metro areas containing at least 15,000 transactions over the last 10 years and ranges from 1 to 275; (3) figures based on a weighted average of Census Division estimates using a seasonally adjusted, purchase-only index; all figures are for the period ending December 31, 2014

Source: Federal Housing Finance Agency, House Price Index, February 26, 2015

Median Single-Family Home Prices

Area	2012	2013	2014p	Percent Change 2013 to 2014
MSA[1]	159.3	175.6	188.3	7.2
U.S. Average	177.2	197.4	209.0	5.9

Note: Figures are median sales prices of existing single-family homes in thousands of dollars; (p) preliminary; n/a not available; (1) Dallas-Fort Worth-Arlington, TX Metropolitan Statistical Area—see Appendix B for areas included

Source: National Association of Realtors, Median Sales Price of Existing Single-Family Homes for Metropolitan Areas, 4th Quarter 2014

Qualifying Income Based on Median Sales Price of Existing Single-Family Homes

Area	With 5% Down ($)	With 10% Down ($)	With 20% Down ($)
MSA[1]	41,665	39,473	35,087
U.S. Average	45,863	43,449	38,621

Note: Figures are preliminary; Qualifying income is based on a mortgage rate of 4.0%. Monthly principal and interest payment is limited to 25% of income; n/a not available; (1) Dallas-Fort Worth-Arlington, TX Metropolitan Statistical Area—see Appendix B for areas included

Source: National Association of Realtors, Qualifying Income Based on Median Sales Price of Existing Single-Family Homes for Metropolitan Areas, 4th Quarter 2014

Median Apartment Condo-Coop Home Prices

Area	2012	2013	2014p	Percent Change 2013 to 2014
MSA[1]	142.1	155.7	152.3	-2.2
U.S. Average	173.7	194.9	205.1	5.2

Note: Figures are median sales prices of existing apartment condo-coop homes in thousands of dollars; (p) preliminary; n/a not available; (1) Dallas-Fort Worth-Arlington, TX Metropolitan Statistical Area—see Appendix B for areas included

Source: National Association of Realtors, Median Sales Price of Existing Apartment Condo-Coop Homes for Metropolitan Areas, 4th Quarter 2014

Gross Monthly Rent

Area	Under $200	$200 -299	$300 -499	$500 -749	$750 -999	$1,000 -1,499	$1,500 and up	Median ($)
City	1.4	1.7	5.8	28.1	27.9	26.0	9.1	851
MSA[1]	0.9	1.3	3.7	25.0	30.4	27.9	10.9	896
U.S.	1.7	3.2	7.8	22.1	24.3	26.0	14.9	900

Note: Figures are percentages except for Median; Gross rent is the contract rent plus the estimated average monthly cost of utilities (electricity, gas, and water and sewer) and fuels (oil, coal, kerosene, wood, etc.) if these are paid by the renter (or paid for the renter by someone else); (1) Figures cover the Dallas-Fort Worth-Arlington, TX Metropolitan Statistical Area—see Appendix B for areas included

Source: U.S. Census Bureau, 2011-2013 American Community Survey 3-Year Estimates

Homeownership Rate

Area	2007 (%)	2008 (%)	2009 (%)	2010 (%)	2011 (%)	2012 (%)	2013 (%)	2014 (%)
MSA[1]	60.9	60.9	61.6	63.8	62.6	61.8	59.9	57.7
U.S.	68.1	67.8	67.4	66.9	66.1	65.4	65.1	64.5

Note: (1) Figures cover the Dallas-Fort Worth-Arlington, TX Metropolitan Statistical Area—see Appendix B for areas included
Source: U.S. Census Bureau, Housing Vacancies and Homeownership Annual Statistics: 2014

Year Housing Structure Built

Area	2010 or Later	2000 -2009	1990 -1999	1980 -1989	1970 -1979	1960 -1969	1950 -1959	1940 -1949	Before 1940	Median Year
City	1.9	27.1	11.2	15.2	10.7	9.3	12.3	5.8	6.5	1984
MSA[1]	1.7	23.2	16.6	19.6	15.5	9.5	7.7	3.1	3.0	1986
U.S.	0.9	15.0	13.9	13.8	15.8	11.0	10.9	5.4	13.3	1976

Note: Figures are percentages except for Median Year; (1) Figures cover the Dallas-Fort Worth-Arlington, TX Metropolitan Statistical Area—see Appendix B for areas included
Source: U.S. Census Bureau, 2011-2013 American Community Survey 3-Year Estimates

HEALTH

Health Risk Data

Category	MD[1] (%)	U.S. (%)
Adults aged 18–64 who have any kind of health care coverage	70.7	79.6
Adults who reported being in good or excellent health	84.3	83.1
Adults who are current smokers	20.5	19.6
Adults who are heavy drinkers[2]	7.1	6.1
Adults who are binge drinkers[3]	17.5	16.9
Adults who are overweight (BMI 25.0 - 29.9)	37.2	35.8
Adults who are obese (BMI 30.0 - 99.8)	30.0	27.6
Adults who participated in any physical activities in the past month	71.2	77.1
Adults 50+ who have ever had a sigmoidoscopy or colonoscopy	67.3	67.3
Women aged 40+ who have had a mammogram within the past two years	73.2	74.0
Men aged 40+ who have had a PSA test within the past two years	43.7	45.2
Adults aged 65+ who have had flu shot within the past year	60.0	60.1
Adults who always wear a seatbelt	97.2	93.8

Note: Data as of 2012 unless otherwise noted; (1) Figures cover the Fort Worth-Arlington, TX Metropolitan Division—see Appendix B for areas included; (2) Heavy drinkers are classified as males having more than two drinks per day or females having more than one drink per day; (3) Binge drinkers are classified as males having five or more drinks on one occasion or females having four or more drinks on one occasion
Source: Centers for Disease Control and Prevention, Behaviorial Risk Factor Surveillance System, SMART: Selected Metropolitan/Micropolitan Area Risk Trends, 2012 (Note: the CDC has discontinued this dataset but will be releasing a replacement in late 2015)

Chronic Health Indicators

Category	MD[1] (%)	U.S. (%)
Adults who have ever been told they had a heart attack	4.0	4.5
Adults who have ever been told they had a stroke	2.7	2.9
Adults who have been told they currently have asthma	7.2	8.9
Adults who have ever been told they have arthritis	21.3	25.7
Adults who have ever been told they have diabetes[2]	9.7	9.7
Adults who have ever been told they had skin cancer	5.9	5.7
Adults who have ever been told they had any other types of cancer	4.6	6.5
Adults who have ever been told they have COPD	5.4	6.2
Adults who have ever been told they have kidney disease	2.1	2.5
Adults who have ever been told they have a form of depression	13.8	18.0

Note: Data as of 2012 unless otherwise noted; (1) Figures cover the Fort Worth-Arlington, TX Metropolitan Division—see Appendix B for areas included; (2) Figures do not include pregnancy-related, borderline, or pre-diabetes
Source: Centers for Disease Control and Prevention, Behaviorial Risk Factor Surveillance System, SMART: Selected Metropolitan/Micropolitan Area Risk Trends, 2012 (Note: the CDC has discontinued this dataset but will be releasing a replacement in late 2015)

Mortality Rates for the Top 10 Causes of Death in the U.S.

ICD-10[a] Sub-Chapter	ICD-10[a] Code	Age-Adjusted Mortality Rate[1] per 100,000 population	
		County[2]	U.S.
Malignant neoplasms	C00-C97	160.0	166.2
Ischaemic heart diseases	I20-I25	94.4	105.7
Other forms of heart disease	I30-I51	49.7	49.3
Chronic lower respiratory diseases	J40-J47	45.6	42.1
Organic, including symptomatic, mental disorders	F01-F09	58.2	38.1
Cerebrovascular diseases	I60-I69	42.4	37.0
Other external causes of accidental injury	W00-X59	18.2	26.9
Other degenerative diseases of the nervous system	G30-G31	25.8	25.6
Diabetes mellitus	E10-E14	21.1	21.3
Hypertensive diseases	I10-I15	26.8	19.4

Note: (a) ICD-10 = International Classification of Diseases 10th Revision; (1) Mortality rates are a three year average covering 2011-2013; (2) Figures cover Tarrant County
Source: Centers for Disease Control and Prevention, National Center for Health Statistics. Compressed Mortality File 1999-2013 on CDC WONDER Online Database, released October 2014. Data are compiled from the Compressed Mortality File 1999-2013, Series 20 No. 2S, 2014.

Mortality Rates for Selected Causes of Death

ICD-10[a] Sub-Chapter	ICD-10[a] Code	Age-Adjusted Mortality Rate[1] per 100,000 population	
		County[2]	U.S.
Assault	X85-Y09	5.1	5.2
Diseases of the liver	K70-K76	15.1	13.2
Human immunodeficiency virus (HIV) disease	B20-B24	2.4	2.2
Influenza and pneumonia	J09-J18	13.5	15.4
Intentional self-harm	X60-X84	11.1	12.5
Malnutrition	E40-E46	1.6	0.9
Obesity and other hyperalimentation	E65-E68	1.6	1.8
Renal failure	N17-N19	16.0	13.1
Transport accidents	V01-V99	11.2	11.7
Viral hepatitis	B15-B19	2.5	2.2

Note: (a) ICD-10 = International Classification of Diseases 10th Revision; (1) Mortality rates are a three year average covering 2011-2013; (2) Figures cover Tarrant County
Source: Centers for Disease Control and Prevention, National Center for Health Statistics. Compressed Mortality File 1999-2013 on CDC WONDER Online Database, released October 2014. Data are compiled from the Compressed Mortality File 1999-2013, Series 20 No. 2S, 2014.

Health Insurance Coverage

Area	With Health Insurance	With Private Health Insurance	With Public Health Insurance	Without Health Insurance	Population Under Age 18 Without Health Insurance
City	75.9	54.3	27.7	24.1	12.9
MSA[1]	78.1	60.8	24.3	21.9	12.9
U.S.	85.2	65.2	31.0	14.8	7.3

Note: Figures are percentages that cover the civilian noninstitutionalized population; (1) Figures cover the Dallas-Fort Worth-Arlington, TX Metropolitan Statistical Area—see Appendix B for areas included
Source: U.S. Census Bureau, 2011-2013 American Community Survey 3-Year Estimates

Number of Medical Professionals

Area[1]	MDs[2]	DOs[2,3]	Dentists	Podiatrists	Chiropractors	Optometrists
Local (number)	3,251	708	1,017	78	437	258
Local (rate[4])	172.7	37.6	53.1	4.1	22.8	13.5
U.S. (rate[4])	270.0	20.2	63.1	5.7	25.2	14.9

Note: Data as of 2013 unless noted; (1) Local data covers Tarrant County; (2) Data as of 2012 and includes all active, non-federal physicians; (3) Doctor of Osteopathic Medicine; (4) rate per 100,000 population
Source: U.S. Department of Health and Human Services, Health Resources and Services Administration, Bureau of Health Professions, Area Resource File (ARF) 2013-2014

Best Hospitals

According to *U.S. News,* the Fort Worth-Arlington, TX metro area is home to one of the best children's hospitals in the U.S.: **Cook Children's Medical Center** (7 specialties). The hospital listed was highly ranked in at least one pediatric specialty. Eighty-nine children's hospitals in the U.S. were nationally ranked in at least one specialty. Ten children's hospitals in the U.S. made the Honor Roll with high scores in at least three specialties. *U.S. News Online, "America's Best Children's Hospitals 2014-15"*

EDUCATION

Public School District Statistics

District Name	Schls	Pupils	Pupil/ Teacher Ratio	Minority Pupils[1] (%)	Free Lunch Eligible[2] (%)	IEP[3] (%)
Castleberry ISD	7	3,814	17.4	78.6	77.8	7.6
Eagle Mt-Saginaw ISD	26	17,728	16.3	52.2	32.3	8.2
Fort Worth ISD	144	83,503	16.8	86.7	71.6	7.5
Harmony Science Academy (Ft Worth)	5	3,422	17.6	76.2	39.0	3.6

Note: Table includes school districts with 2,000 or more students; (1) Percentage of students that are not non-Hispanic white; (2) Percentage of students that are eligible for the free lunch program; (3) Percentage of students that have an Individualized Education Program.
Source: U.S. Department of Education, National Center for Education Statistics, Common Core of Data, Local Education Agency (School District) Universe Survey: School Year 2012-2013; U.S. Department of Education, National Center for Education Statistics, Common Core of Data, Public Elementary/Secondary School Universe Survey: School Year 2012-2013

Best High Schools

According to *The Daily Beast,* Fort Worth is home to one of the best high schools in the U.S.: **Fort Worth Academy of Fine Arts** (#91); *The Daily Beast* used six indicators culled from school surveys to compare public high schools in the U.S., with graduation and college acceptance rates weighed most heavily. Other criteria included: college-level courses/exams and SAT/ACT scores. *The Daily Beast, "Top High Schools 2014"*

Highest Level of Education

Area	Less than H.S.	H.S. Diploma	Some College, No Deg.	Associate Degree	Bachelor's Degree	Master's Degree	Prof. School Degree	Doctorate Degree
City	20.2	24.4	23.1	5.7	17.7	6.7	1.2	0.9
MSA[1]	15.9	22.8	22.9	6.6	21.3	7.9	1.6	1.0
U.S.	13.7	28.0	21.2	7.9	18.2	7.7	1.9	1.3

Note: Figures cover persons age 25 and over; (1) Figures cover the Dallas-Fort Worth-Arlington, TX Metropolitan Statistical Area—see Appendix B for areas included
Source: U.S. Census Bureau, 2011-2013 American Community Survey 3-Year Estimates

Educational Attainment by Race

Area	High School Graduate or Higher (%)					Bachelor's Degree or Higher (%)				
	Total	White	Black	Asian	Hisp.[2]	Total	White	Black	Asian	Hisp.[2]
City	79.8	81.0	85.9	78.9	53.0	26.6	30.6	16.8	36.2	9.4
MSA[1]	84.1	85.3	88.8	88.0	55.2	31.9	33.4	23.7	55.9	11.0
U.S.	86.3	88.3	83.1	85.7	64.0	29.1	30.4	18.8	50.7	13.7

Note: Figures shown cover persons 25 years old and over; (1) Figures cover the Dallas-Fort Worth-Arlington, TX Metropolitan Statistical Area—see Appendix B for areas included; (2) People of Hispanic origin can be of any race
Source: U.S. Census Bureau, 2011-2013 American Community Survey 3-Year Estimates

School Enrollment by Grade and Control

Area	Preschool (%)		Kindergarten (%)		Grades 1 - 4 (%)		Grades 5 - 8 (%)		Grades 9 - 12 (%)	
	Public	Private	Public	Private	Public	Private	Public	Private	Public	Private
City	62.7	37.3	92.6	7.4	93.6	6.4	92.2	7.8	93.8	6.2
MSA[1]	56.4	43.6	89.9	10.1	92.6	7.4	92.2	7.8	92.4	7.6
U.S.	57.7	42.3	87.9	12.1	89.9	10.1	90.0	10.0	90.7	9.3

Note: Figures shown cover persons 3 years old and over; (1) Figures cover the Dallas-Fort Worth-Arlington, TX Metropolitan Statistical Area—see Appendix B for areas included
Source: U.S. Census Bureau, 2011-2013 American Community Survey 3-Year Estimates

Average Salaries of Public School Classroom Teachers

Area	2013-14 Dollars	2013-14 Rank[1]	2014-15 Dollars	2014-15 Rank[1]	Percent Change 2013-14 to 2014-15	Percent Change 2004-05 to 2014-15
TEXAS	49,690	30	50,576	29	1.78	23.3
U.S. Average	56,610	–	57,379	–	1.36	20.8

Note: (1) State rank ranges from 1 to 51 where 1 indicates highest salary.
Source: National Education Association, Rankings & Estimates: Rankings of the States 2014 and Estimates of School Statistics 2015, March 2015

Higher Education

Four-Year Colleges			Two-Year Colleges			Medical Schools[1]	Law Schools[2]	Voc/ Tech[3]
Public	Private Non-profit	Private For-profit	Public	Private Non-profit	Private For-profit			
1	3	2	1	1	3	1	1	2

Note: Figures cover institutions located within the city limits and include main campuses only; (1) includes schools accredited by the Liaison Committee on Medical Education and the American Osteopathic Association's Commission on Osteopathic College Accreditation; (2) includes ABA-accredited schools, schools with provisional ABA accreditation, and state accredited schools; (3) includes all schools with programs that are less than 2 years.
Source: National Center for Education Statistics, Integrated Postsecondary Education System (IPEDS), 2013-14; Association of American Medical Colleges, Member List, May 1, 2015; American Osteopathic Association, Member List, May 1, 2015; Law School Admission Council, Official Guide to ABA-Approved Law Schools Online, May 1, 2015; Wikipedia, List of Medical Schools in the United States, May 1, 2015; Wikipedia, List of Law Schools in the United States, May 1, 2015

According to *U.S. News & World Report,* the Fort Worth-Arlington, TX metro division is home to one of the best national universities in the U.S.: **Texas Christian University** (#76). The indicators used to capture academic quality fall into a number of categories: assessment by administrators at peer institutions; retention of students; faculty resources; student selectivity; financial resources; alumni giving; high school counselor ratings of colleges; and graduation rate. *U.S. News & World Report, "America's Best Colleges 2015"*

According to *U.S. News & World Report,* the Fort Worth-Arlington, TX metro division is home to one of the top 75 business schools in the U.S.: **Texas Christian University (Neeley)** (#63). The rankings are based on a weighted average of the following nine measures: quality assessment; peer assessment; recruiter assessment; placement success; mean starting salary and bonus; student selectivity; mean GMAT and GRE scores; mean undergraduate GPA; and acceptance rate. *U.S. News & World Report, "America's Best Graduate Schools, Business, 2016"*

PRESIDENTIAL ELECTION

2012 Presidential Election Results

Area	Obama (%)	Romney (%)	Other (%)
Tarrant County	41.4	57.1	1.4
U.S.	51.0	47.2	1.8

Note: Results may not add to 100% due to rounding
Source: Dave Leip's Atlas of U.S. Presidential Elections

EMPLOYERS

Major Employers

Company Name	Industry
AMR Corporation	Air transportation, scheduled
Associates First Capital Corporation	Mortgage bankers
Baylor University Medical Center	General medical and surgical hospitals
Children's Medical Center Dallas	Specialty hospitals, except psychiatric
Combat Support Associates	Engineering services
County of Dallas	County supervisors' and executives' office
Dallas County Hospital District	General medical and surgical hospitals
Fort Worth Independent School District	Public elementary and secondary schools
Housewares Holding Company	Toasters, electric: household
HP Enterprise Services	Computer integrated systems design
J.C. Penney Company	Department stores
JCP Publications Corp.	Department stores
L-3 Communications Corporation	Business economic service
Odyssey HealthCare	Home health care services
Romano's Macaroni Grill	Italian restaurant
SFG Management Limited Liability	Milk processing (pasteurizing, homogenizing, bottling)
Texas Instruments Incorporated	Semiconductors and related devices
University of North Texas	Colleges and universities
University of Texas SW Medical Center	Accident and health insurance
Verizon Business Global	Telephone communication, except radio

Note: Companies shown are located within the Dallas-Fort Worth-Arlington, TX Metropolitan Statistical Area.
Source: Hoovers.com; Wikipedia

Best Companies to Work For

BNSF Railway, headquartered in Fort Worth, is among the "100 Best Places to Work in IT." To qualify, companies, both public and private, had to have a minimum of 50 IT employees and were selected based on average salary and bonus increases, the percentage of IT staffers promoted, IT staff turnover rates, training and development programs, and the percentage of women and minorities in IT staff and management positions. In addition, *Computerworld* looked at retention efforts, programs for recognizing and rewarding outstanding performances, and benefits such as flextime, elder care and child care, and reimbursement for college tuition and the cost of pursuing technology certifications. *Computerworld, "100 Best Places to Work in IT 2014"*

PUBLIC SAFETY

Crime Rate

Area	All Crimes	Violent Crimes				Property Crimes		
		Murder	Forcible Rape	Robbery	Aggrav. Assault	Burglary	Larceny -Theft	Motor Vehicle Theft
City	4,903.7	6.1	66.3	159.2	328.6	1,053.9	2,985.5	304.0
Suburbs[1]	3,047.6	2.8	21.3	65.1	169.9	563.3	2,057.7	167.6
Metro[2]	3,682.2	3.9	36.7	97.3	224.1	731.0	2,375.0	214.3
U.S.	3,098.6	4.5	25.2	109.1	229.1	610.0	1,899.4	221.3

Note: Figures are crimes per 100,000 population; (1) All areas within the metro area that are located outside the city limits; (2) Figures cover the Fort Worth-Arlington, TX Metropolitan Division—see Appendix B for areas included
Source: FBI Uniform Crime Reports, 2013

Hate Crimes

Area	Number of Quarters Reported	Number of Incidents per Bias Motivation						
		Race	Religion	Sexual Orientation	Ethnicity	Disability	Gender	Gender Identity
City	4	9	0	2	5	0	0	0
U.S.	4	2,871	1,031	1,233	655	83	18	31

Source: Federal Bureau of Investigation, Hate Crime Statistics 2013

Identity Theft Consumer Complaints

Area	Complaints	Complaints per 100,000 Population	Rank[2]
MSA[1]	8,158	119.8	27
U.S.	332,646	104.3	-

Note: (1) Figures cover the Dallas-Fort Worth-Arlington, TX Metropolitan Statistical Area—see Appendix B for areas included; (2) Rank ranges from 1 to 380 where 1 indicates greatest number of identity theft complaints per 100,000 population
Source: Federal Trade Commission, Consumer Sentinel Network Data Book for January–December 2014

Fraud and Other Consumer Complaints

Area	Complaints	Complaints per 100,000 Population	Rank[2]
MSA[1]	32,064	470.8	35
U.S.	2,250,205	705.7	-

Note: (1) Figures cover the Dallas-Fort Worth-Arlington, TX Metropolitan Statistical Area—see Appendix B for areas included; (2) Rank ranges from 1 to 380 where 1 indicates greatest number of identity theft complaints per 100,000 population
Source: Federal Trade Commission, Consumer Sentinel Network Data Book for January–December 2014

RECREATION

Culture

Dance[1]	Theatre[1]	Instrumental Music[1]	Vocal Music[1]	Series and Festivals	Museums and Art Galleries[2]	Zoos and Aquariums[3]
3	9	3	5	3	49	1

Note: (1) Professional perfoming groups; (2) Based on organizations with SIC code 8412; (3) AZA-accredited
Source: The Grey House Performing Arts Directory, 2015-16; Association of Zoos & Aquariums, AZA Member Zoos & Aquariums, April 2015; www.AccuLeads.com, April 2015

Professional Sports Teams

Team Name	League	Year Established
Dallas Cowboys	National Football League (NFL)	1960
Dallas Mavericks	National Basketball Association (NBA)	1980
Dallas Stars	National Hockey League (NHL)	1993
FC Dallas	Major League Soccer (MLS)	1996
Texas Rangers	Major League Baseball (MLB)	1972

Note: Includes teams located in the Dallas-Fort Worth-Arlington, TX Metropolitan Statistical Area.
Source: Wikipedia, Major Professional Sports Teams of the United States and Canada, April 2015

CLIMATE

Average and Extreme Temperatures

Temperature	Jan	Feb	Mar	Apr	May	Jun	Jul	Aug	Sep	Oct	Nov	Dec	Yr.
Extreme High (°F)	88	88	96	98	103	113	110	108	107	106	89	90	113
Average High (°F)	54	59	67	76	83	92	96	96	88	79	67	58	76
Average Temp. (°F)	44	49	57	66	73	81	85	85	78	68	56	47	66
Average Low (°F)	33	38	45	54	63	71	75	74	67	56	45	37	55
Extreme Low (°F)	4	6	11	29	41	51	59	56	43	29	19	-1	-1

Note: Figures cover the years 1953-1990
Source: National Climatic Data Center, International Station Meteorological Climate Summary, 9/96

Average Precipitation/Snowfall/Humidity

Precip./Humidity	Jan	Feb	Mar	Apr	May	Jun	Jul	Aug	Sep	Oct	Nov	Dec	Yr.
Avg. Precip. (in.)	1.8	2.2	2.6	3.7	4.9	2.8	2.1	1.9	3.0	3.3	2.1	1.7	32.3
Avg. Snowfall (in.)	1	1	Tr	0	0	0	0	0	0	0	Tr	Tr	3
Avg. Rel. Hum. 6am (%)	79	79	79	81	86	85	80	79	83	82	80	79	81
Avg. Rel. Hum. 3pm (%)	52	51	48	50	53	47	42	41	46	47	49	51	48

Note: Figures cover the years 1953-1990; Tr = Trace amounts (<0.05 in. of rain; <0.5 in. of snow)
Source: National Climatic Data Center, International Station Meteorological Climate Summary, 9/96

Weather Conditions

Temperature			Daytime Sky			Precipitation		
10°F & below	32°F & below	90°F & above	Clear	Partly cloudy	Cloudy	0.01 inch or more precip.	0.1 inch or more snow/ice	Thunder-storms
1	40	100	123	136	106	79	3	47

Note: Figures are average number of days per year and cover the years 1953-1990
Source: National Climatic Data Center, International Station Meteorological Climate Summary, 9/96

HAZARDOUS WASTE

Superfund Sites

Fort Worth has one hazardous waste site on the EPA's Superfund Final National Priorities List: **Air Force Plant #4 (General Dynamics)**. There are a total of 1,322 Superfund sites on the list in the U.S. *U.S. Environmental Protection Agency, Final National Priorities List, April 14, 2015*

AIR & WATER QUALITY

Air Quality Trends: Ozone

	2004	2005	2006	2007	2008	2009	2010	2011	2012	2013
MSA[1]	0.087	0.093	0.089	0.081	0.077	0.080	0.076	0.085	0.083	0.078

Note: (1) Data covers the Dallas-Fort Worth-Arlington, TX Metropolitan Statistical Area—see Appendix B for areas included. The values shown are the composite ozone concentration averages among trend sites based on the highest fourth daily maximum 8-hour concentration in parts per million. These trends are based on sites having an adequate record of monitoring data during the trend period. Data from exceptional events are included.
Source: U.S. Environmental Protection Agency, Air Quality Monitoring Information, "Air Quality Trends by City, 2000-2013"

Air Quality Index

Area	Percent of Days when Air Quality was...[2]					AQI Statistics[2]	
	Good	Moderate	Unhealthy for Sensitive Groups	Unhealthy	Very Unhealthy	Maximum	Median
MSA[1]	53.2	43.0	3.8	0.0	0.0	132	49

Note: (1) Data covers the Dallas-Fort Worth-Arlington, TX Metropolitan Statistical Area—see Appendix B for areas included; (2) Based on 365 days with AQI data in 2014. Air Quality Index (AQI) is an index for reporting daily air quality. EPA calculates the AQI for five major air pollutants regulated by the Clean Air Act: ground-level ozone, particle pollution (aka particulate matter), carbon monoxide, sulfur dioxide, and nitrogen dioxide. The AQI runs from 0 to 500. The higher the AQI value, the greater the level of air pollution and the greater the health concern. There are six AQI categories: "Good" AQI is between 0 and 50. Air quality is considered satisfactory; "Moderate" AQI is between 51 and 100. Air quality is acceptable; "Unhealthy for Sensitive Groups" When AQI values are between 101 and 150, members of sensitive groups may experience health effects; "Unhealthy" When AQI values are between 151 and 200 everyone may begin to experience health effects; "Very Unhealthy" AQI values between 201 and 300 trigger a health alert; "Hazardous" AQI values over 300 trigger warnings of emergency conditions (not shown).
Source: U.S. Environmental Protection Agency, Air Quality Index Report, 2014

Air Quality Index Pollutants

Area	Percent of Days when AQI Pollutant was...[2]					
	Carbon Monoxide	Nitrogen Dioxide	Ozone	Sulfur Dioxide	Particulate Matter 2.5	Particulate Matter 10
MSA[1]	0.0	6.8	41.9	0.3	50.1	0.8

Note: (1) Data covers the Dallas-Fort Worth-Arlington, TX Metropolitan Statistical Area—see Appendix B for areas included; (2) Based on 365 days with AQI data in 2014. The Air Quality Index (AQI) is an index for reporting daily air quality. EPA calculates the AQI for five major air pollutants regulated by the Clean Air Act: ground-level ozone, particle pollution (also known as particulate matter), carbon monoxide, sulfur dioxide, and nitrogen dioxide. The AQI runs from 0 to 500. The higher the AQI value, the greater the level of air pollution and the greater the health concern.
Source: U.S. Environmental Protection Agency, Air Quality Index Report, 2014

Maximum Air Pollutant Concentrations: Particulate Matter, Ozone, CO and Lead

	Particulate Matter 10 (ug/m^3)	Particulate Matter 2.5 Wtd AM (ug/m^3)	Particulate Matter 2.5 24-Hr (ug/m^3)	Ozone (ppm)	Carbon Monoxide (ppm)	Lead (ug/m^3)
MSA[1] Level	93	10.6	26	0.085	2	0.08
NAAQS[2]	150	15	35	0.075	9	0.15
Met NAAQS[2]	Yes	Yes	Yes	No	Yes	Yes

Note: (1) Data covers the Dallas-Fort Worth-Arlington, TX Metropolitan Statistical Area—see Appendix B for areas included; Data from exceptional events are included; (2) National Ambient Air Quality Standards; ppm = parts per million; ug/m^3 = micrograms per cubic meter; n/a not available.
Concentrations: Particulate Matter 10 (coarse particulate)—highest second maximum 24-hour concentration; Particulate Matter 2.5 Wtd AM (fine particulate)—highest weighted annual mean concentration; Particulate Matter 2.5 24-Hour (fine particulate)—highest 98th percentile 24-hour concentration; Ozone—highest fourth daily maximum 8-hour concentration; Carbon Monoxide—highest second maximum non-overlapping 8-hour concentration; Lead—maximum running 3-month average
Source: U.S. Environmental Protection Agency, Air Quality Monitoring Information, "Air Quality Statistics by City, 2013"

Maximum Air Pollutant Concentrations: Nitrogen Dioxide and Sulfur Dioxide

	Nitrogen Dioxide AM (ppb)	Nitrogen Dioxide 1-Hr (ppb)	Sulfur Dioxide AM (ppb)	Sulfur Dioxide 1-Hr (ppb)	Sulfur Dioxide 24-Hr (ppb)
MSA[1] Level	12	49	n/a	16	n/a
NAAQS[2]	53	100	30	75	140
Met NAAQS[2]	Yes	Yes	n/a	Yes	n/a

Note: (1) Data covers the Dallas-Fort Worth-Arlington, TX Metropolitan Statistical Area—see Appendix B for areas included; Data from exceptional events are included; (2) National Ambient Air Quality Standards; ppm = parts per million; ug/m^3 = micrograms per cubic meter; n/a not available.
Concentrations: Nitrogen Dioxide AM—highest arithmetic mean concentration; Nitrogen Dioxide 1-Hr—highest 98th percentile 1-hour daily maximum concentration; Sulfur Dioxide AM—highest annual mean concentration; Sulfur Dioxide 1-Hr—highest 99th percentile 1-hour daily maximum concentration; Sulfur Dioxide 24-Hr—highest second maximum 24-hour concentration
Source: U.S. Environmental Protection Agency, Air Quality Monitoring Information, "Air Quality Statistics by City, 2013"

Drinking Water

Water System Name	Pop. Served	Primary Water Source Type	Violations[1]	
			Health Based	Monitoring/ Reporting
City of Fort Worth	748,450	Surface	0	1

Note: (1) Based on violation data from January 1, 2014 to December 31, 2014 (includes unresolved violations from earlier years)
Source: U.S. Environmental Protection Agency, Office of Ground Water and Drinking Water, Safe Drinking Water Information System (based on data extracted January 27, 2015)

Gainesville, Florida

Background

Gainesville is the cultural and educational hub of North Florida, located partway between the Atlantic Ocean and Gulf of Mexico. Alachua County's largest city has grown with a population drawn to its subtropical locale and its heartbeat and largest employer, the colossal University of Florida (UF). Innovation is the name of the game when it comes to the region's push for businesses emerging from the university's numerous research centers. In addition, Gainesville is only a short drive to rural Florida habitat. Ten miles south are the bison, alligators, and 270 bird species found at Paynes Prairie Preserve. Plus, North Florida has the world's largest concentration of freshwater springs.

Originally a Timucuan Indian village, present-day Gainesville was part of a Spanish land grant by 1817. The United States annexed Florida in 1825, and just over a quarter-century later came plans for the Florida Railroad. In 1853, the local citizenry opted to create a new county seat along the railroad line, and Gainesville was founded and named for Seminole Indian War General Edmund P. Gaines. After the Civil War, a Union veteran established a successful cotton shipping station here, and in 1906 UF was founded. Through the years, fire and development has destroyed many of Gainesville's early buildings; a few remain including the Hippodrome State Theatre which was once the local Federal Building.

Emerging from the University of Florida (the nation's fifth largest university), are projects from dozens of research centers and institutes. An early success was Gatorade, invented in 1965 to hydrate the Gator football team. Alternative energy research draws accolades, and the city proper became the nation's first to implement a solar feed-in tariff, which means consumers who invest in the appropriate technology can sell their electricity back to the utility. The university's Sid Martin Biotechnology Incubator was ranked "World's Best University Biotechnology Incubator" by an international study conducted by the Sweden-based research group UBI in 2013. The university's annual economic impact is more than $8.76 billion, and state-wide its activities are estimated to generate more than 106,000 jobs.

In addition to the biotechnology incubator, the city is also home to the Florida Innovation Hub, the first building of the 40-acre Innovation Square package situated as a bridge between the campus and Gainesville's downtown. Eventually, over five million square feet of space will be filled with residences, retail, hotels and open space. The Hub is a 48,000 square-foot facility that incubates start-up companies that emerge from university research. Its Office of Technology Licensing aids the push to grow new business. Also at the square: the UF Innovation Academy, an undergraduate program focusing on entrepreneurial-minded students.

A long list of rankings lauds Gainesville's quality of life for young people and retirees. As with many college towns, there's long been a happening music scene. Tom Petty and the Heartbreakers emerged from Gainesville. Cultural resources include the Florida Museum of Natural History, founded in 1891, fueled by donations from interested professors. In addition to its central museum and collections, it operates the Randell Research Center (a significant Calusa Indian archaeological site-and an ancient ecological site-in Lee County northwest of Fort Myers) and the McGuire Center for Lepidoptera and Biodiversity that boasts one of the world's largest butterfly and moth collections. Public exhibitions include the 6800 square-foot living Butterfly Rainforest.

In addition, UF's Harn Museum of Art exhibits traveling shows and collections of photography and Ancient American, Asian, African, modern and contemporary art. Also in the city are the Hippodrome State Theatre, showcasing cinema and traveling theater, and the Curtis M. Phillips Center for Performing Arts.

Famously humid, Gainesville's subtropical climate means freezes are not unheard of in winter, with December through February average highs in the 50s. June through August is notably wet, averaging more than six inches of rain the first two months of summer and eight inches in August. Equally notable, Gainesville's inland location tends to mitigate the threat of hurricanes that face Florida's coasts. Temperatures often climb into the 90s from April to October.

Rankings

Business/Finance Rankings

- Using data from the Council for Community and Economic Research's 2013 Annual Report, NerdWallet ranked the 100 U.S. cities with the most expensive cost of living. Cities in California and in the Northeast topped the list. Of the cities with the highest cost of living, Gainesville ranked #90. *NerdWallet.com, "Most Expensive Cities in America," June 4, 2014*
- Gainesville was identified as one of "America's Hardest-Working Towns." The city ranked #6 out of 25. Criteria: average hours worked per capita; willingness to work during personal time; number of dual income households; local employment rate. *Parade, "What is America's Hardest-Working Town?," April 15, 2012*
- The Gainesville metro area appeared on the Milken Institute "2013 Best Performing Cities" list. Rank: #182 out of 200 large metro areas. Criteria: job growth; wage and salary growth; high-tech output growth. *Milken Institute, "Best-Performing Cities 2014," January 2015*
- *Forbes* ranked the 200 most populous metro areas to determine the nation's "Best Places for Business and Careers." The Gainesville metro area was ranked #83. Criteria: costs (business and living); job growth (past and projected); income growth; educational attainment (college and high school); projected economic growth; cultural and recreational opportunities; net migration patterns; number of highly ranked colleges. *Forbes, "The Best Places for Business and Careers 2014," July 23, 2014*

Dating/Romance Rankings

- Gainesville was selected as one of the most romantic cities in America by Amazon.com. The city ranked #19 of 20. Criteria: cities with 100,000 or more residents were ranked on their per capita sales of romance novels and relationship books, romantic comedy movies, romantic music, and sexual wellness products. *Amazon.com, "Top 20 Most Romantic Cities in America," February 5, 2015*

Education Rankings

- Gainesville was selected as one of the most well-read cities in America by Amazon.com. The city ranked #16 among the top 20. Cities with populations greater than 100,000 were evaluated based on per capita sales of books, magazines and newspapers. *Amazon.com, "The 20 Most Well-Read Cities in America," May 20, 2014*

Environmental Rankings

- The Gainesville metro area came in at #295 for the relative comfort of its climate on Sperling's list of "chill cities," as measured by the Sperling Heat Index. All 361 metro areas are included. Criteria included daytime high temperatures, nighttime low temperatures, dew point, and relative humidity at the high temperatures. *www.bertsperling.com, "Sperling's Chill Cities," July 18, 2013*
- Sperling's BestPlaces assessed 379 metropolitan areas of the United States for the likelihood of dangerously extreme weather events or earthquakes. In general the Southeast and South-Central regions have the highest risk of weather extremes and earthquakes, while the Pacific Northwest enjoys the lowest risk. Of the least risky metropolitan areas, the Gainesville metro area was ranked #291. *www.bestplaces.net, "Safest Places from Natural Disasters," April 2011*
- Gainesville was highlighted as one of the cleanest metro areas for ozone air pollution in the U.S. during 2011 through 2013. The list represents cities with no monitored ozone air pollution in unhealthful ranges. *American Lung Association, State of the Air 2015*

Health/Fitness Rankings

- The Gainesville metro area appeared in the 2013 Gallup-Healthways Well-Being Index. The area ranked #112 out of 189. The Gallup-Healthways Well-Being Index score is an average of six sub-indexes, which individually examine life evaluation, emotional health, work environment, physical health, healthy behaviors, and access to basic necessities. Results are based on telephone interviews conducted as part of the Gallup-Healthways Well-Being Index survey January 2–December 29, 2012, and January 2–December 30, 2013, with a random sample of 531,630 adults, aged 18 and older, living in metropolitan areas in the 50 U.S. states and the District of Columbia. *Gallup-Healthways, "State of American Well-Being," March 25, 2014*

Real Estate Rankings

- Gainesville was ranked #101 out of 226 metro areas in terms of housing affordability in 2014 by the National Association of Home Builders (#1 = most affordable). The NAHB-Wells Fargo Housing Opportunity Index (HOI) for a given area is defined as the share of homes sold in that area that would have been affordable to a family earning the local median income, based on standard mortgage underwriting criteria. *National Association of Home Builders®, NAHB-Wells Fargo Housing Opportunity Index, 4th Quarter 2014*

Safety Rankings

- The National Insurance Crime Bureau ranked 380 metro areas in the U.S. in terms of per capita rates of vehicle theft. The Gainesville metro area ranked #212 (#1 = highest rate). Criteria: number of vehicle theft offenses per 100,000 inhabitants in 2012. *National Insurance Crime Bureau, "Hot Spots 2012," June 26, 2013*

Seniors/Retirement Rankings

- From its Best Cities for Successful Aging indexes, the Milken Institute generated rankings for metropolitan areas, weighing data in eight categories—health care, wellness, living arrangements, transportation, financial characteristics, education and employment opportunities, community engagement, and overall livability. The Gainesville metro area was ranked #12 overall in the small metro area category. *Milken Institute, "Best Cities for Successful Aging, 2014"*
- The AARP named Gainesville one of the "10 Best Places to Live on $100 a Day." Analysts looked at 200 cities to arrive at their 10-best list. Criteria includes: cost of living; quality-of-life; arts and culture; educational institutions; restaurants; community life; health care; natural setting; sunny days per year; and overall vibe. *AARP The Magazine, "10 Best Places to Live on $100 a Day," July 2012*
- Gainesville was identified as one of the most popular places to retire by *Topretirements.com*. The list reflects the 100 cities (out of 900+ total cities reviewed) that visitors to the website are most interested in for retirement. *Topretirements.com, "Most Popular Places to Retire for 2014," February 25, 2014*

Sports/Recreation Rankings

- Gainesville was chosen as a bicycle friendly community by the League of American Bicyclists. A "Bicycle Friendly Community" welcomes cyclists by providing safe accommodation for cycling and encouraging people to bike for transportation and recreation. There are four award levels: Platinum; Gold; Silver; and Bronze. The community achieved an award level of Silver. *League of American Bicyclists, "Bicycle Friendly Community Master List," Fall 2013*
- Gainesville was chosen as one of America's best cities for bicycling. The city ranked #37 out of 50. Criteria: robust cycling infrastructure; vibrant bike culture. The editors only considered cities with populations of 95,000 or more. *Bicycling, "America's Top 50 Bike-Friendly Cities," May 23, 2012*

Miscellaneous Rankings

- Using Musicmetric's Digital Music Index (DMI), CNBC ranked results for music piracy by way of the file-sharing protocol BitTorrent. Gainesville was ranked #1 among American cities. *CNBC.com, "Florida City Named 'Pirate Capital' of Music World," October 8, 2012*

Business Environment

CITY FINANCES

City Government Finances

Component	2012 ($000)	2012 ($ per capita)
Total Revenues	550,565	4,427
Total Expenditures	549,235	4,417
Debt Outstanding	1,189,870	9,568
Cash and Securities[1]	880,335	7,079

Note: (1) Cash and security holdings of a government at the close of its fiscal year, including those of its dependent agencies, utilities, and liquor stores.
Source: U.S Census Bureau, State & Local Government Finances 2012

City Government Revenue by Source

Source	2012 ($000)	2012 ($ per capita)
General Revenue		
From Federal Government	9,461	76
From State Government	11,449	92
From Local Governments	3,271	26
Taxes		
Property	26,834	216
Sales and Gross Receipts	33,733	271
Personal Income	0	0
Corporate Income	0	0
Motor Vehicle License	0	0
Other Taxes	3,866	31
Current Charges	68,007	547
Liquor Store	0	0
Utility	333,517	2,682
Employee Retirement	10,772	87

Source: U.S Census Bureau, State & Local Government Finances 2012

City Government Expenditures by Function

Function	2012 ($000)	2012 ($ per capita)	2012 (%)
General Direct Expenditures			
Air Transportation	0	0	0.0
Corrections	0	0	0.0
Education	0	0	0.0
Employment Security Administration	0	0	0.0
Financial Administration	6,611	53	1.2
Fire Protection	18,908	152	3.4
General Public Buildings	2,362	19	0.4
Governmental Administration, Other	4,891	39	0.9
Health	285	2	0.1
Highways	17,848	144	3.2
Hospitals	0	0	0.0
Housing and Community Development	7,552	61	1.4
Interest on General Debt	16,288	131	3.0
Judicial and Legal	1,535	12	0.3
Libraries	0	0	0.0
Parking	509	4	0.1
Parks and Recreation	16,449	132	3.0
Police Protection	37,500	302	6.8
Public Welfare	1,362	11	0.2
Sewerage	26,968	217	4.9
Solid Waste Management	8,678	70	1.6
Veterans' Services	0	0	0.0
Liquor Store	0	0	0.0
Utility	305,383	2,456	55.6
Employee Retirement	35,685	287	6.5

Source: U.S Census Bureau, State & Local Government Finances 2012

DEMOGRAPHICS

Population Growth

Area	1990 Census	2000 Census	2010 Census	Population Growth (%) 1990-2000	Population Growth (%) 2000-2010
City	90,519	95,447	124,354	5.4	30.3
MSA[1]	191,263	232,392	264,275	21.5	13.7
U.S.	248,709,873	281,421,906	308,745,538	13.2	9.7

Note: (1) Figures cover the Gainesville, FL Metropolitan Statistical Area—see Appendix B for areas included
Source: U.S. Census Bureau, Census 1990, 2000, 2010

Household Size

Area	Persons in Household (%)							Average Household Size
	One	Two	Three	Four	Five	Six	Seven or More	
City	37.7	35.3	14.9	9.1	1.9	1.0	0.1	2.35
MSA[1]	32.8	35.9	15.2	10.7	3.5	1.1	0.7	2.47
U.S.	27.7	33.6	15.7	13.1	6.0	2.3	1.5	2.64

Note: (1) Figures cover the Gainesville, FL Metropolitan Statistical Area—see Appendix B for areas included
Source: U.S. Census Bureau, 2011-2013 American Community Survey 3-Year Estimates

Race

Area	White Alone[2] (%)	Black Alone[2] (%)	Asian Alone[2] (%)	AIAN[3] Alone[2] (%)	NHOPI[4] Alone[2] (%)	Other Race Alone[2] (%)	Two or More Races (%)
City	65.5	23.0	6.8	0.3	0.1	1.0	3.3
MSA[1]	71.5	19.2	5.1	0.3	0.1	1.0	2.8
U.S.	73.9	12.6	5.0	0.8	0.2	4.7	2.9

Note: (1) Figures cover the Gainesville, FL Metropolitan Statistical Area—see Appendix B for areas included; (2) Alone is defined as not being in combination with one or more other races; (3) American Indian and Alaska Native; (4) Native Hawaiian and Other Pacific Islander
Source: U.S. Census Bureau, 2011-2013 American Community Survey 3-Year Estimates

Hispanic or Latino Origin

Area	Total (%)	Mexican (%)	Puerto Rican (%)	Cuban (%)	Other (%)
City	10.1	1.1	2.5	2.8	3.8
MSA[1]	8.5	1.4	2.3	2.0	2.8
U.S.	16.9	10.8	1.6	0.6	3.8

Note: Persons of Hispanic or Latino origin can be of any race; (1) Figures cover the Gainesville, FL Metropolitan Statistical Area—see Appendix B for areas included
Source: U.S. Census Bureau, 2011-2013 American Community Survey 3-Year Estimates

Segregation

Type	Segregation Indices[1]				Percent Change		
	1990	2000	2010	2010 Rank[2]	1990-2000	1990-2010	2000-2010
Black/White	n/a	n/a	n/a	n/a	n/a	n/a	n/a
Asian/White	n/a	n/a	n/a	n/a	n/a	n/a	n/a
Hispanic/White	n/a	n/a	n/a	n/a	n/a	n/a	n/a

Note: All figures cover the Metropolitan Statistical Area—see Appendix B for areas included; Figures are based on an analysis of 1990, 2000, and 2010 Census Decennial Census tract data by William H. Frey, Brookings Institution and the University of Michigan Social Science Data Analysis Network. In this analysis all racial groups (whites, blacks, and asians) are non-Hispanic members of those races. Hispanics are shown as a separate category;
(1) Segregation Indices are Dissimilarity Indices that measure the degree to which the minority group is distributed differently than whites across census tracts. They range from 0 (complete integration) to 100 (complete segregation) where the value indicates the percentage of the minority group that needs to move to be distributed exactly like whites; (2) Ranges from 1 (most segregated) to 102 (least segregated); n/a not available.
Source: www.CensusScope.org

Ancestry

Area	German	Irish	English	American	Italian	Polish	French[2]	Scottish	Dutch
City	11.5	10.6	8.4	4.2	5.9	3.0	2.5	2.5	1.0
MSA[1]	12.7	11.2	9.8	6.1	4.8	2.5	2.6	2.2	1.3
U.S.	14.9	10.8	8.0	7.4	5.5	3.0	2.7	1.7	1.4

Note: Figures are the percentage of the total population reporting a particular ancestry. The nine most commonly reported ancestries in the U.S. are shown. Figures include multiple ancestries (e.g. if a person reported being Irish and Italian, they were included in both columns); (1) Figures cover the Gainesville, FL Metropolitan Statistical Area—see Appendix B for areas included; (2) Excludes Basque
Source: U.S. Census Bureau, 2011-2013 American Community Survey 3-Year Estimates

Foreign-Born Population

Area	Percent of Population Born in								
	Any Foreign Country	Mexico	Asia	Europe	Carribean	South America	Central America[2]	Africa	Canada
City	12.5	0.4	5.3	1.5	2.1	1.9	0.3	0.6	0.4
MSA[1]	9.9	0.5	3.7	1.4	1.7	1.4	0.3	0.5	0.4
U.S.	13.0	3.7	3.8	1.5	1.2	0.9	1.0	0.6	0.3

Note: (1) Figures cover the Gainesville, FL Metropolitan Statistical Area—see Appendix B for areas included; (2) Excludes Mexico.
Source: U.S. Census Bureau, 2011-2013 American Community Survey 3-Year Estimates

Marital Status

Area	Never Married	Now Married[2]	Separated	Widowed	Divorced
City	62.2	24.0	2.0	3.9	7.8
MSA[1]	46.0	37.2	1.9	5.2	9.8
U.S.	32.7	48.1	2.2	6.0	11.0

Note: Figures are percentages and cover the population 15 years of age and older; (1) Figures cover the Gainesville, FL Metropolitan Statistical Area—see Appendix B for areas included; (2) Excludes separated
Source: U.S. Census Bureau, 2011-2013 American Community Survey 3-Year Estimates

Disability Status

Area	All Ages	Under 18 Years Old	18 to 64 Years Old	65 Years and Over
City	9.4	4.5	7.2	38.6
MSA[1]	11.0	3.7	8.6	37.0
U.S.	12.3	4.1	10.2	36.3

Note: Figures show percent of the civilian noninstitutionalized population that reported having a disability. Disability status is determined from from six types of difficulty: vision, hearing, cognitive, ambulatory, self-care, and independent living. For children under 5 years old, hearing and vision difficulty are used to determine disability status. For children between the ages of 5 and 14, disability status is determined from hearing, vision, cognitive, ambulatory, and self-care difficulties. For people aged 15 years and older, they are considered to have a disability if they have difficulty with any one of the six difficulty types; (1) Figures cover the Gainesville, FL Metropolitan Statistical Area—see Appendix B for areas included.
Source: U.S. Census Bureau, 2011-2013 American Community Survey 3-Year Estimates

Age

Area	Percent of Population									Median Age
	Under Age 5	Age 5–19	Age 20–34	Age 35–44	Age 45–54	Age 55–64	Age 65–74	Age 75–84	Age 85+	
City	4.5	17.7	43.9	8.4	8.0	9.1	4.2	3.0	1.2	25.1
MSA[1]	5.5	18.2	31.3	10.3	11.3	11.5	6.7	3.6	1.5	31.0
U.S.	6.4	19.9	20.7	12.9	14.1	12.3	7.6	4.2	1.9	37.4

Note: (1) Figures cover the Gainesville, FL Metropolitan Statistical Area—see Appendix B for areas included
Source: U.S. Census Bureau, 2011-2013 American Community Survey 3-Year Estimates

Gender

Area	Males	Females	Males per 100 Females
City	60,742	65,911	92.2
MSA[1]	130,829	137,730	95.0
U.S.	154,451,010	159,410,713	96.9

Note: (1) Figures cover the Gainesville, FL Metropolitan Statistical Area—see Appendix B for areas included
Source: U.S. Census Bureau, 2011-2013 American Community Survey 3-Year Estimates

Religious Groups by Family

Area	Catholic	Baptist	Non-Den.	Methodist[2]	Lutheran	LDS[3]	Pente-costal	Presby-terian[4]	Muslim[5]	Judaism
MSA[1]	7.6	12.3	4.3	6.4	0.5	1.0	3.5	1.1	1.1	0.4
U.S.	19.1	9.3	4.0	4.0	2.3	2.0	1.9	1.6	0.8	0.7

Note: Figures are the number of adherents as a percentage of the total population; (1) Figures cover the Gainesville, FL Metropolitan Statistical Area—see Appendix B for areas included; (2) Methodist/Pietist; (3) Latter Day Saints; (4) Reformed; (5) Figures are estimates
Source: Association of Statisticians of American Religious Bodies, 2010 U.S. Religion Census: Religious Congregations & Membership Study

Religious Groups by Tradition

Area	Catholic	Evangelical Protestant	Mainline Protestant	Other Tradition	Black Protestant	Orthodox
MSA[1]	7.6	20.4	7.0	4.2	2.2	0.1
U.S.	19.1	16.2	7.3	4.3	1.6	0.3

Note: Figures are the number of adherents as a percentage of the total population; (1) Figures cover the Gainesville, FL Metropolitan Statistical Area—see Appendix B for areas included
Source: Association of Statisticians of American Religious Bodies, 2010 U.S. Religion Census: Religious Congregations & Membership Study

ECONOMY

Gross Metropolitan Product

Area	2012	2013	2014	2015	Rank[2]
MSA[1]	10.5	10.7	11.1	11.6	174

Note: Figures are in billions of dollars; (1) Figures cover the Gainesville, FL Metropolitan Statistical Area—see Appendix B for areas included; (2) Rank is based on 2015 data and ranges from 1 to 363
Source: The U.S. Conference of Mayors, U.S. Metro Economies: GMP and Employment 2013-2015, June 2014

Economic Growth

Area	2010-12 (%)	2013 (%)	2014 (%)	2015 (%)	Rank[2]
MSA[1]	-0.3	1.3	2.0	2.3	285
U.S.	2.1	2.0	2.3	3.2	–

Note: Figures are real gross metropolitan product (GMP) growth rates and represent annual average percent change; (1) Figures cover the Gainesville, FL Metropolitan Statistical Area—see Appendix B for areas included; (2) Rank is based on 2015 data and ranges from 1 to 363
Source: The U.S. Conference of Mayors, U.S. Metro Economies: GMP and Employment 2013-2015, June 2014

Metropolitan Area Exports

Area	2008	2009	2010	2011	2012	2013	Rank[2]
MSA[1]	285.5	233.2	277.7	305.1	348.6	295.0	270

Note: Figures are in millions of dollars; (1) Figures cover the Gainesville, FL Metropolitan Statistical Area—see Appendix B for areas included; (2) Rank is based on 2013 data and ranges from 1 to 387
Source: U.S. Department of Commerce, International Trade Administration, Office of Trade & Industry Information, Manufacturing & Services, data extracted April 3, 2015

Building Permits

Area	Single-Family			Multi-Family			Total		
	2013	2014	Pct. Chg.	2013	2014	Pct. Chg.	2013	2014	Pct. Chg.
City	63	67	6.3	240	263	9.6	303	330	8.9
MSA[1]	558	536	-3.9	242	263	8.7	800	799	-0.1
U.S.	620,802	634,597	2.2	370,020	411,766	11.3	990,822	1,046,363	5.6

Note: (1) Figures cover the Gainesville, FL Metropolitan Statistical Area—see Appendix B for areas included; Figures represent new, privately-owned housing units authorized (unadjusted data); All permit data are based on estimates with imputation.
Source: U.S. Census Bureau, Manufacturing, Mining, and Construction Statistics, Building Permits, 2013, 2014

Bankruptcy Filings

Area	Business Filings			Nonbusiness Filings		
	2013	2014	% Chg.	2013	2014	% Chg.
Alachua County	30	15	-50.0	297	314	5.7
U.S.	33,212	26,983	-18.8	1,038,720	909,812	-12.4

Note: Business filings include Chapter 7, Chapter 11, Chapter 12, and Chapter 13; Nonbusiness filings include Chapter 7, Chapter 11, and Chapter 13
Source: Administrative Office of the U.S. Courts, Business and Nonbusiness Bankruptcy, County Cases Commenced by Chapter of the Bankruptcy Code, During the 12- Month Period Ending December 31, 2013 and Business and Nonbusiness Bankruptcy, County Cases Commenced by Chapter of the Bankruptcy Code, During the 12- Month Period Ending December 31, 2014

Housing Vacancy Rates

Area	Gross Vacancy Rate[2] (%)			Year-Round Vacancy Rate[3] (%)			Rental Vacancy Rate[4] (%)			Homeowner Vacancy Rate[5] (%)		
	2012	2013	2014	2012	2013	2014	2012	2013	2014	2012	2013	2014
MSA[1]	n/a	n/a	n/a	n/a	n/a	n/a	n/a	n/a	n/a	n/a	n/a	n/a
U.S.	13.8	13.6	13.4	10.8	10.7	10.4	8.7	8.3	7.6	2.0	2.0	1.9

Note: (1) Figures cover the Gainesville, FL Metropolitan Statistical Area—see Appendix B for areas included; (2) The percentage of the total housing inventory that is vacant; (3) The percentage of the housing inventory (excluding seasonal units) that is year-round vacant; (4) The percentage of rental inventory that is vacant for rent; (5) The percentage of homeowner inventory that is vacant for sale; n/a not available
Source: U.S. Census Bureau, Housing Vacancies and Homeownership Annual Statistics: 2014

INCOME

Income

Area	Per Capita ($)	Median Household ($)	Average Household ($)
City	19,235	31,584	47,358
MSA[1]	24,234	41,211	60,668
U.S.	27,884	52,176	72,897

Note: (1) Figures cover the Gainesville, FL Metropolitan Statistical Area—see Appendix B for areas included
Source: U.S. Census Bureau, 2011-2013 American Community Survey 3-Year Estimates

Household Income Distribution

Area	Percent of Households Earning							
	Under $15,000	$15,000 -24,999	$25,000 -34,999	$35,000 -49,999	$50,000 -74,999	$75,000 -99,000	$100,000 -149,999	$150,000 and up
City	28.1	12.4	13.4	12.7	15.2	7.8	6.3	4.1
MSA[1]	20.7	11.4	11.9	13.3	16.2	10.3	9.1	7.1
U.S.	13.0	10.9	10.3	13.6	17.9	11.9	12.7	9.6

Note: (1) Figures cover the Gainesville, FL Metropolitan Statistical Area—see Appendix B for areas included
Source: U.S. Census Bureau, 2011-2013 American Community Survey 3-Year Estimates

Poverty Rate

Area	All Ages	Under 18 Years Old	18 to 64 Years Old	65 Years and Over
City	36.4	30.7	40.3	10.8
MSA[1]	25.5	25.1	28.4	9.8
U.S.	15.9	22.4	14.8	9.5

Note: Figures are percentage of people whose income during the past 12 months was below the poverty level; (1) Figures cover the Gainesville, FL Metropolitan Statistical Area—see Appendix B for areas included
Source: U.S. Census Bureau, 2011-2013 American Community Survey 3-Year Estimates

EMPLOYMENT

Labor Force and Employment

Area	Civilian Labor Force			Workers Employed		
	Dec. 2013	Dec. 2014	% Chg.	Dec. 2013	Dec. 2014	% Chg.
City	63,864	65,155	2.0	60,490	62,150	2.7
MSA[1]	134,410	137,132	2.0	127,340	130,889	2.8
U.S.	154,408,000	155,521,000	0.7	144,423,000	147,190,000	1.9

Note: Data is not seasonally adjusted and covers workers 16 years of age and older; (1) Figures cover the Gainesville, FL Metropolitan Statistical Area—see Appendix B for areas included
Source: Bureau of Labor Statistics, Local Area Unemployment Statistics

Unemployment Rate

Area	2014											
	Jan.	Feb.	Mar.	Apr.	May	Jun.	Jul.	Aug.	Sep.	Oct.	Nov.	Dec.
City	5.5	5.4	5.3	4.5	5.2	5.9	6.2	5.8	5.3	4.9	5.0	4.6
MSA[1]	5.6	5.5	5.4	4.7	5.2	5.6	5.9	5.7	5.1	4.8	4.9	4.6
U.S.	7.0	7.0	6.8	5.9	6.1	6.3	6.5	6.3	5.7	5.5	5.5	5.4

Note: Data is not seasonally adjusted and covers workers 16 years of age and older; (1) Figures cover the Gainesville, FL Metropolitan Statistical Area—see Appendix B for areas included
Source: Bureau of Labor Statistics, Local Area Unemployment Statistics

Employment by Occupation

Occupation Classification	City (%)	MSA[1] (%)	U.S. (%)
Management, Business, Science, and Arts	45.2	44.5	36.2
Natural Resources, Construction, and Maintenance	4.2	5.8	9.0
Production, Transportation, and Material Moving	5.1	6.2	12.1
Sales and Office	25.3	24.3	24.4
Service	20.3	19.2	18.3

Note: Figures cover employed civilians 16 years of age and older; (1) Figures cover the Gainesville, FL Metropolitan Statistical Area—see Appendix B for areas included
Source: U.S. Census Bureau, 2011-2013 American Community Survey 3-Year Estimates

Employment by Industry

Sector	MSA[1]		U.S.
	Number of Employees	Percent of Total	Percent of Total
Construction, Mining, and Logging	4,500	3.3	5.0
Education and Health Services	24,400	18.0	15.5
Financial Activities	6,200	4.6	5.7
Government	42,500	31.4	15.8
Information	1,500	1.1	2.0
Leisure and Hospitality	14,600	10.8	10.3
Manufacturing	4,300	3.2	8.7
Other Services	4,300	3.2	4.0
Professional and Business Services	13,000	9.6	13.8
Retail Trade	14,500	10.7	11.4
Transportation, Warehousing, and Utilities	2,900	2.1	3.9
Wholesale Trade	2,800	2.1	4.2

Note: Figures are non-farm employment as of December 2014. Figures are not seasonally adjusted and include workers 16 years of age and older; (1) Figures cover the Gainesville, FL Metropolitan Statistical Area—see Appendix B for areas included; n/a not available
Source: Bureau of Labor Statistics, Current Employment Statistics, Employment, Hours, and Earnings

Occupations with Greatest Projected Employment Growth: 2012 – 2022

Occupation[1]	2012 Employment	2022 Projected Employment	Numeric Employment Change	Percent Employment Change
Retail Salespersons	326,380	380,120	53,740	16.5
Combined Food Preparation and Serving Workers, Including Fast Food	196,980	237,340	40,360	20.5
Customer Service Representatives	191,210	228,620	37,410	19.6
Registered Nurses	164,020	201,140	37,120	22.6
Waiters and Waitresses	191,370	227,810	36,440	19.0
Office Clerks, General	142,710	170,300	27,590	19.3
Cashiers	206,660	230,190	23,530	11.4
Landscaping and Groundskeeping Workers	92,510	115,540	23,030	24.9
Receptionists and Information Clerks	75,780	95,680	19,900	26.2
Nursing Assistants	86,990	106,200	19,210	22.1

Note: Projections cover Florida; (1) Sorted by numeric employment change
Source: www.projectionscentral.com, State Occupational Projections, 2012–2022 Long-Term Projections

Fastest Growing Occupations: 2012 – 2022

Occupation[1]	2012 Employment	2022 Projected Employment	Numeric Employment Change	Percent Employment Change
Helpers—Carpenters	1,280	2,450	1,170	90.7
Helpers—Brickmasons, Blockmasons, Stonemasons, and Tile and Marble Setters	1,050	1,890	840	79.5
Biomedical Engineers	760	1,300	540	70.7
Reinforcing Iron and Rebar Workers	520	870	350	67.5
Glaziers	2,890	4,710	1,820	62.8
Solar Photovoltaic Installers	170	270	100	58.7
Brickmasons and Blockmasons	2,820	4,430	1,610	57.1
Stonemasons	450	710	260	56.4
Helpers—Pipelayers, Plumbers, Pipefitters, and Steamfitters	2,420	3,750	1,330	54.8
Cement Masons and Concrete Finishers	10,390	16,050	5,660	54.4

Note: Projections cover Florida; (1) Sorted by percent employment change and excludes occupations with numeric employment change less than 100
Source: www.projectionscentral.com, State Occupational Projections, 2012–2022 Long-Term Projections

Average Wages

Occupation	$/Hr.	Occupation	$/Hr.
Accountants and Auditors	29.10	Maids and Housekeeping Cleaners	9.86
Automotive Mechanics	18.61	Maintenance and Repair Workers	17.14
Bookkeepers	16.71	Marketing Managers	62.12
Carpenters	16.67	Nuclear Medicine Technologists	n/a
Cashiers	9.19	Nurses, Licensed Practical	20.12
Clerks, General Office	12.50	Nurses, Registered	29.16
Clerks, Receptionists/Information	11.65	Nursing Assistants	10.93
Clerks, Shipping/Receiving	14.56	Packers and Packagers, Hand	9.58
Computer Programmers	28.74	Physical Therapists	37.82
Computer Systems Analysts	37.02	Postal Service Mail Carriers	24.31
Computer User Support Specialists	19.84	Real Estate Brokers	n/a
Cooks, Restaurant	10.17	Retail Salespersons	11.27
Dentists	93.12	Sales Reps., Exc. Tech./Scientific	24.02
Electrical Engineers	33.07	Sales Reps., Tech./Scientific	37.49
Electricians	18.32	Secretaries, Exc. Legal/Med./Exec.	14.25
Financial Managers	64.77	Security Guards	11.33
First-Line Supervisors/Managers, Sales	18.84	Surgeons	124.14
Food Preparation Workers	9.99	Teacher Assistants	9.50
General and Operations Managers	55.68	Teachers, Elementary School	22.10
Hairdressers/Cosmetologists	13.03	Teachers, Secondary School	24.40
Internists	113.85	Telemarketers	9.39
Janitors and Cleaners	10.63	Truck Drivers, Heavy/Tractor-Trailer	14.27
Landscaping/Groundskeeping Workers	10.90	Truck Drivers, Light/Delivery Svcs.	15.92
Lawyers	48.54	Waiters and Waitresses	9.80

Note: Wage data covers the Gainesville, FL Metropolitan Statistical Area—see Appendix B for areas included; Hourly wages for elementary/secondary school teachers and teacher assistants were calculated by the editors from annual wage data assuming a 40 hour work week; n/a not available.
Source: Bureau of Labor Statistics, Metro Area Occupational Employment and Wage Estimates, May 2014

TAXES

State Corporate Income Tax Rates

State	Tax Rate (%)	Income Brackets ($)	Num. of Brackets	Financial Institution Tax Rate (%)[a]	Federal Income Tax Ded.
Florida	5.5 (f)	Flat rate	1	5.5 (f)	No

Note: Tax rates as of January 1, 2015; (a) Rates listed are the corporate income tax rate applied to financial institutions or excise taxes based on income. Some states have other taxes based upon the value of deposits or shares; (f) An exemption of $50,000 is allowed. Florida's Alternative Minimum Tax rate is 3.3%.
Source: Federation of Tax Administrators, "State Corporate Income Tax Rates, 2015"

State Individual Income Tax Rates

State	Tax Rate (%)	Income Brackets ($)	Num. of Brackets	Personal Exempt. ($)[1]		Fed. Inc. Tax Ded.
				Single	Dependents	
Florida	None	–	–	–	–	–

Note: Tax rates as of January 1, 2015; Local- and county-level taxes are not included; n/a not applicable; (1) Married joint filers generally receive double the single exemption
Source: Federation of Tax Administrators, "State Individual Income Tax Rates, 2015"

Various State and Local Tax Rates

State	State and Local Sales and Use (%)	State Sales and Use (%)	Gasoline[1] (¢/gal.)	Cigarette[2] ($/pack)	Spirits[3] ($/gal.)	Wine[4] ($/gal.)	Beer[5] ($/gal.)
Florida	6.0	6.0	36.42	1.339	6.50 (f)	2.25	0.48 (p)

Note: All tax rates as of January 1, 2015; (1) The American Petroleum Institute has developed a methodology for determining the average tax rate on a gallon of fuel. Rates may include any of the following: excise taxes, environmental fees, storage tank fees, other fees or taxes, general sales tax, and local taxes. In states where gasoline is subject to the general sales tax, or where the fuel tax is based on the average sale price, the average rate determined by API is sensitive to changes in the price of gasoline. States that fully or partially apply general sales taxes to gasoline: CA, CO, GA, IL, IN, MI, NY; (2) The federal excise tax of $1.0066 per pack and local taxes are not included; (3) Rates are those applicable to off-premise sales of 40% alcohol by volume (a.b.v.) distilled spirits in 750ml containers. Local excise taxes are excluded; (4) Rates are those applicable to off-premise sales of 11% a.b.v. non-carbonated wine in 750ml containers; (5) Rates are those applicable to off-premise sales of 4.7% a.b.v. beer in 12 ounce containers; (f) Different rates are also applicable according to alcohol content, place of production, size of container, or place purchased (on- or off-premise or onboard airlines); (p) Local excise taxes are excluded.
Source: Tax Foundation, 2015 Facts & Figures: How Does Your State Compare?

State Business Tax Climate Index Rankings

State	Overall Rank	Corporate Tax Index Rank	Individual Income Tax Index Rank	Sales Tax Index Rank	Unemployment Insurance Tax Index Rank	Property Tax Index Rank
Florida	5	14	1	12	3	16

Note: The index is a measure of how each state's tax laws affect economic performance. The lower the rank, the more favorable a state's tax system is for business. States without a given tax are given a ranking of 1. The scores/rankings for the District of Columbia do not affect other states. The 2015 index represents the tax climate as of July 1, 2014.
Source: Tax Foundation, State Business Tax Climate Index 2015

COMMERCIAL UTILITIES

Typical Monthly Electric Bills

Area	Commercial Service ($/month)		Industrial Service ($/month)	
	1,500 kWh	40 kW demand 14,000 kWh	1,000 kW demand 200,000 kWh	50,000 kW demand 32,500,000 kWh
City	n/a	n/a	n/a	n/a
Average[1]	201	1,653	26,124	2,639,743

Note: Figures are based on annualized 2014 rates; (1) Average based on 180 utilities surveyed; n/a not available
Source: Edison Electric Institute, Typical Bills and Average Rates Report, Summer 2014

TRANSPORTATION

Means of Transportation to Work

Area	Car/Truck/Van		Public Transportation			Bicycle	Walked	Other Means	Worked at Home
	Drove Alone	Car-pooled	Bus	Subway	Railroad				
City	64.3	8.9	7.9	0.0	0.0	6.6	5.1	2.7	4.5
MSA[1]	73.4	9.7	4.3	0.0	0.0	3.3	3.1	1.8	4.4
U.S.	76.4	9.6	2.6	1.8	0.6	0.6	2.8	1.3	4.3

Note: Figures are percentages and cover workers 16 years of age and older; (1) Figures cover the Gainesville, FL Metropolitan Statistical Area—see Appendix B for areas included
Source: U.S. Census Bureau, 2011-2013 American Community Survey 3-Year Estimates

Travel Time to Work

Area	Less Than 10 Minutes	10 to 19 Minutes	20 to 29 Minutes	30 to 44 Minutes	45 to 59 Minutes	60 to 89 Minutes	90 Minutes or More
City	18.0	53.7	16.3	8.7	1.8	0.9	0.6
MSA[1]	13.4	40.3	23.3	16.1	3.7	2.1	1.0
U.S.	13.3	29.7	20.9	20.2	7.7	5.7	2.6

Note: Figures are percentages and include workers 16 years old and over; (1) Figures cover the Gainesville, FL Metropolitan Statistical Area—see Appendix B for areas included
Source: U.S. Census Bureau, 2011-2013 American Community Survey 3-Year Estimates

Travel Time Index

Area	1985	1990	1995	2000	2005	2010	2011
Urban Area[1]	n/a	n/a	n/a	n/a	n/a	n/a	n/a
Average[2]	1.09	1.14	1.16	1.19	1.23	1.18	1.18

Note: Travel Time Index—the ratio of travel time in the peak period to the travel time at free-flow conditions. For example, a value of 1.30 indicates a 20-minute free-flow trip takes 26 minutes in the peak. Free-flow speeds (60 mph on freeways and 35 mph on principal arterials) are used as the comparison threshold; (1) Data for the Gainesville, FL urban area was not available; (2) average of 498 urban areas
Source: Texas Transportation Institute, Urban Mobility Report 2012, December 2012

Public Transportation

Agency Name / Mode of Transportation	Vehicles Operated in Maximum Service	Annual Unlinked Passenger Trips (in thous.)	Annual Passenger Miles (in thous.)
Gainesville Regional Transit System (RTS)			
Bus (directly operated)	103	10,832.7	26,540.1
Demand Response (purchased transportation)	35	51.1	469.9

Source: Federal Transit Administration, National Transit Database, 2013

Air Transportation

Airport Name and Code / Type of Service	Passenger Airlines[1]	Passenger Enplanements	Freight Carriers[2]	Freight (lbs.)
Gainesville Regional Airport (GNV)				
Domestic service (U.S. carriers - 2014)	16	206,520	5	8,209
International service (U.S. carriers - 2013)	0	0	0	0

Note: (1) Includes all U.S.-based major, minor and commuter airlines that carried at least one passenger during the year; (2) Includes all U.S.-based airlines and freight carriers that transported at least one lb. of freight during the year.
Source: Bureau of Transportation Statistics, The Intermodal Transportation Database, Air Carriers: T-100 Domestic Market (U.S. Carriers), 2014; Bureau of Transportation Statistics, The Intermodal Transportation Database, Air Carriers: T-100 International Market (U.S. Carriers), 2013

Other Transportation Statistics

Major Highways:	I-75
Amtrak Service:	Yes (train station is located in Waldo
Major Waterways/Ports:	None

Source: Amtrak.com; Google Maps

BUSINESSES

Major Business Headquarters

Company Name	Rankings	
	Fortune[1]	Forbes[2]
No companies listed	-	-

Note: (1) Fortune 500—companies that produce a 10-K are ranked 1 to 500 based on 2013 revenue; (2) all private companies with at least $2 billion in annual revenue through the end of their most current fiscal year are ranked 1 to 221; companies listed are headquartered in the city; dashes indicate no ranking
Source: Fortune, "Fortune 500," June 16, 2014; Forbes, "America's Largest Private Companies," November 5, 2014

Minority- and Women-Owned Businesses

Group	All Firms		Firms with Paid Employees			
	Firms	Sales ($000)	Firms	Sales ($000)	Employees	Payroll ($000)
Asian	407	97,010	152	93,107	583	12,034
Black	919	146,222	122	135,251	587	17,559
Hispanic	753	207,434	193	168,321	856	28,036
Women	3,387	629,433	498	532,285	4,359	114,296
All Firms	10,976	10,487,232	3,219	10,132,351	60,343	2,193,878

Note: Figures cover firms located in the city; minority- and women-owned business are defined as firms in which the corresponding group own 51% or more of the stock or equity of the company
Source: U.S. Census Bureau, 2007 Economic Census, Survey of Business Owners (2012 Survey of Business Owners data will be released starting in June 2015)

HOTELS & CONVENTION CENTERS

Hotels/Motels

Area	5 Star		4 Star		3 Star		2 Star		1 Star		Not Rated	
	Num.	Pct.[3]	Num.	Pct.[3]	Num.	Pct.[3]	Num.	Pct.[3]	Num.	Pct.[3]	Num.	Pct.[3]
City[1]	0	0.0	0	0.0	13	14.9	62	71.3	6	6.9	6	6.9
Total[2]	166	0.9	1,264	7.0	5,718	31.8	9,340	52.0	411	2.3	1,070	6.0

Note: (1) Figures cover Gainesville and vicinity; (2) Figures cover all 100 cities in this book; (3) Percentage of hotels which have a given star rating; Star ratings are determined by expedia.com and offer an indication of the general quality of a particular hotel.
Source: expedia.com, April 2, 2015

Major Convention Centers

Name	Overall Space (sq. ft.)	Exhibit Space (sq. ft.)	Meeting Space (sq. ft.)	Meeting Rooms

There are no major convention centers located in the metro area
Source: Original research

Living Environment

COST OF LIVING

Cost of Living Index

Composite Index	Groceries	Housing	Utilities	Trans-portation	Health Care	Misc. Goods/ Services
97.3	102.8	91.1	99.6	105.7	102.4	95.6

Note: The Cost of Living Index measures regional differences in the cost of consumer goods and services, excluding taxes and non-consumer expenditures, for professional and managerial households in the top income quintile. It is based on more than 50,000 prices covering almost 60 different items for which prices are collected three times a year by chambers of commerce, economic development organizations or university applied economic centers in each participating urban area. The numbers shown should be read as a percentage above or below the national average of 100. For example, a value of 115.4 in the groceries column indicates that grocery prices are 15.4% higher than the national average. Small differences in the index numbers should not be interpreted as significant; Figures cover the Gainesville FL urban area.
Source: The Council for Community and Economic Research, ACCRA Cost of Living Index, 2014

Grocery Prices

Area[1]	T-Bone Steak ($/pound)	Frying Chicken ($/pound)	Whole Milk ($/half gal.)	Eggs ($/dozen)	Orange Juice ($/64 oz.)	Coffee ($/11.5 oz.)
City[2]	11.14	1.47	2.83	1.99	3.57	3.78
Avg.	10.40	1.37	2.40	1.99	3.46	4.27
Min.	8.48	0.93	1.37	1.30	2.83	2.99
Max.	14.20	2.44	3.62	4.02	6.42	6.96

Note: (1) Values for the local area are compared with the average, minimum and maximum values for all 308 areas in the Cost of Living Index; (2) Figures cover the Gainesville FL urban area; **T-Bone Steak** *(price per pound);* **Frying Chicken** *(price per pound, whole fryer);* **Whole Milk** *(half gallon carton);* **Eggs** *(price per dozen, Grade A, large);* **Orange Juice** *(64 oz. Tropicana or Florida Natural);* **Coffee** *(11.5 oz. can, vacuum-packed, Maxwell House, Hills Bros, or Folgers).*
Source: The Council for Community and Economic Research, ACCRA Cost of Living Index, 2014

Housing and Utility Costs

Area[1]	New Home Price ($)	Apartment Rent ($/month)	All Electric ($/month)	Part Electric ($/month)	Other Energy ($/month)	Telephone ($/month)
City[2]	275,745	890	-	124.58	44.11	27.78
Avg.	305,838	919	181.00	93.66	73.14	27.95
Min.	183,142	480	112.00	42.06	23.42	17.16
Max.	1,358,576	3,851	594.00	180.03	440.99	40.42

Note: (1) Values for the local area are compared with the average, minimum and maximum values for all 308 areas in the Cost of Living Index; (2) Figures cover the Gainesville FL urban area; **New Home Price** *(2,400 sf living area, 8,000 sf lot, in urban area with full utilities);* **Apartment Rent** *(950 sf 2 bedroom/1.5 or 2 bath, unfurnished, excluding all utilities except water);* **All Electric** *(average monthly cost for an all-electric home);* **Part Electric** *(average monthly cost for a part-electric home);* **Other Energy** *(average monthly cost for natural gas, fuel oil, coal, wood, and any other forms of energy except electricity);* **Telephone** *(price includes basic monthly rate for a private residential line plus additional local usage charges incurred by a family of four).*
Source: The Council for Community and Economic Research, ACCRA Cost of Living Index, 2014

Health Care, Transportation, and Other Costs

Area[1]	Doctor ($/visit)	Dentist ($/visit)	Optometrist ($/visit)	Gasoline ($/gallon)	Beauty Salon ($/visit)	Men's Shirt ($)
City[2]	88.61	99.78	82.72	3.49	35.00	20.65
Avg.	102.86	87.89	97.66	3.44	34.37	26.74
Min.	67.47	65.78	51.18	3.00	17.43	12.79
Max.	173.50	150.14	235.00	4.33	64.28	49.50

Note: (1) Values for the local area are compared with the average, minimum and maximum values for all 308 areas in the Cost of Living Index; (2) Figures cover the Gainesville FL urban area; **Doctor** *(general practitioners routine exam of an established patient);* **Dentist** *(adult teeth cleaning and periodic oral examination);* **Optometrist** *(full vision eye exam for established adult patient);* **Gasoline** *(one gallon regular unleaded, national brand, including all taxes, cash price at self-service pump if available);* **Beauty Salon** *(woman's shampoo, trim, and blow-dry);* **Men's Shirt** *(cotton/polyester dress shirt, pinpoint weave, long sleeves).*
Source: The Council for Community and Economic Research, ACCRA Cost of Living Index, 2014

HOUSING

House Price Index (HPI)

Area	National Ranking[2]	Quarterly Change (%)	One-Year Change (%)	Five-Year Change (%)
MSA[1]	(a)	n/a	4.19	-12.63
U.S.[3]	–	1.35	4.91	11.59

Note: The HPI is a weighted repeat sales index. It measures average price changes in repeat sales or refinancings on the same properties. This information is obtained by reviewing repeat mortgage transactions on single-family properties whose mortgages have been purchased or securitized by Fannie Mae or Freddie Mac in January 1975; (1) Gainesville Metropolitan Statistical Area—see Appendix B for areas included; (2) Rankings are based on annual percentage change for all metro areas containing at least 15,000 transactions over the last 10 years and ranges from 1 to 275; (3) figures based on a weighted average of Census Division estimates using a seasonally adjusted, purchase-only index; all figures are for the period ending December 31, 2014; n/a not available; (a) Not ranked because of increased index variability due to smaller sample size
Source: Federal Housing Finance Agency, House Price Index, February 26, 2015

Median Single-Family Home Prices

Area	2012	2013	2014p	Percent Change 2013 to 2014
MSA[1]	145.6	167.3	172.3	3.0
U.S. Average	177.2	197.4	209.0	5.9

Note: Figures are median sales prices of existing single-family homes in thousands of dollars; (p) preliminary; n/a not available; (1) Gainesville, FL Metropolitan Statistical Area—see Appendix B for areas included
Source: National Association of Realtors, Median Sales Price of Existing Single-Family Homes for Metropolitan Areas, 4th Quarter 2014

Qualifying Income Based on Median Sales Price of Existing Single-Family Homes

Area	With 5% Down ($)	With 10% Down ($)	With 20% Down ($)
MSA[1]	38,457	36,433	32,385
U.S. Average	45,863	43,449	38,621

Note: Figures are preliminary; Qualifying income is based on a mortgage rate of 4.0%. Monthly principal and interest payment is limited to 25% of income; n/a not available; (1) Gainesville, FL Metropolitan Statistical Area—see Appendix B for areas included
Source: National Association of Realtors, Qualifying Income Based on Median Sales Price of Existing Single-Family Homes for Metropolitan Areas, 4th Quarter 2014

Median Apartment Condo-Coop Home Prices

Area	2012	2013	2014p	Percent Change 2013 to 2014
MSA[1]	n/a	n/a	n/a	n/a
U.S. Average	173.7	194.9	205.1	5.2

Note: Figures are median sales prices of existing apartment condo-coop homes in thousands of dollars; (p) preliminary; n/a not available; (1) Gainesville, FL Metropolitan Statistical Area—see Appendix B for areas included
Source: National Association of Realtors, Median Sales Price of Existing Apartment Condo-Coop Homes for Metropolitan Areas, 4th Quarter 2014

Gross Monthly Rent

Area	Under $200	$200 -299	$300 -499	$500 -749	$750 -999	$1,000 -1,499	$1,500 and up	Median ($)
City	1.4	2.5	5.6	28.7	31.7	22.2	7.9	825
MSA[1]	1.2	2.0	6.5	25.8	31.1	24.3	9.2	852
U.S.	1.7	3.2	7.8	22.1	24.3	26.0	14.9	900

Note: Figures are percentages except for Median; Gross rent is the contract rent plus the estimated average monthly cost of utilities (electricity, gas, and water and sewer) and fuels (oil, coal, kerosene, wood, etc.) if these are paid by the renter (or paid for the renter by someone else); (1) Figures cover the Gainesville, FL Metropolitan Statistical Area—see Appendix B for areas included
Source: U.S. Census Bureau, 2011-2013 American Community Survey 3-Year Estimates

Homeownership Rate

Area	2007 (%)	2008 (%)	2009 (%)	2010 (%)	2011 (%)	2012 (%)	2013 (%)	2014 (%)
MSA[1]	n/a	n/a	n/a	n/a	n/a	n/a	n/a	n/a
U.S.	68.1	67.8	67.4	66.9	66.1	65.4	65.1	64.5

Note: (1) Figures cover the Gainesville, FL Metropolitan Statistical Area—see Appendix B for areas included; n/a not available
Source: U.S. Census Bureau, Housing Vacancies and Homeownership Annual Statistics: 2014

Year Housing Structure Built

Area	2010 or Later	2000 -2009	1990 -1999	1980 -1989	1970 -1979	1960 -1969	1950 -1959	1940 -1949	Before 1940	Median Year
City	0.4	15.5	15.9	19.3	22.7	12.6	7.4	2.5	3.8	1981
MSA[1]	0.7	19.4	20.9	20.6	18.8	9.2	5.7	1.7	3.1	1986
U.S.	0.9	15.0	13.9	13.8	15.8	11.0	10.9	5.4	13.3	1976

Note: Figures are percentages except for Median Year; (1) Figures cover the Gainesville, FL Metropolitan Statistical Area—see Appendix B for areas included
Source: U.S. Census Bureau, 2011-2013 American Community Survey 3-Year Estimates

HEALTH

Health Risk Data

Category	MSA[1] (%)	U.S. (%)
Adults aged 18–64 who have any kind of health care coverage	n/a	79.6
Adults who reported being in good or excellent health	n/a	83.1
Adults who are current smokers	n/a	19.6
Adults who are heavy drinkers[2]	n/a	6.1
Adults who are binge drinkers[3]	n/a	16.9
Adults who are overweight (BMI 25.0 - 29.9)	n/a	35.8
Adults who are obese (BMI 30.0 - 99.8)	n/a	27.6
Adults who participated in any physical activities in the past month	n/a	77.1
Adults 50+ who have ever had a sigmoidoscopy or colonoscopy	n/a	67.3
Women aged 40+ who have had a mammogram within the past two years	n/a	74.0
Men aged 40+ who have had a PSA test within the past two years	n/a	45.2
Adults aged 65+ who have had flu shot within the past year	n/a	60.1
Adults who always wear a seatbelt	n/a	93.8

Note: Data as of 2012 unless otherwise noted; n/a not available; (1) Figures cover the Gainesville, FL Metropolitan Statistical Area—see Appendix B for areas included; (2) Heavy drinkers are classified as males having more than two drinks per day or females having more than one drink per day; (3) Binge drinkers are classified as males having five or more drinks on one occasion or females having four or more drinks on one occasion
Source: Centers for Disease Control and Prevention, Behaviorial Risk Factor Surveillance System, SMART: Selected Metropolitan/Micropolitan Area Risk Trends, 2012 (Note: the CDC has discontinued this dataset but will be releasing a replacement in late 2015)

Chronic Health Indicators

Category	MSA[1] (%)	U.S. (%)
Adults who have ever been told they had a heart attack	n/a	4.5
Adults who have ever been told they had a stroke	n/a	2.9
Adults who have been told they currently have asthma	n/a	8.9
Adults who have ever been told they have arthritis	n/a	25.7
Adults who have ever been told they have diabetes[2]	n/a	9.7
Adults who have ever been told they had skin cancer	n/a	5.7
Adults who have ever been told they had any other types of cancer	n/a	6.5
Adults who have ever been told they have COPD	n/a	6.2
Adults who have ever been told they have kidney disease	n/a	2.5
Adults who have ever been told they have a form of depression	n/a	18.0

Note: Data as of 2012 unless otherwise noted; n/a not available; (1) Figures cover the Gainesville, FL Metropolitan Statistical Area—see Appendix B for areas included; (2) Figures do not include pregnancy-related, borderline, or pre-diabetes
Source: Centers for Disease Control and Prevention, Behaviorial Risk Factor Surveillance System, SMART: Selected Metropolitan/Micropolitan Area Risk Trends, 2012 (Note: the CDC has discontinued this dataset but will be releasing a replacement in late 2015)

Mortality Rates for the Top 10 Causes of Death in the U.S.

ICD-10[a] Sub-Chapter	ICD-10[a] Code	Age-Adjusted Mortality Rate[1] per 100,000 population	
		County[2]	U.S.
Malignant neoplasms	C00-C97	181.9	166.2
Ischaemic heart diseases	I20-I25	93.4	105.7
Other forms of heart disease	I30-I51	35.5	49.3
Chronic lower respiratory diseases	J40-J47	38.9	42.1
Organic, including symptomatic, mental disorders	F01-F09	56.4	38.1
Cerebrovascular diseases	I60-I69	37.3	37.0
Other external causes of accidental injury	W00-X59	31.9	26.9
Other degenerative diseases of the nervous system	G30-G31	18.7	25.6
Diabetes mellitus	E10-E14	27.1	21.3
Hypertensive diseases	I10-I15	21.3	19.4

Note: (a) ICD-10 = International Classification of Diseases 10th Revision; (1) Mortality rates are a three year average covering 2011-2013; (2) Figures cover Alachua County
Source: Centers for Disease Control and Prevention, National Center for Health Statistics. Compressed Mortality File 1999-2013 on CDC WONDER Online Database, released October 2014. Data are compiled from the Compressed Mortality File 1999-2013, Series 20 No. 2S, 2014.

Mortality Rates for Selected Causes of Death

ICD-10[a] Sub-Chapter	ICD-10[a] Code	Age-Adjusted Mortality Rate[1] per 100,000 population	
		County[2]	U.S.
Assault	X85-Y09	5.0	5.2
Diseases of the liver	K70-K76	13.2	13.2
Human immunodeficiency virus (HIV) disease	B20-B24	5.9	2.2
Influenza and pneumonia	J09-J18	8.2	15.4
Intentional self-harm	X60-X84	13.7	12.5
Malnutrition	E40-E46	Suppressed	0.9
Obesity and other hyperalimentation	E65-E68	*2.5	1.8
Renal failure	N17-N19	10.0	13.1
Transport accidents	V01-V99	10.9	11.7
Viral hepatitis	B15-B19	3.0	2.2

Note: (a) ICD-10 = International Classification of Diseases 10th Revision; (1) Mortality rates are a three year average covering 2011-2013; (2) Figures cover Alachua County; (*) Unreliable data as per CDC
Source: Centers for Disease Control and Prevention, National Center for Health Statistics. Compressed Mortality File 1999-2013 on CDC WONDER Online Database, released October 2014. Data are compiled from the Compressed Mortality File 1999-2013, Series 20 No. 2S, 2014.

Health Insurance Coverage

Area	With Health Insurance	With Private Health Insurance	With Public Health Insurance	Without Health Insurance	Population Under Age 18 Without Health Insurance
City	82.9	69.3	20.6	17.1	7.1
MSA[1]	84.2	68.1	25.9	15.8	8.4
U.S.	85.2	65.2	31.0	14.8	7.3

Note: Figures are percentages that cover the civilian noninstitutionalized population; (1) Figures cover the Gainesville, FL Metropolitan Statistical Area—see Appendix B for areas included
Source: U.S. Census Bureau, 2011-2013 American Community Survey 3-Year Estimates

Number of Medical Professionals

Area[1]	MDs[2]	DOs[2,3]	Dentists	Podiatrists	Chiropractors	Optometrists
Local (number)	2,159	62	401	12	65	32
Local (rate[4])	857.7	24.6	158.3	4.7	25.7	12.6
U.S. (rate[4])	270.0	20.2	63.1	5.7	25.2	14.9

Note: Data as of 2013 unless noted; (1) Local data covers Alachua County; (2) Data as of 2012 and includes all active, non-federal physicians; (3) Doctor of Osteopathic Medicine; (4) rate per 100,000 population
Source: U.S. Department of Health and Human Services, Health Resources and Services Administration, Bureau of Health Professions, Area Resource File (ARF) 2013-2014

Best Hospitals

According to *U.S. News,* the Gainesville, FL metro area is home to one of the best hospitals in the U.S.: **UF Health Shands Hospital** (3 specialties). The hospital listed was nationally ranked in at least one adult specialty. Only 144 hospitals nationwide were nationally ranked in one or more specialties. Seventeen hospitals in the U.S. made the Honor Roll with high scores in at least six specialties. *U.S. News Online, "America's Best Children's Hospitals 2014-15"*

According to *U.S. News,* the Gainesville, FL metro area is home to one of the best children's hospitals in the U.S.: **UF Health Shands Children's Hospital** (7 specialties). The hospital listed was highly ranked in at least one pediatric specialty. Eighty-nine children's hospitals in the U.S. were nationally ranked in at least one specialty. Ten children's hospitals in the U.S. made the Honor Roll with high scores in at least three specialties. *U.S. News Online, "America's Best Children's Hospitals 2014-15"*

EDUCATION

Public School District Statistics

District Name	Schls	Pupils	Pupil/ Teacher Ratio	Minority Pupils[1] (%)	Free Lunch Eligible[2] (%)	IEP[3] (%)
Alachua County	70	27,826	15.6	54.3	43.5	14.0

Note: Table includes school districts with 2,000 or more students; (1) Percentage of students that are not non-Hispanic white; (2) Percentage of students that are eligible for the free lunch program; (3) Percentage of students that have an Individualized Education Program.
Source: U.S. Department of Education, National Center for Education Statistics, Common Core of Data, Local Education Agency (School District) Universe Survey: School Year 2012-2013; U.S. Department of Education, National Center for Education Statistics, Common Core of Data, Public Elementary/Secondary School Universe Survey: School Year 2012-2013

Highest Level of Education

Area	Less than H.S.	H.S. Diploma	Some College, No Deg.	Associate Degree	Bachelor's Degree	Master's Degree	Prof. School Degree	Doctorate Degree
City	8.3	20.6	18.1	10.4	21.8	11.2	3.7	5.8
MSA[1]	8.8	22.6	20.0	10.6	20.3	9.6	3.7	4.4
U.S.	13.7	28.0	21.2	7.9	18.2	7.7	1.9	1.3

Note: Figures cover persons age 25 and over; (1) Figures cover the Gainesville, FL Metropolitan Statistical Area—see Appendix B for areas included
Source: U.S. Census Bureau, 2011-2013 American Community Survey 3-Year Estimates

Educational Attainment by Race

Area	High School Graduate or Higher (%)					Bachelor's Degree or Higher (%)				
	Total	White	Black	Asian	Hisp.[2]	Total	White	Black	Asian	Hisp.[2]
City	91.7	94.4	85.4	87.8	93.1	42.5	48.6	18.9	69.7	43.3
MSA[1]	91.2	93.2	83.6	89.3	90.7	38.1	41.1	16.1	70.2	42.2
U.S.	86.3	88.3	83.1	85.7	64.0	29.1	30.4	18.8	50.7	13.7

Note: Figures shown cover persons 25 years old and over; (1) Figures cover the Gainesville, FL Metropolitan Statistical Area—see Appendix B for areas included; (2) People of Hispanic origin can be of any race
Source: U.S. Census Bureau, 2011-2013 American Community Survey 3-Year Estimates

School Enrollment by Grade and Control

Area	Preschool (%)		Kindergarten (%)		Grades 1 - 4 (%)		Grades 5 - 8 (%)		Grades 9 - 12 (%)	
	Public	Private	Public	Private	Public	Private	Public	Private	Public	Private
City	56.4	43.6	69.8	30.2	86.0	14.0	87.5	12.5	89.3	10.7
MSA[1]	50.0	50.0	77.7	22.3	86.1	13.9	88.6	11.4	87.7	12.3
U.S.	57.7	42.3	87.9	12.1	89.9	10.1	90.0	10.0	90.7	9.3

Note: Figures shown cover persons 3 years old and over; (1) Figures cover the Gainesville, FL Metropolitan Statistical Area—see Appendix B for areas included
Source: U.S. Census Bureau, 2011-2013 American Community Survey 3-Year Estimates

Average Salaries of Public School Classroom Teachers

Area	2013-14 Dollars	2013-14 Rank[1]	2014-15 Dollars	2014-15 Rank[1]	Percent Change 2013-14 to 2014-15	Percent Change 2004-05 to 2014-15
FLORIDA	47,780	39	48,992	36	2.54	17.8
U.S. Average	56,610	–	57,379	–	1.36	20.8

Note: (1) State rank ranges from 1 to 51 where 1 indicates highest salary.
Source: National Education Association, Rankings & Estimates: Rankings of the States 2014 and Estimates of School Statistics 2015, March 2015

Higher Education

Four-Year Colleges			Two-Year Colleges			Medical Schools[1]	Law Schools[2]	Voc/ Tech[3]
Public	Private Non-profit	Private For-profit	Public	Private Non-profit	Private For-profit			
2	2	1	0	1	0	1	1	3

Note: Figures cover institutions located within the city limits and include main campuses only; (1) includes schools accredited by the Liaison Committee on Medical Education and the American Osteopathic Association's Commission on Osteopathic College Accreditation; (2) includes ABA-accredited schools, schools with provisional ABA accreditation, and state accredited schools; (3) includes all schools with programs that are less than 2 years.
Source: National Center for Education Statistics, Integrated Postsecondary Education System (IPEDS), 2013-14; Association of American Medical Colleges, Member List, May 1, 2015; American Osteopathic Association, Member List, May 1, 2015; Law School Admission Council, Official Guide to ABA-Approved Law Schools Online, May 1, 2015; Wikipedia, List of Medical Schools in the United States, May 1, 2015; Wikipedia, List of Law Schools in the United States, May 1, 2015

According to *U.S. News & World Report,* the Gainesville, FL metro area is home to one of the best national universities in the U.S.: **University of Florida** (#48). The indicators used to capture academic quality fall into a number of categories: assessment by administrators at peer institutions; retention of students; faculty resources; student selectivity; financial resources; alumni giving; high school counselor ratings of colleges; and graduation rate. *U.S. News & World Report, "America's Best Colleges 2015"*

According to *U.S. News & World Report,* the Gainesville, FL metro area is home to one of the top 100 law schools in the U.S.: **University of Florida (Levin)** (#47). The rankings are based on a weighted average of 12 measures of quality: peer assessment score; assessment score by lawyers/judges; median LSAT scores; median undergrad GPA; acceptance rate; employment rates for graduates; placement success; bar passage rate; faculty resources; expenditures per student; student/faculty ratio; and library resources. *U.S. News & World Report, "America's Best Graduate Schools, Law, 2016"*

According to *U.S. News & World Report,* the Gainesville, FL metro area is home to one of the top 75 medical schools for research in the U.S.: **University of Florida** (#43). The rankings are based on a weighted average of 11 measures of quality: quality assessment; peer assessment score; assessment score by residency directors; research activity; total research activity; average research activity per faculty member; student selectivity; median MCAT total score; median undergraduate GPA; acceptance rate; and faculty resources. *U.S. News & World Report, "America's Best Graduate Schools, Medical, 2016"*

According to *U.S. News & World Report,* the Gainesville, FL metro area is home to one of the top 75 business schools in the U.S.: **University of Florida (Hough)** (#37). The rankings are based on a weighted average of the following nine measures: quality assessment; peer assessment; recruiter assessment; placement success; mean starting salary and bonus; student selectivity; mean GMAT and GRE scores; mean undergraduate GPA; and acceptance rate. *U.S. News & World Report, "America's Best Graduate Schools, Business, 2016"*

PRESIDENTIAL ELECTION

2012 Presidential Election Results

Area	Obama (%)	Romney (%)	Other (%)
Alachua County	57.9	40.5	1.6
U.S.	51.0	47.2	1.8

Note: Results may not add to 100% due to rounding
Source: Dave Leip's Atlas of U.S. Presidential Elections

EMPLOYERS

Major Employers

Company Name	Industry
Alachua County	Government
Alachua County School Board	Public education
AvMed Health Plan	Health plans
City of Gainesville	City government
Cox Communications	Communication
Dollar General Distribution Center	Retail
Driltech Mission	Manufacturing
ESE (Now Mactech)	Management services
Florida Farm Bureau	Agricultural association
Gator Dining Services	Food service
Hunter Marine Corporation	Sailboats
Meridian Behavioral Health Care	Mental healthcare
Nationwide Insurance Company	Insurance
North Florida Regional Medical Center	Healthcare
Publix Supermarkets	Grocery
Regeneration Technologies	Orthopedic/cardio implants
Santa Fe Community College	Education
Shands Hospital	Healthcare
Tower Hill Insurance Group	Insurance
U.S. Postal Services	Government
UF Athletic Association	Athletics
University of Florida	Education
Veterans Affairs Medical Center	Healthcare
Wal-Mart Distribution Center	Grocery
Wal-Mart Stores	Grocery

Note: Companies shown are located within the Gainesville, FL Metropolitan Statistical Area.
Source: Hoovers.com; Wikipedia

PUBLIC SAFETY

Crime Rate

Area	All Crimes	Violent Crimes				Property Crimes		
		Murder	Forcible Rape	Robbery	Aggrav. Assault	Burglary	Larceny -Theft	Motor Vehicle Theft
City	4,575.4	4.7	49.0	122.4	460.5	586.1	3,159.8	192.7
Suburbs[1]	2,558.8	2.8	36.8	57.7	361.3	560.0	1,455.5	84.8
Metro[2]	3,502.5	3.7	42.5	88.0	407.7	572.2	2,253.0	135.3
U.S.	3,098.6	4.5	25.2	109.1	229.1	610.0	1,899.4	221.3

Note: Figures are crimes per 100,000 population; (1) All areas within the metro area that are located outside the city limits; (2) Figures cover the Gainesville, FL Metropolitan Statistical Area—see Appendix B for areas included
Source: FBI Uniform Crime Reports, 2013

Hate Crimes

Area	Number of Quarters Reported	Number of Incidents per Bias Motivation						
		Race	Religion	Sexual Orientation	Ethnicity	Disability	Gender	Gender Identity
City	4	2	0	1	0	0	0	0
U.S.	4	2,871	1,031	1,233	655	83	18	31

Source: Federal Bureau of Investigation, Hate Crime Statistics 2013

Identity Theft Consumer Complaints

Area	Complaints	Complaints per 100,000 Population	Rank[2]
MSA[1]	312	115.4	32
U.S.	332,646	104.3	-

Note: (1) Figures cover the Gainesville, FL Metropolitan Statistical Area—see Appendix B for areas included; (2) Rank ranges from 1 to 380 where 1 indicates greatest number of identity theft complaints per 100,000 population
Source: Federal Trade Commission, Consumer Sentinel Network Data Book for January–December 2014

Fraud and Other Consumer Complaints

Area	Complaints	Complaints per 100,000 Population	Rank[2]
MSA[1]	1,345	497.4	24
U.S.	2,250,205	705.7	-

Note: (1) Figures cover the Gainesville, FL Metropolitan Statistical Area—see Appendix B for areas included; (2) Rank ranges from 1 to 380 where 1 indicates greatest number of identity theft complaints per 100,000 population

Source: Federal Trade Commission, Consumer Sentinel Network Data Book for January–December 2014

RECREATION

Culture

Dance[1]	Theatre[1]	Instrumental Music[1]	Vocal Music[1]	Series and Festivals	Museums and Art Galleries[2]	Zoos and Aquariums[3]
1	1	1	0	0	12	1

Note: (1) Professional perfoming groups; (2) Based on organizations with SIC code 8412; (3) AZA-accredited

Source: The Grey House Performing Arts Directory, 2015-16; Association of Zoos & Aquariums, AZA Member Zoos & Aquariums, April 2015; www.AccuLeads.com, April 2015

Professional Sports Teams

Team Name	League	Year Established
No teams are located in the metro area		

Source: Wikipedia, Major Professional Sports Teams of the United States and Canada, April 2015

CLIMATE

Average and Extreme Temperatures

Temperature	Jan	Feb	Mar	Apr	May	Jun	Jul	Aug	Sep	Oct	Nov	Dec	Yr.
Extreme High (°F)	83	85	90	95	98	102	99	99	95	92	88	85	102
Average High (°F)	66	68	74	81	86	89	90	90	87	81	74	68	79
Average Temp. (°F)	55	57	63	69	75	79	81	81	78	71	63	56	69
Average Low (°F)	43	45	50	56	63	69	71	71	69	60	51	44	58
Extreme Low (°F)	10	19	28	35	42	50	62	62	48	33	28	13	10

Note: Figures cover the years 1962-1995

Source: National Climatic Data Center, International Station Meteorological Climate Summary, 9/96

Average Precipitation/Snowfall/Humidity

Precip./Humidity	Jan	Feb	Mar	Apr	May	Jun	Jul	Aug	Sep	Oct	Nov	Dec	Yr.
Avg. Precip. (in.)	3.7	4.0	3.9	2.3	3.3	6.9	6.5	7.7	5.1	2.8	2.2	2.6	50.9
Avg. Snowfall (in.)	0	Tr	0	0	0	0	0	0	0	0	0	Tr	Tr
Avg. Rel. Hum. 7am (%)	90	90	92	92	91	93	94	96	96	94	94	92	93
Avg. Rel. Hum. 4pm (%)	60	55	52	50	51	61	67	67	67	63	63	61	60

Note: Figures cover the years 1962-1995; Tr = Trace amounts (<0.05 in. of rain; <0.5 in. of snow)

Source: National Climatic Data Center, International Station Meteorological Climate Summary, 9/96

Weather Conditions

Temperature			Daytime Sky			Precipitation		
32°F & below	45°F & below	90°F & above	Clear	Partly cloudy	Cloudy	0.01 inch or more precip.	0.1 inch or more snow/ice	Thunder-storms
16	73	77	88	196	81	119	0	78

Note: Figures are average number of days per year and cover the years 1962-1995

Source: National Climatic Data Center, International Station Meteorological Climate Summary, 9/96

HAZARDOUS WASTE

Superfund Sites

Gainesville has one hazardous waste site on the EPA's Superfund Final National Priorities List: **Cabot/Koppers**. There are a total of 1,322 Superfund sites on the list in the U.S. *U.S. Environmental Protection Agency, Final National Priorities List, April 14, 2015*

AIR & WATER QUALITY

Air Quality Trends: Ozone

	2004	2005	2006	2007	2008	2009	2010	2011	2012	2013
MSA[1]	0.075	0.073	0.075	0.078	0.069	0.056	0.069	0.064	0.064	0.062

Note: (1) Data covers the Gainesville, FL Metropolitan Statistical Area—see Appendix B for areas included. The values shown are the composite ozone concentration averages among trend sites based on the highest fourth daily maximum 8-hour concentration in parts per million. These trends are based on sites having an adequate record of monitoring data during the trend period. Data from exceptional events are included.
Source: U.S. Environmental Protection Agency, Air Quality Monitoring Information, "Air Quality Trends by City, 2000-2013"

Air Quality Index

Area	Percent of Days when Air Quality was...[2]					AQI Statistics[2]	
	Good	Moderate	Unhealthy for Sensitive Groups	Unhealthy	Very Unhealthy	Maximum	Median
MSA[1]	93.4	6.6	0.0	0.0	0.0	64	33

Note: (1) Data covers the Gainesville, FL Metropolitan Statistical Area—see Appendix B for areas included; (2) Based on 364 days with AQI data in 2014. Air Quality Index (AQI) is an index for reporting daily air quality. EPA calculates the AQI for five major air pollutants regulated by the Clean Air Act: ground-level ozone, particle pollution (aka particulate matter), carbon monoxide, sulfur dioxide, and nitrogen dioxide. The AQI runs from 0 to 500. The higher the AQI value, the greater the level of air pollution and the greater the health concern. There are six AQI categories: "Good" AQI is between 0 and 50. Air quality is considered satisfactory; "Moderate" AQI is between 51 and 100. Air quality is acceptable; "Unhealthy for Sensitive Groups" When AQI values are between 101 and 150, members of sensitive groups may experience health effects; "Unhealthy" When AQI values are between 151 and 200 everyone may begin to experience health effects; "Very Unhealthy" AQI values between 201 and 300 trigger a health alert; "Hazardous" AQI values over 300 trigger warnings of emergency conditions (not shown).
Source: U.S. Environmental Protection Agency, Air Quality Index Report, 2014

Air Quality Index Pollutants

Area	Percent of Days when AQI Pollutant was...[2]					
	Carbon Monoxide	Nitrogen Dioxide	Ozone	Sulfur Dioxide	Particulate Matter 2.5	Particulate Matter 10
MSA[1]	0.0	0.0	51.4	0.0	48.6	0.0

Note: (1) Data covers the Gainesville, FL Metropolitan Statistical Area—see Appendix B for areas included; (2) Based on 364 days with AQI data in 2014. The Air Quality Index (AQI) is an index for reporting daily air quality. EPA calculates the AQI for five major air pollutants regulated by the Clean Air Act: ground-level ozone, particle pollution (also known as particulate matter), carbon monoxide, sulfur dioxide, and nitrogen dioxide. The AQI runs from 0 to 500. The higher the AQI value, the greater the level of air pollution and the greater the health concern.
Source: U.S. Environmental Protection Agency, Air Quality Index Report, 2014

Maximum Air Pollutant Concentrations: Particulate Matter, Ozone, CO and Lead

	Particulate Matter 10 (ug/m^3)	Particulate Matter 2.5 Wtd AM (ug/m^3)	Particulate Matter 2.5 24-Hr (ug/m^3)	Ozone (ppm)	Carbon Monoxide (ppm)	Lead (ug/m^3)
MSA[1] Level	n/a	6.9	16	0.062	n/a	n/a
NAAQS[2]	150	15	35	0.075	9	0.15
Met NAAQS[2]	n/a	Yes	Yes	Yes	n/a	n/a

Note: (1) Data covers the Gainesville, FL Metropolitan Statistical Area—see Appendix B for areas included; Data from exceptional events are included; (2) National Ambient Air Quality Standards; ppm = parts per million; ug/m^3 = micrograms per cubic meter; n/a not available.
Concentrations: Particulate Matter 10 (coarse particulate)—highest second maximum 24-hour concentration; Particulate Matter 2.5 Wtd AM (fine particulate)—highest weighted annual mean concentration; Particulate Matter 2.5 24-Hour (fine particulate)—highest 98th percentile 24-hour concentration; Ozone—highest fourth daily maximum 8-hour concentration; Carbon Monoxide—highest second maximum non-overlapping 8-hour concentration; Lead—maximum running 3-month average
Source: U.S. Environmental Protection Agency, Air Quality Monitoring Information, "Air Quality Statistics by City, 2013"

Maximum Air Pollutant Concentrations: Nitrogen Dioxide and Sulfur Dioxide

	Nitrogen Dioxide AM (ppb)	Nitrogen Dioxide 1-Hr (ppb)	Sulfur Dioxide AM (ppb)	Sulfur Dioxide 1-Hr (ppb)	Sulfur Dioxide 24-Hr (ppb)
MSA[1] Level	n/a	n/a	n/a	n/a	n/a
NAAQS[2]	53	100	30	75	140
Met NAAQS[2]	n/a	n/a	n/a	n/a	n/a

Note: (1) Data covers the Gainesville, FL Metropolitan Statistical Area—see Appendix B for areas included; Data from exceptional events are included; (2) National Ambient Air Quality Standards; ppm = parts per million; ug/m^3 = micrograms per cubic meter; n/a not available.
Concentrations: Nitrogen Dioxide AM—highest arithmetic mean concentration; Nitrogen Dioxide 1-Hr—highest 98th percentile 1-hour daily maximum concentration; Sulfur Dioxide AM—highest annual mean concentration; Sulfur Dioxide 1-Hr—highest 99th percentile 1-hour daily maximum concentration; Sulfur Dioxide 24-Hr—highest second maximum 24-hour concentration
Source: U.S. Environmental Protection Agency, Air Quality Monitoring Information, "Air Quality Statistics by City, 2013"

Drinking Water

Water System Name	Pop. Served	Primary Water Source Type	Violations[1]	
			Health Based	Monitoring/ Reporting
GRU - Murphree WTP	181,468	Ground	0	0

Note: (1) Based on violation data from January 1, 2014 to December 31, 2014 (includes unresolved violations from earlier years)
Source: U.S. Environmental Protection Agency, Office of Ground Water and Drinking Water, Safe Drinking Water Information System (based on data extracted January 27, 2015)

Houston, Texas

Background

Back in 1836, brothers John K. and Augustus C. Allen bought a 6,642-acre tract of marshy, mosquito-infested land 56 miles north of the Gulf of Mexico and named it Houston, after the hero of San Jacinto. From that moment on, Houston has experienced continued growth.

By the end of its first year in the Republic of Texas, Houston claimed 1,500 residents, one theater, and interestingly, no churches. The first churches came three years later. By the end of its second year, Houston saw its first steamship, establishing its position as one of the top-ranking ports in the country.

Certainly, Houston owes much to the Houston ship channel, the "golden strip" on which oil refineries, chemical plants, cement factories, and grain elevators conduct their bustling economic activity. The diversity of these industries is a testament to Houston's economy in general.

Tonnage through the Port of Houston has grown to the point of its claim of being number one in the nation for foreign tonnage. The port is important to the cruise industry as well, and the Norwegian Cruise Line has sailed from Houston since 2003.

As Texas' biggest city, Houston has also enjoyed manufacturing expansion in its diversified economy. The city is home to the second largest number of Fortune 500 companies, second only to New York City.

Houston is also one of the major scientific research areas in the world. The presence of the Johnson Space Center has spawned a number of related industries in medical and technological research. The Texas Medical Center oversees a network of 45 medical institutions, including St. Luke's Episcopal Hospital, the Texas Children's Hospital, and the Methodist Hospital. As a city whose reputation rests upon advanced research, Houston is also devoted to education and the arts. Rice University, for example, whose admission standards rank as one of the highest in the nation, is located in Houston, as are Dominican College and the University of St. Thomas.

Today, this relatively young city is home to a diverse range of ethnicities, including Mexican-American, Nigerian, American-Indian and Pakistani.

Houston also is patron to the Museum of Fine Arts, the Contemporary Arts Museum, and the Houston Ballet and Grand Opera. A host of smaller cultural institutions, such as the Gilbert and Sullivan Society, the Virtuoso Quartet, and the Houston Harpsichord Society enliven the scene. Two privately funded museums, the Holocaust Museum Houston and the Houston Museum of Natural Science, are historical and educational attractions, and a new baseball stadium, Minute Maid Park, was completed in 2000 in the city's downtown.

Houstonians are eagerly embracing continued revitalization. This urban comeback has resulted in a virtual explosion of dining and entertainment options in the heart of the city. The opening of the Bayou Place, Houston's largest entertainment complex, has especially generated excitement, providing a variety of restaurants and entertainment options in one facility. A new highly active urban park opened in 2007 on 12 acres in front of the George R. Brown Convention Center. Reliant Stadium, located in downtown Houston, is home to the NFL's Houston Texans. The stadium hosted Superbowl XXXVIII in 2004 and WrestleMania XXV in the spring of 2009. In fact, the city has sports teams for every major professional league except the National Hockey League.

Located in the flat coastal plains, Houston's climate is predominantly marine. The terrain includes many small streams and bayous, which, together with the nearness to Galveston Bay, favor the development of fog. Temperatures are moderated by the influence of winds from the Gulf of Mexico, which is 50 miles away. Mild winters are the norm, as is abundant rainfall. Polar air penetrates the area frequently enough to provide variability in the weather.

Rankings

General Rankings

- Houston appeared on *Business Insider's* list of the "15 Hottest American Cities for 2015." Criteria: job and population growth; demographics; affordability; livability; residents' health and welfare; technological innovation; sustainability; culture favoring youth and creativity. *www.businessinsider.com, "The Fifteen Hottest American Cities for 2015," November 19, 2014*

- The Houston metro area was identified as one of America's fastest-growing areas in terms of population and economy by *Forbes*. The area ranked #1 out of 20. The 100 most populous metro areas in the U.S. were evaluated on the following criteria: estimated population growth; job growth; gross metropolitan product growth; unemployment; median salaries for college-educated workers. *Forbes, "America's Fastest-Growing Cities 2015," January 27, 2015*

- Houston was identified as one of America's fastest-growing major metropolitan areas in terms of population growth by CNNMoney.com. The area ranked #2 out of 10. Criteria: population growth between July 2012 and July 2013. *CNNMoney, "10 Fastest-Growing Cities," March 28, 2014*

- Among the 50 largest U.S. cities, Houston placed #16 in Vocativ's "semi-exhaustive, mostly scientific" city Livability Index for people aged 35 and under. Average salary, unemployment rates, rents, and other living costs were considered, along with crime rates, weather, public transportation, access to music and sports, and "lifestyle metrics" such as the price of dinner at Buffalo Wild Wings and an ounce of high-quality weed. *vocative.com, "The Livability Index: The Best U.S. Cities for People 35 and Under," December 9, 2014*

- Houston was selected as one of America's best cities by *Bloomberg Businessweek*. The city ranked #22 out of 50. Criteria: leisure attributes (the number of restaurants, bars, libraries, museums, professional sports teams, and park acres by population); educational attributes (public school performance, the number of colleges, and graduate degree holders); economic factors (2011 income and June and July 2012 unemployment); crime; and air quality. *Bloomberg BusinessWeek, "America's Best Cities," September 26, 2012*

- The human resources consulting firm Mercer ranked 230 cities worldwide in terms of overall quality of life. Houston ranked #64. Criteria: political, social, economic, and socio-cultural factors; medical and health considerations; schools and education; public services and transportation; recreation; consumer goods; housing; and natural environment. *Mercer, "Mercer 2015 Quality of Living Survey," March 4, 2015*

- The U.S. Conference of Mayors and Waste Management sponsor the City Livability Awards Program. The awards recognize and honor mayors for exemplary leadership in developing and implementing specific programs that improve the quality of life in America's cities. Houston was one of 17 second round finalists in the large cities (population 100,000 or more) category. *U.S. Conference of Mayors, "2015 City Livability Awards"*

Business/Finance Rankings

- To help veterans transition to civilian life, USAA and Hiring Our Heroes worked with Sperlings's BestPlaces and the Institute for Veterans and Military Families at Syracuse University to develop a list of the major metropolitan areas where military-skills-related employment is strongest. Criteria for *mid-career* veterans included veteran wage growth; military skills, defense contractor, and government jobs; recent job growth; supervisor/manager jobs; and accessible health resources. Metro areas with a violent crime rate or high cost of living were excluded. At #1, the Houston metro area made the top ten. *www.usaa.com, "2014 Best Places for Veterans"*

- The finance website Wall St. Cheat Sheet reported on the prospects for high-wage job creation in the nation's largest metro areas over the next five years and ranked them accordingly, drawing on in-depth analysis by CareerBuilder and Economic Modeling Specialists International (EMSI). The Houston metro area placed #4 on the Wall St. Cheat Sheet list. *wallstcheatsheet.com, "Top 10 Cities for High-Wage Job Growth," December 8, 2013*

- Building on the U.S. Department of Labor's Occupational Information Network Data Collection Program, the Brookings Institution defined STEM occupations and job opportunities for STEM workers at various levels of educational attainment. The Houston metro area was placed among the ten large metro areas with the highest demand for high-level STEM knowledge. *www.brookings.edu, "The Hidden Stem Economy," June 10, 2013*
- Analysts for the business website 24/7 Wall Street looked at the local government report "Tax Rates and Tax Burdens in the District of Columbia—A Nationwide Comparison" to determine where a family of three at two different income levels would pay the least and the most in state and local taxes. Among the ten cities with the lowest state and local tax burdens was Houston, at #3. *247wallst.com, American Cities with the Highest (and Lowest) Taxes, February 25, 2013*
- The business website 24/7 Wall Street drew on Brookings Institution research on 50 advanced industries to identify the proportion of workers in the nation's largest metropolitan areas that were employed in jobs requiring knowledge in the science, technology, engineering, or math (STEM) fields. The Houston metro area was #9. *247wallst.com, "15 Cities with the Most High-Tech Jobs," March 13, 2015*
- Based on metro area social media reviews, the employment opinion group Glassdoor surveyed 50 of the largest U.S. metro areas on measures including compensation and benefits, satisfaction with management, business outlook, and number of employers hiring. The Houston metro area was ranked #21 in overall employee satisfaction. *www.glassdoor.com, "Employment Satisfaction Report Card by City," June 13, 2014*
- In a survey of economic confidence in the nation's 50 largest metropolitan areas conducted January–December 2014, the Houston metro area placed #10, according to Gallup's 2014 Economic Confidence Index. *Gallup, "San Jose and San Francisco Lead in Economic Confidence," March 19, 2015*
- Using data from the Council for Community and Economic Research's 2013 Annual Report, NerdWallet ranked the 100 U.S. cities with the most expensive cost of living. Cities in California and in the Northeast topped the list. Of the cities with the highest cost of living, Houston ranked #88. *NerdWallet.com, "Most Expensive Cities in America," June 4, 2014*
- The Brookings Institution ranked the 50 largest cities in the U.S. based on income inequality. Houston was ranked #15. (#1 = greatest ineqality). Criteria: the cities were ranked based on the "95/20 ratio," a figure representing the income at which a household earns more than 95 percent of all other households, divided by the income at which a household earns more than only 20 percent of all other households. *Brookings Institution, "Income Inequality in America's 50 Largest Cities, 2007-2013," March 17, 2015*
- CareerBliss, an employment and careers website, analyzed U.S. Bureau of Labor Statistics data, more than 30,000 company reviews from employees and former employees, and job openings over a 12-month period to arrive at its list of the best and worst places in the United States to look for a job. Houston was #8 among the best places. *CareerBliss.com, "CareerBliss 2013 Best and Worst Cities to Find a Job," January 8, 2013*
- Houston was ranked #12 out of 100 metro areas in terms of economic performance (#1 = best) during the recession and recovery from trough quarter through the second quarter of 2013. Criteria: percent change in employment; percentage point change in unemployment rate; percent change in gross metropolitan product; percent change in House Price Index. *Brookings Institution, MetroMonitor: Tracking Economic Recession and Recovery in America's 100 Largest Metropolitan Areas, September 2013*
- Houston was identified as one of the best places for finding a job by *U.S. News & World Report.* The city ranked #9 out of 10. Criteria: strong job market. *U.S. News & World Report, "The 10 Best Cities to Find Jobs," June 17, 2013*
- Payscale.com ranked the 20 largest metro areas in terms of wage growth. The Houston metro area ranked #14. Criteria: private-sector wage growth between the 1st quarter of 2014 and the 1st quarter of 2015. *PayScale, "Wage Trends by Metro Area," 1st Quarter, 2015*
- The Houston metro area was identified as one of the most debt-ridden places in America by the finance site Credit.com. The metro area was ranked #2. Criteria: residents' average personal debt load and average credit scores. *Credit.com, "The Most Debt-Ridden Cities," May 1, 2014*

- Houston was identified as one of America's most frugal metro areas by *Coupons.com.* The city ranked #21 out of 25. Criteria: Grocery IQ and coupons.com mobile app usage. *Coupons.com, "Top 25 Most On-the-Go Frugal Cities of 2013," April 10, 2014*

- Houston was identified as one of America's "10 Best Cities to Find Jobs" by *U.S. News & World Report.* The city ranked #9. Criteria: Bureau of labor Statistics unemployment rates; employment data from Indeed.com and juju.com. *U.S. News & World Report, "10 Best Cities to Find Jobs," June 17, 2013*

- Houston was cited as one of America's top metros for new and expanded facility projects in 2014. The area ranked #2 in the large metro area category (population over 1 million). *Site Selection, "Top Metros of 2014," March 2015*

- Houston was identified as one of the best cities for college graduates to find work—and live. The city ranked #8 out of 15. Criteria: job availability; average salary; average rent. *CareerBuilder.com, "15 Best Cities for College Grads to Find Work—and Live," June 5, 2012*

- *Forbes* reports that Houston was identified as one of the unhappiest cities to work in by CareerBliss.com, an online community for career advancement. The city ranked #8 out of 10. Criteria: work-life balance; an employee's relationship with his or her boss and co-workers; general work environment; compensation; opportunities for advancement; company culture; and resources. *Forbes.com, "The 10 Happiest and Unhappiest Cities to Work in Right Now," January 16, 2015*

- Houston was identified as one of the happiest cities for young professionals by *CareerBliss.com,* an online community for career advancement. The city ranked #8. Criteria: more than 45,000 young professionals were asked to rate key factors that affect workplace happiness including: work-life balance; compensation; company culture; overall work environment; company reputation; relationships with managers and co-workers; opportunities for growth; job resources; daily tasks; job autonomy. Young professionals are defined as having less than 10 years of work experience. *CareerBliss.com, "Happiest Cities for Young Professionals," April 26, 2013*

- The Houston metro area appeared on the Milken Institute "2013 Best Performing Cities" list. Rank: #7 out of 200 large metro areas. Criteria: job growth; wage and salary growth; high-tech output growth. *Milken Institute, "Best-Performing Cities 2014," January 2015*

- *Forbes* ranked the 200 most populous metro areas to determine the nation's "Best Places for Business and Careers." The Houston metro area was ranked #15. Criteria: costs (business and living); job growth (past and projected); income growth; educational attainment (college and high school); projected economic growth; cultural and recreational opportunities; net migration patterns; number of highly ranked colleges. *Forbes, "The Best Places for Business and Careers 2014," July 23, 2014*

- Mercer Human Resources Consulting ranked 211 urban areas worldwide in terms of cost-of-living. Houston ranked #143 (the lower the ranking, the higher the cost-of-living). The survey measured the comparative cost of over 200 items (such as housing, food, clothing, household goods, transportation, and entertainment) in each location.*Mercer, "2014 Cost of Living Survey," July 10, 2014*

Culture/Performing Arts Rankings

- Houston was selected as one of "America's Favorite Cities." The city ranked #3 in the "Culture: Museums " category. Respondents to an online survey were asked to rate 38 top urban destinations in the U.S. from a visitor's perspective. Criteria: number and quality of museums. *Travelandleisure.com, "America's Favorite Cities," October 7, 2014*

- Houston was selected as one of "America's Favorite Cities." The city ranked #2 in the "Culture: Galleries " category. Respondents to an online survey were asked to rate 38 top urban destinations in the U.S. from a visitor's perspective. Criteria: number and quality of galleries. *Travelandleisure.com, "America's Favorite Cities," October 7, 2014*

- Houston was selected as one of "America's Favorite Cities." The city ranked #5 in the "Culture: Art Scene " category. Respondents to an online survey were asked to rate 38 top urban destinations in the U.S. from a visitor's perspective. Criteria: number and quality of art events. *Travelandleisure.com, "America's Favorite Cities," October 7, 2014*

- Houston was selected as one of "America's Favorite Cities." The city ranked #5 in the "Culture: Concerts " category. Respondents to an online survey were asked to rate 38 top urban destinations in the U.S. from a visitor's perspective. Criteria: number and quality of concerts. *Travelandleisure.com, "America's Favorite Cities," October 7, 2014*

- Houston was selected as one of "America's Favorite Cities." The city ranked #3 in the "Culture: Theater " category. Respondents to an online survey were asked to rate 38 top urban destinations in the U.S. from a visitor's perspective. Criteria: number and quality of theater offerings. *Travelandleisure.com, "America's Favorite Cities," October 7, 2014*

- Houston was selected as one of America's top cities for the arts. The city ranked #22 in the big city (population 500,000 and over) category. Criteria: readers' top choices for arts travel destinations based on the richness and variety of visual arts sites, activities and events. *American Style, "2012 Top 25 Arts Destinations," June 2012*

Dating/Romance Rankings

- A *Cosmopolitan* magazine article surveyed the gender balance and other factors to arrive at a list of the best and worst cities for women to meet single guys. Houston was #3 among the best for single women looking for dates. *www.cosmopolitan.com, "Working the Ratio," October 1, 2013*

- *Forbes* reports that the Houston metro area made Rent.com's Best Cities for Newlyweds survey for 2013, based on Bureau of Labor Statistics and Census Bureau data on number of married couples, percentage of families with children under age six, average annual income, cost of living, and availability of rentals. *www.forbes.com, "The 10 Best Cities for Newlyweds to Live and Work In," May 30, 2013*

- Of the 100 U.S. cities surveyed by *Men's Health* in its quest to identify the nation's best cities for dating and forming relationships, Houston was ranked #16 for online dating (#1 = best). *Men's Health, "The Best and Worst Cities for Online Dating," January 30, 2013*

- Houston was selected as one of America's best cities for singles by the readers of *Travel + Leisure* in their annual "America's Favorite Cities" survey. The city was ranked #2 out of 20. Criteria included good-looking locals, cool shopping, and hipster-magnet coffee bars. *Travel + Leisure, "America's Best Cities for Singles," January 23, 2015*

- Houston was selected as one of the best cities for newlyweds by *Rent.com*. The city ranked #1 of 10. Criteria: cost of living; availability of rental inventory; annual mean wages; percentage of married couples; percentage of children under the age of six. *Rent.com, "10 Best Cities for Newlyweds," May 10, 2013*

Education Rankings

- Personal finance website *WalletHub* analyzed the 150 largest U.S. metropolitan statistical areas to determine where the most educated Americans are choosing to settle. Criteria: educational attainment; percentage of workers with jobs in computer, engineering, and science fields; quality and size of each metro area's universities. Houston was ranked #56 (#1 = most educated city). *www.WalletHub.com, "2014's Most and Least Educated Cities*

- Houston was selected as one of America's most literate cities. The city ranked #60 out of the 77 largest U.S. cities. Criteria: number of booksellers; library resources; Internet resources; educational attainment; periodical publishing resources; newspaper circulation. *Central Connecticut State University, "America's Most Literate Cities, 2014," April 8, 2015*

Environmental Rankings

- The Houston metro area came in at #348 for the relative comfort of its climate on Sperling's list of "chill cities," as measured by the Sperling Heat Index. All 361 metro areas are included. Criteria included daytime high temperatures, nighttime low temperatures, dew point, and relative humidity at the high temperatures. *www.bertsperling.com, "Sperling's Chill Cities," July 18, 2013*

- Sperling's BestPlaces assessed 379 metropolitan areas of the United States for the likelihood of dangerously extreme weather events or earthquakes. In general the Southeast and South-Central regions have the highest risk of weather extremes and earthquakes, while the Pacific Northwest enjoys the lowest risk. Of the least risky metropolitan areas, the Houston metro area was ranked #376. *www.bestplaces.net, "Safest Places from Natural Disasters," April 2011*
- Houston was identified as one of America's dirtiest metro areas by *Forbes.* The area ranked #13 out of 20. Criteria: air quality; water quality; toxic releases; superfund sites. *Forbes, "America's 20 Dirtiest Cities," December 10, 2012*
- The U.S. Environmental Protection Agency (EPA) released a list of large U.S. metropolitan areas with the most ENERGY STAR certified buildings in 2014. The Houston metro area was ranked #8 out of 25. *U.S. Environmental Protection Agency, "Top Cities With the Most ENERGY STAR Certified Buildings in 2014," March 25, 2015*
- Houston was highlighted as one of the 25 most ozone-polluted metro areas in the U.S. during 2011 through 2013. The area ranked #6. *American Lung Association, State of the Air 2015*
- Houston was highlighted as one of the 25 metro areas most polluted by year-round particle pollution (Annual PM 2.5) in the U.S. during 2011 through 2013. The area ranked #20. *American Lung Association, State of the Air 2015*
- Houston was highlighted as one of the top 25 cleanest metro areas for short-term particle pollution (24-hour PM 2.5) in the U.S. during 2011 through 2013. Monitors in these cities reported no days with unhealthful PM 2.5 levels. *American Lung Association, State of the Air 2015*

Food/Drink Rankings

- *Men's Health* ranked 100 major U.S. cities in terms of alcohol intoxication. Houston ranked #50 (#1 = most sober).Criteria: binge drinking; alcohol-related traffic accidents, arrests, and fatalities. *Men's Health, "The Drunkest Cities in America," November 19, 2013*
- Houston was identified as one of the most vegetarian-friendly cities in America by GrubHub.com, the nation's largest food ordering service. The city ranked #4 out of 10. Criteria: percentage of vegetarian restaurants. *GrubHub.com, "Top Vegetarian-Friendly Cities," July 18, 2012*
- Houston was selected as one of America's best cities for hamburgers by the readers of *Travel + Leisure* in their annual America's Favorite Cities survey. The city was ranked #4 out of 10. *Travel + Leisure, "America's Best Burger Cities," August 25, 2013*

Health/Fitness Rankings

- For each of the 50 most populous metro areas in the United States, the American College of Sports Medicine's American Fitness Index evaluated infrastructure, community assets, and policies that encourage healthy and fit lifestyles, including preventive health behaviors, levels of chronic disease conditions, health care access, and community resources and policies that support physical activity. The Houston metro area ranked #43 for "community fitness." Personal health indicators were considered as well as community and environmental indicators. *www.americanfitnessindex.org, "ACSM American Fitness Index Health and Community Fitness Status of the 50 Largest Metropolitan Areas," May 2013*
- The Houston metro area was identified as one of the worst cities for bed bugs in America by pest control company Orkin. The area ranked #16 out of 50 based on the number of bed bug treatments Orkin performed from January to December 2013. *Orkin, "Chicago Tops Bed Bug Cities List for Second Year in a Row," January 16, 2014*
- Houston was identified as one of 15 cities with the highest increase in bed bug activity in the U.S. by pest control provider Terminix. The city ranked #15.Criteria: cities with the largest percentage gains in bed bug customer calls from January–May 2013 compared to the same time period in 2012. *Terminix, "Cities with Highest Increases in Bed Bug Activity," July 9, 2013*

- Houston was selected as one of the 25 fattest cities in America by *Men's Fitness Online*. It ranked #1 out of America's 50 largest cities. Criteria: fitness centers and sport stores; nutrition; sports participation; TV viewing; overweight/sedentary; junk food; air quality; geography; commute; parks and open space; city recreational facilities; access to healthcare; motivation; mayor and city initiatives; state obesity initiatives. *Men's Fitness, "The Fittest and Fattest Cities in America," March 5, 2012*

- Houston was identified as a "2013 Spring Allergy Capital." The area ranked #58 out of 100. Three groups of factors were used to identify the most severe cities for people with allergies during the spring season: annual pollen levels; medicine utilization; access to board-certified allergists. *Asthma and Allergy Foundation of America, "Spring Allergy Capitals 2013"*

- Houston was identified as a "2013 Fall Allergy Capital." The area ranked #32 out of 100. Three groups of factors were used to identify the most severe cities for people with allergies during the fall season: annual pollen levels; medicine utilization; access to board-certified allergists. *Asthma and Allergy Foundation of America, "Fall Allergy Capitals 2013"*

- Houston was identified as a "2013 Asthma Capital." The area ranked #74 out of the nation's 100 largest metropolitan areas. Twelve factors were used to identify the most challenging places to live for people with asthma: estimated prevalence; self-reported prevalence; crude death rate for asthma; annual pollen score; annual air quality; public smoking laws; number of board-certified asthma specialists; school inhaler access laws; rescue medication use; controller medication use; uninsured rate; poverty rate. *Asthma and Allergy Foundation of America, "Asthma Capitals 2013"*

- *Men's Health* ranked 100 major U.S. cities in terms of the best and worst cities for men. Houston ranked #55. Criteria: thirty-three data points were examined covering health, fitness, and quality of life. *Men's Health, "The Best & Worst Cities for Men 2014," December 6, 2013*

- Houston was selected as one of the best metropolitan areas for hospital care in America by *HealthGrades.com.* The rankings are based on a comprehensive study of patient death and complication rates in the nation's nearly 5,000 hospitals. Hospitals performing in the top 5% nationwide across 26 different medical procedures and diagnoses were identified. *HealthGrades.com* then ranked cities by the highest percentage of these Distinguished Hospitals for Clinical Excellence™. The Houston metro area ranked #37. *HealthGrades.com, "America's Top 50 Cities for Hospital Care," January 21, 2012*

- The Houston metro area appeared in the 2013 Gallup-Healthways Well-Being Index. The area ranked #60 out of 189. The Gallup-Healthways Well-Being Index score is an average of six sub-indexes, which individually examine life evaluation, emotional health, work environment, physical health, healthy behaviors, and access to basic necessities. Results are based on telephone interviews conducted as part of the Gallup-Healthways Well-Being Index survey January 2–December 29, 2012, and January 2–December 30, 2013, with a random sample of 531,630 adults, aged 18 and older, living in metropolitan areas in the 50 U.S. states and the District of Columbia. *Gallup-Healthways, "State of American Well-Being," March 25, 2014*

- The Houston metro area was identified as one of "America's Most Stressful Cities" by *Sperling's BestPlaces.* The metro area ranked #26 out of 50. Criteria: unemployment rate; suicide rate; commute time; mental health; poor rest; alcohol use; violent crime rate; property crime rate; cloudy days annually. *Sperling's BestPlaces, www.BestPlaces.net, "Stressful Cities 2012*

Real Estate Rankings

- On the list compiled by Penske Truck Rental, the Houston metro area was named the #8 moving destination in 2014, based on one-way consumer truck rental reservations made through Penske's website and reservations call center. *blog.gopenske.com, "Penske Truck Rental's 2014 Top Moving Destinations List," February 4, 2015*

- The Houston metro area appeared on Realtor.com's list of the hottest housing markets to watch in 2015. Criteria: strong housing growth; affordable prices; and fast-paced sales. *Realtor.com®, "Top 10 Hot Housing Markets to Watch in 2015," December 4, 2014*

- The Houston metro area was identified as one of the top 20 housing markets to invest in for 2015 by *Forbes*. The area ranked #3. Criteria: strong population and job growth; relatively low home prices which are below equilibrium home price (EHP). The EHP is what the average price for a market should be, if speculation, weird distortions in local income, and other factors (like the housing collapse) weren't present in the market. *Forbes.com, "Best Buy Cities: Where to Invest in Housing in 2015," January 9, 2015*

- Houston was ranked #13 out of 275 metro areas in terms of house price appreciation in 2014 (#1 = highest rate). *Federal Housing Finance Agency, House Price Index, 4th Quarter 2014*

- Houston was ranked #178 out of 226 metro areas in terms of housing affordability in 2014 by the National Association of Home Builders (#1 = most affordable). The NAHB-Wells Fargo Housing Opportunity Index (HOI) for a given area is defined as the share of homes sold in that area that would have been affordable to a family earning the local median income, based on standard mortgage underwriting criteria. *National Association of Home Builders®, NAHB-Wells Fargo Housing Opportunity Index, 4th Quarter 2014*

Safety Rankings

- Symantec, in partnership with Sperling's BestPlaces, ranked the 50 largest cities in the U.S. in terms of their vulnerability to cybercrime. The city ranked #24. Criteria: number of cyberattacks and potential infections; level of Internet access; expenditures on smartphones and computer hardware/software; wireless hotspots; broadband connectivity; Internet usage; online purchases. *Symantec, "Riskiest Online Cities of 2012" February 15, 2012*

- Allstate ranked the 200 largest cities in America in terms of driver safety. Houston ranked #158. Allstate researchers analyzed internal property damage claims over a two-year period from January 2011 to December 2012. A weighted average of the two-year numbers determined the annual percentages. *Allstate, "Allstate America's Best Drivers Report, 2014"*

- Houston was identified as one of the most dangerous large cities in America by CQ Press. All 32 cities with populations of 500,000 or more that reported crime rates in 2012 for murder, rape, robbery, aggravated assault, burglary, and motor vehicle thefts were ranked. The city ranked #9 out of the top 10. *CQ Press, City Crime Rankings 2014*

- The National Insurance Crime Bureau ranked 380 metro areas in the U.S. in terms of per capita rates of vehicle theft. The Houston metro area ranked #35 (#1 = highest rate). Criteria: number of vehicle theft offenses per 100,000 inhabitants in 2012. *National Insurance Crime Bureau, "Hot Spots 2012," June 26, 2013*

Seniors/Retirement Rankings

- From its Best Cities for Successful Aging indexes, the Milken Institute generated rankings for metropolitan areas, weighing data in eight categories—health care, wellness, living arrangements, transportation, financial characteristics, education and employment opportunities, community engagement, and overall livability. The Houston metro area was ranked #42 overall in the large metro area category. *Milken Institute, "Best Cities for Successful Aging, 2014"*

Sports/Recreation Rankings

- Houston was selected as one of "America's Most Miserable Sports Cities" by *Forbes*. The city was ranked #8. Criteria: postseason losses; years since last title; ratio of cumulative seasons to championships won. Contenders were limited to cities with at least 75 total seasons of NFL, NBA, NHL and MLB play. *Forbes, "America's Most Miserable Sports Cities," July 31, 2013*

- Houston was chosen as a bicycle friendly community by the League of American Bicyclists. A "Bicycle Friendly Community" welcomes cyclists by providing safe accommodation for cycling and encouraging people to bike for transportation and recreation. There are four award levels: Platinum; Gold; Silver; and Bronze. The community achieved an award level of Bronze. *League of American Bicyclists, "Bicycle Friendly Community Master List," Fall 2013*

Transportation Rankings

- NerdWallet surveyed average annual car insurance premiums in 125 U.S. cities to identify the least expensive U.S. cities in which to insure a car. Locations with no-fault insurance laws was a strong determinant. Houston came in at #28 for the most expensive rates. *www.nerdwallet.com, "Best Cities for Cheap Car Insurance," February 3, 2014*
- Houston appeared on *Trapster.com's* list of the 10 most-active U.S. cities for speed traps. The city ranked #3 of 10. *Trapster.com* is a community platform accessed online and via smartphone app that alerts drivers to traps, hazards and other traffic issues nearby. *Trapster.com, "Speeders Beware: Cities With the Most Speed Traps," February 10, 2012*
- Houston was identified as one of the most congested metro areas in the U.S. The area ranked #6 out of 10. Criteria: yearly delay per auto commuter in hours. *Texas A&M Transportation Institute, "2012 Urban Mobility Report," December 2012*

Women/Minorities Rankings

- *Women's Health* examined U.S. cities and identified the 100 best cities for women. Houston was ranked #46. Criteria: 30 categories were examined from obesity and breast cancer rates to commuting times and hours spent working out. *Women's Health, "Best Cities for Women 2012"*

Miscellaneous Rankings

- *Travel + Leisure* invited readers to rate cities on indicators such as aloofness, "smarty-pants residents," highbrow cultural offerings, high-end shopping, artisanal coffeehouses, conspicuous eco-consciousness, and more in order to identify the nation's snobbiest cities. Cities large and small made the list; among them was Houston, at #17. *www.travelandleisure.com, "America's Snobbiest Cities, June 2013*
- The watchdog site Charity Navigator conducts an annual study of charities in the nation's major markets both to analyze statistical differences in their financial, accountability, and transparency practices and to track year-to-year variations in individual communities. The Houston metro area was ranked #2 among the 30 metro markets. *www.charitynavigator.org, "Metro Market Study 2013," June 1, 2013*
- The Harris Poll's Happiness Index survey revealed that of the top ten U.S. markets, the Houston metro area residents ranked #2 in happiness. Criteria included strong assent to positive statements and strong disagreement with negative ones, and degree of agreement with a series of statements about respondents' personal relationships and general outlook. The online survey was conducted between July 14 and July 30, 2013. *www.harrisinteractive.com, "Dallas/Fort Worth Is "Happiest" City among America's Top Ten Markets," September 4, 2013*
- Energizer Personal Care, the makers of Edge® shave gel, in partnership with Sperling's BestPlaces, ranked 50 major metro areas in terms of everyday irritations. The Houston metro area ranked #8. Criteria: high male-to-female ratio; poor sports team performance and high ticket prices; slow traffic; lack of job availability; unaffordable housing; extreme weather; lack of nightlife and fitness options. *Energizer Personal Care, "Most Irritatng Cities for Guys," August 26, 2013*
- Mars Chocolate North America, the makers of COMBOS®, in partnership with Sperling's BestPlaces, ranked 50 major metro areas in terms of their "manliness." The Houston metro area ranked #6. Criteria: number of professional sports teams; number of nearby NASCAR tracks and racing events; manly lifestyle; concentration of manly retail stores; manly occupations per capita; salty snack sales; "Board of Manliness" rankings. *Mars Chocolate North America, "America's Manliest Cities 2012"*
- The National Alliance to End Homelessness ranked the 100 most populous metro areas in terms the rate of homelessness. The Houston metro area ranked #50. Criteria: number of homeless people per 10,000 population in 2011. *National Alliance to End Homelessness, The State of Homelessness in America 2012*

- The financial education website CreditDonkey compiled a list of the ten "best" cities of the future, based on percentage of housing built in 1990 or later, population change since 2010, and construction jobs as a percentage of population. Also considered were two more futuristic criteria: number of DeLorean cars available for purchase and number of spaceport companies and proposed spaceports. Houston was scored #9. *www.creditDonkey.com, "In the Future, Almost All of America's 'Best' Cities Will Be on the West Coast, Report Says," February 14, 2014*

Business Environment

CITY FINANCES

City Government Finances

Component	2012 ($000)	2012 ($ per capita)
Total Revenues	4,402,538	2,097
Total Expenditures	4,540,802	2,163
Debt Outstanding	13,983,714	6,661
Cash and Securities[1]	11,992,583	5,712

Note: (1) Cash and security holdings of a government at the close of its fiscal year, including those of its dependent agencies, utilities, and liquor stores.
Source: U.S Census Bureau, State & Local Government Finances 2012

City Government Revenue by Source

Source	2012 ($000)	2012 ($ per capita)
General Revenue		
From Federal Government	174,911	83
From State Government	87,791	42
From Local Governments	52,326	25
Taxes		
Property	1,025,312	488
Sales and Gross Receipts	809,401	386
Personal Income	0	0
Corporate Income	0	0
Motor Vehicle License	0	0
Other Taxes	86,639	41
Current Charges	1,034,471	493
Liquor Store	0	0
Utility	476,367	227
Employee Retirement	258,282	123

Source: U.S Census Bureau, State & Local Government Finances 2012

City Government Expenditures by Function

Function	2012 ($000)	2012 ($ per capita)	2012 (%)
General Direct Expenditures			
Air Transportation	397,251	189	8.7
Corrections	22,311	11	0.5
Education	0	0	0.0
Employment Security Administration	0	0	0.0
Financial Administration	70,132	33	1.5
Fire Protection	351,688	168	7.7
General Public Buildings	197,769	94	4.4
Governmental Administration, Other	221,154	105	4.9
Health	111,896	53	2.5
Highways	368,075	175	8.1
Hospitals	0	0	0.0
Housing and Community Development	93,355	44	2.1
Interest on General Debt	492,490	235	10.8
Judicial and Legal	40,230	19	0.9
Libraries	47,776	23	1.1
Parking	6,610	3	0.1
Parks and Recreation	98,096	47	2.2
Police Protection	594,622	283	13.1
Public Welfare	0	0	0.0
Sewerage	189,796	90	4.2
Solid Waste Management	50,296	24	1.1
Veterans' Services	0	0	0.0
Liquor Store	0	0	0.0
Utility	308,526	147	6.8
Employee Retirement	534,365	255	11.8

Source: U.S Census Bureau, State & Local Government Finances 2012

DEMOGRAPHICS

Population Growth

Area	1990 Census	2000 Census	2010 Census	Population Growth (%)	
				1990-2000	2000-2010
City	1,697,610	1,953,631	2,099,451	15.1	7.5
MSA[1]	3,767,335	4,715,407	5,946,800	25.2	26.1
U.S.	248,709,873	281,421,906	308,745,538	13.2	9.7

Note: (1) Figures cover the Houston-Sugar Land-Baytown, TX Metropolitan Statistical Area—see Appendix B for areas included
Source: U.S. Census Bureau, Census 1990, 2000, 2010

Household Size

Area	Persons in Household (%)							Average Household Size
	One	Two	Three	Four	Five	Six	Seven or More	
City	32.2	29.3	15.0	11.8	7.0	2.7	2.1	2.70
MSA[1]	24.4	29.9	16.9	15.3	8.1	3.2	2.1	2.91
U.S.	27.7	33.6	15.7	13.1	6.0	2.3	1.5	2.64

Note: (1) Figures cover the Houston-The Woodlands-Sugar Land, TX Metropolitan Statistical Area—see Appendix B for areas included
Source: U.S. Census Bureau, 2011-2013 American Community Survey 3-Year Estimates

Race

Area	White Alone[2] (%)	Black Alone[2] (%)	Asian Alone[2] (%)	AIAN[3] Alone[2] (%)	NHOPI[4] Alone[2] (%)	Other Race Alone[2] (%)	Two or More Races (%)
City	58.2	23.1	6.2	0.4	0.0	10.1	2.0
MSA[1]	65.7	17.2	6.9	0.4	0.1	7.6	2.2
U.S.	73.9	12.6	5.0	0.8	0.2	4.7	2.9

Note: (1) Figures cover the Houston-The Woodlands-Sugar Land, TX Metropolitan Statistical Area—see Appendix B for areas included; (2) Alone is defined as not being in combination with one or more other races; (3) American Indian and Alaska Native; (4) Native Hawaiian and Other Pacific Islander
Source: U.S. Census Bureau, 2011-2013 American Community Survey 3-Year Estimates

Hispanic or Latino Origin

Area	Total (%)	Mexican (%)	Puerto Rican (%)	Cuban (%)	Other (%)
City	43.8	33.0	0.5	0.3	9.9
MSA[1]	35.9	27.7	0.5	0.3	7.3
U.S.	16.9	10.8	1.6	0.6	3.8

Note: Persons of Hispanic or Latino origin can be of any race; (1) Figures cover the Houston-The Woodlands-Sugar Land, TX Metropolitan Statistical Area—see Appendix B for areas included
Source: U.S. Census Bureau, 2011-2013 American Community Survey 3-Year Estimates

Segregation

Type	Segregation Indices[1]				Percent Change		
	1990	2000	2010	2010 Rank[2]	1990-2000	1990-2010	2000-2010
Black/White	65.5	65.7	61.4	36	0.1	-4.1	-4.2
Asian/White	48.0	51.4	50.4	7	3.4	2.4	-1.0
Hispanic/White	47.8	53.4	52.5	18	5.6	4.7	-0.9

Note: All figures cover the Metropolitan Statistical Area—see Appendix B for areas included; Figures are based on an analysis of 1990, 2000, and 2010 Census Decennial Census tract data by William H. Frey, Brookings Institution and the University of Michigan Social Science Data Analysis Network. In this analysis all racial groups (whites, blacks, and asians) are non-Hispanic members of those races. Hispanics are shown as a separate category;
(1) Segregation Indices are Dissimilarity Indices that measure the degree to which the minority group is distributed differently than whites across census tracts. They range from 0 (complete integration) to 100 (complete segregation) where the value indicates the percentage of the minority group that needs to move to be distributed exactly like whites; (2) Ranges from 1 (most segregated) to 102 (least segregated); n/a not available.
Source: www.CensusScope.org

Ancestry

Area	German	Irish	English	American	Italian	Polish	French[2]	Scottish	Dutch
City	5.3	3.7	3.9	3.8	1.6	0.9	1.7	0.9	0.5
MSA[1]	8.7	6.0	5.4	4.9	2.1	1.3	2.3	1.2	0.7
U.S.	14.9	10.8	8.0	7.4	5.5	3.0	2.7	1.7	1.4

Note: Figures are the percentage of the total population reporting a particular ancestry. The nine most commonly reported ancestries in the U.S. are shown. Figures include multiple ancestries (e.g. if a person reported being Irish and Italian, they were included in both columns); (1) Figures cover the Houston-The Woodlands-Sugar Land, TX Metropolitan Statistical Area—see Appendix B for areas included; (2) Excludes Basque
Source: U.S. Census Bureau, 2011-2013 American Community Survey 3-Year Estimates

Foreign-Born Population

Area	Percent of Population Born in								
	Any Foreign Country	Mexico	Asia	Europe	Carribean	South America	Central America[2]	Africa	Canada
City	28.0	13.1	5.5	1.1	0.6	1.0	5.3	1.2	0.2
MSA[1]	22.3	9.8	5.3	1.0	0.5	1.0	3.3	1.0	0.3
U.S.	13.0	3.7	3.8	1.5	1.2	0.9	1.0	0.6	0.3

Note: (1) Figures cover the Houston-The Woodlands-Sugar Land, TX Metropolitan Statistical Area—see Appendix B for areas included; (2) Excludes Mexico.
Source: U.S. Census Bureau, 2011-2013 American Community Survey 3-Year Estimates

Marital Status

Area	Never Married	Now Married[2]	Separated	Widowed	Divorced
City	39.5	41.5	3.5	4.8	10.6
MSA[1]	32.9	49.6	2.8	4.5	10.1
U.S.	32.7	48.1	2.2	6.0	11.0

Note: Figures are percentages and cover the population 15 years of age and older; (1) Figures cover the Houston-The Woodlands-Sugar Land, TX Metropolitan Statistical Area—see Appendix B for areas included; (2) Excludes separated
Source: U.S. Census Bureau, 2011-2013 American Community Survey 3-Year Estimates

Disability Status

Area	All Ages	Under 18 Years Old	18 to 64 Years Old	65 Years and Over
City	10.1	3.7	8.5	38.3
MSA[1]	9.6	3.5	8.4	37.0
U.S.	12.3	4.1	10.2	36.3

Note: Figures show percent of the civilian noninstitutionalized population that reported having a disability. Disability status is determined from from six types of difficulty: vision, hearing, cognitive, ambulatory, self-care, and independent living. For children under 5 years old, hearing and vision difficulty are used to determine disability status. For children between the ages of 5 and 14, disability status is determined from hearing, vision, cognitive, ambulatory, and self-care difficulties. For people aged 15 years and older, they are considered to have a disability if they have difficulty with any one of the six difficulty types; (1) Figures cover the Houston-The Woodlands-Sugar Land, TX Metropolitan Statistical Area—see Appendix B for areas included.
Source: U.S. Census Bureau, 2011-2013 American Community Survey 3-Year Estimates

Age

Area	Percent of Population									Median Age
	Under Age 5	Age 5–19	Age 20–34	Age 35–44	Age 45–54	Age 55–64	Age 65–74	Age 75–84	Age 85+	
City	7.8	20.1	25.8	14.0	12.6	10.2	5.5	2.9	1.2	32.6
MSA[1]	7.7	22.4	22.0	14.3	13.6	10.8	5.6	2.6	1.0	33.5
U.S.	6.4	19.9	20.7	12.9	14.1	12.3	7.6	4.2	1.9	37.4

Note: (1) Figures cover the Houston-The Woodlands-Sugar Land, TX Metropolitan Statistical Area—see Appendix B for areas included
Source: U.S. Census Bureau, 2011-2013 American Community Survey 3-Year Estimates

Gender

Area	Males	Females	Males per 100 Females
City	1,083,898	1,078,370	100.5
MSA[1]	3,076,211	3,104,755	99.1
U.S.	154,451,010	159,410,713	96.9

Note: (1) Figures cover the Houston-The Woodlands-Sugar Land, TX Metropolitan Statistical Area—see Appendix B for areas included
Source: U.S. Census Bureau, 2011-2013 American Community Survey 3-Year Estimates

Religious Groups by Family

Area	Catholic	Baptist	Non-Den.	Methodist[2]	Lutheran	LDS[3]	Pente-costal	Presby-terian[4]	Muslim[5]	Judaism
MSA[1]	17.1	16.0	7.3	4.9	1.1	1.1	1.5	0.9	2.7	0.4
U.S.	19.1	9.3	4.0	4.0	2.3	2.0	1.9	1.6	0.8	0.7

Note: Figures are the number of adherents as a percentage of the total population; (1) Figures cover the Houston-Sugar Land-Baytown, TX Metropolitan Statistical Area—see Appendix B for areas included; (2) Methodist/Pietist; (3) Latter Day Saints; (4) Reformed; (5) Figures are estimates
Source: Association of Statisticians of American Religious Bodies, 2010 U.S. Religion Census: Religious Congregations & Membership Study

Religious Groups by Tradition

Area	Catholic	Evangelical Protestant	Mainline Protestant	Other Tradition	Black Protestant	Orthodox
MSA[1]	17.1	24.9	6.7	4.9	1.3	0.2
U.S.	19.1	16.2	7.3	4.3	1.6	0.3

Note: Figures are the number of adherents as a percentage of the total population; (1) Figures cover the Houston-Sugar Land-Baytown, TX Metropolitan Statistical Area—see Appendix B for areas included
Source: Association of Statisticians of American Religious Bodies, 2010 U.S. Religion Census: Religious Congregations & Membership Study

ECONOMY

Gross Metropolitan Product

Area	2012	2013	2014	2015	Rank[2]
MSA[1]	449.7	467.5	496.1	523.2	4

Note: Figures are in billions of dollars; (1) Figures cover the Houston-The Woodlands-Sugar Land, TX Metropolitan Statistical Area—see Appendix B for areas included; (2) Rank is based on 2015 data and ranges from 1 to 363
Source: The U.S. Conference of Mayors, U.S. Metro Economies: GMP and Employment 2013-2015, June 2014

Economic Growth

Area	2010-12 (%)	2013 (%)	2014 (%)	2015 (%)	Rank[2]
MSA[1]	4.8	2.8	3.5	4.8	6
U.S.	2.1	2.0	2.3	3.2	–

Note: Figures are real gross metropolitan product (GMP) growth rates and represent annual average percent change; (1) Figures cover the Houston-The Woodlands-Sugar Land, TX Metropolitan Statistical Area—see Appendix B for areas included; (2) Rank is based on 2015 data and ranges from 1 to 363
Source: The U.S. Conference of Mayors, U.S. Metro Economies: GMP and Employment 2013-2015, June 2014

Metropolitan Area Exports

Area	2008	2009	2010	2011	2012	2013	Rank[2]
MSA[1]	80,015.1	65,820.9	80,569.7	104,457.0	110,298.0	114,963.0	1

Note: Figures are in millions of dollars; (1) Figures cover the Houston-The Woodlands-Sugar Land, TX Metropolitan Statistical Area—see Appendix B for areas included; (2) Rank is based on 2013 data and ranges from 1 to 387
Source: U.S. Department of Commerce, International Trade Administration, Office of Trade & Industry Information, Manufacturing & Services, data extracted April 3, 2015

Building Permits

Area	Single-Family			Multi-Family			Total		
	2013	2014	Pct. Chg.	2013	2014	Pct. Chg.	2013	2014	Pct. Chg.
City	5,198	5,398	3.8	8,845	14,906	68.5	14,043	20,304	44.6
MSA[1]	34,542	38,315	10.9	16,791	25,426	51.4	51,333	63,741	24.2
U.S.	620,802	634,597	2.2	370,020	411,766	11.3	990,822	1,046,363	5.6

Note: (1) Figures cover the Houston-The Woodlands-Sugar Land, TX Metropolitan Statistical Area—see Appendix B for areas included; Figures represent new, privately-owned housing units authorized (unadjusted data); All permit data are based on estimates with imputation.
Source: U.S. Census Bureau, Manufacturing, Mining, and Construction Statistics, Building Permits, 2013, 2014

Bankruptcy Filings

Area	Business Filings			Nonbusiness Filings		
	2013	2014	% Chg.	2013	2014	% Chg.
Harris County	388	300	-22.7	5,462	4,832	-11.5
U.S.	33,212	26,983	-18.8	1,038,720	909,812	-12.4

Note: Business filings include Chapter 7, Chapter 11, Chapter 12, and Chapter 13; Nonbusiness filings include Chapter 7, Chapter 11, and Chapter 13
Source: Administrative Office of the U.S. Courts, Business and Nonbusiness Bankruptcy, County Cases Commenced by Chapter of the Bankruptcy Code, During the 12- Month Period Ending December 31, 2013 and Business and Nonbusiness Bankruptcy, County Cases Commenced by Chapter of the Bankruptcy Code, During the 12- Month Period Ending December 31, 2014

Housing Vacancy Rates

Area	Gross Vacancy Rate[2] (%)			Year-Round Vacancy Rate[3] (%)			Rental Vacancy Rate[4] (%)			Homeowner Vacancy Rate[5] (%)		
	2012	2013	2014	2012	2013	2014	2012	2013	2014	2012	2013	2014
MSA[1]	9.8	9.6	8.9	9.4	9.0	8.4	11.4	10.0	8.6	1.9	2.3	1.3
U.S.	13.8	13.6	13.4	10.8	10.7	10.4	8.7	8.3	7.6	2.0	2.0	1.9

Note: (1) Figures cover the Houston-The Woodlands-Sugar Land, TX Metropolitan Statistical Area—see Appendix B for areas included; (2) The percentage of the total housing inventory that is vacant; (3) The percentage of the housing inventory (excluding seasonal units) that is year-round vacant; (4) The percentage of rental inventory that is vacant for rent; (5) The percentage of homeowner inventory that is vacant for sale
Source: U.S. Census Bureau, Housing Vacancies and Homeownership Annual Statistics: 2014

INCOME

Income

Area	Per Capita ($)	Median Household ($)	Average Household ($)
City	27,328	44,451	71,474
MSA[1]	28,849	56,889	81,822
U.S.	27,884	52,176	72,897

Note: (1) Figures cover the Houston-The Woodlands-Sugar Land, TX Metropolitan Statistical Area—see Appendix B for areas included
Source: U.S. Census Bureau, 2011-2013 American Community Survey 3-Year Estimates

Household Income Distribution

Area	Percent of Households Earning							
	Under $15,000	$15,000 -24,999	$25,000 -34,999	$35,000 -49,999	$50,000 -74,999	$75,000 -99,000	$100,000 -149,999	$150,000 and up
City	15.7	13.1	11.6	14.3	15.9	9.5	9.7	10.2
MSA[1]	11.3	10.2	9.8	13.0	17.2	11.8	13.8	12.9
U.S.	13.0	10.9	10.3	13.6	17.9	11.9	12.7	9.6

Note: (1) Figures cover the Houston-The Woodlands-Sugar Land, TX Metropolitan Statistical Area—see Appendix B for areas included
Source: U.S. Census Bureau, 2011-2013 American Community Survey 3-Year Estimates

Poverty Rate

Area	All Ages	Under 18 Years Old	18 to 64 Years Old	65 Years and Over
City	23.3	36.3	19.5	14.4
MSA[1]	16.8	24.7	14.3	10.5
U.S.	15.9	22.4	14.8	9.5

Note: Figures are percentage of people whose income during the past 12 months was below the poverty level; (1) Figures cover the Houston-The Woodlands-Sugar Land, TX Metropolitan Statistical Area—see Appendix B for areas included
Source: U.S. Census Bureau, 2011-2013 American Community Survey 3-Year Estimates

EMPLOYMENT

Labor Force and Employment

Area	Civilian Labor Force			Workers Employed		
	Dec. 2013	Dec. 2014	% Chg.	Dec. 2013	Dec. 2014	% Chg.
City	1,132,953	1,158,089	2.2	1,077,239	1,113,785	3.4
MSA[1]	3,210,505	3,280,203	2.2	3,045,705	3,148,828	3.4
U.S.	154,408,000	155,521,000	0.7	144,423,000	147,190,000	1.9

Note: Data is not seasonally adjusted and covers workers 16 years of age and older; (1) Figures cover the Houston-The Woodlands-Sugar Land, TX Metropolitan Statistical Area—see Appendix B for areas included
Source: Bureau of Labor Statistics, Local Area Unemployment Statistics

Unemployment Rate

Area	2014											
	Jan.	Feb.	Mar.	Apr.	May	Jun.	Jul.	Aug.	Sep.	Oct.	Nov.	Dec.
City	5.3	5.2	5.0	4.4	4.8	5.1	5.2	5.0	4.6	4.3	4.2	3.8
MSA[1]	5.5	5.4	5.2	4.6	4.9	5.3	5.4	5.1	4.7	4.4	4.3	4.0
U.S.	7.0	7.0	6.8	5.9	6.1	6.3	6.5	6.3	5.7	5.5	5.5	5.4

Note: Data is not seasonally adjusted and covers workers 16 years of age and older; (1) Figures cover the Houston-The Woodlands-Sugar Land, TX Metropolitan Statistical Area—see Appendix B for areas included
Source: Bureau of Labor Statistics, Local Area Unemployment Statistics

Employment by Occupation

Occupation Classification	City (%)	MSA[1] (%)	U.S. (%)
Management, Business, Science, and Arts	33.8	36.3	36.2
Natural Resources, Construction, and Maintenance	11.9	11.0	9.0
Production, Transportation, and Material Moving	12.6	12.4	12.1
Sales and Office	22.0	23.7	24.4
Service	19.7	16.7	18.3

Note: Figures cover employed civilians 16 years of age and older; (1) Figures cover the Houston-The Woodlands-Sugar Land, TX Metropolitan Statistical Area—see Appendix B for areas included
Source: U.S. Census Bureau, 2011-2013 American Community Survey 3-Year Estimates

Employment by Industry

Sector	MSA[1] Number of Employees	MSA[1] Percent of Total	U.S. Percent of Total
Construction	208,800	7.0	4.4
Education and Health Services	359,200	12.0	15.5
Financial Activities	149,300	5.0	5.7
Government	383,700	12.8	15.8
Information	32,600	1.1	2.0
Leisure and Hospitality	290,000	9.7	10.3
Manufacturing	258,700	8.6	8.7
Mining and Logging	115,500	3.9	0.6
Other Services	104,300	3.5	4.0
Professional and Business Services	470,400	15.7	13.8
Retail Trade	308,700	10.3	11.4
Transportation, Warehousing, and Utilities	139,000	4.6	3.9
Wholesale Trade	172,400	5.8	4.2

Note: Figures are non-farm employment as of December 2014. Figures are not seasonally adjusted and include workers 16 years of age and older; (1) Figures cover the Houston-The Woodlands-Sugar Land, TX Metropolitan Statistical Area—see Appendix B for areas included
Source: Bureau of Labor Statistics, Current Employment Statistics, Employment, Hours, and Earnings

Occupations with Greatest Projected Employment Growth: 2012 – 2022

Occupation[1]	2012 Employment	2022 Projected Employment	Numeric Employment Change	Percent Employment Change
Combined Food Preparation and Serving Workers, Including Fast Food	285,480	378,000	92,520	32.4
Personal Care Aides	199,230	283,980	84,750	42.5
Retail Salespersons	378,330	439,340	61,010	16.1
Registered Nurses	189,380	242,860	53,480	28.2
Customer Service Representatives	214,240	262,770	48,530	22.7
Waiters and Waitresses	196,390	240,390	44,000	22.4
Janitors and Cleaners, Except Maids and Housekeeping Cleaners	172,120	213,340	41,220	23.9
Laborers and Freight, Stock, and Material Movers, Hand	185,770	226,470	40,700	21.9
Elementary School Teachers, Except Special Education	141,030	180,920	39,890	28.3
Secretaries and Administrative Assistants, Except Legal, Medical, and Executive	190,470	230,220	39,750	20.9

Note: Projections cover Texas; (1) Sorted by numeric employment change
Source: www.projectionscentral.com, State Occupational Projections, 2012–2022 Long-Term Projections

Fastest Growing Occupations: 2012 – 2022

Occupation[1]	2012 Employment	2022 Projected Employment	Numeric Employment Change	Percent Employment Change
Diagnostic Medical Sonographers	4,380	6,900	2,520	57.6
Computer Numerically Controlled Machine Tool Programmers, Metal and Plastic	1,740	2,700	960	54.8
Interpreters and Translators	4,510	6,720	2,210	49.0
Skincare Specialists	5,130	7,620	2,490	48.3
Agents and Business Managers of Artists, Performers, and Athletes	310	450	140	47.4
Petroleum Engineers	19,280	28,010	8,730	45.3
Information Security Analysts	6,640	9,630	2,990	45.0
Insulation Workers, Mechanical	4,460	6,460	2,000	44.6
Cardiovascular Technologists and Technicians	3,950	5,700	1,750	44.3
Physician Assistants	5,470	7,880	2,410	44.2

Note: Projections cover Texas; (1) Sorted by percent employment change and excludes occupations with numeric employment change less than 100
Source: www.projectionscentral.com, State Occupational Projections, 2012–2022 Long-Term Projections

Average Wages

Occupation	$/Hr.	Occupation	$/Hr.
Accountants and Auditors	39.99	Maids and Housekeeping Cleaners	9.07
Automotive Mechanics	19.38	Maintenance and Repair Workers	18.00
Bookkeepers	19.12	Marketing Managers	73.12
Carpenters	16.69	Nuclear Medicine Technologists	34.42
Cashiers	9.70	Nurses, Licensed Practical	23.39
Clerks, General Office	16.52	Nurses, Registered	36.30
Clerks, Receptionists/Information	12.97	Nursing Assistants	12.21
Clerks, Shipping/Receiving	14.63	Packers and Packagers, Hand	10.79
Computer Programmers	37.77	Physical Therapists	43.09
Computer Systems Analysts	49.51	Postal Service Mail Carriers	24.92
Computer User Support Specialists	27.66	Real Estate Brokers	56.32
Cooks, Restaurant	10.61	Retail Salespersons	12.65
Dentists	83.10	Sales Reps., Exc. Tech./Scientific	37.04
Electrical Engineers	52.03	Sales Reps., Tech./Scientific	45.99
Electricians	23.54	Secretaries, Exc. Legal/Med./Exec.	16.42
Financial Managers	71.19	Security Guards	12.12
First-Line Supervisors/Managers, Sales	22.25	Surgeons	106.03
Food Preparation Workers	9.79	Teacher Assistants	10.10
General and Operations Managers	66.54	Teachers, Elementary School	25.40
Hairdressers/Cosmetologists	14.67	Teachers, Secondary School	25.90
Internists	82.70	Telemarketers	12.37
Janitors and Cleaners	10.06	Truck Drivers, Heavy/Tractor-Trailer	23.01
Landscaping/Groundskeeping Workers	11.35	Truck Drivers, Light/Delivery Svcs.	16.33
Lawyers	78.40	Waiters and Waitresses	10.78

Note: Wage data covers the Houston-Sugar Land-Baytown, TX Metropolitan Statistical Area—see Appendix B for areas included; Hourly wages for elementary/secondary school teachers and teacher assistants were calculated by the editors from annual wage data assuming a 40 hour work week; n/a not available.
Source: Bureau of Labor Statistics, Metro Area Occupational Employment and Wage Estimates, May 2014

TAXES

State Corporate Income Tax Rates

State	Tax Rate (%)	Income Brackets ($)	Num. of Brackets	Financial Institution Tax Rate (%)[a]	Federal Income Tax Ded.
Texas	(y)	–	–	(y)	No

Note: Tax rates as of January 1, 2015; (a) Rates listed are the corporate income tax rate applied to financial institutions or excise taxes based on income. Some states have other taxes based upon the value of deposits or shares; (y) Texas imposes a Franchise Tax, otherwise known as margin tax, imposed on entities with more than $1,030,000 total revenues at rate of 1%, or 0.5% for entities primarily engaged in retail or wholesale trade, on lesser of 70% of total revenues or 100%of gross receipts after deductions for either compensation or cost of goods sold.
Source: Federation of Tax Administrators, "State Corporate Income Tax Rates, 2015"

State Individual Income Tax Rates

State	Tax Rate (%)	Income Brackets ($)	Num. of Brackets	Personal Exempt. ($)[1] Single	Personal Exempt. ($)[1] Dependents	Fed. Inc. Tax Ded.
Texas	None	–	–	–	–	–

Note: Tax rates as of January 1, 2015; Local- and county-level taxes are not included; n/a not applicable; (1) Married joint filers generally receive double the single exemption
Source: Federation of Tax Administrators, "State Individual Income Tax Rates, 2015"

Various State and Local Tax Rates

State	State and Local Sales and Use (%)	State Sales and Use (%)	Gasoline[1] (¢/gal.)	Cigarette[2] ($/pack)	Spirits[3] ($/gal.)	Wine[4] ($/gal.)	Beer[5] ($/gal.)
Texas	8.25	6.25	20	1.41	2.40 (f)	0.20	0.20 (p)

Note: All tax rates as of January 1, 2015; (1) The American Petroleum Institute has developed a methodology for determining the average tax rate on a gallon of fuel. Rates may include any of the following: excise taxes, environmental fees, storage tank fees, other fees or taxes, general sales tax, and local taxes. In states where gasoline is subject to the general sales tax, or where the fuel tax is based on the average sale price, the average rate determined by API is sensitive to changes in the price of gasoline. States that fully or partially apply general sales taxes to gasoline: CA, CO, GA, IL, IN, MI, NY; (2) The federal excise tax of $1.0066 per pack and local taxes are not included; (3) Rates are those applicable to off-premise sales of 40% alcohol by volume (a.b.v.) distilled spirits in 750ml containers. Local excise taxes are excluded; (4) Rates are those applicable to off-premise sales of 11% a.b.v. non-carbonated wine in 750ml containers; (5) Rates are those applicable to off-premise sales of 4.7% a.b.v. beer in 12 ounce containers; (f) Different rates are also applicable according to alcohol content, place of production, size of container, or place purchased (on- or off-premise or onboard airlines); (p) Local excise taxes are excluded.
Source: Tax Foundation, 2015 Facts & Figures: How Does Your State Compare?

State Business Tax Climate Index Rankings

State	Overall Rank	Corporate Tax Index Rank	Individual Income Tax Index Rank	Sales Tax Index Rank	Unemployment Insurance Tax Index Rank	Property Tax Index Rank
Texas	10	39	6	36	15	36

Note: The index is a measure of how each state's tax laws affect economic performance. The lower the rank, the more favorable a state's tax system is for business. States without a given tax are given a ranking of 1. The scores/rankings for the District of Columbia do not affect other states. The 2015 index represents the tax climate as of July 1, 2014.
Source: Tax Foundation, State Business Tax Climate Index 2015

COMMERCIAL REAL ESTATE

Office Market

Market Area	Inventory (sq. ft.)	Vacancy Rate (%)	Under Construction (sq. ft.)	YTD Net Absorption (sq. ft.)	Total Average Asking Rent ($/sq. ft./year)
Houston	214,671,087	13.4	10,487,866	4,540,832	27.47
National	4,745,108,508	14.3	71,190,461	51,084,126	27.40

Source: Newmark Grubb Knight Frank, National Office Market Report, 4th Quarter 2014

Industrial/Warehouse/R&D Market

Market Area	Inventory (sq. ft.)	Vacancy Rate (%)	Under Construction (sq. ft.)	YTD Net Absorption (sq. ft.)	Total Average Asking Rent ($/sq. ft./year)
Houston	497,846,760	4.8	8,853,170	9,862,249	6.34
National	14,238,613,765	7.2	134,387,407	185,246,438	5.64

Source: Newmark Grubb Knight Frank, National Industrial Market Report, 4th Quarter 2014

COMMERCIAL UTILITIES

Typical Monthly Electric Bills

Area	Commercial Service ($/month)		Industrial Service ($/month)	
	1,500 kWh	40 kW demand 14,000 kWh	1,000 kW demand 200,000 kWh	50,000 kW demand 32,500,000 kWh
City	n/a	n/a	n/a	n/a
Average[1]	201	1,653	26,124	2,639,743

Note: Figures are based on annualized 2014 rates; (1) Average based on 180 utilities surveyed; n/a not available
Source: Edison Electric Institute, Typical Bills and Average Rates Report, Summer 2014

TRANSPORTATION

Means of Transportation to Work

Area	Car/Truck/Van		Public Transportation			Bicycle	Walked	Other Means	Worked at Home
	Drove Alone	Car-pooled	Bus	Subway	Railroad				
City	75.7	12.1	4.2	0.1	0.1	0.6	2.1	1.8	3.4
MSA[1]	79.9	10.9	2.4	0.0	0.0	0.3	1.4	1.5	3.5
U.S.	76.4	9.6	2.6	1.8	0.6	0.6	2.8	1.3	4.3

Note: Figures are percentages and cover workers 16 years of age and older; (1) Figures cover the Houston-The Woodlands-Sugar Land, TX Metropolitan Statistical Area—see Appendix B for areas included
Source: U.S. Census Bureau, 2011-2013 American Community Survey 3-Year Estimates

Travel Time to Work

Area	Less Than 10 Minutes	10 to 19 Minutes	20 to 29 Minutes	30 to 44 Minutes	45 to 59 Minutes	60 to 89 Minutes	90 Minutes or More
City	8.6	27.9	23.5	25.6	7.2	5.5	1.7
MSA[1]	8.6	24.9	20.8	25.4	10.6	7.6	2.1
U.S.	13.3	29.7	20.9	20.2	7.7	5.7	2.6

Note: Figures are percentages and include workers 16 years old and over; (1) Figures cover the Houston-The Woodlands-Sugar Land, TX Metropolitan Statistical Area—see Appendix B for areas included
Source: U.S. Census Bureau, 2011-2013 American Community Survey 3-Year Estimates

Travel Time Index

Area	1985	1990	1995	2000	2005	2010	2011
Urban Area[1]	1.23	1.22	1.19	1.25	1.31	1.26	1.26
Average[2]	1.09	1.14	1.16	1.19	1.23	1.18	1.18

Note: Travel Time Index—the ratio of travel time in the peak period to the travel time at free-flow conditions. For example, a value of 1.30 indicates a 20-minute free-flow trip takes 26 minutes in the peak. Free-flow speeds (60 mph on freeways and 35 mph on principal arterials) are used as the comparison threshold; (1) Covers the Houston TX urban area; (2) average of 498 urban areas
Source: Texas Transportation Institute, Urban Mobility Report 2012, December 2012

Public Transportation

Agency Name / Mode of Transportation	Vehicles Operated in Maximum Service	Annual Unlinked Passenger Trips (in thous.)	Annual Passenger Miles (in thous.)
Metropolitan Transit Authority of Harris County (METRO)			
Bus (directly operated)	616	48,883.6	254,630.3
Bus (purchased transportation)	150	11,869.0	56,170.0
Commuter Bus (directly operated)	223	6,055.0	111,621.5
Commuter Bus (purchased transportation)	59	1,882.8	36,610.5
Demand Response (purchased transportation)	293	1,568.4	17,653.5
Demand Response Taxi (purchased transportation)	114	181.5	1,589.4
Light Rail (directly operated)	22	11,321.0	26,539.4
Vanpool (purchased transportation)	715	2,474.4	69,413.9

Source: Federal Transit Administration, National Transit Database, 2013

Air Transportation

Airport Name and Code / Type of Service	Passenger Airlines[1]	Passenger Enplanements	Freight Carriers[2]	Freight (lbs.)
George Bush Intercontinental (IAH)				
Domestic service (U.S. carriers - 2014)	33	14,969,657	20	181,028,337
International service (U.S. carriers - 2013)	15	3,375,918	14	74,825,393
William P. Hobby (HOU)				
Domestic service (U.S. carriers - 2014)	25	5,797,585	10	14,456,112
International service (U.S. carriers - 2013)	1	129	0	0

Note: (1) Includes all U.S.-based major, minor and commuter airlines that carried at least one passenger during the year; (2) Includes all U.S.-based airlines and freight carriers that transported at least one lb. of freight during the year.

Source: Bureau of Transportation Statistics, The Intermodal Transportation Database, Air Carriers: T-100 Domestic Market (U.S. Carriers), 2014; Bureau of Transportation Statistics, The Intermodal Transportation Database, Air Carriers: T-100 International Market (U.S. Carriers), 2013

Other Transportation Statistics

Major Highways:	I-10; I-45
Amtrak Service:	Yes
Major Waterways/Ports:	Gulf of Mexico; Port of Houston

Source: Amtrak.com; Google Maps

BUSINESSES

Major Business Headquarters

Company Name	Rankings	
	Fortune[1]	Forbes[2]
Apache Corporation	179	-
Baker Hughes Incorporated	132	-
Buckeye Partners	L.P.	485
Calpine Corporation	414	-
Cameron International Corporation	286	-
CenterPoint Energy	333	-
ConocoPhillips	47	-
EOG Resources	203	-
Enterprise Products Partners	56	-
FMC Technologies	368	-
Fertitta Entertainment	-	175
Grocers Supply	-	131
Group 1 Automotive	307	-
Gulf States Toyota	-	48
Halliburton Company	103	-
KBR	360	-
Kinder Morgan	206	-
MRC Global	478	-
Marathon Oil Corporation	188	-
National Oilwell Varco	131	-
Noble Energy	491	-
Pacific Life	333	-
Phillips 66	6	-
Plains GP Holdings	70	-
Quanta Services	396	-
Republic National Distributing Company	-	71
Spectra Energy Corp	461	-
Sysco Corporation	63	-
Targa Resources Corp.	395	-
Tauber Oil	-	87
Waste Management	207	-

Note: (1) Fortune 500—companies that produce a 10-K are ranked 1 to 500 based on 2013 revenue; (2) all private companies with at least $2 billion in annual revenue through the end of their most current fiscal year are ranked 1 to 221; companies listed are headquartered in the city; dashes indicate no ranking

Source: Fortune, "Fortune 500," June 16, 2014; Forbes, "America's Largest Private Companies," November 5, 2014

Fast-Growing Businesses

According to *Inc.*, Houston is home to four of America's 500 fastest-growing private companies: **PPT Fiberglass** (#229); **EPI Engineering** (#263); **Southern Green Builders** (#284); **Team Trident** (#372). Criteria: must be an independent, privately-held, for-profit, U.S. corporation, proprietorship or partnership; revenues must be at least $100,000 in 2010 and $2 million in 2013; must have four-year operating/sales history. Holding companies, regulated banks, and utilities were excluded. *Inc., "America's 500 Fastest-Growing Private Companies," September 2014*

According to *Fortune*, Houston is home to 11 of the 100 fastest-growing companies in the world: **Carrizo Oil & Gas** (#21); **EOG Resources** (#34); **Rosetta Resources** (#41); **Flotek Industries** (#54); **DXP Enterprises** (#57); **Cabot Oil & Gas** (#64); **Kinder Morgan** (#79); **Quanta Services** (#86); **Adams Resources & Energy** (#87); **Geospace Technologies** (#91); **Kirby** (#100). Companies were ranked by their revenue growth rate; their EPS growth rate; and their three-year annualized total return to investors for the period ending June 30, 2014. Criteria for inclusion: a company, foreign or domestic, must trade on a major U.S. stock exchange; must file quarterly reports with the SEC; must have a minimum market capitalization of $250 million; must have a stock price of at least $5 on June 30, 2014; must have been trading continuously since June 30, 2010; must have revenue and net income for the four quarters ended on or before April 30, 2014, of at least $50 million and $10 million, respectively; and must have posted a compound annual growth in revenue and earnings per share of at least 20% annually over the three years ending on or before April 30, 2014. Real estate investment trusts, limited-liability companies, limited parterships, business development companies, closed end investment firms, and companies that lost money in the quarter ending April 30, 2014 were excluded. *Fortune, "100 Fastest-Growing Companies," August 28, 2014*

According to *Initiative for a Competitive Inner City (ICIC)*, Houston is home to two of America's 100 fastest-growing "inner city" companies: **The Bulsard Group** (#31); **Gulfgate Animal Hospital** (#92). Criteria for inclusion: company must be headquartered in or have 51 percent or more of its physical operations in an economically distressed urban area; must be an independent, for-profit corporation, partnership or proprietorship; must have 10 or more employees and have a five-year sales history that includes sales of at least $200,000 in the base year and at least $1 million in the current year with no decrease in sales over the two most recent years. This year, for the first time in the list's 16-year history, the Inner City 100 consists of 10 fast-growing businesses in 10 industry categories. Companies were ranked overall by revenue growth over the five-year period between 2009 and 2013 as well as within their respective industry categories. *Initiative for a Competitive Inner City (ICIC), "Inner City 100 Companies, 2014"*

According to Deloitte, Houston is home to four of North America's 500 fastest-growing high-technology companies: **VCS** (#279); **Alert Logic** (#295); **Geospace Technologies** (#363); **RigNet** (#430). Companies are ranked by percentage growth in revenue over a five-year period. Criteria for inclusion: company must be headquartered within North America; must own proprietary intellectual property or proprietary technology that contributes to a significant portion of the company's operating revenue, or devote a significant proportion of revenues to research and development of technology; must have been in business for a minumum of five years with 2009 operating revenues of at least $50,000 USD/CD and 2013 operating revenues of at least $5 million USD/CD. *Deloitte Touche Tohmatsu, 2014 Technology Fast 500™*

Minority Business Opportunity

Houston is home to two companies which are on the *Black Enterprise* Industrial/Service 100 list (100 largest companies based on gross sales): **The Lewis Group** (#25); **ChaseSource** (#97). Criteria: operational in previous calendar year; at least 51% black-owned and manufactures/owns the product it sells or provides industrial or consumer services. Brokerages, real estate firms and firms that provide professional services are not eligible. *Black Enterprise, B.E. 100s, 2014*

Houston is home to two companies which are on the *Black Enterprise* Auto Dealer 60 list (60 largest dealers based on gross sales): **J Davis Automotive Group** (#23); **Barnett Auto Group** (#28). Criteria: company must be operational in previous calendar year and be at least 51% black-owned. *Black Enterprise, B.E. 100s, 2014*

Houston is home to one company which is on the *Black Enterprise* Asset Manager 15 list (15 largest asset management firms based on assets under management): **Smith, Graham & Co. Investment Advisors** (#7). Criteria: company must have been operational in previous calendar year and be at least 51% black-owned. *Black Enterprise, B.E. 100s, 2014*

Houston is home to 17 companies which are on the *Hispanic Business* 500 list (500 largest U.S. Hispanic-owned companies based on 2012 revenue): **G&A Partners** (#16); **Petro Amigos Supply** (#20); **The Plaza Group** (#29); **MEI Technologies (MEIT)** (#53); **Tejas Office Products** (#134); **Lopez Negrete Communications** (#167); **Reytec Construction Resources** (#173); **MCA Communications** (#177); **Today's Business Solutions** (#194); **Tube America**

(#273); **Traf-Tex** (#310); **Nino Properties** (#401); **Navarro Insurance Group** (#458); **Translation Source** (#460); **Transfinance Corp.** (#465); **Perches Land Services** (#475); **CapWest Companies** (#490). Companies included must show at least 51 percent ownership by Hispanic U.S. citizens, and must maintain headquarters in one of the 50 states or Washington, D.C. *Hispanic Business, "Hispanic Business 500," June 20, 2013*

Houston is home to five companies which are on the *Hispanic Business* Fastest-Growing 100 list (greatest sales growth from 2008 to 2012): **Tejas Office Products** (#18); **Today's Business Solutions** (#27); **Petro Amigos Supply** (#64); **G&A Partners** (#65); **Translation Source** (#83). Companies included must show at least 51 percent ownership by Hispanic U.S. citizens, and must maintain headquarters in one of the 50 states or Washington, D.C. In addition, companies must have minimum revenues of $200,000 for calendar year 2008. *Hispanic Business, June 20, 2013*

Minority- and Women-Owned Businesses

Group	All Firms		Firms with Paid Employees			
	Firms	Sales ($000)	Firms	Sales ($000)	Employees	Payroll ($000)
Asian	22,826	10,793,503	6,878	10,053,255	47,323	1,317,131
Black	33,061	2,077,993	1,757	1,492,851	27,498	530,585
Hispanic	51,205	10,505,159	4,071	8,548,735	42,665	1,526,879
Women	63,416	17,883,106	7,340	16,317,650	88,123	3,246,910
All Firms	219,284	514,239,417	48,175	505,797,015	1,442,271	76,231,379

Note: Figures cover firms located in the city; minority- and women-owned business are defined as firms in which the corresponding group own 51% or more of the stock or equity of the company
Source: U.S. Census Bureau, 2007 Economic Census, Survey of Business Owners (2012 Survey of Business Owners data will be released starting in June 2015)

HOTELS & CONVENTION CENTERS

Hotels/Motels

Area	5 Star		4 Star		3 Star		2 Star		1 Star		Not Rated	
	Num.	Pct.[3]	Num.	Pct.[3]	Num.	Pct.[3]	Num.	Pct.[3]	Num.	Pct.[3]	Num.	Pct.[3]
City[1]	4	0.7	25	4.2	148	25.1	367	62.3	5	0.8	40	6.8
Total[2]	166	0.9	1,264	7.0	5,718	31.8	9,340	52.0	411	2.3	1,070	6.0

Note: (1) Figures cover Houston and vicinity; (2) Figures cover all 100 cities in this book; (3) Percentage of hotels which have a given star rating; Star ratings are determined by expedia.com and offer an indication of the general quality of a particular hotel.
Source: expedia.com, April 2, 2015

The Houston-The Woodlands-Sugar Land, TX metro area is home to one of the best hotels in the U.S. according to *Travel & Leisure*: **St. Regis Houston**. Criteria: service; location; rooms; food; and value. The list includes the top 236 hotels in the U.S. *Travel & Leisure, "T+L 500, The World's Best Hotels 2015"*

Major Convention Centers

Name	Overall Space (sq. ft.)	Exhibit Space (sq. ft.)	Meeting Space (sq. ft.)	Meeting Rooms
George R. Brown Convention Center	1,200,000	862,000	185,000	100
Reliant Center	1,400,000	706,000	n/a	n/a

Note: Table includes convention centers located in the Houston-The Woodlands-Sugar Land, TX metro area; n/a not available
Source: Original research

Living Environment

COST OF LIVING

Cost of Living Index

Composite Index	Groceries	Housing	Utilities	Transportation	Health Care	Misc. Goods/ Services
98.8	84.3	108.1	99.4	93.7	91.0	99.9

Note: The Cost of Living Index measures regional differences in the cost of consumer goods and services, excluding taxes and non-consumer expenditures, for professional and managerial households in the top income quintile. It is based on more than 50,000 prices covering almost 60 different items for which prices are collected three times a year by chambers of commerce, economic development organizations or university applied economic centers in each participating urban area. The numbers shown should be read as a percentage above or below the national average of 100. For example, a value of 115.4 in the groceries column indicates that grocery prices are 15.4% higher than the national average. Small differences in the index numbers should not be interpreted as significant; Figures cover the Houston TX urban area.
Source: The Council for Community and Economic Research, ACCRA Cost of Living Index, 2014

Grocery Prices

Area[1]	T-Bone Steak ($/pound)	Frying Chicken ($/pound)	Whole Milk ($/half gal.)	Eggs ($/dozen)	Orange Juice ($/64 oz.)	Coffee ($/11.5 oz.)
City[2]	8.77	1.09	2.12	1.83	3.08	3.88
Avg.	10.40	1.37	2.40	1.99	3.46	4.27
Min.	8.48	0.93	1.37	1.30	2.83	2.99
Max.	14.20	2.44	3.62	4.02	6.42	6.96

Note: (1) Values for the local area are compared with the average, minimum and maximum values for all 308 areas in the Cost of Living Index; (2) Figures cover the Houston TX urban area; **T-Bone Steak** *(price per pound);* **Frying Chicken** *(price per pound, whole fryer);* **Whole Milk** *(half gallon carton);* **Eggs** *(price per dozen, Grade A, large);* **Orange Juice** *(64 oz. Tropicana or Florida Natural);* **Coffee** *(11.5 oz. can, vacuum-packed, Maxwell House, Hills Bros, or Folgers).*
Source: The Council for Community and Economic Research, ACCRA Cost of Living Index, 2014

Housing and Utility Costs

Area[1]	New Home Price ($)	Apartment Rent ($/month)	All Electric ($/month)	Part Electric ($/month)	Other Energy ($/month)	Telephone ($/month)
City[2]	273,623	1,427	-	116.14	41.72	30.15
Avg.	305,838	919	181.00	93.66	73.14	27.95
Min.	183,142	480	112.00	42.06	23.42	17.16
Max.	1,358,576	3,851	594.00	180.03	440.99	40.42

Note: (1) Values for the local area are compared with the average, minimum and maximum values for all 308 areas in the Cost of Living Index; (2) Figures cover the Houston TX urban area; **New Home Price** *(2,400 sf living area, 8,000 sf lot, in urban area with full utilities);* **Apartment Rent** *(950 sf 2 bedroom/1.5 or 2 bath, unfurnished, excluding all utilities except water);* **All Electric** *(average monthly cost for an all-electric home);* **Part Electric** *(average monthly cost for a part-electric home);* **Other Energy** *(average monthly cost for natural gas, fuel oil, coal, wood, and any other forms of energy except electricity);* **Telephone** *(price includes basic monthly rate for a private residential line plus additional local usage charges incurred by a family of four).*
Source: The Council for Community and Economic Research, ACCRA Cost of Living Index, 2014

Health Care, Transportation, and Other Costs

Area[1]	Doctor ($/visit)	Dentist ($/visit)	Optometrist ($/visit)	Gasoline ($/gallon)	Beauty Salon ($/visit)	Men's Shirt ($)
City[2]	82.15	83.51	86.81	3.29	49.10	25.91
Avg.	102.86	87.89	97.66	3.44	34.37	26.74
Min.	67.47	65.78	51.18	3.00	17.43	12.79
Max.	173.50	150.14	235.00	4.33	64.28	49.50

Note: (1) Values for the local area are compared with the average, minimum and maximum values for all 308 areas in the Cost of Living Index; (2) Figures cover the Houston TX urban area; **Doctor** *(general practitioners routine exam of an established patient);* **Dentist** *(adult teeth cleaning and periodic oral examination);* **Optometrist** *(full vision eye exam for established adult patient);* **Gasoline** *(one gallon regular unleaded, national brand, including all taxes, cash price at self-service pump if available);* **Beauty Salon** *(woman's shampoo, trim, and blow-dry);* **Men's Shirt** *(cotton/polyester dress shirt, pinpoint weave, long sleeves).*
Source: The Council for Community and Economic Research, ACCRA Cost of Living Index, 2014

HOUSING

House Price Index (HPI)

Area	National Ranking[2]	Quarterly Change (%)	One-Year Change (%)	Five-Year Change (%)
MSA[1]	13	0.87	11.02	23.21
U.S.[3]	–	1.35	4.91	11.59

Note: The HPI is a weighted repeat sales index. It measures average price changes in repeat sales or refinancings on the same properties. This information is obtained by reviewing repeat mortgage transactions on single-family properties whose mortgages have been purchased or securitized by Fannie Mae or Freddie Mac in January 1975; (1) Houston-The Woodlands-Sugar Land Metropolitan Statistical Area—see Appendix B for areas included; (2) Rankings are based on annual percentage change for all metro areas containing at least 15,000 transactions over the last 10 years and ranges from 1 to 275; (3) figures based on a weighted average of Census Division estimates using a seasonally adjusted, purchase-only index; all figures are for the period ending December 31, 2014
Source: Federal Housing Finance Agency, House Price Index, February 26, 2015

Median Single-Family Home Prices

Area	2012	2013	2014p	Percent Change 2013 to 2014
MSA[1]	164.8	181.3	198.4	9.4
U.S. Average	177.2	197.4	209.0	5.9

Note: Figures are median sales prices of existing single-family homes in thousands of dollars; (p) preliminary; n/a not available; (1) Houston-The Woodlands-Sugar Land, TX Metropolitan Statistical Area—see Appendix B for areas included
Source: National Association of Realtors, Median Sales Price of Existing Single-Family Homes for Metropolitan Areas, 4th Quarter 2014

Qualifying Income Based on Median Sales Price of Existing Single-Family Homes

Area	With 5% Down ($)	With 10% Down ($)	With 20% Down ($)
MSA[1]	43,797	41,492	36,882
U.S. Average	45,863	43,449	38,621

Note: Figures are preliminary; Qualifying income is based on a mortgage rate of 4.0%. Monthly principal and interest payment is limited to 25% of income; n/a not available; (1) Houston-The Woodlands-Sugar Land, TX Metropolitan Statistical Area—see Appendix B for areas included
Source: National Association of Realtors, Qualifying Income Based on Median Sales Price of Existing Single-Family Homes for Metropolitan Areas, 4th Quarter 2014

Median Apartment Condo-Coop Home Prices

Area	2012	2013	2014p	Percent Change 2013 to 2014
MSA[1]	134.6	142.0	149.8	5.5
U.S. Average	173.7	194.9	205.1	5.2

Note: Figures are median sales prices of existing apartment condo-coop homes in thousands of dollars; (p) preliminary; n/a not available; (1) Houston-The Woodlands-Sugar Land, TX Metropolitan Statistical Area—see Appendix B for areas included
Source: National Association of Realtors, Median Sales Price of Existing Apartment Condo-Coop Homes for Metropolitan Areas, 4th Quarter 2014

Gross Monthly Rent

Area	Under $200	$200 -299	$300 -499	$500 -749	$750 -999	$1,000 -1,499	$1,500 and up	Median ($)
City	0.9	1.2	4.9	31.5	28.9	23.0	9.6	837
MSA[1]	0.8	1.3	4.5	26.9	29.1	26.6	10.8	885
U.S.	1.7	3.2	7.8	22.1	24.3	26.0	14.9	900

Note: Figures are percentages except for Median; Gross rent is the contract rent plus the estimated average monthly cost of utilities (electricity, gas, and water and sewer) and fuels (oil, coal, kerosene, wood, etc.) if these are paid by the renter (or paid for the renter by someone else); (1) Figures cover the Houston-The Woodlands-Sugar Land, TX Metropolitan Statistical Area—see Appendix B for areas included
Source: U.S. Census Bureau, 2011-2013 American Community Survey 3-Year Estimates

Homeownership Rate

Area	2007 (%)	2008 (%)	2009 (%)	2010 (%)	2011 (%)	2012 (%)	2013 (%)	2014 (%)
MSA[1]	64.5	64.8	63.6	61.4	61.3	62.1	60.5	60.4
U.S.	68.1	67.8	67.4	66.9	66.1	65.4	65.1	64.5

Note: (1) Figures cover the Houston-The Woodlands-Sugar Land, TX Metropolitan Statistical Area—see Appendix B for areas included
Source: U.S. Census Bureau, Housing Vacancies and Homeownership Annual Statistics: 2014

Year Housing Structure Built

Area	2010 or Later	2000 -2009	1990 -1999	1980 -1989	1970 -1979	1960 -1969	1950 -1959	1940 -1949	Before 1940	Median Year
City	1.4	15.8	9.3	13.7	24.6	14.5	11.3	5.0	4.5	1976
MSA[1]	2.3	25.3	14.6	16.1	19.7	9.4	6.8	3.0	2.7	1985
U.S.	0.9	15.0	13.9	13.8	15.8	11.0	10.9	5.4	13.3	1976

Note: Figures are percentages except for Median Year; (1) Figures cover the Houston-The Woodlands-Sugar Land, TX Metropolitan Statistical Area—see Appendix B for areas included
Source: U.S. Census Bureau, 2011-2013 American Community Survey 3-Year Estimates

HEALTH

Health Risk Data

Category	MSA[1] (%)	U.S. (%)
Adults aged 18–64 who have any kind of health care coverage	64.1	79.6
Adults who reported being in good or excellent health	80.9	83.1
Adults who are current smokers	16.6	19.6
Adults who are heavy drinkers[2]	5.6	6.1
Adults who are binge drinkers[3]	15.1	16.9
Adults who are overweight (BMI 25.0 - 29.9)	35.9	35.8
Adults who are obese (BMI 30.0 - 99.8)	26.6	27.6
Adults who participated in any physical activities in the past month	73.0	77.1
Adults 50+ who have ever had a sigmoidoscopy or colonoscopy	65.1	67.3
Women aged 40+ who have had a mammogram within the past two years	69.1	74.0
Men aged 40+ who have had a PSA test within the past two years	41.9	45.2
Adults aged 65+ who have had flu shot within the past year	61.7	60.1
Adults who always wear a seatbelt	97.0	93.8

Note: Data as of 2012 unless otherwise noted; (1) Figures cover the Houston-Sugar Land-Baytown, TX Metropolitan Statistical Area—see Appendix B for areas included; (2) Heavy drinkers are classified as males having more than two drinks per day or females having more than one drink per day; (3) Binge drinkers are classified as males having five or more drinks on one occasion or females having four or more drinks on one occasion
Source: Centers for Disease Control and Prevention, Behaviorial Risk Factor Surveillance System, SMART: Selected Metropolitan/Micropolitan Area Risk Trends, 2012 (Note: the CDC has discontinued this dataset but will be releasing a replacement in late 2015)

Chronic Health Indicators

Category	MSA[1] (%)	U.S. (%)
Adults who have ever been told they had a heart attack	3.0	4.5
Adults who have ever been told they had a stroke	2.7	2.9
Adults who have been told they currently have asthma	5.1	8.9
Adults who have ever been told they have arthritis	19.5	25.7
Adults who have ever been told they have diabetes[2]	10.5	9.7
Adults who have ever been told they had skin cancer	4.5	5.7
Adults who have ever been told they had any other types of cancer	4.9	6.5
Adults who have ever been told they have COPD	5.0	6.2
Adults who have ever been told they have kidney disease	2.2	2.5
Adults who have ever been told they have a form of depression	15.6	18.0

Note: Data as of 2012 unless otherwise noted; (1) Figures cover the Houston-Sugar Land-Baytown, TX Metropolitan Statistical Area—see Appendix B for areas included; (2) Figures do not include pregnancy-related, borderline, or pre-diabetes
Source: Centers for Disease Control and Prevention, Behaviorial Risk Factor Surveillance System, SMART: Selected Metropolitan/Micropolitan Area Risk Trends, 2012 (Note: the CDC has discontinued this dataset but will be releasing a replacement in late 2015)

Mortality Rates for the Top 10 Causes of Death in the U.S.

ICD-10[a] Sub-Chapter	ICD-10[a] Code	Age-Adjusted Mortality Rate[1] per 100,000 population	
		County[2]	U.S.
Malignant neoplasms	C00-C97	160.5	166.2
Ischaemic heart diseases	I20-I25	96.6	105.7
Other forms of heart disease	I30-I51	51.3	49.3
Chronic lower respiratory diseases	J40-J47	32.4	42.1
Organic, including symptomatic, mental disorders	F01-F09	49.7	38.1
Cerebrovascular diseases	I60-I69	41.2	37.0
Other external causes of accidental injury	W00-X59	24.9	26.9
Other degenerative diseases of the nervous system	G30-G31	16.3	25.6
Diabetes mellitus	E10-E14	20.4	21.3
Hypertensive diseases	I10-I15	20.5	19.4

Note: (a) ICD-10 = International Classification of Diseases 10th Revision; (1) Mortality rates are a three year average covering 2011-2013; (2) Figures cover Harris County
Source: Centers for Disease Control and Prevention, National Center for Health Statistics. Compressed Mortality File 1999-2013 on CDC WONDER Online Database, released October 2014. Data are compiled from the Compressed Mortality File 1999-2013, Series 20 No. 2S, 2014.

Mortality Rates for Selected Causes of Death

ICD-10[a] Sub-Chapter	ICD-10[a] Code	Age-Adjusted Mortality Rate[1] per 100,000 population	
		County[2]	U.S.
Assault	X85-Y09	7.7	5.2
Diseases of the liver	K70-K76	14.8	13.2
Human immunodeficiency virus (HIV) disease	B20-B24	4.6	2.2
Influenza and pneumonia	J09-J18	13.9	15.4
Intentional self-harm	X60-X84	10.2	12.5
Malnutrition	E40-E46	1.8	0.9
Obesity and other hyperalimentation	E65-E68	1.5	1.8
Renal failure	N17-N19	16.4	13.1
Transport accidents	V01-V99	11.0	11.7
Viral hepatitis	B15-B19	2.0	2.2

Note: (a) ICD-10 = International Classification of Diseases 10th Revision; (1) Mortality rates are a three year average covering 2011-2013; (2) Figures cover Harris County
Source: Centers for Disease Control and Prevention, National Center for Health Statistics. Compressed Mortality File 1999-2013 on CDC WONDER Online Database, released October 2014. Data are compiled from the Compressed Mortality File 1999-2013, Series 20 No. 2S, 2014.

Health Insurance Coverage

Area	With Health Insurance	With Private Health Insurance	With Public Health Insurance	Without Health Insurance	Population Under Age 18 Without Health Insurance
City	71.4	46.4	30.7	28.6	15.2
MSA[1]	76.5	57.1	25.6	23.5	13.3
U.S.	85.2	65.2	31.0	14.8	7.3

Note: Figures are percentages that cover the civilian noninstitutionalized population; (1) Figures cover the Houston-The Woodlands-Sugar Land, TX Metropolitan Statistical Area—see Appendix B for areas included
Source: U.S. Census Bureau, 2011-2013 American Community Survey 3-Year Estimates

Number of Medical Professionals

Area[1]	MDs[2]	DOs[2,3]	Dentists	Podiatrists	Chiropractors	Optometrists
Local (number)	12,696	405	2,691	196	896	765
Local (rate[4])	297.8	9.5	61.8	4.5	20.6	17.6
U.S. (rate[4])	270.0	20.2	63.1	5.7	25.2	14.9

Note: Data as of 2013 unless noted; (1) Local data covers Harris County; (2) Data as of 2012 and includes all active, non-federal physicians; (3) Doctor of Osteopathic Medicine; (4) rate per 100,000 population
Source: U.S. Department of Health and Human Services, Health Resources and Services Administration, Bureau of Health Professions, Area Resource File (ARF) 2013-2014

Best Hospitals

According to *U.S. News,* the Houston-The Woodlands-Sugar Land, TX metro area is home to six of the best hospitals in the U.S.: **Houston Methodist Hospital** (11 specialties); **Menninger Clinic** (1 specialty); **St. Luke's Episcopal Hospital** (2 specialties); **TIRR Memorial Hermann** (1 specialty); **Texas Heart Institute at St. Luke's Episcopal Hospital** (1 specialty); **University of Texas MD Anderson Cancer Center** (3 specialties). The hospitals listed were nationally ranked in at least one adult specialty. Only 144 hospitals nationwide were nationally ranked in one or more specialties. Seventeen hospitals in the U.S. made the Honor Roll with high scores in at least six specialties. *U.S. News Online, "America's Best Children's Hospitals 2014-15"*

According to *U.S. News,* the Houston-The Woodlands-Sugar Land, TX metro area is home to three of the best children's hospitals in the U.S.: **Children's Cancer Hospital-University of Texas M.D. Anderson** (1 specialty); **Children's Memorial Hermann Hospital** (1 specialty); **Texas Children's Hospital** (Honor Roll/10 specialties). The hospitals listed were highly ranked in at least one pediatric specialty. Eighty-nine children's hospitals in the U.S. were nationally ranked in at least one specialty. Ten children's hospitals in the U.S. made the Honor Roll with high scores in at least three specialties. *U.S. News Online, "America's Best Children's Hospitals 2014-15"*

EDUCATION

Public School District Statistics

District Name	Schls	Pupils	Pupil/ Teacher Ratio	Minority Pupils[1] (%)	Free Lunch Eligible[2] (%)	IEP[3] (%)
Aldine ISD	76	65,684	17.1	98.0	77.5	7.0
Alief ISD	46	45,783	14.8	96.5	74.6	7.6
Cypress-Fairbanks ISD	83	110,013	17.2	71.0	42.0	7.2
Galena Park ISD	24	22,113	14.9	94.1	73.4	8.6
Harmony School of Excellence	6	3,860	17.0	82.8	35.4	3.5
Harmony Science Academy	6	3,481	16.0	84.7	52.8	3.8
Harmony Science Academy (El Paso)	3	2,260	16.8	88.5	46.9	4.2
Houston ISD	276	203,354	18.6	91.8	72.6	7.8
Kipp Inc Charter	15	6,695	18.8	99.0	76.2	3.5
North Forest ISD	11	6,693	18.9	99.1	99.5	8.3
Sheldon ISD	13	7,566	16.5	88.1	69.8	6.6
Spring Branch ISD	49	34,857	16.0	72.1	54.3	7.6
Spring ISD	39	36,098	16.8	87.9	62.9	8.2
Yes Prep Public Schools Inc.	9	5,934	15.3	99.2	68.2	5.2

Note: Table includes school districts with 2,000 or more students; (1) Percentage of students that are not non-Hispanic white; (2) Percentage of students that are eligible for the free lunch program; (3) Percentage of students that have an Individualized Education Program.
Source: U.S. Department of Education, National Center for Education Statistics, Common Core of Data, Local Education Agency (School District) Universe Survey: School Year 2012-2013; U.S. Department of Education, National Center for Education Statistics, Common Core of Data, Public Elementary/Secondary School Universe Survey: School Year 2012-2013

Best High Schools

According to *The Daily Beast,* Houston is home to 10 of the best high schools in the U.S.: **Westchester Academy for International Studies** (#113); **Alief Kerr High School** (#138); **YES Prep Southeast** (#236); **Clear Lake High School** (#283); **Memorial High School** (#302); **YES Prep North Central** (#488); **YES Prep East End** (#515); **YES Prep Southwest** (#516); **KIPP Houston High School** (#562); **Elsik High School** (#698); *The Daily Beast* used six indicators culled from school surveys to compare public high schools in the U.S., with graduation and college acceptance rates weighed most heavily. Other criteria included: college-level courses/exams and SAT/ACT scores. *The Daily Beast, "Top High Schools 2014"*

Highest Level of Education

Area	Less than H.S.	H.S. Diploma	Some College, No Deg.	Associate Degree	Bachelor's Degree	Master's Degree	Prof. School Degree	Doctorate Degree
City	23.8	22.6	19.0	4.6	18.6	7.4	2.4	1.5
MSA[1]	18.6	23.7	21.6	6.3	19.5	7.1	1.9	1.3
U.S.	13.7	28.0	21.2	7.9	18.2	7.7	1.9	1.3

Note: Figures cover persons age 25 and over; (1) Figures cover the Houston-The Woodlands-Sugar Land, TX Metropolitan Statistical Area—see Appendix B for areas included
Source: U.S. Census Bureau, 2011-2013 American Community Survey 3-Year Estimates

Educational Attainment by Race

Area	High School Graduate or Higher (%)					Bachelor's Degree or Higher (%)				
	Total	White	Black	Asian	Hisp.[2]	Total	White	Black	Asian	Hisp.[2]
City	76.2	75.8	85.0	84.8	52.8	30.0	34.3	19.7	56.3	10.7
MSA[1]	81.4	82.1	87.8	86.2	58.2	29.9	30.8	24.4	53.9	12.0
U.S.	86.3	88.3	83.1	85.7	64.0	29.1	30.4	18.8	50.7	13.7

Note: Figures shown cover persons 25 years old and over; (1) Figures cover the Houston-The Woodlands-Sugar Land, TX Metropolitan Statistical Area—see Appendix B for areas included; (2) People of Hispanic origin can be of any race
Source: U.S. Census Bureau, 2011-2013 American Community Survey 3-Year Estimates

School Enrollment by Grade and Control

Area	Preschool (%)		Kindergarten (%)		Grades 1 - 4 (%)		Grades 5 - 8 (%)		Grades 9 - 12 (%)	
	Public	Private	Public	Private	Public	Private	Public	Private	Public	Private
City	66.5	33.5	91.4	8.6	92.8	7.2	93.1	6.9	92.8	7.2
MSA[1]	59.0	41.0	89.8	10.2	93.5	6.5	94.0	6.0	93.6	6.4
U.S.	57.7	42.3	87.9	12.1	89.9	10.1	90.0	10.0	90.7	9.3

Note: Figures shown cover persons 3 years old and over; (1) Figures cover the Houston-The Woodlands-Sugar Land, TX Metropolitan Statistical Area—see Appendix B for areas included
Source: U.S. Census Bureau, 2011-2013 American Community Survey 3-Year Estimates

Average Salaries of Public School Classroom Teachers

Area	2013-14		2014-15		Percent Change 2013-14 to 2014-15	Percent Change 2004-05 to 2014-15
	Dollars	Rank[1]	Dollars	Rank[1]		
TEXAS	49,690	30	50,576	29	1.78	23.3
U.S. Average	56,610	–	57,379	–	1.36	20.8

Note: (1) State rank ranges from 1 to 51 where 1 indicates highest salary.
Source: National Education Association, Rankings & Estimates: Rankings of the States 2014 and Estimates of School Statistics 2015, March 2015

Higher Education

Four-Year Colleges			Two-Year Colleges			Medical Schools[1]	Law Schools[2]	Voc/ Tech[3]
Public	Private Non-profit	Private For-profit	Public	Private Non-profit	Private For-profit			
6	8	9	1	3	13	2	3	32

Note: Figures cover institutions located within the city limits and include main campuses only; (1) includes schools accredited by the Liaison Committee on Medical Education and the American Osteopathic Association's Commission on Osteopathic College Accreditation; (2) includes ABA-accredited schools, schools with provisional ABA accreditation, and state accredited schools; (3) includes all schools with programs that are less than 2 years.
Source: National Center for Education Statistics, Integrated Postsecondary Education System (IPEDS), 2013-14; Association of American Medical Colleges, Member List, May 1, 2015; American Osteopathic Association, Member List, May 1, 2015; Law School Admission Council, Official Guide to ABA-Approved Law Schools Online, May 1, 2015; Wikipedia, List of Medical Schools in the United States, May 1, 2015; Wikipedia, List of Law Schools in the United States, May 1, 2015

According to *U.S. News & World Report,* the Houston-The Woodlands-Sugar Land, TX metro area is home to two of the best national universities in the U.S.: **Rice University** (#19); **University of Houston** (#189). The indicators used to capture academic quality fall into a number of categories: assessment by administrators at peer institutions; retention of students; faculty resources; student selectivity; financial resources; alumni giving; high school counselor ratings of colleges; and graduation rate. *U.S. News & World Report, "America's Best Colleges 2015"*

According to *U.S. News & World Report,* the Houston-The Woodlands-Sugar Land, TX metro area is home to one of the top 100 law schools in the U.S.: **University of Houston** (#59). The rankings are based on a weighted average of 12 measures of quality: peer assessment score; assessment score by lawyers/judges; median LSAT scores; median undergrad GPA; acceptance rate; employment rates for graduates; placement success; bar passage rate; faculty resources; expenditures per student; student/faculty ratio; and library resources. *U.S. News & World Report, "America's Best Graduate Schools, Law, 2016"*

According to *U.S. News & World Report,* the Houston-The Woodlands-Sugar Land, TX metro area is home to two of the top 75 medical schools for research in the U.S.: **Baylor College of Medicine** (#21); **University of Texas Health Science Center-Houston** (#57). The rankings are based on a weighted average of 11 measures of quality: quality assessment; peer assessment score; assessment score by residency directors; research activity; total research activity; average research activity per faculty member; student selectivity; median MCAT total score; median undergraduate GPA; acceptance rate; and faculty resources. *U.S. News & World Report, "America's Best Graduate Schools, Medical, 2016"*

According to *U.S. News & World Report,* the Houston-The Woodlands-Sugar Land, TX metro area is home to one of the top 75 business schools in the U.S.: **Rice University (Jones)** (#33). The rankings are based on a weighted average of the following nine measures: quality assessment; peer assessment; recruiter assessment; placement success; mean starting salary and bonus; student selectivity; mean GMAT and GRE scores; mean undergraduate GPA; and acceptance rate. *U.S. News & World Report, "America's Best Graduate Schools, Business, 2016"*

PRESIDENTIAL ELECTION

2012 Presidential Election Results

Area	Obama (%)	Romney (%)	Other (%)
Harris County	49.4	49.3	1.3
U.S.	51.0	47.2	1.8

Note: Results may not add to 100% due to rounding
Source: Dave Leip's Atlas of U.S. Presidential Elections

EMPLOYERS

Major Employers

Company Name	Industry
Christus Health Gulf Coast	Management consulting services
Conoco Phillips	Petroleum refining
Continental Airlines	Air trans scheduled
Dibellos Dynamic Orthotics & Prosthetics	Surgical appliances and supplies
El Paso E&P Company	Petroleum refining
F Charles Brunicardi MD	Accounting assoc
Grey Wolf	Drilling oil and gas wells
Kellogg Brown &Root	Industrial plant construction
Mustang Engineers and Constructors	Construction management consultant
Philip Industrial Services	Environmental consultant
Philips Petroleum Company	Oil and gas exploration services
Quaker State Corp	Lubricating oils and greases
St Lukes Episcopal Health System	General medical/surgical hospitals
Texas Childrens Hospital	Specialty hosp
The Methodist Hospital	General medical/surgical hospitals
Tracer Industries	Plumbing
Univ of Texas Medical Branch at Galveston	Accident and health ins
University of Houston System	University
University of Texas System	General medical/surgical hospitals
US Dept of Veteran Affairs	Administration of veterans affairs
Veterans Health Administration	Administration of veterans affairs

Note: Companies shown are located within the Houston-The Woodlands-Sugar Land, TX Metropolitan Statistical Area.
Source: Hoovers.com; Wikipedia

Best Companies to Work For

Camden Property Trust; David Weekley Homes; Hilcorp; Houston Methodist, headquartered in Houston, are among "The 100 Best Companies to Work For." To pick the best companies, *Fortune* partnered with the Great Place to Work Institute. Two-thirds of a company's score is based on the results of the Institute's Trust Index survey, which is sent to a random sample of employees from each company. The questions related to attitudes about management's credibility, job satisfaction, and camaraderie. The other third of the scoring is based on the company's responses to the Institute's Culture Audit, which includes detailed questions about pay and benefit programs, and a series of open-ended questions about hiring practices, internal communication, training, recognition programs, and diversity efforts. Any company that is at least five years old with more than 1,000 U.S. employees is eligible. *Fortune, "The 100 Best Companies to Work For," 2015*

MEI Technologies; The University of Texas MD Anderson Cancer Center, headquartered in Houston, are among the "50 Best Employers for Workers Over 50." Criteria: recruiting practices; opportunities for training, education, and career development; workplace accommodations; alternative work options, such as flexible scheduling, job sharing, and phased retirement; employee health and pension benefits; and retiree benefits. Employers with at least 50 employees based in the U.S. are eligible, including for-profit companies, not-for-profit organizations, and government employers. *AARP, "2013 AARP Best Employers for Workers Over 50"*

LINN Energy; Noah Consulting; Transocean, headquartered in Houston, are among the "100 Best Places to Work in IT." To qualify, companies, both public and private, had to have a minimum of 50 IT employees and were selected based on average salary and bonus increases, the percentage of IT staffers promoted, IT staff turnover rates, training and development programs, and the percentage of women and minorities in IT staff and management positions. In addition, *Computerworld* looked at retention efforts, programs for recognizing and rewarding outstanding performances, and benefits such as flextime, elder care and child care, and reimbursement for college tuition and the cost of pursuing technology certifications. *Computerworld, "100 Best Places to Work in IT 2014"*

PUBLIC SAFETY

Crime Rate

Area	All Crimes	Violent Crimes				Property Crimes		
		Murder	Forcible Rape	Robbery	Aggrav. Assault	Burglary	Larceny -Theft	Motor Vehicle Theft
City	6,049.3	9.8	28.3	453.6	471.0	1,088.4	3,374.8	623.5
Suburbs[1]	2,983.4	3.9	20.1	116.2	204.2	631.7	1,770.7	236.6
Metro[2]	4,047.8	5.9	22.9	233.3	296.8	790.3	2,327.6	370.9
U.S.	3,098.6	4.5	25.2	109.1	229.1	610.0	1,899.4	221.3

Note: Figures are crimes per 100,000 population; (1) All areas within the metro area that are located outside the city limits; (2) Figures cover the Houston-The Woodlands-Sugar Land, TX Metropolitan Statistical Area—see Appendix B for areas included
Source: FBI Uniform Crime Reports, 2013

Hate Crimes

Area	Number of Quarters Reported	Number of Incidents per Bias Motivation						
		Race	Religion	Sexual Orientation	Ethnicity	Disability	Gender	Gender Identity
City	4	4	0	5	4	0	0	0
U.S.	4	2,871	1,031	1,233	655	83	18	31

Source: Federal Bureau of Investigation, Hate Crime Statistics 2013

Identity Theft Consumer Complaints

Area	Complaints	Complaints per 100,000 Population	Rank[2]
MSA[1]	7,076	112.1	37
U.S.	332,646	104.3	-

Note: (1) Figures cover the Houston-The Woodlands-Sugar Land, TX Metropolitan Statistical Area—see Appendix B for areas included; (2) Rank ranges from 1 to 380 where 1 indicates greatest number of identity theft complaints per 100,000 population
Source: Federal Trade Commission, Consumer Sentinel Network Data Book for January–December 2014

Fraud and Other Consumer Complaints

Area	Complaints	Complaints per 100,000 Population	Rank[2]
MSA[1]	24,932	394.9	144
U.S.	2,250,205	705.7	-

Note: (1) Figures cover the Houston-The Woodlands-Sugar Land, TX Metropolitan Statistical Area—see Appendix B for areas included; (2) Rank ranges from 1 to 380 where 1 indicates greatest number of identity theft complaints per 100,000 population
Source: Federal Trade Commission, Consumer Sentinel Network Data Book for January–December 2014

RECREATION

Culture

Dance[1]	Theatre[1]	Instrumental Music[1]	Vocal Music[1]	Series and Festivals	Museums and Art Galleries[2]	Zoos and Aquariums[3]
8	11	7	6	11	101	2

Note: (1) Professional perfoming groups; (2) Based on organizations with SIC code 8412; (3) AZA-accredited
Source: The Grey House Performing Arts Directory, 2015-16; Association of Zoos & Aquariums, AZA Member Zoos & Aquariums, April 2015; www.AccuLeads.com, April 2015

Professional Sports Teams

Team Name	League	Year Established
Houston Astros	Major League Baseball (MLB)	1962
Houston Dynamo	Major League Soccer (MLS)	2006
Houston Rockets	National Basketball Association (NBA)	1971
Houston Texans	National Football League (NFL)	2002

Note: Includes teams located in the Houston-The Woodlands-Sugar Land, TX Metropolitan Statistical Area.
Source: Wikipedia, Major Professional Sports Teams of the United States and Canada, April 2015

CLIMATE

Average and Extreme Temperatures

Temperature	Jan	Feb	Mar	Apr	May	Jun	Jul	Aug	Sep	Oct	Nov	Dec	Yr.
Extreme High (°F)	84	91	91	95	97	103	104	107	102	94	89	83	107
Average High (°F)	61	65	73	79	85	91	93	93	89	81	72	65	79
Average Temp. (°F)	51	54	62	69	75	81	83	83	79	70	61	54	69
Average Low (°F)	41	43	51	58	65	71	73	73	68	58	50	43	58
Extreme Low (°F)	12	20	22	31	44	52	62	62	48	32	19	7	7

Note: Figures cover the years 1969-1990
Source: National Climatic Data Center, International Station Meteorological Climate Summary, 9/96

Average Precipitation/Snowfall/Humidity

Precip./Humidity	Jan	Feb	Mar	Apr	May	Jun	Jul	Aug	Sep	Oct	Nov	Dec	Yr.
Avg. Precip. (in.)	3.3	2.7	3.3	3.3	5.6	4.9	3.7	3.7	4.8	4.7	3.7	3.3	46.9
Avg. Snowfall (in.)	Tr	Tr	0	0	0	0	0	0	0	0	Tr	Tr	Tr
Avg. Rel. Hum. 6am (%)	85	86	87	89	91	92	93	93	93	91	89	86	90
Avg. Rel. Hum. 3pm (%)	58	55	54	54	57	56	55	55	57	53	55	57	55

Note: Figures cover the years 1969-1990; Tr = Trace amounts (<0.05 in. of rain; <0.5 in. of snow)
Source: National Climatic Data Center, International Station Meteorological Climate Summary, 9/96

Weather Conditions

Temperature			Daytime Sky			Precipitation		
32°F & below	45°F & below	90°F & above	Clear	Partly cloudy	Cloudy	0.01 inch or more precip.	0.1 inch or more snow/ice	Thunder-storms
21	87	96	83	168	114	101	1	62

Note: Figures are average number of days per year and cover the years 1969-1990
Source: National Climatic Data Center, International Station Meteorological Climate Summary, 9/96

HAZARDOUS WASTE

Superfund Sites

Houston has seven hazardous waste sites on the EPA's Superfund Final National Priorities List: **Crystal Chemical Co.; Geneva Industries/Fuhrmann Energy; Jones Road Ground Water Plume; Many Diversified Interests, Inc.; North Cavalcade Street; Sol Lynn/Industrial Transformers; South Cavalcade Street**. There are a total of 1,322 Superfund sites on the list in the U.S. *U.S. Environmental Protection Agency, Final National Priorities List, April 14, 2015*

AIR & WATER QUALITY

Air Quality Trends: Ozone

	2004	2005	2006	2007	2008	2009	2010	2011	2012	2013
MSA[1]	0.092	0.087	0.090	0.079	0.074	0.079	0.078	0.082	0.081	0.074

Note: (1) Data covers the Houston-The Woodlands-Sugar Land, TX Metropolitan Statistical Area—see Appendix B for areas included. The values shown are the composite ozone concentration averages among trend sites based on the highest fourth daily maximum 8-hour concentration in parts per million. These trends are based on sites having an adequate record of monitoring data during the trend period. Data from exceptional events are included.
Source: U.S. Environmental Protection Agency, Air Quality Monitoring Information, "Air Quality Trends by City, 2000-2013"

Air Quality Index

Area	Percent of Days when Air Quality was...[2]					AQI Statistics[2]	
	Good	Moderate	Unhealthy for Sensitive Groups	Unhealthy	Very Unhealthy	Maximum	Median
MSA[1]	43.6	54.5	1.9	0.0	0.0	150	53

Note: (1) Data covers the Houston-The Woodlands-Sugar Land, TX Metropolitan Statistical Area—see Appendix B for areas included; (2) Based on 365 days with AQI data in 2014. Air Quality Index (AQI) is an index for reporting daily air quality. EPA calculates the AQI for five major air pollutants regulated by the Clean Air Act: ground-level ozone, particle pollution (aka particulate matter), carbon monoxide, sulfur dioxide, and nitrogen dioxide. The AQI runs from 0 to 500. The higher the AQI value, the greater the level of air pollution and the greater the health concern. There are six AQI categories: "Good" AQI is between 0 and 50. Air quality is considered satisfactory; "Moderate" AQI is between 51 and 100. Air quality is acceptable; "Unhealthy for Sensitive Groups" When AQI values are between 101 and 150, members of sensitive groups may experience health effects; "Unhealthy" When AQI values are between 151 and 200 everyone may begin to experience health effects; "Very Unhealthy" AQI values between 201 and 300 trigger a health alert; "Hazardous" AQI values over 300 trigger warnings of emergency conditions (not shown).
Source: U.S. Environmental Protection Agency, Air Quality Index Report, 2014

Air Quality Index Pollutants

Area	Percent of Days when AQI Pollutant was...[2]					
	Carbon Monoxide	Nitrogen Dioxide	Ozone	Sulfur Dioxide	Particulate Matter 2.5	Particulate Matter 10
MSA[1]	0.0	5.8	22.2	0.8	65.8	5.5

Note: (1) Data covers the Houston-The Woodlands-Sugar Land, TX Metropolitan Statistical Area—see Appendix B for areas included; (2) Based on 365 days with AQI data in 2014. The Air Quality Index (AQI) is an index for reporting daily air quality. EPA calculates the AQI for five major air pollutants regulated by the Clean Air Act: ground-level ozone, particle pollution (also known as particulate matter), carbon monoxide, sulfur dioxide, and nitrogen dioxide. The AQI runs from 0 to 500. The higher the AQI value, the greater the level of air pollution and the greater the health concern.
Source: U.S. Environmental Protection Agency, Air Quality Index Report, 2014

Maximum Air Pollutant Concentrations: Particulate Matter, Ozone, CO and Lead

	Particulate Matter 10 (ug/m^3)	Particulate Matter 2.5 Wtd AM (ug/m^3)	Particulate Matter 2.5 24-Hr (ug/m^3)	Ozone (ppm)	Carbon Monoxide (ppm)	Lead (ug/m^3)
MSA[1] Level	80	11.3	27	0.084	2	0.01
NAAQS[2]	150	15	35	0.075	9	0.15
Met NAAQS[2]	Yes	Yes	Yes	No	Yes	Yes

Note: (1) Data covers the Houston-The Woodlands-Sugar Land, TX Metropolitan Statistical Area—see Appendix B for areas included; Data from exceptional events are included; (2) National Ambient Air Quality Standards; ppm = parts per million; ug/m^3 = micrograms per cubic meter; n/a not available.
Concentrations: Particulate Matter 10 (coarse particulate)—highest second maximum 24-hour concentration; Particulate Matter 2.5 Wtd AM (fine particulate)—highest weighted annual mean concentration; Particulate Matter 2.5 24-Hour (fine particulate)—highest 98th percentile 24-hour concentration; Ozone—highest fourth daily maximum 8-hour concentration; Carbon Monoxide—highest second maximum non-overlapping 8-hour concentration; Lead—maximum running 3-month average
Source: U.S. Environmental Protection Agency, Air Quality Monitoring Information, "Air Quality Statistics by City, 2013"

Maximum Air Pollutant Concentrations: Nitrogen Dioxide and Sulfur Dioxide

	Nitrogen Dioxide AM (ppb)	Nitrogen Dioxide 1-Hr (ppb)	Sulfur Dioxide AM (ppb)	Sulfur Dioxide 1-Hr (ppb)	Sulfur Dioxide 24-Hr (ppb)
MSA[1] Level	13	58	n/a	35	n/a
NAAQS[2]	53	100	30	75	140
Met NAAQS[2]	Yes	Yes	n/a	Yes	n/a

Note: (1) Data covers the Houston-The Woodlands-Sugar Land, TX Metropolitan Statistical Area—see Appendix B for areas included; Data from exceptional events are included; (2) National Ambient Air Quality Standards; ppm = parts per million; ug/m^3 = micrograms per cubic meter; n/a not available.
Concentrations: Nitrogen Dioxide AM—highest arithmetic mean concentration; Nitrogen Dioxide 1-Hr—highest 98th percentile 1-hour daily maximum concentration; Sulfur Dioxide AM—highest annual mean concentration; Sulfur Dioxide 1-Hr—highest 99th percentile 1-hour daily maximum concentration; Sulfur Dioxide 24-Hr—highest second maximum 24-hour concentration
Source: U.S. Environmental Protection Agency, Air Quality Monitoring Information, "Air Quality Statistics by City, 2013"

Drinking Water

Water System Name	Pop. Served	Primary Water Source Type	Violations[1] Health Based	Violations[1] Monitoring/ Reporting
City of Houston	2,201,027	Surface	0	0

Note: (1) Based on violation data from January 1, 2014 to December 31, 2014 (includes unresolved violations from earlier years)
Source: U.S. Environmental Protection Agency, Office of Ground Water and Drinking Water, Safe Drinking Water Information System (based on data extracted January 27, 2015)

Huntsville, Alabama

Background

The seat of Madison County, Huntsville is richly evocative of the antebellum Deep South. It is also a uniquely cosmopolitan town that remains one of the South's fastest growing, with the highest per capita income in the Southeast.

Huntsville became the seat of Madison County, named for President James Madison, when that jurisdiction was created in 1808. Originally home to Cherokee and Chickasaw Indians, the Huntsville area was rich in forests and game animals. The town itself is named for John Hunt, a Virginia Revolutionary War veteran who built a cabin in 1805 on what is now the corner of Bank Street and Oak Avenue.

The fertility of the valley began to attract both smaller farmers and wealthy plantation investors. Leroy Pope, having donated land to the embryonic municipality, wished to rename it Twickenham, after a London suburb that was home to his relative, the poet Alexander Pope. However, resentment against all things British, which surged following the War of 1812, was sufficient to reestablish Huntsville under its original moniker.

Huntsville was the largest town in the Alabama Territory by 1819, the same year Alabama received statehood. The town was the site of the state's first constitutional convention and briefly served as the state capital. It quickly became a major hub for the sale and processing of corn, tobacco, and cotton, with the last crop becoming the economic mainstay. The establishment of textile mills allowed the town to benefit from both primary production and finished products. In 1852, the last leg of the Memphis and Charleston Railway was completed, establishing Huntsville as a major center in a larger regional marketplace. By the middle of the nineteenth century, the region's planters, merchants, and shippers had transformed Huntsville into one of the main commercial cities in the South.

Because many wealthy residents had remained loyal to the Union at the outset of the Civil War, the town was largely undamaged by occupying forces and, as a result, Huntsville boasts one of the largest collections of undamaged antebellum houses in the South. Walking tours of the Twickenham historic district offer the charms of the 1819 Weeden House Museum and the 1860 Huntsville Depot Museum. Restored nineteenth-century cabins and farm buildings are displayed at the mountaintop Burritt Museum and Park.

Huntsville's U.S. Space and Rocket Center, the state's largest tourist attraction, showcases space technology. It is also the home of Space Camp, providing residential and day camp educational opportunities for children and adults designed to promote science, engineering, aviation and exploration. The Huntsville Botanical Garden, features year-long floral and aquatic gardens, and the Huntsville Museum of Art features both contemporary and classical exhibits.

The city's modern Von Braun Center hosts national and international trade shows and conventions and local sports teams; it also has a concert hall and playhouse. The city also has an outstanding symphony orchestra.

Institutions of higher learning include the University of Alabama in Huntsville (established 1950), and Oakwood College (1896), while Alabama A&M University (1875) is in nearby Normal, Alabama.

Redstone Arsenal, home to the U.S. Army Aviation and Missile Command, is the main engine that propelled Huntsville into the high-tech hub it is today, and is the United States' most crucial strategic and research site for the development and implementation of rocketry, aviation, and related programs. In 1950, German rocket scientists, most notably the famous Wernher von Braun, came to the Redstone Arsenal to develop rockets for the U.S. Army. Within the decade, the Redstone complex had developed the rocket that launched America's first satellite into space, and later, the rockets that put astronauts into space and eventually landed them on the moon.

Despite the economic downturn of the early 1990s, Huntsville has seen progress on the manufacturing front. More than forty Fortune 500 companies have operations in Huntsville.

Huntsville enjoys a mild, temperate climate. Only four to five weeks during the middle of winter see temperatures below freezing. While substantial winter weather and blizzards were frequent in the 1990s, Huntsville has now gone over 13 years without significant snowfall. Rainfall is fairly abundant.

Rankings

Business/Finance Rankings

- The Huntsville metro area appeared on the Milken Institute "2013 Best Performing Cities" list. Rank: #66 out of 200 large metro areas. Criteria: job growth; wage and salary growth; high-tech output growth. *Milken Institute, "Best-Performing Cities 2014," January 2015*
- *Forbes* ranked the 200 most populous metro areas to determine the nation's "Best Places for Business and Careers." The Huntsville metro area was ranked #90. Criteria: costs (business and living); job growth (past and projected); income growth; educational attainment (college and high school); projected economic growth; cultural and recreational opportunities; net migration patterns; number of highly ranked colleges. *Forbes, "The Best Places for Business and Careers 2014," July 23, 2014*

Education Rankings

- Personal finance website *WalletHub* analyzed the 150 largest U.S. metropolitan statistical areas to determine where the most educated Americans are choosing to settle. Criteria: educational attainment; percentage of workers with jobs in computer, engineering, and science fields; quality and size of each metro area's universities. Huntsville was ranked #25 (#1 = most educated city). *www.WalletHub.com, "2014's Most and Least Educated Cities*

Environmental Rankings

- The Huntsville metro area came in at #258 for the relative comfort of its climate on Sperling's list of "chill cities," as measured by the Sperling Heat Index. All 361 metro areas are included. Criteria included daytime high temperatures, nighttime low temperatures, dew point, and relative humidity at the high temperatures. *www.bertsperling.com, "Sperling's Chill Cities," July 18, 2013*
- Sperling's BestPlaces assessed 379 metropolitan areas of the United States for the likelihood of dangerously extreme weather events or earthquakes. In general the Southeast and South-Central regions have the highest risk of weather extremes and earthquakes, while the Pacific Northwest enjoys the lowest risk. Of the least risky metropolitan areas, the Huntsville metro area was ranked #351. *www.bestplaces.net, "Safest Places from Natural Disasters," April 2011*
- Huntsville was highlighted as one of the top 25 cleanest metro areas for short-term particle pollution (24-hour PM 2.5) in the U.S. during 2011 through 2013. Monitors in these cities reported no days with unhealthful PM 2.5 levels. *American Lung Association, State of the Air 2015*

Health/Fitness Rankings

- The Huntsville metro area appeared in the 2013 Gallup-Healthways Well-Being Index. The area ranked #81 out of 189. The Gallup-Healthways Well-Being Index score is an average of six sub-indexes, which individually examine life evaluation, emotional health, work environment, physical health, healthy behaviors, and access to basic necessities. Results are based on telephone interviews conducted as part of the Gallup-Healthways Well-Being Index survey January 2–December 29, 2012, and January 2–December 30, 2013, with a random sample of 531,630 adults, aged 18 and older, living in metropolitan areas in the 50 U.S. states and the District of Columbia. *Gallup-Healthways, "State of American Well-Being," March 25, 2014*

Real Estate Rankings

- Huntsville was ranked #125 out of 275 metro areas in terms of house price appreciation in 2014 (#1 = highest rate). *Federal Housing Finance Agency, House Price Index, 4th Quarter 2014*

Safety Rankings

- Allstate ranked the 200 largest cities in America in terms of driver safety. Huntsville ranked #5. Allstate researchers analyzed internal property damage claims over a two-year period from January 2011 to December 2012. A weighted average of the two-year numbers determined the annual percentages. *Allstate, "Allstate America's Best Drivers Report, 2014"*
- The National Insurance Crime Bureau ranked 380 metro areas in the U.S. in terms of per capita rates of vehicle theft. The Huntsville metro area ranked #168 (#1 = highest rate). Criteria: number of vehicle theft offenses per 100,000 inhabitants in 2012. *National Insurance Crime Bureau, "Hot Spots 2012," June 26, 2013*

Seniors/Retirement Rankings

- From its Best Cities for Successful Aging indexes, the Milken Institute generated rankings for metropolitan areas, weighing data in eight categories—health care, wellness, living arrangements, transportation, financial characteristics, education and employment opportunities, community engagement, and overall livability. The Huntsville metro area was ranked #124 overall in the small metro area category. *Milken Institute, "Best Cities for Successful Aging, 2014"*
- Huntsville was chosen in the "College Town" category of CNNMoney's list of the 25 best places to retire." Criteria include: type of location (big city, small town, resort area, college town); median home prices; top state income tax rate. *CNNMoney, "25 Best Places to Retire," December 17, 2012*

Sports/Recreation Rankings

- Huntsville was selected as one of the most playful cities in the U.S. by KaBOOM! The organization's Playful City USA initiative honors cities and towns across the nation for a vision, plan and commitment to creating an agenda for play. Criteria: creating a local play commission or task force; designing an annual action plan for play; conducting a play space audit; outlining a financial investment in play for the current fiscal year; and proclaiming and celebrating an annual "play day." *KaBOOM! National Campaign for Play, "2013 Playful City USA Communities"*

Business Environment

CITY FINANCES

City Government Finances

Component	2012 ($000)	2012 ($ per capita)
Total Revenues	899,541	4,995
Total Expenditures	897,059	4,981
Debt Outstanding	774,765	4,302
Cash and Securities[1]	374,519	2,079

Note: (1) Cash and security holdings of a government at the close of its fiscal year, including those of its dependent agencies, utilities, and liquor stores.
Source: U.S Census Bureau, State & Local Government Finances 2012

City Government Revenue by Source

Source	2012 ($000)	2012 ($ per capita)
General Revenue		
From Federal Government	1,895	11
From State Government	26,351	146
From Local Governments	0	0
Taxes		
Property	58,862	327
Sales and Gross Receipts	156,008	866
Personal Income	0	0
Corporate Income	0	0
Motor Vehicle License	0	0
Other Taxes	3,069	17
Current Charges	62,706	348
Liquor Store	0	0
Utility	570,591	3,168
Employee Retirement	0	0

Source: U.S Census Bureau, State & Local Government Finances 2012

City Government Expenditures by Function

Function	2012 ($000)	2012 ($ per capita)	2012 (%)
General Direct Expenditures			
Air Transportation	0	0	0.0
Corrections	0	0	0.0
Education	0	0	0.0
Employment Security Administration	0	0	0.0
Financial Administration	10,185	57	1.1
Fire Protection	28,811	160	3.2
General Public Buildings	0	0	0.0
Governmental Administration, Other	11,200	62	1.2
Health	2,648	15	0.3
Highways	22,189	123	2.5
Hospitals	0	0	0.0
Housing and Community Development	7,913	44	0.9
Interest on General Debt	27,275	151	3.0
Judicial and Legal	4,524	25	0.5
Libraries	5,639	31	0.6
Parking	1,642	9	0.2
Parks and Recreation	30,324	168	3.4
Police Protection	41,685	231	4.6
Public Welfare	614	3	0.1
Sewerage	29,708	165	3.3
Solid Waste Management	0	0	0.0
Veterans' Services	0	0	0.0
Liquor Store	0	0	0.0
Utility	559,642	3,107	62.4
Employee Retirement	0	0	0.0

Source: U.S Census Bureau, State & Local Government Finances 2012

DEMOGRAPHICS

Population Growth

Area	1990 Census	2000 Census	2010 Census	Population Growth (%)	
				1990-2000	2000-2010
City	161,842	158,216	180,105	-2.2	13.8
MSA[1]	293,047	342,376	417,593	16.8	22.0
U.S.	248,709,873	281,421,906	308,745,538	13.2	9.7

Note: (1) Figures cover the Huntsville, AL Metropolitan Statistical Area—see Appendix B for areas included
Source: U.S. Census Bureau, Census 1990, 2000, 2010

Household Size

Area	Persons in Household (%)							Average Household Size
	One	Two	Three	Four	Five	Six	Seven or More	
City	37.1	33.0	13.8	9.9	4.2	1.2	0.8	2.31
MSA[1]	29.3	34.6	15.9	12.7	5.0	1.4	0.9	2.50
U.S.	27.7	33.6	15.7	13.1	6.0	2.3	1.5	2.64

Note: (1) Figures cover the Huntsville, AL Metropolitan Statistical Area—see Appendix B for areas included
Source: U.S. Census Bureau, 2011-2013 American Community Survey 3-Year Estimates

Race

Area	White Alone[2] (%)	Black Alone[2] (%)	Asian Alone[2] (%)	AIAN[3] Alone[2] (%)	NHOPI[4] Alone[2] (%)	Other Race Alone[2] (%)	Two or More Races (%)
City	62.3	31.0	2.1	0.5	0.1	1.2	2.9
MSA[1]	71.5	22.0	2.2	0.6	0.1	1.1	2.5
U.S.	73.9	12.6	5.0	0.8	0.2	4.7	2.9

Note: (1) Figures cover the Huntsville, AL Metropolitan Statistical Area—see Appendix B for areas included; (2) Alone is defined as not being in combination with one or more other races; (3) American Indian and Alaska Native; (4) Native Hawaiian and Other Pacific Islander
Source: U.S. Census Bureau, 2011-2013 American Community Survey 3-Year Estimates

Hispanic or Latino Origin

Area	Total (%)	Mexican (%)	Puerto Rican (%)	Cuban (%)	Other (%)
City	5.8	3.9	0.8	0.1	1.0
MSA[1]	4.9	3.5	0.6	0.1	0.7
U.S.	16.9	10.8	1.6	0.6	3.8

Note: Persons of Hispanic or Latino origin can be of any race; (1) Figures cover the Huntsville, AL Metropolitan Statistical Area—see Appendix B for areas included
Source: U.S. Census Bureau, 2011-2013 American Community Survey 3-Year Estimates

Segregation

Type	Segregation Indices[1]				Percent Change		
	1990	2000	2010	2010 Rank[2]	1990-2000	1990-2010	2000-2010
Black/White	n/a	n/a	n/a	n/a	n/a	n/a	n/a
Asian/White	n/a	n/a	n/a	n/a	n/a	n/a	n/a
Hispanic/White	n/a	n/a	n/a	n/a	n/a	n/a	n/a

Note: All figures cover the Metropolitan Statistical Area—see Appendix B for areas included; Figures are based on an analysis of 1990, 2000, and 2010 Census Decennial Census tract data by William H. Frey, Brookings Institution and the University of Michigan Social Science Data Analysis Network. In this analysis all racial groups (whites, blacks, and asians) are non-Hispanic members of those races. Hispanics are shown as a separate category;
(1) Segregation Indices are Dissimilarity Indices that measure the degree to which the minority group is distributed differently than whites across census tracts. They range from 0 (complete integration) to 100 (complete segregation) where the value indicates the percentage of the minority group that needs to move to be distributed exactly like whites; (2) Ranges from 1 (most segregated) to 102 (least segregated); n/a not available.
Source: www.CensusScope.org

Ancestry

Area	German	Irish	English	American	Italian	Polish	French[2]	Scottish	Dutch
City	10.7	8.8	9.6	9.9	2.7	1.0	1.9	2.3	1.0
MSA[1]	10.1	9.0	9.3	14.7	2.1	1.0	1.8	2.0	0.9
U.S.	14.9	10.8	8.0	7.4	5.5	3.0	2.7	1.7	1.4

Note: Figures are the percentage of the total population reporting a particular ancestry. The nine most commonly reported ancestries in the U.S. are shown. Figures include multiple ancestries (e.g. if a person reported being Irish and Italian, they were included in both columns); (1) Figures cover the Huntsville, AL Metropolitan Statistical Area—see Appendix B for areas included; (2) Excludes Basque
Source: U.S. Census Bureau, 2011-2013 American Community Survey 3-Year Estimates

Foreign-Born Population

Area	Percent of Population Born in								
	Any Foreign Country	Mexico	Asia	Europe	Carribean	South America	Central America[2]	Africa	Canada
City	6.3	1.7	2.0	0.9	0.4	0.2	0.2	0.7	0.1
MSA[1]	5.2	1.5	1.9	0.8	0.3	0.1	0.1	0.4	0.1
U.S.	13.0	3.7	3.8	1.5	1.2	0.9	1.0	0.6	0.3

Note: (1) Figures cover the Huntsville, AL Metropolitan Statistical Area—see Appendix B for areas included; (2) Excludes Mexico.
Source: U.S. Census Bureau, 2011-2013 American Community Survey 3-Year Estimates

Marital Status

Area	Never Married	Now Married[2]	Separated	Widowed	Divorced
City	35.7	42.0	2.5	6.0	13.8
MSA[1]	29.7	50.5	2.0	5.7	12.1
U.S.	32.7	48.1	2.2	6.0	11.0

Note: Figures are percentages and cover the population 15 years of age and older; (1) Figures cover the Huntsville, AL Metropolitan Statistical Area—see Appendix B for areas included; (2) Excludes separated
Source: U.S. Census Bureau, 2011-2013 American Community Survey 3-Year Estimates

Disability Status

Area	All Ages	Under 18 Years Old	18 to 64 Years Old	65 Years and Over
City	13.2	4.2	11.0	37.7
MSA[1]	12.2	3.5	10.2	37.8
U.S.	12.3	4.1	10.2	36.3

Note: Figures show percent of the civilian noninstitutionalized population that reported having a disability. Disability status is determined from from six types of difficulty: vision, hearing, cognitive, ambulatory, self-care, and independent living. For children under 5 years old, hearing and vision difficulty are used to determine disability status. For children between the ages of 5 and 14, disability status is determined from hearing, vision, cognitive, ambulatory, and self-care difficulties. For people aged 15 years and older, they are considered to have a disability if they have difficulty with any one of the six difficulty types; (1) Figures cover the Huntsville, AL Metropolitan Statistical Area—see Appendix B for areas included.
Source: U.S. Census Bureau, 2011-2013 American Community Survey 3-Year Estimates

Age

Area	Percent of Population									Median Age
	Under Age 5	Age 5–19	Age 20–34	Age 35–44	Age 45–54	Age 55–64	Age 65–74	Age 75–84	Age 85+	
City	6.2	18.5	22.8	12.0	14.7	11.7	7.7	4.5	1.8	36.7
MSA[1]	6.1	19.8	20.4	13.0	15.8	12.1	7.4	4.0	1.4	37.9
U.S.	6.4	19.9	20.7	12.9	14.1	12.3	7.6	4.2	1.9	37.4

Note: (1) Figures cover the Huntsville, AL Metropolitan Statistical Area—see Appendix B for areas included
Source: U.S. Census Bureau, 2011-2013 American Community Survey 3-Year Estimates

Gender

Area	Males	Females	Males per 100 Females
City	89,776	93,926	95.6
MSA[1]	211,831	218,536	96.9
U.S.	154,451,010	159,410,713	96.9

Note: (1) Figures cover the Huntsville, AL Metropolitan Statistical Area—see Appendix B for areas included
Source: U.S. Census Bureau, 2011-2013 American Community Survey 3-Year Estimates

Religious Groups by Family

Area	Catholic	Baptist	Non-Den.	Methodist[2]	Lutheran	LDS[3]	Pente-costal	Presby-terian[4]	Muslim[5]	Judaism
MSA[1]	4.0	27.6	3.2	7.5	0.7	1.2	1.2	1.7	0.2	0.2
U.S.	19.1	9.3	4.0	4.0	2.3	2.0	1.9	1.6	0.8	0.7

Note: Figures are the number of adherents as a percentage of the total population; (1) Figures cover the Huntsville, AL Metropolitan Statistical Area—see Appendix B for areas included; (2) Methodist/Pietist; (3) Latter Day Saints; (4) Reformed; (5) Figures are estimates
Source: Association of Statisticians of American Religious Bodies, 2010 U.S. Religion Census: Religious Congregations & Membership Study

Religious Groups by Tradition

Area	Catholic	Evangelical Protestant	Mainline Protestant	Other Tradition	Black Protestant	Orthodox
MSA[1]	4.0	33.3	9.7	1.9	1.8	0.1
U.S.	19.1	16.2	7.3	4.3	1.6	0.3

Note: Figures are the number of adherents as a percentage of the total population; (1) Figures cover the Huntsville, AL Metropolitan Statistical Area—see Appendix B for areas included
Source: Association of Statisticians of American Religious Bodies, 2010 U.S. Religion Census: Religious Congregations & Membership Study

ECONOMY

Gross Metropolitan Product

Area	2012	2013	2014	2015	Rank[2]
MSA[1]	21.7	22.1	22.9	24.1	99

Note: Figures are in billions of dollars; (1) Figures cover the Huntsville, AL Metropolitan Statistical Area—see Appendix B for areas included; (2) Rank is based on 2015 data and ranges from 1 to 363
Source: The U.S. Conference of Mayors, U.S. Metro Economies: GMP and Employment 2013-2015, June 2014

Economic Growth

Area	2010-12 (%)	2013 (%)	2014 (%)	2015 (%)	Rank[2]
MSA[1]	0.4	0.6	2.1	3.3	102
U.S.	2.1	2.0	2.3	3.2	-

Note: Figures are real gross metropolitan product (GMP) growth rates and represent annual average percent change; (1) Figures cover the Huntsville, AL Metropolitan Statistical Area—see Appendix B for areas included; (2) Rank is based on 2015 data and ranges from 1 to 363
Source: The U.S. Conference of Mayors, U.S. Metro Economies: GMP and Employment 2013-2015, June 2014

Metropolitan Area Exports

Area	2008	2009	2010	2011	2012	2013	Rank[2]
MSA[1]	1,079.3	1,136.5	986.8	1,293.3	1,491.5	1,518.7	123

Note: Figures are in millions of dollars; (1) Figures cover the Huntsville, AL Metropolitan Statistical Area—see Appendix B for areas included; (2) Rank is based on 2013 data and ranges from 1 to 387
Source: U.S. Department of Commerce, International Trade Administration, Office of Trade & Industry Information, Manufacturing & Services, data extracted April 3, 2015

Building Permits

Area	Single-Family			Multi-Family			Total		
	2013	2014	Pct. Chg.	2013	2014	Pct. Chg.	2013	2014	Pct. Chg.
City	1,000	897	-10.3	306	977	219.3	1,306	1,874	43.5
MSA[1]	1,944	1,784	-8.2	306	1,033	237.6	2,250	2,817	25.2
U.S.	620,802	634,597	2.2	370,020	411,766	11.3	990,822	1,046,363	5.6

Note: (1) Figures cover the Huntsville, AL Metropolitan Statistical Area—see Appendix B for areas included; Figures represent new, privately-owned housing units authorized (unadjusted data); All permit data are based on estimates with imputation.
Source: U.S. Census Bureau, Manufacturing, Mining, and Construction Statistics, Building Permits, 2013, 2014

Bankruptcy Filings

Area	Business Filings			Nonbusiness Filings		
	2013	2014	% Chg.	2013	2014	% Chg.
Madison County	40	35	-12.5	1,425	1,334	-6.4
U.S.	33,212	26,983	-18.8	1,038,720	909,812	-12.4

Note: Business filings include Chapter 7, Chapter 11, Chapter 12, and Chapter 13; Nonbusiness filings include Chapter 7, Chapter 11, and Chapter 13
Source: Administrative Office of the U.S. Courts, Business and Nonbusiness Bankruptcy, County Cases Commenced by Chapter of the Bankruptcy Code, During the 12- Month Period Ending December 31, 2013 and Business and Nonbusiness Bankruptcy, County Cases Commenced by Chapter of the Bankruptcy Code, During the 12- Month Period Ending December 31, 2014

Housing Vacancy Rates

Area	Gross Vacancy Rate[2] (%)			Year-Round Vacancy Rate[3] (%)			Rental Vacancy Rate[4] (%)			Homeowner Vacancy Rate[5] (%)		
	2012	2013	2014	2012	2013	2014	2012	2013	2014	2012	2013	2014
MSA[1]	n/a	n/a	n/a	n/a	n/a	n/a	n/a	n/a	n/a	n/a	n/a	n/a
U.S.	13.8	13.6	13.4	10.8	10.7	10.4	8.7	8.3	7.6	2.0	2.0	1.9

Note: (1) Figures cover the Huntsville, AL Metropolitan Statistical Area—see Appendix B for areas included; (2) The percentage of the total housing inventory that is vacant; (3) The percentage of the housing inventory (excluding seasonal units) that is year-round vacant; (4) The percentage of rental inventory that is vacant for rent; (5) The percentage of homeowner inventory that is vacant for sale; n/a not available
Source: U.S. Census Bureau, Housing Vacancies and Homeownership Annual Statistics: 2014

INCOME

Income

Area	Per Capita ($)	Median Household ($)	Average Household ($)
City	29,649	47,575	68,995
MSA[1]	29,792	54,838	74,829
U.S.	27,884	52,176	72,897

Note: (1) Figures cover the Huntsville, AL Metropolitan Statistical Area—see Appendix B for areas included
Source: U.S. Census Bureau, 2011-2013 American Community Survey 3-Year Estimates

Household Income Distribution

Area	Percent of Households Earning							
	Under $15,000	$15,000 -24,999	$25,000 -34,999	$35,000 -49,999	$50,000 -74,999	$75,000 -99,000	$100,000 -149,999	$150,000 and up
City	15.5	11.9	10.2	13.9	15.8	10.6	12.9	9.2
MSA[1]	12.5	9.8	10.2	13.5	16.7	12.1	15.2	10.3
U.S.	13.0	10.9	10.3	13.6	17.9	11.9	12.7	9.6

Note: (1) Figures cover the Huntsville, AL Metropolitan Statistical Area—see Appendix B for areas included
Source: U.S. Census Bureau, 2011-2013 American Community Survey 3-Year Estimates

Poverty Rate

Area	All Ages	Under 18 Years Old	18 to 64 Years Old	65 Years and Over
City	17.6	26.5	17.0	6.8
MSA[1]	13.6	19.1	12.8	7.6
U.S.	15.9	22.4	14.8	9.5

Note: Figures are percentage of people whose income during the past 12 months was below the poverty level; (1) Figures cover the Huntsville, AL Metropolitan Statistical Area—see Appendix B for areas included
Source: U.S. Census Bureau, 2011-2013 American Community Survey 3-Year Estimates

EMPLOYMENT

Labor Force and Employment

Area	Civilian Labor Force			Workers Employed		
	Dec. 2013	Dec. 2014	% Chg.	Dec. 2013	Dec. 2014	% Chg.
City	90,673	89,429	-1.4	85,404	84,932	-0.6
MSA[1]	209,521	206,534	-1.4	197,294	196,222	-0.5
U.S.	154,408,000	155,521,000	0.7	144,423,000	147,190,000	1.9

Note: Data is not seasonally adjusted and covers workers 16 years of age and older; (1) Figures cover the Huntsville, AL Metropolitan Statistical Area—see Appendix B for areas included
Source: Bureau of Labor Statistics, Local Area Unemployment Statistics

Unemployment Rate

Area	2014											
	Jan.	Feb.	Mar.	Apr.	May	Jun.	Jul.	Aug.	Sep.	Oct.	Nov.	Dec.
City	6.7	7.1	6.8	5.7	6.0	6.9	7.1	6.4	5.6	5.4	5.2	5.0
MSA[1]	6.8	7.2	6.8	5.7	6.0	6.8	6.9	6.5	5.6	5.4	5.1	5.0
U.S.	7.0	7.0	6.8	5.9	6.1	6.3	6.5	6.3	5.7	5.5	5.5	5.4

Note: Data is not seasonally adjusted and covers workers 16 years of age and older; (1) Figures cover the Huntsville, AL Metropolitan Statistical Area—see Appendix B for areas included
Source: Bureau of Labor Statistics, Local Area Unemployment Statistics

Employment by Occupation

Occupation Classification	City (%)	MSA[1] (%)	U.S. (%)
Management, Business, Science, and Arts	41.1	41.9	36.2
Natural Resources, Construction, and Maintenance	6.1	8.0	9.0
Production, Transportation, and Material Moving	10.0	11.3	12.1
Sales and Office	25.0	23.6	24.4
Service	17.8	15.2	18.3

Note: Figures cover employed civilians 16 years of age and older; (1) Figures cover the Huntsville, AL Metropolitan Statistical Area—see Appendix B for areas included
Source: U.S. Census Bureau, 2011-2013 American Community Survey 3-Year Estimates

Employment by Industry

Sector	MSA[1]		U.S.
	Number of Employees	Percent of Total	Percent of Total
Construction, Mining, and Logging	7,800	3.6	5.0
Education and Health Services	20,500	9.4	15.5
Financial Activities	6,200	2.8	5.7
Government	49,100	22.5	15.8
Information	2,700	1.2	2.0
Leisure and Hospitality	18,800	8.6	10.3
Manufacturing	23,300	10.7	8.7
Other Services	7,100	3.2	4.0
Professional and Business Services	49,400	22.6	13.8
Retail Trade	24,800	11.4	11.4
Transportation, Warehousing, and Utilities	3,000	1.4	3.9
Wholesale Trade	5,800	2.7	4.2

Note: Figures are non-farm employment as of December 2014. Figures are not seasonally adjusted and include workers 16 years of age and older; (1) Figures cover the Huntsville, AL Metropolitan Statistical Area—see Appendix B for areas included; n/a not available
Source: Bureau of Labor Statistics, Current Employment Statistics, Employment, Hours, and Earnings

Occupations with Greatest Projected Employment Growth: 2012 – 2022

Occupation[1]	2012 Employment	2022 Projected Employment	Numeric Employment Change	Percent Employment Change
Registered Nurses	46,040	54,670	8,630	18.7
Team Assemblers	29,770	36,190	6,420	21.6
Retail Salespersons	59,400	65,790	6,390	10.8
Secretaries and Administrative Assistants, Except Legal, Medical, and Executive	42,330	48,520	6,190	14.6
Combined Food Preparation and Serving Workers, Including Fast Food	40,870	46,690	5,820	14.2
Personal Care Aides	10,730	15,650	4,920	45.9
Laborers and Freight, Stock, and Material Movers, Hand	34,790	38,910	4,120	11.8
Customer Service Representatives	30,640	34,660	4,020	13.1
Heavy and Tractor-Trailer Truck Drivers	31,860	35,690	3,830	12.0
Janitors and Cleaners, Except Maids and Housekeeping Cleaners	27,930	31,490	3,560	12.7

Note: Projections cover Alabama; (1) Sorted by numeric employment change
Source: www.projectionscentral.com, State Occupational Projections, 2012–2022 Long-Term Projections

Fastest Growing Occupations: 2012 – 2022

Occupation[1]	2012 Employment	2022 Projected Employment	Numeric Employment Change	Percent Employment Change
Engine and Other Machine Assemblers	2,150	3,430	1,280	59.7
Occupational Therapy Assistants	360	530	170	49.6
Personal Care Aides	10,730	15,650	4,920	45.9
Diagnostic Medical Sonographers	1,130	1,630	500	44.5
Physical Therapist Assistants	1,870	2,680	810	43.4
Computer Numerically Controlled Machine Tool Programmers, Metal and Plastic	290	410	120	42.3
Helpers—Brickmasons, Blockmasons, Stonemasons, and Tile and Marble Setters	340	490	150	42.0
Biological Science Teachers, Postsecondary	1,730	2,460	730	41.9
Insulation Workers, Mechanical	550	770	220	40.6
Home Health Aides	8,340	11,710	3,370	40.4

Note: Projections cover Alabama; (1) Sorted by percent employment change and excludes occupations with numeric employment change less than 100
Source: www.projectionscentral.com, State Occupational Projections, 2012–2022 Long-Term Projections

Average Wages

Occupation	$/Hr.	Occupation	$/Hr.
Accountants and Auditors	34.54	Maids and Housekeeping Cleaners	8.33
Automotive Mechanics	17.01	Maintenance and Repair Workers	19.40
Bookkeepers	17.38	Marketing Managers	63.98
Carpenters	16.42	Nuclear Medicine Technologists	24.87
Cashiers	9.01	Nurses, Licensed Practical	17.96
Clerks, General Office	11.37	Nurses, Registered	27.18
Clerks, Receptionists/Information	12.05	Nursing Assistants	11.48
Clerks, Shipping/Receiving	15.12	Packers and Packagers, Hand	10.90
Computer Programmers	43.72	Physical Therapists	39.13
Computer Systems Analysts	42.61	Postal Service Mail Carriers	24.20
Computer User Support Specialists	22.75	Real Estate Brokers	29.62
Cooks, Restaurant	9.92	Retail Salespersons	11.95
Dentists	89.18	Sales Reps., Exc. Tech./Scientific	29.32
Electrical Engineers	47.11	Sales Reps., Tech./Scientific	44.28
Electricians	21.89	Secretaries, Exc. Legal/Med./Exec.	17.41
Financial Managers	59.17	Security Guards	12.99
First-Line Supervisors/Managers, Sales	20.18	Surgeons	n/a
Food Preparation Workers	8.61	Teacher Assistants	8.90
General and Operations Managers	64.51	Teachers, Elementary School	24.50
Hairdressers/Cosmetologists	12.68	Teachers, Secondary School	24.60
Internists	n/a	Telemarketers	n/a
Janitors and Cleaners	10.21	Truck Drivers, Heavy/Tractor-Trailer	17.32
Landscaping/Groundskeeping Workers	10.31	Truck Drivers, Light/Delivery Svcs.	14.71
Lawyers	66.26	Waiters and Waitresses	9.69

Note: Wage data covers the Huntsville, AL Metropolitan Statistical Area—see Appendix B for areas included; Hourly wages for elementary/secondary school teachers and teacher assistants were calculated by the editors from annual wage data assuming a 40 hour work week; n/a not available.
Source: Bureau of Labor Statistics, Metro Area Occupational Employment and Wage Estimates, May 2014

TAXES

State Corporate Income Tax Rates

State	Tax Rate (%)	Income Brackets ($)	Num. of Brackets	Financial Institution Tax Rate (%)[a]	Federal Income Tax Ded.
Alabama	6.5	Flat rate	1	6.5	Yes

Note: Tax rates as of January 1, 2015; (a) Rates listed are the corporate income tax rate applied to financial institutions or excise taxes based on income. Some states have other taxes based upon the value of deposits or shares.
Source: Federation of Tax Administrators, "State Corporate Income Tax Rates, 2015"

State Individual Income Tax Rates

State	Tax Rate (%)	Income Brackets ($)	Num. of Brackets	Personal Exempt. ($)[1] Single	Personal Exempt. ($)[1] Dependents	Fed. Inc. Tax Ded.
Alabama	2.0 - 5.0	500 (b) - 3,001 (b)	3	1,500	500 (e)	Yes

Note: Tax rates as of January 1, 2015; Local- and county-level taxes are not included; n/a not applicable; (1) Married joint filers generally receive double the single exemption; (b) For joint returns, taxes are twice the tax on half the couple's income; (e) In Alabama, the per-dependent exemption is $1,000 for taxpayers with state AGI of $20,000 or less, $500 with AGI from $20,001 to $100,000, and $300 with AGI over $100,000.
Source: Federation of Tax Administrators, "State Individual Income Tax Rates, 2015"

Various State and Local Tax Rates

State	State and Local Sales and Use (%)	State Sales and Use (%)	Gasoline[1] (¢/gal.)	Cigarette[2] ($/pack)	Spirits[3] ($/gal.)	Wine[4] ($/gal.)	Beer[5] ($/gal.)
Alabama	9.0	4.0	20.87	0.425	18.22 (g)	1.70	1.05 (q)

Note: All tax rates as of January 1, 2015; (1) The American Petroleum Institute has developed a methodology for determining the average tax rate on a gallon of fuel. Rates may include any of the following: excise taxes, environmental fees, storage tank fees, other fees or taxes, general sales tax, and local taxes. In states where gasoline is subject to the general sales tax, or where the fuel tax is based on the average sale price, the average rate determined by API is sensitive to changes in the price of gasoline. States that fully or partially apply general sales taxes to gasoline: CA, CO, GA, IL, IN, MI, NY; (2) The federal excise tax of $1.0066 per pack and local taxes are not included; (3) Rates are those applicable to off-premise sales of 40% alcohol by volume (a.b.v.) distilled spirits in 750ml containers. Local excise taxes are excluded; (4) Rates are those applicable to off-premise sales of 11% a.b.v. non-carbonated wine in 750ml containers; (5) Rates are those applicable to off-premise sales of 4.7% a.b.v. beer in 12 ounce containers; (g) States where the government controls sales. In these "control states," products are subject to ad valorem mark-up and excise taxes. The excise tax rate is calculated using a methodology developed by the Distilled Spirits Council of the United States; (q) Includes statewide local tax in Alabama ($0.52) and Georgia ($0.53).
Source: Tax Foundation, 2015 Facts & Figures: How Does Your State Compare?

State Business Tax Climate Index Rankings

State	Overall Rank	Corporate Tax Index Rank	Individual Income Tax Index Rank	Sales Tax Index Rank	Unemployment Insurance Tax Index Rank	Property Tax Index Rank
Alabama	28	27	23	41	25	10

Note: The index is a measure of how each state's tax laws affect economic performance. The lower the rank, the more favorable a state's tax system is for business. States without a given tax are given a ranking of 1. The scores/rankings for the District of Columbia do not affect other states. The 2015 index represents the tax climate as of July 1, 2014.
Source: Tax Foundation, State Business Tax Climate Index 2015

COMMERCIAL UTILITIES

Typical Monthly Electric Bills

Area	Commercial Service ($/month)		Industrial Service ($/month)	
	40 kW demand 5,000 kWh	500 kW demand 100,000 kWh	5,000 kW demand 1,500,000 kWh	70,000 kW demand 50,000,000 kWh
City	538	11,111	141,894	2,504,350

Note: Figures are based on rates in effect January 2, 2014
Source: Memphis Light, Gas and Water, 2014 Utility Bill Comparisons for Selected U.S. Cities

TRANSPORTATION

Means of Transportation to Work

Area	Car/Truck/Van		Public Transportation			Bicycle	Walked	Other Means	Worked at Home
	Drove Alone	Car-pooled	Bus	Subway	Railroad				
City	86.0	6.8	0.4	0.0	0.0	0.2	1.5	2.2	2.8
MSA[1]	86.9	7.7	0.3	0.1	0.0	0.1	1.1	1.3	2.6
U.S.	76.4	9.6	2.6	1.8	0.6	0.6	2.8	1.3	4.3

Note: Figures are percentages and cover workers 16 years of age and older; (1) Figures cover the Huntsville, AL Metropolitan Statistical Area—see Appendix B for areas included
Source: U.S. Census Bureau, 2011-2013 American Community Survey 3-Year Estimates

Travel Time to Work

Area	Less Than 10 Minutes	10 to 19 Minutes	20 to 29 Minutes	30 to 44 Minutes	45 to 59 Minutes	60 to 89 Minutes	90 Minutes or More
City	15.4	44.0	24.9	12.1	1.6	1.1	1.0
MSA[1]	11.9	33.7	26.9	19.8	4.5	2.0	1.3
U.S.	13.3	29.7	20.9	20.2	7.7	5.7	2.6

Note: Figures are percentages and include workers 16 years old and over; (1) Figures cover the Huntsville, AL Metropolitan Statistical Area—see Appendix B for areas included
Source: U.S. Census Bureau, 2011-2013 American Community Survey 3-Year Estimates

Travel Time Index

Area	1985	1990	1995	2000	2005	2010	2011
Urban Area[1]	n/a	n/a	n/a	n/a	n/a	n/a	n/a
Average[2]	1.09	1.14	1.16	1.19	1.23	1.18	1.18

Note: Travel Time Index—the ratio of travel time in the peak period to the travel time at free-flow conditions. For example, a value of 1.30 indicates a 20-minute free-flow trip takes 26 minutes in the peak. Free-flow speeds (60 mph on freeways and 35 mph on principal arterials) are used as the comparison threshold; (1) Data for the Huntsville, AL urban area was not available; (2) average of 498 urban areas
Source: Texas Transportation Institute, Urban Mobility Report 2012, December 2012

Public Transportation

Agency Name / Mode of Transportation	Vehicles Operated in Maximum Service	Annual Unlinked Passenger Trips (in thous.)	Annual Passenger Miles (in thous.)
City of Huntsville - Public Transportation Division			
Bus (directly operated)	13	449.5	2,322.4
Demand Response (directly operated)	16	89.8	749.8

Source: Federal Transit Administration, National Transit Database, 2013

Air Transportation

Airport Name and Code / Type of Service	Passenger Airlines[1]	Passenger Enplanements	Freight Carriers[2]	Freight (lbs.)
Huntsville International (HSV)				
Domestic service (U.S. carriers - 2014)	16	517,709	12	16,570,025
International service (U.S. carriers - 2013)	1	30	6	67,480,208

Note: (1) Includes all U.S.-based major, minor and commuter airlines that carried at least one passenger during the year; (2) Includes all U.S.-based airlines and freight carriers that transported at least one lb. of freight during the year.
Source: Bureau of Transportation Statistics, The Intermodal Transportation Database, Air Carriers: T-100 Domestic Market (U.S. Carriers), 2014; Bureau of Transportation Statistics, The Intermodal Transportation Database, Air Carriers: T-100 International Market (U.S. Carriers), 2013

Other Transportation Statistics

Major Highways:	I-65
Amtrak Service:	No
Major Waterways/Ports:	Near the Tennessee River (12 miles)

Source: Amtrak.com; Google Maps

BUSINESSES

Major Business Headquarters

Company Name	Rankings	
	Fortune[1]	Forbes[2]
No companies listed	-	-

Note: (1) Fortune 500—companies that produce a 10-K are ranked 1 to 500 based on 2013 revenue; (2) all private companies with at least $2 billion in annual revenue through the end of their most current fiscal year are ranked 1 to 221; companies listed are headquartered in the city; dashes indicate no ranking
Source: Fortune, "Fortune 500," June 16, 2014; Forbes, "America's Largest Private Companies," November 5, 2014

Fast-Growing Businesses

According to *Inc.*, Huntsville is home to two of America's 500 fastest-growing private companies: **Thompson Gray** (#43); **Gideon Services** (#67). Criteria: must be an independent, privately-held, for-profit, U.S. corporation, proprietorship or partnership; revenues must be at least $100,000 in 2010 and $2 million in 2013; must have four-year operating/sales history. Holding companies, regulated banks, and utilities were excluded. *Inc., "America's 500 Fastest-Growing Private Companies," September 2014*

Minority Business Opportunity

Huntsville is home to one company which is on the *Black Enterprise* Auto Dealer 60 list (60 largest dealers based on gross sales): **Lexus of Huntsville** (#50). Criteria: company must be operational in previous calendar year and be at least 51% black-owned. *Black Enterprise, B.E. 100s, 2014*

Huntsville is home to two companies which are on the *Hispanic Business* 500 list (500 largest U.S. Hispanic-owned companies based on 2012 revenue): **COLSA Corp.** (#37); **SEI Group** (#236). Companies included must show at least 51 percent ownership by Hispanic U.S. citizens, and must maintain headquarters in one of the 50 states or Washington, D.C. *Hispanic Business, "Hispanic Business 500," June 20, 2013*

Minority- and Women-Owned Businesses

Group	All Firms		Firms with Paid Employees			
	Firms	Sales ($000)	Firms	Sales ($000)	Employees	Payroll ($000)
Asian	576	413,879	256	390,751	3,129	137,158
Black	2,007	268,991	157	243,092	1,821	77,246
Hispanic	207	260,684	45	254,977	1,705	111,457
Women	4,347	1,211,336	649	1,117,014	7,744	276,445
All Firms	14,555	28,244,278	4,604	27,652,214	122,186	5,233,410

Note: Figures cover firms located in the city; minority- and women-owned business are defined as firms in which the corresponding group own 51% or more of the stock or equity of the company
Source: U.S. Census Bureau, 2007 Economic Census, Survey of Business Owners (2012 Survey of Business Owners data will be released starting in June 2015)

HOTELS & CONVENTION CENTERS

Hotels/Motels

Area	5 Star		4 Star		3 Star		2 Star		1 Star		Not Rated	
	Num.	Pct.[3]	Num.	Pct.[3]	Num.	Pct.[3]	Num.	Pct.[3]	Num.	Pct.[3]	Num.	Pct.[3]
City[1]	0	0.0	1	1.2	15	17.4	63	73.3	3	3.5	4	4.7
Total[2]	166	0.9	1,264	7.0	5,718	31.8	9,340	52.0	411	2.3	1,070	6.0

Note: (1) Figures cover Huntsville and vicinity; (2) Figures cover all 100 cities in this book; (3) Percentage of hotels which have a given star rating; Star ratings are determined by expedia.com and offer an indication of the general quality of a particular hotel.
Source: expedia.com, April 2, 2015

Major Convention Centers

Name	Overall Space (sq. ft.)	Exhibit Space (sq. ft.)	Meeting Space (sq. ft.)	Meeting Rooms
Von Braun Center	n/a	n/a	170,000	n/a

Note: Table includes convention centers located in the Huntsville, AL metro area; n/a not available
Source: Original research

Living Environment

COST OF LIVING

Cost of Living Index

Composite Index	Groceries	Housing	Utilities	Transportation	Health Care	Misc. Goods/ Services
94.2	100.6	79.1	105.0	100.1	96.6	98.5

Note: The Cost of Living Index measures regional differences in the cost of consumer goods and services, excluding taxes and non-consumer expenditures, for professional and managerial households in the top income quintile. It is based on more than 50,000 prices covering almost 60 different items for which prices are collected three times a year by chambers of commerce, economic development organizations or university applied economic centers in each participating urban area. The numbers shown should be read as a percentage above or below the national average of 100. For example, a value of 115.4 in the groceries column indicates that grocery prices are 15.4% higher than the national average. Small differences in the index numbers should not be interpreted as significant; Figures cover the Huntsville AL urban area.
Source: The Council for Community and Economic Research, ACCRA Cost of Living Index, 2014

Grocery Prices

Area[1]	T-Bone Steak ($/pound)	Frying Chicken ($/pound)	Whole Milk ($/half gal.)	Eggs ($/dozen)	Orange Juice ($/64 oz.)	Coffee ($/11.5 oz.)
City[2]	10.87	1.30	2.37	1.98	3.29	4.15
Avg.	10.40	1.37	2.40	1.99	3.46	4.27
Min.	8.48	0.93	1.37	1.30	2.83	2.99
Max.	14.20	2.44	3.62	4.02	6.42	6.96

Note: (1) Values for the local area are compared with the average, minimum and maximum values for all 308 areas in the Cost of Living Index; (2) Figures cover the Huntsville AL urban area; **T-Bone Steak** *(price per pound);* **Frying Chicken** *(price per pound, whole fryer);* **Whole Milk** *(half gallon carton);* **Eggs** *(price per dozen, Grade A, large);* **Orange Juice** *(64 oz. Tropicana or Florida Natural);* **Coffee** *(11.5 oz. can, vacuum-packed, Maxwell House, Hills Bros, or Folgers).*
Source: The Council for Community and Economic Research, ACCRA Cost of Living Index, 2014

Housing and Utility Costs

Area[1]	New Home Price ($)	Apartment Rent ($/month)	All Electric ($/month)	Part Electric ($/month)	Other Energy ($/month)	Telephone ($/month)
City[2]	229,687	836	151.00	-	-	35.51
Avg.	305,838	919	181.00	93.66	73.14	27.95
Min.	183,142	480	112.00	42.06	23.42	17.16
Max.	1,358,576	3,851	594.00	180.03	440.99	40.42

Note: (1) Values for the local area are compared with the average, minimum and maximum values for all 308 areas in the Cost of Living Index; (2) Figures cover the Huntsville AL urban area; **New Home Price** *(2,400 sf living area, 8,000 sf lot, in urban area with full utilities);* **Apartment Rent** *(950 sf 2 bedroom/1.5 or 2 bath, unfurnished, excluding all utilities except water);* **All Electric** *(average monthly cost for an all-electric home);* **Part Electric** *(average monthly cost for a part-electric home);* **Other Energy** *(average monthly cost for natural gas, fuel oil, coal, wood, and any other forms of energy except electricity);* **Telephone** *(price includes basic monthly rate for a private residential line plus additional local usage charges incurred by a family of four).*
Source: The Council for Community and Economic Research, ACCRA Cost of Living Index, 2014

Health Care, Transportation, and Other Costs

Area[1]	Doctor ($/visit)	Dentist ($/visit)	Optometrist ($/visit)	Gasoline ($/gallon)	Beauty Salon ($/visit)	Men's Shirt ($)
City[2]	80.83	90.64	108.06	3.35	31.92	30.07
Avg.	102.86	87.89	97.66	3.44	34.37	26.74
Min.	67.47	65.78	51.18	3.00	17.43	12.79
Max.	173.50	150.14	235.00	4.33	64.28	49.50

Note: (1) Values for the local area are compared with the average, minimum and maximum values for all 308 areas in the Cost of Living Index; (2) Figures cover the Huntsville AL urban area; **Doctor** *(general practitioners routine exam of an established patient);* **Dentist** *(adult teeth cleaning and periodic oral examination);* **Optometrist** *(full vision eye exam for established adult patient);* **Gasoline** *(one gallon regular unleaded, national brand, including all taxes, cash price at self-service pump if available);* **Beauty Salon** *(woman's shampoo, trim, and blow-dry);* **Men's Shirt** *(cotton/polyester dress shirt, pinpoint weave, long sleeves).*
Source: The Council for Community and Economic Research, ACCRA Cost of Living Index, 2014

HOUSING

House Price Index (HPI)

Area	National Ranking[2]	Quarterly Change (%)	One-Year Change (%)	Five-Year Change (%)
MSA[1]	125	0.99	4.51	-1.26
U.S.[3]	–	1.35	4.91	11.59

Note: The HPI is a weighted repeat sales index. It measures average price changes in repeat sales or refinancings on the same properties. This information is obtained by reviewing repeat mortgage transactions on single-family properties whose mortgages have been purchased or securitized by Fannie Mae or Freddie Mac in January 1975; (1) Huntsville Metropolitan Statistical Area—see Appendix B for areas included; (2) Rankings are based on annual percentage change for all metro areas containing at least 15,000 transactions over the last 10 years and ranges from 1 to 275; (3) figures based on a weighted average of Census Division estimates using a seasonally adjusted, purchase-only index; all figures are for the period ending December 31, 2014
Source: Federal Housing Finance Agency, House Price Index, February 26, 2015

Median Single-Family Home Prices

Area	2012	2013	2014p	Percent Change 2013 to 2014
MSA[1]	173.6	171.6	171.1	-0.3
U.S. Average	177.2	197.4	209.0	5.9

Note: Figures are median sales prices of existing single-family homes in thousands of dollars; (p) preliminary; n/a not available; (1) Huntsville, AL Metropolitan Statistical Area—see Appendix B for areas included
Source: National Association of Realtors, Median Sales Price of Existing Single-Family Homes for Metropolitan Areas, 4th Quarter 2014

Qualifying Income Based on Median Sales Price of Existing Single-Family Homes

Area	With 5% Down ($)	With 10% Down ($)	With 20% Down ($)
MSA[1]	38,281	36,266	32,237
U.S. Average	45,863	43,449	38,621

Note: Figures are preliminary; Qualifying income is based on a mortgage rate of 4.0%. Monthly principal and interest payment is limited to 25% of income; n/a not available; (1) Huntsville, AL Metropolitan Statistical Area—see Appendix B for areas included
Source: National Association of Realtors, Qualifying Income Based on Median Sales Price of Existing Single-Family Homes for Metropolitan Areas, 4th Quarter 2014

Median Apartment Condo-Coop Home Prices

Area	2012	2013	2014p	Percent Change 2013 to 2014
MSA[1]	n/a	n/a	n/a	n/a
U.S. Average	173.7	194.9	205.1	5.2

Note: Figures are median sales prices of existing apartment condo-coop homes in thousands of dollars; (p) preliminary; n/a not available; (1) Huntsville, AL Metropolitan Statistical Area—see Appendix B for areas included
Source: National Association of Realtors, Median Sales Price of Existing Apartment Condo-Coop Homes for Metropolitan Areas, 4th Quarter 2014

Gross Monthly Rent

Area	Under $200	$200 -299	$300 -499	$500 -749	$750 -999	$1,000 -1,499	$1,500 and up	Median ($)
City	1.1	4.0	12.6	38.3	25.1	15.5	3.4	715
MSA[1]	1.0	4.6	11.6	37.1	24.2	16.8	4.7	723
U.S.	1.7	3.2	7.8	22.1	24.3	26.0	14.9	900

Note: Figures are percentages except for Median; Gross rent is the contract rent plus the estimated average monthly cost of utilities (electricity, gas, and water and sewer) and fuels (oil, coal, kerosene, wood, etc.) if these are paid by the renter (or paid for the renter by someone else); (1) Figures cover the Huntsville, AL Metropolitan Statistical Area—see Appendix B for areas included
Source: U.S. Census Bureau, 2011-2013 American Community Survey 3-Year Estimates

HEALTH

Homeownership Rate

Area	2007 (%)	2008 (%)	2009 (%)	2010 (%)	2011 (%)	2012 (%)	2013 (%)	2014 (%)
MSA[1]	n/a	n/a	n/a	n/a	n/a	n/a	n/a	n/a
U.S.	68.1	67.8	67.4	66.9	66.1	65.4	65.1	64.5

Note: (1) Figures cover the Huntsville, AL Metropolitan Statistical Area—see Appendix B for areas included; n/a not available
Source: U.S. Census Bureau, Housing Vacancies and Homeownership Annual Statistics: 2014

Year Housing Structure Built

Area	2010 or Later	2000 -2009	1990 -1999	1980 -1989	1970 -1979	1960 -1969	1950 -1959	1940 -1949	Before 1940	Median Year
City	1.8	15.0	11.6	14.6	16.3	22.7	11.0	3.3	3.7	1976
MSA[1]	2.6	21.8	19.8	15.7	12.8	14.2	7.4	2.4	3.4	1986
U.S.	0.9	15.0	13.9	13.8	15.8	11.0	10.9	5.4	13.3	1976

Note: Figures are percentages except for Median Year; (1) Figures cover the Huntsville, AL Metropolitan Statistical Area—see Appendix B for areas included
Source: U.S. Census Bureau, 2011-2013 American Community Survey 3-Year Estimates

Health Risk Data

Category	MSA[1] (%)	U.S. (%)
Adults aged 18–64 who have any kind of health care coverage	81.3	79.6
Adults who reported being in good or excellent health	78.8	83.1
Adults who are current smokers	22.0	19.6
Adults who are heavy drinkers[2]	4.1	6.1
Adults who are binge drinkers[3]	11.4	16.9
Adults who are overweight (BMI 25.0 - 29.9)	36.8	35.8
Adults who are obese (BMI 30.0 - 99.8)	29.4	27.6
Adults who participated in any physical activities in the past month	73.8	77.1
Adults 50+ who have ever had a sigmoidoscopy or colonoscopy	68.0	67.3
Women aged 40+ who have had a mammogram within the past two years	81.8	74.0
Men aged 40+ who have had a PSA test within the past two years	44.7	45.2
Adults aged 65+ who have had flu shot within the past year	54.8	60.1
Adults who always wear a seatbelt	94.8	93.8

Note: Data as of 2012 unless otherwise noted; (1) Figures cover the Huntsville, AL Metropolitan Statistical Area—see Appendix B for areas included; (2) Heavy drinkers are classified as males having more than two drinks per day or females having more than one drink per day; (3) Binge drinkers are classified as males having five or more drinks on one occasion or females having four or more drinks on one occasion
Source: Centers for Disease Control and Prevention, Behaviorial Risk Factor Surveillance System, SMART: Selected Metropolitan/Micropolitan Area Risk Trends, 2012 (Note: the CDC has discontinued this dataset but will be releasing a replacement in late 2015)

Chronic Health Indicators

Category	MSA[1] (%)	U.S. (%)
Adults who have ever been told they had a heart attack	3.9	4.5
Adults who have ever been told they had a stroke	n/a	2.9
Adults who have been told they currently have asthma	8.6	8.9
Adults who have ever been told they have arthritis	29.9	25.7
Adults who have ever been told they have diabetes[2]	8.8	9.7
Adults who have ever been told they had skin cancer	8.1	5.7
Adults who have ever been told they had any other types of cancer	6.4	6.5
Adults who have ever been told they have COPD	6.8	6.2
Adults who have ever been told they have kidney disease	1.8	2.5
Adults who have ever been told they have a form of depression	20.8	18.0

Note: Data as of 2012 unless otherwise noted; n/a not available; (1) Figures cover the Huntsville, AL Metropolitan Statistical Area—see Appendix B for areas included; (2) Figures do not include pregnancy-related, borderline, or pre-diabetes
Source: Centers for Disease Control and Prevention, Behaviorial Risk Factor Surveillance System, SMART: Selected Metropolitan/Micropolitan Area Risk Trends, 2012 (Note: the CDC has discontinued this dataset but will be releasing a replacement in late 2015)

Mortality Rates for the Top 10 Causes of Death in the U.S.

ICD-10[a] Sub-Chapter	ICD-10[a] Code	Age-Adjusted Mortality Rate[1] per 100,000 population	
		County[2]	U.S.
Malignant neoplasms	C00-C97	156.5	166.2
Ischaemic heart diseases	I20-I25	59.8	105.7
Other forms of heart disease	I30-I51	116.3	49.3
Chronic lower respiratory diseases	J40-J47	42.9	42.1
Organic, including symptomatic, mental disorders	F01-F09	43.6	38.1
Cerebrovascular diseases	I60-I69	40.6	37.0
Other external causes of accidental injury	W00-X59	21.5	26.9
Other degenerative diseases of the nervous system	G30-G31	27.1	25.6
Diabetes mellitus	E10-E14	15.4	21.3
Hypertensive diseases	I10-I15	11.8	19.4

Note: (a) ICD-10 = International Classification of Diseases 10th Revision; (1) Mortality rates are a three year average covering 2011-2013; (2) Figures cover Madison County
Source: Centers for Disease Control and Prevention, National Center for Health Statistics. Compressed Mortality File 1999-2013 on CDC WONDER Online Database, released October 2014. Data are compiled from the Compressed Mortality File 1999-2013, Series 20 No. 2S, 2014.

Mortality Rates for Selected Causes of Death

ICD-10[a] Sub-Chapter	ICD-10[a] Code	Age-Adjusted Mortality Rate[1] per 100,000 population	
		County[2]	U.S.
Assault	X85-Y09	6.3	5.2
Diseases of the liver	K70-K76	12.3	13.2
Human immunodeficiency virus (HIV) disease	B20-B24	2.4	2.2
Influenza and pneumonia	J09-J18	13.5	15.4
Intentional self-harm	X60-X84	13.3	12.5
Malnutrition	E40-E46	*1.6	0.9
Obesity and other hyperalimentation	E65-E68	*1.3	1.8
Renal failure	N17-N19	19.3	13.1
Transport accidents	V01-V99	15.3	11.7
Viral hepatitis	B15-B19	*1.4	2.2

Note: (a) ICD-10 = International Classification of Diseases 10th Revision; (1) Mortality rates are a three year average covering 2011-2013; (2) Figures cover Madison County; (*) Unreliable data as per CDC
Source: Centers for Disease Control and Prevention, National Center for Health Statistics. Compressed Mortality File 1999-2013 on CDC WONDER Online Database, released October 2014. Data are compiled from the Compressed Mortality File 1999-2013, Series 20 No. 2S, 2014.

Health Insurance Coverage

Area	With Health Insurance	With Private Health Insurance	With Public Health Insurance	Without Health Insurance	Population Under Age 18 Without Health Insurance
City	84.2	68.5	29.4	15.8	4.8
MSA[1]	87.2	72.9	27.0	12.8	3.4
U.S.	85.2	65.2	31.0	14.8	7.3

Note: Figures are percentages that cover the civilian noninstitutionalized population; (1) Figures cover the Huntsville, AL Metropolitan Statistical Area—see Appendix B for areas included
Source: U.S. Census Bureau, 2011-2013 American Community Survey 3-Year Estimates

Number of Medical Professionals

Area[1]	MDs[2]	DOs[2,3]	Dentists	Podiatrists	Chiropractors	Optometrists
Local (number)	903	36	190	13	76	61
Local (rate[4])	263.4	10.5	54.7	3.7	21.9	17.6
U.S. (rate[4])	270.0	20.2	63.1	5.7	25.2	14.9

Note: Data as of 2013 unless noted; (1) Local data covers Madison County; (2) Data as of 2012 and includes all active, non-federal physicians; (3) Doctor of Osteopathic Medicine; (4) rate per 100,000 population
Source: U.S. Department of Health and Human Services, Health Resources and Services Administration, Bureau of Health Professions, Area Resource File (ARF) 2013-2014

EDUCATION

Public School District Statistics

District Name	Schls	Pupils	Pupil/ Teacher Ratio	Minority Pupils[1] (%)	Free Lunch Eligible[2] (%)	IEP[3] (%)
Huntsville City	50	23,437	13.9	54.2	45.4	9.7
Madison County	29	19,764	14.6	31.2	28.5	10.3

Note: Table includes school districts with 2,000 or more students; (1) Percentage of students that are not non-Hispanic white; (2) Percentage of students that are eligible for the free lunch program; (3) Percentage of students that have an Individualized Education Program.
Source: U.S. Department of Education, National Center for Education Statistics, Common Core of Data, Local Education Agency (School District) Universe Survey: School Year 2012-2013; U.S. Department of Education, National Center for Education Statistics, Common Core of Data, Public Elementary/Secondary School Universe Survey: School Year 2012-2013

Highest Level of Education

Area	Less than H.S.	H.S. Diploma	Some College, No Deg.	Associate Degree	Bachelor's Degree	Master's Degree	Prof. School Degree	Doctorate Degree
City	9.9	20.5	23.0	7.8	24.1	11.0	1.9	1.9
MSA[1]	11.0	23.6	22.2	7.8	22.5	10.2	1.3	1.5
U.S.	13.7	28.0	21.2	7.9	18.2	7.7	1.9	1.3

Note: Figures cover persons age 25 and over; (1) Figures cover the Huntsville, AL Metropolitan Statistical Area—see Appendix B for areas included
Source: U.S. Census Bureau, 2011-2013 American Community Survey 3-Year Estimates

Educational Attainment by Race

Area	High School Graduate or Higher (%)					Bachelor's Degree or Higher (%)				
	Total	White	Black	Asian	Hisp.[2]	Total	White	Black	Asian	Hisp.[2]
City	90.1	92.9	84.1	90.2	71.4	38.9	45.3	22.8	57.1	24.1
MSA[1]	89.0	90.2	85.9	88.7	68.8	35.5	37.9	26.0	53.8	24.3
U.S.	86.3	88.3	83.1	85.7	64.0	29.1	30.4	18.8	50.7	13.7

Note: Figures shown cover persons 25 years old and over; (1) Figures cover the Huntsville, AL Metropolitan Statistical Area—see Appendix B for areas included; (2) People of Hispanic origin can be of any race
Source: U.S. Census Bureau, 2011-2013 American Community Survey 3-Year Estimates

School Enrollment by Grade and Control

Area	Preschool (%)		Kindergarten (%)		Grades 1 - 4 (%)		Grades 5 - 8 (%)		Grades 9 - 12 (%)	
	Public	Private	Public	Private	Public	Private	Public	Private	Public	Private
City	40.1	59.9	83.3	16.7	86.0	14.0	85.0	15.0	88.0	12.0
MSA[1]	44.8	55.2	85.5	14.5	87.5	12.5	88.1	11.9	88.8	11.2
U.S.	57.7	42.3	87.9	12.1	89.9	10.1	90.0	10.0	90.7	9.3

Note: Figures shown cover persons 3 years old and over; (1) Figures cover the Huntsville, AL Metropolitan Statistical Area—see Appendix B for areas included
Source: U.S. Census Bureau, 2011-2013 American Community Survey 3-Year Estimates

Average Salaries of Public School Classroom Teachers

Area	2013-14		2014-15		Percent Change 2013-14 to 2014-15	Percent Change 2004-05 to 2014-15
	Dollars	Rank[1]	Dollars	Rank[1]		
ALABAMA	48,720	35	49,497	35	1.59	29.6
U.S. Average	56,610	–	57,379	–	1.36	20.8

Note: (1) State rank ranges from 1 to 51 where 1 indicates highest salary.
Source: National Education Association, Rankings & Estimates: Rankings of the States 2014 and Estimates of School Statistics 2015, March 2015

Higher Education

Four-Year Colleges			Two-Year Colleges			Medical Schools[1]	Law Schools[2]	Voc/ Tech[3]
Public	Private Non-profit	Private For-profit	Public	Private Non-profit	Private For-profit			
1	2	1	1	0	0	0	0	1

Note: Figures cover institutions located within the city limits and include main campuses only; (1) includes schools accredited by the Liaison Committee on Medical Education and the American Osteopathic Association's Commission on Osteopathic College Accreditation; (2) includes ABA-accredited schools, schools with provisional ABA accreditation, and state accredited schools; (3) includes all schools with programs that are less than 2 years.
Source: National Center for Education Statistics, Integrated Postsecondary Education System (IPEDS), 2013-14; Association of American Medical Colleges, Member List, May 1, 2015; American Osteopathic Association, Member List, May 1, 2015; Law School Admission Council, Official Guide to ABA-Approved Law Schools Online, May 1, 2015; Wikipedia, List of Medical Schools in the United States, May 1, 2015; Wikipedia, List of Law Schools in the United States, May 1, 2015

According to *U.S. News & World Report,* the Huntsville, AL metro area is home to one of the best national universities in the U.S.: **University of Alabama-Huntsville** (#181). The indicators used to capture academic quality fall into a number of categories: assessment by administrators at peer institutions; retention of students; faculty resources; student selectivity; financial resources; alumni giving; high school counselor ratings of colleges; and graduation rate. *U.S. News & World Report, "America's Best Colleges 2015"*

PRESIDENTIAL ELECTION

2012 Presidential Election Results

Area	Obama (%)	Romney (%)	Other (%)
Madison County	40.0	58.6	1.4
U.S.	51.0	47.2	1.8

Note: Results may not add to 100% due to rounding
Source: Dave Leip's Atlas of U.S. Presidential Elections

EMPLOYERS

Major Employers

Company Name	Industry
Avocent Corporation	Computer peripheral equip
City of Huntsville	Town council
City of Huntsville	Mayor's office
COLSA Corporation	Commercial research laboratory
County of Madison	Executive offices
Dynetics	Engineering laboratory/except testing
General Dynamics C4 Systems	Defense systems equipment
Healthcare Auth - City of Huntsville	General governement
Intergraph Process & Bldg Solutions	Systems software development
Qualitest Products	Drugs and drug proprietaries
Science Applications Int'l Corporation	Computer processing services
Science Applications Int'l Corporation	Commercial research laboratory
Teledyne brown Engineering	Energy research
The Army, United States Department of	Army
The Boeing Company	Aircraft
The Boeing Company	Guided missiles/space vehicles
United States Department of the Army	Army

Note: Companies shown are located within the Huntsville, AL Metropolitan Statistical Area.
Source: Hoovers.com; Wikipedia

PUBLIC SAFETY

Crime Rate

Area	All Crimes	Violent Crimes				Property Crimes		
		Murder	Forcible Rape	Robbery	Aggrav. Assault	Burglary	Larceny -Theft	Motor Vehicle Theft
City	5,804.4	13.0	47.1	211.7	544.0	1,019.8	3,588.3	380.5
Suburbs[1]	2,385.9	1.2	40.0	30.0	166.6	522.9	1,507.0	118.1
Metro[2]	3,839.4	6.2	43.0	107.2	327.0	734.2	2,391.9	229.7
U.S.	3,098.6	4.5	25.2	109.1	229.1	610.0	1,899.4	221.3

Note: Figures are crimes per 100,000 population; (1) All areas within the metro area that are located outside the city limits; (2) Figures cover the Huntsville, AL Metropolitan Statistical Area—see Appendix B for areas included
Source: FBI Uniform Crime Reports, 2013

Hate Crimes

Area	Number of Quarters Reported	Number of Incidents per Bias Motivation						
		Race	Religion	Sexual Orientation	Ethnicity	Disability	Gender	Gender Identity
City	4	0	0	0	0	0	0	0
U.S.	4	2,871	1,031	1,233	655	83	18	31

Source: Federal Bureau of Investigation, Hate Crime Statistics 2013

Identity Theft Consumer Complaints

Area	Complaints	Complaints per 100,000 Population	Rank[2]
MSA[1]	322	73.9	159
U.S.	332,646	104.3	-

Note: (1) Figures cover the Huntsville, AL Metropolitan Statistical Area—see Appendix B for areas included; (2) Rank ranges from 1 to 380 where 1 indicates greatest number of identity theft complaints per 100,000 population
Source: Federal Trade Commission, Consumer Sentinel Network Data Book for January–December 2014

Fraud and Other Consumer Complaints

Area	Complaints	Complaints per 100,000 Population	Rank[2]
MSA[1]	1,760	403.9	129
U.S.	2,250,205	705.7	-

Note: (1) Figures cover the Huntsville, AL Metropolitan Statistical Area—see Appendix B for areas included; (2) Rank ranges from 1 to 380 where 1 indicates greatest number of identity theft complaints per 100,000 population
Source: Federal Trade Commission, Consumer Sentinel Network Data Book for January–December 2014

RECREATION

Culture

Dance[1]	Theatre[1]	Instrumental Music[1]	Vocal Music[1]	Series and Festivals	Museums and Art Galleries[2]	Zoos and Aquariums[3]
1	1	3	1	2	19	0

Note: (1) Professional perfoming groups; (2) Based on organizations with SIC code 8412; (3) AZA-accredited
Source: The Grey House Performing Arts Directory, 2015-16; Association of Zoos & Aquariums, AZA Member Zoos & Aquariums, April 2015; www.AccuLeads.com, April 2015

Professional Sports Teams

Team Name	League	Year Established
No teams are located in the metro area		

Source: Wikipedia, Major Professional Sports Teams of the United States and Canada, April 2015

CLIMATE

Average and Extreme Temperatures

Temperature	Jan	Feb	Mar	Apr	May	Jun	Jul	Aug	Sep	Oct	Nov	Dec	Yr.
Extreme High (°F)	76	82	88	92	96	101	104	103	101	91	84	77	104
Average High (°F)	49	54	63	73	80	87	90	89	83	73	62	52	71
Average Temp. (°F)	39	44	52	61	69	76	80	79	73	62	51	43	61
Average Low (°F)	30	33	41	49	58	65	69	68	62	50	40	33	50
Extreme Low (°F)	-11	5	6	26	36	45	53	52	37	28	15	-3	-11

Note: Figures cover the years 1958-1995
Source: National Climatic Data Center, International Station Meteorological Climate Summary, 9/96

Average Precipitation/Snowfall/Humidity

Precip./Humidity	Jan	Feb	Mar	Apr	May	Jun	Jul	Aug	Sep	Oct	Nov	Dec	Yr.
Avg. Precip. (in.)	5.0	5.0	6.6	4.8	5.1	4.3	4.6	3.5	4.1	3.3	4.7	5.7	56.8
Avg. Snowfall (in.)	2	1	1	Tr	0	0	0	0	0	Tr	Tr	1	4
Avg. Rel. Hum. 7am (%)	82	81	79	78	79	81	84	86	85	86	84	81	82
Avg. Rel. Hum. 4pm (%)	60	56	51	46	51	53	56	55	54	51	55	60	54

Note: Figures cover the years 1958-1995; Tr = Trace amounts (<0.05 in. of rain; <0.5 in. of snow)
Source: National Climatic Data Center, International Station Meteorological Climate Summary, 9/96

Weather Conditions

Temperature			Daytime Sky			Precipitation		
10°F & below	32°F & below	90°F & above	Clear	Partly cloudy	Cloudy	0.01 inch or more precip.	0.1 inch or more snow/ice	Thunder-storms
2	66	49	70	118	177	116	2	54

Note: Figures are average number of days per year and cover the years 1958-1995
Source: National Climatic Data Center, International Station Meteorological Climate Summary, 9/96

HAZARDOUS WASTE

Superfund Sites

Huntsville has one hazardous waste site on the EPA's Superfund Final National Priorities List: **Redstone Arsenal (USARMY/NASA)**. There are a total of 1,322 Superfund sites on the list in the U.S. *U.S. Environmental Protection Agency, Final National Priorities List, April 14, 2015*

AIR & WATER QUALITY

Air Quality Trends: Ozone

	2004	2005	2006	2007	2008	2009	2010	2011	2012	2013
MSA[1]	0.077	0.075	0.079	0.082	0.073	0.066	0.071	0.072	0.076	0.064

Note: (1) Data covers the Huntsville, AL Metropolitan Statistical Area—see Appendix B for areas included. The values shown are the composite ozone concentration averages among trend sites based on the highest fourth daily maximum 8-hour concentration in parts per million. These trends are based on sites having an adequate record of monitoring data during the trend period. Data from exceptional events are included.
Source: U.S. Environmental Protection Agency, Air Quality Monitoring Information, "Air Quality Trends by City, 2000-2013"

Air Quality Index

Area	Percent of Days when Air Quality was...[2]					AQI Statistics[2]	
	Good	Moderate	Unhealthy for Sensitive Groups	Unhealthy	Very Unhealthy	Maximum	Median
MSA[1]	88.8	11.2	0.0	0.0	0.0	87	36

Note: (1) Data covers the Huntsville, AL Metropolitan Statistical Area—see Appendix B for areas included; (2) Based on 338 days with AQI data in 2014. Air Quality Index (AQI) is an index for reporting daily air quality. EPA calculates the AQI for five major air pollutants regulated by the Clean Air Act: ground-level ozone, particle pollution (aka particulate matter), carbon monoxide, sulfur dioxide, and nitrogen dioxide. The AQI runs from 0 to 500. The higher the AQI value, the greater the level of air pollution and the greater the health concern. There are six AQI categories: "Good" AQI is between 0 and 50. Air quality is considered satisfactory; "Moderate" AQI is between 51 and 100. Air quality is acceptable; "Unhealthy for Sensitive Groups" When AQI values are between 101 and 150, members of sensitive groups may experience health effects; "Unhealthy" When AQI values are between 151 and 200 everyone may begin to experience health effects; "Very Unhealthy" AQI values between 201 and 300 trigger a health alert; "Hazardous" AQI values over 300 trigger warnings of emergency conditions (not shown).
Source: U.S. Environmental Protection Agency, Air Quality Index Report, 2014

Air Quality Index Pollutants

Area	Percent of Days when AQI Pollutant was...[2]					
	Carbon Monoxide	Nitrogen Dioxide	Ozone	Sulfur Dioxide	Particulate Matter 2.5	Particulate Matter 10
MSA[1]	0.0	0.0	60.7	0.0	22.8	16.6

Note: (1) Data covers the Huntsville, AL Metropolitan Statistical Area—see Appendix B for areas included; (2) Based on 338 days with AQI data in 2014. The Air Quality Index (AQI) is an index for reporting daily air quality. EPA calculates the AQI for five major air pollutants regulated by the Clean Air Act: ground-level ozone, particle pollution (also known as particulate matter), carbon monoxide, sulfur dioxide, and nitrogen dioxide. The AQI runs from 0 to 500. The higher the AQI value, the greater the level of air pollution and the greater the health concern.
Source: U.S. Environmental Protection Agency, Air Quality Index Report, 2014

Maximum Air Pollutant Concentrations: Particulate Matter, Ozone, CO and Lead

	Particulate Matter 10 (ug/m^3)	Particulate Matter 2.5 Wtd AM (ug/m^3)	Particulate Matter 2.5 24-Hr (ug/m^3)	Ozone (ppm)	Carbon Monoxide (ppm)	Lead (ug/m^3)
MSA[1] Level	37	8.6	16	0.064	n/a	n/a
NAAQS[2]	150	15	35	0.075	9	0.15
Met NAAQS[2]	Yes	Yes	Yes	Yes	n/a	n/a

Note: (1) Data covers the Huntsville, AL Metropolitan Statistical Area—see Appendix B for areas included; Data from exceptional events are included; (2) National Ambient Air Quality Standards; ppm = parts per million; ug/m^3 = micrograms per cubic meter; n/a not available.
Concentrations: Particulate Matter 10 (coarse particulate)—highest second maximum 24-hour concentration; Particulate Matter 2.5 Wtd AM (fine particulate)—highest weighted annual mean concentration; Particulate Matter 2.5 24-Hour (fine particulate)—highest 98th percentile 24-hour concentration; Ozone—highest fourth daily maximum 8-hour concentration; Carbon Monoxide—highest second maximum non-overlapping 8-hour concentration; Lead—maximum running 3-month average
Source: U.S. Environmental Protection Agency, Air Quality Monitoring Information, "Air Quality Statistics by City, 2013"

Maximum Air Pollutant Concentrations: Nitrogen Dioxide and Sulfur Dioxide

	Nitrogen Dioxide AM (ppb)	Nitrogen Dioxide 1-Hr (ppb)	Sulfur Dioxide AM (ppb)	Sulfur Dioxide 1-Hr (ppb)	Sulfur Dioxide 24-Hr (ppb)
MSA[1] Level	n/a	n/a	n/a	n/a	n/a
NAAQS[2]	53	100	30	75	140
Met NAAQS[2]	n/a	n/a	n/a	n/a	n/a

Note: (1) Data covers the Huntsville, AL Metropolitan Statistical Area—see Appendix B for areas included; Data from exceptional events are included; (2) National Ambient Air Quality Standards; ppm = parts per million; ug/m^3 = micrograms per cubic meter; n/a not available.
Concentrations: Nitrogen Dioxide AM—highest arithmetic mean concentration; Nitrogen Dioxide 1-Hr—highest 98th percentile 1-hour daily maximum concentration; Sulfur Dioxide AM—highest annual mean concentration; Sulfur Dioxide 1-Hr—highest 99th percentile 1-hour daily maximum concentration; Sulfur Dioxide 24-Hr—highest second maximum 24-hour concentration
Source: U.S. Environmental Protection Agency, Air Quality Monitoring Information, "Air Quality Statistics by City, 2013"

Drinking Water

Water System Name	Pop. Served	Primary Water Source Type	Violations[1]	
			Health Based	Monitoring/ Reporting
Huntsville Utilities	219,168	Surface	0	0

Note: (1) Based on violation data from January 1, 2014 to December 31, 2014 (includes unresolved violations from earlier years)
Source: U.S. Environmental Protection Agency, Office of Ground Water and Drinking Water, Safe Drinking Water Information System (based on data extracted January 27, 2015)

Jacksonville, Florida

Background

Modern day Jacksonville is largely a product of the reconstruction that occurred during the 1940s after a fire had razed 147 city blocks a few decades earlier. Lying under the modern structures, however, is a history that dates back earlier than the settlement of Plymouth by the Pilgrims.

Located in the northeast part of Florida on the St. John's River, Jacksonville, the largest city in land area in the contiguous United States, was settled by English, Spanish, and French explorers from the sixteenth through the eighteenth centuries. Sites commemorating their presence include: Fort Caroline National Monument, marking the French settlement led by René de Goulaine Laudonniére in 1564; Spanish Pond one-quarter of a mile east of Fort Caroline, where Spanish forces led by Pedro Menendez captured the Fort; and Fort George Island, from which General James Oglethorpe led English attacks against the Spanish during the eighteenth century.

Jacksonville was attractive to these early settlers because of its easy access to the Atlantic Ocean, which meant a favorable port.

Today, Jacksonville remains an advantageous port and is home to Naval Air Station Jacksonville, a major employer in the area. Jacksonville is the financial hub of Florida, and many companies have headquarters here.

On the cultural front, Jacksonville boasts a range of options, including the Children's Museum, the Jacksonville Symphony Orchestra, the Gator Bowl, and beach facilities. In 2005, the city hosted Super Bowl XXXIX at the former Alltel Stadium (now Jacksonville Municipal Stadium), home of the NFL's Jacksonville Jaguars. The city also boasts the largest urban park system in the United States, providing services at more than 337 locations on more than 80,000 acres located throughout the city. The Jacksonville Jazz Festival, held every April, is the second-largest jazz festival in the nation. The city is home to several theaters, including Little Theatre, which, operating since 1919, is one of the oldest operating community theaters in the nation.

Jacksonville has more than 80,000 acres of parkland throughout the city, and is renowned for its outdoor recreational facilities. The city's most recent park, The Jacksonville Arboretum and Gardens, was opened in the fall of 2008.

Summers are long, warm, and relatively humid. Winters are generally mild, although periodic invasions of cold northern air bring the temperature down. Temperatures along the beaches rarely rise above 90 degrees. Summer coastal thunderstorms usually occur before noon, and move inland in the afternoons. The greatest rainfall, as localized thundershowers, occurs during the summer months. Although the area is in the hurricane belt, this section of the coast has been very fortunate in escaping hurricane-force winds.

Rankings

General Rankings

- The U.S. Conference of Mayors and Waste Management sponsor the City Livability Awards Program. The awards recognize and honor mayors for exemplary leadership in developing and implementing specific programs that improve the quality of life in America's cities. Jacksonville was one of 17 second round finalists in the large cities (population 100,000 or more) category. *U.S. Conference of Mayors, "2015 City Livability Awards"*

Business/Finance Rankings

- Analysts for the business website 24/7 Wall Street looked at the local government report "Tax Rates and Tax Burdens in the District of Columbia—A Nationwide Comparison" to determine where a family of three at two different income levels would pay the least and the most in state and local taxes. Among the ten cities with the lowest state and local tax burdens was Jacksonville, at #5. *247wallst.com, American Cities with the Highest (and Lowest) Taxes, February 25, 2013*
- Based on metro area social media reviews, the employment opinion group Glassdoor surveyed 50 of the largest U.S. metro areas on measures including compensation and benefits, satisfaction with management, business outlook, and number of employers hiring. The Jacksonville metro area was ranked #19 in overall employee satisfaction. *www.glassdoor.com, "Employment Satisfaction Report Card by City," June 13, 2014*
- In a survey of economic confidence in the nation's 50 largest metropolitan areas conducted January–December 2014, the Jacksonville metro area placed #40, according to Gallup's 2014 Economic Confidence Index. *Gallup, "San Jose and San Francisco Lead in Economic Confidence," March 19, 2015*
- The Brookings Institution ranked the 50 largest cities in the U.S. based on income inequality. Jacksonville was ranked #40. (#1 = greatest ineqality). Criteria: the cities were ranked based on the "95/20 ratio," a figure representing the income at which a household earns more than 95 percent of all other households, divided by the income at which a household earns more than only 20 percent of all other households. *Brookings Institution, "Income Inequality in America's 50 Largest Cities, 2007-2013," March 17, 2015*
- Jacksonville was ranked #37 out of 100 metro areas in terms of economic performance (#1 = best) during the recession and recovery from trough quarter through the second quarter of 2013. Criteria: percent change in employment; percentage point change in unemployment rate; percent change in gross metropolitan product; percent change in House Price Index. *Brookings Institution, MetroMonitor: Tracking Economic Recession and Recovery in America's 100 Largest Metropolitan Areas, September 2013*
- The Jacksonville metro area appeared on the Milken Institute "2013 Best Performing Cities" list. Rank: #64 out of 200 large metro areas. Criteria: job growth; wage and salary growth; high-tech output growth. *Milken Institute, "Best-Performing Cities 2014," January 2015*
- *Forbes* ranked the 200 most populous metro areas to determine the nation's "Best Places for Business and Careers." The Jacksonville metro area was ranked #75. Criteria: costs (business and living); job growth (past and projected); income growth; educational attainment (college and high school); projected economic growth; cultural and recreational opportunities; net migration patterns; number of highly ranked colleges. *Forbes, "The Best Places for Business and Careers 2014," July 23, 2014*

Culture/Performing Arts Rankings

- Jacksonville was selected as one of America's top cities for the arts. The city ranked #15 in the big city (population 500,000 and over) category. Criteria: readers' top choices for arts travel destinations based on the richness and variety of visual arts sites, activities and events. *American Style, "2012 Top 25 Arts Destinations," June 2012*

Dating/Romance Rankings

- Of the 100 U.S. cities surveyed by *Men's Health* in its quest to identify the nation's best cities for dating and forming relationships, Jacksonville was ranked #21 for online dating (#1 = best). *Men's Health, "The Best and Worst Cities for Online Dating," January 30, 2013*

Education Rankings

- Personal finance website *WalletHub* analyzed the 150 largest U.S. metropolitan statistical areas to determine where the most educated Americans are choosing to settle. Criteria: educational attainment; percentage of workers with jobs in computer, engineering, and science fields; quality and size of each metro area's universities. Jacksonville was ranked #92 (#1 = most educated city). *www.WalletHub.com, "2014's Most and Least Educated Cities*

- Jacksonville was selected as one of America's most literate cities. The city ranked #56 out of the 77 largest U.S. cities. Criteria: number of booksellers; library resources; Internet resources; educational attainment; periodical publishing resources; newspaper circulation. *Central Connecticut State University, "America's Most Literate Cities, 2014," April 8, 2015*

Environmental Rankings

- The Jacksonville metro area came in at #314 for the relative comfort of its climate on Sperling's list of "chill cities," as measured by the Sperling Heat Index. All 361 metro areas are included. Criteria included daytime high temperatures, nighttime low temperatures, dew point, and relative humidity at the high temperatures. *www.bertsperling.com, "Sperling's Chill Cities," July 18, 2013*

- Sperling's BestPlaces assessed 379 metropolitan areas of the United States for the likelihood of dangerously extreme weather events or earthquakes. In general the Southeast and South-Central regions have the highest risk of weather extremes and earthquakes, while the Pacific Northwest enjoys the lowest risk. Of the least risky metropolitan areas, the Jacksonville metro area was ranked #330. *www.bestplaces.net, "Safest Places from Natural Disasters," April 2011*

- The U.S. Environmental Protection Agency (EPA) released a list of mid-size U.S. metropolitan areas with the most ENERGY STAR certified buildings in 2014. The Jacksonville metro area was ranked #10 out of 10. *U.S. Environmental Protection Agency, "Top Cities With the Most ENERGY STAR Certified Buildings in 2014," March 25, 2015*

Food/Drink Rankings

- *Men's Health* ranked 100 major U.S. cities in terms of alcohol intoxication. Jacksonville ranked #65 (#1 = most sober).Criteria: binge drinking; alcohol-related traffic accidents, arrests, and fatalities. *Men's Health, "The Drunkest Cities in America," November 19, 2013*

Health/Fitness Rankings

- For each of the 50 most populous metro areas in the United States, the American College of Sports Medicine's American Fitness Index evaluated infrastructure, community assets, and policies that encourage healthy and fit lifestyles, including preventive health behaviors, levels of chronic disease conditions, health care access, and community resources and policies that support physical activity. The Jacksonville metro area ranked #37 for "community fitness." Personal health indicators were considered as well as community and environmental indicators. *www.americanfitnessindex.org, "ACSM American Fitness Index Health and Community Fitness Status of the 50 Largest Metropolitan Areas," May 2013*

- Jacksonville was given "Well City USA" status by The Wellness Councils of America, whose objective is to engage entire business communities in building healthy workforces. Well City status is met when a minimum of 20 employers who collectively employ at least 20% of the city's workforce become designated Well Workplaces within a three-year period. To date, eleven communities have achieved Well City USA status. *The Wellness Councils of America, "Well City USA, 2014"*

- Jacksonville was selected as one of the 25 fittest cities in America by *Men's Fitness Online*. It ranked #20 out of America's 50 largest cities. Criteria: fitness centers and sport stores; nutrition; sports participation; TV viewing; overweight/sedentary; junk food; air quality; geography; commute; parks and open space; city recreational facilities; access to healthcare; motivation; mayor and city initiatives; state obesity initiatives. *Men's Fitness, "The Fittest and Fattest Cities in America," March 5, 2012*

- Jacksonville was identified as a "2013 Spring Allergy Capital." The area ranked #52 out of 100. Three groups of factors were used to identify the most severe cities for people with allergies during the spring season: annual pollen levels; medicine utilization; access to board-certified allergists. *Asthma and Allergy Foundation of America, "Spring Allergy Capitals 2013"*

- Jacksonville was identified as a "2013 Fall Allergy Capital." The area ranked #59 out of 100. Three groups of factors were used to identify the most severe cities for people with allergies during the fall season: annual pollen levels; medicine utilization; access to board-certified allergists. *Asthma and Allergy Foundation of America, "Fall Allergy Capitals 2013"*

- Jacksonville was identified as a "2013 Asthma Capital." The area ranked #48 out of the nation's 100 largest metropolitan areas. Twelve factors were used to identify the most challenging places to live for people with asthma: estimated prevalence; self-reported prevalence; crude death rate for asthma; annual pollen score; annual air quality; public smoking laws; number of board-certified asthma specialists; school inhaler access laws; rescue medication use; controller medication use; uninsured rate; poverty rate. *Asthma and Allergy Foundation of America, "Asthma Capitals 2013"*

- *Men's Health* ranked 100 major U.S. cities in terms of the best and worst cities for men. Jacksonville ranked #79. Criteria: thirty-three data points were examined covering health, fitness, and quality of life. *Men's Health, "The Best & Worst Cities for Men 2014," December 6, 2013*

- Jacksonville was selected as one of the best metropolitan areas for hospital care in America by *HealthGrades.com.* The rankings are based on a comprehensive study of patient death and complication rates in the nation's nearly 5,000 hospitals. Hospitals performing in the top 5% nationwide across 26 different medical procedures and diagnoses were identified. *HealthGrades.com* then ranked cities by the highest percentage of these Distinguished Hospitals for Clinical Excellence™. The Jacksonville metro area ranked #40. *HealthGrades.com, "America's Top 50 Cities for Hospital Care," January 21, 2012*

- The Jacksonville metro area appeared in the 2013 Gallup-Healthways Well-Being Index. The area ranked #159 out of 189. The Gallup-Healthways Well-Being Index score is an average of six sub-indexes, which individually examine life evaluation, emotional health, work environment, physical health, healthy behaviors, and access to basic necessities. Results are based on telephone interviews conducted as part of the Gallup-Healthways Well-Being Index survey January 2–December 29, 2012, and January 2–December 30, 2013, with a random sample of 531,630 adults, aged 18 and older, living in metropolitan areas in the 50 U.S. states and the District of Columbia. *Gallup-Healthways, "State of American Well-Being," March 25, 2014*

- The Jacksonville metro area was identified as one of "America's Most Stressful Cities" by *Sperling's BestPlaces.* The metro area ranked #4 out of 50. Criteria: unemployment rate; suicide rate; commute time; mental health; poor rest; alcohol use; violent crime rate; property crime rate; cloudy days annually. *Sperling's BestPlaces, www.BestPlaces.net, "Stressful Cities 2012*

Real Estate Rankings

- The Jacksonville metro area was identified as one of the top 20 housing markets to invest in for 2015 by *Forbes*. The area ranked #16. Criteria: strong population and job growth; relatively low home prices which are below equilibrium home price (EHP). The EHP is what the average price for a market should be, if speculation, weird distortions in local income, and other factors (like the housing collapse) weren't present in the market. *Forbes.com, "Best Buy Cities: Where to Invest in Housing in 2015," January 9, 2015*

- Jacksonville was ranked #51 out of 275 metro areas in terms of house price appreciation in 2014 (#1 = highest rate). *Federal Housing Finance Agency, House Price Index, 4th Quarter 2014*

- The Jacksonville metro area was identified as one of the 20 best housing markets in the U.S. in 2014. The area ranked #11 out of 178 markets with a home price appreciation of 12.6%. Criteria: year-over-year change of median sales price of existing single-family homes between the 4th quarter of 2013 and the 4th quarter of 2014. *National Association of Realtors®, Median Sales Price of Existing Single-Family Homes for Metropolitan Areas, 4th Quarter 2014*
- Jacksonville was ranked #97 out of 226 metro areas in terms of housing affordability in 2014 by the National Association of Home Builders (#1 = most affordable). The NAHB-Wells Fargo Housing Opportunity Index (HOI) for a given area is defined as the share of homes sold in that area that would have been affordable to a family earning the local median income, based on standard mortgage underwriting criteria. *National Association of Home Builders®, NAHB-Wells Fargo Housing Opportunity Index, 4th Quarter 2014*
- The nation's largest metro areas were analyzed in terms of the percentage of households entering some stage of foreclosure in 2013. The Jacksonville metro area ranked #2 out of 10 (#1 = highest foreclosure rate). *RealtyTrac, "2013 Year-End U.S. Foreclosure Market Report™," January 16, 2014*

Safety Rankings

- Symantec, in partnership with Sperling's BestPlaces, ranked the 50 largest cities in the U.S. in terms of their vulnerability to cybercrime. The city ranked #40. Criteria: number of cyberattacks and potential infections; level of Internet access; expenditures on smartphones and computer hardware/software; wireless hotspots; broadband connectivity; Internet usage; online purchases. *Symantec, "Riskiest Online Cities of 2012" February 15, 2012*
- Allstate ranked the 200 largest cities in America in terms of driver safety. Jacksonville ranked #54. Allstate researchers analyzed internal property damage claims over a two-year period from January 2011 to December 2012. A weighted average of the two-year numbers determined the annual percentages. *Allstate, "Allstate America's Best Drivers Report, 2014"*
- The National Insurance Crime Bureau ranked 380 metro areas in the U.S. in terms of per capita rates of vehicle theft. The Jacksonville metro area ranked #155 (#1 = highest rate). Criteria: number of vehicle theft offenses per 100,000 inhabitants in 2012. *National Insurance Crime Bureau, "Hot Spots 2012," June 26, 2013*

Seniors/Retirement Rankings

- From its Best Cities for Successful Aging indexes, the Milken Institute generated rankings for metropolitan areas, weighing data in eight categories—health care, wellness, living arrangements, transportation, financial characteristics, education and employment opportunities, community engagement, and overall livability. The Jacksonville metro area was ranked #71 overall in the large metro area category. *Milken Institute, "Best Cities for Successful Aging, 2014"*
- Jacksonville was identified as one of the most popular places to retire by *Topretirements.com*. The list reflects the 100 cities (out of 900+ total cities reviewed) that visitors to the website are most interested in for retirement. *Topretirements.com, "Most Popular Places to Retire for 2014," February 25, 2014*

Women/Minorities Rankings

- *Women's Health* examined U.S. cities and identified the 100 best cities for women. Jacksonville was ranked #77. Criteria: 30 categories were examined from obesity and breast cancer rates to commuting times and hours spent working out. *Women's Health, "Best Cities for Women 2012"*

Miscellaneous Rankings

- Jacksonville was selected as a 2013 Digital Cities Survey winner. The city ranked #3 in the large city (250,000 or more population) category. The survey examined and assessed how city governments are utilizing information technology to operate and deliver quality service to their customers and citizens. Survey questions focused on implementation and adoption of online service delivery; planning and governance; and the infrastructure and architecture that make the transformation to digital government possible. *Center for Digital Government, "2013 Digital Cities Survey," November 7, 2013*
- Mars Chocolate North America, the makers of COMBOS®, in partnership with Sperling's BestPlaces, ranked 50 major metro areas in terms of their "manliness." The Jacksonville metro area ranked #21. Criteria: number of professional sports teams; number of nearby NASCAR tracks and racing events; manly lifestyle; concentration of manly retail stores; manly occupations per capita; salty snack sales; "Board of Manliness" rankings. *Mars Chocolate North America, "America's Manliest Cities 2012"*
- The National Alliance to End Homelessness ranked the 100 most populous metro areas in terms the rate of homelessness. The Jacksonville metro area ranked #14. Criteria: number of homeless people per 10,000 population in 2011. *National Alliance to End Homelessness, The State of Homelessness in America 2012*

Business Environment

CITY FINANCES

City Government Finances

Component	2012 ($000)	2012 ($ per capita)
Total Revenues	3,929,970	4,782
Total Expenditures	4,266,035	5,191
Debt Outstanding	10,439,029	12,703
Cash and Securities[1]	5,672,691	6,903

Note: (1) Cash and security holdings of a government at the close of its fiscal year, including those of its dependent agencies, utilities, and liquor stores.
Source: U.S Census Bureau, State & Local Government Finances 2012

City Government Revenue by Source

Source	2012 ($000)	2012 ($ per capita)
General Revenue		
From Federal Government	95,869	117
From State Government	149,645	182
From Local Governments	0	0
Taxes		
Property	498,507	607
Sales and Gross Receipts	366,013	445
Personal Income	0	0
Corporate Income	0	0
Motor Vehicle License	0	0
Other Taxes	59,839	73
Current Charges	548,306	667
Liquor Store	0	0
Utility	1,913,412	2,328
Employee Retirement	69,707	85

Source: U.S Census Bureau, State & Local Government Finances 2012

City Government Expenditures by Function

Function	2012 ($000)	2012 ($ per capita)	2012 (%)
General Direct Expenditures			
Air Transportation	62,278	76	1.5
Corrections	61,128	74	1.4
Education	0	0	0.0
Employment Security Administration	0	0	0.0
Financial Administration	71,050	86	1.7
Fire Protection	162,641	198	3.8
General Public Buildings	11,833	14	0.3
Governmental Administration, Other	19,568	24	0.5
Health	31,784	39	0.7
Highways	70,319	86	1.6
Hospitals	0	0	0.0
Housing and Community Development	4,794	6	0.1
Interest on General Debt	161,694	197	3.8
Judicial and Legal	27,095	33	0.6
Libraries	39,791	48	0.9
Parking	3,876	5	0.1
Parks and Recreation	80,566	98	1.9
Police Protection	299,212	364	7.0
Public Welfare	45,958	56	1.1
Sewerage	129,510	158	3.0
Solid Waste Management	64,794	79	1.5
Veterans' Services	0	0	0.0
Liquor Store	0	0	0.0
Utility	2,152,368	2,619	50.5
Employee Retirement	225,608	275	5.3

Source: U.S Census Bureau, State & Local Government Finances 2012

DEMOGRAPHICS

Population Growth

Area	1990 Census	2000 Census	2010 Census	Population Growth (%) 1990-2000	Population Growth (%) 2000-2010
City	635,221	735,617	821,784	15.8	11.7
MSA[1]	925,213	1,122,750	1,345,596	21.4	19.8
U.S.	248,709,873	281,421,906	308,745,538	13.2	9.7

Note: (1) Figures cover the Jacksonville, FL Metropolitan Statistical Area—see Appendix B for areas included
Source: U.S. Census Bureau, Census 1990, 2000, 2010

Household Size

Area	Persons in Household (%) One	Two	Three	Four	Five	Six	Seven or More	Average Household Size
City	31.2	33.2	16.4	11.7	4.7	1.6	1.3	2.62
MSA[1]	28.4	34.9	16.2	12.5	5.1	1.8	1.0	2.65
U.S.	27.7	33.6	15.7	13.1	6.0	2.3	1.5	2.64

Note: (1) Figures cover the Jacksonville, FL Metropolitan Statistical Area—see Appendix B for areas included
Source: U.S. Census Bureau, 2011-2013 American Community Survey 3-Year Estimates

Race

Area	White Alone[2] (%)	Black Alone[2] (%)	Asian Alone[2] (%)	AIAN[3] Alone[2] (%)	NHOPI[4] Alone[2] (%)	Other Race Alone[2] (%)	Two or More Races (%)
City	60.4	30.5	4.4	0.3	0.1	1.0	3.3
MSA[1]	70.8	21.5	3.5	0.3	0.1	0.9	2.9
U.S.	73.9	12.6	5.0	0.8	0.2	4.7	2.9

Note: (1) Figures cover the Jacksonville, FL Metropolitan Statistical Area—see Appendix B for areas included; (2) Alone is defined as not being in combination with one or more other races; (3) American Indian and Alaska Native; (4) Native Hawaiian and Other Pacific Islander
Source: U.S. Census Bureau, 2011-2013 American Community Survey 3-Year Estimates

Hispanic or Latino Origin

Area	Total (%)	Mexican (%)	Puerto Rican (%)	Cuban (%)	Other (%)
City	8.2	1.8	2.7	1.0	2.7
MSA[1]	7.4	1.7	2.4	0.9	2.5
U.S.	16.9	10.8	1.6	0.6	3.8

Note: Persons of Hispanic or Latino origin can be of any race; (1) Figures cover the Jacksonville, FL Metropolitan Statistical Area—see Appendix B for areas included
Source: U.S. Census Bureau, 2011-2013 American Community Survey 3-Year Estimates

Segregation

Type	Segregation Indices[1] 1990	2000	2010	2010 Rank[2]	Percent Change 1990-2000	1990-2010	2000-2010
Black/White	57.5	53.9	53.1	59	-3.6	-4.4	-0.8
Asian/White	34.2	37.0	37.5	71	2.8	3.2	0.4
Hispanic/White	22.1	26.6	27.6	98	4.6	5.5	1.0

Note: All figures cover the Metropolitan Statistical Area—see Appendix B for areas included; Figures are based on an analysis of 1990, 2000, and 2010 Census Decennial Census tract data by William H. Frey, Brookings Institution and the University of Michigan Social Science Data Analysis Network. In this analysis all racial groups (whites, blacks, and asians) are non-Hispanic members of those races. Hispanics are shown as a separate category;
(1) Segregation Indices are Dissimilarity Indices that measure the degree to which the minority group is distributed differently than whites across census tracts. They range from 0 (complete integration) to 100 (complete segregation) where the value indicates the percentage of the minority group that needs to move to be distributed exactly like whites; (2) Ranges from 1 (most segregated) to 102 (least segregated); n/a not available.
Source: www.CensusScope.org

Ancestry

Area	German	Irish	English	American	Italian	Polish	French[2]	Scottish	Dutch
City	9.6	9.7	8.2	6.0	4.0	1.6	2.1	1.8	0.8
MSA[1]	11.2	11.4	9.6	8.4	4.8	2.1	2.6	2.3	1.0
U.S.	14.9	10.8	8.0	7.4	5.5	3.0	2.7	1.7	1.4

Note: Figures are the percentage of the total population reporting a particular ancestry. The nine most commonly reported ancestries in the U.S. are shown. Figures include multiple ancestries (e.g. if a person reported being Irish and Italian, they were included in both columns); (1) Figures cover the Jacksonville, FL Metropolitan Statistical Area—see Appendix B for areas included; (2) Excludes Basque
Source: U.S. Census Bureau, 2011-2013 American Community Survey 3-Year Estimates

Foreign-Born Population

Area	Percent of Population Born in								
	Any Foreign Country	Mexico	Asia	Europe	Carribean	South America	Central America[2]	Africa	Canada
City	9.6	0.5	3.7	1.7	1.4	1.0	0.6	0.5	0.2
MSA[1]	7.9	0.4	2.9	1.6	1.1	0.8	0.4	0.4	0.2
U.S.	13.0	3.7	3.8	1.5	1.2	0.9	1.0	0.6	0.3

Note: (1) Figures cover the Jacksonville, FL Metropolitan Statistical Area—see Appendix B for areas included; (2) Excludes Mexico.
Source: U.S. Census Bureau, 2011-2013 American Community Survey 3-Year Estimates

Marital Status

Area	Never Married	Now Married[2]	Separated	Widowed	Divorced
City	34.5	42.9	2.7	5.8	14.1
MSA[1]	31.2	46.8	2.4	5.8	13.8
U.S.	32.7	48.1	2.2	6.0	11.0

Note: Figures are percentages and cover the population 15 years of age and older; (1) Figures cover the Jacksonville, FL Metropolitan Statistical Area—see Appendix B for areas included; (2) Excludes separated
Source: U.S. Census Bureau, 2011-2013 American Community Survey 3-Year Estimates

Disability Status

Area	All Ages	Under 18 Years Old	18 to 64 Years Old	65 Years and Over
City	12.6	4.2	11.2	38.1
MSA[1]	12.7	4.4	10.8	36.6
U.S.	12.3	4.1	10.2	36.3

Note: Figures show percent of the civilian noninstitutionalized population that reported having a disability. Disability status is determined from from six types of difficulty: vision, hearing, cognitive, ambulatory, self-care, and independent living. For children under 5 years old, hearing and vision difficulty are used to determine disability status. For children between the ages of 5 and 14, disability status is determined from hearing, vision, cognitive, ambulatory, and self-care difficulties. For people aged 15 years and older, they are considered to have a disability if they have difficulty with any one of the six difficulty types; (1) Figures cover the Jacksonville, FL Metropolitan Statistical Area—see Appendix B for areas included.
Source: U.S. Census Bureau, 2011-2013 American Community Survey 3-Year Estimates

Age

Area	Percent of Population									Median Age
	Under Age 5	Age 5–19	Age 20–34	Age 35–44	Age 45–54	Age 55–64	Age 65–74	Age 75–84	Age 85+	
City	7.0	18.9	23.2	13.1	14.1	12.0	6.8	3.4	1.5	35.7
MSA[1]	6.3	19.5	20.7	13.1	14.7	12.7	7.7	3.8	1.7	37.7
U.S.	6.4	19.9	20.7	12.9	14.1	12.3	7.6	4.2	1.9	37.4

Note: (1) Figures cover the Jacksonville, FL Metropolitan Statistical Area—see Appendix B for areas included
Source: U.S. Census Bureau, 2011-2013 American Community Survey 3-Year Estimates

Gender

Area	Males	Females	Males per 100 Females
City	405,350	430,737	94.1
MSA[1]	670,928	707,065	94.9
U.S.	154,451,010	159,410,713	96.9

Note: (1) Figures cover the Jacksonville, FL Metropolitan Statistical Area—see Appendix B for areas included
Source: U.S. Census Bureau, 2011-2013 American Community Survey 3-Year Estimates

Religious Groups by Family

Area	Catholic	Baptist	Non-Den.	Methodist[2]	Lutheran	LDS[3]	Pente-costal	Presby-terian[4]	Muslim[5]	Judaism
MSA[1]	9.9	18.5	7.8	4.5	0.7	1.1	1.9	1.6	0.6	0.4
U.S.	19.1	9.3	4.0	4.0	2.3	2.0	1.9	1.6	0.8	0.7

Note: Figures are the number of adherents as a percentage of the total population; (1) Figures cover the Jacksonville, FL Metropolitan Statistical Area—see Appendix B for areas included; (2) Methodist/Pietist; (3) Latter Day Saints; (4) Reformed; (5) Figures are estimates
Source: Association of Statisticians of American Religious Bodies, 2010 U.S. Religion Census: Religious Congregations & Membership Study

Religious Groups by Tradition

Area	Catholic	Evangelical Protestant	Mainline Protestant	Other Tradition	Black Protestant	Orthodox
MSA[1]	9.9	27.1	5.7	2.9	4.2	0.3
U.S.	19.1	16.2	7.3	4.3	1.6	0.3

Note: Figures are the number of adherents as a percentage of the total population; (1) Figures cover the Jacksonville, FL Metropolitan Statistical Area—see Appendix B for areas included
Source: Association of Statisticians of American Religious Bodies, 2010 U.S. Religion Census: Religious Congregations & Membership Study

ECONOMY

Gross Metropolitan Product

Area	2012	2013	2014	2015	Rank[2]
MSA[1]	62.3	65.1	68.1	71.9	47

Note: Figures are in billions of dollars; (1) Figures cover the Jacksonville, FL Metropolitan Statistical Area—see Appendix B for areas included; (2) Rank is based on 2015 data and ranges from 1 to 363
Source: The U.S. Conference of Mayors, U.S. Metro Economies: GMP and Employment 2013-2015, June 2014

Economic Growth

Area	2010-12 (%)	2013 (%)	2014 (%)	2015 (%)	Rank[2]
MSA[1]	1.4	3.2	3.0	3.5	74
U.S.	2.1	2.0	2.3	3.2	–

Note: Figures are real gross metropolitan product (GMP) growth rates and represent annual average percent change; (1) Figures cover the Jacksonville, FL Metropolitan Statistical Area—see Appendix B for areas included; (2) Rank is based on 2015 data and ranges from 1 to 363
Source: The U.S. Conference of Mayors, U.S. Metro Economies: GMP and Employment 2013-2015, June 2014

Metropolitan Area Exports

Area	2008	2009	2010	2011	2012	2013	Rank[2]
MSA[1]	1,973.5	1,634.4	1,940.5	2,385.2	2,595.0	2,467.8	91

Note: Figures are in millions of dollars; (1) Figures cover the Jacksonville, FL Metropolitan Statistical Area—see Appendix B for areas included; (2) Rank is based on 2013 data and ranges from 1 to 387
Source: U.S. Department of Commerce, International Trade Administration, Office of Trade & Industry Information, Manufacturing & Services, data extracted April 3, 2015

Building Permits

Area	Single-Family			Multi-Family			Total		
	2013	2014	Pct. Chg.	2013	2014	Pct. Chg.	2013	2014	Pct. Chg.
City	1,844	2,106	14.2	709	1,196	68.7	2,553	3,302	29.3
MSA[1]	6,281	6,299	0.3	1,077	1,482	37.6	7,358	7,781	5.7
U.S.	620,802	634,597	2.2	370,020	411,766	11.3	990,822	1,046,363	5.6

Note: (1) Figures cover the Jacksonville, FL Metropolitan Statistical Area—see Appendix B for areas included; Figures represent new, privately-owned housing units authorized (unadjusted data); All permit data are based on estimates with imputation.
Source: U.S. Census Bureau, Manufacturing, Mining, and Construction Statistics, Building Permits, 2013, 2014

Bankruptcy Filings

Area	Business Filings			Nonbusiness Filings		
	2013	2014	% Chg.	2013	2014	% Chg.
Duval County	137	106	-22.6	3,773	2,917	-22.7
U.S.	33,212	26,983	-18.8	1,038,720	909,812	-12.4

Note: Business filings include Chapter 7, Chapter 11, Chapter 12, and Chapter 13; Nonbusiness filings include Chapter 7, Chapter 11, and Chapter 13
Source: Administrative Office of the U.S. Courts, Business and Nonbusiness Bankruptcy, County Cases Commenced by Chapter of the Bankruptcy Code, During the 12- Month Period Ending December 31, 2013 and Business and Nonbusiness Bankruptcy, County Cases Commenced by Chapter of the Bankruptcy Code, During the 12- Month Period Ending December 31, 2014

Housing Vacancy Rates

Area	Gross Vacancy Rate[2] (%)			Year-Round Vacancy Rate[3] (%)			Rental Vacancy Rate[4] (%)			Homeowner Vacancy Rate[5] (%)		
	2012	2013	2014	2012	2013	2014	2012	2013	2014	2012	2013	2014
MSA[1]	15.4	14.2	16.6	14.4	12.7	14.0	11.7	8.4	11.1	1.9	1.5	2.6
U.S.	13.8	13.6	13.4	10.8	10.7	10.4	8.7	8.3	7.6	2.0	2.0	1.9

Note: (1) Figures cover the Jacksonville, FL Metropolitan Statistical Area—see Appendix B for areas included; (2) The percentage of the total housing inventory that is vacant; (3) The percentage of the housing inventory (excluding seasonal units) that is year-round vacant; (4) The percentage of rental inventory that is vacant for rent; (5) The percentage of homeowner inventory that is vacant for sale
Source: U.S. Census Bureau, Housing Vacancies and Homeownership Annual Statistics: 2014

INCOME

Income

Area	Per Capita ($)	Median Household ($)	Average Household ($)
City	24,870	45,978	62,959
MSA[1]	27,340	51,016	70,192
U.S.	27,884	52,176	72,897

Note: (1) Figures cover the Jacksonville, FL Metropolitan Statistical Area—see Appendix B for areas included
Source: U.S. Census Bureau, 2011-2013 American Community Survey 3-Year Estimates

Household Income Distribution

Area	Percent of Households Earning							
	Under $15,000	$15,000 -24,999	$25,000 -34,999	$35,000 -49,999	$50,000 -74,999	$75,000 -99,000	$100,000 -149,999	$150,000 and up
City	15.1	11.7	11.5	14.9	18.6	11.0	10.8	6.3
MSA[1]	13.1	10.6	10.6	14.5	19.2	11.7	12.0	8.1
U.S.	13.0	10.9	10.3	13.6	17.9	11.9	12.7	9.6

Note: (1) Figures cover the Jacksonville, FL Metropolitan Statistical Area—see Appendix B for areas included
Source: U.S. Census Bureau, 2011-2013 American Community Survey 3-Year Estimates

Poverty Rate

Area	All Ages	Under 18 Years Old	18 to 64 Years Old	65 Years and Over
City	18.0	26.5	16.2	10.2
MSA[1]	15.2	21.2	14.3	8.4
U.S.	15.9	22.4	14.8	9.5

Note: Figures are percentage of people whose income during the past 12 months was below the poverty level; (1) Figures cover the Jacksonville, FL Metropolitan Statistical Area—see Appendix B for areas included
Source: U.S. Census Bureau, 2011-2013 American Community Survey 3-Year Estimates

EMPLOYMENT

Labor Force and Employment

Area	Civilian Labor Force			Workers Employed		
	Dec. 2013	Dec. 2014	% Chg.	Dec. 2013	Dec. 2014	% Chg.
City	429,171	434,184	1.2	401,740	410,048	2.1
MSA[1]	706,767	715,342	1.2	663,622	677,314	2.1
U.S.	154,408,000	155,521,000	0.7	144,423,000	147,190,000	1.9

Note: Data is not seasonally adjusted and covers workers 16 years of age and older; (1) Figures cover the Jacksonville, FL Metropolitan Statistical Area—see Appendix B for areas included
Source: Bureau of Labor Statistics, Local Area Unemployment Statistics

Unemployment Rate

Area	2014											
	Jan.	Feb.	Mar.	Apr.	May	Jun.	Jul.	Aug.	Sep.	Oct.	Nov.	Dec.
City	6.8	6.9	6.8	6.2	6.6	6.8	7.1	7.1	6.4	6.0	6.0	5.6
MSA[1]	6.5	6.5	6.5	5.9	6.2	6.4	6.8	6.7	6.1	5.8	5.7	5.3
U.S.	7.0	7.0	6.8	5.9	6.1	6.3	6.5	6.3	5.7	5.5	5.5	5.4

Note: Data is not seasonally adjusted and covers workers 16 years of age and older; (1) Figures cover the Jacksonville, FL Metropolitan Statistical Area—see Appendix B for areas included
Source: Bureau of Labor Statistics, Local Area Unemployment Statistics

Employment by Occupation

Occupation Classification	City (%)	MSA[1] (%)	U.S. (%)
Management, Business, Science, and Arts	34.4	36.0	36.2
Natural Resources, Construction, and Maintenance	7.9	8.0	9.0
Production, Transportation, and Material Moving	10.8	10.3	12.1
Sales and Office	28.3	27.3	24.4
Service	18.6	18.4	18.3

Note: Figures cover employed civilians 16 years of age and older; (1) Figures cover the Jacksonville, FL Metropolitan Statistical Area—see Appendix B for areas included
Source: U.S. Census Bureau, 2011-2013 American Community Survey 3-Year Estimates

Employment by Industry

Sector	MSA[1] Number of Employees	MSA[1] Percent of Total	U.S. Percent of Total
Construction	33,200	5.2	4.4
Education and Health Services	95,600	14.9	15.5
Financial Activities	62,100	9.7	5.7
Government	76,000	11.9	15.8
Information	9,100	1.4	2.0
Leisure and Hospitality	76,500	12.0	10.3
Manufacturing	28,100	4.4	8.7
Mining and Logging	400	0.1	0.6
Other Services	22,200	3.5	4.0
Professional and Business Services	101,000	15.8	13.8
Retail Trade	78,100	12.2	11.4
Transportation, Warehousing, and Utilities	33,500	5.2	3.9
Wholesale Trade	23,700	3.7	4.2

Note: Figures are non-farm employment as of December 2014. Figures are not seasonally adjusted and include workers 16 years of age and older; (1) Figures cover the Jacksonville, FL Metropolitan Statistical Area—see Appendix B for areas included
Source: Bureau of Labor Statistics, Current Employment Statistics, Employment, Hours, and Earnings

Occupations with Greatest Projected Employment Growth: 2012 – 2022

Occupation[1]	2012 Employment	2022 Projected Employment	Numeric Employment Change	Percent Employment Change
Retail Salespersons	326,380	380,120	53,740	16.5
Combined Food Preparation and Serving Workers, Including Fast Food	196,980	237,340	40,360	20.5
Customer Service Representatives	191,210	228,620	37,410	19.6
Registered Nurses	164,020	201,140	37,120	22.6
Waiters and Waitresses	191,370	227,810	36,440	19.0
Office Clerks, General	142,710	170,300	27,590	19.3
Cashiers	206,660	230,190	23,530	11.4
Landscaping and Groundskeeping Workers	92,510	115,540	23,030	24.9
Receptionists and Information Clerks	75,780	95,680	19,900	26.2
Nursing Assistants	86,990	106,200	19,210	22.1

Note: Projections cover Florida; (1) Sorted by numeric employment change
Source: www.projectionscentral.com, State Occupational Projections, 2012–2022 Long-Term Projections

Fastest Growing Occupations: 2012 – 2022

Occupation[1]	2012 Employment	2022 Projected Employment	Numeric Employment Change	Percent Employment Change
Helpers—Carpenters	1,280	2,450	1,170	90.7
Helpers—Brickmasons, Blockmasons, Stonemasons, and Tile and Marble Setters	1,050	1,890	840	79.5
Biomedical Engineers	760	1,300	540	70.7
Reinforcing Iron and Rebar Workers	520	870	350	67.5
Glaziers	2,890	4,710	1,820	62.8
Solar Photovoltaic Installers	170	270	100	58.7
Brickmasons and Blockmasons	2,820	4,430	1,610	57.1
Stonemasons	450	710	260	56.4
Helpers—Pipelayers, Plumbers, Pipefitters, and Steamfitters	2,420	3,750	1,330	54.8
Cement Masons and Concrete Finishers	10,390	16,050	5,660	54.4

Note: Projections cover Florida; (1) Sorted by percent employment change and excludes occupations with numeric employment change less than 100
Source: www.projectionscentral.com, State Occupational Projections, 2012–2022 Long-Term Projections

Average Wages

Occupation	$/Hr.	Occupation	$/Hr.
Accountants and Auditors	32.77	Maids and Housekeeping Cleaners	9.35
Automotive Mechanics	18.31	Maintenance and Repair Workers	17.52
Bookkeepers	17.44	Marketing Managers	57.64
Carpenters	15.42	Nuclear Medicine Technologists	35.62
Cashiers	9.38	Nurses, Licensed Practical	20.15
Clerks, General Office	13.05	Nurses, Registered	30.30
Clerks, Receptionists/Information	12.94	Nursing Assistants	11.49
Clerks, Shipping/Receiving	15.15	Packers and Packagers, Hand	9.70
Computer Programmers	36.13	Physical Therapists	45.60
Computer Systems Analysts	36.86	Postal Service Mail Carriers	25.15
Computer User Support Specialists	21.05	Real Estate Brokers	n/a
Cooks, Restaurant	11.36	Retail Salespersons	11.63
Dentists	81.76	Sales Reps., Exc. Tech./Scientific	27.56
Electrical Engineers	40.80	Sales Reps., Tech./Scientific	37.64
Electricians	20.58	Secretaries, Exc. Legal/Med./Exec.	15.06
Financial Managers	64.14	Security Guards	10.72
First-Line Supervisors/Managers, Sales	19.99	Surgeons	111.20
Food Preparation Workers	10.04	Teacher Assistants	12.70
General and Operations Managers	58.38	Teachers, Elementary School	24.60
Hairdressers/Cosmetologists	15.99	Teachers, Secondary School	24.80
Internists	107.64	Telemarketers	10.16
Janitors and Cleaners	11.55	Truck Drivers, Heavy/Tractor-Trailer	19.07
Landscaping/Groundskeeping Workers	12.18	Truck Drivers, Light/Delivery Svcs.	16.18
Lawyers	52.18	Waiters and Waitresses	10.17

Note: Wage data covers the Jacksonville, FL Metropolitan Statistical Area—see Appendix B for areas included; Hourly wages for elementary/secondary school teachers and teacher assistants were calculated by the editors from annual wage data assuming a 40 hour work week; n/a not available.
Source: Bureau of Labor Statistics, Metro Area Occupational Employment and Wage Estimates, May 2014

TAXES

State Corporate Income Tax Rates

State	Tax Rate (%)	Income Brackets ($)	Num. of Brackets	Financial Institution Tax Rate (%)[a]	Federal Income Tax Ded.
Florida	5.5 (f)	Flat rate	1	5.5 (f)	No

Note: Tax rates as of January 1, 2015; (a) Rates listed are the corporate income tax rate applied to financial institutions or excise taxes based on income. Some states have other taxes based upon the value of deposits or shares; (f) An exemption of $50,000 is allowed. Florida's Alternative Minimum Tax rate is 3.3%.
Source: Federation of Tax Administrators, "State Corporate Income Tax Rates, 2015"

State Individual Income Tax Rates

State	Tax Rate (%)	Income Brackets ($)	Num. of Brackets	Personal Exempt. ($)[1]		Fed. Inc. Tax Ded.
				Single	Dependents	
Florida	None			–	–	–

Note: Tax rates as of January 1, 2015; Local- and county-level taxes are not included; n/a not applicable; (1) Married joint filers generally receive double the single exemption
Source: Federation of Tax Administrators, "State Individual Income Tax Rates, 2015"

Various State and Local Tax Rates

State	State and Local Sales and Use (%)	State Sales and Use (%)	Gasoline[1] (¢/gal.)	Cigarette[2] ($/pack)	Spirits[3] ($/gal.)	Wine[4] ($/gal.)	Beer[5] ($/gal.)
Florida	7.0	6.0	36.42	1.339	6.50 (f)	2.25	0.48 (p)

Note: All tax rates as of January 1, 2015; (1) The American Petroleum Institute has developed a methodology for determining the average tax rate on a gallon of fuel. Rates may include any of the following: excise taxes, environmental fees, storage tank fees, other fees or taxes, general sales tax, and local taxes. In states where gasoline is subject to the general sales tax, or where the fuel tax is based on the average sale price, the average rate determined by API is sensitive to changes in the price of gasoline. States that fully or partially apply general sales taxes to gasoline: CA, CO, GA, IL, IN, MI, NY; (2) The federal excise tax of $1.0066 per pack and local taxes are not included; (3) Rates are those applicable to off-premise sales of 40% alcohol by volume (a.b.v.) distilled spirits in 750ml containers. Local excise taxes are excluded; (4) Rates are those applicable to off-premise sales of 11% a.b.v. non-carbonated wine in 750ml containers; (5) Rates are those applicable to off-premise sales of 4.7% a.b.v. beer in 12 ounce containers; (f) Different rates are also applicable according to alcohol content, place of production, size of container, or place purchased (on- or off-premise or onboard airlines); (p) Local excise taxes are excluded.
Source: Tax Foundation, 2015 Facts & Figures: How Does Your State Compare?

State Business Tax Climate Index Rankings

State	Overall Rank	Corporate Tax Index Rank	Individual Income Tax Index Rank	Sales Tax Index Rank	Unemployment Insurance Tax Index Rank	Property Tax Index Rank
Florida	5	14	1	12	3	16

Note: The index is a measure of how each state's tax laws affect economic performance. The lower the rank, the more favorable a state's tax system is for business. States without a given tax are given a ranking of 1. The scores/rankings for the District of Columbia do not affect other states. The 2015 index represents the tax climate as of July 1, 2014.
Source: Tax Foundation, State Business Tax Climate Index 2015

COMMERCIAL REAL ESTATE

Office Market

Market Area	Inventory (sq. ft.)	Vacancy Rate (%)	Under Construction (sq. ft.)	YTD Net Absorption (sq. ft.)	Total Average Asking Rent ($/sq. ft./year)
Jacksonville	31,559,191	17.4	234,041	381,012	17.72
National	4,745,108,508	14.3	71,190,461	51,084,126	27.40

Source: Newmark Grubb Knight Frank, National Office Market Report, 4th Quarter 2014

Industrial/Warehouse/R&D Market

Market Area	Inventory (sq. ft.)	Vacancy Rate (%)	Under Construction (sq. ft.)	YTD Net Absorption (sq. ft.)	Total Average Asking Rent ($/sq. ft./year)
Jacksonville	118,953,591	9.3	367,546	1,365,416	3.91
National	14,238,613,765	7.2	134,387,407	185,246,438	5.64

Source: Newmark Grubb Knight Frank, National Industrial Market Report, 4th Quarter 2014

COMMERCIAL UTILITIES

Typical Monthly Electric Bills

Area	Commercial Service ($/month)		Industrial Service ($/month)	
	40 kW demand 5,000 kWh	500 kW demand 100,000 kWh	5,000 kW demand 1,500,000 kWh	70,000 kW demand 50,000,000 kWh
City	566	12,742	170,357	3,524,892

Note: Figures are based on rates in effect January 2, 2014
Source: Memphis Light, Gas and Water, 2014 Utility Bill Comparisons for Selected U.S. Cities

TRANSPORTATION

Means of Transportation to Work

Area	Car/Truck/Van		Public Transportation			Bicycle	Walked	Other Means	Worked at Home
	Drove Alone	Car-pooled	Bus	Subway	Railroad				
City	80.3	10.0	1.9	0.0	0.0	0.4	1.2	1.5	4.6
MSA[1]	80.8	9.8	1.3	0.0	0.0	0.6	1.2	1.4	4.9
U.S.	76.4	9.6	2.6	1.8	0.6	0.6	2.8	1.3	4.3

Note: Figures are percentages and cover workers 16 years of age and older; (1) Figures cover the Jacksonville, FL Metropolitan Statistical Area—see Appendix B for areas included
Source: U.S. Census Bureau, 2011-2013 American Community Survey 3-Year Estimates

Travel Time to Work

Area	Less Than 10 Minutes	10 to 19 Minutes	20 to 29 Minutes	30 to 44 Minutes	45 to 59 Minutes	60 to 89 Minutes	90 Minutes or More
City	7.8	30.1	30.9	22.3	4.9	2.7	1.3
MSA[1]	9.2	27.6	26.3	23.7	7.8	3.9	1.5
U.S.	13.3	29.7	20.9	20.2	7.7	5.7	2.6

Note: Figures are percentages and include workers 16 years old and over; (1) Figures cover the Jacksonville, FL Metropolitan Statistical Area—see Appendix B for areas included
Source: U.S. Census Bureau, 2011-2013 American Community Survey 3-Year Estimates

Travel Time Index

Area	1985	1990	1995	2000	2005	2010	2011
Urban Area[1]	1.11	1.17	1.25	1.20	1.26	1.14	1.14
Average[2]	1.09	1.14	1.16	1.19	1.23	1.18	1.18

Note: Travel Time Index—the ratio of travel time in the peak period to the travel time at free-flow conditions. For example, a value of 1.30 indicates a 20-minute free-flow trip takes 26 minutes in the peak. Free-flow speeds (60 mph on freeways and 35 mph on principal arterials) are used as the comparison threshold; (1) Covers the Jacksonville FL urban area; (2) average of 498 urban areas
Source: Texas Transportation Institute, Urban Mobility Report 2012, December 2012

Public Transportation

Agency Name / Mode of Transportation	Vehicles Operated in Maximum Service	Annual Unlinked Passenger Trips (in thous.)	Annual Passenger Miles (in thous.)
Jacksonville Transportation Authority (JTA)			
Bus (directly operated)	138	11,220.2	74,120.2
Demand Response (purchased transportation)	82	378.5	4,769.3
Monorail and Automated Guideway (directly operated)	5	1,079.2	495.1

Source: Federal Transit Administration, National Transit Database, 2013

Air Transportation

Airport Name and Code / Type of Service	Passenger Airlines[1]	Passenger Enplanements	Freight Carriers[2]	Freight (lbs.)
Jacksonville International (JAX)				
Domestic service (U.S. carriers - 2014)	27	2,587,961	16	75,594,096
International service (U.S. carriers - 2013)	5	264	2	14,889

Note: (1) Includes all U.S.-based major, minor and commuter airlines that carried at least one passenger during the year; (2) Includes all U.S.-based airlines and freight carriers that transported at least one lb. of freight during the year.
Source: Bureau of Transportation Statistics, The Intermodal Transportation Database, Air Carriers: T-100 Domestic Market (U.S. Carriers), 2014; Bureau of Transportation Statistics, The Intermodal Transportation Database, Air Carriers: T-100 International Market (U.S. Carriers), 2013

Other Transportation Statistics

Major Highways:	I-10; I-95
Amtrak Service:	Yes
Major Waterways/Ports:	St. Johns River

Source: Amtrak.com; Google Maps

BUSINESSES

Major Business Headquarters

Company Name	Rankings	
	Fortune[1]	Forbes[2]
CSX Corporation	231	-
Fidelity National Financial	316	-
Fidelity National Information Services	426	-

Note: (1) Fortune 500—companies that produce a 10-K are ranked 1 to 500 based on 2013 revenue; (2) all private companies with at least $2 billion in annual revenue through the end of their most current fiscal year are ranked 1 to 221; companies listed are headquartered in the city; dashes indicate no ranking
Source: Fortune, "Fortune 500," June 16, 2014; Forbes, "America's Largest Private Companies," November 5, 2014

Fast-Growing Businesses

According to *Inc.*, Jacksonville is home to four of America's 500 fastest-growing private companies: **The HCI Group** (#13); **Early Upgrade** (#94); **Dakenna Development** (#184); **ShayCore Enterprises** (#431). Criteria: must be an independent, privately-held, for-profit, U.S. corporation, proprietorship or partnership; revenues must be at least $100,000 in 2010 and $2 million in 2013; must have four-year operating/sales history. Holding companies, regulated banks, and utilities were excluded. *Inc., "America's 500 Fastest-Growing Private Companies," September 2014*

According to Deloitte, Jacksonville is home to one of North America's 500 fastest-growing high-technology companies: **Web.com Group** (#267). Companies are ranked by percentage growth in revenue over a five-year period. Criteria for inclusion: company must be headquartered within North America; must own proprietary intellectual property or proprietary technology that contributes to a significant portion of the company's operating revenue, or devote a significant proportion of revenues to research and development of technology; must have been in business for a minumum of five years with 2009 operating revenues of at least $50,000 USD/CD and 2013 operating revenues of at least $5 million USD/CD. *Deloitte Touche Tohmatsu, 2014 Technology Fast 500™*

Minority Business Opportunity

Jacksonville is home to one company which is on the *Black Enterprise* Industrial/Service 100 list (100 largest companies based on gross sales): **Raven Transport Co.** (#39). Criteria: operational in previous calendar year; at least 51% black-owned and manufactures/owns the product it sells or provides industrial or consumer services. Brokerages, real estate firms and firms that provide professional services are not eligible. *Black Enterprise, B.E. 100s, 2014*

Jacksonville is home to one company which is on the *Hispanic Business* 500 list (500 largest U.S. Hispanic-owned companies based on 2012 revenue): **Information and Computing Services** (#209). Companies included must show at least 51 percent ownership by Hispanic U.S. citizens, and must maintain headquarters in one of the 50 states or Washington, D.C. *Hispanic Business, "Hispanic Business 500," June 20, 2013*

Jacksonville is home to one company which is on the *Hispanic Business* Fastest-Growing 100 list (greatest sales growth from 2008 to 2012): **Information & Computing Services** (#99). Companies included must show at least 51 percent ownership by Hispanic U.S. citizens, and must maintain headquarters in one of the 50 states or Washington, D.C. In addition, companies must have minimum revenues of $200,000 for calendar year 2008. *Hispanic Business, June 20, 2013*

Minority- and Women-Owned Businesses

Group	All Firms		Firms with Paid Employees			
	Firms	Sales ($000)	Firms	Sales ($000)	Employees	Payroll ($000)
Asian	3,275	683,318	873	590,497	5,392	124,476
Black	9,718	373,933	650	208,344	3,220	66,134
Hispanic	4,175	800,765	611	627,534	4,024	117,669
Women	19,155	3,802,252	3,059	3,403,581	22,636	698,117
All Firms	64,101	109,406,895	17,474	107,422,420	431,635	17,490,879

Note: Figures cover firms located in the city; minority- and women-owned business are defined as firms in which the corresponding group own 51% or more of the stock or equity of the company
Source: U.S. Census Bureau, 2007 Economic Census, Survey of Business Owners (2012 Survey of Business Owners data will be released starting in June 2015)

HOTELS & CONVENTION CENTERS

Hotels/Motels

Area	5 Star		4 Star		3 Star		2 Star		1 Star		Not Rated	
	Num.	Pct.[3]	Num.	Pct.[3]	Num.	Pct.[3]	Num.	Pct.[3]	Num.	Pct.[3]	Num.	Pct.[3]
City[1]	1	0.5	9	4.9	56	30.4	107	58.2	4	2.2	7	3.8
Total[2]	166	0.9	1,264	7.0	5,718	31.8	9,340	52.0	411	2.3	1,070	6.0

Note: (1) Figures cover Jacksonville and vicinity; (2) Figures cover all 100 cities in this book; (3) Percentage of hotels which have a given star rating; Star ratings are determined by expedia.com and offer an indication of the general quality of a particular hotel.
Source: expedia.com, April 2, 2015

The Jacksonville, FL metro area is home to four of the best hotels in the U.S. according to *Travel & Leisure*: **Ritz-Carlton, Amelia Island**; **One Ocean Resort**; **Lodge & Club at Ponte Vedra Beach**; **Ponte Vedra Inn & Club**. Criteria: service; location; rooms; food; and value. The list includes the top 236 hotels in the U.S. *Travel & Leisure, "T+L 500, The World's Best Hotels 2015"*

Major Convention Centers

Name	Overall Space (sq. ft.)	Exhibit Space (sq. ft.)	Meeting Space (sq. ft.)	Meeting Rooms
Prime F. Osborn III Convention Center	296,000	100,000	48,000	22

Note: Table includes convention centers located in the Jacksonville, FL metro area; n/a not available
Source: Original research

Living Environment

COST OF LIVING

Cost of Living Index

Composite Index	Groceries	Housing	Utilities	Trans- portation	Health Care	Misc. Goods/ Services
98.1	102.3	85.4	107.4	103.8	89.6	103.3

Note: The Cost of Living Index measures regional differences in the cost of consumer goods and services, excluding taxes and non-consumer expenditures, for professional and managerial households in the top income quintile. It is based on more than 50,000 prices covering almost 60 different items for which prices are collected three times a year by chambers of commerce, economic development organizations or university applied economic centers in each participating urban area. The numbers shown should be read as a percentage above or below the national average of 100. For example, a value of 115.4 in the groceries column indicates that grocery prices are 15.4% higher than the national average. Small differences in the index numbers should not be interpreted as significant; Figures cover the Jacksonville FL urban area.
Source: The Council for Community and Economic Research, ACCRA Cost of Living Index, 2014

Grocery Prices

Area[1]	T-Bone Steak ($/pound)	Frying Chicken ($/pound)	Whole Milk ($/half gal.)	Eggs ($/dozen)	Orange Juice ($/64 oz.)	Coffee ($/11.5 oz.)
City[2]	10.84	1.45	2.75	1.92	3.39	3.96
Avg.	10.40	1.37	2.40	1.99	3.46	4.27
Min.	8.48	0.93	1.37	1.30	2.83	2.99
Max.	14.20	2.44	3.62	4.02	6.42	6.96

Note: (1) Values for the local area are compared with the average, minimum and maximum values for all 308 areas in the Cost of Living Index; (2) Figures cover the Jacksonville FL urban area; **T-Bone Steak** *(price per pound);* **Frying Chicken** *(price per pound, whole fryer);* **Whole Milk** *(half gallon carton);* **Eggs** *(price per dozen, Grade A, large);* **Orange Juice** *(64 oz. Tropicana or Florida Natural);* **Coffee** *(11.5 oz. can, vacuum-packed, Maxwell House, Hills Bros, or Folgers).*
Source: The Council for Community and Economic Research, ACCRA Cost of Living Index, 2014

Housing and Utility Costs

Area[1]	New Home Price ($)	Apartment Rent ($/month)	All Electric ($/month)	Part Electric ($/month)	Other Energy ($/month)	Telephone ($/month)
City[2]	229,363	1,069	170.00	-	-	32.75
Avg.	305,838	919	181.00	93.66	73.14	27.95
Min.	183,142	480	112.00	42.06	23.42	17.16
Max.	1,358,576	3,851	594.00	180.03	440.99	40.42

Note: (1) Values for the local area are compared with the average, minimum and maximum values for all 308 areas in the Cost of Living Index; (2) Figures cover the Jacksonville FL urban area; **New Home Price** *(2,400 sf living area, 8,000 sf lot, in urban area with full utilities);* **Apartment Rent** *(950 sf 2 bedroom/1.5 or 2 bath, unfurnished, excluding all utilities except water);* **All Electric** *(average monthly cost for an all-electric home);* **Part Electric** *(average monthly cost for a part-electric home);* **Other Energy** *(average monthly cost for natural gas, fuel oil, coal, wood, and any other forms of energy except electricity);* **Telephone** *(price includes basic monthly rate for a private residential line plus additional local usage charges incurred by a family of four).*
Source: The Council for Community and Economic Research, ACCRA Cost of Living Index, 2014

Health Care, Transportation, and Other Costs

Area[1]	Doctor ($/visit)	Dentist ($/visit)	Optometrist ($/visit)	Gasoline ($/gallon)	Beauty Salon ($/visit)	Men's Shirt ($)
City[2]	67.47	91.07	74.07	3.41	57.78	21.33
Avg.	102.86	87.89	97.66	3.44	34.37	26.74
Min.	67.47	65.78	51.18	3.00	17.43	12.79
Max.	173.50	150.14	235.00	4.33	64.28	49.50

Note: (1) Values for the local area are compared with the average, minimum and maximum values for all 308 areas in the Cost of Living Index; (2) Figures cover the Jacksonville FL urban area; **Doctor** *(general practitioners routine exam of an established patient);* **Dentist** *(adult teeth cleaning and periodic oral examination);* **Optometrist** *(full vision eye exam for established adult patient);* **Gasoline** *(one gallon regular unleaded, national brand, including all taxes, cash price at self-service pump if available);* **Beauty Salon** *(woman's shampoo, trim, and blow-dry);* **Men's Shirt** *(cotton/polyester dress shirt, pinpoint weave, long sleeves).*
Source: The Council for Community and Economic Research, ACCRA Cost of Living Index, 2014

HOUSING

House Price Index (HPI)

Area	National Ranking[2]	Quarterly Change (%)	One-Year Change (%)	Five-Year Change (%)
MSA[1]	51	1.61	8.13	-0.80
U.S.[3]	–	1.35	4.91	11.59

Note: The HPI is a weighted repeat sales index. It measures average price changes in repeat sales or refinancings on the same properties. This information is obtained by reviewing repeat mortgage transactions on single-family properties whose mortgages have been purchased or securitized by Fannie Mae or Freddie Mac in January 1975; (1) Jacksonville Metropolitan Statistical Area—see Appendix B for areas included; (2) Rankings are based on annual percentage change for all metro areas containing at least 15,000 transactions over the last 10 years and ranges from 1 to 275; (3) figures based on a weighted average of Census Division estimates using a seasonally adjusted, purchase-only index; all figures are for the period ending December 31, 2014
Source: Federal Housing Finance Agency, House Price Index, February 26, 2015

Median Single-Family Home Prices

Area	2012	2013	2014p	Percent Change 2013 to 2014
MSA[1]	128.2	160.8	181.1	12.6
U.S. Average	177.2	197.4	209.0	5.9

Note: Figures are median sales prices of existing single-family homes in thousands of dollars; (p) preliminary; n/a not available; (1) Jacksonville, FL Metropolitan Statistical Area—see Appendix B for areas included
Source: National Association of Realtors, Median Sales Price of Existing Single-Family Homes for Metropolitan Areas, 4th Quarter 2014

Qualifying Income Based on Median Sales Price of Existing Single-Family Homes

Area	With 5% Down ($)	With 10% Down ($)	With 20% Down ($)
MSA[1]	41,248	39,077	34,735
U.S. Average	45,863	43,449	38,621

Note: Figures are preliminary; Qualifying income is based on a mortgage rate of 4.0%. Monthly principal and interest payment is limited to 25% of income; n/a not available; (1) Jacksonville, FL Metropolitan Statistical Area—see Appendix B for areas included
Source: National Association of Realtors, Qualifying Income Based on Median Sales Price of Existing Single-Family Homes for Metropolitan Areas, 4th Quarter 2014

Median Apartment Condo-Coop Home Prices

Area	2012	2013	2014p	Percent Change 2013 to 2014
MSA[1]	75.8	102.9	115.3	12.1
U.S. Average	173.7	194.9	205.1	5.2

Note: Figures are median sales prices of existing apartment condo-coop homes in thousands of dollars; (p) preliminary; n/a not available; (1) Jacksonville, FL Metropolitan Statistical Area—see Appendix B for areas included
Source: National Association of Realtors, Median Sales Price of Existing Apartment Condo-Coop Homes for Metropolitan Areas, 4th Quarter 2014

Gross Monthly Rent

Area	Under $200	$200 -299	$300 -499	$500 -749	$750 -999	$1,000 -1,499	$1,500 and up	Median ($)
City	1.7	2.5	4.6	20.3	31.1	32.5	7.4	915
MSA[1]	1.4	2.3	4.2	18.7	29.5	34.2	9.8	947
U.S.	1.7	3.2	7.8	22.1	24.3	26.0	14.9	900

Note: Figures are percentages except for Median; Gross rent is the contract rent plus the estimated average monthly cost of utilities (electricity, gas, and water and sewer) and fuels (oil, coal, kerosene, wood, etc.) if these are paid by the renter (or paid for the renter by someone else); (1) Figures cover the Jacksonville, FL Metropolitan Statistical Area—see Appendix B for areas included
Source: U.S. Census Bureau, 2011-2013 American Community Survey 3-Year Estimates

Homeownership Rate

Area	2007 (%)	2008 (%)	2009 (%)	2010 (%)	2011 (%)	2012 (%)	2013 (%)	2014 (%)
MSA[1]	70.9	72.1	72.6	70.0	68.0	66.6	69.9	65.3
U.S.	68.1	67.8	67.4	66.9	66.1	65.4	65.1	64.5

Note: (1) Figures cover the Jacksonville, FL Metropolitan Statistical Area—see Appendix B for areas included
Source: U.S. Census Bureau, Housing Vacancies and Homeownership Annual Statistics: 2014

Year Housing Structure Built

Area	2010 or Later	2000 -2009	1990 -1999	1980 -1989	1970 -1979	1960 -1969	1950 -1959	1940 -1949	Before 1940	Median Year
City	0.9	20.9	14.4	16.2	14.3	11.0	11.7	5.4	5.2	1981
MSA[1]	1.1	24.4	16.9	17.9	13.8	8.9	8.8	4.0	4.1	1986
U.S.	0.9	15.0	13.9	13.8	15.8	11.0	10.9	5.4	13.3	1976

Note: Figures are percentages except for Median Year; (1) Figures cover the Jacksonville, FL Metropolitan Statistical Area—see Appendix B for areas included
Source: U.S. Census Bureau, 2011-2013 American Community Survey 3-Year Estimates

HEALTH

Health Risk Data

Category	MSA[1] (%)	U.S. (%)
Adults aged 18–64 who have any kind of health care coverage	80.8	79.6
Adults who reported being in good or excellent health	81.4	83.1
Adults who are current smokers	20.9	19.6
Adults who are heavy drinkers[2]	9.7	6.1
Adults who are binge drinkers[3]	19.3	16.9
Adults who are overweight (BMI 25.0 - 29.9)	36.7	35.8
Adults who are obese (BMI 30.0 - 99.8)	29.2	27.6
Adults who participated in any physical activities in the past month	81.5	77.1
Adults 50+ who have ever had a sigmoidoscopy or colonoscopy	70.4	67.3
Women aged 40+ who have had a mammogram within the past two years	67.8	74.0
Men aged 40+ who have had a PSA test within the past two years	38.7	45.2
Adults aged 65+ who have had flu shot within the past year	55.5	60.1
Adults who always wear a seatbelt	n/a	93.8

Note: Data as of 2012 unless otherwise noted; n/a not available; (1) Figures cover the Jacksonville, FL Metropolitan Statistical Area—see Appendix B for areas included; (2) Heavy drinkers are classified as males having more than two drinks per day or females having more than one drink per day; (3) Binge drinkers are classified as males having five or more drinks on one occasion or females having four or more drinks on one occasion
Source: Centers for Disease Control and Prevention, Behaviorial Risk Factor Surveillance System, SMART: Selected Metropolitan/Micropolitan Area Risk Trends, 2012 (Note: the CDC has discontinued this dataset but will be releasing a replacement in late 2015)

Chronic Health Indicators

Category	MSA[1] (%)	U.S. (%)
Adults who have ever been told they had a heart attack	4.5	4.5
Adults who have ever been told they had a stroke	3.1	2.9
Adults who have been told they currently have asthma	10.3	8.9
Adults who have ever been told they have arthritis	26.6	25.7
Adults who have ever been told they have diabetes[2]	11.6	9.7
Adults who have ever been told they had skin cancer	8.5	5.7
Adults who have ever been told they had any other types of cancer	6.2	6.5
Adults who have ever been told they have COPD	7.7	6.2
Adults who have ever been told they have kidney disease	n/a	2.5
Adults who have ever been told they have a form of depression	18.7	18.0

Note: Data as of 2012 unless otherwise noted; n/a not available; (1) Figures cover the Jacksonville, FL Metropolitan Statistical Area—see Appendix B for areas included; (2) Figures do not include pregnancy-related, borderline, or pre-diabetes
Source: Centers for Disease Control and Prevention, Behaviorial Risk Factor Surveillance System, SMART: Selected Metropolitan/Micropolitan Area Risk Trends, 2012 (Note: the CDC has discontinued this dataset but will be releasing a replacement in late 2015)

Mortality Rates for the Top 10 Causes of Death in the U.S.

ICD-10[a] Sub-Chapter	ICD-10[a] Code	Age-Adjusted Mortality Rate[1] per 100,000 population	
		County[2]	U.S.
Malignant neoplasms	C00-C97	183.0	166.2
Ischaemic heart diseases	I20-I25	116.1	105.7
Other forms of heart disease	I30-I51	53.2	49.3
Chronic lower respiratory diseases	J40-J47	54.8	42.1
Organic, including symptomatic, mental disorders	F01-F09	52.7	38.1
Cerebrovascular diseases	I60-I69	38.5	37.0
Other external causes of accidental injury	W00-X59	31.5	26.9
Other degenerative diseases of the nervous system	G30-G31	19.9	25.6
Diabetes mellitus	E10-E14	27.8	21.3
Hypertensive diseases	I10-I15	27.9	19.4

Note: (a) ICD-10 = International Classification of Diseases 10th Revision; (1) Mortality rates are a three year average covering 2011-2013; (2) Figures cover Duval County
Source: Centers for Disease Control and Prevention, National Center for Health Statistics. Compressed Mortality File 1999-2013 on CDC WONDER Online Database, released October 2014. Data are compiled from the Compressed Mortality File 1999-2013, Series 20 No. 2S, 2014.

Mortality Rates for Selected Causes of Death

ICD-10[a] Sub-Chapter	ICD-10[a] Code	Age-Adjusted Mortality Rate[1] per 100,000 population	
		County[2]	U.S.
Assault	X85-Y09	11.4	5.2
Diseases of the liver	K70-K76	16.3	13.2
Human immunodeficiency virus (HIV) disease	B20-B24	7.9	2.2
Influenza and pneumonia	J09-J18	16.3	15.4
Intentional self-harm	X60-X84	15.7	12.5
Malnutrition	E40-E46	1.4	0.9
Obesity and other hyperalimentation	E65-E68	2.2	1.8
Renal failure	N17-N19	17.8	13.1
Transport accidents	V01-V99	14.0	11.7
Viral hepatitis	B15-B19	3.6	2.2

Note: (a) ICD-10 = International Classification of Diseases 10th Revision; (1) Mortality rates are a three year average covering 2011-2013; (2) Figures cover Duval County
Source: Centers for Disease Control and Prevention, National Center for Health Statistics. Compressed Mortality File 1999-2013 on CDC WONDER Online Database, released October 2014. Data are compiled from the Compressed Mortality File 1999-2013, Series 20 No. 2S, 2014.

Health Insurance Coverage

Area	With Health Insurance	With Private Health Insurance	With Public Health Insurance	Without Health Insurance	Population Under Age 18 Without Health Insurance
City	82.6	61.5	30.9	17.4	8.4
MSA[1]	84.2	65.3	30.0	15.8	8.0
U.S.	85.2	65.2	31.0	14.8	7.3

Note: Figures are percentages that cover the civilian noninstitutionalized population; (1) Figures cover the Jacksonville, FL Metropolitan Statistical Area—see Appendix B for areas included
Source: U.S. Census Bureau, 2011-2013 American Community Survey 3-Year Estimates

Number of Medical Professionals

Area[1]	MDs[2]	DOs[2,3]	Dentists	Podiatrists	Chiropractors	Optometrists
Local (number)	2,998	207	617	67	190	131
Local (rate[4])	340.5	23.5	69.5	7.6	21.4	14.8
U.S. (rate[4])	270.0	20.2	63.1	5.7	25.2	14.9

Note: Data as of 2013 unless noted; (1) Local data covers Duval County; (2) Data as of 2012 and includes all active, non-federal physicians; (3) Doctor of Osteopathic Medicine; (4) rate per 100,000 population
Source: U.S. Department of Health and Human Services, Health Resources and Services Administration, Bureau of Health Professions, Area Resource File (ARF) 2013-2014

Best Hospitals

According to *U.S. News,* the Jacksonville, FL metro area is home to one of the best hospitals in the U.S.: **Baptist Medical Center** (1 specialty). The hospital listed was nationally ranked in at least one adult specialty. Only 144 hospitals nationwide were nationally ranked in one or more specialties. Seventeen hospitals in the U.S. made the Honor Roll with high scores in at least six specialties. *U.S. News Online, "America's Best Children's Hospitals 2014-15"*

According to *U.S. News,* the Jacksonville, FL metro area is home to one of the best children's hospitals in the U.S.: **Wolfson Children's Hospital** (1 specialty). The hospital listed was highly ranked in at least one pediatric specialty. Eighty-nine children's hospitals in the U.S. were nationally ranked in at least one specialty. Ten children's hospitals in the U.S. made the Honor Roll with high scores in at least three specialties. *U.S. News Online, "America's Best Children's Hospitals 2014-15"*

EDUCATION

Public School District Statistics

District Name	Schls	Pupils	Pupil/ Teacher Ratio	Minority Pupils[1] (%)	Free Lunch Eligible[2] (%)	IEP[3] (%)
Duval County	197	125,686	16.5	61.5	45.0	13.5

Note: Table includes school districts with 2,000 or more students; (1) Percentage of students that are not non-Hispanic white; (2) Percentage of students that are eligible for the free lunch program; (3) Percentage of students that have an Individualized Education Program.
Source: U.S. Department of Education, National Center for Education Statistics, Common Core of Data, Local Education Agency (School District) Universe Survey: School Year 2012-2013; U.S. Department of Education, National Center for Education Statistics, Common Core of Data, Public Elementary/Secondary School Universe Survey: School Year 2012-2013

Best High Schools

According to *The Daily Beast,* Jacksonville is home to two of the best high schools in the U.S.: **Stanton College Preparatory School** (#6); **Douglas Anderson School of the Arts** (#184); *The Daily Beast* used six indicators culled from school surveys to compare public high schools in the U.S., with graduation and college acceptance rates weighed most heavily. Other criteria included: college-level courses/exams and SAT/ACT scores. *The Daily Beast, "Top High Schools 2014"*

Highest Level of Education

Area	Less than H.S.	H.S. Diploma	Some College, No Deg.	Associate Degree	Bachelor's Degree	Master's Degree	Prof. School Degree	Doctorate Degree
City	12.1	29.4	23.3	9.6	17.8	5.5	1.5	0.8
MSA[1]	10.8	28.6	23.4	9.5	19.0	6.2	1.6	0.9
U.S.	13.7	28.0	21.2	7.9	18.2	7.7	1.9	1.3

Note: Figures cover persons age 25 and over; (1) Figures cover the Jacksonville, FL Metropolitan Statistical Area—see Appendix B for areas included
Source: U.S. Census Bureau, 2011-2013 American Community Survey 3-Year Estimates

Educational Attainment by Race

Area	High School Graduate or Higher (%)					Bachelor's Degree or Higher (%)				
	Total	White	Black	Asian	Hisp.[2]	Total	White	Black	Asian	Hisp.[2]
City	87.9	89.6	84.7	85.1	84.3	25.7	28.4	16.5	44.8	23.6
MSA[1]	89.2	90.4	84.8	87.0	85.2	27.7	29.7	17.0	46.1	25.3
U.S.	86.3	88.3	83.1	85.7	64.0	29.1	30.4	18.8	50.7	13.7

Note: Figures shown cover persons 25 years old and over; (1) Figures cover the Jacksonville, FL Metropolitan Statistical Area—see Appendix B for areas included; (2) People of Hispanic origin can be of any race
Source: U.S. Census Bureau, 2011-2013 American Community Survey 3-Year Estimates

School Enrollment by Grade and Control

Area	Preschool (%)		Kindergarten (%)		Grades 1 - 4 (%)		Grades 5 - 8 (%)		Grades 9 - 12 (%)	
	Public	Private	Public	Private	Public	Private	Public	Private	Public	Private
City	58.5	41.5	86.1	13.9	83.7	16.3	84.6	15.4	84.5	15.5
MSA[1]	54.8	45.2	86.2	13.8	85.8	14.2	87.2	12.8	86.5	13.5
U.S.	57.7	42.3	87.9	12.1	89.9	10.1	90.0	10.0	90.7	9.3

Note: Figures shown cover persons 3 years old and over; (1) Figures cover the Jacksonville, FL Metropolitan Statistical Area—see Appendix B for areas included
Source: U.S. Census Bureau, 2011-2013 American Community Survey 3-Year Estimates

Average Salaries of Public School Classroom Teachers

Area	2013-14		2014-15		Percent Change 2013-14 to 2014-15	Percent Change 2004-05 to 2014-15
	Dollars	Rank[1]	Dollars	Rank[1]		
FLORIDA	47,780	39	48,992	36	2.54	17.8
U.S. Average	56,610	–	57,379	–	1.36	20.8

Note: (1) State rank ranges from 1 to 51 where 1 indicates highest salary.
Source: National Education Association, Rankings & Estimates: Rankings of the States 2014 and Estimates of School Statistics 2015, March 2015

Higher Education

Four-Year Colleges			Two-Year Colleges			Medical Schools[1]	Law Schools[2]	Voc/ Tech[3]
Public	Private Non-profit	Private For-profit	Public	Private Non-profit	Private For-profit			
2	4	6	0	0	8	0	1	10

Note: Figures cover institutions located within the city limits and include main campuses only; (1) includes schools accredited by the Liaison Committee on Medical Education and the American Osteopathic Association's Commission on Osteopathic College Accreditation; (2) includes ABA-accredited schools, schools with provisional ABA accreditation, and state accredited schools; (3) includes all schools with programs that are less than 2 years.
Source: National Center for Education Statistics, Integrated Postsecondary Education System (IPEDS), 2013-14; Association of American Medical Colleges, Member List, May 1, 2015; American Osteopathic Association, Member List, May 1, 2015; Law School Admission Council, Official Guide to ABA-Approved Law Schools Online, May 1, 2015; Wikipedia, List of Medical Schools in the United States, May 1, 2015; Wikipedia, List of Law Schools in the United States, May 1, 2015

PRESIDENTIAL ELECTION

2012 Presidential Election Results

Area	Obama (%)	Romney (%)	Other (%)
Duval County	47.8	51.4	0.8
U.S.	51.0	47.2	1.8

Note: Results may not add to 100% due to rounding
Source: Dave Leip's Atlas of U.S. Presidential Elections

EMPLOYERS

Major Employers

Company Name	Industry
Baptist Health System	Hospital management
Baptist Health System	General medical/surgical hospitals
Baptist Health System Foundation	Individual and family services
Blue Cross Blue Shield of Florida	Hospital and medical service plans
Fidelity National Information Services	Prepackaged software
Jacksonville Electric Authority	Electric services
Kelley Clark	Food brokers
Mayo Clinic Jacksonville	General medical/surgical hospitals
Shands Jacksonville Medical Center	General medical/surgical hospitals
Southern Baptist Hospital of Florida	Hospital medical school affiliated with residency

Note: Companies shown are located within the Jacksonville, FL Metropolitan Statistical Area.
Source: Hoovers.com; Wikipedia

Best Companies to Work For

CSX, headquartered in Jacksonville, is among the "100 Best Places to Work in IT." To qualify, companies, both public and private, had to have a minimum of 50 IT employees and were selected based on average salary and bonus increases, the percentage of IT staffers promoted, IT staff turnover rates, training and development programs, and the percentage of women and minorities in IT staff and management positions. In addition, *Computerworld* looked at retention efforts, programs for recognizing and rewarding outstanding performances, and benefits such as flextime, elder care and child care, and reimbursement for college tuition and the cost of pursuing technology certifications. *Computerworld, "100 Best Places to Work in IT 2014"*

PUBLIC SAFETY

Crime Rate

Area	All Crimes	Violent Crimes				Property Crimes		
		Murder	Forcible Rape	Robbery	Aggrav. Assault	Burglary	Larceny -Theft	Motor Vehicle Theft
City	4,523.0	11.0	53.4	168.4	387.5	835.8	2,880.4	186.5
Suburbs[1]	2,490.1	1.1	23.9	40.6	237.4	435.7	1,666.2	85.2
Metro[2]	3,724.4	7.1	41.9	118.2	328.5	678.6	2,403.5	146.7
U.S.	3,098.6	4.5	25.2	109.1	229.1	610.0	1,899.4	221.3

Note: Figures are crimes per 100,000 population; (1) All areas within the metro area that are located outside the city limits; (2) Figures cover the Jacksonville, FL Metropolitan Statistical Area—see Appendix B for areas included
Source: FBI Uniform Crime Reports, 2013

Hate Crimes

Area	Number of Quarters Reported	Number of Incidents per Bias Motivation						
		Race	Religion	Sexual Orientation	Ethnicity	Disability	Gender	Gender Identity
City	4	5	0	0	0	0	0	0
U.S.	4	2,871	1,031	1,233	655	83	18	31

Source: Federal Bureau of Investigation, Hate Crime Statistics 2013

Identity Theft Consumer Complaints

Area	Complaints	Complaints per 100,000 Population	Rank[2]
MSA[1]	2,156	154.6	9
U.S.	332,646	104.3	-

Note: (1) Figures cover the Jacksonville, FL Metropolitan Statistical Area—see Appendix B for areas included; (2) Rank ranges from 1 to 380 where 1 indicates greatest number of identity theft complaints per 100,000 population
Source: Federal Trade Commission, Consumer Sentinel Network Data Book for January–December 2014

Fraud and Other Consumer Complaints

Area	Complaints	Complaints per 100,000 Population	Rank[2]
MSA[1]	7,799	559.2	11
U.S.	2,250,205	705.7	-

Note: (1) Figures cover the Jacksonville, FL Metropolitan Statistical Area—see Appendix B for areas included; (2) Rank ranges from 1 to 380 where 1 indicates greatest number of identity theft complaints per 100,000 population
Source: Federal Trade Commission, Consumer Sentinel Network Data Book for January–December 2014

RECREATION

Culture

Dance[1]	Theatre[1]	Instrumental Music[1]	Vocal Music[1]	Series and Festivals	Museums and Art Galleries[2]	Zoos and Aquariums[3]
2	3	1	0	4	29	1

Note: (1) Professional perfoming groups; (2) Based on organizations with SIC code 8412; (3) AZA-accredited
Source: The Grey House Performing Arts Directory, 2015-16; Association of Zoos & Aquariums, AZA Member Zoos & Aquariums, April 2015; www.AccuLeads.com, April 2015

Professional Sports Teams

Team Name	League	Year Established
Jacksonville Jaguars	National Football League (NFL)	1995

Note: Includes teams located in the Jacksonville, FL Metropolitan Statistical Area.
Source: Wikipedia, Major Professional Sports Teams of the United States and Canada, April 2015

CLIMATE

Average and Extreme Temperatures

Temperature	Jan	Feb	Mar	Apr	May	Jun	Jul	Aug	Sep	Oct	Nov	Dec	Yr.
Extreme High (°F)	84	88	91	95	100	103	103	102	98	96	88	84	103
Average High (°F)	65	68	74	80	86	90	92	91	87	80	73	67	79
Average Temp. (°F)	54	57	62	69	75	80	83	82	79	71	62	56	69
Average Low (°F)	43	45	51	57	64	70	73	73	70	61	51	44	58
Extreme Low (°F)	7	22	23	34	45	47	61	63	48	36	21	11	7

Note: Figures cover the years 1948-1990
Source: National Climatic Data Center, International Station Meteorological Climate Summary, 9/96

Average Precipitation/Snowfall/Humidity

Precip./Humidity	Jan	Feb	Mar	Apr	May	Jun	Jul	Aug	Sep	Oct	Nov	Dec	Yr.
Avg. Precip. (in.)	3.0	3.7	3.8	3.0	3.6	5.3	6.2	7.4	7.8	3.7	2.0	2.6	52.0
Avg. Snowfall (in.)	Tr	Tr	Tr	0	0	0	0	0	0	0	0	Tr	0
Avg. Rel. Hum. 7am (%)	86	86	87	86	86	88	89	91	92	91	89	88	88
Avg. Rel. Hum. 4pm (%)	56	53	50	49	54	61	64	65	66	62	58	58	58

Note: Figures cover the years 1948-1990; Tr = Trace amounts (<0.05 in. of rain; <0.5 in. of snow)
Source: National Climatic Data Center, International Station Meteorological Climate Summary, 9/96

Weather Conditions

Temperature			Daytime Sky			Precipitation		
10°F & below	32°F & below	90°F & above	Clear	Partly cloudy	Cloudy	0.01 inch or more precip.	0.1 inch or more snow/ice	Thunder-storms
<1	16	83	86	181	98	114	1	65

Note: Figures are average number of days per year and cover the years 1948-1990
Source: National Climatic Data Center, International Station Meteorological Climate Summary, 9/96

HAZARDOUS WASTE

Superfund Sites

Jacksonville has five hazardous waste sites on the EPA's Superfund Final National Priorities List: **Cecil Field Naval Air Station; Fairfax St. Wood Treaters; Jacksonville Naval Air Station; Kerr-McGee Chemical Corp - Jacksonville; Pickettville Road Landfill**. There are a total of 1,322 Superfund sites on the list in the U.S. *U.S. Environmental Protection Agency, Final National Priorities List, April 14, 2015*

AIR & WATER QUALITY

Air Quality Trends: Ozone

	2004	2005	2006	2007	2008	2009	2010	2011	2012	2013
MSA[1]	0.074	0.072	0.074	0.073	0.069	0.061	0.067	0.066	0.060	0.057

Note: (1) Data covers the Jacksonville, FL Metropolitan Statistical Area—see Appendix B for areas included. The values shown are the composite ozone concentration averages among trend sites based on the highest fourth daily maximum 8-hour concentration in parts per million. These trends are based on sites having an adequate record of monitoring data during the trend period. Data from exceptional events are included.
Source: U.S. Environmental Protection Agency, Air Quality Monitoring Information, "Air Quality Trends by City, 2000-2013"

Air Quality Index

Area	Percent of Days when Air Quality was...[2]					AQI Statistics[2]	
	Good	Moderate	Unhealthy for Sensitive Groups	Unhealthy	Very Unhealthy	Maximum	Median
MSA[1]	70.1	29.0	0.8	0.0	0.0	106	43

Note: (1) Data covers the Jacksonville, FL Metropolitan Statistical Area—see Appendix B for areas included; (2) Based on 365 days with AQI data in 2014. Air Quality Index (AQI) is an index for reporting daily air quality. EPA calculates the AQI for five major air pollutants regulated by the Clean Air Act: ground-level ozone, particle pollution (aka particulate matter), carbon monoxide, sulfur dioxide, and nitrogen dioxide. The AQI runs from 0 to 500. The higher the AQI value, the greater the level of air pollution and the greater the health concern. There are six AQI categories: "Good" AQI is between 0 and 50. Air quality is considered satisfactory; "Moderate" AQI is between 51 and 100. Air quality is acceptable; "Unhealthy for Sensitive Groups" When AQI values are between 101 and 150, members of sensitive groups may experience health effects; "Unhealthy" When AQI values are between 151 and 200 everyone may begin to experience health effects; "Very Unhealthy" AQI values between 201 and 300 trigger a health alert; "Hazardous" AQI values over 300 trigger warnings of emergency conditions (not shown).
Source: U.S. Environmental Protection Agency, Air Quality Index Report, 2014

Air Quality Index Pollutants

Area	Percent of Days when AQI Pollutant was...[2]					
	Carbon Monoxide	Nitrogen Dioxide	Ozone	Sulfur Dioxide	Particulate Matter 2.5	Particulate Matter 10
MSA[1]	0.0	1.1	32.9	7.9	58.1	0.0

Note: (1) Data covers the Jacksonville, FL Metropolitan Statistical Area—see Appendix B for areas included; (2) Based on 365 days with AQI data in 2014. The Air Quality Index (AQI) is an index for reporting daily air quality. EPA calculates the AQI for five major air pollutants regulated by the Clean Air Act: ground-level ozone, particle pollution (also known as particulate matter), carbon monoxide, sulfur dioxide, and nitrogen dioxide. The AQI runs from 0 to 500. The higher the AQI value, the greater the level of air pollution and the greater the health concern.
Source: U.S. Environmental Protection Agency, Air Quality Index Report, 2014

Maximum Air Pollutant Concentrations: Particulate Matter, Ozone, CO and Lead

	Particulate Matter 10 (ug/m^3)	Particulate Matter 2.5 Wtd AM (ug/m^3)	Particulate Matter 2.5 24-Hr (ug/m^3)	Ozone (ppm)	Carbon Monoxide (ppm)	Lead (ug/m^3)
MSA[1] Level	47	6.3	16	0.06	1	n/a
NAAQS[2]	150	15	35	0.075	9	0.15
Met NAAQS[2]	Yes	Yes	Yes	Yes	Yes	n/a

Note: (1) Data covers the Jacksonville, FL Metropolitan Statistical Area—see Appendix B for areas included; Data from exceptional events are included; (2) National Ambient Air Quality Standards; ppm = parts per million; ug/m^3 = micrograms per cubic meter; n/a not available.
Concentrations: Particulate Matter 10 (coarse particulate)—highest second maximum 24-hour concentration; Particulate Matter 2.5 Wtd AM (fine particulate)—highest weighted annual mean concentration; Particulate Matter 2.5 24-Hour (fine particulate)—highest 98th percentile 24-hour concentration; Ozone—highest fourth daily maximum 8-hour concentration; Carbon Monoxide—highest second maximum non-overlapping 8-hour concentration; Lead—maximum running 3-month average
Source: U.S. Environmental Protection Agency, Air Quality Monitoring Information, "Air Quality Statistics by City, 2013"

Maximum Air Pollutant Concentrations: Nitrogen Dioxide and Sulfur Dioxide

	Nitrogen Dioxide AM (ppb)	Nitrogen Dioxide 1-Hr (ppb)	Sulfur Dioxide AM (ppb)	Sulfur Dioxide 1-Hr (ppb)	Sulfur Dioxide 24-Hr (ppb)
MSA[1] Level	8	38	n/a	60	n/a
NAAQS[2]	53	100	30	75	140
Met NAAQS[2]	Yes	Yes	n/a	Yes	n/a

Note: (1) Data covers the Jacksonville, FL Metropolitan Statistical Area—see Appendix B for areas included; Data from exceptional events are included; (2) National Ambient Air Quality Standards; ppm = parts per million; ug/m^3 = micrograms per cubic meter; n/a not available.
Concentrations: Nitrogen Dioxide AM—highest arithmetic mean concentration; Nitrogen Dioxide 1-Hr—highest 98th percentile 1-hour daily maximum concentration; Sulfur Dioxide AM—highest annual mean concentration; Sulfur Dioxide 1-Hr—highest 99th percentile 1-hour daily maximum concentration; Sulfur Dioxide 24-Hr—highest second maximum 24-hour concentration
Source: U.S. Environmental Protection Agency, Air Quality Monitoring Information, "Air Quality Statistics by City, 2013"

Drinking Water

Water System Name	Pop. Served	Primary Water Source Type	Violations[1]	
			Health Based	Monitoring/ Reporting
JEA Major Grid	703,750	Ground	0	0

Note: (1) Based on violation data from January 1, 2014 to December 31, 2014 (includes unresolved violations from earlier years)
Source: U.S. Environmental Protection Agency, Office of Ground Water and Drinking Water, Safe Drinking Water Information System (based on data extracted January 27, 2015)

Lafayette, Louisiana

Background

Lafayette's cultural origins originated far north of the city, to Nova Scotia, Canada. In 1755, the British governor, Charles Lawrence, expelled the entire population of Canadians known as the Acadians, whose roots were French and Catholic, when they refused to pledge loyalty to the British crown. Many lost their lives in their quest for a new home, as they settled all along the eastern seaboard of the United States. A large majority of Acadians settled in southern Louisiana, in the area surrounding New Orleans.

Prior to the Acadian expulsion, southern Louisiana had remained fairly unsettled. The first known inhabitants were the Attakapas, a much-feared and brutal tribe of Native Americans. A sparse population of French trappers, traders, and ranchers occupied the region until the Spanish occupation of 1766. The 1789 French Revolution brought teams of French immigrants fleeing the brutal conditions at home. In 1803, the French sold the Louisiana territory to the United States—a transaction known as the Louisiana Purchase.

The most important early event for Lafayette was the donation of land by an Acadian named Jean Mouton, to the Catholic Church. The population began to grow in the parish then known as St. John the Evangelist of Vermillion. Lafayette's original name was Vermillionville, but it was renamed in 1884 in honor of the French Marquis de Lafayette, a Frenchman who fought under General George Washington in the American Revolution. Lafayette has been credited with bringing some of the ideals of the American Revolution to the French, partly precipitating the French Revolution. By his death, Lafayette had visited all 24 of the United States, and was an American citizen.

The word "cajun," is derived from the early Acadian settlers. In French, "Les Acadians" became "le Cadiens," which later became just "'Cadien." The French pronunciation was difficult for non-French Americans to say, so Cadien became Cajun. A primary characteristic of the Acadian/Cajun culture is what's known as "joie de vivre"—joy of living. The Cajun reputation is one of hard work and hard play, full of passion that can turn on a dime. Their greatest contribution to the fabric of America has been their food and their music—both are decidedly spicy.

Geographically, Lafayette is about 40 miles north of the Gulf of Mexico, and 100 miles west of New Orleans. The city is often referred to as the center of Cajun culture not because of its geography, but because of the strong Cajun influence in everyday life. Celebration is a major part of the Cajun culture, and this is reflected in Lafayette's many festivals and cultural traditions. The most famous of dozens of annual festivals is Mari Gras. The Festival International de Louisiana celebrates the French-speaking heritage of much of the population. Festival Acadians celebrates everything that is uniquely Cajun.

While Lafayette is known for its oil and natural gas industries, with over 600 oil-related businesses in Lafayette Parish alone, jobs in healthcare are not far behind. Education is also a big industry in Lafayette, home of the University of Louisiana's Ragin' Cajuns. UL started out as a small agricultural college with about 100 students, and today, over 17,000 students roam the 1,300-acre campus. It is the second largest public university in the state. The university's main focus is hands-on research—dubbed "research for a reason"—meaning that all students are given the opportunity to have a meaningful impact in their area of study. The University of Louisiana is considered among the top universities in computer science, engineering and nursing.

Lafayette's climate is humid and subtropical. It is typical of areas along the Gulf of Mexico with hot, humid summers and mild winters.

Rankings

Business/Finance Rankings

- According to data published by the U.S. Conference of Mayors and produced by IHS Global Insight, the Lafayette metro area was on the list of metro areas with the fastest-shrinking GMP (gross metro product) and negative employment trends, at #4. *247wallst.com, "America's Fastest Growing (and Shrinking) Economies," January 31, 2014*
- To identify the metro areas with the largest gap in income between rich and poor residents, the 24/7 Wall Street research team used the U.S. Census Bureau's 2012 American Community Survey, an index of income disparity, additional income, poverty, and home-value data. The Lafayette metro area placed #7 among metro areas with the widest wealth gap between rich and poor. *247wallst.com, "Cities with the Widest Gap between Rich and Poor," November 4, 2013*
- The Lafayette metro area was identified as one of 10 places with the highest projected job growth through 2015. The metro area was ranked #4. Criteria: 384 metropolitan areas were ranked by projected job growth for first-quarter 2012 through fourth-quarter 2015. *USAToday.com, "Jobs Rebound Will Be Slow," March 7, 2012*
- The Lafayette metro area appeared on the Milken Institute "2013 Best Performing Cities" list. Rank: #19 out of 200 large metro areas. Criteria: job growth; wage and salary growth; high-tech output growth. *Milken Institute, "Best-Performing Cities 2014," January 2015*
- *Forbes* ranked the 200 most populous metro areas to determine the nation's "Best Places for Business and Careers." The Lafayette metro area was ranked #144. Criteria: costs (business and living); job growth (past and projected); income growth; educational attainment (college and high school); projected economic growth; cultural and recreational opportunities; net migration patterns; number of highly ranked colleges. *Forbes, "The Best Places for Business and Careers 2014," July 23, 2014*

Environmental Rankings

- The Lafayette metro area came in at #322 for the relative comfort of its climate on Sperling's list of "chill cities," as measured by the Sperling Heat Index. All 361 metro areas are included. Criteria included daytime high temperatures, nighttime low temperatures, dew point, and relative humidity at the high temperatures. *www.bertsperling.com, "Sperling's Chill Cities," July 18, 2013*
- Sperling's BestPlaces assessed 379 metropolitan areas of the United States for the likelihood of dangerously extreme weather events or earthquakes. In general the Southeast and South-Central regions have the highest risk of weather extremes and earthquakes, while the Pacific Northwest enjoys the lowest risk. Of the least risky metropolitan areas, the Lafayette metro area was ranked #363. *www.bestplaces.net, "Safest Places from Natural Disasters," April 2011*
- Lafayette was highlighted as one of the top 25 cleanest metro areas for short-term particle pollution (24-hour PM 2.5) in the U.S. during 2011 through 2013. Monitors in these cities reported no days with unhealthful PM 2.5 levels. *American Lung Association, State of the Air 2015*

Food/Drink Rankings

- In compiling its list of "Top 10 Foodie Cities 2013," the lifestyle website Livability excluded "well-known food-lovers' cities like New York, Chicago, San Francisco and New Orleans" and focused on cities of fewer than 250,000 with "unexpected epicurean delights." Looking at food festivals, farmers' markets, cooking schools, ratio of top-rated restaurants to residents, and more, Livability chose Lafayette as the #6 American foodie town. *livability.com, "Top 10 Foodie Cities 2013: A Second Helping," August 2, 2013*

Health/Fitness Rankings

- The Gallup-Healthways Well-Being Index tracks Americans' optimism about their communities in addition to their satisfaction with the metro areas in which they live. Gallup researchers asked at least 300 adult residents in each of 189 U.S. metropolitan areas whether their metro was improving. The Lafayette metro area placed among the top ten in the percentage of residents who were optimistic about their metro area. *www.gallup.com, "City Satisfaction Highest in Fort Collins-Loveland, Colo.," April 11, 2014*
- The Lafayette metro area appeared in the 2013 Gallup-Healthways Well-Being Index. The area ranked #86 out of 189. The Gallup-Healthways Well-Being Index score is an average of six sub-indexes, which individually examine life evaluation, emotional health, work environment, physical health, healthy behaviors, and access to basic necessities. Results are based on telephone interviews conducted as part of the Gallup-Healthways Well-Being Index survey January 2–December 29, 2012, and January 2–December 30, 2013, with a random sample of 531,630 adults, aged 18 and older, living in metropolitan areas in the 50 U.S. states and the District of Columbia. *Gallup-Healthways, "State of American Well-Being," March 25, 2014*

Real Estate Rankings

- Lafayette was ranked #153 out of 275 metro areas in terms of house price appreciation in 2014 (#1 = highest rate). *Federal Housing Finance Agency, House Price Index, 4th Quarter 2014*

Safety Rankings

- The National Insurance Crime Bureau ranked 380 metro areas in the U.S. in terms of per capita rates of vehicle theft. The Lafayette metro area ranked #240 (#1 = highest rate). Criteria: number of vehicle theft offenses per 100,000 inhabitants in 2012. *National Insurance Crime Bureau, "Hot Spots 2012," June 26, 2013*

Seniors/Retirement Rankings

- From its Best Cities for Successful Aging indexes, the Milken Institute generated rankings for metropolitan areas, weighing data in eight categories—health care, wellness, living arrangements, transportation, financial characteristics, education and employment opportunities, community engagement, and overall livability. The Lafayette metro area was ranked #61 overall in the small metro area category. *Milken Institute, "Best Cities for Successful Aging, 2014"*
- *Forbes* selected the Lafayette metro area as one of 25 "Best Places for a Working Retirement." Criteria: affordability; improving, above-average economies and job prospects; and a favorable tax climate for retirees. *Forbes.com, "Best Places for a Working Retirement in 2013," February 4, 2013*

Business Environment

CITY FINANCES

City Government Finances

Component	2012 ($000)	2012 ($ per capita)
Total Revenues	679,288	5,631
Total Expenditures	701,034	5,812
Debt Outstanding	1,132,601	9,390
Cash and Securities[1]	840,167	6,965

Note: (1) Cash and security holdings of a government at the close of its fiscal year, including those of its dependent agencies, utilities, and liquor stores.
Source: U.S Census Bureau, State & Local Government Finances 2012

City Government Revenue by Source

Source	2012 ($000)	2012 ($ per capita)
General Revenue		
From Federal Government	32,947	273
From State Government	33,091	274
From Local Governments	4,210	35
Taxes		
Property	102,073	846
Sales and Gross Receipts	94,058	780
Personal Income	0	0
Corporate Income	0	0
Motor Vehicle License	0	0
Other Taxes	4,997	41
Current Charges	97,202	806
Liquor Store	0	0
Utility	276,903	2,296
Employee Retirement	0	0

Source: U.S Census Bureau, State & Local Government Finances 2012

City Government Expenditures by Function

Function	2012 ($000)	2012 ($ per capita)	2012 (%)
General Direct Expenditures			
Air Transportation	22,288	185	3.2
Corrections	23,505	195	3.4
Education	0	0	0.0
Employment Security Administration	0	0	0.0
Financial Administration	14,794	123	2.1
Fire Protection	18,398	153	2.6
General Public Buildings	3,637	30	0.5
Governmental Administration, Other	9,617	80	1.4
Health	6,102	51	0.9
Highways	33,668	279	4.8
Hospitals	0	0	0.0
Housing and Community Development	22,389	186	3.2
Interest on General Debt	38,881	322	5.5
Judicial and Legal	24,997	207	3.6
Libraries	7,653	63	1.1
Parking	701	6	0.1
Parks and Recreation	26,793	222	3.8
Police Protection	56,499	468	8.1
Public Welfare	751	6	0.1
Sewerage	28,033	232	4.0
Solid Waste Management	12,342	102	1.8
Veterans' Services	0	0	0.0
Liquor Store	0	0	0.0
Utility	257,595	2,136	36.7
Employee Retirement	0	0	0.0

Source: U.S Census Bureau, State & Local Government Finances 2012

DEMOGRAPHICS

Population Growth

Area	1990 Census	2000 Census	2010 Census	Population Growth (%) 1990-2000	Population Growth (%) 2000-2010
City	104,735	110,257	120,623	5.3	9.4
MSA[1]	208,740	239,086	273,738	14.5	14.5
U.S.	248,709,873	281,421,906	308,745,538	13.2	9.7

Note: (1) Figures cover the Lafayette, LA Metropolitan Statistical Area—see Appendix B for areas included
Source: U.S. Census Bureau, Census 1990, 2000, 2010

Household Size

Area	Persons in Household (%)							Average Household Size
	One	Two	Three	Four	Five	Six	Seven or More	
City	35.2	32.6	14.8	11.4	4.3	0.7	1.0	2.40
MSA[1]	27.9	32.2	17.8	12.9	5.8	2.1	1.3	2.63
U.S.	27.7	33.6	15.7	13.1	6.0	2.3	1.5	2.64

Note: (1) Figures cover the Lafayette, LA Metropolitan Statistical Area—see Appendix B for areas included
Source: U.S. Census Bureau, 2011-2013 American Community Survey 3-Year Estimates

Race

Area	White Alone[2] (%)	Black Alone[2] (%)	Asian Alone[2] (%)	AIAN[3] Alone[2] (%)	NHOPI[4] Alone[2] (%)	Other Race Alone[2] (%)	Two or More Races (%)
City	64.2	30.9	2.0	0.3	0.0	0.7	1.8
MSA[1]	70.8	24.4	1.4	0.4	0.0	0.6	2.2
U.S.	73.9	12.6	5.0	0.8	0.2	4.7	2.9

Note: (1) Figures cover the Lafayette, LA Metropolitan Statistical Area—see Appendix B for areas included; (2) Alone is defined as not being in combination with one or more other races; (3) American Indian and Alaska Native; (4) Native Hawaiian and Other Pacific Islander
Source: U.S. Census Bureau, 2011-2013 American Community Survey 3-Year Estimates

Hispanic or Latino Origin

Area	Total (%)	Mexican (%)	Puerto Rican (%)	Cuban (%)	Other (%)
City	4.4	2.0	0.3	0.2	2.0
MSA[1]	3.4	1.8	0.2	0.1	1.3
U.S.	16.9	10.8	1.6	0.6	3.8

Note: Persons of Hispanic or Latino origin can be of any race; (1) Figures cover the Lafayette, LA Metropolitan Statistical Area—see Appendix B for areas included
Source: U.S. Census Bureau, 2011-2013 American Community Survey 3-Year Estimates

Segregation

Type	Segregation Indices[1]				Percent Change		
	1990	2000	2010	2010 Rank[2]	1990-2000	1990-2010	2000-2010
Black/White	n/a	n/a	n/a	n/a	n/a	n/a	n/a
Asian/White	n/a	n/a	n/a	n/a	n/a	n/a	n/a
Hispanic/White	n/a	n/a	n/a	n/a	n/a	n/a	n/a

Note: All figures cover the Metropolitan Statistical Area—see Appendix B for areas included; Figures are based on an analysis of 1990, 2000, and 2010 Census Decennial Census tract data by William H. Frey, Brookings Institution and the University of Michigan Social Science Data Analysis Network. In this analysis all racial groups (whites, blacks, and asians) are non-Hispanic members of those races. Hispanics are shown as a separate category;
(1) Segregation Indices are Dissimilarity Indices that measure the degree to which the minority group is distributed differently than whites across census tracts. They range from 0 (complete integration) to 100 (complete segregation) where the value indicates the percentage of the minority group that needs to move to be distributed exactly like whites; (2) Ranges from 1 (most segregated) to 102 (least segregated); n/a not available.
Source: www.CensusScope.org

Ancestry

Area	German	Irish	English	American	Italian	Polish	French[2]	Scottish	Dutch
City	9.2	6.6	5.9	7.7	3.4	0.7	20.1	1.3	0.7
MSA[1]	8.0	4.6	4.2	10.7	2.5	0.4	21.0	0.7	0.3
U.S.	14.9	10.8	8.0	7.4	5.5	3.0	2.7	1.7	1.4

Note: Figures are the percentage of the total population reporting a particular ancestry. The nine most commonly reported ancestries in the U.S. are shown. Figures include multiple ancestries (e.g. if a person reported being Irish and Italian, they were included in both columns); (1) Figures cover the Lafayette, LA Metropolitan Statistical Area—see Appendix B for areas included; (2) Excludes Basque
Source: U.S. Census Bureau, 2011-2013 American Community Survey 3-Year Estimates

Foreign-Born Population

Area	Percent of Population Born in								
	Any Foreign Country	Mexico	Asia	Europe	Carribean	South America	Central America[2]	Africa	Canada
City	n/a	n/a	n/a	n/a	n/a	n/a	n/a	n/a	n/a
MSA[1]	n/a	n/a	n/a	n/a	n/a	n/a	n/a	n/a	n/a
U.S.	13.0	3.7	3.8	1.5	1.2	0.9	1.0	0.6	0.3

Note: (1) Figures cover the Lafayette, LA Metropolitan Statistical Area—see Appendix B for areas included; (2) Excludes Mexico.
Source: U.S. Census Bureau, 2011-2013 American Community Survey 3-Year Estimates

Marital Status

Area	Never Married	Now Married[2]	Separated	Widowed	Divorced
City	40.6	39.1	2.5	6.1	11.8
MSA[1]	33.1	46.2	2.7	6.1	11.9
U.S.	32.7	48.1	2.2	6.0	11.0

Note: Figures are percentages and cover the population 15 years of age and older; (1) Figures cover the Lafayette, LA Metropolitan Statistical Area—see Appendix B for areas included; (2) Excludes separated
Source: U.S. Census Bureau, 2011-2013 American Community Survey 3-Year Estimates

Disability Status

Area	All Ages	Under 18 Years Old	18 to 64 Years Old	65 Years and Over
City	12.3	4.8	10.9	34.1
MSA[1]	13.8	5.0	12.5	40.7
U.S.	12.3	4.1	10.2	36.3

Note: Figures show percent of the civilian noninstitutionalized population that reported having a disability. Disability status is determined from from six types of difficulty: vision, hearing, cognitive, ambulatory, self-care, and independent living. For children under 5 years old, hearing and vision difficulty are used to determine disability status. For children between the ages of 5 and 14, disability status is determined from hearing, vision, cognitive, ambulatory, and self-care difficulties. For people aged 15 years and older, they are considered to have a disability if they have difficulty with any one of the six difficulty types; (1) Figures cover the Lafayette, LA Metropolitan Statistical Area—see Appendix B for areas included.
Source: U.S. Census Bureau, 2011-2013 American Community Survey 3-Year Estimates

Age

Area	Percent of Population									Median Age
	Under Age 5	Age 5–19	Age 20–34	Age 35–44	Age 45–54	Age 55–64	Age 65–74	Age 75–84	Age 85+	
City	5.5	19.4	26.8	11.7	13.2	11.5	6.6	4.0	1.4	33.7
MSA[1]	7.1	20.8	22.1	12.3	14.0	11.8	6.7	3.8	1.4	35.0
U.S.	6.4	19.9	20.7	12.9	14.1	12.3	7.6	4.2	1.9	37.4

Note: (1) Figures cover the Lafayette, LA Metropolitan Statistical Area—see Appendix B for areas included
Source: U.S. Census Bureau, 2011-2013 American Community Survey 3-Year Estimates

Gender

Area	Males	Females	Males per 100 Females
City	59,888	63,109	94.9
MSA[1]	231,522	243,048	95.3
U.S.	154,451,010	159,410,713	96.9

Note: (1) Figures cover the Lafayette, LA Metropolitan Statistical Area—see Appendix B for areas included
Source: U.S. Census Bureau, 2011-2013 American Community Survey 3-Year Estimates

Religious Groups by Family

Area	Catholic	Baptist	Non-Den.	Methodist[2]	Lutheran	LDS[3]	Pente-costal	Presby-terian[4]	Muslim[5]	Judaism
MSA[1]	47.0	14.8	4.0	2.6	0.2	0.4	2.9	0.2	0.1	0.1
U.S.	19.1	9.3	4.0	4.0	2.3	2.0	1.9	1.6	0.8	0.7

Note: Figures are the number of adherents as a percentage of the total population; (1) Figures cover the Lafayette, LA Metropolitan Statistical Area—see Appendix B for areas included; (2) Methodist/Pietist; (3) Latter Day Saints; (4) Reformed; (5) Figures are estimates
Source: Association of Statisticians of American Religious Bodies, 2010 U.S. Religion Census: Religious Congregations & Membership Study

Religious Groups by Tradition

Area	Catholic	Evangelical Protestant	Mainline Protestant	Other Tradition	Black Protestant	Orthodox
MSA[1]	47.0	12.8	3.2	0.8	9.3	0.1
U.S.	19.1	16.2	7.3	4.3	1.6	0.3

Note: Figures are the number of adherents as a percentage of the total population; (1) Figures cover the Lafayette, LA Metropolitan Statistical Area—see Appendix B for areas included
Source: Association of Statisticians of American Religious Bodies, 2010 U.S. Religion Census: Religious Congregations & Membership Study

ECONOMY

Gross Metropolitan Product

Area	2012	2013	2014	2015	Rank[2]
MSA[1]	17.7	17.8	18.8	19.6	123

Note: Figures are in billions of dollars; (1) Figures cover the Lafayette, LA Metropolitan Statistical Area—see Appendix B for areas included; (2) Rank is based on 2015 data and ranges from 1 to 363
Source: The U.S. Conference of Mayors, U.S. Metro Economies: GMP and Employment 2013-2015, June 2014

Economic Growth

Area	2010-12 (%)	2013 (%)	2014 (%)	2015 (%)	Rank[2]
MSA[1]	-3.6	-1.3	2.9	3.8	47
U.S.	2.1	2.0	2.3	3.2	–

Note: Figures are real gross metropolitan product (GMP) growth rates and represent annual average percent change; (1) Figures cover the Lafayette, LA Metropolitan Statistical Area—see Appendix B for areas included; (2) Rank is based on 2015 data and ranges from 1 to 363
Source: The U.S. Conference of Mayors, U.S. Metro Economies: GMP and Employment 2013-2015, June 2014

Metropolitan Area Exports

Area	2008	2009	2010	2011	2012	2013	Rank[2]
MSA[1]	762.7	657.0	488.1	655.9	726.0	1,261.8	139

Note: Figures are in millions of dollars; (1) Figures cover the Lafayette, LA Metropolitan Statistical Area—see Appendix B for areas included; (2) Rank is based on 2013 data and ranges from 1 to 387
Source: U.S. Department of Commerce, International Trade Administration, Office of Trade & Industry Information, Manufacturing & Services, data extracted April 3, 2015

Building Permits

Area	Single-Family			Multi-Family			Total		
	2013	2014	Pct. Chg.	2013	2014	Pct. Chg.	2013	2014	Pct. Chg.
City	n/a	n/a	n/a	n/a	n/a	n/a	n/a	n/a	n/a
MSA[1]	1,399	2,224	59.0	155	138	-11.0	1,554	2,362	52.0
U.S.	620,802	634,597	2.2	370,020	411,766	11.3	990,822	1,046,363	5.6

Note: (1) Figures cover the Lafayette, LA Metropolitan Statistical Area—see Appendix B for areas included; Figures represent new, privately-owned housing units authorized (unadjusted data); All permit data are based on estimates with imputation.
Source: U.S. Census Bureau, Manufacturing, Mining, and Construction Statistics, Building Permits, 2013, 2014

Bankruptcy Filings

Area	Business Filings			Nonbusiness Filings		
	2013	2014	% Chg.	2013	2014	% Chg.
Lafayette Parish	20	40	100.0	495	516	4.2
U.S.	33,212	26,983	-18.8	1,038,720	909,812	-12.4

Note: Business filings include Chapter 7, Chapter 11, Chapter 12, and Chapter 13; Nonbusiness filings include Chapter 7, Chapter 11, and Chapter 13
Source: Administrative Office of the U.S. Courts, Business and Nonbusiness Bankruptcy, County Cases Commenced by Chapter of the Bankruptcy Code, During the 12- Month Period Ending December 31, 2013 and Business and Nonbusiness Bankruptcy, County Cases Commenced by Chapter of the Bankruptcy Code, During the 12- Month Period Ending December 31, 2014

Housing Vacancy Rates

Area	Gross Vacancy Rate[2] (%)			Year-Round Vacancy Rate[3] (%)			Rental Vacancy Rate[4] (%)			Homeowner Vacancy Rate[5] (%)		
	2012	2013	2014	2012	2013	2014	2012	2013	2014	2012	2013	2014
MSA[1]	n/a	n/a	n/a	n/a	n/a	n/a	n/a	n/a	n/a	n/a	n/a	n/a
U.S.	13.8	13.6	13.4	10.8	10.7	10.4	8.7	8.3	7.6	2.0	2.0	1.9

Note: (1) Figures cover the Lafayette, LA Metropolitan Statistical Area—see Appendix B for areas included; (2) The percentage of the total housing inventory that is vacant; (3) The percentage of the housing inventory (excluding seasonal units) that is year-round vacant; (4) The percentage of rental inventory that is vacant for rent; (5) The percentage of homeowner inventory that is vacant for sale; n/a not available
Source: U.S. Census Bureau, Housing Vacancies and Homeownership Annual Statistics: 2014

INCOME

Income

Area	Per Capita ($)	Median Household ($)	Average Household ($)
City	28,454	45,317	67,042
MSA[1]	25,649	46,222	65,919
U.S.	27,884	52,176	72,897

Note: (1) Figures cover the Lafayette, LA Metropolitan Statistical Area—see Appendix B for areas included
Source: U.S. Census Bureau, 2011-2013 American Community Survey 3-Year Estimates

Household Income Distribution

Area	Percent of Households Earning							
	Under $15,000	$15,000 -24,999	$25,000 -34,999	$35,000 -49,999	$50,000 -74,999	$75,000 -99,000	$100,000 -149,999	$150,000 and up
City	18.5	12.4	9.4	14.3	14.6	9.9	12.0	8.9
MSA[1]	16.8	12.5	10.4	13.4	15.8	11.4	11.8	7.9
U.S.	13.0	10.9	10.3	13.6	17.9	11.9	12.7	9.6

Note: (1) Figures cover the Lafayette, LA Metropolitan Statistical Area—see Appendix B for areas included
Source: U.S. Census Bureau, 2011-2013 American Community Survey 3-Year Estimates

Poverty Rate

Area	All Ages	Under 18 Years Old	18 to 64 Years Old	65 Years and Over
City	19.1	26.4	18.4	9.9
MSA[1]	17.6	23.7	15.9	13.1
U.S.	15.9	22.4	14.8	9.5

Note: Figures are percentage of people whose income during the past 12 months was below the poverty level; (1) Figures cover the Lafayette, LA Metropolitan Statistical Area—see Appendix B for areas included
Source: U.S. Census Bureau, 2011-2013 American Community Survey 3-Year Estimates

EMPLOYMENT

Labor Force and Employment

Area	Civilian Labor Force			Workers Employed		
	Dec. 2013	Dec. 2014	% Chg.	Dec. 2013	Dec. 2014	% Chg.
City	64,366	66,367	3.1	61,853	63,005	1.9
MSA[1]	226,804	234,554	3.4	217,493	221,842	2.0
U.S.	154,408,000	155,521,000	0.7	144,423,000	147,190,000	1.9

Note: Data is not seasonally adjusted and covers workers 16 years of age and older; (1) Figures cover the Lafayette, LA Metropolitan Statistical Area—see Appendix B for areas included
Source: Bureau of Labor Statistics, Local Area Unemployment Statistics

Unemployment Rate

Area	2014											
	Jan.	Feb.	Mar.	Apr.	May	Jun.	Jul.	Aug.	Sep.	Oct.	Nov.	Dec.
City	4.6	4.0	4.4	4.0	5.0	5.7	5.9	6.0	5.5	5.6	5.5	5.1
MSA[1]	4.9	4.3	4.7	4.2	5.1	5.9	6.1	6.2	5.8	5.8	5.8	5.4
U.S.	7.0	7.0	6.8	5.9	6.1	6.3	6.5	6.3	5.7	5.5	5.5	5.4

Note: Data is not seasonally adjusted and covers workers 16 years of age and older; (1) Figures cover the Lafayette, LA Metropolitan Statistical Area—see Appendix B for areas included
Source: Bureau of Labor Statistics, Local Area Unemployment Statistics

Employment by Occupation

Occupation Classification	City (%)	MSA[1] (%)	U.S. (%)
Management, Business, Science, and Arts	36.1	30.2	36.2
Natural Resources, Construction, and Maintenance	8.4	13.3	9.0
Production, Transportation, and Material Moving	10.2	13.4	12.1
Sales and Office	24.1	25.0	24.4
Service	21.2	18.1	18.3

Note: Figures cover employed civilians 16 years of age and older; (1) Figures cover the Lafayette, LA Metropolitan Statistical Area—see Appendix B for areas included
Source: U.S. Census Bureau, 2011-2013 American Community Survey 3-Year Estimates

Employment by Industry

Sector	MSA[1] Number of Employees	MSA[1] Percent of Total	U.S. Percent of Total
Construction	11,000	4.9	4.4
Education and Health Services	29,700	13.3	15.5
Financial Activities	12,400	5.6	5.7
Government	26,500	11.9	15.8
Information	2,900	1.3	2.0
Leisure and Hospitality	21,500	9.6	10.3
Manufacturing	20,200	9.1	8.7
Mining and Logging	23,000	10.3	0.6
Other Services	6,800	3.1	4.0
Professional and Business Services	23,100	10.4	13.8
Retail Trade	28,700	12.9	11.4
Transportation, Warehousing, and Utilities	6,800	3.1	3.9
Wholesale Trade	10,300	4.6	4.2

Note: Figures are non-farm employment as of December 2014. Figures are not seasonally adjusted and include workers 16 years of age and older; (1) Figures cover the Lafayette, LA Metropolitan Statistical Area—see Appendix B for areas included
Source: Bureau of Labor Statistics, Current Employment Statistics, Employment, Hours, and Earnings

Occupations with Greatest Projected Employment Growth: 2012 – 2022

Occupation[1]	2012 Employment	2022 Projected Employment	Numeric Employment Change	Percent Employment Change
Personal Care Aides	24,990	35,060	10,070	40.3
Retail Salespersons	58,870	67,040	8,170	13.9
Registered Nurses	41,270	48,690	7,420	18.0
Laborers and Freight, Stock, and Material Movers, Hand	39,440	45,610	6,170	15.7
Secretaries and Administrative Assistants, Except Legal, Medical, and Executive	40,400	46,010	5,610	13.9
Combined Food Preparation and Serving Workers, Including Fast Food	27,780	33,030	5,250	18.9
General and Operations Managers	31,060	35,860	4,800	15.4
Home Health Aides	11,560	16,250	4,690	40.6
Licensed Practical and Licensed Vocational Nurses	22,930	27,360	4,430	19.3
Cashiers	68,250	72,430	4,180	6.1

Note: Projections cover Louisiana; (1) Sorted by numeric employment change
Source: www.projectionscentral.com, State Occupational Projections, 2012–2022 Long-Term Projections

Fastest Growing Occupations: 2012 – 2022

Occupation[1]	2012 Employment	2022 Projected Employment	Numeric Employment Change	Percent Employment Change
Software Developers, Systems Software	1,110	2,010	900	80.6
Software Developers, Applications	1,220	2,100	880	72.3
Interpreters and Translators	440	710	270	62.5
Computer Systems Analysts	3,460	5,070	1,610	46.6
Home Health Aides	11,560	16,250	4,690	40.6
Personal Care Aides	24,990	35,060	10,070	40.3
Computer Numerically Controlled Machine Tool Programmers, Metal and Plastic	240	340	100	39.8
Information Security Analysts	530	740	210	39.6
Skincare Specialists	410	570	160	39.2
Diagnostic Medical Sonographers	890	1,230	340	38.8

Note: Projections cover Louisiana; (1) Sorted by percent employment change and excludes occupations with numeric employment change less than 100
Source: www.projectionscentral.com, State Occupational Projections, 2012–2022 Long-Term Projections

Average Wages

Occupation	$/Hr.	Occupation	$/Hr.
Accountants and Auditors	32.05	Maids and Housekeeping Cleaners	8.66
Automotive Mechanics	18.85	Maintenance and Repair Workers	18.33
Bookkeepers	17.31	Marketing Managers	35.31
Carpenters	17.64	Nuclear Medicine Technologists	27.19
Cashiers	9.07	Nurses, Licensed Practical	17.44
Clerks, General Office	11.76	Nurses, Registered	28.28
Clerks, Receptionists/Information	11.09	Nursing Assistants	9.35
Clerks, Shipping/Receiving	14.93	Packers and Packagers, Hand	9.76
Computer Programmers	25.02	Physical Therapists	34.68
Computer Systems Analysts	31.63	Postal Service Mail Carriers	25.04
Computer User Support Specialists	22.34	Real Estate Brokers	26.33
Cooks, Restaurant	9.84	Retail Salespersons	11.55
Dentists	39.93	Sales Reps., Exc. Tech./Scientific	27.68
Electrical Engineers	n/a	Sales Reps., Tech./Scientific	33.19
Electricians	21.25	Secretaries, Exc. Legal/Med./Exec.	14.63
Financial Managers	42.95	Security Guards	11.78
First-Line Supervisors/Managers, Sales	18.38	Surgeons	70.64
Food Preparation Workers	8.85	Teacher Assistants	10.30
General and Operations Managers	57.52	Teachers, Elementary School	24.10
Hairdressers/Cosmetologists	11.58	Teachers, Secondary School	24.80
Internists	n/a	Telemarketers	n/a
Janitors and Cleaners	9.81	Truck Drivers, Heavy/Tractor-Trailer	18.12
Landscaping/Groundskeeping Workers	10.85	Truck Drivers, Light/Delivery Svcs.	14.34
Lawyers	48.67	Waiters and Waitresses	8.98

Note: Wage data covers the Lafayette, LA Metropolitan Statistical Area—see Appendix B for areas included; Hourly wages for elementary/secondary school teachers and teacher assistants were calculated by the editors from annual wage data assuming a 40 hour work week; n/a not available.
Source: Bureau of Labor Statistics, Metro Area Occupational Employment and Wage Estimates, May 2014

TAXES

State Corporate Income Tax Rates

State	Tax Rate (%)	Income Brackets ($)	Num. of Brackets	Financial Institution Tax Rate (%)[a]	Federal Income Tax Ded.
Louisiana	4.0 - 8.0	25,000 - 200,001	5	4.0 - 8.0	Yes

Note: Tax rates as of January 1, 2015; (a) Rates listed are the corporate income tax rate applied to financial institutions or excise taxes based on income. Some states have other taxes based upon the value of deposits or shares.
Source: Federation of Tax Administrators, "State Corporate Income Tax Rates, 2015"

State Individual Income Tax Rates

State	Tax Rate (%)	Income Brackets ($)	Num. of Brackets	Personal Exempt. ($)[1] Single	Personal Exempt. ($)[1] Dependents	Fed. Inc. Tax Ded.
Louisiana	2.0 - 6.0	12,500 - 50,001 (b)	3	4,500 (k)	1,000	Yes

Note: Tax rates as of January 1, 2015; Local- and county-level taxes are not included; n/a not applicable; (1) Married joint filers generally receive double the single exemption; (b) For joint returns, taxes are twice the tax on half the couple's income; (k) The amounts reported for Louisiana are a combined personal exemption-standard deduction.
Source: Federation of Tax Administrators, "State Individual Income Tax Rates, 2015"

Various State and Local Tax Rates

State	State and Local Sales and Use (%)	State Sales and Use (%)	Gasoline[1] (¢/gal.)	Cigarette[2] ($/pack)	Spirits[3] ($/gal.)	Wine[4] ($/gal.)	Beer[5] ($/gal.)
Louisiana	8.0	4.0	20.01	0.36	2.50 (f)	0.11	0.32

Note: All tax rates as of January 1, 2015; (1) The American Petroleum Institute has developed a methodology for determining the average tax rate on a gallon of fuel. Rates may include any of the following: excise taxes, environmental fees, storage tank fees, other fees or taxes, general sales tax, and local taxes. In states where gasoline is subject to the general sales tax, or where the fuel tax is based on the average sale price, the average rate determined by API is sensitive to changes in the price of gasoline. States that fully or partially apply general sales taxes to gasoline: CA, CO, GA, IL, IN, MI, NY; (2) The federal excise tax of $1.0066 per pack and local taxes are not included; (3) Rates are those applicable to off-premise sales of 40% alcohol by volume (a.b.v.) distilled spirits in 750ml containers. Local excise taxes are excluded; (4) Rates are those applicable to off-premise sales of 11% a.b.v. non-carbonated wine in 750ml containers; (5) Rates are those applicable to off-premise sales of 4.7% a.b.v. beer in 12 ounce containers; (f) Different rates are also applicable according to alcohol content, place of production, size of container, or place purchased (on- or off-premise or onboard airlines).
Source: Tax Foundation, 2015 Facts & Figures: How Does Your State Compare?

State Business Tax Climate Index Rankings

State	Overall Rank	Corporate Tax Index Rank	Individual Income Tax Index Rank	Sales Tax Index Rank	Unemployment Insurance Tax Index Rank	Property Tax Index Rank
Louisiana	35	23	27	50	6	24

Note: The index is a measure of how each state's tax laws affect economic performance. The lower the rank, the more favorable a state's tax system is for business. States without a given tax are given a ranking of 1. The scores/rankings for the District of Columbia do not affect other states. The 2015 index represents the tax climate as of July 1, 2014.
Source: Tax Foundation, State Business Tax Climate Index 2015

COMMERCIAL UTILITIES

Typical Monthly Electric Bills

Area	Commercial Service ($/month)		Industrial Service ($/month)	
	1,500 kWh	40 kW demand 14,000 kWh	1,000 kW demand 200,000 kWh	50,000 kW demand 32,500,000 kWh
City	213	1,701	20,968	2,532,363
Average[1]	201	1,653	26,124	2,639,743

Note: Figures are based on annualized 2014 rates; (1) Average based on 180 utilities surveyed
Source: Edison Electric Institute, Typical Bills and Average Rates Report, Summer 2014

TRANSPORTATION

Means of Transportation to Work

Area	Car/Truck/Van		Public Transportation			Bicycle	Walked	Other Means	Worked at Home
	Drove Alone	Car-pooled	Bus	Subway	Railroad				
City	81.2	10.1	0.8	0.0	0.0	1.1	2.4	1.5	2.9
MSA[1]	82.7	10.8	0.5	0.0	0.0	0.4	1.9	1.6	2.1
U.S.	76.4	9.6	2.6	1.8	0.6	0.6	2.8	1.3	4.3

Note: Figures are percentages and cover workers 16 years of age and older; (1) Figures cover the Lafayette, LA Metropolitan Statistical Area—see Appendix B for areas included
Source: U.S. Census Bureau, 2011-2013 American Community Survey 3-Year Estimates

Travel Time to Work

Area	Less Than 10 Minutes	10 to 19 Minutes	20 to 29 Minutes	30 to 44 Minutes	45 to 59 Minutes	60 to 89 Minutes	90 Minutes or More
City	18.1	44.6	17.6	11.5	1.8	3.3	3.0
MSA[1]	16.6	34.2	19.7	17.1	4.4	3.6	4.4
U.S.	13.3	29.7	20.9	20.2	7.7	5.7	2.6

Note: Figures are percentages and include workers 16 years old and over; (1) Figures cover the Lafayette, LA Metropolitan Statistical Area—see Appendix B for areas included
Source: U.S. Census Bureau, 2011-2013 American Community Survey 3-Year Estimates

Travel Time Index

Area	1985	1990	1995	2000	2005	2010	2011
Urban Area[1]	n/a	n/a	n/a	n/a	n/a	n/a	n/a
Average[2]	1.09	1.14	1.16	1.19	1.23	1.18	1.18

Note: Travel Time Index—the ratio of travel time in the peak period to the travel time at free-flow conditions. For example, a value of 1.30 indicates a 20-minute free-flow trip takes 26 minutes in the peak. Free-flow speeds (60 mph on freeways and 35 mph on principal arterials) are used as the comparison threshold; (1) Data for the Lafayette, LA urban area was not available; (2) average of 498 urban areas

Source: Texas Transportation Institute, Urban Mobility Report 2012, December 2012

Public Transportation

Agency Name / Mode of Transportation	Vehicles Operated in Maximum Service	Annual Unlinked Passenger Trips (in thous.)	Annual Passenger Miles (in thous.)
Lafayette Transit System			
Bus (directly operated)	13	1,437.0	7,157.9
Bus (purchased transportation)	4	30.3	450.4
Demand Response (purchased transportation)	5	24.9	154.9

Source: Federal Transit Administration, National Transit Database, 2013

Air Transportation

Airport Name and Code / Type of Service	Passenger Airlines[1]	Passenger Enplanements	Freight Carriers[2]	Freight (lbs.)
Lafayette Regional Airport (LFT)				
Domestic service (U.S. carriers - 2014)	8	246,680	5	11,220,944
International service (U.S. carriers - 2013)	1	166	0	0

Note: (1) Includes all U.S.-based major, minor and commuter airlines that carried at least one passenger during the year; (2) Includes all U.S.-based airlines and freight carriers that transported at least one lb. of freight during the year.

Source: Bureau of Transportation Statistics, The Intermodal Transportation Database, Air Carriers: T-100 Domestic Market (U.S. Carriers), 2014; Bureau of Transportation Statistics, The Intermodal Transportation Database, Air Carriers: T-100 International Market (U.S. Carriers), 2013

Other Transportation Statistics

Major Highways:	I-10
Amtrak Service:	Yes
Major Waterways/Ports:	Gulf of Mexico (40 miles)

Source: Amtrak.com; Google Maps

BUSINESSES

Major Business Headquarters

Company Name	Rankings	
	Fortune[1]	Forbes[2]
No companies listed	-	-

Note: (1) Fortune 500—companies that produce a 10-K are ranked 1 to 500 based on 2013 revenue; (2) all private companies with at least $2 billion in annual revenue through the end of their most current fiscal year are ranked 1 to 221; companies listed are headquartered in the city; dashes indicate no ranking

Source: Fortune, "Fortune 500," June 16, 2014; Forbes, "America's Largest Private Companies," November 5, 2014

Minority- and Women-Owned Businesses

Group	All Firms		Firms with Paid Employees			
	Firms	Sales ($000)	Firms	Sales ($000)	Employees	Payroll ($000)
Asian	396	90,192	144	80,346	1,739	23,430
Black	2,131	108,455	151	72,640	1,525	31,327
Hispanic	443	137,108	68	123,280	659	24,084
Women	3,517	833,991	665	756,160	6,398	172,600
All Firms	15,659	16,255,682	4,787	15,627,640	89,598	2,969,477

Note: Figures cover firms located in the city; minority- and women-owned business are defined as firms in which the corresponding group own 51% or more of the stock or equity of the company
Source: U.S. Census Bureau, 2007 Economic Census, Survey of Business Owners (2012 Survey of Business Owners data will be released starting in June 2015)

HOTELS & CONVENTION CENTERS

Hotels/Motels

Area	5 Star		4 Star		3 Star		2 Star		1 Star		Not Rated	
	Num.	Pct.[3]	Num.	Pct.[3]	Num.	Pct.[3]	Num.	Pct.[3]	Num.	Pct.[3]	Num.	Pct.[3]
City[1]	0	0.0	1	1.1	18	19.6	67	72.8	2	2.2	4	4.3
Total[2]	166	0.9	1,264	7.0	5,718	31.8	9,340	52.0	411	2.3	1,070	6.0

Note: (1) Figures cover Lafayette and vicinity; (2) Figures cover all 100 cities in this book; (3) Percentage of hotels which have a given star rating; Star ratings are determined by expedia.com and offer an indication of the general quality of a particular hotel.
Source: expedia.com, April 2, 2015

Major Convention Centers

Name	Overall Space (sq. ft.)	Exhibit Space (sq. ft.)	Meeting Space (sq. ft.)	Meeting Rooms
Cajundome and Convention Center	72,000	37,300	20,000	n/a

Note: Table includes convention centers located in the Lafayette, LA metro area; n/a not available
Source: Original research

Living Environment

COST OF LIVING

Cost of Living Index

Composite Index	Groceries	Housing	Utilities	Transportation	Health Care	Misc. Goods/ Services
95.7	94.2	93.5	92.9	100.8	86.8	98.5

Note: The Cost of Living Index measures regional differences in the cost of consumer goods and services, excluding taxes and non-consumer expenditures, for professional and managerial households in the top income quintile. It is based on more than 50,000 prices covering almost 60 different items for which prices are collected three times a year by chambers of commerce, economic development organizations or university applied economic centers in each participating urban area. The numbers shown should be read as a percentage above or below the national average of 100. For example, a value of 115.4 in the groceries column indicates that grocery prices are 15.4% higher than the national average. Small differences in the index numbers should not be interpreted as significant; Figures cover the Lafayette LA urban area.
Source: The Council for Community and Economic Research, ACCRA Cost of Living Index, 2014

Grocery Prices

Area[1]	T-Bone Steak ($/pound)	Frying Chicken ($/pound)	Whole Milk ($/half gal.)	Eggs ($/dozen)	Orange Juice ($/64 oz.)	Coffee ($/11.5 oz.)
City[2]	9.74	1.15	2.75	1.84	3.45	3.67
Avg.	10.40	1.37	2.40	1.99	3.46	4.27
Min.	8.48	0.93	1.37	1.30	2.83	2.99
Max.	14.20	2.44	3.62	4.02	6.42	6.96

Note: (1) Values for the local area are compared with the average, minimum and maximum values for all 308 areas in the Cost of Living Index; (2) Figures cover the Lafayette LA urban area; **T-Bone Steak** *(price per pound);* **Frying Chicken** *(price per pound, whole fryer);* **Whole Milk** *(half gallon carton);* **Eggs** *(price per dozen, Grade A, large);* **Orange Juice** *(64 oz. Tropicana or Florida Natural);* **Coffee** *(11.5 oz. can, vacuum-packed, Maxwell House, Hills Bros, or Folgers).*
Source: The Council for Community and Economic Research, ACCRA Cost of Living Index, 2014

Housing and Utility Costs

Area[1]	New Home Price ($)	Apartment Rent ($/month)	All Electric ($/month)	Part Electric ($/month)	Other Energy ($/month)	Telephone ($/month)
City[2]	272,388	907	-	95.47	49.71	28.73
Avg.	305,838	919	181.00	93.66	73.14	27.95
Min.	183,142	480	112.00	42.06	23.42	17.16
Max.	1,358,576	3,851	594.00	180.03	440.99	40.42

Note: (1) Values for the local area are compared with the average, minimum and maximum values for all 308 areas in the Cost of Living Index; (2) Figures cover the Lafayette LA urban area; **New Home Price** *(2,400 sf living area, 8,000 sf lot, in urban area with full utilities);* **Apartment Rent** *(950 sf 2 bedroom/1.5 or 2 bath, unfurnished, excluding all utilities except water);* **All Electric** *(average monthly cost for an all-electric home);* **Part Electric** *(average monthly cost for a part-electric home);* **Other Energy** *(average monthly cost for natural gas, fuel oil, coal, wood, and any other forms of energy except electricity);* **Telephone** *(price includes basic monthly rate for a private residential line plus additional local usage charges incurred by a family of four).*
Source: The Council for Community and Economic Research, ACCRA Cost of Living Index, 2014

Health Care, Transportation, and Other Costs

Area[1]	Doctor ($/visit)	Dentist ($/visit)	Optometrist ($/visit)	Gasoline ($/gallon)	Beauty Salon ($/visit)	Men's Shirt ($)
City[2]	75.97	76.38	72.87	3.20	33.93	28.99
Avg.	102.86	87.89	97.66	3.44	34.37	26.74
Min.	67.47	65.78	51.18	3.00	17.43	12.79
Max.	173.50	150.14	235.00	4.33	64.28	49.50

Note: (1) Values for the local area are compared with the average, minimum and maximum values for all 308 areas in the Cost of Living Index; (2) Figures cover the Lafayette LA urban area; **Doctor** *(general practitioners routine exam of an established patient);* **Dentist** *(adult teeth cleaning and periodic oral examination);* **Optometrist** *(full vision eye exam for established adult patient);* **Gasoline** *(one gallon regular unleaded, national brand, including all taxes, cash price at self-service pump if available);* **Beauty Salon** *(woman's shampoo, trim, and blow-dry);* **Men's Shirt** *(cotton/polyester dress shirt, pinpoint weave, long sleeves).*
Source: The Council for Community and Economic Research, ACCRA Cost of Living Index, 2014

HOUSING

House Price Index (HPI)

Area	National Ranking[2]	Quarterly Change (%)	One-Year Change (%)	Five-Year Change (%)
MSA[1]	153	1.69	3.88	6.75
U.S.[3]	–	1.35	4.91	11.59

Note: The HPI is a weighted repeat sales index. It measures average price changes in repeat sales or refinancings on the same properties. This information is obtained by reviewing repeat mortgage transactions on single-family properties whose mortgages have been purchased or securitized by Fannie Mae or Freddie Mac in January 1975; (1) Lafayette Metropolitan Statistical Area—see Appendix B for areas included; (2) Rankings are based on annual percentage change for all metro areas containing at least 15,000 transactions over the last 10 years and ranges from 1 to 275; (3) figures based on a weighted average of Census Division estimates using a seasonally adjusted, purchase-only index; all figures are for the period ending December 31, 2014
Source: Federal Housing Finance Agency, House Price Index, February 26, 2015

Median Single-Family Home Prices

Area	2012	2013	2014p	Percent Change 2013 to 2014
MSA[1]	n/a	n/a	n/a	n/a
U.S. Average	177.2	197.4	209.0	5.9

Note: Figures are median sales prices of existing single-family homes in thousands of dollars; (p) preliminary; n/a not available; (1) Lafayette, LA Metropolitan Statistical Area—see Appendix B for areas included
Source: National Association of Realtors, Median Sales Price of Existing Single-Family Homes for Metropolitan Areas, 4th Quarter 2014

Qualifying Income Based on Median Sales Price of Existing Single-Family Homes

Area	With 5% Down ($)	With 10% Down ($)	With 20% Down ($)
MSA[1]	n/a	n/a	n/a
U.S. Average	45,863	43,449	38,621

Note: Figures are preliminary; Qualifying income is based on a mortgage rate of 4.0%. Monthly principal and interest payment is limited to 25% of income; n/a not available; (1) Lafayette, LA Metropolitan Statistical Area—see Appendix B for areas included
Source: National Association of Realtors, Qualifying Income Based on Median Sales Price of Existing Single-Family Homes for Metropolitan Areas, 4th Quarter 2014

Median Apartment Condo-Coop Home Prices

Area	2012	2013	2014p	Percent Change 2013 to 2014
MSA[1]	n/a	n/a	n/a	n/a
U.S. Average	173.7	194.9	205.1	5.2

Note: Figures are median sales prices of existing apartment condo-coop homes in thousands of dollars; (p) preliminary; n/a not available; (1) Lafayette, LA Metropolitan Statistical Area—see Appendix B for areas included
Source: National Association of Realtors, Median Sales Price of Existing Apartment Condo-Coop Homes for Metropolitan Areas, 4th Quarter 2014

Gross Monthly Rent

Area	Under $200	$200 -299	$300 -499	$500 -749	$750 -999	$1,000 -1,499	$1,500 and up	Median ($)
City	2.9	3.5	7.4	30.5	30.0	19.8	5.8	787
MSA[1]	3.0	5.2	16.1	33.7	24.6	13.8	3.5	696
U.S.	1.7	3.2	7.8	22.1	24.3	26.0	14.9	900

Note: Figures are percentages except for Median; Gross rent is the contract rent plus the estimated average monthly cost of utilities (electricity, gas, and water and sewer) and fuels (oil, coal, kerosene, wood, etc.) if these are paid by the renter (or paid for the renter by someone else); (1) Figures cover the Lafayette, LA Metropolitan Statistical Area—see Appendix B for areas included
Source: U.S. Census Bureau, 2011-2013 American Community Survey 3-Year Estimates

Homeownership Rate

Area	2007 (%)	2008 (%)	2009 (%)	2010 (%)	2011 (%)	2012 (%)	2013 (%)	2014 (%)
MSA[1]	n/a	n/a	n/a	n/a	n/a	n/a	n/a	n/a
U.S.	68.1	67.8	67.4	66.9	66.1	65.4	65.1	64.5

Note: (1) Figures cover the Lafayette, LA Metropolitan Statistical Area—see Appendix B for areas included; n/a not available
Source: U.S. Census Bureau, Housing Vacancies and Homeownership Annual Statistics: 2014

Year Housing Structure Built

Area	2010 or Later	2000 -2009	1990 -1999	1980 -1989	1970 -1979	1960 -1969	1950 -1959	1940 -1949	Before 1940	Median Year
City	1.4	14.0	11.2	17.8	21.0	15.6	11.0	4.1	4.0	1977
MSA[1]	2.5	17.9	13.9	16.7	18.2	11.7	9.2	4.3	5.7	1981
U.S.	0.9	15.0	13.9	13.8	15.8	11.0	10.9	5.4	13.3	1976

Note: Figures are percentages except for Median Year; (1) Figures cover the Lafayette, LA Metropolitan Statistical Area—see Appendix B for areas included
Source: U.S. Census Bureau, 2011-2013 American Community Survey 3-Year Estimates

HEALTH

Health Risk Data

Category	MSA[1] (%)	U.S. (%)
Adults aged 18–64 who have any kind of health care coverage	72.6	79.6
Adults who reported being in good or excellent health	83.9	83.1
Adults who are current smokers	26.0	19.6
Adults who are heavy drinkers[2]	9.0	6.1
Adults who are binge drinkers[3]	18.2	16.9
Adults who are overweight (BMI 25.0 - 29.9)	35.0	35.8
Adults who are obese (BMI 30.0 - 99.8)	29.6	27.6
Adults who participated in any physical activities in the past month	74.0	77.1
Adults 50+ who have ever had a sigmoidoscopy or colonoscopy	52.4	67.3
Women aged 40+ who have had a mammogram within the past two years	73.5	74.0
Men aged 40+ who have had a PSA test within the past two years	53.3	45.2
Adults aged 65+ who have had flu shot within the past year	60.5	60.1
Adults who always wear a seatbelt	n/a	93.8

Note: Data as of 2012 unless otherwise noted; n/a not available; (1) Figures cover the Lafayette, LA Metropolitan Statistical Area—see Appendix B for areas included; (2) Heavy drinkers are classified as males having more than two drinks per day or females having more than one drink per day; (3) Binge drinkers are classified as males having five or more drinks on one occasion or females having four or more drinks on one occasion
Source: Centers for Disease Control and Prevention, Behaviorial Risk Factor Surveillance System, SMART: Selected Metropolitan/Micropolitan Area Risk Trends, 2012 (Note: the CDC has discontinued this dataset but will be releasing a replacement in late 2015)

Chronic Health Indicators

Category	MSA[1] (%)	U.S. (%)
Adults who have ever been told they had a heart attack	3.4	4.5
Adults who have ever been told they had a stroke	3.0	2.9
Adults who have been told they currently have asthma	6.8	8.9
Adults who have ever been told they have arthritis	25.1	25.7
Adults who have ever been told they have diabetes[2]	10.3	9.7
Adults who have ever been told they had skin cancer	5.7	5.7
Adults who have ever been told they had any other types of cancer	8.2	6.5
Adults who have ever been told they have COPD	6.4	6.2
Adults who have ever been told they have kidney disease	n/a	2.5
Adults who have ever been told they have a form of depression	13.8	18.0

Note: Data as of 2012 unless otherwise noted; n/a not available; (1) Figures cover the Lafayette, LA Metropolitan Statistical Area—see Appendix B for areas included; (2) Figures do not include pregnancy-related, borderline, or pre-diabetes
Source: Centers for Disease Control and Prevention, Behaviorial Risk Factor Surveillance System, SMART: Selected Metropolitan/Micropolitan Area Risk Trends, 2012 (Note: the CDC has discontinued this dataset but will be releasing a replacement in late 2015)

Mortality Rates for the Top 10 Causes of Death in the U.S.

ICD-10[a] Sub-Chapter	ICD-10[a] Code	Age-Adjusted Mortality Rate[1] per 100,000 population	
		County[2]	U.S.
Malignant neoplasms	C00-C97	183.8	166.2
Ischaemic heart diseases	I20-I25	129.6	105.7
Other forms of heart disease	I30-I51	58.4	49.3
Chronic lower respiratory diseases	J40-J47	38.0	42.1
Organic, including symptomatic, mental disorders	F01-F09	47.0	38.1
Cerebrovascular diseases	I60-I69	38.6	37.0
Other external causes of accidental injury	W00-X59	26.9	26.9
Other degenerative diseases of the nervous system	G30-G31	38.8	25.6
Diabetes mellitus	E10-E14	29.3	21.3
Hypertensive diseases	I10-I15	27.4	19.4

Note: (a) ICD-10 = International Classification of Diseases 10th Revision; (1) Mortality rates are a three year average covering 2011-2013; (2) Figures cover Lafayette Parish
Source: Centers for Disease Control and Prevention, National Center for Health Statistics. Compressed Mortality File 1999-2013 on CDC WONDER Online Database, released October 2014. Data are compiled from the Compressed Mortality File 1999-2013, Series 20 No. 2S, 2014.

Mortality Rates for Selected Causes of Death

ICD-10[a] Sub-Chapter	ICD-10[a] Code	Age-Adjusted Mortality Rate[1] per 100,000 population	
		County[2]	U.S.
Assault	X85-Y09	4.9	5.2
Diseases of the liver	K70-K76	10.8	13.2
Human immunodeficiency virus (HIV) disease	B20-B24	*2.0	2.2
Influenza and pneumonia	J09-J18	12.2	15.4
Intentional self-harm	X60-X84	13.2	12.5
Malnutrition	E40-E46	Suppressed	0.9
Obesity and other hyperalimentation	E65-E68	4.8	1.8
Renal failure	N17-N19	20.3	13.1
Transport accidents	V01-V99	12.8	11.7
Viral hepatitis	B15-B19	2.7	2.2

Note: (a) ICD-10 = International Classification of Diseases 10th Revision; (1) Mortality rates are a three year average covering 2011-2013; (2) Figures cover Lafayette Parish; (*) Unreliable data as per CDC
Source: Centers for Disease Control and Prevention, National Center for Health Statistics. Compressed Mortality File 1999-2013 on CDC WONDER Online Database, released October 2014. Data are compiled from the Compressed Mortality File 1999-2013, Series 20 No. 2S, 2014.

Health Insurance Coverage

Area	With Health Insurance	With Private Health Insurance	With Public Health Insurance	Without Health Insurance	Population Under Age 18 Without Health Insurance
City	82.7	63.8	28.9	17.3	4.0
MSA[1]	83.5	62.0	31.8	16.5	4.4
U.S.	85.2	65.2	31.0	14.8	7.3

Note: Figures are percentages that cover the civilian noninstitutionalized population; (1) Figures cover the Lafayette, LA Metropolitan Statistical Area—see Appendix B for areas included
Source: U.S. Census Bureau, 2011-2013 American Community Survey 3-Year Estimates

Number of Medical Professionals

Area[1]	MDs[2]	DOs[2,3]	Dentists	Podiatrists	Chiropractors	Optometrists
Local (number)	810	13	147	9	69	32
Local (rate[4])	356.7	5.7	63.6	3.9	29.8	13.8
U.S. (rate[4])	270.0	20.2	63.1	5.7	25.2	14.9

Note: Data as of 2013 unless noted; (1) Local data covers Lafayette Parish; (2) Data as of 2012 and includes all active, non-federal physicians; (3) Doctor of Osteopathic Medicine; (4) rate per 100,000 population
Source: U.S. Department of Health and Human Services, Health Resources and Services Administration, Bureau of Health Professions, Area Resource File (ARF) 2013-2014

EDUCATION

Public School District Statistics

District Name	Schls	Pupils	Pupil/ Teacher Ratio	Minority Pupils[1] (%)	Free Lunch Eligible[2] (%)	IEP[3] (%)
Lafayette Parish	41	30,723	15.2	51.0	53.3	8.8

Note: Table includes school districts with 2,000 or more students; (1) Percentage of students that are not non-Hispanic white; (2) Percentage of students that are eligible for the free lunch program; (3) Percentage of students that have an Individualized Education Program.
Source: U.S. Department of Education, National Center for Education Statistics, Common Core of Data, Local Education Agency (School District) Universe Survey: School Year 2012-2013; U.S. Department of Education, National Center for Education Statistics, Common Core of Data, Public Elementary/Secondary School Universe Survey: School Year 2012-2013

Highest Level of Education

Area	Less than H.S.	H.S. Diploma	Some College, No Deg.	Associate Degree	Bachelor's Degree	Master's Degree	Prof. School Degree	Doctorate Degree
City	13.6	25.2	22.9	5.4	21.6	7.0	2.3	1.8
MSA[1]	19.5	35.0	20.1	5.3	14.1	4.1	1.1	0.8
U.S.	13.7	28.0	21.2	7.9	18.2	7.7	1.9	1.3

Note: Figures cover persons age 25 and over; (1) Figures cover the Lafayette, LA Metropolitan Statistical Area—see Appendix B for areas included
Source: U.S. Census Bureau, 2011-2013 American Community Survey 3-Year Estimates

Educational Attainment by Race

Area	High School Graduate or Higher (%)					Bachelor's Degree or Higher (%)				
	Total	White	Black	Asian	Hisp.[2]	Total	White	Black	Asian	Hisp.[2]
City	86.4	91.8	73.4	85.9	74.3	32.8	39.4	14.8	55.7	27.4
MSA[1]	80.5	84.3	69.3	60.9	64.5	20.0	22.7	11.1	24.0	15.6
U.S.	86.3	88.3	83.1	85.7	64.0	29.1	30.4	18.8	50.7	13.7

Note: Figures shown cover persons 25 years old and over; (1) Figures cover the Lafayette, LA Metropolitan Statistical Area—see Appendix B for areas included; (2) People of Hispanic origin can be of any race
Source: U.S. Census Bureau, 2011-2013 American Community Survey 3-Year Estimates

School Enrollment by Grade and Control

Area	Preschool (%)		Kindergarten (%)		Grades 1 - 4 (%)		Grades 5 - 8 (%)		Grades 9 - 12 (%)	
	Public	Private	Public	Private	Public	Private	Public	Private	Public	Private
City	52.9	47.1	80.2	19.8	82.3	17.7	73.9	26.1	76.0	24.0
MSA[1]	58.7	41.3	81.0	19.0	79.6	20.4	77.6	22.4	78.4	21.6
U.S.	57.7	42.3	87.9	12.1	89.9	10.1	90.0	10.0	90.7	9.3

Note: Figures shown cover persons 3 years old and over; (1) Figures cover the Lafayette, LA Metropolitan Statistical Area—see Appendix B for areas included
Source: U.S. Census Bureau, 2011-2013 American Community Survey 3-Year Estimates

Average Salaries of Public School Classroom Teachers

Area	2013-14		2014-15		Percent Change 2013-14 to 2014-15	Percent Change 2004-05 to 2014-15
	Dollars	Rank[1]	Dollars	Rank[1]		
LOUISIANA	49,067	34	47,886	41	-2.41	22.7
U.S. Average	56,610	-	57,379	-	1.36	20.8

Note: (1) State rank ranges from 1 to 51 where 1 indicates highest salary.
Source: National Education Association, Rankings & Estimates: Rankings of the States 2014 and Estimates of School Statistics 2015, March 2015

Higher Education

Four-Year Colleges			Two-Year Colleges			Medical Schools[1]	Law Schools[2]	Voc/ Tech[3]
Public	Private Non-profit	Private For-profit	Public	Private Non-profit	Private For-profit			
1	0	1	2	1	0	0	0	4

Note: Figures cover institutions located within the city limits and include main campuses only; (1) includes schools accredited by the Liaison Committee on Medical Education and the American Osteopathic Association's Commission on Osteopathic College Accreditation; (2) includes ABA-accredited schools, schools with provisional ABA accreditation, and state accredited schools; (3) includes all schools with programs that are less than 2 years.
Source: National Center for Education Statistics, Integrated Postsecondary Education System (IPEDS), 2013-14; Association of American Medical Colleges, Member List, May 1, 2015; American Osteopathic Association, Member List, May 1, 2015; Law School Admission Council, Official Guide to ABA-Approved Law Schools Online, May 1, 2015; Wikipedia, List of Medical Schools in the United States, May 1, 2015; Wikipedia, List of Law Schools in the United States, May 1, 2015

PRESIDENTIAL ELECTION

2012 Presidential Election Results

Area	Obama (%)	Romney (%)	Other (%)
Lafayette Parish	32.2	65.9	1.9
U.S.	51.0	47.2	1.8

Note: Results may not add to 100% due to rounding
Source: Dave Leip's Atlas of U.S. Presidential Elections

EMPLOYERS

Major Employers

Company Name	Industry
Acadian Ambulance & Air Med Services	Healthcare/transportation
Cingular Wireless	Telecommunications
ESS Support Services Worldwide	Retail trade
Frank's Casing Crew	Oil and gas
Haliburton Energy SVC	Oil and gas
Island Operating Company	Oil and gas
Lafayette Consolidated Government	Government
Lafayette General Medical Center	Healthcare
Lafayette Parish Government	Government
Mac-Laff	Service
Moncla Well Service	Oil and gas
Omni Energy Services, Corp.	Oil and gas
Our Lady of Lourdes Reg. Med. Ctr.	Healthcare
School Board Lafayette Parish	Education
Stuller	Manufacturing
The Ace Group	Transportation
Univ of LA Lafayette	Education
University Medical Ctr	Healthcare
Walmart Stores	Retail
Women's & Children's Hospital	Healthcare

Note: Companies shown are located within the Lafayette, LA Metropolitan Statistical Area.
Source: Hoovers.com; Wikipedia

PUBLIC SAFETY

Crime Rate

Area	All Crimes	Violent Crimes				Property Crimes		
		Murder	Forcible Rape	Robbery	Aggrav. Assault	Burglary	Larceny -Theft	Motor Vehicle Theft
City	6,835.8	6.5	13.8	220.4	462.7	1,034.0	4,857.8	240.7
Suburbs[1]	3,019.1	4.5	19.2	68.1	285.0	717.5	1,718.5	206.4
Metro[2]	4,006.3	5.0	17.8	107.5	330.9	799.3	2,530.4	215.2
U.S.	3,098.6	4.5	25.2	109.1	229.1	610.0	1,899.4	221.3

Note: Figures are crimes per 100,000 population; (1) All areas within the metro area that are located outside the city limits; (2) Figures cover the Lafayette, LA Metropolitan Statistical Area—see Appendix B for areas included
Source: FBI Uniform Crime Reports, 2013

Hate Crimes

Area	Number of Quarters Reported	Number of Incidents per Bias Motivation						
		Race	Religion	Sexual Orientation	Ethnicity	Disability	Gender	Gender Identity
City	1	0	0	0	0	0	0	0
U.S.	4	2,871	1,031	1,233	655	83	18	31

Source: Federal Bureau of Investigation, Hate Crime Statistics 2013

Identity Theft Consumer Complaints

Area	Complaints	Complaints per 100,000 Population	Rank[2]
MSA[1]	248	51.8	305
U.S.	332,646	104.3	-

Note: (1) Figures cover the Lafayette, LA Metropolitan Statistical Area—see Appendix B for areas included; (2) Rank ranges from 1 to 380 where 1 indicates greatest number of identity theft complaints per 100,000 population
Source: Federal Trade Commission, Consumer Sentinel Network Data Book for January–December 2014

Fraud and Other Consumer Complaints

Area	Complaints	Complaints per 100,000 Population	Rank[2]
MSA[1]	1,440	300.6	324
U.S.	2,250,205	705.7	-

Note: (1) Figures cover the Lafayette, LA Metropolitan Statistical Area—see Appendix B for areas included; (2) Rank ranges from 1 to 380 where 1 indicates greatest number of identity theft complaints per 100,000 population
Source: Federal Trade Commission, Consumer Sentinel Network Data Book for January–December 2014

RECREATION

Culture

Dance[1]	Theatre[1]	Instrumental Music[1]	Vocal Music[1]	Series and Festivals	Museums and Art Galleries[2]	Zoos and Aquariums[3]
0	0	1	0	5	12	0

Note: (1) Professional perfoming groups; (2) Based on organizations with SIC code 8412; (3) AZA-accredited
Source: The Grey House Performing Arts Directory, 2015-16; Association of Zoos & Aquariums, AZA Member Zoos & Aquariums, April 2015; www.AccuLeads.com, April 2015

Professional Sports Teams

Team Name	League	Year Established
No teams are located in the metro area		

Source: Wikipedia, Major Professional Sports Teams of the United States and Canada, April 2015

CLIMATE

Average and Extreme Temperatures

Temperature	Jan	Feb	Mar	Apr	May	Jun	Jul	Aug	Sep	Oct	Nov	Dec	Yr.
Extreme High (°F)	82	85	91	92	98	103	101	102	99	94	87	85	103
Average High (°F)	61	65	71	79	85	90	91	91	87	80	70	64	78
Average Temp. (°F)	51	54	61	68	75	81	82	82	78	69	59	53	68
Average Low (°F)	41	44	50	57	64	70	73	72	68	57	48	43	57
Extreme Low (°F)	9	13	20	32	44	53	58	59	43	30	21	8	8

Note: Figures cover the years 1948-1995
Source: National Climatic Data Center, International Station Meteorological Climate Summary, 9/96

Average Precipitation/Snowfall/Humidity

Precip./Humidity	Jan	Feb	Mar	Apr	May	Jun	Jul	Aug	Sep	Oct	Nov	Dec	Yr.
Avg. Precip. (in.)	4.9	5.1	4.8	5.5	5.0	4.4	6.6	5.4	4.1	3.1	4.2	5.3	58.5
Avg. Snowfall (in.)	Tr	Tr	Tr	0	0	0	0	0	0	0	Tr	Tr	Tr
Avg. Rel. Hum. 6am (%)	85	85	86	89	91	91	92	93	91	89	88	86	89
Avg. Rel. Hum. 3pm (%)	59	55	52	52	54	57	62	61	59	51	53	57	56

Note: Figures cover the years 1948-1995; Tr = Trace amounts (<0.05 in. of rain; <0.5 in. of snow)
Source: National Climatic Data Center, International Station Meteorological Climate Summary, 9/96

Weather Conditions

Temperature			Daytime Sky			Precipitation		
10°F & below	32°F & below	90°F & above	Clear	Partly cloudy	Cloudy	0.01 inch or more precip.	0.1 inch or more snow/ice	Thunder-storms
< 1	21	86	99	150	116	113	< 1	73

Note: Figures are average number of days per year and cover the years 1948-1995
Source: National Climatic Data Center, International Station Meteorological Climate Summary, 9/96

HAZARDOUS WASTE

Superfund Sites

Lafayette has no sites on the EPA's Superfund Final National Priorities List. There are a total of 1,322 Superfund sites on the list in the U.S. *U.S. Environmental Protection Agency, Final National Priorities List, April 14, 2015*

AIR & WATER QUALITY

Air Quality Trends: Ozone

	2004	2005	2006	2007	2008	2009	2010	2011	2012	2013
MSA[1]	n/a	n/a	n/a	n/a	n/a	n/a	n/a	n/a	n/a	n/a

Note: (1) Data covers the Lafayette, LA Metropolitan Statistical Area—see Appendix B for areas included; n/a not available. The values shown are the composite ozone concentration averages among trend sites based on the highest fourth daily maximum 8-hour concentration in parts per million. These trends are based on sites having an adequate record of monitoring data during the trend period. Data from exceptional events are included.
Source: U.S. Environmental Protection Agency, Air Quality Monitoring Information, "Air Quality Trends by City, 2000-2013"

Air Quality Index

Area	Percent of Days when Air Quality was...[2]					AQI Statistics[2]	
	Good	Moderate	Unhealthy for Sensitive Groups	Unhealthy	Very Unhealthy	Maximum	Median
MSA[1]	62.9	37.1	0.0	0.0	0.0	96	44.5

Note: (1) Data covers the Lafayette, LA Metropolitan Statistical Area—see Appendix B for areas included; (2) Based on 364 days with AQI data in 2014. Air Quality Index (AQI) is an index for reporting daily air quality. EPA calculates the AQI for five major air pollutants regulated by the Clean Air Act: ground-level ozone, particle pollution (aka particulate matter), carbon monoxide, sulfur dioxide, and nitrogen dioxide. The AQI runs from 0 to 500. The higher the AQI value, the greater the level of air pollution and the greater the health concern. There are six AQI categories: "Good" AQI is between 0 and 50. Air quality is considered satisfactory; "Moderate" AQI is between 51 and 100. Air quality is acceptable; "Unhealthy for Sensitive Groups" When AQI values are between 101 and 150, members of sensitive groups may experience health effects; "Unhealthy" When AQI values are between 151 and 200 everyone may begin to experience health effects; "Very Unhealthy" AQI values between 201 and 300 trigger a health alert; "Hazardous" AQI values over 300 trigger warnings of emergency conditions (not shown).
Source: U.S. Environmental Protection Agency, Air Quality Index Report, 2014

Air Quality Index Pollutants

Area	Percent of Days when AQI Pollutant was...[2]					
	Carbon Monoxide	Nitrogen Dioxide	Ozone	Sulfur Dioxide	Particulate Matter 2.5	Particulate Matter 10
MSA[1]	0.0	0.0	22.8	0.0	76.9	0.3

Note: (1) Data covers the Lafayette, LA Metropolitan Statistical Area—see Appendix B for areas included; (2) Based on 364 days with AQI data in 2014. The Air Quality Index (AQI) is an index for reporting daily air quality. EPA calculates the AQI for five major air pollutants regulated by the Clean Air Act: ground-level ozone, particle pollution (also known as particulate matter), carbon monoxide, sulfur dioxide, and nitrogen dioxide. The AQI runs from 0 to 500. The higher the AQI value, the greater the level of air pollution and the greater the health concern.
Source: U.S. Environmental Protection Agency, Air Quality Index Report, 2014

Maximum Air Pollutant Concentrations: Particulate Matter, Ozone, CO and Lead

	Particulate Matter 10 (ug/m^3)	Particulate Matter 2.5 Wtd AM (ug/m^3)	Particulate Matter 2.5 24-Hr (ug/m^3)	Ozone (ppm)	Carbon Monoxide (ppm)	Lead (ug/m^3)
MSA[1] Level	74	7.9	18	0.066	n/a	n/a
NAAQS[2]	150	15	35	0.075	9	0.15
Met NAAQS[2]	Yes	Yes	Yes	Yes	n/a	n/a

Note: (1) Data covers the Lafayette, LA Metropolitan Statistical Area—see Appendix B for areas included; Data from exceptional events are included; (2) National Ambient Air Quality Standards; ppm = parts per million; ug/m^3 = micrograms per cubic meter; n/a not available.
Concentrations: Particulate Matter 10 (coarse particulate)—highest second maximum 24-hour concentration; Particulate Matter 2.5 Wtd AM (fine particulate)—highest weighted annual mean concentration; Particulate Matter 2.5 24-Hour (fine particulate)—highest 98th percentile 24-hour concentration; Ozone—highest fourth daily maximum 8-hour concentration; Carbon Monoxide—highest second maximum non-overlapping 8-hour concentration; Lead—maximum running 3-month average
Source: U.S. Environmental Protection Agency, Air Quality Monitoring Information, "Air Quality Statistics by City, 2013"

Maximum Air Pollutant Concentrations: Nitrogen Dioxide and Sulfur Dioxide

	Nitrogen Dioxide AM (ppb)	Nitrogen Dioxide 1-Hr (ppb)	Sulfur Dioxide AM (ppb)	Sulfur Dioxide 1-Hr (ppb)	Sulfur Dioxide 24-Hr (ppb)
MSA[1] Level	n/a	n/a	n/a	n/a	n/a
NAAQS[2]	53	100	30	75	140
Met NAAQS[2]	n/a	n/a	n/a	n/a	n/a

Note: (1) Data covers the Lafayette, LA Metropolitan Statistical Area—see Appendix B for areas included; Data from exceptional events are included; (2) National Ambient Air Quality Standards; ppm = parts per million; ug/m^3 = micrograms per cubic meter; n/a not available.
Concentrations: Nitrogen Dioxide AM—highest arithmetic mean concentration; Nitrogen Dioxide 1-Hr—highest 98th percentile 1-hour daily maximum concentration; Sulfur Dioxide AM—highest annual mean concentration; Sulfur Dioxide 1-Hr—highest 99th percentile 1-hour daily maximum concentration; Sulfur Dioxide 24-Hr—highest second maximum 24-hour concentration
Source: U.S. Environmental Protection Agency, Air Quality Monitoring Information, "Air Quality Statistics by City, 2013"

Drinking Water

Water System Name	Pop. Served	Primary Water Source Type	Violations[1]	
			Health Based	Monitoring/ Reporting
Lafayette Utilities Water System	145,629	Ground	0	0

Note: (1) Based on violation data from January 1, 2014 to December 31, 2014 (includes unresolved violations from earlier years)
Source: U.S. Environmental Protection Agency, Office of Ground Water and Drinking Water, Safe Drinking Water Information System (based on data extracted January 27, 2015)

Lubbock, Texas

Background

Rarely are the words *West Texas* and *Quaker* used in the same context; however, one of the first settlers in the Lubbock area was a Quaker—Paris Cox, who was looking for farm and ranch land. Originally, the area comprised prime buffalo hunting ground for the Comanche Native Americans, but after the herds were decimated, there was little left for them. Spanish explorers like Francisco Vaquez de Coronado, camped on their way through, looking for the illusive cities of gold.

The Civil War bought a new kind of migration to the country. One way to escape the devastation wrought by the war was to leave the east for new land. And land was ripe for the taking, with the government offering 320 acres to anyone willing to work the land in Texas. It turned out the land was ripe indeed. Draught-resistant soil made for a bounty of cotton.

Lubbock derives its name from a former Texas Ranger and Confederate Officer, Thomas S. Lubbock. It was incorporated in 1909, and soon thereafter, the Santa Fe Railroad helped make Lubbock an important market center, sometimes referred to as the "Hub of the Plains." (To this day, Lubbock's nickname is "Hub City.") A farmer named S. S. Rush is credited with bringing cotton to Texas—an important crop for Lubbock's economy—and a town cotton gin was erected. Cotton production in Lubbock went from four bales in 1902, to over 100,000 by 1932. By 1977, 60% of the state's cotton would come from the Lubbock area, the largest contiguous cotton field in the world.

The Second World War also brought a boon to Lubbock's economy when the U.S. Government developed Lubbock Army Air Field—an advanced training school for would-be pilots, later re-named Reese Air Base. A second base, the South Plains Army Airfield, became a school for training glider pilots, who were charged with silently air dropping supplies to the Allied troops of Europe. Today Lubbock's unique Silent Wings Museum tells their story. The war also increased the demand for cotton, which Lubbock was glad to provide.

Lubbock is a surprising wellspring of music innovation. Rock and Roll legend Buddy Holley was born and raised in Lubbock. Today the Buddy Holly Center highlights his life and his contribution to rock and roll. Though Holly's career was short-lived (Holly died in a plane crash after only a year and a half in the public spotlight), many of today's rock legends, including such greats as Paul McCartney, Keith Richards, Bob Dylan, and Elvis Costello, tribute Holly as one of the greatest influencers in the industry. *Rolling Stone* acknowledged him as one of the top 20 innovators in the history of rock and roll.

With Lubbock's rich music history, comes a rich nightlife. The Depot District, located in the area that surrounds the old railroad depot, is dedicated to music and entertainment. The area is filled with theaters, pubs, nightclubs, upscale restaurants, and cultural attractions, including a winery and radio station. The Buddy Holly Center is also located in the Depot District. Each year, the Lubbock Music Festival, brings a wide variety of top bands and entertainers to the area.

Many institutions of higher learning call Lubbock home. Founded in 1923, Texas Technical University is the only school in Texas to feature an undergraduate university, a medical school, and a Law school at one location. TTU is highly regarded for its research in medicine and technology. The Tech Red Raiders are members of the Division 1, Big 12 Conference for varsity sports.

Lubbock is also the site of one of the first credible UFO sightings. In 1951, numerous residents witnessed the "Lubbock lights," some of whom were highly-regarded Texas Tech scientists. The U.S. Airforce launched an official investigation and concluded that they were not a hoax, though the study failed to explain them. Photographs of these UFO events were published in *Life Magazine*.

Lubbock sits at the southern edge of the western high plains. The climate in Lubbock is semi-arid, and usually warm and dry, but in 1970 a devastating tornado tore through town, destroying over three square miles of the city, and killing 26 people. Damage was estimated to be well over $135 million.

Rankings

General Rankings

- Among the 50 largest U.S. cities, Lubbock placed #15 in Vocativ's "semi-exhaustive, mostly scientific" city Livability Index for people aged 35 and under. Average salary, unemployment rates, rents, and other living costs were considered, along with crime rates, weather, public transportation, access to music and sports, and "lifestyle metrics" such as the price of dinner at Buffalo Wild Wings and an ounce of high-quality weed. *vocative.com, "The Livability Index: The Best U.S. Cities for People 35 and Under," December 9, 2014*

Business/Finance Rankings

- Using data from the Council for Community and Economic Research's 2013 Annual Report, NerdWallet ranked the 100 most affordable cities in America. States from the central and southern United States dominate the list. On the affordability scale, Lubbock ranked #49. *NerdWallet.com, "Most Affordable Cities in America," June 4, 2014*
- The Lubbock metro area appeared on the Milken Institute "2013 Best Performing Cities" list. Rank: #20 out of 200 large metro areas. Criteria: job growth; wage and salary growth; high-tech output growth. *Milken Institute, "Best-Performing Cities 2014," January 2015*
- *Forbes* ranked the 200 most populous metro areas to determine the nation's "Best Places for Business and Careers." The Lubbock metro area was ranked #40. Criteria: costs (business and living); job growth (past and projected); income growth; educational attainment (college and high school); projected economic growth; cultural and recreational opportunities; net migration patterns; number of highly ranked colleges. *Forbes, "The Best Places for Business and Careers 2014," July 23, 2014*

Children/Family Rankings

- Lubbock was chosen as one of America's 100 best communities for young people. The winners were selected based upon detailed information provided about each community's efforts to fulfill five essential promises critical to the well-being of young people: caring adults who are actively involved in their lives; safe places in which to learn and grow; a healthy start toward adulthood; an effective education that builds marketable skills; and opportunities to help others. *America's Promise Alliance, "100 Best Communities for Young People, 2012"*

Dating/Romance Rankings

- Of the 100 U.S. cities surveyed by *Men's Health* in its quest to identify the nation's best cities for dating and forming relationships, Lubbock was ranked #90 for online dating (#1 = best). *Men's Health, "The Best and Worst Cities for Online Dating," January 30, 2013*

Environmental Rankings

- The Lubbock metro area came in at #261 for the relative comfort of its climate on Sperling's list of "chill cities," as measured by the Sperling Heat Index. All 361 metro areas are included. Criteria included daytime high temperatures, nighttime low temperatures, dew point, and relative humidity at the high temperatures. *www.bertsperling.com, "Sperling's Chill Cities," July 18, 2013*
- Sperling's BestPlaces assessed 379 metropolitan areas of the United States for the likelihood of dangerously extreme weather events or earthquakes. In general the Southeast and South-Central regions have the highest risk of weather extremes and earthquakes, while the Pacific Northwest enjoys the lowest risk. Of the least risky metropolitan areas, the Lubbock metro area was ranked #312. *www.bestplaces.net, "Safest Places from Natural Disasters," April 2011*
- The Lubbock metro area was identified as one of nine cities running out of water by *24/7 Wall St.* The area ranked #1. Based on data provided by the U.S. Drought Monitor, a joint program produced by academic and government organizations, *24/7 Wall St.* identified large U.S. urban areas that have been under persistent, serious drought for months. *24/7 Wall St., "Nine Cities Running Out of Water," August 1, 2013*

Food/Drink Rankings

- *Men's Health* ranked 100 major U.S. cities in terms of alcohol intoxication. Lubbock ranked #69 (#1 = most sober).Criteria: binge drinking; alcohol-related traffic accidents, arrests, and fatalities. *Men's Health, "The Drunkest Cities in America," November 19, 2013*

Health/Fitness Rankings

- *Men's Health* ranked 100 major U.S. cities in terms of the best and worst cities for men. Lubbock ranked #64. Criteria: thirty-three data points were examined covering health, fitness, and quality of life. *Men's Health, "The Best & Worst Cities for Men 2014," December 6, 2013*
- Lubbock was selected as one of the "20 Most Livable U.S. Cities for Wheelchair Users" by the Christopher & Dana Reeve Foundation. The city ranked #10. Criteria: Medicaid eligibility and spending; access to physicians and rehabilitation facilities; access to fitness facilities and recreation; access to paratransit; percentage of people living with disabilities who are employed; clean air; climate. *Christopher & Dana Reeve Foundation, "20 Most Livable U.S. Cities for Wheelchair Users," July 26, 2010*

Real Estate Rankings

- Lubbock was ranked #143 out of 275 metro areas in terms of house price appreciation in 2014 (#1 = highest rate). *Federal Housing Finance Agency, House Price Index, 4th Quarter 2014*

Safety Rankings

- Allstate ranked the 200 largest cities in America in terms of driver safety. Lubbock ranked #40. Allstate researchers analyzed internal property damage claims over a two-year period from January 2011 to December 2012. A weighted average of the two-year numbers determined the annual percentages. *Allstate, "Allstate America's Best Drivers Report, 2014"*
- The National Insurance Crime Bureau ranked 380 metro areas in the U.S. in terms of per capita rates of vehicle theft. The Lubbock metro area ranked #56 (#1 = highest rate). Criteria: number of vehicle theft offenses per 100,000 inhabitants in 2012. *National Insurance Crime Bureau, "Hot Spots 2012," June 26, 2013*

Seniors/Retirement Rankings

- From its Best Cities for Successful Aging indexes, the Milken Institute generated rankings for metropolitan areas, weighing data in eight categories—health care, wellness, living arrangements, transportation, financial characteristics, education and employment opportunities, community engagement, and overall livability. The Lubbock metro area was ranked #14 overall in the small metro area category. *Milken Institute, "Best Cities for Successful Aging, 2014"*

Women/Minorities Rankings

- Movoto chose five objective criteria to identify the best places for professional women among the largest 100 American cities. Lubbock was among the top ten, at #1, based on commute time, recent job growth, unemployment rank, professional women's groups per capita, and average earnings adjusted for the cost of living. *www.movoto.com, "These Are America's Best Cities for Professional Women," March 5, 2014*
- *Women's Health* examined U.S. cities and identified the 100 best cities for women. Lubbock was ranked #63. Criteria: 30 categories were examined from obesity and breast cancer rates to commuting times and hours spent working out. *Women's Health, "Best Cities for Women 2012"*

Business Environment

CITY FINANCES

City Government Finances

Component	2012 ($000)	2012 ($ per capita)
Total Revenues	556,835	2,426
Total Expenditures	762,515	3,321
Debt Outstanding	1,342,067	5,846
Cash and Securities[1]	891,162	3,882

Note: (1) Cash and security holdings of a government at the close of its fiscal year, including those of its dependent agencies, utilities, and liquor stores.
Source: U.S Census Bureau, State & Local Government Finances 2012

City Government Revenue by Source

Source	2012 ($000)	2012 ($ per capita)
General Revenue		
From Federal Government	26,875	117
From State Government	11,495	50
From Local Governments	0	0
Taxes		
Property	57,784	252
Sales and Gross Receipts	67,167	293
Personal Income	0	0
Corporate Income	0	0
Motor Vehicle License	0	0
Other Taxes	2,076	9
Current Charges	82,556	360
Liquor Store	0	0
Utility	281,684	1,227
Employee Retirement	4,451	19

Source: U.S Census Bureau, State & Local Government Finances 2012

City Government Expenditures by Function

Function	2012 ($000)	2012 ($ per capita)	2012 (%)
General Direct Expenditures			
Air Transportation	23,887	104	3.1
Corrections	0	0	0.0
Education	0	0	0.0
Employment Security Administration	0	0	0.0
Financial Administration	2,414	11	0.3
Fire Protection	34,832	152	4.6
General Public Buildings	3,018	13	0.4
Governmental Administration, Other	8,544	37	1.1
Health	5,658	25	0.7
Highways	22,554	98	3.0
Hospitals	0	0	0.0
Housing and Community Development	4,442	19	0.6
Interest on General Debt	31,738	138	4.2
Judicial and Legal	3,432	15	0.5
Libraries	5,144	22	0.7
Parking	0	0	0.0
Parks and Recreation	16,143	70	2.1
Police Protection	50,302	219	6.6
Public Welfare	0	0	0.0
Sewerage	34,527	150	4.5
Solid Waste Management	22,708	99	3.0
Veterans' Services	0	0	0.0
Liquor Store	0	0	0.0
Utility	441,585	1,924	57.9
Employee Retirement	10,640	46	1.4

Source: U.S Census Bureau, State & Local Government Finances 2012

DEMOGRAPHICS

Population Growth

Area	1990 Census	2000 Census	2010 Census	Population Growth (%) 1990-2000	Population Growth (%) 2000-2010
City	187,170	199,564	229,573	6.6	15.0
MSA[1]	229,940	249,700	284,890	8.6	14.1
U.S.	248,709,873	281,421,906	308,745,538	13.2	9.7

Note: (1) Figures cover the Lubbock, TX Metropolitan Statistical Area—see Appendix B for areas included
Source: U.S. Census Bureau, Census 1990, 2000, 2010

Household Size

Area	Persons in Household (%)							Average Household Size
	One	Two	Three	Four	Five	Six	Seven or More	
City	29.5	33.1	15.2	13.4	5.1	2.3	1.3	2.55
MSA[1]	27.7	33.8	15.5	13.4	5.9	2.3	1.5	2.61
U.S.	27.7	33.6	15.7	13.1	6.0	2.3	1.5	2.64

Note: (1) Figures cover the Lubbock, TX Metropolitan Statistical Area—see Appendix B for areas included
Source: U.S. Census Bureau, 2011-2013 American Community Survey 3-Year Estimates

Race

Area	White Alone[2] (%)	Black Alone[2] (%)	Asian Alone[2] (%)	AIAN[3] Alone[2] (%)	NHOPI[4] Alone[2] (%)	Other Race Alone[2] (%)	Two or More Races (%)
City	77.6	8.0	2.3	0.6	0.1	8.1	3.4
MSA[1]	79.9	6.9	1.9	0.5	0.1	7.6	3.2
U.S.	73.9	12.6	5.0	0.8	0.2	4.7	2.9

Note: (1) Figures cover the Lubbock, TX Metropolitan Statistical Area—see Appendix B for areas included; (2) Alone is defined as not being in combination with one or more other races; (3) American Indian and Alaska Native; (4) Native Hawaiian and Other Pacific Islander
Source: U.S. Census Bureau, 2011-2013 American Community Survey 3-Year Estimates

Hispanic or Latino Origin

Area	Total (%)	Mexican (%)	Puerto Rican (%)	Cuban (%)	Other (%)
City	33.6	29.3	0.2	0.0	4.0
MSA[1]	33.8	29.8	0.2	0.0	3.7
U.S.	16.9	10.8	1.6	0.6	3.8

Note: Persons of Hispanic or Latino origin can be of any race; (1) Figures cover the Lubbock, TX Metropolitan Statistical Area—see Appendix B for areas included
Source: U.S. Census Bureau, 2011-2013 American Community Survey 3-Year Estimates

Segregation

Type	Segregation Indices[1] 1990	2000	2010	2010 Rank[2]	Percent Change 1990-2000	1990-2010	2000-2010
Black/White	n/a	n/a	n/a	n/a	n/a	n/a	n/a
Asian/White	n/a	n/a	n/a	n/a	n/a	n/a	n/a
Hispanic/White	n/a	n/a	n/a	n/a	n/a	n/a	n/a

Note: All figures cover the Metropolitan Statistical Area—see Appendix B for areas included; Figures are based on an analysis of 1990, 2000, and 2010 Census Decennial Census tract data by William H. Frey, Brookings Institution and the University of Michigan Social Science Data Analysis Network. In this analysis all racial groups (whites, blacks, and asians) are non-Hispanic members of those races. Hispanics are shown as a separate category;
(1) Segregation Indices are Dissimilarity Indices that measure the degree to which the minority group is distributed differently than whites across census tracts. They range from 0 (complete integration) to 100 (complete segregation) where the value indicates the percentage of the minority group that needs to move to be distributed exactly like whites; (2) Ranges from 1 (most segregated) to 102 (least segregated); n/a not available.
Source: www.CensusScope.org

Ancestry

Area	German	Irish	English	American	Italian	Polish	French[2]	Scottish	Dutch
City	11.8	8.0	7.4	7.5	1.7	0.9	1.6	1.5	0.9
MSA[1]	11.8	8.4	7.2	8.0	1.5	0.8	1.6	1.6	0.9
U.S.	14.9	10.8	8.0	7.4	5.5	3.0	2.7	1.7	1.4

Note: Figures are the percentage of the total population reporting a particular ancestry. The nine most commonly reported ancestries in the U.S. are shown. Figures include multiple ancestries (e.g. if a person reported being Irish and Italian, they were included in both columns); (1) Figures cover the Lubbock, TX Metropolitan Statistical Area—see Appendix B for areas included; (2) Excludes Basque
Source: U.S. Census Bureau, 2011-2013 American Community Survey 3-Year Estimates

Foreign-Born Population

Area	Percent of Population Born in								
	Any Foreign Country	Mexico	Asia	Europe	Carribean	South America	Central America[2]	Africa	Canada
City	5.9	2.3	2.0	0.6	0.1	0.2	0.2	0.4	0.1
MSA[1]	5.6	2.6	1.7	0.5	0.1	0.2	0.2	0.3	0.1
U.S.	13.0	3.7	3.8	1.5	1.2	0.9	1.0	0.6	0.3

Note: (1) Figures cover the Lubbock, TX Metropolitan Statistical Area—see Appendix B for areas included; (2) Excludes Mexico.
Source: U.S. Census Bureau, 2011-2013 American Community Survey 3-Year Estimates

Marital Status

Area	Never Married	Now Married[2]	Separated	Widowed	Divorced
City	40.1	41.2	2.2	5.2	11.3
MSA[1]	37.0	44.3	2.3	5.4	11.0
U.S.	32.7	48.1	2.2	6.0	11.0

Note: Figures are percentages and cover the population 15 years of age and older; (1) Figures cover the Lubbock, TX Metropolitan Statistical Area—see Appendix B for areas included; (2) Excludes separated
Source: U.S. Census Bureau, 2011-2013 American Community Survey 3-Year Estimates

Disability Status

Area	All Ages	Under 18 Years Old	18 to 64 Years Old	65 Years and Over
City	13.7	5.2	12.1	42.4
MSA[1]	14.1	5.4	12.3	43.0
U.S.	12.3	4.1	10.2	36.3

Note: Figures show percent of the civilian noninstitutionalized population that reported having a disability. Disability status is determined from from six types of difficulty: vision, hearing, cognitive, ambulatory, self-care, and independent living. For children under 5 years old, hearing and vision difficulty are used to determine disability status. For children between the ages of 5 and 14, disability status is determined from hearing, vision, cognitive, ambulatory, and self-care difficulties. For people aged 15 years and older, they are considered to have a disability if they have difficulty with any one of the six difficulty types; (1) Figures cover the Lubbock, TX Metropolitan Statistical Area—see Appendix B for areas included.
Source: U.S. Census Bureau, 2011-2013 American Community Survey 3-Year Estimates

Age

Area	Percent of Population									Median Age
	Under Age 5	Age 5–19	Age 20–34	Age 35–44	Age 45–54	Age 55–64	Age 65–74	Age 75–84	Age 85+	
City	7.1	21.7	29.2	10.5	11.1	9.5	5.8	4.0	1.2	29.2
MSA[1]	7.1	21.7	26.9	11.0	11.6	10.2	6.3	4.0	1.3	31.0
U.S.	6.4	19.9	20.7	12.9	14.1	12.3	7.6	4.2	1.9	37.4

Note: (1) Figures cover the Lubbock, TX Metropolitan Statistical Area—see Appendix B for areas included
Source: U.S. Census Bureau, 2011-2013 American Community Survey 3-Year Estimates

Gender

Area	Males	Females	Males per 100 Females
City	116,283	120,205	96.7
MSA[1]	148,268	151,160	98.1
U.S.	154,451,010	159,410,713	96.9

Note: (1) Figures cover the Lubbock, TX Metropolitan Statistical Area—see Appendix B for areas included
Source: U.S. Census Bureau, 2011-2013 American Community Survey 3-Year Estimates

Religious Groups by Family

Area	Catholic	Baptist	Non-Den.	Methodist[2]	Lutheran	LDS[3]	Pente-costal	Presby-terian[4]	Muslim[5]	Judaism
MSA[1]	13.4	22.4	7.3	6.6	0.5	1.4	1.9	0.8	1.8	0.1
U.S.	19.1	9.3	4.0	4.0	2.3	2.0	1.9	1.6	0.8	0.7

Note: Figures are the number of adherents as a percentage of the total population; (1) Figures cover the Lubbock, TX Metropolitan Statistical Area—see Appendix B for areas included; (2) Methodist/Pietist; (3) Latter Day Saints; (4) Reformed; (5) Figures are estimates
Source: Association of Statisticians of American Religious Bodies, 2010 U.S. Religion Census: Religious Congregations & Membership Study

Religious Groups by Tradition

Area	Catholic	Evangelical Protestant	Mainline Protestant	Other Tradition	Black Protestant	Orthodox
MSA[1]	13.4	31.5	8.6	4.0	0.7	0.1
U.S.	19.1	16.2	7.3	4.3	1.6	0.3

Note: Figures are the number of adherents as a percentage of the total population; (1) Figures cover the Lubbock, TX Metropolitan Statistical Area—see Appendix B for areas included
Source: Association of Statisticians of American Religious Bodies, 2010 U.S. Religion Census: Religious Congregations & Membership Study

ECONOMY

Gross Metropolitan Product

Area	2012	2013	2014	2015	Rank[2]
MSA[1]	10.9	11.3	11.7	12.1	172

Note: Figures are in billions of dollars; (1) Figures cover the Lubbock, TX Metropolitan Statistical Area—see Appendix B for areas included; (2) Rank is based on 2015 data and ranges from 1 to 363
Source: The U.S. Conference of Mayors, U.S. Metro Economies: GMP and Employment 2013-2015, June 2014

Economic Growth

Area	2010-12 (%)	2013 (%)	2014 (%)	2015 (%)	Rank[2]
MSA[1]	0.8	2.7	1.0	1.9	332
U.S.	2.1	2.0	2.3	3.2	–

Note: Figures are real gross metropolitan product (GMP) growth rates and represent annual average percent change; (1) Figures cover the Lubbock, TX Metropolitan Statistical Area—see Appendix B for areas included; (2) Rank is based on 2015 data and ranges from 1 to 363
Source: The U.S. Conference of Mayors, U.S. Metro Economies: GMP and Employment 2013-2015, June 2014

Metropolitan Area Exports

Area	2008	2009	2010	2011	2012	2013	Rank[2]
MSA[1]	1,016.6	530.4	772.8	966.9	657.9	536.8	209

Note: Figures are in millions of dollars; (1) Figures cover the Lubbock, TX Metropolitan Statistical Area—see Appendix B for areas included; (2) Rank is based on 2013 data and ranges from 1 to 387
Source: U.S. Department of Commerce, International Trade Administration, Office of Trade & Industry Information, Manufacturing & Services, data extracted April 3, 2015

Building Permits

Area	Single-Family			Multi-Family			Total		
	2013	2014	Pct. Chg.	2013	2014	Pct. Chg.	2013	2014	Pct. Chg.
City	938	888	-5.3	1,039	1,161	11.7	1,977	2,049	3.6
MSA[1]	1,009	975	-3.4	1,039	1,161	11.7	2,048	2,136	4.3
U.S.	620,802	634,597	2.2	370,020	411,766	11.3	990,822	1,046,363	5.6

Note: (1) Figures cover the Lubbock, TX Metropolitan Statistical Area—see Appendix B for areas included; Figures represent new, privately-owned housing units authorized (unadjusted data); All permit data are based on estimates with imputation.
Source: U.S. Census Bureau, Manufacturing, Mining, and Construction Statistics, Building Permits, 2013, 2014

Bankruptcy Filings

Area	Business Filings			Nonbusiness Filings		
	2013	2014	% Chg.	2013	2014	% Chg.
Lubbock County	25	12	-52.0	253	177	-30.0
U.S.	33,212	26,983	-18.8	1,038,720	909,812	-12.4

Note: Business filings include Chapter 7, Chapter 11, Chapter 12, and Chapter 13; Nonbusiness filings include Chapter 7, Chapter 11, and Chapter 13
Source: Administrative Office of the U.S. Courts, Business and Nonbusiness Bankruptcy, County Cases Commenced by Chapter of the Bankruptcy Code, During the 12- Month Period Ending December 31, 2013 and Business and Nonbusiness Bankruptcy, County Cases Commenced by Chapter of the Bankruptcy Code, During the 12- Month Period Ending December 31, 2014

Housing Vacancy Rates

Area	Gross Vacancy Rate[2] (%)			Year-Round Vacancy Rate[3] (%)			Rental Vacancy Rate[4] (%)			Homeowner Vacancy Rate[5] (%)		
	2012	2013	2014	2012	2013	2014	2012	2013	2014	2012	2013	2014
MSA[1]	n/a	n/a	n/a	n/a	n/a	n/a	n/a	n/a	n/a	n/a	n/a	n/a
U.S.	13.8	13.6	13.4	10.8	10.7	10.4	8.7	8.3	7.6	2.0	2.0	1.9

Note: (1) Figures cover the Lubbock, TX Metropolitan Statistical Area—see Appendix B for areas included; (2) The percentage of the total housing inventory that is vacant; (3) The percentage of the housing inventory (excluding seasonal units) that is year-round vacant; (4) The percentage of rental inventory that is vacant for rent; (5) The percentage of homeowner inventory that is vacant for sale; n/a not available
Source: U.S. Census Bureau, Housing Vacancies and Homeownership Annual Statistics: 2014

INCOME

Income

Area	Per Capita ($)	Median Household ($)	Average Household ($)
City	23,537	43,413	60,480
MSA[1]	23,840	44,523	62,415
U.S.	27,884	52,176	72,897

Note: (1) Figures cover the Lubbock, TX Metropolitan Statistical Area—see Appendix B for areas included
Source: U.S. Census Bureau, 2011-2013 American Community Survey 3-Year Estimates

Household Income Distribution

Area	Percent of Households Earning							
	Under $15,000	$15,000 -24,999	$25,000 -34,999	$35,000 -49,999	$50,000 -74,999	$75,000 -99,000	$100,000 -149,999	$150,000 and up
City	16.8	12.8	12.2	14.1	17.5	10.9	9.5	6.2
MSA[1]	15.9	12.7	12.0	14.4	17.4	11.0	10.2	6.6
U.S.	13.0	10.9	10.3	13.6	17.9	11.9	12.7	9.6

Note: (1) Figures cover the Lubbock, TX Metropolitan Statistical Area—see Appendix B for areas included
Source: U.S. Census Bureau, 2011-2013 American Community Survey 3-Year Estimates

Poverty Rate

Area	All Ages	Under 18 Years Old	18 to 64 Years Old	65 Years and Over
City	21.4	26.8	21.7	7.7
MSA[1]	20.3	26.5	20.2	7.7
U.S.	15.9	22.4	14.8	9.5

Note: Figures are percentage of people whose income during the past 12 months was below the poverty level; (1) Figures cover the Lubbock, TX Metropolitan Statistical Area—see Appendix B for areas included
Source: U.S. Census Bureau, 2011-2013 American Community Survey 3-Year Estimates

EMPLOYMENT

Labor Force and Employment

Area	Civilian Labor Force			Workers Employed		
	Dec. 2013	Dec. 2014	% Chg.	Dec. 2013	Dec. 2014	% Chg.
City	123,688	124,204	0.4	118,815	120,508	1.4
MSA[1]	153,418	153,908	0.3	147,248	149,220	1.3
U.S.	154,408,000	155,521,000	0.7	144,423,000	147,190,000	1.9

Note: Data is not seasonally adjusted and covers workers 16 years of age and older; (1) Figures cover the Lubbock, TX Metropolitan Statistical Area—see Appendix B for areas included
Source: Bureau of Labor Statistics, Local Area Unemployment Statistics

Unemployment Rate

Area	2014											
	Jan.	Feb.	Mar.	Apr.	May	Jun.	Jul.	Aug.	Sep.	Oct.	Nov.	Dec.
City	4.2	4.2	4.0	3.4	3.8	4.5	4.6	4.1	3.7	3.5	3.4	3.0
MSA[1]	4.3	4.3	4.1	3.5	3.8	4.5	4.7	4.2	3.8	3.5	3.4	3.0
U.S.	7.0	7.0	6.8	5.9	6.1	6.3	6.5	6.3	5.7	5.5	5.5	5.4

Note: Data is not seasonally adjusted and covers workers 16 years of age and older; (1) Figures cover the Lubbock, TX Metropolitan Statistical Area—see Appendix B for areas included
Source: Bureau of Labor Statistics, Local Area Unemployment Statistics

Employment by Occupation

Occupation Classification	City (%)	MSA[1] (%)	U.S. (%)
Management, Business, Science, and Arts	34.3	34.0	36.2
Natural Resources, Construction, and Maintenance	8.7	10.3	9.0
Production, Transportation, and Material Moving	9.1	9.7	12.1
Sales and Office	27.1	25.8	24.4
Service	20.7	20.2	18.3

Note: Figures cover employed civilians 16 years of age and older; (1) Figures cover the Lubbock, TX Metropolitan Statistical Area—see Appendix B for areas included
Source: U.S. Census Bureau, 2011-2013 American Community Survey 3-Year Estimates

Employment by Industry

Sector	MSA[1]		U.S.
	Number of Employees	Percent of Total	Percent of Total
Construction, Mining, and Logging	6,300	4.5	5.0
Education and Health Services	22,300	16.0	15.5
Financial Activities	7,700	5.5	5.7
Government	29,300	21.1	15.8
Information	3,800	2.7	2.0
Leisure and Hospitality	17,200	12.4	10.3
Manufacturing	4,900	3.5	8.7
Other Services	5,600	4.0	4.0
Professional and Business Services	11,000	7.9	13.8
Retail Trade	18,600	13.4	11.4
Transportation, Warehousing, and Utilities	5,300	3.8	3.9
Wholesale Trade	7,000	5.0	4.2

Note: Figures are non-farm employment as of December 2014. Figures are not seasonally adjusted and include workers 16 years of age and older; (1) Figures cover the Lubbock, TX Metropolitan Statistical Area—see Appendix B for areas included; n/a not available
Source: Bureau of Labor Statistics, Current Employment Statistics, Employment, Hours, and Earnings

Occupations with Greatest Projected Employment Growth: 2012 – 2022

Occupation[1]	2012 Employment	2022 Projected Employment	Numeric Employment Change	Percent Employment Change
Combined Food Preparation and Serving Workers, Including Fast Food	285,480	378,000	92,520	32.4
Personal Care Aides	199,230	283,980	84,750	42.5
Retail Salespersons	378,330	439,340	61,010	16.1
Registered Nurses	189,380	242,860	53,480	28.2
Customer Service Representatives	214,240	262,770	48,530	22.7
Waiters and Waitresses	196,390	240,390	44,000	22.4
Janitors and Cleaners, Except Maids and Housekeeping Cleaners	172,120	213,340	41,220	23.9
Laborers and Freight, Stock, and Material Movers, Hand	185,770	226,470	40,700	21.9
Elementary School Teachers, Except Special Education	141,030	180,920	39,890	28.3
Secretaries and Administrative Assistants, Except Legal, Medical, and Executive	190,470	230,220	39,750	20.9

Note: Projections cover Texas; (1) Sorted by numeric employment change
Source: www.projectionscentral.com, State Occupational Projections, 2012–2022 Long-Term Projections

Fastest Growing Occupations: 2012 – 2022

Occupation[1]	2012 Employment	2022 Projected Employment	Numeric Employment Change	Percent Employment Change
Diagnostic Medical Sonographers	4,380	6,900	2,520	57.6
Computer Numerically Controlled Machine Tool Programmers, Metal and Plastic	1,740	2,700	960	54.8
Interpreters and Translators	4,510	6,720	2,210	49.0
Skincare Specialists	5,130	7,620	2,490	48.3
Agents and Business Managers of Artists, Performers, and Athletes	310	450	140	47.4
Petroleum Engineers	19,280	28,010	8,730	45.3
Information Security Analysts	6,640	9,630	2,990	45.0
Insulation Workers, Mechanical	4,460	6,460	2,000	44.6
Cardiovascular Technologists and Technicians	3,950	5,700	1,750	44.3
Physician Assistants	5,470	7,880	2,410	44.2

Note: Projections cover Texas; (1) Sorted by percent employment change and excludes occupations with numeric employment change less than 100
Source: www.projectionscentral.com, State Occupational Projections, 2012–2022 Long-Term Projections

Average Wages

Occupation	$/Hr.	Occupation	$/Hr.
Accountants and Auditors	31.54	Maids and Housekeeping Cleaners	8.78
Automotive Mechanics	16.42	Maintenance and Repair Workers	15.46
Bookkeepers	14.49	Marketing Managers	57.30
Carpenters	15.54	Nuclear Medicine Technologists	35.94
Cashiers	8.84	Nurses, Licensed Practical	21.03
Clerks, General Office	14.34	Nurses, Registered	29.11
Clerks, Receptionists/Information	11.31	Nursing Assistants	11.44
Clerks, Shipping/Receiving	13.02	Packers and Packagers, Hand	8.57
Computer Programmers	28.20	Physical Therapists	40.80
Computer Systems Analysts	34.05	Postal Service Mail Carriers	25.31
Computer User Support Specialists	18.18	Real Estate Brokers	n/a
Cooks, Restaurant	9.46	Retail Salespersons	11.44
Dentists	67.89	Sales Reps., Exc. Tech./Scientific	27.57
Electrical Engineers	35.65	Sales Reps., Tech./Scientific	37.38
Electricians	19.63	Secretaries, Exc. Legal/Med./Exec.	13.80
Financial Managers	51.82	Security Guards	11.53
First-Line Supervisors/Managers, Sales	21.88	Surgeons	n/a
Food Preparation Workers	9.29	Teacher Assistants	9.50
General and Operations Managers	50.12	Teachers, Elementary School	22.00
Hairdressers/Cosmetologists	10.76	Teachers, Secondary School	23.20
Internists	n/a	Telemarketers	n/a
Janitors and Cleaners	10.11	Truck Drivers, Heavy/Tractor-Trailer	18.50
Landscaping/Groundskeeping Workers	11.28	Truck Drivers, Light/Delivery Svcs.	15.05
Lawyers	65.52	Waiters and Waitresses	9.39

Note: Wage data covers the Lubbock, TX Metropolitan Statistical Area—see Appendix B for areas included; Hourly wages for elementary/secondary school teachers and teacher assistants were calculated by the editors from annual wage data assuming a 40 hour work week; n/a not available.
Source: Bureau of Labor Statistics, Metro Area Occupational Employment and Wage Estimates, May 2014

TAXES

State Corporate Income Tax Rates

State	Tax Rate (%)	Income Brackets ($)	Num. of Brackets	Financial Institution Tax Rate (%)[a]	Federal Income Tax Ded.
Texas	(y)	–	–	(y)	No

Note: Tax rates as of January 1, 2015; (a) Rates listed are the corporate income tax rate applied to financial institutions or excise taxes based on income. Some states have other taxes based upon the value of deposits or shares; (y) Texas imposes a Franchise Tax, otherwise known as margin tax, imposed on entities with more than $1,030,000 total revenues at rate of 1%, or 0.5% for entities primarily engaged in retail or wholesale trade, on lesser of 70% of total revenues or 100%of gross receipts after deductions for either compensation or cost of goods sold.
Source: Federation of Tax Administrators, "State Corporate Income Tax Rates, 2015"

State Individual Income Tax Rates

State	Tax Rate (%)	Income Brackets ($)	Num. of Brackets	Personal Exempt. ($)[1]		Fed. Inc. Tax Ded.
				Single	Dependents	
Texas	None	–	–	–	–	–

Note: Tax rates as of January 1, 2015; Local- and county-level taxes are not included; n/a not applicable; (1) Married joint filers generally receive double the single exemption
Source: Federation of Tax Administrators, "State Individual Income Tax Rates, 2015"

Various State and Local Tax Rates

State	State and Local Sales and Use (%)	State Sales and Use (%)	Gasoline[1] (¢/gal.)	Cigarette[2] ($/pack)	Spirits[3] ($/gal.)	Wine[4] ($/gal.)	Beer[5] ($/gal.)
Texas	8.25	6.25	20	1.41	2.40 (f)	0.20	0.20 (p)

Note: All tax rates as of January 1, 2015; (1) The American Petroleum Institute has developed a methodology for determining the average tax rate on a gallon of fuel. Rates may include any of the following: excise taxes, environmental fees, storage tank fees, other fees or taxes, general sales tax, and local taxes. In states where gasoline is subject to the general sales tax, or where the fuel tax is based on the average sale price, the average rate determined by API is sensitive to changes in the price of gasoline. States that fully or partially apply general sales taxes to gasoline: CA, CO, GA, IL, IN, MI, NY; (2) The federal excise tax of $1.0066 per pack and local taxes are not included; (3) Rates are those applicable to off-premise sales of 40% alcohol by volume (a.b.v.) distilled spirits in 750ml containers. Local excise taxes are excluded; (4) Rates are those applicable to off-premise sales of 11% a.b.v. non-carbonated wine in 750ml containers; (5) Rates are those applicable to off-premise sales of 4.7% a.b.v. beer in 12 ounce containers; (f) Different rates are also applicable according to alcohol content, place of production, size of container, or place purchased (on- or off-premise or onboard airlines); (p) Local excise taxes are excluded.
Source: Tax Foundation, 2015 Facts & Figures: How Does Your State Compare?

State Business Tax Climate Index Rankings

State	Overall Rank	Corporate Tax Index Rank	Individual Income Tax Index Rank	Sales Tax Index Rank	Unemployment Insurance Tax Index Rank	Property Tax Index Rank
Texas	10	39	6	36	15	36

Note: The index is a measure of how each state's tax laws affect economic performance. The lower the rank, the more favorable a state's tax system is for business. States without a given tax are given a ranking of 1. The scores/rankings for the District of Columbia do not affect other states. The 2015 index represents the tax climate as of July 1, 2014.
Source: Tax Foundation, State Business Tax Climate Index 2015

COMMERCIAL UTILITIES

Typical Monthly Electric Bills

Area	Commercial Service ($/month)		Industrial Service ($/month)	
	1,500 kWh	40 kW demand 14,000 kWh	1,000 kW demand 200,000 kWh	50,000 kW demand 32,500,000 kWh
City	n/a	n/a	n/a	n/a
Average[1]	201	1,653	26,124	2,639,743

Note: Figures are based on annualized 2014 rates; (1) Average based on 180 utilities surveyed; n/a not available
Source: Edison Electric Institute, Typical Bills and Average Rates Report, Summer 2014

TRANSPORTATION

Means of Transportation to Work

Area	Car/Truck/Van		Public Transportation			Bicycle	Walked	Other Means	Worked at Home
	Drove Alone	Car-pooled	Bus	Subway	Railroad				
City	82.9	10.0	0.8	0.0	0.0	0.6	2.2	0.9	2.6
MSA[1]	82.9	10.0	0.7	0.0	0.0	0.5	2.1	1.0	2.7
U.S.	76.4	9.6	2.6	1.8	0.6	0.6	2.8	1.3	4.3

Note: Figures are percentages and cover workers 16 years of age and older; (1) Figures cover the Lubbock, TX Metropolitan Statistical Area—see Appendix B for areas included
Source: U.S. Census Bureau, 2011-2013 American Community Survey 3-Year Estimates

Travel Time to Work

Area	Less Than 10 Minutes	10 to 19 Minutes	20 to 29 Minutes	30 to 44 Minutes	45 to 59 Minutes	60 to 89 Minutes	90 Minutes or More
City	20.4	58.3	12.7	4.9	1.9	1.1	0.7
MSA[1]	20.0	52.5	15.6	7.5	2.3	1.2	0.8
U.S.	13.3	29.7	20.9	20.2	7.7	5.7	2.6

Note: Figures are percentages and include workers 16 years old and over; (1) Figures cover the Lubbock, TX Metropolitan Statistical Area—see Appendix B for areas included
Source: U.S. Census Bureau, 2011-2013 American Community Survey 3-Year Estimates

Travel Time Index

Area	1985	1990	1995	2000	2005	2010	2011
Urban Area[1]	n/a	n/a	n/a	n/a	n/a	n/a	n/a
Average[2]	1.09	1.14	1.16	1.19	1.23	1.18	1.18

Note: Travel Time Index—the ratio of travel time in the peak period to the travel time at free-flow conditions. For example, a value of 1.30 indicates a 20-minute free-flow trip takes 26 minutes in the peak. Free-flow speeds (60 mph on freeways and 35 mph on principal arterials) are used as the comparison threshold; (1) Data for the Lubbock, TX urban area was not available; (2) average of 498 urban areas
Source: Texas Transportation Institute, Urban Mobility Report 2012, December 2012

Public Transportation

Agency Name / Mode of Transportation	Vehicles Operated in Maximum Service	Annual Unlinked Passenger Trips (in thous.)	Annual Passenger Miles (in thous.)
Citybus	n/a	n/a	n/a

Source: Federal Transit Administration, National Transit Database, 2013

Air Transportation

Airport Name and Code / Type of Service	Passenger Airlines[1]	Passenger Enplanements	Freight Carriers[2]	Freight (lbs.)
Lubbock Preston Smith International Airport (LBB)				
Domestic service (U.S. carriers - 2014)	16	447,104	7	45,543,256
International service (U.S. carriers - 2013)	0	0	1	31

Note: (1) Includes all U.S.-based major, minor and commuter airlines that carried at least one passenger during the year; (2) Includes all U.S.-based airlines and freight carriers that transported at least one lb. of freight during the year.
Source: Bureau of Transportation Statistics, The Intermodal Transportation Database, Air Carriers: T-100 Domestic Market (U.S. Carriers), 2014; Bureau of Transportation Statistics, The Intermodal Transportation Database, Air Carriers: T-100 International Market (U.S. Carriers), 2013

Other Transportation Statistics

Major Highways:	I-27
Amtrak Service:	No
Major Waterways/Ports:	None

Source: Amtrak.com; Google Maps

BUSINESSES

Major Business Headquarters

Company Name	Rankings	
	Fortune[1]	Forbes[2]
No companies listed	-	-

Note: (1) Fortune 500—companies that produce a 10-K are ranked 1 to 500 based on 2013 revenue; (2) all private companies with at least $2 billion in annual revenue through the end of their most current fiscal year are ranked 1 to 221; companies listed are headquartered in the city; dashes indicate no ranking
Source: Fortune, "Fortune 500," June 16, 2014; Forbes, "America's Largest Private Companies," November 5, 2014

Minority- and Women-Owned Businesses

Group	All Firms		Firms with Paid Employees			
	Firms	Sales ($000)	Firms	Sales ($000)	Employees	Payroll ($000)
Asian	449	99,426	(s)	(s)	(s)	(s)
Black	(s)	(s)	(s)	(s)	(s)	(s)
Hispanic	2,464	155,002	223	65,531	729	12,191
Women	4,332	672,719	667	595,008	5,840	145,700
All Firms	19,350	19,394,134	5,426	18,631,615	93,151	2,700,414

Note: Figures cover firms located in the city; minority- and women-owned business are defined as firms in which the corresponding group own 51% or more of the stock or equity of the company; (s) estimates are suppressed when publication standards are not met
Source: U.S. Census Bureau, 2007 Economic Census, Survey of Business Owners (2012 Survey of Business Owners data will be released starting in June 2015)

HOTELS & CONVENTION CENTERS

Hotels/Motels

Area	5 Star		4 Star		3 Star		2 Star		1 Star		Not Rated	
	Num.	Pct.[3]	Num.	Pct.[3]	Num.	Pct.[3]	Num.	Pct.[3]	Num.	Pct.[3]	Num.	Pct.[3]
City[1]	0	0.0	0	0.0	10	16.9	46	78.0	2	3.4	1	1.7
Total[2]	166	0.9	1,264	7.0	5,718	31.8	9,340	52.0	411	2.3	1,070	6.0

Note: (1) Figures cover Lubbock and vicinity; (2) Figures cover all 100 cities in this book; (3) Percentage of hotels which have a given star rating; Star ratings are determined by expedia.com and offer an indication of the general quality of a particular hotel.
Source: expedia.com, April 2, 2015

Major Convention Centers

Name	Overall Space (sq. ft.)	Exhibit Space (sq. ft.)	Meeting Space (sq. ft.)	Meeting Rooms
Lubbock Civic Center	300,000	40,000	n/a	12

Note: Table includes convention centers located in the Lubbock, TX metro area; n/a not available
Source: Original research

Living Environment

COST OF LIVING

Cost of Living Index

Composite Index	Groceries	Housing	Utilities	Trans-portation	Health Care	Misc. Goods/ Services
89.1	93.8	82.3	79.2	94.4	96.7	93.1

Note: The Cost of Living Index measures regional differences in the cost of consumer goods and services, excluding taxes and non-consumer expenditures, for professional and managerial households in the top income quintile. It is based on more than 50,000 prices covering almost 60 different items for which prices are collected three times a year by chambers of commerce, economic development organizations or university applied economic centers in each participating urban area. The numbers shown should be read as a percentage above or below the national average of 100. For example, a value of 115.4 in the groceries column indicates that grocery prices are 15.4% higher than the national average. Small differences in the index numbers should not be interpreted as significant; Figures cover the Lubbock TX urban area.
Source: The Council for Community and Economic Research, ACCRA Cost of Living Index, 2014

Grocery Prices

Area[1]	T-Bone Steak ($/pound)	Frying Chicken ($/pound)	Whole Milk ($/half gal.)	Eggs ($/dozen)	Orange Juice ($/64 oz.)	Coffee ($/11.5 oz.)
City[2]	9.75	1.16	2.69	2.13	3.21	3.86
Avg.	10.40	1.37	2.40	1.99	3.46	4.27
Min.	8.48	0.93	1.37	1.30	2.83	2.99
Max.	14.20	2.44	3.62	4.02	6.42	6.96

Note: (1) Values for the local area are compared with the average, minimum and maximum values for all 308 areas in the Cost of Living Index; (2) Figures cover the Lubbock TX urban area; **T-Bone Steak** *(price per pound);* **Frying Chicken** *(price per pound, whole fryer);* **Whole Milk** *(half gallon carton);* **Eggs** *(price per dozen, Grade A, large);* **Orange Juice** *(64 oz. Tropicana or Florida Natural);* **Coffee** *(11.5 oz. can, vacuum-packed, Maxwell House, Hills Bros, or Folgers).*
Source: The Council for Community and Economic Research, ACCRA Cost of Living Index, 2014

Housing and Utility Costs

Area[1]	New Home Price ($)	Apartment Rent ($/month)	All Electric ($/month)	Part Electric ($/month)	Other Energy ($/month)	Telephone ($/month)
City[2]	241,638	811	-	81.85	44.15	24.01
Avg.	305,838	919	181.00	93.66	73.14	27.95
Min.	183,142	480	112.00	42.06	23.42	17.16
Max.	1,358,576	3,851	594.00	180.03	440.99	40.42

Note: (1) Values for the local area are compared with the average, minimum and maximum values for all 308 areas in the Cost of Living Index; (2) Figures cover the Lubbock TX urban area; **New Home Price** *(2,400 sf living area, 8,000 sf lot, in urban area with full utilities);* **Apartment Rent** *(950 sf 2 bedroom/1.5 or 2 bath, unfurnished, excluding all utilities except water);* **All Electric** *(average monthly cost for an all-electric home);* **Part Electric** *(average monthly cost for a part-electric home);* **Other Energy** *(average monthly cost for natural gas, fuel oil, coal, wood, and any other forms of energy except electricity);* **Telephone** *(price includes basic monthly rate for a private residential line plus additional local usage charges incurred by a family of four).*
Source: The Council for Community and Economic Research, ACCRA Cost of Living Index, 2014

Health Care, Transportation, and Other Costs

Area[1]	Doctor ($/visit)	Dentist ($/visit)	Optometrist ($/visit)	Gasoline ($/gallon)	Beauty Salon ($/visit)	Men's Shirt ($)
City[2]	102.87	78.39	98.87	3.18	35.33	29.71
Avg.	102.86	87.89	97.66	3.44	34.37	26.74
Min.	67.47	65.78	51.18	3.00	17.43	12.79
Max.	173.50	150.14	235.00	4.33	64.28	49.50

Note: (1) Values for the local area are compared with the average, minimum and maximum values for all 308 areas in the Cost of Living Index; (2) Figures cover the Lubbock TX urban area; **Doctor** *(general practitioners routine exam of an established patient);* **Dentist** *(adult teeth cleaning and periodic oral examination);* **Optometrist** *(full vision eye exam for established adult patient);* **Gasoline** *(one gallon regular unleaded, national brand, including all taxes, cash price at self-service pump if available);* **Beauty Salon** *(woman's shampoo, trim, and blow-dry);* **Men's Shirt** *(cotton/polyester dress shirt, pinpoint weave, long sleeves).*
Source: The Council for Community and Economic Research, ACCRA Cost of Living Index, 2014

HOUSING

House Price Index (HPI)

Area	National Ranking[2]	Quarterly Change (%)	One-Year Change (%)	Five-Year Change (%)
MSA[1]	143	0.37	4.07	11.65
U.S.[3]	–	1.35	4.91	11.59

Note: The HPI is a weighted repeat sales index. It measures average price changes in repeat sales or refinancings on the same properties. This information is obtained by reviewing repeat mortgage transactions on single-family properties whose mortgages have been purchased or securitized by Fannie Mae or Freddie Mac in January 1975; (1) Lubbock Metropolitan Statistical Area—see Appendix B for areas included; (2) Rankings are based on annual percentage change for all metro areas containing at least 15,000 transactions over the last 10 years and ranges from 1 to 275; (3) figures based on a weighted average of Census Division estimates using a seasonally adjusted, purchase-only index; all figures are for the period ending December 31, 2014
Source: Federal Housing Finance Agency, House Price Index, February 26, 2015

Median Single-Family Home Prices

Area	2012	2013	2014p	Percent Change 2013 to 2014
MSA[1]	n/a	n/a	n/a	n/a
U.S. Average	177.2	197.4	209.0	5.9

Note: Figures are median sales prices of existing single-family homes in thousands of dollars; (p) preliminary; n/a not available; (1) Lubbock, TX Metropolitan Statistical Area—see Appendix B for areas included
Source: National Association of Realtors, Median Sales Price of Existing Single-Family Homes for Metropolitan Areas, 4th Quarter 2014

Qualifying Income Based on Median Sales Price of Existing Single-Family Homes

Area	With 5% Down ($)	With 10% Down ($)	With 20% Down ($)
MSA[1]	n/a	n/a	n/a
U.S. Average	45,863	43,449	38,621

Note: Figures are preliminary; Qualifying income is based on a mortgage rate of 4.0%. Monthly principal and interest payment is limited to 25% of income; n/a not available; (1) Lubbock, TX Metropolitan Statistical Area—see Appendix B for areas included
Source: National Association of Realtors, Qualifying Income Based on Median Sales Price of Existing Single-Family Homes for Metropolitan Areas, 4th Quarter 2014

Median Apartment Condo-Coop Home Prices

Area	2012	2013	2014p	Percent Change 2013 to 2014
MSA[1]	n/a	n/a	n/a	n/a
U.S. Average	173.7	194.9	205.1	5.2

Note: Figures are median sales prices of existing apartment condo-coop homes in thousands of dollars; (p) preliminary; n/a not available; (1) Lubbock, TX Metropolitan Statistical Area—see Appendix B for areas included
Source: National Association of Realtors, Median Sales Price of Existing Apartment Condo-Coop Homes for Metropolitan Areas, 4th Quarter 2014

Gross Monthly Rent

Area	Under $200	$200 -299	$300 -499	$500 -749	$750 -999	$1,000 -1,499	$1,500 and up	Median ($)
City	1.1	1.6	8.4	32.3	28.3	21.2	7.1	799
MSA[1]	1.2	2.3	9.2	32.2	28.3	20.1	6.7	787
U.S.	1.7	3.2	7.8	22.1	24.3	26.0	14.9	900

Note: Figures are percentages except for Median; Gross rent is the contract rent plus the estimated average monthly cost of utilities (electricity, gas, and water and sewer) and fuels (oil, coal, kerosene, wood, etc.) if these are paid by the renter (or paid for the renter by someone else); (1) Figures cover the Lubbock, TX Metropolitan Statistical Area—see Appendix B for areas included
Source: U.S. Census Bureau, 2011-2013 American Community Survey 3-Year Estimates

Homeownership Rate

Area	2007 (%)	2008 (%)	2009 (%)	2010 (%)	2011 (%)	2012 (%)	2013 (%)	2014 (%)
MSA[1]	n/a	n/a	n/a	n/a	n/a	n/a	n/a	n/a
U.S.	68.1	67.8	67.4	66.9	66.1	65.4	65.1	64.5

Note: (1) Figures cover the Lubbock, TX Metropolitan Statistical Area—see Appendix B for areas included; n/a not available
Source: U.S. Census Bureau, Housing Vacancies and Homeownership Annual Statistics: 2014

Year Housing Structure Built

Area	2010 or Later	2000 -2009	1990 -1999	1980 -1989	1970 -1979	1960 -1969	1950 -1959	1940 -1949	Before 1940	Median Year
City	1.9	16.5	11.7	15.0	18.7	15.0	13.4	4.7	3.1	1977
MSA[1]	1.8	16.4	12.4	15.1	17.8	14.1	13.5	5.2	3.7	1978
U.S.	0.9	15.0	13.9	13.8	15.8	11.0	10.9	5.4	13.3	1976

Note: Figures are percentages except for Median Year; (1) Figures cover the Lubbock, TX Metropolitan Statistical Area—see Appendix B for areas included
Source: U.S. Census Bureau, 2011-2013 American Community Survey 3-Year Estimates

HEALTH

Health Risk Data

Category	MSA[1] (%)	U.S. (%)
Adults aged 18–64 who have any kind of health care coverage	n/a	79.6
Adults who reported being in good or excellent health	n/a	83.1
Adults who are current smokers	n/a	19.6
Adults who are heavy drinkers[2]	n/a	6.1
Adults who are binge drinkers[3]	n/a	16.9
Adults who are overweight (BMI 25.0 - 29.9)	n/a	35.8
Adults who are obese (BMI 30.0 - 99.8)	n/a	27.6
Adults who participated in any physical activities in the past month	n/a	77.1
Adults 50+ who have ever had a sigmoidoscopy or colonoscopy	n/a	67.3
Women aged 40+ who have had a mammogram within the past two years	n/a	74.0
Men aged 40+ who have had a PSA test within the past two years	n/a	45.2
Adults aged 65+ who have had flu shot within the past year	n/a	60.1
Adults who always wear a seatbelt	n/a	93.8

Note: Data as of 2012 unless otherwise noted; n/a not available; (1) Figures cover the Lubbock, TX Metropolitan Statistical Area—see Appendix B for areas included; (2) Heavy drinkers are classified as males having more than two drinks per day or females having more than one drink per day; (3) Binge drinkers are classified as males having five or more drinks on one occasion or females having four or more drinks on one occasion
Source: Centers for Disease Control and Prevention, Behaviorial Risk Factor Surveillance System, SMART: Selected Metropolitan/Micropolitan Area Risk Trends, 2012 (Note: the CDC has discontinued this dataset but will be releasing a replacement in late 2015)

Chronic Health Indicators

Category	MSA[1] (%)	U.S. (%)
Adults who have ever been told they had a heart attack	n/a	4.5
Adults who have ever been told they had a stroke	n/a	2.9
Adults who have been told they currently have asthma	n/a	8.9
Adults who have ever been told they have arthritis	n/a	25.7
Adults who have ever been told they have diabetes[2]	n/a	9.7
Adults who have ever been told they had skin cancer	n/a	5.7
Adults who have ever been told they had any other types of cancer	n/a	6.5
Adults who have ever been told they have COPD	n/a	6.2
Adults who have ever been told they have kidney disease	n/a	2.5
Adults who have ever been told they have a form of depression	n/a	18.0

Note: Data as of 2012 unless otherwise noted; n/a not available; (1) Figures cover the Lubbock, TX Metropolitan Statistical Area—see Appendix B for areas included; (2) Figures do not include pregnancy-related, borderline, or pre-diabetes
Source: Centers for Disease Control and Prevention, Behaviorial Risk Factor Surveillance System, SMART: Selected Metropolitan/Micropolitan Area Risk Trends, 2012 (Note: the CDC has discontinued this dataset but will be releasing a replacement in late 2015)

Mortality Rates for the Top 10 Causes of Death in the U.S.

ICD-10[a] Sub-Chapter	ICD-10[a] Code	Age-Adjusted Mortality Rate[1] per 100,000 population	
		County[2]	U.S.
Malignant neoplasms	C00-C97	158.7	166.2
Ischaemic heart diseases	I20-I25	110.0	105.7
Other forms of heart disease	I30-I51	55.8	49.3
Chronic lower respiratory diseases	J40-J47	65.3	42.1
Organic, including symptomatic, mental disorders	F01-F09	59.6	38.1
Cerebrovascular diseases	I60-I69	42.1	37.0
Other external causes of accidental injury	W00-X59	31.7	26.9
Other degenerative diseases of the nervous system	G30-G31	19.8	25.6
Diabetes mellitus	E10-E14	35.1	21.3
Hypertensive diseases	I10-I15	20.9	19.4

Note: (a) ICD-10 = International Classification of Diseases 10th Revision; (1) Mortality rates are a three year average covering 2011-2013; (2) Figures cover Lubbock County
Source: Centers for Disease Control and Prevention, National Center for Health Statistics. Compressed Mortality File 1999-2013 on CDC WONDER Online Database, released October 2014. Data are compiled from the Compressed Mortality File 1999-2013, Series 20 No. 2S, 2014.

Mortality Rates for Selected Causes of Death

ICD-10[a] Sub-Chapter	ICD-10[a] Code	Age-Adjusted Mortality Rate[1] per 100,000 population	
		County[2]	U.S.
Assault	X85-Y09	4.4	5.2
Diseases of the liver	K70-K76	24.8	13.2
Human immunodeficiency virus (HIV) disease	B20-B24	2.6	2.2
Influenza and pneumonia	J09-J18	16.8	15.4
Intentional self-harm	X60-X84	13.3	12.5
Malnutrition	E40-E46	*1.2	0.9
Obesity and other hyperalimentation	E65-E68	3.1	1.8
Renal failure	N17-N19	14.9	13.1
Transport accidents	V01-V99	14.3	11.7
Viral hepatitis	B15-B19	3.0	2.2

Note: (a) ICD-10 = International Classification of Diseases 10th Revision; (1) Mortality rates are a three year average covering 2011-2013; (2) Figures cover Lubbock County; (*) Unreliable data as per CDC
Source: Centers for Disease Control and Prevention, National Center for Health Statistics. Compressed Mortality File 1999-2013 on CDC WONDER Online Database, released October 2014. Data are compiled from the Compressed Mortality File 1999-2013, Series 20 No. 2S, 2014.

Health Insurance Coverage

Area	With Health Insurance	With Private Health Insurance	With Public Health Insurance	Without Health Insurance	Population Under Age 18 Without Health Insurance
City	81.7	63.0	28.0	18.3	9.6
MSA[1]	80.9	61.5	28.7	19.1	10.4
U.S.	85.2	65.2	31.0	14.8	7.3

Note: Figures are percentages that cover the civilian noninstitutionalized population; (1) Figures cover the Lubbock, TX Metropolitan Statistical Area—see Appendix B for areas included
Source: U.S. Census Bureau, 2011-2013 American Community Survey 3-Year Estimates

Number of Medical Professionals

Area[1]	MDs[2]	DOs[2,3]	Dentists	Podiatrists	Chiropractors	Optometrists
Local (number)	1,032	48	148	9	47	43
Local (rate[4])	360.7	16.8	51.0	3.1	16.2	14.8
U.S. (rate[4])	270.0	20.2	63.1	5.7	25.2	14.9

Note: Data as of 2013 unless noted; (1) Local data covers Lubbock County; (2) Data as of 2012 and includes all active, non-federal physicians; (3) Doctor of Osteopathic Medicine; (4) rate per 100,000 population
Source: U.S. Department of Health and Human Services, Health Resources and Services Administration, Bureau of Health Professions, Area Resource File (ARF) 2013-2014

EDUCATION

Public School District Statistics

District Name	Schls	Pupils	Pupil/ Teacher Ratio	Minority Pupils[1] (%)	Free Lunch Eligible[2] (%)	IEP[3] (%)
Lubbock ISD	54	29,219	15.3	73.4	57.9	11.1
Lubbock-Cooper ISD	7	4,633	13.8	38.6	28.4	8.7

Note: Table includes school districts with 2,000 or more students; (1) Percentage of students that are not non-Hispanic white; (2) Percentage of students that are eligible for the free lunch program; (3) Percentage of students that have an Individualized Education Program.

Source: U.S. Department of Education, National Center for Education Statistics, Common Core of Data, Local Education Agency (School District) Universe Survey: School Year 2012-2013; U.S. Department of Education, National Center for Education Statistics, Common Core of Data, Public Elementary/Secondary School Universe Survey: School Year 2012-2013

Best High Schools

According to *The Daily Beast,* Lubbock is home to one of the best high schools in the U.S.: **Lubbock High School** (#672); *The Daily Beast* used six indicators culled from school surveys to compare public high schools in the U.S., with graduation and college acceptance rates weighed most heavily. Other criteria included: college-level courses/exams and SAT/ACT scores. *The Daily Beast, "Top High Schools 2014"*

Highest Level of Education

Area	Less than H.S.	H.S. Diploma	Some College, No Deg.	Associate Degree	Bachelor's Degree	Master's Degree	Prof. School Degree	Doctorate Degree
City	14.6	24.5	25.9	6.2	18.3	6.7	2.1	1.7
MSA[1]	16.2	25.5	25.3	6.1	17.3	6.3	1.8	1.5
U.S.	13.7	28.0	21.2	7.9	18.2	7.7	1.9	1.3

Note: Figures cover persons age 25 and over; (1) Figures cover the Lubbock, TX Metropolitan Statistical Area—see Appendix B for areas included

Source: U.S. Census Bureau, 2011-2013 American Community Survey 3-Year Estimates

Educational Attainment by Race

Area	High School Graduate or Higher (%)					Bachelor's Degree or Higher (%)				
	Total	White	Black	Asian	Hisp.[2]	Total	White	Black	Asian	Hisp.[2]
City	85.4	88.2	81.0	90.3	67.1	28.8	31.2	12.1	73.9	9.8
MSA[1]	83.8	86.6	79.1	90.6	63.9	27.0	29.0	11.6	73.3	8.7
U.S.	86.3	88.3	83.1	85.7	64.0	29.1	30.4	18.8	50.7	13.7

Note: Figures shown cover persons 25 years old and over; (1) Figures cover the Lubbock, TX Metropolitan Statistical Area—see Appendix B for areas included; (2) People of Hispanic origin can be of any race

Source: U.S. Census Bureau, 2011-2013 American Community Survey 3-Year Estimates

School Enrollment by Grade and Control

Area	Preschool (%)		Kindergarten (%)		Grades 1 - 4 (%)		Grades 5 - 8 (%)		Grades 9 - 12 (%)	
	Public	Private	Public	Private	Public	Private	Public	Private	Public	Private
City	65.9	34.1	89.1	10.9	93.5	6.5	94.5	5.5	95.8	4.2
MSA[1]	65.4	34.6	88.7	11.3	93.0	7.0	94.1	5.9	94.8	5.2
U.S.	57.7	42.3	87.9	12.1	89.9	10.1	90.0	10.0	90.7	9.3

Note: Figures shown cover persons 3 years old and over; (1) Figures cover the Lubbock, TX Metropolitan Statistical Area—see Appendix B for areas included

Source: U.S. Census Bureau, 2011-2013 American Community Survey 3-Year Estimates

Average Salaries of Public School Classroom Teachers

Area	2013-14		2014-15		Percent Change 2013-14 to 2014-15	Percent Change 2004-05 to 2014-15
	Dollars	Rank[1]	Dollars	Rank[1]		
TEXAS	49,690	30	50,576	29	1.78	23.3
U.S. Average	56,610	–	57,379	–	1.36	20.8

Note: (1) State rank ranges from 1 to 51 where 1 indicates highest salary.

Source: National Education Association, Rankings & Estimates: Rankings of the States 2014 and Estimates of School Statistics 2015, March 2015

Higher Education

Four-Year Colleges			Two-Year Colleges			Medical Schools[1]	Law Schools[2]	Voc/ Tech[3]
Public	Private Non-profit	Private For-profit	Public	Private Non-profit	Private For-profit			
2	1	0	0	1	2	1	1	1

Note: Figures cover institutions located within the city limits and include main campuses only; (1) includes schools accredited by the Liaison Committee on Medical Education and the American Osteopathic Association's Commission on Osteopathic College Accreditation; (2) includes ABA-accredited schools, schools with provisional ABA accreditation, and state accredited schools; (3) includes all schools with programs that are less than 2 years.
Source: National Center for Education Statistics, Integrated Postsecondary Education System (IPEDS), 2013-14; Association of American Medical Colleges, Member List, May 1, 2015; American Osteopathic Association, Member List, May 1, 2015; Law School Admission Council, Official Guide to ABA-Approved Law Schools Online, May 1, 2015; Wikipedia, List of Medical Schools in the United States, May 1, 2015; Wikipedia, List of Law Schools in the United States, May 1, 2015

According to *U.S. News & World Report,* the Lubbock, TX metro area is home to one of the best national universities in the U.S.: **Texas Tech University** (#156). The indicators used to capture academic quality fall into a number of categories: assessment by administrators at peer institutions; retention of students; faculty resources; student selectivity; financial resources; alumni giving; high school counselor ratings of colleges; and graduation rate. *U.S. News & World Report, "America's Best Colleges 2015"*

PRESIDENTIAL ELECTION

2012 Presidential Election Results

Area	Obama (%)	Romney (%)	Other (%)
Lubbock County	28.8	69.6	1.6
U.S.	51.0	47.2	1.8

Note: Results may not add to 100% due to rounding
Source: Dave Leip's Atlas of U.S. Presidential Elections

EMPLOYERS

Major Employers

Company Name	Industry
American State Bank	Finance
Caprock Home Health Services	Healthcare
City of Lubbock	Government
Convergys Corporation	Call center
Covenant Health System	Healthcare
Frenship ISD	Education
G Boren Services	Recruiting
Interim Healthcare of West Texas	Home health care
Lubbock Christian University	Education
Lubbock Cooper ISD	Education
Lubbock County	Government
Lubbock Independent School District	Education
Lubbock MHMR Center	Government agency
Lubbock State Supported Living Center	Residential care
Messer Auto Group	Vehicle sales and service
Sonic Drive In	Restaurants
SuddenLink Communications	Cable tv services & internet
Texas Dept. of Criminal Justice	Psychiatric/medical facility
Texas Tech University	Education
Texas Tech University Health Sci Ctr	Health sciences
UMC Physician Network Services	Physicians practice management
United Supermarkets	supermarkets
University Medical Center	Healthcare
Walmart	Retail
Wells Fargo Bank	Finance

Note: Companies shown are located within the Lubbock, TX Metropolitan Statistical Area.
Source: Hoovers.com; Wikipedia

PUBLIC SAFETY

Crime Rate

Area	All Crimes	Violent Crimes				Property Crimes		
		Murder	Forcible Rape	Robbery	Aggrav. Assault	Burglary	Larceny -Theft	Motor Vehicle Theft
City	5,627.3	2.1	37.0	163.1	566.7	1,096.4	3,406.4	355.6
Suburbs[1]	2,175.1	6.4	44.5	3.2	184.4	518.3	1,279.9	138.3
Metro[2]	4,905.4	3.0	38.6	129.7	486.8	975.5	2,961.7	310.2
U.S.	3,098.6	4.5	25.2	109.1	229.1	610.0	1,899.4	221.3

Note: Figures are crimes per 100,000 population; (1) All areas within the metro area that are located outside the city limits; (2) Figures cover the Lubbock, TX Metropolitan Statistical Area—see Appendix B for areas included
Source: FBI Uniform Crime Reports, 2013

Hate Crimes

Area	Number of Quarters Reported	Number of Incidents per Bias Motivation						
		Race	Religion	Sexual Orientation	Ethnicity	Disability	Gender	Gender Identity
City	4	0	0	0	0	0	0	0
U.S.	4	2,871	1,031	1,233	655	83	18	31

Source: Federal Bureau of Investigation, Hate Crime Statistics 2013

Identity Theft Consumer Complaints

Area	Complaints	Complaints per 100,000 Population	Rank[2]
MSA[1]	193	64.1	227
U.S.	332,646	104.3	-

Note: (1) Figures cover the Lubbock, TX Metropolitan Statistical Area—see Appendix B for areas included; (2) Rank ranges from 1 to 380 where 1 indicates greatest number of identity theft complaints per 100,000 population
Source: Federal Trade Commission, Consumer Sentinel Network Data Book for January–December 2014

Fraud and Other Consumer Complaints

Area	Complaints	Complaints per 100,000 Population	Rank[2]
MSA[1]	1,174	390.0	153
U.S.	2,250,205	705.7	-

Note: (1) Figures cover the Lubbock, TX Metropolitan Statistical Area—see Appendix B for areas included; (2) Rank ranges from 1 to 380 where 1 indicates greatest number of identity theft complaints per 100,000 population
Source: Federal Trade Commission, Consumer Sentinel Network Data Book for January–December 2014

RECREATION

Culture

Dance[1]	Theatre[1]	Instrumental Music[1]	Vocal Music[1]	Series and Festivals	Museums and Art Galleries[2]	Zoos and Aquariums[3]
0	0	1	0	3	10	0

Note: (1) Professional perfoming groups; (2) Based on organizations with SIC code 8412; (3) AZA-accredited
Source: The Grey House Performing Arts Directory, 2015-16; Association of Zoos & Aquariums, AZA Member Zoos & Aquariums, April 2015; www.AccuLeads.com, April 2015

Professional Sports Teams

Team Name	League	Year Established
No teams are located in the metro area		

Source: Wikipedia, Major Professional Sports Teams of the United States and Canada, April 2015

CLIMATE

Average and Extreme Temperatures

Temperature	Jan	Feb	Mar	Apr	May	Jun	Jul	Aug	Sep	Oct	Nov	Dec	Yr.
Extreme High (°F)	83	87	95	100	104	110	108	106	103	98	86	81	110
Average High (°F)	53	58	66	75	83	91	92	90	84	75	63	55	74
Average Temp. (°F)	39	43	51	61	69	78	80	78	71	61	49	41	60
Average Low (°F)	25	29	36	46	55	64	68	66	59	48	35	27	47
Extreme Low (°F)	-16	-8	2	22	30	45	51	52	33	20	-1	-2	-16

Note: Figures cover the years 1948-1992
Source: National Climatic Data Center, International Station Meteorological Climate Summary, 9/96

Average Precipitation/Snowfall/Humidity

Precip./Humidity	Jan	Feb	Mar	Apr	May	Jun	Jul	Aug	Sep	Oct	Nov	Dec	Yr.
Avg. Precip. (in.)	0.5	0.6	0.8	1.0	2.6	2.9	2.3	2.1	2.3	1.9	0.6	0.5	18.4
Avg. Snowfall (in.)	3	3	2	Tr	0	0	0	0	0	Tr	1	2	10
Avg. Rel. Hum. 6am (%)	73	72	67	68	76	78	75	78	81	78	73	72	74
Avg. Rel. Hum. 3pm (%)	41	40	32	30	35	36	39	41	44	39	38	40	38

Note: Figures cover the years 1948-1992; Tr = Trace amounts (<0.05 in. of rain; <0.5 in. of snow)
Source: National Climatic Data Center, International Station Meteorological Climate Summary, 9/96

Weather Conditions

Temperature			Daytime Sky			Precipitation		
10°F & below	32°F & below	90°F & above	Clear	Partly cloudy	Cloudy	0.01 inch or more precip.	0.1 inch or more snow/ice	Thunder-storms
5	93	79	134	150	81	62	8	48

Note: Figures are average number of days per year and cover the years 1948-1992
Source: National Climatic Data Center, International Station Meteorological Climate Summary, 9/96

HAZARDOUS WASTE

Superfund Sites

Lubbock has no sites on the EPA's Superfund Final National Priorities List. There are a total of 1,322 Superfund sites on the list in the U.S. *U.S. Environmental Protection Agency, Final National Priorities List, April 14, 2015*

AIR & WATER QUALITY

Air Quality Trends: Ozone

	2004	2005	2006	2007	2008	2009	2010	2011	2012	2013
MSA[1]	n/a	n/a	n/a	n/a	n/a	n/a	n/a	n/a	n/a	n/a

Note: (1) Data covers the Lubbock, TX Metropolitan Statistical Area—see Appendix B for areas included; n/a not available. The values shown are the composite ozone concentration averages among trend sites based on the highest fourth daily maximum 8-hour concentration in parts per million. These trends are based on sites having an adequate record of monitoring data during the trend period. Data from exceptional events are included.
Source: U.S. Environmental Protection Agency, Air Quality Monitoring Information, "Air Quality Trends by City, 2000-2013"

Air Quality Index

Area	Percent of Days when Air Quality was...[2]					AQI Statistics[2]	
	Good	Moderate	Unhealthy for Sensitive Groups	Unhealthy	Very Unhealthy	Maximum	Median
MSA[1]	87.5	12.5	0.0	0.0	0.0	100	28

Note: (1) Data covers the Lubbock, TX Metropolitan Statistical Area—see Appendix B for areas included; (2) Based on 265 days with AQI data in 2014. Air Quality Index (AQI) is an index for reporting daily air quality. EPA calculates the AQI for five major air pollutants regulated by the Clean Air Act: ground-level ozone, particle pollution (aka particulate matter), carbon monoxide, sulfur dioxide, and nitrogen dioxide. The AQI runs from 0 to 500. The higher the AQI value, the greater the level of air pollution and the greater the health concern. There are six AQI categories: "Good" AQI is between 0 and 50. Air quality is considered satisfactory; "Moderate" AQI is between 51 and 100. Air quality is acceptable; "Unhealthy for Sensitive Groups" When AQI values are between 101 and 150, members of sensitive groups may experience health effects; "Unhealthy" When AQI values are between 151 and 200 everyone may begin to experience health effects; "Very Unhealthy" AQI values between 201 and 300 trigger a health alert; "Hazardous" AQI values over 300 trigger warnings of emergency conditions (not shown).
Source: U.S. Environmental Protection Agency, Air Quality Index Report, 2014

Air Quality Index Pollutants

Area	Percent of Days when AQI Pollutant was...[2]					
	Carbon Monoxide	Nitrogen Dioxide	Ozone	Sulfur Dioxide	Particulate Matter 2.5	Particulate Matter 10
MSA[1]	0.0	0.0	0.0	0.0	100.0	0.0

Note: (1) Data covers the Lubbock, TX Metropolitan Statistical Area—see Appendix B for areas included; (2) Based on 265 days with AQI data in 2014. The Air Quality Index (AQI) is an index for reporting daily air quality. EPA calculates the AQI for five major air pollutants regulated by the Clean Air Act: ground-level ozone, particle pollution (also known as particulate matter), carbon monoxide, sulfur dioxide, and nitrogen dioxide. The AQI runs from 0 to 500. The higher the AQI value, the greater the level of air pollution and the greater the health concern.
Source: U.S. Environmental Protection Agency, Air Quality Index Report, 2014

Maximum Air Pollutant Concentrations: Particulate Matter, Ozone, CO and Lead

	Particulate Matter 10 (ug/m^3)	Particulate Matter 2.5 Wtd AM (ug/m^3)	Particulate Matter 2.5 24-Hr (ug/m^3)	Ozone (ppm)	Carbon Monoxide (ppm)	Lead (ug/m^3)
MSA[1] Level	n/a	n/a	n/a	n/a	n/a	n/a
NAAQS[2]	150	15	35	0.075	9	0.15
Met NAAQS[2]	Yes	Yes	Yes	Yes	Yes	Yes

Note: (1) Data covers the Lubbock, TX Metropolitan Statistical Area—see Appendix B for areas included; Data from exceptional events are included; (2) National Ambient Air Quality Standards; ppm = parts per million; ug/m^3 = micrograms per cubic meter; n/a not available.
Concentrations: Particulate Matter 10 (coarse particulate)—highest second maximum 24-hour concentration; Particulate Matter 2.5 Wtd AM (fine particulate)—highest weighted annual mean concentration; Particulate Matter 2.5 24-Hour (fine particulate)—highest 98th percentile 24-hour concentration; Ozone—highest fourth daily maximum 8-hour concentration; Carbon Monoxide—highest second maximum non-overlapping 8-hour concentration; Lead—maximum running 3-month average
Source: U.S. Environmental Protection Agency, Air Quality Monitoring Information, "Air Quality Statistics by City, 2013"

Maximum Air Pollutant Concentrations: Nitrogen Dioxide and Sulfur Dioxide

	Nitrogen Dioxide AM (ppb)	Nitrogen Dioxide 1-Hr (ppb)	Sulfur Dioxide AM (ppb)	Sulfur Dioxide 1-Hr (ppb)	Sulfur Dioxide 24-Hr (ppb)
MSA[1] Level	n/a	n/a	n/a	n/a	n/a
NAAQS[2]	53	100	30	75	140
Met NAAQS[2]	Yes	Yes	Yes	Yes	Yes

Note: (1) Data covers the Lubbock, TX Metropolitan Statistical Area—see Appendix B for areas included; Data from exceptional events are included; (2) National Ambient Air Quality Standards; ppm = parts per million; ug/m^3 = micrograms per cubic meter; n/a not available.
Concentrations: Nitrogen Dioxide AM—highest arithmetic mean concentration; Nitrogen Dioxide 1-Hr—highest 98th percentile 1-hour daily maximum concentration; Sulfur Dioxide AM—highest annual mean concentration; Sulfur Dioxide 1-Hr—highest 99th percentile 1-hour daily maximum concentration; Sulfur Dioxide 24-Hr—highest second maximum 24-hour concentration
Source: U.S. Environmental Protection Agency, Air Quality Monitoring Information, "Air Quality Statistics by City, 2013"

Drinking Water

Water System Name	Pop. Served	Primary Water Source Type	Violations[1]	
			Health Based	Monitoring/ Reporting
Lubbock Public Water System	218,327	Surface	0	0

Note: (1) Based on violation data from January 1, 2014 to December 31, 2014 (includes unresolved violations from earlier years)
Source: U.S. Environmental Protection Agency, Office of Ground Water and Drinking Water, Safe Drinking Water Information System (based on data extracted January 27, 2015)

McAllen, Texas

Background

The largest city in Hidalgo County, Texas, McAllen is located near the tip of southern Texas, across the Rio Grande from Reynosa, Mexico, a location that has been the key to its commercial transformation. The city had begun to grow while agriculture and petroleum were still its economic mainstays, but since the ratification of the North American Free Trade Agreement in 1994, international trade, health care, government administration, and tourism have become its economic engines. Tourism in McAllen has fueled the highest retail spending per capita in Texas.

In 1904 John McAllen, together with his son, James, and other partners, established a town site 8 miles north of the county seat, Hidalgo. In 1907, two miles to the east, William Briggs, O. Jones, and John Closner founded a settlement called East McAllen, while the original town came to be called West McAllen. By 1911 East McAllen had a thousand residents and West McAllen had withered, and the larger town incorporated as the city of McAllen.

John McAllen experimented with growing sugarcane, cotton, alfalfa, broom corn, citrus fruits, grapes, and figs. Eventually farming, mostly by Anglo interests and dependent on the railroad and irrigation systems, displaced ranching as the primary economic activity. By the 1920s the city had some 6,000 residents.

From 1926 McAllen was linked to Reynosa by bridge. The McAllen-Hidalgo-Reynosa International Bridge proved crucial to McAllen after oil was discovered near Reynosa in the late 1940s. The bridge became the second-most-important port of entry into Mexico. Tourism and retail businesses flourished, bolstered by the cheap labor supply.

McAllen's population grew sporadically over the next several decades. In the 1970s and 1980s, however, the population boomed, owing to the *maquiladora* economy (in which U.S. companies take advantage of low labor costs in Mexico, shipping components of manufactured goods across the border to be assembled and shipped back). The McAllen Foreign-Trade Zone (FTZ), created in 1973, was the first inland U.S. foreign trade zone; there is also an FTZ site at McAllen-Miller International Airport. Anzaldúas International Bridge opened in 2009. Today the city is more than three-quarters Hispanic. Thanks to international trade, cross-border commerce, and its concentration of major health-care facilities, McAllen is the U.S. city ranked highest for long-term job growth, according to the U.S. Bureau of Labor Statistics.

South Texas College was founded in 1993. Three of its five campuses are in McAllen, including the Technical Campus. Edinburg-based University of Texas–Pan American has a branch in McAllen.

McAllen's cultural institutions include Quinta Mazatlan, a Spanish Revival Style hacienda built in 1935 and now a sanctuary known for its environmental stewardship programs. Quinta Mazatlan is one of nine Rio Grande Valley preserves administered by the World Birding Center. The oldest stand of native forest in the area is preserved in the McAllen Botanical Garden. Nearby nature preserves include the Edinburg Scenic Wetlands, Santa Ana National Wildlife Refuge, and Bentsen State Park.

McAllen has several notable museums: the International Museum of Art & Science, the Museum of South Texas History, and the McAllen Heritage Center. The Valley Symphony Orchestra and Chorale and two VSO-affiliated youth orchestras perform in McAllen and at the University of Texas–Pan American. An arts scene is coalescing, thanks to the city's Creative Arts Incubator, which sponsors a public art program, studio space for artists and performers, a monthly Artwalk, and a music series. Notable among the region's yearly festivals are the February Borderfest, at Hidalgo, and the mid-March Rio Grande Valley Livestock Show, in Mercedes. The 18.5-acre McAllen Convention Center complex opened in 2007.

The Rio Grande Valley Vipers won the National Basketball Association Development League championship in 2010 and again in 2013. Like the Vipers, the Rio Grande Valley Flash indoor soccer team plays at State Farm Arena in Hidalgo. The Edinburg Roadrunners play at Edinburg Baseball Stadium, which they share with the McAllen Thunder baseball team.

The City of Palms, as McAllen has been known since the 1940s, has sunshine and a warm climate year-round.

Rankings

Business/Finance Rankings

- TransUnion ranked the nation's metro areas by average credit score, calculated on the VantageScore system, developed by the three major credit-reporting bureaus—TransUnion, Experian, and Equifax. The McAllen metro area was among the ten cities with the lowest collective credit score, meaning that its residents posed the highest average consumer credit risk. *www.usatoday.com, "Metro Areas' Average Credit Rating Revealed," February 7, 2013*
- Building on the U.S. Department of Labor's Occupational Information Network Data Collection Program, the Brookings Institution defined STEM occupations and job opportunities for STEM workers at various levels of educational attainment. The McAllen metro area was one of the ten metro areas where workers in low-education-level STEM jobs earn the lowest relative wages. *www.brookings.edu, "The Hidden Stem Economy," June 10, 2013*
- Building on the U.S. Department of Labor's Occupational Information Network Data Collection Program, the Brookings Institution defined STEM occupations and job opportunities for STEM workers at various levels of educational attainment. The McAllen metro area was placed among the ten large metro areas with the lowest demand for high-level STEM knowledge. *www.brookings.edu, "The Hidden Stem Economy," June 10, 2013*
- To identify the metro areas with the largest gap in income between rich and poor residents, the 24/7 Wall Street research team used the U.S. Census Bureau's 2012 American Community Survey, an index of income disparity, additional income, poverty, and home-value data. The McAllen metro area placed #10 among metro areas with the widest wealth gap between rich and poor. *247wallst.com, "Cities with the Widest Gap between Rich and Poor," November 4, 2013*
- Using data from the Council for Community and Economic Research's 2013 Annual Report, NerdWallet ranked the 100 most affordable cities in America. States from the central and southern United States dominate the list. On the affordability scale, McAllen ranked #24. *NerdWallet.com, "Most Affordable Cities in America," June 4, 2014*
- McAllen was ranked #43 out of 100 metro areas in terms of economic performance (#1 = best) during the recession and recovery from trough quarter through the second quarter of 2013. Criteria: percent change in employment; percentage point change in unemployment rate; percent change in gross metropolitan product; percent change in House Price Index. *Brookings Institution, MetroMonitor: Tracking Economic Recession and Recovery in America's 100 Largest Metropolitan Areas, September 2013*
- The finance site *24/7 Wall St.* identified the metropolitan areas that have the smallest and largest pay disparities between men and women, comparing the median earnings for the past 12 months of both men and women working full-time in the country's 100 largest metropolitan statistical areas. Of the ten best-paying metros for women, the McAllen metro area ranked #4. *24/7 Wall St., "The Best (and Worst) Paying Cities for Women," March 6, 2015*
- The McAllen metro area was identified as one of the most affordable metropolitan areas in America by *Forbes.* The area ranked #17 out of 20. Criteria: the 100 largest metro areas in the U.S. were analyzed based on the National Association of Home Builders/Wells Fargo Housing Affordability Index and Sperling's Best Places' cost-of-living index. Some major cities were omitted for lack of data. *Forbes.com, "America's Most Affordable Cities in 2015," March 12, 2015*
- McAllen was identified as one of "America's Least Expensive Cities" in 2012. The city ranked #4 out of 5. Criteria: prices of 60 consumer goods and services were compared to the average annual income of professional and managerial households in the top fifth income level. *CNBC, "America's Least Expensive Cities, 2012," January 17, 2012*
- The McAllen metro area appeared on the Milken Institute "2013 Best Performing Cities" list. Rank: #35 out of 200 large metro areas. Criteria: job growth; wage and salary growth; high-tech output growth. *Milken Institute, "Best-Performing Cities 2014," January 2015*

- *Forbes* ranked the 200 most populous metro areas to determine the nation's "Best Places for Business and Careers." The McAllen metro area was ranked #93. Criteria: costs (business and living); job growth (past and projected); income growth; educational attainment (college and high school); projected economic growth; cultural and recreational opportunities; net migration patterns; number of highly ranked colleges. *Forbes, "The Best Places for Business and Careers 2014," July 23, 2014*

Education Rankings

- Personal finance website *WalletHub* analyzed the 150 largest U.S. metropolitan statistical areas to determine where the most educated Americans are choosing to settle. Criteria: educational attainment; percentage of workers with jobs in computer, engineering, and science fields; quality and size of each metro area's universities. McAllen was ranked #142 (#1 = most educated city). *www.WalletHub.com, "2014's Most and Least Educated Cities*

Environmental Rankings

- The McAllen metro area came in at #357 for the relative comfort of its climate on Sperling's list of "chill cities," as measured by the Sperling Heat Index. All 361 metro areas are included. Criteria included daytime high temperatures, nighttime low temperatures, dew point, and relative humidity at the high temperatures. *www.bertsperling.com, "Sperling's Chill Cities," July 18, 2013*

- Sperling's BestPlaces assessed 379 metropolitan areas of the United States for the likelihood of dangerously extreme weather events or earthquakes. In general the Southeast and South-Central regions have the highest risk of weather extremes and earthquakes, while the Pacific Northwest enjoys the lowest risk. Of the least risky metropolitan areas, the McAllen metro area was ranked #314. *www.bestplaces.net, "Safest Places from Natural Disasters," April 2011*

- The McAllen metro area was identified as one of nine cities running out of water by *24/7 Wall St.* The area ranked #3. Based on data provided by the U.S. Drought Monitor, a joint program produced by academic and government organizations, *24/7 Wall St.* identified large U.S. urban areas that have been under persistent, serious drought for months. *24/7 Wall St., "Nine Cities Running Out of Water," August 1, 2013*

- McAllen was highlighted as one of the cleanest metro areas for ozone air pollution in the U.S. during 2011 through 2013. The list represents cities with no monitored ozone air pollution in unhealthful ranges. *American Lung Association, State of the Air 2015*

- McAllen was highlighted as one of the top 25 cleanest metro areas for short-term particle pollution (24-hour PM 2.5) in the U.S. during 2011 through 2013. Monitors in these cities reported no days with unhealthful PM 2.5 levels. *American Lung Association, State of the Air 2015*

Health/Fitness Rankings

- The Gallup-Healthways Well-Being Index tracks Americans' optimism about their communities in addition to their satisfaction with the metro areas in which they live. Gallup researchers asked at least 300 adult residents in each of 189 U.S. metropolitan areas whether their metro was improving. The McAllen metro area placed among the top ten in the percentage of residents who were optimistic about their metro area. *www.gallup.com, "City Satisfaction Highest in Fort Collins-Loveland, Colo.," April 11, 2014*

- Analysts who tracked obesity rates in 189 of the nation's metro areas found that the McAllen metro area was one of the ten communities where residents were most likely to be obese, defined as a BMI score of 30 or above. *www.gallup.com, "Boulder, Colo., Residents Still Least Likely to Be Obese," April 4, 2014*

- McAllen was identified as a "2013 Spring Allergy Capital." The area ranked #4 out of 100. Three groups of factors were used to identify the most severe cities for people with allergies during the spring season: annual pollen levels; medicine utilization; access to board-certified allergists. *Asthma and Allergy Foundation of America, "Spring Allergy Capitals 2013"*

- McAllen was identified as a "2013 Fall Allergy Capital." The area ranked #6 out of 100. Three groups of factors were used to identify the most severe cities for people with allergies during the fall season: annual pollen levels; medicine utilization; access to board-certified allergists. *Asthma and Allergy Foundation of America, "Fall Allergy Capitals 2013"*
- McAllen was identified as a "2013 Asthma Capital." The area ranked #8 out of the nation's 100 largest metropolitan areas. Twelve factors were used to identify the most challenging places to live for people with asthma: estimated prevalence; self-reported prevalence; crude death rate for asthma; annual pollen score; annual air quality; public smoking laws; number of board-certified asthma specialists; school inhaler access laws; rescue medication use; controller medication use; uninsured rate; poverty rate. *Asthma and Allergy Foundation of America, "Asthma Capitals 2013"*
- The McAllen metro area appeared in the 2013 Gallup-Healthways Well-Being Index. The area ranked #147 out of 189. The Gallup-Healthways Well-Being Index score is an average of six sub-indexes, which individually examine life evaluation, emotional health, work environment, physical health, healthy behaviors, and access to basic necessities. Results are based on telephone interviews conducted as part of the Gallup-Healthways Well-Being Index survey January 2–December 29, 2012, and January 2–December 30, 2013, with a random sample of 531,630 adults, aged 18 and older, living in metropolitan areas in the 50 U.S. states and the District of Columbia. *Gallup-Healthways, "State of American Well-Being," March 25, 2014*

Real Estate Rankings

- McAllen was ranked #176 out of 226 metro areas in terms of housing affordability in 2014 by the National Association of Home Builders (#1 = most affordable). The NAHB-Wells Fargo Housing Opportunity Index (HOI) for a given area is defined as the share of homes sold in that area that would have been affordable to a family earning the local median income, based on standard mortgage underwriting criteria. *National Association of Home Builders®, NAHB-Wells Fargo Housing Opportunity Index, 4th Quarter 2014*

Safety Rankings

- Allstate ranked the 200 largest cities in America in terms of driver safety. McAllen ranked #51. Allstate researchers analyzed internal property damage claims over a two-year period from January 2011 to December 2012. A weighted average of the two-year numbers determined the annual percentages. *Allstate, "Allstate America's Best Drivers Report, 2014"*
- The National Insurance Crime Bureau ranked 380 metro areas in the U.S. in terms of per capita rates of vehicle theft. The McAllen metro area ranked #90 (#1 = highest rate). Criteria: number of vehicle theft offenses per 100,000 inhabitants in 2012. *National Insurance Crime Bureau, "Hot Spots 2012," June 26, 2013*

Seniors/Retirement Rankings

- From its Best Cities for Successful Aging indexes, the Milken Institute generated rankings for metropolitan areas, weighing data in eight categories—health care, wellness, living arrangements, transportation, financial characteristics, education and employment opportunities, community engagement, and overall livability. The McAllen metro area was ranked #59 overall in the large metro area category. *Milken Institute, "Best Cities for Successful Aging, 2014"*

Sports/Recreation Rankings

- McAllen was selected as one of the most playful cities in the U.S. by KaBOOM! The organization's Playful City USA initiative honors cities and towns across the nation for a vision, plan and commitment to creating an agenda for play. Criteria: creating a local play commission or task force; designing an annual action plan for play; conducting a play space audit; outlining a financial investment in play for the current fiscal year; and proclaiming and celebrating an annual "play day." *KaBOOM! National Campaign for Play, "2013 Playful City USA Communities"*

Business Environment

CITY FINANCES

City Government Finances

Component	2012 ($000)	2012 ($ per capita)
Total Revenues	206,225	1,588
Total Expenditures	237,926	1,832
Debt Outstanding	182,611	1,406
Cash and Securities[1]	256,528	1,975

Note: (1) Cash and security holdings of a government at the close of its fiscal year, including those of its dependent agencies, utilities, and liquor stores.
Source: U.S Census Bureau, State & Local Government Finances 2012

City Government Revenue by Source

Source	2012 ($000)	2012 ($ per capita)
General Revenue		
From Federal Government	15,676	121
From State Government	4,282	33
From Local Governments	0	0
Taxes		
Property	32,810	253
Sales and Gross Receipts	64,259	495
Personal Income	0	0
Corporate Income	0	0
Motor Vehicle License	0	0
Other Taxes	1,375	11
Current Charges	56,765	437
Liquor Store	0	0
Utility	17,571	135
Employee Retirement	3,395	26

Source: U.S Census Bureau, State & Local Government Finances 2012

City Government Expenditures by Function

Function	2012 ($000)	2012 ($ per capita)	2012 (%)
General Direct Expenditures			
Air Transportation	7,878	61	3.3
Corrections	0	0	0.0
Education	0	0	0.0
Employment Security Administration	0	0	0.0
Financial Administration	5,312	41	2.2
Fire Protection	15,402	119	6.5
General Public Buildings	1,223	9	0.5
Governmental Administration, Other	5,020	39	2.1
Health	1,679	13	0.7
Highways	23,121	178	9.7
Hospitals	0	0	0.0
Housing and Community Development	3,372	26	1.4
Interest on General Debt	5,143	40	2.2
Judicial and Legal	3,564	27	1.5
Libraries	15,576	120	6.5
Parking	791	6	0.3
Parks and Recreation	20,970	161	8.8
Police Protection	33,209	256	14.0
Public Welfare	1,147	9	0.5
Sewerage	31,955	246	13.4
Solid Waste Management	12,642	97	5.3
Veterans' Services	0	0	0.0
Liquor Store	0	0	0.0
Utility	34,180	263	14.4
Employee Retirement	2,334	18	1.0

Source: U.S Census Bureau, State & Local Government Finances 2012

DEMOGRAPHICS

Population Growth

Area	1990 Census	2000 Census	2010 Census	Population Growth (%) 1990-2000	2000-2010
City	86,145	106,414	129,877	23.5	22.0
MSA[1]	383,545	569,463	774,769	48.5	36.1
U.S.	248,709,873	281,421,906	308,745,538	13.2	9.7

Note: (1) Figures cover the McAllen-Edinburg-Mission, TX Metropolitan Statistical Area—see Appendix B for areas included
Source: U.S. Census Bureau, Census 1990, 2000, 2010

Household Size

Area	Persons in Household (%) One	Two	Three	Four	Five	Six	Seven or More	Average Household Size
City	21.9	25.1	18.8	15.5	11.1	5.0	2.6	3.20
MSA[1]	15.9	23.7	17.8	17.4	13.0	6.7	5.6	3.60
U.S.	27.7	33.6	15.7	13.1	6.0	2.3	1.5	2.64

Note: (1) Figures cover the McAllen-Edinburg-Mission, TX Metropolitan Statistical Area—see Appendix B for areas included
Source: U.S. Census Bureau, 2011-2013 American Community Survey 3-Year Estimates

Race

Area	White Alone[2] (%)	Black Alone[2] (%)	Asian Alone[2] (%)	AIAN[3] Alone[2] (%)	NHOPI[4] Alone[2] (%)	Other Race Alone[2] (%)	Two or More Races (%)
City	87.9	0.8	2.6	0.5	0.0	6.8	1.4
MSA[1]	92.3	0.6	1.0	0.3	0.0	5.0	0.7
U.S.	73.9	12.6	5.0	0.8	0.2	4.7	2.9

Note: (1) Figures cover the McAllen-Edinburg-Mission, TX Metropolitan Statistical Area—see Appendix B for areas included; (2) Alone is defined as not being in combination with one or more other races; (3) American Indian and Alaska Native; (4) Native Hawaiian and Other Pacific Islander
Source: U.S. Census Bureau, 2011-2013 American Community Survey 3-Year Estimates

Hispanic or Latino Origin

Area	Total (%)	Mexican (%)	Puerto Rican (%)	Cuban (%)	Other (%)
City	84.8	80.5	0.4	0.1	3.8
MSA[1]	90.9	88.4	0.2	0.1	2.2
U.S.	16.9	10.8	1.6	0.6	3.8

Note: Persons of Hispanic or Latino origin can be of any race; (1) Figures cover the McAllen-Edinburg-Mission, TX Metropolitan Statistical Area—see Appendix B for areas included
Source: U.S. Census Bureau, 2011-2013 American Community Survey 3-Year Estimates

Segregation

Type	Segregation Indices[1] 1990	2000	2010	2010 Rank[2]	Percent Change 1990-2000	1990-2010	2000-2010
Black/White	33.9	48.8	40.7	90	14.8	6.8	-8.1
Asian/White	40.3	41.2	46.7	17	0.9	6.4	5.6
Hispanic/White	37.9	39.5	39.2	69	1.6	1.3	-0.4

Note: All figures cover the Metropolitan Statistical Area—see Appendix B for areas included; Figures are based on an analysis of 1990, 2000, and 2010 Census Decennial Census tract data by William H. Frey, Brookings Institution and the University of Michigan Social Science Data Analysis Network. In this analysis all racial groups (whites, blacks, and asians) are non-Hispanic members of those races. Hispanics are shown as a separate category;
(1) Segregation Indices are Dissimilarity Indices that measure the degree to which the minority group is distributed differently than whites across census tracts. They range from 0 (complete integration) to 100 (complete segregation) where the value indicates the percentage of the minority group that needs to move to be distributed exactly like whites; (2) Ranges from 1 (most segregated) to 102 (least segregated); n/a not available.
Source: www.CensusScope.org

Ancestry

Area	German	Irish	English	American	Italian	Polish	French[2]	Scottish	Dutch
City	4.3	2.6	2.8	2.5	1.4	0.2	3.1	0.3	0.4
MSA[1]	2.6	1.3	1.2	1.6	0.6	0.2	0.9	0.3	0.2
U.S.	14.9	10.8	8.0	7.4	5.5	3.0	2.7	1.7	1.4

Note: Figures are the percentage of the total population reporting a particular ancestry. The nine most commonly reported ancestries in the U.S. are shown. Figures include multiple ancestries (e.g. if a person reported being Irish and Italian, they were included in both columns); (1) Figures cover the McAllen-Edinburg-Mission, TX Metropolitan Statistical Area—see Appendix B for areas included; (2) Excludes Basque

Source: U.S. Census Bureau, 2011-2013 American Community Survey 3-Year Estimates

Foreign-Born Population

Area	Percent of Population Born in								
	Any Foreign Country	Mexico	Asia	Europe	Carribean	South America	Central America[2]	Africa	Canada
City	n/a	n/a	n/a	n/a	n/a	n/a	n/a	n/a	n/a
MSA[1]	n/a	n/a	n/a	n/a	n/a	n/a	n/a	n/a	n/a
U.S.	13.0	3.7	3.8	1.5	1.2	0.9	1.0	0.6	0.3

Note: (1) Figures cover the McAllen-Edinburg-Mission, TX Metropolitan Statistical Area—see Appendix B for areas included; (2) Excludes Mexico.

Source: U.S. Census Bureau, 2011-2013 American Community Survey 3-Year Estimates

Marital Status

Area	Never Married	Now Married[2]	Separated	Widowed	Divorced
City	29.9	52.1	3.6	5.9	8.5
MSA[1]	31.5	52.4	4.1	5.1	6.8
U.S.	32.7	48.1	2.2	6.0	11.0

Note: Figures are percentages and cover the population 15 years of age and older; (1) Figures cover the McAllen-Edinburg-Mission, TX Metropolitan Statistical Area—see Appendix B for areas included; (2) Excludes separated

Source: U.S. Census Bureau, 2011-2013 American Community Survey 3-Year Estimates

Disability Status

Area	All Ages	Under 18 Years Old	18 to 64 Years Old	65 Years and Over
City	12.2	4.4	9.6	48.7
MSA[1]	13.6	6.0	12.0	50.3
U.S.	12.3	4.1	10.2	36.3

Note: Figures show percent of the civilian noninstitutionalized population that reported having a disability. Disability status is determined from from six types of difficulty: vision, hearing, cognitive, ambulatory, self-care, and independent living. For children under 5 years old, hearing and vision difficulty are used to determine disability status. For children between the ages of 5 and 14, disability status is determined from hearing, vision, cognitive, ambulatory, and self-care difficulties. For people aged 15 years and older, they are considered to have a disability if they have difficulty with any one of the six difficulty types; (1) Figures cover the McAllen-Edinburg-Mission, TX Metropolitan Statistical Area—see Appendix B for areas included.

Source: U.S. Census Bureau, 2011-2013 American Community Survey 3-Year Estimates

Age

Area	Percent of Population									Median Age
	Under Age 5	Age 5–19	Age 20–34	Age 35–44	Age 45–54	Age 55–64	Age 65–74	Age 75–84	Age 85+	
City	7.5	24.4	21.3	13.9	11.8	10.1	6.4	3.0	1.6	32.7
MSA[1]	9.6	27.8	21.2	13.2	10.4	8.0	5.4	3.2	1.1	28.5
U.S.	6.4	19.9	20.7	12.9	14.1	12.3	7.6	4.2	1.9	37.4

Note: (1) Figures cover the McAllen-Edinburg-Mission, TX Metropolitan Statistical Area—see Appendix B for areas included

Source: U.S. Census Bureau, 2011-2013 American Community Survey 3-Year Estimates

Gender

Area	Males	Females	Males per 100 Females
City	66,239	68,893	96.1
MSA[1]	393,607	411,890	95.6
U.S.	154,451,010	159,410,713	96.9

Note: (1) Figures cover the McAllen-Edinburg-Mission, TX Metropolitan Statistical Area—see Appendix B for areas included
Source: U.S. Census Bureau, 2011-2013 American Community Survey 3-Year Estimates

Religious Groups by Family

Area	Catholic	Baptist	Non-Den.	Methodist[2]	Lutheran	LDS[3]	Pente-costal	Presby-terian[4]	Muslim[5]	Judaism
MSA[1]	34.7	4.5	2.8	1.3	0.4	1.3	1.2	0.2	1.0	<0.1
U.S.	19.1	9.3	4.0	4.0	2.3	2.0	1.9	1.6	0.8	0.7

Note: Figures are the number of adherents as a percentage of the total population; (1) Figures cover the McAllen-Edinburg-Mission, TX Metropolitan Statistical Area—see Appendix B for areas included; (2) Methodist/Pietist; (3) Latter Day Saints; (4) Reformed; (5) Figures are estimates
Source: Association of Statisticians of American Religious Bodies, 2010 U.S. Religion Census: Religious Congregations & Membership Study

Religious Groups by Tradition

Area	Catholic	Evangelical Protestant	Mainline Protestant	Other Tradition	Black Protestant	Orthodox
MSA[1]	34.7	9.7	1.9	2.4	<0.1	<0.1
U.S.	19.1	16.2	7.3	4.3	1.6	0.3

Note: Figures are the number of adherents as a percentage of the total population; (1) Figures cover the McAllen-Edinburg-Mission, TX Metropolitan Statistical Area—see Appendix B for areas included
Source: Association of Statisticians of American Religious Bodies, 2010 U.S. Religion Census: Religious Congregations & Membership Study

ECONOMY

Gross Metropolitan Product

Area	2012	2013	2014	2015	Rank[2]
MSA[1]	16.0	16.6	17.4	18.4	128

Note: Figures are in billions of dollars; (1) Figures cover the McAllen-Edinburg-Mission, TX Metropolitan Statistical Area—see Appendix B for areas included; (2) Rank is based on 2015 data and ranges from 1 to 363
Source: The U.S. Conference of Mayors, U.S. Metro Economies: GMP and Employment 2013-2015, June 2014

Economic Growth

Area	2010-12 (%)	2013 (%)	2014 (%)	2015 (%)	Rank[2]
MSA[1]	1.5	2.0	2.5	4.6	10
U.S.	2.1	2.0	2.3	3.2	–

Note: Figures are real gross metropolitan product (GMP) growth rates and represent annual average percent change; (1) Figures cover the McAllen-Edinburg-Mission, TX Metropolitan Statistical Area—see Appendix B for areas included; (2) Rank is based on 2015 data and ranges from 1 to 363
Source: The U.S. Conference of Mayors, U.S. Metro Economies: GMP and Employment 2013-2015, June 2014

Metropolitan Area Exports

Area	2008	2009	2010	2011	2012	2013	Rank[2]
MSA[1]	4,578.5	3,736.1	4,527.1	4,676.1	5,198.5	5,265.5	54

Note: Figures are in millions of dollars; (1) Figures cover the McAllen-Edinburg-Mission, TX Metropolitan Statistical Area—see Appendix B for areas included; (2) Rank is based on 2013 data and ranges from 1 to 387
Source: U.S. Department of Commerce, International Trade Administration, Office of Trade & Industry Information, Manufacturing & Services, data extracted April 3, 2015

Building Permits

Area	Single-Family			Multi-Family			Total		
	2013	2014	Pct. Chg.	2013	2014	Pct. Chg.	2013	2014	Pct. Chg.
City	374	412	10.2	145	196	35.2	519	608	17.1
MSA[1]	2,545	2,840	11.6	749	633	-15.5	3,294	3,473	5.4
U.S.	620,802	634,597	2.2	370,020	411,766	11.3	990,822	1,046,363	5.6

Note: (1) Figures cover the McAllen-Edinburg-Mission, TX Metropolitan Statistical Area—see Appendix B for areas included; Figures represent new, privately-owned housing units authorized (unadjusted data); All permit data are based on estimates with imputation.
Source: U.S. Census Bureau, Manufacturing, Mining, and Construction Statistics, Building Permits, 2013, 2014

Bankruptcy Filings

Area	Business Filings			Nonbusiness Filings		
	2013	2014	% Chg.	2013	2014	% Chg.
Hidalgo County	47	45	-4.3	627	649	3.5
U.S.	33,212	26,983	-18.8	1,038,720	909,812	-12.4

Note: Business filings include Chapter 7, Chapter 11, Chapter 12, and Chapter 13; Nonbusiness filings include Chapter 7, Chapter 11, and Chapter 13
Source: Administrative Office of the U.S. Courts, Business and Nonbusiness Bankruptcy, County Cases Commenced by Chapter of the Bankruptcy Code, During the 12- Month Period Ending December 31, 2013 and Business and Nonbusiness Bankruptcy, County Cases Commenced by Chapter of the Bankruptcy Code, During the 12- Month Period Ending December 31, 2014

Housing Vacancy Rates

Area	Gross Vacancy Rate[2] (%)			Year-Round Vacancy Rate[3] (%)			Rental Vacancy Rate[4] (%)			Homeowner Vacancy Rate[5] (%)		
	2012	2013	2014	2012	2013	2014	2012	2013	2014	2012	2013	2014
MSA[1]	n/a	n/a	n/a	n/a	n/a	n/a	n/a	n/a	n/a	n/a	n/a	n/a
U.S.	13.8	13.6	13.4	10.8	10.7	10.4	8.7	8.3	7.6	2.0	2.0	1.9

Note: (1) Figures cover the McAllen-Edinburg-Mission, TX Metropolitan Statistical Area—see Appendix B for areas included; (2) The percentage of the total housing inventory that is vacant; (3) The percentage of the housing inventory (excluding seasonal units) that is year-round vacant; (4) The percentage of rental inventory that is vacant for rent; (5) The percentage of homeowner inventory that is vacant for sale; n/a not available
Source: U.S. Census Bureau, Housing Vacancies and Homeownership Annual Statistics: 2014

INCOME

Income

Area	Per Capita ($)	Median Household ($)	Average Household ($)
City	21,205	40,651	65,383
MSA[1]	14,274	33,845	49,333
U.S.	27,884	52,176	72,897

Note: (1) Figures cover the McAllen-Edinburg-Mission, TX Metropolitan Statistical Area—see Appendix B for areas included
Source: U.S. Census Bureau, 2011-2013 American Community Survey 3-Year Estimates

Household Income Distribution

Area	Percent of Households Earning							
	Under $15,000	$15,000 -24,999	$25,000 -34,999	$35,000 -49,999	$50,000 -74,999	$75,000 -99,000	$100,000 -149,999	$150,000 and up
City	20.0	14.3	10.3	13.5	14.8	9.8	10.2	7.1
MSA[1]	24.0	15.5	11.5	14.2	15.1	8.5	7.7	3.4
U.S.	13.0	10.9	10.3	13.6	17.9	11.9	12.7	9.6

Note: (1) Figures cover the McAllen-Edinburg-Mission, TX Metropolitan Statistical Area—see Appendix B for areas included
Source: U.S. Census Bureau, 2011-2013 American Community Survey 3-Year Estimates

Poverty Rate

Area	All Ages	Under 18 Years Old	18 to 64 Years Old	65 Years and Over
City	28.0	36.0	24.5	26.9
MSA[1]	35.5	46.7	30.2	26.5
U.S.	15.9	22.4	14.8	9.5

Note: Figures are percentage of people whose income during the past 12 months was below the poverty level; (1) Figures cover the McAllen-Edinburg-Mission, TX Metropolitan Statistical Area—see Appendix B for areas included
Source: U.S. Census Bureau, 2011-2013 American Community Survey 3-Year Estimates

EMPLOYMENT

Labor Force and Employment

Area	Civilian Labor Force			Workers Employed		
	Dec. 2013	Dec. 2014	% Chg.	Dec. 2013	Dec. 2014	% Chg.
City	63,415	63,736	0.5	59,732	60,846	1.9
MSA[1]	337,227	336,129	-0.3	305,062	310,751	1.9
U.S.	154,408,000	155,521,000	0.7	144,423,000	147,190,000	1.9

Note: Data is not seasonally adjusted and covers workers 16 years of age and older; (1) Figures cover the McAllen-Edinburg-Mission, TX Metropolitan Statistical Area—see Appendix B for areas included
Source: Bureau of Labor Statistics, Local Area Unemployment Statistics

Unemployment Rate

Area	2014											
	Jan.	Feb.	Mar.	Apr.	May	Jun.	Jul.	Aug.	Sep.	Oct.	Nov.	Dec.
City	6.3	6.2	6.0	5.4	5.7	6.1	6.2	6.0	5.4	5.0	4.8	4.5
MSA[1]	10.2	9.7	9.3	8.4	8.3	9.3	9.5	9.1	8.0	7.3	7.7	7.6
U.S.	7.0	7.0	6.8	5.9	6.1	6.3	6.5	6.3	5.7	5.5	5.5	5.4

Note: Data is not seasonally adjusted and covers workers 16 years of age and older; (1) Figures cover the McAllen-Edinburg-Mission, TX Metropolitan Statistical Area—see Appendix B for areas included
Source: Bureau of Labor Statistics, Local Area Unemployment Statistics

Employment by Occupation

Occupation Classification	City (%)	MSA[1] (%)	U.S. (%)
Management, Business, Science, and Arts	35.0	25.7	36.2
Natural Resources, Construction, and Maintenance	6.6	13.5	9.0
Production, Transportation, and Material Moving	8.2	11.5	12.1
Sales and Office	27.6	25.8	24.4
Service	22.6	23.5	18.3

Note: Figures cover employed civilians 16 years of age and older; (1) Figures cover the McAllen-Edinburg-Mission, TX Metropolitan Statistical Area—see Appendix B for areas included
Source: U.S. Census Bureau, 2011-2013 American Community Survey 3-Year Estimates

Employment by Industry

Sector	MSA[1] Number of Employees	MSA[1] Percent of Total	U.S. Percent of Total
Construction, Mining, and Logging	10,100	4.0	5.0
Education and Health Services	65,800	26.3	15.5
Financial Activities	9,100	3.6	5.7
Government	56,800	22.7	15.8
Information	2,300	0.9	2.0
Leisure and Hospitality	22,100	8.8	10.3
Manufacturing	6,300	2.5	8.7
Other Services	6,200	2.5	4.0
Professional and Business Services	15,700	6.3	13.8
Retail Trade	39,100	15.7	11.4
Transportation, Warehousing, and Utilities	8,400	3.4	3.9
Wholesale Trade	7,900	3.2	4.2

Note: Figures are non-farm employment as of December 2014. Figures are not seasonally adjusted and include workers 16 years of age and older; (1) Figures cover the McAllen-Edinburg-Mission, TX Metropolitan Statistical Area—see Appendix B for areas included; n/a not available
Source: Bureau of Labor Statistics, Current Employment Statistics, Employment, Hours, and Earnings

Occupations with Greatest Projected Employment Growth: 2012 – 2022

Occupation[1]	2012 Employment	2022 Projected Employment	Numeric Employment Change	Percent Employment Change
Combined Food Preparation and Serving Workers, Including Fast Food	285,480	378,000	92,520	32.4
Personal Care Aides	199,230	283,980	84,750	42.5
Retail Salespersons	378,330	439,340	61,010	16.1
Registered Nurses	189,380	242,860	53,480	28.2
Customer Service Representatives	214,240	262,770	48,530	22.7
Waiters and Waitresses	196,390	240,390	44,000	22.4
Janitors and Cleaners, Except Maids and Housekeeping Cleaners	172,120	213,340	41,220	23.9
Laborers and Freight, Stock, and Material Movers, Hand	185,770	226,470	40,700	21.9
Elementary School Teachers, Except Special Education	141,030	180,920	39,890	28.3
Secretaries and Administrative Assistants, Except Legal, Medical, and Executive	190,470	230,220	39,750	20.9

Note: Projections cover Texas; (1) Sorted by numeric employment change
Source: www.projectionscentral.com, State Occupational Projections, 2012–2022 Long-Term Projections

Fastest Growing Occupations: 2012 – 2022

Occupation[1]	2012 Employment	2022 Projected Employment	Numeric Employment Change	Percent Employment Change
Diagnostic Medical Sonographers	4,380	6,900	2,520	57.6
Computer Numerically Controlled Machine Tool Programmers, Metal and Plastic	1,740	2,700	960	54.8
Interpreters and Translators	4,510	6,720	2,210	49.0
Skincare Specialists	5,130	7,620	2,490	48.3
Agents and Business Managers of Artists, Performers, and Athletes	310	450	140	47.4
Petroleum Engineers	19,280	28,010	8,730	45.3
Information Security Analysts	6,640	9,630	2,990	45.0
Insulation Workers, Mechanical	4,460	6,460	2,000	44.6
Cardiovascular Technologists and Technicians	3,950	5,700	1,750	44.3
Physician Assistants	5,470	7,880	2,410	44.2

Note: Projections cover Texas; (1) Sorted by percent employment change and excludes occupations with numeric employment change less than 100
Source: www.projectionscentral.com, State Occupational Projections, 2012–2022 Long-Term Projections

Average Wages

Occupation	$/Hr.	Occupation	$/Hr.
Accountants and Auditors	29.71	Maids and Housekeeping Cleaners	8.56
Automotive Mechanics	15.33	Maintenance and Repair Workers	11.44
Bookkeepers	14.22	Marketing Managers	n/a
Carpenters	14.17	Nuclear Medicine Technologists	n/a
Cashiers	9.10	Nurses, Licensed Practical	22.31
Clerks, General Office	11.99	Nurses, Registered	31.38
Clerks, Receptionists/Information	9.71	Nursing Assistants	9.65
Clerks, Shipping/Receiving	10.83	Packers and Packagers, Hand	9.22
Computer Programmers	32.26	Physical Therapists	45.05
Computer Systems Analysts	30.92	Postal Service Mail Carriers	24.89
Computer User Support Specialists	17.82	Real Estate Brokers	n/a
Cooks, Restaurant	9.80	Retail Salespersons	10.10
Dentists	106.15	Sales Reps., Exc. Tech./Scientific	23.55
Electrical Engineers	42.65	Sales Reps., Tech./Scientific	n/a
Electricians	15.82	Secretaries, Exc. Legal/Med./Exec.	12.11
Financial Managers	45.16	Security Guards	10.48
First-Line Supervisors/Managers, Sales	20.37	Surgeons	n/a
Food Preparation Workers	8.91	Teacher Assistants	10.90
General and Operations Managers	40.70	Teachers, Elementary School	24.10
Hairdressers/Cosmetologists	12.47	Teachers, Secondary School	25.40
Internists	n/a	Telemarketers	10.52
Janitors and Cleaners	10.24	Truck Drivers, Heavy/Tractor-Trailer	16.33
Landscaping/Groundskeeping Workers	9.75	Truck Drivers, Light/Delivery Svcs.	11.43
Lawyers	52.56	Waiters and Waitresses	9.42

Note: Wage data covers the McAllen-Edinburg-Mission, TX Metropolitan Statistical Area—see Appendix B for areas included; Hourly wages for elementary/secondary school teachers and teacher assistants were calculated by the editors from annual wage data assuming a 40 hour work week; n/a not available.
Source: Bureau of Labor Statistics, Metro Area Occupational Employment and Wage Estimates, May 2014

TAXES

State Corporate Income Tax Rates

State	Tax Rate (%)	Income Brackets ($)	Num. of Brackets	Financial Institution Tax Rate (%)[a]	Federal Income Tax Ded.
Texas	(y)	–	–	(y)	No

Note: Tax rates as of January 1, 2015; (a) Rates listed are the corporate income tax rate applied to financial institutions or excise taxes based on income. Some states have other taxes based upon the value of deposits or shares; (y) Texas imposes a Franchise Tax, otherwise known as margin tax, imposed on entities with more than $1,030,000 total revenues at rate of 1%, or 0.5% for entities primarily engaged in retail or wholesale trade, on lesser of 70% of total revenues or 100%of gross receipts after deductions for either compensation or cost of goods sold.
Source: Federation of Tax Administrators, "State Corporate Income Tax Rates, 2015"

State Individual Income Tax Rates

State	Tax Rate (%)	Income Brackets ($)	Num. of Brackets	Personal Exempt. ($)[1] Single	Personal Exempt. ($)[1] Dependents	Fed. Inc. Tax Ded.
Texas	None	–	–	–	–	–

Note: Tax rates as of January 1, 2015; Local- and county-level taxes are not included; n/a not applicable; (1) Married joint filers generally receive double the single exemption
Source: Federation of Tax Administrators, "State Individual Income Tax Rates, 2015"

Various State and Local Tax Rates

State	State and Local Sales and Use (%)	State Sales and Use (%)	Gasoline[1] (¢/gal.)	Cigarette[2] ($/pack)	Spirits[3] ($/gal.)	Wine[4] ($/gal.)	Beer[5] ($/gal.)
Texas	8.25	6.25	20	1.41	2.40 (f)	0.20	0.20 (p)

Note: All tax rates as of January 1, 2015; (1) The American Petroleum Institute has developed a methodology for determining the average tax rate on a gallon of fuel. Rates may include any of the following: excise taxes, environmental fees, storage tank fees, other fees or taxes, general sales tax, and local taxes. In states where gasoline is subject to the general sales tax, or where the fuel tax is based on the average sale price, the average rate determined by API is sensitive to changes in the price of gasoline. States that fully or partially apply general sales taxes to gasoline: CA, CO, GA, IL, IN, MI, NY; (2) The federal excise tax of $1.0066 per pack and local taxes are not included; (3) Rates are those applicable to off-premise sales of 40% alcohol by volume (a.b.v.) distilled spirits in 750ml containers. Local excise taxes are excluded; (4) Rates are those applicable to off-premise sales of 11% a.b.v. non-carbonated wine in 750ml containers; (5) Rates are those applicable to off-premise sales of 4.7% a.b.v. beer in 12 ounce containers; (f) Different rates are also applicable according to alcohol content, place of production, size of container, or place purchased (on- or off-premise or onboard airlines); (p) Local excise taxes are excluded.
Source: Tax Foundation, 2015 Facts & Figures: How Does Your State Compare?

State Business Tax Climate Index Rankings

State	Overall Rank	Corporate Tax Index Rank	Individual Income Tax Index Rank	Sales Tax Index Rank	Unemployment Insurance Tax Index Rank	Property Tax Index Rank
Texas	10	39	6	36	15	36

Note: The index is a measure of how each state's tax laws affect economic performance. The lower the rank, the more favorable a state's tax system is for business. States without a given tax are given a ranking of 1. The scores/rankings for the District of Columbia do not affect other states. The 2015 index represents the tax climate as of July 1, 2014.
Source: Tax Foundation, State Business Tax Climate Index 2015

COMMERCIAL UTILITIES

Typical Monthly Electric Bills

Area	Commercial Service ($/month)		Industrial Service ($/month)	
	1,500 kWh	40 kW demand 14,000 kWh	1,000 kW demand 200,000 kWh	50,000 kW demand 32,500,000 kWh
City	n/a	n/a	n/a	n/a
Average[1]	201	1,653	26,124	2,639,743

Note: Figures are based on annualized 2014 rates; (1) Average based on 180 utilities surveyed; n/a not available
Source: Edison Electric Institute, Typical Bills and Average Rates Report, Summer 2014

TRANSPORTATION

Means of Transportation to Work

Area	Car/Truck/Van		Public Transportation			Bicycle	Walked	Other Means	Worked at Home
	Drove Alone	Car-pooled	Bus	Subway	Railroad				
City	74.0	9.7	0.6	0.0	0.0	0.2	0.9	8.0	6.8
MSA[1]	78.9	11.0	0.2	0.0	0.0	0.1	1.2	4.0	4.5
U.S.	76.4	9.6	2.6	1.8	0.6	0.6	2.8	1.3	4.3

Note: Figures are percentages and cover workers 16 years of age and older; (1) Figures cover the McAllen-Edinburg-Mission, TX Metropolitan Statistical Area—see Appendix B for areas included
Source: U.S. Census Bureau, 2011-2013 American Community Survey 3-Year Estimates

Travel Time to Work

Area	Less Than 10 Minutes	10 to 19 Minutes	20 to 29 Minutes	30 to 44 Minutes	45 to 59 Minutes	60 to 89 Minutes	90 Minutes or More
City	17.2	43.8	21.7	10.6	2.5	1.2	3.0
MSA[1]	13.7	38.2	24.0	17.3	2.7	1.8	2.2
U.S.	13.3	29.7	20.9	20.2	7.7	5.7	2.6

Note: Figures are percentages and include workers 16 years old and over; (1) Figures cover the McAllen-Edinburg-Mission, TX Metropolitan Statistical Area—see Appendix B for areas included
Source: U.S. Census Bureau, 2011-2013 American Community Survey 3-Year Estimates

Travel Time Index

Area	1985	1990	1995	2000	2005	2010	2011
Urban Area[1]	1.02	1.02	1.05	1.11	1.13	1.16	1.16
Average[2]	1.09	1.14	1.16	1.19	1.23	1.18	1.18

Note: Travel Time Index—the ratio of travel time in the peak period to the travel time at free-flow conditions. For example, a value of 1.30 indicates a 20-minute free-flow trip takes 26 minutes in the peak. Free-flow speeds (60 mph on freeways and 35 mph on principal arterials) are used as the comparison threshold; (1) Covers the McAllen TX urban area; (2) average of 498 urban areas

Source: Texas Transportation Institute, Urban Mobility Report 2012, December 2012

Public Transportation

Agency Name / Mode of Transportation	Vehicles Operated in Maximum Service	Annual Unlinked Passenger Trips (in thous.)	Annual Passenger Miles (in thous.)
City of McAllen - McAllen Express Transit			
Bus (directly operated)	8	713.6	n/a
Demand Response (directly operated)	2	12.4	n/a

Source: Federal Transit Administration, National Transit Database, 2013

Air Transportation

Airport Name and Code / Type of Service	Passenger Airlines[1]	Passenger Enplanements	Freight Carriers[2]	Freight (lbs.)
McAllen-Miller International Airport (MFE)				
Domestic service (U.S. carriers - 2014)	10	377,778	7	6,136,400
International service (U.S. carriers - 2013)	2	29	2	14,777

Note: (1) Includes all U.S.-based major, minor and commuter airlines that carried at least one passenger during the year; (2) Includes all U.S.-based airlines and freight carriers that transported at least one lb. of freight during the year.

Source: Bureau of Transportation Statistics, The Intermodal Transportation Database, Air Carriers: T-100 Domestic Market (U.S. Carriers), 2014; Bureau of Transportation Statistics, The Intermodal Transportation Database, Air Carriers: T-100 International Market (U.S. Carriers), 2013

Other Transportation Statistics

Major Highways:	Expressway 83E
Amtrak Service:	No
Major Waterways/Ports:	Rio Grande

Source: Amtrak.com; Google Maps

BUSINESSES

Major Business Headquarters

Company Name	Rankings	
	Fortune[1]	Forbes[2]
No companies listed	-	-

Note: (1) Fortune 500—companies that produce a 10-K are ranked 1 to 500 based on 2013 revenue; (2) all private companies with at least $2 billion in annual revenue through the end of their most current fiscal year are ranked 1 to 221; companies listed are headquartered in the city; dashes indicate no ranking

Source: Fortune, "Fortune 500," June 16, 2014; Forbes, "America's Largest Private Companies," November 5, 2014

Minority Business Opportunity

McAllen is home to one company which is on the *Hispanic Business* 500 list (500 largest U.S. Hispanic-owned companies based on 2012 revenue): **Galvotec Alloys** (#135). Companies included must show at least 51 percent ownership by Hispanic U.S. citizens, and must maintain headquarters in one of the 50 states or Washington, D.C. *Hispanic Business, "Hispanic Business 500," June 20, 2013*

McAllen is home to one company which is on the *Hispanic Business* Fastest-Growing 100 list (greatest sales growth from 2008 to 2012): **Galvotec Alloys** (#92). Companies included must show at least 51 percent ownership by Hispanic U.S. citizens, and must maintain headquarters in one of the 50 states or Washington, D.C. In addition, companies must have minimum revenues of $200,000 for calendar year 2008. *Hispanic Business, June 20, 2013*

Minority- and Women-Owned Businesses

Group	All Firms		Firms with Paid Employees			
	Firms	Sales ($000)	Firms	Sales ($000)	Employees	Payroll ($000)
Asian	567	245,168	248	229,744	2,094	67,958
Black	(s)	(s)	(s)	(s)	(s)	(s)
Hispanic	8,453	1,632,256	1,344	1,327,110	12,835	272,650
Women	4,346	668,696	686	586,224	6,503	128,807
All Firms	15,161	10,809,367	3,662	10,224,956	60,682	1,514,388

Note: Figures cover firms located in the city; minority- and women-owned business are defined as firms in which the corresponding group own 51% or more of the stock or equity of the company; (s) estimates are suppressed when publication standards are not met
Source: U.S. Census Bureau, 2007 Economic Census, Survey of Business Owners (2012 Survey of Business Owners data will be released starting in June 2015)

HOTELS & CONVENTION CENTERS

Hotels/Motels

Area	5 Star		4 Star		3 Star		2 Star		1 Star		Not Rated	
	Num.	Pct.[3]	Num.	Pct.[3]	Num.	Pct.[3]	Num.	Pct.[3]	Num.	Pct.[3]	Num.	Pct.[3]
City[1]	0	0.0	0	0.0	15	17.9	61	72.6	3	3.6	5	6.0
Total[2]	166	0.9	1,264	7.0	5,718	31.8	9,340	52.0	411	2.3	1,070	6.0

Note: (1) Figures cover McAllen and vicinity; (2) Figures cover all 100 cities in this book; (3) Percentage of hotels which have a given star rating; Star ratings are determined by expedia.com and offer an indication of the general quality of a particular hotel.
Source: expedia.com, April 2, 2015

Major Convention Centers

Name	Overall Space (sq. ft.)	Exhibit Space (sq. ft.)	Meeting Space (sq. ft.)	Meeting Rooms
McAllen Convention Center	n/a	60,000	25,000	16

Note: Table includes convention centers located in the McAllen-Edinburg-Mission, TX metro area; n/a not available
Source: Original research

Living Environment

COST OF LIVING

Cost of Living Index

Composite Index	Groceries	Housing	Utilities	Trans-portation	Health Care	Misc. Goods/ Services
84.1	83.4	76.6	92.4	94.6	82.7	84.4

Note: The Cost of Living Index measures regional differences in the cost of consumer goods and services, excluding taxes and non-consumer expenditures, for professional and managerial households in the top income quintile. It is based on more than 50,000 prices covering almost 60 different items for which prices are collected three times a year by chambers of commerce, economic development organizations or university applied economic centers in each participating urban area. The numbers shown should be read as a percentage above or below the national average of 100. For example, a value of 115.4 in the groceries column indicates that grocery prices are 15.4% higher than the national average. Small differences in the index numbers should not be interpreted as significant; Figures cover the McAllen TX urban area.
Source: The Council for Community and Economic Research, ACCRA Cost of Living Index, 2014

Grocery Prices

Area[1]	T-Bone Steak ($/pound)	Frying Chicken ($/pound)	Whole Milk ($/half gal.)	Eggs ($/dozen)	Orange Juice ($/64 oz.)	Coffee ($/11.5 oz.)
City[2]	9.47	1.02	2.42	1.79	3.03	3.34
Avg.	10.40	1.37	2.40	1.99	3.46	4.27
Min.	8.48	0.93	1.37	1.30	2.83	2.99
Max.	14.20	2.44	3.62	4.02	6.42	6.96

Note: (1) Values for the local area are compared with the average, minimum and maximum values for all 308 areas in the Cost of Living Index; (2) Figures cover the McAllen TX urban area; **T-Bone Steak** *(price per pound);* **Frying Chicken** *(price per pound, whole fryer);* **Whole Milk** *(half gallon carton);* **Eggs** *(price per dozen, Grade A, large);* **Orange Juice** *(64 oz. Tropicana or Florida Natural);* **Coffee** *(11.5 oz. can, vacuum-packed, Maxwell House, Hills Bros, or Folgers).*
Source: The Council for Community and Economic Research, ACCRA Cost of Living Index, 2014

Housing and Utility Costs

Area[1]	New Home Price ($)	Apartment Rent ($/month)	All Electric ($/month)	Part Electric ($/month)	Other Energy ($/month)	Telephone ($/month)
City[2]	227,081	768	-	139.08	38.11	21.01
Avg.	305,838	919	181.00	93.66	73.14	27.95
Min.	183,142	480	112.00	42.06	23.42	17.16
Max.	1,358,576	3,851	594.00	180.03	440.99	40.42

Note: (1) Values for the local area are compared with the average, minimum and maximum values for all 308 areas in the Cost of Living Index; (2) Figures cover the McAllen TX urban area; **New Home Price** *(2,400 sf living area, 8,000 sf lot, in urban area with full utilities);* **Apartment Rent** *(950 sf 2 bedroom/1.5 or 2 bath, unfurnished, excluding all utilities except water);* **All Electric** *(average monthly cost for an all-electric home);* **Part Electric** *(average monthly cost for a part-electric home);* **Other Energy** *(average monthly cost for natural gas, fuel oil, coal, wood, and any other forms of energy except electricity);* **Telephone** *(price includes basic monthly rate for a private residential line plus additional local usage charges incurred by a family of four).*
Source: The Council for Community and Economic Research, ACCRA Cost of Living Index, 2014

Health Care, Transportation, and Other Costs

Area[1]	Doctor ($/visit)	Dentist ($/visit)	Optometrist ($/visit)	Gasoline ($/gallon)	Beauty Salon ($/visit)	Men's Shirt ($)
City[2]	71.67	68.33	68.22	3.23	29.11	19.16
Avg.	102.86	87.89	97.66	3.44	34.37	26.74
Min.	67.47	65.78	51.18	3.00	17.43	12.79
Max.	173.50	150.14	235.00	4.33	64.28	49.50

Note: (1) Values for the local area are compared with the average, minimum and maximum values for all 308 areas in the Cost of Living Index; (2) Figures cover the McAllen TX urban area; **Doctor** *(general practitioners routine exam of an established patient);* **Dentist** *(adult teeth cleaning and periodic oral examination);* **Optometrist** *(full vision eye exam for established adult patient);* **Gasoline** *(one gallon regular unleaded, national brand, including all taxes, cash price at self-service pump if available);* **Beauty Salon** *(woman's shampoo, trim, and blow-dry);* **Men's Shirt** *(cotton/polyester dress shirt, pinpoint weave, long sleeves).*
Source: The Council for Community and Economic Research, ACCRA Cost of Living Index, 2014

HOUSING

House Price Index (HPI)

Area	National Ranking[2]	Quarterly Change (%)	One-Year Change (%)	Five-Year Change (%)
MSA[1]	(a)	n/a	8.85	6.64
U.S.[3]	–	1.35	4.91	11.59

Note: The HPI is a weighted repeat sales index. It measures average price changes in repeat sales or refinancings on the same properties. This information is obtained by reviewing repeat mortgage transactions on single-family properties whose mortgages have been purchased or securitized by Fannie Mae or Freddie Mac in January 1975; (1) McAllen-Edinburg-Mission Metropolitan Statistical Area—see Appendix B for areas included; (2) Rankings are based on annual percentage change for all metro areas containing at least 15,000 transactions over the last 10 years and ranges from 1 to 275; (3) figures based on a weighted average of Census Division estimates using a seasonally adjusted, purchase-only index; all figures are for the period ending December 31, 2014; n/a not available; (a) Not ranked because of increased index variability due to smaller sample size

Source: Federal Housing Finance Agency, House Price Index, February 26, 2015

Median Single-Family Home Prices

Area	2012	2013	2014p	Percent Change 2013 to 2014
MSA[1]	n/a	n/a	n/a	n/a
U.S. Average	177.2	197.4	209.0	5.9

Note: Figures are median sales prices of existing single-family homes in thousands of dollars; (p) preliminary; n/a not available; (1) McAllen-Edinburg-Mission, TX Metropolitan Statistical Area—see Appendix B for areas included

Source: National Association of Realtors, Median Sales Price of Existing Single-Family Homes for Metropolitan Areas, 4th Quarter 2014

Qualifying Income Based on Median Sales Price of Existing Single-Family Homes

Area	With 5% Down ($)	With 10% Down ($)	With 20% Down ($)
MSA[1]	n/a	n/a	n/a
U.S. Average	45,863	43,449	38,621

Note: Figures are preliminary; Qualifying income is based on a mortgage rate of 4.0%. Monthly principal and interest payment is limited to 25% of income; n/a not available; (1) McAllen-Edinburg-Mission, TX Metropolitan Statistical Area—see Appendix B for areas included

Source: National Association of Realtors, Qualifying Income Based on Median Sales Price of Existing Single-Family Homes for Metropolitan Areas, 4th Quarter 2014

Median Apartment Condo-Coop Home Prices

Area	2012	2013	2014p	Percent Change 2013 to 2014
MSA[1]	n/a	n/a	n/a	n/a
U.S. Average	173.7	194.9	205.1	5.2

Note: Figures are median sales prices of existing apartment condo-coop homes in thousands of dollars; (p) preliminary; n/a not available; (1) McAllen-Edinburg-Mission, TX Metropolitan Statistical Area—see Appendix B for areas included

Source: National Association of Realtors, Median Sales Price of Existing Apartment Condo-Coop Homes for Metropolitan Areas, 4th Quarter 2014

Gross Monthly Rent

Area	Under $200	$200 -299	$300 -499	$500 -749	$750 -999	$1,000 -1,499	$1,500 and up	Median ($)
City	1.5	3.4	11.6	38.4	28.0	13.9	3.3	722
MSA[1]	3.2	5.5	19.0	40.8	20.7	8.4	2.4	644
U.S.	1.7	3.2	7.8	22.1	24.3	26.0	14.9	900

Note: Figures are percentages except for Median; Gross rent is the contract rent plus the estimated average monthly cost of utilities (electricity, gas, and water and sewer) and fuels (oil, coal, kerosene, wood, etc.) if these are paid by the renter (or paid for the renter by someone else); (1) Figures cover the McAllen-Edinburg-Mission, TX Metropolitan Statistical Area—see Appendix B for areas included

Source: U.S. Census Bureau, 2011-2013 American Community Survey 3-Year Estimates

Homeownership Rate

Area	2007 (%)	2008 (%)	2009 (%)	2010 (%)	2011 (%)	2012 (%)	2013 (%)	2014 (%)
MSA[1]	n/a	n/a	n/a	n/a	n/a	n/a	n/a	n/a
U.S.	68.1	67.8	67.4	66.9	66.1	65.4	65.1	64.5

Note: (1) Figures cover the McAllen-Edinburg-Mission, TX Metropolitan Statistical Area—see Appendix B for areas included; n/a not available
Source: U.S. Census Bureau, Housing Vacancies and Homeownership Annual Statistics: 2014

Year Housing Structure Built

Area	2010 or Later	2000 -2009	1990 -1999	1980 -1989	1970 -1979	1960 -1969	1950 -1959	1940 -1949	Before 1940	Median Year
City	2.2	27.3	19.0	20.2	17.1	6.2	5.2	1.1	1.9	1989
MSA[1]	2.4	31.3	23.6	18.4	12.6	4.8	3.6	1.6	1.8	1993
U.S.	0.9	15.0	13.9	13.8	15.8	11.0	10.9	5.4	13.3	1976

Note: Figures are percentages except for Median Year; (1) Figures cover the McAllen-Edinburg-Mission, TX Metropolitan Statistical Area—see Appendix B for areas included
Source: U.S. Census Bureau, 2011-2013 American Community Survey 3-Year Estimates

HEALTH

Health Risk Data

Category	MSA[1] (%)	U.S. (%)
Adults aged 18–64 who have any kind of health care coverage	35.4	79.6
Adults who reported being in good or excellent health	71.9	83.1
Adults who are current smokers	14.1	19.6
Adults who are heavy drinkers[2]	n/a	6.1
Adults who are binge drinkers[3]	17.6	16.9
Adults who are overweight (BMI 25.0 - 29.9)	31.2	35.8
Adults who are obese (BMI 30.0 - 99.8)	44.5	27.6
Adults who participated in any physical activities in the past month	63.4	77.1
Adults 50+ who have ever had a sigmoidoscopy or colonoscopy	53.8	67.3
Women aged 40+ who have had a mammogram within the past two years	64.4	74.0
Men aged 40+ who have had a PSA test within the past two years	41.8	45.2
Adults aged 65+ who have had flu shot within the past year	63.8	60.1
Adults who always wear a seatbelt	n/a	93.8

Note: Data as of 2012 unless otherwise noted; n/a not available; (1) Figures cover the McAllen-Edinburg-Mission, TX Metropolitan Statistical Area—see Appendix B for areas included; (2) Heavy drinkers are classified as males having more than two drinks per day or females having more than one drink per day; (3) Binge drinkers are classified as males having five or more drinks on one occasion or females having four or more drinks on one occasion
Source: Centers for Disease Control and Prevention, Behaviorial Risk Factor Surveillance System, SMART: Selected Metropolitan/Micropolitan Area Risk Trends, 2012 (Note: the CDC has discontinued this dataset but will be releasing a replacement in late 2015)

Chronic Health Indicators

Category	MSA[1] (%)	U.S. (%)
Adults who have ever been told they had a heart attack	4.3	4.5
Adults who have ever been told they had a stroke	n/a	2.9
Adults who have been told they currently have asthma	3.1	8.9
Adults who have ever been told they have arthritis	21.6	25.7
Adults who have ever been told they have diabetes[2]	13.4	9.7
Adults who have ever been told they had skin cancer	2.6	5.7
Adults who have ever been told they had any other types of cancer	3.8	6.5
Adults who have ever been told they have COPD	3.3	6.2
Adults who have ever been told they have kidney disease	n/a	2.5
Adults who have ever been told they have a form of depression	14.4	18.0

Note: Data as of 2012 unless otherwise noted; n/a not available; (1) Figures cover the McAllen-Edinburg-Mission, TX Metropolitan Statistical Area—see Appendix B for areas included; (2) Figures do not include pregnancy-related, borderline, or pre-diabetes
Source: Centers for Disease Control and Prevention, Behaviorial Risk Factor Surveillance System, SMART: Selected Metropolitan/Micropolitan Area Risk Trends, 2012 (Note: the CDC has discontinued this dataset but will be releasing a replacement in late 2015)

Mortality Rates for the Top 10 Causes of Death in the U.S.

ICD-10[a] Sub-Chapter	ICD-10[a] Code	Age-Adjusted Mortality Rate[1] per 100,000 population	
		County[2]	U.S.
Malignant neoplasms	C00-C97	125.9	166.2
Ischaemic heart diseases	I20-I25	111.0	105.7
Other forms of heart disease	I30-I51	31.7	49.3
Chronic lower respiratory diseases	J40-J47	21.1	42.1
Organic, including symptomatic, mental disorders	F01-F09	19.9	38.1
Cerebrovascular diseases	I60-I69	28.2	37.0
Other external causes of accidental injury	W00-X59	10.1	26.9
Other degenerative diseases of the nervous system	G30-G31	18.5	25.6
Diabetes mellitus	E10-E14	23.2	21.3
Hypertensive diseases	I10-I15	8.1	19.4

Note: (a) ICD-10 = International Classification of Diseases 10th Revision; (1) Mortality rates are a three year average covering 2011-2013; (2) Figures cover Hidalgo County
Source: Centers for Disease Control and Prevention, National Center for Health Statistics. Compressed Mortality File 1999-2013 on CDC WONDER Online Database, released October 2014. Data are compiled from the Compressed Mortality File 1999-2013, Series 20 No. 2S, 2014.

Mortality Rates for Selected Causes of Death

ICD-10[a] Sub-Chapter	ICD-10[a] Code	Age-Adjusted Mortality Rate[1] per 100,000 population	
		County[2]	U.S.
Assault	X85-Y09	3.4	5.2
Diseases of the liver	K70-K76	22.4	13.2
Human immunodeficiency virus (HIV) disease	B20-B24	2.2	2.2
Influenza and pneumonia	J09-J18	16.1	15.4
Intentional self-harm	X60-X84	5.6	12.5
Malnutrition	E40-E46	1.8	0.9
Obesity and other hyperalimentation	E65-E68	*0.9	1.8
Renal failure	N17-N19	16.9	13.1
Transport accidents	V01-V99	12.7	11.7
Viral hepatitis	B15-B19	1.1	2.2

Note: (a) ICD-10 = International Classification of Diseases 10th Revision; (1) Mortality rates are a three year average covering 2011-2013; (2) Figures cover Hidalgo County; (*) Unreliable data as per CDC
Source: Centers for Disease Control and Prevention, National Center for Health Statistics. Compressed Mortality File 1999-2013 on CDC WONDER Online Database, released October 2014. Data are compiled from the Compressed Mortality File 1999-2013, Series 20 No. 2S, 2014.

Health Insurance Coverage

Area	With Health Insurance	With Private Health Insurance	With Public Health Insurance	Without Health Insurance	Population Under Age 18 Without Health Insurance
City	65.3	40.2	29.5	34.7	18.8
MSA[1]	63.4	30.9	37.0	36.6	17.3
U.S.	85.2	65.2	31.0	14.8	7.3

Note: Figures are percentages that cover the civilian noninstitutionalized population; (1) Figures cover the McAllen-Edinburg-Mission, TX Metropolitan Statistical Area—see Appendix B for areas included
Source: U.S. Census Bureau, 2011-2013 American Community Survey 3-Year Estimates

Number of Medical Professionals

Area[1]	MDs[2]	DOs[2,3]	Dentists	Podiatrists	Chiropractors	Optometrists
Local (number)	865	23	198	9	69	49
Local (rate[4])	107.1	2.8	24.2	1.1	8.4	6.0
U.S. (rate[4])	270.0	20.2	63.1	5.7	25.2	14.9

Note: Data as of 2013 unless noted; (1) Local data covers Hidalgo County; (2) Data as of 2012 and includes all active, non-federal physicians; (3) Doctor of Osteopathic Medicine; (4) rate per 100,000 population
Source: U.S. Department of Health and Human Services, Health Resources and Services Administration, Bureau of Health Professions, Area Resource File (ARF) 2013-2014

EDUCATION

Public School District Statistics

District Name	Schls	Pupils	Pupil/ Teacher Ratio	Minority Pupils[1] (%)	Free Lunch Eligible[2] (%)	IEP[3] (%)
McAllen ISD	34	24,931	15.6	95.5	55.6	7.8

Note: Table includes school districts with 2,000 or more students; (1) Percentage of students that are not non-Hispanic white; (2) Percentage of students that are eligible for the free lunch program; (3) Percentage of students that have an Individualized Education Program.

Source: U.S. Department of Education, National Center for Education Statistics, Common Core of Data, Local Education Agency (School District) Universe Survey: School Year 2012-2013; U.S. Department of Education, National Center for Education Statistics, Common Core of Data, Public Elementary/Secondary School Universe Survey: School Year 2012-2013

Highest Level of Education

Area	Less than H.S.	H.S. Diploma	Some College, No Deg.	Associate Degree	Bachelor's Degree	Master's Degree	Prof. School Degree	Doctorate Degree
City	27.3	19.7	20.6	5.9	18.5	5.0	2.3	0.7
MSA[1]	37.8	24.0	17.6	4.4	11.5	3.4	1.0	0.4
U.S.	13.7	28.0	21.2	7.9	18.2	7.7	1.9	1.3

Note: Figures cover persons age 25 and over; (1) Figures cover the McAllen-Edinburg-Mission, TX Metropolitan Statistical Area—see Appendix B for areas included

Source: U.S. Census Bureau, 2011-2013 American Community Survey 3-Year Estimates

Educational Attainment by Race

Area	High School Graduate or Higher (%)					Bachelor's Degree or Higher (%)				
	Total	White	Black	Asian	Hisp.[2]	Total	White	Black	Asian	Hisp.[2]
City	72.7	73.6	n/a	94.8	68.1	26.5	26.2	n/a	65.9	22.3
MSA[1]	62.2	62.4	77.0	94.3	58.2	16.2	15.8	28.8	65.0	13.9
U.S.	86.3	88.3	83.1	85.7	64.0	29.1	30.4	18.8	50.7	13.7

Note: Figures shown cover persons 25 years old and over; (1) Figures cover the McAllen-Edinburg-Mission, TX Metropolitan Statistical Area—see Appendix B for areas included; (2) People of Hispanic origin can be of any race

Source: U.S. Census Bureau, 2011-2013 American Community Survey 3-Year Estimates

School Enrollment by Grade and Control

Area	Preschool (%)		Kindergarten (%)		Grades 1 - 4 (%)		Grades 5 - 8 (%)		Grades 9 - 12 (%)	
	Public	Private	Public	Private	Public	Private	Public	Private	Public	Private
City	82.0	18.0	86.6	13.4	96.1	3.9	93.7	6.3	94.8	5.2
MSA[1]	91.8	8.2	94.9	5.1	97.9	2.1	97.8	2.2	97.7	2.3
U.S.	57.7	42.3	87.9	12.1	89.9	10.1	90.0	10.0	90.7	9.3

Note: Figures shown cover persons 3 years old and over; (1) Figures cover the McAllen-Edinburg-Mission, TX Metropolitan Statistical Area—see Appendix B for areas included

Source: U.S. Census Bureau, 2011-2013 American Community Survey 3-Year Estimates

Average Salaries of Public School Classroom Teachers

Area	2013-14		2014-15		Percent Change 2013-14 to 2014-15	Percent Change 2004-05 to 2014-15
	Dollars	Rank[1]	Dollars	Rank[1]		
TEXAS	49,690	30	50,576	29	1.78	23.3
U.S. Average	56,610	–	57,379	–	1.36	20.8

Note: (1) State rank ranges from 1 to 51 where 1 indicates highest salary.

Source: National Education Association, Rankings & Estimates: Rankings of the States 2014 and Estimates of School Statistics 2015, March 2015

Higher Education

Four-Year Colleges			Two-Year Colleges			Medical Schools[1]	Law Schools[2]	Voc/ Tech[3]
Public	Private Non-profit	Private For-profit	Public	Private Non-profit	Private For-profit			
1	0	0	0	0	1	0	0	4

Note: Figures cover institutions located within the city limits and include main campuses only; (1) includes schools accredited by the Liaison Committee on Medical Education and the American Osteopathic Association's Commission on Osteopathic College Accreditation; (2) includes ABA-accredited schools, schools with provisional ABA accreditation, and state accredited schools; (3) includes all schools with programs that are less than 2 years.

Source: National Center for Education Statistics, Integrated Postsecondary Education System (IPEDS), 2013-14; Association of American Medical Colleges, Member List, May 1, 2015; American Osteopathic Association, Member List, May 1, 2015; Law School Admission Council, Official Guide to ABA-Approved Law Schools Online, May 1, 2015; Wikipedia, List of Medical Schools in the United States, May 1, 2015; Wikipedia, List of Law Schools in the United States, May 1, 2015

PRESIDENTIAL ELECTION

2012 Presidential Election Results

Area	Obama (%)	Romney (%)	Other (%)
Hidalgo County	70.4	28.6	1.0
U.S.	51.0	47.2	1.8

Note: Results may not add to 100% due to rounding
Source: Dave Leip's Atlas of U.S. Presidential Elections

EMPLOYERS

Major Employers

Company Name	Industry
Am-Mex Products	Motor vehicle parts and accessories
City of McAllen	City and town managers' office
County of Hidalgo	Executive offices
Donna Independent School District	Public elementary school
Edcouch-Elsa Independent School District	Public elementary and secondary schools
Edinburg Consol. Ind. School District	Public elementary and secondary schools
Knapp Medical Center	Business services at non-commercial site
La Joya Independent School District	Public elementary and secondary schools
McAllen Independent School District	Public elementary school
McAllen Medical Center	General medical and surgical hospitals
Mercedes Independent School District	Public senior high school
Mid Valley Health System	Investment holding companies, except banks
Mission Consolidated Ind. School District	Public elementary school
Panasonic Industrial Devices Corporation	Audio electronic systems
Pharr-San Juan-Alamo Ind. School District	Public elementary and secondary schools
Sharyland Isb	Public elementary and secondary schools
South Texas College	Junior colleges
Tex-Best Travel Centers	Fast-food restaurant, chain
Texas Regional Delaware Inc.	State commercial banks
TST NA Trim	Personal service agents, brokers, and bureaus
University of Texas - Pan American	College, except junior
Weslaco Independent School District	Public elementary school
Woodcrafters Home Products Holding	Vanities, bathroom: wood

Note: Companies shown are located within the McAllen-Edinburg-Mission, TX Metropolitan Statistical Area.
Source: Hoovers.com; Wikipedia

PUBLIC SAFETY

Crime Rate

Area	All Crimes	Violent Crimes				Property Crimes		
		Murder	Forcible Rape	Robbery	Aggrav. Assault	Burglary	Larceny -Theft	Motor Vehicle Theft
City	4,108.9	1.5	4.4	61.0	58.8	393.6	3,416.3	173.3
Suburbs[1]	3,955.7	2.9	28.0	56.5	231.5	860.9	2,581.5	194.4
Metro[2]	3,981.2	2.7	24.0	57.2	202.7	783.3	2,720.3	190.9
U.S.	3,098.6	4.5	25.2	109.1	229.1	610.0	1,899.4	221.3

Note: Figures are crimes per 100,000 population; (1) All areas within the metro area that are located outside the city limits; (2) Figures cover the McAllen-Edinburg-Mission, TX Metropolitan Statistical Area—see Appendix B for areas included
Source: FBI Uniform Crime Reports, 2013

Hate Crimes

Area	Number of Quarters Reported	Number of Incidents per Bias Motivation						
		Race	Religion	Sexual Orientation	Ethnicity	Disability	Gender	Gender Identity
City	4	0	0	1	0	0	0	0
U.S.	4	2,871	1,031	1,233	655	83	18	31

Source: Federal Bureau of Investigation, Hate Crime Statistics 2013

Identity Theft Consumer Complaints

Area	Complaints	Complaints per 100,000 Population	Rank[2]
MSA[1]	602	73.8	162
U.S.	332,646	104.3	-

Note: (1) Figures cover the McAllen-Edinburg-Mission, TX Metropolitan Statistical Area—see Appendix B for areas included; (2) Rank ranges from 1 to 380 where 1 indicates greatest number of identity theft complaints per 100,000 population
Source: Federal Trade Commission, Consumer Sentinel Network Data Book for January–December 2014

Fraud and Other Consumer Complaints

Area	Complaints	Complaints per 100,000 Population	Rank[2]
MSA[1]	1,194	146.3	380
U.S.	2,250,205	705.7	-

Note: (1) Figures cover the McAllen-Edinburg-Mission, TX Metropolitan Statistical Area—see Appendix B for areas included; (2) Rank ranges from 1 to 380 where 1 indicates greatest number of identity theft complaints per 100,000 population
Source: Federal Trade Commission, Consumer Sentinel Network Data Book for January–December 2014

RECREATION

Culture

Dance[1]	Theatre[1]	Instrumental Music[1]	Vocal Music[1]	Series and Festivals	Museums and Art Galleries[2]	Zoos and Aquariums[3]
1	0	0	0	2	4	0

Note: (1) Professional perfoming groups; (2) Based on organizations with SIC code 8412; (3) AZA-accredited
Source: The Grey House Performing Arts Directory, 2015-16; Association of Zoos & Aquariums, AZA Member Zoos & Aquariums, April 2015; www.AccuLeads.com, April 2015

Professional Sports Teams

Team Name	League	Year Established
No teams are located in the metro area		

Source: Wikipedia, Major Professional Sports Teams of the United States and Canada, April 2015

CLIMATE

Average and Extreme Temperatures

Temperature	Jan	Feb	Mar	Apr	May	Jun	Jul	Aug	Sep	Oct	Nov	Dec	Yr.
Extreme High (°F)	93	94	106	102	102	102	101	102	99	96	97	94	106
Average High (°F)	70	73	78	83	87	91	93	93	90	85	78	72	83
Average Temp. (°F)	60	63	69	75	80	83	84	85	82	76	68	63	74
Average Low (°F)	51	53	59	66	72	75	76	76	73	66	59	53	65
Extreme Low (°F)	19	22	32	38	52	60	67	63	56	40	33	16	16

Note: Figures cover the years 1948-1990
Source: National Climatic Data Center, International Station Meteorological Climate Summary, 9/96

Average Precipitation/Snowfall/Humidity

Precip./Humidity	Jan	Feb	Mar	Apr	May	Jun	Jul	Aug	Sep	Oct	Nov	Dec	Yr.
Avg. Precip. (in.)	1.4	1.4	0.6	1.5	2.5	2.8	1.8	2.6	5.6	3.2	1.5	1.1	25.8
Avg. Snowfall (in.)	Tr	Tr	0	0	0	0	0	0	0	0	Tr	Tr	Tr
Avg. Rel. Hum. 6am (%)	88	89	88	89	90	91	92	92	91	89	87	87	89
Avg. Rel. Hum. 3pm (%)	62	60	57	58	60	59	54	55	60	58	59	61	59

Note: Figures cover the years 1948-1990; Tr = Trace amounts (<0.05 in. of rain; <0.5 in. of snow)
Source: National Climatic Data Center, International Station Meteorological Climate Summary, 9/96

Weather Conditions

Temperature			Daytime Sky			Precipitation		
32°F & below	45°F & below	90°F & above	Clear	Partly cloudy	Cloudy	0.01 inch or more precip.	0.1 inch or more snow/ice	Thunder-storms
2	30	116	86	180	99	72	0	27

Note: Figures are average number of days per year and cover the years 1948-1990
Source: National Climatic Data Center, International Station Meteorological Climate Summary, 9/96

HAZARDOUS WASTE

Superfund Sites

McAllen has no sites on the EPA's Superfund Final National Priorities List. There are a total of 1,322 Superfund sites on the list in the U.S. *U.S. Environmental Protection Agency, Final National Priorities List, April 14, 2015*

AIR & WATER QUALITY

Air Quality Trends: Ozone

	2004	2005	2006	2007	2008	2009	2010	2011	2012	2013
MSA[1]	0.070	0.069	0.060	0.055	0.058	0.060	0.065	0.062	0.061	0.055

Note: (1) Data covers the McAllen-Edinburg-Mission, TX Metropolitan Statistical Area—see Appendix B for areas included. The values shown are the composite ozone concentration averages among trend sites based on the highest fourth daily maximum 8-hour concentration in parts per million. These trends are based on sites having an adequate record of monitoring data during the trend period. Data from exceptional events are included.
Source: U.S. Environmental Protection Agency, Air Quality Monitoring Information, "Air Quality Trends by City, 2000-2013"

Air Quality Index

Area	Percent of Days when Air Quality was...[2]					AQI Statistics[2]	
	Good	Moderate	Unhealthy for Sensitive Groups	Unhealthy	Very Unhealthy	Maximum	Median
MSA[1]	75.3	24.7	0.0	0.0	0.0	88	37

Note: (1) Data covers the McAllen-Edinburg-Mission, TX Metropolitan Statistical Area—see Appendix B for areas included; (2) Based on 365 days with AQI data in 2014. Air Quality Index (AQI) is an index for reporting daily air quality. EPA calculates the AQI for five major air pollutants regulated by the Clean Air Act: ground-level ozone, particle pollution (aka particulate matter), carbon monoxide, sulfur dioxide, and nitrogen dioxide. The AQI runs from 0 to 500. The higher the AQI value, the greater the level of air pollution and the greater the health concern. There are six AQI categories: "Good" AQI is between 0 and 50. Air quality is considered satisfactory; "Moderate" AQI is between 51 and 100. Air quality is acceptable; "Unhealthy for Sensitive Groups" When AQI values are between 101 and 150, members of sensitive groups may experience health effects; "Unhealthy" When AQI values are between 151 and 200 everyone may begin to experience health effects; "Very Unhealthy" AQI values between 201 and 300 trigger a health alert; "Hazardous" AQI values over 300 trigger warnings of emergency conditions (not shown).
Source: U.S. Environmental Protection Agency, Air Quality Index Report, 2014

Air Quality Index Pollutants

Area	Percent of Days when AQI Pollutant was...[2]					
	Carbon Monoxide	Nitrogen Dioxide	Ozone	Sulfur Dioxide	Particulate Matter 2.5	Particulate Matter 10
MSA[1]	0.0	0.0	27.7	0.0	71.5	0.8

Note: (1) Data covers the McAllen-Edinburg-Mission, TX Metropolitan Statistical Area—see Appendix B for areas included; (2) Based on 365 days with AQI data in 2014. The Air Quality Index (AQI) is an index for reporting daily air quality. EPA calculates the AQI for five major air pollutants regulated by the Clean Air Act: ground-level ozone, particle pollution (also known as particulate matter), carbon monoxide, sulfur dioxide, and nitrogen dioxide. The AQI runs from 0 to 500. The higher the AQI value, the greater the level of air pollution and the greater the health concern.
Source: U.S. Environmental Protection Agency, Air Quality Index Report, 2014

Maximum Air Pollutant Concentrations: Particulate Matter, Ozone, CO and Lead

	Particulate Matter 10 (ug/m³)	Particulate Matter 2.5 Wtd AM (ug/m³)	Particulate Matter 2.5 24-Hr (ug/m³)	Ozone (ppm)	Carbon Monoxide (ppm)	Lead (ug/m³)
MSA[1] Level	88	n/a	n/a	0.055	n/a	n/a
NAAQS[2]	150	15	35	0.075	9	0.15
Met NAAQS[2]	Yes	n/a	n/a	Yes	n/a	n/a

Note: (1) Data covers the McAllen-Edinburg-Mission, TX Metropolitan Statistical Area—see Appendix B for areas included; Data from exceptional events are included; (2) National Ambient Air Quality Standards; ppm = parts per million; ug/m³ = micrograms per cubic meter; n/a not available.
Concentrations: Particulate Matter 10 (coarse particulate)—highest second maximum 24-hour concentration; Particulate Matter 2.5 Wtd AM (fine particulate)—highest weighted annual mean concentration; Particulate Matter 2.5 24-Hour (fine particulate)—highest 98th percentile 24-hour concentration; Ozone—highest fourth daily maximum 8-hour concentration; Carbon Monoxide—highest second maximum non-overlapping 8-hour concentration; Lead—maximum running 3-month average
Source: U.S. Environmental Protection Agency, Air Quality Monitoring Information, "Air Quality Statistics by City, 2013"

Maximum Air Pollutant Concentrations: Nitrogen Dioxide and Sulfur Dioxide

	Nitrogen Dioxide AM (ppb)	Nitrogen Dioxide 1-Hr (ppb)	Sulfur Dioxide AM (ppb)	Sulfur Dioxide 1-Hr (ppb)	Sulfur Dioxide 24-Hr (ppb)
MSA[1] Level	n/a	n/a	n/a	n/a	n/a
NAAQS[2]	53	100	30	75	140
Met NAAQS[2]	n/a	n/a	n/a	n/a	n/a

Note: (1) Data covers the McAllen-Edinburg-Mission, TX Metropolitan Statistical Area—see Appendix B for areas included; Data from exceptional events are included; (2) National Ambient Air Quality Standards; ppm = parts per million; ug/m³ = micrograms per cubic meter; n/a not available.
Concentrations: Nitrogen Dioxide AM—highest arithmetic mean concentration; Nitrogen Dioxide 1-Hr—highest 98th percentile 1-hour daily maximum concentration; Sulfur Dioxide AM—highest annual mean concentration; Sulfur Dioxide 1-Hr—highest 99th percentile 1-hour daily maximum concentration; Sulfur Dioxide 24-Hr—highest second maximum 24-hour concentration
Source: U.S. Environmental Protection Agency, Air Quality Monitoring Information, "Air Quality Statistics by City, 2013"

Drinking Water

Water System Name	Pop. Served	Primary Water Source Type	Violations[1]	
			Health Based	Monitoring/ Reporting
McAllen Public Utility	157,125	Surface	0	0

Note: (1) Based on violation data from January 1, 2014 to December 31, 2014 (includes unresolved violations from earlier years)

Source: U.S. Environmental Protection Agency, Office of Ground Water and Drinking Water, Safe Drinking Water Information System (based on data extracted January 27, 2015)

Miami, Florida

Background

While the majority of Miami's residents used to be Caucasian of European descent, the rapidly growing city now consists of a majority of Latinos. The number of Cubans, Puerto Ricans, and Haitians give the city a flavorful mix with a Latin American and Caribbean accent. The City of Miami has three official languages: English, Spanish, and Haitian Creole.

Thanks to early pioneer Julia Tuttle, railroad magnate Henry Flagler extended the East Coast Railroad beyond Palm Beach. Within 15 years of that decision, Miami became known as the "Gold Coast." The land boom of the 1920s brought wealthy socialites, as well as African-Americans in search of work. Pink- and aquamarine-hued art deco hotels were squeezed onto a tiny tract of land called Miami Beach, and the population of the Miami metro area swelled.

Given Miami's origins in a tourist-oriented economy, many of the activities in which residents engage are "leisurely," including swimming, scuba diving, golf, tennis, and boating. For those who enjoy professional sports, the city is host to the following teams: the Miami Dolphins, football; the Florida Marlins, baseball; the Miami Heat, basketball; and the Florida Panthers, hockey. Cultural activities range from the Miami City Ballet and the Coconut Grove Playhouse to numerous art galleries and museums, including the Bass Museum of Art. Visits to the Villa Vizcaya, a gorgeous palazzo built by industrialist James Deering in the Italian Renaissance style, and to the Miami MetroZoo are popular pastimes.

Miami's prime location on Biscayne Bay in the southeastern United States makes it a perfect nexus for travel and trade. The Port of Miami is a bustling center for many cruise and cargo ships. The Port is also a base for the National Oceanic and Atmospheric Administration. The Miami International Airport is a busy destination point to and from many Latin-American and Caribbean countries.

Miami is still at the trading crossroads of the Western Hemisphere as the chief shipment point for exports and imports with Latin America and the Caribbean. One out of every three North American cruise passengers sails from Miami. Miami was also the host city of the 2003 Free Trade Area of the Americas negotiations, and is one of the leading candidates to become the trading bloc's headquarters.

The sultry, subtropical climate against a backdrop of Spanish, art deco, and modern architecture makes Miami a uniquely cosmopolitan city. The Art Deco Historic District, known as South Beach and located on the tip of Miami Beach, has an international reputation in the fashion, film, and music industries. Greater Miami is now a national center for film, television, and print production.

In recent years Miami has witnessed its largest real estate boom since the 1920s, especially in the newly created midtown, north of downtown and south of the Design District. Nearly 25,000 new residential units have been added to the downtown skyline since 2005.

Long, warm summers are typical, as are mild, dry winters. The marine influence is evidenced by the narrow daily range of temperature and the rapid warming of cold air masses. During the summer months, rainfall occurs in early morning near the ocean and in early afternoon further inland. Hurricanes occasionally affect the Miami area, usually in September and October, while destructive tornadoes are quite rare. Funnel clouds are occasionally sighted and a few touch the ground briefly, but significant destruction is unusual. Waterspouts are visible from the beaches during the summer months but seldom cause any damage. During June, July, and August, there are numerous beautiful, but dangerous, lightning events.

Rankings

General Rankings

- The human resources consulting firm Mercer ranked 230 cities worldwide in terms of overall quality of life. Miami ranked #65. Criteria: political, social, economic, and socio-cultural factors; medical and health considerations; schools and education; public services and transportation; recreation; consumer goods; housing; and natural environment. *Mercer, "Mercer 2015 Quality of Living Survey," March 4, 2015*

Business/Finance Rankings

- The personal finance site NerdWallet scored the nation's 50 largest American cities according to how friendly a business climate they offer to would-be entrepreneurs. Criteria included access to funding, human capital, local economy, and business-friendliness as judged by small business owners. On the resulting list of most welcoming cities, Miami ranked #2. *www.nerdwallet.com, "Best Cities to Start a Business," May 7, 2014*
- Recognizing the sizeable percentage of American workers who are self-employed, NerdWallet editors assessed the country's cities according to percentage of freelancers, median rental costs, and affordability of median healthcare costs. By these criteria, Miami placed #3 among the best cities for independent workers. *www.nerdwallet.com, "Best Cities for Freelancers," February 25, 2014*
- Building on the U.S. Department of Labor's Occupational Information Network Data Collection Program, the Brookings Institution defined STEM occupations and job opportunities for STEM workers at various levels of educational attainment. The Miami metro area was placed among the ten large metro areas with the lowest demand for high-level STEM knowledge. *www.brookings.edu, "The Hidden Stem Economy," June 10, 2013*
- To identify the metro areas with the largest gap in income between rich and poor residents, the 24/7 Wall Street research team used the U.S. Census Bureau's 2012 American Community Survey, an index of income disparity, additional income, poverty, and home-value data. The Miami metro area placed #8 among metro areas with the widest wealth gap between rich and poor. *247wallst.com, "Cities with the Widest Gap between Rich and Poor," November 4, 2013*
- Based on metro area social media reviews, the employment opinion group Glassdoor surveyed 50 of the largest U.S. metro areas on measures including compensation and benefits, satisfaction with management, business outlook, and number of employers hiring. The Miami metro area was ranked #26 in overall employee satisfaction. *www.glassdoor.com, "Employment Satisfaction Report Card by City," June 13, 2014*
- In a survey of economic confidence in the nation's 50 largest metropolitan areas conducted January–December 2014, the Miami metro area placed #5, according to Gallup's 2014 Economic Confidence Index. *Gallup, "San Jose and San Francisco Lead in Economic Confidence," March 19, 2015*
- Using data from the Council for Community and Economic Research's 2013 Annual Report, NerdWallet ranked the 100 U.S. cities with the most expensive cost of living. Cities in California and in the Northeast topped the list. Of the cities with the highest cost of living, Miami ranked #47. *NerdWallet.com, "Most Expensive Cities in America," June 4, 2014*
- The Brookings Institution ranked the 50 largest cities in the U.S. based on income inequality. Miami was ranked #4. (#1 = greatest ineqality). Criteria: the cities were ranked based on the "95/20 ratio," a figure representing the income at which a household earns more than 95 percent of all other households, divided by the income at which a household earns more than only 20 percent of all other households. *Brookings Institution, "Income Inequality in America's 50 Largest Cities, 2007-2013," March 17, 2015*
- Miami was ranked #26 out of 100 metro areas in terms of economic performance (#1 = best) during the recession and recovery from trough quarter through the second quarter of 2013. Criteria: percent change in employment; percentage point change in unemployment rate; percent change in gross metropolitan product; percent change in House Price Index. *Brookings Institution, MetroMonitor: Tracking Economic Recession and Recovery in America's 100 Largest Metropolitan Areas, September 2013*

- The finance site *24/7 Wall St.* identified the metropolitan areas that have the smallest and largest pay disparities between men and women, comparing the median earnings for the past 12 months of both men and women working full-time in the country's 100 largest metropolitan statistical areas. Of the ten best-paying metros for women, the Miami metro area ranked #6. *24/7 Wall St., "The Best (and Worst) Paying Cities for Women," March 6, 2015*

- Payscale.com ranked the 20 largest metro areas in terms of wage growth. The Miami metro area ranked #2. Criteria: private-sector wage growth between the 1st quarter of 2014 and the 1st quarter of 2015. *PayScale, "Wage Trends by Metro Area," 1st Quarter, 2015*

- *Forbes* reports that Miami was identified as one of the happiest cities to work in by CareerBliss.com, an online community for career advancement. The city ranked #1 out of 10. Criteria: work-life balance; an employee's relationship with his or her boss and co-workers; general work environment; compensation; opportunities for advancement; company culture; and resources. *Forbes.com, "The 10 Happiest and Unhappiest Cities to Work in Right Now," January 16, 2015*

- The Miami metro area appeared on the Milken Institute "2013 Best Performing Cities" list. Rank: #85 out of 200 large metro areas. Criteria: job growth; wage and salary growth; high-tech output growth. *Milken Institute, "Best-Performing Cities 2014," January 2015*

- *Forbes* ranked the 200 most populous metro areas to determine the nation's "Best Places for Business and Careers." The Miami metro area was ranked #113. Criteria: costs (business and living); job growth (past and projected); income growth; educational attainment (college and high school); projected economic growth; cultural and recreational opportunities; net migration patterns; number of highly ranked colleges. *Forbes, "The Best Places for Business and Careers 2014," July 23, 2014*

- Mercer Human Resources Consulting ranked 211 urban areas worldwide in terms of cost-of-living. Miami ranked #98 (the lower the ranking, the higher the cost-of-living). The survey measured the comparative cost of over 200 items (such as housing, food, clothing, household goods, transportation, and entertainment) in each location.*Mercer, "2014 Cost of Living Survey," July 10, 2014*

Culture/Performing Arts Rankings

- Miami was selected as one of America's top cities for the arts. The city ranked #7 in the mid-sized city (population 100,000 to 499,999) category. Criteria: readers' top choices for arts travel destinations based on the richness and variety of visual arts sites, activities and events. *American Style, "2012 Top 25 Arts Destinations," June 2012*

Dating/Romance Rankings

- Gizmodo reported on data that Facebook collected on the best American cities for singles. Criteria included highest percentage of single people, the widest single female-to-single male ratio (and vice versa), and the best probability of relationship formation. Among the top 50 American population centers Miami ranked #4. *gizmodo.com, "The Best Places to Find Hot Singles (According to Facebook)," February 13, 2014*

- Of the 100 U.S. cities surveyed by *Men's Health* in its quest to identify the nation's best cities for dating and forming relationships, Miami was ranked #7 for online dating (#1 = best). *Men's Health, "The Best and Worst Cities for Online Dating," January 30, 2013*

- Miami was selected as one of America's best cities for singles by the readers of *Travel + Leisure* in their annual "America's Favorite Cities" survey. The city was ranked #1 out of 20. Criteria included good-looking locals, cool shopping, and hipster-magnet coffee bars. *Travel + Leisure, "America's Best Cities for Singles," January 23, 2015*

- Miami was selected as one of the most romantic cities in America by Amazon.com. The city ranked #2 of 20. Criteria: cities with 100,000 or more residents were ranked on their per capita sales of romance novels and relationship books, romantic comedy movies, romantic music, and sexual wellness products. *Amazon.com, "Top 20 Most Romantic Cities in America," February 5, 2015*

- Miami was selected as one of "America's Best Cities for Dating" by *Yahoo! Travel*. Criteria: high proportion of singles; excellent dating venues and/or stunning natural settings. *Yahoo! Travel, "America's Best Cities for Dating," February 7, 2012*

Education Rankings

- Personal finance website *WalletHub* analyzed the 150 largest U.S. metropolitan statistical areas to determine where the most educated Americans are choosing to settle. Criteria: educational attainment; percentage of workers with jobs in computer, engineering, and science fields; quality and size of each metro area's universities. Miami was ranked #107 (#1 = most educated city). *www.WalletHub.com, "2014's Most and Least Educated Cities*
- Miami was selected as one of the most well-read cities in America by Amazon.com. The city ranked #2 among the top 20. Cities with populations greater than 100,000 were evaluated based on per capita sales of books, magazines and newspapers. *Amazon.com, "The 20 Most Well-Read Cities in America," May 20, 2014*
- The real estate website *MovoTo.com* selected Miami as one of the "Nerdiest Cities in America." The city ranked #8 among the top 10 derived from data on the 50 most populous cities in the United States. Criteria: Number of annual comic book, video game, anime, and sci-fi/fantasy conventions; people per comic book store, video game store, and traditional gaming store; people per LARPing ("live action role-playing") group; people per science museum. Also factored in: distance to the nearest Renaissance faire. *MovoTo.com, "The 10 Nerdiest Cities in America," April 10, 2013*
- Miami was selected as one of America's most literate cities. The city ranked #43 out of the 77 largest U.S. cities. Criteria: number of booksellers; library resources; Internet resources; educational attainment; periodical publishing resources; newspaper circulation. *Central Connecticut State University, "America's Most Literate Cities, 2014," April 8, 2015*

Environmental Rankings

- The Miami metro area came in at #342 for the relative comfort of its climate on Sperling's list of "chill cities," as measured by the Sperling Heat Index. All 361 metro areas are included. Criteria included daytime high temperatures, nighttime low temperatures, dew point, and relative humidity at the high temperatures. *www.bertsperling.com, "Sperling's Chill Cities," July 18, 2013*
- Sperling's BestPlaces assessed 379 metropolitan areas of the United States for the likelihood of dangerously extreme weather events or earthquakes. In general the Southeast and South-Central regions have the highest risk of weather extremes and earthquakes, while the Pacific Northwest enjoys the lowest risk. Of the least risky metropolitan areas, the Miami metro area was ranked #313. *www.bestplaces.net, "Safest Places from Natural Disasters," April 2011*
- The U.S. Environmental Protection Agency (EPA) released a list of large U.S. metropolitan areas with the most ENERGY STAR certified buildings in 2014. The Miami metro area was ranked #18 out of 25. *U.S. Environmental Protection Agency, "Top Cities With the Most ENERGY STAR Certified Buildings in 2014," March 25, 2015*
- Miami was highlighted as one of the top 25 cleanest metro areas for year-round particle pollution (Annual PM 2.5) in the U.S. during 2011 through 2013. The area ranked #23. *American Lung Association, State of the Air 2015*

Food/Drink Rankings

- *Men's Health* ranked 100 major U.S. cities in terms of alcohol intoxication. Miami ranked #6 (#1 = most sober).Criteria: binge drinking; alcohol-related traffic accidents, arrests, and fatalities. *Men's Health, "The Drunkest Cities in America," November 19, 2013*

Health/Fitness Rankings

- Analysts who tracked obesity rates in the nation's largest metro areas (those with populations above one million) found that the Miami metro area was one of the ten major metros where residents were least likely to be obese, defined as a BMI score of 30 or above. *www.gallup.com, "Boulder, Colo., Residents Still Least Likely to Be Obese," April 4, 2014*

- For each of the 50 most populous metro areas in the United States, the American College of Sports Medicine's American Fitness Index evaluated infrastructure, community assets, and policies that encourage healthy and fit lifestyles, including preventive health behaviors, levels of chronic disease conditions, health care access, and community resources and policies that support physical activity. The Miami metro area ranked #42 for "community fitness." Personal health indicators were considered as well as community and environmental indicators. *www.americanfitnessindex.org, "ACSM American Fitness Index Health and Community Fitness Status of the 50 Largest Metropolitan Areas," May 2013*
- Miami was identified as one of the 10 most walkable cities in the U.S. by Walk Score, a Seattle-based service that rates the convenience and transit access of 10,000 neighborhoods in 3,000 cities. The area ranked #5 out of the 50 largest U.S. cities. Walk Score measures walkability by analyzing hundreds of walking routes to nearby amenities. Walk Score also measures pedestrian friendliness by analyzing population density and road metrics such as block length and intersection density. *WalkScore.com, March 20, 2014*
- The Miami metro area was identified as one of the worst cities for bed bugs in America by pest control company Orkin. The area ranked #22 out of 50 based on the number of bed bug treatments Orkin performed from January to December 2013. *Orkin, "Chicago Tops Bed Bug Cities List for Second Year in a Row," January 16, 2014*
- Miami was selected as one of the 25 fattest cities in America by *Men's Fitness Online*. It ranked #12 out of America's 50 largest cities. Criteria: fitness centers and sport stores; nutrition; sports participation; TV viewing; overweight/sedentary; junk food; air quality; geography; commute; parks and open space; city recreational facilities; access to healthcare; motivation; mayor and city initiatives; state obesity initiatives. *Men's Fitness, "The Fittest and Fattest Cities in America," March 5, 2012*
- Miami was identified as a "2013 Spring Allergy Capital." The area ranked #71 out of 100. Three groups of factors were used to identify the most severe cities for people with allergies during the spring season: annual pollen levels; medicine utilization; access to board-certified allergists. *Asthma and Allergy Foundation of America, "Spring Allergy Capitals 2013"*
- Miami was identified as a "2013 Fall Allergy Capital." The area ranked #67 out of 100. Three groups of factors were used to identify the most severe cities for people with allergies during the fall season: annual pollen levels; medicine utilization; access to board-certified allergists. *Asthma and Allergy Foundation of America, "Fall Allergy Capitals 2013"*
- Miami was identified as a "2013 Asthma Capital." The area ranked #64 out of the nation's 100 largest metropolitan areas. Twelve factors were used to identify the most challenging places to live for people with asthma: estimated prevalence; self-reported prevalence; crude death rate for asthma; annual pollen score; annual air quality; public smoking laws; number of board-certified asthma specialists; school inhaler access laws; rescue medication use; controller medication use; uninsured rate; poverty rate. *Asthma and Allergy Foundation of America, "Asthma Capitals 2013"*
- *Men's Health* ranked 100 major U.S. cities in terms of the best and worst cities for men. Miami ranked #68. Criteria: thirty-three data points were examined covering health, fitness, and quality of life. *Men's Health, "The Best & Worst Cities for Men 2014," December 6, 2013*
- Miami was selected as one of the best metropolitan areas for hospital care in America by *HealthGrades.com.* The rankings are based on a comprehensive study of patient death and complication rates in the nation's nearly 5,000 hospitals. Hospitals performing in the top 5% nationwide across 26 different medical procedures and diagnoses were identified. *HealthGrades.com* then ranked cities by the highest percentage of these Distinguished Hospitals for Clinical Excellence™. The Miami metro area ranked #16. *HealthGrades.com, "America's Top 50 Cities for Hospital Care," January 21, 2012*
- The Miami metro area appeared in the 2013 Gallup-Healthways Well-Being Index. The area ranked #124 out of 189. The Gallup-Healthways Well-Being Index score is an average of six sub-indexes, which individually examine life evaluation, emotional health, work environment, physical health, healthy behaviors, and access to basic necessities. Results are based on telephone interviews conducted as part of the Gallup-Healthways Well-Being Index survey January 2–December 29, 2012, and January 2–December 30, 2013, with a random sample of 531,630 adults, aged 18 and older, living in metropolitan areas in the 50 U.S. states and the District of Columbia. *Gallup-Healthways, "State of American Well-Being," March 25, 2014*

- The Miami metro area was identified as one of "America's Most Stressful Cities" by *Sperling's BestPlaces.* The metro area ranked #3 out of 50. Criteria: unemployment rate; suicide rate; commute time; mental health; poor rest; alcohol use; violent crime rate; property crime rate; cloudy days annually. *Sperling's BestPlaces, www.BestPlaces.net, "Stressful Cities 2012*
- Miami was selected as one of the "20 Most Livable U.S. Cities for Wheelchair Users" by the Christopher & Dana Reeve Foundation. The city ranked #11. Criteria: Medicaid eligibility and spending; access to physicians and rehabilitation facilities; access to fitness facilities and recreation; access to paratransit; percentage of people living with disabilities who are employed; clean air; climate. *Christopher & Dana Reeve Foundation, "20 Most Livable U.S. Cities for Wheelchair Users," July 26, 2010*

Pet Rankings

- Miami was selected as one of the best cities for dogs by real estate website Estately.com. The city was ranked #14. Criteria: weather; walkability; yard sizes; dog activities; meetup groups; availability of dogsitters. *Estately.com, "17 Best U.S. Cities for Dogs," May 14, 2013*

Real Estate Rankings

- The Miami metro area was identified as #5 among the ten housing markets with the highest percentage of distressed property sales, based on the findings of the housing data website RealtyTrac. Criteria included being sold "short"—for less than the outstanding mortgage balance—or in a foreclosure auction, income and poverty figures, and unemployment data. *247wallst.com, "Cities Selling the Most Distressed Homes," January 23, 2014*
- Miami was ranked #7 out of 275 metro areas in terms of house price appreciation in 2014 (#1 = highest rate). *Federal Housing Finance Agency, House Price Index, 4th Quarter 2014*
- The Miami metro area was identified as one of the 15 worst housing markets for the next five years." Criteria: projected annualized change in home prices between the fourth quarter 2012 and the fourth quarter 2017. *The Business Insider, "The 15 Worst Housing Markets for the Next Five Years," May 22, 2013*
- The Miami metro area was identified as one of the 20 least affordable housing markets in the U.S. in 2014. The area ranked #10 out of 178 markets. Criteria: whether or not a typical family could qualify for a mortgage loan on a typical home. *National Association of Realtors®, Affordability Index of Existing Single-Family Homes for Metropolitan Areas, 2014*
- Miami was ranked #208 out of 226 metro areas in terms of housing affordability in 2014 by the National Association of Home Builders (#1 = most affordable). The NAHB-Wells Fargo Housing Opportunity Index (HOI) for a given area is defined as the share of homes sold in that area that would have been affordable to a family earning the local median income, based on standard mortgage underwriting criteria. *National Association of Home Builders®, NAHB-Wells Fargo Housing Opportunity Index, 4th Quarter 2014*
- The nation's largest metro areas were analyzed in terms of the percentage of households entering some stage of foreclosure in 2013. The Miami metro area ranked #1 out of 10 (#1 = highest foreclosure rate). *RealtyTrac, "2013 Year-End U.S. Foreclosure Market Report™," January 16, 2014*

Safety Rankings

- Symantec, in partnership with Sperling's BestPlaces, ranked the 50 largest cities in the U.S. in terms of their vulnerability to cybercrime. The city ranked #23. Criteria: number of cyberattacks and potential infections; level of Internet access; expenditures on smartphones and computer hardware/software; wireless hotspots; broadband connectivity; Internet usage; online purchases. *Symantec, "Riskiest Online Cities of 2012" February 15, 2012*
- Allstate ranked the 200 largest cities in America in terms of driver safety. Miami ranked #186. Allstate researchers analyzed internal property damage claims over a two-year period from January 2011 to December 2012. A weighted average of the two-year numbers determined the annual percentages. *Allstate, "Allstate America's Best Drivers Report, 2014"*

- Miami was identified as one of the most dangerous cities in America by *The Business Insider.* Criteria: cities with 100,000 residents or more were ranked by violent crime rate in 2011. Violent crimes include for murder, rape, robbery, and aggravated assault. The city ranked #17 out of 25. *The Business Insider, "The 25 Most Dangerous Cities in America," November 4, 2012*

- The National Insurance Crime Bureau ranked 380 metro areas in the U.S. in terms of per capita rates of vehicle theft. The Miami metro area ranked #65 (#1 = highest rate). Criteria: number of vehicle theft offenses per 100,000 inhabitants in 2012. *National Insurance Crime Bureau, "Hot Spots 2012," June 26, 2013*

Seniors/Retirement Rankings

- The finance website CNNMoney surveyed small U.S. cities that offer exceptional urban amenities at a cost of living somewhat higher than for the top-ten locations but still affordable for retirees. Median home-price figures were supplied by the residential real-estate website Trulia. Miami was among the eight small cities singled out. *money.cnn.com, "Best Places to Retire with a Nice Nest Egg," October 28, 2013*

- From its Best Cities for Successful Aging indexes, the Milken Institute generated rankings for metropolitan areas, weighing data in eight categories—health care, wellness, living arrangements, transportation, financial characteristics, education and employment opportunities, community engagement, and overall livability. The Miami metro area was ranked #76 overall in the large metro area category. *Milken Institute, "Best Cities for Successful Aging, 2014"*

Sports/Recreation Rankings

- According to the personal finance website NerdWallet, the Miami metro area, at #9, is one of the nation's top dozen metro areas for sports fans. Criteria included the presence of all four major sports—MLB, NFL, NHL, and NBA, fan enthusiasm (as measured by game attendance), ticket affordability, and "sports culture," that is, number of sports bars. *www.nerdwallet.com, "Best Cities for Sports Fans," May 5, 2013*

- Miami was chosen as one of America's best cities for bicycling. The city ranked #34 out of 50. Criteria: robust cycling infrastructure; vibrant bike culture. The editors only considered cities with populations of 95,000 or more. *Bicycling, "America's Top 50 Bike-Friendly Cities," May 23, 2012*

Transportation Rankings

- NerdWallet surveyed average annual car insurance premiums in 125 U.S. cities to identify the least expensive U.S. cities in which to insure a car. Locations with no-fault insurance laws was a strong determinant. Miami came in at #9 for the most expensive rates. *www.nerdwallet.com, "Best Cities for Cheap Car Insurance," February 3, 2014*

Women/Minorities Rankings

- *Women's Health* examined U.S. cities and identified the 100 best cities for women. Miami was ranked #56. Criteria: 30 categories were examined from obesity and breast cancer rates to commuting times and hours spent working out. *Women's Health, "Best Cities for Women 2012"*

Miscellaneous Rankings

- The watchdog site Charity Navigator conducts an annual study of charities in the nation's major markets both to analyze statistical differences in their financial, accountability, and transparency practices and to track year-to-year variations in individual communities. The Miami metro area was ranked #26 among the 30 metro markets. *www.charitynavigator.org, "Metro Market Study 2013," June 1, 2013*

- Business Insider reports on the 2013 Trick-or-Treat Index compiled by the real estate site Zillow, which used its own Home Value Index and Walk Score along with population density and local crime stats to determine that Miami ranked #14 for "how much candy it gives out versus how far kids have to walk to get it." Zillow also zeroes in on the best neighborhoods in its top 20 cities. *www.businessinsider.com, "These Are the Best Cities for Trick-or-Treating," October 15, 2013*

- Miami was selected as one of the 10 worst run cities in America by *24/7 Wall St.* The city ranked #4. Criteria: the 100 largest cities in the U.S. were ranked in terms of economy, job market, crime, and the welfare of its residents. *24/7 Wall St., "The Best and Worst Run Cities in America," January 15, 2013*

- Miami appeared on *Travel + Leisure's* list of America's least attractive people. Criteria: cities were selected by readers in their annual America's Favorite Cities survey. The city ranked #6 out of 10. *Travel + Leisure, "America's Most and Least Attractive People," November 2013*

- Scarborough Research, a leading market research firm, identified the top local markets for lottery ticket purchasers. The Miami DMA (Designated Market Area) ranked in the top 13 with 48% of adults 18+ reporting that they purchased lottery tickets in the past 30 days. *Scarborough Research, January 30, 2012*

- Mars Chocolate North America, the makers of COMBOS®, in partnership with Sperling's BestPlaces, ranked 50 major metro areas in terms of their "manliness." The Miami metro area ranked #36. Criteria: number of professional sports teams; number of nearby NASCAR tracks and racing events; manly lifestyle; concentration of manly retail stores; manly occupations per capita; salty snack sales; "Board of Manliness" rankings. *Mars Chocolate North America, "America's Manliest Cities 2012"*

- Miami was selected as one of the most tattooed cities in America by *Lovelyish.com.* The city was ranked #1. Criteria: number of tattoo shops per capita. *Lovelyish.com, "Top Ten: Most Tattooed Cities in America," October 17, 2012*

- The National Alliance to End Homelessness ranked the 100 most populous metro areas in terms the rate of homelessness. The Miami metro area ranked #38. Criteria: number of homeless people per 10,000 population in 2011. *National Alliance to End Homelessness, The State of Homelessness in America 2012*

- The financial education website CreditDonkey compiled a list of the ten "best" cities of the future, based on percentage of housing built in 1990 or later, population change since 2010, and construction jobs as a percentage of population. Also considered were two more futuristic criteria: number of DeLorean cars available for purchase and number of spaceport companies and proposed spaceports. Miami was scored #6. *www.creditDonkey.com, "In the Future, Almost All of America's 'Best' Cities Will Be on the West Coast, Report Says," February 14, 2014*

Business Environment

CITY FINANCES

City Government Finances

Component	2012 ($000)	2012 ($ per capita)
Total Revenues	903,371	2,261
Total Expenditures	944,249	2,364
Debt Outstanding	873,238	2,186
Cash and Securities[1]	2,430,733	6,085

Note: (1) Cash and security holdings of a government at the close of its fiscal year, including those of its dependent agencies, utilities, and liquor stores.
Source: U.S Census Bureau, State & Local Government Finances 2012

City Government Revenue by Source

Source	2012 ($000)	2012 ($ per capita)
General Revenue		
From Federal Government	79,889	200
From State Government	53,881	135
From Local Governments	38,426	96
Taxes		
Property	265,821	665
Sales and Gross Receipts	78,416	196
Personal Income	0	0
Corporate Income	0	0
Motor Vehicle License	0	0
Other Taxes	62,638	157
Current Charges	115,058	288
Liquor Store	0	0
Utility	0	0
Employee Retirement	181,098	453

Source: U.S Census Bureau, State & Local Government Finances 2012

City Government Expenditures by Function

Function	2012 ($000)	2012 ($ per capita)	2012 (%)
General Direct Expenditures			
Air Transportation	0	0	0.0
Corrections	0	0	0.0
Education	0	0	0.0
Employment Security Administration	0	0	0.0
Financial Administration	30,073	75	3.2
Fire Protection	85,757	215	9.1
General Public Buildings	0	0	0.0
Governmental Administration, Other	9,738	24	1.0
Health	0	0	0.0
Highways	20,594	52	2.2
Hospitals	0	0	0.0
Housing and Community Development	40,112	100	4.2
Interest on General Debt	39,648	99	4.2
Judicial and Legal	4,328	11	0.5
Libraries	0	0	0.0
Parking	27,496	69	2.9
Parks and Recreation	110,390	276	11.7
Police Protection	137,044	343	14.5
Public Welfare	1,381	3	0.1
Sewerage	2,712	7	0.3
Solid Waste Management	21,012	53	2.2
Veterans' Services	0	0	0.0
Liquor Store	0	0	0.0
Utility	162	< 1	< 0.1
Employee Retirement	203,372	509	21.5

Source: U.S Census Bureau, State & Local Government Finances 2012

DEMOGRAPHICS

Population Growth

Area	1990 Census	2000 Census	2010 Census	Population Growth (%)	
				1990-2000	2000-2010
City	358,843	362,470	399,457	1.0	10.2
MSA[1]	4,056,100	5,007,564	5,564,635	23.5	11.1
U.S.	248,709,873	281,421,906	308,745,538	13.2	9.7

Note: (1) Figures cover the Miami-Fort Lauderdale-Pompano Beach, FL Metropolitan Statistical Area—see Appendix B for areas included
Source: U.S. Census Bureau, Census 1990, 2000, 2010

Household Size

Area	Persons in Household (%)							Average Household Size
	One	Two	Three	Four	Five	Six	Seven or More	
City	36.5	30.3	15.4	10.3	4.2	1.8	1.4	2.66
MSA[1]	29.1	32.1	16.3	13.3	5.7	2.1	1.3	2.81
U.S.	27.7	33.6	15.7	13.1	6.0	2.3	1.5	2.64

Note: (1) Figures cover the Miami-Fort Lauderdale-West Palm Beach, FL Metropolitan Statistical Area—see Appendix B for areas included
Source: U.S. Census Bureau, 2011-2013 American Community Survey 3-Year Estimates

Race

Area	White Alone[2] (%)	Black Alone[2] (%)	Asian Alone[2] (%)	AIAN[3] Alone[2] (%)	NHOPI[4] Alone[2] (%)	Other Race Alone[2] (%)	Two or More Races (%)
City	75.4	19.8	1.0	0.2	0.0	2.6	1.1
MSA[1]	71.7	21.3	2.4	0.2	0.0	2.5	1.9
U.S.	73.9	12.6	5.0	0.8	0.2	4.7	2.9

Note: (1) Figures cover the Miami-Fort Lauderdale-West Palm Beach, FL Metropolitan Statistical Area—see Appendix B for areas included; (2) Alone is defined as not being in combination with one or more other races; (3) American Indian and Alaska Native; (4) Native Hawaiian and Other Pacific Islander
Source: U.S. Census Bureau, 2011-2013 American Community Survey 3-Year Estimates

Hispanic or Latino Origin

Area	Total (%)	Mexican (%)	Puerto Rican (%)	Cuban (%)	Other (%)
City	70.3	2.0	3.3	34.4	30.6
MSA[1]	42.2	2.4	3.7	18.2	17.8
U.S.	16.9	10.8	1.6	0.6	3.8

Note: Persons of Hispanic or Latino origin can be of any race; (1) Figures cover the Miami-Fort Lauderdale-West Palm Beach, FL Metropolitan Statistical Area—see Appendix B for areas included
Source: U.S. Census Bureau, 2011-2013 American Community Survey 3-Year Estimates

Segregation

Type	Segregation Indices[1]				Percent Change		
	1990	2000	2010	2010 Rank[2]	1990-2000	1990-2010	2000-2010
Black/White	71.4	69.2	64.8	23	-2.3	-6.6	-4.3
Asian/White	26.8	33.3	34.2	80	6.4	7.3	0.9
Hispanic/White	32.5	59.0	57.4	8	26.5	24.8	-1.6

Note: All figures cover the Metropolitan Statistical Area—see Appendix B for areas included; Figures are based on an analysis of 1990, 2000, and 2010 Census Decennial Census tract data by William H. Frey, Brookings Institution and the University of Michigan Social Science Data Analysis Network. In this analysis all racial groups (whites, blacks, and asians) are non-Hispanic members of those races. Hispanics are shown as a separate category;
(1) Segregation Indices are Dissimilarity Indices that measure the degree to which the minority group is distributed differently than whites across census tracts. They range from 0 (complete integration) to 100 (complete segregation) where the value indicates the percentage of the minority group that needs to move to be distributed exactly like whites; (2) Ranges from 1 (most segregated) to 102 (least segregated); n/a not available.
Source: www.CensusScope.org

Ancestry

Area	German	Irish	English	American	Italian	Polish	French[2]	Scottish	Dutch
City	2.0	1.5	1.1	4.7	2.3	0.8	0.8	0.3	0.3
MSA[1]	5.2	5.1	3.3	6.1	5.4	2.2	1.4	0.7	0.5
U.S.	14.9	10.8	8.0	7.4	5.5	3.0	2.7	1.7	1.4

Note: Figures are the percentage of the total population reporting a particular ancestry. The nine most commonly reported ancestries in the U.S. are shown. Figures include multiple ancestries (e.g. if a person reported being Irish and Italian, they were included in both columns); (1) Figures cover the Miami-Fort Lauderdale-West Palm Beach, FL Metropolitan Statistical Area—see Appendix B for areas included; (2) Excludes Basque
Source: U.S. Census Bureau, 2011-2013 American Community Survey 3-Year Estimates

Foreign-Born Population

Area	Percent of Population Born in								
	Any Foreign Country	Mexico	Asia	Europe	Carribean	South America	Central America[2]	Africa	Canada
City	57.0	1.0	1.0	1.7	32.7	7.8	12.2	0.2	0.2
MSA[1]	38.5	1.1	2.0	2.3	20.4	7.6	4.2	0.4	0.6
U.S.	13.0	3.7	3.8	1.5	1.2	0.9	1.0	0.6	0.3

Note: (1) Figures cover the Miami-Fort Lauderdale-West Palm Beach, FL Metropolitan Statistical Area—see Appendix B for areas included; (2) Excludes Mexico.
Source: U.S. Census Bureau, 2011-2013 American Community Survey 3-Year Estimates

Marital Status

Area	Never Married	Now Married[2]	Separated	Widowed	Divorced
City	41.0	34.2	4.6	6.6	13.6
MSA[1]	34.3	43.0	3.1	6.9	12.7
U.S.	32.7	48.1	2.2	6.0	11.0

Note: Figures are percentages and cover the population 15 years of age and older; (1) Figures cover the Miami-Fort Lauderdale-West Palm Beach, FL Metropolitan Statistical Area—see Appendix B for areas included; (2) Excludes separated
Source: U.S. Census Bureau, 2011-2013 American Community Survey 3-Year Estimates

Disability Status

Area	All Ages	Under 18 Years Old	18 to 64 Years Old	65 Years and Over
City	12.4	3.1	8.8	38.8
MSA[1]	10.9	2.9	7.5	34.6
U.S.	12.3	4.1	10.2	36.3

Note: Figures show percent of the civilian noninstitutionalized population that reported having a disability. Disability status is determined from from six types of difficulty: vision, hearing, cognitive, ambulatory, self-care, and independent living. For children under 5 years old, hearing and vision difficulty are used to determine disability status. For children between the ages of 5 and 14, disability status is determined from hearing, vision, cognitive, ambulatory, and self-care difficulties. For people aged 15 years and older, they are considered to have a disability if they have difficulty with any one of the six difficulty types; (1) Figures cover the Miami-Fort Lauderdale-West Palm Beach, FL Metropolitan Statistical Area—see Appendix B for areas included.
Source: U.S. Census Bureau, 2011-2013 American Community Survey 3-Year Estimates

Age

Area	Percent of Population									Median Age
	Under Age 5	Age 5–19	Age 20–34	Age 35–44	Age 45–54	Age 55–64	Age 65–74	Age 75–84	Age 85+	
City	6.3	14.4	23.2	14.8	14.2	11.2	7.9	5.5	2.5	39.0
MSA[1]	5.7	17.8	19.6	13.6	14.9	11.9	8.3	5.5	2.6	40.2
U.S.	6.4	19.9	20.7	12.9	14.1	12.3	7.6	4.2	1.9	37.4

Note: (1) Figures cover the Miami-Fort Lauderdale-West Palm Beach, FL Metropolitan Statistical Area—see Appendix B for areas included
Source: U.S. Census Bureau, 2011-2013 American Community Survey 3-Year Estimates

Gender

Area	Males	Females	Males per 100 Females
City	207,228	206,916	100.2
MSA[1]	2,796,261	2,963,665	94.4
U.S.	154,451,010	159,410,713	96.9

Note: (1) Figures cover the Miami-Fort Lauderdale-West Palm Beach, FL Metropolitan Statistical Area—see Appendix B for areas included
Source: U.S. Census Bureau, 2011-2013 American Community Survey 3-Year Estimates

Religious Groups by Family

Area	Catholic	Baptist	Non-Den.	Methodist[2]	Lutheran	LDS[3]	Pente-costal	Presby-terian[4]	Muslim[5]	Judaism
MSA[1]	18.6	5.4	4.2	1.3	0.5	0.5	1.8	0.7	0.9	1.6
U.S.	19.1	9.3	4.0	4.0	2.3	2.0	1.9	1.6	0.8	0.7

Note: Figures are the number of adherents as a percentage of the total population; (1) Figures cover the Miami-Fort Lauderdale-Pompano Beach, FL Metropolitan Statistical Area—see Appendix B for areas included; (2) Methodist/Pietist; (3) Latter Day Saints; (4) Reformed; (5) Figures are estimates
Source: Association of Statisticians of American Religious Bodies, 2010 U.S. Religion Census: Religious Congregations & Membership Study

Religious Groups by Tradition

Area	Catholic	Evangelical Protestant	Mainline Protestant	Other Tradition	Black Protestant	Orthodox
MSA[1]	18.6	11.4	2.5	3.5	1.7	0.3
U.S.	19.1	16.2	7.3	4.3	1.6	0.3

Note: Figures are the number of adherents as a percentage of the total population; (1) Figures cover the Miami-Fort Lauderdale-Pompano Beach, FL Metropolitan Statistical Area—see Appendix B for areas included
Source: Association of Statisticians of American Religious Bodies, 2010 U.S. Religion Census: Religious Congregations & Membership Study

ECONOMY

Gross Metropolitan Product

Area	2012	2013	2014	2015	Rank[2]
MSA[1]	274.1	284.9	298.8	315.6	11

Note: Figures are in billions of dollars; (1) Figures cover the Miami-Fort Lauderdale-West Palm Beach, FL Metropolitan Statistical Area—see Appendix B for areas included; (2) Rank is based on 2015 data and ranges from 1 to 363
Source: The U.S. Conference of Mayors, U.S. Metro Economies: GMP and Employment 2013-2015, June 2014

Economic Growth

Area	2010-12 (%)	2013 (%)	2014 (%)	2015 (%)	Rank[2]
MSA[1]	2.4	2.7	3.2	3.6	61
U.S.	2.1	2.0	2.3	3.2	–

Note: Figures are real gross metropolitan product (GMP) growth rates and represent annual average percent change; (1) Figures cover the Miami-Fort Lauderdale-West Palm Beach, FL Metropolitan Statistical Area—see Appendix B for areas included; (2) Rank is based on 2015 data and ranges from 1 to 363
Source: The U.S. Conference of Mayors, U.S. Metro Economies: GMP and Employment 2013-2015, June 2014

Metropolitan Area Exports

Area	2008	2009	2010	2011	2012	2013	Rank[2]
MSA[1]	33,411.5	31,175.0	35,866.9	43,129.9	47,858.7	41,771.5	7

Note: Figures are in millions of dollars; (1) Figures cover the Miami-Fort Lauderdale-West Palm Beach, FL Metropolitan Statistical Area—see Appendix B for areas included; (2) Rank is based on 2013 data and ranges from 1 to 387
Source: U.S. Department of Commerce, International Trade Administration, Office of Trade & Industry Information, Manufacturing & Services, data extracted April 3, 2015

Building Permits

Area	Single-Family			Multi-Family			Total		
	2013	2014	Pct. Chg.	2013	2014	Pct. Chg.	2013	2014	Pct. Chg.
City	115	72	-37.4	4,371	3,714	-15.0	4,486	3,786	-15.6
MSA[1]	6,369	5,791	-9.1	13,552	9,468	-30.1	19,921	15,259	-23.4
U.S.	620,802	634,597	2.2	370,020	411,766	11.3	990,822	1,046,363	5.6

Note: (1) Figures cover the Miami-Fort Lauderdale-West Palm Beach, FL Metropolitan Statistical Area—see Appendix B for areas included; Figures represent new, privately-owned housing units authorized (unadjusted data); All permit data are based on estimates with imputation.
Source: U.S. Census Bureau, Manufacturing, Mining, and Construction Statistics, Building Permits, 2013, 2014

Bankruptcy Filings

Area	Business Filings			Nonbusiness Filings		
	2013	2014	% Chg.	2013	2014	% Chg.
Miami-Dade County	379	266	-29.8	16,145	14,486	-10.3
U.S.	33,212	26,983	-18.8	1,038,720	909,812	-12.4

Note: Business filings include Chapter 7, Chapter 11, Chapter 12, and Chapter 13; Nonbusiness filings include Chapter 7, Chapter 11, and Chapter 13
Source: Administrative Office of the U.S. Courts, Business and Nonbusiness Bankruptcy, County Cases Commenced by Chapter of the Bankruptcy Code, During the 12- Month Period Ending December 31, 2013 and Business and Nonbusiness Bankruptcy, County Cases Commenced by Chapter of the Bankruptcy Code, During the 12- Month Period Ending December 31, 2014

Housing Vacancy Rates

Area	Gross Vacancy Rate[2] (%)			Year-Round Vacancy Rate[3] (%)			Rental Vacancy Rate[4] (%)			Homeowner Vacancy Rate[5] (%)		
	2012	2013	2014	2012	2013	2014	2012	2013	2014	2012	2013	2014
MSA[1]	20.1	20.2	19.6	10.1	10.3	10.4	8.2	6.7	7.0	0.9	1.7	1.8
U.S.	13.8	13.6	13.4	10.8	10.7	10.4	8.7	8.3	7.6	2.0	2.0	1.9

Note: (1) Figures cover the Miami-Fort Lauderdale-West Palm Beach, FL Metropolitan Statistical Area—see Appendix B for areas included; (2) The percentage of the total housing inventory that is vacant; (3) The percentage of the housing inventory (excluding seasonal units) that is year-round vacant; (4) The percentage of rental inventory that is vacant for rent; (5) The percentage of homeowner inventory that is vacant for sale
Source: U.S. Census Bureau, Housing Vacancies and Homeownership Annual Statistics: 2014

INCOME

Income

Area	Per Capita ($)	Median Household ($)	Average Household ($)
City	21,416	30,126	52,271
MSA[1]	26,619	46,982	70,524
U.S.	27,884	52,176	72,897

Note: (1) Figures cover the Miami-Fort Lauderdale-West Palm Beach, FL Metropolitan Statistical Area—see Appendix B for areas included
Source: U.S. Census Bureau, 2011-2013 American Community Survey 3-Year Estimates

Household Income Distribution

Area	Percent of Households Earning							
	Under $15,000	$15,000 -24,999	$25,000 -34,999	$35,000 -49,999	$50,000 -74,999	$75,000 -99,000	$100,000 -149,999	$150,000 and up
City	26.9	16.4	12.5	12.8	12.5	6.3	6.6	6.0
MSA[1]	14.9	12.2	11.1	14.1	17.2	10.4	11.1	9.0
U.S.	13.0	10.9	10.3	13.6	17.9	11.9	12.7	9.6

Note: (1) Figures cover the Miami-Fort Lauderdale-West Palm Beach, FL Metropolitan Statistical Area—see Appendix B for areas included
Source: U.S. Census Bureau, 2011-2013 American Community Survey 3-Year Estimates

Poverty Rate

Area	All Ages	Under 18 Years Old	18 to 64 Years Old	65 Years and Over
City	30.3	44.9	25.8	31.8
MSA[1]	17.7	24.6	16.0	15.2
U.S.	15.9	22.4	14.8	9.5

Note: Figures are percentage of people whose income during the past 12 months was below the poverty level; (1) Figures cover the Miami-Fort Lauderdale-West Palm Beach, FL Metropolitan Statistical Area—see Appendix B for areas included
Source: U.S. Census Bureau, 2011-2013 American Community Survey 3-Year Estimates

EMPLOYMENT

Labor Force and Employment

Area	Civilian Labor Force			Workers Employed		
	Dec. 2013	Dec. 2014	% Chg.	Dec. 2013	Dec. 2014	% Chg.
City	204,318	209,288	2.4	190,542	196,787	3.3
MD[1]	1,292,935	1,322,890	2.3	1,205,792	1,245,316	3.3
U.S.	154,408,000	155,521,000	0.7	144,423,000	147,190,000	1.9

Note: Data is not seasonally adjusted and covers workers 16 years of age and older; (1) Figures cover the Miami-Miami Beach-Kendall, FL Metropolitan Division—see Appendix B for areas included
Source: Bureau of Labor Statistics, Local Area Unemployment Statistics

Unemployment Rate

Area	2014											
	Jan.	Feb.	Mar.	Apr.	May	Jun.	Jul.	Aug.	Sep.	Oct.	Nov.	Dec.
City	6.9	7.3	7.7	7.3	7.4	7.1	7.3	7.7	7.2	6.5	6.0	6.0
MD[1]	6.9	7.1	7.5	6.9	7.1	6.9	7.1	7.3	6.8	6.3	5.8	5.9
U.S.	7.0	7.0	6.8	5.9	6.1	6.3	6.5	6.3	5.7	5.5	5.5	5.4

Note: Data is not seasonally adjusted and covers workers 16 years of age and older; (1) Figures cover the Miami-Miami Beach-Kendall, FL Metropolitan Division—see Appendix B for areas included
Source: Bureau of Labor Statistics, Local Area Unemployment Statistics

Employment by Occupation

Occupation Classification	City (%)	MSA[1] (%)	U.S. (%)
Management, Business, Science, and Arts	28.0	33.2	36.2
Natural Resources, Construction, and Maintenance	11.1	8.7	9.0
Production, Transportation, and Material Moving	10.9	8.9	12.1
Sales and Office	24.7	28.2	24.4
Service	25.3	21.1	18.3

Note: Figures cover employed civilians 16 years of age and older; (1) Figures cover the Miami-Fort Lauderdale-West Palm Beach, FL Metropolitan Statistical Area—see Appendix B for areas included
Source: U.S. Census Bureau, 2011-2013 American Community Survey 3-Year Estimates

Employment by Industry

Sector	MD[1] Number of Employees	MD[1] Percent of Total	U.S. Percent of Total
Construction	37,100	3.3	4.4
Education and Health Services	172,900	15.4	15.5
Financial Activities	77,800	6.9	5.7
Government	139,500	12.5	15.8
Information	19,300	1.7	2.0
Leisure and Hospitality	133,600	11.9	10.3
Manufacturing	37,800	3.4	8.7
Mining and Logging	400	<0.1	0.6
Other Services	50,500	4.5	4.0
Professional and Business Services	158,000	14.1	13.8
Retail Trade	151,000	13.5	11.4
Transportation, Warehousing, and Utilities	67,400	6.0	3.9
Wholesale Trade	74,300	6.6	4.2

Note: Figures are non-farm employment as of December 2014. Figures are not seasonally adjusted and include workers 16 years of age and older; (1) Figures cover the Miami-Miami Beach-Kendall, FL Metropolitan Division—see Appendix B for areas included
Source: Bureau of Labor Statistics, Current Employment Statistics, Employment, Hours, and Earnings

Occupations with Greatest Projected Employment Growth: 2012 – 2022

Occupation[1]	2012 Employment	2022 Projected Employment	Numeric Employment Change	Percent Employment Change
Retail Salespersons	326,380	380,120	53,740	16.5
Combined Food Preparation and Serving Workers, Including Fast Food	196,980	237,340	40,360	20.5
Customer Service Representatives	191,210	228,620	37,410	19.6
Registered Nurses	164,020	201,140	37,120	22.6
Waiters and Waitresses	191,370	227,810	36,440	19.0
Office Clerks, General	142,710	170,300	27,590	19.3
Cashiers	206,660	230,190	23,530	11.4
Landscaping and Groundskeeping Workers	92,510	115,540	23,030	24.9
Receptionists and Information Clerks	75,780	95,680	19,900	26.2
Nursing Assistants	86,990	106,200	19,210	22.1

Note: Projections cover Florida; (1) Sorted by numeric employment change
Source: www.projectionscentral.com, State Occupational Projections, 2012–2022 Long-Term Projections

Fastest Growing Occupations: 2012 – 2022

Occupation[1]	2012 Employment	2022 Projected Employment	Numeric Employment Change	Percent Employment Change
Helpers—Carpenters	1,280	2,450	1,170	90.7
Helpers—Brickmasons, Blockmasons, Stonemasons, and Tile and Marble Setters	1,050	1,890	840	79.5
Biomedical Engineers	760	1,300	540	70.7
Reinforcing Iron and Rebar Workers	520	870	350	67.5
Glaziers	2,890	4,710	1,820	62.8
Solar Photovoltaic Installers	170	270	100	58.7
Brickmasons and Blockmasons	2,820	4,430	1,610	57.1
Stonemasons	450	710	260	56.4
Helpers—Pipelayers, Plumbers, Pipefitters, and Steamfitters	2,420	3,750	1,330	54.8
Cement Masons and Concrete Finishers	10,390	16,050	5,660	54.4

Note: Projections cover Florida; (1) Sorted by percent employment change and excludes occupations with numeric employment change less than 100
Source: www.projectionscentral.com, State Occupational Projections, 2012–2022 Long-Term Projections

Average Wages

Occupation	$/Hr.	Occupation	$/Hr.
Accountants and Auditors	33.67	Maids and Housekeeping Cleaners	9.97
Automotive Mechanics	17.39	Maintenance and Repair Workers	15.64
Bookkeepers	17.29	Marketing Managers	52.20
Carpenters	16.85	Nuclear Medicine Technologists	35.69
Cashiers	9.44	Nurses, Licensed Practical	20.67
Clerks, General Office	13.81	Nurses, Registered	30.72
Clerks, Receptionists/Information	12.67	Nursing Assistants	11.29
Clerks, Shipping/Receiving	13.34	Packers and Packagers, Hand	9.44
Computer Programmers	45.10	Physical Therapists	34.48
Computer Systems Analysts	48.37	Postal Service Mail Carriers	25.43
Computer User Support Specialists	24.29	Real Estate Brokers	n/a
Cooks, Restaurant	11.87	Retail Salespersons	11.35
Dentists	77.55	Sales Reps., Exc. Tech./Scientific	26.12
Electrical Engineers	43.09	Sales Reps., Tech./Scientific	34.36
Electricians	25.09	Secretaries, Exc. Legal/Med./Exec.	14.84
Financial Managers	66.96	Security Guards	10.96
First-Line Supervisors/Managers, Sales	20.92	Surgeons	n/a
Food Preparation Workers	10.53	Teacher Assistants	11.60
General and Operations Managers	65.16	Teachers, Elementary School	24.60
Hairdressers/Cosmetologists	12.07	Teachers, Secondary School	28.60
Internists	95.49	Telemarketers	11.87
Janitors and Cleaners	10.25	Truck Drivers, Heavy/Tractor-Trailer	17.57
Landscaping/Groundskeeping Workers	11.04	Truck Drivers, Light/Delivery Svcs.	14.33
Lawyers	71.66	Waiters and Waitresses	10.36

Note: Wage data covers the Miami-Miami Beach-Kendall, FL Metropolitan Division—see Appendix B for areas included; Hourly wages for elementary/secondary school teachers and teacher assistants were calculated by the editors from annual wage data assuming a 40 hour work week; n/a not available.
Source: Bureau of Labor Statistics, Metro Area Occupational Employment and Wage Estimates, May 2014

TAXES

State Corporate Income Tax Rates

State	Tax Rate (%)	Income Brackets ($)	Num. of Brackets	Financial Institution Tax Rate (%)[a]	Federal Income Tax Ded.
Florida	5.5 (f)	Flat rate	1	5.5 (f)	No

Note: Tax rates as of January 1, 2015; (a) Rates listed are the corporate income tax rate applied to financial institutions or excise taxes based on income. Some states have other taxes based upon the value of deposits or shares; (f) An exemption of $50,000 is allowed. Florida's Alternative Minimum Tax rate is 3.3%.
Source: Federation of Tax Administrators, "State Corporate Income Tax Rates, 2015"

State Individual Income Tax Rates

State	Tax Rate (%)	Income Brackets ($)	Num. of Brackets	Personal Exempt. ($)[1]		Fed. Inc. Tax Ded.
				Single	Dependents	
Florida	None	–	–	–	–	–

Note: Tax rates as of January 1, 2015; Local- and county-level taxes are not included; n/a not applicable; (1) Married joint filers generally receive double the single exemption
Source: Federation of Tax Administrators, "State Individual Income Tax Rates, 2015"

Various State and Local Tax Rates

State	State and Local Sales and Use (%)	State Sales and Use (%)	Gasoline[1] (¢/gal.)	Cigarette[2] ($/pack)	Spirits[3] ($/gal.)	Wine[4] ($/gal.)	Beer[5] ($/gal.)
Florida	7.0	6.0	36.42	1.339	6.50 (f)	2.25	0.48 (p)

Note: All tax rates as of January 1, 2015; (1) The American Petroleum Institute has developed a methodology for determining the average tax rate on a gallon of fuel. Rates may include any of the following: excise taxes, environmental fees, storage tank fees, other fees or taxes, general sales tax, and local taxes. In states where gasoline is subject to the general sales tax, or where the fuel tax is based on the average sale price, the average rate determined by API is sensitive to changes in the price of gasoline. States that fully or partially apply general sales taxes to gasoline: CA, CO, GA, IL, IN, MI, NY; (2) The federal excise tax of $1.0066 per pack and local taxes are not included; (3) Rates are those applicable to off-premise sales of 40% alcohol by volume (a.b.v.) distilled spirits in 750ml containers. Local excise taxes are excluded; (4) Rates are those applicable to off-premise sales of 11% a.b.v. non-carbonated wine in 750ml containers; (5) Rates are those applicable to off-premise sales of 4.7% a.b.v. beer in 12 ounce containers; (f) Different rates are also applicable according to alcohol content, place of production, size of container, or place purchased (on- or off-premise or onboard airlines); (p) Local excise taxes are excluded.
Source: Tax Foundation, 2015 Facts & Figures: How Does Your State Compare?

State Business Tax Climate Index Rankings

State	Overall Rank	Corporate Tax Index Rank	Individual Income Tax Index Rank	Sales Tax Index Rank	Unemployment Insurance Tax Index Rank	Property Tax Index Rank
Florida	5	14	1	12	3	16

Note: The index is a measure of how each state's tax laws affect economic performance. The lower the rank, the more favorable a state's tax system is for business. States without a given tax are given a ranking of 1. The scores/rankings for the District of Columbia do not affect other states. The 2015 index represents the tax climate as of July 1, 2014.
Source: Tax Foundation, State Business Tax Climate Index 2015

COMMERCIAL REAL ESTATE

Office Market

Market Area	Inventory (sq. ft.)	Vacancy Rate (%)	Under Construction (sq. ft.)	YTD Net Absorption (sq. ft.)	Total Average Asking Rent ($/sq. ft./year)
Miami	46,985,645	14.9	230,083	805,917	30.79
National	4,745,108,508	14.3	71,190,461	51,084,126	27.40

Source: Newmark Grubb Knight Frank, National Office Market Report, 4th Quarter 2014

Industrial/Warehouse/R&D Market

Market Area	Inventory (sq. ft.)	Vacancy Rate (%)	Under Construction (sq. ft.)	YTD Net Absorption (sq. ft.)	Total Average Asking Rent ($/sq. ft./year)
Miami	204,002,857	5.7	656,186	1,420,504	6.50
National	14,238,613,765	7.2	134,387,407	185,246,438	5.64

Source: Newmark Grubb Knight Frank, National Industrial Market Report, 4th Quarter 2014

COMMERCIAL UTILITIES

Typical Monthly Electric Bills

Area	Commercial Service ($/month)		Industrial Service ($/month)	
	1,500 kWh	40 kW demand 14,000 kWh	1,000 kW demand 200,000 kWh	50,000 kW demand 32,500,000 kWh
City	156	1,255	27,158	1,691,463
Average[1]	201	1,653	26,124	2,639,743

Note: Figures are based on annualized 2014 rates; (1) Average based on 180 utilities surveyed
Source: Edison Electric Institute, Typical Bills and Average Rates Report, Summer 2014

TRANSPORTATION

Means of Transportation to Work

Area	Car/Truck/Van: Drove Alone	Car/Truck/Van: Car-pooled	Public Transportation: Bus	Public Transportation: Subway	Public Transportation: Railroad	Bicycle	Walked	Other Means	Worked at Home
City	68.9	9.6	10.4	0.7	0.3	0.9	4.7	1.2	3.3
MSA[1]	77.9	9.6	3.6	0.2	0.2	0.6	1.8	1.3	4.8
U.S.	76.4	9.6	2.6	1.8	0.6	0.6	2.8	1.3	4.3

Note: Figures are percentages and cover workers 16 years of age and older; (1) Figures cover the Miami-Fort Lauderdale-West Palm Beach, FL Metropolitan Statistical Area—see Appendix B for areas included
Source: U.S. Census Bureau, 2011-2013 American Community Survey 3-Year Estimates

Travel Time to Work

Area	Less Than 10 Minutes	10 to 19 Minutes	20 to 29 Minutes	30 to 44 Minutes	45 to 59 Minutes	60 to 89 Minutes	90 Minutes or More
City	7.1	26.6	27.0	25.8	7.2	4.4	2.0
MSA[1]	7.5	24.9	23.2	27.5	9.0	5.9	2.0
U.S.	13.3	29.7	20.9	20.2	7.7	5.7	2.6

Note: Figures are percentages and include workers 16 years old and over; (1) Figures cover the Miami-Fort Lauderdale-West Palm Beach, FL Metropolitan Statistical Area—see Appendix B for areas included
Source: U.S. Census Bureau, 2011-2013 American Community Survey 3-Year Estimates

Travel Time Index

Area	1985	1990	1995	2000	2005	2010	2011
Urban Area[1]	1.11	1.20	1.21	1.29	1.33	1.25	1.25
Average[2]	1.09	1.14	1.16	1.19	1.23	1.18	1.18

Note: Travel Time Index—the ratio of travel time in the peak period to the travel time at free-flow conditions. For example, a value of 1.30 indicates a 20-minute free-flow trip takes 26 minutes in the peak. Free-flow speeds (60 mph on freeways and 35 mph on principal arterials) are used as the comparison threshold; (1) Covers the Miami FL urban area; (2) average of 498 urban areas
Source: Texas Transportation Institute, Urban Mobility Report 2012, December 2012

Public Transportation

Agency Name / Mode of Transportation	Vehicles Operated in Maximum Service	Annual Unlinked Passenger Trips (in thous.)	Annual Passenger Miles (in thous.)
Miami-Dade Transit (MDT)			
Bus (directly operated)	692	78,500.8	414,639.9
Bus (purchased transportation)	7	392.1	27,661.3
Demand Response (purchased transportation)	336	1,706.9	21,753.9
Heavy Rail (directly operated)	78	21,198.7	155,169.1
Monorail and Automated Guideway (directly operated)	21	9,643.7	9,472.3
South Florida Regional Transportation Authority (TRI-Rail)			
Bus (purchased transportation)	21	921.6	3,617.8
Commuter Rail (purchased transportation)	40	4,201.0	116,122.4

Source: Federal Transit Administration, National Transit Database, 2013

Air Transportation

Airport Name and Code / Type of Service	Passenger Airlines[1]	Passenger Enplanements	Freight Carriers[2]	Freight (lbs.)
Miami International (MIA)				
Domestic service (U.S. carriers - 2014)	25	9,416,132	22	215,135,314
International service (U.S. carriers - 2013)	14	6,190,892	19	804,809,441

Note: (1) Includes all U.S.-based major, minor and commuter airlines that carried at least one passenger during the year; (2) Includes all U.S.-based airlines and freight carriers that transported at least one lb. of freight during the year.
Source: Bureau of Transportation Statistics, The Intermodal Transportation Database, Air Carriers: T-100 Domestic Market (U.S. Carriers), 2014; Bureau of Transportation Statistics, The Intermodal Transportation Database, Air Carriers: T-100 International Market (U.S. Carriers), 2013

Other Transportation Statistics

Major Highways:	I-95
Amtrak Service:	Yes
Major Waterways/Ports:	Port of Miami; Atlantic Intracoastal Waterway

Source: Amtrak.com; Google Maps

BUSINESSES

Major Business Headquarters

Company Name	Rankings	
	Fortune[1]	Forbes[2]
Lennar Corporation	431	-
Ryder System	406	-
Southern Wine & Spirits	-	28
World Fuel Services Corporation	71	-

Note: (1) Fortune 500—companies that produce a 10-K are ranked 1 to 500 based on 2013 revenue; (2) all private companies with at least $2 billion in annual revenue through the end of their most current fiscal year are ranked 1 to 221; companies listed are headquartered in the city; dashes indicate no ranking
Source: Fortune, "Fortune 500," June 16, 2014; Forbes, "America's Largest Private Companies," November 5, 2014

Fast-Growing Businesses

According to *Inc.*, Miami is home to eight of America's 500 fastest-growing private companies: **Showroom Logic** (#26); **SmackTom.com** (#125); **CareCloud** (#127); **3A/WorldWide** (#175); **Cinium Financial Services** (#265); **Whet Travel** (#288); **VSI Nearshore Outsourcing** (#295); **EveryMundo** (#309). Criteria: must be an independent, privately-held, for-profit, U.S. corporation, proprietorship or partnership; revenues must be at least $100,000 in 2010 and $2 million in 2013; must have four-year operating/sales history. Holding companies, regulated banks, and utilities were excluded. *Inc., "America's 500 Fastest-Growing Private Companies," September 2014*

According to *Fortune*, Miami is home to one of the 100 fastest-growing companies in the world: **Lennar** (#35). Companies were ranked by their revenue growth rate; their EPS growth rate; and their three-year annualized total return to investors for the period ending June 30, 2014. Criteria for inclusion: a company, foreign or domestic, must trade on a major U.S. stock exchange; must file quarterly reports with the SEC; must have a minimum market capitalization of $250 million; must have a stock price of at least $5 on June 30, 2014; must have been trading continuously since June 30, 2010; must have revenue and net income for the four quarters ended on or before April 30, 2014, of at least $50 million and $10 million, respectively; and must have posted a compound annual growth in revenue and earnings per share of at least 20% annually over the three years ending on or before April 30, 2014. Real estate investment trusts, limited-liability companies, limited parterships, business development companies, closed end investment firms, and companies that lost money in the quarter ending April 30, 2014 were excluded. *Fortune, "100 Fastest-Growing Companies," August 28, 2014*

According to Deloitte, Miami is home to two of North America's 500 fastest-growing high-technology companies: **OPKO Health** (#65); **Emerging Markets Communications** (#492). Companies are ranked by percentage growth in revenue over a five-year period. Criteria for inclusion: company must be headquartered within North America; must own proprietary intellectual property or proprietary technology that contributes to a significant portion of the company's operating revenue, or devote a significant proportion of revenues to research and development of technology; must have been in business for a minumum of five years with 2009 operating revenues of at least $50,000 USD/CD and 2013 operating revenues of at least $5 million USD/CD. *Deloitte Touche Tohmatsu, 2014 Technology Fast 500™*

Minority Business Opportunity

Miami is home to 57 companies which are on the *Hispanic Business* 500 list (500 largest U.S. Hispanic-owned companies based on 2012 revenue): **Brightstar Corp.** (#1); **The Related Group** (#4); **Quirch Foods** (#8); **First Equity Mortgage Bankers** (#27); **BMI Financial Group** (#31); **Precision Trading Corp.** (#40); **MCM** (#44); **El Dorado Furniture Corp.** (#45); **Headquarter Toyota** (#48); **Miami Automotive Retail** (#49); **Refricenter of Miami** (#59); **Machado Garcia Serra** (#72); **Metro Ford** (#89); **Transnational Foods** (#91); **Link Construction Group** (#92); **South Dade Automotive** (#94); **Century Metals & Supplies** (#103); **CSA Holdings** (#111); **John Keeler & Co.** (#120); **Softech International** (#121); **Everglades Steel, Medley Steel, Metallic Products** (#132); **Adonel Concrete Pumping & Finishing of S. Florida** (#139); **Solo Printing** (#142); **Ascendant Commercial Insurance Co.** (#144); **Metric Engineering** (#146);

Gancedo Lumber Co. (#163); **The Intermarket Group** (#171); **Roach Busters Bug Killers of America** (#185); **Fru-Veg Marketing** (#189); **Express Travel** (#192); **Original Impressions** (#201); **Protec** (#206); **Nital Trading Co.** (#214); **Future Force Personnel** (#235); **Vina & Sons Food Distributor Corp.** (#237); **Bermello, Ajamil & Partners** (#246); **AZF Automotive Group** (#286); **X-EETO** (#287); **American Fasteners Corp.** (#294); **Interamerican Bank** (#304); **EnviroWaste Services Group** (#308); **Republica** (#311); **EYMAQ** (#324); **Wendium of Florida** (#327); **Hispanic Group** (#329); **Farma International** (#334); **Cherokee Enterprises** (#343); **Amtec Sales** (#351); **South Florida Trading Corp.** (#362); **T&S Roofing Systems** (#368); **F.R. Aleman & Associates** (#396); **A-1 Property Services Group** (#404); **Gomez Ossa International** (#433); **Honshy Electric Co.** (#434); **Hernandez & Tacoronte PA** (#447); **Decorative Sales Assoc.** (#484); **Dynamic Turbo** (#486). Companies included must show at least 51 percent ownership by Hispanic U.S. citizens, and must maintain headquarters in one of the 50 states or Washington, D.C. *Hispanic Business, "Hispanic Business 500," June 20, 2013*

Miami is home to 12 companies which are on the *Hispanic Business* Fastest-Growing 100 list (greatest sales growth from 2008 to 2012): **Fru-Veg Marketing** (#10); **A-1 Property Services Group** (#13); **Miami Automotive Retail** (#39); **First Equity Mortgage Bankers** (#42); **Link Construction Group** (#43); **Nital Trading Co.** (#56); **Transnational Foods** (#60); **MCM** (#73); **South Florida Trading Corp.** (#84); **Roach Busters Bug Killers of America** (#90); **BMI Financial Group** (#93); **EYMAQ** (#100). Companies included must show at least 51 percent ownership by Hispanic U.S. citizens, and must maintain headquarters in one of the 50 states or Washington, D.C. In addition, companies must have minimum revenues of $200,000 for calendar year 2008. *Hispanic Business, June 20, 2013*

Minority- and Women-Owned Businesses

Group	All Firms		Firms with Paid Employees			
	Firms	Sales ($000)	Firms	Sales ($000)	Employees	Payroll ($000)
Asian	1,738	629,557	579	586,220	2,895	58,879
Black	9,448	492,059	588	337,832	4,470	75,101
Hispanic	53,234	11,975,646	6,317	10,407,324	35,426	1,127,862
Women	24,414	2,443,049	2,705	1,920,188	14,331	420,472
All Firms	85,143	65,730,894	15,127	62,998,520	321,378	15,801,777

Note: Figures cover firms located in the city; minority- and women-owned business are defined as firms in which the corresponding group own 51% or more of the stock or equity of the company
Source: U.S. Census Bureau, 2007 Economic Census, Survey of Business Owners (2012 Survey of Business Owners data will be released starting in June 2015)

HOTELS & CONVENTION CENTERS

Hotels/Motels

Area	5 Star		4 Star		3 Star		2 Star		1 Star		Not Rated	
	Num.	Pct.[3]	Num.	Pct.[3]	Num.	Pct.[3]	Num.	Pct.[3]	Num.	Pct.[3]	Num.	Pct.[3]
City[1]	16	3.5	103	22.3	194	42.0	112	24.2	8	1.7	29	6.3
Total[2]	166	0.9	1,264	7.0	5,718	31.8	9,340	52.0	411	2.3	1,070	6.0

Note: (1) Figures cover Miami and vicinity; (2) Figures cover all 100 cities in this book; (3) Percentage of hotels which have a given star rating; Star ratings are determined by expedia.com and offer an indication of the general quality of a particular hotel.
Source: expedia.com, April 2, 2015

The Miami-Miami Beach-Kendall, FL metro area is home to four of the best hotels in the U.S. according to *Travel & Leisure*: **EPIC, Miami - A Kimpton Hotel; JW Marriott Marquis Miami; Ritz-Carlton, Key Biscayne; Mandarin Oriental, Miami**. Criteria: service; location; rooms; food; and value. The list includes the top 236 hotels in the U.S. *Travel & Leisure, "T+L 500, The World's Best Hotels 2015"*

The Miami-Miami Beach-Kendall, FL metro area is home to one of the best hotels in the world according to *Condé Nast Traveler*: **Metropolitan by COMO, Miami Beach**. The selections are based on editors' picks. The list includes the top 25 hotels in the U.S. *Condé Nast Traveler, "Gold List 2015, The Top Hotels in the World"*

Major Convention Centers

Name	Overall Space (sq. ft.)	Exhibit Space (sq. ft.)	Meeting Space (sq. ft.)	Meeting Rooms
Coconut Grove Convention Center	n/a	150,000	n/a	n/a
Miami Beach Convention Center	1,000,000	500,000	100,000	70

Note: Table includes convention centers located in the Miami-Fort Lauderdale-West Palm Beach, FL metro area; n/a not available
Source: Original research

Living Environment

COST OF LIVING

Cost of Living Index

Composite Index	Groceries	Housing	Utilities	Trans-portation	Health Care	Misc. Goods/ Services
111.1	108.3	125.0	97.9	111.1	103.3	105.4

Note: The Cost of Living Index measures regional differences in the cost of consumer goods and services, excluding taxes and non-consumer expenditures, for professional and managerial households in the top income quintile. It is based on more than 50,000 prices covering almost 60 different items for which prices are collected three times a year by chambers of commerce, economic development organizations or university applied economic centers in each participating urban area. The numbers shown should be read as a percentage above or below the national average of 100. For example, a value of 115.4 in the groceries column indicates that grocery prices are 15.4% higher than the national average. Small differences in the index numbers should not be interpreted as significant; Figures cover the Miami-Dade County FL urban area.
Source: The Council for Community and Economic Research, ACCRA Cost of Living Index, 2014

Grocery Prices

Area[1]	T-Bone Steak ($/pound)	Frying Chicken ($/pound)	Whole Milk ($/half gal.)	Eggs ($/dozen)	Orange Juice ($/64 oz.)	Coffee ($/11.5 oz.)
City[2]	10.50	1.62	2.82	2.17	3.26	3.42
Avg.	10.40	1.37	2.40	1.99	3.46	4.27
Min.	8.48	0.93	1.37	1.30	2.83	2.99
Max.	14.20	2.44	3.62	4.02	6.42	6.96

Note: (1) Values for the local area are compared with the average, minimum and maximum values for all 308 areas in the Cost of Living Index; (2) Figures cover the Miami-Dade County FL urban area; **T-Bone Steak** *(price per pound);* **Frying Chicken** *(price per pound, whole fryer);* **Whole Milk** *(half gallon carton);* **Eggs** *(price per dozen, Grade A, large);* **Orange Juice** *(64 oz. Tropicana or Florida Natural);* **Coffee** *(11.5 oz. can, vacuum-packed, Maxwell House, Hills Bros, or Folgers).*
Source: The Council for Community and Economic Research, ACCRA Cost of Living Index, 2014

Housing and Utility Costs

Area[1]	New Home Price ($)	Apartment Rent ($/month)	All Electric ($/month)	Part Electric ($/month)	Other Energy ($/month)	Telephone ($/month)
City[2]	357,091	1,300	164.00	-	-	27.70
Avg.	305,838	919	181.00	93.66	73.14	27.95
Min.	183,142	480	112.00	42.06	23.42	17.16
Max.	1,358,576	3,851	594.00	180.03	440.99	40.42

Note: (1) Values for the local area are compared with the average, minimum and maximum values for all 308 areas in the Cost of Living Index; (2) Figures cover the Miami-Dade County FL urban area; **New Home Price** *(2,400 sf living area, 8,000 sf lot, in urban area with full utilities);* **Apartment Rent** *(950 sf 2 bedroom/1.5 or 2 bath, unfurnished, excluding all utilities except water);* **All Electric** *(average monthly cost for an all-electric home);* **Part Electric** *(average monthly cost for a part-electric home);* **Other Energy** *(average monthly cost for natural gas, fuel oil, coal, wood, and any other forms of energy except electricity);* **Telephone** *(price includes basic monthly rate for a private residential line plus additional local usage charges incurred by a family of four).*
Source: The Council for Community and Economic Research, ACCRA Cost of Living Index, 2014

Health Care, Transportation, and Other Costs

Area[1]	Doctor ($/visit)	Dentist ($/visit)	Optometrist ($/visit)	Gasoline ($/gallon)	Beauty Salon ($/visit)	Men's Shirt ($)
City[2]	101.25	96.00	92.50	3.63	53.00	22.99
Avg.	102.86	87.89	97.66	3.44	34.37	26.74
Min.	67.47	65.78	51.18	3.00	17.43	12.79
Max.	173.50	150.14	235.00	4.33	64.28	49.50

Note: (1) Values for the local area are compared with the average, minimum and maximum values for all 308 areas in the Cost of Living Index; (2) Figures cover the Miami-Dade County FL urban area; **Doctor** *(general practitioners routine exam of an established patient);* **Dentist** *(adult teeth cleaning and periodic oral examination);* **Optometrist** *(full vision eye exam for established adult patient);* **Gasoline** *(one gallon regular unleaded, national brand, including all taxes, cash price at self-service pump if available);* **Beauty Salon** *(woman's shampoo, trim, and blow-dry);* **Men's Shirt** *(cotton/polyester dress shirt, pinpoint weave, long sleeves).*
Source: The Council for Community and Economic Research, ACCRA Cost of Living Index, 2014

HOUSING

House Price Index (HPI)

Area	National Ranking[2]	Quarterly Change (%)	One-Year Change (%)	Five-Year Change (%)
MD[1]	7	2.71	12.17	21.88
U.S.[3]	–	1.35	4.91	11.59

Note: The HPI is a weighted repeat sales index. It measures average price changes in repeat sales or refinancings on the same properties. This information is obtained by reviewing repeat mortgage transactions on single-family properties whose mortgages have been purchased or securitized by Fannie Mae or Freddie Mac in January 1975; (1) Miami-Miami Beach-Kendall Metropolitan Division—see Appendix B for areas included; (2) Rankings are based on annual percentage change for all metro areas containing at least 15,000 transactions over the last 10 years and ranges from 1 to 275; (3) figures based on a weighted average of Census Division estimates using a seasonally adjusted, purchase-only index; all figures are for the period ending December 31, 2014

Source: Federal Housing Finance Agency, House Price Index, February 26, 2015

Median Single-Family Home Prices

Area	2012	2013	2014p	Percent Change 2013 to 2014
MSA[1]	203.1	246.0	266.0	8.1
U.S. Average	177.2	197.4	209.0	5.9

Note: Figures are median sales prices of existing single-family homes in thousands of dollars; (p) preliminary; n/a not available; (1) Miami-Fort Lauderdale-West Palm Beach, FL Metropolitan Statistical Area—see Appendix B for areas included

Source: National Association of Realtors, Median Sales Price of Existing Single-Family Homes for Metropolitan Areas, 4th Quarter 2014

Qualifying Income Based on Median Sales Price of Existing Single-Family Homes

Area	With 5% Down ($)	With 10% Down ($)	With 20% Down ($)
MSA[1]	58,235	55,170	49,040
U.S. Average	45,863	43,449	38,621

Note: Figures are preliminary; Qualifying income is based on a mortgage rate of 4.0%. Monthly principal and interest payment is limited to 25% of income; n/a not available; (1) Miami-Fort Lauderdale-West Palm Beach, FL Metropolitan Statistical Area—see Appendix B for areas included

Source: National Association of Realtors, Qualifying Income Based on Median Sales Price of Existing Single-Family Homes for Metropolitan Areas, 4th Quarter 2014

Median Apartment Condo-Coop Home Prices

Area	2012	2013	2014p	Percent Change 2013 to 2014
MSA[1]	101.3	129.5	144.3	11.4
U.S. Average	173.7	194.9	205.1	5.2

Note: Figures are median sales prices of existing apartment condo-coop homes in thousands of dollars; (p) preliminary; n/a not available; (1) Miami-Fort Lauderdale-West Palm Beach, FL Metropolitan Statistical Area—see Appendix B for areas included

Source: National Association of Realtors, Median Sales Price of Existing Apartment Condo-Coop Homes for Metropolitan Areas, 4th Quarter 2014

Gross Monthly Rent

Area	Under $200	$200 -299	$300 -499	$500 -749	$750 -999	$1,000 -1,499	$1,500 and up	Median ($)
City	3.7	4.3	4.8	18.3	25.5	25.1	18.4	936
MSA[1]	1.6	2.2	2.9	9.9	23.2	38.0	22.3	1,113
U.S.	1.7	3.2	7.8	22.1	24.3	26.0	14.9	900

Note: Figures are percentages except for Median; Gross rent is the contract rent plus the estimated average monthly cost of utilities (electricity, gas, and water and sewer) and fuels (oil, coal, kerosene, wood, etc.) if these are paid by the renter (or paid for the renter by someone else); (1) Figures cover the Miami-Fort Lauderdale-West Palm Beach, FL Metropolitan Statistical Area—see Appendix B for areas included

Source: U.S. Census Bureau, 2011-2013 American Community Survey 3-Year Estimates

Homeownership Rate

Area	2007 (%)	2008 (%)	2009 (%)	2010 (%)	2011 (%)	2012 (%)	2013 (%)	2014 (%)
MSA[1]	66.6	66.0	67.1	63.8	64.2	61.8	60.1	58.8
U.S.	68.1	67.8	67.4	66.9	66.1	65.4	65.1	64.5

Note: (1) Figures cover the Miami-Fort Lauderdale-West Palm Beach, FL Metropolitan Statistical Area—see Appendix B for areas included
Source: U.S. Census Bureau, Housing Vacancies and Homeownership Annual Statistics: 2014

Year Housing Structure Built

Area	2010 or Later	2000 -2009	1990 -1999	1980 -1989	1970 -1979	1960 -1969	1950 -1959	1940 -1949	Before 1940	Median Year
City	1.2	20.1	5.9	7.7	13.1	10.0	16.1	15.3	10.5	1968
MSA[1]	0.5	14.1	14.8	20.0	21.9	12.8	10.4	3.2	2.3	1980
U.S.	0.9	15.0	13.9	13.8	15.8	11.0	10.9	5.4	13.3	1976

Note: Figures are percentages except for Median Year; (1) Figures cover the Miami-Fort Lauderdale-West Palm Beach, FL Metropolitan Statistical Area—see Appendix B for areas included
Source: U.S. Census Bureau, 2011-2013 American Community Survey 3-Year Estimates

HEALTH

Health Risk Data

Category	MSA[1] (%)	U.S. (%)
Adults aged 18–64 who have any kind of health care coverage	67.9	79.6
Adults who reported being in good or excellent health	81.0	83.1
Adults who are current smokers	13.2	19.6
Adults who are heavy drinkers[2]	4.6	6.1
Adults who are binge drinkers[3]	15.4	16.9
Adults who are overweight (BMI 25.0 - 29.9)	38.8	35.8
Adults who are obese (BMI 30.0 - 99.8)	23.1	27.6
Adults who participated in any physical activities in the past month	74.7	77.1
Adults 50+ who have ever had a sigmoidoscopy or colonoscopy	61.7	67.3
Women aged 40+ who have had a mammogram within the past two years	75.7	74.0
Men aged 40+ who have had a PSA test within the past two years	51.1	45.2
Adults aged 65+ who have had flu shot within the past year	53.0	60.1
Adults who always wear a seatbelt	92.8	93.8

Note: Data as of 2012 unless otherwise noted; (1) Figures cover the Miami-Fort Lauderdale-Miami Beach, FL Metropolitan Statistical Area—see Appendix B for areas included; (2) Heavy drinkers are classified as males having more than two drinks per day or females having more than one drink per day; (3) Binge drinkers are classified as males having five or more drinks on one occasion or females having four or more drinks on one occasion
Source: Centers for Disease Control and Prevention, Behaviorial Risk Factor Surveillance System, SMART: Selected Metropolitan/Micropolitan Area Risk Trends, 2012 (Note: the CDC has discontinued this dataset but will be releasing a replacement in late 2015)

Chronic Health Indicators

Category	MSA[1] (%)	U.S. (%)
Adults who have ever been told they had a heart attack	3.8	4.5
Adults who have ever been told they had a stroke	2.4	2.9
Adults who have been told they currently have asthma	5.3	8.9
Adults who have ever been told they have arthritis	21.4	25.7
Adults who have ever been told they have diabetes[2]	10.5	9.7
Adults who have ever been told they had skin cancer	5.9	5.7
Adults who have ever been told they had any other types of cancer	5.7	6.5
Adults who have ever been told they have COPD	6.2	6.2
Adults who have ever been told they have kidney disease	4.0	2.5
Adults who have ever been told they have a form of depression	13.4	18.0

Note: Data as of 2012 unless otherwise noted; (1) Figures cover the Miami-Fort Lauderdale-Miami Beach, FL Metropolitan Statistical Area—see Appendix B for areas included; (2) Figures do not include pregnancy-related, borderline, or pre-diabetes
Source: Centers for Disease Control and Prevention, Behaviorial Risk Factor Surveillance System, SMART: Selected Metropolitan/Micropolitan Area Risk Trends, 2012 (Note: the CDC has discontinued this dataset but will be releasing a replacement in late 2015)

Mortality Rates for the Top 10 Causes of Death in the U.S.

ICD-10[a] Sub-Chapter	ICD-10[a] Code	Age-Adjusted Mortality Rate[1] per 100,000 population	
		County[2]	U.S.
Malignant neoplasms	C00-C97	135.5	166.2
Ischaemic heart diseases	I20-I25	104.8	105.7
Other forms of heart disease	I30-I51	35.9	49.3
Chronic lower respiratory diseases	J40-J47	27.6	42.1
Organic, including symptomatic, mental disorders	F01-F09	30.5	38.1
Cerebrovascular diseases	I60-I69	27.9	37.0
Other external causes of accidental injury	W00-X59	13.6	26.9
Other degenerative diseases of the nervous system	G30-G31	28.9	25.6
Diabetes mellitus	E10-E14	20.3	21.3
Hypertensive diseases	I10-I15	20.0	19.4

Note: (a) ICD-10 = International Classification of Diseases 10th Revision; (1) Mortality rates are a three year average covering 2011-2013; (2) Figures cover Miami-Dade County
Source: Centers for Disease Control and Prevention, National Center for Health Statistics. Compressed Mortality File 1999-2013 on CDC WONDER Online Database, released October 2014. Data are compiled from the Compressed Mortality File 1999-2013, Series 20 No. 2S, 2014.

Mortality Rates for Selected Causes of Death

ICD-10[a] Sub-Chapter	ICD-10[a] Code	Age-Adjusted Mortality Rate[1] per 100,000 population	
		County[2]	U.S.
Assault	X85-Y09	8.7	5.2
Diseases of the liver	K70-K76	10.2	13.2
Human immunodeficiency virus (HIV) disease	B20-B24	8.0	2.2
Influenza and pneumonia	J09-J18	8.3	15.4
Intentional self-harm	X60-X84	8.0	12.5
Malnutrition	E40-E46	0.3	0.9
Obesity and other hyperalimentation	E65-E68	1.5	1.8
Renal failure	N17-N19	11.8	13.1
Transport accidents	V01-V99	9.9	11.7
Viral hepatitis	B15-B19	1.9	2.2

Note: (a) ICD-10 = International Classification of Diseases 10th Revision; (1) Mortality rates are a three year average covering 2011-2013; (2) Figures cover Miami-Dade County
Source: Centers for Disease Control and Prevention, National Center for Health Statistics. Compressed Mortality File 1999-2013 on CDC WONDER Online Database, released October 2014. Data are compiled from the Compressed Mortality File 1999-2013, Series 20 No. 2S, 2014.

Health Insurance Coverage

Area	With Health Insurance	With Private Health Insurance	With Public Health Insurance	Without Health Insurance	Population Under Age 18 Without Health Insurance
City	66.2	33.2	36.1	33.8	12.4
MSA[1]	74.9	51.1	31.1	25.1	13.0
U.S.	85.2	65.2	31.0	14.8	7.3

Note: Figures are percentages that cover the civilian noninstitutionalized population; (1) Figures cover the Miami-Fort Lauderdale-West Palm Beach, FL Metropolitan Statistical Area—see Appendix B for areas included
Source: U.S. Census Bureau, 2011-2013 American Community Survey 3-Year Estimates

Number of Medical Professionals

Area[1]	MDs[2]	DOs[2,3]	Dentists	Podiatrists	Chiropractors	Optometrists
Local (number)	8,363	402	1,494	236	444	303
Local (rate[4])	320.3	15.4	56.6	8.9	16.8	11.5
U.S. (rate[4])	270.0	20.2	63.1	5.7	25.2	14.9

Note: Data as of 2013 unless noted; (1) Local data covers Miami-Dade County; (2) Data as of 2012 and includes all active, non-federal physicians; (3) Doctor of Osteopathic Medicine; (4) rate per 100,000 population
Source: U.S. Department of Health and Human Services, Health Resources and Services Administration, Bureau of Health Professions, Area Resource File (ARF) 2013-2014

Best Hospitals

According to *U.S. News,* the Miami-Miami Beach-Kendall, FL metro area is home to one of the best hospitals in the U.S.: **Bascom Palmer Eye Institute-Anne Bates Leach Eye Hospital** (1 specialty). The hospital listed was nationally ranked in at least one adult specialty. Only 144 hospitals nationwide were nationally ranked in one or more specialties. Seventeen hospitals in the U.S. made the Honor Roll with high scores in at least six specialties. *U.S. News Online, "America's Best Children's Hospitals 2014-15"*

According to *U.S. News,* the Miami-Miami Beach-Kendall, FL metro area is home to two of the best children's hospitals in the U.S.: **Holtz Children's Hospital at UM-Jackson Memorial Medical Ctr** (7 specialties); **Miami Children's Hospital** (9 specialties). The hospitals listed were highly ranked in at least one pediatric specialty. Eighty-nine children's hospitals in the U.S. were nationally ranked in at least one specialty. Ten children's hospitals in the U.S. made the Honor Roll with high scores in at least three specialties. *U.S. News Online, "America's Best Children's Hospitals 2014-15"*

EDUCATION

Public School District Statistics

District Name	Schls	Pupils	Pupil/ Teacher Ratio	Minority Pupils[1] (%)	Free Lunch Eligible[2] (%)	IEP[3] (%)
Miami-Dade County	529	354,262	16.5	92.0	64.7	10.1

Note: Table includes school districts with 2,000 or more students; (1) Percentage of students that are not non-Hispanic white; (2) Percentage of students that are eligible for the free lunch program; (3) Percentage of students that have an Individualized Education Program.
Source: U.S. Department of Education, National Center for Education Statistics, Common Core of Data, Local Education Agency (School District) Universe Survey: School Year 2012-2013; U.S. Department of Education, National Center for Education Statistics, Common Core of Data, Public Elementary/Secondary School Universe Survey: School Year 2012-2013

Best High Schools

According to *The Daily Beast,* Miami is home to five of the best high schools in the U.S.: **School for Advanced Studies** (#11); **Archimedean Upper Conservatory** (#67); **Coral Reef Senior High School** (#121); **International Studies Charter High School** (#235); **Mater Lakes Academy Charter High School** (#646); *The Daily Beast* used six indicators culled from school surveys to compare public high schools in the U.S., with graduation and college acceptance rates weighed most heavily. Other criteria included: college-level courses/exams and SAT/ACT scores. *The Daily Beast, "Top High Schools 2014"*

Highest Level of Education

Area	Less than H.S.	H.S. Diploma	Some College, No Deg.	Associate Degree	Bachelor's Degree	Master's Degree	Prof. School Degree	Doctorate Degree
City	28.0	29.9	11.9	6.9	14.4	5.1	3.0	0.8
MSA[1]	15.8	27.9	18.4	8.8	18.6	6.8	2.7	1.2
U.S.	13.7	28.0	21.2	7.9	18.2	7.7	1.9	1.3

Note: Figures cover persons age 25 and over; (1) Figures cover the Miami-Fort Lauderdale-West Palm Beach, FL Metropolitan Statistical Area—see Appendix B for areas included
Source: U.S. Census Bureau, 2011-2013 American Community Survey 3-Year Estimates

Educational Attainment by Race

Area	High School Graduate or Higher (%)					Bachelor's Degree or Higher (%)				
	Total	White	Black	Asian	Hisp.[2]	Total	White	Black	Asian	Hisp.[2]
City	72.0	73.4	66.3	80.4	68.7	23.3	25.7	10.4	58.5	19.3
MSA[1]	84.2	85.7	79.1	87.1	77.3	29.2	31.7	17.2	49.7	23.8
U.S.	86.3	88.3	83.1	85.7	64.0	29.1	30.4	18.8	50.7	13.7

Note: Figures shown cover persons 25 years old and over; (1) Figures cover the Miami-Fort Lauderdale-West Palm Beach, FL Metropolitan Statistical Area—see Appendix B for areas included; (2) People of Hispanic origin can be of any race
Source: U.S. Census Bureau, 2011-2013 American Community Survey 3-Year Estimates

School Enrollment by Grade and Control

Area	Preschool (%)		Kindergarten (%)		Grades 1 - 4 (%)		Grades 5 - 8 (%)		Grades 9 - 12 (%)	
	Public	Private	Public	Private	Public	Private	Public	Private	Public	Private
City	59.3	40.7	81.2	18.8	85.6	14.4	90.6	9.4	89.5	10.5
MSA[1]	49.0	51.0	82.2	17.8	86.3	13.7	88.1	11.9	87.7	12.3
U.S.	57.7	42.3	87.9	12.1	89.9	10.1	90.0	10.0	90.7	9.3

Note: Figures shown cover persons 3 years old and over; (1) Figures cover the Miami-Fort Lauderdale-West Palm Beach, FL Metropolitan Statistical Area—see Appendix B for areas included
Source: U.S. Census Bureau, 2011-2013 American Community Survey 3-Year Estimates

Average Salaries of Public School Classroom Teachers

Area	2013-14		2014-15		Percent Change 2013-14 to 2014-15	Percent Change 2004-05 to 2014-15
	Dollars	Rank[1]	Dollars	Rank[1]		
FLORIDA	47,780	39	48,992	36	2.54	17.8
U.S. Average	56,610	–	57,379	–	1.36	20.8

Note: (1) State rank ranges from 1 to 51 where 1 indicates highest salary.
Source: National Education Association, Rankings & Estimates: Rankings of the States 2014 and Estimates of School Statistics 2015, March 2015

Higher Education

Four-Year Colleges			Two-Year Colleges			Medical Schools[1]	Law Schools[2]	Voc/ Tech[3]
Public	Private Non-profit	Private For-profit	Public	Private Non-profit	Private For-profit			
2	5	7	4	1	9	2	2	17

Note: Figures cover institutions located within the city limits and include main campuses only; (1) includes schools accredited by the Liaison Committee on Medical Education and the American Osteopathic Association's Commission on Osteopathic College Accreditation; (2) includes ABA-accredited schools, schools with provisional ABA accreditation, and state accredited schools; (3) includes all schools with programs that are less than 2 years.
Source: National Center for Education Statistics, Integrated Postsecondary Education System (IPEDS), 2013-14; Association of American Medical Colleges, Member List, May 1, 2015; American Osteopathic Association, Member List, May 1, 2015; Law School Admission Council, Official Guide to ABA-Approved Law Schools Online, May 1, 2015; Wikipedia, List of Medical Schools in the United States, May 1, 2015; Wikipedia, List of Law Schools in the United States, May 1, 2015

According to *U.S. News & World Report,* the Miami-Miami Beach-Kendall, FL metro division is home to one of the best national universities in the U.S.: **University of Miami** (#48). The indicators used to capture academic quality fall into a number of categories: assessment by administrators at peer institutions; retention of students; faculty resources; student selectivity; financial resources; alumni giving; high school counselor ratings of colleges; and graduation rate. *U.S. News & World Report, "America's Best Colleges 2015"*

According to *U.S. News & World Report,* the Miami-Miami Beach-Kendall, FL metro division is home to one of the top 100 law schools in the U.S.: **University of Miami** (#63). The rankings are based on a weighted average of 12 measures of quality: peer assessment score; assessment score by lawyers/judges; median LSAT scores; median undergrad GPA; acceptance rate; employment rates for graduates; placement success; bar passage rate; faculty resources; expenditures per student; student/faculty ratio; and library resources. *U.S. News & World Report, "America's Best Graduate Schools, Law, 2016"*

According to *U.S. News & World Report,* the Miami-Miami Beach-Kendall, FL metro division is home to one of the top 75 medical schools for research in the U.S.: **University of Miami (Miller)** (#45). The rankings are based on a weighted average of 11 measures of quality: quality assessment; peer assessment score; assessment score by residency directors; research activity; total research activity; average research activity per faculty member; student selectivity; median MCAT total score; median undergraduate GPA; acceptance rate; and faculty resources. *U.S. News & World Report, "America's Best Graduate Schools, Medical, 2016"*

PRESIDENTIAL ELECTION

2012 Presidential Election Results

Area	Obama (%)	Romney (%)	Other (%)
Miami-Dade County	61.6	37.9	0.4
U.S.	51.0	47.2	1.8

Note: Results may not add to 100% due to rounding
Source: Dave Leip's Atlas of U.S. Presidential Elections

EMPLOYERS

Major Employers

Company Name	Industry
Baptist Health South Florida	General medical and surgical hospitals
Baptist Hospital of Miami	General medical and surgical hospitals
County of Miami-Dade	Police protection, county government
County of Miami-Dade	Regulation, administration of transportation
County of, Palm Beach	County supervisors' and executives' office
Florida International University	Colleges and universities
Intercoastal Health Systems	Management services
Miami Dade College	Community college
Mount Sinai Medical Center of Florida	General medical and surgical hospitals
North Broward Hospital District	Hospital, ama approved residency
North Broward Hospital District	General and family practice, physician/surgeon
Royal Caribbean Cruises Ltd.	Computer processing services
Royal Caribbean Cruises Ltd.	Deep sea passenger transportation, except ferry
School Board of Palm Beach County	Public elementary and secondary schools
Style View Products	Storm doors of windows, metal
The Answer Group	Custom computer programming services
University of Miami	Colleges and universities
Veterans Health Administration	General medical and surgical hospitals

Note: Companies shown are located within the Miami-Fort Lauderdale-West Palm Beach, FL Metropolitan Statistical Area.
Source: Hoovers.com; Wikipedia

Best Companies to Work For

Independent Purchasing Cooperative; Miami Children's Hospital, headquartered in Miami, are among the "100 Best Places to Work in IT." To qualify, companies, both public and private, had to have a minimum of 50 IT employees and were selected based on average salary and bonus increases, the percentage of IT staffers promoted, IT staff turnover rates, training and development programs, and the percentage of women and minorities in IT staff and management positions. In addition, *Computerworld* looked at retention efforts, programs for recognizing and rewarding outstanding performances, and benefits such as flextime, elder care and child care, and reimbursement for college tuition and the cost of pursuing technology certifications. *Computerworld, "100 Best Places to Work in IT 2014"*

PUBLIC SAFETY

Crime Rate

Area	All Crimes	Violent Crimes				Property Crimes		
		Murder	Forcible Rape	Robbery	Aggrav. Assault	Burglary	Larceny -Theft	Motor Vehicle Theft
City	6,183.9	17.0	22.9	529.6	612.3	954.4	3,590.2	457.5
Suburbs[1]	4,571.9	7.1	32.4	187.8	328.8	675.8	3,049.9	290.1
Metro[2]	4,828.3	8.7	30.9	242.2	373.9	720.1	3,135.8	316.7
U.S.	3,098.6	4.5	25.2	109.1	229.1	610.0	1,899.4	221.3

Note: Figures are crimes per 100,000 population; (1) All areas within the metro area that are located outside the city limits; (2) Figures cover the Miami-Miami Beach-Kendall, FL Metropolitan Division—see Appendix B for areas included
Source: FBI Uniform Crime Reports, 2013

Hate Crimes

Area	Number of Quarters Reported	Number of Incidents per Bias Motivation						
		Race	Religion	Sexual Orientation	Ethnicity	Disability	Gender	Gender Identity
City	4	0	0	0	0	0	0	0
U.S.	4	2,871	1,031	1,233	655	83	18	31

Source: Federal Bureau of Investigation, Hate Crime Statistics 2013

Identity Theft Consumer Complaints

Area	Complaints	Complaints per 100,000 Population	Rank[2]
MSA[1]	18,428	316.2	1
U.S.	332,646	104.3	-

Note: (1) Figures cover the Miami-Fort Lauderdale-West Palm Beach, FL Metropolitan Statistical Area—see Appendix B for areas included; (2) Rank ranges from 1 to 380 where 1 indicates greatest number of identity theft complaints per 100,000 population
Source: Federal Trade Commission, Consumer Sentinel Network Data Book for January–December 2014

Fraud and Other Consumer Complaints

Area	Complaints	Complaints per 100,000 Population	Rank[2]
MSA[1]	31,010	532.1	14
U.S.	2,250,205	705.7	-

Note: (1) Figures cover the Miami-Fort Lauderdale-West Palm Beach, FL Metropolitan Statistical Area—see Appendix B for areas included; (2) Rank ranges from 1 to 380 where 1 indicates greatest number of identity theft complaints per 100,000 population
Source: Federal Trade Commission, Consumer Sentinel Network Data Book for January–December 2014

RECREATION

Culture

Dance[1]	Theatre[1]	Instrumental Music[1]	Vocal Music[1]	Series and Festivals	Museums and Art Galleries[2]	Zoos and Aquariums[3]
3	3	4	2	4	80	1

Note: (1) Professional perfoming groups; (2) Based on organizations with SIC code 8412; (3) AZA-accredited
Source: The Grey House Performing Arts Directory, 2015-16; Association of Zoos & Aquariums, AZA Member Zoos & Aquariums, April 2015; www.AccuLeads.com, April 2015

Professional Sports Teams

Team Name	League	Year Established
Florida Panthers	National Hockey League (NHL)	1993
Miami Dolphins	National Football League (NFL)	1966
Miami Heat	National Basketball Association (NBA)	1988
Miami Marlins	Major League Baseball (MLB)	1993

Note: Includes teams located in the Miami-Fort Lauderdale-West Palm Beach, FL Metropolitan Statistical Area.
Source: Wikipedia, Major Professional Sports Teams of the United States and Canada, April 2015

CLIMATE

Average and Extreme Temperatures

Temperature	Jan	Feb	Mar	Apr	May	Jun	Jul	Aug	Sep	Oct	Nov	Dec	Yr.
Extreme High (°F)	88	89	92	96	95	98	98	98	97	95	89	87	98
Average High (°F)	75	77	79	82	85	88	89	90	88	85	80	77	83
Average Temp. (°F)	68	69	72	75	79	82	83	83	82	78	73	69	76
Average Low (°F)	59	60	64	68	72	75	76	76	76	72	66	61	69
Extreme Low (°F)	30	35	32	42	55	60	69	68	68	53	39	30	30

Note: Figures cover the years 1948-1990
Source: National Climatic Data Center, International Station Meteorological Climate Summary, 9/96

Average Precipitation/Snowfall/Humidity

Precip./Humidity	Jan	Feb	Mar	Apr	May	Jun	Jul	Aug	Sep	Oct	Nov	Dec	Yr.
Avg. Precip. (in.)	1.9	2.0	2.3	3.0	6.2	8.7	6.1	7.5	8.2	6.6	2.7	1.8	57.1
Avg. Snowfall (in.)	0	0	0	0	0	0	0	0	0	0	0	0	0
Avg. Rel. Hum. 7am (%)	84	84	82	80	81	84	84	86	88	87	85	84	84
Avg. Rel. Hum. 4pm (%)	59	57	57	57	62	68	66	67	69	65	63	60	63

Note: Figures cover the years 1948-1990; Tr = Trace amounts (<0.05 in. of rain; <0.5 in. of snow)
Source: National Climatic Data Center, International Station Meteorological Climate Summary, 9/96

Weather Conditions

Temperature			Daytime Sky			Precipitation		
32°F & below	45°F & below	90°F & above	Clear	Partly cloudy	Cloudy	0.01 inch or more precip.	0.1 inch or more snow/ice	Thunder-storms
< 1	7	55	48	263	54	128	0	74

Note: Figures are average number of days per year and cover the years 1948-1990
Source: National Climatic Data Center, International Station Meteorological Climate Summary, 9/96

HAZARDOUS WASTE

Superfund Sites

Miami has three hazardous waste sites on the EPA's Superfund Final National Priorities List: **Airco Plating Co.; Continental Cleaners; Miami Drum Services.** There are a total of 1,322 Superfund sites on the list in the U.S. *U.S. Environmental Protection Agency, Final National Priorities List, April 14, 2015*

AIR & WATER QUALITY

Air Quality Trends: Ozone

	2004	2005	2006	2007	2008	2009	2010	2011	2012	2013
MSA[1]	0.063	0.064	0.074	0.066	0.067	0.062	0.064	0.060	0.062	0.061

Note: (1) Data covers the Miami-Fort Lauderdale-West Palm Beach, FL Metropolitan Statistical Area—see Appendix B for areas included. The values shown are the composite ozone concentration averages among trend sites based on the highest fourth daily maximum 8-hour concentration in parts per million. These trends are based on sites having an adequate record of monitoring data during the trend period. Data from exceptional events are included.
Source: U.S. Environmental Protection Agency, Air Quality Monitoring Information, "Air Quality Trends by City, 2000-2013"

Air Quality Index

Area	Percent of Days when Air Quality was...[2]					AQI Statistics[2]	
	Good	Moderate	Unhealthy for Sensitive Groups	Unhealthy	Very Unhealthy	Maximum	Median
MSA[1]	74.0	25.2	0.8	0.0	0.0	123	43

Note: (1) Data covers the Miami-Fort Lauderdale-West Palm Beach, FL Metropolitan Statistical Area—see Appendix B for areas included; (2) Based on 365 days with AQI data in 2014. Air Quality Index (AQI) is an index for reporting daily air quality. EPA calculates the AQI for five major air pollutants regulated by the Clean Air Act: ground-level ozone, particle pollution (aka particulate matter), carbon monoxide, sulfur dioxide, and nitrogen dioxide. The AQI runs from 0 to 500. The higher the AQI value, the greater the level of air pollution and the greater the health concern. There are six AQI categories: "Good" AQI is between 0 and 50. Air quality is considered satisfactory; "Moderate" AQI is between 51 and 100. Air quality is acceptable; "Unhealthy for Sensitive Groups" When AQI values are between 101 and 150, members of sensitive groups may experience health effects; "Unhealthy" When AQI values are between 151 and 200 everyone may begin to experience health effects; "Very Unhealthy" AQI values between 201 and 300 trigger a health alert; "Hazardous" AQI values over 300 trigger warnings of emergency conditions (not shown).
Source: U.S. Environmental Protection Agency, Air Quality Index Report, 2014

Air Quality Index Pollutants

Area	Percent of Days when AQI Pollutant was...[2]					
	Carbon Monoxide	Nitrogen Dioxide	Ozone	Sulfur Dioxide	Particulate Matter 2.5	Particulate Matter 10
MSA[1]	0.0	2.7	26.3	0.0	71.0	0.0

Note: (1) Data covers the Miami-Fort Lauderdale-West Palm Beach, FL Metropolitan Statistical Area—see Appendix B for areas included; (2) Based on 365 days with AQI data in 2014. The Air Quality Index (AQI) is an index for reporting daily air quality. EPA calculates the AQI for five major air pollutants regulated by the Clean Air Act: ground-level ozone, particle pollution (also known as particulate matter), carbon monoxide, sulfur dioxide, and nitrogen dioxide. The AQI runs from 0 to 500. The higher the AQI value, the greater the level of air pollution and the greater the health concern.

Source: U.S. Environmental Protection Agency, Air Quality Index Report, 2014

Maximum Air Pollutant Concentrations: Particulate Matter, Ozone, CO and Lead

	Particulate Matter 10 (ug/m^3)	Particulate Matter 2.5 Wtd AM (ug/m^3)	Particulate Matter 2.5 24-Hr (ug/m^3)	Ozone (ppm)	Carbon Monoxide (ppm)	Lead (ug/m^3)
MSA[1] Level	62	5.8	14	0.068	1	n/a
NAAQS[2]	150	15	35	0.075	9	0.15
Met NAAQS[2]	Yes	Yes	Yes	Yes	Yes	n/a

Note: (1) Data covers the Miami-Fort Lauderdale-West Palm Beach, FL Metropolitan Statistical Area—see Appendix B for areas included; Data from exceptional events are included; (2) National Ambient Air Quality Standards; ppm = parts per million; ug/m^3 = micrograms per cubic meter; n/a not available.

Concentrations: Particulate Matter 10 (coarse particulate)—highest second maximum 24-hour concentration; Particulate Matter 2.5 Wtd AM (fine particulate)—highest weighted annual mean concentration; Particulate Matter 2.5 24-Hour (fine particulate)—highest 98th percentile 24-hour concentration; Ozone—highest fourth daily maximum 8-hour concentration; Carbon Monoxide—highest second maximum non-overlapping 8-hour concentration; Lead—maximum running 3-month average

Source: U.S. Environmental Protection Agency, Air Quality Monitoring Information, "Air Quality Statistics by City, 2013"

Maximum Air Pollutant Concentrations: Nitrogen Dioxide and Sulfur Dioxide

	Nitrogen Dioxide AM (ppb)	Nitrogen Dioxide 1-Hr (ppb)	Sulfur Dioxide AM (ppb)	Sulfur Dioxide 1-Hr (ppb)	Sulfur Dioxide 24-Hr (ppb)
MSA[1] Level	8	44	n/a	3	n/a
NAAQS[2]	53	100	30	75	140
Met NAAQS[2]	Yes	Yes	n/a	Yes	n/a

Note: (1) Data covers the Miami-Fort Lauderdale-West Palm Beach, FL Metropolitan Statistical Area—see Appendix B for areas included; Data from exceptional events are included; (2) National Ambient Air Quality Standards; ppm = parts per million; ug/m^3 = micrograms per cubic meter; n/a not available.

Concentrations: Nitrogen Dioxide AM—highest arithmetic mean concentration; Nitrogen Dioxide 1-Hr—highest 98th percentile 1-hour daily maximum concentration; Sulfur Dioxide AM—highest annual mean concentration; Sulfur Dioxide 1-Hr—highest 99th percentile 1-hour daily maximum concentration; Sulfur Dioxide 24-Hr—highest second maximum 24-hour concentration

Source: U.S. Environmental Protection Agency, Air Quality Monitoring Information, "Air Quality Statistics by City, 2013"

Drinking Water

Water System Name	Pop. Served	Primary Water Source Type	Violations[1]	
			Health Based	Monitoring/ Reporting
MDWASA - Main System	2,100,000	Ground	0	0

Note: (1) Based on violation data from January 1, 2014 to December 31, 2014 (includes unresolved violations from earlier years)

Source: U.S. Environmental Protection Agency, Office of Ground Water and Drinking Water, Safe Drinking Water Information System (based on data extracted January 27, 2015)

Midland, Texas

Background

In 1881, when Midland Texas might have appeared as a dot on a map, it would have been called the middle of nowhere. In fact, Midland was almost exactly at the midpoint between Fort Worth Texas and El Paso. Today the locals like to tease that Midland is "in the middle of somewhere." Barely a whistle-stop, Midland provided a small shelter where Texas and Pacific Railroad crews could rest and store maintenance equipment. Within ten years, it would become a vital shipping center for the cattle trade.

Little is known about the first inhabitants in the region, though they left plenty of evidence of their existence. The Pecos Trail region is rich with petroglyphs and pictographs. Anthropologists refer to these communities as the Karankawas (hunter-gatherers), and surmise these early scribes are the ancestors of the Comanche, Apache, Kiowa, and Kickapoo nations.

The first westerner to make Midland his permanent home in 1882 was Herman Garrett, a sheep rancher from California. Midland grew quickly. Within three years, 100 families lived there, and by 1900, the population was 1,000. Midland became known as the "Windmill Town," as individual homes built windmills to pump water. After several devastating fires in 1905 and 1909, the town put in a municipal water system and a fire department.

Midland would remain a center of ranching and shipping until May 27, 1923, when a new industry would overrun the town. At 6:00 a.m., in an area just southeast of Midland, the Santa Rita No. 1 "blew." From that time on, Midland's economy and culture would be defined by the price of oil, and its roller coaster ride of market highs and lows. By 1929, there were thirty-six oil companies in Midland. Roads were paved and streetlights were raised as Midland's skyline began to rise from the wide-open landscape. The new Hogal Building was twelve stories high. By 1930, the population blossomed to 5,484. When the Great Depression hit, the demand for petroleum decreased and prices plummeted. By 1932, one third of Midland's workers were unemployed.

World War II brought an increase in oil prices, along with the new Midland Army Air Force Base, a training ground for bomber pilots, giving Midland's economy a much-needed boost. By 1950, 250 oil companies had set up shop in Midland.

In 1972, Midland Community College was founded, and later, a satellite campus in Fort Stockton opened. Twice a year, Midland College hosts free lectures by world-renowned speakers—a Who's Who list of past guest lecturers including such luminaries as Ken Burns, Bill Moyers, Sandra Day O'Connor, Richard Rodriguez, John Updike and Neil deGrasse Tyson.

In recent years, Midland has grabbed headlines due to its association with the Bush family. Laura Bush was born and raised in Midland. Both former presidents George W. Bush, and George H.W. Bush, as well as Barbara and Jeb Bush, lived in Midland. In April of 2006, the George Bush Childhood Home Museum was officially dedicated and has since received over 30,000 visitors.

Midland is a cultural mecca with six museums, as well as a community theater that offers fifteen shows each year. The Midland-Odessa Symphony & Chorale performs eighteen venues each year, with four masterworks, four Pops Concerts, six Chamber Concerts, two Chorale concerts and a youth concert. The Marian Blakemore planetarium offers educational shows and lectures about the history of astronomy.

Midland features a semi-arid climate with long, hot summers and short, moderate winters. The city is occasionally subject to cold waves during the winter, but it rarely sees extended periods of below-freezing cold. Midland receives approximately 14.6 inches of precipitation per year, much of which falls in the summer. Highs exceed 90 °F (32 °C) on 101 days per year, and 100 °F (38 °C) on 16 days.

Rankings

Business/Finance Rankings

- According to data published by the U.S. Conference of Mayors and produced by IHS Global Insight, the Midland metro area was among the metro areas with the fastest-growing GMP (gross metro product) and positive employment trends, at #1. *247wallst.com, "America's Fastest Growing (and Shrinking) Economies," January 31, 2014*
- Based on the Bureau of Labor Statistics (BLS) quarterly reports on employment and wages over fourth-quarter 2011–2012, researchers at 24/7 Wall Street listed the Midland metro area as the #3 metro area for wage growth. *247wallst.com, "American Cities Where Wages Are Soaring," July 15, 2013*
- Using data from the Council for Community and Economic Research's 2013 Annual Report, NerdWallet ranked the 100 U.S. cities with the most expensive cost of living. Cities in California and in the Northeast topped the list. Of the cities with the highest cost of living, Midland ranked #82. *NerdWallet.com, "Most Expensive Cities in America," June 4, 2014*
- Midland was cited as one of America's top metros for new and expanded facility projects in 2014. The area ranked #7 in the small metro area category (population under 200,000). *Site Selection, "Top Metros of 2014," March 2015*
- The Midland metro area appeared on the Milken Institute "2013 Best Performing Cities" list. Rank: #6 out of 179 small metro areas. Criteria: job growth; wage and salary growth; high-tech output growth.*Milken Institute, "Best-Performing Cities 2014," January 2015*
- *Forbes* ranked 184 smaller metro areas to determine the nation's "Best Small Places for Business and Careers." The Midland metro area was ranked #60. Criteria: costs (business and living); job growth (past and projected); income growth; educational attainment (college and high school); projected economic growth; cultural and recreational opportunities; net migration patterns; number of highly ranked colleges. *Forbes, "The Best Small Places for Business and Careers 2014," July 23, 2014*

Dating/Romance Rankings

- Midland was selected as one of the least romantic cities in the U.S. by video-rental kiosk company Redbox. The city ranked #2 out of 10. Criteria: number of romance-related rentals in 2014. *Redbox, "10 Most/Least Romantic Cities," January 29, 2015*

Environmental Rankings

- The Midland metro area came in at #298 for the relative comfort of its climate on Sperling's list of "chill cities," as measured by the Sperling Heat Index. All 361 metro areas are included. Criteria included daytime high temperatures, nighttime low temperatures, dew point, and relative humidity at the high temperatures. *www.bertsperling.com, "Sperling's Chill Cities," July 18, 2013*
- Sperling's BestPlaces assessed 379 metropolitan areas of the United States for the likelihood of dangerously extreme weather events or earthquakes. In general the Southeast and South-Central regions have the highest risk of weather extremes and earthquakes, while the Pacific Northwest enjoys the lowest risk. Of the least risky metropolitan areas, the Midland metro area was ranked #258. *www.bestplaces.net, "Safest Places from Natural Disasters," April 2011*

Real Estate Rankings

- The Midland metro area was identified as one of the 15 worst housing markets for the next five years." Criteria: projected annualized change in home prices between the fourth quarter 2012 and the fourth quarter 2017. *The Business Insider, "The 15 Worst Housing Markets for the Next Five Years," May 22, 2013*

- Midland was ranked #195 out of 226 metro areas in terms of housing affordability in 2014 by the National Association of Home Builders (#1 = most affordable). The NAHB-Wells Fargo Housing Opportunity Index (HOI) for a given area is defined as the share of homes sold in that area that would have been affordable to a family earning the local median income, based on standard mortgage underwriting criteria. *National Association of Home Builders®, NAHB-Wells Fargo Housing Opportunity Index, 4th Quarter 2014*

Safety Rankings

- Farmers Insurance, in partnership with Sperling's BestPlaces, ranked metro areas in the U.S. and identified the "Most Secure Places to Live." The Midland metro area ranked #2 out of the top 20 in the small town category (fewer than 150,000 residents). Criteria: economic stability; crime statistics; extreme weather; risk of natural disasters; housing depreciation; foreclosures; air quality; environmental hazards; life expectancy; motor vehicle fatalities; and employment numbers. *Farmers Insurance Group of Companies, "Most Secure U.S. Places to Live in the U.S.," June 25, 2013*
- The National Insurance Crime Bureau ranked 380 metro areas in the U.S. in terms of per capita rates of vehicle theft. The Midland metro area ranked #133 (#1 = highest rate). Criteria: number of vehicle theft offenses per 100,000 inhabitants in 2012. *National Insurance Crime Bureau, "Hot Spots 2012," June 26, 2013*

Seniors/Retirement Rankings

- From its Best Cities for Successful Aging indexes, the Milken Institute generated rankings for metropolitan areas, weighing data in eight categories—health care, wellness, living arrangements, transportation, financial characteristics, education and employment opportunities, community engagement, and overall livability. The Midland metro area was ranked #11 overall in the small metro area category. *Milken Institute, "Best Cities for Successful Aging, 2014"*

Business Environment

CITY FINANCES

City Government Finances

Component	2012 ($000)	2012 ($ per capita)
Total Revenues	184,662	1,661
Total Expenditures	163,419	1,470
Debt Outstanding	125,335	1,128
Cash and Securities[1]	252,691	2,273

Note: (1) Cash and security holdings of a government at the close of its fiscal year, including those of its dependent agencies, utilities, and liquor stores.
Source: U.S Census Bureau, State & Local Government Finances 2012

City Government Revenue by Source

Source	2012 ($000)	2012 ($ per capita)
General Revenue		
From Federal Government	4,566	41
From State Government	2,837	26
From Local Governments	0	0
Taxes		
Property	32,749	295
Sales and Gross Receipts	59,835	538
Personal Income	0	0
Corporate Income	0	0
Motor Vehicle License	0	0
Other Taxes	1,991	18
Current Charges	33,702	303
Liquor Store	0	0
Utility	33,579	302
Employee Retirement	3,811	34

Source: U.S Census Bureau, State & Local Government Finances 2012

City Government Expenditures by Function

Function	2012 ($000)	2012 ($ per capita)	2012 (%)
General Direct Expenditures			
Air Transportation	8,860	80	5.4
Corrections	0	0	0.0
Education	0	0	0.0
Employment Security Administration	0	0	0.0
Financial Administration	6,491	58	4.0
Fire Protection	18,783	169	11.5
General Public Buildings	1,206	11	0.7
Governmental Administration, Other	2,149	19	1.3
Health	4,123	37	2.5
Highways	6,765	61	4.1
Hospitals	0	0	0.0
Housing and Community Development	720	6	0.4
Interest on General Debt	2,936	26	1.8
Judicial and Legal	2,252	20	1.4
Libraries	0	0	0.0
Parking	0	0	0.0
Parks and Recreation	16,926	152	10.4
Police Protection	21,416	193	13.1
Public Welfare	0	0	0.0
Sewerage	9,628	87	5.9
Solid Waste Management	10,373	93	6.3
Veterans' Services	0	0	0.0
Liquor Store	0	0	0.0
Utility	32,266	290	19.7
Employee Retirement	5,145	46	3.1

Source: U.S Census Bureau, State & Local Government Finances 2012

DEMOGRAPHICS

Population Growth

Area	1990 Census	2000 Census	2010 Census	Population Growth (%) 1990-2000	Population Growth (%) 2000-2010
City	89,358	94,996	111,147	6.3	17.0
MSA[1]	106,611	116,009	136,872	8.8	18.0
U.S.	248,709,873	281,421,906	308,745,538	13.2	9.7

Note: (1) Figures cover the Midland, TX Metropolitan Statistical Area—see Appendix B for areas included
Source: U.S. Census Bureau, Census 1990, 2000, 2010

Household Size

Area	Persons in Household (%)							Average Household Size
	One	Two	Three	Four	Five	Six	Seven or More	
City	24.3	32.7	18.4	13.5	6.7	2.6	1.9	2.80
MSA[1]	24.2	32.9	17.4	14.0	7.1	2.4	1.9	2.81
U.S.	27.7	33.6	15.7	13.1	6.0	2.3	1.5	2.64

Note: (1) Figures cover the Midland, TX Metropolitan Statistical Area—see Appendix B for areas included
Source: U.S. Census Bureau, 2011-2013 American Community Survey 3-Year Estimates

Race

Area	White Alone[2] (%)	Black Alone[2] (%)	Asian Alone[2] (%)	AIAN[3] Alone[2] (%)	NHOPI[4] Alone[2] (%)	Other Race Alone[2] (%)	Two or More Races (%)
City	79.0	7.8	1.6	0.3	0.1	9.1	2.0
MSA[1]	81.1	6.5	1.5	0.4	0.1	8.8	1.8
U.S.	73.9	12.6	5.0	0.8	0.2	4.7	2.9

Note: (1) Figures cover the Midland, TX Metropolitan Statistical Area—see Appendix B for areas included; (2) Alone is defined as not being in combination with one or more other races; (3) American Indian and Alaska Native; (4) Native Hawaiian and Other Pacific Islander
Source: U.S. Census Bureau, 2011-2013 American Community Survey 3-Year Estimates

Hispanic or Latino Origin

Area	Total (%)	Mexican (%)	Puerto Rican (%)	Cuban (%)	Other (%)
City	39.9	37.9	0.1	0.3	1.7
MSA[1]	40.1	37.8	0.3	0.2	1.7
U.S.	16.9	10.8	1.6	0.6	3.8

Note: Persons of Hispanic or Latino origin can be of any race; (1) Figures cover the Midland, TX Metropolitan Statistical Area—see Appendix B for areas included
Source: U.S. Census Bureau, 2011-2013 American Community Survey 3-Year Estimates

Segregation

Type	Segregation Indices[1] 1990	2000	2010	2010 Rank[2]	Percent Change 1990-2000	1990-2010	2000-2010
Black/White	n/a	n/a	n/a	n/a	n/a	n/a	n/a
Asian/White	n/a	n/a	n/a	n/a	n/a	n/a	n/a
Hispanic/White	n/a	n/a	n/a	n/a	n/a	n/a	n/a

Note: All figures cover the Metropolitan Statistical Area—see Appendix B for areas included; Figures are based on an analysis of 1990, 2000, and 2010 Census Decennial Census tract data by William H. Frey, Brookings Institution and the University of Michigan Social Science Data Analysis Network. In this analysis all racial groups (whites, blacks, and asians) are non-Hispanic members of those races. Hispanics are shown as a separate category;
(1) Segregation Indices are Dissimilarity Indices that measure the degree to which the minority group is distributed differently than whites across census tracts. They range from 0 (complete integration) to 100 (complete segregation) where the value indicates the percentage of the minority group that needs to move to be distributed exactly like whites; (2) Ranges from 1 (most segregated) to 102 (least segregated); n/a not available.
Source: www.CensusScope.org

Ancestry

Area	German	Irish	English	American	Italian	Polish	French[2]	Scottish	Dutch
City	11.6	8.3	7.1	6.5	1.2	0.6	1.3	1.5	0.8
MSA[1]	11.3	8.2	6.9	6.3	1.1	0.6	1.3	1.8	0.9
U.S.	14.9	10.8	8.0	7.4	5.5	3.0	2.7	1.7	1.4

Note: Figures are the percentage of the total population reporting a particular ancestry. The nine most commonly reported ancestries in the U.S. are shown. Figures include multiple ancestries (e.g. if a person reported being Irish and Italian, they were included in both columns); (1) Figures cover the Midland, TX Metropolitan Statistical Area—see Appendix B for areas included; (2) Excludes Basque
Source: U.S. Census Bureau, 2011-2013 American Community Survey 3-Year Estimates

Foreign-Born Population

Area	Percent of Population Born in								
	Any Foreign Country	Mexico	Asia	Europe	Carribean	South America	Central America[2]	Africa	Canada
City	n/a	n/a	n/a	n/a	n/a	n/a	n/a	n/a	n/a
MSA[1]	n/a	n/a	n/a	n/a	n/a	n/a	n/a	n/a	n/a
U.S.	13.0	3.7	3.8	1.5	1.2	0.9	1.0	0.6	0.3

Note: (1) Figures cover the Midland, TX Metropolitan Statistical Area—see Appendix B for areas included; (2) Excludes Mexico.
Source: U.S. Census Bureau, 2011-2013 American Community Survey 3-Year Estimates

Marital Status

Area	Never Married	Now Married[2]	Separated	Widowed	Divorced
City	30.3	51.6	1.9	5.4	10.9
MSA[1]	29.6	52.8	1.8	5.1	10.6
U.S.	32.7	48.1	2.2	6.0	11.0

Note: Figures are percentages and cover the population 15 years of age and older; (1) Figures cover the Midland, TX Metropolitan Statistical Area—see Appendix B for areas included; (2) Excludes separated
Source: U.S. Census Bureau, 2011-2013 American Community Survey 3-Year Estimates

Disability Status

Area	All Ages	Under 18 Years Old	18 to 64 Years Old	65 Years and Over
City	11.9	4.4	9.7	44.0
MSA[1]	12.1	4.8	9.9	44.6
U.S.	12.3	4.1	10.2	36.3

Note: Figures show percent of the civilian noninstitutionalized population that reported having a disability. Disability status is determined from from six types of difficulty: vision, hearing, cognitive, ambulatory, self-care, and independent living. For children under 5 years old, hearing and vision difficulty are used to determine disability status. For children between the ages of 5 and 14, disability status is determined from hearing, vision, cognitive, ambulatory, and self-care difficulties. For people aged 15 years and older, they are considered to have a disability if they have difficulty with any one of the six difficulty types; (1) Figures cover the Midland, TX Metropolitan Statistical Area—see Appendix B for areas included.
Source: U.S. Census Bureau, 2011-2013 American Community Survey 3-Year Estimates

Age

Area	Percent of Population									Median Age
	Under Age 5	Age 5–19	Age 20–34	Age 35–44	Age 45–54	Age 55–64	Age 65–74	Age 75–84	Age 85+	
City	8.5	21.8	23.7	12.0	12.2	11.0	5.4	3.7	1.8	31.9
MSA[1]	8.2	22.1	23.1	11.9	12.9	11.2	5.5	3.5	1.6	32.4
U.S.	6.4	19.9	20.7	12.9	14.1	12.3	7.6	4.2	1.9	37.4

Note: (1) Figures cover the Midland, TX Metropolitan Statistical Area—see Appendix B for areas included
Source: U.S. Census Bureau, 2011-2013 American Community Survey 3-Year Estimates

Gender

Area	Males	Females	Males per 100 Females
City	58,026	61,145	94.9
MSA[1]	74,592	75,892	98.3
U.S.	154,451,010	159,410,713	96.9

Note: (1) Figures cover the Midland, TX Metropolitan Statistical Area—see Appendix B for areas included
Source: U.S. Census Bureau, 2011-2013 American Community Survey 3-Year Estimates

Religious Groups by Family

Area	Catholic	Baptist	Non-Den.	Methodist[2]	Lutheran	LDS[3]	Pente-costal	Presby-terian[4]	Muslim[5]	Judaism
MSA[1]	22.4	25.3	8.8	4.2	0.7	1.2	1.6	1.9	3.7	<0.1
U.S.	19.1	9.3	4.0	4.0	2.3	2.0	1.9	1.6	0.8	0.7

Note: Figures are the number of adherents as a percentage of the total population; (1) Figures cover the Midland, TX Metropolitan Statistical Area—see Appendix B for areas included; (2) Methodist/Pietist; (3) Latter Day Saints; (4) Reformed; (5) Figures are estimates
Source: Association of Statisticians of American Religious Bodies, 2010 U.S. Religion Census: Religious Congregations & Membership Study

Religious Groups by Tradition

Area	Catholic	Evangelical Protestant	Mainline Protestant	Other Tradition	Black Protestant	Orthodox
MSA[1]	22.4	35.5	7.2	5.4	1.0	<0.1
U.S.	19.1	16.2	7.3	4.3	1.6	0.3

Note: Figures are the number of adherents as a percentage of the total population; (1) Figures cover the Midland, TX Metropolitan Statistical Area—see Appendix B for areas included
Source: Association of Statisticians of American Religious Bodies, 2010 U.S. Religion Census: Religious Congregations & Membership Study

ECONOMY

Gross Metropolitan Product

Area	2012	2013	2014	2015	Rank[2]
MSA[1]	16.2	17.9	20.0	21.3	114

Note: Figures are in billions of dollars; (1) Figures cover the Midland, TX Metropolitan Statistical Area—see Appendix B for areas included; (2) Rank is based on 2015 data and ranges from 1 to 363
Source: The U.S. Conference of Mayors, U.S. Metro Economies: GMP and Employment 2013-2015, June 2014

Economic Growth

Area	2010-12 (%)	2013 (%)	2014 (%)	2015 (%)	Rank[2]
MSA[1]	10.3	8.5	7.1	8.4	1
U.S.	2.1	2.0	2.3	3.2	–

Note: Figures are real gross metropolitan product (GMP) growth rates and represent annual average percent change; (1) Figures cover the Midland, TX Metropolitan Statistical Area—see Appendix B for areas included; (2) Rank is based on 2015 data and ranges from 1 to 363
Source: The U.S. Conference of Mayors, U.S. Metro Economies: GMP and Employment 2013-2015, June 2014

Metropolitan Area Exports

Area	2008	2009	2010	2011	2012	2013	Rank[2]
MSA[1]	93.5	75.6	87.2	81.1	104.4	164.1	316

Note: Figures are in millions of dollars; (1) Figures cover the Midland, TX Metropolitan Statistical Area—see Appendix B for areas included; (2) Rank is based on 2013 data and ranges from 1 to 387
Source: U.S. Department of Commerce, International Trade Administration, Office of Trade & Industry Information, Manufacturing & Services, data extracted April 3, 2015

Building Permits

Area	Single-Family			Multi-Family			Total		
	2013	2014	Pct. Chg.	2013	2014	Pct. Chg.	2013	2014	Pct. Chg.
City	732	917	25.3	1,092	636	-41.8	1,824	1,553	-14.9
MSA[1]	732	920	25.7	1,092	636	-41.8	1,824	1,556	-14.7
U.S.	620,802	634,597	2.2	370,020	411,766	11.3	990,822	1,046,363	5.6

Note: (1) Figures cover the Midland, TX Metropolitan Statistical Area—see Appendix B for areas included; Figures represent new, privately-owned housing units authorized (unadjusted data); All permit data are based on estimates with imputation.
Source: U.S. Census Bureau, Manufacturing, Mining, and Construction Statistics, Building Permits, 2013, 2014

Bankruptcy Filings

Area	Business Filings			Nonbusiness Filings		
	2013	2014	% Chg.	2013	2014	% Chg.
Midland County	8	8	0.0	49	53	8.2
U.S.	33,212	26,983	-18.8	1,038,720	909,812	-12.4

Note: Business filings include Chapter 7, Chapter 11, Chapter 12, and Chapter 13; Nonbusiness filings include Chapter 7, Chapter 11, and Chapter 13
Source: Administrative Office of the U.S. Courts, Business and Nonbusiness Bankruptcy, County Cases Commenced by Chapter of the Bankruptcy Code, During the 12- Month Period Ending December 31, 2013 and Business and Nonbusiness Bankruptcy, County Cases Commenced by Chapter of the Bankruptcy Code, During the 12- Month Period Ending December 31, 2014

Housing Vacancy Rates

Area	Gross Vacancy Rate[2] (%)			Year-Round Vacancy Rate[3] (%)			Rental Vacancy Rate[4] (%)			Homeowner Vacancy Rate[5] (%)		
	2012	2013	2014	2012	2013	2014	2012	2013	2014	2012	2013	2014
MSA[1]	n/a	n/a	n/a	n/a	n/a	n/a	n/a	n/a	n/a	n/a	n/a	n/a
U.S.	13.8	13.6	13.4	10.8	10.7	10.4	8.7	8.3	7.6	2.0	2.0	1.9

Note: (1) Figures cover the Midland, TX Metropolitan Statistical Area—see Appendix B for areas included; (2) The percentage of the total housing inventory that is vacant; (3) The percentage of the housing inventory (excluding seasonal units) that is year-round vacant; (4) The percentage of rental inventory that is vacant for rent; (5) The percentage of homeowner inventory that is vacant for sale; n/a not available
Source: U.S. Census Bureau, Housing Vacancies and Homeownership Annual Statistics: 2014

INCOME

Income

Area	Per Capita ($)	Median Household ($)	Average Household ($)
City	34,306	63,819	94,266
MSA[1]	33,571	63,581	92,348
U.S.	27,884	52,176	72,897

Note: (1) Figures cover the Midland, TX Metropolitan Statistical Area—see Appendix B for areas included
Source: U.S. Census Bureau, 2011-2013 American Community Survey 3-Year Estimates

Household Income Distribution

Area	Percent of Households Earning							
	Under $15,000	$15,000 -24,999	$25,000 -34,999	$35,000 -49,999	$50,000 -74,999	$75,000 -99,000	$100,000 -149,999	$150,000 and up
City	8.4	8.7	8.6	12.9	19.2	12.7	15.9	13.5
MSA[1]	8.0	8.7	9.6	13.3	17.9	13.0	16.3	13.2
U.S.	13.0	10.9	10.3	13.6	17.9	11.9	12.7	9.6

Note: (1) Figures cover the Midland, TX Metropolitan Statistical Area—see Appendix B for areas included
Source: U.S. Census Bureau, 2011-2013 American Community Survey 3-Year Estimates

Poverty Rate

Area	All Ages	Under 18 Years Old	18 to 64 Years Old	65 Years and Over
City	10.3	15.0	8.2	10.4
MSA[1]	9.5	13.0	8.0	9.4
U.S.	15.9	22.4	14.8	9.5

Note: Figures are percentage of people whose income during the past 12 months was below the poverty level; (1) Figures cover the Midland, TX Metropolitan Statistical Area—see Appendix B for areas included
Source: U.S. Census Bureau, 2011-2013 American Community Survey 3-Year Estimates

EMPLOYMENT

Labor Force and Employment

Area	Civilian Labor Force			Workers Employed		
	Dec. 2013	Dec. 2014	% Chg.	Dec. 2013	Dec. 2014	% Chg.
City	71,357	76,671	7.4	69,168	74,970	8.4
MSA[1]	89,915	96,559	7.4	87,140	94,394	8.3
U.S.	154,408,000	155,521,000	0.7	144,423,000	147,190,000	1.9

Note: Data is not seasonally adjusted and covers workers 16 years of age and older; (1) Figures cover the Midland, TX Metropolitan Statistical Area—see Appendix B for areas included
Source: Bureau of Labor Statistics, Local Area Unemployment Statistics

Unemployment Rate

Area	2014											
	Jan.	Feb.	Mar.	Apr.	May	Jun.	Jul.	Aug.	Sep.	Oct.	Nov.	Dec.
City	3.2	3.2	3.0	2.6	2.9	3.1	3.1	2.9	2.8	2.6	2.4	2.2
MSA[1]	3.2	3.2	3.1	2.6	2.9	3.2	3.2	2.9	2.8	2.6	2.4	2.2
U.S.	7.0	7.0	6.8	5.9	6.1	6.3	6.5	6.3	5.7	5.5	5.5	5.4

Note: Data is not seasonally adjusted and covers workers 16 years of age and older; (1) Figures cover the Midland, TX Metropolitan Statistical Area—see Appendix B for areas included
Source: Bureau of Labor Statistics, Local Area Unemployment Statistics

Employment by Occupation

Occupation Classification	City (%)	MSA[1] (%)	U.S. (%)
Management, Business, Science, and Arts	32.3	31.7	36.2
Natural Resources, Construction, and Maintenance	15.1	16.1	9.0
Production, Transportation, and Material Moving	11.0	11.9	12.1
Sales and Office	27.8	26.3	24.4
Service	13.8	14.0	18.3

Note: Figures cover employed civilians 16 years of age and older; (1) Figures cover the Midland, TX Metropolitan Statistical Area—see Appendix B for areas included
Source: U.S. Census Bureau, 2011-2013 American Community Survey 3-Year Estimates

Employment by Industry

Sector	MSA[1]		U.S.
	Number of Employees	Percent of Total	Percent of Total
Construction, Mining, and Logging	29,800	30.2	5.0
Education and Health Services	7,000	7.1	15.5
Financial Activities	4,600	4.7	5.7
Government	9,500	9.6	15.8
Information	900	0.9	2.0
Leisure and Hospitality	8,900	9.0	10.3
Manufacturing	4,100	4.1	8.7
Other Services	3,200	3.2	4.0
Professional and Business Services	9,800	9.9	13.8
Retail Trade	10,200	10.3	11.4
Transportation, Warehousing, and Utilities	4,600	4.7	3.9
Wholesale Trade	6,200	6.3	4.2

Note: Figures are non-farm employment as of December 2014. Figures are not seasonally adjusted and include workers 16 years of age and older; (1) Figures cover the Midland, TX Metropolitan Statistical Area—see Appendix B for areas included; n/a not available
Source: Bureau of Labor Statistics, Current Employment Statistics, Employment, Hours, and Earnings

Occupations with Greatest Projected Employment Growth: 2012 – 2022

Occupation[1]	2012 Employment	2022 Projected Employment	Numeric Employment Change	Percent Employment Change
Combined Food Preparation and Serving Workers, Including Fast Food	285,480	378,000	92,520	32.4
Personal Care Aides	199,230	283,980	84,750	42.5
Retail Salespersons	378,330	439,340	61,010	16.1
Registered Nurses	189,380	242,860	53,480	28.2
Customer Service Representatives	214,240	262,770	48,530	22.7
Waiters and Waitresses	196,390	240,390	44,000	22.4
Janitors and Cleaners, Except Maids and Housekeeping Cleaners	172,120	213,340	41,220	23.9
Laborers and Freight, Stock, and Material Movers, Hand	185,770	226,470	40,700	21.9
Elementary School Teachers, Except Special Education	141,030	180,920	39,890	28.3
Secretaries and Administrative Assistants, Except Legal, Medical, and Executive	190,470	230,220	39,750	20.9

Note: Projections cover Texas; (1) Sorted by numeric employment change
Source: www.projectionscentral.com, State Occupational Projections, 2012–2022 Long-Term Projections

Fastest Growing Occupations: 2012 – 2022

Occupation[1]	2012 Employment	2022 Projected Employment	Numeric Employment Change	Percent Employment Change
Diagnostic Medical Sonographers	4,380	6,900	2,520	57.6
Computer Numerically Controlled Machine Tool Programmers, Metal and Plastic	1,740	2,700	960	54.8
Interpreters and Translators	4,510	6,720	2,210	49.0
Skincare Specialists	5,130	7,620	2,490	48.3
Agents and Business Managers of Artists, Performers, and Athletes	310	450	140	47.4
Petroleum Engineers	19,280	28,010	8,730	45.3
Information Security Analysts	6,640	9,630	2,990	45.0
Insulation Workers, Mechanical	4,460	6,460	2,000	44.6
Cardiovascular Technologists and Technicians	3,950	5,700	1,750	44.3
Physician Assistants	5,470	7,880	2,410	44.2

Note: Projections cover Texas; (1) Sorted by percent employment change and excludes occupations with numeric employment change less than 100
Source: www.projectionscentral.com, State Occupational Projections, 2012–2022 Long-Term Projections

Average Wages

Occupation	$/Hr.	Occupation	$/Hr.
Accountants and Auditors	37.18	Maids and Housekeeping Cleaners	10.06
Automotive Mechanics	23.24	Maintenance and Repair Workers	20.01
Bookkeepers	19.42	Marketing Managers	67.96
Carpenters	17.94	Nuclear Medicine Technologists	n/a
Cashiers	10.45	Nurses, Licensed Practical	21.64
Clerks, General Office	17.65	Nurses, Registered	31.16
Clerks, Receptionists/Information	13.86	Nursing Assistants	12.46
Clerks, Shipping/Receiving	n/a	Packers and Packagers, Hand	12.63
Computer Programmers	37.84	Physical Therapists	36.67
Computer Systems Analysts	33.98	Postal Service Mail Carriers	25.43
Computer User Support Specialists	22.48	Real Estate Brokers	n/a
Cooks, Restaurant	11.31	Retail Salespersons	16.03
Dentists	74.78	Sales Reps., Exc. Tech./Scientific	31.12
Electrical Engineers	n/a	Sales Reps., Tech./Scientific	38.87
Electricians	22.50	Secretaries, Exc. Legal/Med./Exec.	15.96
Financial Managers	71.96	Security Guards	13.54
First-Line Supervisors/Managers, Sales	25.03	Surgeons	n/a
Food Preparation Workers	10.84	Teacher Assistants	8.80
General and Operations Managers	62.58	Teachers, Elementary School	24.30
Hairdressers/Cosmetologists	15.33	Teachers, Secondary School	24.80
Internists	n/a	Telemarketers	n/a
Janitors and Cleaners	11.45	Truck Drivers, Heavy/Tractor-Trailer	22.62
Landscaping/Groundskeeping Workers	14.20	Truck Drivers, Light/Delivery Svcs.	15.44
Lawyers	n/a	Waiters and Waitresses	10.06

Note: Wage data covers the Midland, TX Metropolitan Statistical Area—see Appendix B for areas included; Hourly wages for elementary/secondary school teachers and teacher assistants were calculated by the editors from annual wage data assuming a 40 hour work week; n/a not available.
Source: Bureau of Labor Statistics, Metro Area Occupational Employment and Wage Estimates, May 2014

TAXES

State Corporate Income Tax Rates

State	Tax Rate (%)	Income Brackets ($)	Num. of Brackets	Financial Institution Tax Rate (%)[a]	Federal Income Tax Ded.
Texas	(y)	–	–	(y)	No

Note: Tax rates as of January 1, 2015; (a) Rates listed are the corporate income tax rate applied to financial institutions or excise taxes based on income. Some states have other taxes based upon the value of deposits or shares; (y) Texas imposes a Franchise Tax, otherwise known as margin tax, imposed on entities with more than $1,030,000 total revenues at rate of 1%, or 0.5% for entities primarily engaged in retail or wholesale trade, on lesser of 70% of total revenues or 100%of gross receipts after deductions for either compensation or cost of goods sold.
Source: Federation of Tax Administrators, "State Corporate Income Tax Rates, 2015"

State Individual Income Tax Rates

State	Tax Rate (%)	Income Brackets ($)	Num. of Brackets	Personal Exempt. ($)[1]		Fed. Inc. Tax Ded.
				Single	Dependents	
Texas	None	–	–	–	–	–

Note: Tax rates as of January 1, 2015; Local- and county-level taxes are not included; n/a not applicable; (1) Married joint filers generally receive double the single exemption
Source: Federation of Tax Administrators, "State Individual Income Tax Rates, 2015"

Various State and Local Tax Rates

State	State and Local Sales and Use (%)	State Sales and Use (%)	Gasoline[1] (¢/gal.)	Cigarette[2] ($/pack)	Spirits[3] ($/gal.)	Wine[4] ($/gal.)	Beer[5] ($/gal.)
Texas	8.25	6.25	20	1.41	2.40 (f)	0.20	0.20 (p)

Note: All tax rates as of January 1, 2015; (1) The American Petroleum Institute has developed a methodology for determining the average tax rate on a gallon of fuel. Rates may include any of the following: excise taxes, environmental fees, storage tank fees, other fees or taxes, general sales tax, and local taxes. In states where gasoline is subject to the general sales tax, or where the fuel tax is based on the average sale price, the average rate determined by API is sensitive to changes in the price of gasoline. States that fully or partially apply general sales taxes to gasoline: CA, CO, GA, IL, IN, MI, NY; (2) The federal excise tax of $1.0066 per pack and local taxes are not included; (3) Rates are those applicable to off-premise sales of 40% alcohol by volume (a.b.v.) distilled spirits in 750ml containers. Local excise taxes are excluded; (4) Rates are those applicable to off-premise sales of 11% a.b.v. non-carbonated wine in 750ml containers; (5) Rates are those applicable to off-premise sales of 4.7% a.b.v. beer in 12 ounce containers; (f) Different rates are also applicable according to alcohol content, place of production, size of container, or place purchased (on- or off-premise or onboard airlines); (p) Local excise taxes are excluded.
Source: Tax Foundation, 2015 Facts & Figures: How Does Your State Compare?

State Business Tax Climate Index Rankings

State	Overall Rank	Corporate Tax Index Rank	Individual Income Tax Index Rank	Sales Tax Index Rank	Unemployment Insurance Tax Index Rank	Property Tax Index Rank
Texas	10	39	6	36	15	36

Note: The index is a measure of how each state's tax laws affect economic performance. The lower the rank, the more favorable a state's tax system is for business. States without a given tax are given a ranking of 1. The scores/rankings for the District of Columbia do not affect other states. The 2015 index represents the tax climate as of July 1, 2014.
Source: Tax Foundation, State Business Tax Climate Index 2015

COMMERCIAL UTILITIES

Typical Monthly Electric Bills

Area	Commercial Service ($/month)		Industrial Service ($/month)	
	1,500 kWh	40 kW demand 14,000 kWh	1,000 kW demand 200,000 kWh	50,000 kW demand 32,500,000 kWh
City	n/a	n/a	n/a	n/a
Average[1]	201	1,653	26,124	2,639,743

Note: Figures are based on annualized 2014 rates; (1) Average based on 180 utilities surveyed; n/a not available
Source: Edison Electric Institute, Typical Bills and Average Rates Report, Summer 2014

TRANSPORTATION

Means of Transportation to Work

Area	Car/Truck/Van		Public Transportation			Bicycle	Walked	Other Means	Worked at Home
	Drove Alone	Car-pooled	Bus	Subway	Railroad				
City	83.3	11.2	0.2	0.0	0.0	0.2	1.0	1.7	2.5
MSA[1]	82.9	10.4	0.2	0.0	0.0	0.1	0.8	2.3	3.3
U.S.	76.4	9.6	2.6	1.8	0.6	0.6	2.8	1.3	4.3

Note: Figures are percentages and cover workers 16 years of age and older; (1) Figures cover the Midland, TX Metropolitan Statistical Area—see Appendix B for areas included
Source: U.S. Census Bureau, 2011-2013 American Community Survey 3-Year Estimates

Travel Time to Work

Area	Less Than 10 Minutes	10 to 19 Minutes	20 to 29 Minutes	30 to 44 Minutes	45 to 59 Minutes	60 to 89 Minutes	90 Minutes or More
City	18.3	47.2	16.8	11.4	1.6	2.7	2.0
MSA[1]	17.8	44.9	18.2	12.1	2.0	2.7	2.4
U.S.	13.3	29.7	20.9	20.2	7.7	5.7	2.6

Note: Figures are percentages and include workers 16 years old and over; (1) Figures cover the Midland, TX Metropolitan Statistical Area—see Appendix B for areas included
Source: U.S. Census Bureau, 2011-2013 American Community Survey 3-Year Estimates

Travel Time Index

Area	1985	1990	1995	2000	2005	2010	2011
Urban Area[1]	n/a	n/a	n/a	n/a	n/a	n/a	n/a
Average[2]	1.09	1.14	1.16	1.19	1.23	1.18	1.18

Note: Travel Time Index—the ratio of travel time in the peak period to the travel time at free-flow conditions. For example, a value of 1.30 indicates a 20-minute free-flow trip takes 26 minutes in the peak. Free-flow speeds (60 mph on freeways and 35 mph on principal arterials) are used as the comparison threshold; (1) Data for the Midland, TX urban area was not available; (2) average of 498 urban areas
Source: Texas Transportation Institute, Urban Mobility Report 2012, December 2012

Public Transportation

Agency Name / Mode of Transportation	Vehicles Operated in Maximum Service	Annual Unlinked Passenger Trips (in thous.)	Annual Passenger Miles (in thous.)
Midland-Odessa Urban Transit District			
Bus (directly operated)	12	399.6	n/a
Commuter Bus (purchased transportation)	2	5.5	n/a
Demand Response (directly operated)	6	24.3	n/a

Source: Federal Transit Administration, National Transit Database, 2013

Air Transportation

Airport Name and Code / Type of Service	Passenger Airlines[1]	Passenger Enplanements	Freight Carriers[2]	Freight (lbs.)
Midland International Airport (MAF)				
Domestic service (U.S. carriers - 2014)	9	547,322	6	3,830,784
International service (U.S. carriers - 2013)	0	0	0	0

Note: (1) Includes all U.S.-based major, minor and commuter airlines that carried at least one passenger during the year; (2) Includes all U.S.-based airlines and freight carriers that transported at least one lb. of freight during the year.
Source: Bureau of Transportation Statistics, The Intermodal Transportation Database, Air Carriers: T-100 Domestic Market (U.S. Carriers), 2014; Bureau of Transportation Statistics, The Intermodal Transportation Database, Air Carriers: T-100 International Market (U.S. Carriers), 2013

Other Transportation Statistics

Major Highways:	I-20
Amtrak Service:	No
Major Waterways/Ports:	None

Source: Amtrak.com; Google Maps

BUSINESSES

Major Business Headquarters

Company Name	Rankings	
	Fortune[1]	Forbes[2]
No companies listed	-	-

Note: (1) Fortune 500—companies that produce a 10-K are ranked 1 to 500 based on 2013 revenue; (2) all private companies with at least $2 billion in annual revenue through the end of their most current fiscal year are ranked 1 to 221; companies listed are headquartered in the city; dashes indicate no ranking
Source: Fortune, "Fortune 500," June 16, 2014; Forbes, "America's Largest Private Companies," November 5, 2014

Minority- and Women-Owned Businesses

Group	All Firms		Firms with Paid Employees			
	Firms	Sales ($000)	Firms	Sales ($000)	Employees	Payroll ($000)
Asian	447	119,053	128	79,440	960	22,455
Black	382	27,258	(s)	(s)	(s)	(s)
Hispanic	(s)	(s)	(s)	(s)	(s)	(s)
Women	3,332	554,300	(s)	(s)	(s)	(s)
All Firms	13,791	17,850,108	3,152	16,941,762	54,240	1,932,582

Note: Figures cover firms located in the city; minority- and women-owned business are defined as firms in which the corresponding group own 51% or more of the stock or equity of the company; (s) estimates are suppressed when publication standards are not met
Source: U.S. Census Bureau, 2007 Economic Census, Survey of Business Owners (2012 Survey of Business Owners data will be released starting in June 2015)

HOTELS & CONVENTION CENTERS

Hotels/Motels

Area	5 Star		4 Star		3 Star		2 Star		1 Star		Not Rated	
	Num.	Pct.[3]	Num.	Pct.[3]	Num.	Pct.[3]	Num.	Pct.[3]	Num.	Pct.[3]	Num.	Pct.[3]
City[1]	0	0.0	0	0.0	15	18.8	48	60.0	6	7.5	11	13.8
Total[2]	166	0.9	1,264	7.0	5,718	31.8	9,340	52.0	411	2.3	1,070	6.0

Note: (1) Figures cover Midland and vicinity; (2) Figures cover all 100 cities in this book; (3) Percentage of hotels which have a given star rating; Star ratings are determined by expedia.com and offer an indication of the general quality of a particular hotel.
Source: expedia.com, April 2, 2015

Major Convention Centers

Name	Overall Space (sq. ft.)	Exhibit Space (sq. ft.)	Meeting Space (sq. ft.)	Meeting Rooms
Midland Center	n/a	12,500	n/a	n/a

Note: Table includes convention centers located in the Midland, TX metro area; n/a not available
Source: Original research

Living Environment

COST OF LIVING

Cost of Living Index

Composite Index	Groceries	Housing	Utilities	Transportation	Health Care	Misc. Goods/ Services
96.8	91.1	97.3	91.8	101.9	97.4	98.5

Note: The Cost of Living Index measures regional differences in the cost of consumer goods and services, excluding taxes and non-consumer expenditures, for professional and managerial households in the top income quintile. It is based on more than 50,000 prices covering almost 60 different items for which prices are collected three times a year by chambers of commerce, economic development organizations or university applied economic centers in each participating urban area. The numbers shown should be read as a percentage above or below the national average of 100. For example, a value of 115.4 in the groceries column indicates that grocery prices are 15.4% higher than the national average. Small differences in the index numbers should not be interpreted as significant; Figures cover the Midland TX urban area.
Source: The Council for Community and Economic Research, ACCRA Cost of Living Index, 2014

Grocery Prices

Area[1]	T-Bone Steak ($/pound)	Frying Chicken ($/pound)	Whole Milk ($/half gal.)	Eggs ($/dozen)	Orange Juice ($/64 oz.)	Coffee ($/11.5 oz.)
City[2]	10.45	1.16	2.06	1.82	3.08	3.70
Avg.	10.40	1.37	2.40	1.99	3.46	4.27
Min.	8.48	0.93	1.37	1.30	2.83	2.99
Max.	14.20	2.44	3.62	4.02	6.42	6.96

Note: (1) Values for the local area are compared with the average, minimum and maximum values for all 308 areas in the Cost of Living Index; (2) Figures cover the Midland TX urban area; **T-Bone Steak** *(price per pound);* **Frying Chicken** *(price per pound, whole fryer);* **Whole Milk** *(half gallon carton);* **Eggs** *(price per dozen, Grade A, large);* **Orange Juice** *(64 oz. Tropicana or Florida Natural);* **Coffee** *(11.5 oz. can, vacuum-packed, Maxwell House, Hills Bros, or Folgers).*
Source: The Council for Community and Economic Research, ACCRA Cost of Living Index, 2014

Housing and Utility Costs

Area[1]	New Home Price ($)	Apartment Rent ($/month)	All Electric ($/month)	Part Electric ($/month)	Other Energy ($/month)	Telephone ($/month)
City[2]	252,485	1,281	-	115.55	42.96	24.95
Avg.	305,838	919	181.00	93.66	73.14	27.95
Min.	183,142	480	112.00	42.06	23.42	17.16
Max.	1,358,576	3,851	594.00	180.03	440.99	40.42

Note: (1) Values for the local area are compared with the average, minimum and maximum values for all 308 areas in the Cost of Living Index; (2) Figures cover the Midland TX urban area; **New Home Price** *(2,400 sf living area, 8,000 sf lot, in urban area with full utilities);* **Apartment Rent** *(950 sf 2 bedroom/1.5 or 2 bath, unfurnished, excluding all utilities except water);* **All Electric** *(average monthly cost for an all-electric home);* **Part Electric** *(average monthly cost for a part-electric home);* **Other Energy** *(average monthly cost for natural gas, fuel oil, coal, wood, and any other forms of energy except electricity);* **Telephone** *(price includes basic monthly rate for a private residential line plus additional local usage charges incurred by a family of four).*
Source: The Council for Community and Economic Research, ACCRA Cost of Living Index, 2014

Health Care, Transportation, and Other Costs

Area[1]	Doctor ($/visit)	Dentist ($/visit)	Optometrist ($/visit)	Gasoline ($/gallon)	Beauty Salon ($/visit)	Men's Shirt ($)
City[2]	96.00	86.00	99.00	3.30	35.00	15.08
Avg.	102.86	87.89	97.66	3.44	34.37	26.74
Min.	67.47	65.78	51.18	3.00	17.43	12.79
Max.	173.50	150.14	235.00	4.33	64.28	49.50

Note: (1) Values for the local area are compared with the average, minimum and maximum values for all 308 areas in the Cost of Living Index; (2) Figures cover the Midland TX urban area; **Doctor** *(general practitioners routine exam of an established patient);* **Dentist** *(adult teeth cleaning and periodic oral examination);* **Optometrist** *(full vision eye exam for established adult patient);* **Gasoline** *(one gallon regular unleaded, national brand, including all taxes, cash price at self-service pump if available);* **Beauty Salon** *(woman's shampoo, trim, and blow-dry);* **Men's Shirt** *(cotton/polyester dress shirt, pinpoint weave, long sleeves).*
Source: The Council for Community and Economic Research, ACCRA Cost of Living Index, 2014

HOUSING

House Price Index (HPI)

Area	National Ranking[2]	Quarterly Change (%)	One-Year Change (%)	Five-Year Change (%)
MSA[1]	(a)	n/a	8.78	40.53
U.S.[3]	–	1.35	4.91	11.59

Note: The HPI is a weighted repeat sales index. It measures average price changes in repeat sales or refinancings on the same properties. This information is obtained by reviewing repeat mortgage transactions on single-family properties whose mortgages have been purchased or securitized by Fannie Mae or Freddie Mac in January 1975; (1) Midland Metropolitan Statistical Area—see Appendix B for areas included; (2) Rankings are based on annual percentage change for all metro areas containing at least 15,000 transactions over the last 10 years and ranges from 1 to 275; (3) figures based on a weighted average of Census Division estimates using a seasonally adjusted, purchase-only index; all figures are for the period ending December 31, 2014; n/a not available; (a) Not ranked because of increased index variability due to smaller sample size
Source: Federal Housing Finance Agency, House Price Index, February 26, 2015

Median Single-Family Home Prices

Area	2012	2013	2014p	Percent Change 2013 to 2014
MSA[1]	n/a	n/a	n/a	n/a
U.S. Average	177.2	197.4	209.0	5.9

Note: Figures are median sales prices of existing single-family homes in thousands of dollars; (p) preliminary; n/a not available; (1) Midland, TX Metropolitan Statistical Area—see Appendix B for areas included
Source: National Association of Realtors, Median Sales Price of Existing Single-Family Homes for Metropolitan Areas, 4th Quarter 2014

Qualifying Income Based on Median Sales Price of Existing Single-Family Homes

Area	With 5% Down ($)	With 10% Down ($)	With 20% Down ($)
MSA[1]	n/a	n/a	n/a
U.S. Average	45,863	43,449	38,621

Note: Figures are preliminary; Qualifying income is based on a mortgage rate of 4.0%. Monthly principal and interest payment is limited to 25% of income; n/a not available; (1) Midland, TX Metropolitan Statistical Area—see Appendix B for areas included
Source: National Association of Realtors, Qualifying Income Based on Median Sales Price of Existing Single-Family Homes for Metropolitan Areas, 4th Quarter 2014

Median Apartment Condo-Coop Home Prices

Area	2012	2013	2014p	Percent Change 2013 to 2014
MSA[1]	n/a	n/a	n/a	n/a
U.S. Average	173.7	194.9	205.1	5.2

Note: Figures are median sales prices of existing apartment condo-coop homes in thousands of dollars; (p) preliminary; n/a not available; (1) Midland, TX Metropolitan Statistical Area—see Appendix B for areas included
Source: National Association of Realtors, Median Sales Price of Existing Apartment Condo-Coop Homes for Metropolitan Areas, 4th Quarter 2014

Gross Monthly Rent

Area	Under $200	$200 -299	$300 -499	$500 -749	$750 -999	$1,000 -1,499	$1,500 and up	Median ($)
City	0.5	0.7	3.2	15.8	30.7	32.3	16.7	991
MSA[1]	0.6	0.7	4.4	17.1	30.0	31.0	16.2	975
U.S.	1.7	3.2	7.8	22.1	24.3	26.0	14.9	900

Note: Figures are percentages except for Median; Gross rent is the contract rent plus the estimated average monthly cost of utilities (electricity, gas, and water and sewer) and fuels (oil, coal, kerosene, wood, etc.) if these are paid by the renter (or paid for the renter by someone else); (1) Figures cover the Midland, TX Metropolitan Statistical Area—see Appendix B for areas included
Source: U.S. Census Bureau, 2011-2013 American Community Survey 3-Year Estimates

Homeownership Rate

Area	2007 (%)	2008 (%)	2009 (%)	2010 (%)	2011 (%)	2012 (%)	2013 (%)	2014 (%)
MSA[1]	n/a	n/a	n/a	n/a	n/a	n/a	n/a	n/a
U.S.	68.1	67.8	67.4	66.9	66.1	65.4	65.1	64.5

Note: (1) Figures cover the Midland, TX Metropolitan Statistical Area—see Appendix B for areas included; n/a not available
Source: U.S. Census Bureau, Housing Vacancies and Homeownership Annual Statistics: 2014

Year Housing Structure Built

Area	2010 or Later	2000 -2009	1990 -1999	1980 -1989	1970 -1979	1960 -1969	1950 -1959	1940 -1949	Before 1940	Median Year
City	1.8	11.2	9.5	22.4	17.1	12.3	19.4	4.4	1.8	1977
MSA[1]	2.6	12.4	12.1	22.5	16.0	11.2	16.7	4.2	2.2	1980
U.S.	0.9	15.0	13.9	13.8	15.8	11.0	10.9	5.4	13.3	1976

Note: Figures are percentages except for Median Year; (1) Figures cover the Midland, TX Metropolitan Statistical Area—see Appendix B for areas included
Source: U.S. Census Bureau, 2011-2013 American Community Survey 3-Year Estimates

HEALTH

Health Risk Data

Category	MSA[1] (%)	U.S. (%)
Adults aged 18–64 who have any kind of health care coverage	n/a	79.6
Adults who reported being in good or excellent health	n/a	83.1
Adults who are current smokers	n/a	19.6
Adults who are heavy drinkers[2]	n/a	6.1
Adults who are binge drinkers[3]	n/a	16.9
Adults who are overweight (BMI 25.0 - 29.9)	n/a	35.8
Adults who are obese (BMI 30.0 - 99.8)	n/a	27.6
Adults who participated in any physical activities in the past month	n/a	77.1
Adults 50+ who have ever had a sigmoidoscopy or colonoscopy	n/a	67.3
Women aged 40+ who have had a mammogram within the past two years	n/a	74.0
Men aged 40+ who have had a PSA test within the past two years	n/a	45.2
Adults aged 65+ who have had flu shot within the past year	n/a	60.1
Adults who always wear a seatbelt	n/a	93.8

Note: Data as of 2012 unless otherwise noted; n/a not available; (1) Figures cover the Midland, TX Metropolitan Statistical Area—see Appendix B for areas included; (2) Heavy drinkers are classified as males having more than two drinks per day or females having more than one drink per day; (3) Binge drinkers are classified as males having five or more drinks on one occasion or females having four or more drinks on one occasion
Source: Centers for Disease Control and Prevention, Behaviorial Risk Factor Surveillance System, SMART: Selected Metropolitan/Micropolitan Area Risk Trends, 2012 (Note: the CDC has discontinued this dataset but will be releasing a replacement in late 2015)

Chronic Health Indicators

Category	MSA[1] (%)	U.S. (%)
Adults who have ever been told they had a heart attack	n/a	4.5
Adults who have ever been told they had a stroke	n/a	2.9
Adults who have been told they currently have asthma	n/a	8.9
Adults who have ever been told they have arthritis	n/a	25.7
Adults who have ever been told they have diabetes[2]	n/a	9.7
Adults who have ever been told they had skin cancer	n/a	5.7
Adults who have ever been told they had any other types of cancer	n/a	6.5
Adults who have ever been told they have COPD	n/a	6.2
Adults who have ever been told they have kidney disease	n/a	2.5
Adults who have ever been told they have a form of depression	n/a	18.0

Note: Data as of 2012 unless otherwise noted; n/a not available; (1) Figures cover the Midland, TX Metropolitan Statistical Area—see Appendix B for areas included; (2) Figures do not include pregnancy-related, borderline, or pre-diabetes
Source: Centers for Disease Control and Prevention, Behaviorial Risk Factor Surveillance System, SMART: Selected Metropolitan/Micropolitan Area Risk Trends, 2012 (Note: the CDC has discontinued this dataset but will be releasing a replacement in late 2015)

Mortality Rates for the Top 10 Causes of Death in the U.S.

ICD-10[a] Sub-Chapter	ICD-10[a] Code	Age-Adjusted Mortality Rate[1] per 100,000 population	
		County[2]	U.S.
Malignant neoplasms	C00-C97	149.5	166.2
Ischaemic heart diseases	I20-I25	124.9	105.7
Other forms of heart disease	I30-I51	38.0	49.3
Chronic lower respiratory diseases	J40-J47	50.0	42.1
Organic, including symptomatic, mental disorders	F01-F09	9.3	38.1
Cerebrovascular diseases	I60-I69	47.1	37.0
Other external causes of accidental injury	W00-X59	20.7	26.9
Other degenerative diseases of the nervous system	G30-G31	42.4	25.6
Diabetes mellitus	E10-E14	18.2	21.3
Hypertensive diseases	I10-I15	10.8	19.4

Note: (a) ICD-10 = International Classification of Diseases 10th Revision; (1) Mortality rates are a three year average covering 2011-2013; (2) Figures cover Midland County
Source: Centers for Disease Control and Prevention, National Center for Health Statistics. Compressed Mortality File 1999-2013 on CDC WONDER Online Database, released October 2014. Data are compiled from the Compressed Mortality File 1999-2013, Series 20 No. 2S, 2014.

Mortality Rates for Selected Causes of Death

ICD-10[a] Sub-Chapter	ICD-10[a] Code	Age-Adjusted Mortality Rate[1] per 100,000 population	
		County[2]	U.S.
Assault	X85-Y09	*4.1	5.2
Diseases of the liver	K70-K76	20.7	13.2
Human immunodeficiency virus (HIV) disease	B20-B24	Suppressed	2.2
Influenza and pneumonia	J09-J18	31.2	15.4
Intentional self-harm	X60-X84	16.4	12.5
Malnutrition	E40-E46	Suppressed	0.9
Obesity and other hyperalimentation	E65-E68	Suppressed	1.8
Renal failure	N17-N19	11.0	13.1
Transport accidents	V01-V99	21.8	11.7
Viral hepatitis	B15-B19	Suppressed	2.2

Note: (a) ICD-10 = International Classification of Diseases 10th Revision; (1) Mortality rates are a three year average covering 2011-2013; (2) Figures cover Midland County; (*) Unreliable data as per CDC
Source: Centers for Disease Control and Prevention, National Center for Health Statistics. Compressed Mortality File 1999-2013 on CDC WONDER Online Database, released October 2014. Data are compiled from the Compressed Mortality File 1999-2013, Series 20 No. 2S, 2014.

Health Insurance Coverage

Area	With Health Insurance	With Private Health Insurance	With Public Health Insurance	Without Health Insurance	Population Under Age 18 Without Health Insurance
City	79.4	66.2	22.1	20.6	16.3
MSA[1]	77.5	64.9	21.1	22.5	21.6
U.S.	85.2	65.2	31.0	14.8	7.3

Note: Figures are percentages that cover the civilian noninstitutionalized population; (1) Figures cover the Midland, TX Metropolitan Statistical Area—see Appendix B for areas included
Source: U.S. Census Bureau, 2011-2013 American Community Survey 3-Year Estimates

Number of Medical Professionals

Area[1]	MDs[2]	DOs[2,3]	Dentists	Podiatrists	Chiropractors	Optometrists
Local (number)	237	7	75	4	23	18
Local (rate[4])	161.1	4.8	49.4	2.6	15.1	11.8
U.S. (rate[4])	270.0	20.2	63.1	5.7	25.2	14.9

Note: Data as of 2013 unless noted; (1) Local data covers Midland County; (2) Data as of 2012 and includes all active, non-federal physicians; (3) Doctor of Osteopathic Medicine; (4) rate per 100,000 population
Source: U.S. Department of Health and Human Services, Health Resources and Services Administration, Bureau of Health Professions, Area Resource File (ARF) 2013-2014

EDUCATION

Public School District Statistics

District Name	Schls	Pupils	Pupil/ Teacher Ratio	Minority Pupils[1] (%)	Free Lunch Eligible[2] (%)	IEP[3] (%)
Midland ISD	35	23,319	16.3	70.0	38.4	6.8

Note: Table includes school districts with 2,000 or more students; (1) Percentage of students that are not non-Hispanic white; (2) Percentage of students that are eligible for the free lunch program; (3) Percentage of students that have an Individualized Education Program.
Source: U.S. Department of Education, National Center for Education Statistics, Common Core of Data, Local Education Agency (School District) Universe Survey: School Year 2012-2013; U.S. Department of Education, National Center for Education Statistics, Common Core of Data, Public Elementary/Secondary School Universe Survey: School Year 2012-2013

Highest Level of Education

Area	Less than H.S.	H.S. Diploma	Some College, No Deg.	Associate Degree	Bachelor's Degree	Master's Degree	Prof. School Degree	Doctorate Degree
City	18.3	22.9	27.4	6.0	18.2	5.4	1.3	0.4
MSA[1]	18.3	23.4	27.0	6.3	17.6	5.8	1.3	0.4
U.S.	13.7	28.0	21.2	7.9	18.2	7.7	1.9	1.3

Note: Figures cover persons age 25 and over; (1) Figures cover the Midland, TX Metropolitan Statistical Area—see Appendix B for areas included
Source: U.S. Census Bureau, 2011-2013 American Community Survey 3-Year Estimates

Educational Attainment by Race

Area	High School Graduate or Higher (%)					Bachelor's Degree or Higher (%)				
	Total	White	Black	Asian	Hisp.[2]	Total	White	Black	Asian	Hisp.[2]
City	81.7	84.1	80.6	79.4	61.4	25.4	27.8	15.6	43.1	9.1
MSA[1]	81.7	83.9	80.7	81.5	61.3	25.0	27.1	15.1	47.0	9.6
U.S.	86.3	88.3	83.1	85.7	64.0	29.1	30.4	18.8	50.7	13.7

Note: Figures shown cover persons 25 years old and over; (1) Figures cover the Midland, TX Metropolitan Statistical Area—see Appendix B for areas included; (2) People of Hispanic origin can be of any race
Source: U.S. Census Bureau, 2011-2013 American Community Survey 3-Year Estimates

School Enrollment by Grade and Control

Area	Preschool (%)		Kindergarten (%)		Grades 1 - 4 (%)		Grades 5 - 8 (%)		Grades 9 - 12 (%)	
	Public	Private	Public	Private	Public	Private	Public	Private	Public	Private
City	42.0	58.0	77.3	22.7	87.5	12.5	85.9	14.1	88.8	11.2
MSA[1]	46.0	54.0	81.5	18.5	90.2	9.8	87.9	12.1	89.3	10.7
U.S.	57.7	42.3	87.9	12.1	89.9	10.1	90.0	10.0	90.7	9.3

Note: Figures shown cover persons 3 years old and over; (1) Figures cover the Midland, TX Metropolitan Statistical Area—see Appendix B for areas included
Source: U.S. Census Bureau, 2011-2013 American Community Survey 3-Year Estimates

Average Salaries of Public School Classroom Teachers

Area	2013-14		2014-15		Percent Change 2013-14 to 2014-15	Percent Change 2004-05 to 2014-15
	Dollars	Rank[1]	Dollars	Rank[1]		
TEXAS	49,690	30	50,576	29	1.78	23.3
U.S. Average	56,610	–	57,379	–	1.36	20.8

Note: (1) State rank ranges from 1 to 51 where 1 indicates highest salary.
Source: National Education Association, Rankings & Estimates: Rankings of the States 2014 and Estimates of School Statistics 2015, March 2015

Higher Education

Four-Year Colleges			Two-Year Colleges			Medical Schools[1]	Law Schools[2]	Voc/ Tech[3]
Public	Private Non-profit	Private For-profit	Public	Private Non-profit	Private For-profit			
1	0	0	0	0	0	0	0	0

Note: Figures cover institutions located within the city limits and include main campuses only; (1) includes schools accredited by the Liaison Committee on Medical Education and the American Osteopathic Association's Commission on Osteopathic College Accreditation; (2) includes ABA-accredited schools, schools with provisional ABA accreditation, and state accredited schools; (3) includes all schools with programs that are less than 2 years.
Source: National Center for Education Statistics, Integrated Postsecondary Education System (IPEDS), 2013-14; Association of American Medical Colleges, Member List, May 1, 2015; American Osteopathic Association, Member List, May 1, 2015; Law School Admission Council, Official Guide to ABA-Approved Law Schools Online, May 1, 2015; Wikipedia, List of Medical Schools in the United States, May 1, 2015; Wikipedia, List of Law Schools in the United States, May 1, 2015

PRESIDENTIAL ELECTION

2012 Presidential Election Results

Area	Obama (%)	Romney (%)	Other (%)
Midland County	18.6	80.1	1.4
U.S.	51.0	47.2	1.8

Note: Results may not add to 100% due to rounding
Source: Dave Leip's Atlas of U.S. Presidential Elections

EMPLOYERS

Major Employers

Company Name	Industry
Albertson's	Grocery
Bobby Cox Companies	Retail/ restaurants
City of Odessa	City government
Cudd Energy	Oil & gas
Dixie Electric	Electric
Ector County	Government
Ector County I.S.D.	Public education
Family Dollar	Distribution
Halliburton Services	Oil & gas
HEB	Grocery
Holloman Construction	Oil field construction
Investment Corp. of America	Financial
Lithia Motors	Automotive
Medical Center Hospital	County hospital
Nurses Unlimited	Medical
Odessa College	Education
Odessa Regional Medical Center	Medical
REXtac	Manufacturer
Saulsbury Companies	Electric & construction
Sewell Family of Dealerships	Automotive
Southwest Convenience Stores	Retail/ service
Texas Tech Univ Health Sciences Ctr	Education/ medical
The University of Texas Permian Basin	Education
Walmart	Retail
Weatherford	Oil & gas

Note: Companies shown are located within the Midland, TX Metropolitan Statistical Area.
Source: Hoovers.com; Wikipedia

PUBLIC SAFETY

Crime Rate

Area	All Crimes	Violent Crimes				Property Crimes		
		Murder	Forcible Rape	Robbery	Aggrav. Assault	Burglary	Larceny -Theft	Motor Vehicle Theft
City	2,896.3	4.1	18.0	51.5	212.7	464.6	2,011.3	134.1
Suburbs[1]	3,001.3	3.0	9.0	20.9	226.7	656.3	1,781.1	304.3
Metro[2]	2,918.9	3.9	16.0	44.9	215.7	505.8	1,961.8	170.8
U.S.	3,098.6	4.5	25.2	109.1	229.1	610.0	1,899.4	221.3

Note: Figures are crimes per 100,000 population; (1) All areas within the metro area that are located outside the city limits; (2) Figures cover the Midland, TX Metropolitan Statistical Area—see Appendix B for areas included

Source: FBI Uniform Crime Reports, 2013

Hate Crimes

Area	Number of Quarters Reported	Number of Incidents per Bias Motivation						
		Race	Religion	Sexual Orientation	Ethnicity	Disability	Gender	Gender Identity
City	4	0	0	0	0	0	0	0
U.S.	4	2,871	1,031	1,233	655	83	18	31

Source: Federal Bureau of Investigation, Hate Crime Statistics 2013

Identity Theft Consumer Complaints

Area	Complaints	Complaints per 100,000 Population	Rank[2]
MSA[1]	107	68.2	200
U.S.	332,646	104.3	-

Note: (1) Figures cover the Midland, TX Metropolitan Statistical Area—see Appendix B for areas included; (2) Rank ranges from 1 to 380 where 1 indicates greatest number of identity theft complaints per 100,000 population

Source: Federal Trade Commission, Consumer Sentinel Network Data Book for January–December 2014

Fraud and Other Consumer Complaints

Area	Complaints	Complaints per 100,000 Population	Rank[2]
MSA[1]	569	362.9	208
U.S.	2,250,205	705.7	-

Note: (1) Figures cover the Midland, TX Metropolitan Statistical Area—see Appendix B for areas included; (2) Rank ranges from 1 to 380 where 1 indicates greatest number of identity theft complaints per 100,000 population

Source: Federal Trade Commission, Consumer Sentinel Network Data Book for January–December 2014

RECREATION

Culture

Dance[1]	Theatre[1]	Instrumental Music[1]	Vocal Music[1]	Series and Festivals	Museums and Art Galleries[2]	Zoos and Aquariums[3]
0	0	1	1	0	9	0

Note: (1) Professional perfoming groups; (2) Based on organizations with SIC code 8412; (3) AZA-accredited

Source: The Grey House Performing Arts Directory, 2015-16; Association of Zoos & Aquariums, AZA Member Zoos & Aquariums, April 2015; www.AccuLeads.com, April 2015

Professional Sports Teams

Team Name	League	Year Established
No teams are located in the metro area		

Source: Wikipedia, Major Professional Sports Teams of the United States and Canada, April 2015

CLIMATE

Average and Extreme Temperatures

Temperature	Jan	Feb	Mar	Apr	May	Jun	Jul	Aug	Sep	Oct	Nov	Dec	Yr.
Extreme High (°F)	84	90	95	101	108	116	112	107	107	100	89	85	116
Average High (°F)	57	62	70	79	86	93	94	93	86	78	66	59	77
Average Temp. (°F)	43	48	55	64	73	80	82	81	74	65	53	46	64
Average Low (°F)	30	34	40	49	59	67	69	68	62	51	39	32	50
Extreme Low (°F)	-8	-11	9	20	34	47	53	54	36	24	13	-1	-11

Note: Figures cover the years 1948-1995
Source: National Climatic Data Center, International Station Meteorological Climate Summary, 9/96

Average Precipitation/Snowfall/Humidity

Precip./Humidity	Jan	Feb	Mar	Apr	May	Jun	Jul	Aug	Sep	Oct	Nov	Dec	Yr.
Avg. Precip. (in.)	0.6	0.6	0.5	0.8	2.1	1.6	1.9	1.7	2.1	1.6	0.6	0.5	14.6
Avg. Snowfall (in.)	2	1	Tr	Tr	0	0	0	0	0	Tr	Tr	1	4
Avg. Rel. Hum. 6am (%)	72	72	65	67	75	76	73	74	79	78	74	71	73
Avg. Rel. Hum. 3pm (%)	38	35	27	27	31	32	34	34	40	37	35	37	34

Note: Figures cover the years 1948-1995; Tr = Trace amounts (<0.05 in. of rain; <0.5 in. of snow)
Source: National Climatic Data Center, International Station Meteorological Climate Summary, 9/96

Weather Conditions

Temperature			Daytime Sky			Precipitation		
10°F & below	32°F & below	90°F & above	Clear	Partly cloudy	Cloudy	0.01 inch or more precip.	0.1 inch or more snow/ice	Thunder-storms
1	62	102	144	138	83	52	3	38

Note: Figures are average number of days per year and cover the years 1948-1995
Source: National Climatic Data Center, International Station Meteorological Climate Summary, 9/96

HAZARDOUS WASTE

Superfund Sites

Midland has one hazardous waste site on the EPA's Superfund Final National Priorities List: **West County Road 112 Ground Water**. There are a total of 1,322 Superfund sites on the list in the U.S. *U.S. Environmental Protection Agency, Final National Priorities List, April 14, 2015*

AIR & WATER QUALITY

Air Quality Trends: Ozone

	2004	2005	2006	2007	2008	2009	2010	2011	2012	2013
MSA[1]	n/a	n/a	n/a	n/a	n/a	n/a	n/a	n/a	n/a	n/a

Note: (1) Data covers the Midland, TX Metropolitan Statistical Area—see Appendix B for areas included; n/a not available. The values shown are the composite ozone concentration averages among trend sites based on the highest fourth daily maximum 8-hour concentration in parts per million. These trends are based on sites having an adequate record of monitoring data during the trend period. Data from exceptional events are included.
Source: U.S. Environmental Protection Agency, Air Quality Monitoring Information, "Air Quality Trends by City, 2000-2013"

Air Quality Index

Area	Percent of Days when Air Quality was...[2]					AQI Statistics[2]	
	Good	Moderate	Unhealthy for Sensitive Groups	Unhealthy	Very Unhealthy	Maximum	Median
MSA[1]	n/a	n/a	n/a	n/a	n/a	n/a	n/a

Note: (1) Data covers the Midland, TX Metropolitan Statistical Area—see Appendix B for areas included; (2) Based on days with AQI data in 2014. Air Quality Index (AQI) is an index for reporting daily air quality. EPA calculates the AQI for five major air pollutants regulated by the Clean Air Act: ground-level ozone, particle pollution (aka particulate matter), carbon monoxide, sulfur dioxide, and nitrogen dioxide. The AQI runs from 0 to 500. The higher the AQI value, the greater the level of air pollution and the greater the health concern. There are six AQI categories: "Good" AQI is between 0 and 50. Air quality is considered satisfactory; "Moderate" AQI is between 51 and 100. Air quality is acceptable; "Unhealthy for Sensitive Groups" When AQI values are between 101 and 150, members of sensitive groups may experience health effects; "Unhealthy" When AQI values are between 151 and 200 everyone may begin to experience health effects; "Very Unhealthy" AQI values between 201 and 300 trigger a health alert; "Hazardous" AQI values over 300 trigger warnings of emergency conditions (not shown).
Source: U.S. Environmental Protection Agency, Air Quality Index Report, 2014

Air Quality Index Pollutants

Area	Percent of Days when AQI Pollutant was...[2]					
	Carbon Monoxide	Nitrogen Dioxide	Ozone	Sulfur Dioxide	Particulate Matter 2.5	Particulate Matter 10
MSA[1]	n/a	n/a	n/a	n/a	n/a	n/a

Note: (1) Data covers the Midland, TX Metropolitan Statistical Area—see Appendix B for areas included; (2) Based on days with AQI data in 2014. The Air Quality Index (AQI) is an index for reporting daily air quality. EPA calculates the AQI for five major air pollutants regulated by the Clean Air Act: ground-level ozone, particle pollution (also known as particulate matter), carbon monoxide, sulfur dioxide, and nitrogen dioxide. The AQI runs from 0 to 500. The higher the AQI value, the greater the level of air pollution and the greater the health concern.
Source: U.S. Environmental Protection Agency, Air Quality Index Report, 2014

Maximum Air Pollutant Concentrations: Particulate Matter, Ozone, CO and Lead

	Particulate Matter 10 (ug/m^3)	Particulate Matter 2.5 Wtd AM (ug/m^3)	Particulate Matter 2.5 24-Hr (ug/m^3)	Ozone (ppm)	Carbon Monoxide (ppm)	Lead (ug/m^3)
MSA[1] Level	n/a	n/a	n/a	n/a	n/a	n/a
NAAQS[2]	150	15	35	0.075	9	0.15
Met NAAQS[2]	Yes	Yes	Yes	Yes	Yes	Yes

Note: (1) Data covers the Midland, TX Metropolitan Statistical Area—see Appendix B for areas included; Data from exceptional events are included; (2) National Ambient Air Quality Standards; ppm = parts per million; ug/m^3 = micrograms per cubic meter; n/a not available.
Concentrations: Particulate Matter 10 (coarse particulate)—highest second maximum 24-hour concentration; Particulate Matter 2.5 Wtd AM (fine particulate)—highest weighted annual mean concentration; Particulate Matter 2.5 24-Hour (fine particulate)—highest 98th percentile 24-hour concentration; Ozone—highest fourth daily maximum 8-hour concentration; Carbon Monoxide—highest second maximum non-overlapping 8-hour concentration; Lead—maximum running 3-month average
Source: U.S. Environmental Protection Agency, Air Quality Monitoring Information, "Air Quality Statistics by City, 2013"

Maximum Air Pollutant Concentrations: Nitrogen Dioxide and Sulfur Dioxide

	Nitrogen Dioxide AM (ppb)	Nitrogen Dioxide 1-Hr (ppb)	Sulfur Dioxide AM (ppb)	Sulfur Dioxide 1-Hr (ppb)	Sulfur Dioxide 24-Hr (ppb)
MSA[1] Level	n/a	n/a	n/a	n/a	n/a
NAAQS[2]	53	100	30	75	140
Met NAAQS[2]	Yes	Yes	Yes	Yes	Yes

Note: (1) Data covers the Midland, TX Metropolitan Statistical Area—see Appendix B for areas included; Data from exceptional events are included; (2) National Ambient Air Quality Standards; ppm = parts per million; ug/m^3 = micrograms per cubic meter; n/a not available.
Concentrations: Nitrogen Dioxide AM—highest arithmetic mean concentration; Nitrogen Dioxide 1-Hr—highest 98th percentile 1-hour daily maximum concentration; Sulfur Dioxide AM—highest annual mean concentration; Sulfur Dioxide 1-Hr—highest 99th percentile 1-hour daily maximum concentration; Sulfur Dioxide 24-Hr—highest second maximum 24-hour concentration
Source: U.S. Environmental Protection Agency, Air Quality Monitoring Information, "Air Quality Statistics by City, 2013"

Drinking Water

Water System Name	Pop. Served	Primary Water Source Type	Violations[1]	
			Health Based	Monitoring/ Reporting
City of Midland Water Purification	119,385	Surface	20	0

Note: (1) Based on violation data from January 1, 2014 to December 31, 2014 (includes unresolved violations from earlier years)
Source: U.S. Environmental Protection Agency, Office of Ground Water and Drinking Water, Safe Drinking Water Information System (based on data extracted January 27, 2015)

Nashville, Tennessee

Background

Nashville, the capital of Tennessee, was founded on Christmas Day in 1779 by James Robertson and John Donelson, and sits in the minds of millions as the country music capital of the world. This is the place to record if you want to make it into the country music industry, and where the Grand Ole Opry—the longest-running radio show in the country—still captures the hearts of millions of devoted listeners. It is no wonder, given how profoundly this industry has touched people, names like Dolly, Chet, Loretta, Hank, and Johnny are more familiar than the city's true native sons: Andrew, James, and Sam. Jackson, Polk, and Houston, that is.

Nashville is home to Music Row, an area just to the southwest of downtown with hundreds of businesses related to the country music, gospel music, and contemporary Christian music industries. The USA Network's Nashville Star, a country music singing competition, is also held in the Acuff Theatre. The magnitude of Nashville's recording industry is impressive, but other industries are important to the city, such as health care management, automobile production, and printing and publishing.

Nashville is also a devoted patron of education. The Davidson Academy, forerunner of the George Peabody College for Teachers, was founded in Nashville, as were Vanderbilt and Fisk universities, the latter being the first private black university in the United States. Vanderbilt University and Medical Center is the region's largest non-governmental employer.

Nashville citizens take pride in their numerous museums, including the Adventure Science Center, with its Sudekum Planetarium; the Aaron Douglas Gallery at Fisk University, which features a remarkable collection of African-American art; and the Carl Van Vechten Gallery, also at Fisk University, home to works by Alfred Stieglitz, Picasso, Cezanne, and Georgia O'Keefe. The Cheekwood Botanical Garden and Museum of Art includes 55 acres of gardens and contemporary art galleries.

Gracing the city are majestic mansions and plantations that testify to the mid nineteenth-century splendor for which the South came to be famous. Known as the "Queen of the Tennessee Plantations," the Belle Meade Plantation is an 1853 Greek Revival mansion crowning a 5,400-acre thoroughbred stud farm and nursery. The Belmont Mansion, built in 1850 by Adelicia Acklen, one of the wealthiest women in America, is constructed in the style of an Italian villa and was originally intended to be the summer home of the Acklens. Travelers' Rest Plantation served as a haven for weary travelers, past and present, and is Nashville's oldest plantation home open to the public. It features docents dressed in period costume who explain and demonstrate life in the plantations' heyday. Carnton Plantation was the site of the Civil War's Battle of Franklin, and The Hermitage was the home of Andrew Jackson, the seventh president of the United States. Tennessee's historic State Capitol Building, completed in 1859, has had much of its interior restored to its nineteenth-century appearance.

The Nashville area comprises many urban, suburban, rural, and historic districts, which can differ immensely from each other. Most of the best restaurants, clubs, and shops are on the west side of the Cumberland River, however, the east side encompasses fine neighborhoods, interesting homes, plenty of shopping, and good food, as well. Outdoor activities include camping, fishing, hiking, and biking at the many scenic and accessible lakes in the region.

Located on the Cumberland River in central Tennessee, Nashville's average relative humidity is moderate, as is its weather, with great temperature extremes a rarity. The city is not in the most common path of storms that cross the country, but is in a zone of moderate frequency for thunderstorms.

Rankings

General Rankings

- Nashville appeared on *Business Insider's* list of the "15 Hottest American Cities for 2015." Criteria: job and population growth; demographics; affordability; livability; residents' health and welfare; technological innovation; sustainability; culture favoring youth and creativity. *www.businessinsider.com, "The Fifteen Hottest American Cities for 2015," November 19, 2014*
- The Nashville metro area was identified as one of America's fastest-growing areas in terms of population and economy by *Forbes*. The area ranked #20 out of 20. The 100 most populous metro areas in the U.S. were evaluated on the following criteria: estimated population growth; job growth; gross metropolitan product growth; unemployment; median salaries for college-educated workers. *Forbes, "America's Fastest-Growing Cities 2015," January 27, 2015*
- Nashville was identified as one of America's fastest-growing major metropolitan areas in terms of population growth by CNNMoney.com. The area ranked #7 out of 10. Criteria: population growth between July 2012 and July 2013. *CNNMoney, "10 Fastest-Growing Cities," March 28, 2014*
- Nashville was selected as one of America's best cities by *Bloomberg Businessweek*. The city ranked #13 out of 50. Criteria: leisure attributes (the number of restaurants, bars, libraries, museums, professional sports teams, and park acres by population); educational attributes (public school performance, the number of colleges, and graduate degree holders); economic factors (2011 income and June and July 2012 unemployment); crime; and air quality. *Bloomberg BusinessWeek, "America's Best Cities," September 26, 2012*
- Nashville was selected as one of America's best river towns by *Outside Magazine*. Criteria: cost of living; cultural vibrancy; job prospects; environmental stewardship; access to the outdoors. *Outside Magazine, "Best River Towns 2012," October 2012*
- Nashville was selected as one the best places to live in America by *Outside Magazine*. The city ranked #14. Criteria included nearby adventure, healthy eating options, bike lanes, green spaces, number of outfitters and bike shops, miles of trails, median income, and unemployment rate. *Outside Magazine, "Outside's Best 16 Best Places to Live in the U.S. 2014," September 2014*
- Nashville was selected as one of the "10 Best Places to Live Now" by *Men's Journal*. Nashville ranked #2. *Men's Journal, "10 Best Places to Live Now," April 2015*

Business/Finance Rankings

- The personal finance site NerdWallet scored the nation's 50 largest American cities according to how friendly a business climate they offer to would-be entrepreneurs. Criteria included access to funding, human capital, local economy, and business-friendliness as judged by small business owners. On the resulting list of most welcoming cities, Nashville ranked #5. *www.nerdwallet.com, "Best Cities to Start a Business," May 7, 2014*
- Recognizing the sizeable percentage of American workers who are self-employed, NerdWallet editors assessed the country's cities according to percentage of freelancers, median rental costs, and affordability of median healthcare costs. By these criteria, Nashville placed #5 among the best cities for independent workers. *www.nerdwallet.com, "Best Cities for Freelancers," February 25, 2014*
- The editors of *Kiplinger's Personal Finance Magazine* named Nashville to their list of ten of the best metro areas for start-ups. The area rank #3.Criteria: well-educated workforce; low living costs for self-employed people, as measured by the Council for Community and Economic Research; a strong existing community of small business; low unemployment; low business costs. *www.kiplinger.com, "10 Great Cities for Starting a Business," October 2014*
- Based on metro area social media reviews, the employment opinion group Glassdoor surveyed 50 of the largest U.S. metro areas on measures including compensation and benefits, satisfaction with management, business outlook, and number of employers hiring. The Nashville metro area was ranked #40 in overall employee satisfaction. *www.glassdoor.com, "Employment Satisfaction Report Card by City," June 13, 2014*

- In a survey of economic confidence in the nation's 50 largest metropolitan areas conducted January–December 2014, the Nashville metro area placed #35, according to Gallup's 2014 Economic Confidence Index. *Gallup, "San Jose and San Francisco Lead in Economic Confidence," March 19, 2015*

- Using data from the Council for Community and Economic Research's 2013 Annual Report, NerdWallet ranked the 100 most affordable cities in America. States from the central and southern United States dominate the list. On the affordability scale, Nashville ranked #18. *NerdWallet.com, "Most Affordable Cities in America," June 4, 2014*

- The Brookings Institution ranked the 50 largest cities in the U.S. based on income inequality. Nashville was ranked #45. (#1 = greatest ineqality). Criteria: the cities were ranked based on the "95/20 ratio," a figure representing the income at which a household earns more than 95 percent of all other households, divided by the income at which a household earns more than only 20 percent of all other households. *Brookings Institution, "Income Inequality in America's 50 Largest Cities, 2007-2013," March 17, 2015*

- Nashville was ranked #11 out of 100 metro areas in terms of economic performance (#1 = best) during the recession and recovery from trough quarter through the second quarter of 2013. Criteria: percent change in employment; percentage point change in unemployment rate; percent change in gross metropolitan product; percent change in House Price Index. *Brookings Institution, MetroMonitor: Tracking Economic Recession and Recovery in America's 100 Largest Metropolitan Areas, September 2013*

- Nashville was identified as one of America's most frugal metro areas by *Coupons.com.* The city ranked #4 out of 25. Criteria: online coupon usage. *Coupons.com, "Top 25 Most Frugal Cities of 2013," April 10, 2014*

- Nashville was identified as one of America's most frugal metro areas by *Coupons.com.* The city ranked #10 out of 25. Criteria: Grocery IQ and coupons.com mobile app usage. *Coupons.com, "Top 25 Most On-the-Go Frugal Cities of 2013," April 10, 2014*

- The Nashville metro area appeared on the Milken Institute "2013 Best Performing Cities" list. Rank: #15 out of 200 large metro areas. Criteria: job growth; wage and salary growth; high-tech output growth. *Milken Institute, "Best-Performing Cities 2014," January 2015*

- *Forbes* ranked the 200 most populous metro areas to determine the nation's "Best Places for Business and Careers." The Nashville metro area was ranked #10. Criteria: costs (business and living); job growth (past and projected); income growth; educational attainment (college and high school); projected economic growth; cultural and recreational opportunities; net migration patterns; number of highly ranked colleges. *Forbes, "The Best Places for Business and Careers 2014," July 23, 2014*

Children/Family Rankings

- Nashville was selected as one of the best cities for families to live by *Parenting* magazine. The city ranked #3 out of 100. Criteria: education ratings; FBI crime statistics, Bureau of Labor statistics, U.S. Census data. *Parenting.com, " Top Ten Best Cities for Families 2014"*

- Nashville was chosen as one of America's 100 best communities for young people. The winners were selected based upon detailed information provided about each community's efforts to fulfill five essential promises critical to the well-being of young people: caring adults who are actively involved in their lives; safe places in which to learn and grow; a healthy start toward adulthood; an effective education that builds marketable skills; and opportunities to help others. *America's Promise Alliance, "100 Best Communities for Young People, 2012"*

Culture/Performing Arts Rankings

- Nashville was selected as one of "America's Favorite Cities." The city ranked #1 in the "Culture: Concerts " category. Respondents to an online survey were asked to rate 38 top urban destinations in the U.S. from a visitor's perspective. Criteria: number and quality of concerts. *Travelandleisure.com, "America's Favorite Cities," October 7, 2014*

- Nashville was selected as one of "America's Favorite Cities." The city ranked #1 in the "Culture: Music Scene " category. Respondents to an online survey were asked to rate 38 top urban destinations in the U.S. from a visitor's perspective. *Travelandleisure.com, "America's Favorite Cities," October 7, 2014*

- Nashville was selected as one of America's top cities for the arts. The city ranked #16 in the big city (population 500,000 and over) category. Criteria: readers' top choices for arts travel destinations based on the richness and variety of visual arts sites, activities and events. *American Style, "2012 Top 25 Arts Destinations," June 2012*

Dating/Romance Rankings

- Of the 100 U.S. cities surveyed by *Men's Health* in its quest to identify the nation's best cities for dating and forming relationships, Nashville was ranked #42 for online dating (#1 = best). *Men's Health, "The Best and Worst Cities for Online Dating," January 30, 2013*
- Nashville was selected as one of America's best cities for singles by the readers of *Travel + Leisure* in their annual "America's Favorite Cities" survey. The city was ranked #7 out of 20. Criteria included good-looking locals, cool shopping, and hipster-magnet coffee bars. *Travel + Leisure, "America's Best Cities for Singles," January 23, 2015*

Education Rankings

- Personal finance website *WalletHub* analyzed the 150 largest U.S. metropolitan statistical areas to determine where the most educated Americans are choosing to settle. Criteria: educational attainment; percentage of workers with jobs in computer, engineering, and science fields; quality and size of each metro area's universities. Nashville was ranked #30 (#1 = most educated city). *www.WalletHub.com, "2014's Most and Least Educated Cities*
- Nashville was selected as one of America's most literate cities. The city ranked #26 out of the 77 largest U.S. cities. Criteria: number of booksellers; library resources; Internet resources; educational attainment; periodical publishing resources; newspaper circulation. *Central Connecticut State University, "America's Most Literate Cities, 2014," April 8, 2015*

Environmental Rankings

- The Nashville metro area came in at #230 for the relative comfort of its climate on Sperling's list of "chill cities," as measured by the Sperling Heat Index. All 361 metro areas are included. Criteria included daytime high temperatures, nighttime low temperatures, dew point, and relative humidity at the high temperatures. *www.bertsperling.com, "Sperling's Chill Cities," July 18, 2013*
- Sperling's BestPlaces assessed 379 metropolitan areas of the United States for the likelihood of dangerously extreme weather events or earthquakes. In general the Southeast and South-Central regions have the highest risk of weather extremes and earthquakes, while the Pacific Northwest enjoys the lowest risk. Of the least risky metropolitan areas, the Nashville metro area was ranked #234. *www.bestplaces.net, "Safest Places from Natural Disasters," April 2011*
- The U.S. Environmental Protection Agency (EPA) released a list of mid-size U.S. metropolitan areas with the most ENERGY STAR certified buildings in 2014. The Nashville metro area was ranked #8 out of 10. *U.S. Environmental Protection Agency, "Top Cities With the Most ENERGY STAR Certified Buildings in 2014," March 25, 2015*

Food/Drink Rankings

- *Men's Health* ranked 100 major U.S. cities in terms of alcohol intoxication. Nashville ranked #87 (#1 = most sober).Criteria: binge drinking; alcohol-related traffic accidents, arrests, and fatalities. *Men's Health, "The Drunkest Cities in America," November 19, 2013*
- Nashville was selected as one of the seven best cities for barbeque by *U.S. News & World Report.* The city was ranked #6. *U.S. New & World Report, "America's Best BBQ Cities," February 29, 2012*

Health/Fitness Rankings

- For each of the 50 most populous metro areas in the United States, the American College of Sports Medicine's American Fitness Index evaluated infrastructure, community assets, and policies that encourage healthy and fit lifestyles, including preventive health behaviors, levels of chronic disease conditions, health care access, and community resources and policies that support physical activity. The Nashville metro area ranked #32 for "community fitness." Personal health indicators were considered as well as community and environmental indicators. *www.americanfitnessindex.org, "ACSM American Fitness Index Health and Community Fitness Status of the 50 Largest Metropolitan Areas," May 2013*

- The Nashville metro area was identified as one of the worst cities for bed bugs in America by pest control company Orkin. The area ranked #23 out of 50 based on the number of bed bug treatments Orkin performed from January to December 2013. *Orkin, "Chicago Tops Bed Bug Cities List for Second Year in a Row," January 16, 2014*

- Nashville was identified as one of 15 cities with the highest increase in bed bug activity in the U.S. by pest control provider Terminix. The city ranked #14.Criteria: cities with the largest percentage gains in bed bug customer calls from January–May 2013 compared to the same time period in 2012. *Terminix, "Cities with Highest Increases in Bed Bug Activity," July 9, 2013*

- Nashville was selected as one of the 25 fittest cities in America by *Men's Fitness Online*. It ranked #24 out of America's 50 largest cities. Criteria: fitness centers and sport stores; nutrition; sports participation; TV viewing; overweight/sedentary; junk food; air quality; geography; commute; parks and open space; city recreational facilities; access to healthcare; motivation; mayor and city initiatives; state obesity initiatives. *Men's Fitness, "The Fittest and Fattest Cities in America," March 5, 2012*

- Nashville was identified as a "2013 Spring Allergy Capital." The area ranked #36 out of 100. Three groups of factors were used to identify the most severe cities for people with allergies during the spring season: annual pollen levels; medicine utilization; access to board-certified allergists. *Asthma and Allergy Foundation of America, "Spring Allergy Capitals 2013"*

- Nashville was identified as a "2013 Fall Allergy Capital." The area ranked #24 out of 100. Three groups of factors were used to identify the most severe cities for people with allergies during the fall season: annual pollen levels; medicine utilization; access to board-certified allergists. *Asthma and Allergy Foundation of America, "Fall Allergy Capitals 2013"*

- Nashville was identified as a "2013 Asthma Capital." The area ranked #32 out of the nation's 100 largest metropolitan areas. Twelve factors were used to identify the most challenging places to live for people with asthma: estimated prevalence; self-reported prevalence; crude death rate for asthma; annual pollen score; annual air quality; public smoking laws; number of board-certified asthma specialists; school inhaler access laws; rescue medication use; controller medication use; uninsured rate; poverty rate. *Asthma and Allergy Foundation of America, "Asthma Capitals 2013"*

- *Men's Health* ranked 100 major U.S. cities in terms of the best and worst cities for men. Nashville ranked #41. Criteria: thirty-three data points were examined covering health, fitness, and quality of life. *Men's Health, "The Best & Worst Cities for Men 2014," December 6, 2013*

- The Nashville metro area appeared in the 2013 Gallup-Healthways Well-Being Index. The area ranked #72 out of 189. The Gallup-Healthways Well-Being Index score is an average of six sub-indexes, which individually examine life evaluation, emotional health, work environment, physical health, healthy behaviors, and access to basic necessities. Results are based on telephone interviews conducted as part of the Gallup-Healthways Well-Being Index survey January 2–December 29, 2012, and January 2–December 30, 2013, with a random sample of 531,630 adults, aged 18 and older, living in metropolitan areas in the 50 U.S. states and the District of Columbia. *Gallup-Healthways, "State of American Well-Being," March 25, 2014*

- The Nashville metro area was identified as one of "America's Most Stressful Cities" by *Sperling's BestPlaces.* The metro area ranked #30 out of 50. Criteria: unemployment rate; suicide rate; commute time; mental health; poor rest; alcohol use; violent crime rate; property crime rate; cloudy days annually. *Sperling's BestPlaces, www.BestPlaces.net, "Stressful Cities 2012*

Real Estate Rankings

- Nashville was ranked #58 out of 275 metro areas in terms of house price appreciation in 2014 (#1 = highest rate). *Federal Housing Finance Agency, House Price Index, 4th Quarter 2014*
- The Nashville metro area was identified as one of the 15 worst housing markets for the next five years." Criteria: projected annualized change in home prices between the fourth quarter 2012 and the fourth quarter 2017. *The Business Insider, "The 15 Worst Housing Markets for the Next Five Years," May 22, 2013*

Safety Rankings

- Symantec, in partnership with Sperling's BestPlaces, ranked the 50 largest cities in the U.S. in terms of their vulnerability to cybercrime. The city ranked #36. Criteria: number of cyberattacks and potential infections; level of Internet access; expenditures on smartphones and computer hardware/software; wireless hotspots; broadband connectivity; Internet usage; online purchases. *Symantec, "Riskiest Online Cities of 2012" February 15, 2012*
- Allstate ranked the 200 largest cities in America in terms of driver safety. Nashville ranked #63. Allstate researchers analyzed internal property damage claims over a two-year period from January 2011 to December 2012. A weighted average of the two-year numbers determined the annual percentages. *Allstate, "Allstate America's Best Drivers Report, 2014"*
- Nashville was identified as one of the most dangerous cities in America by *The Business Insider.* Criteria: cities with 100,000 residents or more were ranked by violent crime rate in 2011. Violent crimes include for murder, rape, robbery, and aggravated assault. The city ranked #19 out of 25. *The Business Insider, "The 25 Most Dangerous Cities in America," November 4, 2012*
- The National Insurance Crime Bureau ranked 380 metro areas in the U.S. in terms of per capita rates of vehicle theft. The Nashville metro area ranked #211 (#1 = highest rate). Criteria: number of vehicle theft offenses per 100,000 inhabitants in 2012. *National Insurance Crime Bureau, "Hot Spots 2012," June 26, 2013*

Seniors/Retirement Rankings

- From its Best Cities for Successful Aging indexes, the Milken Institute generated rankings for metropolitan areas, weighing data in eight categories—health care, wellness, living arrangements, transportation, financial characteristics, education and employment opportunities, community engagement, and overall livability. The Nashville metro area was ranked #23 overall in the large metro area category. *Milken Institute, "Best Cities for Successful Aging, 2014"*
- *Forbes* selected the Nashville metro area as one of 25 "Best Places for a Working Retirement." Criteria: affordability; improving, above-average economies and job prospects; and a favorable tax climate for retirees. *Forbes.com, "Best Places for a Working Retirement in 2013," February 4, 2013*

Sports/Recreation Rankings

- *24/7 Wall St.* analysts isolated the ten cities that spent the most public money per capita on sports stadiums, according to 2010 data. Nashville ranked #9. *24/7 Wall St., "Cities Paying the Most for Sports Teams," January 30, 2013*

Women/Minorities Rankings

- *Women's Health* examined U.S. cities and identified the 100 best cities for women. Nashville was ranked #64. Criteria: 30 categories were examined from obesity and breast cancer rates to commuting times and hours spent working out. *Women's Health, "Best Cities for Women 2012"*

Miscellaneous Rankings

- *Travel + Leisure* invited readers to rate cities on indicators such as aloofness, "smarty-pants residents," highbrow cultural offerings, high-end shopping, artisanal coffeehouses, conspicuous eco-consciousness, and more in order to identify the nation's snobbiest cities. Cities large and small made the list; among them was Nashville, at #13. *www.travelandleisure.com, "America's Snobbiest Cities, June 2013*
- The watchdog site Charity Navigator conducts an annual study of charities in the nation's major markets both to analyze statistical differences in their financial, accountability, and transparency practices and to track year-to-year variations in individual communities. The Nashville metro area was ranked #28 among the 30 metro markets. *www.charitynavigator.org, "Metro Market Study 2013," June 1, 2013*
- Nashville appeared on *Travel + Leisure's* list of America's most attractive people. Criteria: cities were selected by readers in their annual America's Favorite Cities survey. The city ranked #3 out of 10. *Travel + Leisure, "America's Most and Least Attractive People," November 2013*
- The Nashville metro area was selected as one of "The Best U.S. Cities for Bargain Shopping" by *Forbes.* The area ranked #9 out of 10. Criteria: number of outlet stores; gross leasable retail space in major malls; low consumer price index; low sales tax rate. Indicators were examined in the nation's 50 largest metropolitan areas. *Forbes, "The Best U.S. Cities for Bargain Shopping," January 20, 2012*
- Mars Chocolate North America, the makers of COMBOS®, in partnership with Sperling's BestPlaces, ranked 50 major metro areas in terms of their "manliness." The Nashville metro area ranked #4. Criteria: number of professional sports teams; number of nearby NASCAR tracks and racing events; manly lifestyle; concentration of manly retail stores; manly occupations per capita; salty snack sales; "Board of Manliness" rankings. *Mars Chocolate North America, "America's Manliest Cities 2012"*
- Nashville was selected as one of "America's Best Cities for Hipsters" by *Travel + Leisure.* The city was ranked #8 out of 20. Criteria: live music; coffee bars; independent boutiques; best microbrews; offbeat and tech-savvy locals. *Travel + Leisure, "America's Best Cities for Hipsters," November 2013*
- The National Alliance to End Homelessness ranked the 100 most populous metro areas in terms the rate of homelessness. The Nashville metro area ranked #59. Criteria: number of homeless people per 10,000 population in 2011. *National Alliance to End Homelessness, The State of Homelessness in America 2012*

Business Environment

CITY FINANCES

City Government Finances

Component	2012 ($000)	2012 ($ per capita)
Total Revenues	3,786,875	6,299
Total Expenditures	3,941,120	6,555
Debt Outstanding	4,895,022	8,142
Cash and Securities[1]	4,527,122	7,530

Note: (1) Cash and security holdings of a government at the close of its fiscal year, including those of its dependent agencies, utilities, and liquor stores.
Source: U.S Census Bureau, State & Local Government Finances 2012

City Government Revenue by Source

Source	2012 ($000)	2012 ($ per capita)
General Revenue		
From Federal Government	12,679	21
From State Government	611,671	1,017
From Local Governments	0	0
Taxes		
Property	787,882	1,310
Sales and Gross Receipts	363,043	604
Personal Income	0	0
Corporate Income	0	0
Motor Vehicle License	27,358	46
Other Taxes	42,328	70
Current Charges	320,142	532
Liquor Store	0	0
Utility	1,280,165	2,129
Employee Retirement	108,000	180

Source: U.S Census Bureau, State & Local Government Finances 2012

City Government Expenditures by Function

Function	2012 ($000)	2012 ($ per capita)	2012 (%)
General Direct Expenditures			
Air Transportation	0	0	0.0
Corrections	63,217	105	1.6
Education	845,888	1,407	21.5
Employment Security Administration	0	0	0.0
Financial Administration	21,913	36	0.6
Fire Protection	108,609	181	2.8
General Public Buildings	0	0	0.0
Governmental Administration, Other	26,010	43	0.7
Health	85,976	143	2.2
Highways	39,232	65	1.0
Hospitals	144,343	240	3.7
Housing and Community Development	0	0	0.0
Interest on General Debt	169,870	283	4.3
Judicial and Legal	53,575	89	1.4
Libraries	21,178	35	0.5
Parking	0	0	0.0
Parks and Recreation	81,001	135	2.1
Police Protection	193,910	323	4.9
Public Welfare	31,618	53	0.8
Sewerage	137,857	229	3.5
Solid Waste Management	20,036	33	0.5
Veterans' Services	0	0	0.0
Liquor Store	0	0	0.0
Utility	1,318,174	2,192	33.4
Employee Retirement	191,662	319	4.9

Source: U.S Census Bureau, State & Local Government Finances 2012

DEMOGRAPHICS

Population Growth

Area	1990 Census	2000 Census	2010 Census	Population Growth (%) 1990-2000	Population Growth (%) 2000-2010
City	488,364	545,524	601,222	11.7	10.2
MSA[1]	1,048,218	1,311,789	1,589,934	25.1	21.2
U.S.	248,709,873	281,421,906	308,745,538	13.2	9.7

Note: (1) Figures cover the Nashville-Davidson—Murfreesboro—Franklin, TN Metropolitan Statistical Area—see Appendix B for areas included
Source: U.S. Census Bureau, Census 1990, 2000, 2010

Household Size

Area	Persons in Household (%)							Average Household Size
	One	Two	Three	Four	Five	Six	Seven or More	
City	36.8	32.2	13.8	10.3	4.0	1.6	1.1	2.41
MSA[1]	28.2	34.1	15.7	13.2	5.6	1.9	1.2	2.60
U.S.	27.7	33.6	15.7	13.1	6.0	2.3	1.5	2.64

Note: (1) Figures cover the Nashville-Davidson—Murfreesboro—Franklin, TN Metropolitan Statistical Area—see Appendix B for areas included
Source: U.S. Census Bureau, 2011-2013 American Community Survey 3-Year Estimates

Race

Area	White Alone[2] (%)	Black Alone[2] (%)	Asian Alone[2] (%)	AIAN[3] Alone[2] (%)	NHOPI[4] Alone[2] (%)	Other Race Alone[2] (%)	Two or More Races (%)
City	60.9	28.4	3.2	0.3	0.1	4.9	2.3
MSA[1]	77.7	15.3	2.3	0.3	0.0	2.5	1.9
U.S.	73.9	12.6	5.0	0.8	0.2	4.7	2.9

Note: (1) Figures cover the Nashville-Davidson—Murfreesboro—Franklin, TN Metropolitan Statistical Area—see Appendix B for areas included; (2) Alone is defined as not being in combination with one or more other races; (3) American Indian and Alaska Native; (4) Native Hawaiian and Other Pacific Islander
Source: U.S. Census Bureau, 2011-2013 American Community Survey 3-Year Estimates

Hispanic or Latino Origin

Area	Total (%)	Mexican (%)	Puerto Rican (%)	Cuban (%)	Other (%)
City	10.1	6.1	0.6	0.4	3.1
MSA[1]	6.7	4.2	0.5	0.2	1.7
U.S.	16.9	10.8	1.6	0.6	3.8

Note: Persons of Hispanic or Latino origin can be of any race; (1) Figures cover the Nashville-Davidson—Murfreesboro—Franklin, TN Metropolitan Statistical Area—see Appendix B for areas included
Source: U.S. Census Bureau, 2011-2013 American Community Survey 3-Year Estimates

Segregation

Type	Segregation Indices[1]				Percent Change		
	1990	2000	2010	2010 Rank[2]	1990-2000	1990-2010	2000-2010
Black/White	60.7	58.1	56.2	49	-2.6	-4.4	-1.9
Asian/White	45.2	44.4	41.0	51	-0.8	-4.2	-3.4
Hispanic/White	24.3	46.0	47.9	34	21.6	23.5	1.9

Note: All figures cover the Metropolitan Statistical Area—see Appendix B for areas included; Figures are based on an analysis of 1990, 2000, and 2010 Census Decennial Census tract data by William H. Frey, Brookings Institution and the University of Michigan Social Science Data Analysis Network. In this analysis all racial groups (whites, blacks, and asians) are non-Hispanic members of those races. Hispanics are shown as a separate category;
(1) Segregation Indices are Dissimilarity Indices that measure the degree to which the minority group is distributed differently than whites across census tracts. They range from 0 (complete integration) to 100 (complete segregation) where the value indicates the percentage of the minority group that needs to move to be distributed exactly like whites; (2) Ranges from 1 (most segregated) to 102 (least segregated); n/a not available.
Source: www.CensusScope.org

Ancestry

Area	German	Irish	English	American	Italian	Polish	French[2]	Scottish	Dutch
City	9.2	8.9	8.1	7.7	2.4	1.0	2.0	1.9	0.9
MSA[1]	10.8	11.0	10.3	14.0	2.6	1.2	2.2	2.3	1.0
U.S.	14.9	10.8	8.0	7.4	5.5	3.0	2.7	1.7	1.4

Note: Figures are the percentage of the total population reporting a particular ancestry. The nine most commonly reported ancestries in the U.S. are shown. Figures include multiple ancestries (e.g. if a person reported being Irish and Italian, they were included in both columns); (1) Figures cover the Nashville-Davidson—Murfreesboro—Franklin, TN Metropolitan Statistical Area—see Appendix B for areas included; (2) Excludes Basque

Source: U.S. Census Bureau, 2011-2013 American Community Survey 3-Year Estimates

Foreign-Born Population

Area	Percent of Population Born in								
	Any Foreign Country	Mexico	Asia	Europe	Carribean	South America	Central America[2]	Africa	Canada
City	12.0	3.1	3.6	0.9	0.4	0.5	1.6	1.7	0.2
MSA[1]	7.3	2.0	2.2	0.7	0.2	0.3	0.8	0.8	0.2
U.S.	13.0	3.7	3.8	1.5	1.2	0.9	1.0	0.6	0.3

Note: (1) Figures cover the Nashville-Davidson—Murfreesboro—Franklin, TN Metropolitan Statistical Area—see Appendix B for areas included; (2) Excludes Mexico.

Source: U.S. Census Bureau, 2011-2013 American Community Survey 3-Year Estimates

Marital Status

Area	Never Married	Now Married[2]	Separated	Widowed	Divorced
City	40.4	39.1	2.6	5.1	12.9
MSA[1]	30.8	49.4	2.0	5.4	12.4
U.S.	32.7	48.1	2.2	6.0	11.0

Note: Figures are percentages and cover the population 15 years of age and older; (1) Figures cover the Nashville-Davidson—Murfreesboro—Franklin, TN Metropolitan Statistical Area—see Appendix B for areas included; (2) Excludes separated

Source: U.S. Census Bureau, 2011-2013 American Community Survey 3-Year Estimates

Disability Status

Area	All Ages	Under 18 Years Old	18 to 64 Years Old	65 Years and Over
City	11.3	3.5	9.8	37.9
MSA[1]	11.5	3.8	10.0	36.7
U.S.	12.3	4.1	10.2	36.3

Note: Figures show percent of the civilian noninstitutionalized population that reported having a disability. Disability status is determined from from six types of difficulty: vision, hearing, cognitive, ambulatory, self-care, and independent living. For children under 5 years old, hearing and vision difficulty are used to determine disability status. For children between the ages of 5 and 14, disability status is determined from hearing, vision, cognitive, ambulatory, and self-care difficulties. For people aged 15 years and older, they are considered to have a disability if they have difficulty with any one of the six difficulty types; (1) Figures cover the Nashville-Davidson—Murfreesboro—Franklin, TN Metropolitan Statistical Area—see Appendix B for areas included.

Source: U.S. Census Bureau, 2011-2013 American Community Survey 3-Year Estimates

Age

Area	Percent of Population									Median Age
	Under Age 5	Age 5–19	Age 20–34	Age 35–44	Age 45–54	Age 55–64	Age 65–74	Age 75–84	Age 85+	
City	7.1	17.4	27.2	13.8	12.9	11.1	5.8	3.3	1.3	33.8
MSA[1]	6.7	20.0	21.8	14.0	14.3	11.8	6.7	3.4	1.3	36.1
U.S.	6.4	19.9	20.7	12.9	14.1	12.3	7.6	4.2	1.9	37.4

Note: (1) Figures cover the Nashville-Davidson—Murfreesboro—Franklin, TN Metropolitan Statistical Area—see Appendix B for areas included

Source: U.S. Census Bureau, 2011-2013 American Community Survey 3-Year Estimates

Gender

Area	Males	Females	Males per 100 Females
City	302,021	321,874	93.8
MSA[1]	843,798	883,814	95.5
U.S.	154,451,010	159,410,713	96.9

Note: (1) Figures cover the Nashville-Davidson—Murfreesboro—Franklin, TN Metropolitan Statistical Area—see Appendix B for areas included
Source: U.S. Census Bureau, 2011-2013 American Community Survey 3-Year Estimates

Religious Groups by Family

Area	Catholic	Baptist	Non-Den.	Methodist[2]	Lutheran	LDS[3]	Pente-costal	Presby-terian[4]	Muslim[5]	Judaism
MSA[1]	4.1	25.3	5.8	6.1	0.4	0.8	2.2	2.1	0.4	0.2
U.S.	19.1	9.3	4.0	4.0	2.3	2.0	1.9	1.6	0.8	0.7

Note: Figures are the number of adherents as a percentage of the total population; (1) Figures cover the Nashville-Davidson—Murfreesboro—Franklin, TN Metropolitan Statistical Area—see Appendix B for areas included; (2) Methodist/Pietist; (3) Latter Day Saints; (4) Reformed; (5) Figures are estimates
Source: Association of Statisticians of American Religious Bodies, 2010 U.S. Religion Census: Religious Congregations & Membership Study

Religious Groups by Tradition

Area	Catholic	Evangelical Protestant	Mainline Protestant	Other Tradition	Black Protestant	Orthodox
MSA[1]	4.1	33.0	8.0	1.7	3.4	0.5
U.S.	19.1	16.2	7.3	4.3	1.6	0.3

Note: Figures are the number of adherents as a percentage of the total population; (1) Figures cover the Nashville-Davidson—Murfreesboro—Franklin, TN Metropolitan Statistical Area—see Appendix B for areas included
Source: Association of Statisticians of American Religious Bodies, 2010 U.S. Religion Census: Religious Congregations & Membership Study

ECONOMY

Gross Metropolitan Product

Area	2012	2013	2014	2015	Rank[2]
MSA[1]	91.1	96.3	100.8	106.2	35

Note: Figures are in billions of dollars; (1) Figures cover the Nashville-Davidson—Murfreesboro—Franklin, TN Metropolitan Statistical Area—see Appendix B for areas included; (2) Rank is based on 2015 data and ranges from 1 to 363
Source: The U.S. Conference of Mayors, U.S. Metro Economies: GMP and Employment 2013-2015, June 2014

Economic Growth

Area	2010-12 (%)	2013 (%)	2014 (%)	2015 (%)	Rank[2]
MSA[1]	4.5	4.2	3.1	3.4	88
U.S.	2.1	2.0	2.3	3.2	–

Note: Figures are real gross metropolitan product (GMP) growth rates and represent annual average percent change; (1) Figures cover the Nashville-Davidson—Murfreesboro—Franklin, TN Metropolitan Statistical Area—see Appendix B for areas included; (2) Rank is based on 2015 data and ranges from 1 to 363
Source: The U.S. Conference of Mayors, U.S. Metro Economies: GMP and Employment 2013-2015, June 2014

Metropolitan Area Exports

Area	2008	2009	2010	2011	2012	2013	Rank[2]
MSA[1]	5,259.5	4,406.6	5,748.5	5,878.7	6,402.1	8,702.8	39

Note: Figures are in millions of dollars; (1) Figures cover the Nashville-Davidson—Murfreesboro—Franklin, TN Metropolitan Statistical Area—see Appendix B for areas included; (2) Rank is based on 2013 data and ranges from 1 to 387
Source: U.S. Department of Commerce, International Trade Administration, Office of Trade & Industry Information, Manufacturing & Services, data extracted April 3, 2015

Building Permits

Area	Single-Family			Multi-Family			Total		
	2013	2014	Pct. Chg.	2013	2014	Pct. Chg.	2013	2014	Pct. Chg.
City	1,824	2,538	39.1	2,142	3,829	78.8	3,966	6,367	60.5
MSA[1]	7,020	9,075	29.3	3,869	5,869	51.7	10,889	14,944	37.2
U.S.	620,802	634,597	2.2	370,020	411,766	11.3	990,822	1,046,363	5.6

Note: (1) Figures cover the Nashville-Davidson—Murfreesboro—Franklin, TN Metropolitan Statistical Area—see Appendix B for areas included; Figures represent new, privately-owned housing units authorized (unadjusted data); All permit data are based on estimates with imputation.
Source: U.S. Census Bureau, Manufacturing, Mining, and Construction Statistics, Building Permits, 2013, 2014

Bankruptcy Filings

Area	Business Filings			Nonbusiness Filings		
	2013	2014	% Chg.	2013	2014	% Chg.
Davidson County	78	70	-10.3	3,434	3,124	-9.0
U.S.	33,212	26,983	-18.8	1,038,720	909,812	-12.4

Note: Business filings include Chapter 7, Chapter 11, Chapter 12, and Chapter 13; Nonbusiness filings include Chapter 7, Chapter 11, and Chapter 13
Source: Administrative Office of the U.S. Courts, Business and Nonbusiness Bankruptcy, County Cases Commenced by Chapter of the Bankruptcy Code, During the 12- Month Period Ending December 31, 2013 and Business and Nonbusiness Bankruptcy, County Cases Commenced by Chapter of the Bankruptcy Code, During the 12- Month Period Ending December 31, 2014

Housing Vacancy Rates

Area	Gross Vacancy Rate[2] (%)			Year-Round Vacancy Rate[3] (%)			Rental Vacancy Rate[4] (%)			Homeowner Vacancy Rate[5] (%)		
	2012	2013	2014	2012	2013	2014	2012	2013	2014	2012	2013	2014
MSA[1]	8.7	6.6	7.0	8.2	6.4	6.7	8.4	5.3	4.0	1.6	0.9	2.4
U.S.	13.8	13.6	13.4	10.8	10.7	10.4	8.7	8.3	7.6	2.0	2.0	1.9

Note: (1) Figures cover the Nashville-Davidson—Murfreesboro—Franklin, TN Metropolitan Statistical Area—see Appendix B for areas included; (2) The percentage of the total housing inventory that is vacant; (3) The percentage of the housing inventory (excluding seasonal units) that is year-round vacant; (4) The percentage of rental inventory that is vacant for rent; (5) The percentage of homeowner inventory that is vacant for sale
Source: U.S. Census Bureau, Housing Vacancies and Homeownership Annual Statistics: 2014

INCOME

Income

Area	Per Capita ($)	Median Household ($)	Average Household ($)
City	26,976	45,542	63,645
MSA[1]	27,929	51,825	71,398
U.S.	27,884	52,176	72,897

Note: (1) Figures cover the Nashville-Davidson—Murfreesboro—Franklin, TN Metropolitan Statistical Area—see Appendix B for areas included
Source: U.S. Census Bureau, 2011-2013 American Community Survey 3-Year Estimates

Household Income Distribution

Area	Percent of Households Earning							
	Under $15,000	$15,000 -24,999	$25,000 -34,999	$35,000 -49,999	$50,000 -74,999	$75,000 -99,000	$100,000 -149,999	$150,000 and up
City	13.8	12.2	12.2	16.0	18.3	11.0	9.8	6.7
MSA[1]	11.3	10.8	10.9	15.2	19.0	12.4	12.0	8.5
U.S.	13.0	10.9	10.3	13.6	17.9	11.9	12.7	9.6

Note: (1) Figures cover the Nashville-Davidson—Murfreesboro—Franklin, TN Metropolitan Statistical Area—see Appendix B for areas included
Source: U.S. Census Bureau, 2011-2013 American Community Survey 3-Year Estimates

Poverty Rate

Area	All Ages	Under 18 Years Old	18 to 64 Years Old	65 Years and Over
City	19.0	30.9	16.6	8.9
MSA[1]	14.3	20.8	13.0	8.0
U.S.	15.9	22.4	14.8	9.5

Note: Figures are percentage of people whose income during the past 12 months was below the poverty level; (1) Figures cover the Nashville-Davidson—Murfreesboro—Franklin, TN Metropolitan Statistical Area—see Appendix B for areas included
Source: U.S. Census Bureau, 2011-2013 American Community Survey 3-Year Estimates

EMPLOYMENT

Labor Force and Employment

Area	Civilian Labor Force			Workers Employed		
	Dec. 2013	Dec. 2014	% Chg.	Dec. 2013	Dec. 2014	% Chg.
City	353,381	351,800	-0.4	336,639	335,389	-0.4
MSA[1]	901,839	896,903	-0.5	857,621	854,219	-0.4
U.S.	154,408,000	155,521,000	0.7	144,423,000	147,190,000	1.9

Note: Data is not seasonally adjusted and covers workers 16 years of age and older; (1) Figures cover the Nashville-Davidson—Murfreesboro—Franklin, TN Metropolitan Statistical Area—see Appendix B for areas included
Source: Bureau of Labor Statistics, Local Area Unemployment Statistics

Unemployment Rate

Area	2014											
	Jan.	Feb.	Mar.	Apr.	May	Jun.	Jul.	Aug.	Sep.	Oct.	Nov.	Dec.
City	4.8	5.0	5.1	4.5	5.0	5.4	5.7	5.6	5.1	4.9	4.9	4.7
MSA[1]	5.0	5.2	5.3	4.6	5.1	5.7	6.0	5.8	5.3	5.1	5.0	4.8
U.S.	7.0	7.0	6.8	5.9	6.1	6.3	6.5	6.3	5.7	5.5	5.5	5.4

Note: Data is not seasonally adjusted and covers workers 16 years of age and older; (1) Figures cover the Nashville-Davidson—Murfreesboro—Franklin, TN Metropolitan Statistical Area—see Appendix B for areas included
Source: Bureau of Labor Statistics, Local Area Unemployment Statistics

Employment by Occupation

Occupation Classification	City (%)	MSA[1] (%)	U.S. (%)
Management, Business, Science, and Arts	39.0	37.4	36.2
Natural Resources, Construction, and Maintenance	6.9	8.0	9.0
Production, Transportation, and Material Moving	10.5	12.2	12.1
Sales and Office	26.7	26.7	24.4
Service	16.9	15.6	18.3

Note: Figures cover employed civilians 16 years of age and older; (1) Figures cover the Nashville-Davidson—Murfreesboro—Franklin, TN Metropolitan Statistical Area—see Appendix B for areas included
Source: U.S. Census Bureau, 2011-2013 American Community Survey 3-Year Estimates

Employment by Industry

Sector	MSA[1]		U.S.
	Number of Employees	Percent of Total	Percent of Total
Construction, Mining, and Logging	37,200	4.1	5.0
Education and Health Services	138,500	15.4	15.5
Financial Activities	56,700	6.3	5.7
Government	114,200	12.7	15.8
Information	20,800	2.3	2.0
Leisure and Hospitality	95,200	10.6	10.3
Manufacturing	79,800	8.9	8.7
Other Services	37,400	4.2	4.0
Professional and Business Services	138,300	15.4	13.8
Retail Trade	97,300	10.8	11.4
Transportation, Warehousing, and Utilities	41,200	4.6	3.9
Wholesale Trade	42,800	4.8	4.2

Note: Figures are non-farm employment as of December 2014. Figures are not seasonally adjusted and include workers 16 years of age and older; (1) Figures cover the Nashville-Davidson—Murfreesboro—Franklin, TN Metropolitan Statistical Area—see Appendix B for areas included; n/a not available
Source: Bureau of Labor Statistics, Current Employment Statistics, Employment, Hours, and Earnings

Occupations with Greatest Projected Employment Growth: 2012 – 2022

Occupation[1]	2012 Employment	2022 Projected Employment	Numeric Employment Change	Percent Employment Change
Combined Food Preparation and Serving Workers, Including Fast Food	57,280	69,200	11,920	20.8
Laborers and Freight, Stock, and Material Movers, Hand	73,340	84,450	11,110	15.1
Heavy and Tractor-Trailer Truck Drivers	58,030	66,640	8,610	14.8
Janitors and Cleaners, Except Maids and Housekeeping Cleaners	44,250	52,850	8,600	19.4
Customer Service Representatives	48,050	56,410	8,360	17.4
Team Assemblers	39,680	47,700	8,020	20.2
Registered Nurses	56,400	64,290	7,890	14.0
Security Guards	22,050	29,280	7,230	32.8
Secretaries and Administrative Assistants, Except Legal, Medical, and Executive	42,120	49,220	7,100	16.8
General and Operations Managers	40,120	46,280	6,160	15.4

Note: Projections cover Tennessee; (1) Sorted by numeric employment change
Source: www.projectionscentral.com, State Occupational Projections, 2012–2022 Long-Term Projections

Fastest Growing Occupations: 2012 – 2022

Occupation[1]	2012 Employment	2022 Projected Employment	Numeric Employment Change	Percent Employment Change
Computer Numerically Controlled Machine Tool Programmers, Metal and Plastic	490	740	250	49.8
Paralegals and Legal Assistants	4,820	7,170	2,350	48.7
Skincare Specialists	560	830	270	46.5
Physician Assistants	1,300	1,880	580	44.6
Interpreters and Translators	690	1,000	310	44.4
Diagnostic Medical Sonographers	1,450	2,060	610	42.0
Ambulance Drivers and Attendants, Except Emergency Medical Technicians	270	380	110	41.6
Meeting, Convention, and Event Planners	1,180	1,670	490	41.1
Veterinary Technologists and Technicians	1,620	2,250	630	39.4
Helpers—Brickmasons, Blockmasons, Stonemasons, and Tile and Marble Setters	420	580	160	39.0

Note: Projections cover Tennessee; (1) Sorted by percent employment change and excludes occupations with numeric employment change less than 100
Source: www.projectionscentral.com, State Occupational Projections, 2012–2022 Long-Term Projections

Average Wages

Occupation	$/Hr.	Occupation	$/Hr.
Accountants and Auditors	33.06	Maids and Housekeeping Cleaners	9.85
Automotive Mechanics	19.39	Maintenance and Repair Workers	18.10
Bookkeepers	18.33	Marketing Managers	47.41
Carpenters	16.83	Nuclear Medicine Technologists	29.91
Cashiers	9.69	Nurses, Licensed Practical	18.71
Clerks, General Office	15.41	Nurses, Registered	28.51
Clerks, Receptionists/Information	13.95	Nursing Assistants	11.12
Clerks, Shipping/Receiving	14.52	Packers and Packagers, Hand	10.64
Computer Programmers	37.14	Physical Therapists	38.94
Computer Systems Analysts	35.56	Postal Service Mail Carriers	25.03
Computer User Support Specialists	22.31	Real Estate Brokers	n/a
Cooks, Restaurant	10.66	Retail Salespersons	13.10
Dentists	82.20	Sales Reps., Exc. Tech./Scientific	29.39
Electrical Engineers	37.82	Sales Reps., Tech./Scientific	36.34
Electricians	22.65	Secretaries, Exc. Legal/Med./Exec.	15.64
Financial Managers	52.35	Security Guards	14.21
First-Line Supervisors/Managers, Sales	19.69	Surgeons	n/a
Food Preparation Workers	9.33	Teacher Assistants	11.50
General and Operations Managers	55.29	Teachers, Elementary School	25.00
Hairdressers/Cosmetologists	14.48	Teachers, Secondary School	25.00
Internists	82.28	Telemarketers	13.27
Janitors and Cleaners	10.76	Truck Drivers, Heavy/Tractor-Trailer	19.95
Landscaping/Groundskeeping Workers	12.02	Truck Drivers, Light/Delivery Svcs.	15.94
Lawyers	57.91	Waiters and Waitresses	8.95

Note: Wage data covers the Nashville-Davidson—Murfreesboro—Franklin, TN Metropolitan Statistical Area—see Appendix B for areas included; Hourly wages for elementary/secondary school teachers and teacher assistants were calculated by the editors from annual wage data assuming a 40 hour work week; n/a not available.
Source: Bureau of Labor Statistics, Metro Area Occupational Employment and Wage Estimates, May 2014

TAXES

State Corporate Income Tax Rates

State	Tax Rate (%)	Income Brackets ($)	Num. of Brackets	Financial Institution Tax Rate (%)[a]	Federal Income Tax Ded.
Tennessee	6.5	Flat rate	1	6.5	No

Note: Tax rates as of January 1, 2015; (a) Rates listed are the corporate income tax rate applied to financial institutions or excise taxes based on income. Some states have other taxes based upon the value of deposits or shares.
Source: Federation of Tax Administrators, "State Corporate Income Tax Rates, 2015"

State Individual Income Tax Rates

State	Tax Rate (%)	Income Brackets ($)	Num. of Brackets	Personal Exempt. ($)[1] Single	Personal Exempt. ($)[1] Dependents	Fed. Inc. Tax Ded.
Tennessee	State income tax of 6% on dividends and interest income only					

Note: Tax rates as of January 1, 2015; Local- and county-level taxes are not included; n/a not applicable; (1) Married joint filers generally receive double the single exemption
Source: Federation of Tax Administrators, "State Individual Income Tax Rates, 2015"

Various State and Local Tax Rates

State	State and Local Sales and Use (%)	State Sales and Use (%)	Gasoline[1] (¢/gal.)	Cigarette[2] ($/pack)	Spirits[3] ($/gal.)	Wine[4] ($/gal.)	Beer[5] ($/gal.)
Tennessee	9.25	7.0	21.4	0.62	4.46 (i)	1.27 (m)	1.29 (t)

Note: All tax rates as of January 1, 2015; (1) The American Petroleum Institute has developed a methodology for determining the average tax rate on a gallon of fuel. Rates may include any of the following: excise taxes, environmental fees, storage tank fees, other fees or taxes, general sales tax, and local taxes. In states where gasoline is subject to the general sales tax, or where the fuel tax is based on the average sale price, the average rate determined by API is sensitive to changes in the price of gasoline. States that fully or partially apply general sales taxes to gasoline: CA, CO, GA, IL, IN, MI, NY; (2) The federal excise tax of $1.0066 per pack and local taxes are not included; (3) Rates are those applicable to off-premise sales of 40% alcohol by volume (a.b.v.) distilled spirits in 750ml containers. Local excise taxes are excluded; (4) Rates are those applicable to off-premise sales of 11% a.b.v. non-carbonated wine in 750ml containers; (5) Rates are those applicable to off-premise sales of 4.7% a.b.v. beer in 12 ounce containers; (i) Includes case fees and/or bottle fees which may vary with the size of container; (m) Includes case fees and/or bottle fees which may vary with size of container; (t) Includes the wholesale tax rate of 17%, converted into a gallonage excise tax rate.
Source: Tax Foundation, 2015 Facts & Figures: How Does Your State Compare?

State Business Tax Climate Index Rankings

State	Overall Rank	Corporate Tax Index Rank	Individual Income Tax Index Rank	Sales Tax Index Rank	Unemployment Insurance Tax Index Rank	Property Tax Index Rank
Tennessee	15	15	8	47	26	37

Note: The index is a measure of how each state's tax laws affect economic performance. The lower the rank, the more favorable a state's tax system is for business. States without a given tax are given a ranking of 1. The scores/rankings for the District of Columbia do not affect other states. The 2015 index represents the tax climate as of July 1, 2014.
Source: Tax Foundation, State Business Tax Climate Index 2015

COMMERCIAL REAL ESTATE

Office Market

Market Area	Inventory (sq. ft.)	Vacancy Rate (%)	Under Construction (sq. ft.)	YTD Net Absorption (sq. ft.)	Total Average Asking Rent ($/sq. ft./year)
Nashville	49,542,536	8.4	673,695	769,041	21.39
National	4,745,108,508	14.3	71,190,461	51,084,126	27.40

Source: Newmark Grubb Knight Frank, National Office Market Report, 4th Quarter 2014

Industrial/Warehouse/R&D Market

Market Area	Inventory (sq. ft.)	Vacancy Rate (%)	Under Construction (sq. ft.)	YTD Net Absorption (sq. ft.)	Total Average Asking Rent ($/sq. ft./year)
Nashville	216,195,963	7.3	1,145,541	3,468,782	3.73
National	14,238,613,765	7.2	134,387,407	185,246,438	5.64

Source: Newmark Grubb Knight Frank, National Industrial Market Report, 4th Quarter 2014

COMMERCIAL UTILITIES

Typical Monthly Electric Bills

Area	Commercial Service ($/month)		Industrial Service ($/month)	
	40 kW demand 5,000 kWh	500 kW demand 100,000 kWh	5,000 kW demand 1,500,000 kWh	70,000 kW demand 50,000,000 kWh
City	573	12,891	165,074	3,224,600

Note: Figures are based on rates in effect January 2, 2014
Source: Memphis Light, Gas and Water, 2014 Utility Bill Comparisons for Selected U.S. Cities

TRANSPORTATION

Means of Transportation to Work

Area	Car/Truck/Van		Public Transportation			Bicycle	Walked	Other Means	Worked at Home
	Drove Alone	Car-pooled	Bus	Subway	Railroad				
City	80.1	9.9	2.1	0.0	0.1	0.3	2.1	1.1	4.4
MSA[1]	82.5	9.4	1.1	0.0	0.1	0.2	1.3	0.9	4.5
U.S.	76.4	9.6	2.6	1.8	0.6	0.6	2.8	1.3	4.3

Note: Figures are percentages and cover workers 16 years of age and older; (1) Figures cover the Nashville-Davidson—Murfreesboro—Franklin, TN Metropolitan Statistical Area—see Appendix B for areas included
Source: U.S. Census Bureau, 2011-2013 American Community Survey 3-Year Estimates

Travel Time to Work

Area	Less Than 10 Minutes	10 to 19 Minutes	20 to 29 Minutes	30 to 44 Minutes	45 to 59 Minutes	60 to 89 Minutes	90 Minutes or More
City	8.9	31.0	28.0	23.7	5.1	2.2	1.2
MSA[1]	9.8	27.6	22.7	23.7	9.4	5.0	1.7
U.S.	13.3	29.7	20.9	20.2	7.7	5.7	2.6

Note: Figures are percentages and include workers 16 years old and over; (1) Figures cover the Nashville-Davidson—Murfreesboro—Franklin, TN Metropolitan Statistical Area—see Appendix B for areas included
Source: U.S. Census Bureau, 2011-2013 American Community Survey 3-Year Estimates

Travel Time Index

Area	1985	1990	1995	2000	2005	2010	2011
Urban Area[1]	1.13	1.16	1.19	1.23	1.25	1.23	1.23
Average[2]	1.09	1.14	1.16	1.19	1.23	1.18	1.18

Note: Travel Time Index—the ratio of travel time in the peak period to the travel time at free-flow conditions. For example, a value of 1.30 indicates a 20-minute free-flow trip takes 26 minutes in the peak. Free-flow speeds (60 mph on freeways and 35 mph on principal arterials) are used as the comparison threshold; (1) Covers the Nashville-Davidson TN urban area; (2) average of 498 urban areas
Source: Texas Transportation Institute, Urban Mobility Report 2012, December 2012

Public Transportation

Agency Name / Mode of Transportation	Vehicles Operated in Maximum Service	Annual Unlinked Passenger Trips (in thous.)	Annual Passenger Miles (in thous.)
Metropolitan Transit Authority (MTA)			
Bus (directly operated)	137	9,489.1	54,531.7
Demand Response (directly operated)	50	279.0	4,589.9
Demand Response Taxi (purchased transportation)	57	106.3	794.8

Source: Federal Transit Administration, National Transit Database, 2013

Air Transportation

Airport Name and Code / Type of Service	Passenger Airlines[1]	Passenger Enplanements	Freight Carriers[2]	Freight (lbs.)
Nashville International (BNA)				
Domestic service (U.S. carriers - 2014)	37	5,359,238	14	48,626,625
International service (U.S. carriers - 2013)	7	2,899	1	21,914

Note: (1) Includes all U.S.-based major, minor and commuter airlines that carried at least one passenger during the year; (2) Includes all U.S.-based airlines and freight carriers that transported at least one lb. of freight during the year.
Source: Bureau of Transportation Statistics, The Intermodal Transportation Database, Air Carriers: T-100 Domestic Market (U.S. Carriers), 2014; Bureau of Transportation Statistics, The Intermodal Transportation Database, Air Carriers: T-100 International Market (U.S. Carriers), 2013

Other Transportation Statistics

Major Highways:	I-24; I-40; I-65
Amtrak Service:	Bus connection
Major Waterways/Ports:	Cumberland River; Port of Nashville

Source: Amtrak.com; Google Maps

BUSINESSES

Major Business Headquarters

Company Name	Rankings	
	Fortune[1]	Forbes[2]
Ardent Health Services	-	197
HCA Holdings	79	-
Ingram Industries	-	216
Vanguard Health Systems	388	-

Note: (1) Fortune 500—companies that produce a 10-K are ranked 1 to 500 based on 2013 revenue; (2) all private companies with at least $2 billion in annual revenue through the end of their most current fiscal year are ranked 1 to 221; companies listed are headquartered in the city; dashes indicate no ranking
Source: Fortune, "Fortune 500," June 16, 2014; Forbes, "America's Largest Private Companies," November 5, 2014

Fast-Growing Businesses

According to *Inc.*, Nashville is home to one of America's 500 fastest-growing private companies: **InQuicker** (#291). Criteria: must be an independent, privately-held, for-profit, U.S. corporation, proprietorship or partnership; revenues must be at least $100,000 in 2010 and $2 million in 2013; must have four-year operating/sales history. Holding companies, regulated banks, and utilities were excluded. *Inc., "America's 500 Fastest-Growing Private Companies," September 2014*

According to *Initiative for a Competitive Inner City (ICIC)*, Nashville is home to one of America's 100 fastest-growing "inner city" companies: **Concept Technology** (#60). Criteria for inclusion: company must be headquartered in or have 51 percent or more of its physical operations in an economically distressed urban area; must be an independent, for-profit corporation, partnership or proprietorship; must have 10 or more employees and have a five-year sales history that includes sales of at least $200,000 in the base year and at least $1 million in the current year with no decrease in sales over the two most recent years. This year, for the first time in the list's 16-year history, the Inner City 100 consists of 10 fast-growing businesses in 10 industry categories. Companies were ranked overall by revenue growth over the five-year period between 2009 and 2013 as well as within their respective industry categories. *Initiative for a Competitive Inner City (ICIC), "Inner City 100 Companies, 2014"*

Minority Business Opportunity

Nashville is home to one company which is on the *Black Enterprise* Industrial/Service 100 list (100 largest companies based on gross sales): **Zycron** (#68). Criteria: operational in previous calendar year; at least 51% black-owned and manufactures/owns the product it sells or provides industrial or consumer services. Brokerages, real estate firms and firms that provide professional services are not eligible. *Black Enterprise, B.E. 100s, 2014*

Nashville is home to one company which is on the *Black Enterprise* Bank 20 list (20 largest banks based on total assets, capital, deposits and loans, including mortgage-backed securities for the calendar year): **Citizens Savings Bank & Trust Co.** (#14). Only commercial banks or savings and loans that are classified by the Federal Reserve as black institutions and have been fully operational for the previous calendar year were considered. *Black Enterprise, B.E. 100s, 2014*

Minority- and Women-Owned Businesses

Group	All Firms		Firms with Paid Employees			
	Firms	Sales ($000)	Firms	Sales ($000)	Employees	Payroll ($000)
Asian	2,147	605,394	603	527,918	3,935	95,615
Black	7,005	414,476	417	258,896	2,878	74,329
Hispanic	1,868	236,570	199	133,356	1,381	36,780
Women	16,501	5,688,845	1,744	5,198,533	16,705	536,402
All Firms	61,668	80,576,131	13,323	77,992,495	375,494	15,429,858

Note: Figures cover firms located in the city; minority- and women-owned business are defined as firms in which the corresponding group own 51% or more of the stock or equity of the company
Source: U.S. Census Bureau, 2007 Economic Census, Survey of Business Owners (2012 Survey of Business Owners data will be released starting in June 2015)

HOTELS & CONVENTION CENTERS

Hotels/Motels

Area	5 Star		4 Star		3 Star		2 Star		1 Star		Not Rated	
	Num.	Pct.[3]	Num.	Pct.[3]	Num.	Pct.[3]	Num.	Pct.[3]	Num.	Pct.[3]	Num.	Pct.[3]
City[1]	0	0.0	11	4.1	61	22.6	175	64.8	7	2.6	16	5.9
Total[2]	166	0.9	1,264	7.0	5,718	31.8	9,340	52.0	411	2.3	1,070	6.0

Note: (1) Figures cover Nashville and vicinity; (2) Figures cover all 100 cities in this book; (3) Percentage of hotels which have a given star rating; Star ratings are determined by expedia.com and offer an indication of the general quality of a particular hotel.
Source: expedia.com, April 2, 2015

The Nashville-Davidson—Murfreesboro—Franklin, TN metro area is home to two of the best hotels in the U.S. according to *Travel & Leisure*: **Hermitage Hotel**; **Loews Vanderbilt Hotel**. Criteria: service; location; rooms; food; and value. The list includes the top 236 hotels in the U.S. *Travel & Leisure, "T+L 500, The World's Best Hotels 2015"*

Major Convention Centers

Name	Overall Space (sq. ft.)	Exhibit Space (sq. ft.)	Meeting Space (sq. ft.)	Meeting Rooms
Mid-TN Expo Convention Center	40,000	n/a	n/a	n/a
Nashville Convention Center	n/a	118,675	n/a	25

Note: Table includes convention centers located in the Nashville-Davidson—Murfreesboro—Franklin, TN metro area; n/a not available
Source: Original research

Living Environment

COST OF LIVING

Cost of Living Index

Composite Index	Groceries	Housing	Utilities	Trans-portation	Health Care	Misc. Goods/ Services
90.0	95.2	76.4	92.2	93.3	84.3	98.6

Note: The Cost of Living Index measures regional differences in the cost of consumer goods and services, excluding taxes and non-consumer expenditures, for professional and managerial households in the top income quintile. It is based on more than 50,000 prices covering almost 60 different items for which prices are collected three times a year by chambers of commerce, economic development organizations or university applied economic centers in each participating urban area. The numbers shown should be read as a percentage above or below the national average of 100. For example, a value of 115.4 in the groceries column indicates that grocery prices are 15.4% higher than the national average. Small differences in the index numbers should not be interpreted as significant; Figures cover the Nashville-Franklin TN urban area.
Source: The Council for Community and Economic Research, ACCRA Cost of Living Index, 2014

Grocery Prices

Area[1]	T-Bone Steak ($/pound)	Frying Chicken ($/pound)	Whole Milk ($/half gal.)	Eggs ($/dozen)	Orange Juice ($/64 oz.)	Coffee ($/11.5 oz.)
City[2]	10.75	1.28	2.07	1.91	3.24	4.04
Avg.	10.40	1.37	2.40	1.99	3.46	4.27
Min.	8.48	0.93	1.37	1.30	2.83	2.99
Max.	14.20	2.44	3.62	4.02	6.42	6.96

Note: (1) Values for the local area are compared with the average, minimum and maximum values for all 308 areas in the Cost of Living Index; (2) Figures cover the Nashville-Franklin TN urban area; **T-Bone Steak** *(price per pound);* **Frying Chicken** *(price per pound, whole fryer);* **Whole Milk** *(half gallon carton);* **Eggs** *(price per dozen, Grade A, large);* **Orange Juice** *(64 oz. Tropicana or Florida Natural);* **Coffee** *(11.5 oz. can, vacuum-packed, Maxwell House, Hills Bros, or Folgers).*
Source: The Council for Community and Economic Research, ACCRA Cost of Living Index, 2014

Housing and Utility Costs

Area[1]	New Home Price ($)	Apartment Rent ($/month)	All Electric ($/month)	Part Electric ($/month)	Other Energy ($/month)	Telephone ($/month)
City[2]	211,580	870	-	97.85	63.67	24.50
Avg.	305,838	919	181.00	93.66	73.14	27.95
Min.	183,142	480	112.00	42.06	23.42	17.16
Max.	1,358,576	3,851	594.00	180.03	440.99	40.42

Note: (1) Values for the local area are compared with the average, minimum and maximum values for all 308 areas in the Cost of Living Index; (2) Figures cover the Nashville-Franklin TN urban area; **New Home Price** *(2,400 sf living area, 8,000 sf lot, in urban area with full utilities);* **Apartment Rent** *(950 sf 2 bedroom/1.5 or 2 bath, unfurnished, excluding all utilities except water);* **All Electric** *(average monthly cost for an all-electric home);* **Part Electric** *(average monthly cost for a part-electric home);* **Other Energy** *(average monthly cost for natural gas, fuel oil, coal, wood, and any other forms of energy except electricity);* **Telephone** *(price includes basic monthly rate for a private residential line plus additional local usage charges incurred by a family of four).*
Source: The Council for Community and Economic Research, ACCRA Cost of Living Index, 2014

Health Care, Transportation, and Other Costs

Area[1]	Doctor ($/visit)	Dentist ($/visit)	Optometrist ($/visit)	Gasoline ($/gallon)	Beauty Salon ($/visit)	Men's Shirt ($)
City[2]	80.53	78.65	67.17	3.33	31.13	23.67
Avg.	102.86	87.89	97.66	3.44	34.37	26.74
Min.	67.47	65.78	51.18	3.00	17.43	12.79
Max.	173.50	150.14	235.00	4.33	64.28	49.50

Note: (1) Values for the local area are compared with the average, minimum and maximum values for all 308 areas in the Cost of Living Index; (2) Figures cover the Nashville-Franklin TN urban area; **Doctor** *(general practitioners routine exam of an established patient);* **Dentist** *(adult teeth cleaning and periodic oral examination);* **Optometrist** *(full vision eye exam for established adult patient);* **Gasoline** *(one gallon regular unleaded, national brand, including all taxes, cash price at self-service pump if available);* **Beauty Salon** *(woman's shampoo, trim, and blow-dry);* **Men's Shirt** *(cotton/polyester dress shirt, pinpoint weave, long sleeves).*
Source: The Council for Community and Economic Research, ACCRA Cost of Living Index, 2014

HOUSING

House Price Index (HPI)

Area	National Ranking[2]	Quarterly Change (%)	One-Year Change (%)	Five-Year Change (%)
MSA[1]	58	1.18	7.74	12.51
U.S.[3]	–	1.35	4.91	11.59

Note: The HPI is a weighted repeat sales index. It measures average price changes in repeat sales or refinancings on the same properties. This information is obtained by reviewing repeat mortgage transactions on single-family properties whose mortgages have been purchased or securitized by Fannie Mae or Freddie Mac in January 1975; (1) Nashville-Davidson—Murfreesboro—Franklin Metropolitan Statistical Area—see Appendix B for areas included; (2) Rankings are based on annual percentage change for all metro areas containing at least 15,000 transactions over the last 10 years and ranges from 1 to 275; (3) figures based on a weighted average of Census Division estimates using a seasonally adjusted, purchase-only index; all figures are for the period ending December 31, 2014
Source: Federal Housing Finance Agency, House Price Index, February 26, 2015

Median Single-Family Home Prices

Area	2012	2013	2014p	Percent Change 2013 to 2014
MSA[1]	160.6	176.4	183.0	3.7
U.S. Average	177.2	197.4	209.0	5.9

Note: Figures are median sales prices of existing single-family homes in thousands of dollars; (p) preliminary; n/a not available; (1) Nashville-Davidson—Murfreesboro—Franklin, TN Metropolitan Statistical Area—see Appendix B for areas included
Source: National Association of Realtors, Median Sales Price of Existing Single-Family Homes for Metropolitan Areas, 4th Quarter 2014

Qualifying Income Based on Median Sales Price of Existing Single-Family Homes

Area	With 5% Down ($)	With 10% Down ($)	With 20% Down ($)
MSA[1]	41,138	38,973	34,643
U.S. Average	45,863	43,449	38,621

Note: Figures are preliminary; Qualifying income is based on a mortgage rate of 4.0%. Monthly principal and interest payment is limited to 25% of income; n/a not available;
(1) Nashville-Davidson—Murfreesboro—Franklin, TN Metropolitan Statistical Area—see Appendix B for areas included
Source: National Association of Realtors, Qualifying Income Based on Median Sales Price of Existing Single-Family Homes for Metropolitan Areas, 4th Quarter 2014

Median Apartment Condo-Coop Home Prices

Area	2012	2013	2014p	Percent Change 2013 to 2014
MSA[1]	n/a	n/a	n/a	n/a
U.S. Average	173.7	194.9	205.1	5.2

Note: Figures are median sales prices of existing apartment condo-coop homes in thousands of dollars; (p) preliminary; n/a not available; (1) Nashville-Davidson—Murfreesboro—Franklin, TN Metropolitan Statistical Area—see Appendix B for areas included
Source: National Association of Realtors, Median Sales Price of Existing Apartment Condo-Coop Homes for Metropolitan Areas, 4th Quarter 2014

Gross Monthly Rent

Area	Under $200	$200 -299	$300 -499	$500 -749	$750 -999	$1,000 -1,499	$1,500 and up	Median ($)
City	2.9	3.3	5.0	26.7	32.1	23.8	6.2	833
MSA[1]	2.4	3.1	6.4	26.3	31.9	23.2	6.6	835
U.S.	1.7	3.2	7.8	22.1	24.3	26.0	14.9	900

Note: Figures are percentages except for Median; Gross rent is the contract rent plus the estimated average monthly cost of utilities (electricity, gas, and water and sewer) and fuels (oil, coal, kerosene, wood, etc.) if these are paid by the renter (or paid for the renter by someone else); (1) Figures cover the Nashville-Davidson—Murfreesboro—Franklin, TN Metropolitan Statistical Area—see Appendix B for areas included
Source: U.S. Census Bureau, 2011-2013 American Community Survey 3-Year Estimates

Homeownership Rate

Area	2007 (%)	2008 (%)	2009 (%)	2010 (%)	2011 (%)	2012 (%)	2013 (%)	2014 (%)
MSA[1]	70.0	71.3	71.8	70.4	69.6	64.9	63.9	67.1
U.S.	68.1	67.8	67.4	66.9	66.1	65.4	65.1	64.5

Note: (1) Figures cover the Nashville-Davidson—Murfreesboro—Franklin, TN Metropolitan Statistical Area—see Appendix B for areas included
Source: U.S. Census Bureau, Housing Vacancies and Homeownership Annual Statistics: 2014

Year Housing Structure Built

Area	2010 or Later	2000 -2009	1990 -1999	1980 -1989	1970 -1979	1960 -1969	1950 -1959	1940 -1949	Before 1940	Median Year
City	1.1	15.8	11.9	17.3	16.7	13.8	12.0	5.0	6.4	1978
MSA[1]	1.6	22.0	18.9	16.1	14.9	10.3	7.7	3.3	5.2	1985
U.S.	0.9	15.0	13.9	13.8	15.8	11.0	10.9	5.4	13.3	1976

Note: Figures are percentages except for Median Year; (1) Figures cover the Nashville-Davidson—Murfreesboro—Franklin, TN Metropolitan Statistical Area—see Appendix B for areas included
Source: U.S. Census Bureau, 2011-2013 American Community Survey 3-Year Estimates

HEALTH

Health Risk Data

Category	MSA[1] (%)	U.S. (%)
Adults aged 18–64 who have any kind of health care coverage	82.0	79.6
Adults who reported being in good or excellent health	84.7	83.1
Adults who are current smokers	23.7	19.6
Adults who are heavy drinkers[2]	4.5	6.1
Adults who are binge drinkers[3]	16.0	16.9
Adults who are overweight (BMI 25.0 - 29.9)	34.3	35.8
Adults who are obese (BMI 30.0 - 99.8)	29.1	27.6
Adults who participated in any physical activities in the past month	74.3	77.1
Adults 50+ who have ever had a sigmoidoscopy or colonoscopy	71.6	67.3
Women aged 40+ who have had a mammogram within the past two years	75.3	74.0
Men aged 40+ who have had a PSA test within the past two years	53.8	45.2
Adults aged 65+ who have had flu shot within the past year	71.9	60.1
Adults who always wear a seatbelt	94.6	93.8

Note: Data as of 2012 unless otherwise noted; (1) Figures cover the Nashville-Davidson—Murfreesboro, TN Metropolitan Statistical Area—see Appendix B for areas included; (2) Heavy drinkers are classified as males having more than two drinks per day or females having more than one drink per day; (3) Binge drinkers are classified as males having five or more drinks on one occasion or females having four or more drinks on one occasion
Source: Centers for Disease Control and Prevention, Behaviorial Risk Factor Surveillance System, SMART: Selected Metropolitan/Micropolitan Area Risk Trends, 2012 (Note: the CDC has discontinued this dataset but will be releasing a replacement in late 2015)

Chronic Health Indicators

Category	MSA[1] (%)	U.S. (%)
Adults who have ever been told they had a heart attack	5.4	4.5
Adults who have ever been told they had a stroke	2.9	2.9
Adults who have been told they currently have asthma	6.7	8.9
Adults who have ever been told they have arthritis	25.2	25.7
Adults who have ever been told they have diabetes[2]	9.4	9.7
Adults who have ever been told they had skin cancer	6.4	5.7
Adults who have ever been told they had any other types of cancer	6.4	6.5
Adults who have ever been told they have COPD	7.3	6.2
Adults who have ever been told they have kidney disease	1.5	2.5
Adults who have ever been told they have a form of depression	16.6	18.0

Note: Data as of 2012 unless otherwise noted; (1) Figures cover the Nashville-Davidson—Murfreesboro, TN Metropolitan Statistical Area—see Appendix B for areas included; (2) Figures do not include pregnancy-related, borderline, or pre-diabetes
Source: Centers for Disease Control and Prevention, Behaviorial Risk Factor Surveillance System, SMART: Selected Metropolitan/Micropolitan Area Risk Trends, 2012 (Note: the CDC has discontinued this dataset but will be releasing a replacement in late 2015)

Mortality Rates for the Top 10 Causes of Death in the U.S.

ICD-10[a] Sub-Chapter	ICD-10[a] Code	Age-Adjusted Mortality Rate[1] per 100,000 population	
		County[2]	U.S.
Malignant neoplasms	C00-C97	186.5	166.2
Ischaemic heart diseases	I20-I25	122.7	105.7
Other forms of heart disease	I30-I51	38.6	49.3
Chronic lower respiratory diseases	J40-J47	47.8	42.1
Organic, including symptomatic, mental disorders	F01-F09	49.6	38.1
Cerebrovascular diseases	I60-I69	40.5	37.0
Other external causes of accidental injury	W00-X59	42.4	26.9
Other degenerative diseases of the nervous system	G30-G31	31.3	25.6
Diabetes mellitus	E10-E14	25.9	21.3
Hypertensive diseases	I10-I15	32.1	19.4

Note: (a) ICD-10 = International Classification of Diseases 10th Revision; (1) Mortality rates are a three year average covering 2011-2013; (2) Figures cover Davidson County
Source: Centers for Disease Control and Prevention, National Center for Health Statistics. Compressed Mortality File 1999-2013 on CDC WONDER Online Database, released October 2014. Data are compiled from the Compressed Mortality File 1999-2013, Series 20 No. 2S, 2014.

Mortality Rates for Selected Causes of Death

ICD-10[a] Sub-Chapter	ICD-10[a] Code	Age-Adjusted Mortality Rate[1] per 100,000 population	
		County[2]	U.S.
Assault	X85-Y09	7.4	5.2
Diseases of the liver	K70-K76	14.0	13.2
Human immunodeficiency virus (HIV) disease	B20-B24	4.6	2.2
Influenza and pneumonia	J09-J18	13.8	15.4
Intentional self-harm	X60-X84	12.1	12.5
Malnutrition	E40-E46	*0.8	0.9
Obesity and other hyperalimentation	E65-E68	2.0	1.8
Renal failure	N17-N19	11.7	13.1
Transport accidents	V01-V99	10.6	11.7
Viral hepatitis	B15-B19	4.9	2.2

Note: (a) ICD-10 = International Classification of Diseases 10th Revision; (1) Mortality rates are a three year average covering 2011-2013; (2) Figures cover Davidson County; (*) Unreliable data as per CDC
Source: Centers for Disease Control and Prevention, National Center for Health Statistics. Compressed Mortality File 1999-2013 on CDC WONDER Online Database, released October 2014. Data are compiled from the Compressed Mortality File 1999-2013, Series 20 No. 2S, 2014.

Health Insurance Coverage

Area	With Health Insurance	With Private Health Insurance	With Public Health Insurance	Without Health Insurance	Population Under Age 18 Without Health Insurance
City	83.1	63.1	28.5	16.9	7.6
MSA[1]	86.4	68.7	27.1	13.6	5.8
U.S.	85.2	65.2	31.0	14.8	7.3

Note: Figures are percentages that cover the civilian noninstitutionalized population; (1) Figures cover the Nashville-Davidson—Murfreesboro—Franklin, TN Metropolitan Statistical Area—see Appendix B for areas included
Source: U.S. Census Bureau, 2011-2013 American Community Survey 3-Year Estimates

Number of Medical Professionals

Area[1]	MDs[2]	DOs[2,3]	Dentists	Podiatrists	Chiropractors	Optometrists
Local (number)	3,909	60	470	26	137	89
Local (rate[4])	602.2	9.2	71.3	3.9	20.8	13.5
U.S. (rate[4])	270.0	20.2	63.1	5.7	25.2	14.9

Note: Data as of 2013 unless noted; (1) Local data covers Davidson County; (2) Data as of 2012 and includes all active, non-federal physicians; (3) Doctor of Osteopathic Medicine; (4) rate per 100,000 population
Source: U.S. Department of Health and Human Services, Health Resources and Services Administration, Bureau of Health Professions, Area Resource File (ARF) 2013-2014

Best Hospitals

According to *U.S. News,* the Nashville-Davidson—Murfreesboro—Franklin, TN metro area is home to one of the best hospitals in the U.S.: **Vanderbilt University Medical Center** (6 specialties). The hospital listed was nationally ranked in at least one adult specialty. Only 144 hospitals nationwide were nationally ranked in one or more specialties. Seventeen hospitals in the U.S. made the Honor Roll with high scores in at least six specialties. *U.S. News Online, "America's Best Children's Hospitals 2014-15"*

According to *U.S. News,* the Nashville-Davidson—Murfreesboro—Franklin, TN metro area is home to one of the best children's hospitals in the U.S.: **Monroe Carell Jr. Children's Hospital at Vanderbilt** (9 specialties). The hospital listed was highly ranked in at least one pediatric specialty. Eighty-nine children's hospitals in the U.S. were nationally ranked in at least one specialty. Ten children's hospitals in the U.S. made the Honor Roll with high scores in at least three specialties. *U.S. News Online, "America's Best Children's Hospitals 2014-15"*

EDUCATION

Public School District Statistics

District Name	Schls	Pupils	Pupil/ Teacher Ratio	Minority Pupils[1] (%)	Free Lunch Eligible[2] (%)	IEP[3] (%)
Davidson County	155	81,134	14.7	67.1	65.7	11.7

Note: Table includes school districts with 2,000 or more students; (1) Percentage of students that are not non-Hispanic white; (2) Percentage of students that are eligible for the free lunch program; (3) Percentage of students that have an Individualized Education Program.
Source: U.S. Department of Education, National Center for Education Statistics, Common Core of Data, Local Education Agency (School District) Universe Survey: School Year 2012-2013; U.S. Department of Education, National Center for Education Statistics, Common Core of Data, Public Elementary/Secondary School Universe Survey: School Year 2012-2013

Best High Schools

According to *The Daily Beast,* Nashville is home to two of the best high schools in the U.S.: **Hume-Fogg Academic High School** (#36); **Martin Luther King Magnet** (#89); *The Daily Beast* used six indicators culled from school surveys to compare public high schools in the U.S., with graduation and college acceptance rates weighed most heavily. Other criteria included: college-level courses/exams and SAT/ACT scores. *The Daily Beast, "Top High Schools 2014"*

Highest Level of Education

Area	Less than H.S.	H.S. Diploma	Some College, No Deg.	Associate Degree	Bachelor's Degree	Master's Degree	Prof. School Degree	Doctorate Degree
City	13.3	24.6	20.6	5.8	22.9	8.4	2.5	2.0
MSA[1]	12.2	29.1	21.1	6.3	20.7	7.3	1.9	1.5
U.S.	13.7	28.0	21.2	7.9	18.2	7.7	1.9	1.3

Note: Figures cover persons age 25 and over; (1) Figures cover the Nashville-Davidson—Murfreesboro—Franklin, TN Metropolitan Statistical Area—see Appendix B for areas included
Source: U.S. Census Bureau, 2011-2013 American Community Survey 3-Year Estimates

Educational Attainment by Race

Area	High School Graduate or Higher (%)					Bachelor's Degree or Higher (%)				
	Total	White	Black	Asian	Hisp.[2]	Total	White	Black	Asian	Hisp.[2]
City	86.7	90.1	85.6	79.0	56.7	35.7	41.0	24.3	51.2	12.9
MSA[1]	87.8	89.3	85.2	83.7	60.3	31.4	32.7	24.1	50.0	12.9
U.S.	86.3	88.3	83.1	85.7	64.0	29.1	30.4	18.8	50.7	13.7

Note: Figures shown cover persons 25 years old and over; (1) Figures cover the Nashville-Davidson—Murfreesboro—Franklin, TN Metropolitan Statistical Area—see Appendix B for areas included; (2) People of Hispanic origin can be of any race
Source: U.S. Census Bureau, 2011-2013 American Community Survey 3-Year Estimates

School Enrollment by Grade and Control

Area	Preschool (%)		Kindergarten (%)		Grades 1 - 4 (%)		Grades 5 - 8 (%)		Grades 9 - 12 (%)	
	Public	Private	Public	Private	Public	Private	Public	Private	Public	Private
City	60.3	39.7	87.5	12.5	88.3	11.7	81.9	18.1	82.1	17.9
MSA[1]	51.8	48.2	88.4	11.6	89.3	10.7	86.2	13.8	85.3	14.7
U.S.	57.7	42.3	87.9	12.1	89.9	10.1	90.0	10.0	90.7	9.3

Note: Figures shown cover persons 3 years old and over; (1) Figures cover the Nashville-Davidson—Murfreesboro—Franklin, TN Metropolitan Statistical Area—see Appendix B for areas included
Source: U.S. Census Bureau, 2011-2013 American Community Survey 3-Year Estimates

Average Salaries of Public School Classroom Teachers

Area	2013-14		2014-15		Percent Change 2013-14 to 2014-15	Percent Change 2004-05 to 2014-15
	Dollars	Rank[1]	Dollars	Rank[1]		
TENNESSEE	47,742	40	48,503	39	1.59	15.3
U.S. Average	56,610	–	57,379	–	1.36	20.8

Note: (1) State rank ranges from 1 to 51 where 1 indicates highest salary.
Source: National Education Association, Rankings & Estimates: Rankings of the States 2014 and Estimates of School Statistics 2015, March 2015

Higher Education

Four-Year Colleges			Two-Year Colleges			Medical Schools[1]	Law Schools[2]	Voc/ Tech[3]
Public	Private Non-profit	Private For-profit	Public	Private Non-profit	Private For-profit			
1	10	6	2	2	6	2	3	4

Note: Figures cover institutions located within the city limits and include main campuses only; (1) includes schools accredited by the Liaison Committee on Medical Education and the American Osteopathic Association's Commission on Osteopathic College Accreditation; (2) includes ABA-accredited schools, schools with provisional ABA accreditation, and state accredited schools; (3) includes all schools with programs that are less than 2 years.
Source: National Center for Education Statistics, Integrated Postsecondary Education System (IPEDS), 2013-14; Association of American Medical Colleges, Member List, May 1, 2015; American Osteopathic Association, Member List, May 1, 2015; Law School Admission Council, Official Guide to ABA-Approved Law Schools Online, May 1, 2015; Wikipedia, List of Medical Schools in the United States, May 1, 2015; Wikipedia, List of Law Schools in the United States, May 1, 2015

According to *U.S. News & World Report,* the Nashville-Davidson—Murfreesboro—Franklin, TN metro area is home to one of the best national universities in the U.S.: **Vanderbilt University** (#16). The indicators used to capture academic quality fall into a number of categories: assessment by administrators at peer institutions; retention of students; faculty resources; student selectivity; financial resources; alumni giving; high school counselor ratings of colleges; and graduation rate. *U.S. News & World Report, "America's Best Colleges 2015"*

According to *U.S. News & World Report,* the Nashville-Davidson—Murfreesboro—Franklin, TN metro area is home to one of the best liberal arts colleges in the U.S.: **Fisk University** (#165). The indicators used to capture academic quality fall into a number of categories: assessment by administrators at peer institutions; retention of students; faculty resources; student selectivity; financial resources; alumni giving; high school counselor ratings of colleges; and graduation rate. *U.S. News & World Report, "America's Best Colleges 2015"*

According to *U.S. News & World Report,* the Nashville-Davidson—Murfreesboro—Franklin, TN metro area is home to one of the top 100 law schools in the U.S.: **Vanderbilt University** (#17). The rankings are based on a weighted average of 12 measures of quality: peer assessment score; assessment score by lawyers/judges; median LSAT scores; median undergrad GPA; acceptance rate; employment rates for graduates; placement success; bar passage rate; faculty resources; expenditures per student; student/faculty ratio; and library resources. *U.S. News & World Report, "America's Best Graduate Schools, Law, 2016"*

According to *U.S. News & World Report,* the Nashville-Davidson—Murfreesboro—Franklin, TN metro area is home to one of the top 75 medical schools for research in the U.S.: **Vanderbilt University** (#14). The rankings are based on a weighted average of 11 measures of quality: quality assessment; peer assessment score; assessment score by residency directors; research activity; total research activity; average research activity per faculty member; student selectivity; median MCAT total score; median undergraduate GPA; acceptance rate; and faculty resources. *U.S. News & World Report, "America's Best Graduate Schools, Medical, 2016"*

According to *U.S. News & World Report,* the Nashville-Davidson—Murfreesboro—Franklin, TN metro area is home to one of the top 75 business schools in the U.S.: **Vanderbilt University (Owen)** (#27). The rankings are based on a weighted average of the following nine measures: quality assessment; peer assessment; recruiter assessment; placement success; mean starting salary and bonus; student selectivity; mean GMAT and GRE scores; mean undergraduate GPA; and acceptance rate. *U.S. News & World Report, "America's Best Graduate Schools, Business, 2016"*

PRESIDENTIAL ELECTION

2012 Presidential Election Results

Area	Obama (%)	Romney (%)	Other (%)
Davidson County	58.4	39.9	1.7
U.S.	51.0	47.2	1.8

Note: Results may not add to 100% due to rounding
Source: Dave Leip's Atlas of U.S. Presidential Elections

EMPLOYERS

Major Employers

Company Name	Industry
AHOM Holdings	Home health care services
Asurion Corporation	Business services nec
Baptist Hospital	General medical/surgical hospitals
Cannon County Knitting Mills	Apparel and outerwear broadwoven fabrics
County of Rutherford	Public elementary and secondary schools
County of Sumner	Executive offices, local government
Gaylord Entertainment Company	Hotels/motels
Gaylord Opryland USA	Hotels
Ingram Book Company	Books, periodicals, and newspapers
International Automotive	Automotive storage garage
LifeWay Christian Resources of the SBC	Religious organizations
Middle Tennessee State University	Colleges/universities
Newspaper Printing Corporation	Newspapers
Nissan North America	Motor vehicles/car bodies
Primus Automotive Financial Services	Automobile loans including insurance
Psychiatric Solutions	Psychiatric clinic
State Industries	Hot water heaters, household
State of Tennessee	Mentally handicapped home
Tennesee Department of Transportation	Regulation, administration of transportation
Vanderbilt Childrens Hospital	General medical/surgical hospitals
Vanderbilt University	Colleges/universities

Note: Companies shown are located within the Nashville-Davidson—Murfreesboro—Franklin, TN Metropolitan Statistical Area.
Source: Hoovers.com; Wikipedia

Best Companies to Work For

HCA, headquartered in Nashville, is among the "100 Best Places to Work in IT." To qualify, companies, both public and private, had to have a minimum of 50 IT employees and were selected based on average salary and bonus increases, the percentage of IT staffers promoted, IT staff turnover rates, training and development programs, and the percentage of women and minorities in IT staff and management positions. In addition, *Computerworld* looked at retention efforts, programs for recognizing and rewarding outstanding performances, and benefits such as flextime, elder care and child care, and reimbursement for college tuition and the cost of pursuing technology certifications. *Computerworld, "100 Best Places to Work in IT 2014"*

PUBLIC SAFETY

Crime Rate

Area	All Crimes	Violent Crimes				Property Crimes		
		Murder	Forcible Rape	Robbery	Aggrav. Assault	Burglary	Larceny -Theft	Motor Vehicle Theft
City	4,888.0	5.5	68.7	253.4	712.5	883.0	2,776.6	188.3
Suburbs[1]	2,412.8	2.2	27.9	36.2	275.4	419.6	1,556.2	95.3
Metro[2]	3,314.2	3.4	42.8	115.3	434.6	588.3	2,000.6	129.2
U.S.	3,098.6	4.5	25.2	109.1	229.1	610.0	1,899.4	221.3

Note: Figures are crimes per 100,000 population; (1) All areas within the metro area that are located outside the city limits; (2) Figures cover the Nashville-Davidson—Murfreesboro—Franklin, TN Metropolitan Statistical Area—see Appendix B for areas included
Source: FBI Uniform Crime Reports, 2013

Hate Crimes

Area	Number of Quarters Reported	Number of Incidents per Bias Motivation						
		Race	Religion	Sexual Orientation	Ethnicity	Disability	Gender	Gender Identity
City	4	4	0	1	1	0	0	0
U.S.	4	2,871	1,031	1,233	655	83	18	31

Source: Federal Bureau of Investigation, Hate Crime Statistics 2013

Identity Theft Consumer Complaints

Area	Complaints	Complaints per 100,000 Population	Rank[2]
MSA[1]	1,377	78.3	133
U.S.	332,646	104.3	-

Note: (1) Figures cover the Nashville-Davidson—Murfreesboro—Franklin, TN Metropolitan Statistical Area—see Appendix B for areas included; (2) Rank ranges from 1 to 380 where 1 indicates greatest number of identity theft complaints per 100,000 population
Source: Federal Trade Commission, Consumer Sentinel Network Data Book for January–December 2014

Fraud and Other Consumer Complaints

Area	Complaints	Complaints per 100,000 Population	Rank[2]
MSA[1]	7,846	446.3	65
U.S.	2,250,205	705.7	-

Note: (1) Figures cover the Nashville-Davidson—Murfreesboro—Franklin, TN Metropolitan Statistical Area—see Appendix B for areas included; (2) Rank ranges from 1 to 380 where 1 indicates greatest number of identity theft complaints per 100,000 population
Source: Federal Trade Commission, Consumer Sentinel Network Data Book for January–December 2014

RECREATION

Culture

Dance[1]	Theatre[1]	Instrumental Music[1]	Vocal Music[1]	Series and Festivals	Museums and Art Galleries[2]	Zoos and Aquariums[3]
2	9	1	2	5	48	1

Note: (1) Professional perfoming groups; (2) Based on organizations with SIC code 8412; (3) AZA-accredited
Source: The Grey House Performing Arts Directory, 2015-16; Association of Zoos & Aquariums, AZA Member Zoos & Aquariums, April 2015; www.AccuLeads.com, April 2015

Professional Sports Teams

Team Name	League	Year Established
Nashville Predators	National Hockey League (NHL)	1998
Tennessee Titans	National Football League (NFL)	1997

Note: Includes teams located in the Nashville-Davidson—Murfreesboro—Franklin, TN Metropolitan Statistical Area.
Source: Wikipedia, Major Professional Sports Teams of the United States and Canada, April 2015

CLIMATE

Average and Extreme Temperatures

Temperature	Jan	Feb	Mar	Apr	May	Jun	Jul	Aug	Sep	Oct	Nov	Dec	Yr.
Extreme High (°F)	78	84	86	91	95	106	107	104	105	94	84	79	107
Average High (°F)	47	51	60	71	79	87	90	89	83	72	60	50	70
Average Temp. (°F)	38	41	50	60	68	76	80	79	72	61	49	41	60
Average Low (°F)	28	31	39	48	57	65	69	68	61	48	39	31	49
Extreme Low (°F)	-17	-13	2	23	34	42	54	49	36	26	-1	-10	-17

Note: Figures cover the years 1948-1990
Source: National Climatic Data Center, International Station Meteorological Climate Summary, 9/96

Average Precipitation/Snowfall/Humidity

Precip./Humidity	Jan	Feb	Mar	Apr	May	Jun	Jul	Aug	Sep	Oct	Nov	Dec	Yr.
Avg. Precip. (in.)	4.4	4.2	5.0	4.1	4.6	3.7	3.8	3.3	3.2	2.6	3.9	4.6	47.4
Avg. Snowfall (in.)	4	3	1	Tr	0	0	0	0	0	Tr	1	1	11
Avg. Rel. Hum. 6am (%)	81	81	80	81	86	86	88	90	90	87	83	82	85
Avg. Rel. Hum. 3pm (%)	61	57	51	48	52	52	54	53	52	49	55	59	54

Note: Figures cover the years 1948-1990; Tr = Trace amounts (<0.05 in. of rain; <0.5 in. of snow)
Source: National Climatic Data Center, International Station Meteorological Climate Summary, 9/96

Weather Conditions

Temperature			Daytime Sky			Precipitation		
10°F & below	32°F & below	90°F & above	Clear	Partly cloudy	Cloudy	0.01 inch or more precip.	0.1 inch or more snow/ice	Thunder-storms
5	76	51	98	135	132	119	8	54

Note: Figures are average number of days per year and cover the years 1948-1990
Source: National Climatic Data Center, International Station Meteorological Climate Summary, 9/96

HAZARDOUS WASTE

Superfund Sites

Nashville has no sites on the EPA's Superfund Final National Priorities List. There are a total of 1,322 Superfund sites on the list in the U.S. *U.S. Environmental Protection Agency, Final National Priorities List, April 14, 2015*

AIR & WATER QUALITY

Air Quality Trends: Ozone

	2004	2005	2006	2007	2008	2009	2010	2011	2012	2013
MSA[1]	0.072	0.078	0.078	0.083	0.072	0.064	0.073	0.071	0.077	0.065

Note: (1) Data covers the Nashville-Davidson—Murfreesboro—Franklin, TN Metropolitan Statistical Area—see Appendix B for areas included. The values shown are the composite ozone concentration averages among trend sites based on the highest fourth daily maximum 8-hour concentration in parts per million. These trends are based on sites having an adequate record of monitoring data during the trend period. Data from exceptional events are included.
Source: U.S. Environmental Protection Agency, Air Quality Monitoring Information, "Air Quality Trends by City, 2000-2013"

Air Quality Index

Area	Percent of Days when Air Quality was...[2]					AQI Statistics[2]	
	Good	Moderate	Unhealthy for Sensitive Groups	Unhealthy	Very Unhealthy	Maximum	Median
MSA[1]	61.1	38.4	0.5	0.0	0.0	119	45

Note: (1) Data covers the Nashville-Davidson—Murfreesboro—Franklin, TN Metropolitan Statistical Area—see Appendix B for areas included; (2) Based on 365 days with AQI data in 2014. Air Quality Index (AQI) is an index for reporting daily air quality. EPA calculates the AQI for five major air pollutants regulated by the Clean Air Act: ground-level ozone, particle pollution (aka particulate matter), carbon monoxide, sulfur dioxide, and nitrogen dioxide. The AQI runs from 0 to 500. The higher the AQI value, the greater the level of air pollution and the greater the health concern. There are six AQI categories: "Good" AQI is between 0 and 50. Air quality is considered satisfactory; "Moderate" AQI is between 51 and 100. Air quality is acceptable; "Unhealthy for Sensitive Groups" When AQI values are between 101 and 150, members of sensitive groups may experience health effects; "Unhealthy" When AQI values are between 151 and 200 everyone may begin to experience health effects; "Very Unhealthy" AQI values between 201 and 300 trigger a health alert; "Hazardous" AQI values over 300 trigger warnings of emergency conditions (not shown).
Source: U.S. Environmental Protection Agency, Air Quality Index Report, 2014

Air Quality Index Pollutants

Area	Percent of Days when AQI Pollutant was...[2]					
	Carbon Monoxide	Nitrogen Dioxide	Ozone	Sulfur Dioxide	Particulate Matter 2.5	Particulate Matter 10
MSA[1]	0.0	5.5	23.0	0.3	71.2	0.0

Note: (1) Data covers the Nashville-Davidson—Murfreesboro—Franklin, TN Metropolitan Statistical Area—see Appendix B for areas included; (2) Based on 365 days with AQI data in 2014. The Air Quality Index (AQI) is an index for reporting daily air quality. EPA calculates the AQI for five major air pollutants regulated by the Clean Air Act: ground-level ozone, particle pollution (also known as particulate matter), carbon monoxide, sulfur dioxide, and nitrogen dioxide. The AQI runs from 0 to 500. The higher the AQI value, the greater the level of air pollution and the greater the health concern.
Source: U.S. Environmental Protection Agency, Air Quality Index Report, 2014

Maximum Air Pollutant Concentrations: Particulate Matter, Ozone, CO and Lead

	Particulate Matter 10 (ug/m^3)	Particulate Matter 2.5 Wtd AM (ug/m^3)	Particulate Matter 2.5 24-Hr (ug/m^3)	Ozone (ppm)	Carbon Monoxide (ppm)	Lead (ug/m^3)
MSA[1] Level	29	10.1	20	0.068	1	n/a
NAAQS[2]	150	15	35	0.075	9	0.15
Met NAAQS[2]	Yes	Yes	Yes	Yes	Yes	n/a

Note: (1) Data covers the Nashville-Davidson—Murfreesboro—Franklin, TN Metropolitan Statistical Area—see Appendix B for areas included; Data from exceptional events are included; (2) National Ambient Air Quality Standards; ppm = parts per million; ug/m^3 = micrograms per cubic meter; n/a not available.
Concentrations: Particulate Matter 10 (coarse particulate)—highest second maximum 24-hour concentration; Particulate Matter 2.5 Wtd AM (fine particulate)—highest weighted annual mean concentration; Particulate Matter 2.5 24-Hour (fine particulate)—highest 98th percentile 24-hour concentration; Ozone—highest fourth daily maximum 8-hour concentration; Carbon Monoxide—highest second maximum non-overlapping 8-hour concentration; Lead—maximum running 3-month average
Source: U.S. Environmental Protection Agency, Air Quality Monitoring Information, "Air Quality Statistics by City, 2013"

Maximum Air Pollutant Concentrations: Nitrogen Dioxide and Sulfur Dioxide

	Nitrogen Dioxide AM (ppb)	Nitrogen Dioxide 1-Hr (ppb)	Sulfur Dioxide AM (ppb)	Sulfur Dioxide 1-Hr (ppb)	Sulfur Dioxide 24-Hr (ppb)
MSA[1] Level	10	42	n/a	10	n/a
NAAQS[2]	53	100	30	75	140
Met NAAQS[2]	Yes	Yes	n/a	Yes	n/a

Note: (1) Data covers the Nashville-Davidson—Murfreesboro—Franklin, TN Metropolitan Statistical Area—see Appendix B for areas included; Data from exceptional events are included; (2) National Ambient Air Quality Standards; ppm = parts per million; ug/m^3 = micrograms per cubic meter; n/a not available.
Concentrations: Nitrogen Dioxide AM—highest arithmetic mean concentration; Nitrogen Dioxide 1-Hr—highest 98th percentile 1-hour daily maximum concentration; Sulfur Dioxide AM—highest annual mean concentration; Sulfur Dioxide 1-Hr—highest 99th percentile 1-hour daily maximum concentration; Sulfur Dioxide 24-Hr—highest second maximum 24-hour concentration
Source: U.S. Environmental Protection Agency, Air Quality Monitoring Information, "Air Quality Statistics by City, 2013"

Drinking Water

Water System Name	Pop. Served	Primary Water Source Type	Violations[1]	
			Health Based	Monitoring/ Reporting
Nashville Water Dept #1	616,468	Surface	0	0

Note: (1) Based on violation data from January 1, 2014 to December 31, 2014 (includes unresolved violations from earlier years)

Source: U.S. Environmental Protection Agency, Office of Ground Water and Drinking Water, Safe Drinking Water Information System (based on data extracted January 27, 2015)

New Orleans, Louisiana

Background

New Orleans, the old port city upriver from the mouth of the Mississippi River, is on a par with San Francisco and New York City as one of the United States' most interesting cities. The birthplace of jazz is rich in unique local history, distinctive neighborhoods, and an unmistakably individual character.

The failure of the federal levees following Hurricane Katrina in 2005 put 80 percent of the city under floodwaters for weeks. The Crescent City's revival since then is a testament to her unique spirit, an influx of federal dollars, and an outpouring from volunteers ranging from church groups to spring breakers who returned year after year to help rebuild.

New Orleans was founded on behalf of France by the brothers Le Moyne, Sieurs d'Iberville, and de Bienville, in 1718. Despite disease, starvation, and an unwilling working class, New Orleans emerged as a genteel antebellum slave society, fashioning itself after the rigid social hierarchy of Versailles. Even after New Orleans was ceded to Spain after the French & Indian War, this unequal lifestyle, however gracious, persisted.

The port city briefly returned to French control, then became a crown jewel in the 1803 Louisiana Purchase to the U.S. The transfer of control changed New Orleans's Old World isolation. American settlers introduced aggressive business acumen to the area, as well as the idea of respect for the self-made man. As trade opened up with countries around the world, this made for a happy union. New Orleans became "Queen City of the South," growing prosperous from adventurous riverboat traders and speculators, as well as the cotton trade.

Today, much of the city's Old World charm remains, resulting from Southern, Creole, African-American, and European cultures. New Orleans' cuisine, indigenous music, unique festivals, and sultry, pleasing atmosphere, drew more than eight million visitors in 2010.

A major pillar of the city's economy is the enormous tourism trade that includes the Ernest N. Morial Convention Center's numerous convention goers who fill more than 35,000 rooms. A second economic pillar is the Port of New Orleans, one of the nation's leading general cargo ports. In recent years, it has seen $400 million invested in new facilities.

In addition, an influx of mostly young people who arrived after Hurricane Katrina is giving rise to a new start-up spirit. Plus, state tax breaks have helped to turn New Orleans into "Hollywood South," where 35 films were produced in the last few years. New Orleans has given birth to a mother lode of cultural phenomena: Dixieland jazz, musicians Louis Armstrong, Mahalia Jackson, Dr. John, and chefs Emeril Lagasse and John Besh. The city is well aware of its "cultural economy," which employs 12.5 percent of the local workforce. Popular tourist draws include the annual Mardi Gras celebration—which spans two long weekends leading up to Fat Tuesday—and the annual New Orleans Jazz & Heritage Festival. The Louisiana Superdome—renovated and renamed to the Mercedes Benz Superdome, is home to the 2010 Super Bowl champion New Orleans Saints, and hosted the 2013 Super Bowl. A new, nearly $75 million Consolidated Rental Car Facility project is expanding rental capacity and bring scattered facilities under one roof at the Louis Armstrong New Orleans International Airport.

In addition, an effort to boost a medical economy that suffered after Hurricane Katrina is underway with the near completion of a new Louisiana State University teaching hospital.

In his 2011 state of the city address, Mayor Mitch Landrieu said more than $13 billion in investments would unfold in coming years for bridge, airport, road and hospital repairs. School rebuilding was set for a $1.8 billion influx. Since Katrina, the majority of New Orleans public schools have become charter schools—a major experiment that is seeing some success. Higher education campuses include Tulane University (including a medical school and law school), Loyola University, and the University of New Orleans. Louisiana State University has a medical school campus downtown.

Cultural amenities include the New Orleans Museum of Art located in the live-oak filled City Park, the Ogden Museum of Southern Art, and Audubon Park, designed by John Charles Olmsted with its golf course and the Audubon Zoo.

The New Orleans metro area is virtually surrounded by water, which influences its climate. Between mid-June and September, temperatures are kept down by near-daily sporadic thunderstorms. Cold spells sometimes reach the area in winter but seldom last. Frequent and sometimes heavy rains are typical. Hurricane season officially runs from June 1 to November 30 but typically reaches its height in late summer.

Rankings

General Rankings

- New Orleans was selected as one of America's best cities by *Bloomberg Businessweek.* The city ranked #14 out of 50. Criteria: leisure attributes (the number of restaurants, bars, libraries, museums, professional sports teams, and park acres by population); educational attributes (public school performance, the number of colleges, and graduate degree holders); economic factors (2011 income and June and July 2012 unemployment); crime; and air quality. *Bloomberg BusinessWeek, "America's Best Cities," September 26, 2012*
- New Orleans was selected as one of "America's Favorite Cities." The city ranked #4 in the "Type of Trip: Gay-friendly Vacation" category. Respondents to an online survey were asked to rate 38 top urban destinations in the United States from a visitor's perspective. Criteria: gay-friendly. *Travel + Leisure, "America's Favorite Cities 20143"*
- New Orleans was selected as one of the "10 Best Places to Live Now" by *Men's Journal*. New Orleans ranked #6. *Men's Journal, "10 Best Places to Live Now," April 2015*
- New Orleans appeared on *Travel + Leisure's* list of the ten best cities in the United States and Canada. The city was ranked #2. Criteria: activities/attractions; culture/arts; restaurants/food; people; and value. *Travel + Leisure, "The World's Best Awards 2014"*
- Based on nearly 77,000 responses, *Condé Nast Traveler* ranked its readers' favorite cities worldwide. New Orleans ranked #17. *Condé Nast Traveler, Readers' Choice Awards 2014, "Top 10 Cities in the World"*

Business/Finance Rankings

- Building on the U.S. Department of Labor's Occupational Information Network Data Collection Program, the Brookings Institution defined STEM occupations and job opportunities for STEM workers at various levels of educational attainment. The New Orleans metro area was one of the ten metro areas where workers in low-education-level STEM jobs earn the highest relative wages. *www.brookings.edu, "The Hidden Stem Economy," June 10, 2013*
- Based on metro area social media reviews, the employment opinion group Glassdoor surveyed 50 of the largest U.S. metro areas on measures including compensation and benefits, satisfaction with management, business outlook, and number of employers hiring. The New Orleans metro area was ranked #16 in overall employee satisfaction. *www.glassdoor.com, "Employment Satisfaction Report Card by City," June 13, 2014*
- In a survey of economic confidence in the nation's 50 largest metropolitan areas conducted January–December 2014, the New Orleans metro area placed #46, according to Gallup's 2014 Economic Confidence Index. *Gallup, "San Jose and San Francisco Lead in Economic Confidence," March 19, 2015*
- Using data from the Council for Community and Economic Research's 2013 Annual Report, NerdWallet ranked the 100 U.S. cities with the most expensive cost of living. Cities in California and in the Northeast topped the list. Of the cities with the highest cost of living, New Orleans ranked #91. *NerdWallet.com, "Most Expensive Cities in America," June 4, 2014*
- New Orleans was ranked #6 out of 100 metro areas in terms of economic performance (#1 = best) during the recession and recovery from trough quarter through the second quarter of 2013. Criteria: percent change in employment; percentage point change in unemployment rate; percent change in gross metropolitan product; percent change in House Price Index. *Brookings Institution, MetroMonitor: Tracking Economic Recession and Recovery in America's 100 Largest Metropolitan Areas, September 2013*
- The New Orleans metro area appeared on the Milken Institute "2013 Best Performing Cities" list. Rank: #67 out of 200 large metro areas. Criteria: job growth; wage and salary growth; high-tech output growth. *Milken Institute, "Best-Performing Cities 2014," January 2015*

- *Forbes* ranked the 200 most populous metro areas to determine the nation's "Best Places for Business and Careers." The New Orleans metro area was ranked #65. Criteria: costs (business and living); job growth (past and projected); income growth; educational attainment (college and high school); projected economic growth; cultural and recreational opportunities; net migration patterns; number of highly ranked colleges. *Forbes, "The Best Places for Business and Careers 2014," July 23, 2014*

Culture/Performing Arts Rankings

- New Orleans was selected as one of the ten best small U.S. cities in which to be a moviemaker. Of cities with a population between 100,000 and 400,000, the city was ranked #2. Criteria: film community; access to new films; access to equipment; cost of living; tax incentives. *MovieMaker Magazine, "Best Places to Live and Work as a Moviemaker: 2013," January 22, 2015*
- New Orleans was selected as one of "America's Favorite Cities." The city ranked #3 in the "Culture: Music Scene " category. Respondents to an online survey were asked to rate 38 top urban destinations in the U.S. from a visitor's perspective. *Travelandleisure.com, "America's Favorite Cities," October 7, 2014*
- New Orleans was selected as one of "America's Favorite Cities." The city ranked #5 in the "Culture: Historical Sites " category. Respondents to an online survey were asked to rate 38 top urban destinations in the U.S. from a visitor's perspective. *Travelandleisure.com, "America's Favorite Cities," October 7, 2014*
- New Orleans was selected as one of America's top cities for the arts. The city ranked #5 in the mid-sized city (population 100,000 to 499,999) category. Criteria: readers' top choices for arts travel destinations based on the richness and variety of visual arts sites, activities and events. *American Style, "2012 Top 25 Arts Destinations," June 2012*

Dating/Romance Rankings

- Of the 100 U.S. cities surveyed by *Men's Health* in its quest to identify the nation's best cities for dating and forming relationships, New Orleans was ranked #70 for online dating (#1 = best). *Men's Health, "The Best and Worst Cities for Online Dating," January 30, 2013*
- New Orleans was selected as one of America's best cities for singles by the readers of *Travel + Leisure* in their annual "America's Favorite Cities" survey. The city was ranked #3 out of 20. Criteria included good-looking locals, cool shopping, and hipster-magnet coffee bars. *Travel + Leisure, "America's Best Cities for Singles," January 23, 2015*
- New Orleans was selected as one of "America's Best Cities for Dating" by *Yahoo! Travel*. Criteria: high proportion of singles; excellent dating venues and/or stunning natural settings. *Yahoo! Travel, "America's Best Cities for Dating," February 7, 2012*

Education Rankings

- Personal finance website *WalletHub* analyzed the 150 largest U.S. metropolitan statistical areas to determine where the most educated Americans are choosing to settle. Criteria: educational attainment; percentage of workers with jobs in computer, engineering, and science fields; quality and size of each metro area's universities. New Orleans was ranked #88 (#1 = most educated city). *www.WalletHub.com, "2014's Most and Least Educated Cities*
- New Orleans was selected as one of America's most literate cities. The city ranked #27 out of the 77 largest U.S. cities. Criteria: number of booksellers; library resources; Internet resources; educational attainment; periodical publishing resources; newspaper circulation. *Central Connecticut State University, "America's Most Literate Cities, 2014," April 8, 2015*

Environmental Rankings

- The New Orleans metro area came in at #336 for the relative comfort of its climate on Sperling's list of "chill cities," as measured by the Sperling Heat Index. All 361 metro areas are included. Criteria included daytime high temperatures, nighttime low temperatures, dew point, and relative humidity at the high temperatures. *www.bertsperling.com, "Sperling's Chill Cities," July 18, 2013*

- Sperling's BestPlaces assessed 379 metropolitan areas of the United States for the likelihood of dangerously extreme weather events or earthquakes. In general the Southeast and South-Central regions have the highest risk of weather extremes and earthquakes, while the Pacific Northwest enjoys the lowest risk. Of the least risky metropolitan areas, the New Orleans metro area was ranked #326. *www.bestplaces.net, "Safest Places from Natural Disasters," April 2011*

- New Orleans was highlighted as one of the top 25 cleanest metro areas for short-term particle pollution (24-hour PM 2.5) in the U.S. during 2011 through 2013. Monitors in these cities reported no days with unhealthful PM 2.5 levels. *American Lung Association, State of the Air 2015*

Food/Drink Rankings

- *Men's Health* ranked 100 major U.S. cities in terms of alcohol intoxication. New Orleans ranked #15 (#1 = most sober).Criteria: binge drinking; alcohol-related traffic accidents, arrests, and fatalities. *Men's Health, "The Drunkest Cities in America," November 19, 2013*

Health/Fitness Rankings

- Analysts who tracked obesity rates in the nation's largest metro areas (those with populations above one million) found that the New Orleans metro area was one of the ten major metros where residents were most likely to be obese, defined as a BMI score of 30 or above. *www.gallup.com, "Boulder, Colo., Residents Still Least Likely to Be Obese," April 4, 2014*

- For each of the 50 most populous metro areas in the United States, the American College of Sports Medicine's American Fitness Index evaluated infrastructure, community assets, and policies that encourage healthy and fit lifestyles, including preventive health behaviors, levels of chronic disease conditions, health care access, and community resources and policies that support physical activity. The New Orleans metro area ranked #38 for "community fitness." Personal health indicators were considered as well as community and environmental indicators. *www.americanfitnessindex.org, "ACSM American Fitness Index Health and Community Fitness Status of the 50 Largest Metropolitan Areas," May 2013*

- The New Orleans metro area was identified as one of the worst cities for bed bugs in America by pest control company Orkin. The area ranked #49 out of 50 based on the number of bed bug treatments Orkin performed from January to December 2013. *Orkin, "Chicago Tops Bed Bug Cities List for Second Year in a Row," January 16, 2014*

- New Orleans was selected as one of the 25 fattest cities in America by *Men's Fitness Online*. It ranked #19 out of America's 50 largest cities. Criteria: fitness centers and sport stores; nutrition; sports participation; TV viewing; overweight/sedentary; junk food; air quality; geography; commute; parks and open space; city recreational facilities; access to healthcare; motivation; mayor and city initiatives; state obesity initiatives. *Men's Fitness, "The Fittest and Fattest Cities in America," March 5, 2012*

- New Orleans was identified as a "2013 Spring Allergy Capital." The area ranked #13 out of 100. Three groups of factors were used to identify the most severe cities for people with allergies during the spring season: annual pollen levels; medicine utilization; access to board-certified allergists. *Asthma and Allergy Foundation of America, "Spring Allergy Capitals 2013"*

- New Orleans was identified as a "2013 Fall Allergy Capital." The area ranked #11 out of 100. Three groups of factors were used to identify the most severe cities for people with allergies during the fall season: annual pollen levels; medicine utilization; access to board-certified allergists. *Asthma and Allergy Foundation of America, "Fall Allergy Capitals 2013"*

- New Orleans was identified as a "2013 Asthma Capital." The area ranked #24 out of the nation's 100 largest metropolitan areas. Twelve factors were used to identify the most challenging places to live for people with asthma: estimated prevalence; self-reported prevalence; crude death rate for asthma; annual pollen score; annual air quality; public smoking laws; number of board-certified asthma specialists; school inhaler access laws; rescue medication use; controller medication use; uninsured rate; poverty rate. *Asthma and Allergy Foundation of America, "Asthma Capitals 2013"*

- *Men's Health* ranked 100 major U.S. cities in terms of the best and worst cities for men. New Orleans ranked #77. Criteria: thirty-three data points were examined covering health, fitness, and quality of life. *Men's Health, "The Best & Worst Cities for Men 2014," December 6, 2013*
- The New Orleans metro area appeared in the 2013 Gallup-Healthways Well-Being Index. The area ranked #120 out of 189. The Gallup-Healthways Well-Being Index score is an average of six sub-indexes, which individually examine life evaluation, emotional health, work environment, physical health, healthy behaviors, and access to basic necessities. Results are based on telephone interviews conducted as part of the Gallup-Healthways Well-Being Index survey January 2–December 29, 2012, and January 2–December 30, 2013, with a random sample of 531,630 adults, aged 18 and older, living in metropolitan areas in the 50 U.S. states and the District of Columbia. *Gallup-Healthways, "State of American Well-Being," March 25, 2014*
- New Orleans was selected as one of the "20 Most Livable U.S. Cities for Wheelchair Users" by the Christopher & Dana Reeve Foundation. The city ranked #18. Criteria: Medicaid eligibility and spending; access to physicians and rehabilitation facilities; access to fitness facilities and recreation; access to paratransit; percentage of people living with disabilities who are employed; clean air; climate. *Christopher & Dana Reeve Foundation, "20 Most Livable U.S. Cities for Wheelchair Users," July 26, 2010*

Real Estate Rankings

- Based on the home-price forecasts compiled by the real-estate valuation firm CoreLogic Case-Shiller, the finance website CNNMoney reported that in 2014, the New Orleans metro area is expected to place #3 among American metro areas in terms of increases in residential real estate prices. *money.cnn.com, "10 Hottest Housing Markets for 2014," January 23, 2014*
- The New Orleans metro area was identified as one of the nations's 20 hottest housing markets in 2015. Criteria: listing views relative to the number of listings. The area ranked #2. *Realtor.com, "These Are the 20 Hottest Housing Markets in the U.S. Right Now," April 8, 2015*
- New Orleans was ranked #127 out of 275 metro areas in terms of house price appreciation in 2014 (#1 = highest rate). *Federal Housing Finance Agency, House Price Index, 4th Quarter 2014*

Safety Rankings

- Business Insider looked at the FBI's Uniform Crime Report to identify the U.S. cities with the most violent crime per capita, excluding localities with fewer than 100,000 residents. To judge by its relatively high murder, rape, and robbery data, New Orleans was ranked #5 (#1 = worst) among the 25 most dangerous cities. *www.businessinsider.com, "The 25 Most Dangerous Cities in America," June 13, 2013*
- Allstate ranked the 200 largest cities in America in terms of driver safety. New Orleans ranked #181. Allstate researchers analyzed internal property damage claims over a two-year period from January 2011 to December 2012. A weighted average of the two-year numbers determined the annual percentages. *Allstate, "Allstate America's Best Drivers Report, 2014"*
- New Orleans was identified as one of the most dangerous mid-size cities in America by CQ Press. All 252 cities with populations of 100,000 to 499,999 that reported crime rates in 2012 for murder, rape, robbery, aggravated assault, burglary, and motor vehicle thefts were ranked. The city ranked #9 out of the top 10. *CQ Press, City Crime Rankings 2014*
- The National Insurance Crime Bureau ranked 380 metro areas in the U.S. in terms of per capita rates of vehicle theft. The New Orleans metro area ranked #51 (#1 = highest rate). Criteria: number of vehicle theft offenses per 100,000 inhabitants in 2012. *National Insurance Crime Bureau, "Hot Spots 2012," June 26, 2013*

Seniors/Retirement Rankings

- From its Best Cities for Successful Aging indexes, the Milken Institute generated rankings for metropolitan areas, weighing data in eight categories—health care, wellness, living arrangements, transportation, financial characteristics, education and employment opportunities, community engagement, and overall livability. The New Orleans metro area was ranked #38 overall in the large metro area category. *Milken Institute, "Best Cities for Successful Aging, 2014"*

Sports/Recreation Rankings

- *24/7 Wall St.* analysts isolated the ten cities that spent the most public money per capita on sports stadiums, according to 2010 data. New Orleans ranked #8. *24/7 Wall St., "Cities Paying the Most for Sports Teams," January 30, 2013*
- New Orleans was selected as one of the most playful cities in the U.S. by KaBOOM! The organization's Playful City USA initiative honors cities and towns across the nation for a vision, plan and commitment to creating an agenda for play. Criteria: creating a local play commission or task force; designing an annual action plan for play; conducting a play space audit; outlining a financial investment in play for the current fiscal year; and proclaiming and celebrating an annual "play day." *KaBOOM! National Campaign for Play, "2013 Playful City USA Communities"*
- New Orleans was chosen as one of America's best cities for bicycling. The city ranked #43 out of 50. Criteria: robust cycling infrastructure; vibrant bike culture. The editors only considered cities with populations of 95,000 or more. *Bicycling, "America's Top 50 Bike-Friendly Cities," May 23, 2012*

Transportation Rankings

- NerdWallet surveyed average annual car insurance premiums in 125 U.S. cities to identify the least expensive U.S. cities in which to insure a car. Locations with no-fault insurance laws was a strong determinant. New Orleans came in at #2 for the most expensive rates. *www.nerdwallet.com, "Best Cities for Cheap Car Insurance," February 3, 2014*

Women/Minorities Rankings

- The Daily Beast surveyed the nation's cities for highest percentage of singles and lowest divorce rate, plus other measures, to determine "emotional intelligence"—happiness, confidence, kindness—which, researchers say, has a strong correlation with people's satisfaction with their romantic relationships. New Orleans placed #19. *www.thedailybeast.com, "Best Cities to Find Love and Stay in Love," February 14, 2014*
- *Women's Health* examined U.S. cities and identified the 100 best cities for women. New Orleans was ranked #70. Criteria: 30 categories were examined from obesity and breast cancer rates to commuting times and hours spent working out. *Women's Health, "Best Cities for Women 2012"*

Miscellaneous Rankings

- The New Orleans metro area was selected as one of "The Best U.S. Cities for Bargain Shopping" by *Forbes*. The area ranked #10 out of 10. Criteria: number of outlet stores; gross leasable retail space in major malls; low consumer price index; low sales tax rate. Indicators were examined in the nation's 50 largest metropolitan areas. *Forbes, "The Best U.S. Cities for Bargain Shopping," January 20, 2012*
- Mars Chocolate North America, the makers of COMBOS®, in partnership with Sperling's BestPlaces, ranked 50 major metro areas in terms of their "manliness." The New Orleans metro area ranked #14. Criteria: number of professional sports teams; number of nearby NASCAR tracks and racing events; manly lifestyle; concentration of manly retail stores; manly occupations per capita; salty snack sales; "Board of Manliness" rankings. *Mars Chocolate North America, "America's Manliest Cities 2012"*

- New Orleans was selected as one of "America's Best Cities for Hipsters" by *Travel + Leisure.* The city was ranked #2 out of 20. Criteria: live music; coffee bars; independent boutiques; best microbrews; offbeat and tech-savvy locals. *Travel + Leisure, "America's Best Cities for Hipsters," November 2013*
- The National Alliance to End Homelessness ranked the 100 most populous metro areas in terms the rate of homelessness. The New Orleans metro area ranked #2. Criteria: number of homeless people per 10,000 population in 2011. *National Alliance to End Homelessness, The State of Homelessness in America 2012*

Business Environment

CITY FINANCES

City Government Finances

Component	2012 ($000)	2012 ($ per capita)
Total Revenues	1,598,967	4,650
Total Expenditures	1,761,547	5,123
Debt Outstanding	2,018,886	5,872
Cash and Securities[1]	1,910,232	5,556

Note: (1) Cash and security holdings of a government at the close of its fiscal year, including those of its dependent agencies, utilities, and liquor stores.
Source: U.S Census Bureau, State & Local Government Finances 2012

City Government Revenue by Source

Source	2012 ($000)	2012 ($ per capita)
General Revenue		
From Federal Government	297,472	865
From State Government	236,446	688
From Local Governments	1,725	5
Taxes		
Property	256,208	745
Sales and Gross Receipts	213,690	622
Personal Income	0	0
Corporate Income	0	0
Motor Vehicle License	2,462	7
Other Taxes	26,991	79
Current Charges	329,346	958
Liquor Store	0	0
Utility	64,320	187
Employee Retirement	29,531	86

Source: U.S Census Bureau, State & Local Government Finances 2012

City Government Expenditures by Function

Function	2012 ($000)	2012 ($ per capita)	2012 (%)
General Direct Expenditures			
Air Transportation	131,891	384	7.5
Corrections	129,001	375	7.3
Education	0	0	0.0
Employment Security Administration	0	0	0.0
Financial Administration	45,701	133	2.6
Fire Protection	89,338	260	5.1
General Public Buildings	16,624	48	0.9
Governmental Administration, Other	61,851	180	3.5
Health	10,785	31	0.6
Highways	121,900	355	6.9
Hospitals	1,498	4	0.1
Housing and Community Development	248,903	724	14.1
Interest on General Debt	95,072	277	5.4
Judicial and Legal	46,718	136	2.7
Libraries	26,651	78	1.5
Parking	2,289	7	0.1
Parks and Recreation	88,260	257	5.0
Police Protection	143,572	418	8.2
Public Welfare	2,746	8	0.2
Sewerage	182,903	532	10.4
Solid Waste Management	36,830	107	2.1
Veterans' Services	0	0	0.0
Liquor Store	0	0	0.0
Utility	85,790	250	4.9
Employee Retirement	71,382	208	4.1

Source: U.S Census Bureau, State & Local Government Finances 2012

DEMOGRAPHICS

Population Growth

Area	1990 Census	2000 Census	2010 Census	Population Growth (%)	
				1990-2000	2000-2010
City	496,938	484,674	343,829	-2.5	-29.1
MSA[1]	1,264,391	1,316,510	1,167,764	4.1	-11.3
U.S.	248,709,873	281,421,906	308,745,538	13.2	9.7

Note: (1) Figures cover the New Orleans-Metairie-Kenner, LA Metropolitan Statistical Area—see Appendix B for areas included
Source: U.S. Census Bureau, Census 1990, 2000, 2010

Household Size

Area	Persons in Household (%)							Average Household Size
	One	Two	Three	Four	Five	Six	Seven or More	
City	40.6	29.9	14.4	8.5	4.2	1.3	1.1	2.35
MSA[1]	31.4	32.5	16.3	11.8	5.3	1.6	1.1	2.56
U.S.	27.7	33.6	15.7	13.1	6.0	2.3	1.5	2.64

Note: (1) Figures cover the New Orleans-Metairie, LA Metropolitan Statistical Area—see Appendix B for areas included
Source: U.S. Census Bureau, 2011-2013 American Community Survey 3-Year Estimates

Race

Area	White Alone[2] (%)	Black Alone[2] (%)	Asian Alone[2] (%)	AIAN[3] Alone[2] (%)	NHOPI[4] Alone[2] (%)	Other Race Alone[2] (%)	Two or More Races (%)
City	34.1	59.8	3.0	0.3	0.0	1.5	1.4
MSA[1]	58.5	34.7	2.8	0.4	0.0	1.9	1.6
U.S.	73.9	12.6	5.0	0.8	0.2	4.7	2.9

Note: (1) Figures cover the New Orleans-Metairie, LA Metropolitan Statistical Area—see Appendix B for areas included; (2) Alone is defined as not being in combination with one or more other races; (3) American Indian and Alaska Native; (4) Native Hawaiian and Other Pacific Islander
Source: U.S. Census Bureau, 2011-2013 American Community Survey 3-Year Estimates

Hispanic or Latino Origin

Area	Total (%)	Mexican (%)	Puerto Rican (%)	Cuban (%)	Other (%)
City	5.4	1.2	0.4	0.3	3.5
MSA[1]	8.1	1.8	0.5	0.6	5.2
U.S.	16.9	10.8	1.6	0.6	3.8

Note: Persons of Hispanic or Latino origin can be of any race; (1) Figures cover the New Orleans-Metairie, LA Metropolitan Statistical Area—see Appendix B for areas included
Source: U.S. Census Bureau, 2011-2013 American Community Survey 3-Year Estimates

Segregation

Type	Segregation Indices[1]				Percent Change		
	1990	2000	2010	2010 Rank[2]	1990-2000	1990-2010	2000-2010
Black/White	68.3	69.2	63.9	28	0.9	-4.4	-5.3
Asian/White	49.6	50.4	48.6	9	0.8	-1.0	-1.8
Hispanic/White	31.1	35.6	38.3	74	4.5	7.2	2.7

Note: All figures cover the Metropolitan Statistical Area—see Appendix B for areas included; Figures are based on an analysis of 1990, 2000, and 2010 Census Decennial Census tract data by William H. Frey, Brookings Institution and the University of Michigan Social Science Data Analysis Network. In this analysis all racial groups (whites, blacks, and asians) are non-Hispanic members of those races. Hispanics are shown as a separate category;
(1) Segregation Indices are Dissimilarity Indices that measure the degree to which the minority group is distributed differently than whites across census tracts. They range from 0 (complete integration) to 100 (complete segregation) where the value indicates the percentage of the minority group that needs to move to be distributed exactly like whites; (2) Ranges from 1 (most segregated) to 102 (least segregated); n/a not available.
Source: www.CensusScope.org

Ancestry

Area	German	Irish	English	American	Italian	Polish	French[2]	Scottish	Dutch
City	6.8	6.0	4.2	3.4	4.1	0.8	6.2	1.0	0.4
MSA[1]	10.8	8.5	4.9	6.2	8.9	0.7	14.3	1.0	0.5
U.S.	14.9	10.8	8.0	7.4	5.5	3.0	2.7	1.7	1.4

Note: Figures are the percentage of the total population reporting a particular ancestry. The nine most commonly reported ancestries in the U.S. are shown. Figures include multiple ancestries (e.g. if a person reported being Irish and Italian, they were included in both columns); (1) Figures cover the New Orleans-Metairie, LA Metropolitan Statistical Area—see Appendix B for areas included; (2) Excludes Basque
Source: U.S. Census Bureau, 2011-2013 American Community Survey 3-Year Estimates

Foreign-Born Population

Area	Percent of Population Born in								
	Any Foreign Country	Mexico	Asia	Europe	Carribean	South America	Central America[2]	Africa	Canada
City	5.9	0.4	2.2	0.7	0.2	0.4	1.7	0.2	0.1
MSA[1]	7.1	0.6	2.0	0.6	0.7	0.4	2.5	0.2	0.1
U.S.	13.0	3.7	3.8	1.5	1.2	0.9	1.0	0.6	0.3

Note: (1) Figures cover the New Orleans-Metairie, LA Metropolitan Statistical Area—see Appendix B for areas included; (2) Excludes Mexico.
Source: U.S. Census Bureau, 2011-2013 American Community Survey 3-Year Estimates

Marital Status

Area	Never Married	Now Married[2]	Separated	Widowed	Divorced
City	48.8	30.1	3.0	6.1	12.1
MSA[1]	37.3	41.5	2.5	6.6	12.1
U.S.	32.7	48.1	2.2	6.0	11.0

Note: Figures are percentages and cover the population 15 years of age and older; (1) Figures cover the New Orleans-Metairie, LA Metropolitan Statistical Area—see Appendix B for areas included; (2) Excludes separated
Source: U.S. Census Bureau, 2011-2013 American Community Survey 3-Year Estimates

Disability Status

Area	All Ages	Under 18 Years Old	18 to 64 Years Old	65 Years and Over
City	13.9	4.7	12.4	40.3
MSA[1]	13.9	5.5	11.7	40.0
U.S.	12.3	4.1	10.2	36.3

Note: Figures show percent of the civilian noninstitutionalized population that reported having a disability. Disability status is determined from from six types of difficulty: vision, hearing, cognitive, ambulatory, self-care, and independent living. For children under 5 years old, hearing and vision difficulty are used to determine disability status. For children between the ages of 5 and 14, disability status is determined from hearing, vision, cognitive, ambulatory, and self-care difficulties. For people aged 15 years and older, they are considered to have a disability if they have difficulty with any one of the six difficulty types; (1) Figures cover the New Orleans-Metairie, LA Metropolitan Statistical Area—see Appendix B for areas included.
Source: U.S. Census Bureau, 2011-2013 American Community Survey 3-Year Estimates

Age

Area	Percent of Population									Median Age
	Under Age 5	Age 5–19	Age 20–34	Age 35–44	Age 45–54	Age 55–64	Age 65–74	Age 75–84	Age 85+	
City	6.3	17.3	26.3	12.4	13.5	12.8	6.5	3.4	1.5	35.0
MSA[1]	6.4	19.0	21.8	12.6	14.4	13.1	7.4	3.9	1.6	37.2
U.S.	6.4	19.9	20.7	12.9	14.1	12.3	7.6	4.2	1.9	37.4

Note: (1) Figures cover the New Orleans-Metairie, LA Metropolitan Statistical Area—see Appendix B for areas included
Source: U.S. Census Bureau, 2011-2013 American Community Survey 3-Year Estimates

Gender

Area	Males	Females	Males per 100 Females
City	177,685	192,080	92.5
MSA[1]	595,635	631,894	94.3
U.S.	154,451,010	159,410,713	96.9

Note: (1) Figures cover the New Orleans-Metairie, LA Metropolitan Statistical Area—see Appendix B for areas included
Source: U.S. Census Bureau, 2011-2013 American Community Survey 3-Year Estimates

Religious Groups by Family

Area	Catholic	Baptist	Non-Den.	Methodist[2]	Lutheran	LDS[3]	Pente-costal	Presby-terian[4]	Muslim[5]	Judaism
MSA[1]	31.6	8.4	3.7	2.7	0.8	0.6	2.1	0.5	0.5	0.5
U.S.	19.1	9.3	4.0	4.0	2.3	2.0	1.9	1.6	0.8	0.7

Note: Figures are the number of adherents as a percentage of the total population; (1) Figures cover the New Orleans-Metairie-Kenner, LA Metropolitan Statistical Area—see Appendix B for areas included; (2) Methodist/Pietist; (3) Latter Day Saints; (4) Reformed; (5) Figures are estimates
Source: Association of Statisticians of American Religious Bodies, 2010 U.S. Religion Census: Religious Congregations & Membership Study

Religious Groups by Tradition

Area	Catholic	Evangelical Protestant	Mainline Protestant	Other Tradition	Black Protestant	Orthodox
MSA[1]	31.6	12.7	4.0	2.1	3.0	0.1
U.S.	19.1	16.2	7.3	4.3	1.6	0.3

Note: Figures are the number of adherents as a percentage of the total population; (1) Figures cover the New Orleans-Metairie-Kenner, LA Metropolitan Statistical Area—see Appendix B for areas included
Source: Association of Statisticians of American Religious Bodies, 2010 U.S. Religion Census: Religious Congregations & Membership Study

ECONOMY

Gross Metropolitan Product

Area	2012	2013	2014	2015	Rank[2]
MSA[1]	80.2	83.7	87.4	91.0	40

Note: Figures are in billions of dollars; (1) Figures cover the New Orleans-Metairie, LA Metropolitan Statistical Area—see Appendix B for areas included; (2) Rank is based on 2015 data and ranges from 1 to 363
Source: The U.S. Conference of Mayors, U.S. Metro Economies: GMP and Employment 2013-2015, June 2014

Economic Growth

Area	2010-12 (%)	2013 (%)	2014 (%)	2015 (%)	Rank[2]
MSA[1]	0.8	3.9	2.2	3.0	155
U.S.	2.1	2.0	2.3	3.2	–

Note: Figures are real gross metropolitan product (GMP) growth rates and represent annual average percent change; (1) Figures cover the New Orleans-Metairie, LA Metropolitan Statistical Area—see Appendix B for areas included; (2) Rank is based on 2015 data and ranges from 1 to 363
Source: The U.S. Conference of Mayors, U.S. Metro Economies: GMP and Employment 2013-2015, June 2014

Metropolitan Area Exports

Area	2008	2009	2010	2011	2012	2013	Rank[2]
MSA[1]	12,664.5	10,145.1	13,964.9	20,336.9	24,359.5	30,030.9	8

Note: Figures are in millions of dollars; (1) Figures cover the New Orleans-Metairie, LA Metropolitan Statistical Area—see Appendix B for areas included; (2) Rank is based on 2013 data and ranges from 1 to 387
Source: U.S. Department of Commerce, International Trade Administration, Office of Trade & Industry Information, Manufacturing & Services, data extracted April 3, 2015

Building Permits

Area	Single-Family			Multi-Family			Total		
	2013	2014	Pct. Chg.	2013	2014	Pct. Chg.	2013	2014	Pct. Chg.
City	736	574	-22.0	159	452	184.3	895	1,026	14.6
MSA[1]	2,441	2,440	0.0	175	551	214.9	2,616	2,991	14.3
U.S.	620,802	634,597	2.2	370,020	411,766	11.3	990,822	1,046,363	5.6

Note: (1) Figures cover the New Orleans-Metairie, LA Metropolitan Statistical Area—see Appendix B for areas included; Figures represent new, privately-owned housing units authorized (unadjusted data); All permit data are based on estimates with imputation.
Source: U.S. Census Bureau, Manufacturing, Mining, and Construction Statistics, Building Permits, 2013, 2014

Bankruptcy Filings

Area	Business Filings			Nonbusiness Filings		
	2013	2014	% Chg.	2013	2014	% Chg.
Orleans Parish	40	45	12.5	704	674	-4.3
U.S.	33,212	26,983	-18.8	1,038,720	909,812	-12.4

Note: Business filings include Chapter 7, Chapter 11, Chapter 12, and Chapter 13; Nonbusiness filings include Chapter 7, Chapter 11, and Chapter 13
Source: Administrative Office of the U.S. Courts, Business and Nonbusiness Bankruptcy, County Cases Commenced by Chapter of the Bankruptcy Code, During the 12- Month Period Ending December 31, 2013 and Business and Nonbusiness Bankruptcy, County Cases Commenced by Chapter of the Bankruptcy Code, During the 12- Month Period Ending December 31, 2014

Housing Vacancy Rates

Area	Gross Vacancy Rate[2] (%)			Year-Round Vacancy Rate[3] (%)			Rental Vacancy Rate[4] (%)			Homeowner Vacancy Rate[5] (%)		
	2012	2013	2014	2012	2013	2014	2012	2013	2014	2012	2013	2014
MSA[1]	13.6	13.3	13.0	13.4	12.7	12.3	15.9	11.1	8.5	2.9	1.9	1.6
U.S.	13.8	13.6	13.4	10.8	10.7	10.4	8.7	8.3	7.6	2.0	2.0	1.9

Note: (1) Figures cover the New Orleans-Metairie, LA Metropolitan Statistical Area—see Appendix B for areas included; (2) The percentage of the total housing inventory that is vacant; (3) The percentage of the housing inventory (excluding seasonal units) that is year-round vacant; (4) The percentage of rental inventory that is vacant for rent; (5) The percentage of homeowner inventory that is vacant for sale
Source: U.S. Census Bureau, Housing Vacancies and Homeownership Annual Statistics: 2014

INCOME

Income

Area	Per Capita ($)	Median Household ($)	Average Household ($)
City	26,348	35,837	60,632
MSA[1]	26,502	45,592	65,898
U.S.	27,884	52,176	72,897

Note: (1) Figures cover the New Orleans-Metairie, LA Metropolitan Statistical Area—see Appendix B for areas included
Source: U.S. Census Bureau, 2011-2013 American Community Survey 3-Year Estimates

Household Income Distribution

Area	Percent of Households Earning							
	Under $15,000	$15,000 -24,999	$25,000 -34,999	$35,000 -49,999	$50,000 -74,999	$75,000 -99,000	$100,000 -149,999	$150,000 and up
City	24.8	13.8	10.5	12.5	13.7	8.4	8.7	7.6
MSA[1]	17.1	12.0	11.0	13.3	16.4	10.8	11.3	8.1
U.S.	13.0	10.9	10.3	13.6	17.9	11.9	12.7	9.6

Note: (1) Figures cover the New Orleans-Metairie, LA Metropolitan Statistical Area—see Appendix B for areas included
Source: U.S. Census Bureau, 2011-2013 American Community Survey 3-Year Estimates

Poverty Rate

Area	All Ages	Under 18 Years Old	18 to 64 Years Old	65 Years and Over
City	28.1	41.5	25.9	16.7
MSA[1]	19.4	28.3	17.7	12.1
U.S.	15.9	22.4	14.8	9.5

Note: Figures are percentage of people whose income during the past 12 months was below the poverty level; (1) Figures cover the New Orleans-Metairie, LA Metropolitan Statistical Area—see Appendix B for areas included
Source: U.S. Census Bureau, 2011-2013 American Community Survey 3-Year Estimates

EMPLOYMENT

Labor Force and Employment

Area	Civilian Labor Force			Workers Employed		
	Dec. 2013	Dec. 2014	% Chg.	Dec. 2013	Dec. 2014	% Chg.
City	173,364	179,735	3.7	163,628	167,131	2.1
MSA[1]	581,922	603,346	3.7	552,417	564,490	2.2
U.S.	154,408,000	155,521,000	0.7	144,423,000	147,190,000	1.9

Note: Data is not seasonally adjusted and covers workers 16 years of age and older; (1) Figures cover the New Orleans-Metairie, LA Metropolitan Statistical Area—see Appendix B for areas included
Source: Bureau of Labor Statistics, Local Area Unemployment Statistics

Unemployment Rate

Area	2014											
	Jan.	Feb.	Mar.	Apr.	May	Jun.	Jul.	Aug.	Sep.	Oct.	Nov.	Dec.
City	6.4	5.8	6.1	5.5	6.5	7.6	8.0	8.2	7.9	7.5	7.4	7.0
MSA[1]	5.8	5.2	5.5	5.0	5.9	6.9	7.2	7.4	7.1	6.9	6.8	6.4
U.S.	7.0	7.0	6.8	5.9	6.1	6.3	6.5	6.3	5.7	5.5	5.5	5.4

Note: Data is not seasonally adjusted and covers workers 16 years of age and older; (1) Figures cover the New Orleans-Metairie, LA Metropolitan Statistical Area—see Appendix B for areas included
Source: Bureau of Labor Statistics, Local Area Unemployment Statistics

Employment by Occupation

Occupation Classification	City (%)	MSA[1] (%)	U.S. (%)
Management, Business, Science, and Arts	41.1	34.4	36.2
Natural Resources, Construction, and Maintenance	7.1	11.6	9.0
Production, Transportation, and Material Moving	8.4	10.5	12.1
Sales and Office	19.9	23.9	24.4
Service	23.5	19.7	18.3

Note: Figures cover employed civilians 16 years of age and older; (1) Figures cover the New Orleans-Metairie, LA Metropolitan Statistical Area—see Appendix B for areas included
Source: U.S. Census Bureau, 2011-2013 American Community Survey 3-Year Estimates

Employment by Industry

Sector	MSA[1] Number of Employees	MSA[1] Percent of Total	U.S. Percent of Total
Construction	29,700	5.2	4.4
Education and Health Services	91,000	16.0	15.5
Financial Activities	28,000	4.9	5.7
Government	74,300	13.0	15.8
Information	8,300	1.5	2.0
Leisure and Hospitality	83,500	14.7	10.3
Manufacturing	30,000	5.3	8.7
Mining and Logging	8,000	1.4	0.6
Other Services	23,300	4.1	4.0
Professional and Business Services	74,400	13.1	13.8
Retail Trade	65,800	11.6	11.4
Transportation, Warehousing, and Utilities	29,200	5.1	3.9
Wholesale Trade	24,000	4.2	4.2

Note: Figures are non-farm employment as of December 2014. Figures are not seasonally adjusted and include workers 16 years of age and older; (1) Figures cover the New Orleans-Metairie, LA Metropolitan Statistical Area—see Appendix B for areas included
Source: Bureau of Labor Statistics, Current Employment Statistics, Employment, Hours, and Earnings

Occupations with Greatest Projected Employment Growth: 2012 – 2022

Occupation[1]	2012 Employment	2022 Projected Employment	Numeric Employment Change	Percent Employment Change
Personal Care Aides	24,990	35,060	10,070	40.3
Retail Salespersons	58,870	67,040	8,170	13.9
Registered Nurses	41,270	48,690	7,420	18.0
Laborers and Freight, Stock, and Material Movers, Hand	39,440	45,610	6,170	15.7
Secretaries and Administrative Assistants, Except Legal, Medical, and Executive	40,400	46,010	5,610	13.9
Combined Food Preparation and Serving Workers, Including Fast Food	27,780	33,030	5,250	18.9
General and Operations Managers	31,060	35,860	4,800	15.4
Home Health Aides	11,560	16,250	4,690	40.6
Licensed Practical and Licensed Vocational Nurses	22,930	27,360	4,430	19.3
Cashiers	68,250	72,430	4,180	6.1

Note: Projections cover Louisiana; (1) Sorted by numeric employment change
Source: www.projectionscentral.com, State Occupational Projections, 2012–2022 Long-Term Projections

Fastest Growing Occupations: 2012 – 2022

Occupation[1]	2012 Employment	2022 Projected Employment	Numeric Employment Change	Percent Employment Change
Software Developers, Systems Software	1,110	2,010	900	80.6
Software Developers, Applications	1,220	2,100	880	72.3
Interpreters and Translators	440	710	270	62.5
Computer Systems Analysts	3,460	5,070	1,610	46.6
Home Health Aides	11,560	16,250	4,690	40.6
Personal Care Aides	24,990	35,060	10,070	40.3
Computer Numerically Controlled Machine Tool Programmers, Metal and Plastic	240	340	100	39.8
Information Security Analysts	530	740	210	39.6
Skincare Specialists	410	570	160	39.2
Diagnostic Medical Sonographers	890	1,230	340	38.8

Note: Projections cover Louisiana; (1) Sorted by percent employment change and excludes occupations with numeric employment change less than 100
Source: www.projectionscentral.com, State Occupational Projections, 2012–2022 Long-Term Projections

Average Wages

Occupation	$/Hr.	Occupation	$/Hr.
Accountants and Auditors	30.95	Maids and Housekeeping Cleaners	9.66
Automotive Mechanics	19.11	Maintenance and Repair Workers	17.75
Bookkeepers	17.27	Marketing Managers	52.86
Carpenters	18.71	Nuclear Medicine Technologists	31.41
Cashiers	9.09	Nurses, Licensed Practical	19.51
Clerks, General Office	11.95	Nurses, Registered	31.38
Clerks, Receptionists/Information	12.10	Nursing Assistants	11.00
Clerks, Shipping/Receiving	15.60	Packers and Packagers, Hand	10.63
Computer Programmers	34.05	Physical Therapists	40.05
Computer Systems Analysts	30.86	Postal Service Mail Carriers	24.54
Computer User Support Specialists	22.56	Real Estate Brokers	n/a
Cooks, Restaurant	11.06	Retail Salespersons	12.46
Dentists	102.62	Sales Reps., Exc. Tech./Scientific	31.07
Electrical Engineers	50.88	Sales Reps., Tech./Scientific	41.18
Electricians	23.93	Secretaries, Exc. Legal/Med./Exec.	15.49
Financial Managers	49.32	Security Guards	14.39
First-Line Supervisors/Managers, Sales	19.47	Surgeons	116.86
Food Preparation Workers	8.67	Teacher Assistants	11.40
General and Operations Managers	52.92	Teachers, Elementary School	23.80
Hairdressers/Cosmetologists	12.40	Teachers, Secondary School	25.10
Internists	116.99	Telemarketers	14.37
Janitors and Cleaners	11.24	Truck Drivers, Heavy/Tractor-Trailer	19.52
Landscaping/Groundskeeping Workers	10.71	Truck Drivers, Light/Delivery Svcs.	16.85
Lawyers	64.02	Waiters and Waitresses	9.73

Note: Wage data covers the New Orleans-Metairie-Kenner, LA Metropolitan Statistical Area—see Appendix B for areas included; Hourly wages for elementary/secondary school teachers and teacher assistants were calculated by the editors from annual wage data assuming a 40 hour work week; n/a not available.
Source: Bureau of Labor Statistics, Metro Area Occupational Employment and Wage Estimates, May 2014

TAXES

State Corporate Income Tax Rates

State	Tax Rate (%)	Income Brackets ($)	Num. of Brackets	Financial Institution Tax Rate (%)[a]	Federal Income Tax Ded.
Louisiana	4.0 - 8.0	25,000 - 200,001	5	4.0 - 8.0	Yes

Note: Tax rates as of January 1, 2015; (a) Rates listed are the corporate income tax rate applied to financial institutions or excise taxes based on income. Some states have other taxes based upon the value of deposits or shares.
Source: Federation of Tax Administrators, "State Corporate Income Tax Rates, 2015"

State Individual Income Tax Rates

State	Tax Rate (%)	Income Brackets ($)	Num. of Brackets	Personal Exempt. ($)[1]		Fed. Inc. Tax Ded.
				Single	Dependents	
Louisiana	2.0 - 6.0	12,500 - 50,001 (b)	3	4,500 (k)	1,000	Yes

Note: Tax rates as of January 1, 2015; Local- and county-level taxes are not included; n/a not applicable; (1) Married joint filers generally receive double the single exemption; (b) For joint returns, taxes are twice the tax on half the couple's income; (k) The amounts reported for Louisiana are a combined personal exemption-standard deduction.
Source: Federation of Tax Administrators, "State Individual Income Tax Rates, 2015"

Various State and Local Tax Rates

State	State and Local Sales and Use (%)	State Sales and Use (%)	Gasoline[1] (¢/gal.)	Cigarette[2] ($/pack)	Spirits[3] ($/gal.)	Wine[4] ($/gal.)	Beer[5] ($/gal.)
Louisiana	8.75	4.0	20.01	0.36	2.50 (f)	0.11	0.32

Note: All tax rates as of January 1, 2015; (1) The American Petroleum Institute has developed a methodology for determining the average tax rate on a gallon of fuel. Rates may include any of the following: excise taxes, environmental fees, storage tank fees, other fees or taxes, general sales tax, and local taxes. In states where gasoline is subject to the general sales tax, or where the fuel tax is based on the average sale price, the average rate determined by API is sensitive to changes in the price of gasoline. States that fully or partially apply general sales taxes to gasoline: CA, CO, GA, IL, IN, MI, NY; (2) The federal excise tax of $1.0066 per pack and local taxes are not included; (3) Rates are those applicable to off-premise sales of 40% alcohol by volume (a.b.v.) distilled spirits in 750ml containers. Local excise taxes are excluded; (4) Rates are those applicable to off-premise sales of 11% a.b.v. non-carbonated wine in 750ml containers; (5) Rates are those applicable to off-premise sales of 4.7% a.b.v. beer in 12 ounce containers; (f) Different rates are also applicable according to alcohol content, place of production, size of container, or place purchased (on- or off-premise or onboard airlines).
Source: Tax Foundation, 2015 Facts & Figures: How Does Your State Compare?

State Business Tax Climate Index Rankings

State	Overall Rank	Corporate Tax Index Rank	Individual Income Tax Index Rank	Sales Tax Index Rank	Unemployment Insurance Tax Index Rank	Property Tax Index Rank
Louisiana	35	23	27	50	6	24

Note: The index is a measure of how each state's tax laws affect economic performance. The lower the rank, the more favorable a state's tax system is for business. States without a given tax are given a ranking of 1. The scores/rankings for the District of Columbia do not affect other states. The 2015 index represents the tax climate as of July 1, 2014.
Source: Tax Foundation, State Business Tax Climate Index 2015

COMMERCIAL UTILITIES

Typical Monthly Electric Bills

Area	Commercial Service ($/month)		Industrial Service ($/month)	
	1,500 kWh	40 kW demand 14,000 kWh	1,000 kW demand 200,000 kWh	50,000 kW demand 32,500,000 kWh
City	165	1,444	22,571	2,724,890
Average[1]	201	1,653	26,124	2,639,743

Note: Figures are based on annualized 2014 rates; (1) Average based on 180 utilities surveyed
Source: Edison Electric Institute, Typical Bills and Average Rates Report, Summer 2014

TRANSPORTATION

Means of Transportation to Work

Area	Car/Truck/Van		Public Transportation			Bicycle	Walked	Other Means	Worked at Home
	Drove Alone	Car-pooled	Bus	Subway	Railroad				
City	70.0	9.7	6.3	0.0	0.0	2.8	5.0	2.4	3.7
MSA[1]	79.1	10.3	2.4	0.0	0.0	1.1	2.5	2.0	2.6
U.S.	76.4	9.6	2.6	1.8	0.6	0.6	2.8	1.3	4.3

Note: Figures are percentages and cover workers 16 years of age and older; (1) Figures cover the New Orleans-Metairie, LA Metropolitan Statistical Area—see Appendix B for areas included
Source: U.S. Census Bureau, 2011-2013 American Community Survey 3-Year Estimates

Travel Time to Work

Area	Less Than 10 Minutes	10 to 19 Minutes	20 to 29 Minutes	30 to 44 Minutes	45 to 59 Minutes	60 to 89 Minutes	90 Minutes or More
City	10.5	34.9	25.5	19.3	4.3	3.6	1.8
MSA[1]	11.3	30.8	21.7	20.7	7.4	5.7	2.4
U.S.	13.3	29.7	20.9	20.2	7.7	5.7	2.6

Note: Figures are percentages and include workers 16 years old and over; (1) Figures cover the New Orleans-Metairie, LA Metropolitan Statistical Area—see Appendix B for areas included
Source: U.S. Census Bureau, 2011-2013 American Community Survey 3-Year Estimates

Travel Time Index

Area	1985	1990	1995	2000	2005	2010	2011
Urban Area[1]	1.21	1.21	1.22	1.22	1.22	1.20	1.20
Average[2]	1.09	1.14	1.16	1.19	1.23	1.18	1.18

Note: Travel Time Index—the ratio of travel time in the peak period to the travel time at free-flow conditions. For example, a value of 1.30 indicates a 20-minute free-flow trip takes 26 minutes in the peak. Free-flow speeds (60 mph on freeways and 35 mph on principal arterials) are used as the comparison threshold; (1) Covers the New Orleans LA urban area; (2) average of 498 urban areas
Source: Texas Transportation Institute, Urban Mobility Report 2012, December 2012

Public Transportation

Agency Name / Mode of Transportation	Vehicles Operated in Maximum Service	Annual Unlinked Passenger Trips (in thous.)	Annual Passenger Miles (in thous.)
New Orleans Regional Transit Authority (NORTA)			
Bus (purchased transportation)	77	12,915.7	42,191.3
Demand Response (purchased transportation)	34	219.2	1,607.7
Streetcar Rail (purchased transportation)	24	8,650.4	15,441.1

Source: Federal Transit Administration, National Transit Database, 2013

Air Transportation

Airport Name and Code / Type of Service	Passenger Airlines[1]	Passenger Enplanements	Freight Carriers[2]	Freight (lbs.)
New Orleans International (MSY)				
Domestic service (U.S. carriers - 2014)	27	4,842,470	13	42,088,665
International service (U.S. carriers - 2013)	10	2,583	1	10

Note: (1) Includes all U.S.-based major, minor and commuter airlines that carried at least one passenger during the year; (2) Includes all U.S.-based airlines and freight carriers that transported at least one lb. of freight during the year.
Source: Bureau of Transportation Statistics, The Intermodal Transportation Database, Air Carriers: T-100 Domestic Market (U.S. Carriers), 2014; Bureau of Transportation Statistics, The Intermodal Transportation Database, Air Carriers: T-100 International Market (U.S. Carriers), 2013

Other Transportation Statistics

Major Highways:	I-10; I-59
Amtrak Service:	Yes
Major Waterways/Ports:	Port of New Orleans; Mississippi River

Source: Amtrak.com; Google Maps

BUSINESSES

Major Business Headquarters

Company Name	Rankings	
	Fortune[1]	Forbes[2]
Entergy Corporation	242	-

Note: (1) Fortune 500—companies that produce a 10-K are ranked 1 to 500 based on 2013 revenue; (2) all private companies with at least $2 billion in annual revenue through the end of their most current fiscal year are ranked 1 to 221; companies listed are headquartered in the city; dashes indicate no ranking
Source: Fortune, "Fortune 500," June 16, 2014; Forbes, "America's Largest Private Companies," November 5, 2014

Fast-Growing Businesses

According to *Inc.*, New Orleans is home to two of America's 500 fastest-growing private companies: **Pontchartrain Partners** (#38); **MaxHome** (#52). Criteria: must be an independent, privately-held, for-profit, U.S. corporation, proprietorship or partnership; revenues must be at least $100,000 in 2010 and $2 million in 2013; must have four-year operating/sales history. Holding companies, regulated banks, and utilities were excluded. *Inc., "America's 500 Fastest-Growing Private Companies," September 2014*

According to *Initiative for a Competitive Inner City (ICIC)*, New Orleans is home to two of America's 100 fastest-growing "inner city" companies: **QCS Logistics** (#70); **Finn McCool's Irish Pub** (#96). Criteria for inclusion: company must be headquartered in or have 51 percent or more of its physical operations in an economically distressed urban area; must be an independent, for-profit corporation, partnership or proprietorship; must have 10 or more employees and have a five-year sales history that includes sales of at least $200,000 in the base year and at least $1 million in the current year with no decrease in sales over the two most recent years. This year, for the first time in the list's 16-year history, the Inner City 100 consists of 10 fast-growing businesses in 10 industry categories. Companies were ranked overall by revenue growth over the five-year period between 2009 and 2013 as well as within their respective industry categories. *Initiative for a Competitive Inner City (ICIC), "Inner City 100 Companies, 2014"*

Minority Business Opportunity

New Orleans is home to one company which is on the *Black Enterprise* Bank 20 list (20 largest banks based on total assets, capital, deposits and loans, including mortgage-backed securities for the calendar year): **Liberty Bank and Trust Co.** (#4). Only commercial banks or savings and loans that are classified by the Federal Reserve as black institutions and have been fully operational for the previous calendar year were considered. *Black Enterprise, B.E. 100s, 2014*

New Orleans is home to two companies which are on the *Hispanic Business* 500 list (500 largest U.S. Hispanic-owned companies based on 2012 revenue): **Pan-American Life Insurance Group** (#15); **Atlantis International** (#184). Companies included must show at least 51 percent ownership by Hispanic U.S. citizens, and must maintain headquarters in one of the 50 states or Washington, D.C. *Hispanic Business, "Hispanic Business 500," June 20, 2013*

New Orleans is home to one company which is on the *Hispanic Business* Fastest-Growing 100 list (greatest sales growth from 2008 to 2012): **Pan-American Life Insurance Group** (#86). Companies included must show at least 51 percent ownership by Hispanic U.S. citizens, and must maintain headquarters in one of the 50 states or Washington, D.C. In addition, companies must have minimum revenues of $200,000 for calendar year 2008. *Hispanic Business, June 20, 2013*

Minority- and Women-Owned Businesses

Group	All Firms		Firms with Paid Employees			
	Firms	Sales ($000)	Firms	Sales ($000)	Employees	Payroll ($000)
Asian	1,403	310,414	388	268,702	1,755	39,419
Black	7,843	497,070	391	345,949	4,728	104,339
Hispanic	1,103	107,771	137	77,257	970	23,102
Women	8,245	1,418,443	1,048	1,236,470	9,907	300,668
All Firms	27,165	28,788,251	6,587	27,896,926	136,637	6,059,640

Note: Figures cover firms located in the city; minority- and women-owned business are defined as firms in which the corresponding group own 51% or more of the stock or equity of the company
Source: U.S. Census Bureau, 2007 Economic Census, Survey of Business Owners (2012 Survey of Business Owners data will be released starting in June 2015)

HOTELS & CONVENTION CENTERS

Hotels/Motels

Area	5 Star		4 Star		3 Star		2 Star		1 Star		Not Rated	
	Num.	Pct.³	Num.	Pct.³	Num.	Pct.³	Num.	Pct.³	Num.	Pct.³	Num.	Pct.³
City¹	0	0.0	26	9.6	107	39.6	109	40.4	7	2.6	21	7.8
Total²	166	0.9	1,264	7.0	5,718	31.8	9,340	52.0	411	2.3	1,070	6.0

Note: (1) Figures cover New Orleans and vicinity; (2) Figures cover all 100 cities in this book; (3) Percentage of hotels which have a given star rating; Star ratings are determined by expedia.com and offer an indication of the general quality of a particular hotel.
Source: expedia.com, April 2, 2015

The New Orleans-Metairie, LA metro area is home to two of the best hotels in the U.S. according to *Travel & Leisure*: **The Roosevelt Hotel, New Orleans; Windsor Court Hotel**. Criteria: service; location; rooms; food; and value. The list includes the top 236 hotels in the U.S. *Travel & Leisure, "T+L 500, The World's Best Hotels 2015"*

Major Convention Centers

Name	Overall Space (sq. ft.)	Exhibit Space (sq. ft.)	Meeting Space (sq. ft.)	Meeting Rooms
Ernest N. Morial Convention Center	3,000,000	1,100,000	n/a	n/a

Note: Table includes convention centers located in the New Orleans-Metairie, LA metro area; n/a not available
Source: Original research

Living Environment

COST OF LIVING

Cost of Living Index

Composite Index	Groceries	Housing	Utilities	Trans-portation	Health Care	Misc. Goods/ Services
96.8	100.6	95.5	84.2	102.7	100.5	97.5

Note: The Cost of Living Index measures regional differences in the cost of consumer goods and services, excluding taxes and non-consumer expenditures, for professional and managerial households in the top income quintile. It is based on more than 50,000 prices covering almost 60 different items for which prices are collected three times a year by chambers of commerce, economic development organizations or university applied economic centers in each participating urban area. The numbers shown should be read as a percentage above or below the national average of 100. For example, a value of 115.4 in the groceries column indicates that grocery prices are 15.4% higher than the national average. Small differences in the index numbers should not be interpreted as significant; Figures cover the New Orleans LA urban area.
Source: The Council for Community and Economic Research, ACCRA Cost of Living Index, 2014

Grocery Prices

Area[1]	T-Bone Steak ($/pound)	Frying Chicken ($/pound)	Whole Milk ($/half gal.)	Eggs ($/dozen)	Orange Juice ($/64 oz.)	Coffee ($/11.5 oz.)
City[2]	10.80	1.14	2.54	2.08	3.38	3.60
Avg.	10.40	1.37	2.40	1.99	3.46	4.27
Min.	8.48	0.93	1.37	1.30	2.83	2.99
Max.	14.20	2.44	3.62	4.02	6.42	6.96

Note: (1) Values for the local area are compared with the average, minimum and maximum values for all 308 areas in the Cost of Living Index; (2) Figures cover the New Orleans LA urban area; **T-Bone Steak** *(price per pound);* **Frying Chicken** *(price per pound, whole fryer);* **Whole Milk** *(half gallon carton);* **Eggs** *(price per dozen, Grade A, large);* **Orange Juice** *(64 oz. Tropicana or Florida Natural);* **Coffee** *(11.5 oz. can, vacuum-packed, Maxwell House, Hills Bros, or Folgers).*
Source: The Council for Community and Economic Research, ACCRA Cost of Living Index, 2014

Housing and Utility Costs

Area[1]	New Home Price ($)	Apartment Rent ($/month)	All Electric ($/month)	Part Electric ($/month)	Other Energy ($/month)	Telephone ($/month)
City[2]	285,368	908	-	90.13	40.75	26.23
Avg.	305,838	919	181.00	93.66	73.14	27.95
Min.	183,142	480	112.00	42.06	23.42	17.16
Max.	1,358,576	3,851	594.00	180.03	440.99	40.42

Note: (1) Values for the local area are compared with the average, minimum and maximum values for all 308 areas in the Cost of Living Index; (2) Figures cover the New Orleans LA urban area; **New Home Price** *(2,400 sf living area, 8,000 sf lot, in urban area with full utilities);* **Apartment Rent** *(950 sf 2 bedroom/1.5 or 2 bath, unfurnished, excluding all utilities except water);* **All Electric** *(average monthly cost for an all-electric home);* **Part Electric** *(average monthly cost for a part-electric home);* **Other Energy** *(average monthly cost for natural gas, fuel oil, coal, wood, and any other forms of energy except electricity);* **Telephone** *(price includes basic monthly rate for a private residential line plus additional local usage charges incurred by a family of four).*
Source: The Council for Community and Economic Research, ACCRA Cost of Living Index, 2014

Health Care, Transportation, and Other Costs

Area[1]	Doctor ($/visit)	Dentist ($/visit)	Optometrist ($/visit)	Gasoline ($/gallon)	Beauty Salon ($/visit)	Men's Shirt ($)
City[2]	81.90	96.78	73.45	3.29	44.67	22.43
Avg.	102.86	87.89	97.66	3.44	34.37	26.74
Min.	67.47	65.78	51.18	3.00	17.43	12.79
Max.	173.50	150.14	235.00	4.33	64.28	49.50

Note: (1) Values for the local area are compared with the average, minimum and maximum values for all 308 areas in the Cost of Living Index; (2) Figures cover the New Orleans LA urban area; **Doctor** *(general practitioners routine exam of an established patient);* **Dentist** *(adult teeth cleaning and periodic oral examination);* **Optometrist** *(full vision eye exam for established adult patient);* **Gasoline** *(one gallon regular unleaded, national brand, including all taxes, cash price at self-service pump if available);* **Beauty Salon** *(woman's shampoo, trim, and blow-dry);* **Men's Shirt** *(cotton/polyester dress shirt, pinpoint weave, long sleeves).*
Source: The Council for Community and Economic Research, ACCRA Cost of Living Index, 2014

HOUSING

House Price Index (HPI)

Area	National Ranking[2]	Quarterly Change (%)	One-Year Change (%)	Five-Year Change (%)
MSA[1]	127	0.86	4.43	6.89
U.S.[3]	–	1.35	4.91	11.59

Note: The HPI is a weighted repeat sales index. It measures average price changes in repeat sales or refinancings on the same properties. This information is obtained by reviewing repeat mortgage transactions on single-family properties whose mortgages have been purchased or securitized by Fannie Mae or Freddie Mac in January 1975; (1) New Orleans-Metairie Metropolitan Statistical Area—see Appendix B for areas included; (2) Rankings are based on annual percentage change for all metro areas containing at least 15,000 transactions over the last 10 years and ranges from 1 to 275; (3) figures based on a weighted average of Census Division estimates using a seasonally adjusted, purchase-only index; all figures are for the period ending December 31, 2014
Source: Federal Housing Finance Agency, House Price Index, February 26, 2015

Median Single-Family Home Prices

Area	2012	2013	2014p	Percent Change 2013 to 2014
MSA[1]	156.2	164.7	165.0	0.2
U.S. Average	177.2	197.4	209.0	5.9

Note: Figures are median sales prices of existing single-family homes in thousands of dollars; (p) preliminary; n/a not available; (1) New Orleans-Metairie, LA Metropolitan Statistical Area—see Appendix B for areas included
Source: National Association of Realtors, Median Sales Price of Existing Single-Family Homes for Metropolitan Areas, 4th Quarter 2014

Qualifying Income Based on Median Sales Price of Existing Single-Family Homes

Area	With 5% Down ($)	With 10% Down ($)	With 20% Down ($)
MSA[1]	36,062	34,164	30,368
U.S. Average	45,863	43,449	38,621

Note: Figures are preliminary; Qualifying income is based on a mortgage rate of 4.0%. Monthly principal and interest payment is limited to 25% of income; n/a not available; (1) New Orleans-Metairie, LA Metropolitan Statistical Area—see Appendix B for areas included
Source: National Association of Realtors, Qualifying Income Based on Median Sales Price of Existing Single-Family Homes for Metropolitan Areas, 4th Quarter 2014

Median Apartment Condo-Coop Home Prices

Area	2012	2013	2014p	Percent Change 2013 to 2014
MSA[1]	186.7	187.3	193.1	3.1
U.S. Average	173.7	194.9	205.1	5.2

Note: Figures are median sales prices of existing apartment condo-coop homes in thousands of dollars; (p) preliminary; n/a not available; (1) New Orleans-Metairie, LA Metropolitan Statistical Area—see Appendix B for areas included
Source: National Association of Realtors, Median Sales Price of Existing Apartment Condo-Coop Homes for Metropolitan Areas, 4th Quarter 2014

Gross Monthly Rent

Area	Under $200	$200 -299	$300 -499	$500 -749	$750 -999	$1,000 -1,499	$1,500 and up	Median ($)
City	2.5	4.4	6.5	18.5	28.1	29.1	10.9	910
MSA[1]	1.4	3.0	6.3	21.0	30.3	29.1	8.9	903
U.S.	1.7	3.2	7.8	22.1	24.3	26.0	14.9	900

Note: Figures are percentages except for Median; Gross rent is the contract rent plus the estimated average monthly cost of utilities (electricity, gas, and water and sewer) and fuels (oil, coal, kerosene, wood, etc.) if these are paid by the renter (or paid for the renter by someone else); (1) Figures cover the New Orleans-Metairie, LA Metropolitan Statistical Area—see Appendix B for areas included
Source: U.S. Census Bureau, 2011-2013 American Community Survey 3-Year Estimates

Homeownership Rate

Area	2007 (%)	2008 (%)	2009 (%)	2010 (%)	2011 (%)	2012 (%)	2013 (%)	2014 (%)
MSA[1]	67.8	68.0	68.2	66.9	63.9	62.4	61.4	60.6
U.S.	68.1	67.8	67.4	66.9	66.1	65.4	65.1	64.5

Note: (1) Figures cover the New Orleans-Metairie, LA Metropolitan Statistical Area—see Appendix B for areas included
Source: U.S. Census Bureau, Housing Vacancies and Homeownership Annual Statistics: 2014

Year Housing Structure Built

Area	2010 or Later	2000 -2009	1990 -1999	1980 -1989	1970 -1979	1960 -1969	1950 -1959	1940 -1949	Before 1940	Median Year
City	1.5	8.6	3.9	7.8	14.3	10.6	12.5	10.4	30.3	1957
MSA[1]	1.2	13.1	9.6	14.6	19.4	13.4	10.1	5.9	12.8	1974
U.S.	0.9	15.0	13.9	13.8	15.8	11.0	10.9	5.4	13.3	1976

Note: Figures are percentages except for Median Year; (1) Figures cover the New Orleans-Metairie, LA Metropolitan Statistical Area—see Appendix B for areas included
Source: U.S. Census Bureau, 2011-2013 American Community Survey 3-Year Estimates

HEALTH

Health Risk Data

Category	MSA[1] (%)	U.S. (%)
Adults aged 18–64 who have any kind of health care coverage	76.1	79.6
Adults who reported being in good or excellent health	80.7	83.1
Adults who are current smokers	22.8	19.6
Adults who are heavy drinkers[2]	7.9	6.1
Adults who are binge drinkers[3]	19.0	16.9
Adults who are overweight (BMI 25.0 - 29.9)	35.9	35.8
Adults who are obese (BMI 30.0 - 99.8)	28.7	27.6
Adults who participated in any physical activities in the past month	73.8	77.1
Adults 50+ who have ever had a sigmoidoscopy or colonoscopy	66.1	67.3
Women aged 40+ who have had a mammogram within the past two years	79.3	74.0
Men aged 40+ who have had a PSA test within the past two years	49.2	45.2
Adults aged 65+ who have had flu shot within the past year	66.4	60.1
Adults who always wear a seatbelt	95.7	93.8

Note: Data as of 2012 unless otherwise noted; (1) Figures cover the New Orleans-Metairie-Kenner, LA Metropolitan Statistical Area—see Appendix B for areas included; (2) Heavy drinkers are classified as males having more than two drinks per day or females having more than one drink per day; (3) Binge drinkers are classified as males having five or more drinks on one occasion or females having four or more drinks on one occasion
Source: Centers for Disease Control and Prevention, Behaviorial Risk Factor Surveillance System, SMART: Selected Metropolitan/Micropolitan Area Risk Trends, 2012 (Note: the CDC has discontinued this dataset but will be releasing a replacement in late 2015)

Chronic Health Indicators

Category	MSA[1] (%)	U.S. (%)
Adults who have ever been told they had a heart attack	4.4	4.5
Adults who have ever been told they had a stroke	3.1	2.9
Adults who have been told they currently have asthma	6.1	8.9
Adults who have ever been told they have arthritis	25.3	25.7
Adults who have ever been told they have diabetes[2]	12.3	9.7
Adults who have ever been told they had skin cancer	5.4	5.7
Adults who have ever been told they had any other types of cancer	5.7	6.5
Adults who have ever been told they have COPD	5.7	6.2
Adults who have ever been told they have kidney disease	1.7	2.5
Adults who have ever been told they have a form of depression	15.3	18.0

Note: Data as of 2012 unless otherwise noted; (1) Figures cover the New Orleans-Metairie-Kenner, LA Metropolitan Statistical Area—see Appendix B for areas included; (2) Figures do not include pregnancy-related, borderline, or pre-diabetes
Source: Centers for Disease Control and Prevention, Behaviorial Risk Factor Surveillance System, SMART: Selected Metropolitan/Micropolitan Area Risk Trends, 2012 (Note: the CDC has discontinued this dataset but will be releasing a replacement in late 2015)

Mortality Rates for the Top 10 Causes of Death in the U.S.

ICD-10[a] Sub-Chapter	ICD-10[a] Code	Age-Adjusted Mortality Rate[1] per 100,000 population	
		County[2]	U.S.
Malignant neoplasms	C00-C97	189.0	166.2
Ischaemic heart diseases	I20-I25	84.3	105.7
Other forms of heart disease	I30-I51	64.8	49.3
Chronic lower respiratory diseases	J40-J47	27.3	42.1
Organic, including symptomatic, mental disorders	F01-F09	43.3	38.1
Cerebrovascular diseases	I60-I69	40.7	37.0
Other external causes of accidental injury	W00-X59	31.3	26.9
Other degenerative diseases of the nervous system	G30-G31	19.1	25.6
Diabetes mellitus	E10-E14	29.0	21.3
Hypertensive diseases	I10-I15	55.4	19.4

Note: (a) ICD-10 = International Classification of Diseases 10th Revision; (1) Mortality rates are a three year average covering 2011-2013; (2) Figures cover Orleans Parish
Source: Centers for Disease Control and Prevention, National Center for Health Statistics. Compressed Mortality File 1999-2013 on CDC WONDER Online Database, released October 2014. Data are compiled from the Compressed Mortality File 1999-2013, Series 20 No. 2S, 2014.

Mortality Rates for Selected Causes of Death

ICD-10[a] Sub-Chapter	ICD-10[a] Code	Age-Adjusted Mortality Rate[1] per 100,000 population	
		County[2]	U.S.
Assault	X85-Y09	40.8	5.2
Diseases of the liver	K70-K76	15.8	13.2
Human immunodeficiency virus (HIV) disease	B20-B24	11.1	2.2
Influenza and pneumonia	J09-J18	10.4	15.4
Intentional self-harm	X60-X84	8.7	12.5
Malnutrition	E40-E46	Suppressed	0.9
Obesity and other hyperalimentation	E65-E68	*1.6	1.8
Renal failure	N17-N19	22.2	13.1
Transport accidents	V01-V99	16.1	11.7
Viral hepatitis	B15-B19	1.8	2.2

Note: (a) ICD-10 = International Classification of Diseases 10th Revision; (1) Mortality rates are a three year average covering 2011-2013; (2) Figures cover Orleans Parish; (*) Unreliable data as per CDC
Source: Centers for Disease Control and Prevention, National Center for Health Statistics. Compressed Mortality File 1999-2013 on CDC WONDER Online Database, released October 2014. Data are compiled from the Compressed Mortality File 1999-2013, Series 20 No. 2S, 2014.

Health Insurance Coverage

Area	With Health Insurance	With Private Health Insurance	With Public Health Insurance	Without Health Insurance	Population Under Age 18 Without Health Insurance
City	81.8	52.2	37.1	18.2	5.3
MSA[1]	83.4	58.5	33.5	16.6	4.5
U.S.	85.2	65.2	31.0	14.8	7.3

Note: Figures are percentages that cover the civilian noninstitutionalized population; (1) Figures cover the New Orleans-Metairie, LA Metropolitan Statistical Area—see Appendix B for areas included
Source: U.S. Census Bureau, 2011-2013 American Community Survey 3-Year Estimates

Number of Medical Professionals

Area[1]	MDs[2]	DOs[2,3]	Dentists	Podiatrists	Chiropractors	Optometrists
Local (number)	2,643	49	238	13	27	23
Local (rate[4])	714.0	13.2	62.8	3.4	7.1	6.1
U.S. (rate[4])	270.0	20.2	63.1	5.7	25.2	14.9

Note: Data as of 2013 unless noted; (1) Local data covers Orleans Parish; (2) Data as of 2012 and includes all active, non-federal physicians; (3) Doctor of Osteopathic Medicine; (4) rate per 100,000 population
Source: U.S. Department of Health and Human Services, Health Resources and Services Administration, Bureau of Health Professions, Area Resource File (ARF) 2013-2014

Best Hospitals

According to *U.S. News,* the New Orleans-Metairie, LA metro area is home to one of the best hospitals in the U.S.: **Ochsner Medical Center** (9 specialties). The hospital listed was nationally ranked in at least one adult specialty. Only 144 hospitals nationwide were nationally ranked in one or more specialties. Seventeen hospitals in the U.S. made the Honor Roll with high scores in at least six specialties. *U.S. News Online, "America's Best Children's Hospitals 2014-15"*

EDUCATION

Public School District Statistics

District Name	Schls	Pupils	Pupil/ Teacher Ratio	Minority Pupils[1] (%)	Free Lunch Eligible[2] (%)	IEP[3] (%)
Orleans Parish	19	13,707	18.6	86.0	56.1	8.2
RSD-Algiers Charter Schools	6	3,550	16.6	99.2	75.5	10.1
RSD-Firstline Schools	5	2,563	13.8	98.7	90.6	16.4
RSD-Knowledge Is Power Program	6	3,211	15.7	98.2	92.0	11.6
RSD-New Beginnings Schools	4	2,014	17.9	98.8	86.7	5.8
RSD-Renew-Reinventing Education	5	2,431	16.7	99.9	93.1	11.1
Recovery School District-LDE	23	6,500	n/a	99.4	90.6	11.8

Note: Table includes school districts with 2,000 or more students; (1) Percentage of students that are not non-Hispanic white; (2) Percentage of students that are eligible for the free lunch program; (3) Percentage of students that have an Individualized Education Program.

Source: U.S. Department of Education, National Center for Education Statistics, Common Core of Data, Local Education Agency (School District) Universe Survey: School Year 2012-2013; U.S. Department of Education, National Center for Education Statistics, Common Core of Data, Public Elementary/Secondary School Universe Survey: School Year 2012-2013

Best High Schools

According to *The Daily Beast,* New Orleans is home to one of the best high schools in the U.S.: **Edna Karr High School** (#708); *The Daily Beast* used six indicators culled from school surveys to compare public high schools in the U.S., with graduation and college acceptance rates weighed most heavily. Other criteria included: college-level courses/exams and SAT/ACT scores. *The Daily Beast, "Top High Schools 2014"*

Highest Level of Education

Area	Less than H.S.	H.S. Diploma	Some College, No Deg.	Associate Degree	Bachelor's Degree	Master's Degree	Prof. School Degree	Doctorate Degree
City	15.5	23.5	22.3	4.4	19.5	8.4	4.2	2.2
MSA[1]	15.3	29.3	23.1	5.6	16.9	5.9	2.6	1.2
U.S.	13.7	28.0	21.2	7.9	18.2	7.7	1.9	1.3

Note: Figures cover persons age 25 and over; (1) Figures cover the New Orleans-Metairie, LA Metropolitan Statistical Area—see Appendix B for areas included

Source: U.S. Census Bureau, 2011-2013 American Community Survey 3-Year Estimates

Educational Attainment by Race

Area	High School Graduate or Higher (%)					Bachelor's Degree or Higher (%)				
	Total	White	Black	Asian	Hisp.[2]	Total	White	Black	Asian	Hisp.[2]
City	84.5	94.8	78.9	66.8	74.1	34.2	60.7	16.2	33.9	31.9
MSA[1]	84.7	89.1	78.6	70.9	72.9	26.6	32.5	15.3	35.2	20.3
U.S.	86.3	88.3	83.1	85.7	64.0	29.1	30.4	18.8	50.7	13.7

Note: Figures shown cover persons 25 years old and over; (1) Figures cover the New Orleans-Metairie, LA Metropolitan Statistical Area—see Appendix B for areas included; (2) People of Hispanic origin can be of any race

Source: U.S. Census Bureau, 2011-2013 American Community Survey 3-Year Estimates

School Enrollment by Grade and Control

Area	Preschool (%)		Kindergarten (%)		Grades 1 - 4 (%)		Grades 5 - 8 (%)		Grades 9 - 12 (%)	
	Public	Private	Public	Private	Public	Private	Public	Private	Public	Private
City	60.2	39.8	77.7	22.3	81.5	18.5	78.2	21.8	81.2	18.8
MSA[1]	55.4	44.6	75.9	24.1	77.4	22.6	76.1	23.9	76.0	24.0
U.S.	57.7	42.3	87.9	12.1	89.9	10.1	90.0	10.0	90.7	9.3

Note: Figures shown cover persons 3 years old and over; (1) Figures cover the New Orleans-Metairie, LA Metropolitan Statistical Area—see Appendix B for areas included
Source: U.S. Census Bureau, 2011-2013 American Community Survey 3-Year Estimates

Average Salaries of Public School Classroom Teachers

Area	2013-14		2014-15		Percent Change 2013-14 to 2014-15	Percent Change 2004-05 to 2014-15
	Dollars	Rank[1]	Dollars	Rank[1]		
LOUISIANA	49,067	34	47,886	41	-2.41	22.7
U.S. Average	56,610	–	57,379	–	1.36	20.8

Note: (1) State rank ranges from 1 to 51 where 1 indicates highest salary.
Source: National Education Association, Rankings & Estimates: Rankings of the States 2014 and Estimates of School Statistics 2015, March 2015

Higher Education

Four-Year Colleges			Two-Year Colleges			Medical Schools[1]	Law Schools[2]	Voc/ Tech[3]
Public	Private Non-profit	Private For-profit	Public	Private Non-profit	Private For-profit			
3	7	0	1	0	1	2	2	5

Note: Figures cover institutions located within the city limits and include main campuses only; (1) includes schools accredited by the Liaison Committee on Medical Education and the American Osteopathic Association's Commission on Osteopathic College Accreditation; (2) includes ABA-accredited schools, schools with provisional ABA accreditation, and state accredited schools; (3) includes all schools with programs that are less than 2 years.
Source: National Center for Education Statistics, Integrated Postsecondary Education System (IPEDS), 2013-14; Association of American Medical Colleges, Member List, May 1, 2015; American Osteopathic Association, Member List, May 1, 2015; Law School Admission Council, Official Guide to ABA-Approved Law Schools Online, May 1, 2015; Wikipedia, List of Medical Schools in the United States, May 1, 2015; Wikipedia, List of Law Schools in the United States, May 1, 2015

According to *U.S. News & World Report,* the New Orleans-Metairie, LA metro area is home to one of the best national universities in the U.S.: **Tulane University** (#54). The indicators used to capture academic quality fall into a number of categories: assessment by administrators at peer institutions; retention of students; faculty resources; student selectivity; financial resources; alumni giving; high school counselor ratings of colleges; and graduation rate. *U.S. News & World Report, "America's Best Colleges 2015"*

According to *U.S. News & World Report,* the New Orleans-Metairie, LA metro area is home to one of the best liberal arts colleges in the U.S.: **Xavier University of Louisiana** (#178). The indicators used to capture academic quality fall into a number of categories: assessment by administrators at peer institutions; retention of students; faculty resources; student selectivity; financial resources; alumni giving; high school counselor ratings of colleges; and graduation rate. *U.S. News & World Report, "America's Best Colleges 2015"*

According to *U.S. News & World Report,* the New Orleans-Metairie, LA metro area is home to one of the top 100 law schools in the U.S.: **Tulane University** (#50). The rankings are based on a weighted average of 12 measures of quality: peer assessment score; assessment score by lawyers/judges; median LSAT scores; median undergrad GPA; acceptance rate; employment rates for graduates; placement success; bar passage rate; faculty resources; expenditures per student; student/faculty ratio; and library resources. *U.S. News & World Report, "America's Best Graduate Schools, Law, 2016"*

According to *U.S. News & World Report,* the New Orleans-Metairie, LA metro area is home to one of the top 75 business schools in the U.S.: **Tulane University (Freeman)** (#61). The rankings are based on a weighted average of the following nine measures: quality assessment; peer assessment; recruiter assessment; placement success; mean starting salary and bonus; student selectivity; mean GMAT and GRE scores; mean undergraduate GPA; and acceptance rate. *U.S. News & World Report, "America's Best Graduate Schools, Business, 2016"*

PRESIDENTIAL ELECTION

2012 Presidential Election Results

Area	Obama (%)	Romney (%)	Other (%)
Orleans Parish	80.3	17.7	2.0
U.S.	51.0	47.2	1.8

Note: Results may not add to 100% due to rounding
Source: Dave Leip's Atlas of U.S. Presidential Elections

EMPLOYERS

Major Employers

Company Name	Industry
Alton Ochsner Medical Foundation	Home health care services
Avondale Industries of New York	Barges, building and repair
Capital One, National Association	National commercial banks
Chevron USA	Filling stations, gasoline
Childrens Hospital	Childrens hospital
East Jefferson Hospital	General medical/surgical hospitals
Jazz Casino Company LJC	Casino hotel
Lockheed Martin Corporation	Tanks, standard or custom fabricated metal plate 0
Louisiana State University System	University
Medical Ctr of Louisiana at New Orleans	General medical/surgical hospitals
NASA George C Marshall Space Flight Ctr	Space flight operations
Ochsner Clinic Foundation	General medical/surgical hospitals
Ochsner Foundation Hospital	General medical/surgical hospitals
St Tammany Parish Hospital	General medical/surgical hospitals
Tulane University	Colleges/universities
United States Department of the Army	Army
United States Dept of Agriculture	Regulation of agricultural marketing
United States Postal Service	Us postal service
University Healthcare System	General medical/surgical hospitals
US Army Corps of Engineers	Army
West Jefferson Medical Center	General medical/surgical hospitals

Note: Companies shown are located within the New Orleans-Metairie, LA Metropolitan Statistical Area.
Source: Hoovers.com; Wikipedia

Best Companies to Work For

Ochsner Health System, headquartered in New Orleans, is among the "50 Best Employers for Workers Over 50." Criteria: recruiting practices; opportunities for training, education, and career development; workplace accommodations; alternative work options, such as flexible scheduling, job sharing, and phased retirement; employee health and pension benefits; and retiree benefits. Employers with at least 50 employees based in the U.S. are eligible, including for-profit companies, not-for-profit organizations, and government employers. *AARP, "2013 AARP Best Employers for Workers Over 50"*

PUBLIC SAFETY

Crime Rate

Area	All Crimes	Violent Crimes: Murder	Violent Crimes: Forcible Rape	Violent Crimes: Robbery	Violent Crimes: Aggrav. Assault	Property Crimes: Burglary	Property Crimes: Larceny -Theft	Property Crimes: Motor Vehicle Theft
City	4,639.0	41.4	46.7	301.8	396.5	849.6	2,434.6	568.4
Suburbs[1]	3,183.0	9.2	16.8	77.4	233.8	539.4	2,145.6	160.9
Metro[2]	3,626.0	19.0	25.9	145.7	283.3	633.8	2,233.5	284.9
U.S.	3,098.6	4.5	25.2	109.1	229.1	610.0	1,899.4	221.3

Note: Figures are crimes per 100,000 population; (1) All areas within the metro area that are located outside the city limits; (2) Figures cover the New Orleans-Metairie, LA Metropolitan Statistical Area—see Appendix B for areas included
Source: FBI Uniform Crime Reports, 2013

Hate Crimes

Area	Number of Quarters Reported	Number of Incidents per Bias Motivation						
		Race	Religion	Sexual Orientation	Ethnicity	Disability	Gender	Gender Identity
City	4	1	1	5	1	0	0	0
U.S.	4	2,871	1,031	1,233	655	83	18	31

Source: Federal Bureau of Investigation, Hate Crime Statistics 2013

Identity Theft Consumer Complaints

Area	Complaints	Complaints per 100,000 Population	Rank[2]
MSA[1]	1,058	85.3	104
U.S.	332,646	104.3	-

Note: (1) Figures cover the New Orleans-Metairie, LA Metropolitan Statistical Area—see Appendix B for areas included; (2) Rank ranges from 1 to 380 where 1 indicates greatest number of identity theft complaints per 100,000 population
Source: Federal Trade Commission, Consumer Sentinel Network Data Book for January–December 2014

Fraud and Other Consumer Complaints

Area	Complaints	Complaints per 100,000 Population	Rank[2]
MSA[1]	5,325	429.1	94
U.S.	2,250,205	705.7	-

Note: (1) Figures cover the New Orleans-Metairie, LA Metropolitan Statistical Area—see Appendix B for areas included; (2) Rank ranges from 1 to 380 where 1 indicates greatest number of identity theft complaints per 100,000 population
Source: Federal Trade Commission, Consumer Sentinel Network Data Book for January–December 2014

RECREATION

Culture

Dance[1]	Theatre[1]	Instrumental Music[1]	Vocal Music[1]	Series and Festivals	Museums and Art Galleries[2]	Zoos and Aquariums[3]
1	6	3	2	4	63	2

Note: (1) Professional perfoming groups; (2) Based on organizations with SIC code 8412; (3) AZA-accredited
Source: The Grey House Performing Arts Directory, 2015-16; Association of Zoos & Aquariums, AZA Member Zoos & Aquariums, April 2015; www.AccuLeads.com, April 2015

Professional Sports Teams

Team Name	League	Year Established
New Orleans Pelicans	National Basketball Association (NBA)	2002
New Orleans Saints	National Football League (NFL)	1967

Note: Includes teams located in the New Orleans-Metairie, LA Metropolitan Statistical Area.
Source: Wikipedia, Major Professional Sports Teams of the United States and Canada, April 2015

CLIMATE

Average and Extreme Temperatures

Temperature	Jan	Feb	Mar	Apr	May	Jun	Jul	Aug	Sep	Oct	Nov	Dec	Yr.
Extreme High (°F)	83	85	89	92	96	100	101	102	101	92	87	84	102
Average High (°F)	62	65	71	78	85	89	91	90	87	80	71	64	78
Average Temp. (°F)	53	56	62	69	75	81	82	82	79	70	61	55	69
Average Low (°F)	43	46	52	59	66	71	73	73	70	59	51	45	59
Extreme Low (°F)	14	19	25	32	41	50	60	60	42	35	24	11	11

Note: Figures cover the years 1948-1990
Source: National Climatic Data Center, International Station Meteorological Climate Summary, 9/96

Average Precipitation/Snowfall/Humidity

Precip./Humidity	Jan	Feb	Mar	Apr	May	Jun	Jul	Aug	Sep	Oct	Nov	Dec	Yr.
Avg. Precip. (in.)	4.7	5.6	5.2	4.7	4.4	5.4	6.4	5.9	5.5	2.8	4.4	5.5	60.6
Avg. Snowfall (in.)	Tr	Tr	Tr	0	0	0	0	0	0	0	0	Tr	Tr
Avg. Rel. Hum. 6am (%)	85	84	84	88	89	89	91	91	89	87	86	85	88
Avg. Rel. Hum. 3pm (%)	62	59	57	57	58	61	66	65	63	56	59	62	60

Note: Figures cover the years 1948-1990; Tr = Trace amounts (<0.05 in. of rain; <0.5 in. of snow)
Source: National Climatic Data Center, International Station Meteorological Climate Summary, 9/96

Weather Conditions

Temperature			Daytime Sky			Precipitation		
10°F & below	32°F & below	90°F & above	Clear	Partly cloudy	Cloudy	0.01 inch or more precip.	0.1 inch or more snow/ice	Thunderstorms
0	13	70	90	169	106	114	1	69

Note: Figures are average number of days per year and cover the years 1948-1990
Source: National Climatic Data Center, International Station Meteorological Climate Summary, 9/96

HAZARDOUS WASTE

Superfund Sites

New Orleans has one hazardous waste site on the EPA's Superfund Final National Priorities List: **Agriculture Street Landfill**. There are a total of 1,322 Superfund sites on the list in the U.S. *U.S. Environmental Protection Agency, Final National Priorities List, April 14, 2015*

AIR & WATER QUALITY

Air Quality Trends: Ozone

	2004	2005	2006	2007	2008	2009	2010	2011	2012	2013
MSA[1]	0.076	0.076	0.078	0.079	0.070	0.073	0.075	0.073	0.072	0.064

Note: (1) Data covers the New Orleans-Metairie, LA Metropolitan Statistical Area—see Appendix B for areas included. The values shown are the composite ozone concentration averages among trend sites based on the highest fourth daily maximum 8-hour concentration in parts per million. These trends are based on sites having an adequate record of monitoring data during the trend period. Data from exceptional events are included.
Source: U.S. Environmental Protection Agency, Air Quality Monitoring Information, "Air Quality Trends by City, 2000-2013"

Air Quality Index

Area	Percent of Days when Air Quality was...[2]					AQI Statistics[2]	
	Good	Moderate	Unhealthy for Sensitive Groups	Unhealthy	Very Unhealthy	Maximum	Median
MSA[1]	53.2	43.8	3.0	0.0	0.0	132	48

Note: (1) Data covers the New Orleans-Metairie, LA Metropolitan Statistical Area—see Appendix B for areas included; (2) Based on 365 days with AQI data in 2014. Air Quality Index (AQI) is an index for reporting daily air quality. EPA calculates the AQI for five major air pollutants regulated by the Clean Air Act: ground-level ozone, particle pollution (aka particulate matter), carbon monoxide, sulfur dioxide, and nitrogen dioxide. The AQI runs from 0 to 500. The higher the AQI value, the greater the level of air pollution and the greater the health concern. There are six AQI categories: "Good" AQI is between 0 and 50. Air quality is considered satisfactory; "Moderate" AQI is between 51 and 100. Air quality is acceptable; "Unhealthy for Sensitive Groups" When AQI values are between 101 and 150, members of sensitive groups may experience health effects; "Unhealthy" When AQI values are between 151 and 200 everyone may begin to experience health effects; "Very Unhealthy" AQI values between 201 and 300 trigger a health alert; "Hazardous" AQI values over 300 trigger warnings of emergency conditions (not shown).
Source: U.S. Environmental Protection Agency, Air Quality Index Report, 2014

Air Quality Index Pollutants

Area	Percent of Days when AQI Pollutant was...[2]					
	Carbon Monoxide	Nitrogen Dioxide	Ozone	Sulfur Dioxide	Particulate Matter 2.5	Particulate Matter 10
MSA[1]	0.0	1.4	28.8	10.4	59.5	0.0

Note: (1) Data covers the New Orleans-Metairie, LA Metropolitan Statistical Area—see Appendix B for areas included; (2) Based on 365 days with AQI data in 2014. The Air Quality Index (AQI) is an index for reporting daily air quality. EPA calculates the AQI for five major air pollutants regulated by the Clean Air Act: ground-level ozone, particle pollution (also known as particulate matter), carbon monoxide, sulfur dioxide, and nitrogen dioxide. The AQI runs from 0 to 500. The higher the AQI value, the greater the level of air pollution and the greater the health concern.
Source: U.S. Environmental Protection Agency, Air Quality Index Report, 2014

Maximum Air Pollutant Concentrations: Particulate Matter, Ozone, CO and Lead

	Particulate Matter 10 (ug/m^3)	Particulate Matter 2.5 Wtd AM (ug/m^3)	Particulate Matter 2.5 24-Hr (ug/m^3)	Ozone (ppm)	Carbon Monoxide (ppm)	Lead (ug/m^3)
MSA[1] Level	52	7.9	18	0.071	n/a	0.08
NAAQS[2]	150	15	35	0.075	9	0.15
Met NAAQS[2]	Yes	Yes	Yes	Yes	n/a	Yes

Note: (1) Data covers the New Orleans-Metairie, LA Metropolitan Statistical Area—see Appendix B for areas included; Data from exceptional events are included; (2) National Ambient Air Quality Standards; ppm = parts per million; ug/m^3 = micrograms per cubic meter; n/a not available.
Concentrations: Particulate Matter 10 (coarse particulate)—highest second maximum 24-hour concentration; Particulate Matter 2.5 Wtd AM (fine particulate)—highest weighted annual mean concentration; Particulate Matter 2.5 24-Hour (fine particulate)—highest 98th percentile 24-hour concentration; Ozone—highest fourth daily maximum 8-hour concentration; Carbon Monoxide—highest second maximum non-overlapping 8-hour concentration; Lead—maximum running 3-month average
Source: U.S. Environmental Protection Agency, Air Quality Monitoring Information, "Air Quality Statistics by City, 2013"

Maximum Air Pollutant Concentrations: Nitrogen Dioxide and Sulfur Dioxide

	Nitrogen Dioxide AM (ppb)	Nitrogen Dioxide 1-Hr (ppb)	Sulfur Dioxide AM (ppb)	Sulfur Dioxide 1-Hr (ppb)	Sulfur Dioxide 24-Hr (ppb)
MSA[1] Level	6	46	n/a	181	n/a
NAAQS[2]	53	100	30	75	140
Met NAAQS[2]	Yes	Yes	n/a	No	n/a

Note: (1) Data covers the New Orleans-Metairie, LA Metropolitan Statistical Area—see Appendix B for areas included; Data from exceptional events are included; (2) National Ambient Air Quality Standards; ppm = parts per million; ug/m^3 = micrograms per cubic meter; n/a not available.
Concentrations: Nitrogen Dioxide AM—highest arithmetic mean concentration; Nitrogen Dioxide 1-Hr—highest 98th percentile 1-hour daily maximum concentration; Sulfur Dioxide AM—highest annual mean concentration; Sulfur Dioxide 1-Hr—highest 99th percentile 1-hour daily maximum concentration; Sulfur Dioxide 24-Hr—highest second maximum 24-hour concentration
Source: U.S. Environmental Protection Agency, Air Quality Monitoring Information, "Air Quality Statistics by City, 2013"

Drinking Water

Water System Name	Pop. Served	Primary Water Source Type	Violations[1]	
			Health Based	Monitoring/ Reporting
New Orleans Algiers Water Works	52,785	Surface	0	0
New Orleans Carrollton WW	291,044	Surface	0	0

Note: (1) Based on violation data from January 1, 2014 to December 31, 2014 (includes unresolved violations from earlier years)
Source: U.S. Environmental Protection Agency, Office of Ground Water and Drinking Water, Safe Drinking Water Information System (based on data extracted January 27, 2015)

Orlando, Florida

Background

The city of Orlando can hold the viewer aghast with its rampant tourism. Not only is it home to the worldwide tourist attractions of Disney World, Epcot Center, and Sea World, but Orlando and its surrounding area also host such institutions as Medieval Times Dinner & Tournament, Wet-N-Wild, Ripley's Believe It or Not Museum, and Sleuths Mystery Dinner Shows, as well as thousands of T-shirt, citrus, and shell vendor shacks.

Orlando has its own high-tech corridor because of the University of Central Florida's College of Optics and Photonics. Manufacturing, government, business service, health care, high-tech research, and tourism supply significant numbers of jobs.

Aside from the glitz that pumps most of the money into its economy, Orlando is also called "The City Beautiful." The warm climate and abundant rains produce a variety of lush flora and fauna, which provide an attractive setting for the many young people who settle in the area, spending their nights in the numerous jazz clubs, restaurants, and pubs along Orange Avenue and Church Street. Stereotypically the land of orange juice and sunshine, Orlando is becoming the city for young job seekers and professionals.

This genteel setting is a far cry from Orlando's rough-and-tumble origins. The city started out as a makeshift campsite in the middle of a cotton plantation. The Civil War and devastating rains brought an end to the cotton trade, and its settlers turned to raising livestock. The transition to a new livelihood did not insure any peace and serenity. Rustling, chaotic brawls, and senseless shootings were everyday occurrences. Martial law had to be imposed by a few large ranch families.

The greatest impetus toward modernity came from the installation of Cape Canaveral, 50 miles away, which brought missile assembly and electronic component production to the area, and Walt Disney World, created out of 27,000 acres of unexplored swampland, which set the tone for Orlando as a tourist-oriented economy.

Orlando is also a major film production site. Nickelodeon, the world's largest teleproduction studio dedicated to children's television programming, is based there, as are the Golf Channel, Sun Sports, House of Moves, and the America Channel. Disney's biggest theme-park competitor, Universal Studios, is also based in Orlando.

The city is also home to a variety of arts and entertainment facilities, including the Amway Arena, part of the Orlando Centroplex, home to the NBA's Orlando Magic and the Orlando Sharks of the Indoor Soccer League. The city vies with Chicago and Las Vegas for hosting the most convention attendees in the United States.

Orlando is surrounded by many lakes. Its relative humidity remains high year-round, though in winter the humidity may drop. June through September is the rainy season, during which time, scattered afternoon thunderstorms are an almost daily occurrence. During the winter months rainfall is light and the afternoons are most pleasant. Hurricanes are not usually considered a threat to the area.

Rankings

General Rankings

- The Orlando metro area was identified as one of America's fastest-growing areas in terms of population and economy by *Forbes*. The area ranked #13 out of 20. The 100 most populous metro areas in the U.S. were evaluated on the following criteria: estimated population growth; job growth; gross metropolitan product growth; unemployment; median salaries for college-educated workers. *Forbes, "America's Fastest-Growing Cities 2015," January 27, 2015*
- Orlando was identified as one of America's fastest-growing major metropolitan areas in terms of population growth by CNNMoney.com. The area ranked #4 out of 10. Criteria: population growth between July 2012 and July 2013. *CNNMoney, "10 Fastest-Growing Cities," March 28, 2014*
- The U.S. Conference of Mayors and Waste Management sponsor the City Livability Awards Program. The awards recognize and honor mayors for exemplary leadership in developing and implementing specific programs that improve the quality of life in America's cities. Orlando was one of 17 second round finalists in the large cities (population 100,000 or more) category. *U.S. Conference of Mayors, "2015 City Livability Awards"*
- In their second annual survey, analysts for the small- and mid-sized city lifestyle site Livability.com looked at data for more than 2,000 U.S. cities to determine the rankings for Livability's "Top 100 Best Places to Live" in 2015. Orlando ranked #86. Criteria: vibrant economy; low cost of living; abundant lifestyle amenities. *Livability.com, "Top 100 Best Places to Live 2015"*

Business/Finance Rankings

- The finance website Wall St. Cheat Sheet reported on the prospects for high-wage job creation in the nation's largest metro areas over the next five years and ranked them accordingly, drawing on in-depth analysis by CareerBuilder and Economic Modeling Specialists International (EMSI). The Orlando metro area placed #7 on the Wall St. Cheat Sheet list. *wallstcheatsheet.com, "Top 10 Cities for High-Wage Job Growth," December 8, 2013*
- Looking at February 2012–2013, 24/7 Wall Street's analysts focused on metro areas where jobs were being added at a faster rate than the labor force was growing to identify the metro areas with the biggest real declines in unemployment. The #7 metro area for gains posted in employment was the Orlando metro area. *247wallst.com, "Cities Where Unemployment Has Fallen the Most," April 16, 2013*
- Based on metro area social media reviews, the employment opinion group Glassdoor surveyed 50 of the largest U.S. metro areas on measures including compensation and benefits, satisfaction with management, business outlook, and number of employers hiring. The Orlando metro area was ranked #24 in overall employee satisfaction. *www.glassdoor.com, "Employment Satisfaction Report Card by City," June 13, 2014*
- In its Competitive Alternatives report, consulting firm KPMG analyzed the 27 largest metropolitan statistical areas according to 26 cost components (such as taxes, labor costs, and utilities) and 30 non-cost-related variables (such as crime rates and number of universities). The business website 24/7 Wall Street examined the KPMG findings, adding to the mix current unemployment rates, GDP, median income, and employment decline during the last recession and "projected" recovery. It identified the Orlando metro area as #3 among the ten best American cities for business. *247wallst.com, "Best American Cities for Business," April 4, 2012*
- In a survey of economic confidence in the nation's 50 largest metropolitan areas conducted January–December 2014, the Orlando metro area placed #19, according to Gallup's 2014 Economic Confidence Index. *Gallup, "San Jose and San Francisco Lead in Economic Confidence," March 19, 2015*

- Orlando was ranked #22 out of 100 metro areas in terms of economic performance (#1 = best) during the recession and recovery from trough quarter through the second quarter of 2013. Criteria: percent change in employment; percentage point change in unemployment rate; percent change in gross metropolitan product; percent change in House Price Index. *Brookings Institution, MetroMonitor: Tracking Economic Recession and Recovery in America's 100 Largest Metropolitan Areas, September 2013*
- Orlando was identified as one of America's most frugal metro areas by *Coupons.com.* The city ranked #1 out of 25. Criteria: online coupon usage. *Coupons.com, "Top 25 Most Frugal Cities of 2013," April 10, 2014*
- Orlando was identified as one of America's most frugal metro areas by *Coupons.com.* The city ranked #1 out of 25. Criteria: Grocery IQ and coupons.com mobile app usage. *Coupons.com, "Top 25 Most On-the-Go Frugal Cities of 2013," April 10, 2014*
- *Forbes* reports that Orlando was identified as one of the happiest cities to work in by CareerBliss.com, an online community for career advancement. The city ranked #4 out of 10. Criteria: work-life balance; an employee's relationship with his or her boss and co-workers; general work environment; compensation; opportunities for advancement; company culture; and resources. *Forbes.com, "The 10 Happiest and Unhappiest Cities to Work in Right Now," January 16, 2015*
- The Orlando metro area appeared on the Milken Institute "2013 Best Performing Cities" list. Rank: #56 out of 200 large metro areas. Criteria: job growth; wage and salary growth; high-tech output growth. *Milken Institute, "Best-Performing Cities 2014," January 2015*
- *Forbes* ranked the 200 most populous metro areas to determine the nation's "Best Places for Business and Careers." The Orlando metro area was ranked #67. Criteria: costs (business and living); job growth (past and projected); income growth; educational attainment (college and high school); projected economic growth; cultural and recreational opportunities; net migration patterns; number of highly ranked colleges. *Forbes, "The Best Places for Business and Careers 2014," July 23, 2014*

Culture/Performing Arts Rankings

- Orlando was selected as one of the ten best small U.S. cities in which to be a moviemaker. Of cities with a population between 100,000 and 400,000, the city was ranked #5. Criteria: film community; access to new films; access to equipment; cost of living; tax incentives. *MovieMaker Magazine, "Best Places to Live and Work as a Moviemaker: 2013," January 22, 2015*

Dating/Romance Rankings

- Of the 100 U.S. cities surveyed by *Men's Health* in its quest to identify the nation's best cities for dating and forming relationships, Orlando was ranked #4 for online dating (#1 = best). *Men's Health, "The Best and Worst Cities for Online Dating," January 30, 2013*
- Orlando was selected as one of the most romantic cities in America by Amazon.com. The city ranked #3 of 20. Criteria: cities with 100,000 or more residents were ranked on their per capita sales of romance novels and relationship books, romantic comedy movies, romantic music, and sexual wellness products. *Amazon.com, "Top 20 Most Romantic Cities in America," February 5, 2015*

Education Rankings

- Personal finance website *WalletHub* analyzed the 150 largest U.S. metropolitan statistical areas to determine where the most educated Americans are choosing to settle. Criteria: educational attainment; percentage of workers with jobs in computer, engineering, and science fields; quality and size of each metro area's universities. Orlando was ranked #86 (#1 = most educated city). *www.WalletHub.com, "2014's Most and Least Educated Cities*
- Orlando was selected as one of the most well-read cities in America by Amazon.com. The city ranked #5 among the top 20. Cities with populations greater than 100,000 were evaluated based on per capita sales of books, magazines and newspapers. *Amazon.com, "The 20 Most Well-Read Cities in America," May 20, 2014*

- Orlando was selected as one of America's most literate cities. The city ranked #18 out of the 77 largest U.S. cities. Criteria: number of booksellers; library resources; Internet resources; educational attainment; periodical publishing resources; newspaper circulation. *Central Connecticut State University, "America's Most Literate Cities, 2014," April 8, 2015*

Environmental Rankings

- The Orlando metro area came in at #333 for the relative comfort of its climate on Sperling's list of "chill cities," as measured by the Sperling Heat Index. All 361 metro areas are included. Criteria included daytime high temperatures, nighttime low temperatures, dew point, and relative humidity at the high temperatures. *www.bertsperling.com, "Sperling's Chill Cities," July 18, 2013*
- Sperling's BestPlaces assessed 379 metropolitan areas of the United States for the likelihood of dangerously extreme weather events or earthquakes. In general the Southeast and South-Central regions have the highest risk of weather extremes and earthquakes, while the Pacific Northwest enjoys the lowest risk. Of the least risky metropolitan areas, the Orlando metro area was ranked #341. *www.bestplaces.net, "Safest Places from Natural Disasters," April 2011*
- Orlando was highlighted as one of the top 25 cleanest metro areas for year-round particle pollution (Annual PM 2.5) in the U.S. during 2011 through 2013. The area ranked #19. *American Lung Association, State of the Air 2015*

Food/Drink Rankings

- *Men's Health* ranked 100 major U.S. cities in terms of alcohol intoxication. Orlando ranked #33 (#1 = most sober).Criteria: binge drinking; alcohol-related traffic accidents, arrests, and fatalities. *Men's Health, "The Drunkest Cities in America," November 19, 2013*

Health/Fitness Rankings

- For each of the 50 most populous metro areas in the United States, the American College of Sports Medicine's American Fitness Index evaluated infrastructure, community assets, and policies that encourage healthy and fit lifestyles, including preventive health behaviors, levels of chronic disease conditions, health care access, and community resources and policies that support physical activity. The Orlando metro area ranked #34 for "community fitness." Personal health indicators were considered as well as community and environmental indicators. *www.americanfitnessindex.org, "ACSM American Fitness Index Health and Community Fitness Status of the 50 Largest Metropolitan Areas," May 2013*
- Orlando was identified as a "2013 Spring Allergy Capital." The area ranked #86 out of 100. Three groups of factors were used to identify the most severe cities for people with allergies during the spring season: annual pollen levels; medicine utilization; access to board-certified allergists. *Asthma and Allergy Foundation of America, "Spring Allergy Capitals 2013"*
- Orlando was identified as a "2013 Fall Allergy Capital." The area ranked #79 out of 100. Three groups of factors were used to identify the most severe cities for people with allergies during the fall season: annual pollen levels; medicine utilization; access to board-certified allergists. *Asthma and Allergy Foundation of America, "Fall Allergy Capitals 2013"*
- Orlando was identified as a "2013 Asthma Capital." The area ranked #62 out of the nation's 100 largest metropolitan areas. Twelve factors were used to identify the most challenging places to live for people with asthma: estimated prevalence; self-reported prevalence; crude death rate for asthma; annual pollen score; annual air quality; public smoking laws; number of board-certified asthma specialists; school inhaler access laws; rescue medication use; controller medication use; uninsured rate; poverty rate. *Asthma and Allergy Foundation of America, "Asthma Capitals 2013"*
- *Men's Health* ranked 100 major U.S. cities in terms of the best and worst cities for men. Orlando ranked #36. Criteria: thirty-three data points were examined covering health, fitness, and quality of life. *Men's Health, "The Best & Worst Cities for Men 2014," December 6, 2013*

- The Orlando metro area appeared in the 2013 Gallup-Healthways Well-Being Index. The area ranked #62 out of 189. The Gallup-Healthways Well-Being Index score is an average of six sub-indexes, which individually examine life evaluation, emotional health, work environment, physical health, healthy behaviors, and access to basic necessities. Results are based on telephone interviews conducted as part of the Gallup-Healthways Well-Being Index survey January 2–December 29, 2012, and January 2–December 30, 2013, with a random sample of 531,630 adults, aged 18 and older, living in metropolitan areas in the 50 U.S. states and the District of Columbia. *Gallup-Healthways, "State of American Well-Being," March 25, 2014*
- The Orlando metro area was identified as one of "America's Most Stressful Cities" by *Sperling's BestPlaces.* The metro area ranked #6 out of 50. Criteria: unemployment rate; suicide rate; commute time; mental health; poor rest; alcohol use; violent crime rate; property crime rate; cloudy days annually. *Sperling's BestPlaces, www.BestPlaces.net, "Stressful Cities 2012*
- Orlando was selected as one of the "20 Most Livable U.S. Cities for Wheelchair Users" by the Christopher & Dana Reeve Foundation. The city ranked #9. Criteria: Medicaid eligibility and spending; access to physicians and rehabilitation facilities; access to fitness facilities and recreation; access to paratransit; percentage of people living with disabilities who are employed; clean air; climate. *Christopher & Dana Reeve Foundation, "20 Most Livable U.S. Cities for Wheelchair Users," July 26, 2010*

Real Estate Rankings

- On the list compiled by Penske Truck Rental, the Orlando metro area was named the #5 moving destination in 2014, based on one-way consumer truck rental reservations made through Penske's website and reservations call center. *blog.gopenske.com, "Penske Truck Rental's 2014 Top Moving Destinations List," February 4, 2015*
- The Orlando metro area was identified as #2 among the ten housing markets with the highest percentage of distressed property sales, based on the findings of the housing data website RealtyTrac. Criteria included being sold "short"—for less than the outstanding mortgage balance—or in a foreclosure auction, income and poverty figures, and unemployment data. *247wallst.com, "Cities Selling the Most Distressed Homes," January 23, 2014*
- The Orlando metro area was identified as one of the top 20 housing markets to invest in for 2015 by *Forbes*. The area ranked #4. Criteria: strong population and job growth; relatively low home prices which are below equilibrium home price (EHP). The EHP is what the average price for a market should be, if speculation, weird distortions in local income, and other factors (like the housing collapse) weren't present in the market. *Forbes.com, "Best Buy Cities: Where to Invest in Housing in 2015," January 9, 2015*
- Orlando was ranked #26 out of 275 metro areas in terms of house price appreciation in 2014 (#1 = highest rate). *Federal Housing Finance Agency, House Price Index, 4th Quarter 2014*
- The Orlando metro area was identified as one of the 20 best housing markets in the U.S. in 2014. The area ranked #12 out of 178 markets with a home price appreciation of 12.2%. Criteria: year-over-year change of median sales price of existing single-family homes between the 4th quarter of 2013 and the 4th quarter of 2014. *National Association of Realtors®, Median Sales Price of Existing Single-Family Homes for Metropolitan Areas, 4th Quarter 2014*
- Orlando was ranked #142 out of 226 metro areas in terms of housing affordability in 2014 by the National Association of Home Builders (#1 = most affordable). The NAHB-Wells Fargo Housing Opportunity Index (HOI) for a given area is defined as the share of homes sold in that area that would have been affordable to a family earning the local median income, based on standard mortgage underwriting criteria. *National Association of Home Builders®, NAHB-Wells Fargo Housing Opportunity Index, 4th Quarter 2014*
- The nation's largest metro areas were analyzed in terms of the percentage of households entering some stage of foreclosure in 2013. The Orlando metro area ranked #3 out of 10 (#1 = highest foreclosure rate). *RealtyTrac, "2013 Year-End U.S. Foreclosure Market Report™," January 16, 2014*

Safety Rankings

- Allstate ranked the 200 largest cities in America in terms of driver safety. Orlando ranked #128. Allstate researchers analyzed internal property damage claims over a two-year period from January 2011 to December 2012. A weighted average of the two-year numbers determined the annual percentages. *Allstate, "Allstate America's Best Drivers Report, 2014"*

- Orlando was identified as one of the most dangerous cities in America by *The Business Insider.* Criteria: cities with 100,000 residents or more were ranked by violent crime rate in 2011. Violent crimes include for murder, rape, robbery, and aggravated assault. The city ranked #24 out of 25. *The Business Insider, "The 25 Most Dangerous Cities in America," November 4, 2012*

- The National Insurance Crime Bureau ranked 380 metro areas in the U.S. in terms of per capita rates of vehicle theft. The Orlando metro area ranked #113 (#1 = highest rate). Criteria: number of vehicle theft offenses per 100,000 inhabitants in 2012. *National Insurance Crime Bureau, "Hot Spots 2012," June 26, 2013*

Seniors/Retirement Rankings

- From its Best Cities for Successful Aging indexes, the Milken Institute generated rankings for metropolitan areas, weighing data in eight categories—health care, wellness, living arrangements, transportation, financial characteristics, education and employment opportunities, community engagement, and overall livability. The Orlando metro area was ranked #85 overall in the large metro area category. *Milken Institute, "Best Cities for Successful Aging, 2014"*

- Orlando was identified as one of the most popular places to retire by *Topretirements.com*. The list reflects the 100 cities (out of 900+ total cities reviewed) that visitors to the website are most interested in for retirement. *Topretirements.com, "Most Popular Places to Retire for 2014," February 25, 2014*

Sports/Recreation Rankings

- The sports site Bleacher Report named Orlando as one of the nation's top ten golf cities. Criteria included the concentration of public and private golf courses in a given city and the favored locations of PGA tour events. *BleacherReport.com, "Top 10 U.S. Cities for Golf," September 16, 2013*

- Orlando was selected as one of the most playful cities in the U.S. by KaBOOM! The organization's Playful City USA initiative honors cities and towns across the nation for a vision, plan and commitment to creating an agenda for play. Criteria: creating a local play commission or task force; designing an annual action plan for play; conducting a play space audit; outlining a financial investment in play for the current fiscal year; and proclaiming and celebrating an annual "play day." *KaBOOM! National Campaign for Play, "2013 Playful City USA Communities"*

- Orlando was chosen as one of America's best cities for bicycling. The city ranked #49 out of 50. Criteria: robust cycling infrastructure; vibrant bike culture. The editors only considered cities with populations of 95,000 or more. *Bicycling, "America's Top 50 Bike-Friendly Cities," May 23, 2012*

Transportation Rankings

- Orlando appeared on *Trapster.com's* list of the 10 most-active U.S. cities for speed traps. The city ranked #7 of 10. *Trapster.com* is a community platform accessed online and via smartphone app that alerts drivers to traps, hazards and other traffic issues nearby. *Trapster.com, "Speeders Beware: Cities With the Most Speed Traps," February 10, 2012*

Women/Minorities Rankings

- *Women's Health* examined U.S. cities and identified the 100 best cities for women. Orlando was ranked #52. Criteria: 30 categories were examined from obesity and breast cancer rates to commuting times and hours spent working out. *Women's Health, "Best Cities for Women 2012"*

- Orlando was selected as one of the gayest cities in America by *The Advocate*. The city ranked #13 out of 15. This year's criteria include points for a city's LGBT elected officials (and fractional points for the state's elected officials), points for the percentage of the population comprised by lesbian-coupled households, a point for a gay rodeo association, points for bars listed in *Out* magazine's 200 Best Bars list, a point per women's college, and points for concert performances by Mariah Carey, Pink, Lady Gaga, or the Jonas Brothers. The raw score is divided by the population to provide a ranking based on a per capita LGBT quotient. *The Advocate, "2014's Gayest Cities in America" January 6, 2014*

Miscellaneous Rankings

- The watchdog site Charity Navigator conducts an annual study of charities in the nation's major markets both to analyze statistical differences in their financial, accountability, and transparency practices and to track year-to-year variations in individual communities. The Orlando metro area was ranked #29 among the 30 metro markets. *www.charitynavigator.org, "Metro Market Study 2013," June 1, 2013*
- Market analyst Scarborough Research surveyed adults who had done volunteer work over the previous 12 months to find out where volunteers are concentrated. The Orlando metro area made the list for highest volunteer participation. *Scarborough Research, "Salt Lake City, UT; Minneapolis, MN; and Des Moines, IA Lend a Helping Hand," November 27, 2012*
- Orlando appeared on *Travel + Leisure's* list of America's least attractive people. Criteria: cities were selected by readers in their annual America's Favorite Cities survey. The city ranked #8 out of 10. *Travel + Leisure, "America's Most and Least Attractive People," November 2013*
- Scarborough Research, a leading market research firm, identified the top local markets for lottery ticket purchasers. The Orlando DMA (Designated Market Area) ranked in the top 13 with 48% of adults 18+ reporting that they purchased lottery tickets in the past 30 days. *Scarborough Research, January 30, 2012*
- The Orlando metro area was selected as one of "The Best U.S. Cities for Bargain Shopping" by *Forbes*. The area ranked #1 out of 10. Criteria: number of outlet stores; gross leasable retail space in major malls; low consumer price index; low sales tax rate. Indicators were examined in the nation's 50 largest metropolitan areas. *Forbes, "The Best U.S. Cities for Bargain Shopping," January 20, 2012*
- Mars Chocolate North America, the makers of COMBOS®, in partnership with Sperling's BestPlaces, ranked 50 major metro areas in terms of their "manliness." The Orlando metro area ranked #28. Criteria: number of professional sports teams; number of nearby NASCAR tracks and racing events; manly lifestyle; concentration of manly retail stores; manly occupations per capita; salty snack sales; "Board of Manliness" rankings. *Mars Chocolate North America, "America's Manliest Cities 2012"*
- The National Alliance to End Homelessness ranked the 100 most populous metro areas in terms the rate of homelessness. The Orlando metro area ranked #17. Criteria: number of homeless people per 10,000 population in 2011. *National Alliance to End Homelessness, The State of Homelessness in America 2012*
- The financial education website CreditDonkey compiled a list of the ten "best" cities of the future, based on percentage of housing built in 1990 or later, population change since 2010, and construction jobs as a percentage of population. Also considered were two more futuristic criteria: number of DeLorean cars available for purchase and number of spaceport companies and proposed spaceports. Orlando was scored #4. *www.creditDonkey.com, "In the Future, Almost All of America's 'Best' Cities Will Be on the West Coast, Report Says," February 14, 2014*

Business Environment

CITY FINANCES

City Government Finances

Component	2012 ($000)	2012 ($ per capita)
Total Revenues	708,206	2,972
Total Expenditures	712,915	2,992
Debt Outstanding	1,055,430	4,429
Cash and Securities[1]	1,422,971	5,971

Note: (1) Cash and security holdings of a government at the close of its fiscal year, including those of its dependent agencies, utilities, and liquor stores.
Source: U.S Census Bureau, State & Local Government Finances 2012

City Government Revenue by Source

Source	2012 ($000)	2012 ($ per capita)
General Revenue		
From Federal Government	30,515	128
From State Government	52,746	221
From Local Governments	89,435	375
Taxes		
Property	104,215	437
Sales and Gross Receipts	56,248	236
Personal Income	0	0
Corporate Income	0	0
Motor Vehicle License	0	0
Other Taxes	63,311	266
Current Charges	170,593	716
Liquor Store	0	0
Utility	49	0
Employee Retirement	32,482	136

Source: U.S Census Bureau, State & Local Government Finances 2012

City Government Expenditures by Function

Function	2012 ($000)	2012 ($ per capita)	2012 (%)
General Direct Expenditures			
Air Transportation	0	0	0.0
Corrections	0	0	0.0
Education	0	0	0.0
Employment Security Administration	0	0	0.0
Financial Administration	32,607	137	4.6
Fire Protection	91,085	382	12.8
General Public Buildings	0	0	0.0
Governmental Administration, Other	19,190	81	2.7
Health	6,738	28	0.9
Highways	43,661	183	6.1
Hospitals	0	0	0.0
Housing and Community Development	11,134	47	1.6
Interest on General Debt	45,365	190	6.4
Judicial and Legal	3,542	15	0.5
Libraries	0	0	0.0
Parking	16,490	69	2.3
Parks and Recreation	83,149	349	11.7
Police Protection	123,681	519	17.3
Public Welfare	0	0	0.0
Sewerage	64,574	271	9.1
Solid Waste Management	23,555	99	3.3
Veterans' Services	0	0	0.0
Liquor Store	0	0	0.0
Utility	16,490	69	2.3
Employee Retirement	51,632	217	7.2

Source: U.S Census Bureau, State & Local Government Finances 2012

DEMOGRAPHICS

Population Growth

Area	1990 Census	2000 Census	2010 Census	Population Growth (%) 1990-2000	2000-2010
City	161,172	185,951	238,300	15.4	28.2
MSA[1]	1,224,852	1,644,561	2,134,411	34.3	29.8
U.S.	248,709,873	281,421,906	308,745,538	13.2	9.7

Note: (1) Figures cover the Orlando-Kissimmee-Sanford, FL Metropolitan Statistical Area—see Appendix B for areas included
Source: U.S. Census Bureau, Census 1990, 2000, 2010

Household Size

Area	Persons in Household (%) One	Two	Three	Four	Five	Six	Seven or More	Average Household Size
City	37.7	32.9	13.6	10.5	3.4	1.2	0.6	2.41
MSA[1]	26.5	35.1	16.5	13.1	5.7	1.9	1.1	2.82
U.S.	27.7	33.6	15.7	13.1	6.0	2.3	1.5	2.64

Note: (1) Figures cover the Orlando-Kissimmee-Sanford, FL Metropolitan Statistical Area—see Appendix B for areas included
Source: U.S. Census Bureau, 2011-2013 American Community Survey 3-Year Estimates

Race

Area	White Alone[2] (%)	Black Alone[2] (%)	Asian Alone[2] (%)	AIAN[3] Alone[2] (%)	NHOPI[4] Alone[2] (%)	Other Race Alone[2] (%)	Two or More Races (%)
City	59.3	27.6	3.6	0.3	0.0	6.5	2.7
MSA[1]	71.7	16.1	4.1	0.3	0.1	4.8	2.9
U.S.	73.9	12.6	5.0	0.8	0.2	4.7	2.9

Note: (1) Figures cover the Orlando-Kissimmee-Sanford, FL Metropolitan Statistical Area—see Appendix B for areas included; (2) Alone is defined as not being in combination with one or more other races; (3) American Indian and Alaska Native; (4) Native Hawaiian and Other Pacific Islander
Source: U.S. Census Bureau, 2011-2013 American Community Survey 3-Year Estimates

Hispanic or Latino Origin

Area	Total (%)	Mexican (%)	Puerto Rican (%)	Cuban (%)	Other (%)
City	27.7	2.7	14.8	1.5	8.7
MSA[1]	26.7	3.4	13.5	1.9	7.9
U.S.	16.9	10.8	1.6	0.6	3.8

Note: Persons of Hispanic or Latino origin can be of any race; (1) Figures cover the Orlando-Kissimmee-Sanford, FL Metropolitan Statistical Area—see Appendix B for areas included
Source: U.S. Census Bureau, 2011-2013 American Community Survey 3-Year Estimates

Segregation

Type	Segregation Indices[1] 1990	2000	2010	2010 Rank[2]	Percent Change 1990-2000	1990-2010	2000-2010
Black/White	59.1	55.9	50.7	69	-3.2	-8.4	-5.2
Asian/White	29.4	35.4	33.9	81	6.0	4.6	-1.4
Hispanic/White	29.2	38.7	40.2	64	9.5	11.0	1.5

Note: All figures cover the Metropolitan Statistical Area—see Appendix B for areas included; Figures are based on an analysis of 1990, 2000, and 2010 Census Decennial Census tract data by William H. Frey, Brookings Institution and the University of Michigan Social Science Data Analysis Network. In this analysis all racial groups (whites, blacks, and asians) are non-Hispanic members of those races. Hispanics are shown as a separate category;
(1) Segregation Indices are Dissimilarity Indices that measure the degree to which the minority group is distributed differently than whites across census tracts. They range from 0 (complete integration) to 100 (complete segregation) where the value indicates the percentage of the minority group that needs to move to be distributed exactly like whites; (2) Ranges from 1 (most segregated) to 102 (least segregated); n/a not available.
Source: www.CensusScope.org

Ancestry

Area	German	Irish	English	American	Italian	Polish	French[2]	Scottish	Dutch
City	7.9	6.5	5.6	7.4	3.7	1.5	1.5	1.3	0.7
MSA[1]	10.4	8.5	7.2	8.8	5.1	2.3	2.2	1.6	0.9
U.S.	14.9	10.8	8.0	7.4	5.5	3.0	2.7	1.7	1.4

Note: Figures are the percentage of the total population reporting a particular ancestry. The nine most commonly reported ancestries in the U.S. are shown. Figures include multiple ancestries (e.g. if a person reported being Irish and Italian, they were included in both columns); (1) Figures cover the Orlando-Kissimmee-Sanford, FL Metropolitan Statistical Area—see Appendix B for areas included; (2) Excludes Basque

Source: U.S. Census Bureau, 2011-2013 American Community Survey 3-Year Estimates

Foreign-Born Population

Area	Percent of Population Born in								
	Any Foreign Country	Mexico	Asia	Europe	Carribean	South America	Central America[2]	Africa	Canada
City	18.4	1.3	2.9	1.3	5.7	5.6	0.7	0.5	0.3
MSA[1]	16.2	1.4	2.9	1.6	4.9	3.7	0.9	0.5	0.4
U.S.	13.0	3.7	3.8	1.5	1.2	0.9	1.0	0.6	0.3

Note: (1) Figures cover the Orlando-Kissimmee-Sanford, FL Metropolitan Statistical Area—see Appendix B for areas included; (2) Excludes Mexico.

Source: U.S. Census Bureau, 2011-2013 American Community Survey 3-Year Estimates

Marital Status

Area	Never Married	Now Married[2]	Separated	Widowed	Divorced
City	43.9	33.8	3.6	5.3	13.5
MSA[1]	35.0	44.9	2.6	5.5	12.0
U.S.	32.7	48.1	2.2	6.0	11.0

Note: Figures are percentages and cover the population 15 years of age and older; (1) Figures cover the Orlando-Kissimmee-Sanford, FL Metropolitan Statistical Area—see Appendix B for areas included; (2) Excludes separated

Source: U.S. Census Bureau, 2011-2013 American Community Survey 3-Year Estimates

Disability Status

Area	All Ages	Under 18 Years Old	18 to 64 Years Old	65 Years and Over
City	9.5	4.5	7.5	35.4
MSA[1]	11.2	4.4	8.9	35.0
U.S.	12.3	4.1	10.2	36.3

Note: Figures show percent of the civilian noninstitutionalized population that reported having a disability. Disability status is determined from from six types of difficulty: vision, hearing, cognitive, ambulatory, self-care, and independent living. For children under 5 years old, hearing and vision difficulty are used to determine disability status. For children between the ages of 5 and 14, disability status is determined from hearing, vision, cognitive, ambulatory, and self-care difficulties. For people aged 15 years and older, they are considered to have a disability if they have difficulty with any one of the six difficulty types; (1) Figures cover the Orlando-Kissimmee-Sanford, FL Metropolitan Statistical Area—see Appendix B for areas included.

Source: U.S. Census Bureau, 2011-2013 American Community Survey 3-Year Estimates

Age

Area	Percent of Population									Median Age
	Under Age 5	Age 5–19	Age 20–34	Age 35–44	Age 45–54	Age 55–64	Age 65–74	Age 75–84	Age 85+	
City	7.3	16.8	29.0	14.9	12.8	9.4	5.4	3.1	1.3	32.9
MSA[1]	6.0	19.6	22.2	13.6	14.1	11.3	7.4	4.0	1.6	36.5
U.S.	6.4	19.9	20.7	12.9	14.1	12.3	7.6	4.2	1.9	37.4

Note: (1) Figures cover the Orlando-Kissimmee-Sanford, FL Metropolitan Statistical Area—see Appendix B for areas included

Source: U.S. Census Bureau, 2011-2013 American Community Survey 3-Year Estimates

Gender

Area	Males	Females	Males per 100 Females
City	120,322	129,452	92.9
MSA[1]	1,088,197	1,133,645	96.0
U.S.	154,451,010	159,410,713	96.9

Note: (1) Figures cover the Orlando-Kissimmee-Sanford, FL Metropolitan Statistical Area—see Appendix B for areas included
Source: U.S. Census Bureau, 2011-2013 American Community Survey 3-Year Estimates

Religious Groups by Family

Area	Catholic	Baptist	Non-Den.	Methodist[2]	Lutheran	LDS[3]	Pente-costal	Presby-terian[4]	Muslim[5]	Judaism
MSA[1]	13.2	7.0	5.7	3.0	0.9	1.0	3.2	1.4	1.3	0.3
U.S.	19.1	9.3	4.0	4.0	2.3	2.0	1.9	1.6	0.8	0.7

Note: Figures are the number of adherents as a percentage of the total population; (1) Figures cover the Orlando-Kissimmee-Sanford, FL Metropolitan Statistical Area—see Appendix B for areas included; (2) Methodist/Pietist; (3) Latter Day Saints; (4) Reformed; (5) Figures are estimates
Source: Association of Statisticians of American Religious Bodies, 2010 U.S. Religion Census: Religious Congregations & Membership Study

Religious Groups by Tradition

Area	Catholic	Evangelical Protestant	Mainline Protestant	Other Tradition	Black Protestant	Orthodox
MSA[1]	13.2	17.8	4.8	3.3	1.2	0.3
U.S.	19.1	16.2	7.3	4.3	1.6	0.3

Note: Figures are the number of adherents as a percentage of the total population; (1) Figures cover the Orlando-Kissimmee-Sanford, FL Metropolitan Statistical Area—see Appendix B for areas included
Source: Association of Statisticians of American Religious Bodies, 2010 U.S. Religion Census: Religious Congregations & Membership Study

ECONOMY

Gross Metropolitan Product

Area	2012	2013	2014	2015	Rank[2]
MSA[1]	106.1	110.7	117.0	124.5	28

Note: Figures are in billions of dollars; (1) Figures cover the Orlando-Kissimmee-Sanford, FL Metropolitan Statistical Area—see Appendix B for areas included; (2) Rank is based on 2015 data and ranges from 1 to 363
Source: The U.S. Conference of Mayors, U.S. Metro Economies: GMP and Employment 2013-2015, June 2014

Economic Growth

Area	2010-12 (%)	2013 (%)	2014 (%)	2015 (%)	Rank[2]
MSA[1]	2.4	3.0	4.1	4.4	16
U.S.	2.1	2.0	2.3	3.2	–

Note: Figures are real gross metropolitan product (GMP) growth rates and represent annual average percent change; (1) Figures cover the Orlando-Kissimmee-Sanford, FL Metropolitan Statistical Area—see Appendix B for areas included; (2) Rank is based on 2015 data and ranges from 1 to 363
Source: The U.S. Conference of Mayors, U.S. Metro Economies: GMP and Employment 2013-2015, June 2014

Metropolitan Area Exports

Area	2008	2009	2010	2011	2012	2013	Rank[2]
MSA[1]	3,388.0	2,947.1	3,453.6	3,230.0	3,850.6	3,227.7	76

Note: Figures are in millions of dollars; (1) Figures cover the Orlando-Kissimmee-Sanford, FL Metropolitan Statistical Area—see Appendix B for areas included; (2) Rank is based on 2013 data and ranges from 1 to 387
Source: U.S. Department of Commerce, International Trade Administration, Office of Trade & Industry Information, Manufacturing & Services, data extracted April 3, 2015

Building Permits

Area	Single-Family			Multi-Family			Total		
	2013	2014	Pct. Chg.	2013	2014	Pct. Chg.	2013	2014	Pct. Chg.
City	1,037	915	-11.8	1,850	1,934	4.5	2,887	2,849	-1.3
MSA[1]	9,222	9,806	6.3	6,341	6,309	-0.5	15,563	16,115	3.5
U.S.	620,802	634,597	2.2	370,020	411,766	11.3	990,822	1,046,363	5.6

Note: (1) Figures cover the Orlando-Kissimmee-Sanford, FL Metropolitan Statistical Area—see Appendix B for areas included; Figures represent new, privately-owned housing units authorized (unadjusted data); All permit data are based on estimates with imputation.
Source: U.S. Census Bureau, Manufacturing, Mining, and Construction Statistics, Building Permits, 2013, 2014

Bankruptcy Filings

Area	Business Filings			Nonbusiness Filings		
	2013	2014	% Chg.	2013	2014	% Chg.
Orange County	354	192	-45.8	5,776	5,383	-6.8
U.S.	33,212	26,983	-18.8	1,038,720	909,812	-12.4

Note: Business filings include Chapter 7, Chapter 11, Chapter 12, and Chapter 13; Nonbusiness filings include Chapter 7, Chapter 11, and Chapter 13
Source: Administrative Office of the U.S. Courts, Business and Nonbusiness Bankruptcy, County Cases Commenced by Chapter of the Bankruptcy Code, During the 12- Month Period Ending December 31, 2013 and Business and Nonbusiness Bankruptcy, County Cases Commenced by Chapter of the Bankruptcy Code, During the 12- Month Period Ending December 31, 2014

Housing Vacancy Rates

Area	Gross Vacancy Rate[2] (%)			Year-Round Vacancy Rate[3] (%)			Rental Vacancy Rate[4] (%)			Homeowner Vacancy Rate[5] (%)		
	2012	2013	2014	2012	2013	2014	2012	2013	2014	2012	2013	2014
MSA[1]	21.2	20.5	18.8	14.3	15.5	15.2	18.5	14.7	14.6	2.2	2.8	3.1
U.S.	13.8	13.6	13.4	10.8	10.7	10.4	8.7	8.3	7.6	2.0	2.0	1.9

Note: (1) Figures cover the Orlando-Kissimmee-Sanford, FL Metropolitan Statistical Area—see Appendix B for areas included; (2) The percentage of the total housing inventory that is vacant; (3) The percentage of the housing inventory (excluding seasonal units) that is year-round vacant; (4) The percentage of rental inventory that is vacant for rent; (5) The percentage of homeowner inventory that is vacant for sale
Source: U.S. Census Bureau, Housing Vacancies and Homeownership Annual Statistics: 2014

INCOME

Income

Area	Per Capita ($)	Median Household ($)	Average Household ($)
City	25,083	42,026	57,912
MSA[1]	24,095	47,119	64,638
U.S.	27,884	52,176	72,897

Note: (1) Figures cover the Orlando-Kissimmee-Sanford, FL Metropolitan Statistical Area—see Appendix B for areas included
Source: U.S. Census Bureau, 2011-2013 American Community Survey 3-Year Estimates

Household Income Distribution

Area	Percent of Households Earning							
	Under $15,000	$15,000 -24,999	$25,000 -34,999	$35,000 -49,999	$50,000 -74,999	$75,000 -99,000	$100,000 -149,999	$150,000 and up
City	15.0	14.7	12.8	16.1	18.8	8.6	8.4	5.6
MSA[1]	12.5	12.0	12.5	15.5	19.0	10.9	10.7	6.8
U.S.	13.0	10.9	10.3	13.6	17.9	11.9	12.7	9.6

Note: (1) Figures cover the Orlando-Kissimmee-Sanford, FL Metropolitan Statistical Area—see Appendix B for areas included
Source: U.S. Census Bureau, 2011-2013 American Community Survey 3-Year Estimates

Poverty Rate

Area	All Ages	Under 18 Years Old	18 to 64 Years Old	65 Years and Over
City	20.9	33.8	17.5	15.0
MSA[1]	16.6	24.0	15.4	9.6
U.S.	15.9	22.4	14.8	9.5

Note: Figures are percentage of people whose income during the past 12 months was below the poverty level; (1) Figures cover the Orlando-Kissimmee-Sanford, FL Metropolitan Statistical Area—see Appendix B for areas included
Source: U.S. Census Bureau, 2011-2013 American Community Survey 3-Year Estimates

EMPLOYMENT

Labor Force and Employment

Area	Civilian Labor Force			Workers Employed		
	Dec. 2013	Dec. 2014	% Chg.	Dec. 2013	Dec. 2014	% Chg.
City	147,553	151,977	3.0	139,444	144,840	3.9
MSA[1]	1,177,275	1,211,468	2.9	1,106,175	1,149,268	3.9
U.S.	154,408,000	155,521,000	0.7	144,423,000	147,190,000	1.9

Note: Data is not seasonally adjusted and covers workers 16 years of age and older; (1) Figures cover the Orlando-Kissimmee-Sanford, FL Metropolitan Statistical Area—see Appendix B for areas included
Source: Bureau of Labor Statistics, Local Area Unemployment Statistics

Unemployment Rate

Area	2014											
	Jan.	Feb.	Mar.	Apr.	May	Jun.	Jul.	Aug.	Sep.	Oct.	Nov.	Dec.
City	5.8	5.8	5.7	5.2	5.5	5.5	5.9	5.8	5.4	5.2	5.1	4.7
MSA[1]	6.3	6.3	6.2	5.7	5.9	6.1	6.4	6.3	5.8	5.5	5.5	5.1
U.S.	7.0	7.0	6.8	5.9	6.1	6.3	6.5	6.3	5.7	5.5	5.5	5.4

Note: Data is not seasonally adjusted and covers workers 16 years of age and older; (1) Figures cover the Orlando-Kissimmee-Sanford, FL Metropolitan Statistical Area—see Appendix B for areas included
Source: Bureau of Labor Statistics, Local Area Unemployment Statistics

Employment by Occupation

Occupation Classification	City (%)	MSA[1] (%)	U.S. (%)
Management, Business, Science, and Arts	36.8	34.0	36.2
Natural Resources, Construction, and Maintenance	5.6	7.6	9.0
Production, Transportation, and Material Moving	7.5	8.8	12.1
Sales and Office	27.4	28.3	24.4
Service	22.7	21.3	18.3

Note: Figures cover employed civilians 16 years of age and older; (1) Figures cover the Orlando-Kissimmee-Sanford, FL Metropolitan Statistical Area—see Appendix B for areas included
Source: U.S. Census Bureau, 2011-2013 American Community Survey 3-Year Estimates

Employment by Industry

Sector	MSA[1] Number of Employees	MSA[1] Percent of Total	U.S. Percent of Total
Construction	58,700	5.1	4.4
Education and Health Services	138,600	12.1	15.5
Financial Activities	72,600	6.3	5.7
Government	120,100	10.5	15.8
Information	24,600	2.1	2.0
Leisure and Hospitality	239,400	20.9	10.3
Manufacturing	40,300	3.5	8.7
Mining and Logging	300	<0.1	0.6
Other Services	37,900	3.3	4.0
Professional and Business Services	187,600	16.4	13.8
Retail Trade	145,900	12.7	11.4
Transportation, Warehousing, and Utilities	35,000	3.1	3.9
Wholesale Trade	44,200	3.9	4.2

Note: Figures are non-farm employment as of December 2014. Figures are not seasonally adjusted and include workers 16 years of age and older; (1) Figures cover the Orlando-Kissimmee-Sanford, FL Metropolitan Statistical Area—see Appendix B for areas included
Source: Bureau of Labor Statistics, Current Employment Statistics, Employment, Hours, and Earnings

Occupations with Greatest Projected Employment Growth: 2012 – 2022

Occupation[1]	2012 Employment	2022 Projected Employment	Numeric Employment Change	Percent Employment Change
Retail Salespersons	326,380	380,120	53,740	16.5
Combined Food Preparation and Serving Workers, Including Fast Food	196,980	237,340	40,360	20.5
Customer Service Representatives	191,210	228,620	37,410	19.6
Registered Nurses	164,020	201,140	37,120	22.6
Waiters and Waitresses	191,370	227,810	36,440	19.0
Office Clerks, General	142,710	170,300	27,590	19.3
Cashiers	206,660	230,190	23,530	11.4
Landscaping and Groundskeeping Workers	92,510	115,540	23,030	24.9
Receptionists and Information Clerks	75,780	95,680	19,900	26.2
Nursing Assistants	86,990	106,200	19,210	22.1

Note: Projections cover Florida; (1) Sorted by numeric employment change
Source: www.projectionscentral.com, State Occupational Projections, 2012–2022 Long-Term Projections

Fastest Growing Occupations: 2012 – 2022

Occupation[1]	2012 Employment	2022 Projected Employment	Numeric Employment Change	Percent Employment Change
Helpers—Carpenters	1,280	2,450	1,170	90.7
Helpers—Brickmasons, Blockmasons, Stonemasons, and Tile and Marble Setters	1,050	1,890	840	79.5
Biomedical Engineers	760	1,300	540	70.7
Reinforcing Iron and Rebar Workers	520	870	350	67.5
Glaziers	2,890	4,710	1,820	62.8
Solar Photovoltaic Installers	170	270	100	58.7
Brickmasons and Blockmasons	2,820	4,430	1,610	57.1
Stonemasons	450	710	260	56.4
Helpers—Pipelayers, Plumbers, Pipefitters, and Steamfitters	2,420	3,750	1,330	54.8
Cement Masons and Concrete Finishers	10,390	16,050	5,660	54.4

Note: Projections cover Florida; (1) Sorted by percent employment change and excludes occupations with numeric employment change less than 100
Source: www.projectionscentral.com, State Occupational Projections, 2012–2022 Long-Term Projections

Average Wages

Occupation	$/Hr.	Occupation	$/Hr.
Accountants and Auditors	31.76	Maids and Housekeeping Cleaners	9.98
Automotive Mechanics	18.27	Maintenance and Repair Workers	15.68
Bookkeepers	16.61	Marketing Managers	54.52
Carpenters	16.98	Nuclear Medicine Technologists	35.88
Cashiers	9.30	Nurses, Licensed Practical	19.09
Clerks, General Office	13.27	Nurses, Registered	29.53
Clerks, Receptionists/Information	12.79	Nursing Assistants	11.66
Clerks, Shipping/Receiving	13.49	Packers and Packagers, Hand	10.63
Computer Programmers	36.45	Physical Therapists	41.89
Computer Systems Analysts	41.93	Postal Service Mail Carriers	25.19
Computer User Support Specialists	20.75	Real Estate Brokers	55.07
Cooks, Restaurant	11.81	Retail Salespersons	11.53
Dentists	96.90	Sales Reps., Exc. Tech./Scientific	27.45
Electrical Engineers	42.16	Sales Reps., Tech./Scientific	35.16
Electricians	18.52	Secretaries, Exc. Legal/Med./Exec.	15.27
Financial Managers	62.39	Security Guards	11.32
First-Line Supervisors/Managers, Sales	19.97	Surgeons	n/a
Food Preparation Workers	10.60	Teacher Assistants	11.80
General and Operations Managers	55.63	Teachers, Elementary School	22.70
Hairdressers/Cosmetologists	11.82	Teachers, Secondary School	22.30
Internists	105.54	Telemarketers	10.88
Janitors and Cleaners	10.25	Truck Drivers, Heavy/Tractor-Trailer	18.65
Landscaping/Groundskeeping Workers	11.57	Truck Drivers, Light/Delivery Svcs.	15.77
Lawyers	70.01	Waiters and Waitresses	10.52

Note: Wage data covers the Orlando-Kissimmee-Sanford, FL Metropolitan Statistical Area—see Appendix B for areas included; Hourly wages for elementary/secondary school teachers and teacher assistants were calculated by the editors from annual wage data assuming a 40 hour work week; n/a not available.
Source: Bureau of Labor Statistics, Metro Area Occupational Employment and Wage Estimates, May 2014

TAXES

State Corporate Income Tax Rates

State	Tax Rate (%)	Income Brackets ($)	Num. of Brackets	Financial Institution Tax Rate (%)[a]	Federal Income Tax Ded.
Florida	5.5 (f)	Flat rate	1	5.5 (f)	No

Note: Tax rates as of January 1, 2015; (a) Rates listed are the corporate income tax rate applied to financial institutions or excise taxes based on income. Some states have other taxes based upon the value of deposits or shares; (f) An exemption of $50,000 is allowed. Florida's Alternative Minimum Tax rate is 3.3%.
Source: Federation of Tax Administrators, "State Corporate Income Tax Rates, 2015"

State Individual Income Tax Rates

State	Tax Rate (%)	Income Brackets ($)	Num. of Brackets	Personal Exempt. ($)[1]		Fed. Inc. Tax Ded.
				Single	Dependents	
Florida	None	–	–	–	–	–

Note: Tax rates as of January 1, 2015; Local- and county-level taxes are not included; n/a not applicable; (1) Married joint filers generally receive double the single exemption
Source: Federation of Tax Administrators, "State Individual Income Tax Rates, 2015"

Various State and Local Tax Rates

State	State and Local Sales and Use (%)	State Sales and Use (%)	Gasoline[1] (¢/gal.)	Cigarette[2] ($/pack)	Spirits[3] ($/gal.)	Wine[4] ($/gal.)	Beer[5] ($/gal.)
Florida	6.5	6.0	36.42	1.339	6.50 (f)	2.25	0.48 (p)

Note: All tax rates as of January 1, 2015; (1) The American Petroleum Institute has developed a methodology for determining the average tax rate on a gallon of fuel. Rates may include any of the following: excise taxes, environmental fees, storage tank fees, other fees or taxes, general sales tax, and local taxes. In states where gasoline is subject to the general sales tax, or where the fuel tax is based on the average sale price, the average rate determined by API is sensitive to changes in the price of gasoline. States that fully or partially apply general sales taxes to gasoline: CA, CO, GA, IL, IN, MI, NY; (2) The federal excise tax of $1.0066 per pack and local taxes are not included; (3) Rates are those applicable to off-premise sales of 40% alcohol by volume (a.b.v.) distilled spirits in 750ml containers. Local excise taxes are excluded; (4) Rates are those applicable to off-premise sales of 11% a.b.v. non-carbonated wine in 750ml containers; (5) Rates are those applicable to off-premise sales of 4.7% a.b.v. beer in 12 ounce containers; (f) Different rates are also applicable according to alcohol content, place of production, size of container, or place purchased (on- or off-premise or onboard airlines); (p) Local excise taxes are excluded.
Source: Tax Foundation, 2015 Facts & Figures: How Does Your State Compare?

State Business Tax Climate Index Rankings

State	Overall Rank	Corporate Tax Index Rank	Individual Income Tax Index Rank	Sales Tax Index Rank	Unemployment Insurance Tax Index Rank	Property Tax Index Rank
Florida	5	14	1	12	3	16

Note: The index is a measure of how each state's tax laws affect economic performance. The lower the rank, the more favorable a state's tax system is for business. States without a given tax are given a ranking of 1. The scores/rankings for the District of Columbia do not affect other states. The 2015 index represents the tax climate as of July 1, 2014.
Source: Tax Foundation, State Business Tax Climate Index 2015

COMMERCIAL REAL ESTATE

Office Market

Market Area	Inventory (sq. ft.)	Vacancy Rate (%)	Under Construction (sq. ft.)	YTD Net Absorption (sq. ft.)	Total Average Asking Rent ($/sq. ft./year)
Orlando	68,123,552	11.6	40,000	291,686	19.97
National	4,745,108,508	14.3	71,190,461	51,084,126	27.40

Source: Newmark Grubb Knight Frank, National Office Market Report, 4th Quarter 2014

Industrial/Warehouse/R&D Market

Market Area	Inventory (sq. ft.)	Vacancy Rate (%)	Under Construction (sq. ft.)	YTD Net Absorption (sq. ft.)	Total Average Asking Rent ($/sq. ft./year)
Orlando	163,921,459	8.7	1,896,502	2,433,568	5.28
National	14,238,613,765	7.2	134,387,407	185,246,438	5.64

Source: Newmark Grubb Knight Frank, National Industrial Market Report, 4th Quarter 2014

COMMERCIAL UTILITIES

Typical Monthly Electric Bills

Area	Commercial Service ($/month)		Industrial Service ($/month)	
	1,500 kWh	40 kW demand 14,000 kWh	1,000 kW demand 200,000 kWh	50,000 kW demand 32,500,000 kWh
City	156	1,255	27,158	1,691,463
Average[1]	201	1,653	26,124	2,639,743

Note: Figures are based on annualized 2014 rates; (1) Average based on 180 utilities surveyed
Source: Edison Electric Institute, Typical Bills and Average Rates Report, Summer 2014

TRANSPORTATION

Means of Transportation to Work

Area	Car/Truck/Van		Public Transportation			Bicycle	Walked	Other Means	Worked at Home
	Drove Alone	Car-pooled	Bus	Subway	Railroad				
City	79.2	7.9	5.2	0.0	0.0	0.6	2.2	1.5	3.5
MSA[1]	80.7	9.4	2.0	0.0	0.0	0.5	1.2	1.6	4.6
U.S.	76.4	9.6	2.6	1.8	0.6	0.6	2.8	1.3	4.3

Note: Figures are percentages and cover workers 16 years of age and older; (1) Figures cover the Orlando-Kissimmee-Sanford, FL Metropolitan Statistical Area—see Appendix B for areas included
Source: U.S. Census Bureau, 2011-2013 American Community Survey 3-Year Estimates

Travel Time to Work

Area	Less Than 10 Minutes	10 to 19 Minutes	20 to 29 Minutes	30 to 44 Minutes	45 to 59 Minutes	60 to 89 Minutes	90 Minutes or More
City	8.3	34.0	26.1	20.5	5.3	3.1	2.6
MSA[1]	7.2	27.6	23.7	25.4	9.6	4.5	2.0
U.S.	13.3	29.7	20.9	20.2	7.7	5.7	2.6

Note: Figures are percentages and include workers 16 years old and over; (1) Figures cover the Orlando-Kissimmee-Sanford, FL Metropolitan Statistical Area—see Appendix B for areas included
Source: U.S. Census Bureau, 2011-2013 American Community Survey 3-Year Estimates

Travel Time Index

Area	1985	1990	1995	2000	2005	2010	2011
Urban Area[1]	1.12	1.20	1.21	1.25	1.24	1.20	1.20
Average[2]	1.09	1.14	1.16	1.19	1.23	1.18	1.18

Note: Travel Time Index—the ratio of travel time in the peak period to the travel time at free-flow conditions. For example, a value of 1.30 indicates a 20-minute free-flow trip takes 26 minutes in the peak. Free-flow speeds (60 mph on freeways and 35 mph on principal arterials) are used as the comparison threshold; (1) Covers the Orlando FL urban area; (2) average of 498 urban areas
Source: Texas Transportation Institute, Urban Mobility Report 2012, December 2012

Public Transportation

Agency Name / Mode of Transportation	Vehicles Operated in Maximum Service	Annual Unlinked Passenger Trips (in thous.)	Annual Passenger Miles (in thous.)
Central Florida Regional Transportation Authority (Lynx)			
Bus (directly operated)	226	27,846.6	146,407.1
Bus (purchased transportation)	14	145.1	1,235.0
Bus Rapid Transit (directly operated)	7	844.5	615.8
Demand Response (purchased transportation)	236	770.1	9,816.5
Vanpool (purchased transportation)	88	246.7	9,225.2

Source: Federal Transit Administration, National Transit Database, 2013

Air Transportation

Airport Name and Code / Type of Service	Passenger Airlines[1]	Passenger Enplanements	Freight Carriers[2]	Freight (lbs.)
Orlando International (MCO)				
Domestic service (U.S. carriers - 2014)	28	15,137,590	16	132,825,632
International service (U.S. carriers - 2013)	12	319,063	6	65,470

Note: (1) Includes all U.S.-based major, minor and commuter airlines that carried at least one passenger during the year; (2) Includes all U.S.-based airlines and freight carriers that transported at least one lb. of freight during the year.
Source: Bureau of Transportation Statistics, The Intermodal Transportation Database, Air Carriers: T-100 Domestic Market (U.S. Carriers), 2014; Bureau of Transportation Statistics, The Intermodal Transportation Database, Air Carriers: T-100 International Market (U.S. Carriers), 2013

Other Transportation Statistics

Major Highways:	I-4
Amtrak Service:	Yes
Major Waterways/Ports:	None

Source: Amtrak.com; Google Maps

BUSINESSES

Major Business Headquarters

Company Name	Rankings	
	Fortune[1]	Forbes[2]
Darden Restaurants	319	-

Note: (1) Fortune 500—companies that produce a 10-K are ranked 1 to 500 based on 2013 revenue; (2) all private companies with at least $2 billion in annual revenue through the end of their most current fiscal year are ranked 1 to 221; companies listed are headquartered in the city; dashes indicate no ranking
Source: Fortune, "Fortune 500," June 16, 2014; Forbes, "America's Largest Private Companies," November 5, 2014

Fast-Growing Businesses

According to *Inc.*, Orlando is home to three of America's 500 fastest-growing private companies: **Loyal Source Government Services** (#134); **uBreakiFix** (#197); **Overstocks Trading** (#384). Criteria: must be an independent, privately-held, for-profit, U.S. corporation, proprietorship or partnership; revenues must be at least $100,000 in 2010 and $2 million in 2013; must have four-year operating/sales history. Holding companies, regulated banks, and utilities were excluded. *Inc., "America's 500 Fastest-Growing Private Companies," September 2014*

According to Deloitte, Orlando is home to two of North America's 500 fastest-growing high-technology companies: **API Technologies Corp.** (#83); **ActivEngage** (#117). Companies are ranked by percentage growth in revenue over a five-year period. Criteria for inclusion: company must be headquartered within North America; must own proprietary intellectual property or proprietary technology that contributes to a significant portion of the company's operating revenue, or devote a significant proportion of revenues to research and development of technology; must have been in business for a minumum of five years with 2009 operating revenues of at least $50,000 USD/CD and 2013 operating revenues of at least $5 million USD/CD. *Deloitte Touche Tohmatsu, 2014 Technology Fast 500™*

Minority Business Opportunity

Orlando is home to one company which is on the *Black Enterprise* Auto Dealer 60 list (60 largest dealers based on gross sales): **Boyland Auto Group** (#3). Criteria: company must be operational in previous calendar year and be at least 51% black-owned. *Black Enterprise, B.E. 100s, 2014*

Orlando is home to five companies which are on the *Hispanic Business* 500 list (500 largest U.S. Hispanic-owned companies based on 2012 revenue): **Greenway Ford** (#3); **Jardon & Howard Technologies** (#170); **Advanced Xerographics Imaging Systems** (#179); **T&G Constructors** (#202); **US Aluminum Services Corp.** (#361). Companies included must show at least 51 percent ownership by Hispanic U.S. citizens, and must maintain headquarters in one of the 50 states or Washington, D.C. *Hispanic Business, "Hispanic Business 500," June 20, 2013*

Orlando is home to two companies which are on the *Hispanic Business* Fastest-Growing 100 list (greatest sales growth from 2008 to 2012): **US Aluminum Services Corp.** (#16); **Greenway Ford** (#22). Companies included must show at least 51 percent ownership by Hispanic U.S. citizens, and must maintain headquarters in one of the 50 states or Washington, D.C. In addition, companies must have minimum revenues of $200,000 for calendar year 2008. *Hispanic Business, June 20, 2013*

Minority- and Women-Owned Businesses

Group	All Firms		Firms with Paid Employees			
	Firms	Sales ($000)	Firms	Sales ($000)	Employees	Payroll ($000)
Asian	1,522	774,833	467	715,806	2,957	77,699
Black	3,685	676,406	267	594,074	4,180	237,447
Hispanic	5,698	763,059	625	612,670	4,149	111,111
Women	8,731	1,491,871	1,376	1,231,467	9,795	283,759
All Firms	30,564	47,965,704	9,019	46,886,322	239,814	9,467,514

Note: Figures cover firms located in the city; minority- and women-owned business are defined as firms in which the corresponding group own 51% or more of the stock or equity of the company
Source: U.S. Census Bureau, 2007 Economic Census, Survey of Business Owners (2012 Survey of Business Owners data will be released starting in June 2015)

HOTELS & CONVENTION CENTERS

Hotels/Motels

Area	5 Star		4 Star		3 Star		2 Star		1 Star		Not Rated	
	Num.	Pct.[3]	Num.	Pct.[3]	Num.	Pct.[3]	Num.	Pct.[3]	Num.	Pct.[3]	Num.	Pct.[3]
City[1]	5	0.7	73	10.1	390	53.8	205	28.3	8	1.1	44	6.1
Total[2]	166	0.9	1,264	7.0	5,718	31.8	9,340	52.0	411	2.3	1,070	6.0

Note: (1) Figures cover Orlando and vicinity; (2) Figures cover all 100 cities in this book; (3) Percentage of hotels which have a given star rating; Star ratings are determined by expedia.com and offer an indication of the general quality of a particular hotel.
Source: expedia.com, April 2, 2015

The Orlando-Kissimmee-Sanford, FL metro area is home to three of the best hotels in the U.S. according to *Travel & Leisure*: **Disney's Animal Kingdom Lodge**; **Disney's Polynesian Resort**; **Loews Royal Pacific Resort at Universal Orlando**. Criteria: service; location; rooms; food; and value. The list includes the top 236 hotels in the U.S. *Travel & Leisure, "T+L 500, The World's Best Hotels 2015"*

Major Convention Centers

Name	Overall Space (sq. ft.)	Exhibit Space (sq. ft.)	Meeting Space (sq. ft.)	Meeting Rooms
Orange County Convention Center	n/a	2,100,000	n/a	74

Note: Table includes convention centers located in the Orlando-Kissimmee-Sanford, FL metro area; n/a not available
Source: Original research

Living Environment

COST OF LIVING

Cost of Living Index

Composite Index	Groceries	Housing	Utilities	Transportation	Health Care	Misc. Goods/ Services
99.8	101.3	93.0	108.6	99.1	93.2	103.5

Note: The Cost of Living Index measures regional differences in the cost of consumer goods and services, excluding taxes and non-consumer expenditures, for professional and managerial households in the top income quintile. It is based on more than 50,000 prices covering almost 60 different items for which prices are collected three times a year by chambers of commerce, economic development organizations or university applied economic centers in each participating urban area. The numbers shown should be read as a percentage above or below the national average of 100. For example, a value of 115.4 in the groceries column indicates that grocery prices are 15.4% higher than the national average. Small differences in the index numbers should not be interpreted as significant; Figures cover the Orlando FL urban area.
Source: The Council for Community and Economic Research, ACCRA Cost of Living Index, 2014

Grocery Prices

Area[1]	T-Bone Steak ($/pound)	Frying Chicken ($/pound)	Whole Milk ($/half gal.)	Eggs ($/dozen)	Orange Juice ($/64 oz.)	Coffee ($/11.5 oz.)
City[2]	11.07	1.45	2.69	1.92	3.55	4.09
Avg.	10.40	1.37	2.40	1.99	3.46	4.27
Min.	8.48	0.93	1.37	1.30	2.83	2.99
Max.	14.20	2.44	3.62	4.02	6.42	6.96

Note: (1) Values for the local area are compared with the average, minimum and maximum values for all 308 areas in the Cost of Living Index; (2) Figures cover the Orlando FL urban area; **T-Bone Steak** *(price per pound);* **Frying Chicken** *(price per pound, whole fryer);* **Whole Milk** *(half gallon carton);* **Eggs** *(price per dozen, Grade A, large);* **Orange Juice** *(64 oz. Tropicana or Florida Natural);* **Coffee** *(11.5 oz. can, vacuum-packed, Maxwell House, Hills Bros, or Folgers).*
Source: The Council for Community and Economic Research, ACCRA Cost of Living Index, 2014

Housing and Utility Costs

Area[1]	New Home Price ($)	Apartment Rent ($/month)	All Electric ($/month)	Part Electric ($/month)	Other Energy ($/month)	Telephone ($/month)
City[2]	274,673	889	190.00	-	-	28.88
Avg.	305,838	919	181.00	93.66	73.14	27.95
Min.	183,142	480	112.00	42.06	23.42	17.16
Max.	1,358,576	3,851	594.00	180.03	440.99	40.42

Note: (1) Values for the local area are compared with the average, minimum and maximum values for all 308 areas in the Cost of Living Index; (2) Figures cover the Orlando FL urban area; **New Home Price** *(2,400 sf living area, 8,000 sf lot, in urban area with full utilities);* **Apartment Rent** *(950 sf 2 bedroom/1.5 or 2 bath, unfurnished, excluding all utilities except water);* **All Electric** *(average monthly cost for an all-electric home);* **Part Electric** *(average monthly cost for a part-electric home);* **Other Energy** *(average monthly cost for natural gas, fuel oil, coal, wood, and any other forms of energy except electricity);* **Telephone** *(price includes basic monthly rate for a private residential line plus additional local usage charges incurred by a family of four).*
Source: The Council for Community and Economic Research, ACCRA Cost of Living Index, 2014

Health Care, Transportation, and Other Costs

Area[1]	Doctor ($/visit)	Dentist ($/visit)	Optometrist ($/visit)	Gasoline ($/gallon)	Beauty Salon ($/visit)	Men's Shirt ($)
City[2]	84.90	83.18	63.41	3.42	45.04	25.52
Avg.	102.86	87.89	97.66	3.44	34.37	26.74
Min.	67.47	65.78	51.18	3.00	17.43	12.79
Max.	173.50	150.14	235.00	4.33	64.28	49.50

Note: (1) Values for the local area are compared with the average, minimum and maximum values for all 308 areas in the Cost of Living Index; (2) Figures cover the Orlando FL urban area; **Doctor** *(general practitioners routine exam of an established patient);* **Dentist** *(adult teeth cleaning and periodic oral examination);* **Optometrist** *(full vision eye exam for established adult patient);* **Gasoline** *(one gallon regular unleaded, national brand, including all taxes, cash price at self-service pump if available);* **Beauty Salon** *(woman's shampoo, trim, and blow-dry);* **Men's Shirt** *(cotton/polyester dress shirt, pinpoint weave, long sleeves).*
Source: The Council for Community and Economic Research, ACCRA Cost of Living Index, 2014

HOUSING

House Price Index (HPI)

Area	National Ranking[2]	Quarterly Change (%)	One-Year Change (%)	Five-Year Change (%)
MSA[1]	26	3.18	9.84	5.81
U.S.[3]	–	1.35	4.91	11.59

Note: The HPI is a weighted repeat sales index. It measures average price changes in repeat sales or refinancings on the same properties. This information is obtained by reviewing repeat mortgage transactions on single-family properties whose mortgages have been purchased or securitized by Fannie Mae or Freddie Mac in January 1975; (1) Orlando-Kissimmee-Sanford Metropolitan Statistical Area—see Appendix B for areas included; (2) Rankings are based on annual percentage change for all metro areas containing at least 15,000 transactions over the last 10 years and ranges from 1 to 275; (3) figures based on a weighted average of Census Division estimates using a seasonally adjusted, purchase-only index; all figures are for the period ending December 31, 2014

Source: Federal Housing Finance Agency, House Price Index, February 26, 2015

Median Single-Family Home Prices

Area	2012	2013	2014p	Percent Change 2013 to 2014
MSA[1]	134.0	160.4	180.0	12.2
U.S. Average	177.2	197.4	209.0	5.9

Note: Figures are median sales prices of existing single-family homes in thousands of dollars; (p) preliminary; n/a not available; (1) Orlando-Kissimmee-Sanford, FL Metropolitan Statistical Area—see Appendix B for areas included

Source: National Association of Realtors, Median Sales Price of Existing Single-Family Homes for Metropolitan Areas, 4th Quarter 2014

Qualifying Income Based on Median Sales Price of Existing Single-Family Homes

Area	With 5% Down ($)	With 10% Down ($)	With 20% Down ($)
MSA[1]	39,556	37,474	33,310
U.S. Average	45,863	43,449	38,621

Note: Figures are preliminary; Qualifying income is based on a mortgage rate of 4.0%. Monthly principal and interest payment is limited to 25% of income; n/a not available; (1) Orlando-Kissimmee-Sanford, FL Metropolitan Statistical Area—see Appendix B for areas included

Source: National Association of Realtors, Qualifying Income Based on Median Sales Price of Existing Single-Family Homes for Metropolitan Areas, 4th Quarter 2014

Median Apartment Condo-Coop Home Prices

Area	2012	2013	2014p	Percent Change 2013 to 2014
MSA[1]	n/a	n/a	n/a	n/a
U.S. Average	173.7	194.9	205.1	5.2

Note: Figures are median sales prices of existing apartment condo-coop homes in thousands of dollars; (p) preliminary; n/a not available; (1) Orlando-Kissimmee-Sanford, FL Metropolitan Statistical Area—see Appendix B for areas included

Source: National Association of Realtors, Median Sales Price of Existing Apartment Condo-Coop Homes for Metropolitan Areas, 4th Quarter 2014

Gross Monthly Rent

Area	Under $200	$200 -299	$300 -499	$500 -749	$750 -999	$1,000 -1,499	$1,500 and up	Median ($)
City	0.3	1.2	3.1	13.9	35.1	36.0	10.4	976
MSA[1]	0.4	1.0	2.5	14.2	32.6	38.1	11.1	994
U.S.	1.7	3.2	7.8	22.1	24.3	26.0	14.9	900

Note: Figures are percentages except for Median; Gross rent is the contract rent plus the estimated average monthly cost of utilities (electricity, gas, and water and sewer) and fuels (oil, coal, kerosene, wood, etc.) if these are paid by the renter (or paid for the renter by someone else); (1) Figures cover the Orlando-Kissimmee-Sanford, FL Metropolitan Statistical Area—see Appendix B for areas included

Source: U.S. Census Bureau, 2011-2013 American Community Survey 3-Year Estimates

Homeownership Rate

Area	2007 (%)	2008 (%)	2009 (%)	2010 (%)	2011 (%)	2012 (%)	2013 (%)	2014 (%)
MSA[1]	71.8	70.5	72.4	70.8	68.6	68.0	65.5	62.3
U.S.	68.1	67.8	67.4	66.9	66.1	65.4	65.1	64.5

Note: (1) Figures cover the Orlando-Kissimmee-Sanford, FL Metropolitan Statistical Area—see Appendix B for areas included
Source: U.S. Census Bureau, Housing Vacancies and Homeownership Annual Statistics: 2014

Year Housing Structure Built

Area	2010 or Later	2000 -2009	1990 -1999	1980 -1989	1970 -1979	1960 -1969	1950 -1959	1940 -1949	Before 1940	Median Year
City	0.4	24.7	17.4	18.2	13.4	8.1	10.5	3.9	3.5	1986
MSA[1]	0.9	26.8	21.3	22.0	13.8	6.5	5.8	1.4	1.7	1990
U.S.	0.9	15.0	13.9	13.8	15.8	11.0	10.9	5.4	13.3	1976

Note: Figures are percentages except for Median Year; (1) Figures cover the Orlando-Kissimmee-Sanford, FL Metropolitan Statistical Area—see Appendix B for areas included
Source: U.S. Census Bureau, 2011-2013 American Community Survey 3-Year Estimates

HEALTH

Health Risk Data

Category	MSA[1] (%)	U.S. (%)
Adults aged 18–64 who have any kind of health care coverage	73.0	79.6
Adults who reported being in good or excellent health	76.8	83.1
Adults who are current smokers	18.7	19.6
Adults who are heavy drinkers[2]	5.7	6.1
Adults who are binge drinkers[3]	17.6	16.9
Adults who are overweight (BMI 25.0 - 29.9)	35.7	35.8
Adults who are obese (BMI 30.0 - 99.8)	28.1	27.6
Adults who participated in any physical activities in the past month	77.7	77.1
Adults 50+ who have ever had a sigmoidoscopy or colonoscopy	72.5	67.3
Women aged 40+ who have had a mammogram within the past two years	76.9	74.0
Men aged 40+ who have had a PSA test within the past two years	53.4	45.2
Adults aged 65+ who have had flu shot within the past year	54.6	60.1
Adults who always wear a seatbelt	94.5	93.8

Note: Data as of 2012 unless otherwise noted; (1) Figures cover the Orlando-Kissimmee, FL Metropolitan Statistical Area—see Appendix B for areas included; (2) Heavy drinkers are classified as males having more than two drinks per day or females having more than one drink per day; (3) Binge drinkers are classified as males having five or more drinks on one occasion or females having four or more drinks on one occasion
Source: Centers for Disease Control and Prevention, Behaviorial Risk Factor Surveillance System, SMART: Selected Metropolitan/Micropolitan Area Risk Trends, 2012 (Note: the CDC has discontinued this dataset but will be releasing a replacement in late 2015)

Chronic Health Indicators

Category	MSA[1] (%)	U.S. (%)
Adults who have ever been told they had a heart attack	6.6	4.5
Adults who have ever been told they had a stroke	n/a	2.9
Adults who have been told they currently have asthma	9.5	8.9
Adults who have ever been told they have arthritis	21.9	25.7
Adults who have ever been told they have diabetes[2]	10.2	9.7
Adults who have ever been told they had skin cancer	5.7	5.7
Adults who have ever been told they had any other types of cancer	7.3	6.5
Adults who have ever been told they have COPD	5.9	6.2
Adults who have ever been told they have kidney disease	2.8	2.5
Adults who have ever been told they have a form of depression	18.2	18.0

Note: Data as of 2012 unless otherwise noted; n/a not available; (1) Figures cover the Orlando-Kissimmee, FL Metropolitan Statistical Area—see Appendix B for areas included; (2) Figures do not include pregnancy-related, borderline, or pre-diabetes
Source: Centers for Disease Control and Prevention, Behaviorial Risk Factor Surveillance System, SMART: Selected Metropolitan/Micropolitan Area Risk Trends, 2012 (Note: the CDC has discontinued this dataset but will be releasing a replacement in late 2015)

Mortality Rates for the Top 10 Causes of Death in the U.S.

ICD-10[a] Sub-Chapter	ICD-10[a] Code	Age-Adjusted Mortality Rate[1] per 100,000 population	
		County[2]	U.S.
Malignant neoplasms	C00-C97	158.1	166.2
Ischaemic heart diseases	I20-I25	98.3	105.7
Other forms of heart disease	I30-I51	36.2	49.3
Chronic lower respiratory diseases	J40-J47	37.2	42.1
Organic, including symptomatic, mental disorders	F01-F09	36.4	38.1
Cerebrovascular diseases	I60-I69	34.5	37.0
Other external causes of accidental injury	W00-X59	22.9	26.9
Other degenerative diseases of the nervous system	G30-G31	22.1	25.6
Diabetes mellitus	E10-E14	24.3	21.3
Hypertensive diseases	I10-I15	19.3	19.4

Note: (a) ICD-10 = International Classification of Diseases 10th Revision; (1) Mortality rates are a three year average covering 2011-2013; (2) Figures cover Orange County
Source: Centers for Disease Control and Prevention, National Center for Health Statistics. Compressed Mortality File 1999-2013 on CDC WONDER Online Database, released October 2014. Data are compiled from the Compressed Mortality File 1999-2013, Series 20 No. 2S, 2014.

Mortality Rates for Selected Causes of Death

ICD-10[a] Sub-Chapter	ICD-10[a] Code	Age-Adjusted Mortality Rate[1] per 100,000 population	
		County[2]	U.S.
Assault	X85-Y09	6.6	5.2
Diseases of the liver	K70-K76	11.0	13.2
Human immunodeficiency virus (HIV) disease	B20-B24	5.2	2.2
Influenza and pneumonia	J09-J18	12.2	15.4
Intentional self-harm	X60-X84	10.4	12.5
Malnutrition	E40-E46	*0.3	0.9
Obesity and other hyperalimentation	E65-E68	1.1	1.8
Renal failure	N17-N19	11.6	13.1
Transport accidents	V01-V99	10.2	11.7
Viral hepatitis	B15-B19	1.6	2.2

Note: (a) ICD-10 = International Classification of Diseases 10th Revision; (1) Mortality rates are a three year average covering 2011-2013; (2) Figures cover Orange County; (*) Unreliable data as per CDC
Source: Centers for Disease Control and Prevention, National Center for Health Statistics. Compressed Mortality File 1999-2013 on CDC WONDER Online Database, released October 2014. Data are compiled from the Compressed Mortality File 1999-2013, Series 20 No. 2S, 2014.

Health Insurance Coverage

Area	With Health Insurance	With Private Health Insurance	With Public Health Insurance	Without Health Insurance	Population Under Age 18 Without Health Insurance
City	76.3	55.2	26.8	23.7	12.3
MSA[1]	79.2	59.5	28.4	20.8	12.1
U.S.	85.2	65.2	31.0	14.8	7.3

Note: Figures are percentages that cover the civilian noninstitutionalized population; (1) Figures cover the Orlando-Kissimmee-Sanford, FL Metropolitan Statistical Area—see Appendix B for areas included
Source: U.S. Census Bureau, 2011-2013 American Community Survey 3-Year Estimates

Number of Medical Professionals

Area[1]	MDs[2]	DOs[2,3]	Dentists	Podiatrists	Chiropractors	Optometrists
Local (number)	3,300	234	545	49	287	150
Local (rate[4])	274.5	19.5	44.4	4.0	23.4	12.2
U.S. (rate[4])	270.0	20.2	63.1	5.7	25.2	14.9

Note: Data as of 2013 unless noted; (1) Local data covers Orange County; (2) Data as of 2012 and includes all active, non-federal physicians; (3) Doctor of Osteopathic Medicine; (4) rate per 100,000 population
Source: U.S. Department of Health and Human Services, Health Resources and Services Administration, Bureau of Health Professions, Area Resource File (ARF) 2013-2014

Best Hospitals

According to *U.S. News,* the Orlando-Kissimmee-Sanford, FL metro area is home to one of the best hospitals in the U.S.: **Florida Hospital Orlando** (10 specialties). The hospital listed was nationally ranked in at least one adult specialty. Only 144 hospitals nationwide were nationally ranked in one or more specialties. Seventeen hospitals in the U.S. made the Honor Roll with high scores in at least six specialties. *U.S. News Online, "America's Best Children's Hospitals 2014-15"*

According to *U.S. News,* the Orlando-Kissimmee-Sanford, FL metro area is home to one of the best children's hospitals in the U.S.: **Arnold Palmer Medical Center** (8 specialties). The hospital listed was highly ranked in at least one pediatric specialty. Eighty-nine children's hospitals in the U.S. were nationally ranked in at least one specialty. Ten children's hospitals in the U.S. made the Honor Roll with high scores in at least three specialties. *U.S. News Online, "America's Best Children's Hospitals 2014-15"*

EDUCATION

Public School District Statistics

District Name	Schls	Pupils	Pupil/ Teacher Ratio	Minority Pupils[1] (%)	Free Lunch Eligible[2] (%)	IEP[3] (%)
Florida Virtual	4	5,101	2.6	33.8	n/a	4.0
Orange County	249	183,066	16.0	69.5	56.1	11.4

Note: Table includes school districts with 2,000 or more students; (1) Percentage of students that are not non-Hispanic white; (2) Percentage of students that are eligible for the free lunch program; (3) Percentage of students that have an Individualized Education Program.
Source: U.S. Department of Education, National Center for Education Statistics, Common Core of Data, Local Education Agency (School District) Universe Survey: School Year 2012-2013; U.S. Department of Education, National Center for Education Statistics, Common Core of Data, Public Elementary/Secondary School Universe Survey: School Year 2012-2013

Highest Level of Education

Area	Less than H.S.	H.S. Diploma	Some College, No Deg.	Associate Degree	Bachelor's Degree	Master's Degree	Prof. School Degree	Doctorate Degree
City	11.1	25.1	19.0	11.1	22.5	7.9	2.2	1.1
MSA[1]	12.4	28.4	21.0	9.8	19.0	6.7	1.6	1.0
U.S.	13.7	28.0	21.2	7.9	18.2	7.7	1.9	1.3

Note: Figures cover persons age 25 and over; (1) Figures cover the Orlando-Kissimmee-Sanford, FL Metropolitan Statistical Area—see Appendix B for areas included
Source: U.S. Census Bureau, 2011-2013 American Community Survey 3-Year Estimates

Educational Attainment by Race

Area	High School Graduate or Higher (%)					Bachelor's Degree or Higher (%)				
	Total	White	Black	Asian	Hisp.[2]	Total	White	Black	Asian	Hisp.[2]
City	88.9	92.3	81.4	90.7	82.6	33.7	39.6	17.2	59.7	23.4
MSA[1]	87.6	89.5	83.1	85.6	79.2	28.3	29.9	19.1	47.6	18.9
U.S.	86.3	88.3	83.1	85.7	64.0	29.1	30.4	18.8	50.7	13.7

Note: Figures shown cover persons 25 years old and over; (1) Figures cover the Orlando-Kissimmee-Sanford, FL Metropolitan Statistical Area—see Appendix B for areas included; (2) People of Hispanic origin can be of any race
Source: U.S. Census Bureau, 2011-2013 American Community Survey 3-Year Estimates

School Enrollment by Grade and Control

Area	Preschool (%)		Kindergarten (%)		Grades 1 - 4 (%)		Grades 5 - 8 (%)		Grades 9 - 12 (%)	
	Public	Private	Public	Private	Public	Private	Public	Private	Public	Private
City	54.2	45.8	82.0	18.0	91.0	9.0	92.2	7.8	91.9	8.1
MSA[1]	51.0	49.0	87.6	12.4	89.1	10.9	88.9	11.1	91.2	8.8
U.S.	57.7	42.3	87.9	12.1	89.9	10.1	90.0	10.0	90.7	9.3

Note: Figures shown cover persons 3 years old and over; (1) Figures cover the Orlando-Kissimmee-Sanford, FL Metropolitan Statistical Area—see Appendix B for areas included
Source: U.S. Census Bureau, 2011-2013 American Community Survey 3-Year Estimates

Average Salaries of Public School Classroom Teachers

Area	2013-14 Dollars	2013-14 Rank[1]	2014-15 Dollars	2014-15 Rank[1]	Percent Change 2013-14 to 2014-15	Percent Change 2004-05 to 2014-15
FLORIDA	47,780	39	48,992	36	2.54	17.8
U.S. Average	56,610	–	57,379	–	1.36	20.8

Note: (1) State rank ranges from 1 to 51 where 1 indicates highest salary.
Source: National Education Association, Rankings & Estimates: Rankings of the States 2014 and Estimates of School Statistics 2015, March 2015

Higher Education

Four-Year Colleges			Two-Year Colleges			Medical Schools[1]	Law Schools[2]	Voc/ Tech[3]
Public	Private Non-profit	Private For-profit	Public	Private Non-profit	Private For-profit			
2	2	7	2	0	8	1	2	2

Note: Figures cover institutions located within the city limits and include main campuses only; (1) includes schools accredited by the Liaison Committee on Medical Education and the American Osteopathic Association's Commission on Osteopathic College Accreditation; (2) includes ABA-accredited schools, schools with provisional ABA accreditation, and state accredited schools; (3) includes all schools with programs that are less than 2 years.
Source: National Center for Education Statistics, Integrated Postsecondary Education System (IPEDS), 2013-14; Association of American Medical Colleges, Member List, May 1, 2015; American Osteopathic Association, Member List, May 1, 2015; Law School Admission Council, Official Guide to ABA-Approved Law Schools Online, May 1, 2015; Wikipedia, List of Medical Schools in the United States, May 1, 2015; Wikipedia, List of Law Schools in the United States, May 1, 2015

According to *U.S. News & World Report,* the Orlando-Kissimmee-Sanford, FL metro area is home to one of the best national universities in the U.S.: **University of Central Florida** (#173). The indicators used to capture academic quality fall into a number of categories: assessment by administrators at peer institutions; retention of students; faculty resources; student selectivity; financial resources; alumni giving; high school counselor ratings of colleges; and graduation rate. *U.S. News & World Report, "America's Best Colleges 2015"*

PRESIDENTIAL ELECTION

2012 Presidential Election Results

Area	Obama (%)	Romney (%)	Other (%)
Orange County	58.7	40.4	0.9
U.S.	51.0	47.2	1.8

Note: Results may not add to 100% due to rounding
Source: Dave Leip's Atlas of U.S. Presidential Elections

EMPLOYERS

Major Employers

Company Name	Industry
Adventist Health System/Sunbelt	General medical and surgical hospitals
Airtran Airways	Air passenger carrier, scheduled
Central Florida Health Alliance	Hospital management
Children & Families, Florida Department	Individual and family services
Cnl Lifestyle Properties	Real estate agents and managers
Connextions	Communication services, nec
Florida Hospital Medical Center	General medical and surgical hospitals
Gaylord Palms Resort & Conv Ctr	Hotel franchised
Leesburg Regional Medical Center	General medical and surgical hospitals
Lockheed Martin Corporation	Aircraft
Marriott International	Hotels and motels
Orlando Health	General medical and surgical hospitals
Rosen 9939	Hotels
Sea World of Florida	Theme park, amusement
Sears Termite & Pest Control	Pest control in structures
Siemens Energy	Power plant construction
Universal City Florida Partners	Amusement parks
University of Central Florida	Colleges and universities
Winter Park Healthcare Group, Ltd	Hospital affiliated with ama residency

Note: Companies shown are located within the Orlando-Kissimmee-Sanford, FL Metropolitan Statistical Area.
Source: Hoovers.com; Wikipedia

Best Companies to Work For

Darden Restaurants, headquartered in Orlando, is among the "Best Companies for Multicultural Women." *Working Mother* selected 25 companies based on a detailed application completed by public and private firms based in the United States, excluding government agencies, companies in the human resources field and non-autonomous divisions. Companies supplied data about the hiring, pay, and promotion of multicultural employees. Applications focused on representation of multicultural women, recruitment, retention and advancement programs, and company culture. *Working Mother, "2014 Best Companies for Multicultural Women"*

PUBLIC SAFETY

Crime Rate

Area	All Crimes	Violent Crimes				Property Crimes		
		Murder	Forcible Rape	Robbery	Aggrav. Assault	Burglary	Larceny -Theft	Motor Vehicle Theft
City	7,425.8	6.7	49.8	226.3	631.8	1,376.2	4,732.3	402.8
Suburbs[1]	3,523.1	3.6	40.5	110.3	338.5	820.1	2,033.1	177.0
Metro[2]	3,960.2	3.9	41.5	123.3	371.3	882.4	2,335.4	202.3
U.S.	3,098.6	4.5	25.2	109.1	229.1	610.0	1,899.4	221.3

Note: Figures are crimes per 100,000 population; (1) All areas within the metro area that are located outside the city limits; (2) Figures cover the Orlando-Kissimmee-Sanford, FL Metropolitan Statistical Area—see Appendix B for areas included
Source: FBI Uniform Crime Reports, 2013

Hate Crimes

Area	Number of Quarters Reported	Number of Incidents per Bias Motivation						
		Race	Religion	Sexual Orientation	Ethnicity	Disability	Gender	Gender Identity
City	4	1	0	1	0	0	0	0
U.S.	4	2,871	1,031	1,233	655	83	18	31

Source: Federal Bureau of Investigation, Hate Crime Statistics 2013

Identity Theft Consumer Complaints

Area	Complaints	Complaints per 100,000 Population	Rank[2]
MSA[1]	3,124	137.8	17
U.S.	332,646	104.3	-

Note: (1) Figures cover the Orlando-Kissimmee-Sanford, FL Metropolitan Statistical Area—see Appendix B for areas included; (2) Rank ranges from 1 to 380 where 1 indicates greatest number of identity theft complaints per 100,000 population
Source: Federal Trade Commission, Consumer Sentinel Network Data Book for January–December 2014

Fraud and Other Consumer Complaints

Area	Complaints	Complaints per 100,000 Population	Rank[2]
MSA[1]	10,934	482.1	30
U.S.	2,250,205	705.7	-

Note: (1) Figures cover the Orlando-Kissimmee-Sanford, FL Metropolitan Statistical Area—see Appendix B for areas included; (2) Rank ranges from 1 to 380 where 1 indicates greatest number of identity theft complaints per 100,000 population
Source: Federal Trade Commission, Consumer Sentinel Network Data Book for January–December 2014

RECREATION

Culture

Dance[1]	Theatre[1]	Instrumental Music[1]	Vocal Music[1]	Series and Festivals	Museums and Art Galleries[2]	Zoos and Aquariums[3]
3	7	3	1	1	30	3

Note: (1) Professional perfoming groups; (2) Based on organizations with SIC code 8412; (3) AZA-accredited
Source: The Grey House Performing Arts Directory, 2015-16; Association of Zoos & Aquariums, AZA Member Zoos & Aquariums, April 2015; www.AccuLeads.com, April 2015

Professional Sports Teams

Team Name	League	Year Established
Orlando City SC	Major League Soccer (MLS)	2015
Orlando Magic	National Basketball Association (NBA)	1989

Note: Includes teams located in the Orlando-Kissimmee-Sanford, FL Metropolitan Statistical Area.
Source: Wikipedia, Major Professional Sports Teams of the United States and Canada, April 2015

CLIMATE

Average and Extreme Temperatures

Temperature	Jan	Feb	Mar	Apr	May	Jun	Jul	Aug	Sep	Oct	Nov	Dec	Yr.
Extreme High (°F)	86	89	90	95	100	100	99	100	98	95	89	90	100
Average High (°F)	70	72	77	82	87	90	91	91	89	83	78	72	82
Average Temp. (°F)	59	62	67	72	77	81	82	82	81	75	68	62	72
Average Low (°F)	48	51	56	60	66	71	73	74	72	66	58	51	62
Extreme Low (°F)	19	29	25	38	51	53	64	65	57	44	32	20	19

Note: Figures cover the years 1952-1990
Source: National Climatic Data Center, International Station Meteorological Climate Summary, 9/96

Average Precipitation/Snowfall/Humidity

Precip./Humidity	Jan	Feb	Mar	Apr	May	Jun	Jul	Aug	Sep	Oct	Nov	Dec	Yr.
Avg. Precip. (in.)	2.3	2.8	3.4	2.0	3.2	7.0	7.2	5.8	5.8	2.7	3.5	2.0	47.7
Avg. Snowfall (in.)	Tr	0	0	0	0	0	0	0	0	0	0	0	Tr
Avg. Rel. Hum. 7am (%)	87	87	88	87	88	89	90	92	92	89	89	87	89
Avg. Rel. Hum. 4pm (%)	53	51	49	47	51	61	65	66	66	59	56	55	57

Note: Figures cover the years 1952-1990; Tr = Trace amounts (<0.05 in. of rain; <0.5 in. of snow)
Source: National Climatic Data Center, International Station Meteorological Climate Summary, 9/96

Weather Conditions

Temperature			Daytime Sky			Precipitation		
32°F & below	45°F & below	90°F & above	Clear	Partly cloudy	Cloudy	0.01 inch or more precip.	0.1 inch or more snow/ice	Thunder-storms
3	35	90	76	208	81	115	0	80

Note: Figures are average number of days per year and cover the years 1952-1990
Source: National Climatic Data Center, International Station Meteorological Climate Summary, 9/96

HAZARDOUS WASTE

Superfund Sites

Orlando has two hazardous waste sites on the EPA's Superfund Final National Priorities List: **Chevron Chemical Co. (Ortho Division); City Industries, Inc.** There are a total of 1,322 Superfund sites on the list in the U.S. *U.S. Environmental Protection Agency, Final National Priorities List, April 14, 2015*

AIR & WATER QUALITY

Air Quality Trends: Ozone

	2004	2005	2006	2007	2008	2009	2010	2011	2012	2013
MSA[1]	0.074	0.080	0.078	0.075	0.069	0.064	0.068	0.072	0.069	0.063

Note: (1) Data covers the Orlando-Kissimmee-Sanford, FL Metropolitan Statistical Area—see Appendix B for areas included. The values shown are the composite ozone concentration averages among trend sites based on the highest fourth daily maximum 8-hour concentration in parts per million. These trends are based on sites having an adequate record of monitoring data during the trend period. Data from exceptional events are included.
Source: U.S. Environmental Protection Agency, Air Quality Monitoring Information, "Air Quality Trends by City, 2000-2013"

Air Quality Index

Area	Percent of Days when Air Quality was...[2]					AQI Statistics[2]	
	Good	Moderate	Unhealthy for Sensitive Groups	Unhealthy	Very Unhealthy	Maximum	Median
MSA[1]	85.5	14.2	0.3	0.0	0.0	106	38

Note: (1) Data covers the Orlando-Kissimmee-Sanford, FL Metropolitan Statistical Area—see Appendix B for areas included; (2) Based on 365 days with AQI data in 2014. Air Quality Index (AQI) is an index for reporting daily air quality. EPA calculates the AQI for five major air pollutants regulated by the Clean Air Act: ground-level ozone, particle pollution (aka particulate matter), carbon monoxide, sulfur dioxide, and nitrogen dioxide. The AQI runs from 0 to 500. The higher the AQI value, the greater the level of air pollution and the greater the health concern. There are six AQI categories: "Good" AQI is between 0 and 50. Air quality is considered satisfactory; "Moderate" AQI is between 51 and 100. Air quality is acceptable; "Unhealthy for Sensitive Groups" When AQI values are between 101 and 150, members of sensitive groups may experience health effects; "Unhealthy" When AQI values are between 151 and 200 everyone may begin to experience health effects; "Very Unhealthy" AQI values between 201 and 300 trigger a health alert; "Hazardous" AQI values over 300 trigger warnings of emergency conditions (not shown).
Source: U.S. Environmental Protection Agency, Air Quality Index Report, 2014

Air Quality Index Pollutants

Area	Percent of Days when AQI Pollutant was...[2]					
	Carbon Monoxide	Nitrogen Dioxide	Ozone	Sulfur Dioxide	Particulate Matter 2.5	Particulate Matter 10
MSA[1]	0.0	0.5	56.4	0.0	43.0	0.0

Note: (1) Data covers the Orlando-Kissimmee-Sanford, FL Metropolitan Statistical Area—see Appendix B for areas included; (2) Based on 365 days with AQI data in 2014. The Air Quality Index (AQI) is an index for reporting daily air quality. EPA calculates the AQI for five major air pollutants regulated by the Clean Air Act: ground-level ozone, particle pollution (also known as particulate matter), carbon monoxide, sulfur dioxide, and nitrogen dioxide. The AQI runs from 0 to 500. The higher the AQI value, the greater the level of air pollution and the greater the health concern.
Source: U.S. Environmental Protection Agency, Air Quality Index Report, 2014

Maximum Air Pollutant Concentrations: Particulate Matter, Ozone, CO and Lead

	Particulate Matter 10 (ug/m³)	Particulate Matter 2.5 Wtd AM (ug/m³)	Particulate Matter 2.5 24-Hr (ug/m³)	Ozone (ppm)	Carbon Monoxide (ppm)	Lead (ug/m³)
MSA[1] Level	62	6.3	16	0.065	1	n/a
NAAQS[2]	150	15	35	0.075	9	0.15
Met NAAQS[2]	Yes	Yes	Yes	Yes	Yes	n/a

Note: (1) Data covers the Orlando-Kissimmee-Sanford, FL Metropolitan Statistical Area—see Appendix B for areas included; Data from exceptional events are included; (2) National Ambient Air Quality Standards; ppm = parts per million; ug/m³ = micrograms per cubic meter; n/a not available.
Concentrations: Particulate Matter 10 (coarse particulate)—highest second maximum 24-hour concentration; Particulate Matter 2.5 Wtd AM (fine particulate)—highest weighted annual mean concentration; Particulate Matter 2.5 24-Hour (fine particulate)—highest 98th percentile 24-hour concentration; Ozone—highest fourth daily maximum 8-hour concentration; Carbon Monoxide—highest second maximum non-overlapping 8-hour concentration; Lead—maximum running 3-month average
Source: U.S. Environmental Protection Agency, Air Quality Monitoring Information, "Air Quality Statistics by City, 2013"

Maximum Air Pollutant Concentrations: Nitrogen Dioxide and Sulfur Dioxide

	Nitrogen Dioxide AM (ppb)	Nitrogen Dioxide 1-Hr (ppb)	Sulfur Dioxide AM (ppb)	Sulfur Dioxide 1-Hr (ppb)	Sulfur Dioxide 24-Hr (ppb)
MSA[1] Level	5	34	n/a	3	n/a
NAAQS[2]	53	100	30	75	140
Met NAAQS[2]	Yes	Yes	n/a	Yes	n/a

Note: (1) Data covers the Orlando-Kissimmee-Sanford, FL Metropolitan Statistical Area—see Appendix B for areas included; Data from exceptional events are included; (2) National Ambient Air Quality Standards; ppm = parts per million; ug/m³ = micrograms per cubic meter; n/a not available.
Concentrations: Nitrogen Dioxide AM—highest arithmetic mean concentration; Nitrogen Dioxide 1-Hr—highest 98th percentile 1-hour daily maximum concentration; Sulfur Dioxide AM—highest annual mean concentration; Sulfur Dioxide 1-Hr—highest 99th percentile 1-hour daily maximum concentration; Sulfur Dioxide 24-Hr—highest second maximum 24-hour concentration
Source: U.S. Environmental Protection Agency, Air Quality Monitoring Information, "Air Quality Statistics by City, 2013"

Drinking Water

Water System Name	Pop. Served	Primary Water Source Type	Violations[1]	
			Health Based	Monitoring/ Reporting
Orlando Utilities Commission	425,520	Ground	0	0

Note: (1) Based on violation data from January 1, 2014 to December 31, 2014 (includes unresolved violations from earlier years)
Source: U.S. Environmental Protection Agency, Office of Ground Water and Drinking Water, Safe Drinking Water Information System (based on data extracted January 27, 2015)

Palm Bay, Florida

Background

Palm Bay is located on the east central coast of Florida in Brevard County. The Timucan Indians are thought to be the first inhabitants of the area. They were drawn to the Turkey Creek section of the Indian River's fresh water springs, fishing and wildlife. When the first European settlers arrived in the late 1800s, the area became known as Tillman after local businessman John Tillman. In 1842, Congress enacted the Armed Occupation Act which gave settlers 160 acres of unoccupied Florida land in exchange for defending that land against Indians. In the mid 19th century, the area's economy depended on orange groves, winter vegetable packing houses, and lumber and paper industries. The Melbourne-Tillman Drainage District was formed in 1922 and developed a 180 mile grid of canals to aid agriculture and development to expand westward.

In 1925 the name Palm Bay replaced Tillman to reflect the beauty of the area that was lined with palm trees along the mouth of Turkey Creek. A residential expansion project called Port Malabar in 1959 by the Mackle Brothers and the General Development Corporation acquired 42,000 acres and vastly expanded Palm Bay's borders. Palm Bay was officially incorporated in 1960 and it's population grew from 2,808 to nearly 105,000 by 2013. It is now the most populated and one of the safest cities in Brevard County.

Today, the City of Palm Bay is a fast growing, culturally diverse community. Situated between Jacksonville and Miami, Palm Bay is home to Eastern Florida State College, The University of Central Florida and Webster University. It is home to Lockheed Martin, Harris Corporation and the Florida Institute of Technology.

Palm Bay's transit system is provided by the Space Coast Area Transit Company which operates throughout Brevard County. The buses are customer friendly, with wheelchair access as well as room for bicycles and surf boards. Scenic U.S. 1 encircles Palm Bay's Indian River Lagoon. Orlando and Disney World are an hour away. Palm Bay is served by Melourne International Airport, 12 miles away.

Recreation in Palm Bay takes on many forms: Theater is provided by the Maxwell C. King Company of Palm Bay, and fishing is abundant on the St John's River, known as the "bass fishing capital of the world." The Turkey Creek Sanctuary provides not only a magnificent nature preserve for many endangered plants and animals, but also a perfect kayaking waterway. A trip to Goode Park allows up close inspection of manatees and dolphins. The Indian River provides opportunity for all water sports, and the city has over 70 miles of beach coastline. Also, major league baseball spring training homes for the Washington Nationals and the Milwaukee Brewers are a 20-minute drive away.

Rankings

Business/Finance Rankings

- Building on the U.S. Department of Labor's Occupational Information Network Data Collection Program, the Brookings Institution defined STEM occupations and job opportunities for STEM workers at various levels of educational attainment. The Palm Bay metro area was one of the ten metro areas where workers in low-education-level STEM jobs earn the highest relative wages. *www.brookings.edu, "The Hidden Stem Economy," June 10, 2013*
- Building on the U.S. Department of Labor's Occupational Information Network Data Collection Program, the Brookings Institution defined STEM occupations and job opportunities for STEM workers at various levels of educational attainment. The Palm Bay metro area was placed among the ten large metro areas with the highest demand for high-level STEM knowledge. *www.brookings.edu, "The Hidden Stem Economy," June 10, 2013*
- The business website 24/7 Wall Street drew on Brookings Institution research on 50 advanced industries to identify the proportion of workers in the nation's largest metropolitan areas that were employed in jobs requiring knowledge in the science, technology, engineering, or math (STEM) fields. The Palm Bay metro area was #7. *247wallst.com, "15 Cities with the Most High-Tech Jobs," March 13, 2015*
- Palm Bay was ranked #60 out of 100 metro areas in terms of economic performance (#1 = best) during the recession and recovery from trough quarter through the second quarter of 2013. Criteria: percent change in employment; percentage point change in unemployment rate; percent change in gross metropolitan product; percent change in House Price Index. *Brookings Institution, MetroMonitor: Tracking Economic Recession and Recovery in America's 100 Largest Metropolitan Areas, September 2013*
- The Palm Bay metro area appeared on the Milken Institute "2013 Best Performing Cities" list. Rank: #195 out of 200 large metro areas. Criteria: job growth; wage and salary growth; high-tech output growth. *Milken Institute, "Best-Performing Cities 2014," January 2015*
- *Forbes* ranked the 200 most populous metro areas to determine the nation's "Best Places for Business and Careers." The Palm Bay metro area was ranked #164. Criteria: costs (business and living); job growth (past and projected); income growth; educational attainment (college and high school); projected economic growth; cultural and recreational opportunities; net migration patterns; number of highly ranked colleges. *Forbes, "The Best Places for Business and Careers 2014," July 23, 2014*

Education Rankings

- Personal finance website *WalletHub* analyzed the 150 largest U.S. metropolitan statistical areas to determine where the most educated Americans are choosing to settle. Criteria: educational attainment; percentage of workers with jobs in computer, engineering, and science fields; quality and size of each metro area's universities. Palm Bay was ranked #53 (#1 = most educated city). *www.WalletHub.com, "2014's Most and Least Educated Cities*

Environmental Rankings

- The Palm Bay metro area came in at #316 for the relative comfort of its climate on Sperling's list of "chill cities," as measured by the Sperling Heat Index. All 361 metro areas are included. Criteria included daytime high temperatures, nighttime low temperatures, dew point, and relative humidity at the high temperatures. *www.bertsperling.com, "Sperling's Chill Cities," July 18, 2013*
- Sperling's BestPlaces assessed 379 metropolitan areas of the United States for the likelihood of dangerously extreme weather events or earthquakes. In general the Southeast and South-Central regions have the highest risk of weather extremes and earthquakes, while the Pacific Northwest enjoys the lowest risk. Of the least risky metropolitan areas, the Palm Bay metro area was ranked #320. *www.bestplaces.net, "Safest Places from Natural Disasters," April 2011*

- Palm Bay was highlighted as one of the top 25 cleanest metro areas for year-round particle pollution (Annual PM 2.5) in the U.S. during 2011 through 2013. The area ranked #6. *American Lung Association, State of the Air 2015*
- Palm Bay was highlighted as one of the top 25 cleanest metro areas for short-term particle pollution (24-hour PM 2.5) in the U.S. during 2011 through 2013. Monitors in these cities reported no days with unhealthful PM 2.5 levels. *American Lung Association, State of the Air 2015*

Health/Fitness Rankings

- Palm Bay was identified as a "2013 Spring Allergy Capital." The area ranked #95 out of 100. Three groups of factors were used to identify the most severe cities for people with allergies during the spring season: annual pollen levels; medicine utilization; access to board-certified allergists. *Asthma and Allergy Foundation of America, "Spring Allergy Capitals 2013"*
- Palm Bay was identified as a "2013 Fall Allergy Capital." The area ranked #89 out of 100. Three groups of factors were used to identify the most severe cities for people with allergies during the fall season: annual pollen levels; medicine utilization; access to board-certified allergists. *Asthma and Allergy Foundation of America, "Fall Allergy Capitals 2013"*
- Palm Bay was identified as a "2013 Asthma Capital." The area ranked #97 out of the nation's 100 largest metropolitan areas. Twelve factors were used to identify the most challenging places to live for people with asthma: estimated prevalence; self-reported prevalence; crude death rate for asthma; annual pollen score; annual air quality; public smoking laws; number of board-certified asthma specialists; school inhaler access laws; rescue medication use; controller medication use; uninsured rate; poverty rate. *Asthma and Allergy Foundation of America, "Asthma Capitals 2013"*
- The Palm Bay metro area appeared in the 2013 Gallup-Healthways Well-Being Index. The area ranked #139 out of 189. The Gallup-Healthways Well-Being Index score is an average of six sub-indexes, which individually examine life evaluation, emotional health, work environment, physical health, healthy behaviors, and access to basic necessities. Results are based on telephone interviews conducted as part of the Gallup-Healthways Well-Being Index survey January 2–December 29, 2012, and January 2–December 30, 2013, with a random sample of 531,630 adults, aged 18 and older, living in metropolitan areas in the 50 U.S. states and the District of Columbia. *Gallup-Healthways, "State of American Well-Being," March 25, 2014*

Real Estate Rankings

- Palm Bay was ranked #43 out of 275 metro areas in terms of house price appreciation in 2014 (#1 = highest rate). *Federal Housing Finance Agency, House Price Index, 4th Quarter 2014*
- Palm Bay was ranked #74 out of 226 metro areas in terms of housing affordability in 2014 by the National Association of Home Builders (#1 = most affordable). The NAHB-Wells Fargo Housing Opportunity Index (HOI) for a given area is defined as the share of homes sold in that area that would have been affordable to a family earning the local median income, based on standard mortgage underwriting criteria. *National Association of Home Builders®, NAHB-Wells Fargo Housing Opportunity Index, 4th Quarter 2014*
- The nation's largest metro areas were analyzed in terms of the percentage of households entering some stage of foreclosure in 2013. The Palm Bay metro area ranked #4 out of 10 (#1 = highest foreclosure rate). *RealtyTrac, "2013 Year-End U.S. Foreclosure Market Report™," January 16, 2014*

Safety Rankings

- The National Insurance Crime Bureau ranked 380 metro areas in the U.S. in terms of per capita rates of vehicle theft. The Palm Bay metro area ranked #241 (#1 = highest rate). Criteria: number of vehicle theft offenses per 100,000 inhabitants in 2012. *National Insurance Crime Bureau, "Hot Spots 2012," June 26, 2013*

Seniors/Retirement Rankings

- From its Best Cities for Successful Aging indexes, the Milken Institute generated rankings for metropolitan areas, weighing data in eight categories—health care, wellness, living arrangements, transportation, financial characteristics, education and employment opportunities, community engagement, and overall livability. The Palm Bay metro area was ranked #92 overall in the large metro area category. *Milken Institute, "Best Cities for Successful Aging, 2014"*

Sports/Recreation Rankings

- Palm Bay was selected as one of the most playful cities in the U.S. by KaBOOM! The organization's Playful City USA initiative honors cities and towns across the nation for a vision, plan and commitment to creating an agenda for play. Criteria: creating a local play commission or task force; designing an annual action plan for play; conducting a play space audit; outlining a financial investment in play for the current fiscal year; and proclaiming and celebrating an annual "play day." *KaBOOM! National Campaign for Play, "2013 Playful City USA Communities"*

Women/Minorities Rankings

- *24/7 Wall St.* compared median earnings over a 12-month period for men and women who worked full-time, year-round, and employment composition by sector to identify the worst-paying cities for women. Of the largest 100 U.S. metropolitan areas, Palm Bay was ranked #5 in pay disparity. *24/7 Wall St., "The Worst-Paying Cities for Women," March 8, 2013*

Miscellaneous Rankings

- The National Alliance to End Homelessness ranked the 100 most populous metro areas in terms the rate of homelessness. The Palm Bay metro area ranked #11. Criteria: number of homeless people per 10,000 population in 2011. *National Alliance to End Homelessness, The State of Homelessness in America 2012*

Business Environment

CITY FINANCES

City Government Finances

Component	2012 ($000)	2012 ($ per capita)
Total Revenues	111,693	1,082
Total Expenditures	109,857	1,065
Debt Outstanding	157,796	1,529
Cash and Securities[1]	167,366	1,622

Note: (1) Cash and security holdings of a government at the close of its fiscal year, including those of its dependent agencies, utilities, and liquor stores.
Source: U.S Census Bureau, State & Local Government Finances 2012

City Government Revenue by Source

Source	2012 ($000)	2012 ($ per capita)
General Revenue		
From Federal Government	13,682	133
From State Government	8,528	83
From Local Governments	325	3
Taxes		
Property	24,607	238
Sales and Gross Receipts	12,760	124
Personal Income	0	0
Corporate Income	0	0
Motor Vehicle License	0	0
Other Taxes	6,465	63
Current Charges	21,452	208
Liquor Store	0	0
Utility	14,067	136
Employee Retirement	2,140	21

Source: U.S Census Bureau, State & Local Government Finances 2012

City Government Expenditures by Function

Function	2012 ($000)	2012 ($ per capita)	2012 (%)
General Direct Expenditures			
Air Transportation	0	0	0.0
Corrections	0	0	0.0
Education	0	0	0.0
Employment Security Administration	0	0	0.0
Financial Administration	3,690	36	3.4
Fire Protection	13,152	127	12.0
General Public Buildings	0	0	0.0
Governmental Administration, Other	4,562	44	4.2
Health	0	0	0.0
Highways	9,950	96	9.1
Hospitals	0	0	0.0
Housing and Community Development	3,797	37	3.5
Interest on General Debt	4,518	44	4.1
Judicial and Legal	965	9	0.9
Libraries	0	0	0.0
Parking	0	0	0.0
Parks and Recreation	3,494	34	3.2
Police Protection	20,523	199	18.7
Public Welfare	0	0	0.0
Sewerage	11,915	115	10.8
Solid Waste Management	6,571	64	6.0
Veterans' Services	0	0	0.0
Liquor Store	0	0	0.0
Utility	9,809	95	8.9
Employee Retirement	3,692	36	3.4

Source: U.S Census Bureau, State & Local Government Finances 2012

DEMOGRAPHICS

Population Growth

Area	1990 Census	2000 Census	2010 Census	Population Growth (%) 1990-2000	Population Growth (%) 2000-2010
City	62,587	79,413	103,190	26.9	29.9
MSA[1]	398,978	476,230	543,376	19.4	14.1
U.S.	248,709,873	281,421,906	308,745,538	13.2	9.7

Note: (1) Figures cover the Palm Bay-Melbourne-Titusville, FL Metropolitan Statistical Area—see Appendix B for areas included
Source: U.S. Census Bureau, Census 1990, 2000, 2010

Household Size

Area	Persons in Household (%)							Average Household Size
	One	Two	Three	Four	Five	Six	Seven or More	
City	26.4	37.5	16.2	10.2	5.8	2.0	1.9	2.76
MSA[1]	30.5	39.9	13.4	10.0	4.1	1.1	1.0	2.48
U.S.	27.7	33.6	15.7	13.1	6.0	2.3	1.5	2.64

Note: (1) Figures cover the Palm Bay-Melbourne-Titusville, FL Metropolitan Statistical Area—see Appendix B for areas included
Source: U.S. Census Bureau, 2011-2013 American Community Survey 3-Year Estimates

Race

Area	White Alone[2] (%)	Black Alone[2] (%)	Asian Alone[2] (%)	AIAN[3] Alone[2] (%)	NHOPI[4] Alone[2] (%)	Other Race Alone[2] (%)	Two or More Races (%)
City	75.3	17.6	1.4	0.5	0.0	2.0	3.3
MSA[1]	83.4	10.2	2.1	0.2	0.1	1.3	2.6
U.S.	73.9	12.6	5.0	0.8	0.2	4.7	2.9

Note: (1) Figures cover the Palm Bay-Melbourne-Titusville, FL Metropolitan Statistical Area—see Appendix B for areas included; (2) Alone is defined as not being in combination with one or more other races; (3) American Indian and Alaska Native; (4) Native Hawaiian and Other Pacific Islander
Source: U.S. Census Bureau, 2011-2013 American Community Survey 3-Year Estimates

Hispanic or Latino Origin

Area	Total (%)	Mexican (%)	Puerto Rican (%)	Cuban (%)	Other (%)
City	13.6	1.2	6.9	1.6	3.8
MSA[1]	8.7	1.5	3.4	1.1	2.7
U.S.	16.9	10.8	1.6	0.6	3.8

Note: Persons of Hispanic or Latino origin can be of any race; (1) Figures cover the Palm Bay-Melbourne-Titusville, FL Metropolitan Statistical Area—see Appendix B for areas included
Source: U.S. Census Bureau, 2011-2013 American Community Survey 3-Year Estimates

Segregation

Type	Segregation Indices[1]				Percent Change		
	1990	2000	2010	2010 Rank[2]	1990-2000	1990-2010	2000-2010
Black/White	52.6	48.9	47.2	79	-3.7	-5.4	-1.8
Asian/White	22.8	21.0	20.6	101	-1.8	-2.1	-0.3
Hispanic/White	19.7	22.6	25.0	101	2.9	5.3	2.4

Note: All figures cover the Metropolitan Statistical Area—see Appendix B for areas included; Figures are based on an analysis of 1990, 2000, and 2010 Census Decennial Census tract data by William H. Frey, Brookings Institution and the University of Michigan Social Science Data Analysis Network. In this analysis all racial groups (whites, blacks, and asians) are non-Hispanic members of those races. Hispanics are shown as a separate category;
(1) Segregation Indices are Dissimilarity Indices that measure the degree to which the minority group is distributed differently than whites across census tracts. They range from 0 (complete integration) to 100 (complete segregation) where the value indicates the percentage of the minority group that needs to move to be distributed exactly like whites; (2) Ranges from 1 (most segregated) to 102 (least segregated); n/a not available.
Source: www.CensusScope.org

Ancestry

Area	German	Irish	English	American	Italian	Polish	French[2]	Scottish	Dutch
City	14.2	12.1	10.9	12.1	8.7	3.2	3.3	1.9	1.1
MSA[1]	15.8	14.0	11.1	11.9	8.5	3.3	3.4	2.4	1.7
U.S.	14.9	10.8	8.0	7.4	5.5	3.0	2.7	1.7	1.4

Note: Figures are the percentage of the total population reporting a particular ancestry. The nine most commonly reported ancestries in the U.S. are shown. Figures include multiple ancestries (e.g. if a person reported being Irish and Italian, they were included in both columns); (1) Figures cover the Palm Bay-Melbourne-Titusville, FL Metropolitan Statistical Area—see Appendix B for areas included; (2) Excludes Basque

Source: U.S. Census Bureau, 2011-2013 American Community Survey 3-Year Estimates

Foreign-Born Population

Area	Percent of Population Born in								
	Any Foreign Country	Mexico	Asia	Europe	Carribean	South America	Central America[2]	Africa	Canada
City	n/a	n/a	n/a	n/a	n/a	n/a	n/a	n/a	n/a
MSA[1]	8.6	0.5	1.8	1.9	2.2	0.9	0.6	0.2	0.6
U.S.	13.0	3.7	3.8	1.5	1.2	0.9	1.0	0.6	0.3

Note: (1) Figures cover the Palm Bay-Melbourne-Titusville, FL Metropolitan Statistical Area—see Appendix B for areas included; (2) Excludes Mexico.

Source: U.S. Census Bureau, 2011-2013 American Community Survey 3-Year Estimates

Marital Status

Area	Never Married	Now Married[2]	Separated	Widowed	Divorced
City	27.2	47.5	3.1	8.3	13.9
MSA[1]	26.6	48.0	2.3	8.6	14.5
U.S.	32.7	48.1	2.2	6.0	11.0

Note: Figures are percentages and cover the population 15 years of age and older; (1) Figures cover the Palm Bay-Melbourne-Titusville, FL Metropolitan Statistical Area—see Appendix B for areas included; (2) Excludes separated

Source: U.S. Census Bureau, 2011-2013 American Community Survey 3-Year Estimates

Disability Status

Area	All Ages	Under 18 Years Old	18 to 64 Years Old	65 Years and Over
City	14.5	3.5	12.3	38.2
MSA[1]	15.3	3.9	12.0	34.7
U.S.	12.3	4.1	10.2	36.3

Note: Figures show percent of the civilian noninstitutionalized population that reported having a disability. Disability status is determined from from six types of difficulty: vision, hearing, cognitive, ambulatory, self-care, and independent living. For children under 5 years old, hearing and vision difficulty are used to determine disability status. For children between the ages of 5 and 14, disability status is determined from hearing, vision, cognitive, ambulatory, and self-care difficulties. For people aged 15 years and older, they are considered to have a disability if they have difficulty with any one of the six difficulty types; (1) Figures cover the Palm Bay-Melbourne-Titusville, FL Metropolitan Statistical Area—see Appendix B for areas included.

Source: U.S. Census Bureau, 2011-2013 American Community Survey 3-Year Estimates

Age

Area	Percent of Population									Median Age
	Under Age 5	Age 5–19	Age 20–34	Age 35–44	Age 45–54	Age 55–64	Age 65–74	Age 75–84	Age 85+	
City	5.9	19.4	17.0	11.1	16.3	13.7	9.3	5.2	2.1	41.8
MSA[1]	4.8	16.6	16.1	10.7	15.8	14.6	11.3	7.5	2.7	46.4
U.S.	6.4	19.9	20.7	12.9	14.1	12.3	7.6	4.2	1.9	37.4

Note: (1) Figures cover the Palm Bay-Melbourne-Titusville, FL Metropolitan Statistical Area—see Appendix B for areas included

Source: U.S. Census Bureau, 2011-2013 American Community Survey 3-Year Estimates

Gender

Area	Males	Females	Males per 100 Females
City	47,695	56,485	84.4
MSA[1]	267,572	279,831	95.6
U.S.	154,451,010	159,410,713	96.9

Note: (1) Figures cover the Palm Bay-Melbourne-Titusville, FL Metropolitan Statistical Area—see Appendix B for areas included
Source: U.S. Census Bureau, 2011-2013 American Community Survey 3-Year Estimates

Religious Groups by Family

Area	Catholic	Baptist	Non-Den.	Methodist[2]	Lutheran	LDS[3]	Pente-costal	Presby-terian[4]	Muslim[5]	Judaism
MSA[1]	11.9	6.5	5.3	4.0	1.2	1.0	1.0	1.3	0.8	0.1
U.S.	19.1	9.3	4.0	4.0	2.3	2.0	1.9	1.6	0.8	0.7

Note: Figures are the number of adherents as a percentage of the total population; (1) Figures cover the Palm Bay-Melbourne-Titusville, FL Metropolitan Statistical Area—see Appendix B for areas included; (2) Methodist/Pietist; (3) Latter Day Saints; (4) Reformed; (5) Figures are estimates
Source: Association of Statisticians of American Religious Bodies, 2010 U.S. Religion Census: Religious Congregations & Membership Study

Religious Groups by Tradition

Area	Catholic	Evangelical Protestant	Mainline Protestant	Other Tradition	Black Protestant	Orthodox
MSA[1]	11.9	14.0	5.7	2.0	1.0	0.2
U.S.	19.1	16.2	7.3	4.3	1.6	0.3

Note: Figures are the number of adherents as a percentage of the total population; (1) Figures cover the Palm Bay-Melbourne-Titusville, FL Metropolitan Statistical Area—see Appendix B for areas included
Source: Association of Statisticians of American Religious Bodies, 2010 U.S. Religion Census: Religious Congregations & Membership Study

ECONOMY

Gross Metropolitan Product

Area	2012	2013	2014	2015	Rank[2]
MSA[1]	18.1	18.5	19.1	20.2	118

Note: Figures are in billions of dollars; (1) Figures cover the Palm Bay-Melbourne-Titusville, FL Metropolitan Statistical Area—see Appendix B for areas included; (2) Rank is based on 2015 data and ranges from 1 to 363
Source: The U.S. Conference of Mayors, U.S. Metro Economies: GMP and Employment 2013-2015, June 2014

Economic Growth

Area	2010-12 (%)	2013 (%)	2014 (%)	2015 (%)	Rank[2]
MSA[1]	-1.7	0.7	1.8	3.6	61
U.S.	2.1	2.0	2.3	3.2	–

Note: Figures are real gross metropolitan product (GMP) growth rates and represent annual average percent change; (1) Figures cover the Palm Bay-Melbourne-Titusville, FL Metropolitan Statistical Area—see Appendix B for areas included; (2) Rank is based on 2015 data and ranges from 1 to 363
Source: The U.S. Conference of Mayors, U.S. Metro Economies: GMP and Employment 2013-2015, June 2014

Metropolitan Area Exports

Area	2008	2009	2010	2011	2012	2013	Rank[2]
MSA[1]	782.6	555.5	858.3	1,162.8	982.3	984.3	158

Note: Figures are in millions of dollars; (1) Figures cover the Palm Bay-Melbourne-Titusville, FL Metropolitan Statistical Area—see Appendix B for areas included; (2) Rank is based on 2013 data and ranges from 1 to 387
Source: U.S. Department of Commerce, International Trade Administration, Office of Trade & Industry Information, Manufacturing & Services, data extracted April 3, 2015

Building Permits

Area	Single-Family			Multi-Family			Total		
	2013	2014	Pct. Chg.	2013	2014	Pct. Chg.	2013	2014	Pct. Chg.
City	157	162	3.2	0	0	-	157	162	3.2
MSA[1]	1,349	1,241	-8.0	24	45	87.5	1,373	1,286	-6.3
U.S.	620,802	634,597	2.2	370,020	411,766	11.3	990,822	1,046,363	5.6

Note: (1) Figures cover the Palm Bay-Melbourne-Titusville, FL Metropolitan Statistical Area—see Appendix B for areas included; Figures represent new, privately-owned housing units authorized (unadjusted data); All permit data are based on estimates with imputation.
Source: U.S. Census Bureau, Manufacturing, Mining, and Construction Statistics, Building Permits, 2013, 2014

Bankruptcy Filings

Area	Business Filings			Nonbusiness Filings		
	2013	2014	% Chg.	2013	2014	% Chg.
Brevard County	58	49	-15.5	1,992	1,581	-20.6
U.S.	33,212	26,983	-18.8	1,038,720	909,812	-12.4

Note: Business filings include Chapter 7, Chapter 11, Chapter 12, and Chapter 13; Nonbusiness filings include Chapter 7, Chapter 11, and Chapter 13
Source: Administrative Office of the U.S. Courts, Business and Nonbusiness Bankruptcy, County Cases Commenced by Chapter of the Bankruptcy Code, During the 12- Month Period Ending December 31, 2013 and Business and Nonbusiness Bankruptcy, County Cases Commenced by Chapter of the Bankruptcy Code, During the 12- Month Period Ending December 31, 2014

Housing Vacancy Rates

Area	Gross Vacancy Rate[2] (%)			Year-Round Vacancy Rate[3] (%)			Rental Vacancy Rate[4] (%)			Homeowner Vacancy Rate[5] (%)		
	2012	2013	2014	2012	2013	2014	2012	2013	2014	2012	2013	2014
MSA[1]	n/a	n/a	n/a	n/a	n/a	n/a	n/a	n/a	n/a	n/a	n/a	n/a
U.S.	13.8	13.6	13.4	10.8	10.7	10.4	8.7	8.3	7.6	2.0	2.0	1.9

Note: (1) Figures cover the Palm Bay-Melbourne-Titusville, FL Metropolitan Statistical Area—see Appendix B for areas included; (2) The percentage of the total housing inventory that is vacant; (3) The percentage of the housing inventory (excluding seasonal units) that is year-round vacant; (4) The percentage of rental inventory that is vacant for rent; (5) The percentage of homeowner inventory that is vacant for sale; n/a not available
Source: U.S. Census Bureau, Housing Vacancies and Homeownership Annual Statistics: 2014

INCOME

Income

Area	Per Capita ($)	Median Household ($)	Average Household ($)
City	20,122	41,540	51,765
MSA[1]	26,305	47,076	62,678
U.S.	27,884	52,176	72,897

Note: (1) Figures cover the Palm Bay-Melbourne-Titusville, FL Metropolitan Statistical Area—see Appendix B for areas included
Source: U.S. Census Bureau, 2011-2013 American Community Survey 3-Year Estimates

Household Income Distribution

Area	Percent of Households Earning							
	Under $15,000	$15,000 -24,999	$25,000 -34,999	$35,000 -49,999	$50,000 -74,999	$75,000 -99,000	$100,000 -149,999	$150,000 and up
City	13.6	14.1	14.4	15.6	20.6	11.4	7.6	2.6
MSA[1]	12.9	11.8	12.3	15.6	19.0	11.1	11.1	6.2
U.S.	13.0	10.9	10.3	13.6	17.9	11.9	12.7	9.6

Note: (1) Figures cover the Palm Bay-Melbourne-Titusville, FL Metropolitan Statistical Area—see Appendix B for areas included
Source: U.S. Census Bureau, 2011-2013 American Community Survey 3-Year Estimates

Poverty Rate

Area	All Ages	Under 18 Years Old	18 to 64 Years Old	65 Years and Over
City	19.3	32.6	17.6	7.2
MSA[1]	14.6	22.8	14.5	7.4
U.S.	15.9	22.4	14.8	9.5

Note: Figures are percentage of people whose income during the past 12 months was below the poverty level; (1) Figures cover the Palm Bay-Melbourne-Titusville, FL Metropolitan Statistical Area—see Appendix B for areas included
Source: U.S. Census Bureau, 2011-2013 American Community Survey 3-Year Estimates

EMPLOYMENT

Labor Force and Employment

Area	Civilian Labor Force			Workers Employed		
	Dec. 2013	Dec. 2014	% Chg.	Dec. 2013	Dec. 2014	% Chg.
City	49,117	49,484	0.7	45,486	46,412	2.0
MSA[1]	254,921	256,415	0.6	236,334	241,147	2.0
U.S.	154,408,000	155,521,000	0.7	144,423,000	147,190,000	1.9

Note: Data is not seasonally adjusted and covers workers 16 years of age and older; (1) Figures cover the Palm Bay-Melbourne-Titusville, FL Metropolitan Statistical Area—see Appendix B for areas included
Source: Bureau of Labor Statistics, Local Area Unemployment Statistics

Unemployment Rate

Area	2014											
	Jan.	Feb.	Mar.	Apr.	May	Jun.	Jul.	Aug.	Sep.	Oct.	Nov.	Dec.
City	7.8	7.8	7.9	7.4	7.5	7.7	7.8	7.5	6.9	6.7	6.9	6.2
MSA[1]	7.6	7.5	7.4	6.7	7.0	7.0	7.3	7.3	6.7	6.4	6.4	6.0
U.S.	7.0	7.0	6.8	5.9	6.1	6.3	6.5	6.3	5.7	5.5	5.5	5.4

Note: Data is not seasonally adjusted and covers workers 16 years of age and older; (1) Figures cover the Palm Bay-Melbourne-Titusville, FL Metropolitan Statistical Area—see Appendix B for areas included
Source: Bureau of Labor Statistics, Local Area Unemployment Statistics

Employment by Occupation

Occupation Classification	City (%)	MSA[1] (%)	U.S. (%)
Management, Business, Science, and Arts	26.3	34.8	36.2
Natural Resources, Construction, and Maintenance	8.8	8.8	9.0
Production, Transportation, and Material Moving	13.2	9.6	12.1
Sales and Office	28.8	26.6	24.4
Service	22.9	20.3	18.3

Note: Figures cover employed civilians 16 years of age and older; (1) Figures cover the Palm Bay-Melbourne-Titusville, FL Metropolitan Statistical Area—see Appendix B for areas included
Source: U.S. Census Bureau, 2011-2013 American Community Survey 3-Year Estimates

Employment by Industry

Sector	MSA[1] Number of Employees	MSA[1] Percent of Total	U.S. Percent of Total
Construction, Mining, and Logging	10,100	5.0	5.0
Education and Health Services	33,800	16.8	15.5
Financial Activities	7,500	3.7	5.7
Government	28,600	14.2	15.8
Information	1,900	0.9	2.0
Leisure and Hospitality	24,600	12.2	10.3
Manufacturing	20,100	10.0	8.7
Other Services	8,100	4.0	4.0
Professional and Business Services	30,200	15.0	13.8
Retail Trade	27,100	13.5	11.4
Transportation, Warehousing, and Utilities	3,500	1.7	3.9
Wholesale Trade	5,500	2.7	4.2

Note: Figures are non-farm employment as of December 2014. Figures are not seasonally adjusted and include workers 16 years of age and older; (1) Figures cover the Palm Bay-Melbourne-Titusville, FL Metropolitan Statistical Area—see Appendix B for areas included; n/a not available
Source: Bureau of Labor Statistics, Current Employment Statistics, Employment, Hours, and Earnings

Occupations with Greatest Projected Employment Growth: 2012 – 2022

Occupation[1]	2012 Employment	2022 Projected Employment	Numeric Employment Change	Percent Employment Change
Retail Salespersons	326,380	380,120	53,740	16.5
Combined Food Preparation and Serving Workers, Including Fast Food	196,980	237,340	40,360	20.5
Customer Service Representatives	191,210	228,620	37,410	19.6
Registered Nurses	164,020	201,140	37,120	22.6
Waiters and Waitresses	191,370	227,810	36,440	19.0
Office Clerks, General	142,710	170,300	27,590	19.3
Cashiers	206,660	230,190	23,530	11.4
Landscaping and Groundskeeping Workers	92,510	115,540	23,030	24.9
Receptionists and Information Clerks	75,780	95,680	19,900	26.2
Nursing Assistants	86,990	106,200	19,210	22.1

Note: Projections cover Florida; (1) Sorted by numeric employment change
Source: www.projectionscentral.com, State Occupational Projections, 2012–2022 Long-Term Projections

Fastest Growing Occupations: 2012 – 2022

Occupation[1]	2012 Employment	2022 Projected Employment	Numeric Employment Change	Percent Employment Change
Helpers—Carpenters	1,280	2,450	1,170	90.7
Helpers—Brickmasons, Blockmasons, Stonemasons, and Tile and Marble Setters	1,050	1,890	840	79.5
Biomedical Engineers	760	1,300	540	70.7
Reinforcing Iron and Rebar Workers	520	870	350	67.5
Glaziers	2,890	4,710	1,820	62.8
Solar Photovoltaic Installers	170	270	100	58.7
Brickmasons and Blockmasons	2,820	4,430	1,610	57.1
Stonemasons	450	710	260	56.4
Helpers—Pipelayers, Plumbers, Pipefitters, and Steamfitters	2,420	3,750	1,330	54.8
Cement Masons and Concrete Finishers	10,390	16,050	5,660	54.4

Note: Projections cover Florida; (1) Sorted by percent employment change and excludes occupations with numeric employment change less than 100
Source: www.projectionscentral.com, State Occupational Projections, 2012–2022 Long-Term Projections

Average Wages

Occupation	$/Hr.	Occupation	$/Hr.
Accountants and Auditors	31.02	Maids and Housekeeping Cleaners	10.32
Automotive Mechanics	17.49	Maintenance and Repair Workers	16.43
Bookkeepers	16.28	Marketing Managers	60.20
Carpenters	15.44	Nuclear Medicine Technologists	32.09
Cashiers	9.52	Nurses, Licensed Practical	20.37
Clerks, General Office	14.05	Nurses, Registered	29.36
Clerks, Receptionists/Information	13.21	Nursing Assistants	11.54
Clerks, Shipping/Receiving	13.03	Packers and Packagers, Hand	9.56
Computer Programmers	44.22	Physical Therapists	42.97
Computer Systems Analysts	36.29	Postal Service Mail Carriers	24.96
Computer User Support Specialists	24.22	Real Estate Brokers	25.52
Cooks, Restaurant	10.53	Retail Salespersons	12.10
Dentists	67.43	Sales Reps., Exc. Tech./Scientific	25.05
Electrical Engineers	41.57	Sales Reps., Tech./Scientific	39.33
Electricians	19.63	Secretaries, Exc. Legal/Med./Exec.	14.49
Financial Managers	58.11	Security Guards	11.97
First-Line Supervisors/Managers, Sales	19.96	Surgeons	112.98
Food Preparation Workers	10.24	Teacher Assistants	11.60
General and Operations Managers	56.20	Teachers, Elementary School	21.10
Hairdressers/Cosmetologists	13.29	Teachers, Secondary School	21.50
Internists	n/a	Telemarketers	10.27
Janitors and Cleaners	11.28	Truck Drivers, Heavy/Tractor-Trailer	16.39
Landscaping/Groundskeeping Workers	11.76	Truck Drivers, Light/Delivery Svcs.	14.19
Lawyers	47.11	Waiters and Waitresses	10.45

Note: Wage data covers the Palm Bay-Melbourne-Titusville, FL Metropolitan Statistical Area—see Appendix B for areas included; Hourly wages for elementary/secondary school teachers and teacher assistants were calculated by the editors from annual wage data assuming a 40 hour work week; n/a not available.
Source: Bureau of Labor Statistics, Metro Area Occupational Employment and Wage Estimates, May 2014

TAXES

State Corporate Income Tax Rates

State	Tax Rate (%)	Income Brackets ($)	Num. of Brackets	Financial Institution Tax Rate (%)[a]	Federal Income Tax Ded.
Florida	5.5 (f)	Flat rate	1	5.5 (f)	No

Note: Tax rates as of January 1, 2015; (a) Rates listed are the corporate income tax rate applied to financial institutions or excise taxes based on income. Some states have other taxes based upon the value of deposits or shares; (f) An exemption of $50,000 is allowed. Florida's Alternative Minimum Tax rate is 3.3%.
Source: Federation of Tax Administrators, "State Corporate Income Tax Rates, 2015"

State Individual Income Tax Rates

State	Tax Rate (%)	Income Brackets ($)	Num. of Brackets	Personal Exempt. ($)[1]		Fed. Inc. Tax Ded.
				Single	Dependents	
Florida	None	–	–	–	–	–

Note: Tax rates as of January 1, 2015; Local- and county-level taxes are not included; n/a not applicable; (1) Married joint filers generally receive double the single exemption
Source: Federation of Tax Administrators, "State Individual Income Tax Rates, 2015"

Various State and Local Tax Rates

State	State and Local Sales and Use (%)	State Sales and Use (%)	Gasoline[1] (¢/gal.)	Cigarette[2] ($/pack)	Spirits[3] ($/gal.)	Wine[4] ($/gal.)	Beer[5] ($/gal.)
Florida	6.5	6.0	36.42	1.339	6.50 (f)	2.25	0.48 (p)

Note: All tax rates as of January 1, 2015; (1) The American Petroleum Institute has developed a methodology for determining the average tax rate on a gallon of fuel. Rates may include any of the following: excise taxes, environmental fees, storage tank fees, other fees or taxes, general sales tax, and local taxes. In states where gasoline is subject to the general sales tax, or where the fuel tax is based on the average sale price, the average rate determined by API is sensitive to changes in the price of gasoline. States that fully or partially apply general sales taxes to gasoline: CA, CO, GA, IL, IN, MI, NY; (2) The federal excise tax of $1.0066 per pack and local taxes are not included; (3) Rates are those applicable to off-premise sales of 40% alcohol by volume (a.b.v.) distilled spirits in 750ml containers. Local excise taxes are excluded; (4) Rates are those applicable to off-premise sales of 11% a.b.v. non-carbonated wine in 750ml containers; (5) Rates are those applicable to off-premise sales of 4.7% a.b.v. beer in 12 ounce containers; (f) Different rates are also applicable according to alcohol content, place of production, size of container, or place purchased (on- or off-premise or onboard airlines); (p) Local excise taxes are excluded.
Source: Tax Foundation, 2015 Facts & Figures: How Does Your State Compare?

State Business Tax Climate Index Rankings

State	Overall Rank	Corporate Tax Index Rank	Individual Income Tax Index Rank	Sales Tax Index Rank	Unemployment Insurance Tax Index Rank	Property Tax Index Rank
Florida	5	14	1	12	3	16

Note: The index is a measure of how each state's tax laws affect economic performance. The lower the rank, the more favorable a state's tax system is for business. States without a given tax are given a ranking of 1. The scores/rankings for the District of Columbia do not affect other states. The 2015 index represents the tax climate as of July 1, 2014.
Source: Tax Foundation, State Business Tax Climate Index 2015

COMMERCIAL UTILITIES

Typical Monthly Electric Bills

Area	Commercial Service ($/month)		Industrial Service ($/month)	
	1,500 kWh	40 kW demand 14,000 kWh	1,000 kW demand 200,000 kWh	50,000 kW demand 32,500,000 kWh
City	156	1,255	27,158	1,691,463
Average[1]	201	1,653	26,124	2,639,743

Note: Figures are based on annualized 2014 rates; (1) Average based on 180 utilities surveyed
Source: Edison Electric Institute, Typical Bills and Average Rates Report, Summer 2014

TRANSPORTATION

Means of Transportation to Work

Area	Car/Truck/Van		Public Transportation			Bicycle	Walked	Other Means	Worked at Home
	Drove Alone	Car-pooled	Bus	Subway	Railroad				
City	83.6	10.5	0.2	0.1	0.0	0.7	1.2	1.4	2.4
MSA[1]	82.7	8.5	0.6	0.0	0.0	0.6	1.1	1.9	4.6
U.S.	76.4	9.6	2.6	1.8	0.6	0.6	2.8	1.3	4.3

Note: Figures are percentages and cover workers 16 years of age and older; (1) Figures cover the Palm Bay-Melbourne-Titusville, FL Metropolitan Statistical Area—see Appendix B for areas included
Source: U.S. Census Bureau, 2011-2013 American Community Survey 3-Year Estimates

Travel Time to Work

Area	Less Than 10 Minutes	10 to 19 Minutes	20 to 29 Minutes	30 to 44 Minutes	45 to 59 Minutes	60 to 89 Minutes	90 Minutes or More
City	7.4	26.9	30.4	22.9	5.4	3.9	3.2
MSA[1]	12.5	32.3	24.9	18.8	5.5	3.8	2.3
U.S.	13.3	29.7	20.9	20.2	7.7	5.7	2.6

Note: Figures are percentages and include workers 16 years old and over; (1) Figures cover the Palm Bay-Melbourne-Titusville, FL Metropolitan Statistical Area—see Appendix B for areas included
Source: U.S. Census Bureau, 2011-2013 American Community Survey 3-Year Estimates

Travel Time Index

Area	1985	1990	1995	2000	2005	2010	2011
Urban Area[1]	n/a	n/a	n/a	n/a	n/a	n/a	n/a
Average[2]	1.09	1.14	1.16	1.19	1.23	1.18	1.18

Note: Travel Time Index—the ratio of travel time in the peak period to the travel time at free-flow conditions. For example, a value of 1.30 indicates a 20-minute free-flow trip takes 26 minutes in the peak. Free-flow speeds (60 mph on freeways and 35 mph on principal arterials) are used as the comparison threshold; (1) Data for the Palm Bay-Melbourne-Titusville, FL urban area was not available; (2) average of 498 urban areas

Source: Texas Transportation Institute, Urban Mobility Report 2012, December 2012

Public Transportation

Agency Name / Mode of Transportation	Vehicles Operated in Maximum Service	Annual Unlinked Passenger Trips (in thous.)	Annual Passenger Miles (in thous.)
Space Coast Area Transit (SCAT)			
Bus (directly operated)	24	2,284.8	13,264.4
Demand Response (directly operated)	33	124.8	1,411.4
Demand Response (purchased transportation)	59	316.2	4,036.9
Vanpool (purchased transportation)	50	157.5	7,189.3

Source: Federal Transit Administration, National Transit Database, 2013

Air Transportation

Airport Name and Code / Type of Service	Passenger Airlines[1]	Passenger Enplanements	Freight Carriers[2]	Freight (lbs.)
Melbourne International Airport (MLB)				
Domestic service (U.S. carriers - 2014)	6	214,688	2	175,650
International service (U.S. carriers - 2013)	1	56	1	1

Note: (1) Includes all U.S.-based major, minor and commuter airlines that carried at least one passenger during the year; (2) Includes all U.S.-based airlines and freight carriers that transported at least one lb. of freight during the year.

Source: Bureau of Transportation Statistics, The Intermodal Transportation Database, Air Carriers: T-100 Domestic Market (U.S. Carriers), 2014; Bureau of Transportation Statistics, The Intermodal Transportation Database, Air Carriers: T-100 International Market (U.S. Carriers), 2013

Other Transportation Statistics

Major Highways:	I-95
Amtrak Service:	No
Major Waterways/Ports:	Atlantic Ocean

Source: Amtrak.com; Google Maps

BUSINESSES

Major Business Headquarters

Company Name	Rankings	
	Fortune[1]	Forbes[2]
No companies listed	-	-

Note: (1) Fortune 500—companies that produce a 10-K are ranked 1 to 500 based on 2013 revenue; (2) all private companies with at least $2 billion in annual revenue through the end of their most current fiscal year are ranked 1 to 221; companies listed are headquartered in the city; dashes indicate no ranking

Source: Fortune, "Fortune 500," June 16, 2014; Forbes, "America's Largest Private Companies," November 5, 2014

Minority- and Women-Owned Businesses

Group	All Firms		Firms with Paid Employees			
	Firms	Sales ($000)	Firms	Sales ($000)	Employees	Payroll ($000)
Asian	202	21,182	(s)	(s)	(s)	(s)
Black	1,174	28,688	(s)	(s)	(s)	(s)
Hispanic	1,016	38,265	37	13,623	135	3,216
Women	2,672	92,912	230	52,688	854	16,453
All Firms	8,020	4,796,196	1,468	4,604,189	24,130	936,577

Note: Figures cover firms located in the city; minority- and women-owned business are defined as firms in which the corresponding group own 51% or more of the stock or equity of the company; (s) estimates are suppressed when publication standards are not met
Source: U.S. Census Bureau, 2007 Economic Census, Survey of Business Owners (2012 Survey of Business Owners data will be released starting in June 2015)

HOTELS & CONVENTION CENTERS

Hotels/Motels

Area	5 Star		4 Star		3 Star		2 Star		1 Star		Not Rated	
	Num.	Pct.[3]	Num.	Pct.[3]	Num.	Pct.[3]	Num.	Pct.[3]	Num.	Pct.[3]	Num.	Pct.[3]
City[1]	0	0.0	0	0.0	14	25.5	29	52.7	0	0.0	12	21.8
Total[2]	166	0.9	1,264	7.0	5,718	31.8	9,340	52.0	411	2.3	1,070	6.0

Note: (1) Figures cover Palm Bay and vicinity; (2) Figures cover all 100 cities in this book; (3) Percentage of hotels which have a given star rating; Star ratings are determined by expedia.com and offer an indication of the general quality of a particular hotel.
Source: expedia.com, April 2, 2015

Major Convention Centers

Name	Overall Space (sq. ft.)	Exhibit Space (sq. ft.)	Meeting Space (sq. ft.)	Meeting Rooms
Eau Gallie Civic Center (Melbourne)	16,000	n/a	8,000	2

Note: Table includes convention centers located in the Palm Bay-Melbourne-Titusville, FL metro area; n/a not available
Source: Original research

Living Environment

COST OF LIVING

Cost of Living Index

Composite Index	Groceries	Housing	Utilities	Transportation	Health Care	Misc. Goods/Services
n/a	n/a	n/a	n/a	n/a	n/a	n/a

Note: The Cost of Living Index measures regional differences in the cost of consumer goods and services, excluding taxes and non-consumer expenditures, for professional and managerial households in the top income quintile. It is based on more than 50,000 prices covering almost 60 different items for which prices are collected three times a year by chambers of commerce, economic development organizations or university applied economic centers in each participating urban area. The numbers shown should be read as a percentage above or below the national average of 100. For example, a value of 115.4 in the groceries column indicates that grocery prices are 15.4% higher than the national average. Small differences in the index numbers should not be interpreted as significant; n/a not available.
Source: The Council for Community and Economic Research, ACCRA Cost of Living Index, 2014

Grocery Prices

Area[1]	T-Bone Steak ($/pound)	Frying Chicken ($/pound)	Whole Milk ($/half gal.)	Eggs ($/dozen)	Orange Juice ($/64 oz.)	Coffee ($/11.5 oz.)
City[2]	n/a	n/a	n/a	n/a	n/a	n/a
Avg.	10.40	1.37	2.40	1.99	3.46	4.27
Min.	8.48	0.93	1.37	1.30	2.83	2.99
Max.	14.20	2.44	3.62	4.02	6.42	6.96

Note: (1) Values for the local area are compared with the average, minimum and maximum values for all 308 areas in the Cost of Living Index; (2) Figures cover the urban area; n/a not available; **T-Bone Steak** *(price per pound);* **Frying Chicken** *(price per pound, whole fryer);* **Whole Milk** *(half gallon carton);* **Eggs** *(price per dozen, Grade A, large);* **Orange Juice** *(64 oz. Tropicana or Florida Natural);* **Coffee** *(11.5 oz. can, vacuum-packed, Maxwell House, Hills Bros, or Folgers).*
Source: The Council for Community and Economic Research, ACCRA Cost of Living Index, 2014

Housing and Utility Costs

Area[1]	New Home Price ($)	Apartment Rent ($/month)	All Electric ($/month)	Part Electric ($/month)	Other Energy ($/month)	Telephone ($/month)
City[2]	n/a	n/a	n/a	n/a	n/a	n/a
Avg.	305,838	919	181.00	93.66	73.14	27.95
Min.	183,142	480	112.00	42.06	23.42	17.16
Max.	1,358,576	3,851	594.00	180.03	440.99	40.42

Note: (1) Values for the local area are compared with the average, minimum and maximum values for all 308 areas in the Cost of Living Index; (2) Figures cover the urban area; n/a not available; **New Home Price** *(2,400 sf living area, 8,000 sf lot, in urban area with full utilities);* **Apartment Rent** *(950 sf 2 bedroom/1.5 or 2 bath, unfurnished, excluding all utilities except water);* **All Electric** *(average monthly cost for an all-electric home);* **Part Electric** *(average monthly cost for a part-electric home);* **Other Energy** *(average monthly cost for natural gas, fuel oil, coal, wood, and any other forms of energy except electricity);* **Telephone** *(price includes basic monthly rate for a private residential line plus additional local usage charges incurred by a family of four).*
Source: The Council for Community and Economic Research, ACCRA Cost of Living Index, 2014

Health Care, Transportation, and Other Costs

Area[1]	Doctor ($/visit)	Dentist ($/visit)	Optometrist ($/visit)	Gasoline ($/gallon)	Beauty Salon ($/visit)	Men's Shirt ($)
City[2]	n/a	n/a	n/a	n/a	n/a	n/a
Avg.	102.86	87.89	97.66	3.44	34.37	26.74
Min.	67.47	65.78	51.18	3.00	17.43	12.79
Max.	173.50	150.14	235.00	4.33	64.28	49.50

Note: (1) Values for the local area are compared with the average, minimum and maximum values for all 308 areas in the Cost of Living Index; (2) Figures cover the urban area; n/a not available; **Doctor** *(general practitioners routine exam of an established patient);* **Dentist** *(adult teeth cleaning and periodic oral examination);* **Optometrist** *(full vision eye exam for established adult patient);* **Gasoline** *(one gallon regular unleaded, national brand, including all taxes, cash price at self-service pump if available);* **Beauty Salon** *(woman's shampoo, trim, and blow-dry);* **Men's Shirt** *(cotton/polyester dress shirt, pinpoint weave, long sleeves).*
Source: The Council for Community and Economic Research, ACCRA Cost of Living Index, 2014

HOUSING

House Price Index (HPI)

Area	National Ranking[2]	Quarterly Change (%)	One-Year Change (%)	Five-Year Change (%)
MSA[1]	43	3.61	8.69	7.88
U.S.[3]	–	1.35	4.91	11.59

Note: The HPI is a weighted repeat sales index. It measures average price changes in repeat sales or refinancings on the same properties. This information is obtained by reviewing repeat mortgage transactions on single-family properties whose mortgages have been purchased or securitized by Fannie Mae or Freddie Mac in January 1975; (1) Palm Bay-Melbourne-Titusville Metropolitan Statistical Area—see Appendix B for areas included; (2) Rankings are based on annual percentage change for all metro areas containing at least 15,000 transactions over the last 10 years and ranges from 1 to 275; (3) figures based on a weighted average of Census Division estimates using a seasonally adjusted, purchase-only index; all figures are for the period ending December 31, 2014

Source: Federal Housing Finance Agency, House Price Index, February 26, 2015

Median Single-Family Home Prices

Area	2012	2013	2014p	Percent Change 2013 to 2014
MSA[1]	116.5	126.2	137.6	9.0
U.S. Average	177.2	197.4	209.0	5.9

Note: Figures are median sales prices of existing single-family homes in thousands of dollars; (p) preliminary; n/a not available; (1) Palm Bay-Melbourne-Titusville, FL Metropolitan Statistical Area—see Appendix B for areas included

Source: National Association of Realtors, Median Sales Price of Existing Single-Family Homes for Metropolitan Areas, 4th Quarter 2014

Qualifying Income Based on Median Sales Price of Existing Single-Family Homes

Area	With 5% Down ($)	With 10% Down ($)	With 20% Down ($)
MSA[1]	30,546	28,938	25,723
U.S. Average	45,863	43,449	38,621

Note: Figures are preliminary; Qualifying income is based on a mortgage rate of 4.0%. Monthly principal and interest payment is limited to 25% of income; n/a not available; (1) Palm Bay-Melbourne-Titusville, FL Metropolitan Statistical Area—see Appendix B for areas included

Source: National Association of Realtors, Qualifying Income Based on Median Sales Price of Existing Single-Family Homes for Metropolitan Areas, 4th Quarter 2014

Median Apartment Condo-Coop Home Prices

Area	2012	2013	2014p	Percent Change 2013 to 2014
MSA[1]	106.9	108.7	120.8	11.1
U.S. Average	173.7	194.9	205.1	5.2

Note: Figures are median sales prices of existing apartment condo-coop homes in thousands of dollars; (p) preliminary; n/a not available; (1) Palm Bay-Melbourne-Titusville, FL Metropolitan Statistical Area—see Appendix B for areas included

Source: National Association of Realtors, Median Sales Price of Existing Apartment Condo-Coop Homes for Metropolitan Areas, 4th Quarter 2014

Gross Monthly Rent

Area	Under $200	$200 -299	$300 -499	$500 -749	$750 -999	$1,000 -1,499	$1,500 and up	Median ($)
City	0.3	0.3	1.1	23.8	40.3	30.8	3.4	888
MSA[1]	0.7	2.2	4.9	23.4	32.4	28.4	8.0	877
U.S.	1.7	3.2	7.8	22.1	24.3	26.0	14.9	900

Note: Figures are percentages except for Median; Gross rent is the contract rent plus the estimated average monthly cost of utilities (electricity, gas, and water and sewer) and fuels (oil, coal, kerosene, wood, etc.) if these are paid by the renter (or paid for the renter by someone else); (1) Figures cover the Palm Bay-Melbourne-Titusville, FL Metropolitan Statistical Area—see Appendix B for areas included

Source: U.S. Census Bureau, 2011-2013 American Community Survey 3-Year Estimates

Homeownership Rate

Area	2007 (%)	2008 (%)	2009 (%)	2010 (%)	2011 (%)	2012 (%)	2013 (%)	2014 (%)
MSA[1]	n/a	n/a	n/a	n/a	n/a	n/a	n/a	n/a
U.S.	68.1	67.8	67.4	66.9	66.1	65.4	65.1	64.5

Note: (1) Figures cover the Palm Bay-Melbourne-Titusville, FL Metropolitan Statistical Area—see Appendix B for areas included; n/a not available
Source: U.S. Census Bureau, Housing Vacancies and Homeownership Annual Statistics: 2014

Year Housing Structure Built

Area	2010 or Later	2000 -2009	1990 -1999	1980 -1989	1970 -1979	1960 -1969	1950 -1959	1940 -1949	Before 1940	Median Year
City	0.1	29.4	15.1	37.4	12.4	3.8	1.5	0.1	0.2	1989
MSA[1]	0.6	20.2	16.3	25.7	13.8	15.4	6.5	0.8	0.9	1985
U.S.	0.9	15.0	13.9	13.8	15.8	11.0	10.9	5.4	13.3	1976

Note: Figures are percentages except for Median Year; (1) Figures cover the Palm Bay-Melbourne-Titusville, FL Metropolitan Statistical Area—see Appendix B for areas included
Source: U.S. Census Bureau, 2011-2013 American Community Survey 3-Year Estimates

HEALTH

Health Risk Data

Category	MSA[1] (%)	U.S. (%)
Adults aged 18–64 who have any kind of health care coverage	n/a	79.6
Adults who reported being in good or excellent health	n/a	83.1
Adults who are current smokers	n/a	19.6
Adults who are heavy drinkers[2]	n/a	6.1
Adults who are binge drinkers[3]	n/a	16.9
Adults who are overweight (BMI 25.0 - 29.9)	n/a	35.8
Adults who are obese (BMI 30.0 - 99.8)	n/a	27.6
Adults who participated in any physical activities in the past month	n/a	77.1
Adults 50+ who have ever had a sigmoidoscopy or colonoscopy	n/a	67.3
Women aged 40+ who have had a mammogram within the past two years	n/a	74.0
Men aged 40+ who have had a PSA test within the past two years	n/a	45.2
Adults aged 65+ who have had flu shot within the past year	n/a	60.1
Adults who always wear a seatbelt	n/a	93.8

Note: Data as of 2012 unless otherwise noted; n/a not available; (1) Figures cover the Palm Bay-Melbourne-Titusville, FL Metropolitan Statistical Area—see Appendix B for areas included; (2) Heavy drinkers are classified as males having more than two drinks per day or females having more than one drink per day; (3) Binge drinkers are classified as males having five or more drinks on one occasion or females having four or more drinks on one occasion
Source: Centers for Disease Control and Prevention, Behaviorial Risk Factor Surveillance System, SMART: Selected Metropolitan/Micropolitan Area Risk Trends, 2012 (Note: the CDC has discontinued this dataset but will be releasing a replacement in late 2015)

Chronic Health Indicators

Category	MSA[1] (%)	U.S. (%)
Adults who have ever been told they had a heart attack	n/a	4.5
Adults who have ever been told they had a stroke	n/a	2.9
Adults who have been told they currently have asthma	n/a	8.9
Adults who have ever been told they have arthritis	n/a	25.7
Adults who have ever been told they have diabetes[2]	n/a	9.7
Adults who have ever been told they had skin cancer	n/a	5.7
Adults who have ever been told they had any other types of cancer	n/a	6.5
Adults who have ever been told they have COPD	n/a	6.2
Adults who have ever been told they have kidney disease	n/a	2.5
Adults who have ever been told they have a form of depression	n/a	18.0

Note: Data as of 2012 unless otherwise noted; n/a not available; (1) Figures cover the Palm Bay-Melbourne-Titusville, FL Metropolitan Statistical Area—see Appendix B for areas included; (2) Figures do not include pregnancy-related, borderline, or pre-diabetes
Source: Centers for Disease Control and Prevention, Behaviorial Risk Factor Surveillance System, SMART: Selected Metropolitan/Micropolitan Area Risk Trends, 2012 (Note: the CDC has discontinued this dataset but will be releasing a replacement in late 2015)

Mortality Rates for the Top 10 Causes of Death in the U.S.

ICD-10[a] Sub-Chapter	ICD-10[a] Code	Age-Adjusted Mortality Rate[1] per 100,000 population	
		County[2]	U.S.
Malignant neoplasms	C00-C97	181.4	166.2
Ischaemic heart diseases	I20-I25	108.3	105.7
Other forms of heart disease	I30-I51	39.5	49.3
Chronic lower respiratory diseases	J40-J47	44.1	42.1
Organic, including symptomatic, mental disorders	F01-F09	36.9	38.1
Cerebrovascular diseases	I60-I69	30.1	37.0
Other external causes of accidental injury	W00-X59	35.3	26.9
Other degenerative diseases of the nervous system	G30-G31	25.4	25.6
Diabetes mellitus	E10-E14	18.4	21.3
Hypertensive diseases	I10-I15	14.1	19.4

Note: (a) ICD-10 = International Classification of Diseases 10th Revision; (1) Mortality rates are a three year average covering 2011-2013; (2) Figures cover Brevard County
Source: Centers for Disease Control and Prevention, National Center for Health Statistics. Compressed Mortality File 1999-2013 on CDC WONDER Online Database, released October 2014. Data are compiled from the Compressed Mortality File 1999-2013, Series 20 No. 2S, 2014.

Mortality Rates for Selected Causes of Death

ICD-10[a] Sub-Chapter	ICD-10[a] Code	Age-Adjusted Mortality Rate[1] per 100,000 population	
		County[2]	U.S.
Assault	X85-Y09	6.1	5.2
Diseases of the liver	K70-K76	19.1	13.2
Human immunodeficiency virus (HIV) disease	B20-B24	2.3	2.2
Influenza and pneumonia	J09-J18	11.9	15.4
Intentional self-harm	X60-X84	20.2	12.5
Malnutrition	E40-E46	Suppressed	0.9
Obesity and other hyperalimentation	E65-E68	2.4	1.8
Renal failure	N17-N19	12.8	13.1
Transport accidents	V01-V99	14.4	11.7
Viral hepatitis	B15-B19	2.4	2.2

Note: (a) ICD-10 = International Classification of Diseases 10th Revision; (1) Mortality rates are a three year average covering 2011-2013; (2) Figures cover Brevard County
Source: Centers for Disease Control and Prevention, National Center for Health Statistics. Compressed Mortality File 1999-2013 on CDC WONDER Online Database, released October 2014. Data are compiled from the Compressed Mortality File 1999-2013, Series 20 No. 2S, 2014.

Health Insurance Coverage

Area	With Health Insurance	With Private Health Insurance	With Public Health Insurance	Without Health Insurance	Population Under Age 18 Without Health Insurance
City	82.8	55.9	38.8	17.2	8.6
MSA[1]	83.2	62.3	37.7	16.8	10.9
U.S.	85.2	65.2	31.0	14.8	7.3

Note: Figures are percentages that cover the civilian noninstitutionalized population; (1) Figures cover the Palm Bay-Melbourne-Titusville, FL Metropolitan Statistical Area—see Appendix B for areas included
Source: U.S. Census Bureau, 2011-2013 American Community Survey 3-Year Estimates

Number of Medical Professionals

Area[1]	MDs[2]	DOs[2,3]	Dentists	Podiatrists	Chiropractors	Optometrists
Local (number)	1,175	102	303	36	133	81
Local (rate[4])	214.5	18.6	54.9	6.5	24.1	14.7
U.S. (rate[4])	270.0	20.2	63.1	5.7	25.2	14.9

Note: Data as of 2013 unless noted; (1) Local data covers Brevard County; (2) Data as of 2012 and includes all active, non-federal physicians; (3) Doctor of Osteopathic Medicine; (4) rate per 100,000 population
Source: U.S. Department of Health and Human Services, Health Resources and Services Administration, Bureau of Health Professions, Area Resource File (ARF) 2013-2014

EDUCATION

Public School District Statistics

District Name	Schls	Pupils	Pupil/ Teacher Ratio	Minority Pupils[1] (%)	Free Lunch Eligible[2] (%)	IEP[3] (%)
Brevard County	124	71,228	14.5	36.6	40.1	16.4

Note: Table includes school districts with 2,000 or more students; (1) Percentage of students that are not non-Hispanic white; (2) Percentage of students that are eligible for the free lunch program; (3) Percentage of students that have an Individualized Education Program.
Source: U.S. Department of Education, National Center for Education Statistics, Common Core of Data, Local Education Agency (School District) Universe Survey: School Year 2012-2013; U.S. Department of Education, National Center for Education Statistics, Common Core of Data, Public Elementary/Secondary School Universe Survey: School Year 2012-2013

Highest Level of Education

Area	Less than H.S.	H.S. Diploma	Some College, No Deg.	Associate Degree	Bachelor's Degree	Master's Degree	Prof. School Degree	Doctorate Degree
City	13.7	32.3	24.2	12.0	12.0	5.1	0.4	0.3
MSA[1]	10.3	28.5	23.5	11.4	16.5	7.4	1.4	1.1
U.S.	13.7	28.0	21.2	7.9	18.2	7.7	1.9	1.3

Note: Figures cover persons age 25 and over; (1) Figures cover the Palm Bay-Melbourne-Titusville, FL Metropolitan Statistical Area—see Appendix B for areas included
Source: U.S. Census Bureau, 2011-2013 American Community Survey 3-Year Estimates

Educational Attainment by Race

Area	High School Graduate or Higher (%)					Bachelor's Degree or Higher (%)				
	Total	White	Black	Asian	Hisp.[2]	Total	White	Black	Asian	Hisp.[2]
City	86.3	88.7	77.7	90.2	82.3	17.9	18.4	14.9	25.4	15.3
MSA[1]	89.7	91.0	79.2	85.6	85.2	26.4	27.1	15.6	38.9	23.7
U.S.	86.3	88.3	83.1	85.7	64.0	29.1	30.4	18.8	50.7	13.7

Note: Figures shown cover persons 25 years old and over; (1) Figures cover the Palm Bay-Melbourne-Titusville, FL Metropolitan Statistical Area—see Appendix B for areas included; (2) People of Hispanic origin can be of any race
Source: U.S. Census Bureau, 2011-2013 American Community Survey 3-Year Estimates

School Enrollment by Grade and Control

Area	Preschool (%)		Kindergarten (%)		Grades 1 - 4 (%)		Grades 5 - 8 (%)		Grades 9 - 12 (%)	
	Public	Private	Public	Private	Public	Private	Public	Private	Public	Private
City	47.0	53.0	93.4	6.6	89.6	10.4	87.1	12.9	86.4	13.6
MSA[1]	51.4	48.6	90.0	10.0	89.9	10.1	87.8	12.2	90.0	10.0
U.S.	57.7	42.3	87.9	12.1	89.9	10.1	90.0	10.0	90.7	9.3

Note: Figures shown cover persons 3 years old and over; (1) Figures cover the Palm Bay-Melbourne-Titusville, FL Metropolitan Statistical Area—see Appendix B for areas included
Source: U.S. Census Bureau, 2011-2013 American Community Survey 3-Year Estimates

Average Salaries of Public School Classroom Teachers

Area	2013-14		2014-15		Percent Change 2013-14 to 2014-15	Percent Change 2004-05 to 2014-15
	Dollars	Rank[1]	Dollars	Rank[1]		
FLORIDA	47,780	39	48,992	36	2.54	17.8
U.S. Average	56,610	–	57,379	–	1.36	20.8

Note: (1) State rank ranges from 1 to 51 where 1 indicates highest salary.
Source: National Education Association, Rankings & Estimates: Rankings of the States 2014 and Estimates of School Statistics 2015, March 2015

Higher Education

Four-Year Colleges			Two-Year Colleges			Medical Schools[1]	Law Schools[2]	Voc/ Tech[3]
Public	Private Non-profit	Private For-profit	Public	Private Non-profit	Private For-profit			
0	0	0	0	0	0	0	0	0

Note: Figures cover institutions located within the city limits and include main campuses only; (1) includes schools accredited by the Liaison Committee on Medical Education and the American Osteopathic Association's Commission on Osteopathic College Accreditation; (2) includes ABA-accredited schools, schools with provisional ABA accreditation, and state accredited schools; (3) includes all schools with programs that are less than 2 years.
Source: National Center for Education Statistics, Integrated Postsecondary Education System (IPEDS), 2013-14; Association of American Medical Colleges, Member List, May 1, 2015; American Osteopathic Association, Member List, May 1, 2015; Law School Admission Council, Official Guide to ABA-Approved Law Schools Online, May 1, 2015; Wikipedia, List of Medical Schools in the United States, May 1, 2015; Wikipedia, List of Law Schools in the United States, May 1, 2015

According to *U.S. News & World Report,* the Palm Bay-Melbourne-Titusville, FL metro area is home to one of the best national universities in the U.S.: **Florida Institute of Technology** (#173). The indicators used to capture academic quality fall into a number of categories: assessment by administrators at peer institutions; retention of students; faculty resources; student selectivity; financial resources; alumni giving; high school counselor ratings of colleges; and graduation rate. *U.S. News & World Report, "America's Best Colleges 2015"*

PRESIDENTIAL ELECTION

2012 Presidential Election Results

Area	Obama (%)	Romney (%)	Other (%)
Brevard County	43.1	55.8	1.1
U.S.	51.0	47.2	1.8

Note: Results may not add to 100% due to rounding
Source: Dave Leip's Atlas of U.S. Presidential Elections

EMPLOYERS

Major Employers

Company Name	Industry
City of Palm Bay	Government
DRS Optronics	Electrical components, imaging and visual systems
Harris Corporation	Business center
Holmes Regional Medical Center	Healthcare
Intersil	Manufacturer
MC Assembly	Electronic manufacturing
Palm Bay Community Hospital	Healthcare
Publix Supermarkets	Retail grocery
Walmart	Retail
Winn Dixie Supermarkets	Retail grocery

Note: Companies shown are located within the Palm Bay-Melbourne-Titusville, FL Metropolitan Statistical Area.
Source: Hoovers.com; Wikipedia

Best Companies to Work For

School Board of Brevard County (Viera), headquartered in Palm Bay, is among the "50 Best Employers for Workers Over 50." Criteria: recruiting practices; opportunities for training, education, and career development; workplace accommodations; alternative work options, such as flexible scheduling, job sharing, and phased retirement; employee health and pension benefits; and retiree benefits. Employers with at least 50 employees based in the U.S. are eligible, including for-profit companies, not-for-profit organizations, and government employers. *AARP, "2013 AARP Best Employers for Workers Over 50"*

PUBLIC SAFETY

Crime Rate

Area	All Crimes	Violent Crimes: Murder	Violent Crimes: Forcible Rape	Violent Crimes: Robbery	Violent Crimes: Aggrav. Assault	Property Crimes: Burglary	Property Crimes: Larceny -Theft	Property Crimes: Motor Vehicle Theft
City	2,307.7	2.9	20.1	41.2	367.8	495.3	1,270.2	110.2
Suburbs[1]	3,558.1	3.8	57.4	95.7	389.6	724.9	2,157.8	128.9
Metro[2]	3,321.0	3.6	50.3	85.4	385.5	681.4	1,989.5	125.3
U.S.	3,098.6	4.5	25.2	109.1	229.1	610.0	1,899.4	221.3

Note: Figures are crimes per 100,000 population; (1) All areas within the metro area that are located outside the city limits; (2) Figures cover the Palm Bay-Melbourne-Titusville, FL Metropolitan Statistical Area—see Appendix B for areas included
Source: FBI Uniform Crime Reports, 2013

Hate Crimes

Area	Number of Quarters Reported	Race	Religion	Sexual Orientation	Ethnicity	Disability	Gender	Gender Identity
		Number of Incidents per Bias Motivation						
City	4	0	1	0	1	0	0	0
U.S.	4	2,871	1,031	1,233	655	83	18	31

Source: Federal Bureau of Investigation, Hate Crime Statistics 2013

Identity Theft Consumer Complaints

Area	Complaints	Complaints per 100,000 Population	Rank[2]
MSA[1]	602	109.3	41
U.S.	332,646	104.3	-

Note: (1) Figures cover the Palm Bay-Melbourne-Titusville, FL Metropolitan Statistical Area—see Appendix B for areas included; (2) Rank ranges from 1 to 380 where 1 indicates greatest number of identity theft complaints per 100,000 population
Source: Federal Trade Commission, Consumer Sentinel Network Data Book for January–December 2014

Fraud and Other Consumer Complaints

Area	Complaints	Complaints per 100,000 Population	Rank[2]
MSA[1]	2,923	530.7	15
U.S.	2,250,205	705.7	-

Note: (1) Figures cover the Palm Bay-Melbourne-Titusville, FL Metropolitan Statistical Area—see Appendix B for areas included; (2) Rank ranges from 1 to 380 where 1 indicates greatest number of identity theft complaints per 100,000 population
Source: Federal Trade Commission, Consumer Sentinel Network Data Book for January–December 2014

RECREATION

Culture

Dance[1]	Theatre[1]	Instrumental Music[1]	Vocal Music[1]	Series and Festivals	Museums and Art Galleries[2]	Zoos and Aquariums[3]
0	0	0	0	0	0	0

Note: (1) Professional perfoming groups; (2) Based on organizations with SIC code 8412; (3) AZA-accredited
Source: The Grey House Performing Arts Directory, 2015-16; Association of Zoos & Aquariums, AZA Member Zoos & Aquariums, April 2015; www.AccuLeads.com, April 2015

Professional Sports Teams

Team Name	League	Year Established
No teams are located in the metro area		

Source: Wikipedia, Major Professional Sports Teams of the United States and Canada, April 2015

CLIMATE

Average and Extreme Temperatures

Temperature	Jan	Feb	Mar	Apr	May	Jun	Jul	Aug	Sep	Oct	Nov	Dec	Yr.
Extreme High (°F)	88	88	91	94	98	100	98	98	95	94	91	87	100
Average High (°F)	73	74	77	81	85	89	90	90	88	84	78	74	82
Average Temp. (°F)	64	65	68	72	77	81	82	82	81	77	70	64	74
Average Low (°F)	54	55	59	62	68	72	73	74	73	69	61	55	65
Extreme Low (°F)	21	28	32	36	51	57	67	64	65	46	33	23	21

Note: Figures cover the years 1949-1995
Source: National Climatic Data Center, International Station Meteorological Climate Summary, 9/96

Average Precipitation/Snowfall/Humidity

Precip./Humidity	Jan	Feb	Mar	Apr	May	Jun	Jul	Aug	Sep	Oct	Nov	Dec	Yr.
Avg. Precip. (in.)	2.2	3.0	3.5	2.8	3.1	4.8	5.7	6.1	7.1	6.6	3.5	2.0	50.5
Avg. Snowfall (in.)	0	0	0	0	0	0	0	0	0	0	0	0	0
Avg. Rel. Hum. 7am (%)	89	88	86	84	83	86	88	90	90	87	87	88	87
Avg. Rel. Hum. 4pm (%)	63	60	59	58	62	69	69	70	70	68	66	64	65

Note: Figures cover the years 1949-1995; Tr = Trace amounts (<0.05 in. of rain; <0.5 in. of snow)
Source: National Climatic Data Center, International Station Meteorological Climate Summary, 9/96

Weather Conditions

Temperature			Daytime Sky			Precipitation		
32°F & below	45°F & below	90°F & above	Clear	Partly cloudy	Cloudy	0.01 inch or more precip.	0.1 inch or more snow/ice	Thunder-storms
1	21	59	75	228	62	124	0	73

Note: Figures are average number of days per year and cover the years 1949-1995
Source: National Climatic Data Center, International Station Meteorological Climate Summary, 9/96

HAZARDOUS WASTE

Superfund Sites

Palm Bay has one hazardous waste site on the EPA's Superfund Final National Priorities List: **Harris Corp. (Palm Bay Plant)**. There are a total of 1,322 Superfund sites on the list in the U.S.
U.S. Environmental Protection Agency, Final National Priorities List, April 14, 2015

AIR & WATER QUALITY

Air Quality Trends: Ozone

	2004	2005	2006	2007	2008	2009	2010	2011	2012	2013
MSA[1]	0.067	0.070	0.076	0.068	0.068	0.063	0.064	0.066	0.065	0.063

Note: (1) Data covers the Palm Bay-Melbourne-Titusville, FL Metropolitan Statistical Area—see Appendix B for areas included. The values shown are the composite ozone concentration averages among trend sites based on the highest fourth daily maximum 8-hour concentration in parts per million. These trends are based on sites having an adequate record of monitoring data during the trend period. Data from exceptional events are included.
Source: U.S. Environmental Protection Agency, Air Quality Monitoring Information, "Air Quality Trends by City, 2000-2013"

Air Quality Index

Area	Percent of Days when Air Quality was...[2]					AQI Statistics[2]	
	Good	Moderate	Unhealthy for Sensitive Groups	Unhealthy	Very Unhealthy	Maximum	Median
MSA[1]	89.3	10.7	0.0	0.0	0.0	77	36

Note: (1) Data covers the Palm Bay-Melbourne-Titusville, FL Metropolitan Statistical Area—see Appendix B for areas included; (2) Based on 365 days with AQI data in 2014. Air Quality Index (AQI) is an index for reporting daily air quality. EPA calculates the AQI for five major air pollutants regulated by the Clean Air Act: ground-level ozone, particle pollution (aka particulate matter), carbon monoxide, sulfur dioxide, and nitrogen dioxide. The AQI runs from 0 to 500. The higher the AQI value, the greater the level of air pollution and the greater the health concern. There are six AQI categories: "Good" AQI is between 0 and 50. Air quality is considered satisfactory; "Moderate" AQI is between 51 and 100. Air quality is acceptable; "Unhealthy for Sensitive Groups" When AQI values are between 101 and 150, members of sensitive groups may experience health effects; "Unhealthy" When AQI values are between 151 and 200 everyone may begin to experience health effects; "Very Unhealthy" AQI values between 201 and 300 trigger a health alert; "Hazardous" AQI values over 300 trigger warnings of emergency conditions (not shown).
Source: U.S. Environmental Protection Agency, Air Quality Index Report, 2014

Air Quality Index Pollutants

Area	Percent of Days when AQI Pollutant was...[2]					
	Carbon Monoxide	Nitrogen Dioxide	Ozone	Sulfur Dioxide	Particulate Matter 2.5	Particulate Matter 10
MSA[1]	0.0	0.0	62.5	0.0	37.5	0.0

Note: (1) Data covers the Palm Bay-Melbourne-Titusville, FL Metropolitan Statistical Area—see Appendix B for areas included; (2) Based on 365 days with AQI data in 2014. The Air Quality Index (AQI) is an index for reporting daily air quality. EPA calculates the AQI for five major air pollutants regulated by the Clean Air Act: ground-level ozone, particle pollution (also known as particulate matter), carbon monoxide, sulfur dioxide, and nitrogen dioxide. The AQI runs from 0 to 500. The higher the AQI value, the greater the level of air pollution and the greater the health concern.
Source: U.S. Environmental Protection Agency, Air Quality Index Report, 2014

Maximum Air Pollutant Concentrations: Particulate Matter, Ozone, CO and Lead

	Particulate Matter 10 (ug/m^3)	Particulate Matter 2.5 Wtd AM (ug/m^3)	Particulate Matter 2.5 24-Hr (ug/m^3)	Ozone (ppm)	Carbon Monoxide (ppm)	Lead (ug/m^3)
MSA[1] Level	54	5.8	21	0.063	n/a	n/a
NAAQS[2]	150	15	35	0.075	9	0.15
Met NAAQS[2]	Yes	Yes	Yes	Yes	n/a	n/a

Note: (1) Data covers the Palm Bay-Melbourne-Titusville, FL Metropolitan Statistical Area—see Appendix B for areas included; Data from exceptional events are included; (2) National Ambient Air Quality Standards; ppm = parts per million; ug/m^3 = micrograms per cubic meter; n/a not available.
Concentrations: Particulate Matter 10 (coarse particulate)—highest second maximum 24-hour concentration; Particulate Matter 2.5 Wtd AM (fine particulate)—highest weighted annual mean concentration; Particulate Matter 2.5 24-Hour (fine particulate)—highest 98th percentile 24-hour concentration; Ozone—highest fourth daily maximum 8-hour concentration; Carbon Monoxide—highest second maximum non-overlapping 8-hour concentration; Lead—maximum running 3-month average
Source: U.S. Environmental Protection Agency, Air Quality Monitoring Information, "Air Quality Statistics by City, 2013"

Maximum Air Pollutant Concentrations: Nitrogen Dioxide and Sulfur Dioxide

	Nitrogen Dioxide AM (ppb)	Nitrogen Dioxide 1-Hr (ppb)	Sulfur Dioxide AM (ppb)	Sulfur Dioxide 1-Hr (ppb)	Sulfur Dioxide 24-Hr (ppb)
MSA[1] Level	n/a	n/a	n/a	n/a	n/a
NAAQS[2]	53	100	30	75	140
Met NAAQS[2]	n/a	n/a	n/a	n/a	n/a

Note: (1) Data covers the Palm Bay-Melbourne-Titusville, FL Metropolitan Statistical Area—see Appendix B for areas included; Data from exceptional events are included; (2) National Ambient Air Quality Standards; ppm = parts per million; ug/m^3 = micrograms per cubic meter; n/a not available.
Concentrations: Nitrogen Dioxide AM—highest arithmetic mean concentration; Nitrogen Dioxide 1-Hr—highest 98th percentile 1-hour daily maximum concentration; Sulfur Dioxide AM—highest annual mean concentration; Sulfur Dioxide 1-Hr—highest 99th percentile 1-hour daily maximum concentration; Sulfur Dioxide 24-Hr—highest second maximum 24-hour concentration
Source: U.S. Environmental Protection Agency, Air Quality Monitoring Information, "Air Quality Statistics by City, 2013"

Drinking Water

Water System Name	Pop. Served	Primary Water Source Type	Violations[1]	
			Health Based	Monitoring/ Reporting
City of Palm Bay	112,025	Ground	0	0

Note: (1) Based on violation data from January 1, 2014 to December 31, 2014 (includes unresolved violations from earlier years)
Source: U.S. Environmental Protection Agency, Office of Ground Water and Drinking Water, Safe Drinking Water Information System (based on data extracted January 27, 2015)

San Antonio, Texas

Background

San Antonio is a charming preservation of its Mexican-Spanish heritage. Walking along its famous Paseo Del Rio at night, with cream-colored stucco structures, sea shell ornamented facades, and gently illuminating tiny lights is very romantic.

Emotional intensity is nothing new to San Antonio. The city began in the early eighteenth century as a cohesion of different Spanish missions, whose zealous aim was to convert the Coahuiltecan natives to Christianity, and to European ways of farming. A debilitating epidemic, however, killed most of the natives, as well as the missions' goal, causing the city to be abandoned.

In 1836, San Antonio became the site of interest again, when a small band of American soldiers were unable to successfully defend themselves against an army of 4,000 Mexican soldiers, led by General Antonio de Lopez Santa Anna. Fighting desperately from within the walls of the Mission San Antonio de Valero, or The Alamo, all 183 men were killed. This inspired the cry "Remember the Alamo" from the throats of every American soldier led by General Sam Houston, who was determined to wrest Texas territory and independence from Mexico.

Despite the Anglo victory over the Mexicans more than 150 years ago, the Mexican culture and its influence remain strong. We see evidence of this in the architecture, the Franciscan educational system, the variety of Spanish-language media, and the racial composition of the population, in which over half the city's residents are Latino.

This picturesque and practical blend of old and new makes San Antonio unique among American cities.

The city continues to draw tourists who come to visit not just the Alamo, but the nearby theme parks like Six Flags Fiesta Texas and SeaWorld, or to take in the famed River Walk, the charming promenade of shops, restaurants, and pubs. In addition, the city has used ingenuity to diversify its traditional economy. For instance, Kelly Air Force Base, which was decommissioned in 2001, was developed into a successful, nearly 5,000-acre business park, called Kelly USA. The name has since changed to Port San Antonio and a warehouse on the site was used to house refugees from Hurricane Katrina. Businesses at the port receive favorable property tax and pay no state, city or corporate income taxes. Toyota is a major employer in the city.

San Antonio's location on the edge of the Gulf Coastal Plains exposes it to a modified subtropical climate. Summers are hot, although extremely high temperatures are rare. Winters are mild. Since the city is only 140 miles from the Gulf of Mexico, tropical storms occasionally occur, bringing strong winds and heavy rains. Relative humidity is high in the morning, but tends to drop by late afternoon.

Rankings

General Rankings

- The San Antonio metro area was identified as one of America's fastest-growing areas in terms of population and economy by *Forbes*. The area ranked #10 out of 20. The 100 most populous metro areas in the U.S. were evaluated on the following criteria: estimated population growth; job growth; gross metropolitan product growth; unemployment; median salaries for college-educated workers. *Forbes, "America's Fastest-Growing Cities 2015," January 27, 2015*
- San Antonio was identified as one of America's fastest-growing major metropolitan areas in terms of population growth by CNNMoney.com. The area ranked #5 out of 10. Criteria: population growth between July 2012 and July 2013. *CNNMoney, "10 Fastest-Growing Cities," March 28, 2014*
- San Antonio was selected as one of America's best cities by *Bloomberg Businessweek*. The city ranked #30 out of 50. Criteria: leisure attributes (the number of restaurants, bars, libraries, museums, professional sports teams, and park acres by population); educational attributes (public school performance, the number of colleges, and graduate degree holders); economic factors (2011 income and June and July 2012 unemployment); crime; and air quality. *Bloomberg BusinessWeek, "America's Best Cities," September 26, 2012*

Business/Finance Rankings

- To help veterans transition to civilian life, USAA and Hiring Our Heroes worked with Sperlings's BestPlaces and the Institute for Veterans and Military Families at Syracuse University to develop a list of the major metropolitan areas where military-skills-related employment is strongest. Criteria for veterans *starting out* included G.I. Bill enrollment, job prospects, unemployment rate, military skills jobs and certification/license transfers, recent job growth, and accessible health resources. Metro areas with a violent crime rate or high cost of living were excluded. At #4, the San Antonio metro area made the top ten. *www.usaa.com, "2014 Best Places for Veterans"*
- To help veterans transition to civilian life, USAA and Hiring Our Heroes worked with Sperlings's BestPlaces and the Institute for Veterans and Military Families at Syracuse University to develop a list of the major metropolitan areas where military-skills-related employment is strongest. Criteria for *mid-career* veterans included veteran wage growth; military skills, defense contractor, and government jobs; recent job growth; supervisor/manager jobs; and accessible health resources. Metro areas with a violent crime rate or high cost of living were excluded. At #2, the San Antonio metro area made the top ten. *www.usaa.com, "2014 Best Places for Veterans"*
- The finance website Wall St. Cheat Sheet reported on the prospects for high-wage job creation in the nation's largest metro areas over the next five years and ranked them accordingly, drawing on in-depth analysis by CareerBuilder and Economic Modeling Specialists International (EMSI). The San Antonio metro area placed #1 on the Wall St. Cheat Sheet list. *wallstcheatsheet.com, "Top 10 Cities for High-Wage Job Growth," December 8, 2013*
- Based on metro area social media reviews, the employment opinion group Glassdoor surveyed 50 of the largest U.S. metro areas on measures including compensation and benefits, satisfaction with management, business outlook, and number of employers hiring. The San Antonio metro area was ranked #9 in overall employee satisfaction. *www.glassdoor.com, "Employment Satisfaction Report Card by City," June 13, 2014*
- In a survey of economic confidence in the nation's 50 largest metropolitan areas conducted January–December 2014, the San Antonio metro area placed #24, according to Gallup's 2014 Economic Confidence Index. *Gallup, "San Jose and San Francisco Lead in Economic Confidence," March 19, 2015*
- Using data from the Council for Community and Economic Research's 2013 Annual Report, NerdWallet ranked the 100 most affordable cities in America. States from the central and southern United States dominate the list. On the affordability scale, San Antonio ranked #34. *NerdWallet.com, "Most Affordable Cities in America," June 4, 2014*

- The Brookings Institution ranked the 50 largest cities in the U.S. based on income inequality. San Antonio was ranked #33. (#1 = greatest ineqality). Criteria: the cities were ranked based on the "95/20 ratio," a figure representing the income at which a household earns more than 95 percent of all other households, divided by the income at which a household earns more than only 20 percent of all other households. *Brookings Institution, "Income Inequality in America's 50 Largest Cities, 2007-2013," March 17, 2015*

- San Antonio was ranked #36 out of 100 metro areas in terms of economic performance (#1 = best) during the recession and recovery from trough quarter through the second quarter of 2013. Criteria: percent change in employment; percentage point change in unemployment rate; percent change in gross metropolitan product; percent change in House Price Index. *Brookings Institution, MetroMonitor: Tracking Economic Recession and Recovery in America's 100 Largest Metropolitan Areas, September 2013*

- The San Antonio metro area was identified as one of the most affordable metropolitan areas in America by *Forbes.* The area ranked #20 out of 20. Criteria: the 100 largest metro areas in the U.S. were analyzed based on the National Association of Home Builders/Wells Fargo Housing Affordability Index and Sperling's Best Places' cost-of-living index. Some major cities were omitted for lack of data. *Forbes.com, "America's Most Affordable Cities in 2015," March 12, 2015*

- San Antonio was identified as one of America's most frugal metro areas by *Coupons.com.* The city ranked #18 out of 25. Criteria: Grocery IQ and coupons.com mobile app usage. *Coupons.com, "Top 25 Most On-the-Go Frugal Cities of 2013," April 10, 2014*

- *Forbes* reports that San Antonio was identified as one of the happiest cities to work in by CareerBliss.com, an online community for career advancement. The city ranked #8 out of 10. Criteria: work-life balance; an employee's relationship with his or her boss and co-workers; general work environment; compensation; opportunities for advancement; company culture; and resources. *Forbes.com, "The 10 Happiest and Unhappiest Cities to Work in Right Now," January 16, 2015*

- The San Antonio metro area appeared on the Milken Institute "2013 Best Performing Cities" list. Rank: #10 out of 200 large metro areas. Criteria: job growth; wage and salary growth; high-tech output growth. *Milken Institute, "Best-Performing Cities 2014," January 2015*

- *Forbes* ranked the 200 most populous metro areas to determine the nation's "Best Places for Business and Careers." The San Antonio metro area was ranked #16. Criteria: costs (business and living); job growth (past and projected); income growth; educational attainment (college and high school); projected economic growth; cultural and recreational opportunities; net migration patterns; number of highly ranked colleges. *Forbes, "The Best Places for Business and Careers 2014," July 23, 2014*

Culture/Performing Arts Rankings

- San Antonio was selected as one of the ten best large U.S. cities in which to be a moviemaker. Of cities with a population over 400,000, the city was ranked #10. Criteria: film community; access to new films; access to equipment; cost of living; tax incentives. *MovieMaker Magazine, "Best Places to Live and Work as a Moviemaker: 2013," January 22, 2015*

- San Antonio was selected as one of America's top cities for the arts. The city ranked #21 in the big city (population 500,000 and over) category. Criteria: readers' top choices for arts travel destinations based on the richness and variety of visual arts sites, activities and events. *American Style, "2012 Top 25 Arts Destinations," June 2012*

Dating/Romance Rankings

- A *Cosmopolitan* magazine article surveyed the gender balance and other factors to arrive at a list of the best and worst cities for women to meet single guys. San Antonio was #9 among the best for single women looking for dates. *www.cosmopolitan.com, "Working the Ratio," October 1, 2013*

- Of the 100 U.S. cities surveyed by *Men's Health* in its quest to identify the nation's best cities for dating and forming relationships, San Antonio was ranked #28 for online dating (#1 = best). *Men's Health, "The Best and Worst Cities for Online Dating," January 30, 2013*

Education Rankings

- Personal finance website *WalletHub* analyzed the 150 largest U.S. metropolitan statistical areas to determine where the most educated Americans are choosing to settle. Criteria: educational attainment; percentage of workers with jobs in computer, engineering, and science fields; quality and size of each metro area's universities. San Antonio was ranked #96 (#1 = most educated city). *www.WalletHub.com, "2014's Most and Least Educated Cities*
- San Antonio was selected as one of America's most literate cities. The city ranked #70 out of the 77 largest U.S. cities. Criteria: number of booksellers; library resources; Internet resources; educational attainment; periodical publishing resources; newspaper circulation. *Central Connecticut State University, "America's Most Literate Cities, 2014," April 8, 2015*

Environmental Rankings

- The San Antonio metro area came in at #345 for the relative comfort of its climate on Sperling's list of "chill cities," as measured by the Sperling Heat Index. All 361 metro areas are included. Criteria included daytime high temperatures, nighttime low temperatures, dew point, and relative humidity at the high temperatures. *www.bertsperling.com, "Sperling's Chill Cities," July 18, 2013*
- Sperling's BestPlaces assessed 379 metropolitan areas of the United States for the likelihood of dangerously extreme weather events or earthquakes. In general the Southeast and South-Central regions have the highest risk of weather extremes and earthquakes, while the Pacific Northwest enjoys the lowest risk. Of the least risky metropolitan areas, the San Antonio metro area was ranked #356. *www.bestplaces.net, "Safest Places from Natural Disasters," April 2011*
- San Antonio was highlighted as one of the top 25 cleanest metro areas for short-term particle pollution (24-hour PM 2.5) in the U.S. during 2011 through 2013. Monitors in these cities reported no days with unhealthful PM 2.5 levels. *American Lung Association, State of the Air 2015*

Food/Drink Rankings

- *Men's Health* ranked 100 major U.S. cities in terms of alcohol intoxication. San Antonio ranked #99 (#1 = most sober).Criteria: binge drinking; alcohol-related traffic accidents, arrests, and fatalities. *Men's Health, "The Drunkest Cities in America," November 19, 2013*

Health/Fitness Rankings

- Analysts who tracked obesity rates in the nation's largest metro areas (those with populations above one million) found that the San Antonio metro area was one of the ten major metros where residents were most likely to be obese, defined as a BMI score of 30 or above. *www.gallup.com, "Boulder, Colo., Residents Still Least Likely to Be Obese," April 4, 2014*
- For each of the 50 most populous metro areas in the United States, the American College of Sports Medicine's American Fitness Index evaluated infrastructure, community assets, and policies that encourage healthy and fit lifestyles, including preventive health behaviors, levels of chronic disease conditions, health care access, and community resources and policies that support physical activity. The San Antonio metro area ranked #48 for "community fitness." Personal health indicators were considered as well as community and environmental indicators. *www.americanfitnessindex.org, "ACSM American Fitness Index Health and Community Fitness Status of the 50 Largest Metropolitan Areas," May 2013*
- San Antonio was selected as one of the 25 fittest cities in America by *Men's Fitness Online*. It ranked #25 out of America's 50 largest cities. Criteria: fitness centers and sport stores; nutrition; sports participation; TV viewing; overweight/sedentary; junk food; air quality; geography; commute; parks and open space; city recreational facilities; access to healthcare; motivation; mayor and city initiatives; state obesity initiatives. *Men's Fitness, "The Fittest and Fattest Cities in America," March 5, 2012*

- San Antonio was identified as a "2013 Spring Allergy Capital." The area ranked #24 out of 100. Three groups of factors were used to identify the most severe cities for people with allergies during the spring season: annual pollen levels; medicine utilization; access to board-certified allergists. *Asthma and Allergy Foundation of America, "Spring Allergy Capitals 2013"*
- San Antonio was identified as a "2013 Fall Allergy Capital." The area ranked #23 out of 100. Three groups of factors were used to identify the most severe cities for people with allergies during the fall season: annual pollen levels; medicine utilization; access to board-certified allergists. *Asthma and Allergy Foundation of America, "Fall Allergy Capitals 2013"*
- San Antonio was identified as a "2013 Asthma Capital." The area ranked #66 out of the nation's 100 largest metropolitan areas. Twelve factors were used to identify the most challenging places to live for people with asthma: estimated prevalence; self-reported prevalence; crude death rate for asthma; annual pollen score; annual air quality; public smoking laws; number of board-certified asthma specialists; school inhaler access laws; rescue medication use; controller medication use; uninsured rate; poverty rate. *Asthma and Allergy Foundation of America, "Asthma Capitals 2013"*
- *Men's Health* ranked 100 major U.S. cities in terms of the best and worst cities for men. San Antonio ranked #62. Criteria: thirty-three data points were examined covering health, fitness, and quality of life. *Men's Health, "The Best & Worst Cities for Men 2014," December 6, 2013*
- The San Antonio metro area appeared in the 2013 Gallup-Healthways Well-Being Index. The area ranked #75 out of 189. The Gallup-Healthways Well-Being Index score is an average of six sub-indexes, which individually examine life evaluation, emotional health, work environment, physical health, healthy behaviors, and access to basic necessities. Results are based on telephone interviews conducted as part of the Gallup-Healthways Well-Being Index survey January 2–December 29, 2012, and January 2–December 30, 2013, with a random sample of 531,630 adults, aged 18 and older, living in metropolitan areas in the 50 U.S. states and the District of Columbia. *Gallup-Healthways, "State of American Well-Being," March 25, 2014*
- The San Antonio metro area was identified as one of "America's Most Stressful Cities" by *Sperling's BestPlaces.* The metro area ranked #40 out of 50. Criteria: unemployment rate; suicide rate; commute time; mental health; poor rest; alcohol use; violent crime rate; property crime rate; cloudy days annually. *Sperling's BestPlaces, www.BestPlaces.net, "Stressful Cities 2012*

Real Estate Rankings

- The San Antonio metro area was identified as one of the top 20 housing markets to invest in for 2015 by *Forbes*. The area ranked #6. Criteria: strong population and job growth; relatively low home prices which are below equilibrium home price (EHP). The EHP is what the average price for a market should be, if speculation, weird distortions in local income, and other factors (like the housing collapse) weren't present in the market. *Forbes.com, "Best Buy Cities: Where to Invest in Housing in 2015," January 9, 2015*
- San Antonio was ranked #96 out of 275 metro areas in terms of house price appreciation in 2014 (#1 = highest rate). *Federal Housing Finance Agency, House Price Index, 4th Quarter 2014*
- San Antonio was ranked #170 out of 226 metro areas in terms of housing affordability in 2014 by the National Association of Home Builders (#1 = most affordable). The NAHB-Wells Fargo Housing Opportunity Index (HOI) for a given area is defined as the share of homes sold in that area that would have been affordable to a family earning the local median income, based on standard mortgage underwriting criteria. *National Association of Home Builders®, NAHB-Wells Fargo Housing Opportunity Index, 4th Quarter 2014*

Safety Rankings

- Symantec, in partnership with Sperling's BestPlaces, ranked the 50 largest cities in the U.S. in terms of their vulnerability to cybercrime. The city ranked #43. Criteria: number of cyberattacks and potential infections; level of Internet access; expenditures on smartphones and computer hardware/software; wireless hotspots; broadband connectivity; Internet usage; online purchases. *Symantec, "Riskiest Online Cities of 2012" February 15, 2012*

- Allstate ranked the 200 largest cities in America in terms of driver safety. San Antonio ranked #142. Allstate researchers analyzed internal property damage claims over a two-year period from January 2011 to December 2012. A weighted average of the two-year numbers determined the annual percentages. *Allstate, "Allstate America's Best Drivers Report, 2014"*

- San Antonio was identified as one of the safest large cities in America by CQ Press. All 32 cities with populations of 500,000 or more that reported crime rates in 2012 for murder, rape, robbery, aggravated assault, burglary, and motor vehicle thefts were ranked. The city ranked #10 out of the top 10. *CQ Press, City Crime Rankings 2014*

- The National Insurance Crime Bureau ranked 380 metro areas in the U.S. in terms of per capita rates of vehicle theft. The San Antonio metro area ranked #45 (#1 = highest rate). Criteria: number of vehicle theft offenses per 100,000 inhabitants in 2012. *National Insurance Crime Bureau, "Hot Spots 2012," June 26, 2013*

Seniors/Retirement Rankings

- For *U.S. News & World Report's* Best Places rankings, the editors sought out affordable cities where retirees spend the least on housing and can live on $75 a day while still having easy access to amenities they want and need, such as recreation, services for seniors, and medical facilities. San Antonio was among the ten cities that best satisfied their criteria. *money.usnews.com, "The Best Places to Retire on $75 a Day," October 15, 2013*

- From its Best Cities for Successful Aging indexes, the Milken Institute generated rankings for metropolitan areas, weighing data in eight categories—health care, wellness, living arrangements, transportation, financial characteristics, education and employment opportunities, community engagement, and overall livability. The San Antonio metro area was ranked #54 overall in the large metro area category. *Milken Institute, "Best Cities for Successful Aging, 2014"*

- The AARP named San Antonio one of the "10 Best Places to Live on $100 a Day." Analysts looked at 200 cities to arrive at their 10-best list. Criteria includes: cost of living; quality-of-life; arts and culture; educational institutions; restaurants; community life; health care; natural setting; sunny days per year; and overall vibe. *AARP The Magazine, "10 Best Places to Live on $100 a Day," July 2012*

- *U.S. News & World Report* listed the best places to retire on an income of $40,000 per year. San Antonio was among the ten cities selected. Criteria: low cost of living; affordable housing; quality of life; accessible major medical facilities; services for seniors; educational institutions; outdoor recreational activities. *U.S. News & World Report, "Best Places to Retire for Under $40,000," October 15, 2012*

- San Antonio was identified as one of the most popular places to retire by *Topretirements.com*. The list reflects the 100 cities (out of 900+ total cities reviewed) that visitors to the website are most interested in for retirement. *Topretirements.com, "Most Popular Places to Retire for 2014," February 25, 2014*

Sports/Recreation Rankings

- San Antonio was chosen as a bicycle friendly community by the League of American Bicyclists. A "Bicycle Friendly Community" welcomes cyclists by providing safe accommodation for cycling and encouraging people to bike for transportation and recreation. There are four award levels: Platinum; Gold; Silver; and Bronze. The community achieved an award level of Bronze. *League of American Bicyclists, "Bicycle Friendly Community Master List," Fall 2013*

- San Antonio was selected as one of the most playful cities in the U.S. by KaBOOM! The organization's Playful City USA initiative honors cities and towns across the nation for a vision, plan and commitment to creating an agenda for play. Criteria: creating a local play commission or task force; designing an annual action plan for play; conducting a play space audit; outlining a financial investment in play for the current fiscal year; and proclaiming and celebrating an annual "play day." *KaBOOM! National Campaign for Play, "2013 Playful City USA Communities"*

- San Antonio was chosen as one of America's best cities for bicycling. The city ranked #47 out of 50. Criteria: robust cycling infrastructure; vibrant bike culture. The editors only considered cities with populations of 95,000 or more. *Bicycling, "America's Top 50 Bike-Friendly Cities," May 23, 2012*

Women/Minorities Rankings

- *Women's Health* examined U.S. cities and identified the 100 best cities for women. San Antonio was ranked #44. Criteria: 30 categories were examined from obesity and breast cancer rates to commuting times and hours spent working out. *Women's Health, "Best Cities for Women 2012"*
- San Antonio was selected as one of the best cities for young Latinos in 2013 by mun2, a national cable television broadcast network. The city ranked #1. Criteria: U.S. cities with populations over 500,000 residents were evaluated on the following criteria: number of young latinos; jobs; friendliness; cost of living; fun. *mun2.tv, "Best Cities for Young Latinos 2013*

Miscellaneous Rankings

- San Antonio was selected as one of "America's Best Cities for Hipsters" by *Travel + Leisure.* The city was ranked #16 out of 20. Criteria: live music; coffee bars; independent boutiques; best microbrews; offbeat and tech-savvy locals. *Travel + Leisure, "America's Best Cities for Hipsters," November 2013*
- The National Alliance to End Homelessness ranked the 100 most populous metro areas in terms the rate of homelessness. The San Antonio metro area ranked #51. Criteria: number of homeless people per 10,000 population in 2011. *National Alliance to End Homelessness, The State of Homelessness in America 2012*

Business Environment

CITY FINANCES

City Government Finances

Component	2012 ($000)	2012 ($ per capita)
Total Revenues	4,043,206	3,046
Total Expenditures	4,261,688	3,211
Debt Outstanding	8,830,926	6,653
Cash and Securities[1]	3,951,950	2,977

Note: (1) Cash and security holdings of a government at the close of its fiscal year, including those of its dependent agencies, utilities, and liquor stores.
Source: U.S Census Bureau, State & Local Government Finances 2012

City Government Revenue by Source

Source	2012 ($000)	2012 ($ per capita)
General Revenue		
From Federal Government	89,996	68
From State Government	154,110	116
From Local Governments	56,430	43
Taxes		
Property	380,985	287
Sales and Gross Receipts	323,835	244
Personal Income	0	0
Corporate Income	0	0
Motor Vehicle License	0	0
Other Taxes	35,489	27
Current Charges	563,948	425
Liquor Store	0	0
Utility	2,196,118	1,654
Employee Retirement	98,523	74

Source: U.S Census Bureau, State & Local Government Finances 2012

City Government Expenditures by Function

Function	2012 ($000)	2012 ($ per capita)	2012 (%)
General Direct Expenditures			
Air Transportation	90,166	68	2.1
Corrections	0	0	0.0
Education	0	0	0.0
Employment Security Administration	0	0	0.0
Financial Administration	19,318	15	0.5
Fire Protection	226,022	170	5.3
General Public Buildings	16,464	12	0.4
Governmental Administration, Other	9,688	7	0.2
Health	32,995	25	0.8
Highways	111,473	84	2.6
Hospitals	0	0	0.0
Housing and Community Development	51,313	39	1.2
Interest on General Debt	28,217	21	0.7
Judicial and Legal	20,684	16	0.5
Libraries	32,976	25	0.8
Parking	5,862	4	0.1
Parks and Recreation	136,182	103	3.2
Police Protection	308,881	233	7.2
Public Welfare	135,802	102	3.2
Sewerage	249,081	188	5.8
Solid Waste Management	93,353	70	2.2
Veterans' Services	0	0	0.0
Liquor Store	0	0	0.0
Utility	2,425,616	1,827	56.9
Employee Retirement	92,790	70	2.2

Source: U.S Census Bureau, State & Local Government Finances 2012

DEMOGRAPHICS

Population Growth

Area	1990 Census	2000 Census	2010 Census	Population Growth (%) 1990-2000	Population Growth (%) 2000-2010
City	997,258	1,144,646	1,327,407	14.8	16.0
MSA[1]	1,407,745	1,711,703	2,142,508	21.6	25.2
U.S.	248,709,873	281,421,906	308,745,538	13.2	9.7

Note: (1) Figures cover the San Antonio-New Braunfels, TX Metropolitan Statistical Area—see Appendix B for areas included
Source: U.S. Census Bureau, Census 1990, 2000, 2010

Household Size

Area	Persons in Household (%)							Average Household Size
	One	Two	Three	Four	Five	Six	Seven or More	
City	28.5	29.1	16.5	13.2	7.4	3.0	2.3	2.82
MSA[1]	25.4	30.9	16.7	14.1	7.4	3.0	2.3	2.86
U.S.	27.7	33.6	15.7	13.1	6.0	2.3	1.5	2.64

Note: (1) Figures cover the San Antonio-New Braunfels, TX Metropolitan Statistical Area—see Appendix B for areas included
Source: U.S. Census Bureau, 2011-2013 American Community Survey 3-Year Estimates

Race

Area	White Alone[2] (%)	Black Alone[2] (%)	Asian Alone[2] (%)	AIAN[3] Alone[2] (%)	NHOPI[4] Alone[2] (%)	Other Race Alone[2] (%)	Two or More Races (%)
City	76.2	6.9	2.4	0.7	0.1	10.9	2.7
MSA[1]	78.8	6.5	2.2	0.6	0.1	8.7	3.1
U.S.	73.9	12.6	5.0	0.8	0.2	4.7	2.9

Note: (1) Figures cover the San Antonio-New Braunfels, TX Metropolitan Statistical Area—see Appendix B for areas included; (2) Alone is defined as not being in combination with one or more other races; (3) American Indian and Alaska Native; (4) Native Hawaiian and Other Pacific Islander
Source: U.S. Census Bureau, 2011-2013 American Community Survey 3-Year Estimates

Hispanic or Latino Origin

Area	Total (%)	Mexican (%)	Puerto Rican (%)	Cuban (%)	Other (%)
City	63.0	57.1	1.0	0.2	4.6
MSA[1]	54.4	48.9	1.0	0.2	4.3
U.S.	16.9	10.8	1.6	0.6	3.8

Note: Persons of Hispanic or Latino origin can be of any race; (1) Figures cover the San Antonio-New Braunfels, TX Metropolitan Statistical Area—see Appendix B for areas included
Source: U.S. Census Bureau, 2011-2013 American Community Survey 3-Year Estimates

Segregation

Type	Segregation Indices[1]				Percent Change		
	1990	2000	2010	2010 Rank[2]	1990-2000	1990-2010	2000-2010
Black/White	56.1	52.8	49.0	73	-3.3	-7.1	-3.8
Asian/White	33.8	35.4	38.3	66	1.6	4.5	2.9
Hispanic/White	52.1	49.7	46.1	43	-2.4	-6.0	-3.6

Note: All figures cover the Metropolitan Statistical Area—see Appendix B for areas included; Figures are based on an analysis of 1990, 2000, and 2010 Census Decennial Census tract data by William H. Frey, Brookings Institution and the University of Michigan Social Science Data Analysis Network. In this analysis all racial groups (whites, blacks, and asians) are non-Hispanic members of those races. Hispanics are shown as a separate category;
(1) Segregation Indices are Dissimilarity Indices that measure the degree to which the minority group is distributed differently than whites across census tracts. They range from 0 (complete integration) to 100 (complete segregation) where the value indicates the percentage of the minority group that needs to move to be distributed exactly like whites; (2) Ranges from 1 (most segregated) to 102 (least segregated); n/a not available.
Source: www.CensusScope.org

Ancestry

Area	German	Irish	English	American	Italian	Polish	French[2]	Scottish	Dutch
City	8.5	4.6	4.0	3.8	1.9	1.1	1.5	0.9	0.5
MSA[1]	12.1	5.9	5.5	4.4	2.0	1.6	1.9	1.2	0.6
U.S.	14.9	10.8	8.0	7.4	5.5	3.0	2.7	1.7	1.4

Note: Figures are the percentage of the total population reporting a particular ancestry. The nine most commonly reported ancestries in the U.S. are shown. Figures include multiple ancestries (e.g. if a person reported being Irish and Italian, they were included in both columns); (1) Figures cover the San Antonio-New Braunfels, TX Metropolitan Statistical Area—see Appendix B for areas included; (2) Excludes Basque
Source: U.S. Census Bureau, 2011-2013 American Community Survey 3-Year Estimates

Foreign-Born Population

Area	Percent of Population Born in								
	Any Foreign Country	Mexico	Asia	Europe	Carribean	South America	Central America[2]	Africa	Canada
City	14.1	9.7	2.2	0.6	0.2	0.2	0.8	0.3	0.1
MSA[1]	11.8	7.8	1.9	0.7	0.1	0.3	0.6	0.3	0.1
U.S.	13.0	3.7	3.8	1.5	1.2	0.9	1.0	0.6	0.3

Note: (1) Figures cover the San Antonio-New Braunfels, TX Metropolitan Statistical Area—see Appendix B for areas included; (2) Excludes Mexico.
Source: U.S. Census Bureau, 2011-2013 American Community Survey 3-Year Estimates

Marital Status

Area	Never Married	Now Married[2]	Separated	Widowed	Divorced
City	36.1	42.8	3.3	5.4	12.4
MSA[1]	32.6	47.7	2.8	5.4	11.5
U.S.	32.7	48.1	2.2	6.0	11.0

Note: Figures are percentages and cover the population 15 years of age and older; (1) Figures cover the San Antonio-New Braunfels, TX Metropolitan Statistical Area—see Appendix B for areas included; (2) Excludes separated
Source: U.S. Census Bureau, 2011-2013 American Community Survey 3-Year Estimates

Disability Status

Area	All Ages	Under 18 Years Old	18 to 64 Years Old	65 Years and Over
City	13.9	5.2	12.3	44.9
MSA[1]	13.3	4.8	11.7	42.2
U.S.	12.3	4.1	10.2	36.3

Note: Figures show percent of the civilian noninstitutionalized population that reported having a disability. Disability status is determined from from six types of difficulty: vision, hearing, cognitive, ambulatory, self-care, and independent living. For children under 5 years old, hearing and vision difficulty are used to determine disability status. For children between the ages of 5 and 14, disability status is determined from hearing, vision, cognitive, ambulatory, and self-care difficulties. For people aged 15 years and older, they are considered to have a disability if they have difficulty with any one of the six difficulty types; (1) Figures cover the San Antonio-New Braunfels, TX Metropolitan Statistical Area—see Appendix B for areas included.
Source: U.S. Census Bureau, 2011-2013 American Community Survey 3-Year Estimates

Age

Area	Percent of Population									Median Age
	Under Age 5	Age 5–19	Age 20–34	Age 35–44	Age 45–54	Age 55–64	Age 65–74	Age 75–84	Age 85+	
City	7.4	21.8	23.7	13.0	12.9	10.3	6.1	3.5	1.4	32.8
MSA[1]	7.1	22.1	21.7	13.2	13.3	10.9	6.6	3.5	1.4	34.2
U.S.	6.4	19.9	20.7	12.9	14.1	12.3	7.6	4.2	1.9	37.4

Note: (1) Figures cover the San Antonio-New Braunfels, TX Metropolitan Statistical Area—see Appendix B for areas included
Source: U.S. Census Bureau, 2011-2013 American Community Survey 3-Year Estimates

Gender

Area	Males	Females	Males per 100 Females
City	675,440	708,276	95.4
MSA[1]	1,100,400	1,134,484	97.0
U.S.	154,451,010	159,410,713	96.9

Note: (1) Figures cover the San Antonio-New Braunfels, TX Metropolitan Statistical Area—see Appendix B for areas included
Source: U.S. Census Bureau, 2011-2013 American Community Survey 3-Year Estimates

Religious Groups by Family

Area	Catholic	Baptist	Non-Den.	Methodist[2]	Lutheran	LDS[3]	Pente-costal	Presby-terian[4]	Muslim[5]	Judaism
MSA[1]	28.4	8.5	6.0	3.1	1.7	1.4	1.3	0.8	1.0	0.2
U.S.	19.1	9.3	4.0	4.0	2.3	2.0	1.9	1.6	0.8	0.7

Note: Figures are the number of adherents as a percentage of the total population; (1) Figures cover the San Antonio-New Braunfels, TX Metropolitan Statistical Area—see Appendix B for areas included; (2) Methodist/Pietist; (3) Latter Day Saints; (4) Reformed; (5) Figures are estimates
Source: Association of Statisticians of American Religious Bodies, 2010 U.S. Religion Census: Religious Congregations & Membership Study

Religious Groups by Tradition

Area	Catholic	Evangelical Protestant	Mainline Protestant	Other Tradition	Black Protestant	Orthodox
MSA[1]	28.4	17.0	5.0	3.2	0.4	0.1
U.S.	19.1	16.2	7.3	4.3	1.6	0.3

Note: Figures are the number of adherents as a percentage of the total population; (1) Figures cover the San Antonio-New Braunfels, TX Metropolitan Statistical Area—see Appendix B for areas included
Source: Association of Statisticians of American Religious Bodies, 2010 U.S. Religion Census: Religious Congregations & Membership Study

ECONOMY

Gross Metropolitan Product

Area	2012	2013	2014	2015	Rank[2]
MSA[1]	92.0	95.1	99.9	105.4	36

Note: Figures are in billions of dollars; (1) Figures cover the San Antonio-New Braunfels, TX Metropolitan Statistical Area—see Appendix B for areas included; (2) Rank is based on 2015 data and ranges from 1 to 363
Source: The U.S. Conference of Mayors, U.S. Metro Economies: GMP and Employment 2013-2015, June 2014

Economic Growth

Area	2010-12 (%)	2013 (%)	2014 (%)	2015 (%)	Rank[2]
MSA[1]	3.8	1.8	3.0	4.0	29
U.S.	2.1	2.0	2.3	3.2	–

Note: Figures are real gross metropolitan product (GMP) growth rates and represent annual average percent change; (1) Figures cover the San Antonio-New Braunfels, TX Metropolitan Statistical Area—see Appendix B for areas included; (2) Rank is based on 2015 data and ranges from 1 to 363
Source: The U.S. Conference of Mayors, U.S. Metro Economies: GMP and Employment 2013-2015, June 2014

Metropolitan Area Exports

Area	2008	2009	2010	2011	2012	2013	Rank[2]
MSA[1]	5,049.5	4,390.0	6,416.2	10,506.5	14,010.2	19,287.6	16

Note: Figures are in millions of dollars; (1) Figures cover the San Antonio-New Braunfels, TX Metropolitan Statistical Area—see Appendix B for areas included; (2) Rank is based on 2013 data and ranges from 1 to 387
Source: U.S. Department of Commerce, International Trade Administration, Office of Trade & Industry Information, Manufacturing & Services, data extracted April 3, 2015

Building Permits

Area	Single-Family 2013	Single-Family 2014	Single-Family Pct. Chg.	Multi-Family 2013	Multi-Family 2014	Multi-Family Pct. Chg.	Total 2013	Total 2014	Total Pct. Chg.
City	2,102	2,270	8.0	16	3,368	20,950.0	2,118	5,638	166.2
MSA[1]	5,827	6,220	6.7	301	4,112	1,266.1	6,128	10,332	68.6
U.S.	620,802	634,597	2.2	370,020	411,766	11.3	990,822	1,046,363	5.6

Note: (1) Figures cover the San Antonio-New Braunfels, TX Metropolitan Statistical Area—see Appendix B for areas included; Figures represent new, privately-owned housing units authorized (unadjusted data); All permit data are based on estimates with imputation.
Source: U.S. Census Bureau, Manufacturing, Mining, and Construction Statistics, Building Permits, 2013, 2014

Bankruptcy Filings

Area	Business Filings 2013	Business Filings 2014	Business Filings % Chg.	Nonbusiness Filings 2013	Nonbusiness Filings 2014	Nonbusiness Filings % Chg.
Bexar County	157	124	-21.0	2,696	2,497	-7.4
U.S.	33,212	26,983	-18.8	1,038,720	909,812	-12.4

Note: Business filings include Chapter 7, Chapter 11, Chapter 12, and Chapter 13; Nonbusiness filings include Chapter 7, Chapter 11, and Chapter 13
Source: Administrative Office of the U.S. Courts, Business and Nonbusiness Bankruptcy, County Cases Commenced by Chapter of the Bankruptcy Code, During the 12- Month Period Ending December 31, 2013 and Business and Nonbusiness Bankruptcy, County Cases Commenced by Chapter of the Bankruptcy Code, During the 12- Month Period Ending December 31, 2014

Housing Vacancy Rates

Area	Gross Vacancy Rate[2] (%) 2012	2013	2014	Year-Round Vacancy Rate[3] (%) 2012	2013	2014	Rental Vacancy Rate[4] (%) 2012	2013	2014	Homeowner Vacancy Rate[5] (%) 2012	2013	2014
MSA[1]	11.3	9.0	8.6	10.4	8.3	8.2	9.0	9.1	7.3	2.7	1.4	1.2
U.S.	13.8	13.6	13.4	10.8	10.7	10.4	8.7	8.3	7.6	2.0	2.0	1.9

Note: (1) Figures cover the San Antonio-New Braunfels, TX Metropolitan Statistical Area—see Appendix B for areas included; (2) The percentage of the total housing inventory that is vacant; (3) The percentage of the housing inventory (excluding seasonal units) that is year-round vacant; (4) The percentage of rental inventory that is vacant for rent; (5) The percentage of homeowner inventory that is vacant for sale
Source: U.S. Census Bureau, Housing Vacancies and Homeownership Annual Statistics: 2014

INCOME

Income

Area	Per Capita ($)	Median Household ($)	Average Household ($)
City	22,311	45,253	60,746
MSA[1]	24,742	51,401	68,839
U.S.	27,884	52,176	72,897

Note: (1) Figures cover the San Antonio-New Braunfels, TX Metropolitan Statistical Area—see Appendix B for areas included
Source: U.S. Census Bureau, 2011-2013 American Community Survey 3-Year Estimates

Household Income Distribution

Area	Percent of Households Earning: Under $15,000	$15,000 -24,999	$25,000 -34,999	$35,000 -49,999	$50,000 -74,999	$75,000 -99,000	$100,000 -149,999	$150,000 and up
City	15.3	12.5	11.6	15.2	18.7	10.3	10.3	6.2
MSA[1]	12.7	11.0	10.3	14.6	18.9	11.9	12.4	8.1
U.S.	13.0	10.9	10.3	13.6	17.9	11.9	12.7	9.6

Note: (1) Figures cover the San Antonio-New Braunfels, TX Metropolitan Statistical Area—see Appendix B for areas included
Source: U.S. Census Bureau, 2011-2013 American Community Survey 3-Year Estimates

Poverty Rate

Area	All Ages	Under 18 Years Old	18 to 64 Years Old	65 Years and Over
City	20.5	29.5	18.1	12.8
MSA[1]	16.8	24.2	14.9	10.6
U.S.	15.9	22.4	14.8	9.5

Note: Figures are percentage of people whose income during the past 12 months was below the poverty level; (1) Figures cover the San Antonio-New Braunfels, TX Metropolitan Statistical Area—see Appendix B for areas included
Source: U.S. Census Bureau, 2011-2013 American Community Survey 3-Year Estimates

EMPLOYMENT

Labor Force and Employment

Area	Civilian Labor Force			Workers Employed		
	Dec. 2013	Dec. 2014	% Chg.	Dec. 2013	Dec. 2014	% Chg.
City	665,217	676,837	1.7	633,279	652,731	3.1
MSA[1]	1,078,143	1,096,505	1.7	1,025,485	1,056,403	3.0
U.S.	154,408,000	155,521,000	0.7	144,423,000	147,190,000	1.9

Note: Data is not seasonally adjusted and covers workers 16 years of age and older; (1) Figures cover the San Antonio-New Braunfels, TX Metropolitan Statistical Area—see Appendix B for areas included
Source: Bureau of Labor Statistics, Local Area Unemployment Statistics

Unemployment Rate

Area	2014											
	Jan.	Feb.	Mar.	Apr.	May	Jun.	Jul.	Aug.	Sep.	Oct.	Nov.	Dec.
City	5.1	5.1	4.8	4.2	4.5	4.9	5.0	4.7	4.4	4.1	3.9	3.6
MSA[1]	5.2	5.2	4.9	4.3	4.6	4.9	5.0	4.8	4.5	4.2	4.0	3.7
U.S.	7.0	7.0	6.8	5.9	6.1	6.3	6.5	6.3	5.7	5.5	5.5	5.4

Note: Data is not seasonally adjusted and covers workers 16 years of age and older; (1) Figures cover the San Antonio-New Braunfels, TX Metropolitan Statistical Area—see Appendix B for areas included
Source: Bureau of Labor Statistics, Local Area Unemployment Statistics

Employment by Occupation

Occupation Classification	City (%)	MSA[1] (%)	U.S. (%)
Management, Business, Science, and Arts	32.9	34.5	36.2
Natural Resources, Construction, and Maintenance	10.0	10.1	9.0
Production, Transportation, and Material Moving	9.8	9.9	12.1
Sales and Office	26.8	26.2	24.4
Service	20.6	19.3	18.3

Note: Figures cover employed civilians 16 years of age and older; (1) Figures cover the San Antonio-New Braunfels, TX Metropolitan Statistical Area—see Appendix B for areas included
Source: U.S. Census Bureau, 2011-2013 American Community Survey 3-Year Estimates

Employment by Industry

Sector	MSA[1] Number of Employees	MSA[1] Percent of Total	U.S. Percent of Total
Construction	47,300	4.9	4.4
Education and Health Services	149,200	15.5	15.5
Financial Activities	83,100	8.6	5.7
Government	165,600	17.2	15.8
Information	21,900	2.3	2.0
Leisure and Hospitality	114,900	11.9	10.3
Manufacturing	45,700	4.7	8.7
Mining and Logging	8,500	0.9	0.6
Other Services	34,700	3.6	4.0
Professional and Business Services	123,400	12.8	13.8
Retail Trade	110,800	11.5	11.4
Transportation, Warehousing, and Utilities	26,000	2.7	3.9
Wholesale Trade	34,200	3.5	4.2

Note: Figures are non-farm employment as of December 2014. Figures are not seasonally adjusted and include workers 16 years of age and older; (1) Figures cover the San Antonio-New Braunfels, TX Metropolitan Statistical Area—see Appendix B for areas included
Source: Bureau of Labor Statistics, Current Employment Statistics, Employment, Hours, and Earnings

Occupations with Greatest Projected Employment Growth: 2012 – 2022

Occupation[1]	2012 Employment	2022 Projected Employment	Numeric Employment Change	Percent Employment Change
Combined Food Preparation and Serving Workers, Including Fast Food	285,480	378,000	92,520	32.4
Personal Care Aides	199,230	283,980	84,750	42.5
Retail Salespersons	378,330	439,340	61,010	16.1
Registered Nurses	189,380	242,860	53,480	28.2
Customer Service Representatives	214,240	262,770	48,530	22.7
Waiters and Waitresses	196,390	240,390	44,000	22.4
Janitors and Cleaners, Except Maids and Housekeeping Cleaners	172,120	213,340	41,220	23.9
Laborers and Freight, Stock, and Material Movers, Hand	185,770	226,470	40,700	21.9
Elementary School Teachers, Except Special Education	141,030	180,920	39,890	28.3
Secretaries and Administrative Assistants, Except Legal, Medical, and Executive	190,470	230,220	39,750	20.9

Note: Projections cover Texas; (1) Sorted by numeric employment change
Source: www.projectionscentral.com, State Occupational Projections, 2012–2022 Long-Term Projections

Fastest Growing Occupations: 2012 – 2022

Occupation[1]	2012 Employment	2022 Projected Employment	Numeric Employment Change	Percent Employment Change
Diagnostic Medical Sonographers	4,380	6,900	2,520	57.6
Computer Numerically Controlled Machine Tool Programmers, Metal and Plastic	1,740	2,700	960	54.8
Interpreters and Translators	4,510	6,720	2,210	49.0
Skincare Specialists	5,130	7,620	2,490	48.3
Agents and Business Managers of Artists, Performers, and Athletes	310	450	140	47.4
Petroleum Engineers	19,280	28,010	8,730	45.3
Information Security Analysts	6,640	9,630	2,990	45.0
Insulation Workers, Mechanical	4,460	6,460	2,000	44.6
Cardiovascular Technologists and Technicians	3,950	5,700	1,750	44.3
Physician Assistants	5,470	7,880	2,410	44.2

Note: Projections cover Texas; (1) Sorted by percent employment change and excludes occupations with numeric employment change less than 100
Source: www.projectionscentral.com, State Occupational Projections, 2012–2022 Long-Term Projections

Average Wages

Occupation	$/Hr.	Occupation	$/Hr.
Accountants and Auditors	33.59	Maids and Housekeeping Cleaners	9.40
Automotive Mechanics	18.94	Maintenance and Repair Workers	15.50
Bookkeepers	17.96	Marketing Managers	52.16
Carpenters	17.92	Nuclear Medicine Technologists	32.74
Cashiers	9.58	Nurses, Licensed Practical	20.65
Clerks, General Office	15.01	Nurses, Registered	31.91
Clerks, Receptionists/Information	11.89	Nursing Assistants	11.64
Clerks, Shipping/Receiving	13.54	Packers and Packagers, Hand	10.73
Computer Programmers	38.96	Physical Therapists	41.87
Computer Systems Analysts	37.89	Postal Service Mail Carriers	25.09
Computer User Support Specialists	21.15	Real Estate Brokers	32.39
Cooks, Restaurant	10.09	Retail Salespersons	12.78
Dentists	84.92	Sales Reps., Exc. Tech./Scientific	32.89
Electrical Engineers	43.18	Sales Reps., Tech./Scientific	36.78
Electricians	21.23	Secretaries, Exc. Legal/Med./Exec.	15.32
Financial Managers	61.53	Security Guards	11.61
First-Line Supervisors/Managers, Sales	22.05	Surgeons	116.16
Food Preparation Workers	9.76	Teacher Assistants	11.20
General and Operations Managers	54.74	Teachers, Elementary School	27.10
Hairdressers/Cosmetologists	12.44	Teachers, Secondary School	27.70
Internists	n/a	Telemarketers	10.63
Janitors and Cleaners	10.45	Truck Drivers, Heavy/Tractor-Trailer	18.18
Landscaping/Groundskeeping Workers	12.21	Truck Drivers, Light/Delivery Svcs.	14.56
Lawyers	60.15	Waiters and Waitresses	9.36

Note: Wage data covers the San Antonio-New Braunfels, TX Metropolitan Statistical Area—see Appendix B for areas included; Hourly wages for elementary/secondary school teachers and teacher assistants were calculated by the editors from annual wage data assuming a 40 hour work week; n/a not available.
Source: Bureau of Labor Statistics, Metro Area Occupational Employment and Wage Estimates, May 2014

TAXES

State Corporate Income Tax Rates

State	Tax Rate (%)	Income Brackets ($)	Num. of Brackets	Financial Institution Tax Rate (%)[a]	Federal Income Tax Ded.
Texas	(y)	–	–	(y)	No

Note: Tax rates as of January 1, 2015; (a) Rates listed are the corporate income tax rate applied to financial institutions or excise taxes based on income. Some states have other taxes based upon the value of deposits or shares; (y) Texas imposes a Franchise Tax, otherwise known as margin tax, imposed on entities with more than $1,030,000 total revenues at rate of 1%, or 0.5% for entities primarily engaged in retail or wholesale trade, on lesser of 70% of total revenues or 100%of gross receipts after deductions for either compensation or cost of goods sold.
Source: Federation of Tax Administrators, "State Corporate Income Tax Rates, 2015"

State Individual Income Tax Rates

State	Tax Rate (%)	Income Brackets ($)	Num. of Brackets	Personal Exempt. ($)[1] Single	Personal Exempt. ($)[1] Dependents	Fed. Inc. Tax Ded.
Texas	None			–	–	–

Note: Tax rates as of January 1, 2015; Local- and county-level taxes are not included; n/a not applicable; (1) Married joint filers generally receive double the single exemption
Source: Federation of Tax Administrators, "State Individual Income Tax Rates, 2015"

Various State and Local Tax Rates

State	State and Local Sales and Use (%)	State Sales and Use (%)	Gasoline[1] (¢/gal.)	Cigarette[2] ($/pack)	Spirits[3] ($/gal.)	Wine[4] ($/gal.)	Beer[5] ($/gal.)
Texas	8.25	6.25	20	1.41	2.40 (f)	0.20	0.20 (p)

Note: All tax rates as of January 1, 2015; (1) The American Petroleum Institute has developed a methodology for determining the average tax rate on a gallon of fuel. Rates may include any of the following: excise taxes, environmental fees, storage tank fees, other fees or taxes, general sales tax, and local taxes. In states where gasoline is subject to the general sales tax, or where the fuel tax is based on the average sale price, the average rate determined by API is sensitive to changes in the price of gasoline. States that fully or partially apply general sales taxes to gasoline: CA, CO, GA, IL, IN, MI, NY; (2) The federal excise tax of $1.0066 per pack and local taxes are not included; (3) Rates are those applicable to off-premise sales of 40% alcohol by volume (a.b.v.) distilled spirits in 750ml containers. Local excise taxes are excluded; (4) Rates are those applicable to off-premise sales of 11% a.b.v. non-carbonated wine in 750ml containers; (5) Rates are those applicable to off-premise sales of 4.7% a.b.v. beer in 12 ounce containers; (f) Different rates are also applicable according to alcohol content, place of production, size of container, or place purchased (on- or off-premise or onboard airlines); (p) Local excise taxes are excluded.
Source: Tax Foundation, 2015 Facts & Figures: How Does Your State Compare?

State Business Tax Climate Index Rankings

State	Overall Rank	Corporate Tax Index Rank	Individual Income Tax Index Rank	Sales Tax Index Rank	Unemployment Insurance Tax Index Rank	Property Tax Index Rank
Texas	10	39	6	36	15	36

Note: The index is a measure of how each state's tax laws affect economic performance. The lower the rank, the more favorable a state's tax system is for business. States without a given tax are given a ranking of 1. The scores/rankings for the District of Columbia do not affect other states. The 2015 index represents the tax climate as of July 1, 2014.
Source: Tax Foundation, State Business Tax Climate Index 2015

COMMERCIAL REAL ESTATE

Office Market

Market Area	Inventory (sq. ft.)	Vacancy Rate (%)	Under Construction (sq. ft.)	YTD Net Absorption (sq. ft.)	Total Average Asking Rent ($/sq. ft./year)
San Antonio	43,488,325	13.4	536,876	894,367	19.85
National	4,745,108,508	14.3	71,190,461	51,084,126	27.40

Source: Newmark Grubb Knight Frank, National Office Market Report, 4th Quarter 2014

Industrial/Warehouse/R&D Market

Market Area	Inventory (sq. ft.)	Vacancy Rate (%)	Under Construction (sq. ft.)	YTD Net Absorption (sq. ft.)	Total Average Asking Rent ($/sq. ft./year)
San Antonio	102,131,196	6.9	813,028	493,609	5.82
National	14,238,613,765	7.2	134,387,407	185,246,438	5.64

Source: Newmark Grubb Knight Frank, National Industrial Market Report, 4th Quarter 2014

COMMERCIAL UTILITIES

Typical Monthly Electric Bills

Area	Commercial Service ($/month)		Industrial Service ($/month)	
	1,500 kWh	40 kW demand 14,000 kWh	1,000 kW demand 200,000 kWh	50,000 kW demand 32,500,000 kWh
City	n/a	n/a	n/a	n/a
Average[1]	201	1,653	26,124	2,639,743

Note: Figures are based on annualized 2014 rates; (1) Average based on 180 utilities surveyed; n/a not available
Source: Edison Electric Institute, Typical Bills and Average Rates Report, Summer 2014

TRANSPORTATION

Means of Transportation to Work

Area	Car/Truck/Van		Public Transportation			Bicycle	Walked	Other Means	Worked at Home
	Drove Alone	Car-pooled	Bus	Subway	Railroad				
City	79.2	11.0	3.4	0.0	0.0	0.3	1.9	1.0	3.2
MSA[1]	79.3	11.0	2.3	0.0	0.0	0.2	1.8	1.1	4.3
U.S.	76.4	9.6	2.6	1.8	0.6	0.6	2.8	1.3	4.3

Note: Figures are percentages and cover workers 16 years of age and older; (1) Figures cover the San Antonio-New Braunfels, TX Metropolitan Statistical Area—see Appendix B for areas included
Source: U.S. Census Bureau, 2011-2013 American Community Survey 3-Year Estimates

Travel Time to Work

Area	Less Than 10 Minutes	10 to 19 Minutes	20 to 29 Minutes	30 to 44 Minutes	45 to 59 Minutes	60 to 89 Minutes	90 Minutes or More
City	10.5	31.7	27.6	20.9	4.7	2.8	1.8
MSA[1]	10.9	28.9	25.0	22.2	7.0	3.9	2.0
U.S.	13.3	29.7	20.9	20.2	7.7	5.7	2.6

Note: Figures are percentages and include workers 16 years old and over; (1) Figures cover the San Antonio-New Braunfels, TX Metropolitan Statistical Area—see Appendix B for areas included
Source: U.S. Census Bureau, 2011-2013 American Community Survey 3-Year Estimates

Travel Time Index

Area	1985	1990	1995	2000	2005	2010	2011
Urban Area[1]	1.06	1.06	1.09	1.19	1.22	1.19	1.19
Average[2]	1.09	1.14	1.16	1.19	1.23	1.18	1.18

Note: Travel Time Index—the ratio of travel time in the peak period to the travel time at free-flow conditions. For example, a value of 1.30 indicates a 20-minute free-flow trip takes 26 minutes in the peak. Free-flow speeds (60 mph on freeways and 35 mph on principal arterials) are used as the comparison threshold; (1) Covers the San Antonio TX urban area; (2) average of 498 urban areas
Source: Texas Transportation Institute, Urban Mobility Report 2012, December 2012

Public Transportation

Agency Name / Mode of Transportation	Vehicles Operated in Maximum Service	Annual Unlinked Passenger Trips (in thous.)	Annual Passenger Miles (in thous.)
VIA Metropolitan Transit (VIA)			
Bus (directly operated)	352	45,484.4	195,735.8
Demand Response (directly operated)	102	488.8	5,254.0
Demand Response (purchased transportation)	103	570.3	6,579.7
Vanpool (purchased transportation)	166	419.7	17,663.7

Source: Federal Transit Administration, National Transit Database, 2013

Air Transportation

Airport Name and Code / Type of Service	Passenger Airlines[1]	Passenger Enplanements	Freight Carriers[2]	Freight (lbs.)
San Antonio International (SAT)				
Domestic service (U.S. carriers - 2014)	30	3,807,401	15	100,950,338
International service (U.S. carriers - 2013)	14	64,219	5	12,920,778

Note: (1) Includes all U.S.-based major, minor and commuter airlines that carried at least one passenger during the year; (2) Includes all U.S.-based airlines and freight carriers that transported at least one lb. of freight during the year.
Source: Bureau of Transportation Statistics, The Intermodal Transportation Database, Air Carriers: T-100 Domestic Market (U.S. Carriers), 2014; Bureau of Transportation Statistics, The Intermodal Transportation Database, Air Carriers: T-100 International Market (U.S. Carriers), 2013

Other Transportation Statistics

Major Highways:	I-10; I-35; I-37
Amtrak Service:	Yes
Major Waterways/Ports:	None

Source: Amtrak.com; Google Maps

BUSINESSES

Major Business Headquarters

Company Name	Rankings	
	Fortune[1]	Forbes[2]
CC Media Holdings	419	-
CST Brands	266	-
HE Butt Grocery	-	15
Tesoro Corporation	75	-
United Services Automobile Association	141	-
Valero Energy	10	-

Note: (1) Fortune 500—companies that produce a 10-K are ranked 1 to 500 based on 2013 revenue; (2) all private companies with at least $2 billion in annual revenue through the end of their most current fiscal year are ranked 1 to 221; companies listed are headquartered in the city; dashes indicate no ranking
Source: Fortune, "Fortune 500," June 16, 2014; Forbes, "America's Largest Private Companies," November 5, 2014

Fast-Growing Businesses

According to *Inc.*, San Antonio is home to one of America's 500 fastest-growing private companies: **Culture.Service.Growth.** (#198). Criteria: must be an independent, privately-held, for-profit, U.S. corporation, proprietorship or partnership; revenues must be at least $100,000 in 2010 and $2 million in 2013; must have four-year operating/sales history. Holding companies, regulated banks, and utilities were excluded. *Inc., "America's 500 Fastest-Growing Private Companies," September 2014*

According to Deloitte, San Antonio is home to one of North America's 500 fastest-growing high-technology companies: **Rackspace Hosting** (#482). Companies are ranked by percentage growth in revenue over a five-year period. Criteria for inclusion: company must be headquartered within North America; must own proprietary intellectual property or proprietary technology that contributes to a significant portion of the company's operating revenue, or devote a significant proportion of revenues to research and development of technology; must have been in business for a minumum of five years with 2009 operating revenues of at least $50,000 USD/CD and 2013 operating revenues of at least $5 million USD/CD. *Deloitte Touche Tohmatsu, 2014 Technology Fast 500™*

Minority Business Opportunity

San Antonio is home to one company which is on the *Black Enterprise* Industrial/Service 100 list (100 largest companies based on gross sales): **Millennium Steel of Texas L.P.** (#17). Criteria: operational in previous calendar year; at least 51% black-owned and manufactures/owns the product it sells or provides industrial or consumer services. Brokerages, real estate firms and firms that provide professional services are not eligible. *Black Enterprise, B.E. 100s, 2014*

San Antonio is home to 13 companies which are on the *Hispanic Business* 500 list (500 largest U.S. Hispanic-owned companies based on 2012 revenue): **Genesis Networks Telecom Services** (#6); **Ancira Enterprises** (#7); **The Alamo Travel Group LP** (#65); **InGenesis** (#74); **Maldonado Nursery & Landscaping** (#172); **P3S Corp.** (#191); **Davila Pharmacy** (#248);

Garcia Foods (#256); **Munoz & Co.** (#280); **LuLu's Dessert Corp.** (#387); **IDC** (#407); **J.R. Ramon & Sons** (#412); **Inventiva** (#457). Companies included must show at least 51 percent ownership by Hispanic U.S. citizens, and must maintain headquarters in one of the 50 states or Washington, D.C. *Hispanic Business, "Hispanic Business 500," June 20, 2013*

San Antonio is home to three companies which are on the *Hispanic Business* Fastest-Growing 100 list (greatest sales growth from 2008 to 2012): **InGenesis** (#2); **IDC** (#38); **Visual Net Design** (#55). Companies included must show at least 51 percent ownership by Hispanic U.S. citizens, and must maintain headquarters in one of the 50 states or Washington, D.C. In addition, companies must have minimum revenues of $200,000 for calendar year 2008. *Hispanic Business, June 20, 2013*

Minority- and Women-Owned Businesses

Group	All Firms		Firms with Paid Employees			
	Firms	Sales ($000)	Firms	Sales ($000)	Employees	Payroll ($000)
Asian	3,893	1,370,455	1,258	1,273,871	7,827	226,171
Black	3,870	247,723	405	185,861	3,241	73,771
Hispanic	43,099	5,679,041	4,527	4,390,071	49,857	1,143,331
Women	30,581	5,468,661	3,714	4,750,495	40,585	944,051
All Firms	109,186	116,493,946	20,843	112,708,202	560,683	21,250,657

Note: Figures cover firms located in the city; minority- and women-owned business are defined as firms in which the corresponding group own 51% or more of the stock or equity of the company
Source: U.S. Census Bureau, 2007 Economic Census, Survey of Business Owners (2012 Survey of Business Owners data will be released starting in June 2015)

HOTELS & CONVENTION CENTERS

Hotels/Motels

Area	5 Star		4 Star		3 Star		2 Star		1 Star		Not Rated	
	Num.	Pct.[3]	Num.	Pct.[3]	Num.	Pct.[3]	Num.	Pct.[3]	Num.	Pct.[3]	Num.	Pct.[3]
City[1]	0	0.0	17	5.3	92	28.7	190	59.2	9	2.8	13	4.0
Total[2]	166	0.9	1,264	7.0	5,718	31.8	9,340	52.0	411	2.3	1,070	6.0

Note: (1) Figures cover San Antonio and vicinity; (2) Figures cover all 100 cities in this book; (3) Percentage of hotels which have a given star rating; Star ratings are determined by expedia.com and offer an indication of the general quality of a particular hotel.
Source: expedia.com, April 2, 2015

The San Antonio-New Braunfels, TX metro area is home to two of the best hotels in the U.S. according to *Travel & Leisure*: **JW Marriott San Antonio Hill Country Resort & Spa**; **Omni La Mansión del Rio**. Criteria: service; location; rooms; food; and value. The list includes the top 236 hotels in the U.S. *Travel & Leisure, "T+L 500, The World's Best Hotels 2015"*

Major Convention Centers

Name	Overall Space (sq. ft.)	Exhibit Space (sq. ft.)	Meeting Space (sq. ft.)	Meeting Rooms
Henry B. Gonzalez Convention Center	1,300,000	440,000	n/a	59

Note: Table includes convention centers located in the San Antonio-New Braunfels, TX metro area; n/a not available
Source: Original research

Living Environment

COST OF LIVING

Cost of Living Index

Composite Index	Groceries	Housing	Utilities	Transportation	Health Care	Misc. Goods/Services
92.1	89.3	79.8	84.0	96.7	97.1	104.5

Note: The Cost of Living Index measures regional differences in the cost of consumer goods and services, excluding taxes and non-consumer expenditures, for professional and managerial households in the top income quintile. It is based on more than 50,000 prices covering almost 60 different items for which prices are collected three times a year by chambers of commerce, economic development organizations or university applied economic centers in each participating urban area. The numbers shown should be read as a percentage above or below the national average of 100. For example, a value of 115.4 in the groceries column indicates that grocery prices are 15.4% higher than the national average. Small differences in the index numbers should not be interpreted as significant; Figures cover the San Antonio TX urban area.
Source: The Council for Community and Economic Research, ACCRA Cost of Living Index, 2014

Grocery Prices

Area[1]	T-Bone Steak ($/pound)	Frying Chicken ($/pound)	Whole Milk ($/half gal.)	Eggs ($/dozen)	Orange Juice ($/64 oz.)	Coffee ($/11.5 oz.)
City[2]	9.29	1.35	2.47	2.17	2.96	3.76
Avg.	10.40	1.37	2.40	1.99	3.46	4.27
Min.	8.48	0.93	1.37	1.30	2.83	2.99
Max.	14.20	2.44	3.62	4.02	6.42	6.96

Note: (1) Values for the local area are compared with the average, minimum and maximum values for all 308 areas in the Cost of Living Index; (2) Figures cover the San Antonio TX urban area; **T-Bone Steak** *(price per pound);* **Frying Chicken** *(price per pound, whole fryer);* **Whole Milk** *(half gallon carton);* **Eggs** *(price per dozen, Grade A, large);* **Orange Juice** *(64 oz. Tropicana or Florida Natural);* **Coffee** *(11.5 oz. can, vacuum-packed, Maxwell House, Hills Bros, or Folgers).*
Source: The Council for Community and Economic Research, ACCRA Cost of Living Index, 2014

Housing and Utility Costs

Area[1]	New Home Price ($)	Apartment Rent ($/month)	All Electric ($/month)	Part Electric ($/month)	Other Energy ($/month)	Telephone ($/month)
City[2]	225,397	855	-	96.27	37.03	25.51
Avg.	305,838	919	181.00	93.66	73.14	27.95
Min.	183,142	480	112.00	42.06	23.42	17.16
Max.	1,358,576	3,851	594.00	180.03	440.99	40.42

Note: (1) Values for the local area are compared with the average, minimum and maximum values for all 308 areas in the Cost of Living Index; (2) Figures cover the San Antonio TX urban area; **New Home Price** *(2,400 sf living area, 8,000 sf lot, in urban area with full utilities);* **Apartment Rent** *(950 sf 2 bedroom/1.5 or 2 bath, unfurnished, excluding all utilities except water);* **All Electric** *(average monthly cost for an all-electric home);* **Part Electric** *(average monthly cost for a part-electric home);* **Other Energy** *(average monthly cost for natural gas, fuel oil, coal, wood, and any other forms of energy except electricity);* **Telephone** *(price includes basic monthly rate for a private residential line plus additional local usage charges incurred by a family of four).*
Source: The Council for Community and Economic Research, ACCRA Cost of Living Index, 2014

Health Care, Transportation, and Other Costs

Area[1]	Doctor ($/visit)	Dentist ($/visit)	Optometrist ($/visit)	Gasoline ($/gallon)	Beauty Salon ($/visit)	Men's Shirt ($)
City[2]	96.30	84.33	87.56	3.32	34.15	32.08
Avg.	102.86	87.89	97.66	3.44	34.37	26.74
Min.	67.47	65.78	51.18	3.00	17.43	12.79
Max.	173.50	150.14	235.00	4.33	64.28	49.50

Note: (1) Values for the local area are compared with the average, minimum and maximum values for all 308 areas in the Cost of Living Index; (2) Figures cover the San Antonio TX urban area; **Doctor** *(general practitioners routine exam of an established patient);* **Dentist** *(adult teeth cleaning and periodic oral examination);* **Optometrist** *(full vision eye exam for established adult patient);* **Gasoline** *(one gallon regular unleaded, national brand, including all taxes, cash price at self-service pump if available);* **Beauty Salon** *(woman's shampoo, trim, and blow-dry);* **Men's Shirt** *(cotton/polyester dress shirt, pinpoint weave, long sleeves).*
Source: The Council for Community and Economic Research, ACCRA Cost of Living Index, 2014

HOUSING

House Price Index (HPI)

Area	National Ranking[2]	Quarterly Change (%)	One-Year Change (%)	Five-Year Change (%)
MSA[1]	96	0.35	5.61	11.65
U.S.[3]	–	1.35	4.91	11.59

Note: The HPI is a weighted repeat sales index. It measures average price changes in repeat sales or refinancings on the same properties. This information is obtained by reviewing repeat mortgage transactions on single-family properties whose mortgages have been purchased or securitized by Fannie Mae or Freddie Mac in January 1975; (1) San Antonio-New Braunfels Metropolitan Statistical Area—see Appendix B for areas included; (2) Rankings are based on annual percentage change for all metro areas containing at least 15,000 transactions over the last 10 years and ranges from 1 to 275; (3) figures based on a weighted average of Census Division estimates using a seasonally adjusted, purchase-only index; all figures are for the period ending December 31, 2014

Source: Federal Housing Finance Agency, House Price Index, February 26, 2015

Median Single-Family Home Prices

Area	2012	2013	2014p	Percent Change 2013 to 2014
MSA[1]	159.5	171.0	182.1	6.5
U.S. Average	177.2	197.4	209.0	5.9

Note: Figures are median sales prices of existing single-family homes in thousands of dollars; (p) preliminary; n/a not available; (1) San Antonio-New Braunfels, TX Metropolitan Statistical Area—see Appendix B for areas included

Source: National Association of Realtors, Median Sales Price of Existing Single-Family Homes for Metropolitan Areas, 4th Quarter 2014

Qualifying Income Based on Median Sales Price of Existing Single-Family Homes

Area	With 5% Down ($)	With 10% Down ($)	With 20% Down ($)
MSA[1]	40,764	38,619	34,328
U.S. Average	45,863	43,449	38,621

Note: Figures are preliminary; Qualifying income is based on a mortgage rate of 4.0%. Monthly principal and interest payment is limited to 25% of income; n/a not available; (1) San Antonio-New Braunfels, TX Metropolitan Statistical Area—see Appendix B for areas included

Source: National Association of Realtors, Qualifying Income Based on Median Sales Price of Existing Single-Family Homes for Metropolitan Areas, 4th Quarter 2014

Median Apartment Condo-Coop Home Prices

Area	2012	2013	2014p	Percent Change 2013 to 2014
MSA[1]	n/a	n/a	n/a	n/a
U.S. Average	173.7	194.9	205.1	5.2

Note: Figures are median sales prices of existing apartment condo-coop homes in thousands of dollars; (p) preliminary; n/a not available; (1) San Antonio-New Braunfels, TX Metropolitan Statistical Area—see Appendix B for areas included

Source: National Association of Realtors, Median Sales Price of Existing Apartment Condo-Coop Homes for Metropolitan Areas, 4th Quarter 2014

Gross Monthly Rent

Area	Under $200	$200 -299	$300 -499	$500 -749	$750 -999	$1,000 -1,499	$1,500 and up	Median ($)
City	1.9	3.1	7.0	28.9	30.3	22.6	6.3	817
MSA[1]	1.7	2.8	6.9	27.1	29.1	24.9	7.5	842
U.S.	1.7	3.2	7.8	22.1	24.3	26.0	14.9	900

Note: Figures are percentages except for Median; Gross rent is the contract rent plus the estimated average monthly cost of utilities (electricity, gas, and water and sewer) and fuels (oil, coal, kerosene, wood, etc.) if these are paid by the renter (or paid for the renter by someone else); (1) Figures cover the San Antonio-New Braunfels, TX Metropolitan Statistical Area—see Appendix B for areas included

Source: U.S. Census Bureau, 2011-2013 American Community Survey 3-Year Estimates

Homeownership Rate

Area	2007 (%)	2008 (%)	2009 (%)	2010 (%)	2011 (%)	2012 (%)	2013 (%)	2014 (%)
MSA[1]	62.4	66.1	69.8	70.1	66.5	67.5	70.1	70.2
U.S.	68.1	67.8	67.4	66.9	66.1	65.4	65.1	64.5

Note: (1) Figures cover the San Antonio-New Braunfels, TX Metropolitan Statistical Area—see Appendix B for areas included
Source: U.S. Census Bureau, Housing Vacancies and Homeownership Annual Statistics: 2014

Year Housing Structure Built

Area	2010 or Later	2000 -2009	1990 -1999	1980 -1989	1970 -1979	1960 -1969	1950 -1959	1940 -1949	Before 1940	Median Year
City	1.3	18.6	12.6	17.4	17.5	11.3	10.3	5.5	5.6	1980
MSA[1]	2.2	24.1	14.7	16.1	15.9	9.5	8.1	4.5	4.9	1984
U.S.	0.9	15.0	13.9	13.8	15.8	11.0	10.9	5.4	13.3	1976

Note: Figures are percentages except for Median Year; (1) Figures cover the San Antonio-New Braunfels, TX Metropolitan Statistical Area—see Appendix B for areas included
Source: U.S. Census Bureau, 2011-2013 American Community Survey 3-Year Estimates

HEALTH

Health Risk Data

Category	MSA[1] (%)	U.S. (%)
Adults aged 18–64 who have any kind of health care coverage	68.3	79.6
Adults who reported being in good or excellent health	81.0	83.1
Adults who are current smokers	17.7	19.6
Adults who are heavy drinkers[2]	7.3	6.1
Adults who are binge drinkers[3]	20.7	16.9
Adults who are overweight (BMI 25.0 - 29.9)	38.5	35.8
Adults who are obese (BMI 30.0 - 99.8)	28.5	27.6
Adults who participated in any physical activities in the past month	74.7	77.1
Adults 50+ who have ever had a sigmoidoscopy or colonoscopy	66.1	67.3
Women aged 40+ who have had a mammogram within the past two years	69.4	74.0
Men aged 40+ who have had a PSA test within the past two years	40.8	45.2
Adults aged 65+ who have had flu shot within the past year	63.6	60.1
Adults who always wear a seatbelt	96.8	93.8

Note: Data as of 2012 unless otherwise noted; (1) Figures cover the San Antonio, TX Metropolitan Statistical Area—see Appendix B for areas included; (2) Heavy drinkers are classified as males having more than two drinks per day or females having more than one drink per day; (3) Binge drinkers are classified as males having five or more drinks on one occasion or females having four or more drinks on one occasion
Source: Centers for Disease Control and Prevention, Behaviorial Risk Factor Surveillance System, SMART: Selected Metropolitan/Micropolitan Area Risk Trends, 2012 (Note: the CDC has discontinued this dataset but will be releasing a replacement in late 2015)

Chronic Health Indicators

Category	MSA[1] (%)	U.S. (%)
Adults who have ever been told they had a heart attack	3.6	4.5
Adults who have ever been told they had a stroke	2.5	2.9
Adults who have been told they currently have asthma	6.2	8.9
Adults who have ever been told they have arthritis	22.1	25.7
Adults who have ever been told they have diabetes[2]	10.3	9.7
Adults who have ever been told they had skin cancer	4.4	5.7
Adults who have ever been told they had any other types of cancer	6.7	6.5
Adults who have ever been told they have COPD	3.3	6.2
Adults who have ever been told they have kidney disease	2.3	2.5
Adults who have ever been told they have a form of depression	16.0	18.0

Note: Data as of 2012 unless otherwise noted; (1) Figures cover the San Antonio, TX Metropolitan Statistical Area—see Appendix B for areas included; (2) Figures do not include pregnancy-related, borderline, or pre-diabetes
Source: Centers for Disease Control and Prevention, Behaviorial Risk Factor Surveillance System, SMART: Selected Metropolitan/Micropolitan Area Risk Trends, 2012 (Note: the CDC has discontinued this dataset but will be releasing a replacement in late 2015)

Mortality Rates for the Top 10 Causes of Death in the U.S.

ICD-10[a] Sub-Chapter	ICD-10[a] Code	Age-Adjusted Mortality Rate[1] per 100,000 population	
		County[2]	U.S.
Malignant neoplasms	C00-C97	156.6	166.2
Ischaemic heart diseases	I20-I25	105.2	105.7
Other forms of heart disease	I30-I51	52.7	49.3
Chronic lower respiratory diseases	J40-J47	34.9	42.1
Organic, including symptomatic, mental disorders	F01-F09	53.0	38.1
Cerebrovascular diseases	I60-I69	40.6	37.0
Other external causes of accidental injury	W00-X59	30.3	26.9
Other degenerative diseases of the nervous system	G30-G31	20.2	25.6
Diabetes mellitus	E10-E14	26.9	21.3
Hypertensive diseases	I10-I15	15.7	19.4

Note: (a) ICD-10 = International Classification of Diseases 10th Revision; (1) Mortality rates are a three year average covering 2011-2013; (2) Figures cover Bexar County
Source: Centers for Disease Control and Prevention, National Center for Health Statistics. Compressed Mortality File 1999-2013 on CDC WONDER Online Database, released October 2014. Data are compiled from the Compressed Mortality File 1999-2013, Series 20 No. 2S, 2014.

Mortality Rates for Selected Causes of Death

ICD-10[a] Sub-Chapter	ICD-10[a] Code	Age-Adjusted Mortality Rate[1] per 100,000 population	
		County[2]	U.S.
Assault	X85-Y09	5.8	5.2
Diseases of the liver	K70-K76	24.1	13.2
Human immunodeficiency virus (HIV) disease	B20-B24	3.0	2.2
Influenza and pneumonia	J09-J18	11.2	15.4
Intentional self-harm	X60-X84	10.6	12.5
Malnutrition	E40-E46	1.8	0.9
Obesity and other hyperalimentation	E65-E68	1.4	1.8
Renal failure	N17-N19	15.9	13.1
Transport accidents	V01-V99	11.4	11.7
Viral hepatitis	B15-B19	2.7	2.2

Note: (a) ICD-10 = International Classification of Diseases 10th Revision; (1) Mortality rates are a three year average covering 2011-2013; (2) Figures cover Bexar County
Source: Centers for Disease Control and Prevention, National Center for Health Statistics. Compressed Mortality File 1999-2013 on CDC WONDER Online Database, released October 2014. Data are compiled from the Compressed Mortality File 1999-2013, Series 20 No. 2S, 2014.

Health Insurance Coverage

Area	With Health Insurance	With Private Health Insurance	With Public Health Insurance	Without Health Insurance	Population Under Age 18 Without Health Insurance
City	78.8	56.7	31.7	21.2	10.3
MSA[1]	80.6	61.0	30.1	19.4	10.0
U.S.	85.2	65.2	31.0	14.8	7.3

Note: Figures are percentages that cover the civilian noninstitutionalized population; (1) Figures cover the San Antonio-New Braunfels, TX Metropolitan Statistical Area—see Appendix B for areas included
Source: U.S. Census Bureau, 2011-2013 American Community Survey 3-Year Estimates

Number of Medical Professionals

Area[1]	MDs[2]	DOs[2,3]	Dentists	Podiatrists	Chiropractors	Optometrists
Local (number)	5,649	335	1,402	96	269	249
Local (rate[4])	315.8	18.7	76.9	5.3	14.8	13.7
U.S. (rate[4])	270.0	20.2	63.1	5.7	25.2	14.9

Note: Data as of 2013 unless noted; (1) Local data covers Bexar County; (2) Data as of 2012 and includes all active, non-federal physicians; (3) Doctor of Osteopathic Medicine; (4) rate per 100,000 population
Source: U.S. Department of Health and Human Services, Health Resources and Services Administration, Bureau of Health Professions, Area Resource File (ARF) 2013-2014

Best Hospitals

According to *U.S. News,* the San Antonio-New Braunfels, TX metro area is home to one of the best hospitals in the U.S.: **University Hospital** (1 specialty). The hospital listed was nationally ranked in at least one adult specialty. Only 144 hospitals nationwide were nationally ranked in one or more specialties. Seventeen hospitals in the U.S. made the Honor Roll with high scores in at least six specialties. *U.S. News Online, "America's Best Children's Hospitals 2014-15"*

EDUCATION

Public School District Statistics

District Name	Schls	Pupils	Pupil/ Teacher Ratio	Minority Pupils[1] (%)	Free Lunch Eligible[2] (%)	IEP[3] (%)
Alamo Heights ISD	6	4,808	14.5	45.0	17.4	6.9
East Central ISD	15	9,603	17.3	79.5	56.4	11.0
Edgewood ISD	19	11,937	16.9	99.5	95.3	9.6
Harlandale ISD	30	15,175	15.6	97.8	87.6	9.4
Harmony Science Acad. (San Antonio)	3	2,148	16.3	86.3	46.3	4.9
Jubilee Academic Center	8	2,378	13.2	94.5	62.2	6.8
North East ISD	77	67,901	15.8	70.1	38.0	9.0
Northside ISD	112	100,159	16.8	80.9	44.4	11.3
San Antonio ISD	99	54,268	16.1	98.0	84.6	10.2
South San Antonio ISD	19	9,842	15.7	98.2	87.9	7.5
Southside ISD	9	5,128	15.2	91.3	70.9	9.9
Southwest ISD	17	13,024	17.0	94.8	72.2	10.3

Note: Table includes school districts with 2,000 or more students; (1) Percentage of students that are not non-Hispanic white; (2) Percentage of students that are eligible for the free lunch program; (3) Percentage of students that have an Individualized Education Program.
Source: U.S. Department of Education, National Center for Education Statistics, Common Core of Data, Local Education Agency (School District) Universe Survey: School Year 2012-2013; U.S. Department of Education, National Center for Education Statistics, Common Core of Data, Public Elementary/Secondary School Universe Survey: School Year 2012-2013

Best High Schools

According to *The Daily Beast,* San Antonio is home to five of the best high schools in the U.S.: **Communications Arts High School** (#71); **Alamo Heights High School** (#181); **Tom C. Clark High School** (#368); **Business Careers High School** (#415); **Earl Warren High School** (#689); *The Daily Beast* used six indicators culled from school surveys to compare public high schools in the U.S., with graduation and college acceptance rates weighed most heavily. Other criteria included: college-level courses/exams and SAT/ACT scores. *The Daily Beast, "Top High Schools 2014"*

Highest Level of Education

Area	Less than H.S.	H.S. Diploma	Some College, No Deg.	Associate Degree	Bachelor's Degree	Master's Degree	Prof. School Degree	Doctorate Degree
City	18.8	25.6	23.3	7.1	16.2	6.3	1.7	0.9
MSA[1]	16.6	25.8	23.6	7.5	17.2	6.8	1.6	1.0
U.S.	13.7	28.0	21.2	7.9	18.2	7.7	1.9	1.3

Note: Figures cover persons age 25 and over; (1) Figures cover the San Antonio-New Braunfels, TX Metropolitan Statistical Area—see Appendix B for areas included
Source: U.S. Census Bureau, 2011-2013 American Community Survey 3-Year Estimates

Educational Attainment by Race

Area	High School Graduate or Higher (%)					Bachelor's Degree or Higher (%)				
	Total	White	Black	Asian	Hisp.[2]	Total	White	Black	Asian	Hisp.[2]
City	81.2	82.6	88.5	84.1	72.4	25.1	26.4	22.6	52.1	14.4
MSA[1]	83.4	84.7	89.9	82.4	73.2	26.5	27.7	24.7	48.7	14.9
U.S.	86.3	88.3	83.1	85.7	64.0	29.1	30.4	18.8	50.7	13.7

Note: Figures shown cover persons 25 years old and over; (1) Figures cover the San Antonio-New Braunfels, TX Metropolitan Statistical Area—see Appendix B for areas included; (2) People of Hispanic origin can be of any race
Source: U.S. Census Bureau, 2011-2013 American Community Survey 3-Year Estimates

School Enrollment by Grade and Control

Area	Preschool (%)		Kindergarten (%)		Grades 1 - 4 (%)		Grades 5 - 8 (%)		Grades 9 - 12 (%)	
	Public	Private	Public	Private	Public	Private	Public	Private	Public	Private
City	69.3	30.7	90.3	9.7	93.1	6.9	92.2	7.8	93.6	6.4
MSA[1]	65.5	34.5	91.1	8.9	92.3	7.7	92.7	7.3	93.6	6.4
U.S.	57.7	42.3	87.9	12.1	89.9	10.1	90.0	10.0	90.7	9.3

Note: Figures shown cover persons 3 years old and over; (1) Figures cover the San Antonio-New Braunfels, TX Metropolitan Statistical Area—see Appendix B for areas included
Source: U.S. Census Bureau, 2011-2013 American Community Survey 3-Year Estimates

Average Salaries of Public School Classroom Teachers

Area	2013-14		2014-15		Percent Change 2013-14 to 2014-15	Percent Change 2004-05 to 2014-15
	Dollars	Rank[1]	Dollars	Rank[1]		
TEXAS	49,690	30	50,576	29	1.78	23.3
U.S. Average	56,610	–	57,379	–	1.36	20.8

Note: (1) State rank ranges from 1 to 51 where 1 indicates highest salary.
Source: National Education Association, Rankings & Estimates: Rankings of the States 2014 and Estimates of School Statistics 2015, March 2015

Higher Education

Four-Year Colleges			Two-Year Colleges			Medical Schools[1]	Law Schools[2]	Voc/ Tech[3]
Public	Private Non-profit	Private For-profit	Public	Private Non-profit	Private For-profit			
2	7	8	4	0	7	1	1	19

Note: Figures cover institutions located within the city limits and include main campuses only; (1) includes schools accredited by the Liaison Committee on Medical Education and the American Osteopathic Association's Commission on Osteopathic College Accreditation; (2) includes ABA-accredited schools, schools with provisional ABA accreditation, and state accredited schools; (3) includes all schools with programs that are less than 2 years.
Source: National Center for Education Statistics, Integrated Postsecondary Education System (IPEDS), 2013-14; Association of American Medical Colleges, Member List, May 1, 2015; American Osteopathic Association, Member List, May 1, 2015; Law School Admission Council, Official Guide to ABA-Approved Law Schools Online, May 1, 2015; Wikipedia, List of Medical Schools in the United States, May 1, 2015; Wikipedia, List of Law Schools in the United States, May 1, 2015

According to *U.S. News & World Report,* the San Antonio-New Braunfels, TX metro area is home to one of the top 75 medical schools for research in the U.S.: **University of Texas Health Science Center-San Antonio (#55).** The rankings are based on a weighted average of 11 measures of quality: quality assessment; peer assessment score; assessment score by residency directors; research activity; total research activity; average research activity per faculty member; student selectivity; median MCAT total score; median undergraduate GPA; acceptance rate; and faculty resources. *U.S. News & World Report, "America's Best Graduate Schools, Medical, 2016"*

PRESIDENTIAL ELECTION

2012 Presidential Election Results

Area	Obama (%)	Romney (%)	Other (%)
Bexar County	51.6	47.0	1.4
U.S.	51.0	47.2	1.8

Note: Results may not add to 100% due to rounding
Source: Dave Leip's Atlas of U.S. Presidential Elections

EMPLOYERS

Major Employers

Company Name	Industry
Air Force, United States Dept of the	Air force
Baptist Health Systems	Hospital, ama approved residency
Baptist Health Systems	Hospital, med school affiliated with nursing & residency
Boeing Aerospace Operations	Aviation school
Boeing Aerospace Operations	Aircraft and heavy equipment repair services
Christus Santa Rosa Health Care Corp	General medical and surgical hospitals
Continental Automotive Systems	Semiconductors and related devices
Diamond Shamrock Refining & Marketing Co	Gasoline service stations
Northside Independent School District	Personal service agents, brokers and bureaus
Pacific Telesis Group	Telephone communication, except radio
Season Group USA	Electronic circuits
Southwest Research Institute	Commercial physical research
The Scooter Store, Ltd	Medical and hospital equipment
Toyota Motor Manufacturing, Texas	Motor vehicles and car bodies
U of Texas Health Science Center	University
University Health System	General medical and surgical hospitals
University of Texas at San Antonio	University
USAA	Fire, marine, and casualty insurance
Valero Services	Petroleum refining
Veterans Health Administration	Administration of veterans' affairs

Note: Companies shown are located within the San Antonio-New Braunfels, TX Metropolitan Statistical Area.
Source: Hoovers.com; Wikipedia

Best Companies to Work For

NuStar Energy; USAA, headquartered in San Antonio, are among "The 100 Best Companies to Work For." To pick the best companies, *Fortune* partnered with the Great Place to Work Institute. Two-thirds of a company's score is based on the results of the Institute's Trust Index survey, which is sent to a random sample of employees from each company. The questions related to attitudes about management's credibility, job satisfaction, and camaraderie. The other third of the scoring is based on the company's responses to the Institute's Culture Audit, which includes detailed questions about pay and benefit programs, and a series of open-ended questions about hiring practices, internal communication, training, recognition programs, and diversity efforts. Any company that is at least five years old with more than 1,000 U.S. employees is eligible. *Fortune, "The 100 Best Companies to Work For," 2015*

GlobalScape; USAA, headquartered in San Antonio, are among the "100 Best Places to Work in IT." To qualify, companies, both public and private, had to have a minimum of 50 IT employees and were selected based on average salary and bonus increases, the percentage of IT staffers promoted, IT staff turnover rates, training and development programs, and the percentage of women and minorities in IT staff and management positions. In addition, *Computerworld* looked at retention efforts, programs for recognizing and rewarding outstanding performances, and benefits such as flextime, elder care and child care, and reimbursement for college tuition and the cost of pursuing technology certifications. *Computerworld, "100 Best Places to Work in IT 2014"*

PUBLIC SAFETY

Crime Rate

Area	All Crimes	Violent Crimes				Property Crimes		
		Murder	Forcible Rape	Robbery	Aggrav. Assault	Burglary	Larceny -Theft	Motor Vehicle Theft
City	6,345.7	5.1	47.4	156.6	421.6	1,060.9	4,184.2	469.9
Suburbs[1]	2,511.9	3.8	25.9	27.3	127.9	510.2	1,687.4	129.5
Metro[2]	4,874.8	4.6	39.1	107.0	308.9	849.6	3,226.3	339.3
U.S.	3,098.6	4.5	25.2	109.1	229.1	610.0	1,899.4	221.3

Note: Figures are crimes per 100,000 population; (1) All areas within the metro area that are located outside the city limits; (2) Figures cover the San Antonio-New Braunfels, TX Metropolitan Statistical Area—see Appendix B for areas included
Source: FBI Uniform Crime Reports, 2013

Hate Crimes

Area	Number of Quarters Reported	Number of Incidents per Bias Motivation						
		Race	Religion	Sexual Orientation	Ethnicity	Disability	Gender	Gender Identity
City	4	3	0	7	1	0	0	0
U.S.	4	2,871	1,031	1,233	655	83	18	31

Source: Federal Bureau of Investigation, Hate Crime Statistics 2013

Identity Theft Consumer Complaints

Area	Complaints	Complaints per 100,000 Population	Rank[2]
MSA[1]	2,128	93.4	76
U.S.	332,646	104.3	-

Note: (1) Figures cover the San Antonio-New Braunfels, TX Metropolitan Statistical Area—see Appendix B for areas included; (2) Rank ranges from 1 to 380 where 1 indicates greatest number of identity theft complaints per 100,000 population
Source: Federal Trade Commission, Consumer Sentinel Network Data Book for January–December 2014

Fraud and Other Consumer Complaints

Area	Complaints	Complaints per 100,000 Population	Rank[2]
MSA[1]	8,628	378.8	178
U.S.	2,250,205	705.7	-

Note: (1) Figures cover the San Antonio-New Braunfels, TX Metropolitan Statistical Area—see Appendix B for areas included; (2) Rank ranges from 1 to 380 where 1 indicates greatest number of identity theft complaints per 100,000 population
Source: Federal Trade Commission, Consumer Sentinel Network Data Book for January–December 2014

RECREATION

Culture

Dance[1]	Theatre[1]	Instrumental Music[1]	Vocal Music[1]	Series and Festivals	Museums and Art Galleries[2]	Zoos and Aquariums[3]
1	4	3	1	5	55	2

Note: (1) Professional perfoming groups; (2) Based on organizations with SIC code 8412; (3) AZA-accredited
Source: The Grey House Performing Arts Directory, 2015-16; Association of Zoos & Aquariums, AZA Member Zoos & Aquariums, April 2015; www.AccuLeads.com, April 2015

Professional Sports Teams

Team Name	League	Year Established
San Antonio Spurs	National Basketball Association (NBA)	1973

Note: Includes teams located in the San Antonio-New Braunfels, TX Metropolitan Statistical Area.
Source: Wikipedia, Major Professional Sports Teams of the United States and Canada, April 2015

CLIMATE

Average and Extreme Temperatures

Temperature	Jan	Feb	Mar	Apr	May	Jun	Jul	Aug	Sep	Oct	Nov	Dec	Yr.
Extreme High (°F)	89	97	100	100	103	105	106	108	103	98	94	90	108
Average High (°F)	62	66	74	80	86	92	95	95	90	82	71	64	80
Average Temp. (°F)	51	55	62	70	76	82	85	85	80	71	60	53	69
Average Low (°F)	39	43	50	58	66	72	74	74	69	59	49	41	58
Extreme Low (°F)	0	6	19	31	43	53	62	61	46	33	21	6	0

Note: Figures cover the years 1948-1990
Source: National Climatic Data Center, International Station Meteorological Climate Summary, 9/96

Average Precipitation/Snowfall/Humidity

Precip./Humidity	Jan	Feb	Mar	Apr	May	Jun	Jul	Aug	Sep	Oct	Nov	Dec	Yr.
Avg. Precip. (in.)	1.5	1.8	1.5	2.6	3.8	3.6	2.0	2.5	3.3	3.2	2.3	1.4	29.6
Avg. Snowfall (in.)	1	Tr	Tr	0	0	0	0	0	0	0	Tr	Tr	1
Avg. Rel. Hum. 6am (%)	79	80	79	82	87	87	87	86	85	83	81	79	83
Avg. Rel. Hum. 3pm (%)	51	48	45	48	51	48	43	42	47	46	48	49	47

Note: Figures cover the years 1948-1990; Tr = Trace amounts (<0.05 in. of rain; <0.5 in. of snow)
Source: National Climatic Data Center, International Station Meteorological Climate Summary, 9/96

Weather Conditions

Temperature			Daytime Sky			Precipitation		
32°F & below	45°F & below	90°F & above	Clear	Partly cloudy	Cloudy	0.01 inch or more precip.	0.1 inch or more snow/ice	Thunder-storms
23	91	112	97	153	115	81	1	36

Note: Figures are average number of days per year and cover the years 1948-1990
Source: National Climatic Data Center, International Station Meteorological Climate Summary, 9/96

HAZARDOUS WASTE

Superfund Sites

San Antonio has no sites on the EPA's Superfund Final National Priorities List. There are a total of 1,322 Superfund sites on the list in the U.S. *U.S. Environmental Protection Agency, Final National Priorities List, April 14, 2015*

AIR & WATER QUALITY

Air Quality Trends: Ozone

	2004	2005	2006	2007	2008	2009	2010	2011	2012	2013
MSA[1]	0.085	0.082	0.083	0.071	0.075	0.070	0.072	0.075	0.079	0.076

Note: (1) Data covers the San Antonio-New Braunfels, TX Metropolitan Statistical Area—see Appendix B for areas included. The values shown are the composite ozone concentration averages among trend sites based on the highest fourth daily maximum 8-hour concentration in parts per million. These trends are based on sites having an adequate record of monitoring data during the trend period. Data from exceptional events are included.
Source: U.S. Environmental Protection Agency, Air Quality Monitoring Information, "Air Quality Trends by City, 2000-2013"

Air Quality Index

Area	Percent of Days when Air Quality was...[2]					AQI Statistics[2]	
	Good	Moderate	Unhealthy for Sensitive Groups	Unhealthy	Very Unhealthy	Maximum	Median
MSA[1]	60.0	39.2	0.8	0.0	0.0	125	46

Note: (1) Data covers the San Antonio-New Braunfels, TX Metropolitan Statistical Area—see Appendix B for areas included; (2) Based on 365 days with AQI data in 2014. Air Quality Index (AQI) is an index for reporting daily air quality. EPA calculates the AQI for five major air pollutants regulated by the Clean Air Act: ground-level ozone, particle pollution (aka particulate matter), carbon monoxide, sulfur dioxide, and nitrogen dioxide. The AQI runs from 0 to 500. The higher the AQI value, the greater the level of air pollution and the greater the health concern. There are six AQI categories: "Good" AQI is between 0 and 50. Air quality is considered satisfactory; "Moderate" AQI is between 51 and 100. Air quality is acceptable; "Unhealthy for Sensitive Groups" When AQI values are between 101 and 150, members of sensitive groups may experience health effects; "Unhealthy" When AQI values are between 151 and 200 everyone may begin to experience health effects; "Very Unhealthy" AQI values between 201 and 300 trigger a health alert; "Hazardous" AQI values over 300 trigger warnings of emergency conditions (not shown).
Source: U.S. Environmental Protection Agency, Air Quality Index Report, 2014

Air Quality Index Pollutants

Area	Percent of Days when AQI Pollutant was...[2]					
	Carbon Monoxide	Nitrogen Dioxide	Ozone	Sulfur Dioxide	Particulate Matter 2.5	Particulate Matter 10
MSA[1]	0.0	4.1	37.5	0.0	58.1	0.3

Note: (1) Data covers the San Antonio-New Braunfels, TX Metropolitan Statistical Area—see Appendix B for areas included; (2) Based on 365 days with AQI data in 2014. The Air Quality Index (AQI) is an index for reporting daily air quality. EPA calculates the AQI for five major air pollutants regulated by the Clean Air Act: ground-level ozone, particle pollution (also known as particulate matter), carbon monoxide, sulfur dioxide, and nitrogen dioxide. The AQI runs from 0 to 500. The higher the AQI value, the greater the level of air pollution and the greater the health concern.
Source: U.S. Environmental Protection Agency, Air Quality Index Report, 2014

Maximum Air Pollutant Concentrations: Particulate Matter, Ozone, CO and Lead

	Particulate Matter 10 (ug/m^3)	Particulate Matter 2.5 Wtd AM (ug/m^3)	Particulate Matter 2.5 24-Hr (ug/m^3)	Ozone (ppm)	Carbon Monoxide (ppm)	Lead (ug/m^3)
MSA[1] Level	71	8.3	26	0.083	n/a	0.02
NAAQS[2]	150	15	35	0.075	9	0.15
Met NAAQS[2]	Yes	Yes	Yes	No	n/a	Yes

Note: (1) Data covers the San Antonio-New Braunfels, TX Metropolitan Statistical Area—see Appendix B for areas included; Data from exceptional events are included; (2) National Ambient Air Quality Standards; ppm = parts per million; ug/m^3 = micrograms per cubic meter; n/a not available.
Concentrations: Particulate Matter 10 (coarse particulate)—highest second maximum 24-hour concentration; Particulate Matter 2.5 Wtd AM (fine particulate)—highest weighted annual mean concentration; Particulate Matter 2.5 24-Hour (fine particulate)—highest 98th percentile 24-hour concentration; Ozone—highest fourth daily maximum 8-hour concentration; Carbon Monoxide—highest second maximum non-overlapping 8-hour concentration; Lead—maximum running 3-month average
Source: U.S. Environmental Protection Agency, Air Quality Monitoring Information, "Air Quality Statistics by City, 2013"

Maximum Air Pollutant Concentrations: Nitrogen Dioxide and Sulfur Dioxide

	Nitrogen Dioxide AM (ppb)	Nitrogen Dioxide 1-Hr (ppb)	Sulfur Dioxide AM (ppb)	Sulfur Dioxide 1-Hr (ppb)	Sulfur Dioxide 24-Hr (ppb)
MSA[1] Level	5	35	n/a	15	n/a
NAAQS[2]	53	100	30	75	140
Met NAAQS[2]	Yes	Yes	n/a	Yes	n/a

Note: (1) Data covers the San Antonio-New Braunfels, TX Metropolitan Statistical Area—see Appendix B for areas included; Data from exceptional events are included; (2) National Ambient Air Quality Standards; ppm = parts per million; ug/m^3 = micrograms per cubic meter; n/a not available.
Concentrations: Nitrogen Dioxide AM—highest arithmetic mean concentration; Nitrogen Dioxide 1-Hr—highest 98th percentile 1-hour daily maximum concentration; Sulfur Dioxide AM—highest annual mean concentration; Sulfur Dioxide 1-Hr—highest 99th percentile 1-hour daily maximum concentration; Sulfur Dioxide 24-Hr—highest second maximum 24-hour concentration
Source: U.S. Environmental Protection Agency, Air Quality Monitoring Information, "Air Quality Statistics by City, 2013"

Drinking Water

Water System Name	Pop. Served	Primary Water Source Type	Violations[1]	
			Health Based	Monitoring/ Reporting
San Antonio Water System	1,596,714	Purchased Surface	0	0

Note: (1) Based on violation data from January 1, 2014 to December 31, 2014 (includes unresolved violations from earlier years)
Source: U.S. Environmental Protection Agency, Office of Ground Water and Drinking Water, Safe Drinking Water Information System (based on data extracted January 27, 2015)

Savannah, Georgia

Background

Savannah, at the mouth of the Savannah River on the border between Georgia and South Carolina, is Georgia's second fastest-growing city. It was established in 1733 when General James Oglethorpe landed with a group of settlers in the sailing vessel Anne, after a voyage of more than three months. City Hall now stands at the spot where Oglethorpe and his followers first camped on a small bluff overlooking the river.

Savannah is unique among American cities in that it was extensively planned while Oglethorpe was still in England. Each new settler was given a package of property, including a town lot, a garden space, and an outlying farm area. The town was planned in quadrants, the north and south for residences, and the east and west for public buildings.

The quadrant design was inspired in part by considerations of public defense, given the unsettled character of relations with Native Americans, but in fact an early treaty between the settlers and the Creek Indian Chief Tomochichi allowed Savannah to develop quite peacefully, with little of the hostility between Europeans and Indians that marred much of the development elsewhere in the colonies.

Savannah was taken by the British during the American Revolution, and in the patriotic siege that followed, many lives were lost. Count Pulaski, among other Revolutionary heroes, lost his life during the battle, but Savannah was eventually retaken in 1782 by the American Generals Nathaniel Greene and Anthony Wayne.

In the post-Revolutionary period, Savannah grew dramatically, its economic strength being driven in large part by Eli Whitney's cotton gin. As the world's leader in the cotton trade, Savannah also hosted a great development in export activity, and the first American steamboat built in the United States to cross the Atlantic was launched in its busy port.

Savannah's physical structure had been saved from the worst ravages of war, but the destruction of the area's infrastructure slowed its further development for an extended period, and "sleepy" became a common adjective applied to the once-vibrant economic center. In the long period of slow recovery that followed, one of the great Savannah success stories was the establishment of the Girl Scouts in 1912 by Juliette Gordon Low.

In 1954, an extensive fire destroyed a large portion of the historic City Market, and the area was bulldozed to make room for a parking garage. The Historic Savannah Foundation has worked unceasingly since then to maintain and improve Savannah's considerable architectural charms.

As a result, Savannah's Historic District was designated a Registered National Historic Landmark. Savannah has also been one of the favored sites for movie makers for decades. More than forty major movies have been filmed in Savannah including *Roots* (1976), *East of Eden* (1980), *Forrest Gump* (1994), *Midnight in the Garden of Good and Evil* (1997) and *The Legend of Bagger Vance* (2000), and a segment of the Colbert Report (2005).

Tourism, military services, port operations, and arts & culture industries are major employers in the city. Savannah's port facilities, operated by the Georgia Ports Authority, have seen notable growth in container tonnage in recent years. Garden City Terminal is the fourth largest container port in the United States, and the largest single-terminal operation in North America. Military installations in the area include Hunter Army Airfield and Fort Stewart military bases, employing a combined 42,000 people. Museums include Juliette Gordon Low Museum, Telfair Museum of Art and the Mighty 8th Air Forth Museum.

In addition, the city's beauty draws not just tourists, but conventioneers. The Savannah International Trade & Convention Center is a state-of-the-art facility with more than 100,000 square feet of exhibition space, accommodating nearly 10,000 people.

Colleges and universities in the city include the Savannah College of Art and Design, Savannah State University, and South University.

Savannah's climate is subtropical, with hot summers and mild winters, making the city an ideal locale for all-year outside activities.

Rankings

General Rankings

- Savannah appeared on *Travel + Leisure's* list of the ten best cities in the United States and Canada. The city was ranked #3. Criteria: activities/attractions; culture/arts; restaurants/food; people; and value. *Travel + Leisure, "The World's Best Awards 2014"*

Business/Finance Rankings

- The Savannah metro area appeared on the Milken Institute "2013 Best Performing Cities" list. Rank: #58 out of 200 large metro areas. Criteria: job growth; wage and salary growth; high-tech output growth. *Milken Institute, "Best-Performing Cities 2014," January 2015*

- *Forbes* ranked the 200 most populous metro areas to determine the nation's "Best Places for Business and Careers." The Savannah metro area was ranked #78. Criteria: costs (business and living); job growth (past and projected); income growth; educational attainment (college and high school); projected economic growth; cultural and recreational opportunities; net migration patterns; number of highly ranked colleges. *Forbes, "The Best Places for Business and Careers 2014," July 23, 2014*

Culture/Performing Arts Rankings

- Savannah was selected as one of the ten best small U.S. cities in which to be a moviemaker. Of cities with a population between 100,000 and 400,000, the city was ranked #3. Criteria: film community; access to new films; access to equipment; cost of living; tax incentives. *MovieMaker Magazine, "Best Places to Live and Work as a Moviemaker: 2013," January 22, 2015*

- Savannah was selected as one of America's top cities for the arts. The city ranked #6 in the mid-sized city (population 100,000 to 499,999) category. Criteria: readers' top choices for arts travel destinations based on the richness and variety of visual arts sites, activities and events. *American Style, "2012 Top 25 Arts Destinations," June 2012*

Education Rankings

- Personal finance website *WalletHub* analyzed the 150 largest U.S. metropolitan statistical areas to determine where the most educated Americans are choosing to settle. Criteria: educational attainment; percentage of workers with jobs in computer, engineering, and science fields; quality and size of each metro area's universities. Savannah was ranked #118 (#1 = most educated city). *www.WalletHub.com, "2014's Most and Least Educated Cities*

Environmental Rankings

- The Savannah metro area came in at #330 for the relative comfort of its climate on Sperling's list of "chill cities," as measured by the Sperling Heat Index. All 361 metro areas are included. Criteria included daytime high temperatures, nighttime low temperatures, dew point, and relative humidity at the high temperatures. *www.bertsperling.com, "Sperling's Chill Cities," July 18, 2013*

- Sperling's BestPlaces assessed 379 metropolitan areas of the United States for the likelihood of dangerously extreme weather events or earthquakes. In general the Southeast and South-Central regions have the highest risk of weather extremes and earthquakes, while the Pacific Northwest enjoys the lowest risk. Of the least risky metropolitan areas, the Savannah metro area was ranked #266. *www.bestplaces.net, "Safest Places from Natural Disasters," April 2011*

- Savannah was highlighted as one of the cleanest metro areas for ozone air pollution in the U.S. during 2011 through 2013. The list represents cities with no monitored ozone air pollution in unhealthful ranges. *American Lung Association, State of the Air 2015*

Health/Fitness Rankings

- The Savannah metro area appeared in the 2013 Gallup-Healthways Well-Being Index. The area ranked #89 out of 189. The Gallup-Healthways Well-Being Index score is an average of six sub-indexes, which individually examine life evaluation, emotional health, work environment, physical health, healthy behaviors, and access to basic necessities. Results are based on telephone interviews conducted as part of the Gallup-Healthways Well-Being Index survey January 2–December 29, 2012, and January 2–December 30, 2013, with a random sample of 531,630 adults, aged 18 and older, living in metropolitan areas in the 50 U.S. states and the District of Columbia. *Gallup-Healthways, "State of American Well-Being," March 25, 2014*

Real Estate Rankings

- Using data from the housing-market research firm RealtyTrac, Yahoo! Finance researchers listed the housing markets in which housing affordability is improving most, factoring in interest rates as well as median home prices. The Savannah metro area was among the most affordable housing markets according to the percentage difference in the income required to buy a home in December 2013 as opposed to in December 2012. *news.yahoo.com, "10 Cities Where Ordinary People Can No Longer Afford Homes," March 5, 2014*

- Savannah was ranked #236 out of 275 metro areas in terms of house price appreciation in 2014 (#1 = highest rate). *Federal Housing Finance Agency, House Price Index, 4th Quarter 2014*

Safety Rankings

- Allstate ranked the 200 largest cities in America in terms of driver safety. Savannah ranked #149. Allstate researchers analyzed internal property damage claims over a two-year period from January 2011 to December 2012. A weighted average of the two-year numbers determined the annual percentages. *Allstate, "Allstate America's Best Drivers Report, 2014"*
- The National Insurance Crime Bureau ranked 380 metro areas in the U.S. in terms of per capita rates of vehicle theft. The Savannah metro area ranked #84 (#1 = highest rate). Criteria: number of vehicle theft offenses per 100,000 inhabitants in 2012. *National Insurance Crime Bureau, "Hot Spots 2012," June 26, 2013*

Seniors/Retirement Rankings

- From its Best Cities for Successful Aging indexes, the Milken Institute generated rankings for metropolitan areas, weighing data in eight categories—health care, wellness, living arrangements, transportation, financial characteristics, education and employment opportunities, community engagement, and overall livability. The Savannah metro area was ranked #126 overall in the small metro area category. *Milken Institute, "Best Cities for Successful Aging, 2014"*

- Savannah was identified as one of the most popular places to retire by *Topretirements.com*. The list reflects the 100 cities (out of 900+ total cities reviewed) that visitors to the website are most interested in for retirement. *Topretirements.com, "Most Popular Places to Retire for 2014," February 25, 2014*

Sports/Recreation Rankings

- Savannah was chosen as a bicycle friendly community by the League of American Bicyclists. A "Bicycle Friendly Community" welcomes cyclists by providing safe accommodation for cycling and encouraging people to bike for transportation and recreation. There are four award levels: Platinum; Gold; Silver; and Bronze. The community achieved an award level of Bronze. *League of American Bicyclists, "Bicycle Friendly Community Master List," Fall 2013*

- Savannah was selected as one of the most playful cities in the U.S. by KaBOOM! The organization's Playful City USA initiative honors cities and towns across the nation for a vision, plan and commitment to creating an agenda for play. Criteria: creating a local play commission or task force; designing an annual action plan for play; conducting a play space audit; outlining a financial investment in play for the current fiscal year; and proclaiming and celebrating an annual "play day." *KaBOOM! National Campaign for Play, "2013 Playful City USA Communities"*

Miscellaneous Rankings

- *Travel + Leisure* invited readers to rate cities on indicators such as aloofness, "smarty-pants residents," highbrow cultural offerings, high-end shopping, artisanal coffeehouses, conspicuous eco-consciousness, and more in order to identify the nation's snobbiest cities. Cities large and small made the list; among them was Savannah, at #12. *www.travelandleisure.com, "America's Snobbiest Cities, June 2013*
- Now an international phenomenon, public St. Patrick's Day celebrations of "everything Irish" typically call forth parades and music and green in unexpected places. In its not-particularly-scientific survey of the St. Patrick's Day scene, the Huffington Post chose the festivities in Savannah as among the world's five best. *www.huffingtonpost.com, "The 5 Best Places to Celebrate St. Patrick's Day," March 10, 2014*
- In *Condé Nast Traveler* magazine's 2013 Readers' Choice Survey, Savannah made the top ten list of friendliest American cities, at #3. *www.cntraveler.com, "The Friendliest and Unfriendliest Cities in the U.S.," July 30, 2013*
- Savannah appeared on *Travel + Leisure's* list of America's most attractive people. Criteria: cities were selected by readers in their annual America's Favorite Cities survey. The city ranked #5 out of 10. *Travel + Leisure, "America's Most and Least Attractive People," November 2013*
- Savannah was selected as one of "America's Best Cities for Hipsters" by *Travel + Leisure.* The city was ranked #13 out of 20. Criteria: live music; coffee bars; independent boutiques; best microbrews; offbeat and tech-savvy locals. *Travel + Leisure, "America's Best Cities for Hipsters," November 2013*
- Savannah was selected as one of America's best-mannered cities. The area ranked #2. The general public determined the winners by casting votes online. *The Charleston School of Protocol and Etiquette, "2012 Most Mannerly City in America Contest," January 31, 2013*

Business Environment

CITY FINANCES

City Government Finances

Component	2012 ($000)	2012 ($ per capita)
Total Revenues	410,102	3,009
Total Expenditures	368,016	2,700
Debt Outstanding	184,328	1,353
Cash and Securities[1]	582,183	4,272

Note: (1) Cash and security holdings of a government at the close of its fiscal year, including those of its dependent agencies, utilities, and liquor stores.
Source: U.S Census Bureau, State & Local Government Finances 2012

City Government Revenue by Source

Source	2012 ($000)	2012 ($ per capita)
General Revenue		
From Federal Government	27,848	204
From State Government	9,828	72
From Local Governments	88,953	653
Taxes		
Property	59,464	436
Sales and Gross Receipts	36,314	266
Personal Income	0	0
Corporate Income	0	0
Motor Vehicle License	0	0
Other Taxes	9,331	68
Current Charges	90,709	666
Liquor Store	0	0
Utility	37,296	274
Employee Retirement	27,237	200

Source: U.S Census Bureau, State & Local Government Finances 2012

City Government Expenditures by Function

Function	2012 ($000)	2012 ($ per capita)	2012 (%)
General Direct Expenditures			
Air Transportation	26,231	192	7.1
Corrections	0	0	0.0
Education	0	0	0.0
Employment Security Administration	0	0	0.0
Financial Administration	4,970	36	1.4
Fire Protection	24,572	180	6.7
General Public Buildings	11,459	84	3.1
Governmental Administration, Other	6,004	44	1.6
Health	0	0	0.0
Highways	13,931	102	3.8
Hospitals	0	0	0.0
Housing and Community Development	33,113	243	9.0
Interest on General Debt	4,475	33	1.2
Judicial and Legal	2,149	16	0.6
Libraries	0	0	0.0
Parking	6,422	47	1.7
Parks and Recreation	21,368	157	5.8
Police Protection	62,497	459	17.0
Public Welfare	871	6	0.2
Sewerage	33,130	243	9.0
Solid Waste Management	21,313	156	5.8
Veterans' Services	0	0	0.0
Liquor Store	0	0	0.0
Utility	36,712	269	10.0
Employee Retirement	23,809	175	6.5

Source: U.S Census Bureau, State & Local Government Finances 2012

DEMOGRAPHICS

Population Growth

Area	1990 Census	2000 Census	2010 Census	Population Growth (%) 1990-2000	Population Growth (%) 2000-2010
City	138,038	131,510	136,286	-4.7	3.6
MSA[1]	258,060	293,000	347,611	13.5	18.6
U.S.	248,709,873	281,421,906	308,745,538	13.2	9.7

Note: (1) Figures cover the Savannah, GA Metropolitan Statistical Area—see Appendix B for areas included
Source: U.S. Census Bureau, Census 1990, 2000, 2010

Household Size

Area	Persons in Household (%)							Average Household Size
	One	Two	Three	Four	Five	Six	Seven or More	
City	35.4	31.6	15.3	9.3	5.1	2.1	1.1	2.54
MSA[1]	28.4	33.9	16.1	13.3	5.4	2.1	1.0	2.64
U.S.	27.7	33.6	15.7	13.1	6.0	2.3	1.5	2.64

Note: (1) Figures cover the Savannah, GA Metropolitan Statistical Area—see Appendix B for areas included
Source: U.S. Census Bureau, 2011-2013 American Community Survey 3-Year Estimates

Race

Area	White Alone[2] (%)	Black Alone[2] (%)	Asian Alone[2] (%)	AIAN[3] Alone[2] (%)	NHOPI[4] Alone[2] (%)	Other Race Alone[2] (%)	Two or More Races (%)
City	41.9	53.4	1.7	0.3	0.1	0.8	1.7
MSA[1]	60.9	33.5	2.2	0.3	0.1	0.9	2.3
U.S.	73.9	12.6	5.0	0.8	0.2	4.7	2.9

Note: (1) Figures cover the Savannah, GA Metropolitan Statistical Area—see Appendix B for areas included; (2) Alone is defined as not being in combination with one or more other races; (3) American Indian and Alaska Native; (4) Native Hawaiian and Other Pacific Islander
Source: U.S. Census Bureau, 2011-2013 American Community Survey 3-Year Estimates

Hispanic or Latino Origin

Area	Total (%)	Mexican (%)	Puerto Rican (%)	Cuban (%)	Other (%)
City	5.7	2.7	1.1	0.2	1.7
MSA[1]	5.5	2.8	1.1	0.2	1.3
U.S.	16.9	10.8	1.6	0.6	3.8

Note: Persons of Hispanic or Latino origin can be of any race; (1) Figures cover the Savannah, GA Metropolitan Statistical Area—see Appendix B for areas included
Source: U.S. Census Bureau, 2011-2013 American Community Survey 3-Year Estimates

Segregation

Type	Segregation Indices[1]				Percent Change		
	1990	2000	2010	2010 Rank[2]	1990-2000	1990-2010	2000-2010
Black/White	n/a	n/a	n/a	n/a	n/a	n/a	n/a
Asian/White	n/a	n/a	n/a	n/a	n/a	n/a	n/a
Hispanic/White	n/a	n/a	n/a	n/a	n/a	n/a	n/a

Note: All figures cover the Metropolitan Statistical Area—see Appendix B for areas included; Figures are based on an analysis of 1990, 2000, and 2010 Census Decennial Census tract data by William H. Frey, Brookings Institution and the University of Michigan Social Science Data Analysis Network. In this analysis all racial groups (whites, blacks, and asians) are non-Hispanic members of those races. Hispanics are shown as a separate category;
(1) Segregation Indices are Dissimilarity Indices that measure the degree to which the minority group is distributed differently than whites across census tracts. They range from 0 (complete integration) to 100 (complete segregation) where the value indicates the percentage of the minority group that needs to move to be distributed exactly like whites; (2) Ranges from 1 (most segregated) to 102 (least segregated); n/a not available.
Source: www.CensusScope.org

Ancestry

Area	German	Irish	English	American	Italian	Polish	French[2]	Scottish	Dutch
City	6.1	6.5	5.5	4.2	2.2	1.3	1.4	1.6	0.6
MSA[1]	9.5	9.5	7.8	7.3	2.8	1.5	1.9	2.0	0.9
U.S.	14.9	10.8	8.0	7.4	5.5	3.0	2.7	1.7	1.4

Note: Figures are the percentage of the total population reporting a particular ancestry. The nine most commonly reported ancestries in the U.S. are shown. Figures include multiple ancestries (e.g. if a person reported being Irish and Italian, they were included in both columns); (1) Figures cover the Savannah, GA Metropolitan Statistical Area—see Appendix B for areas included; (2) Excludes Basque
Source: U.S. Census Bureau, 2011-2013 American Community Survey 3-Year Estimates

Foreign-Born Population

Area	Percent of Population Born in								
	Any Foreign Country	Mexico	Asia	Europe	Carribean	South America	Central America[2]	Africa	Canada
City	5.7	1.7	1.2	0.7	0.4	0.6	0.2	0.4	0.2
MSA[1]	5.9	1.4	1.8	0.8	0.5	0.4	0.2	0.5	0.2
U.S.	13.0	3.7	3.8	1.5	1.2	0.9	1.0	0.6	0.3

Note: (1) Figures cover the Savannah, GA Metropolitan Statistical Area—see Appendix B for areas included; (2) Excludes Mexico.
Source: U.S. Census Bureau, 2011-2013 American Community Survey 3-Year Estimates

Marital Status

Area	Never Married	Now Married[2]	Separated	Widowed	Divorced
City	45.2	31.7	2.8	7.0	13.4
MSA[1]	34.5	44.4	2.4	5.9	12.8
U.S.	32.7	48.1	2.2	6.0	11.0

Note: Figures are percentages and cover the population 15 years of age and older; (1) Figures cover the Savannah, GA Metropolitan Statistical Area—see Appendix B for areas included; (2) Excludes separated
Source: U.S. Census Bureau, 2011-2013 American Community Survey 3-Year Estimates

Disability Status

Area	All Ages	Under 18 Years Old	18 to 64 Years Old	65 Years and Over
City	13.1	4.1	11.0	40.5
MSA[1]	11.5	3.2	9.8	37.3
U.S.	12.3	4.1	10.2	36.3

Note: Figures show percent of the civilian noninstitutionalized population that reported having a disability. Disability status is determined from from six types of difficulty: vision, hearing, cognitive, ambulatory, self-care, and independent living. For children under 5 years old, hearing and vision difficulty are used to determine disability status. For children between the ages of 5 and 14, disability status is determined from hearing, vision, cognitive, ambulatory, and self-care difficulties. For people aged 15 years and older, they are considered to have a disability if they have difficulty with any one of the six difficulty types; (1) Figures cover the Savannah, GA Metropolitan Statistical Area—see Appendix B for areas included.
Source: U.S. Census Bureau, 2011-2013 American Community Survey 3-Year Estimates

Age

Area	Percent of Population									Median Age
	Under Age 5	Age 5–19	Age 20–34	Age 35–44	Age 45–54	Age 55–64	Age 65–74	Age 75–84	Age 85+	
City	6.8	19.8	27.6	11.0	11.6	10.7	6.7	3.8	2.0	31.9
MSA[1]	6.9	20.0	23.7	12.7	13.1	11.4	7.1	3.6	1.5	34.6
U.S.	6.4	19.9	20.7	12.9	14.1	12.3	7.6	4.2	1.9	37.4

Note: (1) Figures cover the Savannah, GA Metropolitan Statistical Area—see Appendix B for areas included
Source: U.S. Census Bureau, 2011-2013 American Community Survey 3-Year Estimates

Gender

Area	Males	Females	Males per 100 Females
City	67,265	74,521	90.3
MSA[1]	175,117	186,378	94.0
U.S.	154,451,010	159,410,713	96.9

Note: (1) Figures cover the Savannah, GA Metropolitan Statistical Area—see Appendix B for areas included
Source: U.S. Census Bureau, 2011-2013 American Community Survey 3-Year Estimates

Religious Groups by Family

Area	Catholic	Baptist	Non-Den.	Methodist[2]	Lutheran	LDS[3]	Pente-costal	Presby-terian[4]	Muslim[5]	Judaism
MSA[1]	7.1	19.7	6.9	8.9	1.6	1.0	2.4	1.0	0.2	0.8
U.S.	19.1	9.3	4.0	4.0	2.3	2.0	1.9	1.6	0.8	0.7

Note: Figures are the number of adherents as a percentage of the total population; (1) Figures cover the Savannah, GA Metropolitan Statistical Area—see Appendix B for areas included; (2) Methodist/Pietist; (3) Latter Day Saints; (4) Reformed; (5) Figures are estimates
Source: Association of Statisticians of American Religious Bodies, 2010 U.S. Religion Census: Religious Congregations & Membership Study

Religious Groups by Tradition

Area	Catholic	Evangelical Protestant	Mainline Protestant	Other Tradition	Black Protestant	Orthodox
MSA[1]	7.1	25.1	9.5	2.6	8.6	0.1
U.S.	19.1	16.2	7.3	4.3	1.6	0.3

Note: Figures are the number of adherents as a percentage of the total population; (1) Figures cover the Savannah, GA Metropolitan Statistical Area—see Appendix B for areas included
Source: Association of Statisticians of American Religious Bodies, 2010 U.S. Religion Census: Religious Congregations & Membership Study

ECONOMY

Gross Metropolitan Product

Area	2012	2013	2014	2015	Rank[2]
MSA[1]	14.1	14.6	15.1	15.9	145

Note: Figures are in billions of dollars; (1) Figures cover the Savannah, GA Metropolitan Statistical Area—see Appendix B for areas included; (2) Rank is based on 2015 data and ranges from 1 to 363
Source: The U.S. Conference of Mayors, U.S. Metro Economies: GMP and Employment 2013-2015, June 2014

Economic Growth

Area	2010-12 (%)	2013 (%)	2014 (%)	2015 (%)	Rank[2]
MSA[1]	2.3	1.9	2.1	3.1	134
U.S.	2.1	2.0	2.3	3.2	–

Note: Figures are real gross metropolitan product (GMP) growth rates and represent annual average percent change; (1) Figures cover the Savannah, GA Metropolitan Statistical Area—see Appendix B for areas included; (2) Rank is based on 2015 data and ranges from 1 to 363
Source: The U.S. Conference of Mayors, U.S. Metro Economies: GMP and Employment 2013-2015, June 2014

Metropolitan Area Exports

Area	2008	2009	2010	2011	2012	2013	Rank[2]
MSA[1]	3,598.5	2,724.7	3,459.1	4,140.2	4,116.5	5,436.4	52

Note: Figures are in millions of dollars; (1) Figures cover the Savannah, GA Metropolitan Statistical Area—see Appendix B for areas included; (2) Rank is based on 2013 data and ranges from 1 to 387
Source: U.S. Department of Commerce, International Trade Administration, Office of Trade & Industry Information, Manufacturing & Services, data extracted April 3, 2015

Building Permits

Area	Single-Family			Multi-Family			Total		
	2013	2014	Pct. Chg.	2013	2014	Pct. Chg.	2013	2014	Pct. Chg.
City	265	341	28.7	18	23	27.8	283	364	28.6
MSA[1]	1,517	1,857	22.4	233	354	51.9	1,750	2,211	26.3
U.S.	620,802	634,597	2.2	370,020	411,766	11.3	990,822	1,046,363	5.6

Note: (1) Figures cover the Savannah, GA Metropolitan Statistical Area—see Appendix B for areas included; Figures represent new, privately-owned housing units authorized (unadjusted data); All permit data are based on estimates with imputation.
Source: U.S. Census Bureau, Manufacturing, Mining, and Construction Statistics, Building Permits, 2013, 2014

Bankruptcy Filings

Area	Business Filings			Nonbusiness Filings		
	2013	2014	% Chg.	2013	2014	% Chg.
Chatham County	42	24	-42.9	1,517	1,390	-8.4
U.S.	33,212	26,983	-18.8	1,038,720	909,812	-12.4

Note: Business filings include Chapter 7, Chapter 11, Chapter 12, and Chapter 13; Nonbusiness filings include Chapter 7, Chapter 11, and Chapter 13
Source: Administrative Office of the U.S. Courts, Business and Nonbusiness Bankruptcy, County Cases Commenced by Chapter of the Bankruptcy Code, During the 12- Month Period Ending December 31, 2013 and Business and Nonbusiness Bankruptcy, County Cases Commenced by Chapter of the Bankruptcy Code, During the 12- Month Period Ending December 31, 2014

Housing Vacancy Rates

Area	Gross Vacancy Rate[2] (%)			Year-Round Vacancy Rate[3] (%)			Rental Vacancy Rate[4] (%)			Homeowner Vacancy Rate[5] (%)		
	2012	2013	2014	2012	2013	2014	2012	2013	2014	2012	2013	2014
MSA[1]	n/a	n/a	n/a	n/a	n/a	n/a	n/a	n/a	n/a	n/a	n/a	n/a
U.S.	13.8	13.6	13.4	10.8	10.7	10.4	8.7	8.3	7.6	2.0	2.0	1.9

Note: (1) Figures cover the Savannah, GA Metropolitan Statistical Area—see Appendix B for areas included; (2) The percentage of the total housing inventory that is vacant; (3) The percentage of the housing inventory (excluding seasonal units) that is year-round vacant; (4) The percentage of rental inventory that is vacant for rent; (5) The percentage of homeowner inventory that is vacant for sale; n/a not available
Source: U.S. Census Bureau, Housing Vacancies and Homeownership Annual Statistics: 2014

INCOME

Income

Area	Per Capita ($)	Median Household ($)	Average Household ($)
City	19,928	36,144	49,971
MSA[1]	25,036	48,852	65,120
U.S.	27,884	52,176	72,897

Note: (1) Figures cover the Savannah, GA Metropolitan Statistical Area—see Appendix B for areas included
Source: U.S. Census Bureau, 2011-2013 American Community Survey 3-Year Estimates

Household Income Distribution

Area	Percent of Households Earning							
	Under $15,000	$15,000 -24,999	$25,000 -34,999	$35,000 -49,999	$50,000 -74,999	$75,000 -99,000	$100,000 -149,999	$150,000 and up
City	22.6	14.3	11.5	15.4	17.1	8.2	6.7	4.3
MSA[1]	14.8	11.3	10.0	14.8	18.2	12.0	11.4	7.5
U.S.	13.0	10.9	10.3	13.6	17.9	11.9	12.7	9.6

Note: (1) Figures cover the Savannah, GA Metropolitan Statistical Area—see Appendix B for areas included
Source: U.S. Census Bureau, 2011-2013 American Community Survey 3-Year Estimates

Poverty Rate

Area	All Ages	Under 18 Years Old	18 to 64 Years Old	65 Years and Over
City	26.7	41.8	24.3	11.5
MSA[1]	17.9	27.1	16.3	8.6
U.S.	15.9	22.4	14.8	9.5

Note: Figures are percentage of people whose income during the past 12 months was below the poverty level; (1) Figures cover the Savannah, GA Metropolitan Statistical Area—see Appendix B for areas included
Source: U.S. Census Bureau, 2011-2013 American Community Survey 3-Year Estimates

EMPLOYMENT

Labor Force and Employment

Area	Civilian Labor Force			Workers Employed		
	Dec. 2013	Dec. 2014	% Chg.	Dec. 2013	Dec. 2014	% Chg.
City	63,923	64,485	0.9	58,614	59,872	2.1
MSA[1]	170,618	172,492	1.1	158,457	161,896	2.2
U.S.	154,408,000	155,521,000	0.7	144,423,000	147,190,000	1.9

Note: Data is not seasonally adjusted and covers workers 16 years of age and older; (1) Figures cover the Savannah, GA Metropolitan Statistical Area—see Appendix B for areas included
Source: Bureau of Labor Statistics, Local Area Unemployment Statistics

Unemployment Rate

Area	2014											
	Jan.	Feb.	Mar.	Apr.	May	Jun.	Jul.	Aug.	Sep.	Oct.	Nov.	Dec.
City	8.5	8.3	8.6	7.3	8.1	9.0	9.3	8.8	7.9	7.4	6.9	7.2
MSA[1]	7.4	7.3	7.4	6.5	7.1	7.6	7.9	7.6	6.8	6.6	6.1	6.1
U.S.	7.0	7.0	6.8	5.9	6.1	6.3	6.5	6.3	5.7	5.5	5.5	5.4

Note: Data is not seasonally adjusted and covers workers 16 years of age and older; (1) Figures cover the Savannah, GA Metropolitan Statistical Area—see Appendix B for areas included
Source: Bureau of Labor Statistics, Local Area Unemployment Statistics

Employment by Occupation

Occupation Classification	City (%)	MSA[1] (%)	U.S. (%)
Management, Business, Science, and Arts	30.3	33.8	36.2
Natural Resources, Construction, and Maintenance	7.1	9.3	9.0
Production, Transportation, and Material Moving	12.6	13.2	12.1
Sales and Office	24.6	23.9	24.4
Service	25.4	19.8	18.3

Note: Figures cover employed civilians 16 years of age and older; (1) Figures cover the Savannah, GA Metropolitan Statistical Area—see Appendix B for areas included
Source: U.S. Census Bureau, 2011-2013 American Community Survey 3-Year Estimates

Employment by Industry

Sector	MSA[1]		U.S.
	Number of Employees	Percent of Total	Percent of Total
Construction, Mining, and Logging	6,000	3.6	5.0
Education and Health Services	24,400	14.5	15.5
Financial Activities	6,400	3.8	5.7
Government	23,400	13.9	15.8
Information	2,000	1.2	2.0
Leisure and Hospitality	24,200	14.4	10.3
Manufacturing	16,500	9.8	8.7
Other Services	7,200	4.3	4.0
Professional and Business Services	20,300	12.1	13.8
Retail Trade	20,500	12.2	11.4
Transportation, Warehousing, and Utilities	10,900	6.5	3.9
Wholesale Trade	6,500	3.9	4.2

Note: Figures are non-farm employment as of December 2014. Figures are not seasonally adjusted and include workers 16 years of age and older; (1) Figures cover the Savannah, GA Metropolitan Statistical Area—see Appendix B for areas included; n/a not available
Source: Bureau of Labor Statistics, Current Employment Statistics, Employment, Hours, and Earnings

Occupations with Greatest Projected Employment Growth: 2012 – 2022

Occupation[1]	2012 Employment	2022 Projected Employment	Numeric Employment Change	Percent Employment Change
Combined Food Preparation and Serving Workers, Including Fast Food	169,450	192,830	23,380	13.8
Customer Service Representatives	95,900	115,410	19,510	20.3
Laborers and Freight, Stock, and Material Movers, Hand	85,460	104,150	18,690	21.9
Elementary School Teachers, Except Special Education	42,300	56,170	13,870	32.8
General and Operations Managers	71,410	84,890	13,480	18.9
Sales Representatives, Wholesale and Manufacturing, Except Technical and Scientific Products	56,220	67,450	11,230	20.0
Secretaries and Administrative Assistants, Except Legal, Medical, and Executive	51,850	63,030	11,180	21.6
Office Clerks, General	79,920	91,010	11,090	13.9
Janitors and Cleaners, Except Maids and Housekeeping Cleaners	52,860	63,600	10,740	20.3
Childcare Workers	37,650	48,280	10,630	28.2

Note: Projections cover Georgia; (1) Sorted by numeric employment change
Source: www.projectionscentral.com, State Occupational Projections, 2012–2022 Long-Term Projections

Fastest Growing Occupations: 2012 – 2022

Occupation[1]	2012 Employment	2022 Projected Employment	Numeric Employment Change	Percent Employment Change
Physician Assistants	2,820	4,740	1,920	67.9
Health Specialties Teachers, Postsecondary	4,870	8,060	3,190	65.5
Agents and Business Managers of Artists, Performers, and Athletes	430	700	270	62.6
Personal Care Aides	16,440	26,630	10,190	62.0
Interpreters and Translators	1,650	2,630	980	58.9
Nursing Instructors and Teachers, Postsecondary	1,420	2,200	780	55.5
Psychiatric Aides	1,390	2,150	760	55.3
Home Health Aides	7,950	12,340	4,390	55.1
Nurse Practitioners	3,260	5,010	1,750	53.9
Nurse Midwives	250	380	130	53.6

Note: Projections cover Georgia; (1) Sorted by percent employment change and excludes occupations with numeric employment change less than 100
Source: www.projectionscentral.com, State Occupational Projections, 2012–2022 Long-Term Projections

Average Wages

Occupation	$/Hr.	Occupation	$/Hr.
Accountants and Auditors	34.28	Maids and Housekeeping Cleaners	8.65
Automotive Mechanics	21.01	Maintenance and Repair Workers	18.60
Bookkeepers	17.36	Marketing Managers	46.64
Carpenters	20.03	Nuclear Medicine Technologists	n/a
Cashiers	9.50	Nurses, Licensed Practical	18.62
Clerks, General Office	13.20	Nurses, Registered	29.37
Clerks, Receptionists/Information	13.21	Nursing Assistants	10.62
Clerks, Shipping/Receiving	17.97	Packers and Packagers, Hand	9.38
Computer Programmers	n/a	Physical Therapists	42.35
Computer Systems Analysts	35.28	Postal Service Mail Carriers	25.20
Computer User Support Specialists	26.00	Real Estate Brokers	21.46
Cooks, Restaurant	10.28	Retail Salespersons	11.45
Dentists	106.56	Sales Reps., Exc. Tech./Scientific	28.34
Electrical Engineers	45.37	Sales Reps., Tech./Scientific	29.44
Electricians	22.22	Secretaries, Exc. Legal/Med./Exec.	16.68
Financial Managers	60.86	Security Guards	13.44
First-Line Supervisors/Managers, Sales	16.71	Surgeons	n/a
Food Preparation Workers	10.03	Teacher Assistants	9.90
General and Operations Managers	43.56	Teachers, Elementary School	26.70
Hairdressers/Cosmetologists	11.24	Teachers, Secondary School	23.60
Internists	n/a	Telemarketers	14.79
Janitors and Cleaners	10.21	Truck Drivers, Heavy/Tractor-Trailer	18.16
Landscaping/Groundskeeping Workers	10.35	Truck Drivers, Light/Delivery Svcs.	13.78
Lawyers	45.27	Waiters and Waitresses	9.66

Note: Wage data covers the Savannah, GA Metropolitan Statistical Area—see Appendix B for areas included; Hourly wages for elementary/secondary school teachers and teacher assistants were calculated by the editors from annual wage data assuming a 40 hour work week; n/a not available.
Source: Bureau of Labor Statistics, Metro Area Occupational Employment and Wage Estimates, May 2014

TAXES

State Corporate Income Tax Rates

State	Tax Rate (%)	Income Brackets ($)	Num. of Brackets	Financial Institution Tax Rate (%)[a]	Federal Income Tax Ded.
Georgia	6.0	Flat rate	1	6.0	No

Note: Tax rates as of January 1, 2015; (a) Rates listed are the corporate income tax rate applied to financial institutions or excise taxes based on income. Some states have other taxes based upon the value of deposits or shares.
Source: Federation of Tax Administrators, "State Corporate Income Tax Rates, 2015"

State Individual Income Tax Rates

State	Tax Rate (%)	Income Brackets ($)	Num. of Brackets	Personal Exempt. ($)[1]		Fed. Inc. Tax Ded.
				Single	Dependents	
Georgia	1.0 - 6.0	750 - 7,001 (h)	6	2,700	3,000	No

Note: Tax rates as of January 1, 2015; Local- and county-level taxes are not included; n/a not applicable; (1) Married joint filers generally receive double the single exemption; (h) The Georgia income brackets reported are for single individuals. For married couples filing jointly, the same tax rates apply to income brackets ranging from $1,000, to $10,000.
Source: Federation of Tax Administrators, "State Individual Income Tax Rates, 2015"

Various State and Local Tax Rates

State	State and Local Sales and Use (%)	State Sales and Use (%)	Gasoline[1] (¢/gal.)	Cigarette[2] ($/pack)	Spirits[3] ($/gal.)	Wine[4] ($/gal.)	Beer[5] ($/gal.)
Georgia	7.0	4.0	26.53	0.37	3.79 (f)	1.51	1.01 (q)

Note: All tax rates as of January 1, 2015; (1) The American Petroleum Institute has developed a methodology for determining the average tax rate on a gallon of fuel. Rates may include any of the following: excise taxes, environmental fees, storage tank fees, other fees or taxes, general sales tax, and local taxes. In states where gasoline is subject to the general sales tax, or where the fuel tax is based on the average sale price, the average rate determined by API is sensitive to changes in the price of gasoline. States that fully or partially apply general sales taxes to gasoline: CA, CO, GA, IL, IN, MI, NY; (2) The federal excise tax of $1.0066 per pack and local taxes are not included; (3) Rates are those applicable to off-premise sales of 40% alcohol by volume (a.b.v.) distilled spirits in 750ml containers. Local excise taxes are excluded; (4) Rates are those applicable to off-premise sales of 11% a.b.v. non-carbonated wine in 750ml containers; (5) Rates are those applicable to off-premise sales of 4.7% a.b.v. beer in 12 ounce containers; (f) Different rates are also applicable according to alcohol content, place of production, size of container, or place purchased (on- or off-premise or onboard airlines); (q) Includes statewide local tax in Alabama ($0.52) and Georgia ($0.53).
Source: Tax Foundation, 2015 Facts & Figures: How Does Your State Compare?

State Business Tax Climate Index Rankings

State	Overall Rank	Corporate Tax Index Rank	Individual Income Tax Index Rank	Sales Tax Index Rank	Unemployment Insurance Tax Index Rank	Property Tax Index Rank
Georgia	36	8	42	17	36	30

Note: The index is a measure of how each state's tax laws affect economic performance. The lower the rank, the more favorable a state's tax system is for business. States without a given tax are given a ranking of 1. The scores/rankings for the District of Columbia do not affect other states. The 2015 index represents the tax climate as of July 1, 2014.
Source: Tax Foundation, State Business Tax Climate Index 2015

COMMERCIAL UTILITIES

Typical Monthly Electric Bills

Area	Commercial Service ($/month)		Industrial Service ($/month)	
	1,500 kWh	40 kW demand 14,000 kWh	1,000 kW demand 200,000 kWh	50,000 kW demand 32,500,000 kWh
City	254	1,610	31,246	2,340,613
Average[1]	201	1,653	26,124	2,639,743

Note: Figures are based on annualized 2014 rates; (1) Average based on 180 utilities surveyed
Source: Edison Electric Institute, Typical Bills and Average Rates Report, Summer 2014

TRANSPORTATION

Means of Transportation to Work

Area	Car/Truck/Van		Public Transportation			Bicycle	Walked	Other Means	Worked at Home
	Drove Alone	Car-pooled	Bus	Subway	Railroad				
City	76.5	10.3	3.4	0.0	0.0	1.7	4.0	0.9	3.3
MSA[1]	82.1	8.9	1.8	0.0	0.0	0.7	2.2	1.0	3.5
U.S.	76.4	9.6	2.6	1.8	0.6	0.6	2.8	1.3	4.3

Note: Figures are percentages and cover workers 16 years of age and older; (1) Figures cover the Savannah, GA Metropolitan Statistical Area—see Appendix B for areas included
Source: U.S. Census Bureau, 2011-2013 American Community Survey 3-Year Estimates

Travel Time to Work

Area	Less Than 10 Minutes	10 to 19 Minutes	20 to 29 Minutes	30 to 44 Minutes	45 to 59 Minutes	60 to 89 Minutes	90 Minutes or More
City	14.1	40.0	25.9	13.7	3.7	1.5	1.1
MSA[1]	10.1	30.2	28.1	21.5	6.6	2.3	1.2
U.S.	13.3	29.7	20.9	20.2	7.7	5.7	2.6

Note: Figures are percentages and include workers 16 years old and over; (1) Figures cover the Savannah, GA Metropolitan Statistical Area—see Appendix B for areas included
Source: U.S. Census Bureau, 2011-2013 American Community Survey 3-Year Estimates

Travel Time Index

Area	1985	1990	1995	2000	2005	2010	2011
Urban Area[1]	n/a	n/a	n/a	n/a	n/a	n/a	n/a
Average[2]	1.09	1.14	1.16	1.19	1.23	1.18	1.18

Note: Travel Time Index—the ratio of travel time in the peak period to the travel time at free-flow conditions. For example, a value of 1.30 indicates a 20-minute free-flow trip takes 26 minutes in the peak. Free-flow speeds (60 mph on freeways and 35 mph on principal arterials) are used as the comparison threshold; (1) Data for the Savannah, GA urban area was not available; (2) average of 498 urban areas
Source: Texas Transportation Institute, Urban Mobility Report 2012, December 2012

Public Transportation

Agency Name / Mode of Transportation	Vehicles Operated in Maximum Service	Annual Unlinked Passenger Trips (in thous.)	Annual Passenger Miles (in thous.)
Chatham Area Transit Authority (CAT)			
Bus (directly operated)	52	425.4	1,744.4
Bus (purchased transportation)	52	3,207.7	12,152.8
Demand Response (directly operated)	20	10.5	85.3
Demand Response (purchased transportation)	20	70.8	594.7
Ferryboat (directly operated)	1	106.5	43.2
Ferryboat (purchased transportation)	1	571.0	225.3

Source: Federal Transit Administration, National Transit Database, 2013

Air Transportation

Airport Name and Code / Type of Service	Passenger Airlines[1]	Passenger Enplanements	Freight Carriers[2]	Freight (lbs.)
Savannah International (SAV)				
Domestic service (U.S. carriers - 2014)	24	931,961	11	6,298,214
International service (U.S. carriers - 2013)	1	9	0	0

Note: (1) Includes all U.S.-based major, minor and commuter airlines that carried at least one passenger during the year; (2) Includes all U.S.-based airlines and freight carriers that transported at least one lb. of freight during the year.
Source: Bureau of Transportation Statistics, The Intermodal Transportation Database, Air Carriers: T-100 Domestic Market (U.S. Carriers), 2014; Bureau of Transportation Statistics, The Intermodal Transportation Database, Air Carriers: T-100 International Market (U.S. Carriers), 2013

Other Transportation Statistics

Major Highways:	I-16; I-95
Amtrak Service:	Yes
Major Waterways/Ports:	Savannah River (Atlantic Ocean)

Source: Amtrak.com; Google Maps

BUSINESSES

Major Business Headquarters

Company Name	Rankings	
	Fortune[1]	Forbes[2]
Colonial Group	-	161

Note: (1) Fortune 500—companies that produce a 10-K are ranked 1 to 500 based on 2013 revenue; (2) all private companies with at least $2 billion in annual revenue through the end of their most current fiscal year are ranked 1 to 221; companies listed are headquartered in the city; dashes indicate no ranking
Source: Fortune, "Fortune 500," June 16, 2014; Forbes, "America's Largest Private Companies," November 5, 2014

Minority Business Opportunity

Savannah is home to one company which is on the *Black Enterprise* Bank 20 list (20 largest banks based on total assets, capital, deposits and loans, including mortgage-backed securities for the calendar year): **Carver State Bank** (#20). Only commercial banks or savings and loans that are classified by the Federal Reserve as black institutions and have been fully operational for the previous calendar year were considered. *Black Enterprise, B.E. 100s, 2014*

Minority- and Women-Owned Businesses

Group	All Firms		Firms with Paid Employees			
	Firms	Sales ($000)	Firms	Sales ($000)	Employees	Payroll ($000)
Asian	639	240,363	290	222,341	3,076	38,001
Black	4,185	316,962	211	193,454	839	21,492
Hispanic	139	47,330	39	39,932	727	6,988
Women	4,332	717,594	628	633,948	7,500	147,281
All Firms	13,717	14,667,749	3,975	14,215,679	89,726	2,944,187

Note: Figures cover firms located in the city; minority- and women-owned business are defined as firms in which the corresponding group own 51% or more of the stock or equity of the company
Source: U.S. Census Bureau, 2007 Economic Census, Survey of Business Owners (2012 Survey of Business Owners data will be released starting in June 2015)

HOTELS & CONVENTION CENTERS

Hotels/Motels

Area	5 Star		4 Star		3 Star		2 Star		1 Star		Not Rated	
	Num.	Pct.[3]	Num.	Pct.[3]	Num.	Pct.[3]	Num.	Pct.[3]	Num.	Pct.[3]	Num.	Pct.[3]
City[1]	1	0.6	16	8.9	55	30.7	94	52.5	4	2.2	9	5.0
Total[2]	166	0.9	1,264	7.0	5,718	31.8	9,340	52.0	411	2.3	1,070	6.0

Note: (1) Figures cover Savannah and vicinity; (2) Figures cover all 100 cities in this book; (3) Percentage of hotels which have a given star rating; Star ratings are determined by expedia.com and offer an indication of the general quality of a particular hotel.
Source: expedia.com, April 2, 2015

The Savannah, GA metro area is home to one of the best hotels in the U.S. according to *Travel & Leisure*: **Bohemian Hotel Savannah Riverfront**. Criteria: service; location; rooms; food; and value. The list includes the top 236 hotels in the U.S. *Travel & Leisure, "T+L 500, The World's Best Hotels 2015"*

Major Convention Centers

Name	Overall Space (sq. ft.)	Exhibit Space (sq. ft.)	Meeting Space (sq. ft.)	Meeting Rooms
Savannah Intl Trade & Convention Center	330,000	100,000	50,000	13

Note: Table includes convention centers located in the Savannah, GA metro area; n/a not available
Source: Original research

Living Environment

COST OF LIVING

Cost of Living Index

Composite Index	Groceries	Housing	Utilities	Trans-portation	Health Care	Misc. Goods/ Services
91.3	97.7	69.6	106.8	98.9	98.7	98.6

Note: The Cost of Living Index measures regional differences in the cost of consumer goods and services, excluding taxes and non-consumer expenditures, for professional and managerial households in the top income quintile. It is based on more than 50,000 prices covering almost 60 different items for which prices are collected three times a year by chambers of commerce, economic development organizations or university applied economic centers in each participating urban area. The numbers shown should be read as a percentage above or below the national average of 100. For example, a value of 115.4 in the groceries column indicates that grocery prices are 15.4% higher than the national average. Small differences in the index numbers should not be interpreted as significant; Figures cover the Savannah GA urban area.
Source: The Council for Community and Economic Research, ACCRA Cost of Living Index, 2014

Grocery Prices

Area[1]	T-Bone Steak ($/pound)	Frying Chicken ($/pound)	Whole Milk ($/half gal.)	Eggs ($/dozen)	Orange Juice ($/64 oz.)	Coffee ($/11.5 oz.)
City[2]	10.66	1.42	2.72	1.82	3.20	4.15
Avg.	10.40	1.37	2.40	1.99	3.46	4.27
Min.	8.48	0.93	1.37	1.30	2.83	2.99
Max.	14.20	2.44	3.62	4.02	6.42	6.96

Note: (1) Values for the local area are compared with the average, minimum and maximum values for all 308 areas in the Cost of Living Index; (2) Figures cover the Savannah GA urban area; **T-Bone Steak** *(price per pound);* **Frying Chicken** *(price per pound, whole fryer);* **Whole Milk** *(half gallon carton);* **Eggs** *(price per dozen, Grade A, large);* **Orange Juice** *(64 oz. Tropicana or Florida Natural);* **Coffee** *(11.5 oz. can, vacuum-packed, Maxwell House, Hills Bros, or Folgers).*
Source: The Council for Community and Economic Research, ACCRA Cost of Living Index, 2014

Housing and Utility Costs

Area[1]	New Home Price ($)	Apartment Rent ($/month)	All Electric ($/month)	Part Electric ($/month)	Other Energy ($/month)	Telephone ($/month)
City[2]	198,491	767	164.00	-	-	33.80
Avg.	305,838	919	181.00	93.66	73.14	27.95
Min.	183,142	480	112.00	42.06	23.42	17.16
Max.	1,358,576	3,851	594.00	180.03	440.99	40.42

Note: (1) Values for the local area are compared with the average, minimum and maximum values for all 308 areas in the Cost of Living Index; (2) Figures cover the Savannah GA urban area; **New Home Price** *(2,400 sf living area, 8,000 sf lot, in urban area with full utilities);* **Apartment Rent** *(950 sf 2 bedroom/1.5 or 2 bath, unfurnished, excluding all utilities except water);* **All Electric** *(average monthly cost for an all-electric home);* **Part Electric** *(average monthly cost for a part-electric home);* **Other Energy** *(average monthly cost for natural gas, fuel oil, coal, wood, and any other forms of energy except electricity);* **Telephone** *(price includes basic monthly rate for a private residential line plus additional local usage charges incurred by a family of four).*
Source: The Council for Community and Economic Research, ACCRA Cost of Living Index, 2014

Health Care, Transportation, and Other Costs

Area[1]	Doctor ($/visit)	Dentist ($/visit)	Optometrist ($/visit)	Gasoline ($/gallon)	Beauty Salon ($/visit)	Men's Shirt ($)
City[2]	110.33	81.99	71.91	3.36	35.32	23.38
Avg.	102.86	87.89	97.66	3.44	34.37	26.74
Min.	67.47	65.78	51.18	3.00	17.43	12.79
Max.	173.50	150.14	235.00	4.33	64.28	49.50

Note: (1) Values for the local area are compared with the average, minimum and maximum values for all 308 areas in the Cost of Living Index; (2) Figures cover the Savannah GA urban area; **Doctor** *(general practitioners routine exam of an established patient);* **Dentist** *(adult teeth cleaning and periodic oral examination);* **Optometrist** *(full vision eye exam for established adult patient);* **Gasoline** *(one gallon regular unleaded, national brand, including all taxes, cash price at self-service pump if available);* **Beauty Salon** *(woman's shampoo, trim, and blow-dry);* **Men's Shirt** *(cotton/polyester dress shirt, pinpoint weave, long sleeves).*
Source: The Council for Community and Economic Research, ACCRA Cost of Living Index, 2014

HOUSING

House Price Index (HPI)

Area	National Ranking[2]	Quarterly Change (%)	One-Year Change (%)	Five-Year Change (%)
MSA[1]	236	-1.71	1.64	-6.77
U.S.[3]	–	1.35	4.91	11.59

Note: The HPI is a weighted repeat sales index. It measures average price changes in repeat sales or refinancings on the same properties. This information is obtained by reviewing repeat mortgage transactions on single-family properties whose mortgages have been purchased or securitized by Fannie Mae or Freddie Mac in January 1975; (1) Savannah Metropolitan Statistical Area—see Appendix B for areas included; (2) Rankings are based on annual percentage change for all metro areas containing at least 15,000 transactions over the last 10 years and ranges from 1 to 275; (3) figures based on a weighted average of Census Division estimates using a seasonally adjusted, purchase-only index; all figures are for the period ending December 31, 2014
Source: Federal Housing Finance Agency, House Price Index, February 26, 2015

Median Single-Family Home Prices

Area	2012	2013	2014p	Percent Change 2013 to 2014
MSA[1]	n/a	n/a	n/a	n/a
U.S. Average	177.2	197.4	209.0	5.9

Note: Figures are median sales prices of existing single-family homes in thousands of dollars; (p) preliminary; n/a not available; (1) Savannah, GA Metropolitan Statistical Area—see Appendix B for areas included
Source: National Association of Realtors, Median Sales Price of Existing Single-Family Homes for Metropolitan Areas, 4th Quarter 2014

Qualifying Income Based on Median Sales Price of Existing Single-Family Homes

Area	With 5% Down ($)	With 10% Down ($)	With 20% Down ($)
MSA[1]	n/a	n/a	n/a
U.S. Average	45,863	43,449	38,621

Note: Figures are preliminary; Qualifying income is based on a mortgage rate of 4.0%. Monthly principal and interest payment is limited to 25% of income; n/a not available; (1) Savannah, GA Metropolitan Statistical Area—see Appendix B for areas included
Source: National Association of Realtors, Qualifying Income Based on Median Sales Price of Existing Single-Family Homes for Metropolitan Areas, 4th Quarter 2014

Median Apartment Condo-Coop Home Prices

Area	2012	2013	2014p	Percent Change 2013 to 2014
MSA[1]	n/a	n/a	n/a	n/a
U.S. Average	173.7	194.9	205.1	5.2

Note: Figures are median sales prices of existing apartment condo-coop homes in thousands of dollars; (p) preliminary; n/a not available; (1) Savannah, GA Metropolitan Statistical Area—see Appendix B for areas included
Source: National Association of Realtors, Median Sales Price of Existing Apartment Condo-Coop Homes for Metropolitan Areas, 4th Quarter 2014

Gross Monthly Rent

Area	Under $200	$200 -299	$300 -499	$500 -749	$750 -999	$1,000 -1,499	$1,500 and up	Median ($)
City	2.5	2.8	6.1	17.9	35.0	28.8	6.9	884
MSA[1]	1.9	1.8	5.7	16.9	32.5	32.7	8.5	926
U.S.	1.7	3.2	7.8	22.1	24.3	26.0	14.9	900

Note: Figures are percentages except for Median; Gross rent is the contract rent plus the estimated average monthly cost of utilities (electricity, gas, and water and sewer) and fuels (oil, coal, kerosene, wood, etc.) if these are paid by the renter (or paid for the renter by someone else); (1) Figures cover the Savannah, GA Metropolitan Statistical Area—see Appendix B for areas included
Source: U.S. Census Bureau, 2011-2013 American Community Survey 3-Year Estimates

Homeownership Rate

Area	2007 (%)	2008 (%)	2009 (%)	2010 (%)	2011 (%)	2012 (%)	2013 (%)	2014 (%)
MSA[1]	n/a	n/a	n/a	n/a	n/a	n/a	n/a	n/a
U.S.	68.1	67.8	67.4	66.9	66.1	65.4	65.1	64.5

Note: (1) Figures cover the Savannah, GA Metropolitan Statistical Area—see Appendix B for areas included; n/a not available
Source: U.S. Census Bureau, Housing Vacancies and Homeownership Annual Statistics: 2014

Year Housing Structure Built

Area	2010 or Later	2000 -2009	1990 -1999	1980 -1989	1970 -1979	1960 -1969	1950 -1959	1940 -1949	Before 1940	Median Year
City	1.9	10.6	7.6	10.4	15.5	13.2	15.6	7.5	17.7	1967
MSA[1]	1.7	23.8	15.8	14.8	12.8	8.6	8.9	4.7	8.8	1984
U.S.	0.9	15.0	13.9	13.8	15.8	11.0	10.9	5.4	13.3	1976

Note: Figures are percentages except for Median Year; (1) Figures cover the Savannah, GA Metropolitan Statistical Area—see Appendix B for areas included
Source: U.S. Census Bureau, 2011-2013 American Community Survey 3-Year Estimates

HEALTH

Health Risk Data

Category	MSA[1] (%)	U.S. (%)
Adults aged 18–64 who have any kind of health care coverage	n/a	79.6
Adults who reported being in good or excellent health	n/a	83.1
Adults who are current smokers	n/a	19.6
Adults who are heavy drinkers[2]	n/a	6.1
Adults who are binge drinkers[3]	n/a	16.9
Adults who are overweight (BMI 25.0 - 29.9)	n/a	35.8
Adults who are obese (BMI 30.0 - 99.8)	n/a	27.6
Adults who participated in any physical activities in the past month	n/a	77.1
Adults 50+ who have ever had a sigmoidoscopy or colonoscopy	n/a	67.3
Women aged 40+ who have had a mammogram within the past two years	n/a	74.0
Men aged 40+ who have had a PSA test within the past two years	n/a	45.2
Adults aged 65+ who have had flu shot within the past year	n/a	60.1
Adults who always wear a seatbelt	n/a	93.8

Note: Data as of 2012 unless otherwise noted; n/a not available; (1) Figures cover the Savannah, GA Metropolitan Statistical Area—see Appendix B for areas included; (2) Heavy drinkers are classified as males having more than two drinks per day or females having more than one drink per day; (3) Binge drinkers are classified as males having five or more drinks on one occasion or females having four or more drinks on one occasion
Source: Centers for Disease Control and Prevention, Behaviorial Risk Factor Surveillance System, SMART: Selected Metropolitan/Micropolitan Area Risk Trends, 2012 (Note: the CDC has discontinued this dataset but will be releasing a replacement in late 2015)

Chronic Health Indicators

Category	MSA[1] (%)	U.S. (%)
Adults who have ever been told they had a heart attack	n/a	4.5
Adults who have ever been told they had a stroke	n/a	2.9
Adults who have been told they currently have asthma	n/a	8.9
Adults who have ever been told they have arthritis	n/a	25.7
Adults who have ever been told they have diabetes[2]	n/a	9.7
Adults who have ever been told they had skin cancer	n/a	5.7
Adults who have ever been told they had any other types of cancer	n/a	6.5
Adults who have ever been told they have COPD	n/a	6.2
Adults who have ever been told they have kidney disease	n/a	2.5
Adults who have ever been told they have a form of depression	n/a	18.0

Note: Data as of 2012 unless otherwise noted; n/a not available; (1) Figures cover the Savannah, GA Metropolitan Statistical Area—see Appendix B for areas included; (2) Figures do not include pregnancy-related, borderline, or pre-diabetes
Source: Centers for Disease Control and Prevention, Behaviorial Risk Factor Surveillance System, SMART: Selected Metropolitan/Micropolitan Area Risk Trends, 2012 (Note: the CDC has discontinued this dataset but will be releasing a replacement in late 2015)

Mortality Rates for the Top 10 Causes of Death in the U.S.

ICD-10[a] Sub-Chapter	ICD-10[a] Code	Age-Adjusted Mortality Rate[1] per 100,000 population	
		County[2]	U.S.
Malignant neoplasms	C00-C97	168.2	166.2
Ischaemic heart diseases	I20-I25	94.0	105.7
Other forms of heart disease	I30-I51	61.4	49.3
Chronic lower respiratory diseases	J40-J47	41.1	42.1
Organic, including symptomatic, mental disorders	F01-F09	48.8	38.1
Cerebrovascular diseases	I60-I69	42.5	37.0
Other external causes of accidental injury	W00-X59	25.1	26.9
Other degenerative diseases of the nervous system	G30-G31	22.1	25.6
Diabetes mellitus	E10-E14	18.1	21.3
Hypertensive diseases	I10-I15	25.2	19.4

Note: (a) ICD-10 = International Classification of Diseases 10th Revision; (1) Mortality rates are a three year average covering 2011-2013; (2) Figures cover Chatham County
Source: Centers for Disease Control and Prevention, National Center for Health Statistics. Compressed Mortality File 1999-2013 on CDC WONDER Online Database, released October 2014. Data are compiled from the Compressed Mortality File 1999-2013, Series 20 No. 2S, 2014.

Mortality Rates for Selected Causes of Death

ICD-10[a] Sub-Chapter	ICD-10[a] Code	Age-Adjusted Mortality Rate[1] per 100,000 population	
		County[2]	U.S.
Assault	X85-Y09	10.3	5.2
Diseases of the liver	K70-K76	12.2	13.2
Human immunodeficiency virus (HIV) disease	B20-B24	5.7	2.2
Influenza and pneumonia	J09-J18	15.0	15.4
Intentional self-harm	X60-X84	11.9	12.5
Malnutrition	E40-E46	Suppressed	0.9
Obesity and other hyperalimentation	E65-E68	*1.8	1.8
Renal failure	N17-N19	15.0	13.1
Transport accidents	V01-V99	12.0	11.7
Viral hepatitis	B15-B19	*1.2	2.2

Note: (a) ICD-10 = International Classification of Diseases 10th Revision; (1) Mortality rates are a three year average covering 2011-2013; (2) Figures cover Chatham County; (*) Unreliable data as per CDC
Source: Centers for Disease Control and Prevention, National Center for Health Statistics. Compressed Mortality File 1999-2013 on CDC WONDER Online Database, released October 2014. Data are compiled from the Compressed Mortality File 1999-2013, Series 20 No. 2S, 2014.

Health Insurance Coverage

Area	With Health Insurance	With Private Health Insurance	With Public Health Insurance	Without Health Insurance	Population Under Age 18 Without Health Insurance
City	78.5	56.2	31.7	21.5	8.8
MSA[1]	81.2	64.2	27.0	18.8	8.9
U.S.	85.2	65.2	31.0	14.8	7.3

Note: Figures are percentages that cover the civilian noninstitutionalized population; (1) Figures cover the Savannah, GA Metropolitan Statistical Area—see Appendix B for areas included
Source: U.S. Census Bureau, 2011-2013 American Community Survey 3-Year Estimates

Number of Medical Professionals

Area[1]	MDs[2]	DOs[2,3]	Dentists	Podiatrists	Chiropractors	Optometrists
Local (number)	949	48	173	18	46	36
Local (rate[4])	343.0	17.3	62.1	6.5	16.5	12.9
U.S. (rate[4])	270.0	20.2	63.1	5.7	25.2	14.9

Note: Data as of 2013 unless noted; (1) Local data covers Chatham County; (2) Data as of 2012 and includes all active, non-federal physicians; (3) Doctor of Osteopathic Medicine; (4) rate per 100,000 population
Source: U.S. Department of Health and Human Services, Health Resources and Services Administration, Bureau of Health Professions, Area Resource File (ARF) 2013-2014

EDUCATION

Public School District Statistics

District Name	Schls	Pupils	Pupil/ Teacher Ratio	Minority Pupils[1] (%)	Free Lunch Eligible[2] (%)	IEP[3] (%)
Chatham County	56	36,610	14.4	71.3	57.6	10.1

Note: Table includes school districts with 2,000 or more students; (1) Percentage of students that are not non-Hispanic white; (2) Percentage of students that are eligible for the free lunch program; (3) Percentage of students that have an Individualized Education Program.
Source: U.S. Department of Education, National Center for Education Statistics, Common Core of Data, Local Education Agency (School District) Universe Survey: School Year 2012-2013; U.S. Department of Education, National Center for Education Statistics, Common Core of Data, Public Elementary/Secondary School Universe Survey: School Year 2012-2013

Highest Level of Education

Area	Less than H.S.	H.S. Diploma	Some College, No Deg.	Associate Degree	Bachelor's Degree	Master's Degree	Prof. School Degree	Doctorate Degree
City	14.0	29.5	24.0	5.1	17.5	6.7	1.9	1.4
MSA[1]	11.9	27.9	23.5	7.0	18.9	7.6	1.9	1.4
U.S.	13.7	28.0	21.2	7.9	18.2	7.7	1.9	1.3

Note: Figures cover persons age 25 and over; (1) Figures cover the Savannah, GA Metropolitan Statistical Area—see Appendix B for areas included
Source: U.S. Census Bureau, 2011-2013 American Community Survey 3-Year Estimates

Educational Attainment by Race

Area	High School Graduate or Higher (%)					Bachelor's Degree or Higher (%)				
	Total	White	Black	Asian	Hisp.[2]	Total	White	Black	Asian	Hisp.[2]
City	86.0	91.4	81.6	79.4	62.2	27.4	38.8	16.4	45.9	26.4
MSA[1]	88.1	90.1	84.5	83.0	69.0	29.8	33.9	19.8	45.6	25.4
U.S.	86.3	88.3	83.1	85.7	64.0	29.1	30.4	18.8	50.7	13.7

Note: Figures shown cover persons 25 years old and over; (1) Figures cover the Savannah, GA Metropolitan Statistical Area—see Appendix B for areas included; (2) People of Hispanic origin can be of any race
Source: U.S. Census Bureau, 2011-2013 American Community Survey 3-Year Estimates

School Enrollment by Grade and Control

Area	Preschool (%)		Kindergarten (%)		Grades 1 - 4 (%)		Grades 5 - 8 (%)		Grades 9 - 12 (%)	
	Public	Private	Public	Private	Public	Private	Public	Private	Public	Private
City	73.0	27.0	89.4	10.6	92.7	7.3	87.8	12.2	82.5	17.5
MSA[1]	62.2	37.8	88.6	11.4	88.7	11.3	85.9	14.1	83.5	16.5
U.S.	57.7	42.3	87.9	12.1	89.9	10.1	90.0	10.0	90.7	9.3

Note: Figures shown cover persons 3 years old and over; (1) Figures cover the Savannah, GA Metropolitan Statistical Area—see Appendix B for areas included
Source: U.S. Census Bureau, 2011-2013 American Community Survey 3-Year Estimates

Average Salaries of Public School Classroom Teachers

Area	2013-14		2014-15		Percent Change 2013-14 to 2014-15	Percent Change 2004-05 to 2014-15
	Dollars	Rank[1]	Dollars	Rank[1]		
GEORGIA	52,924	24	53,382	24	0.87	14.7
U.S. Average	56,610	–	57,379	–	1.36	20.8

Note: (1) State rank ranges from 1 to 51 where 1 indicates highest salary.
Source: National Education Association, Rankings & Estimates: Rankings of the States 2014 and Estimates of School Statistics 2015, March 2015

Higher Education

Four-Year Colleges			Two-Year Colleges			Medical Schools[1]	Law Schools[2]	Voc/ Tech[3]
Public	Private Non-profit	Private For-profit	Public	Private Non-profit	Private For-profit			
2	1	4	1	0	1	0	1	1

Note: Figures cover institutions located within the city limits and include main campuses only; (1) includes schools accredited by the Liaison Committee on Medical Education and the American Osteopathic Association's Commission on Osteopathic College Accreditation; (2) includes ABA-accredited schools, schools with provisional ABA accreditation, and state accredited schools; (3) includes all schools with programs that are less than 2 years.

Source: National Center for Education Statistics, Integrated Postsecondary Education System (IPEDS), 2013-14; Association of American Medical Colleges, Member List, May 1, 2015; American Osteopathic Association, Member List, May 1, 2015; Law School Admission Council, Official Guide to ABA-Approved Law Schools Online, May 1, 2015; Wikipedia, List of Medical Schools in the United States, May 1, 2015; Wikipedia, List of Law Schools in the United States, May 1, 2015

PRESIDENTIAL ELECTION

2012 Presidential Election Results

Area	Obama (%)	Romney (%)	Other (%)
Chatham County	55.5	43.5	1.0
U.S.	51.0	47.2	1.8

Note: Results may not add to 100% due to rounding

Source: Dave Leip's Atlas of U.S. Presidential Elections

EMPLOYERS

Major Employers

Company Name	Industry
Armstrong Atlantic State University	University
Candler Hospital	General medical and surgical hospitals
City of Savannah	City and town managers' office
City of Savannah	Police protection, local government
Georgia Dept of Public Health	Administration of public health programs
Great Dane Trailers	Trailer parts and accessories
Gulfstream Aerospace Corporation	Aircraft
Honeywell International	Aircraft/aerospace flight instruments & guidance systems
International Paper Company	Paper mills
Kapstone Paper and Packaging Corporation	Stationery stores
Memorial Health University Medical Center	General medical and surgical hospitals
Netjets International	Air transportation, nonscheduled
Saint Joseph's Hospital	General medical and surgical hospitals
Savannah College of Art & Design	Professional schools
Savannah State University	University
St Joseph's/Candler Health System	General medical and surgical hospitals
The Sullivan Group	Employment agencies
United Parcel Service	Mailing and messenger services
Wal-Mart Stores	Department stores, discount
Wells Fargo Insurance Services USA	Insurance brokers, nec

Note: Companies shown are located within the Savannah, GA Metropolitan Statistical Area.

Source: Hoovers.com; Wikipedia

PUBLIC SAFETY

Crime Rate

Area	All Crimes	Violent Crimes				Property Crimes		
		Murder	Forcible Rape	Robbery	Aggrav. Assault	Burglary	Larceny -Theft	Motor Vehicle Theft
City	3,957.9	12.8	20.8	176.0	152.2	903.5	2,384.4	308.2
Suburbs[1]	2,349.7	4.6	14.5	65.5	149.3	555.2	1,450.2	110.4
Metro[2]	3,381.8	9.8	18.6	136.4	151.2	778.7	2,049.7	237.4
U.S.	3,098.6	4.5	25.2	109.1	229.1	610.0	1,899.4	221.3

Note: Figures are crimes per 100,000 population; (1) All areas within the metro area that are located outside the city limits; (2) Figures cover the Savannah, GA Metropolitan Statistical Area—see Appendix B for areas included

Source: FBI Uniform Crime Reports, 2013

Hate Crimes

Area	Number of Quarters Reported	Number of Incidents per Bias Motivation						
		Race	Religion	Sexual Orientation	Ethnicity	Disability	Gender	Gender Identity
City	4	0	0	0	0	0	0	0
U.S.	4	2,871	1,031	1,233	655	83	18	31

Source: Federal Bureau of Investigation, Hate Crime Statistics 2013

Identity Theft Consumer Complaints

Area	Complaints	Complaints per 100,000 Population	Rank[2]
MSA[1]	337	92.1	80
U.S.	332,646	104.3	-

Note: (1) Figures cover the Savannah, GA Metropolitan Statistical Area—see Appendix B for areas included; (2) Rank ranges from 1 to 380 where 1 indicates greatest number of identity theft complaints per 100,000 population
Source: Federal Trade Commission, Consumer Sentinel Network Data Book for January–December 2014

Fraud and Other Consumer Complaints

Area	Complaints	Complaints per 100,000 Population	Rank[2]
MSA[1]	1,650	450.8	58
U.S.	2,250,205	705.7	-

Note: (1) Figures cover the Savannah, GA Metropolitan Statistical Area—see Appendix B for areas included; (2) Rank ranges from 1 to 380 where 1 indicates greatest number of identity theft complaints per 100,000 population
Source: Federal Trade Commission, Consumer Sentinel Network Data Book for January–December 2014

RECREATION

Culture

Dance[1]	Theatre[1]	Instrumental Music[1]	Vocal Music[1]	Series and Festivals	Museums and Art Galleries[2]	Zoos and Aquariums[3]
0	0	0	0	3	27	0

Note: (1) Professional perfoming groups; (2) Based on organizations with SIC code 8412; (3) AZA-accredited
Source: The Grey House Performing Arts Directory, 2015-16; Association of Zoos & Aquariums, AZA Member Zoos & Aquariums, April 2015; www.AccuLeads.com, April 2015

Professional Sports Teams

Team Name	League	Year Established
No teams are located in the metro area		

Source: Wikipedia, Major Professional Sports Teams of the United States and Canada, April 2015

CLIMATE

Average and Extreme Temperatures

Temperature	Jan	Feb	Mar	Apr	May	Jun	Jul	Aug	Sep	Oct	Nov	Dec	Yr.
Extreme High (°F)	84	86	91	95	100	104	105	104	98	97	89	83	105
Average High (°F)	60	64	70	78	84	89	92	90	86	78	70	62	77
Average Temp. (°F)	49	53	59	66	74	79	82	81	77	68	59	52	67
Average Low (°F)	38	41	48	54	62	69	72	72	68	57	47	40	56
Extreme Low (°F)	3	14	20	32	39	51	61	57	43	28	15	9	3

Note: Figures cover the years 1950-1995
Source: National Climatic Data Center, International Station Meteorological Climate Summary, 9/96

Average Precipitation/Snowfall/Humidity

Precip./Humidity	Jan	Feb	Mar	Apr	May	Jun	Jul	Aug	Sep	Oct	Nov	Dec	Yr.
Avg. Precip. (in.)	3.5	3.1	3.9	3.2	4.2	5.6	6.8	7.2	5.0	2.9	2.2	2.7	50.3
Avg. Snowfall (in.)	Tr	Tr	Tr	0	0	0	0	0	0	0	Tr	Tr	Tr
Avg. Rel. Hum. 7am (%)	83	82	83	84	85	87	88	91	91	88	86	83	86
Avg. Rel. Hum. 4pm (%)	53	50	49	48	52	58	61	63	62	55	53	54	55

Note: Figures cover the years 1950-1995; Tr = Trace amounts (<0.05 in. of rain; <0.5 in. of snow)
Source: National Climatic Data Center, International Station Meteorological Climate Summary, 9/96

Weather Conditions

Temperature			Daytime Sky			Precipitation		
10°F & below	32°F & below	90°F & above	Clear	Partly cloudy	Cloudy	0.01 inch or more precip.	0.1 inch or more snow/ice	Thunder-storms
< 1	29	70	97	155	113	111	< 1	63

Note: Figures are average number of days per year and cover the years 1950-1995
Source: National Climatic Data Center, International Station Meteorological Climate Summary, 9/96

HAZARDOUS WASTE

Superfund Sites

Savannah has no sites on the EPA's Superfund Final National Priorities List. There are a total of 1,322 Superfund sites on the list in the U.S. *U.S. Environmental Protection Agency, Final National Priorities List, April 14, 2015*

AIR & WATER QUALITY

Air Quality Trends: Ozone

	2004	2005	2006	2007	2008	2009	2010	2011	2012	2013
MSA[1]	0.071	0.068	0.069	0.065	0.067	0.062	0.065	0.065	0.063	0.059

Note: (1) Data covers the Savannah, GA Metropolitan Statistical Area—see Appendix B for areas included. The values shown are the composite ozone concentration averages among trend sites based on the highest fourth daily maximum 8-hour concentration in parts per million. These trends are based on sites having an adequate record of monitoring data during the trend period. Data from exceptional events are included.
Source: U.S. Environmental Protection Agency, Air Quality Monitoring Information, "Air Quality Trends by City, 2000-2013"

Air Quality Index

Area	Percent of Days when Air Quality was...[2]					AQI Statistics[2]	
	Good	Moderate	Unhealthy for Sensitive Groups	Unhealthy	Very Unhealthy	Maximum	Median
MSA[1]	69.9	29.6	0.5	0.0	0.0	114	43

Note: (1) Data covers the Savannah, GA Metropolitan Statistical Area—see Appendix B for areas included; (2) Based on 365 days with AQI data in 2014. Air Quality Index (AQI) is an index for reporting daily air quality. EPA calculates the AQI for five major air pollutants regulated by the Clean Air Act: ground-level ozone, particle pollution (aka particulate matter), carbon monoxide, sulfur dioxide, and nitrogen dioxide. The AQI runs from 0 to 500. The higher the AQI value, the greater the level of air pollution and the greater the health concern. There are six AQI categories: "Good" AQI is between 0 and 50. Air quality is considered satisfactory; "Moderate" AQI is between 51 and 100. Air quality is acceptable; "Unhealthy for Sensitive Groups" When AQI values are between 101 and 150, members of sensitive groups may experience health effects; "Unhealthy" When AQI values are between 151 and 200 everyone may begin to experience health effects; "Very Unhealthy" AQI values between 201 and 300 trigger a health alert; "Hazardous" AQI values over 300 trigger warnings of emergency conditions (not shown).
Source: U.S. Environmental Protection Agency, Air Quality Index Report, 2014

Air Quality Index Pollutants

Area	Percent of Days when AQI Pollutant was...[2]					
	Carbon Monoxide	Nitrogen Dioxide	Ozone	Sulfur Dioxide	Particulate Matter 2.5	Particulate Matter 10
MSA[1]	0.0	0.0	9.9	25.5	64.7	0.0

Note: (1) Data covers the Savannah, GA Metropolitan Statistical Area—see Appendix B for areas included; (2) Based on 365 days with AQI data in 2014. The Air Quality Index (AQI) is an index for reporting daily air quality. EPA calculates the AQI for five major air pollutants regulated by the Clean Air Act: ground-level ozone, particle pollution (also known as particulate matter), carbon monoxide, sulfur dioxide, and nitrogen dioxide. The AQI runs from 0 to 500. The higher the AQI value, the greater the level of air pollution and the greater the health concern.
Source: U.S. Environmental Protection Agency, Air Quality Index Report, 2014

Maximum Air Pollutant Concentrations: Particulate Matter, Ozone, CO and Lead

	Particulate Matter 10 (ug/m^3)	Particulate Matter 2.5 Wtd AM (ug/m^3)	Particulate Matter 2.5 24-Hr (ug/m^3)	Ozone (ppm)	Carbon Monoxide (ppm)	Lead (ug/m^3)
MSA[1] Level	n/a	9	18	0.059	n/a	n/a
NAAQS[2]	150	15	35	0.075	9	0.15
Met NAAQS[2]	n/a	Yes	Yes	Yes	n/a	n/a

Note: (1) Data covers the Savannah, GA Metropolitan Statistical Area—see Appendix B for areas included; Data from exceptional events are included; (2) National Ambient Air Quality Standards; ppm = parts per million; ug/m^3 = micrograms per cubic meter; n/a not available.

Concentrations: Particulate Matter 10 (coarse particulate)—highest second maximum 24-hour concentration; Particulate Matter 2.5 Wtd AM (fine particulate)—highest weighted annual mean concentration; Particulate Matter 2.5 24-Hour (fine particulate)—highest 98th percentile 24-hour concentration; Ozone—highest fourth daily maximum 8-hour concentration; Carbon Monoxide—highest second maximum non-overlapping 8-hour concentration; Lead—maximum running 3-month average

Source: U.S. Environmental Protection Agency, Air Quality Monitoring Information, "Air Quality Statistics by City, 2013"

Maximum Air Pollutant Concentrations: Nitrogen Dioxide and Sulfur Dioxide

	Nitrogen Dioxide AM (ppb)	Nitrogen Dioxide 1-Hr (ppb)	Sulfur Dioxide AM (ppb)	Sulfur Dioxide 1-Hr (ppb)	Sulfur Dioxide 24-Hr (ppb)
MSA[1] Level	n/a	n/a	n/a	93	n/a
NAAQS[2]	53	100	30	75	140
Met NAAQS[2]	n/a	n/a	n/a	No	n/a

Note: (1) Data covers the Savannah, GA Metropolitan Statistical Area—see Appendix B for areas included; Data from exceptional events are included; (2) National Ambient Air Quality Standards; ppm = parts per million; ug/m^3 = micrograms per cubic meter; n/a not available.

Concentrations: Nitrogen Dioxide AM—highest arithmetic mean concentration; Nitrogen Dioxide 1-Hr—highest 98th percentile 1-hour daily maximum concentration; Sulfur Dioxide AM—highest annual mean concentration; Sulfur Dioxide 1-Hr—highest 99th percentile 1-hour daily maximum concentration; Sulfur Dioxide 24-Hr—highest second maximum 24-hour concentration

Source: U.S. Environmental Protection Agency, Air Quality Monitoring Information, "Air Quality Statistics by City, 2013"

Drinking Water

Water System Name	Pop. Served	Primary Water Source Type	Violations[1]	
			Health Based	Monitoring/ Reporting
Savannah-Main	168,958	Ground	0	0

Note: (1) Based on violation data from January 1, 2014 to December 31, 2014 (includes unresolved violations from earlier years)

Source: U.S. Environmental Protection Agency, Office of Ground Water and Drinking Water, Safe Drinking Water Information System (based on data extracted January 27, 2015)

Tallahassee, Florida

Background

Tallahassee is the capital of Florida and located in the northern panhandle of the state in Leon County. In addition to the state government, the city is primarily known as home to Florida State University, with its 40,000 students and 16 colleges. The presence of FSU, as well as other smaller universities, has shaped development of Tallahassee from a small, rural settlement to the modern metropolis that it is today.

After the state of Florida was ceded to United States from Spain in 1821, a governing body was set up to preside over the new territory. The group initially alternated between meetings in St. Augustine and Pensacola-the territory's two largest cities at the time. Eventually Governor William Pope Duval appointed a committee to choose a more central, permanent location for the government. Tallahassee, located between St. Augustine and Pensacola, was incorporated in 1824. The word Tallahassee means "old town" in the language of the Creek Native American tribe that inhabited the area during the 18th century.

Florida State University was founded in 1851, establishing Tallahassee as a city known for education. During the Civil War, Tallahassee was the only Confederate capital city east of the Mississippi not captured by the Union Army. After the war, much of the industry in the southern United States changed. What was once a prosperous region for cotton and tobacco production suffered without slave labor. New industries emerged, including citrus production, cattle ranching and tourism, all of which were well suited to the climate and geography of Tallahassee. The first airport in the city opened in 1929. The 200-acre facility was named Dale Mabry Field after an Army Captain who had grown up in the city.

In 1961, the Tallahassee Regional Airport opened with limited service. In 1989, major passenger service was offered and in 2000, the terminal was renamed Ivan Monroe Terminal. Monroe, the first Tallahassee resident to own his own plane, was also the first manager of Dale Mabry Field-the city's original airport, and adjacent to the site of the present-day Tallahassee Regional. Other transportation services in the city include the StarMetro bus lines and the CSX railroad.

Economic and population growth in recent decades has created the need for more land in the city. During this time, approximately seventy-five square miles have been added to the city by voluntary annexation, in which property owners actively petition for their land to become part of the city. A 25-year-old program to fund new infrastructure and transportation projects via a one cent sales tax has yielded such public gems as the Capital Cascades Park which, at its foundation, is a two-pond storm-water management facility but is also a gathering place with venues such as the Capital City Amphitheater and the 5.2 mile Capital Cascades Trail.

Today, economic activity in Tallahassee is centered primarily on education and research. In addition to Florida State University, the city is home to Florida A&M University, the state's only historically black university that has 11,000 students. In 2014, the 126-year-old institution saw its first woman president, Dr. Elmira Magnum, take the helm. Also here is Tallahassee Community College, home to an Advanced Manufacturing Training Center, a 16,000 square foot facility geared toward high tech and precision manufacturing training, and the Ghazvini Center for Healthcare Education, an 85,000-square foot facility that houses programs in diagnostic medical sonography, nursing, radiologic technology, respiratory care, and emergency medical services. Other higher education offerings in Tallahassee include campuses of Barry University, Embry Riddle Aeronautical University, and Flagler College, among others.

The high-tech industry has grown significantly in recent decades. Recent arrivals include companies such as Bing Energy and SunnyLand Solar that are interested in working with university-based researchers. Also located here are manufacturing facilities for General Dynamics, Land Systems and Danfoss Turbocor.

Major attractions in the Tallahassee area include the Alfred B. Maclay Gardens State Park, the Florida State Capitol, the Lake Jackson Mounds Archaeological State Park, the Mary Brogan Museum of Art and Science and the Tallahassee Museum. Although the city does not host any major professional sports teams, students and residents alike flock to the games of the college teams. The most popular is the division 1 FSU Seminoles football team.

Despite being located in the northern part of the state, Tallahassee is generally hotter in the summer than cities in located on the Florida peninsula. The summer season also brings scattered, severe thunderstorms that develop on the Gulf of Mexico. Winters in the city are usually much cooler than in the rest of Florida. The city does receive occasional snow, but it's usually very light and only occurs once every few years. The city's location near the Gulf of Mexico also means that it sees its share of hurricane activity, but the last direct hit was Hurricane Kate in 1985.

Rankings

Business/Finance Rankings

- Using data from the Council for Community and Economic Research's 2013 Annual Report, NerdWallet ranked the 100 U.S. cities with the most expensive cost of living. Cities in California and in the Northeast topped the list. Of the cities with the highest cost of living, Tallahassee ranked #95. *NerdWallet.com, "Most Expensive Cities in America," June 4, 2014*
- The Tallahassee metro area appeared on the Milken Institute "2013 Best Performing Cities" list. Rank: #194 out of 200 large metro areas. Criteria: job growth; wage and salary growth; high-tech output growth. *Milken Institute, "Best-Performing Cities 2014," January 2015*
- *Forbes* ranked the 200 most populous metro areas to determine the nation's "Best Places for Business and Careers." The Tallahassee metro area was ranked #165. Criteria: costs (business and living); job growth (past and projected); income growth; educational attainment (college and high school); projected economic growth; cultural and recreational opportunities; net migration patterns; number of highly ranked colleges. *Forbes, "The Best Places for Business and Careers 2014," July 23, 2014*

Education Rankings

- Personal finance website *WalletHub* analyzed the 150 largest U.S. metropolitan statistical areas to determine where the most educated Americans are choosing to settle. Criteria: educational attainment; percentage of workers with jobs in computer, engineering, and science fields; quality and size of each metro area's universities. Tallahassee was ranked #12 (#1 = most educated city). *www.WalletHub.com, "2014's Most and Least Educated Cities*
- Tallahassee was selected as one of the most well-read cities in America by Amazon.com. The city ranked #20 among the top 20. Cities with populations greater than 100,000 were evaluated based on per capita sales of books, magazines and newspapers. *Amazon.com, "The 20 Most Well-Read Cities in America," May 20, 2014*

Environmental Rankings

- The Tallahassee metro area came in at #300 for the relative comfort of its climate on Sperling's list of "chill cities," as measured by the Sperling Heat Index. All 361 metro areas are included. Criteria included daytime high temperatures, nighttime low temperatures, dew point, and relative humidity at the high temperatures. *www.bertsperling.com, "Sperling's Chill Cities," July 18, 2013*
- Sperling's BestPlaces assessed 379 metropolitan areas of the United States for the likelihood of dangerously extreme weather events or earthquakes. In general the Southeast and South-Central regions have the highest risk of weather extremes and earthquakes, while the Pacific Northwest enjoys the lowest risk. Of the least risky metropolitan areas, the Tallahassee metro area was ranked #304. *www.bestplaces.net, "Safest Places from Natural Disasters," April 2011*
- Tallahassee was highlighted as one of the cleanest metro areas for ozone air pollution in the U.S. during 2011 through 2013. The list represents cities with no monitored ozone air pollution in unhealthful ranges. *American Lung Association, State of the Air 2015*
- Tallahassee was highlighted as one of the top 25 cleanest metro areas for short-term particle pollution (24-hour PM 2.5) in the U.S. during 2011 through 2013. Monitors in these cities reported no days with unhealthful PM 2.5 levels. *American Lung Association, State of the Air 2015*

Health/Fitness Rankings

- Tallahassee was identified as one of the top running towns in the southern U.S. by *Running Journal.* The city ranked #2 out of seven. Criteria: training venues; access to running clubs; quality of local running events; specialty running stores; overall social scene. *Running Journal, "Top Running Towns of the South," March 13, 2012*

- The Tallahassee metro area appeared in the 2013 Gallup-Healthways Well-Being Index. The area ranked #125 out of 189. The Gallup-Healthways Well-Being Index score is an average of six sub-indexes, which individually examine life evaluation, emotional health, work environment, physical health, healthy behaviors, and access to basic necessities. Results are based on telephone interviews conducted as part of the Gallup-Healthways Well-Being Index survey January 2–December 29, 2012, and January 2–December 30, 2013, with a random sample of 531,630 adults, aged 18 and older, living in metropolitan areas in the 50 U.S. states and the District of Columbia. *Gallup-Healthways, "State of American Well-Being," March 25, 2014*

Real Estate Rankings

- Using data from the housing-market research firm RealtyTrac, Yahoo! Finance researchers listed the housing markets in which housing affordability is deteriorating most, factoring in interest rates as well as median home prices. The Tallahassee metro area was among the least affordable housing markets according to the percentage difference in the income required to buy a home in December 2013 as opposed to in December 2012. *news.yahoo.com, "10 Cities Where Ordinary People Can No Longer Afford Homes," March 5, 2014*
- Tallahassee was ranked #220 out of 275 metro areas in terms of house price appreciation in 2014 (#1 = highest rate). *Federal Housing Finance Agency, House Price Index, 4th Quarter 2014*
- The Tallahassee metro area was identified as one of the 20 worst housing markets in the U.S. in 2014. The area ranked #14 out of 178 markets with a home price appreciation of -2.6%. Criteria: year-over-year change of median sales price of existing single-family homes between the 4th quarter of 2013 and the 4th quarter of 2014. *National Association of Realtors®, Median Sales Price of Existing Single-Family Homes for Metropolitan Areas, 4th Quarter 2014*
- Tallahassee was ranked #51 out of 226 metro areas in terms of housing affordability in 2014 by the National Association of Home Builders (#1 = most affordable). The NAHB-Wells Fargo Housing Opportunity Index (HOI) for a given area is defined as the share of homes sold in that area that would have been affordable to a family earning the local median income, based on standard mortgage underwriting criteria. *National Association of Home Builders®, NAHB-Wells Fargo Housing Opportunity Index, 4th Quarter 2014*

Safety Rankings

- Allstate ranked the 200 largest cities in America in terms of driver safety. Tallahassee ranked #44. Allstate researchers analyzed internal property damage claims over a two-year period from January 2011 to December 2012. A weighted average of the two-year numbers determined the annual percentages. *Allstate, "Allstate America's Best Drivers Report, 2014"*
- The National Insurance Crime Bureau ranked 380 metro areas in the U.S. in terms of per capita rates of vehicle theft. The Tallahassee metro area ranked #154 (#1 = highest rate). Criteria: number of vehicle theft offenses per 100,000 inhabitants in 2012. *National Insurance Crime Bureau, "Hot Spots 2012," June 26, 2013*

Seniors/Retirement Rankings

- From its Best Cities for Successful Aging indexes, the Milken Institute generated rankings for metropolitan areas, weighing data in eight categories—health care, wellness, living arrangements, transportation, financial characteristics, education and employment opportunities, community engagement, and overall livability. The Tallahassee metro area was ranked #97 overall in the small metro area category. *Milken Institute, "Best Cities for Successful Aging, 2014"*

Sports/Recreation Rankings

- Tallahassee was chosen as a bicycle friendly community by the League of American Bicyclists. A "Bicycle Friendly Community" welcomes cyclists by providing safe accommodation for cycling and encouraging people to bike for transportation and recreation. There are four award levels: Platinum; Gold; Silver; and Bronze. The community achieved an award level of Bronze. *League of American Bicyclists, "Bicycle Friendly Community Master List," Fall 2013*

Miscellaneous Rankings

- Bustle.com, a news, entertainment, and lifestyle site for women, studied binge- and heavy drinking rates among nonalcoholics to determine the nation's ten "drunkest" cities. Tallahassee made the list, at #8. *www.bustle.com, "38 Million Americans Have a Problem with Alcohol: The 10 Drunkest American Cities," January 2014*

- Using Musicmetric's Digital Music Index (DMI), CNBC ranked results for music piracy by way of the file-sharing protocol BitTorrent. Tallahassee was ranked #5 among American cities. *CNBC.com, "Florida City Named 'Pirate Capital' of Music World," October 8, 2012*

Business Environment

CITY FINANCES

City Government Finances

Component	2012 ($000)	2012 ($ per capita)
Total Revenues	765,208	4,219
Total Expenditures	814,789	4,492
Debt Outstanding	1,263,362	6,965
Cash and Securities[1]	1,898,733	10,468

Note: (1) Cash and security holdings of a government at the close of its fiscal year, including those of its dependent agencies, utilities, and liquor stores.
Source: U.S Census Bureau, State & Local Government Finances 2012

City Government Revenue by Source

Source	2012 ($000)	2012 ($ per capita)
General Revenue		
From Federal Government	18,970	105
From State Government	20,205	111
From Local Governments	12,792	71
Taxes		
Property	34,433	190
Sales and Gross Receipts	57,931	319
Personal Income	0	0
Corporate Income	0	0
Motor Vehicle License	0	0
Other Taxes	13,361	74
Current Charges	144,707	798
Liquor Store	0	0
Utility	382,471	2,109
Employee Retirement	43,297	239

Source: U.S Census Bureau, State & Local Government Finances 2012

City Government Expenditures by Function

Function	2012 ($000)	2012 ($ per capita)	2012 (%)
General Direct Expenditures			
Air Transportation	17,402	96	2.1
Corrections	0	0	0.0
Education	0	0	0.0
Employment Security Administration	0	0	0.0
Financial Administration	4,231	23	0.5
Fire Protection	31,598	174	3.9
General Public Buildings	0	0	0.0
Governmental Administration, Other	5,960	33	0.7
Health	0	0	0.0
Highways	55,945	308	6.9
Hospitals	0	0	0.0
Housing and Community Development	6,842	38	0.8
Interest on General Debt	8,699	48	1.1
Judicial and Legal	2,014	11	0.2
Libraries	0	0	0.0
Parking	0	0	0.0
Parks and Recreation	20,780	115	2.6
Police Protection	48,910	270	6.0
Public Welfare	0	0	0.0
Sewerage	96,735	533	11.9
Solid Waste Management	19,884	110	2.4
Veterans' Services	0	0	0.0
Liquor Store	0	0	0.0
Utility	359,534	1,982	44.1
Employee Retirement	84,381	465	10.4

Source: U.S Census Bureau, State & Local Government Finances 2012

DEMOGRAPHICS

Population Growth

Area	1990 Census	2000 Census	2010 Census	Population Growth (%) 1990-2000	Population Growth (%) 2000-2010
City	128,014	150,624	181,376	17.7	20.4
MSA[1]	259,096	320,304	367,413	23.6	14.7
U.S.	248,709,873	281,421,906	308,745,538	13.2	9.7

Note: (1) Figures cover the Tallahassee, FL Metropolitan Statistical Area—see Appendix B for areas included
Source: U.S. Census Bureau, Census 1990, 2000, 2010

Household Size

Area	Persons in Household (%)							Average Household Size
	One	Two	Three	Four	Five	Six	Seven or More	
City	32.7	34.3	17.9	10.4	3.2	1.0	0.5	2.34
MSA[1]	28.9	35.0	18.0	11.8	4.0	1.5	0.9	2.46
U.S.	27.7	33.6	15.7	13.1	6.0	2.3	1.5	2.64

Note: (1) Figures cover the Tallahassee, FL Metropolitan Statistical Area—see Appendix B for areas included
Source: U.S. Census Bureau, 2011-2013 American Community Survey 3-Year Estimates

Race

Area	White Alone[2] (%)	Black Alone[2] (%)	Asian Alone[2] (%)	AIAN[3] Alone[2] (%)	NHOPI[4] Alone[2] (%)	Other Race Alone[2] (%)	Two or More Races (%)
City	56.6	35.8	3.9	0.3	0.0	1.2	2.3
MSA[1]	61.0	32.9	2.4	0.3	0.0	1.4	2.0
U.S.	73.9	12.6	5.0	0.8	0.2	4.7	2.9

Note: (1) Figures cover the Tallahassee, FL Metropolitan Statistical Area—see Appendix B for areas included; (2) Alone is defined as not being in combination with one or more other races; (3) American Indian and Alaska Native; (4) Native Hawaiian and Other Pacific Islander
Source: U.S. Census Bureau, 2011-2013 American Community Survey 3-Year Estimates

Hispanic or Latino Origin

Area	Total (%)	Mexican (%)	Puerto Rican (%)	Cuban (%)	Other (%)
City	6.6	1.5	1.5	1.5	2.2
MSA[1]	6.2	1.9	1.2	1.1	2.0
U.S.	16.9	10.8	1.6	0.6	3.8

Note: Persons of Hispanic or Latino origin can be of any race; (1) Figures cover the Tallahassee, FL Metropolitan Statistical Area—see Appendix B for areas included
Source: U.S. Census Bureau, 2011-2013 American Community Survey 3-Year Estimates

Segregation

Type	Segregation Indices[1]				Percent Change		
	1990	2000	2010	2010 Rank[2]	1990-2000	1990-2010	2000-2010
Black/White	n/a	n/a	n/a	n/a	n/a	n/a	n/a
Asian/White	n/a	n/a	n/a	n/a	n/a	n/a	n/a
Hispanic/White	n/a	n/a	n/a	n/a	n/a	n/a	n/a

Note: All figures cover the Metropolitan Statistical Area—see Appendix B for areas included; Figures are based on an analysis of 1990, 2000, and 2010 Census Decennial Census tract data by William H. Frey, Brookings Institution and the University of Michigan Social Science Data Analysis Network. In this analysis all racial groups (whites, blacks, and asians) are non-Hispanic members of those races. Hispanics are shown as a separate category;
(1) Segregation Indices are Dissimilarity Indices that measure the degree to which the minority group is distributed differently than whites across census tracts. They range from 0 (complete integration) to 100 (complete segregation) where the value indicates the percentage of the minority group that needs to move to be distributed exactly like whites; (2) Ranges from 1 (most segregated) to 102 (least segregated); n/a not available.
Source: www.CensusScope.org

Ancestry

Area	German	Irish	English	American	Italian	Polish	French[2]	Scottish	Dutch
City	9.8	9.7	8.8	4.3	4.5	2.1	1.9	2.3	0.9
MSA[1]	9.8	9.9	8.8	5.9	4.0	1.6	2.0	2.5	1.1
U.S.	14.9	10.8	8.0	7.4	5.5	3.0	2.7	1.7	1.4

Note: Figures are the percentage of the total population reporting a particular ancestry. The nine most commonly reported ancestries in the U.S. are shown. Figures include multiple ancestries (e.g. if a person reported being Irish and Italian, they were included in both columns); (1) Figures cover the Tallahassee, FL Metropolitan Statistical Area—see Appendix B for areas included; (2) Excludes Basque
Source: U.S. Census Bureau, 2011-2013 American Community Survey 3-Year Estimates

Foreign-Born Population

Area	Percent of Population Born in								
	Any Foreign Country	Mexico	Asia	Europe	Carribean	South America	Central America[2]	Africa	Canada
City	7.9	0.4	2.8	0.9	2.0	0.8	0.3	0.6	0.2
MSA[1]	6.3	0.6	1.9	0.8	1.3	0.6	0.3	0.4	0.2
U.S.	13.0	3.7	3.8	1.5	1.2	0.9	1.0	0.6	0.3

Note: (1) Figures cover the Tallahassee, FL Metropolitan Statistical Area—see Appendix B for areas included; (2) Excludes Mexico.
Source: U.S. Census Bureau, 2011-2013 American Community Survey 3-Year Estimates

Marital Status

Area	Never Married	Now Married[2]	Separated	Widowed	Divorced
City	55.8	30.0	1.5	3.6	9.2
MSA[1]	43.0	39.6	1.9	4.5	11.1
U.S.	32.7	48.1	2.2	6.0	11.0

Note: Figures are percentages and cover the population 15 years of age and older; (1) Figures cover the Tallahassee, FL Metropolitan Statistical Area—see Appendix B for areas included; (2) Excludes separated
Source: U.S. Census Bureau, 2011-2013 American Community Survey 3-Year Estimates

Disability Status

Area	All Ages	Under 18 Years Old	18 to 64 Years Old	65 Years and Over
City	8.9	4.2	6.9	35.9
MSA[1]	11.0	4.6	8.9	35.4
U.S.	12.3	4.1	10.2	36.3

Note: Figures show percent of the civilian noninstitutionalized population that reported having a disability. Disability status is determined from from six types of difficulty: vision, hearing, cognitive, ambulatory, self-care, and independent living. For children under 5 years old, hearing and vision difficulty are used to determine disability status. For children between the ages of 5 and 14, disability status is determined from hearing, vision, cognitive, ambulatory, and self-care difficulties. For people aged 15 years and older, they are considered to have a disability if they have difficulty with any one of the six difficulty types; (1) Figures cover the Tallahassee, FL Metropolitan Statistical Area—see Appendix B for areas included.
Source: U.S. Census Bureau, 2011-2013 American Community Survey 3-Year Estimates

Age

Area	Percent of Population									Median Age
	Under Age 5	Age 5–19	Age 20–34	Age 35–44	Age 45–54	Age 55–64	Age 65–74	Age 75–84	Age 85+	
City	5.1	19.8	39.0	9.9	9.2	8.6	4.5	2.7	1.3	26.1
MSA[1]	5.5	19.3	28.2	11.6	12.3	11.9	6.6	3.3	1.3	32.3
U.S.	6.4	19.9	20.7	12.9	14.1	12.3	7.6	4.2	1.9	37.4

Note: (1) Figures cover the Tallahassee, FL Metropolitan Statistical Area—see Appendix B for areas included
Source: U.S. Census Bureau, 2011-2013 American Community Survey 3-Year Estimates

Gender

Area	Males	Females	Males per 100 Females
City	89,007	96,668	92.1
MSA[1]	181,396	191,849	94.6
U.S.	154,451,010	159,410,713	96.9

Note: (1) Figures cover the Tallahassee, FL Metropolitan Statistical Area—see Appendix B for areas included
Source: U.S. Census Bureau, 2011-2013 American Community Survey 3-Year Estimates

Religious Groups by Family

Area	Catholic	Baptist	Non-Den.	Methodist[2]	Lutheran	LDS[3]	Pente-costal	Presby-terian[4]	Muslim[5]	Judaism
MSA[1]	4.8	16.1	6.8	9.2	0.5	1.0	2.2	1.6	0.9	0.4
U.S.	19.1	9.3	4.0	4.0	2.3	2.0	1.9	1.6	0.8	0.7

Note: Figures are the number of adherents as a percentage of the total population; (1) Figures cover the Tallahassee, FL Metropolitan Statistical Area—see Appendix B for areas included; (2) Methodist/Pietist; (3) Latter Day Saints; (4) Reformed; (5) Figures are estimates
Source: Association of Statisticians of American Religious Bodies, 2010 U.S. Religion Census: Religious Congregations & Membership Study

Religious Groups by Tradition

Area	Catholic	Evangelical Protestant	Mainline Protestant	Other Tradition	Black Protestant	Orthodox
MSA[1]	4.8	21.9	6.4	3.0	9.2	0.2
U.S.	19.1	16.2	7.3	4.3	1.6	0.3

Note: Figures are the number of adherents as a percentage of the total population; (1) Figures cover the Tallahassee, FL Metropolitan Statistical Area—see Appendix B for areas included
Source: Association of Statisticians of American Religious Bodies, 2010 U.S. Religion Census: Religious Congregations & Membership Study

ECONOMY

Gross Metropolitan Product

Area	2012	2013	2014	2015	Rank[2]
MSA[1]	13.4	13.7	14.2	14.9	150

Note: Figures are in billions of dollars; (1) Figures cover the Tallahassee, FL Metropolitan Statistical Area—see Appendix B for areas included; (2) Rank is based on 2015 data and ranges from 1 to 363
Source: The U.S. Conference of Mayors, U.S. Metro Economies: GMP and Employment 2013-2015, June 2014

Economic Growth

Area	2010-12 (%)	2013 (%)	2014 (%)	2015 (%)	Rank[2]
MSA[1]	-0.8	1.3	1.9	2.8	194
U.S.	2.1	2.0	2.3	3.2	–

Note: Figures are real gross metropolitan product (GMP) growth rates and represent annual average percent change; (1) Figures cover the Tallahassee, FL Metropolitan Statistical Area—see Appendix B for areas included; (2) Rank is based on 2015 data and ranges from 1 to 363
Source: The U.S. Conference of Mayors, U.S. Metro Economies: GMP and Employment 2013-2015, June 2014

Metropolitan Area Exports

Area	2008	2009	2010	2011	2012	2013	Rank[2]
MSA[1]	119.1	108.1	117.8	118.1	130.8	122.5	337

Note: Figures are in millions of dollars; (1) Figures cover the Tallahassee, FL Metropolitan Statistical Area—see Appendix B for areas included; (2) Rank is based on 2013 data and ranges from 1 to 387
Source: U.S. Department of Commerce, International Trade Administration, Office of Trade & Industry Information, Manufacturing & Services, data extracted April 3, 2015

Building Permits

Area	Single-Family			Multi-Family			Total		
	2013	2014	Pct. Chg.	2013	2014	Pct. Chg.	2013	2014	Pct. Chg.
City	293	271	-7.5	648	632	-2.5	941	903	-4.0
MSA[1]	628	628	0.0	652	632	-3.1	1,280	1,260	-1.6
U.S.	620,802	634,597	2.2	370,020	411,766	11.3	990,822	1,046,363	5.6

Note: (1) Figures cover the Tallahassee, FL Metropolitan Statistical Area—see Appendix B for areas included; Figures represent new, privately-owned housing units authorized (unadjusted data); All permit data are based on estimates with imputation.
Source: U.S. Census Bureau, Manufacturing, Mining, and Construction Statistics, Building Permits, 2013, 2014

Bankruptcy Filings

Area	Business Filings			Nonbusiness Filings		
	2013	2014	% Chg.	2013	2014	% Chg.
Leon County	53	44	-17.0	441	427	-3.2
U.S.	33,212	26,983	-18.8	1,038,720	909,812	-12.4

Note: Business filings include Chapter 7, Chapter 11, Chapter 12, and Chapter 13; Nonbusiness filings include Chapter 7, Chapter 11, and Chapter 13
Source: Administrative Office of the U.S. Courts, Business and Nonbusiness Bankruptcy, County Cases Commenced by Chapter of the Bankruptcy Code, During the 12- Month Period Ending December 31, 2013 and Business and Nonbusiness Bankruptcy, County Cases Commenced by Chapter of the Bankruptcy Code, During the 12- Month Period Ending December 31, 2014

Housing Vacancy Rates

Area	Gross Vacancy Rate[2] (%)			Year-Round Vacancy Rate[3] (%)			Rental Vacancy Rate[4] (%)			Homeowner Vacancy Rate[5] (%)		
	2012	2013	2014	2012	2013	2014	2012	2013	2014	2012	2013	2014
MSA[1]	n/a	n/a	n/a	n/a	n/a	n/a	n/a	n/a	n/a	n/a	n/a	n/a
U.S.	13.8	13.6	13.4	10.8	10.7	10.4	8.7	8.3	7.6	2.0	2.0	1.9

Note: (1) Figures cover the Tallahassee, FL Metropolitan Statistical Area—see Appendix B for areas included; (2) The percentage of the total housing inventory that is vacant; (3) The percentage of the housing inventory (excluding seasonal units) that is year-round vacant; (4) The percentage of rental inventory that is vacant for rent; (5) The percentage of homeowner inventory that is vacant for sale; n/a not available
Source: U.S. Census Bureau, Housing Vacancies and Homeownership Annual Statistics: 2014

INCOME

Income

Area	Per Capita ($)	Median Household ($)	Average Household ($)
City	23,752	39,868	57,997
MSA[1]	24,467	45,683	62,453
U.S.	27,884	52,176	72,897

Note: (1) Figures cover the Tallahassee, FL Metropolitan Statistical Area—see Appendix B for areas included
Source: U.S. Census Bureau, 2011-2013 American Community Survey 3-Year Estimates

Household Income Distribution

Area	Percent of Households Earning							
	Under $15,000	$15,000 -24,999	$25,000 -34,999	$35,000 -49,999	$50,000 -74,999	$75,000 -99,000	$100,000 -149,999	$150,000 and up
City	22.6	11.9	10.8	14.2	15.3	9.2	9.1	6.8
MSA[1]	17.5	11.4	10.9	13.9	17.5	11.0	11.0	6.8
U.S.	13.0	10.9	10.3	13.6	17.9	11.9	12.7	9.6

Note: (1) Figures cover the Tallahassee, FL Metropolitan Statistical Area—see Appendix B for areas included
Source: U.S. Census Bureau, 2011-2013 American Community Survey 3-Year Estimates

Poverty Rate

Area	All Ages	Under 18 Years Old	18 to 64 Years Old	65 Years and Over
City	29.8	27.1	33.0	8.7
MSA[1]	22.3	25.1	23.7	8.5
U.S.	15.9	22.4	14.8	9.5

Note: Figures are percentage of people whose income during the past 12 months was below the poverty level; (1) Figures cover the Tallahassee, FL Metropolitan Statistical Area—see Appendix B for areas included
Source: U.S. Census Bureau, 2011-2013 American Community Survey 3-Year Estimates

EMPLOYMENT

Labor Force and Employment

Area	Civilian Labor Force			Workers Employed		
	Dec. 2013	Dec. 2014	% Chg.	Dec. 2013	Dec. 2014	% Chg.
City	96,950	99,198	2.3	91,539	94,333	3.1
MSA[1]	185,716	189,921	2.3	175,128	180,393	3.0
U.S.	154,408,000	155,521,000	0.7	144,423,000	147,190,000	1.9

Note: Data is not seasonally adjusted and covers workers 16 years of age and older; (1) Figures cover the Tallahassee, FL Metropolitan Statistical Area—see Appendix B for areas included
Source: Bureau of Labor Statistics, Local Area Unemployment Statistics

Unemployment Rate

Area	2014											
	Jan.	Feb.	Mar.	Apr.	May	Jun.	Jul.	Aug.	Sep.	Oct.	Nov.	Dec.
City	5.9	5.8	5.7	5.2	5.8	6.3	6.6	6.3	5.7	5.3	5.4	4.9
MSA[1]	6.0	5.9	5.9	5.2	5.8	6.1	6.5	6.3	5.7	5.4	5.4	5.0
U.S.	7.0	7.0	6.8	5.9	6.1	6.3	6.5	6.3	5.7	5.5	5.5	5.4

Note: Data is not seasonally adjusted and covers workers 16 years of age and older; (1) Figures cover the Tallahassee, FL Metropolitan Statistical Area—see Appendix B for areas included
Source: Bureau of Labor Statistics, Local Area Unemployment Statistics

Employment by Occupation

Occupation Classification	City (%)	MSA[1] (%)	U.S. (%)
Management, Business, Science, and Arts	43.4	41.0	36.2
Natural Resources, Construction, and Maintenance	5.2	7.6	9.0
Production, Transportation, and Material Moving	5.0	6.2	12.1
Sales and Office	27.4	27.4	24.4
Service	19.1	17.8	18.3

Note: Figures cover employed civilians 16 years of age and older; (1) Figures cover the Tallahassee, FL Metropolitan Statistical Area—see Appendix B for areas included
Source: U.S. Census Bureau, 2011-2013 American Community Survey 3-Year Estimates

Employment by Industry

Sector	MSA[1]		U.S.
	Number of Employees	Percent of Total	Percent of Total
Construction, Mining, and Logging	6,300	3.6	5.0
Education and Health Services	21,000	11.9	15.5
Financial Activities	7,200	4.1	5.7
Government	62,400	35.2	15.8
Information	3,900	2.2	2.0
Leisure and Hospitality	19,100	10.8	10.3
Manufacturing	2,900	1.6	8.7
Other Services	9,300	5.3	4.0
Professional and Business Services	20,000	11.3	13.8
Retail Trade	19,700	11.1	11.4
Transportation, Warehousing, and Utilities	2,000	1.1	3.9
Wholesale Trade	3,300	1.9	4.2

Note: Figures are non-farm employment as of December 2014. Figures are not seasonally adjusted and include workers 16 years of age and older; (1) Figures cover the Tallahassee, FL Metropolitan Statistical Area—see Appendix B for areas included; n/a not available
Source: Bureau of Labor Statistics, Current Employment Statistics, Employment, Hours, and Earnings

Occupations with Greatest Projected Employment Growth: 2012 – 2022

Occupation[1]	2012 Employment	2022 Projected Employment	Numeric Employment Change	Percent Employment Change
Retail Salespersons	326,380	380,120	53,740	16.5
Combined Food Preparation and Serving Workers, Including Fast Food	196,980	237,340	40,360	20.5
Customer Service Representatives	191,210	228,620	37,410	19.6
Registered Nurses	164,020	201,140	37,120	22.6
Waiters and Waitresses	191,370	227,810	36,440	19.0
Office Clerks, General	142,710	170,300	27,590	19.3
Cashiers	206,660	230,190	23,530	11.4
Landscaping and Groundskeeping Workers	92,510	115,540	23,030	24.9
Receptionists and Information Clerks	75,780	95,680	19,900	26.2
Nursing Assistants	86,990	106,200	19,210	22.1

Note: Projections cover Florida; (1) Sorted by numeric employment change
Source: www.projectionscentral.com, State Occupational Projections, 2012–2022 Long-Term Projections

Fastest Growing Occupations: 2012 – 2022

Occupation[1]	2012 Employment	2022 Projected Employment	Numeric Employment Change	Percent Employment Change
Helpers—Carpenters	1,280	2,450	1,170	90.7
Helpers—Brickmasons, Blockmasons, Stonemasons, and Tile and Marble Setters	1,050	1,890	840	79.5
Biomedical Engineers	760	1,300	540	70.7
Reinforcing Iron and Rebar Workers	520	870	350	67.5
Glaziers	2,890	4,710	1,820	62.8
Solar Photovoltaic Installers	170	270	100	58.7
Brickmasons and Blockmasons	2,820	4,430	1,610	57.1
Stonemasons	450	710	260	56.4
Helpers—Pipelayers, Plumbers, Pipefitters, and Steamfitters	2,420	3,750	1,330	54.8
Cement Masons and Concrete Finishers	10,390	16,050	5,660	54.4

Note: Projections cover Florida; (1) Sorted by percent employment change and excludes occupations with numeric employment change less than 100
Source: www.projectionscentral.com, State Occupational Projections, 2012–2022 Long-Term Projections

Average Wages

Occupation	$/Hr.	Occupation	$/Hr.
Accountants and Auditors	26.61	Maids and Housekeeping Cleaners	9.18
Automotive Mechanics	16.97	Maintenance and Repair Workers	14.86
Bookkeepers	16.12	Marketing Managers	41.02
Carpenters	19.58	Nuclear Medicine Technologists	n/a
Cashiers	9.31	Nurses, Licensed Practical	19.21
Clerks, General Office	12.01	Nurses, Registered	27.68
Clerks, Receptionists/Information	11.78	Nursing Assistants	10.98
Clerks, Shipping/Receiving	12.10	Packers and Packagers, Hand	9.23
Computer Programmers	28.15	Physical Therapists	40.52
Computer Systems Analysts	42.25	Postal Service Mail Carriers	24.74
Computer User Support Specialists	17.87	Real Estate Brokers	n/a
Cooks, Restaurant	10.68	Retail Salespersons	10.95
Dentists	104.55	Sales Reps., Exc. Tech./Scientific	25.49
Electrical Engineers	43.20	Sales Reps., Tech./Scientific	35.94
Electricians	18.66	Secretaries, Exc. Legal/Med./Exec.	14.52
Financial Managers	52.43	Security Guards	12.86
First-Line Supervisors/Managers, Sales	20.41	Surgeons	124.29
Food Preparation Workers	9.56	Teacher Assistants	12.30
General and Operations Managers	56.30	Teachers, Elementary School	20.50
Hairdressers/Cosmetologists	13.10	Teachers, Secondary School	20.60
Internists	n/a	Telemarketers	13.57
Janitors and Cleaners	10.15	Truck Drivers, Heavy/Tractor-Trailer	15.64
Landscaping/Groundskeeping Workers	10.80	Truck Drivers, Light/Delivery Svcs.	15.75
Lawyers	51.85	Waiters and Waitresses	10.54

Note: Wage data covers the Tallahassee, FL Metropolitan Statistical Area—see Appendix B for areas included; Hourly wages for elementary/secondary school teachers and teacher assistants were calculated by the editors from annual wage data assuming a 40 hour work week; n/a not available.
Source: Bureau of Labor Statistics, Metro Area Occupational Employment and Wage Estimates, May 2014

TAXES

State Corporate Income Tax Rates

State	Tax Rate (%)	Income Brackets ($)	Num. of Brackets	Financial Institution Tax Rate (%)[a]	Federal Income Tax Ded.
Florida	5.5 (f)	Flat rate	1	5.5 (f)	No

Note: Tax rates as of January 1, 2015; (a) Rates listed are the corporate income tax rate applied to financial institutions or excise taxes based on income. Some states have other taxes based upon the value of deposits or shares; (f) An exemption of $50,000 is allowed. Florida's Alternative Minimum Tax rate is 3.3%.
Source: Federation of Tax Administrators, "State Corporate Income Tax Rates, 2015"

State Individual Income Tax Rates

State	Tax Rate (%)	Income Brackets ($)	Num. of Brackets	Personal Exempt. ($)[1]		Fed. Inc. Tax Ded.
				Single	Dependents	
Florida	None	–	–	–	–	–

Note: Tax rates as of January 1, 2015; Local- and county-level taxes are not included; n/a not applicable; (1) Married joint filers generally receive double the single exemption
Source: Federation of Tax Administrators, "State Individual Income Tax Rates, 2015"

Various State and Local Tax Rates

State	State and Local Sales and Use (%)	State Sales and Use (%)	Gasoline[1] (¢/gal.)	Cigarette[2] ($/pack)	Spirits[3] ($/gal.)	Wine[4] ($/gal.)	Beer[5] ($/gal.)
Florida	7.5	6.0	36.42	1.339	6.50 (f)	2.25	0.48 (p)

Note: All tax rates as of January 1, 2015; (1) The American Petroleum Institute has developed a methodology for determining the average tax rate on a gallon of fuel. Rates may include any of the following: excise taxes, environmental fees, storage tank fees, other fees or taxes, general sales tax, and local taxes. In states where gasoline is subject to the general sales tax, or where the fuel tax is based on the average sale price, the average rate determined by API is sensitive to changes in the price of gasoline. States that fully or partially apply general sales taxes to gasoline: CA, CO, GA, IL, IN, MI, NY; (2) The federal excise tax of $1.0066 per pack and local taxes are not included; (3) Rates are those applicable to off-premise sales of 40% alcohol by volume (a.b.v.) distilled spirits in 750ml containers. Local excise taxes are excluded; (4) Rates are those applicable to off-premise sales of 11% a.b.v. non-carbonated wine in 750ml containers; (5) Rates are those applicable to off-premise sales of 4.7% a.b.v. beer in 12 ounce containers; (f) Different rates are also applicable according to alcohol content, place of production, size of container, or place purchased (on- or off-premise or onboard airlines); (p) Local excise taxes are excluded.
Source: Tax Foundation, 2015 Facts & Figures: How Does Your State Compare?

State Business Tax Climate Index Rankings

State	Overall Rank	Corporate Tax Index Rank	Individual Income Tax Index Rank	Sales Tax Index Rank	Unemployment Insurance Tax Index Rank	Property Tax Index Rank
Florida	5	14	1	12	3	16

Note: The index is a measure of how each state's tax laws affect economic performance. The lower the rank, the more favorable a state's tax system is for business. States without a given tax are given a ranking of 1. The scores/rankings for the District of Columbia do not affect other states. The 2015 index represents the tax climate as of July 1, 2014.
Source: Tax Foundation, State Business Tax Climate Index 2015

COMMERCIAL UTILITIES

Typical Monthly Electric Bills

Area	Commercial Service ($/month)		Industrial Service ($/month)	
	1,500 kWh	40 kW demand 14,000 kWh	1,000 kW demand 200,000 kWh	50,000 kW demand 32,500,000 kWh
City	n/a	n/a	n/a	n/a
Average[1]	201	1,653	26,124	2,639,743

Note: Figures are based on annualized 2014 rates; (1) Average based on 180 utilities surveyed; n/a not available
Source: Edison Electric Institute, Typical Bills and Average Rates Report, Summer 2014

TRANSPORTATION

Means of Transportation to Work

Area	Car/Truck/Van		Public Transportation			Bicycle	Walked	Other Means	Worked at Home
	Drove Alone	Car-pooled	Bus	Subway	Railroad				
City	81.4	7.9	2.4	0.0	0.0	0.9	3.0	1.1	3.2
MSA[1]	82.1	9.7	1.4	0.0	0.0	0.5	1.9	1.1	3.3
U.S.	76.4	9.6	2.6	1.8	0.6	0.6	2.8	1.3	4.3

Note: Figures are percentages and cover workers 16 years of age and older; (1) Figures cover the Tallahassee, FL Metropolitan Statistical Area—see Appendix B for areas included
Source: U.S. Census Bureau, 2011-2013 American Community Survey 3-Year Estimates

Travel Time to Work

Area	Less Than 10 Minutes	10 to 19 Minutes	20 to 29 Minutes	30 to 44 Minutes	45 to 59 Minutes	60 to 89 Minutes	90 Minutes or More
City	15.8	43.8	24.2	12.1	1.7	1.4	0.9
MSA[1]	11.9	34.0	25.4	20.4	5.2	2.1	1.0
U.S.	13.3	29.7	20.9	20.2	7.7	5.7	2.6

Note: Figures are percentages and include workers 16 years old and over; (1) Figures cover the Tallahassee, FL Metropolitan Statistical Area—see Appendix B for areas included
Source: U.S. Census Bureau, 2011-2013 American Community Survey 3-Year Estimates

Travel Time Index

Area	1985	1990	1995	2000	2005	2010	2011
Urban Area[1]	n/a	n/a	n/a	n/a	n/a	n/a	n/a
Average[2]	1.09	1.14	1.16	1.19	1.23	1.18	1.18

Note: Travel Time Index—the ratio of travel time in the peak period to the travel time at free-flow conditions. For example, a value of 1.30 indicates a 20-minute free-flow trip takes 26 minutes in the peak. Free-flow speeds (60 mph on freeways and 35 mph on principal arterials) are used as the comparison threshold; (1) Data for the Tallahassee, FL urban area was not available; (2) average of 498 urban areas
Source: Texas Transportation Institute, Urban Mobility Report 2012, December 2012

Public Transportation

Agency Name / Mode of Transportation	Vehicles Operated in Maximum Service	Annual Unlinked Passenger Trips (in thous.)	Annual Passenger Miles (in thous.)
City of Tallahassee (StarMetro)			
Bus (directly operated)	58	4,432.1	13,724.5
Demand Response (directly operated)	15	86.5	575.1

Source: Federal Transit Administration, National Transit Database, 2013

Air Transportation

Airport Name and Code / Type of Service	Passenger Airlines[1]	Passenger Enplanements	Freight Carriers[2]	Freight (lbs.)
Tallahassee Regional (TLH)				
Domestic service (U.S. carriers - 2014)	19	338,880	6	8,988,681
International service (U.S. carriers - 2013)	0	0	1	9,070

Note: (1) Includes all U.S.-based major, minor and commuter airlines that carried at least one passenger during the year; (2) Includes all U.S.-based airlines and freight carriers that transported at least one lb. of freight during the year.
Source: Bureau of Transportation Statistics, The Intermodal Transportation Database, Air Carriers: T-100 Domestic Market (U.S. Carriers), 2014; Bureau of Transportation Statistics, The Intermodal Transportation Database, Air Carriers: T-100 International Market (U.S. Carriers), 2013

Other Transportation Statistics

Major Highways:	I-10
Amtrak Service:	No
Major Waterways/Ports:	None

Source: Amtrak.com; Google Maps

BUSINESSES

Major Business Headquarters

Company Name	Rankings	
	Fortune[1]	Forbes[2]
No companies listed	-	-

Note: (1) Fortune 500—companies that produce a 10-K are ranked 1 to 500 based on 2013 revenue; (2) all private companies with at least $2 billion in annual revenue through the end of their most current fiscal year are ranked 1 to 221; companies listed are headquartered in the city; dashes indicate no ranking
Source: Fortune, "Fortune 500," June 16, 2014; Forbes, "America's Largest Private Companies," November 5, 2014

Minority- and Women-Owned Businesses

Group	All Firms		Firms with Paid Employees			
	Firms	Sales ($000)	Firms	Sales ($000)	Employees	Payroll ($000)
Asian	541	104,534	155	76,732	1,222	15,117
Black	2,581	114,987	(s)	(s)	(s)	(s)
Hispanic	765	88,113	186	73,230	881	21,731
Women	4,816	609,031	921	526,609	5,438	129,271
All Firms	15,791	12,932,947	4,959	12,337,448	86,866	3,001,106

Note: Figures cover firms located in the city; minority- and women-owned business are defined as firms in which the corresponding group own 51% or more of the stock or equity of the company; (s) estimates are suppressed when publication standards are not met
Source: U.S. Census Bureau, 2007 Economic Census, Survey of Business Owners (2012 Survey of Business Owners data will be released starting in June 2015)

HOTELS & CONVENTION CENTERS

Hotels/Motels

Area	5 Star		4 Star		3 Star		2 Star		1 Star		Not Rated	
	Num.	Pct.[3]	Num.	Pct.[3]	Num.	Pct.[3]	Num.	Pct.[3]	Num.	Pct.[3]	Num.	Pct.[3]
City[1]	0	0.0	2	2.3	18	20.7	63	72.4	3	3.4	1	1.1
Total[2]	166	0.9	1,264	7.0	5,718	31.8	9,340	52.0	411	2.3	1,070	6.0

Note: (1) Figures cover Tallahassee and vicinity; (2) Figures cover all 100 cities in this book; (3) Percentage of hotels which have a given star rating; Star ratings are determined by expedia.com and offer an indication of the general quality of a particular hotel.
Source: expedia.com, April 2, 2015

Major Convention Centers

Name	Overall Space (sq. ft.)	Exhibit Space (sq. ft.)	Meeting Space (sq. ft.)	Meeting Rooms
Donald L. Tucker Civic Center at FSU	n/a	54,000	n/a	n/a

Note: Table includes convention centers located in the Tallahassee, FL metro area; n/a not available
Source: Original research

Living Environment

COST OF LIVING

Cost of Living Index

Composite Index	Groceries	Housing	Utilities	Trans-portation	Health Care	Misc. Goods/ Services
n/a	n/a	n/a	n/a	n/a	n/a	n/a

Note: The Cost of Living Index measures regional differences in the cost of consumer goods and services, excluding taxes and non-consumer expenditures, for professional and managerial households in the top income quintile. It is based on more than 50,000 prices covering almost 60 different items for which prices are collected three times a year by chambers of commerce, economic development organizations or university applied economic centers in each participating urban area. The numbers shown should be read as a percentage above or below the national average of 100. For example, a value of 115.4 in the groceries column indicates that grocery prices are 15.4% higher than the national average. Small differences in the index numbers should not be interpreted as significant; n/a not available.
Source: The Council for Community and Economic Research, ACCRA Cost of Living Index, 2014

Grocery Prices

Area[1]	T-Bone Steak ($/pound)	Frying Chicken ($/pound)	Whole Milk ($/half gal.)	Eggs ($/dozen)	Orange Juice ($/64 oz.)	Coffee ($/11.5 oz.)
City[2]	n/a	n/a	n/a	n/a	n/a	n/a
Avg.	10.40	1.37	2.40	1.99	3.46	4.27
Min.	8.48	0.93	1.37	1.30	2.83	2.99
Max.	14.20	2.44	3.62	4.02	6.42	6.96

Note: (1) Values for the local area are compared with the average, minimum and maximum values for all 308 areas in the Cost of Living Index; (2) Figures cover the Tallahassee FL urban area; n/a not available; **T-Bone Steak** *(price per pound);* **Frying Chicken** *(price per pound, whole fryer);* **Whole Milk** *(half gallon carton);* **Eggs** *(price per dozen, Grade A, large);* **Orange Juice** *(64 oz. Tropicana or Florida Natural);* **Coffee** *(11.5 oz. can, vacuum-packed, Maxwell House, Hills Bros, or Folgers).*
Source: The Council for Community and Economic Research, ACCRA Cost of Living Index, 2014

Housing and Utility Costs

Area[1]	New Home Price ($)	Apartment Rent ($/month)	All Electric ($/month)	Part Electric ($/month)	Other Energy ($/month)	Telephone ($/month)
City[2]	n/a	n/a	n/a	n/a	n/a	n/a
Avg.	305,838	919	181.00	93.66	73.14	27.95
Min.	183,142	480	112.00	42.06	23.42	17.16
Max.	1,358,576	3,851	594.00	180.03	440.99	40.42

Note: (1) Values for the local area are compared with the average, minimum and maximum values for all 308 areas in the Cost of Living Index; (2) Figures cover the Tallahassee FL urban area; n/a not available; **New Home Price** *(2,400 sf living area, 8,000 sf lot, in urban area with full utilities);* **Apartment Rent** *(950 sf 2 bedroom/1.5 or 2 bath, unfurnished, excluding all utilities except water);* **All Electric** *(average monthly cost for an all-electric home);* **Part Electric** *(average monthly cost for a part-electric home);* **Other Energy** *(average monthly cost for natural gas, fuel oil, coal, wood, and any other forms of energy except electricity);* **Telephone** *(price includes basic monthly rate for a private residential line plus additional local usage charges incurred by a family of four).*
Source: The Council for Community and Economic Research, ACCRA Cost of Living Index, 2014

Health Care, Transportation, and Other Costs

Area[1]	Doctor ($/visit)	Dentist ($/visit)	Optometrist ($/visit)	Gasoline ($/gallon)	Beauty Salon ($/visit)	Men's Shirt ($)
City[2]	n/a	n/a	n/a	n/a	n/a	n/a
Avg.	102.86	87.89	97.66	3.44	34.37	26.74
Min.	67.47	65.78	51.18	3.00	17.43	12.79
Max.	173.50	150.14	235.00	4.33	64.28	49.50

Note: (1) Values for the local area are compared with the average, minimum and maximum values for all 308 areas in the Cost of Living Index; (2) Figures cover the Tallahassee FL urban area; n/a not available; **Doctor** *(general practitioners routine exam of an established patient);* **Dentist** *(adult teeth cleaning and periodic oral examination);* **Optometrist** *(full vision eye exam for established adult patient);* **Gasoline** *(one gallon regular unleaded, national brand, including all taxes, cash price at self-service pump if available);* **Beauty Salon** *(woman's shampoo, trim, and blow-dry);* **Men's Shirt** *(cotton/polyester dress shirt, pinpoint weave, long sleeves).*
Source: The Council for Community and Economic Research, ACCRA Cost of Living Index, 2014

HOUSING

House Price Index (HPI)

Area	National Ranking[2]	Quarterly Change (%)	One-Year Change (%)	Five-Year Change (%)
MSA[1]	220	-1.36	2.06	-10.88
U.S.[3]	–	1.35	4.91	11.59

Note: The HPI is a weighted repeat sales index. It measures average price changes in repeat sales or refinancings on the same properties. This information is obtained by reviewing repeat mortgage transactions on single-family properties whose mortgages have been purchased or securitized by Fannie Mae or Freddie Mac in January 1975; (1) Tallahassee Metropolitan Statistical Area—see Appendix B for areas included; (2) Rankings are based on annual percentage change for all metro areas containing at least 15,000 transactions over the last 10 years and ranges from 1 to 275; (3) figures based on a weighted average of Census Division estimates using a seasonally adjusted, purchase-only index; all figures are for the period ending December 31, 2014
Source: Federal Housing Finance Agency, House Price Index, February 26, 2015

Median Single-Family Home Prices

Area	2012	2013	2014p	Percent Change 2013 to 2014
MSA[1]	144.9	171.9	167.5	-2.6
U.S. Average	177.2	197.4	209.0	5.9

Note: Figures are median sales prices of existing single-family homes in thousands of dollars; (p) preliminary; n/a not available; (1) Tallahassee, FL Metropolitan Statistical Area—see Appendix B for areas included
Source: National Association of Realtors, Median Sales Price of Existing Single-Family Homes for Metropolitan Areas, 4th Quarter 2014

Qualifying Income Based on Median Sales Price of Existing Single-Family Homes

Area	With 5% Down ($)	With 10% Down ($)	With 20% Down ($)
MSA[1]	37,358	35,392	31,460
U.S. Average	45,863	43,449	38,621

Note: Figures are preliminary; Qualifying income is based on a mortgage rate of 4.0%. Monthly principal and interest payment is limited to 25% of income; n/a not available; (1) Tallahassee, FL Metropolitan Statistical Area—see Appendix B for areas included
Source: National Association of Realtors, Qualifying Income Based on Median Sales Price of Existing Single-Family Homes for Metropolitan Areas, 4th Quarter 2014

Median Apartment Condo-Coop Home Prices

Area	2012	2013	2014p	Percent Change 2013 to 2014
MSA[1]	68.7	77.8	80.9	4.0
U.S. Average	173.7	194.9	205.1	5.2

Note: Figures are median sales prices of existing apartment condo-coop homes in thousands of dollars; (p) preliminary; n/a not available; (1) Tallahassee, FL Metropolitan Statistical Area—see Appendix B for areas included
Source: National Association of Realtors, Median Sales Price of Existing Apartment Condo-Coop Homes for Metropolitan Areas, 4th Quarter 2014

Gross Monthly Rent

Area	Under $200	$200 -299	$300 -499	$500 -749	$750 -999	$1,000 -1,499	$1,500 and up	Median ($)
City	1.1	1.7	5.1	22.6	32.1	26.4	11.1	906
MSA[1]	1.1	1.9	6.8	22.8	31.4	26.4	9.7	882
U.S.	1.7	3.2	7.8	22.1	24.3	26.0	14.9	900

Note: Figures are percentages except for Median; Gross rent is the contract rent plus the estimated average monthly cost of utilities (electricity, gas, and water and sewer) and fuels (oil, coal, kerosene, wood, etc.) if these are paid by the renter (or paid for the renter by someone else); (1) Figures cover the Tallahassee, FL Metropolitan Statistical Area—see Appendix B for areas included
Source: U.S. Census Bureau, 2011-2013 American Community Survey 3-Year Estimates

Homeownership Rate

Area	2007 (%)	2008 (%)	2009 (%)	2010 (%)	2011 (%)	2012 (%)	2013 (%)	2014 (%)
MSA[1]	n/a	n/a	n/a	n/a	n/a	n/a	n/a	n/a
U.S.	68.1	67.8	67.4	66.9	66.1	65.4	65.1	64.5

Note: (1) Figures cover the Tallahassee, FL Metropolitan Statistical Area—see Appendix B for areas included; n/a not available
Source: U.S. Census Bureau, Housing Vacancies and Homeownership Annual Statistics: 2014

Year Housing Structure Built

Area	2010 or Later	2000 -2009	1990 -1999	1980 -1989	1970 -1979	1960 -1969	1950 -1959	1940 -1949	Before 1940	Median Year
City	1.0	20.3	17.9	18.2	18.5	10.8	8.0	3.5	1.8	1984
MSA[1]	0.9	20.2	21.6	20.1	16.7	8.4	6.5	2.9	2.7	1986
U.S.	0.9	15.0	13.9	13.8	15.8	11.0	10.9	5.4	13.3	1976

Note: Figures are percentages except for Median Year; (1) Figures cover the Tallahassee, FL Metropolitan Statistical Area—see Appendix B for areas included
Source: U.S. Census Bureau, 2011-2013 American Community Survey 3-Year Estimates

HEALTH

Health Risk Data

Category	MSA[1] (%)	U.S. (%)
Adults aged 18–64 who have any kind of health care coverage	n/a	79.6
Adults who reported being in good or excellent health	n/a	83.1
Adults who are current smokers	n/a	19.6
Adults who are heavy drinkers[2]	n/a	6.1
Adults who are binge drinkers[3]	n/a	16.9
Adults who are overweight (BMI 25.0 - 29.9)	n/a	35.8
Adults who are obese (BMI 30.0 - 99.8)	n/a	27.6
Adults who participated in any physical activities in the past month	n/a	77.1
Adults 50+ who have ever had a sigmoidoscopy or colonoscopy	n/a	67.3
Women aged 40+ who have had a mammogram within the past two years	n/a	74.0
Men aged 40+ who have had a PSA test within the past two years	n/a	45.2
Adults aged 65+ who have had flu shot within the past year	n/a	60.1
Adults who always wear a seatbelt	n/a	93.8

Note: Data as of 2012 unless otherwise noted; n/a not available; (1) Figures cover the Tallahassee, FL Metropolitan Statistical Area—see Appendix B for areas included; (2) Heavy drinkers are classified as males having more than two drinks per day or females having more than one drink per day; (3) Binge drinkers are classified as males having five or more drinks on one occasion or females having four or more drinks on one occasion
Source: Centers for Disease Control and Prevention, Behaviorial Risk Factor Surveillance System, SMART: Selected Metropolitan/Micropolitan Area Risk Trends, 2012 (Note: the CDC has discontinued this dataset but will be releasing a replacement in late 2015)

Chronic Health Indicators

Category	MSA[1] (%)	U.S. (%)
Adults who have ever been told they had a heart attack	n/a	4.5
Adults who have ever been told they had a stroke	n/a	2.9
Adults who have been told they currently have asthma	n/a	8.9
Adults who have ever been told they have arthritis	n/a	25.7
Adults who have ever been told they have diabetes[2]	n/a	9.7
Adults who have ever been told they had skin cancer	n/a	5.7
Adults who have ever been told they had any other types of cancer	n/a	6.5
Adults who have ever been told they have COPD	n/a	6.2
Adults who have ever been told they have kidney disease	n/a	2.5
Adults who have ever been told they have a form of depression	n/a	18.0

Note: Data as of 2012 unless otherwise noted; n/a not available; (1) Figures cover the Tallahassee, FL Metropolitan Statistical Area—see Appendix B for areas included; (2) Figures do not include pregnancy-related, borderline, or pre-diabetes
Source: Centers for Disease Control and Prevention, Behaviorial Risk Factor Surveillance System, SMART: Selected Metropolitan/Micropolitan Area Risk Trends, 2012 (Note: the CDC has discontinued this dataset but will be releasing a replacement in late 2015)

Mortality Rates for the Top 10 Causes of Death in the U.S.

ICD-10[a] Sub-Chapter	ICD-10[a] Code	Age-Adjusted Mortality Rate[1] per 100,000 population	
		County[2]	U.S.
Malignant neoplasms	C00-C97	152.9	166.2
Ischaemic heart diseases	I20-I25	88.3	105.7
Other forms of heart disease	I30-I51	48.9	49.3
Chronic lower respiratory diseases	J40-J47	37.0	42.1
Organic, including symptomatic, mental disorders	F01-F09	61.9	38.1
Cerebrovascular diseases	I60-I69	38.1	37.0
Other external causes of accidental injury	W00-X59	24.8	26.9
Other degenerative diseases of the nervous system	G30-G31	22.5	25.6
Diabetes mellitus	E10-E14	20.1	21.3
Hypertensive diseases	I10-I15	23.4	19.4

Note: (a) ICD-10 = International Classification of Diseases 10th Revision; (1) Mortality rates are a three year average covering 2011-2013; (2) Figures cover Leon County
Source: Centers for Disease Control and Prevention, National Center for Health Statistics. Compressed Mortality File 1999-2013 on CDC WONDER Online Database, released October 2014. Data are compiled from the Compressed Mortality File 1999-2013, Series 20 No. 2S, 2014.

Mortality Rates for Selected Causes of Death

ICD-10[a] Sub-Chapter	ICD-10[a] Code	Age-Adjusted Mortality Rate[1] per 100,000 population	
		County[2]	U.S.
Assault	X85-Y09	6.2	5.2
Diseases of the liver	K70-K76	10.9	13.2
Human immunodeficiency virus (HIV) disease	B20-B24	5.8	2.2
Influenza and pneumonia	J09-J18	13.1	15.4
Intentional self-harm	X60-X84	13.8	12.5
Malnutrition	E40-E46	Suppressed	0.9
Obesity and other hyperalimentation	E65-E68	3.7	1.8
Renal failure	N17-N19	7.7	13.1
Transport accidents	V01-V99	10.0	11.7
Viral hepatitis	B15-B19	2.7	2.2

Note: (a) ICD-10 = International Classification of Diseases 10th Revision; (1) Mortality rates are a three year average covering 2011-2013; (2) Figures cover Leon County
Source: Centers for Disease Control and Prevention, National Center for Health Statistics. Compressed Mortality File 1999-2013 on CDC WONDER Online Database, released October 2014. Data are compiled from the Compressed Mortality File 1999-2013, Series 20 No. 2S, 2014.

Health Insurance Coverage

Area	With Health Insurance	With Private Health Insurance	With Public Health Insurance	Without Health Insurance	Population Under Age 18 Without Health Insurance
City	85.8	72.8	20.9	14.2	5.0
MSA[1]	85.8	69.6	26.0	14.2	6.9
U.S.	85.2	65.2	31.0	14.8	7.3

Note: Figures are percentages that cover the civilian noninstitutionalized population; (1) Figures cover the Tallahassee, FL Metropolitan Statistical Area—see Appendix B for areas included
Source: U.S. Census Bureau, 2011-2013 American Community Survey 3-Year Estimates

Number of Medical Professionals

Area[1]	MDs[2]	DOs[2,3]	Dentists	Podiatrists	Chiropractors	Optometrists
Local (number)	737	24	104	11	53	50
Local (rate[4])	259.6	8.5	36.9	3.9	18.8	17.7
U.S. (rate[4])	270.0	20.2	63.1	5.7	25.2	14.9

Note: Data as of 2013 unless noted; (1) Local data covers Leon County; (2) Data as of 2012 and includes all active, non-federal physicians; (3) Doctor of Osteopathic Medicine; (4) rate per 100,000 population
Source: U.S. Department of Health and Human Services, Health Resources and Services Administration, Bureau of Health Professions, Area Resource File (ARF) 2013-2014

EDUCATION

Public School District Statistics

District Name	Schls	Pupils	Pupil/ Teacher Ratio	Minority Pupils[1] (%)	Free Lunch Eligible[2] (%)	IEP[3] (%)
FSU Laboratory School	3	2,381	13.2	58.7	n/a	8.2
Leon County	61	33,432	15.7	54.3	40.5	15.9

Note: Table includes school districts with 2,000 or more students; (1) Percentage of students that are not non-Hispanic white; (2) Percentage of students that are eligible for the free lunch program; (3) Percentage of students that have an Individualized Education Program.
Source: U.S. Department of Education, National Center for Education Statistics, Common Core of Data, Local Education Agency (School District) Universe Survey: School Year 2012-2013; U.S. Department of Education, National Center for Education Statistics, Common Core of Data, Public Elementary/Secondary School Universe Survey: School Year 2012-2013

Best High Schools

According to *The Daily Beast,* Tallahassee is home to two of the best high schools in the U.S.: **Florida State University Schools** (#627); **Lincoln High School** (#685); *The Daily Beast* used six indicators culled from school surveys to compare public high schools in the U.S., with graduation and college acceptance rates weighed most heavily. Other criteria included: college-level courses/exams and SAT/ACT scores. *The Daily Beast, "Top High Schools 2014"*

Highest Level of Education

Area	Less than H.S.	H.S. Diploma	Some College, No Deg.	Associate Degree	Bachelor's Degree	Master's Degree	Prof. School Degree	Doctorate Degree
City	7.7	16.4	19.2	9.1	26.0	13.8	3.9	3.9
MSA[1]	10.8	23.8	20.3	8.3	21.1	10.6	2.6	2.6
U.S.	13.7	28.0	21.2	7.9	18.2	7.7	1.9	1.3

Note: Figures cover persons age 25 and over; (1) Figures cover the Tallahassee, FL Metropolitan Statistical Area—see Appendix B for areas included
Source: U.S. Census Bureau, 2011-2013 American Community Survey 3-Year Estimates

Educational Attainment by Race

Area	High School Graduate or Higher (%)					Bachelor's Degree or Higher (%)				
	Total	White	Black	Asian	Hisp.[2]	Total	White	Black	Asian	Hisp.[2]
City	92.3	96.3	85.1	93.6	90.0	47.5	56.6	28.3	78.0	41.9
MSA[1]	89.2	93.0	81.5	91.9	80.8	36.9	42.7	22.5	73.6	32.9
U.S.	86.3	88.3	83.1	85.7	64.0	29.1	30.4	18.8	50.7	13.7

Note: Figures shown cover persons 25 years old and over; (1) Figures cover the Tallahassee, FL Metropolitan Statistical Area—see Appendix B for areas included; (2) People of Hispanic origin can be of any race
Source: U.S. Census Bureau, 2011-2013 American Community Survey 3-Year Estimates

School Enrollment by Grade and Control

Area	Preschool (%)		Kindergarten (%)		Grades 1 - 4 (%)		Grades 5 - 8 (%)		Grades 9 - 12 (%)	
	Public	Private	Public	Private	Public	Private	Public	Private	Public	Private
City	55.3	44.7	91.6	8.4	90.8	9.2	89.0	11.0	90.8	9.2
MSA[1]	63.3	36.7	86.1	13.9	90.8	9.2	87.6	12.4	88.7	11.3
U.S.	57.7	42.3	87.9	12.1	89.9	10.1	90.0	10.0	90.7	9.3

Note: Figures shown cover persons 3 years old and over; (1) Figures cover the Tallahassee, FL Metropolitan Statistical Area—see Appendix B for areas included
Source: U.S. Census Bureau, 2011-2013 American Community Survey 3-Year Estimates

Average Salaries of Public School Classroom Teachers

Area	2013-14		2014-15		Percent Change 2013-14 to 2014-15	Percent Change 2004-05 to 2014-15
	Dollars	Rank[1]	Dollars	Rank[1]		
FLORIDA	47,780	39	48,992	36	2.54	17.8
U.S. Average	56,610	–	57,379	–	1.36	20.8

Note: (1) State rank ranges from 1 to 51 where 1 indicates highest salary.
Source: National Education Association, Rankings & Estimates: Rankings of the States 2014 and Estimates of School Statistics 2015, March 2015

Higher Education

Four-Year Colleges			Two-Year Colleges			Medical Schools[1]	Law Schools[2]	Voc/ Tech[3]
Public	Private Non-profit	Private For-profit	Public	Private Non-profit	Private For-profit			
2	1	1	1	0	0	1	1	3

Note: Figures cover institutions located within the city limits and include main campuses only; (1) includes schools accredited by the Liaison Committee on Medical Education and the American Osteopathic Association's Commission on Osteopathic College Accreditation; (2) includes ABA-accredited schools, schools with provisional ABA accreditation, and state accredited schools; (3) includes all schools with programs that are less than 2 years.
Source: National Center for Education Statistics, Integrated Postsecondary Education System (IPEDS), 2013-14; Association of American Medical Colleges, Member List, May 1, 2015; American Osteopathic Association, Member List, May 1, 2015; Law School Admission Council, Official Guide to ABA-Approved Law Schools Online, May 1, 2015; Wikipedia, List of Medical Schools in the United States, May 1, 2015; Wikipedia, List of Law Schools in the United States, May 1, 2015

According to *U.S. News & World Report,* the Tallahassee, FL metro area is home to one of the best national universities in the U.S.: **Florida State University** (#95). The indicators used to capture academic quality fall into a number of categories: assessment by administrators at peer institutions; retention of students; faculty resources; student selectivity; financial resources; alumni giving; high school counselor ratings of colleges; and graduation rate. *U.S. News & World Report, "America's Best Colleges 2015"*

According to *U.S. News & World Report,* the Tallahassee, FL metro area is home to one of the top 100 law schools in the U.S.: **Florida State University** (#50). The rankings are based on a weighted average of 12 measures of quality: peer assessment score; assessment score by lawyers/judges; median LSAT scores; median undergrad GPA; acceptance rate; employment rates for graduates; placement success; bar passage rate; faculty resources; expenditures per student; student/faculty ratio; and library resources. *U.S. News & World Report, "America's Best Graduate Schools, Law, 2016"*

PRESIDENTIAL ELECTION

2012 Presidential Election Results

Area	Obama (%)	Romney (%)	Other (%)
Leon County	61.3	37.6	1.1
U.S.	51.0	47.2	1.8

Note: Results may not add to 100% due to rounding
Source: Dave Leip's Atlas of U.S. Presidential Elections

EMPLOYERS

Major Employers

Company Name	Industry
ACS, A Xerox Company	Print services
Big Bend Hospice	Healthcare
Capital City Bank group	Finance
Capital Health Plan	Healthcare
Capital Regional Medical Center	Healthcare
CenturyLink	Telecommunications
City of Tallahassee	Government
Comcast Cable	Telecommunications & internet
Dale Earnhardt Jr. Chevrolet	Auto dealer
Danfoss Turbocor	Hvac industry
Florida A&M University	Education
Florida Bar	Regulatory agency for lawyers
Florida State University	Education
General Dynamics Land Systems	Manufacturer
Leon County	Government
Leon County Schools	Education
Publix Supermarket	Supermarket
St. Marks Powder	Manufacturer
State of Florida	Government
Tallahassee Community College	Education
Tallahassee Democrat	Newspaper
Tallahassee Memorial HealthCare	Healthcare
Tallahassee Primary Care Associates	Healthcare
Walmart Stores	Retail
Westminister Oaks	Senior care

Note: Companies shown are located within the Tallahassee, FL Metropolitan Statistical Area.
Source: Hoovers.com; Wikipedia

PUBLIC SAFETY

Crime Rate

Area	All Crimes	Violent Crimes				Property Crimes		
		Murder	Forcible Rape	Robbery	Aggrav. Assault	Burglary	Larceny -Theft	Motor Vehicle Theft
City	5,041.5	5.8	84.8	205.1	445.1	1,103.3	2,964.3	233.2
Suburbs[1]	2,919.3	3.2	33.1	35.8	352.9	617.9	1,788.6	87.8
Metro[2]	3,976.4	4.5	58.9	120.1	398.8	859.7	2,374.2	160.2
U.S.	3,098.6	4.5	25.2	109.1	229.1	610.0	1,899.4	221.3

Note: Figures are crimes per 100,000 population; (1) All areas within the metro area that are located outside the city limits; (2) Figures cover the Tallahassee, FL Metropolitan Statistical Area—see Appendix B for areas included
Source: FBI Uniform Crime Reports, 2013

Hate Crimes

Area	Number of Quarters Reported	Number of Incidents per Bias Motivation						
		Race	Religion	Sexual Orientation	Ethnicity	Disability	Gender	Gender Identity
City	4	1	0	0	0	0	0	0
U.S.	4	2,871	1,031	1,233	655	83	18	31

Source: Federal Bureau of Investigation, Hate Crime Statistics 2013

Identity Theft Consumer Complaints

Area	Complaints	Complaints per 100,000 Population	Rank[2]
MSA[1]	706	189.1	4
U.S.	332,646	104.3	-

Note: (1) Figures cover the Tallahassee, FL Metropolitan Statistical Area—see Appendix B for areas included; (2) Rank ranges from 1 to 380 where 1 indicates greatest number of identity theft complaints per 100,000 population
Source: Federal Trade Commission, Consumer Sentinel Network Data Book for January–December 2014

Fraud and Other Consumer Complaints

Area	Complaints	Complaints per 100,000 Population	Rank[2]
MSA[1]	1,638	438.8	72
U.S.	2,250,205	705.7	-

Note: (1) Figures cover the Tallahassee, FL Metropolitan Statistical Area—see Appendix B for areas included; (2) Rank ranges from 1 to 380 where 1 indicates greatest number of identity theft complaints per 100,000 population
Source: Federal Trade Commission, Consumer Sentinel Network Data Book for January–December 2014

RECREATION

Culture

Dance[1]	Theatre[1]	Instrumental Music[1]	Vocal Music[1]	Series and Festivals	Museums and Art Galleries[2]	Zoos and Aquariums[3]
1	2	2	1	1	24	0

Note: (1) Professional perfoming groups; (2) Based on organizations with SIC code 8412; (3) AZA-accredited
Source: The Grey House Performing Arts Directory, 2015-16; Association of Zoos & Aquariums, AZA Member Zoos & Aquariums, April 2015; www.AccuLeads.com, April 2015

Professional Sports Teams

Team Name	League	Year Established
No teams are located in the metro area		

Source: Wikipedia, Major Professional Sports Teams of the United States and Canada, April 2015

CLIMATE

Average and Extreme Temperatures

Temperature	Jan	Feb	Mar	Apr	May	Jun	Jul	Aug	Sep	Oct	Nov	Dec	Yr.
Extreme High (°F)	83	89	90	95	102	103	103	102	99	94	88	84	103
Average High (°F)	64	67	73	80	86	90	91	91	88	81	72	66	79
Average Temp. (°F)	52	55	61	67	74	80	81	81	78	69	60	54	68
Average Low (°F)	40	42	48	53	62	69	71	72	68	57	47	41	56
Extreme Low (°F)	6	14	20	29	34	46	57	61	40	30	13	10	6

Note: Figures cover the years 1948-1990
Source: National Climatic Data Center, International Station Meteorological Climate Summary, 9/96

Average Precipitation/Snowfall/Humidity

Precip./Humidity	Jan	Feb	Mar	Apr	May	Jun	Jul	Aug	Sep	Oct	Nov	Dec	Yr.
Avg. Precip. (in.)	4.2	5.1	6.0	4.2	4.5	6.8	8.8	7.1	5.7	2.9	3.5	4.5	63.3
Avg. Snowfall (in.)	Tr	Tr	Tr	0	0	0	0	0	0	0	0	Tr	Tr
Avg. Rel. Hum. 7am (%)	86	87	88	89	89	91	93	94	93	90	89	87	90
Avg. Rel. Hum. 4pm (%)	54	51	49	46	50	58	66	64	60	51	52	55	55

Note: Figures cover the years 1948-1990; Tr = Trace amounts (<0.05 in. of rain; <0.5 in. of snow)
Source: National Climatic Data Center, International Station Meteorological Climate Summary, 9/96

Weather Conditions

Temperature			Daytime Sky			Precipitation		
10°F & below	32°F & below	90°F & above	Clear	Partly cloudy	Cloudy	0.01 inch or more precip.	0.1 inch or more snow/ice	Thunder-storms
< 1	31	86	93	175	97	114	1	83

Note: Figures are average number of days per year and cover the years 1948-1990
Source: National Climatic Data Center, International Station Meteorological Climate Summary, 9/96

HAZARDOUS WASTE

Superfund Sites

Tallahassee has no sites on the EPA's Superfund Final National Priorities List. There are a total of 1,322 Superfund sites on the list in the U.S. *U.S. Environmental Protection Agency, Final National Priorities List, April 14, 2015*

AIR & WATER QUALITY

Air Quality Trends: Ozone

	2004	2005	2006	2007	2008	2009	2010	2011	2012	2013
MSA[1]	0.071	0.070	0.071	0.072	0.071	0.058	0.066	0.065	0.066	0.061

Note: (1) Data covers the Tallahassee, FL Metropolitan Statistical Area—see Appendix B for areas included. The values shown are the composite ozone concentration averages among trend sites based on the highest fourth daily maximum 8-hour concentration in parts per million. These trends are based on sites having an adequate record of monitoring data during the trend period. Data from exceptional events are included.
Source: U.S. Environmental Protection Agency, Air Quality Monitoring Information, "Air Quality Trends by City, 2000-2013"

Air Quality Index

Area	Percent of Days when Air Quality was...[2]					AQI Statistics[2]	
	Good	Moderate	Unhealthy for Sensitive Groups	Unhealthy	Very Unhealthy	Maximum	Median
MSA[1]	69.6	30.1	0.0	0.3	0.0	157	42

Note: (1) Data covers the Tallahassee, FL Metropolitan Statistical Area—see Appendix B for areas included; (2) Based on 365 days with AQI data in 2014. Air Quality Index (AQI) is an index for reporting daily air quality. EPA calculates the AQI for five major air pollutants regulated by the Clean Air Act: ground-level ozone, particle pollution (aka particulate matter), carbon monoxide, sulfur dioxide, and nitrogen dioxide. The AQI runs from 0 to 500. The higher the AQI value, the greater the level of air pollution and the greater the health concern. There are six AQI categories: "Good" AQI is between 0 and 50. Air quality is considered satisfactory; "Moderate" AQI is between 51 and 100. Air quality is acceptable; "Unhealthy for Sensitive Groups" When AQI values are between 101 and 150, members of sensitive groups may experience health effects; "Unhealthy" When AQI values are between 151 and 200 everyone may begin to experience health effects; "Very Unhealthy" AQI values between 201 and 300 trigger a health alert; "Hazardous" AQI values over 300 trigger warnings of emergency conditions (not shown).
Source: U.S. Environmental Protection Agency, Air Quality Index Report, 2014

Air Quality Index Pollutants

Area	Percent of Days when AQI Pollutant was...[2]					
	Carbon Monoxide	Nitrogen Dioxide	Ozone	Sulfur Dioxide	Particulate Matter 2.5	Particulate Matter 10
MSA[1]	0.0	0.0	23.8	0.0	76.2	0.0

Note: (1) Data covers the Tallahassee, FL Metropolitan Statistical Area—see Appendix B for areas included; (2) Based on 365 days with AQI data in 2014. The Air Quality Index (AQI) is an index for reporting daily air quality. EPA calculates the AQI for five major air pollutants regulated by the Clean Air Act: ground-level ozone, particle pollution (also known as particulate matter), carbon monoxide, sulfur dioxide, and nitrogen dioxide. The AQI runs from 0 to 500. The higher the AQI value, the greater the level of air pollution and the greater the health concern.
Source: U.S. Environmental Protection Agency, Air Quality Index Report, 2014

Maximum Air Pollutant Concentrations: Particulate Matter, Ozone, CO and Lead

	Particulate Matter 10 (ug/m^3)	Particulate Matter 2.5 Wtd AM (ug/m^3)	Particulate Matter 2.5 24-Hr (ug/m^3)	Ozone (ppm)	Carbon Monoxide (ppm)	Lead (ug/m^3)
MSA[1] Level	n/a	7.9	20	0.062	n/a	n/a
NAAQS[2]	150	15	35	0.075	9	0.15
Met NAAQS[2]	n/a	Yes	Yes	Yes	n/a	n/a

Note: (1) Data covers the Tallahassee, FL Metropolitan Statistical Area—see Appendix B for areas included; Data from exceptional events are included; (2) National Ambient Air Quality Standards; ppm = parts per million; ug/m^3 = micrograms per cubic meter; n/a not available.
Concentrations: Particulate Matter 10 (coarse particulate)—highest second maximum 24-hour concentration; Particulate Matter 2.5 Wtd AM (fine particulate)—highest weighted annual mean concentration; Particulate Matter 2.5 24-Hour (fine particulate)—highest 98th percentile 24-hour concentration; Ozone—highest fourth daily maximum 8-hour concentration; Carbon Monoxide—highest second maximum non-overlapping 8-hour concentration; Lead—maximum running 3-month average
Source: U.S. Environmental Protection Agency, Air Quality Monitoring Information, "Air Quality Statistics by City, 2013"

Maximum Air Pollutant Concentrations: Nitrogen Dioxide and Sulfur Dioxide

	Nitrogen Dioxide AM (ppb)	Nitrogen Dioxide 1-Hr (ppb)	Sulfur Dioxide AM (ppb)	Sulfur Dioxide 1-Hr (ppb)	Sulfur Dioxide 24-Hr (ppb)
MSA[1] Level	n/a	n/a	n/a	n/a	n/a
NAAQS[2]	53	100	30	75	140
Met NAAQS[2]	n/a	n/a	n/a	n/a	n/a

Note: (1) Data covers the Tallahassee, FL Metropolitan Statistical Area—see Appendix B for areas included; Data from exceptional events are included; (2) National Ambient Air Quality Standards; ppm = parts per million; ug/m^3 = micrograms per cubic meter; n/a not available.
Concentrations: Nitrogen Dioxide AM—highest arithmetic mean concentration; Nitrogen Dioxide 1-Hr—highest 98th percentile 1-hour daily maximum concentration; Sulfur Dioxide AM—highest annual mean concentration; Sulfur Dioxide 1-Hr—highest 99th percentile 1-hour daily maximum concentration; Sulfur Dioxide 24-Hr—highest second maximum 24-hour concentration
Source: U.S. Environmental Protection Agency, Air Quality Monitoring Information, "Air Quality Statistics by City, 2013"

Drinking Water

Water System Name	Pop. Served	Primary Water Source Type	Violations[1]	
			Health Based	Monitoring/ Reporting
City of Tallahassee	193,927	Ground	0	0

Note: (1) Based on violation data from January 1, 2014 to December 31, 2014 (includes unresolved violations from earlier years)
Source: U.S. Environmental Protection Agency, Office of Ground Water and Drinking Water, Safe Drinking Water Information System (based on data extracted January 27, 2015)

Tampa, Florida

Background

Although Tampa was visited by Spanish explorers, such as Ponce de Leon and Hernando de Soto as early as 1521, this city, located on the mouth of the Hillsborough River on Tampa Bay, did not see significant growth until the mid-nineteenth century.

Like many cities in northern Florida such as Jacksonville, Tampa was a fort during the Seminole War, and during the Civil War it was captured by the Union Army. Later, Tampa enjoyed prosperity and development when the railroad transported tourists from up north to enjoy the warmth and sunshine of Florida.

Two historical events in the late nineteenth century set Tampa apart from other Florida cities. First, Tampa played a significant role during the Spanish-American War in 1898 as a chief port of embarkation for American troops to Cuba. During that time, Colonel Theodore Roosevelt occupied a Tampa hotel as his military headquarters. Second, a cigar factory in nearby Ybor City, named after owner Vicente Martinez Ybor, was the site where Jose Marti (the George Washington of Cuba) exhorted workers to take up arms against the tyranny of Spanish rule in the late 1800s.

Today, Tampa enjoys its role as a U.S. port and is host to many cruise ships. Major industries in and around Tampa include services, retail trade, government and finance, insurance and real estate. Like most of Florida, its economy is also heavily based on tourism. Significant employers include the Hillsborough County School District, WellCare Health Plan, Raymond James Financial, the University of South Florida, Hillsborough County Government, and MacDill Air Force Base. It is also home to servers at Wikipedia, the online encyclopedia.

The city boasts NFL's Tampa Bay Buccaneers, the Devil Rays baseball team, and the NHL's Lightning. Other attractions include Florida's Latin Quarter known as Ybor City (a National Historic Landmark District), Busch Gardens, and a Museum of Science and Industry. MacDill Air Force Base also hosts a popular air show every year. Tampa hosted the 2012 Republican National Convention.

Tampa has received high marks in various surveys throughout the years, including being top cleanest and outdoor cities, as well as the best place for 20-somethings.

Winters are mild, while summers are long, warm, and humid. Freezing temperatures occur on one or two mornings per year during November through March. A dramatic feature of the Tampa climate is the summer thunderstorm season. Most occur during the late afternoon, sometimes causing temperatures to drop dramatically. The area is vulnerable to tidal surges, as the land has an elevation of less than 15 feet above sea level. The city has not experienced a direct hit from a hurricane since the 1930s.

Rankings

General Rankings

- Tampa was selected as one of America's best cities by *Bloomberg Businessweek.* The city ranked #34 out of 50. Criteria: leisure attributes (the number of restaurants, bars, libraries, museums, professional sports teams, and park acres by population); educational attributes (public school performance, the number of colleges, and graduate degree holders); economic factors (2011 income and June and July 2012 unemployment); crime; and air quality. *Bloomberg BusinessWeek, "America's Best Cities," September 26, 2012*
- Tampa was selected as one of "America's Favorite Cities." The city ranked #5 in the "Quality of Life: Cleanliness" category. Respondents to an online survey were asked to rate 38 top urban destinations in the United States from a visitor's perspective. Criteria: cleanliness. *Travel + Leisure, "America's Favorite Cities 2014"*
- In their second annual survey, analysts for the small- and mid-sized city lifestyle site Livability.com looked at data for more than 2,000 U.S. cities to determine the rankings for Livability's "Top 100 Best Places to Live" in 2015. Tampa ranked #71. Criteria: vibrant economy; low cost of living; abundant lifestyle amenities. *Livability.com, "Top 100 Best Places to Live 2015"*

Business/Finance Rankings

- Based on metro area social media reviews, the employment opinion group Glassdoor surveyed 50 of the largest U.S. metro areas on measures including compensation and benefits, satisfaction with management, business outlook, and number of employers hiring. The Tampa metro area was ranked #47 in overall employee satisfaction. *www.glassdoor.com, "Employment Satisfaction Report Card by City," June 13, 2014*
- In its Competitive Alternatives report, consulting firm KPMG analyzed the 27 largest metropolitan statistical areas according to 26 cost components (such as taxes, labor costs, and utilities) and 30 non-cost-related variables (such as crime rates and number of universities). The business website 24/7 Wall Street examined the KPMG findings, adding to the mix current unemployment rates, GDP, median income, and employment decline during the last recession and "projected" recovery. It identified the Tampa metro area as #4 among the ten best American cities for business. *247wallst.com, "Best American Cities for Business," April 4, 2012*
- In a survey of economic confidence in the nation's 50 largest metropolitan areas conducted January–December 2014, the Tampa metro area placed #39, according to Gallup's 2014 Economic Confidence Index. *Gallup, "San Jose and San Francisco Lead in Economic Confidence," March 19, 2015*
- Tampa was ranked #21 out of 100 metro areas in terms of economic performance (#1 = best) during the recession and recovery from trough quarter through the second quarter of 2013. Criteria: percent change in employment; percentage point change in unemployment rate; percent change in gross metropolitan product; percent change in House Price Index. *Brookings Institution, MetroMonitor: Tracking Economic Recession and Recovery in America's 100 Largest Metropolitan Areas, September 2013*
- Payscale.com ranked the 20 largest metro areas in terms of wage growth. The Tampa metro area ranked #12. Criteria: private-sector wage growth between the 1st quarter of 2014 and the 1st quarter of 2015. *PayScale, "Wage Trends by Metro Area," 1st Quarter, 2015*
- Tampa was identified as one of America's most frugal metro areas by *Coupons.com.* The city ranked #2 out of 25. Criteria: online coupon usage. *Coupons.com, "Top 25 Most Frugal Cities of 2013," April 10, 2014*
- Tampa was identified as one of America's most frugal metro areas by *Coupons.com.* The city ranked #7 out of 25. Criteria: Grocery IQ and coupons.com mobile app usage. *Coupons.com, "Top 25 Most On-the-Go Frugal Cities of 2013," April 10, 2014*
- The Tampa metro area appeared on the Milken Institute "2013 Best Performing Cities" list. Rank: #86 out of 200 large metro areas. Criteria: job growth; wage and salary growth; high-tech output growth. *Milken Institute, "Best-Performing Cities 2014," January 2015*

- *Forbes* ranked the 200 most populous metro areas to determine the nation's "Best Places for Business and Careers." The Tampa metro area was ranked #72. Criteria: costs (business and living); job growth (past and projected); income growth; educational attainment (college and high school); projected economic growth; cultural and recreational opportunities; net migration patterns; number of highly ranked colleges. *Forbes, "The Best Places for Business and Careers 2014," July 23, 2014*

Children/Family Rankings

- Tampa was chosen as one of America's 100 best communities for young people. The winners were selected based upon detailed information provided about each community's efforts to fulfill five essential promises critical to the well-being of young people: caring adults who are actively involved in their lives; safe places in which to learn and grow; a healthy start toward adulthood; an effective education that builds marketable skills; and opportunities to help others. *America's Promise Alliance, "100 Best Communities for Young People, 2012"*

Culture/Performing Arts Rankings

- Tampa was selected as one of America's top cities for the arts. The city ranked #3 in the mid-sized city (population 100,000 to 499,999) category. Criteria: readers' top choices for arts travel destinations based on the richness and variety of visual arts sites, activities and events. *American Style, "2012 Top 25 Arts Destinations," June 2012*

Dating/Romance Rankings

- Of the 100 U.S. cities surveyed by *Men's Health* in its quest to identify the nation's best cities for dating and forming relationships, Tampa was ranked #12 for online dating (#1 = best). *Men's Health, "The Best and Worst Cities for Online Dating," January 30, 2013*
- Tampa was selected as one of America's best cities for singles by the readers of *Travel + Leisure* in their annual "America's Favorite Cities" survey. The city was ranked #17 out of 20. Criteria included good-looking locals, cool shopping, and hipster-magnet coffee bars. *Travel + Leisure, "America's Best Cities for Singles," January 23, 2015*

Education Rankings

- Personal finance website *WalletHub* analyzed the 150 largest U.S. metropolitan statistical areas to determine where the most educated Americans are choosing to settle. Criteria: educational attainment; percentage of workers with jobs in computer, engineering, and science fields; quality and size of each metro area's universities. Tampa was ranked #98 (#1 = most educated city). *www.WalletHub.com, "2014's Most and Least Educated Cities*
- Tampa was selected as one of America's most literate cities. The city ranked #29 out of the 77 largest U.S. cities. Criteria: number of booksellers; library resources; Internet resources; educational attainment; periodical publishing resources; newspaper circulation. *Central Connecticut State University, "America's Most Literate Cities, 2014," April 8, 2015*

Environmental Rankings

- The Tampa metro area came in at #329 for the relative comfort of its climate on Sperling's list of "chill cities," as measured by the Sperling Heat Index. All 361 metro areas are included. Criteria included daytime high temperatures, nighttime low temperatures, dew point, and relative humidity at the high temperatures. *www.bertsperling.com, "Sperling's Chill Cities," July 18, 2013*
- Sperling's BestPlaces assessed 379 metropolitan areas of the United States for the likelihood of dangerously extreme weather events or earthquakes. In general the Southeast and South-Central regions have the highest risk of weather extremes and earthquakes, while the Pacific Northwest enjoys the lowest risk. Of the least risky metropolitan areas, the Tampa metro area was ranked #334. *www.bestplaces.net, "Safest Places from Natural Disasters," April 2011*

- The U.S. Environmental Protection Agency (EPA) released a list of large U.S. metropolitan areas with the most ENERGY STAR certified buildings in 2014. The Tampa metro area was ranked #24 out of 25. *U.S. Environmental Protection Agency, "Top Cities With the Most ENERGY STAR Certified Buildings in 2014," March 25, 2015*
- Tampa was highlighted as one of the top 25 cleanest metro areas for year-round particle pollution (Annual PM 2.5) in the U.S. during 2011 through 2013. The area ranked #23. *American Lung Association, State of the Air 2015*
- Tampa was highlighted as one of the top 25 cleanest metro areas for short-term particle pollution (24-hour PM 2.5) in the U.S. during 2011 through 2013. Monitors in these cities reported no days with unhealthful PM 2.5 levels. *American Lung Association, State of the Air 2015*

Food/Drink Rankings

- *Men's Health* ranked 100 major U.S. cities in terms of alcohol intoxication. Tampa ranked #73 (#1 = most sober).Criteria: binge drinking; alcohol-related traffic accidents, arrests, and fatalities. *Men's Health, "The Drunkest Cities in America," November 19, 2013*

Health/Fitness Rankings

- For each of the 50 most populous metro areas in the United States, the American College of Sports Medicine's American Fitness Index evaluated infrastructure, community assets, and policies that encourage healthy and fit lifestyles, including preventive health behaviors, levels of chronic disease conditions, health care access, and community resources and policies that support physical activity. The Tampa metro area ranked #40 for "community fitness." Personal health indicators were considered as well as community and environmental indicators. *www.americanfitnessindex.org, "ACSM American Fitness Index Health and Community Fitness Status of the 50 Largest Metropolitan Areas," May 2013*
- Tampa was selected as one of the 25 fattest cities in America by *Men's Fitness Online*. It ranked #5 out of America's 50 largest cities. Criteria: fitness centers and sport stores; nutrition; sports participation; TV viewing; overweight/sedentary; junk food; air quality; geography; commute; parks and open space; city recreational facilities; access to healthcare; motivation; mayor and city initiatives; state obesity initiatives. *Men's Fitness, "The Fittest and Fattest Cities in America," March 5, 2012*
- Tampa was identified as a "2013 Spring Allergy Capital." The area ranked #76 out of 100. Three groups of factors were used to identify the most severe cities for people with allergies during the spring season: annual pollen levels; medicine utilization; access to board-certified allergists. *Asthma and Allergy Foundation of America, "Spring Allergy Capitals 2013"*
- Tampa was identified as a "2013 Fall Allergy Capital." The area ranked #71 out of 100. Three groups of factors were used to identify the most severe cities for people with allergies during the fall season: annual pollen levels; medicine utilization; access to board-certified allergists. *Asthma and Allergy Foundation of America, "Fall Allergy Capitals 2013"*
- Tampa was identified as a "2013 Asthma Capital." The area ranked #57 out of the nation's 100 largest metropolitan areas. Twelve factors were used to identify the most challenging places to live for people with asthma: estimated prevalence; self-reported prevalence; crude death rate for asthma; annual pollen score; annual air quality; public smoking laws; number of board-certified asthma specialists; school inhaler access laws; rescue medication use; controller medication use; uninsured rate; poverty rate. *Asthma and Allergy Foundation of America, "Asthma Capitals 2013"*
- *Men's Health* ranked 100 major U.S. cities in terms of the best and worst cities for men. Tampa ranked #54. Criteria: thirty-three data points were examined covering health, fitness, and quality of life. *Men's Health, "The Best & Worst Cities for Men 2014," December 6, 2013*

- The Tampa metro area appeared in the 2013 Gallup-Healthways Well-Being Index. The area ranked #152 out of 189. The Gallup-Healthways Well-Being Index score is an average of six sub-indexes, which individually examine life evaluation, emotional health, work environment, physical health, healthy behaviors, and access to basic necessities. Results are based on telephone interviews conducted as part of the Gallup-Healthways Well-Being Index survey January 2–December 29, 2012, and January 2–December 30, 2013, with a random sample of 531,630 adults, aged 18 and older, living in metropolitan areas in the 50 U.S. states and the District of Columbia. *Gallup-Healthways, "State of American Well-Being," March 25, 2014*

- The Tampa metro area was identified as one of "America's Most Stressful Cities" by *Sperling's BestPlaces.* The metro area ranked #1 out of 50. Criteria: unemployment rate; suicide rate; commute time; mental health; poor rest; alcohol use; violent crime rate; property crime rate; cloudy days annually. *Sperling's BestPlaces, www.BestPlaces.net, "Stressful Cities 2012*

- Tampa was selected as one of the "20 Most Livable U.S. Cities for Wheelchair Users" by the Christopher & Dana Reeve Foundation. The city ranked #12. Criteria: Medicaid eligibility and spending; access to physicians and rehabilitation facilities; access to fitness facilities and recreation; access to paratransit; percentage of people living with disabilities who are employed; clean air; climate. *Christopher & Dana Reeve Foundation, "20 Most Livable U.S. Cities for Wheelchair Users," July 26, 2010*

Real Estate Rankings

- Based on the home-price forecasts compiled by the real-estate valuation firm CoreLogic Case-Shiller, the finance website CNNMoney reported that in 2014, the Tampa metro area is expected to place #6 among American metro areas in terms of increases in residential real estate prices. *money.cnn.com, "10 Hottest Housing Markets for 2014," January 23, 2014*

- On the list compiled by Penske Truck Rental, the Tampa metro area was named the #2 moving destination in 2014, based on one-way consumer truck rental reservations made through Penske's website and reservations call center. *blog.gopenske.com, "Penske Truck Rental's 2014 Top Moving Destinations List," February 4, 2015*

- The Tampa metro area was identified as #4 among the ten housing markets with the highest percentage of distressed property sales, based on the findings of the housing data website RealtyTrac. Criteria included being sold "short"—for less than the outstanding mortgage balance—or in a foreclosure auction, income and poverty figures, and unemployment data. *247wallst.com, "Cities Selling the Most Distressed Homes," January 23, 2014*

- The Tampa metro area was identified as one of the nations's 20 hottest housing markets in 2015. Criteria: listing views relative to the number of listings. The area ranked #18. *Realtor.com, "These Are the 20 Hottest Housing Markets in the U.S. Right Now," April 8, 2015*

- Tampa was ranked #46 out of 275 metro areas in terms of house price appreciation in 2014 (#1 = highest rate). *Federal Housing Finance Agency, House Price Index, 4th Quarter 2014*

- The Tampa metro area was identified as one of the 10 best condo markets in the U.S. in 2014. The area ranked #4 out of 66 markets with a price appreciation of 16.6%. Criteria: year-over-year change of median sales price of existing apartment condo-coop homes between the 4th quarter of 2013 and the 4th quarter of 2014. *National Association of Realtors®, Median Sales Price of Existing Apartment Condo-Coop Homes for Metropolitan Areas, 4th Quarter 2014*

- Tampa was ranked #107 out of 226 metro areas in terms of housing affordability in 2014 by the National Association of Home Builders (#1 = most affordable). The NAHB-Wells Fargo Housing Opportunity Index (HOI) for a given area is defined as the share of homes sold in that area that would have been affordable to a family earning the local median income, based on standard mortgage underwriting criteria. *National Association of Home Builders®, NAHB-Wells Fargo Housing Opportunity Index, 4th Quarter 2014*

- The nation's largest metro areas were analyzed in terms of the percentage of households entering some stage of foreclosure in 2013. The Tampa metro area ranked #6 out of 10 (#1 = highest foreclosure rate). *RealtyTrac, "2013 Year-End U.S. Foreclosure Market Report™," January 16, 2014*

Safety Rankings

- Allstate ranked the 200 largest cities in America in terms of driver safety. Tampa ranked #160. Allstate researchers analyzed internal property damage claims over a two-year period from January 2011 to December 2012. A weighted average of the two-year numbers determined the annual percentages. *Allstate, "Allstate America's Best Drivers Report, 2014"*
- The National Insurance Crime Bureau ranked 380 metro areas in the U.S. in terms of per capita rates of vehicle theft. The Tampa metro area ranked #159 (#1 = highest rate). Criteria: number of vehicle theft offenses per 100,000 inhabitants in 2012. *National Insurance Crime Bureau, "Hot Spots 2012," June 26, 2013*

Seniors/Retirement Rankings

- From its Best Cities for Successful Aging indexes, the Milken Institute generated rankings for metropolitan areas, weighing data in eight categories—health care, wellness, living arrangements, transportation, financial characteristics, education and employment opportunities, community engagement, and overall livability. The Tampa metro area was ranked #86 overall in the large metro area category. *Milken Institute, "Best Cities for Successful Aging, 2014"*
- Tampa was identified as one of the most popular places to retire by *Topretirements.com*. The list reflects the 100 cities (out of 900+ total cities reviewed) that visitors to the website are most interested in for retirement. *Topretirements.com, "Most Popular Places to Retire for 2014," February 25, 2014*

Sports/Recreation Rankings

- Tampa was selected as one of the most playful cities in the U.S. by KaBOOM! The organization's Playful City USA initiative honors cities and towns across the nation for a vision, plan and commitment to creating an agenda for play. Criteria: creating a local play commission or task force; designing an annual action plan for play; conducting a play space audit; outlining a financial investment in play for the current fiscal year; and proclaiming and celebrating an annual "play day." *KaBOOM! National Campaign for Play, "2013 Playful City USA Communities"*

Transportation Rankings

- NerdWallet surveyed average annual car insurance premiums in 125 U.S. cities to identify the least expensive U.S. cities in which to insure a car. Locations with no-fault insurance laws was a strong determinant. Tampa came in at #15 for the most expensive rates. *www.nerdwallet.com, "Best Cities for Cheap Car Insurance," February 3, 2014*

Women/Minorities Rankings

- *Women's Health* examined U.S. cities and identified the 100 best cities for women. Tampa was ranked #74. Criteria: 30 categories were examined from obesity and breast cancer rates to commuting times and hours spent working out. *Women's Health, "Best Cities for Women 2012"*

Miscellaneous Rankings

- The watchdog site Charity Navigator conducts an annual study of charities in the nation's major markets both to analyze statistical differences in their financial, accountability, and transparency practices and to track year-to-year variations in individual communities. The Tampa metro area was ranked #24 among the 30 metro markets. *www.charitynavigator.org, "Metro Market Study 2013," June 1, 2013*
- Mars Chocolate North America, the makers of COMBOS®, in partnership with Sperling's BestPlaces, ranked 50 major metro areas in terms of their "manliness." The Tampa metro area ranked #23. Criteria: number of professional sports teams; number of nearby NASCAR tracks and racing events; manly lifestyle; concentration of manly retail stores; manly occupations per capita; salty snack sales; "Board of Manliness" rankings. *Mars Chocolate North America, "America's Manliest Cities 2012"*

- The National Alliance to End Homelessness ranked the 100 most populous metro areas in terms the rate of homelessness. The Tampa metro area ranked #1. Criteria: number of homeless people per 10,000 population in 2011. *National Alliance to End Homelessness, The State of Homelessness in America 2012*

Business Environment

CITY FINANCES

City Government Finances

Component	2012 ($000)	2012 ($ per capita)
Total Revenues	781,450	2,328
Total Expenditures	774,533	2,307
Debt Outstanding	1,376,995	4,102
Cash and Securities[1]	2,518,708	7,503

Note: (1) Cash and security holdings of a government at the close of its fiscal year, including those of its dependent agencies, utilities, and liquor stores.
Source: U.S Census Bureau, State & Local Government Finances 2012

City Government Revenue by Source

Source	2012 ($000)	2012 ($ per capita)
General Revenue		
From Federal Government	49,808	148
From State Government	51,495	153
From Local Governments	34,597	103
Taxes		
Property	122,036	364
Sales and Gross Receipts	105,820	315
Personal Income	0	0
Corporate Income	0	0
Motor Vehicle License	0	0
Other Taxes	42,227	126
Current Charges	207,186	617
Liquor Store	0	0
Utility	88,538	264
Employee Retirement	49,744	148

Source: U.S Census Bureau, State & Local Government Finances 2012

City Government Expenditures by Function

Function	2012 ($000)	2012 ($ per capita)	2012 (%)
General Direct Expenditures			
Air Transportation	0	0	0.0
Corrections	0	0	0.0
Education	0	0	0.0
Employment Security Administration	0	0	0.0
Financial Administration	27,288	81	3.5
Fire Protection	74,056	221	9.6
General Public Buildings	17,815	53	2.3
Governmental Administration, Other	3,441	10	0.4
Health	0	0	0.0
Highways	55,033	164	7.1
Hospitals	0	0	0.0
Housing and Community Development	34,121	102	4.4
Interest on General Debt	25,772	77	3.3
Judicial and Legal	4,170	12	0.5
Libraries	0	0	0.0
Parking	13,709	41	1.8
Parks and Recreation	56,142	167	7.2
Police Protection	151,200	450	19.5
Public Welfare	0	0	0.0
Sewerage	76,564	228	9.9
Solid Waste Management	57,609	172	7.4
Veterans' Services	0	0	0.0
Liquor Store	0	0	0.0
Utility	75,348	224	9.7
Employee Retirement	65,031	194	8.4

Source: U.S Census Bureau, State & Local Government Finances 2012

DEMOGRAPHICS

Population Growth

Area	1990 Census	2000 Census	2010 Census	Population Growth (%) 1990-2000	2000-2010
City	279,960	303,447	335,709	8.4	10.6
MSA[1]	2,067,959	2,395,997	2,783,243	15.9	16.2
U.S.	248,709,873	281,421,906	308,745,538	13.2	9.7

Note: (1) Figures cover the Tampa-St. Petersburg-Clearwater, FL Metropolitan Statistical Area—see Appendix B for areas included
Source: U.S. Census Bureau, Census 1990, 2000, 2010

Household Size

Area	Persons in Household (%) One	Two	Three	Four	Five	Six	Seven or More	Average Household Size
City	37.4	31.3	14.7	10.6	3.9	1.3	0.9	2.40
MSA[1]	32.0	36.0	14.3	10.9	4.2	1.5	0.9	2.49
U.S.	27.7	33.6	15.7	13.1	6.0	2.3	1.5	2.64

Note: (1) Figures cover the Tampa-St. Petersburg-Clearwater, FL Metropolitan Statistical Area—see Appendix B for areas included
Source: U.S. Census Bureau, 2011-2013 American Community Survey 3-Year Estimates

Race

Area	White Alone[2] (%)	Black Alone[2] (%)	Asian Alone[2] (%)	AIAN[3] Alone[2] (%)	NHOPI[4] Alone[2] (%)	Other Race Alone[2] (%)	Two or More Races (%)
City	64.0	25.9	3.9	0.3	0.1	2.9	3.0
MSA[1]	79.5	12.0	3.0	0.4	0.1	2.5	2.6
U.S.	73.9	12.6	5.0	0.8	0.2	4.7	2.9

Note: (1) Figures cover the Tampa-St. Petersburg-Clearwater, FL Metropolitan Statistical Area—see Appendix B for areas included; (2) Alone is defined as not being in combination with one or more other races; (3) American Indian and Alaska Native; (4) Native Hawaiian and Other Pacific Islander
Source: U.S. Census Bureau, 2011-2013 American Community Survey 3-Year Estimates

Hispanic or Latino Origin

Area	Total (%)	Mexican (%)	Puerto Rican (%)	Cuban (%)	Other (%)
City	22.6	2.5	7.4	6.5	6.2
MSA[1]	17.0	3.5	5.6	3.3	4.6
U.S.	16.9	10.8	1.6	0.6	3.8

Note: Persons of Hispanic or Latino origin can be of any race; (1) Figures cover the Tampa-St. Petersburg-Clearwater, FL Metropolitan Statistical Area—see Appendix B for areas included
Source: U.S. Census Bureau, 2011-2013 American Community Survey 3-Year Estimates

Segregation

Type	Segregation Indices[1] 1990	2000	2010	2010 Rank[2]	Percent Change 1990-2000	1990-2010	2000-2010
Black/White	69.7	64.6	56.2	50	-5.1	-13.5	-8.3
Asian/White	33.8	35.4	35.3	78	1.6	1.5	-0.1
Hispanic/White	45.3	44.4	40.7	62	-0.9	-4.6	-3.7

Note: All figures cover the Metropolitan Statistical Area—see Appendix B for areas included; Figures are based on an analysis of 1990, 2000, and 2010 Census Decennial Census tract data by William H. Frey, Brookings Institution and the University of Michigan Social Science Data Analysis Network. In this analysis all racial groups (whites, blacks, and asians) are non-Hispanic members of those races. Hispanics are shown as a separate category;
(1) Segregation Indices are Dissimilarity Indices that measure the degree to which the minority group is distributed differently than whites across census tracts. They range from 0 (complete integration) to 100 (complete segregation) where the value indicates the percentage of the minority group that needs to move to be distributed exactly like whites; (2) Ranges from 1 (most segregated) to 102 (least segregated); n/a not available.
Source: www.CensusScope.org

Ancestry

Area	German	Irish	English	American	Italian	Polish	French[2]	Scottish	Dutch
City	8.7	8.0	5.8	5.7	6.0	1.9	2.0	1.5	1.0
MSA[1]	12.9	11.6	8.6	9.7	7.7	3.0	2.9	1.8	1.2
U.S.	14.9	10.8	8.0	7.4	5.5	3.0	2.7	1.7	1.4

Note: Figures are the percentage of the total population reporting a particular ancestry. The nine most commonly reported ancestries in the U.S. are shown. Figures include multiple ancestries (e.g. if a person reported being Irish and Italian, they were included in both columns); (1) Figures cover the Tampa-St. Petersburg-Clearwater, FL Metropolitan Statistical Area—see Appendix B for areas included; (2) Excludes Basque

Source: U.S. Census Bureau, 2011-2013 American Community Survey 3-Year Estimates

Foreign-Born Population

Area	Percent of Population Born in								
	Any Foreign Country	Mexico	Asia	Europe	Carribean	South America	Central America[2]	Africa	Canada
City	15.2	1.0	3.2	1.5	5.8	1.6	1.1	0.6	0.2
MSA[1]	12.7	1.4	2.5	2.3	3.1	1.6	0.7	0.4	0.7
U.S.	13.0	3.7	3.8	1.5	1.2	0.9	1.0	0.6	0.3

Note: (1) Figures cover the Tampa-St. Petersburg-Clearwater, FL Metropolitan Statistical Area—see Appendix B for areas included; (2) Excludes Mexico.

Source: U.S. Census Bureau, 2011-2013 American Community Survey 3-Year Estimates

Marital Status

Area	Never Married	Now Married[2]	Separated	Widowed	Divorced
City	41.6	36.6	3.1	5.7	13.0
MSA[1]	30.1	46.2	2.4	7.4	13.9
U.S.	32.7	48.1	2.2	6.0	11.0

Note: Figures are percentages and cover the population 15 years of age and older; (1) Figures cover the Tampa-St. Petersburg-Clearwater, FL Metropolitan Statistical Area—see Appendix B for areas included; (2) Excludes separated

Source: U.S. Census Bureau, 2011-2013 American Community Survey 3-Year Estimates

Disability Status

Area	All Ages	Under 18 Years Old	18 to 64 Years Old	65 Years and Over
City	12.9	5.1	11.2	38.4
MSA[1]	14.0	4.5	11.2	34.6
U.S.	12.3	4.1	10.2	36.3

Note: Figures show percent of the civilian noninstitutionalized population that reported having a disability. Disability status is determined from from six types of difficulty: vision, hearing, cognitive, ambulatory, self-care, and independent living. For children under 5 years old, hearing and vision difficulty are used to determine disability status. For children between the ages of 5 and 14, disability status is determined from hearing, vision, cognitive, ambulatory, and self-care difficulties. For people aged 15 years and older, they are considered to have a disability if they have difficulty with any one of the six difficulty types; (1) Figures cover the Tampa-St. Petersburg-Clearwater, FL Metropolitan Statistical Area—see Appendix B for areas included.

Source: U.S. Census Bureau, 2011-2013 American Community Survey 3-Year Estimates

Age

Area	Percent of Population									Median Age
	Under Age 5	Age 5–19	Age 20–34	Age 35–44	Age 45–54	Age 55–64	Age 65–74	Age 75–84	Age 85+	
City	6.1	19.2	24.4	13.6	14.3	11.1	6.0	3.8	1.5	35.2
MSA[1]	5.5	17.6	18.6	12.6	14.6	13.2	9.5	5.8	2.6	41.7
U.S.	6.4	19.9	20.7	12.9	14.1	12.3	7.6	4.2	1.9	37.4

Note: (1) Figures cover the Tampa-St. Petersburg-Clearwater, FL Metropolitan Statistical Area—see Appendix B for areas included

Source: U.S. Census Bureau, 2011-2013 American Community Survey 3-Year Estimates

Gender

Area	Males	Females	Males per 100 Females
City	170,731	178,698	95.5
MSA[1]	1,379,741	1,468,026	94.0
U.S.	154,451,010	159,410,713	96.9

Note: (1) Figures cover the Tampa-St. Petersburg-Clearwater, FL Metropolitan Statistical Area—see Appendix B for areas included
Source: U.S. Census Bureau, 2011-2013 American Community Survey 3-Year Estimates

Religious Groups by Family

Area	Catholic	Baptist	Non-Den.	Methodist[2]	Lutheran	LDS[3]	Pente-costal	Presby-terian[4]	Muslim[5]	Judaism
MSA[1]	10.9	7.1	3.8	3.5	1.0	0.6	2.1	1.0	1.3	0.5
U.S.	19.1	9.3	4.0	4.0	2.3	2.0	1.9	1.6	0.8	0.7

Note: Figures are the number of adherents as a percentage of the total population; (1) Figures cover the Tampa-St. Petersburg-Clearwater, FL Metropolitan Statistical Area—see Appendix B for areas included; (2) Methodist/Pietist; (3) Latter Day Saints; (4) Reformed; (5) Figures are estimates
Source: Association of Statisticians of American Religious Bodies, 2010 U.S. Religion Census: Religious Congregations & Membership Study

Religious Groups by Tradition

Area	Catholic	Evangelical Protestant	Mainline Protestant	Other Tradition	Black Protestant	Orthodox
MSA[1]	10.9	13.6	5.2	3.1	1.2	0.8
U.S.	19.1	16.2	7.3	4.3	1.6	0.3

Note: Figures are the number of adherents as a percentage of the total population; (1) Figures cover the Tampa-St. Petersburg-Clearwater, FL Metropolitan Statistical Area—see Appendix B for areas included
Source: Association of Statisticians of American Religious Bodies, 2010 U.S. Religion Census: Religious Congregations & Membership Study

ECONOMY

Gross Metropolitan Product

Area	2012	2013	2014	2015	Rank[2]
MSA[1]	119.9	125.7	131.7	139.0	23

Note: Figures are in billions of dollars; (1) Figures cover the Tampa-St. Petersburg-Clearwater, FL Metropolitan Statistical Area—see Appendix B for areas included; (2) Rank is based on 2015 data and ranges from 1 to 363
Source: The U.S. Conference of Mayors, U.S. Metro Economies: GMP and Employment 2013-2015, June 2014

Economic Growth

Area	2010-12 (%)	2013 (%)	2014 (%)	2015 (%)	Rank[2]
MSA[1]	2.3	3.5	3.1	3.6	61
U.S.	2.1	2.0	2.3	3.2	-

Note: Figures are real gross metropolitan product (GMP) growth rates and represent annual average percent change; (1) Figures cover the Tampa-St. Petersburg-Clearwater, FL Metropolitan Statistical Area—see Appendix B for areas included; (2) Rank is based on 2015 data and ranges from 1 to 363
Source: The U.S. Conference of Mayors, U.S. Metro Economies: GMP and Employment 2013-2015, June 2014

Metropolitan Area Exports

Area	2008	2009	2010	2011	2012	2013	Rank[2]
MSA[1]	7,153.5	6,463.6	6,633.6	7,736.7	7,190.0	6,673.0	43

Note: Figures are in millions of dollars; (1) Figures cover the Tampa-St. Petersburg-Clearwater, FL Metropolitan Statistical Area—see Appendix B for areas included; (2) Rank is based on 2013 data and ranges from 1 to 387
Source: U.S. Department of Commerce, International Trade Administration, Office of Trade & Industry Information, Manufacturing & Services, data extracted April 3, 2015

Building Permits

Area	Single-Family			Multi-Family			Total		
	2013	2014	Pct. Chg.	2013	2014	Pct. Chg.	2013	2014	Pct. Chg.
City	686	712	3.8	1,168	1,843	57.8	1,854	2,555	37.8
MSA[1]	7,314	7,267	-0.6	4,838	5,119	5.8	12,152	12,386	1.9
U.S.	620,802	634,597	2.2	370,020	411,766	11.3	990,822	1,046,363	5.6

Note: (1) Figures cover the Tampa-St. Petersburg-Clearwater, FL Metropolitan Statistical Area—see Appendix B for areas included; Figures represent new, privately-owned housing units authorized (unadjusted data); All permit data are based on estimates with imputation.
Source: U.S. Census Bureau, Manufacturing, Mining, and Construction Statistics, Building Permits, 2013, 2014

Bankruptcy Filings

Area	Business Filings			Nonbusiness Filings		
	2013	2014	% Chg.	2013	2014	% Chg.
Hillsborough County	185	206	11.4	4,632	3,876	-16.3
U.S.	33,212	26,983	-18.8	1,038,720	909,812	-12.4

Note: Business filings include Chapter 7, Chapter 11, Chapter 12, and Chapter 13; Nonbusiness filings include Chapter 7, Chapter 11, and Chapter 13
Source: Administrative Office of the U.S. Courts, Business and Nonbusiness Bankruptcy, County Cases Commenced by Chapter of the Bankruptcy Code, During the 12- Month Period Ending December 31, 2013 and Business and Nonbusiness Bankruptcy, County Cases Commenced by Chapter of the Bankruptcy Code, During the 12- Month Period Ending December 31, 2014

Housing Vacancy Rates

Area	Gross Vacancy Rate[2] (%)			Year-Round Vacancy Rate[3] (%)			Rental Vacancy Rate[4] (%)			Homeowner Vacancy Rate[5] (%)		
	2012	2013	2014	2012	2013	2014	2012	2013	2014	2012	2013	2014
MSA[1]	20.8	18.4	18.3	14.2	12.1	11.5	13.0	9.2	8.4	2.0	2.1	2.4
U.S.	13.8	13.6	13.4	10.8	10.7	10.4	8.7	8.3	7.6	2.0	2.0	1.9

Note: (1) Figures cover the Tampa-St. Petersburg-Clearwater, FL Metropolitan Statistical Area—see Appendix B for areas included; (2) The percentage of the total housing inventory that is vacant; (3) The percentage of the housing inventory (excluding seasonal units) that is year-round vacant; (4) The percentage of rental inventory that is vacant for rent; (5) The percentage of homeowner inventory that is vacant for sale
Source: U.S. Census Bureau, Housing Vacancies and Homeownership Annual Statistics: 2014

INCOME

Income

Area	Per Capita ($)	Median Household ($)	Average Household ($)
City	28,945	41,927	68,704
MSA[1]	26,573	45,492	63,858
U.S.	27,884	52,176	72,897

Note: (1) Figures cover the Tampa-St. Petersburg-Clearwater, FL Metropolitan Statistical Area—see Appendix B for areas included
Source: U.S. Census Bureau, 2011-2013 American Community Survey 3-Year Estimates

Household Income Distribution

Area	Percent of Households Earning							
	Under $15,000	$15,000 -24,999	$25,000 -34,999	$35,000 -49,999	$50,000 -74,999	$75,000 -99,000	$100,000 -149,999	$150,000 and up
City	18.8	13.0	11.5	13.1	15.6	8.6	9.5	9.9
MSA[1]	14.1	12.9	12.0	15.1	18.0	10.7	10.3	7.0
U.S.	13.0	10.9	10.3	13.6	17.9	11.9	12.7	9.6

Note: (1) Figures cover the Tampa-St. Petersburg-Clearwater, FL Metropolitan Statistical Area—see Appendix B for areas included
Source: U.S. Census Bureau, 2011-2013 American Community Survey 3-Year Estimates

Poverty Rate

Area	All Ages	Under 18 Years Old	18 to 64 Years Old	65 Years and Over
City	22.7	31.9	20.6	17.6
MSA[1]	16.1	23.2	15.6	9.4
U.S.	15.9	22.4	14.8	9.5

Note: Figures are percentage of people whose income during the past 12 months was below the poverty level; (1) Figures cover the Tampa-St. Petersburg-Clearwater, FL Metropolitan Statistical Area—see Appendix B for areas included
Source: U.S. Census Bureau, 2011-2013 American Community Survey 3-Year Estimates

EMPLOYMENT

Labor Force and Employment

Area	Civilian Labor Force			Workers Employed		
	Dec. 2013	Dec. 2014	% Chg.	Dec. 2013	Dec. 2014	% Chg.
City	182,483	184,674	1.2	171,471	175,032	2.1
MSA[1]	1,413,617	1,430,638	1.2	1,327,059	1,355,252	2.1
U.S.	154,408,000	155,521,000	0.7	144,423,000	147,190,000	1.9

Note: Data is not seasonally adjusted and covers workers 16 years of age and older; (1) Figures cover the Tampa-St. Petersburg-Clearwater, FL Metropolitan Statistical Area—see Appendix B for areas included
Source: Bureau of Labor Statistics, Local Area Unemployment Statistics

Unemployment Rate

Area	2014											
	Jan.	Feb.	Mar.	Apr.	May	Jun.	Jul.	Aug.	Sep.	Oct.	Nov.	Dec.
City	6.3	6.2	6.2	5.6	5.9	6.1	6.4	6.3	5.8	5.6	5.6	5.2
MSA[1]	6.5	6.4	6.4	5.7	6.1	6.2	6.5	6.4	5.9	5.7	5.7	5.3
U.S.	7.0	7.0	6.8	5.9	6.1	6.3	6.5	6.3	5.7	5.5	5.5	5.4

Note: Data is not seasonally adjusted and covers workers 16 years of age and older; (1) Figures cover the Tampa-St. Petersburg-Clearwater, FL Metropolitan Statistical Area—see Appendix B for areas included
Source: Bureau of Labor Statistics, Local Area Unemployment Statistics

Employment by Occupation

Occupation Classification	City (%)	MSA[1] (%)	U.S. (%)
Management, Business, Science, and Arts	40.1	36.3	36.2
Natural Resources, Construction, and Maintenance	6.3	8.4	9.0
Production, Transportation, and Material Moving	7.9	8.5	12.1
Sales and Office	26.8	28.3	24.4
Service	18.9	18.5	18.3

Note: Figures cover employed civilians 16 years of age and older; (1) Figures cover the Tampa-St. Petersburg-Clearwater, FL Metropolitan Statistical Area—see Appendix B for areas included
Source: U.S. Census Bureau, 2011-2013 American Community Survey 3-Year Estimates

Employment by Industry

Sector	MSA[1] Number of Employees	MSA[1] Percent of Total	U.S. Percent of Total
Construction	59,200	4.8	4.4
Education and Health Services	192,900	15.6	15.5
Financial Activities	103,500	8.4	5.7
Government	155,700	12.6	15.8
Information	25,800	2.1	2.0
Leisure and Hospitality	142,000	11.5	10.3
Manufacturing	61,200	5.0	8.7
Mining and Logging	500	<0.1	0.6
Other Services	45,400	3.7	4.0
Professional and Business Services	205,700	16.7	13.8
Retail Trade	160,000	13.0	11.4
Transportation, Warehousing, and Utilities	30,200	2.4	3.9
Wholesale Trade	50,900	4.1	4.2

Note: Figures are non-farm employment as of December 2014. Figures are not seasonally adjusted and include workers 16 years of age and older; (1) Figures cover the Tampa-St. Petersburg-Clearwater, FL Metropolitan Statistical Area—see Appendix B for areas included
Source: Bureau of Labor Statistics, Current Employment Statistics, Employment, Hours, and Earnings

Occupations with Greatest Projected Employment Growth: 2012 – 2022

Occupation[1]	2012 Employment	2022 Projected Employment	Numeric Employment Change	Percent Employment Change
Retail Salespersons	326,380	380,120	53,740	16.5
Combined Food Preparation and Serving Workers, Including Fast Food	196,980	237,340	40,360	20.5
Customer Service Representatives	191,210	228,620	37,410	19.6
Registered Nurses	164,020	201,140	37,120	22.6
Waiters and Waitresses	191,370	227,810	36,440	19.0
Office Clerks, General	142,710	170,300	27,590	19.3
Cashiers	206,660	230,190	23,530	11.4
Landscaping and Groundskeeping Workers	92,510	115,540	23,030	24.9
Receptionists and Information Clerks	75,780	95,680	19,900	26.2
Nursing Assistants	86,990	106,200	19,210	22.1

Note: Projections cover Florida; (1) Sorted by numeric employment change
Source: www.projectionscentral.com, State Occupational Projections, 2012–2022 Long-Term Projections

Fastest Growing Occupations: 2012 – 2022

Occupation[1]	2012 Employment	2022 Projected Employment	Numeric Employment Change	Percent Employment Change
Helpers—Carpenters	1,280	2,450	1,170	90.7
Helpers—Brickmasons, Blockmasons, Stonemasons, and Tile and Marble Setters	1,050	1,890	840	79.5
Biomedical Engineers	760	1,300	540	70.7
Reinforcing Iron and Rebar Workers	520	870	350	67.5
Glaziers	2,890	4,710	1,820	62.8
Solar Photovoltaic Installers	170	270	100	58.7
Brickmasons and Blockmasons	2,820	4,430	1,610	57.1
Stonemasons	450	710	260	56.4
Helpers—Pipelayers, Plumbers, Pipefitters, and Steamfitters	2,420	3,750	1,330	54.8
Cement Masons and Concrete Finishers	10,390	16,050	5,660	54.4

Note: Projections cover Florida; (1) Sorted by percent employment change and excludes occupations with numeric employment change less than 100
Source: www.projectionscentral.com, State Occupational Projections, 2012–2022 Long-Term Projections

Average Wages

Occupation	$/Hr.	Occupation	$/Hr.
Accountants and Auditors	33.01	Maids and Housekeeping Cleaners	9.46
Automotive Mechanics	18.87	Maintenance and Repair Workers	15.83
Bookkeepers	16.07	Marketing Managers	55.62
Carpenters	16.31	Nuclear Medicine Technologists	36.51
Cashiers	9.42	Nurses, Licensed Practical	20.11
Clerks, General Office	13.31	Nurses, Registered	30.68
Clerks, Receptionists/Information	13.08	Nursing Assistants	11.61
Clerks, Shipping/Receiving	13.49	Packers and Packagers, Hand	9.28
Computer Programmers	35.31	Physical Therapists	37.77
Computer Systems Analysts	38.92	Postal Service Mail Carriers	25.12
Computer User Support Specialists	22.25	Real Estate Brokers	20.90
Cooks, Restaurant	11.91	Retail Salespersons	12.17
Dentists	84.08	Sales Reps., Exc. Tech./Scientific	31.31
Electrical Engineers	43.77	Sales Reps., Tech./Scientific	34.58
Electricians	19.04	Secretaries, Exc. Legal/Med./Exec.	14.85
Financial Managers	62.50	Security Guards	10.62
First-Line Supervisors/Managers, Sales	21.17	Surgeons	121.64
Food Preparation Workers	10.01	Teacher Assistants	10.40
General and Operations Managers	62.54	Teachers, Elementary School	21.30
Hairdressers/Cosmetologists	13.63	Teachers, Secondary School	21.60
Internists	105.04	Telemarketers	12.64
Janitors and Cleaners	10.50	Truck Drivers, Heavy/Tractor-Trailer	16.66
Landscaping/Groundskeeping Workers	11.19	Truck Drivers, Light/Delivery Svcs.	16.98
Lawyers	56.02	Waiters and Waitresses	10.26

Note: Wage data covers the Tampa-St. Petersburg-Clearwater, FL Metropolitan Statistical Area—see Appendix B for areas included; Hourly wages for elementary/secondary school teachers and teacher assistants were calculated by the editors from annual wage data assuming a 40 hour work week; n/a not available.
Source: Bureau of Labor Statistics, Metro Area Occupational Employment and Wage Estimates, May 2014

TAXES

State Corporate Income Tax Rates

State	Tax Rate (%)	Income Brackets ($)	Num. of Brackets	Financial Institution Tax Rate (%)[a]	Federal Income Tax Ded.
Florida	5.5 (f)	Flat rate	1	5.5 (f)	No

Note: Tax rates as of January 1, 2015; (a) Rates listed are the corporate income tax rate applied to financial institutions or excise taxes based on income. Some states have other taxes based upon the value of deposits or shares; (f) An exemption of $50,000 is allowed. Florida's Alternative Minimum Tax rate is 3.3%.
Source: Federation of Tax Administrators, "State Corporate Income Tax Rates, 2015"

State Individual Income Tax Rates

State	Tax Rate (%)	Income Brackets ($)	Num. of Brackets	Personal Exempt. ($)[1] Single	Personal Exempt. ($)[1] Dependents	Fed. Inc. Tax Ded.
Florida	None	–	–	–	–	–

Note: Tax rates as of January 1, 2015; Local- and county-level taxes are not included; n/a not applicable; (1) Married joint filers generally receive double the single exemption
Source: Federation of Tax Administrators, "State Individual Income Tax Rates, 2015"

Various State and Local Tax Rates

State	State and Local Sales and Use (%)	State Sales and Use (%)	Gasoline[1] (¢/gal.)	Cigarette[2] ($/pack)	Spirits[3] ($/gal.)	Wine[4] ($/gal.)	Beer[5] ($/gal.)
Florida	7.0	6.0	36.42	1.339	6.50 (f)	2.25	0.48 (p)

Note: All tax rates as of January 1, 2015; (1) The American Petroleum Institute has developed a methodology for determining the average tax rate on a gallon of fuel. Rates may include any of the following: excise taxes, environmental fees, storage tank fees, other fees or taxes, general sales tax, and local taxes. In states where gasoline is subject to the general sales tax, or where the fuel tax is based on the average sale price, the average rate determined by API is sensitive to changes in the price of gasoline. States that fully or partially apply general sales taxes to gasoline: CA, CO, GA, IL, IN, MI, NY; (2) The federal excise tax of $1.0066 per pack and local taxes are not included; (3) Rates are those applicable to off-premise sales of 40% alcohol by volume (a.b.v.) distilled spirits in 750ml containers. Local excise taxes are excluded; (4) Rates are those applicable to off-premise sales of 11% a.b.v. non-carbonated wine in 750ml containers; (5) Rates are those applicable to off-premise sales of 4.7% a.b.v. beer in 12 ounce containers; (f) Different rates are also applicable according to alcohol content, place of production, size of container, or place purchased (on- or off-premise or onboard airlines); (p) Local excise taxes are excluded.
Source: Tax Foundation, 2015 Facts & Figures: How Does Your State Compare?

State Business Tax Climate Index Rankings

State	Overall Rank	Corporate Tax Index Rank	Individual Income Tax Index Rank	Sales Tax Index Rank	Unemployment Insurance Tax Index Rank	Property Tax Index Rank
Florida	5	14	1	12	3	16

Note: The index is a measure of how each state's tax laws affect economic performance. The lower the rank, the more favorable a state's tax system is for business. States without a given tax are given a ranking of 1. The scores/rankings for the District of Columbia do not affect other states. The 2015 index represents the tax climate as of July 1, 2014.
Source: Tax Foundation, State Business Tax Climate Index 2015

COMMERCIAL REAL ESTATE

Office Market

Market Area	Inventory (sq. ft.)	Vacancy Rate (%)	Under Construction (sq. ft.)	YTD Net Absorption (sq. ft.)	Total Average Asking Rent ($/sq. ft./year)
Tampa-Saint Petersburg	64,184,143	15.4	0	1,081,095	20.99
National	4,745,108,508	14.3	71,190,461	51,084,126	27.40

Source: Newmark Grubb Knight Frank, National Office Market Report, 4th Quarter 2014

Industrial/Warehouse/R&D Market

Market Area	Inventory (sq. ft.)	Vacancy Rate (%)	Under Construction (sq. ft.)	YTD Net Absorption (sq. ft.)	Total Average Asking Rent ($/sq. ft./year)
Tampa-Saint Petersburg	247,611,020	8.5	166,000	6,131,753	4.74
National	14,238,613,765	7.2	134,387,407	185,246,438	5.64

Source: Newmark Grubb Knight Frank, National Industrial Market Report, 4th Quarter 2014

COMMERCIAL UTILITIES

Typical Monthly Electric Bills

Area	Commercial Service ($/month)		Industrial Service ($/month)	
	1,500 kWh	40 kW demand 14,000 kWh	1,000 kW demand 200,000 kWh	50,000 kW demand 32,500,000 kWh
City	169	1,333	23,385	2,546,569
Average[1]	201	1,653	26,124	2,639,743

Note: Figures are based on annualized 2014 rates; (1) Average based on 180 utilities surveyed
Source: Edison Electric Institute, Typical Bills and Average Rates Report, Summer 2014

TRANSPORTATION

Means of Transportation to Work

Area	Car/Truck/Van: Drove Alone	Car/Truck/Van: Car-pooled	Public Transportation: Bus	Public Transportation: Subway	Public Transportation: Railroad	Bicycle	Walked	Other Means	Worked at Home
City	78.7	8.2	2.5	0.0	0.0	1.4	2.4	1.6	5.1
MSA[1]	80.8	9.0	1.2	0.0	0.0	0.8	1.5	1.4	5.2
U.S.	76.4	9.6	2.6	1.8	0.6	0.6	2.8	1.3	4.3

Note: Figures are percentages and cover workers 16 years of age and older; (1) Figures cover the Tampa-St. Petersburg-Clearwater, FL Metropolitan Statistical Area—see Appendix B for areas included
Source: U.S. Census Bureau, 2011-2013 American Community Survey 3-Year Estimates

Travel Time to Work

Area	Less Than 10 Minutes	10 to 19 Minutes	20 to 29 Minutes	30 to 44 Minutes	45 to 59 Minutes	60 to 89 Minutes	90 Minutes or More
City	12.6	33.5	23.9	19.2	6.1	3.2	1.7
MSA[1]	10.6	28.2	22.9	22.6	9.0	4.9	1.7
U.S.	13.3	29.7	20.9	20.2	7.7	5.7	2.6

Note: Figures are percentages and include workers 16 years old and over; (1) Figures cover the Tampa-St. Petersburg-Clearwater, FL Metropolitan Statistical Area—see Appendix B for areas included
Source: U.S. Census Bureau, 2011-2013 American Community Survey 3-Year Estimates

Travel Time Index

Area	1985	1990	1995	2000	2005	2010	2011
Urban Area[1]	1.17	1.21	1.22	1.19	1.22	1.20	1.20
Average[2]	1.09	1.14	1.16	1.19	1.23	1.18	1.18

Note: Travel Time Index—the ratio of travel time in the peak period to the travel time at free-flow conditions. For example, a value of 1.30 indicates a 20-minute free-flow trip takes 26 minutes in the peak. Free-flow speeds (60 mph on freeways and 35 mph on principal arterials) are used as the comparison threshold; (1) Covers the Tampa-St. Petersburg FL urban area; (2) average of 498 urban areas
Source: Texas Transportation Institute, Urban Mobility Report 2012, December 2012

Public Transportation

Agency Name / Mode of Transportation	Vehicles Operated in Maximum Service	Annual Unlinked Passenger Trips (in thous.)	Annual Passenger Miles (in thous.)
Hillsborough Area Regional Transit Authority (HART)			
Bus (directly operated)	158	14,732.5	73,720.7
Demand Response (directly operated)	36	141.2	1,002.7
Streetcar Rail (directly operated)	3	295.9	516.1

Source: Federal Transit Administration, National Transit Database, 2013

Air Transportation

Airport Name and Code / Type of Service	Passenger Airlines[1]	Passenger Enplanements	Freight Carriers[2]	Freight (lbs.)
Tampa International (TPA)				
Domestic service (U.S. carriers - 2014)	27	8,251,442	14	85,128,798
International service (U.S. carriers - 2013)	11	26,876	1	251,206

Note: (1) Includes all U.S.-based major, minor and commuter airlines that carried at least one passenger during the year; (2) Includes all U.S.-based airlines and freight carriers that transported at least one lb. of freight during the year.
Source: Bureau of Transportation Statistics, The Intermodal Transportation Database, Air Carriers: T-100 Domestic Market (U.S. Carriers), 2014; Bureau of Transportation Statistics, The Intermodal Transportation Database, Air Carriers: T-100 International Market (U.S. Carriers), 2013

Other Transportation Statistics

Major Highways:	I-4; I-75
Amtrak Service:	Yes
Major Waterways/Ports:	Port of Tampa

Source: Amtrak.com; Google Maps

BUSINESSES

Major Business Headquarters

Company Name	Rankings	
	Fortune[1]	Forbes[2]
WellCare Health Plans	294	-

Note: (1) Fortune 500—companies that produce a 10-K are ranked 1 to 500 based on 2013 revenue; (2) all private companies with at least $2 billion in annual revenue through the end of their most current fiscal year are ranked 1 to 221; companies listed are headquartered in the city; dashes indicate no ranking
Source: Fortune, "Fortune 500," June 16, 2014; Forbes, "America's Largest Private Companies," November 5, 2014

Fast-Growing Businesses

According to *Inc.*, Tampa is home to three of America's 500 fastest-growing private companies: **MedHOK** (#25); **LabTech Software** (#354); **Convene (Tampa, FL)** (#430). Criteria: must be an independent, privately-held, for-profit, U.S. corporation, proprietorship or partnership; revenues must be at least $100,000 in 2010 and $2 million in 2013; must have four-year operating/sales history. Holding companies, regulated banks, and utilities were excluded. *Inc., "America's 500 Fastest-Growing Private Companies," September 2014*

According to *Fortune*, Tampa is home to one of the 100 fastest-growing companies in the world: **HCI Group** (#2). Companies were ranked by their revenue growth rate; their EPS growth rate; and their three-year annualized total return to investors for the period ending June 30, 2014. Criteria for inclusion: a company, foreign or domestic, must trade on a major U.S. stock exchange; must file quarterly reports with the SEC; must have a minimum market capitalization of $250 million; must have a stock price of at least $5 on June 30, 2014; must have been trading continuously since June 30, 2010; must have revenue and net income for the four quarters ended on or before April 30, 2014, of at least $50 million and $10 million, respectively; and must have posted a compound annual growth in revenue and earnings per share of at least 20% annually over the three years ending on or before April 30, 2014. Real estate investment trusts, limited-liability companies, limited parterships, business development companies, closed end investment firms, and companies that lost money in the quarter ending April 30, 2014 were excluded. *Fortune, "100 Fastest-Growing Companies," August 28, 2014*

Minority Business Opportunity

Tampa is home to one company which is on the *Black Enterprise* Industrial/Service 100 list (100 largest companies based on gross sales): **Sun State International Trucks** (#34). Criteria: operational in previous calendar year; at least 51% black-owned and manufactures/owns the product it sells or provides industrial or consumer services. Brokerages, real estate firms and firms that provide professional services are not eligible. *Black Enterprise, B.E. 100s, 2014*

Tampa is home to one company which is on the *Black Enterprise* Auto Dealer 60 list (60 largest dealers based on gross sales): **March Hodge Automotive Group** (#2). Criteria: company must be operational in previous calendar year and be at least 51% black-owned. *Black Enterprise, B.E. 100s, 2014*

Tampa is home to three companies which are on the *Hispanic Business* 500 list (500 largest U.S. Hispanic-owned companies based on 2012 revenue): **Merchandise Partners** (#174); **MarkMaster** (#297); **Diverse ID Products of Florida** (#301). Companies included must show at least 51 percent ownership by Hispanic U.S. citizens, and must maintain headquarters in one of the 50 states or Washington, D.C. *Hispanic Business, "Hispanic Business 500," June 20, 2013*

Minority- and Women-Owned Businesses

Group	All Firms		Firms with Paid Employees			
	Firms	Sales ($000)	Firms	Sales ($000)	Employees	Payroll ($000)
Asian	1,552	605,434	521	483,557	3,663	95,944
Black	4,378	455,594	338	351,483	2,814	63,365
Hispanic	7,947	1,642,003	1,395	1,338,467	7,318	288,902
Women	10,798	3,708,549	1,626	3,373,231	13,263	369,989
All Firms	38,662	67,668,675	11,085	66,207,395	301,427	13,045,436

Note: Figures cover firms located in the city; minority- and women-owned business are defined as firms in which the corresponding group own 51% or more of the stock or equity of the company
Source: U.S. Census Bureau, 2007 Economic Census, Survey of Business Owners (2012 Survey of Business Owners data will be released starting in June 2015)

HOTELS & CONVENTION CENTERS

Hotels/Motels

Area	5 Star		4 Star		3 Star		2 Star		1 Star		Not Rated	
	Num.	Pct.[3]	Num.	Pct.[3]	Num.	Pct.[3]	Num.	Pct.[3]	Num.	Pct.[3]	Num.	Pct.[3]
City[1]	0	0.0	9	5.7	56	35.2	81	50.9	6	3.8	7	4.4
Total[2]	166	0.9	1,264	7.0	5,718	31.8	9,340	52.0	411	2.3	1,070	6.0

Note: (1) Figures cover Tampa and vicinity; (2) Figures cover all 100 cities in this book; (3) Percentage of hotels which have a given star rating; Star ratings are determined by expedia.com and offer an indication of the general quality of a particular hotel.
Source: expedia.com, April 2, 2015

The Tampa-St. Petersburg-Clearwater, FL metro area is home to two of the best hotels in the U.S. according to *Travel & Leisure*: **Sandpearl Resort**; **Vinoy Renaissance St. Petersburg Resort & Golf Club**. Criteria: service; location; rooms; food; and value. The list includes the top 236 hotels in the U.S. *Travel & Leisure, "T+L 500, The World's Best Hotels 2015"*

Major Convention Centers

Name	Overall Space (sq. ft.)	Exhibit Space (sq. ft.)	Meeting Space (sq. ft.)	Meeting Rooms
Tampa Convention Center	600,000	200,000	42,000	36

Note: Table includes convention centers located in the Tampa-St. Petersburg-Clearwater, FL metro area; n/a not available
Source: Original research

Living Environment

COST OF LIVING

Cost of Living Index

Composite Index	Groceries	Housing	Utilities	Transportation	Health Care	Misc. Goods/ Services
92.1	98.5	75.9	103.9	102.1	91.2	96.1

Note: The Cost of Living Index measures regional differences in the cost of consumer goods and services, excluding taxes and non-consumer expenditures, for professional and managerial households in the top income quintile. It is based on more than 50,000 prices covering almost 60 different items for which prices are collected three times a year by chambers of commerce, economic development organizations or university applied economic centers in each participating urban area. The numbers shown should be read as a percentage above or below the national average of 100. For example, a value of 115.4 in the groceries column indicates that grocery prices are 15.4% higher than the national average. Small differences in the index numbers should not be interpreted as significant; Figures cover the Tampa FL urban area.
Source: The Council for Community and Economic Research, ACCRA Cost of Living Index, 2014

Grocery Prices

Area[1]	T-Bone Steak ($/pound)	Frying Chicken ($/pound)	Whole Milk ($/half gal.)	Eggs ($/dozen)	Orange Juice ($/64 oz.)	Coffee ($/11.5 oz.)
City[2]	10.60	1.43	2.69	2.04	3.38	3.56
Avg.	10.40	1.37	2.40	1.99	3.46	4.27
Min.	8.48	0.93	1.37	1.30	2.83	2.99
Max.	14.20	2.44	3.62	4.02	6.42	6.96

Note: (1) Values for the local area are compared with the average, minimum and maximum values for all 308 areas in the Cost of Living Index; (2) Figures cover the Tampa FL urban area; **T-Bone Steak** *(price per pound);* **Frying Chicken** *(price per pound, whole fryer);* **Whole Milk** *(half gallon carton);* **Eggs** *(price per dozen, Grade A, large);* **Orange Juice** *(64 oz. Tropicana or Florida Natural);* **Coffee** *(11.5 oz. can, vacuum-packed, Maxwell House, Hills Bros, or Folgers).*
Source: The Council for Community and Economic Research, ACCRA Cost of Living Index, 2014

Housing and Utility Costs

Area[1]	New Home Price ($)	Apartment Rent ($/month)	All Electric ($/month)	Part Electric ($/month)	Other Energy ($/month)	Telephone ($/month)
City[2]	212,792	843	161.00	-	-	32.47
Avg.	305,838	919	181.00	93.66	73.14	27.95
Min.	183,142	480	112.00	42.06	23.42	17.16
Max.	1,358,576	3,851	594.00	180.03	440.99	40.42

Note: (1) Values for the local area are compared with the average, minimum and maximum values for all 308 areas in the Cost of Living Index; (2) Figures cover the Tampa FL urban area; **New Home Price** *(2,400 sf living area, 8,000 sf lot, in urban area with full utilities);* **Apartment Rent** *(950 sf 2 bedroom/1.5 or 2 bath, unfurnished, excluding all utilities except water);* **All Electric** *(average monthly cost for an all-electric home);* **Part Electric** *(average monthly cost for a part-electric home);* **Other Energy** *(average monthly cost for natural gas, fuel oil, coal, wood, and any other forms of energy except electricity);* **Telephone** *(price includes basic monthly rate for a private residential line plus additional local usage charges incurred by a family of four).*
Source: The Council for Community and Economic Research, ACCRA Cost of Living Index, 2014

Health Care, Transportation, and Other Costs

Area[1]	Doctor ($/visit)	Dentist ($/visit)	Optometrist ($/visit)	Gasoline ($/gallon)	Beauty Salon ($/visit)	Men's Shirt ($)
City[2]	85.10	76.28	92.33	3.40	32.07	22.35
Avg.	102.86	87.89	97.66	3.44	34.37	26.74
Min.	67.47	65.78	51.18	3.00	17.43	12.79
Max.	173.50	150.14	235.00	4.33	64.28	49.50

Note: (1) Values for the local area are compared with the average, minimum and maximum values for all 308 areas in the Cost of Living Index; (2) Figures cover the Tampa FL urban area; **Doctor** *(general practitioners routine exam of an established patient);* **Dentist** *(adult teeth cleaning and periodic oral examination);* **Optometrist** *(full vision eye exam for established adult patient);* **Gasoline** *(one gallon regular unleaded, national brand, including all taxes, cash price at self-service pump if available);* **Beauty Salon** *(woman's shampoo, trim, and blow-dry);* **Men's Shirt** *(cotton/polyester dress shirt, pinpoint weave, long sleeves).*
Source: The Council for Community and Economic Research, ACCRA Cost of Living Index, 2014

HOUSING

House Price Index (HPI)

Area	National Ranking[2]	Quarterly Change (%)	One-Year Change (%)	Five-Year Change (%)
MSA[1]	46	1.25	8.46	8.55
U.S.[3]	–	1.35	4.91	11.59

Note: The HPI is a weighted repeat sales index. It measures average price changes in repeat sales or refinancings on the same properties. This information is obtained by reviewing repeat mortgage transactions on single-family properties whose mortgages have been purchased or securitized by Fannie Mae or Freddie Mac in January 1975; (1) Tampa-St. Petersburg-Clearwater Metropolitan Statistical Area—see Appendix B for areas included; (2) Rankings are based on annual percentage change for all metro areas containing at least 15,000 transactions over the last 10 years and ranges from 1 to 275; (3) figures based on a weighted average of Census Division estimates using a seasonally adjusted, purchase-only index; all figures are for the period ending December 31, 2014

Source: Federal Housing Finance Agency, House Price Index, February 26, 2015

Median Single-Family Home Prices

Area	2012	2013	2014p	Percent Change 2013 to 2014
MSA[1]	133.9	142.8	151.5	6.1
U.S. Average	177.2	197.4	209.0	5.9

Note: Figures are median sales prices of existing single-family homes in thousands of dollars; (p) preliminary; n/a not available; (1) Tampa-St. Petersburg-Clearwater, FL Metropolitan Statistical Area—see Appendix B for areas included

Source: National Association of Realtors, Median Sales Price of Existing Single-Family Homes for Metropolitan Areas, 4th Quarter 2014

Qualifying Income Based on Median Sales Price of Existing Single-Family Homes

Area	With 5% Down ($)	With 10% Down ($)	With 20% Down ($)
MSA[1]	35,161	33,310	29,609
U.S. Average	45,863	43,449	38,621

Note: Figures are preliminary; Qualifying income is based on a mortgage rate of 4.0%. Monthly principal and interest payment is limited to 25% of income; n/a not available; (1) Tampa-St. Petersburg-Clearwater, FL Metropolitan Statistical Area—see Appendix B for areas included

Source: National Association of Realtors, Qualifying Income Based on Median Sales Price of Existing Single-Family Homes for Metropolitan Areas, 4th Quarter 2014

Median Apartment Condo-Coop Home Prices

Area	2012	2013	2014p	Percent Change 2013 to 2014
MSA[1]	84.0	91.6	106.8	16.6
U.S. Average	173.7	194.9	205.1	5.2

Note: Figures are median sales prices of existing apartment condo-coop homes in thousands of dollars; (p) preliminary; n/a not available; (1) Tampa-St. Petersburg-Clearwater, FL Metropolitan Statistical Area—see Appendix B for areas included

Source: National Association of Realtors, Median Sales Price of Existing Apartment Condo-Coop Homes for Metropolitan Areas, 4th Quarter 2014

Gross Monthly Rent

Area	Under $200	$200 -299	$300 -499	$500 -749	$750 -999	$1,000 -1,499	$1,500 and up	Median ($)
City	1.9	3.5	5.8	19.2	27.4	28.1	14.1	929
MSA[1]	1.0	1.5	4.7	20.8	31.5	29.2	11.3	922
U.S.	1.7	3.2	7.8	22.1	24.3	26.0	14.9	900

Note: Figures are percentages except for Median; Gross rent is the contract rent plus the estimated average monthly cost of utilities (electricity, gas, and water and sewer) and fuels (oil, coal, kerosene, wood, etc.) if these are paid by the renter (or paid for the renter by someone else); (1) Figures cover the Tampa-St. Petersburg-Clearwater, FL Metropolitan Statistical Area—see Appendix B for areas included

Source: U.S. Census Bureau, 2011-2013 American Community Survey 3-Year Estimates

Homeownership Rate

Area	2007 (%)	2008 (%)	2009 (%)	2010 (%)	2011 (%)	2012 (%)	2013 (%)	2014 (%)
MSA[1]	72.9	70.5	68.3	68.3	68.3	67.0	65.3	64.9
U.S.	68.1	67.8	67.4	66.9	66.1	65.4	65.1	64.5

Note: (1) Figures cover the Tampa-St. Petersburg-Clearwater, FL Metropolitan Statistical Area—see Appendix B for areas included
Source: U.S. Census Bureau, Housing Vacancies and Homeownership Annual Statistics: 2014

Year Housing Structure Built

Area	2010 or Later	2000 -2009	1990 -1999	1980 -1989	1970 -1979	1960 -1969	1950 -1959	1940 -1949	Before 1940	Median Year
City	1.4	19.9	10.9	13.0	11.4	12.6	15.9	6.0	8.8	1976
MSA[1]	1.0	17.3	14.3	21.3	21.7	11.0	8.7	2.0	2.8	1982
U.S.	0.9	15.0	13.9	13.8	15.8	11.0	10.9	5.4	13.3	1976

Note: Figures are percentages except for Median Year; (1) Figures cover the Tampa-St. Petersburg-Clearwater, FL Metropolitan Statistical Area—see Appendix B for areas included
Source: U.S. Census Bureau, 2011-2013 American Community Survey 3-Year Estimates

HEALTH

Health Risk Data

Category	MSA[1] (%)	U.S. (%)
Adults aged 18–64 who have any kind of health care coverage	76.7	79.6
Adults who reported being in good or excellent health	81.0	83.1
Adults who are current smokers	20.3	19.6
Adults who are heavy drinkers[2]	8.3	6.1
Adults who are binge drinkers[3]	18.9	16.9
Adults who are overweight (BMI 25.0 - 29.9)	32.5	35.8
Adults who are obese (BMI 30.0 - 99.8)	25.1	27.6
Adults who participated in any physical activities in the past month	75.5	77.1
Adults 50+ who have ever had a sigmoidoscopy or colonoscopy	67.2	67.3
Women aged 40+ who have had a mammogram within the past two years	71.4	74.0
Men aged 40+ who have had a PSA test within the past two years	50.7	45.2
Adults aged 65+ who have had flu shot within the past year	56.0	60.1
Adults who always wear a seatbelt	95.0	93.8

Note: Data as of 2012 unless otherwise noted; (1) Figures cover the Tampa-St. Petersburg-Clearwater, FL Metropolitan Statistical Area—see Appendix B for areas included; (2) Heavy drinkers are classified as males having more than two drinks per day or females having more than one drink per day; (3) Binge drinkers are classified as males having five or more drinks on one occasion or females having four or more drinks on one occasion
Source: Centers for Disease Control and Prevention, Behaviorial Risk Factor Surveillance System, SMART: Selected Metropolitan/Micropolitan Area Risk Trends, 2012 (Note: the CDC has discontinued this dataset but will be releasing a replacement in late 2015)

Chronic Health Indicators

Category	MSA[1] (%)	U.S. (%)
Adults who have ever been told they had a heart attack	5.9	4.5
Adults who have ever been told they had a stroke	2.5	2.9
Adults who have been told they currently have asthma	8.8	8.9
Adults who have ever been told they have arthritis	28.2	25.7
Adults who have ever been told they have diabetes[2]	11.5	9.7
Adults who have ever been told they had skin cancer	7.2	5.7
Adults who have ever been told they had any other types of cancer	7.6	6.5
Adults who have ever been told they have COPD	7.2	6.2
Adults who have ever been told they have kidney disease	1.9	2.5
Adults who have ever been told they have a form of depression	16.6	18.0

Note: Data as of 2012 unless otherwise noted; (1) Figures cover the Tampa-St. Petersburg-Clearwater, FL Metropolitan Statistical Area—see Appendix B for areas included; (2) Figures do not include pregnancy-related, borderline, or pre-diabetes
Source: Centers for Disease Control and Prevention, Behaviorial Risk Factor Surveillance System, SMART: Selected Metropolitan/Micropolitan Area Risk Trends, 2012 (Note: the CDC has discontinued this dataset but will be releasing a replacement in late 2015)

Mortality Rates for the Top 10 Causes of Death in the U.S.

ICD-10[a] Sub-Chapter	ICD-10[a] Code	Age-Adjusted Mortality Rate[1] per 100,000 population	
		County[2]	U.S.
Malignant neoplasms	C00-C97	163.6	166.2
Ischaemic heart diseases	I20-I25	105.1	105.7
Other forms of heart disease	I30-I51	32.7	49.3
Chronic lower respiratory diseases	J40-J47	40.8	42.1
Organic, including symptomatic, mental disorders	F01-F09	45.3	38.1
Cerebrovascular diseases	I60-I69	32.2	37.0
Other external causes of accidental injury	W00-X59	32.3	26.9
Other degenerative diseases of the nervous system	G30-G31	23.7	25.6
Diabetes mellitus	E10-E14	22.3	21.3
Hypertensive diseases	I10-I15	33.5	19.4

Note: (a) ICD-10 = International Classification of Diseases 10th Revision; (1) Mortality rates are a three year average covering 2011-2013; (2) Figures cover Hillsborough County
Source: Centers for Disease Control and Prevention, National Center for Health Statistics. Compressed Mortality File 1999-2013 on CDC WONDER Online Database, released October 2014. Data are compiled from the Compressed Mortality File 1999-2013, Series 20 No. 2S, 2014.

Mortality Rates for Selected Causes of Death

ICD-10[a] Sub-Chapter	ICD-10[a] Code	Age-Adjusted Mortality Rate[1] per 100,000 population	
		County[2]	U.S.
Assault	X85-Y09	5.3	5.2
Diseases of the liver	K70-K76	11.9	13.2
Human immunodeficiency virus (HIV) disease	B20-B24	4.7	2.2
Influenza and pneumonia	J09-J18	10.7	15.4
Intentional self-harm	X60-X84	12.5	12.5
Malnutrition	E40-E46	0.5	0.9
Obesity and other hyperalimentation	E65-E68	1.5	1.8
Renal failure	N17-N19	10.3	13.1
Transport accidents	V01-V99	13.1	11.7
Viral hepatitis	B15-B19	2.1	2.2

Note: (a) ICD-10 = International Classification of Diseases 10th Revision; (1) Mortality rates are a three year average covering 2011-2013; (2) Figures cover Hillsborough County
Source: Centers for Disease Control and Prevention, National Center for Health Statistics. Compressed Mortality File 1999-2013 on CDC WONDER Online Database, released October 2014. Data are compiled from the Compressed Mortality File 1999-2013, Series 20 No. 2S, 2014.

Health Insurance Coverage

Area	With Health Insurance	With Private Health Insurance	With Public Health Insurance	Without Health Insurance	Population Under Age 18 Without Health Insurance
City	81.9	57.3	32.0	18.1	8.2
MSA[1]	82.4	59.6	34.6	17.6	9.2
U.S.	85.2	65.2	31.0	14.8	7.3

Note: Figures are percentages that cover the civilian noninstitutionalized population; (1) Figures cover the Tampa-St. Petersburg-Clearwater, FL Metropolitan Statistical Area—see Appendix B for areas included
Source: U.S. Census Bureau, 2011-2013 American Community Survey 3-Year Estimates

Number of Medical Professionals

Area[1]	MDs[2]	DOs[2,3]	Dentists	Podiatrists	Chiropractors	Optometrists
Local (number)	4,048	327	656	65	302	147
Local (rate[4])	315.7	25.5	50.7	5.0	23.3	11.4
U.S. (rate[4])	270.0	20.2	63.1	5.7	25.2	14.9

Note: Data as of 2013 unless noted; (1) Local data covers Hillsborough County; (2) Data as of 2012 and includes all active, non-federal physicians; (3) Doctor of Osteopathic Medicine; (4) rate per 100,000 population
Source: U.S. Department of Health and Human Services, Health Resources and Services Administration, Bureau of Health Professions, Area Resource File (ARF) 2013-2014

Best Hospitals

According to *U.S. News,* the Tampa-St. Petersburg-Clearwater, FL metro area is home to two of the best hospitals in the U.S.: **Moffitt Cancer Center** (1 specialty); **Tampa General Hospital** (4 specialties). The hospitals listed were nationally ranked in at least one adult specialty. Only 144 hospitals nationwide were nationally ranked in one or more specialties. Seventeen hospitals in the U.S. made the Honor Roll with high scores in at least six specialties. *U.S. News Online, "America's Best Children's Hospitals 2014-15"*

According to *U.S. News,* the Tampa-St. Petersburg-Clearwater, FL metro area is home to one of the best children's hospitals in the U.S.: **All Children's Hospital** (3 specialties). The hospital listed was highly ranked in at least one pediatric specialty. Eighty-nine children's hospitals in the U.S. were nationally ranked in at least one specialty. Ten children's hospitals in the U.S. made the Honor Roll with high scores in at least three specialties. *U.S. News Online, "America's Best Children's Hospitals 2014-15"*

EDUCATION

Public School District Statistics

District Name	Schls	Pupils	Pupil/ Teacher Ratio	Minority Pupils[1] (%)	Free Lunch Eligible[2] (%)	IEP[3] (%)
Hillsborough County	311	200,466	14.5	62.3	50.1	14.2

Note: Table includes school districts with 2,000 or more students; (1) Percentage of students that are not non-Hispanic white; (2) Percentage of students that are eligible for the free lunch program; (3) Percentage of students that have an Individualized Education Program.
Source: U.S. Department of Education, National Center for Education Statistics, Common Core of Data, Local Education Agency (School District) Universe Survey: School Year 2012-2013; U.S. Department of Education, National Center for Education Statistics, Common Core of Data, Public Elementary/Secondary School Universe Survey: School Year 2012-2013

Highest Level of Education

Area	Less than H.S.	H.S. Diploma	Some College, No Deg.	Associate Degree	Bachelor's Degree	Master's Degree	Prof. School Degree	Doctorate Degree
City	13.5	26.6	18.2	7.8	20.7	8.4	3.2	1.7
MSA[1]	12.0	30.8	21.1	9.5	17.3	6.4	1.8	1.0
U.S.	13.7	28.0	21.2	7.9	18.2	7.7	1.9	1.3

Note: Figures cover persons age 25 and over; (1) Figures cover the Tampa-St. Petersburg-Clearwater, FL Metropolitan Statistical Area—see Appendix B for areas included
Source: U.S. Census Bureau, 2011-2013 American Community Survey 3-Year Estimates

Educational Attainment by Race

Area	High School Graduate or Higher (%)					Bachelor's Degree or Higher (%)				
	Total	White	Black	Asian	Hisp.[2]	Total	White	Black	Asian	Hisp.[2]
City	86.5	89.5	79.3	85.4	76.3	33.9	40.2	13.4	54.7	18.8
MSA[1]	88.0	89.2	83.6	84.2	77.3	26.6	27.0	18.4	48.7	18.4
U.S.	86.3	88.3	83.1	85.7	64.0	29.1	30.4	18.8	50.7	13.7

Note: Figures shown cover persons 25 years old and over; (1) Figures cover the Tampa-St. Petersburg-Clearwater, FL Metropolitan Statistical Area—see Appendix B for areas included; (2) People of Hispanic origin can be of any race
Source: U.S. Census Bureau, 2011-2013 American Community Survey 3-Year Estimates

School Enrollment by Grade and Control

Area	Preschool (%)		Kindergarten (%)		Grades 1 - 4 (%)		Grades 5 - 8 (%)		Grades 9 - 12 (%)	
	Public	Private	Public	Private	Public	Private	Public	Private	Public	Private
City	54.6	45.4	91.9	8.1	90.2	9.8	87.2	12.8	90.8	9.2
MSA[1]	57.6	42.4	88.3	11.7	89.4	10.6	88.8	11.2	91.5	8.5
U.S.	57.7	42.3	87.9	12.1	89.9	10.1	90.0	10.0	90.7	9.3

Note: Figures shown cover persons 3 years old and over; (1) Figures cover the Tampa-St. Petersburg-Clearwater, FL Metropolitan Statistical Area—see Appendix B for areas included
Source: U.S. Census Bureau, 2011-2013 American Community Survey 3-Year Estimates

Average Salaries of Public School Classroom Teachers

Area	2013-14		2014-15		Percent Change 2013-14 to 2014-15	Percent Change 2004-05 to 2014-15
	Dollars	Rank[1]	Dollars	Rank[1]		
FLORIDA	47,780	39	48,992	36	2.54	17.8
U.S. Average	56,610	–	57,379	–	1.36	20.8

Note: (1) State rank ranges from 1 to 51 where 1 indicates highest salary.
Source: National Education Association, Rankings & Estimates: Rankings of the States 2014 and Estimates of School Statistics 2015, March 2015

Higher Education

Four-Year Colleges			Two-Year Colleges			Medical Schools[1]	Law Schools[2]	Voc/ Tech[3]
Public	Private Non-profit	Private For-profit	Public	Private Non-profit	Private For-profit			
1	2	8	3	0	4	1	0	6

Note: Figures cover institutions located within the city limits and include main campuses only; (1) includes schools accredited by the Liaison Committee on Medical Education and the American Osteopathic Association's Commission on Osteopathic College Accreditation; (2) includes ABA-accredited schools, schools with provisional ABA accreditation, and state accredited schools; (3) includes all schools with programs that are less than 2 years.
Source: National Center for Education Statistics, Integrated Postsecondary Education System (IPEDS), 2013-14; Association of American Medical Colleges, Member List, May 1, 2015; American Osteopathic Association, Member List, May 1, 2015; Law School Admission Council, Official Guide to ABA-Approved Law Schools Online, May 1, 2015; Wikipedia, List of Medical Schools in the United States, May 1, 2015; Wikipedia, List of Law Schools in the United States, May 1, 2015

According to *U.S. News & World Report,* the Tampa-St. Petersburg-Clearwater, FL metro area is home to one of the best national universities in the U.S.: **University of South Florida** (#161). The indicators used to capture academic quality fall into a number of categories: assessment by administrators at peer institutions; retention of students; faculty resources; student selectivity; financial resources; alumni giving; high school counselor ratings of colleges; and graduation rate. *U.S. News & World Report, "America's Best Colleges 2015"*

According to *U.S. News & World Report,* the Tampa-St. Petersburg-Clearwater, FL metro area is home to one of the best liberal arts colleges in the U.S.: **Eckerd College** (#124). The indicators used to capture academic quality fall into a number of categories: assessment by administrators at peer institutions; retention of students; faculty resources; student selectivity; financial resources; alumni giving; high school counselor ratings of colleges; and graduation rate. *U.S. News & World Report, "America's Best Colleges 2015"*

PRESIDENTIAL ELECTION

2012 Presidential Election Results

Area	Obama (%)	Romney (%)	Other (%)
Hillsborough County	52.8	46.2	1.0
U.S.	51.0	47.2	1.8

Note: Results may not add to 100% due to rounding
Source: Dave Leip's Atlas of U.S. Presidential Elections

EMPLOYERS

Major Employers

Company Name	Industry
American Staff Management	Employee leasing service
City of Tampa	County supervisor of education, except school board
Diversified Maintenance Systems	Building and maintenance services, nec
Florida Hospital Tampa Bay Division	General medical and surgical hospitals
Granite Services International	Help supply services
H. Lee Moffitt Cancer Center	Physicians' office, including specialists
Honeywell International	Aircraft engines and engine parts
JPMorgan Chase Bank National Association	National commerical banks
Morton Plant Hospital Association	General medical and surgical hospitals
Raymond James & Associates	Security brokers and dealers
Seven-One-Seven Parking Services	Valet parking
SHC Holding	Convalescent home with continuous care
Sykes Enterprisesorporated	Business services, nec
Tech Data Corporation	Computers, peripherals, and software
United States Postal Service	Us postal service
University of South Florida	Colleges and universities
Usani Sub	Television broadcasting stations
Verizon Data Services	Data processing service
Veterans Health Administration	Administration of veterans' affairs
Veterans Health Administration	General medical and surgical hospitals

Note: Companies shown are located within the Tampa-St. Petersburg-Clearwater, FL Metropolitan Statistical Area.
Source: Hoovers.com; Wikipedia

Best Companies to Work For

Moffitt Cancer Center, headquartered in Tampa, is among the "100 Best Companies for Working Mothers." Criteria: leave policies, workforce representation, benefits, child care, advancement programs, and flexibility policies. This year *Working Mother* gave particular weight to representation of women, advancement programs and flex. *Working Mother, "100 Best Companies 2014"*

PUBLIC SAFETY

Crime Rate

Area	All Crimes	Violent Crimes				Property Crimes		
		Murder	Forcible Rape	Robbery	Aggrav. Assault	Burglary	Larceny -Theft	Motor Vehicle Theft
City	3,108.3	8.0	22.2	165.1	401.6	555.1	1,799.0	157.4
Suburbs[1]	3,131.4	3.8	32.2	80.4	252.2	628.5	1,981.3	153.0
Metro[2]	3,128.6	4.3	31.0	90.8	270.5	619.5	1,959.0	153.6
U.S.	3,098.6	4.5	25.2	109.1	229.1	610.0	1,899.4	221.3

Note: Figures are crimes per 100,000 population; (1) All areas within the metro area that are located outside the city limits; (2) Figures cover the Tampa-St. Petersburg-Clearwater, FL Metropolitan Statistical Area—see Appendix B for areas included
Source: FBI Uniform Crime Reports, 2013

Hate Crimes

Area	Number of Quarters Reported	Number of Incidents per Bias Motivation						
		Race	Religion	Sexual Orientation	Ethnicity	Disability	Gender	Gender Identity
City	4	0	0	0	0	0	0	0
U.S.	4	2,871	1,031	1,233	655	83	18	31

Source: Federal Bureau of Investigation, Hate Crime Statistics 2013

Identity Theft Consumer Complaints

Area	Complaints	Complaints per 100,000 Population	Rank[2]
MSA[1]	3,956	137.8	17
U.S.	332,646	104.3	-

Note: (1) Figures cover the Tampa-St. Petersburg-Clearwater, FL Metropolitan Statistical Area—see Appendix B for areas included; (2) Rank ranges from 1 to 380 where 1 indicates greatest number of identity theft complaints per 100,000 population
Source: Federal Trade Commission, Consumer Sentinel Network Data Book for January–December 2014

Fraud and Other Consumer Complaints

Area	Complaints	Complaints per 100,000 Population	Rank[2]
MSA[1]	14,966	521.4	18
U.S.	2,250,205	705.7	-

Note: (1) Figures cover the Tampa-St. Petersburg-Clearwater, FL Metropolitan Statistical Area—see Appendix B for areas included; (2) Rank ranges from 1 to 380 where 1 indicates greatest number of identity theft complaints per 100,000 population
Source: Federal Trade Commission, Consumer Sentinel Network Data Book for January–December 2014

RECREATION

Culture

Dance[1]	Theatre[1]	Instrumental Music[1]	Vocal Music[1]	Series and Festivals	Museums and Art Galleries[2]	Zoos and Aquariums[3]
0	5	0	2	0	32	3

Note: (1) Professional perfoming groups; (2) Based on organizations with SIC code 8412; (3) AZA-accredited
Source: The Grey House Performing Arts Directory, 2015-16; Association of Zoos & Aquariums, AZA Member Zoos & Aquariums, April 2015; www.AccuLeads.com, April 2015

Professional Sports Teams

Team Name	League	Year Established
Tampa Bay Buccaneers	National Football League (NFL)	1976
Tampa Bay Lightning	National Hockey League (NHL)	1993
Tampa Bay Rays	Major League Baseball (MLB)	1998

Note: Includes teams located in the Tampa-St. Petersburg-Clearwater, FL Metropolitan Statistical Area.
Source: Wikipedia, Major Professional Sports Teams of the United States and Canada, April 2015

CLIMATE

Average and Extreme Temperatures

Temperature	Jan	Feb	Mar	Apr	May	Jun	Jul	Aug	Sep	Oct	Nov	Dec	Yr.
Extreme High (°F)	85	88	91	93	98	99	97	98	96	94	90	86	99
Average High (°F)	70	72	76	82	87	90	90	90	89	84	77	72	82
Average Temp. (°F)	60	62	67	72	78	81	82	83	81	75	68	62	73
Average Low (°F)	50	52	56	61	67	73	74	74	73	66	57	52	63
Extreme Low (°F)	21	24	29	40	49	53	63	67	57	40	23	18	18

Note: Figures cover the years 1948-1990
Source: National Climatic Data Center, International Station Meteorological Climate Summary, 9/96

Average Precipitation/Snowfall/Humidity

Precip./Humidity	Jan	Feb	Mar	Apr	May	Jun	Jul	Aug	Sep	Oct	Nov	Dec	Yr.
Avg. Precip. (in.)	2.1	2.8	3.5	1.8	3.0	5.6	7.3	7.9	6.5	2.3	1.8	2.1	46.7
Avg. Snowfall (in.)	Tr	Tr	Tr	0	0	0	0	0	0	0	0	Tr	Tr
Avg. Rel. Hum. 7am (%)	87	87	86	86	85	86	88	90	91	89	88	87	88
Avg. Rel. Hum. 4pm (%)	56	55	54	51	52	60	65	66	64	57	56	57	58

Note: Figures cover the years 1948-1990; Tr = Trace amounts (<0.05 in. of rain; <0.5 in. of snow)
Source: National Climatic Data Center, International Station Meteorological Climate Summary, 9/96

Weather Conditions

Temperature			Daytime Sky			Precipitation		
32°F & below	45°F & below	90°F & above	Clear	Partly cloudy	Cloudy	0.01 inch or more precip.	0.1 inch or more snow/ice	Thunder-storms
3	35	85	81	204	80	107	< 1	87

Note: Figures are average number of days per year and cover the years 1948-1990
Source: National Climatic Data Center, International Station Meteorological Climate Summary, 9/96

HAZARDOUS WASTE

Superfund Sites

Tampa has eight hazardous waste sites on the EPA's Superfund Final National Priorities List: **Alaric Area Ground Water Plume; Helena Chemical Co. (Tampa Plant); MRI Corp (Tampa); Peak Oil Co./Bay Drum Co.; Raleigh Street Dump; Reeves Southeastern Galvanizing Corp.; Southern Solvents, Inc.; Stauffer Chemical Co (Tampa)**. There are a total of 1,322 Superfund sites on the list in the U.S. *U.S. Environmental Protection Agency, Final National Priorities List, April 14, 2015*

AIR & WATER QUALITY

Air Quality Trends: Ozone

	2004	2005	2006	2007	2008	2009	2010	2011	2012	2013
MSA[1]	0.074	0.075	0.074	0.076	0.075	0.064	0.067	0.071	0.066	0.066

Note: (1) Data covers the Tampa-St. Petersburg-Clearwater, FL Metropolitan Statistical Area—see Appendix B for areas included. The values shown are the composite ozone concentration averages among trend sites based on the highest fourth daily maximum 8-hour concentration in parts per million. These trends are based on sites having an adequate record of monitoring data during the trend period. Data from exceptional events are included.
Source: U.S. Environmental Protection Agency, Air Quality Monitoring Information, "Air Quality Trends by City, 2000-2013"

Air Quality Index

Area	Percent of Days when Air Quality was...[2]					AQI Statistics[2]	
	Good	Moderate	Unhealthy for Sensitive Groups	Unhealthy	Very Unhealthy	Maximum	Median
MSA[1]	64.1	35.6	0.3	0.0	0.0	112	45

Note: (1) Data covers the Tampa-St. Petersburg-Clearwater, FL Metropolitan Statistical Area—see Appendix B for areas included; (2) Based on 365 days with AQI data in 2014. Air Quality Index (AQI) is an index for reporting daily air quality. EPA calculates the AQI for five major air pollutants regulated by the Clean Air Act: ground-level ozone, particle pollution (aka particulate matter), carbon monoxide, sulfur dioxide, and nitrogen dioxide. The AQI runs from 0 to 500. The higher the AQI value, the greater the level of air pollution and the greater the health concern. There are six AQI categories: "Good" AQI is between 0 and 50. Air quality is considered satisfactory; "Moderate" AQI is between 51 and 100. Air quality is acceptable; "Unhealthy for Sensitive Groups" When AQI values are between 101 and 150, members of sensitive groups may experience health effects; "Unhealthy" When AQI values are between 151 and 200 everyone may begin to experience health effects; "Very Unhealthy" AQI values between 201 and 300 trigger a health alert; "Hazardous" AQI values over 300 trigger warnings of emergency conditions (not shown).
Source: U.S. Environmental Protection Agency, Air Quality Index Report, 2014

Air Quality Index Pollutants

Area	Percent of Days when AQI Pollutant was...[2]					
	Carbon Monoxide	Nitrogen Dioxide	Ozone	Sulfur Dioxide	Particulate Matter 2.5	Particulate Matter 10
MSA[1]	0.0	0.5	35.9	5.8	57.8	0.0

Note: (1) Data covers the Tampa-St. Petersburg-Clearwater, FL Metropolitan Statistical Area—see Appendix B for areas included; (2) Based on 365 days with AQI data in 2014. The Air Quality Index (AQI) is an index for reporting daily air quality. EPA calculates the AQI for five major air pollutants regulated by the Clean Air Act: ground-level ozone, particle pollution (also known as particulate matter), carbon monoxide, sulfur dioxide, and nitrogen dioxide. The AQI runs from 0 to 500. The higher the AQI value, the greater the level of air pollution and the greater the health concern.
Source: U.S. Environmental Protection Agency, Air Quality Index Report, 2014

Maximum Air Pollutant Concentrations: Particulate Matter, Ozone, CO and Lead

	Particulate Matter 10 (ug/m^3)	Particulate Matter 2.5 Wtd AM (ug/m^3)	Particulate Matter 2.5 24-Hr (ug/m^3)	Ozone (ppm)	Carbon Monoxide (ppm)	Lead (ug/m^3)
MSA[1] Level	49	6.5	15	0.07	1	0.49
NAAQS[2]	150	15	35	0.075	9	0.15
Met NAAQS[2]	Yes	Yes	Yes	Yes	Yes	No

Note: (1) Data covers the Tampa-St. Petersburg-Clearwater, FL Metropolitan Statistical Area—see Appendix B for areas included; Data from exceptional events are included; (2) National Ambient Air Quality Standards; ppm = parts per million; ug/m^3 = micrograms per cubic meter; n/a not available.

Concentrations: Particulate Matter 10 (coarse particulate)—highest second maximum 24-hour concentration; Particulate Matter 2.5 Wtd AM (fine particulate)—highest weighted annual mean concentration; Particulate Matter 2.5 24-Hour (fine particulate)—highest 98th percentile 24-hour concentration; Ozone—highest fourth daily maximum 8-hour concentration; Carbon Monoxide—highest second maximum non-overlapping 8-hour concentration; Lead—maximum running 3-month average

Source: U.S. Environmental Protection Agency, Air Quality Monitoring Information, "Air Quality Statistics by City, 2013"

Maximum Air Pollutant Concentrations: Nitrogen Dioxide and Sulfur Dioxide

	Nitrogen Dioxide AM (ppb)	Nitrogen Dioxide 1-Hr (ppb)	Sulfur Dioxide AM (ppb)	Sulfur Dioxide 1-Hr (ppb)	Sulfur Dioxide 24-Hr (ppb)
MSA[1] Level	5	34	n/a	68	n/a
NAAQS[2]	53	100	30	75	140
Met NAAQS[2]	Yes	Yes	n/a	Yes	n/a

Note: (1) Data covers the Tampa-St. Petersburg-Clearwater, FL Metropolitan Statistical Area—see Appendix B for areas included; Data from exceptional events are included; (2) National Ambient Air Quality Standards; ppm = parts per million; ug/m^3 = micrograms per cubic meter; n/a not available.

Concentrations: Nitrogen Dioxide AM—highest arithmetic mean concentration; Nitrogen Dioxide 1-Hr—highest 98th percentile 1-hour daily maximum concentration; Sulfur Dioxide AM—highest annual mean concentration; Sulfur Dioxide 1-Hr—highest 99th percentile 1-hour daily maximum concentration; Sulfur Dioxide 24-Hr—highest second maximum 24-hour concentration

Source: U.S. Environmental Protection Agency, Air Quality Monitoring Information, "Air Quality Statistics by City, 2013"

Drinking Water

Water System Name	Pop. Served	Primary Water Source Type	Violations[1] Health Based	Violations[1] Monitoring/ Reporting
City of Tampa Water Department	588,000	Surface	0	0

Note: (1) Based on violation data from January 1, 2014 to December 31, 2014 (includes unresolved violations from earlier years)

Source: U.S. Environmental Protection Agency, Office of Ground Water and Drinking Water, Safe Drinking Water Information System (based on data extracted January 27, 2015)

Tyler, Texas

Background

Just 90 miles east of Dallas Fort Worth, Texas lies the city of Tyler, named after the 10th President of the United States. President John Tyler was instrumental in admitting Texas to the Union, as the 48th state, in 1845. The town of Tyler was incorporated in 1850. In 1860 over 350 of the 1,021 residents were slaves, on which the town's economy depended on. During the Civil War, Tyler was the largest Confederate ordnance plant and the home of Camp Ford, one of the largest prison camps. Post war brought challenges to Tyler due to both the loss of slaves and the fact that the railroad company bypassed the town. In 1874, the Hudson & Great Northern Railway began service to Tyler. Tyler then "tapped" the Texas Pacific Railway and created a connection to Fergerson in 1877 known as the "Tyler Tap". The Tyler Tap Railroad later became the St. Louis Southwestern Railway.

With the influx of railroad service, Tyler grew at steady pace and by 1890 its population tripled. With agriculture, and especially cotton, to fuel it's economy, Tyler continued to prosper. Sixty percent of Tyler's agricultural income came from the production of cotton. The St. Louis Western Railroad referred to its line as The Cotton Belt Route. In the late 1890s, the emergence of fruit trees, mostly peaches, became increasingly important to the county's economy. Unfortunately, there was a peach blight that nearly destroy all the peach orchard. Tyler's farmers converted their orchards to produce roses, and the perfect combination of rich soil and good climate attributed to Tyler's booming rose industry. The Tyler Rose Festival became a major event in 1933. By 1940, more than half of all rose bushes sold in the United States came from Tyler and its surrounding area.

While roses were fueling the economy, Tyler's good fortune continued with the discovery of oil fields in the mid 1930s. The new oil industry propelled Tyler's economy once again and the population continued to grow to over 28,000 by 1940. Soon oil companies and developers were flocking to Tyler, and it became a regional leader in the oil and gas production industry. In the late 1940s, Tyler economic growth continued in agriculture, manufacturing, and retail. Through the 1970s, Tyler's oil industry continued to dominate its economy. With the continued growth came other strong industries such as furniture, clothing and metal fabricating. In 2013, the population of Tyler was over 110,000.

Today, the Texas Rose Festival is still an annual event in Tyler. The Rose Parade is a major attraction, drawing thousands of tourists. Tyler, now called the Rose Capitol of America, still supplies over one third of the country's rose bushes.

Other attractions in Tyler include the Cotton Belt Depot Museum, housed in the original 1905 depot station. On display at the museum are all things from the "Cotton Belt" era including railroad artifacts and paintings. Lionel Electric Trains houses its "Brag Train Collection" at the museum featuring over 1600 cars and 200 locomotives. Even though the Depot is not active, visitors can still experience the Union Pacific Railroad passing by the station.

The Smith County Historical Society manages Camp Ford Historic Park, where tourists can visit the site of the largest Confederate Army's POW camp. On July 4th of 1865, the original prison was destroyed, but the park offers a reproduction of the prison's gate, cabins and a history of the site. The Tyler Sons of Confederate Veterans Camp sponsor an annual "living event" demonstrating a soldier's life within the prison camp.

Tyler Rose Museum also showcases Tyler's history, with costumes and memorabilia that were part of previous Festivals. Theater presentations and animations enhance the importance of roses in Tyler's history.

Rankings

Business/Finance Rankings

- The Tyler metro area appeared on the Milken Institute "2013 Best Performing Cities" list. Rank: #46 out of 179 small metro areas. Criteria: job growth; wage and salary growth; high-tech output growth.*Milken Institute, "Best-Performing Cities 2014," January 2015*
- *Forbes* ranked 184 smaller metro areas to determine the nation's "Best Small Places for Business and Careers." The Tyler metro area was ranked #79. Criteria: costs (business and living); job growth (past and projected); income growth; educational attainment (college and high school); projected economic growth; cultural and recreational opportunities; net migration patterns; number of highly ranked colleges. *Forbes, "The Best Small Places for Business and Careers 2014," July 23, 2014*

Environmental Rankings

- The Tyler metro area came in at #323 for the relative comfort of its climate on Sperling's list of "chill cities," as measured by the Sperling Heat Index. All 361 metro areas are included. Criteria included daytime high temperatures, nighttime low temperatures, dew point, and relative humidity at the high temperatures. *www.bertsperling.com, "Sperling's Chill Cities," July 18, 2013*
- Sperling's BestPlaces assessed 379 metropolitan areas of the United States for the likelihood of dangerously extreme weather events or earthquakes. In general the Southeast and South-Central regions have the highest risk of weather extremes and earthquakes, while the Pacific Northwest enjoys the lowest risk. Of the least risky metropolitan areas, the Tyler metro area was ranked #353. *www.bestplaces.net, "Safest Places from Natural Disasters," April 2011*

Real Estate Rankings

- Tyler was ranked #125 out of 226 metro areas in terms of housing affordability in 2014 by the National Association of Home Builders (#1 = most affordable). The NAHB-Wells Fargo Housing Opportunity Index (HOI) for a given area is defined as the share of homes sold in that area that would have been affordable to a family earning the local median income, based on standard mortgage underwriting criteria. *National Association of Home Builders®, NAHB-Wells Fargo Housing Opportunity Index, 4th Quarter 2014*

Safety Rankings

- The National Insurance Crime Bureau ranked 380 metro areas in the U.S. in terms of per capita rates of vehicle theft. The Tyler metro area ranked #152 (#1 = highest rate). Criteria: number of vehicle theft offenses per 100,000 inhabitants in 2012. *National Insurance Crime Bureau, "Hot Spots 2012," June 26, 2013*

Seniors/Retirement Rankings

- From its Best Cities for Successful Aging indexes, the Milken Institute generated rankings for metropolitan areas, weighing data in eight categories—health care, wellness, living arrangements, transportation, financial characteristics, education and employment opportunities, community engagement, and overall livability. The Tyler metro area was ranked #43 overall in the small metro area category. *Milken Institute, "Best Cities for Successful Aging, 2014"*

Business Environment

CITY FINANCES

City Government Finances

Component	2012 ($000)	2012 ($ per capita)
Total Revenues	162,437	1,676
Total Expenditures	149,250	1,540
Debt Outstanding	428,220	4,419
Cash and Securities[1]	456,109	4,707

Note: (1) Cash and security holdings of a government at the close of its fiscal year, including those of its dependent agencies, utilities, and liquor stores.
Source: U.S Census Bureau, State & Local Government Finances 2012

City Government Revenue by Source

Source	2012 ($000)	2012 ($ per capita)
General Revenue		
From Federal Government	12,895	133
From State Government	2,052	21
From Local Governments	5	0
Taxes		
Property	14,141	146
Sales and Gross Receipts	46,647	481
Personal Income	0	0
Corporate Income	0	0
Motor Vehicle License	0	0
Other Taxes	1,134	12
Current Charges	25,974	268
Liquor Store	0	0
Utility	23,109	238
Employee Retirement	10,451	108

Source: U.S Census Bureau, State & Local Government Finances 2012

City Government Expenditures by Function

Function	2012 ($000)	2012 ($ per capita)	2012 (%)
General Direct Expenditures			
Air Transportation	3,078	32	2.1
Corrections	0	0	0.0
Education	0	0	0.0
Employment Security Administration	0	0	0.0
Financial Administration	1,029	11	0.7
Fire Protection	14,892	154	10.0
General Public Buildings	0	0	0.0
Governmental Administration, Other	4,502	46	3.0
Health	0	0	0.0
Highways	13,531	140	9.1
Hospitals	0	0	0.0
Housing and Community Development	8,000	83	5.4
Interest on General Debt	17,619	182	11.8
Judicial and Legal	3,086	32	2.1
Libraries	1,516	16	1.0
Parking	0	0	0.0
Parks and Recreation	4,206	43	2.8
Police Protection	22,245	230	14.9
Public Welfare	0	0	0.0
Sewerage	9,807	101	6.6
Solid Waste Management	10,763	111	7.2
Veterans' Services	0	0	0.0
Liquor Store	0	0	0.0
Utility	26,216	271	17.6
Employee Retirement	2,885	30	1.9

Source: U.S Census Bureau, State & Local Government Finances 2012

DEMOGRAPHICS

Population Growth

Area	1990 Census	2000 Census	2010 Census	Population Growth (%) 1990-2000	Population Growth (%) 2000-2010
City	77,653	83,650	96,900	7.7	15.8
MSA[1]	151,309	174,706	209,714	15.5	20.0
U.S.	248,709,873	281,421,906	308,745,538	13.2	9.7

Note: (1) Figures cover the Tyler, TX Metropolitan Statistical Area—see Appendix B for areas included
Source: U.S. Census Bureau, Census 1990, 2000, 2010

Household Size

Area	Persons in Household (%) One	Two	Three	Four	Five	Six	Seven or More	Average Household Size
City	32.7	32.0	16.5	11.2	3.4	2.0	2.1	2.49
MSA[1]	26.7	34.9	15.6	12.3	5.9	2.5	2.1	2.65
U.S.	27.7	33.6	15.7	13.1	6.0	2.3	1.5	2.64

Note: (1) Figures cover the Tyler, TX Metropolitan Statistical Area—see Appendix B for areas included
Source: U.S. Census Bureau, 2011-2013 American Community Survey 3-Year Estimates

Race

Area	White Alone[2] (%)	Black Alone[2] (%)	Asian Alone[2] (%)	AIAN[3] Alone[2] (%)	NHOPI[4] Alone[2] (%)	Other Race Alone[2] (%)	Two or More Races (%)
City	69.3	23.9	2.1	0.4	0.0	2.5	1.8
MSA[1]	76.7	18.1	1.3	0.3	0.0	2.1	1.5
U.S.	73.9	12.6	5.0	0.8	0.2	4.7	2.9

Note: (1) Figures cover the Tyler, TX Metropolitan Statistical Area—see Appendix B for areas included; (2) Alone is defined as not being in combination with one or more other races; (3) American Indian and Alaska Native; (4) Native Hawaiian and Other Pacific Islander
Source: U.S. Census Bureau, 2011-2013 American Community Survey 3-Year Estimates

Hispanic or Latino Origin

Area	Total (%)	Mexican (%)	Puerto Rican (%)	Cuban (%)	Other (%)
City	22.8	20.8	0.2	0.1	1.8
MSA[1]	18.0	16.3	0.2	0.1	1.4
U.S.	16.9	10.8	1.6	0.6	3.8

Note: Persons of Hispanic or Latino origin can be of any race; (1) Figures cover the Tyler, TX Metropolitan Statistical Area—see Appendix B for areas included
Source: U.S. Census Bureau, 2011-2013 American Community Survey 3-Year Estimates

Segregation

Type	Segregation Indices[1] 1990	2000	2010	2010 Rank[2]	Percent Change 1990-2000	1990-2010	2000-2010
Black/White	n/a	n/a	n/a	n/a	n/a	n/a	n/a
Asian/White	n/a	n/a	n/a	n/a	n/a	n/a	n/a
Hispanic/White	n/a	n/a	n/a	n/a	n/a	n/a	n/a

Note: All figures cover the Metropolitan Statistical Area—see Appendix B for areas included; Figures are based on an analysis of 1990, 2000, and 2010 Census Decennial Census tract data by William H. Frey, Brookings Institution and the University of Michigan Social Science Data Analysis Network. In this analysis all racial groups (whites, blacks, and asians) are non-Hispanic members of those races. Hispanics are shown as a separate category;
(1) Segregation Indices are Dissimilarity Indices that measure the degree to which the minority group is distributed differently than whites across census tracts. They range from 0 (complete integration) to 100 (complete segregation) where the value indicates the percentage of the minority group that needs to move to be distributed exactly like whites; (2) Ranges from 1 (most segregated) to 102 (least segregated); n/a not available.
Source: www.CensusScope.org

Ancestry

Area	German	Irish	English	American	Italian	Polish	French[2]	Scottish	Dutch
City	9.0	9.2	8.2	7.1	2.3	0.8	2.5	1.6	0.9
MSA[1]	10.5	11.1	9.2	9.4	1.9	1.0	3.1	2.0	1.2
U.S.	14.9	10.8	8.0	7.4	5.5	3.0	2.7	1.7	1.4

Note: Figures are the percentage of the total population reporting a particular ancestry. The nine most commonly reported ancestries in the U.S. are shown. Figures include multiple ancestries (e.g. if a person reported being Irish and Italian, they were included in both columns); (1) Figures cover the Tyler, TX Metropolitan Statistical Area—see Appendix B for areas included; (2) Excludes Basque
Source: U.S. Census Bureau, 2011-2013 American Community Survey 3-Year Estimates

Foreign-Born Population

Area	Percent of Population Born in								
	Any Foreign Country	Mexico	Asia	Europe	Carribean	South America	Central America[2]	Africa	Canada
City	n/a	n/a	n/a	n/a	n/a	n/a	n/a	n/a	n/a
MSA[1]	n/a	n/a	n/a	n/a	n/a	n/a	n/a	n/a	n/a
U.S.	13.0	3.7	3.8	1.5	1.2	0.9	1.0	0.6	0.3

Note: (1) Figures cover the Tyler, TX Metropolitan Statistical Area—see Appendix B for areas included; (2) Excludes Mexico.
Source: U.S. Census Bureau, 2011-2013 American Community Survey 3-Year Estimates

Marital Status

Area	Never Married	Now Married[2]	Separated	Widowed	Divorced
City	34.0	42.3	3.2	7.4	13.1
MSA[1]	27.2	50.8	2.6	7.1	12.2
U.S.	32.7	48.1	2.2	6.0	11.0

Note: Figures are percentages and cover the population 15 years of age and older; (1) Figures cover the Tyler, TX Metropolitan Statistical Area—see Appendix B for areas included; (2) Excludes separated
Source: U.S. Census Bureau, 2011-2013 American Community Survey 3-Year Estimates

Disability Status

Area	All Ages	Under 18 Years Old	18 to 64 Years Old	65 Years and Over
City	12.5	4.9	10.1	35.2
MSA[1]	13.1	5.2	11.2	34.6
U.S.	12.3	4.1	10.2	36.3

Note: Figures show percent of the civilian noninstitutionalized population that reported having a disability. Disability status is determined from from six types of difficulty: vision, hearing, cognitive, ambulatory, self-care, and independent living. For children under 5 years old, hearing and vision difficulty are used to determine disability status. For children between the ages of 5 and 14, disability status is determined from hearing, vision, cognitive, ambulatory, and self-care difficulties. For people aged 15 years and older, they are considered to have a disability if they have difficulty with any one of the six difficulty types; (1) Figures cover the Tyler, TX Metropolitan Statistical Area—see Appendix B for areas included.
Source: U.S. Census Bureau, 2011-2013 American Community Survey 3-Year Estimates

Age

Area	Percent of Population									Median Age
	Under Age 5	Age 5–19	Age 20–34	Age 35–44	Age 45–54	Age 55–64	Age 65–74	Age 75–84	Age 85+	
City	6.2	20.4	25.0	11.5	11.0	10.8	7.1	5.4	2.6	33.7
MSA[1]	7.0	21.1	20.8	12.0	12.6	11.7	8.1	4.8	1.9	35.9
U.S.	6.4	19.9	20.7	12.9	14.1	12.3	7.6	4.2	1.9	37.4

Note: (1) Figures cover the Tyler, TX Metropolitan Statistical Area—see Appendix B for areas included
Source: U.S. Census Bureau, 2011-2013 American Community Survey 3-Year Estimates

Gender

Area	Males	Females	Males per 100 Females
City	46,121	53,283	86.6
MSA[1]	103,615	110,914	93.4
U.S.	154,451,010	159,410,713	96.9

Note: (1) Figures cover the Tyler, TX Metropolitan Statistical Area—see Appendix B for areas included
Source: U.S. Census Bureau, 2011-2013 American Community Survey 3-Year Estimates

Religious Groups by Family

Area	Catholic	Baptist	Non-Den.	Methodist[2]	Lutheran	LDS[3]	Pente-costal	Presby-terian[4]	Muslim[5]	Judaism
MSA[1]	12.2	33.6	9.0	6.4	0.6	1.2	5.1	0.7	0.4	0.1
U.S.	19.1	9.3	4.0	4.0	2.3	2.0	1.9	1.6	0.8	0.7

Note: Figures are the number of adherents as a percentage of the total population; (1) Figures cover the Tyler, TX Metropolitan Statistical Area—see Appendix B for areas included; (2) Methodist/Pietist; (3) Latter Day Saints; (4) Reformed; (5) Figures are estimates
Source: Association of Statisticians of American Religious Bodies, 2010 U.S. Religion Census: Religious Congregations & Membership Study

Religious Groups by Tradition

Area	Catholic	Evangelical Protestant	Mainline Protestant	Other Tradition	Black Protestant	Orthodox
MSA[1]	12.2	45.5	7.4	1.7	4.1	<0.1
U.S.	19.1	16.2	7.3	4.3	1.6	0.3

Note: Figures are the number of adherents as a percentage of the total population; (1) Figures cover the Tyler, TX Metropolitan Statistical Area—see Appendix B for areas included
Source: Association of Statisticians of American Religious Bodies, 2010 U.S. Religion Census: Religious Congregations & Membership Study

ECONOMY

Gross Metropolitan Product

Area	2012	2013	2014	2015	Rank[2]
MSA[1]	9.4	9.7	10.1	10.5	194

Note: Figures are in billions of dollars; (1) Figures cover the Tyler, TX Metropolitan Statistical Area—see Appendix B for areas included; (2) Rank is based on 2015 data and ranges from 1 to 363
Source: The U.S. Conference of Mayors, U.S. Metro Economies: GMP and Employment 2013-2015, June 2014

Economic Growth

Area	2010-12 (%)	2013 (%)	2014 (%)	2015 (%)	Rank[2]
MSA[1]	1.7	2.2	1.2	3.9	35
U.S.	2.1	2.0	2.3	3.2	–

Note: Figures are real gross metropolitan product (GMP) growth rates and represent annual average percent change; (1) Figures cover the Tyler, TX Metropolitan Statistical Area—see Appendix B for areas included; (2) Rank is based on 2015 data and ranges from 1 to 363
Source: The U.S. Conference of Mayors, U.S. Metro Economies: GMP and Employment 2013-2015, June 2014

Metropolitan Area Exports

Area	2008	2009	2010	2011	2012	2013	Rank[2]
MSA[1]	147.1	130.1	184.4	249.6	221.1	219.6	302

Note: Figures are in millions of dollars; (1) Figures cover the Tyler, TX Metropolitan Statistical Area—see Appendix B for areas included; (2) Rank is based on 2013 data and ranges from 1 to 387
Source: U.S. Department of Commerce, International Trade Administration, Office of Trade & Industry Information, Manufacturing & Services, data extracted April 3, 2015

Building Permits

Area	Single-Family			Multi-Family			Total		
	2013	2014	Pct. Chg.	2013	2014	Pct. Chg.	2013	2014	Pct. Chg.
City	271	268	-1.1	0	12	-	271	280	3.3
MSA[1]	373	377	1.1	0	12	-	373	389	4.3
U.S.	620,802	634,597	2.2	370,020	411,766	11.3	990,822	1,046,363	5.6

Note: (1) Figures cover the Tyler, TX Metropolitan Statistical Area—see Appendix B for areas included; Figures represent new, privately-owned housing units authorized (unadjusted data); All permit data are based on estimates with imputation.
Source: U.S. Census Bureau, Manufacturing, Mining, and Construction Statistics, Building Permits, 2013, 2014

Bankruptcy Filings

Area	Business Filings			Nonbusiness Filings		
	2013	2014	% Chg.	2013	2014	% Chg.
Smith County	20	14	-30.0	312	307	-1.6
U.S.	33,212	26,983	-18.8	1,038,720	909,812	-12.4

Note: Business filings include Chapter 7, Chapter 11, Chapter 12, and Chapter 13; Nonbusiness filings include Chapter 7, Chapter 11, and Chapter 13
Source: Administrative Office of the U.S. Courts, Business and Nonbusiness Bankruptcy, County Cases Commenced by Chapter of the Bankruptcy Code, During the 12- Month Period Ending December 31, 2013 and Business and Nonbusiness Bankruptcy, County Cases Commenced by Chapter of the Bankruptcy Code, During the 12- Month Period Ending December 31, 2014

Housing Vacancy Rates

Area	Gross Vacancy Rate[2] (%)			Year-Round Vacancy Rate[3] (%)			Rental Vacancy Rate[4] (%)			Homeowner Vacancy Rate[5] (%)		
	2012	2013	2014	2012	2013	2014	2012	2013	2014	2012	2013	2014
MSA[1]	n/a	n/a	n/a	n/a	n/a	n/a	n/a	n/a	n/a	n/a	n/a	n/a
U.S.	13.8	13.6	13.4	10.8	10.7	10.4	8.7	8.3	7.6	2.0	2.0	1.9

Note: (1) Figures cover the Tyler, TX Metropolitan Statistical Area—see Appendix B for areas included; (2) The percentage of the total housing inventory that is vacant; (3) The percentage of the housing inventory (excluding seasonal units) that is year-round vacant; (4) The percentage of rental inventory that is vacant for rent; (5) The percentage of homeowner inventory that is vacant for sale; n/a not available
Source: U.S. Census Bureau, Housing Vacancies and Homeownership Annual Statistics: 2014

INCOME

Income

Area	Per Capita ($)	Median Household ($)	Average Household ($)
City	26,733	43,239	66,559
MSA[1]	24,846	46,436	65,051
U.S.	27,884	52,176	72,897

Note: (1) Figures cover the Tyler, TX Metropolitan Statistical Area—see Appendix B for areas included
Source: U.S. Census Bureau, 2011-2013 American Community Survey 3-Year Estimates

Household Income Distribution

Area	Percent of Households Earning							
	Under $15,000	$15,000 -24,999	$25,000 -34,999	$35,000 -49,999	$50,000 -74,999	$75,000 -99,000	$100,000 -149,999	$150,000 and up
City	14.8	14.0	12.0	15.2	17.6	9.5	9.2	7.6
MSA[1]	13.2	12.5	12.8	14.2	18.4	11.9	10.3	6.7
U.S.	13.0	10.9	10.3	13.6	17.9	11.9	12.7	9.6

Note: (1) Figures cover the Tyler, TX Metropolitan Statistical Area—see Appendix B for areas included
Source: U.S. Census Bureau, 2011-2013 American Community Survey 3-Year Estimates

Poverty Rate

Area	All Ages	Under 18 Years Old	18 to 64 Years Old	65 Years and Over
City	20.8	29.9	19.5	11.6
MSA[1]	17.4	24.3	15.9	11.3
U.S.	15.9	22.4	14.8	9.5

Note: Figures are percentage of people whose income during the past 12 months was below the poverty level; (1) Figures cover the Tyler, TX Metropolitan Statistical Area—see Appendix B for areas included
Source: U.S. Census Bureau, 2011-2013 American Community Survey 3-Year Estimates

EMPLOYMENT

Labor Force and Employment

Area	Civilian Labor Force			Workers Employed		
	Dec. 2013	Dec. 2014	% Chg.	Dec. 2013	Dec. 2014	% Chg.
City	48,500	49,440	1.9	45,914	47,496	3.4
MSA[1]	101,802	103,643	1.8	96,086	99,397	3.4
U.S.	154,408,000	155,521,000	0.7	144,423,000	147,190,000	1.9

Note: Data is not seasonally adjusted and covers workers 16 years of age and older; (1) Figures cover the Tyler, TX Metropolitan Statistical Area—see Appendix B for areas included
Source: Bureau of Labor Statistics, Local Area Unemployment Statistics

Unemployment Rate

Area	2014											
	Jan.	Feb.	Mar.	Apr.	May	Jun.	Jul.	Aug.	Sep.	Oct.	Nov.	Dec.
City	5.9	5.8	5.4	4.7	5.0	5.4	5.5	5.1	5.0	4.7	4.5	3.9
MSA[1]	6.1	6.0	5.6	4.9	5.1	5.4	5.5	5.2	5.0	4.7	4.6	4.1
U.S.	7.0	7.0	6.8	5.9	6.1	6.3	6.5	6.3	5.7	5.5	5.5	5.4

Note: Data is not seasonally adjusted and covers workers 16 years of age and older; (1) Figures cover the Tyler, TX Metropolitan Statistical Area—see Appendix B for areas included
Source: Bureau of Labor Statistics, Local Area Unemployment Statistics

Employment by Occupation

Occupation Classification	City (%)	MSA[1] (%)	U.S. (%)
Management, Business, Science, and Arts	36.6	35.3	36.2
Natural Resources, Construction, and Maintenance	9.1	11.1	9.0
Production, Transportation, and Material Moving	11.8	12.5	12.1
Sales and Office	22.9	23.6	24.4
Service	19.6	17.6	18.3

Note: Figures cover employed civilians 16 years of age and older; (1) Figures cover the Tyler, TX Metropolitan Statistical Area—see Appendix B for areas included
Source: U.S. Census Bureau, 2011-2013 American Community Survey 3-Year Estimates

Employment by Industry

Sector	MSA[1]		U.S.
	Number of Employees	Percent of Total	Percent of Total
Construction, Mining, and Logging	6,600	6.5	5.0
Education and Health Services	23,000	22.7	15.5
Financial Activities	4,500	4.4	5.7
Government	13,600	13.4	15.8
Information	2,300	2.3	2.0
Leisure and Hospitality	11,100	11.0	10.3
Manufacturing	5,700	5.6	8.7
Other Services	4,000	4.0	4.0
Professional and Business Services	9,100	9.0	13.8
Retail Trade	13,400	13.2	11.4
Transportation, Warehousing, and Utilities	4,600	4.5	3.9
Wholesale Trade	3,300	3.3	4.2

Note: Figures are non-farm employment as of December 2014. Figures are not seasonally adjusted and include workers 16 years of age and older; (1) Figures cover the Tyler, TX Metropolitan Statistical Area—see Appendix B for areas included; n/a not available
Source: Bureau of Labor Statistics, Current Employment Statistics, Employment, Hours, and Earnings

Occupations with Greatest Projected Employment Growth: 2012 – 2022

Occupation[1]	2012 Employment	2022 Projected Employment	Numeric Employment Change	Percent Employment Change
Combined Food Preparation and Serving Workers, Including Fast Food	285,480	378,000	92,520	32.4
Personal Care Aides	199,230	283,980	84,750	42.5
Retail Salespersons	378,330	439,340	61,010	16.1
Registered Nurses	189,380	242,860	53,480	28.2
Customer Service Representatives	214,240	262,770	48,530	22.7
Waiters and Waitresses	196,390	240,390	44,000	22.4
Janitors and Cleaners, Except Maids and Housekeeping Cleaners	172,120	213,340	41,220	23.9
Laborers and Freight, Stock, and Material Movers, Hand	185,770	226,470	40,700	21.9
Elementary School Teachers, Except Special Education	141,030	180,920	39,890	28.3
Secretaries and Administrative Assistants, Except Legal, Medical, and Executive	190,470	230,220	39,750	20.9

Note: Projections cover Texas; (1) Sorted by numeric employment change
Source: www.projectionscentral.com, State Occupational Projections, 2012–2022 Long-Term Projections

Fastest Growing Occupations: 2012 – 2022

Occupation[1]	2012 Employment	2022 Projected Employment	Numeric Employment Change	Percent Employment Change
Diagnostic Medical Sonographers	4,380	6,900	2,520	57.6
Computer Numerically Controlled Machine Tool Programmers, Metal and Plastic	1,740	2,700	960	54.8
Interpreters and Translators	4,510	6,720	2,210	49.0
Skincare Specialists	5,130	7,620	2,490	48.3
Agents and Business Managers of Artists, Performers, and Athletes	310	450	140	47.4
Petroleum Engineers	19,280	28,010	8,730	45.3
Information Security Analysts	6,640	9,630	2,990	45.0
Insulation Workers, Mechanical	4,460	6,460	2,000	44.6
Cardiovascular Technologists and Technicians	3,950	5,700	1,750	44.3
Physician Assistants	5,470	7,880	2,410	44.2

Note: Projections cover Texas; (1) Sorted by percent employment change and excludes occupations with numeric employment change less than 100
Source: www.projectionscentral.com, State Occupational Projections, 2012–2022 Long-Term Projections

Average Wages

Occupation	$/Hr.	Occupation	$/Hr.
Accountants and Auditors	33.97	Maids and Housekeeping Cleaners	8.46
Automotive Mechanics	21.27	Maintenance and Repair Workers	16.32
Bookkeepers	17.66	Marketing Managers	n/a
Carpenters	15.54	Nuclear Medicine Technologists	n/a
Cashiers	9.11	Nurses, Licensed Practical	20.58
Clerks, General Office	14.60	Nurses, Registered	28.16
Clerks, Receptionists/Information	11.40	Nursing Assistants	9.85
Clerks, Shipping/Receiving	13.28	Packers and Packagers, Hand	11.68
Computer Programmers	29.42	Physical Therapists	44.11
Computer Systems Analysts	31.67	Postal Service Mail Carriers	25.16
Computer User Support Specialists	20.99	Real Estate Brokers	n/a
Cooks, Restaurant	10.26	Retail Salespersons	12.78
Dentists	85.74	Sales Reps., Exc. Tech./Scientific	26.77
Electrical Engineers	53.16	Sales Reps., Tech./Scientific	51.68
Electricians	19.66	Secretaries, Exc. Legal/Med./Exec.	14.99
Financial Managers	53.28	Security Guards	13.71
First-Line Supervisors/Managers, Sales	19.90	Surgeons	n/a
Food Preparation Workers	9.03	Teacher Assistants	11.70
General and Operations Managers	54.59	Teachers, Elementary School	21.50
Hairdressers/Cosmetologists	14.38	Teachers, Secondary School	23.10
Internists	n/a	Telemarketers	n/a
Janitors and Cleaners	9.79	Truck Drivers, Heavy/Tractor-Trailer	18.50
Landscaping/Groundskeeping Workers	10.75	Truck Drivers, Light/Delivery Svcs.	15.84
Lawyers	55.31	Waiters and Waitresses	9.01

Note: Wage data covers the Tyler, TX Metropolitan Statistical Area—see Appendix B for areas included; Hourly wages for elementary/secondary school teachers and teacher assistants were calculated by the editors from annual wage data assuming a 40 hour work week; n/a not available.
Source: Bureau of Labor Statistics, Metro Area Occupational Employment and Wage Estimates, May 2014

TAXES

State Corporate Income Tax Rates

State	Tax Rate (%)	Income Brackets ($)	Num. of Brackets	Financial Institution Tax Rate (%)[a]	Federal Income Tax Ded.
Texas	(y)	–	–	(y)	No

Note: Tax rates as of January 1, 2015; (a) Rates listed are the corporate income tax rate applied to financial institutions or excise taxes based on income. Some states have other taxes based upon the value of deposits or shares; (y) Texas imposes a Franchise Tax, otherwise known as margin tax, imposed on entities with more than $1,030,000 total revenues at rate of 1%, or 0.5% for entities primarily engaged in retail or wholesale trade, on lesser of 70% of total revenues or 100%of gross receipts after deductions for either compensation or cost of goods sold.
Source: Federation of Tax Administrators, "State Corporate Income Tax Rates, 2015"

State Individual Income Tax Rates

State	Tax Rate (%)	Income Brackets ($)	Num. of Brackets	Personal Exempt. ($)[1]		Fed. Inc. Tax Ded.
				Single	Dependents	
Texas	None	–	–	–	–	–

Note: Tax rates as of January 1, 2015; Local- and county-level taxes are not included; n/a not applicable; (1) Married joint filers generally receive double the single exemption
Source: Federation of Tax Administrators, "State Individual Income Tax Rates, 2015"

Various State and Local Tax Rates

State	State and Local Sales and Use (%)	State Sales and Use (%)	Gasoline[1] (¢/gal.)	Cigarette[2] ($/pack)	Spirits[3] ($/gal.)	Wine[4] ($/gal.)	Beer[5] ($/gal.)
Texas	8.25	6.25	20	1.41	2.40 (f)	0.20	0.20 (p)

Note: All tax rates as of January 1, 2015; (1) The American Petroleum Institute has developed a methodology for determining the average tax rate on a gallon of fuel. Rates may include any of the following: excise taxes, environmental fees, storage tank fees, other fees or taxes, general sales tax, and local taxes. In states where gasoline is subject to the general sales tax, or where the fuel tax is based on the average sale price, the average rate determined by API is sensitive to changes in the price of gasoline. States that fully or partially apply general sales taxes to gasoline: CA, CO, GA, IL, IN, MI, NY; (2) The federal excise tax of $1.0066 per pack and local taxes are not included; (3) Rates are those applicable to off-premise sales of 40% alcohol by volume (a.b.v.) distilled spirits in 750ml containers. Local excise taxes are excluded; (4) Rates are those applicable to off-premise sales of 11% a.b.v. non-carbonated wine in 750ml containers; (5) Rates are those applicable to off-premise sales of 4.7% a.b.v. beer in 12 ounce containers; (f) Different rates are also applicable according to alcohol content, place of production, size of container, or place purchased (on- or off-premise or onboard airlines); (p) Local excise taxes are excluded.
Source: Tax Foundation, 2015 Facts & Figures: How Does Your State Compare?

State Business Tax Climate Index Rankings

State	Overall Rank	Corporate Tax Index Rank	Individual Income Tax Index Rank	Sales Tax Index Rank	Unemployment Insurance Tax Index Rank	Property Tax Index Rank
Texas	10	39	6	36	15	36

Note: The index is a measure of how each state's tax laws affect economic performance. The lower the rank, the more favorable a state's tax system is for business. States without a given tax are given a ranking of 1. The scores/rankings for the District of Columbia do not affect other states. The 2015 index represents the tax climate as of July 1, 2014.
Source: Tax Foundation, State Business Tax Climate Index 2015

COMMERCIAL UTILITIES

Typical Monthly Electric Bills

Area	Commercial Service ($/month)		Industrial Service ($/month)	
	1,500 kWh	40 kW demand 14,000 kWh	1,000 kW demand 200,000 kWh	50,000 kW demand 32,500,000 kWh
City	n/a	n/a	n/a	n/a
Average[1]	201	1,653	26,124	2,639,743

Note: Figures are based on annualized 2014 rates; (1) Average based on 180 utilities surveyed; n/a not available
Source: Edison Electric Institute, Typical Bills and Average Rates Report, Summer 2014

TRANSPORTATION

Means of Transportation to Work

Area	Car/Truck/Van		Public Transportation			Bicycle	Walked	Other Means	Worked at Home
	Drove Alone	Car-pooled	Bus	Subway	Railroad				
City	82.0	10.3	0.3	0.0	0.0	0.2	1.7	2.2	3.2
MSA[1]	83.0	10.2	0.3	0.0	0.0	0.1	1.4	1.6	3.3
U.S.	76.4	9.6	2.6	1.8	0.6	0.6	2.8	1.3	4.3

Note: Figures are percentages and cover workers 16 years of age and older; (1) Figures cover the Tyler, TX Metropolitan Statistical Area—see Appendix B for areas included
Source: U.S. Census Bureau, 2011-2013 American Community Survey 3-Year Estimates

Travel Time to Work

Area	Less Than 10 Minutes	10 to 19 Minutes	20 to 29 Minutes	30 to 44 Minutes	45 to 59 Minutes	60 to 89 Minutes	90 Minutes or More
City	21.5	44.2	16.8	11.4	2.5	1.4	2.2
MSA[1]	15.8	35.1	21.1	18.6	3.7	3.0	2.7
U.S.	13.3	29.7	20.9	20.2	7.7	5.7	2.6

Note: Figures are percentages and include workers 16 years old and over; (1) Figures cover the Tyler, TX Metropolitan Statistical Area—see Appendix B for areas included
Source: U.S. Census Bureau, 2011-2013 American Community Survey 3-Year Estimates

Travel Time Index

Area	1985	1990	1995	2000	2005	2010	2011
Urban Area[1]	n/a	n/a	n/a	n/a	n/a	n/a	n/a
Average[2]	1.09	1.14	1.16	1.19	1.23	1.18	1.18

Note: Travel Time Index—the ratio of travel time in the peak period to the travel time at free-flow conditions. For example, a value of 1.30 indicates a 20-minute free-flow trip takes 26 minutes in the peak. Free-flow speeds (60 mph on freeways and 35 mph on principal arterials) are used as the comparison threshold; (1) Data for the Tyler, TX urban area was not available; (2) average of 498 urban areas
Source: Texas Transportation Institute, Urban Mobility Report 2012, December 2012

Public Transportation

Agency Name / Mode of Transportation	Vehicles Operated in Maximum Service	Annual Unlinked Passenger Trips (in thous.)	Annual Passenger Miles (in thous.)
City of Tyler (COT)			
Bus (directly operated)	6	161.6	n/a
Demand Response Taxi (purchased transportation)	24	32.2	n/a

Source: Federal Transit Administration, National Transit Database, 2013

Air Transportation

Airport Name and Code / Type of Service	Passenger Airlines[1]	Passenger Enplanements	Freight Carriers[2]	Freight (lbs.)
Tyler Pounds Regional Airport (TYR)				
Domestic service (U.S. carriers - 2014)	3	86,615	2	956
International service (U.S. carriers - 2013)	0	0	0	0

Note: (1) Includes all U.S.-based major, minor and commuter airlines that carried at least one passenger during the year; (2) Includes all U.S.-based airlines and freight carriers that transported at least one lb. of freight during the year.
Source: Bureau of Transportation Statistics, The Intermodal Transportation Database, Air Carriers: T-100 Domestic Market (U.S. Carriers), 2014; Bureau of Transportation Statistics, The Intermodal Transportation Database, Air Carriers: T-100 International Market (U.S. Carriers), 2013

Other Transportation Statistics

Major Highways:	I-20 via US-69 and US-271
Amtrak Service:	Bus connection
Major Waterways/Ports:	None

Source: Amtrak.com; Google Maps

BUSINESSES

Major Business Headquarters

Company Name	Rankings: Fortune[1]	Rankings: Forbes[2]
Brookshire Grocery	-	187

Note: (1) Fortune 500—companies that produce a 10-K are ranked 1 to 500 based on 2013 revenue; (2) all private companies with at least $2 billion in annual revenue through the end of their most current fiscal year are ranked 1 to 221; companies listed are headquartered in the city; dashes indicate no ranking
Source: Fortune, "Fortune 500," June 16, 2014; Forbes, "America's Largest Private Companies," November 5, 2014

Fast-Growing Businesses

According to *Inc.*, Tyler is home to one of America's 500 fastest-growing private companies: **Innovative Surveillance Solutions** (#45). Criteria: must be an independent, privately-held, for-profit, U.S. corporation, proprietorship or partnership; revenues must be at least $100,000 in 2010 and $2 million in 2013; must have four-year operating/sales history. Holding companies, regulated banks, and utilities were excluded. *Inc., "America's 500 Fastest-Growing Private Companies," September 2014*

Minority Business Opportunity

Tyler is home to one company which is on the *Hispanic Business* 500 list (500 largest U.S. Hispanic-owned companies based on 2012 revenue): **Mentoring Minds** (#226). Companies included must show at least 51 percent ownership by Hispanic U.S. citizens, and must maintain headquarters in one of the 50 states or Washington, D.C. *Hispanic Business, "Hispanic Business 500," June 20, 2013*

Tyler is home to one company which is on the *Hispanic Business* Fastest-Growing 100 list (greatest sales growth from 2008 to 2012): **Mentoring Minds** (#37). Companies included must show at least 51 percent ownership by Hispanic U.S. citizens, and must maintain headquarters in one of the 50 states or Washington, D.C. In addition, companies must have minimum revenues of $200,000 for calendar year 2008. *Hispanic Business, June 20, 2013*

Minority- and Women-Owned Businesses

Group	All Firms		Firms with Paid Employees			
	Firms	Sales ($000)	Firms	Sales ($000)	Employees	Payroll ($000)
Asian	(s)	(s)	(s)	(s)	(s)	(s)
Black	1,019	26,858	(s)	(s)	(s)	(s)
Hispanic	(s)	(s)	(s)	(s)	(s)	(s)
Women	2,605	400,941	359	348,466	3,125	79,550
All Firms	11,044	13,505,117	3,116	13,124,941	59,648	2,194,286

Note: Figures cover firms located in the city; minority- and women-owned business are defined as firms in which the corresponding group own 51% or more of the stock or equity of the company; (s) estimates are suppressed when publication standards are not met
Source: U.S. Census Bureau, 2007 Economic Census, Survey of Business Owners (2012 Survey of Business Owners data will be released starting in June 2015)

HOTELS & CONVENTION CENTERS

Hotels/Motels

Area	5 Star		4 Star		3 Star		2 Star		1 Star		Not Rated	
	Num.	Pct.[3]	Num.	Pct.[3]	Num.	Pct.[3]	Num.	Pct.[3]	Num.	Pct.[3]	Num.	Pct.[3]
City[1]	0	0.0	0	0.0	10	17.9	40	71.4	2	3.6	4	7.1
Total[2]	166	0.9	1,264	7.0	5,718	31.8	9,340	52.0	411	2.3	1,070	6.0

Note: (1) Figures cover Tyler and vicinity; (2) Figures cover all 100 cities in this book; (3) Percentage of hotels which have a given star rating; Star ratings are determined by expedia.com and offer an indication of the general quality of a particular hotel.
Source: expedia.com, April 2, 2015

Major Convention Centers

Name	Overall Space (sq. ft.)	Exhibit Space (sq. ft.)	Meeting Space (sq. ft.)	Meeting Rooms
Harvey Convention Center	n/a	n/a	27,667	3

Note: Table includes convention centers located in the Tyler, TX metro area; n/a not available
Source: Original research

Living Environment

COST OF LIVING

Cost of Living Index

Composite Index	Groceries	Housing	Utilities	Transportation	Health Care	Misc. Goods/ Services
95.3	93.0	95.8	94.0	96.3	90.7	96.6

Note: The Cost of Living Index measures regional differences in the cost of consumer goods and services, excluding taxes and non-consumer expenditures, for professional and managerial households in the top income quintile. It is based on more than 50,000 prices covering almost 60 different items for which prices are collected three times a year by chambers of commerce, economic development organizations or university applied economic centers in each participating urban area. The numbers shown should be read as a percentage above or below the national average of 100. For example, a value of 115.4 in the groceries column indicates that grocery prices are 15.4% higher than the national average. Small differences in the index numbers should not be interpreted as significant; Figures cover the Tyler TX urban area.
Source: The Council for Community and Economic Research, ACCRA Cost of Living Index, 2014

Grocery Prices

Area[1]	T-Bone Steak ($/pound)	Frying Chicken ($/pound)	Whole Milk ($/half gal.)	Eggs ($/dozen)	Orange Juice ($/64 oz.)	Coffee ($/11.5 oz.)
City[2]	9.48	1.12	2.78	2.03	3.26	3.44
Avg.	10.40	1.37	2.40	1.99	3.46	4.27
Min.	8.48	0.93	1.37	1.30	2.83	2.99
Max.	14.20	2.44	3.62	4.02	6.42	6.96

Note: (1) Values for the local area are compared with the average, minimum and maximum values for all 308 areas in the Cost of Living Index; (2) Figures cover the Tyler TX urban area; **T-Bone Steak** *(price per pound);* **Frying Chicken** *(price per pound, whole fryer);* **Whole Milk** *(half gallon carton);* **Eggs** *(price per dozen, Grade A, large);* **Orange Juice** *(64 oz. Tropicana or Florida Natural);* **Coffee** *(11.5 oz. can, vacuum-packed, Maxwell House, Hills Bros, or Folgers).*
Source: The Council for Community and Economic Research, ACCRA Cost of Living Index, 2014

Housing and Utility Costs

Area[1]	New Home Price ($)	Apartment Rent ($/month)	All Electric ($/month)	Part Electric ($/month)	Other Energy ($/month)	Telephone ($/month)
City[2]	268,261	1,071	-	121.67	44.31	24.72
Avg.	305,838	919	181.00	93.66	73.14	27.95
Min.	183,142	480	112.00	42.06	23.42	17.16
Max.	1,358,576	3,851	594.00	180.03	440.99	40.42

Note: (1) Values for the local area are compared with the average, minimum and maximum values for all 308 areas in the Cost of Living Index; (2) Figures cover the Tyler TX urban area; **New Home Price** *(2,400 sf living area, 8,000 sf lot, in urban area with full utilities);* **Apartment Rent** *(950 sf 2 bedroom/1.5 or 2 bath, unfurnished, excluding all utilities except water);* **All Electric** *(average monthly cost for an all-electric home);* **Part Electric** *(average monthly cost for a part-electric home);* **Other Energy** *(average monthly cost for natural gas, fuel oil, coal, wood, and any other forms of energy except electricity);* **Telephone** *(price includes basic monthly rate for a private residential line plus additional local usage charges incurred by a family of four).*
Source: The Council for Community and Economic Research, ACCRA Cost of Living Index, 2014

Health Care, Transportation, and Other Costs

Area[1]	Doctor ($/visit)	Dentist ($/visit)	Optometrist ($/visit)	Gasoline ($/gallon)	Beauty Salon ($/visit)	Men's Shirt ($)
City[2]	78.96	84.22	97.50	3.27	41.93	27.84
Avg.	102.86	87.89	97.66	3.44	34.37	26.74
Min.	67.47	65.78	51.18	3.00	17.43	12.79
Max.	173.50	150.14	235.00	4.33	64.28	49.50

Note: (1) Values for the local area are compared with the average, minimum and maximum values for all 308 areas in the Cost of Living Index; (2) Figures cover the Tyler TX urban area; **Doctor** *(general practitioners routine exam of an established patient);* **Dentist** *(adult teeth cleaning and periodic oral examination);* **Optometrist** *(full vision eye exam for established adult patient);* **Gasoline** *(one gallon regular unleaded, national brand, including all taxes, cash price at self-service pump if available);* **Beauty Salon** *(woman's shampoo, trim, and blow-dry);* **Men's Shirt** *(cotton/polyester dress shirt, pinpoint weave, long sleeves).*
Source: The Council for Community and Economic Research, ACCRA Cost of Living Index, 2014

HOUSING

House Price Index (HPI)

Area	National Ranking[2]	Quarterly Change (%)	One-Year Change (%)	Five-Year Change (%)
MSA[1]	(a)	n/a	3.73	5.11
U.S.[3]	–	1.35	4.91	11.59

Note: The HPI is a weighted repeat sales index. It measures average price changes in repeat sales or refinancings on the same properties. This information is obtained by reviewing repeat mortgage transactions on single-family properties whose mortgages have been purchased or securitized by Fannie Mae or Freddie Mac in January 1975; (1) Tyler Metropolitan Statistical Area—see Appendix B for areas included; (2) Rankings are based on annual percentage change for all metro areas containing at least 15,000 transactions over the last 10 years and ranges from 1 to 275; (3) figures based on a weighted average of Census Division estimates using a seasonally adjusted, purchase-only index; all figures are for the period ending December 31, 2014; n/a not available; (a) Not ranked because of increased index variability due to smaller sample size
Source: Federal Housing Finance Agency, House Price Index, February 26, 2015

Median Single-Family Home Prices

Area	2012	2013	2014p	Percent Change 2013 to 2014
MSA[1]	n/a	n/a	n/a	n/a
U.S. Average	177.2	197.4	209.0	5.9

Note: Figures are median sales prices of existing single-family homes in thousands of dollars; (p) preliminary; n/a not available; (1) Tyler, TX Metropolitan Statistical Area—see Appendix B for areas included
Source: National Association of Realtors, Median Sales Price of Existing Single-Family Homes for Metropolitan Areas, 4th Quarter 2014

Qualifying Income Based on Median Sales Price of Existing Single-Family Homes

Area	With 5% Down ($)	With 10% Down ($)	With 20% Down ($)
MSA[1]	n/a	n/a	n/a
U.S. Average	45,863	43,449	38,621

Note: Figures are preliminary; Qualifying income is based on a mortgage rate of 4.0%. Monthly principal and interest payment is limited to 25% of income; n/a not available; (1) Tyler, TX Metropolitan Statistical Area—see Appendix B for areas included
Source: National Association of Realtors, Qualifying Income Based on Median Sales Price of Existing Single-Family Homes for Metropolitan Areas, 4th Quarter 2014

Median Apartment Condo-Coop Home Prices

Area	2012	2013	2014p	Percent Change 2013 to 2014
MSA[1]	n/a	n/a	n/a	n/a
U.S. Average	173.7	194.9	205.1	5.2

Note: Figures are median sales prices of existing apartment condo-coop homes in thousands of dollars; (p) preliminary; n/a not available; (1) Tyler, TX Metropolitan Statistical Area—see Appendix B for areas included
Source: National Association of Realtors, Median Sales Price of Existing Apartment Condo-Coop Homes for Metropolitan Areas, 4th Quarter 2014

Gross Monthly Rent

Area	Under $200	$200 -299	$300 -499	$500 -749	$750 -999	$1,000 -1,499	$1,500 and up	Median ($)
City	0.8	1.8	5.1	32.1	29.6	21.4	9.2	810
MSA[1]	1.0	2.0	6.2	30.0	30.4	22.8	7.7	822
U.S.	1.7	3.2	7.8	22.1	24.3	26.0	14.9	900

Note: Figures are percentages except for Median; Gross rent is the contract rent plus the estimated average monthly cost of utilities (electricity, gas, and water and sewer) and fuels (oil, coal, kerosene, wood, etc.) if these are paid by the renter (or paid for the renter by someone else); (1) Figures cover the Tyler, TX Metropolitan Statistical Area—see Appendix B for areas included
Source: U.S. Census Bureau, 2011-2013 American Community Survey 3-Year Estimates

Homeownership Rate

Area	2007 (%)	2008 (%)	2009 (%)	2010 (%)	2011 (%)	2012 (%)	2013 (%)	2014 (%)
MSA[1]	n/a	n/a	n/a	n/a	n/a	n/a	n/a	n/a
U.S.	68.1	67.8	67.4	66.9	66.1	65.4	65.1	64.5

Note: (1) Figures cover the Tyler, TX Metropolitan Statistical Area—see Appendix B for areas included; n/a not available
Source: U.S. Census Bureau, Housing Vacancies and Homeownership Annual Statistics: 2014

Year Housing Structure Built

Area	2010 or Later	2000 -2009	1990 -1999	1980 -1989	1970 -1979	1960 -1969	1950 -1959	1940 -1949	Before 1940	Median Year
City	1.7	17.7	9.7	15.8	17.6	12.4	14.5	6.4	4.2	1977
MSA[1]	1.7	20.1	15.2	18.0	17.6	10.2	9.3	4.3	3.6	1983
U.S.	0.9	15.0	13.9	13.8	15.8	11.0	10.9	5.4	13.3	1976

Note: Figures are percentages except for Median Year; (1) Figures cover the Tyler, TX Metropolitan Statistical Area—see Appendix B for areas included
Source: U.S. Census Bureau, 2011-2013 American Community Survey 3-Year Estimates

HEALTH

Health Risk Data

Category	MSA[1] (%)	U.S. (%)
Adults aged 18–64 who have any kind of health care coverage	n/a	79.6
Adults who reported being in good or excellent health	n/a	83.1
Adults who are current smokers	n/a	19.6
Adults who are heavy drinkers[2]	n/a	6.1
Adults who are binge drinkers[3]	n/a	16.9
Adults who are overweight (BMI 25.0 - 29.9)	n/a	35.8
Adults who are obese (BMI 30.0 - 99.8)	n/a	27.6
Adults who participated in any physical activities in the past month	n/a	77.1
Adults 50+ who have ever had a sigmoidoscopy or colonoscopy	n/a	67.3
Women aged 40+ who have had a mammogram within the past two years	n/a	74.0
Men aged 40+ who have had a PSA test within the past two years	n/a	45.2
Adults aged 65+ who have had flu shot within the past year	n/a	60.1
Adults who always wear a seatbelt	n/a	93.8

Note: Data as of 2012 unless otherwise noted; n/a not available; (1) Figures cover the Tyler, TX Metropolitan Statistical Area—see Appendix B for areas included; (2) Heavy drinkers are classified as males having more than two drinks per day or females having more than one drink per day; (3) Binge drinkers are classified as males having five or more drinks on one occasion or females having four or more drinks on one occasion
Source: Centers for Disease Control and Prevention, Behaviorial Risk Factor Surveillance System, SMART: Selected Metropolitan/Micropolitan Area Risk Trends, 2012 (Note: the CDC has discontinued this dataset but will be releasing a replacement in late 2015)

Chronic Health Indicators

Category	MSA[1] (%)	U.S. (%)
Adults who have ever been told they had a heart attack	n/a	4.5
Adults who have ever been told they had a stroke	n/a	2.9
Adults who have been told they currently have asthma	n/a	8.9
Adults who have ever been told they have arthritis	n/a	25.7
Adults who have ever been told they have diabetes[2]	n/a	9.7
Adults who have ever been told they had skin cancer	n/a	5.7
Adults who have ever been told they had any other types of cancer	n/a	6.5
Adults who have ever been told they have COPD	n/a	6.2
Adults who have ever been told they have kidney disease	n/a	2.5
Adults who have ever been told they have a form of depression	n/a	18.0

Note: Data as of 2012 unless otherwise noted; n/a not available; (1) Figures cover the Tyler, TX Metropolitan Statistical Area—see Appendix B for areas included; (2) Figures do not include pregnancy-related, borderline, or pre-diabetes
Source: Centers for Disease Control and Prevention, Behaviorial Risk Factor Surveillance System, SMART: Selected Metropolitan/Micropolitan Area Risk Trends, 2012 (Note: the CDC has discontinued this dataset but will be releasing a replacement in late 2015)

Mortality Rates for the Top 10 Causes of Death in the U.S.

ICD-10[a] Sub-Chapter	ICD-10[a] Code	Age-Adjusted Mortality Rate[1] per 100,000 population	
		County[2]	U.S.
Malignant neoplasms	C00-C97	152.6	166.2
Ischaemic heart diseases	I20-I25	103.4	105.7
Other forms of heart disease	I30-I51	53.4	49.3
Chronic lower respiratory diseases	J40-J47	44.7	42.1
Organic, including symptomatic, mental disorders	F01-F09	47.6	38.1
Cerebrovascular diseases	I60-I69	39.8	37.0
Other external causes of accidental injury	W00-X59	26.7	26.9
Other degenerative diseases of the nervous system	G30-G31	21.4	25.6
Diabetes mellitus	E10-E14	21.3	21.3
Hypertensive diseases	I10-I15	9.5	19.4

Note: (a) ICD-10 = International Classification of Diseases 10th Revision; (1) Mortality rates are a three year average covering 2011-2013; (2) Figures cover Smith County
Source: Centers for Disease Control and Prevention, National Center for Health Statistics. Compressed Mortality File 1999-2013 on CDC WONDER Online Database, released October 2014. Data are compiled from the Compressed Mortality File 1999-2013, Series 20 No. 2S, 2014.

Mortality Rates for Selected Causes of Death

ICD-10[a] Sub-Chapter	ICD-10[a] Code	Age-Adjusted Mortality Rate[1] per 100,000 population	
		County[2]	U.S.
Assault	X85-Y09	4.0	5.2
Diseases of the liver	K70-K76	11.4	13.2
Human immunodeficiency virus (HIV) disease	B20-B24	3.5	2.2
Influenza and pneumonia	J09-J18	15.1	15.4
Intentional self-harm	X60-X84	16.6	12.5
Malnutrition	E40-E46	*2.1	0.9
Obesity and other hyperalimentation	E65-E68	3.5	1.8
Renal failure	N17-N19	18.5	13.1
Transport accidents	V01-V99	19.5	11.7
Viral hepatitis	B15-B19	*1.8	2.2

Note: (a) ICD-10 = International Classification of Diseases 10th Revision; (1) Mortality rates are a three year average covering 2011-2013; (2) Figures cover Smith County; (*) Unreliable data as per CDC
Source: Centers for Disease Control and Prevention, National Center for Health Statistics. Compressed Mortality File 1999-2013 on CDC WONDER Online Database, released October 2014. Data are compiled from the Compressed Mortality File 1999-2013, Series 20 No. 2S, 2014.

Health Insurance Coverage

Area	With Health Insurance	With Private Health Insurance	With Public Health Insurance	Without Health Insurance	Population Under Age 18 Without Health Insurance
City	78.5	58.9	30.5	21.5	12.2
MSA[1]	78.9	59.4	30.7	21.1	13.8
U.S.	85.2	65.2	31.0	14.8	7.3

Note: Figures are percentages that cover the civilian noninstitutionalized population; (1) Figures cover the Tyler, TX Metropolitan Statistical Area—see Appendix B for areas included
Source: U.S. Census Bureau, 2011-2013 American Community Survey 3-Year Estimates

Number of Medical Professionals

Area[1]	MDs[2]	DOs[2,3]	Dentists	Podiatrists	Chiropractors	Optometrists
Local (number)	778	51	122	14	52	32
Local (rate[4])	362.0	23.7	56.3	6.5	24.0	14.8
U.S. (rate[4])	270.0	20.2	63.1	5.7	25.2	14.9

Note: Data as of 2013 unless noted; (1) Local data covers Smith County; (2) Data as of 2012 and includes all active, non-federal physicians; (3) Doctor of Osteopathic Medicine; (4) rate per 100,000 population
Source: U.S. Department of Health and Human Services, Health Resources and Services Administration, Bureau of Health Professions, Area Resource File (ARF) 2013-2014

EDUCATION

Public School District Statistics

District Name	Schls	Pupils	Pupil/ Teacher Ratio	Minority Pupils[1] (%)	Free Lunch Eligible[2] (%)	IEP[3] (%)
Chapel Hill ISD	5	3,446	14.8	63.2	64.0	7.3
Tyler ISD	27	18,263	14.3	76.4	63.9	7.5

Note: Table includes school districts with 2,000 or more students; (1) Percentage of students that are not non-Hispanic white; (2) Percentage of students that are eligible for the free lunch program; (3) Percentage of students that have an Individualized Education Program.
Source: U.S. Department of Education, National Center for Education Statistics, Common Core of Data, Local Education Agency (School District) Universe Survey: School Year 2012-2013; U.S. Department of Education, National Center for Education Statistics, Common Core of Data, Public Elementary/Secondary School Universe Survey: School Year 2012-2013

Highest Level of Education

Area	Less than H.S.	H.S. Diploma	Some College, No Deg.	Associate Degree	Bachelor's Degree	Master's Degree	Prof. School Degree	Doctorate Degree
City	15.6	21.1	24.7	9.1	18.6	6.9	2.7	1.3
MSA[1]	15.1	25.4	25.5	9.3	17.0	5.2	1.7	0.8
U.S.	13.7	28.0	21.2	7.9	18.2	7.7	1.9	1.3

Note: Figures cover persons age 25 and over; (1) Figures cover the Tyler, TX Metropolitan Statistical Area—see Appendix B for areas included
Source: U.S. Census Bureau, 2011-2013 American Community Survey 3-Year Estimates

Educational Attainment by Race

Area	High School Graduate or Higher (%)					Bachelor's Degree or Higher (%)				
	Total	White	Black	Asian	Hisp.[2]	Total	White	Black	Asian	Hisp.[2]
City	84.4	84.5	84.9	96.6	46.5	29.6	33.0	16.2	55.4	6.5
MSA[1]	84.9	85.1	85.7	94.5	45.9	24.8	26.7	14.5	53.6	5.8
U.S.	86.3	88.3	83.1	85.7	64.0	29.1	30.4	18.8	50.7	13.7

Note: Figures shown cover persons 25 years old and over; (1) Figures cover the Tyler, TX Metropolitan Statistical Area—see Appendix B for areas included; (2) People of Hispanic origin can be of any race
Source: U.S. Census Bureau, 2011-2013 American Community Survey 3-Year Estimates

School Enrollment by Grade and Control

Area	Preschool (%)		Kindergarten (%)		Grades 1 - 4 (%)		Grades 5 - 8 (%)		Grades 9 - 12 (%)	
	Public	Private	Public	Private	Public	Private	Public	Private	Public	Private
City	68.3	31.7	98.2	1.8	92.8	7.2	89.8	10.2	88.6	11.4
MSA[1]	70.7	29.3	95.0	5.0	93.6	6.4	91.5	8.5	89.8	10.2
U.S.	57.7	42.3	87.9	12.1	89.9	10.1	90.0	10.0	90.7	9.3

Note: Figures shown cover persons 3 years old and over; (1) Figures cover the Tyler, TX Metropolitan Statistical Area—see Appendix B for areas included
Source: U.S. Census Bureau, 2011-2013 American Community Survey 3-Year Estimates

Average Salaries of Public School Classroom Teachers

Area	2013-14		2014-15		Percent Change 2013-14 to 2014-15	Percent Change 2004-05 to 2014-15
	Dollars	Rank[1]	Dollars	Rank[1]		
TEXAS	49,690	30	50,576	29	1.78	23.3
U.S. Average	56,610	–	57,379	–	1.36	20.8

Note: (1) State rank ranges from 1 to 51 where 1 indicates highest salary.
Source: National Education Association, Rankings & Estimates: Rankings of the States 2014 and Estimates of School Statistics 2015, March 2015

Higher Education

Four-Year Colleges			Two-Year Colleges			Medical Schools[1]	Law Schools[2]	Voc/ Tech[3]
Public	Private Non-profit	Private For-profit	Public	Private Non-profit	Private For-profit			
1	1	0	1	0	0	0	0	1

Note: Figures cover institutions located within the city limits and include main campuses only; (1) includes schools accredited by the Liaison Committee on Medical Education and the American Osteopathic Association's Commission on Osteopathic College Accreditation; (2) includes ABA-accredited schools, schools with provisional ABA accreditation, and state accredited schools; (3) includes all schools with programs that are less than 2 years.
Source: National Center for Education Statistics, Integrated Postsecondary Education System (IPEDS), 2013-14; Association of American Medical Colleges, Member List, May 1, 2015; American Osteopathic Association, Member List, May 1, 2015; Law School Admission Council, Official Guide to ABA-Approved Law Schools Online, May 1, 2015; Wikipedia, List of Medical Schools in the United States, May 1, 2015; Wikipedia, List of Law Schools in the United States, May 1, 2015

PRESIDENTIAL ELECTION

2012 Presidential Election Results

Area	Obama (%)	Romney (%)	Other (%)
Smith County	26.1	73.0	1.0
U.S.	51.0	47.2	1.8

Note: Results may not add to 100% due to rounding
Source: Dave Leip's Atlas of U.S. Presidential Elections

EMPLOYERS

Major Employers

Company Name	Industry
Brookshire Grocery Company	Grocery distribution
East Texas Medical Center	Healthcare
ETMC Regional Healthcare System	Healthcare
ETMC Tyler Radiology	Healthcare
Suddenlink	Cable, internet, and phone
Target Distribution Center	Retail distribution
The Trane Co.	Air conditioning units
The University of Texas at Tyler	Education
Trinity Mother Frances	Healthcare
Tyler Independent School District	Education
Tyler Junior College	Education
Tyler Pipe Company	Cast iron pipes, iron fittings
University of Texas Health Science Center at	Education
UT Health Center at Tyler	Medical care and research
Walmart	Retail

Note: Companies shown are located within the Tyler, TX Metropolitan Statistical Area.
Source: Hoovers.com; Wikipedia

PUBLIC SAFETY

Crime Rate

Area	All Crimes	Violent Crimes				Property Crimes		
		Murder	Forcible Rape	Robbery	Aggrav. Assault	Burglary	Larceny -Theft	Motor Vehicle Theft
City	4,490.5	5.0	43.0	53.0	274.9	824.7	3,110.0	179.9
Suburbs[1]	2,198.5	2.6	11.9	22.2	158.7	642.7	1,218.8	141.7
Metro[2]	3,254.1	3.7	26.2	36.4	212.2	726.5	2,089.8	159.3
U.S.	3,098.6	4.5	25.2	109.1	229.1	610.0	1,899.4	221.3

Note: Figures are crimes per 100,000 population; (1) All areas within the metro area that are located outside the city limits; (2) Figures cover the Tyler, TX Metropolitan Statistical Area—see Appendix B for areas included
Source: FBI Uniform Crime Reports, 2013

RECREATION

CLIMATE

Hate Crimes

Area	Number of Quarters Reported	Number of Incidents per Bias Motivation: Race	Religion	Sexual Orientation	Ethnicity	Disability	Gender	Gender Identity
City	4	1	0	3	1	0	0	0
U.S.	4	2,871	1,031	1,233	655	83	18	31

Source: Federal Bureau of Investigation, Hate Crime Statistics 2013

Identity Theft Consumer Complaints

Area	Complaints	Complaints per 100,000 Population	Rank[2]
MSA[1]	151	69.9	182
U.S.	332,646	104.3	-

Note: (1) Figures cover the Tyler, TX Metropolitan Statistical Area—see Appendix B for areas included; (2) Rank ranges from 1 to 380 where 1 indicates greatest number of identity theft complaints per 100,000 population
Source: Federal Trade Commission, Consumer Sentinel Network Data Book for January–December 2014

Fraud and Other Consumer Complaints

Area	Complaints	Complaints per 100,000 Population	Rank[2]
MSA[1]	800	370.2	193
U.S.	2,250,205	705.7	-

Note: (1) Figures cover the Tyler, TX Metropolitan Statistical Area—see Appendix B for areas included; (2) Rank ranges from 1 to 380 where 1 indicates greatest number of identity theft complaints per 100,000 population
Source: Federal Trade Commission, Consumer Sentinel Network Data Book for January–December 2014

Culture

Dance[1]	Theatre[1]	Instrumental Music[1]	Vocal Music[1]	Series and Festivals	Museums and Art Galleries[2]	Zoos and Aquariums[3]
1	0	1	0	2	12	1

Note: (1) Professional perfoming groups; (2) Based on organizations with SIC code 8412; (3) AZA-accredited
Source: The Grey House Performing Arts Directory, 2015-16; Association of Zoos & Aquariums, AZA Member Zoos & Aquariums, April 2015; www.AccuLeads.com, April 2015

Professional Sports Teams

Team Name	League	Year Established
No teams are located in the metro area		

Source: Wikipedia, Major Professional Sports Teams of the United States and Canada, April 2015

Average and Extreme Temperatures

Temperature	Jan	Feb	Mar	Apr	May	Jun	Jul	Aug	Sep	Oct	Nov	Dec	Yr.
Extreme High (°F)	85	90	100	100	101	112	111	109	107	101	91	87	112
Average High (°F)	55	60	68	76	84	92	96	96	89	79	67	58	77
Average Temp. (°F)	45	50	57	66	74	82	86	86	79	68	56	48	67
Average Low (°F)	35	39	47	56	64	72	76	75	68	57	46	38	56
Extreme Low (°F)	-2	9	12	30	39	53	58	58	42	24	16	0	-2

Note: Figures cover the years 1945-1993
Source: National Climatic Data Center, International Station Meteorological Climate Summary, 9/96

Average Precipitation/Snowfall/Humidity

Precip./Humidity	Jan	Feb	Mar	Apr	May	Jun	Jul	Aug	Sep	Oct	Nov	Dec	Yr.
Avg. Precip. (in.)	1.9	2.3	2.6	3.8	4.9	3.4	2.1	2.3	2.9	3.3	2.3	2.1	33.9
Avg. Snowfall (in.)	1	1	Tr	Tr	0	0	0	0	0	Tr	Tr	Tr	3
Avg. Rel. Hum. 6am (%)	78	77	75	77	82	81	77	76	80	79	78	77	78
Avg. Rel. Hum. 3pm (%)	53	51	47	49	51	48	43	41	46	46	48	51	48

Note: Figures cover the years 1945-1993; Tr = Trace amounts (<0.05 in. of rain; <0.5 in. of snow)
Source: National Climatic Data Center, International Station Meteorological Climate Summary, 9/96

Weather Conditions

Temperature			Daytime Sky			Precipitation		
10°F & below	32°F & below	90°F & above	Clear	Partly cloudy	Cloudy	0.01 inch or more precip.	0.1 inch or more snow/ice	Thunder-storms
1	34	102	108	160	97	78	2	49

Note: Figures are average number of days per year and cover the years 1945-1993
Source: National Climatic Data Center, International Station Meteorological Climate Summary, 9/96

HAZARDOUS WASTE

Superfund Sites

Tyler has no sites on the EPA's Superfund Final National Priorities List. There are a total of 1,322 Superfund sites on the list in the U.S. *U.S. Environmental Protection Agency, Final National Priorities List, April 14, 2015*

AIR & WATER QUALITY

Air Quality Trends: Ozone

	2004	2005	2006	2007	2008	2009	2010	2011	2012	2013
MSA[1]	0.081	0.083	0.082	0.077	0.072	0.075	0.072	0.078	0.076	0.071

Note: (1) Data covers the Tyler, TX Metropolitan Statistical Area—see Appendix B for areas included. The values shown are the composite ozone concentration averages among trend sites based on the highest fourth daily maximum 8-hour concentration in parts per million. These trends are based on sites having an adequate record of monitoring data during the trend period. Data from exceptional events are included.
Source: U.S. Environmental Protection Agency, Air Quality Monitoring Information, "Air Quality Trends by City, 2000-2013"

Air Quality Index

Area	Percent of Days when Air Quality was...[2]					AQI Statistics[2]	
	Good	Moderate	Unhealthy for Sensitive Groups	Unhealthy	Very Unhealthy	Maximum	Median
MSA[1]	96.2	3.8	0.0	0.0	0.0	84	31

Note: (1) Data covers the Tyler, TX Metropolitan Statistical Area—see Appendix B for areas included; (2) Based on 365 days with AQI data in 2014. Air Quality Index (AQI) is an index for reporting daily air quality. EPA calculates the AQI for five major air pollutants regulated by the Clean Air Act: ground-level ozone, particle pollution (aka particulate matter), carbon monoxide, sulfur dioxide, and nitrogen dioxide. The AQI runs from 0 to 500. The higher the AQI value, the greater the level of air pollution and the greater the health concern. There are six AQI categories: "Good" AQI is between 0 and 50. Air quality is considered satisfactory; "Moderate" AQI is between 51 and 100. Air quality is acceptable; "Unhealthy for Sensitive Groups" When AQI values are between 101 and 150, members of sensitive groups may experience health effects; "Unhealthy" When AQI values are between 151 and 200 everyone may begin to experience health effects; "Very Unhealthy" AQI values between 201 and 300 trigger a health alert; "Hazardous" AQI values over 300 trigger warnings of emergency conditions (not shown).
Source: U.S. Environmental Protection Agency, Air Quality Index Report, 2014

Air Quality Index Pollutants

Area	Percent of Days when AQI Pollutant was...[2]					
	Carbon Monoxide	Nitrogen Dioxide	Ozone	Sulfur Dioxide	Particulate Matter 2.5	Particulate Matter 10
MSA[1]	0.0	0.5	99.5	0.0	0.0	0.0

Note: (1) Data covers the Tyler, TX Metropolitan Statistical Area—see Appendix B for areas included; (2) Based on 365 days with AQI data in 2014. The Air Quality Index (AQI) is an index for reporting daily air quality. EPA calculates the AQI for five major air pollutants regulated by the Clean Air Act: ground-level ozone, particle pollution (also known as particulate matter), carbon monoxide, sulfur dioxide, and nitrogen dioxide. The AQI runs from 0 to 500. The higher the AQI value, the greater the level of air pollution and the greater the health concern.
Source: U.S. Environmental Protection Agency, Air Quality Index Report, 2014

Maximum Air Pollutant Concentrations: Particulate Matter, Ozone, CO and Lead

	Particulate Matter 10 (ug/m³)	Particulate Matter 2.5 Wtd AM (ug/m³)	Particulate Matter 2.5 24-Hr (ug/m³)	Ozone (ppm)	Carbon Monoxide (ppm)	Lead (ug/m³)
MSA[1] Level	n/a	n/a	n/a	0.071	n/a	n/a
NAAQS[2]	150	15	35	0.075	9	0.15
Met NAAQS[2]	n/a	n/a	n/a	Yes	n/a	n/a

Note: (1) Data covers the Tyler, TX Metropolitan Statistical Area—see Appendix B for areas included; Data from exceptional events are included; (2) National Ambient Air Quality Standards; ppm = parts per million; ug/m³ = micrograms per cubic meter; n/a not available.

Concentrations: Particulate Matter 10 (coarse particulate)—highest second maximum 24-hour concentration; Particulate Matter 2.5 Wtd AM (fine particulate)—highest weighted annual mean concentration; Particulate Matter 2.5 24-Hour (fine particulate)—highest 98th percentile 24-hour concentration; Ozone—highest fourth daily maximum 8-hour concentration; Carbon Monoxide—highest second maximum non-overlapping 8-hour concentration; Lead—maximum running 3-month average

Source: U.S. Environmental Protection Agency, Air Quality Monitoring Information, "Air Quality Statistics by City, 2013"

Maximum Air Pollutant Concentrations: Nitrogen Dioxide and Sulfur Dioxide

	Nitrogen Dioxide AM (ppb)	Nitrogen Dioxide 1-Hr (ppb)	Sulfur Dioxide AM (ppb)	Sulfur Dioxide 1-Hr (ppb)	Sulfur Dioxide 24-Hr (ppb)
MSA[1] Level	3	17	n/a	n/a	n/a
NAAQS[2]	53	100	30	75	140
Met NAAQS[2]	Yes	Yes	n/a	n/a	n/a

Note: (1) Data covers the Tyler, TX Metropolitan Statistical Area—see Appendix B for areas included; Data from exceptional events are included; (2) National Ambient Air Quality Standards; ppm = parts per million; ug/m³ = micrograms per cubic meter; n/a not available.

Concentrations: Nitrogen Dioxide AM—highest arithmetic mean concentration; Nitrogen Dioxide 1-Hr—highest 98th percentile 1-hour daily maximum concentration; Sulfur Dioxide AM—highest annual mean concentration; Sulfur Dioxide 1-Hr—highest 99th percentile 1-hour daily maximum concentration; Sulfur Dioxide 24-Hr—highest second maximum 24-hour concentration

Source: U.S. Environmental Protection Agency, Air Quality Monitoring Information, "Air Quality Statistics by City, 2013"

Drinking Water

Water System Name	Pop. Served	Primary Water Source Type	Violations[1]	
			Health Based	Monitoring/ Reporting
City of Tyler	109,242	Surface	0	4

Note: (1) Based on violation data from January 1, 2014 to December 31, 2014 (includes unresolved violations from earlier years)

Source: U.S. Environmental Protection Agency, Office of Ground Water and Drinking Water, Safe Drinking Water Information System (based on data extracted January 27, 2015)

Appendix A: Comparative Statistics

Population Growth: City

City	1990 Census	2000 Census	2010 Census	Population Growth (%) 1990-2000	Population Growth (%) 2000-2010
Albuquerque, NM	388,375	448,607	545,852	15.5	21.7
Anchorage, AK	226,338	260,283	291,826	15.0	12.1
Ann Arbor, MI	111,018	114,024	113,934	2.7	-0.1
Athens, GA	86,561	100,266	115,452	15.8	15.1
Atlanta, GA	394,092	416,474	420,003	5.7	0.8
Austin, TX	499,053	656,562	790,390	31.6	20.4
Billings, MT	81,812	89,847	104,170	9.8	15.9
Boise City, ID	144,317	185,787	205,671	28.7	10.7
Boston, MA	574,283	589,141	617,594	2.6	4.8
Boulder, CO	87,737	94,673	97,385	7.9	2.9
Cape Coral, FL	75,507	102,286	154,305	35.5	50.9
Cedar Rapids, IA	110,829	120,758	126,326	9.0	4.6
Charleston, SC	96,102	96,650	120,083	0.6	24.2
Charlotte, NC	428,283	540,828	731,424	26.3	35.2
Chicago, IL	2,783,726	2,896,016	2,695,598	4.0	-6.9
Clarksville, TN	78,569	103,455	132,929	31.7	28.5
Colorado Springs, CO	283,798	360,890	416,427	27.2	15.4
Columbia, MO	71,069	84,531	108,500	18.9	28.4
Columbus, OH	648,656	711,470	787,033	9.7	10.6
Dallas, TX	1,006,971	1,188,580	1,197,816	18.0	0.8
Davenport, IA	95,705	98,359	99,685	2.8	1.3
Denver, CO	467,153	554,636	600,158	18.7	8.2
Des Moines, IA	193,569	198,682	203,433	2.6	2.4
Durham, NC	151,737	187,035	228,330	23.3	22.1
El Paso, TX	515,541	563,662	649,121	9.3	15.2
Erie, PA	108,718	103,717	101,786	-4.6	-1.9
Eugene, OR	118,073	137,893	156,185	16.8	13.3
Fargo, ND	74,372	90,599	105,549	21.8	16.5
Fayetteville, NC	118,247	121,015	200,564	2.3	65.7
Fort Collins, CO	89,555	118,652	143,986	32.5	21.4
Fort Wayne, IN	205,671	205,727	253,691	0.0	23.3
Fort Worth, TX	448,311	534,694	741,206	19.3	38.6
Gainesville, FL	90,519	95,447	124,354	5.4	30.3
Grand Rapids, MI	189,145	197,800	188,040	4.6	-4.9
Green Bay, WI	96,466	102,313	104,057	6.1	1.7
Greensboro, NC	193,389	223,891	269,666	15.8	20.4
Honolulu, HI	376,465	371,657	337,256	-1.3	-9.3
Houston, TX	1,697,610	1,953,631	2,099,451	15.1	7.5
Huntsville, AL	161,842	158,216	180,105	-2.2	13.8
Indianapolis, IN	730,993	781,870	820,445	7.0	4.9
Jacksonville, FL	635,221	735,617	821,784	15.8	11.7
Kansas City, MO	434,967	441,545	459,787	1.5	4.1
Lafayette, LA	104,735	110,257	120,623	5.3	9.4
Las Vegas, NV	261,374	478,434	583,756	83.0	22.0
Lexington, KY	225,366	260,512	295,803	15.6	13.5
Lincoln, NE	193,629	225,581	258,379	16.5	14.5
Little Rock, AR	177,519	183,133	193,524	3.2	5.7
Los Angeles, CA	3,487,671	3,694,820	3,792,621	5.9	2.6
Louisville, KY	269,160	256,231	597,337	-4.8	133.1
Lubbock, TX	187,170	199,564	229,573	6.6	15.0
Madison, WI	193,451	208,054	233,209	7.5	12.1
Manchester, NH	99,567	107,006	109,565	7.5	2.4
McAllen, TX	86,145	106,414	129,877	23.5	22.0
Miami, FL	358,843	362,470	399,457	1.0	10.2
Midland, TX	89,358	94,996	111,147	6.3	17.0

Table continued on next page.

City	1990 Census	2000 Census	2010 Census	Population Growth (%)	
				1990-2000	2000-2010
Minneapolis, MN	368,383	382,618	382,578	3.9	0.0
Nashville, TN	488,364	545,524	601,222	11.7	10.2
New Orleans, LA	496,938	484,674	343,829	-2.5	-29.1
New York, NY	7,322,552	8,008,278	8,175,133	9.4	2.1
Oklahoma City, OK	445,065	506,132	579,999	13.7	14.6
Omaha, NE	371,972	390,007	408,958	4.8	4.9
Orlando, FL	161,172	185,951	238,300	15.4	28.2
Oxnard, CA	143,271	170,358	197,899	18.9	16.2
Palm Bay, FL	62,587	79,413	103,190	26.9	29.9
Peoria, IL	114,341	112,936	115,007	-1.2	1.8
Philadelphia, PA	1,585,577	1,517,550	1,526,006	-4.3	0.6
Phoenix, AZ	989,873	1,321,045	1,445,632	33.5	9.4
Pittsburgh, PA	369,785	334,563	305,704	-9.5	-8.6
Portland, OR	485,833	529,121	583,776	8.9	10.3
Providence, RI	160,734	173,618	178,042	8.0	2.5
Provo, UT	87,148	105,166	112,488	20.7	7.0
Raleigh, NC	226,841	276,093	403,892	21.7	46.3
Reno, NV	139,950	180,480	225,221	29.0	24.8
Richmond, VA	202,783	197,790	204,214	-2.5	3.2
Roanoke, VA	96,415	94,911	97,032	-1.6	2.2
Rochester, MN	74,151	85,806	106,769	15.7	24.4
Sacramento, CA	368,923	407,018	466,488	10.3	14.6
Salem, OR	112,046	136,924	154,637	22.2	12.9
Salt Lake City, UT	159,796	181,743	186,440	13.7	2.6
San Antonio, TX	997,258	1,144,646	1,327,407	14.8	16.0
San Diego, CA	1,111,048	1,223,400	1,307,402	10.1	6.9
San Francisco, CA	723,959	776,733	805,235	7.3	3.7
San Jose, CA	784,324	894,943	945,942	14.1	5.7
Santa Rosa, CA	123,297	147,595	167,815	19.7	13.7
Savannah, GA	138,038	131,510	136,286	-4.7	3.6
Seattle, WA	516,262	563,374	608,660	9.1	8.0
Sioux Falls, SD	102,262	123,975	153,888	21.2	24.1
Spokane, WA	178,202	195,629	208,916	9.8	6.8
Springfield, IL	108,997	111,454	116,250	2.3	4.3
Tallahassee, FL	128,014	150,624	181,376	17.7	20.4
Tampa, FL	279,960	303,447	335,709	8.4	10.6
Topeka, KS	121,197	122,377	127,473	1.0	4.2
Tulsa, OK	367,241	393,049	391,906	7.0	-0.3
Tyler, TX	77,653	83,650	96,900	7.7	15.8
Virginia Beach, VA	393,069	425,257	437,994	8.2	3.0
Washington, DC	606,900	572,059	601,723	-5.7	5.2
Wichita, KS	313,693	344,284	382,368	9.8	11.1
Wilmington, NC	64,609	75,838	106,476	17.4	40.4
Winston-Salem, NC	168,139	185,776	229,617	10.5	23.6
Worcester, MA	169,759	172,648	181,045	1.7	4.9
U.S.	248,709,873	281,421,906	308,745,538	13.2	9.7

Source: U.S. Census Bureau, Census 2010, 2000, 1990

Population Growth: Metro Area

Metro Area	1990 Census	2000 Census	2010 Census	Population Growth (%)	
				1990-2000	2000-2010
Albuquerque, NM	599,416	729,649	887,077	21.7	21.6
Anchorage, AK	266,021	319,605	380,821	20.1	19.2
Ann Arbor, MI	282,937	322,895	344,791	14.1	6.8
Athens, GA	136,025	166,079	192,541	22.1	15.9
Atlanta, GA	3,069,411	4,247,981	5,268,860	38.4	24.0
Austin, TX	846,217	1,249,763	1,716,289	47.7	37.3
Billings, MT	121,499	138,904	158,050	14.3	13.8
Boise City, ID	319,596	464,840	616,561	45.4	32.6
Boston, MA	4,133,895	4,391,344	4,552,402	6.2	3.7
Boulder, CO	208,898	269,758	294,567	29.1	9.2
Cape Coral, FL	335,113	440,888	618,754	31.6	40.3
Cedar Rapids, IA	210,640	237,230	257,940	12.6	8.7
Charleston, SC	506,875	549,033	664,607	8.3	21.1
Charlotte, NC	1,024,331	1,330,448	1,758,038	29.9	32.1
Chicago, IL	8,182,076	9,098,316	9,461,105	11.2	4.0
Clarksville, TN	189,277	232,000	273,949	22.6	18.1
Colorado Springs, CO	409,482	537,484	645,613	31.3	20.1
Columbia, MO	122,010	145,666	172,786	19.4	18.6
Columbus, OH	1,405,176	1,612,694	1,836,536	14.8	13.9
Dallas, TX	3,989,294	5,161,544	6,371,773	29.4	23.4
Davenport, IA	368,151	376,019	379,690	2.1	1.0
Denver, CO	1,666,935	2,179,296	2,543,482	30.7	16.7
Des Moines, IA	416,346	481,394	569,633	15.6	18.3
Durham, NC	344,646	426,493	504,357	23.7	18.3
El Paso, TX	591,610	679,622	800,647	14.9	17.8
Erie, PA	275,603	280,843	280,566	1.9	-0.1
Eugene, OR	282,912	322,959	351,715	14.2	8.9
Fargo, ND	153,296	174,367	208,777	13.7	19.7
Fayetteville, NC	297,422	336,609	366,383	13.2	8.8
Fort Collins, CO	186,136	251,494	299,630	35.1	19.1
Fort Wayne, IN	354,435	390,156	416,257	10.1	6.7
Fort Worth, TX	3,989,294	5,161,544	6,371,773	29.4	23.4
Gainesville, FL	191,263	232,392	264,275	21.5	13.7
Grand Rapids, MI	645,914	740,482	774,160	14.6	4.5
Green Bay, WI	243,698	282,599	306,241	16.0	8.4
Greensboro, NC	540,257	643,430	723,801	19.1	12.5
Honolulu, HI	836,231	876,156	953,207	4.8	8.8
Houston, TX	3,767,335	4,715,407	5,946,800	25.2	26.1
Huntsville, AL	293,047	342,376	417,593	16.8	22.0
Indianapolis, IN	1,294,217	1,525,104	1,756,241	17.8	15.2
Jacksonville, FL	925,213	1,122,750	1,345,596	21.4	19.8
Kansas City, MO	1,636,528	1,836,038	2,035,334	12.2	10.9
Lafayette, LA	208,740	239,086	273,738	14.5	14.5
Las Vegas, NV	741,459	1,375,765	1,951,269	85.5	41.8
Lexington, KY	348,428	408,326	472,099	17.2	15.6
Lincoln, NE	229,091	266,787	302,157	16.5	13.3
Little Rock, AR	535,034	610,518	699,757	14.1	14.6
Los Angeles, CA	11,273,720	12,365,627	12,828,837	9.7	3.7
Louisville, KY	1,055,973	1,161,975	1,283,566	10.0	10.5
Lubbock, TX	229,940	249,700	284,890	8.6	14.1
Madison, WI	432,323	501,774	568,593	16.1	13.3
Manchester, NH	336,073	380,841	400,721	13.3	5.2
McAllen, TX	383,545	569,463	774,769	48.5	36.1
Miami, FL	4,056,100	5,007,564	5,564,635	23.5	11.1
Midland, TX	106,611	116,009	136,872	8.8	18.0

Table continued on next page.

Metro Area	1990 Census	2000 Census	2010 Census	Population Growth (%) 1990-2000	Population Growth (%) 2000-2010
Minneapolis, MN	2,538,834	2,968,806	3,279,833	16.9	10.5
Nashville, TN	1,048,218	1,311,789	1,589,934	25.1	21.2
New Orleans, LA	1,264,391	1,316,510	1,167,764	4.1	-11.3
New York, NY	16,845,992	18,323,002	18,897,109	8.8	3.1
Oklahoma City, OK	971,042	1,095,421	1,252,987	12.8	14.4
Omaha, NE	685,797	767,041	865,350	11.8	12.8
Orlando, FL	1,224,852	1,644,561	2,134,411	34.3	29.8
Oxnard, CA	669,016	753,197	823,318	12.6	9.3
Palm Bay, FL	398,978	476,230	543,376	19.4	14.1
Peoria, IL	358,552	366,899	379,186	2.3	3.3
Philadelphia, PA	5,435,470	5,687,147	5,965,343	4.6	4.9
Phoenix, AZ	2,238,480	3,251,876	4,192,887	45.3	28.9
Pittsburgh, PA	2,468,289	2,431,087	2,356,285	-1.5	-3.1
Portland, OR	1,523,741	1,927,881	2,226,009	26.5	15.5
Providence, RI	1,509,789	1,582,997	1,600,852	4.8	1.1
Provo, UT	269,407	376,774	526,810	39.9	39.8
Raleigh, NC	541,081	797,071	1,130,490	47.3	41.8
Reno, NV	257,193	342,885	425,417	33.3	24.1
Richmond, VA	949,244	1,096,957	1,258,251	15.6	14.7
Roanoke, VA	268,465	288,309	308,707	7.4	7.1
Rochester, MN	141,945	163,618	186,011	15.3	13.7
Sacramento, CA	1,481,126	1,796,857	2,149,127	21.3	19.6
Salem, OR	278,024	347,214	390,738	24.9	12.5
Salt Lake City, UT	768,075	968,858	1,124,197	26.1	16.0
San Antonio, TX	1,407,745	1,711,703	2,142,508	21.6	25.2
San Diego, CA	2,498,016	2,813,833	3,095,313	12.6	10.0
San Francisco, CA	3,686,592	4,123,740	4,335,391	11.9	5.1
San Jose, CA	1,534,280	1,735,819	1,836,911	13.1	5.8
Santa Rosa, CA	388,222	458,614	483,878	18.1	5.5
Savannah, GA	258,060	293,000	347,611	13.5	18.6
Seattle, WA	2,559,164	3,043,878	3,439,809	18.9	13.0
Sioux Falls, SD	153,500	187,093	228,261	21.9	22.0
Spokane, WA	361,364	417,939	471,221	15.7	12.7
Springfield, IL	189,550	201,437	210,170	6.3	4.3
Tallahassee, FL	259,096	320,304	367,413	23.6	14.7
Tampa, FL	2,067,959	2,395,997	2,783,243	15.9	16.2
Topeka, KS	210,257	224,551	233,870	6.8	4.2
Tulsa, OK	761,019	859,532	937,478	12.9	9.1
Tyler, TX	151,309	174,706	209,714	15.5	20.0
Virginia Beach, VA	1,449,389	1,576,370	1,671,683	8.8	6.0
Washington, DC	4,122,914	4,796,183	5,582,170	16.3	16.4
Wichita, KS	511,111	571,166	623,061	11.7	9.1
Wilmington, NC	200,124	274,532	362,315	37.2	32.0
Winston-Salem, NC	361,091	421,961	477,717	16.9	13.2
Worcester, MA	709,728	750,963	798,552	5.8	6.3
U.S.	248,709,873	281,421,906	308,745,538	13.2	9.7

Note: Figures cover the Metropolitan Statistical Area (MSA)—see Appendix B for areas included
Source: U.S. Census Bureau, Census 2010, 2000, 1990

Household Size: City

City	Persons in Household (%)							Average Household Size
	One	Two	Three	Four	Five	Six	Seven or More	
Albuquerque, NM	32.4	32.8	15.3	11.5	5.0	2.2	0.8	2.46
Anchorage, AK	26.3	33.1	17.1	13.0	5.7	2.6	2.2	2.77
Ann Arbor, MI	38.3	34.0	13.2	9.0	3.1	1.9	0.5	2.24
Athens, GA	34.3	33.9	14.6	11.5	3.4	1.5	0.8	2.63
Atlanta, GA	46.6	29.9	11.2	7.5	2.9	1.3	0.7	2.26
Austin, TX	33.8	33.1	14.8	10.7	4.7	1.6	1.2	2.46
Billings, MT	32.3	35.5	13.8	10.5	5.9	1.3	0.8	2.38
Boise City, ID	30.6	35.0	16.4	11.1	4.5	1.9	0.6	2.39
Boston, MA	37.7	31.4	14.8	9.7	3.9	1.6	1.0	2.37
Boulder, CO	33.1	36.1	16.0	10.3	3.7	0.7	0.2	2.26
Cape Coral, FL	22.0	41.5	15.7	11.2	6.5	1.8	1.2	2.87
Cedar Rapids, IA	33.0	34.9	13.7	11.7	3.9	1.7	1.1	2.39
Charleston, SC	36.8	35.9	14.1	9.3	2.9	0.5	0.4	2.28
Charlotte, NC	31.5	31.4	16.0	12.6	5.5	2.0	1.1	2.56
Chicago, IL	36.7	28.0	14.1	10.6	5.8	2.6	2.2	2.59
Clarksville, TN	22.0	32.0	19.2	15.5	6.8	2.3	2.0	2.72
Colorado Springs, CO	29.1	34.1	15.0	13.3	5.4	2.1	1.1	2.53
Columbia, MO	33.1	32.9	15.3	12.8	4.2	1.4	0.3	2.37
Columbus, OH	36.7	30.8	14.7	9.8	4.9	1.9	1.3	2.41
Dallas, TX	34.6	28.4	14.0	11.5	6.6	3.0	2.0	2.62
Davenport, IA	34.5	31.7	15.6	9.6	5.7	1.5	1.3	2.44
Denver, CO	40.6	31.5	12.0	8.3	4.2	2.0	1.4	2.30
Des Moines, IA	32.3	29.9	16.2	11.0	6.5	2.4	1.8	2.48
Durham, NC	34.2	33.8	14.4	10.9	4.0	2.0	0.7	2.35
El Paso, TX	23.2	26.6	18.9	16.6	8.9	3.6	2.2	3.01
Erie, PA	36.6	32.0	14.0	9.8	4.3	1.5	1.9	2.33
Eugene, OR	33.0	36.1	15.6	9.4	3.9	1.3	0.7	2.30
Fargo, ND	36.3	34.4	15.0	8.4	4.4	1.3	0.3	2.18
Fayetteville, NC	29.6	35.1	17.0	11.7	4.5	1.3	0.8	2.48
Fort Collins, CO	26.2	36.5	19.0	11.7	4.6	1.5	0.6	2.46
Fort Wayne, IN	33.1	30.6	16.1	11.5	5.3	2.3	1.1	2.46
Fort Worth, TX	27.1	28.4	15.2	15.0	8.3	3.5	2.4	2.87
Gainesville, FL	37.7	35.3	14.9	9.1	1.9	1.0	0.1	2.35
Grand Rapids, MI	33.1	31.5	13.7	11.8	5.8	2.3	1.7	2.51
Green Bay, WI	32.8	33.9	13.5	11.9	4.7	1.7	1.5	2.38
Greensboro, NC	33.9	33.2	15.0	11.2	4.4	1.5	0.8	2.34
Honolulu, HI	33.9	30.9	14.6	10.3	4.6	2.6	3.1	2.59
Houston, TX	32.2	29.3	15.0	11.8	7.0	2.7	2.1	2.70
Huntsville, AL	37.1	33.0	13.8	9.9	4.2	1.2	0.8	2.31
Indianapolis, IN	34.1	31.9	14.7	10.8	5.0	2.2	1.2	2.50
Jacksonville, FL	31.2	33.2	16.4	11.7	4.7	1.6	1.3	2.62
Kansas City, MO	36.3	32.9	13.6	10.2	4.3	1.6	1.1	2.38
Lafayette, LA	35.2	32.6	14.8	11.4	4.3	0.7	1.0	2.40
Las Vegas, NV	28.7	31.4	15.2	13.0	6.6	3.0	2.1	2.78
Lexington, KY	32.8	33.9	15.7	11.2	4.0	1.7	0.6	2.37
Lincoln, NE	31.1	35.2	14.2	11.3	5.1	2.0	1.0	2.38
Little Rock, AR	38.1	35.0	13.7	8.3	3.5	0.7	0.7	2.44
Los Angeles, CA	30.3	27.9	15.4	13.2	7.1	3.2	2.8	2.84
Louisville, KY	32.8	32.5	15.4	11.8	4.9	1.7	0.9	2.43
Lubbock, TX	29.5	33.1	15.2	13.4	5.1	2.3	1.3	2.55
Madison, WI	37.1	35.0	13.3	9.9	3.1	1.2	0.5	2.20
Manchester, NH	32.7	34.8	14.4	10.9	4.8	1.4	0.9	2.36
McAllen, TX	21.9	25.1	18.8	15.5	11.1	5.0	2.6	3.20
Miami, FL	36.5	30.3	15.4	10.3	4.2	1.8	1.4	2.66

Table continued on next page.

City	Persons in Household (%)							Average Household Size
	One	Two	Three	Four	Five	Six	Seven or More	
Midland, TX	24.3	32.7	18.4	13.5	6.7	2.6	1.9	2.80
Minneapolis, MN	40.0	32.4	11.4	8.9	3.8	1.6	1.9	2.27
Nashville, TN	36.8	32.2	13.8	10.3	4.0	1.6	1.1	2.41
New Orleans, LA	40.6	29.9	14.4	8.5	4.2	1.3	1.1	2.35
New York, NY	33.1	27.6	16.1	12.4	6.0	2.6	2.2	2.66
Oklahoma City, OK	31.1	32.2	15.4	11.4	6.1	2.4	1.4	2.57
Omaha, NE	33.9	31.8	13.7	10.7	6.1	2.1	1.7	2.47
Orlando, FL	37.7	32.9	13.6	10.5	3.4	1.2	0.6	2.41
Oxnard, CA	14.7	21.9	16.7	18.4	12.5	6.8	8.9	3.93
Palm Bay, FL	26.4	37.5	16.2	10.2	5.8	2.0	1.9	2.76
Peoria, IL	36.7	31.2	13.1	10.7	4.5	2.5	1.2	2.37
Philadelphia, PA	40.0	27.3	14.7	9.9	4.7	2.0	1.4	2.58
Phoenix, AZ	28.8	30.2	15.0	13.0	6.8	3.4	2.7	2.83
Pittsburgh, PA	41.3	33.2	12.7	8.1	3.2	0.9	0.6	2.14
Portland, OR	35.1	33.8	14.4	10.0	3.8	1.7	1.2	2.34
Providence, RI	30.8	27.0	18.5	14.3	5.9	1.9	1.5	2.67
Provo, UT	14.0	33.1	17.7	16.3	9.0	5.6	4.3	3.30
Raleigh, NC	33.1	32.0	15.4	12.4	4.4	1.8	0.8	2.43
Reno, NV	34.6	32.0	13.7	10.9	5.1	2.3	1.3	2.50
Richmond, VA	40.6	31.4	14.7	8.0	3.6	1.0	0.7	2.34
Roanoke, VA	36.7	33.3	15.1	9.3	3.2	1.0	1.4	2.27
Rochester, MN	31.7	33.5	13.6	12.6	5.6	1.7	1.3	2.45
Sacramento, CA	33.0	29.2	14.2	11.7	5.8	3.2	2.8	2.65
Salem, OR	29.7	32.1	14.9	12.6	6.6	2.7	1.5	2.59
Salt Lake City, UT	36.1	30.4	13.9	10.0	4.8	2.6	2.3	2.48
San Antonio, TX	28.5	29.1	16.5	13.2	7.4	3.0	2.3	2.82
San Diego, CA	29.0	32.4	15.7	12.8	5.7	2.5	1.9	2.73
San Francisco, CA	38.4	33.1	13.0	9.1	3.5	1.5	1.4	2.31
San Jose, CA	19.7	27.6	18.7	18.2	8.7	3.6	3.4	3.12
Santa Rosa, CA	28.9	32.1	15.3	13.2	6.9	1.6	2.0	2.67
Savannah, GA	35.4	31.6	15.3	9.3	5.1	2.1	1.1	2.54
Seattle, WA	41.3	33.2	12.2	8.7	2.9	1.0	0.8	2.12
Sioux Falls, SD	29.6	36.4	14.3	10.6	5.4	2.5	1.2	2.43
Spokane, WA	34.4	34.2	13.2	11.3	4.4	1.6	0.9	2.33
Springfield, IL	37.3	33.0	14.3	9.1	3.6	1.8	0.9	2.24
Tallahassee, FL	32.7	34.3	17.9	10.4	3.2	1.0	0.5	2.34
Tampa, FL	37.4	31.3	14.7	10.6	3.9	1.3	0.9	2.40
Topeka, KS	36.1	33.1	12.4	10.1	4.5	2.3	1.5	2.35
Tulsa, OK	34.8	32.5	14.0	10.3	5.1	2.1	1.2	2.38
Tyler, TX	32.7	32.0	16.5	11.2	3.4	2.0	2.1	2.49
Virginia Beach, VA	24.2	34.1	18.5	14.1	6.1	1.8	1.2	2.64
Washington, DC	44.7	30.1	12.1	7.6	3.4	1.3	0.8	2.21
Wichita, KS	32.5	32.0	14.1	11.6	5.8	2.2	1.8	2.53
Wilmington, NC	36.3	35.1	14.9	10.4	2.1	0.7	0.4	2.20
Winston-Salem, NC	34.8	32.0	13.9	11.3	4.4	2.5	1.1	2.43
Worcester, MA	32.4	29.7	16.3	12.4	6.1	1.9	1.2	2.52
U.S.	27.7	33.6	15.7	13.1	6.0	2.3	1.5	2.64

U.S. Census Bureau, 2011-2013 American Community Survey 3-Year Estimates

Household Size: Metro Area

Metro Area	Persons in Household (%)							Average Household Size
	One	Two	Three	Four	Five	Six	Seven or More	
Albuquerque, NM	29.5	33.8	15.3	12.1	5.6	2.5	1.2	2.59
Anchorage, AK	25.2	34.1	16.7	13.0	5.8	2.8	2.3	2.80
Ann Arbor, MI	31.2	34.3	14.6	12.6	4.8	1.6	0.8	2.44
Athens, GA	29.2	34.5	15.7	13.2	4.6	1.7	1.1	2.70
Atlanta, GA	26.6	31.4	16.6	14.8	6.5	2.5	1.5	2.78
Austin, TX	27.8	33.1	15.9	13.5	6.1	2.3	1.4	2.68
Billings, MT	29.8	37.1	13.4	11.5	5.6	1.5	1.0	2.44
Boise City, ID	24.1	34.7	15.5	13.9	6.8	3.0	1.8	2.71
Boston, MA	28.4	32.5	16.3	14.4	5.8	1.8	0.9	2.54
Boulder, CO	28.2	36.1	15.4	13.2	5.1	1.5	0.6	2.44
Cape Coral, FL	28.1	43.7	11.9	9.6	4.2	1.7	0.8	2.64
Cedar Rapids, IA	29.4	36.1	13.9	12.9	5.0	1.7	1.0	2.45
Charleston, SC	28.3	35.3	16.7	12.5	4.8	1.6	0.8	2.58
Charlotte, NC	26.7	33.8	17.0	13.5	5.9	2.1	1.1	2.66
Chicago, IL	28.5	29.9	15.8	14.2	7.1	2.8	1.8	2.73
Clarksville, TN	22.1	32.9	18.6	14.4	7.1	2.9	2.0	2.72
Colorado Springs, CO	25.7	35.0	15.6	14.2	6.0	2.3	1.2	2.63
Columbia, MO	30.3	34.7	16.0	12.4	4.6	1.4	0.5	2.42
Columbus, OH	29.4	33.2	15.6	12.9	5.7	2.0	1.1	2.55
Dallas, TX	25.2	30.8	16.6	15.0	7.5	3.0	1.8	2.80
Davenport, IA	31.4	35.2	14.1	11.3	5.4	1.6	1.1	2.42
Denver, CO	29.6	33.3	15.0	12.8	5.5	2.3	1.4	2.56
Des Moines, IA	27.0	34.2	15.9	13.6	6.2	2.0	1.1	2.52
Durham, NC	30.7	35.7	15.0	11.7	4.4	1.7	0.7	2.43
El Paso, TX	21.4	25.9	19.1	17.2	9.8	4.0	2.8	3.13
Erie, PA	30.2	35.4	14.6	11.8	5.1	1.8	1.1	2.44
Eugene, OR	29.4	38.0	15.2	10.3	4.4	1.6	1.0	2.39
Fargo, ND	31.8	34.4	15.2	11.4	5.1	1.7	0.5	2.34
Fayetteville, NC	28.0	32.5	18.3	12.9	5.6	1.6	1.1	2.60
Fort Collins, CO	25.4	39.4	16.1	12.2	4.7	1.6	0.7	2.45
Fort Wayne, IN	29.0	32.7	16.0	12.8	5.8	2.3	1.2	2.54
Fort Worth, TX	25.2	30.8	16.6	15.0	7.5	3.0	1.8	2.80
Gainesville, FL	32.8	35.9	15.2	10.7	3.5	1.1	0.7	2.47
Grand Rapids, MI	24.8	34.4	15.5	14.2	7.2	2.6	1.3	2.65
Green Bay, WI	27.6	36.5	14.2	13.7	5.5	1.6	1.0	2.47
Greensboro, NC	28.6	35.2	16.1	12.2	5.0	1.8	1.0	2.47
Honolulu, HI	23.7	30.1	17.1	14.1	7.2	3.4	4.3	3.04
Houston, TX	24.4	29.9	16.9	15.3	8.1	3.2	2.1	2.91
Huntsville, AL	29.3	34.6	15.9	12.7	5.0	1.4	0.9	2.50
Indianapolis, IN	28.6	33.3	15.8	13.2	5.9	2.2	1.0	2.58
Jacksonville, FL	28.4	34.9	16.2	12.5	5.1	1.8	1.0	2.65
Kansas City, MO	28.7	34.0	15.3	12.9	5.8	2.1	1.2	2.54
Lafayette, LA	27.9	32.2	17.8	12.9	5.8	2.1	1.3	2.63
Las Vegas, NV	27.8	32.0	15.4	13.1	6.7	3.2	2.0	2.79
Lexington, KY	29.6	35.0	16.0	12.2	4.5	1.9	0.7	2.45
Lincoln, NE	29.5	35.8	14.2	11.8	5.5	2.1	1.0	2.43
Little Rock, AR	29.7	36.6	15.4	11.4	4.8	1.4	0.6	2.58
Los Angeles, CA	24.9	28.1	16.4	15.4	8.3	3.7	3.2	3.03
Louisville, KY	29.2	34.3	15.8	12.9	5.3	1.7	0.8	2.51
Lubbock, TX	27.7	33.8	15.5	13.4	5.9	2.3	1.5	2.61
Madison, WI	30.2	36.7	14.6	11.8	4.3	1.7	0.7	2.37
Manchester, NH	25.3	35.7	16.0	14.8	5.8	1.5	1.0	2.56
McAllen, TX	15.9	23.7	17.8	17.4	13.0	6.7	5.6	3.60
Miami, FL	29.1	32.1	16.3	13.3	5.7	2.1	1.3	2.81

Table continued on next page.

Metro Area	Persons in Household (%)							Average Household Size
	One	Two	Three	Four	Five	Six	Seven or More	
Midland, TX	24.2	32.9	17.4	14.0	7.1	2.4	1.9	2.81
Minneapolis, MN	27.9	33.8	15.0	13.8	6.0	2.1	1.3	2.54
Nashville, TN	28.2	34.1	15.7	13.2	5.6	1.9	1.2	2.60
New Orleans, LA	31.4	32.5	16.3	11.8	5.3	1.6	1.1	2.56
New York, NY	28.1	28.9	16.9	14.7	6.8	2.6	1.9	2.75
Oklahoma City, OK	28.7	33.9	15.6	12.5	6.0	2.2	1.2	2.60
Omaha, NE	28.8	33.7	14.5	12.8	6.6	2.2	1.4	2.56
Orlando, FL	26.5	35.1	16.5	13.1	5.7	1.9	1.1	2.82
Oxnard, CA	20.7	30.5	17.3	16.0	8.3	3.7	3.5	3.08
Palm Bay, FL	30.5	39.9	13.4	10.0	4.1	1.1	1.0	2.48
Peoria, IL	29.8	36.0	13.6	12.5	5.0	2.0	1.1	2.45
Philadelphia, PA	29.7	31.2	16.4	13.5	6.0	2.1	1.2	2.63
Phoenix, AZ	26.8	34.8	14.3	12.7	6.4	3.0	2.1	2.76
Pittsburgh, PA	32.4	35.3	14.9	11.4	4.2	1.2	0.6	2.33
Portland, OR	27.6	34.6	15.7	13.0	5.6	2.0	1.5	2.57
Providence, RI	29.6	32.9	16.6	13.5	5.1	1.6	0.9	2.49
Provo, UT	12.5	26.4	15.8	17.2	12.5	9.2	6.3	3.64
Raleigh, NC	25.9	32.7	17.0	15.2	6.1	2.0	1.1	2.65
Reno, NV	29.7	34.9	14.3	12.4	5.0	2.3	1.4	2.59
Richmond, VA	28.6	34.1	16.6	13.2	5.1	1.7	0.8	2.60
Roanoke, VA	29.3	37.4	15.2	11.2	4.4	1.2	1.1	2.37
Rochester, MN	27.7	36.1	13.9	13.6	5.9	1.7	1.2	2.51
Sacramento, CA	26.2	32.7	15.9	13.7	6.6	2.9	2.0	2.73
Salem, OR	25.0	34.4	15.4	12.2	7.7	3.1	2.1	2.72
Salt Lake City, UT	22.8	29.5	16.0	14.2	8.8	4.8	3.9	3.04
San Antonio, TX	25.4	30.9	16.7	14.1	7.4	3.0	2.3	2.86
San Diego, CA	24.9	32.7	16.8	14.3	6.5	2.8	2.1	2.86
San Francisco, CA	28.4	31.5	16.3	13.8	5.9	2.4	1.7	2.67
San Jose, CA	21.6	29.2	18.6	17.4	7.7	2.9	2.6	2.94
Santa Rosa, CA	28.3	34.2	15.2	13.2	5.8	1.7	1.5	2.60
Savannah, GA	28.4	33.9	16.1	13.3	5.4	2.1	1.0	2.64
Seattle, WA	28.9	33.5	15.9	13.3	5.1	2.0	1.2	2.54
Sioux Falls, SD	26.9	36.5	14.2	12.2	6.3	2.5	1.4	2.53
Spokane, WA	28.9	37.1	13.7	12.0	5.3	1.9	1.2	2.46
Springfield, IL	31.3	35.1	15.5	10.7	4.8	1.8	0.9	2.36
Tallahassee, FL	28.9	35.0	18.0	11.8	4.0	1.5	0.9	2.46
Tampa, FL	32.0	36.0	14.3	10.9	4.2	1.5	0.9	2.49
Topeka, KS	29.9	36.0	13.2	11.7	5.4	2.3	1.6	2.46
Tulsa, OK	28.1	34.4	15.6	12.5	5.9	2.2	1.3	2.55
Tyler, TX	26.7	34.9	15.6	12.3	5.9	2.5	2.1	2.65
Virginia Beach, VA	26.2	34.3	17.8	12.9	5.8	1.8	1.1	2.62
Washington, DC	27.3	30.6	16.7	14.6	6.6	2.7	1.5	2.73
Wichita, KS	29.3	33.4	14.3	12.5	6.2	2.6	1.6	2.59
Wilmington, NC	30.3	36.8	15.7	11.9	3.4	1.3	0.6	2.41
Winston-Salem, NC	29.3	35.7	15.2	12.0	4.6	2.2	0.9	2.49
Worcester, MA	26.6	32.6	17.2	14.9	6.0	2.0	0.8	2.60
U.S.	27.7	33.6	15.7	13.1	6.0	2.3	1.5	2.64

Note: Figures cover the Metropolitan Statistical Area (MSA)—see Appendix B for areas included
Source: U.S. Census Bureau, 2011-2013 American Community Survey 3-Year Estimates

Race: City

City	White Alone[1] (%)	Black Alone[1] (%)	Asian Alone[1] (%)	AIAN[2] Alone[1] (%)	NHOPI[3] Alone[1] (%)	Other Race Alone[1] (%)	Two or More Races (%)
Albuquerque, NM	72.0	3.5	2.6	4.2	0.1	13.7	3.9
Anchorage, AK	65.9	6.0	8.4	6.7	2.1	1.4	9.5
Ann Arbor, MI	73.7	7.4	14.4	0.2	0.0	0.5	3.7
Athens, GA	65.5	26.4	4.3	0.2	0.0	1.5	2.1
Atlanta, GA	40.5	52.8	3.7	0.2	0.0	1.0	1.7
Austin, TX	74.9	7.7	6.6	0.6	0.1	6.8	3.3
Billings, MT	89.0	1.1	1.1	4.4	0.1	1.7	2.7
Boise City, ID	89.6	1.2	3.6	0.7	0.2	1.4	3.4
Boston, MA	53.4	25.2	9.1	0.4	0.0	7.5	4.5
Boulder, CO	89.4	0.8	4.5	0.2	0.0	2.0	3.0
Cape Coral, FL	91.0	3.4	1.8	0.4	0.0	2.1	1.4
Cedar Rapids, IA	87.3	6.5	1.7	0.3	0.0	1.1	3.1
Charleston, SC	71.8	24.4	1.4	0.2	0.1	0.5	1.6
Charlotte, NC	52.0	35.1	5.3	0.4	0.1	4.4	2.7
Chicago, IL	48.4	31.7	5.8	0.3	0.0	11.5	2.3
Clarksville, TN	66.5	22.7	2.2	1.0	0.4	2.2	5.0
Colorado Springs, CO	80.2	6.2	2.9	0.6	0.3	5.0	4.8
Columbia, MO	79.5	9.7	5.6	0.2	0.0	0.8	4.2
Columbus, OH	61.6	27.7	4.4	0.2	0.0	2.3	3.7
Dallas, TX	58.5	24.6	3.0	0.2	0.0	11.6	2.1
Davenport, IA	81.1	11.3	2.3	0.3	0.0	1.4	3.5
Denver, CO	75.0	9.9	3.5	1.0	0.1	7.0	3.4
Des Moines, IA	77.7	10.5	5.0	0.3	0.1	3.2	3.2
Durham, NC	48.6	40.2	4.8	0.6	0.1	2.5	3.2
El Paso, TX	83.2	3.6	1.2	0.5	0.2	9.1	2.2
Erie, PA	75.6	15.8	2.3	0.4	0.0	1.9	4.0
Eugene, OR	85.7	1.4	4.2	1.1	0.4	2.6	4.5
Fargo, ND	89.6	3.0	2.7	1.4	0.0	0.5	2.7
Fayetteville, NC	47.3	41.1	2.8	0.9	0.5	2.5	4.9
Fort Collins, CO	89.6	1.2	2.9	0.4	0.2	2.0	3.7
Fort Wayne, IN	73.9	16.1	3.3	0.3	0.1	2.8	3.4
Fort Worth, TX	66.2	18.7	3.6	0.8	0.2	7.5	3.0
Gainesville, FL	65.5	23.0	6.8	0.3	0.1	1.0	3.3
Grand Rapids, MI	69.5	20.8	1.9	0.4	0.0	2.7	4.6
Green Bay, WI	82.4	3.8	4.5	2.8	0.0	2.6	3.9
Greensboro, NC	49.1	41.6	3.9	0.4	0.1	2.6	2.2
Honolulu, HI	18.0	1.9	54.2	0.1	8.1	0.7	17.1
Houston, TX	58.2	23.1	6.2	0.4	0.0	10.1	2.0
Huntsville, AL	62.3	31.0	2.1	0.5	0.1	1.2	2.9
Indianapolis, IN	61.5	27.8	2.2	0.3	0.0	5.4	2.8
Jacksonville, FL	60.4	30.5	4.4	0.3	0.1	1.0	3.3
Kansas City, MO	59.7	28.5	2.6	0.5	0.2	4.8	3.6
Lafayette, LA	64.2	30.9	2.0	0.3	0.0	0.7	1.8
Las Vegas, NV	65.3	11.6	6.6	0.6	0.6	10.9	4.4
Lexington, KY	76.2	14.6	3.6	0.3	0.0	2.9	2.5
Lincoln, NE	86.8	4.1	4.1	0.7	0.1	1.2	3.1
Little Rock, AR	51.6	42.3	3.0	0.3	0.0	1.1	1.6
Los Angeles, CA	52.4	9.1	11.4	0.5	0.2	22.8	3.5
Louisville, KY	71.1	22.7	2.3	0.1	0.0	0.8	2.9
Lubbock, TX	77.6	8.0	2.3	0.6	0.1	8.1	3.4
Madison, WI	79.9	7.2	8.0	0.4	0.0	1.5	3.0
Manchester, NH	85.8	4.7	4.5	0.1	0.0	2.4	2.5
McAllen, TX	87.9	0.8	2.6	0.5	0.0	6.8	1.4
Miami, FL	75.4	19.8	1.0	0.2	0.0	2.6	1.1

Table continued on next page.

City	White Alone[1] (%)	Black Alone[1] (%)	Asian Alone[1] (%)	AIAN[2] Alone[1] (%)	NHOPI[3] Alone[1] (%)	Other Race Alone[1] (%)	Two or More Races (%)
Midland, TX	79.0	7.8	1.6	0.3	0.1	9.1	2.0
Minneapolis, MN	66.2	17.9	5.8	1.4	0.0	3.8	4.8
Nashville, TN	60.9	28.4	3.2	0.3	0.1	4.9	2.3
New Orleans, LA	34.1	59.8	3.0	0.3	0.0	1.5	1.4
New York, NY	43.7	24.7	13.2	0.4	0.1	14.9	3.1
Oklahoma City, OK	68.0	14.2	4.2	3.1	0.0	3.9	6.6
Omaha, NE	76.2	12.9	2.8	0.6	0.0	4.5	2.9
Orlando, FL	59.3	27.6	3.6	0.3	0.0	6.5	2.7
Oxnard, CA	73.8	2.8	8.0	0.9	0.2	10.5	3.8
Palm Bay, FL	75.3	17.6	1.4	0.5	0.0	2.0	3.3
Peoria, IL	62.5	27.1	5.3	0.5	0.0	1.2	3.4
Philadelphia, PA	41.4	43.0	6.6	0.3	0.1	6.0	2.6
Phoenix, AZ	76.6	6.8	3.2	2.0	0.2	8.4	2.8
Pittsburgh, PA	66.6	24.9	5.0	0.2	0.0	0.4	2.9
Portland, OR	77.8	6.1	7.6	0.7	0.5	2.9	4.4
Providence, RI	50.7	16.1	6.6	1.1	0.1	21.6	3.8
Provo, UT	87.1	0.9	3.1	0.5	1.4	3.7	3.3
Raleigh, NC	60.3	29.6	4.4	0.2	0.1	3.2	2.1
Reno, NV	78.6	2.8	6.5	0.9	0.8	6.9	3.4
Richmond, VA	43.4	49.0	2.2	0.3	0.0	1.5	3.6
Roanoke, VA	64.9	27.1	2.1	0.4	0.2	0.8	4.5
Rochester, MN	82.4	6.5	6.9	0.2	0.0	1.0	3.0
Sacramento, CA	49.8	14.1	18.6	0.8	1.4	8.4	6.9
Salem, OR	80.4	1.2	3.0	0.8	1.0	8.8	4.8
Salt Lake City, UT	73.7	2.9	5.2	1.2	2.4	11.9	2.7
San Antonio, TX	76.2	6.9	2.4	0.7	0.1	10.9	2.7
San Diego, CA	64.1	6.7	16.7	0.6	0.4	6.7	4.8
San Francisco, CA	49.5	5.8	33.4	0.4	0.4	6.1	4.4
San Jose, CA	45.8	3.0	32.9	0.7	0.4	12.5	4.7
Santa Rosa, CA	74.6	2.4	4.9	1.8	0.7	11.2	4.5
Savannah, GA	41.9	53.4	1.7	0.3	0.1	0.8	1.7
Seattle, WA	70.0	7.6	14.0	0.7	0.3	1.8	5.7
Sioux Falls, SD	86.1	4.6	2.2	2.8	0.0	2.3	2.1
Spokane, WA	87.7	2.6	2.9	1.5	0.3	0.9	4.0
Springfield, IL	75.1	19.2	2.4	0.2	0.0	0.7	2.3
Tallahassee, FL	56.6	35.8	3.9	0.3	0.0	1.2	2.3
Tampa, FL	64.0	25.9	3.9	0.3	0.1	2.9	3.0
Topeka, KS	78.2	10.6	1.4	1.0	0.0	2.7	6.1
Tulsa, OK	66.4	15.1	2.5	4.2	0.1	4.2	7.5
Tyler, TX	69.3	23.9	2.1	0.4	0.0	2.5	1.8
Virginia Beach, VA	68.3	19.3	6.5	0.3	0.1	1.2	4.3
Washington, DC	40.2	49.4	3.6	0.3	0.0	4.0	2.5
Wichita, KS	76.0	11.3	4.8	1.0	0.0	2.6	4.4
Wilmington, NC	75.4	19.6	1.7	0.4	0.0	1.5	1.2
Winston-Salem, NC	58.6	34.4	1.9	0.2	0.2	2.7	1.9
Worcester, MA	72.2	12.7	6.5	0.3	0.1	4.2	4.1
U.S.	73.9	12.6	5.0	0.8	0.2	4.7	2.9

Note: (1) Alone is defined as not being in combination with one or more other races; (2) American Indian and Alaska Native; (3) Native Hawaiian and Other Pacific Islander

Source: U.S. Census Bureau, 2011-2013 American Community Survey 3-Year Estimates

Race: Metro Area

Metro Area	White Alone[1] (%)	Black Alone[1] (%)	Asian Alone[1] (%)	AIAN[2] Alone[1] (%)	NHOPI[3] Alone[1] (%)	Other Race Alone[1] (%)	Two or More Races (%)
Albuquerque, NM	71.8	2.8	1.9	5.5	0.1	14.1	3.8
Anchorage, AK	70.3	4.8	6.7	6.4	1.7	1.3	8.8
Ann Arbor, MI	74.4	12.2	8.1	0.2	0.0	1.0	4.2
Athens, GA	73.4	19.5	3.4	0.3	0.0	1.4	2.0
Atlanta, GA	56.2	32.9	5.1	0.3	0.0	3.4	2.2
Austin, TX	78.6	7.3	4.9	0.5	0.1	5.7	2.9
Billings, MT	90.7	0.8	0.8	3.9	0.1	1.4	2.4
Boise City, ID	91.6	0.7	2.0	0.6	0.2	2.1	2.8
Boston, MA	78.1	7.8	6.9	0.2	0.0	4.1	2.9
Boulder, CO	88.3	1.0	4.1	0.5	0.1	3.2	2.9
Cape Coral, FL	84.1	8.3	1.6	0.4	0.0	3.9	1.7
Cedar Rapids, IA	91.4	3.7	1.6	0.4	0.0	0.8	2.1
Charleston, SC	67.3	27.2	1.7	0.4	0.1	1.2	2.2
Charlotte, NC	69.4	22.1	3.0	0.4	0.0	3.0	2.1
Chicago, IL	66.7	17.0	5.9	0.2	0.0	7.9	2.2
Clarksville, TN	73.0	18.5	1.7	0.6	0.4	1.6	4.2
Colorado Springs, CO	81.6	5.8	2.7	0.6	0.3	3.8	5.1
Columbia, MO	82.8	8.3	4.0	0.1	0.1	0.8	3.9
Columbus, OH	78.0	14.4	3.2	0.2	0.0	1.3	2.9
Dallas, TX	69.6	15.0	5.6	0.5	0.1	6.5	2.7
Davenport, IA	86.4	7.3	1.8	0.3	0.0	1.8	2.5
Denver, CO	81.9	5.6	3.8	0.8	0.1	4.4	3.5
Des Moines, IA	87.5	4.8	3.4	0.2	0.1	1.8	2.3
Durham, NC	62.8	26.8	4.5	0.5	0.0	2.7	2.7
El Paso, TX	82.1	3.4	1.1	0.6	0.2	10.4	2.2
Erie, PA	88.1	7.0	1.3	0.3	0.0	0.9	2.4
Eugene, OR	88.4	1.0	2.6	1.1	0.3	2.4	4.3
Fargo, ND	91.5	2.2	2.0	1.1	0.0	0.4	2.6
Fayetteville, NC	51.5	36.0	2.1	2.3	0.3	2.4	5.3
Fort Collins, CO	90.8	0.8	2.0	0.5	0.1	2.7	3.1
Fort Wayne, IN	82.2	10.3	2.4	0.3	0.1	2.0	2.7
Fort Worth, TX	69.6	15.0	5.6	0.5	0.1	6.5	2.7
Gainesville, FL	71.5	19.2	5.1	0.3	0.1	1.0	2.8
Grand Rapids, MI	86.1	6.5	2.2	0.5	0.0	1.9	2.9
Green Bay, WI	89.4	2.2	2.5	2.0	0.0	1.3	2.6
Greensboro, NC	65.6	26.1	3.2	0.5	0.0	2.5	2.0
Honolulu, HI	21.5	2.6	43.1	0.2	9.3	1.0	22.4
Houston, TX	65.7	17.2	6.9	0.4	0.1	7.6	2.2
Huntsville, AL	71.5	22.0	2.2	0.6	0.1	1.1	2.5
Indianapolis, IN	77.6	14.6	2.2	0.2	0.0	2.9	2.4
Jacksonville, FL	70.8	21.5	3.5	0.3	0.1	0.9	2.9
Kansas City, MO	79.1	12.5	2.5	0.5	0.1	2.5	2.9
Lafayette, LA	70.8	24.4	1.4	0.4	0.0	0.6	2.2
Las Vegas, NV	64.9	10.7	9.0	0.6	0.7	9.8	4.4
Lexington, KY	81.5	11.1	2.5	0.2	0.0	2.3	2.3
Lincoln, NE	88.2	3.6	3.6	0.7	0.1	1.1	2.8
Little Rock, AR	72.6	22.6	1.5	0.3	0.0	1.0	1.9
Los Angeles, CA	56.1	6.8	15.0	0.5	0.3	17.7	3.7
Louisville, KY	80.8	14.0	1.7	0.1	0.0	1.0	2.4
Lubbock, TX	79.9	6.9	1.9	0.5	0.1	7.6	3.2
Madison, WI	87.2	4.5	4.2	0.3	0.0	1.4	2.3
Manchester, NH	90.6	2.3	3.4	0.1	0.0	1.4	2.2
McAllen, TX	92.3	0.6	1.0	0.3	0.0	5.0	0.7
Miami, FL	71.7	21.3	2.4	0.2	0.0	2.5	1.9

Table continued on next page.

Metro Area	White Alone[1] (%)	Black Alone[1] (%)	Asian Alone[1] (%)	AIAN[2] Alone[1] (%)	NHOPI[3] Alone[1] (%)	Other Race Alone[1] (%)	Two or More Races (%)
Midland, TX	81.1	6.5	1.5	0.4	0.1	8.8	1.8
Minneapolis, MN	81.2	7.4	5.9	0.6	0.0	1.8	3.0
Nashville, TN	77.7	15.3	2.3	0.3	0.0	2.5	1.9
New Orleans, LA	58.5	34.7	2.8	0.4	0.0	1.9	1.6
New York, NY	59.5	17.2	10.2	0.3	0.0	10.1	2.8
Oklahoma City, OK	74.5	10.1	2.9	3.7	0.1	2.6	6.1
Omaha, NE	84.3	7.7	2.3	0.5	0.1	2.6	2.5
Orlando, FL	71.7	16.1	4.1	0.3	0.1	4.8	2.9
Oxnard, CA	77.7	1.8	6.9	0.6	0.1	8.4	4.3
Palm Bay, FL	83.4	10.2	2.1	0.2	0.1	1.3	2.6
Peoria, IL	85.8	9.2	2.1	0.2	0.0	0.7	2.0
Philadelphia, PA	68.1	20.8	5.2	0.2	0.0	3.2	2.4
Phoenix, AZ	80.5	5.1	3.4	2.2	0.2	5.6	2.9
Pittsburgh, PA	87.5	8.2	1.9	0.1	0.0	0.3	1.9
Portland, OR	82.1	2.9	6.0	0.8	0.5	3.6	4.0
Providence, RI	83.6	5.4	2.8	0.4	0.0	5.1	2.7
Provo, UT	91.9	0.6	1.5	0.5	0.9	2.3	2.3
Raleigh, NC	69.7	20.3	4.7	0.4	0.0	2.8	2.2
Reno, NV	80.7	2.4	5.3	1.6	0.6	5.9	3.5
Richmond, VA	62.0	30.2	3.3	0.4	0.0	1.5	2.5
Roanoke, VA	82.3	12.8	1.7	0.2	0.1	0.4	2.5
Rochester, MN	89.5	3.6	3.9	0.2	0.0	0.7	2.1
Sacramento, CA	66.6	7.2	12.3	0.8	0.7	6.4	5.9
Salem, OR	82.2	0.8	1.9	1.2	0.6	9.0	4.3
Salt Lake City, UT	83.8	1.6	3.3	0.9	1.5	6.3	2.6
San Antonio, TX	78.8	6.5	2.2	0.6	0.1	8.7	3.1
San Diego, CA	71.0	5.1	11.2	0.7	0.5	6.8	4.7
San Francisco, CA	54.3	8.0	23.8	0.5	0.7	7.4	5.4
San Jose, CA	50.6	2.6	32.1	0.5	0.4	9.4	4.5
Santa Rosa, CA	78.1	1.6	3.9	1.2	0.3	10.8	4.1
Savannah, GA	60.9	33.5	2.2	0.3	0.1	0.9	2.3
Seattle, WA	72.7	5.6	11.8	0.9	0.8	2.4	5.7
Sioux Falls, SD	89.5	3.3	1.5	2.1	0.0	1.7	1.8
Spokane, WA	89.4	1.8	2.1	1.7	0.3	0.9	3.7
Springfield, IL	84.0	11.5	1.7	0.2	0.0	0.6	2.0
Tallahassee, FL	61.0	32.9	2.4	0.3	0.0	1.4	2.0
Tampa, FL	79.5	12.0	3.0	0.4	0.1	2.5	2.6
Topeka, KS	85.5	6.1	0.9	1.2	0.0	1.6	4.6
Tulsa, OK	72.7	8.0	1.9	6.9	0.1	2.4	8.0
Tyler, TX	76.7	18.1	1.3	0.3	0.0	2.1	1.5
Virginia Beach, VA	60.4	30.9	3.6	0.3	0.1	1.1	3.6
Washington, DC	56.0	25.4	9.5	0.3	0.1	5.1	3.6
Wichita, KS	82.7	7.5	3.3	0.9	0.0	1.9	3.7
Wilmington, NC	80.0	15.1	1.1	0.5	0.0	1.7	1.6
Winston-Salem, NC	77.1	17.6	1.4	0.3	0.1	2.0	1.5
Worcester, MA	85.9	4.2	3.9	0.2	0.0	3.1	2.7
U.S.	73.9	12.6	5.0	0.8	0.2	4.7	2.9

Note: (1) Figures cover the Metropolitan Statistical Area (MSA)—see Appendix B for areas included; (1) Alone is defined as not being in combination with one or more other races; (2) American Indian and Alaska Native; (3) Native Hawaiian & Other Pacific Islander
Source: U.S. Census Bureau, 2011-2013 American Community Survey 3-Year Estimates

Hispanic Origin: City

City	Hispanic or Latino (%)	Mexican (%)	Puerto Rican (%)	Cuban (%)	Other Hispanic or Latino (%)
Albuquerque, NM	46.9	26.2	0.5	0.6	19.6
Anchorage, AK	8.3	4.5	1.2	0.2	2.3
Ann Arbor, MI	4.4	2.2	0.2	0.1	1.9
Athens, GA	10.6	7.2	0.4	0.4	2.7
Atlanta, GA	5.3	2.8	0.7	0.4	1.5
Austin, TX	33.9	28.5	0.6	0.5	4.3
Billings, MT	5.5	3.9	0.4	0.0	1.1
Boise City, ID	7.6	6.3	0.2	0.1	1.1
Boston, MA	18.5	1.1	5.0	0.4	12.0
Boulder, CO	8.3	5.9	0.3	0.3	1.8
Cape Coral, FL	19.1	1.9	5.3	5.6	6.3
Cedar Rapids, IA	3.7	2.9	0.2	0.0	0.6
Charleston, SC	2.9	1.0	1.0	0.4	0.7
Charlotte, NC	13.4	5.2	1.0	0.3	6.7
Chicago, IL	29.1	21.8	3.8	0.3	3.2
Clarksville, TN	10.2	5.2	2.8	0.1	2.1
Colorado Springs, CO	17.1	11.2	0.9	0.2	4.7
Columbia, MO	3.6	2.1	0.4	0.5	0.7
Columbus, OH	5.8	3.5	0.7	0.1	1.4
Dallas, TX	41.8	37.2	0.4	0.2	4.0
Davenport, IA	8.1	7.1	0.3	0.1	0.6
Denver, CO	31.2	26.3	0.6	0.2	4.0
Des Moines, IA	12.4	9.8	0.2	0.1	2.2
Durham, NC	13.8	8.2	0.7	0.3	4.6
El Paso, TX	79.7	75.7	1.1	0.3	2.7
Erie, PA	6.8	1.0	5.1	0.2	0.5
Eugene, OR	8.3	6.5	0.3	0.1	1.4
Fargo, ND	2.9	2.0	0.2	0.1	0.6
Fayetteville, NC	11.1	4.1	3.8	0.3	2.9
Fort Collins, CO	10.6	7.4	0.8	0.1	2.3
Fort Wayne, IN	8.3	6.4	0.4	0.1	1.4
Fort Worth, TX	34.5	31.1	0.7	0.1	2.6
Gainesville, FL	10.1	1.1	2.5	2.8	3.8
Grand Rapids, MI	15.0	9.0	1.5	0.3	4.2
Green Bay, WI	12.3	9.4	1.4	0.1	1.5
Greensboro, NC	7.4	4.5	0.5	0.2	2.2
Honolulu, HI	6.0	1.6	2.1	0.1	2.1
Houston, TX	43.8	33.0	0.5	0.3	9.9
Huntsville, AL	5.8	3.9	0.8	0.1	1.0
Indianapolis, IN	9.7	7.2	0.5	0.1	1.9
Jacksonville, FL	8.2	1.8	2.7	1.0	2.7
Kansas City, MO	10.0	7.6	0.4	0.3	1.6
Lafayette, LA	4.4	2.0	0.3	0.2	2.0
Las Vegas, NV	31.7	24.5	0.9	0.9	5.3
Lexington, KY	6.9	5.1	0.5	0.2	1.2
Lincoln, NE	6.7	5.0	0.2	0.1	1.4
Little Rock, AR	5.9	4.1	0.2	0.0	1.5
Los Angeles, CA	48.6	32.5	0.5	0.3	15.3
Louisville, KY	4.8	2.2	0.3	1.4	0.9
Lubbock, TX	33.6	29.3	0.2	0.0	4.0
Madison, WI	6.9	4.9	0.8	0.2	1.0
Manchester, NH	8.1	2.6	2.2	0.1	3.2
McAllen, TX	84.8	80.5	0.4	0.1	3.8
Miami, FL	70.3	2.0	3.3	34.4	30.6
Midland, TX	39.9	37.9	0.1	0.3	1.7

Table continued on next page.

City	Hispanic or Latino (%)	Mexican (%)	Puerto Rican (%)	Cuban (%)	Other Hispanic or Latino (%)
Minneapolis, MN	10.1	6.4	0.4	0.2	3.1
Nashville, TN	10.1	6.1	0.6	0.4	3.1
New Orleans, LA	5.4	1.2	0.4	0.3	3.5
New York, NY	28.8	3.9	8.9	0.5	15.5
Oklahoma City, OK	18.3	15.6	0.3	0.1	2.3
Omaha, NE	13.3	10.6	0.3	0.1	2.3
Orlando, FL	27.7	2.7	14.8	1.5	8.7
Oxnard, CA	73.8	69.7	0.4	0.1	3.6
Palm Bay, FL	13.6	1.2	6.9	1.6	3.8
Peoria, IL	5.4	4.2	0.3	0.0	0.8
Philadelphia, PA	13.0	1.1	8.6	0.2	3.1
Phoenix, AZ	40.6	37.4	0.5	0.3	2.4
Pittsburgh, PA	2.5	0.9	0.6	0.2	0.9
Portland, OR	9.6	7.5	0.3	0.2	1.5
Providence, RI	40.0	1.9	8.1	0.3	29.7
Provo, UT	18.2	11.2	0.4	0.4	6.3
Raleigh, NC	11.3	5.1	1.1	0.3	4.8
Reno, NV	25.4	20.1	0.6	0.1	4.6
Richmond, VA	6.3	2.1	0.6	0.1	3.6
Roanoke, VA	5.7	1.8	0.7	0.3	3.0
Rochester, MN	5.5	4.0	0.4	0.1	0.9
Sacramento, CA	27.5	23.8	0.8	0.1	2.7
Salem, OR	20.7	18.8	0.1	0.1	1.7
Salt Lake City, UT	20.2	16.2	0.3	0.0	3.8
San Antonio, TX	63.0	57.1	1.0	0.2	4.6
San Diego, CA	29.9	26.4	0.7	0.2	2.6
San Francisco, CA	15.3	7.6	0.6	0.2	6.9
San Jose, CA	33.4	29.1	0.4	0.2	3.7
Santa Rosa, CA	30.2	26.2	0.6	0.0	3.4
Savannah, GA	5.7	2.7	1.1	0.2	1.7
Seattle, WA	6.8	4.3	0.4	0.2	1.9
Sioux Falls, SD	4.9	2.5	0.1	0.0	2.3
Spokane, WA	5.5	3.6	0.2	0.1	1.7
Springfield, IL	2.5	1.7	0.2	0.0	0.6
Tallahassee, FL	6.6	1.5	1.5	1.5	2.2
Tampa, FL	22.6	2.5	7.4	6.5	6.2
Topeka, KS	13.7	12.0	0.4	0.1	1.2
Tulsa, OK	14.6	12.2	0.5	0.1	1.8
Tyler, TX	22.8	20.8	0.2	0.1	1.8
Virginia Beach, VA	7.2	2.3	2.4	0.2	2.3
Washington, DC	9.9	1.4	0.6	0.3	7.6
Wichita, KS	15.9	14.3	0.5	0.1	1.1
Wilmington, NC	5.2	3.2	0.4	0.1	1.4
Winston-Salem, NC	15.5	11.0	1.3	0.2	3.1
Worcester, MA	20.6	0.9	12.4	0.2	7.1
U.S.	16.9	10.8	1.6	0.6	3.8

Note: Persons of Hispanic or Latino origin can be of any race
Source: U.S. Census Bureau, 2011-2013 American Community Survey 3-Year Estimates

Hispanic Origin: Metro Area

Metro Area	Hispanic or Latino (%)	Mexican (%)	Puerto Rican (%)	Cuban (%)	Other Hispanic or Latino (%)
Albuquerque, NM	47.4	25.6	0.4	0.4	21.0
Anchorage, AK	7.3	4.1	1.1	0.2	2.0
Ann Arbor, MI	4.3	2.2	0.3	0.1	1.7
Athens, GA	8.2	5.6	0.5	0.3	1.9
Atlanta, GA	10.5	6.0	1.0	0.4	3.1
Austin, TX	31.7	26.9	0.6	0.4	3.9
Billings, MT	4.9	3.8	0.3	0.0	0.8
Boise City, ID	12.8	10.9	0.3	0.1	1.5
Boston, MA	9.7	0.6	2.7	0.2	6.1
Boulder, CO	13.6	10.8	0.3	0.2	2.3
Cape Coral, FL	18.9	5.8	4.2	3.5	5.4
Cedar Rapids, IA	2.6	1.8	0.1	0.0	0.6
Charleston, SC	5.3	2.9	0.8	0.1	1.4
Charlotte, NC	9.4	4.5	0.9	0.3	3.7
Chicago, IL	21.2	16.8	2.1	0.2	2.1
Clarksville, TN	7.9	4.4	1.7	0.1	1.7
Colorado Springs, CO	15.3	9.5	1.1	0.2	4.5
Columbia, MO	3.1	1.9	0.3	0.3	0.6
Columbus, OH	3.7	2.2	0.5	0.1	0.9
Dallas, TX	27.8	23.7	0.6	0.2	3.3
Davenport, IA	8.0	7.2	0.3	0.1	0.4
Denver, CO	22.7	18.1	0.5	0.1	3.9
Des Moines, IA	6.9	5.1	0.2	0.1	1.4
Durham, NC	11.3	6.9	0.6	0.2	3.5
El Paso, TX	81.2	77.4	1.0	0.2	2.6
Erie, PA	3.6	0.7	2.4	0.1	0.5
Eugene, OR	7.8	6.3	0.3	0.1	1.2
Fargo, ND	2.7	2.0	0.2	0.1	0.4
Fayetteville, NC	10.6	4.1	3.7	0.3	2.5
Fort Collins, CO	10.8	8.1	0.4	0.1	2.2
Fort Wayne, IN	6.1	4.6	0.4	0.1	1.0
Fort Worth, TX	27.8	23.7	0.6	0.2	3.3
Gainesville, FL	8.5	1.4	2.3	2.0	2.8
Grand Rapids, MI	8.8	6.0	0.8	0.3	1.7
Green Bay, WI	6.6	4.6	0.8	0.1	1.0
Greensboro, NC	7.8	5.5	0.6	0.2	1.5
Honolulu, HI	8.9	2.6	3.1	0.1	3.1
Houston, TX	35.9	27.7	0.5	0.3	7.3
Huntsville, AL	4.9	3.5	0.6	0.1	0.7
Indianapolis, IN	6.2	4.5	0.3	0.1	1.3
Jacksonville, FL	7.4	1.7	2.4	0.9	2.5
Kansas City, MO	8.5	6.5	0.3	0.2	1.4
Lafayette, LA	3.4	1.8	0.2	0.1	1.3
Las Vegas, NV	29.7	22.7	1.0	1.1	5.0
Lexington, KY	5.6	4.2	0.4	0.1	0.9
Lincoln, NE	6.0	4.5	0.2	0.1	1.2
Little Rock, AR	4.9	3.7	0.2	0.0	1.0
Los Angeles, CA	44.8	34.9	0.5	0.4	9.0
Louisville, KY	4.2	2.2	0.3	0.7	0.9
Lubbock, TX	33.8	29.8	0.2	0.0	3.7
Madison, WI	5.4	4.0	0.5	0.1	0.9
Manchester, NH	5.6	1.8	1.5	0.1	2.2
McAllen, TX	90.9	88.4	0.2	0.1	2.2
Miami, FL	42.2	2.4	3.7	18.2	17.8
Midland, TX	40.1	37.8	0.3	0.2	1.7

Table continued on next page.

Metro Area	Hispanic or Latino (%)	Mexican (%)	Puerto Rican (%)	Cuban (%)	Other Hispanic or Latino (%)
Minneapolis, MN	5.5	3.7	0.3	0.1	1.4
Nashville, TN	6.7	4.2	0.5	0.2	1.7
New Orleans, LA	8.1	1.8	0.5	0.6	5.2
New York, NY	23.2	3.0	6.4	0.7	13.1
Oklahoma City, OK	11.9	10.0	0.3	0.1	1.6
Omaha, NE	9.4	7.4	0.3	0.1	1.6
Orlando, FL	26.7	3.4	13.5	1.9	7.9
Oxnard, CA	41.2	36.6	0.5	0.2	3.9
Palm Bay, FL	8.7	1.5	3.4	1.1	2.7
Peoria, IL	3.1	2.3	0.3	0.0	0.4
Philadelphia, PA	8.3	1.7	4.3	0.2	2.1
Phoenix, AZ	29.8	26.8	0.6	0.2	2.2
Pittsburgh, PA	1.4	0.5	0.4	0.0	0.5
Portland, OR	11.2	9.2	0.3	0.1	1.5
Providence, RI	10.9	0.7	3.6	0.1	6.5
Provo, UT	10.8	7.1	0.2	0.1	3.4
Raleigh, NC	10.3	5.9	1.0	0.3	3.1
Reno, NV	22.8	18.0	0.5	0.1	4.1
Richmond, VA	5.4	1.8	1.0	0.2	2.4
Roanoke, VA	3.4	1.3	0.4	0.3	1.3
Rochester, MN	4.0	3.0	0.3	0.1	0.6
Sacramento, CA	20.6	17.0	0.7	0.2	2.8
Salem, OR	22.6	20.7	0.2	0.0	1.7
Salt Lake City, UT	17.1	12.8	0.3	0.1	4.0
San Antonio, TX	54.4	48.9	1.0	0.2	4.3
San Diego, CA	32.7	29.1	0.7	0.2	2.7
San Francisco, CA	21.8	14.7	0.7	0.2	6.3
San Jose, CA	27.7	23.7	0.4	0.1	3.5
Santa Rosa, CA	25.5	21.7	0.5	0.1	3.2
Savannah, GA	5.5	2.8	1.1	0.2	1.3
Seattle, WA	9.3	6.8	0.5	0.1	1.9
Sioux Falls, SD	3.7	1.9	0.1	0.0	1.7
Spokane, WA	4.7	3.3	0.2	0.1	1.1
Springfield, IL	2.0	1.4	0.1	0.0	0.4
Tallahassee, FL	6.2	1.9	1.2	1.1	2.0
Tampa, FL	17.0	3.5	5.6	3.3	4.6
Topeka, KS	9.3	8.1	0.4	0.0	0.9
Tulsa, OK	8.7	7.2	0.4	0.1	1.1
Tyler, TX	18.0	16.3	0.2	0.1	1.4
Virginia Beach, VA	5.8	2.0	1.8	0.2	1.8
Washington, DC	14.4	2.2	0.9	0.3	11.0
Wichita, KS	11.9	10.6	0.4	0.1	0.8
Wilmington, NC	5.6	4.0	0.5	0.2	0.9
Winston-Salem, NC	9.6	6.7	0.7	0.2	2.0
Worcester, MA	9.9	0.7	5.8	0.1	3.3
U.S.	16.9	10.8	1.6	0.6	3.8

Note: Persons of Hispanic or Latino origin can be of any race; Figures cover the Metropolitan Statistical Area (MSA)—see Appendix B for areas included

Source: U.S. Census Bureau, 2011-2013 American Community Survey 3-Year Estimates

Age: City

City	Percent of Population							
	Under Age 5	Age 5–19	Age 20–34	Age 35–44	Age 45–54	Age 55–64	Age 65–74	Age 75–84
Albuquerque, NM	6.7	19.3	23.1	12.7	13.3	12.0	7.1	4.0
Anchorage, AK	7.5	20.5	25.4	12.9	14.0	11.7	5.2	2.2
Ann Arbor, MI	4.2	19.5	37.9	9.5	9.2	9.5	5.5	3.1
Athens, GA	5.9	21.3	36.8	10.3	8.8	8.2	5.0	2.5
Atlanta, GA	6.2	16.3	30.7	14.8	12.3	9.6	5.7	3.0
Austin, TX	6.8	18.1	31.0	15.4	12.1	9.3	4.2	2.1
Billings, MT	6.6	18.7	21.6	12.0	13.3	12.9	7.8	4.7
Boise City, ID	5.9	18.7	23.9	13.3	13.9	12.6	6.5	3.4
Boston, MA	5.4	15.9	34.9	12.4	11.3	9.6	5.6	3.2
Boulder, CO	3.9	19.8	36.0	10.7	10.5	9.4	5.4	2.7
Cape Coral, FL	5.7	19.8	14.8	12.3	14.5	14.2	10.9	5.4
Cedar Rapids, IA	6.9	19.3	23.3	12.4	12.8	12.1	6.6	4.5
Charleston, SC	6.2	15.6	30.0	12.1	11.6	11.7	7.5	3.6
Charlotte, NC	7.4	20.3	24.6	15.5	13.3	10.0	5.1	2.7
Chicago, IL	6.8	18.3	27.3	14.2	12.4	10.2	5.9	3.3
Clarksville, TN	9.2	21.4	30.4	13.3	10.9	7.7	4.2	2.1
Colorado Springs, CO	7.1	20.3	23.6	12.4	13.8	11.4	6.4	3.6
Columbia, MO	6.2	20.2	36.1	10.0	9.9	8.8	4.4	2.9
Columbus, OH	7.7	18.6	29.1	13.5	12.2	10.1	5.0	2.7
Dallas, TX	8.1	20.2	26.4	14.0	12.4	9.8	5.1	2.8
Davenport, IA	7.2	19.8	23.1	12.2	12.8	12.4	6.5	3.7
Denver, CO	7.0	16.3	28.6	15.3	11.7	10.5	5.8	3.1
Des Moines, IA	8.0	20.2	24.5	12.8	12.8	10.9	6.0	3.3
Durham, NC	7.5	18.5	28.1	14.3	12.0	10.3	5.4	2.5
El Paso, TX	7.9	23.3	22.4	12.5	12.5	10.0	6.2	3.9
Erie, PA	7.0	19.8	24.3	11.5	12.8	11.4	6.6	4.2
Eugene, OR	4.7	17.8	28.7	11.9	11.3	12.2	7.2	3.8
Fargo, ND	6.4	18.0	32.8	11.1	10.9	10.2	4.8	3.7
Fayetteville, NC	8.4	19.6	28.7	11.6	11.5	9.8	5.7	3.7
Fort Collins, CO	5.5	19.6	33.0	11.5	11.7	9.8	5.0	2.5
Fort Wayne, IN	7.5	21.1	21.4	12.5	13.0	11.8	6.6	4.0
Fort Worth, TX	8.6	23.2	23.4	14.3	12.5	9.3	4.8	2.6
Gainesville, FL	4.5	17.7	43.9	8.4	8.0	9.1	4.2	3.0
Grand Rapids, MI	7.9	20.0	28.0	11.8	10.9	10.0	5.2	3.8
Green Bay, WI	7.7	19.1	24.3	11.8	13.3	11.8	5.8	4.0
Greensboro, NC	6.5	19.6	25.1	12.8	12.9	11.1	6.5	4.0
Honolulu, HI	5.4	14.9	22.7	12.6	13.5	13.0	8.3	6.0
Houston, TX	7.8	20.1	25.8	14.0	12.6	10.2	5.5	2.9
Huntsville, AL	6.2	18.5	22.8	12.0	14.7	11.7	7.7	4.5
Indianapolis, IN	7.5	19.9	24.2	13.0	13.4	11.3	5.9	3.3
Jacksonville, FL	7.0	18.9	23.2	13.1	14.1	12.0	6.8	3.4
Kansas City, MO	7.2	18.7	24.1	13.2	13.6	11.8	6.4	3.5
Lafayette, LA	5.5	19.4	26.8	11.7	13.2	11.5	6.6	4.0
Las Vegas, NV	6.8	20.5	20.6	14.2	13.6	11.3	7.7	4.1
Lexington, KY	6.3	18.3	26.9	13.3	12.9	11.2	6.2	3.2
Lincoln, NE	7.0	19.7	27.4	12.0	11.7	11.0	6.0	3.6
Little Rock, AR	6.8	18.4	23.1	13.6	13.1	12.4	7.0	3.7
Los Angeles, CA	6.5	18.7	25.4	14.8	13.3	10.5	5.9	3.4
Louisville, KY	6.7	19.1	21.2	12.8	14.2	12.8	7.0	4.3
Lubbock, TX	7.1	21.7	29.2	10.5	11.1	9.5	5.8	4.0
Madison, WI	5.7	16.6	34.9	11.5	11.2	10.1	5.3	3.1
Manchester, NH	5.6	17.6	24.2	14.0	13.8	11.8	7.0	3.8
McAllen, TX	7.5	24.4	21.3	13.9	11.8	10.1	6.4	3.0
Miami, FL	6.3	14.4	23.2	14.8	14.2	11.2	7.9	5.5

Table continued on next page.

City	Percent of Population							
	Under Age 5	Age 5–19	Age 20–34	Age 35–44	Age 45–54	Age 55–64	Age 65–74	Age 75–84
Midland, TX	8.5	21.8	23.7	12.0	12.2	11.0	5.4	3.7
Minneapolis, MN	6.9	17.2	31.8	13.3	11.9	10.4	4.8	2.3
Nashville, TN	7.1	17.4	27.2	13.8	12.9	11.1	5.8	3.3
New Orleans, LA	6.3	17.3	26.3	12.4	13.5	12.8	6.5	3.4
New York, NY	6.6	17.2	25.1	14.0	13.3	11.3	6.8	3.9
Oklahoma City, OK	8.0	19.9	24.1	12.6	12.7	11.5	6.2	3.5
Omaha, NE	7.4	20.5	23.7	12.3	13.1	11.5	6.2	3.7
Orlando, FL	7.3	16.8	29.0	14.9	12.8	9.4	5.4	3.1
Oxnard, CA	8.6	22.8	25.2	13.5	11.8	9.4	5.0	2.8
Palm Bay, FL	5.9	19.4	17.0	11.1	16.3	13.7	9.3	5.2
Peoria, IL	7.1	21.5	23.8	11.8	11.3	11.4	6.8	3.8
Philadelphia, PA	6.9	18.7	26.4	12.2	12.6	11.1	6.5	3.9
Phoenix, AZ	7.7	22.1	23.2	14.2	13.5	10.2	5.3	2.6
Pittsburgh, PA	5.0	16.4	30.9	10.4	11.4	12.0	6.7	4.5
Portland, OR	5.8	15.0	26.6	16.7	12.9	12.2	6.3	2.9
Providence, RI	5.9	23.0	30.3	12.1	11.1	8.9	4.5	2.5
Provo, UT	8.7	22.6	44.7	7.5	5.4	5.2	2.7	1.9
Raleigh, NC	6.9	20.1	27.7	15.2	12.3	9.1	4.9	2.6
Reno, NV	6.7	19.3	24.7	12.4	13.1	11.5	7.2	3.5
Richmond, VA	6.4	16.3	30.4	11.5	12.4	11.8	6.0	3.5
Roanoke, VA	7.3	16.7	21.8	13.0	13.9	13.1	7.3	4.0
Rochester, MN	7.4	19.4	22.6	12.5	13.4	11.3	6.9	4.4
Sacramento, CA	7.1	19.7	24.9	13.1	12.6	11.3	6.1	3.4
Salem, OR	7.4	20.9	21.6	12.9	12.5	11.7	7.1	3.8
Salt Lake City, UT	7.4	17.7	31.0	13.4	11.2	9.4	5.2	3.1
San Antonio, TX	7.4	21.8	23.7	13.0	12.9	10.3	6.1	3.5
San Diego, CA	6.4	18.1	27.5	13.5	13.0	10.4	6.2	3.4
San Francisco, CA	4.5	10.8	28.4	16.4	13.7	12.2	7.1	4.6
San Jose, CA	6.8	19.7	22.0	15.4	14.3	10.8	6.0	3.5
Santa Rosa, CA	6.1	20.0	20.2	13.1	14.1	12.7	7.0	4.3
Savannah, GA	6.8	19.8	27.6	11.0	11.6	10.7	6.7	3.8
Seattle, WA	5.3	13.1	30.1	15.7	12.7	11.7	6.4	3.1
Sioux Falls, SD	8.2	18.4	25.0	12.6	12.9	11.7	5.9	3.4
Spokane, WA	7.1	17.9	24.6	11.9	12.4	12.1	7.2	4.6
Springfield, IL	6.3	18.5	20.7	11.6	14.1	13.7	7.6	4.5
Tallahassee, FL	5.1	19.8	39.0	9.9	9.2	8.6	4.5	2.7
Tampa, FL	6.1	19.2	24.4	13.6	14.3	11.1	6.0	3.8
Topeka, KS	7.6	19.1	21.5	11.5	13.1	12.4	7.3	4.9
Tulsa, OK	7.6	19.6	23.1	12.0	13.0	12.0	6.8	4.0
Tyler, TX	6.2	20.4	25.0	11.5	11.0	10.8	7.1	5.4
Virginia Beach, VA	6.7	19.1	24.2	13.1	14.2	11.2	6.5	3.4
Washington, DC	6.1	14.5	31.6	13.7	12.0	10.7	6.2	3.5
Wichita, KS	8.0	20.8	22.2	12.2	13.1	11.6	6.3	3.8
Wilmington, NC	4.9	18.0	27.6	11.6	12.1	12.1	7.5	4.4
Winston-Salem, NC	7.3	20.9	22.4	12.7	12.9	11.1	6.8	4.3
Worcester, MA	6.8	19.8	25.5	12.0	13.0	10.9	6.1	3.6
U.S.	6.4	19.9	20.7	12.9	14.1	12.3	7.6	4.2

Source: U.S. Census Bureau, 2011-2013 American Community Survey 3-Year Estimates

Age: Metro Area

Metro Area	Percent of Population							
	Under Age 5	Age 5–19	Age 20–34	Age 35–44	Age 45–54	Age 55–64	Age 65–74	Age 75–84
Albuquerque, NM	6.5	20.1	21.2	12.5	13.8	12.7	7.7	4.0
Anchorage, AK	7.5	21.1	23.9	13.0	14.2	12.0	5.3	2.3
Ann Arbor, MI	5.3	20.2	26.6	12.2	13.1	11.7	6.4	3.1
Athens, GA	5.7	21.4	28.6	11.6	11.5	10.3	6.5	3.1
Atlanta, GA	6.9	21.8	20.6	15.2	14.6	11.0	6.1	2.8
Austin, TX	7.1	20.6	25.0	15.4	13.0	10.2	5.3	2.5
Billings, MT	6.3	19.1	19.3	12.1	14.1	13.8	8.0	4.7
Boise City, ID	7.0	22.7	20.4	13.5	13.1	11.4	7.0	3.4
Boston, MA	5.6	18.6	21.4	13.1	15.1	12.5	7.3	4.2
Boulder, CO	5.3	19.9	23.7	13.3	14.1	12.5	6.5	3.2
Cape Coral, FL	5.1	16.2	16.0	10.9	12.8	14.1	14.0	7.8
Cedar Rapids, IA	6.3	20.4	19.8	12.8	14.2	12.4	7.4	4.7
Charleston, SC	6.6	18.9	23.3	12.8	13.8	12.2	7.5	3.5
Charlotte, NC	6.7	21.0	19.9	14.9	14.5	11.4	6.9	3.4
Chicago, IL	6.5	20.7	21.1	13.7	14.2	11.8	6.7	3.7
Clarksville, TN	8.8	21.4	27.1	12.8	11.4	9.1	5.5	2.9
Colorado Springs, CO	7.0	21.4	22.7	12.6	14.0	11.6	6.4	3.3
Columbia, MO	6.1	20.0	31.1	11.1	11.7	10.4	5.3	3.0
Columbus, OH	6.8	20.4	22.1	13.8	14.0	11.7	6.5	3.4
Dallas, TX	7.4	22.4	21.4	14.7	14.0	10.4	5.7	2.8
Davenport, IA	6.3	19.5	18.8	12.1	14.0	13.5	8.5	4.8
Denver, CO	6.7	19.9	21.9	14.7	14.1	11.9	6.4	3.1
Des Moines, IA	7.3	21.0	21.2	13.8	13.7	11.4	6.4	3.5
Durham, NC	6.3	19.1	23.6	13.6	13.2	12.0	7.0	3.6
El Paso, TX	8.2	24.3	22.4	12.8	12.1	9.6	5.7	3.5
Erie, PA	5.9	19.8	20.2	11.7	14.0	13.6	7.8	4.9
Eugene, OR	5.0	17.8	22.3	11.4	12.8	14.4	9.1	4.8
Fargo, ND	6.8	19.6	28.3	11.9	11.9	10.7	5.4	3.6
Fayetteville, NC	8.5	21.2	26.0	12.4	12.2	10.1	5.7	3.0
Fort Collins, CO	5.6	19.1	24.6	12.0	13.0	12.9	7.5	3.8
Fort Wayne, IN	7.1	21.8	19.6	12.6	13.7	12.4	7.0	4.0
Fort Worth, TX	7.4	22.4	21.4	14.7	14.0	10.4	5.7	2.8
Gainesville, FL	5.5	18.2	31.3	10.3	11.3	11.5	6.7	3.6
Grand Rapids, MI	6.8	21.7	21.0	12.3	14.0	11.9	6.7	3.8
Green Bay, WI	6.5	20.1	19.5	12.7	15.2	12.8	7.1	4.1
Greensboro, NC	6.0	20.0	19.8	13.4	14.3	12.5	7.9	4.4
Honolulu, HI	6.5	17.7	23.1	12.7	13.0	11.9	7.8	4.7
Houston, TX	7.7	22.4	22.0	14.3	13.6	10.8	5.6	2.6
Huntsville, AL	6.1	19.8	20.4	13.0	15.8	12.1	7.4	4.0
Indianapolis, IN	7.0	21.1	20.5	13.6	14.4	11.7	6.6	3.6
Jacksonville, FL	6.3	19.5	20.7	13.1	14.7	12.7	7.7	3.8
Kansas City, MO	6.9	20.7	20.0	13.3	14.3	12.2	7.0	3.8
Lafayette, LA	7.1	20.8	22.1	12.3	14.0	11.8	6.7	3.8
Las Vegas, NV	6.7	20.1	21.6	14.4	13.5	11.4	7.6	3.5
Lexington, KY	6.3	19.3	23.6	13.4	13.6	11.9	6.7	3.5
Lincoln, NE	6.8	20.3	25.4	11.9	12.3	11.5	6.3	3.7
Little Rock, AR	6.8	20.0	21.9	13.0	13.4	11.9	7.5	4.0
Los Angeles, CA	6.4	20.0	22.6	14.2	14.0	10.9	6.4	3.6
Louisville, KY	6.3	19.5	19.7	13.2	14.7	13.1	7.6	4.2
Lubbock, TX	7.1	21.7	26.9	11.0	11.6	10.2	6.3	4.0
Madison, WI	6.0	18.8	24.2	12.9	14.0	12.3	6.6	3.6
Manchester, NH	5.7	19.5	18.6	13.5	16.8	13.2	7.1	4.0
McAllen, TX	9.6	27.8	21.2	13.2	10.4	8.0	5.4	3.2
Miami, FL	5.7	17.8	19.6	13.6	14.9	11.9	8.3	5.5

Table continued on next page.

Metro Area	Percent of Population							
	Under Age 5	Age 5–19	Age 20–34	Age 35–44	Age 45–54	Age 55–64	Age 65–74	Age 75–84
Midland, TX	8.2	22.1	23.1	11.9	12.9	11.2	5.5	3.5
Minneapolis, MN	6.7	20.4	21.0	13.4	15.0	12.0	6.4	3.5
Nashville, TN	6.7	20.0	21.8	14.0	14.3	11.8	6.7	3.4
New Orleans, LA	6.4	19.0	21.8	12.6	14.4	13.1	7.4	3.9
New York, NY	6.2	18.9	21.2	13.6	14.7	12.0	7.3	4.2
Oklahoma City, OK	7.2	20.5	22.8	12.6	13.1	11.7	6.9	3.7
Omaha, NE	7.4	21.2	21.5	12.9	13.7	11.7	6.3	3.6
Orlando, FL	6.0	19.6	22.2	13.6	14.1	11.3	7.4	4.0
Oxnard, CA	6.5	21.3	20.0	12.9	14.6	12.0	7.0	3.8
Palm Bay, FL	4.8	16.6	16.1	10.7	15.8	14.6	11.3	7.5
Peoria, IL	6.4	19.7	19.3	12.4	13.7	13.2	8.1	4.9
Philadelphia, PA	6.1	19.5	20.5	12.6	14.8	12.6	7.4	4.4
Phoenix, AZ	7.0	21.3	21.1	13.5	13.0	11.0	7.6	4.0
Pittsburgh, PA	5.1	17.3	18.7	11.8	15.0	14.6	8.8	5.9
Portland, OR	6.2	19.2	21.3	14.6	13.8	12.7	7.1	3.4
Providence, RI	5.3	18.9	20.0	12.6	15.2	13.0	7.8	4.6
Provo, UT	10.7	28.7	27.4	11.6	8.3	6.5	3.9	2.2
Raleigh, NC	6.8	21.6	20.7	15.7	14.6	10.7	5.9	2.8
Reno, NV	6.3	19.1	21.3	12.7	13.9	13.2	8.3	3.6
Richmond, VA	6.0	19.4	20.6	13.3	14.9	12.8	7.4	3.7
Roanoke, VA	5.6	17.9	17.4	12.8	14.7	14.4	9.4	5.2
Rochester, MN	7.0	20.3	19.2	12.3	14.5	12.5	7.5	4.6
Sacramento, CA	6.4	20.6	21.1	12.8	14.0	12.1	7.2	3.9
Salem, OR	6.9	21.8	20.4	12.4	12.4	12.3	7.7	4.1
Salt Lake City, UT	8.4	23.2	24.2	13.7	11.6	9.8	5.2	2.7
San Antonio, TX	7.1	22.1	21.7	13.2	13.3	10.9	6.6	3.5
San Diego, CA	6.6	19.2	24.3	13.3	13.5	11.1	6.4	3.7
San Francisco, CA	5.8	17.3	21.6	14.8	14.7	12.5	7.3	4.0
San Jose, CA	6.7	19.5	21.4	15.2	14.6	10.9	6.4	3.6
Santa Rosa, CA	5.5	18.5	19.5	12.2	14.5	14.6	8.6	4.4
Savannah, GA	6.9	20.0	23.7	12.7	13.1	11.4	7.1	3.6
Seattle, WA	6.4	18.4	22.4	14.5	14.6	12.3	6.6	3.3
Sioux Falls, SD	7.8	20.6	22.0	13.0	13.5	11.7	6.0	3.5
Spokane, WA	6.1	19.6	20.8	11.9	13.7	13.5	8.2	4.4
Springfield, IL	6.1	19.4	18.8	12.4	14.7	13.9	7.9	4.4
Tallahassee, FL	5.5	19.3	28.2	11.6	12.3	11.9	6.6	3.3
Tampa, FL	5.5	17.6	18.6	12.6	14.6	13.2	9.5	5.8
Topeka, KS	6.6	20.4	18.0	11.6	14.1	13.7	8.4	4.9
Tulsa, OK	7.0	20.8	20.1	12.7	13.6	12.3	7.7	4.2
Tyler, TX	7.0	21.1	20.8	12.0	12.6	11.7	8.1	4.8
Virginia Beach, VA	6.4	19.6	23.6	12.3	14.3	11.7	6.9	3.7
Washington, DC	6.7	19.4	22.1	14.6	14.9	11.5	6.3	3.0
Wichita, KS	7.5	21.7	20.5	12.0	13.5	12.2	6.7	4.0
Wilmington, NC	5.5	18.2	22.0	13.0	13.5	13.0	8.8	4.5
Winston-Salem, NC	6.1	19.9	18.1	13.3	14.7	12.9	8.4	4.7
Worcester, MA	5.6	20.0	18.8	13.2	16.1	12.9	7.2	4.1
U.S.	6.4	19.9	20.7	12.9	14.1	12.3	7.6	4.2

Note: Figures cover the Metropolitan Statistical Area (MSA)—see Appendix B for areas included
Source: U.S. Census Bureau, 2011-2013 American Community Survey 3-Year Estimates

Segregation

Area	Black/White		Asian/White		Hispanic/White	
	Index[1]	Rank[2]	Index[1]	Rank[2]	Index[1]	Rank[2]
Albuquerque, NM	30.9	99	28.5	93	36.4	79
Anchorage, AK	n/a	n/a	n/a	n/a	n/a	n/a
Ann Arbor, MI	n/a	n/a	n/a	n/a	n/a	n/a
Athens, GA	n/a	n/a	n/a	n/a	n/a	n/a
Atlanta, GA	59.0	41	48.5	10	49.5	27
Austin, TX	50.1	70	41.2	49	43.2	51
Billings, MT	n/a	n/a	n/a	n/a	n/a	n/a
Boise City, ID	30.2	101	27.6	95	36.2	80
Boston, MA	64.0	27	45.4	23	59.6	5
Boulder, CO	n/a	n/a	n/a	n/a	n/a	n/a
Cape Coral, FL	61.6	35	25.3	96	40.2	63
Cedar Rapids, IA	n/a	n/a	n/a	n/a	n/a	n/a
Charleston, SC	41.5	88	33.4	84	39.8	66
Charlotte, NC	53.8	56	43.6	34	47.6	35
Chicago, IL	76.4	3	44.9	26	56.3	10
Clarksville, TN	n/a	n/a	n/a	n/a	n/a	n/a
Colorado Springs, CO	39.3	92	24.1	98	30.3	95
Columbia, MO	n/a	n/a	n/a	n/a	n/a	n/a
Columbus, OH	62.2	33	43.3	35	41.5	59
Dallas, TX	56.6	48	46.6	19	50.3	24
Davenport, IA	n/a	n/a	n/a	n/a	n/a	n/a
Denver, CO	62.6	31	33.4	83	48.8	31
Des Moines, IA	51.6	66	35.5	76	46.7	40
Durham, NC	48.1	75	44.0	30	48.0	33
El Paso, TX	30.7	100	22.2	100	43.3	50
Erie, PA	n/a	n/a	n/a	n/a	n/a	n/a
Eugene, OR	n/a	n/a	n/a	n/a	n/a	n/a
Fargo, ND	n/a	n/a	n/a	n/a	n/a	n/a
Fayetteville, NC	n/a	n/a	n/a	n/a	n/a	n/a
Fort Collins, CO	n/a	n/a	n/a	n/a	n/a	n/a
Fort Wayne, IN	n/a	n/a	n/a	n/a	n/a	n/a
Fort Worth, TX	56.6	48	46.6	19	50.3	24
Gainesville, FL	n/a	n/a	n/a	n/a	n/a	n/a
Grand Rapids, MI	64.3	26	43.2	37	50.4	23
Green Bay, WI	n/a	n/a	n/a	n/a	n/a	n/a
Greensboro, NC	54.7	53	47.7	14	41.1	61
Honolulu, HI	36.9	95	42.1	44	31.9	91
Houston, TX	61.4	36	50.4	7	52.5	18
Huntsville, AL	n/a	n/a	n/a	n/a	n/a	n/a
Indianapolis, IN	66.4	15	41.6	47	47.3	37
Jacksonville, FL	53.1	59	37.5	71	27.6	98
Kansas City, MO	61.2	39	38.4	65	44.4	48
Lafayette, LA	n/a	n/a	n/a	n/a	n/a	n/a
Las Vegas, NV	37.6	94	28.8	92	42.0	58
Lexington, KY	n/a	n/a	n/a	n/a	n/a	n/a
Lincoln, NE	n/a	n/a	n/a	n/a	n/a	n/a
Little Rock, AR	58.8	42	39.7	59	39.7	68
Los Angeles, CA	67.8	10	48.4	12	62.2	2
Louisville, KY	58.1	43	42.2	43	38.7	73
Lubbock, TX	n/a	n/a	n/a	n/a	n/a	n/a
Madison, WI	49.6	71	44.2	29	40.1	65
Manchester, NH	n/a	n/a	n/a	n/a	n/a	n/a
McAllen, TX	40.7	90	46.7	17	39.2	69
Miami, FL	64.8	23	34.2	80	57.4	8
Midland, TX	n/a	n/a	n/a	n/a	n/a	n/a

Table continued on next page.

Area	Black/White		Asian/White		Hispanic/White	
	Index[1]	Rank[2]	Index[1]	Rank[2]	Index[1]	Rank[2]
Minneapolis, MN	52.9	60	42.8	39	42.5	54
Nashville, TN	56.2	49	41.0	51	47.9	34
New Orleans, LA	63.9	28	48.6	9	38.3	74
New York, NY	78.0	2	51.9	3	62.0	3
Oklahoma City, OK	51.4	67	39.2	60	47.0	38
Omaha, NE	61.3	38	36.3	74	48.8	30
Orlando, FL	50.7	69	33.9	81	40.2	64
Oxnard, CA	39.9	91	31.2	87	54.6	13
Palm Bay, FL	47.2	79	20.6	101	25.0	101
Peoria, IL	n/a	n/a	n/a	n/a	n/a	n/a
Philadelphia, PA	68.4	9	42.3	42	55.1	12
Phoenix, AZ	43.6	86	32.7	85	49.3	28
Pittsburgh, PA	65.8	17	52.4	2	28.6	97
Portland, OR	46.0	81	35.8	75	34.3	83
Providence, RI	53.5	57	40.1	55	60.1	4
Provo, UT	21.9	102	28.2	94	30.9	93
Raleigh, NC	42.1	87	46.7	16	37.1	76
Reno, NV	n/a	n/a	n/a	n/a	n/a	n/a
Richmond, VA	52.4	63	43.9	32	44.9	46
Roanoke, VA	n/a	n/a	n/a	n/a	n/a	n/a
Rochester, MN	n/a	n/a	n/a	n/a	n/a	n/a
Sacramento, CA	56.9	46	49.9	8	38.9	71
Salem, OR	n/a	n/a	n/a	n/a	n/a	n/a
Salt Lake City, UT	39.3	93	31.0	88	42.9	53
San Antonio, TX	49.0	73	38.3	66	46.1	43
San Diego, CA	51.2	68	48.2	13	49.6	25
San Francisco, CA	62.0	34	46.6	18	49.6	26
San Jose, CA	40.9	89	45.0	25	47.6	36
Santa Rosa, CA	n/a	n/a	n/a	n/a	n/a	n/a
Savannah, GA	n/a	n/a	n/a	n/a	n/a	n/a
Seattle, WA	49.1	72	37.6	69	32.8	87
Sioux Falls, SD	n/a	n/a	n/a	n/a	n/a	n/a
Spokane, WA	n/a	n/a	n/a	n/a	n/a	n/a
Springfield, IL	n/a	n/a	n/a	n/a	n/a	n/a
Tallahassee, FL	n/a	n/a	n/a	n/a	n/a	n/a
Tampa, FL	56.2	50	35.3	78	40.7	62
Topeka, KS	n/a	n/a	n/a	n/a	n/a	n/a
Tulsa, OK	56.6	47	42.6	40	45.3	45
Tyler, TX	n/a	n/a	n/a	n/a	n/a	n/a
Virginia Beach, VA	47.8	76	34.3	79	32.2	90
Washington, DC	62.3	32	38.9	64	48.3	32
Wichita, KS	58.0	44	46.5	20	42.3	56
Wilmington, NC	n/a	n/a	n/a	n/a	n/a	n/a
Winston-Salem, NC	n/a	n/a	n/a	n/a	n/a	n/a
Worcester, MA	52.6	61	45.8	22	52.7	17

Note: Figures are based on an analysis of 1990, 2000, and 2010 Census Decennial Census tract data by William H. Frey, Brookings Institution and the University of Michigan Social Science Data Analysis Network. In this analysis all racial groups (whites, blacks, and asians) are non-Hispanic members of those races. Hispanics are shown as a separate category; All figures cover the Metropolitan Statistical Area (see Appendix B for areas included); (1) Segregation Indices are Dissimilarity Indices that measure the degree to which the minority group is distributed differently than whites across census tracts. They range from 0 (complete integration) to 100 (complete [segregation) where the value indicates the percentage of the minority group that needs to move to be distributed exactly like whites; (2) Ranges from 1 (most segregated) to 102 (least segregated); n/a not available.
Source: www.CensusScope.org

Religious Groups by Family

Area[1]	Catholic	Baptist	Non-Den.	Methodist[2]	Lutheran	LDS[3]	Pentecostal	Presbyterian[4]	Muslim[5]	Judaism
Albuquerque, NM	27.2	3.8	4.2	1.5	1.0	2.4	1.5	1.1	0.2	0.3
Anchorage, AK	6.9	5.0	6.4	1.4	1.9	5.1	1.9	0.7	0.2	0.1
Ann Arbor, MI	12.4	2.2	1.6	3.1	2.9	0.9	1.9	3.0	1.3	0.9
Athens, GA	4.4	16.3	2.3	8.4	0.4	0.8	2.8	2.0	0.4	0.2
Atlanta, GA	7.5	17.5	6.9	7.9	0.5	0.8	2.6	1.8	0.8	0.6
Austin, TX	16.0	10.3	4.5	3.6	2.0	1.2	0.8	1.1	1.2	0.3
Billings, MT	12.1	2.5	3.8	2.1	6.1	4.9	4.1	1.8	<0.1	0.1
Boise City, ID	8.0	2.9	4.2	2.1	1.2	15.9	2.3	0.6	0.1	0.1
Boston, MA	44.4	1.2	1.0	1.0	0.4	0.4	0.6	1.6	0.4	1.4
Boulder, CO	20.1	2.4	4.8	1.8	3.1	3.0	0.5	2.0	0.1	0.8
Cape Coral, FL	16.2	5.0	3.0	2.5	1.2	0.5	4.4	1.4	0.9	0.2
Cedar Rapids, IA	18.8	2.4	3.0	7.3	11.3	0.9	1.8	3.3	0.5	0.1
Charleston, SC	6.2	12.4	7.1	10.0	1.1	1.0	2.0	2.4	0.2	0.3
Charlotte, NC	5.9	17.3	6.8	8.6	1.3	0.8	3.3	4.5	0.2	0.3
Chicago, IL	34.2	3.2	4.5	1.9	3.0	0.4	1.2	1.9	3.3	0.8
Clarksville, TN	4.1	30.9	2.3	6.2	0.6	1.5	1.8	1.1	0.1	<0.1
Colorado Springs, CO	8.4	4.3	7.4	2.4	2.0	3.0	1.1	2.1	0.1	0.1
Columbia, MO	6.6	14.7	5.4	4.3	1.7	1.4	1.1	2.3	0.3	0.3
Columbus, OH	11.8	5.3	3.6	4.7	2.4	0.7	2.0	2.0	0.8	0.5
Dallas, TX	13.3	18.7	7.8	5.3	0.8	1.2	2.2	1.0	2.4	0.4
Davenport, IA	14.9	5.0	2.7	5.3	8.7	0.8	1.4	3.0	0.9	0.1
Denver, CO	16.1	3.0	4.6	1.7	2.1	2.4	1.2	1.6	0.6	0.6
Des Moines, IA	13.6	4.8	3.3	7.0	8.2	1.0	2.4	3.0	0.3	0.3
Durham, NC	5.1	13.9	5.6	8.1	0.5	0.8	1.4	2.5	0.5	0.6
El Paso, TX	43.2	3.8	5.0	0.9	0.3	1.6	1.4	0.2	0.1	0.2
Erie, PA	33.5	2.2	1.7	5.7	3.0	0.6	2.2	2.1	0.7	0.2
Eugene, OR	6.2	3.1	1.9	0.9	1.4	3.7	3.3	0.6	0.1	0.4
Fargo, ND	17.4	0.4	0.5	3.3	32.5	0.6	1.5	1.9	0.1	<0.1
Fayetteville, NC	2.6	14.1	10.5	6.2	0.2	1.4	4.9	2.1	0.2	<0.1
Fort Collins, CO	11.8	2.2	6.4	4.4	3.5	3.0	4.7	1.9	0.1	<0.1
Fort Wayne, IN	14.2	6.1	6.8	5.1	8.5	0.4	1.5	1.7	0.3	0.1
Fort Worth, TX	13.3	18.7	7.8	5.3	0.8	1.2	2.2	1.0	2.4	0.4
Gainesville, FL	7.6	12.3	4.3	6.4	0.5	1.0	3.5	1.1	1.1	0.4
Grand Rapids, MI	17.2	1.7	8.4	3.1	2.1	0.6	1.1	10.0	1.1	0.1
Green Bay, WI	42.0	0.7	3.4	2.2	12.7	0.4	0.6	1.0	0.1	0.1
Greensboro, NC	2.7	12.8	7.4	9.9	0.7	0.8	2.5	3.2	0.6	0.4
Honolulu, HI	18.2	1.9	2.2	0.8	0.3	5.1	4.2	1.5	<0.1	0.1
Houston, TX	17.1	16.0	7.3	4.9	1.1	1.1	1.5	0.9	2.7	0.4
Huntsville, AL	4.0	27.6	3.2	7.5	0.7	1.2	1.2	1.7	0.2	0.2
Indianapolis, IN	10.5	10.3	7.2	5.0	1.7	0.7	1.6	1.7	0.2	0.4
Jacksonville, FL	9.9	18.5	7.8	4.5	0.7	1.1	1.9	1.6	0.6	0.4
Kansas City, MO	12.7	13.2	5.2	5.9	2.3	2.5	2.6	1.6	0.3	0.4
Lafayette, LA	47.0	14.8	4.0	2.6	0.2	0.4	2.9	0.2	0.1	0.1
Las Vegas, NV	18.1	3.0	3.1	0.4	0.7	6.4	1.5	0.2	0.1	0.3
Lexington, KY	6.8	24.9	2.4	5.9	0.4	1.1	2.1	1.4	0.1	0.3
Lincoln, NE	14.8	2.4	1.9	7.2	11.3	1.2	1.4	3.9	0.2	0.2
Little Rock, AR	4.5	25.9	6.1	7.3	0.5	0.9	2.9	0.9	0.1	0.1
Los Angeles, CA	33.8	2.8	3.6	1.1	0.7	1.7	1.8	0.9	0.7	1.0
Louisville, KY	13.7	25.1	1.7	3.7	0.6	0.8	1.0	1.2	0.5	0.4
Lubbock, TX	13.4	22.4	7.3	6.6	0.5	1.4	1.9	0.8	1.8	0.1
Madison, WI	21.8	1.1	1.6	3.7	12.8	0.5	0.4	2.2	0.5	0.5
Manchester, NH	31.2	1.4	2.4	1.2	0.5	0.6	0.5	2.0	0.3	0.5
McAllen, TX	34.7	4.5	2.8	1.3	0.4	1.3	1.2	0.2	1.0	<0.1
Miami, FL	18.6	5.4	4.2	1.3	0.5	0.5	1.8	0.7	0.9	1.6
Midland, TX	22.4	25.3	8.8	4.2	0.7	1.2	1.6	1.9	3.7	<0.1

Table continued on next page.

Area[1]	Catholic	Baptist	Non-Den.	Methodist[2]	Lutheran	LDS[3]	Pente-costal	Presby-terian[4]	Muslim[5]	Judaism
Minneapolis, MN	21.7	2.5	3.0	2.8	14.5	0.6	1.8	1.9	0.4	0.7
Nashville, TN	4.1	25.3	5.8	6.1	0.4	0.8	2.2	2.1	0.4	0.2
New Orleans, LA	31.6	8.4	3.7	2.7	0.8	0.6	2.1	0.5	0.5	0.5
New York, NY	36.9	1.9	1.8	1.3	0.8	0.4	0.9	1.1	2.3	4.8
Oklahoma City, OK	6.4	25.4	7.1	10.6	0.7	1.3	3.2	1.0	0.2	0.1
Omaha, NE	21.6	4.6	1.8	3.9	7.9	1.8	1.3	2.3	0.5	0.4
Orlando, FL	13.2	7.0	5.7	3.0	0.9	1.0	3.2	1.4	1.3	0.3
Oxnard, CA	28.2	1.9	4.1	1.1	1.5	2.5	1.3	0.7	0.4	0.7
Palm Bay, FL	11.9	6.5	5.3	4.0	1.2	1.0	1.0	1.3	0.8	0.1
Peoria, IL	11.5	5.5	5.3	5.0	6.1	0.5	1.5	2.8	5.2	0.1
Philadelphia, PA	33.5	3.9	2.9	3.0	1.9	0.3	0.9	2.1	1.3	1.4
Phoenix, AZ	13.4	3.5	5.2	1.0	1.6	6.1	2.9	0.6	0.2	0.3
Pittsburgh, PA	32.8	2.3	2.8	5.7	3.4	0.4	1.1	4.7	0.3	0.7
Portland, OR	10.6	2.3	4.5	1.0	1.6	3.8	2.0	1.0	0.1	0.3
Providence, RI	47.0	1.4	1.2	0.8	0.5	0.3	0.6	1.0	0.1	0.7
Provo, UT	1.3	0.1	0.1	0.2	<0.1	88.6	0.1	0.1	<0.1	<0.1
Raleigh, NC	9.2	12.1	6.0	6.7	0.9	0.9	2.3	2.3	0.9	0.3
Reno, NV	14.3	1.5	3.2	0.9	0.8	4.6	2.0	0.4	0.1	0.2
Richmond, VA	6.0	19.9	5.5	6.1	0.6	1.0	1.8	2.1	2.8	0.4
Roanoke, VA	3.7	22.4	4.6	7.3	1.4	1.1	2.8	2.5	2.2	0.3
Rochester, MN	23.4	1.7	4.7	4.9	21.1	1.1	1.3	2.9	0.3	0.2
Sacramento, CA	16.2	3.2	4.0	1.8	0.8	3.4	2.0	0.8	0.8	0.3
Salem, OR	16.7	2.2	3.0	1.2	1.7	3.9	3.4	0.7	<0.1	0.1
Salt Lake City, UT	8.9	0.8	0.5	0.5	0.5	58.9	0.7	0.4	0.4	0.1
San Antonio, TX	28.4	8.5	6.0	3.1	1.7	1.4	1.3	0.8	1.0	0.2
San Diego, CA	25.9	2.0	4.8	1.1	1.0	2.3	1.0	0.9	0.7	0.5
San Francisco, CA	20.8	2.5	2.5	2.0	0.6	1.6	1.2	1.1	1.2	0.9
San Jose, CA	26.0	1.4	4.3	1.1	0.6	1.4	1.2	0.7	1.0	0.7
Santa Rosa, CA	22.3	1.4	1.5	0.9	1.0	1.9	0.7	0.9	0.5	0.4
Savannah, GA	7.1	19.7	6.9	8.9	1.6	1.0	2.4	1.0	0.2	0.8
Seattle, WA	12.3	2.2	5.0	1.2	2.1	3.3	2.8	1.4	0.5	0.5
Sioux Falls, SD	14.9	3.0	1.5	3.9	21.4	0.7	1.1	6.2	0.3	0.1
Spokane, WA	13.1	1.9	4.3	1.0	2.9	5.2	2.9	1.5	0.1	0.2
Springfield, IL	15.6	11.7	2.7	6.8	5.6	0.8	5.0	2.0	1.6	0.2
Tallahassee, FL	4.8	16.1	6.8	9.2	0.5	1.0	2.2	1.6	0.9	0.4
Tampa, FL	10.9	7.1	3.8	3.5	1.0	0.6	2.1	1.0	1.3	0.5
Topeka, KS	12.8	9.1	4.1	7.3	3.6	1.5	2.0	1.7	0.1	0.1
Tulsa, OK	5.8	22.9	7.6	9.2	0.8	1.2	3.3	1.3	0.3	0.3
Tyler, TX	12.2	33.6	9.0	6.4	0.6	1.2	5.1	0.7	0.4	0.1
Virginia Beach, VA	6.4	11.6	6.2	5.3	0.7	0.9	1.9	2.0	2.1	0.4
Washington, DC	14.5	7.3	4.9	4.5	1.3	1.2	1.1	1.4	2.4	1.2
Wichita, KS	14.5	13.5	3.2	7.2	1.8	1.4	2.0	1.7	0.2	<0.1
Wilmington, NC	6.2	14.5	4.6	8.5	0.9	1.0	1.1	2.5	0.3	0.1
Winston-Salem, NC	3.6	17.5	9.4	12.4	0.7	0.7	2.6	2.2	0.3	0.1
Worcester, MA	38.4	1.2	1.8	1.0	0.9	0.3	1.1	2.1	0.1	0.5
U.S.	19.1	9.3	4.0	4.0	2.3	2.0	1.9	1.6	0.8	0.7

Note: Figures are the number of adherents as a percentage of the total population; (1) Figures cover the Metropolitan Statistical Area—see Appendix B for areas included; (2) Methodist/Pietist; (3) Latter Day Saints; (4) Reformed; (5) Figures are estimates
Source: Association of Statisticians of American Religious Bodies, 2010 U.S. Religion Census: Religious Congregations & Membership Study

Religious Groups by Tradition

Area	Catholic	Evangelical Protestant	Mainline Protestant	Other Tradition	Black Protestant	Orthodox
Albuquerque, NM	27.2	11.3	3.3	3.9	0.2	0.2
Anchorage, AK	6.9	15.7	3.6	6.8	0.3	0.6
Ann Arbor, MI	12.4	7.3	7.5	3.8	1.6	0.3
Athens, GA	4.4	21.1	9.8	1.7	2.5	0.1
Atlanta, GA	7.5	26.1	9.8	2.9	3.2	0.3
Austin, TX	16.0	16.1	6.3	3.9	1.4	0.1
Billings, MT	12.1	13.7	8.2	5.2	0.1	0.1
Boise City, ID	8.0	13.0	4.4	16.7	<0.1	0.1
Boston, MA	44.4	3.2	4.5	3.4	0.2	1.1
Boulder, CO	20.1	9.8	6.5	4.9	<0.1	0.2
Cape Coral, FL	16.2	14.3	4.6	2.0	0.3	0.2
Cedar Rapids, IA	18.8	13.7	17.5	2.0	0.2	0.2
Charleston, SC	6.2	19.7	11.2	1.9	7.3	0.1
Charlotte, NC	5.9	27.6	13.3	1.7	2.8	0.5
Chicago, IL	34.2	9.8	5.1	5.1	2.1	0.9
Clarksville, TN	4.1	35.4	7.3	1.7	2.4	<0.1
Colorado Springs, CO	8.4	15.2	5.4	3.7	0.4	0.1
Columbia, MO	6.6	19.9	10.5	2.3	0.5	0.1
Columbus, OH	11.8	11.9	9.5	3.1	1.1	0.3
Dallas, TX	13.3	28.3	7.0	4.8	1.8	0.2
Davenport, IA	14.9	11.4	15.1	2.4	1.6	0.1
Denver, CO	16.1	11.1	4.5	4.6	0.4	0.3
Des Moines, IA	13.6	12.4	16.8	1.9	0.9	0.1
Durham, NC	5.1	19.4	11.7	2.9	3.1	0.1
El Paso, TX	43.2	10.9	1.3	2.1	0.2	0.1
Erie, PA	33.5	8.4	11.7	1.6	0.9	0.3
Eugene, OR	6.2	9.7	3.4	5.5	0.1	0.1
Fargo, ND	17.4	10.7	30.8	0.9	<0.1	<0.1
Fayetteville, NC	2.6	26.7	7.9	1.8	4.3	0.1
Fort Collins, CO	11.8	18.8	5.9	4.0	<0.1	0.1
Fort Wayne, IN	14.2	24.6	9.2	1.0	2.4	0.2
Fort Worth, TX	13.3	28.3	7.0	4.8	1.8	0.2
Gainesville, FL	7.6	20.4	7.0	4.2	2.2	0.1
Grand Rapids, MI	17.2	20.7	7.6	2.2	1.1	0.2
Green Bay, WI	42.0	14.1	8.1	0.6	<0.1	<0.1
Greensboro, NC	2.7	23.2	14.0	2.2	2.6	0.1
Honolulu, HI	18.2	9.7	2.9	8.4	<0.1	<0.1
Houston, TX	17.1	24.9	6.7	4.9	1.3	0.2
Huntsville, AL	4.0	33.3	9.7	1.9	1.8	0.1
Indianapolis, IN	10.5	18.3	9.6	1.7	1.9	0.3
Jacksonville, FL	9.9	27.1	5.7	2.9	4.2	0.3
Kansas City, MO	12.7	20.6	10.0	3.7	2.6	0.1
Lafayette, LA	47.0	12.8	3.2	0.8	9.3	0.1
Las Vegas, NV	18.1	7.7	1.4	7.6	0.4	0.4
Lexington, KY	6.8	28.3	10.3	1.7	2.1	0.2
Lincoln, NE	14.8	14.8	16.2	2.0	0.1	0.1
Little Rock, AR	4.5	33.9	8.2	1.7	3.5	0.1
Los Angeles, CA	33.8	9.0	2.4	4.6	0.9	0.6
Louisville, KY	13.7	24.5	7.1	2.0	3.0	0.1
Lubbock, TX	13.4	31.5	8.6	4.0	0.7	0.1
Madison, WI	21.8	7.3	15.4	2.3	0.1	0.1
Manchester, NH	31.2	5.1	4.4	1.8	<0.1	0.7
McAllen, TX	34.7	9.7	1.9	2.4	<0.1	<0.1
Miami, FL	18.6	11.4	2.5	3.5	1.7	0.3
Midland, TX	22.4	35.5	7.2	5.4	1.0	<0.1

Table continued on next page.

Area	Catholic	Evangelical Protestant	Mainline Protestant	Other Tradition	Black Protestant	Orthodox
Minneapolis, MN	21.7	12.9	14.5	2.3	0.5	0.2
Nashville, TN	4.1	33.0	8.0	1.7	3.4	0.5
New Orleans, LA	31.6	12.7	4.0	2.1	3.0	0.1
New York, NY	36.9	4.0	4.1	8.4	1.2	1.0
Oklahoma City, OK	6.4	39.1	9.9	2.8	1.9	0.2
Omaha, NE	21.6	12.1	10.8	3.3	1.5	0.1
Orlando, FL	13.2	17.8	4.8	3.3	1.2	0.3
Oxnard, CA	28.2	8.9	2.7	4.5	0.2	0.2
Palm Bay, FL	11.9	14.0	5.7	2.0	1.0	0.2
Peoria, IL	11.5	18.9	11.1	6.2	0.9	0.1
Philadelphia, PA	33.5	6.3	8.9	3.7	1.8	0.4
Phoenix, AZ	13.4	13.2	2.6	7.8	0.2	0.3
Pittsburgh, PA	32.8	7.4	13.8	2.1	0.9	0.7
Portland, OR	10.6	11.7	3.7	5.2	0.2	0.3
Providence, RI	47.0	2.8	4.7	1.6	0.1	0.6
Provo, UT	1.3	0.5	0.1	88.9	<0.1	<0.1
Raleigh, NC	9.2	19.9	10.1	3.3	1.7	0.2
Reno, NV	14.3	7.7	1.9	5.1	0.2	0.1
Richmond, VA	6.0	23.7	13.3	4.6	2.4	0.2
Roanoke, VA	3.7	31.7	13.2	4.0	1.2	0.2
Rochester, MN	23.4	19.0	21.1	2.1	<0.1	0.1
Sacramento, CA	16.2	11.4	2.2	5.8	0.6	0.3
Salem, OR	16.7	14.1	3.8	4.2	<0.1	<0.1
Salt Lake City, UT	8.9	2.6	1.3	60.1	0.1	0.5
San Antonio, TX	28.4	17.0	5.0	3.2	0.4	0.1
San Diego, CA	25.9	9.8	2.4	5.2	0.4	0.3
San Francisco, CA	20.8	6.2	3.8	5.2	1.1	0.7
San Jose, CA	26.0	8.2	2.5	6.9	0.1	0.4
Santa Rosa, CA	22.3	5.3	2.4	4.8	<0.1	0.3
Savannah, GA	7.1	25.1	9.5	2.6	8.6	0.1
Seattle, WA	12.3	11.9	4.7	5.9	0.4	0.4
Sioux Falls, SD	14.9	12.9	28.1	1.2	0.1	0.1
Spokane, WA	13.1	12.4	4.9	6.3	0.1	0.2
Springfield, IL	15.6	21.5	11.7	3.2	2.1	0.1
Tallahassee, FL	4.8	21.9	6.4	3.0	9.2	0.2
Tampa, FL	10.9	13.6	5.2	3.1	1.2	0.8
Topeka, KS	12.8	15.5	12.9	1.8	2.8	<0.1
Tulsa, OK	5.8	34.6	11.3	2.2	1.6	0.1
Tyler, TX	12.2	45.5	7.4	1.7	4.1	<0.1
Virginia Beach, VA	6.4	18.0	9.4	4.0	2.3	0.3
Washington, DC	14.5	12.4	8.8	5.9	2.3	0.6
Wichita, KS	14.5	20.7	11.1	2.4	1.9	0.2
Wilmington, NC	6.2	20.4	10.8	1.7	3.1	0.1
Winston-Salem, NC	3.6	29.2	15.7	1.3	2.3	0.3
Worcester, MA	38.4	4.7	5.4	2.4	0.1	1.0
U.S.	19.1	16.2	7.3	4.3	1.6	0.3

Note: Figures are the number of adherents as a percentage of the total population; (1) Figures cover the Metropolitan Statistical Area—see Appendix B for areas included; Source: Association of Statisticians of American Religious Bodies, 2010 U.S. Religion Census: Religious Congregations & Membership Study

Ancestry: City

City	German	Irish	English	American	Italian	Polish	French[1]	Scottish	Dutch
Albuquerque, NM	10.4	7.4	6.7	4.0	3.2	1.2	2.0	1.7	1.0
Anchorage, AK	16.7	10.1	8.6	5.7	3.2	1.8	2.8	3.0	1.7
Ann Arbor, MI	18.0	10.0	10.2	5.4	5.0	6.6	3.2	2.9	2.4
Athens, GA	9.2	7.9	9.1	8.6	2.5	1.8	1.5	3.2	0.7
Atlanta, GA	5.9	5.2	6.7	7.4	2.1	1.2	1.4	2.2	0.6
Austin, TX	12.8	8.4	8.3	4.2	3.0	1.6	3.0	2.2	0.9
Billings, MT	26.2	12.1	9.8	14.5	3.7	2.0	3.2	2.4	1.8
Boise City, ID	18.0	10.5	14.2	6.9	4.6	1.8	2.5	3.8	2.2
Boston, MA	4.7	14.6	5.0	6.0	8.0	2.6	1.9	1.3	0.5
Boulder, CO	22.4	14.0	12.9	5.1	6.6	4.1	4.4	3.1	2.0
Cape Coral, FL	18.9	14.5	8.6	9.9	11.1	4.5	3.3	1.4	1.0
Cedar Rapids, IA	37.0	15.7	8.8	5.3	2.2	1.8	2.8	1.8	1.8
Charleston, SC	12.0	11.4	11.4	13.9	4.2	2.1	2.7	3.2	1.0
Charlotte, NC	9.7	7.7	7.4	5.2	3.4	1.8	1.5	2.2	0.7
Chicago, IL	7.4	7.5	2.2	2.0	4.0	6.0	0.9	0.6	0.6
Clarksville, TN	13.6	11.5	6.9	7.0	3.3	2.5	2.2	1.6	1.3
Colorado Springs, CO	22.4	13.0	10.2	5.8	5.8	2.4	3.0	2.9	2.1
Columbia, MO	27.2	13.3	11.3	5.3	3.9	2.5	3.1	2.9	1.7
Columbus, OH	20.2	11.6	6.7	5.4	5.3	2.2	1.9	1.5	1.0
Dallas, TX	5.9	4.4	5.0	3.2	1.4	0.9	1.4	1.1	0.5
Davenport, IA	31.6	15.0	6.4	6.3	2.3	2.4	2.2	1.1	2.3
Denver, CO	14.9	10.1	7.8	3.3	4.2	2.5	2.5	2.2	1.4
Des Moines, IA	21.1	11.8	7.5	5.2	3.5	1.2	2.0	1.7	3.3
Durham, NC	6.8	5.5	7.5	4.3	2.7	1.6	1.3	1.8	0.8
El Paso, TX	3.5	2.9	1.7	4.2	1.0	0.4	0.6	0.4	0.2
Erie, PA	24.3	15.7	5.1	2.9	11.5	11.6	1.8	0.8	1.3
Eugene, OR	19.0	13.3	12.0	4.9	4.2	2.6	3.7	2.8	2.2
Fargo, ND	40.1	9.6	5.1	2.1	1.4	2.5	3.1	1.6	1.1
Fayetteville, NC	10.4	7.5	5.0	5.2	2.6	1.4	1.4	1.8	0.6
Fort Collins, CO	26.3	14.2	11.6	4.1	6.8	3.6	3.9	2.9	2.6
Fort Wayne, IN	26.7	9.3	6.8	11.3	2.6	2.2	3.5	1.5	1.6
Fort Worth, TX	8.9	7.1	5.4	6.8	1.9	1.2	1.5	1.5	0.7
Gainesville, FL	11.5	10.6	8.4	4.2	5.9	3.0	2.5	2.5	1.0
Grand Rapids, MI	15.3	8.9	6.8	3.2	3.0	7.0	3.0	1.3	15.0
Green Bay, WI	33.0	8.8	3.4	4.0	2.1	9.8	5.0	0.9	4.0
Greensboro, NC	7.4	5.8	7.9	5.6	2.3	1.1	1.1	2.1	0.6
Honolulu, HI	4.3	3.2	2.8	1.5	2.0	0.6	1.3	0.9	0.4
Houston, TX	5.3	3.7	3.9	3.8	1.6	0.9	1.7	0.9	0.5
Huntsville, AL	10.7	8.8	9.6	9.9	2.7	1.0	1.9	2.3	1.0
Indianapolis, IN	16.2	10.0	6.5	7.5	2.1	1.5	1.8	1.6	1.1
Jacksonville, FL	9.6	9.7	8.2	6.0	4.0	1.6	2.1	1.8	0.8
Kansas City, MO	17.4	11.7	7.5	9.4	3.3	1.4	2.2	1.6	1.3
Lafayette, LA	9.2	6.6	5.9	7.7	3.4	0.7	20.1	1.3	0.7
Las Vegas, NV	9.8	8.2	5.7	3.8	6.2	2.3	2.2	1.3	0.7
Lexington, KY	13.6	12.5	11.5	15.1	3.2	1.3	2.0	2.6	1.2
Lincoln, NE	40.0	13.4	9.4	4.6	2.0	2.6	2.8	1.7	2.0
Little Rock, AR	8.1	7.4	7.6	6.3	1.4	0.7	1.6	1.9	0.6
Los Angeles, CA	4.3	3.7	3.1	3.0	2.6	1.6	1.2	0.8	0.5
Louisville, KY	16.4	12.4	8.5	14.7	2.4	0.8	2.0	1.5	1.2
Lubbock, TX	11.8	8.0	7.4	7.5	1.7	0.9	1.6	1.5	0.9
Madison, WI	33.3	13.3	8.8	3.0	4.2	5.2	2.7	1.7	2.1
Manchester, NH	7.1	19.5	9.3	3.4	8.0	4.8	17.4	1.9	0.5
McAllen, TX	4.3	2.6	2.8	2.5	1.4	0.2	3.1	0.3	0.4
Miami, FL	2.0	1.5	1.1	4.7	2.3	0.8	0.8	0.3	0.3
Midland, TX	11.6	8.3	7.1	6.5	1.2	0.6	1.3	1.5	0.8
Minneapolis, MN	22.2	10.7	5.8	2.3	2.3	3.9	2.9	1.4	1.4

Table continued on next page.

City	German	Irish	English	American	Italian	Polish	French[1]	Scottish	Dutch
Nashville, TN	9.2	8.9	8.1	7.7	2.4	1.0	2.0	1.9	0.9
New Orleans, LA	6.8	6.0	4.2	3.4	4.1	0.8	6.2	1.0	0.4
New York, NY	3.0	4.7	1.7	4.5	6.8	2.5	0.8	0.4	0.3
Oklahoma City, OK	12.7	9.5	7.2	7.2	1.6	0.9	2.1	1.9	1.2
Omaha, NE	27.4	14.6	7.1	3.5	4.7	4.1	2.4	1.2	1.7
Orlando, FL	7.9	6.5	5.6	7.4	3.7	1.5	1.5	1.3	0.7
Oxnard, CA	4.1	3.4	2.4	1.5	1.7	0.5	0.9	0.6	0.5
Palm Bay, FL	14.2	12.1	10.9	12.1	8.7	3.2	3.3	1.9	1.1
Peoria, IL	20.5	9.4	7.3	5.0	3.2	2.0	1.9	1.3	0.9
Philadelphia, PA	7.2	11.8	2.6	2.5	7.9	3.4	0.7	0.6	0.4
Phoenix, AZ	11.8	8.1	6.2	4.2	4.0	2.2	1.9	1.4	1.1
Pittsburgh, PA	19.6	16.3	5.0	3.9	12.7	7.5	1.6	1.6	0.7
Portland, OR	17.3	12.1	10.7	5.7	4.5	2.4	3.1	3.3	1.9
Providence, RI	3.3	8.5	3.9	2.6	9.9	1.8	3.1	1.1	0.4
Provo, UT	10.6	5.4	23.1	4.6	2.7	0.5	2.6	4.4	1.6
Raleigh, NC	9.9	8.1	9.9	10.0	3.8	1.8	1.7	2.5	0.9
Reno, NV	14.1	11.8	8.0	5.1	6.4	1.6	2.8	2.2	1.7
Richmond, VA	7.3	6.7	8.5	4.0	2.5	1.0	1.6	1.9	0.6
Roanoke, VA	11.2	10.1	10.1	11.8	2.2	1.2	2.0	1.6	1.4
Rochester, MN	32.4	10.2	6.2	4.3	1.9	3.8	2.7	1.1	2.1
Sacramento, CA	8.3	6.7	5.4	2.4	3.8	0.9	1.6	1.4	0.8
Salem, OR	19.6	11.5	11.1	4.4	3.5	1.1	3.4	2.8	2.1
Salt Lake City, UT	10.8	6.5	16.1	4.0	2.8	1.1	1.9	3.8	2.1
San Antonio, TX	8.5	4.6	4.0	3.8	1.9	1.1	1.5	0.9	0.5
San Diego, CA	9.3	7.6	5.9	3.2	4.1	1.8	2.1	1.4	0.9
San Francisco, CA	7.9	7.9	4.9	2.8	5.0	1.7	2.2	1.4	0.9
San Jose, CA	5.9	4.8	4.1	1.8	4.2	0.9	1.3	0.9	0.7
Santa Rosa, CA	12.6	11.0	9.3	4.5	8.0	1.4	3.4	2.5	1.6
Savannah, GA	6.1	6.5	5.5	4.2	2.2	1.3	1.4	1.6	0.6
Seattle, WA	16.4	11.4	11.0	3.4	4.4	2.4	3.3	3.1	1.8
Sioux Falls, SD	36.8	10.8	4.6	3.9	1.1	1.6	2.4	0.8	7.2
Spokane, WA	22.0	13.5	10.6	5.3	5.1	1.8	3.4	2.7	1.8
Springfield, IL	23.5	13.8	9.1	6.6	5.3	2.1	2.1	1.5	1.1
Tallahassee, FL	9.8	9.7	8.8	4.3	4.5	2.1	1.9	2.3	0.9
Tampa, FL	8.7	8.0	5.8	5.7	6.0	1.9	2.0	1.5	1.0
Topeka, KS	26.0	13.6	10.2	4.9	2.8	1.0	3.2	2.0	1.8
Tulsa, OK	13.5	11.2	8.7	8.2	1.8	1.0	2.5	2.2	1.5
Tyler, TX	9.0	9.2	8.2	7.1	2.3	0.8	2.5	1.6	0.9
Virginia Beach, VA	13.2	11.4	9.3	14.1	6.1	2.9	2.6	2.3	1.1
Washington, DC	6.6	6.5	5.2	2.7	3.8	2.1	1.4	1.4	0.5
Wichita, KS	21.6	10.3	8.2	8.7	1.8	0.9	2.3	1.8	1.5
Wilmington, NC	10.9	9.7	10.2	21.4	4.5	1.6	2.1	3.8	1.4
Winston-Salem, NC	8.8	6.0	9.2	5.2	2.4	1.2	1.4	2.6	0.8
Worcester, MA	3.1	15.9	4.8	3.0	9.6	4.5	7.6	1.2	0.4
U.S.	14.9	10.8	8.0	7.4	5.5	3.0	2.7	1.7	1.4

Note: Figures are the percentage of the total population reporting a particular ancestry. The nine most commonly reported ancestries in the U.S. are shown. Figures include multiple ancestries (e.g. if a person reported being Irish and Italian, they were included in both columns); (1) Excludes Basque
Source: U.S. Census Bureau, 2011-2013 American Community Survey 3-Year Estimates

Ancestry: Metro Area

Metro Area	German	Irish	English	American	Italian	Polish	French[1]	Scottish	Dutch
Albuquerque, NM	10.6	7.2	6.8	4.8	3.1	1.5	1.8	1.6	1.0
Anchorage, AK	18.1	10.8	8.7	5.6	3.2	1.9	3.0	3.0	1.8
Ann Arbor, MI	20.8	11.1	10.3	7.6	5.0	6.7	3.1	2.7	2.0
Athens, GA	9.3	8.9	9.7	13.0	2.5	1.3	1.6	2.9	0.7
Atlanta, GA	7.5	7.6	7.4	10.2	2.5	1.3	1.5	1.7	0.8
Austin, TX	14.6	8.7	8.8	5.1	3.0	1.6	2.8	2.2	1.0
Billings, MT	28.1	11.8	10.0	15.2	3.1	1.9	3.0	2.6	2.0
Boise City, ID	17.0	8.8	13.9	10.4	3.3	1.5	2.2	3.2	2.0
Boston, MA	6.3	23.4	10.5	4.9	14.8	3.7	5.7	2.5	0.6
Boulder, CO	22.4	13.6	13.5	5.5	5.8	3.8	4.0	3.4	2.3
Cape Coral, FL	15.5	11.9	9.0	13.6	7.7	3.5	3.1	1.5	1.3
Cedar Rapids, IA	40.7	16.4	9.2	6.3	2.0	1.5	2.7	1.6	2.1
Charleston, SC	11.4	10.4	9.0	13.5	3.6	1.7	2.6	2.6	1.0
Charlotte, NC	12.0	9.2	8.3	10.1	3.7	1.8	1.6	2.3	1.0
Chicago, IL	15.4	11.8	4.4	3.0	7.1	9.3	1.5	1.0	1.3
Clarksville, TN	12.4	10.5	8.2	13.2	3.0	2.0	1.8	1.9	1.3
Colorado Springs, CO	22.2	13.2	10.1	6.3	5.4	2.6	3.2	2.9	2.1
Columbia, MO	27.4	13.5	11.5	6.5	3.5	1.9	3.0	2.8	1.5
Columbus, OH	25.5	14.0	9.4	8.1	5.5	2.3	2.2	2.1	1.7
Dallas, TX	10.3	8.2	7.5	6.9	2.2	1.1	2.0	1.7	0.9
Davenport, IA	28.7	14.8	8.6	6.6	2.7	2.2	2.3	1.5	2.1
Denver, CO	19.7	11.9	9.9	5.1	5.3	2.7	2.8	2.4	1.6
Des Moines, IA	28.5	13.8	9.4	5.5	3.2	1.4	2.3	1.6	3.9
Durham, NC	9.4	7.9	10.6	7.0	3.0	2.0	1.9	2.3	0.9
El Paso, TX	3.3	2.6	1.6	3.9	1.0	0.4	0.6	0.4	0.2
Erie, PA	28.9	17.7	8.3	4.7	12.4	12.1	1.8	1.6	1.5
Eugene, OR	19.0	13.6	12.0	5.9	4.2	2.3	3.4	3.0	2.3
Fargo, ND	39.8	8.4	4.5	2.1	1.3	2.7	3.2	1.2	1.1
Fayetteville, NC	9.4	7.5	5.2	7.9	2.8	1.2	1.3	1.9	0.8
Fort Collins, CO	28.2	13.9	12.6	4.7	5.8	3.1	4.0	3.1	2.5
Fort Wayne, IN	30.4	9.1	7.7	12.4	2.5	2.3	3.5	1.6	1.6
Fort Worth, TX	10.3	8.2	7.5	6.9	2.2	1.1	2.0	1.7	0.9
Gainesville, FL	12.7	11.2	9.8	6.1	4.8	2.5	2.6	2.2	1.3
Grand Rapids, MI	21.5	11.1	9.9	5.1	3.2	6.9	3.7	1.9	20.6
Green Bay, WI	38.4	9.6	3.6	4.4	2.5	10.4	4.9	0.9	5.0
Greensboro, NC	9.0	7.0	9.6	10.2	2.3	0.9	1.3	2.1	0.8
Honolulu, HI	5.2	4.0	3.3	1.5	2.0	0.8	1.1	0.8	0.6
Houston, TX	8.7	6.0	5.4	4.9	2.1	1.3	2.3	1.2	0.7
Huntsville, AL	10.1	9.0	9.3	14.7	2.1	1.0	1.8	2.0	0.9
Indianapolis, IN	20.4	11.7	9.1	9.8	2.6	1.9	2.1	2.0	1.7
Jacksonville, FL	11.2	11.4	9.6	8.4	4.8	2.1	2.6	2.3	1.0
Kansas City, MO	23.1	13.4	10.1	8.3	3.4	1.8	2.6	2.0	1.5
Lafayette, LA	8.0	4.6	4.2	10.7	2.5	0.4	21.0	0.7	0.3
Las Vegas, NV	10.5	8.2	6.1	4.2	6.0	2.4	2.1	1.4	0.9
Lexington, KY	14.1	12.6	11.9	19.0	2.9	1.3	1.9	2.7	1.2
Lincoln, NE	41.3	13.1	9.2	4.8	2.0	2.5	2.8	1.7	2.1
Little Rock, AR	10.9	10.4	10.2	10.5	1.7	0.9	2.2	2.0	1.1
Los Angeles, CA	6.0	4.9	4.3	3.5	3.0	1.3	1.4	1.0	0.7
Louisville, KY	18.7	12.8	9.5	18.1	2.3	1.0	2.1	1.8	1.2
Lubbock, TX	11.8	8.4	7.2	8.0	1.5	0.8	1.6	1.6	0.9
Madison, WI	40.3	13.7	8.8	3.6	3.3	4.8	2.7	1.5	2.0
Manchester, NH	8.1	21.2	13.3	4.3	9.7	4.8	14.7	3.2	0.9
McAllen, TX	2.6	1.3	1.2	1.6	0.6	0.2	0.9	0.3	0.2
Miami, FL	5.2	5.1	3.3	6.1	5.4	2.2	1.4	0.7	0.5
Midland, TX	11.3	8.2	6.9	6.3	1.1	0.6	1.3	1.8	0.9
Minneapolis, MN	32.4	11.9	5.9	3.5	2.8	4.7	3.7	1.3	1.6

Table continued on next page.

Metro Area	German	Irish	English	American	Italian	Polish	French[1]	Scottish	Dutch
Nashville, TN	10.8	11.0	10.3	14.0	2.6	1.2	2.2	2.3	1.0
New Orleans, LA	10.8	8.5	4.9	6.2	8.9	0.7	14.3	1.0	0.5
New York, NY	7.2	10.7	3.1	4.7	13.7	4.2	1.1	0.7	0.6
Oklahoma City, OK	14.1	11.2	8.3	9.1	1.7	1.0	2.2	1.9	1.5
Omaha, NE	32.0	15.2	8.6	4.4	4.6	4.0	2.5	1.3	2.0
Orlando, FL	10.4	8.5	7.2	8.8	5.1	2.3	2.2	1.6	0.9
Oxnard, CA	11.6	8.7	8.3	3.6	5.1	1.9	2.5	1.9	1.1
Palm Bay, FL	15.8	14.0	11.1	11.9	8.5	3.3	3.4	2.4	1.7
Peoria, IL	31.1	12.6	10.0	8.4	4.3	2.3	2.6	1.8	1.7
Philadelphia, PA	16.4	20.1	7.5	3.8	14.0	5.3	1.5	1.3	1.0
Phoenix, AZ	14.4	9.4	8.3	6.4	4.6	2.6	2.3	1.7	1.4
Pittsburgh, PA	28.6	19.1	8.3	4.6	16.4	9.0	1.9	1.9	1.3
Portland, OR	19.7	11.6	11.1	5.3	3.9	2.0	3.2	3.1	2.2
Providence, RI	5.1	18.7	11.1	3.3	15.4	4.2	11.1	1.9	0.5
Provo, UT	11.8	5.4	28.8	5.8	2.4	0.7	2.1	5.5	1.9
Raleigh, NC	11.1	10.0	11.2	11.7	4.6	2.2	1.9	2.8	1.2
Reno, NV	14.8	11.7	9.2	5.5	6.6	1.8	3.1	2.4	1.6
Richmond, VA	9.7	8.7	11.8	8.5	3.6	1.6	1.9	2.2	0.8
Roanoke, VA	14.5	12.4	13.0	15.1	2.5	1.4	2.1	2.0	1.3
Rochester, MN	38.3	10.9	6.2	4.4	1.6	3.4	2.6	1.1	2.4
Sacramento, CA	13.2	9.7	8.8	3.7	5.3	1.5	2.6	2.0	1.3
Salem, OR	19.7	10.1	10.9	4.5	3.1	1.3	3.1	2.7	2.2
Salt Lake City, UT	11.4	6.2	21.9	5.2	2.9	1.0	1.8	4.0	2.4
San Antonio, TX	12.1	5.9	5.5	4.4	2.0	1.6	1.9	1.2	0.6
San Diego, CA	10.6	8.3	8.3	3.2	4.4	1.8	2.2	1.5	1.0
San Francisco, CA	8.5	7.9	6.3	2.9	5.3	1.5	2.0	1.6	0.9
San Jose, CA	7.1	5.6	5.2	2.2	4.5	1.2	1.6	1.1	0.8
Santa Rosa, CA	14.1	12.6	10.7	4.5	9.2	1.8	3.5	2.5	1.7
Savannah, GA	9.5	9.5	7.8	7.3	2.8	1.5	1.9	2.0	0.9
Seattle, WA	16.6	10.9	10.4	4.5	3.7	1.9	3.2	2.8	1.8
Sioux Falls, SD	40.2	10.4	4.7	4.4	1.1	1.4	2.2	0.8	7.8
Spokane, WA	23.1	13.4	11.0	5.5	4.7	1.8	3.6	2.9	1.9
Springfield, IL	25.7	14.5	10.4	8.0	5.6	2.0	2.1	1.8	1.4
Tallahassee, FL	9.8	9.9	8.8	5.9	4.0	1.6	2.0	2.5	1.1
Tampa, FL	12.9	11.6	8.6	9.7	7.7	3.0	2.9	1.8	1.2
Topeka, KS	29.7	14.4	10.3	6.8	2.6	1.3	3.2	2.0	1.9
Tulsa, OK	15.0	12.5	8.6	9.4	1.9	1.0	2.5	2.0	1.7
Tyler, TX	10.5	11.1	9.2	9.4	1.9	1.0	3.1	2.0	1.2
Virginia Beach, VA	10.9	9.5	9.6	11.0	4.5	2.0	2.2	2.1	1.0
Washington, DC	10.6	9.4	7.6	4.9	4.5	2.3	1.7	1.8	0.8
Wichita, KS	25.7	11.4	9.0	10.3	1.9	1.1	2.6	2.1	1.9
Wilmington, NC	11.8	11.3	11.3	19.5	4.6	2.0	2.2	3.0	1.2
Winston-Salem, NC	12.3	8.0	10.3	11.8	2.1	1.1	1.3	2.4	1.1
Worcester, MA	6.6	20.2	10.5	4.3	13.4	6.5	14.6	2.3	0.8
U.S.	14.9	10.8	8.0	7.4	5.5	3.0	2.7	1.7	1.4

Note: Figures are the percentage of the total population reporting a particular ancestry. The nine most commonly reported ancestries in the U.S. are shown. Figures include multiple ancestries (e.g. if a person reported being Irish and Italian, they were included in both columns); Figures cover the Metropolitan Statistical Area—see Appendix B for areas included; (1) Excludes Basque
Source: U.S. Census Bureau, 2011-2013 American Community Survey 3-Year Estimates

Foreign-Born Population: City

City	Percent of Population Born in								
	Any Foreign Country	Mexico	Asia	Europe	Carribean	South America	Central America[1]	Africa	Canada
Albuquerque, NM	10.6	6.0	2.2	1.0	0.4	0.4	0.3	0.2	0.2
Anchorage, AK	9.4	0.9	5.6	1.1	0.4	0.3	0.2	0.3	0.3
Ann Arbor, MI	17.2	0.7	10.7	3.2	0.1	0.6	0.3	0.7	0.7
Athens, GA	n/a	n/a	n/a	n/a	n/a	n/a	n/a	n/a	n/a
Atlanta, GA	7.8	1.4	2.7	1.3	0.6	0.4	0.3	0.7	0.1
Austin, TX	18.3	8.7	5.0	1.2	0.4	0.5	1.6	0.6	0.3
Billings, MT	n/a	n/a	n/a	n/a	n/a	n/a	n/a	n/a	n/a
Boise City, ID	7.4	1.4	3.3	1.5	0.0	0.1	0.3	0.4	0.4
Boston, MA	26.9	0.5	6.7	3.6	7.9	2.2	3.0	2.6	0.4
Boulder, CO	9.7	1.8	3.6	3.0	0.1	0.4	0.1	0.1	0.4
Cape Coral, FL	n/a	n/a	n/a	n/a	n/a	n/a	n/a	n/a	n/a
Cedar Rapids, IA	n/a	n/a	n/a	n/a	n/a	n/a	n/a	n/a	n/a
Charleston, SC	n/a	n/a	n/a	n/a	n/a	n/a	n/a	n/a	n/a
Charlotte, NC	15.3	2.9	4.2	1.5	1.0	1.3	2.6	1.6	0.2
Chicago, IL	21.4	9.7	4.6	3.8	0.4	1.0	0.9	0.8	0.2
Clarksville, TN	n/a	n/a	n/a	n/a	n/a	n/a	n/a	n/a	n/a
Colorado Springs, CO	8.2	2.5	2.1	1.7	0.3	0.4	0.5	0.4	0.3
Columbia, MO	n/a	n/a	n/a	n/a	n/a	n/a	n/a	n/a	n/a
Columbus, OH	11.1	1.8	3.9	0.9	0.3	0.4	0.4	3.3	0.1
Dallas, TX	24.4	16.8	2.6	0.8	0.1	0.4	2.0	1.4	0.2
Davenport, IA	n/a	n/a	n/a	n/a	n/a	n/a	n/a	n/a	n/a
Denver, CO	15.8	9.0	2.8	1.4	0.2	0.4	0.5	1.2	0.3
Des Moines, IA	n/a	n/a	n/a	n/a	n/a	n/a	n/a	n/a	n/a
Durham, NC	14.6	4.5	3.6	1.1	0.4	0.7	2.5	1.4	0.3
El Paso, TX	24.9	22.2	1.0	0.5	0.2	0.3	0.4	0.1	0.1
Erie, PA	n/a	n/a	n/a	n/a	n/a	n/a	n/a	n/a	n/a
Eugene, OR	7.9	2.0	3.5	1.1	0.1	0.2	0.2	0.2	0.4
Fargo, ND	n/a	n/a	n/a	n/a	n/a	n/a	n/a	n/a	n/a
Fayetteville, NC	5.9	0.6	2.2	1.0	0.7	0.4	0.8	0.2	0.0
Fort Collins, CO	6.1	1.2	2.5	1.2	0.1	0.4	0.2	0.2	0.3
Fort Wayne, IN	7.8	2.4	2.9	1.1	0.2	0.3	0.5	0.4	0.2
Fort Worth, TX	17.8	11.5	3.2	0.7	0.2	0.4	0.8	0.7	0.2
Gainesville, FL	12.5	0.4	5.3	1.5	2.1	1.9	0.3	0.6	0.4
Grand Rapids, MI	9.6	3.2	1.9	0.7	0.6	0.2	1.7	0.8	0.5
Green Bay, WI	n/a	n/a	n/a	n/a	n/a	n/a	n/a	n/a	n/a
Greensboro, NC	10.4	2.3	3.5	0.9	0.4	0.8	0.7	1.7	0.2
Honolulu, HI	27.8	0.2	23.2	1.1	0.1	0.2	0.0	0.1	0.3
Houston, TX	28.0	13.1	5.5	1.1	0.6	1.0	5.3	1.2	0.2
Huntsville, AL	6.3	1.7	2.0	0.9	0.4	0.2	0.2	0.7	0.1
Indianapolis, IN	8.3	3.4	2.0	0.5	0.3	0.2	0.8	1.0	0.1
Jacksonville, FL	9.6	0.5	3.7	1.7	1.4	1.0	0.6	0.5	0.2
Kansas City, MO	7.7	2.4	2.1	0.7	0.4	0.3	0.4	1.1	0.1
Lafayette, LA	n/a	n/a	n/a	n/a	n/a	n/a	n/a	n/a	n/a
Las Vegas, NV	21.3	10.1	5.1	1.5	0.8	0.8	2.0	0.4	0.4
Lexington, KY	9.0	2.7	3.3	0.8	0.2	0.3	0.5	0.8	0.2
Lincoln, NE	7.6	1.4	3.8	1.0	0.1	0.2	0.3	0.6	0.1
Little Rock, AR	n/a	n/a	n/a	n/a	n/a	n/a	n/a	n/a	n/a
Los Angeles, CA	38.6	13.9	11.1	2.4	0.3	1.1	8.6	0.7	0.3
Louisville, KY	6.9	1.0	2.2	0.9	1.4	0.2	0.2	1.0	0.1
Lubbock, TX	5.9	2.3	2.0	0.6	0.1	0.2	0.2	0.4	0.1
Madison, WI	10.8	2.0	5.8	1.3	0.1	0.5	0.2	0.6	0.3
Manchester, NH	13.2	1.3	4.2	2.2	1.3	1.2	0.5	1.3	1.1
McAllen, TX	n/a	n/a	n/a	n/a	n/a	n/a	n/a	n/a	n/a
Miami, FL	57.0	1.0	1.0	1.7	32.7	7.8	12.2	0.2	0.2

Table continued on next page.

City	Percent of Population Born in: Any Foreign Country	Mexico	Asia	Europe	Carribean	South America	Central America[1]	Africa	Canada
Midland, TX	n/a	n/a	n/a	n/a	n/a	n/a	n/a	n/a	n/a
Minneapolis, MN	15.0	3.0	3.8	1.1	0.2	1.6	0.6	4.4	0.2
Nashville, TN	12.0	3.1	3.6	0.9	0.4	0.5	1.6	1.7	0.2
New Orleans, LA	5.9	0.4	2.2	0.7	0.2	0.4	1.7	0.2	0.1
New York, NY	37.3	2.2	10.4	5.7	10.4	5.1	1.5	1.6	0.3
Oklahoma City, OK	12.5	6.9	3.2	0.4	0.1	0.2	1.0	0.4	0.1
Omaha, NE	9.9	4.4	2.4	0.6	0.2	0.2	1.0	1.0	0.1
Orlando, FL	18.4	1.3	2.9	1.3	5.7	5.6	0.7	0.5	0.3
Oxnard, CA	n/a	n/a	n/a	n/a	n/a	n/a	n/a	n/a	n/a
Palm Bay, FL	n/a	n/a	n/a	n/a	n/a	n/a	n/a	n/a	n/a
Peoria, IL	n/a	n/a	n/a	n/a	n/a	n/a	n/a	n/a	n/a
Philadelphia, PA	12.4	0.5	4.9	2.2	2.1	0.8	0.5	1.3	0.1
Phoenix, AZ	20.1	13.1	3.0	1.5	0.3	0.4	0.8	0.7	0.4
Pittsburgh, PA	7.9	0.1	4.4	1.9	0.2	0.3	0.1	0.7	0.1
Portland, OR	14.1	3.1	5.6	2.9	0.2	0.3	0.4	0.9	0.4
Providence, RI	29.6	0.5	4.7	2.1	10.2	1.6	7.3	2.9	0.2
Provo, UT	n/a	n/a	n/a	n/a	n/a	n/a	n/a	n/a	n/a
Raleigh, NC	13.1	3.0	3.7	1.2	0.8	0.9	1.8	1.5	0.3
Reno, NV	17.0	8.0	5.0	1.3	0.0	0.3	1.8	0.2	0.2
Richmond, VA	6.5	1.1	1.2	0.7	0.3	0.4	1.9	0.8	0.1
Roanoke, VA	n/a	n/a	n/a	n/a	n/a	n/a	n/a	n/a	n/a
Rochester, MN	12.6	1.7	5.1	1.4	0.2	0.4	0.1	3.0	0.5
Sacramento, CA	22.5	7.0	10.8	1.6	0.2	0.3	0.6	0.5	0.1
Salem, OR	n/a	n/a	n/a	n/a	n/a	n/a	n/a	n/a	n/a
Salt Lake City, UT	17.5	6.7	4.1	2.4	0.3	1.0	0.7	1.0	0.4
San Antonio, TX	14.1	9.7	2.2	0.6	0.2	0.2	0.8	0.3	0.1
San Diego, CA	26.3	9.3	12.0	2.3	0.2	0.6	0.5	0.9	0.4
San Francisco, CA	35.8	2.8	22.9	4.7	0.2	1.1	2.9	0.3	0.6
San Jose, CA	38.7	10.3	23.5	2.1	0.1	0.5	1.1	0.6	0.4
Santa Rosa, CA	18.8	10.8	3.5	1.3	0.1	0.3	0.9	1.0	0.4
Savannah, GA	5.7	1.7	1.2	0.7	0.4	0.6	0.2	0.4	0.2
Seattle, WA	18.3	1.4	9.8	2.6	0.2	0.3	0.4	2.4	0.9
Sioux Falls, SD	n/a	n/a	n/a	n/a	n/a	n/a	n/a	n/a	n/a
Spokane, WA	n/a	n/a	n/a	n/a	n/a	n/a	n/a	n/a	n/a
Springfield, IL	n/a	n/a	n/a	n/a	n/a	n/a	n/a	n/a	n/a
Tallahassee, FL	7.9	0.4	2.8	0.9	2.0	0.8	0.3	0.6	0.2
Tampa, FL	15.2	1.0	3.2	1.5	5.8	1.6	1.1	0.6	0.2
Topeka, KS	n/a	n/a	n/a	n/a	n/a	n/a	n/a	n/a	n/a
Tulsa, OK	10.1	5.6	2.2	0.6	0.1	0.2	0.8	0.3	0.1
Tyler, TX	n/a	n/a	n/a	n/a	n/a	n/a	n/a	n/a	n/a
Virginia Beach, VA	8.6	0.3	4.7	1.5	0.6	0.5	0.4	0.5	0.2
Washington, DC	14.2	0.4	2.7	2.6	1.4	1.3	3.1	2.2	0.3
Wichita, KS	10.5	4.7	3.8	0.5	0.1	0.2	0.3	0.7	0.1
Wilmington, NC	n/a	n/a	n/a	n/a	n/a	n/a	n/a	n/a	n/a
Winston-Salem, NC	10.7	5.6	1.5	0.8	0.4	0.5	1.4	0.2	0.1
Worcester, MA	21.8	0.4	5.8	4.2	3.1	2.4	0.9	4.8	0.2
U.S.	13.0	3.7	3.8	1.5	1.2	0.9	1.0	0.6	0.3

Note: (1) Excludes Mexico
Source: U.S. Census Bureau, 2011-2013 American Community Survey 3-Year Estimates

Foreign-Born Population: Metro Area

Metro Area	Any Foreign Country	Mexico	Asia	Europe	Carribean	South America	Central America[1]	Africa	Canada
	Percent of Population Born in								
Albuquerque, NM	9.6	6.0	1.6	0.8	0.3	0.3	0.3	0.1	0.1
Anchorage, AK	8.1	0.7	4.5	1.2	0.3	0.2	0.2	0.3	0.3
Ann Arbor, MI	11.4	0.6	6.5	1.9	0.2	0.5	0.5	0.6	0.5
Athens, GA	7.5	2.6	2.6	0.7	0.2	0.4	0.7	0.2	0.1
Atlanta, GA	13.2	3.1	3.9	1.2	1.5	0.9	1.0	1.3	0.2
Austin, TX	14.8	7.3	3.7	1.1	0.3	0.4	1.1	0.5	0.3
Billings, MT	n/a	n/a	n/a	n/a	n/a	n/a	n/a	n/a	n/a
Boise City, ID	6.6	2.8	1.6	1.1	0.0	0.2	0.2	0.2	0.3
Boston, MA	16.9	0.2	5.3	3.3	3.0	1.8	1.4	1.4	0.5
Boulder, CO	10.5	3.7	3.2	2.3	0.1	0.3	0.3	0.3	0.4
Cape Coral, FL	15.1	2.7	1.2	2.2	4.4	1.8	1.6	0.1	1.0
Cedar Rapids, IA	n/a	n/a	n/a	n/a	n/a	n/a	n/a	n/a	n/a
Charleston, SC	5.2	1.4	1.3	1.0	0.3	0.4	0.4	0.1	0.2
Charlotte, NC	9.4	2.4	2.2	1.1	0.6	0.8	1.3	0.7	0.2
Chicago, IL	17.8	7.0	4.7	3.9	0.3	0.6	0.5	0.5	0.2
Clarksville, TN	n/a	n/a	n/a	n/a	n/a	n/a	n/a	n/a	n/a
Colorado Springs, CO	7.1	1.8	2.0	1.7	0.3	0.3	0.4	0.3	0.3
Columbia, MO	n/a	n/a	n/a	n/a	n/a	n/a	n/a	n/a	n/a
Columbus, OH	6.9	0.9	2.6	0.8	0.2	0.2	0.2	1.6	0.2
Dallas, TX	17.5	9.1	4.3	0.8	0.2	0.5	1.3	1.0	0.2
Davenport, IA	4.7	1.6	1.4	0.7	0.1	0.1	0.1	0.5	0.1
Denver, CO	12.1	5.5	2.9	1.5	0.1	0.4	0.4	0.9	0.3
Des Moines, IA	7.6	1.9	2.5	1.4	0.0	0.2	0.5	0.9	0.1
Durham, NC	12.1	3.7	3.3	1.3	0.3	0.5	1.8	0.9	0.3
El Paso, TX	25.8	23.4	0.9	0.4	0.2	0.2	0.4	0.1	0.1
Erie, PA	4.1	0.1	1.4	1.6	0.2	0.1	0.1	0.4	0.1
Eugene, OR	5.8	1.8	2.0	0.9	0.0	0.2	0.2	0.1	0.4
Fargo, ND	5.1	0.1	2.4	0.8	0.0	0.1	0.0	1.2	0.3
Fayetteville, NC	5.3	0.9	1.7	0.9	0.6	0.3	0.7	0.2	0.1
Fort Collins, CO	5.3	1.8	1.6	1.0	0.0	0.3	0.2	0.2	0.2
Fort Wayne, IN	5.6	1.6	2.1	0.9	0.1	0.2	0.3	0.2	0.2
Fort Worth, TX	17.5	9.1	4.3	0.8	0.2	0.5	1.3	1.0	0.2
Gainesville, FL	9.9	0.5	3.7	1.4	1.7	1.4	0.3	0.5	0.4
Grand Rapids, MI	6.4	1.8	1.8	1.0	0.3	0.2	0.5	0.4	0.3
Green Bay, WI	4.4	1.9	1.4	0.4	0.2	0.1	0.2	0.1	0.1
Greensboro, NC	8.4	2.8	2.6	0.7	0.2	0.4	0.5	0.9	0.2
Honolulu, HI	19.3	0.2	15.8	0.7	0.1	0.2	0.1	0.1	0.3
Houston, TX	22.3	9.8	5.3	1.0	0.5	1.0	3.3	1.0	0.3
Huntsville, AL	5.2	1.5	1.9	0.8	0.3	0.1	0.1	0.4	0.1
Indianapolis, IN	6.0	1.9	1.9	0.6	0.2	0.2	0.4	0.6	0.1
Jacksonville, FL	7.9	0.4	2.9	1.6	1.1	0.8	0.4	0.4	0.2
Kansas City, MO	6.4	2.1	2.0	0.6	0.2	0.2	0.4	0.6	0.1
Lafayette, LA	n/a	n/a	n/a	n/a	n/a	n/a	n/a	n/a	n/a
Las Vegas, NV	21.8	9.0	6.7	1.7	0.9	0.7	1.8	0.6	0.4
Lexington, KY	6.7	2.1	2.3	0.7	0.2	0.2	0.4	0.5	0.2
Lincoln, NE	6.8	1.2	3.3	0.9	0.1	0.2	0.3	0.5	0.1
Little Rock, AR	3.8	1.3	1.4	0.4	0.0	0.1	0.3	0.1	0.1
Los Angeles, CA	33.8	13.2	12.4	1.7	0.3	0.9	4.3	0.5	0.3
Louisville, KY	5.1	1.0	1.5	0.7	0.8	0.2	0.2	0.6	0.1
Lubbock, TX	5.6	2.6	1.7	0.5	0.1	0.2	0.2	0.3	0.1
Madison, WI	6.9	1.7	3.0	1.0	0.1	0.3	0.2	0.4	0.2
Manchester, NH	8.8	0.7	3.0	1.7	0.7	0.9	0.4	0.6	1.0
McAllen, TX	n/a	n/a	n/a	n/a	n/a	n/a	n/a	n/a	n/a
Miami, FL	38.5	1.1	2.0	2.3	20.4	7.6	4.2	0.4	0.6

Table continued on next page.

Metro Area	Any Foreign Country	Mexico	Asia	Europe	Carribean	South America	Central America[1]	Africa	Canada
	Percent of Population Born in								
Midland, TX	n/a	n/a	n/a	n/a	n/a	n/a	n/a	n/a	n/a
Minneapolis, MN	9.7	1.4	3.9	1.1	0.1	0.5	0.4	2.0	0.2
Nashville, TN	7.3	2.0	2.2	0.7	0.2	0.3	0.8	0.8	0.2
New Orleans, LA	7.1	0.6	2.0	0.6	0.7	0.4	2.5	0.2	0.1
New York, NY	28.5	1.7	8.0	4.7	6.5	4.3	1.9	1.2	0.2
Oklahoma City, OK	8.1	4.0	2.3	0.4	0.1	0.2	0.6	0.4	0.1
Omaha, NE	6.9	2.8	2.0	0.6	0.1	0.1	0.6	0.6	0.1
Orlando, FL	16.2	1.4	2.9	1.6	4.9	3.7	0.9	0.5	0.4
Oxnard, CA	22.6	13.1	5.3	1.6	0.1	0.6	1.2	0.2	0.5
Palm Bay, FL	8.6	0.5	1.8	1.9	2.2	0.9	0.6	0.2	0.6
Peoria, IL	3.6	0.6	1.8	0.6	0.1	0.2	0.0	0.1	0.1
Philadelphia, PA	9.9	0.9	4.0	2.0	1.1	0.5	0.4	0.9	0.1
Phoenix, AZ	14.4	7.9	2.9	1.4	0.2	0.3	0.5	0.4	0.7
Pittsburgh, PA	3.5	0.1	1.7	1.0	0.1	0.1	0.1	0.2	0.1
Portland, OR	12.5	3.8	4.4	2.4	0.1	0.3	0.4	0.4	0.5
Providence, RI	12.9	0.2	2.1	4.4	1.8	1.0	1.6	1.4	0.2
Provo, UT	7.2	2.7	1.1	0.6	0.1	1.3	0.5	0.1	0.5
Raleigh, NC	11.6	3.1	3.8	1.1	0.5	0.7	1.1	0.9	0.3
Reno, NV	15.0	7.2	4.0	1.2	0.1	0.3	1.4	0.2	0.3
Richmond, VA	7.2	0.8	2.6	1.1	0.4	0.4	1.1	0.6	0.1
Roanoke, VA	4.7	0.6	1.5	0.8	0.6	0.1	0.5	0.5	0.1
Rochester, MN	7.3	1.1	2.9	0.9	0.1	0.2	0.1	1.6	0.3
Sacramento, CA	18.0	4.9	8.0	2.8	0.1	0.3	0.6	0.4	0.3
Salem, OR	12.0	7.9	1.5	1.3	0.1	0.3	0.3	0.1	0.3
Salt Lake City, UT	11.9	4.9	2.7	1.4	0.1	1.1	0.6	0.4	0.3
San Antonio, TX	11.8	7.8	1.9	0.7	0.1	0.3	0.6	0.3	0.1
San Diego, CA	23.4	10.6	8.7	1.9	0.2	0.5	0.5	0.6	0.4
San Francisco, CA	29.8	5.6	16.3	2.9	0.1	1.0	2.5	0.6	0.4
San Jose, CA	36.8	8.2	22.8	2.9	0.1	0.6	0.9	0.5	0.5
Santa Rosa, CA	16.8	9.6	2.8	2.0	0.0	0.3	0.9	0.6	0.3
Savannah, GA	5.9	1.4	1.8	0.8	0.5	0.4	0.2	0.5	0.2
Seattle, WA	17.2	2.5	8.5	2.8	0.1	0.4	0.5	1.3	0.8
Sioux Falls, SD	n/a	n/a	n/a	n/a	n/a	n/a	n/a	n/a	n/a
Spokane, WA	5.4	0.4	1.9	2.0	0.0	0.1	0.1	0.3	0.4
Springfield, IL	3.3	0.2	1.6	0.6	0.2	0.1	0.0	0.5	0.1
Tallahassee, FL	6.3	0.6	1.9	0.8	1.3	0.6	0.3	0.4	0.2
Tampa, FL	12.7	1.4	2.5	2.3	3.1	1.6	0.7	0.4	0.7
Topeka, KS	n/a	n/a	n/a	n/a	n/a	n/a	n/a	n/a	n/a
Tulsa, OK	5.9	2.9	1.5	0.5	0.1	0.2	0.4	0.2	0.1
Tyler, TX	n/a	n/a	n/a	n/a	n/a	n/a	n/a	n/a	n/a
Virginia Beach, VA	6.2	0.4	2.7	1.1	0.5	0.3	0.5	0.5	0.2
Washington, DC	21.9	0.8	7.8	1.9	1.1	2.3	4.6	3.1	0.2
Wichita, KS	7.4	3.2	2.6	0.5	0.1	0.2	0.2	0.5	0.1
Wilmington, NC	5.3	1.9	0.9	1.0	0.2	0.2	0.7	0.1	0.2
Winston-Salem, NC	6.8	3.3	1.1	0.6	0.2	0.3	0.9	0.2	0.1
Worcester, MA	10.6	0.3	3.2	2.3	1.0	1.3	0.5	1.4	0.5
U.S.	13.0	3.7	3.8	1.5	1.2	0.9	1.0	0.6	0.3

Note: Figures cover the Metropolitan Statistical Area—see Appendix B for areas included; (1) Excludes Mexico
Source: U.S. Census Bureau, 2011-2013 American Community Survey 3-Year Estimates

Marital Status: City

City	Never Married	Now Married[1]	Separated	Widowed	Divorced
Albuquerque, NM	35.7	43.1	1.9	5.2	14.0
Anchorage, AK	35.3	47.4	1.6	3.6	12.1
Ann Arbor, MI	55.8	31.9	0.7	3.6	8.2
Athens, GA	56.8	29.6	1.4	4.3	7.8
Atlanta, GA	54.0	27.3	2.4	5.4	10.9
Austin, TX	43.6	39.1	2.4	3.4	11.5
Billings, MT	30.5	45.8	1.3	6.7	15.7
Boise City, ID	33.1	47.2	0.9	4.8	14.1
Boston, MA	56.6	28.3	2.9	4.3	7.9
Boulder, CO	55.7	32.8	0.7	2.7	8.1
Cape Coral, FL	24.6	52.6	2.3	6.9	13.6
Cedar Rapids, IA	34.5	45.8	1.9	6.2	11.6
Charleston, SC	42.5	38.5	2.5	5.3	11.2
Charlotte, NC	39.9	42.3	3.1	4.6	10.1
Chicago, IL	48.9	34.5	2.5	5.4	8.6
Clarksville, TN	28.1	52.8	3.3	3.9	12.0
Colorado Springs, CO	29.3	51.0	2.0	4.6	12.9
Columbia, MO	51.5	35.5	1.2	3.3	8.5
Columbus, OH	43.8	36.5	2.6	4.5	12.5
Dallas, TX	40.9	39.6	3.5	4.8	11.2
Davenport, IA	35.4	42.5	1.5	6.4	14.1
Denver, CO	41.8	38.5	2.3	4.4	13.0
Des Moines, IA	34.7	43.1	2.2	6.0	14.0
Durham, NC	41.8	40.2	2.8	4.6	10.6
El Paso, TX	31.9	47.0	3.8	5.7	11.6
Erie, PA	43.5	35.9	3.0	6.4	11.2
Eugene, OR	43.2	37.1	1.4	5.2	13.1
Fargo, ND	43.6	41.3	1.2	4.4	9.4
Fayetteville, NC	32.5	45.7	4.0	5.4	12.4
Fort Collins, CO	44.0	42.3	0.7	3.4	9.6
Fort Wayne, IN	34.4	44.0	1.7	6.1	13.9
Fort Worth, TX	33.9	46.1	3.0	4.6	12.5
Gainesville, FL	62.2	24.0	2.0	3.9	7.8
Grand Rapids, MI	44.8	36.7	2.6	5.3	10.6
Green Bay, WI	37.4	44.0	1.5	5.2	11.9
Greensboro, NC	41.3	39.5	3.0	5.4	10.8
Honolulu, HI	36.7	44.5	1.4	7.3	10.2
Houston, TX	39.5	41.5	3.5	4.8	10.6
Huntsville, AL	35.7	42.0	2.5	6.0	13.8
Indianapolis, IN	39.0	39.5	2.4	5.3	13.8
Jacksonville, FL	34.5	42.9	2.7	5.8	14.1
Kansas City, MO	39.0	39.6	2.4	5.6	13.3
Lafayette, LA	40.6	39.1	2.5	6.1	11.8
Las Vegas, NV	33.1	43.3	3.1	5.5	15.0
Lexington, KY	38.1	43.2	1.8	4.5	12.4
Lincoln, NE	37.5	45.8	1.3	4.3	11.1
Little Rock, AR	39.0	39.1	2.6	5.5	13.8
Los Angeles, CA	45.7	38.2	2.9	4.7	8.5
Louisville, KY	35.3	42.0	2.7	6.5	13.6
Lubbock, TX	40.1	41.2	2.2	5.2	11.3
Madison, WI	48.3	37.6	1.2	3.5	9.4
Manchester, NH	38.0	40.2	2.1	5.5	14.3
McAllen, TX	29.9	52.1	3.6	5.9	8.5
Miami, FL	41.0	34.2	4.6	6.6	13.6
Midland, TX	30.3	51.6	1.9	5.4	10.9
Minneapolis, MN	51.8	33.2	1.7	3.3	10.0

Table continued on next page.

City	Never Married	Now Married[1]	Separated	Widowed	Divorced
Nashville, TN	40.4	39.1	2.6	5.1	12.9
New Orleans, LA	48.8	30.1	3.0	6.1	12.1
New York, NY	44.1	38.6	3.4	5.7	8.1
Oklahoma City, OK	31.9	47.3	2.5	5.5	12.9
Omaha, NE	36.8	43.7	1.8	5.5	12.2
Orlando, FL	43.9	33.8	3.6	5.3	13.5
Oxnard, CA	38.3	45.5	2.7	4.4	9.1
Palm Bay, FL	27.2	47.5	3.1	8.3	13.9
Peoria, IL	41.8	40.5	1.2	6.3	10.2
Philadelphia, PA	52.2	28.7	3.4	6.7	9.0
Phoenix, AZ	38.9	41.7	2.5	4.2	12.7
Pittsburgh, PA	51.2	30.9	2.3	6.5	9.0
Portland, OR	40.7	40.5	1.9	4.3	12.6
Providence, RI	54.7	28.6	3.3	4.7	8.6
Provo, UT	46.9	44.6	0.8	2.2	5.5
Raleigh, NC	42.4	40.5	2.8	3.9	10.3
Reno, NV	35.8	42.1	2.3	4.8	15.0
Richmond, VA	52.0	25.7	4.3	6.0	12.1
Roanoke, VA	34.7	39.5	3.0	7.4	15.3
Rochester, MN	32.3	51.3	1.3	4.8	10.3
Sacramento, CA	40.3	39.2	2.8	5.4	12.3
Salem, OR	32.7	44.7	2.6	5.1	14.8
Salt Lake City, UT	41.3	41.0	1.8	4.3	11.6
San Antonio, TX	36.1	42.8	3.3	5.4	12.4
San Diego, CA	40.7	42.8	2.0	4.6	10.0
San Francisco, CA	46.5	38.1	1.6	5.1	8.6
San Jose, CA	34.6	50.9	1.9	4.5	8.2
Santa Rosa, CA	34.3	44.0	2.2	5.6	13.9
Savannah, GA	45.2	31.7	2.8	7.0	13.4
Seattle, WA	44.2	39.5	1.4	4.0	10.9
Sioux Falls, SD	34.0	48.4	1.3	5.0	11.4
Spokane, WA	34.3	42.6	1.7	5.9	15.6
Springfield, IL	34.4	41.2	1.8	7.5	15.1
Tallahassee, FL	55.8	30.0	1.5	3.6	9.2
Tampa, FL	41.6	36.6	3.1	5.7	13.0
Topeka, KS	31.3	44.3	1.9	6.4	16.1
Tulsa, OK	33.5	42.9	2.7	6.0	15.0
Tyler, TX	34.0	42.3	3.2	7.4	13.1
Virginia Beach, VA	31.6	49.5	2.7	4.8	11.4
Washington, DC	57.5	26.0	2.3	4.7	9.6
Wichita, KS	31.9	46.9	2.2	5.7	13.3
Wilmington, NC	42.9	37.5	2.9	5.1	11.7
Winston-Salem, NC	40.0	40.1	3.1	6.4	10.4
Worcester, MA	43.8	35.5	2.8	6.3	11.6
U.S.	32.7	48.1	2.2	6.0	11.0

Note: Figures are percentages and cover the population 15 years of age and older; (1) Excludes separated
Source: U.S. Census Bureau, 2011-2013 American Community Survey 3-Year Estimates

Marital Status: Metro Area

Metro Area	Never Married	Now Married[1]	Separated	Widowed	Divorced
Albuquerque, NM	33.9	45.4	1.8	5.3	13.6
Anchorage, AK	33.4	49.0	1.6	3.7	12.3
Ann Arbor, MI	41.8	43.8	1.0	4.3	9.1
Athens, GA	44.7	39.4	1.6	5.4	8.9
Atlanta, GA	34.4	47.4	2.3	4.8	11.2
Austin, TX	35.9	47.4	2.1	3.6	11.0
Billings, MT	27.5	50.1	1.3	6.4	14.7
Boise City, ID	27.5	53.8	1.2	4.8	12.6
Boston, MA	36.4	47.3	1.9	5.4	9.0
Boulder, CO	37.2	47.7	1.1	3.5	10.6
Cape Coral, FL	26.0	50.3	2.1	8.2	13.4
Cedar Rapids, IA	28.8	51.7	1.7	6.0	11.7
Charleston, SC	33.7	45.9	3.2	5.9	11.2
Charlotte, NC	31.6	49.6	3.0	5.5	10.2
Chicago, IL	36.4	46.9	1.9	5.6	9.1
Clarksville, TN	26.8	54.2	2.7	5.1	11.2
Colorado Springs, CO	28.1	53.9	1.8	4.3	11.9
Columbia, MO	43.3	42.0	1.6	3.8	9.2
Columbus, OH	33.6	47.5	2.0	5.1	11.8
Dallas, TX	31.4	50.4	2.5	4.5	11.2
Davenport, IA	28.7	50.3	1.3	6.9	12.8
Denver, CO	31.9	49.5	1.8	4.3	12.5
Des Moines, IA	28.7	53.2	1.6	5.0	11.5
Durham, NC	37.2	45.4	2.3	4.9	10.1
El Paso, TX	32.5	47.4	3.9	5.4	10.9
Erie, PA	34.7	46.6	2.3	6.4	10.0
Eugene, OR	33.3	45.1	1.6	5.9	14.1
Fargo, ND	37.9	47.2	1.0	4.5	9.3
Fayetteville, NC	31.6	47.6	3.7	5.3	11.8
Fort Collins, CO	33.6	50.9	1.0	4.0	10.5
Fort Wayne, IN	29.8	50.1	1.5	5.8	12.7
Fort Worth, TX	31.4	50.4	2.5	4.5	11.2
Gainesville, FL	46.0	37.2	1.9	5.2	9.8
Grand Rapids, MI	31.5	52.4	1.3	4.8	10.0
Green Bay, WI	30.2	53.4	1.0	5.2	10.2
Greensboro, NC	32.1	47.4	3.3	6.2	11.0
Honolulu, HI	33.8	50.2	1.3	6.2	8.6
Houston, TX	32.9	49.6	2.8	4.5	10.1
Huntsville, AL	29.7	50.5	2.0	5.7	12.1
Indianapolis, IN	31.3	48.8	1.8	5.3	12.9
Jacksonville, FL	31.2	46.8	2.4	5.8	13.8
Kansas City, MO	29.7	50.3	1.8	5.6	12.6
Lafayette, LA	33.1	46.2	2.7	6.1	11.9
Las Vegas, NV	33.6	44.7	2.7	5.2	13.9
Lexington, KY	33.4	47.1	2.2	4.9	12.5
Lincoln, NE	35.6	48.3	1.2	4.2	10.7
Little Rock, AR	30.5	48.0	2.1	5.7	13.6
Los Angeles, CA	39.8	44.0	2.6	5.0	8.6
Louisville, KY	30.6	47.4	2.1	6.4	13.4
Lubbock, TX	37.0	44.3	2.3	5.4	11.0
Madison, WI	35.4	49.1	1.2	4.3	10.0
Manchester, NH	30.5	51.3	1.4	5.0	11.9
McAllen, TX	31.5	52.4	4.1	5.1	6.8
Miami, FL	34.3	43.0	3.1	6.9	12.7
Midland, TX	29.6	52.8	1.8	5.1	10.6
Minneapolis, MN	32.9	51.2	1.3	4.4	10.1

Table continued on next page.

Metro Area	Never Married	Now Married[1]	Separated	Widowed	Divorced
Nashville, TN	30.8	49.4	2.0	5.4	12.4
New Orleans, LA	37.3	41.5	2.5	6.6	12.1
New York, NY	37.9	45.5	2.6	6.0	8.0
Oklahoma City, OK	29.9	49.3	2.2	5.8	12.8
Omaha, NE	31.4	50.9	1.5	5.2	11.1
Orlando, FL	35.0	44.9	2.6	5.5	12.0
Oxnard, CA	32.2	50.4	1.9	5.1	10.4
Palm Bay, FL	26.6	48.0	2.3	8.6	14.5
Peoria, IL	29.6	51.7	1.3	6.3	11.0
Philadelphia, PA	37.3	44.9	2.3	6.4	9.0
Phoenix, AZ	33.3	47.5	1.9	5.0	12.3
Pittsburgh, PA	31.6	48.5	2.0	8.1	9.8
Portland, OR	31.5	49.3	1.8	4.8	12.5
Providence, RI	35.0	45.3	2.0	6.5	11.2
Provo, UT	31.9	58.2	1.1	2.6	6.3
Raleigh, NC	31.7	51.7	2.8	4.4	9.5
Reno, NV	31.6	46.7	2.0	4.9	14.7
Richmond, VA	34.5	45.5	2.9	6.0	11.2
Roanoke, VA	26.5	51.7	2.3	7.1	12.4
Rochester, MN	28.1	56.2	1.1	5.1	9.5
Sacramento, CA	33.2	47.2	2.4	5.4	11.7
Salem, OR	30.2	50.0	2.4	5.2	12.2
Salt Lake City, UT	31.1	52.4	2.0	3.9	10.7
San Antonio, TX	32.6	47.7	2.8	5.4	11.5
San Diego, CA	35.9	47.0	1.9	5.0	10.3
San Francisco, CA	36.0	47.3	1.9	5.2	9.6
San Jose, CA	32.6	53.1	1.7	4.4	8.1
Santa Rosa, CA	32.2	46.6	2.0	5.4	13.7
Savannah, GA	34.5	44.4	2.4	5.9	12.8
Seattle, WA	32.4	49.5	1.6	4.4	12.0
Sioux Falls, SD	30.9	52.6	1.1	5.0	10.4
Spokane, WA	29.8	49.4	1.4	5.6	13.8
Springfield, IL	30.2	48.1	1.7	6.8	13.2
Tallahassee, FL	43.0	39.6	1.9	4.5	11.1
Tampa, FL	30.1	46.2	2.4	7.4	13.9
Topeka, KS	26.7	52.0	1.4	6.2	13.7
Tulsa, OK	27.2	51.1	2.1	6.1	13.5
Tyler, TX	27.2	50.8	2.6	7.1	12.2
Virginia Beach, VA	33.6	46.6	3.0	5.5	11.2
Washington, DC	36.2	48.2	2.3	4.4	9.0
Wichita, KS	28.7	51.2	1.7	5.8	12.6
Wilmington, NC	33.4	47.0	2.7	5.5	11.4
Winston-Salem, NC	29.5	50.0	2.9	6.6	11.1
Worcester, MA	33.3	47.8	1.9	5.9	11.0
U.S.	32.7	48.1	2.2	6.0	11.0

Note: Figures are percentages and cover the population 15 years of age and older; Figures cover the Metropolitan Statistical Area—see Appendix B for areas included; (1) Excludes separated
Source: U.S. Census Bureau, 2011-2013 American Community Survey 3-Year Estimates

Disability Status: City

City	All Ages	Under 18 Years Old	18 to 64 Years Old	65 Years and Over
Albuquerque, NM	12.8	4.0	10.8	39.2
Anchorage, AK	9.8	2.9	9.1	37.5
Ann Arbor, MI	6.6	2.0	4.7	27.6
Athens, GA	9.9	2.9	8.6	34.5
Atlanta, GA	11.4	3.3	9.6	39.4
Austin, TX	9.2	4.3	8.1	35.5
Billings, MT	13.8	5.0	11.6	36.8
Boise City, ID	11.3	4.1	9.4	36.0
Boston, MA	12.0	5.5	9.3	42.2
Boulder, CO	6.7	1.4	5.4	25.4
Cape Coral, FL	12.8	2.9	10.6	31.9
Cedar Rapids, IA	11.4	5.2	9.2	33.5
Charleston, SC	10.1	2.9	7.8	32.9
Charlotte, NC	8.8	3.1	7.5	34.5
Chicago, IL	11.0	3.4	9.0	40.7
Clarksville, TN	13.8	5.8	14.2	42.8
Colorado Springs, CO	12.0	4.2	10.8	36.2
Columbia, MO	9.4	2.9	8.1	34.7
Columbus, OH	12.2	5.3	10.9	40.2
Dallas, TX	9.4	2.9	8.0	38.1
Davenport, IA	10.9	2.9	9.7	33.2
Denver, CO	9.8	2.7	8.1	35.7
Des Moines, IA	12.9	4.4	12.8	33.6
Durham, NC	9.7	2.9	8.4	36.6
El Paso, TX	12.6	3.6	10.6	45.3
Erie, PA	18.1	9.3	16.7	40.5
Eugene, OR	13.2	4.6	10.3	39.5
Fargo, ND	9.1	2.2	8.2	28.9
Fayetteville, NC	13.8	3.9	13.1	41.9
Fort Collins, CO	7.5	1.9	5.9	33.2
Fort Wayne, IN	12.3	4.7	10.9	36.0
Fort Worth, TX	10.6	3.4	10.1	39.8
Gainesville, FL	9.4	4.5	7.2	38.6
Grand Rapids, MI	12.6	4.9	11.1	39.1
Green Bay, WI	13.3	3.5	12.4	38.4
Greensboro, NC	9.7	2.6	7.8	33.8
Honolulu, HI	11.1	2.5	7.2	33.5
Houston, TX	10.1	3.7	8.5	38.3
Huntsville, AL	13.2	4.2	11.0	37.7
Indianapolis, IN	13.2	5.3	12.2	39.0
Jacksonville, FL	12.6	4.2	11.2	38.1
Kansas City, MO	12.6	3.9	11.7	36.1
Lafayette, LA	12.3	4.8	10.9	34.1
Las Vegas, NV	12.7	3.9	11.2	36.6
Lexington, KY	11.5	4.6	9.4	38.0
Lincoln, NE	9.5	3.0	7.6	34.1
Little Rock, AR	12.0	3.2	10.4	36.8
Los Angeles, CA	9.7	2.7	7.2	39.4
Louisville, KY	15.1	5.9	13.7	38.9
Lubbock, TX	13.7	5.2	12.1	42.4
Madison, WI	8.5	3.7	6.7	31.0
Manchester, NH	13.3	5.7	11.1	37.1
McAllen, TX	12.2	4.4	9.6	48.7
Miami, FL	12.4	3.1	8.8	38.8
Midland, TX	11.9	4.4	9.7	44.0

Table continued on next page.

City	All Ages	Under 18 Years Old	18 to 64 Years Old	65 Years and Over
Minneapolis, MN	10.3	4.6	9.2	35.0
Nashville, TN	11.3	3.5	9.8	37.9
New Orleans, LA	13.9	4.7	12.4	40.3
New York, NY	10.3	3.2	7.7	36.8
Oklahoma City, OK	13.0	4.5	11.7	40.9
Omaha, NE	10.9	3.9	9.6	34.3
Orlando, FL	9.5	4.5	7.5	35.4
Oxnard, CA	10.5	4.4	9.1	41.1
Palm Bay, FL	14.5	3.5	12.3	38.2
Peoria, IL	11.7	4.7	10.1	33.6
Philadelphia, PA	15.9	6.4	14.5	41.7
Phoenix, AZ	9.5	3.2	8.5	35.7
Pittsburgh, PA	14.0	5.6	11.4	37.7
Portland, OR	12.1	4.1	10.3	37.6
Providence, RI	11.8	4.3	10.9	40.8
Provo, UT	7.4	4.2	6.1	36.7
Raleigh, NC	7.8	3.6	6.1	32.9
Reno, NV	11.1	3.2	9.6	34.0
Richmond, VA	15.7	7.1	14.0	41.3
Roanoke, VA	17.6	7.0	16.6	39.0
Rochester, MN	9.4	2.5	7.7	30.4
Sacramento, CA	13.2	4.1	11.5	42.1
Salem, OR	14.2	5.0	13.9	34.3
Salt Lake City, UT	11.4	3.7	10.1	38.1
San Antonio, TX	13.9	5.2	12.3	44.9
San Diego, CA	8.7	3.0	6.2	34.9
San Francisco, CA	10.5	1.7	6.9	38.2
San Jose, CA	8.3	2.6	5.9	36.0
Santa Rosa, CA	11.9	3.4	9.5	38.1
Savannah, GA	13.1	4.1	11.0	40.5
Seattle, WA	9.1	2.4	6.8	34.0
Sioux Falls, SD	10.0	2.3	9.3	31.7
Spokane, WA	15.6	5.0	14.1	39.9
Springfield, IL	16.1	6.0	15.1	36.2
Tallahassee, FL	8.9	4.2	6.9	35.9
Tampa, FL	12.9	5.1	11.2	38.4
Topeka, KS	16.5	3.6	16.4	39.1
Tulsa, OK	14.1	5.2	13.0	36.8
Tyler, TX	12.5	4.9	10.1	35.2
Virginia Beach, VA	10.0	3.9	7.9	34.0
Washington, DC	11.2	5.1	9.0	34.6
Wichita, KS	12.5	3.5	11.2	39.3
Wilmington, NC	13.7	4.6	10.7	40.9
Winston-Salem, NC	11.0	3.8	9.3	34.1
Worcester, MA	13.7	5.9	11.6	41.5
U.S.	12.3	4.1	10.2	36.3

Note: Figures show percent of the civilian noninstitutionalized population that reported having a disability. Disability status is determined from from six types of difficulty: vision, hearing, cognitive, ambulatory, self-care, and independent living. For children under 5 years old, hearing and vision difficulty are used to determine disability status. For children between the ages of 5 and 14, disability status is determined from hearing, vision, cognitive, ambulatory, and self-care difficulties. For people aged 15 years and older, they are considered to have a disability if they have difficulty with any one of the six difficulty types.
Source: U.S. Census Bureau, 2011-2013 American Community Survey 3-Year Estimates

Disability Status: Metro Area

Metro Area	All Ages	Under 18 Years Old	18 to 64 Years Old	65 Years and Over
Albuquerque, NM	13.3	4.0	11.6	38.6
Anchorage, AK	10.2	3.0	9.5	38.1
Ann Arbor, MI	8.6	2.7	6.8	30.8
Athens, GA	11.4	3.2	9.8	36.8
Atlanta, GA	9.9	3.3	8.7	35.1
Austin, TX	9.5	4.0	8.5	33.1
Billings, MT	14.1	5.5	11.9	37.1
Boise City, ID	11.6	4.5	10.0	36.2
Boston, MA	10.5	4.0	7.9	33.7
Boulder, CO	8.3	2.9	7.0	26.7
Cape Coral, FL	14.2	3.6	10.8	29.8
Cedar Rapids, IA	10.5	4.8	8.4	29.5
Charleston, SC	11.4	3.5	9.6	35.7
Charlotte, NC	11.0	3.5	9.5	35.7
Chicago, IL	9.8	3.1	7.8	35.1
Clarksville, TN	13.9	5.1	14.1	38.9
Colorado Springs, CO	11.6	4.3	10.7	34.1
Columbia, MO	10.2	3.7	9.1	33.0
Columbus, OH	11.9	4.7	10.4	36.7
Dallas, TX	9.5	3.3	8.2	35.8
Davenport, IA	11.6	3.8	9.1	33.6
Denver, CO	9.3	3.2	7.8	32.4
Des Moines, IA	10.1	3.1	9.2	31.9
Durham, NC	10.5	3.1	8.7	33.9
El Paso, TX	12.6	3.7	11.1	46.2
Erie, PA	14.8	6.7	12.6	36.8
Eugene, OR	15.6	5.4	13.1	37.9
Fargo, ND	9.4	2.8	8.1	32.0
Fayetteville, NC	13.8	4.3	13.4	43.2
Fort Collins, CO	9.4	2.8	7.4	30.7
Fort Wayne, IN	11.8	4.8	10.1	35.2
Fort Worth, TX	9.5	3.3	8.2	35.8
Gainesville, FL	11.0	3.7	8.6	37.0
Grand Rapids, MI	11.4	4.5	9.8	34.2
Green Bay, WI	10.9	3.7	9.2	33.0
Greensboro, NC	12.0	3.5	10.2	34.7
Honolulu, HI	10.6	3.0	7.6	34.1
Houston, TX	9.6	3.5	8.4	37.0
Huntsville, AL	12.2	3.5	10.2	37.8
Indianapolis, IN	12.1	4.7	10.7	36.4
Jacksonville, FL	12.7	4.4	10.8	36.6
Kansas City, MO	11.6	3.6	10.2	35.3
Lafayette, LA	13.8	5.0	12.5	40.7
Las Vegas, NV	11.7	3.8	10.2	35.2
Lexington, KY	12.8	4.8	11.1	38.2
Lincoln, NE	9.5	2.9	7.5	34.0
Little Rock, AR	14.0	5.4	12.4	38.5
Los Angeles, CA	9.3	2.7	6.8	36.5
Louisville, KY	14.4	5.3	12.8	38.3
Lubbock, TX	14.1	5.4	12.3	43.0
Madison, WI	9.4	4.0	7.4	30.7
Manchester, NH	10.8	4.6	8.8	33.1
McAllen, TX	13.6	6.0	12.0	50.3
Miami, FL	10.9	2.9	7.5	34.6
Midland, TX	12.1	4.8	9.9	44.6

Table continued on next page.

Metro Area	All Ages	Under 18 Years Old	18 to 64 Years Old	65 Years and Over
Minneapolis, MN	9.2	3.5	7.6	30.7
Nashville, TN	11.5	3.8	10.0	36.7
New Orleans, LA	13.9	5.5	11.7	40.0
New York, NY	9.8	3.1	7.3	33.6
Oklahoma City, OK	13.3	4.3	11.8	40.3
Omaha, NE	10.3	3.6	9.0	33.3
Orlando, FL	11.2	4.4	8.9	35.0
Oxnard, CA	10.2	3.9	7.8	35.2
Palm Bay, FL	15.3	3.9	12.0	34.7
Peoria, IL	10.9	3.9	8.4	32.6
Philadelphia, PA	12.1	4.5	10.0	34.3
Phoenix, AZ	10.3	3.2	8.5	32.6
Pittsburgh, PA	14.0	5.1	11.0	35.1
Portland, OR	11.9	4.1	10.1	36.6
Providence, RI	13.0	4.6	10.7	35.5
Provo, UT	7.2	2.9	6.6	34.7
Raleigh, NC	8.4	3.3	6.9	32.2
Reno, NV	11.6	3.7	9.8	33.6
Richmond, VA	12.1	4.4	10.1	35.5
Roanoke, VA	14.8	5.1	12.6	35.2
Rochester, MN	9.0	2.7	7.0	29.9
Sacramento, CA	12.1	4.1	9.9	38.1
Salem, OR	14.2	4.9	13.2	36.2
Salt Lake City, UT	9.1	3.4	8.2	34.5
San Antonio, TX	13.3	4.8	11.7	42.2
San Diego, CA	9.5	2.8	7.0	35.7
San Francisco, CA	9.6	2.7	7.0	33.5
San Jose, CA	7.7	2.4	5.2	33.1
Santa Rosa, CA	11.1	3.1	8.5	33.4
Savannah, GA	11.5	3.2	9.8	37.3
Seattle, WA	10.9	3.6	9.1	35.7
Sioux Falls, SD	9.6	2.9	8.5	31.6
Spokane, WA	14.9	5.0	13.0	38.9
Springfield, IL	14.1	6.2	12.4	34.6
Tallahassee, FL	11.0	4.6	8.9	35.4
Tampa, FL	14.0	4.5	11.2	34.6
Topeka, KS	14.6	3.9	13.8	35.7
Tulsa, OK	14.4	4.8	13.1	38.7
Tyler, TX	13.1	5.2	11.2	34.6
Virginia Beach, VA	10.9	3.9	9.1	33.7
Washington, DC	8.0	2.8	6.3	30.6
Wichita, KS	12.1	3.9	10.6	37.6
Wilmington, NC	13.7	4.2	11.3	37.7
Winston-Salem, NC	13.1	4.7	11.1	34.8
Worcester, MA	11.7	5.0	9.5	34.3
U.S.	12.3	4.1	10.2	36.3

Note: Figures show percent of the civilian noninstitutionalized population that reported having a disability. Disability status is determined from from six types of difficulty: vision, hearing, cognitive, ambulatory, self-care, and independent living. For children under 5 years old, hearing and vision difficulty are used to determine disability status. For children between the ages of 5 and 14, disability status is determined from hearing, vision, cognitive, ambulatory, and self-care difficulties. For people aged 15 years and older, they are considered to have a disability if they have difficulty with any one of the six difficulty types; Figures cover the Metropolitan Statistical Area—see Appendix B for areas included

Source: U.S. Census Bureau, 2011-2013 American Community Survey 3-Year Estimates

Male/Female Ratio: City

City	Males	Females	Males per 100 Females
Albuquerque, NM	269,222	285,083	94.4
Anchorage, AK	151,980	146,404	103.8
Ann Arbor, MI	58,168	58,005	100.3
Athens, GA	56,490	62,221	90.8
Atlanta, GA	220,467	220,597	99.9
Austin, TX	434,273	428,603	101.3
Billings, MT	51,432	55,776	92.2
Boise City, ID	104,867	107,013	98.0
Boston, MA	304,699	332,926	91.5
Boulder, CO	51,017	50,854	100.3
Cape Coral, FL	79,085	82,607	95.7
Cedar Rapids, IA	62,690	65,432	95.8
Charleston, SC	59,351	66,304	89.5
Charlotte, NC	371,347	403,086	92.1
Chicago, IL	1,318,892	1,393,100	94.7
Clarksville, TN	69,555	71,073	97.9
Colorado Springs, CO	215,263	218,356	98.6
Columbia, MO	54,336	58,880	92.3
Columbus, OH	395,555	414,832	95.4
Dallas, TX	621,146	618,122	100.5
Davenport, IA	49,731	51,590	96.4
Denver, CO	317,325	317,360	100.0
Des Moines, IA	101,802	104,769	97.2
Durham, NC	113,327	126,339	89.7
El Paso, TX	324,421	346,637	93.6
Erie, PA	49,740	51,343	96.9
Eugene, OR	77,877	80,292	97.0
Fargo, ND	55,020	55,454	99.2
Fayetteville, NC	99,138	103,438	95.8
Fort Collins, CO	73,780	75,195	98.1
Fort Wayne, IN	122,638	131,968	92.9
Fort Worth, TX	377,614	399,898	94.4
Gainesville, FL	60,742	65,911	92.2
Grand Rapids, MI	92,894	97,664	95.1
Green Bay, WI	51,307	53,316	96.2
Greensboro, NC	130,638	145,673	89.7
Honolulu, HI	170,480	174,427	97.7
Houston, TX	1,083,898	1,078,370	100.5
Huntsville, AL	89,776	93,926	95.6
Indianapolis, IN	402,096	431,804	93.1
Jacksonville, FL	405,350	430,737	94.1
Kansas City, MO	225,947	238,501	94.7
Lafayette, LA	59,888	63,109	94.9
Las Vegas, NV	301,119	294,787	102.1
Lexington, KY	149,904	155,094	96.7
Lincoln, NE	132,892	132,578	100.2
Little Rock, AR	93,837	102,598	91.5
Los Angeles, CA	1,914,874	1,937,942	98.8
Louisville, KY	292,181	313,248	93.3
Lubbock, TX	116,283	120,205	96.7
Madison, WI	118,531	121,770	97.3
Manchester, NH	55,100	55,068	100.1
McAllen, TX	66,239	68,893	96.1
Miami, FL	207,228	206,916	100.2
Midland, TX	58,026	61,145	94.9

Table continued on next page.

City	Males	Females	Males per 100 Females
Minneapolis, MN	198,752	194,909	102.0
Nashville, TN	302,021	321,874	93.8
New Orleans, LA	177,685	192,080	92.5
New York, NY	3,975,566	4,365,556	91.1
Oklahoma City, OK	295,559	304,485	97.1
Omaha, NE	209,768	219,013	95.8
Orlando, FL	120,322	129,452	92.9
Oxnard, CA	102,516	98,864	103.7
Palm Bay, FL	47,695	56,485	84.4
Peoria, IL	54,981	60,833	90.4
Philadelphia, PA	730,467	816,303	89.5
Phoenix, AZ	745,057	743,612	100.2
Pittsburgh, PA	148,248	157,751	94.0
Portland, OR	298,719	304,328	98.2
Providence, RI	86,711	91,428	94.8
Provo, UT	57,216	58,211	98.3
Raleigh, NC	203,584	219,614	92.7
Reno, NV	117,408	113,377	103.6
Richmond, VA	100,088	110,365	90.7
Roanoke, VA	46,584	51,070	91.2
Rochester, MN	53,066	56,258	94.3
Sacramento, CA	230,879	244,657	94.4
Salem, OR	77,965	80,744	96.6
Salt Lake City, UT	97,585	92,016	106.1
San Antonio, TX	675,440	708,276	95.4
San Diego, CA	674,569	662,953	101.8
San Francisco, CA	420,456	406,170	103.5
San Jose, CA	495,022	488,753	101.3
Santa Rosa, CA	84,919	85,574	99.2
Savannah, GA	67,265	74,521	90.3
Seattle, WA	316,940	319,330	99.3
Sioux Falls, SD	80,030	80,518	99.4
Spokane, WA	102,789	107,087	96.0
Springfield, IL	56,324	60,684	92.8
Tallahassee, FL	89,007	96,668	92.1
Tampa, FL	170,731	178,698	95.5
Topeka, KS	61,217	66,694	91.8
Tulsa, OK	191,759	203,450	94.3
Tyler, TX	46,121	53,283	86.6
Virginia Beach, VA	218,702	226,859	96.4
Washington, DC	299,718	333,449	89.9
Wichita, KS	190,463	194,691	97.8
Wilmington, NC	51,873	58,206	89.1
Winston-Salem, NC	109,996	124,235	88.5
Worcester, MA	87,241	95,145	91.7
U.S.	154,451,010	159,410,713	96.9

Source: U.S. Census Bureau, 2011-2013 American Community Survey 3-Year Estimates

Male/Female Ratio: Metro Area

Metro Area	Males	Females	Males per 100 Females
Albuquerque, NM	443,025	457,019	96.9
Anchorage, AK	200,581	191,444	104.8
Ann Arbor, MI	173,332	178,013	97.4
Athens, GA	94,417	101,892	92.7
Atlanta, GA	2,648,950	2,801,341	94.6
Austin, TX	918,435	914,909	100.4
Billings, MT	79,631	83,411	95.5
Boise City, ID	318,282	320,228	99.4
Boston, MA	2,250,752	2,392,619	94.1
Boulder, CO	153,103	152,181	100.6
Cape Coral, FL	316,615	329,066	96.2
Cedar Rapids, IA	129,627	132,007	98.2
Charleston, SC	341,017	356,099	95.8
Charlotte, NC	1,115,779	1,179,924	94.6
Chicago, IL	4,652,858	4,861,354	95.7
Clarksville, TN	135,821	134,884	100.7
Colorado Springs, CO	335,926	333,190	100.8
Columbia, MO	81,563	86,820	93.9
Columbus, OH	956,827	988,980	96.7
Dallas, TX	3,301,095	3,393,794	97.3
Davenport, IA	188,146	194,300	96.8
Denver, CO	1,318,148	1,329,879	99.1
Des Moines, IA	290,333	299,670	96.9
Durham, NC	252,398	272,977	92.5
El Paso, TX	405,065	423,307	95.7
Erie, PA	138,217	142,462	97.0
Eugene, OR	174,253	180,485	96.5
Fargo, ND	109,338	108,318	100.9
Fayetteville, NC	182,311	192,352	94.8
Fort Collins, CO	154,721	155,883	99.3
Fort Wayne, IN	206,410	215,343	95.9
Fort Worth, TX	3,301,095	3,393,794	97.3
Gainesville, FL	130,829	137,730	95.0
Grand Rapids, MI	496,436	509,598	97.4
Green Bay, WI	155,064	155,643	99.6
Greensboro, NC	353,362	382,528	92.4
Honolulu, HI	491,583	483,100	101.8
Houston, TX	3,076,211	3,104,755	99.1
Huntsville, AL	211,831	218,536	96.9
Indianapolis, IN	944,327	986,738	95.7
Jacksonville, FL	670,928	707,065	94.9
Kansas City, MO	1,000,116	1,039,202	96.2
Lafayette, LA	231,522	243,048	95.3
Las Vegas, NV	1,003,453	993,918	101.0
Lexington, KY	237,743	246,503	96.4
Lincoln, NE	155,726	154,585	100.7
Little Rock, AR	348,536	369,164	94.4
Los Angeles, CA	6,433,666	6,602,204	97.4
Louisville, KY	610,951	641,909	95.2
Lubbock, TX	148,268	151,160	98.1
Madison, WI	308,430	312,225	98.8
Manchester, NH	199,795	203,184	98.3
McAllen, TX	393,607	411,890	95.6
Miami, FL	2,796,261	2,963,665	94.4
Midland, TX	74,592	75,892	98.3

Table continued on next page.

Metro Area	Males	Females	Males per 100 Females
Minneapolis, MN	1,691,801	1,731,624	97.7
Nashville, TN	843,798	883,814	95.5
New Orleans, LA	595,635	631,894	94.3
New York, NY	9,588,708	10,250,992	93.5
Oklahoma City, OK	640,103	657,728	97.3
Omaha, NE	437,416	448,403	97.5
Orlando, FL	1,088,197	1,133,645	96.0
Oxnard, CA	414,557	420,323	98.6
Palm Bay, FL	267,572	279,831	95.6
Peoria, IL	186,544	194,515	95.9
Philadelphia, PA	2,905,084	3,111,882	93.4
Phoenix, AZ	2,151,086	2,175,269	98.9
Pittsburgh, PA	1,144,050	1,216,496	94.0
Portland, OR	1,130,628	1,157,386	97.7
Providence, RI	775,445	826,242	93.9
Provo, UT	277,155	273,824	101.2
Raleigh, NC	580,255	608,423	95.4
Reno, NV	218,347	215,262	101.4
Richmond, VA	595,906	636,733	93.6
Roanoke, VA	149,362	160,766	92.9
Rochester, MN	103,661	106,336	97.5
Sacramento, CA	1,075,677	1,119,301	96.1
Salem, OR	196,381	200,953	97.7
Salt Lake City, UT	564,875	559,027	101.0
San Antonio, TX	1,100,400	1,134,484	97.0
San Diego, CA	1,595,328	1,579,985	101.0
San Francisco, CA	2,199,538	2,255,873	97.5
San Jose, CA	951,310	942,011	101.0
Santa Rosa, CA	241,429	249,628	96.7
Savannah, GA	175,117	186,378	94.0
Seattle, WA	1,772,064	1,781,242	99.5
Sioux Falls, SD	119,034	118,946	100.1
Spokane, WA	264,607	268,120	98.7
Springfield, IL	101,637	110,147	92.3
Tallahassee, FL	181,396	191,849	94.6
Tampa, FL	1,379,741	1,468,026	94.0
Topeka, KS	114,781	119,775	95.8
Tulsa, OK	467,985	485,135	96.5
Tyler, TX	103,615	110,914	93.4
Virginia Beach, VA	834,506	863,039	96.7
Washington, DC	2,860,283	3,001,035	95.3
Wichita, KS	314,540	320,772	98.1
Wilmington, NC	128,681	135,148	95.2
Winston-Salem, NC	311,623	335,810	92.8
Worcester, MA	455,895	468,049	97.4
U.S.	154,451,010	159,410,713	96.9

Note: Figures cover the Metropolitan Statistical Area (MSA)—see Appendix B for areas included
Source: U.S. Census Bureau, 2011-2013 American Community Survey 3-Year Estimates

Gross Metropolitan Product

MSA[1]	2012	2013	2014	2015	Rank[2]
Albuquerque, NM	38.8	39.9	41.5	43.3	62
Anchorage, AK	28.6	29.3	30.4	31.8	83
Ann Arbor, MI	19.3	19.8	20.6	21.6	111
Athens, GA	6.8	7.1	7.4	7.7	224
Atlanta, GA	294.0	306.2	321.1	339.9	10
Austin, TX	98.7	104.4	110.6	117.5	31
Billings, MT	8.5	8.7	8.9	9.4	205
Boise City, ID	27.5	28.3	29.5	31.1	85
Boston, MA	336.2	347.0	361.2	379.4	9
Boulder, CO	20.3	21.1	21.8	22.9	107
Cape Coral, FL	20.9	21.9	23.1	24.6	95
Cedar Rapids, IA	14.8	15.3	15.8	16.5	142
Charleston, SC	31.0	31.9	33.3	35.2	74
Charlotte, NC	125.2	131.7	138.1	146.3	22
Chicago, IL	571.0	588.6	611.5	641.0	3
Clarksville, TN	11.8	11.8	12.2	12.7	167
Colorado Springs, CO	28.0	28.6	29.6	31.2	84
Columbia, MO	7.3	7.6	7.8	8.3	219
Columbus, OH	99.8	102.8	106.4	112.1	32
Dallas, TX	418.6	440.1	464.7	491.4	6
Davenport, IA	18.6	18.9	19.5	20.4	116
Denver, CO	167.9	174.8	182.6	192.6	18
Des Moines, IA	42.1	44.0	45.6	47.9	57
Durham, NC	39.7	41.5	43.6	46.3	58
El Paso, TX	29.6	29.9	31.1	32.6	78
Erie, PA	10.0	10.1	10.3	10.8	186
Eugene, OR	12.2	12.6	13.0	13.6	160
Fargo, ND	13.2	13.9	14.5	15.3	146
Fayetteville, NC	18.7	18.8	19.4	20.3	117
Fort Collins, CO	12.4	12.8	13.3	14.0	155
Fort Wayne, IN	19.0	19.5	20.3	21.2	115
Fort Worth, TX	418.6	440.1	464.7	491.4	6
Gainesville, FL	10.5	10.7	11.1	11.6	174
Grand Rapids, MI	35.3	36.8	39.0	40.9	65
Green Bay, WI	15.9	16.4	17.1	17.9	133
Greensboro, NC	36.9	38.1	39.4	41.4	64
Honolulu, HI	56.6	57.8	59.8	62.2	51
Houston, TX	449.7	467.5	496.1	523.2	4
Huntsville, AL	21.7	22.1	22.9	24.1	99
Indianapolis, IN	112.8	116.5	120.8	126.5	27
Jacksonville, FL	62.3	65.1	68.1	71.9	47
Kansas City, MO	113.8	117.2	121.3	127.5	26
Lafayette, LA	17.7	17.8	18.8	19.6	123
Las Vegas, NV	95.6	98.7	103.2	109.5	34
Lexington, KY	23.9	24.8	25.7	27.1	90
Lincoln, NE	15.9	16.5	17.4	18.3	130
Little Rock, AR	34.4	35.5	36.9	38.7	68
Los Angeles, CA	765.7	792.2	822.9	865.2	2
Louisville, KY	63.8	66.6	69.0	72.5	46
Lubbock, TX	10.9	11.3	11.7	12.1	172
Madison, WI	38.0	39.3	41.0	43.2	63
Manchester, NH	22.2	22.4	23.2	24.3	98
McAllen, TX	16.0	16.6	17.4	18.4	128
Miami, FL	274.1	284.9	298.8	315.6	11
Midland, TX	16.2	17.9	20.0	21.3	114
Minneapolis, MN	218.5	228.6	237.6	249.8	13

Table continued on next page.

MSA[1]	2012	2013	2014	2015	Rank[2]
Nashville, TN	91.1	96.3	100.8	106.2	35
New Orleans, LA	80.2	83.7	87.4	91.0	40
New York, NY	1,335.1	1,386.0	1,433.2	1,500.4	1
Oklahoma City, OK	63.3	65.0	67.7	70.5	49
Omaha, NE	51.9	52.9	55.0	57.8	52
Orlando, FL	106.1	110.7	117.0	124.5	28
Oxnard, CA	39.1	39.7	41.3	43.5	61
Palm Bay, FL	18.1	18.5	19.1	20.2	118
Peoria, IL	21.3	21.5	22.1	23.0	104
Philadelphia, PA	364.0	375.3	387.7	406.2	8
Phoenix, AZ	201.7	210.9	221.0	234.5	14
Pittsburgh, PA	123.6	126.7	130.9	137.1	24
Portland, OR	147.0	153.8	161.5	171.5	20
Providence, RI	69.5	71.5	74.2	77.5	44
Provo, UT	17.0	17.8	18.7	19.9	120
Raleigh, NC	61.4	63.7	67.4	71.8	48
Reno, NV	20.4	20.9	21.7	22.8	108
Richmond, VA	70.1	72.2	75.0	78.7	43
Roanoke, VA	13.7	14.1	14.5	15.1	148
Rochester, MN	9.7	10.0	10.3	10.9	184
Sacramento, CA	97.6	100.4	104.6	110.7	33
Salem, OR	12.7	13.1	13.6	14.3	152
Salt Lake City, UT	74.8	77.7	81.2	85.9	42
San Antonio, TX	92.0	95.1	99.9	105.4	36
San Diego, CA	177.4	182.7	190.8	201.8	17
San Francisco, CA	360.4	379.4	395.6	417.8	7
San Jose, CA	173.9	182.7	192.2	203.2	16
Santa Rosa, CA	20.3	20.9	21.9	23.0	104
Savannah, GA	14.1	14.6	15.1	15.9	145
Seattle, WA	258.8	269.5	279.8	293.8	12
Sioux Falls, SD	16.6	17.7	18.4	19.4	125
Spokane, WA	19.3	19.9	20.5	21.5	112
Springfield, IL	10.0	10.0	10.3	10.7	190
Tallahassee, FL	13.4	13.7	14.2	14.9	150
Tampa, FL	119.9	125.7	131.7	139.0	23
Topeka, KS	9.9	10.0	10.2	10.6	192
Tulsa, OK	47.9	48.5	50.5	52.9	54
Tyler, TX	9.4	9.7	10.1	10.5	194
Virginia Beach, VA	85.2	87.3	90.0	93.8	39
Washington, DC	447.0	458.1	475.5	501.7	5
Wichita, KS	29.4	29.7	30.7	32.3	82
Wilmington, NC	15.4	16.1	17.0	18.0	132
Winston-Salem, NC	23.0	23.5	24.3	25.4	92
Worcester, MA	30.5	31.5	32.6	34.0	75

Note: Figures are in billions of dollars; (1) Metropolitan Statistical Area—see Appendix B for areas included; (2) Rank is based on 2015 data and ranges from 1 to 363.
Source: The U.S. Conference of Mayors, U.S. Metro Economies: GMP and Employment 2013-2015, June 2014

Economic Growth

Area	2010-12 (%)	2013 (%)	2014 (%)	2015 (%)	Rank[2]
Albuquerque, NM	0.6	1.2	2.2	2.7	220
Anchorage, AK	1.6	1.1	1.1	3.7	54
Ann Arbor, MI	1.4	1.2	2.6	2.9	172
Athens, GA	0.2	2.8	2.1	2.7	220
Atlanta, GA	2.6	2.7	3.3	3.9	35
Austin, TX	5.1	4.6	3.9	4.7	8
Billings, MT	4.2	1.0	1.6	2.7	220
Boise City, ID	1.3	1.5	2.7	3.4	88
Boston, MA	2.2	1.9	2.5	3.0	155
Boulder, CO	3.7	2.4	1.9	2.9	172
Cape Coral, FL	1.3	3.4	3.8	4.3	19
Cedar Rapids, IA	1.4	1.4	1.7	2.7	220
Charleston, SC	3.5	1.6	2.7	3.6	61
Charlotte, NC	3.3	3.8	3.3	3.9	35
Chicago, IL	2.2	1.8	2.3	2.9	172
Clarksville, TN	3.6	-1.1	1.2	2.8	194
Colorado Springs, CO	2.1	0.7	1.8	3.1	134
Columbia, MO	2.8	3.3	1.2	3.3	102
Columbus, OH	2.9	1.7	1.9	3.3	102
Dallas, TX	3.8	3.7	3.3	4.5	14
Davenport, IA	1.8	0.2	1.9	2.5	254
Denver, CO	2.1	2.8	2.6	3.8	47
Des Moines, IA	2.9	2.3	2.1	3.1	134
Durham, NC	-0.4	3.1	3.5	4.1	25
El Paso, TX	2.4	-0.3	1.9	3.1	134
Erie, PA	3.1	-0.1	1.1	2.0	321
Eugene, OR	1.8	1.6	1.8	2.9	172
Fargo, ND	4.3	3.4	2.5	3.9	35
Fayetteville, NC	0.8	-0.9	1.4	2.4	270
Fort Collins, CO	2.5	1.8	2.0	3.3	102
Fort Wayne, IN	2.4	1.6	2.7	2.5	254
Fort Worth, TX	3.8	3.7	3.3	4.5	14
Gainesville, FL	-0.3	1.3	2.0	2.3	285
Grand Rapids, MI	3.9	3.0	4.4	2.9	172
Green Bay, WI	1.3	1.9	2.4	3.1	134
Greensboro, NC	2.1	1.8	2.1	3.1	134
Honolulu, HI	2.3	0.8	1.8	1.9	332
Houston, TX	4.8	2.8	3.5	4.8	6
Huntsville, AL	0.4	0.6	2.1	3.3	102
Indianapolis, IN	2.5	2.1	2.1	2.8	194
Jacksonville, FL	1.4	3.2	3.0	3.5	74
Kansas City, MO	1.8	1.5	1.9	3.2	119
Lafayette, LA	-3.6	-1.3	2.9	3.8	47
Las Vegas, NV	1.3	1.8	2.9	4.0	29
Lexington, KY	0.9	2.2	2.2	3.5	74
Lincoln, NE	2.3	2.4	3.8	2.8	194
Little Rock, AR	1.4	1.7	2.5	3.0	155
Los Angeles, CA	2.1	2.3	2.3	3.3	102
Louisville, KY	3.2	3.0	2.0	3.1	134
Lubbock, TX	0.8	2.7	1.0	1.9	332
Madison, WI	1.9	1.9	2.8	3.2	119
Manchester, NH	1.7	0.1	2.1	2.9	172
McAllen, TX	1.5	2.0	2.5	4.6	10
Miami, FL	2.4	2.7	3.2	3.6	61
Midland, TX	10.3	8.5	7.1	8.4	1
Minneapolis, MN	3.2	3.2	2.4	3.2	119

Table continued on next page.

Area	2010-12 (%)	2013 (%)	2014 (%)	2015 (%)	Rank[2]
Nashville, TN	4.5	4.2	3.1	3.4	88
New Orleans, LA	0.8	3.9	2.2	3.0	155
New York, NY	1.3	2.7	1.8	2.6	239
Oklahoma City, OK	2.4	1.3	2.0	2.9	172
Omaha, NE	1.5	0.3	2.4	3.1	134
Orlando, FL	2.4	3.0	4.1	4.4	16
Oxnard, CA	1.8	0.5	2.2	3.6	61
Palm Bay, FL	-1.7	0.7	1.8	3.6	61
Peoria, IL	8.7	-0.4	1.2	2.5	254
Philadelphia, PA	1.3	1.8	1.7	2.7	220
Phoenix, AZ	2.6	3.3	3.2	4.0	29
Pittsburgh, PA	2.8	1.3	1.7	2.6	239
Portland, OR	4.9	3.2	3.5	4.3	19
Providence, RI	1.0	1.7	2.1	2.5	254
Provo, UT	4.1	3.7	3.4	4.6	10
Raleigh, NC	2.3	2.3	4.1	4.5	14
Reno, NV	0.8	1.0	2.5	3.0	155
Richmond, VA	2.1	1.6	2.3	2.8	194
Roanoke, VA	1.4	1.1	1.1	2.3	285
Rochester, MN	0.3	0.8	1.7	3.3	102
Sacramento, CA	1.8	1.5	2.4	3.9	35
Salem, OR	-0.4	1.6	1.7	3.2	119
Salt Lake City, UT	3.6	2.9	2.9	3.9	35
San Antonio, TX	3.8	1.8	3.0	4.0	29
San Diego, CA	2.4	1.8	2.7	3.8	47
San Francisco, CA	3.8	4.1	2.6	3.7	54
San Jose, CA	5.2	4.3	3.7	3.9	35
Santa Rosa, CA	0.4	1.6	2.9	3.3	102
Savannah, GA	2.3	1.9	2.1	3.1	134
Seattle, WA	4.0	2.8	2.3	3.1	134
Sioux Falls, SD	2.7	4.3	2.0	3.3	102
Spokane, WA	1.6	1.9	1.4	2.9	172
Springfield, IL	-0.3	-0.9	1.0	1.8	339
Tallahassee, FL	-0.8	1.3	1.9	2.8	194
Tampa, FL	2.3	3.5	3.1	3.6	61
Topeka, KS	1.4	-0.7	0.8	2.3	285
Tulsa, OK	1.4	0.2	2.1	3.3	102
Tyler, TX	1.7	2.2	1.2	3.9	35
Virginia Beach, VA	1.2	1.0	1.5	2.2	301
Washington, DC	1.1	1.2	2.1	3.4	88
Wichita, KS	2.6	-0.2	1.6	3.4	88
Wilmington, NC	1.3	3.1	3.7	4.1	25
Winston-Salem, NC	-0.7	0.8	1.7	2.8	194
Worcester, MA	0.9	1.8	1.8	2.3	285
U.S.	2.1	2.0	2.3	3.2	–

Note: Figures are real gross metropolitan product (GMP) growth rates and represent annual average percent change.(1) Metropolitan Statistical Area—see Appendix B for areas included; (2) Rank is based on 2015 data and ranges from 1 to 363
Source: The U.S. Conference of Mayors, U.S. Metro Economies: GMP and Employment 2013-2015, June 2014

Metropolitan Area Exports

Area	2008	2009	2010	2011	2012	2013	Rank[2]
Albuquerque, NM	474.9	357.6	519.9	951.9	1,790.6	1,389.6	129
Anchorage, AK	245.8	213.9	n/a	n/a	416.4	518.0	211
Ann Arbor, MI	1,084.6	903.4	1,050.8	1,129.5	1,053.4	1,156.2	145
Athens, GA	171.4	214.6	194.6	221.6	229.7	286.0	271
Atlanta, GA	14,432.9	13,405.9	15,009.7	17,229.1	18,169.1	18,827.9	18
Austin, TX	7,405.5	5,963.7	8,867.8	8,626.3	8,976.6	8,870.8	38
Billings, MT	88.6	70.7	86.7	102.1	141.4	139.8	326
Boise City, ID	3,851.2	2,849.7	3,647.7	4,131.5	4,088.2	3,657.9	68
Boston, MA	22,955.2	18,972.6	21,804.5	22,292.8	21,234.8	22,212.8	14
Boulder, CO	891.7	727.2	1,058.7	946.7	1,128.0	1,046.0	153
Cape Coral, FL	282.8	237.5	298.0	305.1	509.8	442.6	225
Cedar Rapids, IA	909.9	734.8	749.5	880.8	889.1	930.2	161
Charleston, SC	2,005.5	1,455.7	2,120.0	2,299.4	2,429.8	3,464.3	71
Charlotte, NC	5,036.3	4,133.4	5,424.6	6,253.3	6,322.6	10,684.1	31
Chicago, IL	35,554.7	28,196.6	33,672.0	39,522.4	40,568.0	44,910.6	6
Clarksville, TN	311.4	158.4	238.3	328.8	326.3	315.9	263
Colorado Springs, CO	1,932.4	1,281.1	1,193.1	1,118.7	1,044.6	1,065.4	149
Columbia, MO	234.8	211.1	255.6	281.6	296.6	423.9	230
Columbus, OH	3,881.8	2,872.7	3,554.4	4,327.5	5,488.6	5,731.4	48
Dallas, TX	22,503.7	19,881.8	22,500.4	26,648.7	27,820.9	27,596.0	9
Davenport, IA	5,255.0	3,542.6	4,792.8	6,725.9	7,926.1	7,141.2	42
Denver, CO	4,633.5	4,309.8	4,990.9	3,771.3	3,355.8	3,618.4	69
Des Moines, IA	1,034.6	782.3	767.9	970.1	1,183.2	1,279.4	138
Durham, NC	2,688.4	2,656.1	2,736.6	2,640.3	2,723.2	2,971.7	80
El Paso, TX	9,390.5	7,748.0	10,315.9	11,615.9	12,796.9	14,359.7	22
Erie, PA	1,861.9	1,407.8	1,063.3	1,577.7	1,854.2	1,808.1	106
Eugene, OR	781.3	314.4	415.5	464.5	482.2	476.0	218
Fargo, ND	677.2	465.9	548.6	730.8	785.9	817.9	175
Fayetteville, NC	300.4	218.4	260.1	307.7	322.3	344.0	251
Fort Collins, CO	631.5	584.0	694.1	812.7	861.7	986.1	157
Fort Wayne, IN	1,142.8	916.8	1,059.2	1,283.8	1,353.5	1,441.8	127
Fort Worth, TX	22,503.7	19,881.8	22,500.4	26,648.7	27,820.9	27,596.0	9
Gainesville, FL	285.5	233.2	277.7	305.1	348.6	295.0	270
Grand Rapids, MI	2,993.7	2,408.5	2,474.0	2,791.9	3,156.4	5,314.8	53
Green Bay, WI	622.1	496.1	669.9	1,023.2	1,031.6	914.8	163
Greensboro, NC	3,687.9	3,168.6	4,007.8	4,054.1	4,281.9	4,278.3	61
Honolulu, HI	546.0	357.9	439.5	375.3	306.3	323.2	257
Houston, TX	80,015.1	65,820.9	80,569.7	104,457.0	110,298.0	114,963.0	1
Huntsville, AL	1,079.3	1,136.5	986.8	1,293.3	1,491.5	1,518.7	123
Indianapolis, IN	8,590.0	8,030.9	9,446.7	9,560.7	10,436.0	9,747.5	34
Jacksonville, FL	1,973.5	1,634.4	1,940.5	2,385.2	2,595.0	2,467.8	91
Kansas City, MO	7,799.7	5,888.9	7,374.1	7,958.9	7,880.8	8,012.1	41
Lafayette, LA	762.7	657.0	488.1	655.9	726.0	1,261.8	139
Las Vegas, NV	1,167.7	1,022.7	1,187.8	1,667.6	1,811.5	2,008.2	100
Lexington, KY	2,490.6	2,260.2	2,400.4	2,170.5	2,462.1	2,294.0	92
Lincoln, NE	733.4	682.8	722.7	922.1	904.7	818.4	174
Little Rock, AR	1,411.0	1,693.8	790.2	892.4	2,418.9	2,497.5	90
Los Angeles, CA	59,985.6	51,528.4	62,167.6	72,688.9	75,007.5	76,305.7	3
Louisville, KY	5,662.1	5,316.1	6,187.8	6,756.6	7,706.7	8,898.0	36
Lubbock, TX	1,016.6	530.4	772.8	966.9	657.9	536.8	209
Madison, WI	1,595.5	1,571.6	1,906.5	1,958.1	2,168.7	2,292.1	93
Manchester, NH	2,005.6	1,743.0	2,612.1	2,494.1	1,634.9	1,445.8	126
McAllen, TX	4,578.5	3,736.1	4,527.1	4,676.1	5,198.5	5,265.5	54
Miami, FL	33,411.5	31,175.0	35,866.9	43,129.9	47,858.7	41,771.5	7
Midland, TX	93.5	75.6	87.2	81.1	104.4	164.1	316
Minneapolis, MN	25,212.2	20,096.7	23,192.8	26,189.1	25,155.7	23,747.5	12

Table continued on next page.

Area	2008	2009	2010	2011	2012	2013	Rank[2]
Nashville, TN	5,259.5	4,406.6	5,748.5	5,878.7	6,402.1	8,702.8	39
New Orleans, LA	12,664.5	10,145.1	13,964.9	20,336.9	24,359.5	30,030.9	8
New York, NY	95,244.3	69,990.3	85,081.2	105,102.0	102,298.0	106,923.0	2
Oklahoma City, OK	1,233.8	987.6	1,196.1	1,592.8	1,574.6	1,581.7	120
Omaha, NE	2,317.1	1,924.4	2,079.4	2,658.0	3,529.3	4,255.9	62
Orlando, FL	3,388.0	2,947.1	3,453.6	3,230.0	3,850.6	3,227.7	76
Oxnard, CA	2,579.1	2,483.8	2,611.2	2,919.8	2,854.6	2,893.9	82
Palm Bay, FL	782.6	555.5	858.3	1,162.8	982.3	984.3	158
Peoria, IL	14,230.0	7,846.5	11,104.0	15,182.3	17,838.0	12,184.5	25
Philadelphia, PA	21,683.2	19,067.4	22,710.0	26,155.8	22,991.6	24,929.2	11
Phoenix, AZ	12,623.6	7,947.5	9,342.7	10,914.4	10,834.3	11,473.5	27
Pittsburgh, PA	11,309.0	8,343.0	12,160.7	15,165.5	14,134.7	10,444.4	32
Portland, OR	19,477.1	15,482.4	18,544.9	20,875.7	20,337.7	17,606.8	20
Providence, RI	5,382.0	5,392.0	5,791.9	7,139.1	5,830.8	6,609.0	44
Provo, UT	2,218.0	1,772.8	2,024.6	2,056.4	2,058.1	2,789.2	83
Raleigh, NC	2,076.7	1,799.5	1,912.4	2,254.4	2,308.1	2,280.6	95
Reno, NV	1,317.0	1,233.8	1,511.9	1,687.4	2,019.0	2,117.4	97
Richmond, VA	5,162.4	4,096.8	4,606.5	5,072.8	4,328.1	4,337.2	60
Roanoke, VA	669.3	582.4	709.8	659.8	716.6	746.5	182
Rochester, MN	938.2	779.7	984.5	842.6	1,023.7	1,061.0	151
Sacramento, CA	3,608.0	3,502.0	4,070.5	4,686.0	5,194.6	5,777.1	47
Salem, OR	331.9	325.2	453.8	508.7	437.3	414.4	232
Salt Lake City, UT	7,799.0	7,783.5	10,719.2	15,579.2	15,990.0	11,867.2	26
San Antonio, TX	5,049.5	4,390.0	6,416.2	10,506.5	14,010.2	19,287.6	16
San Diego, CA	15,855.9	13,418.6	16,464.3	17,410.5	17,183.3	17,885.5	19
San Francisco, CA	20,470.4	16,040.3	21,355.4	23,573.8	23,031.7	25,305.3	10
San Jose, CA	27,048.6	21,405.8	26,333.0	26,712.1	26,687.7	23,413.1	13
Santa Rosa, CA	1,117.8	880.1	992.4	1,132.2	1,059.1	1,044.8	154
Savannah, GA	3,598.5	2,724.7	3,459.1	4,140.2	4,116.5	5,436.4	52
Seattle, WA	46,911.2	36,942.3	35,409.6	41,117.5	50,301.7	56,686.4	4
Sioux Falls, SD	234.1	202.8	330.3	457.8	439.5	433.0	229
Spokane, WA	894.8	662.2	727.4	761.4	873.5	862.4	172
Springfield, IL	86.8	87.0	148.6	158.0	99.5	97.5	350
Tallahassee, FL	119.1	108.1	117.8	118.1	130.8	122.5	337
Tampa, FL	7,153.5	6,463.6	6,633.6	7,736.7	7,190.0	6,673.0	43
Topeka, KS	446.2	441.8	478.1	483.2	265.0	303.3	265
Tulsa, OK	2,878.1	2,441.1	2,741.8	3,123.6	3,578.9	3,818.0	65
Tyler, TX	147.1	130.1	184.4	249.6	221.1	219.6	302
Virginia Beach, VA	2,278.8	2,004.5	2,450.7	2,594.6	2,735.0	2,539.2	88
Washington, DC	9,879.4	9,226.1	11,082.9	10,237.9	14,609.7	16,225.0	21
Wichita, KS	6,845.9	4,954.8	5,512.0	4,169.2	4,250.3	3,785.5	66
Wilmington, NC	1,138.8	1,078.6	1,161.9	951.6	923.5	766.7	179
Winston-Salem, NC	1,855.1	1,741.5	1,554.6	1,268.3	1,148.1	1,660.1	117
Worcester, MA	2,863.5	2,035.9	2,355.7	2,397.0	2,966.2	3,393.6	73

Note: Figures are in millions of dollars; (1) Metropolitan Statistical Area—see Appendix B for areas included; (2) Rank is based on 2013 data and ranges from 1 to 387; n/a not available

Source: U.S. Department of Commerce, International Trade Administration, Office of Trade & Industry Information, Manufacturing & Services, data extracted April 3, 2015

Building Permits: City

City	Single-Family 2013	Single-Family 2014	Single-Family Pct. Chg.	Multi-Family 2013	Multi-Family 2014	Multi-Family Pct. Chg.	Total 2013	Total 2014	Total Pct. Chg.
Albuquerque, NM	434	1,110	155.8	1,040	306	-70.6	1,474	1,416	-3.9
Anchorage, AK	475	572	20.4	58	198	241.4	533	770	44.5
Ann Arbor, MI	27	22	-18.5	198	2	-99.0	225	24	-89.3
Athens, GA	143	116	-18.9	351	422	20.2	494	538	8.9
Atlanta, GA	473	545	15.2	5,070	3,960	-21.9	5,543	4,505	-18.7
Austin, TX	2,573	2,800	8.8	9,261	6,642	-28.3	11,834	9,442	-20.2
Billings, MT	481	473	-1.7	558	132	-76.3	1,039	605	-41.8
Boise City, ID	498	467	-6.2	222	793	257.2	720	1,260	75.0
Boston, MA	34	48	41.2	2,527	2,793	10.5	2,561	2,841	10.9
Boulder, CO	89	104	16.9	789	504	-36.1	878	608	-30.8
Cape Coral, FL	492	663	34.8	6	0	-100.0	498	663	33.1
Cedar Rapids, IA	242	325	34.3	245	124	-49.4	487	449	-7.8
Charleston, SC	576	600	4.2	351	378	7.7	927	978	5.5
Charlotte, NC	n/a	n/a	n/a	n/a	n/a	n/a	n/a	n/a	n/a
Chicago, IL	448	536	19.6	2,577	5,214	102.3	3,025	5,750	90.1
Clarksville, TN	779	850	9.1	580	137	-76.4	1,359	987	-27.4
Colorado Springs, CO	n/a	n/a	n/a	n/a	n/a	n/a	n/a	n/a	n/a
Columbia, MO	631	444	-29.6	378	739	95.5	1,009	1,183	17.2
Columbus, OH	770	724	-6.0	3,565	2,918	-18.1	4,335	3,642	-16.0
Dallas, TX	1,075	1,181	9.9	7,559	6,675	-11.7	8,634	7,856	-9.0
Davenport, IA	114	90	-21.1	16	30	87.5	130	120	-7.7
Denver, CO	1,284	1,710	33.2	4,586	4,248	-7.4	5,870	5,958	1.5
Des Moines, IA	184	116	-37.0	559	167	-70.1	743	283	-61.9
Durham, NC	1,112	1,154	3.8	2,636	360	-86.3	3,748	1,514	-59.6
El Paso, TX	2,271	2,021	-11.0	1,408	777	-44.8	3,679	2,798	-23.9
Erie, PA	2	3	50.0	0	0	-	2	3	50.0
Eugene, OR	182	224	23.1	733	808	10.2	915	1,032	12.8
Fargo, ND	509	377	-25.9	1,146	1,793	56.5	1,655	2,170	31.1
Fayetteville, NC	437	346	-20.8	288	77	-73.3	725	423	-41.7
Fort Collins, CO	612	742	21.2	779	410	-47.4	1,391	1,152	-17.2
Fort Wayne, IN	n/a	n/a	n/a	n/a	n/a	n/a	n/a	n/a	n/a
Fort Worth, TX	3,321	3,121	-6.0	2,334	2,802	20.1	5,655	5,923	4.7
Gainesville, FL	63	67	6.3	240	263	9.6	303	330	8.9
Grand Rapids, MI	59	75	27.1	96	128	33.3	155	203	31.0
Green Bay, WI	71	70	-1.4	105	110	4.8	176	180	2.3
Greensboro, NC	354	415	17.2	614	814	32.6	968	1,229	27.0
Honolulu, HI	n/a	n/a	n/a	n/a	n/a	n/a	n/a	n/a	n/a
Houston, TX	5,198	5,398	3.8	8,845	14,906	68.5	14,043	20,304	44.6
Huntsville, AL	1,000	897	-10.3	306	977	219.3	1,306	1,874	43.5
Indianapolis, IN	562	572	1.8	671	554	-17.4	1,233	1,126	-8.7
Jacksonville, FL	1,844	2,106	14.2	709	1,196	68.7	2,553	3,302	29.3
Kansas City, MO	703	656	-6.7	827	2,078	151.3	1,530	2,734	78.7
Lafayette, LA	n/a	n/a	n/a	n/a	n/a	n/a	n/a	n/a	n/a
Las Vegas, NV	1,517	1,453	-4.2	0	0	-	1,517	1,453	-4.2
Lexington, KY	676	687	1.6	223	538	141.3	899	1,225	36.3
Lincoln, NE	844	854	1.2	531	938	76.6	1,375	1,792	30.3
Little Rock, AR	356	338	-5.1	252	441	75.0	608	779	28.1
Los Angeles, CA	1,144	1,668	45.8	7,248	9,596	32.4	8,392	11,264	34.2
Louisville, KY	938	964	2.8	1,289	1,449	12.4	2,227	2,413	8.4
Lubbock, TX	938	888	-5.3	1,039	1,161	11.7	1,977	2,049	3.6
Madison, WI	217	235	8.3	1,018	1,445	41.9	1,235	1,680	36.0
Manchester, NH	49	104	112.2	38	10	-73.7	87	114	31.0
McAllen, TX	374	412	10.2	145	196	35.2	519	608	17.1
Miami, FL	115	72	-37.4	4,371	3,714	-15.0	4,486	3,786	-15.6

Table continued on next page.

City	Single-Family			Multi-Family			Total		
	2013	2014	Pct. Chg.	2013	2014	Pct. Chg.	2013	2014	Pct. Chg.
Midland, TX	732	917	25.3	1,092	636	-41.8	1,824	1,553	-14.9
Minneapolis, MN	146	138	-5.5	3,176	1,821	-42.7	3,322	1,959	-41.0
Nashville, TN	1,824	2,538	39.1	2,142	3,829	78.8	3,966	6,367	60.5
New Orleans, LA	736	574	-22.0	159	452	184.3	895	1,026	14.6
New York, NY	402	541	34.6	17,593	19,346	10.0	17,995	19,887	10.5
Oklahoma City, OK	3,609	3,306	-8.4	804	1,155	43.7	4,413	4,461	1.1
Omaha, NE	1,567	1,306	-16.7	1,003	1,147	14.4	2,570	2,453	-4.6
Orlando, FL	1,037	915	-11.8	1,850	1,934	4.5	2,887	2,849	-1.3
Oxnard, CA	94	71	-24.5	276	431	56.2	370	502	35.7
Palm Bay, FL	157	162	3.2	0	0	-	157	162	3.2
Peoria, IL	147	51	-65.3	6	0	-100.0	153	51	-66.7
Philadelphia, PA	632	756	19.6	2,183	3,217	47.4	2,815	3,973	41.1
Phoenix, AZ	1,673	1,608	-3.9	1,458	3,530	142.1	3,131	5,138	64.1
Pittsburgh, PA	100	89	-11.0	0	249	-	100	338	238.0
Portland, OR	763	792	3.8	2,992	4,224	41.2	3,755	5,016	33.6
Providence, RI	16	14	-12.5	26	13	-50.0	42	27	-35.7
Provo, UT	136	128	-5.9	51	163	219.6	187	291	55.6
Raleigh, NC	1,662	1,318	-20.7	2,138	3,337	56.1	3,800	4,655	22.5
Reno, NV	687	858	24.9	426	699	64.1	1,113	1,557	39.9
Richmond, VA	106	182	71.7	743	369	-50.3	849	551	-35.1
Roanoke, VA	65	35	-46.2	161	14	-91.3	226	49	-78.3
Rochester, MN	323	352	9.0	44	134	204.5	367	486	32.4
Sacramento, CA	232	256	10.3	27	25	-7.4	259	281	8.5
Salem, OR	283	270	-4.6	294	21	-92.9	577	291	-49.6
Salt Lake City, UT	80	95	18.8	178	245	37.6	258	340	31.8
San Antonio, TX	2,102	2,270	8.0	16	3,368	20,950.0	2,118	5,638	166.2
San Diego, CA	821	712	-13.3	4,487	2,031	-54.7	5,308	2,743	-48.3
San Francisco, CA	54	35	-35.2	4,420	2,676	-39.5	4,474	2,711	-39.4
San Jose, CA	274	384	40.1	3,429	4,061	18.4	3,703	4,445	20.0
Santa Rosa, CA	138	184	33.3	347	64	-81.6	485	248	-48.9
Savannah, GA	265	341	28.7	18	23	27.8	283	364	28.6
Seattle, WA	822	898	9.2	5,855	6,547	11.8	6,677	7,445	11.5
Sioux Falls, SD	1,025	842	-17.9	986	1,036	5.1	2,011	1,878	-6.6
Spokane, WA	321	223	-30.5	142	296	108.5	463	519	12.1
Springfield, IL	81	89	9.9	46	137	197.8	127	226	78.0
Tallahassee, FL	293	271	-7.5	648	632	-2.5	941	903	-4.0
Tampa, FL	686	712	3.8	1,168	1,843	57.8	1,854	2,555	37.8
Topeka, KS	84	86	2.4	2	28	1,300.0	86	114	32.6
Tulsa, OK	436	402	-7.8	164	963	487.2	600	1,365	127.5
Tyler, TX	271	268	-1.1	0	12	-	271	280	3.3
Virginia Beach, VA	733	688	-6.1	929	520	-44.0	1,662	1,208	-27.3
Washington, DC	333	288	-13.5	2,922	3,901	33.5	3,255	4,189	28.7
Wichita, KS	536	550	2.6	200	182	-9.0	736	732	-0.5
Wilmington, NC	n/a	n/a	n/a	n/a	n/a	n/a	n/a	n/a	n/a
Winston-Salem, NC	476	514	8.0	502	269	-46.4	978	783	-19.9
Worcester, MA	53	88	66.0	8	16	100.0	61	104	70.5
U.S.	620,802	634,597	2.2	370,020	411,766	11.3	990,822	1,046,363	5.6

Note: Figures represent new, privately-owned housing units authorized (unadjusted data); All permit data are based on estimates with imputation

Source: U.S. Census Bureau, Manufacturing, Mining, and Construction Statistics, Building Permits, 2013, 2014

Building Permits: Metro Area

Metro Area	Single-Family			Multi-Family			Total		
	2013	2014	Pct. Chg.	2013	2014	Pct. Chg.	2013	2014	Pct. Chg.
Albuquerque, NM	1,456	2,128	46.2	1,150	415	-63.9	2,606	2,543	-2.4
Anchorage, AK	500	671	34.2	76	216	184.2	576	887	54.0
Ann Arbor, MI	394	385	-2.3	364	185	-49.2	758	570	-24.8
Athens, GA	698	502	-28.1	381	428	12.3	1,079	930	-13.8
Atlanta, GA	14,824	16,984	14.6	9,473	9,699	2.4	24,297	26,683	9.8
Austin, TX	8,941	11,515	28.8	11,911	8,434	-29.2	20,852	19,949	-4.3
Billings, MT	974	517	-46.9	1,128	134	-88.1	2,102	651	-69.0
Boise City, ID	3,522	3,481	-1.2	843	1,702	101.9	4,365	5,183	18.7
Boston, MA	4,953	4,991	0.8	7,068	7,033	-0.5	12,021	12,024	0.0
Boulder, CO	591	560	-5.2	1,034	811	-21.6	1,625	1,371	-15.6
Cape Coral, FL	2,531	3,112	23.0	645	983	52.4	3,176	4,095	28.9
Cedar Rapids, IA	625	644	3.0	324	237	-26.9	949	881	-7.2
Charleston, SC	3,779	4,144	9.7	1,638	2,011	22.8	5,417	6,155	13.6
Charlotte, NC	8,792	11,306	28.6	5,217	7,231	38.6	14,009	18,537	32.3
Chicago, IL	7,261	7,723	6.4	4,366	7,956	82.2	11,627	15,679	34.8
Clarksville, TN	1,256	1,276	1.6	586	231	-60.6	1,842	1,507	-18.2
Colorado Springs, CO	2,885	2,662	-7.7	702	1,011	44.0	3,587	3,673	2.4
Columbia, MO	836	663	-20.7	396	751	89.6	1,232	1,414	14.8
Columbus, OH	3,495	3,497	0.1	4,868	3,547	-27.1	8,363	7,044	-15.8
Dallas, TX	21,224	22,550	6.2	16,686	18,868	13.1	37,910	41,418	9.3
Davenport, IA	510	458	-10.2	107	197	84.1	617	655	6.2
Denver, CO	6,965	8,064	15.8	8,510	7,703	-9.5	15,475	15,767	1.9
Des Moines, IA	3,307	2,952	-10.7	1,614	1,484	-8.1	4,921	4,436	-9.9
Durham, NC	1,969	2,167	10.1	2,725	420	-84.6	4,694	2,587	-44.9
El Paso, TX	2,613	2,260	-13.5	1,484	783	-47.2	4,097	3,043	-25.7
Erie, PA	258	166	-35.7	209	155	-25.8	467	321	-31.3
Eugene, OR	506	506	0.0	743	810	9.0	1,249	1,316	5.4
Fargo, ND	1,395	1,242	-11.0	1,698	2,524	48.6	3,093	3,766	21.8
Fayetteville, NC	1,269	1,012	-20.3	621	77	-87.6	1,890	1,089	-42.4
Fort Collins, CO	1,489	1,627	9.3	888	871	-1.9	2,377	2,498	5.1
Fort Wayne, IN	960	883	-8.0	75	362	382.7	1,035	1,245	20.3
Fort Worth, TX	21,224	22,550	6.2	16,686	18,868	13.1	37,910	41,418	9.3
Gainesville, FL	558	536	-3.9	242	263	8.7	800	799	-0.1
Grand Rapids, MI	1,319	2,273	72.3	162	898	454.3	1,481	3,171	114.1
Green Bay, WI	719	641	-10.8	551	363	-34.1	1,270	1,004	-20.9
Greensboro, NC	1,416	1,470	3.8	616	1,162	88.6	2,032	2,632	29.5
Honolulu, HI	1,137	875	-23.0	1,504	703	-53.3	2,641	1,578	-40.2
Houston, TX	34,542	38,315	10.9	16,791	25,426	51.4	51,333	63,741	24.2
Huntsville, AL	1,944	1,784	-8.2	306	1,033	237.6	2,250	2,817	25.2
Indianapolis, IN	5,014	4,965	-1.0	3,137	3,041	-3.1	8,151	8,006	-1.8
Jacksonville, FL	6,281	6,299	0.3	1,077	1,482	37.6	7,358	7,781	5.7
Kansas City, MO	4,229	4,170	-1.4	3,303	4,031	22.0	7,532	8,201	8.9
Lafayette, LA	1,399	2,224	59.0	155	138	-11.0	1,554	2,362	52.0
Las Vegas, NV	7,067	6,809	-3.7	1,506	3,227	114.3	8,573	10,036	17.1
Lexington, KY	1,335	1,319	-1.2	319	569	78.4	1,654	1,888	14.1
Lincoln, NE	1,052	1,052	0.0	535	942	76.1	1,587	1,994	25.6
Little Rock, AR	1,681	1,514	-9.9	814	568	-30.2	2,495	2,082	-16.6
Los Angeles, CA	7,509	8,300	10.5	17,689	18,650	5.4	25,198	26,950	7.0
Louisville, KY	2,551	2,390	-6.3	1,466	1,621	10.6	4,017	4,011	-0.1
Lubbock, TX	1,009	975	-3.4	1,039	1,161	11.7	2,048	2,136	4.3
Madison, WI	1,212	1,243	2.6	1,754	2,562	46.1	2,966	3,805	28.3
Manchester, NH	468	464	-0.9	99	504	409.1	567	968	70.7
McAllen, TX	2,545	2,840	11.6	749	633	-15.5	3,294	3,473	5.4
Miami, FL	6,369	5,791	-9.1	13,552	9,468	-30.1	19,921	15,259	-23.4

Table continued on next page.

Metro Area	Single-Family			Multi-Family			Total		
	2013	2014	Pct. Chg.	2013	2014	Pct. Chg.	2013	2014	Pct. Chg.
Midland, TX	732	920	25.7	1,092	636	-41.8	1,824	1,556	-14.7
Minneapolis, MN	7,174	6,689	-6.8	4,859	4,736	-2.5	12,033	11,425	-5.1
Nashville, TN	7,020	9,075	29.3	3,869	5,869	51.7	10,889	14,944	37.2
New Orleans, LA	2,441	2,440	0.0	175	551	214.9	2,616	2,991	14.3
New York, NY	10,139	11,799	16.4	29,685	36,185	21.9	39,824	47,984	20.5
Oklahoma City, OK	6,359	5,959	-6.3	1,146	1,911	66.8	7,505	7,870	4.9
Omaha, NE	3,039	2,639	-13.2	1,425	1,553	9.0	4,464	4,192	-6.1
Orlando, FL	9,222	9,806	6.3	6,341	6,309	-0.5	15,563	16,115	3.5
Oxnard, CA	430	536	24.7	571	778	36.3	1,001	1,314	31.3
Palm Bay, FL	1,349	1,241	-8.0	24	45	87.5	1,373	1,286	-6.3
Peoria, IL	538	835	55.2	80	55	-31.3	618	890	44.0
Philadelphia, PA	6,252	6,379	2.0	4,965	7,252	46.1	11,217	13,631	21.5
Phoenix, AZ	12,959	11,557	-10.8	5,778	8,784	52.0	18,737	20,341	8.6
Pittsburgh, PA	3,251	3,082	-5.2	1,312	1,108	-15.5	4,563	4,190	-8.2
Portland, OR	5,717	5,462	-4.5	6,013	6,894	14.7	11,730	12,356	5.3
Providence, RI	1,465	1,441	-1.6	509	334	-34.4	1,974	1,775	-10.1
Provo, UT	2,675	2,679	0.1	748	2,616	249.7	3,423	5,295	54.7
Raleigh, NC	8,034	7,680	-4.4	3,397	3,967	16.8	11,431	11,647	1.9
Reno, NV	1,243	1,507	21.2	477	709	48.6	1,720	2,216	28.8
Richmond, VA	3,555	3,181	-10.5	1,450	1,131	-22.0	5,005	4,312	-13.8
Roanoke, VA	476	425	-10.7	209	86	-58.9	685	511	-25.4
Rochester, MN	594	621	4.5	44	211	379.5	638	832	30.4
Sacramento, CA	3,539	3,694	4.4	650	465	-28.5	4,189	4,159	-0.7
Salem, OR	646	712	10.2	304	232	-23.7	950	944	-0.6
Salt Lake City, UT	3,447	3,159	-8.4	2,081	2,159	3.7	5,528	5,318	-3.8
San Antonio, TX	5,827	6,220	6.7	301	4,112	1,266.1	6,128	10,332	68.6
San Diego, CA	2,565	2,487	-3.0	5,699	4,388	-23.0	8,264	6,875	-16.8
San Francisco, CA	3,659	3,716	1.6	7,263	6,285	-13.5	10,922	10,001	-8.4
San Jose, CA	1,870	1,861	-0.5	5,894	8,176	38.7	7,764	10,037	29.3
Santa Rosa, CA	453	419	-7.5	593	244	-58.9	1,046	663	-36.6
Savannah, GA	1,517	1,857	22.4	233	354	51.9	1,750	2,211	26.3
Seattle, WA	8,773	8,665	-1.2	10,744	13,288	23.7	19,517	21,953	12.5
Sioux Falls, SD	1,330	1,134	-14.7	1,079	1,196	10.8	2,409	2,330	-3.3
Spokane, WA	1,299	1,135	-12.6	335	825	146.3	1,634	1,960	20.0
Springfield, IL	276	300	8.7	64	155	142.2	340	455	33.8
Tallahassee, FL	628	628	0.0	652	632	-3.1	1,280	1,260	-1.6
Tampa, FL	7,314	7,267	-0.6	4,838	5,119	5.8	12,152	12,386	1.9
Topeka, KS	272	285	4.8	10	30	200.0	282	315	11.7
Tulsa, OK	3,008	3,022	0.5	717	1,511	110.7	3,725	4,533	21.7
Tyler, TX	373	377	1.1	0	12	-	373	389	4.3
Virginia Beach, VA	4,104	3,766	-8.2	3,273	1,949	-40.5	7,377	5,715	-22.5
Washington, DC	13,274	12,411	-6.5	10,759	12,393	15.2	24,033	24,804	3.2
Wichita, KS	1,163	1,177	1.2	341	337	-1.2	1,504	1,514	0.7
Wilmington, NC	3,141	1,367	-56.5	916	841	-8.2	4,057	2,208	-45.6
Winston-Salem, NC	1,001	1,424	42.3	502	661	31.7	1,503	2,085	38.7
Worcester, MA	1,164	1,274	9.5	177	110	-37.9	1,341	1,384	3.2
U.S.	620,802	634,597	2.2	370,020	411,766	11.3	990,822	1,046,363	5.6

Note: Figures cover the Metropolitan Statistical Area—see Appendix B for areas included; Figures represent new, privately-owned housing units authorized (unadjusted data); All permit data are based on estimates with imputation
Source: U.S. Census Bureau, Manufacturing, Mining, and Construction Statistics, Building Permits, 2013, 2014

Housing Vacancy Rates

Metro Area[1]	Gross Vacancy Rate[2] (%)			Year-Round Vacancy Rate[3] (%)			Rental Vacancy Rate[4] (%)			Homeowner Vacancy Rate[5] (%)		
	2012	2013	2014	2012	2013	2014	2012	2013	2014	2012	2013	2014
Albuquerque, NM	7.1	8.4	8.6	6.5	7.7	7.3	5.1	7.8	7.5	2.2	2.4	1.9
Anchorage, AK	n/a	n/a	n/a	n/a	n/a	n/a	n/a	n/a	n/a	n/a	n/a	n/a
Ann Arbor, MI	n/a	n/a	n/a	n/a	n/a	n/a	n/a	n/a	n/a	n/a	n/a	n/a
Athens, GA	n/a	n/a	n/a	n/a	n/a	n/a	n/a	n/a	n/a	n/a	n/a	n/a
Atlanta, GA	12.5	12.4	11.0	12.2	11.8	10.3	10.6	10.2	8.8	2.6	2.1	2.5
Austin, TX	12.7	12.5	12.4	11.9	11.9	11.6	9.6	12.1	10.9	1.3	1.1	0.8
Billings, MT	n/a	n/a	n/a	n/a	n/a	n/a	n/a	n/a	n/a	n/a	n/a	n/a
Boise City, ID	n/a	n/a	n/a	n/a	n/a	n/a	n/a	n/a	n/a	n/a	n/a	n/a
Boston, MA	8.6	7.8	9.2	6.9	6.2	6.4	5.9	6.8	4.9	1.3	1.1	0.8
Boulder, CO	n/a	n/a	n/a	n/a	n/a	n/a	n/a	n/a	n/a	n/a	n/a	n/a
Cape Coral, FL	n/a	n/a	n/a	n/a	n/a	n/a	n/a	n/a	n/a	n/a	n/a	n/a
Cedar Rapids, IA	n/a	n/a	n/a	n/a	n/a	n/a	n/a	n/a	n/a	n/a	n/a	n/a
Charleston, SC	n/a	n/a	n/a	n/a	n/a	n/a	n/a	n/a	n/a	n/a	n/a	n/a
Charlotte, NC	8.0	9.3	7.9	7.7	8.7	7.8	6.4	6.4	6.0	1.3	3.5	1.7
Chicago, IL	10.8	10.5	10.3	10.6	10.3	10.2	9.7	10.9	9.1	2.8	2.8	2.6
Clarksville, TN	n/a	n/a	n/a	n/a	n/a	n/a	n/a	n/a	n/a	n/a	n/a	n/a
Colorado Springs, CO	n/a	n/a	n/a	n/a	n/a	n/a	n/a	n/a	n/a	n/a	n/a	n/a
Columbia, MO	n/a	n/a	n/a	n/a	n/a	n/a	n/a	n/a	n/a	n/a	n/a	n/a
Columbus, OH	13.7	9.8	10.2	13.7	9.8	9.9	8.3	6.3	7.0	2.3	1.1	1.7
Dallas, TX	8.7	9.0	9.2	8.4	8.8	9.0	9.2	8.2	9.8	2.1	1.9	1.5
Davenport, IA	n/a	n/a	n/a	n/a	n/a	n/a	n/a	n/a	n/a	n/a	n/a	n/a
Denver, CO	6.3	6.3	6.1	5.9	5.5	5.1	4.7	5.3	3.3	1.5	1.2	0.8
Des Moines, IA	n/a	n/a	n/a	n/a	n/a	n/a	n/a	n/a	n/a	n/a	n/a	n/a
Durham, NC	n/a	n/a	n/a	n/a	n/a	n/a	n/a	n/a	n/a	n/a	n/a	n/a
El Paso, TX	4.3	8.8	9.3	4.3	8.6	8.4	8.2	7.9	9.2	0.1	2.9	1.5
Erie, PA	n/a	n/a	n/a	n/a	n/a	n/a	n/a	n/a	n/a	n/a	n/a	n/a
Eugene, OR	n/a	n/a	n/a	n/a	n/a	n/a	n/a	n/a	n/a	n/a	n/a	n/a
Fargo, ND	n/a	n/a	n/a	n/a	n/a	n/a	n/a	n/a	n/a	n/a	n/a	n/a
Fayetteville, NC	n/a	n/a	n/a	n/a	n/a	n/a	n/a	n/a	n/a	n/a	n/a	n/a
Fort Collins, CO	n/a	n/a	n/a	n/a	n/a	n/a	n/a	n/a	n/a	n/a	n/a	n/a
Fort Wayne, IN	n/a	n/a	n/a	n/a	n/a	n/a	n/a	n/a	n/a	n/a	n/a	n/a
Fort Worth, TX	8.7	9.0	9.2	8.4	8.8	9.0	9.2	8.2	9.8	2.1	1.9	1.5
Gainesville, FL	n/a	n/a	n/a	n/a	n/a	n/a	n/a	n/a	n/a	n/a	n/a	n/a
Grand Rapids, MI	8.8	7.2	6.5	6.4	6.2	5.8	5.6	5.1	3.7	2.4	2.5	1.6
Green Bay, WI	n/a	n/a	n/a	n/a	n/a	n/a	n/a	n/a	n/a	n/a	n/a	n/a
Greensboro, NC	12.1	12.5	11.4	12.0	12.4	10.9	7.6	9.6	8.6	3.5	3.0	2.0
Honolulu, HI	10.2	10.9	12.3	8.8	8.6	10.2	6.3	6.0	5.6	1.3	0.9	1.1
Houston, TX	9.8	9.6	8.9	9.4	9.0	8.4	11.4	10.0	8.6	1.9	2.3	1.3
Huntsville, AL	n/a	n/a	n/a	n/a	n/a	n/a	n/a	n/a	n/a	n/a	n/a	n/a
Indianapolis, IN	10.5	9.2	8.8	9.5	8.7	8.7	11.1	10.9	10.9	1.8	1.5	2.2
Jacksonville, FL	15.4	14.2	16.6	14.4	12.7	14.0	11.7	8.4	11.1	1.9	1.5	2.6
Kansas City, MO	10.5	10.8	9.0	10.3	10.4	8.6	11.2	10.1	9.5	1.6	2.0	1.5
Lafayette, LA	n/a	n/a	n/a	n/a	n/a	n/a	n/a	n/a	n/a	n/a	n/a	n/a
Las Vegas, NV	16.2	16.6	14.3	15.0	15.5	13.4	12.8	14.1	10.1	3.4	3.0	2.9
Lexington, KY	n/a	n/a	n/a	n/a	n/a	n/a	n/a	n/a	n/a	n/a	n/a	n/a
Lincoln, NE	n/a	n/a	n/a	n/a	n/a	n/a	n/a	n/a	n/a	n/a	n/a	n/a
Little Rock, AR	n/a	n/a	n/a	n/a	n/a	n/a	n/a	n/a	n/a	n/a	n/a	n/a
Los Angeles, CA	6.2	6.2	5.8	5.9	5.7	5.5	4.9	4.2	4.6	1.3	1.2	0.8
Louisville, KY	10.6	11.0	10.3	10.6	11.0	9.8	7.2	7.8	5.5	2.4	0.8	2.2
Lubbock, TX	n/a	n/a	n/a	n/a	n/a	n/a	n/a	n/a	n/a	n/a	n/a	n/a
Madison, WI	n/a	n/a	n/a	n/a	n/a	n/a	n/a	n/a	n/a	n/a	n/a	n/a
Manchester, NH	n/a	n/a	n/a	n/a	n/a	n/a	n/a	n/a	n/a	n/a	n/a	n/a
McAllen, TX	n/a	n/a	n/a	n/a	n/a	n/a	n/a	n/a	n/a	n/a	n/a	n/a
Miami, FL	20.1	20.2	19.6	10.1	10.3	10.4	8.2	6.7	7.0	0.9	1.7	1.8

Table continued on next page.

Metro Area[1]	Gross Vacancy Rate[2] (%)			Year-Round Vacancy Rate[3] (%)			Rental Vacancy Rate[4] (%)			Homeowner Vacancy Rate[5] (%)		
	2012	2013	2014	2012	2013	2014	2012	2013	2014	2012	2013	2014
Midland, TX	n/a	n/a	n/a	n/a	n/a	n/a	n/a	n/a	n/a	n/a	n/a	n/a
Minneapolis, MN	5.8	5.7	5.7	5.2	5.1	5.3	5.3	5.4	4.4	1.2	0.9	1.4
Nashville, TN	8.7	6.6	7.0	8.2	6.4	6.7	8.4	5.3	4.0	1.6	0.9	2.4
New Orleans, LA	13.6	13.3	13.0	13.4	12.7	12.3	15.9	11.1	8.5	2.9	1.9	1.6
New York, NY	9.8	9.5	9.2	8.4	8.1	7.9	6.4	5.4	4.6	2.2	2.1	1.6
Oklahoma City, OK	12.8	13.0	13.4	12.6	12.6	12.9	10.2	8.7	10.1	2.5	2.0	1.7
Omaha, NE	8.3	7.5	7.7	7.9	6.5	7.0	9.5	6.1	5.5	1.2	1.3	1.8
Orlando, FL	21.2	20.5	18.8	14.3	15.5	15.2	18.5	14.7	14.6	2.2	2.8	3.1
Oxnard, CA	5.5	7.4	8.4	4.6	5.6	8.1	2.3	5.3	2.5	0.5	1.7	2.1
Palm Bay, FL	n/a	n/a	n/a	n/a	n/a	n/a	n/a	n/a	n/a	n/a	n/a	n/a
Peoria, IL	n/a	n/a	n/a	n/a	n/a	n/a	n/a	n/a	n/a	n/a	n/a	n/a
Philadelphia, PA	10.2	10.4	10.2	9.8	10.2	10.0	12.6	11.6	9.7	1.9	1.6	2.0
Phoenix, AZ	16.6	18.4	17.5	9.8	11.5	11.3	10.3	9.7	9.7	2.7	2.4	2.9
Pittsburgh, PA	14.4	12.7	12.2	14.1	12.5	11.7	6.4	7.8	6.1	1.3	1.7	1.2
Portland, OR	7.0	6.5	6.3	6.6	6.1	6.2	5.0	3.1	3.6	1.9	1.2	1.3
Providence, RI	13.8	12.3	13.2	10.9	8.9	9.9	8.0	6.6	6.8	2.9	2.3	1.6
Provo, UT	n/a	n/a	n/a	n/a	n/a	n/a	n/a	n/a	n/a	n/a	n/a	n/a
Raleigh, NC	8.5	7.3	6.4	8.2	7.2	6.4	8.8	6.9	5.3	1.9	1.8	0.6
Reno, NV	n/a	n/a	n/a	n/a	n/a	n/a	n/a	n/a	n/a	n/a	n/a	n/a
Richmond, VA	13.8	14.5	11.8	13.0	13.6	11.5	17.5	11.4	12.0	1.4	2.4	1.9
Roanoke, VA	n/a	n/a	n/a	n/a	n/a	n/a	n/a	n/a	n/a	n/a	n/a	n/a
Rochester, MN	n/a	n/a	n/a	n/a	n/a	n/a	n/a	n/a	n/a	n/a	n/a	n/a
Sacramento, CA	8.5	9.7	10.2	7.6	8.4	7.6	5.7	7.0	6.5	2.3	1.2	1.0
Salem, OR	n/a	n/a	n/a	n/a	n/a	n/a	n/a	n/a	n/a	n/a	n/a	n/a
Salt Lake City, UT	7.9	7.4	7.8	7.3	6.8	7.6	7.3	6.7	9.8	0.8	1.5	1.8
San Antonio, TX	11.3	9.0	8.6	10.4	8.3	8.2	9.0	9.1	7.3	2.7	1.4	1.2
San Diego, CA	9.1	7.8	7.7	8.6	7.4	7.3	7.1	5.5	4.8	1.4	1.2	1.3
San Francisco, CA	6.9	6.5	5.9	6.8	6.4	5.9	3.2	3.9	3.2	1.0	1.1	0.4
San Jose, CA	3.8	5.0	4.7	3.7	4.9	4.5	3.8	3.0	2.9	0.9	0.6	0.6
Santa Rosa, CA	n/a	n/a	n/a	n/a	n/a	n/a	n/a	n/a	n/a	n/a	n/a	n/a
Savannah, GA	n/a	n/a	n/a	n/a	n/a	n/a	n/a	n/a	n/a	n/a	n/a	n/a
Seattle, WA	8.1	6.9	6.9	8.0	6.6	6.7	5.7	4.3	4.4	2.3	1.7	1.2
Sioux Falls, SD	n/a	n/a	n/a	n/a	n/a	n/a	n/a	n/a	n/a	n/a	n/a	n/a
Spokane, WA	n/a	n/a	n/a	n/a	n/a	n/a	n/a	n/a	n/a	n/a	n/a	n/a
Springfield, IL	n/a	n/a	n/a	n/a	n/a	n/a	n/a	n/a	n/a	n/a	n/a	n/a
Tallahassee, FL	n/a	n/a	n/a	n/a	n/a	n/a	n/a	n/a	n/a	n/a	n/a	n/a
Tampa, FL	20.8	18.4	18.3	14.2	12.1	11.5	13.0	9.2	8.4	2.0	2.1	2.4
Topeka, KS	n/a	n/a	n/a	n/a	n/a	n/a	n/a	n/a	n/a	n/a	n/a	n/a
Tulsa, OK	13.3	12.0	11.0	12.8	11.5	10.5	9.5	10.5	9.7	2.4	2.4	1.2
Tyler, TX	n/a	n/a	n/a	n/a	n/a	n/a	n/a	n/a	n/a	n/a	n/a	n/a
Virginia Beach, VA	10.8	9.6	9.4	9.5	8.7	8.4	8.7	7.0	6.6	2.9	2.5	2.0
Washington, DC	8.1	8.3	7.8	7.9	8.2	7.5	6.4	7.2	6.7	1.3	1.3	1.4
Wichita, KS	n/a	n/a	n/a	n/a	n/a	n/a	n/a	n/a	n/a	n/a	n/a	n/a
Wilmington, NC	n/a	n/a	n/a	n/a	n/a	n/a	n/a	n/a	n/a	n/a	n/a	n/a
Winston-Salem, NC	n/a	n/a	n/a	n/a	n/a	n/a	n/a	n/a	n/a	n/a	n/a	n/a
Worcester, MA	10.3	10.8	11.0	9.5	8.6	6.8	3.7	6.4	4.5	2.4	3.1	1.9
U.S.	13.8	13.6	13.4	10.8	10.7	10.4	8.7	8.3	7.6	2.0	2.0	1.9

Note: (1) Metropolitan Statistical Area—see Appendix B for areas included; (2) The percentage of the total housing inventory that is vacant; (3) The percentage of the housing inventory (excluding seasonal units) that is year-round vacant; (4) The percentage of rental inventory that is vacant for rent; (5) The percentage of homeowner inventory that is vacant for sale; n/a not available
Source: U.S. Census Bureau, Housing Vacancies and Homeownership Annual Statistics: 2014

Bankruptcy Filings

City	Area Covered	Business Filings			Nonbusiness Filings		
		2013	2014	% Chg.	2013	2014	% Chg.
Albuquerque, NM	Bernalillo County	64	50	-21.9	1,668	1,399	-16.1
Anchorage, AK	Anchorage Borough	19	17	-10.5	268	210	-21.6
Ann Arbor, MI	Washtenaw County	22	16	-27.3	939	848	-9.7
Athens, GA	Clarke County	18	7	-61.1	383	381	-0.5
Atlanta, GA	Fulton County	256	161	-37.1	5,143	5,080	-1.2
Austin, TX	Travis County	141	112	-20.6	1,062	838	-21.1
Billings, MT	Yellowstone County	13	17	30.8	296	263	-11.1
Boise City, ID	Ada County	60	47	-21.7	1,494	1,177	-21.2
Boston, MA	Suffolk County	30	31	3.3	946	764	-19.2
Boulder, CO	Boulder County	46	33	-28.3	708	544	-23.2
Cape Coral, FL	Lee County	79	74	-6.3	1,833	1,619	-11.7
Cedar Rapids, IA	Linn County	10	5	-50.0	407	347	-14.7
Charleston, SC	Charleston County	22	29	31.8	480	448	-6.7
Charlotte, NC	Mecklenburg County	70	63	-10.0	1,653	1,326	-19.8
Chicago, IL	Cook County	794	569	-28.3	35,315	33,968	-3.8
Clarksville, TN	Montgomery County	14	14	0.0	773	808	4.5
Colorado Springs, CO	El Paso County	51	40	-21.6	2,641	2,126	-19.5
Columbia, MO	Boone County	8	10	25.0	577	419	-27.4
Columbus, OH	Franklin County	82	82	0.0	5,271	4,806	-8.8
Dallas, TX	Dallas County	310	379	22.3	5,162	4,779	-7.4
Davenport, IA	Scott County	22	12	-45.5	357	379	6.2
Denver, CO	Denver County	126	69	-45.2	2,829	2,203	-22.1
Des Moines, IA	Polk County	55	39	-29.1	1,110	978	-11.9
Durham, NC	Durham County	12	18	50.0	575	533	-7.3
El Paso, TX	El Paso County	82	68	-17.1	2,108	2,035	-3.5
Erie, PA	Erie County	17	13	-23.5	664	491	-26.1
Eugene, OR	Lane County	29	18	-37.9	1,174	1,025	-12.7
Fargo, ND	Cass County	12	9	-25.0	292	257	-12.0
Fayetteville, NC	Cumberland County	12	12	0.0	838	822	-1.9
Fort Collins, CO	Larimer County	49	29	-40.8	1,077	857	-20.4
Fort Wayne, IN	Allen County	35	19	-45.7	2,101	1,710	-18.6
Fort Worth, TX	Tarrant County	214	177	-17.3	4,694	4,302	-8.4
Gainesville, FL	Alachua County	30	15	-50.0	297	314	5.7
Grand Rapids, MI	Kent County	86	55	-36.0	1,841	1,532	-16.8
Green Bay, WI	Brown County	28	20	-28.6	776	731	-5.8
Greensboro, NC	Guilford County	65	32	-50.8	880	782	-11.1
Honolulu, HI	Honolulu County	54	44	-18.5	1,231	1,057	-14.1
Houston, TX	Harris County	388	300	-22.7	5,462	4,832	-11.5
Huntsville, AL	Madison County	40	35	-12.5	1,425	1,334	-6.4
Indianapolis, IN	Marion County	119	85	-28.6	5,633	4,942	-12.3
Jacksonville, FL	Duval County	137	106	-22.6	3,773	2,917	-22.7
Kansas City, MO	Jackson County	61	45	-26.2	3,110	2,916	-6.2
Lafayette, LA	Lafayette Parish	20	40	100.0	495	516	4.2
Las Vegas, NV	Clark County	408	327	-19.9	10,814	8,554	-20.9
Lexington, KY	Fayette County	40	39	-2.5	1,010	942	-6.7
Lincoln, NE	Lancaster County	22	20	-9.1	804	771	-4.1
Little Rock, AR	Pulaski County	49	23	-53.1	2,456	2,455	0.0
Los Angeles, CA	Los Angeles County	1,456	1,212	-16.8	37,662	29,341	-22.1
Louisville, KY	Jefferson County	66	65	-1.5	3,579	3,353	-6.3
Lubbock, TX	Lubbock County	25	12	-52.0	253	177	-30.0
Madison, WI	Dane County	47	40	-14.9	1,199	991	-17.3
Manchester, NH	Hillsborough County	69	78	13.0	942	750	-20.4
McAllen, TX	Hidalgo County	47	45	-4.3	627	649	3.5
Miami, FL	Miami-Dade County	379	266	-29.8	16,145	14,486	-10.3
Midland, TX	Midland County	8	8	0.0	49	53	8.2

Table continued on next page.

City	Area Covered	Business Filings			Nonbusiness Filings		
		2013	2014	% Chg.	2013	2014	% Chg.
Minneapolis, MN	Hennepin County	106	110	3.8	3,267	2,625	-19.7
Nashville, TN	Davidson County	78	70	-10.3	3,434	3,124	-9.0
New Orleans, LA	Orleans Parish	40	45	12.5	704	674	-4.3
New York, NY	Bronx County	69	43	-37.7	2,389	2,057	-13.9
New York, NY	Kings County	196	140	-28.6	2,790	2,484	-11.0
New York, NY	New York County	248	301	21.4	1,470	1,110	-24.5
New York, NY	Queens County	127	145	14.2	3,719	3,058	-17.8
New York, NY	Richmond County	39	29	-25.6	863	725	-16.0
Oklahoma City, OK	Oklahoma County	56	57	1.8	2,452	2,365	-3.5
Omaha, NE	Douglas County	62	44	-29.0	1,788	1,514	-15.3
Orlando, FL	Orange County	354	192	-45.8	5,776	5,383	-6.8
Oxnard, CA	Ventura County	101	84	-16.8	2,483	1,935	-22.1
Palm Bay, FL	Brevard County	58	49	-15.5	1,992	1,581	-20.6
Peoria, IL	Peoria County	13	8	-38.5	676	631	-6.7
Philadelphia, PA	Philadelphia County	103	89	-13.6	3,129	2,879	-8.0
Phoenix, AZ	Maricopa County	705	545	-22.7	15,679	13,283	-15.3
Pittsburgh, PA	Allegheny County	129	88	-31.8	2,807	2,209	-21.3
Portland, OR	Multnomah County	74	49	-33.8	2,429	2,213	-8.9
Providence, RI	Providence County	70	46	-34.3	2,207	1,830	-17.1
Provo, UT	Utah County	57	43	-24.6	2,083	2,003	-3.8
Raleigh, NC	Wake County	138	110	-20.3	1,927	1,823	-5.4
Reno, NV	Washoe County	87	64	-26.4	1,615	1,454	-10.0
Richmond, VA	Richmond city	11	25	127.3	951	1,009	6.1
Roanoke, VA	Roanoke city	6	5	-16.7	387	307	-20.7
Rochester, MN	Olmsted County	12	2	-83.3	252	224	-11.1
Sacramento, CA	Sacramento County	207	128	-38.2	6,736	5,064	-24.8
Salem, OR	Marion County	25	19	-24.0	1,334	1,219	-8.6
Salt Lake City, UT	Salt Lake County	127	114	-10.2	6,361	5,837	-8.2
San Antonio, TX	Bexar County	157	124	-21.0	2,696	2,497	-7.4
San Diego, CA	San Diego County	467	378	-19.1	11,822	9,544	-19.3
San Francisco, CA	San Francisco County	113	89	-21.2	980	694	-29.2
San Jose, CA	Santa Clara County	199	147	-26.1	4,248	3,173	-25.3
Santa Rosa, CA	Sonoma County	43	48	11.6	1,258	930	-26.1
Savannah, GA	Chatham County	42	24	-42.9	1,517	1,390	-8.4
Seattle, WA	King County	218	185	-15.1	5,624	4,752	-15.5
Sioux Falls, SD	Minnehaha County	25	13	-48.0	391	379	-3.1
Spokane, WA	Spokane County	51	30	-41.2	1,786	1,654	-7.4
Springfield, IL	Sangamon County	20	12	-40.0	649	551	-15.1
Tallahassee, FL	Leon County	53	44	-17.0	441	427	-3.2
Tampa, FL	Hillsborough County	185	206	11.4	4,632	3,876	-16.3
Topeka, KS	Shawnee County	15	7	-53.3	926	854	-7.8
Tulsa, OK	Tulsa County	56	53	-5.4	1,838	1,656	-9.9
Tyler, TX	Smith County	20	14	-30.0	312	307	-1.6
Virginia Beach, VA	Virginia Beach city	40	31	-22.5	1,779	1,712	-3.8
Washington, DC	District of Columbia	67	68	1.5	756	706	-6.6
Wichita, KS	Sedgwick County	74	43	-41.9	1,873	1,597	-14.7
Wilmington, NC	New Hanover County	33	22	-33.3	429	295	-31.2
Winston-Salem, NC	Forsyth County	24	21	-12.5	622	574	-7.7
Worcester, MA	Worcester County	46	52	13.0	1,860	1,561	-16.1
U.S.	U.S.	33,212	26,983	-18.8	1,038,720	909,812	-12.4

Note: Business filings include Chapter 7, Chapter 11, Chapter 12, and Chapter 13; Nonbusiness filings include Chapter 7, Chapter 11, and Chapter 13

Source: Administrative Office of the U.S. Courts, Business and Nonbusiness Bankruptcy, County Cases Commenced by Chapter of the Bankruptcy Code, During the 12- Month Period Ending December 31, 2013 and Business and Nonbusiness Bankruptcy, County Cases Commenced by Chapter of the Bankruptcy Code, During the 12- Month Period Ending December 31, 2014

Income: City

City	Per Capita ($)	Median Household ($)	Average Household ($)
Albuquerque, NM	26,403	46,668	63,418
Anchorage, AK	35,769	76,159	96,249
Ann Arbor, MI	34,905	53,458	77,948
Athens, GA	18,885	31,884	49,581
Atlanta, GA	36,091	46,783	82,895
Austin, TX	32,091	54,331	77,898
Billings, MT	27,024	47,196	64,341
Boise City, ID	27,616	46,757	65,336
Boston, MA	33,565	52,465	80,025
Boulder, CO	37,315	57,012	88,752
Cape Coral, FL	22,251	48,095	59,217
Cedar Rapids, IA	27,993	51,338	66,289
Charleston, SC	32,832	52,066	75,238
Charlotte, NC	31,262	51,271	78,433
Chicago, IL	27,979	46,014	70,505
Clarksville, TN	21,017	46,100	55,585
Colorado Springs, CO	28,854	53,619	72,046
Columbia, MO	26,555	42,945	66,161
Columbus, OH	23,998	43,441	56,932
Dallas, TX	27,380	42,026	69,885
Davenport, IA	23,740	45,323	57,396
Denver, CO	33,654	50,728	75,906
Des Moines, IA	23,359	44,830	57,515
Durham, NC	28,758	48,046	69,050
El Paso, TX	19,895	41,657	58,012
Erie, PA	18,383	32,672	43,093
Eugene, OR	25,688	40,628	59,964
Fargo, ND	29,475	45,227	65,810
Fayetteville, NC	22,842	44,770	55,955
Fort Collins, CO	28,766	53,435	72,215
Fort Wayne, IN	22,911	42,309	55,904
Fort Worth, TX	24,059	51,168	67,578
Gainesville, FL	19,235	31,584	47,358
Grand Rapids, MI	20,358	39,308	51,270
Green Bay, WI	24,054	42,088	57,746
Greensboro, NC	25,496	40,415	60,551
Honolulu, HI	30,378	59,490	77,842
Houston, TX	27,328	44,451	71,474
Huntsville, AL	29,649	47,575	68,995
Indianapolis, IN	23,722	41,154	57,910
Jacksonville, FL	24,870	45,978	62,959
Kansas City, MO	26,546	44,613	61,958
Lafayette, LA	28,454	45,317	67,042
Las Vegas, NV	24,945	48,676	66,092
Lexington, KY	29,203	47,977	70,104
Lincoln, NE	26,047	48,329	64,180
Little Rock, AR	28,976	44,911	68,114
Los Angeles, CA	27,345	47,812	75,509
Louisville, KY	26,043	43,963	62,879
Lubbock, TX	23,537	43,413	60,480
Madison, WI	31,208	51,833	70,350
Manchester, NH	26,965	52,462	63,747
McAllen, TX	21,205	40,651	65,383
Miami, FL	21,416	30,126	52,271
Midland, TX	34,306	63,819	94,266
Minneapolis, MN	31,616	49,777	72,720

Table continued on next page.

City	Per Capita ($)	Median Household ($)	Average Household ($)
Nashville, TN	26,976	45,542	63,645
New Orleans, LA	26,348	35,837	60,632
New York, NY	31,746	51,526	82,008
Oklahoma City, OK	25,085	45,073	63,367
Omaha, NE	26,700	47,275	65,560
Orlando, FL	25,083	42,026	57,912
Oxnard, CA	20,438	59,465	75,180
Palm Bay, FL	20,122	41,540	51,765
Peoria, IL	25,937	42,214	62,309
Philadelphia, PA	21,902	36,222	53,661
Phoenix, AZ	23,367	45,775	63,762
Pittsburgh, PA	27,159	39,527	60,305
Portland, OR	31,812	52,421	73,563
Providence, RI	21,500	36,700	58,248
Provo, UT	16,496	38,542	55,455
Raleigh, NC	30,174	54,088	74,854
Reno, NV	25,716	46,348	62,934
Richmond, VA	26,307	39,469	60,519
Roanoke, VA	23,049	37,710	51,923
Rochester, MN	32,709	62,105	79,970
Sacramento, CA	24,952	48,807	64,943
Salem, OR	22,242	44,773	58,617
Salt Lake City, UT	28,892	45,774	71,057
San Antonio, TX	22,311	45,253	60,746
San Diego, CA	32,658	63,258	86,740
San Francisco, CA	48,861	74,559	110,996
San Jose, CA	34,059	80,609	104,333
Santa Rosa, CA	29,133	58,908	76,326
Savannah, GA	19,928	36,144	49,971
Seattle, WA	42,929	65,454	92,113
Sioux Falls, SD	27,527	51,099	66,919
Spokane, WA	23,781	41,200	55,686
Springfield, IL	28,023	47,571	63,512
Tallahassee, FL	23,752	39,868	57,997
Tampa, FL	28,945	41,927	68,704
Topeka, KS	23,305	40,323	55,106
Tulsa, OK	27,071	41,162	63,845
Tyler, TX	26,733	43,239	66,559
Virginia Beach, VA	31,665	64,771	82,655
Washington, DC	45,851	66,950	102,656
Wichita, KS	24,236	44,532	60,298
Wilmington, NC	29,410	41,724	66,019
Winston-Salem, NC	24,319	38,566	60,142
Worcester, MA	23,935	44,553	60,978
U.S.	27,884	52,176	72,897

Source: U.S. Census Bureau, 2011-2013 American Community Survey 3-Year Estimates

Income: Metro Area

Metro Area	Per Capita ($)	Median Household ($)	Average Household ($)
Albuquerque, NM	25,525	47,754	64,396
Anchorage, AK	34,228	74,830	93,213
Ann Arbor, MI	33,495	58,254	81,651
Athens, GA	21,588	39,291	57,764
Atlanta, GA	28,166	55,295	76,582
Austin, TX	31,255	60,443	82,338
Billings, MT	27,609	50,472	66,897
Boise City, ID	23,630	48,755	63,335
Boston, MA	38,552	72,543	98,859
Boulder, CO	37,871	69,260	93,227
Cape Coral, FL	26,690	46,587	66,302
Cedar Rapids, IA	29,230	56,875	71,523
Charleston, SC	27,162	51,580	68,685
Charlotte, NC	27,924	51,264	72,780
Chicago, IL	30,787	60,140	82,611
Clarksville, TN	21,868	46,183	58,156
Colorado Springs, CO	29,097	57,110	75,630
Columbia, MO	26,893	48,302	67,075
Columbus, OH	28,576	53,914	72,580
Dallas, TX	29,110	57,630	80,048
Davenport, IA	27,302	50,868	65,946
Denver, CO	33,364	62,229	83,895
Des Moines, IA	30,477	60,410	76,654
Durham, NC	30,332	51,565	75,434
El Paso, TX	18,563	40,595	56,031
Erie, PA	24,092	44,639	59,400
Eugene, OR	23,915	41,936	57,134
Fargo, ND	29,135	52,391	69,495
Fayetteville, NC	21,837	44,185	55,886
Fort Collins, CO	30,422	57,316	74,915
Fort Wayne, IN	24,763	48,377	62,511
Fort Worth, TX	29,110	57,630	80,048
Gainesville, FL	24,234	41,211	60,668
Grand Rapids, MI	25,405	52,348	67,685
Green Bay, WI	27,301	52,442	67,946
Greensboro, NC	24,211	42,822	59,885
Honolulu, HI	30,002	71,728	89,208
Houston, TX	28,849	56,889	81,822
Huntsville, AL	29,792	54,838	74,829
Indianapolis, IN	27,356	51,601	70,125
Jacksonville, FL	27,340	51,016	70,192
Kansas City, MO	29,429	55,664	73,931
Lafayette, LA	25,649	46,222	65,919
Las Vegas, NV	25,354	50,498	67,454
Lexington, KY	28,014	49,044	69,062
Lincoln, NE	27,029	51,337	67,656
Little Rock, AR	25,562	48,472	64,010
Los Angeles, CA	28,785	58,569	84,766
Louisville, KY	26,931	50,039	67,010
Lubbock, TX	23,840	44,523	62,415
Madison, WI	32,231	59,981	77,083
Manchester, NH	34,090	69,024	87,185
McAllen, TX	14,274	33,845	49,333
Miami, FL	26,619	46,982	70,524
Midland, TX	33,571	63,581	92,348
Minneapolis, MN	33,687	66,489	85,723

Table continued on next page.

Metro Area	Per Capita ($)	Median Household ($)	Average Household ($)
Nashville, TN	27,929	51,825	71,398
New Orleans, LA	26,502	45,592	65,898
New York, NY	35,258	65,253	95,316
Oklahoma City, OK	26,164	49,552	67,160
Omaha, NE	28,664	55,901	72,996
Orlando, FL	24,095	47,119	64,638
Oxnard, CA	32,489	75,536	97,897
Palm Bay, FL	26,305	47,076	62,678
Peoria, IL	27,894	52,544	68,367
Philadelphia, PA	32,069	60,683	83,695
Phoenix, AZ	26,247	51,923	70,448
Pittsburgh, PA	29,593	51,059	68,999
Portland, OR	29,978	57,732	76,085
Providence, RI	29,778	55,313	74,418
Provo, UT	20,470	60,215	73,641
Raleigh, NC	30,770	61,390	81,319
Reno, NV	28,115	51,916	70,915
Richmond, VA	29,784	57,646	76,580
Roanoke, VA	26,610	48,673	63,727
Rochester, MN	32,088	62,638	80,275
Sacramento, CA	28,234	57,217	76,121
Salem, OR	21,769	46,763	59,174
Salt Lake City, UT	25,911	60,322	76,812
San Antonio, TX	24,742	51,401	68,839
San Diego, CA	30,031	61,382	83,467
San Francisco, CA	41,528	76,767	109,045
San Jose, CA	41,294	90,434	120,427
Santa Rosa, CA	32,554	61,479	83,455
Savannah, GA	25,036	48,852	65,120
Seattle, WA	35,186	66,750	88,361
Sioux Falls, SD	27,867	55,755	70,171
Spokane, WA	24,924	48,116	61,566
Springfield, IL	29,517	54,500	70,117
Tallahassee, FL	24,467	45,683	62,453
Tampa, FL	26,573	45,492	63,858
Topeka, KS	25,376	49,442	62,629
Tulsa, OK	26,110	48,184	65,783
Tyler, TX	24,846	46,436	65,051
Virginia Beach, VA	28,389	57,148	73,663
Washington, DC	42,965	89,605	115,614
Wichita, KS	25,197	49,943	64,352
Wilmington, NC	28,107	48,645	67,933
Winston-Salem, NC	24,548	43,042	60,886
Worcester, MA	30,579	62,221	79,777
U.S.	27,884	52,176	72,897

Note: Figures cover the Metropolitan Statistical Area (MSA)—see Appendix B for areas included
Source: U.S. Census Bureau, 2011-2013 American Community Survey 3-Year Estimates

Household Income Distribution: City

City	Percent of Households Earning							
	Under $15,000	$15,000 -24,999	$25,000 -34,999	$35,000 -49,999	$50,000 -74,999	$75,000 -99,000	$100,000 -149,999	$150,000 and up
Albuquerque, NM	15.2	12.1	11.3	13.9	18.0	11.4	11.4	6.7
Anchorage, AK	5.5	6.2	6.3	12.9	18.1	15.2	19.1	16.7
Ann Arbor, MI	16.5	9.4	9.6	11.8	15.7	10.4	13.9	12.8
Athens, GA	28.6	13.2	11.7	12.4	14.0	8.3	6.6	5.4
Atlanta, GA	20.5	10.8	9.5	11.2	15.1	9.2	10.4	13.3
Austin, TX	12.5	9.5	10.2	14.3	17.7	11.6	13.2	11.0
Billings, MT	14.5	12.3	10.3	15.0	18.4	11.5	11.2	6.7
Boise City, ID	13.7	11.5	12.1	15.5	17.1	11.6	10.6	7.8
Boston, MA	19.8	9.9	7.2	11.1	15.0	10.5	13.5	13.0
Boulder, CO	16.7	9.2	8.9	10.4	14.7	9.8	12.5	17.9
Cape Coral, FL	11.2	11.9	12.8	16.1	21.6	11.7	9.8	5.0
Cedar Rapids, IA	12.2	9.8	11.5	14.8	19.3	13.4	12.5	6.3
Charleston, SC	17.2	9.4	9.3	12.2	17.2	11.6	11.6	11.5
Charlotte, NC	12.4	10.1	11.5	14.8	17.8	10.6	11.9	11.0
Chicago, IL	18.0	11.6	10.6	12.8	16.1	10.4	10.8	9.7
Clarksville, TN	13.4	10.8	12.1	17.6	23.2	11.2	8.7	2.9
Colorado Springs, CO	10.6	11.1	10.5	14.2	18.7	12.8	13.5	8.8
Columbia, MO	19.5	12.2	10.0	13.9	14.7	9.6	11.3	9.0
Columbus, OH	16.8	12.0	11.7	15.5	18.6	10.9	9.8	4.7
Dallas, TX	16.3	13.2	12.4	14.9	16.6	8.5	8.9	9.3
Davenport, IA	14.9	12.2	12.1	15.5	18.1	11.9	11.6	3.6
Denver, CO	14.6	10.4	10.7	13.5	16.6	11.3	11.4	11.4
Des Moines, IA	14.8	11.8	12.1	15.9	20.3	11.8	9.5	4.0
Durham, NC	13.4	12.3	12.3	13.9	17.0	10.9	11.1	9.1
El Paso, TX	17.2	13.7	11.7	15.6	17.3	9.9	9.2	5.4
Erie, PA	22.9	16.7	12.6	16.9	15.2	8.7	5.0	2.0
Eugene, OR	22.0	11.3	11.3	14.0	17.2	8.1	10.0	6.2
Fargo, ND	13.7	11.5	12.8	16.2	18.1	10.7	9.7	7.4
Fayetteville, NC	14.5	11.0	12.7	17.5	20.9	10.7	8.7	4.0
Fort Collins, CO	13.8	11.2	8.6	13.5	17.3	13.1	13.4	9.2
Fort Wayne, IN	15.3	13.0	12.8	16.6	18.8	10.6	9.1	3.8
Fort Worth, TX	13.5	11.0	10.9	13.4	19.3	12.4	12.1	7.4
Gainesville, FL	28.1	12.4	13.4	12.7	15.2	7.8	6.3	4.1
Grand Rapids, MI	18.7	13.4	12.0	17.2	18.3	9.5	7.7	3.1
Green Bay, WI	16.2	11.9	13.3	17.2	19.1	10.4	6.9	4.8
Greensboro, NC	16.3	13.9	13.4	15.3	16.7	9.5	8.7	6.3
Honolulu, HI	11.8	8.3	8.6	13.2	19.8	13.1	14.1	11.3
Houston, TX	15.7	13.1	11.6	14.3	15.9	9.5	9.7	10.2
Huntsville, AL	15.5	11.9	10.2	13.9	15.8	10.6	12.9	9.2
Indianapolis, IN	17.3	13.0	12.5	15.2	17.6	10.4	9.1	4.9
Jacksonville, FL	15.1	11.7	11.5	14.9	18.6	11.0	10.8	6.3
Kansas City, MO	16.6	11.8	11.5	14.7	17.9	10.7	10.4	6.4
Lafayette, LA	18.5	12.4	9.4	14.3	14.6	9.9	12.0	8.9
Las Vegas, NV	12.9	11.3	11.3	15.6	18.8	11.8	11.0	7.3
Lexington, KY	15.6	11.1	10.4	14.4	16.7	10.8	12.1	8.8
Lincoln, NE	13.1	11.0	11.6	15.8	18.5	12.0	11.4	6.6
Little Rock, AR	16.9	13.3	10.4	13.9	15.8	10.0	10.0	9.7
Los Angeles, CA	15.9	12.3	10.4	13.0	15.8	10.2	11.3	11.0
Louisville, KY	16.4	12.8	11.7	14.5	17.4	10.7	9.9	6.6
Lubbock, TX	16.8	12.8	12.2	14.1	17.5	10.9	9.5	6.2
Madison, WI	14.3	10.1	10.3	13.7	18.0	12.0	12.9	8.7
Manchester, NH	13.0	11.1	11.0	12.6	21.0	12.8	13.0	5.3
McAllen, TX	20.0	14.3	10.3	13.5	14.8	9.8	10.2	7.1
Miami, FL	26.9	16.4	12.5	12.8	12.5	6.3	6.6	6.0

Table continued on next page.

City	Percent of Households Earning							
	Under $15,000	$15,000 -24,999	$25,000 -34,999	$35,000 -49,999	$50,000 -74,999	$75,000 -99,000	$100,000 -149,999	$150,000 and up
Midland, TX	8.4	8.7	8.6	12.9	19.2	12.7	15.9	13.5
Minneapolis, MN	17.0	10.7	9.3	13.2	16.3	11.5	12.5	9.7
Nashville, TN	13.8	12.2	12.2	16.0	18.3	11.0	9.8	6.7
New Orleans, LA	24.8	13.8	10.5	12.5	13.7	8.4	8.7	7.6
New York, NY	17.0	10.9	9.1	11.6	15.6	10.7	12.4	12.6
Oklahoma City, OK	14.4	12.0	12.4	15.5	17.7	11.1	10.7	6.3
Omaha, NE	14.0	12.3	11.8	14.3	18.4	11.5	10.6	7.1
Orlando, FL	15.0	14.7	12.8	16.1	18.8	8.6	8.4	5.6
Oxnard, CA	8.0	10.0	8.7	14.9	20.1	14.3	15.1	8.9
Palm Bay, FL	13.6	14.1	14.4	15.6	20.6	11.4	7.6	2.6
Peoria, IL	17.6	13.8	11.2	13.7	15.2	11.5	10.9	6.1
Philadelphia, PA	23.4	13.6	11.7	13.8	15.4	9.0	8.2	5.0
Phoenix, AZ	15.0	12.1	11.4	15.1	17.5	10.9	10.9	7.2
Pittsburgh, PA	20.9	13.1	11.6	13.2	16.8	9.2	8.2	7.0
Portland, OR	14.9	9.7	10.0	13.5	16.7	12.4	13.1	9.7
Providence, RI	25.7	12.7	9.9	12.6	15.4	8.6	8.3	6.7
Provo, UT	18.8	13.8	13.3	15.6	16.9	9.8	7.2	4.6
Raleigh, NC	11.1	8.9	10.9	14.6	19.4	12.2	12.7	10.0
Reno, NV	15.7	13.0	10.6	13.5	18.4	10.5	11.3	7.0
Richmond, VA	21.5	11.8	11.9	14.9	16.2	8.9	8.0	6.8
Roanoke, VA	17.5	15.4	14.0	14.4	19.0	8.9	6.9	3.9
Rochester, MN	9.4	8.6	8.9	13.2	18.9	14.8	15.3	10.9
Sacramento, CA	16.3	11.0	10.3	13.3	18.7	11.2	11.7	7.6
Salem, OR	15.8	11.7	12.0	15.5	18.6	11.3	10.3	4.8
Salt Lake City, UT	16.3	12.2	10.9	13.3	17.6	10.5	9.6	9.5
San Antonio, TX	15.3	12.5	11.6	15.2	18.7	10.3	10.3	6.2
San Diego, CA	10.8	8.8	8.3	12.1	17.0	12.8	15.6	14.7
San Francisco, CA	13.4	8.0	6.7	8.7	13.4	10.4	15.8	23.7
San Jose, CA	8.1	7.2	7.2	10.1	14.7	12.2	18.0	22.5
Santa Rosa, CA	8.6	9.8	9.1	14.8	19.9	12.9	14.5	10.5
Savannah, GA	22.6	14.3	11.5	15.4	17.1	8.2	6.7	4.3
Seattle, WA	12.3	7.5	8.2	11.3	16.4	12.2	15.7	16.5
Sioux Falls, SD	9.7	10.4	12.3	16.5	20.0	13.4	10.9	6.9
Spokane, WA	17.1	13.6	12.6	14.2	18.0	11.7	8.3	4.6
Springfield, IL	16.3	11.1	11.0	14.0	17.9	11.2	11.5	7.0
Tallahassee, FL	22.6	11.9	10.8	14.2	15.3	9.2	9.1	6.8
Tampa, FL	18.8	13.0	11.5	13.1	15.6	8.6	9.5	9.9
Topeka, KS	16.1	13.1	14.3	16.0	18.1	10.2	8.3	4.0
Tulsa, OK	16.7	13.4	12.8	15.1	17.5	8.5	8.7	7.4
Tyler, TX	14.8	14.0	12.0	15.2	17.6	9.5	9.2	7.6
Virginia Beach, VA	7.2	6.7	8.7	13.8	21.6	14.5	16.4	11.2
Washington, DC	15.0	7.6	6.8	10.1	14.5	10.4	15.6	19.9
Wichita, KS	14.2	12.9	12.6	15.0	18.3	11.5	10.2	5.4
Wilmington, NC	17.7	12.9	12.7	13.9	16.9	8.5	9.2	8.0
Winston-Salem, NC	17.9	14.9	13.4	14.3	15.6	8.3	8.7	6.8
Worcester, MA	19.1	12.0	10.3	13.3	17.5	10.3	10.7	6.8
U.S.	13.0	10.9	10.3	13.6	17.9	11.9	12.7	9.6

Source: U.S. Census Bureau, 2011-2013 American Community Survey 3-Year Estimates

Household Income Distribution: Metro Area

Metro Area	Percent of Households Earning							
	Under $15,000	$15,000 -24,999	$25,000 -34,999	$35,000 -49,999	$50,000 -74,999	$75,000 -99,000	$100,000 -149,999	$150,000 and up
Albuquerque, NM	15.0	12.1	11.1	13.6	18.1	11.3	11.6	7.3
Anchorage, AK	6.2	6.7	6.4	12.2	18.6	15.4	19.0	15.5
Ann Arbor, MI	12.6	9.5	9.7	12.4	15.4	11.8	15.3	13.3
Athens, GA	21.7	12.7	11.3	13.2	15.5	10.0	9.2	6.7
Atlanta, GA	11.9	9.8	10.0	13.7	18.5	12.0	13.4	10.7
Austin, TX	10.3	8.7	9.2	13.7	18.1	12.8	15.1	12.2
Billings, MT	13.2	11.4	10.4	14.5	19.1	12.7	12.0	6.8
Boise City, ID	12.3	11.2	11.9	15.6	20.2	12.1	10.4	6.3
Boston, MA	10.7	7.8	7.2	10.1	15.7	12.6	17.5	18.5
Boulder, CO	10.9	8.0	7.8	11.3	15.4	12.2	16.3	18.2
Cape Coral, FL	12.0	12.5	12.6	16.0	18.9	10.7	9.8	7.4
Cedar Rapids, IA	10.0	9.1	10.7	13.5	20.2	14.7	14.3	7.5
Charleston, SC	13.6	10.6	10.1	14.1	19.2	12.4	12.0	8.1
Charlotte, NC	12.5	10.8	10.9	14.6	18.1	11.7	12.0	9.4
Chicago, IL	11.6	9.4	9.1	12.3	17.6	12.8	14.7	12.5
Clarksville, TN	13.6	11.8	12.1	16.2	21.5	11.6	9.0	4.1
Colorado Springs, CO	9.4	10.0	9.8	14.1	19.3	13.4	14.5	9.7
Columbia, MO	16.5	11.5	10.2	13.6	17.1	11.6	11.3	8.2
Columbus, OH	12.4	10.1	10.2	13.8	18.7	12.2	13.4	9.2
Dallas, TX	10.4	9.5	10.1	13.5	18.3	12.1	14.5	11.6
Davenport, IA	12.0	10.7	11.4	15.0	19.8	12.4	12.3	6.5
Denver, CO	9.7	8.5	9.1	12.8	18.4	13.2	15.5	12.8
Des Moines, IA	9.7	8.6	9.7	13.3	19.9	14.4	15.2	9.2
Durham, NC	13.0	11.3	10.6	13.7	17.3	10.9	12.2	11.0
El Paso, TX	17.7	13.9	12.2	15.5	17.4	9.7	8.7	4.9
Erie, PA	15.3	12.5	11.5	15.9	18.5	11.7	9.7	4.8
Eugene, OR	17.5	12.9	11.9	14.7	18.5	10.5	9.2	4.7
Fargo, ND	11.5	10.5	11.6	14.3	19.3	12.6	12.5	7.6
Fayetteville, NC	15.0	12.1	12.5	15.8	19.8	11.4	9.3	4.2
Fort Collins, CO	10.7	10.6	9.7	13.2	18.7	13.4	14.1	9.7
Fort Wayne, IN	11.9	11.4	11.8	16.5	20.4	12.4	10.6	5.0
Fort Worth, TX	10.4	9.5	10.1	13.5	18.3	12.1	14.5	11.6
Gainesville, FL	20.7	11.4	11.9	13.3	16.2	10.3	9.1	7.1
Grand Rapids, MI	10.8	10.7	11.2	14.9	20.7	12.8	12.4	6.5
Green Bay, WI	10.9	10.8	10.8	15.0	20.6	13.4	12.0	6.6
Greensboro, NC	15.3	13.1	12.5	15.2	17.7	10.8	9.7	5.6
Honolulu, HI	8.5	6.3	7.0	11.7	18.9	14.2	19.1	14.5
Houston, TX	11.3	10.2	9.8	13.0	17.2	11.8	13.8	12.9
Huntsville, AL	12.5	9.8	10.2	13.5	16.7	12.1	15.2	10.3
Indianapolis, IN	12.3	10.6	10.7	14.7	18.8	12.4	12.6	7.9
Jacksonville, FL	13.1	10.6	10.6	14.5	19.2	11.7	12.0	8.1
Kansas City, MO	11.3	9.6	10.1	14.1	18.7	13.2	13.9	9.1
Lafayette, LA	16.8	12.5	10.4	13.4	15.8	11.4	11.8	7.9
Las Vegas, NV	11.5	10.7	11.5	15.6	19.9	12.2	11.3	7.2
Lexington, KY	14.8	10.9	11.0	14.1	17.2	11.8	12.4	7.9
Lincoln, NE	12.2	10.3	11.0	15.2	18.8	12.7	12.5	7.2
Little Rock, AR	13.4	12.0	11.2	14.7	18.8	12.1	11.4	6.4
Los Angeles, CA	11.8	10.2	9.1	12.3	16.7	11.8	14.3	13.7
Louisville, KY	13.5	11.3	10.6	14.5	18.9	12.3	11.9	6.9
Lubbock, TX	15.9	12.7	12.0	14.4	17.4	11.0	10.2	6.6
Madison, WI	10.2	8.6	9.7	13.4	19.3	13.8	15.4	9.6
Manchester, NH	8.1	8.3	8.2	11.6	17.4	14.3	18.8	13.4
McAllen, TX	24.0	15.5	11.5	14.2	15.1	8.5	7.7	3.4
Miami, FL	14.9	12.2	11.1	14.1	17.2	10.4	11.1	9.0

Table continued on next page.

Metro Area	Percent of Households Earning Under $15,000	$15,000 -24,999	$25,000 -34,999	$35,000 -49,999	$50,000 -74,999	$75,000 -99,000	$100,000 -149,999	$150,000 and up
Midland, TX	8.0	8.7	9.6	13.3	17.9	13.0	16.3	13.2
Minneapolis, MN	8.8	8.0	8.2	12.2	18.6	14.4	17.1	12.6
Nashville, TN	11.3	10.8	10.9	15.2	19.0	12.4	12.0	8.5
New Orleans, LA	17.1	12.0	11.0	13.3	16.4	10.8	11.3	8.1
New York, NY	12.2	9.0	8.1	10.7	15.5	11.8	15.5	17.2
Oklahoma City, OK	12.9	11.1	11.4	15.0	18.8	12.1	11.6	7.0
Omaha, NE	10.8	9.8	10.2	13.9	19.6	13.4	13.7	8.5
Orlando, FL	12.5	12.0	12.5	15.5	19.0	10.9	10.7	6.8
Oxnard, CA	7.2	7.7	7.1	11.1	16.5	13.6	18.4	18.3
Palm Bay, FL	12.9	11.8	12.3	15.6	19.0	11.1	11.1	6.2
Peoria, IL	11.3	10.8	10.6	14.5	19.0	13.6	13.5	6.6
Philadelphia, PA	12.1	9.3	8.8	12.0	16.9	12.3	15.3	13.3
Phoenix, AZ	11.8	10.7	10.8	14.7	18.7	12.2	12.8	8.5
Pittsburgh, PA	13.2	11.6	10.8	13.3	18.6	12.1	12.3	8.0
Portland, OR	11.0	9.3	9.4	13.6	18.8	13.7	14.5	9.7
Providence, RI	13.6	10.4	9.1	12.6	17.3	12.3	14.4	10.3
Provo, UT	9.4	8.4	9.0	14.5	21.6	15.0	14.5	7.8
Raleigh, NC	9.2	8.2	9.8	13.4	18.4	13.0	15.6	12.3
Reno, NV	12.7	11.5	10.2	13.5	19.2	11.6	13.5	7.8
Richmond, VA	10.9	8.7	9.5	13.9	19.0	12.9	14.8	10.2
Roanoke, VA	12.6	12.2	11.8	14.6	19.7	12.2	10.8	6.2
Rochester, MN	8.9	8.3	9.0	13.5	19.1	15.4	15.4	10.5
Sacramento, CA	11.8	9.8	9.6	13.0	17.9	12.4	14.5	11.0
Salem, OR	13.7	11.6	11.7	15.4	20.2	11.9	10.9	4.4
Salt Lake City, UT	9.0	9.1	9.1	13.6	21.1	14.3	14.4	9.2
San Antonio, TX	12.7	11.0	10.3	14.6	18.9	11.9	12.4	8.1
San Diego, CA	11.1	8.9	9.0	12.4	17.3	12.6	15.2	13.5
San Francisco, CA	9.6	7.6	6.8	9.9	15.1	11.7	17.0	22.3
San Jose, CA	7.2	6.4	6.4	8.9	13.8	11.6	18.6	27.0
Santa Rosa, CA	8.5	10.0	8.7	13.4	18.1	12.6	16.2	12.6
Savannah, GA	14.8	11.3	10.0	14.8	18.2	12.0	11.4	7.5
Seattle, WA	9.4	7.7	8.2	12.1	18.0	13.5	16.9	14.3
Sioux Falls, SD	8.8	9.2	11.3	15.6	20.2	15.4	12.5	7.1
Spokane, WA	14.3	11.7	11.6	14.2	19.3	12.6	10.7	5.7
Springfield, IL	12.7	10.0	9.9	13.8	18.3	13.2	13.9	8.4
Tallahassee, FL	17.5	11.4	10.9	13.9	17.5	11.0	11.0	6.8
Tampa, FL	14.1	12.9	12.0	15.1	18.0	10.7	10.3	7.0
Topeka, KS	12.2	10.9	12.0	15.5	19.7	12.7	11.7	5.3
Tulsa, OK	13.5	11.5	11.4	15.2	19.1	11.3	11.2	6.8
Tyler, TX	13.2	12.5	12.8	14.2	18.4	11.9	10.3	6.7
Virginia Beach, VA	10.3	8.9	9.8	14.2	19.9	13.4	14.6	8.9
Washington, DC	6.4	5.2	5.5	9.2	15.7	13.2	20.0	24.9
Wichita, KS	12.1	11.6	11.2	15.2	19.4	12.6	12.3	5.6
Wilmington, NC	13.8	11.2	11.7	14.6	18.0	11.6	11.8	7.3
Winston-Salem, NC	15.0	13.3	13.0	14.9	17.7	10.5	9.7	5.9
Worcester, MA	10.8	9.7	8.8	11.6	17.1	13.4	16.2	12.4
U.S.	13.0	10.9	10.3	13.6	17.9	11.9	12.7	9.6

Note: Figures cover the Metropolitan Statistical Area (MSA)—see Appendix B for areas included
Source: Source: U.S. Census Bureau, 2011-2013 American Community Survey 3-Year Estimates

Poverty Rate: City

City	All Ages	Under 18 Years Old	18 to 64 Years Old	65 Years and Over
Albuquerque, NM	18.6	26.1	17.9	8.1
Anchorage, AK	7.7	10.6	7.0	4.2
Ann Arbor, MI	24.1	13.7	28.9	6.1
Athens, GA	36.9	37.0	40.2	11.6
Atlanta, GA	25.4	38.7	22.9	16.9
Austin, TX	19.0	26.6	17.7	8.9
Billings, MT	15.2	19.6	14.8	10.2
Boise City, ID	15.9	18.9	16.6	6.3
Boston, MA	22.1	30.3	20.5	19.7
Boulder, CO	23.8	8.8	29.2	6.0
Cape Coral, FL	14.9	21.3	14.6	7.9
Cedar Rapids, IA	12.4	14.4	12.9	6.5
Charleston, SC	20.1	26.0	20.4	10.1
Charlotte, NC	17.7	24.4	16.2	9.8
Chicago, IL	23.5	35.0	20.6	17.6
Clarksville, TN	18.1	26.7	15.5	7.9
Colorado Springs, CO	14.1	19.1	13.3	8.2
Columbia, MO	25.1	20.5	28.8	6.2
Columbus, OH	22.5	33.0	20.4	10.6
Dallas, TX	24.4	38.1	20.2	15.9
Davenport, IA	17.8	26.9	16.1	8.5
Denver, CO	18.7	28.3	16.9	11.2
Des Moines, IA	20.0	30.6	17.8	8.3
Durham, NC	20.6	27.6	19.6	11.0
El Paso, TX	21.7	30.4	18.3	18.6
Erie, PA	28.1	43.7	25.4	13.9
Eugene, OR	26.7	23.9	31.0	8.7
Fargo, ND	16.7	15.6	18.4	6.9
Fayetteville, NC	18.2	26.1	16.2	10.4
Fort Collins, CO	18.5	11.4	22.2	6.1
Fort Wayne, IN	20.5	31.0	18.5	8.2
Fort Worth, TX	20.1	27.8	17.4	12.9
Gainesville, FL	36.4	30.7	40.3	10.8
Grand Rapids, MI	27.1	37.4	26.1	9.9
Green Bay, WI	18.5	26.4	16.6	12.9
Greensboro, NC	20.4	27.1	19.8	11.0
Honolulu, HI	12.3	16.8	11.9	9.4
Houston, TX	23.3	36.3	19.5	14.4
Huntsville, AL	17.6	26.5	17.0	6.8
Indianapolis, IN	21.6	32.4	19.3	10.6
Jacksonville, FL	18.0	26.5	16.2	10.2
Kansas City, MO	19.8	30.0	17.9	9.8
Lafayette, LA	19.1	26.4	18.4	9.9
Las Vegas, NV	18.6	27.1	17.0	9.9
Lexington, KY	18.5	21.8	19.2	8.2
Lincoln, NE	16.3	19.8	16.9	5.7
Little Rock, AR	18.5	26.9	17.4	8.0
Los Angeles, CA	22.9	33.5	20.5	16.3
Louisville, KY	18.9	27.9	17.3	10.1
Lubbock, TX	21.4	26.8	21.7	7.7
Madison, WI	20.2	22.7	21.7	4.4
Manchester, NH	15.4	23.9	14.0	9.1
McAllen, TX	28.0	36.0	24.5	26.9
Miami, FL	30.3	44.9	25.8	31.8
Midland, TX	10.3	15.0	8.2	10.4

Table continued on next page.

City	All Ages	Under 18 Years Old	18 to 64 Years Old	65 Years and Over
Minneapolis, MN	22.4	30.1	21.1	14.6
Nashville, TN	19.0	30.9	16.6	8.9
New Orleans, LA	28.1	41.5	25.9	16.7
New York, NY	21.0	30.3	18.4	19.0
Oklahoma City, OK	18.9	28.3	16.9	8.3
Omaha, NE	17.6	25.3	16.1	8.8
Orlando, FL	20.9	33.8	17.5	15.0
Oxnard, CA	17.1	26.7	14.0	9.0
Palm Bay, FL	19.3	32.6	17.6	7.2
Peoria, IL	24.9	37.7	22.7	9.8
Philadelphia, PA	27.2	37.5	25.4	17.3
Phoenix, AZ	23.4	34.1	20.7	11.1
Pittsburgh, PA	22.8	31.8	22.5	13.4
Portland, OR	18.5	23.7	18.3	10.9
Providence, RI	31.1	43.2	28.2	19.4
Provo, UT	31.7	29.4	34.6	7.8
Raleigh, NC	16.1	23.0	14.8	7.2
Reno, NV	18.5	23.2	18.3	11.0
Richmond, VA	26.2	40.1	24.0	15.9
Roanoke, VA	21.7	32.1	20.7	10.4
Rochester, MN	10.1	10.7	10.5	6.8
Sacramento, CA	23.2	33.6	21.3	12.1
Salem, OR	20.5	29.5	18.9	10.2
Salt Lake City, UT	20.2	25.3	19.6	12.3
San Antonio, TX	20.5	29.5	18.1	12.8
San Diego, CA	15.7	21.7	14.8	9.5
San Francisco, CA	14.2	14.0	14.1	15.2
San Jose, CA	12.6	15.3	11.8	10.8
Santa Rosa, CA	13.2	17.7	12.8	7.0
Savannah, GA	26.7	41.8	24.3	11.5
Seattle, WA	14.4	15.9	14.1	14.6
Sioux Falls, SD	11.6	15.7	10.6	7.6
Spokane, WA	19.5	23.3	20.2	10.5
Springfield, IL	19.7	29.6	19.0	7.6
Tallahassee, FL	29.8	27.1	33.0	8.7
Tampa, FL	22.7	31.9	20.6	17.6
Topeka, KS	20.6	29.0	20.2	8.0
Tulsa, OK	20.1	31.0	18.0	9.5
Tyler, TX	20.8	29.9	19.5	11.6
Virginia Beach, VA	8.7	13.7	7.4	5.8
Washington, DC	18.8	28.5	17.1	14.0
Wichita, KS	18.3	26.8	16.4	8.7
Wilmington, NC	22.0	30.5	22.8	7.5
Winston-Salem, NC	25.7	39.9	23.4	9.3
Worcester, MA	23.3	33.9	21.1	14.9
U.S.	15.9	22.4	14.8	9.5

Note: Figures are percentage of people whose income during the past 12 months was below the poverty level
Source: U.S. Census Bureau, 2011-2013 American Community Survey 3-Year Estimates

Poverty Rate: Metro Area

Metro Area	All Ages	Under 18 Years Old	18 to 64 Years Old	65 Years and Over
Albuquerque, NM	19.3	27.2	18.2	9.9
Anchorage, AK	8.2	11.1	7.5	4.3
Ann Arbor, MI	16.6	16.5	18.4	6.0
Athens, GA	27.0	26.1	30.1	10.1
Atlanta, GA	16.3	23.0	14.6	9.6
Austin, TX	15.0	19.4	14.4	6.8
Billings, MT	12.8	16.3	12.4	9.1
Boise City, ID	16.2	20.7	15.7	8.9
Boston, MA	10.6	13.2	10.0	8.9
Boulder, CO	14.5	13.2	16.3	5.9
Cape Coral, FL	16.0	27.1	16.3	6.8
Cedar Rapids, IA	10.0	11.7	10.1	6.6
Charleston, SC	16.1	23.1	14.9	8.9
Charlotte, NC	15.5	21.4	14.3	9.0
Chicago, IL	14.5	20.9	13.0	9.4
Clarksville, TN	17.8	25.8	15.5	8.8
Colorado Springs, CO	12.1	16.1	11.4	7.3
Columbia, MO	20.1	17.9	22.7	6.9
Columbus, OH	15.2	21.2	14.2	7.3
Dallas, TX	15.1	21.8	13.1	9.1
Davenport, IA	13.0	20.2	12.0	6.5
Denver, CO	12.6	17.6	11.5	7.3
Des Moines, IA	11.5	15.3	10.8	6.7
Durham, NC	17.9	23.2	18.0	7.5
El Paso, TX	23.6	32.7	19.8	19.4
Erie, PA	17.0	26.0	15.6	9.3
Eugene, OR	22.0	25.2	24.4	8.5
Fargo, ND	13.0	12.4	14.3	6.3
Fayetteville, NC	18.1	25.7	16.0	10.9
Fort Collins, CO	14.0	13.0	16.1	5.0
Fort Wayne, IN	15.9	24.3	14.3	6.5
Fort Worth, TX	15.1	21.8	13.1	9.1
Gainesville, FL	25.5	25.1	28.4	9.8
Grand Rapids, MI	14.2	18.9	13.9	6.4
Green Bay, WI	11.4	15.2	10.3	9.0
Greensboro, NC	18.7	26.2	17.8	10.1
Honolulu, HI	9.9	13.5	9.3	7.2
Houston, TX	16.8	24.7	14.3	10.5
Huntsville, AL	13.6	19.1	12.8	7.6
Indianapolis, IN	14.7	20.8	13.5	7.5
Jacksonville, FL	15.2	21.2	14.3	8.4
Kansas City, MO	12.9	18.5	11.9	6.5
Lafayette, LA	17.6	23.7	15.9	13.1
Las Vegas, NV	16.3	23.5	15.0	9.2
Lexington, KY	16.9	20.8	17.0	8.5
Lincoln, NE	14.7	17.5	15.4	5.6
Little Rock, AR	15.1	20.7	14.4	7.6
Los Angeles, CA	17.4	24.7	15.7	12.2
Louisville, KY	15.1	21.9	13.9	8.8
Lubbock, TX	20.3	26.5	20.2	7.7
Madison, WI	12.8	14.9	13.3	5.4
Manchester, NH	9.3	13.2	8.5	5.9
McAllen, TX	35.5	46.7	30.2	26.5
Miami, FL	17.7	24.6	16.0	15.2
Midland, TX	9.5	13.0	8.0	9.4

Table continued on next page.

Metro Area	All Ages	Under 18 Years Old	18 to 64 Years Old	65 Years and Over
Minneapolis, MN	10.7	13.9	10.1	7.1
Nashville, TN	14.3	20.8	13.0	8.0
New Orleans, LA	19.4	28.3	17.7	12.1
New York, NY	14.5	20.5	13.0	11.8
Oklahoma City, OK	15.8	22.0	14.9	8.0
Omaha, NE	12.7	17.8	11.4	7.7
Orlando, FL	16.6	24.0	15.4	9.6
Oxnard, CA	11.6	17.4	10.3	7.0
Palm Bay, FL	14.6	22.8	14.5	7.4
Peoria, IL	13.9	20.7	13.0	6.8
Philadelphia, PA	13.4	18.2	12.7	9.0
Phoenix, AZ	17.4	25.2	16.1	8.0
Pittsburgh, PA	12.5	18.1	12.0	8.0
Portland, OR	14.2	18.5	13.8	8.0
Providence, RI	13.9	19.8	12.8	9.9
Provo, UT	14.1	12.9	15.8	5.5
Raleigh, NC	12.3	17.2	11.1	7.2
Reno, NV	15.5	21.3	15.0	8.2
Richmond, VA	12.6	17.4	12.0	7.6
Roanoke, VA	13.7	19.4	13.2	8.2
Rochester, MN	9.0	10.4	8.7	7.6
Sacramento, CA	16.5	22.0	15.9	8.9
Salem, OR	19.7	29.1	18.6	7.5
Salt Lake City, UT	13.1	17.2	12.1	6.8
San Antonio, TX	16.8	24.2	14.9	10.6
San Diego, CA	15.1	19.4	14.6	9.3
San Francisco, CA	11.7	14.1	11.5	9.0
San Jose, CA	10.6	12.6	10.1	9.0
Santa Rosa, CA	12.2	16.1	12.4	6.3
Savannah, GA	17.9	27.1	16.3	8.6
Seattle, WA	12.0	15.9	11.3	8.8
Sioux Falls, SD	9.8	12.7	9.0	7.8
Spokane, WA	16.0	19.3	16.6	8.1
Springfield, IL	15.8	24.6	14.6	6.6
Tallahassee, FL	22.3	25.1	23.7	8.5
Tampa, FL	16.1	23.2	15.6	9.4
Topeka, KS	14.5	20.1	14.3	6.3
Tulsa, OK	15.0	21.9	13.6	8.6
Tyler, TX	17.4	24.3	15.9	11.3
Virginia Beach, VA	12.7	18.9	11.4	7.0
Washington, DC	8.4	10.9	7.8	7.1
Wichita, KS	15.1	21.8	13.6	7.9
Wilmington, NC	18.0	24.6	18.0	8.7
Winston-Salem, NC	18.8	29.0	17.2	9.4
Worcester, MA	12.1	16.8	11.2	8.5
U.S.	15.9	22.4	14.8	9.5

Note: Figures are percentage of people whose income during the past 12 months was below the poverty level; Figures cover the Metropolitan Statistical Area—see Appendix B for areas included
Source: U.S. Census Bureau, 2011-2013 American Community Survey 3-Year Estimates

Employment by Industry

Metro Area[1]	(A)	(B)	(C)	(D)	(E)	(F)	(G)	(H)	(I)	(J)	(K)	(L)	(M)	(N)
Albuquerque, NM	5.6	n/a	16.0	4.7	21.7	2.0	10.4	4.3	n/a	3.1	15.0	11.5	2.7	3.1
Anchorage, AK	n/a	5.5	16.5	4.7	20.0	2.5	10.5	1.3	2.1	3.9	11.6	12.3	6.3	2.7
Ann Arbor, MI	1.7	n/a	12.4	3.6	38.1	2.3	7.0	6.6	n/a	3.1	13.1	8.0	1.6	2.4
Athens, GA	n/a	n/a	n/a	n/a	33.1	n/a	10.5	n/a	n/a	n/a	7.7	11.3	n/a	n/a
Atlanta, GA	n/a	4.0	12.2	6.4	12.8	3.5	10.3	6.0	0.1	3.8	18.4	11.1	5.5	6.1
Austin, TX	5.4	n/a	11.8	5.7	18.4	2.8	11.4	6.2	n/a	4.3	16.4	10.9	1.8	5.0
Billings, MT	n/a	n/a	17.0	n/a	11.7	n/a	12.5	n/a	n/a	n/a	10.4	n/a	n/a	n/a
Boise City, ID	6.2	n/a	15.1	5.6	15.9	1.5	9.2	8.7	n/a	3.6	14.1	12.2	3.2	4.7
Boston, MA[4]	3.3	n/a	22.6	8.1	11.4	3.2	9.6	4.7	n/a	3.8	19.0	8.6	2.3	3.3
Boulder, CO	2.8	n/a	12.9	4.2	20.0	4.6	10.3	9.9	n/a	3.2	18.2	9.7	1.0	3.1
Cape Coral, FL	8.9	n/a	11.4	4.9	16.8	1.3	16.4	2.2	n/a	4.1	12.7	16.5	2.0	2.9
Cedar Rapids, IA	5.6	n/a	14.2	7.6	11.8	3.3	8.0	14.3	n/a	3.7	9.0	12.0	6.5	4.0
Charleston, SC	4.9	n/a	11.4	4.2	19.2	1.6	12.7	7.7	n/a	4.1	15.3	12.3	4.2	2.5
Charlotte, NC	5.0	n/a	10.3	7.6	14.1	2.3	10.9	9.2	n/a	3.4	16.3	11.6	4.3	5.0
Chicago, IL[2]	n/a	3.1	15.7	6.8	11.7	2.0	9.4	7.7	<0.1	4.3	18.6	10.2	5.2	5.3
Clarksville, TN	3.6	n/a	13.0	3.5	22.7	1.3	12.4	11.3	n/a	3.4	10.4	13.2	2.7	n/a
Colorado Springs, CO	5.3	n/a	13.1	6.1	18.6	2.6	12.2	4.5	n/a	5.9	15.8	12.1	1.8	2.0
Columbia, MO	n/a	n/a	n/a	n/a	31.5	n/a	n/a	n/a	n/a	n/a	n/a	11.9	n/a	n/a
Columbus, OH	3.5	n/a	14.4	7.3	16.2	1.7	9.5	6.7	n/a	3.8	17.5	10.4	4.9	4.2
Dallas, TX[2]	5.4	n/a	12.2	9.1	11.8	2.9	9.6	7.0	n/a	3.3	18.6	10.1	3.8	6.2
Davenport, IA	n/a	n/a	n/a	n/a	n/a	n/a	n/a	n/a	n/a	n/a	n/a	n/a	n/a	n/a
Denver, CO	6.9	n/a	12.6	7.2	13.9	3.2	10.8	4.8	n/a	3.9	17.8	9.9	3.9	5.0
Des Moines, IA	5.0	n/a	13.6	15.7	12.9	1.9	8.3	5.7	n/a	4.0	13.1	11.5	3.1	5.2
Durham, NC	2.3	n/a	20.3	4.7	22.8	1.4	8.8	10.3	n/a	3.5	12.5	8.7	1.5	3.3
El Paso, TX	4.2	n/a	14.0	4.0	23.2	2.0	10.9	5.7	n/a	3.2	10.7	13.7	4.8	3.7
Erie, PA	3.1	n/a	21.7	4.9	12.3	0.9	10.3	17.0	n/a	4.6	7.7	12.2	2.5	2.8
Eugene, OR	n/a	3.7	15.7	4.8	20.3	2.3	10.0	8.6	0.6	3.2	10.2	14.2	2.4	4.0
Fargo, ND	5.8	n/a	15.3	7.5	13.5	2.3	10.4	7.3	n/a	3.8	11.3	12.4	3.7	6.6
Fayetteville, NC	3.5	n/a	11.4	3.0	31.0	1.1	12.0	6.1	n/a	3.6	9.6	13.3	3.6	1.9
Fort Collins, CO	6.5	n/a	10.2	4.2	24.2	1.7	12.4	8.4	n/a	3.7	12.8	11.4	2.0	2.6
Fort Wayne, IN	4.3	n/a	18.2	5.4	10.2	1.4	9.0	16.3	n/a	5.2	9.9	10.7	4.2	5.1
Fort Worth, TX[2]	7.3	n/a	12.6	5.7	13.3	1.3	10.8	9.7	n/a	3.7	11.6	11.6	7.6	4.8
Gainesville, FL	3.3	n/a	18.0	4.6	31.4	1.1	10.8	3.2	n/a	3.2	9.6	10.7	2.1	2.1
Grand Rapids, MI	3.6	n/a	16.3	4.8	8.9	1.0	8.5	20.0	n/a	4.1	15.1	9.4	2.7	5.6
Green Bay, WI	4.0	n/a	13.4	7.0	12.6	1.3	9.5	16.7	n/a	4.6	11.5	10.3	4.6	4.5
Greensboro, NC	3.7	n/a	13.8	5.0	12.9	1.4	9.1	15.1	n/a	3.6	14.6	10.8	4.7	5.2
Honolulu, HI	5.2	n/a	13.4	4.5	21.4	1.6	14.6	2.4	n/a	4.5	14.2	10.6	4.7	3.1
Houston, TX	n/a	7.0	12.0	5.0	12.8	1.1	9.7	8.6	3.9	3.5	15.7	10.3	4.6	5.8
Huntsville, AL	3.6	n/a	9.4	2.8	22.5	1.2	8.6	10.7	n/a	3.2	22.6	11.4	1.4	2.7
Indianapolis, IN	n/a	4.3	14.4	6.2	12.8	1.7	9.9	9.0	0.1	4.4	15.6	11.0	6.2	4.7
Jacksonville, FL	n/a	5.2	14.9	9.7	11.9	1.4	12.0	4.4	0.1	3.5	15.8	12.2	5.2	3.7
Kansas City, MO	4.3	n/a	13.7	7.2	14.2	2.8	9.7	7.0	n/a	4.0	16.7	10.7	4.5	5.1
Lafayette, LA	n/a	4.9	13.3	5.6	11.9	1.3	9.6	9.1	10.3	3.1	10.4	12.9	3.1	4.6
Las Vegas, NV	n/a	5.4	9.3	4.9	10.9	1.1	31.1	2.4	<0.1	2.9	13.1	12.1	4.3	2.4
Lexington, KY	4.0	n/a	12.7	3.5	18.9	2.1	10.6	11.4	n/a	3.3	14.6	11.3	4.0	3.6
Lincoln, NE	4.1	n/a	15.8	7.9	21.6	1.4	9.2	7.6	n/a	3.7	9.7	11.0	5.9	2.1
Little Rock, AR	4.9	n/a	14.8	5.9	20.5	1.9	9.2	5.8	n/a	4.6	12.7	11.2	4.1	4.3
Los Angeles, CA[2]	n/a	2.8	17.8	4.9	13.2	4.6	10.9	8.4	0.1	3.5	14.3	10.1	3.9	5.3
Louisville, KY	4.4	n/a	13.3	7.1	12.5	1.5	10.2	11.6	n/a	3.8	13.2	10.3	7.6	4.4
Lubbock, TX	4.5	n/a	16.0	5.5	21.1	2.7	12.4	3.5	n/a	4.0	7.9	13.4	3.8	5.0
Madison, WI	3.8	n/a	11.7	6.0	22.9	3.8	8.3	8.8	n/a	4.8	12.5	11.0	2.4	3.9
Manchester, NH[3]	4.5	n/a	19.8	7.2	10.9	2.7	8.3	7.1	n/a	4.7	14.8	12.9	2.6	4.5
McAllen, TX	4.0	n/a	26.3	3.6	22.7	0.9	8.8	2.5	n/a	2.5	6.3	15.7	3.4	3.2
Miami, FL[2]	n/a	3.3	15.4	6.9	12.5	1.7	11.9	3.4	<0.1	4.5	14.1	13.5	6.0	6.6
Midland, TX	30.2	n/a	7.1	4.7	9.6	0.9	9.0	4.1	n/a	3.2	9.9	10.3	4.7	6.3
Minneapolis, MN	3.6	n/a	16.0	7.6	13.0	2.1	8.9	10.1	n/a	4.2	16.0	9.8	3.6	5.1

Table continued on next page.

Metro Area[1]	(A)	(B)	(C)	(D)	(E)	(F)	(G)	(H)	(I)	(J)	(K)	(L)	(M)	(N)
Nashville, TN	4.1	n/a	15.4	6.3	12.7	2.3	10.6	8.9	n/a	4.2	15.4	10.8	4.6	4.8
New Orleans, LA	n/a	5.2	16.0	4.9	13.0	1.5	14.7	5.3	1.4	4.1	13.1	11.6	5.1	4.2
New York, NY[2]	3.5	n/a	19.7	8.9	13.5	3.5	9.3	3.1	n/a	4.3	16.0	10.4	3.6	4.2
Oklahoma City, OK	n/a	4.4	14.3	5.3	20.4	1.3	10.2	6.0	3.4	3.6	13.1	10.9	2.7	4.4
Omaha, NE	5.0	n/a	16.1	8.8	13.5	2.3	9.4	6.5	n/a	3.6	14.6	11.0	5.7	3.6
Orlando, FL	n/a	5.1	12.1	6.3	10.5	2.1	20.9	3.5	<0.1	3.3	16.4	12.7	3.1	3.9
Oxnard, CA	n/a	4.6	13.8	6.2	15.1	1.9	11.9	10.2	0.4	3.3	12.2	13.9	2.2	4.4
Palm Bay, FL	5.0	n/a	16.8	3.7	14.2	0.9	12.2	10.0	n/a	4.0	15.0	13.5	1.7	2.7
Peoria, IL	4.4	n/a	19.3	4.3	11.9	1.2	9.7	15.0	n/a	4.4	11.2	10.4	4.1	4.1
Philadelphia, PA[2]	2.3	n/a	29.7	6.3	13.9	1.5	9.7	3.9	n/a	4.4	13.2	8.4	3.9	2.7
Phoenix, AZ	n/a	5.1	14.6	8.7	12.7	1.8	10.6	6.1	0.2	3.5	16.8	12.3	3.6	4.1
Pittsburgh, PA	n/a	4.6	20.9	5.9	10.3	1.6	9.5	7.7	1.1	4.4	14.8	11.5	4.0	3.8
Portland, OR	n/a	4.9	14.6	5.9	13.7	2.2	9.9	10.9	0.1	3.5	15.1	10.8	3.5	5.0
Providence, RI[3]	n/a	3.6	22.0	6.1	12.6	1.8	10.8	9.1	<0.1	4.7	11.7	11.4	2.5	3.6
Provo, UT	7.6	n/a	21.9	3.1	13.7	4.6	8.1	8.5	n/a	2.2	13.4	12.6	1.5	2.9
Raleigh, NC	5.7	n/a	11.7	4.7	16.4	3.3	11.1	5.5	n/a	4.1	19.8	11.5	2.1	4.0
Reno, NV	n/a	5.3	11.6	4.7	14.4	1.0	17.2	6.3	0.1	2.8	13.8	11.0	7.4	4.5
Richmond, VA	5.2	n/a	14.4	7.7	17.4	1.2	9.2	4.8	n/a	4.8	15.8	11.8	3.3	4.3
Roanoke, VA	5.0	n/a	16.4	5.2	13.9	1.0	8.4	10.3	n/a	4.7	13.3	11.4	5.7	4.5
Rochester, MN	3.4	n/a	39.5	2.4	11.2	1.7	8.4	9.4	n/a	3.2	5.1	10.8	2.7	2.3
Sacramento, CA	n/a	5.0	15.1	5.5	25.3	1.5	10.1	3.9	0.1	3.4	13.4	11.4	2.7	2.7
Salem, OR	n/a	5.1	15.9	4.7	27.6	0.7	8.9	7.6	0.8	3.5	8.3	11.8	2.6	2.6
Salt Lake City, UT	5.3	n/a	11.2	7.9	15.7	2.8	8.2	8.0	n/a	3.0	17.3	10.9	4.9	4.7
San Antonio, TX	n/a	4.9	15.5	8.6	17.2	2.3	11.9	4.7	0.9	3.6	12.8	11.5	2.7	3.5
San Diego, CA	n/a	4.6	13.9	5.1	17.2	1.8	13.0	7.1	<0.1	3.9	17.2	11.1	2.0	3.2
San Francisco, CA[2]	n/a	3.4	12.6	7.0	11.8	5.4	13.1	3.5	<0.1	3.9	24.8	8.1	3.9	2.5
San Jose, CA	n/a	3.9	14.8	3.5	9.3	6.8	8.9	15.6	<0.1	2.5	20.7	8.8	1.6	3.6
Santa Rosa, CA	n/a	5.3	16.8	3.9	16.4	1.4	12.5	10.4	0.2	3.5	10.3	13.0	2.3	4.1
Savannah, GA	3.6	n/a	14.5	3.8	13.9	1.2	14.4	9.8	n/a	4.3	12.1	12.2	6.5	3.9
Seattle, WA[2]	n/a	5.2	12.9	5.5	13.3	5.8	9.4	10.7	<0.1	3.6	14.9	10.9	3.2	4.5
Sioux Falls, SD	4.9	n/a	20.4	10.9	9.1	1.8	9.1	9.4	n/a	3.2	9.0	13.0	3.7	5.5
Spokane, WA	4.6	n/a	20.8	6.1	17.1	1.3	9.0	7.2	n/a	4.1	10.2	12.2	3.0	4.4
Springfield, IL	3.6	n/a	18.2	6.3	26.9	1.5	9.5	2.7	n/a	5.7	9.3	11.1	2.0	3.1
Tallahassee, FL	3.6	n/a	11.9	4.1	35.2	2.2	10.8	1.6	n/a	5.3	11.3	11.1	1.1	1.9
Tampa, FL	n/a	4.8	15.6	8.4	12.6	2.1	11.5	5.0	<0.1	3.7	16.7	13.0	2.4	4.1
Topeka, KS	5.2	n/a	16.3	6.7	24.4	1.3	7.5	6.4	n/a	3.8	11.4	10.0	3.9	3.0
Tulsa, OK	n/a	5.0	15.5	5.1	13.4	1.7	9.0	11.7	1.8	3.8	13.5	11.3	4.7	3.6
Tyler, TX	6.5	n/a	22.7	4.4	13.4	2.3	11.0	5.6	n/a	4.0	9.0	13.2	4.5	3.3
Virginia Beach, VA	4.5	n/a	13.8	5.0	20.7	1.5	10.9	7.3	n/a	4.8	13.8	11.9	3.2	2.7
Washington, DC[2]	4.5	n/a	12.8	4.4	22.9	2.5	9.6	1.3	n/a	6.3	22.7	8.7	2.4	2.0
Wichita, KS	5.5	n/a	15.6	3.7	13.5	1.5	10.2	17.7	n/a	3.2	11.4	11.2	3.3	3.1
Wilmington, NC	5.4	n/a	12.0	4.9	19.2	2.4	14.8	4.9	n/a	3.9	12.5	14.2	2.4	3.4
Winston-Salem, NC	3.5	n/a	20.5	5.0	12.7	0.9	9.6	12.0	n/a	3.7	13.7	11.1	3.9	3.4
Worcester, MA[3]	3.3	n/a	23.3	5.1	15.8	1.2	8.4	9.8	n/a	3.7	9.7	11.3	4.5	3.8
U.S.	5.0	4.4	15.5	5.7	15.8	2.0	10.3	8.7	0.6	4.0	13.8	11.4	3.9	4.2

Note: All figures are percentages covering non-farm employment as of December 2014 and are not seasonally adjusted; (1) Figures cover the Metropolitan Statistical Area (MSA) except where noted. See Appendix B for areas included; (2) Metropolitan Division; (3) New England City and Town Area; (4) New England City and Town Area Division; (A) Construction, Mining, and Logging (some areas report Construction separate from Mining and Logging); (B) Construction; (C) Education and Health Services; (D) Financial Activities; (E) Government; (F) Information; (G) Leisure and Hospitality; (H) Manufacturing; (I) Mining and Logging; (J) Other Services; (K) Professional and Business Services; (L) Retail Trade; (M) Transportation and Utilities; (N) Wholesale Trade; n/a not available
Source: Bureau of Labor Statistics, Current Employment Statistics, Employment, Hours, and Earnings

Labor Force, Employment and Job Growth: City

City	Civilian Labor Force			Workers Employed		
	Dec. 2013	Dec. 2014	% Chg.	Dec. 2013	Dec. 2014	% Chg.
Albuquerque, NM	269,058	268,681	-0.1	253,374	255,366	0.8
Anchorage, AK	161,364	162,186	0.5	153,539	154,675	0.7
Ann Arbor, MI	61,458	62,527	1.7	58,959	60,807	3.1
Athens, GA	58,098	58,233	0.2	54,164	54,791	1.2
Atlanta, GA	230,075	232,034	0.9	211,965	215,889	1.9
Austin, TX	520,901	531,265	2.0	501,106	515,399	2.9
Billings, MT	56,312	56,686	0.7	54,003	54,802	1.5
Boise City, ID	115,170	115,344	0.2	110,221	111,964	1.6
Boston, MA	349,305	356,708	2.1	330,598	340,962	3.1
Boulder, CO	59,422	59,883	0.8	56,735	58,038	2.3
Cape Coral, FL	80,176	82,969	3.5	75,135	78,825	4.9
Cedar Rapids, IA	71,883	71,495	-0.5	68,424	68,269	-0.2
Charleston, SC	66,385	68,271	2.8	63,572	65,182	2.5
Charlotte, NC	421,260	425,392	1.0	398,670	408,035	2.3
Chicago, IL	1,358,761	1,361,612	0.2	1,237,219	1,278,994	3.4
Clarksville, TN	56,955	56,613	-0.6	53,150	53,062	-0.2
Colorado Springs, CO	215,051	214,044	-0.5	200,273	203,493	1.6
Columbia, MO	65,992	67,687	2.6	63,612	65,689	3.3
Columbus, OH	435,341	440,795	1.3	412,078	424,206	2.9
Dallas, TX	628,877	644,851	2.5	594,858	618,008	3.9
Davenport, IA	51,448	51,607	0.3	48,411	48,548	0.3
Denver, CO	364,755	371,168	1.8	343,595	356,126	3.6
Des Moines, IA	111,116	113,143	1.8	104,874	107,217	2.2
Durham, NC	127,698	128,389	0.5	121,870	123,469	1.3
El Paso, TX	291,236	288,097	-1.1	272,823	274,124	0.5
Erie, PA	45,629	45,264	-0.8	42,213	42,773	1.3
Eugene, OR	77,207	78,708	1.9	72,364	74,184	2.5
Fargo, ND	63,513	65,858	3.7	61,885	64,193	3.7
Fayetteville, NC	74,063	72,860	-1.6	69,330	69,164	-0.2
Fort Collins, CO	86,406	87,583	1.4	82,460	84,643	2.6
Fort Wayne, IN	119,899	120,503	0.5	112,064	113,482	1.3
Fort Worth, TX	386,122	393,410	1.9	366,908	377,987	3.0
Gainesville, FL	63,864	65,155	2.0	60,490	62,150	2.7
Grand Rapids, MI	97,774	99,110	1.4	90,984	94,402	3.8
Green Bay, WI	55,640	55,446	-0.3	51,059	52,867	3.5
Greensboro, NC	137,883	137,084	-0.6	129,397	130,458	0.8
Honolulu, HI	460,385	469,161	1.9	442,022	452,749	2.4
Houston, TX	1,132,953	1,158,089	2.2	1,077,239	1,113,785	3.4
Huntsville, AL	90,673	89,429	-1.4	85,404	84,932	-0.6
Indianapolis, IN	425,221	430,205	1.2	396,167	404,120	2.0
Jacksonville, FL	429,171	434,184	1.2	401,740	410,048	2.1
Kansas City, MO	244,157	252,292	3.3	227,582	238,398	4.8
Lafayette, LA	64,366	66,367	3.1	61,853	63,005	1.9
Las Vegas, NV	288,653	293,421	1.7	263,230	272,820	3.6
Lexington, KY	169,676	164,945	-2.8	161,353	159,074	-1.4
Lincoln, NE	153,110	153,680	0.4	148,712	149,851	0.8
Little Rock, AR	92,969	93,816	0.9	87,363	89,201	2.1
Los Angeles, CA	2,001,203	2,023,204	1.1	1,820,275	1,862,132	2.3
Louisville, KY	380,412	374,238	-1.6	355,415	357,039	0.5
Lubbock, TX	123,688	124,204	0.4	118,815	120,508	1.4
Madison, WI	148,233	151,368	2.1	142,540	146,937	3.1
Manchester, NH	62,090	62,556	0.8	59,058	60,098	1.8
McAllen, TX	63,415	63,736	0.5	59,732	60,846	1.9
Miami, FL	204,318	209,288	2.4	190,542	196,787	3.3
Midland, TX	71,357	76,671	7.4	69,168	74,970	8.4

Table continued on next page.

City	Civilian Labor Force			Workers Employed		
	Dec. 2013	Dec. 2014	% Chg.	Dec. 2013	Dec. 2014	% Chg.
Minneapolis, MN	226,735	226,378	-0.2	217,650	219,575	0.9
Nashville, TN	353,381	351,800	-0.4	336,639	335,389	-0.4
New Orleans, LA	173,364	179,735	3.7	163,628	167,131	2.1
New York, NY	4,082,835	4,121,481	0.9	3,766,200	3,865,586	2.6
Oklahoma City, OK	302,302	300,796	-0.5	289,357	291,008	0.6
Omaha, NE	228,426	229,167	0.3	220,129	221,984	0.8
Orlando, FL	147,553	151,977	3.0	139,444	144,840	3.9
Oxnard, CA	100,705	99,409	-1.3	92,898	92,730	-0.2
Palm Bay, FL	49,117	49,484	0.7	45,486	46,412	2.0
Peoria, IL	55,482	54,130	-2.4	50,191	50,552	0.7
Philadelphia, PA	683,240	682,563	-0.1	624,523	639,820	2.4
Phoenix, AZ	729,162	750,178	2.9	683,046	707,507	3.6
Pittsburgh, PA	155,623	155,259	-0.2	146,953	148,458	1.0
Portland, OR	336,471	345,730	2.8	317,062	327,696	3.4
Providence, RI	86,679	85,407	-1.5	78,364	79,120	1.0
Provo, UT	61,667	63,496	3.0	59,690	61,968	3.8
Raleigh, NC	225,384	230,215	2.1	215,331	221,676	2.9
Reno, NV	119,781	119,949	0.1	110,144	112,134	1.8
Richmond, VA	110,682	111,203	0.5	103,904	105,357	1.4
Roanoke, VA	49,677	49,641	-0.1	46,779	47,151	0.8
Rochester, MN	60,497	60,446	-0.1	58,346	58,757	0.7
Sacramento, CA	224,686	225,924	0.6	206,006	210,607	2.2
Salem, OR	72,077	74,276	3.1	66,723	69,347	3.9
Salt Lake City, UT	107,003	107,929	0.9	103,241	104,692	1.4
San Antonio, TX	665,217	676,837	1.7	633,279	652,731	3.1
San Diego, CA	690,196	695,388	0.8	645,688	659,330	2.1
San Francisco, CA	522,913	540,603	3.4	498,846	520,640	4.4
San Jose, CA	523,072	539,145	3.1	490,669	512,941	4.5
Santa Rosa, CA	87,121	87,301	0.2	81,415	82,474	1.3
Savannah, GA	63,923	64,485	0.9	58,614	59,872	2.1
Seattle, WA	403,307	409,272	1.5	386,941	393,826	1.8
Sioux Falls, SD	94,854	96,535	1.8	91,799	93,526	1.9
Spokane, WA	99,937	101,944	2.0	92,391	93,991	1.7
Springfield, IL	58,425	58,602	0.3	54,132	55,356	2.3
Tallahassee, FL	96,950	99,198	2.3	91,539	94,333	3.1
Tampa, FL	182,483	184,674	1.2	171,471	175,032	2.1
Topeka, KS	63,322	63,837	0.8	60,042	61,045	1.7
Tulsa, OK	194,398	193,757	-0.3	185,103	186,890	1.0
Tyler, TX	48,500	49,440	1.9	45,914	47,496	3.4
Virginia Beach, VA	229,693	228,187	-0.7	218,263	218,127	-0.1
Washington, DC	371,236	382,019	2.9	343,031	353,654	3.1
Wichita, KS	185,773	187,025	0.7	175,819	178,296	1.4
Wilmington, NC	55,703	55,690	0.0	52,580	53,198	1.2
Winston-Salem, NC	110,060	109,175	-0.8	103,650	104,072	0.4
Worcester, MA	89,535	91,328	2.0	82,975	86,013	3.7
U.S.	154,408,000	155,521,000	0.7	144,423,000	147,190,000	1.9

Note: Data is not seasonally adjusted and covers workers 16 years of age and older
Source: Bureau of Labor Statistics, Local Area Unemployment Statistics

Labor Force, Employment and Job Growth: Metro Area

Metro Area[1]	Civilian Labor Force			Workers Employed		
	Dec. 2013	Dec. 2014	% Chg.	Dec. 2013	Dec. 2014	% Chg.
Albuquerque, NM	415,650	414,520	-0.3	389,105	391,974	0.7
Anchorage, AK	206,084	206,927	0.4	194,694	196,055	0.7
Ann Arbor, MI	184,281	186,936	1.4	175,187	180,678	3.1
Athens, GA	94,913	95,298	0.4	88,840	90,012	1.3
Atlanta, GA	2,791,270	2,815,375	0.9	2,598,666	2,647,261	1.9
Austin, TX	1,032,725	1,052,087	1.9	988,473	1,016,673	2.9
Billings, MT	85,366	85,903	0.6	81,779	82,995	1.5
Boise City, ID	312,188	313,572	0.4	296,477	300,918	1.5
Boston, MA[4]	1,520,594	1,552,222	2.1	1,443,823	1,488,588	3.1
Boulder, CO	175,574	177,034	0.8	167,341	171,184	2.3
Cape Coral, FL	304,065	315,307	3.7	285,502	299,521	4.9
Cedar Rapids, IA	144,731	144,082	-0.4	137,729	137,538	-0.1
Charleston, SC	338,882	348,192	2.7	321,313	329,245	2.5
Charlotte, NC	1,174,230	1,184,609	0.9	1,099,106	1,125,541	2.4
Chicago, IL[2]	3,758,317	3,777,331	0.5	3,450,135	3,567,076	3.4
Clarksville, TN	108,531	107,539	-0.9	100,928	101,055	0.1
Colorado Springs, CO	317,531	315,991	-0.5	295,202	299,942	1.6
Columbia, MO	97,963	100,486	2.6	94,189	97,265	3.3
Columbus, OH	1,020,830	1,034,102	1.3	966,006	994,183	2.9
Dallas, TX[2]	2,331,802	2,392,061	2.6	2,210,843	2,296,944	3.9
Davenport, IA	194,454	194,082	-0.2	181,649	182,541	0.5
Denver, CO	1,470,470	1,497,400	1.8	1,386,478	1,437,876	3.7
Des Moines, IA	334,297	340,970	2.0	319,616	326,880	2.3
Durham, NC	270,301	271,289	0.4	256,766	259,905	1.2
El Paso, TX	350,534	346,011	-1.3	326,299	327,831	0.5
Erie, PA	133,865	132,990	-0.7	124,960	126,617	1.3
Eugene, OR	168,275	171,408	1.9	156,388	160,322	2.5
Fargo, ND	126,236	131,007	3.8	122,617	127,473	4.0
Fayetteville, NC	146,200	142,889	-2.3	134,082	133,752	-0.2
Fort Collins, CO	173,690	175,415	1.0	164,957	169,324	2.6
Fort Wayne, IN	203,906	205,369	0.7	191,667	194,314	1.4
Fort Worth, TX[2]	1,177,281	1,198,013	1.8	1,117,300	1,150,482	3.0
Gainesville, FL	134,410	137,132	2.0	127,340	130,889	2.8
Grand Rapids, MI	531,709	541,925	1.9	502,841	521,839	3.8
Green Bay, WI	168,435	171,803	2.0	158,852	164,440	3.5
Greensboro, NC	357,367	353,721	-1.0	332,708	335,400	0.8
Honolulu, HI	460,385	469,161	1.9	442,022	452,749	2.4
Houston, TX	3,210,505	3,280,203	2.2	3,045,705	3,148,828	3.4
Huntsville, AL	209,521	206,534	-1.4	197,294	196,222	-0.5
Indianapolis, IN	981,345	996,479	1.5	922,753	942,497	2.1
Jacksonville, FL	706,767	715,342	1.2	663,622	677,314	2.1
Kansas City, MO	1,071,183	1,107,078	3.4	1,011,658	1,055,730	4.4
Lafayette, LA	226,804	234,554	3.4	217,493	221,842	2.0
Las Vegas, NV	1,005,346	1,023,287	1.8	918,649	952,117	3.6
Lexington, KY	263,030	255,792	-2.8	249,550	246,382	-1.3
Lincoln, NE	179,125	179,760	0.4	173,816	175,145	0.8
Little Rock, AR	335,097	338,366	1.0	315,108	321,765	2.1
Los Angeles, CA[2]	4,988,880	5,047,001	1.2	4,562,492	4,667,406	2.3
Louisville, KY	629,438	626,503	-0.5	590,084	597,380	1.2
Lubbock, TX	153,418	153,908	0.3	147,248	149,220	1.3
Madison, WI	368,745	376,562	2.1	353,230	364,184	3.1
Manchester, NH[3]	114,919	115,941	0.9	109,798	111,785	1.8
McAllen, TX	337,227	336,129	-0.3	305,062	310,751	1.9
Miami, FL[2]	1,292,935	1,322,890	2.3	1,205,792	1,245,316	3.3
Midland, TX	89,915	96,559	7.4	87,140	94,394	8.3

Table continued on next page.

Metro Area[1]	Civilian Labor Force			Workers Employed		
	Dec. 2013	Dec. 2014	% Chg.	Dec. 2013	Dec. 2014	% Chg.
Minneapolis, MN	1,904,505	1,905,506	0.1	1,824,770	1,843,783	1.0
Nashville, TN	901,839	896,903	-0.5	857,621	854,219	-0.4
New Orleans, LA	581,922	603,346	3.7	552,417	564,490	2.2
New York, NY[2]	6,959,013	7,017,636	0.8	6,466,641	6,611,164	2.2
Oklahoma City, OK	648,737	646,136	-0.4	620,148	624,543	0.7
Omaha, NE	476,219	478,096	0.4	458,544	462,809	0.9
Orlando, FL	1,177,275	1,211,468	2.9	1,106,175	1,149,268	3.9
Oxnard, CA	432,764	427,575	-1.2	401,909	401,181	-0.2
Palm Bay, FL	254,921	256,415	0.6	236,334	241,147	2.0
Peoria, IL	187,911	184,654	-1.7	171,896	173,229	0.8
Philadelphia, PA[2]	970,794	971,041	0.0	895,703	916,043	2.3
Phoenix, AZ	2,080,302	2,140,674	2.9	1,953,680	2,023,418	3.6
Pittsburgh, PA	1,200,870	1,195,363	-0.5	1,130,540	1,141,244	0.9
Portland, OR	1,185,566	1,215,428	2.5	1,108,886	1,143,702	3.1
Providence, RI[3]	680,750	675,936	-0.7	625,230	634,087	1.4
Provo, UT	257,646	265,249	3.0	248,594	258,088	3.8
Raleigh, NC	618,124	629,675	1.9	586,865	604,111	2.9
Reno, NV	224,477	224,562	0.0	206,330	210,050	1.8
Richmond, VA	648,143	651,865	0.6	612,891	621,055	1.3
Roanoke, VA	159,624	159,655	0.0	151,479	152,525	0.7
Rochester, MN	115,978	116,698	0.6	111,656	113,108	1.3
Sacramento, CA	1,039,207	1,046,596	0.7	959,164	980,489	2.2
Salem, OR	180,148	185,317	2.9	166,202	172,750	3.9
Salt Lake City, UT	605,373	609,378	0.7	582,348	590,573	1.4
San Antonio, TX	1,078,143	1,096,505	1.7	1,025,485	1,056,403	3.0
San Diego, CA	1,541,159	1,551,683	0.7	1,436,717	1,467,071	2.1
San Francisco, CA[2]	945,703	977,381	3.3	902,803	942,144	4.4
San Jose, CA	1,006,995	1,039,234	3.2	949,768	992,810	4.5
Santa Rosa, CA	253,990	254,794	0.3	239,042	242,150	1.3
Savannah, GA	170,618	172,492	1.1	158,457	161,896	2.2
Seattle, WA[2]	1,535,809	1,556,437	1.3	1,463,517	1,489,804	1.8
Sioux Falls, SD	140,284	142,640	1.7	136,077	138,463	1.8
Spokane, WA	249,497	253,873	1.8	229,979	233,898	1.7
Springfield, IL	109,228	109,836	0.6	101,716	104,024	2.3
Tallahassee, FL	185,716	189,921	2.3	175,128	180,393	3.0
Tampa, FL	1,413,617	1,430,638	1.2	1,327,059	1,355,252	2.1
Topeka, KS	119,934	120,948	0.8	114,262	116,056	1.6
Tulsa, OK	464,674	463,735	-0.2	441,252	445,953	1.1
Tyler, TX	101,802	103,643	1.8	96,086	99,397	3.4
Virginia Beach, VA	836,154	829,722	-0.8	788,797	787,936	-0.1
Washington, DC[2]	2,566,590	2,576,993	0.4	2,436,513	2,459,715	1.0
Wichita, KS	307,119	309,464	0.8	291,865	295,832	1.4
Wilmington, NC	132,318	131,612	-0.5	123,743	125,184	1.2
Winston-Salem, NC	310,079	306,441	-1.2	290,747	291,862	0.4
Worcester, MA[3]	340,358	348,073	2.3	318,232	329,698	3.6
U.S.	154,408,000	155,521,000	0.7	144,423,000	147,190,000	1.9

Note: Data is not seasonally adjusted and covers workers 16 years of age and older; (1) Figures cover the Metropolitan Statistical Area (MSA) except where noted. See Appendix B for areas included; (2) Metropolitan Division; (3) New England City and Town Area; (4) New England City and Town Area Division

Source: Bureau of Labor Statistics, Local Area Unemployment Statistics

Unemployment Rate: City

City	2014											
	Jan.	Feb.	Mar.	Apr.	May	Jun.	Jul.	Aug.	Sep.	Oct.	Nov.	Dec.
Albuquerque, NM	6.3	6.2	6.1	5.5	5.7	6.6	6.4	6.0	5.7	5.5	5.3	5.0
Anchorage, AK	5.4	5.7	5.5	5.3	5.2	5.6	5.0	4.9	4.9	4.7	4.8	4.6
Ann Arbor, MI	4.1	4.3	4.3	3.7	4.4	4.5	5.2	4.1	3.8	3.3	3.0	2.8
Athens, GA	6.8	6.8	6.9	6.3	7.0	8.0	8.2	7.6	6.9	6.4	6.1	5.9
Atlanta, GA	8.0	8.0	7.9	7.2	7.8	8.3	8.6	8.3	7.5	7.4	7.1	7.0
Austin, TX	4.1	4.0	3.8	3.3	3.6	3.9	4.0	3.9	3.6	3.4	3.3	3.0
Billings, MT	4.5	4.3	4.4	3.5	3.3	3.9	3.6	3.6	3.3	3.2	3.4	3.3
Boise City, ID	4.8	4.6	4.4	4.1	3.9	4.1	4.0	4.1	3.7	3.4	3.3	2.9
Boston, MA	5.9	5.5	5.2	4.9	5.3	5.8	5.9	5.5	5.5	4.8	4.7	4.4
Boulder, CO	5.0	5.1	4.8	4.2	4.0	4.5	4.4	3.8	3.3	3.3	3.5	3.1
Cape Coral, FL	6.5	6.4	6.4	5.7	6.1	6.3	6.6	6.5	5.9	5.6	5.5	5.0
Cedar Rapids, IA	5.4	5.2	5.0	4.4	4.3	4.5	4.6	4.5	4.4	4.0	4.2	4.5
Charleston, SC	4.5	4.3	4.2	3.8	4.4	5.1	5.2	5.5	5.1	4.8	4.8	4.5
Charlotte, NC	5.5	5.6	5.4	4.8	5.3	5.4	5.7	5.5	4.8	4.6	4.4	4.1
Chicago, IL	9.3	9.3	8.5	7.7	7.7	7.9	8.1	7.6	6.9	6.8	6.5	6.1
Clarksville, TN	6.6	6.7	6.7	6.0	6.6	7.6	7.9	7.6	6.9	6.9	6.7	6.3
Colorado Springs, CO	7.4	7.2	7.2	6.5	5.8	6.1	5.9	5.5	5.0	4.7	4.9	4.9
Columbia, MO	4.2	4.6	4.6	3.7	4.1	4.7	4.4	4.2	3.7	3.1	3.3	3.0
Columbus, OH	6.0	5.7	5.3	4.3	4.6	5.0	5.1	4.8	4.5	4.1	4.1	3.8
Dallas, TX	5.8	5.8	5.5	5.0	5.3	5.5	5.6	5.5	5.0	4.7	4.6	4.2
Davenport, IA	6.6	6.4	6.2	5.4	5.5	5.9	5.9	5.7	5.6	5.4	5.6	5.9
Denver, CO	6.2	6.1	6.0	5.2	4.8	4.9	4.7	4.5	4.1	3.9	4.0	4.1
Des Moines, IA	6.4	6.2	6.0	5.1	4.8	4.8	4.8	4.9	4.6	4.6	4.7	5.2
Durham, NC	4.7	4.8	4.7	4.1	4.7	4.8	5.2	4.9	4.2	4.2	4.1	3.8
El Paso, TX	6.7	6.7	6.3	5.7	5.9	6.4	6.5	6.3	5.8	5.5	5.3	4.9
Erie, PA	8.2	8.3	8.1	6.6	7.1	7.1	7.5	7.1	6.1	5.7	5.8	5.5
Eugene, OR	6.9	6.8	6.7	5.9	5.9	6.5	6.9	6.8	6.0	5.9	5.9	5.7
Fargo, ND	3.0	2.9	2.9	2.5	2.2	2.7	2.3	2.3	2.1	2.0	2.2	2.5
Fayetteville, NC	6.6	6.8	6.5	5.7	6.5	6.6	7.2	6.9	5.9	5.6	5.5	5.1
Fort Collins, CO	5.3	5.3	5.0	4.4	3.9	4.2	4.1	3.8	3.4	3.3	3.4	3.4
Fort Wayne, IN	6.6	6.9	6.6	5.6	5.9	6.0	6.9	6.0	5.5	5.6	6.0	5.8
Fort Worth, TX	5.4	5.4	5.2	4.6	4.9	5.3	5.4	5.2	4.7	4.4	4.3	3.9
Gainesville, FL	5.5	5.4	5.3	4.5	5.2	5.9	6.2	5.8	5.3	4.9	5.0	4.6
Grand Rapids, MI	7.3	7.6	7.5	6.0	6.9	7.1	8.2	6.5	5.8	5.2	4.9	4.8
Green Bay, WI	6.6	7.0	6.7	5.8	5.6	5.7	5.5	5.1	4.8	4.6	4.7	4.7
Greensboro, NC	6.5	6.4	6.2	5.6	6.3	6.4	6.9	6.5	5.5	5.2	5.1	4.8
Honolulu, HI	4.4	4.2	4.1	4.0	4.0	4.6	4.1	3.9	4.1	3.9	3.9	3.5
Houston, TX	5.3	5.2	5.0	4.4	4.8	5.1	5.2	5.0	4.6	4.3	4.2	3.8
Huntsville, AL	6.7	7.1	6.8	5.7	6.0	6.9	7.1	6.4	5.6	5.4	5.2	5.0
Indianapolis, IN	6.8	7.3	7.0	6.3	6.5	6.4	6.6	6.6	6.0	6.1	6.3	6.1
Jacksonville, FL	6.8	6.9	6.8	6.2	6.6	6.8	7.1	7.1	6.4	6.0	6.0	5.6
Kansas City, MO	7.3	7.5	7.4	6.1	7.0	6.8	7.5	7.2	6.6	6.0	5.7	5.5
Lafayette, LA	4.6	4.0	4.4	4.0	5.0	5.7	5.9	6.0	5.5	5.6	5.5	5.1
Las Vegas, NV	9.0	8.6	8.6	8.2	8.0	8.3	8.3	7.8	7.6	7.3	7.2	7.0
Lexington, KY	5.6	6.0	5.8	4.8	5.1	5.2	5.1	4.6	4.2	3.9	4.0	3.6
Lincoln, NE	3.5	3.4	3.2	2.8	2.9	3.1	3.1	2.7	2.6	2.4	2.2	2.5
Little Rock, AR	6.3	6.2	5.8	5.3	5.6	5.6	5.9	5.6	5.3	4.9	4.8	4.9
Los Angeles, CA	9.5	9.2	9.0	8.2	8.4	8.7	9.5	9.1	8.5	8.4	8.3	8.0
Louisville, KY	7.4	7.7	7.4	6.2	6.4	6.4	6.2	5.8	5.3	4.8	4.9	4.6
Lubbock, TX	4.2	4.2	4.0	3.4	3.8	4.5	4.6	4.1	3.7	3.5	3.4	3.0
Madison, WI	3.9	4.2	4.1	3.5	3.8	4.1	3.9	3.6	3.4	3.2	3.2	2.9
Manchester, NH	5.5	5.4	5.3	4.8	4.5	4.7	4.5	4.4	4.2	4.0	4.1	3.9
McAllen, TX	6.3	6.2	6.0	5.4	5.7	6.1	6.2	6.0	5.4	5.0	4.8	4.5
Miami, FL	6.9	7.3	7.7	7.3	7.4	7.1	7.3	7.7	7.2	6.5	6.0	6.0
Midland, TX	3.2	3.2	3.0	2.6	2.9	3.1	3.1	2.9	2.8	2.6	2.4	2.2

Table continued on next page.

City	2014											
	Jan.	Feb.	Mar.	Apr.	May	Jun.	Jul.	Aug.	Sep.	Oct.	Nov.	Dec.
Minneapolis, MN	4.6	4.5	4.4	3.7	3.7	4.1	3.9	3.7	3.5	3.0	3.0	3.0
Nashville, TN	4.8	5.0	5.1	4.5	5.0	5.4	5.7	5.6	5.1	4.9	4.9	4.7
New Orleans, LA	6.4	5.8	6.1	5.5	6.5	7.6	8.0	8.2	7.9	7.5	7.4	7.0
New York, NY	8.3	8.5	8.1	7.1	7.3	7.2	7.6	7.1	6.5	6.6	6.6	6.2
Oklahoma City, OK	4.6	4.5	4.2	3.5	3.9	4.2	3.9	3.8	3.7	3.6	3.4	3.3
Omaha, NE	4.3	4.1	4.1	3.4	3.4	3.8	3.8	3.4	3.2	3.1	3.0	3.1
Orlando, FL	5.8	5.8	5.7	5.2	5.5	5.5	5.9	5.8	5.4	5.2	5.1	4.7
Oxnard, CA	8.1	7.9	7.7	6.6	6.6	6.9	7.7	7.6	7.1	7.0	7.2	6.7
Palm Bay, FL	7.8	7.8	7.9	7.4	7.5	7.7	7.8	7.5	6.9	6.7	6.9	6.2
Peoria, IL	9.5	9.4	8.7	7.2	7.7	7.9	8.2	8.0	7.2	7.1	7.1	6.6
Philadelphia, PA	9.2	9.0	8.8	7.5	8.5	8.4	8.8	8.4	7.3	7.0	6.8	6.3
Phoenix, AZ	6.5	6.3	6.3	5.6	5.9	6.4	6.5	6.6	6.2	6.0	5.8	5.7
Pittsburgh, PA	6.3	6.2	6.1	5.0	6.0	6.0	6.4	6.1	5.0	4.8	4.8	4.4
Portland, OR	6.4	6.6	6.4	5.8	5.7	5.9	6.0	6.0	5.5	5.6	5.5	5.2
Providence, RI	10.9	10.3	10.2	9.3	9.2	8.8	9.4	9.0	8.3	7.8	7.7	7.4
Provo, UT	3.8	3.9	3.5	2.9	3.3	4.1	3.7	3.6	3.1	3.0	2.5	2.4
Raleigh, NC	4.7	4.8	4.7	4.2	4.8	4.8	5.1	4.9	4.2	4.1	4.0	3.7
Reno, NV	8.9	8.5	8.3	7.8	7.5	7.6	7.4	7.1	6.9	6.7	6.6	6.5
Richmond, VA	6.7	6.6	6.5	5.8	6.2	6.4	6.6	6.6	6.0	5.5	5.4	5.3
Roanoke, VA	6.5	6.4	6.2	5.6	5.9	6.2	6.2	6.5	5.6	5.1	5.2	5.0
Rochester, MN	4.4	4.4	4.4	3.6	3.4	3.6	3.4	3.1	2.9	2.6	2.7	2.8
Sacramento, CA	8.7	8.7	8.7	7.4	7.4	7.6	8.1	7.8	7.2	7.2	7.2	6.8
Salem, OR	8.0	8.3	8.1	7.2	7.0	7.3	7.6	7.3	6.5	6.7	6.8	6.6
Salt Lake City, UT	3.9	3.9	3.9	3.1	3.4	3.8	3.7	3.7	3.3	3.3	3.0	3.0
San Antonio, TX	5.1	5.1	4.8	4.2	4.5	4.9	5.0	4.7	4.4	4.1	3.9	3.6
San Diego, CA	6.8	6.8	6.7	5.8	5.8	6.1	6.5	6.3	5.8	5.7	5.7	5.2
San Francisco, CA	5.0	4.9	4.9	4.1	4.2	4.3	4.6	4.5	4.1	4.1	4.1	3.7
San Jose, CA	6.5	6.5	6.5	5.5	5.6	5.8	6.2	6.0	5.5	5.4	5.4	4.9
Santa Rosa, CA	7.0	7.0	7.0	5.9	5.8	6.1	6.6	6.3	5.7	5.7	5.9	5.5
Savannah, GA	8.5	8.3	8.6	7.3	8.1	9.0	9.3	8.8	7.9	7.4	6.9	7.2
Seattle, WA	4.2	4.4	4.3	3.7	3.9	4.4	4.4	4.3	4.2	4.0	4.1	3.8
Sioux Falls, SD	3.7	3.7	3.7	3.1	2.9	2.8	2.6	2.7	2.6	2.6	2.8	3.1
Spokane, WA	8.0	8.6	7.9	6.8	7.0	6.6	7.0	7.3	6.8	6.8	7.1	7.8
Springfield, IL	7.5	7.7	7.1	5.7	6.0	6.4	6.8	6.5	5.9	5.8	6.0	5.5
Tallahassee, FL	5.9	5.8	5.7	5.2	5.8	6.3	6.6	6.3	5.7	5.3	5.4	4.9
Tampa, FL	6.3	6.2	6.2	5.6	5.9	6.1	6.4	6.3	5.8	5.6	5.6	5.2
Topeka, KS	6.0	6.1	5.9	4.9	5.0	5.3	5.5	5.3	4.8	4.5	4.5	4.4
Tulsa, OK	5.1	5.0	4.7	3.9	4.4	4.5	4.2	4.1	4.0	3.9	3.7	3.5
Tyler, TX	5.9	5.8	5.4	4.7	5.0	5.4	5.5	5.1	5.0	4.7	4.5	3.9
Virginia Beach, VA	5.3	5.3	5.2	4.6	5.0	5.1	5.2	5.2	4.8	4.6	4.5	4.4
Washington, DC	8.1	8.1	7.9	7.2	7.4	8.0	8.1	8.1	8.0	7.7	7.6	7.4
Wichita, KS	6.2	6.2	6.0	5.2	5.5	6.0	6.4	5.8	5.4	5.0	4.8	4.7
Wilmington, NC	6.2	6.1	5.7	4.9	5.3	5.5	5.9	5.7	4.9	4.7	4.5	4.5
Winston-Salem, NC	6.1	6.1	6.0	5.3	6.0	6.2	6.5	6.1	5.0	4.8	4.8	4.7
Worcester, MA	8.1	7.7	7.4	6.7	7.1	7.6	7.8	7.1	7.0	6.1	6.1	5.8
U.S.	7.0	7.0	6.8	5.9	6.1	6.3	6.5	6.3	5.7	5.5	5.5	5.4

Note: Data is not seasonally adjusted and covers workers 16 years of age and older; All figures are percentages
Source: Bureau of Labor Statistics, Local Area Unemployment Statistics

Unemployment Rate: Metro Area

Metro Area[1]	2014											
	Jan.	Feb.	Mar.	Apr.	May	Jun.	Jul.	Aug.	Sep.	Oct.	Nov.	Dec.
Albuquerque, NM	6.9	6.7	6.6	6.1	6.3	7.2	7.1	6.6	6.2	5.9	5.8	5.4
Anchorage, AK	6.2	6.5	6.3	6.0	5.8	6.2	5.6	5.4	5.4	5.2	5.4	5.3
Ann Arbor, MI	5.0	5.3	5.2	4.5	5.3	5.5	6.3	5.0	4.6	4.1	3.6	3.3
Athens, GA	6.5	6.5	6.5	5.9	6.6	7.4	7.7	7.1	6.4	6.0	5.7	5.5
Atlanta, GA	7.1	7.1	7.0	6.4	6.9	7.3	7.6	7.3	6.7	6.5	6.1	6.0
Austin, TX	4.6	4.6	4.4	3.8	4.1	4.4	4.5	4.4	4.1	3.8	3.7	3.4
Billings, MT	4.6	4.4	4.5	3.6	3.4	3.9	3.7	3.6	3.3	3.2	3.6	3.4
Boise City, ID	5.7	5.4	5.2	4.7	4.4	4.6	4.6	4.7	4.2	4.0	4.2	4.0
Boston, MA[4]	5.6	5.3	5.0	4.6	4.8	5.3	5.3	4.9	5.0	4.4	4.3	4.1
Boulder, CO	5.1	5.2	5.0	4.2	4.0	4.3	4.2	3.8	3.4	3.3	3.4	3.3
Cape Coral, FL	6.3	6.2	6.1	5.5	6.0	6.3	6.7	6.6	6.0	5.6	5.4	5.0
Cedar Rapids, IA	5.7	5.5	5.3	4.5	4.3	4.5	4.5	4.5	4.3	4.0	4.1	4.5
Charleston, SC	5.3	5.3	5.0	4.5	5.1	5.8	6.0	6.3	5.9	5.7	5.6	5.4
Charlotte, NC	6.6	6.6	6.3	5.7	6.2	6.3	6.6	6.5	5.7	5.5	5.3	5.0
Chicago, IL[2]	8.8	8.8	8.1	7.1	7.0	7.3	7.4	6.9	6.2	6.1	5.8	5.6
Clarksville, TN	7.2	7.4	7.3	6.4	6.9	7.5	7.8	7.3	6.7	6.5	6.4	6.0
Colorado Springs, CO	7.6	7.4	7.3	6.5	5.9	6.2	6.0	5.5	5.0	4.8	5.0	5.1
Columbia, MO	4.6	5.1	4.8	3.8	4.1	4.7	4.7	4.3	3.7	3.2	3.4	3.2
Columbus, OH	6.1	5.8	5.3	4.4	4.6	5.1	5.2	4.8	4.4	4.2	4.1	3.9
Dallas, TX[2]	5.6	5.6	5.4	4.8	5.0	5.3	5.4	5.2	4.8	4.5	4.4	4.0
Davenport, IA	7.6	7.4	7.0	5.7	5.9	6.0	6.3	5.9	6.0	5.8	5.8	5.9
Denver, CO	6.1	6.1	5.9	5.2	4.8	4.9	4.8	4.5	4.0	3.9	4.0	4.0
Des Moines, IA	5.1	4.9	4.8	4.1	3.9	4.1	4.0	4.1	3.9	4.0	3.8	4.1
Durham, NC	5.3	5.3	5.2	4.5	5.1	5.2	5.6	5.4	4.7	4.6	4.5	4.2
El Paso, TX	7.3	7.2	6.8	6.2	6.5	7.0	7.1	6.8	6.3	5.9	5.7	5.3
Erie, PA	7.5	7.5	7.3	5.9	6.2	6.4	6.6	6.2	5.2	4.9	5.0	4.8
Eugene, OR	7.8	7.9	7.7	6.9	6.6	7.0	7.3	7.3	6.6	6.7	6.7	6.5
Fargo, ND	3.5	3.5	3.3	2.8	2.4	2.9	2.6	2.5	2.2	2.1	2.2	2.7
Fayetteville, NC	8.5	8.6	8.2	7.4	8.0	8.2	8.7	8.4	7.2	7.0	6.9	6.4
Fort Collins, CO	5.6	5.6	5.3	4.5	4.1	4.3	4.2	3.9	3.4	3.4	3.5	3.5
Fort Wayne, IN	6.2	6.4	6.2	5.2	5.5	5.5	6.5	5.5	5.0	5.2	5.5	5.4
Fort Worth, TX[2]	5.6	5.5	5.3	4.7	4.9	5.3	5.4	5.2	4.7	4.5	4.4	4.0
Gainesville, FL	5.6	5.5	5.4	4.7	5.2	5.6	5.9	5.7	5.1	4.8	4.9	4.6
Grand Rapids, MI	5.7	6.0	5.9	4.6	5.3	5.4	6.3	4.9	4.4	4.0	3.8	3.7
Green Bay, WI	6.1	6.4	6.2	5.3	5.0	5.2	5.1	4.8	4.3	4.1	4.3	4.3
Greensboro, NC	7.2	7.2	6.9	6.2	6.7	6.9	7.2	6.9	5.9	5.7	5.6	5.2
Honolulu, HI	4.4	4.2	4.1	4.0	4.0	4.6	4.1	3.9	4.1	3.9	3.9	3.5
Houston, TX	5.5	5.4	5.2	4.6	4.9	5.3	5.4	5.1	4.7	4.4	4.3	4.0
Huntsville, AL	6.8	7.2	6.8	5.7	6.0	6.8	6.9	6.5	5.6	5.4	5.1	5.0
Indianapolis, IN	6.1	6.5	6.2	5.4	5.7	5.7	5.8	5.7	5.2	5.4	5.6	5.4
Jacksonville, FL	6.5	6.5	6.5	5.9	6.2	6.4	6.8	6.7	6.1	5.8	5.7	5.3
Kansas City, MO	6.3	6.6	6.3	5.1	5.8	5.7	6.1	5.7	5.4	4.9	4.8	4.6
Lafayette, LA	4.9	4.3	4.7	4.2	5.1	5.9	6.1	6.2	5.8	5.8	5.8	5.4
Las Vegas, NV	8.8	8.5	8.4	8.0	7.8	8.0	8.0	7.6	7.4	7.1	7.0	7.0
Lexington, KY	5.9	6.3	6.0	4.9	5.3	5.3	5.3	4.7	4.3	4.0	4.1	3.7
Lincoln, NE	3.6	3.5	3.3	2.8	2.9	3.2	3.2	2.8	2.6	2.4	2.3	2.6
Little Rock, AR	6.5	6.3	5.8	5.2	5.6	5.6	5.8	5.4	5.2	4.8	4.8	4.9
Los Angeles, CA[2]	9.0	8.7	8.5	7.8	8.0	8.2	9.0	8.6	8.1	8.0	7.9	7.5
Louisville, KY	7.0	7.3	7.0	5.8	6.1	6.1	5.9	5.6	5.1	4.8	4.9	4.6
Lubbock, TX	4.3	4.3	4.1	3.5	3.8	4.5	4.7	4.2	3.8	3.5	3.4	3.0
Madison, WI	4.6	4.9	4.8	4.0	4.0	4.2	4.0	3.8	3.5	3.3	3.4	3.3
Manchester, NH[3]	5.0	5.0	4.8	4.3	4.2	4.3	4.1	4.0	3.9	3.6	3.8	3.6
McAllen, TX	10.2	9.7	9.3	8.4	8.3	9.3	9.5	9.1	8.0	7.3	7.7	7.6
Miami, FL[2]	6.9	7.1	7.5	6.9	7.1	6.9	7.1	7.3	6.8	6.3	5.8	5.9
Midland, TX	3.2	3.2	3.1	2.6	2.9	3.2	3.2	2.9	2.8	2.6	2.4	2.2

Table continued on next page.

Metro Area[1]	2014											
	Jan.	Feb.	Mar.	Apr.	May	Jun.	Jul.	Aug.	Sep.	Oct.	Nov.	Dec.
Minneapolis, MN	4.9	4.9	4.8	3.9	3.7	4.0	3.9	3.6	3.5	3.0	3.1	3.2
Nashville, TN	5.0	5.2	5.3	4.6	5.1	5.7	6.0	5.8	5.3	5.1	5.0	4.8
New Orleans, LA	5.8	5.2	5.5	5.0	5.9	6.9	7.2	7.4	7.1	6.9	6.8	6.4
New York, NY[2]	7.7	7.8	7.5	6.5	6.7	6.7	7.1	6.7	6.2	6.2	6.1	5.8
Oklahoma City, OK	4.7	4.7	4.3	3.6	4.1	4.3	4.0	3.9	3.7	3.7	3.5	3.3
Omaha, NE	4.4	4.3	4.2	3.5	3.5	3.9	3.9	3.5	3.3	3.1	3.1	3.2
Orlando, FL	6.3	6.3	6.2	5.7	5.9	6.1	6.4	6.3	5.8	5.5	5.5	5.1
Oxnard, CA	7.5	7.3	7.1	6.1	6.1	6.4	7.0	7.0	6.6	6.4	6.6	6.2
Palm Bay, FL	7.6	7.5	7.4	6.7	7.0	7.0	7.3	7.3	6.7	6.4	6.4	6.0
Peoria, IL	8.9	9.1	8.4	6.6	6.8	7.0	7.3	7.0	6.2	6.2	6.3	6.2
Philadelphia, PA[2]	8.3	8.2	8.0	6.8	7.6	7.6	8.0	7.7	6.6	6.4	6.2	5.7
Phoenix, AZ	6.3	6.2	6.2	5.5	5.8	6.2	6.3	6.4	6.0	5.8	5.6	5.5
Pittsburgh, PA	6.7	6.6	6.4	5.1	5.7	5.9	6.2	5.9	4.9	4.6	4.7	4.5
Portland, OR	7.0	7.2	6.9	6.3	6.2	6.3	6.5	6.5	6.0	6.1	6.1	5.9
Providence, RI[3]	9.4	9.0	8.7	7.7	7.5	7.2	7.7	7.3	6.8	6.3	6.3	6.2
Provo, UT	4.1	4.2	3.9	3.2	3.4	4.0	3.8	3.7	3.2	3.1	2.7	2.7
Raleigh, NC	5.3	5.3	5.2	4.6	5.1	5.2	5.5	5.3	4.6	4.4	4.3	4.1
Reno, NV	9.0	8.6	8.4	7.8	7.4	7.5	7.3	7.0	6.9	6.6	6.5	6.5
Richmond, VA	5.9	5.9	5.8	5.2	5.5	5.7	5.8	5.8	5.3	5.0	4.9	4.7
Roanoke, VA	5.7	5.7	5.5	4.8	5.2	5.4	5.5	5.6	5.0	4.7	4.6	4.5
Rochester, MN	4.8	4.8	4.7	3.9	3.4	3.6	3.5	3.1	2.9	2.6	2.7	3.1
Sacramento, CA	8.1	8.1	8.1	6.9	6.8	7.0	7.5	7.2	6.6	6.6	6.7	6.3
Salem, OR	8.5	8.6	8.3	7.3	7.0	7.2	7.5	7.3	6.5	6.7	6.9	6.8
Salt Lake City, UT	4.3	4.4	4.2	3.4	3.6	4.0	3.9	3.9	3.4	3.4	3.1	3.1
San Antonio, TX	5.2	5.2	4.9	4.3	4.6	4.9	5.0	4.8	4.5	4.2	4.0	3.7
San Diego, CA	7.2	7.1	7.1	6.1	6.1	6.4	6.9	6.6	6.1	6.0	6.0	5.5
San Francisco, CA[2]	4.9	4.8	4.8	4.0	4.1	4.3	4.6	4.4	4.1	4.0	4.0	3.6
San Jose, CA	6.0	6.0	6.0	5.1	5.1	5.3	5.7	5.4	5.0	5.0	4.9	4.5
Santa Rosa, CA	6.3	6.3	6.3	5.3	5.2	5.5	5.9	5.6	5.1	5.2	5.3	5.0
Savannah, GA	7.4	7.3	7.4	6.5	7.1	7.6	7.9	7.6	6.8	6.6	6.1	6.1
Seattle, WA[2]	5.0	5.1	5.1	4.3	4.5	5.0	5.0	4.8	4.6	4.5	4.6	4.3
Sioux Falls, SD	3.5	3.5	3.5	2.9	2.8	2.7	2.4	2.5	2.5	2.4	2.6	2.9
Spokane, WA	8.5	8.8	8.2	6.9	6.9	6.5	6.9	7.2	6.7	6.7	7.1	7.9
Springfield, IL	7.3	7.5	6.9	5.3	5.6	5.8	6.1	5.9	5.4	5.4	5.5	5.3
Tallahassee, FL	6.0	5.9	5.9	5.2	5.8	6.1	6.5	6.3	5.7	5.4	5.4	5.0
Tampa, FL	6.5	6.4	6.4	5.7	6.1	6.2	6.5	6.4	5.9	5.7	5.7	5.3
Topeka, KS	5.6	5.8	5.4	4.4	4.6	4.9	5.0	4.8	4.4	4.1	4.1	4.0
Tulsa, OK	5.4	5.2	4.8	4.1	4.6	4.7	4.4	4.3	4.2	4.1	4.0	3.8
Tyler, TX	6.1	6.0	5.6	4.9	5.1	5.4	5.5	5.2	5.0	4.7	4.6	4.1
Virginia Beach, VA	6.2	6.1	5.9	5.3	5.7	5.8	5.9	5.9	5.5	5.2	5.2	5.0
Washington, DC[2]	5.4	5.5	5.4	4.8	5.2	5.4	5.5	5.5	5.1	4.8	4.7	4.6
Wichita, KS	5.8	5.8	5.6	4.9	5.1	5.5	6.0	5.4	5.0	4.7	4.5	4.4
Wilmington, NC	7.2	7.1	6.5	5.7	6.1	6.2	6.5	6.2	5.4	5.2	5.1	4.9
Winston-Salem, NC	6.5	6.5	6.3	5.6	6.1	6.2	6.5	6.3	5.4	5.2	5.1	4.8
Worcester, MA[3]	7.3	7.1	6.8	6.0	6.1	6.4	6.6	6.2	6.0	5.4	5.4	5.3
U.S.	7.0	7.0	6.8	5.9	6.1	6.3	6.5	6.3	5.7	5.5	5.5	5.4

Note: Data is not seasonally adjusted and covers workers 16 years of age and older; All figures are percentages; (1) Figures cover the Metropolitan Statistical Area (MSA) except where noted. See Appendix B for areas included; (2) Metropolitan Division; (3) New England City and Town Area; (4) New England City and Town Area Division
Source: Bureau of Labor Statistics, Local Area Unemployment Statistics

Average Hourly Wages: Occupations A – C

Metro Area[1]	Accountants/ Auditors	Automotive Mechanics	Book-keepers	Carpenters	Cashiers	Clerks, Gen. Office	Clerks, Recep./Info.
Albuquerque, NM	30.53	19.82	17.21	18.35	10.07	12.62	12.30
Anchorage, AK	38.15	23.62	21.70	31.91	12.05	20.64	15.67
Ann Arbor, MI	29.52	18.68	18.55	26.96	10.51	15.37	13.17
Athens, GA	27.70	17.29	15.39	14.66	9.12	12.14	12.72
Atlanta, GA	37.98	19.46	18.75	20.59	9.33	13.71	13.81
Austin, TX	32.55	18.74	19.22	18.19	10.31	16.13	13.51
Billings, MT	29.56	20.43	16.29	19.33	10.05	14.68	13.27
Boise City, ID	31.21	19.95	16.67	16.83	10.18	13.70	12.93
Boston, MA[4]	39.60	23.35	22.08	29.83	10.63	18.04	15.35
Boulder, CO	36.66	20.61	18.94	19.33	11.16	19.42	14.09
Cape Coral, FL	32.71	19.81	16.61	18.60	9.83	13.22	13.00
Cedar Rapids, IA	29.57	17.30	17.24	19.96	9.12	16.12	12.75
Charleston, SC	28.39	19.80	16.44	18.76	9.48	12.52	13.73
Charlotte, NC	36.72	20.80	18.06	17.22	9.38	13.83	13.58
Chicago, IL[2]	35.71	21.80	19.50	30.94	10.55	15.74	14.16
Clarksville, TN	27.33	19.77	15.70	17.69	9.16	13.49	11.35
Colorado Springs, CO	31.59	20.26	16.46	21.37	10.46	15.97	13.32
Columbia, MO	31.60	17.20	18.81	21.09	9.36	14.08	12.60
Columbus, OH	33.16	18.54	20.54	21.88	9.74	15.02	12.95
Dallas, TX[2]	37.39	20.77	19.04	14.87	9.56	16.19	13.04
Davenport, IA	31.93	18.18	16.18	22.41	9.51	14.33	12.53
Denver, CO	37.01	20.60	19.12	20.42	10.56	17.84	15.02
Des Moines, IA	33.01	19.91	17.48	20.80	9.38	16.03	13.65
Durham, NC	36.57	18.65	18.91	18.57	9.55	14.16	13.64
El Paso, TX	28.34	15.87	15.25	13.88	8.96	12.73	10.04
Erie, PA	28.00	15.20	14.38	18.87	8.90	13.44	11.24
Eugene, OR	29.42	17.85	17.43	21.32	10.76	14.38	13.22
Fargo, ND	27.33	19.01	17.41	18.55	9.65	12.99	12.50
Fayetteville, NC	32.71	17.05	15.84	16.03	9.27	12.96	11.43
Fort Collins, CO	30.38	20.72	17.74	19.23	10.12	15.89	13.73
Fort Wayne, IN	31.40	18.64	16.30	19.02	9.03	12.71	13.08
Fort Worth, TX[2]	34.66	19.75	18.03	15.44	9.96	15.42	12.59
Gainesville, FL	29.10	18.61	16.71	16.67	9.19	12.50	11.65
Grand Rapids, MI	30.22	18.74	17.52	20.67	9.34	15.12	14.25
Green Bay, WI	30.01	19.28	17.07	21.98	8.91	14.66	13.82
Greensboro, NC	33.47	19.53	17.37	15.00	9.02	12.48	12.78
Honolulu, HI	29.42	21.49	18.39	34.11	10.72	15.52	13.84
Houston, TX	39.99	19.38	19.12	16.69	9.70	16.52	12.97
Huntsville, AL	34.54	17.01	17.38	16.42	9.01	11.37	12.05
Indianapolis, IN	33.67	22.69	18.45	21.30	9.36	14.01	13.37
Jacksonville, FL	32.77	18.31	17.44	15.42	9.38	13.05	12.94
Kansas City, MO	32.02	19.02	18.37	23.43	9.72	14.93	13.85
Lafayette, LA	32.05	18.85	17.31	17.64	9.07	11.76	11.09
Las Vegas, NV	30.63	19.99	18.00	23.76	10.72	15.19	12.91
Lexington, KY	32.60	16.37	17.23	18.86	9.18	14.41	12.93
Lincoln, NE	30.36	19.48	16.08	15.99	9.29	11.75	12.79
Little Rock, AR	31.83	16.88	17.02	16.60	9.06	12.07	11.45
Los Angeles, CA[2]	36.68	18.59	20.19	26.08	10.49	15.32	14.37
Louisville, KY	29.75	17.38	17.21	18.27	9.45	14.15	12.88
Lubbock, TX	31.54	16.42	14.49	15.54	8.84	14.34	11.31
Madison, WI	33.54	18.96	18.53	26.80	9.47	16.01	13.45
Manchester, NH[3]	34.98	20.55	19.94	22.05	9.43	17.02	13.61
McAllen, TX	29.71	15.33	14.22	14.17	9.10	11.99	9.71
Miami, FL[2]	33.67	17.39	17.29	16.85	9.44	13.81	12.67
Midland, TX	37.18	23.24	19.42	17.94	10.45	17.65	13.86

Table continued on next page.

Metro Area[1]	Accountants/ Auditors	Automotive Mechanics	Book-keepers	Carpenters	Cashiers	Clerks, Gen. Office	Clerks, Recep./Info.
Minneapolis, MN	33.66	19.29	19.40	25.79	10.39	15.99	14.21
Nashville, TN	33.06	19.39	18.33	16.83	9.69	15.41	13.95
New Orleans, LA	30.95	19.11	17.27	18.71	9.09	11.95	12.10
New York, NY[2]	46.51	20.77	21.12	32.32	10.63	15.49	14.92
Oklahoma City, OK	32.22	19.09	16.90	17.16	9.21	13.54	13.08
Omaha, NE	33.29	19.98	17.17	18.19	9.20	13.17	12.95
Orlando, FL	31.76	18.27	16.61	16.98	9.30	13.27	12.79
Oxnard, CA	36.91	20.91	21.42	24.04	11.80	15.59	13.92
Palm Bay, FL	31.02	17.49	16.28	15.44	9.52	14.05	13.21
Peoria, IL	36.00	17.24	16.77	24.90	9.64	14.05	12.57
Philadelphia, PA[2]	37.07	19.79	19.77	26.27	10.10	16.50	13.49
Phoenix, AZ	31.92	20.45	17.99	19.02	10.25	15.98	13.20
Pittsburgh, PA	32.36	17.79	17.24	22.79	9.21	14.44	12.57
Portland, OR	32.74	20.59	19.25	20.89	11.91	16.34	14.05
Providence, RI[3]	37.07	19.06	18.81	21.67	10.22	16.17	14.27
Provo, UT	31.81	16.78	16.74	18.13	9.40	12.53	12.05
Raleigh, NC	32.43	21.65	18.04	16.10	9.26	14.05	13.55
Reno, NV	30.67	19.61	19.01	21.98	10.42	17.04	13.73
Richmond, VA	35.28	20.20	18.64	18.87	9.38	14.75	13.28
Roanoke, VA	32.34	16.30	16.80	15.59	9.47	13.46	12.15
Rochester, MN	30.62	17.81	19.08	20.47	9.47	14.44	12.09
Sacramento, CA	32.79	22.50	19.80	22.94	12.17	16.11	14.09
Salem, OR	30.82	20.50	18.36	20.36	11.35	15.81	13.99
Salt Lake City, UT	33.89	18.70	17.43	18.39	9.62	13.78	12.73
San Antonio, TX	33.59	18.94	17.96	17.92	9.58	15.01	11.89
San Diego, CA	37.51	20.62	19.99	21.74	10.98	15.79	14.15
San Francisco, CA[2]	42.23	26.07	24.04	31.17	13.01	19.40	17.28
San Jose, CA	44.69	24.99	23.84	29.18	12.19	19.36	17.32
Santa Rosa, CA	34.61	23.44	21.37	29.72	12.52	17.87	16.81
Savannah, GA	34.28	21.01	17.36	20.03	9.50	13.20	13.21
Seattle, WA[2]	37.33	22.27	20.90	26.09	13.31	16.27	15.67
Sioux Falls, SD	30.61	19.04	14.98	16.81	9.41	11.65	12.21
Spokane, WA	29.41	21.09	18.66	23.53	12.08	14.69	13.93
Springfield, IL	31.43	19.61	19.85	22.18	9.67	n/a	13.07
Tallahassee, FL	26.61	16.97	16.12	19.58	9.31	12.01	11.78
Tampa, FL	33.01	18.87	16.07	16.31	9.42	13.31	13.08
Topeka, KS	27.87	17.35	16.16	18.40	8.88	14.19	12.20
Tulsa, OK	32.20	18.18	17.09	15.76	9.21	13.41	12.93
Tyler, TX	33.97	21.27	17.66	15.54	9.11	14.60	11.40
Virginia Beach, VA	34.29	20.37	17.41	18.66	9.20	14.10	12.41
Washington, DC[2]	41.96	24.13	21.90	22.41	10.61	17.86	14.91
Wichita, KS	31.23	18.25	16.89	17.35	9.15	13.29	12.49
Wilmington, NC	34.46	20.81	16.38	16.74	9.17	13.12	11.94
Winston-Salem, NC	32.70	19.81	17.41	16.62	8.93	13.87	12.81
Worcester, MA[3]	36.25	19.23	19.10	23.74	10.35	15.93	15.08

Notes: (1) Figures cover the Metropolitan Statistical Area (MSA) except where noted. See Appendix B for areas included; (2) Metropolitan Division; (3) New England City and Town Area; (4) New England City and Town Area Division; n/a not available

Source: Bureau of Labor Statistics, May 2014 Metro Area Occupational Employment and Wage Estimates

Average Hourly Wages: Occupations C – E

Metro Area	Clerks, Ship./Rec.	Computer Programmers	Computer Systems Analysts	Comp. User Support Specialists	Cooks, Restaurant	Dentists	Electrical Engineers
Albuquerque, NM	14.19	47.67	35.95	21.40	10.54	90.64	51.12
Anchorage, AK	18.30	38.79	37.89	25.59	14.45	105.67	53.37
Ann Arbor, MI	18.11	33.36	39.04	20.08	11.24	88.92	46.61
Athens, GA	14.88	26.72	28.85	19.61	9.20	n/a	37.44
Atlanta, GA	14.24	47.23	39.53	25.60	11.41	91.62	42.31
Austin, TX	13.79	42.31	38.17	24.07	10.96	82.77	52.24
Billings, MT	13.31	27.50	35.04	21.03	10.31	73.25	36.65
Boise City, ID	13.54	31.15	37.77	20.70	9.81	85.84	44.74
Boston, MA[4]	17.40	42.97	42.53	31.18	13.84	87.92	50.23
Boulder, CO	15.58	45.70	42.22	26.32	11.59	89.92	47.38
Cape Coral, FL	12.90	45.16	40.73	19.77	11.59	50.97	32.32
Cedar Rapids, IA	15.78	33.92	36.20	20.36	10.03	102.47	40.70
Charleston, SC	14.81	35.48	33.17	23.47	11.26	88.43	36.59
Charlotte, NC	15.20	40.21	43.76	24.76	10.79	92.52	47.05
Chicago, IL[2]	15.77	35.72	40.12	26.17	11.37	62.67	45.60
Clarksville, TN	16.19	24.00	36.80	18.85	9.70	n/a	36.18
Colorado Springs, CO	14.48	37.28	46.56	23.66	11.63	100.65	50.76
Columbia, MO	13.19	30.91	36.36	18.16	10.06	70.98	n/a
Columbus, OH	13.57	34.92	38.29	24.48	11.45	91.59	37.92
Dallas, TX[2]	14.53	39.61	41.45	23.89	11.58	107.16	44.24
Davenport, IA	14.59	33.42	n/a	19.16	10.14	n/a	40.87
Denver, CO	16.05	46.46	46.48	27.55	11.63	79.78	46.18
Des Moines, IA	17.45	34.60	38.43	22.06	9.90	92.50	33.13
Durham, NC	15.05	38.84	42.10	26.85	10.04	77.76	42.12
El Paso, TX	11.36	36.58	32.53	21.75	9.26	107.28	45.16
Erie, PA	13.92	29.66	33.79	19.39	9.72	87.57	41.52
Eugene, OR	15.02	27.98	36.63	21.02	11.04	92.36	42.35
Fargo, ND	15.12	27.39	n/a	22.53	11.61	87.72	40.55
Fayetteville, NC	14.62	36.84	39.11	23.26	9.25	106.04	38.58
Fort Collins, CO	13.49	43.50	42.95	25.95	11.24	67.22	46.14
Fort Wayne, IN	13.07	32.59	32.07	20.13	9.83	85.46	36.45
Fort Worth, TX[2]	14.49	39.65	42.08	23.54	11.18	80.18	45.23
Gainesville, FL	14.56	28.74	37.02	19.84	10.17	93.12	33.07
Grand Rapids, MI	14.92	33.48	33.93	24.39	10.28	103.95	40.50
Green Bay, WI	15.31	33.82	33.58	21.09	10.31	104.38	31.93
Greensboro, NC	14.81	36.97	40.19	22.57	10.07	114.43	45.78
Honolulu, HI	16.27	33.81	38.30	23.78	12.56	83.04	41.55
Houston, TX	14.63	37.77	49.51	27.66	10.61	83.10	52.03
Huntsville, AL	15.12	43.72	42.61	22.75	9.92	89.18	47.11
Indianapolis, IN	14.65	32.36	35.84	25.76	10.90	56.85	40.58
Jacksonville, FL	15.15	36.13	36.86	21.05	11.36	81.76	40.80
Kansas City, MO	15.03	35.03	37.81	24.88	10.77	75.41	44.15
Lafayette, LA	14.93	25.02	31.63	22.34	9.84	39.93	n/a
Las Vegas, NV	16.42	38.46	38.43	24.36	14.21	62.06	42.42
Lexington, KY	15.05	28.97	36.61	16.06	10.77	84.48	41.85
Lincoln, NE	15.40	31.15	32.72	19.91	10.95	94.10	45.32
Little Rock, AR	14.19	33.28	33.64	21.92	9.72	98.56	41.75
Los Angeles, CA[2]	14.56	43.18	45.36	26.63	11.48	70.52	53.36
Louisville, KY	15.49	30.08	32.91	21.82	10.48	76.18	39.58
Lubbock, TX	13.02	28.20	34.05	18.18	9.46	67.89	35.65
Madison, WI	15.00	37.01	33.61	23.21	11.16	89.41	38.63
Manchester, NH[3]	14.98	30.68	38.89	24.08	12.12	94.00	43.36
McAllen, TX	10.83	32.26	30.92	17.82	9.80	106.15	42.65
Miami, FL[2]	13.34	45.10	48.37	24.29	11.87	77.55	43.09
Midland, TX	n/a	37.84	33.98	22.48	11.31	74.78	n/a

Table continued on next page.

Metro Area	Clerks, Ship./Rec.	Computer Programmers	Computer Systems Analysts	Comp. User Support Specialists	Cooks, Restaurant	Dentists	Electrical Engineers
Minneapolis, MN	16.57	38.76	42.18	25.81	12.03	91.00	44.80
Nashville, TN	14.52	37.14	35.56	22.31	10.66	82.20	37.82
New Orleans, LA	15.60	34.05	30.86	22.56	11.06	102.62	50.88
New York, NY[2]	16.99	43.94	48.44	29.01	13.41	74.04	47.29
Oklahoma City, OK	15.23	32.75	36.34	20.86	10.38	73.03	40.37
Omaha, NE	15.13	39.24	36.34	23.50	11.15	74.64	36.31
Orlando, FL	13.49	36.45	41.93	20.75	11.81	96.90	42.16
Oxnard, CA	16.02	48.02	49.88	24.80	12.52	59.61	51.41
Palm Bay, FL	13.03	44.22	36.29	24.22	10.53	67.43	41.57
Peoria, IL	14.99	30.57	44.75	23.18	10.97	n/a	46.47
Philadelphia, PA[2]	16.71	41.28	45.48	25.98	12.29	86.68	46.36
Phoenix, AZ	15.64	39.60	43.35	24.36	11.20	64.84	49.47
Pittsburgh, PA	15.68	33.59	35.62	24.09	11.56	73.25	42.15
Portland, OR	15.53	35.50	42.01	23.81	11.62	73.12	42.95
Providence, RI[3]	15.60	37.19	37.62	24.00	12.07	81.94	45.59
Provo, UT	12.56	36.64	37.74	19.41	10.58	55.54	39.85
Raleigh, NC	14.37	39.08	41.91	24.93	10.73	100.91	40.24
Reno, NV	15.22	37.15	31.60	20.80	12.08	102.52	40.30
Richmond, VA	15.59	38.24	40.17	25.49	11.00	71.36	41.94
Roanoke, VA	13.48	41.29	35.35	21.65	10.04	91.70	41.55
Rochester, MN	15.64	44.65	31.04	23.50	12.35	97.47	42.60
Sacramento, CA	15.07	36.53	38.26	27.84	11.34	88.71	50.64
Salem, OR	14.60	36.39	37.11	24.03	11.49	81.34	45.32
Salt Lake City, UT	14.54	38.16	35.14	21.90	11.92	68.03	43.92
San Antonio, TX	13.54	38.96	37.89	21.15	10.09	84.92	43.18
San Diego, CA	16.29	40.29	44.11	26.32	11.89	82.71	53.45
San Francisco, CA[2]	17.84	50.37	50.86	34.05	14.21	90.43	56.55
San Jose, CA	17.31	45.20	52.16	36.30	12.92	75.07	61.65
Santa Rosa, CA	16.40	37.30	37.04	27.87	12.49	89.30	48.52
Savannah, GA	17.97	n/a	35.28	26.00	10.28	106.56	45.37
Seattle, WA[2]	17.89	57.58	49.01	28.74	13.08	88.07	50.78
Sioux Falls, SD	13.74	27.33	31.92	17.72	10.99	76.94	38.62
Spokane, WA	15.46	26.47	34.89	22.37	12.06	95.08	41.46
Springfield, IL	15.39	32.75	47.97	21.52	11.18	n/a	41.27
Tallahassee, FL	12.10	28.15	42.25	17.87	10.68	104.55	43.20
Tampa, FL	13.49	35.31	38.92	22.25	11.91	84.08	43.77
Topeka, KS	20.25	34.10	30.26	21.04	9.42	89.78	n/a
Tulsa, OK	15.41	32.24	37.74	23.20	10.75	71.50	39.11
Tyler, TX	13.28	29.42	31.67	20.99	10.26	85.74	53.16
Virginia Beach, VA	15.57	31.62	38.76	23.31	11.30	74.67	39.15
Washington, DC[2]	16.60	44.45	49.88	28.89	12.93	72.78	52.36
Wichita, KS	14.73	33.11	36.89	16.61	9.70	88.39	41.58
Wilmington, NC	13.97	40.02	38.53	22.05	10.64	96.76	55.91
Winston-Salem, NC	14.75	37.18	41.46	21.38	10.04	99.23	44.38
Worcester, MA[3]	16.82	40.41	42.44	26.87	12.25	94.14	45.39

Notes: (1) Figures cover the Metropolitan Statistical Area (MSA) except where noted. See Appendix B for areas included; (2) Metropolitan Division; (3) New England City and Town Area; (4) New England City and Town Area Division; n/a not available
Source: Bureau of Labor Statistics, May 2014 Metro Area Occupational Employment and Wage Estimates

Average Hourly Wages: Occupations E – I

Metro Area	Electricians	Financial Managers	First-Line Supervisors/ Mgrs., Sales	Food Preparation Workers	General/ Operations Managers	Hairdressers/ Cosmetologists	Internists
Albuquerque, NM	20.63	52.39	17.47	10.11	47.54	12.41	n/a
Anchorage, AK	37.67	57.37	20.58	11.77	52.07	15.62	87.17
Ann Arbor, MI	34.13	52.36	21.31	10.91	58.44	12.74	n/a
Athens, GA	21.17	52.53	18.71	9.46	44.55	13.01	n/a
Atlanta, GA	22.92	64.95	20.49	9.97	58.17	13.23	125.05
Austin, TX	22.44	65.24	20.91	10.58	57.92	16.16	n/a
Billings, MT	28.93	55.25	19.30	9.55	47.00	18.62	n/a
Boise City, ID	22.22	48.15	18.16	9.20	39.82	11.79	n/a
Boston, MA[4]	32.26	65.97	22.79	12.12	69.66	15.82	97.42
Boulder, CO	22.87	66.19	24.57	10.82	62.75	15.89	101.78
Cape Coral, FL	18.53	51.28	21.86	9.84	55.15	15.98	99.55
Cedar Rapids, IA	27.91	58.49	19.19	9.99	47.50	11.92	n/a
Charleston, SC	21.15	53.06	19.67	10.77	48.40	12.98	95.46
Charlotte, NC	19.05	73.64	21.93	10.08	62.61	14.14	n/a
Chicago, IL[2]	35.99	62.95	20.26	10.17	53.12	13.44	74.91
Clarksville, TN	19.36	29.83	18.14	10.10	39.05	11.03	n/a
Colorado Springs, CO	22.45	66.96	23.33	10.18	54.42	12.65	n/a
Columbia, MO	24.83	49.17	18.87	9.20	34.34	14.11	n/a
Columbus, OH	22.22	62.76	17.92	10.72	54.06	12.37	87.88
Dallas, TX[2]	19.95	67.69	22.06	9.68	66.25	12.48	82.59
Davenport, IA	29.18	46.43	17.65	9.68	42.34	11.50	n/a
Denver, CO	23.46	73.42	20.81	10.87	64.10	13.60	104.45
Des Moines, IA	26.17	60.19	18.93	9.49	51.39	15.76	102.12
Durham, NC	19.86	63.65	20.19	11.24	66.10	12.94	n/a
El Paso, TX	18.67	48.33	20.84	8.55	50.94	8.93	118.46
Erie, PA	25.09	48.18	19.36	10.85	48.75	11.84	n/a
Eugene, OR	29.10	43.83	18.18	10.61	40.22	12.34	n/a
Fargo, ND	26.64	50.52	20.34	12.29	50.18	14.31	n/a
Fayetteville, NC	19.38	56.53	18.43	9.70	59.24	12.81	n/a
Fort Collins, CO	22.15	61.03	20.77	11.18	47.71	12.67	n/a
Fort Wayne, IN	26.12	50.86	18.86	9.87	53.12	10.88	n/a
Fort Worth, TX[2]	20.19	59.62	23.34	9.79	56.63	12.43	102.25
Gainesville, FL	18.32	64.77	18.84	9.99	55.68	13.03	113.85
Grand Rapids, MI	22.61	48.24	19.28	10.13	53.57	12.90	38.10
Green Bay, WI	23.51	50.91	17.79	10.23	47.34	11.41	122.85
Greensboro, NC	18.85	60.86	20.92	9.23	62.90	13.38	110.75
Honolulu, HI	31.86	48.00	22.63	10.93	49.10	18.81	91.52
Houston, TX	23.54	71.19	22.25	9.79	66.54	14.67	82.70
Huntsville, AL	21.89	59.17	20.18	8.61	64.51	12.68	n/a
Indianapolis, IN	26.18	54.52	20.39	9.13	55.79	13.67	122.48
Jacksonville, FL	20.58	64.14	19.99	10.04	58.38	15.99	107.64
Kansas City, MO	27.72	58.18	19.61	9.82	52.19	12.54	112.97
Lafayette, LA	21.25	42.95	18.38	8.85	57.52	11.58	n/a
Las Vegas, NV	27.13	49.10	20.58	13.01	49.24	11.31	84.91
Lexington, KY	21.06	47.58	18.05	10.39	44.05	14.22	84.01
Lincoln, NE	21.64	63.78	17.32	9.17	51.18	11.26	n/a
Little Rock, AR	22.27	53.33	16.62	9.12	43.64	12.53	103.98
Los Angeles, CA[2]	28.71	73.35	20.59	9.99	61.38	13.23	84.61
Louisville, KY	24.69	50.81	18.04	9.97	46.38	12.56	95.90
Lubbock, TX	19.63	51.82	21.88	9.29	50.12	10.76	n/a
Madison, WI	26.74	54.80	18.79	10.16	53.76	13.91	122.70
Manchester, NH[3]	24.92	56.64	21.18	13.27	57.08	12.97	n/a
McAllen, TX	15.82	45.16	20.37	8.91	40.70	12.47	n/a
Miami, FL[2]	25.09	66.96	20.92	10.53	65.16	12.07	95.49
Midland, TX	22.50	71.96	25.03	10.84	62.58	15.33	n/a

Table continued on next page.

Metro Area	Electricians	Financial Managers	First-Line Supervisors/ Mgrs., Sales	Food Preparation Workers	General/ Operations Managers	Hairdressers/ Cosmetologists	Internists
Minneapolis, MN	29.39	64.61	19.66	12.02	54.47	12.93	107.43
Nashville, TN	22.65	52.35	19.69	9.33	55.29	14.48	82.28
New Orleans, LA	23.93	49.32	19.47	8.67	52.92	12.40	116.99
New York, NY[2]	36.31	90.14	24.85	12.00	77.14	16.02	88.73
Oklahoma City, OK	22.89	48.69	19.01	9.33	49.86	10.94	89.29
Omaha, NE	23.27	65.65	21.01	9.11	53.30	13.54	94.13
Orlando, FL	18.52	62.39	19.97	10.60	55.63	11.82	105.54
Oxnard, CA	27.04	57.20	21.66	11.67	58.42	12.46	99.51
Palm Bay, FL	19.63	58.11	19.96	10.24	56.20	13.29	n/a
Peoria, IL	29.24	54.23	17.75	9.78	47.99	9.58	113.32
Philadelphia, PA[2]	31.88	75.01	24.43	10.99	66.30	13.51	100.69
Phoenix, AZ	21.77	56.97	19.42	10.37	52.50	12.16	84.25
Pittsburgh, PA	26.48	67.54	21.36	10.08	55.92	11.92	103.20
Portland, OR	35.00	52.99	19.22	11.00	51.85	14.59	102.98
Providence, RI[3]	24.15	63.15	22.35	11.05	64.63	13.60	90.20
Provo, UT	22.83	54.02	18.10	9.39	40.93	12.66	n/a
Raleigh, NC	18.56	60.35	20.97	9.86	65.27	14.38	114.03
Reno, NV	27.35	47.23	20.07	9.78	48.92	10.52	n/a
Richmond, VA	22.42	64.04	21.49	9.63	59.09	16.57	96.24
Roanoke, VA	20.74	57.00	20.41	9.37	52.94	13.69	85.77
Rochester, MN	31.43	50.08	18.30	10.90	41.83	14.36	n/a
Sacramento, CA	29.07	56.32	20.02	10.14	53.55	11.88	108.61
Salem, OR	27.80	44.82	17.97	10.78	42.99	12.30	102.69
Salt Lake City, UT	23.08	54.45	19.38	9.67	46.68	14.02	93.65
San Antonio, TX	21.23	61.53	22.05	9.76	54.74	12.44	n/a
San Diego, CA	31.91	65.07	22.26	10.31	58.68	15.36	98.53
San Francisco, CA[2]	41.67	85.60	23.94	11.58	72.35	18.36	80.03
San Jose, CA	35.29	79.99	23.58	11.48	74.72	11.55	110.04
Santa Rosa, CA	33.78	55.30	21.77	10.87	55.98	11.54	113.18
Savannah, GA	22.22	60.86	16.71	10.03	43.56	11.24	n/a
Seattle, WA[2]	34.96	59.47	22.25	11.93	63.37	18.24	98.11
Sioux Falls, SD	21.56	63.66	21.93	9.32	60.49	14.51	117.25
Spokane, WA	28.19	47.12	22.00	10.77	46.30	13.64	76.87
Springfield, IL	32.10	47.83	18.50	10.13	46.32	19.15	63.16
Tallahassee, FL	18.66	52.43	20.41	9.56	56.30	13.10	n/a
Tampa, FL	19.04	62.50	21.17	10.01	62.54	13.63	105.04
Topeka, KS	24.24	50.04	19.33	8.97	42.57	13.24	n/a
Tulsa, OK	22.46	54.15	18.57	9.22	50.31	11.63	98.48
Tyler, TX	19.66	53.28	19.90	9.03	54.59	14.38	n/a
Virginia Beach, VA	22.14	57.19	19.47	9.99	57.52	16.63	81.30
Washington, DC[2]	27.07	71.05	22.49	10.93	69.97	16.97	n/a
Wichita, KS	23.64	42.88	19.10	8.85	49.24	12.55	123.92
Wilmington, NC	19.73	53.29	20.77	9.61	57.79	12.69	n/a
Winston-Salem, NC	24.18	64.03	20.02	9.74	60.54	13.99	n/a
Worcester, MA[3]	31.42	53.53	22.14	10.87	56.52	16.28	n/a

Notes: (1) Figures cover the Metropolitan Statistical Area (MSA) except where noted. See Appendix B for areas included; (2) Metropolitan Division; (3) New England City and Town Area; (4) New England City and Town Area Division; n/a not available
Source: Bureau of Labor Statistics, May 2014 Metro Area Occupational Employment and Wage Estimates

Average Hourly Wages: Occupations J – N

Metro Area	Janitors/ Cleaners	Landscapers	Lawyers	Maids/ House-keepers	Main-tenance Repairers	Marketing Managers	Nuclear Medicine Techs
Albuquerque, NM	10.84	11.39	43.13	9.06	17.34	43.67	35.06
Anchorage, AK	13.96	15.76	57.05	11.80	22.16	43.16	n/a
Ann Arbor, MI	14.49	13.30	66.46	10.25	19.27	56.03	33.16
Athens, GA	10.90	13.31	48.77	9.44	16.76	52.97	n/a
Atlanta, GA	11.63	12.39	66.91	9.24	18.51	65.68	35.15
Austin, TX	10.70	11.84	63.59	9.32	17.30	68.82	35.23
Billings, MT	12.51	11.85	35.98	10.18	15.40	n/a	n/a
Boise City, ID	10.63	12.63	50.07	10.54	15.46	51.47	n/a
Boston, MA[4]	15.55	16.67	72.96	13.80	22.05	67.44	37.99
Boulder, CO	13.26	13.43	59.33	9.78	18.72	70.60	37.63
Cape Coral, FL	11.93	11.41	42.74	10.18	16.36	54.42	31.55
Cedar Rapids, IA	13.76	13.01	49.81	10.03	21.56	55.01	n/a
Charleston, SC	10.36	11.51	48.27	9.55	18.73	50.87	33.40
Charlotte, NC	10.29	11.30	59.02	8.90	18.67	66.37	33.35
Chicago, IL[2]	13.87	13.49	60.77	11.62	20.70	59.32	35.08
Clarksville, TN	10.97	11.95	38.00	9.53	18.16	36.81	n/a
Colorado Springs, CO	12.21	12.34	53.13	9.60	17.93	66.67	n/a
Columbia, MO	12.44	11.28	55.59	9.62	16.07	50.54	n/a
Columbus, OH	12.46	12.19	56.31	10.05	19.08	63.69	32.86
Dallas, TX[2]	10.05	11.91	69.58	9.34	17.74	68.82	33.63
Davenport, IA	12.36	12.55	53.98	9.97	17.80	43.57	n/a
Denver, CO	11.61	13.64	65.99	10.24	19.12	67.90	38.70
Des Moines, IA	11.57	15.15	60.72	10.23	17.75	60.13	32.20
Durham, NC	11.28	13.65	51.42	10.30	20.29	76.12	n/a
El Paso, TX	9.89	10.00	71.19	8.55	13.50	57.93	n/a
Erie, PA	10.59	11.18	50.10	8.87	15.52	54.91	n/a
Eugene, OR	12.54	14.20	42.01	10.36	18.32	33.62	n/a
Fargo, ND	12.69	11.47	49.31	9.46	17.41	53.29	n/a
Fayetteville, NC	10.17	10.01	48.40	8.53	15.92	n/a	28.39
Fort Collins, CO	11.76	13.24	66.59	9.99	17.29	67.14	n/a
Fort Wayne, IN	11.12	11.69	62.69	8.71	19.18	47.72	30.53
Fort Worth, TX[2]	10.54	11.63	56.57	9.40	16.75	56.57	34.54
Gainesville, FL	10.63	10.90	48.54	9.86	17.14	62.12	n/a
Grand Rapids, MI	11.84	12.17	46.77	10.06	17.89	44.94	n/a
Green Bay, WI	11.92	13.42	41.62	9.78	18.70	51.21	n/a
Greensboro, NC	9.70	11.75	60.88	9.04	19.02	62.43	31.89
Honolulu, HI	12.01	14.13	50.53	15.83	20.38	44.45	42.17
Houston, TX	10.06	11.35	78.40	9.07	18.00	73.12	34.42
Huntsville, AL	10.21	10.31	66.26	8.33	19.40	63.98	24.87
Indianapolis, IN	12.18	11.68	53.41	9.10	18.03	52.22	34.40
Jacksonville, FL	11.55	12.18	52.18	9.35	17.52	57.64	35.62
Kansas City, MO	12.23	12.79	63.28	9.66	17.70	57.69	33.60
Lafayette, LA	9.81	10.85	48.67	8.66	18.33	35.31	27.19
Las Vegas, NV	14.03	12.39	60.83	15.39	22.63	55.16	36.22
Lexington, KY	11.24	11.28	48.19	9.28	16.48	45.66	n/a
Lincoln, NE	10.82	12.17	52.83	9.26	18.90	46.17	31.55
Little Rock, AR	10.17	10.77	46.55	8.60	15.42	52.58	31.74
Los Angeles, CA[2]	13.07	13.57	82.27	12.17	20.92	68.97	48.08
Louisville, KY	10.99	12.11	46.23	9.28	18.81	54.06	28.80
Lubbock, TX	10.11	11.28	65.52	8.78	15.46	57.30	35.94
Madison, WI	12.11	13.38	51.62	10.06	19.03	51.71	n/a
Manchester, NH[3]	11.79	16.75	60.87	10.39	20.69	50.53	n/a
McAllen, TX	10.24	9.75	52.56	8.56	11.44	n/a	n/a
Miami, FL[2]	10.25	11.04	71.66	9.97	15.64	52.20	35.69
Midland, TX	11.45	14.20	n/a	10.06	20.01	67.96	n/a

Table continued on next page.

Metro Area	Janitors/ Cleaners	Landscapers	Lawyers	Maids/ House-keepers	Main-tenance Repairers	Marketing Managers	Nuclear Medicine Techs
Minneapolis, MN	12.90	14.13	64.40	10.77	21.40	63.45	36.95
Nashville, TN	10.76	12.02	57.91	9.85	18.10	47.41	29.91
New Orleans, LA	11.24	10.71	64.02	9.66	17.75	52.86	31.41
New York, NY[2]	15.81	15.96	80.56	17.82	21.32	86.43	40.07
Oklahoma City, OK	10.49	12.31	50.19	9.20	16.73	44.40	33.51
Omaha, NE	11.42	12.68	47.82	9.43	18.04	51.81	31.60
Orlando, FL	10.25	11.57	70.01	9.98	15.68	54.52	35.88
Oxnard, CA	14.13	13.29	74.13	11.15	19.73	71.68	47.69
Palm Bay, FL	11.28	11.76	47.11	10.32	16.43	60.20	32.09
Peoria, IL	11.53	13.40	61.57	10.26	18.12	56.35	32.53
Philadelphia, PA[2]	13.68	15.11	66.04	11.72	20.02	80.96	35.05
Phoenix, AZ	10.94	11.61	60.06	9.99	17.50	57.16	37.02
Pittsburgh, PA	12.33	12.49	66.20	10.27	19.11	70.82	28.46
Portland, OR	12.93	14.39	58.93	11.94	20.32	52.74	40.06
Providence, RI[3]	13.84	14.21	56.50	12.18	19.61	62.61	40.69
Provo, UT	9.91	11.47	57.38	9.40	16.71	56.40	n/a
Raleigh, NC	10.01	11.64	61.58	9.28	18.62	65.26	32.48
Reno, NV	10.58	13.08	54.03	10.09	18.67	45.79	n/a
Richmond, VA	10.74	12.31	61.69	9.84	18.58	66.50	31.36
Roanoke, VA	10.62	11.97	56.54	9.07	16.31	69.20	31.39
Rochester, MN	13.91	13.55	48.97	10.88	18.71	59.53	n/a
Sacramento, CA	12.91	13.80	61.90	13.54	19.83	56.13	50.94
Salem, OR	13.69	13.45	57.07	11.45	17.47	36.40	n/a
Salt Lake City, UT	10.28	12.22	60.92	9.48	17.96	62.31	32.12
San Antonio, TX	10.45	12.21	60.15	9.40	15.50	52.16	32.74
San Diego, CA	12.96	13.22	69.45	10.97	19.46	70.12	37.17
San Francisco, CA[2]	14.03	18.40	82.65	16.90	25.10	86.40	54.17
San Jose, CA	13.63	15.69	96.75	14.64	22.42	90.33	57.46
Santa Rosa, CA	13.77	15.00	77.19	13.96	22.42	64.87	n/a
Savannah, GA	10.21	10.35	45.27	8.65	18.60	46.64	n/a
Seattle, WA[2]	14.27	16.23	63.11	12.07	21.05	68.07	42.69
Sioux Falls, SD	11.01	12.41	49.13	9.11	16.04	53.54	26.13
Spokane, WA	13.73	13.07	47.57	10.98	18.08	52.77	35.89
Springfield, IL	13.55	14.52	51.79	10.22	19.49	41.03	35.33
Tallahassee, FL	10.15	10.80	51.85	9.18	14.86	41.02	n/a
Tampa, FL	10.50	11.19	56.02	9.46	15.83	55.62	36.51
Topeka, KS	11.82	13.09	38.39	9.01	18.03	60.82	n/a
Tulsa, OK	10.55	11.43	68.76	9.24	17.33	48.13	28.15
Tyler, TX	9.79	10.75	55.31	8.46	16.32	n/a	n/a
Virginia Beach, VA	10.54	11.80	58.75	9.86	17.20	54.08	31.30
Washington, DC[2]	12.72	13.10	77.76	12.18	21.78	74.74	37.71
Wichita, KS	11.51	12.29	46.25	9.00	16.84	57.47	n/a
Wilmington, NC	10.22	11.32	47.06	9.61	18.53	51.98	n/a
Winston-Salem, NC	9.50	11.96	67.84	8.74	18.25	60.61	34.61
Worcester, MA[3]	14.97	15.31	58.44	11.17	20.59	60.16	n/a

Notes: (1) Figures cover the Metropolitan Statistical Area (MSA) except where noted. See Appendix B for areas included; (2) Metropolitan Division; (3) New England City and Town Area; (4) New England City and Town Area Division; n/a not available
Source: Bureau of Labor Statistics, May 2014 Metro Area Occupational Employment and Wage Estimates

Average Hourly Wages: Occupations N – R

Metro Area	Nurses, Licensed Practical	Nurses, Registered	Nursing Assistants	Packers/ Packagers	Physical Therapists	Postal Mail Carriers	R.E. Brokers
Albuquerque, NM	23.04	32.08	13.56	9.38	42.05	25.32	n/a
Anchorage, AK	25.37	41.46	17.75	13.44	48.61	25.82	42.45
Ann Arbor, MI	22.53	33.45	14.39	10.01	38.02	25.07	n/a
Athens, GA	19.18	29.28	10.65	10.21	39.78	23.71	n/a
Atlanta, GA	19.12	31.27	11.22	11.08	39.00	25.21	54.71
Austin, TX	22.40	31.42	11.92	11.54	36.27	25.51	56.11
Billings, MT	19.04	31.34	12.31	11.20	35.01	25.15	22.10
Boise City, ID	20.09	29.51	11.14	12.24	36.62	24.83	n/a
Boston, MA[4]	26.04	43.69	14.98	11.46	39.63	26.31	60.84
Boulder, CO	22.06	34.99	13.61	10.50	35.24	25.32	31.66
Cape Coral, FL	20.35	30.64	12.52	9.31	44.59	24.80	22.86
Cedar Rapids, IA	18.31	25.86	11.88	8.96	33.84	25.01	n/a
Charleston, SC	19.89	31.98	11.57	10.97	38.61	24.42	27.17
Charlotte, NC	19.74	28.49	11.21	10.95	38.61	24.80	30.80
Chicago, IL[2]	23.40	35.35	12.34	11.25	38.00	25.38	47.43
Clarksville, TN	18.91	27.70	12.03	9.71	37.99	24.87	n/a
Colorado Springs, CO	21.39	31.03	12.49	10.75	36.99	25.15	n/a
Columbia, MO	18.14	27.18	11.68	9.72	32.87	24.69	n/a
Columbus, OH	20.22	31.29	12.03	11.41	36.56	24.53	40.25
Dallas, TX[2]	23.73	34.57	12.31	10.63	47.84	25.37	n/a
Davenport, IA	18.17	26.30	11.75	11.01	34.98	24.40	n/a
Denver, CO	23.98	34.76	14.69	11.03	36.46	25.20	40.15
Des Moines, IA	19.74	27.38	12.29	9.98	36.71	25.06	n/a
Durham, NC	22.08	32.29	12.43	10.10	36.88	24.86	29.05
El Paso, TX	21.28	31.21	10.30	9.13	46.97	24.27	n/a
Erie, PA	19.14	27.49	12.45	11.44	37.54	24.01	n/a
Eugene, OR	22.53	38.61	13.86	10.83	42.09	24.68	32.09
Fargo, ND	18.22	29.24	13.58	10.53	34.16	24.49	n/a
Fayetteville, NC	19.54	29.96	11.07	9.20	38.19	24.55	18.48
Fort Collins, CO	21.75	31.50	13.68	9.53	34.13	25.41	30.37
Fort Wayne, IN	19.31	25.50	11.11	10.68	38.43	25.11	n/a
Fort Worth, TX[2]	22.81	34.32	11.86	11.20	40.58	25.27	42.75
Gainesville, FL	20.12	29.16	10.93	9.58	37.82	24.31	n/a
Grand Rapids, MI	19.55	28.62	12.70	9.88	37.45	24.45	n/a
Green Bay, WI	18.61	28.57	12.59	11.68	40.13	24.11	n/a
Greensboro, NC	20.09	29.50	10.67	9.81	34.96	24.58	21.37
Honolulu, HI	23.19	43.39	14.28	10.66	38.79	26.41	72.67
Houston, TX	23.39	36.30	12.21	10.79	43.09	24.92	56.32
Huntsville, AL	17.96	27.18	11.48	10.90	39.13	24.20	29.62
Indianapolis, IN	20.40	30.02	12.27	10.65	39.56	24.58	47.92
Jacksonville, FL	20.15	30.30	11.49	9.70	45.60	25.15	n/a
Kansas City, MO	19.27	30.18	12.02	11.86	36.91	24.73	n/a
Lafayette, LA	17.44	28.28	9.35	9.76	34.68	25.04	26.33
Las Vegas, NV	25.70	39.82	16.84	11.10	68.02	25.25	57.87
Lexington, KY	18.81	28.46	12.21	9.95	38.70	25.07	n/a
Lincoln, NE	18.46	26.80	12.07	10.19	35.07	24.98	n/a
Little Rock, AR	18.20	29.00	11.10	9.47	37.53	24.64	n/a
Los Angeles, CA[2]	24.02	45.26	14.15	10.44	42.21	26.10	48.11
Louisville, KY	19.16	29.21	12.16	10.55	38.60	24.57	n/a
Lubbock, TX	21.03	29.11	11.44	8.57	40.80	25.31	n/a
Madison, WI	21.50	35.93	13.89	15.33	37.19	24.91	21.81
Manchester, NH[3]	24.35	32.53	14.74	10.52	36.56	25.52	n/a
McAllen, TX	22.31	31.38	9.65	9.22	45.05	24.89	n/a
Miami, FL[2]	20.67	30.72	11.29	9.44	34.48	25.43	n/a
Midland, TX	21.64	31.16	12.46	12.63	36.67	25.43	n/a

Table continued on next page.

Metro Area	Nurses, Licensed Practical	Nurses, Registered	Nursing Assistants	Packers/ Packagers	Physical Therapists	Postal Mail Carriers	R.E. Brokers
Minneapolis, MN	21.36	36.33	14.48	11.53	36.46	24.83	n/a
Nashville, TN	18.71	28.51	11.12	10.64	38.94	25.03	n/a
New Orleans, LA	19.51	31.38	11.00	10.63	40.05	24.54	n/a
New York, NY[2]	25.00	41.35	16.33	11.24	43.86	25.71	56.08
Oklahoma City, OK	19.06	28.17	11.01	11.72	37.49	24.88	n/a
Omaha, NE	19.68	28.70	12.39	10.15	35.03	24.99	n/a
Orlando, FL	19.09	29.53	11.66	10.63	41.89	25.19	55.07
Oxnard, CA	25.10	41.29	14.21	11.19	41.46	25.87	n/a
Palm Bay, FL	20.37	29.36	11.54	9.56	42.97	24.96	25.52
Peoria, IL	20.98	27.02	11.51	11.30	37.14	24.78	n/a
Philadelphia, PA[2]	23.83	35.66	14.18	11.30	39.61	25.18	57.53
Phoenix, AZ	25.13	35.15	13.85	11.08	40.31	25.45	n/a
Pittsburgh, PA	19.95	30.03	13.28	12.20	39.16	25.07	n/a
Portland, OR	24.14	41.08	13.90	12.01	38.57	24.92	41.83
Providence, RI[3]	24.48	36.37	13.65	10.71	39.30	25.21	26.78
Provo, UT	19.71	27.91	11.36	10.80	35.82	24.99	n/a
Raleigh, NC	21.05	28.98	11.64	10.62	35.90	24.64	27.57
Reno, NV	24.00	36.23	13.75	10.16	44.27	24.92	27.65
Richmond, VA	19.13	30.66	11.41	11.78	39.91	24.19	54.12
Roanoke, VA	19.04	28.45	11.55	9.55	50.52	24.57	n/a
Rochester, MN	22.02	31.56	14.89	10.59	39.81	25.51	n/a
Sacramento, CA	27.59	50.67	15.59	12.78	45.28	25.51	n/a
Salem, OR	22.33	37.43	14.19	10.39	39.98	24.05	26.23
Salt Lake City, UT	22.81	30.51	11.94	10.79	37.89	25.44	35.96
San Antonio, TX	20.65	31.91	11.64	10.73	41.87	25.09	32.39
San Diego, CA	24.22	41.23	13.66	11.08	43.10	25.62	43.87
San Francisco, CA[2]	29.61	61.63	19.20	13.17	50.54	26.78	40.04
San Jose, CA	28.63	58.57	16.50	11.96	48.82	26.71	40.86
Santa Rosa, CA	24.38	49.36	15.35	10.94	43.46	25.51	50.54
Savannah, GA	18.62	29.37	10.62	9.38	42.35	25.20	21.46
Seattle, WA[2]	25.95	40.52	15.24	13.77	40.65	25.61	42.63
Sioux Falls, SD	16.88	26.30	11.64	10.65	32.70	24.51	38.96
Spokane, WA	21.72	35.14	12.71	11.56	38.63	24.97	n/a
Springfield, IL	18.68	30.04	12.42	10.89	32.64	24.54	n/a
Tallahassee, FL	19.21	27.68	10.98	9.23	40.52	24.74	n/a
Tampa, FL	20.11	30.68	11.61	9.28	37.77	25.12	20.90
Topeka, KS	19.49	30.01	11.19	13.93	43.51	24.04	n/a
Tulsa, OK	19.13	28.79	10.94	10.21	39.09	24.94	n/a
Tyler, TX	20.58	28.16	9.85	11.68	44.11	25.16	n/a
Virginia Beach, VA	18.87	28.99	11.40	10.44	39.89	25.11	35.85
Washington, DC[2]	23.48	36.65	13.53	10.19	39.93	25.08	39.18
Wichita, KS	19.17	25.37	11.26	9.63	36.33	24.75	n/a
Wilmington, NC	19.14	27.14	10.78	9.87	43.24	24.02	27.20
Winston-Salem, NC	19.86	29.33	11.23	11.20	39.34	24.21	24.66
Worcester, MA[3]	26.14	43.44	14.74	10.31	37.04	24.65	n/a

Notes: (1) Figures cover the Metropolitan Statistical Area (MSA) except where noted. See Appendix B for areas included; (2) Metropolitan Division; (3) New England City and Town Area; (4) New England City and Town Area Division; n/a not available
Source: Bureau of Labor Statistics, May 2014 Metro Area Occupational Employment and Wage Estimates

Average Hourly Wages: Occupations R – T

Metro Area	Retail Salespersons	Sales Reps., Except Tech./Scien.	Sales Reps., Tech./Scien.	Secretaries, Exc. Leg./ Med./Exec.	Security Guards	Surgeons	Teacher Assistants
Albuquerque, NM	11.93	25.47	32.08	15.01	13.09	n/a	9.80
Anchorage, AK	12.99	28.46	37.22	16.96	14.72	n/a	17.70
Ann Arbor, MI	12.87	34.07	37.02	17.93	16.86	n/a	13.70
Athens, GA	10.84	25.40	26.49	15.47	13.58	n/a	8.80
Atlanta, GA	12.20	30.23	38.88	17.11	11.76	119.43	10.60
Austin, TX	13.21	31.05	39.30	16.04	12.59	102.01	10.50
Billings, MT	13.67	25.53	n/a	14.85	11.70	n/a	13.70
Boise City, ID	12.38	28.69	30.79	14.58	13.16	n/a	11.90
Boston, MA[4]	12.52	40.91	46.95	21.58	15.10	123.81	14.50
Boulder, CO	14.72	38.65	36.38	17.54	15.25	103.98	15.50
Cape Coral, FL	11.99	26.37	43.19	14.95	11.25	n/a	13.30
Cedar Rapids, IA	12.01	32.42	39.84	14.48	n/a	n/a	13.10
Charleston, SC	11.27	29.99	34.28	15.48	13.90	131.24	11.10
Charlotte, NC	12.45	34.71	41.36	17.12	11.54	122.15	11.00
Chicago, IL[2]	12.51	34.23	36.30	17.77	14.44	121.53	13.70
Clarksville, TN	12.04	22.17	44.78	13.70	14.07	n/a	11.00
Colorado Springs, CO	13.47	32.60	36.45	15.92	13.45	113.24	11.90
Columbia, MO	10.41	25.25	32.47	14.86	12.17	n/a	11.50
Columbus, OH	11.64	32.86	40.03	16.63	12.42	108.75	13.10
Dallas, TX[2]	12.97	36.59	35.52	16.76	13.07	107.42	10.90
Davenport, IA	12.90	29.86	32.49	15.06	11.86	113.22	11.90
Denver, CO	12.90	34.55	47.66	18.22	14.70	115.12	13.30
Des Moines, IA	13.39	35.00	37.34	16.84	17.65	104.00	10.80
Durham, NC	11.52	30.76	48.15	17.74	12.61	114.66	12.50
El Paso, TX	11.34	21.16	37.74	13.05	10.13	116.07	11.00
Erie, PA	11.42	27.80	30.04	14.02	11.21	122.52	10.20
Eugene, OR	13.26	23.83	37.87	16.13	12.67	n/a	13.10
Fargo, ND	13.08	30.35	38.20	16.52	11.74	n/a	14.30
Fayetteville, NC	10.63	23.83	n/a	14.89	16.12	n/a	10.00
Fort Collins, CO	12.51	28.50	33.51	16.40	11.03	102.71	12.70
Fort Wayne, IN	11.68	28.94	47.60	15.93	15.50	n/a	11.20
Fort Worth, TX[2]	12.49	34.57	35.89	14.87	13.96	123.79	9.20
Gainesville, FL	11.27	24.02	37.49	14.25	11.33	124.14	9.50
Grand Rapids, MI	12.13	29.54	40.88	15.68	10.68	n/a	12.70
Green Bay, WI	11.50	31.92	38.67	16.31	11.69	n/a	13.60
Greensboro, NC	12.57	36.10	34.25	15.84	11.25	n/a	10.80
Honolulu, HI	12.09	22.95	34.42	18.61	13.23	n/a	13.10
Houston, TX	12.65	37.04	45.99	16.42	12.12	106.03	10.10
Huntsville, AL	11.95	29.32	44.28	17.41	12.99	n/a	8.90
Indianapolis, IN	12.37	33.02	44.66	16.78	13.24	n/a	11.00
Jacksonville, FL	11.63	27.56	37.64	15.06	10.72	111.20	12.70
Kansas City, MO	11.83	32.28	47.71	16.22	14.14	118.85	11.60
Lafayette, LA	11.55	27.68	33.19	14.63	11.78	70.64	10.30
Las Vegas, NV	12.87	30.00	42.07	17.97	13.08	126.61	15.50
Lexington, KY	12.15	26.55	32.51	16.26	10.14	108.58	14.90
Lincoln, NE	11.58	26.81	31.96	15.94	15.82	n/a	12.10
Little Rock, AR	13.22	27.97	31.22	14.56	12.32	95.23	9.60
Los Angeles, CA[2]	12.89	30.21	40.43	18.49	12.86	119.27	14.20
Louisville, KY	11.81	32.36	46.31	15.70	12.33	n/a	14.10
Lubbock, TX	11.44	27.57	37.38	13.80	11.53	n/a	9.50
Madison, WI	12.15	30.12	35.85	17.54	11.61	119.57	12.80
Manchester, NH[3]	12.05	31.88	43.36	15.85	13.39	n/a	13.00
McAllen, TX	10.10	23.55	n/a	12.11	10.48	n/a	10.90
Miami, FL[2]	11.35	26.12	34.36	14.84	10.96	n/a	11.60
Midland, TX	16.03	31.12	38.87	15.96	13.54	n/a	8.80

Table continued on next page.

Metro Area	Retail Salespersons	Sales Reps., Except Tech./Scien.	Sales Reps., Tech./Scien.	Secretaries, Exc. Leg./ Med./Exec.	Security Guards	Surgeons	Teacher Assistants
Minneapolis, MN	11.58	36.90	48.32	19.12	14.70	n/a	15.40
Nashville, TN	13.10	29.39	36.34	15.64	14.21	n/a	11.50
New Orleans, LA	12.46	31.07	41.18	15.49	14.39	116.86	11.40
New York, NY[2]	12.88	37.87	49.43	19.19	15.53	104.98	14.10
Oklahoma City, OK	12.60	28.10	34.62	14.86	13.95	114.86	9.00
Omaha, NE	12.29	28.11	34.71	15.91	13.87	n/a	10.30
Orlando, FL	11.53	27.45	35.16	15.27	11.32	n/a	11.80
Oxnard, CA	12.76	n/a	46.05	18.59	15.68	121.08	14.70
Palm Bay, FL	12.10	25.05	39.33	14.49	11.97	112.98	11.60
Peoria, IL	11.80	26.80	32.35	14.79	14.82	n/a	11.30
Philadelphia, PA[2]	13.03	33.11	52.02	17.66	12.30	n/a	12.60
Phoenix, AZ	11.97	28.59	44.41	16.47	13.71	117.17	11.80
Pittsburgh, PA	12.62	31.62	38.90	15.77	11.77	114.66	11.30
Portland, OR	13.04	32.68	38.75	17.62	15.19	n/a	14.50
Providence, RI[3]	12.95	32.08	41.03	18.15	13.03	125.75	14.80
Provo, UT	12.25	32.49	38.50	14.58	14.09	100.95	11.30
Raleigh, NC	11.72	29.57	48.22	16.55	12.95	n/a	11.00
Reno, NV	12.99	28.94	38.90	17.84	11.83	116.44	12.80
Richmond, VA	12.17	34.63	45.81	16.69	13.10	113.16	11.40
Roanoke, VA	11.93	28.59	36.15	15.72	10.76	94.20	11.60
Rochester, MN	12.67	27.65	34.68	18.13	12.53	n/a	12.30
Sacramento, CA	12.79	31.85	41.20	17.72	12.75	n/a	14.40
Salem, OR	12.94	21.91	39.34	16.38	13.67	n/a	16.20
Salt Lake City, UT	12.82	36.15	48.29	16.23	14.80	n/a	11.50
San Antonio, TX	12.78	32.89	36.78	15.32	11.61	116.16	11.20
San Diego, CA	13.34	27.73	41.16	18.46	14.56	105.25	14.30
San Francisco, CA[2]	15.30	29.54	48.03	21.58	15.87	94.79	17.50
San Jose, CA	13.40	35.32	54.47	21.31	14.33	113.16	15.50
Santa Rosa, CA	13.49	29.47	45.85	19.44	14.70	114.81	13.30
Savannah, GA	11.45	28.34	29.44	16.68	13.44	n/a	9.90
Seattle, WA[2]	14.35	35.28	43.16	19.95	16.33	104.00	15.90
Sioux Falls, SD	12.95	27.44	47.04	13.39	12.84	n/a	10.80
Spokane, WA	14.27	25.66	n/a	16.31	13.32	n/a	12.90
Springfield, IL	12.00	25.58	38.91	17.31	20.37	92.52	11.10
Tallahassee, FL	10.95	25.49	35.94	14.52	12.86	124.29	12.30
Tampa, FL	12.17	31.31	34.58	14.85	10.62	121.64	10.40
Topeka, KS	11.31	29.02	41.78	14.44	10.57	n/a	11.30
Tulsa, OK	12.77	29.62	37.57	14.36	13.21	79.73	11.00
Tyler, TX	12.78	26.77	51.68	14.99	13.71	n/a	11.70
Virginia Beach, VA	11.55	29.08	41.92	15.72	13.77	119.18	12.10
Washington, DC[2]	12.20	36.98	52.11	20.79	18.20	103.94	14.40
Wichita, KS	13.03	32.52	41.09	14.76	12.44	122.05	12.30
Wilmington, NC	12.47	27.18	41.51	15.70	11.87	n/a	11.90
Winston-Salem, NC	12.84	28.37	n/a	16.42	12.91	n/a	10.70
Worcester, MA[3]	12.12	33.20	43.15	19.49	13.56	126.96	14.00

Notes: (1) Figures cover the Metropolitan Statistical Area (MSA) except where noted. See Appendix B for areas included; (2) Metropolitan Division; (3) New England City and Town Area; (4) New England City and Town Area Division; n/a not available
Source: Bureau of Labor Statistics, May 2014 Metro Area Occupational Employment and Wage Estimates

Average Hourly Wages: Occupations T – Z

Metro Area	Teachers, Elementary School	Teachers, Secondary School	Tele-marketers	Truck Driv., Heavy/ Trac. Trail.	Truck Drivers, Light	Waiters/ Waitresses
Albuquerque, NM	21.10	22.80	10.63	18.93	14.78	10.44
Anchorage, AK	33.20	33.30	n/a	26.53	18.71	13.45
Ann Arbor, MI	28.10	29.90	n/a	19.35	16.82	11.24
Athens, GA	26.10	27.70	n/a	21.06	16.84	8.47
Atlanta, GA	25.90	26.90	14.51	20.07	16.69	9.20
Austin, TX	23.00	23.70	11.84	18.81	17.42	9.85
Billings, MT	24.10	26.70	13.17	23.71	17.24	9.33
Boise City, ID	24.50	24.20	12.08	18.12	14.55	8.96
Boston, MA[4]	35.30	36.10	14.91	23.78	17.42	13.88
Boulder, CO	26.90	27.30	12.13	21.50	16.76	11.02
Cape Coral, FL	23.80	24.60	10.01	17.41	15.51	9.55
Cedar Rapids, IA	24.70	24.60	10.64	20.70	16.51	8.78
Charleston, SC	24.50	25.50	9.50	20.52	14.54	9.67
Charlotte, NC	21.20	21.70	13.37	19.22	15.72	9.95
Chicago, IL[2]	29.70	36.30	13.61	23.57	18.56	10.38
Clarksville, TN	27.40	26.40	n/a	15.19	13.62	8.80
Colorado Springs, CO	22.10	22.40	11.94	18.92	14.73	9.56
Columbia, MO	n/a	n/a	n/a	19.81	14.74	9.61
Columbus, OH	30.20	30.50	11.19	20.65	16.53	10.34
Dallas, TX[2]	25.40	26.10	14.68	20.00	15.74	10.42
Davenport, IA	25.60	29.00	10.88	19.82	15.19	9.85
Denver, CO	25.60	27.10	14.69	22.34	16.52	10.01
Des Moines, IA	26.10	26.60	14.55	21.57	17.04	8.69
Durham, NC	20.70	21.60	12.38	18.04	17.96	9.57
El Paso, TX	24.40	24.70	10.43	17.44	12.44	8.85
Erie, PA	26.60	26.00	n/a	17.45	17.12	8.76
Eugene, OR	26.40	26.20	n/a	19.12	17.16	11.02
Fargo, ND	25.20	24.00	9.84	19.73	15.83	10.07
Fayetteville, NC	19.50	19.60	n/a	15.03	15.83	8.73
Fort Collins, CO	23.60	23.80	13.69	16.93	17.08	10.10
Fort Wayne, IN	24.30	24.80	10.23	18.83	15.78	9.69
Fort Worth, TX[2]	26.00	26.60	11.23	18.98	15.83	9.08
Gainesville, FL	22.10	24.40	9.39	14.27	15.92	9.80
Grand Rapids, MI	34.10	29.30	13.61	18.10	15.91	9.81
Green Bay, WI	25.50	24.90	12.96	19.44	15.69	8.96
Greensboro, NC	21.20	21.70	10.97	19.10	15.60	9.23
Honolulu, HI	26.30	26.80	12.13	20.79	14.96	14.19
Houston, TX	25.40	25.90	12.37	23.01	16.33	10.78
Huntsville, AL	24.50	24.60	n/a	17.32	14.71	9.69
Indianapolis, IN	25.00	26.30	16.03	22.03	17.09	10.53
Jacksonville, FL	24.60	24.80	10.16	19.07	16.18	10.17
Kansas City, MO	23.00	24.00	12.75	21.28	16.69	9.66
Lafayette, LA	24.10	24.80	n/a	18.12	14.34	8.98
Las Vegas, NV	25.20	25.60	13.83	21.71	16.57	11.33
Lexington, KY	25.00	25.20	13.05	20.97	15.77	9.24
Lincoln, NE	25.70	25.90	11.10	n/a	14.00	8.75
Little Rock, AR	22.40	24.30	8.66	18.54	13.70	8.31
Los Angeles, CA[2]	34.60	35.30	13.05	20.06	16.61	11.81
Louisville, KY	27.20	26.90	12.12	21.09	17.94	9.46
Lubbock, TX	22.00	23.20	n/a	18.50	15.05	9.39
Madison, WI	24.90	27.10	12.56	21.52	15.95	11.31
Manchester, NH[3]	26.90	26.60	15.41	19.39	15.72	11.23
McAllen, TX	24.10	25.40	10.52	16.33	11.43	9.42
Miami, FL[2]	24.60	28.60	11.87	17.57	14.33	10.36
Midland, TX	24.30	24.80	n/a	22.62	15.44	10.06

Table continued on next page.

Metro Area	Teachers, Elementary School	Teachers, Secondary School	Tele-marketers	Truck Driv., Heavy/ Trac. Trail.	Truck Drivers, Light	Waiters/ Waitresses
Minneapolis, MN	31.10	31.70	14.88	21.88	18.21	9.24
Nashville, TN	25.00	25.00	13.27	19.95	15.94	8.95
New Orleans, LA	23.80	25.10	14.37	19.52	16.85	9.73
New York, NY[2]	36.20	38.20	15.89	22.71	18.22	13.21
Oklahoma City, OK	19.70	20.90	10.22	18.92	15.91	9.72
Omaha, NE	22.70	23.70	10.99	19.87	14.70	8.79
Orlando, FL	22.70	22.30	10.88	18.65	15.77	10.52
Oxnard, CA	33.30	33.30	16.20	22.71	18.52	11.45
Palm Bay, FL	21.10	21.50	10.27	16.39	14.19	10.45
Peoria, IL	22.70	30.00	12.20	18.58	16.70	10.16
Philadelphia, PA[2]	32.00	31.50	14.12	21.75	17.00	10.19
Phoenix, AZ	21.00	23.60	11.67	20.02	16.12	10.41
Pittsburgh, PA	27.70	29.40	13.19	20.51	16.15	9.45
Portland, OR	28.50	28.60	12.59	19.88	16.94	11.45
Providence, RI[3]	33.50	32.60	16.78	19.94	18.33	9.95
Provo, UT	26.80	29.00	12.88	23.28	13.67	10.89
Raleigh, NC	21.70	22.30	17.13	20.09	15.93	9.98
Reno, NV	25.40	24.80	13.77	22.83	16.06	9.97
Richmond, VA	26.60	27.40	12.40	19.39	15.86	10.39
Roanoke, VA	22.50	23.30	15.62	18.42	16.08	10.16
Rochester, MN	26.60	26.50	n/a	21.57	15.86	8.39
Sacramento, CA	32.40	33.30	15.40	19.39	17.86	11.79
Salem, OR	28.80	27.10	10.69	17.54	18.65	10.85
Salt Lake City, UT	27.90	26.90	12.23	20.09	15.54	11.09
San Antonio, TX	27.10	27.70	10.63	18.18	14.56	9.36
San Diego, CA	31.60	35.00	12.15	19.56	16.71	12.44
San Francisco, CA[2]	33.10	35.00	15.57	22.44	19.39	12.63
San Jose, CA	34.40	36.10	14.43	22.34	18.59	12.02
Santa Rosa, CA	23.70	32.50	13.12	21.96	17.73	12.08
Savannah, GA	26.70	23.60	14.79	18.16	13.78	9.66
Seattle, WA[2]	29.50	31.10	13.49	22.18	17.66	14.45
Sioux Falls, SD	20.40	20.20	14.22	20.16	15.48	8.70
Spokane, WA	29.20	30.30	11.51	19.94	17.33	12.73
Springfield, IL	29.30	30.30	15.10	18.92	14.56	9.49
Tallahassee, FL	20.50	20.60	13.57	15.64	15.75	10.54
Tampa, FL	21.30	21.60	12.64	16.66	16.98	10.26
Topeka, KS	24.20	24.40	n/a	18.40	15.87	8.48
Tulsa, OK	22.50	22.50	10.63	20.67	15.12	9.09
Tyler, TX	21.50	23.10	n/a	18.50	15.84	9.01
Virginia Beach, VA	27.80	28.10	11.94	18.63	16.64	11.46
Washington, DC[2]	33.00	33.80	11.65	20.74	18.52	11.74
Wichita, KS	21.50	22.90	11.47	18.16	14.14	8.87
Wilmington, NC	19.60	19.90	9.73	17.23	14.51	9.14
Winston-Salem, NC	20.60	20.90	15.27	19.53	15.87	9.27
Worcester, MA[3]	31.90	33.00	15.33	24.01	18.22	11.70

Notes: (1) Figures cover the Metropolitan Statistical Area (MSA) except where noted. See Appendix B for areas included; (2) Metropolitan Division; (3) New England City and Town Area; (4) New England City and Town Area Division; Hourly wages for elementary and secondary school teachers were calculated by the editors from annual wage data assuming a 40 hour work week; n/a not available
Source: Bureau of Labor Statistics, May 2014 Metro Area Occupational Employment and Wage Estimates

Means of Transportation to Work: City

City	Car/Truck/Van		Public Transportation			Bicycle	Walked	Other Means	Worked at Home
	Drove Alone	Car-pooled	Bus	Subway	Railroad				
Albuquerque, NM	79.6	9.7	1.7	0.0	0.1	1.3	2.1	1.5	3.8
Anchorage, AK	74.4	12.1	2.2	0.0	0.0	1.2	3.4	2.8	4.0
Ann Arbor, MI	57.4	5.9	10.3	0.1	0.0	5.1	14.4	0.5	6.3
Athens, GA	76.3	9.6	3.1	0.0	0.0	1.7	5.1	1.6	2.5
Atlanta, GA	68.5	7.5	6.2	3.0	0.1	0.9	4.9	1.2	7.7
Austin, TX	73.3	10.3	3.9	0.0	0.1	1.6	2.6	1.5	6.6
Billings, MT	78.5	10.5	1.1	0.0	0.0	1.2	3.6	0.9	4.1
Boise City, ID	78.9	7.6	0.7	0.0	0.0	2.5	3.2	1.4	5.6
Boston, MA	38.7	6.5	13.5	17.6	1.4	1.9	14.8	1.9	3.6
Boulder, CO	51.3	5.2	9.0	0.1	0.0	10.8	10.5	1.6	11.5
Cape Coral, FL	83.2	9.3	0.5	0.0	0.0	0.4	0.8	1.5	4.4
Cedar Rapids, IA	81.9	8.9	1.2	0.0	0.0	0.5	3.0	1.2	3.3
Charleston, SC	76.5	6.5	2.2	0.0	0.0	2.5	5.8	1.5	4.9
Charlotte, NC	76.1	10.2	3.5	0.3	0.1	0.2	2.2	1.4	6.0
Chicago, IL	50.0	8.9	14.2	11.0	1.8	1.4	6.7	1.7	4.3
Clarksville, TN	84.0	9.2	0.9	0.0	0.0	0.1	2.8	1.1	1.9
Colorado Springs, CO	79.5	10.3	0.9	0.0	0.0	0.6	2.1	1.3	5.3
Columbia, MO	76.3	10.4	1.0	0.0	0.0	1.6	6.0	1.0	3.7
Columbus, OH	80.1	8.8	3.2	0.0	0.0	0.8	2.9	1.0	3.3
Dallas, TX	76.6	11.2	3.3	0.3	0.4	0.2	1.9	1.8	4.3
Davenport, IA	85.4	7.5	0.8	0.0	0.0	0.4	2.2	1.2	2.6
Denver, CO	69.6	8.8	6.0	0.6	0.2	2.4	4.8	1.3	6.3
Des Moines, IA	81.3	10.4	1.4	0.0	0.0	0.3	2.8	1.0	2.8
Durham, NC	73.8	11.7	4.2	0.0	0.0	1.1	3.2	1.5	4.4
El Paso, TX	79.2	11.3	2.0	0.0	0.0	0.1	2.0	2.5	2.8
Erie, PA	74.9	10.5	4.5	0.0	0.0	0.4	5.7	1.5	2.3
Eugene, OR	65.7	8.2	3.9	0.0	0.0	8.0	7.0	0.9	6.4
Fargo, ND	80.8	8.4	1.0	0.0	0.0	1.0	4.7	1.3	2.8
Fayetteville, NC	81.7	8.9	0.8	0.1	0.0	0.1	5.0	1.0	2.4
Fort Collins, CO	71.2	7.9	1.3	0.0	0.0	7.4	4.0	1.3	6.8
Fort Wayne, IN	84.5	8.4	0.9	0.0	0.0	0.4	1.3	1.1	3.4
Fort Worth, TX	81.9	11.1	0.7	0.0	0.2	0.2	1.2	1.6	3.2
Gainesville, FL	64.3	8.9	7.9	0.0	0.0	6.6	5.1	2.7	4.5
Grand Rapids, MI	75.2	11.5	3.7	0.0	0.0	0.9	3.2	0.7	4.9
Green Bay, WI	79.3	9.9	1.6	0.0	0.0	0.8	3.4	2.2	2.9
Greensboro, NC	81.3	8.9	1.8	0.0	0.0	0.3	2.1	1.2	4.2
Honolulu, HI	57.5	12.6	12.1	0.0	0.0	1.9	8.9	3.5	3.5
Houston, TX	75.7	12.1	4.2	0.1	0.1	0.6	2.1	1.8	3.4
Huntsville, AL	86.0	6.8	0.4	0.0	0.0	0.2	1.5	2.2	2.8
Indianapolis, IN	81.5	10.0	2.2	0.0	0.0	0.4	2.1	1.0	2.7
Jacksonville, FL	80.3	10.0	1.9	0.0	0.0	0.4	1.2	1.5	4.6
Kansas City, MO	79.5	9.3	3.3	0.0	0.0	0.4	2.2	1.2	4.0
Lafayette, LA	81.2	10.1	0.8	0.0	0.0	1.1	2.4	1.5	2.9
Las Vegas, NV	78.1	11.4	3.9	0.0	0.0	0.4	1.7	1.4	3.0
Lexington, KY	79.2	9.3	1.7	0.0	0.0	1.2	3.8	0.8	4.0
Lincoln, NE	81.1	9.1	1.4	0.0	0.0	1.8	2.7	0.7	3.2
Little Rock, AR	84.8	8.9	1.3	0.0	0.0	0.1	1.3	0.9	2.7
Los Angeles, CA	67.2	9.8	10.2	0.6	0.1	1.1	3.7	1.6	5.7
Louisville, KY	82.1	8.2	3.0	0.0	0.0	0.3	2.3	1.3	2.8
Lubbock, TX	82.9	10.0	0.8	0.0	0.0	0.6	2.2	0.9	2.6
Madison, WI	63.5	8.3	9.0	0.0	0.0	5.2	9.5	0.7	3.8
Manchester, NH	80.6	10.2	1.3	0.1	0.0	0.2	3.4	0.8	3.4
McAllen, TX	74.0	9.7	0.6	0.0	0.0	0.2	0.9	8.0	6.8
Miami, FL	68.9	9.6	10.4	0.7	0.3	0.9	4.7	1.2	3.3

Table continued on next page.

City	Car/Truck/Van		Public Transportation			Bicycle	Walked	Other Means	Worked at Home
	Drove Alone	Car-pooled	Bus	Subway	Railroad				
Midland, TX	83.3	11.2	0.2	0.0	0.0	0.2	1.0	1.7	2.5
Minneapolis, MN	62.2	8.2	11.9	0.4	0.4	3.9	6.5	1.1	5.4
Nashville, TN	80.1	9.9	2.1	0.0	0.1	0.3	2.1	1.1	4.4
New Orleans, LA	70.0	9.7	6.3	0.0	0.0	2.8	5.0	2.4	3.7
New York, NY	22.0	4.7	11.4	42.8	1.7	1.0	10.2	2.3	4.0
Oklahoma City, OK	81.8	11.6	0.5	0.0	0.0	0.2	1.6	0.9	3.3
Omaha, NE	81.2	10.1	1.5	0.0	0.0	0.2	2.7	0.9	3.3
Orlando, FL	79.2	7.9	5.2	0.0	0.0	0.6	2.2	1.5	3.5
Oxnard, CA	72.6	20.5	1.3	0.0	0.1	0.7	1.3	1.0	2.5
Palm Bay, FL	83.6	10.5	0.2	0.1	0.0	0.7	1.2	1.4	2.4
Peoria, IL	81.3	8.8	3.4	0.0	0.0	0.5	2.9	0.8	2.4
Philadelphia, PA	50.1	8.9	18.2	4.9	2.8	2.1	8.5	1.6	3.0
Phoenix, AZ	75.0	12.0	3.5	0.1	0.1	0.7	1.9	2.1	4.7
Pittsburgh, PA	55.7	9.7	16.2	0.3	0.0	1.8	11.1	1.6	3.8
Portland, OR	58.0	9.1	9.4	0.8	0.2	6.1	5.9	2.8	7.6
Providence, RI	59.7	11.7	7.7	0.1	0.9	1.2	11.2	3.1	4.4
Provo, UT	60.2	15.0	1.1	0.1	0.5	3.6	12.7	1.5	5.4
Raleigh, NC	79.3	9.6	2.1	0.0	0.0	0.5	1.9	1.2	5.3
Reno, NV	76.6	10.1	3.2	0.0	0.0	1.0	3.8	2.0	3.2
Richmond, VA	70.1	10.9	5.4	0.1	0.0	2.1	5.2	1.6	4.7
Roanoke, VA	80.4	9.3	3.2	0.1	0.0	0.1	2.8	1.3	2.8
Rochester, MN	74.6	11.0	5.4	0.1	0.0	0.7	4.1	0.9	3.1
Sacramento, CA	71.8	12.5	3.1	0.4	0.4	2.3	3.3	1.5	4.7
Salem, OR	75.5	11.8	1.8	0.0	0.0	1.8	4.7	0.8	3.6
Salt Lake City, UT	67.1	12.8	5.3	0.2	0.3	2.9	4.9	2.7	3.7
San Antonio, TX	79.2	11.0	3.4	0.0	0.0	0.3	1.9	1.0	3.2
San Diego, CA	74.9	9.3	3.7	0.0	0.1	0.9	3.1	1.4	6.5
San Francisco, CA	36.7	7.3	22.4	6.7	1.3	3.7	10.2	4.6	7.1
San Jose, CA	77.2	11.1	2.6	0.2	0.8	0.9	1.6	1.6	4.0
Santa Rosa, CA	78.9	10.0	1.8	0.0	0.0	1.1	3.4	1.0	3.8
Savannah, GA	76.5	10.3	3.4	0.0	0.0	1.7	4.0	0.9	3.3
Seattle, WA	51.0	8.6	18.6	0.4	0.1	3.7	9.3	1.6	6.7
Sioux Falls, SD	84.5	8.1	1.0	0.0	0.0	0.5	2.4	1.3	2.3
Spokane, WA	76.0	9.9	4.0	0.0	0.0	0.6	3.7	0.6	5.2
Springfield, IL	80.1	9.9	1.9	0.2	0.0	0.2	3.4	0.8	3.5
Tallahassee, FL	81.4	7.9	2.4	0.0	0.0	0.9	3.0	1.1	3.2
Tampa, FL	78.7	8.2	2.5	0.0	0.0	1.4	2.4	1.6	5.1
Topeka, KS	80.3	12.3	1.0	0.0	0.0	0.3	2.1	1.2	2.8
Tulsa, OK	81.7	10.6	1.0	0.0	0.0	0.2	1.8	1.3	3.4
Tyler, TX	82.0	10.3	0.3	0.0	0.0	0.2	1.7	2.2	3.2
Virginia Beach, VA	82.0	8.2	0.7	0.1	0.0	0.6	2.5	1.1	4.7
Washington, DC	33.1	5.8	16.5	21.6	0.4	4.0	12.6	1.4	4.5
Wichita, KS	84.8	8.7	0.6	0.0	0.0	0.3	1.4	1.1	3.0
Wilmington, NC	76.4	9.4	1.5	0.0	0.0	1.6	3.4	1.7	6.1
Winston-Salem, NC	81.1	8.2	2.0	0.0	0.0	0.1	2.2	2.1	4.3
Worcester, MA	74.2	11.1	2.6	0.2	0.5	0.3	6.4	1.1	3.5
U.S.	76.4	9.6	2.6	1.8	0.6	0.6	2.8	1.3	4.3

Note: Figures are percentages and cover workers 16 years of age and older
Source: U.S. Census Bureau, 2011-2013 American Community Survey 3-Year Estimates

Means of Transportation to Work: Metro Area

Metro Area	Car/Truck/Van		Public Transportation			Bicycle	Walked	Other Means	Worked at Home
	Drove Alone	Car-pooled	Bus	Subway	Railroad				
Albuquerque, NM	80.0	9.6	1.3	0.0	0.3	1.0	1.9	1.6	4.4
Anchorage, AK	73.8	12.4	2.0	0.0	0.0	1.0	3.1	3.5	4.3
Ann Arbor, MI	73.0	7.7	5.2	0.0	0.0	2.0	6.2	0.7	5.3
Athens, GA	80.1	8.9	1.9	0.0	0.0	1.1	3.4	1.3	3.3
Atlanta, GA	77.9	10.4	2.2	0.7	0.1	0.2	1.4	1.3	5.8
Austin, TX	76.0	10.6	2.2	0.0	0.1	0.9	1.9	1.4	6.9
Billings, MT	78.7	10.8	1.0	0.0	0.0	0.9	3.5	1.0	4.0
Boise City, ID	79.0	8.7	0.4	0.0	0.0	1.1	2.0	1.9	6.8
Boston, MA	68.5	7.5	4.1	5.7	2.0	0.9	5.4	1.3	4.5
Boulder, CO	64.1	8.0	5.5	0.0	0.0	4.4	5.1	1.8	11.1
Cape Coral, FL	77.8	11.1	1.1	0.0	0.0	0.7	1.0	2.6	5.7
Cedar Rapids, IA	82.8	8.2	0.8	0.0	0.0	0.3	2.7	1.1	4.0
Charleston, SC	80.5	9.2	1.5	0.0	0.0	0.9	2.7	0.9	4.3
Charlotte, NC	80.2	10.0	1.6	0.1	0.1	0.1	1.4	1.1	5.3
Chicago, IL	70.9	8.5	4.7	3.6	3.1	0.6	3.1	1.1	4.2
Clarksville, TN	81.2	9.9	0.7	0.0	0.0	0.1	4.1	1.6	2.3
Colorado Springs, CO	77.5	10.4	0.7	0.0	0.0	0.4	4.1	1.1	5.8
Columbia, MO	78.4	10.7	0.8	0.0	0.0	1.1	4.5	1.0	3.5
Columbus, OH	82.5	8.0	1.7	0.0	0.0	0.4	2.2	1.0	4.2
Dallas, TX	80.8	10.2	1.0	0.2	0.3	0.2	1.2	1.4	4.8
Davenport, IA	84.4	8.4	0.9	0.0	0.0	0.3	1.8	1.2	3.0
Denver, CO	75.9	9.0	3.7	0.4	0.2	1.0	2.2	1.2	6.4
Des Moines, IA	84.0	8.5	0.8	0.0	0.0	0.2	1.7	0.8	4.0
Durham, NC	73.6	10.7	4.2	0.0	0.0	1.0	3.2	1.7	5.5
El Paso, TX	78.7	11.3	1.7	0.0	0.0	0.1	2.4	2.8	3.0
Erie, PA	80.1	9.5	1.8	0.0	0.0	0.3	3.8	1.0	3.4
Eugene, OR	70.9	10.0	2.8	0.0	0.0	4.5	4.7	0.8	6.3
Fargo, ND	81.1	8.3	0.8	0.0	0.0	0.7	4.3	1.0	3.7
Fayetteville, NC	83.3	9.2	0.7	0.0	0.0	0.2	3.4	1.2	2.1
Fort Collins, CO	74.3	8.3	1.0	0.0	0.0	4.3	3.0	1.5	7.6
Fort Wayne, IN	84.9	7.8	0.6	0.0	0.0	0.4	1.3	1.0	4.0
Fort Worth, TX	80.8	10.2	1.0	0.2	0.3	0.2	1.2	1.4	4.8
Gainesville, FL	73.4	9.7	4.3	0.0	0.0	3.3	3.1	1.8	4.4
Grand Rapids, MI	82.1	9.3	1.4	0.0	0.0	0.5	2.0	0.7	3.9
Green Bay, WI	82.4	8.2	0.7	0.0	0.0	0.4	2.7	1.2	4.3
Greensboro, NC	82.8	9.5	1.0	0.0	0.0	0.2	1.6	0.9	4.0
Honolulu, HI	64.4	14.8	8.0	0.0	0.0	1.2	5.2	2.9	3.5
Houston, TX	79.9	10.9	2.4	0.0	0.0	0.3	1.4	1.5	3.5
Huntsville, AL	86.9	7.7	0.3	0.1	0.0	0.1	1.1	1.3	2.6
Indianapolis, IN	83.7	8.9	1.1	0.0	0.0	0.3	1.6	0.9	3.6
Jacksonville, FL	80.8	9.8	1.3	0.0	0.0	0.6	1.2	1.4	4.9
Kansas City, MO	83.2	9.0	1.2	0.0	0.0	0.2	1.3	0.9	4.2
Lafayette, LA	82.7	10.8	0.5	0.0	0.0	0.4	1.9	1.6	2.1
Las Vegas, NV	78.9	10.6	3.7	0.0	0.0	0.3	1.8	1.6	2.9
Lexington, KY	80.3	9.7	1.2	0.0	0.0	0.8	3.2	0.7	4.1
Lincoln, NE	81.2	8.9	1.3	0.0	0.0	1.6	2.7	0.7	3.7
Little Rock, AR	85.5	9.0	0.7	0.0	0.0	0.1	1.1	0.9	2.8
Los Angeles, CA	73.9	10.1	5.4	0.3	0.2	0.9	2.7	1.3	5.1
Louisville, KY	83.8	8.5	1.8	0.0	0.0	0.2	1.7	1.0	3.0
Lubbock, TX	82.9	10.0	0.7	0.0	0.0	0.5	2.1	1.0	2.7
Madison, WI	74.0	8.6	4.4	0.0	0.0	2.4	5.3	0.7	4.5
Manchester, NH	81.6	8.4	0.7	0.1	0.1	0.1	2.2	0.8	6.1
McAllen, TX	78.9	11.0	0.2	0.0	0.0	0.1	1.2	4.0	4.5
Miami, FL	77.9	9.6	3.6	0.2	0.2	0.6	1.8	1.3	4.8

Table continued on next page.

Metro Area	Car/Truck/Van: Drove Alone	Car/Truck/Van: Car-pooled	Public Transportation: Bus	Public Transportation: Subway	Public Transportation: Railroad	Bicycle	Walked	Other Means	Worked at Home
Midland, TX	82.9	10.4	0.2	0.0	0.0	0.1	0.8	2.3	3.3
Minneapolis, MN	78.4	8.4	4.2	0.1	0.2	0.9	2.2	0.8	4.9
Nashville, TN	82.5	9.4	1.1	0.0	0.1	0.2	1.3	0.9	4.5
New Orleans, LA	79.1	10.3	2.4	0.0	0.0	1.1	2.5	2.0	2.6
New York, NY	50.5	6.8	7.9	18.6	3.6	0.6	6.1	1.9	4.1
Oklahoma City, OK	83.1	10.2	0.5	0.0	0.0	0.3	1.6	1.0	3.2
Omaha, NE	83.1	9.5	0.9	0.0	0.0	0.2	1.9	0.9	3.6
Orlando, FL	80.7	9.4	2.0	0.0	0.0	0.5	1.2	1.6	4.6
Oxnard, CA	76.7	12.7	0.9	0.0	0.3	0.7	2.0	1.0	5.6
Palm Bay, FL	82.7	8.5	0.6	0.0	0.0	0.6	1.1	1.9	4.6
Peoria, IL	84.4	8.7	1.2	0.0	0.0	0.3	2.0	0.6	2.7
Philadelphia, PA	73.3	7.8	5.5	1.7	2.3	0.7	3.8	0.9	4.0
Phoenix, AZ	76.5	11.3	2.1	0.0	0.0	0.9	1.5	1.9	5.8
Pittsburgh, PA	77.5	8.9	4.8	0.2	0.0	0.3	3.4	1.2	3.7
Portland, OR	70.9	9.7	4.7	0.6	0.3	2.3	3.6	1.7	6.4
Providence, RI	80.6	8.7	1.8	0.1	0.9	0.3	3.2	1.1	3.3
Provo, UT	72.4	13.5	1.2	0.2	0.3	1.3	4.2	1.1	6.0
Raleigh, NC	80.5	9.4	1.0	0.0	0.0	0.2	1.3	1.2	6.4
Reno, NV	78.1	10.4	2.4	0.0	0.0	0.7	2.7	1.9	3.8
Richmond, VA	81.8	8.9	1.5	0.0	0.0	0.5	1.6	1.1	4.6
Roanoke, VA	83.2	8.6	1.3	0.0	0.0	0.1	2.3	1.1	3.4
Rochester, MN	75.9	11.2	3.7	0.0	0.0	0.5	3.3	0.9	4.4
Sacramento, CA	75.2	11.3	1.9	0.3	0.2	1.9	2.2	1.3	5.8
Salem, OR	74.4	13.9	1.3	0.0	0.0	1.3	4.2	1.0	4.0
Salt Lake City, UT	75.2	12.5	2.5	0.3	0.4	0.8	1.9	1.8	4.7
San Antonio, TX	79.3	11.0	2.3	0.0	0.0	0.2	1.8	1.1	4.3
San Diego, CA	76.1	9.8	2.6	0.0	0.2	0.7	2.9	1.4	6.4
San Francisco, CA	60.6	10.0	7.7	5.9	1.0	1.9	4.4	2.3	6.1
San Jose, CA	76.3	10.4	2.3	0.2	1.1	1.8	2.0	1.5	4.5
Santa Rosa, CA	76.5	9.7	1.7	0.0	0.0	1.0	3.2	1.3	6.6
Savannah, GA	82.1	8.9	1.8	0.0	0.0	0.7	2.2	1.0	3.5
Seattle, WA	70.0	10.2	8.0	0.2	0.4	1.0	3.6	1.2	5.4
Sioux Falls, SD	84.1	8.0	0.7	0.0	0.0	0.4	2.3	1.2	3.4
Spokane, WA	76.7	10.5	2.5	0.0	0.0	0.5	3.0	0.9	5.9
Springfield, IL	81.8	10.1	1.2	0.1	0.0	0.2	2.4	0.9	3.3
Tallahassee, FL	82.1	9.7	1.4	0.0	0.0	0.5	1.9	1.1	3.3
Tampa, FL	80.8	9.0	1.2	0.0	0.0	0.8	1.5	1.4	5.2
Topeka, KS	81.5	11.7	0.6	0.0	0.0	0.2	1.8	0.8	3.3
Tulsa, OK	83.5	9.9	0.6	0.0	0.0	0.2	1.4	1.1	3.4
Tyler, TX	83.0	10.2	0.3	0.0	0.0	0.1	1.4	1.6	3.3
Virginia Beach, VA	81.3	8.4	1.7	0.0	0.0	0.4	2.7	1.2	4.2
Washington, DC	66.0	9.9	5.5	7.9	0.7	0.8	3.3	0.9	4.9
Wichita, KS	85.2	8.4	0.4	0.0	0.0	0.3	1.5	1.0	3.2
Wilmington, NC	77.5	11.1	0.9	0.0	0.0	0.9	2.0	1.6	6.1
Winston-Salem, NC	83.4	8.9	0.8	0.0	0.0	0.1	1.4	1.3	4.0
Worcester, MA	82.1	8.7	0.7	0.2	0.6	0.1	2.9	0.6	4.1
U.S.	76.4	9.6	2.6	1.8	0.6	0.6	2.8	1.3	4.3

Note: Figures are percentages and cover workers 16 years of age and older; (1) Figures cover the Metropolitan Statistical Area—see Appendix B for areas included
Source: U.S. Census Bureau, 2011-2013 American Community Survey 3-Year Estimates

Travel Time to Work: City

City	Less Than 10 Minutes	10 to 19 Minutes	20 to 29 Minutes	30 to 44 Minutes	45 to 59 Minutes	60 to 89 Minutes	90 Minutes or More
Albuquerque, NM	11.5	36.8	28.7	16.5	3.1	2.0	1.4
Anchorage, AK	15.3	44.4	22.1	12.0	2.8	1.4	1.9
Ann Arbor, MI	15.3	45.0	18.4	12.5	5.0	3.3	0.5
Athens, GA	17.8	48.7	16.6	8.2	3.3	3.5	1.9
Atlanta, GA	9.0	31.4	27.6	19.4	6.1	4.3	2.3
Austin, TX	10.6	33.9	24.5	21.4	5.0	3.1	1.5
Billings, MT	19.6	51.2	19.2	5.0	1.8	1.2	2.0
Boise City, ID	17.3	44.9	24.2	9.7	1.3	1.3	1.3
Boston, MA	7.9	22.0	20.2	28.6	10.6	8.7	1.9
Boulder, CO	20.8	42.7	16.2	11.4	4.9	2.5	1.5
Cape Coral, FL	7.2	25.3	19.5	30.1	11.0	4.6	2.3
Cedar Rapids, IA	20.2	47.4	17.1	10.1	2.1	1.8	1.3
Charleston, SC	14.7	35.3	26.5	16.5	3.6	2.4	1.1
Charlotte, NC	10.4	31.0	25.4	23.0	5.5	2.8	2.0
Chicago, IL	5.2	18.1	18.6	29.2	13.6	11.6	3.6
Clarksville, TN	12.7	34.5	27.0	15.7	5.4	4.0	0.7
Colorado Springs, CO	13.3	38.3	27.2	14.5	2.7	2.5	1.5
Columbia, MO	21.6	52.7	12.7	7.7	3.0	1.3	1.1
Columbus, OH	10.0	34.5	31.1	18.6	3.1	1.5	1.2
Dallas, TX	9.0	29.0	22.8	25.2	7.3	4.8	2.0
Davenport, IA	17.5	48.1	22.3	7.0	2.5	1.7	1.0
Denver, CO	9.9	30.2	24.8	23.1	6.5	3.9	1.5
Des Moines, IA	16.0	41.7	26.6	10.9	2.5	1.3	1.0
Durham, NC	11.3	42.0	23.4	15.9	3.3	2.4	1.7
El Paso, TX	8.8	34.0	28.9	21.2	3.6	2.0	1.5
Erie, PA	21.3	50.1	16.4	7.7	2.2	1.6	0.7
Eugene, OR	17.5	50.6	19.9	7.2	1.9	2.1	0.8
Fargo, ND	22.4	56.4	13.7	3.6	1.2	1.9	1.0
Fayetteville, NC	15.1	41.6	23.7	12.3	3.2	2.1	2.0
Fort Collins, CO	17.9	45.2	18.5	10.7	3.2	2.7	1.9
Fort Wayne, IN	11.8	42.6	28.4	11.3	2.7	1.6	1.5
Fort Worth, TX	9.3	29.1	23.1	23.1	8.1	5.6	1.7
Gainesville, FL	18.0	53.7	16.3	8.7	1.8	0.9	0.6
Grand Rapids, MI	16.9	42.2	23.5	9.6	3.4	2.9	1.4
Green Bay, WI	16.2	51.0	17.5	8.8	3.1	2.1	1.2
Greensboro, NC	12.6	45.9	21.9	13.6	2.2	1.8	2.1
Honolulu, HI	8.4	35.9	24.7	22.0	5.0	3.2	0.8
Houston, TX	8.6	27.9	23.5	25.6	7.2	5.5	1.7
Huntsville, AL	15.4	44.0	24.9	12.1	1.6	1.1	1.0
Indianapolis, IN	11.1	30.3	29.4	21.1	4.4	2.6	1.1
Jacksonville, FL	7.8	30.1	30.9	22.3	4.9	2.7	1.3
Kansas City, MO	12.4	34.6	26.9	19.4	3.7	1.8	1.1
Lafayette, LA	18.1	44.6	17.6	11.5	1.8	3.3	3.0
Las Vegas, NV	7.1	26.1	29.2	28.5	4.5	2.8	1.8
Lexington, KY	13.0	43.0	25.0	13.0	2.9	2.0	1.1
Lincoln, NE	16.2	47.2	23.2	8.2	2.5	1.8	1.0
Little Rock, AR	13.6	41.3	30.0	10.4	2.4	1.6	0.8
Los Angeles, CA	7.2	24.3	20.3	26.9	9.5	8.6	3.2
Louisville, KY	10.2	33.1	30.2	19.0	3.8	2.2	1.4
Lubbock, TX	20.4	58.3	12.7	4.9	1.9	1.1	0.7
Madison, WI	15.0	41.4	25.0	12.5	3.1	2.3	0.7
Manchester, NH	13.2	40.6	21.0	13.7	4.8	4.2	2.6
McAllen, TX	17.2	43.8	21.7	10.6	2.5	1.2	3.0
Miami, FL	7.1	26.6	27.0	25.8	7.2	4.4	2.0
Midland, TX	18.3	47.2	16.8	11.4	1.6	2.7	2.0

Table continued on next page.

City	Less Than 10 Minutes	10 to 19 Minutes	20 to 29 Minutes	30 to 44 Minutes	45 to 59 Minutes	60 to 89 Minutes	90 Minutes or More
Minneapolis, MN	8.6	34.9	29.7	19.2	3.9	2.5	1.2
Nashville, TN	8.9	31.0	28.0	23.7	5.1	2.2	1.2
New Orleans, LA	10.5	34.9	25.5	19.3	4.3	3.6	1.8
New York, NY	4.3	13.6	14.5	27.7	15.4	17.9	6.6
Oklahoma City, OK	13.1	36.7	29.0	16.1	2.4	1.4	1.3
Omaha, NE	14.9	42.9	26.5	11.7	1.7	1.3	0.9
Orlando, FL	8.3	34.0	26.1	20.5	5.3	3.1	2.6
Oxnard, CA	9.2	34.1	25.8	21.1	4.5	3.3	2.1
Palm Bay, FL	7.4	26.9	30.4	22.9	5.4	3.9	3.2
Peoria, IL	16.5	46.6	24.2	7.2	2.2	2.4	0.9
Philadelphia, PA	6.3	20.7	20.0	27.2	12.7	9.6	3.5
Phoenix, AZ	9.1	29.2	25.0	25.4	6.6	3.4	1.4
Pittsburgh, PA	10.2	33.2	25.6	21.1	5.6	3.1	1.2
Portland, OR	9.2	31.1	26.3	21.1	6.1	4.2	1.9
Providence, RI	15.5	42.4	18.9	12.4	4.3	4.5	2.0
Provo, UT	23.7	45.0	16.8	7.3	3.2	2.5	1.4
Raleigh, NC	11.9	35.9	27.2	17.6	4.1	2.1	1.2
Reno, NV	14.3	45.4	22.9	9.6	3.2	3.1	1.5
Richmond, VA	12.0	38.4	25.7	15.5	3.9	2.5	2.0
Roanoke, VA	14.3	48.5	21.4	10.7	2.3	1.7	1.1
Rochester, MN	20.6	56.6	11.9	5.6	2.0	2.2	1.1
Sacramento, CA	10.2	35.2	25.2	18.7	4.6	3.0	3.2
Salem, OR	16.6	41.9	19.3	12.2	4.0	4.2	1.8
Salt Lake City, UT	14.5	44.8	21.2	11.9	3.7	2.4	1.5
San Antonio, TX	10.5	31.7	27.6	20.9	4.7	2.8	1.8
San Diego, CA	8.5	34.7	29.0	19.7	4.0	2.5	1.6
San Francisco, CA	4.9	21.5	21.8	28.3	11.2	10.0	2.4
San Jose, CA	6.6	27.6	25.8	24.8	7.5	5.7	1.9
Santa Rosa, CA	14.6	42.8	19.2	12.8	3.9	4.3	2.6
Savannah, GA	14.1	40.0	25.9	13.7	3.7	1.5	1.1
Seattle, WA	8.4	27.4	24.6	25.8	8.5	3.9	1.5
Sioux Falls, SD	16.2	53.8	20.9	4.6	1.7	2.0	0.8
Spokane, WA	16.2	40.0	23.3	14.5	2.7	1.7	1.5
Springfield, IL	20.4	51.3	17.6	6.5	1.5	1.3	1.3
Tallahassee, FL	15.8	43.8	24.2	12.1	1.7	1.4	0.9
Tampa, FL	12.6	33.5	23.9	19.2	6.1	3.2	1.7
Topeka, KS	18.7	55.0	14.6	7.0	1.2	2.3	1.2
Tulsa, OK	16.3	43.7	24.7	10.9	1.9	1.4	1.1
Tyler, TX	21.5	44.2	16.8	11.4	2.5	1.4	2.2
Virginia Beach, VA	11.2	32.5	26.0	21.3	5.4	2.4	1.3
Washington, DC	5.7	19.9	23.0	31.2	11.0	6.8	2.4
Wichita, KS	14.3	47.2	25.3	9.8	1.5	1.1	0.8
Wilmington, NC	18.9	49.5	18.0	7.8	2.7	1.8	1.3
Winston-Salem, NC	14.8	47.3	20.6	10.6	3.0	2.1	1.5
Worcester, MA	12.7	38.8	19.8	15.5	5.8	5.2	2.0
U.S.	13.3	29.7	20.9	20.2	7.7	5.7	2.6

Note: Figures are percentages and include workers 16 years old and over
Source: U.S. Census Bureau, 2011-2013 American Community Survey 3-Year Estimates

Travel Time to Work: Metro Area

Metro Area	Less Than 10 Minutes	10 to 19 Minutes	20 to 29 Minutes	30 to 44 Minutes	45 to 59 Minutes	60 to 89 Minutes	90 Minutes or More
Albuquerque, NM	11.9	32.4	25.7	19.7	5.5	3.1	1.7
Anchorage, AK	15.0	41.1	20.7	11.8	4.5	4.4	2.4
Ann Arbor, MI	12.2	34.8	23.3	18.2	6.6	3.8	1.0
Athens, GA	14.2	40.8	21.2	13.4	4.1	3.7	2.6
Atlanta, GA	8.0	23.5	20.4	24.9	11.8	8.5	2.9
Austin, TX	10.8	28.9	22.2	23.0	8.2	5.0	2.0
Billings, MT	18.2	43.6	22.6	9.0	2.4	1.7	2.5
Boise City, ID	14.4	34.8	26.3	17.6	3.8	2.0	1.2
Boston, MA	10.4	23.8	18.4	24.2	11.1	9.2	2.8
Boulder, CO	15.7	34.5	21.1	16.7	6.3	4.0	1.6
Cape Coral, FL	8.4	27.5	20.7	26.4	9.4	4.9	2.7
Cedar Rapids, IA	20.0	38.7	20.5	13.3	4.0	2.4	1.2
Charleston, SC	10.5	30.1	24.3	22.9	7.7	3.0	1.4
Charlotte, NC	10.6	29.7	22.8	22.9	8.2	4.0	2.0
Chicago, IL	9.0	22.5	18.8	24.8	11.7	9.9	3.2
Clarksville, TN	15.9	32.6	24.3	16.3	5.6	4.0	1.1
Colorado Springs, CO	13.0	35.4	25.9	16.7	4.5	2.9	1.6
Columbia, MO	17.6	47.4	18.1	11.4	3.4	1.1	1.0
Columbus, OH	11.7	30.3	26.7	21.5	5.6	2.9	1.4
Dallas, TX	9.9	26.5	21.2	24.8	9.8	5.9	1.9
Davenport, IA	17.6	38.5	24.3	13.0	3.5	2.0	1.2
Denver, CO	9.1	26.1	23.8	25.4	8.7	5.0	1.9
Des Moines, IA	15.8	36.6	27.6	14.5	3.0	1.5	1.0
Durham, NC	11.1	35.3	24.2	19.0	6.0	2.9	1.4
El Paso, TX	9.6	32.3	27.8	22.0	4.0	2.6	1.6
Erie, PA	19.8	38.9	21.8	13.4	3.2	1.8	1.1
Eugene, OR	17.0	43.5	21.7	11.0	2.8	2.6	1.3
Fargo, ND	21.3	49.4	16.8	7.5	1.9	2.1	1.0
Fayetteville, NC	12.6	35.1	25.4	18.3	4.2	2.5	2.0
Fort Collins, CO	16.0	38.5	19.8	13.8	5.1	4.5	2.3
Fort Wayne, IN	13.1	36.5	29.5	14.0	3.9	1.5	1.5
Fort Worth, TX	9.9	26.5	21.2	24.8	9.8	5.9	1.9
Gainesville, FL	13.4	40.3	23.3	16.1	3.7	2.1	1.0
Grand Rapids, MI	15.5	35.0	24.3	16.1	4.9	2.5	1.6
Green Bay, WI	17.2	40.4	22.5	13.2	3.6	1.9	1.2
Greensboro, NC	12.3	38.4	24.0	16.6	4.5	2.1	2.1
Honolulu, HI	9.9	25.8	20.5	25.5	9.3	6.9	2.3
Houston, TX	8.6	24.9	20.8	25.4	10.6	7.6	2.1
Huntsville, AL	11.9	33.7	26.9	19.8	4.5	2.0	1.3
Indianapolis, IN	11.9	27.5	24.4	23.9	7.5	3.5	1.4
Jacksonville, FL	9.2	27.6	26.3	23.7	7.8	3.9	1.5
Kansas City, MO	13.2	31.3	24.7	21.3	5.9	2.3	1.2
Lafayette, LA	16.6	34.2	19.7	17.1	4.4	3.6	4.4
Las Vegas, NV	8.3	29.0	29.5	24.6	4.3	2.6	1.8
Lexington, KY	14.8	37.4	23.8	16.4	4.2	2.0	1.4
Lincoln, NE	16.2	44.0	24.0	10.2	2.8	1.8	1.0
Little Rock, AR	12.9	33.3	24.1	19.7	6.0	2.8	1.2
Los Angeles, CA	8.1	26.2	20.4	24.8	9.1	8.3	3.1
Louisville, KY	10.6	30.4	27.7	21.3	5.6	2.9	1.4
Lubbock, TX	20.0	52.5	15.6	7.5	2.3	1.2	0.8
Madison, WI	16.2	33.2	24.4	17.5	4.8	2.7	1.1
Manchester, NH	11.8	30.0	21.1	19.1	8.3	6.8	2.8
McAllen, TX	13.7	38.2	24.0	17.3	2.7	1.8	2.2
Miami, FL	7.5	24.9	23.2	27.5	9.0	5.9	2.0
Midland, TX	17.8	44.9	18.2	12.1	2.0	2.7	2.4

Table continued on next page.

Metro Area	Less Than 10 Minutes	10 to 19 Minutes	20 to 29 Minutes	30 to 44 Minutes	45 to 59 Minutes	60 to 89 Minutes	90 Minutes or More
Minneapolis, MN	10.9	28.2	24.9	22.8	7.7	4.1	1.3
Nashville, TN	9.8	27.6	22.7	23.7	9.4	5.0	1.7
New Orleans, LA	11.3	30.8	21.7	20.7	7.4	5.7	2.4
New York, NY	7.8	19.9	16.6	23.6	12.0	14.0	6.1
Oklahoma City, OK	14.1	32.9	25.6	19.1	4.6	2.2	1.6
Omaha, NE	14.5	37.2	26.7	15.7	3.2	1.6	1.0
Orlando, FL	7.2	27.6	23.7	25.4	9.6	4.5	2.0
Oxnard, CA	13.6	31.3	20.8	19.3	6.5	5.5	2.8
Palm Bay, FL	12.5	32.3	24.9	18.8	5.5	3.8	2.3
Peoria, IL	16.6	35.1	26.0	15.4	3.3	2.2	1.3
Philadelphia, PA	10.1	25.5	20.5	23.1	10.4	7.5	2.8
Phoenix, AZ	9.9	27.2	23.4	24.8	8.6	4.6	1.5
Pittsburgh, PA	12.5	27.6	21.5	21.7	9.0	5.8	1.9
Portland, OR	11.5	29.3	23.2	21.6	7.9	4.5	1.9
Providence, RI	13.0	31.8	21.9	18.2	7.0	5.4	2.6
Provo, UT	18.2	35.2	21.0	14.6	6.0	3.5	1.5
Raleigh, NC	10.5	29.4	25.5	22.4	7.3	3.3	1.7
Reno, NV	12.5	39.4	25.4	14.1	3.4	3.0	2.1
Richmond, VA	9.3	31.1	27.0	21.8	5.9	2.9	2.0
Roanoke, VA	13.8	36.0	24.5	16.4	5.1	3.0	1.2
Rochester, MN	19.4	42.6	19.1	11.2	3.6	2.5	1.5
Sacramento, CA	11.7	30.2	22.5	21.8	6.9	3.8	3.1
Salem, OR	17.9	33.6	21.7	15.1	5.3	4.4	2.0
Salt Lake City, UT	10.8	33.3	26.6	20.2	5.1	2.5	1.4
San Antonio, TX	10.9	28.9	25.0	22.2	7.0	3.9	2.0
San Diego, CA	9.1	31.8	26.0	21.1	6.2	3.7	2.0
San Francisco, CA	7.8	24.9	19.0	24.2	11.2	9.9	3.0
San Jose, CA	8.4	29.4	25.5	22.2	7.3	5.4	1.9
Santa Rosa, CA	15.5	33.6	19.7	15.3	5.8	6.5	3.5
Savannah, GA	10.1	30.2	28.1	21.5	6.6	2.3	1.2
Seattle, WA	8.9	25.2	22.1	24.9	9.8	6.7	2.4
Sioux Falls, SD	17.1	45.0	23.9	8.8	2.4	1.8	1.1
Spokane, WA	15.1	34.4	24.1	17.4	4.7	2.5	1.7
Springfield, IL	17.1	41.7	23.6	12.4	2.4	1.7	1.1
Tallahassee, FL	11.9	34.0	25.4	20.4	5.2	2.1	1.0
Tampa, FL	10.6	28.2	22.9	22.6	9.0	4.9	1.7
Topeka, KS	15.9	42.6	20.8	12.3	3.9	3.1	1.4
Tulsa, OK	14.7	34.2	25.7	17.5	4.4	2.2	1.2
Tyler, TX	15.8	35.1	21.1	18.6	3.7	3.0	2.7
Virginia Beach, VA	10.7	32.7	23.9	20.9	6.7	3.5	1.5
Washington, DC	6.3	19.5	17.9	25.7	13.8	12.5	4.4
Wichita, KS	16.7	39.1	25.3	14.2	2.6	1.3	0.8
Wilmington, NC	12.9	40.1	22.5	15.0	4.4	3.0	2.1
Winston-Salem, NC	12.6	35.7	24.3	17.9	4.9	2.6	2.0
Worcester, MA	12.5	26.8	19.7	20.5	9.6	7.9	2.9
U.S.	13.3	29.7	20.9	20.2	7.7	5.7	2.6

Note: Figures are percentages and include workers 16 years old and over; Figures cover the Metropolitan Statistical Area—see Appendix B for areas included

Source: U.S. Census Bureau, 2011-2013 American Community Survey 3-Year Estimates

2012 Presidential Election Results

City	Area Covered	Obama	Romney	Other
Albuquerque, NM	Bernalillo County	55.6	39.3	5.1
Anchorage, AK	Districts 18 – 32	41.5	54.5	4.0
Ann Arbor, MI	Washtenaw County	67.0	31.3	1.7
Athens, GA	Clarke County	63.3	34.4	2.4
Atlanta, GA	Fulton County	64.3	34.5	1.2
Austin, TX	Travis County	60.1	36.2	3.6
Billings, MT	Yellowstone County	38.4	58.9	2.8
Boise City, ID	Ada County	42.7	54.0	3.2
Boston, MA	Suffolk County	77.6	20.8	1.6
Boulder, CO	Boulder County	69.7	27.9	2.4
Cape Coral, FL	Lee County	41.4	57.9	0.7
Cedar Rapids, IA	Linn County	57.9	40.2	1.9
Charleston, SC	Charleston County	50.4	48.0	1.6
Charlotte, NC	Mecklenburg County	60.7	38.2	1.1
Chicago, IL	Cook County	74.0	24.6	1.3
Clarksville, TN	Montgomery County	44.0	54.5	1.5
Colorado Springs, CO	El Paso County	38.1	59.4	2.5
Columbia, MO	Boone County	50.2	47.1	2.7
Columbus, OH	Franklin County	60.1	38.4	1.5
Dallas, TX	Dallas County	57.1	41.7	1.2
Davenport, IA	Scott County	56.1	42.4	1.5
Denver, CO	Denver County	73.5	24.4	2.1
Des Moines, IA	Polk County	56.1	42.0	1.9
Durham, NC	Durham County	75.8	23.0	1.2
El Paso, TX	El Paso County	65.6	33.0	1.3
Erie, PA	Erie County	57.4	41.3	1.3
Eugene, OR	Lane County	59.7	36.4	3.9
Fargo, ND	Cass County	47.0	49.9	3.1
Fayetteville, NC	Cumberland County	59.4	39.7	0.9
Fort Collins, CO	Larimer County	51.4	45.8	2.7
Fort Wayne, IN	Allen County	40.9	57.6	1.5
Fort Worth, TX	Tarrant County	41.4	57.1	1.4
Gainesville, FL	Alachua County	57.9	40.5	1.6
Grand Rapids, MI	Kent County	45.5	53.4	1.0
Green Bay, WI	Brown County	48.6	50.4	1.0
Greensboro, NC	Guilford County	57.7	41.2	1.1
Honolulu, HI	Honolulu County	68.9	29.8	1.3
Houston, TX	Harris County	49.4	49.3	1.3
Huntsville, AL	Madison County	40.0	58.6	1.4
Indianapolis, IN	Marion County	60.2	38.1	1.7
Jacksonville, FL	Duval County	47.8	51.4	0.8
Kansas City, MO	Jackson County	58.7	39.7	1.6
Lafayette, LA	Lafayette Parish	32.2	65.9	1.9
Las Vegas, NV	Clark County	56.4	41.9	1.8
Lexington, KY	Fayette County	49.3	48.3	2.3
Lincoln, NE	Lancaster County	49.0	49.3	1.7
Little Rock, AR	Pulaski County	54.7	43.3	2.0
Los Angeles, CA	Los Angeles County	68.6	29.1	2.3
Louisville, KY	Jefferson County	54.8	43.7	1.4
Lubbock, TX	Lubbock County	28.8	69.6	1.6
Madison, WI	Dane County	71.1	27.6	1.3
Manchester, NH	Hillsborough County	49.7	48.6	1.6
McAllen, TX	Hidalgo County	70.4	28.6	1.0
Miami, FL	Miami-Dade County	61.6	37.9	0.4
Midland, TX	Midland County	18.6	80.1	1.4
Minneapolis, MN	Hennepin County	62.3	35.3	2.4

Table continued on next page.

City	Area Covered	Obama	Romney	Other
Nashville, TN	Davidson County	58.4	39.9	1.7
New Orleans, LA	Orleans Parish	80.3	17.7	2.0
New York, NY	Bronx County	91.4	8.1	0.5
New York, NY	Kings County	82.0	16.9	1.1
New York, NY	New York County	83.7	14.9	1.3
New York, NY	Queens County	79.1	19.9	1.0
New York, NY	Richmond County	50.7	48.1	1.2
Oklahoma City, OK	Oklahoma County	41.7	58.3	0.0
Omaha, NE	Douglas County	47.2	51.4	1.4
Orlando, FL	Orange County	58.7	40.4	0.9
Oxnard, CA	Ventura County	51.7	46.1	2.2
Palm Bay, FL	Brevard County	43.1	55.8	1.1
Peoria, IL	Peoria County	51.3	46.9	1.8
Philadelphia, PA	Philadelphia County	85.3	14.0	0.7
Phoenix, AZ	Maricopa County	43.1	54.9	2.0
Pittsburgh, PA	Allegheny County	56.6	42.2	1.2
Portland, OR	Multnomah County	75.3	20.7	4.0
Providence, RI	Providence County	66.5	31.6	1.9
Provo, UT	Utah County	9.8	88.3	2.0
Raleigh, NC	Wake County	54.9	43.5	1.6
Reno, NV	Washoe County	50.7	47.2	2.1
Richmond, VA	Richmond City	77.0	21.4	1.6
Roanoke, VA	Roanoke City	59.1	37.6	3.3
Rochester, MN	Olmsted County	50.2	47.0	2.7
Sacramento, CA	Sacramento County	57.5	40.0	2.5
Salem, OR	Marion County	46.7	50.2	3.1
Salt Lake City, UT	Salt Lake County	38.8	58.2	3.0
San Antonio, TX	Bexar County	51.6	47.0	1.4
San Diego, CA	San Diego County	51.7	46.2	2.1
San Francisco, CA	San Francisco County	83.4	13.3	3.3
San Jose, CA	Santa Clara County	69.9	27.6	2.5
Santa Rosa, CA	Sonoma County	70.8	26.0	3.2
Savannah, GA	Chatham County	55.5	43.5	1.0
Seattle, WA	King County	68.8	28.8	2.3
Sioux Falls, SD	Minnehaha County	45.3	52.7	2.0
Spokane, WA	Spokane County	45.6	51.6	2.8
Springfield, IL	Sangamon County	44.6	53.3	2.1
Tallahassee, FL	Leon County	61.3	37.6	1.1
Tampa, FL	Hillsborough County	52.8	46.2	1.0
Topeka, KS	Shawnee County	48.0	49.7	2.2
Tulsa, OK	Tulsa County	36.3	63.7	0.0
Tyler, TX	Smith County	26.1	73.0	1.0
Virginia Beach, VA	Virginia Beach City	48.0	50.5	1.6
Washington, DC	District of Columbia	91.1	7.1	1.8
Wichita, KS	Sedgwick County	39.0	58.7	2.3
Wilmington, NC	New Hanover County	47.0	51.5	1.5
Winston-Salem, NC	Forsyth County	53.0	45.8	1.1
Worcester, MA	Worcester County	53.7	44.5	1.8
U.S.	U.S.	51.0	47.2	1.8

Note: Results are percentages and may not add to 100% due to rounding
Source: Dave Leip's Atlas of U.S. Presidential Elections

House Price Index (HPI)

Metro Area[1]	National Ranking[3]	Quarterly Change (%)	One-Year Change (%)	Five-Year Change (%)
Albuquerque, NM	187	0.19	3.13	-4.10
Anchorage, AK	248	-1.16	1.26	7.37
Ann Arbor, MI	75	-0.13	6.59	18.50
Athens, GA	82	-0.57	6.20	-2.89
Atlanta, GA	40	0.55	8.87	2.55
Austin, TX	18	1.20	10.57	27.37
Billings, MT	154	-1.43	3.86	11.67
Boise City, ID	65	0.31	7.45	8.86
Boston, MA[2]	91	1.10	5.92	9.51
Boulder, CO	34	1.67	9.27	19.39
Cape Coral, FL	14	4.12	10.98	30.10
Cedar Rapids, IA	213	-0.19	2.22	2.64
Charleston, SC	60	0.93	7.63	4.92
Charlotte, NC	114	1.14	4.86	2.39
Chicago, IL[2]	99	0.58	5.46	-3.39
Clarksville, TN	n/r	n/a	2.66	1.19
Colorado Springs, CO	147	-0.33	4.01	4.01
Columbia, MO	210	-0.91	2.44	6.37
Columbus, OH	124	-0.12	4.51	4.48
Dallas, TX[2]	32	1.10	9.51	17.75
Davenport, IA	241	-1.18	1.56	4.99
Denver, CO	24	1.73	10.18	24.67
Des Moines, IA	144	1.09	4.06	5.16
Durham, NC	141	-0.26	4.16	3.18
El Paso, TX	222	-0.06	1.99	-0.86
Erie, PA	n/r	n/a	-3.32	3.79
Eugene, OR	135	-0.05	4.33	-0.31
Fargo, ND	70	-0.71	6.81	19.60
Fayetteville, NC	270	-1.16	-0.38	-3.72
Fort Collins, CO	63	0.78	7.53	19.30
Fort Wayne, IN	224	1.30	1.96	3.73
Fort Worth, TX[2]	74	0.28	6.65	11.53
Gainesville, FL	n/r	n/a	4.19	-12.63
Grand Rapids, MI	69	-0.38	6.97	10.95
Green Bay, WI	177	-0.55	3.36	-1.17
Greensboro, NC	233	1.38	1.79	-1.71
Honolulu, HI	97	1.94	5.54	20.20
Houston, TX	13	0.87	11.02	23.21
Huntsville, AL	125	0.99	4.51	-1.26
Indianapolis, IN	155	-0.31	3.85	3.89
Jacksonville, FL	51	1.61	8.13	-0.80
Kansas City, MO	117	0.34	4.69	1.41
Lafayette, LA	153	1.69	3.88	6.75
Las Vegas, NV	6	1.44	12.66	23.87
Lexington, KY	152	-0.24	3.88	1.74
Lincoln, NE	164	0.87	3.67	9.23
Little Rock, AR	225	1.15	1.94	2.82
Los Angeles, CA[2]	56	1.22	7.85	21.79
Louisville, KY	161	0.90	3.72	4.39
Lubbock, TX	143	0.37	4.07	11.65
Madison, WI	192	0.19	2.95	1.61
Manchester, NH	166	-0.16	3.65	-0.77
McAllen, TX	n/r	n/a	8.85	6.64
Miami, FL[2]	7	2.71	12.17	21.88
Midland, TX	n/r	n/a	8.78	40.53

Table continued on next page.

Metro Area[1]	National Ranking[3]	Quarterly Change (%)	One-Year Change (%)	Five-Year Change (%)
Minneapolis, MN	108	-0.26	5.11	5.36
Nashville, TN	58	1.18	7.74	12.51
New Orleans, LA	127	0.86	4.43	6.89
New York, NY[2]	175	0.37	3.47	0.02
Oklahoma City, OK	72	1.86	6.73	10.20
Omaha, NE	180	0.02	3.30	5.32
Orlando, FL	26	3.18	9.84	5.81
Oxnard, CA	77	0.71	6.55	17.96
Palm Bay, FL	43	3.61	8.69	7.88
Peoria, IL	231	0.08	1.83	1.89
Philadelphia, PA[2]	194	0.41	2.90	0.63
Phoenix, AZ	68	1.15	7.05	21.42
Pittsburgh, PA	138	-0.68	4.17	11.17
Portland, OR	39	1.44	9.03	12.08
Providence, RI	129	0.12	4.42	-2.37
Provo, UT	95	2.06	5.66	12.34
Raleigh, NC	93	0.29	5.78	4.43
Reno, NV	4	0.27	13.11	15.60
Richmond, VA	132	0.90	4.36	-3.34
Roanoke, VA	184	1.59	3.27	-5.01
Rochester, MN	169	0.17	3.62	3.05
Sacramento, CA	67	0.91	7.14	21.20
Salem, OR	73	1.24	6.72	-2.31
Salt Lake City, UT	106	0.58	5.11	12.00
San Antonio, TX	96	0.35	5.61	11.65
San Diego, CA	86	0.62	6.05	22.50
San Francisco, CA[2]	11	1.37	11.15	33.82
San Jose, CA	21	1.21	10.28	37.27
Santa Rosa, CA	31	1.35	9.59	24.69
Savannah, GA	236	-1.71	1.64	-6.77
Seattle, WA[2]	49	0.31	8.22	10.57
Sioux Falls, SD	113	1.17	4.90	9.95
Spokane, WA	133	-0.72	4.34	-5.75
Springfield, IL	212	0.44	2.37	6.80
Tallahassee, FL	220	-1.36	2.06	-10.88
Tampa, FL	46	1.25	8.46	8.55
Topeka, KS	253	1.01	1.05	0.94
Tulsa, OK	140	0.12	4.16	3.12
Tyler, TX	n/r	n/a	3.73	5.11
Virginia Beach, VA	123	1.84	4.52	-5.15
Washington, DC[2]	94	1.48	5.71	13.58
Wichita, KS	198	0.19	2.85	1.16
Wilmington, NC	103	-1.02	5.25	-8.59
Winston-Salem, NC	215	0.83	2.17	-4.09
Worcester, MA	157	0.78	3.83	-0.11
U.S.[4]	–	1.35	4.91	11.59

Note: The HPI is a weighted repeat sales index. It measures average price changes in repeat sales or refinancings on the same properties. This information is obtained by reviewing repeat mortgage transactions on single-family properties whose mortgages have been purchased or securitized by Fannie Mae or Freddie Mac in January 1975; (1) figures cover the Metropolitan Statistical Area (MSA) unless noted otherwise—see Appendix B for areas included; (2) Metropolitan Division—see Appendix B for areas included;
(3) Rankings are based on annual percentage change, for all MSAs containing at least 15,000 transactions over the last 10 years and ranges from 1 to 275; (4) figures based on a weighted division average; all figures are for the period ended December 31, 2014; n/a not available; n/r not ranked
Source: Federal Housing Finance Agency, House Price Index, February 26, 2015

Homeownership Rate

Metro Area	2007	2008	2009	2010	2011	2012	2013	2014
Albuquerque, NM	70.5	68.2	65.7	65.5	67.1	62.8	65.9	64.4
Anchorage, AK	n/a	n/a	n/a	n/a	n/a	n/a	n/a	n/a
Ann Arbor, MI	n/a	n/a	n/a	n/a	n/a	n/a	n/a	n/a
Athens, GA	n/a	n/a	n/a	n/a	n/a	n/a	n/a	n/a
Atlanta, GA	66.4	67.5	67.7	67.2	65.8	62.1	61.6	61.6
Austin, TX	66.4	65.5	64.0	65.8	58.4	60.1	59.6	61.1
Billings, MT	n/a	n/a	n/a	n/a	n/a	n/a	n/a	n/a
Boise City, ID	n/a	n/a	n/a	n/a	n/a	n/a	n/a	n/a
Boston, MA	64.8	66.2	65.5	66.0	65.5	66.0	66.3	62.8
Boulder, CO	n/a	n/a	n/a	n/a	n/a	n/a	n/a	n/a
Cape Coral, FL	n/a	n/a	n/a	n/a	n/a	n/a	n/a	n/a
Cedar Rapids, IA	n/a	n/a	n/a	n/a	n/a	n/a	n/a	n/a
Charleston, SC	n/a	n/a	n/a	n/a	n/a	n/a	n/a	n/a
Charlotte, NC	66.5	65.4	66.1	66.1	63.6	58.3	58.9	58.1
Chicago, IL	69.0	68.4	69.2	68.2	67.7	67.1	68.2	66.3
Clarksville, TN	n/a	n/a	n/a	n/a	n/a	n/a	n/a	n/a
Colorado Springs, CO	n/a	n/a	n/a	n/a	n/a	n/a	n/a	n/a
Columbia, MO	n/a	n/a	n/a	n/a	n/a	n/a	n/a	n/a
Columbus, OH	66.1	61.2	61.5	62.2	59.7	60.7	60.5	60.0
Dallas, TX	60.9	60.9	61.6	63.8	62.6	61.8	59.9	57.7
Davenport, IA	n/a	n/a	n/a	n/a	n/a	n/a	n/a	n/a
Denver, CO	69.5	66.9	65.3	65.7	63.0	61.8	61.0	61.9
Des Moines, IA	n/a	n/a	n/a	n/a	n/a	n/a	n/a	n/a
Durham, NC	n/a	n/a	n/a	n/a	n/a	n/a	n/a	n/a
El Paso, TX	68.2	64.8	63.8	70.1	72.0	67.4	69.3	66.7
Erie, PA	n/a	n/a	n/a	n/a	n/a	n/a	n/a	n/a
Eugene, OR	n/a	n/a	n/a	n/a	n/a	n/a	n/a	n/a
Fargo, ND	n/a	n/a	n/a	n/a	n/a	n/a	n/a	n/a
Fayetteville, NC	n/a	n/a	n/a	n/a	n/a	n/a	n/a	n/a
Fort Collins, CO	n/a	n/a	n/a	n/a	n/a	n/a	n/a	n/a
Fort Wayne, IN	n/a	n/a	n/a	n/a	n/a	n/a	n/a	n/a
Fort Worth, TX	60.9	60.9	61.6	63.8	62.6	61.8	59.9	57.7
Gainesville, FL	n/a	n/a	n/a	n/a	n/a	n/a	n/a	n/a
Grand Rapids, MI	78.6	77.6	75.6	76.4	76.4	76.9	73.7	71.6
Green Bay, WI	n/a	n/a	n/a	n/a	n/a	n/a	n/a	n/a
Greensboro, NC	62.1	68.0	70.7	68.8	62.7	64.9	67.9	68.1
Honolulu, HI	58.8	57.2	57.6	54.9	54.1	56.1	57.9	58.2
Houston, TX	64.5	64.8	63.6	61.4	61.3	62.1	60.5	60.4
Huntsville, AL	n/a	n/a	n/a	n/a	n/a	n/a	n/a	n/a
Indianapolis, IN	75.9	75.0	71.0	68.8	68.3	67.1	67.5	66.9
Jacksonville, FL	70.9	72.1	72.6	70.0	68.0	66.6	69.9	65.3
Kansas City, MO	71.3	70.2	69.5	68.8	68.5	65.1	65.6	66.1
Lafayette, LA	n/a	n/a	n/a	n/a	n/a	n/a	n/a	n/a
Las Vegas, NV	60.5	60.3	59.0	55.7	52.9	52.6	52.8	53.2
Lexington, KY	n/a	n/a	n/a	n/a	n/a	n/a	n/a	n/a
Lincoln, NE	n/a	n/a	n/a	n/a	n/a	n/a	n/a	n/a
Little Rock, AR	n/a	n/a	n/a	n/a	n/a	n/a	n/a	n/a
Los Angeles, CA	52.3	52.1	50.4	49.7	50.1	49.9	48.7	49.0
Louisville, KY	67.2	67.9	67.7	63.4	61.7	63.3	64.5	68.9
Lubbock, TX	n/a	n/a	n/a	n/a	n/a	n/a	n/a	n/a
Madison, WI	n/a	n/a	n/a	n/a	n/a	n/a	n/a	n/a
Manchester, NH	n/a	n/a	n/a	n/a	n/a	n/a	n/a	n/a
McAllen, TX	n/a	n/a	n/a	n/a	n/a	n/a	n/a	n/a
Miami, FL	66.6	66.0	67.1	63.8	64.2	61.8	60.1	58.8
Midland, TX	n/a	n/a	n/a	n/a	n/a	n/a	n/a	n/a
Minneapolis, MN	70.7	69.9	70.9	71.2	69.1	70.8	71.7	69.7

Table continued on next page.

Metro Area	2007	2008	2009	2010	2011	2012	2013	2014
Nashville, TN	70.0	71.3	71.8	70.4	69.6	64.9	63.9	67.1
New Orleans, LA	67.8	68.0	68.2	66.9	63.9	62.4	61.4	60.6
New York, NY	53.8	52.6	51.7	51.6	50.9	51.5	50.6	50.7
Oklahoma City, OK	68.2	69.5	69.0	70.0	69.6	67.3	67.6	65.7
Omaha, NE	67.9	72.5	73.1	73.2	71.6	72.4	70.6	68.7
Orlando, FL	71.8	70.5	72.4	70.8	68.6	68.0	65.5	62.3
Oxnard, CA	71.4	71.7	73.1	67.1	67.0	66.1	66.8	64.5
Palm Bay, FL	n/a	n/a	n/a	n/a	n/a	n/a	n/a	n/a
Peoria, IL	n/a	n/a	n/a	n/a	n/a	n/a	n/a	n/a
Philadelphia, PA	73.1	71.8	69.7	70.7	69.7	69.5	69.1	67.0
Phoenix, AZ	70.8	70.2	69.8	66.5	63.3	63.1	62.2	61.9
Pittsburgh, PA	73.6	73.2	71.7	70.4	70.3	67.9	68.3	69.1
Portland, OR	61.2	62.6	64.0	63.7	63.7	63.9	60.9	59.8
Providence, RI	64.1	63.9	61.7	61.0	61.3	61.7	60.1	61.6
Provo, UT	n/a	n/a	n/a	n/a	n/a	n/a	n/a	n/a
Raleigh, NC	72.8	70.7	65.7	65.9	66.7	67.7	65.5	65.5
Reno, NV	n/a	n/a	n/a	n/a	n/a	n/a	n/a	n/a
Richmond, VA	72.7	72.4	72.2	68.1	65.2	67.0	65.4	72.6
Roanoke, VA	n/a	n/a	n/a	n/a	n/a	n/a	n/a	n/a
Rochester, MN	n/a	n/a	n/a	n/a	n/a	n/a	n/a	n/a
Sacramento, CA	60.8	61.1	64.3	61.1	57.2	58.6	60.4	60.1
Salem, OR	n/a	n/a	n/a	n/a	n/a	n/a	n/a	n/a
Salt Lake City, UT	71.8	72.0	68.8	65.5	66.4	66.9	66.8	68.2
San Antonio, TX	62.4	66.1	69.8	70.1	66.5	67.5	70.1	70.2
San Diego, CA	59.6	57.1	56.4	54.4	55.2	55.4	55.0	57.4
San Francisco, CA	58.0	56.4	57.3	58.0	56.1	53.2	55.2	54.6
San Jose, CA	57.6	54.6	57.2	58.9	60.4	58.6	56.4	56.4
Santa Rosa, CA	n/a	n/a	n/a	n/a	n/a	n/a	n/a	n/a
Savannah, GA	n/a	n/a	n/a	n/a	n/a	n/a	n/a	n/a
Seattle, WA	62.8	61.3	61.2	60.9	60.7	60.4	61.0	61.3
Sioux Falls, SD	n/a	n/a	n/a	n/a	n/a	n/a	n/a	n/a
Spokane, WA	n/a	n/a	n/a	n/a	n/a	n/a	n/a	n/a
Springfield, IL	n/a	n/a	n/a	n/a	n/a	n/a	n/a	n/a
Tallahassee, FL	n/a	n/a	n/a	n/a	n/a	n/a	n/a	n/a
Tampa, FL	72.9	70.5	68.3	68.3	68.3	67.0	65.3	64.9
Topeka, KS	n/a	n/a	n/a	n/a	n/a	n/a	n/a	n/a
Tulsa, OK	66.7	66.8	67.8	64.2	64.4	66.5	64.1	65.3
Tyler, TX	n/a	n/a	n/a	n/a	n/a	n/a	n/a	n/a
Virginia Beach, VA	66.0	63.9	63.5	61.4	62.3	62.0	63.3	64.1
Washington, DC	69.2	68.1	67.2	67.3	67.6	66.9	66.0	65.0
Wichita, KS	n/a	n/a	n/a	n/a	n/a	n/a	n/a	n/a
Wilmington, NC	n/a	n/a	n/a	n/a	n/a	n/a	n/a	n/a
Winston-Salem, NC	n/a	n/a	n/a	n/a	n/a	n/a	n/a	n/a
Worcester, MA	67.8	68.5	64.4	64.1	65.8	61.9	63.3	62.5
U.S.	68.1	67.8	67.4	66.9	66.1	65.4	65.1	64.5

Note: Figures are percentages and cover the Metropolitan Statistical Area—see Appendix B for areas included
Source: U.S. Census Bureau, Housing Vacancies and Homeownership Annual Statistics: 2014

Year Housing Structure Built: City

City	2010 or Later	2000 -2009	1990 -1999	1980 -1989	1970 -1979	1960 -1969	1950 -1959	1940 -1949	Before 1940	Median Year
Albuquerque, NM	0.6	18.3	15.1	15.1	20.5	10.5	12.4	4.5	3.1	1980
Anchorage, AK	0.6	13.8	11.2	24.4	29.5	12.2	6.3	1.7	0.4	1980
Ann Arbor, MI	0.1	8.0	10.1	10.9	16.4	18.9	13.7	6.9	14.9	1968
Athens, GA	0.8	18.3	19.5	19.3	17.9	10.4	6.2	3.1	4.5	1984
Atlanta, GA	1.2	24.9	10.8	8.4	8.6	13.4	12.3	6.8	13.7	1974
Austin, TX	1.5	22.7	16.2	21.1	19.0	8.1	5.8	2.7	3.0	1985
Billings, MT	1.4	14.7	10.3	11.6	20.1	10.1	16.1	6.7	8.8	1974
Boise City, ID	0.7	12.6	22.2	14.6	22.4	7.7	8.0	4.7	7.0	1980
Boston, MA	0.5	6.8	3.8	5.8	7.2	7.9	7.5	5.8	54.7	<1940
Boulder, CO	1.2	9.8	9.8	16.9	23.6	18.2	9.1	2.1	9.3	1975
Cape Coral, FL	0.5	43.3	14.4	22.7	11.9	5.9	0.8	0.3	0.2	1996
Cedar Rapids, IA	1.0	14.7	14.8	6.4	14.3	13.2	13.1	5.2	17.3	1971
Charleston, SC	1.4	24.7	12.8	13.1	10.9	10.9	7.1	4.3	14.7	1982
Charlotte, NC	1.3	25.2	20.7	15.7	13.6	10.3	7.1	3.0	3.2	1988
Chicago, IL	0.4	8.7	4.4	3.9	6.9	9.8	12.3	8.3	45.3	1946
Clarksville, TN	3.9	28.4	21.2	13.3	13.0	9.1	5.9	2.5	2.7	1992
Colorado Springs, CO	0.9	18.3	15.1	19.6	18.9	11.2	7.6	2.2	6.2	1982
Columbia, MO	1.1	25.9	18.7	13.4	13.5	13.1	5.6	2.6	6.0	1987
Columbus, OH	1.0	12.8	14.9	13.2	15.6	13.3	11.5	5.2	12.5	1975
Dallas, TX	1.1	12.5	9.3	17.4	19.6	14.6	13.4	6.3	5.8	1975
Davenport, IA	0.4	8.7	7.5	6.3	11.9	12.6	14.5	17.2	20.8	1958
Denver, CO	1.3	13.8	6.9	8.5	14.0	11.9	16.0	7.0	20.6	1965
Des Moines, IA	0.9	7.4	7.4	6.8	12.7	10.9	16.9	8.9	28.1	1958
Durham, NC	2.1	20.9	18.9	17.5	11.0	11.2	7.8	4.7	5.9	1985
El Paso, TX	2.8	16.9	12.8	14.8	18.3	12.9	12.7	4.1	4.7	1979
Erie, PA	0.2	3.8	2.9	4.3	9.5	8.0	19.2	11.4	40.7	1948
Eugene, OR	0.9	13.4	17.8	8.7	22.6	13.7	9.3	6.0	7.7	1976
Fargo, ND	2.2	18.5	20.0	14.0	16.7	7.3	8.1	2.2	11.1	1983
Fayetteville, NC	1.9	16.8	17.7	16.9	19.2	14.4	8.6	2.6	1.9	1982
Fort Collins, CO	0.9	20.3	21.7	17.4	20.4	8.0	3.4	2.0	5.8	1986
Fort Wayne, IN	0.3	6.7	14.1	12.5	14.6	16.6	12.3	7.0	15.9	1969
Fort Worth, TX	1.9	27.1	11.2	15.2	10.7	9.3	12.3	5.8	6.5	1984
Gainesville, FL	0.4	15.5	15.9	19.3	22.7	12.6	7.4	2.5	3.8	1981
Grand Rapids, MI	0.3	5.1	6.0	6.7	8.4	10.3	17.3	9.2	36.7	1952
Green Bay, WI	0.6	6.6	10.1	11.6	16.2	12.1	16.1	7.8	18.9	1966
Greensboro, NC	0.8	15.2	18.7	17.1	16.7	12.1	10.0	4.3	5.1	1981
Honolulu, HI	0.9	7.1	8.2	10.6	26.5	22.2	13.4	5.6	5.4	1971
Houston, TX	1.4	15.8	9.3	13.7	24.6	14.5	11.3	5.0	4.5	1976
Huntsville, AL	1.8	15.0	11.6	14.6	16.3	22.7	11.0	3.3	3.7	1976
Indianapolis, IN	0.6	10.6	12.7	11.8	13.4	13.6	13.9	7.1	16.2	1969
Jacksonville, FL	0.9	20.9	14.4	16.2	14.3	11.0	11.7	5.4	5.2	1981
Kansas City, MO	0.5	11.4	8.7	8.5	12.1	14.9	15.2	7.1	21.6	1964
Lafayette, LA	1.4	14.0	11.2	17.8	21.0	15.6	11.0	4.1	4.0	1977
Las Vegas, NV	1.1	24.1	32.4	17.8	11.0	7.3	4.9	1.1	0.4	1992
Lexington, KY	1.2	17.4	16.3	14.2	16.3	13.4	10.0	3.4	7.6	1979
Lincoln, NE	0.9	16.5	15.0	11.0	15.8	10.8	12.0	3.3	14.8	1976
Little Rock, AR	0.8	11.8	14.9	18.8	20.3	12.5	9.3	4.6	7.0	1978
Los Angeles, CA	0.6	6.6	5.7	10.2	13.6	14.2	18.0	10.5	20.6	1961
Louisville, KY	0.4	13.0	10.9	6.7	14.1	13.8	15.3	7.4	18.4	1966
Lubbock, TX	1.9	16.5	11.7	15.0	18.7	15.0	13.4	4.7	3.1	1977
Madison, WI	1.3	17.1	13.3	10.6	15.1	12.1	12.2	4.7	13.6	1975
Manchester, NH	0.2	6.1	6.2	14.4	10.5	7.2	9.0	7.7	38.6	1954
McAllen, TX	2.2	27.3	19.0	20.2	17.1	6.2	5.2	1.1	1.9	1989
Miami, FL	1.2	20.1	5.9	7.7	13.1	10.0	16.1	15.3	10.5	1968
Midland, TX	1.8	11.2	9.5	22.4	17.1	12.3	19.4	4.4	1.8	1977

Table continued on next page.

City	2010 or Later	2000 -2009	1990 -1999	1980 -1989	1970 -1979	1960 -1969	1950 -1959	1940 -1949	Before 1940	Median Year
Minneapolis, MN	0.5	7.4	3.4	6.5	9.3	7.6	9.8	7.8	47.7	1943
Nashville, TN	1.1	15.8	11.9	17.3	16.7	13.8	12.0	5.0	6.4	1978
New Orleans, LA	1.5	8.6	3.9	7.8	14.3	10.6	12.5	10.4	30.3	1957
New York, NY	0.6	6.3	3.6	4.5	7.2	12.5	13.7	10.3	41.3	1948
Oklahoma City, OK	2.1	14.5	9.8	15.5	17.1	14.1	11.3	6.3	9.2	1975
Omaha, NE	0.5	5.7	10.0	10.3	17.6	14.9	12.9	5.5	22.6	1966
Orlando, FL	0.4	24.7	17.4	18.2	13.4	8.1	10.5	3.9	3.5	1986
Oxnard, CA	0.4	14.1	10.3	11.0	21.2	21.0	15.0	4.5	2.6	1973
Palm Bay, FL	0.1	29.4	15.1	37.4	12.4	3.8	1.5	0.1	0.2	1989
Peoria, IL	0.9	9.2	7.5	6.0	15.8	13.3	15.8	9.4	22.0	1962
Philadelphia, PA	0.4	3.6	2.8	4.1	7.0	10.9	16.5	15.5	39.1	1947
Phoenix, AZ	0.7	18.0	16.2	18.8	20.7	9.6	10.6	3.3	2.1	1982
Pittsburgh, PA	0.3	3.8	2.9	4.5	5.8	7.8	13.2	9.1	52.6	<1940
Portland, OR	0.7	12.1	8.2	5.5	11.6	9.5	12.6	9.1	30.7	1958
Providence, RI	0.1	5.8	3.9	5.6	7.9	6.9	9.0	7.9	52.8	<1940
Provo, UT	0.6	13.4	19.4	13.2	19.6	10.5	8.5	5.9	9.0	1978
Raleigh, NC	1.7	28.6	21.4	18.4	10.9	8.4	5.4	2.3	3.0	1991
Reno, NV	1.2	22.6	17.6	14.2	20.4	9.9	6.3	3.3	4.4	1984
Richmond, VA	0.8	5.8	4.7	6.1	11.7	12.8	16.1	9.3	32.8	1955
Roanoke, VA	0.1	6.2	5.7	6.8	13.4	13.0	19.5	11.5	23.8	1958
Rochester, MN	1.3	19.9	15.1	13.4	13.7	13.2	10.9	4.4	8.1	1980
Sacramento, CA	0.2	16.3	7.6	14.8	15.6	12.3	13.2	8.5	11.5	1973
Salem, OR	0.4	14.5	16.4	11.9	21.9	10.1	9.5	6.1	9.1	1977
Salt Lake City, UT	0.6	6.3	5.6	8.0	13.6	9.4	15.1	10.4	31.2	1956
San Antonio, TX	1.3	18.6	12.6	17.4	17.5	11.3	10.3	5.5	5.6	1980
San Diego, CA	0.6	10.5	11.4	18.0	22.0	13.0	12.7	4.9	6.9	1976
San Francisco, CA	0.4	7.3	4.1	5.0	7.1	8.1	9.3	10.2	48.5	1942
San Jose, CA	0.5	10.3	10.1	13.7	25.2	19.3	12.4	3.2	5.3	1974
Santa Rosa, CA	0.3	14.4	13.9	17.3	23.2	12.4	7.4	5.1	5.8	1978
Savannah, GA	1.9	10.6	7.6	10.4	15.5	13.2	15.6	7.5	17.7	1967
Seattle, WA	1.3	15.3	8.0	7.6	9.0	9.2	11.4	9.5	28.6	1961
Sioux Falls, SD	3.1	21.9	15.4	11.5	16.0	8.5	9.0	5.1	9.5	1982
Spokane, WA	0.6	8.7	8.3	8.5	15.0	6.7	15.2	9.8	27.2	1959
Springfield, IL	0.2	9.5	13.1	10.6	14.7	14.8	11.3	7.6	18.2	1969
Tallahassee, FL	1.0	20.3	17.9	18.2	18.5	10.8	8.0	3.5	1.8	1984
Tampa, FL	1.4	19.9	10.9	13.0	11.4	12.6	15.9	6.0	8.8	1976
Topeka, KS	0.5	8.4	8.4	10.8	14.0	17.6	15.6	7.1	17.8	1965
Tulsa, OK	0.7	6.4	8.0	14.3	21.9	14.4	16.9	7.8	9.7	1971
Tyler, TX	1.7	17.7	9.7	15.8	17.6	12.4	14.5	6.4	4.2	1977
Virginia Beach, VA	0.9	11.5	14.2	28.6	22.2	13.2	6.5	1.6	1.2	1982
Washington, DC	1.0	8.7	3.1	4.6	8.2	12.4	13.4	13.0	35.7	1951
Wichita, KS	0.6	11.5	12.4	12.1	13.8	8.8	20.8	8.9	11.1	1970
Wilmington, NC	0.7	16.0	22.9	15.5	10.7	9.3	8.1	6.2	10.5	1983
Winston-Salem, NC	0.7	14.7	11.4	12.6	15.5	15.7	14.3	6.0	9.1	1973
Worcester, MA	0.6	4.8	4.5	9.1	9.0	6.3	10.0	8.3	47.4	1943
U.S.	0.9	15.0	13.9	13.8	15.8	11.0	10.9	5.4	13.3	1976

Note: Figures are percentages except for Median Year
Source: U.S. Census Bureau, 2011-2013 American Community Survey 3-Year Estimates

Year Housing Structure Built: Metro Area

Metro Area	2010 or Later	2000 -2009	1990 -1999	1980 -1989	1970 -1979	1960 -1969	1950 -1959	1940 -1949	Before 1940	Median Year
Albuquerque, NM	0.7	19.4	17.8	17.2	18.6	9.4	9.9	3.7	3.3	1983
Anchorage, AK	1.0	19.1	12.8	24.7	25.5	9.9	5.0	1.5	0.5	1983
Ann Arbor, MI	0.4	14.4	16.3	10.9	16.8	12.8	11.1	5.2	12.0	1975
Athens, GA	0.8	20.2	20.2	18.7	17.4	9.6	5.5	2.7	5.0	1985
Atlanta, GA	0.9	26.9	22.6	18.2	13.1	8.0	5.1	2.1	3.3	1990
Austin, TX	2.4	30.7	19.4	19.1	14.3	5.5	4.1	2.0	2.6	1991
Billings, MT	1.5	16.1	11.2	12.1	21.1	8.3	12.9	5.7	11.1	1976
Boise City, ID	1.2	27.9	22.2	10.4	18.1	5.4	5.1	3.7	5.9	1991
Boston, MA	0.6	8.1	7.2	10.6	11.0	10.4	11.2	5.7	35.2	1958
Boulder, CO	0.8	13.9	19.9	17.0	21.9	11.8	5.3	1.7	7.7	1981
Cape Coral, FL	0.5	34.4	17.9	21.8	15.8	5.5	2.8	0.6	0.7	1992
Cedar Rapids, IA	1.2	16.2	15.8	6.7	14.3	11.4	11.0	4.4	19.0	1973
Charleston, SC	1.7	26.5	15.9	17.4	15.6	9.3	6.0	2.8	4.7	1987
Charlotte, NC	1.4	26.2	20.4	14.9	12.6	9.2	7.2	3.5	4.6	1989
Chicago, IL	0.4	11.9	10.9	8.9	14.0	12.0	13.5	5.9	22.4	1967
Clarksville, TN	3.0	23.7	21.3	12.9	14.7	10.2	6.9	2.6	4.8	1988
Colorado Springs, CO	1.3	21.1	16.6	18.5	17.9	10.1	6.9	1.9	5.7	1984
Columbia, MO	1.0	23.2	19.2	14.2	17.8	12.2	4.9	2.2	5.3	1985
Columbus, OH	1.0	15.5	16.6	12.1	14.5	12.2	10.8	4.3	12.9	1977
Dallas, TX	1.7	23.2	16.6	19.6	15.5	9.5	7.7	3.1	3.0	1986
Davenport, IA	0.8	8.2	7.8	6.8	14.5	13.9	14.1	10.8	23.2	1961
Denver, CO	0.9	18.6	15.7	15.2	19.0	10.4	10.0	3.1	7.2	1980
Des Moines, IA	2.2	18.6	14.8	8.9	14.3	9.4	10.1	4.9	16.8	1976
Durham, NC	1.9	20.5	19.7	17.5	13.1	10.7	7.1	4.0	5.5	1985
El Paso, TX	3.1	18.6	14.1	15.8	17.6	11.6	11.2	3.7	4.3	1981
Erie, PA	0.4	7.1	9.0	8.6	14.4	9.8	15.3	8.1	27.3	1960
Eugene, OR	0.8	12.5	16.0	9.5	23.0	14.2	9.4	7.1	7.6	1975
Fargo, ND	2.4	20.7	16.5	11.4	18.1	7.6	9.2	2.8	11.2	1981
Fayetteville, NC	3.0	20.9	20.2	16.4	16.9	11.4	6.9	2.2	2.1	1986
Fort Collins, CO	1.5	20.3	20.7	14.3	21.6	8.3	4.0	2.2	7.3	1985
Fort Wayne, IN	0.9	11.4	14.9	11.5	14.7	13.8	10.8	5.9	16.0	1972
Fort Worth, TX	1.7	23.2	16.6	19.6	15.5	9.5	7.7	3.1	3.0	1986
Gainesville, FL	0.7	19.4	20.9	20.6	18.8	9.2	5.7	1.7	3.1	1986
Grand Rapids, MI	0.6	13.8	16.3	12.3	14.2	9.9	11.4	5.1	16.3	1975
Green Bay, WI	1.3	16.1	16.5	11.4	15.7	9.7	9.7	4.9	14.7	1977
Greensboro, NC	1.0	16.2	19.1	15.3	15.7	11.5	10.2	5.0	6.1	1981
Honolulu, HI	1.2	11.1	12.6	12.8	24.9	19.0	11.1	4.1	3.3	1975
Houston, TX	2.3	25.3	14.6	16.1	19.7	9.4	6.8	3.0	2.7	1985
Huntsville, AL	2.6	21.8	19.8	15.7	12.8	14.2	7.4	2.4	3.4	1986
Indianapolis, IN	1.3	17.3	16.7	10.7	13.3	11.6	11.1	5.1	12.9	1977
Jacksonville, FL	1.1	24.4	16.9	17.9	13.8	8.9	8.8	4.0	4.1	1986
Kansas City, MO	0.6	15.1	14.4	12.4	15.7	12.5	12.5	4.8	11.9	1975
Lafayette, LA	2.5	17.9	13.9	16.7	18.2	11.7	9.2	4.3	5.7	1981
Las Vegas, NV	1.3	34.3	27.9	15.3	12.5	5.2	2.6	0.7	0.3	1995
Lexington, KY	1.2	18.9	17.7	13.9	16.0	11.5	8.8	3.3	8.8	1981
Lincoln, NE	1.1	16.8	15.0	10.6	16.1	10.3	11.1	3.3	15.7	1976
Little Rock, AR	2.3	19.6	19.0	16.8	17.7	10.2	7.2	3.4	3.9	1985
Los Angeles, CA	0.5	7.0	7.6	12.6	16.5	15.9	19.0	8.8	12.2	1966
Louisville, KY	0.7	15.0	13.9	9.3	16.3	12.4	12.6	6.3	13.4	1973
Lubbock, TX	1.8	16.4	12.4	15.1	17.8	14.1	13.5	5.2	3.7	1978
Madison, WI	1.1	18.0	15.6	11.0	16.3	10.0	9.3	3.8	14.9	1977
Manchester, NH	0.4	10.4	9.9	20.9	15.8	9.6	7.2	3.8	22.0	1975
McAllen, TX	2.4	31.3	23.6	18.4	12.6	4.8	3.6	1.6	1.8	1993
Miami, FL	0.5	14.1	14.8	20.0	21.9	12.8	10.4	3.2	2.3	1980
Midland, TX	2.6	12.4	12.1	22.5	16.0	11.2	16.7	4.2	2.2	1980

Table continued on next page.

Metro Area	2010 or Later	2000 -2009	1990 -1999	1980 -1989	1970 -1979	1960 -1969	1950 -1959	1940 -1949	Before 1940	Median Year
Minneapolis, MN	0.7	15.2	14.7	14.7	15.5	10.0	10.2	4.1	14.9	1977
Nashville, TN	1.6	22.0	18.9	16.1	14.9	10.3	7.7	3.3	5.2	1985
New Orleans, LA	1.2	13.1	9.6	14.6	19.4	13.4	10.1	5.9	12.8	1974
New York, NY	0.6	7.4	6.0	7.8	9.9	13.8	16.5	9.3	28.7	1957
Oklahoma City, OK	2.1	16.3	11.0	15.8	18.4	13.3	10.6	5.5	7.0	1977
Omaha, NE	1.5	15.4	12.5	10.3	15.6	12.2	9.7	4.2	18.5	1973
Orlando, FL	0.9	26.8	21.3	22.0	13.8	6.5	5.8	1.4	1.7	1990
Oxnard, CA	0.4	11.3	10.8	16.7	23.2	20.6	10.5	2.9	3.6	1975
Palm Bay, FL	0.6	20.2	16.3	25.7	13.8	15.4	6.5	0.8	0.9	1985
Peoria, IL	0.7	10.0	8.4	5.8	17.8	12.8	16.2	8.8	19.6	1964
Philadelphia, PA	0.6	8.5	9.0	10.1	12.4	12.4	16.0	9.1	21.8	1962
Phoenix, AZ	0.9	28.1	20.8	18.2	17.2	6.8	5.4	1.5	1.0	1990
Pittsburgh, PA	0.5	6.6	7.7	7.5	12.1	11.1	16.8	9.6	28.1	1957
Portland, OR	0.9	16.5	18.8	11.3	18.2	9.1	7.4	5.1	12.6	1979
Providence, RI	0.4	6.8	7.9	10.4	12.3	10.5	11.7	6.8	33.3	1958
Provo, UT	2.1	30.2	21.1	9.4	16.1	5.4	6.2	3.6	5.9	1992
Raleigh, NC	2.0	30.3	25.6	16.6	10.5	6.4	4.1	1.8	2.8	1993
Reno, NV	1.0	23.9	19.4	15.5	20.5	9.0	5.1	2.4	3.1	1986
Richmond, VA	1.3	16.0	15.2	16.0	16.8	10.9	9.9	4.3	9.6	1979
Roanoke, VA	0.6	12.3	12.7	13.3	17.6	12.3	12.4	6.1	12.7	1974
Rochester, MN	1.1	19.2	14.7	11.6	13.9	10.9	8.8	4.0	15.9	1977
Sacramento, CA	0.6	18.9	14.2	16.5	19.7	11.1	10.7	3.9	4.5	1980
Salem, OR	1.0	14.6	18.7	10.2	23.5	10.2	7.7	4.7	9.3	1978
Salt Lake City, UT	1.5	17.0	16.4	13.3	20.2	9.0	9.9	4.0	8.6	1979
San Antonio, TX	2.2	24.1	14.7	16.1	15.9	9.5	8.1	4.5	4.9	1984
San Diego, CA	0.6	11.9	12.3	20.0	23.7	12.6	10.8	3.8	4.3	1978
San Francisco, CA	0.5	8.4	7.9	10.7	15.5	13.3	14.6	8.5	20.5	1965
San Jose, CA	0.6	9.7	10.4	12.9	22.7	18.7	15.7	4.2	5.1	1973
Santa Rosa, CA	0.4	11.2	13.5	18.6	21.7	11.3	8.8	5.3	9.3	1977
Savannah, GA	1.7	23.8	15.8	14.8	12.8	8.6	8.9	4.7	8.8	1984
Seattle, WA	1.3	16.9	15.9	15.4	15.2	11.5	7.9	4.8	11.0	1980
Sioux Falls, SD	2.7	22.3	15.9	10.1	15.1	7.7	8.3	4.8	13.1	1981
Spokane, WA	1.0	15.4	14.2	10.7	19.2	7.1	11.1	6.2	15.2	1975
Springfield, IL	0.6	10.8	13.7	10.0	16.2	13.3	11.8	7.0	16.5	1971
Tallahassee, FL	0.9	20.2	21.6	20.1	16.7	8.4	6.5	2.9	2.7	1986
Tampa, FL	1.0	17.3	14.3	21.3	21.7	11.0	8.7	2.0	2.8	1982
Topeka, KS	0.5	10.3	11.3	11.0	16.5	15.3	11.6	5.6	17.8	1970
Tulsa, OK	1.3	15.3	12.1	15.1	20.5	11.2	11.3	5.7	7.6	1977
Tyler, TX	1.7	20.1	15.2	18.0	17.6	10.2	9.3	4.3	3.6	1983
Virginia Beach, VA	1.2	13.9	14.7	19.4	16.3	12.7	10.6	5.4	5.8	1980
Washington, DC	1.2	15.7	14.3	16.6	15.1	12.9	10.0	5.5	8.7	1979
Wichita, KS	0.9	12.8	13.9	12.2	14.1	8.3	18.4	7.2	12.3	1973
Wilmington, NC	1.1	22.4	25.1	16.3	12.2	7.4	5.8	3.8	5.8	1989
Winston-Salem, NC	0.8	16.8	17.4	14.7	15.9	12.5	10.2	5.0	6.7	1980
Worcester, MA	0.6	9.0	9.1	12.6	11.4	8.4	10.6	6.0	32.2	1961
U.S.	0.9	15.0	13.9	13.8	15.8	11.0	10.9	5.4	13.3	1976

Note: Figures are percentages except for Median Year; Figures cover the Metropolitan Statistical Area—see Appendix B for areas included
Source: U.S. Census Bureau, 2011-2013 American Community Survey 3-Year Estimates

Highest Level of Education: City

City	Less than H.S.	H.S. Diploma	Some College, No Deg.	Associate Degree	Bachelors Degree	Masters Degree	Profess. School Degree	Doctorate Degree
Albuquerque, NM	10.8	23.3	24.4	8.0	18.7	10.2	2.3	2.3
Anchorage, AK	7.5	24.5	27.3	8.3	20.3	8.4	2.4	1.3
Ann Arbor, MI	3.7	8.5	12.6	4.8	28.7	24.4	6.4	10.9
Athens, GA	13.6	22.6	20.2	4.8	19.0	11.9	2.5	5.3
Atlanta, GA	11.1	19.5	16.6	4.6	28.3	12.9	4.8	2.2
Austin, TX	12.9	16.4	19.5	5.3	29.3	11.5	2.8	2.2
Billings, MT	7.4	29.5	26.8	7.3	20.1	5.8	2.0	1.1
Boise City, ID	5.9	20.5	25.8	9.0	24.7	10.2	2.4	1.6
Boston, MA	15.2	22.2	14.4	4.4	24.0	12.6	4.3	2.9
Boulder, CO	3.5	7.2	11.8	3.9	35.3	23.7	5.1	9.6
Cape Coral, FL	9.0	38.9	23.6	7.9	13.5	5.2	1.0	0.8
Cedar Rapids, IA	7.1	27.5	24.1	10.9	20.4	7.0	1.7	1.1
Charleston, SC	6.9	18.5	18.4	7.4	30.4	11.1	4.4	2.9
Charlotte, NC	11.4	19.8	21.1	7.2	27.9	9.5	2.2	1.0
Chicago, IL	18.6	23.3	18.1	5.6	20.7	9.4	2.9	1.4
Clarksville, TN	8.6	29.0	28.9	9.4	16.6	6.0	0.8	0.8
Colorado Springs, CO	6.7	20.9	25.0	10.7	22.3	11.1	1.9	1.3
Columbia, MO	6.4	14.5	18.3	5.7	30.8	14.0	4.0	6.3
Columbus, OH	11.8	26.4	21.9	6.9	21.7	8.1	1.8	1.4
Dallas, TX	25.8	22.0	18.1	4.6	18.5	7.3	2.7	1.1
Davenport, IA	10.0	30.1	21.4	12.1	18.1	6.1	1.4	0.7
Denver, CO	13.9	18.2	18.4	5.3	26.9	11.5	3.9	1.9
Des Moines, IA	12.3	31.1	22.2	9.2	17.8	5.2	1.4	0.8
Durham, NC	13.2	16.3	18.6	5.7	24.7	12.8	3.7	4.9
El Paso, TX	22.7	23.5	23.4	7.5	15.6	5.5	1.2	0.7
Erie, PA	13.6	41.7	16.0	7.1	14.7	5.0	0.8	1.1
Eugene, OR	6.1	18.8	29.0	7.8	22.0	10.6	2.5	3.2
Fargo, ND	5.5	19.8	23.3	12.8	26.0	7.8	2.7	2.2
Fayetteville, NC	9.3	24.8	30.8	10.9	16.0	6.0	1.2	1.1
Fort Collins, CO	4.7	14.0	20.5	9.1	31.8	13.7	2.4	3.8
Fort Wayne, IN	12.2	28.5	24.7	9.4	16.9	6.2	1.4	0.8
Fort Worth, TX	20.2	24.4	23.1	5.7	17.7	6.7	1.2	0.9
Gainesville, FL	8.3	20.6	18.1	10.4	21.8	11.2	3.7	5.8
Grand Rapids, MI	15.4	24.0	23.4	7.2	19.4	7.7	1.7	1.2
Green Bay, WI	13.1	33.5	19.6	10.6	17.2	4.3	1.1	0.6
Greensboro, NC	11.7	22.7	22.3	6.5	23.8	9.5	1.9	1.5
Honolulu, HI	12.0	24.6	19.3	9.0	22.4	8.2	2.6	1.9
Houston, TX	23.8	22.6	19.0	4.6	18.6	7.4	2.4	1.5
Huntsville, AL	9.9	20.5	23.0	7.8	24.1	11.0	1.9	1.9
Indianapolis, IN	15.2	29.2	21.2	7.1	17.9	6.7	1.8	1.0
Jacksonville, FL	12.1	29.4	23.3	9.6	17.8	5.5	1.5	0.8
Kansas City, MO	12.0	26.0	23.3	6.8	20.0	8.4	2.3	1.1
Lafayette, LA	13.6	25.2	22.9	5.4	21.6	7.0	2.3	1.8
Las Vegas, NV	17.0	29.2	24.4	7.7	14.2	5.2	1.6	0.7
Lexington, KY	10.9	20.6	20.5	7.4	23.3	10.8	3.5	3.1
Lincoln, NE	6.9	22.2	23.3	10.9	23.8	8.3	1.9	2.7
Little Rock, AR	9.4	25.2	21.7	5.2	23.7	8.9	3.9	2.0
Los Angeles, CA	25.2	19.6	18.0	5.9	20.9	6.6	2.6	1.2
Louisville, KY	13.1	29.9	22.8	7.3	15.7	8.0	2.0	1.3
Lubbock, TX	14.6	24.5	25.9	6.2	18.3	6.7	2.1	1.7
Madison, WI	5.1	15.9	17.2	8.1	29.4	15.5	3.9	5.0
Manchester, NH	12.9	32.7	18.8	9.3	18.4	6.1	0.8	0.9
McAllen, TX	27.3	19.7	20.6	5.9	18.5	5.0	2.3	0.7
Miami, FL	28.0	29.9	11.9	6.9	14.4	5.1	3.0	0.8
Midland, TX	18.3	22.9	27.4	6.0	18.2	5.4	1.3	0.4

Table continued on next page.

City	Less than H.S.	H.S. Diploma	Some College, No Deg.	Associate Degree	Bachelors Degree	Masters Degree	Profess. School Degree	Doctorate Degree
Minneapolis, MN	11.4	16.9	18.2	6.6	29.3	11.7	3.8	2.3
Nashville, TN	13.3	24.6	20.6	5.8	22.9	8.4	2.5	2.0
New Orleans, LA	15.5	23.5	22.3	4.4	19.5	8.4	4.2	2.2
New York, NY	20.1	24.4	14.4	6.3	20.6	9.9	3.0	1.4
Oklahoma City, OK	15.6	25.2	24.4	6.5	18.9	6.4	2.0	1.0
Omaha, NE	12.4	23.3	24.2	6.8	21.6	7.7	2.6	1.4
Orlando, FL	11.1	25.1	19.0	11.1	22.5	7.9	2.2	1.1
Oxnard, CA	34.7	21.2	20.4	7.8	11.7	3.1	0.7	0.4
Palm Bay, FL	13.7	32.3	24.2	12.0	12.0	5.1	0.4	0.3
Peoria, IL	11.8	26.9	19.8	9.2	19.9	8.6	2.7	1.2
Philadelphia, PA	18.6	34.2	17.8	5.1	14.3	6.6	2.2	1.3
Phoenix, AZ	19.4	23.7	22.8	7.6	17.2	6.5	1.9	0.9
Pittsburgh, PA	8.8	29.2	16.7	8.0	18.8	11.3	3.5	3.7
Portland, OR	9.1	17.2	22.3	7.0	26.4	12.3	3.6	2.1
Providence, RI	26.7	22.5	16.7	5.3	15.2	7.8	3.0	2.9
Provo, UT	10.2	13.1	29.7	8.3	26.4	8.3	1.5	2.6
Raleigh, NC	10.5	16.3	19.1	7.1	31.1	11.1	2.7	2.0
Reno, NV	14.5	22.8	26.2	6.8	18.6	6.8	2.4	1.9
Richmond, VA	18.2	23.2	18.8	5.0	21.2	9.3	2.8	1.4
Roanoke, VA	17.7	30.2	21.7	7.4	14.3	6.1	1.9	0.8
Rochester, MN	6.3	21.1	19.8	11.0	24.9	9.7	4.6	2.7
Sacramento, CA	16.9	21.1	24.3	8.5	18.5	6.6	2.7	1.3
Salem, OR	13.4	25.2	27.2	7.6	16.2	7.3	1.9	1.2
Salt Lake City, UT	13.5	16.9	20.6	6.2	24.5	10.3	4.2	3.8
San Antonio, TX	18.8	25.6	23.3	7.1	16.2	6.3	1.7	0.9
San Diego, CA	12.7	16.6	21.1	7.6	25.0	10.6	3.4	3.0
San Francisco, CA	13.5	13.1	15.2	5.3	32.1	13.5	4.9	2.4
San Jose, CA	17.5	18.3	18.9	7.7	23.3	10.7	1.6	1.9
Santa Rosa, CA	14.3	20.6	25.9	9.2	18.9	6.8	3.0	1.2
Savannah, GA	14.0	29.5	24.0	5.1	17.5	6.7	1.9	1.4
Seattle, WA	6.8	11.7	17.0	6.8	34.5	15.0	4.9	3.4
Sioux Falls, SD	9.1	27.5	20.4	10.5	21.8	7.4	1.9	1.4
Spokane, WA	9.2	26.1	25.8	10.4	17.6	7.4	2.3	1.3
Springfield, IL	9.1	26.6	22.4	7.6	20.3	10.0	2.8	1.2
Tallahassee, FL	7.7	16.4	19.2	9.1	26.0	13.8	3.9	3.9
Tampa, FL	13.5	26.6	18.2	7.8	20.7	8.4	3.2	1.7
Topeka, KS	12.1	32.3	22.7	6.5	16.7	6.7	2.0	1.0
Tulsa, OK	13.1	25.3	23.4	7.8	20.2	6.6	2.5	1.1
Tyler, TX	15.6	21.1	24.7	9.1	18.6	6.9	2.7	1.3
Virginia Beach, VA	6.0	22.9	27.4	10.0	21.9	8.8	2.0	1.0
Washington, DC	11.4	18.2	13.9	3.0	23.0	18.1	8.5	3.9
Wichita, KS	12.4	26.8	26.2	6.3	19.0	7.1	1.4	0.9
Wilmington, NC	10.7	19.3	20.0	9.9	25.9	9.8	2.4	2.1
Winston-Salem, NC	15.6	24.4	20.6	6.5	20.3	8.1	2.5	2.0
Worcester, MA	15.3	29.7	16.9	8.3	18.4	8.1	1.7	1.6
U.S.	13.7	28.0	21.2	7.9	18.2	7.7	1.9	1.3

Note: Figures cover persons age 25 and over
Source: U.S. Census Bureau, 2011-2013 American Community Survey 3-Year Estimates

Highest Level of Education: Metro Area

Metro Area	Less than H.S.	H.S. Diploma	Some College, No Deg.	Associate Degree	Bachelors Degree	Masters Degree	Profess. School Degree	Doctorate Degree
Albuquerque, NM	12.5	25.1	24.2	8.1	16.9	9.2	2.0	2.0
Anchorage, AK	7.5	26.2	28.1	8.4	18.8	7.6	2.2	1.2
Ann Arbor, MI	5.8	16.2	19.9	6.7	24.9	16.3	4.4	5.8
Athens, GA	14.1	26.5	20.6	5.2	17.1	10.4	2.5	3.7
Atlanta, GA	12.2	24.8	20.8	7.1	22.7	8.9	2.2	1.3
Austin, TX	11.8	19.3	21.5	6.5	26.9	9.9	2.3	1.7
Billings, MT	7.7	31.1	26.6	7.1	19.4	5.2	1.9	0.9
Boise City, ID	10.0	25.2	26.7	8.3	20.4	6.8	1.6	1.0
Boston, MA	9.2	24.3	15.6	7.2	24.3	13.4	3.2	2.8
Boulder, CO	6.2	12.6	17.2	5.6	31.1	18.1	3.4	5.7
Cape Coral, FL	13.2	32.5	21.5	7.8	15.8	6.2	1.9	1.2
Cedar Rapids, IA	6.5	28.9	23.2	12.4	20.1	6.5	1.6	0.9
Charleston, SC	11.5	25.8	22.4	8.8	20.1	7.9	2.0	1.3
Charlotte, NC	13.2	25.4	21.8	8.4	21.6	7.3	1.5	0.9
Chicago, IL	13.2	25.0	20.2	6.8	21.3	9.7	2.5	1.2
Clarksville, TN	11.4	31.2	26.9	8.9	14.7	5.3	1.0	0.6
Colorado Springs, CO	6.1	21.5	26.1	11.3	21.5	10.6	1.7	1.3
Columbia, MO	6.3	20.1	19.6	6.7	27.5	11.8	3.4	4.5
Columbus, OH	9.9	29.2	20.5	7.2	21.4	8.4	2.0	1.4
Dallas, TX	15.9	22.8	22.9	6.6	21.3	7.9	1.6	1.0
Davenport, IA	9.9	31.0	23.2	10.5	17.0	6.6	1.2	0.7
Denver, CO	10.1	20.8	21.8	7.7	25.5	10.3	2.5	1.4
Des Moines, IA	7.3	26.4	21.1	10.1	25.1	7.0	1.9	1.1
Durham, NC	12.4	19.4	18.1	6.3	22.8	12.3	3.7	5.0
El Paso, TX	25.2	23.8	22.8	7.3	14.3	5.0	1.0	0.7
Erie, PA	9.6	40.8	16.3	8.1	16.3	6.3	1.4	1.2
Eugene, OR	8.6	25.5	29.8	8.3	16.8	7.4	1.7	1.9
Fargo, ND	5.6	22.0	23.5	13.7	25.0	6.7	1.8	1.7
Fayetteville, NC	11.0	27.3	29.1	10.9	14.7	5.4	0.9	0.7
Fort Collins, CO	5.4	18.6	23.6	8.9	27.2	11.6	2.1	2.7
Fort Wayne, IN	10.7	31.5	23.6	9.4	16.1	6.4	1.5	0.7
Fort Worth, TX	15.9	22.8	22.9	6.6	21.3	7.9	1.6	1.0
Gainesville, FL	8.8	22.6	20.0	10.6	20.3	9.6	3.7	4.4
Grand Rapids, MI	10.1	28.4	22.9	8.9	19.6	7.5	1.6	0.9
Green Bay, WI	9.4	34.0	19.8	11.5	18.2	5.3	1.2	0.6
Greensboro, NC	14.9	28.6	21.6	7.9	18.3	6.5	1.3	1.0
Honolulu, HI	9.5	26.4	21.7	10.3	21.2	7.4	2.3	1.4
Houston, TX	18.6	23.7	21.6	6.3	19.5	7.1	1.9	1.3
Huntsville, AL	11.0	23.6	22.2	7.8	22.5	10.2	1.3	1.5
Indianapolis, IN	11.2	29.6	20.8	7.7	19.9	7.5	2.0	1.2
Jacksonville, FL	10.8	28.6	23.4	9.5	19.0	6.2	1.6	0.9
Kansas City, MO	9.1	26.6	23.4	7.5	21.4	8.8	2.1	1.0
Lafayette, LA	19.5	35.0	20.1	5.3	14.1	4.1	1.1	0.8
Las Vegas, NV	15.9	29.5	25.0	7.5	14.8	5.0	1.5	0.7
Lexington, KY	12.3	24.7	20.6	7.4	20.6	9.4	2.8	2.3
Lincoln, NE	6.6	22.8	23.1	11.3	23.5	8.1	1.9	2.6
Little Rock, AR	10.9	31.0	23.6	6.2	18.3	6.8	1.9	1.3
Los Angeles, CA	21.5	20.0	19.9	7.1	20.6	7.2	2.4	1.3
Louisville, KY	12.2	31.0	22.4	7.7	16.1	7.5	1.9	1.1
Lubbock, TX	16.2	25.5	25.3	6.1	17.3	6.3	1.8	1.5
Madison, WI	5.7	23.1	19.7	9.8	24.6	11.1	3.0	2.9
Manchester, NH	8.9	27.3	18.6	9.6	23.0	9.9	1.3	1.4
McAllen, TX	37.8	24.0	17.6	4.4	11.5	3.4	1.0	0.4
Miami, FL	15.8	27.9	18.4	8.8	18.6	6.8	2.7	1.2
Midland, TX	18.3	23.4	27.0	6.3	17.6	5.8	1.3	0.4

Table continued on next page.

Metro Area	Less than H.S.	H.S. Diploma	Some College, No Deg.	Associate Degree	Bachelors Degree	Masters Degree	Profess. School Degree	Doctorate Degree
Minneapolis, MN	7.0	22.9	21.5	9.8	25.9	9.1	2.4	1.4
Nashville, TN	12.2	29.1	21.1	6.3	20.7	7.3	1.9	1.5
New Orleans, LA	15.3	29.3	23.1	5.6	16.9	5.9	2.6	1.2
New York, NY	14.9	25.9	15.7	6.6	21.7	10.8	2.9	1.5
Oklahoma City, OK	12.7	27.5	24.8	6.8	18.6	6.7	1.8	1.2
Omaha, NE	9.1	25.3	24.4	8.2	21.8	7.9	2.2	1.1
Orlando, FL	12.4	28.4	21.0	9.8	19.0	6.7	1.6	1.0
Oxnard, CA	17.0	19.1	23.8	8.8	19.8	7.9	2.3	1.3
Palm Bay, FL	10.3	28.5	23.5	11.4	16.5	7.4	1.4	1.1
Peoria, IL	8.8	31.8	23.3	9.8	17.7	6.5	1.4	0.7
Philadelphia, PA	10.9	30.8	17.8	6.6	20.5	9.3	2.5	1.7
Phoenix, AZ	13.6	23.9	25.1	8.4	18.7	7.5	1.8	1.1
Pittsburgh, PA	7.9	35.3	16.6	9.5	18.9	8.4	2.0	1.5
Portland, OR	9.2	22.0	25.4	8.6	21.9	9.0	2.3	1.5
Providence, RI	15.4	28.1	18.3	8.6	18.2	8.3	1.8	1.3
Provo, UT	6.9	17.3	28.9	10.6	25.1	7.8	1.4	2.0
Raleigh, NC	10.4	19.8	19.0	8.5	27.6	10.8	2.0	2.0
Reno, NV	13.7	24.1	26.6	7.6	17.9	6.5	2.2	1.5
Richmond, VA	12.7	26.7	21.0	6.9	20.5	8.9	2.1	1.3
Roanoke, VA	13.2	30.4	21.8	8.5	17.1	6.5	1.6	1.0
Rochester, MN	6.4	26.3	21.2	11.8	21.4	7.8	3.3	1.8
Sacramento, CA	11.9	21.8	26.3	9.6	19.7	6.9	2.4	1.4
Salem, OR	15.1	26.5	27.2	8.2	14.9	5.8	1.5	0.8
Salt Lake City, UT	10.6	23.0	26.3	8.8	20.4	7.4	2.0	1.5
San Antonio, TX	16.6	25.8	23.6	7.5	17.2	6.8	1.6	1.0
San Diego, CA	14.4	19.3	22.3	9.5	21.3	8.6	2.6	2.0
San Francisco, CA	12.1	17.1	19.1	6.9	27.0	11.7	3.6	2.5
San Jose, CA	13.5	15.7	17.4	7.1	25.5	14.8	2.6	3.3
Santa Rosa, CA	12.9	20.5	25.6	9.1	20.6	7.2	2.8	1.2
Savannah, GA	11.9	27.9	23.5	7.0	18.9	7.6	1.9	1.4
Seattle, WA	8.3	21.3	23.1	9.1	24.3	9.7	2.4	1.7
Sioux Falls, SD	8.2	29.1	20.7	11.4	21.2	6.5	1.7	1.1
Spokane, WA	7.7	27.0	27.0	11.4	17.4	6.7	1.8	1.0
Springfield, IL	7.9	29.1	22.8	8.0	20.1	8.7	2.3	1.1
Tallahassee, FL	10.8	23.8	20.3	8.3	21.1	10.6	2.6	2.6
Tampa, FL	12.0	30.8	21.1	9.5	17.3	6.4	1.8	1.0
Topeka, KS	9.2	34.1	23.8	6.8	17.1	6.6	1.6	0.9
Tulsa, OK	11.5	30.0	23.8	8.6	18.0	5.7	1.6	0.8
Tyler, TX	15.1	25.4	25.5	9.3	17.0	5.2	1.7	0.8
Virginia Beach, VA	9.9	26.1	26.0	9.0	18.3	8.1	1.6	1.0
Washington, DC	9.8	19.2	17.4	5.6	25.0	15.8	4.3	2.9
Wichita, KS	10.4	27.6	26.5	7.2	19.3	7.0	1.2	0.8
Wilmington, NC	10.7	23.6	23.3	9.3	22.2	7.5	2.0	1.5
Winston-Salem, NC	16.0	29.9	20.9	7.9	16.9	5.8	1.5	1.1
Worcester, MA	10.5	29.8	18.3	9.0	19.7	9.5	1.6	1.5
U.S.	13.7	28.0	21.2	7.9	18.2	7.7	1.9	1.3

Note: Figures cover persons age 25 and over; Figures cover the Metropolitan Statistical Area—see Appendix B for areas included
Source: U.S. Census Bureau, 2011-2013 American Community Survey 3-Year Estimates

School Enrollment by Grade and Control: City

City	Preschool (%)		Kindergarten (%)		Grades 1 - 4 (%)		Grades 5 - 8 (%)		Grades 9 - 12 (%)	
	Public	Private	Public	Private	Public	Private	Public	Private	Public	Private
Albuquerque, NM	57.0	43.0	90.0	10.0	89.8	10.2	88.3	11.7	88.8	11.2
Anchorage, AK	41.1	58.9	91.3	8.7	92.5	7.5	93.1	6.9	91.4	8.6
Ann Arbor, MI	23.9	76.1	85.8	14.2	91.1	8.9	84.4	15.6	89.4	10.6
Athens, GA	67.4	32.6	84.6	15.4	93.5	6.5	90.1	9.9	89.3	10.7
Atlanta, GA	55.1	44.9	81.2	18.8	84.3	15.7	83.7	16.3	78.2	21.8
Austin, TX	47.4	52.6	87.8	12.2	91.3	8.7	90.2	9.8	92.6	7.4
Billings, MT	45.4	54.6	90.3	9.7	94.6	5.4	91.2	8.8	91.2	8.8
Boise City, ID	52.4	47.6	92.8	7.2	92.6	7.4	93.3	6.7	92.8	7.2
Boston, MA	53.1	46.9	85.0	15.0	86.9	13.1	85.9	14.1	87.0	13.0
Boulder, CO	24.7	75.3	85.4	14.6	86.0	14.0	86.2	13.8	93.2	6.8
Cape Coral, FL	64.1	35.9	94.4	5.6	94.1	5.9	95.7	4.3	93.0	7.0
Cedar Rapids, IA	55.7	44.3	87.6	12.4	85.5	14.5	89.3	10.7	87.9	12.1
Charleston, SC	39.3	60.7	79.4	20.6	77.8	22.2	72.7	27.3	82.1	17.9
Charlotte, NC	42.2	57.8	90.3	9.7	90.1	9.9	88.6	11.4	90.0	10.0
Chicago, IL	65.1	34.9	82.8	17.2	85.5	14.5	86.8	13.2	88.4	11.6
Clarksville, TN	67.0	33.0	96.4	3.6	94.5	5.5	94.8	5.2	90.8	9.2
Colorado Springs, CO	59.5	40.5	89.5	10.5	93.0	7.0	93.4	6.6	93.1	6.9
Columbia, MO	38.3	61.7	83.9	16.1	84.4	15.6	80.2	19.8	94.3	5.7
Columbus, OH	55.0	45.0	89.8	10.2	88.8	11.2	88.0	12.0	88.0	12.0
Dallas, TX	70.4	29.6	89.5	10.5	92.3	7.7	89.6	10.4	90.7	9.3
Davenport, IA	66.4	33.6	86.2	13.8	91.1	8.9	86.9	13.1	91.1	8.9
Denver, CO	58.9	41.1	88.4	11.6	88.7	11.3	86.8	13.2	90.2	9.8
Des Moines, IA	69.9	30.1	89.1	10.9	91.5	8.5	90.3	9.7	91.6	8.4
Durham, NC	51.4	48.6	86.5	13.5	91.2	8.8	89.5	10.5	92.1	7.9
El Paso, TX	81.6	18.4	94.1	5.9	95.0	5.0	94.3	5.7	96.7	3.3
Erie, PA	42.7	57.3	86.3	13.7	87.7	12.3	89.3	10.7	85.2	14.8
Eugene, OR	36.0	64.0	81.2	18.8	85.8	14.2	87.3	12.7	90.9	9.1
Fargo, ND	57.7	42.3	82.5	17.5	79.1	20.9	88.3	11.7	85.1	14.9
Fayetteville, NC	72.2	27.8	90.7	9.3	89.6	10.4	89.6	10.4	90.0	10.0
Fort Collins, CO	31.5	68.5	92.1	7.9	90.1	9.9	90.1	9.9	97.4	2.6
Fort Wayne, IN	52.6	47.4	80.8	19.2	84.5	15.5	81.1	18.9	87.7	12.3
Fort Worth, TX	62.7	37.3	92.6	7.4	93.6	6.4	92.2	7.8	93.8	6.2
Gainesville, FL	56.4	43.6	69.8	30.2	86.0	14.0	87.5	12.5	89.3	10.7
Grand Rapids, MI	67.9	32.1	81.1	18.9	79.5	20.5	86.8	13.2	85.9	14.1
Green Bay, WI	79.4	20.6	87.0	13.0	88.9	11.1	91.6	8.4	90.5	9.5
Greensboro, NC	57.9	42.1	91.9	8.1	92.4	7.6	90.4	9.6	91.6	8.4
Honolulu, HI	41.3	58.7	86.7	13.3	81.9	18.1	80.8	19.2	74.1	25.9
Houston, TX	66.5	33.5	91.4	8.6	92.8	7.2	93.1	6.9	92.8	7.2
Huntsville, AL	40.1	59.9	83.3	16.7	86.0	14.0	85.0	15.0	88.0	12.0
Indianapolis, IN	43.0	57.0	83.6	16.4	89.2	10.8	89.1	10.9	88.0	12.0
Jacksonville, FL	58.5	41.5	86.1	13.9	83.7	16.3	84.6	15.4	84.5	15.5
Kansas City, MO	53.3	46.7	84.4	15.6	84.5	15.5	85.3	14.7	88.0	12.0
Lafayette, LA	52.9	47.1	80.2	19.8	82.3	17.7	73.9	26.1	76.0	24.0
Las Vegas, NV	50.7	49.3	86.9	13.1	92.9	7.1	91.9	8.1	94.7	5.3
Lexington, KY	46.1	53.9	82.5	17.5	85.7	14.3	87.6	12.4	88.2	11.8
Lincoln, NE	48.0	52.0	81.7	18.3	84.3	15.7	83.6	16.4	88.1	11.9
Little Rock, AR	60.3	39.7	86.8	13.2	80.1	19.9	73.1	26.9	81.2	18.8
Los Angeles, CA	61.5	38.5	86.7	13.3	89.1	10.9	88.8	11.2	89.5	10.5
Louisville, KY	50.2	49.8	84.6	15.4	82.5	17.5	81.3	18.7	82.1	17.9
Lubbock, TX	65.9	34.1	89.1	10.9	93.5	6.5	94.5	5.5	95.8	4.2
Madison, WI	44.4	55.6	89.5	10.5	92.4	7.6	88.5	11.5	94.1	5.9
Manchester, NH	41.7	58.3	75.4	24.6	92.1	7.9	89.4	10.6	95.7	4.3
McAllen, TX	82.0	18.0	86.6	13.4	96.1	3.9	93.7	6.3	94.8	5.2
Miami, FL	59.3	40.7	81.2	18.8	85.6	14.4	90.6	9.4	89.5	10.5
Midland, TX	42.0	58.0	77.3	22.7	87.5	12.5	85.9	14.1	88.8	11.2

Table continued on next page.

City	Preschool (%)		Kindergarten (%)		Grades 1 - 4 (%)		Grades 5 - 8 (%)		Grades 9 - 12 (%)	
	Public	Private	Public	Private	Public	Private	Public	Private	Public	Private
Minneapolis, MN	59.5	40.5	86.2	13.8	88.6	11.4	86.7	13.3	89.9	10.1
Nashville, TN	60.3	39.7	87.5	12.5	88.3	11.7	81.9	18.1	82.1	17.9
New Orleans, LA	60.2	39.8	77.7	22.3	81.5	18.5	78.2	21.8	81.2	18.8
New York, NY	54.4	45.6	79.1	20.9	83.3	16.7	82.8	17.2	83.2	16.8
Oklahoma City, OK	68.4	31.6	92.1	7.9	91.0	9.0	91.5	8.5	91.5	8.5
Omaha, NE	57.1	42.9	81.1	18.9	85.1	14.9	86.1	13.9	86.8	13.2
Orlando, FL	54.2	45.8	82.0	18.0	91.0	9.0	92.2	7.8	91.9	8.1
Oxnard, CA	74.8	25.2	94.1	5.9	93.9	6.1	94.6	5.4	93.3	6.7
Palm Bay, FL	47.0	53.0	93.4	6.6	89.6	10.4	87.1	12.9	86.4	13.6
Peoria, IL	70.8	29.2	78.5	21.5	83.1	16.9	74.6	25.4	85.3	14.7
Philadelphia, PA	57.0	43.0	82.1	17.9	81.3	18.7	79.4	20.6	81.7	18.3
Phoenix, AZ	57.3	42.7	92.8	7.2	94.1	5.9	94.1	5.9	93.7	6.3
Pittsburgh, PA	63.0	37.0	81.6	18.4	80.4	19.6	78.0	22.0	79.1	20.9
Portland, OR	35.1	64.9	83.8	16.2	88.7	11.3	90.9	9.1	86.9	13.1
Providence, RI	71.3	28.7	79.1	20.9	89.7	10.3	88.3	11.7	86.5	13.5
Provo, UT	41.2	58.8	91.5	8.5	97.1	2.9	93.0	7.0	91.6	8.4
Raleigh, NC	35.4	64.6	90.4	9.6	90.8	9.2	89.6	10.4	92.2	7.8
Reno, NV	63.8	36.2	89.3	10.7	93.6	6.4	93.2	6.8	96.8	3.2
Richmond, VA	54.7	45.3	82.3	17.7	86.2	13.8	85.3	14.7	89.7	10.3
Roanoke, VA	58.2	41.8	93.3	6.7	95.2	4.8	91.5	8.5	95.9	4.1
Rochester, MN	45.7	54.3	82.8	17.2	83.6	16.4	83.9	16.1	91.1	8.9
Sacramento, CA	69.7	30.3	90.9	9.1	93.1	6.9	93.4	6.6	90.2	9.8
Salem, OR	68.9	31.1	89.8	10.2	93.1	6.9	92.2	7.8	94.4	5.6
Salt Lake City, UT	42.8	57.2	85.4	14.6	90.1	9.9	90.0	10.0	91.7	8.3
San Antonio, TX	69.3	30.7	90.3	9.7	93.1	6.9	92.2	7.8	93.6	6.4
San Diego, CA	54.5	45.5	89.9	10.1	91.9	8.1	92.1	7.9	93.7	6.3
San Francisco, CA	35.0	65.0	70.4	29.6	71.2	28.8	69.6	30.4	77.7	22.3
San Jose, CA	44.4	55.6	82.5	17.5	89.5	10.5	89.7	10.3	89.9	10.1
Santa Rosa, CA	50.5	49.5	91.4	8.6	97.1	2.9	97.3	2.7	90.8	9.2
Savannah, GA	73.0	27.0	89.4	10.6	92.7	7.3	87.8	12.2	82.5	17.5
Seattle, WA	34.9	65.1	73.8	26.2	78.1	21.9	77.7	22.3	79.1	20.9
Sioux Falls, SD	57.5	42.5	86.7	13.3	87.5	12.5	92.1	7.9	90.7	9.3
Spokane, WA	32.1	67.9	83.1	16.9	87.9	12.1	93.5	6.5	93.5	6.5
Springfield, IL	67.8	32.2	80.3	19.7	85.3	14.7	85.8	14.2	83.9	16.1
Tallahassee, FL	55.3	44.7	91.6	8.4	90.8	9.2	89.0	11.0	90.8	9.2
Tampa, FL	54.6	45.4	91.9	8.1	90.2	9.8	87.2	12.8	90.8	9.2
Topeka, KS	72.1	27.9	97.5	2.5	89.2	10.8	89.3	10.7	88.6	11.4
Tulsa, OK	71.7	28.3	89.3	10.7	89.4	10.6	85.7	14.3	86.3	13.7
Tyler, TX	68.3	31.7	98.2	1.8	92.8	7.2	89.8	10.2	88.6	11.4
Virginia Beach, VA	33.2	66.8	85.9	14.1	90.1	9.9	91.1	8.9	93.3	6.7
Washington, DC	73.9	26.1	88.4	11.6	81.6	18.4	81.6	18.4	83.2	16.8
Wichita, KS	69.3	30.7	84.0	16.0	86.6	13.4	86.6	13.4	83.2	16.8
Wilmington, NC	55.9	44.1	90.4	9.6	86.8	13.2	77.6	22.4	87.7	12.3
Winston-Salem, NC	53.8	46.2	90.1	9.9	91.9	8.1	91.9	8.1	93.2	6.8
Worcester, MA	75.0	25.0	95.3	4.7	92.3	7.7	91.3	8.7	89.9	10.1
U.S.	57.7	42.3	87.9	12.1	89.9	10.1	90.0	10.0	90.7	9.3

Note: Figures shown cover persons 3 years old and over
Source: U.S. Census Bureau, 2011-2013 American Community Survey 3-Year Estimates

School Enrollment by Grade and Control: Metro Area

Metro Area	Preschool (%)		Kindergarten (%)		Grades 1 - 4 (%)		Grades 5 - 8 (%)		Grades 9 - 12 (%)	
	Public	Private	Public	Private	Public	Private	Public	Private	Public	Private
Albuquerque, NM	61.8	38.2	89.1	10.9	90.7	9.3	89.4	10.6	89.7	10.3
Anchorage, AK	47.7	52.3	89.9	10.1	91.0	9.0	90.8	9.2	90.9	9.1
Ann Arbor, MI	51.7	48.3	87.1	12.9	89.6	10.4	88.4	11.6	89.7	10.3
Athens, GA	67.9	32.1	88.5	11.5	93.3	6.7	89.8	10.2	87.4	12.6
Atlanta, GA	54.0	46.0	87.6	12.4	90.5	9.5	89.9	10.1	90.6	9.4
Austin, TX	50.2	49.8	88.8	11.2	92.2	7.8	92.2	7.8	93.5	6.5
Billings, MT	44.8	55.2	91.7	8.3	95.0	5.0	90.4	9.6	89.5	10.5
Boise City, ID	47.1	52.9	90.3	9.7	92.9	7.1	94.1	5.9	93.6	6.4
Boston, MA	42.9	57.1	86.2	13.8	90.1	9.9	89.1	10.9	86.8	13.2
Boulder, CO	42.9	57.1	92.9	7.1	90.1	9.9	91.7	8.3	95.2	4.8
Cape Coral, FL	59.9	40.1	94.5	5.5	94.1	5.9	91.5	8.5	93.6	6.4
Cedar Rapids, IA	59.5	40.5	86.0	14.0	87.0	13.0	90.4	9.6	90.5	9.5
Charleston, SC	44.5	55.5	84.8	15.2	88.3	11.7	88.2	11.8	89.8	10.2
Charlotte, NC	46.7	53.3	90.9	9.1	91.3	8.7	90.3	9.7	90.9	9.1
Chicago, IL	57.7	42.3	86.0	14.0	88.5	11.5	89.1	10.9	90.9	9.1
Clarksville, TN	71.4	28.6	94.8	5.2	90.8	9.2	92.3	7.7	90.2	9.8
Colorado Springs, CO	62.2	37.8	90.7	9.3	93.3	6.7	92.9	7.1	93.4	6.6
Columbia, MO	38.3	61.7	87.7	12.3	88.0	12.0	84.4	15.6	92.3	7.7
Columbus, OH	50.7	49.3	87.7	12.3	89.3	10.7	89.2	10.8	89.1	10.9
Dallas, TX	56.4	43.6	89.9	10.1	92.6	7.4	92.2	7.8	92.4	7.6
Davenport, IA	66.9	33.1	90.5	9.5	91.2	8.8	90.6	9.4	93.1	6.9
Denver, CO	56.1	43.9	90.4	9.6	92.9	7.1	91.6	8.4	92.6	7.4
Des Moines, IA	62.1	37.9	88.8	11.2	91.0	9.0	91.5	8.5	91.5	8.5
Durham, NC	45.1	54.9	88.7	11.3	91.2	8.8	90.2	9.8	90.7	9.3
El Paso, TX	84.6	15.4	95.2	4.8	95.9	4.1	95.3	4.7	97.2	2.8
Erie, PA	45.0	55.0	85.8	14.2	88.1	11.9	90.2	9.8	88.5	11.5
Eugene, OR	53.0	47.0	83.8	16.2	89.4	10.6	89.7	10.3	92.8	7.2
Fargo, ND	62.9	37.1	87.3	12.7	86.0	14.0	90.7	9.3	89.3	10.7
Fayetteville, NC	70.0	30.0	91.7	8.3	91.5	8.5	91.2	8.8	91.7	8.3
Fort Collins, CO	38.2	61.8	86.5	13.5	91.5	8.5	90.6	9.4	95.9	4.1
Fort Wayne, IN	47.5	52.5	76.8	23.2	82.1	17.9	79.2	20.8	88.2	11.8
Fort Worth, TX	56.4	43.6	89.9	10.1	92.6	7.4	92.2	7.8	92.4	7.6
Gainesville, FL	50.0	50.0	77.7	22.3	86.1	13.9	88.6	11.4	87.7	12.3
Grand Rapids, MI	64.2	35.8	84.5	15.5	84.2	15.8	85.7	14.3	87.2	12.8
Green Bay, WI	73.2	26.8	84.1	15.9	89.0	11.0	91.3	8.7	92.6	7.4
Greensboro, NC	58.2	41.8	90.6	9.4	91.5	8.5	91.2	8.8	90.3	9.7
Honolulu, HI	39.7	60.3	84.0	16.0	82.6	17.4	79.0	21.0	75.1	24.9
Houston, TX	59.0	41.0	89.8	10.2	93.5	6.5	94.0	6.0	93.6	6.4
Huntsville, AL	44.8	55.2	85.5	14.5	87.5	12.5	88.1	11.9	88.8	11.2
Indianapolis, IN	47.0	53.0	83.1	16.9	88.9	11.1	90.0	10.0	89.3	10.7
Jacksonville, FL	54.8	45.2	86.2	13.8	85.8	14.2	87.2	12.8	86.5	13.5
Kansas City, MO	52.6	47.4	85.7	14.3	88.5	11.5	88.7	11.3	89.7	10.3
Lafayette, LA	58.7	41.3	81.0	19.0	79.6	20.4	77.6	22.4	78.4	21.6
Las Vegas, NV	55.8	44.2	90.3	9.7	93.4	6.6	94.5	5.5	95.3	4.7
Lexington, KY	46.6	53.4	84.5	15.5	85.8	14.2	86.5	13.5	87.2	12.8
Lincoln, NE	49.2	50.8	79.1	20.9	83.6	16.4	83.3	16.7	88.8	11.2
Little Rock, AR	60.1	39.9	87.5	12.5	86.1	13.9	85.7	14.3	87.3	12.7
Los Angeles, CA	59.0	41.0	87.9	12.1	90.3	9.7	90.6	9.4	91.8	8.2
Louisville, KY	49.9	50.1	85.8	14.2	84.3	15.7	83.2	16.8	84.1	15.9
Lubbock, TX	65.4	34.6	88.7	11.3	93.0	7.0	94.1	5.9	94.8	5.2
Madison, WI	53.4	46.6	90.9	9.1	90.8	9.2	90.0	10.0	94.9	5.1
Manchester, NH	38.3	61.7	74.7	25.3	90.6	9.4	90.2	9.8	91.1	8.9
McAllen, TX	91.8	8.2	94.9	5.1	97.9	2.1	97.8	2.2	97.7	2.3
Miami, FL	49.0	51.0	82.2	17.8	86.3	13.7	88.1	11.9	87.7	12.3
Midland, TX	46.0	54.0	81.5	18.5	90.2	9.8	87.9	12.1	89.3	10.7

Table continued on next page.

Metro Area	Preschool (%)		Kindergarten (%)		Grades 1 - 4 (%)		Grades 5 - 8 (%)		Grades 9 - 12 (%)	
	Public	Private	Public	Private	Public	Private	Public	Private	Public	Private
Minneapolis, MN	54.8	45.2	86.2	13.8	87.5	12.5	88.8	11.2	91.4	8.6
Nashville, TN	51.8	48.2	88.4	11.6	89.3	10.7	86.2	13.8	85.3	14.7
New Orleans, LA	55.4	44.6	75.9	24.1	77.4	22.6	76.1	23.9	76.0	24.0
New York, NY	49.5	50.5	81.6	18.4	86.5	13.5	86.6	13.4	86.1	13.9
Oklahoma City, OK	73.1	26.9	89.9	10.1	91.2	8.8	91.7	8.3	92.0	8.0
Omaha, NE	56.3	43.7	84.5	15.5	86.6	13.4	87.6	12.4	87.5	12.5
Orlando, FL	51.0	49.0	87.6	12.4	89.1	10.9	88.9	11.1	91.2	8.8
Oxnard, CA	53.3	46.7	90.2	9.8	91.1	8.9	90.2	9.8	90.2	9.8
Palm Bay, FL	51.4	48.6	90.0	10.0	89.9	10.1	87.8	12.2	90.0	10.0
Peoria, IL	62.4	37.6	85.6	14.4	86.4	13.6	86.5	13.5	91.1	8.9
Philadelphia, PA	43.1	56.9	79.9	20.1	84.8	15.2	83.9	16.1	83.7	16.3
Phoenix, AZ	57.4	42.6	92.2	7.8	92.9	7.1	94.2	5.8	94.1	5.9
Pittsburgh, PA	47.8	52.2	85.7	14.3	87.9	12.1	87.9	12.1	89.7	10.3
Portland, OR	38.1	61.9	83.4	16.6	89.6	10.4	90.8	9.2	91.9	8.1
Providence, RI	51.1	48.9	85.8	14.2	90.0	10.0	90.4	9.6	87.8	12.2
Provo, UT	41.4	58.6	91.6	8.4	95.2	4.8	95.1	4.9	95.7	4.3
Raleigh, NC	36.9	63.1	88.3	11.7	89.7	10.3	88.7	11.3	91.5	8.5
Reno, NV	55.2	44.8	89.9	10.1	93.0	7.0	92.6	7.4	94.9	5.1
Richmond, VA	40.0	60.0	88.4	11.6	89.9	10.1	91.0	9.0	92.0	8.0
Roanoke, VA	50.7	49.3	92.9	7.1	92.3	7.7	90.7	9.3	95.5	4.5
Rochester, MN	58.9	41.1	86.3	13.7	87.0	13.0	87.6	12.4	92.3	7.7
Sacramento, CA	55.9	44.1	89.4	10.6	92.0	8.0	92.4	7.6	91.2	8.8
Salem, OR	59.1	40.9	90.5	9.5	91.3	8.7	91.2	8.8	92.1	7.9
Salt Lake City, UT	50.2	49.8	91.1	8.9	92.8	7.2	93.4	6.6	93.5	6.5
San Antonio, TX	65.5	34.5	91.1	8.9	92.3	7.7	92.7	7.3	93.6	6.4
San Diego, CA	55.1	44.9	90.7	9.3	92.3	7.7	92.3	7.7	93.4	6.6
San Francisco, CA	40.8	59.2	83.4	16.6	86.0	14.0	86.0	14.0	88.3	11.7
San Jose, CA	35.4	64.6	83.2	16.8	87.7	12.3	87.6	12.4	89.1	10.9
Santa Rosa, CA	45.9	54.1	87.3	12.7	92.0	8.0	92.1	7.9	90.9	9.1
Savannah, GA	62.2	37.8	88.6	11.4	88.7	11.3	85.9	14.1	83.5	16.5
Seattle, WA	42.6	57.4	82.2	17.8	88.9	11.1	89.0	11.0	91.2	8.8
Sioux Falls, SD	55.8	44.2	88.7	11.3	87.9	12.1	91.7	8.3	90.8	9.2
Spokane, WA	40.4	59.6	84.1	15.9	89.6	10.4	90.9	9.1	93.0	7.0
Springfield, IL	68.9	31.1	89.0	11.0	88.9	11.1	88.0	12.0	87.3	12.7
Tallahassee, FL	63.3	36.7	86.1	13.9	90.8	9.2	87.6	12.4	88.7	11.3
Tampa, FL	57.6	42.4	88.3	11.7	89.4	10.6	88.8	11.2	91.5	8.5
Topeka, KS	72.4	27.6	91.6	8.4	88.2	11.8	88.1	11.9	89.8	10.2
Tulsa, OK	69.8	30.2	89.7	10.3	89.9	10.1	88.4	11.6	88.8	11.2
Tyler, TX	70.7	29.3	95.0	5.0	93.6	6.4	91.5	8.5	89.8	10.2
Virginia Beach, VA	54.3	45.7	87.4	12.6	90.5	9.5	91.2	8.8	93.3	6.7
Washington, DC	40.7	59.3	84.3	15.7	88.3	11.7	88.1	11.9	89.0	11.0
Wichita, KS	67.2	32.8	85.3	14.7	87.8	12.2	88.2	11.8	87.0	13.0
Wilmington, NC	53.6	46.4	90.3	9.7	90.2	9.8	88.1	11.9	92.6	7.4
Winston-Salem, NC	52.5	47.5	90.4	9.6	90.8	9.2	91.3	8.7	93.6	6.4
Worcester, MA	60.5	39.5	89.4	10.6	92.7	7.3	91.4	8.6	91.2	8.8
U.S.	57.7	42.3	87.9	12.1	89.9	10.1	90.0	10.0	90.7	9.3

Note: Figures shown cover persons 3 years old and over; Figures cover the Metropolitan Statistical Area—see Appendix B for areas included

Source: U.S. Census Bureau, 2011-2013 American Community Survey 3-Year Estimates

Educational Attainment by Race: City

City	High School Graduate or Higher (%)					Bachelor's Degree or Higher (%)				
	Total	White	Black	Asian	Hisp.[1]	Total	White	Black	Asian	Hisp.[1]
Albuquerque, NM	89.2	91.4	90.8	82.8	80.2	33.6	37.3	30.3	44.9	18.6
Anchorage, AK	92.5	95.9	86.0	76.0	87.8	32.4	37.8	22.4	22.0	22.9
Ann Arbor, MI	96.3	97.1	89.7	96.8	89.0	70.4	70.9	40.5	85.0	55.5
Athens, GA	86.4	90.3	80.0	91.5	53.0	38.7	50.5	10.5	69.9	9.9
Atlanta, GA	88.9	96.5	82.0	96.8	76.8	48.2	74.1	23.3	82.5	42.0
Austin, TX	87.1	89.0	88.1	92.0	64.6	45.8	49.0	21.6	67.8	19.6
Billings, MT	92.6	93.5	n/a	n/a	82.6	29.0	30.3	n/a	n/a	12.5
Boise City, ID	94.1	95.0	n/a	82.1	81.4	38.9	39.4	n/a	50.2	17.9
Boston, MA	84.8	91.7	80.1	77.2	65.4	43.8	59.1	17.9	47.5	16.7
Boulder, CO	96.5	97.6	n/a	96.0	70.0	73.6	75.8	n/a	68.2	39.1
Cape Coral, FL	91.0	91.2	93.1	79.5	76.0	20.6	20.9	11.2	24.5	17.3
Cedar Rapids, IA	92.9	93.3	87.8	95.3	67.8	30.3	30.3	18.9	65.2	10.9
Charleston, SC	93.1	96.7	81.3	n/a	89.4	48.7	58.8	15.5	n/a	32.2
Charlotte, NC	88.6	92.0	87.6	84.8	58.9	40.6	51.4	23.7	54.7	15.6
Chicago, IL	81.4	85.4	82.0	85.9	60.0	34.4	45.5	18.0	57.6	12.9
Clarksville, TN	91.4	92.9	88.0	84.2	86.2	24.1	26.4	16.6	26.3	18.7
Colorado Springs, CO	93.3	95.0	91.7	86.1	79.2	36.6	39.2	22.9	35.9	16.4
Columbia, MO	93.6	94.7	86.3	91.4	81.1	55.2	58.1	24.8	74.3	42.6
Columbus, OH	88.2	90.3	85.1	86.1	61.6	33.0	37.8	17.6	61.5	16.2
Dallas, TX	74.2	74.6	82.9	84.1	45.4	29.6	37.2	16.0	58.9	8.4
Davenport, IA	90.0	91.8	82.9	69.1	70.8	26.4	27.9	10.6	41.5	11.4
Denver, CO	86.1	88.5	87.3	76.8	60.8	44.1	49.4	23.9	46.8	11.0
Des Moines, IA	87.7	89.9	85.1	68.7	57.4	25.3	27.4	15.5	20.9	7.1
Durham, NC	86.8	87.9	87.2	90.9	42.1	46.1	57.3	30.3	72.5	12.7
El Paso, TX	77.3	77.6	92.0	89.6	72.2	23.0	22.8	27.9	48.4	18.6
Erie, PA	86.4	88.7	80.3	51.7	70.4	21.6	23.7	11.2	20.7	6.9
Eugene, OR	93.9	94.6	96.3	95.5	68.5	38.3	38.8	31.3	57.3	18.0
Fargo, ND	94.5	95.5	83.5	87.0	77.3	38.7	38.9	36.7	55.8	14.6
Fayetteville, NC	90.7	93.1	88.7	81.2	89.6	24.2	27.9	19.9	34.0	16.6
Fort Collins, CO	95.3	96.1	87.5	96.0	75.7	51.7	52.8	23.5	65.2	25.9
Fort Wayne, IN	87.8	91.0	81.6	61.7	57.6	25.3	27.6	13.7	27.7	12.6
Fort Worth, TX	79.8	81.0	85.9	78.9	53.0	26.6	30.6	16.8	36.2	9.4
Gainesville, FL	91.7	94.4	85.4	87.8	93.1	42.5	48.6	18.9	69.7	43.3
Grand Rapids, MI	84.6	88.2	75.7	69.5	50.0	30.0	35.4	11.7	32.4	9.0
Green Bay, WI	86.9	88.4	89.6	73.8	47.5	23.2	24.7	6.7	21.5	7.0
Greensboro, NC	88.3	92.4	86.4	61.2	58.8	36.7	47.2	23.6	29.1	12.2
Honolulu, HI	88.0	96.6	95.6	84.6	93.1	35.0	51.5	33.0	33.3	27.0
Houston, TX	76.2	75.8	85.0	84.8	52.8	30.0	34.3	19.7	56.3	10.7
Huntsville, AL	90.1	92.9	84.1	90.2	71.4	38.9	45.3	22.8	57.1	24.1
Indianapolis, IN	84.8	87.5	83.8	81.2	52.9	27.3	32.5	15.1	51.5	8.7
Jacksonville, FL	87.9	89.6	84.7	85.1	84.3	25.7	28.4	16.5	44.8	23.6
Kansas City, MO	88.0	92.2	83.3	76.6	64.9	31.9	40.0	14.9	42.0	15.1
Lafayette, LA	86.4	91.8	73.4	85.9	74.3	32.8	39.4	14.8	55.7	27.4
Las Vegas, NV	83.0	85.6	85.8	89.5	59.2	21.7	23.1	16.8	39.0	7.4
Lexington, KY	89.1	91.4	84.9	88.7	53.0	40.7	44.2	18.5	73.0	14.2
Lincoln, NE	93.1	94.9	88.3	77.7	62.4	36.7	38.2	18.1	37.8	13.8
Little Rock, AR	90.6	93.9	86.1	92.8	70.7	38.4	50.2	20.0	62.8	15.5
Los Angeles, CA	74.8	79.1	86.2	89.5	51.2	31.3	36.6	23.0	51.7	9.8
Louisville, KY	86.9	88.0	83.5	78.3	74.3	27.0	29.3	16.1	56.0	21.0
Lubbock, TX	85.4	88.2	81.0	90.3	67.1	28.8	31.2	12.1	73.9	9.8
Madison, WI	94.9	96.2	87.7	88.0	78.5	53.7	55.3	23.2	67.4	32.2
Manchester, NH	87.1	88.6	76.2	66.3	65.1	26.3	26.9	11.0	32.5	10.5
McAllen, TX	72.7	73.6	n/a	94.8	68.1	26.5	26.2	n/a	65.9	22.3
Miami, FL	72.0	73.4	66.3	80.4	68.7	23.3	25.7	10.4	58.5	19.3
Midland, TX	81.7	84.1	80.6	79.4	61.4	25.4	27.8	15.6	43.1	9.1

Table continued on next page.

City	High School Graduate or Higher (%)					Bachelor's Degree or Higher (%)				
	Total	White	Black	Asian	Hisp.[1]	Total	White	Black	Asian	Hisp.[1]
Minneapolis, MN	88.6	94.1	75.5	74.7	53.4	47.0	55.9	16.5	45.2	15.8
Nashville, TN	86.7	90.1	85.6	79.0	56.7	35.7	41.0	24.3	51.2	12.9
New Orleans, LA	84.5	94.8	78.9	66.8	74.1	34.2	60.7	16.2	33.9	31.9
New York, NY	79.9	86.6	80.6	74.3	64.2	34.9	46.3	21.4	41.1	15.7
Oklahoma City, OK	84.4	86.0	88.2	78.4	47.3	28.3	31.4	18.5	35.6	8.4
Omaha, NE	87.6	90.6	83.8	73.9	46.7	33.3	36.3	17.7	52.0	10.2
Orlando, FL	88.9	92.3	81.4	90.7	82.6	33.7	39.6	17.2	59.7	23.4
Oxnard, CA	65.3	62.2	86.9	87.9	51.8	15.9	14.6	19.4	32.1	8.2
Palm Bay, FL	86.3	88.7	77.7	90.2	82.3	17.9	18.4	14.9	25.4	15.3
Peoria, IL	88.2	91.1	79.0	93.8	67.6	32.4	35.8	11.4	79.3	15.2
Philadelphia, PA	81.4	86.7	80.7	67.6	62.6	24.4	34.5	13.6	33.6	11.4
Phoenix, AZ	80.6	82.3	86.2	83.8	56.7	26.5	28.0	16.5	51.2	8.7
Pittsburgh, PA	91.2	92.7	85.9	92.7	86.8	37.3	42.3	14.8	78.1	48.2
Portland, OR	90.9	93.8	87.2	75.4	62.5	44.4	48.1	16.6	36.0	20.6
Providence, RI	73.3	80.3	74.9	66.8	56.4	28.8	40.9	17.1	39.1	7.8
Provo, UT	89.8	91.6	n/a	86.3	66.3	38.8	39.9	n/a	52.7	17.0
Raleigh, NC	89.5	92.7	89.0	83.0	47.2	47.0	56.8	29.5	43.8	13.2
Reno, NV	85.5	87.6	86.0	88.4	53.2	29.7	31.6	19.4	39.4	8.2
Richmond, VA	81.8	90.2	74.0	88.7	46.0	34.7	55.9	13.6	62.0	14.4
Roanoke, VA	82.3	85.2	77.4	56.1	51.2	23.0	27.9	11.3	25.5	7.4
Rochester, MN	93.7	95.1	77.8	88.9	71.5	41.8	42.2	24.4	53.4	26.1
Sacramento, CA	83.1	86.8	88.6	77.4	65.2	29.2	34.3	18.2	32.8	13.6
Salem, OR	86.6	90.1	86.7	88.0	52.3	26.6	28.4	29.9	28.5	10.7
Salt Lake City, UT	86.5	92.5	80.0	88.0	51.3	42.8	47.1	24.7	65.6	15.0
San Antonio, TX	81.2	82.6	88.5	84.1	72.4	25.1	26.4	22.6	52.1	14.4
San Diego, CA	87.3	89.5	89.0	87.5	66.3	41.9	45.3	20.7	48.0	17.4
San Francisco, CA	86.5	94.5	86.0	76.4	73.6	52.9	66.5	23.4	41.4	29.5
San Jose, CA	82.5	85.2	92.6	84.0	64.0	37.6	36.2	27.8	49.7	12.1
Santa Rosa, CA	85.7	90.1	82.0	80.9	58.3	29.9	32.5	22.5	40.4	9.6
Savannah, GA	86.0	91.4	81.6	79.4	62.2	27.4	38.8	16.4	45.9	26.4
Seattle, WA	93.2	96.8	81.7	82.0	79.8	57.8	64.3	22.2	47.8	39.2
Sioux Falls, SD	90.9	93.4	68.0	69.8	56.1	32.5	34.1	14.8	39.3	13.0
Spokane, WA	90.8	91.8	85.4	76.7	81.1	28.5	29.5	18.0	24.3	20.8
Springfield, IL	90.9	92.1	84.2	94.0	90.1	34.4	36.9	17.2	69.9	40.7
Tallahassee, FL	92.3	96.3	85.1	93.6	90.0	47.5	56.6	28.3	78.0	41.9
Tampa, FL	86.5	89.5	79.3	85.4	76.3	33.9	40.2	13.4	54.7	18.8
Topeka, KS	87.9	89.4	81.3	85.7	61.6	26.4	28.2	11.4	63.1	9.4
Tulsa, OK	86.9	89.0	87.5	78.6	53.2	30.4	34.7	16.6	41.0	8.5
Tyler, TX	84.4	84.5	84.9	96.6	46.5	29.6	33.0	16.2	55.4	6.5
Virginia Beach, VA	94.0	95.1	90.6	92.0	92.6	33.7	35.5	24.7	39.8	21.9
Washington, DC	88.6	96.6	82.7	90.1	70.0	53.5	85.9	23.5	75.2	40.1
Wichita, KS	87.6	89.2	88.4	75.4	58.7	28.3	30.5	16.6	30.3	11.6
Wilmington, NC	89.3	92.6	79.4	72.1	54.6	40.1	47.0	13.3	42.5	17.4
Winston-Salem, NC	84.4	85.3	85.2	87.4	41.4	32.9	40.4	18.1	63.0	8.4
Worcester, MA	84.7	87.2	88.2	71.4	66.5	29.8	32.9	20.4	30.9	11.8
U.S.	86.3	88.3	83.1	85.7	64.0	29.1	30.4	18.8	50.7	13.7

Note: Figures shown cover persons 25 years old and over; (1) People of Hispanic origin can be of any race
Source: U.S. Census Bureau, 2011-2013 American Community Survey 3-Year Estimates

Educational Attainment by Race: Metro Area

Metro Area	High School Graduate or Higher (%)					Bachelor's Degree or Higher (%)				
	Total	White	Black	Asian	Hisp.[1]	Total	White	Black	Asian	Hisp.[1]
Albuquerque, NM	87.5	89.9	91.1	83.9	77.7	30.1	33.8	30.6	44.5	16.4
Anchorage, AK	92.5	95.2	86.0	75.9	88.1	29.7	33.5	21.9	21.7	22.6
Ann Arbor, MI	94.2	95.1	89.2	96.0	83.6	51.5	53.4	23.1	80.4	30.4
Athens, GA	85.9	88.7	78.2	88.7	53.6	33.5	39.0	10.9	63.1	10.3
Atlanta, GA	87.8	89.0	88.4	86.5	60.0	35.1	38.7	27.4	52.9	15.6
Austin, TX	88.2	89.7	89.0	92.1	67.1	40.8	42.6	24.1	65.8	17.8
Billings, MT	92.3	92.9	n/a	n/a	79.7	27.4	28.3	n/a	n/a	11.5
Boise City, ID	90.0	90.9	91.0	83.3	63.2	29.9	30.3	25.3	48.4	10.4
Boston, MA	90.8	93.5	81.6	84.6	69.3	43.7	45.9	23.8	57.7	19.6
Boulder, CO	93.8	95.1	86.8	95.0	62.3	58.3	60.0	38.1	69.9	21.8
Cape Coral, FL	86.8	89.1	73.1	86.0	63.2	25.0	26.5	12.6	34.9	11.9
Cedar Rapids, IA	93.5	93.8	87.9	96.3	75.0	29.1	28.7	19.2	69.5	18.1
Charleston, SC	88.5	91.8	81.1	81.6	69.4	31.4	38.2	13.7	34.3	20.9
Charlotte, NC	86.8	88.6	85.1	85.3	59.1	31.2	33.8	22.0	52.3	14.6
Chicago, IL	86.8	89.9	85.3	90.1	61.9	34.8	38.1	20.2	62.2	12.4
Clarksville, TN	88.6	89.3	86.2	84.5	81.9	21.6	23.0	14.8	32.5	15.8
Colorado Springs, CO	93.9	95.3	92.8	84.3	82.1	35.1	37.2	22.6	35.2	17.1
Columbia, MO	93.7	94.4	89.0	90.5	81.2	47.2	48.5	24.6	72.2	37.5
Columbus, OH	90.1	91.2	85.6	89.3	66.7	33.2	34.4	19.7	67.2	19.7
Dallas, TX	84.1	85.3	88.8	88.0	55.2	31.9	33.4	23.7	55.9	11.0
Davenport, IA	90.1	91.3	81.2	82.7	68.0	25.5	25.9	14.4	58.2	12.4
Denver, CO	89.9	91.5	89.5	84.7	66.3	39.7	41.7	25.3	46.7	13.0
Des Moines, IA	92.7	94.0	85.8	82.2	61.0	35.1	36.3	16.9	43.3	14.1
Durham, NC	87.6	89.8	85.1	90.1	47.5	43.7	50.1	26.2	74.8	12.3
El Paso, TX	74.8	75.4	92.6	90.6	69.5	21.0	20.9	28.3	48.9	16.7
Erie, PA	90.4	91.6	79.7	66.3	75.1	25.1	26.0	11.8	39.3	10.9
Eugene, OR	91.4	92.2	94.2	87.3	69.5	27.9	28.2	30.0	45.7	14.2
Fargo, ND	94.4	95.2	82.5	85.9	80.4	35.2	35.6	27.0	48.7	11.1
Fayetteville, NC	89.0	90.8	88.0	81.3	85.2	21.7	24.1	18.9	29.4	15.9
Fort Collins, CO	94.6	95.6	85.4	95.9	74.1	43.6	44.4	18.4	60.3	21.2
Fort Wayne, IN	89.3	91.4	81.8	68.6	60.4	24.8	25.9	14.6	33.7	12.6
Fort Worth, TX	84.1	85.3	88.8	88.0	55.2	31.9	33.4	23.7	55.9	11.0
Gainesville, FL	91.2	93.2	83.6	89.3	90.7	38.1	41.1	16.1	70.2	42.2
Grand Rapids, MI	89.9	91.7	79.0	71.4	60.6	29.6	31.0	13.3	36.5	12.3
Green Bay, WI	90.6	91.5	85.6	81.1	54.2	25.3	25.6	17.5	35.4	14.8
Greensboro, NC	85.1	86.9	84.7	68.6	52.6	27.1	29.4	21.1	34.0	10.5
Honolulu, HI	90.5	96.7	96.3	87.6	90.9	32.2	44.2	28.2	33.1	21.6
Houston, TX	81.4	82.1	87.8	86.2	58.2	29.9	30.8	24.4	53.9	12.0
Huntsville, AL	89.0	90.2	85.9	88.7	68.8	35.5	37.9	26.0	53.8	24.3
Indianapolis, IN	88.8	90.5	84.8	86.1	59.1	30.6	32.7	17.6	57.3	13.5
Jacksonville, FL	89.2	90.4	84.8	87.0	85.2	27.7	29.7	17.0	46.1	25.3
Kansas City, MO	90.9	92.7	85.9	83.1	66.0	33.4	36.0	17.1	50.3	15.8
Lafayette, LA	80.5	84.3	69.3	60.9	64.5	20.0	22.7	11.1	24.0	15.6
Las Vegas, NV	84.1	86.3	86.8	87.9	61.8	22.1	23.1	16.5	35.2	8.6
Lexington, KY	87.7	89.2	84.8	88.9	52.5	35.1	36.9	17.7	72.2	13.1
Lincoln, NE	93.4	94.9	88.4	77.7	63.4	36.1	37.3	18.7	38.1	14.9
Little Rock, AR	89.1	90.3	86.0	88.6	70.0	28.3	30.1	20.4	56.2	12.9
Los Angeles, CA	78.5	81.1	88.3	87.2	57.4	31.6	33.3	24.1	49.9	10.9
Louisville, KY	87.8	88.5	84.2	82.0	71.0	26.6	27.7	16.8	55.8	18.9
Lubbock, TX	83.8	86.6	79.1	90.6	63.9	27.0	29.0	11.6	73.3	8.7
Madison, WI	94.3	95.3	86.7	87.4	70.0	41.7	41.9	22.0	62.8	25.0
Manchester, NH	91.1	91.8	81.9	85.0	70.1	35.5	35.2	26.7	57.2	16.9
McAllen, TX	62.2	62.4	77.0	94.3	58.2	16.2	15.8	28.8	65.0	13.9
Miami, FL	84.2	85.7	79.1	87.1	77.3	29.2	31.7	17.2	49.7	23.8
Midland, TX	81.7	83.9	80.7	81.5	61.3	25.0	27.1	15.1	47.0	9.6

Table continued on next page.

Metro Area	High School Graduate or Higher (%)					Bachelor's Degree or Higher (%)				
	Total	White	Black	Asian	Hisp.[1]	Total	White	Black	Asian	Hisp.[1]
Minneapolis, MN	93.0	95.3	81.5	79.9	64.7	38.8	40.5	20.0	43.7	18.3
Nashville, TN	87.8	89.3	85.2	83.7	60.3	31.4	32.7	24.1	50.0	12.9
New Orleans, LA	84.7	89.1	78.6	70.9	72.9	26.6	32.5	15.3	35.2	20.3
New York, NY	85.1	89.6	82.7	82.3	67.5	36.8	41.7	22.2	52.9	16.5
Oklahoma City, OK	87.3	88.6	89.2	80.9	54.1	28.2	29.8	20.2	41.3	10.0
Omaha, NE	90.9	92.8	85.5	77.5	53.0	33.0	34.3	19.9	50.9	12.1
Orlando, FL	87.6	89.5	83.1	85.6	79.2	28.3	29.9	19.1	47.6	18.9
Oxnard, CA	83.0	84.0	93.0	91.5	59.7	31.3	31.3	33.6	55.2	11.3
Palm Bay, FL	89.7	91.0	79.2	85.6	85.2	26.4	27.1	15.6	38.9	23.7
Peoria, IL	91.2	92.3	79.6	93.6	72.5	26.3	26.3	11.7	78.3	15.8
Philadelphia, PA	89.1	91.9	84.3	82.2	67.8	33.9	37.7	18.0	53.5	15.4
Phoenix, AZ	86.4	87.8	88.6	86.9	62.9	29.0	29.8	22.5	53.3	10.5
Pittsburgh, PA	92.1	92.6	87.9	89.0	85.3	30.8	31.1	16.8	71.0	36.1
Portland, OR	90.8	92.7	87.8	84.6	61.2	34.8	35.7	21.0	44.5	14.8
Providence, RI	84.6	86.3	77.0	78.7	63.0	29.5	30.9	19.2	44.5	12.1
Provo, UT	93.1	94.0	81.2	91.4	69.7	36.3	36.8	40.6	57.7	17.7
Raleigh, NC	89.6	91.9	86.4	90.5	51.5	42.4	46.1	26.6	66.7	15.0
Reno, NV	86.3	88.1	87.8	87.7	54.5	28.0	29.4	21.3	37.8	9.2
Richmond, VA	87.3	90.5	81.3	87.5	62.6	32.7	38.2	18.7	59.0	18.0
Roanoke, VA	86.8	88.1	80.5	80.6	62.0	26.2	27.5	15.0	57.4	8.3
Rochester, MN	93.6	94.4	79.2	88.4	71.4	34.2	33.9	25.0	52.1	23.3
Sacramento, CA	88.1	91.0	88.4	81.9	69.5	30.4	32.0	19.3	39.7	13.7
Salem, OR	84.9	88.2	80.9	90.7	50.7	23.0	24.6	35.0	32.9	7.8
Salt Lake City, UT	89.4	92.2	82.5	82.9	62.9	31.3	32.4	22.5	50.5	12.0
San Antonio, TX	83.4	84.7	89.9	82.4	73.2	26.5	27.7	24.7	48.7	14.9
San Diego, CA	85.6	86.9	89.7	87.8	64.2	34.5	35.7	21.1	45.6	14.9
San Francisco, CA	87.9	91.2	89.8	85.3	67.9	44.8	49.3	23.4	50.5	18.4
San Jose, CA	86.5	88.2	92.5	89.0	65.2	46.2	43.7	29.2	61.2	13.6
Santa Rosa, CA	87.1	90.8	83.3	84.3	57.9	31.9	34.2	29.4	43.8	10.5
Savannah, GA	88.1	90.1	84.5	83.0	69.0	29.8	33.9	19.8	45.6	25.4
Seattle, WA	91.7	93.7	87.4	86.1	70.6	38.1	39.1	20.3	47.9	18.6
Sioux Falls, SD	91.8	93.6	69.5	71.3	58.4	30.6	31.6	15.1	37.4	14.5
Spokane, WA	92.3	93.0	84.0	82.9	80.4	26.9	27.6	15.7	27.5	18.8
Springfield, IL	92.1	93.0	83.2	91.1	89.0	32.2	33.2	17.7	61.4	41.4
Tallahassee, FL	89.2	93.0	81.5	91.9	80.8	36.9	42.7	22.5	73.6	32.9
Tampa, FL	88.0	89.2	83.6	84.2	77.3	26.6	27.0	18.4	48.7	18.4
Topeka, KS	90.8	91.9	82.5	84.2	65.9	26.1	27.2	12.1	59.3	10.3
Tulsa, OK	88.5	89.7	88.2	82.3	58.0	26.1	28.1	18.0	37.5	10.8
Tyler, TX	84.9	85.1	85.7	94.5	45.9	24.8	26.7	14.5	53.6	5.8
Virginia Beach, VA	90.1	92.6	84.8	89.5	84.1	29.0	32.9	18.9	43.7	20.2
Washington, DC	90.2	93.1	89.6	90.5	66.1	48.1	55.6	31.0	62.2	23.6
Wichita, KS	89.6	90.9	87.7	76.5	62.4	28.3	29.7	16.7	30.3	12.1
Wilmington, NC	89.3	92.1	79.3	77.8	55.8	33.2	37.2	13.1	44.4	13.4
Winston-Salem, NC	84.0	84.8	84.5	79.8	47.0	25.4	26.6	18.3	48.0	9.3
Worcester, MA	89.5	90.9	87.8	82.5	67.6	32.4	32.9	23.4	53.3	14.3
U.S.	86.3	88.3	83.1	85.7	64.0	29.1	30.4	18.8	50.7	13.7

Note: Figures shown cover persons 25 years old and over; Figures cover the Metropolitan Statistical Area—see Appendix B for areas included; (1) People of Hispanic origin can be of any race
Source: U.S. Census Bureau, 2011-2013 American Community Survey 3-Year Estimates

Cost of Living Index

Urban Area	Composite	Groceries	Housing	Utilities	Transp.	Health	Misc.
Albuquerque, NM[1]	92.7	89.8	82.6	89.1	99.9	97.8	99.4
Anchorage, AK	125.7	112.6	154.1	98.9	107.0	139.0	121.8
Ann Arbor, MI	101.7	85.8	112.7	106.6	105.0	99.2	97.0
Athens, GA	n/a	n/a	n/a	n/a	n/a	n/a	n/a
Atlanta, GA	94.9	91.2	87.1	92.0	102.0	102.5	99.6
Austin, TX	92.9	84.0	86.0	91.1	97.2	99.4	99.8
Billings, MT	n/a	n/a	n/a	n/a	n/a	n/a	n/a
Boise City, ID	93.2	85.6	86.7	87.9	103.7	103.8	97.3
Boston, MA	139.1	125.5	175.3	144.3	104.1	126.1	129.7
Boulder, CO	n/a	n/a	n/a	n/a	n/a	n/a	n/a
Cape Coral, FL	97.4	91.9	93.2	98.1	109.1	98.1	98.3
Cedar Rapids, IA	91.6	86.5	82.1	102.2	94.6	101.5	95.2
Charleston, SC	99.8	104.9	88.8	113.5	95.7	103.0	103.4
Charlotte, NC	95.4	101.6	83.7	106.6	98.4	98.2	97.0
Chicago, IL	114.8	98.1	135.3	98.9	124.1	97.7	109.2
Clarksville, TN	n/a	n/a	n/a	n/a	n/a	n/a	n/a
Colorado Springs, CO	95.7	93.5	94.4	101.0	94.4	102.4	95.6
Columbia, MO	95.6	91.3	88.3	98.0	94.3	101.7	102.1
Columbus, OH	86.9	86.5	77.1	96.4	96.2	95.1	87.2
Dallas, TX	95.6	92.3	75.5	106.9	102.2	99.1	106.2
Davenport, IA	95.4	86.6	100.2	85.5	111.2	94.9	92.1
Denver, CO	103.8	93.4	115.5	101.3	94.8	103.7	103.0
Des Moines, IA	90.0	85.2	85.4	89.5	96.1	93.6	92.8
Durham, NC	92.3	100.4	80.2	83.5	98.6	101.7	97.5
El Paso, TX	91.2	90.8	84.0	87.2	97.5	89.9	96.1
Erie, PA	97.8	97.5	94.8	97.1	100.5	94.6	99.9
Eugene, OR	n/a	n/a	n/a	n/a	n/a	n/a	n/a
Fargo, ND	93.5	97.6	83.6	89.4	95.6	111.8	97.4
Fayetteville, NC	n/a	n/a	n/a	n/a	n/a	n/a	n/a
Fort Collins, CO	n/a	n/a	n/a	n/a	n/a	n/a	n/a
Fort Wayne, IN	91.3	82.5	85.0	89.5	104.3	95.8	94.7
Fort Worth, TX	97.1	93.6	85.6	99.6	101.8	104.1	103.9
Gainesville, FL	98.7	97.3	94.1	106.1	104.1	101.2	98.1
Grand Rapids, MI	92.7	84.4	77.6	99.4	106.6	91.8	100.9
Green Bay, WI	93.3	86.4	83.9	101.2	99.5	106.1	96.9
Greensboro, NC[2]	88.1	98.0	69.5	100.3	85.3	102.9	94.0
Honolulu, HI	168.3	154.7	262.4	171.4	126.5	111.3	123.1
Houston, TX	98.8	79.5	107.3	103.2	95.4	96.4	100.2
Huntsville, AL	94.2	89.4	79.1	103.7	98.7	96.2	103.2
Indianapolis, IN	91.6	85.5	80.9	91.3	99.4	115.7	96.1
Jacksonville, FL	94.9	95.2	83.3	105.7	104.7	85.1	98.4
Kansas City, MO	98.9	95.6	91.7	110.6	98.2	96.3	102.9
Lafayette, LA	95.9	90.5	101.5	87.8	104.1	84.8	94.6
Las Vegas, NV	100.4	96.5	99.7	85.3	100.9	103.4	106.4
Lexington, KY	89.4	86.1	75.6	101.0	97.9	94.3	94.1
Lincoln, NE	89.3	87.6	75.6	92.3	96.6	95.0	96.3
Little Rock, AR	97.9	89.2	96.6	110.3	93.3	83.9	102.5
Los Angeles, CA	129.8	102.8	196.8	108.0	111.0	109.5	104.8
Louisville, KY	91.0	85.3	81.6	87.2	101.0	91.2	98.1
Lubbock, TX	89.2	90.4	81.4	78.4	95.0	95.6	95.0
Madison, WI	105.2	90.5	110.4	104.2	106.1	123.9	104.2
Manchester, NH	120.2	98.5	137.9	122.7	101.2	117.7	121.9
McAllen, TX	87.9	83.3	78.8	99.9	94.6	88.6	90.5
Miami, FL	107.2	99.9	118.0	95.7	110.4	104.4	104.3
Midland, TX	99.4	88.3	100.2	93.2	104.7	95.0	103.7
Minneapolis, MN	109.7	115.4	116.5	97.8	103.6	98.9	109.4

Table continued on next page.

Urban Area	Composite	Groceries	Housing	Utilities	Transp.	Health	Misc.
Nashville, TN	87.3	87.8	74.3	87.0	94.1	81.4	95.8
New Orleans, LA	98.4	97.9	95.1	91.3	100.0	103.2	102.1
New York, NY	170.7	118.7	320.3	124.0	111.9	110.3	119.2
Oklahoma City, OK	89.9	87.8	82.2	91.6	98.9	98.1	91.7
Omaha, NE	86.9	84.3	78.4	91.1	96.6	100.6	87.6
Orlando, FL	96.0	96.7	78.6	104.4	98.5	99.3	105.6
Oxnard, CA	n/a	n/a	n/a	n/a	n/a	n/a	n/a
Palm Bay, TX	n/a	n/a	n/a	n/a	n/a	n/a	n/a
Peoria, IL	99.2	89.0	100.0	95.9	108.2	95.8	100.8
Philadelphia, PA	120.8	112.8	141.9	128.2	105.1	100.0	114.3
Phoenix, AZ	95.6	93.4	96.2	97.6	95.5	95.8	95.4
Pittsburgh, PA	93.6	94.2	79.3	94.9	104.2	100.9	99.1
Portland, OR	117.1	102.7	142.3	96.6	115.1	117.2	110.1
Providence, RI	125.2	106.9	138.8	133.1	104.2	118.2	128.4
Provo, UT	95.5	88.3	87.1	91.0	111.3	93.1	100.8
Raleigh, NC	93.3	101.7	76.1	105.7	97.8	101.7	96.6
Reno, NV	89.8	90.1	88.1	73.0	103.1	93.3	90.4
Richmond, VA	101.4	98.2	89.4	107.6	99.7	106.5	110.1
Roanoke, VA	999.0	91.0	89.3	98.9	91.3	96.7	89.7
Rochester, MN	100.6	95.9	99.3	101.8	101.9	104.8	102.0
Sacramento, CA	999.0	116.1	117.4	114.7	110.7	111.8	106.5
Salem, OR	n/a	n/a	n/a	n/a	n/a	n/a	n/a
Salt Lake City, UT	94.1	88.4	90.0	84.2	98.8	96.7	100.5
San Antonio, TX	88.4	81.4	79.5	82.6	95.5	93.7	96.6
San Diego, CA	129.4	101.6	199.0	97.7	113.3	109.7	104.5
San Francisco, CA	160.8	119.2	293.5	95.0	114.9	119.9	116.4
San Jose, CA	148.6	110.4	255.6	123.2	112.1	114.6	106.5
Santa Rosa, CA	n/a	n/a	n/a	n/a	n/a	n/a	n/a
Savannah, GA	92.5	91.2	71.5	111.5	102.0	100.1	99.2
Seattle, WA	118.6	102.6	140.1	97.0	118.3	118.9	114.7
Sioux Falls, SD	97.1	86.3	92.5	107.1	93.7	101.3	102.8
Spokane, WA	95.6	91.8	88.4	91.2	99.5	109.8	100.5
Springfield, IL	999.0	95.4	80.4	76.8	101.5	105.1	87.2
Tallahassee, FL	98.1	99.2	98.2	88.7	101.1	101.4	98.6
Tampa, FL	92.8	92.7	78.4	93.9	102.3	95.6	99.8
Topeka, KS	93.4	87.5	91.4	84.0	94.3	91.8	100.2
Tulsa, OK	88.0	85.5	65.0	96.5	96.3	95.5	100.3
Tyler, TX	999.0	93.0	95.8	94.0	96.3	90.7	96.6
Virginia Beach, VA[3]	n/a	n/a	n/a	n/a	n/a	n/a	n/a
Washington, DC	139.4	107.9	247.5	104.1	105.6	98.6	96.6
Wichita, KS	91.6	88.2	75.6	107.7	96.9	94.8	98.2
Wilmington, NC	98.2	104.8	84.9	107.8	97.8	107.4	102.0
Winston-Salem, NC	999.0	102.4	66.8	105.9	96.5	106.5	97.8
Worcester, MA[4]	104.2	94.3	97.7	117.6	103.8	123.4	106.6
U.S.	100.0	100.0	100.0	100.0	100.0	100.0	100.0

Note: The Cost of Living Index measures regional differences in the cost of consumer goods and services, excluding taxes and non-consumer expenditures, for professional and managerial households in the top income quintile. It is based on more than 50,000 prices covering almost 60 different items for which prices are collected three times a year by chambers of commerce, economic development organizations or university applied economic centers in each participating urban area. The numbers shown should be read as a percentage above or below the national average of 100. For example, a value of 115.4 in the groceries column indicates that grocery prices are 15.4% higher than the national average. Small differences in the index numbers should not be interpreted as significant. In cases where data is not available for the city, data for the metro area or for a neighboring city has been provided and noted as follows: (1) Rio Rancho, NM; (2) Winston-Salem, NC; (3) Hampton Roads-SE Virginia; (4) Fitchburg-Leominster, MA

Source: The Council for Community and Economic Research (formerly ACCRA), Cost of Living Index, 2014

Grocery Prices

Urban Area	T-Bone Steak ($/pound)	Frying Chicken ($/pound)	Whole Milk ($/half gal.)	Eggs ($/dozen)	Orange Juice ($/64 oz.)	Coffee ($/11.5 oz.)
Albuquerque, NM[1]	10.88	1.06	2.52	2.04	3.48	4.79
Anchorage, AK	11.85	1.39	2.53	2.29	4.54	5.49
Ann Arbor, MI	10.58	1.17	2.22	1.80	3.05	3.75
Athens, GA	n/a	n/a	n/a	n/a	n/a	n/a
Atlanta, GA	11.61	1.26	2.45	1.80	3.48	4.84
Austin, TX	9.82	1.09	2.18	1.95	3.22	3.79
Billings, MT	n/a	n/a	n/a	n/a	n/a	n/a
Boise City, ID	8.98	1.29	1.72	1.35	3.52	4.75
Boston, MA	11.29	1.76	2.79	2.72	3.92	4.75
Boulder, CO	n/a	n/a	n/a	n/a	n/a	n/a
Cape Coral, FL	11.36	1.42	2.83	2.11	3.84	4.12
Cedar Rapids, IA	9.85	1.41	2.32	1.88	3.20	3.97
Charleston, SC	11.45	1.44	2.72	1.98	3.72	4.48
Charlotte, NC	10.21	1.37	2.62	1.92	3.41	3.98
Chicago, IL	10.81	1.54	1.93	1.87	3.88	5.43
Clarksville, TN	n/a	n/a	n/a	n/a	n/a	n/a
Colorado Springs, CO	10.56	1.09	2.00	2.07	3.14	4.64
Columbia, MO	10.36	1.28	2.46	1.95	3.28	4.15
Columbus, OH	11.65	1.11	2.06	1.86	3.20	4.55
Dallas, TX	9.53	1.35	2.34	1.81	4.01	4.09
Davenport, IA	9.49	1.52	2.43	1.89	3.15	4.28
Denver, CO	10.29	1.35	2.05	2.10	3.66	5.13
Des Moines, IA	9.21	1.55	2.24	1.88	3.11	4.16
Durham, NC	9.90	1.32	2.58	2.09	3.46	4.01
El Paso, TX	10.65	1.30	2.26	1.78	3.22	4.43
Erie, PA	10.11	1.63	2.19	1.90	3.45	4.08
Eugene, OR	n/a	n/a	n/a	n/a	n/a	n/a
Fargo, ND	10.26	1.83	2.96	2.01	3.50	4.35
Fayetteville, NC	n/a	n/a	n/a	n/a	n/a	n/a
Fort Collins, CO	n/a	n/a	n/a	n/a	n/a	n/a
Fort Wayne, IN	10.26	1.10	2.06	1.77	3.58	4.84
Fort Worth, TX	10.05	1.13	2.01	1.89	3.53	4.12
Gainesville, FL	11.14	1.47	2.83	1.99	3.57	3.78
Grand Rapids, MI	11.49	1.13	2.36	1.92	3.30	3.78
Green Bay, WI	10.99	1.63	2.48	1.76	3.19	3.96
Greensboro, NC[2]	11.31	1.34	2.69	2.08	3.34	3.89
Honolulu, HI	11.62	2.42	3.62	3.58	4.92	6.96
Houston, TX	8.77	1.09	2.12	1.83	3.08	3.88
Huntsville, AL	10.87	1.30	2.37	1.98	3.29	4.15
Indianapolis, IN	9.97	1.20	2.17	1.78	3.30	3.97
Jacksonville, FL	10.84	1.45	2.75	1.92	3.39	3.96
Kansas City, MO	10.45	1.82	2.44	2.04	3.57	3.93
Lafayette, LA	9.74	1.15	2.75	1.84	3.45	3.67
Las Vegas, NV	8.83	1.61	2.17	2.02	3.95	4.81
Lexington, KY	10.90	1.21	2.36	1.93	3.54	4.28
Lincoln, NE	10.03	1.18	2.49	1.71	3.63	4.84
Little Rock, AR	10.46	1.13	2.17	1.78	3.22	4.02
Los Angeles, CA	9.88	1.53	2.51	2.46	3.20	5.09
Louisville, KY	9.26	1.04	2.06	1.84	3.24	4.51
Lubbock, TX	9.75	1.16	2.69	2.13	3.21	3.86
Madison, WI	10.55	1.67	2.38	1.75	3.44	4.45
Manchester, NH	9.61	1.43	2.11	1.96	2.96	3.60
McAllen, TX	9.47	1.02	2.42	1.79	3.03	3.34
Miami, FL	10.50	1.62	2.82	2.17	3.26	3.42
Midland, TX	10.45	1.16	2.06	1.82	3.08	3.70

Table continued on next page.

Urban Area	T-Bone Steak ($/pound)	Frying Chicken ($/pound)	Whole Milk ($/half gal.)	Eggs ($/dozen)	Orange Juice ($/64 oz.)	Coffee ($/11.5 oz.)
Minneapolis, MN	14.20	1.80	2.23	1.91	3.83	4.66
Nashville, TN	10.75	1.28	2.07	1.91	3.24	4.04
New Orleans, LA	10.80	1.14	2.54	2.08	3.38	3.60
New York, NY	11.75	1.60	2.06	2.49	4.32	4.73
Oklahoma City, OK	10.13	1.18	2.32	1.80	3.47	4.06
Omaha, NE	10.11	1.29	2.27	1.85	3.38	4.15
Orlando, FL	11.07	1.45	2.69	1.92	3.55	4.09
Oxnard, CA	n/a	n/a	n/a	n/a	n/a	n/a
Palm Bay, TX	n/a	n/a	n/a	n/a	n/a	n/a
Peoria, IL	9.99	1.02	2.31	2.00	3.40	4.31
Philadelphia, PA	10.95	1.70	2.24	2.47	3.84	4.05
Phoenix, AZ	10.45	1.99	1.83	2.06	3.61	4.76
Pittsburgh, PA	11.35	1.56	2.13	1.82	3.41	4.08
Portland, OR	10.13	2.23	1.98	2.09	3.90	5.42
Providence, RI	11.24	1.58	2.95	2.69	3.57	4.89
Provo, UT	9.56	1.47	2.13	1.65	3.30	5.31
Raleigh, NC	10.94	1.39	2.48	2.14	3.52	4.07
Reno, NV	10.12	1.45	2.29	1.85	3.70	4.70
Richmond, VA	9.82	1.46	2.26	1.90	3.24	4.02
Roanoke, VA	9.76	1.11	2.30	1.94	3.12	3.89
Rochester, MN	n/a	n/a	n/a	n/a	n/a	n/a
Sacramento, CA	9.80	1.52	2.45	2.29	3.98	5.34
Salem, OR	n/a	n/a	n/a	n/a	n/a	n/a
Salt Lake City, UT	10.69	1.40	2.28	1.66	3.71	4.98
San Antonio, TX	9.29	1.35	2.47	2.17	2.96	3.76
San Diego, CA	10.04	1.40	2.58	2.67	3.27	5.09
San Francisco, CA	10.74	1.72	2.81	3.15	4.34	5.78
San Jose, CA	11.28	1.43	2.53	2.53	4.11	6.32
Santa Rosa, CA	n/a	n/a	n/a	n/a	n/a	n/a
Savannah, GA	10.66	1.42	2.72	1.82	3.20	4.15
Seattle, WA	11.38	1.72	1.97	2.02	3.78	5.48
Sioux Falls, SD	10.05	1.89	2.40	1.81	3.10	4.24
Spokane, WA	10.80	1.51	1.89	1.93	3.00	4.55
Springfield, IL	10.04	1.29	2.31	1.95	3.03	3.80
Tallahassee, FL	n/a	n/a	n/a	n/a	n/a	n/a
Tampa, FL	10.60	1.43	2.69	2.04	3.38	3.56
Topeka, KS	10.30	1.49	2.43	1.90	3.31	4.34
Tulsa, OK	10.30	1.19	2.40	1.95	3.67	3.55
Tyler, TX	9.48	1.12	2.78	2.03	3.26	3.44
Virginia Beach, VA[3]	10.03	1.19	2.47	1.88	3.70	3.85
Washington, DC	11.28	1.69	2.67	2.13	3.57	4.79
Wichita, KS	9.39	1.44	2.24	1.69	3.39	3.86
Wilmington, NC	10.14	1.46	2.72	2.11	3.32	3.96
Winston-Salem, NC	11.31	1.34	2.69	2.08	3.34	3.89
Worcester, MA[4]	9.78	1.45	1.82	1.82	2.96	3.48
Average*	10.40	1.37	2.40	1.99	3.46	4.27
Minimum*	8.48	0.93	1.37	1.30	2.83	2.99
Maximum*	14.20	2.44	3.62	4.02	6.42	6.96

*Note: **T-Bone Steak** (price per pound); **Frying Chicken** (price per pound, whole fryer); **Whole Milk** (half gallon carton); **Eggs** (price per dozen, Grade A, large); **Orange Juice** (64 oz. Tropicana or Florida Natural); **Coffee** (11.5 oz. can, vacuum-packed, Maxwell House, Hills Bros, or Folgers); (*) Values for the local area are compared with the average, minimum, and maximum values for all 308 areas in the Cost of Living Index report; n/a not available; In cases where data is not available for the city, data for the metro area or for a neighboring city has been provided and noted as follows: (1) Rio Rancho, NM; (2) Winston-Salem, NC; (3) Hampton Roads-SE Virginia; (4) Fitchburg-Leominster, MA*

Source: The Council for Community and Economic Research (formerly ACCRA), Cost of Living Index, 2014

Housing and Utility Costs

Urban Area	New Home Price ($)	Apartment Rent ($/month)	All Electric ($/month)	Part Electric ($/month)	Other Energy ($/month)	Telephone ($/month)
Albuquerque, NM[1]	234,773	747	-	103.86	59.10	22.15
Anchorage, AK	493,524	1,280	-	82.78	85.24	26.34
Ann Arbor, MI	357,512	1,013	-	112.83	70.62	27.02
Athens, GA	n/a	n/a	n/a	n/a	n/a	n/a
Atlanta, GA	286,196	948	-	92.54	62.77	25.06
Austin, TX	239,151	1,037	-	103.58	41.87	35.66
Billings, MT	n/a	n/a	n/a	n/a	n/a	n/a
Boise City, ID	266,916	730	-	83.64	65.94	24.98
Boston, MA	487,661	1,940	-	106.16	122.55	38.25
Boulder, CO	n/a	n/a	n/a	n/a	n/a	n/a
Cape Coral, FL	260,323	925	165.00	-	-	19.97
Cedar Rapids, IA	266,293	752	-	100.61	69.98	29.99
Charleston, SC	263,355	1,078	202.00	-	-	28.92
Charlotte, NC	253,000	859	175.00	-	-	31.26
Chicago, IL	428,069	1,149	-	86.13	79.96	30.02
Clarksville, TN	n/a	n/a	n/a	n/a	n/a	n/a
Colorado Springs, CO	285,348	963	-	73.42	61.97	31.64
Columbia, MO	272,145	751	-	88.84	66.60	29.28
Columbus, OH	231,144	821	-	81.41	76.30	27.99
Dallas, TX	214,204	825	-	126.22	50.81	28.15
Davenport, IA	320,560	747	-	75.39	70.86	24.52
Denver, CO	377,658	1,158	-	96.13	68.50	27.60
Des Moines, IA	277,543	638	-	76.85	71.31	28.50
Durham, NC	220,534	794	169.00	-	-	20.50
El Paso, TX	244,332	930	-	99.97	39.65	26.95
Erie, PA	261,665	735	-	89.20	81.87	21.95
Eugene, OR	n/a	n/a	n/a	n/a	n/a	n/a
Fargo, ND	247,098	820	-	66.58	71.58	29.95
Fayetteville, NC	n/a	n/a	n/a	n/a	n/a	n/a
Fort Collins, CO	n/a	n/a	n/a	n/a	n/a	n/a
Fort Wayne, IN	242,584	620	-	69.95	68.49	30.99
Fort Worth, TX	228,573	1,332	-	125.46	51.44	23.97
Gainesville, FL	275,745	890	-	124.58	44.11	27.78
Grand Rapids, MI	224,700	801	-	87.26	75.22	25.98
Green Bay, WI	258,349	659	-	77.19	73.74	35.08
Greensboro, NC[2]	203,576	620	170.00	-	-	31.73
Honolulu, HI	752,644	2,975	498.00	-	-	28.95
Houston, TX	273,623	1,427	-	116.14	41.72	30.15
Huntsville, AL	229,687	836	151.00	-	-	35.51
Indianapolis, IN	233,436	903	-	81.78	83.73	25.68
Jacksonville, FL	229,363	1,069	170.00	-	-	32.75
Kansas City, MO	281,080	824	-	91.74	70.92	34.11
Lafayette, LA	272,388	907	-	95.47	49.71	28.73
Las Vegas, NV	334,773	911	-	133.02	49.81	18.66
Lexington, KY	207,741	848	-	68.99	67.19	32.67
Lincoln, NE	227,531	727	-	71.46	85.52	26.84
Little Rock, AR	298,117	777	-	81.80	63.66	39.30
Los Angeles, CA	574,972	2,289	-	112.12	69.90	33.30
Louisville, KY	236,192	808	-	52.85	71.13	29.18
Lubbock, TX	241,638	811	-	81.85	44.15	24.01
Madison, WI	367,067	911	-	103.82	84.76	23.99
Manchester, NH	376,734	1,309	-	107.64	98.01	36.12
McAllen, TX	227,081	768	-	139.08	38.11	21.01
Miami, FL	357,091	1,300	164.00	-	-	27.70
Midland, TX	252,485	1,281	-	115.55	42.96	24.95

Table continued on next page.

Urban Area	New Home Price ($)	Apartment Rent ($/month)	All Electric ($/month)	Part Electric ($/month)	Other Energy ($/month)	Telephone ($/month)
Minneapolis, MN	343,961	1,118	-	85.84	74.83	25.07
Nashville, TN	211,580	870	-	97.85	63.67	24.50
New Orleans, LA	285,368	908	-	90.13	40.75	26.23
New York, NY	936,793	2,221	-	127.59	111.72	30.33
Oklahoma City, OK	246,396	779	-	81.43	66.90	28.01
Omaha, NE	236,764	732	-	83.52	77.29	26.68
Orlando, FL	274,673	889	190.00	-	-	28.88
Oxnard, CA	n/a	n/a	n/a	n/a	n/a	n/a
Palm Bay, TX	n/a	n/a	n/a	n/a	n/a	n/a
Peoria, IL	334,061	698	-	93.06	63.51	29.18
Philadelphia, PA	406,468	1,283	-	121.67	65.97	38.50
Phoenix, AZ	283,722	827	188.00	-	-	21.32
Pittsburgh, PA	241,321	986	-	94.00	87.20	25.98
Portland, OR	404,703	2,196	-	80.86	74.95	25.01
Providence, RI	386,111	1,394	-	102.86	103.42	36.19
Provo, UT	260,061	783	-	65.05	74.80	24.80
Raleigh, NC	236,443	713	-	91.07	63.74	32.22
Reno, NV	248,538	930	-	80.67	72.32	19.43
Richmond, VA	260,500	867	-	88.12	77.82	34.01
Roanoke, VA	281,983	746	178.00	-	-	25.25
Rochester, MN	n/a	n/a	n/a	n/a	n/a	n/a
Sacramento, CA	371,449	1,028	-	165.81	38.42	29.74
Salem, OR	n/a	n/a	n/a	n/a	n/a	n/a
Salt Lake City, UT	278,495	865	-	71.14	71.90	29.99
San Antonio, TX	225,397	855	-	96.27	37.03	25.51
San Diego, CA	634,116	1,754	-	123.00	56.46	33.30
San Francisco, CA	920,224	3,072	-	118.94	71.93	24.12
San Jose, CA	813,571	1,778	-	178.34	70.10	26.98
Santa Rosa, CA	n/a	n/a	n/a	n/a	n/a	n/a
Savannah, GA	198,491	767	164.00	-	-	33.80
Seattle, WA	472,833	1,821	173.00	-	-	25.95
Sioux Falls, SD	299,389	755	-	78.88	68.21	35.59
Spokane, WA	274,248	740	-	55.87	77.90	22.09
Springfield, IL	250,588	722	-	84.90	63.73	17.16
Tallahassee, FL	n/a	n/a	n/a	n/a	n/a	n/a
Tampa, FL	212,792	843	161.00	-	-	32.47
Topeka, KS	249,762	808	-	82.02	77.34	22.99
Tulsa, OK	197,493	592	-	79.44	58.96	32.13
Tyler, TX	268,261	1,071	-	121.67	44.31	24.72
Virginia Beach, VA[3]	270,044	968	-	90.92	70.55	34.99
Washington, DC	784,280	1,973	-	78.99	84.64	27.32
Wichita, KS	220,755	678	-	92.01	70.07	36.77
Wilmington, NC	285,525	708	172.00	-	-	29.98
Winston-Salem, NC	203,576	620	170.00	-	-	31.73
Worcester, MA[4]	314,699	991	-	91.53	120.26	29.33
Average*	305,838	919	181.00	93.66	73.14	27.95
Minimum*	183,142	480	112.00	42.06	23.42	17.16
Maximum*	1,358,576	3,851	594.00	180.03	440.99	40.42

*Note: **New Home Price** (2,400 sf living area, 8,000 sf lot, in urban area with full utilities); **Apartment Rent** (950 sf 2 bedroom/1.5 or 2 bath, unfurnished, excluding all utilities except water); **All Electric** (average monthly cost for an all-electric home); **Part Electric** (average monthly cost for a part-electric home); **Other Energy** (average monthly cost for natural gas, fuel oil, coal, wood, and any other forms of energy except electricity); **Telephone** (price includes basic monthly rate for a private residential line plus additional local usage charges incurred by a family of four); (*) Values for the local area are compared with the average, minimum, and maximum values for all 308 areas in the Cost of Living Index report; n/a not available; In cases where data is not available for the city, data for the metro area or for a neighboring city has been provided noted as follows: (1) Rio Rancho, NM; (2) Winston-Salem, NC; (3) Hampton Roads-SE Virginia; (4) Fitchburg-Leominster, MA*
Source: The Council for Community and Economic Research (formerly ACCRA), Cost of Living Index, 2014

Health Care, Transportation, and Other Costs

Urban Area	Doctor ($/visit)	Dentist ($/visit)	Optometrist ($/visit)	Gasoline ($/gallon)	Beauty Salon ($/visit)	Men's Shirt ($)
Albuquerque, NM[1]	96.44	93.30	99.33	3.28	25.89	33.77
Anchorage, AK	167.20	129.47	164.89	3.76	48.53	27.39
Ann Arbor, MI	102.40	90.29	89.73	3.50	34.04	22.67
Athens, GA	n/a	n/a	n/a	n/a	n/a	n/a
Atlanta, GA	97.13	100.61	83.70	3.44	42.80	24.27
Austin, TX	89.86	91.64	122.67	3.33	41.49	29.72
Billings, MT	n/a	n/a	n/a	n/a	n/a	n/a
Boise City, ID	123.82	83.40	110.75	3.48	28.39	30.38
Boston, MA	149.67	105.07	121.77	3.60	50.67	40.32
Boulder, CO	n/a	n/a	n/a	n/a	n/a	n/a
Cape Coral, FL	107.90	92.31	93.93	3.58	39.87	23.17
Cedar Rapids, IA	127.22	76.53	119.95	3.27	36.04	20.67
Charleston, SC	108.95	101.00	97.24	3.31	35.29	33.13
Charlotte, NC	100.20	90.87	118.61	3.46	36.30	24.22
Chicago, IL	94.00	96.67	91.53	4.16	42.33	22.05
Clarksville, TN	n/a	n/a	n/a	n/a	n/a	n/a
Colorado Springs, CO	115.00	90.05	107.03	3.32	34.60	23.58
Columbia, MO	118.50	87.62	76.89	3.19	31.20	25.84
Columbus, OH	103.46	79.79	59.89	3.54	32.33	24.90
Dallas, TX	100.80	86.99	102.48	3.36	39.23	31.16
Davenport, IA	93.34	95.40	98.33	3.43	28.25	28.39
Denver, CO	120.48	85.30	99.71	3.46	36.43	29.58
Des Moines, IA	115.93	77.19	83.75	3.32	28.41	18.52
Durham, NC	92.23	83.08	119.00	3.51	44.25	20.23
El Paso, TX	83.67	79.14	75.22	3.31	32.50	24.55
Erie, PA	83.59	80.79	95.25	3.19	41.26	36.26
Eugene, OR	n/a	n/a	n/a	n/a	n/a	n/a
Fargo, ND	146.17	92.47	79.17	3.30	27.40	26.75
Fayetteville, NC	n/a	n/a	n/a	n/a	n/a	n/a
Fort Collins, CO	n/a	n/a	n/a	n/a	n/a	n/a
Fort Wayne, IN	86.33	82.00	85.28	3.52	22.37	22.66
Fort Worth, TX	98.71	97.50	90.58	3.44	44.90	35.77
Gainesville, FL	88.61	99.78	82.72	3.49	35.00	20.65
Grand Rapids, MI	90.90	78.31	84.00	3.41	34.78	22.59
Green Bay, WI	138.69	84.75	63.17	3.32	29.65	35.70
Greensboro, NC[2]	125.36	82.29	99.82	3.44	35.67	36.54
Honolulu, HI	110.28	92.34	142.51	4.21	52.93	37.57
Houston, TX	82.15	83.51	86.81	3.29	49.10	25.91
Huntsville, AL	80.83	90.64	108.06	3.35	31.92	30.07
Indianapolis, IN	97.32	86.70	86.96	3.45	29.63	30.41
Jacksonville, FL	67.47	91.07	74.07	3.41	57.78	21.33
Kansas City, MO	99.61	86.63	95.86	3.37	27.37	40.23
Lafayette, LA	75.97	76.38	72.87	3.20	33.93	28.99
Las Vegas, NV	114.52	88.96	98.47	3.57	49.06	43.20
Lexington, KY	85.60	83.67	73.13	3.40	39.80	38.14
Lincoln, NE	110.11	77.67	94.67	3.38	27.95	30.96
Little Rock, AR	92.19	66.00	81.67	3.33	41.33	31.51
Los Angeles, CA	97.18	108.13	124.85	4.01	63.24	27.74
Louisville, KY	87.77	87.47	82.00	3.69	32.80	30.67
Lubbock, TX	102.87	78.39	98.87	3.18	35.33	29.71
Madison, WI	158.67	92.44	61.00	3.44	43.78	27.44
Manchester, NH	144.42	103.07	99.49	3.45	37.50	27.89
McAllen, TX	71.67	68.33	68.22	3.23	29.11	19.16
Miami, FL	101.25	96.00	92.50	3.63	53.00	22.99
Midland, TX	96.00	86.00	99.00	3.30	35.00	15.08

Table continued on next page.

Urban Area	Doctor ($/visit)	Dentist ($/visit)	Optometrist ($/visit)	Gasoline ($/gallon)	Beauty Salon ($/visit)	Men's Shirt ($)
Minneapolis, MN	127.48	83.29	80.70	3.42	33.73	28.37
Nashville, TN	80.53	78.65	67.17	3.33	31.13	23.67
New Orleans, LA	81.90	96.78	73.45	3.29	44.67	22.43
New York, NY	108.70	112.67	92.65	3.72	58.68	26.11
Oklahoma City, OK	85.39	99.85	98.73	3.09	36.21	27.03
Omaha, NE	129.98	73.06	97.32	3.23	28.05	19.90
Orlando, FL	84.90	83.18	63.41	3.42	45.04	25.52
Oxnard, CA	n/a	n/a	n/a	n/a	n/a	n/a
Palm Bay, TX	n/a	n/a	n/a	n/a	n/a	n/a
Peoria, IL	97.38	74.95	94.46	3.52	24.99	25.38
Philadelphia, PA	118.19	92.59	102.22	3.60	52.14	40.74
Phoenix, AZ	105.67	98.33	76.00	3.42	25.00	21.66
Pittsburgh, PA	101.66	86.88	107.00	3.65	34.71	25.50
Portland, OR	131.34	104.55	110.90	3.84	44.20	29.59
Providence, RI	149.00	97.78	127.22	3.60	40.00	37.21
Provo, UT	98.95	75.26	89.10	3.13	30.99	20.62
Raleigh, NC	94.33	102.23	97.06	3.45	35.43	21.43
Reno, NV	78.40	91.03	110.56	3.73	33.74	22.02
Richmond, VA	100.07	97.80	118.13	3.28	45.00	19.96
Roanoke, VA	76.92	99.07	77.67	3.15	31.46	15.33
Rochester, MN	n/a	n/a	n/a	n/a	n/a	n/a
Sacramento, CA	110.82	103.23	113.80	3.75	43.78	27.65
Salem, OR	n/a	n/a	n/a	n/a	n/a	n/a
Salt Lake City, UT	98.89	75.78	86.83	3.33	38.92	19.77
San Antonio, TX	96.30	84.33	87.56	3.32	34.15	32.08
San Diego, CA	106.91	106.67	103.63	4.08	56.71	26.86
San Francisco, CA	127.18	117.15	120.63	3.73	60.47	33.81
San Jose, CA	110.69	113.79	129.54	3.82	50.49	25.17
Santa Rosa, CA	n/a	n/a	n/a	n/a	n/a	n/a
Savannah, GA	110.33	81.99	71.91	3.36	35.32	23.38
Seattle, WA	103.22	119.44	139.00	3.78	55.89	22.52
Sioux Falls, SD	114.70	84.04	107.03	3.34	28.62	23.71
Spokane, WA	126.67	97.88	118.51	3.59	30.50	22.41
Springfield, IL	129.22	82.72	82.91	3.49	35.79	17.19
Tallahassee, FL	n/a	n/a	n/a	n/a	n/a	n/a
Tampa, FL	85.10	76.28	92.33	3.40	32.07	22.35
Topeka, KS	87.70	79.95	127.53	3.22	27.33	31.73
Tulsa, OK	106.78	73.80	78.86	3.11	33.89	22.11
Tyler, TX	78.96	84.22	97.50	3.27	41.93	27.84
Virginia Beach, VA[3]	115.08	98.11	92.11	3.34	38.87	24.74
Washington, DC	87.41	89.46	70.67	3.57	51.29	27.45
Wichita, KS	95.75	79.28	134.52	3.28	39.50	37.09
Wilmington, NC	125.22	96.67	108.61	3.48	34.44	41.18
Winston-Salem, NC	125.36	82.29	99.82	3.44	35.67	36.54
Worcester, MA[4]	154.80	98.73	108.75	3.99	32.11	26.60
Average*	102.86	87.89	97.66	3.44	34.37	26.74
Minimum*	67.47	65.78	51.18	3.00	17.43	12.79
Maximum*	173.50	150.14	235.00	4.33	64.28	49.50

*Note: **Doctor** (general practitioners routine exam of an established patient); **Dentist** (adult teeth cleaning and periodic oral examination); **Optometrist** (full vision eye exam for established adult patient); **Gasoline** (one gallon regular unleaded, national brand, including all taxes, cash price at self-service pump if available); **Beauty Salon** (woman's shampoo, trim, and blow-dry); **Men's Shirt** (cotton/polyester dress shirt, pinpoint weave, long sleeves); (*) Values for the local area are compared with the average, minimum, and maximum values for all 308 areas in the Cost of Living Index report; n/a not available; In cases where data is not available for the city, data for the metro area or for a neighboring city has been provided and noted as follows: (1) Rio Rancho, NM; (2) Winston-Salem, NC; (3) Hampton Roads-SE Virginia; (4) Fitchburg-Leominster, MA*

Source: The Council for Community and Economic Research (formerly ACCRA), Cost of Living Index, 2014

Number of Medical Professionals

City	Area Covered	MDs[1]	DOs[1,2]	Dentists	Podiatrists	Chiropractors	Optometrists
Albuquerque, NM	Bernalillo County	419.0	19.9	74.7	8.1	22.8	15.9
Anchorage, AK	Anchorage (B) Borough	310.4	27.5	104.1	4.3	46.7	24.2
Ann Arbor, MI	Washtenaw County	1,145.7	33.0	150.7	5.4	22.3	15.0
Athens, GA	Clarke County	278.5	9.1	54.5	5.0	19.8	17.3
Atlanta, GA	Fulton County	482.4	10.0	65.1	4.1	47.1	13.9
Austin, TX	Travis County	295.7	15.9	64.2	4.9	30.1	15.1
Billings, MT	Yellowstone County	339.7	19.8	83.1	7.1	32.5	24.0
Boise City, ID	Ada County	278.3	20.5	79.7	3.4	50.7	17.8
Boston, MA	Suffolk County	1,350.0	12.4	174.2	8.6	14.3	29.2
Boulder, CO	Boulder County	361.4	23.2	91.5	4.5	67.0	23.2
Cape Coral, FL	Lee County	178.3	26.4	45.4	7.4	26.3	13.3
Cedar Rapids, IA	Linn County	191.0	17.2	68.5	7.4	53.2	16.2
Charleston, SC	Charleston County	780.4	23.5	102.2	5.1	41.8	19.0
Charlotte, NC	Mecklenburg County	301.1	9.2	64.8	3.3	30.7	13.3
Chicago, IL	Cook County	408.2	21.6	79.9	10.9	24.6	17.6
Clarksville, TN	Montgomery County	107.9	19.4	40.6	2.2	15.2	14.1
Colorado Springs, CO	El Paso County	185.2	27.4	96.6	3.8	37.8	21.8
Columbia, MO	Boone County	755.7	40.9	59.1	5.3	27.5	22.8
Columbus, OH	Franklin County	405.5	60.6	82.2	6.5	22.7	24.4
Dallas, TX	Dallas County	308.9	19.6	74.5	3.9	31.8	12.0
Davenport, IA	Scott County	220.9	50.3	67.4	3.5	158.9	15.2
Denver, CO	Denver County	562.1	25.7	65.4	6.6	30.7	14.3
Des Moines, IA	Polk County	227.5	106.5	64.8	9.7	44.3	22.1
Durham, NC	Durham County	1,121.1	12.0	70.8	5.2	16.0	14.2
El Paso, TX	El Paso County	175.4	13.8	37.0	3.6	8.1	7.8
Erie, PA	Erie County	170.6	100.4	62.6	11.4	35.7	15.0
Eugene, OR	Lane County	242.3	11.6	64.9	2.8	26.4	16.6
Fargo, ND	Cass County	413.2	10.2	71.1	3.7	57.0	28.2
Fayetteville, NC	Cumberland County	197.8	17.0	91.0	5.2	10.4	17.8
Fort Collins, CO	Larimer County	231.3	24.1	74.9	4.1	49.6	19.9
Fort Wayne, IN	Allen County	251.1	17.7	58.0	5.0	18.4	21.5
Fort Worth, TX	Tarrant County	172.7	37.6	53.1	4.1	22.8	13.5
Gainesville, FL	Alachua County	857.7	24.6	158.3	4.7	25.7	12.6
Grand Rapids, MI	Kent County	298.9	54.2	67.2	4.8	28.0	21.7
Green Bay, WI	Brown County	227.3	19.0	64.8	3.5	38.9	17.7
Greensboro, NC	Guilford County	257.1	7.8	53.7	4.1	14.4	10.3
Honolulu, HI	Honolulu County	323.5	13.7	90.1	2.9	16.2	21.0
Houston, TX	Harris County	297.8	9.5	61.8	4.5	20.6	17.6
Huntsville, AL	Madison County	263.4	10.5	54.7	3.7	21.9	17.6
Indianapolis, IN	Marion County	423.9	16.4	78.5	6.1	14.6	17.3
Jacksonville, FL	Duval County	340.5	23.5	69.5	7.6	21.4	14.8
Kansas City, MO	Jackson County	275.2	59.9	77.6	5.7	39.0	16.9
Lafayette, LA	Lafayette Parish	356.7	5.7	63.6	3.9	29.8	13.8
Las Vegas, NV	Clark County	172.1	25.1	56.2	3.6	19.1	11.6
Lexington, KY	Fayette County	676.8	27.8	127.8	7.8	21.4	17.5
Lincoln, NE	Lancaster County	216.7	9.5	90.8	4.4	36.3	19.8
Little Rock, AR	Pulaski County	680.6	11.3	69.2	4.3	17.9	17.4
Los Angeles, CA	Los Angeles County	281.9	10.6	77.4	5.7	26.2	15.1
Louisville, KY	Jefferson County	461.3	12.2	93.6	7.8	27.7	12.7
Lubbock, TX	Lubbock County	360.7	16.8	51.0	3.1	16.2	14.8
Madison, WI	Dane County	567.3	16.5	65.1	4.9	40.2	18.6
Manchester, NH	Hillsborough County	231.5	21.9	74.1	4.7	23.5	17.1
McAllen, TX	Hidalgo County	107.1	2.8	24.2	1.1	8.4	6.0
Miami, FL	Miami-Dade County	320.3	15.4	56.6	8.9	16.8	11.5
Midland, TX	Midland County	161.1	4.8	49.4	2.6	15.1	11.8
Minneapolis, MN	Hennepin County	479.3	13.6	87.3	3.7	63.9	18.0

Table continued on next page.

City	Area Covered	MDs[1]	DOs[1,2]	Dentists	Podiatrists	Chiropractors	Optometrists
Nashville, TN	Davidson County	602.2	9.2	71.3	3.9	20.8	13.5
New Orleans, LA	Orleans Parish	714.0	13.2	62.8	3.4	7.1	6.1
New York, NY	New York City County	460.1	13.9	81.1	12.3	14.6	13.8
Oklahoma City, OK	Oklahoma County	387.9	41.3	93.3	4.9	24.7	17.7
Omaha, NE	Douglas County	511.9	24.1	83.2	4.5	35.2	17.3
Orlando, FL	Orange County	274.5	19.5	44.4	4.0	23.4	12.2
Oxnard, CA	Ventura County	218.0	8.5	79.8	5.1	34.2	14.9
Palm Bay, FL	Brevard County	214.5	18.6	54.9	6.5	24.1	14.7
Peoria, IL	Peoria County	501.6	39.0	67.9	7.4	45.1	18.6
Philadelphia, PA	Philadelphia County	506.8	42.2	65.2	16.8	14.9	14.7
Phoenix, AZ	Maricopa County	235.5	32.1	62.8	5.8	33.1	13.6
Pittsburgh, PA	Allegheny County	609.7	35.6	86.2	10.4	39.7	18.0
Portland, OR	Multnomah County	577.5	30.2	89.7	5.2	63.4	20.0
Providence, RI	Providence County	454.6	16.0	58.2	9.7	18.2	17.5
Provo, UT	Utah County	120.6	14.6	63.4	3.4	23.6	9.6
Raleigh, NC	Wake County	267.7	7.5	65.2	3.1	24.1	15.7
Reno, NV	Washoe County	268.7	20.0	63.2	4.1	24.9	18.4
Richmond, VA	Richmond City	668.9	16.1	122.0	9.8	6.5	12.1
Roanoke, VA	Roanoke City	493.5	41.9	60.7	14.2	14.2	22.3
Rochester, MN	Olmsted County	2,262.2	53.7	80.4	6.0	36.9	17.4
Sacramento, CA	Sacramento County	288.5	11.6	71.9	4.3	21.7	16.6
Salem, OR	Marion County	179.3	12.2	75.4	4.3	29.8	15.5
Salt Lake City, UT	Salt Lake County	350.8	11.6	72.3	5.5	25.4	12.4
San Antonio, TX	Bexar County	315.8	18.7	76.9	5.3	14.8	13.7
San Diego, CA	San Diego County	299.1	15.1	78.9	3.9	30.8	15.8
San Francisco, CA	San Francisco County	782.3	10.6	138.9	10.2	36.1	23.7
San Jose, CA	Santa Clara County	389.7	7.3	105.4	5.8	37.6	23.3
Santa Rosa, CA	Sonoma County	249.8	12.2	85.8	6.1	35.7	14.9
Savannah, GA	Chatham County	343.0	17.3	62.1	6.5	16.5	12.9
Seattle, WA	King County	463.8	13.7	100.9	6.3	42.2	19.6
Sioux Falls, SD	Minnehaha County	333.3	22.2	51.7	5.0	52.3	20.0
Spokane, WA	Spokane County	271.6	19.5	73.6	4.8	27.7	18.4
Springfield, IL	Sangamon County	578.2	14.1	67.8	5.0	33.7	21.1
Tallahassee, FL	Leon County	259.6	8.5	36.9	3.9	18.8	17.7
Tampa, FL	Hillsborough County	315.7	25.5	50.7	5.0	23.3	11.4
Topeka, KS	Shawnee County	209.6	23.5	59.9	5.6	24.1	26.3
Tulsa, OK	Tulsa County	274.4	104.0	65.5	3.7	36.1	20.1
Tyler, TX	Smith County	362.0	23.7	56.3	6.5	24.0	14.8
Virginia Beach, VA	Virginia Beach City	250.6	12.3	70.1	6.9	25.8	14.0
Washington, DC	District of Columbia	767.7	15.1	116.0	8.2	7.4	13.2
Wichita, KS	Sedgwick County	255.6	37.7	54.9	2.6	37.3	24.3
Wilmington, NC	New Hanover County	354.8	21.5	71.8	6.6	32.4	17.8
Winston-Salem, NC	Forsyth County	606.8	28.2	60.3	6.1	14.4	16.6
Worcester, MA	Worcester County	354.7	18.0	65.0	6.3	20.0	17.2
U.S.	U.S.	270.0	20.2	63.1	5.7	25.2	14.9

Note: All figures are rates per 100,000 population; Data as of 2013 unless noted; (1) Data as of 2012; (2) Doctor of Osteopathic Medicine; Source: U.S. Department of Health and Human Services, Health Resources and Services Administration, Bureau of Health Professions, Area Resource File (ARF) 2013-2014

Health Insurance Coverage: City

City	With Health Insurance	With Private Health Insurance	With Public Health Insurance	Without Health Insurance	Population Under Age 18 Without Health Insurance
Albuquerque, NM	84.2	59.5	35.2	15.8	6.2
Anchorage, AK	83.1	67.9	23.9	16.9	11.1
Ann Arbor, MI	93.8	85.9	17.5	6.2	2.9
Athens, GA	82.4	66.8	23.1	17.6	9.5
Atlanta, GA	81.7	61.6	27.6	18.3	7.1
Austin, TX	80.3	64.5	22.3	19.7	9.3
Billings, MT	83.3	65.1	30.8	16.7	10.4
Boise City, ID	86.4	72.9	24.5	13.6	7.0
Boston, MA	95.0	65.9	36.4	5.0	1.6
Boulder, CO	92.0	85.0	14.2	8.0	7.1
Cape Coral, FL	79.6	56.1	35.9	20.4	10.5
Cedar Rapids, IA	91.5	74.6	29.4	8.5	3.6
Charleston, SC	87.2	73.4	24.8	12.8	8.7
Charlotte, NC	81.7	63.8	25.2	18.3	7.4
Chicago, IL	80.2	52.4	33.9	19.8	4.7
Clarksville, TN	86.4	69.3	29.8	13.6	4.5
Colorado Springs, CO	86.0	69.3	28.4	14.0	6.9
Columbia, MO	91.1	80.9	18.2	8.9	5.6
Columbus, OH	84.5	62.6	29.4	15.5	7.1
Dallas, TX	69.6	44.9	30.5	30.4	15.9
Davenport, IA	88.4	68.1	32.5	11.6	5.1
Denver, CO	83.4	60.8	30.0	16.6	8.9
Des Moines, IA	89.0	63.0	37.8	11.0	3.5
Durham, NC	82.4	64.4	26.0	17.6	8.5
El Paso, TX	73.7	48.3	32.7	26.3	12.7
Erie, PA	89.2	56.6	45.7	10.8	3.1
Eugene, OR	85.6	68.1	28.8	14.4	5.0
Fargo, ND	89.6	78.2	21.7	10.4	5.3
Fayetteville, NC	86.0	65.3	34.5	14.0	5.0
Fort Collins, CO	89.8	79.8	18.7	10.2	3.7
Fort Wayne, IN	82.8	60.7	31.5	17.2	10.9
Fort Worth, TX	75.9	54.3	27.7	24.1	12.9
Gainesville, FL	82.9	69.3	20.6	17.1	7.1
Grand Rapids, MI	86.8	59.5	38.2	13.2	2.4
Green Bay, WI	87.4	61.6	36.4	12.6	6.7
Greensboro, NC	83.1	63.0	28.7	16.9	6.2
Honolulu, HI	93.2	75.8	31.5	6.8	2.6
Houston, TX	71.4	46.4	30.7	28.6	15.2
Huntsville, AL	84.2	68.5	29.4	15.8	4.8
Indianapolis, IN	82.6	58.0	33.8	17.4	8.4
Jacksonville, FL	82.6	61.5	30.9	17.4	8.4
Kansas City, MO	82.6	63.3	28.6	17.4	8.2
Lafayette, LA	82.7	63.8	28.9	17.3	4.0
Las Vegas, NV	76.7	58.7	27.3	23.3	16.6
Lexington, KY	86.4	71.9	24.0	13.6	5.7
Lincoln, NE	88.4	74.4	23.9	11.6	6.0
Little Rock, AR	84.2	63.2	31.2	15.8	5.7
Los Angeles, CA	74.9	48.7	31.8	25.1	9.0
Louisville, KY	85.6	65.7	32.1	14.4	4.7
Lubbock, TX	81.7	63.0	28.0	18.3	9.6
Madison, WI	92.5	80.5	21.9	7.5	2.9
Manchester, NH	85.5	64.4	31.3	14.5	3.6
McAllen, TX	65.3	40.2	29.5	34.7	18.8
Miami, FL	66.2	33.2	36.1	33.8	12.4
Midland, TX	79.4	66.2	22.1	20.6	16.3

Table continued on next page.

City	With Health Insurance	With Private Health Insurance	With Public Health Insurance	Without Health Insurance	Population Under Age 18 Without Health Insurance
Minneapolis, MN	87.8	65.1	29.9	12.2	7.0
Nashville, TN	83.1	63.1	28.5	16.9	7.6
New Orleans, LA	81.8	52.2	37.1	18.2	5.3
New York, NY	86.0	54.0	39.6	14.0	4.1
Oklahoma City, OK	79.5	58.9	30.4	20.5	10.3
Omaha, NE	85.8	67.0	28.7	14.2	6.2
Orlando, FL	76.3	55.2	26.8	23.7	12.3
Oxnard, CA	75.6	48.1	34.2	24.4	10.4
Palm Bay, FL	82.8	55.9	38.8	17.2	8.6
Peoria, IL	88.7	61.0	39.2	11.3	2.0
Philadelphia, PA	85.5	54.4	41.1	14.5	5.1
Phoenix, AZ	77.1	51.5	32.0	22.9	14.7
Pittsburgh, PA	90.1	69.7	32.4	9.9	3.8
Portland, OR	84.6	67.3	26.6	15.4	4.1
Providence, RI	80.4	50.3	36.3	19.6	5.8
Provo, UT	83.8	72.6	18.6	16.2	13.1
Raleigh, NC	84.4	69.3	22.7	15.6	8.9
Reno, NV	76.8	61.9	23.5	23.2	18.7
Richmond, VA	82.4	58.5	33.2	17.6	4.3
Roanoke, VA	83.4	57.7	35.9	16.6	4.8
Rochester, MN	92.7	78.9	25.8	7.3	4.8
Sacramento, CA	83.8	57.3	35.5	16.2	5.8
Salem, OR	83.3	61.5	33.7	16.7	6.9
Salt Lake City, UT	80.9	64.5	23.9	19.1	14.7
San Antonio, TX	78.8	56.7	31.7	21.2	10.3
San Diego, CA	83.3	66.2	25.5	16.7	8.2
San Francisco, CA	89.7	70.9	27.2	10.3	3.4
San Jose, CA	86.3	66.6	26.6	13.7	4.5
Santa Rosa, CA	84.3	63.1	32.5	15.7	7.9
Savannah, GA	78.5	56.2	31.7	21.5	8.8
Seattle, WA	88.6	76.6	20.6	11.4	4.9
Sioux Falls, SD	88.9	74.7	24.8	11.1	5.9
Spokane, WA	85.4	60.9	36.0	14.6	5.5
Springfield, IL	88.2	66.4	36.1	11.8	3.5
Tallahassee, FL	85.8	72.8	20.9	14.2	5.0
Tampa, FL	81.9	57.3	32.0	18.1	8.2
Topeka, KS	84.5	64.6	33.8	15.5	7.2
Tulsa, OK	78.4	56.3	32.6	21.6	10.7
Tyler, TX	78.5	58.9	30.5	21.5	12.2
Virginia Beach, VA	89.3	79.7	21.1	10.7	4.3
Washington, DC	93.4	69.6	35.1	6.6	2.6
Wichita, KS	83.8	64.4	29.7	16.2	7.0
Wilmington, NC	83.3	65.2	30.3	16.7	5.7
Winston-Salem, NC	81.7	58.2	33.6	18.3	7.0
Worcester, MA	95.1	61.5	43.1	4.9	1.4
U.S.	85.2	65.2	31.0	14.8	7.3

Note: Figures are percentages that cover the civilian noninstitutionalized population
Source: U.S. Census Bureau, 2011-2013 American Community Survey 3-Year Estimates

Health Insurance Coverage: Metro Area

Metro Area	With Health Insurance	With Private Health Insurance	With Public Health Insurance	Without Health Insurance	Population Under Age 18 Without Health Insurance
Albuquerque, NM	83.8	58.3	36.1	16.2	6.6
Anchorage, AK	82.3	66.6	24.6	17.7	11.6
Ann Arbor, MI	92.7	81.3	22.9	7.3	2.8
Athens, GA	83.8	67.2	25.1	16.2	7.2
Atlanta, GA	81.2	64.9	24.3	18.8	9.6
Austin, TX	81.9	68.0	22.0	18.1	9.9
Billings, MT	83.7	67.1	29.4	16.3	10.3
Boise City, ID	84.7	68.1	27.2	15.3	7.4
Boston, MA	95.6	76.8	30.1	4.4	1.7
Boulder, CO	89.4	79.2	18.8	10.6	6.8
Cape Coral, FL	79.2	56.0	40.4	20.8	13.2
Cedar Rapids, IA	92.9	77.5	28.3	7.1	2.9
Charleston, SC	83.4	66.6	28.0	16.6	9.3
Charlotte, NC	83.8	65.7	27.5	16.2	7.0
Chicago, IL	86.0	66.1	28.7	14.0	4.0
Clarksville, TN	85.7	68.7	29.6	14.3	6.5
Colorado Springs, CO	87.1	72.0	26.7	12.9	6.7
Columbia, MO	90.6	79.0	20.4	9.4	4.8
Columbus, OH	88.3	70.7	27.2	11.7	5.3
Dallas, TX	78.1	60.8	24.3	21.9	12.9
Davenport, IA	90.5	73.0	32.6	9.5	3.8
Denver, CO	85.3	69.4	24.5	14.7	8.9
Des Moines, IA	92.3	76.7	27.1	7.7	3.4
Durham, NC	85.2	68.6	26.7	14.8	7.8
El Paso, TX	72.2	45.7	33.0	27.8	13.2
Erie, PA	91.3	69.2	36.5	8.7	2.5
Eugene, OR	85.0	64.5	34.7	15.0	5.9
Fargo, ND	91.3	80.0	22.0	8.7	4.8
Fayetteville, NC	85.7	64.0	34.1	14.3	5.1
Fort Collins, CO	88.2	75.1	24.0	11.8	6.4
Fort Wayne, IN	85.2	66.7	28.4	14.8	10.0
Fort Worth, TX	78.1	60.8	24.3	21.9	12.9
Gainesville, FL	84.2	68.1	25.9	15.8	8.4
Grand Rapids, MI	90.3	73.8	28.7	9.7	3.4
Green Bay, WI	91.3	72.3	29.9	8.7	4.0
Greensboro, NC	83.4	62.2	31.2	16.6	7.8
Honolulu, HI	94.3	78.9	29.4	5.7	2.7
Houston, TX	76.5	57.1	25.6	23.5	13.3
Huntsville, AL	87.2	72.9	27.0	12.8	3.4
Indianapolis, IN	86.5	68.6	28.0	13.5	6.7
Jacksonville, FL	84.2	65.3	30.0	15.8	8.0
Kansas City, MO	86.9	72.4	25.3	13.1	6.7
Lafayette, LA	83.5	62.0	31.8	16.5	4.4
Las Vegas, NV	77.8	61.8	24.9	22.2	15.7
Lexington, KY	87.1	71.5	25.8	12.9	4.8
Lincoln, NE	89.2	76.0	23.4	10.8	5.5
Little Rock, AR	85.8	65.6	31.7	14.2	4.8
Los Angeles, CA	79.2	56.0	29.5	20.8	8.4
Louisville, KY	87.3	70.5	29.3	12.7	5.2
Lubbock, TX	80.9	61.5	28.7	19.1	10.4
Madison, WI	93.0	81.0	23.6	7.0	3.5
Manchester, NH	90.0	75.5	24.7	10.0	3.0
McAllen, TX	63.4	30.9	37.0	36.6	17.3
Miami, FL	74.9	51.1	31.1	25.1	13.0
Midland, TX	77.5	64.9	21.1	22.5	21.6

Table continued on next page.

Metro Area	With Health Insurance	With Private Health Insurance	With Public Health Insurance	Without Health Insurance	Population Under Age 18 Without Health Insurance
Minneapolis, MN	91.8	77.5	24.8	8.2	5.1
Nashville, TN	86.4	68.7	27.1	13.6	5.8
New Orleans, LA	83.4	58.5	33.5	16.6	4.5
New York, NY	87.2	64.8	31.8	12.8	4.4
Oklahoma City, OK	82.7	64.4	29.1	17.3	9.3
Omaha, NE	89.0	74.0	25.5	11.0	5.1
Orlando, FL	79.2	59.5	28.4	20.8	12.1
Oxnard, CA	83.8	66.4	26.9	16.2	7.6
Palm Bay, FL	83.2	62.3	37.7	16.8	10.9
Peoria, IL	90.6	72.1	32.3	9.4	3.2
Philadelphia, PA	90.1	71.8	30.0	9.9	4.1
Phoenix, AZ	82.6	61.5	31.0	17.4	12.0
Pittsburgh, PA	92.1	75.4	32.5	7.9	3.1
Portland, OR	86.1	70.0	26.9	13.9	5.7
Providence, RI	91.2	70.4	33.5	8.8	3.5
Provo, UT	86.7	76.5	17.6	13.3	9.1
Raleigh, NC	85.8	71.9	22.3	14.2	7.7
Reno, NV	79.6	64.4	24.8	20.4	17.0
Richmond, VA	87.6	73.0	25.7	12.4	5.5
Roanoke, VA	88.5	69.8	32.1	11.5	4.2
Rochester, MN	92.8	79.2	26.3	7.2	5.2
Sacramento, CA	86.2	66.3	30.8	13.8	5.9
Salem, OR	83.5	61.4	34.9	16.5	6.7
Salt Lake City, UT	84.2	71.9	20.1	15.8	11.6
San Antonio, TX	80.6	61.0	30.1	19.4	10.0
San Diego, CA	83.2	65.4	26.6	16.8	8.4
San Francisco, CA	88.5	71.9	26.4	11.5	4.8
San Jose, CA	88.5	72.3	23.9	11.5	3.9
Santa Rosa, CA	85.7	68.0	30.1	14.3	6.9
Savannah, GA	81.2	64.2	27.0	18.8	8.9
Seattle, WA	87.2	72.7	24.5	12.8	5.3
Sioux Falls, SD	90.6	78.2	23.1	9.4	4.6
Spokane, WA	86.2	64.4	34.8	13.8	6.0
Springfield, IL	90.8	71.9	33.0	9.2	2.9
Tallahassee, FL	85.8	69.6	26.0	14.2	6.9
Tampa, FL	82.4	59.6	34.6	17.6	9.2
Topeka, KS	88.0	71.6	31.1	12.0	6.2
Tulsa, OK	82.6	63.7	30.4	17.4	9.2
Tyler, TX	78.9	59.4	30.7	21.1	13.8
Virginia Beach, VA	87.9	73.8	26.2	12.1	4.6
Washington, DC	88.4	76.7	21.4	11.6	5.0
Wichita, KS	86.5	69.6	27.8	13.5	6.2
Wilmington, NC	83.3	66.6	30.1	16.7	7.2
Winston-Salem, NC	84.7	63.3	33.4	15.3	6.1
Worcester, MA	95.5	73.6	33.6	4.5	1.7
U.S.	85.2	65.2	31.0	14.8	7.3

Note: Figures are percentages that cover the civilian noninstitutionalized population; Figures cover the Metropolitan Statistical Area (MSA)—see Appendix B for areas included
Source: U.S. Census Bureau, 2011-2013 American Community Survey 3-Year Estimates

Crime Rate: City

City	All Crimes	Violent Crimes				Property Crimes		
		Murder	Forcible Rape	Robbery	Aggrav. Assault	Burglary	Larceny -Theft	Motor Vehicle Theft
Albuquerque, NM	6,244.7	6.6	78.7	187.4	502.2	1,307.3	3,624.2	538.4
Anchorage, AK	4,831.1	4.7	136.2	174.3	497.9	440.1	3,287.6	290.2
Ann Arbor, MI	2,373.3	2.6	41.1	42.0	125.9	351.0	1,730.3	80.5
Athens, GA	3,727.9	1.7	30.8	104.1	199.8	805.0	2,424.2	162.3
Atlanta, GA	7,326.7	18.6	23.3	523.9	657.4	1,316.6	3,804.3	982.7
Austin, TX	5,213.1	3.0	25.3	88.8	246.4	762.4	3,834.8	252.5
Billings, MT	5,532.4	3.7	36.2	75.1	218.9	917.4	3,779.2	501.8
Boise City, ID	2,492.0	1.4	57.4	21.0	200.2	384.9	1,727.7	99.4
Boston, MA	3,555.5	6.1	43.3	290.2	442.8	480.9	2,042.1	250.1
Boulder, CO	3,078.9	0.0	37.0	38.9	136.1	595.2	2,174.5	97.2
Cape Coral, FL	2,185.2	1.8	4.3	24.5	89.9	491.2	1,484.8	88.7
Cedar Rapids, IA	3,963.7	3.1	35.8	70.0	195.9	759.5	2,668.6	230.9
Charleston, SC	2,690.9	5.5	22.8	56.6	96.7	239.8	2,142.2	127.4
Charlotte, NC	4,257.4	7.0	27.5	215.5	358.0	768.7	2,659.1	221.6
Chicago, IL	n/a	15.2	n/a	434.3	n/a	653.4	2,407.5	464.5
Clarksville, TN	3,357.9	4.1	57.7	79.0	372.9	700.6	2,036.4	107.1
Colorado Springs, CO	4,601.6	6.0	84.8	95.8	247.4	854.4	2,871.1	442.1
Columbia, MO	4,167.1	4.4	58.5	97.7	202.5	613.5	3,045.7	144.9
Columbus, OH	6,885.1	11.0	71.7	411.9	163.7	1,926.0	3,841.9	459.0
Dallas, TX	4,828.9	11.4	43.3	334.8	274.3	1,156.6	2,420.2	588.4
Davenport, IA	4,813.7	2.0	86.4	164.0	389.9	943.7	2,993.1	234.7
Denver, CO	4,283.3	6.2	79.2	174.4	370.0	757.8	2,358.5	537.3
Des Moines, IA	5,323.8	5.3	43.4	101.7	344.3	1,114.3	3,304.9	409.9
Durham, NC[1]	5,089.5	8.9	26.7	261.1	429.2	1,394.1	2,670.6	298.9
El Paso, TX	2,660.0	1.5	25.9	67.2	276.4	260.6	1,911.6	116.8
Erie, PA	3,635.4	3.0	59.5	173.6	217.2	1,008.8	2,076.1	97.2
Eugene, OR	5,250.5	0.0	42.9	123.0	87.7	971.0	3,642.3	383.6
Fargo, ND	3,289.8	2.7	63.9	52.2	282.6	631.0	2,108.0	149.4
Fayetteville, NC	6,631.8	12.3	32.1	289.3	243.9	1,619.1	4,123.5	311.6
Fort Collins, CO	2,775.4	0.0	38.0	24.7	175.3	353.8	2,090.4	93.3
Fort Wayne, IN	4,221.0	12.2	37.3	175.4	147.6	940.3	2,756.8	151.5
Fort Worth, TX	4,903.7	6.1	66.3	159.2	328.6	1,053.9	2,985.5	304.0
Gainesville, FL	4,575.4	4.7	49.0	122.4	460.5	586.1	3,159.8	192.7
Grand Rapids, MI	3,929.6	8.9	42.9	246.3	395.4	847.7	2,256.6	131.8
Green Bay, WI	3,019.8	1.9	49.5	75.2	349.2	547.1	1,903.8	93.2
Greensboro, NC	4,648.8	9.7	25.1	177.6	306.4	1,063.9	2,886.4	179.7
Honolulu, HI	n/a	n/a	n/a	n/a	n/a	n/a	n/a	n/a
Houston, TX	6,049.3	9.8	28.3	453.6	471.0	1,088.4	3,374.8	623.5
Huntsville, AL	5,804.4	13.0	47.1	211.7	544.0	1,019.8	3,588.3	380.5
Indianapolis, IN	6,478.9	15.2	77.2	446.9	693.2	1,581.4	3,076.4	588.7
Jacksonville, FL	4,523.0	11.0	53.4	168.4	387.5	835.8	2,880.4	186.5
Kansas City, MO	6,554.5	21.3	81.0	357.0	800.4	1,377.4	2,996.5	920.9
Lafayette, LA	6,835.8	6.5	13.8	220.4	462.7	1,034.0	4,857.8	240.7
Las Vegas, NV	3,954.9	6.5	47.0	271.4	433.2	985.4	1,769.3	442.2
Lexington, KY	4,338.3	5.8	43.4	151.3	105.9	833.8	2,928.9	269.2
Lincoln, NE	3,866.0	1.9	53.1	79.2	235.8	531.8	2,849.8	114.4
Little Rock, AR	9,273.6	17.7	60.3	478.2	850.6	1,922.0	5,397.7	547.1
Los Angeles, CA	2,639.2	6.5	19.7	203.3	196.6	405.5	1,436.9	370.8
Louisville, KY	4,831.3	7.2	23.8	212.6	299.4	1,031.1	2,955.5	301.7
Lubbock, TX	5,627.3	2.1	37.0	163.1	566.7	1,096.4	3,406.4	355.6
Madison, WI	3,551.4	2.1	31.3	122.1	209.1	569.8	2,512.8	104.3
Manchester, NH	4,475.1	3.6	82.4	267.2	323.3	809.7	2,844.8	144.0
McAllen, TX	4,108.9	1.5	4.4	61.0	58.8	393.6	3,416.3	173.3
Miami, FL	6,183.9	17.0	22.9	529.6	612.3	954.4	3,590.2	457.5

Table continued on next page.

City	All Crimes	Violent Crimes				Property Crimes		
		Murder	Forcible Rape	Robbery	Aggrav. Assault	Burglary	Larceny -Theft	Motor Vehicle Theft
Midland, TX	2,896.3	4.1	18.0	51.5	212.7	464.6	2,011.3	134.1
Minneapolis, MN	5,905.0	9.1	97.2	468.4	444.5	1,161.3	3,327.1	397.5
Nashville, TN	4,888.0	5.5	68.7	253.4	712.5	883.0	2,776.6	188.3
New Orleans, LA	4,639.0	41.4	46.7	301.8	396.5	849.6	2,434.6	568.4
New York, NY	2,314.8	4.0	13.2	228.3	378.4	197.8	1,404.6	88.5
Oklahoma City, OK	6,194.2	10.2	74.4	196.8	544.6	1,324.9	3,369.6	673.7
Omaha, NE	5,071.3	9.9	43.3	168.9	354.1	825.5	2,945.1	724.6
Orlando, FL	7,425.8	6.7	49.8	226.3	631.8	1,376.2	4,732.3	402.8
Oxnard, CA	2,825.8	7.4	4.9	161.9	147.1	480.8	1,696.0	327.7
Palm Bay, FL	2,307.7	2.9	20.1	41.2	367.8	495.3	1,270.2	110.2
Peoria, IL	4,483.7	13.8	20.7	237.2	404.5	968.5	2,671.8	167.3
Philadelphia, PA	4,540.8	15.9	82.3	486.9	514.2	670.1	2,398.5	372.9
Phoenix, AZ	4,631.9	7.9	42.3	215.2	366.5	1,114.9	2,462.0	423.1
Pittsburgh, PA	4,000.2	14.6	25.4	310.8	383.6	706.4	2,359.3	200.2
Portland, OR	5,347.6	2.3	38.4	150.5	291.6	677.7	3,647.1	539.9
Providence, RI	5,080.9	6.7	54.2	204.0	358.3	1,021.9	2,897.9	537.8
Provo, UT	2,539.8	0.9	70.1	18.0	47.9	281.3	2,029.3	92.4
Raleigh, NC	3,455.3	2.8	18.4	141.0	230.1	735.9	2,162.7	164.3
Reno, NV	3,583.6	6.0	29.2	131.1	329.8	606.7	2,107.4	373.2
Richmond, VA	4,713.2	17.4	20.2	293.2	292.7	853.7	2,795.2	440.7
Roanoke, VA	5,004.7	9.2	44.9	145.0	267.5	641.3	3,713.0	183.8
Rochester, MN	2,527.5	0.0	45.6	49.2	100.3	391.2	1,847.3	93.9
Sacramento, CA	4,416.1	7.1	19.9	242.2	386.9	812.7	2,349.1	598.3
Salem, OR	4,614.7	4.4	29.7	87.2	207.3	621.2	3,250.2	414.6
Salt Lake City, UT	7,850.9	3.7	107.2	221.8	442.6	1,087.0	5,002.5	986.1
San Antonio, TX	6,345.7	5.1	47.4	156.6	421.6	1,060.9	4,184.2	469.9
San Diego, CA	2,744.4	2.9	23.4	107.9	258.8	471.0	1,425.2	455.3
San Francisco, CA	6,642.3	5.8	19.3	503.9	318.2	711.3	4,380.5	703.5
San Jose, CA	2,895.2	3.8	27.2	110.4	182.6	521.4	1,250.9	798.9
Santa Rosa, CA	2,358.9	1.7	24.5	61.2	227.9	371.9	1,491.6	180.1
Savannah, GA	3,957.9	12.8	20.8	176.0	152.2	903.5	2,384.4	308.2
Seattle, WA	6,166.8	3.0	23.8	249.1	308.8	1,148.7	3,763.0	670.5
Sioux Falls, SD	3,441.0	1.9	85.3	41.4	264.6	537.9	2,346.8	163.2
Spokane, WA	10,008.9	5.2	79.2	247.2	355.6	1,856.1	6,372.5	1,093.0
Springfield, IL	6,046.8	3.4	60.5	244.6	706.4	1,107.8	3,782.7	141.5
Tallahassee, FL	5,041.5	5.8	84.8	205.1	445.1	1,103.3	2,964.3	233.2
Tampa, FL	3,108.3	8.0	22.2	165.1	401.6	555.1	1,799.0	157.4
Topeka, KS	5,544.9	8.6	25.8	134.4	309.4	967.1	3,655.2	444.5
Tulsa, OK	6,287.7	15.2	94.6	252.0	608.4	1,504.4	3,207.6	605.6
Tyler, TX	4,490.5	5.0	43.0	53.0	274.9	824.7	3,110.0	179.9
Virginia Beach, VA	2,652.8	3.8	31.1	67.5	59.7	312.2	2,079.9	98.7
Washington, DC	5,793.0	15.9	60.8	566.2	576.1	512.6	3,574.6	486.8
Wichita, KS	6,175.4	3.9	63.1	121.1	604.9	1,017.6	3,851.4	513.3
Wilmington, NC	5,618.8	6.3	35.1	228.0	349.6	1,482.2	3,215.7	301.8
Winston-Salem, NC	6,055.3	6.4	33.9	186.2	378.3	1,646.7	3,544.8	259.1
Worcester, MA	4,354.8	4.9	12.0	263.3	673.7	1,044.4	2,139.0	217.5
U.S.	3,098.6	4.5	25.2	109.1	229.1	610.0	1,899.4	221.3

Note: Figures are crimes per 100,000 population in 2013 except where noted; n/a not available; (1) 2012 data
Source: FBI Uniform Crime Reports, 2013

Crime Rate: Suburbs

Suburbs[1]	All Crimes	Violent Crimes: Murder	Violent Crimes: Forcible Rape	Violent Crimes: Robbery	Violent Crimes: Aggrav. Assault	Property Crimes: Burglary	Property Crimes: Larceny -Theft	Property Crimes: Motor Vehicle Theft
Albuquerque, NM	3,575.1	4.6	38.9	56.0	589.9	886.3	1,754.3	245.0
Anchorage, AK	7,133.4	6.6	72.9	39.7	291.4	529.9	5,808.7	384.2
Ann Arbor, MI	2,418.0	3.4	58.8	47.4	242.4	464.5	1,482.3	119.3
Athens, GA	2,766.6	0.0	19.4	11.6	141.0	539.4	1,953.0	102.2
Atlanta, GA	3,398.5	4.7	19.2	125.5	165.3	763.9	2,040.0	279.9
Austin, TX	1,964.6	2.5	21.6	23.3	146.3	341.6	1,349.4	79.8
Billings, MT	1,868.7	0.0	17.5	5.3	115.7	380.4	1,155.2	194.6
Boise City, ID	1,644.6	0.7	43.8	9.0	143.2	340.9	1,034.1	72.9
Boston, MA	2,119.7	1.8	29.0	82.0	251.7	370.1	1,291.6	93.6
Boulder, CO	2,202.8	1.0	59.8	16.4	134.9	298.8	1,579.7	112.3
Cape Coral, FL	2,640.5	4.5	29.0	109.0	260.8	603.9	1,497.8	135.6
Cedar Rapids, IA	1,222.7	0.0	20.7	6.7	81.5	309.8	742.5	61.5
Charleston, SC	3,688.7	7.5	29.6	74.2	286.8	705.4	2,321.0	264.2
Charlotte, NC	2,895.6	4.2	20.4	57.7	207.7	638.6	1,850.1	116.9
Chicago, IL	n/a	1.8	n/a	59.7	n/a	299.3	1,392.6	82.8
Clarksville, TN	2,365.5	6.0	36.8	36.8	132.0	602.3	1,460.3	91.5
Colorado Springs, CO	1,921.2	6.6	52.7	19.0	173.5	429.3	1,115.3	124.8
Columbia, MO	2,504.6	0.0	19.6	28.5	222.7	331.3	1,793.8	108.7
Columbus, OH	2,783.7	1.6	24.5	49.9	64.8	593.9	1,979.6	69.3
Dallas, TX	2,583.7	2.2	24.0	54.8	103.5	504.5	1,722.1	172.7
Davenport, IA	2,160.6	1.8	20.2	28.4	209.6	362.8	1,486.7	51.1
Denver, CO	2,691.8	2.9	44.7	48.6	136.8	369.5	1,866.6	222.9
Des Moines, IA	1,810.8	0.8	17.7	9.3	119.0	314.9	1,261.7	87.4
Durham, NC[2]	2,848.2	2.1	16.6	38.9	120.7	845.7	1,724.3	99.8
El Paso, TX	1,953.6	1.2	36.9	24.0	185.8	364.8	1,238.2	102.7
Erie, PA	2,065.8	0.6	16.1	29.5	81.8	386.3	1,509.2	42.3
Eugene, OR	2,815.7	2.0	18.7	23.8	101.6	512.1	1,956.3	201.2
Fargo, ND	1,783.6	0.9	19.8	9.9	79.2	357.4	1,217.3	99.0
Fayetteville, NC	3,979.7	2.8	12.0	103.1	271.2	1,273.2	2,173.3	144.1
Fort Collins, CO	1,985.6	1.2	48.8	17.5	106.7	243.0	1,503.9	64.5
Fort Wayne, IN	1,651.3	1.8	17.1	30.7	56.7	320.8	1,147.3	76.8
Fort Worth, TX	3,047.6	2.8	21.3	65.1	169.9	563.3	2,057.7	167.6
Gainesville, FL	2,558.8	2.8	36.8	57.7	361.3	560.0	1,455.5	84.8
Grand Rapids, MI	1,866.4	0.9	71.9	22.4	115.7	348.5	1,248.4	58.7
Green Bay, WI	1,511.6	0.0	11.6	12.5	45.3	216.2	1,190.9	35.2
Greensboro, NC	3,276.5	1.7	14.3	64.8	158.6	924.9	1,967.1	145.0
Honolulu, HI	n/a	n/a	n/a	n/a	n/a	n/a	n/a	n/a
Houston, TX	2,983.4	3.9	20.1	116.2	204.2	631.7	1,770.7	236.6
Huntsville, AL	2,385.9	1.2	40.0	30.0	166.6	522.9	1,507.0	118.1
Indianapolis, IN	1,134.2	1.7	13.8	33.0	n/a	345.7	1,608.4	136.0
Jacksonville, FL	2,490.1	1.1	23.9	40.6	237.4	435.7	1,666.2	85.2
Kansas City, MO	2,890.6	3.3	30.6	45.4	156.6	469.2	1,926.0	259.5
Lafayette, LA	3,019.1	4.5	19.2	68.1	285.0	717.5	1,718.5	206.4
Las Vegas, NV	2,951.8	3.6	28.5	122.6	294.6	720.0	1,475.8	306.6
Lexington, KY	3,366.8	3.3	28.2	64.8	75.3	687.6	2,404.0	103.5
Lincoln, NE	1,550.7	0.0	21.7	4.3	63.1	269.7	1,148.3	43.5
Little Rock, AR	4,175.7	4.0	33.3	62.0	301.9	996.1	2,534.9	243.5
Los Angeles, CA	2,709.0	4.8	16.1	144.8	222.7	528.1	1,392.9	399.6
Louisville, KY	1,826.6	2.4	18.9	53.6	n/a	531.2	1,776.8	140.4
Lubbock, TX	2,175.1	6.4	44.5	3.2	184.4	518.3	1,279.9	138.3
Madison, WI	1,802.0	1.6	23.5	19.0	79.8	251.1	1,379.8	47.2
Manchester, NH	1,882.3	2.0	31.0	30.3	69.5	258.9	1,439.1	51.4
McAllen, TX	3,955.7	2.9	28.0	56.5	231.5	860.9	2,581.5	194.4
Miami, FL	4,571.9	7.1	32.4	187.8	328.8	675.8	3,049.9	290.1

Table continued on next page.

Suburbs[1]	All Crimes	Violent Crimes: Murder	Violent Crimes: Forcible Rape	Violent Crimes: Robbery	Violent Crimes: Aggrav. Assault	Property Crimes: Burglary	Property Crimes: Larceny -Theft	Property Crimes: Motor Vehicle Theft
Midland, TX	3,001.3	3.0	9.0	20.9	226.7	656.3	1,781.1	304.3
Minneapolis, MN	2,475.7	1.7	27.5	48.5	99.7	341.5	1,812.6	144.3
Nashville, TN	2,412.8	2.2	27.9	36.2	275.4	419.6	1,556.2	95.3
New Orleans, LA	3,183.0	9.2	16.8	77.4	233.8	539.4	2,145.6	160.9
New York, NY	1,772.8	2.0	7.7	86.8	115.7	287.2	1,182.9	90.5
Oklahoma City, OK	2,980.6	2.3	34.5	33.6	157.5	681.2	1,880.4	191.1
Omaha, NE	2,327.4	1.1	33.7	28.4	153.0	423.2	1,473.3	214.7
Orlando, FL	3,523.1	3.6	40.5	110.3	338.5	820.1	2,033.1	177.0
Oxnard, CA	1,928.3	3.0	11.8	43.7	94.8	350.4	1,293.6	131.0
Palm Bay, FL	3,558.1	3.8	57.4	95.7	389.6	724.9	2,157.8	128.9
Peoria, IL	1,874.2	2.3	23.0	21.5	149.1	401.0	1,238.0	39.3
Philadelphia, PA	2,740.7	5.5	32.4	143.4	309.1	356.8	1,774.1	119.4
Phoenix, AZ	-1,815.2	3.3	22.8	63.2	178.3	531.2	2,093.0	n/a
Pittsburgh, PA	1,872.0	2.5	14.1	49.7	160.4	316.4	1,270.5	58.4
Portland, OR	2,490.7	1.1	28.2	46.0	92.9	402.9	1,709.7	209.9
Providence, RI	2,398.8	2.0	41.1	65.1	194.3	487.6	1,460.8	148.0
Provo, UT	1,790.4	1.1	16.2	6.3	29.0	217.5	1,442.1	78.1
Raleigh, NC	1,979.2	2.7	9.6	27.5	84.4	489.1	1,292.3	73.6
Reno, NV	2,287.5	4.4	33.0	41.8	165.2	531.1	1,343.5	168.6
Richmond, VA	2,210.8	3.9	20.0	49.0	92.5	361.0	1,591.1	93.4
Roanoke, VA	1,616.7	3.3	25.3	14.5	90.4	223.1	1,192.1	67.9
Rochester, MN	997.4	0.0	14.8	2.0	69.0	280.9	590.3	40.4
Sacramento, CA	2,842.6	3.3	21.6	97.4	227.6	622.0	1,550.7	320.1
Salem, OR	2,682.3	2.9	22.0	31.6	114.7	440.0	1,868.4	202.7
Salt Lake City, UT	4,075.5	1.4	47.3	57.0	167.2	600.3	2,808.9	393.5
San Antonio, TX	2,511.9	3.8	25.9	27.3	127.9	510.2	1,687.4	129.5
San Diego, CA	2,392.3	1.7	19.0	86.1	209.6	410.1	1,389.7	276.2
San Francisco, CA	2,375.5	1.5	17.9	77.4	154.4	429.3	1,471.9	223.1
San Jose, CA	2,311.4	2.1	15.6	47.5	104.8	410.5	1,477.0	254.0
Santa Rosa, CA	1,841.3	1.9	26.0	42.4	313.6	360.7	969.4	127.4
Savannah, GA	2,349.7	4.6	14.5	65.5	149.3	555.2	1,450.2	110.4
Seattle, WA	3,691.4	1.6	30.0	69.3	96.2	729.1	2,310.5	454.7
Sioux Falls, SD	1,075.2	0.0	26.3	1.3	58.8	339.2	583.3	66.3
Spokane, WA	3,607.3	2.8	26.7	43.3	87.8	779.1	2,348.3	319.4
Springfield, IL	2,951.5	32.6	91.5	67.3	271.5	483.0	1,330.0	675.5
Tallahassee, FL	2,919.3	3.2	33.1	35.8	352.9	617.9	1,788.6	87.8
Tampa, FL	3,131.4	3.8	32.2	80.4	252.2	628.5	1,981.3	153.0
Topeka, KS	1,903.2	1.9	15.0	3.8	173.6	423.2	1,175.9	109.8
Tulsa, OK	2,054.8	0.7	33.9	17.5	148.5	442.7	1,256.7	154.7
Tyler, TX	2,198.5	2.6	11.9	22.2	158.7	642.7	1,218.8	141.7
Virginia Beach, VA	3,558.7	8.0	33.6	97.9	214.7	611.3	2,425.9	167.2
Washington, DC	2,188.1	2.6	19.2	93.8	117.5	261.4	1,525.3	168.3
Wichita, KS	2,436.9	2.8	35.1	12.4	171.5	491.4	1,605.3	118.5
Wilmington, NC	2,737.9	1.3	16.7	28.9	132.1	656.9	1,806.4	95.6
Winston-Salem, NC	2,696.6	1.9	14.9	44.0	178.8	805.8	1,540.8	110.3
Worcester, MA	1,888.6	0.7	36.6	31.8	207.5	368.2	1,170.2	73.5
U.S.	3,098.6	4.5	25.2	109.1	229.1	610.0	1,899.4	221.3

Note: Figures are crimes per 100,000 population in 2013 except where noted; n/a not available; (1) All areas within the metro area that are located outside the city limits; (2) 2012 data

Source: FBI Uniform Crime Reports, 2013

Crime Rate: Metro Area

Metro Area[1]	All Crimes	Violent Crimes				Property Crimes		
		Murder	Forcible Rape	Robbery	Aggrav. Assault	Burglary	Larceny -Theft	Motor Vehicle Theft
Albuquerque, NM	5,226.0	5.9	63.5	137.3	535.7	1,146.7	2,910.6	426.4
Anchorage, AK	4,941.6	4.8	133.2	167.9	488.0	444.4	3,408.6	294.7
Ann Arbor, MI	2,403.2	3.1	52.9	45.6	203.9	427.0	1,564.3	106.5
Athens, GA	3,351.4	1.0	26.3	67.9	176.8	701.0	2,239.7	138.8
Atlanta, GA	3,719.9	5.9	19.5	158.1	205.6	809.1	2,184.4	337.4
Austin, TX	3,449.8	2.8	23.3	53.3	192.0	534.0	2,485.7	158.7
Billings, MT	4,264.6	2.4	29.7	51.0	183.2	731.6	2,871.2	395.5
Boise City, ID	1,925.0	0.9	48.3	13.0	162.1	355.5	1,263.5	81.7
Boston, MA[2]	2,595.6	3.2	33.8	151.0	315.0	406.8	1,540.4	145.4
Boulder, CO	2,493.1	0.6	52.2	23.8	135.3	397.0	1,776.8	107.3
Cape Coral, FL	2,527.1	3.8	22.9	87.9	218.2	575.9	1,494.6	123.9
Cedar Rapids, IA	2,560.4	1.5	28.1	37.6	137.3	529.2	1,682.6	144.2
Charleston, SC	3,510.2	7.2	28.4	71.0	252.8	622.1	2,289.0	239.7
Charlotte, NC	3,385.4	5.2	23.0	114.4	261.8	685.4	2,141.0	154.6
Chicago, IL[2]	n/a	6.8	n/a	198.7	n/a	430.7	1,769.2	224.4
Clarksville, TN	2,883.5	5.0	47.7	58.8	257.8	653.6	1,761.0	99.7
Colorado Springs, CO	3,643.2	6.2	73.4	68.4	221.0	702.4	2,243.3	328.7
Columbia, MO	3,620.5	2.9	45.7	75.0	209.1	520.7	2,634.1	133.0
Columbus, OH	4,541.3	5.7	44.7	205.0	107.2	1,164.8	2,777.7	236.3
Dallas, TX[2]	3,209.0	4.7	29.4	132.8	151.1	686.1	1,916.5	288.4
Davenport, IA	2,864.5	1.8	37.8	64.4	257.4	516.9	1,886.4	99.8
Denver, CO	3,075.3	3.7	53.0	78.9	193.0	463.1	1,985.1	298.6
Des Moines, IA	3,032.5	2.3	26.7	41.4	197.4	592.9	1,972.2	199.5
Durham, NC[3]	3,867.3	5.2	21.2	139.9	261.0	1,095.0	2,154.6	190.3
El Paso, TX	2,523.7	1.4	28.0	58.9	258.9	280.7	1,781.6	114.1
Erie, PA	2,630.1	1.4	31.7	81.3	130.5	610.1	1,713.0	62.0
Eugene, OR	3,898.7	1.1	29.5	67.9	95.4	716.2	2,706.3	282.3
Fargo, ND	2,536.8	1.8	41.9	31.1	180.9	494.2	1,662.7	124.2
Fayetteville, NC	5,400.4	7.9	22.7	202.9	256.6	1,458.5	3,217.9	233.8
Fort Collins, CO	2,360.8	0.6	43.7	20.9	139.3	295.7	1,782.5	78.2
Fort Wayne, IN	3,195.4	8.0	29.2	117.7	111.3	693.0	2,114.5	121.7
Fort Worth, TX[2]	3,682.2	3.9	36.7	97.3	224.1	731.0	2,375.0	214.3
Gainesville, FL	3,502.5	3.7	42.5	88.0	407.7	572.2	2,253.0	135.3
Grand Rapids, MI	2,256.2	2.4	66.4	64.7	168.6	442.8	1,438.8	72.5
Green Bay, WI	2,018.4	0.6	24.3	33.6	147.4	327.4	1,430.4	54.7
Greensboro, NC	3,793.1	4.7	18.3	107.3	214.3	977.2	2,313.2	158.1
Honolulu, HI	n/a	n/a	n/a	n/a	n/a	n/a	n/a	n/a
Houston, TX	4,047.8	5.9	22.9	233.3	296.8	790.3	2,327.6	370.9
Huntsville, AL	3,839.4	6.2	43.0	107.2	327.0	734.2	2,391.9	229.7
Indianapolis, IN	3,468.6	7.6	41.5	213.8	n/a	885.4	2,249.6	333.7
Jacksonville, FL	3,724.4	7.1	41.9	118.2	328.5	678.6	2,403.5	146.7
Kansas City, MO	3,722.8	7.4	42.1	116.2	302.8	675.5	2,169.2	409.7
Lafayette, LA	4,006.3	5.0	17.8	107.5	330.9	799.3	2,530.4	215.2
Las Vegas, NV	3,694.8	5.7	42.2	232.8	397.3	916.5	1,693.2	407.0
Lexington, KY	3,979.7	4.9	37.8	119.3	94.6	779.8	2,735.2	208.0
Lincoln, NE	3,526.4	1.6	48.5	68.3	210.5	493.4	2,600.3	104.0
Little Rock, AR	5,567.3	7.7	40.7	175.6	451.6	1,248.9	3,316.4	326.4
Los Angeles, CA[2]	2,682.0	5.4	17.5	167.5	212.6	480.6	1,410.0	388.5
Louisville, KY	3,430.4	4.9	21.6	138.5	n/a	798.0	2,405.9	226.5
Lubbock, TX	4,905.4	3.0	38.6	129.7	486.8	975.5	2,961.7	310.2
Madison, WI	2,479.7	1.8	26.5	58.9	129.9	374.6	1,818.7	69.3
Manchester, NH	2,590.9	2.5	45.1	95.1	138.9	409.4	1,823.3	76.7
McAllen, TX	3,981.2	2.7	24.0	57.2	202.7	783.3	2,720.3	190.9
Miami, FL[2]	4,828.3	8.7	30.9	242.2	373.9	720.1	3,135.8	316.7

Table continued on next page.

Metro Area[1]	All Crimes	Violent Crimes: Murder	Forcible Rape	Robbery	Aggrav. Assault	Property Crimes: Burglary	Larceny -Theft	Motor Vehicle Theft
Midland, TX	2,918.9	3.9	16.0	44.9	215.7	505.8	1,961.8	170.8
Minneapolis, MN	2,868.9	2.5	35.5	96.7	139.2	435.5	1,986.2	173.3
Nashville, TN	3,314.2	3.4	42.8	115.3	434.6	588.3	2,000.6	129.2
New Orleans, LA	3,626.0	19.0	25.9	145.7	283.3	633.8	2,233.5	284.9
New York, NY[2]	2,093.6	3.2	11.0	170.6	271.2	234.3	1,314.1	89.3
Oklahoma City, OK	4,458.6	5.9	52.8	108.7	335.5	977.3	2,565.3	413.1
Omaha, NE	3,632.6	5.3	38.3	95.2	248.6	614.6	2,173.4	457.2
Orlando, FL	3,960.2	3.9	41.5	123.3	371.3	882.4	2,335.4	202.3
Oxnard, CA	2,144.6	4.0	10.1	72.2	107.4	381.8	1,390.5	178.4
Palm Bay, FL	3,321.0	3.6	50.3	85.4	385.5	681.4	1,989.5	125.3
Peoria, IL	2,668.8	5.8	22.3	87.2	226.9	573.8	1,674.6	78.3
Philadelphia, PA[2]	4,062.9	13.1	69.1	395.7	459.7	586.9	2,232.8	305.6
Phoenix, AZ	392.3	4.8	29.5	115.3	242.8	731.0	2,219.4	n/a
Pittsburgh, PA	2,149.4	4.1	15.5	83.7	189.5	367.2	1,412.4	76.9
Portland, OR	3,242.3	1.4	30.9	73.5	145.2	475.2	2,219.4	296.8
Providence, RI	2,697.8	2.5	42.6	80.6	212.6	547.1	1,621.0	191.4
Provo, UT	1,946.5	1.1	27.4	8.7	32.9	230.8	1,564.4	81.0
Raleigh, NC	2,502.6	2.7	12.7	67.8	136.0	576.6	1,600.9	105.8
Reno, NV	2,975.1	5.2	31.0	89.2	252.5	571.2	1,748.7	277.2
Richmond, VA	2,639.5	6.2	20.0	90.8	126.8	445.4	1,797.4	152.9
Roanoke, VA	2,682.4	5.1	31.5	55.6	146.1	354.6	1,985.1	104.4
Rochester, MN	1,792.2	0.0	30.8	26.5	85.3	338.2	1,243.2	68.2
Sacramento, CA	3,182.5	4.1	21.2	128.7	262.0	663.2	1,723.2	380.2
Salem, OR	3,448.8	3.5	25.1	53.6	151.4	511.9	2,416.5	286.8
Salt Lake City, UT	4,704.6	1.8	57.3	84.4	213.1	681.4	3,174.4	492.2
San Antonio, TX	4,874.8	4.6	39.1	107.0	308.9	849.6	3,226.3	339.3
San Diego, CA	2,540.5	2.2	20.8	95.3	230.3	435.7	1,404.6	351.6
San Francisco, CA[2]	4,626.3	3.7	18.7	302.4	240.8	578.0	3,006.2	476.5
San Jose, CA	2,613.9	3.0	21.6	80.1	145.1	467.9	1,359.9	536.3
Santa Rosa, CA	2,020.8	1.8	25.5	48.9	283.9	364.5	1,150.4	145.7
Savannah, GA	3,381.8	9.8	18.6	136.4	151.2	778.7	2,049.7	237.4
Seattle, WA[2]	4,264.0	1.9	28.6	110.9	145.3	826.2	2,646.5	504.6
Sioux Falls, SD	2,658.9	1.2	65.8	28.1	196.6	472.2	1,763.8	131.2
Spokane, WA	6,113.6	3.7	47.3	123.1	192.7	1,200.7	3,923.8	622.2
Springfield, IL	4,661.8	16.5	74.4	165.3	511.8	828.2	2,685.2	380.4
Tallahassee, FL	3,976.4	4.5	58.9	120.1	398.8	859.7	2,374.2	160.2
Tampa, FL	3,128.6	4.3	31.0	90.8	270.5	619.5	1,959.0	153.6
Topeka, KS	3,890.6	5.5	20.9	75.0	247.7	720.1	2,528.9	292.5
Tulsa, OK	3,794.1	6.7	58.8	113.8	337.5	879.0	2,058.3	340.0
Tyler, TX	3,254.1	3.7	26.2	36.4	212.2	726.5	2,089.8	159.3
Virginia Beach, VA	3,320.0	6.9	32.9	89.9	173.9	532.5	2,334.8	149.2
Washington, DC[2]	2,685.6	4.4	24.9	158.9	180.8	296.1	1,808.1	212.3
Wichita, KS	4,704.4	3.5	52.1	78.3	434.4	810.6	2,967.6	358.0
Wilmington, NC	3,936.0	3.4	24.4	111.7	222.6	1,000.1	2,392.5	181.4
Winston-Salem, NC	3,911.7	3.5	21.8	95.4	251.0	1,110.0	2,265.8	164.2
Worcester, MA	2,419.0	1.6	31.3	81.6	307.8	513.7	1,378.6	104.5
U.S.	3,098.6	4.5	25.2	109.1	229.1	610.0	1,899.4	221.3

Note: Figures are crimes per 100,000 population in 2013 except where noted; n/a not available; (1) Figures cover the Metropolitan Statistical Area except where noted; (2) Metropolitan Division (MD); (3) 2012 data

Source: FBI Uniform Crime Reports, 2013

Temperature & Precipitation: Yearly Averages and Extremes

City	Extreme Low (°F)	Average Low (°F)	Average Temp. (°F)	Average High (°F)	Extreme High (°F)	Average Precip. (in.)	Average Snow (in.)
Albuquerque, NM	-17	43	57	70	105	8.5	11
Anchorage, AK	-34	29	36	43	85	15.7	71
Ann Arbor, MI	-21	39	49	58	104	32.4	41
Athens, GA	-8	52	62	72	105	49.8	2
Atlanta, GA	-8	52	62	72	105	49.8	2
Austin, TX	-2	58	69	79	109	31.1	1
Billings, MT	-32	36	47	59	105	14.6	59
Boise City, ID	-25	39	51	63	111	11.8	22
Boston, MA	-12	44	52	59	102	42.9	41
Boulder, CO	-25	37	51	64	103	15.5	63
Cape Coral, FL	26	65	75	84	103	53.9	0
Cedar Rapids, IA	-34	36	47	57	105	34.4	33
Charleston, SC	6	55	66	76	104	52.1	1
Charlotte, NC	-5	50	61	71	104	42.8	6
Chicago, IL	-27	40	49	59	104	35.4	39
Clarksville, TN	-17	49	60	70	107	47.4	11
Colorado Springs, CO	-24	36	49	62	99	17.0	48
Columbia, MO	-20	44	54	64	111	40.6	25
Columbus, OH	-19	42	52	62	104	37.9	28
Dallas, TX	-2	56	67	77	112	33.9	3
Davenport, IA	-24	40	50	60	108	31.8	33
Denver, CO	-25	37	51	64	103	15.5	63
Des Moines, IA	-24	40	50	60	108	31.8	33
Durham, NC	-9	48	60	71	105	42.0	8
El Paso, TX	-8	50	64	78	114	8.6	6
Erie, PA	-18	41	49	57	100	40.5	83
Eugene, OR	-12	42	53	63	108	47.3	7
Fargo, ND	-36	31	41	52	106	19.6	40
Fayetteville, NC	-9	48	60	71	105	42.0	8
Fort Collins, CO	-25	37	51	64	103	15.5	63
Fort Wayne, IN	-22	40	50	60	106	35.9	33
Fort Worth, TX	-1	55	66	76	113	32.3	3
Gainesville, FL	10	58	69	79	102	50.9	Trace
Grand Rapids, MI	-22	38	48	57	102	34.7	73
Green Bay, WI	-31	34	44	54	99	28.3	46
Greensboro, NC	-8	47	58	69	103	42.5	10
Honolulu, HI	52	70	77	84	94	22.4	0
Houston, TX	7	58	69	79	107	46.9	Trace
Huntsville, AL	-11	50	61	71	104	56.8	4
Indianapolis, IN	-23	42	53	62	104	40.2	25
Jacksonville, FL	7	58	69	79	103	52.0	0
Kansas City, MO	-23	44	54	64	109	38.1	21
Lafayette, LA	8	57	68	78	103	58.5	Trace
Las Vegas, NV	8	53	67	80	116	4.0	1
Lexington, KY	-21	45	55	65	103	45.1	17
Lincoln, NE	-33	39	51	62	108	29.1	27
Little Rock, AR	-5	51	62	73	112	50.7	5
Los Angeles, CA	27	55	63	70	110	11.3	Trace
Louisville, KY	-20	46	57	67	105	43.9	17
Lubbock, TX	-16	47	60	74	110	18.4	10
Madison, WI	-37	35	46	57	104	31.1	42
Manchester, NH	-33	34	46	57	102	36.9	63
McAllen, TX	16	65	74	83	106	25.8	Trace
Miami, FL	30	69	76	83	98	57.1	0
Midland, TX	-11	50	64	77	116	14.6	4

Table continued on next page.

City	Extreme Low (°F)	Average Low (°F)	Average Temp. (°F)	Average High (°F)	Extreme High (°F)	Average Precip. (in.)	Average Snow (in.)
Minneapolis, MN	-34	35	45	54	105	27.1	52
Nashville, TN	-17	49	60	70	107	47.4	11
New Orleans, LA	11	59	69	78	102	60.6	Trace
New York, NY	-2	47	55	62	104	47.0	23
Oklahoma City, OK	-8	49	60	71	110	32.8	10
Omaha, NE	-23	40	51	62	110	30.1	29
Orlando, FL	19	62	72	82	100	47.7	Trace
Oxnard, CA	27	51	60	68	105	12.0	0
Palm Bay, FL	21	65	74	82	100	50.5	0
Peoria, IL	-26	41	51	61	113	35.4	23
Philadelphia, PA	-7	45	55	64	104	41.4	22
Phoenix, AZ	17	59	72	86	122	7.3	Trace
Pittsburgh, PA	-18	41	51	60	103	37.1	43
Portland, OR	-3	45	54	62	107	37.5	7
Providence, RI	-13	42	51	60	104	45.3	35
Provo, UT	-22	40	52	64	107	15.6	63
Raleigh, NC	-9	48	60	71	105	42.0	8
Reno, NV	-16	33	50	67	105	7.2	24
Richmond, VA	-8	48	58	69	105	43.0	13
Roanoke, VA	-11	46	57	67	105	40.8	23
Rochester, MN	-40	34	44	54	102	29.4	47
Sacramento, CA	18	48	61	73	115	17.3	Trace
Salem, OR	-12	41	52	63	108	40.2	7
Salt Lake City, UT	-22	40	52	64	107	15.6	63
San Antonio, TX	0	58	69	80	108	29.6	1
San Diego, CA	29	57	64	71	111	9.5	Trace
San Francisco, CA	24	49	57	65	106	19.3	Trace
San Jose, CA	21	50	59	68	105	13.5	Trace
Santa Rosa, CA	23	42	57	71	109	29.0	n/a
Savannah, GA	3	56	67	77	105	50.3	Trace
Seattle, WA	0	44	52	59	99	38.4	13
Sioux Falls, SD	-36	35	46	57	110	24.6	38
Spokane, WA	-25	37	47	57	108	17.0	51
Springfield, IL	-24	44	54	63	112	34.9	21
Tallahassee, FL	6	56	68	79	103	63.3	Trace
Tampa, FL	18	63	73	82	99	46.7	Trace
Topeka, KS	-26	43	55	66	110	34.4	21
Tulsa, OK	-8	50	61	71	112	38.9	10
Tyler, TX	-2	56	67	77	112	33.9	3
Virginia Beach, VA	-3	51	60	69	104	44.8	8
Washington, DC	-5	49	58	67	104	39.5	18
Wichita, KS	-21	45	57	68	113	29.3	17
Wilmington, NC	0	53	64	74	104	55.0	2
Winston-Salem, NC	-8	47	58	69	103	42.5	10
Worcester, MA	-13	38	47	56	99	47.6	62

Source: National Climatic Data Center, International Station Meteorological Climate Summary, 9/96

Weather Conditions

City	Temperature			Daytime Sky			Precipitation		
	10°F & below	32°F & below	90°F & above	Clear	Partly cloudy	Cloudy	0.01 inch or more precip.	1.0 inch or more snow/ice	Thunder-storms
Albuquerque, NM	4	114	65	140	161	64	60	9	38
Anchorage, AK	n/a	194	n/a	50	115	200	113	49	2
Ann Arbor, MI	n/a	136	12	74	134	157	135	38	32
Athens, GA	1	49	38	98	147	120	116	3	48
Atlanta, GA	1	49	38	98	147	120	116	3	48
Austin, TX	< 1	20	111	105	148	112	83	1	41
Billings, MT	n/a	149	29	75	163	127	97	41	27
Boise City, ID	n/a	124	45	106	133	126	91	22	14
Boston, MA	n/a	97	12	88	127	150	253	48	18
Boulder, CO	24	155	33	99	177	89	90	38	39
Cape Coral, FL	n/a	n/a	115	93	220	52	110	0	92
Cedar Rapids, IA	n/a	156	16	89	132	144	109	28	42
Charleston, SC	< 1	33	53	89	162	114	114	1	59
Charlotte, NC	1	65	44	98	142	125	113	3	41
Chicago, IL	n/a	132	17	83	136	146	125	31	38
Clarksville, TN	5	76	51	98	135	132	119	8	54
Colorado Springs, CO	21	161	18	108	157	100	98	33	49
Columbia, MO	17	108	36	99	127	139	110	17	52
Columbus, OH	n/a	118	19	72	137	156	136	29	40
Dallas, TX	1	34	102	108	160	97	78	2	49
Davenport, IA	n/a	137	26	99	129	137	106	25	46
Denver, CO	24	155	33	99	177	89	90	38	39
Des Moines, IA	n/a	137	26	99	129	137	106	25	46
Durham, NC	n/a	n/a	39	98	143	124	110	3	42
El Paso, TX	1	59	106	147	164	54	49	3	35
Erie, PA	n/a	124	3	57	128	180	165	55	36
Eugene, OR	n/a	n/a	15	75	115	175	136	4	3
Fargo, ND	n/a	180	15	81	145	139	100	38	31
Fayetteville, NC	n/a	n/a	39	98	143	124	110	3	42
Fort Collins, CO	24	155	33	99	177	89	90	38	39
Fort Wayne, IN	n/a	131	16	75	140	150	131	31	39
Fort Worth, TX	1	40	100	123	136	106	79	3	47
Gainesville, FL	n/a	n/a	77	88	196	81	119	0	78
Grand Rapids, MI	n/a	146	11	67	119	179	142	57	34
Green Bay, WI	n/a	163	7	86	125	154	120	40	33
Greensboro, NC	3	85	32	94	143	128	113	5	43
Honolulu, HI	n/a	n/a	23	25	286	54	98	0	7
Houston, TX	n/a	n/a	96	83	168	114	101	1	62
Huntsville, AL	2	66	49	70	118	177	116	2	54
Indianapolis, IN	19	119	19	83	128	154	127	24	43
Jacksonville, FL	< 1	16	83	86	181	98	114	0	65
Kansas City, MO	22	110	39	112	134	119	103	17	51
Lafayette, LA	< 1	21	86	99	150	116	113	< 1	73
Las Vegas, NV	< 1	37	134	185	132	48	27	2	13
Lexington, KY	11	96	22	86	136	143	129	17	44
Lincoln, NE	n/a	145	40	108	135	122	94	19	46
Little Rock, AR	1	57	73	110	142	113	104	4	57
Los Angeles, CA	0	< 1	5	131	125	109	34	0	1
Louisville, KY	8	90	35	82	143	140	125	15	45
Lubbock, TX	5	93	79	134	150	81	62	8	48
Madison, WI	n/a	161	14	88	119	158	118	38	40
Manchester, NH	n/a	171	12	87	131	147	125	32	19
McAllen, TX	n/a	n/a	116	86	180	99	72	0	27
Miami, FL	n/a	n/a	55	48	263	54	128	0	74

Table continued on next page.

City	Temperature			Daytime Sky			Precipitation		
	10°F & below	32°F & below	90°F & above	Clear	Partly cloudy	Cloudy	0.01 inch or more precip.	1.0 inch or more snow/ice	Thunder-storms
Midland, TX	1	62	102	144	138	83	52	3	38
Minneapolis, MN	n/a	156	16	93	125	147	113	41	37
Nashville, TN	5	76	51	98	135	132	119	8	54
New Orleans, LA	0	13	70	90	169	106	114	1	69
New York, NY	n/a	n/a	18	85	166	114	120	11	20
Oklahoma City, OK	5	79	70	124	131	110	80	8	50
Omaha, NE	n/a	139	35	100	142	123	97	20	46
Orlando, FL	n/a	n/a	90	76	208	81	115	0	80
Oxnard, CA	0	1	2	114	155	96	34	< 1	1
Palm Bay, FL	n/a	n/a	59	75	228	62	124	0	73
Peoria, IL	n/a	127	27	89	127	149	115	22	49
Philadelphia, PA	5	94	23	81	146	138	117	14	27
Phoenix, AZ	0	10	167	186	125	54	37	< 1	23
Pittsburgh, PA	n/a	121	8	62	137	166	154	42	35
Portland, OR	n/a	37	11	67	116	182	152	4	7
Providence, RI	n/a	117	9	85	134	146	123	21	21
Provo, UT	n/a	128	56	94	152	119	92	38	38
Raleigh, NC	n/a	n/a	39	98	143	124	110	3	42
Reno, NV	14	178	50	143	139	83	50	17	14
Richmond, VA	3	79	41	90	147	128	115	7	43
Roanoke, VA	4	89	31	90	152	123	119	11	35
Rochester, MN	n/a	165	9	87	126	152	114	40	41
Sacramento, CA	0	21	73	175	111	79	58	< 1	2
Salem, OR	n/a	66	16	78	119	168	146	6	5
Salt Lake City, UT	n/a	128	56	94	152	119	92	38	38
San Antonio, TX	n/a	n/a	112	97	153	115	81	1	36
San Diego, CA	0	< 1	4	115	126	124	40	0	5
San Francisco, CA	0	6	4	136	130	99	63	< 1	5
San Jose, CA	0	5	5	106	180	79	57	< 1	6
Santa Rosa, CA	n/a	43	30	n/a	365	n/a	n/a	n/a	2
Savannah, GA	< 1	29	70	97	155	113	111	< 1	63
Seattle, WA	n/a	38	3	57	121	187	157	8	8
Sioux Falls, SD	n/a	n/a	n/a	95	136	134	n/a	n/a	n/a
Spokane, WA	n/a	140	18	78	135	152	113	37	11
Springfield, IL	19	111	34	96	126	143	111	18	49
Tallahassee, FL	< 1	31	86	93	175	97	114	1	83
Tampa, FL	n/a	n/a	85	81	204	80	107	< 1	87
Topeka, KS	20	123	45	110	128	127	96	15	54
Tulsa, OK	6	78	74	117	141	107	88	8	50
Tyler, TX	1	34	102	108	160	97	78	2	49
Virginia Beach, VA	< 1	53	33	89	149	127	115	5	38
Washington, DC	2	71	34	84	144	137	112	9	30
Wichita, KS	13	110	63	117	132	116	87	13	54
Wilmington, NC	< 1	42	46	96	150	119	115	1	47
Winston-Salem, NC	3	85	32	94	143	128	113	5	43
Worcester, MA	n/a	141	4	81	144	140	131	32	23

Note: Figures are average number of days per year
Source: National Climatic Data Center, International Station Meteorological Climate Summary, 9/96

Air Quality Index

MSA[1] (Days[2])	Percent of Days when Air Quality was...					AQI Statistics	
	Good	Moderate	Unhealthy for Sensitive Groups	Unhealthy	Very Unhealthy	Maximum	Median
Albuquerque, NM (365)	64.1	35.3	0.5	0.0	0.0	105	47
Anchorage, AK (365)	67.4	29.0	2.7	0.5	0.3	231	34
Ann Arbor, MI (365)	71.0	28.8	0.3	0.0	0.0	106	41
Athens, GA (358)	70.1	29.9	0.0	0.0	0.0	92	41
Atlanta, GA (365)	38.4	58.9	2.5	0.0	0.3	214	54
Austin, TX (365)	71.8	28.2	0.0	0.0	0.0	93	42
Billings, MT (365)	81.4	16.4	2.2	0.0	0.0	125	27
Boise City, ID (365)	87.9	11.8	0.0	0.3	0.0	156	37
Boston, MA (365)	58.1	41.9	0.0	0.0	0.0	97	47
Boulder, CO (362)	84.3	15.2	0.6	0.0	0.0	126	41
Cape Coral, FL (365)	88.5	11.5	0.0	0.0	0.0	81	35
Cedar Rapids, IA (365)	61.6	35.3	3.0	0.0	0.0	149	44
Charleston, SC (365)	80.8	19.2	0.0	0.0	0.0	74	39
Charlotte, NC (365)	69.3	30.7	0.0	0.0	0.0	100	45
Chicago, IL (365)	16.4	79.2	4.1	0.3	0.0	155	62
Clarksville, TN (365)	75.1	24.9	0.0	0.0	0.0	87	42
Colorado Springs, CO (365)	84.9	14.8	0.3	0.0	0.0	104	42
Columbia, MO (214)	96.3	3.7	0.0	0.0	0.0	71	35
Columbus, OH (365)	62.2	37.5	0.3	0.0	0.0	102	45
Dallas, TX (365)	53.2	43.0	3.8	0.0	0.0	132	49
Davenport, IA (365)	33.2	65.8	1.1	0.0	0.0	111	56
Denver, CO (365)	45.2	51.8	2.7	0.3	0.0	152	51
Des Moines, IA (365)	79.7	20.3	0.0	0.0	0.0	91	37
Durham, NC (365)	86.0	14.0	0.0	0.0	0.0	84	37
El Paso, TX (365)	55.3	43.6	0.8	0.3	0.0	158	48
Erie, PA (359)	65.5	34.5	0.0	0.0	0.0	99	43
Eugene, OR (365)	69.6	25.8	4.7	0.0	0.0	135	39
Fargo, ND (365)	89.9	9.9	0.3	0.0	0.0	113	33
Fayetteville, NC (314)	78.0	22.0	0.0	0.0	0.0	80	41
Fort Collins, CO (365)	74.2	24.7	1.1	0.0	0.0	116	45
Fort Wayne, IN (365)	52.6	45.8	1.6	0.0	0.0	147	49
Fort Worth, TX (365)	53.2	43.0	3.8	0.0	0.0	132	49
Gainesville, FL (364)	93.4	6.6	0.0	0.0	0.0	64	33
Grand Rapids, MI (365)	71.2	28.5	0.3	0.0	0.0	121	40
Green Bay, WI (365)	68.8	29.0	2.2	0.0	0.0	114	40
Greensboro, NC (363)	79.3	20.7	0.0	0.0	0.0	87	42
Honolulu, HI (360)	97.5	2.2	0.0	0.3	0.0	195	27
Houston, TX (365)	43.6	54.5	1.9	0.0	0.0	150	53
Huntsville, AL (338)	88.8	11.2	0.0	0.0	0.0	87	36
Indianapolis, IN (365)	35.3	56.4	7.9	0.3	0.0	191	58
Jacksonville, FL (365)	70.1	29.0	0.8	0.0	0.0	106	43
Kansas City, MO (365)	26.6	58.9	14.5	0.0	0.0	150	61
Lafayette, LA (364)	62.9	37.1	0.0	0.0	0.0	96	44.5
Las Vegas, NV (365)	46.3	51.8	1.6	0.3	0.0	158	51
Lexington, KY (365)	80.8	19.2	0.0	0.0	0.0	83	40
Lincoln, NE (265)	90.2	9.4	0.4	0.0	0.0	109	34
Little Rock, AR (365)	63.8	35.9	0.3	0.0	0.0	108	43
Los Angeles, CA (365)	6.8	69.0	20.8	3.3	0.0	187	76
Louisville, KY (365)	30.1	61.9	7.9	0.0	0.0	145	56
Lubbock, TX (265)	87.5	12.5	0.0	0.0	0.0	100	28
Madison, WI (365)	72.6	27.1	0.3	0.0	0.0	112	40
Manchester, NH (365)	92.3	7.4	0.3	0.0	0.0	109	36
McAllen, TX (365)	75.3	24.7	0.0	0.0	0.0	88	37
Miami, FL (365)	74.0	25.2	0.8	0.0	0.0	123	43

Table continued on next page.

MSA[1] (Days[2])	Percent of Days when Air Quality was...					AQI Statistics	
	Good	Moderate	Unhealthy for Sensitive Groups	Unhealthy	Very Unhealthy	Maximum	Median
Midland, TX (n/a)	n/a	n/a	n/a	n/a	n/a	n/a	n/a
Minneapolis, MN (365)	60.0	39.5	0.5	0.0	0.0	130	46
Nashville, TN (365)	61.1	38.4	0.5	0.0	0.0	119	45
New Orleans, LA (365)	53.2	43.8	3.0	0.0	0.0	132	48
New York, NY (365)	38.9	58.1	2.7	0.3	0.0	161	54
Oklahoma City, OK (365)	66.0	34.0	0.0	0.0	0.0	100	45
Omaha, NE (365)	61.4	37.8	0.8	0.0	0.0	114	44
Orlando, FL (365)	85.5	14.2	0.3	0.0	0.0	106	38
Oxnard, CA (365)	49.0	49.0	1.9	0.0	0.0	124	51
Palm Bay, FL (365)	89.3	10.7	0.0	0.0	0.0	77	36
Peoria, IL (365)	62.7	29.6	6.6	1.1	0.0	185	43
Philadelphia, PA (365)	25.2	70.7	3.6	0.5	0.0	152	57
Phoenix, AZ (365)	8.5	66.0	20.3	3.6	1.6	825	77
Pittsburgh, PA (365)	29.6	65.5	4.7	0.3	0.0	155	58
Portland, OR (365)	77.3	20.5	1.9	0.3	0.0	153	36
Providence, RI (365)	74.0	25.8	0.3	0.0	0.0	121	42
Provo, UT (365)	74.5	23.6	1.9	0.0	0.0	120	42
Raleigh, NC (365)	70.4	29.6	0.0	0.0	0.0	84	42
Reno, NV (365)	60.0	36.7	1.1	0.8	1.4	891	47
Richmond, VA (365)	79.7	20.0	0.3	0.0	0.0	104	41
Roanoke, VA (365)	82.5	17.3	0.3	0.0	0.0	108	38
Rochester, MN (365)	85.5	14.2	0.3	0.0	0.0	103	35
Sacramento, CA (365)	46.8	43.6	8.8	0.5	0.3	240	53
Salem, OR (365)	87.4	12.3	0.0	0.3	0.0	154	29
Salt Lake City, UT (365)	77.0	18.4	4.1	0.5	0.0	154	42
San Antonio, TX (365)	60.0	39.2	0.8	0.0	0.0	125	46
San Diego, CA (365)	29.9	65.2	4.7	0.3	0.0	165	58
San Francisco, CA (365)	56.4	41.6	1.9	0.0	0.0	119	48
San Jose, CA (365)	73.7	24.9	1.1	0.3	0.0	154	41
Santa Rosa, CA (365)	87.9	12.1	0.0	0.0	0.0	81	35
Savannah, GA (365)	69.9	29.6	0.5	0.0	0.0	114	43
Seattle, WA (365)	66.0	32.3	1.6	0.0	0.0	133	43
Sioux Falls, SD (363)	83.5	16.3	0.3	0.0	0.0	104	36
Spokane, WA (365)	80.0	19.5	0.5	0.0	0.0	105	35
Springfield, IL (365)	93.4	6.6	0.0	0.0	0.0	78	31
Tallahassee, FL (365)	69.6	30.1	0.0	0.3	0.0	157	42
Tampa, FL (365)	64.1	35.6	0.3	0.0	0.0	112	45
Topeka, KS (365)	89.9	9.9	0.3	0.0	0.0	105	35
Tulsa, OK (365)	65.8	34.2	0.0	0.0	0.0	97	43
Tyler, TX (365)	96.2	3.8	0.0	0.0	0.0	84	31
Virginia Beach, VA (365)	77.8	22.2	0.0	0.0	0.0	87	40
Washington, DC (365)	57.5	41.4	1.1	0.0	0.0	129	48
Wichita, KS (365)	80.8	18.4	0.8	0.0	0.0	140	39
Wilmington, NC (365)	86.6	13.4	0.0	0.0	0.0	77	36
Winston-Salem, NC (365)	70.1	29.9	0.0	0.0	0.0	91	44
Worcester, MA (365)	83.0	17.0	0.0	0.0	0.0	100	36

Note: The Air Quality Index (AQI) is an index for reporting daily air quality. EPA calculates the AQI for five major air pollutants regulated by the Clean Air Act: ground-level ozone, particle pollution (also known as particulate matter), carbon monoxide, sulfur dioxide, and nitrogen dioxide. The AQI runs from 0 to 500. The higher the AQI value, the greater the level of air pollution and the greater the health concern. There are six AQI categories: "Good" The AQI is between 0 and 50. Air quality is considered satisfactory; "Moderate" The AQI is between 51 and 100. Air quality is acceptable; "Unhealthy for Sensitive Groups" When AQI values are between 101 and 150, members of sensitive groups may experience health effects; "Unhealthy" When AQI values are between 151 and 200 everyone may begin to experience health effects; "Very Unhealthy" AQI values between 201 and 300 trigger a health alert; "Hazardous" AQI values over 300 trigger health warnings of emergency conditions; Data covers the entire county unless noted otherwise; (1) Data covers the Metropolitan Statistical Area—see Appendix B for areas included; (2) Number of days with AQI data in 2014

Source: U.S. Environmental Protection Agency, Air Quality Index Report, 2014

Air Quality Index Pollutants

MSA[1] (Days[2])	Percent of Days when AQI Pollutant was...					
	Carbon Monoxide	Nitrogen Dioxide	Ozone	Sulfur Dioxide	Particulate Matter 2.5	Particulate Matter 10
Albuquerque, NM (365)	0.0	1.1	57.3	0.8	20.0	20.8
Anchorage, AK (365)	0.3	0.0	14.8	0.0	55.1	29.9
Ann Arbor, MI (365)	0.0	0.0	38.1	0.0	61.9	0.0
Athens, GA (358)	0.0	0.0	21.8	0.0	78.2	0.0
Atlanta, GA (365)	0.0	1.1	22.2	0.0	76.7	0.0
Austin, TX (365)	0.0	3.6	40.3	0.0	55.9	0.3
Billings, MT (365)	0.0	0.0	0.0	43.8	56.2	0.0
Boise City, ID (365)	0.3	18.4	63.0	0.0	10.4	7.9
Boston, MA (365)	0.0	4.4	21.9	0.8	72.3	0.5
Boulder, CO (362)	0.0	0.0	92.0	0.0	7.7	0.3
Cape Coral, FL (365)	0.0	0.0	55.9	0.0	42.7	1.4
Cedar Rapids, IA (365)	0.0	0.0	23.0	15.9	60.3	0.8
Charleston, SC (365)	0.0	0.8	23.3	0.3	75.6	0.0
Charlotte, NC (365)	0.0	2.2	40.0	0.0	57.8	0.0
Chicago, IL (365)	0.0	3.3	7.4	2.5	81.1	5.8
Clarksville, TN (365)	0.0	0.0	48.2	2.2	49.6	0.0
Colorado Springs, CO (365)	0.0	0.0	86.6	11.2	2.2	0.0
Columbia, MO (214)	0.0	0.0	100.0	0.0	0.0	0.0
Columbus, OH (365)	0.0	4.9	26.0	0.3	68.5	0.3
Dallas, TX (365)	0.0	6.8	41.9	0.3	50.1	0.8
Davenport, IA (365)	0.0	0.0	6.6	0.0	64.1	29.3
Denver, CO (365)	0.0	26.8	46.3	0.3	23.3	3.3
Des Moines, IA (365)	0.0	7.4	28.8	0.0	63.0	0.8
Durham, NC (365)	0.0	0.0	50.7	0.5	48.8	0.0
El Paso, TX (365)	0.0	9.9	32.1	0.0	55.3	2.7
Erie, PA (359)	0.0	0.3	33.4	0.0	66.0	0.3
Eugene, OR (365)	0.0	0.0	26.0	0.0	74.0	0.0
Fargo, ND (365)	0.0	2.2	59.7	0.0	32.1	6.0
Fayetteville, NC (314)	0.0	0.0	40.8	0.0	59.2	0.0
Fort Collins, CO (365)	0.0	0.0	95.1	0.0	4.1	0.8
Fort Wayne, IN (365)	0.0	0.8	13.4	0.5	85.2	0.0
Fort Worth, TX (365)	0.0	6.8	41.9	0.3	50.1	0.8
Gainesville, FL (364)	0.0	0.0	51.4	0.0	48.6	0.0
Grand Rapids, MI (365)	0.0	0.0	31.8	0.0	68.2	0.0
Green Bay, WI (365)	0.0	0.0	34.5	12.1	53.4	0.0
Greensboro, NC (363)	0.0	0.0	40.5	2.8	56.7	0.0
Honolulu, HI (360)	0.0	0.3	52.5	1.7	38.9	6.7
Houston, TX (365)	0.0	5.8	22.2	0.8	65.8	5.5
Huntsville, AL (338)	0.0	0.0	60.7	0.0	22.8	16.6
Indianapolis, IN (365)	0.0	1.4	12.3	23.8	62.2	0.3
Jacksonville, FL (365)	0.0	1.1	32.9	7.9	58.1	0.0
Kansas City, MO (365)	0.0	2.2	14.0	26.8	54.8	2.2
Lafayette, LA (364)	0.0	0.0	22.8	0.0	76.9	0.3
Las Vegas, NV (365)	0.0	1.4	58.1	0.0	37.3	3.3
Lexington, KY (365)	0.0	12.3	39.7	0.0	47.9	0.0
Lincoln, NE (265)	0.0	0.0	67.5	0.0	32.5	0.0
Little Rock, AR (365)	0.0	3.0	27.1	0.0	69.9	0.0
Los Angeles, CA (365)	1.1	4.9	33.7	0.0	58.9	1.4
Louisville, KY (365)	0.0	0.8	9.0	17.8	72.3	0.0
Lubbock, TX (265)	0.0	0.0	0.0	0.0	100.0	0.0
Madison, WI (365)	0.0	0.0	37.8	0.0	61.9	0.3
Manchester, NH (365)	0.0	0.0	82.7	0.0	17.3	0.0
McAllen, TX (365)	0.0	0.0	27.7	0.0	71.5	0.8
Miami, FL (365)	0.0	2.7	26.3	0.0	71.0	0.0

Table continued on next page.

MSA[1] (Days[2])	Percent of Days when AQI Pollutant was...					
	Carbon Monoxide	Nitrogen Dioxide	Ozone	Sulfur Dioxide	Particulate Matter 2.5	Particulate Matter 10
Midland, TX (n/a)	n/a	n/a	n/a	n/a	n/a	n/a
Minneapolis, MN (365)	0.0	2.2	22.5	0.8	72.6	1.9
Nashville, TN (365)	0.0	5.5	23.0	0.3	71.2	0.0
New Orleans, LA (365)	0.0	1.4	28.8	10.4	59.5	0.0
New York, NY (365)	0.0	20.8	23.0	0.3	55.9	0.0
Oklahoma City, OK (365)	0.0	6.3	49.9	0.0	42.2	1.6
Omaha, NE (365)	0.0	0.0	30.4	4.9	45.2	19.5
Orlando, FL (365)	0.0	0.5	56.4	0.0	43.0	0.0
Oxnard, CA (365)	0.0	0.3	48.8	0.0	49.0	1.9
Palm Bay, FL (365)	0.0	0.0	62.5	0.0	37.5	0.0
Peoria, IL (365)	0.0	0.0	33.7	20.3	46.0	0.0
Philadelphia, PA (365)	0.0	0.8	18.4	0.3	80.5	0.0
Phoenix, AZ (365)	0.0	1.6	19.7	0.0	20.5	58.1
Pittsburgh, PA (365)	0.0	0.3	10.4	10.4	78.9	0.0
Portland, OR (365)	0.0	1.6	41.6	0.0	56.7	0.0
Providence, RI (365)	0.0	9.3	38.6	0.0	51.5	0.5
Provo, UT (365)	0.0	19.2	59.7	0.0	18.9	2.2
Raleigh, NC (365)	0.0	5.2	40.3	0.0	54.5	0.0
Reno, NV (365)	0.0	3.8	59.5	0.0	26.0	10.7
Richmond, VA (365)	0.0	8.5	48.5	1.4	41.6	0.0
Roanoke, VA (365)	0.3	2.7	30.4	0.0	66.6	0.0
Rochester, MN (365)	0.0	0.0	49.9	0.8	49.3	0.0
Sacramento, CA (365)	0.0	0.3	65.5	0.0	33.4	0.8
Salem, OR (365)	0.0	0.0	35.3	0.0	64.7	0.0
Salt Lake City, UT (365)	0.0	16.7	60.8	0.0	21.4	1.1
San Antonio, TX (365)	0.0	4.1	37.5	0.0	58.1	0.3
San Diego, CA (365)	0.0	5.8	41.6	0.0	48.2	4.4
San Francisco, CA (365)	0.0	5.2	18.6	0.0	76.2	0.0
San Jose, CA (365)	0.0	3.0	61.9	0.0	34.5	0.5
Santa Rosa, CA (365)	0.0	0.0	54.0	0.0	45.2	0.8
Savannah, GA (365)	0.0	0.0	9.9	25.5	64.7	0.0
Seattle, WA (365)	0.0	18.9	36.2	0.0	44.9	0.0
Sioux Falls, SD (363)	0.0	0.6	60.3	0.0	34.7	4.4
Spokane, WA (365)	0.8	0.0	24.1	0.0	60.8	14.2
Springfield, IL (365)	0.0	0.0	86.0	2.7	11.2	0.0
Tallahassee, FL (365)	0.0	0.0	23.8	0.0	76.2	0.0
Tampa, FL (365)	0.0	0.5	35.9	5.8	57.8	0.0
Topeka, KS (365)	0.0	0.0	79.2	0.0	14.8	6.0
Tulsa, OK (365)	0.0	0.5	45.8	0.3	52.9	0.5
Tyler, TX (365)	0.0	0.5	99.5	0.0	0.0	0.0
Virginia Beach, VA (365)	0.0	5.2	42.2	4.7	47.9	0.0
Washington, DC (365)	0.0	5.8	37.3	0.0	57.0	0.0
Wichita, KS (365)	0.0	6.3	66.8	0.0	14.8	12.1
Wilmington, NC (365)	0.0	0.0	45.8	5.5	48.8	0.0
Winston-Salem, NC (365)	0.0	3.0	33.7	0.0	63.3	0.0
Worcester, MA (365)	0.0	5.8	58.9	0.0	34.2	1.1

Note: The Air Quality Index (AQI) is an index for reporting daily air quality. EPA calculates the AQI for five major air pollutants regulated by the Clean Air Act: ground-level ozone, particle pollution (also known as particulate matter), carbon monoxide, sulfur dioxide, and nitrogen dioxide. The AQI runs from 0 to 500. The higher the AQI value, the greater the level of air pollution and the greater the health concern; (1) Data covers the Metropolitan Statistical Area—see Appendix B for areas included; (2) Number of days with AQI data in 2014
Source: U.S. Environmental Protection Agency, Air Quality Index Report, 2014

Air Quality Trends: Ozone

MSA[1]	2004	2005	2006	2007	2008	2009	2010	2011	2012	2013
Albuquerque, NM	0.071	0.074	0.071	0.070	0.066	0.065	0.066	0.070	0.070	0.068
Anchorage, AK	n/a	n/a	n/a	n/a	n/a	n/a	n/a	n/a	n/a	n/a
Ann Arbor, MI	0.071	0.083	0.076	0.077	0.069	0.065	0.066	0.077	0.085	0.065
Athens, GA	0.078	0.082	0.086	0.083	0.077	0.067	0.073	0.075	0.071	0.060
Atlanta, GA	0.081	0.085	0.092	0.091	0.080	0.072	0.074	0.078	0.077	0.065
Austin, TX	0.081	0.081	0.083	0.073	0.072	0.073	0.072	0.074	0.075	0.070
Billings, MT	n/a	n/a	n/a	n/a	n/a	n/a	n/a	n/a	n/a	n/a
Boise City, ID	n/a	n/a	n/a	n/a	n/a	n/a	n/a	n/a	n/a	n/a
Boston, MA	0.075	0.082	0.077	0.081	0.072	0.070	0.069	0.066	0.068	0.067
Boulder, CO	0.068	0.076	0.082	0.085	0.076	0.073	0.072	0.076	0.076	0.079
Cape Coral, FL	0.072	0.070	0.070	0.069	0.068	0.062	0.064	0.062	0.063	0.065
Cedar Rapids, IA	0.063	0.073	0.065	0.076	0.063	0.061	0.064	0.064	0.071	0.060
Charleston, SC	0.072	0.073	0.071	0.065	0.069	0.059	0.067	0.066	0.063	0.059
Charlotte, NC	0.078	0.085	0.084	0.088	0.081	0.067	0.076	0.078	0.076	0.064
Chicago, IL	0.067	0.083	0.069	0.079	0.064	0.065	0.069	0.071	0.081	0.067
Clarksville, TN	n/a	n/a	n/a	n/a	n/a	n/a	n/a	n/a	n/a	n/a
Colorado Springs, CO	0.070	0.077	0.072	0.072	0.070	0.060	0.068	0.074	0.075	0.074
Columbia, MO	n/a	n/a	n/a	n/a	n/a	n/a	n/a	n/a	n/a	n/a
Columbus, OH	0.075	0.085	0.077	0.081	0.073	0.070	0.074	0.078	0.079	0.068
Dallas, TX	0.087	0.093	0.089	0.081	0.077	0.080	0.076	0.085	0.083	0.078
Davenport, IA	0.064	0.071	0.065	0.072	0.061	0.061	0.061	0.059	0.069	0.066
Denver, CO	0.068	0.075	0.080	0.079	0.075	0.070	0.072	0.078	0.080	0.080
Des Moines, IA	0.051	0.072	0.064	0.069	0.059	0.061	0.064	0.063	0.070	0.059
Durham, NC	0.072	0.079	0.073	0.077	0.075	0.064	0.072	0.070	0.068	0.058
El Paso, TX	0.074	0.077	0.077	0.074	0.074	0.068	0.068	0.069	0.067	0.066
Erie, PA	0.074	0.086	0.077	0.084	0.074	0.069	0.075	0.072	0.082	0.068
Eugene, OR	0.066	0.068	0.073	0.060	0.059	0.065	0.058	0.059	0.061	0.055
Fargo, ND	0.056	0.061	0.065	0.055	0.055	0.057	0.063	0.057	0.063	0.059
Fayetteville, NC	0.075	0.088	0.073	0.081	0.075	0.066	0.072	0.075	0.069	0.062
Fort Collins, CO	0.069	0.076	0.077	0.074	0.071	0.066	0.072	0.073	0.077	0.074
Fort Wayne, IN	0.071	0.081	0.072	0.079	0.068	0.065	0.067	0.071	0.076	0.062
Fort Worth, TX	0.087	0.093	0.089	0.081	0.077	0.080	0.076	0.085	0.083	0.078
Gainesville, FL	0.075	0.073	0.075	0.078	0.069	0.056	0.069	0.064	0.064	0.062
Grand Rapids, MI	0.070	0.083	0.082	0.085	0.068	0.069	0.068	0.076	0.080	0.068
Green Bay, WI	0.072	0.084	0.072	0.084	0.064	0.068	0.072	0.068	0.083	0.067
Greensboro, NC	0.074	0.078	0.075	0.082	0.084	0.068	0.074	0.071	0.076	0.062
Honolulu, HI	0.046	0.042	0.040	0.033	0.041	0.048	0.047	0.046	0.043	0.047
Houston, TX	0.092	0.087	0.090	0.079	0.074	0.079	0.078	0.082	0.081	0.074
Huntsville, AL	0.077	0.075	0.079	0.082	0.073	0.066	0.071	0.072	0.076	0.064
Indianapolis, IN	0.071	0.080	0.076	0.081	0.070	0.070	0.068	0.071	0.075	0.063
Jacksonville, FL	0.074	0.072	0.074	0.073	0.069	0.061	0.067	0.066	0.060	0.057
Kansas City, MO	0.066	0.082	0.085	0.076	0.067	0.068	0.068	0.074	0.082	0.066
Lafayette, LA	n/a	n/a	n/a	n/a	n/a	n/a	n/a	n/a	n/a	n/a
Las Vegas, NV	0.078	0.082	0.081	0.081	0.074	0.072	0.071	0.074	0.077	0.073
Lexington, KY	0.064	0.078	0.070	0.079	0.070	0.064	0.070	0.074	0.078	0.061
Lincoln, NE	0.056	0.056	0.056	0.054	0.051	0.053	0.050	0.053	0.058	0.055
Little Rock, AR	0.073	0.083	0.083	0.081	0.068	0.072	0.072	0.078	0.078	0.067
Los Angeles, CA	0.088	0.083	0.088	0.084	0.088	0.085	0.073	0.077	0.078	0.074
Louisville, KY	0.071	0.083	0.076	0.083	0.074	0.068	0.075	0.081	0.085	0.065
Lubbock, TX	n/a	n/a	n/a	n/a	n/a	n/a	n/a	n/a	n/a	n/a
Madison, WI	0.065	0.079	0.066	0.079	0.064	0.063	0.062	0.068	0.074	0.067
Manchester, NH	n/a	n/a	n/a	n/a	n/a	n/a	n/a	n/a	n/a	n/a
McAllen, TX	0.070	0.069	0.060	0.055	0.058	0.060	0.065	0.062	0.061	0.055
Miami, FL	0.063	0.064	0.074	0.066	0.067	0.062	0.064	0.060	0.062	0.061
Midland, TX	n/a	n/a	n/a	n/a	n/a	n/a	n/a	n/a	n/a	n/a
Minneapolis, MN	0.062	0.073	0.068	0.073	0.059	0.062	0.065	0.064	0.069	0.065

Table continued on next page.

MSA[1]	2004	2005	2006	2007	2008	2009	2010	2011	2012	2013
Nashville, TN	0.072	0.078	0.078	0.083	0.072	0.064	0.073	0.071	0.077	0.065
New Orleans, LA	0.076	0.076	0.078	0.079	0.070	0.073	0.075	0.073	0.072	0.064
New York, NY	0.079	0.091	0.087	0.086	0.080	0.071	0.081	0.081	0.079	0.071
Oklahoma City, OK	0.072	0.076	0.081	0.073	0.071	0.072	0.071	0.082	0.078	0.070
Omaha, NE	0.069	0.073	0.071	0.066	0.058	0.060	0.063	0.061	0.073	0.061
Orlando, FL	0.074	0.080	0.078	0.075	0.069	0.064	0.068	0.072	0.069	0.063
Oxnard, CA	0.084	0.080	0.081	0.075	0.079	0.079	0.074	0.074	0.071	0.068
Palm Bay, FL	0.067	0.070	0.076	0.068	0.068	0.063	0.064	0.066	0.065	0.063
Peoria, IL	0.064	0.075	0.069	0.078	0.064	0.061	0.064	0.068	0.072	0.062
Philadelphia, PA	0.080	0.088	0.083	0.086	0.082	0.069	0.082	0.082	0.081	0.067
Phoenix, AZ	0.073	0.078	0.078	0.073	0.076	0.069	0.072	0.076	0.076	0.073
Pittsburgh, PA	0.074	0.085	0.077	0.078	0.075	0.068	0.075	0.072	0.079	0.070
Portland, OR	0.060	0.059	0.067	0.058	0.062	0.064	0.056	0.056	0.059	0.053
Providence, RI	0.081	0.087	0.082	0.084	0.078	0.068	0.076	0.075	0.077	0.076
Provo, UT	0.070	0.079	0.077	0.076	0.073	0.069	0.070	0.065	0.077	0.074
Raleigh, NC	0.076	0.083	0.074	0.081	0.078	0.067	0.072	0.075	0.073	0.061
Reno, NV	0.069	0.067	0.071	0.069	0.074	0.064	0.067	0.064	0.070	0.066
Richmond, VA	0.076	0.082	0.082	0.081	0.082	0.065	0.078	0.076	0.076	0.064
Roanoke, VA	0.071	0.076	0.076	0.076	0.071	0.064	0.073	0.067	0.070	0.057
Rochester, MN	n/a	n/a	n/a	n/a	n/a	n/a	n/a	n/a	n/a	n/a
Sacramento, CA	0.081	0.089	0.094	0.080	0.089	0.083	0.077	0.078	0.082	0.071
Salem, OR	0.062	0.063	0.075	0.060	0.066	0.069	0.057	0.057	0.063	0.055
Salt Lake City, UT	0.072	0.084	0.082	0.081	0.075	0.074	0.072	0.074	0.079	0.076
San Antonio, TX	0.085	0.082	0.083	0.071	0.075	0.070	0.072	0.075	0.079	0.076
San Diego, CA	0.076	0.070	0.073	0.073	0.080	0.071	0.069	0.067	0.066	0.066
San Francisco, CA	0.063	0.058	0.066	0.059	0.067	0.066	0.063	0.062	0.059	0.058
San Jose, CA	0.072	0.066	0.080	0.068	0.074	0.072	0.074	0.066	0.065	0.064
Santa Rosa, CA	0.053	0.049	0.053	0.054	0.058	0.052	0.054	0.050	0.050	0.055
Savannah, GA	0.071	0.068	0.069	0.065	0.067	0.062	0.065	0.065	0.063	0.059
Seattle, WA	0.064	0.054	0.065	0.059	0.056	0.061	0.056	0.053	0.059	0.052
Sioux Falls, SD	n/a	n/a	n/a	n/a	n/a	n/a	n/a	n/a	n/a	n/a
Spokane, WA	0.065	0.063	0.066	0.064	0.058	0.057	0.058	0.056	0.063	0.062
Springfield, IL	n/a	n/a	n/a	n/a	n/a	n/a	n/a	n/a	n/a	n/a
Tallahassee, FL	0.071	0.070	0.071	0.072	0.071	0.058	0.066	0.065	0.066	0.061
Tampa, FL	0.074	0.075	0.074	0.076	0.075	0.064	0.067	0.071	0.066	0.066
Topeka, KS	n/a	n/a	n/a	n/a	n/a	n/a	n/a	n/a	n/a	n/a
Tulsa, OK	0.071	0.080	0.082	0.072	0.071	0.071	0.071	0.083	0.084	0.070
Tyler, TX	0.081	0.083	0.082	0.077	0.072	0.075	0.072	0.078	0.076	0.071
Virginia Beach, VA	0.075	0.078	0.074	0.077	0.078	0.065	0.074	0.075	0.069	0.065
Washington, DC	0.080	0.083	0.086	0.084	0.078	0.067	0.081	0.080	0.079	0.067
Wichita, KS	0.060	0.076	0.077	0.065	0.068	0.073	0.075	0.079	0.081	0.071
Wilmington, NC	0.070	0.075	0.072	0.071	0.063	0.060	0.062	0.064	0.064	0.064
Winston-Salem, NC	0.075	0.077	0.077	0.080	0.079	0.067	0.078	0.073	0.076	0.063
Worcester, MA	0.074	0.085	0.077	0.089	0.081	0.077	0.070	0.065	0.070	0.067

Note: (1) Data covers the Metropolitan Statistical Area—see Appendix B for areas included; n/a not available. The values shown are the composite ozone concentration averages among trend sites based on the highest fourth daily maximum 8-hour concentration in parts per million. These trends are based on sites having an adequate record of monitoring data during the trend period. Data from exceptional events are included.

Source: U.S. Environmental Protection Agency, Air Quality Monitoring Information, "Air Quality Trends by City, 2000-2013"

Maximum Air Pollutant Concentrations: Particulate Matter, Ozone, CO and Lead

Metro Aea	PM 10 (ug/m³)	PM 2.5 Wtd AM (ug/m³)	PM 2.5 24-Hr (ug/m³)	Ozone (ppm)	Carbon Monoxide (ppm)	Lead (ug/m³)
Albuquerque, NM	155	8.7	19	0.072	1	0.01
Anchorage, AK	120	6.4	28	n/a	4	n/a
Ann Arbor, MI	n/a	8.6	19	0.066	n/a	n/a
Athens, GA	n/a	9.7	28	0.06	n/a	n/a
Atlanta, GA	34	9.7	20	0.071	1	0.01
Austin, TX	57	7.2	24	0.07	0	n/a
Billings, MT	n/a	n/a	n/a	n/a	n/a	n/a
Boise City, ID	99	13	89	0.074	1	n/a
Boston, MA	50	9	23	0.073	1	n/a
Boulder, CO	51	7.1	23	0.079	n/a	n/a
Cape Coral, FL	49	5.8	15	0.066	n/a	n/a
Cedar Rapids, IA	55	9.5	22	0.06	1	n/a
Charleston, SC	34	7.1	16	0.059	n/a	n/a
Charlotte, NC	45	8.9	18	0.067	2	n/a
Chicago, IL	121	11.3	27	0.075	1	0.1
Clarksville, TN	26	9.8	22	0.064	n/a	n/a
Colorado Springs, CO	52	6	18	0.074	2	n/a
Columbia, MO	n/a	n/a	n/a	0.062	n/a	n/a
Columbus, OH	41	10.2	24	0.073	1	0.01
Dallas, TX	93	10.6	26	0.085	2	0.08
Davenport, IA	154	10.4	26	0.06	1	n/a
Denver, CO	97	8.2	23	0.085	3	0.02
Des Moines, IA	45	9	22	0.059	1	n/a
Durham, NC	24	7.8	18	0.062	n/a	n/a
El Paso, TX	233	10.8	30	0.073	3	0.03
Erie, PA	31	12.2	26	0.068	1	n/a
Eugene, OR	42	9.8	41	0.056	n/a	n/a
Fargo, ND	62	6.7	18	0.059	0	n/a
Fayetteville, NC	27	8.8	19	0.062	n/a	n/a
Fort Collins, CO	55	6.8	18	0.082	1	n/a
Fort Wayne, IN	n/a	9.5	20	0.062	2	n/a
Fort Worth, TX	93	10.6	26	0.085	2	0.08
Gainesville, FL	n/a	6.9	16	0.062	n/a	n/a
Grand Rapids, MI	29	9	19	0.068	1	0.06
Green Bay, WI	n/a	n/a	n/a	0.068	n/a	n/a
Greensboro, NC	26	8.7	19	0.062	n/a	n/a
Honolulu, HI	39	6.2	13	0.051	1	0
Houston, TX	80	11.3	27	0.084	2	0.01
Huntsville, AL	37	8.6	16	0.064	n/a	n/a
Indianapolis, IN	56	11.5	25	0.069	2	0.02
Jacksonville, FL	47	6.3	16	0.06	1	n/a
Kansas City, MO	95	9.9	22	0.071	2	0.01
Lafayette, LA	74	7.9	18	0.066	n/a	n/a
Las Vegas, NV	169	10.1	26	0.082	3	0.01
Lexington, KY	25	9.4	20	0.061	n/a	n/a
Lincoln, NE	n/a	8.1	20	0.055	n/a	n/a
Little Rock, AR	61	11	29	0.07	1	n/a
Los Angeles, CA	91	12.5	30	0.094	3	0.1
Louisville, KY	36	11.4	23	0.068	1	n/a
Lubbock, TX	n/a	n/a	n/a	n/a	n/a	n/a
Madison, WI	29	9.3	23	0.067	n/a	n/a
Manchester, NH	18	7.5	14	0.068	0	n/a
McAllen, TX	88	n/a	n/a	0.055	n/a	n/a
Miami, FL	62	5.8	14	0.068	1	n/a
Midland, TX	n/a	n/a	n/a	n/a	n/a	n/a

Table continued on next page.

Metro Aea	PM 10 (ug/m³)	PM 2.5 Wtd AM (ug/m³)	PM 2.5 24-Hr (ug/m³)	Ozone (ppm)	Carbon Monoxide (ppm)	Lead (ug/m³)
Minneapolis, MN	70	10.2	23	0.067	3	0.11
Nashville, TN	29	10.1	20	0.068	1	n/a
New Orleans, LA	52	7.9	18	0.071	n/a	0.08
New York, NY	43	10.7	31	0.078	2	0.01
Oklahoma City, OK	62	9.4	21	0.073	1	n/a
Omaha, NE	91	11	24	0.066	2	0.13
Orlando, FL	62	6.3	16	0.065	1	n/a
Oxnard, CA	143	9.3	23	0.077	n/a	n/a
Palm Bay, FL	54	5.8	21	0.063	n/a	n/a
Peoria, IL	n/a	n/a	n/a	0.066	n/a	0.01
Philadelphia, PA	64	11.5	31	0.073	2	0.04
Phoenix, AZ	510	10.6	42	0.079	3	0.04
Pittsburgh, PA	65	12	31	0.078	2	0.22
Portland, OR	43	9.1	56	0.059	2	n/a
Providence, RI	41	8.5	22	0.079	1	n/a
Provo, UT	136	12.5	82	0.077	2	n/a
Raleigh, NC	27	10.6	22	0.062	1	n/a
Reno, NV	999	12.3	41	0.069	2	n/a
Richmond, VA	30	8.1	19	0.066	1	0
Roanoke, VA	n/a	n/a	n/a	0.057	1	n/a
Rochester, MN	n/a	7.9	21	0.064	n/a	n/a
Sacramento, CA	68	11.5	40	0.082	2	n/a
Salem, OR	n/a	n/a	n/a	0.055	n/a	n/a
Salt Lake City, UT	105	12.1	59	0.077	2	0.08
San Antonio, TX	71	8.3	26	0.083	n/a	0.02
San Diego, CA	214	11.1	24	0.078	7	0.01
San Francisco, CA	42	12.8	32	0.069	3	0.22
San Jose, CA	53	11.9	35	0.071	2	0.12
Santa Rosa, CA	30	8.5	23	0.055	1	n/a
Savannah, GA	n/a	9	18	0.059	n/a	n/a
Seattle, WA	28	12.2	34	0.059	1	n/a
Sioux Falls, SD	55	8.9	23	0.067	1	n/a
Spokane, WA	68	9.2	31	0.062	2	n/a
Springfield, IL	n/a	n/a	n/a	0.062	n/a	n/a
Tallahassee, FL	n/a	7.9	20	0.062	n/a	n/a
Tampa, FL	49	6.5	15	0.07	1	0.49
Topeka, KS	54	8.4	20	0.066	n/a	n/a
Tulsa, OK	67	9.3	21	0.072	1	0.01
Tyler, TX	n/a	n/a	n/a	0.071	n/a	n/a
Virginia Beach, VA	21	7.7	18	0.068	1	n/a
Washington, DC	32	9.3	23	0.072	3	0
Wichita, KS	84	9.5	22	0.071	1	n/a
Wilmington, NC	n/a	6.6	15	0.064	n/a	n/a
Winston-Salem, NC	26	8.3	20	0.066	2	n/a
Worcester, MA	47	7.2	18	0.068	1	n/a
NAAQS[1]	150	15	35	0.075	9	0.15

Note: Data from exceptional events are included; Data covers the Metropolitan Statistical Area—see Appendix B for areas included; (1) National Ambient Air Quality Standards; ppm = parts per million; ug/m³ = micrograms per cubic meter; n/a not available
Concentrations: Particulate Matter 10 (coarse particulate)—highest second maximum 24-hour concentration; Particulate Matter 2.5 Wtd AM (fine particulate)—highest weighted annual mean concentration; Particulate Matter 2.5 24-Hour (fine particulate)—highest 98th percentile 24-hour concentration; Ozone—highest fourth daily maximum 8-hour concentration; Carbon Monoxide—highest second maximum non-overlapping 8-hour concentration; Lead—maximum running 3-month average
Source: U.S. Environmental Protection Agency, Air Quality Monitoring Information, "Air Quality Statistics by City, 2013"

Maximum Air Pollutant Concentrations: Nitrogen Dioxide and Sulfur Dioxide

Metro Area	Nitrogen Dioxide AM (ppb)	Nitrogen Dioxide 1-Hr (ppb)	Sulfur Dioxide AM (ppb)	Sulfur Dioxide 1-Hr (ppb)	Sulfur Dioxide 24-Hr (ppb)
Albuquerque, NM	12	45	n/a	4	n/a
Anchorage, AK	n/a	n/a	n/a	n/a	n/a
Ann Arbor, MI	n/a	n/a	n/a	n/a	n/a
Athens, GA	n/a	n/a	n/a	n/a	n/a
Atlanta, GA	9	43	n/a	9	n/a
Austin, TX	5	n/a	n/a	5	n/a
Billings, MT	n/a	n/a	n/a	48	n/a
Boise City, ID	11	n/a	n/a	n/a	n/a
Boston, MA	18	50	n/a	31	n/a
Boulder, CO	n/a	n/a	n/a	n/a	n/a
Cape Coral, FL	n/a	n/a	n/a	n/a	n/a
Cedar Rapids, IA	n/a	n/a	n/a	25	n/a
Charleston, SC	7	37	n/a	15	n/a
Charlotte, NC	8	39	n/a	8	n/a
Chicago, IL	21	64	n/a	73	n/a
Clarksville, TN	n/a	n/a	n/a	28	n/a
Colorado Springs, CO	n/a	n/a	n/a	58	n/a
Columbia, MO	n/a	n/a	n/a	n/a	n/a
Columbus, OH	n/a	n/a	n/a	13	n/a
Dallas, TX	12	49	n/a	16	n/a
Davenport, IA	7	39	n/a	15	n/a
Denver, CO	24	68	n/a	38	n/a
Des Moines, IA	9	37	n/a	1	n/a
Durham, NC	n/a	n/a	n/a	6	n/a
El Paso, TX	14	56	n/a	9	n/a
Erie, PA	6	36	n/a	12	n/a
Eugene, OR	n/a	n/a	n/a	n/a	n/a
Fargo, ND	4	36	n/a	n/a	n/a
Fayetteville, NC	n/a	n/a	n/a	n/a	n/a
Fort Collins, CO	n/a	n/a	n/a	n/a	n/a
Fort Wayne, IN	n/a	n/a	n/a	6	n/a
Fort Worth, TX	12	49	n/a	16	n/a
Gainesville, FL	n/a	n/a	n/a	n/a	n/a
Grand Rapids, MI	n/a	n/a	n/a	9	n/a
Green Bay, WI	n/a	n/a	n/a	76	n/a
Greensboro, NC	n/a	n/a	n/a	n/a	n/a
Honolulu, HI	3	23	n/a	9	n/a
Houston, TX	13	58	n/a	35	n/a
Huntsville, AL	n/a	n/a	n/a	n/a	n/a
Indianapolis, IN	12	44	n/a	78	n/a
Jacksonville, FL	8	38	n/a	60	n/a
Kansas City, MO	13	48	n/a	156	n/a
Lafayette, LA	n/a	n/a	n/a	n/a	n/a
Las Vegas, NV	14	n/a	n/a	7	n/a
Lexington, KY	7	44	n/a	18	n/a
Lincoln, NE	n/a	n/a	n/a	n/a	n/a
Little Rock, AR	10	47	n/a	7	n/a
Los Angeles, CA	23	71	n/a	12	n/a
Louisville, KY	11	43	n/a	117	n/a
Lubbock, TX	n/a	n/a	n/a	n/a	n/a
Madison, WI	n/a	n/a	n/a	8	n/a
Manchester, NH	n/a	n/a	n/a	5	n/a
McAllen, TX	n/a	n/a	n/a	n/a	n/a
Miami, FL	8	44	n/a	3	n/a
Midland, TX	n/a	n/a	n/a	n/a	n/a

Table continued on next page.

Metro Area	Nitrogen Dioxide AM (ppb)	Nitrogen Dioxide 1-Hr (ppb)	Sulfur Dioxide AM (ppb)	Sulfur Dioxide 1-Hr (ppb)	Sulfur Dioxide 24-Hr (ppb)
Minneapolis, MN	9	43	n/a	15	n/a
Nashville, TN	10	42	n/a	10	n/a
New Orleans, LA	6	46	n/a	181	n/a
New York, NY	22	62	n/a	22	n/a
Oklahoma City, OK	9	46	n/a	3	n/a
Omaha, NE	n/a	n/a	n/a	56	n/a
Orlando, FL	5	34	n/a	3	n/a
Oxnard, CA	9	37	n/a	n/a	n/a
Palm Bay, FL	n/a	n/a	n/a	n/a	n/a
Peoria, IL	n/a	n/a	n/a	195	n/a
Philadelphia, PA	17	52	n/a	15	n/a
Phoenix, AZ	25	63	n/a	9	n/a
Pittsburgh, PA	11	40	n/a	81	n/a
Portland, OR	10	33	n/a	5	n/a
Providence, RI	10	43	n/a	62	n/a
Provo, UT	19	75	n/a	n/a	n/a
Raleigh, NC	n/a	n/a	n/a	6	n/a
Reno, NV	16	56	n/a	6	n/a
Richmond, VA	8	41	n/a	30	n/a
Roanoke, VA	6	35	n/a	n/a	n/a
Rochester, MN	n/a	n/a	n/a	n/a	n/a
Sacramento, CA	10	50	n/a	3	n/a
Salem, OR	n/a	n/a	n/a	n/a	n/a
Salt Lake City, UT	18	62	n/a	31	n/a
San Antonio, TX	5	35	n/a	15	n/a
San Diego, CA	19	75	n/a	1	n/a
San Francisco, CA	17	60	n/a	17	n/a
San Jose, CA	15	52	n/a	10	n/a
Santa Rosa, CA	9	37	n/a	n/a	n/a
Savannah, GA	n/a	n/a	n/a	93	n/a
Seattle, WA	n/a	n/a	n/a	n/a	n/a
Sioux Falls, SD	5	34	n/a	3	n/a
Spokane, WA	n/a	n/a	n/a	n/a	n/a
Springfield, IL	n/a	n/a	n/a	12	n/a
Tallahassee, FL	n/a	n/a	n/a	n/a	n/a
Tampa, FL	5	34	n/a	68	n/a
Topeka, KS	n/a	n/a	n/a	n/a	n/a
Tulsa, OK	8	38	n/a	48	n/a
Tyler, TX	3	17	n/a	n/a	n/a
Virginia Beach, VA	8	41	n/a	52	n/a
Washington, DC	13	64	n/a	10	n/a
Wichita, KS	9	40	n/a	6	n/a
Wilmington, NC	n/a	n/a	n/a	45	n/a
Winston-Salem, NC	6	37	n/a	5	n/a
Worcester, MA	12	48	n/a	8	n/a
NAAQS[1]	53	100	30	75	140

Note: Data from exceptional events are included; Data covers the Metropolitan Statistical Area—see Appendix B for areas included; (1) National Ambient Air Quality Standards; ppb = parts per billion; n/a not available
Concentrations: Nitrogen Dioxide AM—highest arithmetic mean concentration; Nitrogen Dioxide 1-Hr—highest 98th percentile 1-hour daily maximum concentration; Sulfur Dioxide AM—highest annual mean concentration; Sulfur Dioxide 1-Hr—highest 99th percentile 1-hour daily maximum concentration; Sulfur Dioxide 24-Hr—highest second maximum 24-hour concentration
Source: U.S. Environmental Protection Agency, Air Quality Monitoring Information, "Air Quality Statistics by City, 2013"

Appendix B: Metropolitan Area Definitions

Metropolitan Statistical Areas (MSA), Metropolitan Divisions (MD), New England City and Town Areas (NECTA), and New England City and Town Area Divisions (NECTAD)

Note: *In February 2013, the Office of Management and Budget (OMB) announced changes to metropolitan and micropolitan statistical area definitions. Both current and historical definitions are shown below. If the change only affected the name of the metro area, the counties included were not repeated.*

Albuquerque, NM MSA
Bernalillo, Sandoval, Torrance, and Valencia Counties

Anchorage, AK MSA
Anchorage Municipality and Matanuska-Susitna Borough

Ann Arbor, MI MSA
Washtenaw County

Athens-Clarke County, GA MSA
Clarke, Madison, Oconee, and Oglethorpe Counties

Atlanta-Sandy Springs-Roswell, GA MSA
Barrow, Bartow, Butts, Carroll, Cherokee, Clayton, Cobb, Coweta, Dawson, DeKalb, Douglas, Fayette, Forsyth, Fulton, Gwinnett, Haralson, Heard, Henry, Jasper, Lamar, Meriwether, Morgan, Newton, Paulding, Pickens, Pike, Rockdale, Spalding, and Walton Counties
Previously Atlanta-Sandy Springs-Marietta, GA MSA
Barrow, Bartow, Butts, Carroll, Cherokee, Clayton, Cobb, Coweta, Dawson, DeKalb, Douglas, Fayette, Forsyth, Fulton, Gwinnett, Haralson, Heard, Henry, Jasper, Lamar, Meriwether, Newton, Paulding, Pickens, Pike, Rockdale, Spalding, and Walton Counties

Austin-Round Rock, TX MSA
Previously Austin-Round Rock-San Marcos, TX MSA
Bastrop, Caldwell, Hays, Travis, and Williamson Counties

Billings, MT MSA
Carbon and Yellowstone Counties

Boise City, ID MSA
Previously Boise City-Nampa, ID MSA
Ada, Boise, Canyon, Gem, and Owyhee Counties

Boston, MA

Boston-Cambridge-Newton, MA-NH MSA
Peviously Boston-Cambridge-Quincy, MA-NH MSA
Essex, Middlesex, Norfolk, Plymouth, and Suffolk Counties, MA; Rockingham and Strafford Counties, NH

Boston, MA MD
Previously Boston-Quincy, MA MD
Norfolk, Plymouth, and Suffolk Counties

Boston-Cambridge-Nashua, MA-NH NECTA
Includes 157 cities and towns in Massachusetts and 34 cities and towns in New Hampshire
Previously Boston-Cambridge-Quincy, MA-NH NECTA
Includes 155 cities and towns in Massachusetts and 38 cities and towns in New Hampshire

Boston-Cambridge-Newton, MA NECTA Division
Includes 92 cities and towns in Massachusetts
Previously Boston-Cambridge-Quincy, MA NECTA Division
Includes 97 cities and towns in Massachusetts

Boulder, CO MSA
Boulder County

Cape Coral-Fort Myers, FL MSA
Lee County

Cedar Rapids, IA, MSA
Benton, Jones, and Linn Counties

Charleston-North Charleston, SC MSA
Previously Charleston-North Charleston- Summerville, SC MSA
Berkeley, Charleston, and Dorchester Counties

Charlotte-Concord-Gastonia, NC-SC MSA
Cabarrus, Gaston, Iredell, Lincoln, Mecklenburg, Rowan, and Union Counties, NC; Chester, Lancaster, and York Counties, SC
Previously Charlotte-Gastonia-Rock Hill, NC-SC MSA
Anson, Cabarrus, Gaston, Mecklenburg, and Union Counties, NC; York County, SC

Chicago, IL

Chicago-Naperville-Elgin, IL-IN-WI MSA
Previously Chicago-Joliet-Naperville, IL-IN-WI MSA
Cook, DeKalb, DuPage, Grundy, Kane, Kendall, Lake, McHenry, and Will Counties, IL; Jasper, Lake, Newton, and Porter Counties, IN; Kenosha County, WI

Chicago-Naperville-Arlington Heights, IL MD
Cook, DuPage, Grundy, Kendall, McHenry, and Will Counties
Previously Chicago-Joliet-Naperville, IL MD
Cook, DeKalb, DuPage, Grundy, Kane, Kendall, McHenry, and Will Counties

Lake County-Kenosha County, IL-WI MD
Lake County, IL; Kenosha County, WI

Clarksville, TN-KY MSA
Mongomery and Stewart Counties, TN; Christian and Trigg Counties, KY

Colorado Springs, CO MSA
El Paso and Teller Counties

Columbia, MO MSA
Boone and Howard Counties

Columbus, OH MSA
Delaware, Fairfield, Franklin, Licking, Madison, Morrow, Pickaway, and Union Counties

Dallas, TX

Dallas-Fort Worth-Arlington, TX MSA
Collin, Dallas, Denton, Ellis, Hunt, Johnson, Kaufman, Parker, Rockwall, Tarrant, and Wise Counties

Dallas-Plano-Irving, TX MD
Collin, Dallas, Denton, Ellis, Hunt, Kaufman, and Rockwall Counties

Davenport-Moline-Rock Island, IA-IL MSA
Henry, Mercer, and Rock Island Counties, IA; Scott County, IL

Denver-Aurora-Lakewood, CO MSA
Previously Denver-Aurora-Broomfield, CO MSA
Adams, Arapahoe, Broomfield, Clear Creek, Denver, Douglas, Elbert, Gilpin, Jefferson, and Park Counties

Des Moines-West Des Moines, IA MSA
Dallas, Guthrie, Madison, Polk, and Warren Counties

Durham-Chapel Hill, NC MSA
Chatham, Durham, Orange, and and Person Counties

El Paso, TX MSA
El Paso County

Erie, PA MSA
Erie County

Eugene, OR MSA
Previously Eugene-Springfield, OR MSA
Lane County

Fargo, ND-MN MSA
Cass County, ND; Clay County, MN

Fayetteville, NC MSA
Cumberland, and Hoke Counties

Fort Collins, CO MSA
Previously Fort Collins-Loveland, CO MSA
Larimer County

Fort Wayne, IN MSA
Allen, Wells, and Whitley Counties

Fort Worth, TX

Dallas-Fort Worth-Arlington, TX MSA
Collin, Dallas, Denton, Ellis, Hunt, Johnson, Kaufman, Parker, Rockwall, Tarrant, and Wise Counties

Fort Worth-Arlington, TX MD
Hood, Johnson, Parker, Somervell, Tarrant, and Wise Counties

Gainesville, FL MSA
Alachua, and Gilchrist Counties

Grand Rapids-Wyoming, MI MSA
Barry, Kent, Montcalm, and Ottawa Counties

Green Bay, WI MSA
Brown, Kewaunee, and Oconto Counties

Greensboro-High Point, NC MSA
Guilford, Randolph, and Rockingham Counties

Honolulu, HI MSA
Honolulu County

Houston-The Woodlands-Sugar Land-Baytown, TX MSA
Austin, Brazoria, Chambers, Fort Bend, Galveston, Harris, Liberty, Montgomery, and Waller Counties
Previously Houston-Sugar Land-Baytown, TX MSA
Austin, Brazoria, Chambers, Fort Bend, Galveston, Harris, Liberty, Montgomery, San Jacinto, and Waller Counties

Huntsville, AL MSA
Limestone and Madison Counties

Indianapolis-Carmel, IN MSA
Boone, Brown, Hamilton, Hancock, Hendricks, Johnson, Marion, Morgan, Putnam, and Shelby Counties

Jacksonville, FL MSA
Baker, Clay, Duval, Nassau, and St. Johns Counties

Kansas City, MO-KS MSA
Franklin, Johnson, Leavenworth, Linn, Miami, and Wyandotte Counties, KS; Bates, Caldwell, Cass, Clay, Clinton, Jackson, Lafayette, Platte, and Ray Counties, MO

Lafayette, LA MSA
Acadia, Iberia, Lafayette, St. Martin, and Vermilion Parishes

Las Vegas-Henderson-Paradise, NV MSA
Previously Las Vegas-Paradise, NV MSA
Clark County

Lexington-Fayette, KY MSA
Bourbon, Clark, Fayette, Jessamine, Scott, and Woodford Counties

Lincoln, NE MSA
Lancaster and Seward Counties

Little Rock-North Little Rock-Conway, AR MSA
Faulkner, Grant, Lonoke, Perry, Pulaski and Saline Counties, AR

Los Angeles, CA

Los Angeles-Long Beach-Anaheim, CA MSA
Previously Los Angeles-Long Beach-Santa Ana, CA MSA
Los Angeles and Orange Counties

Los Angeles-Long Beach-Glendale, CA MD
Los Angeles County

Anaheim-Santa Ana-Irvine, CA MD
Previously Santa Ana-Anaheim-Irvine, CA MD
Orange County

Louisville/Jefferson, KY-IN MSA
Clark, Floyd, Harrison, Scott, and Washington Counties, IN; Bullitt, Henry, Jefferson, Oldham, Shelby, Spencer, and Trimble Counties, KY

Lubbock, TX MSA
Crosby, Lubbock, and Lynn Counties

Madison, WI MSA
Columbia, Dane, and Iowa Counties

Manchester, NH

Manchester-Nashua, NH MSA
Hillsborough County

Manchester, NH NECTA
Includes 11 cities and towns in New Hampshire
Previously Manchester, NH NECTA
Includes 9 cities and towns in New Hampshire

McAllen-Edinburg-Mission, TX
Hidalgo County

Miami, FL

Miami-Fort Lauderdale-West Palm Beach, FL MSA
Previously Miami-Fort Lauderdale-Pompano Beach, FL MSA
Broward, Miami-Dade, and Palm Beach Counties

Miami-Miami Beach-Kendall, FL MD
Miami-Dade County

Midland, TX MSA
Martin, and Midland Counties

Minneapolis-St. Paul-Bloomington, MN-WI MSA
Anoka, Carver, Chisago, Dakota, Hennepin, Isanti, Le Sueur, Mille Lacs, Ramsey, Scott, Sherburne, Sibley, Washington, and Wright Counties, MN; Pierce and St. Croix Counties, WI

Nashville-Davidson-Murfreesboro-Franklin, TN MSA
Cannon, Cheatham, Davidson, Dickson, Hickman, Macon, Robertson, Rutherford, Smith, Sumner, Trousdale, Williamson, and Wilson Counties

New Orleans-Metarie-Kenner, LA MSA
Jefferson, Orleans, Plaquemines, St. Bernard, St. Charles, St. James, St. John the Baptist, and St. Tammany Parish
Previously New Orleans-Metarie-Kenner, LA MSA
Jefferson, Orleans, Plaquemines, St. Bernard, St. Charles, St. John the Baptist, and St. Tammany Parish

New York, NY

New York-Newark-Jersey City, NY-NJ-PA MSA
Bergen, Essex, Hudson, Hunterdon, Middlesex, Monmouth, Morris, Ocean, Passaic, Somerset, Sussex, and Union Counties, NJ; Bronx, Dutchess, Kings, Nassau, New York, Orange, Putnam, Queens, Richmond, Rockland, Suffolk, and Westchester Counties, NY; Pike County, PA
Previously New York-Northern New Jersey-Long Island, NY-NJ-PA MSA
Bergen, Essex, Hudson, Hunterdon, Middlesex, Monmouth, Morris, Ocean, Passaic, Somerset, Sussex, and Union Counties, NJ; Bronx, Kings, Nassau, New York, Putnam, Queens, Richmond, Rockland, Suffolk, and Westchester Counties, NY; Pike County, PA

New York-Jersey City-White Plains, NY-NJ MD
Bergen, Hudson, Middlesex, Monmouth, Ocean, and Passaic Counties, NJ; Bronx, Kings, New York, Putnam, Queens, Richmond, Rockland, and Westchester Counties, NY
Previously New York-Wayne-White Plains, NY-NJ MD
Bergen, Hudson, and Passaic Counties, NJ; Bronx, Kings, New York, Putnam, Queens, Richmond, Rockland, and Westchester Counties, NY

Nassau-Suffolk, NY MD
Nassau and Suffolk Counties

Oklahoma City, OK MSA
Canadian, Cleveland, Grady, Lincoln, Logan, McClain, and Oklahoma Counties

Omaha-Council Bluffs, NE-IA MSA
Harrison, Mills, and Pottawattamie Counties, IA; Cass, Douglas, Sarpy, Saunders, and Washington Counties, NE

Orlando-Kissimmee-Sanford, FL MSA
Lake, Orange, Osceola, and Seminole Counties

Oxnard-Thousand Oaks-Ventura, CA MSA
Ventura County

Palm Bay-Melbourne-Titusville, FL MSA
Brevard County

Peoria, IL MSA
Marshall, Peoria, Stark, Tazewell, and Woodford Counties

Philadelphia, PA

Philadelphia-Camden-Wilmington, PA-NJ-DE-MD MSA
New Castle County, DE; Cecil County, MD; Burlington, Camden, Gloucester, and Salem Counties, NJ; Bucks, Chester, Delaware, Montgomery, and Philadelphia Counties, PA

Philadelphia, PA MD
Delaware and Philadelphia Counties
Previously Philadelphia, PA MD
Bucks, Chester, Delaware, Montgomery, and Philadelphia Counties

Phoenix-Mesa-Scottsdale, AZ MSA
Previously Phoenix-Mesa-Glendale, AZ MSA
Maricopa and Pinal Counties

Pittsburgh, PA MSA
Allegheny, Armstrong, Beaver, Butler, Fayette, Washington, and Westmoreland Counties

Portland-Vancouver-Hillsboro, OR-WA MSA
Clackamas, Columbia, Multnomah, Washington, and Yamhill Counties, OR; Clark and Skamania Counties, WA

Providence, RI

Providence-New Bedford-Fall River, RI-MA MSA
Previously Providence-New Bedford-Fall River, RI-MA MSA
Bristol County, MA; Bristol, Kent, Newport, Providence, and Washington Counties, RI

Providence-Warwick, RI-MA NECTA
Includes 12 cities and towns in Massachusetts and 36 cities and towns in Rhode Island
Previously Providence-Fall River-Warwick, RI-MA NECTA
Includes 12 cities and towns in Massachusetts and 37 cities and towns in Rhode Island

Provo-Orem, UT MSA
Juab and Utah Counties

Raleigh, NC MSA
Previously Raleigh-Cary, NC MSA
Franklin, Johnston, and Wake Counties

Reno, NV MSA
Previously Reno-Sparks, NV MSA
Storey and Washoe Counties

Richmond, VA MSA
Amelia, Caroline, Charles City, Chesterfield, Dinwiddie, Goochland, Hanover, Henrico, King William, New Kent, Powhatan, Prince George, and Sussex Counties; Colonial Heights, Hopewell, Petersburg, and Richmond Cities

Roanoke, VA MSA
Roanoke and Salem cities; Botetourt, Craig, Franklin, and Roanoke Counties

Rochester, MN MSA
Dodge, Fillmore, Olmsted, and Wabasha Counties

Sacramento—Roseville—Arden-Arcade, CA MSA
El Dorado, Placer, Sacramento, and Yolo Counties

Salem, OR MSA
Marion and Polk Counties

Salt Lake City, UT MSA
Salt Lake and Tooele Counties

San Antonio-New Braunfels, TX MSA
Atascosa, Bandera, Bexar, Comal, Guadalupe, Kendall, Medina, and Wilson Counties

San Diego-Carlsbad, CA MSA
Previously San Diego-Carlsbad-San Marcos, CA MSA
San Diego County

San Francisco, CA

San Francisco-Oakland-Hayward, CA MSA
Previously San Francisco-Oakland- Fremont, CA MSA
Alameda, Contra Costa, Marin, San Francisco, and San Mateo Counties

San Francisco-Redwood City-South San Francisco, CA MD
San Francisco and San Mateo Counties

Previously San Francisco-San Mateo-Redwood City, CA MD
Marin, San Francisco, and San Mateo Counties

San Jose-Sunnyvale-Santa Clara, CA MSA
San Benito and Santa Clara Counties

Santa Rosa, CA MSA
Previously Santa Rosa-Petaluma, CA MSA
Sonoma County

Savannah, GA MSA
Bryan, Chatham, and Effingham Counties

Seattle, WA

Seattle-Tacoma-Bellevue, WA MSA
King, Pierce, and Snohomish Counties

Seattle-Bellevue-Everett, WA MD
King and Snohomish Counties

Sioux Falls, SD MSA
Lincoln, McCook, Minnehaha, and Turner Counties

Spokane-Spokane Valley, WA MSA
Pend Oreille, Spokane, and Stevens Counties
Previously Spokane, WA MSA
Spokane County

Springfield, IL MSA
Menard and Sangamon Counties

Tallahassee, FL MSA
Gadsden, Jefferson, Leon, and Wakulla Counties

Tampa-St. Petersburg-Clearwater, FL MSA
Hernando, Hillsborough, Pasco, and Pinellas Counties

Topeka, KS MSA
Jackson, Jefferson, Osage, Shawnee, and Wabaunsee Counties

Tulsa, OK MSA
Creek, Okmulgee, Osage, Pawnee, Rogers, Tulsa, and Wagoner Counties

Tyler, TX MSA
Smith County

Virginia Beach-Norfolk-Newport News, VA-NC MSA
Currituck County, NC; Chesapeake, Hampton, Newport News, Norfolk, Poquoson, Portsmouth, Suffolk, Virginia Beach and Williamsburg cities, VA; Gloucester, Isle of Wight, James City, Mathews, Surry, and York Counties, VA

Washington, DC

Washington-Arlington-Alexandria, DC-VA-MD-WV MSA
District of Columbia; Calvert, Charles, Frederick, Montgomery, and Prince George's Counties, MD; Alexandria, Fairfax, Falls Church, Fredericksburg, Manassas Park, and Manassas cities, VA; Arlington, Clarke, Culpepper, Fairfax, Fauquier, Loudoun, Prince William, Rappahannock, Spotsylvania, Stafford, and Warren Counties, VA; Jefferson County, WV
Previously Washington-Arlington-Alexandria, DC-VA-MD-WV MSA
District of Columbia; Calvert, Charles, Frederick, Montgomery, and Prince George's Counties, MD; Alexandria, Fairfax, Falls Church, Fredericksburg, Manassas Park, and Manassas cities, VA; Arlington, Clarke, Fairfax, Fauquier, Loudoun, Prince William, Spotsylvania, Stafford, and Warren Counties, VA; Jefferson County, WV

Washington-Arlington-Alexandria, DC-VA-MD-WV MD
District of Columbia; Calvert, Charles, and Prince George's Counties, MD; Alexandria, Fairfax, Falls Church, Fredericksburg, Manassas Park, and Manassas cities, VA; Arlington, Clarke, Culpepper, Fairfax, Fauquier, Loudoun, Prince William, Rappahannock, Spotsylvania, Stafford, and Warren Counties, VA; Jefferson County, WV
Previously Washington-Arlington-Alexandria, DC-VA-MD-WV MD
District of Columbia; Calvert, Charles, and Prince George's Counties, MD; Alexandria, Fairfax, Falls Church, Fredericksburg, Manassas Park, and Manassas cities, VA; Arlington, Clarke, Fairfax, Fauquier, Loudoun, Prince William, Spotsylvania, Stafford, and Warren Counties, VA; Jefferson County, WV

Wichita, KS MSA
Butler, Harvey, Kingman, Sedgwick, and Sumner Counties

Wilmington, NC MSA
New Hanover and Pender Counties

Winston-Salem, NC MSA
Davidson, Davie, Forsyth, Stokes, and Yadkin Counties

Worcester, MA

Worcester, MA-CT MSA
Windham County, CT; Worcester County, MA
Previously Worcester, MA MSA
Worcester County

Worcester, MA-CT NECTA
Includes 40 cities and towns in Massachusetts and 8 cities and towns in Connecticut
Previously Worcester, MA-CT NECTA
Includes 37 cities and towns in Massachusetts and 3 cities and towns in Connecticut

Appendix C: Government Type and Primary County

This appendix includes the government structure of each place included in this book. It also includes the county or county equivalent in which each place is located. If a place spans more that one county, the county in which the majority of the population resides is shown.

Albuquerque, NM
Government Type: City
County: Bernalillo

Anchorage, AK
Government Type: Municipality
Borough: Anchorage

Ann Arbor, MI
Government Type: City
County: Washtenaw

Athens, GA
Government Type: Consolidated city-county
County: Clarke

Atlanta, GA
Government Type: City
County: Fulton

Austin, TX
Government Type: City
County: Travis

Billings, MT
Government Type: City
County: Yellowstone

Boise City, ID
Government Type: City
County: Ada

Boston, MA
Government Type: City
County: Suffolk

Boulder, CO
Government Type: City
County: Boulder

Cape Coral, FL
Government Type: City
County: Lee

Cedar Rapids, IA
Government Type: City
County: Linn

Charleston, SC
Government Type: City
County: Charleston

Charlotte, NC
Government Type: City
County: Mecklenburg

Chicago, IL
Government Type: City
County: Cook

Clarksville, TN
Government Type: City
County: Montgomery

Colorado Springs, CO
Government Type: City
County: El Paso

Columbia, MO
Government Type: City
County: Boone

Columbus, OH
Government Type: City
County: Franklin

Dallas, TX
Government Type: City
County: Dallas

Davenport, IA
Government Type: City
County: Scott

Denver, CO
Government Type: City
County: Denver

Des Moines, IA
Government Type: City
County: Polk

Durham, NC
Government Type: City
County: Durham

El Paso, TX
Government Type: City
County: El Paso

Erie, PA
Government Type: City
County: Erie

Eugene, OR
Government Type: City
County: Lane

Fargo, ND
Government Type: City
County: Cass

Fayetteville, NC
Government Type: City
County: Cumberland

Fort Collins, CO
Government Type: City
County: Larimer

Fort Wayne, IN
Government Type: City
County: Allen

Fort Worth, TX
Government Type: City
County: Tarrant

Gainesville, FL
Government Type: City
County: Alachua

Grand Rapids, MI
Government Type: City
County: Kent

Green Bay, WI
Government Type: City
County: Brown

Greensboro, NC
Government Type: City
County: Guilford

Honolulu, HI
Government Type: Census Designated Place (CDP)
County: Honolulu

Houston, TX
Government Type: City
County: Harris

Huntsville, AL
Government Type: City
County: Madison

Indianapolis, IN
Government Type: City
County: Marion

Jacksonville, FL
Government Type: City
County: Duval

Kansas City, MO
Government Type: City
County: Jackson

Lafayette, LA
Government Type: City
Parish: Lafayette

Las Vegas, NV
Government Type: City
County: Clark

Lexington, KY
Government Type: Consolidated city-county
County: Fayette

Lincoln, NE
Government Type: City
County: Lancaster

Little Rock, AR
Government Type: City
County: Pulaski

Los Angeles, CA
Government Type: City
County: Los Angeles

Louisville, KY
Government Type: Consolidated city-county
County: Jefferson

Lubbock, TX
Government Type: City
County: Lubbock

Madison, WI
Government Type: City
County: Dane

Manchester, NH
Government Type: City
County: Hillsborough

McAllen, TX
Government Type: City
County: Hidalgo

Miami, FL
Government Type: City
County: Miami-Dade

Midland, TX
Government Type: City
County: Midland

Minneapolis, MN
Government Type: City
County: Hennepin

Nashville, TN
Government Type: Consolidated city-county
County: Davidson

New Orleans, LA
Government Type: City
Parish: Orleans

New York, NY
Government Type: City
Counties: Bronx; Kings; New York; Queens; Staten Island

Oklahoma City, OK
Government Type: City
County: Oklahoma

Omaha, NE
Government Type: City
County: Douglas

Orlando, FL
Government Type: City
County: Orange

Oxnard, CA
Government Type: City
County: Ventura

Palm Bay, FL
Government Type: City
County: Brevard

Peoria, IL
Government Type: City
County: Peoria

Philadelphia, PA
Government Type: City
County: Philadelphia

Phoenix, AZ
Government Type: City
County: Maricopa

Pittsburgh, PA
Government Type: City
County: Allegheny

Portland, OR
Government Type: City
County: Multnomah

Providence, RI
Government Type: City
County: Providence

Provo, UT
Government Type: City
County: Utah

Raleigh, NC
Government Type: City
County: Wake

Reno, NV
Government Type: City
County: Washoe

Richmond, VA
Government Type: Independent city
County: Richmond city

Roanoke, VA
Government Type: Independent city
County: Roanoke city

Rochester, MN
Government Type: City
County: Olmsted

Sacramento, CA
Government Type: City
County: Sacramento

Salem, OR
Government Type: City
County: Marion

Salt Lake City, UT
Government Type: City
County: Salt Lake

San Antonio, TX
Government Type: City
County: Bexar

San Diego, CA
Government Type: City
County: San Diego

San Francisco, CA
Government Type: City
County: San Francisco

San Jose, CA
Government Type: City
County: Santa Clara

Santa Rosa, CA
Government Type: City
County: Sonoma

Savannah, GA
Government Type: City
County: Chatham

Seattle, WA
Government Type: City
County: King

Sioux Falls, SD
Government Type: City
County: Minnehaha

Spokane, WA
Government Type: City
County: Spokane

Springfield, IL
Government Type: City
County: Sangamon

Tallahassee, FL
Government Type: City
County: Leon

Tampa, FL
Government Type: City
County: Hillsborough

Topeka, KS
Government Type: City
County: Shawnee

Tulsa, OK
Government Type: City
County: Tulsa

Tyler, TX
Government Type: City
County: Smith

Virginia Beach, VA
Government Type: Independent city
County: Virginia Beach city

Washington, DC
Government Type: City
County: District of Columbia

Wichita, KS
Government Type: City
County: Sedgwick

Wilmington, NC
Government Type: City
County: New Hanover

Winston-Salem, NC
Government Type: City
County: Forsyth

Worcester, MA
Government Type: City
County: Worcester

Appendix D: Chambers of Commerce

Albuquerque, NM
Albuquerque Chamber of Commerce
P.O. Box 25100
Albuquerque, NM 87125
Phone: (505) 764-3700
Fax: (505) 764-3714
www.abqchamber.com

Albuquerque Economic Development Dept
851 University Blvd SE
Suite 203
Albuquerque, NM 87106
Phone: (505) 246-6200
Fax: (505) 246-6219
www.cabq.gov/econdev

Anchorage, AK
Anchorage Chamber of Commerce
1016 W Sixth Avenue
Suite 303
Anchorage, AK 99501
Phone: (907) 272-2401
Fax: (907) 272-4117
www.anchoragechamber.org

Anchorage Economic Development Department
900 W 5th Avenue
Suite 300
Anchorage, AK 99501
Phone: (907) 258-3700
Fax: (907) 258-6646
www.aedcweb.com/aedcdig

Ann Arbor, MI
Ann Arbor Area Chamber of Commerce
115 West Huron
3rd Floor
Ann Arbor, MI 48104
Phone: (734) 665-4433
Fax: (734) 665-4191
www.annarborchamber.org

Ann Arbor Economic Development Department
201 S Division
Suite 430
Ann Arbor, MI 48104
Phone: (734) 761-9317
www.annarborspark.org

Athens, GA
Athens Area Chamber of Commerce
246 W Hancock Avenue
Athens, GA 30601
Phone: (706) 549-6800
Fax: (706) 549-5636
www.aacoc.org

Athens-Clarke Economic Development
150 E. Hancock Avenue
P.O. Box 1692
Athens, GA 30603
Phone: (706) 613-3810
Fax: (706) 613-3812
www.athensbusiness.org/contact.aspx

Atlanta, GA
Metro Atlanta Chamber of Commerce
235 Andrew Young International Blvd NW
Atlanta, GA 30303
Phone: (404) 880-9000
Fax: (404) 586-8464
www.metroatlantachamber.com/contact_us.html

Austin, TX
Greater Austin Chamber of Commerce
210 Barton Springs Road
Suite 400
Austin, TX 78704
Phone: (512) 478-9383
Fax: (512) 478-6389
www.austin-chamber.org

Billings, MT
Billings Area Chamber of Commerce
815 S 27th St
Billings, MT 59101
Phone: (406) 245-4111
Fax: (406) 2457333
www.billingschamber.com

Boise City, ID
Boise Metro Chamber of Commerce
250 S 5th Street
Suite 800
Boise City, ID 83701
Phone: (208) 472-5200
Fax: (208) 472-5201
www.boisechamber.org

Boston, MA
Greater Boston Chamber of Commerce
265 Franklin Street
12th Floor
Boston, MA 02110
Phone: (617) 227-4500
Fax: (617) 227-7505
www.bostonchamber.com

Boulder, CO
Boulder Chamber of Commerce
2440 Pearl Street
Boulder, CO 80302
Phone: (303) 442-1044
Fax: (303) 938-8837
www.boulderchamber.com

City of Boulder Economic Vitality Program
P.O. Box 791
Boulder, CO 80306
Phone: (303) 441-3090
www.bouldercolorado.gov

Cape Coral, FL
Chamber of Commerce of Cape Coral
2051 Cape Coral Parkway East
Cape Coral, FL 33904
Phone: (239) 549-6900
Fax: (239) 549-9609
www.capecoralchamber.com

Cedar Rapids, IA
Cedar Rapids Chamber of Commerce
424 First Avenue NE
Cedar Rapids, IA 52401
Phone: (319) 398-5317
Fax: (319) 398-5228
www.cedarrapids.org

Cedar Rapids Economic Development
50 Second Avenue Bridge
Sixth Floor
Cedar Rapids, IA 52401-1256
Phone: (319) 286-5041
Fax: (319) 286-5141
www.cedar-rapids.org

Charleston, SC
Charleston Metro Chamber of Commerce
P.O. Box 975
Charleston, SC 29402
Phone: (843) 577-2510
www.charlestonchamber.net

Charlotte, NC
Charlotte Chamber of Commerce
330 S Tryon Street
P.O. Box 32785
Charlotte, NC 28232
Phone: (704) 378-1300
Fax: (704) 374-1903
www.charlottechamber.com

Charlotte Regional Partnership
1001 Morehead Square Drive
Suite 200
Charlotte, NC 28203
Phone: (704) 347-8942
Fax: (704) 347-8981
www.charlotteusa.com

Chicago, IL
Chicagoland Chamber of Commerce
200 E Randolph Street
Suite 2200
Chicago, IL 60601-6436
Phone: (312) 494-6700
Fax: (312) 861-0660
www.chicagolandchamber.org

City of Chicago Department of Planning and Development
City Hall, Room 1000
121 North La Salle Street
Chicago, IL 60602
Phone: (312) 744-4190
Fax: (312) 744-2271
www.egov.cityofchicago.org

Clarksville, TN
Clarksville Area Chamber of Commerce
25 Jefferson Street
Suite 300
Clarksville, TN 37040
Phone: (931) 647-2331
www.clarksvillechamber.com

Colorado Springs, CO
Greater Colorado Springs Chamber of Commerce
6 S. Tejon Street
Suite 700
Colorado Springs, CO 80903
Phone: (719) 635-1551
Fax: (719) 635-1571
www.gcsco.wliinc3.com

Greater Colorado Springs Economic Development Corp
90 South Cascade Avenue
Suite 1050
Colorado Springs, CO 80903
Phone: (719) 471-8183
Fax: (719) 471-9733
www.coloradosprings.org

Columbia, MO
Columbia Chamber of Commerce
300 South Providence Rd.
PO Box 1016
Columbia, MO 65205-1016
Phone: (573) 874-1132
Fax: (573) 443-3986
www.columbiamochamber.com

Columbus, OH
Greater Columbus Chamber
37 North High Street
Columbus, OH 43215
Phone: (614) 221-1321
Fax: (614) 221-1408
www.columbus.org

Dallas, TX
City of Dallas Economic Development Department
1500 Marilla Street
5C South
Dallas, TX 75201
Phone: (214) 670-1685
Fax: (214) 670-0158
www.dallas-edd.org

Greater Dallas Chamber of Commerce
700 North Pearl Street
Suite1200
Dallas, TX 75201
Phone: (214) 746-6600
Fax: (214) 746-6799
www.dallaschamber.org

Davenport, IA
Quad Cities Chamber
331 W. 3rd St.,
Davenport, IA 52801
Phone: (563) 322-1706
www.quadcitieschamber.com

Denver, CO
Denver Metro Chamber of Commerce
1445 Market Street
Denver, CO 80202
Phone: (303) 534-8500
Fax: (303) 534-3200
www.denverchamber.org

Downtown Denver Partnership
511 16th Street
Suite 200
Denver, CO 80202
Phone: (303) 534-6161
Fax: (303) 534-2803
www.downtowndenver.com

Des Moines, IA
Des Moines Downtown Chamber
301 Grand Ave
Des Moines, IA 50309
Phone: (515) 309-3229
www.desmoinesdowtownchamber.com

Greater Des Moines Partnership
700 Locust Street
Suite 100
Des Moines, IA 50309
Phone: (515) 286-4950
Fax: (515) 286-4974
www.desmoinesmetro.com

Durham, NC
Durham Chamber of Commerce
PO Box 3829
Durham, NC 27702
Phone: (919) 682-2133
Fax: (919) 688-8351
www.durhamchamber.org

North Carolina Institute of Minority Economic Development
114 W Parish Street
Durham, NC 27701
Phone: (919) 956-8889
Fax: (919) 688-7668
www.ncimed.com

El Paso, TX
City of El Paso Department of Economic Development
2 Civic Center Plaza
El Paso, TX 79901
Phone: (915) 541-4000
Fax: (915) 541-1316
www.elpasotexas.gov

Greater El Paso Chamber of Commerce
10 Civic Center Plaza
El Paso, TX 79901
Phone: (915) 534-0500
Fax: (915) 534-0510
www.elpaso.org

Erie, PA
Erie Regional Chamber and Growth Partnership
208 E. Bayfront Parkway
Suite 100
Erie, PA 16507
Phone: (814) 454-7191
www.eriepa.com

Eugene, OR
Eugene Area Chamber of Commerce
1401 Williamette Street
Eugene, OR 97401
Phone: (541) 484-1314
Fax: (541) 484-4942
www.eugenechamber.com

Fargo, ND
Chamber of Commerce of Fargo Moorhead
202 First Avenue North
Fargo, ND 56560
Phone: (218) 233-1100
Fax: (218) 233-1200
www.fmchamber.com

Greater Fargo-Moorhead Economic Development Corporation
51 Broadway, Suite 500
Fargo, ND 58102
Phone: (701) 364-1900
Fax: (701) 293-7819
www.gfmedc.com

Fayetteville, NC
Fayetteville Regional Chamber
1019 Hay Street
Fayetteville, NC 28305
Phone: (910) 483-8133
Fax: (910) 483-0263
www.fayettevillencchamber.org

Fort Collins, CO
Fort Collins Chamber of Commerce
225 South Meldrum
Fort Collins, CO 80521
Phone: (970) 482-3746
Fax: (970) 482-3774
www.fcchamber.org

Fort Wayne, IN
City of Fort Wayne Economic Development
1 Main St
1 Main Street
Fort Wayne, IN 46802
Phone: (260) 427-1111
Fax: (260) 427-1375
www.cityoffortwayne.org

Greater Fort Wayne Chamber of Commerce
826 Ewing Street
Fort Wayne, IN 46802
Phone: (260) 424-1435
Fax: (260) 426-7232
www.fwchamber.org

Fort Worth, TX
City of Fort Worth Economic Development
City Hall
900 Monroe Street, Suite 301
Fort Worth, TX 76102
Phone: (817) 392-6103
Fax: (817) 392-2431
www.fortworthgov.org

Fort Worth Chamber of Commerce
777 Taylor Street
Suite 900
Fort Worth, TX 76102-4997
Phone: (817) 336-2491
Fax: (817) 877-4034
www.fortworthchamber.com

Gainesville, FL
Gainesville Area Chamber of Commerce
300 East University Avenue
Suite 100
Gainesville, FL 32601
Phone: (352) 334-7100
Fax: (352) 334-7141
www.gainesvillechamber.com

Grand Rapids, MI
Grands Rapids Area Chamber of Commerce
111 Pearl Street N.W.
Grand Rapids, MI 49503
Phone: (616) 771-0300
Fax: (616) 771-0318
www.grandrapids.org

Green Bay, WI
Economic Development
100 N Jefferson St
Room 202
Green Bay, WI 54301
Phone: (920) 448-3397
Fax: (920) 448-3063
www.ci.green-bay.wi.us

Green Bay Area Chamber of Commerce
300 N. Broadway
Suite 3A
Green Bay, WI 54305-1660
Phone: (920) 437-8704
Fax: (920) 593-3468
www.titletown.org

Greensboro, NC
Greensboro Area Chamber of Commerce
342 N Elm St.
Greensboro, NC 27401
Phone: (336) 387-8301
Fax: (336) 275-9299
www.greensboro.org

Honolulu, HI
The Chamber of Commerce of Hawaii
1132 Bishop Street
Suite 402
Honolulu, HI 96813
Phone: (808) 545-4300
Fax: (808) 545-4369
www.cochawaii.com

Houston, TX
Greater Houston Partnership
1200 Smith Street
Suite 700
Houston, TX 77002-4400
Phone: (713) 844-3600
Fax: (713) 844-0200
www.houston.org

Huntsville, AL
Chamber of Commerce of
Huntsville/Madison County
225 Church Street
Huntsville, AL 35801
Phone: (256) 535-2000
Fax: (256) 535-2015
www.huntsvillealabamausa.com

Indianapolis, IN
Greater Indianapolis Chamber of Commerce
111 Monument Circle
Suite 1950
Indianapolis, IN 46204
Phone: (317) 464-2222
Fax: (317) 464-2217
www.indychamber.com

The Indy Partnership
111 Monument Circle
Suite 1800
Indianapolis, IN 46204
Phone: (317) 236-6262
Fax: (317) 236-6275
www.indypartnership.com

Jacksonville, FL
Jacksonville Chamber of Commerce
3 Independent Drive
Jacksonville, FL 32202
Phone: (904) 366-6600
Fax: (904) 632-0617
www.myjaxchamber.com

Kansas City, MO
Greater Kansas City Chamber of Commerce
2600 Commerce Tower
911 Main Street
Kansas City, MO 64105
Phone: (816) 221-2424
Fax: (816) 221-7440
www.kcchamber.com

Kansas City Area Development Council
2600 Commerce Tower
911 Main Street
Kansas City, MO 64105
Phone: (816) 221-2121
Fax: (816) 842-2865
www.thinkkc.com

Lafayette, LA
Greater Lafayette Chamber of Commerce
804 East Saint Mary Blvd.
Lafayette, LA 70503
Phone: (337) 233-2705
Fax: (337) 234-8671
www.lafchamber.org

Las Vegas, NV
Las Vegas Chamber of Commerce
6671 Las Vegas Blvd South
Suite 300
Las Vegas, NV 89119
Phone: (702) 735-1616
Fax: (702) 735-0406
www.lvchamber.org

Las Vegas Office of Business Development
400 Stewart Avenue
City Hall
Las Vegas, NV 89101
Phone: (702) 229-6011
Fax: (702) 385-3128
www.lasvegasnevada.gov

Lexington, KY
Greater Lexington Chamber of Commerce
330 East Main Street
Suite 100
Lexington, KY 40507
Phone: (859) 254-4447
Fax: (859) 233-3304
www.commercelexington.com

Lexington Downtown Development
Authority
101 East Vine Street
Suite 500
Lexington, KY 40507
Phone: (859) 425-2296
Fax: (859) 425-2292
www.lexingtondda.com

Lincoln, NE
Lincoln Chamber of Commerce
1135 M Street
Suite 200
Lincoln, NE 68508
Phone: (402) 436-2350
Fax: (402) 436-2360
www.lcoc.com

Little Rock, AR
Little Rock Regional Chamber of
Commerce
One Chamber Plaza
Little Rock, AR 72201-1618
Phone: (501) 374-2001
www.littlerockchamber.com

Los Angeles, CA
Los Angeles Area Chamber of Commerce
350 South Bixel Street
Los Angeles, CA 90017
Phone: (213) 580-7500
Fax: (213) 580-7511
www.lachamber.org

Los Angeles County Economic
Development Corporation
444 South Flower Street
34th Floor
Los Angeles, CA 90071
Phone: (213) 622-4300
Fax: (213) 622-7100
www.laedc.org

Louisville, KY
The Greater Louisville Chamber of
Commerce
614 West Main Street
Suite 6000
Louisville, KY 40202
Phone: (502) 625-0000
Fax: (502) 625-0010
www.greaterlouisville.com

Lubbock, TX
Lubbock Chamber of Commerce
1500 Broadway
Suite 101
Lubbock, TX 79401
Phone: (806) 761-7000
Fax: (806) 761-7013
www.lubbockchamber.com

Madison, WI
Greater Madison Chamber of Commerce
615 East Washington Avenue
P.O. Box 71
Madison, WI 53701-0071
Phone: (608) 256-8348
Fax: (608) 256-0333
www.greatermadisonchamber.com

Manchester, NH
Greater Manchester Chamber of Commerce
889 Elm Street
Manchester, NH 03101
Phone: (603) 666-6600
Fax: (603) 626-0910
www.manchester-chamber.org

Manchester Economic Development Office
One City Hall Plaza
Manchester, NH 03101
Phone: (603) 624-6505
Fax: (603) 624-6308
www.yourmanchesternh.com

Miami, FL
Greater Miami Chamber of Commerce
1601 Biscayne Boulevard
Ballroom Level
Miami, FL 33132-1260
Phone: (305) 350-7700
Fax: (305) 374-6902
www.greatermiami.com

The Beacon Council
80 Southwest 8th Street
Suite 2400
Miami, FL 33130
Phone: (305) 579-1300
Fax: (305) 375-0271
www.beaconcouncil.com

Midland, TX
Midland Chamber of Commerce
109 N. Main
Midland, TX 79701
Phone: (432) 683-3381
Fax: (432) 686-3556
www.midlandtxchamber.com

Minneapolis, MN
Minneapolis Community Development Agency
Crown Roller Mill
105 5th Avenue South, Suite 200
Minneapolis, MN 55401
Phone: (612) 673-5095
Fax: (612) 673-5100
www.ci.minneapolis.mn.us

Minneapolis Regional Chamber
81 South Ninth Street
Suite 200
Minneapolis, MN 55402
Phone: (612) 370-9100
Fax: (612) 370-9195
www.minneapolischamber.org

Nashville, TN
Nashville Area Chamber of Commerce
211 Commerce Street
Suite 100
Nashville, TN 37201
Phone: (615) 743-3000
Fax: (615) 256-3074
www.nashvillechamber.cm

Tennessee Valley Authority Economic Development Corp.
P.O. Box 292409
Nashville, TN 37229-2409
Phone: (615) 232-6225
www.tvaed.com

New Orleans, LA
New Orleans Chamber of Commerce
1515 Poydras St
Suite 1010
New Orleans, LA 70112
Phone: (504) 799-4260
Fax: (504) 799-4259
www.neworleanschamber.org

New York, NY
New York City Economic Development Corporation
110 William Street
New York, NY 10038
Phone: (212) 619-5000
www.nycedc.com

The Partnership for New York City
One Battery Park Plaza
5th Floor
New York, NY 10004
Phone: (212) 493-7400
Fax: (212) 344-3344
www.pfnyc.org

Oklahoma City, OK
Greater Oklahoma City Chamber of Commerce
123 Park Avenue
Oklahoma City, OK 73102
Phone: (405) 297-8900
Fax: (405) 297-8916
www.okcchamber.com

Omaha, NE
Omaha Chamber of Commerce
1301 Harney Street
Omaha, NE 68102
Phone: (402) 346-5000
Fax: (402) 346-7050
www.omahachamber.org

Orlando, FL
Metro Orlando Economic Development Commission of Mid-Florida
301 East Pine Street
Suite 900
Orlando, FL 32801
Phone: (407) 422-7159
Fax: (407) 425.6428
www.orlandoedc.com

Orlando Regional Chamber of Commerce
75 South Ivanhoe Boulevard
PO Box 1234
Orlando, FL 32802
Phone: (407) 425-1234
Fax: (407) 839-5020
www.orlando.org

Oxnard, CA
Oxnard Chamber of Commerce
400 E Esplanade Drive
Suite 302
Oxnard, CA 93036
Phone: (805) 983-6118
Fax: (805) 604-7331
www.oxnardchamber.org

Palm Bay, FL
Greater Palm Bay Chamber of Commerce
4100 Dixie Highway NE
Palm Bay, FL 32905
Phone: (321) 951-9998
www.greaterpalmbaychamber.com

Peoria, IL
Peoria Area Chamber
100 SW Water St.
Peoria, IL 61602
Phone: (309) 495-5900
www.peoriachamber.org

Philadelphia, PA
Greater Philadelphia Chamber of Commerce
200 South Broad Street
Suite 700
Philadelphia, PA 19102
Phone: (215) 545-1234
Fax: (215) 790-3600
www.greaterphilachamber.com

Phoenix, AZ
Greater Phoenix Chamber of Commerce
201 North Central Avenue
27th Floor
Phoenix, AZ 85073
Phone: (602) 495-2195
Fax: (602) 495-8913
www.phoenixchamber.com

Greater Phoenix Economic Council
2 North Central Avenue
Suite 2500
Phoenix, AZ 85004
Phone: (602) 256-7700
Fax: (602) 256-7744
www.gpec.org

Pittsburgh, PA
Allegheny County Industrial Development Authority
425 6th Avenue
Suite 800
Pittsburgh, PA 15219
Phone: (412) 350-1067
Fax: (412) 642-2217
www.alleghenycounty.us

Greater Pittsburgh Chamber of Commerce
425 6th Avenue
12th Floor
Pittsburgh, PA 15219
Phone: (412) 392-4500
Fax: (412) 392-4520
www.alleghenyconference.org

Portland, OR
Portland Business Alliance
200 SW Market Street
Suite 1770
Portland, OR 97201
Phone: (503) 224-8684
Fax: (503) 323-9186
www.portlandalliance.com

Providence, RI
Greater Providence Chamber of Commerce
30 Exchange Terrace
Fourth Floor
Providence, RI 02903
Phone: (401) 521-5000
Fax: (401) 351-2090
www.provchamber.com

Rhode Island Economic Development Corporation
Providence City Hall
25 Dorrance Street
Providence, RI 02903
Phone: (401) 421-7740
Fax: (401) 751-0203
www.providenceri.com

Provo, UT
Provo-Orem Chamber of Commerce
51 South University Avenue
Suite 215
Provo, UT 84601
Phone: (801) 851-2555
Fax: (801) 851-2557
www.thechamber.org

Raleigh, NC
Greater Raleigh Chamber of Commerce
800 South Salisbury Street
Raleigh, NC 27601-2978
Phone: (919) 664-7000
Fax: (919) 664-7099
www.raleighchamber.org

Reno, NV
Greater Reno-Sparks Chamber of Commerce
1 East First Street
16th Floor
Reno, NV 89505
Phone: (775) 337-3030
Fax: (775) 337-3038
www.reno-sparkschamber.org

The Chamber Reno-Sparks-Northern Nevada
449 S. Virginia St.
2nd Floor
Reno, NV 89501
Phone: (775) 636-9550
www.thechambernv.org

Richmond, VA
Greater Richmond Chamber
600 East Main Street
Suite 700
Richmond, VA 23219
Phone: (804) 648-1234
www.grcc.com

Greater Richmond Partnership
901 East Byrd Street
Suite 801
Richmond, VA 23219-4070
Phone: (804) 643-3227
Fax: (804) 343-7167
www.grpva.com

Roanoke, VA
Roanoke Regional Chamber of Commerce
210 S. Jefferson St.
Roanoke, VA 24011-1702
Phone: (540) 983-0700
Fax: (540) 983-0723
www.roanokechamber.org

Rochester, MN
Rochester Area Chamber of Commerce
220 South Broadway
Suite 100
Rochester, MN 55904
Phone: (507) 288-1122
Fax: (507) 282-8960
www.rochestermnchamber.com

Sacramento, CA
Sacramento Metro Chamber of Commerce
One Capitol Mall
Suite 300
Sacramento, CA 95814
Phone: (916) 552-6800
Fax: (916) 443-2672
www.metrochamber.org

Salem, OR
Salem Area Chamber of Commerce
1110 Commercial Street NE
Salem, OR 97301
Phone: (503) 581-1466
Fax: (503) 581-0972
www.salemchamber.org

Salt Lake City, UT
Department of Economic Development
451 South State Street
Room 345
Salt Lake City, UT 84111
Phone: (801) 535-6306
Fax: (801) 535-6331
www.slcgov.com/mayor/ED

Salt Lake Chamber
175 E. University Blvd. (400 S)
Suite 600
Salt Lake City, UT 84111
Phone: (801) 364-3631
www.slchamber.com

San Antonio, TX
San Antonio Economic Development Department
P.O. Box 839966
San Antonio, TX 78283-3966
Phone: (210) 207-8080
Fax: (210) 207-8151
www.sanantonio.gov/edd

The Greater San Antonio Chamber of Commerce
602 E. Commerce Street
San Antonio, TX 78205
Phone: (210) 229-2100
Fax: (210) 229-1600
www.sachamber.org

San Diego, CA
San Diego Economic Development Corporation
401 B Street
Suite 1100
San Diego, CA 92101
Phone: (619) 234-8484
Fax: (619) 234-1935
www.sandiegobusiness.org

San Diego Regional Chamber of Commerce
402 West Broadway
Suite 1000
San Diego, CA 92101-3585
Phone: (619) 544-1300
Fax: (619) 744-7481
www.sdchamber.org

San Francisco, CA
San Francisco Chamber of Commerce
235 Montgomery Street
12th Floor
San Francisco, CA 94104
Phone: (415) 392-4520
Fax: (415) 392-0485
www.sfchamber.com

San Jose, CA
Office of Economic Development
60 South Market Street
Suite 470
San Jose, CA 95113
Phone: (408) 277-5880
Fax: (408) 277-3615
www.sba.gov

San Jose-Silicon Valley Chamber of Commerce
310 South First Street
San Jose, CA 95113
Phone: (408) 291-5250
Fax: (408) 286-5019
www.sjchamber.com

Santa Rosa, CA
Santa Rosa Chamber of Commerce
1260 North Dutton Avenue
Suite 272
Santa Rosa, CA 95401
Phone: (707) 545-1414
www.santarosachamber.com

Savannah, GA
Economic Development Authority
131 Hutchinson Island Road
4th Floor
Savannah, GA 31421
Phone: (912) 447-8450
Fax: (912) 447-8455
www.seda.org

Savannah Chamber of Commerce
101 E. Bay Street
Savannah, GA 31402
Phone: (912) 644-6400
Fax: (912) 644-6499
www.savannahchamber.com

Seattle, WA
Greater Seattle Chamber of Commerce
1301 Fifth Avenue
Suite 2500
Seattle, WA 98101
Phone: (206) 389-7200
Fax: (206) 389-7288
www.seattlechamber.com

Sioux Falls, SD
Sioux Falls Area Chamber of Commerce
200 N. Phillips Avenue
Suite 102
Sioux Falls, SD 57104
Phone: (605) 336-1620
Fax: (605) 336-6499
www.siouxfallschamber.com

Spokane, WA
Greater Spokane
801 W Riverside
Suite 100
Spokane, WA 99201
Phone: (509) 624-1393
Fax: (509) 747-0077
www.spokanechamber.org

Springfield, IL
The Greater Springfield Chamber of Commerce
1011 S. Second St.
Springfield, IL 62704
Phone: (217) 525-1173
Fax: (217) 525-8768
www.gscc.org

Tallahassee, FL
Greater Tallahassee Chamber of Commerce
300 E. Park Avenue
PO Box 1638
Tallahassee, FL 32301
Phone: (850) 224-8116
Fax: (850) 561-3860
www.talchamber.com

Tampa, FL
Greater Tampa Chamber of Commerce
P.O. Box 420
Tampa, FL 33601-0420
Phone: (813) 276-9401
Fax: (813) 229-7855
www.tampachamber.com

Topeka, KS
Greater Topeka Chamber of Commerce/GO Topeka
120 SE Sixth Avenue
Suite 110
Topeka, KS 66603
Phone: (785) 234-2644
Fax: (785) 234-8656
www.topekachamber.org

Tulsa, OK
Tulsa Regional Chamber
1 West 3rd Street
Suite 100
Tulsa, OK 74103
Phone: (918) 585-1201
Fax: (918) 585-8016
www.tulsachamber.com

Tyler, TX
Tyler Area Chamber of Commerce
315 N. Broadway Ave.
Suite 100
Tyler, TX 75702
Phone: (800) 235-5712
Fax: (903) 593-2746
www.tylertexas.com

Virginia Beach, VA
Hampton Roads Chamber of Commerce
500 East Main St
Suite 700
Virginia Beach, VA 23510
Phone: (757) 664-2531
www.hamptonroadschamber.com

Washington, DC
District of Columbia Chamber of Commerce
1213 K Street NW
Washington, DC 20005
Phone: (202) 347-7201
Fax: (202) 638-6762
www.dcchamber.org

District of Columbia Office of Planning and Economic Development
J.A. Wilson Building
1350 Pennsylvania Ave NW, Suite 317
Washington, DC 20004
Phone: (202) 727-6365
Fax: (202) 727-6703
www.dcbiz.dc.gov

Wichita, KS
City of Wichita Economic Development Department
City Hall, 12th Floor
455 North Main Street
Wichita, KS 67202
Phone: (316) 268-4524
Fax: (316) 268-4656
www.wichitagov.org

Wichita Metro Chamber of Commerce
350 West Douglas Avenue
Wichita, KS 67202
Phone: (316) 265-7771
www.wichitachamber.org

Wilmington, NC
Wilmington Chamber of Commerce
One Estell Lee Place
Wilmington, NC 28401
Phone: (910) 762-2611
www.wilmingtonchamber.org

Winston-Salem, NC
Winston-Salem Chamber of Commerce
411 West Fourth Street
Suite 211
Winston-Salem, NC 27101
Phone: (336) 728-9200
www.winstonsalem.com

Worcester, MA
Worcester Regional Chamber of Commerce
446 Main St.
Suite 200
Worcester, MA 01608
Phone: (508) 753-2924
Fax: (508) 754-8560
www.worcesterchamber.org

Appendix E: State Departments of Labor

Alabama
Alabama Department of Labor
P.O. Box 303500
Montgomery, AL 36130-3500
Phone: (334) 242-3072
www.Alalabor.state.al.us

Alaska
Dept of Labor and Workforce Devel.
P.O. Box 11149
Juneau, AK 99822-2249
Phone: (907) 465-2700
www.labor.state.AK.us

Arizona
Arizona Industrial Commission
800 West Washington Street
Phoenix, AZ 85007
Phone: (602) 542-4515
www.ica.state.AZ.us

Arkansas
Department of Labor
10421 West Markham
Little Rock, AR 72205
Phone: (501) 682-4500
www.Arkansas.gov/labor

California
Labor and Workforce Development
445 Golden Gate Ave., 10th Floor
San Francisco, CA 94102
Phone: (916) 263-1811
www.labor.CA.gov

Colorado
Dept of Labor and Employment
633 17th St., 2nd Floor
Denver, CO 80202-3660
Phone: (888) 390-7936
www.COworkforce.com

Connecticut
Department of Labor
200 Folly Brook Blvd.
Wethersfield, CT 06109-1114
Phone: (860) 263-6000
www.CT.gov/dol

Delaware
Department of Labor
4425 N. Market St., 4th Floor
Wilmington, DE 19802
Phone: (302) 451-3423
www.Delawareworks.com

District of Columbia
Employment Services Department
614 New York Ave., NE, Suite 300
Washington, DC 20002
Phone: (202) 671-1900
www.DOES.DC.gov

Florida
Agency for Workforce Innovation
The Caldwell Building
107 East Madison St. Suite 100
Tallahassee, FL 32399-4120
Phone: (800) 342-3450
www.Floridajobs.org

Georgia
Department of Labor
Sussex Place, Room 600
148 Andrew Young Intl Blvd., NE
Atlanta, GA 30303
Phone: (404) 656-3011
www.dol.state.GA.us

Hawaii
Dept of Labor & Industrial Relations
830 Punchbowl Street
Honolulu, HI 96813
Phone: (808) 586-8842
wwwHawaii.gov/labor

Idaho
Department of Labor
317 W. Main St.
Boise, ID 83735-0001
Phone: (208) 332-3579
www.labor.Idaho.gov

Illinois
Department of Labor
160 N. LaSalle Street, 13th Floor
Suite C-1300
Chicago, IL 60601
Phone: (312) 793-2800
www.state.IL.us/agency/idol

Indiana
Indiana Government Center South
402 W. Washington Street
Room W195
Indianapolis, IN 46204
Phone: (317) 232-2655
www.IN.gov/labor

Iowa
Iowa Workforce Development
1000 East Grand Avenue
Des Moines, IA 50319-0209
Phone: (515) 242-5870
www.Iowaworkforce.org/labor

Kansas
Department of Labor
401 S.W. Topeka Blvd.
Topeka, KS 66603-3182
Phone: (785) 296-5000
www.dol.KS.gov

Kentucky
Philip Anderson, Commissioner
Department of Labor
1047 U.S. Hwy 127 South, Suite 4
Frankfort, KY 40601-4381
Phone: (502) 564-3070
www.labor.KY.gov

Louisiana
Department of Labor
P.O. Box 94094
Baton Rouge, LA 70804-9094
Phone: (225) 342-3111
www.LAworks.net

Maine
Department of Labor
45 Commerce Street
Augusta, ME 04330
Phone: (207) 623-7900
www.state.ME.us/labor

Maryland
Department of Labor and Industry
500 N. Calvert Street
Suite 401
Baltimore, MD 21202
Phone: (410) 767-2357
www.dllr.state.MD.us

Massachusetts
Dept of Labor & Work Force Devel.
One Ashburton Place
Room 2112
Boston, MA 02108
Phone: (617) 626-7100
www.Mass.gov/eolwd

Michigan
Dept of Labor & Economic Growth
P.O. Box 30004
Lansing, MI 48909
Phone: (517) 335-0400
www.Michigan.gov/cis

Minnesota
Dept of Labor and Industry
443 Lafayette Road North
Saint Paul, MN 55155
Phone: (651) 284-5070
www.doli.state.MN.us

Mississippi
Dept of Employment Security
P.O. Box 1699
Jackson, MS 39215-1699
Phone: (601) 321-6000
www.mdes.MS.gov

Missouri
Labor and Industrial Relations
P.O. Box 599
3315 W. Truman Boulevard
Jefferson City, MO 65102-0599
Phone: (573) 751-7500
www.dolir.MO.gov/lirc

Montana
Dept of Labor and Industry
P.O. Box 1728
Helena, MT 59624-1728
Phone: (406) 444-9091
www.dli.MT.gov

Nebraska
Department of Labor
550 South 16th Street
Box 94600
Lincoln, NE 68509-4600
Phone: (402) 471-9000
www.Nebraskaworkforce.com

Nevada
Dept of Business and Industry
555 E. Washington Ave.
Suite 4100
Las Vegas, NV 89101-1050
Phone: (702) 486-2650
www.laborcommissioner.com

New Hampshire
Department of Labor
State Office Park South
95 Pleasant Street
Concord, NH 03301
Phone: (603) 271-3176
www.labor.state.NH.us

New Jersey
Department of Labor
John Fitch Plaza, 13th Floor
Suite D
Trenton, NJ 08625-0110
Phone: (609) 777-3200
lwd.dol.state.nj.us/labor

New Mexico
Department of Labor
401 Broadway, NE
Albuquerque, NM 87103-1928
Phone: (505) 841-8450
www.dol.state.NM.us

New York
Department of Labor
State Office Bldg. # 12
W.A. Harriman Campus
Albany, NY 12240
Phone: (518) 457-5519
www.labor.state.NY.us

North Carolina
Department of Labor
4 West Edenton Street
Raleigh, NC 27601-1092
Phone: (919) 733-7166
www.nclabor.com

North Dakota
Department of Labor
State Capitol Building
600 East Boulevard, Dept 406
Bismark, ND 58505-0340
Phone: (701) 328-2660
www.nd.gov/labor

Ohio
Department of Commerce
77 South High Street, 22nd Floor
Columbus, OH 43215
Phone: (614) 644-2239
www.com.state.OH.us

Oklahoma
Department of Labor
4001 N. Lincoln Blvd.
Oklahoma City, OK 73105-5212
Phone: (405) 528-1500
www.state.OK.us/~okdol

Oregon
Bureau of Labor and Industries
800 NE Oregon St., #32
Portland, OR 97232
Phone: (971) 673-0761
www.Oregon.gov/boli

Pennsylvania
Dept of Labor and Industry
1700 Labor and Industry Bldg
7th and Forster Streets
Harrisburg, PA 17120
Phone: (717) 787-5279
www.dli.state.PA.us

Rhode Island
Department of Labor and Training
1511 Pontiac Avenue
Cranston, RI 02920
Phone: (401) 462-8000
www.dlt.state.RI.us

South Carolina
Dept of Labor, Licensing & Regulations
P.O. Box 11329
Columbia, SC 29211-1329
Phone: (803) 896-4300
www.llr.state.SC.us

South Dakota
Department of Labor
700 Governors Drive
Pierre, SD 57501-2291
Phone: (605) 773-3682
www.state.SD.us

Tennessee
Dept of Labor & Workforce Development
Andrew Johnson Tower
710 James Robertson Pkwy
Nashville, TN 37243-0655
Phone: (615) 741-6642
www.state.TN.us/labor-wfd

Texas
Texas Workforce Commission
101 East 15th St.
Austin, TX 78778
Phone: (512) 475-2670
www.twc.state.TX.us

Utah
Utah Labor Commission
P.O. Box 146610
Salt Lake City, UT 84114-6610
Phone: (801) 530-6800
Laborcommission.Utah.gov

Vermont
Department of Labor
5 Green Mountain Drive
P.O. Box 488
Montpelier, VT 05601-0488
Phone: (802) 828-4000
www.labor.verMont.gov

Virginia
Dept of Labor and Industry
Powers-Taylor Building
13 S. 13th Street
Richmond, VA 23219
Phone: (804) 371-2327
www.doli.Virginia.gov

Washington
Dept of Labor and Industries
P.O. Box 44001
Olympia, WA 98504-4001
Phone: (360) 902-4200
www.lni.WA.gov

West Virginia
Division of Labor
State Capitol Complex, Building #6
1900 Kanawha Blvd.
Charleston, WV 25305
Phone: (304) 558-7890
www.labor.state.WV.us

Wisconsin
Dept of Workforce Development
201 E. Washington Ave., #A400
P.O. Box 7946
Madison, WI 53707-7946
Phone: (608) 266-6861
www.dwd.state.WI.us

Wyoming
Department of Employment
1510 East Pershing Blvd.
Cheyenne, WY 82002
Phone: (307) 777-7261
www.doe.state.WY.us

Source: *U.S. Department of Labor*

2015 Title List

Visit www.GreyHouse.com for Product Information, Table of Contents, and Sample Pages.

General Reference

An African Biographical Dictionary
America's College Museums
American Environmental Leaders: From Colonial Times to the Present
Encyclopedia of African-American Writing
Encyclopedia of Constitutional Amendments
Encyclopedia of Gun Control & Gun Rights
An Encyclopedia of Human Rights in the United States
Encyclopedia of Invasions & Conquests
Encyclopedia of Prisoners of War & Internment
Encyclopedia of Religion & Law in America
Encyclopedia of Rural America
Encyclopedia of the Continental Congress
Encyclopedia of the United States Cabinet, 1789-2010
Encyclopedia of War Journalism
Encyclopedia of Warrior Peoples & Fighting Groups
The Environmental Debate: A Documentary History
The Evolution Wars: A Guide to the Debates
From Suffrage to the Senate: America's Political Women
Global Terror & Political Risk Assessment
Media & Communications 1900-2020
Nations of the World
Political Corruption in America
Privacy Rights in the Digital Era
The Religious Right: A Reference Handbook
Speakers of the House of Representatives, 1789-2009
This is Who We Were: 1880-1900
This is Who We Were: A Companion to the 1940 Census
This is Who We Were: In the 1910s
This is Who We Were: In the 1920s
This is Who We Were: In the 1940s
This is Who We Were: In the 1950s
This is Who We Were: In the 1960s
This is Who We Were: In the 1970s
U.S. Land & Natural Resource Policy
The Value of a Dollar 1600-1865: Colonial Era to the Civil War
The Value of a Dollar: 1860-2014
Working Americans 1770-1869 Vol. IX: Revolutionary War to the Civil War
Working Americans 1880-1999 Vol. I: The Working Class
Working Americans 1880-1999 Vol. II: The Middle Class
Working Americans 1880-1999 Vol. III: The Upper Class
Working Americans 1880-1999 Vol. IV: Their Children
Working Americans 1880-2015 Vol. V: Americans At War
Working Americans 1880-2005 Vol. VI: Women at Work
Working Americans 1880-2006 Vol. VII: Social Movements
Working Americans 1880-2007 Vol. VIII: Immigrants
Working Americans 1880-2009 Vol. X: Sports & Recreation
Working Americans 1880-2010 Vol. XI: Inventors & Entrepreneurs
Working Americans 1880-2011 Vol. XII: Our History through Music
Working Americans 1880-2012 Vol. XIII: Education & Educators
World Cultural Leaders of the 20th & 21st Centuries

Education Information

Charter School Movement
Comparative Guide to American Elementary & Secondary Schools
Complete Learning Disabilities Directory
Educators Resource Directory
Special Education: A Reference Book for Policy and Curriculum Development

Health Information

Comparative Guide to American Hospitals
Complete Directory for Pediatric Disorders
Complete Directory for People with Chronic Illness
Complete Directory for People with Disabilities
Complete Mental Health Directory
Diabetes in America: Analysis of an Epidemic
Directory of Drug & Alcohol Residential Rehab Facilities
Directory of Health Care Group Purchasing Organizations
Directory of Hospital Personnel
HMO/PPO Directory
Medical Device Register
Older Americans Information Directory

Business Information

Complete Television, Radio & Cable Industry Directory
Directory of Business Information Resources
Directory of Mail Order Catalogs
Directory of Venture Capital & Private Equity Firms
Environmental Resource Handbook
Food & Beverage Market Place
Grey House Homeland Security Directory
Grey House Performing Arts Directory
Grey House Safety & Security Directory
Grey House Transportation Security Directory
Hudson's Washington News Media Contacts Directory
New York State Directory
Rauch Market Research Guides
Sports Market Place Directory

Statistics & Demographics

American Tally
America's Top-Rated Cities
America's Top-Rated Smaller Cities
America's Top-Rated Small Towns & Cities
Ancestry & Ethnicity in America
The Asian Databook
Comparative Guide to American Suburbs
The Hispanic Databook
Profiles of America
"Profiles of" Series - State Handbooks
Weather America

Financial Ratings Series

TheStreet Ratings' Guide to Bond & Money Market Mutual Funds
TheStreet Ratings' Guide to Common Stocks
TheStreet Ratings' Guide to Exchange-Traded Funds
TheStreet Ratings' Guide to Stock Mutual Funds
TheStreet Ratings' Ultimate Guided Tour of Stock Investing
Weiss Ratings' Consumer Guides
Weiss Ratings' Guide to Banks
Weiss Ratings' Guide to Credit Unions
Weiss Ratings' Guide to Health Insurers
Weiss Ratings' Guide to Life & Annuity Insurers
Weiss Ratings' Guide to Property & Casualty Insurers

Bowker's Books In Print® Titles

American Book Publishing Record® Annual
American Book Publishing Record® Monthly
Books In Print®
Books In Print® Supplement
Books Out Loud™
Bowker's Complete Video Directory™
Children's Books In Print®
El-Hi Textbooks & Serials In Print®
Forthcoming Books®
Large Print Books & Serials™
Law Books & Serials In Print™
Medical & Health Care Books In Print™
Publishers, Distributors & Wholesalers of the US™
Subject Guide to Books In Print®
Subject Guide to Children's Books In Print®

Canadian General Reference

Associations Canada
Canadian Almanac & Directory
Canadian Environmental Resource Guide
Canadian Parliamentary Guide
Canadian Venture Capital & Private Equity Firms
Financial Services Canada
Governments Canada
Health Guide Canada
The History of Canada
Libraries Canada
Major Canadian Cities

SALEM PRESS

2015 Title List

Visit www.SalemPress.com for Product Information, Table of Contents, and Sample Pages.

Science, Careers & Mathematics

Ancient Creatures: Unearthed
Applied Science
Applied Science: Engineering & Mathematics
Applied Science: Science & Medicine
Applied Science: Technology
Biomes and Ecosystems
Careers in Business
Careers in Chemistry
Careers in Communications & Media
Careers in Environment & Conservation
Careers in Healthcare
Careers in Hospitality & Tourism
Careers in Human Services
Careers in Law, Criminal Justice & Emergency Services
Careers in Physics
Careers in Technology Services & Repair
Computer Technology Innovators
Contemporary Biographies in Business
Contemporary Biographies in Chemistry
Contemporary Biographies in Communications & Media
Contemporary Biographies in Environment & Conservation
Contemporary Biographies in Healthcare
Contemporary Biographies in Hospitality & Tourism
Contemporary Biographies in Law & Criminal Justice
Contemporary Biographies in Physics
Earth Science
Earth Science: Earth Materials & Resources
Earth Science: Earth's Surface and History
Earth Science: Physics & Chemistry of the Earth
Earth Science: Weather, Water & Atmosphere
Encyclopedia of Energy
Encyclopedia of Environmental Issues
Encyclopedia of Environmental Issues: Atmosphere and Air Pollution
Encyclopedia of Environmental Issues: Ecology and Ecosystems
Encyclopedia of Environmental Issues: Energy and Energy Use
Encyclopedia of Environmental Issues: Policy and Activism
Encyclopedia of Environmental Issues: Preservation/Wilderness Issues
Encyclopedia of Environmental Issues: Water and Water Pollution
Encyclopedia of Global Resources
Encyclopedia of Global Warming
Encyclopedia of Mathematics & Society
Encyclopedia of Mathematics & Society: Engineering, Tech, Medicine
Encyclopedia of Mathematics & Society: Great Mathematicians
Encyclopedia of Mathematics & Society: Math & Social Sciences
Encyclopedia of Mathematics & Society: Math Development/Concepts
Encyclopedia of Mathematics & Society: Math in Culture & Society
Encyclopedia of Mathematics & Society: Space, Science, Environment
Encyclopedia of the Ancient World
Forensic Science
Geography Basics
Internet Innovators
Inventions and Inventors
Magill's Encyclopedia of Science: Animal Life
Magill's Encyclopedia of Science: Plant life
Notable Natural Disasters
Principles of Chemistry
Science and Scientists
Solar System
Solar System: Great Astronomers
Solar System: Study of the Universe
Solar System: The Inner Planets
Solar System: The Moon and Other Small Bodies
Solar System: The Outer Planets
Solar System: The Sun and Other Stars
World Geography

Literature

American Ethnic Writers
Classics of Science Fiction & Fantasy Literature
Critical Insights: Authors
Critical Insights: New Literary Collection Bundles
Critical Insights: Themes
Critical Insights: Works
Critical Survey of Drama
Critical Survey of Graphic Novels: Heroes & Super Heroes
Critical Survey of Graphic Novels: History, Theme & Technique
Critical Survey of Graphic Novels: Independents/Underground Classics
Critical Survey of Graphic Novels: Manga
Critical Survey of Long Fiction
Critical Survey of Mystery & Detective Fiction
Critical Survey of Mythology and Folklore: Heroes and Heroines
Critical Survey of Mythology and Folklore: Love, Sexuality & Desire
Critical Survey of Mythology and Folklore: World Mythology
Critical Survey of Poetry
Critical Survey of Poetry: American Poets
Critical Survey of Poetry: British, Irish & Commonwealth Poets
Critical Survey of Poetry: Cumulative Index
Critical Survey of Poetry: European Poets
Critical Survey of Poetry: Topical Essays
Critical Survey of Poetry: World Poets
Critical Survey of Shakespeare's Sonnets
Critical Survey of Short Fiction
Critical Survey of Short Fiction: American Writers
Critical Survey of Short Fiction: British, Irish, Commonwealth Writers
Critical Survey of Short Fiction: Cumulative Index
Critical Survey of Short Fiction: European Writers
Critical Survey of Short Fiction: Topical Essays
Critical Survey of Short Fiction: World Writers
Cyclopedia of Literary Characters
Holocaust Literature
Introduction to Literary Context: American Poetry of the 20th Century
Introduction to Literary Context: American Post-Modernist Novels
Introduction to Literary Context: American Short Fiction
Introduction to Literary Context: English Literature
Introduction to Literary Context: Plays
Introduction to Literary Context: World Literature
Magill's Literary Annual 2015
Magill's Survey of American Literature
Magill's Survey of World Literature
Masterplots
Masterplots II: African American Literature
Masterplots II: American Fiction Series
Masterplots II: British & Commonwealth Fiction Series
Masterplots II: Christian Literature
Masterplots II: Drama Series
Masterplots II: Juvenile & Young Adult Literature, Supplement
Masterplots II: Nonfiction Series
Masterplots II: Poetry Series
Masterplots II: Short Story Series
Masterplots II: Women's Literature Series
Notable African American Writers
Notable American Novelists
Notable Playwrights
Notable Poets
Recommended Reading: 500 Classics Reviewed
Short Story Writers

2015 Title List

Visit www.SalemPress.com for Product Information, Table of Contents, and Sample Pages.

History and Social Science

The 2000s in America
50 States
African American History
Agriculture in History
American First Ladies
American Heroes
American Indian Culture
American Indian History
American Indian Tribes
American Presidents
American Villains
America's Historic Sites
Ancient Greece
The Bill of Rights
The Civil Rights Movement
The Cold War
Countries, Peoples & Cultures
Countries, Peoples & Cultures: Central & South America
Countries, Peoples & Cultures: Central, South & Southeast Asia
Countries, Peoples & Cultures: East & South Africa
Countries, Peoples & Cultures: East Asia & the Pacific
Countries, Peoples & Cultures: Eastern Europe
Countries, Peoples & Cultures: Middle East & North Africa
Countries, Peoples & Cultures: North America & the Caribbean
Countries, Peoples & Cultures: West & Central Africa
Countries, Peoples & Cultures: Western Europe
Defining Documents: American Revolution (1754-1805)
Defining Documents: Civil War (1860-1865)
Defining Documents: Emergence of Modern America (1868-1918)
Defining Documents: Exploration & Colonial America (1492-1755)
Defining Documents: Manifest Destiny (1803-1860)
Defining Documents: Post-War 1940s (1945-1949)
Defining Documents: Reconstruction (1865-1880)
Defining Documents: The 1920s
Defining Documents: The 1930s
Defining Documents: The American West (1836-1900)
Defining Documents: The Ancient World (2700 B.C.E.-50 C.E.)
Defining Documents: The Middle Ages (524-1431)
Defining Documents: World War I
Defining Documents: World War II (1939-1946)
The Eighties in America
Encyclopedia of American Immigration
Encyclopedia of Flight
Encyclopedia of the Ancient World
The Fifties in America
The Forties in America
Great Athletes
Great Athletes: Baseball
Great Athletes: Basketball
Great Athletes: Boxing & Soccer
Great Athletes: Cumulative Index
Great Athletes: Football
Great Athletes: Golf & Tennis
Great Athletes: Olympics
Great Athletes: Racing & Individual Sports
Great Events from History: 17th Century
Great Events from History: 18th Century
Great Events from History: 19th Century
Great Events from History: 20th Century (1901-1940)
Great Events from History: 20th Century (1941-1970)
Great Events from History: 20th Century (1971-2000)
Great Events from History: Ancient World
Great Events from History: Cumulative Indexes
Great Events from History: Gay, Lesbian, Bisexual, Transgender Events
Great Events from History: Middle Ages
Great Events from History: Modern Scandals
Great Events from History: Renaissance & Early Modern Era
Great Lives from History: 17th Century
Great Lives from History: 18th Century
Great Lives from History: 19th Century
Great Lives from History: 20th Century
Great Lives from History: African Americans
Great Lives from History: Ancient World
Great Lives from History: Asian & Pacific Islander Americans
Great Lives from History: Cumulative Indexes
Great Lives from History: Incredibly Wealthy
Great Lives from History: Inventors & Inventions
Great Lives from History: Jewish Americans
Great Lives from History: Latinos
Great Lives from History: Middle Ages
Great Lives from History: Notorious Lives
Great Lives from History: Renaissance & Early Modern Era
Great Lives from History: Scientists & Science
Historical Encyclopedia of American Business
Immigration in U.S. History
Magill's Guide to Military History
Milestone Documents in African American History
Milestone Documents in American History
Milestone Documents in World History
Milestone Documents of American Leaders
Milestone Documents of World Religions
Musicians & Composers 20th Century
The Nineties in America
The Seventies in America
The Sixties in America
Survey of American Industry and Careers
The Thirties in America
The Twenties in America
United States at War
U.S.A. in Space
U.S. Court Cases
U.S. Government Leaders
U.S. Laws, Acts, and Treaties
U.S. Legal System
U.S. Supreme Court
Weapons and Warfare
World Conflicts: Asia and the Middle East

Health

Addictions & Substance Abuse
Adolescent Health
Cancer
Complementary & Alternative Medicine
Genetics & Inherited Conditions
Health Issues
Infectious Diseases & Conditions
Magill's Medical Guide
Psychology & Behavioral Health
Psychology Basics

HW WILSON

HW WILSON

2015 Title List

Visit **www.HWWilsonInPrint.com** for Product Information, Table of Contents and Sample Pages

Current Biography
Current Biography Cumulative Index 1946-2013
Current Biography Monthly Magazine
Current Biography Yearbook: 2003
Current Biography Yearbook: 2004
Current Biography Yearbook: 2005
Current Biography Yearbook: 2006
Current Biography Yearbook: 2007
Current Biography Yearbook: 2008
Current Biography Yearbook: 2009
Current Biography Yearbook: 2010
Current Biography Yearbook: 2011
Current Biography Yearbook: 2012
Current Biography Yearbook: 2013
Current Biography Yearbook: 2014
Current Biography Yearbook: 2015

Core Collections
Children's Core Collection
Fiction Core Collection
Middle & Junior High School Core
Public Library Core Collection: Nonfiction
Senior High Core Collection

The Reference Shelf
Aging in America
American Military Presence Overseas
The Arab Spring
The Brain
The Business of Food
Conspiracy Theories
The Digital Age
Dinosaurs
Embracing New Paradigms in Education
Faith & Science
Families: Traditional and New Structures
The Future of U.S. Economic Relations: Mexico, Cuba, and Venezuela
Global Climate Change
Graphic Novels and Comic Books
Immigration in the U.S.
Internet Safety
Marijuana Reform
The News and its Future
The Paranormal
Politics of the Ocean
Reality Television
Representative American Speeches: 2008-2009
Representative American Speeches: 2009-2010
Representative American Speeches: 2010-2011
Representative American Speeches: 2011-2012
Representative American Speeches: 2012-2013
Representative American Speeches: 2013-2014
Representative American Speeches: 2014-2015
Revisiting Gender
Robotics
Russia
Social Networking
Social Services for the Poor
Space Exploration & Development
Sports in America
The Supreme Court
The Transformation of American Cities
U.S. Infrastructure
U.S. National Debate Topic: Surveillance
U.S. National Debate Topic: The Ocean
U.S. National Debate Topic: Transportation Infrastructure
Whistleblowers

Readers' Guide
Abridged Readers' Guide to Periodical Literature
Readers' Guide to Periodical Literature

Indexes
Index to Legal Periodicals & Books
Short Story Index
Book Review Digest

Sears List
Sears List of Subject Headings
Sears: Lista de Encabezamientos de Materia

Facts About Series
Facts About American Immigration
Facts About China
Facts About the 20th Century
Facts About the Presidents
Facts About the World's Languages

Nobel Prize Winners
Nobel Prize Winners: 1901-1986
Nobel Prize Winners: 1987-1991
Nobel Prize Winners: 1992-1996
Nobel Prize Winners: 1997-2001

World Authors
World Authors: 1995-2000
World Authors: 2000-2005

Famous First Facts
Famous First Facts
Famous First Facts About American Politics
Famous First Facts About Sports
Famous First Facts About the Environment
Famous First Facts: International Edition

American Book of Days
The American Book of Days
The International Book of Days

Junior Authors & Illustrators
Tenth Book of Junior Authors & Illustrations

Monographs
The Barnhart Dictionary of Etymology
Celebrate the World
Guide to the Ancient World
Indexing from A to Z
The Poetry Break
Radical Change: Books for Youth in a Digital Age

Wilson Chronology
Wilson Chronology of Asia and the Pacific
Wilson Chronology of Human Rights
Wilson Chronology of Ideas
Wilson Chronology of the Arts
Wilson Chronology of the World's Religions
Wilson Chronology of Women's Achievements